Fodor's 05

FRANCE

Where to Stay and Eat
for All Budgets

Must-See Sights
and Local Secrets

Ratings You Can Trust

Fodor's Travel Publications   New York, Toronto, London, Sydney, Auckland
www.fodors.com

FODOR'S FRANCE
Editor: Robert I. C. Fisher

Editorial Production: Jenna L. Bagnini
Editorial Contributors: Nancy Coons, Thomas Cussans, Sarah Fraser, Ethan Gilsdorf, Simon Hewitt, Rosa Jackson, Nicola Keegan, Christopher Mooney, Christopher Pitts, Mathew Schwartz, George Semler
Maps: David Lindroth *cartographer;* Rebecca Baer and Robert Blake, *map editors*
Design: Fabrizio La Rocca, *creative director;* Guido Caroti, *art director;* Melanie Marin, *senior picture editor*
Cover Design: Moon Sun Kim
Production/Manufacturing: Robert B. Shields
Cover Photo (women in lavender field, Provence): Robb Kendrick/Aurora

ISBN 1-4000-1411-5

ISSN 0532-5692

SPECIAL SALES
This book is available for special discounts for bulk purchases for sales promotions or premiums. Special editions, including personalized covers, excerpts of existing books, and corporate imprints, can be created in large quantities for special needs. For more information, write to Special Markets/Premium Sales, 1745 Broadway, MD 6-2, New York, New York 10019, or e-mail specialmarkets@randomhouse.com.

AN IMPORTANT TIP & AN INVITATION
Although all prices, opening times, and other details in this book are based on information supplied to us at press time, changes occur all the time in the travel world, and Fodor's cannot accept responsibility for facts that become outdated or for inadvertent errors or omissions. So **always confirm information when it matters,** especially if you're making a detour to visit a specific place. Your experiences—positive and negative—matter to us. If we have missed or misstated something, **please write to us.** We follow up on all suggestions. Contact the France editor at editors@fodors.com or c/o Fodor's at 1745 Broadway, New York, NY 10019.

PRINTED IN THE UNITED STATES OF AMERICA

10 9 8 7 6 5 4 3 2 1

DESTINATION FRANCE

Brilliantly radiating 2,000 years of history and culture, France intrigues, provokes, and overwhelms. It is the apex of architectural beauty, artistic expression, and culinary delight—and does it know it. Magisterial as the Arc de Triomphe, quaint as a lace-curtained bistro, alluring as a fairy-tale castle, or as beautiful as a Provençal village, France rarely fails to seduce newcomers. Here is a country where café-lounging is a culture, dining a sacred ritual, and country landscapes look like pop-up Monets. And there is not one France, but many—the Riviera in the south; the medieval cathedrals in the north; the Belle Epoque seaside resorts in the west; the half-timber villages in the east; and central France, home to the storybook Loire Valley and the brilliant poem that is Paris. After tasting the country's many pleasures, you may come to agree with the old saying: "Everyone has two countries, his own and France."

Tim Jarrell, Publisher

CONTENTS

Index

Maps

CloseUps

Taking a trip completely takes you out of yourself. Concerns of life at home are quickly driven away by more immediate thoughts—about, say, what marvels will beguile the next day or where you'll have dinner. That's where Fodor's comes in. We make sure that you have all the right choices and that you don't knowingly miss out on something that's around the next bend just because you didn't know it was there. Always mindful that it's often the things that you didn't come to France expecting to see that end up meaning the most, we guide you to sights large and small all over the country. You might set out to explore the Loire Valley château at Chenonceaux but back at home you find yourself unable to forget that idyllic afternoon spent learning the difference between Sauvignon and Cabernet Franc in the wine cellars of nearby Montlouis or sharing a sunset with the swans at the Domaine des Hauts-de-Loire. With Fodor's at your side, serendipitous discoveries are never far away.

Our success in showing you every corner of France is a credit to our extraordinary writers. While there's no substitute for travel advice from a good friend who knows your style, our contributors are the next best thing—the kind of people you would poll for travel advice if you knew them.

Nancy Coons is based in a 300-year-old farmhouse in Lorraine and covers much of northeastern France while satisfying her long-distance love affair with the luscious south of the country. Author of Fodor's *Provence and the Côte d'Azur,* as well as two of Fodor's color-photograph guide books—*Escape to Provence* and *Escape to the Riviera*—she has become adept at describing the golden light of Arles from under the iron-gray clouds back home.

Thomas Cussans has been passionate about France and the French all his life. Four years ago, he finally found a way to escape the drudgery of desk-bound life in London for the bucolic idyll of the Charente-Maritime. He writes regularly for *The Times* in London. For this edition he updated our Bordeaux, Dordogne, and Poitou-Charentes chapter.

Sarah Fraser spent several years growing up in Central America but re-entry to her native Canadian cold prompted frequent escapes to anywhere hot. So, a university degree and an avid interest in French history and cuisine later, she packed her bags and went in search of the perfect tapenade in the South of France. For this edition, she updated our Provence and Côte D'Azur chapters.

After three years on the Fodor's lodging beat, Ethan Gilsdorf can spot a bathroom's faux marble and a receptionist's fake smile a kilometer away. Ethan arrived in Paris from Vermont with a one-way ticket in 1999. Through a combination of sweet talk and dumb luck, he found himself reviewing restaurants, plays, and films for *Time Out,* critiquing books for the *San Francisco Chronicle,* and writing on travel, arts, and culture for the *Boston Globe* and the *Washington Post.* He has also contributed to the *Los Angeles Times, The Walrus,* and *The Prague Literary Review.*

Simon Hewitt headed to Paris straight from studying French and art history at Oxford. It was a return to base; his grandmother was French, as is his daughter Anaïs. He has been working for Fodor's since 1987, and is a Paris correspondent for several art market magazines, including *Art & Auction.* His main hobby is cricket: he captained France from 1990 to 2001, and is now national coach. For this edition, he updated our chapters on the Ile-de-France, the Loire Valley, Normandy, the North, the Massif Central, and Burgundy.

Rosa Jackson's love affair with French pastries began at age four, when she spent her first year in Paris before returning to the Canadian north. Early experiments with éclairs and croissants led her to enroll in the Paris Cordon Bleu, where she learned that even great chefs make mistakes. A food writer for more than a decade, a Parisian since 1995, and now updater of our Paris Dining section, Rosa has eaten in hundreds of Paris restaurants—and always has room for dessert.

Nicola Keegan was born in Ireland and raised in Iowa. But after spending one year at the Sorbonne, she knew Paris was going to be her home forever. Now famous for her uncanny knowledge of where to purchase absolute necessities from truffle oil to that perfect pair of gold-hue boots, she brings all her hard earned "savoir flair" to the Smart Travel Tips chapter and Paris Shopping section.

Christopher Mooney originally came to Paris to study French philosophy, smoke Gîtanes cigarettes, and hang out in cafés. Thirteen years later he's still there, now happily ensconced as coeditor of the *Paris Ritz Magazine* and the *Paris-Athéné Magazine;* his articles have appeared in *Elle* and *Condé Nast Traveler.* Chris updated our chapters on Brittany and Alsace-Lorraine.

Paris Exploring updater Lisa Pasold first fell in love with the city's architecture and atmosphere in 1989, while dragging her suitcase up seven flights of stairs to a *chambre de bonne.* She writes on travel, food, and architecture for papers like the *Chicago Tribune* and *The Globe and Mail.* She also recently published a book of poetry, *Weave.* As a travel writer, she has been thrown off a train in Belarus and has mushed huskies in the Yukon, but her favorite place to explore remains the fabulous tangle of streets that surrounds her Paris home.

Christopher Pitts, our Paris Nightlife & the Arts updater, left the U.S. at the age of twenty to study Mandarin Chinese. He has lived in Paris since 2001, and, aside from the city's wine bars, is most interested in the nebulous process of cultural adaptation. He has written for several different guidebooks to both France and China.

Freelance writer and photographer Mathew Schwartz followed his wife to France. His work has appeared in such publications as the *Boston Globe, Computerworld,* and *Fortune.* He avidly bikes, plays Ultimate Frisbee, practices yoga, and never passes up a Jean-Luc Godard movie screening. He applied those interests to this year's Paris Sports & the Outdoors section.

George Semler lives over the border in Spain, but he has skied, hiked, fly-fished, and explored every side of the Pyrénées. For this edition, he updated our chapters on Lyon and the Alps, Basque Country, the Midi-Pyrénées, and Corsica. Author of *Fodor's Barcelona to Bilbao,* he also writes for a variety of publications, including *Saveur.*

Robert I. C. Fisher, editor of *Fodor's France 2005,* succeeded in getting one foot in the caviar when he was sent to Paris to write up the noted Ile St-Louis residence of Baron and Baroness Guy de Rothschild for the April 1988 issue of *Town & Country.* His recent trips to the Loire Valley have greatly expanded this edition's coverage of that beautiful realm. His most unforgettable French travel experience? A predawn hike through the streets of Montmartre to the steps of Sacre-Coeur where he watched the sun come up over Paris.

ABOUT THIS BOOK

Once you've learned to find your way around *Fodor's France 2005*'s pages, you'll be in great shape to find your way around your destination.

SELECTION

Our goal is to cover the best properties, sights, and activities in their category, as well as the most interesting communities to visit. We make a point of including local food-lovers' hot spots as well as neighborhood options, and we avoid all that's touristy unless it's really worth your time. It goes without saying that no property mentioned in the book has paid to be included.

RATINGS

Orange stars ★ denote sights and properties that our editors and writers consider Fodor's Choice—the very best in the area covered by the entire book. Black stars ★ highlight the sights and properties we deem Highly Recommended, the don't-miss sights within any region. Use the index to find complete descriptions. In cities, sights pinpointed with numbered map bullets ❶ in the margins tend to be more important than those without bullets.

SPECIAL SPOTS

Pleasures & Pastimes focuses on types of experiences that reveal the spirit of the destination. Watch for Off the Beaten Path sights. Some are out of the way, some are quirky, and all are worth your while. If the munchies hit while you're exploring, look for Need a Break? suggestions.

TIME IT RIGHT

Wondering when to go? Check On the Calendar up front and chapters' Timing sections for weather and crowd overviews and best days and times to visit.

SEE IT ALL

Use Fodor's exclusive Great Itineraries as a model for your trip. (For a good overview of the entire destination, follow those that begin the book, or mix regional itineraries from several chapters.) In cities, Good Walks guide you to important sights in each neighborhood; ▶ indicates the starting points of walks and itineraries in the text and on the map.

BUDGET WELL

Hotel and restaurant price categories from ¢ to $$$$ are defined in the opening pages of each chapter—expect to find a balanced selection for every budget, from amazing bargains to luxurious blowouts. For attractions, we always give standard adult admission fees; reductions are usually available for children, students, and senior citizens.

BASIC INFO

Smart Travel Tips lists travel essentials for the entire area covered by the book; city- and region-specific basics end each chapter in the A to Z sections. To find the best way to get around, see the transportation section; see individual modes of travel ("By Car," "By Train") for details. We assume you'll check Web sites or call for particulars.

ON THE MAPS	Maps throughout the book show you what's where and help you find your way around. Black and orange numbered bullets ❶ ➊ in the text correlate to bullets on maps.
BACKGROUND	In general, we give background information within the chapters in the course of explaining sights as well as in CloseUp boxes and in Understanding France at the end of the book. To get in the mood, review the suggestions in Books & Movies. The glossary can be invaluable.
FIND IT FAST	Within the book, chapters are arranged in a roughly corkscrew direction spiraling out from Paris, the Ile-de-France, and the Loire Valley and encompassing all areas of France. Chapters are divided into small regions, within which towns are covered in logical geographical order; attractive routes and interesting places between towns are flagged as En Route. Heads at the top of each page help you find what you need within a chapter.
DON'T FORGET	Restaurants are open for lunch and dinner daily unless we state otherwise; we mention dress only when there's a specific requirement and reservations only when they're essential or not accepted—it's always best to book ahead. Unless we note otherwise, most hotels have private baths, phone, TVs, and air-conditioning and operate on the European Plan (a.k.a. EP, meaning without meals). We always list facilities but not whether you'll be charged extra to use them, so when pricing accommodations, find out what's included.
SYMBOLS	

Many Listings

- ★ Fodor's Choice
- ★ Highly recommended
- ⊠ Physical address
- ✛ Directions
- ⌖ Mailing address
- ☎ Telephone
- 🖷 Fax
- ⊕ On the Web
- ✉ E-mail
- 🎟 Admission fee
- ☉ Open/closed times
- ► Start of walk/itinerary
- Ⓜ Metro stations
- ▱ Credit cards

Outdoors

- 🏌 Golf
- ⛺ Camping

Hotels & Restaurants

- 🏨 Hotel
- 🛏 Number of rooms
- ⚭ Facilities
- ‖⊙‖ Meal plans
- ✕ Restaurant
- ⚅ Reservations
- 👔 Dress code
- ⚲ Smoking
- 🍷 BYOB
- ✕🏨 Hotel with restaurant that warrants a visit

Other

- ⚘ Family-friendly
- ⚐ Contact information
- ⇨ See also
- ⊠ Branch address
- ☞ Take note

France

La Manche
(English Channel)

ATLANTIC
OCEAN

Bay of Biscay

S P A I N

ANDORRA

Roscoff
Brest
Morlaix
St-Malo
St-Brieuc
BRITTANY
Quimper
Rennes
Lorient
Vannes
Nantes
PAYS-
DE-
LOIRE
Angers
Les Sables
d'Olonne
Niort
La Rochelle
Saintes
Royan
Angoulême
Bordeaux
Langon
AQUITAINE
Bayonne
Biarritz
Pau
Tarbes

Cherbourg
Le Havre
Caen
NORMANDY
Mont St-Michel
Chartres
Le Mans
Blois
Loire
Tours
VAL DE
LOIRE
Poitiers
POITOU–
CHARENTES
Limoges
LIMOUSIN
Périgueux
Brive-la-
Gaillarde
Dordogne
Cahors
Montauban
Toulouse
MIDI-
PYRÉNÉES
Carcassonne

Dieppe
Amien
PIC
Rouen
Seine
Chartres
Orlé
AU
Albi
LANG
ROUS.

0   50 mi
0   75 km

(1) Paris

Paris is one of the most written about, raved about, and spat upon cities in the entire world. Droves of people have come for hundreds of years looking to inject their lives with beauty, glamour, culture, scandal, and romance. They have sung about Paris, painted her, found themselves, lost their religion, and learned how to eat well and smoke too much. Gargoyles leering down from medieval walls, the smell of freshly baked croissants, the pulse of jazz through overcrowded streets, and that first sip of wine to start off the evening are all part of the Parisian obsession with the physical world. Fashionable 85-year-old matrons parade their freshly coiffed Pekingese pooches past boutique windows, spruced-up facades of medieval buildings, and artfully arranged *pâtisserie* (pastry shop) displays. All the while, tourists sweep through town, trying to see in a week what locals haven't seen in a lifetime. The **Eiffel Tower,** needless to say, gives you an overview; the **Louvre,** a good look at the art of the past (with a peek, too, at architecture's present and future). Light a candle at **Notre-Dame,** buy a dress you'll love forever, and eat an unforgettable meal anywhere at all. Open your eyes—there's something beautiful or amusing at every step. Dawdle around the **Latin Quarter,** climb up to **Montmartre** for a peek at **Sacré-Coeur,** spend a morning at the *marché aux puces* (flea market), discover elegant mansion-museums, explore time-machine streets like the **Cour du Commerce St-André,** and sail down the Seine on the **Bateaux Mouches.** *Oui,* Paris is a fête.

(2) Ile-de-France

Kings, clerics, paupers, and ordinary Parisians have long taken refuge from urban life in Ile-de-France, the green surround of Paris. Most have been content to spend a day in the country, which is lushly forested and islanded by meandering rivers, while others have left behind spectacular secular and religious monuments. Biggest and most ostentatious of the Ile's palaces, the **Château de Versailles** is pompous proof that French monarchs lost their heads long before Louis XVI and Marie-Antoinette, the last occupants, walked to the guillotine. Other palatial piles include **Fontainebleau, Vaux-le-Vicomte,** and Napoléon's **Malmaison.** All this worldly froth fades in the stained-glass luster of **Chartres Cathedral,** so sublime its soft limestone hulk has brought the faithful to their knees for centuries. Then skip over the centuries to discover Monet's **Giverny,** Van Gogh's **Auvers,** and Uncle Walt's **Disneyland Paris**—the latter especially if you've been wondering what Donald Duck sounds like speaking French. Today, many Parisians follow in the footsteps of the kings and queens (but wearing Reeboks instead of square-toed heels) and make the Ile's other dazzling sites their weekend retreats. These delights include the ancient régime grace of the park and château de **Rambouillet**—an 18th-century Neoclassical landmark; the gigantic château and park at **St-Germain-en-Laye,** which includes famed gardener Andre Le Nôtre's spectacular Grande Terrasse; the regal elegancies of the château de

Maisons-Laffitte, a masterpiece by architect François Mansart; the lovely medieval town of **Senlis**; and the picturesque forest of **Barbizon,** immortalized by dozens of 19th-century plein-air painters.

(3) The Loire Valley

Sometimes owned by England, and fought over for centuries, this stretch of the Loire southwest of Paris resounds today with the noise of contented tourists, music festivals, and son-et-lumière spectacles at its extraordinary châteaux. This is *la belle France* at its purest and most elegant—just wait until you hear the diamond-sheen of the French spoken hereabouts. Super-stylish château-hotels and lovely country auberges tempt the traveler at nearly every bend in the river. Staying in a château-hotel is a must (a surprising number of them are amazingly affordable). The roll-call of châteaux that are open to the public is legendary. At the **Château de Chenonceau,** Catherine de' Medici built a white pleasure palace to hover over the river Cher. At the **Château de Chambord** it's easy to imagine the days when King François I arrived with a retinue so large it took 12,000 horses to transport them. At magical **Château de Ussé,** Charles Perrault was inspired to write the fairy tale we know as "Sleeping Beauty." The most celebrated gardens are those at the **Château de Villandry,** whose vast Renaissance-style parterres and water terraces are best seen in early July during its Festival of 1,000 Lights. But the Val de Loire is far more than just châteaux. Gorgeous villages like **Saché** (Balzac's favorite) await. Historic manors, such as Leonardo da Vinci's own Clos-Luce in **Amboise,** enchant. **Fontevraud** allures as the largest medieval abbey in France, while storybook **Chinon** has block after block of houses built during the days of Joan of Arc, who went on to capture the city of **Orléans.** You'll find the poppy-covered hillsides and gentle climate throughout the entire region do wonders for your temperament. No wonder so many harried Parisians vacation at least one week a year in the Gallic Shangri-la known as the Val de Loire.

(4) Brittany

"Finistère," or "land's end," is what a part of Brittany is called, and the name suits the entire region. A long arm of rocky land stretching into the Atlantic, Brittany lives to the rhythm of tides and winds, with its own language and legends. The people are Bretons first, rather than French, Celtic rather than Latin, and proud of their difference. They are also proud of their land—with reason. Here you'll find time-defying monuments and customs in awe-inspiring landscapes, such as those at **Pont-Aven,** which once inspired Gauguin. The prehistoric standing stones of **Carnac** are a gateway to the gorgeous sandy peninsula of the **Côte Sauvage,** where birds and flowers abound. The craftspeople in **Quimper** carry on a centuries-old practice of hand-painting delicate-looking faïence wares. Tides bathe the foot of **St-Malo**'s impressive fortifications, still haunted by phantom pirates. A trip across the waters to the aptly named **Belle-Ile,** or "beautiful island," will take you to heaths of yellow broom, fine beaches, and quaint towns. Today **Nantes,** the working-class heart of the province, pumps the economy of the region and provides a daily swig of Breton life, while **Rennes,** the student-fueled mind, gives way to poets and painters, bringing a refreshing breeze to the region. Other sites include the elegant Belle Epoque resort of **Dinard** and the granite splendors of the Corniche Bretonne. Like them, Brittany is a rare gift from the sea.

(5) Normandy

Normandy is a land of fashionable resorts and austere abbeys, warriors and prolific painters, saints and sinners. At **Bayeux,** the town's famous tapestry provides a scene-by-scene look at the Norman invasion of England in 1066 and stars William the Conqueror. Not far away, **Mont-St-Michel** may be the sublimest sight in France, perching dramatically atop its rocky shoreline roost. In **Rouen,** famed for its cathedral immortalized by Monet in paint, medieval rue du Gros-Horloge leads to the spot where Joan of Arc was burned at the stake in 1431. Off to the west at **Omaha Beach,** vast expanses of windswept dunes pay quiet homage to the 10,000 Allied soldiers who lost their lives during 1944's D-Day. Elsewhere lovely seascapes and lush fields allure. Pretty **Honfleur** made Impressionists long to paint the sea and sky. **Étretat** invites a day of ambling along limestone **falaises** (cliffs). Chic **Deauville** and **Trouville** beckon you to stroll along their seafront boardwalks. Of course, indulge in the region's cuisine, ruled and inspired by local cream, butter, eggs, and apples, along with fine lamb sweetened by the salty grasses on which the animals graze. Heady apple brandy, or calvados, is often downed with a meal to make a *trou normand* (Norman hole)—room for more rich food.

(6) The North & Champagne

"Brother, come quickly, I'm drinking stars," exclaimed Dom Pérignon upon first sipping the bubbling beverage that he invented through luck and alchemy. The blind 17th-century monk put **Hautvillers** and an entire region on the world map; he also ensured that vineyards around **Épernay** and elsewhere in the vicinity produce some of the world's finest wine grapes. In towns like **Reims**—once important enough to host the coronation of French kings, with many an amiable monument and spectacular cathedral as proof of its stature—it's perfectly clear what adds extra sparkle to these parts. Besides fine food and drink, there's plenty in the north to capture your attention—the lively city of **Lille** (just an hour from Paris by TGV), the long stretches of empty sand along the Channel coast, and the haunting cemeteries that evoke crucial battles of World War I. The Channel Tunnel, like the traditional ferries, arrives at **Calais;** head inland to admire the palace of **Compiègne**, the picture-perfect storybook castle of **Pierrefonds**, and the awesome cathedrals of **Soissons, Amiens, Noyon, Laon,** and **Beauvais,** the tallest in France.

(7) Alsace-Lorraine

"Let them speak German," said Napoléon of the Alsatians, "as long as they think in French." The emperor would be pleased to know that after centuries of conquest and liberation, Alsace and its neighbor Lorraine are now resolutely and proudly French. Yet there are enough imports from beyond the Rhine to make the region fascinating. **Strasbourg,** capital of Alsace and the cosmopolitan home of the European Parliament, has sophisticated restaurants and fine museums as well as a lacy-spired cathedral, an old quarter known as La Petite France, beer gardens, and winstubs. **Nancy,** capital of Lorraine, adds another element to the region's cultural mix: much of the elegant, easygoing city was laid out with pomp and grandeur by Stanislas Leszczynski, dethroned king of Poland; it was also a center of Art Nouveau architecture in the late 19th century. **Metz** has a grand cathedral, **Domrémy-la-Pucelle** claims the birthplace house of Joan of Arc, and **Ribeauvillé** is famous for its half-timber Renaissance houses. For many, the high point hereabouts will be found in **Colmar**—Grünewald's incomparable 16th-century Issenheim Altarpiece. The **Route du Vin,** running through the green foothills of the **Vosges mountains,** leads to half-timber, impossibly picturesque wine villages such as **Riquewihr.**

(8) Burgundy

Farms, pastures, and fall foliage make Burgundy enticingly, romantically rural. But it's also evident that whether building, ruling, worshiping, dining, or drinking, Burgundians have never embraced life on anything less than a grand scale. From magnificent palaces like the one in the city of **Dijon** and châteaux like the one at **Tanlay,** dukes more powerful than kings once ruled vast tracts of Western Europe. They left behind mighty medieval cathedrals in **Sens** and **Auxerre,** and religious orders built the other Burgundian architectural masterpieces—the Romanesque basilica at **Vézelay** and even more impressive abbeys, such as the Abbaye de **Cluny,** the largest church in the world until the construction of St. Peter's in Rome. **Fontenay** has the best preserved of the famous Cistercian abbeys, **Autun** has some of the greatest Romanesque sculptures in the world in its church. Most likely to evoke a reverential hush, though, is a first sip of one of Burgundy's treasured wines. Follow the **Côte d'Or,** perhaps the world's most famous wine route, out of Dijon, a gastronomic hub and cultural center, and then visit the Marché aux Vins in the wine capital of **Beaune** (with its fabulous Rogier van der Weyden altarpiece). As you sample the bounty of the highly anticipated annual *vendange* (harvest) in such towns as **Clos de Vougeot** and **Nuits-St-Georges,** you'll be introduced to wines so fine that, as the novelist, playwright, and observer of French life Alexandre Dumas once counseled, they should only be drunk on bended knee.

9 Lyon & the Alps

If the very mention of **Lyon** teases the taste buds, give credit to this sophisticated city's chefs—masters who can render even a plate of fruit ethereal. Savor their creations, then enjoy the city's visual delights—Lyon's covered passageways, known as *traboules,* lead to treasure-filled museums and a first-class opera house. Near at hand, seek out more *sportif* amusements: a sail from canal-lined, bridge-bedecked **Annecy** across its breezy and gorgeous lake, perhaps, or a gambol through meadows near **Chamonix,** a resort with a reputation for winter pleasures overshadowed only by its Alpine peaks. Great dining can also be had elsewhere, such as at Pic in **Valence** and Marc Veyrat's Ferme de Mon Père in chic **Megève,** nestled under the shadow of Mont Blanc. Discover the **wine villages of the Beaujolais** and the **Dombes lakes,** then venture down the Rhône to **Vienne** for Roman ruins and Renaissance facades. Pass through **Grenoble** with its fine museums and "Stendhal Itinerary" en route to the Alps.

10 The Massif Central

"Early to bed, early to rise" is the rule of thumb in this craggy, rural heartland at the center of France. You'll want to rise early to venture into the spectacular gorges or tackle the slopes of the highest of the region's 80 dormant volcanoes, the **Puy-de-Dôme.** Early risers in **Bourges,** a medieval city gloriously bypassed by time, have a special reward in store—the sight of the brilliantly hued stained-glass windows of the 13th-century Cathédrale St-Étienne achieving their fullest luster in the morning light. This is also the gateway city to the Loire Valley approached from the south. In the real heart of central France is the famous **Parc des Volcans,** here even the churches are constructed from polychrome lava. Other must-dos in the Massif include the museums and cathedral in **Clermont-Ferrand,** and wonderful medieval towns and villages like **Salers, Ste-Foy,** and sky-kissing **Rocamadour.**

11 Provence

Even the cattle and flamingos wallowing in the salty coastal marshes of the **Camargue** enjoy the sun-drenched good life that Provence provides so generously. In this smiling landscape and in soft-hue, elegant cities, where life still proceeds at an old-fashioned pace, you'll find no end of pleasures. Elegant **Aix-en-Provence** has museums, fountains, and the beautiful Cours Mirabeau boulevard. **Arles** and **Avignon** have bewitched Roman legionnaires, popes, and Vincent van Gogh. The tarnished, exotic, and newly chic port of **Marseille** continues to intrigue sailors and travelers with its hint of mystery. And dusty **Nîmes** headlines the Pont du Gard aqueduct and the beautiful Maison Carrée temple. But the region works its charms most potently in rural places, aided in no small part by cypress trees and vineyards, warm breezes scented with wild rosemary and thyme, and by a cooling glass of pastis. And let's not forget the heavenly lavender fields at the foot of Mont Ventoux or Provence's ocher-color villages, few more enticing than pretty **St-Rémy-de-Provence**, where sunlight really does dapple lanes of plane trees and where you don't have to look hard to find the bounty for a simple and fragrant feast. Other delights include the medieval village of **Aigues-Mortes**, the magnificent Romanesque abbey of **Montmajour**, the craggy towns of **Les-Baux-de-Provence** (home to the famed L'Oustau de la Baumanière hotel) and **Le Barroux**, and the scenic hill-town splendors of **Roussillon** and **Gordes**. Another treat is getting to know the native *Provençaux*—refreshingly friendly and laid-back, these people have sun-worn skin and a song in their voices. You'll get to know them hiking the white-cliffed calanques or exploring the rich landscape of the Route des Vignobles (Vineyard Route) through the region.

12 The Côte d'Azur

Invisible celebrities, pebbly beaches, backed-up traffic, hordes of sunburned bathers—why do people come? Because the medieval hilltop villages (**Mougins and Èze**, to name two), the fields of fragrant flowers that supply the Grasse perfume factories, the wonderful museums, and the lovely, limpid light are still as magnetic as ever. Stylish boutiques, splendid food, exciting nightlife, and spectacular views of crystal bays and cliff-side villas don't hurt either. Great art is also to be had—in the Musée Renoir in **Cagnes-sur-Mer**, the collection at the Musée National Picasso in **Vallauris**, **St-Paul-de-Vence**'s extraordinary Fondation Maeght—filled with Calders and Mirós—or Matisse's sublime Chapelle du Rosaire in **Vence**. For other sorts of aesthetic splendor, explore the lively, cobbled streets of **Nice**'s *Vieille Ville* (Old Town), the pretty, pastel colors of **St-Tropez**, or the millionaire mansions of **Villefrance-sur-Mer** or **St-Jean-Cap-Ferrat**, where you can experience more a true flutter of glamour. If only once in your lifetime you want to sip champagne from a slipper or slink up to a roulette table and go for broke, **Monte Carlo** and **Antibes** are the places to do so. Or you may simply want to enjoy the sun here, yours for the basking on the beach at stylish **Cannes** or in such enchanted seaside retreats as **Beaulieu**.

13 Corsica

For centuries great powers have fought over this strategically placed piece of Mediterranean real estate, leaving behind both architectural and cultural relics that set this stunning island (about 160 km [100 mi] southeast of Monaco) apart from the rest of France. In **Piana** and other ancient stone villages, news from across the sea still seems far removed—delightfully so. Corsica's capital, **Ajaccio**, hometown of the greatest empire builder of them all, Napoléon Bonaparte, is now a port for launching pleasure craft, not naval fleets. Today's spoils are granite peaks, pine forests, and crystalline waters—those around **Bonifacio**, where Ulysses was besieged, are especially inviting. Explore the mountains along the **Scala di Santa Regina**; see **Corte**'s citadel; hear folk songs in **Pigna**; and splurge at the Grand Hôtel de Cala Rossa in the walled town of **Porto-Vecchio.**

⑭ The Midi-Pyrénées & the Languedoc-Roussillon
In the vast stretches of southwest France, the strong sun makes fields of flowers glow and renders the brick buildings of Toulouse-Lautrec's native **Albi** and lively, cosmopolitan, Spanish-flavored **Toulouse** a rosy pink. It reflects on the walled, storybook town of **Carcassonne** and hilltop **Cordes** (so safely high it's known as Cordes-sur-Ciel or "Cordes in the Sky"), medieval villages with long histories of defending the region. It brightens the cloisters at **Moissac** and **St-Guilhem-le-Désert**, and beckons you to climb the Pyrénées' peaks. Along the scenic way, you'll be sure to build up your appetite for the trout, foie gras, and cassoulet, three of the region's many culinary specialties. Forging onward, you'll discover relaxing spa towns and wonderful views enliven the Pyrénées' twisting roads on the way from the rolling plain known as the Roussillon to **Ceret,** heart of the gorgeous "open-air museum" known as the Côte Vermeille (or Vermilion Coast). And when you see picturesque **Collioure**'s stunning Mediterranean setting you'll know why artists such as Matisse and Derain were so inspired.

⑮ The Basque Country, Gascony & Hautes-Pyrénées
At its southwesternmost corner, France eases with grace and dignity toward Spain, separated from it in many ways only by the Pyrénées. Basque country, south from **Bayonne** to the border with Spain, along the coast and in the Pyrénées, is a world of its own. Come here to discover the ancient and mysterious Basque culture, and dine on the incomparable cuisine. Napoléon III and his Spanish wife, Empress Eugénie, put the resort towns of **Eugénie-les-Bains** and **Biarritz** on the map. **Ainhoa, Ste-Engrâce,** and many other towns and villages have a distinctly Basque look and temperament. To the east are Béarn and its capital, the elegant city of **Pau.** The Hautes Pyrénées, the most central and the highest part of the range, hold, among other treasures, two of the region's most famous natural phenomena, the **Cirque de Gavarnie** and the **Brèche de Roland.** The peaks of the Pyrénées are breathtaking, and are spectacular for hiking. When you come back down, the incomparable local cuisine and the wine produced on the vineyard-clad lower slopes taste all the better.

(16) Bordeaux, Dordogne & Poitou-Charentes

Since prehistoric times, this hinterland near the Atlantic coast has had its appeal, as is apparent when you see the cave paintings at the **Grotte de Lascaux** or the storybook villages of the **Dordogne** region, now one of the hottest destinations in all Europe. In the Middle Ages the French and British fought over the area, leaving behind many castles and cathedrals. The continued allure of the rural landscape lies in the opportunity for pleasurable idleness. Float along the waters of Green Venice, as the **Marais Poitevin** near Coulon is known, or explore the fabled vineyards around **Cognac** and **Bordeaux**, perhaps ambling through an estate that rolls right up to the walls of **St-Émilion**, the loveliest of many villages producing wines that are sure to add a memorable note to any day. Come in May to Bordeaux, the regional capital, for the music festival, or any time to sip splendid wines while you indulge in oysters, truffles, foie gras, and caviar. Life is beautiful, *non?*

The Good Life
8 to 11 Days

Great châteaux, fine porcelain, superb wine, brandy, truffles, and foie gras sum up France for many. Beginning in château country, head south and west, through Cognac country into wine country around Bordeaux. Then lose yourself in the Dordogne, a landscape of rolling hills peppered with medieval villages, fortresses, and prehistoric caves.

LOIRE VALLEY CHÂTEAUX

3 or 4 days. Base yourself at the crossroads of Blois, starting with its multi-era château. Then head for the huge château in Chambord. Amboise's château echoes with history, and the neighboring manor, Clos Lucé, was Leonardo da Vinci's final home—or instead of this "town" château, head west to the tiny village of Rigny-Ussé for the "Sleeping Beauty" castle of Ussé. Heading southeast, finish up at Chenonceau—the most magical one of all—then return to the transportation hub city of Tours. ⇨ *The Loire Valley* in *Chapter 3*

COGNAC COUNTRY

1 to 2 days. Cognac's very air is saturated with evaporations of its heady product, enough to grow mushrooms on its black stone walls. Hennessy and Martell give tasting tours. In neighboring Jarnac you can visit Hine and Courvoisier—and François Mitterrand's grave. ⇨ *Charentes* in *Chapter 16*

BORDEAUX WINE COUNTRY

2 days. Pay homage to the great names of Médoc, north of the city of Bordeaux, though the hallowed villages of Margaux, St-Julien, Pauillac, and St-Estèphe aren't much to look at. East of Bordeaux, via the prettier Pomerol vineyards, the village of St-Emilion is everything you'd want a wine

town to be, with ramparts and medieval streets. ⇨ *Bordeaux* in *Chapter 16*

DORDOGNE & PÉRIGORD

2 or 3 days. Follow the famous Dordogne River east to the half-timber market town of Bergerac. Wind through the green, wooded countryside into the region where humans' earliest ancestors left their mark, in the caves in Les Eyzies-de-Tayac and the famous Grotte de Lascaux. Be sure to sample the region's culinary specialties: truffles, foie gras, and preserved duck. Then travel south to the stunning and sky-high village of Rocamadour. ⇨ *Dordogne and Poitou-Charentes* in *Chapter 16*

By Public Transportation

It's easy to get to Blois and Chenonceaux by rail, but you'll need to take a bus to visit other Loire châteaux. Forays farther into Bordeaux country and the Dordogne are difficult by train, involving complex and frequent changes (Limoges is a big railway hub). Further exploration requires a rental car or sometimes sketchy bus routes.

MAP KEY

The Good Life

France from North to South

France from North to South
6 or 9 Days

So, you want to taste France, gaze at its beauty, and inhale its special joie de vivre—all in a one-week to 10-day trip. Let's assume at least that you've seen Paris, and you're ready to venture into the countryside. Here are some itineraries to help you plan your trip. Or create your own route using the suggested itineraries in each chapter. First, zoom from Paris to the heart of historic Burgundy, its rolling green hills traced with hedgerows and etched with vineyards. From here, plunge into the arid beauty of Provence and toward the spectacular coastline of the Côte d'Azur.

BURGUNDY WINE COUNTRY

2 to 3 days. Base yourself in the market town of Beaune and visit its famous Hospices and surrounding vineyards. Make a day trip to the ancient hill town of Vézelay, with its incomparable basilica, stopping in Autun to explore Roman ruins and its celebrated Romanesque cathedral. For more vineyards, follow the Côte d'Or from Beaune to Dijon. Or make a beeline to Dijon, with its charming Vieille Ville and fine museums. From here it's a two-hour drive to Lyon, where you can feast on this city's famous earthy cuisine. Another three hours' push takes you deep into the heart of Provence.
⇨ *Northwest Burgundy and Wine Country* in *Chapter 8* and *Lyon* in *Chapter 9*

ARLES & PROVENCE

2 to 3 days. Arles is the atmospheric, sun-drenched southern town that inspired van Gogh and Gauguin. Make a day trip into grand old Avignon, home to the 14th-century rebel popes, to view their imposing palace. And make a pilgrimage to the Pont du Gard, the famous triple-tiered Roman aqueduct west of Avignon. From here two hours' drive will bring you to the glittering Côte d'Azur.
⇨ *Arles, Avignon, and Pont du Gard* in *Chapter 11*

ANTIBES & THE CÔTE D'AZUR

2 to 3 days. This historic and atmospheric port town is well positioned for day trips. First head west to glamorous Cannes. The next day head east into Nice, with its exotic Vieille Ville and its bounty of modern art. There are ports to explore in Villefranche and St-Jean-Cap-Ferrat, east of Nice. Allow time for a walk out onto the tropical paradise–peninsula of Cap d'Antibes, or for an hour or two lolling on the coast's famous pebble beaches.
⇨ *Cannes, Nice, Villefranche-sur-Mer, St-Jean-Cap-Ferrat,* and *Cap d'Antibes* in *Chapter 12*

By Public Transportation

The high-speed TGV travels from Paris through Burgundy and Lyon then zips through the south to Marseille. Train connections to Beaune from the TGV are easy; getting to Autun from Beaune takes up to two hours, with a change at Chagny. Vézelay can be reached by bus excursion from Dijon or Beaune. Rail connections are easy between Arles and Avignon; you'll need a bus from Avignon to get to the Pont du Gard. Antibes, Cannes, and Nice are easily reached by the scenic rail line, as are most of the resorts and ports along the coast. To squeeze the most daytime out of your trip, take a night train or a plane from Nice back to Paris.

A6

311 km

Vézelay   A6

Dijon

BURGUNDY

Autun   38 km
28 km   Beaune

A6

155 km

Lyon

RHÔNE
VALLEY   A7

200 km

A7

Orange   A9

Pont du Gard   58
Avignon

Nîmes   30 km

Arles   N113

PROVENCE

Nice
Monte Carlo
Antibes   St-Jean-Cap-Ferrat
Cannes   Villefranche
Cap
d'Antibes

A8   235 km

CÔTE D'AZUR

Marseille
Toulon

*M E D I T E R R A N E A N
S E A*

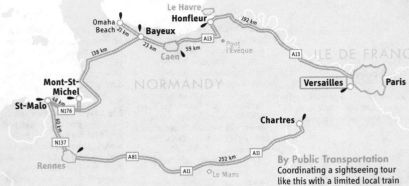

A Child's-Eye View
7 Days

Lead your children (and yourself) wide-eyed through the wonders of Europe, instilling some sense of France's cultural legacy. Make your way through Normandy and Brittany, with enough wonders and evocative topics, from William the Conqueror to D-Day, to inspire any child to put down his computer game and gawk. Short daily drives forestall mutiny, and you'll be in crêperie country, satisfying for casual meals.

VERSAILLES
1 day. Here's an opportunity for a history lesson: With its amazing Baroque extravagance, no other monument so succinctly illustrates what inspired the rage of the French Revolution. Louis XIV's eye-popping château of Versailles pleases the secret monarch in most of us. ⇨ *Southwest from Versailles to Chartres* in *Chapter 2*

HONFLEUR
1 day. From this picture-book seaport lined with skinny half-timber rowhouses and salt-dampened cobblestones, the first French explorers set sail for Canada in the 15th century. ⇨ *Upper Normandy* in *Chapter 5*

BAYEUX
2 days. William the Conqueror's extraordinary invasion of England in 1066 was launched from the shores of Normandy. The famous Bayeux tapestry, showcased in a state-of-the-art museum, spins the tale of the Battle of Hastings. From this home base you can introduce the family to the modern saga of 1944's Allied landings with a visit to the Museum of the Battle of Normandy, then make a pilgrimage to Omaha Beach. ⇨ *Lower Normandy* in *Chapter 5*

MONT-ST-MICHEL
1 day. Rising majestically in a shroud of sea mist over vacillating tidal flats, this mystical peninsula is Gothic in every sense of the word. Though its tiny, steep streets are crammed with visitors and tourist traps, no other sight gives you a stronger sense of the worldly power of medieval monasticism than Mont-St-Michel. ⇨ *Lower Normandy* in *Chapter 5*

ST-MALO
1 day. Even in winter you'll want to brave the Channel winds to beachcomb the shores of this onetime pirate base. In summer, of course, it's mobbed with sunseekers who stroll the old streets, restored to quaintness after World War II. ⇨ *Northeast Brittany and the Channel Coast* in *Chapter 4*

CHARTRES
1 day. Making a beeline on the autoroute back to Paris, stop in Chartres to view the loveliest of all of France's cathedrals. ⇨ *Southwest from Versailles to Chartres* in *Chapter 2*

By Public Transportation
Coordinating a sightseeing tour like this with a limited local train schedule isn't easy, and connections to Mont-St-Michel are especially complicated. Versailles, Chartres, and St-Malo are easy to reach, and Bayeux and Honfleur are doable, if inconvenient. But you'll spend a lot of vacation time waiting along train tracks.

Vintage Sampler
10 Days

Tasting wines in a cool, mossy cave redolent of cork gives vintages new dimensions, and you'll meet vintners of every stripe, from gnarled-fingered grandpas in blue aprons to ascoted gentry in cashmere. Along the way, taste the widely varied wines of eastern France, from Champagne to Alsace to the little-known whites of the Jura, then on to Burgundy, Beaujolais, and the Côtes du Rhône. Take it easy on the *dégustations* (tastings) if you're driving.

REIMS
2 days. At the heart of the green panorama of Champagne country lies Reims, with its magnificent cathedral. There's no shortage of downtown sources of bubbly, but you'll probably also want to venture south down the *Route du Vin* (Wine Road) to Épernay, home to Moët and Chandon. Just northwest is the old-fashioned village of Hautvillers, which claims Dom

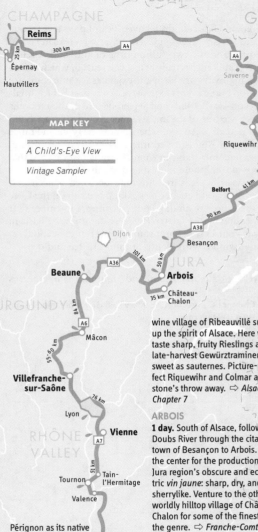

VILLEFRANCHE-SUR-SAÔNE
1 day. Head south along the west bank of the Saône. South of Mâcon, home of the last and lightest of the Burgundies, veer westward and follow the winding southbound Route du Vin through Beaujolais country. Cruise through the famous villages that produce this fruity, Gamay-based red. If you're traveling in autumn, look for the sharp young Beaujolais nouveau: the market-town of Villefranche-sur-Saône celebrates annually with carnival-like festivities. ⇨ *Wine Country* in *Chapter 8* and *Beaujolais and La Dombes* and *The Rhône Valley* in *Chapter 9*

CHÂTEAUNEUF-DU-PAPE
2 days. At Lyon you'll merge into the Rhône Valley. Just north of Valence cross the river at Tournon and pay homage to the vineyards at Tain-l'Hermitage. Press on south past Orange to the famous wine region and village of Châteauneuf-du-Pape, named for the Avignon popes who weekended here. You could continue from here into the region of the "sun wines" of the Côtes de Provence and Languedoc, but you might never get home. ⇨ *Lyon and the Rhône Valley* in *Chapter 9* and *Avignon and the Vaucluse* in *Chapter 11*

By Public Transportation
An abbreviated version of this journey can be worked out via train, leaving out the inaccessible vineyards and villages (which serve as lovely scenery through the train window). Start in Reims, move directly on to Colmar (substituting the atmospheric wine-market center for Ribeauvillé); take the train onward to Beaune. From Beaune the train makes stops along the northbound Côte d'Or route, but the best vineyards are hard to reach on foot. To get closer to the sources, look into package excursions or rent a car.

wine village of Ribeauvillé sums up the spirit of Alsace. Here you'll taste sharp, fruity Rieslings and late-harvest Gewürztraminers as sweet as sauternes. Picture-perfect Riquewihr and Colmar are a stone's throw away. ⇨ *Alsace* in *Chapter 7*

ARBOIS
1 day. South of Alsace, follow the Doubs River through the citadel town of Besançon to Arbois. This is the center for the production of the Jura region's obscure and eccentric *vin jaune*: sharp, dry, and sherrylike. Venture to the otherworldly hilltop village of Château-Chalon for some of the finest of the genre. ⇨ *Franche-Comté* in *Chapter 7*

BEAUNE
2 days. Press westward to Beaune, Burgundy's wine-market town (⇨ *France from North to South* itinerary, *above*). Wine shops abound in the center, but you'll want to cruise along the famous Côte d'Or. ⇨ *Wine Country* in *Chapter 8*

Pérignon as its native son. ⇨ *Champagne and the Ardennes* in *Chapter 6*

RIBEAUVILLÉ
2 days. Head east to Franco-Germanic Strasbourg and south down Alsace's Route du Vin. At the foot of forested Vosges foothills, the tiny

WHEN TO GO

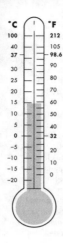

°C | °F
100 | 212
40 | 105
37 | 98.6
30 | 90
25 | 80
20 | 70
15 | 60
10 | 50
5 | 40
0 | 32
−5 | 20
−10 | 10
−15 |
−20 | 0

Keep in mind that French school children have *five* holidays a year: one week at the end of October, two weeks at Christmas, two weeks in February, two weeks in April, and the two full months of July and August. During these times travel in France is truly at its peak season, which means that prices are higher, highways are busier, the queues for museums are long, and transportation is at its most expensive. Your best bet for quality and calm is to travel off-season. June and September are the best months to be in France, as both are free of the midsummer crowds. Try to avoid the second half of July and all of August, when almost everyone in France goes on vacation. July and August in southern France can be stifling. Paris can be stuffy and uncomfortable in August. Many restaurants, theaters, and small shops close, but enough stay open these days to make a low-key, unhurried visit a pleasure. Anytime between March and November will offer you a good chance to soak up the sun on the Côte d'Azur. If Paris and the Loire are among your priorities, remember that the weather is unappealing before Easter. If you're dreaming of Paris in the springtime, May is your best bet, not rainy April. But the capital remains a joy during midwinter, with plenty of things to see and do.

Climate
What follows are average daily maximum and minimum temperatures for Paris and Nice.

🔲 Forecasts **Weather Channel Connection** ☎ 900/932-8437 95¢ per minute from a Touch-Tone phone ⊕ www.weather.com.

NICE

Jan.	55F	13C	May	68F	20C	Sept.	77F	25C
	39	4		55	13		61	16
Feb.	55F	13C	June	75F	24C	Oct.	70F	21C
	41	5		61	16		54	12
Mar.	59F	15C	July	81F	27C	Nov.	63F	17C
	45	7		64	18		46	8
Apr.	64F	18C	Aug.	81F	27C	Dec.	55F	13C
	46	8		64	18		41	5

PARIS

Jan.	43F	6C	May	68F	20C	Sept.	70F	21C
	34	1		49	10		53	12
Feb.	45F	7C	June	73F	23C	Oct.	60F	16C
	34	1		55	13		46	8
Mar.	54F	12C	July	76F	25C	Nov.	50F	10C
	39	4		58	15		40	5
Apr.	60F	16C	Aug.	75F	24C	Dec.	44F	7C
	43	6		58	15		36	2

France is a festival year-round, with special events taking place throughout the country. In Paris check the listings in *Pariscope* (which includes *Time Out,* a section with reviews in English of the week's main events), *L'Officiel des Spectacles,* or *Figaroscope* to find out what's going on around town. The *International Herald Tribune* also lists special events in its weekend edition but not in great detail. The most complete listing of festivals comes in a small pamphlet published by the French Government Tourist Office, or you can consult the official Web site of the *Maison De La France,* which has a list (more than 3,000 strong) of current festivals, seminars, antique fairs, concerts, and temporary exhibits at ⊕ www.franceguide.com.

WINTER

Dec.

On the 24th, a Christmas celebration known as the Shepherds' Festival, featuring midnight Mass and picturesque "living crèches," occurs in Les Baux, Provence. From the end of November through the New Year, Strasbourg mounts its famous Christmas Market, with echoes of German Gemütlichkeit. Christmas in Paris spells celebrations, especially for children, from late December to early January. A giant crèche and a full-size ice-skating rink are set up on the square in front of the Hôtel de Ville.

Jan.

The International Circus Festival, featuring top acts from around the world, and the Monte Carlo Motor Rally, one of the motoring world's most venerable races, take place in Monaco. Wine-producing villages throughout France celebrate St. Vincent's Day with festivities on January 22 in honor of their patron saint. The Tournament St-Vincent, a colorful Burgundy wine festival, takes place on the third weekend in Meursault in 2004; more than 200,000 wine lovers are expected to attend. Angoulême hosts the world's biggest and most popular comic-book festival, the Fête de la Bande Dessinée, from January 24 to January 27.

Feb.

The Carnival de Nice (⊕ www.nicecarnival.com) is a period of parades and revelry in the weeks leading up to Lent. Other cities and villages also have their own smaller versions. The Carnival de Dunkerque, on the weekend before Shrove Tuesday, is the most rambunctious street carnival in northern France. The Festival de Film Fantastique is the international horror film festival, which takes place in Gerardmer. The Fête du Citron (⊕ www.feteducitron.com) is held in the Riviera town of Menton, replete with fruit-filled floats and gardens.

SPRING

Mar.

The Salon de Mars, an art and antiques fair, and the Salon du Livre, France's biggest book festival, take place in Paris. La Foire à la Brocante et au Jambon is an important, high-quality antiques fair held every year in Chatou, a beautiful village outside Paris. Grenoble Jazz

Festival (⊕ www.jazzgrenoble.com) has been going strong for more than 30 years. In late March, the Open-House at the Médoc Vineyards (⊕ www.bordeaux-vineyards.com) is a rare chance to see some great château-vineyards not usually open to the general public.

Apr. The Monte Carlo Open Tennis Championships get under way at the Monte Carlo Country Club. At the end of April, Les Fêtes Musicales (⊕ www.biarritz.tm.fr) are held in Biarritz for the pleasure of all classical-music lovers.

May Complete with cathedral illuminations and religious processions, Les Fêtes Johanniques (⊕ www.ville-orleans.fr), in the first weekend in May, offers a commemoration of the liberation of Orléans from the English by the French troops led by Joan of Arc. The Cannes Film Festival (⊕ www.festival-cannes.fr) sees two weeks of star-studded events. Classical-music festivals get under way throughout the country. The Foire de Paris is a giant fair with food and agricultural products from all over France; it takes place at the Porte de Versailles in Paris. The prestige event of the Formula 1 car circuit is the Monaco Grand Prix (⊕ www.acm.mc) usually held around May 20th. At the end of the month are the French Open Tennis Championships (⊕ www. frenchopen.org) at Roland Garros Stadium, in Paris. Kicking off at the end of May is the extraordinary summer-long Festival des Jardins (⊕ www.chaumont-jardins.com), held in the gardens of the Loire Valley château of Chaumont-sur-Loire.

SUMMER

June From now until September you will find son-et-lumière (sound-and-light) shows—historical pageants featuring special lighting effects—at several châteaux (notably Amboise) and churches in the Loire Valley. Throughout France, there's dancing in the streets during the Fête de la Musique, a free live-music festival on June 21 that lasts all night. From mid-June through the end of August, Paris's Tuileries Gardens hosts a Fête des Tuileries (⊕ www.paris-touristoffice.com) in the shadow of the giant Ferris wheel. In mid-June look for the explosive fireworks festival, the Nuits de Feu (⊕ www.chantilly-tourisme.com), in the gardens of the great château at Chantilly. Strasbourg's Fête de la Musique features concerts in the Cathédrale Notre-Dame and various halls. This is a popular time for horse races: the Prix du Président de la République is run at the Hippodrome de Vincennes, the Grand Steeplechase de Paris is at the Auteuil Racecourse, and the Grand Prix de Paris is at Longchamp Racecourse. The 24 Heures du Mans (⊕ www. lemans.org), the famous 24-hour car race, is held in Le Mans. The Paris Air Show is a display of planes at Le Bourget Airport, near Paris. On the last weekend in June the Fête du Cinéma allows you to take in as many movies as you can for the price of a single ticket. In northern France, Joan of Arc is feted at Reims's Fêtes Johanniques (⊕ www. tourisme.fr/reims), complete with pageants, processions, and a medieval market, all usually held at the end of June.

July	The summer arts festival season gets into full swing, particularly in Provence. Avignon (🌐 www.festival-avignon.com) is one of the biggest celebrations of top-notch theater and avant-garde art, while Aix-en-Provence specializes in opera, Carpentras in religious music, Nice holds a big jazz festival, and Arles mounts a major photography festival. Northern France's spectacular Fête de Gayant (Festival of the Giant, in local patois) is held in Douai on the first Sunday after July 5. The wine hub of France, Bordeaux, hosts its Bordeaux Fête le Vin (🌐 www.bordeaux-tourisme.com) in early July, replete with expositions, tastings, parades, and fireworks. The Tour de France (🌐 www.letour.fr), the world's most famous bicycle race, dominates national attention for three weeks before crossing the finish line on the Champs-Élysées on the last Sunday of the month. Jazz à Juan (🌐 www.antibes-juanlespins.com) has topped the 40-year mark and this jazz festival is usually held in mid-July. The Festival de l'Art Lyrique brings more than 1 million music lovers to Aix-en-Province to hear music spanning several centuries. On Bastille Day (July 14) all of France commemorates the storming of the Bastille in 1789—the start of the French Revolution. Look out for fireworks, free concerts, and street festivities beginning the evening of July 13, with the Bal des Pompiers (Firemen's Ball) organized by local firemen. Head to the Place de la Bastille for the Grand Paris Ball. On July 14th, a military parade goes down the Champs-Élysées, with fireworks after sundown. From July 14th on through summer, Paris Quartiers d'Eté (🌐 www.quartierdete) hosts theater, dance, and concerts in many scenic neighborhood locales throughout Paris. Music aficionados head to Prades in southern France in late July for the famous Annual Pablo Casals Festival (🌐 www.festival-piano.com), held through August at many medieval sites.
Aug.	On Assumption (August 15) many towns, notably Chartres and Lisieux, hold religious festivals and processions dedicated to the Virgin Mary. On the first Sunday following August 15, the Festival de la Force Basque, in St-Palais, brings together participants from eight villages to compete in contests of strength. The most famous annual religious festival in Brittany is the *pardon* in Ste-Anne-la-Palud, near Quimper, on the last Sunday of August. If you want to drive yourself insane, you can always visit the International Mime Festival, held in early August, when the city of Perigueux, in Dordogne, is overtaken by those white-face Marcel Marceau wannabes. The Festival Interceltique (🌐 www.festival-interceltique.com) takes place in Lorient, Brittany, from August 2 to August 11, with a street fair commemorating contemporary expressions of Celtic art, music, and dance. In mid-August, Colmar hosts a big wine fair, the Foire aux Vins (🌐 www.colmar-expo.fr) that attracts hundreds of thousands of wine tasters.

FALL	
Sept.	The vendanges (grape harvests) begin, and festivals take place in the country's wine regions. The Grande Braderie turns Lille into one giant street fair on the month's first weekend. The Fête de Musique de Besançon et Franche-Comté consists of a series of chamber-music concerts in and around Besançon during the month. The Fête d'Automne, a major arts and film festival, opens in Paris and continues until December. France's biggest dance festival—the Biennale de la Danse (⊕ www.biennale-de-lyon.org)—kicks off in mid-September (to early October) in Lyon. The Rencontres Polyphoniques, in Calvi, is an excellent chance to hear authentic Corsican music. The Journée du Patrimoine, on the Sunday nearest September 21, opens the doors of many official and private buildings usually closed to the public. The American Film Festival, in Deauville, is one of the most important international events (second to Cannes) for American film. The Biennale des Antiquaires is held in the Carrousel du Louvre in Paris this month with more than 120 antiques dealers from Europe and the United States. The International Car Salon takes place in the Porte de Versailles from September 28 to October 13 with one of the most impressive car selections in the world (second only to Tokyo).
Oct.	The Prix de l'Arc de Triomphe, horse racing's most prestigious flat race, is held at the Longchamp Racecourse, in Paris, on the first Sunday of the month. A giant contemporary art exhibition called FIAC (⊕ www.fiac.reed-oip.fr) takes place in Paris early in the month. The weeklong Paris Indoor Open attracts the world's top tennis players at the end of the month.
Nov.	Les Trois Glorieuses, Burgundy's biggest wine festival, includes the year's most important wine auction and related merriment, which occurs in several Burgundy locations. The Festiventu, in Calvi (Corsica), is a celebration of wind-related activities ranging from windsurfing to woodwinds. Nationwide Armistice Day ceremonies on November 11 commemorate veterans of World Wars I and II; in Paris there's a military parade down the Champs-Élysées. On the third Thursday in November, France—especially Paris—celebrates the arrival of the Beaujolais Nouveau. The Salon des Caves Particulières is a giant wine fair held in Paris at the end of the month. November is also the Mois de la Photo, with open photography exhibits in most galleries throughout France.

PLEASURES & PASTIMES

Art   It is through the eyes of France's artists that many first get to know the country. No wonder people from across the globe come to find Gauguin's bobbing boats at Pont-Aven, Monet's bridge at Giverny, and the gaslit Moulin Rouge of Toulouse-Lautrec—not framed in gilt and hung in a museum but alive in all their three-dimensional glory. In Arles you can stand on the spot where van Gogh painted and compare his perspective to a placard with his finished work; in Paris you can climb into the garret-atelier where Delacroix created his epic canvases, or wander the redolent streets of Montmartre, once haunted by Renoir, Utrillo, and Modigliani. And, of course, the museums and châteaux hang heavy with masterworks, many of them bringing a telling local insight into *la civilization française*.

Cathedrals   Their extraordinary permanence, their everlasting relevance even in a secular world, and their transcending beauty make the Gothic and Romanesque cathedrals of France a lightning rod if you are in search of the essence of French culture. The product of a peculiarly Gallic mix of mysticism, exquisite taste, and high technology, France's cathedrals provide a thorough grounding in the history of architecture (some say there was nothing new in the art of building between France's Gothic arch and Frank Lloyd Wright's cantilevered slab). Each cathedral imparts its own monumental experience—knee-weakening grandeur, a mighty resonance that touches a chord of awe, and humility in the unbeliever. Even cynics will find satisfaction in the cathedrals' social history—the anonymity of the architects, the solidarity of the artisans, and the astonishing bravery of experiments in suspended stone.

Châteaux   From the humblest feudal ruin to the most delicate Renaissance spires to the grandest of Sun King spreads, the castles, manor houses, and châteaux of France evoke the history of Europe as no museum can. Standing on castellated ramparts overlooking undulating valleys, it's easy to slip into the role of a feudal lord scrambling to protect his patchwork of holdings from the centralized stronghold of kings and dukes. The lovely landscape takes on a strategic air and you find yourself role-playing thus, whether swanning aristocratically over Japanese bridges in the château park or curling a revolutionary lip at the splendid excesses of Versailles. These are, after all, the castles that inspired "Sleeping Beauty," "Beauty and the Beast," and "Snow White," and their fairy-tale magic—rich with history and Disney-free—still holds true.

Cities   Besides being home to the most sophisticated city in the world, France has more to offer than just Paris. Other French cities offer the best of Paris without the staggering crowds, noise, pollution, and traffic. Lille, Lyon, Dijon, Bordeaux, Rennes, Marseille, and Strasbourg all have strong regional identities (and cuisines), as well as historic *Vieilles Villes* (old towns), sidewalk cafés, vast farmers' markets, and fine old parks. As for the arts, France's ministry of culture ensures that even the country's farthest outreaches have top-notch orchestras, stellar operas, and excellent museums.

Dining

Few countries match France's reputation for good food or offer as many fine restaurants. Eating in France can be a memorable experience, from the simplest picnic lunch of baguette, Camembert, and local *jambon* (ham) *sur l'herbe* (on the grass) to the most magnificent haute cuisine in formal splendor. Don't feel guilty if you spend as much of your day in restaurants as in museums and cathedrals: dining is the heart and soul of French culture. Give yourself over to the leisurely meal; two hours for a three-course menu is par, and you may, after relaxing into the routine, feel pressed at less than three.

L'Esprit Sportif

Though the physically inclined would consider walking across Scotland or bicycling across Holland, they often misconstrue France as a sedentary site where one plods from museum to château to restaurant. But it's possible to have a more active approach: imagine pedaling past barges on the Saône River or along slender poplars on a *route départementale* (provincial road); hiking through the dramatic gorges in the Massif Central or over Alpine meadows in the Savoie; or sailing the historic ports of Honfleur or Cap d'Antibes. Experiencing this side of France will take you off the beaten path and into the countryside. As you bike along French country roads or along the extensive network of *Grands Randonnées* (Lengthy Trails) crisscrossing the country, you will have time to tune into the landscape—to study crumbling garden walls, smell the honeysuckle, and chat with a farmer in his *potager* (vegetable garden).

Shopping

Although it's somewhat disconcerting to see Gap stores gracing almost every major street corner in Paris and other urban areas in France, if you take the time to peruse smaller specialty shops, you can find rare original gifts—be it an antique brooch from the 1930s or a modern vase crafted from Parisian rooftop-tile zinc. It's true that the traditional gifts of silk scarves, perfume, and wine can often be purchased for less in the shopping mall back home, but you can make an interesting twist by purchasing a vintage Hermès scarf, or a unique perfume from an artisan perfumer. Bargaining is traditional in outdoor and flea markets, antiques stores, small jewelry shops, and art galleries, for example. If you're thinking of buying several items, or if you're simply in love with something a little bit too expensive, you've nothing to lose by cheerfully suggesting to the proprietor, "*Vous me faites un prix?*" ("How about a discount?"). The small business man will immediately size you up, and you'll have some good-natured fun.

FODOR'S CHOICE

The sights, restaurants, hotels, and other travel experiences listed below are our editors' top picks—the *crème de la crème* chosen from the lists of Fodor's Choices found on the opening pages of regional chapters in this book. They're the best of their type in the area covered by the book. In addition, the list incorporates many of the highly recommended restaurants and hotels our reviewers have come to treasure. In the destination chapters that follow, you will find all the details.

LODGING

$$$$ **L'Hôtel, Paris.** Few can resist the most seductive hotel in town or its many rooms—correction, 19th-century pipe dreams—created by superstar decorator Jacques Garcia.

$$$$ **Les Belles Rives, Juan-les-Pins, Côte d'Azur.** Roaring '20s millionaires loved this Neoclassic-Moderne landmark on the Riviera, now finding a whole new generation of fans.

$$$$ **Château d'Esclimont, Maintenon, Ile de France.** You'll feel like a de la Rochefoucauld overnighting at their former Ile de France seat.

$$$$ **Château Eza, Èze, Côte d'Azur.** Vertiginously perched on the edge of a cliff 3,000 feet above the crouching tiger of St-Jean-Cap-Ferrat, this former residence of Prince William of Sweden is one of the most dramatic hotels on the entire Mediterranean coast.

$$$$ **La Colombe d'Or, St-Paul-de-Vence, Côte d'Azur.** Yes, those are works by Klee, Picasso, Braque, and Utrillo hanging on the wall. Some will quibble that the food has gone downhill, but there is only one Colombe d'Or.

$$$$ **La Cour des Loges, Lyon.** Any hotel that can please both Carl XVI Gustaf of Sweden and the Rolling Stones has to be something special—and this is. Spectacularly renovated around a glassed-in Renaissance courtyard, this former Jesuit convent is now an extravaganza of glowing fireplaces, Baroque credenzas, and antique Lyon silks.

$$$$ **L'Oustau de la Baumanière, Baux-de-Provence.** This veritable museum of Provençal tradition—names like Churchill, Picasso, and Elizabeth Taylor litter the guest book—has been given a nouvelle face-lift (as one bite of lobster cooked in Châteauneuf-du-Pape served up in the famed restaurant will prove).

$$$$ **Le Pavillon de la Reine, Paris.** King Henri IV wouldn't blink an eye upon pulling up to the entryway here—it hasn't changed a bit since it was built on gorgeous place des Vosges in the 17th century.

$$$$ **Les Prés d'Eugénie, Eugénie-les-Bains, Basque Coast.** Founded in the late 1970s by the father of nouvelle cooking, Michel Guérard, this landmark of Basque luxe is still going strong—needless to say, the breakfast here nearly outdoes dinner at most other places.

$$$$ Le Relais Christine, Paris. In St-Germain-des-Pres—the loveliest quartier for tourists in Paris—this luxurious hotel occupies 16th-century abbey cloisters and oozes romantic ambience.

$$$$ Villa Gallici, Aix-en-Provence, Provence. A Provençal dream, shaded by ancient cypress and plane trees and landscaped with jars of laurel and topiary boxwood, this luxurious hilltop garden hotel is right out of the pages of *Maison Française.*

$$$–$$$$ Château de la Bordaisière, Montlouis, Loire Valley. Not one but two princes de Broglie welcome you to this unforgettably idyllic and sumptuous neo-Renaissance retreat—if you want to taste *la vie de château* at its best, head here.

$$$–$$$$ Château des Reaux, Bourgueil, Loire Valley. With its red-and-white chessboard facade, swans in the moat, and the Comtesse de Bouillé in residence, this 17th-century castle is relentlessly, exquisitely picturesque.

$$$–$$$$ Nord-Pinus, Arles, Provence. The adventurer and mail-order genius J. Peterman would feel right at home in this quintessentially Mediterranean hotel on place du Forum; Hemingway certainly did.

$$$–$$$$ Le Vieux Logis, Les Eyzies-de-Tayac, Bordeaux. The Dordogne is known for its storybook houses—this one is particularly alluring, complete with a dining room that may be the prettiest this side of Paris.

$$$–$$$ Le Bon Laboureur, Chenonceau, Loire Valley. That connoisseur of France, Henry James, loved this place—and so will you, especially as it is now renovated, adorably stylish, and has a fabulous chef to boot.

$$–$$$ Château de Colliers, near Chambord, Loire Valley. Keep Chambord and give us this tiny treasure, since it distills all the charm of *la vieille France* into one enchanting package, replete with Rococo salons and a spectacular river terrace.

$$–$$$ Giverny B & Bs, Giverny, Ile-de-France. Just down the road from Monet's famous house and garden you'll find town residences now transformed into alluring B&Bs.

$$–$$$ Caron de Beaumarchais, Paris. The theme of this intimate hotel in the heart of the Marais is the work of Caron de Beaumarchais, who wrote *The Marriage of Figaro* in 1778. Rooms reflect the taste of 18th-century French nobility.

$$–$$$ La Maison Rose, Eugénie-les-Bains, Basque Coast. Michel and Christine Guérard's newest hotel is set in a super-stylish 18th-century farmhouse adorned with old paintings and Pays Basque handicrafts, and comes complete with a spa.

$–$$ **Les Templiers, Collioure.** No visit is complete without a stay at this warm and welcoming hotel filled with more than 2,500 original works of art.

$–$$ **Demeure de la Vignole.** With its enchanting Renaissance-era *château troglodytique,* an elegant 15th-century manor house, and a medieval cave dwelling, this place seems right out of a Perrault fairy-tale.

BUDGET LODGING

$ **Chopin, Paris.** At the end of the historic passage Jouffroy shopping arcade, this 1846 spot has a super location.

$ **Esméralda, Paris.** This quirky, cozy, eccentric place was once any *Vogue* editor's best-kept secret. The lobby is right out of a Flaubert novel.

¢–$ **Le Clos d'Ussé, Rigny-Ussé, Loire Valley.** The whole Duchemin family runs this adorable inn set at the foot of the Chateau d'Ussé—the "Sleeping Beauty" castle—with wife Muriel in charge of this *délicieuse* restaurant.

¢–$ **L'Hostellerie du Vieux Cordes, Cordes.** This old house around a wisteria-draped courtyard is an enchanting place to stay and eat in the opulent crimson dining rooms.

RESTAURANTS

$$$$ **Alain Ducasse, Paris.** Ducasse's reputation is so hot you can practically smell it burning in the kitchen—but some still consider him France's finest chef. And Monaco's, too—his Le Louis XV is the top table there.

$$$$ **L'Auberge de l'Ill, near Sélestat, Alsace.** The showstoppers here—*le homard Prince Wladimir* (lobster with shallots braised in champagne and crème fraîche) or the Germanic-Alsatian truffled *baeckoffa* baker's-oven casserole—are sublime.

$$$$ **Boyer, Reims, Champagne.** Chef Gérard Boyer's innovative cuisine and his extensive wine list draw sophisticated diners (and lodgers) to this opulent restaurant in a 19th-century château.

$$$$ **La Ferme de Mon Père, Megève, Alps.** The talk of foodies everywhere, Marc Veyrat creates peasant-luxe dishes that showcase the best of Haute Savoie cuisine and his Farmhouse Chic decor is an eye-knocker.

$$$$ **La Maison de Marc Veyrat, Annecy, Alps.** Go!

$$$$ **Le Grand Véfour, Paris.** Back when Napoléon dined here, this was the most beautiful restaurant in Paris. Guess what? It still is.

$$$$ **Jean Bardet, Tours, Loire Valley.** In a posh Directoire-style mansion, Bardet—king of Tourangeau chefs—quotes philosophers, harvests his heirloom garden, and creates spectacular dishes.

$$$$ **Les Loges, Lyon.** With dazzlers like roast wild boar with rosemary raisins and poached red pears on his bill of fare, it's little wonder their creator, Nicolas Le Bec, was named Gault-Millau Chef of the Year 2002. Modern art and a medieval hearth make for a stunning setting.

$$$$ **Le Relais de Bracieux, near Chambord, LoireValley.** Chef Bernard Robin shows how it's done with exquisite nouvelle delights, fantasy touches (a miniature mushroom forest on your plate), and an alluring beige salon.

$$$$ **Restaurant de Bacon, Cap d'Antibes, Côte d'Azur.** *The* place for seafood on the Côte d'Azur.

$$$$ **Taillevent, Paris.** A remarkable harmonic alignment of staff, decor, and kitchen make this grande dame—now stunningly revivified—tops in Paris.

$$$$ **La Terrasse at Juana, Juan-les-Pins, Côte d'Azur.** Chef Christian Morisset, with his delicious and exquisitely presented seafood dishes, is on his way to becoming one of France's top chefs.

$$$$ **Troisgros, Roanne, Massif Central.** Book weekends two months in advance at this culinary shrine to celebrate the mainstays of haute cuisine and enjoy the most famous dessert trolley in France.

$$$–$$$$ **Lapérouse, Paris.** Dine with the ghosts of Émile Zola, George Sand, and Victor Hugo—all former regulars—here in this boiserie-graced town house, then fast forward to the future with one bite of lobster flavored with Szechuan pepper and lemon vinaigrette.

$$$–$$$$ **Pic, Valence, Rhône Valley.** Crown jewel of a hotel that is famed as a Drôme-region Xanadu, this restaurant is stronger than ever—don't miss the bass with caviar (served either "avec modération" or "passionnément").

$$$ **La Régalade, Paris.** Yves Camdeborde is the chef of the moment these days in Paris, staking his claim as the leading priest who marries bistro and nouvelle cookery. You'll forget about the dull room once you taste his soup of lentils and puréed chestnuts poured over a mound of foie gras.

$$–$$$ **L'Auberge du XIIᵉ Siècle, Saché, Loire Valley.** Balzac's favorite restaurant, this auberge has a stunningly ambitious menu and a once-upon-a-timefied, wood-beamed dining room.

$$–$$$ **Les Feuillants, Céret, Languedoc-Roussillon.** The cuisine at this restaurant, one of the best in the area, is yet another manifestation of the town's superb artistic endowment.

$$ **La Corde, Toulouse, Midi-Pyrénées.** It's worth finding this doyen of Toulouse restaurants, hidden in a small 15th-century tower in the courtyard of a 16th-century mansion.

$–$$ **L'Ami Fritz, Obernai, Alsace.** With its fireplace, stone-and-beam cellar, and *toile-de-jouy* accents, this place is as succulent as the local specialties and wine served up by the chef.

BUDGET RESTAURANTS

$ **L'Ardoise, Paris.** This minuscule storefront, painted white and decorated with enlargements of old sepia postcards of Paris, is the very model of contemporary bistros making waves in Paris. Who can resist the crab flan in a creamy parsley emulsion?

$ **Chez Yvonne, Strasbourg, Alsace.** This chic yet cozy *winstub* (inn) serves classic Alsatian fare and local wines to hip locals and heads of state.

$ **Les Pipos, Paris.** Bursting with laughter and chatter, this place has everything you could ask for in a Latin Quarter bistro.

¢–$ **Café 203, Lyon.** Fresh, original, fast, inexpensive, delicious—this and a sister bistro, right by the Opéra, are perfect for a quick pre- or post-theater meal.

CHÂTEAUX WE LOVE

Chambord, Loire Valley. Your mouth will drop open at the size and splendor of the "Versailles of the 16th-century," topped with a skyline of dozens and dozens of dazzling white-and-black chimneys and steeples.

Chenonceau, Loire Valley. The most beautiful of them all, with arched galleries spanning the Cher, this magical abode owes its gardens to Queen Catherine de' Medici.

Marqueyssac, Vézac, Dordogne. In the storybook realm of the Dordogne, this domaine has a park as elegant as that of Versailles.

Pierrefonds, Champagne. This huge château, begun in the 12th century, was restored in the 1860s by the fairy-tale imagination of Viollet-le-Duc and the money of Napoléon III.

Ussé, Loire Valley. Motorists often come to a screeching halt when they spot this many-turreted wonder on the straight-arrow road that brings them directly to the door. Perrault, the 17th-century author of "Sleeping Beauty," was inspired to write the tale when he stayed here.

Vaux-le-Vicomte, Ile-de-France. Louis XIV was so jealous on seeing Nicolas Fouquet's new château that he jailed him on the spot and started work on Versailles to show who was boss. The sumptuous gardens and interior remain unchanged.

Versailles, Ile-de-France. The world's grandest palace has it all: paintings, murals, gold-leaf furniture, the Hall of Mirrors, a landscaped park, a faux village, a giant canal, artful fountains, and shady glades.

CHURCHES & MONASTERIES

Basilique, Vézelay. This great pilgrim church, part Romanesque, part Gothic, gazes serenely over the rolling hills of Burgundy. Marvel at the miniature figures on the carved capitals in the nave.

Cathédrale, Chartres. Take your binoculars to survey the world's finest collection of medieval stained-glass windows. The mighty, asymmetric spires dominate the flat grainlands for miles around.

Cathédrale Notre-Dame, Laon. The hilltop setting—known as the Crowned Mountain—is the most spectacular of any French cathedral, bristling with elegant, openwork towers.

Cathédrale Notre-Dame, Paris. Quasimodo's home and the grandest triumph of the Gothic style in central France, this has a spectacular candlelit interior and those stunning gargoyles.

Mont-St-Michel, Normandy. From its silhouette against the horizon to the abbey and gardens at the peak of the rock, you'll never forget this awe-inspiring sight.

Sainte-Chapelle, Paris. A gigantic magic-lantern of medieval stained-glass, this chapel actually is a tiny holy reliquary writ large.

TOWNS & VILLAGES

Ancien Cloître Quarter, Paris. Did you know that there's a medieval "village" hidden in the heart of Paris? Find it nestling under the towers of Notre-Dame.

Chinon, Loire Valley. With its *Vieille Ville* lined with blocks and blocks of half-timbered houses, this is a time-machine back to the Renaissance days of Rabelais.

Collioure, Languedoc-Roussillon. Seaside jewel of the Vermillion Coast, this was a favored home-away-from-home for Matisse. Don't miss its "Chemin de Fauvisme."

Èze, Côte d'Azur. Closer to the sky than the sea, this eagle's village is literally breathtaking.

Roussillon, Provence. The quintessential hilltop cluster, this town is famous for its ochre-red houses and roofs.

Saché, Loire Valley. Beloved of Balzac, this tiny village has a perfect château, auberge, church, and just down the road is the Pont des Ruan, a dream-sequence of a bridge and watermill.

St-Cirq-Lapopie, Dordogne. Artisans, writers, and travelers in search of the perfectly picturesque make this a journey's-end.

St-Remy-de-Provence, Provence. Even Van Gogh was happy here.

WHERE ART COMES FIRST

Fondation Maeght, St-Paul-de-Vence. A small gem of a museum of modern art, it blends its stunning holdings with stylish presentation.

L'Isle-sur-la-Sorgue, Provence. Heaven-on-earth for antiques shoppers.

Louvre, Paris. No matter how many times you've visited, be sure to come again; I. M. Pei's pyramid and the newly opened exhibit rooms are stunning.

Musée Condé, Chantilly. The château houses a remarkable collection of illuminated manuscripts, tapestries, furniture, paintings, Fouquet miniatures, and stained glass.

Musée Nissim de Camondo, Paris. All the luxe of 18th-century France is found here under one roof.

Palais de la Berbie, Albi. The world's greatest collection of works by Henri de Toulouse-Lautrec is housed in this former fortress with gardens designed by André Le Nôtre.

SMART TRAVEL TIPS

Half the fun of traveling is looking forward to your trip—but when you look forward, don't just daydream. There are plans to be made, things to learn about, serious work to be done. After all, finding out about your destination before you leave home means you won't squander time organizing everyday minutiae once you've arrived. You'll be more streetwise when you hit the ground as well, better prepared to explore the aspects of France that drew you here in the first place. The organizations in this section can provide information to supplement this guide; contact them for up-to-the-minute details, and consult the A to Z sections that end each chapter for facts on the various topics as they relate to France's many regions. Happy landings!

ADDRESSES

Addresses in France are fairly straightforward: there are the number and the street name. However, you may see an address with a number plus "bis," for instance, 20 bis rue Vavin: This indicates the next entrance or door down from 20 rue Vavin. In small towns a street number may not be given, as the site will be the dominant (or only) building on the block or square. In rural areas, however, a site may list only a route name, a number near the site, or sometimes just the name of the small village in which it is located.

In Paris a site's location in one of the city's 20 arrondissements is noted by its mailing code or, simply, the last one or two digits of that code (for example, Paris 75010 or 10^e, both of which indicate that the address is in the 10th arrondissement; Paris 75005 or 5e, for another example, indicates the address is in the 5th arrondissement). Because of its large size, Paris's 16th arrondissement has two numbers assigned to it: 75016 and 75116. Note that in France you enter a building on the *rez-de-chaussée* (RC or 0), as the ground floor is known, and you have to go up one floor to reach the first floor, or *premier étage*.

AIR TRAVEL

As one of the premier destinations in the world, Paris is serviced by many international carriers and a surprising number of U.S.–based airlines. **Air France** is the French flag carrier and offers numerous flights (often several per day) between Paris's Charles de Gaulle airport and New York City's JFK airport; Newark, New Jersey; Washington, D.C.'s Reagan airport; as well as the cities of Miami; Chicago; Houston; San Francisco; Los Angeles; Toronto; Montréal; and Mexico City. American-based carriers are usually less expensive but offer, on the whole, fewer nonstop flights. **Delta Airlines** is a popular U.S.–France carrier; departures for Paris leave Atlanta, Cincinnati, and New York City's JFK, although Delta's regional flights link airports throughout the southeastern United States and the Midwest with its main international hub in Atlanta. Travelers in the northeast and southwest of the United States often use **Continental Airlines,** whose nonstop Paris flights generally depart from Newark and Houston; in peak season they often offer daily departures. Another popular carrier is **United Airlines,** with nonstop flights to Paris from Chicago, Washington, D.C., and San Francisco. **American Airlines** also offers daily nonstop flights to Paris's Orly Airport from numerous cities, including New York City's JFK, Boston, Miami, Chicago, and Dallas–Fort Worth. **Northwest** offers a daily departure to Paris from its hub in Detroit; connections from Seattle, Minneapolis, and numerous other airports link up to Detroit. In Canada, Air France and **Air Canada** are the leading choices for departures from Toronto and Montréal; in peak season, departures are often daily. From London, Air France, **British Airways, British Midland,** and **Air U.K.** are the leading carriers, with up to 15 flights daily in peak season. In addition, direct routes link Manchester, Edinburgh, and Southampton with Paris. **Ryan Air,** an Irish charter company that connects Paris, London, and Dublin, is getting raves for its cheaper-than-cheap flights. In order to assure their incredible prices they do not use the main airports that service all the major airlines but the smaller airports located a little bit farther out. In France, Ryan Air flights land at Le Bourget airport, about 45 minutes from Paris; they have a bus waiting to take you into the city for the minimal charge of €15, making the entire trip quite a bargain. A number of charter companies are cashing in on the booming inter-European travel market, offering short flights with no-frills service and exceptional fares. **Buzz** connects London with Paris, Brest, Marseille, and Toulouse among others. **Easyjet** has flights from Paris to Liverpool, London, Nice, and Geneva. It also connects Nice to Amsterdam for less than €30 one way. **Virgin Express** links Nice to Brussels at attractive prices. Options are more limited for travelers to Paris from Australia and New Zealand, who usually wind up taking British Airways and **Qantas** flights to London, then connections to Paris.

There's also the quick and efficient option of using train transport via the Eurostar Express through the Channel Tunnel (⇨ The Channel Tunnel *and* Train Travel to and from Paris).

BOOKING

When you book, look for nonstop flights and remember that "direct" flights stop at least once. Try to avoid connecting flights, which require a change of plane. Two airlines may operate a connecting flight jointly, so ask whether your airline operates every segment of the trip; you may find that the carrier you prefer flies you only part of the way. To find more booking tips and to check prices and make online flight reservations, log on to www.fodors.com.

CARRIERS

▶ Major Airlines **Air Canada** ☎ 800/776-3000 in U.S. and Canada, 08-25-88-08-81 in France. **Air France** ☎ 800/237-2747 in U.S., 08-20-82-08-20 in France ⊕ www.airfrance.com. **American Airlines** ☎ 800/433-7300 in U.S., 08-10-87-28-72 in France ⊕ www.aa.com. **British Airways** ☎ 800/247-9297 in U.S., 0345/222111 in U.K., 08-25-82-54-00 in France ⊕ www.britishairways.com. **Continental** ☎ 800/231-0856 in U.S., 01-42-99-09-09 in France ⊕ www.continental.com. **Delta** ☎ 800/241-4141 in U.S., 01-47-68-92-92 in France ⊕ www.delta.com.

Northwest ☎ 800/225-2525 in U.S., 08-10-55-65-56 in France ⊕ www.klm.com. **Qantas** ☎ 800/227-4500 in U.S., 08-20-82-05-00 in France ⊕ www.qantas.com. **United** ☎ 800/538-2929 in U.S., 08-10-72-72-72 in France ⊕ www.unitedairlines.com. **US Airways** ☎ 800/428-4322 in U.S., 08-10-63-22-22 in France ⊕ www.usairways.com.

🔁 U.K. to France **Air France** ☎ 020/8742-6600 in U.K., 08-20-82-08-20 in France ⊕ www.airfrance.com. **Air U.K.** ☎ 0345/666-777 in U.K., 01-44-56-18-08 in France. **British Airways** ☎ 0345/222-111 in U.K., 08-02-80-29-02 in France ⊕ www.britishairways.com. **British Midland** ☎ 020/8754-7321, 0345/554-554 in U.K., 01-53-43-25-27 in France ⊕ www.flybmi.com. **Buzz** ☎ 01-55-17-42-42 ⊕ www.buzzaway.com. **Easyjet** ☎ 0990/292-929 in U.K., 04-93-21-48-33 in France ⊕ www.easyjet.com runs scheduled services to Nice from Luton. **Ryan Air** ☎ 0990/292-929 in U.K., 08-92-55-56-66 in France ⊕ www.ryanair.com. **Virgin Express** ☎ 08-00-52-85-28 ⊕ www.virginexpress.com.

🔁 Within France **Air France** (⇨ *Carriers, above*).

CHECK-IN & BOARDING

Always **find out your carrier's check-in policy.** Plan to arrive at the airport about two hours before your scheduled departure time for domestic flights and 2½ to 3 hours before international flights. You may need to arrive earlier if you're flying from one of the busier airports or during peak air-traffic times. **Always allot at least an extra hour for the commute (via car, bus, or train) to the main Paris airports** when departing from the capital, since horrendous traffic tie-ups within Charles de Gaulle or Orly airport can seriously add to the time it takes to get to the ticket counter. Once you arrive at the airport from Paris, you'll often need to take the inter-airport bus to shuttle you from one terminal to another, and if there's traffic congestion, a serious case of nail-biting can result.

To avoid delays at airport-security checkpoints, try not to wear any metal. Jewelry, belt and other buckles, steel-toe shoes, barrettes, and underwire bras are among the items that can set off detectors.

Assuming that not everyone with a ticket will show up, airlines routinely overbook planes. When everyone does, airlines ask for volunteers to give up their seats. In return, these volunteers usually get a several-hundred-dollar flight voucher, which can be used toward the purchase of another ticket, and are rebooked on the next flight out. If there are not enough volunteers, the airline must choose who will be denied boarding. The first to get bumped are passengers who checked in late and those flying on discounted tickets, so get to the gate and check in as early as possible, especially during peak periods.

Always **bring a government-issued photo I.D.** to the airport; even when it's not required, a passport is best.

CUTTING COSTS

The least expensive airfares to France are priced for round-trip travel and must usually be purchased in advance. Airlines generally allow you to change your return date for a fee; most low-fare tickets, however, are nonrefundable. It's smart to call a number of airlines and check the Internet; when you are quoted a good price, book it on the spot—the same fare may not be available the next day, or even the next hour. Always check different routings and look into using alternate airports. Also, price off-peak flights, which may be significantly less expensive than others. Travel agents, especially low-fare specialists (⇨ Discounts & Deals), are helpful.

Consolidators are another good source. They buy tickets for scheduled flights at reduced rates from the airlines, then sell them at prices that beat the best fare available directly from the airlines. (Many also offer reduced car-rental and hotel rates.) Sometimes you can even get your money back if you need to return the ticket. Carefully read the fine print detailing penalties for changes and cancellations, purchase the ticket with a credit card, and confirm your consolidator reservation with the airline.

When you fly as a courier, you trade your checked-luggage space for a ticket deeply subsidized by a courier service. There are restrictions on when you can book and how long you can stay. Some courier companies list with membership organizations, such as the Air Courier Association and the International Association of Air Travel Couriers; these require you to become a member before you can book a flight.

🛪 Consolidators **AirlineConsolidator.com** ☎ 888/468-5385 ⊕ www.airlineconsolidator.com, for international tickets. **Best Fares** ☎ 800/880-1234 or 800/576-8255 ⊕ www.bestfares.com; $59.90 annual membership. **Cheap Tickets** ☎ 800/377-1000 or 800/652-4327 ⊕ www.cheaptickets.com. **Expedia** ☎ 800/397-3342 or 404/728-8787 ⊕ www.expedia.com. **Hotwire** ☎ 866/468-9473 or 920/330-9418 ⊕ www.hotwire.com. **Now Voyager Travel** ✉ 45 W. 21st St., Suite 5A New York, NY 10010 ☎ 212/459-1616 🖷 212/243-2711 ⊕ www.nowvoyagertravel.com. **Onetravel.com** ⊕ www.onetravel.com. **Orbitz** ☎ 888/656-4546 ⊕ www.orbitz.com. **Priceline.com** ⊕ www.priceline.com. **Travelocity** ☎ 888/709-5983, 877/282-2925 in Canada, 0870/876-3876 in U.K. ⊕ www.travelocity.com.

🛪 Courier Resources **Air Courier Association/Cheaptrips.com** ☎ 800/280-5973 or 800/282-1202 ⊕ www.aircourier.org or www.cheaptrips.com; $34 annual membership. **International Association of Air Travel Couriers** ☎ 308/632-3273 ⊕ www.courier.org; $45 annual membership.

🛪 Discount Passes **Air France** (⇨ Carriers, *above*).

ENJOYING THE FLIGHT

State your seat preference when purchasing your ticket, and then repeat it when you confirm and when you check in. For more legroom, you can request one of the few emergency-aisle seats at check-in, if you're capable of moving obstacles comparable in weight to an airplane exit door (usually between 35 pounds and 60 pounds)—a Federal Aviation Administration requirement of passengers in these seats. Seats behind a bulkhead also offer more legroom, but they don't have underseat storage. Don't sit in the row in front of the emergency aisle or in front of a bulkhead, where seats may not recline.

Ask the airline whether a snack or meal is served on the flight. If you have dietary concerns, request special meals when booking. These can be vegetarian, low-cholesterol, or kosher, for example. It's a good idea to pack some healthful snacks and a small (plastic) bottle of water in your carry-on bag. On long flights, try to maintain a normal routine, to help fight jet lag. At night, get some sleep. By day, eat light meals, drink water (not alcohol), and **move around the cabin** to stretch your legs. For additional jet-lag tips consult *Fodor's FYI: Travel Fit & Healthy* (available at bookstores everywhere).

Smoking policies vary from carrier to carrier. Many airlines prohibit smoking on all of their flights; others allow smoking only on certain routes or certain departures. Ask your carrier about its policy.

FLYING TIMES

Flying time to Paris is 7½ hours from New York, 9 hours from Chicago, 11 hours from Los Angeles, and 1 hour from London. Flying time between Paris and Nice is one hour.

HOW TO COMPLAIN

If your baggage goes astray or your flight goes awry, complain right away. Most carriers require that you **file a claim immediately.** The Aviation Consumer Protection Division of the Department of Transportation publishes *Fly-Rights,* which discusses airlines and consumer issues and is available online. You can also find articles and information on mytravelrights.com, the Web site of the nonprofit Consumer Travel Rights Center.

🛪 Airline Complaints **Aviation Consumer Protection Division** ✉ U.S. Department of Transportation, Office of Aviation Enforcement and Proceedings, C-75, Room 4107, 400 7th St. SW, Washington, DC 20590 ☎ 202/366-2220 ⊕ airconsumer.ost.dot.gov. **Federal Aviation Administration Consumer Hotline** ✉ For inquiries: FAA, 800 Independence Ave. SW, Washington, DC 20591 ☎ 800/322-7873 ⊕ www.faa.gov.

RECONFIRMING

Check the status of your flight before you leave for the airport. You can do this on your carrier's Web site, by linking to a flight-status checker (many Web booking services offer these), or by calling your carrier or travel agent. Always confirm international flights at least 72 hours ahead of the scheduled departure time.

AIRPORTS

There are two major gateway airports to France, both just outside the capital: Orly, 16 km (10 mi) south of Paris, and Charles de Gaulle—also known as Roissy—26 km (16 mi) northeast of the city. Orly has two terminals: Orly Ouest (domestic flights) and Orly Sud (international, regular, and charter flights). Roissy has three terminals: Aérogare 1 (foreign flights), Aérogare 2 (Air France flights), and Aérogare T-9 (charter flights). Terminal information should be noted on your ticket. The two Orly terminals are connected with a free shuttle service, called the *navette*. At Roissy there's a TGV station (from Terminal 2), where you can connect to trains going all over the country. Many airlines have less frequent flights to Lyon, Nice, Marseille, Bordeaux, and Toulouse. Or you can fly to Paris and get a connecting flight to other destinations in France.

⁊ Airport Information **Charles de Gaulle/Roissy** ☎ 01-48-62-22-80 in English ⊕ www.adp.fr. Orly ☎ 01-49-75-15-15 ⊕ www.adp.fr.

AIRPORT TRANSFERS: PARIS

Charles de Gaulle/Roissy: From Charles de Gaulle airport, **the least expensive way to get into Paris is on the RER-B line,** the suburban express train, which runs from 5 AM to 11:30 PM daily. Each terminal has an exit where the free RER shuttle bus (a white-and-yellow bus with the letters ADP in gray) will pass every 7–15 minutes to take you on the short ride to the nearby RER station: Terminal 2A and Terminal 2C (Exit 8), Terminal 2B and Terminal 2D (Exit 6), Terminal 2E (Exit 2.06), Terminal 2F (Exit 2.08). Trains to central Paris (Les Halles, St-Michel, Luxembourg) depart every 15 minutes. The fare (including métro connection) is €8, and journey time is about 30 minutes.

The **Air France shuttle service** is a comfortable option to get to and from the city— you don't need to have flown the carrier to use this. Line 2 goes from the airport to Paris's Charles de Gaulle Étoile and Porte Maillot from 5:45 AM to 11 PM. It leaves every 15 minutes and costs €11, which you can pay on board. Passengers arriving in Terminal 1 need to take Exit 34; Terminals 2A and 2C, Exit 5; Terminals 2B and 2D, Exit 6; Terminals 2E and 2F, Exit 3. Line 4 goes to Montparnasse and the Gare de Lyon from 7 AM to 9 PM. Buses run every

30 minutes and cost €13. Passengers arriving in Terminal 1 need to look for Exit 34, Terminals 2A and 2C need to take either exit 2 or 2C, Terminals 2B and 2D, Exit 2 or 2B, and Terminals 2E and 2F, Exit 3.

Another option is to take **Roissybus,** operated by the Paris Transit Authority, which runs between Charles de Gaulle and the Opéra every 20 minutes from 6 AM to 11 PM; the cost is €8.20. Note that you have to hail the bus you want—it will not stop automatically—and that rush-hour traffic can make for a slow ride.

Taxis are your least desirable mode of transportation into the city. If you are traveling at peak tourist times, you may have to stand in a very long line with a lot of other disgruntled European travelers (most of whom smoke). Journey times, and as a consequence, prices, are therefore unpredictable. At best, the journey takes 30 minutes but it can take as long as one hour.

Airport Connection is the name of just one of a number of van services that serve both Charles de Gaulle and Orly airports. Prices are set so there are no surprises even if traffic is a snail-paced nightmare. To make a reservation, call or fax your flight details at least one week in advance to the shuttle company and an air-conditioned van with a bilingual chauffeur will be waiting for you upon your arrival. Note these shuttle vans pick up and drop off other passengers.

Orly: From Orly Airport **the most economical way to get into Paris is to take the RER-C or Orlyrail line;** catch the free shuttle bus from the terminal to the train station. Trains to Paris leave every 15 minutes. Passengers arriving in either the South or West Terminal need to use Exit G. The fare is €6, and journey time is about 35 minutes. Another option is to **take the monorail service, Orlyval,** which runs between the Antony RER-B station and Orly Airport daily every four to eight minutes from 6 AM to 11 PM. Passengers arriving in the South Terminal should look for Exit K, those arriving in the West terminal, Exit W. The fare to downtown Paris is €10.

You can also **take an Air France bus** from Orly to Les Invalides on the Left Bank and

Montparnasse; these run every 15 minutes from 6 AM to 11:30 PM (you need not have flown on Air France to use this service). The fare is €8, and journey time is between 30 and 45 minutes, depending on traffic. Those of you arriving in Orly South need to look for Exit K; those arriving in Orly West, Exit D. The Paris Transit Authority's **Orlybus is yet another option**; buses leave every 15 minutes for the Denfert-Rochereau métro station; the cost is €6. You can economize using **Jet Bus,** which shuttles you from the airport to Line 7, métro Villejuif Louis Arragan station for under €5. It operates daily from 6 AM to 10 PM; those arriving in Orly South look for Exit H, Quai 2; those arriving via Orly West need to find Exit C.

⚡ Taxis & Shuttles Air France Bus ☎ 08-92-35-08-20 recorded information in English ⊕ www.cars-airfrance.com. **Airport Connection** ☎ 01-44-18-36-02 ⛿ 01-44-18-36-02 ⊕ www.airport-connection.com. **Paris Airports Service** ☎ 01-55-98-10-80 ⛿ 01-55-98-10-89 ⊕ www.parisairportservice.com.

DUTY-FREE SHOPPING

Duty-free shopping at French airports is no longer available for those traveling *within* the boundaries of the European Community. You can purchase whatever you want at airport stores, of course, but only travelers *leaving* European territory will benefit from the duty-free prices.

BARGE & YACHT TRAVEL

Canal and river trips are popular in France, particularly along the picturesque waterways in Brittany, Burgundy, and the Midi. For further information, contact a travel agent; ask for a "Tourisme Fluvial" brochure at any French tourist office; or get in touch with one of the companies that organize barge trips. It's also possible to rent a barge or crewed sailboat to travel around the coast of France, particularly along the Côte d'Azur.

⚡ Domestic Barge Companies Bourgogne Voies Navigables ✉ 1 quai de la République, 89000 Auxerre ☎ 03-86-72-92-10 ⊕ www.tourisme-yonne.com. **Connoisseur Cruisers** ✉ Halye Nautique, Ile Sauzay, 70100 Gray ☎ 03-84-64-95-20 ⊕ www.connoisseur.fr.

⚡ International Barge Companies Abercrombie & Kent ✉ 1520 Kensington Rd., Oak Brook, IL 60521 ☎ 630/954-2944 or 800/323-7308 ⛿ 630/954-3324. **Étoile de Champagne** ✉ 88 Broad St., Boston, MA 02110 ☎ 800/280-1492 ⛿ 617/426-4689. **European Waterways** ✉ 140 E. 56th St., Suite 4C, New York, NY 10022 ☎ 212/688-9489 or 800/217-4447 ⛿ 212/688-3778 or 800/296-4554. **French Country Waterways** ⌖ Box 2195, Duxbury, MA 02331 ☎ 781/934-2454 or 800/222-1236 ⛿ 781/934-9048. **KD River Cruises of Europe** ✉ 2500 Westchester Ave., Purchase, NY 10577 ☎ 914/696-3600 or 800/346-6525 ⛿ 914/696-0833 ⊕ www.rivercruises.com. **Kemwel's Premier Selections** ✉ 106 Calvert St., Harrison, NY 10528 ☎ 914/835-5555 or 800/234-4000 ⛿ 914/835-5449.

BEACHES

Along the miles of French coast you'll find broad-brimmed hats, parasols, and opaque sunglasses—their modesty and discretion charmingly contradictory in view of (and we mean full view of) the frankly bare flesh that bobbles up and down the same miles of seashore. And not just the famous *seins nus* (topless women), but the bellies of gastronome *pépés* (grandfathers) as well. Naked children crouch over sand châteaux, their unself-consciousness a reflection of their elders' own. For the French the summer beach holiday is a sacred ritual, a counterbalance to the winter ski trip.

To avoid the July and August stampede, **go in June or September.** Ironic as it may be, France's most famous coastline has the country's worst beaches: sand along the Côte d'Azur is in shorter supply than pebbles. By far the finest French beaches are those facing north (toward the Channel) and west (toward the Atlantic). Many are so vast that you can spread out even at the most popular resorts (like Biarritz, Royan, Dinard, or Le Touquet). Brittany's beaches are the most picturesque, though the water can be chilly, even in summer.

If you're planning to devote a lot of time to beaches and haven't tackled the French coast before, get to **know the distinction between private and public.** France's waterfront is carved up into private frontage, often roped off and advertised by color-coordinated awnings, parasols, and mattresses. These private beaches frequently offer full restaurant and bar service and rent mattresses, umbrellas, and lounge chairs by the day and half-day. Dressing rooms and showers are included; some even rent private cabanas. Prices can run from €10 a day to €20 or more. Interspersed between these commercial beaches is plenty of public space.

BIKE TRAVEL

The French are great bicycling enthusiasts—witness the Tour de France—and there are many good bicycling routes in France. For about €8 a day (€12 for a 10-speed touring bike) you can **rent a bike from one of 30 train stations throughout the country**; you need to show your passport and leave a deposit of €155 or a Visa or MasterCard. Mountain bikes (known as VTT, or vélos touts-terrains) can be rented from many shops, as well as from some train stations. Tourist offices supply details on the more than 200 local shops that rent bikes, and the SNCF has a brochure entitled the "Guide du Train et du Vélo," available at any train station. Bikes may be taken as accompanied luggage from any station in France; most trains in rural areas do not charge for bikes (but inquire at the SNCF ticket agencies about which ones do). Free bike space works on a first-come, first-served basis; you must take your bike to the designated compartment for loading yourself, so plan accordingly.

For information about good bike routes, contact the Fédération Française de Cyclotourisme. The yellow Michelin maps (1:200,000 scale) are fine for roads, but for off-road bicycling you may want to get one of the Institut Géographique National's detailed, large-scale maps. Try their blue series (1:25,000) or orange series (1:50,000).

As many travelers have learned, one of the most satisfying ways to explore the French countryside is by bike. Happily, there are many bike-tour companies that truly deliver on their gorgeous *itinéraires* year after year—two of the most successful

are VBT and Butterfield & Robinson. To get a peek into one such bike tour, see the CloseUp Box on biking in the Loire Valley in Chapter 3.

🚲 Bike Maps **Institut Géographique National (IGN)** ✉ 107 rue La Boétie, 75008 Paris 📠 01-42-56-06-68 ⊕ www.ign.fr.
🚲 Bike Rentals **SNCF** (⇨ Train Travel, *below*).
🚲 Bike Routes **Fédération Française du Cyclisme** ✉ 5 rue de Rome, 93561 Rosny-sous-Bois 📠 01-49-35-69-00 ⊕ www.ffc.fr.
🚲 Bike Tours **Backroads** ✉ 801 Cedar St., Berkeley, CA 94710-1800 📠 510/527-1555 or 800/462-2848 🖷 510/527-1444 ⊕ www.backroads.com. **Butterfield & Robinson** ✉ 70 Bond St., Toronto, Ontario M5B 1X3 📠 416/864-1354 or 800/678-1147 🖷 416/864-0541 ⊕ www.butterfield.com. **Chateaux Bike Tours** 🖅 Box 5706, Denver, CO 80217 📠 303/393-6910 or 800/678-2453 🖷 303/393-6801. **Discover France Biking** ✉ 1603 E. Gardenia Ave., Phoenix, AZ 85020 📠 800/960-2221 🖷 602/944-5934 ⊕ www.discoverfrance.com. **Europeds** ✉ 761 Lighthouse Ave., Monterey, CA 93940 📠 800/321-9552 🖷 831/655-4501. **RMF** ✉ 1342 Birchcliff Dr., Oakville, Ontario L6M2A4 📠 905/825-0796 or 800/530-5957 🖷 905/825-4177. **VBT (Vermont Biking Tours)** 🖅 Box 711, Bristol, Vermont 05443 📠 800/245-3868 ⊕ www.vbt.com.

BIKES IN FLIGHT

Most airlines accommodate bikes as luggage, provided they are dismantled and boxed; check with individual airlines about packing requirements. Some airlines sell bike boxes, which are often free at bike shops, for about $20 (bike bags can be considerably more expensive). International travelers often can substitute a bike for a piece of checked luggage at no charge; otherwise, the cost is about $100. Most U.S. and Canadian airlines charge $40–$80 each way.

BOAT & FERRY TRAVEL

BETWEEN THE U.K. & FRANCE

A number of ferry and hovercraft routes link the United Kingdom and France. Driving distances from the French ports to Paris are as follows: from Calais, 290 km (180 mi); from Boulogne, 243 km (151 mi); from Dieppe, 193 km (120 mi); from Dunkerque, 257 km (160 mi). The fastest routes to Paris from each port are via the

N43, A26, and A1 from Calais and the Channel Tunnel; via the N1 from Boulogne; via the N15 from Le Havre; via the D915 and N1 from Dieppe; and via the A25 and A1 from Dunkerque.

🚢 Dover–Calais **Hoverspeed** ⊠ International Hoverport, Marine Parade, Dover CT17 9TG 📠 08702/408070 ⊕ www.hoverspeed.fr operates up to 15 crossings a day by a one-hour fast ferry or a two-hour ferry. **P&O European Ferries** ⊠ Channel House, Channel View Rd., Dover, Kent CT17 9TJ 📠 08702/424999 ⊕ www.poportsmouth.com has up to 3 sailings a day; the crossing takes about 75 minutes. **Seafrance** ⊠ 23 rue Louis le Grand, Paris, France 75002 📠 08-25-04-40-45 ⊕ www.seafrance.net operates up to 15 sailings a day; the crossing takes about 90 minutes.

🚢 Folkestone–Boulogne **Hoverspeed** (⇨ Dover–Calais) is the sole operator on this route, with 10 35-minute crossings a day.

🚢 Newhaven–Dieppe **Seafrance** (⇨ Dover–Calais) has as many as four sailings a day, and the crossing takes four hours.

🚢 Portsmouth–Cherbourg **P&O European Ferries** has up to three sailings a day, and the crossing takes 2¾ hours.

🚢 Portsmouth–Le Havre **P&O European Ferries** (⇨ Dover–Calais) has up to three sailings a day, and the crossing takes 5½ hours by day, 7½ by night.

FARES & SCHEDULES

Note that sample fares are difficult to assess because of the number of variables involved, including destination, season, and number of people traveling. Sample fare (high season): Dover–Calais, round-trip (within five days), €125–€185 for up to five adults plus car (this price doubles if the visit exceeds five days). Schedules and tickets are available at any travel agency throughout France or via the Internet.

BUSINESS HOURS

BANKS & OFFICES

Generally, **banks are open weekdays from 9:00 to 5:00** (note that the Banque de France closes at 3:30), and some banks are also open on Saturday. Most take a one-hour, or even a 90-minute, lunch break, except for those in Paris. In general, government offices and businesses are open 9–5. For information about post office hours, *see* Mail & Shipping, *below*.

GAS STATIONS

Gas stations in cities and towns are generally open 8–8, Monday–Saturday, with the exception of those stations located in the major *portes*, or entryways into each city, which are open 24 hours a day, seven days a week, as are those along the highways.

MUSEUMS & SIGHTS

The usual opening times for museums and other sights are from 9:30 to 5 or 6. Many close for lunch (noon–2). Most are closed one day a week (generally Monday or Tuesday) and on national holidays: **check museum hours before you go.** National museums are free to the public the first Sunday of every month.

PHARMACIES

Pharmacies are generally open Monday–Saturday 8:30–8; on the door of every pharmacy is a list of those closest that are open Sunday or 24 hours.

SHOPS

Large stores in big towns are open from 9 or 9:30 until 7 or 8. Smaller shops often open earlier (8 AM) and close later (8 PM) but take a lengthy lunch break (1–4), particularly in the south of France. Corner groceries frequently stay open until around 10 PM. Some Paris stores are beginning to stay open on Sunday, although it's still uncommon.

BUS TRAVEL

France's excellent train service means that long-distance buses are rare; **regional buses are found mainly where train service is spotty.** Excursions and bus tours are organized by the SNCF and other tour companies. Ask for a brochure at any major travel agent or contact the French Tourism Office (⇨ Visitor Information). Bus tours from the United Kingdom generally depart from London for Paris, the Atlantic Coast, Chamonix and the Alps, Grenoble, Lyon, and the Côte d'Azur. Note that **reservations are necessary on most long-distance buses.**

There's no central bus network servicing France because train service here is considered the best in the world, and if you are traveling off-season or have researched the best rates, train service can be just as economical as bus travel, if not more so. What a bus service saves in money, it often loses in both comfort and time. The largest international operator is Eurolines France, whose main terminal is in the Parisian suburb of Bagnolet (a half-hour métro ride from central Paris, at the end of métro Line 3). Eurolines runs many international routes to over 37 European destinations, including a route from London to Paris, usually departing at 8:30 AM, arriving at 5:30 PM; noon, arriving at 9 PM; and 9:30 PM, arriving at 7:30 AM. Fares are £60 round-trip (under-25 youth pass £56), £35 one-way. Other Eurolines routes include: Amsterdam (7 hours, €70); Barcelona (15 hours, €170); and Berlin (10 hours, €150). There are also international-only arrivals and departures from Avignon, Bordeaux, Lille, Lyon, Toulouse, and Tours. If you are planning a grand tour, there are economical passes to be had—15-day passes run €285, a 30-day pass will cost €425. These passes offer unlimited coach travel to all Eurolines European destinations. Local bus information to the relatively rare rural areas where trains do not have access can be obtained from the SNCF.

🚍 From the U.K. **Eurolines** ✉ 28 av. Général-de-Gaulle, Bagnolet ☎ 08-36-69-52-52 in France, 020/7730-3499 in U.K. ⊕ www.eurolines.fr.

🚍 Within France **Paris Vision** ✉ 1 rue d'Auber, 75009 Paris ☎ 01-47-42-27-40 ⊕ www.parisvision.com. **SNCF** ✉ 88 rue St-Lazare, 75009 Paris ☎ 08-36-35-35-39 in English ⊕ www.sncf.fr.

CAMERAS & PHOTOGRAPHY

If you need to get your camera repaired, your best bet in Paris and other major cities is to go to a FNAC (a book, record, and electronics store). You should be able to find a small camera repair shop in most small towns. Note that you may have to wait some time to get your camera fixed. The *Kodak Guide to Shooting Great Travel Pictures* (available at bookstores everywhere) is loaded with tips.

🚍 Photo Help **Kodak Information Center** ☎ 800/242-2424 ⊕ www.kodak.com.

EQUIPMENT PRECAUTIONS

Don't pack film or equipment in checked luggage, where it is much more susceptible to damage. X-ray machines used to view checked luggage are extremely powerful and therefore are likely to ruin your film. Try to ask for hand inspection of film, which becomes clouded after repeated exposure to airport X-ray machines, and keep videotapes and computer disks away from metal detectors. Always keep film, tape, and computer disks out of the sun. Carry an extra supply of batteries, and be prepared to turn on your camera, camcorder, or laptop to prove to airport security personnel that the device is real.

FILM & DEVELOPING

In Paris and most major cities, the easiest place to get film developed and printed is a FNAC store. If you're in a smaller town and want your film developed, look for a store with a Kodak sign outside its door. Keep in mind that **it's expensive to develop and print film in France**—around $20 per 36-exposure roll.

VIDEOS

France uses SECAM, which is a different system from that used either in the United States (NTSC) or in the United Kingdom (PAL). Therefore, you won't be able to play the videotapes you bring from home on French equipment. In addition, you probably won't be able to use SECAM videotapes in your camera, so it's a good idea to **bring extra videotapes from home.**

CAR RENTAL

Though renting a car in France is expensive—about twice as much as in the United States—as is gas (€.90–€1.25 per liter), it can pay off if you're traveling with two or more people. In addition, renting a car gives you the freedom that trains cannot. Rates in Paris begin at about €35 a day and €200 per week for an economy car with air-conditioning, manual transmission, and unlimited mileage. The price doesn't usually take into account the 19.6% V.A.T. tax or, if you pick it up from the airport, the airport tax. You won't need a car in the capital, so **wait to pick up your rental until the day you leave Paris.**

🚍 Major Agencies **Alamo** ☎ 800/522-9696 ⊕ www.alamo.com. **Avis** ☎ 800/331-1084, 800/879-2847 in Canada, 0870/606-0100 in U.K., 02/

9353-9000 in Australia, 09/526-2847 in New Zealand ⊕ www.avis.com. **Budget** ☎ 800/527-0700, 0870/156-5656 in U.K. ⊕ www.budget.com. **Dollar** ☎ 800/800-6000, 0800/085-4578 in U.K. ⊕ www.dollar.com. **Hertz** ☎ 800/654-3001, 800/263-0600 in Canada, 0870/844-8844 in U.K., 02/9669-2444 in Australia, 09/256-8690 in New Zealand ⊕ www.hertz.com. **National Car Rental** ☎ 800/227-7368, 0870/600-6666 in U.K. ⊕ www.nationalcar.com.

CUTTING COSTS

Renting a car through local French agencies has a number of serious disadvantages, notably price, as they simply cannot compete with the larger international companies. These giants combine bilingual service, the security of name recognition, extensive services (such as 24-hour hot lines), and automatic vehicles. However, Rent-a-car Prestige can be useful if you are interested in luxury cars (convertible BMWs) or large family vans (Renault Espace, for example). Note that the big international agencies like Hertz and Avis offer better prices to those clients who make reservations in their home countries before they arrive in France; if you need to rent a car while in France, it even pays to call home and have a friend take care of it for you from there. So, to get the best deal, **reserve a car before you leave home.**

For a good deal, book through a travel agent who will shop around. Remember to ask about required deposits, cancellation penalties, and drop-off charges if you're planning to pick up the car in one city and leave it in another. If you're traveling during a holiday period, also make sure that a confirmed reservation guarantees you a car.

Do look into wholesalers, companies that do not own fleets but rent in bulk from those that do and often offer better rates than traditional car-rental operations. Prices are best during off-peak periods. Rentals booked through wholesalers often must be paid for before you leave home.

🖪 Local Agencies **ACAR** ✉ 99 bd. Auguste-Blanqui, Bercy/Tolbiac, 75013 Paris ☎ 01-45-88-28-38. **Autorent** ✉ 98 bd. de la Convention, Montpar-

nasse, 75017 Paris ☎ 01-45-54-22-45. **Easycar** ⊕ www.easycar.net. **Europcar** ☎ 08-03-35-23-52 ⊕ www.europcar.fr. **Locabest** ✉ 104 bd. Magenta, République, 75010 Paris ☎ 01-44-72-08-05. **Rent-A-Car** ✉ 79 rue de Bercy, Bercy/Tolbiac, 75012 Paris ☎ 01-43-45-98-99.

🖪 Wholesalers **Auto Europe** ☎ 207/842-2000 or 800/223-5555 🖷 207/842-2222 ⊕ www.autoeurope.com. **Destination Europe Resources** (DER) ✉ 9501 W. Devon Ave., Rosemont, IL 60018 ☎ 800/782-2424 🖷 800/282-7474 ⊕ www.der.com. **Europe by Car** ☎ 212/581-3040 or 800/223-1516 🖷 212/246-1458 ⊕ www.europebycar.com. **Kemwel** ☎ 877/820-0668 or 800/678-0678 🖷 207/842-2147 ⊕ www.kemwel.com.

INSURANCE

When driving a rented car you are generally responsible for any damage to or loss of the vehicle. Collision policies that car-rental companies sell for European rentals typically do not cover stolen vehicles. Before you rent—and purchase collision or theft coverage—see what coverage you already have under the terms of your personal auto-insurance policy and credit cards.

REQUIREMENTS & RESTRICTIONS

In France you must be over 18 to rent a car, though rates may be higher if you're under 25. Foreign drivers should have an international driving licence although this is not required for Canadian and European Union nationals (*see* Rules of the Road *in* Car Travel, *below*).

SURCHARGES

Before you pick up a car in one city and leave it in another, ask about drop-off charges or one-way service fees, which can be substantial. Also inquire about early-return policies; some rental agencies charge extra if you return the car before the time specified in your contract, while others give you a refund for the days not used. To avoid a hefty refueling fee, fill the tank just before you turn in the car, but be aware that gas stations near the rental outlet may overcharge. It's almost never a deal to buy the tank of gas that's in the car when you rent it; the understanding is that you'll return it empty, but some fuel usually remains.

CAR TRAVEL

An unlimited third-party liability insurance policy is compulsory for all automobiles driven in France and will be issued to you automatically as part of your rental agreement. An International Driver's License is valid for temporary, not long term use—less than 90 days—and is not required but can prove useful in emergencies such as traffic violations or auto accidents, particularly when a foreign language is involved. Drivers in France must be over 18 years old to drive, but there is no top age limit (if your faculties are intact).

EMERGENCY SERVICES

If your car breaks down on an expressway, **go to a roadside emergency telephone.** If you have a breakdown anywhere else, find the nearest garage or contact the police. There are also 24-hour assistance hotlines valid throughout France (available through rental agencies and supplied to you when you rent the car), but do not hesitate to call the police in case of any roadside emergency, for they are quick and reliable, and the phone call is free. There are special phones just for this purpose on all highways; you'll see them every few kilometers and they are picked out in bright orange—just pick up the phone and dial 17. The French equivalent of the AAA is the Club Automobile de l'Ile de France, but it only takes care of its members and is of little use to international travelers.
ⓕ Police ☎ 17.

FROM THE U.K.

If you're driving from the United Kingdom to the Continent, you have a choice of either the Channel Tunnel or ferry services. Reservations are essential at peak times and are always a good idea, especially when going via the Chunnel. Cars don't drive in the Chunnel but are loaded onto trains (⇨ Boat & Ferry Travel, *above, and* Channel Tunnel & Train Travel, *below*).

GASOLINE

Gas is expensive, especially on expressways and in rural areas. When possible, **buy gas before you get on the expressway** and keep an eye on pump prices as you go. These vary enormously—anything from €.90 to €1.25 per liter. The cheapest gas can be found at *hypermarchés* (large supermarkets). Credit cards are accepted in every gas station. It's possible to go for miles in the country without passing a gas station—**don't let your tank get too low in rural areas.**

PARKING

Parking is a nightmare in Paris and often difficult in other large towns. Meters and ticket machines (pay and display) are common and work with parking cards (*cartes de stationnements.* Parking cards work like credit cards in the parking meters and come in three denominations: €10, €20, and €30. Since parking in Paris runs a whopping €2 per hour, you should invest in the €30 option if you can. Parking cards are available at any café posting the red TABAC sign. Insert your card into the nearest meter, choose the approximate amount of time you expect to stay, and you'll receive a green receipt, which must be clearly visible to the meter patrol; place it on the dashboard on the inside of the front window on the passenger side.

Parking is free on Sunday, national holidays, and in certain residential areas in August. Parking meters showing a dense yellow circle indicate a free parking zone during the month of August; if you do not see the circle, pay. Parking tickets are expensive, and there's no shortage of the blue-uniformed parking police. Parking lots, indicated by a blue sign with a white P, are usually underground and are generally expensive. In smaller towns, parking may be permitted on one side of the street only—alternating every two weeks—so pay attention to signs. In France, illegally parked cars are likely to be impounded, especially those blocking entrances or fire exits.

ROADS

The French road network is very extensive: 8,000 km of expressway and 808,000 km of main roads. For the fastest roads between two points, **look for roads marked A for *autoroute.*** A *péage* (toll) must be paid on most expressways: the rate varies but can be steep. The N (*route nationale*) roads—which are sometimes di-

vided highways—and D (*route départementale*) roads are usually also wide and
fast. Don't be daunted by smaller (C and
V) roads, either.

There are excellent links between Paris
and most French cities, but poor ones between the provinces (the principal exceptions are A26 from Calais to Reims, A62
between Bordeaux and Toulouse, and A9/
A8 the length of the Mediterranean coast).

Though routes are numbered, **the French
generally guide themselves from city to
city and town to town by destination
name.** When reading a map, keep one eye
on the next big city toward your destination as well as the next small town; most
snap decisions will have to be based on
town names, not road numbers.

When traveling in and out of Paris, note
that there are two major rings that run
parallel to each other and encircle the city:
the *périphérique intérieur,* the inside ring,
also known as the *grands boulevards* (not
to be confused with the major avenue layout in the center of Paris's Right Bank);
and the *périphérique extérieur,* the outside
ring, which is a major highway. From this
ring there are *portes* (gates) that connect
to the major highways of France. The
names of these highways function on the
same principal as the Paris métro, with the
final destination determining which direction you take. These directions are indicated by major cities, and the major
highways connect to Paris at these points.
For instance, heading north, look for Porte
de la Chapelle (direction Lille and Charles
de Gaulle Airport); east, for Porte de Bagnolet (direction Metz and Nancy); south,
for Porte d'Orléans (direction Lyon and
Bordeaux); and west, for Porte d'Auteuil
(direction Rouen and Chartres) or Porte de
St-Cloud. Other portes include Porte de la
Villette; Porte de Pantin; Porte de Bercy
(A4 to Reims); Porte d'Italie; and Porte de
Maillot (A14 to Rouen).

The major expressways into Paris are the
A1, from the north/Great Britain; the A13,
from Rouen, Normandy, and northwestern France; the A6, from Lyon, the French
Alps, the Riviera, and Italy; the A10, from
France's southwest and the Pyrénées; and
the A4, from Nancy and Strasbourg in
eastern France.

ROAD MAPS

If you plan on driving through France, **get
a Michelin or IGN map** for each region
you'll be visiting. The maps are available
from most bookshops, gas stations, and
magazine stores.

RULES OF THE ROAD

Drive on the right and **yield to drivers
coming from streets to the right.** However,
this rule does not necessarily apply at traffic circles, where you should watch out for
just about everyone. You must **wear your
seat belt,** and children under 12 may not
travel in the front seat. Speed limits are
130 kph (80 mph) on expressways (*autoroutes*), 110 kph (70 mph) on divided
highways (*routes nationales*), 90 kph (55
mph) on other roads (*routes*), 50 kph (30
mph) in cities and towns (*villes et villages*).
French drivers break these limits, and police dish out hefty on-the-spot fines with
equal abandon. Do not expect to find traffic lights in the center of the road, as
French lights are usually on the right- and
left-hand sides.

If you are driving through France during
the traditional holiday months (Christmas,
Easter, July–September) you might be
asked to pull over by the Police National
at busy intersections. You will have to
show your papers "papiers"—including
car insurance—and submit to an "al-
cotest" (you guessed it, a Breathalyzer
test). The rules in France have become
stringent due to the high incidence of accidents on the roads; anything above 0.5
grams of alcohol in the blood, which, according to your size, could simply mean
two to three glasses of good wine, and you
are over the limit. This does not necessarily mean a night in the clinker, but your
driving privileges in France will be revoked
on the spot and you will pay a hefty fine.
Don't drink and drive, even if you're just
crossing town to the sleepy little inn on the
river. Local police are notorious for their
vigilance.

Some important traffic terms and signs to
note: SORTIE (exit); SENS UNIQUE (one-way);

STATIONNEMENT INTERDITE (no parking); and IMPASSE (dead end). Blue rectangular signs indicate a highway; green rectangular signs indicate a major direction; triangles carry illustrations of a particular traffic hazard; speed limits are indicated in a circle with the maximum limit circled in red.

⚑ Auto Clubs American Automobile Association ☎ 800/564–6222 ⊕ www.aaany.com/travel/travel services/IDPform2.asp?. **Australian Automobile Association** ☎ 02/6247–7311. **Canadian Automobile Association (CAA)** ☎ 613/247–0117. **New Zealand Automobile Association** ☎ 09/377–4660. **Royal Automobile Club (RAC)** ☎ 0990/722–722 for membership, 0345/121–345 for insurance. **U.K. Automobile Association (AA)** ☎ 0990/500–600.

THE CHANNEL TUNNEL

Short of flying, taking the Eurostar train through the "Chunnel" is the fastest way to cross the English Channel: 3 hours from London's central Waterloo Station to Paris's central Gare du Nord, 35 minutes from Folkestone to Calais, and 60 minutes from motorway to motorway. There's a vast range of prices for Eurostar—round-trip tickets range from €520 for first class to €105 for second class depending on when you travel. It's a good idea to **make a reservation if you're traveling with your car on a Chunnel train**; cars without reservations, if they can get on at all, are charged 20% extra.

⚑ Car Transport Eurotunnel ☎ 0870/535–3535 in U.K., 070/223210 in Belgium, 03–21–00–61–00 in France ⊕ www.eurotunnel.com. **French Motorail/ Rail Europe** ☎ 0870/241–5415 ⊕ www.raileurope. co.uk/frenchmotorail.

⚑ Passenger Service Eurostar ☎ 1233/617575, 0870/518–6186 in U.K. ⊕ www.eurostar.co.uk. **Rail Europe** ☎ 800/942–4866 or 800/274–8724, 0870/ 584–8848 U.K. inquiries and credit-card bookings ⊕ www.raileurope.com.

CHILDREN IN FRANCE

Be sure to plan ahead and **involve your youngsters** as you outline your trip. When packing, include things to keep them busy en route. On sightseeing days try to schedule activities of special interest to your children.

Getting around Paris and other major cities with a stroller can be a challenge, so **take your lightest folding stroller.** Many museums require you to check strollers at the entrance. There are some, like the Louvre in Paris, that will permit you to use one but, chances are, you'll be spending an inordinate amount of time maneuvering through crowds, waiting for one of the tiny elevators, and wishing you brought along a baby back pack or kangaroo pouch. In Paris few métro stations have escalators; you're better off taking the bus in off-peak hours. *Fodor's Around Paris with Kids* (available in bookstores everywhere) can help you plan your days together.

If you are renting a car, don't forget to arrange for a car seat when you reserve. Playgrounds can be found off many highways. Most rest-stop bathrooms have changing tables. For general advice about traveling with children, consult *Fodor's FYI: Travel with Your Baby* (available in bookstores everywhere).

⚑ Family-Friendly Tour Operators Grandtravel ✉ 6900 Wisconsin Ave., Suite 706, Chevy Chase, MD 20815 ☎ 301/986–0790 or 800/247–7651 for people traveling with grandchildren ages 7–17. **Families Welcome!/Great Destinations** ✉ 92 N. Main St., Ashland, OR 97520 ☎ 541/482–6121 or 800/326–0724 ☎ 541/482–0660. **A Touch of France** ✉ 660 King Rd., Fords, NJ 08863 ☎ 800/738–5240.

⚑ Local Information CIDJ ✉ Centre d'Information et de Documentation pour la Jeunesse; 101 quai Branly, 75015 Paris ☎ 01–44–49–12–00 ⊕ www. cidj.asso.fr.

EATING & DRINKING

The best restaurants in France do not welcome small children; except for the traditional family Sunday-noon dinner, fine dining is considered an adult pastime. Aim for more modest *auberges* (country inns), and if there's a choice, **consider having your meal in the café or brasserie** rather than in the linen-and-goblet-filled dining room. In cities, brasseries and cafés offer a casual option and the flexible meal times that children often require. If you get desperate, France has its share of McDonald's, Pizza Huts, and other fast-food restaurants. Very few mainstream restaurants have high chairs, but some do serve children's portions (*menu enfant*), usually spaghetti or the ubiquitous *steak-frîtes*, a mountain of fries with a thin steak or fat patty of ground beef, usually cooked extremely rare. If you're queasy about this, ask for it *bien cuit* (well done) or *à point* (medium). If your children go to bed early, **opt for your hot meal at noon** (there are cheaper prix-fixe menus then, too) and consider having a sandwich, quiche, a *croque monsieur* (a grilled egg-and-cheese sandwich), or pizza at a café or brasserie in the early evening; full-service restaurants usually do not serve before 7 PM.

FLYING

If your children are two or older, ask about children's airfares. As a general rule, infants under two not occupying a seat fly at greatly reduced fares or even for free. But if you want to guarantee a seat for an infant, you have to pay full fare. Consider flying during off-peak days and times; most airlines will grant an infant a seat without a ticket if there are available seats. When booking, confirm carry-on allowances if you're traveling with infants. In general, for babies charged 10% to 50% of the adult fare you are allowed one carry-on bag and a collapsible stroller; if the flight is full, the stroller may have to be checked or you may be limited to less.

Experts agree that it's a good idea to use safety seats aloft for children weighing less than 40 pounds. Airlines set their own policies: if you use a safety seat, U.S. carriers usually require that the child be ticketed, even if he or she is young enough to ride free, because the seats must be strapped into regular seats. And even if you pay the full adult fare for the seat, it may be worth it, especially on longer trips. Do **check your airline's policy about using safety seats during takeoff and landing.** Safety seats are not allowed everywhere in the plane, so get your seat assignments as early as possible.

When reserving, request children's meals or a freestanding bassinet (not available at all airlines) if you need them. But note that bulkhead seats, where you must sit to use the bassinet, may lack an overhead bin or storage space on the floor.

LODGING

If you're planning to stay in hotels, it's essential to book ahead. Many small hotels have only one or two rooms that sleep four (triples are much more common); if there are more of you, you'll have to book two neighboring rooms or a suite. Larger hotels often provide cribs free to guests with young children, which is not usually the case at inns and smaller hotels. Older children are charged at adult rates unless the hotel offers a special family rate. Be sure to **ask about the cutoff age for children's discounts** when booking.

Some hotel chains offer discounts for families and programs for children. Club Med is particularly family friendly: it has a "Baby Club" (from age four months) at its resort in Chamonix, and "Mini Clubs" (for ages 4–6 or 4–8, depending on the resort) and "Kids Clubs" (for ages eight and up during school holidays) at all its resort villages in France except at Val d'Isère. Some clubs are only French-speaking. The Novotel chain allows up to two children under 15 to stay free in their parents' room. Sofitel hotels offer a free second room for children during July and August and over the Christmas period.

Another option: **consider a gîte, a short-term apartment or house rental,** or a home exchange (⇨ Lodging, *below*).

Most hotels in France allow children under a certain age to stay in their parents' room at no extra charge, but others charge for them as extra adults; be sure to find out the cutoff age for children's discounts. **⚄ Best Choices Club Med** ⊠ 40 W. 57th St., New York, NY 10019 ☏ 800/258-2633 ⊕ www.clubmed.com. **Novotel** ☏ 800/221-4542 ⊕ www.novotel.com. **Sofitel** ☏ 800/221-4542 ⊕ www.sofitel.com.

SIGHTS & ATTRACTIONS

Places that are especially appealing to children are indicated by a rubber-duckie icon (🐥) in the margin. There are plenty of diversions for the young, and **almost all museums and movie theaters have discounted rates.**

SUPPLIES & EQUIPMENT

Supermarkets carry several major brands of diapers (*couches*), universally referred to as Pampers (pawm-*paires*). Junior sizes are hard to come by, as the French toilet-train early. Baby formula is available in grocery stores or pharmacies. There are two types of formulas: *lait prémier age,* for infants 0–4 months, and *lait deuxieme age,* for four months or older. French formulas come in powder form and need to be mixed with a pure, low-mineral-content bottled water such as Evian or Volvic (the French *never* mix baby formula with tap water). American formulas are not available in France. If you're looking for treats for your little ones, some items to keep in mind are: *coloriage* (coloring books), *crayons de couleur* (crayons), *pate à modeler* (modeling clay), and *feutres* (magic markers).

TRANSPORTATION

SNCF allows children under four to travel free (provided they don't occupy a seat) or for €8 for a seat, and children 4–12 to travel at half fare with an accompanying adult. The Carte "Enfant Plus" (€63) allows children under 12 and as many as four accompanying adults to make an unlimited number of trips at as much as half the cost (though you are only guaranteed at least 25% off on all trains). This card is worth your while only if you are planning on traveling extensively in France—it is valid for one year.

When traveling by train with children, you may want to travel first class, as there is more space and it's considerably calmer and cleaner than second-class space. Another option is to request an "*espace famille*" ("family space") in second class (when you make reservations), which consists of two sets of seats facing each other. Whatever you do, double—no, *triple*—check your train tickets to make sure your seats are together in a no-smoking train; the SNCF are notorious for bungling the details. For more information, *see* Train Travel, *below.*

COMPUTERS ON THE ROAD

If you use a major Internet provider, getting online in France shouldn't be difficult. Some hotels even have in-room modem lines. You may, however, need an adapter for your computer for the European-style plugs (⇨ Electricity, *below*). As always, if you're traveling with a laptop, carry a spare battery and adapter. **Never plug your computer into any socket before asking about surge protection.** IBM sells a pen-size modem tester that plugs into a telephone jack to check if the line is safe to use.

⌨ Access Numbers in Paris AOL ☏ 01-41-45-81-00. **Compuserve** ☏ 08-03-00-60-00, 08-03-00-80-00, or 08-03-00-90-00.

CONSUMER PROTECTION

Whether you're shopping for gifts or purchasing travel services, **pay with a major credit card** whenever possible, so you can cancel payment or get reimbursed if there's a problem (and you can provide documentation). If you're doing business with a particular company for the first time, contact your local Better Business Bureau and the attorney general's offices in your state and (for U.S. businesses) the company's home state as well. Have any complaints been filed? Finally, if you're buying a package or tour, always consider travel insurance that includes default coverage (⇨ Insurance).

⌨ BBBs Council of Better Business Bureaus ✉ 4200 Wilson Blvd., Suite 800, Arlington, VA 22203 ☏ 703/276-0100 🖷 703/525-8277 ⊕ www.bbb.org.

CUSTOMS & DUTIES

When shopping abroad, keep receipts for all purchases. Upon reentering the country, **be ready to show customs officials what you've bought.** Pack purchases together in an easily accessible place. If you think a duty is incorrect, appeal the assessment. If you object to the way your clearance was handled, note the inspector's badge number. In either case, first ask to see a supervisor. If the problem isn't resolved, write to the appropriate authorities, beginning with the port director at your point of entry.

IN AUSTRALIA

Australian residents who are 18 or older may bring home A$400 worth of souvenirs and gifts (including jewelry), 250 cigarettes or 250 grams of cigars or other tobacco products, and 1,125 ml of alcohol (including wine, beer, and spirits). Residents under 18 may bring back A$200 worth of goods. Members of the same family traveling together may pool their allowances. Prohibited items include meat products. Seeds, plants, and fruits need to be declared upon arrival.

⨎ Australian Customs Service ⌖ Regional Director, Box 8, Sydney, NSW 2001 ☎ 02/9213-2000 or 1300/363263, 02/9364-7222 or 1800/020-504 quarantine-inquiry line 🖷 02/9213-4043 ⊕ www.customs.gov.au.

IN CANADA

Canadian residents who have been out of Canada for at least seven days may bring in C$750 worth of goods duty-free. If you've been away fewer than seven days but more than 48 hours, the duty-free allowance drops to C$200. If your trip lasts 24 to 48 hours, the allowance is C$50. You may not pool allowances with family members. Goods claimed under the C$750 exemption may follow you by mail; those claimed under the lesser exemptions must accompany you. Alcohol and tobacco products may be included in the seven-day and 48-hour exemptions but not in the 24-hour exemption. If you meet the age requirements of the province or territory through which you reenter Canada, you may bring in, duty-free, 1.5 liters of wine *or* 1.14 liters (40 imperial ounces) of liquor *or* 24 12-ounce cans or bottles of beer or ale. Also, if you meet the local age requirement for tobacco products, you may bring in, duty-free, 200 cigarettes and 50 cigars. Check ahead of time with the Canada Customs and Revenue Agency or the Department of Agriculture for policies regarding meat products, seeds, plants, and fruits.

You may send an unlimited number of gifts (only one gift per recipient, however) worth up to C$60 each duty-free to Canada. Label the package UNSOLICITED GIFT—VALUE UNDER $60. Alcohol and tobacco are excluded.

⨎ Canada Customs and Revenue Agency ✉ 2265 St. Laurent Blvd., Ottawa, Ontario K1G 4K3 ☎ 800/461-9999 in Canada, 204/983-3500, 506/636-5064 ⊕ www.ccra.gc.ca.

IN FRANCE

There are two levels of duty-free allowance for travelers entering France: one for goods obtained (tax paid) within another European Union (EU) country and the other for goods obtained anywhere outside the EU or for goods purchased in a duty-free shop within the EU.

In the first category, you may import duty-free: 300 cigarettes or 150 cigarillos or 75 cigars or 400 grams of tobacco; 5 liters of table wine and (1) 1½ liters of alcohol over 22% volume (most spirits), (2) 3 liters of alcohol under 22% by volume (fortified or sparkling wine), or (3) 3 more liters of table wine, 90 milliliters of perfume, 375 milliliters of toilet water, and other goods to the value of €365 (€95 for those under 15).

In the second category, you may import duty-free: 200 cigarettes or 100 cigarillos or 50 cigars or 250 grams of tobacco (these allowances are doubled if you live outside Europe); 2 liters of wine and (1) 1 liter of alcohol over 22% volume (most spirits), (2) 2 liters of alcohol under 22% volume (fortified or sparkling wine), or (3) 2 more liters of table wine, 60 milliliters of perfume, 250 milliliters of toilet water, and other goods to the value of €45 (€25 for those under 15).

⨎ Direction des Douanes ✉ 16 rue Yves Toudic, Paris 10ᵉ ☎ 01-40-40-39-00.

IN NEW ZEALAND

All homeward-bound residents may bring back NZ$700 worth of souvenirs and gifts; passengers may not pool their allowances, and children can claim only the concession on goods intended for their own use. For those 17 or older, the duty-free allowance also includes 4.5 liters of wine or beer; one 1,125-ml bottle of spirits; and either 200 cigarettes, 250 grams of tobacco, 50 cigars, *or* a combination of the three up to 250 grams. Meat products, seeds, plants, and fruits must be declared upon arrival to the Agricultural Services Department.

⨎ New Zealand Customs ✉ Head office: The Customhouse, 17-21 Whitmore St., Box 2218, Wellington ☎ 09/300-5399 or 0800/428-786 ⊕ www.customs.govt.nz.

IN THE U.K.

If you are a U.K. resident and your journey was wholly within the European Union, you probably won't have to pass through customs when you return to the United Kingdom. If you plan to bring back large quantities of alcohol or tobacco, check EU limits beforehand. In most cases, if you bring back more than 200 cigars, 3,200 cigarettes, 400 cigarillos, 10 liters of spirits, 110 liters of beer, 20 liters of fortified wine, and/or 90 liters of wine, you have to declare the goods upon return. Prohibited items include unpasteurized milk, regardless of country of origin.

7 **HM Customs and Excise** ⊠ Portcullis House, 21 Cowbridge Rd. E, Cardiff CF11 9SS ☎ 0845/010–9000, 0208/929–0152 advice service, 0208/929–6731, 0208/910–3602 complaints ⊕ www.hmce.gov.uk.

IN THE U.S.

U.S. residents who have been out of the country for at least 48 hours may bring home, for personal use, $800 worth of foreign goods duty-free, as long as they haven't used the $800 allowance or any part of it in the past 30 days. This exemption may include 1 liter of alcohol (for travelers 21 and older), 200 cigarettes, and 100 non-Cuban cigars. Family members from the same household who are traveling together may pool their $800 personal exemptions. For fewer than 48 hours, the duty-free allowance drops to $200, which may include 50 cigarettes, 10 non-Cuban cigars, and 150 ml of alcohol (or 150 ml of perfume containing alcohol). The $200 allowance cannot be combined with other individuals' exemptions, and if you exceed it, the full value of all the goods will be taxed. Antiques, which U.S. Customs and Border Protection defines as objects more than 100 years old, enter duty-free, as do original works of art done entirely by hand, including paintings, drawings, and sculptures. This doesn't apply to folk art or handicrafts, which are in general dutiable.

You may also send packages home duty-free, with a limit of one parcel per addressee per day (except alcohol or tobacco products or perfume worth more than

$5). You can mail up to $200 worth of goods for personal use; label the package PERSONAL USE and attach a list of its contents and their retail value. If the package contains your used personal belongings, mark it AMERICAN GOODS RETURNED to avoid paying duties. You may send up to $100 worth of goods as a gift; mark the package UNSOLICITED GIFT. Mailed items do not affect your duty-free allowance on your return.

To avoid paying duty on foreign-made high-ticket items you already own and will take on your trip, register them with Customs before you leave the country. Consider filing a Certificate of Registration for laptops, cameras, watches, and other digital devices identified with serial numbers or other permanent markings; you can keep the certificate for other trips. Otherwise, bring a sales receipt or insurance form to show that you owned the item before you left the United States.

For more about duties, restricted items, and other information about international travel, check out U.S. Customs and Border Protection's online brochure, *Know Before You Go.*

7 **U.S. Customs and Border Protection** ⊠ For inquiries and equipment registration, 1300 Pennsylvania Ave. NW, Washington, DC 20229 ⊕ www.cbp. gov ☎ 877/287–8667 or 202/354–1000 ⊠ For complaints, Customer Satisfaction Unit, 1300 Pennsylvania Ave. NW, Room 5.2C, Washington, DC 20229.

DISABILITIES & ACCESSIBILITY

Though the French government is doing much to ensure that public facilities provide for visitors with disabilities, it still has a long way to go.

7 Local Resources **Association des Paralysés de France** ⊠ 22 rue du Père Guerin, 75013 Paris ☎ 01-40-78-69-00 ⊕ www.apf-asso.com for a list of Paris hotels.

LODGING

Only some hotels—particularly more modern ones—are equipped with ramps, elevators, and special toilet facilities. Lists of regional hotels include a symbol to indicate which hotels have rooms accessible to people using wheelchairs.

RESERVATIONS

When discussing accessibility with an operator or reservations agent, ask hard questions. Are there any stairs, inside *or* out? Are there grab bars next to the toilet *and* in the shower/tub? How wide is the doorway to the room? To the bathroom? For the most extensive facilities meeting the latest legal specifications, opt for newer accommodations. If you reserve through a toll-free number, consider also calling the hotel's local number to confirm the information from the central reservations office. Get confirmation in writing when you can.

SIGHTS & ATTRACTIONS

Only some monuments and museums—especially those constructed within the past decade—are equipped with ramps, elevators, and special toilet facilities.

TRANSPORTATION

The SNCF has special accommodations in the first-class compartments (for the usual second-class rate) on non-TGV and mainline rail services that have been reserved exclusively for people using wheelchairs; arrangements can be made for those passengers to be escorted on and off trains and assisted in making connections (this service must be requested in advance at 08–00–05–47–53).

Unfortunately, at this time very few métro stations in Paris and only some RER stations are wheelchair accessible. For information about accessibility, **get the RER and métro access guide,** available at most stations and from the Paris Transit Authority.

The Airhop shuttle company runs adapted vehicles to and from the airports; Orly–Paris costs €35 and Charles de Gaulle–Paris costs €45; this service is available Monday through Friday only. Reservations (in French) must be made in advance. Note that you must pay €2 for every 15 minutes there is a delay.

🗈 Complaints **Aviation Consumer Protection Division** (⇨ Air Travel) for airline-related problems. **Departmental Office of Civil Rights** ✉ For general inquiries, U.S. Department of Transportation, S-30, 400 7th St. SW, Room 10215, Washington, DC 20590 ☎ 202/366-4648 🖷 202/366-9371 🌐 www.

dot.gov/ost/docr/index.htm. **Disability Rights Section** ✉ NYAV, U.S. Department of Justice, Civil Rights Division, 950 Pennsylvania Ave. NW, Washington, DC 20530 🖢 ADA information line 202/514-0301 or 800/514-0301, 202/514-0383 TTY or 800/514-0383 TTY 🌐 www.ada.gov. **U.S. Department of Transportation Hotline** 🖢 For disability-related air-travel problems, 800/778-4838 or 800/455-9880 TTY.

🗈 Local Resources **Airhop** 🖢 01-41-29-01-29. **Paris Transit Authority** ✉ (RATP) kiosk, 54 quai de la Rapée, Cedex 12, 75599 🖢 08-36-68-77-14 🌐 www.ratp.fr.

TRAVEL AGENCIES

In the United States, the Americans with Disabilities Act requires that travel firms serve the needs of all travelers. Some agencies specialize in working with people with disabilities.

🗈 Travelers with Mobility Problems **Access Adventures/B. Roberts Travel** ✉ 206 Chestnut Ridge Rd., Scottsville, NY 14624 🖢 585/889-9096 🌐 www.brobertstravel.com ✍ dltravel@prodigy. net, run by a former physical-rehabilitation counselor. **CareVacations** ✉ No. 5, 5110-50 Ave., Leduc, Alberta, Canada, T9E 6V4 🖢 780/986-6404 or 877/478-7827 🖷 780/986-8332 🌐 www.carevacations. com, for group tours and cruise vacations. **Flying Wheels Travel** ✉ 143 W. Bridge St., Box 382, Owatonna, MN 55060 🖢 507/451-5005 🖷 507/451-1685 🌐 www.flyingwheelstravel.com.

DISCOUNTS & DEALS

Be a smart shopper and compare all your options before making decisions. A plane ticket bought with a promotional coupon from travel clubs, coupon books, and direct-mail offers or purchased on the Internet may not be cheaper than the least expensive fare from a discount ticket agency. And always keep in mind that what you get is just as important as what you save.

DISCOUNT RESERVATIONS

To save money, look into discount reservations services with Web sites and toll-free numbers, which use their buying power to get a better price on hotels, airline tickets (⇨ Air Travel), even car rentals. When booking a room, always **call the hotel's local toll-free number** (if one is available) rather than the central reservations number—you'll often get a better price. Always ask about special packages or corporate rates.

When shopping for the best deal on hotels and car rentals, look for guaranteed exchange rates, which protect you against a falling dollar. With your rate locked in, you won't pay more, even if the price goes up in the local currency.

⁊ Airline Tickets Air 4 Less ☎ 800/AIR4LESS; low-fare specialist.

⁊ Hotel Rooms Accommodations Express ☎ 800/444-7666 or 800/277-1064 ⊕ www.acex. net. **Hotels.com** ☎ 800/246-8357 ⊕ www.hotels. com. **International Marketing & Travel Concepts** ☎ 800/790-4682 ⊕ www.imtc-travel.com. **Steigenberger Reservation Service** ☎ 800/223-5652 ⊕ www.srs-worldhotels.com. **Turbotrip.com** ☎ 800/473-7829 ⊕ www.turbotrip.com.

PACKAGE DEALS

Don't confuse packages and guided tours. When you buy a package, you travel on your own, just as though you had planned the trip yourself. Fly–drive packages, which combine airfare and car rental, are often a good deal. In cities, ask the local visitor's bureau about hotel and local transportation packages that include tickets to major museum exhibits or other special events. If you **buy a rail–drive pass,** you may save on train tickets and car rentals. All Eurailpass holders get a discount on Eurostar fares through the Channel Tunnel and often receive reduced rates for buses, hotels, ferries, sightseeing cruises, and car rentals.

EATING & DRINKING

All establishments must post their menus outside, so study them carefully before deciding to enter. Most restaurants have two basic types of menu: à la carte and fixed-price (prix-fixe or *un menu*). The prix-fixe menu is usually the best value, though choices are more limited. Most menus begin with a first course (*une entrée*), often subdivided into cold and hot starters, followed by fish and poultry, then meat; it's rare today that anyone orders something from all three. The restaurants we review in this book are the cream of the crop in each price category.

A few pointers on French dining etiquette: diners in France don't negotiate their orders much, so don't expect serene smiles when you ask for sauce on the side. Order your coffee after dessert, not with it. When you're ready for the check, ask for it: no professional waiter would dare put a bill on your table while you're still enjoying the last sip of coffee. And don't ask for a doggy bag; it's just not done. The French usually drink wine or mineral water—not soda or coffee—with their food. You may ask for a carafe of tap water, but not always: in general, diners order mineral water if they don't order wine.

COSTS

The following is the price chart used throughout this book to determine price categories for all restaurants. Prices are per person for a main course at dinner, including tax (19.6%) and service; note that if a restaurant offers only prix-fixe (set-price) meals, it is given a price category that reflects the full prix-fixe price.

CATEGORY	ALL REGIONS EXCEPT	CORSICA & BASQUE COUNTRY
$$$$	over €30	over €25
$$$	€23–€30	€18–€25
$$	€17–€23	€12–€18
$	€11–€17	€8–€12
¢	under €11	under €8

MEALS & SPECIALTIES

What's the difference between a bistro and a brasserie? Can you order food at a café? Can you go to a restaurant just for a snack? The following definitions should help.

A **restaurant** traditionally serves a three-course meal (first, main, and dessert) at both lunch and dinner. Although this category includes the most formal, three-star establishments, it also applies to humble neighborhood spots. Don't expect to grab a quick snack. In general, restaurants are what you choose when you want a complete meal and when you have the time to linger over it.

Many say that **bistros** served the world's first fast food. After the fall of Napoléon, the Russian soldiers who occupied Paris were known to bang on zinc-top café bars, crying *"bistro"*—"quickly" in Russian. In the past, bistros were simple places with minimal decor and service. Although nowadays many are quite upscale, with beautiful interiors and chic clientele, most remain cozy establishments serving straightforward, frequently gutsy cooking.

Brasseries—ideal places for quick, one-dish meals—originated when Alsatians fleeing German occupiers after the Franco-Prussian War came to Paris and opened restaurants serving specialties from home. Pork-based dishes, *choucroute* (sauerkraut), and beer (*brasserie* also means brewery) were—and still are—mainstays here. The typical brasserie is convivial and keeps late hours. Some are open 24 hours a day—a good thing to know since many restaurants stop serving at 10:30 PM.

Like bistros and brasseries, **cafés** come in a confusing variety. Often informal neighborhood hangouts, cafés may also be veritable showplaces attracting chic, well-heeled crowds. At most cafés the regulars congregate at the bar, where coffee and drinks are cheaper than at tables. At lunch tables are set, and a limited menu is served. Sandwiches, usually with *jambon* (ham), *fromage* (cheese, often Gruyère or Camembert), or *mixte* (ham and cheese), are served throughout the day. *Casse croûtes* (snacks) are also offered. Cafés are for lingering, for people-watching, and for daydreaming. If none of these options fit the bill, head to the nearest **traiteur** (deli) for picnic fixings.

See the Menu Guide at the end of the book for guidance with menu items that appear frequently on French menus and throughout the reviews in this book.

MEALTIMES

Breakfast is usually served from 7:30 to 10, lunch from noon to 2, and dinner from 8 to 10. Restaurants in Paris usually serve dinner until 10:30 PM. Unless otherwise noted, the restaurants listed in this guide are open daily for lunch and dinner.

PAYING

By French law, prices must include tax and tip (*service compris* or *prix nets*), but pocket change left on the table in basic places, or an additional 5% in better restaurants, is always appreciated. Beware of bills stamped SERVICE NOT INCLUDED in English.

RESERVATIONS & DRESS

Reservations are always a good idea; we mention them only when they're essential or not accepted. Book as far ahead as you can, and reconfirm as soon as you arrive. (Large parties should always call ahead to check the reservations policy.) We mention dress only when men are required to wear a jacket or a jacket and tie.

ELECTRICITY

To use electric-powered equipment purchased in the U.S. or Canada, **bring a converter and adapter.** The electrical current in France is 220 volts, 50 cycles alternating current (AC); wall outlets take continental-type plugs, with two round prongs.

If your appliances are dual-voltage, you'll need only an adapter. Don't use 110-volt outlets marked FOR SHAVERS ONLY for high-wattage appliances such as blow-dryers. Most laptops operate equally well on 110 and 220 volts and so require only an adapter.

EMBASSIES

If you need assistance in an emergency, you can go to your country's embassy. Proof of identity and citizenship are generally required to enter. If your passport has been stolen, get a police report, then contact your embassy for assistance.

🏴 Australia **Australian Embassy** ✉ 4 rue Jean-Rey, Paris, 15ᵉ, Invalides–Eiffel Tower ☎ 01-40-59-33-00 Ⓜ Bir Hakeim ⊙ Weekdays 9:15–12:15.

🏴 Canada **Canadian Embassy** ✉ 35 av. Montaigne, Paris, 8ᵉ, Champs-Élysées Ⓜ Franklin-D.-Roosevelt ☎ 01-44-43-29-00 ⊙ Weekdays 8:30–11.

🏴 New Zealand **New Zealand Embassy** ✉ 7 ter rue Léonardo da Vinci, Paris, 16ᵉ, Trocadéro Ⓜ Victor Hugo ☎ 01-45-00-24-11 ⊙ Weekdays 9–1.

🏴 United Kingdom **British Embassy** ✉ 35 rue du Faubourg-St-Honoré, Paris, 8ᵉ, Louvre–Tuileries ☎ 01-44-51-31-00 Ⓜ Madeleine ⊙ Weekdays 9:30–12:30 and 2:30–5 ✉ 24 av. du Prado, Marseille ☎ 04-91-15-72-10 ⊙ Weekdays 9–noon and 2–5.

🖪 United States **U.S. Embassy** ✉ 2 rue St-Florentin, Paris, 1er, Louvre/Tuileries ☎ 01-43-12-22-22 in English, 01-43-12-23-47 emergencies Ⓜ Concorde ⊘ Weekdays 9–3 ✉ 12 bd. Paul Peytral, Marseille ☎ 04-91-54-92-00 ⊘ Weekdays 8:30–12:30 and 1:30–5:30, until 4:30 Fri.

EMERGENCIES

The National Medical System in France is excellent and was recently ranked number one by the World Health Organization, but there are certain things you must understand to get optimum care. For minor emergencies—the flu, food poisoning, a bad respiratory infection—you should contact a generalist who will actually visit you in your home or hotel, medical bag in hand, at any hour of the day or night, whether you are in the city or on the outskirts of a tiny town. At the moment, hospital emergency rooms are undergoing a crisis and are to be used only for emergencies. They operate on a strict priority system, which could leave you with your high temperature or sprained ankle waiting for hours; in early 2004, a flu epidemic kept hospitals overwhelmed with an average wait of four hours.

France's emergency services are conveniently streamlined and universal and quite simple to use, so no matter where you are in the country you can dial the same phone numbers, listed below. Every town and village has a *médecin de garde* (on-duty doctor) for flus, sprains, tetanus shots, and similar problems. Larger cities have a remarkable service called "SOS Doctor" (or "SOS Dentist" for dental emergencies); just dial information (12) and they will put you through. To find out who's on call on any given evening, call any *généraliste* (general practitioner), and a recording will refer you to the available doctors and specialists. If you need an X-ray or emergency treatment, call an ambulance, and you'll be whisked to the hospital of your choice—or the nearest one. Note that outside Paris it's very difficult to find English-speaking doctors.

Pharmacies have an important role in French culture; they can be very helpful with minor health problems and come equipped with blood pressure machines

and first aid kits. They also can be consulted for a list of practicing doctors in the area, nearby hospitals, private clinics, or health centers. Hotels are required to post emergency exit maps with multilingual instructions to be followed in case of fire on the inside door of every room. On the street the French phrases that may be needed in an emergency are: *Au secours!* (Help!), *urgence* (emergency), *samu* (ambulance), *pompiers* (firemen), *poste de station* (police station), *médecin* (doctor), and *hôpital* (hospital).

See also Emergencies *in* A to Z sections *in* some of the regional chapters for information on local hospitals.

🖪 **Ambulance** ☎ 15. **Fire Department** ☎ 18. **Police** ☎ 17.

ENGLISH-LANGUAGE MEDIA

BOOKS

Paris has many bookstores selling English-language books (⇨ Shopping *in* Chapter 1), and you can probably find at least one bookstore in other major cities with English-language books. However, in most smaller towns you won't have much luck.

NEWSPAPERS & MAGAZINES

Besides a large variety of French newspapers and magazines, all kinds of English-language newspapers and magazines can be found at newsstands in larger cities and even in smaller towns, including: the *International Herald Tribune, USA Today,* the *New York Times,* the *European Financial Times,* the *London Times, Newsweek, The Economist, Vogue,* and *Elle.* In Paris you'll find a number of free English-language magazines with all kinds of listings, including: events, bars, restaurants, shops, films, and museums: Look for *Time Out Paris, FUSAC,* the *Paris Free Voice,* and *Irish Eyes. Pariscope,* the weekly magazine that lists all the new happenings in Paris—music, art, cinema, opera, ballet—has a special section in English worth taking a glance at when you hit the city.

RADIO & TELEVISION

Turn on the television, and you'll notice many American shows dubbed into French (Canal Jimmy, Channel 8, presents American shows in their original, undubbed format). France has both national stations (TF1, France 2, France 3, La Cinq/Arte, and M6) and cable stations (most notably Canal+, France's version of HBO). Every morning at 7:05 AM, ABC News (from the night before) is aired on Channel 4. You can also find CNN, BBC World, and BBC Prime on cable.

You'll find all kinds of music on French radio stations—from rock to jazz to classical, depending on the time of day. For highway information 24/7 tune into 101.7 FM.

ETIQUETTE & BEHAVIOR

SMOKING

The French are smokers—there's no way around it. Just watch them light up their first cigarette after getting off the plane right under the *no smoking* sign at the airport. And they're notorious for disregarding the few no-smoking laws that do exist, with little retribution. Even in restaurants, cafés, and train and métro stations that have no-smoking sections, you'll see people smoking. Even if you ask people to move or not to smoke, don't expect them to respond or respect your request. Your best bet for finding an environment as smoke-free as possible is to stick to the larger cafés and restaurants, where there is a greater likelihood of clearly defined smoking and no-smoking areas, or if you're lucky enough to enjoy good weather, to simply sit at an outside table.

SNCF trains have cars designated for smoking and no-smoking (specify when you make reservations), and these are some of the few places where the laws are respected. Some hotels, too, have designated no-smoking rooms; ask for these when reserving.

GAY & LESBIAN TRAVEL

The largest gay and lesbian communities in France are in Paris. A number of informative newspapers and magazines that cover the Parisian gay and lesbian scene are available at stores and kiosks in the city, notably *Lesbia Magazine* and *Têtu.*

⚑ Gay- & Lesbian-Friendly Travel Agencies Different Roads Travel ✉ 8383 Wilshire Blvd., Suite 520, Beverly Hills, CA 90211 ☎ 323/651-5557 or 800/

429-8747 (Ext. 14 for both) 🖷 323/651-5454 📧 lgernert@tzell.com. **Kennedy Travel** ✉ 130 W. 42nd St., Suite 401, New York, NY 10036 ☎ 212/840-8659 or 800/237-7433 🖷 212/730-2269 ⊕ www. kennedytravel.com. **Now, Voyager** ✉ 4406 18th St., San Francisco, CA 94114 ☎ 415/626-1169 or 800/255-6951 🖷 415/626-8626 ⊕ www.nowvoyager. com. **Skylink Travel and Tour/Flying Dutchmen Travel** ✉ 1455 N. Dutton Ave., Suite A, Santa Rosa, CA 95401 ☎ 707/546-9888 or 800/225-5759 🖷 707/636-0951; serving lesbian travelers.

⚑ Organizations Act Up Paris ✉ 45 rue Sedaine, 11ᵉ ☎ 01-48-06-13-89.

Association des Médecins Gais
☎ 01-48-05-81-71. **Centre Gai et Lesbien** ✉ 3 rue Keller, 11ᵉ ☎ 01-43-57-21-47.

HEALTH

For information about emergencies and hospitals, *see* Emergencies, *above.*

HIKING & WALKING

France has many good places to hike and an extensive network of mapped-out Grandes Randonnées (GRs, or long trails) that range from easy to challenging. For details on hiking in France and guides to GRs in specific areas, contact the Club Alpin Français or the Fédération Française de la Randonnée Pédestre, which also publishes good topographical maps. The IGN maps sold in many bookshops are also invaluable (⇨ Bike Travel, *above*).

⚑ Hiking Organizations Club Alpin Français ✉ 24 av. Laumière, 75019 Paris ☎ 01-53-72-87-00 ⊕ www.clubalpin.com. **Fédération Française de la Randonnée Pédestre** ✉ 14 rue de Riquet, 75019 Paris ☎ 01-44-89-93-93 ⊕ www.ffrp.asso.fr.

⚑ Hiking & Walking Tours Abercrombie & Kent (⇨ Barge Travel, *above*). **BCT Scenic Walking** ✉ 703 Palomar Airport Rd, Suite 200, Carlsbad, CA 92009-1042 ☎ 760/431-7306 🖷 760/431-7782. **Butterfield & Robinson** (⇨ Bike Travel, *above*). **Classic Adventures** (⇨ Bike Travel, *above*). **Country Walkers** 🕮 Box 180, Waterbury, VT 05676-0180 ☎ 802/244-1387 or 800/464-9255 🖷 802/244-5661. **Mountain Travel-Sobek** ✉ 6420 Fairmount Ave., El Cerrito, CA 94530 ☎ 510/527-8100 or 800/227-2384 🖷 510/525-7710. **Wilderness Travel** ✉ 1102 9th St., Berkeley, CA 94710 ☎ 510/558-2488 or 800/368-2794 🖷 510/558-2489 ⊕ www. wildernesstravel.com.

HOLIDAYS

With 11 national *jours feriés* (holidays) and five weeks of paid vacation, the French have their share of repose. In May there is a holiday nearly every week, so be prepared for stores, banks, and museums to shut their doors for days at a time. Be sure to **call museums, restaurants, and hotels in advance to make sure they will be open.**

Note that these dates are for the calendar year 2005: January 1 (New Year's Day); April 11 and 12 (Easter Sunday and Monday); May 1 (Labor Day); May 8 (V.E. Day); May 20 (Ascension); May 30 and 31 (Pentecost Sunday and Monday); July 14 (Bastille Day); August 15 (Assumption); November 1 (All Saints); November 11 (Armistice); December 25 (Christmas).

INSURANCE

The most useful travel-insurance plan is a comprehensive policy that includes coverage for trip cancellation and interruption, default, trip delay, and medical expenses (with a waiver for preexisting conditions).

Without insurance you'll lose all or most of your money if you cancel your trip, regardless of the reason. Default insurance covers you if your tour operator, airline, or cruise line goes out of business—the chances of which have been increasing. Trip-delay covers expenses that arise because of bad weather or mechanical delays. Study the fine print when comparing policies.

If you're traveling internationally, a key component of travel insurance is coverage for medical bills incurred if you get sick on the road. Such expenses aren't generally covered by Medicare or private policies. U.K. residents can buy a travel-insurance policy valid for most vacations taken during the year in which it's purchased (but check preexisting-condition coverage). British and Australian citizens need extra medical coverage when traveling overseas.

Always **buy travel policies directly from the insurance company**; if you buy them from a cruise line, airline, or tour operator that goes out of business you probably won't be covered for the agency or operator's default, a major risk. Before making any purchase, review your existing health and home-owner's policies to find what they cover away from home.

🚩 Travel Insurers In the U.S.: **Access America** ✉ 2805 N. Parham Rd., Richmond, VA 23294 ☎ 800/284-8300 🖷 804/673-1491 or 800/346-9265 ∰ www.accessamerica.com. **Travel Guard International** ✉ 1145 Clark St., Stevens Point, WI 54481 ☎ 715/345-0505 or 800/826-1300 🖷 800/955-8785 ∰ www.travelguard.com.

🚩 In the U.K.: **Association of British Insurers** ✉ 51 Gresham St., London EC2V 7HQ ☎ 020/7600-3333 🖷 020/7696-8999 ∰ www.abi.org.uk. In Canada: **RBC Insurance** ✉ 6880 Financial Dr., Mississauga, Ontario L5N 7Y5 ☎ 800/668-4342 or 905/816-2400 🖷 905/813-4704 ∰ www.rbcinsurance.com. In Australia: **Insurance Council of Australia** ✉ Insurance Enquiries and Complaints, Level 12, Box 561, Collins St. W, Melbourne, VIC 8007 ☎ 1300/780808 or 03/9629-4109 🖷 03/9621-2060 ∰ www.iecltd.com.au. In New Zealand: **Insurance Council of New Zealand** ✉ Level 7, 111-115 Customhouse Quay, Box 474, Wellington ☎ 04/472-5230 🖷 04/473-3011 ∰ www.icnz.org.nz.

LANGUAGE

The truth of the matter is that, although most French people pretend to speak English, they, in fact, do not. So keep in mind that you are in France and France is full of French people who speak French. Needless to say, you'll find personnel in hotels that are mutilingual, but if you find yourself in a small outdoor market in Arles and you want to buy 12 jars of lavender honey for the price of 11, you are going to have to be patient, speak slowly, and smile a lot. This is not to say that English-speaking visitors should shout English words very slowly and loudly in the hope that the French will suddenly understand them. Any effort, even a small one, to say hello, goodbye, or thank you in their language is always greatly appreciated. So even if your own French is terrible, try to master a few words. A simple, friendly *bonjour* (hello) will do, as will asking if the person you are greeting speaks English ("*Parlez-vous anglais?*"). Throwing yourself on their mercy does wonders, so you can always try to begin a conversation with "*Excusez-moi. Mon Française est tres, tres mauvaise.*

Mille pardons. ("Excuse me. My French is very bad. A thousand pardons.") That way, you'll start out by acknowledging your shortcomings—and probably be all the more befriended for them. *See* the French Vocabulary and Menu Guide at the back of the book for more suggestions.

LANGUAGES FOR TRAVELERS

A phrase book and language-tape set can help get you started. *Fodor's French for Travelers* (available at bookstores everywhere) is excellent.

LODGING

The lodgings we list are the cream of the crop in each price category. We always list the facilities available—but we don't specify whether they cost extra: when pricing accommodations, always ask what's included and what costs extra. Properties indicated by a ✕▥ are lodging establishments whose restaurant warrants a special trip.

APARTMENT & HOUSE RENTALS

If you want a home base that's roomy enough for a family and comes with cooking facilities, consider a furnished rental. These can save you money, especially if you're traveling with a group. Renting an apartment or a *gîte rural*—a furnished house in the country—for a week or month can also save you money. Home-exchange directories sometimes list rentals as well as exchanges.

The national rental network, the Fédération Nationale des Gîtes de France, rents all types of accommodations rated by ears of corn (from 1 to 4) based on a stringent criteria of comfort and quality. You can find listings for fabulous stone farmhouses renovated to perfection with lit swimming pools and their own olive groves or simple cottages located in the heart of wine country, in the vineyards themselves if you wish. Gîtes de France has listings for rural gites, B&Bs, lodges, group accommodations for hikers located near hiking paths, and campsites where you can put up your tent in the middle of French farmland with not a soul in sight. Gîtes are nearly always maintained by on-site owners, who greet you on your arrival and provide information on groceries, doctors, and nearby attractions. A nationwide catalog (€16) is available from the Fédération Nationale des Gîtes de France, listing gîtes rent. Called "Nouveaux Gîtes Ruraux," the catalog lists only the newest additions to the network, because a comprehensive nationwide listing of all gîtes would make an unwieldy volume. If you know the region you want to visit, contact the departmental branch directly and order a photo catalog that lists every property. If you specify which dates you plan to visit, the office will narrow down the choice to rentals available for those days, but be sure to plan early, renting gîtes has become one of the most popular ways to discover France.

Individual tourist offices often publish lists of *locations meublés* (furnished rentals); these are often inspected by the tourist office and rated by comfort standards. Usually they are booked directly through the individual owner, which generally requires some knowledge of French. Rentals that are not classified or rated by the tourist office should be undertaken with trepidation, as they can fall well below your minimum standard of comfort.

Vacation rentals in France always book from Saturday to Saturday (with some offering weekend rates off-season). Most do not include bed linens and towels but make them available for an additional fee. Always check on policies on pets and children and specify if you need an enclosed garden for toddlers, a washing machine, a fireplace, etc. If you plan to have overnight guests during your stay, let the owner know; there may be additional charges. Insurance restrictions prohibit loading in guests beyond the specified capacity.

🔢 International Agents **At Home Abroad** ⌂ 163 3rd Ave., No. 319, New York, NY 10003 ☎ 212/421-9165 🖷 212/533-0095 ⊕ www.athomeabroadinc.com. **Drawbridge to Europe** ✉ 98 Granite St., Ashland, OR 97520 ☎ 541/482-7778 or 888/268-1148 🖷 541/482-7779 ⊕ www.drawbridgetoeurope.com. **Hideaways International** ✉ 767 Islington St., Portsmouth, NH 03801 ☎ 603/430-4433 or 800/843-4433 🖷 603/430-4444 ⊕ www.hideaways.com, annual membership $145. **Hometours International** ✉ 1108 Scottie La., Knoxville, TN 37919 ☎ 865/690-

8484 or 866/367-4668 ⊕ thor.he.net/~hometour/.
Interhome ⊠ 1990 N.E. 163rd St., Suite 110, North
Miami Beach, FL 33162 ☎ 305/940-2299 or 800/
882-6864 🖷 305/940-2911 ⊕ www.interhome.us.
Vacation Home Rentals Worldwide ⊠ 235 Kensington Ave., Norwood, NJ 07648 ☎ 201/767-9393 or
800/633-3284 🖷 201/767-5510 ⊕ www.vhrww.com.
Villanet ⊠ 1251 N.W. 116th St., Seattle, WA 98177
☎ 206/417-3444 or 800/964-1891 🖷 206/417-1832
⊕ www.rentavilla.com. **Villas and Apartments
Abroad** ⊠ 183 Madison Ave., Suite 201, New York,
NY 10016 ☎ 212/213-6435 or 800/433-3020 🖷 212/
213-8252 ⊕ www.vaanyc.com. **Villas International**
⊠ 4340 Redwood Hwy., Suite D309, San Rafael, CA
94903 ☎ 415/499-9490 or 800/221-2260 🖷 415/
499-9491 ⊕ www.villasintl.com.

🎦 Local Agents **Fédération Nationale des Gîtes
de France** ⊠ 59 rue St-Lazare, 75009 Paris
☎ 01-49-70-75-75 🖷 01-42-81-28-53 ⊕ www.
gitesdefrance.fr. **French Government Tourist Office**
(⇨ Visitor Information, *below*).

BED & BREAKFASTS

Chambres d'hôtes (bed-and-breakfasts)
can mean simple lodging, usually in the
hosts' home, with breakfast, but can also
mean a beautiful room in an 18th-century
château with gourmet food and a harpsi-
chord in the living room. Chambres
d'hôtes are most common in rural France,
though they are becoming more so in Paris
and other major cities. Check with local
tourist offices or contact Gîtes de France, a
national organization that lists B&Bs all
over the country, or private reservation
agencies. Often table d'hôte dinners (meals
cooked by and eaten with the owners) can
be arranged for an extra, fairly nominal
fee. Note that your hosts at B&Bs, unlike
those at hotels, are more likely to speak
only French.

🎦 Reservation Services **Gîtes de France**
⊠ 59 rue St-Lazare, Cedex 09, 75439 Paris
☎ 01-49-70-75-75 🖷 01-42-81-28-53 ⊕ www.
gitesdefrance.fr. **Paris Bed & Breakfast** ☎ 800/
872-2632.

CAMPING

French campsites have a good reputation
for organization and amenities but are
crowded in July and August. Many campsites welcome reservations, and in summer
it makes sense to book in advance. The

Fédération Française de Camping et de
Caravaning publishes a guide to France's
campsites (€16, plus shipping).

🎦 Campsite Guide **Fédération Française de
Camping et de Caravaning** ⊠ 78 rue de Rivoli,
75004 Paris ☎ 01-42-72-84-08 ⊕ www.
motorpressefrance.fr.

COSTS

The following is the price chart used
throughout this book to determine price
categories for all hotels. Prices are for a
standard double room in high season, including tax (19.6%) and service charge;
rates for any board plans will be higher.

CATEGORY	ALL REGIONS EXCEPT	CORSICA & BASQUE COUNTRY
$$$$	over €190	over €170
$$$	€120–€190	€120–€170
$$	€80–€120	€60–€120
$	€50–€80	€40–€60
¢	under €50	under €40

HOME EXCHANGES

If you would like to exchange your home
for someone else's, join a home-exchange
organization, which will send you its updated listings of available exchanges for a
year and will include your own listing in at
least one of them. It's up to you to make
specific arrangements.

🎦 Exchange Clubs **HomeLink International**
⌖ Box 47747, Tampa, FL 33647 ☎ 813/975-9825 or
800/638-3841 🖷 813/910-8144 ⊕ www.homelink.
org; $110 yearly for a listing, online access, and cata-
log; $70 without catalog. **Intervac U.S.** ⊠ 30 Corte
San Fernando, Tiburon, CA 94920 ☎ 800/756-4663
🖷 415/435-7440 ⊕ www.intervacus.com; $125
yearly for a listing, online access, and a catalog; $65
without catalog.

HOSTELS

No matter what your age, you can save
on lodging costs by staying at hostels. In
some 4,500 locations in more than 70
countries around the world, Hostelling
International (HI), the umbrella group for
a number of national youth-hostel associations, offers single-sex, dorm-style beds
and, at many hostels, rooms for couples
and family accommodations. Membership in any HI national hostel association, open to travelers of all ages, allows

you to stay in HI-affiliated hostels at member rates; one-year membership is about $28 for adults (C$35 for a two-year minimum membership in Canada, £14 in the U.K., A$52 in Australia, and NZ$40 in New Zealand); hostels charge about $10–$30 per night. Members have priority if the hostel is full; they're also eligible for discounts around the world, even on rail and bus travel in some countries.

Paris's major public hostels are run by the Fédération Unie des Auberges de Jeunesse (FUAJ)—for about €20, a bed, sheets, shower, and breakfast are provided, with beds usually three to four to a room. Maisons Internationales des Jeunes Etudiants (MIJE) have the plushest hostels, sometimes in historic mansions. Private hostels have accommodations that run from pleasant, if spartan, double rooms to dormlike arrangements.

🔲 Organizations **Hostelling International–USA** ✉ 8401 Colesville Rd., Suite 600, Silver Spring, MD 20910 ☎ 301/495-1240 🖷 301/495-6697 🌐 www.hiusa.org. **Hostelling International–Canada** ✉ 205 Catherine St., Suite 400, Ottawa, Ontario K2P 1C3 ☎ 613/237-7884 or 800/663-5777 🖷 613/237-7868 🌐 www.hihostels.ca. **YHA England and Wales** ✉ Trevelyan House, Dimple Rd., Matlock, Derbyshire DE4 3YH, U.K. ☎ 0870/870-8808, 0870/770-8868, or 0162/959-2600 🖷 0870/770-6127 🌐 www.yha.org.uk. **YHA Australia** ✉ 422 Kent St., Sydney, NSW 2001 ☎ 02/9261-1111 🖷 02/9261-1969 🌐 www.yha.com.au. **YHA New Zealand** ✉ Level 1, Moorhouse City, 166 Moorhouse Ave., Box 436, Christchurch ☎ 03/379-9970 or 0800/278-299 🖷 03/365-4476 🌐 www.yha.org.nz.

HOTELS & MOTELS

Rates are always by room, not per person. Often a hotel in a certain price category will have a few less-expensive rooms; it's worth asking about. In the off-season—usually November to Easter (except for southern France)—tariffs can be lower. It helps to inquire about promotional specials and weekend deals. Rates must be posted in all rooms (usually on the back of the door), with all extra charges clearly shown. You might try negotiating rates if you're planning on staying for a week or longer.

Assume all hotel rooms have air-conditioning, telephones, TV, and private bath unless otherwise noted. You should always **check what bathroom facilities the price includes.** When making your reservation, state your preference for shower (*douche*) or tub (*baignoire*)—the latter always costs more. Also when booking, **ask for a *grand lit* if you want a double bed.**

If you're counting on air-conditioning you should **make sure, in advance, that your hotel room is climatisé** (air-conditioned). If you throw open the windows, **don't expect screens** (*moustiquaires*). Nowhere in Europe are they standard equipment.

The quality of accommodations, particularly in older properties and even in luxury hotels, can vary greatly from room to room; **if you don't like the room you're given, ask to see another.**

Hotels operate on the European Plan (EP, with no meal provided) unless we note that they offer the Breakfast Plan (BP), Modified American Plan (MAP, with breakfast and dinner daily, known as *demi-pension*), or Full American Plan (FAP, or *pension complète,* with three meals a day); **board plans, which are usually an option offered in addition to the basic room plan, are generally only available with a minimum two- or three-night stay** and are, of course, more expensive than the basic room rate. Many noted hotels—especially those found in Provence, the Côte d'Azur, and the Loire Valley—have superb restaurants and, in such cases, room-and-board plans present an enjoyable game plan (one to be avoided if you wish to explore regional restaurants). Note that the hotel price charts in this book reflect basic room rates only. Inquire about board plans when making your reservations; details and prices are often stated on hotel Web sites.

It's always a good idea to **make hotel reservations in Paris and other major tourist destinations as far in advance as possible,** especially in late spring, summer, or fall. Faxing is the easiest way to contact the hotel (the staff is probably more likely to read English than to understand it spoken over the phone long-distance), though calling also works, while larger, more modern hotels now correspond using their e-mail address (always found on their Web site). But whether by fax, phone, or e-mail, you should specify the exact dates you want to stay at the hotel (don't forget to notify your hotel of a possible late check-in to prevent your room from being given away); the size of the room you want and how many people will be sleeping there; the type of accommodations you want (two twins, double, etc.); and what kind of bathroom (private with shower or bath, or both). You might also ask if a deposit (or your credit-card number) is required, and if so, what happens if you cancel. Request that the hotel fax you back so you have a written confirmation of your reservation.

If you arrive without a reservation, the tourist offices in major train stations and most towns can probably help you find a room.

Many hotels in France are small, often independently owned or family-run establishments. Some are affiliated with hotel groups, such as Logis de France, which can be relied on for comfort, character, and regional cuisine (look for its distinctive yellow-and-green sign). A Logis de France paperback guide is widely available in bookshops or from Logis de France. Two prestigious international groups with numerous converted châteaux and manor houses among its members are Relais & Châteaux and Small Luxury Hotels of the World; booklets listing members are available from these organizations. France also has some hotel chains. Examples in the upper price bracket are Frantel, Novotel, and Sofitel as well as Inter-Continental, Marriott, Hilton, Hyatt, Westin, and Sheraton. The Best Western, Campanile, Climat de France, Ibis, and Timhotel chains are more moderate. Typically, chains offer a consistently acceptable standard of modern features (modern bathrooms, TVs, etc.) but tend to lack atmosphere, with some exceptions (Best Western, for instance, tries to maintain the local character of the hotels it takes over).

RESERVING A ROOM

Here is a sample letter you can use when making a written reservation.

Cher (Dear) *Madame, Monsieur:*

Nous voudrions réserver une chambre pour (We wish to reserve a room for) ___ (number of) *nuit(s)* (nights), *du* (from) ___ (arrival date) *au* ___ (departure date), *à deux lits* (with twin beds), or *à lit-double* (with a double bed), or *une chambre pour une seule personne* (a room for a single person), *avec salle de bains et toilettes privées* (with a bathroom and private toilet). *Si possible, nous voudrains une salle de bains avec une baignoire et aussi une douche.* (If possible, we would prefer a bathroom with a tub as well as a shower—note that a bathroom with a tub can be more expensive than one with just a shower.) *Veuillez confirmer la réservation en nous communicant le prix de la chambre, et le dépot forfaitaire que vous exigez. Dans l'attente de votre lettre, nous vous prions d'agréer, Madame, Monsieur, l'expression de nos sentiments amicales.* (Can you please inform us about availabilties, the rate of room, and if any deposit is needed? With our friendliest greetings, we will wait your confirmation.)

🎫 **Toll-Free Numbers Best Western** ☎ 800/528-1234 ⊕ www.bestwestern.com. **Choice** ☎ 800/424-6423 ⊕ www.choicehotels.com. **Clarion** ☎ 800/424-6423 ⊕ www.choicehotels.com. **Comfort Inn** ☎ 800/424-6423 ⊕ www.choicehotels.com. **Four Seasons** ☎ 800/332-3442 ⊕ www.fourseasons.com. **Hilton** ☎ 800/445-8667 ⊕ www.hilton.com. **Holiday Inn** ☎ 800/465-4329 ⊕ www.ichotelsgroup.com. **Hyatt Hotels & Resorts** ☎ 800/233-1234 ⊕ www.hyatt.com. **Inter-Continental** ☎ 800/327-0200 ⊕ www.ichotelsgroup.com. **Marriott** ☎ 800/228-9290 ⊕ www.marriott.com. **Le Meridien** ☎ 800/543-4300 ⊕ www.lemeridien.com. **Quality Inn** ☎ 800/424-6423 ⊕ www.choicehotels.com. **Renaissance Hotels & Resorts** ☎ 800/468-3571 ⊕ www.renaissancehotels.com/. **Sheraton** ☎ 800/325-3535 ⊕ www.starwood.com/sheraton. **Westin Hotels & Resorts** ☎ 800/228-3000 ⊕ www.starwood.com/westin.

MAIL & SHIPPING

Post offices, or PTT, are found in every town and are recognizable by a yellow LA POSTE sign. They are usually open weekdays 8–7, Saturday 8–noon, but the **main Paris post office** (⊠ 52 rue du Louvre, 1ᵉʳ) is open 24 hours, seven days a week.

OVERNIGHT SERVICES

Sending overnight mail from major cities in France is relatively easy. Besides DHL, Federal Express, and UPS, the French post office has overnight mail service, called Chronopost.

⚡ Major Services DHL ✉ 6 rue des Colonnes, 2ᵉ, Opéra–Grands Boulevards, Paris ☎ 01-55-35-30-30 ✉ 59 rue Iéna, 16ᵉ, Trocadéro, Paris ☎ 01-45-01-91-00 ⊕ www.dhl.com. **Federal Express** ✉ 63 bd. Haussmann, 8ᵉ, Champs-Élysées, Paris ☎ 01-40-06-90-16 ✉ 2 rue 29 Juillet, 1ᵉʳ, Louvre–Tuileries, Paris ☎ 01-49-26-04-6, 08-00-12-38-00 for information about pickups all over France ⊕ www.fedex.com. **UPS** ✉ 34 bd. Malesherbes, 8ᵉ, Champs-Élysées, Paris ✉ 107 rue Réaumur, 2ᵉ, Beaubourg–Les Halles, Paris ☎ 08-00-87-78-77 for information all over France ⊕ www.ups.com.

POSTAL RATES

Letters and postcards to the United States and Canada cost €.75 for 20 grams. Letters and postcards to the United Kingdom cost €.50 for up to 20 grams. Letters and postcards within France cost €.50. Stamps can be bought in post offices and in cafés displaying a red TABAC sign outside. It takes, on the average, five days for a letter to reach the United States, 5–6 days to Australia, 4–5 days to Canada, and three days to any location in Europe.

RECEIVING MAIL

If you're uncertain where you'll be staying, **have mail sent to the local post office,** addressed as "poste restante," or to American Express, but remember that during peak seasons American Express may refuse to accept mail. The French postal service has a €.45 per item service charge.

MONEY MATTERS

The following prices are for Paris; other cities and areas are often cheaper (with the notable exception of the Côte d'Azur). Keep in mind that it's less expensive to eat or drink standing at a café or bar counter than to sit at a table. Two prices are listed, *au comptoir* (at the counter) and *à salle* (at a table; sometimes orders cost even more if you're seated at a terrace table). Coffee in a bar: €1–€1.50 (standing), €1.50–€5 (seated); beer in a bar: €2 (standing), €3–€6 (seated); Coca-Cola: €2–€3 a can; ham sandwich: €3–€5 2-km (1-mi) taxi ride: €6; movie-theater seat: €9 (15%–33% cheaper on Monday and Wednesday); foreign newspaper: €1–€3.

Prices throughout this guide are given for adults. Substantially reduced fees are almost always available for children, students, and senior citizens. For information on taxes, *see* Taxes.

ATMS

Fairly common in Paris, other cities, most towns, and even some villages (as well as in airports and train stations), **ATMs are one of the easiest ways to get euros.** Don't, however, expect to find ATMs in rural areas. Banks usually offer excellent wholesale exchange rates through ATMs.

To get cash at ATMs in France, **your PIN must be four digits long.** Note that the machine will give you two chances to enter your correct PIN number; if you make a mistake on the third try, your card will be held, and you'll have to return to the bank the next morning to retrieve it. You may have better luck with ATMs with a credit or debit card that is also a Visa or MasterCard, rather than just your bank card. Note, too, that you may be charged by your bank for using ATMs overseas; inquire at your bank about charges. Before you go, it's a good idea to **get a list of ATM locations that you can use** in France from your bank.

CREDIT CARDS

France is a credit-card society. Credit cards are used for just about everything, from the automatic gas pumps (now starting to pop up all over the country), to the tolls on highways, payment machines in underground parking lots, stamps at the post office, and even the most minor purchases in the larger department stores. A restaurant or shop would either have to be extremely small or brand-new not to have some credit-card or debit-card capability. However, some of the smaller restaurants and stores do have a credit-card minimum, usually around €15, which normally should be clearly indicated; to be safe, ask before you order. Do not forget to take your credit-card receipt, as fraudulent use of credit-card numbers taken from receipts is on the rise.

Note that American Express isn't always accepted outside the main cities.

Throughout this guide, the following abbreviations are used: **AE,** American Express; **DC,** Diners Club; **MC,** MasterCard; and **V,** Visa.

▨ Reporting Lost Cards **American Express** ☎ 336/939–1111 or 336/668–5309, call collect. **Diners Club** ☎ 303/799–1504, call collect. **MasterCard** ☎ 0800/90–1387. **Visa** ☎ 0800/90–1179, 410/581–9994 collect.

CURRENCY

On January 1, 2002, the new single European Union (EU) currency, the euro (€), became the official currency of the 12 countries participating in the European Monetary Union (with the notable exceptions of Great Britain, Denmark, and Sweden). The first thing you will notice is that the euro system has quite a lot of coins, eight to be exact: 1 and 2 euros, plus 1, 2, 5, 10, 20, and 50 cents. All coins display their value on one side, while the other side is adorned with the national symbol of the issuing country. There are seven colorful notes: 5, 10, 20, 50, 100, 200, and 500 euros. Notes have illustrations of the principal architectural styles from antiquity onward on one side and a map of Europe on the other, and are the same in all countries. The first thing you must do when you change your money is memorize the coins as soon as you can (notes are much easier to grasp, as they start off at €5) and you'll undoubtedly find yourself quickly weighted down with all those coins. This was the first complaint most Europeans had about this new system, and this, in turn, led to the second complaint: euro coins, with their high nickel content, pose a problem for people with an allergic sensitivity to the mineral (if you're one of them, try to handle the coins as little as possible, and if you do come in contact with them, rinse your hands as soon as you can).

The advent of the euro makes any whirlwind grand European tour all the easier.

From France, you'll glide across the borders of Austria, Germany, Italy, Spain, Holland, Ireland, Greece, Belgium, Finland, Luxembourg, and Portugal with no pressing need to run to the local exchange booth to change to yet another currency before you even had the time to become familiar with the last. You'll be able to do what drives many tourists crazy—to assess the value of a purchase (for example, to realize that eating a three-course meal in a small restaurant in Lisbon is cheaper than that ham sandwich you bought on the Champs Élysées). Initially, the euro had another benefit in that it was created as a direct competitor with the U.S. dollar and was envisioned to be, therefore, of nearly equal value. Unfortunately, exchange rates in 2003 and 2004 have seen the euro soar and the dollar take a hit. At press time, one euro equals U.S.$1.25.

Such are the ground rules when it comes to the euro and the old EU currencies. But you still have to **pay close attention to where you change your U.S. dollars and all other currencies that are not part of the EU community**—shop around for the best exchange rates (and also check the rates before leaving home) when it comes to non–EU currencies such as the dollar, the Japanese yen, and the British pound. The rates of conversion between the euro and other local currencies have been irrevocably fixed: 1 euro = 1.95 German marks; 1.39 Canadian dollars; 0.78 Irish punts; 13.76 Austrian schillings; 1.79 Australian dollars; 2.14 New Zealand dollars; 1,936.26 Italian liras; 40.33 Belgian francs; 166.38 Spanish pesetas; 2.20 Dutch guilders; 200.48 Portuguese escudos; 40.33 Luxembourg francs; 5.94 Finnish markkas; and 0.62 British pounds.

CURRENCY EXCHANGE

These days, the **easiest way to get euros is through ATMs**; you can find them in airports, train stations, and throughout the city. ATM rates are excellent because they are based on wholesale rates offered only by major banks. It's a good idea, however, to bring some euros with you from home and always to have some cash and traveler's checks as backup. For the best deal when exchanging currencies not within the Monetary Union purview (the U.S. dollar, the yen, and the British pound are examples), compare rates at banks (which usually have the most favorable rates) and booths and look for exchange booths that clearly state "no commission"; some exchange booths in tourist areas have been adding on a hefty €20—always confirm the rate with the teller before you hand over your money. The best rates are found at the Banque de France, but do expect a wait during busy summer months and be aware of the fact that it closes early (3:30 PM). You won't do as well at exchange booths in airports or rail and bus stations, in hotels, in restaurants, or in stores. To avoid lines at airport exchange booths, **get an initial amount of euros before you leave home.**

🏦 Exchange Services **International Currency Express** ✉ 427 N. Camden Dr., Suite F, Beverly Hills, CA 90210 ☎ 888/278–6628 orders 🖷 310/278–6410 ⊕ www.foreignmoney.com. **Travel Ex Currency Services** ☎ 800/287–7362 orders and retail locations ⊕ www.travelex.com.

TRAVELER'S CHECKS

Do you need traveler's checks? It depends on where you're headed. If you're going to rural areas and small towns, go with cash; traveler's checks are best used in cities. Lost or stolen checks can usually be replaced within 24 hours. To ensure a speedy refund, buy your own traveler's checks—don't let someone else pay for them: irregularities like this can cause delays. The person who bought the checks should make the call to request a refund. Note that with the prevalence of ATM cash machines in even the smallest French towns, you may find little, if no, need for traveler's checks.

PACKING

In your carry-on luggage, pack an extra pair of eyeglasses or contact lenses and enough of any medication you take to last a few days longer than the entire trip. You may also ask your doctor to write a spare prescription using the drug's generic name, as brand names may vary from country to country. In luggage to be checked, **never pack prescription drugs, valuables, or undeveloped film.** And don't forget to carry with you the addresses of offices that handle refunds of lost traveler's checks. Check *Fodor's How to Pack* (available at online retailers and bookstores everywhere) for more tips.

To avoid customs and security delays, carry medications in their original packaging. Don't pack any sharp objects in your carry-on luggage, including knives of any size or material, scissors, nail clippers, and corkscrews, or anything else that might arouse suspicion.

To avoid having your checked luggage chosen for hand inspection, don't cram bags full. The U.S. Transportation Security Administration suggests packing shoes on top and placing personal items you don't want touched in clear plastic bags.

CHECKING LUGGAGE

You're allowed to carry aboard one bag and one personal article, such as a purse or a laptop computer. Make sure what you carry on fits under your seat or in the overhead bin. Get to the gate early, so you can board as soon as possible, before the overhead bins fill up.

Baggage allowances vary by carrier, destination, and ticket class. On international flights, you're usually allowed to check two bags weighing up to 70 pounds (32 kilograms) each, although a few airlines allow checked bags of up to 88 pounds (40 kilograms) in first class. Some international carriers don't allow more than 66 pounds (30 kilograms) per bag in business class and 44 pounds (20 kilograms) in economy. On domestic flights, the limit is usually 50 to 70 pounds (23 to 32 kilograms) per bag. In general, carry-on bags shouldn't exceed 40 pounds (18 kilograms). Most airlines won't accept bags that weigh more than 100 pounds (45 kilograms) on domestic or international flights. Expect to pay a fee for baggage that exceeds weight limits. Check baggage restrictions with your carrier before you pack.

Airline liability for baggage is limited to $2,500 per person on flights within the United States. On international flights it amounts to $9.07 per pound or $20 per kilogram for checked baggage (roughly $640 per 70-pound bag), with a maximum of $634.90 per piece, and $400 per passenger for unchecked baggage. You can buy additional coverage at check-in for about $10 per $1,000 of coverage, but it often excludes a rather extensive list of items, shown on your airline ticket.

Before departure, itemize your bags' contents and their worth, and label the bags with your name, address, and phone number. (If you use your home address, cover it so potential thieves can't see it readily.) Include a label inside each bag and **pack a copy of your itinerary.** At check-in, make sure each bag is correctly tagged with the destination airport's three-letter code. Because some checked bags will be opened for hand inspection, the U.S. Transportation Security Administration recommends that you leave luggage unlocked or use the plastic locks offered at check-in. TSA screeners place an inspection notice inside searched bags, which are re-sealed with a special lock.

If your bag has been searched and contents are missing or damaged, file a claim with the TSA Consumer Response Center as soon as possible. If your bags arrive damaged or fail to arrive at all, file a written report with the airline before leaving the airport.

▨ Complaints U.S. Transportation Security Administration Contact Center ☏ 866/289-9673 ⊕ www.tsa.gov.

PASSPORTS & VISAS

When traveling internationally, carry your passport even if you don't need one (it's always the best form of I.D.) and **make two photocopies of the data page** (one for someone at home and another for you, carried separately from your passport). If you lose your passport, promptly call the nearest embassy or consulate and the local police.

U.S. passport applications for children under age 14 require consent from both parents or legal guardians; both parents must appear together to sign the application. If only one parent appears, he or she must submit a written statement from the

other parent authorizing passport issuance for the child. A parent with sole authority must present evidence of it when applying; acceptable documentation includes the child's certified birth certificate listing only the applying parent, a court order specifically permitting this parent's travel with the child, or a death certificate for the nonapplying parent. Application forms and instructions are available on the Web site of the U.S. State Department's Bureau of Consular Affairs (⊕ travel.state.gov).

ENTERING FRANCE

All Australian, Canadian, New Zealand, U.K., and U.S. citizens, even infants, need only a valid passport to enter France for stays of up to 90 days.

PASSPORT OFFICES

The best time to apply for a passport or to renew is in fall and winter. Before any trip, check your passport's expiration date, and, if necessary, renew it as soon as possible.

▨ Australian Citizens Passports Australia Australian Department of Foreign Affairs and Trade ☏ 131-232 ⊕ www.passports.gov.au.

▨ Canadian Citizens Passport Office ⊠ To mail in applications: 200 Promenade du Portage, Hull, Québec J8X 4B7 ☏ 819/994-3500 or 800/567-6868 ⊕ www.ppt.gc.ca.

▨ New Zealand Citizens New Zealand Passports Office ☏ 0800/22-5050 or 04/474-8100 ⊕ www. passports.govt.nz.

▨ U.K. Citizens U.K. Passport Service ☏ 0870/ 521-0410 ⊕ www.passport.gov.uk.

▨ U.S. Citizens National Passport Information Center ☏ 877/487-2778, 888/874-7793 TDD, TTY ⊕ travel.state.gov.

PUBLIC TRANSPORTATION

For information about public transportation in France, *see* A to Z sections *in* individual chapters.

RESTROOMS

Although most cafés reserve the right to limit use of their bathroom facilities to paying customers, most French are willing to ignore the frustrated glare of the waiter in an emergency. Bathrooms are often downstairs, are usually unisex (which means you may have to walk by urinals in use), are often just holes in the ground with porcelain pads on either side for your feet, and to top it all off, you'll probably have to pay a fee of 50¢. They are not the cleanest places in the world, especially for children, so it is in your best interest to be prepared and always carry a small box of tissues with you. In cities, your best bets may be fast-food chains, large department stores, and hotel lobbies. Do not be alarmed if you don't see any light switches—once the bathroom door is shut and locked, the lights will go on. You can also find pay-per-use toilet units on Parisian streets; these require 50¢ (small children, however, should not use these alone, as the self-sanitizing system works with weight-related sensors that might not sense the presence of a child). There are bathrooms in the larger métro stations and in all train stations for a cost of 50¢. Highway rest stops also have bathrooms, which are equipped with changing tables for babies and even showers during summer months.

SAFETY

Don't wear a waist pack, which pegs you as a tourist. Distribute your cash and any valuables (including your credit cards and passport) between a deep front pocket, an inside jacket or vest pocket, and a hidden money pouch. Do not reach for the money pouch once you're in public.

Beware of petty theft—purse snatching, pickpocketing, and pilfering from automobiles—throughout France, particularly in Paris and along the Côte d'Azur. Use common sense: avoid pulling out a lot of money in public; wear a handbag with long straps that you can sling across your body, bandolier style, with a zippered compartment for your money and passport. It's also a good idea to wear a money belt. When withdrawing money from cash machines, be especially aware of your surroundings and anyone standing uncomfortably close. If you feel uneasy, press the cancel button (*annuler*) and walk to an area where you feel more comfortable. Incidents of credit-card fraud are on the rise in France, especially in urban areas; be sure to collect your receipts, as these have

recently been used by thieves to charge over the Internet, where a PIN number is not mandatory. Men should keep their wallets up front. Car break-ins, especially in isolated parking lots where hikers set off for the day, are on the rise. It makes sense to **take valuables with you or leave your luggage at your hotel.**

Although Paris is as safe as any major city, muggers do occasionally mark tourists in the city's Métro system, especially at the tricky turnstiles; see the Métro Travel section in Paris A to Z in Chapter 1 for details. Note one cultural difference; a friendly smile or steady eye contact is often seen as an invitation to further contact; so, unfortunately, you should avoid being overly friendly with strangers—unless you feel perfectly safe.

SENIOR-CITIZEN TRAVEL

Older travelers (60 and older) can take advantage of many discounts, such as reduced admissions of 20%–50% to museums and movie theaters. For rail travel in France, the Carte Senior entitles travelers 60 years or older to discounts (⇨ Train Travel, *below*).

To qualify for age-related discounts, mention your senior-citizen status up front when booking hotel reservations (not when checking out) and before you're seated in restaurants (not when paying the bill). Be sure to have identification on hand. When renting a car, ask about promotional car-rental discounts, which can be cheaper than senior-citizen rates.
🔢 Educational Programs **Elderhostel** ⊠ 11 Ave. de Lafayette, Boston, MA 02111-1746 ☎ 877/426-8056, 978/323-4141 international callers, 877/426-2167 TTY 🖷 877/426-2166 ⊕ www.elderhostel.org. **Interhostel** ⊠ University of New Hampshire, 6 Garrison Ave., Durham, NH 03824 ☎ 603/862-1147 or 800/733-9753 🖷 603/862-1113 ⊕ www.learn.unh.edu.

SHOPPING

People in France like to bargain when they have a good feeling with the salesperson, even if the prices are clearly marked; it's one of the great pleasures of shopping in a country rich in small local businesses (in fact, the only places people don't bargain are in your typical large shopping center or big-name business). Bargaining is traditional in outdoor and flea markets, antiques stores, small jewelry shops, and art galleries, for example. If you're thinking of buying several items, or if you're simply in love with something a little bit too expensive, you've nothing to lose by cheerfully suggesting to the proprietor, "*Vous me faites un prix?*" ("How about a discount?"). The small business man will immediately size you up, and you'll have some good-natured fun.

SMART SOUVENIRS

When in France, think gourmet. For those who love to cook—or just love to taste—there are some simple gifts available in grocery stores or one of the many city and countryside outdoor markets: delicious mustard in a ceramic jar made following a traditional recipe from the 18th century costs about €4; organic jams made with whole cherries or figs from the south cost about €3 each; organic olive oils (with flavors ranging from thyme to truffle) will run about €15–€25 each; and a pot of organic lavender honey goes for €5. There's even gourmet salt, called *fleur de sel*, which comes from the coast of Brittany. Wonderful liqueurs include cognacs, armagnacs, or calvados—the fiery apple after-dinner *digestif* from Normandy—or one of the various fruit-flavored *eaux de vie* that Hemingway and Fitzgerald loved so much. These liquors can be found in any grocery or small liquor store and cost €16–€45. For the best quality, look for the tall slender bottles with handwritten labels and red-wax seals. For the champagne lover there are wonderful organic champagnes produced by smaller vineyards.

For other unique gift ideas, look to the museums. The Louvre, for example, has a museum shop that sells beautiful reproductions of a variety of masterpieces, from Greek figures to Egyptian heads, and ceramic Buddhas using the original molds. You can also purchase T-shirts here with charming vintage illustrations of Parisian life. Or look—surprise!—in the larger pharmacies for gift ideas from small French companies. For example, you could buy a small pot of all-natural Nuxe honey lip balm or the increasingly popular skin care products by Claudelie made from grape-seed extracts—French actresses swear by these. It's always interesting to look to the past: flea markets and *brocantes* (secondhand shops) sell Art Deco brooches, tiny eau-de-vie glasses, and evocative old copies of *Paris Match*. And there's always the chance of finding a stray bit of Quimper faïence. Another good bet is purchasing regional specialties, though your exports must be legal—madeleines, say, or nougat—as those savory sausages and glass jars of foie gras may be confiscated by customs. And for the hottest gift items going, just consult the latest issues of France's many style magazines, including *Maison Française* and *Vogue*.

STUDENTS IN FRANCE

Studying in France is the perfect way to shake up your perception of the world, make international friends, and improve your language skills. You may choose to study through a U.S.–sponsored program, usually through an American university, or enroll in a program sponsored by a French organization. Do your homework: programs vary greatly in expense, academic quality, exposure to language, amount of contact with locals, and living conditions. Working through your local university is the easiest way to find out about study-abroad programs in France. Most universities have staff members who distribute information on programs at European universities, and they might be able to put you in touch with program participants.

Student bargains can be found almost everywhere—on train and plane fares, and for movie and museum tickets. Note, however, that you must be 26 or under.

🖪 I.D.s & Services **STA Travel** ⊠ 10 Downing St., New York, NY 10014 ☎ 212/627-3111, 800/777-0112 24-hr service center 🖷 212/627-3387 ⊕ www.sta.com. **Travel Cuts** ⊠ 187 College St., Toronto, Ontario M5T 1P7, Canada ☎ 800/592-2887 in the U.S., 416/979-2406 or 866/246-9762 in Canada 🖷 416/979-8167 ⊕ www.travelcuts.com.

🖪 Resources **American Institute for Foreign Study** ⊠ 102 Greenwich Ave., Greenwich, CT 06830 ☎ 203/869-9090 or 800/727-2437 🖷 203/863-

6180. American Council of International Studies (ACIS) ✉ 19 Bay State Rd., Boston, MA 02215 ☎ 617/236-2051 or 800/888-2247. **Council on International Educational Exchange (CIEE)** ✉ 205 E. 42nd St., 15th fl., New York, NY 10017 ☎ 212/822-2600 or 888/268-6245 🖷 212/822-2699. **Institute of International Education (IIE)** ✉ 809 UN Plaza, New York, NY 10017 ☎ 212/984-5413. **World Learning** ✉ Kipling Rd., Box 676, Brattleboro, VT 05302 ☎ 802/257-7751 or 800/336-1616 🖷 802/258-3248.

TAXES

All taxes must be included in posted prices in France. The initials TTC (*toutes taxes comprises*—taxes included) sometimes appear on price lists but, strictly speaking, they are superfluous. By law, **restaurant and hotel prices must include 19.6% taxes and a service charge.** If they show up as extra charges on your bill, complain.

VALUE-ADDED TAX

A number of shops offer V.A.T. refunds to foreign shoppers. You are entitled to an export refund of the 19.6% tax, depending on the item purchased, but it's often applicable only if your purchases in the same store reach a minimum of €430 (for U.K. and EU residents) or €184 (others, including U.S. and Canadian residents). In most instances, you need to fill out a form, which must then be tendered to a customs official at your last port of departure. Remember to **ask for the refund, as some stores—especially larger ones—offer the service only upon request,** and note that V.A.T. refunds can't be processed after you arrive back home. In the end, you often wind up getting a credit on your charge card.

When making a purchase, **ask for a V.A.T. refund form** and find out whether the merchant gives refunds—not all stores do, nor are they required to. Have the form stamped like any customs form by customs officials when you leave the country or, if you're visiting several European Union countries, when you leave the EU. Be ready to show customs officials what you've bought (pack purchases together, in your carry-on luggage); budget extra time for this. After you're through passport control, take the form to a refund-service counter for an on-the-spot refund, or mail it to the address on the form (or the envelope with it) after you arrive home.

A service processes refunds for most shops. You receive the total refund stated on the form. Global Refund is a Europewide service with 210,000 affiliated stores and more than 700 refund counters—located at major airports and border crossings. Its refund form is called a Tax Free Check. The service issues refunds in the form of cash, check, or credit-card adjustment. If you don't have time to wait at the refund counter, you can mail in the form instead.

▣ **V.A.T. Refunds Global Refund** ✉ 99 Main St., Suite 307, Nyack, NY 10960 ☎ 800/566-9828 🖷 845/348-1549 ⊕ www.globalrefund.com.

TELEPHONES

AREA & COUNTRY CODES

The country code for France is 33. The first two digits of French numbers are a prefix determined by zone: Paris and Ile-de-France, 01; the northwest, 02; the northeast, 03; the southeast, 04; and the southwest, 05. Numbers that begin with 06 are for mobile phones (and are notoriously expensive). Pay close attention to the numbers beginning with 08; 08 followed by 00 is a toll-free number but 08–36 numbers are very costly, at least €.35 per minute.

CALLING FRANCE

Note that **when dialing France from abroad, drop the initial 0 from the number.** For instance, to call a telephone number in Paris from the United States, dial 011–33 plus the phone number minus the initial 0 (phone numbers in this book are listed with the full 10 digits, which you use to make local calls). To call France from the United Kingdom, dial 00–33, then dial the number in France minus the initial 0.

DIRECTORY & OPERATOR ASSISTANCE

To find a number **in France, dial 12 for information.** For international inquiries, dial 08–36–59–32–12 (you may request information for two numbers per call for a €3 service charge.

Another source of information is the Minitel, an online network similar to the Internet. You can find one—they look like a small computer terminal—in most post offices. Available free is an online phone book covering the entire country. To find information, hit the *appel* (call) key, then, when prompted, type the name you are looking for and hit *envoi* (return). It's also useful for tracking down services: choose *activité* (activity), tap in *piscine* (swimming pool), then Chartres, for example, and it will give you a list of all the pools in Chartres. Go to other lines or pages by hitting the *suite* (next) key. Newer models will connect automatically when you hit the book-icon key. To disconnect, hit *fin* (end).

INTERNATIONAL CALLS

To make a direct international call out of France, dial 00 and wait for the tone, then dial the country code (1 for the United States and Canada, 44 for the United Kingdom, 61 for Australia, and 64 for New Zealand) and the area code (minus any initial 0) and number.

Telephone rates have decreased recently in France owing to the fact that the French Telecom monopoly finally has some stringent competition. As in most countries, the highest rates fall between 8 AM and 7 PM; you can expect to pay €.25 per minute for a call to the U.S., Canada, or some of the closer European countries such as Great Britain, Belgium, Italy, and Germany. Rates are slashed by almost half when you make that same call between 7 PM and 8 AM, at just €.12 per minute, making it definitely worth the wait. There should be very little to compel you to call home with the help of international directory assistance, as it costs a hefty €6 per call; if this doesn't dissuade you, dial 00–33 plus the code of the country you'd like to call and a bilingual operator will come on line. Try not to make calls directly from your hotel either, unless you're using a phone card; they charge heavily for local calls and slap a service charge on for international calls. Your best bet is to buy a French phone card, a *télécarte,* which can be used from any phone and will end up saving you a bundle.

LOCAL CALLS

To make calls in the same city or town, or in the same region, dial the full 10-digit number.

LONG-DISTANCE CALLS

To call any region in France from another region, just dial the full 10-digit number.

LONG-DISTANCE SERVICES

AT&T, MCI, and Sprint access codes make calling long-distance relatively convenient, but you may find the local access number blocked in many hotel rooms. First ask the hotel operator to connect you. If the hotel operator balks, ask for an international operator, or dial the international operator yourself. One way to improve your odds of getting connected to your long-distance carrier is to travel with more than one company's calling card (a hotel may block Sprint, for example, but not MCI). If all else fails, call from a pay phone.

Access Codes AT&T Direct ☎ 08-00-99-00-11, 08-00-99-01-11, 800/874-4000 for information. **MCI WorldPhone** ☎ 08-00-99-00-19, 800/444-4444 for information. **Sprint International Access** ☎ 08-00-99-87, 800/793-1153 for information.

PHONE CARDS

The rare French person who doesn't have a mobile phone uses *télécartes* (phone cards), which you can buy just about anywhere, from post offices, tabacs, métro stations, magazine kiosks, small grocery stores, or any France Telecom office. These phone cards will save you money because the international rates they offer have been negotiated and are the best you will find. They will also save you time, as it's virtually impossible to find a phone that will take coins nowadays. There are two télécartes available; *une pétite* that costs €8 for 50 units or *une grande* that costs €15 for 120 units. Scratch the card to uncover your personal PIN, dial the toll-free number and the number you wish to reach (be it local or international) and the operator will tell you the exact amount of time you have to chat.

PUBLIC PHONES

Telephone booths can be found in airports, post offices, train stations, on the street, and often in cafés. You can use your own credit card or an international calling card; you must insert your credit card and punch in your PIN. Keep in mind that credit cards work on a €20 minimum—you will have exactly thirty days after the first call you put on your card to use up the credit. If you are using a phone card, simply dial the toll-free number on the back of the card, enter the identification number from the back of the card, and follow the instructions in English. At press time, prices were falling, and a local call made between 8 AM and 7 PM cost €.032 per minute. Low rates of €.016 per minute apply weekdays between 7 PM and 8 AM, all day Saturday and Sunday, and all national holidays.

TIME

The time difference between New York and Paris is six hours (so when it's 1 PM in New York, it's 7 PM in Paris). The time difference between London and Paris is one hour; between Sydney and Paris, 8–9 hours; and between Auckland and Paris, 12 hours. France, like the rest of Europe, uses the 24-hour (or "military") clock, which means that after noon you continue counting forward: 13h00 is 1 PM, 14h00 is 2 PM, 22h30 is 10:30 PM.

TIPPING

The French have a clear idea of when they should be tipped. Bills in bars and restaurants include a service charge, but **it is customary to round out your bill with some small change** unless you're dissatisfied. The amount varies: anywhere from €.50, if you've merely bought a beer, to €5 (or more) after a meal. Tip taxi drivers and hairdressers about 10%. In some theaters and hotels, coat-check attendants may expect nothing (if there is a sign saying POURBOIRE INTERDIT—tips forbidden); otherwise give them €.50–€1. Washroom attendants usually get €.50, though the sum is often posted.

If you stay in a hotel for more than two or three days, it is customary to leave something for the chambermaid—about €1.50 per day. In expensive hotels you may well call on the services of a baggage porter (bellboy) and hotel porter and possibly the telephone receptionist. All expect a tip: plan on about €1.50 per item for the baggage porter, but the other tips will depend on how much you've used their services—common sense must guide you here. In hotels that provide room service, give €1 to the waiter (this does not apply to breakfast served in your room). If the chambermaid does some pressing or laundering for you, give her €1 on top of the charge made. If the concierge has been very helpful, it is customary to leave a tip of €10–€20, depending on the type of hotel and the level of service.

Gas-station attendants get nothing for gas or oil but €.75 or €1.50 for checking tires. Train and airport porters get a fixed €1–€1.50 per bag, but you're better off getting your own baggage cart if you can (a €1 coin—refundable—is necessary in train stations only). Museum guides should get €1–€1.50 after a guided tour, and it is standard practice to tip tour guides (and bus drivers) €2 or more after an excursion, depending on its length.

TOURS & PACKAGES

Because everything is prearranged on a prepackaged tour or independent vacation, you spend less time planning—and often get it all at a good price.

BOOKING WITH AN AGENT

Travel agents are excellent resources. But it's a good idea to collect brochures from several agencies, as some agents' suggestions may be influenced by relationships with tour and package firms that reward them for volume sales. If you have a special interest, find an agent with expertise in that area; the American Society of Travel Agents (ASTA; ⇨ Travel Agencies) has a database of specialists worldwide. You can log on to the group's Web site to find an ASTA travel agent in your neighborhood. Make sure your travel agent knows the accommodations and other services of the place being recommended. Ask about the hotel's location, room size, beds, and whether it has a pool, room service, or programs for children, if you care about these. Has your agent been there in person or sent others whom you can contact? Do some homework on your own, too: local tourism boards can provide information about lesser-known and small-niche operators, some of which may sell only direct.

BUYER BEWARE

Each year consumers are stranded or lose their money when tour operators—even large ones with excellent reputations—go out of business. So check out the operator. Ask several travel agents about its reputation, and try to **book with a company that has a consumer-protection program.** (Look for information in the company's brochure.) In the United States, members of the United States Tour Operators Association are required to set aside funds ($1 million) to help eligible customers cover payments and travel arrangements in the event that the company defaults. It's also a good idea to choose a company that participates in the American Society of Travel Agents' Tour Operator Program; ASTA will act as mediator in any disputes between you and your tour operator.

Remember that the more your package or tour includes, the better you can predict the ultimate cost of your vacation. Make sure you know exactly what is covered, and beware of hidden costs. Are taxes, tips, and transfers included? Entertainment and excursions? These can add up.

🖪 Tour-Operator Recommendations **American Society of Travel Agents** (⇨ Travel Agencies). **National Tour Association (NTA)** ✉ 546 E. Main St., Lexington, KY 40508 ☎ 859/226-4444 or 800/682-8886 🖨 859/226-4404 ⊕ www.ntaonline.com. **United States Tour Operators Association (USTOA)** ✉ 275 Madison Ave., Suite 2014, New York, NY 10016 ☎ 212/599-6599 🖨 212/599-6744 ⊕ www.ustoa.com.

THEME TOURS

The following tour companies specialize in trips to France. The French Government Tourist Office (⇨ Visitor Information, *below*) publishes brochures on theme trips in France including "In the Footsteps of the Painters of Light in Provence" and "France for the Jewish Traveler." Also *see* Barge and Boat Travel, Bike Travel, *and* Children in France, *above*, for more information about theme tours.

🖪 Food & Wine **DuVine Adventures** ✉ 635 Boston Ave., Suite 2, Boston, MA 02144 ☎ 781/395-7440 or 888/396-5383 🖨 781/395-8472 ⊕ www.duvine.com. **European Culinary Adventures** ✉ 5 Ledgewood Way, Suite 6, Peabody, MA 01960 ☎ 978/535-5738 or 800/852-2625. **France In Your Glass** ✉ 814 35th Ave., Seattle, WA 98122 ☎ 206/325-4324 or 800/578-0903 🖨 206/325-1727 or 800/578-7069 ⊕ www.inyourglass.com. **Le Cordon Bleu** ✉ 8 rue Léon Delhomme, 75015 Paris ☎ 01-53-68-22-50 🖨 01-48-56-03-77 ⊕ www.cordonbleu.net. **Ritz-Escoffier** ✉ 15 pl. Vendôme, 75001 Paris ☎ 800/966-5758 ⊕ www.ritzparis.com, in Paris's Ritz hotel. **La Varenne** ☎ Box 25574, Washington, DC 20007 ☎ 202/337-0073 or 800/537-6486 🖨 703/823-5438 ⊕ www.lavarenne.com.

🖪 Music **Dailey-Thorp Travel** ✉ 330 W. 58th St., #610, New York, NY 10019-1817 ☎ 212/307-1555 or 800/998-4677 🖨 212/974-1420.

TRAIN TRAVEL

The SNCF, France's national rail service, is fast, punctual, comfortable, and comprehensive. Traveling across France, you have various options: local trains, overnight trains with sleeping accommodations, and the high-speed TGV, the Trains à Grande Vitesse (very fast trains).

TGVs average 255 kph (160 mph) on the Lyon–southeast line and 300 kph (190 mph) on the Lille and Bordeaux–southwest lines and are the best and the fastest domestic trains. They operate between Paris and Lille/Calais, Paris and Brussels, Paris and Amsterdam, Paris and Lyon–Switzerland–the Côte d'Azur, Paris and Angers–Nantes, and Paris and Tours–Poitiers–Bordeaux. As with other main-line trains, a small supplement may be assessed at peak hours.

It's possible to get from one end of France to the other without traveling overnight, especially on TGVs. Otherwise, you have a choice between high-price *wagons-lit* (sleeping cars) and affordable *couchettes* (bunks, six to a compartment in second class, four to a compartment in first, with sheets and pillow provided, priced at around €15).

Try to **get to the station half an hour before departure** to ensure you'll have a good seat. Before boarding, you must **punch your ticket (but not Eurailpass) in one of the orange machines** at the entrance to the platforms, or else the ticket collector will fine you €15 on the spot.

In Paris there are six international rail stations: Gare du Nord (northern France, northern Europe, and England via Calais or Boulogne); Gare St-Lazare (Normandy and England via Dieppe); Gare de l'Est (Strasbourg, Luxembourg, Basel, and central Europe); Gare de Lyon (Lyon, Marseille, the Côte d'Azur, Geneva, and Italy); and Gare d'Austerlitz (Loire Valley, southwest France, and Spain). Note that Gare Montparnasse has taken over as the main terminus for trains bound for southwest France.

BETWEEN THE U.K. & FRANCE

Short of flying, taking the "Chunnel" by riding the Eurostar train is the fastest way to cross the English Channel: 35 minutes from Folkestone to Calais, 60 minutes from motorway to motorway, or 2 hours and 40 minutes from London's Waterloo Station to Paris's Gare du Nord. For more information, *see* The Channel Tunnel, *above.*

British Rail also has four daily departures from London's Victoria Station, all linking with the Dover–Calais–Boulogne ferry services through to Paris. There's also an overnight service on the Newhaven–Dieppe ferry. Journey time is about eight hours. Credit-card bookings are accepted by phone or in person at a British Rail travel center.

🚗 Car Transport **Le Shuttle** ☎ 0990/353–535 in U.K., 03-21-00-61-00, 01-43-18-62-22 in France ⊕ www.eurotunnel.com.fr.

🚉 Passenger Service In the U.K.: **Eurostar** ☎ 0990/186–186 ⊕ www.eurostar.com. In the U.S.: **BritRail Travel** ☎ 800/677-8585 ⊕ www.britrail.com. **Rail Europe** ☎ 800/942–4866 ⊕ www.raileurope.com.

🚉 Passenger Service In the U.K.: **Eurostar** ☎ 0990/186–186 ⊕ www.eurostar.com. **InterCity Europe** ✉ Victoria Station, London ☎ 0990/848–848 for credit-card bookings. In the U.S.: **BritRail Travel** ☎ 800/677-8585. **Rail Europe** ☎ 800/942–4866 ⊕ www.raileurope.com.

CLASSES

There are two classes of train service in France; first (*première*) or second (*deuxième*). First-class seats offer 50% more legroom, plusher upholstery, private reading lamps, and computer plugs on the TGV, not to mention the hush-hush environment for those of you who want to sleep. The price is also nearly double.

CUTTING COSTS

To save money, **look into rail passes.** But be aware that if you don't plan to cover many miles, you may come out ahead by buying individual tickets.

There are two kinds of rail passes: those you must purchase at home before you leave for France, including the France Rail Pass, the Eurail Selectpass (which replaces the old Europass), and those available in France from SNCF. EurailPasses are available through travel agents and a few authorized organizations, such as Rail Europe (*see* contact information *under* Rail Pass Agents, *below*). SNCF rail passes are available at any train station in France. It's important to note that your rail pass does not guarantee you a seat on the train you wish to ride. You need to **book seats ahead even if you're using a rail pass.**

If you plan to travel outside of Paris by train, **consider purchasing a France Rail Pass,** which allows four days of unlimited train travel in a one-month period. If you travel solo, first class will run you $252, while second class is $218: you can add up to six days on this pass for $32 a day. For two people traveling together on a Saver Pass, the cost is $215, while in second class it is $186 additional days (up to 6) cost $28 each. Another option is the France Rail 'n Drive Pass (combining rail and rental car).

France is one of 17 countries in which **you can use EurailPasses,** which provide unlimited first-class rail travel in all of the participating countries for the duration of the pass. If you plan to rack up the miles, get a standard pass. These are available for 15 days ($588), 21 days ($762), one month ($946), two months ($1,338), and three months ($1,654). If your plans call for only limited train travel between

France and another country, **consider a two-country pass** which costs less money than a EurailPass. With the two-country pass you'll get four flexible travel days between France and Italy, France and Spain, or France and Switzerland for $299. In addition to standard EurailPasses, **ask about special rail-pass plans.** Among these are the Eurail Selectpass Youth (for those under age 26) and the Eurail Selectpass Saver (which gives a discount for two or more people traveling together). Whichever of the above passes you choose, remember that **you must purchase your Eurail passes at home before leaving for France.** Another option is to **purchase one of the discount rail passes available only for sale in France** from SNCF. When traveling together, **two people (who don't have to be a couple) can save money with the Prix Découverte à Deux.** You'll get a 25% discount during "*périodes bleus*" (blue periods: weekdays and not on or near any holidays). Note that you have to be with the person you said you would be traveling with.

You can **get a reduced fare if you're a senior citizen (over 60).** There are two options: for the Prix Découverte Senior, all you have to do is show a valid I.D. with your age and you're entitled to up to a 25% reduction in fares in first and second class. The second, the Carte Senior, is better if you're planning on spending a lot of time traveling; it costs €49, is valid for one year, and entitles you to up to a 50% reduction on most trains with a guaranteed minimum reduction of 25%. It also entitles you to a 30% discount on trips outside of France.

With the Carte Enfant Plus, for €63 **children under 12 and up to four accompanying adults can get up to 50% off on most trains for an unlimited number of trips.** This card is perfect if you're planning on spending a lot of time traveling in France with your children, as it's valid for one year. You can also opt for the Prix Découverte Enfant Plus: when you buy your ticket, simply show a valid I.D. with your child's age and you can get a significant discount for your child

and a 25% reduction for up to four accompanying adults.

If you purchase an individual ticket from SNCF in France and you're under 26, you automatically get a 25% reduction (a valid I.D., such as an ISIC card or your passport, is necessary). If you're going to be using the train quite a bit during your stay in France and **if you're under 26, consider buying the Carte 12–25** (€48), which offers unlimited 50% reductions for one year (provided that there's space available at that price; otherwise you'll just get the standard 25% discount).

If you don't benefit from any of these reductions and **if you plan on traveling at least 200 km (132 mi) round-trip and don't mind staying over a Saturday night, look into the Prix Découverte Séjour.** This ticket gives you a 25% reduction.

▨ Rail Pass Agents CIT Tours Corp. ✉ 15 W. 44th St., 10th fl., New York, NY 10036 ☎ 800/248-7245 for rail, 800/248-8687 for tours and hotels. **DER Travel Services** ✉ 9501 W. Devon Ave., Rosemont, IL 60018 ☎ 800/782-2424. **Rail Europe** ☎ 800/942-4866 in U.S. ⊕ www.raileurope.com.

FARES & SCHEDULES

You can **call for train information from any station or reserve tickets in any station.** Train schedules are available at stations or on the multilingual computerized schedule information network found at many stations. You can also make reservations and buy your ticket at the computer. Go to the Grandes Lignes counter for travel within France and to the Billets Internationaux desk if you're heading out of the country. Note that calling the SNCF's 08 number costs money (€0.34 per minute, and you often have to wait for minutes at a time), so it's better to go to the nearest station.

You must **always make a seat reservation for the TGV**—easily obtained at the ticket window or from an automatic machine. Seat reservations are reassuring but seldom necessary on other main-line French trains, except in summer and at certain busy holiday times. You also need a reservation for sleeping accommodations.

▨ Train Information BritRail Travel ☎ 800/677-8585 in the U.S. ⊕ www.britrail.com. **Eurostar**

☎ 08-36-35-35-39 in France, 0345/881881 in U.K. ⊕ www.eurostar.com. **Rail Europe** ☎ 800/942–4866 in U.S. ⊕ www.raileurope.com. **SNCF** ✉ 88 rue St-Lazare, 75009 Paris ☎ 08-36-35-35-35 ⊕ www.sncf.fr/indexe.htm.

LUGGAGE DELIVERY SERVICE

With an advance arrangement, SNCF will pick up and deliver your luggage at a given time. For instance, if you're planning on spending a weekend in Nice, SNCF will pick up your luggage at your hotel in Paris in the morning before check out and deliver it to your hotel in Nice, where it will be awaiting your arrival. The cost is €15 for the first bag, and €10 for two additional bags, with a maximum of three bags per person.

⌕ **SNCF Luggage Delivery Service** ☎ 08-25-84-58-45 ⊕ www.sncf.fr.

TRAVEL AGENCIES

A good travel agent puts your needs first. Look for an agency that has been in business at least five years, emphasizes customer service, and has someone on staff who specializes in your destination. In addition, **make sure the agency belongs to a professional trade organization.** The American Society of Travel Agents (ASTA)—the largest and most influential in the field with more than 20,000 members in some 140 countries—maintains and enforces a strict code of ethics and will step in to help mediate any agent-client disputes involving ASTA members if necessary. ASTA (whose motto is "Without a travel agent, you're on your own") also maintains a Web site that includes a directory of agents. (If a travel agency is also acting as your tour operator, *see* Buyer Beware *in* Tours & Packages.)

In France there are a number of good local agencies with offices in Paris as well as in other major cities. Nouvelles Frontiéres has offices in France as well as the United States.

⌕ Local Agent Referrals **American Society of Travel Agents** (ASTA) ✉ 1101 King St., Suite 200, Alexandria, VA 22314 ☎ 703/739-2782, 800/965-2782 24-hr hotline 🖷 703/684-8319 ⊕ www.astanet.com. **Association of British Travel Agents** ✉ 68-71 Newman St., London W1T 3AH ☎ 020/

7637-2444 🖷 020/7637-0713 ⊕ www.abta.com. **Association of Canadian Travel Agencies** ✉ 130 Albert St., Suite 1705, Ottawa, Ontario K1P 5G4 ☎ 613/237-3657 🖷 613/237-7052 ⊕ www.acta.ca. **Australian Federation of Travel Agents** ✉ Level 3, 309 Pitt St., Sydney, NSW 2000 ☎ 02/9264-3299 or 1300/363-416 🖷 02/9264-1085 ⊕ www.afta.com.au. **Travel Agents' Association of New Zealand** ✉ Level 5, Tourism and Travel House, 79 Boulcott St., Box 1888, Wellington 6001 ☎ 04/499-0104 🖷 04/499-0786 ⊕ www.taanz.org.nz.

⌕ Local Agencies **Access Voyages** ✉ 6 rue Pierre Lescot, 1e Ⓜ Châtelet-Les Halles ☎ 01-44-76-84-50. **American Express** ✉ 11 rue Scribe, 8e ☎ 01-47-77-77-07 ✉ 38 av. de Wagram, 8e ☎ 01-42-27-58-80. **Nouvelles Frontières** ✉ 5 av. de l'Opéra, 1er Ⓜ Pyramides ☎ 08-03-33-33-33 ✉ 14 av. de Verdun, 06000 Nice ✉ 12 E. 33rd St. New York, NY 10016 🖷 212/779-1007. **Soltours** ✉ 48 rue de Rivoli, 4e Ⓜ Hôtel-de-Ville ☎ 01-42-71-24-34.

VISITOR INFORMATION

Learn more about foreign destinations by checking government-issued travel advisories and country information. For a broader picture, consider information from more than one country.

⌕ France Tourism Information **France On-Call** ☎ 410/286-8310, weekdays 9-7 ⊕ www.francetourism.com. **Chicago** ✉ 676 N. Michigan Ave., Chicago, IL 60611 ✎ fgto@mcs.net. **Los Angeles** ✉ 9454 Wilshire Blvd., Suite 715, Beverly Hills, CA 90212 ✎ fgto@gte.net. **New York City** ✉ 444 Madison Ave., 16th fl., New York, NY 10022 ✎ info@francetourism.com. **Canada** ✉ 1981 Ave. McGill College, Suite 490, Montréal, Québec H3A 2W9. **U.K.** ✉ 178 Piccadilly, London W1V OAL ☎ 171/6399-3500 🖷 171/6493-6594.

⌕ Local Tourist Offices *See* the A to Z sections *in* individual chapters for local tourist office telephone numbers and addresses.

⌕ Government Advisories **U.S. Department of State** ✉ Overseas Citizens Services Office, 2100 Pennsylvania Ave. NW, 4th fl., Washington, DC 20520 ☎ 202/647-5225 interactive hotline, 888/407-4747 ⊕ www.travel.state.gov. **Consular Affairs Bureau of Canada** ☎ 800/267-6788 or 613/944-6788 ⊕ www.voyage.gc.ca. **U.K. Foreign and Commonwealth Office** ✉ Travel Advice Unit, Consular Division, Old Admiralty Bldg., London SW1A 2PA ☎ 0870/606-0290 or 020/7008-1500 ⊕ www.fco.gov.uk/travel. **Australian Department of Foreign**

Affairs and Trade ☎ 300/139–281 travel advice, 02/6261–1299 Consular Travel Advice Faxback Service ⊕ www.dfat.gov.au. **New Zealand Ministry of Foreign Affairs and Trade** ☎ 04/439–8000 ⊕ www.mft.govt.nz.

🔝 Tourism Web Sites **Tourism in France** ⊕ www.tourisme.fr with links to 3,500 tourist offices. **Bordeaux Tourist Office** ⊕ www.bordeaux-tourisme.com is the main site for this southwest France metropolis.**French Government Tourist Office** ⊕ www.francetourism.com is the national site for French tourism. **Lyon Tourist Office** ⊕ www.lyon-france.com is a helpful portal to this important hub of the country. **Monaco Tourist Office** ⊕ www.monaco.mc/usa welcomes you to this glitzy resort in the south of France. **Normandy Tourist Board** ⊕ www.normandy-tourism.org is a great site for the region. **The Office du Tourisme et Congresses de Paris** ⊕ www.paris-touristoffice.com is the main site for the Paris tourist office. **Provence Tourist Office** ⊕ www.visitprovence.com is a helpful site to all things Provençal. **Riviera Tourist Office** ⊕ www.crt-riviera.fr is one of the helpful overview sites devoted to the region. **Strasbourg Tourism Office** ⊕ www.strasbourg.com is devoted to one of the hubs of the Alsace-Lorraine region.

WEB SITES

Do check out the World Wide Web when planning your trip. You'll find everything from weather forecasts to virtual tours of famous cities. Be sure to visit Fodors.com (⊕ www.fodors.com), a complete travel-planning site. You can research prices and book plane tickets, hotel rooms, rental cars, vacation packages, and more. In addition, you can post your pressing questions in the Travel Talk section. Other planning tools include a currency converter and weather reports, and there are loads of links to travel resources.

🔝 Recommended Web Sites The **Centre du Monuments Nationaux** runs 200 monuments—from the Arc de Triomphe to Chambord—and their Web site ⊕ www.monum.fr is chock full of information. If you are château-hopping, log on to ⊕ www.chateauxandcountry.com for brief overview of hundreds of châteaux in France. **Eurail** ⊕ www.eurail.com has all the info about the many railway passes available for travel through France and Europe. **Eurostar** ⊕ www.eurostar.com is the main contact for the Chunnel train that connects Paris and London. **French Embassy** ⊕ www.france.diplomatie.fr is helpful for information on the French government. **French Ministry of Culture** ⊕ www.culture.fr provides a portail to all the cultural happenings and institutions throughout France. **French National Museums** ⊕ www.rmn.fr is the main site for the Réunion des musées nationaux, which administers the biggest and greatest museums in France. **Rail Europe** ⊕ www.raileurope.com gives you the scoop on many different discount rail passes through France and Europe. **SNCF** ⊕ www.sncf.fr/indexe.htm is the main clearinghouse for the French national railway network, invaluable for schedules and prices. **Weather Reports** ⊕ www.meteo.fr helps you track the highly variable weather in France.

PARIS

1

POP YOUR CORK
dining at Le Grand Véfour,
Paris' prettiest restaurant ⇨*p.51*

TRIP THE LIGHT *FANTASTIQUE*
at the Eiffel Tower's nightly show ⇨*p.21*

SHINE YOUR BEST HALF-SMILE
on Mona in the Louvre ⇨*p.10*

MAKE A FACE BACK AT A GARGOYLE
high atop Notre-Dame ⇨*p.12*

PAINT THE TOWN *ROUGE*
at Lapin Agile, Picasso's hangout ⇨*p.46*

CHASE THE PHANTOM'S SHADOWS
at the Opéra Garnier ⇨*p.30*

GREET THE RISING SUN
from Montmartre's Sacré-Coeur ⇨*p.49*

Updated by
Ethan Gilsdorf,
Rosa Jackson,
Nicola
Keegan,
Christopher
Mooney, and
Lisa Pasold

Introduction by
Nancy Coons

IF THERE'S A PROBLEM WITH A TRIP TO PARIS, it's the embarrassment of riches that faces you. No matter which aspect of Paris you choose—touristy, historic, fashion-conscious, pretentious-bourgeois, thrifty, or the legendary bohemian arty Paris of undying attraction—one thing is certain: you will carve out your own Paris, one that is vivid, exciting, ultimately unforgettable. Wherever you head, your itinerary will prove to be a voyage of discovery. But choosing the Paris of your dreams is a bit like choosing a perfume or cologne. Do you want something young and dashing, or elegant and worldly? How about sporty, or perhaps strictly glamorous? No matter: they are all here—be it perfumes, famous museums, legendary churches, or romantic cafés. Whether you spend three days or three months in this city, it will always have something new to offer you, which may explain why the most assiduous explorers of Paris are the Parisians themselves.

Veterans know that Paris is a city of vast, noble perspectives and intimate, ramshackle streets, of formal *espaces vertes* (green open spaces) and quiet squares. This combination of the pompous and the private is one of the secrets of its perennial pull. Another is its size: Paris is relatively small as capitals go, with distances between many of its major sights and museums invariably walkable.

For the first-timer there will always be several must-dos at the top of the list, but getting to know Paris will never be quite as simple as a quick look at Notre-Dame, the Louvre, and the Eiffel Tower. You'll discover that around every corner, down every *ruelle* (little street) lies a resonance-in-waiting. You can stand on the rue du Faubourg St-Honoré at the very spot where Edmond Rostand set Ragueneau's pastry shop in *Cyrano de Bergerac*. You can read the letters of Madame de Sévigné in her actual *hôtel particulier,* or private mansion, now the Musée Carnavalet. You can hear the words of Racine resound in the ringing, hair-raising diction of the Comédie Française. You can breathe in the fumes of hubris before the extravagant onyx tomb Napoléon designed for himself. You can gaze through the gates at the school where Voltaire honed his wit, and you can lay a garland on Oscar Wilde's poignant grave at Père-Lachaise Cemetery.

If this is your first trip, you may want to take a guided tour of the city—a good introduction that will help you get your bearings and provide you with a general impression before you return to explore the sights that particularly interest you. To help track those down, this chapter's exploration of Paris is divided into eight neighborhood walks. Each *quartier,* or neighborhood, has its own personality, which is best discovered by foot power. Ultimately, your route will be marked by your preferences, your curiosity, and your state of fatigue. You can wander for hours without getting bored—though not, perhaps, without getting lost. By the time you have seen only a few neighborhoods, drinking in the rich variety they have to offer, you should not only be culturally replete but downright exhausted—and hungry, too. Again, take your cue from Parisians and think out your next move in a sidewalk café. So you've heard stories of a friend who paid $6 for a coffee at a café. So what? What you're paying for is time, and the opportunity to watch the intricate drama of Parisian street life unfold. Hemingway knew the rules; after all, he would have

1

A visit to Paris will never be quite as simple as a quick look at a few landmarks. Each *quartier* (neighborhood) has its own treasures, and you should be ready to explore them—an enticing prospect in this most elegant of cities. Outlined here are the main areas on which to concentrate, depending on the length of your stay. Bear in mind that the amount of time spent visiting monuments—and museums in particular—is not something you can predict with any certainty, nor would you want to. Just to see the city's larger museums, let alone its smaller ones, would probably take a whole week.

If you have 3 days

On your first day begin at the beginning: the Ile de la Cité, settled more than 2,000 years ago and home to the cathedral of **Notre-Dame** ❶ ⊢. Take a cue from Victor Hugo and climb the 387 steps of one of its towers to the former haunts of its mythic hunchback, Quasimodo—you'll be rewarded by a great view of Paris framed by the stone gargoyles created by Viollet-le-Duc. Descend to explore the enchanting **Ancien Cloître Quartier** ❷, nestled next to the cathedral. Then head several blocks over to marvel at the **Sainte-Chapelle** ❸, a jewel box of Gothic art shimmering with hundreds of stained-glass panels. After visiting the nearby **Conciergerie** ❹— the last abode of Queen Marie-Antoinette—walk over the **Pont Neuf** ❼, which spans the Seine, and turn left to reach the greatest museum in the world— the **Louvre** ❽ (keep in mind it's closed Tuesday), famed showcase for the *Winged Victory,* the *Venus de Milo,* and the haunting, ironic smile of the *Mona Lisa.* Afterward, exit into the calm, green **Jardins des Tuileries** ❿, immortalized by the Impressionists, then head west to the city's heart, place de la Concorde. Walk up the leafy lower reaches of the Champs-Élysées, heading over to the Seine and its most gorgeous bridge—the **Pont Alexandre III** ⓲—just in time for *l'heure bleue,* or dusk.

On Day 2 you're ready to tackle picture-postcard Paris. Start at the **Tour Eiffel** ⓰, then take in some culture at the **Palais de Chaillot** ⓱ museums, or the nearby **Musée Guimet** ⓲ (for great Asian art) and the **Musée d'Art Moderne de la Ville de Paris** ⓴ (for fine modern art). For a blast of the purest Parisian glamour, check out the **Maison de Baccarat** ⓳. At the place de l'Alma opt for a ride on the **Bateaux Mouches** ㉑ up and down the Seine. Head along avenue Montaigne—Dior is here along with numerous other temples of fashion— to the Champs-Élysées and up left to the **Arc de Triomphe** ㉒.

On Day 3 explore the Faubourg St-Honoré, Paris's legendary center of luxe, where world-class shopping and two of Paris's most beautiful urban set pieces— **place Vendôme** ㉗ and the **Palais-Royal** ㉜—await. Continue north to hit the Grands Boulevards, famed for their sidewalk cafés, the glittering **Opéra Garnier** ㊸—still haunted by the Phantom?—and then enjoy a tranquil afternoon in the chic and rich residential neighborhood around **Parc Monceau** ㊳, with a stop at the art-filled mansions of the **Musée Nissim de Camondo** ㊵ and the **Musée Jacquemart-André** ㊶.

If you have
5 days

Follow the three-day itinerary above, then on your fourth day begin at the **Musée d'Orsay** ⑫, where many of the most famous Impressionist paintings in the world are on view. Pay your respects to Napoléon at the nearby church of the **Hôtel des Invalides** ⑭ and then to the great sculptor Rodin, at the **Musée Rodin** ⑮, housed in one of the prettiest *hôtels particuliers* in the city. Head east along the boulevard St-Germain to the picturesque place Furstenberg to visit the **Musée Delacroix** ⑲, the haunt of another great artist and set on gorgeous place Furstenberg. South a few blocks is the **Jardin du Luxembourg** ㉟, perfect for a sylvan time-out. If you're not tired yet, stop in at the extraordinary **Musée National du Moyen-Age** ㊽, which graces the time-stained Hôtel de Cluny.

On your fifth day begin on the **Ile St-Louis** ㉕—the little island sitting next to the larger Ile de la Cité in the Seine. Although there are no major sights to see here, you'll find an enchanting neighborhood that has more than a touch of the time machine to it. Cross over the Seine to the Marais—one of the city's most venerable quarters, studded with great Baroque and Rococo mansions, many of which are now museums, including the **Musée Picasso** ㉖. Nearby is another mecca for modern-art lovers, the **Centre Beaubourg** ㉟, although those with more traditional tastes will make a beeline for the **Musée Carnavalet** ㉓ (the Paris History Museum). Then, to give your less-than-bionic feet a well-deserved rest, head to the magnificent 17th-century square **place des Vosges** ㉔ to enjoy sunset on one of its park benches and dinner at one of the casual cafés lining the square.

If you have
7 days

On your sixth day take a vacation from your Paris vacation by heading out for a day trip to **Versailles,** built in bicep-flexing Baroque splendor. Don't forget to explore its vast park in order to take in the intimate Petit Trianon and Hameau, which was Marie-Antoinette's toy farm.

On your seventh day get up at dawn and hurry up to the Butte (mound) of Montmartre, which graces a dramatic rise over the city. Get here to see the sun rise over the entire city from your perch on place du Parvis, in front of the basilica of the **Sacré-Coeur** ㉑. Track the spirit of Toulouse-Lautrec through the streets and to the **Musée de Montmartre** ㉒. For your last afternoon, descend back into the city to either attack some of the city's "other" museums (the **Musée Cognacq-Jay** ㉒ and the **Musée Maillol** ㉖), to explore Montparnasse, or, for a unique *grande finale* to your trip, visit some "permanent" Parisians ensconced in noble marble splendor at legendary **Cimetière du Père-Lachaise** ㊾. Congratulations are in order: you've just finished a unique cram course in French culture and history.

remained just another unknown sportswriter if the waiters in the cafés had hovered around him impatiently.

Exploring Paris

Updated by
Christopher
Mooney

As world capitals go, Paris is surprisingly compact. With the exceptions of the Bois de Boulogne and Montmartre, you can easily walk from one major sight to the next. The city is divided in two by the River Seine, with two islands (Ile de la Cité and Ile St-Louis) in the middle. Each bank of the Seine has its own personality; the Rive Droite (Right Bank), with its spacious boulevards and formal buildings, generally has a more genteel feel than the carefree Rive Gauche (Left Bank), to the south. The east–west axis from Châtelet to the Arc de Triomphe, via the rue de Rivoli and the Champs-Élysées, is the Right Bank's principal thoroughfare for sightseeing and shopping.

The city is divided into 20 *arrondissements* (districts). The last one or two digits of a city zip code (e.g., 75002) will tell you the arrondissement (in this case, the 2ᵉ, or 2nd). Although the best method of getting to know Paris is on foot, public transportation—particularly the métro system—is excellent. Buy the *Plan de Paris* booklet, a city map and guide with a street-name index that also shows métro stations. Note that all métro stations have detailed neighborhood maps displayed just inside the entrance.

This chapter is divided into eight Paris neighborhood walks. A few monuments and museums close for lunch between noon and 2, and many are closed on either Monday or Tuesday: Check before you set off.

Numbers in the text correspond to numbers in the margin and on the Paris and Montmartre maps.

The Historic Heart: From Notre-Dame to the Place de la Concorde

No matter how you first approach Paris—historically, geographically, emotionally—it is the River Seine that summons all and that harbors two celebrated islands, the Ile de la Cité and the Ile St-Louis, both at the very center of the city. Of the two, it is the Ile de la Cité that forms the historic ground zero of Paris. It was here that the earliest inhabitants of Paris, the Gaulish tribe of the Parisii, settled in about 250 BC, calling their home Lutetia, meaning "settlement surrounded by water." Today it is famed for the great, brooding cathedral of Notre-Dame, the haunted Conciergerie, and the dazzling Sainte-Chapelle. If Notre-Dame represents Church, another major attraction of this walk—the Louvre—symbolizes State. A succession of French rulers was responsible for filling this immense structure with the world's greatest paintings and works of art. It's the largest museum in the world, as well as one of the easiest to get lost in. Beyond the Louvre lie the graceful Tuileries Gardens, the grand place de la Concorde—the very hub of the city—and the Belle Epoque splendor of the Grand Palais and the Pont Alexandre III. All in all, this area comprises some of the most historic and beautiful sights to see in Paris.

a good walk

Place du Parvis—the square regarded by the French as *kilomètre zero,* the spot from which all distances to and from the city are officially measured—makes a fitting setting for **Notre-Dame de Paris** ❶ ☞, familiar and yet regal, like the gracious lady (as the priests will tell you) whose name it bears. Explore the interior, then toil up the steps to the towers for a grand view of the heart of Paris. To escape the crowds, relief is just a short—and magical—stroll away: the **Ancient Cloître** ❷, a nook of medieval Paris that is tucked behind the northern (or left-hand side as you face the cathedral) buttresses of Notre-Dame. Explore this storybook warren of streets, then head behind the cathedral to the Pont de l'Archevêché for the best view of Notre-Dame and proceed to cross over to the quai de la Tournelle (where Leslie Caron and Gene Kelly so memorably pas-de-deux-ed in *An American in Paris*) for a waterside vista.

Walk along the Seine embankment to the Pont au Double, cross over the Seine once again to place du Parvis, then head across the square and along rue de la Cité to rue de Lutèce, where you should make a left and walk to boulevard du Palais and the imposing Palais de Justice, the 19th-century Law Courts, which harbors the medieval **Sainte-Chapelle** ❸—a vision in shimmering stained glass—and the **Conciergerie** ❹, the prison where Marie-Antoinette awaited her appointment with the guillotine. At the end of quai de l'Horloge is the charming **place Dauphine** ❺. Opposite, on the other side of the Pont Neuf, is **square du Vert-Galant** ❻, with its proud equestrian statue of Henri IV. On the quay side of the square, *vedettes* (glass-top motorboats) start their tours along the Seine.

Cross the **Pont Neuf** ❼—the New Bridge, confusingly so called given that it's actually the oldest bridge in Paris—to the Rive Droite and make a left turn toward the **Louvre** ❽, the vast museum on the quai du Louvre, entering through the grand East Front and heading through the Cour Carrée to the I. M. Pei glass-pyramid entry. After viewing some of the greatest artworks in the world, exit through the **Carrousel du Louvre** ❾ complex, a posh underground shopping mall, to the manicured lawns of the **Jardin des Tuileries** ❿, or Tuileries Gardens. Standing sentinel is the **Musée du Jeu de Paume** ⓫, host to outstanding exhibits of contemporary art. At the far end lies one of the world's grandest squares, **place de la Concorde** ⓬, centered by a grand Egyptian obelisk with a gilded top. Continue up the Champs-Élysées to avenue Winston-Churchill to the **Grand Palais** ⓭, whose back half houses the **Palais de la Découverte** ⓮, with Paris's planetarium and exhibits on science and technology. For a romantic finale, head back over to the Seine and the floridly beautiful **Pont Alexandre-III** ⓯.

TIMING   Allowing for toiling up towers, dancing down quays, and musing at *Mona Lisa,* this walk will take a full day—enabling you to reach Pont Alexandre-III just before sundown. Of course, if you want to do full justice to the vast collections of the Louvre, you could easily spend a week there and still not see everything. If you return to ogle the museum, visit in the mornings or late in the day, after 4 PM, when it's less crowded (note that it's closed Tuesday). But if this is your first exploration of Paris's historic heart, plan on spending your morning touring the Ile de la Cité sights, then, after your break for lunch, the afternoon at the Louvre.

What to See

FodorsChoice   ★   ❷ **Ancien Cloître Quarter.** Hidden in the shadows of Notre-Dame, this adorable and often overlooked nook of Paris was thankfully spared when Baron Haussmann knocked down much of the Ile de la Cité in the 19th century. Enter the quarter—originally the area where seminary students boarded with the church canons—by heading north toward the Seine to reach rue Chanoinesse, once the seminary's cloister walk. Here, at No. 10, is the house that was once paradise to those fabled lovers of the Middle Ages, Héloïse and Abélard. That house, unfortunately, is com-

Beyond the Great Museums

Paris's museums range from the ostentatiously grand to the delightfully obscure—the French seem bent on documenting everything any of its citizens have ever done. Not just repositories of masterworks, the city's museums also reveal the endlessly fascinating nuances of French culture. It's fitting that the Musée d'Orsay, a Belle Epoque former train station, houses the city's legacy of art from 1848 to 1914: railroads and other everyday phenomena were—shockingly so at the time—favorite subjects of the period's artists, especially the Impressionists, who enjoy pride of place under the glass-vaulted roof. And it was the French Revolution that opened the Louvre to the masses, so that all can now view the extraordinary collection amassed in good part by seven centuries of monarchs. A proletarian spirit also holds sway at the Centre Pompidou, where the world's largest collection of modern art is displayed; though opened in 1977, it has been so popular that a 2001 renovation means it is looking better than ever. In addition to these big three, other favorites include museums that began life not as museums, but as sumptuous houses. Many of these gilded time-machines are filled with salons aglitter with gilt *boiserie* (carved-wood panels), chandeliers, and flocked red-velvet walls literally oozing Parisian elegance. For these unique peeps into yesteryear, top bets include the decorative arts treasures found at the Musée Nissim de Camondo, the Musée Jacquemart-André, and the Musée Carnavalet. Skip through the centuries at some modern art museums, as both the Musée Rodin and the Musée Picasso are housed in historic hôtels particuliers—mansions built as private homes for the rich and famous. For a true trip back to the 17th, 18th or 19th century, discover overlooked jewels like the Hôtel Lauzun on the Ile St-Louis, the Atelier Delacroix on the place Furstenberg, and the Musée de la Vie Romantique, where the likes of Chopin and George Sand once rendezvoused, at the foot of Montmartre.

Bon Appétit!

As for dining, well . . . the French wrote the book. Paris is one of the world's great food capitals and a bastion of both classic and nouvelle French cuisine. Nonetheless, if you're coming from New York, London, or Los Angeles, where innovative restaurants abound, you may find the French capital a little staid. In fact, a battle is currently being waged here between the traditionalists and a remarkable new generation of chefs who are set on modernizing food preparation—forever changing the French culinary landscape in the process. But all chefs here agree with the French gastronome Anthelme Brillat-Savarin, who proclaimed, "Animals feed, men eat, but only wise men know the art of dining." Join them in the pursuit of this art and don't feel guilty if you spend as much time of your stay in Paris in its restaurants as in its museums. Give yourself over to the leisurely meal; two hours for a three-course menu is par, and you may, after relaxing into the routine, begin to feel pressed at less than three. Whether your dream meal is savoring truffle-studded fois gras served on Limoges china or sharing a baguette with *jambon* (ham) and Brie *sur l'herbe* (on the grass), eating in Paris can be a memorable experience. Needless to say, it's well worth splurging on a dinner of outstanding haute cuisine in historic, time-burnished splendor. But also keep in mind that many famous chefs have opened bistro annexes where you can sample their cooking for less. In addition, younger chefs are setting up shop in more affordable, outlying parts of Paris, where they are serving their own innovative version of bistro classics. End any proper meal with a sublime cheese course, then dessert (the more decadent and creamy the better), then an *express* (taken black, with sugar).

Café Society

Along with air, water, and wine, the café remains one of the basic necessities of life in Paris. You may prefer a posh perch at a renowned spot such as the Deux Magots on boulevard St-Germain or opt for a tiny *café du coin* (corner café), where you can have a quick cup of coffee at the counter. Those on the Grands Boulevards (such as boulevard St-Michel, boulevard St-Germain, and the Champs-Élysées) and in the big tourist spots (near the Louvre, the Opéra, and the Eiffel Tower, for example) will almost always be the most expensive and the least interesting. The more modest establishments (look for nonchalant locals) are the places to really get a feeling for French café culture. And we do mean culture—Les Deux Magots is still milking its reputation as one of the Left Bank's prime meeting places for intelligentsia as the former hangout of Verlaine, Rimbaud, Gide, Picasso, and Breton. In spite of its heart-stopping prices, the Flore still packs them in—you can't help imagining that something profound is being uttered at the next table, any more than you can resist the ultrarich onion soup. At La Closerie des Lilas an expensive drink allows you to rest your derrière on the spots once favored by Baudelaire, Apollinaire, and Hemingway. Delightfully, all these cafés are still crammed with locals, so grab a seat, order a Lillet, and settle in for a round of serious people-watching.

Splendid Shopping

Quotidian activities are elevated to high art in Paris, and shopping is no exception. Sophisticated city dwellers that they are—many natives live by the motto *bon chic, bon genre* ("well dressed, well bred")—Parisians approach this exercise as a ritual, and an elaborate ritual at that. Picking produce at the open-air markets on rue Mouffetard or rue Montorgueil or at the Marché d'Aligre, or searching for haute couture at Jean-Paul Gaultier, Sonia Rykiel, or Christian Dior, they cast a discerning eye on the smallest detail and demand the highest quality—which may explain why the city's shopkeepers are so famously grouchy. Browsing through old books and maps in the stalls of *bouquinistes* (secondhand booksellers) on quai de l'Hôtel de Ville along the Seine, or prowling through castoffs at the Marché aux Puces St-Ouen, Parisians show their practicality, their sense of economy, and their ability to turn even a piece of junk into an inventively chic treasure. The city's lairs of consumerism are celebrated—the fashion salons, venerable antiques shops around the rue de Beaune and rue Jacob, august fashion showrooms, and *grands magasins* (department stores) such as Au Bon Marché, Au Printemps, and the Galeries Lafayette, which flaunt Belle Epoque extravagance and trendy designers.

---

pletely renovated, but there are other houses here that date back to the Middle Ages. Although defaced by a modern police station and garage, this tiny warren of six streets still casts a spell, particularly at the intersection of rue des Ursins and rue des Chantres, where a lovely medieval palace, tiny flower garden, and quayside steps form a cul-de-sac where time seems to be holding its breath. ⊠ *Rue du Cloître-Notre-Dame north to the quai des Fleurs, Ile de la Cité* Ⓜ *Cité.*

❾ Carrousel du Louvre. Part of the early '90s Louvre renovation program, this subterranean shopping complex is centered on an inverted glass pyramid (overlooked by the regional Ile-de-France tourist office) and contains a wide range of stores, spaces for fashion shows, an auditorium, and a huge parking garage. At lunchtime, museum visitors rush to the mall-style food court, where fast food goes international. Note that you can get into or exit from the museum (and avoid some lines) by entering through the mall. ⊠ *Entrances on rue de Rivoli or by Arc du Carrousel, Louvre/Tuileries* Ⓜ *Palais-Royal.*

❹ Conciergerie. Bringing a tear to the eyes of ancien régime devotees, this is the famous prison in which dukes and duchesses, lords and ladies, and, most famously, Queen Marie-Antoinette were imprisoned during the Revolution before being carted off to the guillotine. Originally part of a royal palace, the turreted medieval building still holds Marie-Antoinette's cell; a chapel, embellished with the initials M. A., occupies the true site of her confinement. Out of one of these windows, the queen saw a notorious scene of the Revolution: her best friend, the Comtesse de Lamballe—lover of the arts and daughter of the richest duke in France—torn to pieces by a wild mob, her dismembered limbs then displayed on pikes. Elsewhere are the courtyard and fountain where victims of the Terror spent their final days playing piquet, writing letters to their loved ones, and waiting for the dreaded climb up the staircase to the Chamber of the Revolutionary Council to hear its final verdict. ⊠ *1 quai de l'Horloge, Louvre/Tuileries* ☎ *01–53–40–60–93* ⊕ *www. monum.fr* ▦ *€6.10, joint ticket with Sainte-Chapelle €8* ☉ *Daily 9:30–6* Ⓜ *Cité.*

⓭ Grand Palais (Grand Palace). With its curved glass roof, the Grand Palais is unmistakable when approached from either the Seine or the Champs-Élysées, and forms an attractive duo with the **Petit Palais,** which is closed for restoration until January 2005, on the other side of avenue Winston-Churchill. Today, the adjoining galleries of the Grand Palais play host to major exhibitions, but the giant iron-and-glass interior of the Grand Palais itself is closed for renovation until 2007, when it will re-open as an exhibition space for contemporary art. ⊠ *Av. Winston-Churchill, Champs-Élysées* ☎ *01–44–13–17–30* ⊕ *www.rmn.fr/ galeriesnationalesdugrandpalais* ▦ *€10.10 until 1 PM with reservation, €9 after 1, no reservation* ☉ *Thurs.–Mon. 10–8, Wed. 10–10* Ⓜ *Champs-Élysées–Clemenceau.*

☼ ⓓ Jardin des Tuileries (Tuileries Gardens). Monet and Renoir captured this gracious garden (really more of a long park) with paint and brush, Left Bank songstresses warble about its beauty, and all Parisians know it as a charming place to stroll and survey the surrounding cityscape. A palace once stood here on the site of a clay pit that supplied material for many of the city's tile roofs. (Hence the name *tuileries,* or tile works.) During the Revolution, Louis XVI and his family were kept in the Tuileries under house arrest. Now the Tuileries is a typically French garden: formal and neatly patterned, with statues, rows of trees, fountains with gaping fish, and gravel paths. No wonder the Impressionists liked it here—note how the gray, austere light of Paris makes green trees look even greener. ⊠ *Bordered by quai des Tuileries, pl. de la Concorde, rue de Rivoli, and the Louvre, Louvre/Tuileries* Ⓜ *Tuileries.*

need a break?

Stop off for a snack or lunch at **Dame Tartine** (☎ 01–47–03–94–84), one of the two designer brasseries erected in the Tuileries in the late 1990s (it's on the left as you arrive from the place de la Concorde). With its glass-paneled walls and roof and light wood and aluminum accents, the restaurant is sober and airy. The cuisine is inventive and offers good value—try the lamb flan with tomato puree and a carafe of red Ventoux from the Rhône. You can also eat outdoors in the leafy shade.

❽ Louvre. Leonardo da Vinci's *Mona Lisa* and *Virgin and St. Anne,* Veronese's *Marriage at Cana,* Giorgione's *Concert Champêtre,* Delacroix's *Liberty Guiding the People,* Whistler's *Mother (Arrangement in Black and White)* . . . you get the picture. This is the world's greatest art museum— and the largest. Today, after two decades of renovations, the Louvre is now a coherent, unified structure, and search parties no longer need to be sent in to bring you out. Begun by Philippe-Auguste in the 13th century as a fortress, it was not until the reign of pleasure-loving François I, 300 years later, that the Louvre of today gradually began to take shape. Through the years Henri IV (1589–1610), Louis XIII (1610–43), Louis XIV (1643–1715), Napoléon I (1804–14), and Napoléon III (1852–70) all contributed to its construction. The recent history of the Louvre centers on I. M. Pei's glass pyramid, unveiled in March 1989, and numerous renovations.

FodorśChoice ★

The number one attraction is the Most Famous Painting in the World: Leonardo da Vinci's enigmatic ***Mona Lisa*** (*La Joconde,* to the French), painted in 1503–06. To those who recall Théophile Gautier's words calling her "a sphinx of beauty," the portrait is a bit of a disappointment. Once you get in front of the videotaping tourists, you, too, may find yourself asking, "Is this it?" when faced with this 30″×18″ painting of an eyebrowless woman with yellowing skin and an annoyingly smug smile. However, the story behind her face—one that is still emerging— is fascinating. The portrait of the wife of one Francesco del Giocondo, a 15th-century Florentine millionaire, Leonardo's masterpiece is now believed to have been painted for her husband as a memorial after the lady's death. Some historians now maintain that her black garb is in honor of her baby who died in 1502. If so, however, this may be at odds with the famous smile, which critics point to as another example of Leonardo's famous wit: the family name Giocondo is derived from the Latin word for "jocundity," or humor. On nearby walls, don't miss some other High Renaissance masterworks: Leonardo's *Virgin and St. Anne* and Raphael's *La Belle Jardinière.*

The Louvre is packed with legendary collections, which are divided into seven sections: Asian antiquities; Egyptian antiquities; Greek and Roman

JUMP TO THE HEAD OF THE LINE

Something to consider in the time vs. money balance: the **Carte Musées et Monuments** (Museums and Monuments Pass), which offers unlimited access to more than 65 museums and monuments.

You can get passes for one-, three-, or five-consecutive-day periods; the cost, respectively, is €15, €30, and €45.

Considering that most Paris museums cost under €10, you have to be serious about museum going to make this pay off, but there's one incredible plus: you get to jump to the head of the line by displaying it, a coup when there are 600 people lined up to get into the Musée d'Orsay.

The pass is available at Paris's tourist offices and métro stations and at all participating museums, and it comes with a handy info list of all the museums you can visit.

For more information, see www.intermusees.com.

---

antiquities; sculpture; paintings, prints, and drawings; furniture; and objets d'art. Don't try to see it all at once; try, instead, to make repeat visits—the admission is nearly half price on Sunday and after 3 PM on other days. (Unless you plan on going to a number of museums every day, the one-, three-, and five-day tourist museum passes probably aren't worth your money, since you could easily spend a whole day at the Louvre alone.) Some other highlights of the painting collection are Jan van Eyck's magnificent *The Madonna and Chancellor Rolin,* painted in the early 15th century; *The Lacemaker,* by Jan Vermeer (1632–75); *The Embarkation for Cythera,* by Antoine Watteau (1684–1721); *The Oath of the Horatii,* by Jacques-Louis David (1748–1825); *The Raft of the Medusa,* by Théodore Géricault (1791–1824); and *La Grande Odalisque,* by Jean-Auguste-Dominique Ingres (1780–1867).

The French crown jewels (in the objets d'art section of the Richelieu Wing) include the mind-boggling 186-carat Regent diamond. The Nike, or *Winged Victory of Samothrace,* seems poised for flight at the top of the stairs (remember Audrey Hepburn's high-cheekboned take on this statue in *Funny Face?*), and other much-loved pieces of sculpture are Michelangelo's two *Slaves,* intended for the tomb of Pope Julius II. These can be admired in the Denon Wing, where a medieval and Renaissance sculpture section is housed partly in the former imperial stables. In 1997 new rooms for Persian, Arab, Greek, and Egyptian art were opened, followed in 1999 by rooms for Italian and Spanish painting and French furniture and objets d'art from the period 1815–48. For fans of the Napoléon III style—the apotheosis of 19th-century, red-and-gilt opulence—be sure to see the galleries that once housed the Ministry of Finance. To get into the Louvre, you may have to wait in two long lines: one outside the Pyramide entrance portal and another downstairs at the ticket booths. You can avoid the first by entering through the Carrousel du Louvre, but you can't avoid the second. Your ticket (be sure to hold on to it) will get you into any and all of the wings as many times as you like during one day. Once inside, you should stop by the information desk to pick up a free color-coded map and check which rooms are closed for the day. (Closures rotate through the week, so you can come back if something is temporarily unavailable.) Beyond this, you'll have all you need—shops, a post office, and places to eat. Café Marly may have an enviable location facing into the Cour Napoléon, but its food is decidedly lackluster. For a more soigné lunch, keep your appetite in check until you get to the museum's stylish Café Richelieu, or head outside the palace walls. Remember that the Louvre is closed on Tuesday. ⊠ *Palais du Louvre, Louvre/Tuileries* ☎ *01–40–20–53–17 information* ⊕ *www.louvre. fr* ☞ *€8.50, €6 after 6 PM on Mon. and Wed. and all day Sun. Free 1st Sun. of month, €8.50 for special temporary exhibitions* ☉ *Thurs.–Sun. 9–6, Mon. and Wed. 9 AM–9:45 PM. Some sections closed on certain days* Ⓜ *Palais-Royal.*

⑪ Musée du Jeu de Paume. At the entrance to the Tuileries Gardens, this museum is an ultramodern white-walled showcase for the Centre National de la Photographie, with excellent temporary exhibits of bold contemporary photography, video, and multimedia. Its adjoining sister museum, the **Musé de l'Orangerie**—home to Claude Monet's largest *Water Lilies*—has been closed for renovation. Though it was scheduled to open in fall 2004, workers discovered the ruins of a medieval wall underneath the building and the project was put on pause for further excavation. When it finally reopens, the Orangerie will display its selection of early 20th-century paintings, with works by Renoir, Cézanne, and Matisse, among other masters. ⊠ *1 pl. de la Concorde, Louvre/Tuileries* ☎ *01–47–03–12–51* ☞ *€6* ☉ *Tues., Wed., and Fri. noon–7, Thurs. noon–9:30, weekends 10–7* Ⓜ *Concorde.*

▶ **① Notre-Dame.** Looming above the large, pedestrian place du Parvis is la cathédrale de Notre-Dame, the most enduring symbol of Paris. Begun in 1163, completed in 1345, badly damaged during the Revolution, and restored by Viollet-le-Duc in the 19th century, Notre-Dame may not be France's oldest or largest cathedral, but in terms of beauty and architectural harmony, it has few peers—as you can see by studying the facade from the open square. The doorways seem like hands joined in prayer, and the sculpted kings form a noble procession, while the rose window gleams, to wax poetic, like the eye of divinity. Above, the gallery breaks the lines of the stone vaults, and between the two high towers the flèche soars from the crossing of the transept. The cathedral was conceived by Bishop de Sully, who claimed he had seen the building in a vision. More pragmatically, Sully needed a cathedral in Paris so that he could compete with Abbot Suger's phenomenal cathedral in St-Denis, just north of the city. An army of stonemasons, carpenters, and sculptors came to work and live on the site, which had already seen a Roman temple, an early Christian basilica, and a Romanesque church. The chancel and altar were consecrated in 1182, but the magnificent sculptures surrounding the main doors were not put into position until 1240.

The facade divides neatly into three levels. At the first-floor level are the three main entrances, or portals: the Portal of the Virgin, on the left;

FodorsChoice
★

the Portal of the Last Judgment, in the center; and the Portal of St. Anne, on the right. All three are surmounted by magnificent carvings—most of them 19th-century copies of the originals—of figures, foliage, and biblical scenes. Above these are the restored statues of the kings of Israel, the Galerie des Rois. Above the gallery is the great rose window and, above that, the Grande Galerie, at the base of the twin towers. The south tower houses the great bell of Notre-Dame, as tolled by Quasimodo, Victor Hugo's fictional hunchback. The 387-step climb to the top of the towers is worth the effort for a close-up of the famous gargoyles—most added in the 19th century by Viollet-le-Duc—as they frame an expansive view of the city. If some find both towers a bit top heavy, that's because they were designed to be topped by two needlelike spires, which were never built. The cathedral interior, with its vast proportions, soaring nave, and soft multicolor light dimly filtering through the stained-glass windows, inspires awe—visit early in the morning, when the cathedral is at its lightest and least crowded.

If your interest in the cathedral is not yet sated, duck into the **Musée de Notre-Dame** (⊠ 10 rue du Cloître-Notre-Dame, Ile de la Cité), across the street opposite the North Door. The museum's paintings, engravings, medallions, and other objects and documents chart the history of the cathedral. When it comes to views of Notre-Dame, no visit is complete without a riverside walk past the cathedral through **Square Jean-XXIII.** It offers a breathtaking sight of the east end of the cathedral, ringed by flying buttresses and surmounted by the spire. To put the cathedral in its proper medieval context, explore the super-charming **Ancien Cloître Quarter,** set just to the north of the cathedral. ⊠ *Pl. du Parvis, Ile de la Cité* ☎ *01–53–10–07–00* ⊕ *www.monum.fr* ⊠ *Cathedral free, towers €6.10, crypt €3.30, treasury €2.50, museum €2.50* ⊙ *Cathedral daily 8–7. Towers Apr.–Sept., daily 9:30–7:30; Oct.–Mar., daily 10–5:30. Treasury Mon.–Sat. 9:30–11:30 and 1–5:30. Crypt Tues.–Sun. 10–6. Museum Wed. and weekends 2:30–6* Ⓜ *Cité.*

Ⓒ ⓮ **Palais de la Découverte** (Palace of Discovery). A planetarium, working models, and scientific and technological exhibits on such topics as optics, biology, nuclear physics, and electricity make up this science museum behind the Grand Palais. ⊠ *Av. Franklin-D.-Roosevelt, Champs-Élysées* ☎ *01–56–43–20–21* ⊠ *€5.60, €3.05 extra for planetarium* ⊙ *Tues.–Sat. 9:30–6, Sun. 10–7* Ⓜ *Champs-Élysées–Clemenceau.*

⓬ **Place de la Concorde.** This majestic square at the foot of the Champs-Élysées was laid out in the 1770s, but there was nothing in the way of peace or concord about its early years. Between 1793 and 1795 more than a thousand victims, including Louis XVI and Marie-Antoinette, were sent into oblivion at the guillotine, prompting Madame Roland's famous cry, "Liberty, what crimes are committed in thy name." The top of the 107-foot **Obelisk**—a present from the viceroy of Egypt in 1833—was regilded in 1998. The place continues to have politically symbolic weight. Demonstrations center here, since the Assemblée Nationale is right across the river and the Palais de l'Élysée (the French presidential palace) and the U.S. Embassy are just around the corner. Among the handsome, symmetrical 18th-century buildings facing the square is the Hôtel

Crillon, originally built by Gabriel—architect of the Petit Trianon—as an 18th-century home for three of France's wealthiest families. At the near end of high-walled rue Royale is the legendary Maxim's restaurant, but unless you choose to eat here, you won't be able to see the riot of crimson velvets and florid Art Nouveau furniture inside. ⊠ *Champs-Élysées* Ⓜ *Concorde.*

❺ **Place Dauphine.** The Surrealists loved place Dauphine, which they called "*le sexe de Paris*" because of its location—at the far-western end of the Ile de la Cité—and suggestive V-shape. Its origins were much more proper: built by Henri IV, it was named in homage to his successor, the dauphin, who grew up to become Louis XIII. The triangular square is lined with some charming 17th-century houses that the writer André Maurois felt represented the very quintessence of Paris and France. Take a seat on a park bench, enjoy a picnic, and see if you agree. ⊠ *Ile-de-la-Cité* Ⓜ *Cité.*

⓯ **Pont Alexandre-III** (Alexander III Bridge). No other bridge over the Seine epitomizes the fin-de-siècle frivolity of the Belle Epoque (or Paris itself) like the exuberant, bronze-lamp-lined Pont Alexandre-III. An urban masterstroke that seems as much created of cake frosting and sugar sculptures as stone and iron, it was built, like the Grand and Petit Palais nearby, for the 1900 world's fair and inaugurated by the ill-fated czar Nicholas II, and ingratiatingly named in honor of his father. ⊠ *Invalides* Ⓜ *Invalides.*

❼ **Pont Neuf** (New Bridge). Crossing the Ile de la Cité, just behind square du Vert-Galant, is the oldest bridge in Paris, confusingly called the New Bridge, or Pont Neuf. It was completed in 1607 and was the first bridge in the city to be built without houses lining either side. ⊠ *Ile de la Cité* Ⓜ *Pont-Neuf.*

❸ **Sainte-Chapelle** (Holy Chapel). Not to be missed and one of the most
FodorsChoice magical sights in European medieval art, this chapel was built by Louis
★ IX (1226–70; later canonized as St. Louis) in the 1240s to house what he believed to be Christ's Crown of Thorns, purchased from Emperor Baldwin of Constantinople. A dark lower chapel is a gloomy prelude to the shimmering upper one, whose walls consist of little else but dazzling 13th-century stained glass. Think of it as an enormous magic lantern, illuminating 1,130 figures from the Bible, to create—as one writer put it—"the most marvelous colored and moving air ever held within four walls." Today, the magic of the chapel comes alive during the regular concerts held here; call to check the schedule. ⊠ *4 bd. du Palais, Ile de la Cité* ☎ *01–53–73–78–51* ⊕ *www.monum.fr* 🎟 *€6.10, joint ticket with Conciergerie €8* ⊙ *Daily 9:30–6, entry closes at 5:30* Ⓜ *Cité.*

❻ **Square du Vert-Galant.** The equestrian statue of the Vert-Galant himself—amorous adventurer Henri IV—surveys this leafy square at the western end of the Ile de la Cité. Henri, king of France from 1589 until his assassination in 1610, is probably best remembered for his cynical remark that "*Paris vaut bien une messe*" ("Paris is worth a mass"), a reference to his readiness to renounce Protestantism to gain the throne of predominantly Catholic France. A fine spot to linger on a sunny afternoon, the square is also the departure point for the glass-top *vedettes* (tour boats) on the Seine (at the bottom of the steps to the right). ⊠ *Ile de la Cité* Ⓜ *Pont-Neuf.*

Monuments & Marvels: From the Eiffel Tower to the Arc de Triomphe

The Eiffel Tower (or Tour Eiffel, to use the French) lords over southwest Paris, and from nearly wherever you are on this walk you can see its jutting needle. For years many Parisians felt it was an iron eyesore and called it the Giant Asparagus, a vegetable that weighed 15 million pounds and grew 1,000 feet high. But gradually the tower became part of the Parisian landscape, entering the hearts and souls of Parisians and visitors alike. Thanks to its stunning nighttime illumination, topped by four 6,000-watt projectors creating a lighthouse beacon visible for 80 km (50 mi) around, it continues to make Paris live up to its moniker *La Ville Lumière*—the City of Light.

Water is the second highlight here: fountains playing beneath place du Trocadéro and boat tours along the Seine on a Bateau Mouche. Museums are the third; the area around Trocadéro is full of them. Style is the fourth, and not just because the buildings here are overwhelmingly elegant—but because this is also the center of haute couture, with the top names in fashion all congregated around avenue Montaigne, only a brief walk from the Champs-Élysées, to the north.

The 2-km (1-mi) Champs-Élysées was originally laid out in the 1660s by landscape gardener André Le Nôtre as parkland sweeping away from the Tuileries. In an attempt to reestablish this thoroughfare as one of the world's most beautiful avenues, the city has planted extra trees, broadened sidewalks, refurbished Art Nouveau newsstands, and clamped down on garish storefronts. Site of most French national celebrations, the Champs-Élysées is the last leg of the Tour de France bicycle race, on the third or fourth Sunday in July, and the site of vast ceremonies on Bastille Day (July 14) and Armistice Day (November 11).

a good walk

The verdant expanse of the Champ de Mars, once used as a parade ground by the École Militaire (still in use as a military academy and therefore not open to the public), then as site of the world exhibitions, provides a thrilling approach to the iron symbol of Paris, the **Tour Eiffel** ⑯ ☞. As you get nearer, the Eiffel Tower's colossal bulk (it's far bigger and sturdier than pictures suggest) becomes increasingly evident.

Across the Seine from the Eiffel Tower, above stylish gardens and fountains on the heights of place du Trocadéro, is the Art Deco **Palais de Chaillot** ⑰, a cultural center containing three museums: an anthropology museum, a maritime museum, and a museum of French architecture. The area around place du Trocadéro is a feast for museum lovers. The **Musée Guimet** ⑱, on place d'Iéna, contains three floors of Indo-Chinese and Far Eastern art. If you're interested in glittering crystal, make a detour up avenue d'Iéna to the **Maison de Baccarat** ⑲, a small, Philippe Starck-designed funhouse museum. Otherwise, head down avenue du Président-Wilson, to the **Musée d'Art Moderne de la Ville de Paris** ⑳, which has temporary exhibits as well as a permanent collection of modern art.

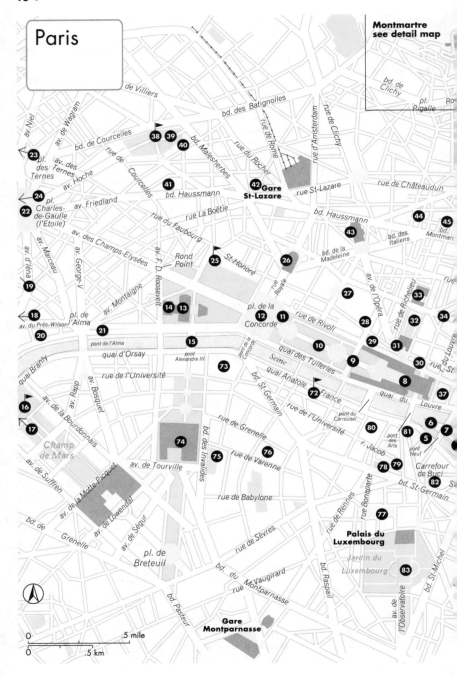

Paris

Montmartre
see detail map

KEY

▶ *Start of walk*

Continue down to bustling place de l'Alma, where a giant golden torch appears to be saluting the memory of Diana, Princess of Wales, who died in a car crash in the tunnel below in 1997 (in fact, this replica of the Statue of Liberty's flame was donated by Paris-based U.S. companies in 1989, in honor of the bicentennial of the French Revolution). Down the sloping side road just beyond the Pont de l'Alma (Alma Bridge) is the embarkation point of the **Bateaux Mouches** ㉑ and their tours of Paris by water. Stylish avenue Montaigne, lined with some of the leading Paris fashion houses, runs up from place de l'Alma toward the Champs-Élysées. At No. 116 is the famous Lido de Paris nightclub, opposite the venerable Le Fouquet's restaurant-café, once frequented by Orson Welles and James Joyce. Local charm is not a highlight of this sector of western Paris, though renovation has gone some way toward restoring the avenue's legendary elegance, particularly as you head up the grand promenade to that icon of Paris, the **Arc de Triomphe** ㉒. Through the arch to the west lies the city's own Manhattan-on-the-Seine— the skyscraper complex of **La Défense** ㉓. For a more tranquil respite, head southwest from the Arc down Avenue Foch—one of Paris's most fashionable addresses—to the sylvan glades of Paris's largest park, the **Bois de Boulogne** ㉔.

TIMING   You can probably cover this walk in a couple of hours, but if you wish to ascend the Eiffel Tower, take a trip along the Seine, or visit any of the myriad museums along the way, you'd be best off allowing most of the day.

What to See

★ ㉒ **Arc de Triomphe.** Set on place Charles-de-Gaulle—known to Parisians as L'Étoile, or the Star (a reference to the streets that fan out from it)— the colossal, 164-foot Arc de Triomphe arch was planned by Napoléon but not finished until 1836, 20 years after the end of his rule. It's decorated with some magnificent sculptures by François Rude, such as the *Departure of the Volunteers,* better known as *La Marseillaise,* to the right of the arch when viewed from the Champs-Élysées. A small museum halfway up the arch is devoted to its history. France's Unknown Soldier is buried beneath the archway; the flame is rekindled every evening at 6:30. ⊠ *Pl. Charles-de-Gaulle, Champs-Élysées* ☎ *01–55–37–73–77* ⊕ *www.monum.fr* ▣ *€7* ☉ *Apr.–Sept., daily 10 AM–11 PM; Oct.–Mar., daily 10 AM–10:30 PM* Ⓜ *Métro or RER: Étoile.*

☾ ㉑ **Bateaux Mouches.** If you want to view Paris in slow motion, hop on one of these famous motorboats, which set off on their hour-long tours of the city waters regularly (every half hour in summer) from place de l'Alma. Their route heads east to the Ile St-Louis and then back west, past the Tour Eiffel, as far as the Allée des Cygnes and its miniature version of the Statue of Liberty. Note that some travelers prefer to take this Seine cruise on the smaller Vedettes du Pont Neuf, which depart from square du Vert-Galant on the Ile de la Cité, as the Vedettes have a guide giving commentary in French and English, while the Bateaux Mouches have a loud recorded spiel in several languages. For the quietest journey, take the city-run Batobus, which has no commentary and allows you to get on and off at its various quay-side stops. ⊠ *Pl. de l'Alma, Trocadéro/*

Eiffel Tower ☎ *01–40–76–99–99* ⊕ *www.bateaux-mouches.fr* ✉ €7 Ⓜ *Alma-Marceau.*

㉔ Bois de Boulogne. Class and style have been associated with this 2,200-acre wood—known to Parisians as simply *Le Bois*—ever since it was landscaped into an upper-class playground by Baron Haussmann in the 1850s. Today the park is a happy escape for rowers, joggers, strollers, riders, and picnickers. Crowds head here for the racetracks of **Longchamp** and **Auteuil,** along with the **Roland Garros** stadium where the French Open tennis tournament is held in late May. After dark, ladies of the night festoon some sections. ✉ *Main entrance at bottom of av. Foch, Bois de Boulogne* Ⓜ *Porte Maillot, Porte Dauphine, Porte d'Auteuil; Bus 244.*

㉓ La Défense. This is the skyscraper district of Paris, just west of the city (thankfully), across the Seine from Neuilly. Crowning the main plaza is the **Grande Arche de La Défense,** an enormous open cube of a building where tubular glass elevators whisk you 360 feet to the top. ✉ *Parvis de La Défense, La Défense* ☎ *01–49–07–27–57* ✉ €7 ☽ *Daily 10–7* Ⓜ *Grande Arche de La Défense.*

⑲ Maison de Baccarat. Famed modernist designer Philippe Starck brought an irreverent, Alice-in-Wonderland approach to the HQ of the venerable Baccarat crystal firm. Opened in 2003, the Baccarat museum plays on its building's Surrealist legacy; Cocteau, Dalí, Buñuel, and Man Ray were all frequent guests of the mansion's onetime owner, Countess Marie-Laure de Noailles. At the entrance, talking heads are projected onto giant crystal urns, and a lit chandelier is submerged in an aquarium. Other fairy-tale touches include a 46-foot-long crystal-legged dinner table and an 8-foot-high chair, perfect for seating a giant princess. Not all the marvels come from Starck though; Baccarat has created exquisite crystal pieces since Louis XV conferred his seal on the glassworks in 1764. Many of the company's masterworks are on display, from the soaring candlesticks made for Czar Nicholas II to the perfume flacon Dalí designed for Schiaparelli. The museum's Cristal Room café–restaurant attracts an appropriately glittering crowd, so book well in advance for lunch or dinner. ✉ *11 pl. des Etats-Unis, Trocadéro/Eiffel Tower* ☎ *01–40–22–11–00* ⊕ *www.baccarat.fr* ✉ €7 ☽ *Mon.–Sat. 10–7* Ⓜ *Trocadéro.*

⑳ Musée d'Art Moderne de la Ville de Paris (City Museum of Modern Art). While the city's modern art museum hasn't attracted a buzz comparable to that of its main Paris competitor, the Centre Georges Pompidou, it can give a more pleasant museum-going experience. Like the Pompidou, it shows temporary exhibits of painting, sculpture, installation and video art, plus a permanent collection of top-tier 20th-century works from around the world—but it happily escapes the Pompidou's overcrowding. At this writing, the Art Nouveau leftover from the Exhibition of 1897 was closed for renovation, due to finish in mid-2005. Once its vast, white-walled galleries are open, they'll again be an ideal backdrop for the bold statements of 20th-century art. The museum takes over, chronologically speaking, where the Musée d'Orsay leaves off; among the earliest works are Fauvist paintings by Vlaminck and Derain, followed by Picasso's early experiments in Cubism. ⊠ *11 av. du Président-Wilson, Trocadéro/Eiffel Tower* ☎ *01–53–67–40–00* ⊕ *www.paris.org* ▱ *Permanent collection free, temporary exhibitions €7* ☉ *Tues.–Fri. 10–5:30, weekends 10–6:45* Ⓜ *Iéna.*

⑱ **Musée Guimet.** Prized by connoisseurs the world over, this museum was founded by Lyonnais industrialist Émile Guimet, who traveled around the world in the late 19th century amassing Indo-Chinese and Far Eastern objets d'art, plus a fabled collection of Cambodian art. Be sure to peer into the delicate round library (where you'd swear Guimet has just stepped out for tea) and toil up to the top floor's 18th-century ivory replica of a Chinese pavilion. ⊠ *6 pl. d'Iéna, Trocadéro/Eiffel Tower* ☎ *01–56–52–53–00* ⊕ *www.museeguimet.fr* ▱ *€7* ☉ *Wed.–Mon. 10–5:45* Ⓜ *Iéna or Boissiére.*

⑰ **Palais de Chaillot** (Chaillot Palace). This honey-color, Art Deco culture center facing the Seine, perched atop tumbling gardens with sculpture and fountains, was built in the 1930s and houses three museums: the **Musée de l'Homme** (Museum of Mankind) with an array of prehistoric artifacts; the **Musée de la Marine** (Maritime Museum), with its salty collection of model ships, marine paintings, and naval paraphernalia; and the **Musée des Monuments Français** (Museum of French Monuments), which is undergoing renovation and will reopen in 2005, when it will share space with the Institut Français d'Architecture. The palace terrace, flanked by gilded statuettes (and often invaded by roller skaters and skateboarders), offers a wonderful picture-postcard view of the Tour Eiffel and is a favorite spot for fashion photographers. ⊠ *Pl. du Trocadéro, Trocadéro/Eiffel Tower* ☎ *01–44–05–72–72 Museum of Mankind, 01–53–65–69–69 Maritime Museum* ⊕ *www.mnhn.fr* ▱ *Museum of Mankind €7, Maritime Museum €7* ☉ *Museum of Mankind Wed.–Mon. 9:45–5:15; Maritime Museum Wed.–Mon. 10–6* Ⓜ *Trocadéro.*

> **need a break?**
>
> You'll get a tremendous view of the Eiffel Tower and the Invalides dome with your ice cream, cocktail, or lunch at **Le Totem** (⊠ Pl. du Trocadéro, Trocadéro/Eiffel Tower ☎ 01–47–27–28–29), an elegant bar and restaurant in the south wing of the Palais de Chaillot.

★ ☻ ⌐ ⑯ **Tour Eiffel** (Eiffel Tower). Known to the French as La Tour Eiffel (pronounced ef-*el*), Paris's most famous landmark was built by Gustave Eiffel for the World Exhibition of 1889, the centennial of the French Revolution, and was still in good shape to celebrate its own 100th birthday. Such was Eiffel's engineering wizardry that even in the strongest winds his tower never sways more than 4½ inches. Since its colossal bulk exudes a feeling of mighty permanence, you may have trouble believing that it nearly became 7,000 tons of scrap iron when its concession expired in 1909. At first many Parisians hated the structure, and only its potential use as a radio antenna saved the day (it still bristles with a forest of radio and television transmitters). Now it is the beloved symbol of Paris. If you're full of energy, stride up the stairs as far as the third deck. If you want to go to the top, you'll have to take the elevator. Today, the Tour is most breathtaking at night, when every girder is highlighted in a sparkling display originally conceived to celebrate the turn of the millennium. The glittering light show was so popular that the 20,000 lights were re-installed for permanent use in 2003; the Tour does its electric shimmy for 10 minutes every hour on the hour, from 9 PM until 1 AM in winter and 2 AM in summer (why not take a seat on the grass of the Champs de Mars from 9 to 10 PM and see the lights dance twice?). If you really want to make an occasion of your visit, plan on reserving a table at Jules Verne, the tower's luxury restaurant, set on the second level. ⊠ *Quai Branly, Trocadéro/Eiffel Tower* ☎ *01–44–11–23–23* ⊕ *www.tour-eiffel.fr* ▱ *By elevator: 2nd fl. €3.70, 3rd fl. €7, 4th fl. €10.20. Climbing: 2nd and 3rd fl. only, €3.30* ⊙ *July and Aug., daily 9 AM–midnight; Sept.–June, daily 9 AM–11 PM, stairs close at dusk in winter* Ⓜ *Bir-Hakeim; RER: Champ de Mars.*

Le Style, C'est Paris: The Faubourg St-Honoré

The Faubourg St-Honoré, north of the Champs-Élysées and the Tuileries, is synonymous with style—as you will see as you progress from the President's Palace, past a wealth of art galleries, to the monumental Madeleine church and on to stately place Vendôme; on this ritzy square, famous boutiques sit side by side with famous banks—but then elegance and finance have never been an unusual combination. It's not surprising to learn that one of the main arteries of the area, rue de Castiglione, was named after one of its former residents—the glamorous fashion-plate Countess de Castiglione, sent to plead the cause of Italian unity with Napoléon III. The emperor was persuaded (he was easily susceptible to feminine charms), and the area became a Kingdom of Woman: famous dressmakers, renowned jewelers, exclusive perfume shops, and the most chic hotel in Paris, the Ritz, made this *faubourg* (district) a symbol of luxury throughout the world. Today the tradition continues, with leading names in fashion found farther east on place des Victoires, close to what was, for centuries, the gastronomic heart of Paris: Les Halles (pronounced "lay-*ahl*"), once the city's main market. These giant glass-and-iron market halls were demolished in 1969 and replaced by a park and a modern shopping mall, the Forum des Halles. The surrounding streets underwent a transformation and are now filled with shops, cafés, restaurants, and chic apartment buildings.

a good walk

Start in front of the most important home in France: the **Palais de l'Élysée** ㉕ ▶, or Presidential Palace. Crash barriers and gold-braided guards keep visitors at bay; in fact, there's more to see in the plethora of art galleries and luxury fashion boutiques lining rue du Faubourg–St-Honoré as you head east. Pass the British Embassy and turn left onto rue Boissy-d'Anglais; then cut right through an archway into Village Royal, a restored courtyard with several trendy boutiques. It leads to rue Royale, a classy street lined with all sorts of tempting stores, including the florist Lachaume, where you might see waist-high vases of perfect long-stemmed roses, and the original branch of Ladurée pâtisserie. (Maxim's, the famed Art Nouveau restaurant, is down at number 3.) Looming to the left is the **Église de La Madeleine** ㉖, a sturdy Neoclassical edifice.

Take boulevard de la Madeleine, to the right as you face the church, then the first right down rue Duphot to Notre-Dame de l'Assomption, noted for its huge dome and solemn interior. Continue left on rue St-Honoré to rue de Castiglione and then head left to **place Vendôme** ㉗, one of the world's most soigné squares. Return to rue St-Honoré and follow it to the mighty church of **St-Roch** ㉘.

Take the next right onto rue des Pyramides and cross the place des Pyramides, with its gilded statue of Joan of Arc on horseback, to the northwest wing of the Louvre, site of the **Union Centrale des Arts Décoratifs** ㉙, with three separate museums dedicated to fashion, publicity, and the decorative arts. Stay on arcaded rue de Rivoli to the place du Palais-Royal. On the far side of the square is the **Louvre des Antiquaires** ㉚, a chic shopping mall housing upscale antiques stores. Just beyond Jean-Michel Othaniel's aluminum and psychedelic glass entrance canopy to the Palais-Royal Métro station, is the **Comédie Française** ㉛, the time-honored house for performances of classical French drama. To the right of the theater is the unobtrusive entrance to the **Palais-Royal** ㉜; its courtyard is an unexpected oasis in the heart of the city. Walk down to the far end of the garden and peek into the glossy 19th-century interior of Le Grand Véfour, one of the swankiest restaurants in the city. One block beyond the north exit of Palais-Royal, on the corner of rue de Richelieu and rue des Petits-Champs, stands what used to be France's main national library, the **Bibliothèque Nationale Richelieu** ㉝, now home to one of the world's largest photography archives. Next door are the connected passages of **Galerie Colbert** and **Galerie Vivienne**, two exquisite shopping arcades built in the mid-19th century, now filled with restaurants, luxury boutiques, and antiquarian booksellers. Continuing eastward on the rue des Petits-Champs brings you to the circular **place des Victoires** ㉞: that's Louis XIV riding the plunging steed in the center of the square. Head south down rue Croix-des-Petits-Champs, past the nondescript Banque de France on your right, and take the second street on the left to the circular **Bourse du Commerce,** or Commercial Exchange. Victor Hugo waggishly likened its roof to a jockey's cap without the peak. Alongside it is the 100-foot-high fluted **Colonne de Ruggieri.**

You don't need to scale Ruggieri's column to spot the bulky outline of the church of **St-Eustache** ㉟, a curious architectural hybrid of Gothic and Classical. The vast site next to St-Eustache is now occupied by a garden, the Jardin des Halles, and the modern **Forum des Halles** ㊱ shopping mall. Rue Berger leads from allée de St-Jean-de-Perse to the Square des Innocents, with its handsome Renaissance fountain. Head south along rue St-Denis from the far end of Square des Innocents to place du Châtelet, with its theaters, fountain, and the Tour St-Jacques, the tower looming up to your left. Turn right along the Seine to reach **St-Germain l'Auxerrois** ㊲, opposite the Louvre, once the French royal family's parish church.

TIMING   With brief visits to churches and monuments, this walk should take from three to four hours. On a nice day you may want to linger in the gardens of the Palais-Royal, and on a cold day you may want to indulge in an unbelievably thick hot chocolate at the Angélina tearoom.

What to See

★ ㉝ **Bibliothèque Nationale Richelieu.** Housed in one of the grandest 17th-century Parisian mansions, France's longtime national library, named for the formidable 17th-century prime minister, Cardinal Richelieu, is shifting its public profile from books to photography. In spring 2003, a large exhibit space opened here to display the library's enormous photography collection. But you can also admire Robert de Cotte's 18th-century courtyard and peep into the magnificent 19th-century reading room (open only to researchers). Original manuscripts, engravings, coins, and prints are still here, and parts of these collections go on display from time to time. ⊠ *58 rue de Richelieu, Opéra/Grands Boulevards* ☏ *01–53–79–59–59* ⊕ *www.bnf.fr* ⊘ *Tues.–Sun. 9–8* Ⓜ *Bourse.*

㉛ **Comédie Française.** This theater is the most celebrated venue for performances of classical French drama. The building itself dates from 1790, but the Comédie Française company was created by that most theatrical of French monarchs, Louis XIV, back in 1680. If you understand French and have a taste for the mannered, declamatory style of French acting—it's a far cry from method acting—you'll appreciate an evening here. ⊠ *Pl. Colette, Louvre/Tuileries* ☏ *01–44–58–15–15* Ⓜ *Palais-Royal.*

㉖ **Église de La Madeleine** (Church of La Madeleine). With its rows of uncompromising columns, this sturdy Neoclassical edifice—designed in 1814 but not consecrated until 1842—looks more like a Greek temple than a Christian church. In fact, La Madeleine, as it is known, was nearly selected as Paris's first train station (the site of the Gare St-Lazare, just up the road, was chosen instead). Inside, the walls are richly and harmoniously decorated; gold glints through the murk. The portico's majestic Corinthian colonnade supports a gigantic pediment with a frieze of the Last Judgment. ⊠ *Pl. de la Madeleine, Opéra/Grands Boulevards* ⊘ *Mon.–Sat. 7:30–7, Sun. 8–7* Ⓜ *Madeleine.*

㊱ **Forum des Halles.** Les Halles, the iron-and-glass halls that made up the central Paris food market, were closed in 1969 and replaced in the late '70s by the Forum des Halles, a mundane shopping mall. Nothing remains of either the market or the rambunctious atmosphere that led 19th-century novelist Émile Zola to dub Les Halles *le ventre de Paris* ("the belly of Paris"), although rue Montorgueil, behind St-Eustache, retains something of its original bustle. For really stylish shopping, wend your way northeast several blocks to rue Dussoubs and rue St-Denis to the 19th-century covered gallery the **Passage du Grand-Cerf**, filled with crafts shops offering innovative selections of jewelry, paintings, and ceramics. ⊠ *Main entrance: rue Pierre-Lescot, Beaubourg/Les Halles* ⊕ *www.forum-des-halles.com* ⊘ *Mon.–Sat. 10–7:30* Ⓜ *Les Halles; RER: Châtelet Les Halles.*

㉚ **Louvre des Antiquaires.** This "shopping mall" of superelegant antiques dealers, off place du Palais-Royal opposite the Louvre, is a minimuseum in itself. Its stylish glass-walled corridors—lined with Louis XVI *boiseries* (antique wood paneling), Charles Dix bureaus, and the pretty sort of bibelots that would have gladdened the heart of Marie-Antoinette— deserve a browse whether you intend to buy or not. Don't wear your flip-flops in here. ✉ *Main entrance: Pl. du Palais-Royal, Louvre/Tuileries* ⊙ *Tues.–Sun. 11–7* Ⓜ *Palais-Royal.*

need a break? Once patronized by Proust, founded in 1903, **Angélina** (✉ 226 rue de Rivoli, Louvre/Tuileries ☎ 01–42–60–82–00) is an elegant *salon de thé* (tearoom), famous for its *chocolat africain,* a jug of incredibly thick hot chocolate served with whipped cream (irresistible even in summer). While it's still among the city's best chocolate hits, Proust would probably sniff at the slightly shopworn air of the place today and reserve his affections for the ever-elegant teas served at historic **Ladurée,** 12 blocks to the east at 16 rue Royale.

▶ ㉕ **Palais de l'Élysée** (Élysée Palace). Madame de Pompadour, Napoléon, Joséphine, the Duke of Wellington, and Queen Victoria all stayed at this "palace," today the official home of the French president. It was originally constructed as a private mansion in 1718 and has housed presidents only since 1873. You can catch a glimpse of the palace forecourt and facade through the Faubourg St-Honoré gateway. ✉ *55 rue du Faubourg St-Honoré, Champs-Élysées* ⊙ *Not open to public* Ⓜ *Miromesnil.*

㉜ **Palais-Royal** (Royal Palace). One of the most Parisian sights in all of Paris, the Palais-Royal is especially loved for its gardens, where children play, lovers whisper, and senior citizens crumble bread for the sparrows, seemingly oblivious to the ghosts of history that haunt this place. The buildings of this former palace—royal only in that all-powerful Cardinal Richelieu (1585–1642) magnanimously bequeathed them to Louis XIII—date from the 1630s. In front of one of its shop fronts Camille Desmoulins gave the first speech calling for the French Revolution in 1789. Today the Palais-Royal is occupied by the French Ministry of Culture and private apartments (Colette and Cocteau were two lucky former owners), and its buildings are not open to the public. You can, however, visit its colonnaded courtyard and classical gardens, a tranquil oasis prized by Parisians. Around the exterior of the complex are famous arcades—notably the Galerie Valois—whose elegant shops have been attracting customers since the days when Thomas Jefferson used to come here for some retail therapy. ✉ *Pl. du Palais-Royal, Louvre/Tuileries* Ⓜ *Palais-Royal.*

㉗ **Place Vendôme.** Snobbish and self-important, this famous square is also gorgeous; property laws have kept away cafés and other such banal establishments, leaving the plaza stately and refined, the perfect home for the rich and famous (Chopin lived and died at No. 12; today's celebs camp out at the Hôtel Ritz, while a lucky few, including the family of the sultan of Brunei, actually own houses here). Mansart's rhythmic, perfectly proportioned example of 17th-century urban architecture still shines in all its golden-stone splendor. Napoléon had the square's central column made from the melted bronze of 1,200 cannons captured at the Battle of Austerlitz in 1805. There he is, perched vigilantly at the top. If you're feeling properly soigné, repair to Hemingway's Bar at the Hôtel Ritz and raise a glass to "Papa" (⇨ CloseUp Box, "Hemingway's Paris," below). Ⓜ *Opéra.*

HEMINGWAY'S PARIS

"**THERE IS NEVER ANY ENDING TO PARIS**," wrote Ernest Hemingway, the legendary author. For the "Lost Generation" after World War I, his aperçu rang particularly true. Disillusioned by America's Depression and Prohibition, lured by favorable exchange rates and a booming artistic scene, many American writers, composers, and painters moved to Paris in the 1920s and 1930s. Heading this impressive list—F. Scott Fitzgerald, Gertrude Stein, Ezra Pound, e. e. cummings, Janet Flanner, and John dos Passos are just a few of the famous figures—was "Papa," who came to epitomize the flamboyant lifestyle of Gertrude Stein's "Lost Generation." He used her phrase—itself a lament made by one French bartender to bemoan the years, and chances, lost to the world war—to preface The Sun Also Rises, but he may or may not have liked it. "The hell with her lost-generation talk and all the dirty, easy labels," he wrote elsewhere.

Hemingway arrived in Paris with his first wife, Hadley, in December 1921, and made for the Left Bank—the Hôtel Jacob et d'Angleterre, to be exact (still operating at 44 rue Jacob). To celebrate their arrival, the couple went to the Café de la Paix for a meal they nearly couldn't afford. In 1922 the couple moved to 74 rue du Cardinal-Lemoine, then in early 1924 the couple and their baby son settled at 113 rue Notre-Dame des Champs. Nearby, he settled in at La Closerie des Lilas café to write much of The Sun Also Rises. The Closerie was "the nearest good café we had"—around the corner from Hemingway's "old friend," the 1853 statue of Marshal Michel ("Mike") Ney. This proved for Hemingway to be a time "when we were very young and very happy," as he wrote in A Moveable Feast. Not happy long. In 1926 Hemingway left Hadley and next year wedded his mistress

Pauline Pfeiffer across town at St-Honoré-d'Eylau, then moved to 6 rue Férou, near the Musée du Luxembourg, whose Cézannes he revered. You can follow the steps of Jake and Bill in The Sun Also Rises as they "circle" the Ile St-Louis before the "steep walking . . . all the way up to the place de la Contrescarpe."

For gossip and books, Papa would visit Shakespeare & Co. at 12 rue de l'Odéon, owned by Sylvia Beach, an early buddy (the bookstore can now be found at 37 rue de la Bûcherie). Hemingway implied his sallies across the Seine to the upmarket Right Bank reflected a need for upmarket cocktails, but his first port of call was invariably the Guaranty Trust Company on 1 rue des Italiens, for money and mail. It was then on to, when flush, the bar of the Hôtel Crillon, or, when poor, either the Caves Mura, at 19 rue d'Antin, or Harry's Bar, still in brisk business at 5 rue Daunou. Hemingway's legendary association with the Hôtel Ritz, where he now has his own bar named for him, dates from the Liberation in 1944, when he strode in at the head of his platoon and "liberated" the joint by ordering 73 dry martinis. Here Hemingway asked Mary Welsh to become his fourth wife, and also righted the world with Jean-Paul Sartre, George Orwell, and Marlene Dietrich. A Moveable Feast tells how Hadley and Hemingway would stop at the Prunier restaurant in rue Duphot on their way back from the races, where you can still feast the night away.

③④ Place des Victoires. This circular square, now home to many of the city's top fashion boutiques, was laid out in 1685 by Jules Hardouin-Mansart in honor of the military victories (*victoires*) of Louis XIV. The Sun King gallops along on a bronze horse in the center. Ⓜ *Sentier.*

③⑤ St-Eustache. This huge church was built as the people's Right Bank reply to Notre-Dame, though St-Eustache dates from a couple of hundred years later. The church is a curious architectural hybrid: with the exception of the feeble west front, added between 1754 and 1788, construction lasted from 1532 to 1637, spanning the decline of the Gothic style and the emergence of the Renaissance. ✉ *2 rue du Jour, Beaubourg/Les Halles* ☎ *01–46–27–89–21 concert information* ☉ *Daily 8–7* Ⓜ *Les Halles; RER: Châtelet–Les Halles.*

③⑦ St-Germain l'Auxerrois. Until 1789, St-Germain was used by the French royal family as its parish church, in the days when the adjacent Louvre was a palace rather than a museum. The facade reveals the influence of 15th-century Flamboyant Gothic style, although the fluted columns around the choir, the area surrounding the altar, demonstrate the triumph of Classicism. ✉ *Pl. du Louvre, Louvre/Tuileries* Ⓜ *Louvre-Rivoli.*

②⑧ St-Roch. Designed by Lemercier in 1653 but completed only in the 1730s, this huge church is almost as long as Notre-Dame (138 yards), thanks to Hardouin-Mansart's domed Lady Chapel at the far end. ✉ *Rue St-Honoré, Louvre/Tuileries* Ⓜ *Tuileries.*

②⑨ Union Centrale des Arts Décoratifs (Decorative Arts Center). A must for lovers of fashion and the decorative arts, this northwestern wing of the Louvre building houses three high-style museums: the **Musée de la Mode,** devoted to costumes and accessories dating from the 16th century to today; the **Musée des Arts Décoratifs,** with furniture, tapestries, glassware, paintings, and other necessities of life from the Middle Ages through Napoléon's time and beyond—a highlight here are the sumptuous period-style rooms (note that until mid-2005, only the medieval and Renaissance rooms will be open to the public, as the rest will be undergoing renovations); and the **Musée de la Publicité,** with temporary exhibits of advertisements and posters. ✉ *107 rue de Rivoli, Louvre/Tuileries* ☎ *01–44–55–57–50* ⊕ *www.ucad.fr* 🎫 *€6* ☉ *Tues.–Sun. 11–6* Ⓜ *Palais-Royal.*

Urban Kaleidoscope: The Grands Boulevards

The French have a word for it: *flâner*—to stroll, promenade, dawdle. Back in the 19th century, the Parisian made this a newly fashionable activity, thanks to the magisterial boulevards Baron Haussmann—the regional prefect who oversaw the reconstruction of the city in the 1850s and 1860s—had designed and laid out. The focal point of this walk is the uninterrupted avenue that runs in almost a straight line from St-Augustin, the city's grandest Second Empire church, to place de la République, whose very name symbolizes the ultimate downfall of the imperial regime. The avenue's name changes six times along the way, which is why Parisians refer to it as the *Grands Boulevards* (plural). The makeup of the neighborhoods along the Grand Boulevards changes steadily as you head east from the posh 8ᵉ arrondissement toward working-class east Paris. The *grands magasins* (department stores) at the start of the walk epitomize upscale Paris shopping and stand on boulevard Haussmann. The opulent Opéra Garnier, just past the grands magasins, is the architectural showpiece of the period (often termed Second Empire and corresponding to the rule of Napoléon III). Although the hurly-burly traffic and neon signs of today have done much to dampen the charm of the Grands Boulevards, look hard and you can still spot aspects of street life that once inspired dozens of Impressionist paintings.

a good walk

Take the métro to Monceau and step through gilt-top iron gates to enter the enchantingly idyllic **Parc Monceau** ㊳ ☞ by the domed Chartres Pavilion. At the middle of the park, head left to avenue Velasquez—lined by some of the most regal mansions in the city—past the **Musée Cernuschi** ㊴, with its distinguished collection of Chinese art from Neolithic pottery to contemporary paintings, to boulevard Malesherbes. Turn right on boulevard Malesherbes and right again on rue de Monceau to reach the **Musée Nissim de Camondo** ㊵, whose aristocratic interior reflects the upscale tone of this haughty part of Paris. More splendor awaits at the **Musée Jacquemart-André** ㊶, a grand 19th-century residence stuffed with antiques and Old Master paintings, which you can find by continuing down rue de Monceau and turning left onto rue de Courcelles, then left again onto boulevard Haussmann.

Continue eastward along the boulevard and cross the square to find the innovative iron-and-stone church of **St-Augustin** ㊷. Cross the square in front and turn left along boulevard Haussmann to Square Louis-XVI, the original burial spot of Louis XVI and Marie-Antoinette—a mausoleum in their honor stands here now. Some 300 yards farther down boulevard Haussmann you'll find the grands magasins, Paris's most renowned department stores. First come the cupolas of Au Printemps, then Galeries Lafayette. Opposite looms the massive bulk of the **Opéra Garnier** ㊸, one of the most sumptuous theaters in the world.

Boulevard des Capucines, lined with cinemas and restaurants, heads east from in front of the Opera, becoming boulevard des Italiens before colliding with boulevard Haussmann. A left here down rue Drouot will take you to the **Hôtel Drouot** ㊹, Paris's central auction house. Rue Rossini leads from Drouot to rue de la Grange-Batelière. Halfway along on the right is the **Passage Jouffroy** ㊺, one of the many covered galleries that honeycomb the center of Paris. At the far end of the passage is the Musée Grévin, a waxworks museum. Cross boulevard Montmartre to passage des Panoramas, one of the city's oldest arcades; it was named for the panoramic scenes painted along the interior. You'll come out on rue St-Marc. Turn right, then left down rue Vivienne, to find the foursquare, colonnaded Bourse, the Paris Stock Exchange.

Head east along rue Réaumur, once the heart of the French newspaper industry—stationery shops still abound—and cross rue Montmartre. Take the second left up rue de Cléry, a narrow street that is the exclusive domain of fabric wholesalers. Continue up rue de Cléry as far as rue des

Degrés—not a street at all but a 14-step stairway—then look for the crooked church tower of **Notre-Dame de Bonne-Nouvelle** ㊻, hemmed in by rickety housing. The porticoed entrance is around the corner on rue de la Lune, which leads back to the Grands Boulevards, by now going under the name of boulevard de Bonne-Nouvelle.

The Porte St-Denis, a triumphal arch, looms up ahead, and a little farther on is the smaller but similar Porte St-Martin. From here take rue St-Martin south past the Musée des Arts et Métiers, a technology museum housed partly in the former church of St-Martin. Then cross rue Réaumur to the high, narrow, late-Gothic church of **St-Nicolas des Champs** ㊼. Head left on rue de Turbigo, past the cloister ruins and Renaissance gateway that embellish the far side of St-Nicolas. Some 400 yards along on the right is the Baroque church of **Ste-Élisabeth** ㊽; shortly after, you'll reach place de la République. It's a short métro ride from here to either the city's most famous cemetery, the **Cimetière du Père-Lachaise** ㊾, or to the **Parc de La Villette** ㊿, with its postmodern science and music museums.

TIMING   The distance between Parc Monceau and place de la République is almost 6 km (4 mi), which will probably take you four hours to walk, including coffee breaks and window-shopping. Allot a few additional hours, if not a whole morning or afternoon, to visit the Père Lachaise Cemetery or the Parc de La Villette. Or return to these on another day.

What to See

㊾ **Cimetière du Père-Lachaise** (Père-Lachaise Cemetery). Cemeteries may not be your idea of the ultimate attraction, but this is the largest and most interesting in Paris. It forms a veritable necropolis, with cobbled avenues and tombs competing in pomposity and originality. Leading incumbents include Jim Morrison, Frédéric Chopin, Marcel Proust, Edith Piaf, and Gertrude Stein. You can get a map at the entrance and track them down. ⊠ *Entrances on rue des Rondeaux, bd. de Ménilmontant, rue de la Réunion, Père Lachaise* ⊕ *www.pere-lachaise.com* ☉ *Apr.–Sept., daily 8–6; Oct.–Mar., daily 8–5* Ⓜ *Gambetta, Philippe-Auguste, Père-Lachaise.*

㊹ **Hôtel Drouot.** Paris's central auction house has everything from stamps and toy soldiers to Renoirs and 18th-century commodes. The 16 salesrooms make for fascinating browsing, and there's no obligation to bid. Although much of the auction action has moved to the Parisian venues of Sotheby's and Christie's, Drouot is still as lively as ever. ⊠ *9 rue Drouot, Opéra/Grands Boulevards* ☏ *01–48–00–20–00* ⊕ *www.gazette-drouot. com* ☉ *Mid-Sept.–mid-July, viewings Mon.–Sat. 11–noon and 2–6, with auctions starting at 2* Ⓜ *Richelieu-Drouot.*

㊴ **Musée Cernuschi.** Reopened in 2004 after an extensive renovation, this Asian art museum is set within an aristocratic town house. A connoisseur's favorite, the collection includes Chinese art from Neolithic pottery (3rd century BC) to funeral statuary, painted 8th-century silks, and contemporary paintings, as well as ancient Persian bronze objects. ⊠ *7 av. Velasquez, Parc Monceau* ☏ *01–45–63–50–75* ⊕ *www.paris.fr/ musees/* ☜ *Free* ☉ *Tues.–Sun. 10–5:40* Ⓜ *Monceau.*

★ ㊶ **Musée Jacquemart-André.** Often compared to New York City's Frick Collection, this was one of the grandest private residences of 19th-century Paris. Built between 1869 and 1875, it found Hollywood fame when used as Gaston Lachaille's mansion in the 1958 musical *Gigi,* as a great stand-in for the floridly opulent home of a sugar millionaire played by Louis Jourdan. Edouard André and his painter-wife, Nélie Jacquemart, the house's actual owners, were rich and cultured, so art from the Italian Renaissance and 18th-century France compete for attention here. Note the freshly restored Tiepolo frescoes in the staircase and on the dining-room ceiling, while salons done in the fashionable "Louis XVI–Empress" style (favored by Empress Eugénie) are hung with great paintings, including Uccello's *Saint George Slaying the Dragon,* Rembrandt's *Pilgrims of Emmaus,* Jean-Marc Nattier's *Mathilde de Canisy,* and Jacques-Louis David's *Comte Antoine-François de Nantes.* You can tour the house with the free English audio guide. The Tiepolo salon now contains a café, so why not lunch here and enjoy the Fragonard, Mantegna, and Chardin salads, named after great painters. ⊠ *158 bd. Haussmann, Parc Monceau* ☎ *01–45–62–11–59* ⊕ *www.musee-jacquemart-andre.com/jandre/* 🔳 *€8* ☉ *Daily 10–6* Ⓜ *St-Philippe-du-Roule or Miromesnil.*

need a break?   Short for *boulangerie-épicerie,* **Be** (⊠ 73 bd. de Courcelles, Monceau ☎ 01–46–22–20–20) is a hybrid bakery and corner store run by superchef Alain Ducasse and renowned baker Eric Kayser. Stocked with gastronomic grocery items like candied tomatoes and walnut oil from the Dordogne, it's also the perfect drop-in spot for delicious soups and sandwiches.

㊵ **Musée Nissim de Camondo.** Molière made fun of the *bourgeois gentilhomme,* the middle-class man who aspired to the class of his royal betters, but the playwright would have been in awe of Comte Moïse de Camondo, whose sense of style, grace, and refinement could have taught the courtiers at Versailles a thing or two. This immensely rich businessman built this grand hôtel particulier in the style of the Petit Trianon and proceeded to furnish it with some of the most exquisite furniture, *boiseries* (carved wood panels), and bibelots of the mid- to late 18th century. His wife and children (the museum is named after his son, who died in combat during World War I) then moved in and lent the house enormous warmth and charm. From ancien régime splendor, however, the family descended to the worst horrors of World War II: after the death of Count Moïse in 1935, the estate left the family's house and treasures to the government, while shortly thereafter family descendants were packed off to Auschwitz by the Nazis, where several of them were murdered. Today, the wealthy matrons of Paris have made this museum their own, and it shines anew with the beauty of the 18th century. No other house in Paris gives you such a sense of high French style as this one. ⊠ *63 rue de Monceau, Parc Monceau* ☎ *01–53–89–06–50* ⊕ *www.ucad.fr* 🔳 *€4.57* ☉ *Wed.–Sun. 10–5* Ⓜ *Villiers.*

Fodor'sChoice
★

46 Notre-Dame de Bonne-Nouvelle. This wide, soberly Neoclassical church, built in 1823–29, is tucked away off the Grands Boulevards. ⊠ *Rue de la Lune, Opéra/Grands Boulevards* Ⓜ *Bonne-Nouvelle.*

43 Opéra Garnier. Haunt of *Phantom of the Opera*, setting for Degas's famous ballet paintings, and still the most opulent theater in the world, the Paris Opéra was begun in 1862 by Charles Garnier at the behest of Napoléon III. But it was not completed until 1875, five years after the emperor's abdication. Awash with Algerian colored marbles and gilt putti, it's said to typify Second Empire architecture: a pompous hodgepodge of styles with about as much subtlety as a Wagnerian cymbal crash. The composer Debussy famously compared it to a Turkish bathhouse, but lovers of pomp and splendor will adore it. To see the theater and lobby, you don't actually have to attend a performance: after paying an entry fee, you can stroll around at leisure and view the auditorium and the Grand Foyer, whose grandeur reminds everyone that this was a theater for Parisians who attended the opera primarily to see and be seen. The **Musée de l'Opéra,** containing a few paintings and theatrical mementos, is unremarkable. Although technically the official home of the Paris Ballet, this auditorium usually mounts one or two full-scale operas a season, although most operas are presented at the drearily modern Opéra de la Bastille. ⊠ *Pl. de l'Opéra, Opéra/Grands Boulevards* ☏ *01–40–01–22–63* ⊕ *www.opera-de-paris.fr* ⊡ *€6* ☉ *Daily 10–5* Ⓜ *Opéra.*

> **need a break?**
>
> Few cafés in Paris are grander than the Belle Epoque **Café de la Paix** (⊠ 5 pl. de l'Opéra, Opéra/Grands Boulevards ☏ 01–40–07–30–10). Once described as "the center of the civilized world," it was a regular meeting place for the glitterati of 19th- and 20th-century Paris; the prices are as grand as the setting.

38 Parc Monceau. The most picturesque gardens on the Right Bank were laid out as a private park in 1778 and retain some of the fanciful elements then in vogue, including mock ruins and a faux pyramid. Today it remains the green heart of one of Paris's most fashionable neighborhoods. ⊠ *Entrances on bd. de Courcelles, av. Velasquez, av. Ruysdaël, av. van Dyck, Parc Monceau* Ⓜ *Monceau.*

50 Parc de La Villette. Usually known simply as La Villette, this ambitiously landscaped, futuristic park has several attractions, including the **Cité de la Musique.** This giant postmodern musical academy also houses the **Musée de la Musique** (Museum of Musical Instruments). At the **Géode** cinema, which looks like a huge silver golf ball, films are shown on an enormous 180-degree curved screen. The science museum, the **Cité des Sciences et de l'Industrie,** contains dozens of interactive exhibits (though most displays are in French only). *Science Museum* ⊠ *30 av. Corentin-Cariou, Parc de la Villette* ☏ *01–40–05–80–00* ⊕ *www.cite-sciences. fr* ⊡ *Museum of Musical Instruments €6.10, Science Museum €7.60* ☉ *Museum of Musical Instruments Tues.–Sat. noon–6, Sun. 10–6; Science Museum Tues.–Sun. 10–6* Ⓜ *Porte de La Villette, Porte de Pantin.*

45 **Passage Jouffroy.** Built in 1846, as its giant clock will tell you, this shops-filled passage was one of the favorite haunts of 19th-century dandies and flâneurs like the author Gérard de Nerval, who often strolled here in top hat and tails, with a large lobster on a pink-ribbon leash. ⊠ *Entrances on bd. Montmartre, rue de la Grange-Batelière, Opéra/Grands Boulevards* Ⓜ *Richelieu Drouot.*

42 **St-Augustin.** This domed church was dexterously constructed in the 1860s within the confines of an awkward V-shape site. It represented a breakthrough in ecclesiastical engineering because the use of metal pillars and girders obviated the need for exterior buttressing. ⊠ *Pl. St-Augustin, Opéra/Grands Boulevards* Ⓜ *St-Augustin.*

48 **Ste-Élisabeth.** This studied essay in Baroque (1628–46) has brightly restored wall paintings and a wide, semicircular apse around the choir. ⊠ *Rue du Temple, République* Ⓜ *Temple.*

47 **St-Nicolas des Champs.** The rounded arches and fluted Doric columns in the chancel of this church date from 1560 to 1587, a full century later than the pointed-arch nave (1420–80). ⊠ *Rue St-Martin, Opéra/Grands Boulevards* Ⓜ *Arts-et-Métiers.*

The Changing Face: The Marais & the Bastille

The Marais is one of the city's most historic and sought-after residential districts. Except for the architecturally whimsical Pompidou Center, the tone here is set by the gracious architecture of the 17th and 18th centuries (the Marais was spared the attentions of Haussmann, the man who rebuilt so much of Paris in the mid-19th century). Today most of the Marais's spectacular *hôtels particuliers*—loosely translated as "mansions," the onetime residences of aristocratic families—have been restored; many are now museums, including the noted Musée Picasso and Musée Carnavalet. There are trendy boutiques and cafés among the kosher shops in what used to be a predominantly Jewish neighborhood around rue des Rosiers, and there's an impressive Jewish Museum on nearby rue du Temple.

On the eastern edge of the Marais is place de la Bastille, site of the infamous prison stormed on July 14, 1789, an event that came to symbolize the beginning of the French Revolution. Largely in commemoration of the bicentennial of the Revolution, the Bastille area was renovated and became one of the trendiest sections of Paris. Galleries, shops, theaters, cafés, restaurants, and bars now fill formerly decrepit buildings and alleys.

a good walk

Make your starting point **place de la Bastille** 51 ▗, easily accessible by the métro. Today the square is dominated by the Colonne de Juillet, the curving glass facade of the modern **Opéra de la Bastille.**

Walk down rue St-Antoine to the **Hôtel de Sully** 52, now housing the Caisse Nationale des Monuments Historiques (National Treasury of Historic Monuments), at No. 62. Cross the road and pause at the mighty Baroque church of **St-Paul–St-Louis** 53. Take the left-hand side door out of the church into narrow passage St-Paul; then turn right onto rue St-Paul, past the grid of courtyards that makes up the Village St-Paul antiques-shops complex. Wend your way through the small streets to the quai de l'Hôtel-de-Ville.

Turn right on quai de l'Hôtel-de-Ville; *bouquinistes* (booksellers) line the Seine to your left. Pause by the Pont Louis-Philippe to admire the dome of the Panthéon floating above the skyline; then take the next right up picturesque rue des Barres to **St-Gervais–St-Protais** 54. Beyond the church stands the Hôtel de Ville, the city hall. From the Hôtel de Ville, cross rue de Rivoli and go up rue du Temple. On your right you'll pass one of the city's most popular department stores, the Bazar de l'Hôtel de Ville, or BHV, as it is known.

Take rue de la Verrerie, the first street on your left. Cross rue du Renard and take the second right past the ornate 16th-century church of St-Merri. Rue St-Martin, which is lined with stores, restaurants, and galleries, leads to the **Centre Pompidou** 55. In front of the Pompidou Center is the **Atelier Brancusi** 56, the reconstituted studio of sculptor Constantin Brancusi. The adjacent Square Igor-Stravinsky merits a stop for its unusual modern fountain.

Cross rue Beaubourg behind the Pompidou Center to rue Rambuteau, then take the first left onto rue du Temple. The stimulating **Musée d'Art et d'Histoire du Judaïsme** 57 is in the Hôtel de St-Aignan, at No. 71. Farther up the street, at No. 79, pause to admire the Hôtel de Montmor, a large-windowed Baroque mansion. Take a right onto rue des Haudriettes. Just to the left at the next corner is the **Musée de la Chasse et de la Nature** 58, the Museum of Hunting and Nature, housed in one of the Marais's most stately mansions. Head right on rue des Archives, crossing rue des Haudriettes, and admire the medieval gateway with two fairytale towers, now part of the **Archives Nationales** 59, the archives museum, entered from rue des Francs-Bourgeois around to the left.

Continue past the Crédit Municipal (the city's grandiose pawnbroking concern), the Dôme du Marais restaurant (housed in a circular 18th-century chamber originally used for auctions), and the church of Notre-Dame des Blancs-Manteaux. A corner turret signals rue Vieille-du-Temple: turn left past the palatial Hôtel de Rohan (now part of the Archives Nationales), then right onto rue de la Perle, and down rue de Thorigny (opposite) to the palatial 17th-century Hôtel Salé, now the **Musée Picasso** 60. Church lovers may wish to detour up rue de Thorigny and along rue du Roi-Doré to admire the severe Neoclassical portico of **St-Denis-du-St-Sacrement** 61 and the Delacroix *Deposition* inside.

Backtrack along rue de Thorigny and cross place de Thorigny to rue Elzévir. Halfway along is the **Musée Cognacq-Jay** 62, a must if you love 18th-century furniture, porcelain, and paintings. Turn left at the end of the street onto rue des Francs-Bourgeois, then right into rue Pavée, past the cheerfully askew facade of the city history library, to reach rue des Rosiers, with its excellent Jewish bakeries and falafel shops. Double back to rue des Francs-Bourgeois and turn right, then left to find rue de Sévigné and the **Musée Carnavalet** 63, the Paris history museum, in perhaps the prettiest edifice in the Marais. A short walk along rue des Francs-Bourgeois takes you to one of Paris's most historic squares, the **place des Vosges** ⑥, lined with pink brick and covered arcades.

TIMING   This walk will comfortably take a morning or an afternoon. If you choose to spend an hour or two in any of the museums along the way, allow a full day. Be prepared to wait in line at the Picasso Museum. Note that some of the museums don't open until the afternoon and that many shops in the Marais don't open until late morning. If you're interested in Judaica, don't plan this tour for a Saturday, when almost all Jewish-owned and -related stores, museums, and restaurants are closed.

What to See

⑤⑨ **Archives Nationales** (National Archives). If you're a serious history buff, you'll be fascinated by the thousands of intricate historical documents, dating from the Merovingian period to the 20th century, at the National Archives. Architecture enthusiasts should also include this on their list as the Archives are housed in the **Hôtel de Soubise,** one of the grandest of all 18th-century Parisian mansions, whose salons were among the first to show the Rococo style in full bloom. ⊠ *60 rue des Francs-Bourgeois, Le Marais* ☎ *01–40–27–62–18* ⊕ *www.archivesnationales.culture. gouv.fr* ⊠ *€3.05* ☉ *Mon. and Wed.–Fri. 10–5:45, weekends 1:45–5:45* Ⓜ *Rambuteau.*

⑤⑥ **Atelier Brancusi** (Brancusi Studio). Romanian-born sculptor Constantin Brancusi settled in Paris in 1898 at age 22. This light, airy museum in front of the Pompidou Center contains four glass-front rooms that re-create Brancusi's studio, crammed with smooth, stylized works from all periods of his career. ⊠ *Pl. Georges-Pompidou, Beaubourg/Les Halles* ☎ *01–44–78–12–33* ⊠ *€7, €10 including Centre Pompidou* ☉ *Wed.–Mon. 2–6* Ⓜ *Rambuteau.*

★ ⑤⑤ **Centre Pompidou.** The futuristic, funnel-top Pompidou Center—known to Parisians as Beaubourg, after the surrounding district—was built in the mid-1970s and named in honor of former French president Georges Pompidou (1911–74). You approach the center across **place Georges-Pompidou,** a sloping piazza, where you'll find (if you look carefully enough) the **Atelier Brancusi.** The **Musée National d'Art Moderne** (Modern Art Museum, entrance on Level 4) has doubled in size to occupy most of the center's top two stories: one devoted to modern art—including major works by Matisse, the Surrealists, Modigliani, Duchamp, and Picasso—the other to contemporary art since the 1960s, including video installations. Also look for rotating exhibits of contemporary art. In addition, there are a public reference library, a language laboratory, an industrial design center, two cinemas, and a rooftop restaurant, Georges, which is noted for its great view of the skyline and Eiffel Tower. ⊠ *Pl. Georges-Pompidou, Beaubourg/Les Halles* ☎ *01–44–78–12–33* ⊕ *www.cnac-gp.fr* ⊠ *€10, including Atelier Brancusi; €7 for permanent collection only; €7–€9 for temporary exhibits; free 1st Sun. of month* ☉ *Wed.–Mon. 11–9* Ⓜ *Rambuteau.*

⑤② **Hôtel de Sully.** This late-Renaissance mansion, begun in 1624, has a stately garden and a majestic courtyard with statues, richly carved pediments, and dormer windows. It is the headquarters of the **Caisse Nationale des Monuments Historiques** (National Treasury of Historic Monuments), responsible for administering France's historic monuments. Guided visits to Paris sites and buildings begin here; all are conducted in French. Millions of photographs also roost here; this **Patrimoine Photographique,** an outpost of the Jeu de Paume museum, holds four major exhibitions a year. ✉ *62 rue St-Antoine, Le Marais* ☎ *01–44–61–20–00* 🌐 *www.monum.fr* Ⓜ *St-Paul.*

(57) **Musée d'Art et d'Histoire du Judaïsme** (Museum of Jewish Art and History). With its clifflike courtyard ringed by giant pilasters, Pierre Le Muet's Hôtel St-Aignan—completed in 1650—is one of the most awesome sights in the Marais. It opened as a museum in 1998 after a 20-year, $35 million restoration. The interior has been remodeled to the point of blandness, but the displays, including 13th-century tombstones excavated in Paris; wooden models of destroyed East European synagogues; a roomful of early Chagalls; and Christian Boltanski's stark, two-part tribute to Shoah (Holocaust) victims, are carefully presented. ✉ *71 rue du Temple, Le Marais* ☎ *01–53–01–86–60* 🌐 *www.mahj.org* 🎫 *€6.10* ⏲ *Sun.–Fri. 11–6* Ⓜ *Rambuteau.*

★ (63) **Musée Carnavalet.** For a potent distillation of Parisian history, head to these two adjacent mansions in the heart of the Marais; the pair holds a fascinating trove of artifacts. Material dating from the city's origins until 1789 is housed in Hôtel Carnavalet, the setting for the most brilliant 17th-century salon in Paris, presided over by Madame de Sévigné, best known for the hundreds of letters she wrote to her daughter; they've become one of the most enduring chronicles of French high society in the 17th century. The section on the Revolution includes riveting models of guillotines and objects associated with the royal family's final days, including the king's razor and the chess set used by the royal prisoners at the approach of their own endgame. Lovers of the decorative arts will enjoy the period rooms here, especially those devoted to that most French of French styles, the 18th-century Rococo. Be sure to see the evocative re-creations of Marcel Proust's cork-lined bedroom, the late-19th-century Fouquet jewelry shop, and a room from the Art Nouveau monument the Café de Paris. ✉ *23 rue de Sévigné, Le Marais* ☎ *01–44–59–58–58* 🌐 *www.paris.fr/musees/musee_carnavalet/* 🎫 *Free* ⏲ *Tues.–Sun. 10–5:30* Ⓜ *St-Paul.*

need a break?

Marais Plus (✉ 20 rue des Francs-Bourgeois, Le Marais ☎ 01–48–87–01–40), on the corner of rue Elzévir and rue des Francs-Bourgeois, is a delightful, artsy gift shop with a cozy *salon de thé* at the rear.

(58) **Musée de la Chasse et de la Nature** (Museum of Hunting and Nature). This museum is in the grandly elegant Hôtel de Guénégaud, designed around 1650 by François Mansart. There's a series of immense 17th- and 18th-century still lifes (notably by Desportes and Oudry) and a wide panoply of swords, guns, muskets, and taxidermy. ✉ *60 rue des Archives, Le Marais* ☎ *01–42–72–86–42* 🎫 *€4.62* ⏲ *Wed.–Mon. 11–6* Ⓜ *Rambuteau.*

⑥② Musée Cognacq-Jay. Another rare opportunity to see how cultured and rich Parisians once lived, this 16th-century mansion contains an outstanding collection of 18th-century artwork in its wood-panel, boiseried rooms. Ernest Cognacq, founder of the department store La Samaritaine, and his wife, Louise Jay, amassed furniture, porcelain, and paintings—notably by Fragonard, Watteau, Boucher, and Tiepolo—to create one of the world's finest private collections of this period. ⊠ *8 rue Elzévir, Le Marais* ☎ *01–40–27–07–21* ⊕ *www.paris.fr/musees/cognacq_jay/* ☜ *Free* ☾ *Tues.–Sun. 10–5:40* Ⓜ *St-Paul.*

★ **⑥⓪ Musée Picasso.** Housed in the 17th-century Hôtel Salé, this museum contains the paintings, sculptures, drawings, prints, ceramics, and assorted works of art given to the government by Picasso's heirs after the painter's death in 1973 in lieu of death duties. There are works from every period of Picasso's life, as well as pieces by Cézanne, Miró, Renoir, Braque, Degas, and Matisse. The scuffed yet regal surroundings of the Hôtel Salé add to the pleasures of a visit. Be warned that peak season weekends here can be uncomfortably crowded. ⊠ *5 rue de Thorigny, Le Marais* ☎ *01–42–71–25–21* ⊕ *www.musee-picasso.fr* ☜ *€5.50, €6.70 for temporary exhibits plus permanent collection, Sun. €4, free 1st Sun. of month* ☾ *Wed.–Mon. 9:30–5:30* Ⓜ *St-Sébastien.*

➤ **⑤① Place de la Bastille.** Nothing remains of the infamous Bastille prison destroyed at the beginning of the French Revolution. In the midst of the large traffic circle is the **Colonne de Juillet** (July Column), commemorating the overthrow of Charles X in July 1830. As part of the countrywide celebrations for July 1989, the bicentennial of the French Revolution, the Opéra de la Bastille was erected, inspiring substantial redevelopment on the surrounding streets, especially along rue de Lappe and rue de la Roquette. What was formerly a humdrum neighborhood rapidly gained art galleries, clubs, and bars. Ⓜ *Bastille.*

⑥④ Place des Vosges. The oldest monumental square in Paris—and probably still its most nobly proportioned—the place des Vosges was laid out by Henri IV at the start of the 17th century. Originally known as place Royale, it has kept its Renaissance beauty nearly intact, although its buildings have been softened by time, their pale pink brick crumbling slightly in the harsh Parisian air and the darker stone facings pitted with age. It was always a highly desirable address, reaching a peak of glamour in the early years of Louis XIV's reign, when the nobility were falling over themselves for the privilege of living here. The two larger buildings on either side of the square were originally the king's and queen's pavilions. The statue in the center is of Louis XIII. It's not the original; that was melted down in the Revolution, the same period when the square's name was changed in honor of the French département of the Vosges, the first in the country to pay the new revolutionary taxes. With its arcades, symmetrical pink-brick town houses, and trim green garden, bisected in the center by gravel paths and edged with plane trees, the square achieves harmony and balance: it's a pleasant place to tarry on a sultry summer afternoon. Better yet, grab an arcade table at one of the many cafés lining the square—even a simple cheese crêpe becomes a feast in this setting. At No. 6 is the **Maison de Victor Hugo** (Victor Hugo's home),

FodorśChoice
★

where the workaholic French author, famed for *Les Misérables* and *The Hunchback of Notre-Dame*, lived between 1832 and 1848. ⊠ *Maison de Victor Hugo, 6 pl. des Vosges, Le Marais* ☎ *01–42–72–10–16* ⊕ *www.paris-france.org/musees* ⊠ *Free* ⊙ *Tues.–Sun. 10–5:45* Ⓜ *St-Paul, Chemin-Vert.*

🟑 **St-Denis-du-St-Sacrement.** This severely Neoclassical edifice, dating from the 1830s, is a formidable example of architectural discipline, oozing restraint and monumental dignity (or banality, according to taste). The grisaille frieze and gilt fresco above the semicircular apse have clout if not subtlety; the Delacroix *Deposition* (1844), in the front right-hand chapel as you enter, has both. ⊠ *Rue de Turenne, Le Marais* Ⓜ *St-Sébastien.*

🟒 **St-Gervais–St-Protais.** This imposing church near the Hôtel de Ville is named after two Roman soldiers martyred by the emperor Nero in the 1st century AD. The church, a riot of Flamboyant style, went up between 1494 and 1598, making it one of the last Gothic constructions in the country; the facade, however, is an essay in 17th-century Classicism. ⊠ *Pl. St-Gervais, Le Marais* ☎ *01–47–26–78–38 concert information* ⊙ *Tues.–Sun. 6:30 AM–8 PM* Ⓜ *Hôtel-de-Ville.*

🟓 **St-Paul–St-Louis.** The leading Baroque church in the Marais, with its elegant dome soaring 180 feet above the crossing, was begun in 1627 by the Jesuits and partly modeled on their Gesù church in Rome. Look for Delacroix's dramatic *Christ on the Mount of Olives* high up in the transept. ⊠ *Rue St-Antoine, Le Marais* Ⓜ *St-Paul.*

Across the Seine: The Ile St-Louis & the Latin Quarter

Set behind the Ile de la Cité is one of the most romantic spots in Paris, tiny Ile St-Louis. Of the two islands in the Seine—the Ile de la Cité is located just to the west—the St-Louis best retains the romance and loveliness of *le Paris traditionnel*. It has remained in the heart of Parisians as it has remained in the heart of every tourist who came upon it by accident, and without warning—a tiny universe unto itself, shaded by trees, bordered by Seine-side quais, and overhung with ancient stone houses. Up until the 1800s it was reputed that some island residents never crossed the bridges to get to Paris proper—and once you discover the island's quiet charm, you may understand why. South of the Ile St-Louis on the Left Bank of the Seine is the bohemian Quartier Latin (Latin Quarter), with its warren of steep, sloping streets, populated largely by Sorbonne students and academics. The name Latin Quarter comes from the old university tradition of studying and speaking in Latin, a tradition that disappeared during the Revolution. The university began as a theology school in the Middle Ages and later became the headquarters of the University of Paris; in 1968 the student revolution here had an explosive effect on French politics, resulting in major reforms in the education system. Most of the district's appeal is less emphatic: Roman ruins, tumbling street markets, the two oldest trees in Paris, and chance glimpses of Notre-Dame all await your discovery.

a good walk

Four bridges link the **Ile St-Louis** ⑥⑤ ▶, the smaller of the city's two is-lands, to the mainland. Rue St-Louis-en-l'Ile runs the length of the is-land, bisecting it. Walk down this street and admire the strange, pierced spire of St-Louis-en-l'Ile, and stop off for an ice cream at Berthillon, at No. 31. In spring and summer walk to the northern edge of the island to quai d'Anjou to visit the historic and opulent **Hôtel de Lauzun** ⑥⑥ (open weekends only from Easter to October).

Head toward the west end of the island, which gloriously overlooks Notre-Dame, and cross the Pont St-Louis. Just across the bridge on the left, at the eastern tip of the Ile de la Cité, is the Mémorial de la Déportation, a starkly moving modern crypt dedicated to the French people who died in Nazi concentration camps. Head through the gardens to the left of Notre-Dame and take the Pont au Double across the Seine to Square René-Viviani. Behind the square are the church of St-Julien-le-Pauvre, built at the same time as Notre-Dame, and the tiny, elegant streets of the Maubert district. Turn left out of St-Julien, then make the first right, and cross rue St-Jacques to the elegantly proportioned church of **St-Séver-in** ⑥⑦. The surrounding streets are for pedestrians only. Take rue St-Séverin, a right on rue Xavier-Privas, and a left on rue de la Huchette to reach place St-Michel. Gabriel Davioud's grandiose 1860 fountain, depicting St. Michael slaying the dragon, is a popular meeting spot at the nerve center of the Left Bank.

Turn left up boulevard St-Michel and cross boulevard St-Germain. To your left, behind some forbidding railings, lurks a garden with ruins that date from Roman times. These belong to the **Musée National du Moyen-Age** ⑥⑧, the National Museum of the Middle Ages. The entrance is down rue Sommerard, the next street on the left. Cross place Paul-Painlevé in front of the museum up toward the **Sorbonne** ⑥⑨, fronted by a small plaza where the Left Bank's student population congregates after classes. Continue uphill until you are confronted, up rue Soufflot on your left, by the menacing domed bulk of the **Panthéon** ⑦⓪. On the far left corner of place du Panthéon is St-Étienne-du-Mont, a church whose facade is a mishmash of architectural styles. Head along rue Clovis to reach rue du Cardinal-Lemoine, which leads into rue des Fosses-St-Bernard, and head back toward the Seine and the glass-facade **Institut du Monde Arabe** ⑦①, a center devoted to Arab culture. End your walk here with a cup of mint tea in the lovely rooftop café, where you'll have a grand view overlooking Paris.

TIMING This walk can be fitted into a morning or afternoon or serve as the basis for a leisurely day's exploring—given that several sites, notably the Musée National du Moyen-Age, deserve a lengthy visit.

What to See

⑥⑥ **Hôtel de Lauzun.** Offering a very rare view inside an Ile St-Louis man-sion, a visit here permits you to see opulent salons that were among the first examples to introduce the 17th-century Baroque style in Paris. Later, the visionary poet Charles Baudelaire (1821–67) had his apart-ment here, where he kept a cache of stuffed snakes and crocodiles and where he wrote a large chunk of *Les Fleurs du Mal* (*The Flowers of Evil*).

In 1848 poet Théophile Gautier moved in, making it the meeting place of the Club des Haschischines (Hashish Eaters' Club); novelist Alexandre Dumas and painter Eugène Delacroix were both members. At this writing, the chances to get in among the gilding are rare; the building is undergoing restoration until spring 2005 and is not generally open to the public except for special tours. ⊠ *17 quai d'Anjou, Ile St-Louis* ☎ *01–43–54–27–14* Ⓜ *Pont-Marie.*

▶ **65** **Ile St-Louis.** One of the more fabled addresses in Paris, this tiny island
Fodor's Choice has long harbored the rich and famous, including Chopin, Daumier, He-
★ lena Rubenstein, Chagall, and the Rothschild family, who still occupy the island's grandest house. In fact, the entire island displays striking architectural unity, stemming from the efforts of a group of early 17th-century property speculators led by Christophe Marie. The group commissioned leading Baroque architect Louis Le Vau (1612–70) to erect a series of imposing town houses. Other than some elegant facades and the island's highly picturesque quays along the Seine, there are no major sights here—just follow your nose and soak in the atmosphere. Study the plaques on the facades of houses describing who lived where when. An especially somber reminder adorns 19 quai de Bourbon: "Here lived Camille Claudel, sculptor, from 1899 to 1913. Then ended her brave career as an artist and began her long night of internment." Rodin's muse, she was committed to an insane asylum by her family where she was forbidden to practice her art. In your tour of the St-Louis, don't miss the views of Notre-Dame from the Quai d'Orleans, the historic Hôtel Lauzun museum, or, *bien sûr,* the Grand-Marnier ice-cream or Pamplemousse Rose sorbet at Berthillon, found on the center street of the island. Ⓜ *Pont-Marie.*

┌─────────┐
│ **need a** │ Cafés all over town sell Berthillon, the haute couture of ice cream,
│ **break?** │ but the **Berthillon** (⊠ 31 rue St-Louis-en-l'Ile, Ile St-Louis
└─────────┘ ☎ 01–43–54–31–61) shop itself is the place to go. More than 30 flavors are served; expect to wait in line. The shop is open Wednesday–Sunday.

71 **Institut du Monde Arabe** (Institute of the Arab World). Jean Nouvel's striking 1988 glass-and-steel edifice adroitly fuses Arabic and European styles. Note the 240 shutterlike apertures that open and close to regulate light exposure. Inside, the institute tries to do for Arab culture what the Pompidou Center does for modern art, with the help of a sound-and-image center, a vast library and documentation center, and an art museum. The top-floor café provides a good view of Paris. ⊠ *1 rue des Fossés-St-Bernard, Quartier Latin* ☎ *01–40–51–38–38* ⊕ *www.imarabe. org* 🎫 *Exhibitions €7, museum €3* ⊙ *Tues.–Sun. 10–6* Ⓜ *Cardinal Lemoine.*

★ **68** **Musée National du Moyen-Age** (National Museum of the Middle Ages). Rivaling New York City's Cloisters as the greatest museum of medieval art in the world, the Musée Cluny—a name that is more popularly used—is housed in the 15th-century Hôtel de Cluny, erstwhile residence of the abbots of Cluny (the famous—but now largely destroyed—abbey in Burgundy). A stunning selection of tapestries, including the exquisite *Dame à la Licorne* (*Lady and the Unicorn*) series, headlines its exhibition of medieval decorative arts. Alongside the mansion are the city's Roman baths and the *Boatmen's Pillar,* Paris's oldest sculpture. ⊠ *6 pl. Paul-Painlevé, Quartier Latin* ☎ *01–53–73–78–00* ⊕ *www.musee-moyenage. fr* 🖹 *€5.50, free 1st Sun. of month, otherwise €4 on Sun.* ☽ *Wed.–Mon. 9:15–5:45* Ⓜ *Cluny–La Sorbonne.*

⑳ Panthéon. Originally commissioned as a church by Louis XV as a mark of gratitude for his recovery from a grave illness in 1744, the Panthéon is now a monument to France's most glorious historical figures, including Voltaire, Zola, Rousseau, and dozens of French statesmen, military heroes, and other thinkers. Germain Soufflot's building was not begun until 1764, and was not completed until 1790, during the French Revolution, whereupon its windows were blocked and it was transformed into the national shrine it is today. Its newest resident is Alexandre Dumas, whose remains were interred there in November of 2002. ⊠ *Pl. du Panthéon, Quartier Latin* ☎ *01–44–32–18–00* ⊕ *www.monum.fr* 🖹 *€7* ☽ *Summer, daily 9:30–6:30; winter, daily 10–6:15* Ⓜ *Cardinal-Lemoine; RER: Luxembourg.*

⑰ St-Séverin. This unusually wide, Flamboyant Gothic church dominates a Left Bank neighborhood filled with squares and pedestrian streets. Note the splendidly deviant spiraling column in the forest of pillars behind the altar. ⊠ *Rue des Prêtres St-Séverin, Latin Quarter* ☽ *Weekdays 11–5:30, Sat. 11–10* Ⓜ *St-Michel.*

⑲ Sorbonne. Named after Robert de Sorbon, a medieval canon who founded a college of theology here in 1253, this is one of the oldest universities in Europe. The church and university buildings were restored by Cardinal Richelieu in the 17th century, and the maze of amphitheaters, lecture rooms, and laboratories, along with the surrounding courtyards and narrow streets, retains a hallowed air. You can visit the main courtyard on rue de la Sorbonne and peek into the main lecture hall, a major meeting point during the tumultuous student upheavals of 1968. The square is dominated by the noble university church with cupola and Corinthian columns. Inside is the white-marble tomb of that ultimate crafty cleric, Cardinal Richelieu himself. ⊠ *Rue de la Sorbonne, Quartier Latin* Ⓜ *Cluny–La Sorbonne.*

Toujours la Politesse: From Orsay to St-Germain-des-Prés

This walk covers the Left Bank, from the Musée d'Orsay in the stately 7ᵉ arrondissement to the chic and colorful area around St-Germain-des-Prés in the 6ᵉ. The Musée d'Orsay, in a daringly converted Belle Epoque rail station on the Seine, houses one of the world's most spectacular arrays of Impressionist paintings. Farther along the river, the 18th-century Palais Bourbon—now home to the National Assembly—sets the tone for the 7ᵉ arrondissement. This is Edith Wharton territory—select, discreet *vieille France,* where all the aristocrats live in gorgeous, sprawling, old-fashioned apartments or *maisons particulières* (*very* private town houses). Embassies—and the Hôtel Matignon, residence of the

French prime minister—line the surrounding streets, their majestic scale in total keeping with the Hôtel des Invalides, whose gold-leaf dome climbs heavenward above the regal tomb of Napoléon. The Rodin Museum—set in a gorgeous 18th-century mansion—is only a short walk away. This remains a district where manners maketh the man.

To the east, away from the splendor of the 7ᵉ, the boulevard St-Michel slices the Left Bank in two: on one side, the Latin Quarter; on the other, the Faubourg St-Germain, named for St-Germain-des-Prés, the oldest church in Paris. Ask Parisians and tourists alike and many venture that this is their favorite district in Paris, stuffed as it is with friendly cafés, soigné boutiques, and adorably quaint streets. The venerable church tower has long acted as a beacon for intellectuals, most famously during the 1950s when Albert Camus, Jean-Paul Sartre, and Simone de Beauvoir ate and drank existentialism in the neighborhood cafés. Today most of the philosophizing is done by tourists, yet a wealth of bookshops, art stores, and antiques galleries ensures that St-Germain, as the area is commonly known, retains its highbrow and very posh appeal. In the southern part of this district is the city's most colorful park, the Jardin du Luxembourg.

a good walk

Start at the **Musée d'Orsay** 72 ⌐, famed for its collection of art from 1848 to 1914. A good meeting point is the pedestrian square outside the museum, where huge bronze statues of an elephant and a rhinoceros disprove the idea that the French take their art *too* seriously. Head west along rue de Lille to the **Palais Bourbon** 73, home of the Assemblée Nationale (French Parliament).

Rue de l'Université leads from the Assemblée to the grassy Esplanade des Invalides and an encounter with the **Hôtel des Invalides** 74, founded by Louis XIV to house invalid, or wounded, war veterans. The most impressive dome in Paris towers over the church at the Invalides—the Église du Dôme. From the church, double back along boulevard des Invalides and take rue de Varenne to the Hôtel Biron, better known as the **Musée Rodin** 75, where you can see a fine collection of Auguste Rodin's emotionally charged statues. The quiet, distinguished 18th-century streets between the Rodin Museum and the Parliament are filled with embassies and ministries.

Continue on to rue du Bac, turn left, then take a right onto rue de Grenelle, to the **Musée Maillol** 76, dedicated to the work of sculptor Aristide Maillol. Continue on rue de Grenelle past Edme Bouchardon's monumental 1730s Fontaine des Quatre Saisons (Four Seasons Fountain) to the carrefour de la Croix-Rouge, with its mighty bronze Centaur by the contemporary sculptor César. Take rue du Vieux-Colombier to place St-Sulpice, a spacious square whose north side is lined with cafés. Looming over the square is the enormous church of **St-Sulpice** 77.

Exit the church, head back across the square, and turn right on rue Bonaparte to reach **St-Germain-des-Prés** 78, Paris's oldest church. Across the cobbled place St-Germain-des-Prés is the café Les Deux Magots, one of the principal haunts of the intelligentsia after World War II. Two doors down boulevard St-Germain is the Café de Flore, another popular spot with the likes of Jean-Paul Sartre and Simone de Beauvoir. Follow rue de l'Abbaye, alongside the far side of the church, to rue de Furstenberg. The street opens out into place Furstenberg—a postcard-perfect square—where you'll find Eugène Delacroix's studio, the **Musée Delacroix** ㉙. Take a left on rue Jacob and turn right down rue Bonaparte to the **École Nationale des Beaux-Arts** ㉚, whose students can often be seen painting and sketching on the nearby quays and bridges.

Continue down to the Seine and turn right along the quay, past the **Institut de France** ㉛. With its distinctive dome, curved facade, and commanding position overlooking the Pont des Arts—a footbridge with delightful views of the Louvre and Ile de la Cité—the institute is one of the city's most impressive waterside sights. Continue along quai de Conti past the Hôtel des Monnaies, the former national mint. Head up rue Dauphine. Just 150 yards up, it's linked by the open-air passage Dauphine to rue Mazarine, which leads left to the carrefour de Buci, where you can find one of the best food markets in Paris. Where rue Dauphine crosses rue St-André-des-Arts, make a left for about a half a block to find the enchanting **Cour de Commerce St-André** ㉜, a relentlessly picturesque alleyway lined with cafés—a time-machine that will hurtle you back to 18th-century Paris. Here you will find the extraordinary Cour de Rohan courtyard, possibly Paris's most magical hideaway. Follow the Cour de Commerce St-André up to busy place de l'Odéon. Cross boulevard St-Germain and climb rue de l'Odéon to the colonnaded Théâtre de l'Odéon. Behind the theater lies the spacious **Jardin du Luxembourg** ㉝, one of the most stylish parks in the city.

TIMING   This walk could take from four hours to a couple of days, depending on how long you spend in the plethora of museums along the way. Aim for an early start—that way you can hit the Musée d'Orsay early, when crowds are smaller, then get to the rue de Buci street market when it's in full swing, in the late afternoon (the stalls are generally closed for lunch until 3 PM). Note that the Hôtel des Invalides is open daily, but Orsay is closed Monday. You might consider returning to one or more museums on another day or night—Orsay is open late on Thursday evening.

What to See

㉜ Cour du Commerce St-André. Like an 18th-century engraving come to
FodorśChoice   life, this exquisite, cobblestone-street arcade is one of Paris's loveliest
★   sights. Although it's been tatted up with some faux cafés, its shop signs, awnings, and outdoor tables make it a most festive tableau, where Napoléon himself still wouldn't look too out of place taking his coffee (as he did back when). One of the restaurants on the Cour is actually Paris's oldest café, **Le Procope** (☎ 01–40–46–79–00), opened in 1686 by an Italian named Francesco Procopio. Many of Paris's most famous literary sons and daughters imbibed here through the centuries, including Voltaire, Balzac, George Sand, Victor Hugo, and even Benjamin Franklin, who popped in whenever business brought him to Paris. The café started out as the Sardi's of its day, because the Comédie-Française was nearby. Racine and Molière were regulars. The place is still going strong, so you, too, can enjoy its period (though now gussied-up) trimmings and traditional menu. Just opposite Procope is that hid-

den 18th-century treasure that some call Paris's most beautiful spot: the **Cour de Rohan,** a series of three cloistered courtyards that found Hollywood immortality when Cecil Beaton picked it as the locale of Gigi's home in the famed Lerner and Loewe 1958 musical film *Gigi* ("Chez Mamita" is the house with the steep staircase directly on your left as you enter). The Cour is comprised of private residences so you may find its gates are sometimes closed. ⊠ *Linking bd. St-Germain and rue St-André-des-Arts, St-Germain-des-Prés* Ⓜ *Odéon.*

⑧⓪ École Nationale des Beaux-Arts (National Fine Arts College). In three large mansions near the Seine, this school—today the breeding ground for painters, sculptors, and architects—was once the site of a convent, founded in 1608. Wander into the courtyard and galleries of the school to see the casts and copies of the statues stored here for safekeeping during the Revolution. ⊠ *14 rue Bonaparte, St-Germain-des-Prés* ☉ *Daily 1–7* Ⓜ *St-Germain-des-Prés.*

> **need a break?**
>
> The popular **La Palette** (⊠ 43 rue de Seine, St-Germain-des-Prés ☎ 01–43–26–68–15), on the corner of rue de Seine and rue Callot, has long been a favorite café haunt of Beaux-Arts students. One of them painted the ungainly portrait of the patron François that presides with mock authority.

★ **⑦④ Hôtel des Invalides.** Famed as the final resting place of Napoléon, Les Invalides, as it is widely known, is an outstanding monumental Baroque ensemble, designed by Libéral Bruand in the 1670s at the behest of Louis XIV to house wounded, or invalid, soldiers. Although no more than a handful of old-timers live at the Invalides these days, the army link remains in the form of the **Musée de l'Armée,** a military museum. The **Musée des Plans-Reliefs,** also housed here, contains a fascinating collection of old scale models of French towns. The 17th-century **Église St-Louis des Invalides** is the Invalides's original church. More impressive is Jules Hardouin-Mansart's **Église du Dôme,** built onto the end of the church of St-Louis but blocked off from it in 1793. The showpiece here is that grandiose monument to glory and hubris, **Napoléon's Tomb.** ⊠ *Pl. des Invalides, Trocadéro/Eiffel Tower* ☎ *01–44–42–37–72 Army and Model museums* ⊕ *www.invalides.org* ☜ *€7* ☉ *Église du Dôme and museums Apr.–Sept., daily 10–6; Oct.–Mar., daily 10–4:30, closed 1st Mon. of month* Ⓜ *La Tour-Maubourg.*

⑧① Institut de France (French Institute). Built to the designs of Louis Le Vau from 1662 to 1674, the institute's curved, dome-top facade is one of the Left Bank's most impressive waterside sights. It also houses one of France's most revered cultural institutions, the Académie Française, created by Cardinal Richelieu in 1635. Unfortunately, the interior is closed to the general public. ⊠ *Pl. de l'Institut, St-Germain-des-Prés* Ⓜ *Pont-Neuf.*

☾ **⑧③ Jardin du Luxembourg** (Luxembourg Gardens). Immortalized in countless paintings, the Luxembourg Gardens possess all that is unique and befuddling about Parisian parks: swarms of pigeons, cookie-cutter trees, ironed-and-pressed dirt walkways, and immaculate lawns meant for admiring, not touching. The tree- and bench-lined paths offer a reprieve from the incessant bustle of the Quartier Latin, as well as an opportunity to discover the dotty old women and smooching university students who once found their way into Doisneau photographs. The park's northern boundary is dominated by the Palais du Luxembourg, surrounded by a handful of well-armed guards; they are protecting the senators who have been deliberating in the palace since 1958. Although the garden may seem purely French, the original 17th-century planning took its inspiration from Italy. When Maria de' Medici, widow of Henri IV, acquired the estate of the deceased Duke of Luxembourg in 1612 she decided to turn his mansion into a version of the Florentine Medici home, the Palazzo Pitti. Today, an adjacent wing of her former palace houses the **Musée de Luxembourg,** open only for special temporary exhibitions. One of the great attractions of the park is the **Théâtre des Marionnettes,** where on Saturday and Sunday at 11 and 3:15, and on Wednesday at 3:15 PM, you can catch one of the classic *guignols* (marionette shows) for a small admission charge. ⊠ *Bordered by bd. St-Michel and rues de Vaugirard, de Médicis, Guynemer, and Auguste-Comte, St-Germain-des-Prés* ⊕ *www.museeduluxembourg.fr* Ⓜ *Odéon; RER: Luxembourg.*

⑦⑨ **Musée Delacroix.** The studio of artist Eugène Delacroix (1798–1863) contains only a small collection of his sketches and drawings. But if you want to pay homage to France's foremost Romantic painter, you'll want to visit this museum. Two other reasons to pay a call: the atelier is set on place Furstenberg, one of the tiniest, most romantic squares in Paris, while just beyond the museum rooms is the backyard garden—an enchanting nook that is sure to bring out the artist in you. ⊠ *6 rue Furstenberg, St-Germain-des-Prés* ☎ *01–44–41–86–50* ⊡ *€4* ⊙ *Wed.–Mon. 9:30–5* Ⓜ *St-Germain-des-Prés.*

Fodor'sChoice ★

⑦⑥ **Musée Maillol.** Drawings, paintings, tapestries, and, above all, bronzes by Art Deco sculptor Aristide Maillol (1861–1944)—whose sleek, stylized nudes adorn the Tuileries—can be admired at this handsome town house, lovingly restored by his former muse, Dina Vierny. ⊠ *61 rue de Grenelle, St-Germain-des-Prés* ☎*01–42–22–59–58* ⊡*€7* ⊙ *Wed.–Mon. 11–6* Ⓜ *Rue du Bac.*

★ ▶ ⑦② **Musée d'Orsay.** In a spectacularly converted Belle Epoque train station, the Orsay Museum—devoted to the arts (mainly French) spanning the period 1848–1914—is one of the city's most popular, thanks to the presence of the world's greatest collection of Impressionist and Postimpressionist paintings. Here you'll find Manet's *Déjeuner sur l'Herbe* (*Lunch on the Grass*), the painting that scandalized Paris in 1863 when it was shown at the Salon des Refusés, an exhibit organized by artists refused permission to show their work at the Academy's official annual salon, as well as the artist's provocative nude, *Olympia.* There is a dazzling rainbow of masterpieces by Renoir (including his beloved *Le Moulin de la Galette*), Sisley, Pissarro, and Monet. The Postimpressionists—Cézanne, van Gogh, Gauguin, and Toulouse-Lautrec—are on the top floor. On the ground floor you'll find the work of Manet, the powerful realism of Courbet, and the delicate nuances of Degas. If you prefer more academic paintings, look for Puvis de Chavannes's larger-than-life classical canvases. And if you're excited by more modern developments, look for the early 20th-century Fauves (meaning "wild beasts," the name given them by an outraged critic in 1905)—particularly Matisse, Derain, and Vlaminck. Thought-provoking sculptures also lurk at every turn. Check out the restaurant here, set in a magnificent hall that was the waiting room of the former station. ⊠ *1 rue de la Légion d'Honneur, St-Germain-des-Prés* ☎ *01–40–49–48–14* ⊕ *www.musee-orsay.fr* ⊡ *€7, Sun. €5* ۞ *Tues., Wed., Fri., and Sat. 10–6, Thurs. 10–9:45, Sun. 9–6* Ⓜ *Solférino; RER: Musée d'Orsay.*

---

need a break?

If those *Déjeuner sur l'Herbe* paintings make you think about lunch, stop at the middle floor's **Musée d'Orsay Restaurant** (☎ 1–45–49–47–03) in the former train station's sumptuous dining room. An elegant lunch is available 11:30–2:30, high tea from 3:30–5:40 (except on Thursday, when dinner is served instead, from 7–9:30 PM). For a simpler snack anytime, visit the top-floor **Café des Hauteurs** and drink in its panoramic view across the Seine toward Montmartre.

★ ❼❺ **Musée Rodin.** The exquisite 18th-century Hôtel Biron makes a gracious stage for the sculpture of Auguste Rodin (1840–1917). You'll doubtless recognize the seated *Le Penseur* (*The Thinker*), with his elbow resting on his knee, and the passionate *Le Baiser* (*The Kiss*). From the upper rooms, which contain some fine if murky paintings by Rodin's friend Eugène Carrière (1849–1906) and some fine sculptures by Rodin's mistress, Camille Claudel (1864–1943), you can see the large garden behind the house. Don't skip the garden: it is exceptional not only for its rosebushes and sculpture, but also its view of the Invalides dome with the Eiffel Tower behind and its superb cafeteria. ⊠ *77 rue de Varenne, Invalides/Eiffel Tower* ☎ *01–44–18–61–10* ⊡ *€5, Sun. €3, gardens only €1* ۞ *Easter–Oct., Tues.–Sun. 9:30–5:45; Nov.–Easter, Tues.–Sun. 9:30–4:45* Ⓜ *Varenne.*

❼❸ **Palais Bourbon.** The most prominent feature of the home of the Assemblée Nationale (French Parliament) is its colonnaded facade, commissioned by Napoléon. ⊠ *Pl. du Palais-Bourbon, Invalides/Eiffel Tower* ۞ *During temporary exhibits only* Ⓜ *Assemblée Nationale.*

❼❽ **St-Germain-des-Prés.** Paris's oldest church was first built to shelter a relic of the true cross brought from Spain in AD 542. The chancel was enlarged and the church then consecrated by Pope Alexander III in 1163; the tall, sturdy tower—a Left Bank landmark—dates from this period. The church stages superb organ concerts and recitals. ⊠ *Pl. St-Germain, St-Germain-des-Prés* ۞ *Weekdays 8–7:30, weekends 8 AM–9 PM* Ⓜ *St-Germain-des-Prés.*

❼❼ **St-Sulpice.** Dubbed the "Cathedral of the Left Bank," this enormous 17th-century church is of note for the powerful Delacroix frescoes in the first chapel on the right. The 18th-century facade was never finished, and its unequal towers add a playful touch to an otherwise sober design. ⊠ *Pl. St-Sulpice, St-Germain-des-Prés* Ⓜ *St-Sulpice.*

Montmartre: The Citadel of Paris

On a dramatic rise above the city is Montmartre, site of the Sacré-Coeur Basilica and home to a once-thriving artist community. This was the quartier that Toulouse-Lautrec and Renoir immortalized with a flash of their brush and a tube of their paint. Although the great painters have long departed, and the fabled nightlife of Old Montmartre has fizzled down to some glitzy nightclubs and skin shows, Montmartre still exudes history and Gallic charm. Windmills once dotted Montmartre (often referred to by Parisians as *La Butte,* meaning "mound"). They were set up here not just because the hill was a good place to catch the wind—at more than 300 feet it's the highest point in the city—but because Montmartre was covered with wheat fields and quarries right up to the end of the 19th century. Today only two of the original 20 windmills remain. Visiting Montmartre means negotiating a lot of steep streets and flights of steps. The crown atop this urban peak, the Sacré-Coeur Basilica, is something of an architectural oddity, with a silhouette that looks more like that of a mosque than a cathedral. No matter: when viewed from afar at dusk or sunrise, it looks like Paris's "sculpted cloud."

Long a draw because of its bohemian–artistic history, Montmartre became even more popular after its starring role in the 2001 smash-hit film *Amélie.* Now you not only have to contend with art lovers seeking out Picasso's studio and Toulouse-Lautrec's favorite brothel, but movie fans looking for Amélie's café and *épicerie.* Yet you can still give the hordes the slip and discover some of Paris's most romantic and picturesque corners.

a good walk

Begin at place Blanche, landmarked by the **Moulin Rouge** ㉞ ▶, the windmill turned dance hall immortalized by Toulouse-Lautrec. Prior to the raucous time of the cancan was the dreamy age of Romanticism; to discover its exquisite 19th-century charm, you need only to visit the lovely **Musée de la Vie Romantique** ㉟, set three blocks south of place Blanche. Heading down rue Blanche until the third left onto rue Chaptal, this country-house-in-the-city was the former haunt of such greats as Georges Sand, Chopin, Ingres, and Delacroix. After savoring its delicate salons, backtrack up to place Blanche and then walk up lively rue Lepic from place Blanche. Few people notice the tiny Lux Bar at No. 12, with its original Art Nouveau woodwork and tiled murals from 1910—most are too busy looking across the street at the Café des Deux Moulins, where Amélie Poulain served coffee and brewed up schemes for helping strangers in the noted 2001 movie. Up rue Lepic you'll find the **Moulin de la Galette** ㊱, atop its leafy hillock opposite rue Tholozé, once a path over the hill. Turn right down rue Tholozé, past Studio 28, the first cinema built expressly for experimental films. Continue down rue Tholozé to rue des Abbesses and turn left toward the triangular **place des Abbesses** ㊲. Follow rue Ravignan as it climbs north, via place Émile-Goudeau, an enchanting little cobbled square, to the "cradle of Cubism," the **Bateau-Lavoir** ㊳, or Boat Wash House, at its northern edge. Painters Picasso and Braque had studios in the original building; this drab concrete edifice was built in its place. Continue up the hill via rue de la Mire to place Jean-Baptiste Clément, where Amedeo Modigliani had a studio.

The upper reaches of rue Lepic lead to rue Norvins, formerly rue des Moulins. At the end of the street to the left is stylish avenue Junot. Continue right past the bars and tourist shops until you reach **place du Tertre** (89). Around the corner on rue Poulbot, the **Espace Dalí** (90) houses works by Salvador Dalí, who once had a studio in the area. Return to place du Tertre. Looming behind is the scaly white dome of the Basilique du **Sacré-Coeur** (91). The cavernous interior is worth visiting for its golden mosaics; climb to the top of the dome for the view of Paris. Walk back toward place du Tertre. Turn right onto rue du Mont-Cenis and left onto rue Cortot, site of the **Musée de Montmartre** (92), which, like the Bateau-Lavoir, once sheltered an illustrious group of painters, writers, and assorted cabaret artists. Another famous Montmartre landmark is at No. 22: the bar-cabaret **Au Lapin Agile** (93). Opposite the Lapin Agile is the tiny Cimetière St-Vincent, where painter Maurice Utrillo is buried.

TIMING Reserve a morning or afternoon (late afternoon if you want to catch Au Lapin Agile open in the early evening) for this walk: many of the streets are steep and slow. Include half an hour each at Sacré-Coeur and the museums (the Dalí museum is open daily, but the Montmartre museum is closed Monday). From Easter through September Montmartre is besieged by tourists. Two hints for avoiding the worst of the rush: come on a gray day, when Montmartre's sullen-tone facades suffer less than most others in the city; or visit during the afternoon and return to place du Tertre (maybe via the funicular) by the early evening, when the tourist buses will have departed.

What to See

(93) **Au Lapin Agile.** One of the most picturesque spots in Paris, this legendary bar-cabaret (sorry—open nights only) is a miraculous survivor from the 19th century. It got its curious name—the Nimble Rabbit—when the owner, André Gill, hung up a sign (now in the Musée du Vieux Montmartre) of a laughing rabbit jumping out of a saucepan clutching a bottle of wine. Founded in 1860, this adorable maison-cottage was a favorite subject of painter Maurice Utrillo. Once owned by Aristide Bruant (immortalized in many Toulouse-Lautrec posters), it became the home-away-from-home for Braque, Modigliani, Apollinaire, and Vlaminck. The most famous habitué, however, was Picasso, who once paid for a meal with one of his paintings, then promptly went out and painted another, which he named after this place (it now hangs in New York's Metropolitan Museum, which purchased it for $50 million). Today the Lapin Agile manages to preserve at least something of its earlier flavor, unlike the Moulin Rouge. ✉ *22 rue des Saules, Montmartre* ☎ *01–46–06–85–87* 🌐 *www.au-lapin-agile.com* €20 ⏲ *Tues.–Sat. 9 PM–2 AM* Ⓜ *Lamarck-Caulaincourt.*

Fodor's Choice ★

(88) **Bateau-Lavoir** (Boat Wash House). Montmartre poet Max Jacob coined the name for the original building on this site (which burned down in

1970), saying it resembled a boat and that the warren of artists' studios within was perpetually paint-splattered and in need of a good hosing down. It was here that Pablo Picasso and Georges Braque made their first bold stabs at the concept of Cubism. The replacement building also contains art studios, but is the epitome of poured-concrete drabness. ⊠ *13 pl. Émile-Goudeau, Montmartre* Ⓜ *Abbesses.*

⑨⓪ Espace Dalí (Dalí Center). Some of Salvador Dalí's less familiar works are among the 25 sculptures and 300 etchings and lithographs housed in this museum, whose atmosphere is meant to approximate the experience of Surrealism. ⊠ *11 rue Poulbot, Montmartre* ☎ *01–42–64–40–10* ⊕ *www.dali-espacemontmartre.com* 🎟 *€6* ☉ *Daily 10–6:30* Ⓜ *Abbesses.*

⑧⑥ Moulin de la Galette (Wafer Windmill). This is one of two remaining windmills in Montmartre. It was once the focal point of an open-air cabaret (made famous in a painting by Renoir). Rumor has it that in 1814 the miller Debray, who had struggled in vain to defend the windmill from invading Cossacks, was then strung up on its sails and spun to death by the invaders. Unfortunately, it's privately owned and can only be admired from the street below. ⊠ *Rue Tholozé, Montmartre* Ⓜ *Abbesses.*

▶ ⑧④ Moulin Rouge (Red Windmill). This world-famous cabaret was built in 1885 as a windmill, then transformed into a dance hall in 1900. Those wild, early days were immortalized by Toulouse-Lautrec in his posters and paintings. It still trades shamelessly on the notion of Paris as a city of sin: if you fancy a gaudy Vegas-style night out—sorry, admirers of the Baz Luhrmann film won't find any of its charm here—this is the place to go. The cancan, by the way—still a regular sight here—was considerably raunchier when Toulouse-Lautrec was around. ⊠ *82 bd. de Clichy, Montmartre* ☎ *01–53–09–82–82* ⊕ *www.moulin-rouge.com* 🎟 *€80–€125* ☉ *Shows nightly at 9 and 11* Ⓜ *Blanche.*

⑨② Musée de Montmartre (Montmartre Museum). In its turn-of-the-20th-century heyday, Montmartre's historical museum was home to an illustrious group of painters, writers, and assorted cabaret artists. Foremost among them were Renoir and Maurice Utrillo. The museum also provides a view of the tiny **vineyard**—the only one in Paris—on neighboring rue des Saules. A token 125 gallons of wine are still produced here every year. ⊠ *12 rue Cortot, Montmartre* ☎ *01–46–06–61–11* ⊕ *www. museedemontmartre.com* 🎟 *€5.50* ☉ *Tues.–Sun. 11–6* Ⓜ *Lamarck-Caulaincourt.*

★ ⑧⑤ Musée de la Vie Romantique. Lovers of all things "romantique" will enjoy visiting this tranquil, 19th-century countrified town house, set in a little park at the foot of Montmartre (head down rue Blanche from place Blanche; the third left is rue Chaptal). For years the site of Friday-evening salons hosted by the Dutch-born painter Ary Scheffer, the house often welcomed such guests as Ingres, Delacroix, Turgenev, Chopin, and Sand. The memory of author George Sand (1804–76)—real name Aurore Dudevant—haunts the museum. Portraits, furniture, and household possessions, right down to her cigarette box, have been moved here from her house in Nohant in the Loire Valley. There's also a selection of Scheffer's competent artistic output on the first floor. Take a moment to enjoy

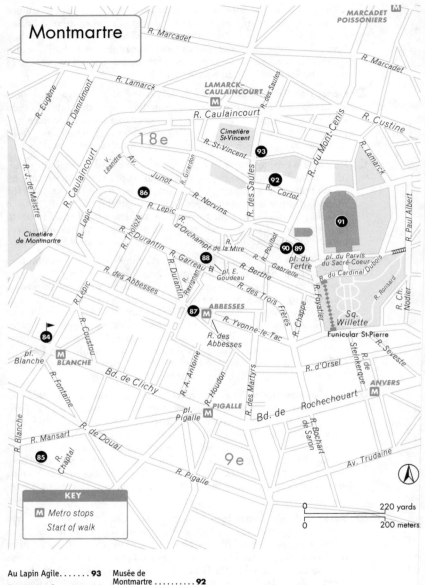

Montmartre

a cup of tea in the garden café. ✉ *16 rue Chaptal, Montmartre* ☎ *01–48–74–95–38* ⊕ *www.paris.fr/musees/* 🎫 *Free for permanent collection, exhibitions €4.50* ⏰ *Tues.–Sun. 10–5:40* Ⓜ *St-Georges.*

87 Place des Abbesses. The triangular square is typical of the picturesque, slightly countrified style that has made Montmartre famous. Now the hub of the local arts and fashion scene, the place is surrounded by trendy shops, sidewalk cafés, and shabby-chic restaurants, a prime habitat for the young, neo-bohemian crowd and a sprinkling of expats. The entrance to the Abbesses métro station, a curving, sensuous mass of delicate iron, is one of only two original Art Nouveau entrance canopies left in Paris. ✉ *Montmartre* Ⓜ *Abbesses.*

89 Place du Tertre. This tumbling square (*tertre* means "hillock") regains its village atmosphere only in the winter, when the branches of the plane trees sketch traceries against the sky. At any other time of year you'll be confronted by crowds of tourists and a swarm of third-rate artists clamoring to do your portrait (if one of them whips up an unsolicited portrait, you are not obliged to buy it). **La Mère Catherine,** on one corner of the square, was a favorite with the Russian Cossacks who occupied Paris in 1814. They couldn't have suspected that by banging on the table and yelling "*bistro*" (Russian for "quickly"), they were inventing a new breed of French restaurant. ✉ *Montmartre* Ⓜ *Abbesses.*

need a break? There are few attractive snack options in this part of town, but **Patachou** (✉ 9 pl. du Tertre, Montmartre ☎ 01–42–51–06–06), serving exquisite if expensive cakes and teas, sounds the one classy note on place du Tertre.

★ **91 Sacré-Coeur.** Often compared to a "sculpted cloud" atop Montmartre, the Sacred Heart Basilica was erected as a sort of national guilt offering in expiation for the blood shed during the Paris Commune and Franco-Prussian War in 1870–71, and was largely financed by French Catholics fearful of an anticlerical backlash under the new republican regime. The basilica was not consecrated until 1919. Stylistically, the Sacré-Coeur borrows elements from Romanesque and Byzantine models. The gloomy, cavernous interior is worth visiting for its golden mosaics; climb to the top of the dome for the view of Paris. ✉ *Pl. du Parvis-du-Sacré-Coeur, Montmartre* ☎ *01–53–41–89–00* 🎫 *Free, dome €4.50* ⏰ *Basilica daily 6:45 AM–11 PM; dome and crypt Oct.–Mar., daily 9–6; Apr.–Sept., daily 10–5* Ⓜ *Anvers.*

WHERE TO EAT

Updated by
Rosa Jackson

Whether you get knee-deep in white truffles at Les Ambassadeurs or merely discover pistachio sausage (the poor man's foie gras) at a classic corner bistro, you'll discover that food in Paris is an obsession, an art, a subject of endless debate. From the edible genius of haute cuisine wizards Eric Frechon and Alain Ducasse to the sublime creations of Pierre Gagnaire (whose marriage of heated foie gras, pressed caviar, and Japanese seaweeds will make you purr), dining in Paris can easily leave you in a pleasurable stupor. And when it all seems a bit overwhelming, you can slip away to a casual little place for an earthy, bubbling cassoulet, have a midnight feast of the world's silkiest oysters, or even opt out of Gaul altogether for superb pasta, couscous, or an herb-bright Vietnamese stir-fry. Once you know where to go, Paris is a city where perfection awaits at all levels of the food chain.

Generally, restaurants are open from noon to about 2 and from 7:30 or 8 to 10 or 10:30. It's best to make reservations, particularly in summer, although the reviews only state when reservations are absolutely essential. If you want no-smoking seating, make this clear; the mandatory no-smoking area is sometimes limited to a very few tables. Brasseries have longer hours and often serve all day and late into the evening; some are open 24 hours. Assume a restaurant is open every day, unless otherwise indicated. Surprisingly, many prestigious restaurants close on Saturday as well as Sunday. July and August are the most common months for annual closings, although Paris in August is no longer the wasteland it once was. For help with the vocabulary of French cooking, see the Menu Guide at the end of this book. Places where a jacket and tie are de rigueur are noted. Otherwise, use common sense—jeans and T-shirts are not suitable in Paris restaurants, nor are shorts or running clothes, except in the most casual bistros and cafés.

Prices & Reservations

By French law, prices must include tax and tip (*service compris* or *prix nets*), but pocket change left on the table in basic places, or an additional 5% in better restaurants, is always appreciated. Beware of bills stamped "Service Not Included" in English or restaurants slyly using American-style credit-card slips, hoping that you'll be confused and add the habitual 15% tip. In neither case should you tip beyond the guidelines suggested above.

Here are a few key sentences for booking, if needed: "*Bonjour madame/ monsieur* (ma'am, sir; say *bonsoir* after 6 PM). *Je voudrais faire une reservation pour X (1, un/une; 2, deux; 4, quatre; 6, six) personnes pour le dîner* (evening)/ *le déjeuner* (lunch) *aujourd'hui à X heures* (today at X o'clock)/*demain à X heures* (tomorrow at X o'clock)/*lundi* (Monday), *mardi* (Tuesday), *mercredi* (Wednesday), *jeudi* (Thursday), *vendredi* (Friday), *samedi* (Saturday), *dimanche* (Sunday) *à X heures* (at X time). *Le nom est* (your own name). *Merci bien.*" Note that most wine bars do not take reservations; reservations are also unnecessary for brasserie and café meals at odd hours.

WHAT IT COSTS In euros				
$$$$	$$$	$$	$	¢
AT DINNER over €30	€23–€30	€17–€23	€11–€17	under €11

Prices are per person for a main course only at dinner, including tax (19.6%) and service; note that if a restaurant offers only prix-fixe (set-price) meals, it is given a price category that reflects the full prix-fixe price.

1ᵉʳ Arrondissement (Louvre/Les Halles)

CONTEMPORARY
$–$$

✕ **Pinxo.** The word Pinxo means "to pinch," which is how the food here is designed to be eaten—often with your fingers, and off your dining companion's plate. (Each dish is served in three portions to allow for sharing.) Alain Dutournier, who also runs the more formal Le Carré des Feuillants nearby, drew on his southwestern French roots to create this welcoming modern spot in black, plum, and dark wood. Diners nibble their way through mini-dishes such as marinated herring with Granny Smith apple and horseradish, cold *pipérade* (spicy scrambled eggs with bell pepper) with fried ham, and squid cooked with ginger and chili pepper, then end, perhaps, with fresh pineapple and a piña colada sorbet. ⊠ *Hôtel Plaza Paris Vendôme, 9 rue d'Alger, Louvre/Tuileries* ☎ *01–40–20–72–00* ▤ *AE, DC, MC, V* Ⓜ *Tuileries.*

FRENCH
$$$$
Fodor'sChoice
★

✕ **Le Grand Véfour.** Victor Hugo could stride in and still recognize this place—in his day, as now, a contender for the prize of most beautiful restaurant in Paris. Originally built in 1784, set in the arcades of the Palais-Royal, it has welcomed everyone from Napoléon to Colette to Jean Cocteau—many seats bear a plaque commemorating a famous patron. The mirrored ceiling and Restoration-era glass paintings of goddesses beguile the foodies as well as the fashionable who gather here to enjoy chef Guy Martin's delights. He hails from Savoie, so you'll find lake fish and mountain cheeses on the menu alongside such luxurious dishes as foie gras–stuffed raviolis. If you can't spring for the extravagant à la carte menu or the 10-course, €250 *menu plaisir,* try the lunchtime prix-fixe for €75. ⊠ *17 rue Beaujolais, Louvre/Tuileries* ☎ *01–42–96–56–27* ✍ *Reservations essential* 🎩 *Jacket and tie* ▤ *AE, DC, MC, V* ☾ *Closed weekends and Aug. No dinner Fri.* Ⓜ *Palais-Royal.*

★ **$$–$$$$**

✕ **Restaurant du Palais-Royal.** Tucked away in the northeast corner of the magnificent Palais-Royal garden, this pleasant bistro offers traditional cuisine with Mediterranean touches and—most appropriate for a prime real-estate situation—a lovely summer terrace. Sole and scallops are beautifully prepared, but juicy steak with fat, symmetrically stacked *frites* is also a favorite of the expense-account lunchers who love this place. Don't miss the mango-in-summer, hazelnut-in-winter *mille-feuille*. Be sure to book in advance, especially in summer, when the terrace tables are hotly sought after. ⊠ *Jardins du Palais-Royal, 110 Galerie Valois, Louvre/Tuileries* ☎ *01–40–20–00–27* ▤ *AE, MC, V* ☾ *Closed Sun. in summer, entirely Oct.–Apr.* Ⓜ *Palais-Royal.*

★ **$$$**

✕ **L'Ardoise.** This minuscule storefront, painted white and decorated with enlargements of old sepia postcards of Paris, is the very model of contemporary bistros making waves in Paris. This one's claim to fame is chef Pierre Jay, who trained at La Tour d'Argent. His first-rate three-course menu for €30 (you can also order à la carte at no extra cost) is adorned with such original dishes as crab flan in a creamy parsley emulsion and fresh cod with grilled chorizo chips, served on a tempting bed of mashed potatoes. Just as enticing are the desserts, such as superb *feuillantine au citron*—caramelized pastry leaves filled with lemon cream and lemon segments. With friendly service and a well-chosen wine-list, L'Ardoise would be perfect if it weren't often crowded and

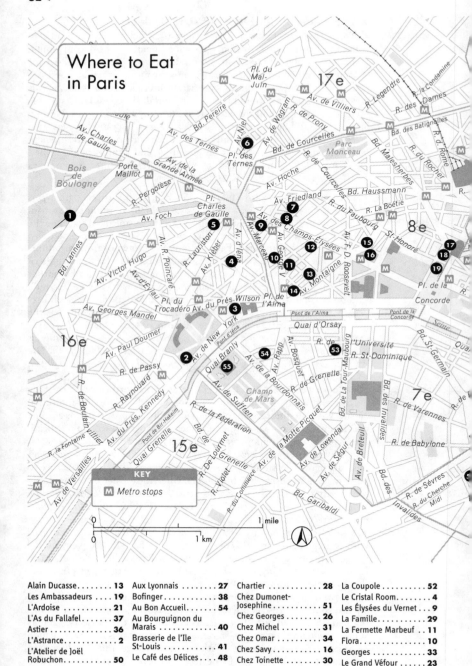

Where to Eat in Paris

noisy. ✉ *28 rue du Mont Thabor, Beaubourg/Les Halles* ☎ *01–42–96–28–18* ⚗ *Reservations essential* ☰ *MC, V* ⊘ *Closed Mon. and Aug.* Ⓜ *Concorde.*

$–$$ ✕ **Willi's Wine Bar.** Don't be fooled by the name—this English-owned spot is no modest watering hole but rather a stylish haunt for Parisian and foreign gourmands. The often original menu changes daily to reflect the market's offerings, and might include fresh scallops, foie gras prepared on the premises, *andouillette* (chitterling sausage), and crème brûlée or a bitter chocolate *terrine* (pudding). Owner Mark Williamson has a passion for Rhône Valley wines, reflected in the extensive list, and for Spanish sherries. ✉ *13 rue des Petits-Champs, Louvre/Tuileries* ☎ *01–42–61–05–09* ☰ *MC, V* ⊘ *Closed Sun.* Ⓜ *Bourse.*

$ ✕ **Le Safran.** Passionate chef Caroll Sinclair works almost exclusively with organic produce, and her small menu changes according to what she finds in the market—creamy shellfish and spinach soup brightened by fresh coriander, red mullet stuffed with cèpe mushrooms, and *gigot de sept heures* (leg of lamb cooked for seven hours) are some signature dishes. Cool it all off with dessert such as black grapes with caramelized pineapple or a saffron crème brûlée. Just don't forget to clean your plate, or you'll have to answer to the attentive chef (and her enormous but very gentle black dog). ✉ *29 rue d'Argenteuil, Louvre/Tuileries* ☎ *01–42–61–25–30* ☰ *MC, V* ⊘ *Closed Sun. and 2 wks in Sept. No lunch Sat.* Ⓜ *Tuileries, Pyramides.*

2ᵉ Arrondissement (La Bourse/Opéra)

FRENCH ✕ **Chez Georges.** When you ask sophisticated Parisians—think bankers, **$$$** aristocrats, or antiques dealers—to name their favorite bistro, many choose Georges. The traditional bistro fare is good—herring, sole, kidneys, steaks, and *frites* (fries)—and the atmosphere is better. A wood-panel entry leads you to an elegant and unpretentious dining room where one long, white-clothed stretch of tables lines the mirrored walls and attentive waiters sweep efficiently along its entire length. ✉ *1 rue du Mail, Louvre/Tuileries* ☎ *01–42–60–07–11* ☰ *AE, DC, MC, V* ⊘ *Closed Sun. and 3 wks in Aug.* Ⓜ *Sentier.*

★ **$$–$$$** ✕ **Aux Lyonnais.** For Alain Ducasse, it's not enough to run three of the world's most expensive restaurants (in Paris, Monte Carlo, and New York) and an ever-expanding string of Spoon, Food & Wine fusion bistros. He also has a passion for the old-fashioned bistro, so he has resurrected this 1890s gem by appointing a terrific young chef to oversee the short, frequently changing menu of Lyonnais specialties. Dandelion salad with crisp potatoes, bacon, and silky poached egg, watercress soup poured over parsleyed frogs' legs, and a sophisticated rendition of coq au vin show he is no bistro dilettante. ✉ *32 rue St-Marc, Opéra/Grands Boulevards* ☎ *01–42–96–65–04* ☰ *MC, V* ⊘ *Closed Sun. and Mon. No lunch Sat.* Ⓜ *Bourse.*

$–$$ ✕ **Le Vaudeville.** One of Jean-Paul Bucher's seven Flo brasseries, Le Vaudeville is filled with journalists, bankers, and locals *d'un certain âge* who come for its good-value assortment of prix-fixe menus. Shellfish, house-smoked salmon, and desserts such as profiteroles are particularly enticing. Enjoy the handsome 1930s decor—almost the entire interior of this intimate dining room is done in real or faux marble—and lively

ON THE MENU

WHAT ARE THE LATEST FASHIONS on the Paris dining scene? Not everyone wants a three-course blow-out every time they go to a restaurant. While meals have long followed a predictable entrée-plat-dessert pattern, this is changing thanks to pioneering chefs such as Joël Robuchon. In his Atelier, the man once voted "chef of the 20th century," encourages dining in small or larger portions, according to your appetite. His opening hours even suggest that it's O.K. to graze outside traditional mealtimes—une révolution. Taking a similar approach are Hélène Darroze, whose modern bistro annex serves tapas-style portions, and Alain Dutournier of Pinxo, who has actually persuaded Parisians to eat with their fingers and steal food off their companions' plates. Chefs are also developing a freer hand with spices, thanks to their experiences abroad. One of the first to successfully incorporate spices into French cuisine without falling into fusion follies was top chef Pascal Barbot at L'Astrance. During a stint in Australia, Barbot learned to juggle Asian flavors, then honed his French technique at L'Arpège. At Ze Kitchen Galerie, chef William Ledeuil puts the emphasis on presentation, drawing on ingredients from Chinatown and Middle Eastern grocery stores. Equally creative is Flora Mikula, who at Flora serves Mediterranean cooking with the occasional Asian twist. Even as their palates grow more adventurous, however, the French are reembracing terroir. Nothing illustrates this better than the purchase of the turn-of-the-century bistro Aux Lyonnais by Alain Ducasse, founder of the Spoon, Food & Wine fusion chain. Never one to miss a trend, Ducasse knows that Parisians will always love earthy regional food when it is prepared with care and served in a gorgeous setting.

dining until 1 AM daily. ⊠ *29 rue Vivienne, Opéra/Grands Boulevards* ☏ *01–40–20–04–62* 🖃 *AE, DC, MC, V* Ⓜ *Bourse.*

3e Arrondissement (Beaubourg/Marais)

FRENCH
★ $$$
✕ **Le Pamphlet.** Chef Alain Carrere's modern and very affordable take on the hearty cooking of the Basque and Béarn regions of southwestern France has made this Marais bistro popular with an artsy crowd. Beyond the delicious, homey food, what many Parisians love is the provincial feel, with a beamed ceiling and faïence that seems to have been borrowed from *grandmère*. The market-fresh menu runs from a carpaccio of duck breast or cream of lentil soup to a juicy pork chop with béarnaise and hand-cut *frites*. Finish up with a slice of sheep's cheese. ⊠ *38 rue Debelleyme, Le Marais* ☏ *01–42–72–39–24* ⌑ *Reservations essential* 🖃 *MC, V* ☉ *Closed Sun., 2 wks in Jan., and 2 wks in Aug. No lunch Mon. and Sat.* Ⓜ *St-Sébastien–Froissart.*

NORTH AFRICAN
$–$$
✕ **Chez Omar.** Popular with a high-voltage fashion crowd—yes, that's Vivienne Westwood having dinner with Alexander McQueen—this is the place to come for couscous with all the trimmings. Order it with grilled skewered lamb, spicy *merguez* sausage, a lamb shank, or chicken—portions are generous—and wash it down with robust Algerian or Mo-

roccan wine. Proprietor Omar Guerida speaks English and is famously friendly. There are no reservations here, so arrive early or be prepared for a mouthwatering wait. ✉ *47 rue de Bretagne, République* ☎ *01–42–72–36–26* ⌂ *Reservations not accepted* ⊟ *No credit cards* ⊘ *No lunch Sun.* Ⓜ *Filles du Calvaire.*

4e Arrondissement (Beaubourg/Marais/Ile St-Louis)

CONTEMPORARY
$$$–$$$$

✕ **Georges.** Decorated in white and gray, with angular chairs and giant metallic shells, Georges stands in stark contrast to its graceful view of Paris from the top floor of the Centre Georges Pompidou. Staff are as sleek as the furniture, and at night the terrace has distinct snob appeal: come snappily dressed or suffer the consequences (you may be relegated to something resembling a dentist's waiting room). The menu headlines predictable Costes comfort food such as macaroni with morel mushrooms, but, sadly, most dishes are considerably less dazzling than the view. The exception are desserts by star pâtissier Stéphane Secco, whose YSL (as in Yves St-Laurent, darling) bitter chocolate cake is an event. ✉ *Centre Pompidou, 6th fl., rue Rambuteau, Beaubourg/Les Halles* ☎ *01–44–78–47–99* ⊟ *AE, DC, MC, V* ⊘ *Closed Tues.* Ⓜ *Rambuteau.*

FRENCH
$–$$$

✕ **Bofinger.** One of the oldest, most beautiful, and most popular brasseries in Paris has generally improved since brasserie maestro Jean-Paul Bucher (of the Flo group) took over. Settle in to one of the tables dressed in crisp white linen under the gorgeous Art Nouveau glass cupola—this part of the dining room is no-smoking—and enjoy classic brasserie fare, such as oysters, grilled sole, or lamb fillet. The prix-fixe includes a decent half bottle of red or white wine. ✉ *5–7 rue de la Bastille, Bastille/Nation* ☎ *01–42–72–87–82* ⊟ *AE, DC, MC, V* Ⓜ *Bastille.*

$–$$$

✕ **Brasserie de l'Ile St-Louis.** Set on picturesque Ile St-Louis and opened in 1870—when Germany took over Alsace-Lorraine and its chefs de-camped to the capital—this outpost of Alsatian cuisine remains a cozy cocoon filled with stuffed animal heads, antique fixtures fashioned from barrels, and folk-art paintings. The food is gemütlich, too: *coq-au-Ries-ling,* omelets with Muenster cheese, onion tarts, and *choucroutes garni* (sauerkraut studded with ham, bacon, and pork loin—one variant is made with smoked haddock). In warm weather, the crowds move out to the terrace overlooking the Seine and Notre-Dame. ✉ *55 quai de Bourbon, Ile St-Louis* ☎ *01–43–54–02–59* ⊘ *Closed Wed. and Aug. No lunch Thurs.* ⊟ *MC, V* Ⓜ *Pont Marie.*

$–$$

✕ **Au Bourguignon du Marais.** The handsome, contemporary look of this Marais bistro and wine bar is the perfect backdrop for the good traditional fare and excellent Burgundies served by the glass and bottle. Always on the menu are Burgundian classics such as *jambon persillé* (ham in parsleyed aspic jelly), escargots, and *oeufs en meurette* (eggs poached in a red wine sauce). The terrace, added in 2003, is hotly sought after in warm weather. ✉ *19 rue de Jouy, Beaubourg/Les Halles* ☎ *01–48–87–15–40* ⊟ *AE, MC, V* ⊘ *Closed Sun. No dinner Sat.* Ⓜ *St-Paul.*

MIDDLE EASTERN
¢–$

✕ **L'As du Fallafel.** Look no farther than the fantastic falafel stands on rue de Rosiers for some of the cheapest and tastiest meals in Paris, with the laurel crown usually awarded to this place. A falafel at L'As ("the Ace") costs €5, but shell out a little extra money for the "spécial" with grilled eggplant, cabbage, hummus, tahini, and hot sauce. Though take-out is popular, you might find that it's quicker, easier, and more entertaining to eat off a plastic plate in the buzzy dining room. ⊠ *34 rue des Rosiers, Le Marais* ☎ *01–48–87–63–60* ▭ *MC, V* ⊘ *Closed Fri. dusk–Sat. dusk* Ⓜ *St-Paul.*

5ᵉ Arrondissement (Latin Quarter)

CONTEMPORARY
★ **$–$$**

✕ **Le Pré Verre.** Chef Philippe Delacourcelle knows his cassia bark from his cinnamon, thanks to a long stint in Asia. He opened this sharp bistro (with purple-gray walls and photos of jazz musicians) in 2003 to showcase his unique culinary style, rejuvenating archetypal French dishes with Asian and Mediterranean spices. His bargain prix-fixe-only menu changes constantly, but crisp salt cod with cassia bark and super-smooth smoked potato purée is a winner, as is an unlikely dessert of roasted figs with olives. ⊠ *8 rue Thénard, Quartier Latin* ☎ *01–43–54–59–47* ▭ *MC, V* Ⓜ *Maubert-Mutualité.*

FRENCH
★ **$$$$**

✕ **La Tour d'Argent.** Beyond the pretty wonderful food (the current chef is Jean-François Sicallac), many factors conspire to make a meal here at this hoary decades-old landmark memorable: the extraordinary wine cellar, considerate service, and, of course, that privileged view across the Seine to Notre-Dame (where nighttime illumination is partly paid for by this establishment). If the price of dinner makes you pause, you can't go wrong with the €65 lunch—you'll even be entitled to succulent slices of one of the restaurant's specially numbered *canard au sang* dishes (the great duck slaughter began in 1919). Try to splurge a little on the wine—for about €80 you can taste a rare vintage Burgundy. The lunch crowd is remarkably casual, although evenings are a more formal affair. ⊠ *15 quai de la Tournelle, Latin Quarter* ☎ *01–43–54–23–31* ⌲ *Reservations essential* 🏛 *Jacket and tie at dinner* ▭ *AE, DC, MC, V* ⊘ *Closed Mon. No lunch Tues.* Ⓜ *Cardinal Lemoine.*

★ **$$$–$$$$**

✕ **Lapérouse.** Emile Zola, George Sand, and Victor Hugo were regulars, and ladies are said to have mercilessly tested the authenticity of their diamonds on the restaurant's mirrors, which still bear the scratches today—all this makes it hard not to fall in love with this 17th-century Seine-side town house. Chef Alain Hacquard seems to have found the right track with a daring (for Paris) spice-infused menu: his lobster, Dublin Bay prawn, and crayfish bisque is flavored with Szechuan pepper and a lemon vinaigrette. For the ultimate romantic meal, reserve a private salon where anything could happen (and probably has). The €30 "business menu," served at lunch in the beamed dining room overlooking the Seine, is a great value. ⊠ *51 quai des Grands Augustins, Latin Quarter* ☎ *01–43–26–68–04* ⌲ *Reservations essential* ▭ *AE, DC, MC, V* ⊘ *Closed Sun., 3 wks in July, 1 wk in Aug. No lunch Sat.* Ⓜ *St-Michel.*

★ **$$**

✕ **Le Reminet.** Chandeliers and mirrors add an unexpected note of elegance at this relaxed and unusually good bistro set in a narrow salon with stone walls. The menu changes regularly and displays the young chef's talent with dishes like a salad of scallops, greens, and sesame seeds, and roasted guinea hen with buttered Savoy cabbage. If it's available, try the luscious caramelized pear with cream. ⊠ *3 rue des Grands-De-*

grés, *Latin Quarter* ☎ *01–44–07–04–24* 🗃 *MC, V* ⊘ *Closed Tues. and Wed., 1 wk in Feb., and 3 wks in Aug.* Ⓜ *Maubert-Mutualité.*

★ $ ╳ **Les Pipos.** The tourist-trap restaurants along romantic rue de la Montagne Ste-Genevieve are enough to make you despair—and then you stumble across this corner bistro, bursting with chatter and laughter. Slang for students of the famous École Polytechnique nearby, Les Pipos is everything you could ask of a Latin Quarter bistro: the space is cramped, the food is substantial (the cheese comes from the Lyon market), and conversation flows as freely as the wine. It gets crowded, so arrive early to snag a table. ✉ *2 rue de L'École Polytechnique, Latin Quarter* ☎ *01–43–54–11–40* 🗃 *No credit cards* ⊘ *Closed Sun. and 2 wks in Aug.* Ⓜ *Maubert-Mutualité.*

6° Arrondissement (St-Germain-des-Prés/ Latin Quarter)

CONTEMPORARY ╳ **Ze Kitchen Galerie.** Baby bistros grow up so fast—now they're even spawn-
$$–$$$ ing their own offshoots. William Ledeuil made his name at the popular Les Bookinistes (a Guy Savoy baby) before opening this pared-down contemporary bistro nearby. If the name isn't exactly inspired, the cooking shows unbridled creativity: expect dishes such as a chicken wing, broccoli, and artichoke soup with lemongrass, or pork ribs with curry jus and white beans. All in all, one of the most mouthtickling kitchens in the city. ✉ *4 quai des Grands-Augustins, Latin Quarter* ☎ *01–44–32–00–32* 🗃 *AE, DC, MC, V* ⊘ *Closed Sun. No lunch Sat.* Ⓜ *St-Michel.*

★ $$ ╳ **Le Café des Délices.** There's a lot to like about this bistro, from the warm Asia-meets-Africa interior, with little pots of spices on each table, to the polished service and lip-smacking food. Drop in for the bargain €14 lunch, or indulge in à la carte dishes such sea bream on white beans cooked with anchovy, lemon, coriander, and chile pepper. Tongue-in-cheek comfort-food desserts tease with ingredients such as Chupa Chups (lollipops) and sugary cereal. ✉ *87 rue d'Assas, Montparnasse* ☎ *01–43–54–70–00* 🗃 *AE, MC, V* ⊘ *Closed Aug.* Ⓜ *Vavin.*

FRENCH ╳ **Hélène Darroze.** Hélène Darroze has won a lot of followers—and
$$$$ two Michelin stars—with her refined take on southwestern French cooking, from the lands around Albi and Toulouse. You know it's not going to be *la même chanson*—the same old song—as soon as you see the contemporary Tse & Tse tableware, and her intriguingly modern touch comes through in such dishes as a sublime duck foie-gras confit served with chutney of exotic fruits, or a blowout of roast wild duck stuffed with foie gras and truffles. Some carp that the portions are small and the service could be much better, but you may forget all that with one bite of the rose-water-flavored crème anglaise. Expect to spend a hefty €350 for two à la carte upstairs, but there's a lunch menu at €58. The livelier downstairs bistro offers similar food in (even) smaller, tapas-style portions—a series of ten tiny dishes costs €53 per person, or €73 with pre-selected wines. ✉ *4 rue d'Assas, St-Germain-des-Prés* ☎ *01–42–22–00–11* 🗃 *AE, DC, MC, V* ⊘ *Closed Sun. and Mon.* Ⓜ *Sèvres Babylone.*

$$$–$$$$ ╳ **Chez Dumonet–Josephine.** Stylish and convivial, this venerable bistro with amber walls, moleskin banquettes, and frosted-glass lamps is pop-

ular with theater people and politicians. Generous portions of classic French cuisine are served; typical are the very good boeuf bourguignon and the roasted saddle of lamb with artichokes. The wine list is excellent but expensive. ⊠ *117 rue du Cherche-Midi, St-Germain-des-Prés* ☎ *01–45–48–52–40* ▤ *AE, MC, V* ⊘ *Closed weekends, Aug., Christmas wk, and 1 wk in Feb.* Ⓜ *Duroc.*

7ᵉ Arrondissement (Invalides/Eiffel Tower)

CONTEMPORARY
$$$–$$$$

✕ **Petrossian.** Twentysomething chef Sebastien Faré took over the helm from Philippe Conticini, who had injected this swish and rather sober-looking Russian-theme restaurant with his wildly imaginative style. Conticini remains a consultant to Petrossian, which is good news for its *gauche caviar* clientele. Smoked fish and caviar star, but another of his winning concoctions is fried frogs' legs and snails in garlic sauce. Don't miss the "drinkable perfumes," an almost magical approach to palate-cleansing. ⊠ *18 bd. de La-Tour-Maubourg, Invalides/Eiffel Tower* ☎ *01–44–11–32–32* ▤ *AE, DC, MC, V* ⊘ *Closed Sun., Mon., and Aug.* Ⓜ *La-Tour-Maubourg, Invalides.*

FRENCH
$$$$

✕ **Jules Verne.** A table at this all-black restaurant on the second level of the Tour Eiffel, 400 feet removed from the gritty reality of Parisian life, is one of the hardest to snag in Paris. At its best, Alain Reix's cooking justifies a wait of two months or more for dinner (lunch is more accessible), but lately his food has been a deflating experience. The wisest approach, then, is to go for the €51 lunch menu and to expect good but not exquisite food, such as pigeon fricassée or squid with duck liver, an intriguing meeting of land and sea. There's always the exceptional view— the highlight of any meal here has to be the ride up the restaurant's private elevator. The restaurant itself is a tired hybrid of *Star Trek* and '70s disco. But who knows? Perhaps these will become the latest fashions again. ⊠ *Eiffel Tower, Invalides/Eiffel Tower* ☎ *01–45–55–61–44* ⌾ *Reservations essential* ⌂ *Jacket and tie* ▤ *AE, DC, MC, V* Ⓜ *Bir-Hakeim.*

★ $$$–$$$$

✕ **L'Atelier de Joël Robuchon.** If you don't like waiting for a table—well, swallow your pride and stand in line, because L'Atelier is the most exciting restaurant to open in Paris in a long time. Legendary chef Joël Robuchon had retired from the restaurant business for several years before opening this red-and-black lacquered space with a bento-box-meets-tapas aesthetic. Seats line up around U-shape bars; this novel plan nudges neighbors to share recommendations and opinions. Robuchon and his devoted kitchen staff whip up "small plates" for grazing (€7–€25) as well as full-sized dishes. The menu changes frequently, but highlights have included an intense tomato jelly topped with avocado purée; thin-crusted mackerel tart; and his (inauthentic, but who's complaining?) take on carbonara with cream and bacon from Alsace. L'Atelier takes reservations only for 11:30 AM and 6:30 PM, and showing up loaded down with Hermès shopping bags won't impress the immovable door staff— they've seen it all before. As if the reservation policy weren't shocking enough, the entire restaurant is smoke-free. ⊠ *5 rue Montalembert, St-Germain-des-Prés* ☎ *01–42–22–56–56* ▤ *MC, V* Ⓜ *Rue du Bac.*

★ $$$

✕ **Au Bon Accueil.** To see what well-heeled Parisians like to eat these days, book a table at this extremely popular bistro as soon as you get to town;

the dining room was redone in 2003 to open up the space, and the sidewalk tables have a Tour Eiffel view. The excellent, reasonably priced *cuisine du marché* (a daily, market-inspired menu, €25 at lunch and €29 at dinner) has made it a hit: typical of the winter fare is roast suckling pig with thyme and endives. ⊠ *14 rue de Montessuy, Trocadéro/Tour Eiffel* ☎ *01–47–05–46–11* ⚐ *Reservations essential* ⊟ *MC, V* ⊘ *Closed weekends* Ⓜ *Pont de l'Alma.*

8° Arrondissement (Champs-Élysées/Louvre)

CONTEMPORARY

$$$$

✕ **Maison Blanche.** The twin Pourcel brothers preside over this "White House," which trumpets a show-off view across Paris from the top floor of the Théâtre du Champs-Élysées. The formerly gray decor has gone fashionably white and the food offers a refreshing taste of the south: hot and iced tomatoes on a pumpkin puree with fresh truffles, scallop carpaccio with sea-urchin coral, and Swiss chard ravioli with tomato confit. Soothe frayed urban nerves with comforting desserts such as a caramel popsicle with pecan cake. ⊠ *15 av. Montaigne, Champs-Élysées* ☎ *01–53–89–93–93* ⊟ *AE, DC, MC, V* ⊘ *No lunch weekends* Ⓜ *Franklin-D.-Roosevelt.*

$$$–$$$$

✕ **Market.** Celebrated New York–based Alsatian chef Jean-Georges Vongerichten (think Vong, Mercer Kitchen, Jean-Georges) set up shop in this strategic neighborhood to much fanfare, as it is his first restaurant in France. Put together with deceptively simple raw materials—burnt pine and stone offset with African masks—the dining room makes a stylish if sometimes noisy setting for well-traveled dishes such as pizza with raw tuna and wasabi cream, Thai-style chicken-coconut soup with galanga, and duck fillet with sesame jus and tamarind confit. ⊠ *15 av. Matignon, Champs-Élysées* ☎ *01–56–43–40–90* ⊟ *AE, MC, V* Ⓜ *Franklin-D.-Roosevelt.*

$$$–$$$$

✕ **Spoon, Food & Wine.** Star chef Alain Ducasse's bistro may be the granddaddy of style-conscious restaurants around the Champs-Élysées, but its popularity shows no signs of waning. What draws the black-clad crowd are the playful Asian- and American-inspired menu, the *Wallpaper*-y decor (white by day, plum by night), and the fact that it's so hard to get a dinner reservation (you can always drop by for a snack at the bar). Fashion folk love this place for its many vegetable and pasta dishes and its irresistible desserts, particularly the TobleSpoon, a take-off on Toblerone. If you've sampled the Spoon concept elsewhere in the world, don't expect the same here; each branch is tailored to a particular city's tastes, and what looks exotic in Paris (bagels and bubble gum ice cream) might seem humdrum in New York. ⊠ *14 rue de Marignan, Champs-Élysées* ☎ *01–40–76–34–44* ⚐ *Reservations essential* ⊟ *AE, MC, V* ⊘ *Closed weekends and 4 wks in July and Aug.* Ⓜ *Franklin-D.-Roosevelt.*

FRENCH

★ **$$$$**

✕ **Alain Ducasse.** You may need to set a steel trap outside his door to actually catch Alain Ducasse in this kitchen—he now has restaurants around the globe (and never cooks on weekends)—but it would probably be worth the wait. The rosy rococo salons in the Plaza Athénée hotel have been draped with metallic organza over the chandeliers and, in a symbolic move, time now stands still since all the clocks have been stopped. Overlooking the prettiest courtyard in Paris, this makes for a setting as delicious as Ducasse's roast lamb garnished with "crumbs" of dried fruit. At these prices, however, the level of presentation—there are few sauce "paintings," orchid blossoms, or other visual adornments on the plate—could be enhanced. All in all, there is still plenty of poetry coming out of the kitchen, so you still need to reserve three weeks in advance. ⊠ *Hotel Plaza-Athénée, 27 av. Montaigne, Champs-Élysées* ☎ *01–53–67–66–65* ⊟ *AE, DC, MC, V* 🔒 *Jacket required* ⊗ *Closed weekends, 2 wks in late Dec., 2 wks in July, and 3 wks in Aug. No lunch Mon.–Wed.* Ⓜ *Alma-Marceau.*

★ **$$$$** ✕ **Les Ambassadeurs.** Looking as if Madame de Pompadour might stroll in the door at any moment, Les Ambassadeurs offers a world of ancien régime splendor with its marble, colored marble, even more colored marble, and gilt chandeliers. The kitchen here likes to mix luxe with more down-to-earth flavors: potato pancakes topped with smoked salmon, caviar-flecked scallops wrapped in bacon with tomato and basil, duck with rutabaga, turbot with cauliflower. The €62 lunch menu is well worth the splurge—especially in summer, when you can while away the rest of the afternoon on the gorgeous terrace. There is even a breakfast—talk about luxury—served from 7 to 10:30 AM. ⊠ *Hôtel Crillon, 10 pl. de la Concorde, Louvre/Tuileries* ☎ *01–44–71–16–16* 🔒 *Jacket and tie* ⊟ *AE, DC, MC, V* Ⓜ *Concorde.*

★ **$$$$** ✕ **Lucas Carton.** Alain Senderens always sips wine while he's cooking, and not to stay relaxed—he's the acknowledged French master of matching wine with food. Each new dish on his menu was inspired by a wine, which is listed next to it as the ideal accompaniment. He dreamed up langoustines in a crunchy vermicelli shell to complement a meursault from Dury, while his *canard à l'Apicius* becomes all the more heavenly with a glass of Banyuls, a sweet wine from southwestern France. Most customers are content to follow his suggestions, and they can be sure the wines will always be served at the optimum temperature—Senderens wants his wines to be as happy as his customers in his sumptuous Art Nouveau landmark dining room. ⊠ *9 pl. de la Madeleine Opéra/Grands Boulevards* ☎ *01–42–65–22–90* ◬ *Reservations essential* ⊟ *AE, DC, MC, V* ⊗ *Closed Sun. and Aug. No lunch Sat. and Mon.* Ⓜ *Madeleine.*

$$$$ ✕ **Maxim's.** Count Danilo sang "I'm going to Maxim's" in Lehar's *The Merry Widow,* Leslie Caron was klieg-lit here by Cecil Beaton for *Gigi,* and Audrey Hepburn adorned one of its banquettes with Peter O'Toole in *How to Steal a Million.* In reality, Maxim's has lost some of its luster—the restaurant had its heyday 100 years ago during La Belle Epoque, when *le tout Paris* swarmed here—but this exuberant Art Nouveau sanctuary still offers a taste of the good life under its breathtaking painted ceiling. Opened in 1893 by Maxime Gaillard, Maxim's has belonged to designer Pierre Cardin since 1981 (who proceeded to clone Maxim's around the world, greatly tarnishing the allure of this home base). It's just a shame that Maxim's is so jaw-droppingly expensive for food that would feel at home in a brasserie, and that—in a fit of cost-cutting not reflected in the menu prices—a lone singing pianist has replaced the orchestra. ⊠ *3 rue Royale, Louvre/Tuileries* ☎ *01–42–65–27–94* ◬ *Reservations essential* ⊟ *AE, DC, MC, V* ⊗ *Closed Sun. and Mon. in July and Aug., Sun. in Sept.–June* Ⓜ *Concorde.*

★ $$$$ ✕ **Pierre Gagnaire.** Legendary chef Pierre Gagnaire's cooking is at once intellectual and poetic—in a single dish at least three or four often unexpected tastes come together in a sensational experience. Just taking in the menu requires concentration, so complex are descriptions such as "suckling lamb from Aveyron: sweetbreads, saddle, and rack; green papaya and turnip velouté thickened with Tarbais beans." Gagnaire remains one of the chefs to beat—foodies consider him a "philosopher" and have made his new London restaurant Europe's hottest culinary shrine. The businesslike gray-and-wood Paris dining room feels refreshingly informal, but uneven service and a scanty wine list are unfortunate drawbacks at this price. ✉ *6 rue de Balzac, Champs-Élysées* ☎ *01–58–36–12–50* ⌕ *Reservations essential* ▭ *AE, DC, MC, V* ⊘ *Closed Sat. and 2 wks in July. No lunch Sun. and Aug.* Ⓜ *Charles-de-Gaulle–Étoile.*

★ $$$$ ✕ **Taillevent.** Once the most traditional of all Paris luxury restaurants, this grande dame has been subtly modernized since the arrival of chef Alain Solivères. He has judiciously revised the menu here, adding creations that sometimes eerily resemble dishes served in modern bistros. Classics such as the *boudin de homard*—an airy sausage-shaped lobster soufflé—offer continuity with the fabled past. Service is flawless, the 19th-century paneled salons *luxe*, the well-priced wine list probably one of the top 10 in the world—all in all, a meal here is usually an event. Reserve a month in advance. ✉ *15 rue Lamennais, Champs-Élysées* ☎ *01–44–95–15–01* ⌕ *Reservations essential* ⌂ *Jacket and tie* ▭ *AE, DC, MC, V* ⊘ *Closed weekends and Aug.* Ⓜ *Charles-de-Gaulle–Étoile.*

★ $$$–$$$$ ✕ **Les Élysées du Vernet.** This is one of the classic choices for a grand blowout in Paris today, thanks to a remarkable harmonic alignment of staff, decor, and kitchen. Eric Briffard found himself out in the cold when Alain Ducasse took over the Plaza Athénée's kitchens—he has now found a suitably grand setting for his talents in the form of this intimate dining room, whose magnificently beautiful *verrière* (glass ceiling) was designed by Gustave Eiffel himself. Briffard is making his mark with dishes such as truffled pig's trotter, foie gras on toast, monkfish with ginger and lime, and potato salad with truffles. This restaurant remains relatively affordable at lunch (€45 or €60 for a set menu), the wine service is outstanding, and all departing women guests are given a rose. ✉ *Hôtel Vernet, 25 rue Vernet, Champs-Élysées* ☎ *01–44–31–98–98* ⌕ *Reservations essential* ▭ *AE, DC, MC, V* ⊘ *Closed weekends, Aug., and 2 wks in Dec.* Ⓜ *George-V.*

$$–$$$ ✕ **La Fermette Marbeuf.** Graced with one of the most mesmerizing Belle Epoque rooms in town—accidentally rediscovered during renovations in the 1970s—this is a favorite haunt of French celebrities who adore the sunflowers, peacocks, and dragonflies of the Art Nouveau mosaic and stained-glass mise-en-scène. The menu rolls out a solid, updated classic cuisine. Try the snails in puff pastry, saddle of lamb with *choron* (a tomato-spiked béarnaise sauce), and bitter-chocolate fondant—but ignore the rather depressing prix-fixe unless you are on a budget. Popular with tourists and businesspeople at lunch, La Fermette becomes truly animated around 9 PM. ✉ *5 rue Marbeuf, Champs-Élysées* ☎ *01–53–23–08–00* ▭ *AE, DC, MC, V* Ⓜ *Franklin-D.-Roosevelt.*

★ **$$–$$$** ✕ **Flora.** Flora Mikula made her name at Les Olivades, a Provençal bistro in the 7ᵉ, before joining a gaggle of ambitious restaurateurs in this platinum-card neck of the woods. Moving away from the bistro register, she's turning out refined food with southern French twists in a setting that feels just a little too staid, despite the ornate plaster moldings. Standout dishes on the frequently changing seasonal menu are a scallop *tarte fine* with truffle vinaigrette, roast sea bass with a potato-olive purée, and a roasted apple mille-feuille with salted-caramel ice cream. Service, like the food, is impeccable. ⊠ *36 av. George V, Champs-Élysées* ☎ *01–40–70–10–49* ☙ *Reservations essential* ⊟ *AE, MC, V* ☉ *Closed Sun. No lunch Sat.* Ⓜ *Franklin-D.-Roosevelt.*

$–$$ ✕ **Chez Savy.** Just off the glitzy avenue Montaigne, Chez Savy exists in its own circa-1930s dimension, oblivious to the area's galloping fashionization. The Art Deco cream-and-burgundy interior looks blissfully intact (avoid the back room unless you're in a large group) and the waiters show not a trace of attitude, even offering to change a wine bottle that's just a touch too chilled. Fill up on rib-sticking specialties from the Auvergne in central France—lentil salad with bacon, beautifully charred lamb with feather-light shoestring frites, poached peach with sorbet—order a celebratory bottle of Mercurey, and feel smug that you've found this place. ⊠ *23 rue Bayard, Champs-Élysées* ☎ *01–47–23–46–98* ⊟ *AE, MC, V* ☉ *Closed weekends and Aug.* Ⓜ *Franklin-D.-Roosevelt.*

9ᵉ Arrondissement (Opéra/Pigalle-Clichy)

FRENCH
$ ✕ **Chartier.** People come here more for the bonhomie than the food, which is often stunningly ordinary. This cavernous 1896 restaurant enjoys a huge following among budget-minded students, solitary bachelors, and tourists. You may find yourself sharing a table with strangers as you study the long, old-fashioned menu of such favorites as hard-boiled eggs with mayonnaise, steak tartare, and roast chicken with fries. ⊠ *7 rue du Faubourg-Montmartre, Opéra/Grands Boulevards* ☎ *01–47–70–86–29* ☙ *Reservations not accepted* ⊟ *MC, V* Ⓜ *Montmartre.*

10ᵉ Arrondissement (République/Gare du Nord)

FRENCH
★ **$$$** ✕ **Chez Michel.** Effusive chef Thierry Breton pulls in a stylish crowd of Parisians and tourists with his wonderful market-inspired cooking, despite the out-of-the-way location in a pretty neighborhood near Gare du Nord. The prix-fixe-only menu changes constantly, but you'll start with a bowl of garlic-seasoned escargots on the table and almost invariably find the Breton specialties *kig ha farz* (a robust pork stew with a bread stuffing) and *kouing aman* (the butteriest cake imaginable). In winter, don't miss Breton's succulent game dishes such as the surprisingly mild-tasting boar chops, served in a cast-iron pot with tiny potatoes and roasted garlic. ⊠ *10 rue Belzunce, République* ☎ *01–44–53–06–20* ☙ *Reservations essential* ⊟ *MC, V* ☉ *Closed weekends and Aug. No lunch Mon.* ☙ *Reservations essential* Ⓜ *Gare du Nord.*

11ᵉ Arrondissement (Bastille/République)

FRENCH
★ **$$–$$$** ✕ **Astier.** The prix-fixe menu (there's no à la carte) at this popular, old-fashioned restaurant must be one of the best values in town. Among the beautifully prepared seasonal dishes are baked eggs topped with truf-

fled foie gras, fricassee of *joue de boeuf* (beef cheeks), rabbit in mustard sauce with fresh tagliatelle, and plum *clafoutis* (a fruit flan). This is a great place to come if you're feeling cheesy, since it's locally famous for having one of the best *plateaux de fromages* (cheese plates) in Paris. ⊠ *44 rue Jean-Pierre Timbaud, République* ☎ *01–43–57–16–35* ⟁ *Reservations essential* ⊟ *MC, V* ⊘ *Closed weekends, Aug., Christmas wk, Easter wk* Ⓜ *Parmentier.*

12ᵉ Arrondissement (Bastille/Nation)

FRENCH ✕ **Le Square Trousseau.** This beautiful Belle Epoque bistro is a favorite ★ $$ of the fashion set. Even models can't resist the peppered country pâté, slow-cooked lamb, or tender baby chicken with mustard and bread-crumb crust. Wines might seem a little pricey, but are lovingly selected from small producers—you can also buy them, along with superb Spanish ham, at the restaurant's small boutique/wine bar next door. ⊠ *1 rue Antoine Vollon, Bastille/Nation* ☎ *01–43–43–06–00* ⊟ *AE, MC, V* ⊘ *Closed Sun. and Mon., and 2 wks at Christmas* Ⓜ *Ledru-Rollin.*

FRENCH ✕ **La Coupole.** This world-renowned, cavernous spot practically defines $–$$$ the term brasserie—and its Art Deco murals are famous, too. La Coupole might have lost its intellectual aura since the Flo group's restoration but it has been popular since the days when Jean-Paul Sartre and Simone de Beauvoir were regulars. Today it attracts a mix of bourgeois families, tourists, and elderly lone diners treating themselves to a dozen oysters. Expect the usual brasserie menu—including perhaps the largest shellfish platter in Paris—choucroute, and some great over-the-top desserts. They don't take reservations after 8:30 PM Monday to Thursday and 8 PM Friday to Sunday, so be prepared for a wait at the bar. ⊠ *102 bd. du Montparnasse, Montparnasse* ☎ *01–43–20–14–20* ⊟ *AE, DC, MC, V* Ⓜ *Vavin.*

16ᵉ Arrondissement (Trocadéro/Bois de Boulogne)

FRENCH ✕ **Le Cristal Room.** Can't get a reservation at the spectacular new restau- $$$ rant in the Maison de Baccarat? You're not alone—a table here is so in demand that at press time they were taking lunch and dinner bookings two months in advance. Its success stems not only from the stunning decor by Philippe Starck—mirrors, patches of exposed brick wall, and chandeliers, including one dramatically immersed in an aquarium—but also from the glittering talent of chef Thierry Burlot. He often plays with textures, as in jellied oysters that are released from their translucent wrap as you pour hot bouillon overtop, or Dublin Bay prawn served both in a "cappuccino" and roasted. Psst, here's a secret: it's easy to get in for breakfast (weekdays 8:30–10 AM), and tea is served on Saturdays only (3–5:30 PM) with no reservations. ⊠ *11 place des Etats-Unis, Trocadéro/Eiffel Tower* ☎ *01–40–22–11–10* ⊟ *AE, MC, V* ⊘ *Closed Sun.* Ⓜ *Iéna.*

★ $$$$ ✕ **Jamin.** At this intimate if rather frilly restaurant, where Joël Robuchon made his name, you can find excellent haute cuisine at almost half the price of other restaurants of its kind: there is a well-priced lunch prix-fixe at just €53 and a pricier €95 menu at dinner. Benoît Guichard, Robuchon's second for many years, is a subtle and accomplished chef and a particularly brilliant *saucier* (sauce maker). The menu changes regularly, but Guichard favors such dishes as sea bass with pistachios in fennel sauce and braised beef with cumin-scented carrots. ⊠ *32 rue de Longchamp, Trocadéro/Eiffel Tower* ☎ *01–45–53–00–07* ⌁ *Reservations essential* ▤ *AE, DC, MC, V* ⊘ *Closed weekends and 3 wks in Aug.* Ⓜ *Iéna.*

$$$$ ✕ **Le Pré Catelan.** Live a Belle Epoque fantasy by dining beneath the chestnut trees on the terrace of this fanciful landmark *pavillon* in the Bois de Boulogne. Among the winning dishes that have appeared on chef Frédéric Anton's menu are spit-roasted squab in a caramelized sauce, sweetbreads with morels and asparagus tips, and roasted pear on a caramelized waffle with bergamot ice cream. For a taste of the good life at a (relatively) gentle price, order the €55 lunch menu and soak up the opulent surroundings along with service that's as polished as the silverware. ⊠ *Bois de Boulogne, rte. de Surèsnes, Bois de Boulogne* ☎ *01–44–14–41–14* ⌁ *Reservations essential* ⌂ *Jacket and tie* ▤ *AE, DC, MC, V* ⊘ *Closed Sun. and Mon., mid-Feb., and 1 wk in Nov.* Ⓜ *Porte Dauphine.*

★ **$$$–$$$$**   ✕ **L'Astrance.** *Le Point* has called L'Astrance "a miracle," while *Le Figaro*'s respected critic François Simon has described it as "perfect." What's all the fuss about? Well, this split-level gray dining room is probably the best place in Paris to part with your hard-earned euros: you get the quality of haute cuisine without the pomposity or the crushing price tag. For a mere €29 at lunch you might feast on an avocado-and-crab millefeuille, ballotine of quail and foie gras, and orange soufflé with marjoram ice cream. A more elaborate dinner menu costs €65. The only catch: you'll need to reserve six weeks ahead for dinner and three weeks in advance for lunch. ⊠ *4 rue Beethoven, Trocadéro/Eiffel Tower* ☎ *01–40–50–84–40* ⌁ *Reservations essential* ⊘ *Closed Mon., 3 wks in Aug., Dec. 22–Jan. 3. No lunch Tues.* ▤ *AE, DC, MC, V* Ⓜ *Passy.*

SEAFOOD   ✕ **Prunier.** Founded in 1925, this seafood restaurant is one of the best, **$$$$** and surely the prettiest, in Paris—even more so following renovations (though the wood-panel upstairs dining room does look a bit saunalike). Now a New York–style caviar house, Maison Prunier doesn't offer much in the way of cooking—a world-weary set from the blasé 16th comes here to feast on Aquitaine caviar (for a cool €100 a tablespoon), chilled oysters with hot, spiced sausages (a Bordeaux specialty), and the so-chic "Christian Dior jellied egg." ⊠ *16 av. Victor-Hugo, Champs-Élysées* ☎ *01–44–17–35–85* ⌂ *Jacket and tie* ▤ *AE, DC, MC, V* ⊘ *Closed Sun. and Aug.* Ⓜ *Étoile.*

17ᵉ Arrondissement (Monceau/Champs-Élysées)

FRENCH   ✕ **Guy Savoy.** Redecorated by Jean-Michel Wilmotte, who dressed up ★ **$$$$** the space with dark African wood, rich leather (like the inside of a Rolls-Royce), and cream-color marble, Guy Savoy's luxury restaurant has stepped gracefully into the 21st century. Come here for a perfectly measured, contemporary haute-cuisine experience. The artichoke soup with black truffles, sea bass with spices, and veal kidneys in mustard-spiked jus reveal the magnitude of Savoy's talent. Half-portions allow you to graze your way through the menu, and reasonably priced wines are available. Best of all, the atmosphere is joyful—Savoy senses that having fun is just as important as eating well. ⊠ *18 rue Troyon, Champs-Élysées*

☎ 01–43–80–40–61 ▤ AE, MC, V ⊘ Closed Sun. and Mon., 3 wks in Aug., and 2 wks at Christmas. No lunch Sat. ⌖ Reservations essential Ⓜ Charles-de-Gaulle–Étoile.

18ᵉ Arrondissement (Montmartre)

FRENCH   ✕ **Chez Toinette.** Between the red lights of Pigalle and the Butte Mont-
$$ martre, this cozy bistro with red walls and candlelight hits the romance nail on the head. In autumn and winter, game comes into play in long-simmered French dishes—choose from *marcassin* (young wild boar), venison, and pheasant. Regulars can't resist the crème brûlée and the raspberry tart. Prices have crept up, but Chez Toinette is still a rare find for this neighborhood. ⊠ *20 rue Germaine Pilon, Montmartre* ☎ 01–42–54–44–36 ▤ MC, V ⊘ Closed Sun. and Mon., Aug., and 2 wks at Christmas. No lunch Ⓜ Pigalle.

$$ ✕ **La Famille.** Inaki Aizpitarte, originally from the Pays Basque, opened this hip restaurant on a street known for its role in the film *Amélie*. Happily, his place is worth visiting for what it brings to the plate, not the screen. The spare space attracts the *bobo* (bohemian bourgeois) residents who are bringing a new energy to Montmartre. Aizpitarte's globetrotting menu might include pan-fried foie gras with miso sauce or chocolate custard with fiery Basque peppers. ⊠ *41 rue des Trois-Frères, Montmartre* ☎ 01–42–52–11–12 ▤ MC, V ⊘ Closed Sun.–Mon. No lunch Ⓜ Abbesses.

Cafés & Salons de Thé

Along with air, water, and wine (Parisians eat fewer and fewer three-course meals), the café remains one of the basic necessities of life in Paris; following is a small selection of cafés and *salons de thé* (tearooms) to whet your appetite. **Au Père Tranquille** (⊠ 16 rue Pierre Lescot, Beaubourg/Les Halles, 1ᵉʳ ☎ 01–45–08–00–34 Ⓜ Les Halles) is one of the best places in Paris for people-watching. **Brasserie Lipp.** (⊠ 151 bd. St-Germain, St-Germain-des-Prés ☎ 01–45–48–53–91 Ⓜ St-Germain-des-Prés), with its turn-of-the-20th-century decor, was a favorite spot of Hemingway's; today television celebrities, journalists, and politicians come here for coffee on the small glassed-in terrace off the main restaurant. **Café Beaubourg** (⊠ 43 rue St-Merri, Beaubourg/Les Halles, 4ᵉ ☎ 01–48–87–63–96 Ⓜ Hôtel-de-Ville), near the Pompidou Center and designed by architect Christian de Portzamparc, is one of the trendiest rendezvous spots for fashion and art types. **Café Marly** (⊠ Cour Napoléon du Louvre, 93 rue de Rivoli, Louvre/Tuileries, 1ᵉʳ ☎ 01–49–26–06–60 Ⓜ Palais-Royal), overlooking the main courtyard of the Louvre, is perfect for an afternoon break or a nightcap, though the food could be better. Note that ordinary café service shuts down during meal hours, when overpriced, mediocre food is served. **La Charlotte en l'Ile** (⊠ 24 rue St-Louis-en-l'Ile, Ile St-Louis, 4ᵉ ☎ 01–43–54–25–83 Ⓜ Pont-Marie) would be fancied by the witch who baked gingerbread children in *Hansel and Gretel*—set with fairy lights, carnival masques, and decoupaged detritus, it's a tiny, storybook spot that offers more than 30 varieties of tea along with a sinfully good hot chocolate. **La Crémaillère** (⊠ 15 pl. du Tertre, Montmartre, 18ᵉ ☎ 01–46–06–58–59 Ⓜ Anvers) is a veritable monument to fin-de-siècle art in Montmartre. **Les Editeurs** (✉ 4 carrefour de l'Odéon, St-Germain-des-Prés, 6ᵉ ☎ 01–43–26–67–76 Ⓜ St-Germain-des-Prés), strategically placed near prestigious Rive Gauche publishing houses, attracts passersby with red velour seats and glossy books on display. The terrace just off the boulevard St-Germain is great for people-watching, but not ideal for catching a waiter's eye. **Le Flore en l'Ile** (✉ 42 quai d'Orléans, Ile St-Louis, 4ᵉ ☎ 01–43–29–88–27 Ⓜ Pont-Marie) is set on the Ile St-Louis and has a magnificent view of the Seine. **Ladurée** (✉ 16 rue Royale, Opéra/Grands Boulevards, 8ᵉ ☎01–42–60–21–79 Ⓜ Madeleine) is pretty enough to bring a tear to Proust's eye—this salon de thé has barely changed since 1862. You'll dote on the signature lemon-and-caramel macaroons (there are other outposts at 75 av. des Champs-Élysées and on the Left Bank at 21 rue Bonaparte). **Ma Bourgogne** (✉ 19 pl. des Vosges, Le Marais, 4ᵉ ☎ 01–42–78–44–64 Ⓜ St-Paul) is a calm oasis for a coffee or a light lunch away from the noisy streets and set on magical place des Vosges. **Mariage Frères** (✉ 30 rue du Bourg-Tibourg, Le Marais, 4ᵉ ☎ 01–42–72–28–11 Ⓜ Hôtel-de-Ville) is an outstanding tea shop serving 500 kinds of tea, along with delicious tarts. **Le Vieux Colombier** (✉ 65 rue de Rennes, St-Germain-des-Prés, 7ᵉ ☎ 01–45–48–53–81 Ⓜ St-Sulpice) is just around the corner from St-Sulpice and the Vieux Colombier Theater.

WHERE TO STAY

Updated by
Ethan Gilsdorf

Winding staircases, flower-filled window boxes, concierges who seem to have stepped from a 19th-century novel—all of these can still be found in Paris hotels, and despite the scales' being tipped in favor of the well-heeled, overall there's good news for travelers of all budgets. Increased competition means the bar for service and amenities has been raised everywhere. Many good-value establishments in the lower-to-middle price ranges have updated their funky '70s wallpaper and "Why should I care, Madame?" attitudes, while still keeping their prices in check. Virtually every hotel is now equipped with cable TV to meet the needs of international guests. Now it's not uncommon for mid-range hotels to have a no-smoking floor, for inexpensive hotels to offer air-conditioning, and even for budget places to have planted an Internet terminal in their little lobbies. So, whatever price you're looking for, compared to most other cities Paris is a paradise for the weary traveler tired of dreary, out-of-date, or cookie-cutter rooms. The best hotels still emanate an unmistakable Paris vibe: weathered beamed ceilings, vaulted stone breakfast crypts, tall windows overlooking zinc rooftops, and leafy courtyards where you can sit and linger over your daily croissant and café.

Despite the huge choice of hotels, you should always reserve well in advance, especially if you're determined to stay in a specific place. You can do this by telephoning, faxing, or e-mailing ahead, then asking for confirmation of your reservation, detailing the duration of your stay, the price, the location and type of your room (single or double, twin beds or double), and the bathroom (shower—*douche*—or bath—*baignoire*—private or shared). Assume that hotel rooms have air-conditioning, TV, telephones, and private bath, unless otherwise noted. Remember that the *very* top Paris hotels retain their ranks among the world's priciest. Room rates at these legendary places can range from €400 to €700—and upward—for a night. These rates can artificially skew our price chart figures for, in truth, a **$$$** hotel listed below can be as reasonable as €160.

Prices

Almost all Paris hotels charge extra for breakfast, with prices ranging from €5 to more than €30 per person in luxury establishments. For anything more than the standard Continental breakfast of café au lait and croissants, the price will be higher. You may be better off finding the nearest café. Occasionally breakfast is included in the hotel rate—this is denoted below with a BP (Breakfast Plan) in the review. If not, presume all hotels reviewed operate on the EP (European Plan), with no breakfast included in the basic room rate. A nominal *séjour* (lodging) tax of €1.07 per person per night is charged to pay for promotion of tourism in Paris.

WHAT IT COSTS In euros				
$$$$	**$$$**	**$$**	**$**	**¢**
FOR 2 PEOPLE over €225	€150–€225	€100–€150	€75–€100	under €75

Prices are for two people in a standard double room in high season, including tax (19.6%) and service charge.

1ᵉʳ Arrondissement (Louvre/Les Halles)

$$$$ **Hôtel Costes.** Jean-Louis and Gilbert Costes's eponymous hotel is the darling of decorating magazines and a magnet for the sunglasses-at-night set. Nearly every room is swathed in enough pomegranate-red, $400-a-yard fabrics, swagging, and braided trim to choke a runway of supermodels. A seductive bar with its labyrinth of secluded nooks is *the* place in Paris to be seen trying not to be seen. For taste, many consider this the top Paris hotel, but better wear thick skin: unless you're an off-duty celeb, the army of perfectly coiffed hosts and hostesses has a knack for making you feel underdressed and unimportant. ☒ *239 rue St-Honoré, Louvre/Tuileries, 75001* ☎ *01–42–44–50–50* 🖷 *01–42–44–50–01* ⊕ *www.hotelcostes.com* ⇨ *77 rooms, 5 suites* ⟁ *Restaurant, room service, in-room data ports, in-room safes, minibars, cable TV, in-room VCRs, indoor pool, gym, sauna, bar, laundry service, meeting rooms, parking (fee), some pets allowed* ⊟ *AE, DC, MC, V* Ⓜ *Tuileries.*

★ **$$$$** **Hôtel Meurice.** One of the finest hotels in the world has become even finer—thanks to the millions of the Sultan of Brunei. The restaurant—a fabled extravaganza of cream boiseries and glittering chandeliers—and the elaborately gilded 18th-century Rococo salons have been entirely restored, while the guest rooms, adorned with Persian carpets, marble mantelpieces, and ormolu clocks, are now more opulent and soigné than ever, if that's possible. Baths are largely white marble, with two sinks and deep, spacious tubs. Goodies are extraordinary: the honey in the minibars is gathered from bees buzzing on the roof of the Opéra, while the health club includes Caudalíe treatments such as grape-based "Sauvignon" massages. ☒ *228 rue de Rivoli, Louvre/Tuileries, 75001* ☎ *01–44–58–10–10* 🖷 *01–44–58–10–15* ⊕ *www.meuricehotel.com*

160 rooms, 36 suites ⅃ 2 restaurants, room service, in-room data ports, in-room safes, minibars, cable TV, health club, bar, laundry service, meeting rooms, no-smoking rooms ☰ *AE, DC, MC, V* Ⓜ *Tuileries, Concorde.*

★ $$$$ 🏨 **Hôtel Ritz.** The majestic and legendary hotel founded in 1896 by Cesar Ritz is festooned with Napoléonic gilt and ormolu, sparkling with crystal chandeliers, and adorned with *qualité de Louvre* antiques. Of course, there are really two Ritzes. The first is the gilded place Vendôme wing with suites named after former residents such as Marcel Proust and Coco Chanel. The glamor quotient declines precipitously in the back wing, where you'll just feel you're staying in a pretty hotel room, not the Ritz. Still, even if you get one of the humbler chambers, you could easily spend days without even venturing out past the main gates because the hotel shops, gardens, bars, clubs, and restaurants could monopolize you. There's the famed Ritz Escoffier cooking school where you can learn the finer points of *gateaux*; the Hemingway Bar, where Colin Field reigns as a world-ranked bartender; and the basement health club—a veritable Louis XIV temple of sweat. ✉ *15 pl. Vendôme, Louvre/Tuileries, 75001* ☎ *01–43–16–30–30* 🖨 *01–43–16–36–68* ⊕ *www.parisritz.com* *107 rooms, 55 suites ⅃ 3 restaurants, room service, in-room data ports, in-room safes, minibars, cable TV, indoor pool, health club, hair salon, 2 bars, shops, baby-sitting, meeting rooms, parking (fee)* ☰ *AE, DC, MC, V* Ⓜ *Opéra.*

$$$$ 🏨 **Hôtel de Vendôme.** In the 19th century this building was the embassy of the Republic of Texas; now it's a hotel with Texas-scaled comforts. Though the entrance is less than grand, the rooms are handsomely done in Second Empire style, with walls and furnishings in muted earth tones and hand-carved wood detailing throughout. Best of all, besides a videophone for checking out visitors at the door, is the fully automated bedside console that controls the lights, curtains, and electronic do-not-disturb sign. ✉ *1 pl. Vendôme, Louvre/Tuileries, 75001* ☎ *01–42–60–32–84* 🖨 *01–49–27–97–89* ⊕ *www.hoteldevendome.com* *20 rooms, 9 suites ⅃ Room service, in-room safes, minibars, cable TV, piano bar, Internet, some pets allowed (fee)* ☰ *AE, DC, MC, V* Ⓜ *Concorde, Opéra.*

★ $$–$$$ 🏨 **Hôtel Brighton.** Many of Paris's most prestigious palace hotels are found facing the Tuileries or Place de la Concorde. The Brighton breathes the same rarified air under the arcades, for a fraction of the price. Inside, you'll find stone columns, chandeliers, and a palatial ambience. Smaller rooms with showers look onto a courtyard; street-facing chambers have balconies and a royal view onto the gardens and Left Bank in the distance. ✉ *218 rue de Rivoli, Louvre/Tuileries 75001* ☎ *01–47–03–61–61* 🖨 *01–42–60–41–78* ⊕ *www.esprit-de-france.com* *65 rooms ⅃ In-room data ports, minibars, cable TV, some pets allowed; no a/c in some rooms* ☰ *AE, DC, MC, V* Ⓜ *Tuileries.*

$–$$ 🏨 **Hôtel Londres St-Honoré.** An appealing combination of character and comfort distinguishes this small, inexpensive hotel, a five-minute walk from the Louvre. Exposed oak beams, statues in niches, and rustic stone walls give this place old-fashioned charm, with new carpets and paint throughout after a 2002 touch-up. Though rooms have floral bedspreads and standard hotel furniture, they are pleasant and the price is

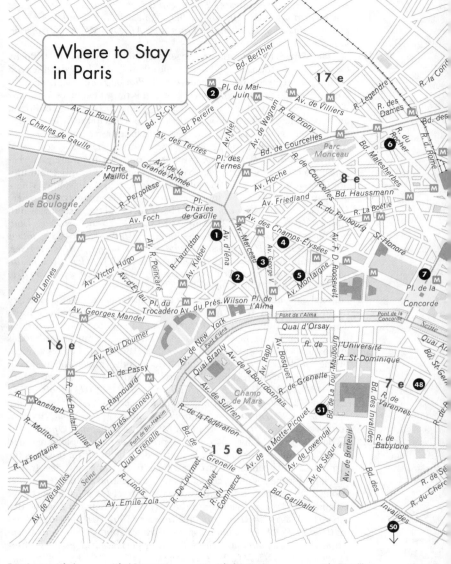

Where to Stay in Paris

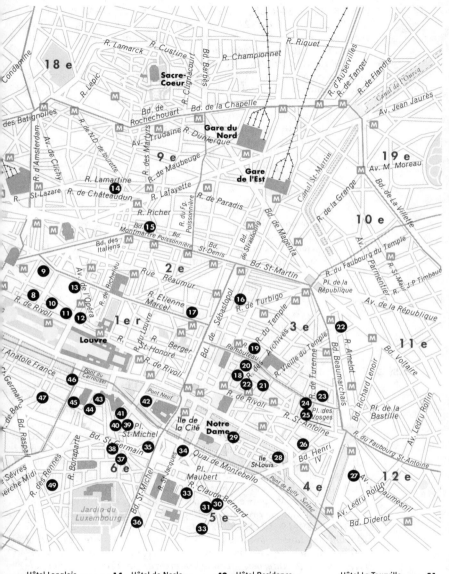

right. ⊠ *13 rue St-Roch, Louvre/Tuileries, 75001* ☎ *01–42–60–15–62*
🖨 *01–42–60–16–00* ⟲ *21 rooms* ◊ *Dining room, minibars, cable TV,
Internet, some pets allowed, no-smoking rooms; no a/c in some rooms*
▤ *AE, DC, MC, V* Ⓜ *Pyramides.*

$ ⛫ **Hôtel Henri IV.** Princes once made the regal Ile de la Cité their home
but even paupers can call it their home, thanks to one of Paris's most
beloved (and popular) budget sleeps. Set in a 400-year-old building that
once housed Henri IV's printing presses, it has a drab lobby and narrow staircase (five flights, no elevator) but guest rooms wear their age
with pride. Nothing beats the top location, set on gorgeous place
Dauphine and just a short stroll to the Louvre and Notre-Dame. Bathrooms are in the hallway; pay a little extra and get a room with private
shower. ⊠ *25 pl. Dauphine, Ile de la Cité, 75001* ☎ *01–43–54–44–53*
⟲ *17 rooms, 7 with shower* ◊ *No a/c, no room phones, no room TVs*
▤ *No credit cards* ⦿ *BP* Ⓜ *Cité, St-Michel, Pont Neuf.*

2e Arrondissement (La Bourse/Les Halles)

¢ ⛫ **Hôtel Tiquetonne.** Just off *marché* Montorgueil and a short hoof
from Les Halles (and the slightly seedy Rue St-Denis), this is one of the
least expensive hotels in the city center. The rooms aren't much to look
at nor do they offer amenities, but they're always clean and some are
downright spacious. Book on one of the top two floors facing the
quiet, pedestrian rue Tiquetonne, not the loud, car-strangled rue Turbigo. ⊠ *6 rue Tiquetonne, Beaubourg/Les Halles, 75002*
☎ *01–42–36–94–58* 🖨 *01–42–36–02–94* ⟲ *45 rooms, 33 with bath*
◊ *Some pets allowed; no a/c, no room TVs* ▤ *AE, MC, V* Ⓜ *Étienne
Marcel.*

3e Arrondissement (Beaubourg/Marais)

★ $$$$ ⛫ **Pavillon de la Reine.** The former hangout of the Marais elite—Madame
de Sévigné, Racine, La Fontaine, and Molière—this gorgeous place des
Vosges mansion dating from 1612 competes with Ritz-level luxury but
on a more intimate scale. *Entrez* through a spectacular courtyard-drive-
way into a luscious lobby that recalls a royal hunting lodge: massive beams
overhead, tapestries, and a salon with the original 300-year-old fireplace.
You can reserve a room in the older section, decorated in classy Louis
XIII style, or opt for the modern yet reserved wing redone in 2001. For
an absolutely royal feeling, ask for a duplex overlooking two flower-
filled courtyards behind the historic Queen's Pavilion. Wireless Internet access has recently been introduced, as has a ground-floor wing of
classy scarlet and gray rooms. ⊠ *28 pl. des Vosges, Le Marais, 75003*
☎ *01–40–29–19–19, 800/447–7462 in U.S.* 🖨 *01–40–29–19–20*
⊕ *www.pavillon-de-la-reine.com* ⟲ *31 rooms, 24 suites* ◊ *Dining
room, room service, in-room safes, minibars, cable TV, bar, laundry service, concierge, Internet, meeting room, free parking, some pets allowed* ▤ *AE, DC, MC, V* Ⓜ *Bastille, St-Paul.*

¢ ⛫ **Hôtel Bellevue et du Chariot d'Or.** Here you have an old Belle Epoque
time traveler, proud to keep its dingy chandeliers and faded gold trim-
ming as is. Budget groups from France and the Netherlands come for
the clean but sans-frills rooms. There may be some quirks, like the hefty
old-fashioned room keys and the bathtub–showers without curtains, but

you're just a few blocks from hipper addresses in the heart of the Marais. Get here before the fashionista crowd turns it into a shabby-chic hangout. ☒ *39 rue de Turbigo, Beaubourg/Les Halles, 75003* ☏ *01–48–87–45–60* ⎙ *01–48–87–95–04* ⊕ *www.hotelbellevue75.com* ⬫ *59 rooms* ⬧ *Dining room, cable TV, bar; no a/c* ▤ *AE, DC, MC, V* Ⓜ *Réaumur-Sébastopol, Arts et Métiers.*

4ᵉ Arrondissement (Marais/Ile St-Louis)

$$$–$$$$ ⌧ **Hôtel du Jeu de Paume.** The showpiece of this lovely 17th-century hotel on the Ile St-Louis is the stone-walled, vaulted lobby-cum–breakfast room. It stands on an erstwhile court where French aristocrats once played *jeu de paume*, an early version of tennis using palm fronds. The bright rooms are nicely done up in butter yellow, with rustic antiques, bric-a-brac, and objets d'art, beamed ceilings, and damask upholstery; however, the starker modern decor in the smaller rooms doesn't quite jibe with the style of the rest of the hotel. The little garden is a haven of sun-drenched tranquillity. ☒ *54 rue St-Louis-en-l'Ile, Ile-St-Louis, 75004* ☏ *01–43–26–14–18* ⎙ *01–40–46–02–76* ⊕ *www.jeudepaumehotel. com* ⬫ *26 rooms, 4 suites* ⬧ *In-room data ports, in-room safes, minibars, cable TV, exercise equipment, sauna, bar, baby-sitting, some pets allowed; no a/c* ▤ *AE, DC, MC, V* Ⓜ *Pont-Marie.*

★ $$$ ⌧ **Hôtel Bourg Tibourg.** Scented candles and subdued lighting announce the designer-du-jour Jacques Garcia's theatrical mix of haremlike romance and Gothic contemplation. Royal blue paint and velvet red fabrics line the claustrophobic halls. The rooms are barely bigger than the beds, and every inch has been upholstered, tasseled, and draped in a cacophony of stripes, florals, and medieval motifs. A stone staircase wends down to an underground nook where you can order drinks and plan your next tryst. A pocket-size garden has room for three tables, leafy plants, and a swath of stars above. ☒ *19 rue Bourg Tibourg, Le Marais, 75004* ☏ *01–42–78–47–39* ⎙ *01–40–29–07–00* ⊕ *www.hoteldubourgtibourg. com* ⬫ *29 rooms, 1 suite* ⬧ *Dining room, in-room safes, minibars, cable TV, laundry service* ▤ *AE, DC, MC, V* Ⓜ *Hôtel de Ville.*

★ $$–$$$ ⌧ **Hôtel Caron de Beaumarchais.** The theme of this intimate jewel is the work of Caron de Beaumarchais, who wrote *The Marriage of Figaro* in 1778. Rooms—some gloriously headlining toile-de-jouy fabrics, Redouté-pastel hues, and Neoclassical wood accents—faithfully reflect the taste of 18th-century French nobility. The second- and fifth-floor rooms with balconies are the largest; those on the sixth floor have beguiling views across Right Bank rooftops. ☒ *12 rue Vieille-du-Temple, Le Marais, 75004* ☏ *01–42–72–34–12* ⎙ *01–42–72–34–63* ⊕ *www. carondebeaumarchais.com* ⬫ *19 rooms* ⬧ *In-room data ports, minibars, cable TV* ▤ *AE, DC, MC, V* Ⓜ *Hôtel de Ville.*

$$ ⌧ **Hôtel de la Bretonnerie.** This small hotel is in a 17th-century *hôtel particulier* (town house) on a tiny street in the Marais, a few minutes' walk from the Centre Pompidou. Rooms are classified as "chambres classiques" or "chambres de charme," the latter being more spacious, and naturally pricier, but with more elaborate furnishings like Louis XIII–style four-poster canopy beds and marble-clad bathtubs. Overall, the establishment is spotless. ☒ *22 rue Ste-Croix-de-la-Bretonnerie, Le Marais, 75004*

☎ *01–48–87–77–63* 🖷 *01–42–77–26–78* ⊕ *www.labretonnerie.com*
🛏 *22 rooms, 7 suites* ⚙ *In-room data ports, minibars, cable TV; no a/c* ☰ *MC, V* Ⓜ *Hôtel de Ville.*

$$ 🏨 **Hôtel de la Place des Vosges.** A loyal, eclectic clientele swears by this small, historic Marais hotel on a delightful street just off place des Vosges. The Louis XIII–style reception area and rooms with oak-beamed ceilings, rough-hewn stone, and a mix of rustic finds from secondhand shops evoke old Marais. ⊠ *12 rue de Birague, Le Marais, 75004* ☎ *01–42–72–60–46* 🖷 *01–42–72–02–64* 🛏 *16 rooms* ⚙ *Minibars, cable TV; no a/c* ☰ *AE, DC, MC, V* Ⓜ *Bastille.*

$$ 🏨 **Hôtel Saint Louis.** Louis XIII–style furniture, oil paintings, exposed beams, bare stone, and various antiques invite speculation about which duke may have owned this 17th-century building on the coveted Ile St-Louis. The older, unrenovated rooms seem worse for wear compared to the fresher ones, so it's best to request the newly remodeled rooms on the fourth and fifth floors. Also, mini-balconies on the upper levels offer Seine views. ⊠ *75 rue St-Louis-en-l'Ile, Ile-St-Louis, 75004* ☎ *01–46–34–04–80* 🖷 *01–46–34–02–13* ⊕ *www.hotelsaintlouis.com* 🛏 *19 rooms* ⚙ *Cable TV* ☰ *MC, V* Ⓜ *Pont Marie.*

$$ 🏨 **Hôtel Saint-Louis Marais.** Once an annex to a local convent, this 18th-century hôtel has retained its stone walls and beams while adding red clay tile floors and antiques. A wooden-banistered stair leads to the small but proper rooms decorated with basic red carpet and green bed spreads. (Those with heavy luggage, beware: no elevator.) The hotel's in Village St-Paul, a little tangle of medieval lanes just south of the well-traveled Marais that has an excellent English-language bookstore and is not yet overrun by tourists. ⊠ *1 rue Charles V Le Marais, 75004* ☎ *01–48–87–87–04* 🖷 *01–48–87–33–26* ⊕ *www.saintlouismarais. com* 🛏 *20 rooms* ⚙ *Dining room, in-room safes, cable TV, laundry service, Internet, some pets allowed; no a/c* ☰ *AE, DC, MC, V* Ⓜ *Sully-Morland and Bastille.*

$$ 🏨 **Hôtel du Vieux Marais.** This pleasing and stylish hotel with a turn-of-the-20th-century facade is on a quiet street in the heart of the Marais. Rooms are bright, impeccably clean, with oak and burgundy leather seating; try to get one overlooking the just-renovated courtyard. The staff is exceptionally courteous. ⊠ *8 rue du Plâtre, Le Marais, 75004* ☎ *01–42–78–47–22* 🖷 *01–42–78–34–32* ⊕ *www.vieuxmarais.com* 🛏 *30 rooms* ⚙ *Cable TV* ☰ *AE, MC, V* Ⓜ *Hôtel de Ville.*

$ 🏨 **Grand Hôtel Jeanne-d'Arc.** If you're on a budget, you're sure to get your money's worth at this hotel in an unbeatable location off the tranquil Place St-Catherine, one of the city's lesser-known pedestrian squares. The 17th-century building has been a hotel for more than a century, and while rooms are on the spartan side, they are well maintained and fairly spacious. The welcoming staff is happy to recount the history of this former market quartier, now home to café life and boutique shopping. It's best to book one to two months in advance. ⊠ *3 rue de Jarente, Le Marais, 75004* ☎ *01–48–87–62–11* ⊕ *www.hoteljeannedarc.com* 🖷 *01–48–87–37–31* 🛏 *36 rooms* ⚙ *Cable TV, some pets allowed; no a/c* ☰ *MC, V* Ⓜ *St-Paul.*

5° Arrondissement (Latin Quarter)

$$ ▦ **Hôtel Familia.** Owner Eric Gaucheron is proud of his hotel's nearly obsessive level of service and pace of renovations at this family-run show. The snug lobby has reproduction antique tapestries and hardwood furniture; rooms are snazzed up with murals of typical city scenes; and bathrooms have modern fixtures and tilework. Balconies give several rooms extra space; Nos. 61 and 62 have clear views to Notre-Dame. Cheaper rooms may strike you as too cramped for large suitcases, but each room has soundproofing and double-pane windows. ⊠ *11 rue des Écoles, Latin Quarter, 75005* ☎ *01–43–54–55–27* ♨ *01–43–29–61–77* ⊕ *www. hotel-paris-familia.com* ↶ *30 rooms* ♣ *Minibars, cable TV; no a/c* ▤ *AE, MC, V* Ⓜ *Cardinal Lemoine.*

$$ ▦ **Hôtel Grandes Écoles.** *Propriétaire* Madame Lefloch takes no chances with security: massive wooden doors protect her castle from invaders while cameras patrol the premises. Divided among a trio of three-story buildings, her baby-blue and white guest rooms and their flowery, Louis-Philippe furnishings and lace bedspreads create a grandmotherly vibe, which may not be to everyone's tastes. But this spot is legendary for its stunning interior cobbled courtyard and garden, your second living room and a perfect breakfast spot when *il fait beau* (Rooms 29 and 30 open directly into the greenery). ⊠ *75 rue du Cardinal Lemoine, Latin Quarter, 75005* ☎ *01–43–26–79–23* ♨ *01–43–25–28–15* ⊕ *www. hotel-grandes-ecoles.com* ↶ *51 rooms* ♣ *Room service, baby-sitting, parking (fee), some pets allowed; no a/c, no room TVs* ▤ *MC, V* Ⓜ *Cardinal Lemoine.*

★ $$ ▦ **Hôtel des Jardin du Luxembourg.** Blessed with a personable staff and a smart, stylish look, this hotel, on an unbelievably calm cul-de-sac just a block from the Luxembourg Gardens, is an oasis for contemplation—even Freud stayed here for six weeks during the winter of 1885–86. A cheery hardwood-floor lobby with fireplace leads to smallish rooms furnished with wrought-iron beds, pastel bathroom tiles and contemporary Provençal fabrics. Ask for one with a balcony overlooking the street; the best room, No. 25, has dormer windows revealing a peekaboo view of the Eiffel Tower. ⊠ *5 impasse Royer-Collard, Latin Quarter, 75005* ☎ *01–40–46–08–88* ♨ *01–40–46–02–28* ↶ *27 rooms* ♣ *In-room safes, minibars, sauna* ▤ *AE, DC, MC, V* Ⓜ *Luxembourg.*

★ $$ ▦ **Hôtel du Lys.** Count on Hôtel du Lys to conjure up an inexpensive medieval fantasy. Just climb the convoluted stairway to your room in this former 17th-century royal residence to discover unique quirks and nooks, weathered antiques, and exposed beams throughout. There's one dollhouse-size room, probably the cutest hotel room in all Paris, that has a beamed, 6-foot ceiling and barely enough space for its bed. The modest but extremely atmospheric lobby dates from the Renaissance. Off on a quiet side street, the hotel is a block away from the bright lights of the Latin Quarter. ⊠ *23 rue Serpente, Latin Quarter 75006* ☎ *01–43–26–97–57* ♨ *01–44–07–34–90* ⊕ *www.hoteldulys.com* ↶ *22 rooms, 16 with bath* ♣ *Cable TV, some pets allowed; no a/c* ▤ *MC, V* ❘◎❘ *BP* Ⓜ *St-Michel, Odéon.*

★ $$ ▦ **Hôtel Minerve.** Fans of the Gaucheron family will be delighted to learn that the Minerve is now part of the Familia fold. Just next door to the

Familia, and twice as big, the hotel has been completely refurbished in the inimitable Gaucheron style: flowers and breakfast tables on the balconies, frescoes in the spacious lobby, tapestries on the walls, and cherry-wood furniture in the rooms. It's less intimate than the Familia—but just as charming. ⊠ *13 rue des Écoles, Latin Quarter, 75005* ☎ *01–43–26–26–04* 🖷 *01–44–07–01–96* ⊕ *www.hotel-paris-minerve. com* 🛏 *54 rooms* ⌂ *Internet; no a/c* ➡ *AE, MC, V* Ⓜ *Cardinal Lemoine.*

★ **$$** 🏨 **Hôtel Saint-Jacques.** In a location convenient to universities, bookshops, and repertory cinemas, this bargain hotel is impressively decorated, nearly every wall bedecked with faux-marble and trompe d'oeil murals. Like many old Paris hotels, each room has unique features, furnishings, and layout, but here the overall emphasis is on customer comfort, with generous amenities for the price. About half the rooms have tiny step-out balconies that give a glimpse of Notre-Dame and the Panthéon. ⊠ *35 rue des Écoles, Latin Quarter, 75005* ☎ *01–44–07–45–45* 🖷 *01–43–25–65–50* ⊕ *www.hotel-saintjacques.com* 🛏 *35 rooms* ⌂ *In-room safes, cable TV, baby-sitting, Internet; no a/c* ➡ *AE, DC, MC, V* Ⓜ *Maubert Mutualité.*

$ 🏨 **Hôtel Esméralda.** A Parisian flea market meets the Renaissance at this legendary shabby-chic hotel with superior views of Notre-Dame if you're lucky enough to get a front room. A vertiginous, ancient spiral staircase (no elevator) leads to a rabbit warren of low corridors, mismatched doors, and even funkier decor. Some rooms surprise with their marble fireplaces and chandeliers; others could be cleaner. The Esméralda's foyer may be its highlight: wood-beamed, strewn with art and tapestries, with classical music playing, it's right out of Flaubert's *Madame Bovary.* You'll decide whether it's "Paris charm" or "low-cost chaos." ⊠ *4 rue St-Julien-le-Pauvre, Latin Quarter, 75005* ☎ *01–43–54–19–20* 🖷 *01–40–51–00–68* 🛏 *19 rooms, 4 without bath* ⌂ *Some pets allowed; no a/c, no room TVs* ➡ *No credit cards* Ⓜ *St-Michel.*

6° Arrondissement (St-Germain)

$$$$ 🏨 **L'Hôtel.** With its baroque mirrors, gold-leaf peacock murals, sinfully
FodorśChoice plush robes, and fax machines in the closets, this eccentric and super-
★ fashionable hotel must be seen to be believed. Once an 18th-century *pavillon d'amour* (inn for trysts), as a hotel it welcomed Oscar Wilde, who in 1900 permanently checked out in Room 16, leaving behind a 2,600-franc bill ("Either this wallpaper goes or I do," were his famous last words). Your jaw drops upon seeing the six-story circular atrium top-lit by a skylight. Decorated by famed designer Jacques Garcia, the rooms deliver 19th-century pipe dreams, their sole downside being their snug size. But for that *style Empire* vibe, they can't be beat—Sarah Bernhardt would feel right at home. The lushly "Oriental"-theme restaurant is another plus. ⊠ *13 rue des Beaux-Arts, St-Germain-des-Prés, 75006* ☎ *01–44–41–99–00* 🖷 *01–43–25–64–81* ⊕ *www.l-hotel.com* 🛏 *16 rooms, 4 suites* ⌂ *Restaurant, cable TV, indoor pool, steam room, bar, baby-sitting, Internet, some pets allowed* ➡ *AE, DC, MC, V* Ⓜ *St-Germain-des-Prés.*

★ **$$$$** 🏨 **Hôtel Relais St-Germain.** With a gracious staff and all the countrified flowers, beams, and flea-market finds you could dream of, the Relais

St-Germain oozes with traditional 17th-century flavor. The rooms, done in bright yellow and red printed fabrics and paints, are at least twice the size of what you find at other hotels for the same price. Top-floor rooms have balconies; some rooms have kitchenettes. Le Comptoir du Relais, an adjacent café and former hangout of Hemingway, Picasso, Joyce, and Matisse, is offered exclusively for hotel guests to breakfast on coffee, croissants, and tartines. ✉ *9 carrefour de l'Odéon, St-Germain-des-Prés, 75006* ☎ *01–43–29–12–05* 🖷 *01–46–33–45–30* ⊕ *www. hotelrsg.com* ➴ *21 rooms, 1 suite* ♿ *Room service, in-room safes, some kitchenettes, minibars, cable TV, bar, some pets allowed* 🚭 *AE, DC, MC, V* ⏺ *BP* Ⓜ *Odéon.*

★ **$$$$** ⛫ **Relais Christine.** Like its mate, the Pavillon de la Reine, Relais Christine excels at dreaming up an opulent yet homey ambiance. The exquisite building was once a 13th-century abbey; the roots of its *Moyen Âge* past can be found in the stone basement breakfast room. The spacious guest rooms are elegant—expect overhead beams, parquet bathrooms, deep colors, rich fabrics, and wooden antiques. The hard-to-reserve ground-level rooms (11 through 17) open onto a garden with private patios, one of the best secluded nooks anywhere. ✉ *3 rue Christine, St-Germain-des-Prés, 75006* ☎ *01–40–51–60–80, 800/447–7462 in U.S.* 🖷 *01–40–51–60–81* ⊕ *www.relais-christine.com* ➴ *33 rooms, 18 suites* ♿ *In-room safes, minibars, cable TV, bar, baby-sitting, Internet, free parking, some pets allowed, no-smoking rooms* 🚭 *AE, DC, MC, V* Ⓜ *Odéon.*

★ **$$$** ⛫ **Hôtel d'Aubusson.** Dapper in their pin-stripe suits, the staff greets you warmly at this 17th-century town house and former literary salon that clings to its "country in the city" past. The showpiece is the stunning salon spanned by massive beams and headed by a gigantic fireplace. Decked out in rich burgundies, greens, or blues, the bedrooms are filled with Louis XV- and Regency-style antiques; even the smallest rooms are a good size by Paris standards. Behind the paved courtyard (where in warmer weather you can have your breakfast or predinner drink) there's a second structure with three apartments handy for families. ✉ *33 rue Dauphine, St-Germain-des-Prés, 75006* ☎ *01–43–29–43–43* 🖷 *01–43–29–12–62* ⊕ *www.hoteldaubusson.com* ➴ *49 rooms* ♿ *Room service, in-room data ports, in-room safes, minibars, cable TV, piano bar, baby-sitting, Internet, parking (fee), no-smoking floors* 🚭 *AE, MC, V* Ⓜ *Odéon.*

$$$ ⛫ **Hôtel de L'Abbaye.** This delightful hotel near St-Sulpice welcomes you with a cobblestone ante-courtyard and vaulted stone entrance. Paneled in bright wood after a makeover in the late 1990s, the rooms are spotless, if a little impersonal. The collision of modern art and country design—fruit baskets and flat-screen TVs—may not be to everyone's taste, but it's all redeemed by the lobby's many-nooked salons, the vestiges of the original 18th-century convent, and the one-of-a-kind spacious garden out back with fountain (which some first-floor rooms face). Upper-floor rooms have oak beams, while duplexes have lovely private terraces. ✉ *10 rue Cassette, St-Germain-des-Prés, 75006* ☎ *01–45–44–38–11* 🖷 *01–45–48–07–86* ⊕ *www.hotel-abbaye.com* ➴ *37 rooms, 7 suites* ♿ *In-room data ports, cable TV, bar, baby-sitting* 🚭 *AE, MC, V* ⏺ *BP* Ⓜ *St-Sulpice.*

$$$ ⊡ **Hôtel Bonaparte.** The congenial staff only makes staying in this intimate place more of a treat. Old-fashioned upholsteries, 19th-century furnishings, and paintings create a quaint feel in the relatively spacious rooms. And the location in the heart of St-Germain is nothing short of fabulous. ⊠ *61 rue Bonaparte, St-Germain-des-Prés, 75006* ☎ *01–43–26–97–37* 🖷 *01–46–33–57–67* 🖙 *29 rooms* � *In-room safes, cable TV* ▭ *MC, V* ⏍ *BP* Ⓜ *St-Germain-des-Prés.*

$$$ ⊡ **Hôtel de Fleurie.** On a quiet side street near place de l'Odéon, a series of statues set into the facade invite you into this spiffy, super-pretty, family-run hotel. Antiques, Oriental rugs, and rich upholsteries fill the 18th-century building. The warm-colored rooms, mostly done in yellows with wood paneling and checked drapes, include amenities such as heated towel racks in the bathroom. Ask the helpful staff about freebies like museum passes that reward long-stays. The location is ideal: equidistant from the Seine and Jardin du Luxembourg. ⊠ *32–34 rue Grégoire-de-Tours, St-Germain-des-Prés, 75006* ☎ *01–53–73–70–00* 🖷 *01–53–73–70–20* ⊕ *www.hotel-de-fleurie.tm.fr* 🖙 *29 rooms* � *In-room data ports, minibars, cable TV, bar, Internet* ▭ *AE, DC, MC, V* Ⓜ *Odéon.*

$$–$$$ ⊡ **Hôtel d'Angleterre.** Is that the spirit of Ernest Hemingway that you hear rustling down the hallways? Or is it the creaky elevator, which, like many things about this beloved spot, has seemingly remained unchanged since the days when "Papa" made this his first Paris pied-à-terre. Set on a street lined with antiques stores and right in the heart of Hemingway Country—why not skip the hotel breakfast for the one at the nearby Café Les Deux Magots?—this has a top location. Lower-end priced guest rooms here are super-snug, so go for the higher-end, often gigantic, rooms complete with wood beams and that special St-Germain-des-Prés ambience. ⊠ *44 rue Jacob, St-Germain-des-Prés, 75006* ☎ *01–42–60–34–72* 🖷 *01–42–60–16–93* 🖙 *27 rooms* � *Bar* ▭ *AE, MC, V* Ⓜ *St-Germain.*

★ **$–$$** ⊡ **Hôtel de Nesle.** The services are bare-bones—no elevator, phones, or breakfast—but if you're on the lookout for a low-cost, one-of-a-kind spot as wondrous as a doll's house, the Hôtel de Nesle will enchant you. The payoff is in the petite rooms cleverly decorated by theme. Sleep in Notre-Dame de Paris, lounge in an Oriental boudoir, spend the night with writer Molière, or steam it up in le Hammam. Decorations include colorful murals, canopy beds, custom lamps, and clay tiles. Most rooms overlook an interior garden oasis. Its dead-end street location keeps the Nesle quiet, despite its being a short walk from boulevard St-Germain in one direction and the Seine in the other. ⊠ *7 rue de Nesle, St-Germain-des-Prés, 75006* ☎ *01–43–54–62–41* 🖷 *01–43–54–31–88* ⊕ *www.hoteldenesle. com* 🖙 *20 rooms, 9 with bath* � *Some pets allowed, no-smoking floors; no a/c, no room phones, no room TVs* ▭ *MC, V* Ⓜ *Odéon.*

7e Arrondissement (Trocadéro/Tour Eiffel & St-Germain-des-Prés)

★ **$$$$** ⊡ **Hôtel Duc de Saint-Simon.** If it's good enough for the notoriously choosy Lauren Bacall, you'll probably fall for the Duc's charms, too. Its hidden location between boulevard St-Germain and rue de Bac is one plus; another is the shady courtyard entry. Rooms, in shades of yellow, green, pink, and blue, teem with antiques and countrified floral and striped fabrics.

Four rooms have spacious terraces overlooking the courtyard and the drooping wisteria. The 16th-century basement lounge is a warren of stone alcoves with a zinc bar and plush seating. To keep the peace, parents are discouraged from bringing children along. ✉ *14 rue de Saint-Simon, St-Germain-des-Prés, 75007* ☎ *01–44–39–20–20* 🖶 *01–45–48–68–25* ⊕ *www.hotelducdesaintsimon.com* 🛏 *29 rooms, 5 suites* ⚶ *Dining room, in-room safes, cable TV, bar, laundry service, parking (fee); no kids, no a/c in some rooms* ⊟ *AE, DC, MC, V* Ⓜ *Rue du Bac.*

$$$$ ▥ **Hôtel Pont Royal.** Once a favorite watering hole of the literary and art world—from Edgar Dégas to T. S. Eliot, F. Scott Fitzgerald to Gabriel García Marquez—this sumptuously refurbished hotel now attracts more businesspeople than writers. It's hard to find a more comfortable hotel, however, or a better location, a quiet street just off boulevard St-Germain. The views from the top floors are magnificent, especially from Suite 801. The library-theme bar resembles a British reading room. The hotel's Atelier de Joël Robuchon is one of the hottest tables in town and attracts well-heeled locals like Antoine Gallimard, whose publishing house is just up the street. Perhaps this will soon become, once again, Paris's "hôtel littéraire." ✉ *7 rue de Montalembert, St-Germain-des-Prés, 75007* ☎ *01–42–84–70–00* 🖶 *01–42–84–71–00* ⊕ *www.hotel-pontroyal.com/hpr* 🛏 *65 rooms, 10 suites* ⚶ *Restaurant, room service, in-room safes, minibars, cable TV with movies, health club, bar, library, Internet, baby-sitting, business services, meeting rooms, some pets allowed, no-smoking rooms* ⊟ *AE, DC, MC, V* Ⓜ *Rue de Bac.*

$$$ ▥ **Hôtel Le Tourville.** Here's a rare find: a cozy, upscale hotel that doesn't cost a fortune. Each room has crisp, milk-white damask upholstery set against pastel or ocher walls, a smattering of antique bureaus and lamps, original artwork, and fabulous old mirrors. The hotel attracts a young, fashionable crowd, especially in the dishy Art Deco bar. The junior suites have hot tubs. The staff couldn't be more helpful. ✉ *16 av. de Tourville, Trocadéro/Tour Eiffel, 75007* ☎ *01–47–05–62–62* 🖶 *01–47–05–43–90* ⊕ *www.hoteltourville.com* 🛏 *27 rooms, 3 suites* ⚶ *Dining room, in-room data ports, some in-room safes, cable TV, bar, laundry service, some pets allowed, no-smoking floor* ⊟ *AE, DC, MC, V* Ⓜ *École Militaire.*

$$ ▥ **Hôtel Verneuil.** The Verneuil's location on a narrow street near the Seine is unbeatable. The rooms may be more petite than you'd hope for, but each is painstakingly decorated. The white-cotton quilts on the beds, framed pressed flowers on the walls, and faux marble trompe d'oeil trim work and stained glass windows in the hall make you feel you've arrived *chez grand-mère*. Fans of Serge Gainsbourg can pilgrimage to his former home directly across the street. ✉ *8 rue de Verneuil, St-Germain-des-Prés, 75007* ☎ *01–42–60–83–14* 🖶 *01–42–61–40–38* ⊕ *www.hotelverneuil.com* 🛏 *26 rooms* ⚶ *Dining room, in-room safes, minibars, cable TV, bar, laundry service, Internet, some pets allowed (fee); no a/c* ⊟ *AE, MC, V* Ⓜ *RER: Musée d'Orsay.*

8ᵉ Arrondissement (Champs-Élysées)

★ **$$$$** ▥ **Four Seasons Hôtel George V Paris.** General Eisenhower's headquarters during the liberation of Paris is now owned by a Saudi prince and managed by the Four Seasons group—with a lineage like this, it is little wonder this place has many aficionados. The original Art Deco detailings and 17th-century tapestries have been restored, the bas-reliefs regilt, and the marble mosaic floors reconstructed stone by stone. Rooms are decked in yards of fabric and Louis XV trimmings; even the cheapest have crystal chandeliers, marble bathrooms, and soaking tubs. The Michelin three-star Le Cinq restaurant is one of Paris's most luxurious tables. ✉ *31 av. George-V, Champs-Élysées, 75008* ☎ *01–49–52–70–00* 🖷 *01–49–52–70–10* ⊕ *www.fourseasons.com* ⇝ *185 rooms, 60 suites* ♵ *2 restaurants, room service, in-room data ports, in-room safes, minibars, cable TV, indoor pool, health club, hair salon, massage, bar, shop, baby-sitting, children's programs, business services, some pets allowed, no-smoking floors* ⊟ *AE, DC, MC, V* Ⓜ *George-V.*

$$$$ ▦ **Hôtel de Crillon.** Home away from home for movie stars and off-duty celebrities, the Crillon has long been one of Paris's greatest hotels. It began life as a regal palace designed for Louis XV in 1758 by Jacques-Ange Gabriel to preside over the north side of the fabled place de la Concorde. In 1909 it became a hostelry and since then has played host to generations of diplomats and refined travelers. Most rooms are lavishly decorated with Rococo and Directoire antiques, crystal-and-gilt wall sconces, and gilt fittings. The sheer quantity of marble downstairs—especially in the highly praised Les Ambassadeurs restaurant—is staggering. ✉ *10 pl. de la Concorde, Champs-Élysées, 75008* ☎ *01–44–71–15–00, 800/ 888–4747 in U.S.* 🖷 *01–44–71–15–02* ⊕ *www.crillon.com* ⇝ *90 rooms, 57 suites* ♵ *2 restaurants, room service, in-room data ports, in-room safes, minibars, cable TV with movies, gym, spa, 2 bars, baby-sitting, children's programs, Internet, business services, meeting rooms, no-smoking rooms* ⊟ *AE, DC, MC, V* Ⓜ *Concorde.*

$$$$ ▦ **Hôtel Plaza-Athenée.** Once the favored Paris address for Grace Kelly and Jackie Kennedy, this 1911 palace hotel has reclaimed the luxury mantle from its peers in the past few years. The renaissance is partly a result of the Le Relais Plaza restaurant's *années 30* restoration and the landing of Alain Ducasse to helm the hotel's flagship Restaurant Plaza Athenée. May to September, all guests repair to the gorgeously red-parasoled La Cour Jardin since this courtyard restaurant has long been one of the prettiest sights in Paris. The Blahnik-heeled crowd likes the fact that they are only a croissant lob from the city's top couture and luxury shops. Most rooms have Regènce and Louis Seize–style accent pieces, while the top two floors go Art Deco. Interact with the unflagging energy of the 460 staff members and you'll see why the Athenée continues to be the choice of the Jagger-Paltrow set. ✉ *25 av. Montaigne, Champs-Élysées, 75008* ☎ *01–53–67–66–65, 866/732–1106 in U.S.* 🖷 *01–53–67–66–66* ⊕ *www.plaza-athenee-paris.com* ⇝ *145 rooms, 43 suites* ♵ *2 restaurants, room service, in-room safes, minibars, cable TV, health club, massage, bar, baby-sitting, business services, meeting rooms, some pets allowed, no-smoking rooms* ⊟ *AE, DC, MC, V* Ⓜ *Alma-Marceau.*

$$$$ ▦ **Pershing Hall.** Formerly an American Legion hall, this circa-2001 boutique hotel quickly became a must-stay address for the dressed-in-black pack. Designed by Andrée Putman, Pershing Hall champions masculine minimalism, with muted surfaces of wood and stone and even cooler attitudes to match. Rooms have stark-white linens, triptych dressing mirrors, slender tubelike lamps and tubs perched on round marble bases. The only trace of lightheartedness is the free minibars. All deluxe rooms and suites face the courtyard dining room whose west wall is a six-story hanging garden with 300 varieties of plants. The lounge bar serves drinks, dinner, and DJ-driven music until 2 AM. ⊠ *49 rue Pierre Charron, Champs-Élysées, 75008* 🕾 *01–58–36–58–00* 🖶 *01–58–36–58–01* ⊕ *www.pershinghall.com* ✂ *20 rooms, 6 suites* △ *Restaurant, room service, in-room data ports, in-room safes, minibars, cable TV, in-room VCRs, health club, bar, baby-sitting, meeting rooms, some pets allowed* ⊟ *AE, DC, MC, V* Ⓜ *George-V, Franklin-D.-Roosevelt.*

$$ 🖾 **Hôtel Résidence Monceau.** Within six blocks of the prim Parc Monceau, one of Paris's most coveted gardens, this friendly and fashionable hotel is an oasis of refined tranquillity. Ivy-covered trellises surround the lovely breakfast garden. Warm tones make rooms cozy; the efficient and professional staff makes your stay easy. In 2004, the hotel refitted guest rooms and added wireless Internet and conference facilities. The management also runs the equally smart and stylish Relais Saint-Sulpice and Jardins du Luxembourg hotels over on the Rive Gauche. ⊠ *85 rue du Rocher, Parc Monceau, 75008* 🕾 *01–45–22–75–11* 🖶 *01–45–22–30–88* ⊕ *monsite.wanadoo.fr/residencemonceau* ✂ *50 rooms, 1 suite* △ *Dining room, in-room data ports, minibars, cable TV, laundry service, no-smoking rooms; no a/c* ⊟ *AE, DC, MC, V* Ⓜ *Villiers.*

9ᵉ Arrondissement (Opéra)

$ 🖾 **Hôtel Chopin.** At the end of the passage Jouffroy—one of the many glass-roof shopping arcades built in Paris in the early 19th century—the Chopin, with its creaky-floor lobby and old wooden trim still recalls its 1846 birth date. The basic but comfortable rooms overlook the arcade's quaint toy shops and bookstores, though plastic plants, salmon walls, green carpets, and modern reproduction furniture don't quite blend with the antique setting. The best rooms are Nos. 409, 310, and 412, while the cheapest are the darker, smaller rooms ending with a 7. Blissful silence reigns throughout, however: the passage gates are closed at dusk, making this possibly the quietest hotel in the city. ⊠ *10 bd. Montmartre (46 passage Jouffroy), Opéra/Grands Boulevards, 75009* 🕾 *01–47–70–58–10* 🖶 *01–42–47–00–70* ✂ *36 rooms* △ *Dining room, in-room safes, cable TV; no a/c* ⊟ *AE, MC, V* Ⓜ *Grands Boulevards.*

★ **$** 🖾 **Hôtel Langlois.** After starring in *The Truth About Charlie* (a remake of *Charade*), this darling hotel gained a reputation as one of the most atmospheric budget sleeps in the city. An impressive Art Nouveau building, the former circa-1870 bank retains its beautiful wood-panel reception area and wrought-iron elevator. The individually decorated and spacious rooms are decked out with original glazed-tile fireplaces and period art. Rooms on the lower floors have the largest bathrooms, but those on the fifth and sixth have wonderful views of Paris rooftops. Nos. 63 and 64 look out upon Sacré-Coeur. ⊠ *63 rue Saint-Lazare, Opéra/Grands Boulevards, 75009* 🕾 *01–48–74–78–24* 🖶 *01–49–95–04–43* ⊕ *www.hotel-langlois.com* ✂ *24 rooms, 3 suites* △ *Dining room, minibars, cable TV, some pets allowed; no a/c* ⊟ *AE, MC, V* Ⓜ *Trinité.*

11ᵉ Arrondissement (Bastille)

$ ⊞ **Hôtel Beaumarchais.** This bold hotel serves as a gateway to the hip student and artist neighborhood of Oberkampf and the 11ᵉ and 20ᵉ arrondissements. Brightly colored vinyl armchairs, an industrial metal staircase, and glass tables mark the lobby. Out back, a small courtyard is decked in hardwood, a look you'll rarely see in Paris. The rooms hum with primary reds and yellows, some with Keith Haring prints on the walls. Kaleidoscopes of ceramic fragments tile the bathrooms. The Beaumarchais lures in artsy budget travelers; for the price and attention to detail, the popularity is justified. ⊠ *3 rue Oberkampf, République, 75011* ☎ *01–53–36–86–86* 🖷 *01–43–38–32–86* ⊕ *www. hotelbeaumarchais.com* ⤶ *31 rooms* ⚒ *Dining room, in-room safes, cable TV, some pets allowed; no a/c in some rooms* ⊟ *AE, MC, V* Ⓜ *Filles du Calvaire, Oberkampf.*

12ᵉArrondissement (Bastille/Gare de Lyon)

$$ ⊞ **Le Pavillon Bastille.** The transformation of this 19th-century *hôtel particulier* (across from the Opéra Bastille) into a mod, colorful, high-design hotel garnered both architectural awards and a fiercely loyal, hip clientele. Some clients take to the hotel's blue and gold color scheme, but others find it brash. ⊠ *65 rue de Lyon, Bastille/Nation, 75012* ☎ *01–43–43–65–65, 800/233–2552 in U.S.* 🖷 *01–43–43–96–52* ⊕ *www.pavillon-bastille.com* ⤶ *24 rooms, 1 suite* ⚒ *In-room data ports, in-room safes, minibars, cable TV, bar, Internet, some pets allowed, no-smoking floors* ⊟ *AE, DC, MC, V* Ⓜ *Bastille.*

14ᵉ Arrondissement (Montparnasse)

$$ ⊞ **Hôtel Lenox-Montparnasse.** Few budget hotels this close to the famous Dôme and Coupole brasseries and the Jardin du Luxembourg offer this level of service and amenities for the price. A smooth head-to-toe face-lift gave the largest (and best) rooms tiled fireplaces, white-painted exposed beams, and violet or beige color schemes. The small standard rooms—there's barely a suitcase-width between the wall and the foot of the bed—follow a more functional contemporary style with rich colors and printed bedspreads. ⊠ *15 rue Delambre, Montparnasse, 75014* ☎ *01–43–35–34–50* 🖷 *01–43–20–46–64* ⊕ *www.hotellenox.com* ⤶ *46 rooms, 6 suites* ⚒ *Dining room, room service, in-room data ports, in-room safes, minibars, cable TV, laundry service, parking (fee), no-smoking rooms* ⊟ *AE, DC, MC, V* Ⓜ *Vavin.*

16ᵉ Arrondissement (Arc de Triomphe/Le Bois)

★ $$$$ ⊞ **Hôtel Raphael.** The landmark and soigné Raphael was built in 1925 to cater to travelers spending a season in Paris, so every space is generously sized for such long, lavish stays—the closets, for instance, have room for ball gowns and plumed hats. Guest rooms, most with king-size beds, are turned out in 18th- and early-19th-century antiques and have 6-foot windows, Oriental rugs, silk damask wallpaper, chandeliers, and ornately carved wood paneling. Bathrooms are remarkably large; most have claw-foot bathtubs and separate massage-jet showers. The roof terrace, topped with a restaurant, has a panoramic view of the city, with the Arc de Triomphe looming in the foreground. ⊠ *17 av. Kléber, Trocadéro Eiffel Tower, 75116* ☎ *01–53–64–32–00* 🖷 *01–53–64–32–01*

⊕ www.raphael-hotel.com ↩ 52 rooms, 38 suites ⌂ 2 restaurants, room service, in-room data ports, in-room safes, some in-room hot tubs, minibars, cable TV with movies, gym, bar, Internet, some pets allowed (fee), no-smoking floors ⊟ AE, DC, MC, V Ⓜ Kléber.

$ ▦ **Hôtel Keppler.** On the border of the 8ᵉ and 16ᵉ arrondissements, near the Champs-Élysées, is this small, modernly outfitted hotel in a 19th-century building. The spacious, airy rooms have simple furnishings and floral upholsteries and upscale amenities (like room safes and an exterior restaurant room service) that you wouldn't expect for the price. Upper-floor rooms face the Eiffel Tower. All in all, a very good deal, given the chic neighborhood. *☒ 12 rue Keppler, Champs-Élysées, 75016 ☎ 01–47–20–65–05 ⊟ 01–47–23–02–29 ⊕ www.hotelkeppler.com ↩ 49 rooms ⌂ Cable TV, bar, no-smoking rooms; no a/c ⊟ AE, MC, V Ⓜ George V.*

NIGHTLIFE & THE ARTS

Updated by
Christopher
Pitts

With a heritage that includes the cancan, the Folies-Bergère, the Moulin Rouge, Mistinguett, and Josephine Baker, Paris is one city where no one has ever had to ask, "Is there any place exciting to go to tonight?" Today the city's nightlife and arts scenes are still filled with pleasures. Hear a chansonnier belt out Piaf, take in a *Victor/Victoria* show, catch a Molière play at the Comédie Française, or perhaps spot Madonna at the Buddha Bar. Information about what's going on in the city can be found in the weekly magazines (published every Wednesday) *Pariscope* (which has an English section), *L'Officiel des Spectacles,* and *Zurban.* Also look for *Aden* and *Figaroscope,* Wednesday supplements to the newspapers *Le Monde* and *Le Figaro* respectively. The **Paris Tourist Office** (☎ 08–36–68–31–12 ⊕ www.parisbienvenu.com) has a 24-hour hotline in English and a Web site listing events.

The best place to buy tickets is at the venue itself; try to purchase in advance, as many of the more popular performances sell out. Also try your hotel or a ticket agency, such as **Opéra Théâtre** (☒ 7 rue de Clichy, Montmartre, 9ᵉ ☎ 01–42–81–98–85 Ⓜ Trinité). Tickets for most concerts can be bought at **FNAC** (☒ 1–5 rue Pierre Lescot, Forum des Halles, 3rd level down, Beaubourg/Les Halles, 1ᵉʳ ☎ 08–92–68–36–22 Ⓜ Châtelet–Les Halles). The **Virgin Megastore** (☒52 av. des Champs-Élysées, Champs-Élysées, 8ᵉ ☎ 01–49–53–50–00 Ⓜ Franklin-D.-Roosevelt) also sells theater and concert tickets. Half-price tickets for many same-day theater performances are available at the **Kiosques Théâtre** (☒ Across from 15 pl. de la Madeleine, Opéra/Grands Boulevards Ⓜ Madeleine ☒ Outside Gare Montparnasse on pl. Raoul Dautry, Montparnasse, 15ᵉ Ⓜ Montparnasse-Bienvenüe); both are open Tuesday–Saturday 1:30–8 and Sunday 12:30–4. Expect to pay a €3 commission per ticket and to wait in line.

The Arts

Classical Music

Classical- and world-music concerts are held at the **Cité de la Musique** (☒ 221 av. Jean-Jaurès, Parc de la Villette, 19ᵉ ☎ 01–44–84–44–84

Ⓜ Porte de Pantin). The **Salle Pleyel** (✉ 252 rue du Faubourg–St-Honoré, Champs-Élysées, 8ᵉ ☎ 08–25–00–02–52 Ⓜ Ternes), a longtime regular venue for the Orchestre de Paris, is undergoing renovations and will be closed until early 2006. The **Théâtre des Champs-Élysées** (✉ 15 av. Montaigne, Champs-Élysées, 8ᵉ ☎ 01–49–52–50–50 Ⓜ Alma-Marceau), an Art Deco temple and famed site of the premiere of Stravinsky's 1913 *Le Sacre du Printemps,* hosts concerts and ballet. **Théâtre du Palais-Royal** (✉ 38 rue Montpensier, Louvre/Tuileries, 1ᵉʳ ☎ 01–42–97–59–81 Ⓜ Palais-Royal) is a sparkling 750-seat Italian theater bedecked in gold and purple. From January until June it's the setting for "Les Concerts du Palais-Royal": a series of performances of Baroque music, vocal recitals, and opera bouffe. Paris has a never-ending stream of inexpensive lunchtime and evening concerts in churches, some scheduled as part of the **Festival d'Art Sacré** (☎ 01–44–70–64–10 for information) between mid-November and Christmas. **Churches** with classical concerts (often free) include: **Notre-Dame, Sainte-Chapelle, St-Eustache, St-Germain-des-Prés, St-Julien-Le-Pauvre, St-Louis-en-l'Ile,** and **St-Roch.**

Dance

★ The **Opéra Garnier** (✉ Pl. de l'Opéra, Opéra/Grands Boulevards, 9ᵉ ☎ 08–92–69–78–68 ⊕ www.opera-de-paris.fr Ⓜ Opéra) is home to the reputable Paris Ballet. The **Opéra de la Bastille** (✉ Pl. de la Bastille, Bastille/Nation, 12ᵉ ☎ 08–92–69–78–68 ⊕ www.opera-de-paris.fr Ⓜ Bastille) occasionally hosts major dance troupes, often modern and avant-garde in tenor. Both here and at the Opéra Garnier venue, ballet production ticket prices usually range from about €4.61 to €60. At the **Théâtre de la Bastille** (✉ 76 rue de la Roquette, Bastille/Nation, 11ᵉ ☎ 01–43–57–42–14 Ⓜ Bastille), innovative modern dance companies perform. At its two houses, the **Théâtre de la Ville** (✉ 2 pl. du Châtelet, Beaubourg/Les Halles, 4ᵉ ☎ 01–42–74–22–77 for both Ⓜ Châtelet ✉ 31 rue des Abbesses, Montmartre, 18ᵉ Ⓜ Abbesses) presents the leading stars of contemporary dance.

Film

Parisians are far more addicted to the cinema as an art form than even Londoners or New Yorkers, as evidenced by the number of movie theaters in the city. Many theaters, especially in principal tourist areas such as the Champs-Élysées, St-Germain-des-Prés, Les Halles, and the boulevard des Italiens near the Opéra, show first-run films in English. Check the weekly guides for a movie of your choice. Look for the initials *v.o.,* which mean *version originale,* that is, not dubbed. Cinema admission runs from €7.50 to €9; many theaters reduce rates slightly on Monday and for some morning shows. Most theaters will post two show times: the first is the *séance,* when commercials, previews, and sometimes short films start, and the second is the actual feature presentation time, which is usually 10–20 minutes later. Paris has many small cinemas showing classic and independent films, especially in the Latin Quarter. Screenings are often organized around retrospectives (check "Festivals" in weekly guides). One of the best venues for the *cinéphile* (movie lover) brought up on Fellini, Bergman, and Resnais is the **Cinémathèque Française** (✉ 42 bd. de Bonne-Nouvelle, Opéra/Grands Boulevards ☎ 01–56–26–01–01

Ⓜ Bonne-Nouvelle ⊠ Palais de Chaillot, 7 av. Albert de Mun, Trocadéro ☎ 01–56–26–01–01 Ⓜ Trocadéro). Its new home, designed by Frank Gehry, is set to open in April 2005 and will include a museum and video library, as well as four theaters. The **Balzac** (⊠ 1 rue Balzac, Champs-Élysées, 8ᵉ ☎ 01–45–61–10–60 Ⓜ George-V) frequently hosts talks by directors before screenings.

★ **La Pagode** (⊠ 57 bis rue de Babylone, Trocadéro/Tour Eiffel, 7ᵉ ☎ 08–92–89–28–92 Ⓜ St-François Xavier)—where else but in Paris would you find movies screened in an antique pagoda? A Far East fantasy, this structure was built in 1896 for the wife of the owner of the Au Bon Marché department store. Who can resist seeing a flick in the silk-and-gilt Salle Japonaise? Come early to have tea in the bamboo-fringed garden.

Opera

Paris offers some of the best opera in the world—and thousands know it. Consequently, getting tickets to a performance of the **Opera National de Paris** at its two main venues, the Opéra de la Bastille and the Opéra Garnier, can be difficult on short notice, so it's a good idea to plan ahead. Bookings by mail begin roughly two months before the date of performance. Buying from scalpers is not recommended, as they have been known to sell counterfeit tickets. For the season's schedule, contact the **Opéra de la Bastille** (⊠ 120 rue de Lyon, Bastille/Nation, 75012) in advance. The **Opéra de la Bastille** (⊠ Pl. de la Bastille, Bastille/Nation, 12ᵉ ☎ 08–92–89–90–90 ⊕ www.opera-de-paris.fr Ⓜ Bastille), a modern auditorium, has taken over the role of Paris's main opera house from the Opéra Garnier. However, nothing beats seeing a grand production of a Verdi or Mozart opera within the 19th-century splendor of the Opéra Garnier, and the good news is that this historic house still hosts a limited number of Opéra National de Paris productions every season (information on these productions is contained within the Opera de Paris Web site listed *above*). Note that if a certain opera is presented, it's only mounted for a minirun of one to two weeks, not in a repertory schedule throughout the season. At both the Bastille and Garnier houses, opera tickets range from about €10 to €114; cheaper seats in the Garnier house are sometimes—and notoriously—view-obstructed (partial-view in French is *visibilité partielle*). The opera season usually runs September through July and the box office is open Monday–Saturday 11–6:30. The Web site is very informative and complete and also allows you to order tickets. For performances at either the Opéra de la Bastille or the Palais Garnier, seats go on sale at the box office two weeks before any given show or a month ahead by phone or online; you must go in person to buy the cheapest tickets. Sometimes rush tickets, if available, are offered 15 minutes before a performance. The box office is open 11 to 6:30 daily. The **Opéra Comique** (⊠ 5 rue Favart, Opéra/Grands Boulevards, 2ᵉ ☎ 08–25–00–00–58 Ⓜ Richelieu-Drouot) is a lofty old hall where comic operas are often performed. **Théâtre Musical de Paris** (⊠ Pl. du Châtelet, Beaubourg/Les Halles, 1ᵉʳ ☎ 01–40–28–28–40 Ⓜ Châtelet), better known as the Théâtre du Châtelet, puts on some of the finest opera productions in the city and regularly attracts international divas like Ce-

cilia Bartoli and Anne-Sofie von Otter. It also plays host to classical concerts, dance performances, and the occasional play.

Theater

A number of theaters line the Grands Boulevards between Opéra and
République, but there's no Paris equivalent of Broadway or the West
End. Shows are mostly in French. Information about performances can
be obtained on a Web site ⊕ www.theatreonline.fr, which lists 170 different theaters, offers critiques, and provides an online reservation service. **Bouffes du Nord** (⊠ 37 bis bd. de la Chapelle, Stalingrad/La Chapelle,
10ᵉ ☎ 01–46–07–34–50 Ⓜ La Chapelle) is the wonderfully atmospheric theater that is home to English director Peter Brook. The **Comédie-
Française** (⊠ Pl. Colette, Louvre/Tuileries, 1ᵉʳ ☎ 01–44–58–15–15
Ⓜ Palais-Royal) is a distinguished venue that stages classical French drama.
The **Théâtre de la Huchette** (⊠ 23 rue de la Huchette, Latin Quarter, 5ᵉ
☎ 01–43–26–38–99 Ⓜ St-Michel), a tiny Left Bank theater, has been
staging Ionesco's *The Bald Soprano* every night since 1950. The **Odéon
Théâtre de l'Europe** (⊠ 8 bd. Berthier, Clichy, 17ᵉ ☎ 01–44–85–40–40
Ⓜ Porte de Clichy) is undergoing extensive renovations at the moment
and has moved to this Clichy address until 2005.

Nightlife

The City of Light truly lights up after dark. So, if you want to paint the
town *rouge* after dutifully pounding the parquet in museums all day,
there's a dazzling array of options to discover. The hottest spots are around
Ménilmontant, the Bastille, and the Marais. The Left Bank is definitely
a lot less happening. The Champs-Élysées is making a comeback, though
the clientele remains predominantly foreign. Take note: the last métro
runs between 12:30 AM and 1 AM (you can take a taxi, but they can be
hard to find, especially on weekend nights). For information about
dates for the dazzling one-night only soirees, keep an eye out for the
free listings mag *Lylo* or flyers in bars.

Bars & Clubs

The famous brasserie **Alcazar** (⊠ 62 rue Mazarine, St-Germain-des-
Prés, 6ᵉ ☎ 01–53–10–19–99 Ⓜ Odéon) was Sir Terence Conran's first
makeover of a Parisian landmark, and comes complete with a stylish
bar on the first floor, where you can sip a glass of wine under the huge
glass roof. From Wednesday to Saturday a DJ spins either lounge or Latin
music. **Les Bains** (⊠ 7 rue du Bourg-l'Abbé, République, 3ᵉ
☎ 01–48–87–01–80 Ⓜ Étienne-Marcel) is very much a Parisian institution. The upstairs bar and restaurant is generally packed wall-to-wall
with stars, while downstairs house music rules on the dance floors. First,
however, you have to get past the particularly selective door policy. **Bar-
rio Latino** (⊠ 46–48 rue du Faubourg-St.-Antoine, Bastille, 12ᵉ
☎ 01–55–78–84–75 Ⓜ Bastille) is a lush cross of casbah, Old Havana,
and SoHo loft that pulls a very mixed crowd of hipsters, including
everyone from threadbare art students to ambitious young lawyers.
Though pricey, it can be a fun scene; it could be more so if the drinks
were better. Alas, the food is even worse. **Batofar** (⊠ 11 quai François
Mauriac, République, 11ᵉ ☎ 01–45–83–33–06 Ⓜ Quai-de-la-Gare) is

an old lighthouse tug, now refitted to include a bar, a club, and a concert venue that's become one of the hippest spots in town. While the Batofar tends to have better music, the neighboring glass-paneled *Guinguette Pirate* and floating garden *El Alamein* edge out the tugboat when it comes to tippling with a view. **Le Bilboquet** (⊠ 13 rue St-Benoît, St-Germain-des-Prés, 6ᵉ ☎ 01–45–48–81–84 Ⓜ St-Germain-des-Prés) is the place to sip cocktails in a ritzy Belle Epoque salon while a jazz combo sets the mood. **Café Charbon** (⊠ 109 rue Oberkampf, Oberkampf, 11ᵉ ☎ 01–43–57–55–13 Ⓜ St-Maur, Parmentier) is a beautifully restored 19th-century café with a trendsetting crowd that has made this place one of the mainstays of trendy Okerkampf. **Chez Prune** (⊠ 71 quai de Valmy, République, 10ᵉ ☎ 01–42–41–30–47 Ⓜ République) is one of the most charming cafés in Paris *and* it has one of the best terraces right in front of the Canal St-Martin. **La Fabrique** (⊠ 53 rue du Faubourg St-Antoine, Bastille/Nation, 11ᵉ ☎ 01–43–07–67–07 Ⓜ Bastille) brews its own beer (look out for the huge copper vats by the entrance) and really gets going after 9 PM, when a DJ hits the turntables. **Le Fumoir** (⊠ 6 rue Amiral de Coligny, Louvre/Tuileries, 1ᵉʳ ☎ 01–42–92–00–24 Ⓜ Louvre), a fashionable spot for cocktails, has a large bar, a library, and comfy leather couches. **Man Ray** (⊠ 34 rue Marbeuf, Champs-Élysées, 8ᵉ ☎ 01–56–88–36–36 Ⓜ Franklin-D.-Roosevelt) keeps its profile high, not surprising given that it is owned by Johnny Depp, Sean Penn, and Simply Red's Mick Hucknall. Man Ray becomes Woman Ray on Monday—an exclusive networking club for women. The ravishing Asian–Art Deco style is reminiscent of a slightly Disneyesque 1930s supper club in Chinatown. **Polo Room** (⊠ 3 rue Lord Byron, Champs-Élysées, 8ᵉ ☎ 01–40–74–07–78 Ⓜ George-V) is the very first martini bar in Paris; there are polo photos on the wall, regular live jazz concerts, and DJs every Friday and Saturday night.

GAY & LESBIAN BARS & CLUBS — Gay and lesbian bars and clubs are mostly concentrated in the Marais and include some of the most happening addresses in the city. **Le Dépôt** (⊠ 10 rue aux Ours, République, 3ᵉ ☎ 01–44–54–96–96 Ⓜ Etienne Marcel) is a bar, club, and backroom for men. The mostly male crowd at **L'Open Café** (⊠ 17 rue des Archives, Le Marais, 4ᵉ ☎ 01–42–72–26–18 Ⓜ Hôtel-de-Ville) comes for the sunny decor and convivial ambience. **Queen** (⊠ 102 av. des Champs-Élysées, Champs-Élysées, 8ᵉ ☎ 01–53–89–08–90 Ⓜ George-V) is one of the hottest nightspots in Paris: although it's predominantly gay, everyone else lines up to get in, too. **Les Scandaleuses** (⊠ 8 rue des Écouffes, Le Marais, 4ᵉ ☎ 01–48–87–39–26 Ⓜ St-Paul) is probably Paris's hippest lesbian hangout. Men are also allowed in (in small numbers), as long as they are accompanied by "scandalous women."

HOTEL BARS — Some of Paris's best hotel bars mix historic pedigrees with hushed elegance—and others go for a modern, edgy luxe. Following are some perennial favorites. **Hôtel Le Bristol** (⊠ 112 rue du Faubourg–St-Honoré, Champs-Élysées, 8ᵉ ☎ 01–53–43–43–42 Ⓜ Miromesnil) attracts the rich and powerful. **Hôtel Costes** (⊠ 239 rue Saint-Honoré, Louvre/Tuileries, 1ᵉʳ ☎ 01–42–44–50–25 Ⓜ Tuileries) draws many big names in the fashion world during Collections weeks. **Hôtel Lutétia** (⊠ 45 bd. Raspail,

Montparnasse, 6ᵉ ☎ 01–49–54–46–09 Ⓜ Sèvres-Babylone) has three soigné bars, one of which, the Saint Germain, is a seductive boîte with live jazz four nights a week. **Hôtel Plaza Athénée** (✉ 25 ave. Montaigne, Champs-Élysées, 8ᵉʳ ☎ 01–53–67–66–00 Ⓜ Alma Marceau) is Paris's perfect chill-out spot; the bar was designed by Starck protegé Patrick Jouin. **Hotel Vernet** (✉ 25 rue Vernet, Champs-Élysées, 8ᵉ ☎ 01–44–31–98–06 Ⓜ George-V) is where you'll find Le Jaipur, a bit of the old Raj in Paris, and wonderful fresh herb-based cocktails. At the **Ritz** (✉ 15 pl. Vendôme, Louvre/Tuileries, 1ᵉʳ ☎ 01–43–16–33–65 Ⓜ Opéra), the Hemingway Bar has Colin Field, the best barman in Paris, and Papa memorabilia (this is where the writer drank to the liberation of Paris), but with a dress code and cognac aux truffles on the menu; however, the Ritz's Vendôme bar is far prettier.

Cabaret

Paris's cabarets are household names, though mostly just tourists go to them these days. Prices range from €40 (simple admission plus one drink) to more than €125 (dinner plus show). **Crazy Horse** (✉ 12 av. George-V, Champs-Élysées, 8ᵉ ☎ 01–47–23–32–32 Ⓜ Alma-Marceau) is one of the best-known cabarets, with pretty dancers and a new risqué routine called "teasing" that involves top hats, fishnets, dark pink lipstick, and little else. **Au Lapin Agile** (✉ 22 rue des Saules, Montmartre, 18ᵉ ☎ 01–46–06–85–87 Ⓜ Lamarck-Caulaincourt), the fabled artists' hangout in Montmartre, considers itself the doyen of cabarets and is a miraculous survivor from the early 20th century; prices at "the Nimble Rabbit" are lower than elsewhere, but then it's more a large bar than a full-blown cabaret. **Lido** (✉ 116 bis av. des Champs-Élysées, Champs-Élysées, 8ᵉ ☎ 01–40–76–56–10 Ⓜ George-V) stars the famous Bluebell Girls; the owners claim that no show in Las Vegas can rival it for special effects.

Le Limonaire (✉ 21 rue Bergère, Opéra/Grands Boulevards, 9ᵉ ☎ 01–45–23–33–33 Ⓜ Grands Boulevards), a small restaurant, simply oozes with Parisian charm. This is the kind of place where you could imagine Edith Piaf belting out "*Je ne regrette rien,*" and, in fact, imagination is often not required at 10 PM, Tuesday to Sunday, when the service stops and a singer takes to the floor. The house specialty is *la chanson française,* and one of its finest guest artists is the modern-day Little Sparrow, Kalifa. That old favorite at the foot of Montmartre, **Moulin Rouge** (✉ 82 bd. de Clichy, Montmartre, 18ᵉ ☎ 01–53–09–82–82 Ⓜ Blanche), mingles the Doriss Girls, the cancan, and a horse in an extravagant (and expensive) spectacle. **Nirvana** (✉ 3 av. Matignon, Champs-Élysées, 8ᵉ ☎ 01–53–89–18–91 Ⓜ Champs-Élysées–Clemenceau) is Claude Challe of Buddha Bar fame's latest offering on the nightlife altar. Nirvana is a haven of mauve and sequins, with "Spiri'tea" in the afternoons presided over by tai-chi and yogi masters. **Paradis Latin** (✉ 28 rue du Cardinal Lemoine, Latin Quarter, 5ᵉ ☎ 01–43–25–28–28 Ⓜ Cardinal Lemoine) is the liveliest and trendiest cabaret on the Left Bank.

Jazz Clubs

For nightly schedules consult the specialty magazines *Jazz Hot, Jazzman,* or *Jazz Magazine*. Nothing gets going 'til 10 PM or 11 PM; entry prices vary widely from about €10 to more than €25. **Caveau de la Huchette** (⌧ 5 rue de la Huchette, Quartier Latin, 5ᵉ ☎ 01–43–26–65–05 Ⓜ St-Michel), one of the only surviving cellar clubs from the 1940s, is a Paris classic, big with swing dancers and Dixieland musicians. At the Méridien Hotel, near Porte Maillot, the **Lionel Hampton Jazz Club** (⌧ 81 bd. Gouvion-St-Cyr, Porte Maillot, 17ᵉ ☎ 01–40–68–30–42 Ⓜ Porte Maillot) hosts a roster of international jazz players. **New Morning** (⌧ 7 rue des Petites-Écuries, Opéra/Grands Boulevards, 10ᵉ ☎ 01–45–23–51–41 Ⓜ Château-d'Eau) is a premier spot for serious fans of avant-garde jazz, as well as folk and world music. The greatest names in French and international jazz have been playing at **Le Petit Journal** (⌧ 71 bd. St-Michel, Latin Quarter, 5ᵉ ☎ 01–43–26–28–59 Ⓜ Luxembourg) for decades; it now specializes in Dixieland jazz (it's closed Sunday).

Rock, Pop & World-Music Venues

Upcoming concerts are posted on boards in FNAC and Virgin Megastores. **L'Élysée Montmartre** is one of the prime venues for emerging French and international rock groups. **L'Olympia** (⌧ 28 bd. des Capucines, Opéra/Grands Boulevards, 9ᵉ ☎ 08–92–69–23–00 Ⓜ Madeleine), a legendary venue once favored by Jacques Brel and Edith Piaf, still plays host to leading French vocalists. **Palais Omnisports de Paris-Bercy** (⌧ 8 bd. de Bercy, Bercy/Tolbiac, 12ᵉ ☎ 08–92–69–23–00 Ⓜ Bercy) is the largest venue in Paris; English and American pop stars shake their spangles here (we see you, Mademoiselle Spears). **Zenith** (⌧ Parc de la Villette, 19ᵉ ☎ 01–42–08–60–00 Ⓜ Porte-de-Pantin) stages large rock shows.

SPORTS & THE OUTDOORS

Bicycling

★ The amazingly popular **Tour de France** (⊕ www.letour.fr) consists of a grueling three weeks of pure physical torture as the world's best cyclists cover more than 2,000 mi of French terrain. The athletes finish in a blaze of adulation, as tradition requires and the winner no doubt merits, on the Champs-Élysées. The race usually begins the end of June or beginning of July and finishes in Paris sometime in July. Maps of Paris's main cycle paths can be found in the free brochure *Paris A Vélo,* available in any city hall or at one of the tourist offices. Paris's two large parks, the Bois de Boulogne and the Bois de Vincennes, are the best places for biking.

The following places rent bikes, and many of these establishments also organize guided excursions. **Bike 'n Roller** (⌧ 38 rue Fabert, Invalides/Eiffel Tower, 7ᵉ ☎ 01–45–50–38–27 ⊕ www.bikenroller.fr Ⓜ La Tour
★ Maubourg) hires bikes for €12 for three hours and €17 for the day. **Fat Tire Bike Tours** (⌧ 24 rue Edgar Faure, Trocadéro/Eiffel Tower 15ᵉ, ☎01–56–58–10–54 ⊕www.FatTireBikeToursParis.com ⒨Dupleix), formerly Mike's Bike Tours, organizes fun guided trips around Paris daily from March to November and by appointment from December to February. Tours are peppered with historical information and give a great overview of the city; tours of Versailles are available, too. Day tours run €24, night tours €28. **Pariscyclo** (⌧ Rond Point de Jardin d'Acclimata-

tion, in the Bois de Boulogne, Bois de Boulogne ☎01–47–47–76–50 Ⓜ Les Sablons) is the perfect place for bike rentals if you want to explore the Bois de Boulogne.

Spectator Sports

Information on upcoming events can be found in the weekly guide *Pariscope,* on posters around the city, or by calling the ticket agencies of **FNAC** (☎ 08–03–80–88–03). You'll find a popular ticket outlet in the **Virgin Megastore** (☎ 08–03–02–30–24). A wide range of sporting events takes place at the **Palais Omnisports de Paris-Bercy** (✉ 8 bd. de Bercy, Bercy/Tolbiac, 12ᵉ ☎ 08–03–03–00–31 Ⓜ Bercy). Details of events are also on their Web site: www.bercy.com. The **Parc des Princes** (✉ 24 rue du Cdt. Guilbaud, Passy-Auteuil, 16ᵉ ☎ 08–25–07–50–78 Ⓜ Porte de Saint-Cloud) is the site of the home matches of the city's soccer team, ★ Paris St-Germain. **Roland-Garros** (✉ 2 av. Gordon Bennett, Bois de Boulogne, 16ᵉ ☎ 01–47–43–48–00 ⊕ www.frenchopen.com Ⓜ Porte d'Auteuil) is the venue for the French Open tennis tournament during the last week of May and first week of June. **Stade de France** (✉ St-Denis ☎ 01–55–93–00–00 ⊕ www.stade-de-france.com Ⓜ La Plaine–Stade de France) is home to the French national soccer and rugby teams.

SHOPPING

Updated by
Nicola Keegan

In the most beautiful city in the world, it's no surprise to discover that the local greengrocer displays his tomatoes as artistically as Cartier does its rubies. The capital of style, Paris has an endless panoply of delights to tempt shop-'til-you-droppers, from grand couturiers like Dior to the funkiest flea markets. Today every neighborhood seems to reflect a unique attitude and style: designer extravagance and haute couture characterize avenue Montaigne and rue Faubourg St-Honoré; classic sophistication pervades St-Germain; avant-garde style dresses up the Marais; while a hip feel suffuses the area around Les Halles.

There's something for everyone and bargains are just not as elusive here as they were of old. Why not try on that little black dress from the 1950s hanging in the window with your name written all over it? Or snag that kitsch-but-cute coffee mug with the famous laughing cow on it for your favorite morning grouch? For you bargain hunters, some words to remember: *soldes,* sale; *fripes,* secondhand clothing; *dépôt vent,* secondhand shop; and *dégriffé,* designer labels, often from last year's collection, for sale at a deep discount. Happy hunting.

If you're from outside the European Union, age 15 and over, and stay in France and/or the European Union for less than six months, you can benefit from Value Added Tax (V.A.T.) reimbursements, known in France as TVA, while the sum remitted to non-EU folk is known as the *détaxe.* To qualify, non-EU residents must spend at least €175 in a single store on a single day. Refunds vary from 13% to 19.6% and are mailed to you by check or credited to your charge card. Remember: If you want to check out—and shop—the latest and greatest that Paris has to offer, pick up the newest issues of style magazines at neighborhood kiosks (or, better yet, back home): *French Vogue, Maison Française,* and *Elle Decor* are just a few of the publications that are filled with the newest finds and *en dit* (gossip).

Shopping by Neighborhood

Avenue Montaigne

Shopping doesn't come much more chic than on avenue Montaigne, with its graceful town mansions housing some of the top names in international fashion: **Chanel, Dior, Céline, Valentino, Krizia, Ungaro, Prada, Dolce & Gabbana,** and many more. Neighboring rue François 1er and avenue George-V are also lined with many designer boutiques: **Versace, Fendi, Givenchy,** and **Balenciaga.**

Champs-Élysées

Cafés and movie theaters keep the once-chic Champs-Élysées active 24 hours a day, but the invasion of exchange banks, car showrooms, and fast-food chains has lowered the tone. Four glitzy 20th-century arcade malls—**Galerie du Lido, Le Rond-Point, Le Claridge,** and **Élysées 26**—capture most of the retail action, not to mention the **Gap** and the **Disney Store. Sephora** has reintroduced a touch of elegance but the cool factor will only soar skyward when the mothership **Louis Vuitton** (on the Champs-Élysées proper) will reopen in winter 2004–05 after a year of renovations.

The Faubourg St-Honoré

This chic shopping and residential area is also quite a political hub. It's home to the Élysée Palace as well as the official residences of the American and British ambassadors. The Paris branches of **Sotheby's** and **Christie's** and renowned antiques galleries such as **Didier Aaron** add artistic flavor. Boutiques include **Hermès, Lanvin, Gucci, Chloé,** and **Christian Lacroix.**

Left Bank

For an array of bedazzling boutiques with hyper-picturesque goods—antique toy theaters, books on gardening—and the most fascinating antiques stores in town, be sure to head to the area around rue Jacob, nearly lined with *antiquaires,* and the streets around super-posh place Furstenberg. After decades of clustering on the Right Bank's venerable shopping avenues, the high-fashion houses have stormed the Rive Gauche. The first to arrive were **Sonia Rykiel** and **Yves St-Laurent** in the late '60s. Some of the more recent arrivals include **Christian Dior, Giorgio Armani,** and **Louis Vuitton.** Rue des St-Pères and rue de Grenelle are lined with designer names.

Louvre–Palais Royal

The elegant and eclectic shops clustered in the 18th-century arcades of the Palais-Royal sell such items as antiques, toy soldiers, cosmetics, jewelry, and vintage designer dresses.

Le Marais

The Marais is a mixture of many moods and many influences; its lovely, impossibly narrow cobblestone streets are filled with some of the most original, small name, nonglobal goods to be had—a true haven for the original gift. Avant-garde designers **Azzedine Alaïa** and Tsumori Chistato have boutiques within a few blocks of stately place des Vosges and the Picasso and Carnavalet museums. The Marais is also one of the few neighborhoods that has a lively Sunday shopping scene.

Opéra to La Madeleine

Two major department stores—**Au Printemps** and **Galeries Lafayette**—dominate boulevard Haussmann, behind Paris's ornate 19th-century Opéra Garnier. Place de la Madeleine tempts many with its two luxurious food stores, **Fauchon** and **Hédiard.**

Place Vendôme & Rue de la Paix

The magnificent 17th-century place Vendôme, home of the Ritz Hotel, and rue de la Paix, leading north from Vendôme, are where you can find the world's most elegant jewelers: **Cartier, Boucheron, Bulgari,** and **Van Cleef and Arpels.** The most exclusive, however, is the discreet **Jar's.**

Place des Victoires & Rue Étienne Marcel

The graceful, circular place des Victoires, near the Palais-Royal, is the playground of fashion icons such as **Kenzo,** while **Comme des Garçons** and Yohji Yamamoto line rue Étienne Marcel. In the nearby oh-so-charming Galerie Vivienne shopping arcade, **Jean-Paul Gaultier** has a shop that has been renovated by Philippe Starck, and definitely worth a stop.

Rue St-Honoré

A fashionable set makes its way to rue St-Honoré to shop at Paris's trendiest boutique, **Colette.** The street is lined with numerous designer names, while on nearby rue Cambon you'll find the wonderfully elegant **Maria Luisa** and the main **Chanel** boutique.

Department Stores

For an overview of Paris *mode,* visit *les grands magasins,* Paris's monolithic department stores. Most are open Monday through Saturday from about 9:30 AM to 7 PM, and some are open until 10 PM one weekday evening.

★ **Au Bon Marché** (✉ 24 rue de Sèvres, St-Germain-des-Prés, 7e ☎ 01–44–39–80–00 Ⓜ Sèvres-Babylone) has undergone a complete facelift and is now Paris's chicest department store, with an impressive array of designers represented for both men and women. La Grande Épicerie is one of the largest groceries in Paris and a gourmand's home away from home. **Bazar de l'Hôtel de Ville** (✉ 52–64 rue de Rivoli, Beaubourg/Les Halles, 4e ☎ 01–42–74–90–00 Ⓜ Hôtel de Ville), better known as BHV, has minimal fashion offerings but is noteworthy for its enormous basement hardware store. **La Samaritaine** (✉ 19 rue de la Monnaie, Louvre/Tuileries, 1er ☎ 01–40–41–20–20 Ⓜ Pont-Neuf or Châtelet) has the Toupary restaurant with magnificent views of the Seine. **Au Printemps** (✉ 64 bd. Haussmann, Opéra/Grands Boulevards, 9e ☎ 01–42–82–50–00 Ⓜ Havre-Caumartin, Opéra, or Auber) has everything plus a whopping six floors dedicated to men's fashion. **Galeries Lafayette** (✉ 40 bd. Haussmann, Opéra/Grands Boulevards, 9e ☎ 01–42–82–34–56 Ⓜ Chaussée d'Antin, Opéra, or Havre-Caumartin) is dangerous—the granddaddy of them all—everything you never even dreamt of and then some.

Budget

Monoprix (✉ 21 av. de l'Opéra, Opéra/Grands Boulevards, 1ᵉʳ
☎ 01–42–61–78–08 Ⓜ Opéra ✉ 6 av. de la Plaine, Nation, 20ᵉ
☎ 01–43–73–17–59 Ⓜ Nation ✉ 50 rue de Rennes, St-Germain-des-
Prés, 6ᵉ ☎ 01–45–48–18–08 Ⓜ St-Germain-des-Prés) is the French
dime store par excellence—with scores of branches throughout the
city—and stocks inexpensive everyday items like toothpaste, groceries,
toys, and paper. It also carries inexpensive children's clothes and makeup
of surprisingly good quality.

Markets

The lively atmosphere that reigns in most of Paris's open-air food markets makes them a sight worth seeing even if you don't want or need to
buy anything. Every neighborhood has one, though many are open
only a few days each week. Sunday morning until 1 PM is usually a good
time to go. Many of the better-known markets are in areas you'd visit
for sightseeing; here's a list of the top bets. **Boulevard Raspail** (✉ Between
rue de Rennes and rue du Cherche-Midi, Latin Quarter, 6ᵉ Ⓜ Rennes),
has a great Sunday organic market. **Rue de Buci** (✉ St-Germain-des-Prés,
6ᵉ Ⓜ Odéon), in the chic and lively St-Germain-des-Prés quarter, is
closed Sunday PM and Monday. **Rue Mouffetard** (✉ Latin Quarter, 5ᵉ
Ⓜ Place Monge), near the Jardin des Plantes, is best on weekends. **Rue
Montorgueuil** (✉ Beaubourg/Les Halles, 1ᵉʳ Ⓜ Châtelet Les Halles) is closed
Monday. **Rue Lepic** (✉ Montmartre, 18ᵉ Ⓜ Blanche or Abbesses) is best
on weekends. The **Marché d'Aligre** (✉ Rue d'Aligre, Bastille/Nation,
12ᵉ Ⓜ Ledru-Rollin), open until 1 PM every day except Monday, is a bit
farther out but is the cheapest market in Paris; on weekends a small flea
market is also held here.

On Paris's northern boundary, the **Marché aux Puces** (Ⓜ Porte de Clig-
nancourt), which takes place Saturday through Monday, is a century-
old labyrinth of alleyways packed with antiques dealers' booths and junk
stalls spreading for more than a square mile; arrive early. On the southern and eastern sides of the city—at **Porte de Vanves** (Ⓜ Porte de Vanves)
and Porte de Montreuil—are other, smaller flea markets. Vanves is a hit
with the fashion set and specializes in smaller objects—mirrors, textiles,
handbags, clothing, and glass. Arrive early if you want to find a bargain, the good stuff goes fast and stalls are liable to be packed up before noon.

Shopping Arcades

Paris's 19th-century commercial arcades, called *passages* or *galeries* are
the forerunners of the modern mall. Glass roofs, decorative pillars, and
mosaic floors give the passages character. The major arcades are on the
Right Bank in central Paris. **Galerie Vivienne** (✉ 4 rue des Petits-Champs,
Opéra/Grands Boulevards, 2ᵉ Ⓜ Bourse) is home to a range of interesting shops, including **Jean-Paul Gautier's** Philippe Starck–designed fan-
★ tasy, an excellent tearoom, and a quality wine shop. **Passage du Grand-Cerf**
(✉ Entrances on rue Dussoubs, rue St-Denis, Beaubourg/Les Halles, 4ᵉ
Ⓜ Étienne-Marcel) is a pretty, glass-roofed gallery filled with crafts

shops offering an innovative selection of jewelry, paintings, and ceramics. **Passage Jouffroy** (✉ 12 bd. Montmartre, Montmartre, 2ᵉ Ⓜ Montmartre) is full of shops selling toys, postcards, antique canes, and perfumes. **Passage des Panoramas** (✉ 11 bd. Montmartre, Montmartre, 2ᵉ Ⓜ Montmartre), built in 1800, is the oldest of them all. The elegant **Galerie Véro-Dodat** (✉ 19 rue Jean-Jacques Rousseau, Louvre/Tuileries, 1ᵉʳ Ⓜ Louvre) has shops selling old-fashioned toys, contemporary art, and stringed instruments. It's best known, however, for its antiques stores.

Specialty Stores

Accessories, Cosmetics & Perfumes

By Terry (✉ Galerie Véro-Dodat, Louvre/Tuileries, 1ᵉʳ ☎ 01–44–76–00–76 Ⓜ Louvre, Palais-Royal) is the brainchild of Yves Saint Laurent's former director of makeup, Terry de Gunzberg; it offers her own brand of "ready-to-wear" cosmetics as well as a personalized cosmetics service. **E. Goyard** (✉ 233 rue St-Honoré, Louvre/Tuileries, 1ᵉʳ ☎ 01–42–60–57–04 Ⓜ Tuileries) has been making the finest luggage since 1853. **Christian Louboutin** (✉ 19 rue Jean-Jacques Rousseau, Louvre/Tuileries, 1ᵉʳ ☎ 01–42–36–05–31 Ⓜ Louvre) is famous for his wacky but elegant shoes, trademark blood-red soles, and impressive client list (Caroline of Monaco, Catherine Deneuve, Elizabeth Taylor). **Sabbia Rosa** (✉ 73 rue des Sts-Pères, St-Germain-des-Prés, 6ᵉ ☎ 01–45–48–88–37 Ⓜ St-Germain-des-Prés) sells French lingerie favored by celebrities like Catherine Deneuve and Claudia Schiffer. **Les Salons du Palais Royal Shiseido** (✉ Jardins du Palais-Royal, 142 Galerie de Valois, 25 rue de Valois, Louvre/Tuileries, 1ᵉʳ ☎ 01–49–27–09–09 Ⓜ Palais-Royal) is a magical place with marble floors and purple walls that exclusively sells the scents Serge Lutens dreams up for the Japanese cosmetics firm.

Bookstores (English-Language)

The scenic open-air bookstalls along the Seine sell secondhand books (mostly in French), prints, and souvenirs. Numerous French-language bookstores—specializing in a wide range of topics, including art, film, literature, and philosophy—are found in the Latin Quarter and around St-Germain-des-Prés. For English-language books try these stores: **Brentano's** (✉ 37 av. de l'Opéra, Opéra/Grands Boulevards, 2ᵉ ☎ 01–42–61–52–50 Ⓜ Opéra) is stocked with everything from classics to children's titles. **Galignani** (✉ 224 rue de Rivoli, Louvre/Tuileries, 1ᵉʳ ☎ 01–42–60–76–07 Ⓜ Tuileries) is especially known for its extensive collection of art and coffee-table books. **The Red Wheelbarrow** (✉ 22 rue St-Paul, Le Marais, 4ᵉ ☎ 01–42–77–42–17 Ⓜ St-Paul ✉ 13 rue St-Charles, Le Marais, 4ᵉ ☎ 01–40–26–76–20 Ⓜ St-Paul) is *the* anglophone bookstore—if it was written in English, they can get it. It also has a complete academic section and every literary review you can think of. **Shakespeare and Company** (✉ 37 rue de la Bûcherie, 5ᵉ, Latin Quarter ☎ 01–43–26–96–50 Ⓜ St-Michel), the sentimental Left Bank favorite, is named after the publishing house that first edited James Joyce's *Ulysses*. Nowadays, it specializes in expatriate literature. The staff tends to be rather pretentious, but the shelves of secondhand books hold real bargains. Poets give readings upstairs on Monday at 8 PM; there are also tea-party talks on Sunday at 4 PM. **Village Voice** (✉ 6 rue Princesse, St-Germain-des-Prés, 6ᵉ ☎ 01–46–33–36–47 Ⓜ Mabillon) hosts regular literary readings.

Clothing

MENSWEAR **Berluti** (✉ 26 rue Marbeuf, Champs-Élysées, 8ᵉ ☎ 01–53–93–97–97 Ⓜ Franklin-D.-Roosevelt) has been making the most exclusive men's shoes for more than a century. **Charvet** (✉ 28 pl. Vendôme, Opéra/Grands Boulevards, 1ᵉʳ ☎ 01–42–60–30–70 Ⓜ Opéra) is the Parisian equivalent of a Savile Row tailor. **Le Printemps de l'Homme** (✉ 61 rue Caumartin, Opéra/Grands Boulevards, 9ᵉ ☎ 01–42–82–50–00 Ⓜ Havre-Caumartin) has six floors of designer suits, sportswear, coats, ties, and accessories.

WOMENSWEAR It doesn't matter, say the French, that fewer and fewer of their top couture houses are still headed by compatriots. It's the chic elegance, the classic ambience, the *je ne sais quoi*, that remains undeniably Gallic. Here are some meccas for Paris chic. **Azzedine Alaïa** (✉ 7 rue de Moussy, Le Marais, 4ᵉ ☎ 01–42–72–19–19 Ⓜ Hôtel-de-Ville) is the undisputed

★ "king of cling" and a supermodel favorite. **Chanel** (✉ 42 av. Montaigne, Champs-Élysées, 8ᵉ ☎ 01–47–23–74–12 Ⓜ Franklin-D.-Roosevelt ✉ 31 rue Cambon, Louvre/Tuileries, 1ᵉʳ ☎ 01–42–86–28–00 Ⓜ Tuileries) is helmed by svelte Karl Lagerfeld who whips together nouvelle takes on all of Coco's favorites: the perfectly tailored tweed suit, a lean, soigné black dress, a quilted bag with the gold chain, a camellia brooch. **Christian Dior** (✉ 30 av. Montaigne, Champs-Élysées, 8ᵉ ☎ 01–40–73–54–44 Ⓜ Franklin-D.-Roosevelt) features the flamboyant John Galliano . . . so what if he pairs full-length body-skimming evening dresses with high-tops and a Davy Crockett raccoon hat? It's

★ just fashion, darling. **Colette** (✉ 213 rue St-Honoré, Louvre/Tuileries, 1ᵉʳ ☎ 01–55–35–33–90 Ⓜ Tuileries) is the most fashionable, most hip, and most hyped store in Paris (and possibly the world). The ground floor, which stocks design objects, gadgets, and makeup, is generally packed with fashion victims and the simply curious. Upstairs are handpicked fashions, accessories, magazines, and books, all of which ooze trendi-

★ ness. **Jean-Paul Gaultier** (✉ 44 av. George V, Champs-Élysées, 8ᵉ ☎ 01–44–43–00–44 Ⓜ George V ✉ 6 Galerie Vivienne, Opéra/Grands Boulevards, 2ᵉ ☎ 01–42–86–05–05 Ⓜ Bourse) first made headlines with his celebrated corset with the ironic i-conic breasts for Madonna, but now sends fashion editors into ecstasy with his sumptuous haute couture creations. Designer Philippe Starck spun an *Alice in Wonderland* fantasy for the boutiques, with quilted cream walls and Murano mirrors. Make no mistake though, it's all about the clothes, dazzlers that make Gaultier a must-see. **Maria Luisa** (✉ 2 rue Cambon, Louvre/Tuileries, 8ᵉ ☎ 01–47–03–96–15 Ⓜ Concorde) is a boudoirlike boutique that has become a legend in its own time; it stocks the likes of Martin Margiela, Jean-Paul Gaultier, Helmut Lang, and Olivier Theyskens. **Sonia Rykiel** (✉ 175 bd. St-Germain, St-Germain-des-Prés, 6ᵉ ☎ 01–49–54–60–60 Ⓜ St-Germain-des-Prés ✉ 70 rue du Faubourg St-Honoré, Louvre/Tuileries, 8ᵉ ☎ 01–42–65–20–81 Ⓜ Concorde) is the queen of French fashion. Since the '60s she's been designing stylish knit separates and has made black her color of preference. **Ungaro** (✉ 2 av. Montaigne, Champs-Élysées, 8ᵉ ☎ 01–53–57–00–22 Ⓜ Alma-Marceau) is once again a hot fashion ticket, with a new generation of devotees, including Jennifer Lopez and Whitney Houston; the boutique is cozy, with sofas, big cushions, and Asian touches.

Antik Batik (✉ 18 rue de Turenne, Le Marais, 4ᵉ ☎ 01–48–87–95–95 Ⓜ St-Paul) sells hippie-chic and ethnic-inspired clothing, bags, and shoes, which has made the label a hit with in-the-know Parisians and supermodels. **Didier Ludot** (✉ Jardins du Palais-Royal, 24 Galerie Montpensier, Louvre/Tuileries, 1ᵉʳ ☎ 01–42–96–06–56 Ⓜ Palais-Royal) is one of the world's most famous vintage clothing dealers; check out the wonderful old Chanel suits, Balenciaga dresses, and Hermès scarves, and bring lots of money.

Gourmet Goodies

Fauchon (✉ 26 pl. de la Madeleine, 8ᵉ, Opéra/Grands Boulevards ☎ 01–47–42–60–11 Ⓜ Madeleine) is the most famous and iconic of all Parisian food stores. **Ladurée** (✉ 21 rue Bonaparte, 6ᵉ, Latin Quarter ☎ 01–44–07–64–87 Ⓜ Odéon), founded in 1862, is a French institution. Its historic tearoom is famed for its chocolates, pastries, macaroons, and sublimely Proustian ambience.

PARIS A TO Z

To research prices, get advice from other travelers, and book travel arrangements, visit www.fodors.com.

AIR TRAVEL TO & FROM PARIS

CARRIERS Major carriers fly daily from the United States; Air France, British Airways, British Midland, and Air U.K. fly regularly from London.

AIRPORTS & TRANSFERS

Paris is served by two international airports: Charles de Gaulle, also known as Roissy, 26 km (16 mi) northeast; and Orly, 16 km (10 mi) south. For telephone numbers, *see* Airports *in* this book's Smart Travel Tips section.

From Charles de Gaulle, the RER-B, the suburban commuter train, beneath Terminal 2, has trains to central Paris (Les Halles, St-Michel, Luxembourg) every 20 minutes; the fare is €8.20, and the journey takes 30 minutes. Note that you have to carry your luggage up from and down to the platform and that trains can be crowded during rush hour. **Remember you must retain the train ticket sold to you at Charles de Gaulle Airport since you will need it at the end of the ride to exit the Métro system** once you are in the city center. Without a ticket stub, you will not be able to get the Métro turnstiles to open to exit the subway system in Paris and you could wind up being ostensibly trapped in the station until a passerby can aid you (also see the note about métro mugging in the Métro Travel section below).

Buses operated by Air France (you need not have flown with the airline) run every 15 minutes between Roissy and western Paris (Porte Maillot and the Arc de Triomphe). The fare is €11, and the trip takes about 40 minutes, though rush-hour traffic may make it longer. Additionally, the Roissybus, operated by the RATP, runs directly between Roissy and rue Scribe by the Opéra every 15 minutes and costs €11. Taxis are readily available; the fare will be around €30–€40, depending on traffic, but traffic jams can make this a frustrating venture. Aeroports Limousine Service can meet you on arrival in a private car and drive you to your destination; reservations should be made two or three days in advance; MasterCard and Visa are accepted—readers report inordinate delays, however. The following minibus services can also meet you on arrival: Airport Shuttle, Paris Airports Service, and Parishuttle.

The RER-C line is one way to get to Paris from Orly Airport; there's a free shuttle bus from the terminal building to the train station, and trains leave every 15 minutes. The fare is €6 (métro included), and the train journey takes about 35 minutes. The Orlyval service is a shuttle train that runs direct from each Orly terminal to the Antony RER-B station every seven minutes; a one-way ticket for the entire trip into Paris is €10. Buses operated by Air France (you need not have flown with the airline) run every 12 minutes between Orly Airport and the Air France air terminal at Les Invalides, on the Left Bank; the fare is €8, and the trip can take from 30 minutes to an hour, depending on traffic. RATP also runs the Orlybus between the Denfert-Rochereau métro station and Orly every 15 minutes, and the trip costs €6. A 20-minute taxi ride costs about €20–€30. With reservations, Aeroports Limousine Service can pick you up at Orly, but readers report delays.

🔽 Taxis & Shuttles **Air France Bus** ☎ 08-92-35-08-20 recorded information in English €.35 per min. ⊕ www.cars-airfrance.com. **Airport Connection** ☎ 01-44-18-36-02 📠 01-45-55-85-19 ⊕ www.airport-connection.com. **Airport Service** ☎ 08-21-80-08-01 📠 01-55-98-10-89 ⊕ www.parisairportservice.com. **RATP (Paris Transit Authority)** ✉ pl. de la Madeleine, 75008 Paris ✉ 53 bis quai des Grands Augustins, 75006 Paris ☎ 08-92-68-41-14 ⊕ www.ratp.com.

BUS TRAVEL TO & FROM PARIS
Long-distance bus journeys within France are uncommon, which may be why Paris has no central bus depot. *See* Bus Travel *in* Smart Travel Tips A to Z for information on traveling to and from Paris by bus.

BUS TRAVEL WITHIN PARIS
Paris buses are marked with the route number and destination in front and with major stopping places along the sides. The brown bus shelters, topped by red-and-yellow circular signs, contain timetables and route maps. Maps are also found in each bus. A recorded message announces the name of the next stop. To get off, press one of the red buttons mounted on all the silver poles that run the length of the bus and the *arrêt demandé* (stop requested) light directly behind the driver will light up. Use the rear door to exit.

TICKETS & SCHEDULES   You can use your métro ticket on buses; if you have individual tickets (as opposed to weekly or monthly tickets), be prepared to validate your ticket in the red-and-gray machines on board the bus. Your best bet is to buy a *carnet* of 10 tickets for €10 at any métro station, or you can buy a single ticket on board (exact change appreciated) for €1.30. You need to show (but not punch) weekly, monthly, and Paris-Visite/Mobilis tickets to the driver. Tickets can be bought on buses, in the métro, or in any bar/tabac store displaying the lime-green métro symbol above its street sign. Most routes operate from 6 AM to 8:30 PM; some continue until midnight. Eighteen *Noctambus,* or night buses, operate hourly (1 AM–6 AM) between Châtelet and various nearby suburbs.

🚍 Bus Information **RATP** ⊠ pl. de la Madeleine, 75008 Paris ⊠ 53 bis quai des Grands Augustins, 75006 Paris ☎ 08-92-68-41-14 ⊕ www.ratp.com.

CAR RENTAL
Cars can be rented at both airports, as well as at locations throughout the city, including the ones listed below.

🚍 Local Agencies **Avis** ⊠ 60 rue de Ponthieu, Champs-Élysées, 8ᵉ ☎ 01-43-59-03-83 Ⓜ St-Philippe du Roule. **Citer** ⊠ 18 rue de Dunkerque, Gare du Nord, 10ᵉ ☎ 01-53-20-06-52 Ⓜ Gare du Nord. **Europcar** ⊠ 60 bd. Diderot, Bastille/Nation, 12ᵉ ☎ 08-03-35-23-52 Ⓜ Gare de Lyon. **Hertz** ⊠ 193 rue de Bercy, Bercy/Tolbiac, 12ᵉ ☎ 01-43-44-06-00 Ⓜ Gare de Lyon.

CAR TRAVEL
In a country as highly centralized as France, it's no surprise that expressways converge on the capital from every direction: A1 from the north (225 km [140 mi] from Lille); A13 from Normandy (225 km [140 mi] from Caen); A4 from the east (500 km [310 mi] from Strasbourg); A10 from the southwest (580 km [360 mi] from Bordeaux); and A7 from the Alps and the Riviera (465 km [290 mi] from Lyon). Each connects with the *périphérique,* the beltway, whose exits into the city are named (as *portes*), not numbered.

CHILDREN IN PARIS
Fodor's Around Paris with Kids (available in bookstores everywhere) can help you plan your days together.

BABY-SITTING   Baby-sitting services can provide English-speaking baby-sitters on just a few hours' notice. The hourly rate is approximately $8 (three-hour minimum) plus an agency fee of around $12.

🚍 Agencies **A. G. Prestige** ⊠ 69 rue Louis Michel, 92300 Levallois ☎ 01-41-40-07-45. **Allo Maman Poule** ⊠ 7 Villa Murat, 16ᵉ ☎ 01-45-20-96-96. **Baby-Sitting Service** ⊠ 18 rue Tronchet, 8ᵉ ☎ 01-46-37-51-24.

EMBASSIES & CONSULATES
🚍 Australia ⊠ 4 rue Jean-Rey, Trocadéro/Eiffel Tower, 15ᵉ ☎ 01-40-59-33-00 Ⓜ Bir Hakeim.

🚍 Canada ⊠ 35 av. Montaigne, Champs-Élysées, 8ᵉ ☎ 01-44-43-29-00 Ⓜ Franklin-D.-Roosevelt.

🚍 New Zealand ⊠ 7 ter rue Léonardo da Vinci, Champs-Élysées, 16ᵉ ☎ 01-45-00-24-11 Ⓜ Victor-Hugo.

🚍 United Kingdom ⊠ 35 rue du Faubourg-St-Honoré, Champs-Élysées, 8ᵉ ☎ 01-44-51-31-00 Ⓜ Concorde.

🚍 United States ⊠ 2 av. Gabriel, Champs-Élysées, 8ᵉ ☎ 01-43-12-22-22 Ⓜ Concorde.

EMERGENCIES

A 24-hour emergency service is available at American Hospital. Hertford British Hospital also has all-night emergency service. This guidebook does not list the major Paris hospitals, as the French government prefers an emergency operator to make the judgment call and assign you the best option. Note that if you are able to walk into a hospital emergency room by yourself, you are often considered "low priority." So if time is of the essence, the best thing to do is to call the fire department (☎ 18); a fully trained team of paramedics will usually arrive within five minutes. You may also dial for a Samu ambulance (☎ 15); there is usually an English-speaking physician available. It's important to check with your insurance company before you leave for your trip to make sure that you are covered internationally.

🎦 Doctors & Dentists **Dentist** ☎ 01-43-37-51-00. **Doctor** ☎ 01-43-07-77-77.

🎦 Emergency Services **Ambulance** ☎ 15 or 01-45-67-50-50. **Police** ☎ 17.

🎦 Hospitals **American Hospital** ⊠ 63 bd. Victor-Hugo, Neuilly ☎ 01-46-41-25-25. **Hertford British Hospital** ⊠ 3 rue Barbès, Levallois-Perret ☎ 01-47-58-13-12.

🎦 Late-Night & 24-Hour Pharmacies **Dhéry** ⊠ Galerie des Champs, 84 bd. des Champs-Élysées, 8ᵉ ☎ 01-45-62-02-41 is open 24 hours. **Pharmacie Internationale** ⊠ 5 pl. Pigalle, 9ᵉ ☎ 01-48-78-38-12. **Pharmacie Matignon** ⊠ rue Jean-Mermoz, at the Rond-Point de Champs-Élysées, 8ᵉ is open daily until 2 AM.

MÉTRO TRAVEL

The métro is by far the quickest and most efficient way to get around. Trains run from 5:30 AM until 1 AM (and be forewarned—this means the famous "last métro" can pass your station anytime after 12:30 AM). Stations are signaled either by a large yellow M within a circle or by their distinctive curly green Art Nouveau railings and archway entrances bearing the subway's full title (Métropolitain). It's essential to **know the name of the last station on the line you take**, as this name appears on all signs. A connection (you can make as many as you like on one ticket) is called a *correspondance*. At junction stations illuminated orange signs bearing the name of the line terminal appear over the correct corridors for correspondance. Illuminated blue signs marked SORTIE indicate the station exit. In general, the métro is safe, although try to avoid Lines 2 and 13 if you're alone late at night. Access to métro platforms is through an automatic ticket barrier. Slide your ticket in and pick it up and retrieve it as it pops up. **Keep your ticket during your journey; you will need it to leave the RER system,** and you'll be glad you have it in case you run into any green-clad inspectors when you are leaving—they can be very unpleasant and will impose a big fine on the spot if you do not have a ticket.

Speaking of unpleasant, many readers have written to us about being mugged in the Métro system. A favorite mode is for muggers to "sandwich" you as you attempt to exit the rather tricky turnstyles; others make their attack on the lengthy escalators at the métro exits. Pickpockets are close enough and nimble-fingered enough (think Oliver Twist) to rob you in a split second. These pickpockets work in groups, never alone—one will divert your attention (think the Artful Dodger) while the other whisks away your wallet or your passport (which should not be in your

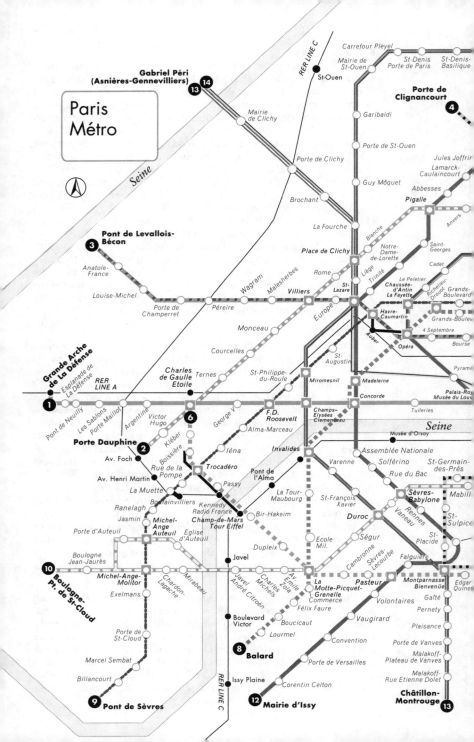

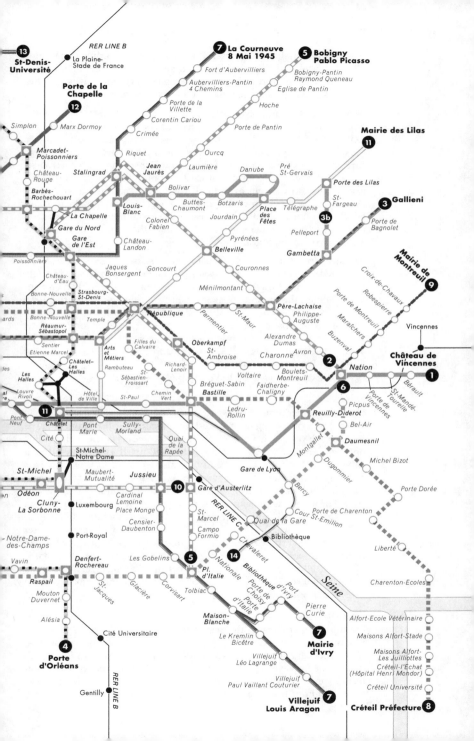

back pocket or shoulder purse). Prevention of petty crime is the same all over the world. Just use discretion and caution while maintaining your physical comfort zone in crowded places. Happily, as large cities go, Paris remains—for the most part—a safe place.

FARES &
SCHEDULES All métro tickets and passes are valid for RER and bus travel as well; tickets cost €1.30 each, but it makes more sense to buy a *carnet* (10 tickets) for €10. If you're staying for a week or more, the best deals are the weekly *coupon jaune* (yellow ticket) or monthly *carte orange* (orange card), sold according to zone. Zones 1 and 2 cover the entire métro network; tickets cost €15 a week or €49 a month. If you plan to take suburban trains to visit places in the Ile-de-France, consider a four-zoner (Versailles, St-Germain-en-Laye; €24 a week) or a six-zoner (Rambouillet, Fontainebleau; €33 a week). Weekly and monthly passes are available from rail and major métro stations; the monthly pass requires a passport-size photograph.

An alternative for métro travel is to purchase two-, three-, or five-day unlimited-travel tickets (*Paris Visite*). Unlike the *coupon jaune* (a weekly pass for unlimited travel beginning on a Monday and ending on a Sunday evening), the unlimited ticket is valid starting any day of the week and gives you discounts on a limited number of museums and tourist attractions. The prices are, respectively, €9, €15, and €28 for Paris only; for Paris and the suburbs, prices are nearly twice as much. The equivalent one-day ticket is called *mobilis* and costs €9 (Paris only) or €9–€18 (Paris plus suburbs).

🚉 **Métro Information RATP** ☎ 08-92-68-41-14 ⊕ www.ratp.fr.

TAXIS

On weekend nights after 11 PM it's nearly impossible to find a free taxi—you are best off asking hotel or restaurant staff to call you one, but, be forewarned; you will have to pay for them to come get you and, depending on where they are, the fare can quickly add up. If you want to hail a cab on your own, look for the taxis with their signs lit up (their signs will be glowing white as opposed to the taxis that are already taken whose signs will be a dull orange). There are taxi stands on almost every major street corner but again, expect a wait if it is a busy weekend night. Taxi stands are marked by a square dark blue sign with a white T in the middle. Daytime rates, A (7 AM–7 PM), within Paris are €.60 per kilometer (½ mi), and nighttime rates, B, are around €1 per kilometer. Suburban zones and airports, C, are €1.20 per kilometer. There is a basic hire charge of €2 for all rides, a €1 supplement per piece of luggage, and a €.75 supplement if you're picked up at an SNCF station. Waiting time is charged at €20 per hour.

TOURS

BOAT TOURS Hour-long boat trips on the Seine can be fun if you're in Paris for the first time; the cost is €6–€1. A few lines (but not the Bateaux Mouches) serve lunch and dinner (for an additional cost); make reservations in advance. The massive, double-decker Bateaux Mouches boats (with commentary in seven languages) depart from the Pont de l'Alma (Right Bank) every half hour from April to September from 10 AM to 10 PM and approximately every hour during the grey winter months from 11 AM to 9 PM. Bateaux Parisiens boats depart every half hour in summer and every hour in winter, starting at 10 AM; the last boat departs at 10 PM (11 PM in summer). Canauxrama organizes half- and full-day barge tours along the canals of east Paris. Vedettes du Pont-Neuf depart every half hour 10–noon, 1:30–6:30, and 9–10:30 from March to October and every 45 minutes 10:30–noon and 1:30–6:30 from November to February. Yachts de Paris organizes romantic 2½-hr "gourmand cruises" (for about €149) year-round. Yachts set off every evening at 7:45 while a team of uniformed officers and crew serve Chef Gérard Besson's three-course meal.

🖪 Fees & Schedules **Bateaux Mouches** ✉ Pont de l'Alma, Trocadéro/Eiffel Tower, 8ᵉ ☎ 01-40-76-99-99 ⊕ www.bateauxmouches.com Ⓜ Alma-Marceau. **Bateaux Parisiens** ✉ Pont d'Iéna, Trocadéro/Eiffel Tower, 7ᵉ ☎ 01-44-11-33-44 ⊕ www.bateauxparisiens. com Ⓜ Trocadéro. Boats depart from **Canauxrama** ✉ 13 quai de la Loire, Gare de l'Est, 19ᵉ ☎ 01-42-39-15-00 ⊕ www.canauxrama.com Ⓜ Jaurès ✉ For information: Bassin de l'Arsenal, opposite 50 bd. de la Bastille, Bastille/Nation, 12ᵉ Ⓜ Bastille ☎ 01-42-39-15-00. **Vedettes du Pont-Neuf** ✉ Below Sq. du Vert-Galant, Ile de la Cité, 1ᵉʳ ☎ 01-46-33-98-38 ⊕ www.vedettesdupontneuf.com Ⓜ Pont Neuf. **Yachts de Paris** ✉ Port de Javel ☎ 01-44-54-14-70 ⊕ www.yachtsdeparis.com.

BUS TOURS For a 2-hr orientation tour by bus, the standard price is about €24. The two largest bus-tour operators are Cityrama and Paris Vision; for a more intimate—albeit expensive—tour of the city, Cityrama also runs several minibus excursions per day with a private multilingual tour operator for €54. Paris Vision runs non-stop two-hour tours with multilingual commentary available via individual headphones with over ten languages for €25. Paris L'Open Tour gives tours in a double-decker bus with an open top; commentary is available in French and English on individual headphones. Get on or off at one of the fifty pickup points indicated by the lime-green sign posts; tickets may be purchased on board and cost €25 for one day. Les Cars Rouges offer double-decker London-style buses with nine stops—a ticket for two consecutive days is available for €22. RATP (Paris Transit Authority) also offers economical, commentary-free excursions; the Montmartrobus departs from meatro Anvers and zips through the winding cobbled streets of Montmartre to the top of the hill for those of you who don't want to brave the walk; the trip is the price of one métro ticket (€1.30). The RATP Balabus Bb line goes from Gare du Lyon to the Grand Arch at La Défense passing by all major tourist attractions on the way for the price of one métro ticket. The Balabus Bb line runs from mid-April to September.

🖪 **Cityrama** ✉ 4 pl. des Pyramides, 1ᵉʳ ☎ 01-44-55-61-00 ⊕ www.cityrama.com. **Les Cars Rouges** ☎ 01-53-95-39-53. **Paris L'Open Tour** ✉ 13 rue Auber, 9ᵉʳ ☎ 01-42-66-56-56 ⊕ www.paris-opentour.com. **Paris Vision** ✉ 214 rue de Rivoli, 1ᵉʳ ☎ 01-42-60-31-25. **RATP** ✉ pl. de la Madeleine, 8ᵉ ✉ 53 bis quai des Grands-Augustins, 6ᵉ ☎ 08-92-68-41-14.

WALKING TOURS The team at Paris Walking Tours offers a wide selection of tours, from neighborhood visits to museum tours and theme tours such as "Hemingway's Paris," "The Marais," "Montmartre," and "The Latin Quarter." A 2-hour tour costs about €10. A list of walking tours is also available from the Caisse Nationale des Monuments Historiques, in the weekly magazines available at any kiosk in the city *Pariscope* and *L'Officiel des Spectacles,* which list walking tours under the heading *"Conférences"* (most are in French, unless otherwise noted).

 Fees & Schedules **Caisse Nationale des Monuments Historiques** ⊠ Bureau des Visites: Hôtel de Sully, 62 rue St-Antoine, Bastille/Nation, 4ᵉ ☎ 01-44-61-20-00 Ⓜ St-Paul. **Paris Walking Tours** ☎ 01-48-09-21-40 ⊕ www.paris-walks.com.

TRAIN TRAVEL

Paris has five international train stations: Gare du Nord (northern France, northern Europe, and England via Calais or the Channel Tunnel); Gare St-Lazare (Normandy and England via Dieppe); Gare de l'Est (Strasbourg, Luxembourg, Basel, and central Europe); Gare de Lyon (Lyon, Marseille, the Riviera, Geneva, Italy); and Gare d'Austerlitz (Loire Valley, southwest France, Spain). The Gare Montparnasse is used by the TGV *Atlantique* bound for Nantes or Bordeaux. Call 08–92–35–35–35 for information.

RER trains travel between Paris and the suburbs. When they go through Paris, they act as a sort of supersonic métro—they connect with the métro network at several points—and can be great time-savers. Access to RER platforms is through the same type of automatic ticket barrier (if you've started your journey on the métro, you can use the same ticket), but you'll need to have the same ticket handy to put through another barrier when you leave the system.

 Train Information **SNCF** ⊠ 1 rue Paturle, Montparnasse ☎ 01-53-90-20-20 ⊕ www.sncf.fr.

TRANSPORTATION AROUND PARIS

To help you find your way around, buy a *Plan de Paris par Arrondissement,* a city guide available at most kiosks, with separate maps of each district, including the whereabouts of métro stations and an index of street names. Maps of the métro/RER network are available free from any métro station and from many hotels. They are also posted on every platform, as are maps of the bus network. Bus routes are also marked at bus stops and on buses. The extensive public transportation system is the best way to get around. Don't use a car in Paris unless you have to. Parking is difficult—and expensive—and traffic can be awesome. Meters and ticket machines (pay and display) are common; make sure you have a supply of coins.

TRAVEL AGENCIES

 Local Agent Referrals **Air France** ⊠ 119 av. des Champs-Élysées, Champs-Élysées, 8ᵉ ☎ 01-42-99-21-01 Ⓜ Charles-de-Gaulle-Étoile. **American Express** ⊠ 11 rue Scribe, Opéra/Grands Boulevards, 8ᵉ ☎ 01-47-77-77-07 Ⓜ Opéra ⊠ 38 av. de Wagram, Champs-Élysées, 8ᵉ ☎ 01-42-27-58-80 Ⓜ Charles-de-Gaulle-Étoile. **Nouvelles Frontières** ⊠ 5 av. de l'Opéra, Louvre/Tuileries, 1ᵉʳ ☎ 08-03-33-33-33 Ⓜ Pyramides. **Sol-tours** ⊠ 46 rue de Rivoli, Le Marais, 4ᵉ ☎ 01-42-71-24-34 Ⓜ Hôtel-de-Ville. **Wagons-Lit** ⊠ 32 rue du Quatre-Septembre, Opéra/Grands Boulevards, 2ᵉ ☎ 01-42-66-15-80 Ⓜ Opéra.

VISITOR INFORMATION

There are over five branches of the Paris tourist office located at key points in the capital. Don't call with a question though—you'll get a host of generic recorded information that will cost you €.34 per minute.

Espace du Tourisme d'Ile-de-France ⊠ Carrousel du Louvre, 99 rue de Rivoli, 75001 Paris Ⓜ Métro: Palais Royale/Musee du Louvre ☎ 08-03-81-80-00 or 01-44-50-19-98. **Office du Tourisme de la Ville de Paris** Opéra - Grands Magasins ⊠ 11, rue Scribe Ⓜ Métro: Opéra ☎ 08-92-68-30-00 €.34 per minute. **Office du Tourisme de la Ville de Paris** Gare du Lyon, Arrivals ⊠ 20, bd Diderot Ⓜ Métro: Gare du Lyon ☎ 08-92-68-30-00, €.34 per minute. **Syndicat d'Initiative de Montmartre** ⊠ 21, place de Tertre ☎ 08-92-68-30-00, €.34 per minute Ⓜ Métro: Abbesses.

ILE-DE-FRANCE

2

TAKE A GILT-TRIP
through the palace of Versailles ⇨*p.110*

PULL MICKEY'S TAIL THREE TIMES
at Disneyland Paris ⇨*p.143*

LIGHTEN UP
under the radiant stained glass
of Chartres Cathedral ⇨*p.124*

PAINT YOURSELF INTO VAN GOGH'S
favorite corner in Auvers-sur-Oise ⇨*p.137*

PLAY PEEK-A-BOO
in the 17th-century halls
of Château de Vaux-le-Vicomte ⇨*p.146*

CHANNEL NAPOLÉON AND JOSEPHINE
at their Malmaison hideaway ⇨*p.129*

STEP INTO A 5-ACRE MONET
at the artist's Giverny garden ⇨*p.133*

Updated by
Simon Hewitt

Introduction by
Nancy Coons

TO SOME OBSERVERS THE ILE-DE-FRANCE is the most heartwarming of all the French provinces. First, there's the pleasure of imagination satisfied: there's something comfortingly familiar about the look of lanes bordered with silvery poplar trees, the golden haze in the air, the gray stone of a village steeple. And no wonder, for scores of painters have immortalized them. Corot began with the forest of Fontainebleau and the village of Barbizon. Pissarro worked at Pontoise. Sisley's famous riverside canvases were painted at Moret-sur-Loing, near Fontainebleau. Monet painted the Epte River. And van Gogh died in Auvers.

Just what is it that makes the Ile-de-France so attractive? Is it that it's so close to the great city of Paris—or perhaps that it's so far removed? Had there not been a world-class cultural hub right nearby, would Monet have retreated to his Japanese gardens at Giverny? Or Cézanne and van Gogh to bucolic Auvers? Counts and kings to the game-rich forests of Fontainebleau, Rambouillet, and Dampierre? Would medieval castles and palaces have sprouted in the towns of Vincennes and St-Germain-en-Laye? Would abbeys and cathedrals have sprung skyward in Chartres, Senlis, and Royaumont?

If you had asked Louis XIV, he wouldn't have minced his words in answering: The city of Paris—yawn—was simply *démodé*—out of fashion. In the 17th century, the new power base was going to be Versailles, once a tiny village in the heart of the Ile-de-France, now the site of a gigantic château from which the Sun King's rays (Louis XIV was known as *le roi soleil*) could radiate, unfettered by rebellious rabble and European arrivistes. Of course, later heirs kept the lines open and restored the grandiose palace as the country retreat it was meant to be—and commuted to Paris, well before the high-speed RER.

That, indeed, is the dream of most Parisians today: to have a foot in both worlds. Paris may be small as capital cities go, with just under 2 million inhabitants, but Ile-de-France, the region around Paris, contains more than 10 million people—a sixth of France's entire population. That's why on closer inspection the once rustic villages of Ile-de-France reveal cosseted gardens, stylishly gentrified cottages, and extraordinary country restaurants no peasant farmer could afford to frequent. And that's why Ile-de-France retains a sophisticated air, along with a glowing patina of history, not found in any of France's other patches of verdure.

The Ile-de-France is the ancient heartland of France, the core from which the French kings gradually extended their power over the rest of a rebellious, individualistic nation. Since the time when it was first wrested from savage Gauls by Julius Caesar, in 52 BC, the region has played a leading role in French history; its towns and villages intimately entwined with the course of national fact and legend. Charlemagne confirmed his power in France after generations had fought against the Romans near Soissons; Joan of Arc, battling for her king's supremacy, was finally captured at Compiègne. There is Versailles, from which the three Louis gloriously reigned until the Revolution dealt the French monarchy a death blow. And Napoléon, after ruling for a time from Malmaison, abdicated in the courtyard at Fontainebleau.

The Ile-de-France is not really an *île* (island), of course. This green-forested buffer that wraps Paris is only vaguely surrounded by the three rivers that meander through its periphery. But France's capital city seems to crown this genteel sprawl of an atoll, peppered with pretty villages, anchored by grandiose châteaux. The spokes of railway and freeway that radiate every which way from the Paris ring road all merge gently into this verdant countryside.

All in all, Ile-de-France strikes a mellow balance, offering a rich and varied cross section of Gallic culture . . . a minisampling of everything you expect from France, and all within easy day trips from Paris. With cathedrals, châteaux, and places immortalized by great painters, what more could you wish for? Well, how about Goofy on parade along Main Street U.S.A.? Pirates of the Caribbean? And Disney's own answer to Versailles, the bubblegum-pink turrets of Sleeping Beauty's Castle? Yes, the much-maligned, now recherché Disneyland Paris has taken root, drawing sellout crowds of Europeans wanting a taste of the American Dream—and of American families stealing a day from their Louvre schedule. It's just another epic vision realized against the green backdrop of Ile-de-France.

Exploring Ile-de-France

A great advantage to exploring Ile-de-France is that all its major monuments are within a half-day's drive from Paris. Though small, Ile-de-France is so rich in treasures that a whole day of fascinating exploration may take you no more than 60 km (35 mi) from the capital. The four tours suggested in the Great Itineraries section include the major points of interest: southwest from Paris to Versailles and Chartres; northwest along the Seine to St-Germain and Giverny; north and east along the Oise Valley via Chantilly to Disneyland; and southeast from Vaux-le-Vicomte to Fontainebleau.

About the Restaurants & Hotels

Not surprisingly, given its proximity to Paris and relatively well-heeled population, the Ile-de-France has no shortage of good restaurants; prices are generally cheaper than those in the capital and eating hours a little earlier—some restaurants will refuse to accept diners who arrive after 9 PM. Be aware that many restaurants popular with the locals, and so not over-reliant on tourist trade, close for up to a month in July and August. Restaurants abound in the larger tourist towns like Versailles, Chartres, and Fontainebleau, but it's best to book ahead in smaller towns, like Chantilly, Senlis, Barbizon, or Auvers-sur-Oise, where choice is limited.

In summer, hotel rooms are at a premium, and making reservations is essential; almost all accommodations in the swankier towns—Versailles, Rambouillet, and Fontainebleau—are on the costly side. Take nothing for granted; picturesque Senlis, for instance, does not have a single hotel in its historic downtown area. Assume that all hotel rooms have air-conditioning, TV, telephones, and private bath, unless otherwise noted. Hotels operate on the European Plan (EP, with no meal provided) unless we note that they use the Breakfast Plan (BP), Modified Ameri-

2

With so many legendary sights in the Ile-de-France—many of which are gratifying human experiences rather than just guidebook necessities—you could spend weeks visiting the region. But if you don't have that much time, try one of the following shorter itineraries. Spend from three to eight days exploring the area or take day trips from Paris—most sites are within easy reach of the capital by car or train.

Numbers in the text correspond to numbers in the margin and on the Ile-de-France, Versailles, and Fontainebleau maps.

If you have 3 days

For a full blast of kingly splendor, first head west from Paris to nearby **St-Germain-en-Laye** 🔲 ⏻ and visit the château and the Prieuré Museum—don't forget to take a promenade on the palace's stately Grande Terrasse. Try to reach 🔲 **Versailles** 🔲–🔲 for lunch and then visit France's largest château and its park. The next morning spend more time in Versailles, then drive 55 km (30 mi) northwest—or return to Paris and train it out—to 🔲 **Giverny** 🔲 to visit Monet's famous home and water-lily garden. For your last day, head south to destinations either spiritual or secular—either the regal châteaux of **Rambouillet** 🔲 or **Maintenon** 🔲 or past the wheat fields of the Beauce to 🔲 **Chartres** 🔲, where you can spend half a day exploring the sublime cathedral and Vieille Ville.

If you have 5 days

Take the expressway north from Paris to **Senlis** 🔲 ⏻, visit the Vieille Ville and cathedral, then head to 🔲 **Chantilly** 🔲 for the afternoon to visit its exquisite château, replete with fabled art collection, grand park, and a regal stable. The next morning follow the Oise Valley, stopping briefly in the painters' village of **Auvers-sur-Oise** 🔲 en route to 🔲 **Versailles** 🔲–🔲. Spend the morning of your third day in Versailles or **Rambouillet** 🔲; try to be in 🔲 **Chartres** 🔲 by early afternoon. Spend the night there and drive to the palace at 🔲 **Fontainebleau** 🔲 –🔲 the following morning, perhaps visiting the romantic forest village of **Barbizon** 🔲 on your way. On Day 5 make sure to visit **Vaux-le-Vicomte** 🔲—the 17th-century château whose splendor inspired the building of Versailles.

If you have 8 days

Spend your first day in medieval **Senlis** 🔲 ⏻ and aristocratic 🔲 **Chantilly** 🔲. On the second day, head down the Oise Valley, via **Auvers-sur-Oise** 🔲 to haunt van Gogh's footsteps and on to 🔲 **St-Germain-en-Laye** 🔲, where the 17th-century palace and gardens await. Head northwest down the Seine Valley to Monet's beloved 🔲 **Giverny** 🔲 on the third day; spend the night here or in nearby 🔲 **Vernon** 🔲. The following day take the expressway to that showstopper, 🔲 **Versailles** 🔲–🔲. On the fifth day, go southwest to feast your eyes (and perhaps your soul) on the sublime cathedral at 🔲 **Chartres** 🔲, with a stop in at *anciéne régime* **Rambouillet** 🔲 or **Maintenon** 🔲 if time allows. On Day 6 head to the painters' forest of **Barbizon** 🔲 and 🔲 **Fontainebleau** 🔲–🔲, Napoléon's favorite palace; make it your base for two nights. On Day 7 don't miss the 17th-century splendor at **Vaux-le-Vicomte** 🔲, and also fit in that Impressionist jewel, **Moret-sur-Loing** 🔲; finish up on Day 8 at **Disneyland Paris** 🔲.

can Plan (MAP, with breakfast and dinner daily, known as *demi-pension*), or Full American Plan (FAP, or *pension complète,* with three meals a day).

WHAT IT COSTS In euros					
	$$$$	**$$$**	**$$**	**$**	**¢**
RESTAURANTS	over €30	€23–€30	€17–€23	€11–€17	under €11
HOTELS	over €190	€120–€190	€80–€120	€50–€80	under €50

Restaurant prices are per person for a main course at dinner, including tax (19.6%) and service; note that if a restaurant offers only prix-fixe (set-price) meals, it has been given the price category that reflects the full prix-fixe price. Hotel prices are for a standard double room in high season, including tax (19.6%) and service charge; higher prices (inquire when booking) prevail for any board plans.

Timing

With its extensive forests, Ile-de-France is especially beautiful in the fall, particularly the month of October. June and July are good months, too, but August can be sultry and crowded. On a Saturday night in summer you can see a son-et-lumière show in Moret-sur-Loing and make a candlelight visit to Vaux-le-Vicomte. Be aware when making your travel plans that some places are closed one or two days a week: the châteaux of Versailles and Auvers are closed on Monday; the Musée Tavet-Delacour in Pontoise is closed both Monday and Tuesday; and the châteaux of Chantilly and Fontainebleau are closed Tuesday. In fact, as a rule, well-touristed towns make their *fermeture hebdomadaire* (weekly closing) on Tuesday, so museums and markets may be closed—call ahead if in doubt. Disneyland Paris gets really crowded on summer weekends. So does Giverny (Monet's garden), which is at its best May through June and, like Vaux-le-Vicomte, is closed November to March.

SOUTHWEST FROM VERSAILLES TO CHARTRES

Not only is majestic Versailles one of the most unforgettable sights in Ile-de-France, it's also within easy reach of Paris, less than 30 minutes distant by either train or car (A13 expressway from Porte d'Auteuil). It's also the starting point for a visit to southwestern Ile-de-France, which is anchored by Chartres to the south and the *Vieille Ville* (Old Town) of Dreux to the west.

Versailles

16 km (10 mi) west of Paris via A13.

You'll need no reminding that you're in the world's grandest palace when you arrive at Versailles—gold, gold, and more gold, multicolor marbles, and acres of Charles Le Brun–painted ceilings will greet your eye. Corridors still warm with the spirits of Louis XIV, Madame de Pompadour, and Marie-Antoinette remind you that this voluptuous glory served as preface to the blood-stained French Revolution. Less a monument than an entire world unto itself, its mere immensity is such that some visi-

The Impressionist Ile

Paris's Musée d'Orsay may have some of the most fabled Monet and van Gogh paintings in the world, but the Ile de France has something (almost) better—the actual landscapes that were rendered into masterpieces by the brushes of many great Impressionist and Post-Impressionist artists. At Giverny, Claude Monet's house and garden is a moving visual link to his finest daubs—its famous lily-pond garden, designed by the artist himself, gave rise to his legendary water-lilies series (some historians feel it was the other way around). Elsewhere, villages like Vétheuil—where the master liked to set up his easel— still look like three-dimensional "Monets." In Auvers-sur-Oise, Vincent van Gogh had a final burst of creativity before ending his life; the famous wheat field where he was attacked by crows and painted his last painting is just outside town. André Derain lived in Chambourcy, Camille Pissarro in Pontoise, Alfred Sisley in Moret-sur-Loing—all were inspired by the silvery sunlight that tumbles over these hills and towns. Earlier, Rousseau, Millet, and Corot paved the way for Impressionism with their penchant for outdoor landscape painting in the village of Barbizon, still surrounded by its quietly dramatic, super-romantic forest. A trip to any of these towns will provide lasting impressions.

La Vie de Châteaux

Dukes and counts began building châteaux in the 11th century, when they needed to watch over parts of the king's lands and protect themselves from each other. Sparse, cold, and uninviting (that being the point), châteaux—the French word for castles—began as drafty stone fortresses. By the 17th century, when the age of feudal wars came to a close, castles began to be seen as pleasure palaces, sumptuous inside and out. The rich and the powerful were mightily attracted to the Ile-de-France partly because its many forests—large portions of which still stand—harbored sufficient game to ensure hunters' satisfaction, even for bloated, pampered monarchs. First Fontainebleau, in manageable Renaissance proportions, then Versailles—the world's most vainglorious palace, designed in minion-crushing Baroque—reflected the royal desire to transform hunting lodges into palatial residences. Other châteaux that exude almost comparable grandeur are at Vaux-le-Vicomte and Chantilly. And there are another dozen châteaux not quite as grandiose but still grand—such as Dampierre, Rambouillet, Maintenon, Maisons-Laffitte, and Thoiry.

Loosen Your Belts

Ile-de-France's fanciest restaurants can be just as pricey as their Parisian counterparts. Little wonder—unlike Normandy's cider, cream, and chicken, or Périgord's truffles and foie gras, Ile-de-France cuisine mirrors that of the big capital. The usual "local delicacies"—lamb stew, *pâté de Pantin* (pastry filled with meat), or pig's trotters—tend to be obsolete; instead, menu highlights consist of sumptuous game and asparagus in season in the south of the region and the soft, creamy cheese of Meaux and Coulommiers to the east.

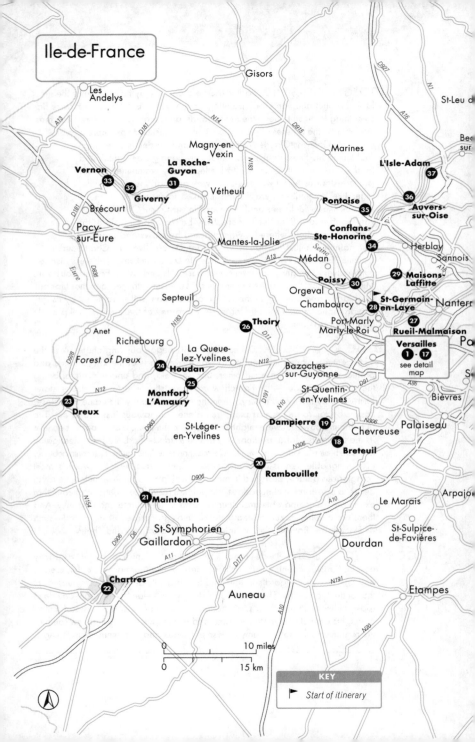

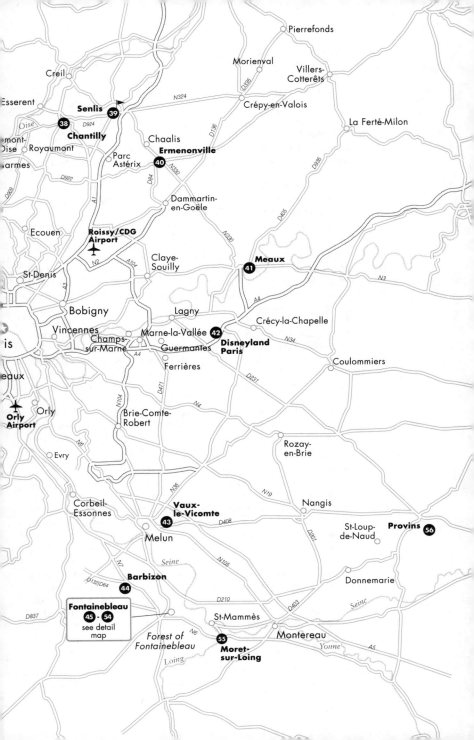

tors consider it more an ordeal than a pleasure. Even the Bourbon kings needed to escape its endless confines, and did so by building one of Europe's largest parks to surround the palace. So take a cue from them and remember: if the grandeur begins to overwhelm, the park outside the palace walls is the best place to come back down to earth.

Psychologically and historically, Versailles may be regarded as the result of a childhood shock suffered by the young king Louis XIV. With his mother, Anne of Austria, he was forced to flee Paris and was captured temporarily by a group of nobles, known as the Frondeurs. Louis developed a hatred for Paris and those Parisians who had sided with the conspirators. He lost no time in casting his cantankerous royal eye over Ile-de-France in search of a site for a new power base. Marshy, inhospitable Versailles became the place of his dreams. Down came his father's modest royal hunting lodge and up, up, and along rose a swank new palace.

❶
FodorśChoice
★

The army of 20,000 noblemen, servants, and sycophants who moved into the huge **Château de Versailles** with Louis is matched today by the battalions of visitors arrayed in front of it. You may be able to avoid the crowds (and lines for tours) if you arrive here at 9 AM. The hard part is figuring out where you're supposed to go once you arrive. There are different lines depending on tour, physical ability, and group status. Frequent guided tours in English visit the private royal apartments. More detailed hour-long tours explore the opera house or Marie-Antoinette's private parlors. You can go through the grandest rooms—including the Hall of Mirrors and Marie-Antoinette's stunning bedchamber—without a group tour (by means of yet another line). To figure out the system, pick up a brochure at the information office or ticket counter. If you plan on spending the day, keep in mind that you can purchase sandwiches in the town of Versailles (whether you can sneak them past the front-door guards is another question) or opt for luncheon at the La Flotille restaurant by the glorious Grand Canal.

Versailles was dreamed up as a gigantic palace flanked by avenues broader than the Champs-Élysées, all in bicep-flexing baroque, on a scale designed by the 23-year-old Louis to dwarf the provocatively lavish château of Vaux-le-Vicomte that had recently been erected by his own finance minister. As time wore on and styles changed, Louis XIV's successors felt out of sync with this architectural inheritance. Louis XV exchanged the heavy red-and-gilt of Italianate Baroque for the lighter, pastel-hue Rococo mode. In doing so, he transformed the daunting royal apartments into places to live rather than pose. The hapless Louis XVI cowered in the Petit Trianon, in the leafy depths of Versailles's gardens, out of the shadow of the mighty château. His queen, Marie-Antoinette, seems to have lost her senses well before she lost her head in 1793, by playing at being a peasant shepherdess amid the ersatz rusticity and perfumed flocks of sheep of the Hameau, a faux farm and village she had created just beyond the precincts of the Petit Trianon.

You enter the château—built between 1662 and 1690 by architects Louis Le Vau and Jules Hardouin-Mansart—through gilt-iron gates from the huge place d'Armes. The center of the vast palace was the living quarters of the king and queen, while the two gigantic wings were occupied by the royal children and princes of the blood. Courtiers had to make do in the attics and distant apartments—while luxurious, Versailles proved to be as crowded and noisy as a tenement, much to the distress of the courtiers who had been commanded to forsake their country homes for this Pentagon-size dwelling. On the first floor of the château, dead center across the sprawling cobbled forecourt beyond the Sun King's statue, is **Louis XIV's bedchamber**, but the real headliner is the sparkling **Galerie des Glaces** (Hall of Mirrors). It was here, after France's capitulation, that Otto von Bismarck proclaimed the unified German Empire in 1871; and here that the Treaty of Versailles, asserting Germany's responsibility for World War I, was signed in 1919. The **Grands Appartements** (state apartments), which flank the Hall of Mirrors, retain most of their original Baroque decoration: gilt stucco, painted ceilings, and marble sculpture. Perhaps the most extravagant is the **Salon d'Apollon** (Apollo Chamber), the former throne room, dedicated to the sun god Apollo, Louis XIV's mythical hero. Equally interesting are the **Petits Appartements** (private apartments), where the royal family and friends lived in relative seclusion.

In the north wing of the château are the solemn white-and-gold **Chapelle** (chapel), completed in 1710; the intimate **Opéra Royal** (Opera House), the first oval-shape hall in France, built by Jacques-Ange Gabriel for Louis XV in 1770 and entirely constructed of wood painted over to look like marble; and, connecting the two, the 17th-century **Galeries,** with exhibits retracing the château's history. The south wing contains the bombastic **Galerie des Batailles** (Hall of Battles), lined with gigantic canvases extolling French military glory. The former state rooms and sumptuous debate chamber of the **Aile du Midi** (South Wing) are also open to the public, with infrared headphones (English commentary available) recounting Versailles's parliamentary history. ✉ *Pl. d'Armes* ☎ *01–30–83–78–00* ⊕ *www.chateauversailles.fr* ✑ *Château €7.50, €5.40 after 3:30, parliament exhibition €3 extra* ☉ *May–Sept., Tues.–Sun. 9–6; Oct.–Apr., Tues.–Sun. 9–5;Galerie des Glaces Tues.–Sun. 9:45–5; Opéra Royal Tues.–Sun. 9:45–3:30. Tours of Opéra Royal and Petits Appartements every 15 mins (€6).*

★ ❷ After the awesome feast of interior pomp, the **Parc de Versailles** (Versailles Park) is an ideal place to catch your breath. The gardens were designed by André Le Nôtre, whose work here represents classical French landscaping at its most formal and sophisticated. The 250-acre grounds include woods, lawns, flower beds, statues, artificial lakes, and fountains galore. An extensive tree-replacement scheme—necessary once a century—was launched in 1998 to recapture the full impact of Le Nôtre's artful vistas; replantings became all the more necessary after 10,000 trees were uprooted by a hurricane in 1999. The cost of that damage came to some $35 million, and American donors contributed 40% of that amount. The distances are vast—the Trianons themselves are more than a mile from the château—so you might want to climb aboard a horse-drawn carriage (round trip from the château to Trianon,

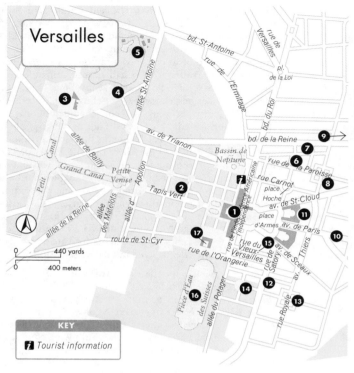

KEY

ℹ️ *Tourist information*

€7, www.calechesversailles.com), take the electric train (€5.20 round-trip), or rent a bike from the **Grille de la Reine** near the Trianon Palace Hotel (€4.50 per hour) or from the **Petite-Venise** (☎ 01–39–66–97–66 🚲 €5.20 per hr, or €26 for 6 hrs) building at the top of the Grand Canal. You can also drive to the Trianons and Canal through the Grille de la Reine (€5.50 per car). The park is at its golden-leafed best in the fall but is also enticing in summer—especially on Sunday afternoons from mid-April through mid-October, when the fountains are in full flow. ☎ 01–30–83–77–88 *for guided tour* 🚲 *Park free; €5 for Sun. fountain displays* ⊙ *Daily 7 AM–8 PM or dusk.*

❸ The **Grand Trianon,** built by Hardouin-Mansart in 1687, is a pink-marble pleasure palace which is occasionally used to entertain visiting heads of state. But most of the time it's open to visitors, who can admire its lavish interior and early 19th-century furnishings. ☎ 01–30–84–75–43 🚲 *Joint ticket with Petit Trianon €5* ⊙ *Tues.–Sun. noon–5:30.*

★❹ Art historians go weak in the knees when they tour the **Petit Trianon**—although you may wonder what all the hubbub is about. That was precisely the point: a bijou palace, this abode—built by the great Gabriel, architect of Paris's Place de la Concorde, upon command of Madame de Pompadour, Louis XV's amour—was a radical statement, since, for

SAVE MARIE-ANTOINETTE

WAS MARIE-ANTOINETTE A luxury-mad butterfly flitting from ball to costume ball? Or was she a misunderstood queen who suffered a loveless marriage and became a prisoner of court etiquette at Versailles? Historians now believe the answer was the latter and point to her private retreats at Versailles as proof. Here, in the northwest part of the royal park, far from the main palace, Marie-Antoinette created a tiny universe of her own: her comparatively dainty mansion called the Petit Trianon and its adjacent "farm," the still extant, still magnificently lovely Hameau ("hamlet"). In a life that took her from royal cradle to throne of France to guillotine, her happiest days were spent at Trianon.

For here she could live a life in the "simplest" possible way; here the queen could enter a salon and the game of cards would not stop; here women wore simple gowns of muslin without a single jewel; here she could be called "Toni." Toinette only wanted to be "Queen of Trianon," not queen of France. And considering the horrible, chamberpot-pungent, gossip-infested corridors of Versailles, you can almost understand why.

From the first, Maria-Antonia (her actual name), was ostracized as an outsider, "l'Autrichienne," an Austrian. Married to Louis XVI—a kind but witless husband—and shamed by her initial failure to deliver a royal heir, she grew to hate overcrowded Versailles and soon escaped to the Trianon, built in 1768 in the English "Adamesque" style by Gabriel for Madame de Pompadour.

Starting in 1774, Toinette refashioned its interior to make it "modern." The gilt trip of the Rococo was banished. Instead, sober neoclassical boiseries (carved wall panels), distinguished Riesener and Carlin bureaus, and walls painted in that most dramatic of new shades—off-white—revealed a sea change in taste. Today her spirit is still present, thanks in part to her bibelots—including the ivory clock fashioned for her by Louis XVI himself—and furniture; her initials still can be seen on the wrought-iron railings of the staircase.

Beyond the Petit Trianon lay the queen's storybook Hameau, a mock-Norman village inspired by the peasant-luxe daydreams caught by Boucher on canvas and by Rousseau in literature. Here Marie-Antoinette lived out her romanticized idyll of "the simple life." With its water mill, genuine lake (Grand Lac), thatched-roof houses built in daub-and-wattle style, pigeon loft, and vegetable plots, this make-believe village was run by Monsieur Valy-Busard, a farmer, and his wife, who often helped the queen—outfitted as a Dresden shepherdess with a Sèvres porcelain crook—tend her flock of perfumed sheep.

As if to destroy any last link with reality, the queen built nearby a jewel-box theater (open by appointment). Here she acted in little plays, sometimes essaying the role of a servant girl. Only the immediate royal family, about seven or so titled friends, and her personal servants were permitted entry; disastrously, the entire officialdom of Versailles society was shut out—a move that only served to infuriate courtiers.

This is how fate and destiny closed the circle. It was at Trianon that a page sent by Monsieur de Saint-Priest found Marie-Antoinette on October 5, 1789, to tell her that Paris was marching on Versailles.

a royal residence, its design was so casual and unassuming. Here *le Bien-Aimé*—the Well-Beloved (as the king was called)—and his consort escaped from the pomp (as in pompous) at Versailles, abandoning royal duties the better to play with lap dogs, translate poetry, and plan gala balls. 🎫 *Joint ticket with Grand Trianon €5* ⊘ *Tues.–Sun. noon–5:30.*

When La Pompadour died, the house passed to Queen Marie-Antoinette, who refurnished it in the Neoclassical style (made fashionable by the rediscovery of Pompeii) while painting its rooms in Redouté pastel hues. Here, across the Petit Lac "Toinette" built her **Hameau** (hamlet), a mock Normandy village where she could live out her idyll of peasant life, pretending to be a shepherdess tending her flock—which happened to be perfumed sheep. Nearby is the tiny jewel-box **Théâtre de la Reine** (☎ 01–30–83–77–43) the queen often used to put on theatricals for her immediate family. The interior is a wonder of 18th-century luxe. Restored in the 1980s, it is now open by appointment only and probably remains the best place to channel the queen's spirit. As she was so happy to take the stage to enact the roles of maids in frothy comedies it is little wonder she lost sight of reality and the first rumblings of revolution (for more on this hapless figure, see the CloseUp box "Marie-Antoinette: Queen of Trianon").

The town of Versailles itself—the capital of France from 1682 to 1789 and again from 1871 to 1879—is easily underestimated, despite its broad, leafy boulevards and majestic buildings. You may feel too tired from exploring the palace and park to spend time visiting the town— but it's worth some effort. Leave the château park by the Bassin de Neptune and turn right onto rue des Réservoirs, past the classical Théâtre Montansier. Up to the right you can make out Louis XIV's equestrian statue in the château courtyard; away in the other direction is the church spire of neighboring Le Chesnay. Rue Carnot, opposite, leads past the stately Écuries de la Reine, once the queen's stables, now the regional law courts, to octagonal place Hoche. Down rue Hoche to the left is the powerful Baroque facade of **Notre-Dame,** built from 1684 to 1686 by Jules Hardouin-Mansart as the parish church for Louis XIV's new town. Around the back of Notre-Dame, on boulevard de la Reine (note the regimented lines of trees), are the elegant Hôtel de Neyret, now used by the Banque de France, and the **Musée Lambinet,** a sumptuous mansion from 1751, furnished with paintings, weapons, fans, and porcelain. ✉ *54 bd. de la Reine* ☎ *01–39–50–30–32* 🎫 *€5* ⊘ *Tues.–Sun. 2–5.*

Take a right onto rue Le Nôtre, then go left and right again into passage de la Geôle, a cobbled alley, lined with quaint antiques shops, that climbs up to **place du Marché-Notre-Dame,** whose open-air morning market on Tuesday, Friday, and Sunday is famed throughout the region; there are also four 19th-century timber-roof halls with fish, meat, and spice stalls. Cross the square and head up rue de la Paroisse to avenue de St-Cloud. Around to the left is the **Lycée Hoche,** whose domed, colonnaded chapel was once part of a convent built for Louis XV's queen, Marie Leszczynska, in 1767.

10 Cross avenue de St-Cloud and head along rue Montbauron to **Avenue de Paris**; its breadth of 120 yards makes it wider than the Champs-Élysées, and its buildings are just as grand and even more historic. Note the mighty doorway at the **Hôtel de Police** on your left and then, at No. 21, the pretty **Hôtel du Barry**. Cross the avenue and return toward the château, past the **Hôtel des Menus-Plaisirs**, where the States General held its first session in May 1789. Just opposite, behind an imposing grille, is the elaborate 19th-century **Préfecture** (the regional government building), confronting the even larger—but uglier—stone-and-brick **Hôtel de Ville** (Town Hall). Avenue de Paris leads down to place d'Armes, a vast sloping plaza usually filled with tourist buses. Facing the château are the Trojan-size

11 royal stables. The **Grandes Écuries** (Grand Stables), to the right, houses the **Musée des Carrosses** (Carriage Museum), open summer weekends only, and the **Manège**, where you can see 28 white horses, and their riders, practicing every morning. ⊠ *1 av. de Paris* ☎*01–39–02–07–14* ⌗*€7* ⊙ *Tues.–Fri., 9–noon, weekends 11–2.*

Cross avenue de Sceaux, pass the imposing chancellery on the corner, and take rue de Satory—a cute pedestrian shopping-street—to the

12 domed **Cathédrale St-Louis,** with its twin-towered facade, built from 1743 to 1754 and enriched with a fine organ and paintings. Turn left

13 down narrow rue du Marché to reach the ramshackle but photogenic **Carrés St-Louis,** a prototype of 18th-century housing development.

14 Rue d'Anjou leads down to the 6-acre **Potager du Roi,** the lovingly restored, split-level royal fruit-and-vegetable garden created in 1683 by Jean-Baptiste de La Quintinye. ⊠ *Entrance at 4 rue Hardy* ☎ *01–39–24–62–62* ⌗ *€6.50* ⊙ *Apr.–Oct., daily 10–6.*

From the Potager du Roi, return up rue de Satory and take rue du Vieux-Versailles, just as old—in parts, actually decrepit—and full of charac-

15 ter as its name suggests. The **Salle du Jeu de Paume,** the indoor tennis court (built in 1686) where the Third Estate swore to transform absolutist France into a constitutional monarchy on June 20, 1789, is off to the right. ⊠ *1 rue du Jeu-de-Paume* ☎ *01–30–83–77–88* ⌗ *Free* ⊙ *Apr.–Oct., weekends 12:30–6:30.*

Rue de l'Indépendance-Américaine leads from the top of rue du Vieux-Versailles up to the château, where Louis XIV, quite uncoincidentally, is clearly visible on his prancing steed. Admire the sculpted porticoes and gilded Sun King emblems on the 17th- and 18th-century state build-

16 ings lining the street. In the other direction, it leads down to the **Pièce d'Eau des Suisses,** a large artificial lake. Opposite the lake is the stately

17 **Orangerie,** erected by Hardouin-Mansart from 1684 to 1686. From November through Easter the Orangerie serves as a hothouse, when it is packed with the orange and palm trees that are artfully arranged in front in summer. Two monumental flights of steps lead up to the château terrace above.

Where to Stay & Eat

★ **$$$$** ✕ **Les Trois Marches.** In the Trianon Palace hotel, celebrated chef Gérard Vié's take on *cuisine bourgeoise* is one of the most *luxe* around—you'll find it hard to wait for your meal after perusing the menu, studded with delights like turbot *galette* (cake) with onions and *pommes Anna,* cassoulet with Codiza sausages, and a sublime duck simmered with turnips and truffles. The restaurant, within the Trianon Palace hotel, has a fetching and huge terrace open in pleasant weather. ⊠ *1 bd. de la Reine* ☎ *01–30–84–52–00* ♨ *Reservations essential* 🏛 *Jacket and tie* ☰ *AE, DC, MC, V* ☉ *Closed Sun., Mon., and Aug.*

$–$$ ✕ **Quai No. 1.** Fish and seafood rule supreme amid the sails, barometers, and model ships of this quaintly decked-out restaurant. Lobster and house-smoked salmon are specialties. Eating à la carte isn't too expensive, and there are good-value prix-fixe menus at €16, €19, and €24. ⊠ *1 av. de St-Cloud* ☎ *01–39–50–42–26* ☰ *MC, V* ☉ *Closed Mon. No dinner Sun.*

★ **$$$$** ✕🏨 **Trianon Palace.** A modern-day Versailles, this deluxe hotel is in a turn-of-the-20th-century creation of imposing size, filled with soaring rooms (including the historic Salle Clemenceau, site of the 1919 Versailles Peace Conference, which brought World War I to an end) and with a huge garden close to the château park. Once faded, the hotel is now aglitter with a health club (alone worth the price of admission—the pool idles beneath a glass pyramid) and Les Trois Marches restaurant, one of France's best. Note that a newer annex, the Pavillon Trianon, has been constructed, but at these prices you should insist on the full treatment in the main building (and ask for one of the even-numbered rooms, which look out over the woods near the Trianons; odd-numbered rooms overlook the modern annex). ⊠ *1 bd. de la Reine, 78000* ☎ *01–30–84–50–00* ⊕ *www.trianonpalace.fr* 🖨 *01–30–84–50–01* ➘ *166 rooms, 26 suites* ♨ *Restaurant, minibars, cable TV, pool, health club, Internet, business services* ☰ *AE, DC, MC, V* ⦿ *BP.*

$ 🏨 **Le Cheval Rouge.** This unpretentious old hotel, built in 1676, is in a corner of the town market square, close to the château and strongly recommended if you plan to explore the town on foot. Some rooms around the old stable courtyard have their original wood beams. ⊠ *18 rue André-Chénier, 78000* ☎ *01–39–50–03–03* 🖨 *01–39–50–61–27* ⊕ *www.chevalrouge.fr.st* ➘ *38 rooms, 7 with bath, 31 with shower* ♨ *Cable TV, bar, some pets allowed (fee); no a/c* ☰ *AE, MC, V* ⦿ *EP.*

¢–$ 🏨 **Home St-Louis.** This family-run, three-story brick hotel is a good, cheap, quiet bet—close to the cathedral and not too far from the château. ⊠ *28 rue St-Louis, 78000* ☎ *01–39–50–23–55* 🖨 *01–39–21–62–45* ➘ *25 rooms, 6 with bath, 19 with shower* ♨ *Some pets allowed; no a/c* ☰ *AE, MC, V* ⦿ *EP.*

Nightlife & the Arts

The largest fountain in Versailles' château park, the Bassin de Neptune, becomes a spectacle of rare grandeur during the **Fêtes de Nuit** (☎ 01–30–83–78–88 for details), a light-and-fireworks show held every Saturday evening in July and September. Directed by Bartabas, the great equine choreographer, the **Académie du Spectacle Equestre** (☎ 01–39–02–07–14) stages hour-long shows on weekend afternoons of horses performing to music—sometimes with riders, sometimes without—in the converted 17th-century Manège (riding school) at the Grandes Ecuries opposite the palace. The **Mois Molière** (☎ 01–30–97–84–48) in June heralds a program of concerts, drama, and exhibits inspired by the famous playwright. The **Théâtre Montansier** (☎ 01–39–24–05–06) has a full program of plays. The **Centre de Musique Baroque** often presents concerts of Baroque music in the château opera and chapel.

Shopping

Aux Colonnes (✉ 14 rue Hoche) is a highly rated *confiserie* (candy shop) with a cornucopia of chocolates and candies; it's closed Monday. **Les Délices du Palais** (✉ 4 rue du Maréchal-Foch) has all the makings for an impromptu picnic (cold cuts, cheese, salads); it's also closed Monday. **Le Gall** (✉ 15 rue Ducis) has a huge choice of cheeses—including one of France's widest selections of goat cheeses; it's closed Sunday afternoon and Monday. **Passage de la Geôle,** which is open Friday–Sunday 9–7 and is close to the town's stupendous market, houses several good antiques shops.

Breteuil

18 *27 km (17 mi) southwest of Versailles, 58 km (35 mi) southwest of Paris, 6 km (4 mi) south of Chevreuse on the N305.*

A textbook example of Neoclassical beauty, the elegant, mansard-roofed **Château de Breteuil,** built in 1610, houses Swedish porcelain, Gobelin tapestries, the richly inlaid Teschen Table encrusted with pearls and precious stones, and dozens of life-size wax figures—including onetime guests English king Edward VII and French novelist Marcel Proust. The vast wooded park has picnic areas, a playground, a pigeon loft, a maze, and more waxwork tableaux representing Puss in Boots, Tom Thumb, and other fairy-tale figures from the works of Charles Perrault. ☎ 01–30–52–05–11 ⊕ *www.chateaudebreteuil.fr* ✍ *Château and grounds €9.90, grounds only €6.80* ☉ *Château Mon.–Sat. 2:30–6, Sun. 11:30–6; grounds daily 10–6.*

The surrounding **Chevreuse Valley** is a scenic region of hills and woods replete with old churches, abbeys, castles, and houses for the well-heeled. Lovers of 17th-century literature may enjoy exploring the **Chemin de Racine** (Racine Route; ⊕ www.parc-naturel-chevreuse.org), which begins in the town of Chevreuse, where the poet and dramatist lived in 1661. Out of boredom he would often walk to neighboring Port-Royal; the path he took through the woods is now marked with panels bearing verses of his poetry. Other sights in Chevreuse are the **Château de la Madeleine,** a hilltop castle, and the 13th-century church of **Notre-Dame de la Roche.**

Dampierre

19 *5 km (3 mi) northwest of Breteuil via D906 and D149, 21 km (13 mi) southwest of Versailles via D91.*

The unspoiled village of Dampierre is adorned with one of the most elegant family seats in Ile-de-France. The stone-and-brick **Château de Dampierre,** surrounded by a moat and set well back from the road, was rebuilt in the 1670s by Hardouin-Mansart for the Duc de Luynes. Much of the interior retains its 17th-century decoration—portraits, wood paneling, furniture, and works of art. But the main staircase, with its trompe-l'oeil murals, and the richly gilded **Salle des Fêtes** (ballroom) date from the 19th century. This second-floor chamber contains a huge wall painting by the celebrated artist Jean-Auguste-Dominique Ingres (1780–1867), an idealized evocation of the mythical Age d'Or (Golden Age)—fitting, perhaps, since this aristocratic family did many good deeds and was even beloved by locals and farmers during the French Revolution. The large park, fronted by gigantic gates, was planned by Versailles landscape architect André Le Nôtre. ⊠ *2 Grande-Rue* ☎ *01–30–52–52–83* ☞ *€8, grounds only €5.20* ◷ *Apr.–mid-Oct., Mon.–Sat. 2–6:30, Sun. 11–noon and 2–6:30.*

Rambouillet

 *16 km (10 mi) southwest of Dampierre via D91 and D906, 32 km (20 mi) southwest of Versailles, 42 km (26 mi) southwest of Paris.*

Haughty Rambouillet, once favored by kings and dukes, is now home to affluent gentry and, occasionally, the French president. The **Château de Rambouillet** is surrounded by a magnificent 30,000-acre forest that remains a great place for biking and walking. Most of the château dates from the early 18th century, but the brawny **Tour François-Ier** (François I Tower), named for the king who died here in 1547, was part of the fortified castle that stood on this site in the 14th century. Highlights include the wood-paneled apartments, especially the **Boudoir de la Comtesse** (Countess's Dressing Room); the marble-wall **Salle de Marbre** (Marble Hall), dating from the Renaissance; and the **Salle de Bains de Napoléon** (Napoléon's Bathroom), adorned with Pompeian-style frescoes. The château's lakeside facade is a sight of unsuspected serenity and, as flowers spill from its balconies, cheerful informality. ☎ *01–34–83–00–25* ⊕ *www.monum.fr* ☞ *€6.10* ◷ *Daily 10–11:30 and 2–5:30.*

An extensive **park,** with a lake with small islands, stretches behind the château, site of the **Laiterie de la Reine** (Queen's Dairy), built for Marie-Antoinette, who, inspired by the writings of Jean-Jacques Rousseau, came here to escape from the pressures of court life, pretending to be a simple milkmaid. It has a small marble temple and grotto and, nearby, the shell-lined Chaumière des Coquillages (Shell Pavilion). The **Bergerie Nationale** (National Sheepfold) is the site of a more serious agricultural venture: the merinos raised here, prized for the quality and yield of their wool, are descendants of sheep imported from Spain by Louis XVI in 1786. A museum alongside tells the tale and evokes shepherd life. The park's exotic, storybook beauty once inspired Jean-Honoré Fragonard to paint one of the greatest landscape paintings of the 18th century, the *Fête at Rambouillet* (now in the Gulbenkian Museum in Lisbon), which tellingly depicts a gilded, courtier-filled barge about to enter a stretch of river torn by raging rapids. *"Apres moi, le deluge,"* indeed. ☞ *Dairy and Shell Pavilion €3, Sheepfold €4* ◷ *Dairy Apr.–Sept., Wed.–Mon. 10–noon and 2–5:30; Oct.–Mar., Wed.–Mon. 10–noon and 2–3:30; Sheepfold mid-Jan.–mid-Dec., Wed.–Sun. 2–5.*

Some 4,000 models, some dating back to 1885, and more than 1,300 feet of track make the **Musée Rambolitrain** a serious model-train museum.

It has historic steam engines, old-time stations, and a realistic points and signaling system. ⊠ *4 pl. Jeanne-d'Arc* ☎ *01–34–83–15–93* ✉ *€3.50* ◷ *Wed.–Sun. 10–noon and 2–5:30.*

Where to Eat

$–$$$ ✕ **La Poste.** You can bank on traditional, unpretentious cooking at this lively former coaching inn right in the center of town. Service is good, as is the selection of prix-fixe menus €20–€32. Chicken fricassee with crayfish is a specialty, along with game in season. ⊠ *101 rue du Général-de-Gaulle* ☎ *01–34–83–03–01* ✉ *AE, MC, V* ◷ *Closed Mon. No dinner Sun. or Thurs.*

Maintenon

㉑ *23 km (14 mi) southwest of Rambouillet via D906, 65 km (41 mi) southwest of Paris.*

Vestiges of Louis XIV, both atmospheric and architectural, make Maintenon an intriguing stopover on the road to Chartres. The **Château de Maintenon** once belonged to Louis XIV's second wife, Françoise Scarron—better known as Madame de Maintenon—whom he married morganatically in 1684 (as social inferiors, neither she nor her children could claim a royal title). She had acquired the château as a young widow 10 years earlier, and her private apartments are the focus of an interior visit. A round brick tower (16th century) and square 12th-century keep give the ensemble a muscular dignity. Mirrored in a canal that contains the waters of the Eure, this remains one of the most picturesque châteaux in France. Inside, lush salons are done up in the Louis XIII style (or rather, in the Second Empire, 19th-century version of it), a homage to royal roots created by the Ducs de Noailles, one of France's most aristocratic families, which has maintained Maintenon as one of its family homes for centuries. ⊠ *Pl. Aristide Briand* ☎ *02–37–23–00–09* ✉ *€6* ◷ *Apr.–Oct., Wed.–Mon. 2–6:30; Nov.–mid-Dec. and late Jan.–Mar., weekends 2–5:30.*

Looming at the back of the château garden and extending through the village almost from the train station to highway D6 are the unlikely ivy-covered arches of a ruined **aqueduct,** one of the Sun King's most outrageous projects. The original scheme aimed to provide the ornamental lakes in the gardens of Versailles (some 50 km [31] mi away) with water from the River Eure. In 1684, 30,000 men were signed up to construct a three-tiered, 5-km (3-mi) aqueduct as part of the project. Many died in the process, and construction was called off in 1689.

Where to Stay & Eat

$$$$ ✕🏨 **Château d'Esclimont.** Graced with pointed turrets, *pièces d'eau*
FodorsChoice (moated pools), and a checkerboard facade, this 19th-century château—
★ built by the de La Rochefoucaulds—is well worth seeking out if you wish to eat and sleep like an aristocrat. This member of the Relais & Châteaux group is replete with luxuriously furnished guest rooms (many are loftily dimensioned, others snug in corner turrets) adorned with reproduction 18th-century French pieces. Carved stone garlands, cordovan leathers, brocades, and period antiques grace the public salons; the superbly

manicured grounds cradle a heated pool. The cuisine is sophisticated: quail, lamb, lobster, and game in season top the menu at the restaurant, La Rochefoucauld (dinner reservations are essential, and a jacket and tie are required, as is a very fat wallet). ⊠ *2 rue du Château-d'Esclimont, 19 km (12 mi) southeast of Maintenon: take D116 to village of Gaillardon, keep an eye out for the imposing church, then turn left, 28700 St-Symphorien-le-Château* ☎ *02–37–31–15–15* 🖷 *02–37–31–57–91* ⊕ *www.esclimont.com* 🛏 *46 rooms, 6 suites* ♨ *Restaurant, minibars, cable TV, 2 tennis courts, pool, fishing, Internet, helipad; no a/c* ⊟ *AE, DC, MC, V* ⏐⦾⏐ *MAP.*

★ ¢ ✕ **Bistrot d'Adeline.** This small, rustic bistro on the main street close to the château in Maintenon offers a cheerful welcome and home cooking with sauces, stews, and *tête de veau* (calf's head) among the specialties. There's a good-value three-course set menu at lunchtime for just €11. ⊠ *3 rue Collin-d'Harleville* ☎ *02–37–23–06–67* ⚏ *Reservations essential* ⊟ *No credit cards* ⊗ *Closed Sun., Mon., and part of Aug.*

Chartres

❷❷ *19 km (12 mi) southwest of Maintenon via D906, 88 km (55 mi) southwest of Paris.*

If Versailles is the climax of French secular architecture, perhaps Chartres is its religious apogee. All the descriptive prose and poetry that have been lavished on this supreme cathedral can only begin to suggest the glory of its 12th- and 13th-century sculpture and stained glass, the strange sense of the numinous that the whole ensemble imparts even to nonbelievers. Notre-Dame de Chartres is an extraordinary fusion of Romanesque and Gothic elements brought together at a moment when the flame of medieval faith burned brightest. The stone and glass of this cathedral are somehow suffused with that same burning mysticism. Chartres is more than a church—it's a nondenominational spiritual experience.

If you arrive from Maintenon across the edge of the Beauce, the richest agrarian plain in France, you can see Chartres's spires rising up from oceans of wheat (at least between early June and late July). The whole town—with its old houses and picturesque streets—is worth leisurely exploration. Ancient streets tumble down from the cathedral to the river; from rue du Pont-St-Hilaire there is an intriguing view of the rooftops below the cathedral. Each year on August 15, pilgrims and tourists flock here for the Procession du Voeu de Louis XIII, a religious procession through the streets commemorating the French monarchy's vow to serve the Virgin Mary.

Fodor'sChoice   Worship on the site of the **Cathédrale Notre-Dame,** better known as Chartres
★   Cathedral, goes back to before the Gallo-Roman period; the crypt contains a well that was the focus of Druid ceremonies. In the late 9th century Charles II (known as the Bald) presented Chartres with what was believed to be the tunic of the Virgin Mary, a precious relic that attracted hordes of pilgrims. The current cathedral, the sixth church on the spot, dates mainly from the 12th and 13th centuries and was erected after the previous building, dating from the 11th century, burned down in 1194.

A well-chronicled outburst of religious fervor followed the discovery that the Virgin Mary's relic had miraculously survived unsinged. Princes and paupers, barons and bourgeois gave their money and their labor to build the new cathedral. Ladies of the manor came to help monks and peasants on the scaffolding in a tremendous resurgence of religious faith that followed the Second Crusade. Just 25 years were needed for Chartres Cathedral to rise again, and it has remained substantially unchanged since.

The lower half of the facade survives from the earlier Romanesque church: this can be seen most clearly in the use of round arches rather than the pointed Gothic type. The **Royal Portal** is richly sculpted with scenes from the life of Christ—these sculpted figures are among the greatest created during the Middle Ages—and the flanking towers are also Romanesque. The taller of the two spires (380 feet versus 350 feet) was built at the start of the 16th century, after its predecessor was destroyed by fire; its fanciful Flamboyant intricacy contrasts sharply with the stumpy solemnity of its Romanesque counterpart (access €3). The **rose window** above the main portal dates from the 13th century, and the three windows below it contain some of the finest examples of 12th-century stained glass in France.

The interior is somber, and your eyes will need time to adjust. The reward is seeing the gemlike richness of the stained glass, with the famous deep Chartres blue predominating. The oldest window is arguably the most beautiful: **Notre-Dame de la Belle Verrière** (Our Lady of the Lovely Window), in the south choir. The cathedral's windows are being gradually cleaned—a lengthy, painstaking process—and the contrast with those still covered in the grime of centuries is staggering. It's worth taking a pair of binoculars along with you to pick out the details. If you wish to know more about stained-glass techniques and the motifs used, visit the small exhibit in the gallery opposite the north porch. For even more detail, try to arrange a tour (in English) with local institution Malcolm Miller, whose knowledge of the cathedral's windows is formidable. (He leads tours twice a day Monday through Saturday; the cost is €5.50. You can reach him at the telephone number below.) The vast black-and-white labyrinth on the floor of the nave is one of the few to have survived from the Middle Ages; the faithful were expected to travel along its entire length (some 300 yards) on their knees. Guided tours of the **Crypte** start from the Maison de la Crypte opposite the south porch. You can also see a 4th-century Gallo-Roman wall and some 12th-century wall paintings. ⊠ *16 cloître Notre-Dame* ☎ *02–37–21–56–33* ⊕ *www.ville-chartres.com* ✆ *Crypt €2.30* ☉ *Cathedral 8:30–7:30, guided tours of crypt Easter–Oct., daily at 11, 2:15, 3:30, 4:30, and 5:15; Nov.–Easter, daily at 11 and 4.*

The **Musée des Beaux-Arts** (Fine Arts Museum) is in a handsome 18th-century building just behind the cathedral that used to serve as the bishop's palace. Its varied collection includes Renaissance enamels, a portrait of Erasmus by Holbein, tapestries, armor, and some fine (mainly French) paintings from the 17th, 18th, and 19th centuries. There's also a room devoted to the forceful 20th-century landscapes of Maurice de Vlaminck, who once lived in the region. ⊠ *29 cloître Notre-Dame* ☎ *02–37–36–41–39* ✆ *€2.50* ☉ *Wed.–Mon. 10–noon and 2–5.*

The Gothic church of **St-Pierre** (⊠ Rue St-Pierre), near the Eure River, has magnificent medieval windows from a period (circa 1300) not represented at the cathedral. The oldest stained glass here, portraying Old Testament worthies, is to the right of the choir and dates from the late 13th century. Exquisite 17th-century stained glass can be admired at the church of **St-Aignan** (⊠ Rue des Grenets), around the corner from St-Pierre.

Where to Stay & Eat

$$$ ✕ **La Vieille Maison.** Just 100 yards from the cathedral, in a pretty 14th-century building with a flower-decked patio, this restaurant is a fine choice for either lunch or dinner. Chef Bruno Letartre regularly changes his menu, but invariably includes such regional specialties as asparagus, rich duck pâté, and superb homemade foie gras. Prices, though justified, can be steep, but the €29 lunch menu is a good bet. ⊠ *5 rue au Lait* ☎ *02–37–34–10–67* ⊕ *www.lavieillemaison.fr.st* ▤ *AE, MC, V* ☯ *Closed Mon. No dinner Sun.*

★ $$–$$$ ✕ **Le Buisson Ardent.** In an attractive old oak-beam building almost within sight of the cathedral's south portal, this popular restaurant has inexpensive prix-fixe menus (especially on weekdays) and a choice of imaginative à la carte dishes. Try the papillote salmon with seafood risotto and the strawberry millefeuille. Service is gratifyingly attentive. ⊠ *10 rue au Lait* ☎ *02–37–34–04–66* ▤ *MC, V* ☯ *Closed Wed. No dinner Sun.*

$$–$$$ ▥ **Le Grand Monarque.** The most popular rooms in this 18th-century coaching inn, part of the Best Western chain, are in a separate turn-of-the-20th-century building overlooking a garden. The most atmospheric are tucked away in the attic. The restaurant, which has prix-fixe menus starting at €29, offers such delicacies as pheasant pie and roast duck with mushrooms. ⊠ *22 pl. des Épars, 28000* ☎ *02–37–18–15–15* ▤ *02–37–36–34–18* ⊕ *www.bw-grand-monarque.com* ⊶ *55 rooms, 47 with bath, 8 with shower* ♨ *Restaurant, minibars, cable TV, bar, Internet, some pets allowed (fee); no a/c in some rooms* ▤ *AE, DC, MC, V* ▮ *BP.*

Shopping

Vitrail (stained glass) being the key to Chartres's fame, you may want to visit the **Galerie du Vitrail** (⊠ 17 cloître Notre-Dame ☎ 02–37–36–10–03 ⊕ www.galerie-du-vitrail.com), which specializes in the noble art. Pieces range from small plaques to entire windows, and there are books on the subject in English and French.

Dreux

㉓ *35 km (22 mi) north of Chartres via N154, 74 km (46 mi) west of Paris.*

Dreux, center of an independent province during the Middle Ages, enjoyed an upsurge in prosperity after being united to the French crown in 1556 (shortly after completion of the beefy belfry on the main square). The early 19th century conferred lasting glory on the town in the form of the burial chapel of the royal House of Orléans.

In 1816 the Orléans family, France's ruling house from 1830 to 1848, began the construction of a circular chapel-mausoleum on the hill behind the town center. The **Chapelle Royale St-Louis** is built in sugary but

★

not unappealing neo-Gothic: superficial ornament rather than structural form recalls the medieval style. The magnificent interior prompts wonder with its Sèvres-manufactured "stained glass"—thin layers of glass coated with painted enamel (an extremely rare, fragile, and vivid technique)—and funereal statuary. Some of the **tombs**—an imploring hand reaching through a window to a loved one or an infant wrapped in a cloak of transparent gauze—may evoke morbid sentimentality, but their technical skill and compositional drama belie any mawkishness. ✉ 2 sq. d'Aumale ☎ 02–37–46–07–06 ⚄ €6 ☉ Apr.–Nov., Wed.–Mon. 9–11:30 and 2:30–6.

The church of **St-Pierre,** across the road from the belfry, is an interesting jumble of styles with pretty stained glass and a 17th-century organ loft. It presents a curious silhouette, with its unfinished classical towers cut off midway. ✉ Pl. Métézeau ☎ 02–37–42–06–89.

Houdan

㉔ 20 km (12 mi) east of Dreux via N12, 54 km (34 mi) west of Paris.

Although fast N12 now skirts around Houdan, the town grew up as a busy stop on the Paris–Dreux road. It's protected by a mighty 12th-century keep rising from the hilltop above two small rivers, the Opton and the Vesgre. Timber-frame houses along the main street (rue de Paris), including several former inns, recall Houdan's bygone status, as does the ornate church, which retains many of its original 17th- and 18th-century elements, including the pulpit, altarpiece, lectern, pews, and organ case. Houdan was also famed for its poultry market, and a succulent local breed of chicken with a fancy plumed crest—the poularde de Houdan—still survives.

Where to Eat

$$ ✕ **La Poularde.** This comfortable restaurant at the foot of the town is named for the local breed of chicken, often served here with truffles or morels. Braised beef and smoked-fish salad are other specialties, and there's a good-value lunch menu. The airy pastel dining room turns its back on the highway outside, looking out on a trim lawn instead. ✉ 24 av. de la République ☎ 01–30–59–60–50 ⊕ www.alapoularde.com ▭ MC, V ☉ Closed Mon., Tues., and part of Aug. No dinner Sun.

Montfort-L'Amaury

㉕ 18 km (11 mi) east of Houdan via N12 and D76, 40 km (25 mi) west of Paris.

Montfort-L'Amaury, with its 17th-century houses and twisting, narrow streets clustered around an old church, is one of the prettiest towns in Ile-de-France. It has a ruined hilltop castle, remnants of medieval ramparts, and a cloister-lined cemetery. Dominating the town square is the bulky Renaissance tower of the church of **St-Pierre–St-Paul.** Note the gargoyles around the far end and, inside, the 37 splendid Renaissance stained-glass windows.

Composer Maurice Ravel lived in Montfort from 1921 until his death in 1937; he composed his famous *Bolero* in 1928 in his Japanese-style garden. His house, now the **Musée Maurice-Ravel** (Ravel Museum), has been reconstituted with many of his mementos and furnishings (including his piano). ☒ *Le Belvédère, 5 rue Maurice-Ravel* ☏ *01–34–86–00–89* 🎟 *€6.10* ☉ *Guided visits only, weekends at 10, 11, 2:30, 3:30, and 4:30, Wed.–Fri. 2:30–5 by appointment.*

Where to Stay & Eat

★ **$$–$$$** ✕🏨 **La Domaine du Verbois.** Greek goddesses set the tone here: bedrooms in this stately late-19th-century mansion in Neauphle-le-Château, 10 km (6 mi) east of Montfort and just a 20-minute drive from Paris, are named after them. The larger rooms are at the front; the smaller rooms at the back are quieter and overlook the pretty, tumbling garden. All rooms have reproduction 18th-century furniture and colorful Chinese rugs. The four-course, €30 set menu in the pink-walled dining room, might include crawfish salad or turbot in champagne sauce. Genial owner Kenneth Boone is half-American. ☒ *38 av. de la République, 10 km (6 mi) east of Montfort via N12–D11, 78640 Neauphle-le-Château* ☏ *01–34–89–11–78* 🖨 *01–34–89–57–33* ⊕ *www.hotelverbois.com* ⤶ *22 rooms* ⚴ *Restaurant, some minibars, cable TV, baby-sitting, Internet, some pets allowed (fee); no a/c* ▭ *AE, DC, MC, V* ☉ *Closed 2 wks Aug. No dinner Sun.* ⦿ *MAP.*

Thoiry

㉖ *11 km (7 mi) north of Montfort-L'Amaury via D76 and D11, 44 km (28 mi) west of Paris.*

Thoiry is most famous for its 16th-century château with beautiful gardens, a wild-animal preserve, and a gastronomy museum. The village makes an excellent day trip from Paris, especially if you're traveling with children. The showpiece remains the **Château de Thoiry,** built by Philibert de l'Orme in 1564. You can see here a handsome Renaissance facade set off by gardens landscaped in the disciplined French fashion by Le Nôtre, in this case with unexpected justification: the château is positioned directly in line with the sun as it sets in the west at the winter solstice (December 21) and as it rises in the east at the summer solstice (June 21). Heightening the effect, the central part of the château appears to be a transparent arch of light because of its huge glass doors and windows. Owners Vicomte Paul de La Panouse and his American wife, Annabelle, have restored the château and park, opening both to the public. The distinguished history of the La Panouse family—a Comte César even fought in the American Revolution—is retraced in the **Musée des Archives** (Archives Museum), where papal bulls and Napoleonic letters mingle with notes from Thomas Jefferson and Benjamin Franklin. You're allowed to wander at leisure, although it's best not to stray too far from the official footpath through the **Parc Zoologique** (animal preserve). Note that the parts of the reserve that contain the wilder beasts—deer, zebra, camels, hippos, bears, elephants, and lions—can be visited only by car. Tigers can be seen from the safety of a raised footbridge. Nearby is a children's play area with a burrow to wriggle through and a huge net-

ted cobweb to bounce around in. ☎ *01–34–87–52–25* ⊕ *www.thoiry.*
tm.fr 🖾 *Château only, €6, park and game reserve €17.80* ⊙ *June–Sept.,*
weekdays 10–6, weekends 10–6:30; Oct.–May, daily 10–5:30.

ALONG THE SEINE TO GIVERNY

Renowned for its beauty as it weaves through Paris, the Seine River is
no less appealing as it flows gently northwest toward Normandy. The
terrace at the château St-Germain-en-Laye, residence of the French
kings before Versailles, provides a memorable view of the valley, soon
to break into a series of chalky cliffs beyond Mantes. Farther on, tucked
away on the bank of the Epte (a tributary of the Seine), are Monet's home
and fabled garden in Giverny.

Rueil-Malmaison

㉗ *8 km (5 mi) west of Paris on N13 via La Défense.*

Rueil-Malmaison is a slightly dreary western suburb of Paris, but the
memory of the legendary pair Napoléon and Joséphine still haunts its
château. Built in 1622, **La Malmaison** was bought by the future empress
Joséphine in 1799 as a love nest for Napoléon and herself (they had married three years earlier). After the childless Joséphine was divorced by
the heir-hungry emperor in 1809, she retired to La Malmaison and died
here on May 29, 1814. The château has 24 rooms furnished with
exquisite tables, chairs, and sofas of the Napoleonic period; of special
note are the library, game room, and dining room. The walls are adorned
with works by artists of the day, such as Jacques-Louis David, Pierre-
Paul Prud'hon, and Baron Gérard. Take time to admire the clothes and
hats that belonged to Napoléon and Joséphine, particularly the empress's
gowns. Their carriage can be seen in one of the garden pavilions, and
another pavilion contains a unique collection of snuffboxes donated by
Prince George of Greece. The gardens themselves are delightful, especially the regimented rows of tulips in spring. 🖾 *15 av. du Château*
☎ *01–41–29–05–55* ⊕ *www.chateau-malmaison.fr/* 🖾 *€4.50*
⊙ *Wed.–Mon. 10–noon and 1:30–5.*

Currently being renovated, the **Bois Préau,** a smaller mansion dating from
the 17th century, is close to La Malmaison (and can be visited on the
same admission ticket). It was acquired by Joséphine in 1810, after her
divorce, but was subsequently reconstructed in the 1850s. Today its 10
rooms, complete with furniture and objects from the Empire period, are
devoted mainly to souvenirs of Napoléon's exile on the island of St. He-
lena. 🖾 *Av. de l'Impératrice* ☎ *01–41–29–05–55* ⊙ *Closed for renovation at this writing.*

St-Germain-en-Laye

㉘ *4 km (2½ mi) north of Marly-le-Roi via N186 and N13, 9 km (5½ mi)*
west of Rueil-Malmaison, 17 km (11 mi) west of Paris.

The elegant town of St-Germain-en-Laye, encircled by forest perched
behind Le Nôtre's Grande Terrace overlooking the Seine, has lost little

FodorśChoice ★

of its original cachet, despite the invasion of wealthy former Parisians who commute to work on the RER.

If you're fond of the swashbuckling novels of Alexandre Dumas (who, incidentally, enjoyed the rare honor of reburial in the Paris Panthéon in 2002), then you'll enjoy the **Château de Monte-Cristo** (Monte Cristo Castle) at Port-Marly on the southern fringe of St-Germain (signposted to your left as you arrive from Marly-le-Roi). You may find that its fanciful exterior, where pilasters, cupolas, and stone carvings compete for attention, has crossed the line from opulence to tastelessness, but—as in the novels, *The Count of Monte Cristo* and *The Three Musketeers*—swagger, not subtlety, is what counts. Dumas built the château after his books' surging popularity made him rich in the 1840s. Construction costs and lavish partying meant he went broke just as quickly, and he skedaddled to a Belgian exile in 1849. The château contains pictures, Dumas mementos, and the luxurious Moorish Chamber, with spellbinding, interlacing plasterwork executed by Arab craftsmen (lent by the Bey of Tunis) and restored thanks to a donation from the late Moroccan king Hassan II. ⊠ *Av. du Président-Kennedy* ☎ *01–39–16–49–49* ⊕ *www. mairie-marlyleroi.fr* 🎫 *€5* ☉ *Apr.–Oct., Tues.–Fri. 10–12:30 and 2–6, weekends 10–6; Nov.–Mar., Sun. 2–5.*

★ Next to the St-Germain RER train station is the stone-and-brick **Château de St-Germain,** with its dry moat, intimidating circular towers, and La Grande Terrasse, one of the most spectacular of all French garden set-pieces; the château itself dates from the 16th and 17th centuries. A royal palace has existed here since the early 12th century, when Louis VI—known as Le Gros (the Fat)—exploited St-Germain's defensive potential in his bid to pacify Ile-de-France. A hundred years later Louis IX (St. Louis) added the elegant **Sainte-Chapelle,** the château's oldest remaining section; note the square-topped, not pointed, side windows and the filled-in rose-window on the back wall. Charles V (1364–80) built a powerful defensive keep in the mid-14th century, but from the 1540s François I and his successors transformed St-Germain into a palace with more of a domestic than warlike vocation. Louis XIV was born here, and it was here that his father, Louis XIII, died. Until 1682—when the court moved to Versailles—it remained the country's foremost royal residence outside Paris; several Molière plays were premiered in the main hall. Since 1867 the château has housed the impressive **Musée des Antiquités Nationales** (Museum of National Antiquities), holding a trove of artifacts, figurines, brooches, and weapons from the Stone Age to the 8th century. Behind the château is Andre Le Nôtre's **Grande Terrasse,** an enormous, terraced promenade lined by century-old lime trees. Directly overlooking the Seine, it was completed in 1673 and has rarely been outdone in terms of sheer grandeur and length. ⊠ *Pl. Charles-de-Gaulle* ☎ *01–39–10–13–00* 🎫 *€4* ☉ *Wed.–Mon. 9–5:15.*

★ The quaint **Musée du Prieuré** (Priory Museum) is devoted to the work of the artist Maurice Denis (1870–1943) and his fellow Symbolists and to Nabis—painters opposed to the naturalism of their 19th-century

Impressionist contemporaries. Denis found the calm of the former Jesuit priory, set above tiered gardens with statues and rose bushes, ideally suited to his spiritual themes, which he expressed in stained glass, ceramics, and frescoes as well as oils. ⊠ *2 bis rue Maurice-Denis* ☎ *01–39–73–77–87* 🖅 *€4* ☉ *Tues.–Fri. 10–5:30, weekends 10–6:30.*

Where to Stay & Eat

$–$$ ✕ **La Feuillantine.** An imaginative, good-value prix-fixe menu has made this wood-beamed restaurant an often-crowded success. Gizzard salad, salmon with endive, and herbed chicken fricassee with morels are among the specialties. Try for a table near the window; those near the back of the restaurant can be a bit gloomy. ⊠ *10 rue des Louviers* ☎ *01–34–51–04–24* ⊕ *www.lafeuillantine.com* ☰ *AE, MC, V.*

★ **$$$$** ✕🖭 **La Forestière.** This hotel, run by Philippe and Isabelle Cazaudehore, is St-Germain's most stylish and a member of the Relais & Châteaux chain. Its forest environs, 18th century–style furniture, and fine restaurant, the Cazaudehore (closed Monday), where chef Jacques Pactol majors in braised monkfish, pig's feet and truffled puree, contribute to a sense of well-being. ⊠ *1 av. du Président-Kennedy, 78100* ☎ *01–30–61–64–64* 🖷 *01–39–73–73–88* ⊕ *www.cazaudehore.fr* 🛏 *25 rooms, 5 suites* ☖ *Restaurant, minibars, cable TV, bar, some pets allowed (fee); no a/c* ☰ *AE, DC, MC, V* ❙◯❙ *BP.*

Nightlife & the Arts

The **Fête des Loges** (Loges Festival) is a giant fair and carnival held in the Forest of St-Germain from July to mid-August. Hordes of fans of cotton candy, roller coasters, and Ferris wheels turn up every year.

Maisons-Laffitte

㉙ *8 km (5 mi) northeast of St-Germain-en-Laye via D157, 16 km (10 mi) northwest of Paris.*

The riverside suburb of Maisons-Laffitte has an unusually high proportion of elegant villas, many of which were built with profits from the town's racetrack by the Seine (with its famous 2,200-yard straight) and training stables; 14 races are held between July and September. The town's steep-roofed, early Baroque **Château de Maisons,** constructed by architect François Mansart from 1634 to 1651, is one of the most elegant but least known châteaux in Ile-de-France. This was not always the case: Sun King Louis XIV came to the housewarming party, and Louis XV, Louis XVI, the 18th-century writer Voltaire, and Napoléon all stayed here. The interior clearly met their exacting standards, thanks to the well-proportioned entrance vestibule with its rich sculpture; the winding **Escalier d'Honneur,** a majestic staircase adorned with paintings and statuary; and the royal apartments above them, with their parquet floors and wall paneling. The **Musée du Cheval de Course** (Racehorse Museum), in the basement, evokes the world of the turf. Unfortunately, the château's once regal grounds have been greatly amputated by encroaching streets and highways. ⊠ *2 av. Carnot* ☎ *01–39–62–01–49* ⊕ *www.monum.fr* 🖅 *€6.10* ☉ *Wed.–Mon. 10–noon and 1:30–5.*

Poissy

30 *8 km (4 mi) west of Maisons-Laffitte via D308, 21 km (13 mi) north-west of Paris.*

Three museums and its historic significance as the birthplace of France's saintly king Louis IX help Poissy—the name comes from *poisson* (fish), as you may deduce from the town's ubiquitous emblem—defy its reputation as an unfashionable industrial town. The remains of the font in which Louis was baptized in 1214 can still be seen in the **Église Notre-Dame,** a medieval church with two striking octagonal towers. The **Musée d'Art et d'Histoire** (Art and History Museum), in a stern brick mansion opposite the church, is packed with tools, sculptures, old postcards, and paintings tracking Poissy's history from its 6th-century origins to its medieval prosperity as a cattle market and vine-growing center to its latter-day position as a center for auto plants. ⊠ *12 rue St-Louis* ☎ *01–39–65–06–06* 🖃 *Free* ⊙ *Wed.–Sun. 9:30–noon and 2–5:30.*

Housed behind the turreted facade of the 14th-century royal priory, the **Musée du Jouet** (Toy Museum) has a collection of historical toys, games, automatons, puppets, electric trains, rocking horses, tin soldiers, and dollhouses. ⊠ *1 enclos de l'Abbaye* ☎ *01–39–65–06–06* 🖃 *€3.20* ⊙ *Tues.–Sun. 9:30–noon and 2–5:30.*

★ Rising on what look like stilts—in fact, slender concrete pillars—above an extensive lawn that stretched over 15 acres until a (not undistinguished) school was built alongside in the 1950s, the **Villa Savoye** is considered one of Le Corbusier's most accomplished designs. Industrialist Pierre Savoye and his wife spent weekends here beginning in 1931, but stopped coming in 1938—fed up with the leaky flat roof. The villa appears as an austere white block; this is intentionally misleading—the ground floor, in fact, curves around to the entrance, at the back. An oval funnel emerges from the roof, harboring a solarium. Inside, the visual teasing continues, with a spiral staircase whose vertical emphasis clashes with the gently sloping ramp that serves as the principal transition from floor to floor. Be warned: the villa's delights are hidden in more ways than one, and advance signposting is terrible. Head up from the Toy Museum and turn right at the lights opposite the cemetery: the villa is 700 yards up, at the crest of the hill on the right. ⊠ *82 rue de Villiers* ☎ *01–39–65–01–06* ⊕ *www.monum.fr* 🖃 *€4* ⊙ *Tues.–Sun. 10–1 and 2–5.*

en route As you begin to enter the region of the Ile-de-France the Impressionists made their own, cross the Seine at Vernouillet and follow D190 to **Mantes-la-Jolie,** approaching across the old bridge from Limay, once painted by Corot. Another painter, the Post-Impressionist Maximilien Luce, is the hero of the fine town museum alongside the vast, 12th-century Église Notre-Dame. The small, circular windows ringing the east end of the church are an unusual local architectural characteristic—you can also see them 11 km (7 mi) north, at the church in **Vétheuil**—a town immortalized in many a magnificent Monet canvas—where the road regains the riverbank beneath impressive chalk cliffs.

La Roche-Guyon

31 *7 km (4 mi) northwest of Vétheuil on D913, 45 km (28 mi) northwest of Poissy via D190 and D147, 69 km (43 mi) northwest of Paris.*

Ruins of a medieval clifftop castle look down on the River Seine and the quaint village of La Roche-Guyon. A steep-climbing stairway, hewn through the rock, links the castle to the classical **château** below, constructed mainly in the 18th century. The château has impressive iron gates incorporating the arms of the owners, the La Rochefoucauld family; its main building is one story higher than ground level, behind an arcaded terrace that towers above the stables and grassy forecourt. An interior highlight is the *Story of Esther* tapestry series. ⊠ *1 rue de l'Audience* ☎ *01–34–79–74–42* ⊕ *www.val-doise-tourisme.fr* ⊠ *€7* ☺ *Daily 10–6; 10–7 on weekends.*

Where to Eat

$$–$$$ ✕ **Le Moulin de Fourges.** Nestled in verdant countryside by the River Epte, 5 km (3 mi) north of La Roche-Guyon, this converted 18th-century water mill has a mouthwatering setting. Stéphane Lebar's cuisine varies from garlic-stuffed lamb roll to fish from the Mediterranean. ⊠ *38 rue du Moulin, Fourges* ☎ *02–32–52–12–12* ⊕ *www.moulin-de-fourges.com* ⚑ *Reservations essential* ☐ *MC, V* ☺ *Closed Mon. and Nov.–Mar. No dinner Sun.*

Giverny

32 *8 km (5 mi) west of La Roche-Guyon on D5, 70 km (44 mi) northwest of Paris.*

The small village of Giverny (pronounced Jeev-an-yee), just beyond the Epte River, which marks the boundary of Ile-de-France, has become a place of pilgrimage for art lovers. It was here that Claude Monet lived for 43 years, until his death at the age of 86 in 1926. Although his house is now prized by connoisseurs of 19th-century interior decoration, it's his garden, with its Japanese-inspired water-lily pond and its bridge, that remains the high point for many—a veritable 5-acre, three-dimensional Impressionist painting through which you can stroll. In addition, Monet immortalized the surrounding countryside's haystacks and poplar trees in oils, but these motifs have often been altered beyond recognition— the wheat fields are still there, but the wheat is now rolled up, while Monet's famous rows of poplar trees along the River Epte, near the village of Limetz, about 3 km (2 mi) south of Giverny, are completely overgrown. It's easy to get to Giverny from Paris—trains leave every couple of hours from the Gare St-Lazare for the 50-minute ride to Vernon; buses meet the trains and whisk you to Giverny. Most make this a day trip, although Giverny has some jewel B&Bs, so you should consider an overnight or two. Vernon itself (*see below*) has a magisterial Gothic church and other medieval treasures.

Fodor's Choice The **Maison et Jardin Claude-Monet** (Monet House and Garden) has been
★ lovingly restored. Monet was brought up in Normandy and, like many of the Impressionists, was captivated by the soft light of the Seine Val-

ley. After several years in Argenteuil, just north of Paris, he moved downriver to Giverny in 1883 along with his two sons, his mistress, Alice Hoschedé (whom he later married), and her six children. By 1890 a prospering Monet was able to buy the house outright. With its pretty pink walls and green shutters, the house has a warm feeling that may come as a welcome change after the stateliness of the French châteaux. Rooms have been restored to Monet's original designs: the kitchen with its blue tiles, the buttercup-yellow dining room, and Monet's bedroom on the second floor. Only in the 1970s was the house fully and glamorously restored, thanks to the millions contributed by fans and patrons (who were often Americans). Reproductions of his works, and some of the Japanese prints he avidly collected, crowd its walls. During this era, French culture had come under the spell of Orientalism and these framed prints were often gifts from visiting Japanese diplomats, whom Monet had befriended in Paris.

Three years after buying his house and cultivating its garden—which the family called the "Clos Normand"—the prospering Monet purchased another plot of land across the lane to continue his gardening experiments, even diverting the Epte to make a pond. The resulting garden *"a la Japonaise"* (reached through a tunnel from the "Clos"), with flowers spilling out across the paths, contains the famous "tea-garden" bridge and water-lily pond, flanked by a mighty willow and rhododendrons. Images of the bridge and the water lilies—in French, *"Les Nymphéas"*—in various seasons appear in much of Monet's later work. Looking across the pond, it's easy to conjure up the grizzled, bearded painter dabbing at his canvases—capturing changes in light and pioneering a breakdown in form that was to have a major influence on 20th-century art.

The garden is a place of wonder, filled with butterflies, roosters, nearly 100,000 plants bedded every year and more than 100,000 perennials. No matter that nearly 500,000 visitors troop through it every year; they fade into the background thanks to all the beautiful roses, purple carnations, lady's slipper, aubrieta, tulips, beaded irises, hollyhocks, poppies, daises, lambs' ears, larkspur, and azaleas, to mention just a few of the blooms (note that the water lilies flower during the latter part of July and the first two weeks of August). Even so, during the height of spring, when the gardens are particularly popular, try to visit during midweek. If you want to pay your respects, Monet is buried in the family vault in Giverny's village church. ⊠ *84 rue Claude-Monet* ☎ *02–32–51–28–21* ⊕ *www.giverny.org* ✑ *Gardens and home €5.50, gardens only €4* ☾ *Apr.–Oct., Tues.–Sun. 10–6.*

After touring the painterly grounds of Monet's house, you may wish to see some real paintings at the airy **Musée Américain** (American Museum), farther along the road. Endowed by Chicago art patrons Daniel and Judith Terra, it displays works by American Impressionists who were influenced by Claude Monet. After the master made Giverny his home, other artists, including Willard Metcalf, Louis Ritter, Theodore Wendel, and John Leslie Breck, "discovered" Giverny, too (truth be known, Monet soon tired of being a cult figure). On-site are a restaurant and *salon de thé* (tearoom), as well as a garden "quoting" some of Monet's plant compositions. Head down the road to visit Giverny's landmark Hotel Baudy (*see below*), now a restaurant and once the stomping grounds and watering hole of many of these 19th-century artists. ⊠ *99 rue Claude-Monet* ☎ *02–32–51–94–65* ⊕ *www.maag.org* ⊠ *€5.50* ⊙ *Apr.–Nov., Tues.–Sun. 10–6.*

Where to Stay & Eat

$–$$ ✕ **Baudy.** Back in Monet's day, this pretty-in-pink villa was the hotel of the American painters' colony. Today the dining room and terrace are more modern than historic, but parts of this old *epicerie-buvette* (notably, the luscious rose gardens and the studio hut where Cézanne once took up residence) are enchanting, and make up for the very simple cuisine and busloads of tour groups. ⊠ *81 rue Claude-Monet* ☎ *02–32–21–10–03* 🖃 *MC, V* ⊙ *No dinner Sun. Closed Mon. and Nov.–Mar.*

$–$$ ✕ **Les Jardins de Giverny.** This tile-floor restaurant, overlooking a rose garden, is a few minutes' walk from Monet's house. Enjoy the €20 menu or choose from a repertoire of inventive dishes such as foie gras spiked with calvados, duck in cider, or scallops with wild mushrooms. ⊠ *Chemin du Roy* ☎ *02–32–21–60–80* ⊕ *www.jardins-giverny.com* 🖃 *AE, MC, V* ⊙ *Closed Mon. and Dec.–Feb. No dinner Sun.–Fri.*

★ $–$$ 🖭 **Giverny B&Bs.** Giverny's dire shortage of hotels is made up for by a plethora of enticing, stylish, and affordable bed-and-breakfasts set up in many of the town's homes. Particularly notable are **Le Clos Fleuri** (⊠ 5 rue de la Dîme ☎☎ 02–32–21–36–51), a Norman manor house set in a lovely garden and run by the Fouché family; **La Réserve** (⊠ Rue Blanche-Hoschedé ☎ 02–32–21–99–09), about a mile outside town, an expansive residence surrounded by orchards and with gorgeous, antiques-adorned and wood-beamed guest apartments, some of which have fireplaces and canopy beds; and the residence of **Marie-Claire Boscher** (⊠ 1 rue du Colombier ☎☎ 02–32–51–39–70), which used to be a hotel-restaurant that Monet frequented. Log onto the Web site www.giverny.org/hotels for all the details.

$–$$ 🖭 **La Musardière.** Just a short stroll from chez Monet, this manor house (the name means "Place To Idle") has a cozy lobby, guest rooms with views overlooking a leafy garden, and its own restaurant-crêperie (no lunch Monday). ⊠ *123 rue Claude-Monet, 27620 Giverny* ☎ *02–32–21–03–18* 🖶 *02–32–21–60–00* ⊲ *10 rooms, 1 suite* ⚭ *Restaurant, tennis court, pool; no a/c* 🖃 *AE, DC, MC, V* ⊙ *Closed Nov.–Mar.* ⏻ *MAP.*

Vernon

③③ *5 km (3 mi) northwest of Giverny on D5, 73 km (46 mi) northwest of Paris.*

The Vieille Ville of Vernon, on the Seine, has a medieval church, which was often painted by Claude Monet, and several fine medieval timber-frame houses (the best one, on rue Carnot, houses the tourist office). The church of **Notre-Dame** (⊠ Rue Carnot), across from the tourist of-fice, has an arresting rose-window facade that, like the high nave, dates from the 15th century. Rounded Romanesque arches in the choir, how-ever, attest to the building's 12th-century origins. The church is a fine sight when viewed from behind: Monet liked to paint it from across the Seine. A few minor Monet canvases, along with other late-19th-century paintings, can be admired in the town museum, the **Musée Poulain.** This rambling old mansion is seldom crowded, and the helpful curators are happy to explain local history. ⊠ *12 rue du Pont* ☎ *02–32–21–28–09* 🖅 *€2.50* ⊘ *Tues.–Fri. 10–12.30 and 2–6, weekends 2–6.*

Where to Stay & Eat

★ **$$$** ✕⬚ **Château de Brécourt.** This 17th-century stone-and-brick château close to the expressway outside Vernon has high-pitched roofs, an imposing forecourt, and extensive grounds. Guest rooms follow the same exuberant turn-of-the-19th-century lines. Even if you're not staying here, you can dine on the inventive food in the august restaurant, Le Grand Siècle. Dishes such as lobster mousse and veal with truffles make it a popular spot—and it's even easy to get to from Giverny, which is just across the Seine from Vernon. As such châteaux-hotels go, a stay here is a relatively good value. ⊠ *Route de Brécourt, 8 km (5 mi) southwest of Vernon on D181–D75, 27120 Douains* ☎ *02–32–52–40–50* 🖅 *02–32–52–69–65* ⊕ *www.chateaudebrecourt.com* 🖅 *25 rooms, 5 suites* ⌂ *Restaurant, in-room hot tubs, minibars, tennis court, pool, sauna, some pets allowed (fee); no a/c* ⊟ *AE, DC, MC, V* ⓘ⚬ *MAP.:*

FROM THE OISE VALLEY TO DISNEYLAND PARIS

This area covers a broad arc, beginning northwest of Paris in Conflans–Ste-Honorine, where the Oise joins the Seine, then heading east along the Oise Valley to Chantilly, and continuing southeast through Meaux. In addition to being the old stomping grounds for several world-famous artists—Pissarro's canvases of Pontoise are among his best-known, while those van Gogh painted in Auvers were his very last—the area is now the domain of Disneyland Paris.

Conflans–Ste-Honorine

❸❹ *28 km (3 mi) northwest of Paris via A15 and D48.*

Conflans is the capital of France's inland waterway network. Barges arrive from as far afield as the ports of Le Havre and Dunkerque, on the Channel coast, and are often moored as many as six abreast along the 1½-km-long (1-mi-long) quayside, near the *conflans* (confluence) of the Rivers Seine and Oise; one, the *Je Sers (I Serve)*, is the boatmen's own church (open daily). From the hilltop church of St-Maclou there is a spectacular view of the boats. The **Musée de la Batellerie** (Waterways Museum) explains the historic role of the barges and waterways with the help of pictures and scale models. ⊠ *3 pl. Jules-Gévelot* ☎ *01–39–72–58–05* 🖅 *€3* ⊘ *Tues. 1:30–6, Wed.–Fri. 9–noon and 1:30–6, weekends 2–6 (Easter–Sept.) or 2–5 (Oct.–Easter).*

Pontoise

❸❺ *8 km (5 mi) north of Conflans-Ste-Honorine via N184 and N14, 29 km (19 mi) northwest of Paris via A15.*

A pleasant Vieille Ville on the banks of the Oise, Pontoise is famous for its link with the Impressionists. The small **Musée Pissarro,** high up in the

Vieille Ville, pays tribute to one of Pontoise's most illustrious past residents, Impressionist painter Camille Pissarro (1830–1903). The collection of prints and drawings is of interest mainly to specialists, but the view across the valley from the museum gardens will appeal to all. ☒ *17 rue du Château* ☎ *01–30–32–06–75* ⊕ *www.ville-pontoise.fr* ☜ *Free* ☺ *Wed.–Sun. 2–6.*

The **Musée Tavet-Delacour,** housed in a turreted mansion in the center of Pontoise, stages good exhibitions and has a permanent collection that ranges from street scenes and landscapes by Norbert Goenutte and other local painters to contemporary art and the intriguing abstractions of Otto Freundlich. ☒ *4 rue Lemercier* ☎ *01–30–38–02–40* ⊕ *www. ville-pontoise.fr* ☜ *€5.25* ☺ *Wed.–Sun. 10–12:30 and 1:30–6.*

Where to Eat

★ ¢ ✕ **Péché Mignon.** You can expect a friendly welcome and simple, copious classics like steak with mashed potato or chicken with french fries at this bustling restaurant near the Tavet-Delacour museum. Fresh flowers on the embroidered tablecloths add a colorful touch. The first set menu is priced at €12. ☒ *19 bd. Jean-Jaurès* ☎ *01–30–38–48–28* ▤ *No credit cards* ☺ *Closed part of Aug. No dinner Sun. and Mon.*

Auvers-sur-Oise

36 7 *km (4 mi) east of Pontoise via D4, 33 km (21 mi) northwest of Paris*
FodorśChoice *via N328.*
★

The tranquil Oise River valley, which runs northeast from Pontoise, retains much of the charm that attracted Camille Pissarro, Paul Cézanne, Camille Corot, Charles-François Daubigny, and Berthe Morisot to Auvers-sur-Oise in the second half of the 19th century. But despite this lofty company, it is the spirit of Vincent van Gogh that haunts every nook and cranny of this pretty riverside village. You can find out about his Vieille Ville haunts and many other Impressionist sites in Auvers by stopping in at the tourist office at Les Colombières, a 14th-century manor house, set on the rue de la Sansonne (closed from 12:30 to 2 PM every day). Short hikes outside the town center—sometimes marked with yellow trail signs—will lead you to rural landscapes once beloved by Pissarro and Cézanne, including the famous site (fairly close to the village cemetery) where van Gogh finished his last painting, *Wheat Fields with Crows* on July 27, 1890. After laying his easel against a haystack, he walked behind the Château d'Auvers, shot himself, then stumbled to the Auberge Ravoux, where the owner sent to Paris for the artist's brother, Thèo. Van Gogh died on July 29th. He is buried next to his brother (who died the following year) in a simple ivy-covered grave in the village cemetery.

Van Gogh moved here from Arles in May 1890 to be nearer his brother. Little has changed here since that summer of 1890, during the last 10 weeks of van Gogh's life, when he painted no fewer than 70 pictures. The whole village is peppered with plaques marking the spots that inspired his art. The plaques bear reproductions of his paintings, enabling you to compare his final works with the scenes as they are today. His last abode has been turned into a shrine. You can also visit the medieval village church, subject of one of van Gogh's most famous paintings, *L'Église d'Auvers,* and admire Osip Zadkine's powerful statue of van Gogh in the village park.

Set opposite the village town hall, the Auberge Ravoux, the inn where van Gogh stayed, is now the **Maison de van Gogh** (Van Gogh House). A dingy staircase leads up to the tiny, Spartan wood-floor attic where van Gogh stored some of modern art's most famous pictures under his bed. A short film retraces van Gogh's time at Auvers, and there is a well-stocked souvenir shop. Stop for a drink or for lunch in the ground-floor restaurant. ⊠ *8 rue de la Sansonne* ☎ *01–30–36–60–60* ⊕ *www.maison-de-van-gogh.com* ⊠ *€5* ⊙ *Mar.–Nov., Tues.–Sun. 10–6.*

A major town landmark opened to the public for the first time in 2004: the house and garden of van Gogh's closest friend in Auvers, Dr. Paul Gachet. Documents and souvenirs at the **Maison du Dr Gachet** evoke van Gogh's stay in Auvers and Gachet's passion for the avant-garde art of his era. The good doctor was himself the subject of one of the artist's most famous portraits (and the world's most expensive painting, sold for $82 million in the late 1980s), the actual painting of which was reenacted in the 1956 Kirk Douglas bio-pic, *Lust for Life.* Friend and patron to many of the artists who settled in and visited Auvers in the 1880s, among them Cézanne (who immortalized the doctor's house in a famous landscape composition), Gachet also taught them about engraving processes. The ivy covering van Gogh's grave in the cemetery across town was provided by Gachet from this house's garden. ⊠ *78 rue du Dr-Gachet* ☎ *01–30–36–60–60* ⊠ *€4* ⊙ *Tues.–Sun. 10–6.*

ↂ The elegant 17th-century village château—also painted in pictures by van Gogh—set above split-level gardens, now houses the **Voyage au Temps des Impressionnistes** (Journey Through the Impressionist Era). You'll receive a set of infrared headphones (English available), with commentary that guides you past various tableaux illustrating life during the Impressionist years. Although there are no Impressionist originals—500 reproductions pop up on screens interspersed between the tableaux—this is one of France's most imaginative, enjoyable, and innovative museums. Some of the special effects—talking mirrors, computerized cabaret dancing girls, and a simulated train ride past Impressionist landscapes—are worthy of Disney. The museum restaurant, Les Canotiers—named after Renoir's famous painting of boaters—offers dishes favored by such artists as Morisot, Degas, and Manet, while more casual fare is offered at a re-creation of a 19th-century *guinguette* (riverbank café). ⊠ *Rue de Léry* ☎ *01–34–48–48–40* ⊕ *www.chateau-auvers.fr* ⊠ *€10* ⊙ *May–Oct., Tues.–Sun. 10–8; Nov.–Apr., Tues.–Sun. 11–4:30.*

The landscape artist Charles-François Daubigny, a precursor of the Impressionists, lived in Auvers from 1861 until his death in 1878. You can visit his studio, the **Maison-Atelier de Daubigny,** and admire the remarkable mural and roof paintings by Daubigny and fellow artists Camille Corot and Honoré Daumier. ⊠ *61 rue Daubigny* ☎ *01–34–48–03–03* ⊠ *€5* ⊙ *Thurs.–Sun. 2–6:30.*

You may also want to visit the modest **Musée Daubigny** to admire the drawings, lithographs, and occasional oils by local 19th-century artists, some of which were collected by Daubigny himself. The museum is opposite the Maison de van Gogh, above the tourist office. ⊠ *Manoir des Colombières, rue de la Sansonne* ☎ *01–30–36–80–20* ⬚ *€3.50* ⊘ *Wed.–Sun. 2–5.*

Where to Eat

★ **$$–$$$** ✕ **Auberge Ravoux.** For total van Gogh immersion, have lunch in the restaurant he patronized regularly more than 100 years ago and where, in fact, he finally expired. The €33, three-course menu changes regularly, but it's the genius loci that makes eating here special, with glasswork, lace curtains, and wall blandishments carefully modeled on the original designs. A magnificently illustrated book, *Van Gogh's Table* (published by Artisan), by culinary historian Alexandra Leaf and Fred Leeman, recalls Vincent's stay at the Auberge and describes in loving detail the dishes served there at the time. ⊠ *52 rue Général-de-Gaulle* ☎ *01–30–36–60–63* ⬚ *Reservations essential* ⊟ *AE, DC, MC, V* ⊘ *Closed Mon. and Nov.–Feb. No dinner Sun.*

L'Isle-Adam

③⑦ *6 km (4 mi) northeast of Auvers-sur-Oise via D4, 40 km (25 mi) north of Paris via N1.*

Residentially exclusive L'Isle-Adam is one of the most picturesque towns in Ile-de-France. Paris lies just 40 km (25 mi) south, but it could be 100 mi and as many years away. The town has a sandy beach along one stretch of the River Oise (via rue de Beaumont); a curious pagodalike folly, the Pavillon Chinois de Cassan; and an unassuming local museum. The **Musée Louis-Senlecq,** on the main street behind the tall-towered town church, features the ceramic figures produced in L'Isle-Adam a century ago, and contains numerous attractive works by Jules Dupré and other local landscapists. ⊠ *46 Grande-Rue* ☎ *01–34–69–45–44* ⊕ *www.ville-isle-adam.fr* ⬚ *€3.10* ⊘ *Wed.–Mon. 2–6.*

Where to Stay & Eat

$–$$ ✕⊡ **Le Cabouillet.** The riverside Cabouillet aptly reflects the quiet charm of L'Isle-Adam, thanks to its pretty views over the Oise. You can savor these from each of its cozy rooms or from the chic restaurant, where the cooking can be inspired—have the crawfish in Sauternes sauce, if it's on the menu. ⊠ *5 quai de l'Oise, 95290* ☎ *01–34–69–00–90* 🖷 *01–34–69–33–88* ⊕ *www.le-cabouillet.com* ⬚ *5 rooms* ⬚ *Restaurant; no a/c* ⊟ *AE, DC, MC, V* ⊘ *Closed Mon. and late Dec.–early Feb. No dinner Sun.* ⦿ *MAP.*

Chantilly

③⑧ *10 km (6 mi) northeast of Royaumont via D909, 23 km (14 mi) east of L'Isle-Adam via D4, 37 km (23 mi) north of Paris via N16.*

Celebrated for lace, cream, and the most beautiful medieval manuscript in the world—*Les Très Riches Heures du Duc de Berry*—romantic

Chantilly has a host of other attractions: a faux Renaissance château with an eye-popping art collection, splendid Baroque stables, a classy racecourse, and a 16,000-acre forest.

Although its lavish exterior may be 19th-century Renaissance pastiche, the **Château de Chantilly,** sitting snugly behind an artificial lake, houses the outstanding **Musée Condé,** with illuminated medieval manuscripts, tapestries, furniture, and paintings. The most famous room, the **Santuario** (sanctuary), contains two celebrated works by Italian painter Raphael (1483–1520)—the *Three Graces* and the *Orleans Virgin*—plus an exquisite ensemble of 15th-century miniatures by the most illustrious French painter of his time, Jean Fouquet (1420–81). Farther on, in the **Cabinet des Livres** (library), is the world-famous book of hours whose title translates as *The Very Rich Hours of the Duc de Berry,* which was illuminated by the Brothers Limbourg with magical pictures of early 15th-century life as lived by one of Burgundy's richest lords (unfortunately, due to their fragility, painted facsimiles of the celebrated calendar illuminations are on display, not the actual pages of the book). Other highlights of this unusual museum are the **Galerie de Psyché** (Psyche Gallery), with 16th-century stained glass and portrait drawings by Flemish artist Jean Clouet II; the **Chapelle,** with sculptures by Jean Goujon and Jacques Sarrazin; and the extensive collection of paintings by 19th-century French artists, headed by Jean-Auguste-Dominique Ingres. In addition, there are grand and smaller salons, all stuffed with palace furniture, family portraits, and Sèvres porcelains, making this an absolute must for lovers of the decorative and applied arts. ☎ 03–44–62–62–62 ⊕ *www.chateaudechantilly.com* ✉ €7, including park ⊙ *Mar.–Oct., daily 10–6; Nov.–Feb., Wed.–Mon. 10:30–12:45 and 2–5.*

Le Nôtre's **park** is based on that familiar French royal combination of formality (neatly planned parterres and a mighty, straight-banked canal) and romantic eccentricity (the waterfall and the Hameau, a mock-Norman village that inspired Marie-Antoinette's version at Versailles). You can explore on foot or on an electric train, and take a **hydrophile** (electric-powered boat) for a glide down the Grand Canal. ☎03–44–57–35–35 ✉ *Park only €3, with boat €8, with train and boat €10; €15 joint ticket including château ⊙ Mar.–Oct., daily 10–6; Nov.–Feb., daily 10:30–12:45 and 2–5.*

★ ☺ The palatial 18th-century **Grandes Écuries** (Grand Stables) by the racetrack, built by Jean Aubert in 1719 to accommodate 240 horses and 500 hounds for stag and boar hunts in the forests nearby, are the grandest stables in France. They're still in use as the home of the **Musée Vivant du Cheval** (Living Horse Museum), with 30 breeds of horses and ponies housed in straw-lined comfort—in between dressage performances in the courtyard or beneath the awe-inspiring central dome. The 31-room museum has a comprehensive collection of equine paraphernalia: everything from saddles, bridles, and stirrups to rocking horses, anatomy displays, and old postcards. There are explanations in English throughout. ⊠ *7 rue du Connétable* ☎ 03–44–57–40–40 ⊕ *www.musee-vivant-du-cheval.fr* ✉ €8 ⊙ *Apr.–Oct., Wed.–Mon. 10:30–5:30; Nov.–Mar., Wed.–Fri. and Mon. 2–6, weekends 10:30–6:30.*

Where to Stay & Eat

$$–$$$ ✕ **La Ferme de Condé.** At the far end of the racetrack, in a building that originally served as an Anglican chapel, is one of the classiest restaurants in Chantilly. Dishes include roast suckling pig, duck with honey and spices, and lobster terrine. A €16 menu makes it a suitable lunch spot. There's a good wine list and choice of wine by the jug. ✉ *42 av. du Maréchal-Joffre* ☎ *03–44–57–32–31* ✍ *Reservations essential* ☰ *AE, DC, MC, V.*

¢–$ ✕ **Capitainerie.** This quaint restaurant is in the château's vaulted medieval basement, adorned with old kitchen utensils. The buffet features a wide choice of salads, cheeses, and desserts, and a selection of hot dishes is also available. ✉ *In Château de Chantilly* ☎ *03–44–57–15–89* ☰ *MC, V* ☽ *Closed Tues.*

$$$$ ▦ **Dolce Chantilly.** Surrounded by forest and its own 18-hole golf course, this luxe, highly restored, and meetings-friendly hotel is set 1½ km (1 mi) northeast of the château. The marble-floor reception hall creates a glitzy impression not quite matched by the guest rooms, which are functional, modern, and a bit small. The De Par En Par brasserie, in the golf clubhouse, serves lunch for €16, and the deluxe Carmontelle has formal dining (pastry chef Hugues Lenté is a master at *crème de Chantilly*). ✉ *Rte. d'Apremont, Vineuil–St-Firmin, 60500* ☎ *03–44–58–47–77* 🖨 *03–44–58–50–11* ⊕ *www.chantilly.dolce.com* ⇆ *202 rooms, 4 suites* ♂ *3 restaurants, minibars, cable TV, golf course, tennis court, pool, health club, baby-sitting, Internet* ☰ *AE, DC, MC, V* ❙⊙❙ *FAP.*

$$ ▦ **Campanile.** This functional, modern motel is in quiet Les Huit Curés, just north of Chantilly, on the edge of the forest (which compensates for the lack of interior atmosphere). There's a grill room for straightforward meals, with a buffet for appetizers, cheese, and desserts. You can dine outside on the terrace in summer. ✉ *Rte. de Creil, on N16 toward Creil, 60500* ☎ *03–44–57–39–24* 🖨 *03–44–58–10–05* ⇆ *45 rooms* ♂ *Restaurant, bar, some pets allowed; no a/c* ☰ *AE, DC, MC, V* ❙⊙❙ *EP.*

Sports & the Outdoors

Since 1834 Chantilly's fabled racetrack, the **Hippodrome des Princes de Condé** (✉ Rte. du Pesage ☎ 03–44–62–41–00 ⊕ www.paristurf.tm.fr/chantil.html), has come into its own each June with two of Europe's most prestigious events: the **Prix du Jockey-Club** (French Derby) on the first Sunday of the month, and the **Prix de Diane** for three-year-old fillies the Sunday after.

Senlis

❸❾ *10 km (6 mi) east of Chantilly via D924, 45 km (28 mi) north of Paris via A1.*

Senlis is an exceptionally well-preserved medieval town with crooked, mazelike streets dominated by the svelte, soaring spire of its Gothic cathedral. Be sure to also inspect the moss-tile church of St-Pierre, with its stumpy crocketed spire. You can enjoy a 40-minute tour of the Vieille Ville by horse and carriage, departing from in front of the cathedral, daily April–December (€30 for up to three people).

★ The **Cathédrale Notre-Dame** (✉ Pl. du Parvis), one of France's oldest and narrowest cathedrals, dates from the second half of the 12th century. The superb spire—arguably the most elegant in France—was added around 1240, and the majestic transept, with its ornate rose windows, in the 16th century.

The town's excellent **Musée d'Art** (Art Museum), built atop an ancient Gallo-Roman residence, displays archaeological finds ranging from Gallo-Roman votive objects unearthed in the neighboring Halatte Forest to the building's own excavated foundations (uncovered in the basement), including some macabre stone heads bathed in half light. Paintings upstairs include works by Manet's teacher Thomas Couture (who lived in Senlis) and a whimsical fried-egg still life by 19th-century realist Théodule Ribot. ✉ *Palais Épiscopal, pl. du Parvis-Notre-Dame* ☎ *03–44–53–00–83* ✏ *€4* ✿ *Thurs.–Mon. 10–noon and 2–6.*

off the beaten path

☾ **PARC ASTÉRIX** – A great alternative to Disneyland, and a wonderful day out for young and old, this Gallic theme park, 10 km (6 mi) south of Senlis via A1, opened in 1989 and takes its cue from a French comic-book figure whose adventures are set during the Roman invasion of France 2,000 years ago. Among the 30 rides and six shows that attract thundering herds of families each year are a mock Gallo-Roman village, costumed druids, performing dolphins, splash-happy water slides, and a giant roller-coaster. ☎ *03–44–62–34–04* ⊕ *www. parcasterix.com* ✏ *€32* ✿ *Apr.–Aug., daily 10–6; Sept.–mid-Oct., Wed. and weekends 10–6.*

Where to Stay & Eat

$$–$$$ ✕ **Le Bourgeois Gentilhomme.** This pink-and-cream restaurant in old Senlis, named for dapper chef Philippe Bourgeois, serves such interesting dishes as pigeon with cabbage and bacon, fricassee of burbot with mushrooms, and crab lasagna with cress, to name but three. ✉ *3 pl. de la Halle* ☎ *03–44–53–13–22* ⊟ *AE, DC, MC, V* ✿ *Closed Mon. and 2 wks in Aug. No lunch Sat., no dinner Sun.*

★ **$** ▦ **L'Hostellerie de la Porte-Bellon.** This old stone house with garden, just a five-minute walk from the cathedral and close to the bus station, is the closest you'll get to spending a night in the historic center of Senlis. ✉ *51 rue Bellon, 60300* ☎ *03–44–53–03–05* ▦ *03–44–53–29–94* ⊕ *www.porte-bellon.com* ⇆ *18 rooms* ♧ *Restaurant, some pets allowed (fee); no a/c* ⊟ *MC, V* ✿ *Closed mid-Dec.–mid-Jan.* ❢⦶ *MAP.*

Ermenonville

➍ *13 km (8 mi) southeast of Senlis via N330, 43 km (27 mi) northeast of Paris.*

A ruined abbey and children's amusement park, both nearby, add to the appeal of the village of Ermenonville, best known as the final haunt of the 18th-century French philosopher Jean-Jacques Rousseau. The Cistercian **Abbaye de Chaalis,** just off N330 as you arrive from Senlis, has photogenic 13th-century ruins, a landscaped park, an orangery, and an 18th-century château. Inside are an eclectic collection of Egyptian antiquities and medieval paintings and three rooms displaying manuscripts and other mementos of Jean-Jacques Rousseau. ⊠ *Just off N330* ☎ *03–44–54–04–02* ⊠ *Abbey and park €6.50; park only €3* ☼ *Mar.–Oct., daily 10:30–12:30 and 2–6; Nov.–Feb., Sun. 10:30–12:30 and 1:30–5:30.*

The **Parc Jean-Jacques Rousseau,** a tranquil oasis in the center of Ermenonville, is famous as the initial resting place of the influential writer, who spent the last three months of his life in Ermenonville in 1778 and was buried on the Ile des Peupliers in the middle of the lake. Rousseau's ideas about natural equality made him a hero of the French Revolution, and in 1794 his body was removed to the Panthéon in Paris. ☎ *€2* ☼ *Daily 2–5:30.*

Where to Stay & Eat

★ **$$$** ╳▦ **Château d'Ermenonville.** Right out of a storybook, this turreted 18th-century château opposite the Parc Jean-Jacques Rousseau has great style—it's surrounded by a lake, the main courtyard has a sculpted pediment and wrought-iron balconies, and the rooms are furnished with fin-de-siècle opulence. The menu changes regularly at the restaurant, La Table du Poète. ⊠ *60950 Ermenonville* ☎ *03–44–54–00–26* ⊟ *03–44–54–01–00* ⊕ *www.chateau-ermenonville.com* ⮩ *38 rooms, 11 suites* ⌂ *Restaurant, minibars, Internet; no a/c* ⊟ *AE, DC, MC, V* ¶◎¶ *MAP.*

Meaux

❹① 24 km (15 mi) southeast of Ermenonville via N330, 40 km (25 mi) east of Paris via N3.

A sturdy cathedral and a well-preserved bishop's palace embellish Meaux, a dignified old market town on the banks of the Marne River. An excellent Brie is produced locally. Above the Marne sits the **Cathédrale St-Étienne,** which took more than 300 years to complete and is, consequently, a bit of a hodgepodge stylistically. The stonework in the soaring interior becomes increasingly decorative as you approach the west end, culminating in a notable Flamboyant Gothic rose window. The exterior is somewhat eroded and looks sadly battered—or pleasingly authentic, according to taste. A son-et-lumière show replete with medieval costumes is staged outside the cathedral most weekends in June, July, and September. ⊠ *Rue St-Étienne* ☎ *01–60–23–40–00 for details about son-et-lumière show* ⊕ *www.feerie.org* ☼ *Daily 8–noon and 2–6.*

Disneyland Paris

☺ ❹② 20 km (13 mi) southwest of Meaux via A140 and A4, 38 km (24 mi)
Fodor'sChoice *east of Paris via A4.*
★

Disneyland Paris (originally called Euro Disney) is probably not what you've traveled to France to experience. But if you have a child in tow, the promise of a day here may get you through an afternoon at Versailles or Fontainebleau. If you're a dyed-in-the-wool Disney fan, you'll want to make a beeline for the park to see how it has been molded to appeal to the tastes of Europeans (Disney's "Imagineers" call it their most lovingly detailed park). And if you've never experienced this particular form of Disney showmanship, you may want to put in an appearance if only to see what all the fuss is about. When it opened, few turned up to do so; today the place is jammed with crowds, and Disneyland Paris is here to stay—and grow, with **Walt Disney Studios** opened alongside it in 2002.

The Disneyland theme park is made up of five "lands": Main Street U.S.A., Frontierland, Adventureland, Fantasyland, and Discoveryland. The central theme of each land is relentlessly echoed in every detail, from attractions to restaurant menus to souvenirs. The park is circled by a railroad, which stops three times along the perimeter. **Main Street U.S.A.** goes under the railroad and past shops and restaurants toward the main plaza; Disney parades are held here every afternoon and, during holiday periods, every evening. Top attractions at **Frontierland** are the chilling Phantom Manor, haunted by holographic spooks, and the thrilling runaway mine train of Big Thunder Mountain, a roller-coaster that plunges wildly through floods and avalanches in a setting meant to evoke Utah's Monument Valley. Whiffs of Arabia, Africa, and the West Indies give **Adventureland** its exotic cachet; the spicy meals and snacks served here rank among the best food in the park. Don't miss the Pirates of the Caribbean, an exciting mise-en-scène populated by eerily humanlike, computer-driven figures, or Indiana Jones and the Temple of Doom, a breathtaking ride that re-creates some of this luckless hero's most exciting moments.

Fantasyland charms the youngest parkgoers with familiar cartoon characters from such classic Disney films as *Snow White, Pinocchio, Dumbo,* and *Peter Pan.* The focal point of Fantasyland, and indeed Disneyland Paris, is Le Château de la Belle au Bois Dormant (Sleeping Beauty's Castle), a 140-foot, bubblegum-pink structure topped with 16 blue- and gold-tipped turrets. Its design was allegedly inspired by illustrations from a medieval *Book of Hours*—if so, it was by way of Beverly Hills. The castle's dungeon conceals a 2-ton scaly green dragon that rumbles in its sleep and occasionally rouses to roar—an impressive feat of engineering, producing an answering chorus of shrieks from younger children. **Discoveryland** is a futuristic eye-knocker for high-tech Disney entertainment. Robots on roller skates welcome you on your way to Star Tours, a pitching, plunging, sense-confounding ride based on the *Star Wars* films. In Le Visionarium, a simulated space journey is presented by 9-Eye, a staggeringly realistic robot. Space Mountain pretends to catapult riders through the Milky Way.

Walt Disney Studios opened next to the Disneyland Park in 2002. The theme park is divided into four "production zones." Beneath imposing entrance gates, and a 100-foot water-tower inspired by the one erected in 1939 at Disney Studios in Burbank, California, **Front Lot** contains shops, a restaurant and a studio recreating the atmosphere of Sunset Boulevard. **Animation Courtyard** has Disney artists demonstrating the various phases of character animation; Animagique brings to life scenes from *Pinocchio* and *The Lion King*; while the Genie from *Aladdin* pilots Flying Carpets over Agrabah. **Production Courtyard** hosts the Walt Disney Television Studios; Cinémagique, a special-effects tribute to U.S. and European cinema; and a behind-the-scenes Studio Tram tour of location sites, movie props, studio décor and costuming, ending with a visit to Catastrophe Canyon in the heart of a film shoot. **Back Lot** majors in stunts. At Armageddon Special Effects you'll confront a flaming meteor shower aboard the Mir space station, then complete your visit at the giant outdoor arena with a Stunt Show Spectacular involving cars, motorbikes, and jet skis. ☎ *01–60–30–60–30* ⊕ *www.disneylandparis. com* ✉ *€39, €105 for 3-day Passport; includes admission to all individual attractions within Disneyland or Walt Disney Studios, but not meals; tickets for Walt Disney Studios are also valid for admission to Disneyland during last 3 opening hrs of same day* ☉ *Disneyland mid-June–mid-Sept., daily 9 AM–10 PM; mid-Sept.–mid-June, weekdays 10–8, weekends 9–8; Dec. 20–Jan. 4, daily 9–8; Walt Disney Studios daily 10–6* ▭ *AE, DC, MC, V.*

Where to Stay & Eat

$–$$$ ✕ **Disneyland Restaurants.** Disneyland Paris is peppered with places to eat, ranging from snack bars and fast-food joints to five full-service restaurants—all with a distinguishing theme. In addition, Walt Disney Studios, Disney Village, and Disney Hotels have restaurants open to the public. But since these are outside the park, it's not recommended that you waste time traveling to them for lunch. Disneyland Paris has relaxed its no-alcohol policy and now serves wine and beer in the park's sit-down restaurants, as well as in the hotels and restaurants outside the park. ☎ *01–60–45–65–40* ▭ *AE, DC, MC, V.*

$$–$$$$ ▥ **Disneyland Hotels.** The resort has 5,000 rooms in six hotels, all a short distance from the park, ranging from the luxurious Disneyland Hotel to the not-so-rustic Camp Davy Crockett. Free transportation to the park is available at every hotel. Packages including Disneyland lodging, entertainment, and admission are available through travel agents in Europe. ✆ *Centre de Réservations, B.P. 100, cedex 4, 77777 Marne-la-Vallée* ☎ *01–60–30–60–30, 407/934–7639 in U.S.* ▤ *01–49–30–71–00* ✐ *All hotels have at least 1 restaurant, café, indoor pool, health club, sauna, bar, Internet* ▭ *AE, DC, MC, V* ▯ *FAP.*

Nightlife & the Arts

Nocturnal entertainment outside the park centers on **Disney Village,** a vast pleasure mall designed by American architect Frank Gehry. Featured are American-style restaurants (crab shack, diner, deli, steak house), including **Billybob's Country Western Saloon** (☎ 01–60–45–70–81). Also in Disney Village is **Buffalo Bill's Wild West Show** (☎ 01–60–45–71–00 for reservations), a two-hour dinner extravaganza with a menu of sausages, spare ribs, and chili; performances by a talented troupe of stunt riders, bronco busters, tribal dancers, and musicians; plus some 50 horses, a dozen buffalo, a bull, and an Annie Oakley–style sharpshooter, with a golden-maned "Buffalo Bill" as emcee. A re-creation of a show that dazzled Parisians 100 years ago, it's corny but great fun. There are two shows nightly, at 6:30 and 9:30; the cost is €52.

en route Aficionados of 18th-century French art and architecture have a soft spot in their hearts for the jewel-like **Château de Champs-sur-Marne** (⊠ 31 rue de Paris, Champs-sur-Marne ☎ 01–60–05–24–43 ⊕ www.monum.fr), to the west of Disneyland, set 8 km (5 mi) west of Guermantes. It's the epitome of *élégance* and set in a magnificent park; it's open daily except Tuesday.

SOUTHEAST TO FONTAINEBLEAU

Fontainebleau forms the hub of this heavily wooded southeast region of Ile-de-France, but no one will want to bypass the grandeur of Vaux-le-Vicomte, a masterpiece of 17th-century architecture and garden design; or the pretty painters' villages of Barbizon and Moret-sur-Loing.

Vaux-le-Vicomte

43 *56 km (35 mi) southeast of Paris via A6, N104, A5, and N36; 5 km (3 mi) northeast of Melun via N36 and D215; 48 km south (30 mi) of Disneyland Paris via N36.*

Fodor's Choice   The quintessence of French 17th-century splendor, the **Château de Vaux-**
★ **le-Vicomte** was built between 1656 and 1661 for finance minister Nicolas Fouquet. The construction of this château was monstrous even for those days: entire villages were razed, 18,000 workmen were called in, and architect Louis Le Vau, painter Charles Le Brun, and landscape architect André Le Nôtre—all biggies of the day—were hired to prove that Fouquet's refined tastes matched his business acumen. The housewarming party was so lavish that star guest Louis XIV, tetchy at the best of times, couldn't contain his envy: he hurled Fouquet in the slammer and promptly began building Versailles to prove just who was top banana.

The high-roofed château, partially surrounded by a moat, is set well back from the road behind iron railings topped with sculpted heads. A cobbled avenue stretches up to the entrance, and stone steps lead to the vestibule, which seems small given the noble scale of the exterior. Charles Le Brun's captivating decoration includes the ceiling of the **Chambre du Roi** (Royal Bedchamber), depicting *Time Bearing Truth Heavenward,* framed by stuccowork by sculptors François Girardon and André Legendre. Along the frieze you can make out small squirrels, the Fouquet family's emblem—even now squirrels are known as *fouquets* in local dialect. But Le Brun's masterwork is the ceiling in the **Salon des Muses** (Hall of Muses), a brilliant allegorical composition painted in glowing, sensuous colors that some feel even surpasses his work at Versailles. On the ground floor the impressive **Grand Salon** (Great Hall), with its unusual oval form and 16 caryatid pillars symbolizing the months and seasons, has harmony and style despite its unfinished state. In the basement, whose cool, dim rooms were used to store food and wine and house the château's staff, you'll find rotating exhibits about the château's past and life-size wax figures illustrating its history.

There's no mistaking the grandeur of Le Nôtre's carefully restored **gardens,** at their best when the fountains are turned on (the second and final

Saturdays of each month from April through October, 3 PM–6 PM). Also visit the **Musée des Équipages** (Carriage Museum) in the stables, and inspect a host of carriages and coaches in wonderful condition. Get to Vaux by training it to Melun, then taking a local bus. ☎ *01–64–14–41–90* ⊕ *www.vaux-le-vicomte.com* ✉ *€12, candlelight château visits €15; gardens only €7* ⊗ *Apr.–Nov. 11, daily 10–6; candlelight visits May–mid-Oct., Sat. 8 PM–midnight.*

Where to Eat

¢–$ ✕ **L'Écureuil.** An imposing barn to the right of the château entrance has been transformed into this self-service cafeteria, where you can enjoy fine steaks (insist yours is cooked enough), coffee, or a snack beneath the ancient rafters of a wood-beam roof. The restaurant is open daily for lunch and tea, and for dinner during candlelight visits. ✉ *Château de Vaux-le-Vicomte* ☎ *01–60–66–95–66* ▭ *MC, V.*

Barbizon

🏵 *17 km (11 mi) southwest of Vaux-le-Vicomte via Melun and D132/D64, 52 km (33 mi) southeast of Paris.*

On the western edge of the 62,000-acre Fontainebleau forest, the village of Barbizon retains its time-stained allure despite the intrusion of art galleries, souvenir shops, and busloads of tourists. The group of landscape painters known as the Barbizon School—Camille Corot, Jean-François Millet, Narcisse Diaz de la Peña, and Théodore Rousseau, among others—lived here from the 1830s on. They paved the way for the Impressionists by their willingness to accept nature on its own terms rather than using it as an idealized base for carefully structured compositions. Sealed to one of the famous sandstone rocks in the forest—which starts, literally, at the far end of the main street—is a bronze medallion by sculptor Henri Chapu, paying homage to Millet and Rousseau.

Corot and company would often repair to the Auberge Ganne after painting to brush up on their social life; the inn is now the **Musée de l'École de Barbizon** (Barbizon School Museum). Here you'll find documents of the village as it was in the 19th century, as well as a few original works. The Barbizon artists painted on every available surface, and even now you can see some originals on the upstairs walls. Two of the ground-floor rooms have been reconstituted as they were in Ganne's time—note the trompe-l'oeil paintings on the buffet doors. There's also a video on the Barbizon School. ✉ *92 Grande-Rue* ☎ *01–60–66–22–27* ✉ *€6, joint admission with Maison-Atelier Théodore-Rousseau* ⊗ *Mon. and Wed.–Fri. 10–12:30 and 2–5, weekends 10–5.*

Though there are no actual Millet works, the **Atelier Jean-François Millet** (Millet's Studio) is cluttered with photographs and mementos evoking his career. It was here that Millet painted some of his most renowned pieces, including *The Gleaners*. ✉ *27 Grande-Rue* ☎ *01–60–66–21–55* ✉ *Free* ⊗ *Wed.–Mon. 9:30–12:30 and 2–5:30.*

By the church, beyond the extraordinary village war memorial featuring a mustached ancient Gaul in a winged helmet, is the **Maison-Atelier**

Théodore-Rousseau (Rousseau's House-cum-Studio), in a converted barn. It doubles as the tourist office and exhibition space for temporary shows. ⊠ *55 Grande-Rue* ☎ *01–60–66–22–38* 🎫 *€6, joint ticket with Barbizon School Museum* ⊙ *Mon. and Wed.–Fri. 10–12:30 and 2–5, weekends 10–5.*

Where to Stay & Eat

$$–$$$ ✕ **Le Relais de Barbizon.** French country specialties are served at this rustic restaurant with a big open fire and a large terrace shaded by lime and chestnut trees. The four-course weekday menu is a good value, but wine here is expensive and cannot be ordered by the *pichet* (pitcher). Reservations are essential on weekends. ⊠ *2 av. Général-de-Gaulle* ☎ *01–60–66–40–28* 🍽 *MC, V* ⊙ *Closed part of Aug., part of Feb., and Wed. No dinner Tues.*

★ **$–$$** ✕🏨 **Les Alouettes.** This delightful, family-run 19th-century inn is set in 2 acres of leafy parkland, which the better rooms overlook. The interior is '30s style, and many rooms have oak beams. Lionel Ménard's rustic restaurant (reservations essential; no dinner Sunday), with its large open terrace, serves traditional French cuisine such as hare with mushrooms and lamb with eggplant. ⊠ *4 rue Antoine-Barye, 77630* ☎ *01–60–66–41–98* 🖨 *01–60–66–20–69* 🛏 *22 rooms* ⚒ *Restaurant, cable TV, bar, Internet, some pets allowed (fee); no a/c* 🍽 *AE, DC, MC, V* 🍴 *MAP.*

Fontainebleau

9 km (6 mi) southeast of Barbizon via N7, 61 km (38 mi) southeast of Paris via A6 and N7.

Like Chambord, in the Loire Valley, or Compiègne, to the north, Fontainebleau was a favorite spot for royal hunting parties long before the construction of one of France's grandest residences. Although not as celebrated as Versailles, Vaux-le-Vicomte, or Chenonceau, this palace is almost as spectacular.

★ ㊺–㊴ The **Château de Fontainebleau** you see today dates from the 16th century, although additions were made by various royal incumbents through the next 300 years. The palace was begun under the flamboyant Renaissance king François I, the French contemporary of England's Henry VIII. The king hired Italian artists Il Rosso (a pupil of Michelangelo) and Primaticcio to embellish his château. In fact, they did much more: by introducing the pagan allegories and elegant lines of Mannerism to France, they revolutionized French decorative art. Their extraordinary frescoes and stuccowork can be admired in the **Galerie François-Ier** (Francis I Gallery) and the jewel of the interior, the **Salle de Bal** (ballroom). Here in the ceremonial ballroom, which is nearly 100 feet long, you can admire the dazzling 16th-century frescoes and gilding. Completed under Henri II, François's successor, it is luxuriantly wood-paneled, with a gleaming parquet floor that reflects the patterns on the ceiling. Like the château as a whole, the room exudes a sense of elegance and style—but on a more intimate, human scale than at Versailles: this is Renaissance, not Baroque. Henri II also added the decorative interlaced initials found

throughout the palace. You might expect to see the royal *H* woven with a *C* (for Catherine de' Médici, his wife). Instead you'll find a *D*—indicating his mistress, Diane de Poitiers.

Napoléon's apartments occupied the first floor. You can see a lock of his hair, his Légion d'Honneur medal, his imperial uniform, the hat he wore on his return from Elba in 1815, and one bed in which he definitely did spend a night (almost every town in France boasts a bed in which the emperor supposedly snoozed). The **Salon Jaune** (Yellow Room) of Joséphine is one of the best examples of the Empire style—the Neoclassical style favored by the emperor. There's also a throne room—Napoléon spurned the one at Versailles, a palace he disliked, establishing his imperial seat in the former King's Bedchamber—and the Queen's Boudoir, also known as the Room of the Six Maries (occupants included ill-fated Marie-Antoinette and Napoléon's second wife, Marie-Louise). The sweeping **Galerie de Diane,** built during the reign of Henri IV (1589–1610), was converted into a library in the 1860s. Other salons have 17th-century tapestries and paintings and frescoes by members of the Fontainebleau School.

Although Louis XIV's architectural fancy was concentrated on Versailles, he commissioned Mansart to design new pavilions and had André

Le Nôtre replant the gardens at Fontainebleau, where he and his court returned faithfully in the fall for the hunting season. But it was Napoléon who made a Versailles, as it were, out of Fontainebleau, spending lavishly to restore it. He held Pope Pius VII here as a captive guest in 1812, signed the second church-state concordat here in 1813, and, in the cobbled **Cour des Adieux** (Farewell Courtyard), said good-bye to his Old Guard on April 20, 1814, as he began his brief exile on the Mediterranean island of Elba. The famous **Horseshoe Staircase** that dominates the Cour des Adieux, once the Cour du Cheval Blanc (White Horse Courtyard), was built by Androuet du Cerceau for Louis XIII (1610–43); it was down this staircase that Napoléon made his way slowly to take the salute of his loyal troops for the last time. Another courtyard—the **Cour de la Fontaine** (Fountain Courtyard)—was commissioned by Napoléon in 1812 and adjoins the Étang des Carpes (Carp Pond). Across from the pond is the formal Parterre (flower garden) and, on the other side, the leafy Jardin Anglais (English Garden).

The **Porte Dauphine** is the most beautiful of the various gateways that connect the complex of buildings; its name commemorates the christening of the dauphin—the heir to the throne, later Louis XIII—under its archway in 1606. The gateway fronts the **Cour Ovale** (Oval Court), shaped like a flattened egg. Opposite the courtyard is the **Cour des Offices** (Offices Court), a large, severe square built at the same time as place des Vosges in Paris (1609). Around the corner is the informal **Jardin de Diane** (Diana's Garden), with peacocks and a statue of the hunting goddess surrounded by mournful hounds. ⊠ *Pl. du Général-de-Gaulle* ☎ *01–60–71–50–70* ⊕ *www.musee-chateau-fontainebleau.fr* ▣ *€5.50, Napoleon's Apartments €3 extra; gardens free* ☉ *Wed.–Mon. 9:30–5; gardens Apr.–Sept., daily 9–8:30; Oct.–Mar., daily 9–5.*

Where to Stay & Eat

$ ✕ **La Route du Beaujolais.** The food is cheap and the welcome cheerful at Giorgio's jolly eatery near the château, where Lyonnais-style cold cuts and bottles of Beaujolais are the mainstays. For something a little more upscale, try the snails or beef fillet with Brie or choose from the wide choice of fish dishes. Prix-fixe meals are priced at €12, €14, and €21. ⊠ *3 rue Montebello* ☎ *01–64–22–27–98* ▤ *AE, MC, V.*

★ **$$$$** ✕▣ **L'Aigle Noir.** This may be Fontainebleau's costliest hotel, but you can't go wrong if you request one of the rooms overlooking either the garden or the palace. They have late-18th- or early 19th-century reproduction furniture, creating a Napoleonic ambience. The restaurant, Le Beauharnais, serves subtle, imaginative cuisine—lamb with thyme and gentian, for instance (dinner only, except Sunday; restaurant closed most of August). There's a tranquil garden for alfresco dining in summer. Reservations are essential and jacket and tie are required. ⊠ *27 pl. Napoléon-Bonaparte, 77300* ☎ *01–60–74–60–00* 🖨 *01–60–74–60–01* ⊕ *www.hotelaiglenoir.fr* ➱ *53 rooms, 3 suites* ♣ *Restaurant, minibars, cable TV, pool, gym, sauna, some pets allowed (fee)* ▤ *AE, DC, MC, V* ⊧ *BP.*

$$-$$$ ✕🖭 **Napoléon.** This former post office close to the palace counts as one of the best local hotels. Pastel-color rooms have modern furniture and marble baths and look out onto terraces or the indoor patio. The plush restaurant, La Table des Maréchaux, with its golden wallpaper and crimson velvet seating, serves satisfying, deftly prepared classics, and the €25 menu is an excellent deal. ⊠ *9 rue Grande, 77300* ☎ *01–60–39–50–50* 🖶 *01–64–22–20–87* ⊕ *www.hotelnapoleon-fontainebleau.com* ⇝ *58 rooms* ⌂ *Restaurant, minibars, cable TV, Internet, some pets allowed (fee); no a/c* 🖃 *AE, DC, MC, V* ¶◯¶ *MAP.*

$$-$$$ 🖭 **Londres.** Established in 1850, the Londres is a small, family-style hotel with Louis XV accents. Some balconies overlook the palace entrance and the Cour des Adieux, where Napoléon bade his troops an emotional farewell. The hotel's prim 19th-century facade is a registered landmark. ⊠ *1 pl. du Général-de-Gaulle, 77300* ☎ *01–64–22–20–21* 🖶 *01–60–72–39–16* ⊕ *www.hoteldelondres.com* ⇝ *12 rooms* ⌂ *Restaurant, cable TV, bar, Internet; no a/c* 🖃 *AE, DC, MC, V* ☉ *Closed 1 wk Aug. and mid-Dec.–early Jan.* ¶◯¶ *BP.*

Sports & the Outdoors

The Forest of Fontainebleau is laced with hiking trails; for more information ask for the *Guide des Sentiers* (trail guide) at the tourist office. Bikes can be rented at the Fontainebleau-Avon train station. The forest is also famed for its fascinating rock formations, where many a novice alpinist first caught the climbing bug; for more information contact the **Club Alpin Français** (⊠ 24 av. Laumière, 75019 Paris ☎ 01–53–72–88–00).

Moret-sur-Loing

⑤⑤ *10 km (6 mi) southeast of Fontainebleau via N6, 72 km (45 mi) southeast of Paris.*

Close to the confluence of the Seine and Yonne rivers is the village of Moret-sur-Loing. It was immortalized by Impressionist painter Alfred Sisley, who lived here for 20 years at 19 rue Montmartre (not open to the public), around the corner from the church. A narrow bridge, one of the oldest in France, leads across the Loing River (boat trips available) and provides a view of the village walls, rooftops, and church tower. If you've a sweet tooth, take note: Moret is renowned for its barley sugar. Truculent World War I leader Georges Clemenceau (1841–1929), known as The Tiger, is the subject of a cozy museum at **La Grange-Batelière,** the thatched house by the Loing where he used to live. His taste for Asian art and his friendship with Impressionist Claude Monet are evoked here. ⊠ *Access via rue du Peintre-Sisley* ☎ *01–60–70–51–21* 🖭 *Guided tours only,* €6 ☉ *Easter–mid-Nov., Sun. at 2:45.*

Nightlife & the Arts

A good time to visit the town is on a Saturday evening in summer (from late June through early September) for the riverside **Festival de Moret,** when 600 locals stage son-et-lumière pageants illustrating the town's history. ☎ *01–60–70–41-66* 🖭 €*12–*€*15.*

Provins

56 *48 km (30 mi) northeast of Moret on N6/D403, 77 km (48 mi) southeast of Paris.*

On the hilltop site of a Roman camp, Provins developed into the third-largest town in France (after Paris and Rouen) in the Middle Ages as capital of the counts of Champagne, acquiring international renown for its fairs and as a rose-growing center. Provins is a UNESCO-listed World Heritage Site with 50 protected monuments bearing witness to its opulent past, including the 12th-century Gothic church of **St-Quiriace** with its incongruous 17th-century classical dome. There's plenty to see underground, too—a guided tour of the **Souterrains** takes in a small part of the 6 mi of tunnels that honeycomb the hill on which Provins is built. Contact the tourist office Web site for details: www.provins.net.

Climb up to the **Tour César,** a round, ivy-covered 11th-century keep atop a sturdy mound, for a panoramic view of the town and some of the best-preserved medieval ramparts in France. ⊠ *7 rue du Palais* ☎ *01–64–01–40–19* ⊠ *€3.40* ⊙ *Apr.–Oct., daily 10–6; Nov.–Mar., daily 2–5.*

The vaulted 13th-century **Grange aux Dîmes** (Tithe Barn), originally used as a covered market, houses a collection of waxwork displays evoking the crafts and merchants who brought medieval Provins wealth and fame, and shows a film retracing the town's history. ⊠ *Rue St-Jean* ⊠ *€3.40* ⊙ *Apr.–Aug., daily 10–6; Sept.–Oct., daily 2–6; Nov.–Mar., weekends 2–5.*

Where to Stay & Eat

$$–$$$$ ╳▣ **Aux Vieux Remparts.** Set, as its name suggests, within the Vieille Ville walls (or ramparts), this thriving establishment (seven new rooms were added in 2002) has plush-carpeted rooms with contemporary furniture overlooking the leafy inner garden, where you can dine outdoors on balmy summer evenings. Otherwise the delectable talents of young chef Lionel Sarre—ranging from grilled scallops to rose-petal soufflé—are showcased in the adjacent half-timber 16th-century restaurant. ⊠ *3 rue Couverte, 77160* ☎ *01–64–08–94–00* ☒ *01–60–67–77–22* ⊕ *www.auxvieuxremparts.com* ⇨ *32 rooms* ⚒ *Restaurant, minibars, cable TV, bar, Internet, some pets allowed (fee); no a/c* ⊟ *AE, DC, MC, V* ⦿ *MAP.*

Nightlife & the Arts

Reconstituted **jousting tournaments** (☎ 01–64–60–26–26) and a mock attack on the town walls using medieval war machines are held most weekend afternoons in summer; call the tourist office for details.

ILE-DE-FRANCE A TO Z

To research prices, get advice from other travelers, and book travel arrangements, visit www.fodors.com.

AIRPORTS

Major airports in the Ile-de-France area are Charles de Gaulle, commonly known as Roissy, 25 km (16 mi) northeast of Paris, and Orly, 16 km

(10 mi) south. Shuttle buses link Disneyland to the airports at Roissy, 56 km (35 mi) away, and Orly, 50 km (31 mi) distant; buses take 45 minutes and run every 45 minutes from Roissy, every 60 minutes from Orly (less frequently in low season), and cost €14.

🔢 Airport Information **Charles de Gaulle** ☎ 01-48-62-22-80. **Orly** ☎ 01-49-75-15-15.

BUS TRAVEL

While many of the major sights in this chapter have train lines connecting them on direct routes with Paris, the lesser towns and destinations pose more of a problem. You often need to take a local bus or taxi after arriving at a train station (for instance, to get to Senlis from Chantilly Gare SNCF, or Fontainebleau and Barbizon from Avon Gare SNCF, or Vaux-le-Vicomte from Melun Gare SNCF, or Giverny from Vernon Gare SNCF). Other buses travel outward from Paris's suburbs—the No. 158A bus, for instance, which goes from La Défense to St-Germain-en-Laye and Rueil-Malmaison.

🔢 Bus Information **SNCF** ☎ 08-36-35-35-35 ⊕ idf.sncf.fr/GB.

CAR RENTAL

Cars can be rented from agencies in Paris or at Orly or Charles de Gaulle airports.

CAR TRAVEL

A13 links Paris (from the Porte d'Auteuil) to Versailles. You can get to Chartres on A10 from Paris (Porte d'Orléans). For Fontainebleau take A6 from Paris (Porte d'Orléans), or for a more attractive route through the Forest of Sénart and the northern part of the Forest of Fontainebleau, take N6 from Paris (Porte de Charenton) via Melun. A4 runs from Paris (Porte de Bercy) to Disneyland. Although a comprehensive rail network ensures that most towns in Ile-de-France can make comfortable day trips from Paris, the only way to crisscross the region without returning to the capital is by car. There's no shortage of expressways or fast highways, but be prepared for delays close to Paris and during the morning and evening rush hours.

EMERGENCIES

The American Hospital and the British Hospital are closer to Paris, and other regional hospitals are listed by town below.

🔢 **Ambulance** ☎ 15. **American Hospital** ⊠ 63 bd. Victor-Hugo ☎ 01-47-45-71-00 in Neuilly. **British Hospital** ⊠ 3 rue Barbès ☎ 01-47-58-13-12 in Levallois-Perret. **Chartres** ⊠ 34 rue du Dr-Maunoury ☎ 02-37-30-30-30. **Melun** ⊠ 2 rue Fréteau-de-Pény ☎ 01-64-71-60-00. **Versailles** ⊠ 177 rue de Versailles, Le Chesnay ☎ 01-39-63-91-33.

TOURS

Cityrama organizes guided excursions to Giverny (€60) from April through October. Cityrama and Paris Vision run half- and full-day trips to Versailles (€ 34–88), Chartres, Vaux-le-Vicomte (€ 55), and Fontainebleau/Barbizon (€55).

🔢 **Cityrama** ⊠ 4 pl. des Pyramides, 1er, Paris ☎ 01-44-55-61-00 ⊕ www.cityrama.com. **Paris Vision** ⊠ 214 rue de Rivoli, 1er, Paris ☎ 01-47-42-72-31 ⊕ www.parisvision.com.

PRIVATE GUIDES   Alliance Autos has bilingual guides who can take you on a private tour around the Paris area in a luxury car or minibus for a minimum of four hours for about €80 an hour (call to check details and prices). Paris Bus Service runs minibus excursions to Versailles (€65) and Giverny (€75). **⊞ Alliance Autos** ✉ 149 rue de Charonne, 75011 Paris Ⓜ Charonne ☎ 01-55-25-23-23. **Paris Bus Service** ⊕ www.touring-france.com/paris-uk; contact your hotel for bookings.

TRAIN TRAVEL

Many sights can be reached by train from Paris. Both regional and main-line (Le Mans–bound) trains leave the Gare Montparnasse for Chartres (50–70 minutes); the former also stop at Versailles, Rambouillet, and Maintenon. Gare Montparnasse is also the terminal for trains to Dreux (Granville line) and for the suburban trains that stop at Montfort-L'A-maury, the nearest station to Thoiry (35 minutes).

Some mainline trains from Gare St-Lazare stop at Mantes-la-Jolie (30 minutes) and Vernon (45 minutes) on their way to Rouen and Le Havre. Suburban trains leave the Gare du Nord for L'Isle-Adam (50 minutes). Chantilly is on the main northbound line from Gare du Nord (the trip takes 25–40 minutes), and Senlis can be reached by bus from Chantilly. Fontainebleau—or, rather, neighboring Avon, 2 km (1½ mi) away (there is frequent bus service)—is 45 minutes from Gare de Lyon. To reach Vaux-le-Vicomte, head first for Melun, then take a taxi or local bus; to reach Giverny, rail it to Vernon, then use the taxi or local bus.

St-Germain-en-Laye is a terminal of the RER-A (commuter train) that tunnels through Paris (main stations at Étoile, Auber, Les Halles, and Gare de Lyon). The RER-A also accesses Poissy and Maisons-Laffitte and, at the other end, the station for Disneyland Paris (called Marne-la-Vallée–Chessy), within 100 yards of the entrance to both the theme park and Disney Village. Journey time is around 40 minutes, and trains operate every 10–30 minutes, depending on the time of day. The handiest of Versailles's three train stations is the one reached by the RER-C line (main stations at Austerlitz, St-Michel, Invalides, and Champ-de-Mars); the trip takes 30–40 minutes. Special *forfait* tickets, combining travel and admission, are available for several regional tourist destinations (including Versailles, Fontainebleau, and Auvers-sur-Oise).

A mainline TGV (Trains à Grande Vitesse) station links Disneyland to Lille, Lyon, Brussels, and London (via Lille and the Channel Tunnel). **⊞ Train Information SNCF** ☎ 08-36-35-35-35 ⊕ idf.sncf.fr/GB. **TGV** ⊕ www.tgv.com.

VISITOR INFORMATION

Contact the Espace du Tourisme d'Ile-de-France (open Wednesday–Monday 10–7, www.pidf.com), under the inverted pyramid in the Carrousel du Louvre, for general information on the area. Information on Disneyland is available from the Disneyland Paris reservations office. Local tourist offices are listed below by town. **⊞ Tourist Information Espace du Tourisme d'Ile-de-France** ✉ Pl. de la Pyramide-Renversée, 99 rue de Rivoli, 75001 Paris ☎ 08-03-81-80-00. **Disneyland Paris reservations office** ✇ B.P. 100, cedex 4, 77777 Marne-la-Vallée ☎ 01-60-30-60-30, 407/824-4321 in U.S. **Barbizon** ✉ 55 Grande-Rue ☎ 01-60-66-41-87 ⊕ www.barbizon-france.com. **Chantilly** ✉ 60 av. du Maréchal-Joffre ☎ 03-44-57-08-58 ⊕ www.ville-de-chantilly.fr. **Chartres** ✉ Pl. de la Cathédrale ☎ 02-37-21-50-00 ⊕ www.ville-chartres.fr. **Fontainebleau** ✉ 4 rue Royale ☎ 01-60-74-99-99 ⊕ www.fontainebleau.online.com. **Rambouillet** ✉ 1 pl. de la Libération ☎ 01-34-83-21-21 ⊕ www.ot-rambouillet.fr. **St-Germain-en-Laye** ✉ 38 rue au Pain ☎ 01-34-51-05-12 ⊕ www.ville-st-germain-en-laye.fr. **Senlis** ✉ Pl. du Parvis Notre-Dame ☎ 03-44-53-06-40 ⊕ www.ville-senlis.fr. **Versailles** ✉ 2 bis av. de Paris ☎ 01-39-24-88-88 ⊕ www.versailles.tourisme.fr.

THE LOIRE VALLEY

3

Updated by
Simon Hewitt

Introduction by
Nancy Coons

A DIAPHANOUS AURA OF SUBTLY SHIFTING LIGHT plays over the luxuriant countryside of the Loire Valley, a region blessedly mild of climate, richly populated with game, and habitually fertile. Although it had always been viewed as prime real estate, the victorious Valois dynasty began to see new possibilities in the territory once the dust from the Hundred Years' War began to settle and the bastions of the Plantagenet kings lost some of their utility. This, they mused, was an ideal spot for a holiday home. Sketching, no doubt, on a tavern napkin at Blois, Louis XII dreamed of a tasteful blend of symmetry and fantasy, of turrets and gargoyles, while Anne of Brittany breathed down his neck for more closet space. In no time at all, the neighboring Joneses had followed suit, and by the 16th century the area was a showplace of fabulous châteaux *d'agrément,* or pleasure castles—palaces for royalty, yes, but also love nests for mistresses and status statements for arrivistes (Chenonceau was built by a tax collector). There were boxwood gardens endlessly receding toward vanishing points, moats graced with swans, parades of delicate cone-topped towers, frescoes, and fancywork ceilings. The glories of the Italian Renaissance, observed by the Valois while making war on their neighbor, were brought to bear on these mega-monuments with all the elegance and proportions characteristic of antiquity.

By the time François I took charge, extravagance knew no bounds: on a 13,000-acre forest estate, hunting parties at Chambord drew A-list crowds from the far reaches of Europe—and the availability of 430 rooms made weekend entertaining a snap. Queen Claudia hired only the most recherché Italian artisans: Chambord's famous double-helix staircase may, in fact, have been Leonardo da Vinci's design (he was a frequent houseguest there when not in residence in a manor on the Amboise grounds). From massive kennels teeming with hunting hounds at Cheverny to luxurious stables at Chaumont-sur-Loire, from endless allées of pollarded lime trees at Villandry to the fairy-tale towers of Ussé—worthy of Sleeping Beauty herself—the Loire Valley became the power base and social center for the New France, allowing the monarchy to go all out in strutting its stuff.

All for good reason. In 1519 Charles V of Spain, at the age of 19, inherited the Holy Roman Empire, leaving François and his New France—as well as England's Henry VIII—out in the cold. It was perhaps no coincidence that in 1519 François, in a grand stab at face-saving one-upmanship, commenced construction on his ultimate declaration of dominion, the gigantic château of Chambord. After a few skirmishes (the Low Countries, Italy), and no doubt a few power breakfasts, François was confident enough to entertain the emperor on his lavish Loire estates, and by 1539 he had married Charles V's sister.

Location is everything, as you realize when you think of Hyannisport, Kennebunkport, and Balmoral: homesteads redolent of dynasty, where natural beauty, idyllic views, an invigorating hunt with the boys, and a barefoot stroll in the great outdoors liberate the mind to think great thoughts and make history's decisions. Perhaps this is why French Revolution have-nots sacked so many of the châteaux of the Loire Valley; today most of the châteaux have been restored, and are maintained as museums in the public domain. Although these châteaux are testimony to France's most fabled age of kings, their pleasures, once restricted to royalty and members of the nobility, are now shared by the populace. Yet the Revolution and the efforts of latter-day socialists have not totally erased a lingering gentility in the people of the region, characterized by an air of refined assurance far removed from the shoulder-shrugging, chest-tapping French stereotypes. Here life proceeds at a pleasingly genteel pace, and you'll find a winning concentration of gracious country inns and discerning chefs, a cornucopia of local produce and game, and the famous, flinty wines of Sancerre—all regional blessings still truly fit for a king, but now available to his subjects as well.

Exploring the Loire Valley

Pick up the Loire River halfway along its course from central France to the Atlantic Ocean. Châteaux and vineyards will accompany you throughout a 340-km (210-mi) westbound course that ranges between the hilltop wine town of Sancerre and the bustling city of Angers. Towns punctuate the route at almost equal distances—Orléans, Blois, Tours, and Saumur—and are useful bases if you're relying on public transportation. But don't let the lack of a car prevent you from visiting and overnighting in the lovely villages of the region because a surprising number can be accessed via train, bus, or comfy taxi. Although you may be rushing around to see as many famous châteaux as possible, try to make time to walk through the poppy-covered hills, picnic along the riverbanks, and sample the famous local wines.

About the Restaurants & Hotels

In summer you will face an appetizing choice of places to eat along the Loire; play safe and book ahead, especially on weekends and in July and August. The off-season (October through Easter) is different—many of the Loire Valley villages that hum with life in the summertime return to hibernation once the tourist season ends. Note that many of the famed château-hotels have their own restaurants; these are usually superb, so if they expect—in summer, sometimes insist—that you eat dinner in their restaurant, by all means, say *oui*. Loire wines are among the most loved in France, and they are varied. Among the best are Savennières, Sancerre, and Cheverny, dry whites; Coteaux du Layon and Montlouis, sweet whites; Cabernet d'Anjou, rosé (often sweet); Bourgueil, Chinon, and Saumur-Champigny, reds; and Vouvray, white—dry, sweet, or sparkling.

Even before the age of the railway, the Loire Valley drew vacationers from far afield, so there are hundreds of hotels of all types. At the higher end are converted châteaux, but even these are not as pricey as you might think. At the lower end are small, traditional inns in towns and villages, usually offering terrific value for the money. The Loire Valley is a very popular destination, so make reservations well in advance. Assume all hotel rooms have air-conditioning, telephones, TV, and private bath, unless otherwise noted.

3

Strung like precious gems along the peaceful Loire and its tributaries, the royal and near-royal châteaux of the region are among the most fabled sights in France. From magical Chenonceau—improbably suspended above the River Cher—to mighty Chambord, from the *Sleeping Beauty* abode of Ussé to the famed gardens of Villandry, this parade of châteaux gloriously epitomizes France's golden age of monarchy. In Orléans, a dramatic chapter in the country's history unfolds: it was here that Joan of Arc had her most rousing successes against the English. With all these treasures, you need two weeks to cover the Loire Valley region in its entirety. But even if you don't have that long, you can still see many of the valley's finest châteaux in three days by concentrating on the area between Blois and Azay-le-Rideau. Six days will give you time to explore these châteaux in depth, as well as to visit Tours and Angers, two of the region's major cities. In 10 days you can follow the Loire from Orléans to Angers.

Numbers in the text correspond to numbers in the margin and on the Loire Valley, Orléans, and Tours maps.

If you have
3 days

Gateway to the central Loire Valley, **Tours ❶ 🚉 – ❽** is the center hub of Touraine. Although there are a few museums to catch and historic place Plumereau beckons, don't tarry in this big city—begin your tour of some of France's choicest real estate by taking an easy train ride away to **Chenonceau ⓬**, everyone's dream of a Loire Valley castle. If you want your own taste of *la vie de château*, backtrack on the train (or by car, of course) to 🚉 **Montlouis-sur-Loire ❿** and the Broglie princes' gorgeous, neo-Renaissance Château de la Bourdaisière (a hotel but also open to day-trippers) or, for a more urban treat, continue on to the north side of the Loire and 🚉 **Blois ⓱**, where you'll find one of the earliest of the great châteaux. Spend the morning of your second day touring Blois, then move inland through the forest to spend the night at 🚉 **Chambord ⓯**—such a vast marble pile it seems more a city than a palace. On your third day, return to Blois, then head downstream to **Amboise ⓫** to take in its massive château and, more delightfully, the Clos-Lucé mansion, the last home of Leonardo da Vinci. If you hustle—and trains can make the journey in around an hour—head instead to the edge of Touraine and spectacular **Chinon ㉓** for an unforgettable dip into the Middle Ages. Connecting trains from Chinon can get you back to Paris via Tours by night.

If you have
6 days

Start by following the three-day itinerary. On the fourth day explore enchanting 🚉 **Chinon ㉓**, then head east to see two of the dreamiest fairy-tale châteaux—the French Renaissance jewel that is **Azay-le-Rideau ⓴** and, a few miles away (buses are rare, so consider a taxi), 🚉 **Ussé ㉒**, which inspired Perrault to write *Sleeping Beauty*. On your fifth day, those without a car will need to return to Azay or Chinon, where you can then wend your way to magical 🚉 **Fontevraud ㉔**, Europe's largest surviving abbey. After marveling at this Romanesque wonder, head to the great river town of **Saumur ㉕**, a posh place with a dramatic clifftop castle and fine train and bus connections.

If you have
10
days Follow the respective three- and six-day itineraries. After exploring Saumur on your sixth day, stop off in adjacent ⌖ **Bourgueil** ㉙ to tour the vineyards or wine caves, making an overnight at the lovely Château de Réaux (save your pennies for this one; it is also open for touring by day-trippers). On your seventh day, a helpful train route can deposit you at the mighty citadel of **Langeais** ㉚ to ogle its sumptuous, tapestried interior. In the afternoon, continue northeast back to Tours, then head out (via bus or taxi if you have no car) to spectacular ⌖ **Villandry** ⑲, famed for its enormous Renaissance château and garden parterres. On your eighth day, backtrack to Tours and train it to ⌖ **Orléans** ㉛–㉞. After exploring this gateway city to the Upper Loire Valley and overnighting here, head out on your ninth morning to explore the region's sights—either the great abbey at **St-Benoît-sur-Loire** ㉝ or the storybook moated castle at **Sully-sur-Loire** ㉚ before ending up in the large town of ⌖ **Gien** ㉟, famed for its earthenware, to spend the night. Or, for a dazzling splurge, head south by car or train to the Franco-Scottish town of ⌖ **Aubigny-sur-Nère** ㊷ and enjoy a stay at the seignorial hotel, the Château de la Verrerie. On your final morning, visit the hilltop wine town of Sancerre. After lunch, head back to Orléans, Paris, and reality.

WHAT IT COSTS In euros					
	$$$$	**$$$**	**$$**	**$**	**¢**
RESTAURANTS	over €30	€23–€30	€17–€23	€11–€17	under €11
HOTELS	over €190	€120–€190	€80–€120	€50–€80	under €50

Restaurant prices are per person for a main course only, including tax (19.6%) and service; note that if a restaurant offers only prix-fixe (set-price) meals, it has been given the price category that reflects the full prix-fixe price. Hotel prices are for a standard double room in high season, including tax (19.6%) and service charge; higher prices (inquire when booking) prevail for any board plans.

Timing

The Loire, the last great European river left undammed, is at its best in May and June, when it still looks like a river; come midsummer, the water level can drop, revealing unsightly sandbanks. The valley divides France in two, both geographically and climatically: north of the Loire, France has the moist, temperate climate of northern Europe; southward lies the drier climate of the Mediterranean. It's striking how changeable the weather can be as you cross the Loire. The valley can be super-sultry in July and August, when most of the son-et-lumière shows take place and the tourist crowds arrive. October is a good off-season option, when all is mist and mellow fruitfulness along the Loire and the mysterious pools of the Sologne, as the trees turn russet and gold. Fall is also the best time to sample regional specialties such as wild mushrooms and game. On Sunday, when most shops are closed, try to avoid the main cities—Orléans, Tours, Angers.

THE CENTRAL LOIRE VALLEY

Halfway along the route of the Loire—the longest river in France—and just outside the city of Orléans, the river takes a wide, westward bend, gliding languidly through low, rich country known as the Val de Loire—or Loire Valley. In this temperate region—a 225-km (140-mi) stretch between Orléans and Angers—scores of châteaux built of local *tufa* (white limestone) rise from the rocky banks of the Loire and its tributaries: the rivers Cher, Indre, Vienne, and Loir (with no *e*).

The Loire is liquid history. For centuries the river was the area's principal means of transportation and an effective barrier against invading armies. Towns arose at strategic bridgeheads, and fortresses—the earliest châteaux—appeared on towering slopes. The Loire Valley was hotly disputed by France and England during the Middle Ages; it belonged to England (under the Anjou Plantagenet family) between 1154 and 1216 and again during the Hundred Years' War (1337–1453). It was the example of Joan of Arc, the Maid of Orléans (so called after the site of her most stirring victories), that crystallized French efforts to expel the English.

The Loire Valley's golden age came under François I (ruled 1515–47), the flamboyant contemporary of England's Henry VIII. His salamander emblem can be seen in many châteaux, including Chambord, the mightiest of them. Although the nation's power base shifted to Paris around 1600, aristocrats continued to erect luxurious palaces along the Loire until the end of the 18th century.

Tours, the capital city of the province of Touraine, is the gateway to the entire region, not only for its central position but because the TGV high-speed train can deposit you there from Paris in little more than an hour. A string of fine châteaux dominates the Loire Valley east of Tours—Blois, Chaumont, and Amboise lead the way—but two of the area's most stunning monuments lie south of the Loire: romantic Chenonceau, with its arches half-straddling the River Cher, and colossal Chambord, its forest of chimneys and turrets visible above the treetops. By heading westward from Tours, on the other hand, you enter a storyland par excellence, address to such fairy-tale châteaux as Ussé and Azay-le-Rideau and the more muscular castles of Chinon and Saumur. At Angers you can drive northeast to explore the winding, intimate Loir Valley all the way to Châteaudun, just south of Chartres and the Ile-de-France; or continue along the Loire as far as Nantes, the southern gateway to Brittany.

Tours

240 km (150 mi) southwest of Paris. See map on p. 168.

Little remains of Tours's own château—one of France's finest cathedrals more than compensates—but the city serves as the transportation hub for the Loire Valley. Trains from Tours (and from its adjacent terminal at St-Pierre-de-Corps) run along the river in both directions, and regular bus services radiate from here; in addition, the city is the starting point for organized bus excursions (many with English-speaking guides). The town has mushroomed into a city of a quarter of a million inhabitants, with an ugly modern sprawl of factories, high-rise blocks, and overhead expressway junctions cluttering up the outskirts. But the timber-frame houses in **Le Vieux Tours** (Old Tours) and the attractive medieval center around place Plumereau were smartly restored after extensive damage in World War II.

Only two sturdy towers—the Tour Charlemagne and the Tour de l'Horloge (Clock Tower)—remain of the great medieval abbey built over the tomb of St. Martin, the city's 4th-century Bishop and patron saint. Most of the abbey, which once dominated the heart of Tours, was razed during the French Revolution. Today's bombastic neo-Byzantine church, ➤ ❶ the **Basilique St-Martin,** was completed in 1924. There's a shrine to St. Martin in the crypt. ⊠ *Rue Descartes.*

❷ Old mosaics and Romanesque sculptures from the former abbey are on display in the **Musée St-Martin,** a small museum housed in a restored 13th-century chapel that adjoined the abbey cloisters. The museum retraces the life of St. Martin and the abbey's history. ⊠ *3 rue Rapin* ☎ *02–47–05–63–87* ⊡ *Free* ☉ *Mid-Mar.–mid-Nov., Wed.–Sun. 9:30–12:30 and 2–5:30.*

North from the Basilique St-Martin to the river is **Le Vieux Tours,** the lovely old medieval quarter. A warren of quaint streets, wood-beam houses, and grand mansions once home to 15th-century merchants, it has been gentrified with chic apartments and pedestrianized streets—Tours's college students and tourists alike love to sit at the cafés lining ❸ **Place Plumereau,** once the town's *carroi aux chapeaux* (hat market). Lining the square, Nos. 1 through 7 form a magnificent series of half-timber houses; note the woodcarvings of royal moneylenders on Nos. 11 and 12. At the top of the square a vaulted passageway leads on to a cute medieval **Place St-Pierre-le-Puellier.** Running off the Place Plumereau are other streets adorned with historic houses, notably rue Briçonnet—No. 16 is the **Maison de Tristan** with a noted medieval staircase. ⊠ *Bordered by rues du Commerce, Briçonnet, de la Monnaie, and du Grand-Marché.*

FodorśChoice
★

❹ The **Musée du Gemmail,** in the imposing 19th-century Hôtel Raimbault, contains an unusual collection of three-dimensional colored-glass window panels. Depicting patterns, figures, and even portraits, the panels are both beautiful and intriguing—most of the gemlike fragments of glass came from broken bottles. Incidentally, Jean Cocteau coined the word *gemmail* by combining *gemme* (gem) with *émail* (enamel). ⊠ *7 rue du Mûrier* ☎ *02–47–61–01–19* ⊕ *www.gemmail.com* ⊡ *€5* ☉ *Apr.–mid-Nov., Tues.–Sun. 10–noon and 2–6:30; mid-Nov.–Dec., weekends 10–noon and 2–6:30.*

❺ The **Hôtel Gouin** (archaeology museum) is set in Tours's most extravagant example of early Renaissance domestic architecture (too bad its immediate vicinity was among the hardest hit by German bombs), its facade covered with carvings that seemed to have grown like topsy. Inside are assorted oddities ranging from ancient Roman finds to the scientific collection of Dupin de Chenonceau (owner of the great château in the 18th century). ⊠ *25 rue du Commerce* ☎ *02–47–66–22–32* ⊡ *€4.50* ☉ *Mid-May–Sept., daily 10–7; mid-Mar.–mid-May, daily 10–12:30 and 2–6:30; Oct. and Nov., Jan.–mid-Mar., daily 10–12:30 and 2–5:30* ☉ *Closed Dec.*

Châteaux Country *Loire* and *château* are almost synonymous; even the word *château*—part fortress, part palace, part mansion—has no English equivalent. There are châteaux in every region of France, but nowhere are they found clustered as thickly as in the Loire. Why? There are several reasons. By the early Middle Ages, strategically sited and prosperous towns had already grown up because of transport on the Loire, and fortresses—the first châteaux—were built by warlords for defense. The region was also a wildly productive land—the part between the Loire and the Cher has long been known as the "garden of France." In few other areas of France is *la douceur de la vie*, the sweetness of life, more alluring. Melons thrive, cattle grow sleek. Feudal lords grew rich; so did monks, building splendid abbeys. The early medieval Plantagenet kings, rulers of France and England, soon arrived (at Chinon and Fontevraud, to be exact). Under the later medieval Valois kings, the Loire became in effect the capital of France. Châteaux sprang up at their command thanks to all the easily worked building stone, tufa, or *tuffeaux*, in the region. The parade of châteaux began with the medieval fortress at Angers, a brooding and muscular fort designed to withstand long sieges. Such castles were meant to look grim, advertising horrid problems for attackers and unpleasant conditions for prisoners in the dungeons. With Saumur, elegance arrived—the Duc de Berry adorned the sturdy fort with a riot of high pointed roofs, gilded steeples, iron weathervanes, and soaring pinnacles, creating a Gothic-style castle that Walt Disney himself would have loved. Decent-sized windows replaced the old cross-bow slits and it is not romantically foolish to think of love-sick princesses leaning out of these windows and of chivalric tournaments, with all the trappings of cloth-of-gold, and banquets with trumpeters. The time has not yet arrived when every rich noble will insist on a decorative drawbridge and defensive tower or two to impress the neighbors. But one can feel it coming.

By the Renaissance—brought to France by Charles VIII at the end of the 15th century—balance, harmony, and grace were brought to the fore by super-rich bankers and officials who wanted to please their wives by building châteaux that were homages to the romantic chivalry of the past. Azay-le-Rideau may look Gothic from a distance, but its moat is actually the river Indre, and its purpose is to provide a pleasing reflection, adding a further symmetry to this jewel of architecture. This was literally a fairy-tale castle, not used to defend territories but to entertain and astonish guests with luxury. This style reached its peak at Chenonceau, the beautiful château that seems moored over the river Cher—designed by ladies, it was used mostly to host gala balls and famous VIPs. By the 17th century the line of great châteaux had come to an end—the locus of power had moved to the Ile de France and Paris. Cheverny, built between 1604 and 1634, seems only an exercise in classical Italianate symmetry. Although it has a wide facade, the building is only one room deep—the château had become a stage curtain and little more.

Son-et-Lumière In summer, concerts, music festivals, fairs, and celebrated *son-et-lumière* (sound-and-light) extravaganzas are held on the grounds of several châteaux. These dramatic spectacles, mounted after dark, can take the form of historical pageants—with huge casts of people, all in period costume, and caparisoned horses, all floodlighted (some shows simulate shadows of flickering flames to conjure up the mobs of the French Revolution) and backed by music and commentary, sometimes in English; Amboise is the top example. Productions are more often shows with spoken commentary and dialogue but no visible figures, as at Chenonceau and Azay-le-Rideau. The most dazzling was at Chambord but was canceled in 2002. Other than at Amboise, don't expect a cast of thousands—most of the special effects are due to slide projections, smoke-machines, torches, and color spotlights, but they are breathtaking and unforgettable. Of course, to truly experience the château in all its splendor, be sure to stay at some of the many gorgeous château-hotels in the region.

---

❻ The **Musée du Compagnonnage** (Guild Museum) and the **Musée du Vin** (Wine Museum) are both in the cloisters of the 13th-century church of St-Julien. *Compagnonnage* is a sort of apprenticeship–cum–trade union system, and here you see the masterpieces of the candidates for guild membership: virtuoso craft work, some of it eccentric (an Eiffel Tower made of slate, for instance, or a château constructed of varnished noodles). ⊠ *8 rue Nationale* 🕾 *02–47–61–07–93* 🖭 *Musée du Compagnonnage €4.20, Musée du Vin €2.60; joint ticket €5* ☉ *Wed.–Mon. 9–noon and 2–6.*

★ ❼ The **Cathédrale St-Gatien,** built between 1239 and 1484, reveals a mixture of architectural styles. The richly sculpted stonework of its majestic, soaring, two-tower facade betrays the Renaissance influence on local château-trained craftsmen. The stained glass dates from the 13th century (if you have binoculars, bring them). Also take a look at the little tomb with kneeling angels built in memory of Charles VIII and Anne of Brittany's two children; and the **Cloître de La Psalette** (cloister), on the south side of the cathedral. ⊠ *Rue Lavoisier* 🕾 *02–47–47–05–19* ☉ *Daily 8–noon and 2–6.*

❽ The **Musée des Beaux-Arts** (Fine Arts Museum), in what was once the archbishop's palace, has an eclectic selection of treasures: furniture, sculpture, wrought-iron work, and pieces by Rubens, Rembrandt, Boucher, Degas, and Calder. It even displays Fritzthe Elephant, stuffed in 1902. ⊠ *18 pl. François-Sicard* 🕾 *02–47–05–68–73* 🖭 *€4* ☉ *Wed.–Mon. 9–12:45 and 2–6.*

Where to Stay & Eat

$–$$ ✕ **Les Tuffeaux.** This restaurant, between the cathedral and the Loire, is the city's best value. Chef Gildas Marsollier wins customers with delicious fennel-perfumed salmon, oysters in an egg sauce seasoned with Roquefort, and remarkable desserts. Gentle lighting and 17th-century wood-beam and stone-wall decor provide a soothing background. ⊠ *19 rue Lavoisier* 🕾 *02–47–47–19–89* 🖃 *AE, MC, V* ☉ *Closed Sun. and part of July. No lunch Mon. or Wed.*

★ **$$$–$$$$** ✕ **Jean Bardet.** King of Tourangeau chefs, Jean Bardet has a propensity for quoting philosophers, is as happy as a rabbit in a garden (his is packed with heirloom blooms and plants), and is celebrated for showcasing exotic fruits and vegetables in his signature creations. Specials served up in his plush yellow dining salon on his eight-course, €110 *menu dégustation* (tasting menu) and on the super-expensive à la carte menu might include pigeon with foie gras in cabbage-leaf papillote, baby eel in red wine, oysters poached in Muscadet on a puree of watercress, or roast lobster with duck gizzards. Reservations are essential (April to October, there is no lunch Saturday, Monday, and Tuesday; November to March, there is no lunch Saturday and Tuesday, no dinner Sunday, and it is closed Monday). If you want to enjoy that ultimate luxury—a breakfast masterminded by Bardet—book one of the guest rooms upstairs at this stately Directoire-style mansion; all luxuriously mix-and-match antiques and modern touches in the distinctive Relais & Châteaux manner. ⊠ *Château Belmont, 57 rue Groison, 37100* ☎ *02–47–41–41–11* 🖨 *02–47–51–68–72* ⊕ *www.jeanbardet.com* 🛏 *16 rooms, 5 suites* ♨ *Restaurant, minibars, cable TV, pool, some pets allowed (fee)* ▤ *AE, DC, MC, V* ☉ *Nov.–Mar., hotel closed Sun. evening and Mon.* ❮○❯ *MAP.*

★ **$$$** ✕ **Domaine de la Tortinière.** South of Tours and set atop a vast, sloping lawn, this storybook, toy-sized, neo-Gothic château comes complete with two fairy-tale donjons (towers) and a heated, terraced pool. Built in 1861, La Tortinière is now nearing perfection in all things bright and beautiful. Guest rooms in the main building convey quiet, rustic luxury; the conversation pieces are those in the two turrets, while others delight with charmingly beamed ceilings. Most beds are so comfy it's a shame to wake up. In recent years the owners have smartly done up the estate "dependencies"—the former stables, warehouses, and servants' quarters (all just a path away from the main building). Replete with Louis XVI chairs, taffeta curtains, chiffonière tables, plate-glass windows, and divine air-conditioning, these are nearly more alluring than the rooms in the main château. Stylish, too, is the rotunda-shape restaurant that looks out over the lawn and showcases Freddy Lefebvre's cuisine, including roast pigeon in spices and lobster bisque with a pastry top (no dinner Sunday, November through March). The picturesque park is covered with cyclamen at times, while the main lawn overlooks the Indre River, bordered by a line of towering oak trees that have been trimmed back to make a "frame" that Mother Nature herself would envy. The sweet life, indeed. ⊠ *10 rte. de Ballan-Miré, 12 km (7 mi) south of Tours, 37250 Veigné* ☎ *02–47–34–35–00* 🖨 *02–47–65–95–70* ⊕ *www. tortiniere.com* 🛏 *30 rooms* ♨ *Restaurant, minibars, cable TV, tennis court, pool; no a/c in some rooms* ▤ *MC, V* ☉ *Closed mid-Dec.–late Feb.* ❮○❯ *MAP.*

$$ **Central.** This Best Western hotel near the Musée du Compagnonnage, set back from the street behind a gravel court and terraced garden, provides a delightfully friendly city-center oasis. Inside, the welcome is vivacious, the lobby daguerrotype-charming, the guest rooms comfortable, and the clientele a pleasant mix of foreign students and happy travelers. ⊠ *21 rue Berthelot, 37000 Tours* ☎ *02–47–05–46–44* 🖨 *02–47–66–10–26* ⊕ *www.bestwesterncentralhoteltours.com/* 🛏 *38*

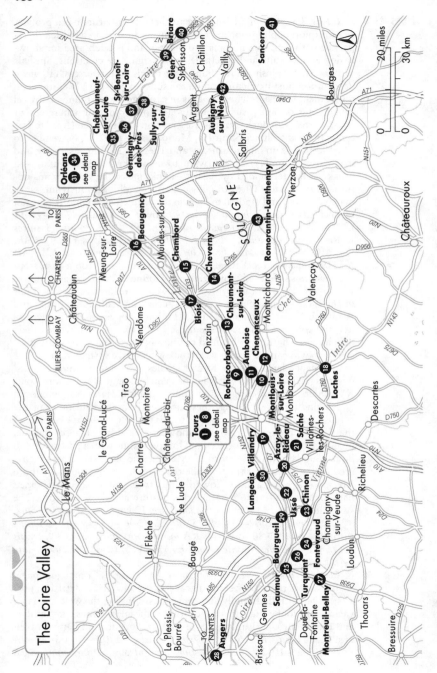

The Loire Valley

rooms ⚴ Minibars, cable TV, bar, free parking, some pets allowed; no a/c in some rooms ⊟ AE, MC, V ⧾⊙⧽ BP.

Rochecorbon

❾ *5 km (3 mi) east of Tours on the north bank of the Loire.*

One of the poshest villages in the Loire, this is a favored forgetaway for Parisians and vacationers. Spread out along the Loire-bank N152 road, with a tiny center set with a church and several fine restaurants, Rochecorbon is overshadowed by its immense cliff studded with curious troglodyte dwellings—caves-cum-cottages sculpted out of tufa, that milky-white porous stone which lines the Loire Valley (and was used to build so many great châteaux). Unfortunately, the town's Manoir des Basses-Rivières—an exquisite, 18th-century rock-face manor—has recently closed for a lengthy renovation. Other than weekend homes for harried urbanites, the town is also address to some of the Val de Loire's most distinctive hotels.Rochecorbon is the only place from which you can actually take

★ a boat-ride excursion out on the Loire. The hour-long **Bateau-Promenade** glides you along a magnificently tranquil stretch of the river. Although the commentary on the boat is in French, the sights alone—riverside caves, deserted towers, distant châteaux (like Moncontour, made famous by Balzac)—make for a most enjoyable outing. ⊠ *Observatoire, 56 quai de la Loire* ☎ *02–47–52–68–88* 🎫 *€8* ☉ *July and Aug., daily 3, 4, and 5 PM; May and June, Sept., weekends 4 and 5 PM.*

Once you find the little town center along the Quai de la Loire embankment, take the road leading into the highlands to discover "upper" Rochecorbon. Past the elegant L'Oubliette restaurant and a gorgeous church (elsewhere in town is the St. George Chapel, with Romaneque frescoes), the road gently mounts the tufa cliff to arrive at a vast plateau studded with vineyards of Vouvray wines. The one attraction hereabouts is found two-thirds up along the route—the **Caves Rupestres,** an abandoned 600-year-old quarry now carved, in a folkloric-modern manner, with 34 wall bas-reliefs detailing the legends of wine in the region, which you can admire with a glass of the grape in your hand. ⊠ *Rue Vaufoynard* 🎫 *€5.30* ☉ *Apr., weekends 2–6; May, June, Sept., and Oct., daily 2–6; July and Aug., daily 10:30–7.*

Rochecorbon makes its own wines and you can explore a vast group of underground galleries at the **Grandes Caves Saint-Roch,** along the main river road. Learn about the extraction of tufa stone, and the methods of cave mushroom-growing and silkworm-production, and taste the Blanc-Foussy whites. ⊠ *65 quai de la Loire* ☎ *02–47–52–57–70* 🎫 *€3.10* ☉ *Call ahead for details.*

Where to Stay & Eat

★ **$$$–$$$$** ✕⛾ **Hôtel des Hautes Roches.** *Extraordinaire* is the word for some of the luxe-troglodyte rooms at this famous hotel, which stud a towering cliff-face with their elegant sash windows, gas-lantern lamps, and finished marble steps. Don't expect decor à la Fred Flintstone: half the guest-room walls are Ice Age, but stylish fabrics, Louis Treize seating, and carved fireplaces are the main allurements. Some prefer rooms in the regular

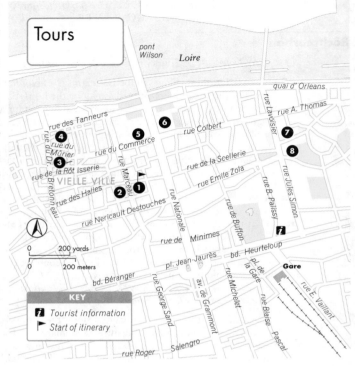

house—no cave-dwelling drama, but exquisitely comfortable and air-conditioned. The restaurant (closed Monday, no lunch Wednesday, no dinner Sunday) has an extremely staid decor, so most everyone repairs to the enchanting terrace to feast on a panoply of various foie gras, fish and duck dishes, and architectonic desserts—certainly one of the best kitchens in the Loire, if not in France (don't forget to order a selection from the gigantic cheese tray brought out—at least one summer afternoon—by a boy who seems half the size of the tray). To top it all off, a sapphire pool tempts all during the Loire's *grandes chaleurs.* ⊠ *86 quai de la Loire, 37210 Rochecorbon* ☎ *02–47–52–88–88* 🖷 *02–47–52–81–30* ⊕ *www. leshautesroches.com/* ⇌ *15 rooms, 3 suites* ♻ *Restaurant, minibars, cable TV, pool, some pets allowed (fee); no a/c in some rooms* 🖃 *AE, DC, MC, V* ☺ *Closed end Jan.–mid-Mar.* ⦿❘ *MAP.*

★ **\$\$–\$\$\$** ✕⛿ **Château de Montgouverne.** If enchantment is what you're after, look no further. More than one Bel Air billionaire must have used this adorable, pint-size château as the model for his California spread. A do-be-impressed driveway leads to the 18th-century building, whose elegance is accented by three perfect fairy-tale turrets and framed by gigantic cedars of Lebanon. Inside, all is *chic et charmant*—benches filled with plants, tables ribboned-and-bowed with sumptuous fabrics, watercolor sketches on the wall, and two of the suavest proprietors around, Laurent Gross and his blonde wife (he's from Switzerland, she's from South Africa). Most guest rooms are soigné charmers—one is a cocoon in 19th-century paisley, another offers a window, complete with picture frame, overlooking vineyards, still another is a *toile-de-jouy* extravaganza. A three-minute ride down the road takes you to the top cave-restaurant, L'Oubliette. ⊠ *37210 Rochecorbon* ☎ *02–47–52–87–59* 🖷 *02–47–52–84–61* ⊕ ➾ *4 rooms, 3 suites* ♨ *Pool; no a/c* ⊟ *AE, MC, V* ⊙ *BP.*

Montlouis-sur-Loire

⑩ *11 km (7 mi) east of Tours on the south bank of the Loire.*

Like Vouvray—its sister town on the north side of the Loire—Montlouis is noted for its white wines. The outskirts of the town are largely suburban but around the river quais are some historic finds—a church begun in the 12th century, the Renaissance-era Ramée Mansion. On place Courtemanche the **Cave Touristique** will allow you to learn all about the fine vintages produced by the wine-growers of Montlouis. On the eastern side of town is one of the most alluring, yet least-known, châteaux of the region, **La Bourdaisière.** Although open to day-trippers for guided tours, this once-royal retreat and birthplace of noted 17th-century courtesan Gabrielle d'Estreaes is today the enchanted hotel–domain of the princes de Broglie.

Where to Stay & Eat

$$$–$$$$
Fodor's Choice
★

✕🏨 **Château de la Bourdaisière.** Few other hotels so magically distill all the grace, warmth, and elan of *la vie de châteaux* as does this 15th-century, 100-carat jewel. Once the favored retreat of two kings, François I and Henri IV, today the presiding spirits are only slightly less royal: brothers Princes Philippe-Maurice and Louis-Albert de Broglie, scions of one of France's top families (two prime ministers and one Nobel Prize winner, at last count). Louis-Albert is one of Paris's most famed gardeners, who here cultivates 400 types of tomatoes in the château's *potager.* It's not surprising, then, to find the three main public salons are suavely done up in shades of tomato red, sumptuously offsetting such accents as an immense marble fireplace and large bouquets designed by the prince. You'll start your gawking, however, at the park entrance—motorists often stop to drink in the view of the neo-Renaissance castle perched atop its picture-perfect hill. Guest rooms range from the grand—*François-Premier* is a timber-roof cottage blown up to ballroom dimensions—to more standard-issue, yet always stylish, salons (garden-view rooms away from the gravel driveway are best). Other rooms are found in the adjoining 17th-century "stables" fitted out with a gardening shop and a tiny eatery that serves up dazzling salads and confections (lunch only, June–September). What more can you ask? What about an enormous secluded pool—a gift from heaven during hot summer days. Life-changingly gracious, La Bourdaisière makes a truly princely base for exploring the Loire. ⊠ *25 rue de la Bourdaisière, 37270* ☎ *02–47–45–16–31* 🖷 *02–47–45–09–11* ⊕ *www.chateaulabourdaisiere. com* ➾ *20 rooms* ♨ *Restaurant, tennis court, pool, shop; no a/c, no room TVs* ⊟ *MC, V* ☉ *Closed Nov. 15–Mar. 15* ⊙ *BP.*

Amboise

🕕 *13 km (8 mi) east of Montlouis via D751, 24 km (15 mi) east of Tours.*

The Da Vinci trail ends here in one of the more popular towns along the river. Site of Leonardo's final home, crowned with a royal château, and jammed with bustling markets and plenty of hotels and restaurants, Amboise is one of the major hubs of the Loire. On hot summer days, however, the plethora of tour-buses turn the Renaissance town into a carbon monoxide nightmare. So why come? The main château is soaked in history (and blood), while Leonardo's Clos-Lucé is a must-do on any Val de Loire itinerary.

The **Château d'Amboise** became a royal palace in the 15th and 16th centuries. Charles VII stayed here, as did the unfortunate Charles VIII, best remembered for banging his head on a low doorway lintel (you will be shown it) and dying as a result. The gigantic **Tour des Minimes** drops down the side of the cliff, enclosing a massive circular ramp designed to lead horses and carriages up the steep hillside. François I, whose long nose appears in so many château paintings, based his court here, inviting Leonardo da Vinci as his guest. The castle was also the stage for the Amboise Conspiracy, an ill-fated Protestant plot against François II; you are shown where the corpses of 1,200 conspirators dangled from the castle walls. This is one reason why the château feels haunted and forlorn—another is the fact that most of its interior furnishings have been lost. But don't miss the lovely grounds, adorned with a Flamboyant Gothic gem, the little chapel of St-Hubert with its carvings of the Virgin and Child, Charles VIII, and Anne of Brittany, and once graced by the tomb of Leonardo. ☎ 02–47–57–00–98 ⊕ *www.chateau-amboise.tm.fr* 🎫 €7.50 ⊙ *Nov.–Mar., daily 9–noon and 2–4:45; Apr.–June, Sept., and Oct., daily 9–6; July and Aug., daily 9–7.*

★ ☾ If you want to see where "the 20th century was born"—as the posters would have it—head to the legendary **Clos Lucé**, about 600 yards up rue Victor-Hugo from the château. Here, in this handsome Renaissance manor, Leonardo da Vinci (1452–1519) spent the last four years of his life, tinkering away at inventions, amusing his patron, King François I, and gazing out over a garden that was planted in the most fashionable Italian manner. The basement contains working models, built by IBM engineers using the detailed sketches in the artist's notebooks, of some of Leonardo's extraordinary inventions; by this time, Leonardo had put away his paint box because of arthritis. Mechanisms on display include three-speed gearboxes, a military tank, a clockwork car, and a flying machine complete with designs for parachutes. Cloux, the house's original name, was given to Anne of Brittany by Charles VIII, who built a chapel for her that is still here. Some of the house's furnishings are authentically 16th century—indeed, thanks to the artist's presence, this house was one of the very first places the Italian Renaissance made inroads in France: Leonardo's *Mona Lisa* and *Virgin of the Rocks,* both of which graced the walls here, were bought by the king, who then moved them to the Louvre. ✉ *2 rue du Clos-Lucé* ☎ 02–47–57–62–88 🎫 €8.50 ⊙ *Sept.–June, daily 9–6; July and Aug., daily 9–7.*

Just 3 km (2 mi) south of Amboise on the road to Chenonceaux, the **Pagode de Chanteloup** is a remarkable sight—a 140-foot, seven-story Chinese-style lakeside pagoda built for the Duke of Choiseul in 1775. Children will adore puffing their way to the top for the vertigo-inducing views, but some adults will find the climb—and the 400-yard walk from the parking lot—a little arduous. Sadly, the adjoining lake and park have become the worse for wear. ⊠ *Rte de Bléré* ☎ *02–47–57–20–97* ⊒ *€6.30* ۞ *Apr.–Sept., daily 10–6:30; Oct.–mid-Nov. and mid-Feb.–Mar., daily 10–noon and 2–5.*

Where to Stay & Eat

★ **$$$–$$$$** ✕▦ **Château de Noizay.** Filled with mystery of the past—this was once the fabled redoubt of the Protestant conspirators in the 1559 Amboise Conspiracy—this château is fitted out with Renaissance chimneys and salons, a parterre garden, and, best of all, one of the finest chefs around. Guest rooms are so regal you may feel like curtsying to the staff, so opt for the adjacent 19th-century "Clock House"—a gracious pastel-hued haven with lush air-conditioning. Noizay itself is a tiny, off-the-beaten-path treasure—don't miss the incredible walk down rue François-Poulenc, an idyllic countryside hike that passes the famous composer's gorgeous 18th-century house, a troglodyte hamlet, and endless poppy fields right out of a Monet painting. ⊠ *Route de Chançay, 8 km (5 mi) west of Tours, 37210 Noizay* ☎ *02–47–52–11–01* ⊟ *02–47–52–04–64* ⊕ *www.chateaudenoizay.com* ➲ *14 rooms* ⌂ *Restaurant, minibars, cable TV, tennis court, pool; no a/c in some rooms* ⊟ *AE, MC, V* ۞ *Closed mid-Jan.–mid-Mar.* �１⊙�１ *FAP.*

★ **$$–$$$$** ✕▦ **Château de Pray.** Fifty years ago Loire Valley guide books praised this domain and, delightfully, things have only gotten better. Like a Rolls Royce Silver Cloud II this hotel keeps purring along, offering many delights—a super-romantic, twin-towered château, a Loire River vista, tranquil guest rooms (four of the less expensive are in a charming "Pavillon Renaissance"), and a truly excellent restaurant. The latter is set in two salons, one in Charles-Dix golds, the other—could this be the most gorgeous dining room in all the Loire?—lit with chandeliers and stained-glass windows, lined with tapestries, and centered around a storybook, sculpted-wood fireplace. Just outside is the lawn terrace, where happy guests assemble to toast their friends with magnums of Veuve Clicquot. ⊠ *Route de Chargé, 4 km (2 mi) east of Amboise, 37400* ☎ *02–47–57–23–67* ⊟ *02–47–57–32–50* ⊕ *www.praycastel.online.fr* ➲ *26 rooms, 2 suites* ⌂ *Restaurant, cable TV, pool; no a/c* ⊟ *AE, MC, V* ۞ *Closed Jan.* �１⊙�１ *MAP.*

$ ✕▦ **Le Blason.** Two blocks behind Château d'Amboise and a five-minute walk from the town center, this small hotel is enlivened by its enthusiastic owners. The old building has rooms of different shapes and sizes: No. 229, for example, has exposed beams and a cathedral ceiling; No. 109 is comfortably spacious and has a good view of the square. In the restaurant, superior, reasonably priced seasonal fare is served—roast lamb with garlic, and salmon carpaccio with mustard dressing, for instance. ⊠ *11 pl. Richelieu, 37400* ☎ *02–47–23–22–41* ⊟ *02–47–57–56–18* ➲ *28 rooms* ⌂ *Restaurant, some pets allowed (fee)* ⊟ *AE, DC, MC, V* ۞ *Closed mid-Jan.–mid-Feb.* �１⊙�１ *MAP.*

★ **$$–$$$** 🖼 **Le Vieux Manoir.** You'll know you're in great hands when you come down to an elegant and inviting breakfast in a glass conservatory filled with purring and laughing fellow guests. An ultimate welcome mat for anyone visiting the Loire Valley, this magnificently lovely hotel is the creation of Gloria Belknap—a Californian whose immense style Edith Wharton (that other great Francophile) would have cottoned to immediately. You'll have a hard time tearing yourself away from your guest room, as Gloria seems to have missed her calling as a decorator extraordinaire: *toile-de-Jouy* screens, gilt-framed paintings, comfy Napoléon III covered-in-jute armchairs, fascinatingly time-worn armoires, and tables adorned with Shaker baskets make this place *House & Garden*-worthy. Each chamber—named after great French ladies, such as Georges Sand, Madame du Barry, and Colette—is a delight: a bleached redbrick chimney and red-and-white calico accent one, while ceiling beams and a French-provincial four-poster bed warm another. Larger groups can move into a separate (and proportionately pricier) 17th-century cottage, a cosseting maison filled with antiques and wood beams. But you'll probably spend more time in the book-filled library or in the main salon—soaking up the wit and wisdom of Gloria and husband Bob— or by the fountain in the leafy garden. ⊠ *13 rue Rabelais, 37400* ☎🖶 *02–47–30–41–27* ⊕ *www.le-vieux-manoir.com* ⛶ *6 rooms, 1 cottage* ⚒ *No a/c, no room TVs* 🖃 *No credit cards* ⏣ *BP.*

Chenonceaux

⑫ *12 km (8 mi) southeast of Amboise via D81, 32 km (20 mi) east of Tours.*

Fodor'sChoice Achingly beautiful, the **Château de Chenonceau** has long been considered
★ the "most romantic" of all the Loire châteaux, thanks in part to its showpiece—a breathtaking *galerie de bal* that spans the River Cher like a bridge (used as an escape point for French Resistance fighters during World War II, since all other crossings had been bombed). Set in the village of Chenonceaux (spelled with an *x*) on the River Cher, this was the fabled retreat for the *dames des Chenonceau*: Diane de Poitiers, Catherine de' Medici, and Mary, Queen of Scots. Happily spending at least half a day wandering through the château and grounds, you'll see that this monument has an undeniable feminine touch (the design was entirely overseen by women). During the peak summer season the château is open—unlike many others—all day. The only drawback is its popularity: if you want to avoid a roomful of schoolchildren, take a stroll on the grounds and come back to the house at lunchtime. Whatever hour, be sure to walk to the most distant point of the largest parterre garden— there you'll find a tiny bridge leading to a river lookout point where you'll find the most beautiful view of France's most glorious château.

More pleasure-palace than fortress, the château was built in 1520 by Thomas Bohier, a wealthy tax collector, for his wife, Catherine Briçonnet. When he went bankrupt, it passed to François I. Later, Henri II gave it to his mistress, Diane de Poitiers. After his death, Henri's not-so-understanding widow, Catherine de' Medici, expelled Diane to nearby Chaumont and took back the château. Before this time, Diane's five-arched bridge over the River Cher was simply meant as a grand ceremonial entryway leading to a gigantic château, a building never constructed. It was to Catherine, and her architect, Philibert de l'Orme, that historians owe the audacious plan to transform the bridge itself into the most unusual château in France. Two stories were constructed, including an enormous gallery that runs from one end of the château to the other—a grand space that became the stage set for some legendary galas. July and August are the peak months at Chenonceau: only then can you escape the maddening crowds by exiting at the far end of the gallery to walk along the opposite bank (weekends only), rent a rowboat to spend an hour just drifting in the river (where Diane used to enjoy her morning dips), and enjoy an evocative **son-et-lumière,** performed in the illuminated château gardens.

Before you go inside, pick up an English-language leaflet at the gate. Then walk around to the right of the main building to see the harmonious, delicate architecture beyond the formal garden—the southern part belonged to Diane de Poitiers, the northern was Catherine's—with the river gliding under the arches (providing superb "air-conditioning" to the rooms above). Inside the château are splendid ceilings, colossal fireplaces, scattered furnishings, and paintings by Rubens, del Sarto, and Correggio. The curatorial staff have delightfully dispensed with velvet ropes and adorned some of the rooms with bouquets designed in 17th-century style. As you tour the salons, be sure to pay your respects to former owner Madame Dupin, tellingly captured in Nattier's charming portrait: thanks to the affection she inspired among her proletarian neighbors, the château and its treasures survived the Revolution intact (her grave is enshrined near the northern embankment). The château's history is illustrated with wax figures in the **Musée des Cires** (Waxwork Museum) in one of the château's outbuildings. A cafeteria, tearoom, and the ambitious Orangerie restaurant handle the crowds' varied appetites. ☎ 02–47–23–90–07 ⊕ www.chenonceau.com 🖃 Château €8, Waxwork Museum €3, son-et-lumière €8 ☉ Feb.–May and Oct.–mid-Nov., daily 9–5:30; June–Sept., daily 9–7; Dec. and Jan., daily 9–4:30.

Where to Stay & Eat

★ $$–$$$ ✕🏨 **Le Bon Laboureur.** In 1882 this ivy-covered inn won Henry James's praise and, happily, the famed author would be even more impressed today. Thanks to four generations of the Jeudi family, this remains one of the most stylish auberges in the Val de Loire. Nearly everywhere, charm is provided in *l'abondance*—many guest rooms are enchantingly accented in *toile-de-jouy* fabrics, rustic wainscotting, tiny lamps, and Redouté pink-and-blue pastels. Those in the main house are comfortably sized (a few overlook the main street—avoid these if you are a light sleeper), those in the former stables are larger (some overlook a lovely vegetable garden) and more renovated, but our favorites are the adorably quaint rooms in the separate patio house near the terrace. Don't lose any time bagging a table in the "old" dining room (book this room, not the more modern ones), whose wood-beamed ceiling, glazed terra-cotta walls, and Louis XVI chairs are almost as elegant as chef Jean-Marie Burnet's cream of crayfish with basil, pike-perch with spices, or turbot with red pepper and fennel. And that is saying something: totally *delicieux*, meals here are marvels. ✉ *6 rue du Dr-Bretonneau, 37150* ☏ *02–47–23–90–02* 📠 *02–47–23–82–01* ⊕ *www.amboise.com/laboureur* 🛏 *24 rooms* ♨ *Restaurant, minibars, cable TV, pool, bicycles, bar, some pets allowed (fee); no a/c in some rooms* ▤ *AE, DC, MC, V* ☯ *Closed Jan.–mid-Feb. and mid-Nov.–mid-Dec.* †○† *MAP.*

★ **$–$$** ✕▦ **La Roseraie.** The Bon Laboureur may be Chenonceaux's most famous hostelry, but this is easily its second for charm, thanks in part to the joyful welcome of its English-speaking hosts, Laurent and Sophie Fiorito. But let's not forget the guest rooms, many of which are designed with florals, checks, and lace, or the copious meals served in the rustic dining room (where foie gras, duck with fruit and honey, and apple tart are among the specialties), or the pretty pool. Try to get a garden-side room, even if too many pink tablecloths and white chairs make the patio less than restful. If car traffic bothers you, be sure to avoid the rooms overlooking the main street. ✉ *7 rue du Dr-Bretonneau, 37150* ☏ *02–47–23–90–09* 📠 *02–47–23–91–59* ⊕ *www.charmingroseraie.com* 🛏 *17 rooms, 14 with bath, 3 with shower* ♨ *Restaurant, cable TV, pool, bar; no a/c* ▤ *AE, DC, MC, V* ☯ *Closed mid-Nov.–late Feb.* †○† *BP.*

Chaumont-sur-Loire

❸ *26 km (16 mi) northeast of Chenonceaux via D176/D62, 21 km (13 mi) southwest of Blois.*

★ Although a favorite of Loire connoisseurs, the **Château de Chaumont** is often overlooked by visitors who are content to ride the conveyor belt of big châteaux like Chambord and Chenonceau, and it's their loss. Set on a dramatic bluff that towers over the river, Chaumont has always cast a spell—perhaps literally so. One of its fabled owners, Catherine de' Medici, occasionally came here with her court "astrologer," the notorious Ruggieri. In one of Chaumont's bell-tower rooms, the queen reputedly practiced sorcery (for her troubles, she foresaw the tragic deaths of all her three sons in a magic mirror, foretelling the historic downfall of the Valois dynasty). Whether Ruggieri still haunts the place (or Nostradamus, another on Catherine's guest list), there seem to be few castles as spirit-warm as this one.

Centerpiece of a gigantic park (a stiff walk up a long path from the little village of Chaumont-sur-Loire; cars and taxis can also leave you off at the top of the hill) and built between 1465 and 1510, the château greets visitors with glorious, twin-tower *châtelets*—twin turrets that frame a double-drawbridge. Originally built by Charles II d'Amboise in the Late Gothic style, the castle became the residence of Henri II and his wife, Catherine. Upon his death, however, the king's widow decided to take her revenge on his mistress, the fabled beauty Diane de Poitiers, and forced her to exchange Chenonceau for Chaumont. Another "refugee" was the late-18th-century writer Madame de Staël. Exiled from Paris by Napoléon, she wrote *De l'Allemagne* (*On Germany*) here, a book that helped kick-start the Romantic movement in France. In the 19th century her descendants, the prince and princess de Broglie, set up regal shop, as you can still see from the stone-and-brick stables, where purebred horses (and one elephant) lived like royalty in velvet-lined stalls.

The couple also renovated many rooms in the glamorous neo-Gothic style of the 1870s. Today, their sense of fantasy is retained in the castle's **Festival International des Jardins** (www.chaumont-jardins.com), held July to October every year in the extensive park and featuring the latest in horticultural inventiveness. ☎02–54–51–26–26 ☒ €6.50 ☉ *Mid-Mar.–mid-Nov., daily 9:30–6; mid-Dec.–mid-Mar., daily 10–5.*

Where to Stay & Eat

★ **$$$–$$$$** ✕☒ **Domaine des Hauts-de-Loire.** Long a landmark of Loire luxe, this aristocratic outpost is across the river from Chaumont (which has a handy bridge) and some 4 km (2 mi) inland. Set in an 18th-century, turreted, vine-covered hunting lodge, it comes with the requisite grand salon furnished with 18th-century antiques, a lovely pool, an adorable swan lake, a helipad, 180 acres of forest for hikes, and the most blissful air-conditioning in all Touraine (a gift from heaven on sweltering summer days). Guest rooms are beige, suave, and tranquil; those in the adjacent carriage houses have spectacular exposed brick walls and gabled ceilings. The restaurant (closed Monday and no lunch Tuesday off-season) glows with mellow lights, white bouquets, and some dazzling dishes, showcased in a €90 menu. Later, contented patrons often repair to the salon for champagne to swap stories and toast their good luck at being here—and *here.* ☒ *Rte. de Mesland, across the Loire from Chaumont, 41150 Onzain* ☎ *02–54–20–72–57* ☒ *02–54–20–77–32* ⊕ *www.domainehautsloire.com* ⤴ *25 rooms, 10 suites* ♨ *Restaurant, minibars, cable TV, tennis court, pool, helipad* ▤ *AE, DC, MC, V* ☉ *Closed Dec.–Feb.* ⅊ *MAP.*

$–$$ ✕☒ **Hostellerie du Château.** Set on a bank of the Loire and directly opposite the road leading up to Chaumont's château, this quaint edifice was—rather uniquely for these parts—built in the early 20th century as a hotel pure and simple. Four-stories tall, fitted out with super-charming half-timbered eaves, the hotel conjures up the grace of earlier days. Today, happily, it's purring along as a very reasonably priced option. The entry hall soars, the restaurant is cozy and friendly, and the staff is Chaumont-courteous. Who cares if the rooms are on the simple side and a bit worse for wear? However: the hotel does front the main road zipping through Chaumont (with loads of traffic) so be sure to bag a room on the side facing the Loire, or, failing that, along the side flanks of the hotel. ☒ *2 rue Maréchal Delatre-de-Tassigny, 41150* ☎ *02–54–20–98–04* ☒ *02–54–20–97–98* ⤴ *28 rooms* ♨ *Restaurant, pool; no room phones* ▤ *MC, V* ☉ *Closed Feb.* ⅊ *EP.*

Cheverny

❶❹ *24 km (15 mi) east of Chaumont, 14 km (9 mi) southeast of Blois.*

Perhaps best remembered as Capitaine Haddock's mansion in the Tintin comic books, the **Château de Cheverny** is also iconic for its restrained 17th-century elegance. One of the last in the area to be built, it was finished in 1634, at a time when the rich and famous had mostly stopped building in the Loire Valley. By then, the taste for quaintly shaped châteaux had given way to disciplined Classicism; so here a white, elegantly proportioned, horizontally coursed, single-block facade greets you across manicured lawns. To emphasize the strict symmetry of the plan, a ruler-straight drive leads to the front entrance. The Louis XIII interior with its stridently painted and gilded rooms, splendid furniture, and rich tapestries depicting the Labors of Hercules is one of the few still intact in the Loire region. Despite the priceless Delft vases and Persian embroideries, it feels lived in. That's because it's one of the rare Loire Valley houses still occupied by a noble family. Elsewhere, you are free to contemplate the antlers of 2,000 stags in the Trophy Room. Hunting, called "venery" in the leaflets, continues vigorously here, with red coats, bugles, and all. In the château's kennels, hordes of hungry hounds lounge around dreaming of their next kill. Feeding times—*la soupe aux chiens*—are posted on a notice board, and you are welcome to watch the "ceremony" (delicate sensibilities beware: the dogs line up like statues and are called, one by one, to wolf down their meal from the trainer). You can visit the château grounds by either boat or electric buggy, or get a bird's-eye view from 500 feet up in a charming hot-air balloon; purchase tickets on the spot. The château's village is officially named Cour-Cheverny. ☎ 02–54–79–96–29 ⊕ *www.chateau-cheverny.fr* ☞ €6.10, €10.80 including boat-and-buggy rides ☉ Apr.–Sept., daily 9:15–6:15; Oct.–Mar., daily 9:45–5.

Chambord

⑮　17 km (11 mi) northeast of Cheverny via D102 and D112, 19 km (12
FodorśChoice　mi) east of Blois, 45 km (28 mi) southwest of Orléans.
★

★ ☾　The "Versailles" of the 16th century and the largest of the Loire châteaux, the **Château de Chambord** is the kind of place William Randolph Hearst might have built if he'd had the money. Variously dubbed "megalomaniacal" and "an enormous film-set extravaganza," this is one of the most extraordinary structures in Europe, set in the middle of a royal game forest, with just a cluster of buildings—barely a village—across the road. As you travel the gigantic highways that converge on the building, you first spot Chambord's incredible towers—19th-century novelist Henry James said they were "more like the spires of a city than the salient points of a single building"—rising above the forest. When the entire château breaks into view, it is an unforgettable sight.

With a facade that is 420 feet long, 440 rooms and 365 chimneys, a wall 32 km (20 mi) long to enclose a 13,000-acre forest (you can wander through 3,000 acres of it; the rest is reserved for wild boar and other game), this is one of the greatest buildings in France. Under François I, building began in 1519, a job that took 12 years and required 1,800 workers. His original grandiose idea was to divert the Loire to form a moat, but someone (perhaps his adviser, Leonardo da Vinci, who some feel may have provided the inspiration behind the entire complex) persuaded him to make do with the River Cosson. François I used the château only for short stays; yet when he came, 12,000 horses were required to transport his luggage, servants, and entourage. Later kings also used Chambord as an occasional retreat, and Louis XIV, the Sun King, had

Molière perform here. In the 18th century Louis XV gave the château to the Maréchal de Saxe as a reward for his victory over the English and Dutch at Fontenoy (southern Belgium) in 1745. When not indulging himself with wine, women, and song, the marshal planted himself on the roof to oversee the exercises of his personal regiment of 1,000 cavalry. Now, after long neglect—all the original furnishings vanished during the French Revolution—Chambord belongs to the state.

There's plenty to see inside. You can wander freely through the vast rooms, filled with exhibits (including a hunting museum)—not all concerned with Chambord, but interesting nonetheless—and lots of Ancien Régime furnishings. The enormous double-helix staircase (probably envisioned by Leonardo, who had a thing about spirals) looks like a single staircase, but an entire regiment could march up one spiral while a second came down the other, and never the twain would meet. But the high point here in more ways than one is the spectacular chimneyscape—the roof terrace whose forest of Italianate towers, turrets, cupolas, gables, and chimneys have been compared to everything from the minarets of Constantinople to a bizarre chessboard. The most eye-popping time to see this roof is at night, when the château is spectacularly illuminated. During the year there's a packed calendar of activities on tap, from performances of 17th-century dressage (horsemanship technique) by Les Ecuries du Maréchal de Saxe to photo-safaris through the game preserve (during deer-rut season) to concerts to boating on the grand moat. Les Metaphorphoses, a super-spectacular light-show, used to be given at night but has now been canceled—hopefully, a new after-hours extravaganza is in the works. A three-story-tall hall has been fitted out to offer lunches and dinners. ☎ *02–54–50–40–28* ⊕ *www.chambord.org* ✉ *€9* ☉ *Apr.–Sept., daily 9–6:15; Oct.–Mar., daily 9–5:15.*

Where to Stay & Eat

★ **$$$–$$$$** ✕ **Relais de Bracieux.** Masterminded by chef Bernard Robin, this is one of the Loire's very top restaurants. Out of the gleaming kitchens comes sumptuous nouvelle cuisine: lobster with dried tomatoes or shepherd's pie with oxtail and truffles. Connoisseurs also savor Robin's simpler fare: carp, game in season, and salmon with beef marrow. Others delight in his opulent details—accompanying your dessert you may find a fairy-tale forest of mushrooms and elves spun in sugar. The dining room is white, traditional-modern, and luxe, while the attentive staff brings delicious tidbits to keep you busy between courses. ⊠ *1 av. de Chambord, 8 km (5 mi) south of Chambord, 9 km (6 mi) northeast of Cour-Cheverny on road to Chambord, Bracieux* ☎ *02–54–46–41–22* ⊕ *www.relaisdebracieux.com* ⚘ *Reservations essential* 🏛 *Jacket and tie* ▭ *AE, DC, MC, V* ☉ *Closed mid-Dec.–mid-Jan. and Wed. No dinner Tues.*

★ **$–$$** ✕🖭 **Grand St-Michel.** The village of Chambord is as tiny as its château is massive. Its leading landmark is this historic hotel, a revamped country house set at the edge of the woods across the lawn from the château. Guest rooms once boasted fabled views of the palace but towering oak trees now block the view from all but two. No matter—this is a most enjoyable hotel, with a cozy lobby, solidly bourgeois guest rooms, and a 19th-century-flavored restaurant. Adorned with mounted deer heads, majolica serving platters, and thick curtains, this room has ambiance to spare. The fare is local, hearty (including deer pâté, pike-perch with fennel, and game in the fall), attractively priced, and there's a pleasant café-terrace facing the château—just the place for reflection while sipping a drink. ✉ *103 pl. St-Michel, 41250* ☎ *02–54–20–31–31* 🖷 *02–54–20–36–40* ➫ *39 rooms, 25 with bath, 13 with shower* ⚴ *Restaurant, tennis court, some pets allowed (fee); no a/c* ▤ *MC, V* ☉ *Closed mid-Nov.–mid-Dec.* ⎸◎⎹ *BP.*

$$–$$$ ▥ **Château de Colliers.** Keep Chenonceau. You can have Chambord. For
Fodor'sChoice a few lucky travelers, the most unforgettable château in the Loire
★ proves to be this tiny, overlooked treasure. Colliers may not have the showy pomp of the Loire's more famous château-hotels, but it has something more precious—*authenticité*. The home of Christian and Marie-France de Gélis (both of whom are charming and speak English), it was sold to their family in 1779 by the Marquis de Vaudreuil, first French governor of Louisiana. At the end of a long allée, this "pavillon Mansart" embraces you in a semicircular layout (the *collier*, or necklace). Ten family descendants study you from gilded Charles-Dix frames in the main salon, a room that is possibly the most beautiful in all the Loire: a confectionery vision of white Rococo moldings, glittering chandelier, with furniture that Madame Bovary would have loved. The breakfast room is covered with quaint 16th-century Italian frescoes (and Madame Gélis's repast is delicious enough to eat for lunch and dinner), each guest room is a bouquet of antiques and comfy furniture, and—unique to this hotel—there is a vast river terrace that overlooks a magnificently pristine stretch of the Loire. The river's ripples will lullaby you to sleep in your bedroom but—trust us—you will undoubtedly already be in a semi-dream state. ✉ *Rue Nationale, Muides-sur-Loire, 8 km (4 mi) northwest of Chambord; 17 km (10 mi) southwest of Blois, 41500* ☎ *02–54–87–50–75* 🖷 *02–54–87–03–64* ✍ *Chcolliers@aol.com* ➫ *5 rooms* ⚴ *Pool; no a/c, no room TVs* ▤ *MC, V* ⎸◎⎹ *BP.*

The Outdoors

Rent a horse from the former stables, **Les Ecuries du Maréchal de Saxe** (✉ On grounds of Château de Chambord ☎ 02–54–20–31–01) and ride through the vast national park surrounding the château. From March through October you can hire a boat to explore the château moat and the **Grand Canal** (☎ 02–54–56–00–43 for details) linking it to the River Cosson.

Beaugency

⑯ *24 km (15 mi) northeast of Chambord via D112 and D951.*

A clutch of historic towers and buildings around a 14th-century bridge over the Loire lends Beaugency its charm. The buildings in this town on the north bank of the river include the massive 11th-century **donjon** (keep), the Romanesque church of **Notre-Dame**, and the **Tour du Diable** (Devil's Tower), overlooking the river. The **Château Dunois** contains a regional museum with traditional costumes and peasant furniture. ⊠ *2 pl. Dunois* ☎ *02–38–44–55–23* ⊘ *Closed for renovation at this writing.*

Blois

⑰ *27 km (17 mi) southwest of Beaugency via N152, 54 km (34 mi) southwest of Orléans, 58 km (36 mi) northeast of Tours.*

Perched on a steep hillside overlooking the Loire, site of one of France's most historic châteaux, and birthplace of those delicious Poulain chocolates and gâteaux (check out the bakeries along the main street of rue Denis-Papin and tour the nearby Poulain factory), the bustling old town of Blois is an alluring and convenient base, well served by train and highway. A signposted route leads you on a walking tour of the **Vieille Ville** (Old Town)—a romantic honeycomb of twisting alleys, cobblestone streets, and half-timber houses—but it is best explored with the help of a map available from the tourist office. The historic highlight is place St-Louis, where you'll find the Maison des Acrobats (note the timbers carved with *jongleurs,* or jugglers), Cathédrale St-Louis, and Hôtel de Villebresme, but unexpected Renaissance-era galleries and staircases also lurk in tucked-away courtyards, such as the one in the Hôtel d'Alluye, built by Florimond Robertet, finance minister to three kings and the last patron to commission a painting from Leonardo da Vinci. The best view of the town, with its château and numerous church spires rising sharply above the river, can be had from across the Loire.

The massive **Château de Blois** spans several architectural periods and is among the valley's finest. Your ticket entitles you to a guided tour—given in English when there are enough visitors who don't understand French—but you are more than welcome to roam around without a guide if you visit between mid-March and August. Before you enter, stand in the courtyard to admire examples of four centuries of architecture. On one side stand the 13th-century hall and tower, the latter offering a stunning view of the town and countryside. The Renaissance begins to flower in the Louis XII wing (built between 1498 and 1503), through which you enter, and comes to full bloom in the François I wing (1515–24). The masterpiece here is the openwork spiral staircase, painstakingly restored. The fourth side consists of the Classical Gaston d'Orléans wing (1635–38). Upstairs in the François I wing is a series of enormous rooms with tremendous fireplaces decorated with the gilded porcupine, emblem of Louis XII, the ermine of Anne of Brittany, and, of course, François I's salamander, breathing fire and surrounded by flickering flames. Many rooms have intricate ceilings and carved, gilt paneling; there's even a sad little picture of Mary, Queen of Scots. In the council room the Duke of Guise was murdered by order of Henri III in 1588. In the **Musée des Beaux-Arts** (Fine Arts Museum), in the Louis XII wing, you'll find royal portraits, including Rubens's puffy portrayal of Maria de' Medici as France Personified. Most evenings May through September, **son-et-lumière** shows are staged (in English on Wednesday). Call 02–54–78–72–76 for details; admission is €10. ☎ *02–54–90–33–33* 🎫 *€6.50* ⊘ *Mid-Mar.–Oct., daily 9–6; Nov.–mid-Mar., daily 9–12:30 and 2–5:30.*

Where to Stay & Eat

$$–$$$ ✕ **L'Espérance.** In a bucolic setting overlooking the Loire, chef Raphaël Guillot serves up inventive cuisine, like fried mangoes with lavender and five different kinds of scallop dishes. ☒ *189 quai Ulysse-Besnard* ☎ *02–54–78–09–01* ▤ *AE, MC, V* ☯ *Closed Mon. and part of Aug. No dinner Sun.*

★ **$$** ✕ **Au Rendez-Vous des Pêcheurs.** This friendly restaurant in an old grocery near the Loire has simple decor but offers excellent value for its creative cooking. Chef Christophe Cosme studied under Burgundy's late Bernard Loiseau and brings inventiveness to his fish and seafood specialties (try the crayfish and parsley flan) and desserts. ☒ *27 rue du Foix* ☎ *02–54–74–67–48* ⌦ *Reservations essential* ▤ *AE, MC, V* ☯ *Closed Sun. and Aug. No lunch Mon.*

$$ ✕🖭 **Le Médicis.** Rooms at this smart little hotel 1 km (½ mi) from the château de Blois are comfortable, air-conditioned, and soundproof; all share a joyous color scheme but are individually decorated. The restaurant alone—done Renaissance-style with a coffered ceiling—makes a stay here worthwhile. Chef-owner Christian Garanger turns his innovative classic dishes into a presentation—*coquilles St-Jacques* (scallops) with bitter *roquette* lettuce, roast pigeon, and thin slices of roast hare with a black-currant sauce. The staff is cheerful and there are 250 wines to choose from (the restaurant does not serve dinner Sunday off-season). ☒ *2 allée François-Ier, 41000* ☎ *02–54–43–94–04* 🖷 *02–54–42–04–05* ⊕ *www.le-medicis.com* ⇆ *12 rooms* ⌂ *Restaurant, minibars* ▤ *AE, DC, MC, V* ☯ *Closed Jan.* ⧖ *MAP.*

Loches

⓲ *39 km (24 mi) southeast of Tours via N143.*

A fascinating detour from the main hub of Tours is to follow one of the "spokes" into the southern reaches of Touraine—via car or the handy rail connection—to picturesque, medieval Loches. On a rocky spur just beside the River Indre, the town is dominated by its famous **Citadelle**, which children thrill to because of its picture-book dungeons. Unlike Chinon's, which stand in ruins, sections of Loches's defensive walls are well preserved and function as part of the town. Inside the **Logis Royaux** (château), on the north end of the citadel, look for the vicious two-man crossbow that could pierce an oak door at 200 yards. There are some interesting pictures, too, including a copy of the well-known portrait showing a disgruntled Charles VII with one of his mistresses, Agnès Sorel, poised as a virtuous Virgin Mary (though semi-topless). Her alabaster image decorates her tomb, guarded by angels and lambs. Agnès died in 1450 at age 28, probably poisoned by Charles's son, the future Louis XI. But invariably the main attractions here are the notorious **dungeons**, which will delight anyone who revels in prison cells and torture chambers—kids love these scarifying precincts. ☒ *Pl. Charles-VII* ☎ *02–47–59–01–32* ▢ *€7* ☯ *Jan.–mid-Mar. and Oct.–Dec., daily 9:30–5; mid-Mar.–June and Sept., daily 9:30–6; July–Aug., daily 9–7.*

Villandry

⑲ *18 km (11 mi) west of Tours via D7, 48 km (30 mi) northwest of Loches.*

To the west of Tours, breathtaking châteaux dot the Indre Valley between the regional capital and the historic town of Chinon on the River Vienne. This is the most glamorous part of the Val de Loire and the beauty pageant begins with the **Château de Villandry.** Green-thumbers get weak in the knees at the mere mention of this grand estate near the Cher River, thanks to its painstakingly re-laid 16th-century **gardens,** now the finest example of Renaissance garden design in France. These were originally planted in 1906 by Dr. Joachim Carvallo and Anne Coleman, his American wife, whose passion resulted in two terraces planted in styles that combine the French monastic garden with Italianate models depicted in historic Du Cerceau etchings. Seen from the cliffside walkway, the terraces look like flowered chessboards blown up to the nth power—a breathtaking sight.

*Fodor's*Choice
★

Beyond the water garden and an ornamental garden depicting symbols of chivalric love is the famous *potager,* or vegetable garden. Organized in square patterns, purple cabbages, pumpkins, and pear trees catch the eye at every turn. In total, there are nearly 150,000 plantings, with two seasonal shows presented—the spring one is a veritable "salad." The fall one comes to fruition in late September or early October and is famed for its pumpkins. Flower lovers will rejoice in the main *jardin à la française* (French-style garden): framed by a canal, it is a vast carpet of rare and colorful blooms planted *en broderie* ("like embroidery"), set into patterns by box hedges and paths. The aromatic and medicinal garden, its plots neatly labeled in three languages, is especially appealing. Below an avenue of 1,500 precisely pruned lime trees lies an ornamental lake that is home to two swans: not a ripple is out of place. The château interior was restored in the mid-19th century; of particular note are the painted and gilt Moorish ceiling from Toledo and the collection of Spanish pictures. Note that the quietest time to visit is usually during the two-hour French lunch break, while the most photogenic is during the **Nuits des Mille Feux** (Nights of a Thousand Lights, usually held in early June), when paths and pergolas are illuminated with myriad lanterns and a dance troupe offers a tableau vivant. There are also a Baroque music festival in late August and a gardening weekend held in early September. ☎ *02–47–50–02–09* ⊕ *www.chateauvillandry.com* ✉ *Château and gardens €7.50, gardens only €5* ⊙ *Château June–Sept., daily 9–6; Oct.–mid-Nov. and mid-Feb.–May, daily 9–5. Gardens June–Sept., daily 9–7:30; Oct.–May, daily 9–5:30.*

Where to Stay & Eat

$ ✕▦ **Cheval Rouge.** Just a half-minute walk from the great chateau of Villandry, this is a fine, comfortable, and casual hotel-restaurant. Since it's set on a major traffic route, book one of the quieter rooms at the back. The restaurant (closed Monday) is popular with locals, who come for the surprisingly good and classic food and wine. Best bets are the terrine of foie gras, the calf sweetbreads, and the wood-fired-grill fare. ✉ *9 rue Principale, 37510* ☎ *02–47–50–02–07* 🖶 *02–47–50–08–77*

⊕ *www.lecheval-rouge.com* ⧁ *32 rooms △ Restaurant, some pets allowed (fee); no room TVs ⊟ MC, V ⊙ Closed Jan. †⊙| BP.*

Azay-le-Rideau

⓴ *11 km (7 mi) south of Villandry via D39, 27 km (17 mi) southwest of Tours.*

In a sylvan dell on the banks of the River Indre, the pleasant town of Azay-le-Rideau is famed for its white-walled Renaissance pleasure palace, called "a faceted diamond set in the Indre Valley" by Honoré de Balzac.
★ The 16th-century **Château d'Azay-le-Rideau** was created as a literal fairy-tale castle. When it was constructed in the Renaissance era (note the Greco-Roman stone detailing), the nouveau-riche treasurer Gilles Berthelot decided he wanted to add tall corner turrets, moat, and machicolations to conjure up the distant seigneurial past when knighthood was in flower and two families, the Azays and the Ridels, ruled this terrain. It was never a serious fortress—it certainly offered no protection to its builder when a financial scandal forced him to flee France shortly after the château's completion in 1529. For centuries the château passed from one private owner to another until it was finally bought by the State in 1905. Though the interior contains an interesting blend of furniture and artwork (one room is a homage to the Marquis de Biencourt who, in the early 20th century, led the way in renovating château interiors in sumptuous fashion—sadly, many of his elegant furnishings were later sold), you may wish to spend most of your time exploring the enchanting gardens, complete with a moatlike lake. Innovative **son-et-lumière** shows are held on the grounds from 10:30 PM, May through September. ☎ 02–47–45–42–04 ⊕ *www.chateau-france.com/azaylerideau.fr* ⛫ €6.10 ⊙ *Apr.–Oct., daily 9:30–6; Nov.–Mar., daily 10–12:30 and 2–5:30.*

Privately tended by Madame de Andia—one of the grandes dames of
★ the Loire—and her staff are the **Jardins de la Chatonnière**, a garden that will make most emerald-green with envy. Framing the private, turreted château are six spectacular visions, with each garden devoted to a theme, including L'Élégance, Le Silence, and L'Abondance. The most extraordinary is in the shape of a gigantic leaf. ⊠ *Route D57, direction Lignières–Langeais, 4 km (2½ mi) north of Azay-le-Rideau* ⛫ €5 ⊙ *Apr.–Oct. 10–7.*

Where to Stay & Eat

$$–$$$ ✕🏨 **Le Grand Monarque.** Very grand and elegant, this famous town landmark is about a three-minute walk from Azay's château. Some complain that its fame brings a captive audience, which can result in offhand service. However, rooms, which vary in size and style, have character; most are simple, with an antique or two, and many have exposed beams. Public salons are alluring, while the restaurant (closed Monday and not serving dinner Sunday) serves high style food. Weekend stays must include dinner. ⊠ *3 pl. de la République, 37190* ☎ 02–47–45–40–08 🖷 02–47–45–46–25 ⊕ *www.legrandmonarque.com* ⧁ *24 rooms, 19 with bath, 5 with shower △ Restaurant, cable TV, bar, some pets allowed (fee); no a/c ⊟ AE, MC, V ⊙ Closed Dec. and Jan. †⊙| MAP.*

★ $ 🏫 **Biencourt.** Charmingly set on the pedestrian street that leads to Azay's château gates, this red-shuttered town house hides an authentic, 19th-century schoolhouse within a delightful courtyard-garden, now fitted out with cozily traditional guest rooms (and the stray blackboard and school desk). No matter if you can't land one of the conversation pieces in "La Classe"—the other chambers are fine enough, decorated in pastels as warm as the delightfully helpful owners, the Mariotons. The town has quite a few restaurant selections—if you just don't want to stroll around and pick, ask Cédric and Emmanuelle for the best. ⊠ *7 rue Balzac, 37190* 🕾 *02–47–45–20–75* 🖶 *02–47–45–91–73* 🛏 *17 rooms, 12 with bath* ♿ *No a/c in some rooms, no room TVs* ☰ *MC, V* ⊗ *Closed mid-Nov.–late Feb.* 🍴❘ *EP.*

The Outdoors

Rent bikes from **Leprovost** (⊠ 13 rue Carnot 🕾 02–47–45–40–94) to ride along the Indre; the area around Azay-le-Rideau is among the most tranquil and scenic in Touraine.

Shopping

Osier (wicker) products have been made for centuries in Villaines-les-Rochers, 6 km (4 mi) southeast of Azay-le-Rideau via D57. Willow reeds are cultivated in nearby fields and dried in the sun each May, before being transformed into sofas, cat baskets, or babies' rattles. In 1849, when the craft was threatened with extinction, the parish priest persuaded 65 small groups of basket weavers to form France's first agricultural workers' cooperative. The **Coopératif de la Vannerie** (⊠ 1 rue de la Cheneil-lère 🕾 02–47–45–43–03), which is open Saturday 10–noon and 2–7 and Sunday 2–7, is still going strong and offers a wide choice of wicker goods for sale.

Saché

🟤 *7 km (4½ mi) east of Azay-le-Rideau via D17.*

Fodor'sChoice
★

A crook in the road, a Gothic church, the centuries-old Auberge du XIIᵉ Siècle, an Alexander Calder stabile (the great American sculptor created a modern atelier nearby), and the country retreat of novelist Honoré de Balzac (1799–1850)—these few but choice elements all add up to Saché, one of the prettiest (and most undiscovered) nooks in the Val de Loire. If you've never read any of Balzac's "Comédie Humaine," you might find little of interest at Saché's **château**; but if you have, and do, you'll return to such novels as *Cousin Bette* and *Eugénie Grandet* with fresh enthusiasm and understanding. Much of the landscape around here, and some of the people back then, found immortality by being fictionalized in many a Balzac novel. The present château, built between the 16th and 18th centuries, is more of a comfortable country house than a fortress. Born in nearby Tours, Balzac came here—to stay with his friends, the Margonnes—during the 1830s, both to write such works as *Le Père Goriot* and to escape his creditors. The château houses substantial exhibits, ranging from photographs to original manuscripts to the coffeepot Balzac used to brew the caffeine that helped to keep him writing up to 16 hours a day. Be sure to study some of the corrected au-

CloseUp

WHEEL ESTATE:
BIKING IN THE LOIRE VALLEY

A FAIRY-TALE REALM PAR EXCELLENCE, the Loire Valley is studded with storybook castles, forests primeval, time-burnished towns, and—bien sûr—the famous châteaux de la Loire, which are strung like a strand of pearls across a countryside so serene it could win the Nobel Peace Prize. With magic at every curve in the road, Cinderella's glass coach might be the optimum way to get around, but the next best thing is to tour the Val de Loire by bike.

A car means you have to stop and get out to look around; on foot you don't cover ground. But the Loire's plateau and châteaux are custom-made for a group bike tour. There's nothing like seeing Chenonceaux with your head pumped full of endorphins, surrounded by 20 new best friends, and knowing you'll be spending the night in a pointed turret bedroom that savors of sleeping princesses. If you want to experience this region at its most blissful—but not blisterful!—take the VBT (Vermont Biking Tours) Loire Valley Tour. Many of the participants found it to be the most wonderful, truly oooooooooolala travel experience they ever had in France.

Every morning, for six days, you sally forth not to kill dragons, but to cycle down village roads that look like Corot paintings, visit feudally luxurious châteaux, explore medieval towns like Chinon, and bike through the "sweet reasonableness" of this lovely landscape at 180 heartbeats a mile. Each day sees from two to four hours of biking (about 19 to 35 miles), with an option of either calling it quits at lunch and returning to your hotel or continuing on with the rack pack for the afternoon.

Our group's Captain Cycle joked that "real men don't ask for directions—at least not in English," but since the instructions and

maps direct you along the route virtually pebble-to-pebble, this faux pas never arose. Just when the route would get too tranquil, a dazzling château was conveniently set around the bend.

In fact, your itinerary reads like the pages of a Perrault fairy tale, studded as it is with such legendary abodes as Azay-le-Rideau, Chenonceaux, Villandry, and Ussé, the latter literally the château that inspired Perrault to write "Sleeping Beauty." Feeling the time for Beauty's awakening was long since past, the Duc de Blacas, Ussé's long-time owner (movie-star handsome and a lawyer who once worked for years in America) has ravishingly renovated this symbol of Old France as a family home open to all. It's a good morning's work to see two châteaux, non?

You'll have an even better evening of it, thanks to VBT's splendid choice of châteaux-hotels. At the 16th-century La Bourdaisière, retreat of King François I, you'll feel a wand has been waved over you as you repair to the Richelieu-red dining room where you enjoy the group's first candlelit supper (our filet de carpe au Bourgueil, was supper-lative). Audrey Hepburn's favorite, the Domaine de la Tortinière, fulfills anyone's "Queen-for-a-day" fantasies. Your final hotel, the Château de Rochecotte, was the 19th-century Xanadu of Prince de Talleyrand-Perigord. After all this, it is little wonder that most of the 20 bikers in the group were in a state of dumb intoxication after six days with **VBT** (✉ 614 Monkton Rd., Bristol, VT 05443 ☎ 800/245–3868 ⊕ www.vbt.com). And we're not talking about all the wine tastings.

— Robert I. C. Fisher

thor proofs on display. Balzac had to pay for corrections and additions beyond a certain limit. Painfully in debt, he made emendations filling all the margins of his proofs, causing dismay to his printers. Their legitimate bills for extra payment meant that some of his books, best-sellers for nearly two centuries, failed to bring him a centime. Several of the château salons have early 19th-century charm, while a pretty park overlooks a tiny vale. Before leaving Saché, be sure to make a small detour 1 mi to the west along the main road to **Pont-de-Ruan**—a dream-sequence of a flower-bedecked bridge, water mill, and lake that is so picturesque it will practically click your camera for you. ☎ 02–47–26–86–50 ⌑ €4.50 ☉ Daily 9:30–12:30 and 2–5:30.

Where to Stay & Eat

★ **\$\$–\$\$\$** ✕ **Auberge du XIIᵉ Siècle.** You half expect Balzac himself to come strolling in the door of this half-timber, delightfully historic auberge, so little has it changed since the 19th century. Still sporting a time-stained painted sign on its exterior, its original exterior staircase, and nearly opposite the great author's country retreat, this inn still retains its centuries-old dining room, now warmed by a fireplace, bouquets, and rich wood tables. Beyond this room is a modern extension—all airy glass and white walls but not exactly what you're looking for in such historic surrounds. Balzac's ample girth attested to his great love of food, and he would no doubt enjoy the nouvelle spins on his classic *géline* chicken favorites served here today. But there's more, much more on tap—chefs Thierry Jimenez and Xavier Aubrun are exceedingly talented, as witness their *aiguillettes de canard rosées en réduction de Chinon* (slices of duck flavored in Chinon wine). Dessert is excellent, and so is the coffee, a refreshment Balzac drank incessantly (little wonder he created more than 2,000 characters). ✉ 1 rue du Château ☎ 02–47–26–88–77 ▬ MC, V ☉ Closed 3 wks in Jan., 1 wk in June, 1 wk in Sept., and Mon. No dinner Sun., no lunch Tues.

\$\$\$ ▦ **Chez Patrick Bernard.** Sadly, there are no hotels in Saché, but you can stay in one of three luxuriously renovated gîtes at an 18th-century farm owned by Patrick Bernard and his Norwegian wife Benny who speaks excellent English. The largest, in a converted barn, has room for six people, with a huge lounge area and mezzanine. The smallest can sleep four. All bedrooms have en suite bathrooms. From Saché, go north on a little road over the Indre river, with a sign pointing to La Sablonnière. The Bernards prefer to rent by the week in summer but call ahead and you may be able to book for a weekend or a night or two. ✉ La Sablonnière, 37190 ☎ 02–47–26–86–92 ✐ baulay@wanadoo.fr ⤳ 3 gîtes with bath ⌂ No a/c ▬ No credit cards ‖⦿‖ EP.

Ussé

㉒ 14 km (9 mi) west of Azay-le-Rideau via D17 and D7.

The most beautiful castle in France is first glimpsed as you approach the **Château d'Ussé** (in the village of Rigny-Ussé) and an astonishing array of blue-slate roofs, dormer windows, delicate towers, and Gothic turrets greets you against the flank of the Forest of Chinon. Literature describes this château, overlooking the banks of the river Indre, as the original *Sleeping Beauty* castle; Charles Perrault—author of this beloved 17th-

Fodor'sChoice
★

century tale—spent time here as a guest of the Count of Saumur and legend has it that Ussé inspired him to write the famous story. Though parts of the castle are from the 1400s, most of it was completed two centuries later. By the 17th century, the region was so secure one fortified wing of the castle was demolished to allow grand vistas over the valley and the castle gardens, newly built in the style Le Nôtre had made so fashionable at Versailles. Only Disney could have outdone this white-tufa marvel: the château is a flamboyant mix of Gothic and Renaissance styles—stylish and romantic, built for fun, not for fighting. Its history supports this playful image: it endured no bloodbaths—no political conquests or conflicts—while a tablet in the chapel indicates that even the French Revolution passed it by. Inside, a tour leads you through several sumptuous period salons, a 19th-century French fashion exhibit, and the Salle de Roi bedchamber built for a visit by King Louis XV (who never arrived—his loss, as the red-silk, canopied four-poster bed here is the stuff of dreams). At the end of the house tour, you can go up the fun spiral staircases to the *chemin de ronde* of the lofty towers; there are pleasant views of the Indre River from the battlements, and you will also find rooms filled with waxwork effigies detailing the fable of Sleeping Beauty herself. Kids will love this.

Before you leave, visit the exquisite Gothic-becomes-Renaissance chapel in the garden, built for Charles d'Espinay and his wife in 1523–35. Note the door decorated with pleasingly sinister skull-and-crossbones carvings. Just a few steps from the chapel are two towering cedars of Lebanon—a gift from the genius-poet of Romanticism, Viscount René de Chateaubriand, to the lady of the house, the Duchess of Duras. When her famous amour died in 1848, she stopped all the clocks in the house—à la Sleeping Beauty—"so as never to hear struck the hours you will not come again." The castle then was inherited by her relations, the Comte et Comtesse de la Rochejacquelin, one of the most dashing couples of the 19th century. Today, Ussé belongs to their descendant, the Duc de Blacas, who is as soigné as his castle. If you do meet him, proffer thanks, as every night his family floodlights the entire château, a vision that is one of the Loire Valley's dreamiest sights. Regarded as a symbol of *la vieille France,* Ussé can't be topped for fairy-tale splendor, so make this a must-do. ☎ 02–47–95–54–05 ⊕ *www.tourisme.fr/usee* ✉ €9.50 ✆ *Mid-Feb.–Mar. and Oct.–mid-Nov., daily 10–noon and 2–5:30; Apr., May, and Sept., daily 9–noon and 2–6:45; June–Aug., daily 9–6:30.*

Where to Stay & Eat

★ $$–$$$ ✕⛆ **Le Castel de Bray & Monts.** A blissfully charming retreat, this handsome 1730s manor is set in the idyllic riverbank village of Bréhémont, on the south bank of the Loire halfway between Azay-le-Rideau and Rigny-Ussé. Here Maxime and Eliane Rochereau run a hotel with a difference—Maxime, once a chef at the Paris Ritz, holds weeklong cooking classes. But you don't need to take the course to sample Maxime's delicious cooking (with local fish at the fore), showcased in three prix-fixe menus starting at €30 and served up in a lovely dining salon. Other standouts include the magnificent hotel staircase, with its neo-Gothic iron banisters, the exquisite and shady rose garden, and the duplex bedroom in the converted former chapel. Most of the guest rooms are redolent of antique charm, replete with *toile-de-jouy* touches and pink-and-white floral accents. ⊠ *10 rue Ridet, 3 km (2 mi) northeast of Rigny-Ussé, 3 km (1½) mi west of Azay-le-Rideau, 37130 Bréhémont* ☎ *02–47–96–70–47* 🖷 *02–47–96–57–36* ⊕ *www.cooking-class-infrance.com* ☝ *9 rooms* △ *Restaurant, some minibars, bicycles, bar, some pets allowed (fee); no a/c, no room TVs* ⊟ *MC, V* ☉ *Closed mid-Nov.–mid-Feb.* ⦿ *EP.*

★ **$** ✕🛏 **Le Clos d'Ussé.** Thank heavens for this delightful inn. The best time to see the great Château d'Ussé is in early morning light or illuminated at night, and the easiest way to do that is to overnight in the village of Rigny-Ussé here at the home of the *famille* Duchemin. Eric runs the place, Muriel is in charge of the extremely cozy restaurant, *grand-mère* offers a warm smile, while Alexandre, their young son, charms everyone. Not surprisingly, families will adore this place, especially as three of the rooms are custom-built for them (and rather stylish, to boot). Best of all, a one-minute walk from the front door takes you to the castle gates. ⊠ *7 rue Principale, Rigny-Ussé* ☎🖷 *02–47–95–55–47* ☝ *8 rooms, 1 with bath, 3 with shower* △ *Restaurant, bar, some pets allowed (fee); no a/c, no room phones* ⊟ *MC, V* ☉ *Closed Nov.–Feb.* ⦿ *EP.*

Chinon

㉓ 13 km (8 mi) southwest of Rigny-Ussé via D7 and D16, 44 km (28 mi)
Fodor'sChoice southwest of Tours.
★

The extraordinary town of Chinon—birthplace of author François Rabelais (1494–1553)—is dominated by the towering ruins of its medieval castle, perched high above the River Vienne. Blessed with a unique medieval quarter, the center of town is a storybook warren of narrow, cobbled streets (some are pedestrian-only) lined with half-timber houses; its fairy-tale allure was effectively used to frame Josette Day when she appeared as Beauty in Jean Cocteau's 1949 film *La Belle et la Bête*. The main road of the historic quarter, rue Haute St-Maurice (a continuation of rue Voltaire, which begins at the central place du Général-de-Gaulle) is a virtual open-air museum; other towns may have one or two or three blocks lined with medieval and Renaissance houses, but this street runs, spectacularly, for more than 15 blocks. While there are some unprepossessing museums in town—the **Musée du Vieux Chinon,** in a medieval town house on rue Haute St-Maurice, the **Maison de la Rivière,** devoted to Chinon's maritime trade and set along the embankment, and the **Musée du Vin** (Wine Museum) on rue Voltaire—the medieval quarter remains the must-do, as a walk here catapults you back to the days of Rabelais. Because both the village and the château are on steep, cobbled slopes, it's a good idea to wear comfortable walking shoes. For a fun side trip in summer, a steam train chugs from Chinon 15 km (10 mi) south to **Richelieu,** the town founded and designed by Louis XIII's notorious cardinal (☎ 02–47–58–12–97 for details).

The vast **Château de Chinon,** a veritable fortress with walls 400 yards long, dates from the time of Henry II of England, who died here in 1189 and was buried at Fontevraud. Two centuries later the castle witnessed an important historic moment: Joan of Arc's recognition of the disguised

Dauphin, later Charles VII; the castle was also one of the domiciles of Henri II and his warring wife, Eleanor of Aquitaine (Kate Hepburn's 1968 film *The Lion in Winter* was set, but not filmed, here). In the early 17th century the castle was partially dismantled by Cardinal Richelieu (1585–1642), who used many of its stones to build himself a new palace—itself now dismantled—in Richelieu, 21 km (13 mi) to the south. At Chinon everything is open to the elements, except the **Logis Royal** (Royal Chambers). Here there is a small museum containing a model of the castle when it was intact, various old tapestries, and precious stones. For a fine view of the region, climb the **Tour Coudray** (Coudray Tower), where in 1307 leading members of the crusading Knights Templar were imprisoned before being taken to Paris, tried, and burned at the stake. The **Tour de l'Horloge** (Clock Tower), whose bell has sounded the hours since 1399, contains the **Musée Jeanne d'Arc** (Joan of Arc Museum). There are sensational views from the ramparts over Chinon and the Vienne Valley. ☎ *02–47–93–13–45* 🔲 *€6* ☉ *Mid-Mar.–June and Sept., daily 9:30–6; July and Aug., daily 9–7; Oct., daily 9–6; Nov.–mid-Mar., daily 9:30–5.*

Where to Stay & Eat

$$$ ✕ **Au Plaisir Gourmand.** Jean-Claude Rigollet's tufa-stone 18th-century restaurant by the Vienne River is the finest in Chinon. Specialties served in the Renaissance-style dining room include crayfish salad, snails in garlic, jellied rabbit, *sandre* (pike-perch) with butter sauce, and braised oxtail in red wine. ⊠ *2 rue Parmentier* ☎ *02–47–93–20–48* 🖃 *AE, MC, V* ☉ *Closed Mon. and Tues.*

$–$$ ✕🏨 **France.** Right on Chinon's most charming square—a picture postcard come to life with splashing fountain and a bevy of cafés—this sweetly agreeable Best Western hotel is set in a 16th-century house just two blocks from the medieval quarter. Many regional notables lived here before the Revolution, when it became the Hôtel Lion d'Or, the first hostelry in the region. Guest rooms are comfortable and cozy; some overlook two tiny, flowerpot-bedecked courtyards, while some take in views that include Chinon's castle ruins. The ground-floor restaurant (closed Tuesday and no lunch Wednesday) serves Italian cuisine. The hotel staff is most congenial. ⊠ *47 pl. du Général-de-Gaulle, 37500* ☎ *02–47–93–33–91* 🖷 *02–47–98–37–03* ⇱ *27 rooms* ⚭ *Restaurant; no a/c in some rooms* 🖃 *AE, DC, MC, V* ☉ *Closed Nov. and mid-Feb.–mid-Mar.* ⨁ *MAP.*

$ 🏨 **Diderot.** With a facade that seems on sabbatical from an 18th-century François Boucher painting—ivy-covered stone, white shutters, mansard roof, dormer windows, rococo spiral staircase—this is Chinon's prettiest hotel. Inside, a corner bar and cozy stone breakfast room create a welcoming air, one strengthened by the Kazamias family, the hotel's owners, who relocated from Cyprus (and brought a bit of it with them, as the olive and laurel trees in the forecourt attest). Guest rooms are standard-issue—avoid those in the separate house on the back street. The hotel is in a nice residential area, about 10 blocks from the medieval quarter. ⊠ *7 rue Diderot, 37500* ☎ *02–47–93–18–87* 🖷 *02–47–93–37–10* ⇱ *28 rooms, including 4 in annex* ⚭ *No a/c, no room TVs* 🖃 *AE, DC, MC, V* ☉ *Closed mid-Dec.–mid-Feb.* ⨁ *EP.*

Nightlife & the Arts

Chinon stages a **Marché à l'Ancienne** on the third Saturday of August, a free wine-tasting extravaganza with stalls, displays, and costumed locals recalling rural life of a hundred years ago. For details, contact the tourist office.

Fontevraud-l'Abbaye

24 *20 km (12 mi) northwest of Chinon via D751.*

A refreshing break from the worldly grandeur of châteaux, the small village of Fontevraud is crowned with the largest abbey in France, a magnificent complex of Romanesque and Renaissance buildings that were of central importance in the history of both England and France. Founded in 1101, the **Abbaye Royale de Fontevraud** had separate churches and living quarters for nuns, monks, lepers, "repentant" female sinners, and the sick. Between 1115 and the French Revolution in 1789, a succession of 39 abbesses—among them a granddaughter of William the Conqueror—directed its operations. The great 12th-century **Église Abbatiale** (Abbey Church) contains the tombs of Henry II of England, his wife Eleanor of Aquitaine, and their son, Richard Coeur de Lion (the Lion-Hearted). Though their bones were scattered during the Revolution, their effigies still lie *en couchant* in the middle of the echoey nave. Napoléon turned the abbey church into a prison, and so it remained until 1963, when historical restoration work—still under way—began. The **Salle Capitulaire** (Chapter House), adjacent to the church, with its collection of 16th-century religious wall paintings (prominent abbesses served as models), is unmistakably Renaissance; the paving stones bear the salamander emblem of François I. Next to the long refectory is the famously octagonal **Cuisine** (kitchen), topped by 20 scaly stone chimneys led by the **Tour d'Evrault.** ⊠ *Pl. des Plantagenêts* ☎ *02–41–51–71–41* ⊕ *www.abbaye-fontevraud.com* ⊠ *€5.50* ☉ *June–Sept., daily 9–6; Oct.–May, daily 10–5.*

After touring the Abbaye Royale, head outside the gates of the complex a few blocks to the north to discover one of the Loire Valley's most time-machine streets, the **Allée Sainte-Catherine.** Bordered by the Fontevraud park, headed by a charming medieval church, and lined with a few scattered houses (which now contain the town tourist office, a gallery that sells medieval illuminated manuscript pages, and the delightful Licorne restaurant), this street still looks like the 14th century aborning.

Where to Stay & Eat

★ **$$$–$$$$** ✕ **La Licorne.** A hanging shop sign adorned with a painted unicorn beckons you to this pretty-as-a-picture town-house restaurant just off Fontevraud's idyllic Allée Sainte-Catherine. Past a flowery garden and table-adorned terrace, tiny salons glow with happy folks feasting on some of the best food in the region: Loire salmon, guineafowl in Layon wine, and lobster with fava beans should make most diners purr with contentment. ⊠ *31 rue Robert-d'Arbrissel* ☎ *02–41–51–72–49* ⚘ *Reservations essential* ☰ *AE, DC, MC, V* ☉ *Closed Mon. No dinner Sun. and Wed.*

★ $$ ✕▦ **Hostellerie du Prieuré St-Lazare.** One of the more unusual hotels in the Loire Valley and set right within the medieval splendor of Fontevraud, this series of outbuildings was once the abbey's lepers' hospice. The entrance gives onto the vast *salle capitulaire* conference room and the cloisters now house an extremely fine restaurant (reservations essential), where such delicacies as swordfish simmered in Saumur-Champigny wine entice. In a snug side wing the erstwhile monks' cells have been transformed into alluring guest rooms, chic and bright in modern checks and fine wood accents. Staying here lets you explore the abbey grounds when its gates are closed to the public—an exceptional experience. ☒ *Abbaye Royale, 49590* ☏ *02–41–51–73–16* 🖷 *02–41–51–75–50* ⊕ *www. hotelfp-fontevraud.com* 🛏 *52 rooms* ♨ *Restaurant, minibars; no a/c* 🖃 *AE, MC, V* ☯ *Closed Nov.–Mar.* ¡◎¡ *MAP.*

Saumur

★ ㉕ *15 km (9 mi) northwest of Fontevraud via D947, 68 km (43 mi) west of Tours.*

Ancient Saumur, dominated by its mighty turreted château high above town and river, is one of the larger towns along the Loire and a key transportation hub for Anjou, the province just to the west of Touraine. Saumur is also known for its riding school and flourishing mushroom industry, which produces 100,000 tons per year. The same cool tunnels in which the mushrooms grow provide an ideal storage place for the local *mousseux* (sparkling wines); many vineyards hereabouts are open to the public for tours.

Regional government offices, wealthy wine producers, and the spiffy riding school all help make Saumur's natives some of the Loire's most stylish, nay, snobbish residents—chances are you'll get a blast of old-time French attitude, not just from the preppy ladies but a greater whiff from shopkeepers and waiters. Little seems to have changed over the centuries: Honoré de Balzac famously wrote up the surly side of the Saumurois in his *Eugénie Grandet*. Putting up with this *snobisme* may be worth it: Saumur's historic center is studded with elegant 19th-century town houses and the magnificent place St-Pierre, lorded over by the vast 14th-century church of St-Pierre and centerpiece of a warren of streets, cafés, and ice-cream parlors. Be sure to spend an hour or two exploring the *centre historique*.

If you arrive in the evening, the sight of the elegant, floodlighted, white 14th-century **Château de Saumur** takes your breath away. Look familiar? Probably because you've seen it in reproductions from the famous *Très Riches Heures* (Book of Hours) painted for the Duc de Berry in 1416 (now in the Musée Condé at Chantilly). Inside it's bright and cheerful, with a fairy-tale gateway and plentiful potted flowers. It houses two museums: the **Musée des Arts Décoratifs** (Decorative Arts Museum), with a fine collection of medieval objets d'art and 18th- and 19th-century porcelain, and the **Musée du Cheval** (Equestrian Museum). After climbing the **Tour de Guet** (watchtower) for impressive views of the many-spired town, take time out at the café or the serious restaurant set up on the castle grounds, then take the exit to the carpark and head over to the cliffside promenade to drink in the thrilling vista of the castle on its bluff against the river backdrop. ⊠ *Esplanade du Château* ☎ *02–41–40–24–40* ⊕ *www.saumur-tourisme.net/chateausaumur.html* ⊠ *€6* ☽ *June–Sept., daily 9–6; Oct.–May, daily 10–1 and 2–5:30.*

The **Cadre Noir de Saumur** (Riding School) is unique in Europe, with its 400 horses, extensive stables, five Olympic-size riding schools, and miles of specially laid tracks. Try for a morning tour, which includes a chance to admire the horses in training. During the **Carrousel de Saumur**, on the last two weekends in July, the horses put on a full gala display for enthusiastic crowds. ⊠ *Rue de l'Abbaye* ☎ *02–41–53–50–60* ⊕ *www.cadrenoir.tm.fr* ⊠ *€7* ☽ *Guided tours only Apr.–Sept., Tues.–Sat. at 9:30, 11, 2, and 4.*

Saumur is the heart of one of the finest wine regions in France. To pay a call on some of the vineyards around the city, first stop into the **Maison du Vin** (House of Wine), for the full scoop on hours and directions; also consult the web site for Loire wines, www.vins-valdeloire.com. ⊠ *Quai Lucien-Gautier* ☎ *02–41–38–45–83* ☽ *Easter–mid-Nov., daily 10–5.*

Here are some of the top vineyards of the Saumur region. Note that Loire wine is not a practical buy—except for instant consumption—but if wine-tasting tours of vineyards inspire you, enterprising wine makers will arrange shipments. For sparkling Saumur wine try **Ackerman** (⊠ 19 rue Léopold-Palustre, St-Hilaire ☎ 02–41–53–30–20). **Veuve Amiot** (⊠ 21 rue Jean-Ackerman, St-Hilaire ☎ 02–41–83–14–14) is a long-established producer of Saumur wines. You can visit the cavernous premises of **Gratien-Meyer** (⊠ Rte. de Montsoreau ☎ 02–41–83–13–32 ⊠ €2.50 ☽ Daily 9–noon and 2–6) on the east side of Saumur daily, April through September. Just southeast of Saumur, in Dampierre-sur-Loire, stop in at the **Château de Chaintres** (⊠ 54 rue de la Croix-de-Chaintre ☎ 02–41–52–90–54), where husky Krishna Lester, a hunky English eccentric, produces the region's finest red and enjoys expounding on the unexpected links between frogs in the throat, toads in the hole, and malolactic fermentation.

Where to Stay & Eat

★ **$$–$$$** ✕ **Les Ménestrels.** Lucien Von cooks fine fare in a restored and delightful 18th-century white-stone mansion up against the castle cliff, on the grounds of the Anne d'Anjou hotel. Specialties include pheasant casserole, fried mushrooms, perch with spring-onion fondue, venison in season, and beef in local red-wine sauce. ⊠ *11 rue Raspail* ☎ *02–41–67–71–10* ⊕ *www.hotel-anneanjou.com* ▭ *AE, DC, MC, V* ☽ *Closed Sun.*

★ **$–$$** ▦ **Saint-Pierre.** At the very epicenter of historic Saumur, this gorgeous little jewel is hidden beneath the medieval walls of the church of St. Pierre—look for the hotel's storybook entrance on one of the pedestrian *passages* that circle the vast nave. Once inside the 15th- to 17th-century house, you'll find a sweet reception area and suave staff to welcome you. Up the Renaissance corkscrew staircase (or modern mini-elevator) you'll find the astonishingly refined guest rooms. Designer fabrics, antique *pont* cabinets (forming a "bridge" over bed headboards), elegant wainscotting,

Persian rugs, tuffeaux fireplaces, and bathrooms replete with Paloma Picasso designs make this a favored home-away-from-home for Saumur's most savvy visitors. The smaller rooms face the church but they also are quieter than those overlooking the road leading up to the castle. There is no restaurant, but just steps away is lovely place St-Pierre, lined with outdoor cafés. ✉ *Rue Haute-Saint-Pierre, 49400* ☎ *02–41–50–33–00* 🖳 *02–41–50–38–68* ⊕ *www.saintpierresaumur.com* ➦ *15 rooms* ⚘ *Minibars, cable TV, some pets allowed (fee)* ➡ *AE, DC, MC, V* ⦿❘ *EP.*

en route

Along the river east of Saumur (that is, on the way back toward Tours) is a particularly scenic stretch of countryside. Here you will find the town of **Montsoreau,** famed for its riverside castle (now a museum devoted to the history of the Loire). Break for a meal at the excellent Diane de Méridor restaurant, just a few steps from the château. One town over is picturesque **Candes-St-Martin,** which perches over the confluence of the Loire and Vienne rivers and huddles within the shadows of its great Gothic church, consecrated to St. Martin of Tours, who died here.

Turquant

㉖
Fodor's Choice
★

6 km (4 mi) west of Saumur via D947.

A treasury of troglodyte dwellings, fairy-tale Turquant is picturesquely arranged around a limestone cliff landmarked by its striking blue windmill, the Moulin de la Herpinière, and the cave-mansion of La Grande Vignolle. Once used to quarry stone for the great châteaux, made into retreats for religious prophets and monks, recycled as storehouses for wines, and, in more recent centuries, transformed into unique houses, the tuffeaux caves that honeycomb the entire Loire Valley are among its most distinctive features. Among the more noted troglodyte towns—Rochecorbon, Rochemenier, Doué-la-Fontaine—the village of Turquant has some of the most amazing of these residences. Growing out of the sheer rock, these houses often boast rock doorways, sash windows, relief sculptures, everything but stone flowers (along the D947 route from Saumur to Turquant look out for the castle, complete with turrets and battlements, emerging from the cliff). Arriving in Turquant, you'll spot **La Grande Vignolle,** landmarked by its historic pigeon-loft tower. Now overseen by the Filleatreau wine company, the "Lordly Dwelling," parts of which date back to the 13th century, comprises several chambers carved out of the living rock, including a chapel, a ballroom, and a kitchen. Best of all is the elegant facade, adorned with horse-shoe staircase and pepper-pot tower. ✉ *Rte. de Montsoreau (D947)* ☎ *02–41–38–16–44* ⊕ *www.chez.com/turquant* ✉ *Free* ⊙ *Easter–Oct., daily 10–6.*

A back road leads from La Grande Vignolle up the cliffside to the Turquant plateau of vineyards—on the way up look for the signs to **Le Val Hulin,** a cave that now holds the Troglo des Pommes Tapées, where you can see how dried and hammered apple slices—*pommes tapées*—are made. These were once the favored taste treat of Georges Clemenceau and the British Royal Navy. ✉ *Le Val Hulin* ☎ *02–41–51–48–30*

✉ *Free* ☺ *July and Aug., Tues.–Sun. 10–noon, 2:30–6:30; June, Sept., Tues.–Sun. 2:30–6:30; Apr., Oct., Nov., weekends only 2:30–6.*

Streets descending from the Turquant plateau are lined with many delightful rockface houses. Once you get back down to ground level, head back to the highway to pass the village church of St-Aubin and the magnificent **Château de la Fessardière** (☏ 02–41–51–48–89), where a small shop is sometimes open to allow you to taste a glass of local wine. For more information on the village, check out the Web site at ⊕ *www.chez.com/turquant.*

Where to Stay

★ **$–$$** ⛉ **Demeure de la Vignole.** A cliffside domain to keep even the most picky atmosphere-hunters happy, this little kingdom—comprising an enchanting Renaissance-era *château troglodytique,* an elegant 15th-century manor house, and a medieval cave dwelling—is adjacent to the noted La Grand Vignolle museum. The manor is a mix of exposed tuffeaux rock face, rustic wood beams, tinkling chandeliers, *Maison Française* fabrics, and piquant antiques. Outside, a terrace framed by a grove of Monet irises overlooks a grand stretch of Saumur-Champigny vineyards. Monique Bartholeyns—blonde, chic, and *très sympathique*—oversees her hotel from her adjacent 1450 rock-château, believed to have once been home to Queen Marguerite d'Anjou. Even this residence may pale when compared to Monique's newest accommodation: the prehistoric "suite troglodyte," a duplex part and parcel (along with a rock ballroom) of the hillside cave dwelling. Upon special request, dinners will be served. Don't miss this delightful place. ✉ *3 impasse Marguerite d'Anjou, 49730* ☏ *02–41–53–67–00* 🖷 *02–41–53–67–09* ⊕ *www.demeurevignole.com* 🕿 *8 rooms* ⌂ *Cable TV, some pets allowed (fee); no a/c* ⊟ *AE, DC, MC, V* ⦿⦿ *MAP.*

Montreuil-Bellay

㉗ *18 km (11 mi) south of Saumur via N147.*

Many people have a special place in their heart for Montreuil-Bellay, a small riverside town with many 18th- and 19th-century houses, lovely public gardens, and a leafy square next to its castle. The 15th-century **Château de Montreuil-Bellay** has a grandiose exterior—majestic towers and pointed roofs—and a fascinating interior, with fine furniture and tapestries, a fully equipped medieval kitchen, and a chapel adorned with frescoes of angelic musicians. For a memorable view, take a stroll in the gardens; graceful white turrets tower high above the trees and rosebushes, and down below, the little River Thouet winds its lazy way to the Loire. ✉ *Pl. des Ormeaux* ☏ *02–41–52–33–06* 🎟€7 ☺ *Apr.–Oct., Wed.–Mon. 10–noon and 2–5:30.*

Angers

㉘ *51 km (32 mi) northwest of Montreuil-Bellay via D761, 45 km (28 mi) northwest of Saumur, 88 km (55 mi) northeast of Nantes.*

The bustling city of Angers, on the banks of the Maine River, just north of the Loire, is famous for its towering castle filled with the extraordinary Apocalypse Tapestry. But it also has a fine Gothic cathedral, a selection of art galleries, and a network of pleasant, traffic-free streets around place Ste-Croix, with its half-timber houses. The town's principal sights lie within a compact square formed by the three main boulevards and the Maine.

★ The banded black-and-white **Château d'Angers,** built by St. Louis (1228–38), glowers over the town from behind turreted moats, now laid out as gardens and overrun with flowers and deer. As you explore the grounds, note the startling contrast between the thick defensive walls, defended by a drawbridge and 17 massive round towers in a distinctive pattern, and the formal garden, with its delicate white-tufa chapel, erected in the 16th century. For a sweeping view of the city and surrounding countryside, climb one of the castle towers. A well-integrated modern gallery on the castle grounds contains the great **Tenture de l'Apocalypse** (Apocalypse Tapestry), woven in Paris in the 1380s for the Duke of Anjou. Measuring 16 feet high and 120 yards long, its many panels show a series of 70 horrifying and humorous scenes from the Book of Revelation. In one, mountains of fire fall from heaven while boats capsize and men struggle in the water. Another has the beast with seven heads. ⊠ *2 promenade du Bout-du-Monde* ☎ *02–41–87–43–47* ⊕ *www.monum.fr* ▨ *€5.50* ⊙ *May–Aug., daily 9:30–6:30; Sept.–Apr., daily 10–5:30.*

The **Cathédrale St-Maurice** (⊠ Pl. Monseigneur-Chappoulie) is a 12th- and 13th-century Gothic cathedral noted for its curious Romanesque facade and original stained-glass windows; bring binoculars to appreciate both fully.

The **Musée David d'Angers,** in a refurbished glass-roof medieval church, has a collection of dramatic sculptures by Jean-Pierre David (1788–1859), the city's favorite son. ⊠ *33 bis rue Toussaint* ☎ *02–41–87–21–03* ▨ *€2* ⊙ *Tues.–Sun. 10–noon and 2–6.*

To learn about the heartwarming liqueur made in Angers since 1849, head to the **Distillerie Cointreau** on the east of the city. It has a museum and offers a guided visit of the distillery, which starts with an introductory film, moves through the bottling plant and alembic room, with its gleaming copper-pot stills, and ends with a tasting. ⊠ *Carrefour Molière, St-Barthélémy d'Anjou* ☎ *02–41–31–50–50* ⊕ *www.cointreau.com* ▨ *€5.50* ⊙ *Tours daily July and Aug. at 10:30, 3:30, and 4:30; May, June, Sept., and Oct., 10:30 and 3; Nov.–Apr. at 3.*

Where to Stay & Eat

$$$ ✕ **La Salamandre.** Chef Danie Louboutin's meticulously prepared classic cuisine ranges from lamb and duck with cranberries to calamari with crab sauce, served amid Renaissance-style allurements and under stained-glass windows. Opt for one of the reasonably priced prix-fixe menus. ⊠ *1 bd. du Maréchal-Foch* ☎ *02–41–88–99–55* ▤ *AE, DC, MC, V* ⊙ *Closed Sun.*

$ ✕ **La Treille.** For traditional, simple fare at affordable prices, try this small two-story mom-and-pop restaurant off place Ste-Croix and across from

Maison d'Adam, Angers's finest timber-frame house. The prix-fixe menu may start with a *salade au chèvre chaud* (warm goat-cheese salad), followed by confit of duck and an apple tart. The upstairs dining room draws a lively crowd; downstairs is quieter. ⊠ *12 rue Montault* ☏ *02–41–88–45–51* ⊟ *MC, V* ⊘ *Closed Sun.*

$$$ ⊡ **Anjou.** In business since 1846, the Anjou, now part of the Best Western chain, has a vaguely 18th-century style, including stained-glass windows in the lobby. The spacious rooms have high ceilings, double doors, and modern bathrooms where terry robes await you. ⊠ *1 bd. du Maréchal-Foch, 49100* ☏ *02–41–88–24–82, 800/528–1324 in U.S.* 🖷 *02–41–87–22–21* ⊕ *www.hoteldanjou.fr* ⇥ *53 rooms, 4 suites* ⚴ *Restaurant, some pets allowed (fee); no a/c* ⊟ *AE, DC, MC, V* ⟨O⟩ *BP.*

$ ⊡ **Mail.** A stately lime tree stands sentinel outside this 17th-century mansion on a calm street between the Hôtel de Ville and the river. The smallish rooms are individually decorated in pastel shades. ⊠ *8 rue des Ursules, 49100* ☏ *02–41–25–05–05* 🖷 *02–41–86–91–20* ⊕ *www. destination-anjou.com/mail* ⇥ *26 rooms, 5 with bath, 17 with shower* ⚴ *Minibars, cable TV, some pets allowed (fee); no a/c* ⊟ *AE, DC, MC, V* ⟨O⟩ *EP.*

Nightlife & the Arts

July and August see the **Angers L'Eté** (Angers Summer) festival, with concerts at the Cloître Toussaint and Chapelle des Ursules; call ☏ 02–41–05–41–48 for details.

en route

Heading 22 km (15 mi) south of Angers, stop off in the charming village of Brissac-Quincé to admire **Château de Brissac,** a towering pile (the tallest château in France) of Mannerist, Baroque, and Classical motifs grafted onto a Gothic castle; inside, all is seignorial splendor, with tapestries, Venetian-glass chandeliers, and even a grand theater (whose crimson interior once hosted such eminences as Gounod, Massenet, and Debussy). ⊕ *www.chateau-brissac.fr.*

Bourgueil

★ ㉙ *66 km (41 mi) southeast of Angers via N147 and D10, 19 km (12 mi) north of Chinon.*

Connoisseurs like to say that Chinon's red wines taste of raspberries, those of Bourgueil—just across the Loire—smell of violets. If you want to test the veracity of such a judgment, explore the caves and vineyards surrounding the quaint market town of Bourgueil; just north of the village in Chevrette is the **Cave Touristique de la Dive Bouteille,** a vast cavern presenting regional wines, open daily 10 to noon and 2 to 6 (a handy Web site for the area wines is www.vinbourgueil.com). Headliner here is the Benedictine **Abbaye de Bourgueil,** where Father Baudry legendarily planted the region's first cabernet franc vine in 1089. Aesthetic attractions—although founded by the Benedictines in the 10th century, most structures here date from the far-from-holy 18th-century—are greatly outweighed by those of the nearby Romanesque abbey of Fontevraud, but there is a **Musée des Arts et Traditions Populaires** to

explore in the abbey. ☎ 02–47–97–72–04   ✍ €5 ⊙ *July and Aug.,*
Wed.–Mon. 2–6; Apr.–June and Sept.–late Oct., weekends 2–6.

Where to Stay

$$$–$$$$ 🏠 **Château des Réaux.** Half-museum, half-hotel, and extravagantly em-
Fodor'sChoice   blazoned with checkered red-and-white brickwork, this historic mon-
★   ument is a must-see for its 15th-century moat, its fortified entrance, and
its fairy-tale, pepper-pot towers (day-trippers can visit for a fee). But it
comes into its own when you overnight as guests of charming Comtesse
Florence de Bouillé, whose family has lived here for more than a cen-
tury. What with period salons dripping with atmosphere (family mem-
orabilia, Louis Quinze sofas, Victorian tric-trac tables), storybook-stylish
guest rooms, and three swans in residence (wait until you hear their nick-
names), this place is an utter delight. ⊠ *Port-Boulet, 5 km (2 mi) south
of Bourgueil, 37140* ☎ *02–47–95–14–40* 🖷 *02–47–95–18–34* ⊕ *www.
chateaux-france.com/reaux* ➷ *12 rooms, 5 suites* ⚹ *Tennis court; no
a/c, no room TVs* ⊟ *AE, DC, MC, V* ⧖| *BP.*

off the
beaten
path   **Le Mans.** Best known for its 24-hour automobile race in June (call
02–43–40–24–75 for details; the Web site is www.lemans.org), Le
Mans (44 km [28 mi] north of Le Lude via D307) is a bustling city
with Gallo-Roman ramparts, a well-preserved Old Quarter, and a
magnificent cathedral—part Gothic, part Romanesque—perched
precariously on a hilltop overlooking the River Sarthe.

Langeais

 19 km (12 mi) northeast of Bourgueil via D35 and N152.

Sometimes overlooked in favor of the more iconic château, the **Château
de Langeais**—a castle in the true sense of the word—will particularly de-
light those who dream of lions rampant, knights in shining armor, and
the chivalric days of yore. Built in the 1460s, bearing a massive portcullis
and gate, and never altered, it has an interior noted for its superb col-
lection of medieval and Renaissance furnishings—fireplaces, tapestries,
chests, and beds. Outside, gardens nestle behind sturdy walls and bat-
tlements. The town itself has other sites, including a Renaissance church
tower, but chances are you won't want to move from the delightful out-
door cafés that face the castle entrance. Do follow the road a bit to the
right (when looking at the entrance) to discover the charming historic
houses grouped around a waterfall and canal. ☎ 02–47–96–72–60
✍ €6.50 ⊙ *Apr.–Sept., daily 9–6:30; Oct.–Mar., daily 10–5:30.*

ORLÉANS & THE EASTERN LOIRE

Orléans probably has the biggest inferiority complex this side of Newark,
New Jersey. The city pales pitifully in comparison with other cities of
central France, so the townfolk cling to the city's finest moment—the
coming of *la pucelle d'Orléans* (the Maid of Orleans), Joan of Arc, in
1429 to liberate the city from the English during the Hundred Years'
War. There's little left from Joan's time, but the city is festooned with

everything from her equestrian monument to a Jeanne d'Arc Dry Cleaners. Orléans remains the gateway to the upper Loire Valley, which has some delightful destinations: the hilltop wine town of Sancerre, the ceramics center of Gien, the ancient abbey of St-Benoît, and the extraordinary canal bridge designed by Gustave Eiffel at Briare. Heading back to the central Loire Valley (or south to Bourges), you can enjoy a grand finale at one of the Loire's most gorgeous hotels—the Comte de Vogüé's Château de la Verrerie (near Aubigny-sur-Nère) and one of the finest restaurants in France, the Lion d'Or, in the moody Sologne region.

Orléans

112 km (70 mi) northeast of Tours, 125 km (78 mi) south of Paris.

Once hallowed by Joan of Arc, Orléans is today a thriving commercial city; sensitive urban renewal has done much to bring it back to life, especially the medieval streets between the Loire and the cathedral. The city has quite a history; as a natural bridgehead over the Loire it was long the focus of hostile confrontations and invasions. In 52 BC Julius Caesar slaughtered its inhabitants and burned it to the ground. Five centuries later Attila and the Huns did much the same. Next came the Normans; then the Valois kings turned it into a secondary capital. The story of the Hundred Years' War, Joan of Arc, and the Siege of Orléans is widely known. In 1429 France had hit rock bottom. The English and their Burgundian allies were carving up the kingdom. Besieged by the English, Orléans was one of the last towns about to yield, when a young Lorraine peasant girl, Joan of Arc, arrived to rally the troops and save the kingdom. During the Wars of Religion (1562–98), much of the cathedral was destroyed. A century ago ham-fisted town planners razed many of the city's fine old buildings. Both German and Allied bombs helped finish the job during World War II.

③ The **Cathédrale Ste-Croix** is a riot of pinnacles and gargoyles, both Gothic and pseudo-Gothic, embellished with 18th-century wedding-cake towers. After most of the cathedral was destroyed in the 16th century during the Wars of Religion, Henry IV and his successors rebuilt it. Novelist Marcel Proust (1871–1922) called it France's ugliest church, but most find it impressive. Inside are vast quantities of stained glass and 18th-century wood carvings, plus the modern **Chapelle de Jeanne d'Arc** (Joan of Arc Chapel), with plaques in memory of British and American war dead. ⊠ *Pl. Ste-Croix* ⊙ *Daily 9–noon and 2–6.*

③ The modern **Musée des Beaux-Arts** (Fine Arts Museum) is across from the cathedral. Take the elevator to the top of the five-story building; then make your way down to see works by such artists as Tintoretto, Velázquez, Watteau, Boucher, Rodin, and Gauguin. The museum's richest collection is its 17th-century French paintings. ⊠ *1 rue Fernand-Rabier* ☎ *02–38–79–21–55* ⊠ *€3.20, joint ticket with History Museum* ⊙ *Tues.–Sat. 9:30–12:15 and 1:30–5:45, Sun. 2–6:30.*

③ The **Musée Historique** (History Museum) is housed in the **Hôtel Cabu**, a Renaissance mansion restored after World War II. It contains works of both "fine" and "popular" art connected with the town's past, in-

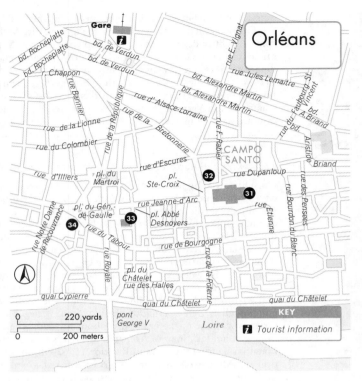

cluding a remarkable collection of pagan bronzes of animals and dancers. These bronzes were hidden from zealous Christian missionaries in the 4th century and discovered in a sandpit near St-Benoît in 1861. ✉ *Square de l'Abbé-Desnoyers* ☎ *02–38–79–25–60* ✉ *€3.20, joint ticket with Arts Museum* ☉ *July and Aug., Tues.–Sun. 10:30–12:15 and 1:30–6; Sept.–June, Wed. and Sun. 1:30–5:30.*

34 During the 10-day Siege of Orléans in 1429, 17-year-old Joan of Arc stayed on the site of the **Maison de Jeanne d'Arc** (Joan of Arc House). This faithful reconstruction of the house she knew contains exhibits about her life and costumes and weapons of her time. Several dioramas modeled by Lucien Harmey recount the main episodes in her life, from the audience at Chinon to the coronation at Reims, her capture at Compiègne, and her burning at the stake at Rouen. ✉ *3 pl. du Général-de-Gaulle* ☎ *02–38–52–99–89* ✉ *€2* ☉ *May–Oct., Tues.–Sun. 10–12:30 and 1:30–6; Nov.–Apr., Tues.–Sun. 1:30–6.*

Where to Stay & Eat

★ **$$–$$$** ✕ **Les Antiquaires.** The understated elegance of this cozy, wood-beamed restaurant close to the river, with its red walls, cane-backed chairs, and brass chandeliers, is in telling contrast to Philippe Bardau's penchant for colorfully presented dishes with a Mediterranean flavor: mullet with eggplant, for instance, or sea bass with artichokes and fennel. ⊠ *4 rue au Lin* ☎ *02–38–53–63–48* ▤ *AE, MC, V* ✆ *Closed Mon. No dinner Sun.*

$$–$$$ ✕▥ **Le Rivage.** This small, white-walled hotel south of Orléans makes a pleasant base. Each of the compact rooms has a little balcony with a view of the tree-lined Loiret River; the bathrooms are tiny. The dining room (no lunch Saturday; no dinner Sunday, November through April) opens onto a terrace facing the river. The menu changes with the season—if you're lucky, chef François Tassin's memorable lobster salad with mango or glazed green-apple soufflé with apple marmalade will be on tap. There's always a huge cheese-board. ⊠ *635 rue de la Reine-Blanche, 5 km (3 mi) south of Orléans, 45160 Olivet* ☎ *02–38–66–02–93* ☎ *02–38–56–31–11* ✎ *17 rooms, 11 with shower, 6 with bath ⚏ Restaurant, minibars, tennis court, bar, some pets allowed (fee)* ▤ *AE, DC, MC, V* ✆ *Closed late Dec.–mid-Jan.* ⍩ *MAP.*

Nightlife & the Arts

The two-day **Fête de Jeanne d'Arc** (Joan of Arc Festival), on May 7 and 8, celebrates the heroic Maid of Orléans with a parade and religious procession.

Châteauneuf-sur-Loire

★ ㉟ *25 km (16 mi) southeast of Orléans via N460.*

The village of Châteauneuf-sur-Loire has a delightful public park with giant tulip trees, magnolias, weeping willows, and rhododendrons, and is especially beautiful in late May and early June. Until the railroad arrived 130 years ago, the Loire was a working river, with boats transporting everything from wheat, salt, wine, and stone to wood, coal, and pottery. The **Musée de la Marine** (Maritime Museum), housed in the former château stables, chronicles that era with documents, old photos, and a reconstituted 19th-century fishing boat equipped with ropes, nets, chests, eel pots, and harpoons. The cynosure remains an astonishingly elegant **octagonal rotunda**—once centerpiece of the château estate and now the town hall, it gracefully overlooks the river. ⊠ *1 pl. Aristide-Briand* ☎ *02–38–46–84–46* ▦ €*3.50* ✆ *Apr.–Oct., Wed.–Mon. 10–6; Nov.–Mar., Wed.–Mon. 2–6.*

Germigny-des-Prés

㊱ *5 km (3 mi) southeast of Châteauneuf-sur-Loire via D60.*

The village of Germigny-des-Prés is famous for its church, one of the oldest in France. Around AD 800, Theodulf, an abbot of St-Benoît, built the tiny **Église de Germigny-des-Prés**—a Byzantine arrangement of round arches on square pillars, with indirect light filtering from smaller arches above the central square. The church was carefully restored to its original condition in the 19th century. Though Theodulf himself brought most of the original mosaics from Italy, only one—covered by plaster and not discovered until 1848—survives. Made of 130,000 cubes of colored glass, it shows the Ark of the Covenant transported by angels with golden halos. The Latin inscription asks us not to forget Theodulf in our prayers. ☎ *02–38–58–27–97* ▦ *Free* ✆ *Daily 9–noon and 2–5.*

St-Benoît-sur-Loire

㊲ *6 km (4 mi) southeast of Germigny-des-Prés.*

The highlight of St-Benoît-sur-Loire is its ancient abbey, which is considered by some to be among the finest Romanesque churches in France. Village signposts refer to it as LA BASILIQUE. St-Benoît (St. Benedict) was the founder of the Benedictine monastic order. In AD 650 a group of monks chose this safe and fertile spot for their new monastery, then returned to Monte Cassino, Italy, to retrieve the bones of St. Benedict with which to bless the site. Despite demands from priests at Monte Cassino for the return of the bones, some of the relics remained here in the 11th-cen-

★ tury **Abbaye St-Benoît.** Following the Hundred Years' War in the 14th and 15th centuries, the monastery fell into decline, and the Wars of Religion (1562–98) wrought further damage. During the French Revolution the monks dispersed, and all the buildings were destroyed except the abbey church itself. Monastic life here began anew in 1944, when the monks rebuilt their monastery and regained the church for their own use. The pillars of the tower porch are noted for their intricately carved capitals, and the choir floor is a gaudy patchwork of multicolor marble. Gregorian chants can be heard daily, at mass or at vespers, and Sunday services attract worshipers and music lovers from all around. ☎ 02–38–35–72–43 📧 *Free* ☉ *Mass and vespers Sun. 11* AM *and 6:15* PM, *Mon.–Sat. noon and 6:15* PM ☞ *Guided English-language tours of monastic bldgs. can be arranged; inquire at monastery shop.*

Sully-sur-Loire

㊳ *8 km (5 mi) southeast of St-Benoît-sur-Loire via D60, 48 km (30 mi) southeast of Orléans.*

An imposing castle with a park, moat, and spectacular medieval roof
★ makes Sully-sur-Loire worth visiting. The **Château de Sully** dates from the first half of the 14th century. Other châteaux have Loire-side perches, but few have the picture-perfect allure of this one, fitted out as it is with turrets and machicolated walkways. It also has a sturdy keep with the finest chestnut roof anywhere along the Loire—a vast structure in the form of an overturned boat, erected in 1400. Great families, including the de Sully and Béthune clans, once called this home; their illustrious friends included Voltaire, who enjoyed putting on plays here. ☎ 02–38–36–36–86 📧 €5 ☉ *Apr.–Sept. daily 10–6; Oct.–May, daily 10–noon and 2–5.*

Gien

㊴ *24 km (15 mi) southeast of Sully-sur-Loire via D951, 70 km (44 mi) southeast of Orléans.*

Ceramics and hunting are the twin historical attractions of the pleasant riverside town of Gien. Its redbrick château, completed in 1484, houses
★ the unexpectedly fine **Musée International de la Chasse** (International Hunting Museum). Exhibits trace the various types of hunt—shooting, trapping, fox-hunting with hounds—and the display of firearms ranges

from harquebuses to rifles. Vast 18th-century hunting pictures by François Desportes and Jean-Baptiste Oudry line the stately hall under its superb beamed roof. ⊠ *Pl. du Château* 🕾 *02–38–67–69–69* 🖼 *€5.60* ⊙ *June–Sept., daily 9–6; Oct.–May, Wed.–Mon. 9–noon and 2–6.*

At the **Musée de la Faïencerie** (Earthenware Factory Museum), in an old paste store, admire local Gien earthenware (both old and new), with its distinctive deep blue glaze and golden decoration. Call ahead to arrange a tour of the factory; there's also a shop. ⊠ *78 pl. de la Victoire* 🕾 *02–38–67–89–99* ⊕ *www.gien.com* 🖼 *€3* ⊙ *May–Sept., daily 9–12:30 and 1:30–6:30; Oct.–Apr., daily 2–6.*

Where to Stay & Eat

$ ✕🏠 **La Poularde.** Some of the bedrooms at this friendly hostelry overlook the Loire; room No. 1 is the largest and lightest. The formal dining room (no lunch Monday, no dinner Sunday), with 18th-century style furniture and local Gien tableware, serves traditional French cuisine, notably *poularde de Bresse,* a succulent fatted chicken, from which the establishment takes its name, often fricasseed *aux morilles* (with morel mushrooms). Weekday menus start at €16, and the copious €22 menu is a good bet for dinner. There's a mountainous cheese board and an extensive selection of local wines. ⊠ *13 quai de Nice, 45500* 🕾 *02–38–37–36–05* 🖼 *02–38–38–18–78* 📞 *9 rooms* ⌂ *Restaurant, some pets allowed (fee)* 🖃 *AE, DC, MC, V* ⊙ *Closed 1st half Jan.* ⦿|*BP.*

Briare

➍ *10 km (6 mi) southeast of Gien via D952.*

The **Pont-Canal de Briare** is one of France's most famous bridges—in fact, a lamp-lined 700-yard aqueduct, held together by a mind-boggling 7 million bolts, built by Gustave Eiffel in 1890 (the year after his Paris tower) to transport the Canal Latéral de la Loire (Loire Side Canal) across the river to join the Canal de Briare. Walk along the span and admire the colorful riverboats along Briare's pretty quay; for those who want to live life along the Loire, there are houseboats available for rent here. (If you're interested in waterways, make a detour 10 km (6 mi) north of Briare to admire the abandoned but spectacular 17th-century seven-rise locks at **Rogny-les-Sept-Écluses.**)

Sancerre

➍ *40 km (25 mi) south of Briare via D951, 120 km (75 mi) southeast of Orléans, 46 km (29 mi) northeast of Bourges.*

The hilltop town of Sancerre is a maze of old cobbled streets offering dramatic views of the mountainous vineyards producing flinty white wines and perky, lesser-known reds and rosés. The local setting challenges the Loire's reputation for soft pastures and gentle hills: the vineyards of Sancerre (like the town itself) stand on rugged, towering mounds and are among the most scenic in France. The main square, Nouvelle Place, was once the site of the grain market; here you'll find the tourist office, which has information about a walking tour of town. From Sancerre visit **Chavignol**, 3 km (2 mi) away, a wine village with a number of producers that have tastings and vintages for sale. Chavignol is also famed for its delicious small, round goat cheese, Crottin de Chavignol, which comes in both hard and soft varieties, depending on the time of year. This famous goat cheese, along with other local cheeses, is celebrated in Sancerre every April during the Fête du Crottin.

Where to Eat

★ ¢ ✕**Auberge Joseph Mellot.** This wood-beam house on the main town square, one of the oldest buildings in Sancerre, has been an inn for over a century and is a splendid setting for a budget meal. You can have an *assiette du pays* platter with local cheese, pâté, or salad from as little as €7; there's a two-course menu at €11 and three courses for €14. Sancerre wine can be ordered by the glass. ⊠ *16 Nouvelle-Place* ☎ *02–48–54–20–53* ⊕ *www.joseph-mellot.fr* ⊟ *No credit cards* ⊘ *Closed Wed. and Feb. No dinner Tues. or Sun.*

Aubigny-sur-Nère

㊷ *42 km (26 mi) northwest of Sancerre via D923, 30 km (18 mi) southwest of Gien.*

Graced with half-timber houses, this town was once the little kingdom of the royal Stuarts of Scotland, who were granted its charter by King Charles VII in 1423. With the noble Darnley family as presiding spirits, the town had been an obvious rallying point for Mary, Queen of Scots. Centuries later the town was made the duchy of the royal courtesan, Louise de Kéroualle, by Louis XIV. The town château now displays her famous tapestries and also contains the **Musée de la Vieille Alliance Franco-Ecossaise,** which details the history of the Auld Alliance and the Scot Jacobite refugees who settled here. A Scottish fête is held every July 14th weekend. ⊠ *Château d'Aubigny* ☎ *02–48–81–50–07* ▨ *€3* ⊘ *Mid-June–mid-Sept., daily 2:30–7; mid-Sept.–mid-Nov. and Apr.–mid-June, weekends 2:30–6; mid-Nov.–Mar., Sun. 2:30–6.*

Where to Stay & Eat

★ $$$–$$$$ ✕▨ **Château de La Verrerie.** Set in the Forêt d'Ivoy next to its own mirror-lake, this turreted abode is the very picture of fairy-tale elegance. Dating from the 15th century and once owned by royal Stuarts, it is now a famously elegant retreat run by Comte Béraud and Comtesse Florence de Vogüé, whose ancestors acquired the place in 1842. Guest rooms are spacious (six have twin beds, six are doubles) with high ceilings, family heirlooms, and sweeping views of the estate. A half-timber 17th-century cottage on the estate has been transformed into the **Maison d'Hélène** restaurant, an excellent spot for light lunches and sumptuous dinners (closed Tuesday, no lunch Wednesday). Don't forget to visit the château's delightful Renaissance chapel, with frescoes dating from 1525. ⊠ *18700 Oizon, 11 km (7 mi) southeast of Aubigny* ☎ *02–48–81–51–60 château, 02–48–58–24–27 restaurant* ▤*02–48–58–21–25* ⊕*www.chateauxfrance. com/verrerie* ⇢ *11 rooms, 1 suite* ⌂ *Restaurant, tennis court, some pets allowed (fee); no a/c, no room TVs* ⊟ *MC, V* ⊘ *Closed mid-Dec.–late Jan.* ¶⊙¶ *BP.*

Romorantin-Lanthenay

43 *60 km (38 mi) southwest of Aubigny-sur-Nère via D924, 45 km (28 mi) southeast of Blois.*

Silence rules in the flat, wooded Sologne region, famed for its game, mushrooms, asparagus, and hidden lakes. Pretty Romorantin-Lanthenay is the area's main town, which saw its heyday in the early 16th century during the turbulent youth of François I (who in 1517 commissioned Leonardo da Vinci to design a palace for his mother here, though it was never built). Some of the great Renaissance houses, including the Hôtel St-Pol where François had his head shaved by doctors after being hit by a burning log (and thereafter grew a beard, starting the fashion for them), are on rue du Milieu and rue de la Résistance.

Where to Stay & Eat

★ **$$$–$$$$** ✕🏠 **Grand Hôtel du Lion d'Or.** Along with Jean Bardet in Tours, this restaurant is considered a mandatory pilgrimage spot by Loire Valley gourmands. The Barrat family has owned this former post house for four decades, welcoming guests to fine accommodations and to chef Didier Clément's renowned restaurant (no lunch Tuesday). This magician is famous for his prawns with the unusual medieval spice called paradise seed; exotic herbs also enliven other dishes, including a *tabac de cuisine* (half a dozen ground spices) garnishing noisettes of lamb. In the inn, pale greens, blues, and pinks plus old stone and warm wood dominate, along with large beds and marble bathrooms; choose one overlooking the delightful courtyard. ⊠ *69 rue Georges-Clemenceau, 41200* ☎ *02–54–94–15–15* 🖷 *02–54–88–24–87* ⊕ *www.hotel-liondor.fr* ⇆ *16 rooms* ⚭ *Restaurant, minibars, cable TV* 🖃 *AE, DC, MC, V* ⊗ *Closed mid-Feb.–late Mar., 2nd half Nov.* ⍾ *BP.*

THE LOIRE VALLEY A TO Z

To research prices, get advice from other travelers, and book travel arrangements, visit www.fodors.com.

AIRPORTS

The closest international airports are Paris's Charles-de-Gaulle and Orly (➪ Air Travel *in* Smart Travel Tips A to Z).

BIKE TRAVEL

With its nearly flat terrain, the Loire Valley is custom-built for traveling by bike; however, a single-day expedition visiting three or more châteaux would be difficult, except for professional bicyclists, considering the distances involved. *Vélos tout-terrain* (mountain bikes) are the sturdiest models. When renting, inquire about bike-repair kits. As Tours is the heart of the region, it is the best base.

🔢 Bike Rentals **Amster Cycles** ⊠ 5 rue du Rempart, Tours ☎ 02–47–61–22–23.

BUS TRAVEL

Local bus services are extensive and reliable, providing a link between train stations and scenic areas off the river; it's possible to reach many villages and châteaux by bus (although many routes are in place to service schoolchildren, meaning service is less frequent in the summer and sometimes all but nonexistent on Sunday). Inquire at tourist offices for information about routes and timetables, available in very handy form. The leading companies are Les Rapides du Val de Loire, originating in Orléans; TLC, serving Chambord and Cheverny from Blois; Touraine Fil Vert, Fil Bleu, and CAT (Compagnies des Autocars de Touraine, which offers buses to Chenonceaux and Amboise from Tours), all of which serve the Touraine region; and Anjou Bus (Anjou region).

🚌 Bus Information **Les Rapides du Val de Loire** ✉ 1 rue Marcel-Proust, Orléans ☎ 02-38-53-94-75. **TLC (Transports du Loir-et-Cher)** ✉ 9 rue Alexandre-Vézin, Blois ☎ 02-54-58-55-44. **Touraine Fil Vert** ✉ Pl. du Général-Leclerc, Tours ☎ 02-47-05-30-49. **Fil Bleu** ✉ Pl. Jean-Jaurès, Tours ☎ 02-47-66-70-70. **Anjou Bus** ✉ Pl. de la Poissonnerie, Angers ☎ 02-41-88-59-25.

CAR RENTAL

🚗 Local Agencies **Avis** ✉ 6 rue Jean-Moulin, Blois ☎ 02-54-74-48-15 ✉ 13 rue Sansonnières, Orléans ☎ 02-38-62-27-04 ✉ Pl. Gal-Leclerc, Tours ☎ 02-47-20-53-27. **Europcar** ✉ 81 rue André-Dessaux, on N20 near Orléans at Fleury-les-Aubrais, ☎ 02-33-73-00-40 ✉ 76 rue Bernard-Palissy, Tours ☎ 02-47-64-47-76. **Hertz** ✉ Chaussée St-Victor [on N7], Blois ☎ 02-54-74-03-03 ✉ 57 rue Marcel-Tribut, Tours ☎ 02-47-75-50-00.

CAR TRAVEL

The Loire Valley is an easy drive from Paris. A10 runs from Paris to Orléans—a distance of around 125 km (80 mi)—and on to Tours, with exits at Meung, Blois, and Amboise. After Tours, A10 veers south, toward Poitiers and Bordeaux. A11 links Paris to Angers and Saumur via Le Mans. Slower but more scenic routes run from the Channel ports down through Normandy into the Loire region.

The easiest way to visit the Loire châteaux is by car; N152 hugs the riverbank and is excellent for sightseeing. You can rent a car in all the large towns in the region, or at train stations in Orléans, Blois, Tours, or Angers, or in Paris.

EMERGENCIES

🚑 Ambulance ☎ 15. **Regional hospitals** ✉ 4 rue Larrey, Angers ☎ 02-41-35-36-37 ✉ 14 av. de l'Hôpital, Orléans ☎ 02-38-51-44-44 ✉ 2 bd. Tonnellé, Tours ☎ 02-47-47-47-47.

TOURS

CHÂTEAU TOURS   Many châteaux insist that you follow one of their tours; try to get a booklet in English before joining, as most are in French. Bus tours of the main châteaux leave daily in summer from Tours, Blois, Angers, Orléans, and Saumur: ask at the relevant tourist office for latest times and prices (*see* Visitor Information, *below*). If you want to do the top châteaux with the convenience of a van tour, readers rave about Acco-Dispo, based in Amboise—usually three are included on the tour (for example, Chambord, Cheverny, and Chenonceau), at a cost of around 30 euros a person, with enticing side-stops and lunch spots provided along the way.

⚑ Acco-Dispo Tours ✉ 18 rue des Vallées, Amboise ☎ 06-82-00-64-51 ⊕ www. accodispo-tours.com.

HELICOPTERS & BALLOONS Jet Systems makes breathtaking helicopter trips over the Loire Valley on Tuesday, Thursday, and weekends from the aerodrome at Dierre, just south of Amboise; cost ranges from €55 (10 minutes) to €225 (50 minutes) per person.

For a more leisurely airborne visit, contact France Montgolfière for details of their balloon trips over the Loire from Chinon; prices run €190–€245.

⚑ Fees & Schedules Jet Systems ☎ 02-47-30-20-21 ⊕ www.jet-systems.fr. **France Montgolfière** ☎ 02-54-71-75-70 ⊕ www.franceballons.com.

PRIVATE GUIDES The tourist offices in Tours and Angers (*see* Visitor Information, *below*) arrange city and regional excursions with personal guides.

WALKING TOURS A walking tour of Tours sets out from the tourist office (⇨ Visitor Information, *below*) every morning at 10 AM from mid-April through October (€6). English-speaking guides show you around Blois on a tour that starts from the château at 4 (€5).

TRAIN TRAVEL

The great writer Henry James used the train system to tour Touraine back in the late 19th century and found it a most convenient way to get around. Things have only gotten better since then. Thanks to superbly organized timetables, you can whisk around from château to château with little worry or stress. True, you may occasionally need to avail yourself of a quick taxi ride from the station to the château door, but compared to renting a car, this adds up to little bother and expense. As gateways to the regions, Tours and Angers are both served by the superfast TGV (Trains à Grande Vitesse) from Paris (Gare Montparnasse). There are also TGV trains from Charles-de-Gaulle Airport direct to the Loire Valley: four per day to Angers (2 hours 10 minutes), one per day (around lunchtime) to Blois (1 hour 50 minutes) and Tours (2 hours 20 minutes). Express trains run every two hours from Paris (Gare d'Austerlitz) to Orléans (usually you must change at nearby Les Aubrais) and Blois. Note that trains for Gien leave from Paris's Gare de Lyon (direction Nevers) and that the nearest station to Sancerre is across the Loire at Tracy.

The Loire region's local train network is magnificent, and it's possible to reach many of the châteaux by train. The main line follows the Loire from Orléans to Angers; there are trains every two hours or so, stopping in Blois, Tours, and Saumur; trains stop less frequently in Onzain (for Chaumont), Amboise, and Langeais. There are branch lines with trains from Tours to Loches, Chenonceaux, Azay-le-Rideau, and Chinon, and to Vendôme and Châteaudun. Ask the SNCF for the brochure *Les Châteaux de la Loire en Train* for more detailed information. Most important, be sure to get the very helpful train-schedule brochures, available at main train stations such as Tours and Orléans.

⚑ Train Information SNCF ☎ 08-36-35-35-35 ⊕ www.ter-sncf.com/uk/paysdelaloire.

TRAVEL AGENCIES

🔲 Local Agent Referrals **Havas–American Express** ✉ 19 av. des Droits-de-l'Homme, Orléans ☎ 02-38-22-15-45. **Carlson Wagonlit** ✉ 9 rue Marceau, Tours ☎ 08-26-82-55-24.

VISITOR INFORMATION

The Loire region has two area tourist offices, both of which are for written inquiries only. For Chinon and points east, contact the Comité Régional du Tourisme Centre-Val de Loire. For Fontevraud and points west, contact the Comité Régional du Tourisme des Pays-de-Loire. Other main tourist offices are listed below by town.

🔲 Tourist Information **Comité Régional du Tourisme Centre-Val de Loire** ✉ 37 av. de Paris, 45000 Orléans ⊕ www.loirevalleytourism.com. **Comité Régional du Tourisme des Pays-de-Loire** ✉ 2 rue de la Loire, 44200 Nantes ⊕ www.paysdelaloire.fr.

Amboise ✉ Quai Général-de-Gaulle ☎ 02-47-57-01-37 ⊕ www.amboise-valdeloire. com. **Angers** ✉ 7 pl. Kennedy ☎ 02-41-23-51-11 ⊕ www.ville-angers.fr. **Blois** ✉ 3 av. du Dr-Jean-Laigret ☎ 02-54-90-41-41 ⊕ www.loiredeschateaux.com. **Fontevraud-L'Abbaye** ✉ Pl. St-Michel ☎ 02-41-51-79-45. **Gien** ✉ Pl. Jean-Jaurès ☎ 02-38-67-25-28 ⊕ www.tourisme.fr/tourist-office/gien.htm. **Montlouis-sur-Loire** ✉ Pl. François-Mitterrand ☎ 02-47-45-00-16 ⊕ www.ville-montlouis37.fr. **Orléans** ✉ 6 rue Albert-Ier ☎ 02-38-24-05-05 ⊕ www.ville-orleans.fr. **Rochecorbon** ✉ Pl. de la Lanterne ☎ 02-47-52-80-22. **Saumur** ✉ Pl. de la Bilange ☎ 02-41-40-20-60 ⊕ www.saumur-tourisme.com. **Tours** ✉ 78 rue Bernard-Palissy ☎ 02-47-70-37-37 ⊕ www.tourisme-touraine.com.

BRITTANY

4

DINE THE BRETON WAY
on Cancale's best oysters ⇨*p.222*

LIFT YOUR SPIRITS
at the Pardon procession
at Ste-Anne-la-Palud ⇨*p.231*

WATCH THE MOON RISE
over Carnac, a Breton Stonehenge ⇨*p.238*

GO HIGHSTEPPING THE CELTIC WAY
at the Festival de Cournouaille ⇨*p.234*

BE A ROAD BUDDY TO GAUGUIN
on the way to Pont-Aven ⇨*p.235*

BE TICKLED PINK
by the rose-hue Corniche Bretonne cliffs ⇨*p.228*

SELECT A CERAMIC TREASURE
at Quimper's famed ateliers ⇨*p.233*

Revised and
updated by
Christopher
Mooney

Introduction by
Nancy Coons

YOU FEEL IT EVEN BEFORE THE SHARP SALT AIR strikes your face from the west—a subliminal rhythm suspended in the mist, a subsonic drone somewhere between a foghorn and a heartbeat, seemingly made up of bagpipes, drums, and the thin, haunting filigree of a tin-whistle tune. This is Brittany, land of the Bretons, where Celtic bloodlines run deep as a Druid's roots into the rocky, sea-swept soil. Wherever you wander—along jagged coastal cliffs, through cobbled seaport streets, into burnished-oak cider pubs—you'll hear this primal pulse of Celtic music. France's most fiercely and determinedly ethnic people, the Bretons delight in celebrating their primeval culture—circle dancing at street fairs, the women donning starched lace-bonnet *coiffes* and the men striped fishermen's shirts at the least sign of a regional celebration. They name their children Erwan and Edwige, carry sacred statues in ceremonial religious processions called *pardons,* pray in Hobbit-scale stone churches decked with elfin, moon-faced gargoyles. And scattered over the mossy hillsides stand Stonehenge-like dolmens and menhirs (prehistoric standing stones), eerie testimony to a primordial culture that predated and has long outlived Frankish France.

Similarities in character, situation, or culture to certain islands across the Channel are by no means coincidental. Indeed, the Celts that migrated to this westernmost outcrop of the French landmass spent much of the Iron Age on the British Isles, where they introduced the indigenes to innovations like the potter's wheel, the rotary millstone, and the compass. This first influx of Continental culture to Great Britain was greeted with typically mixed feelings, and by the 6th century AD the Saxon hordes had sent the Britons packing southward, to the peninsula that became Brittany. So completely did they dominate their new, Cornwall-like peninsula (appropriately named Finistère, from *finis terrae,* or "land's end") that when in 496 they allied themselves with Clovis, the king of the Franks, he felt as if he'd just claimed a little bit of England. Nonetheless the Britons remained independent of France until 1532, only occasionally hiring out as wild and woolly warrior-allies to the Norsemen of Normandy.

Yet the cultural exchange flowed both ways over the Channel. From their days on the British Isles the Britons brought a folklore that shares with England the bittersweet legend of Tristan and Iseult; that weaves mystical tales of the Cornwall/Cornouaille of King Arthur and Merlin. They brought a language that still renders village names unpronounceable: Aber-Wrac'h, Tronoën, Locmariaquer, Poldreuzic, Kerhornaouen. And, too, they brought a way of life with them: half-timber seaside cider bars, their blackened-oak tables softened with prim bits of lace; stone cottages fringed with clumps of hollyhock, hydrangea, and foxglove, damp woolens and rubber boots set to dry in flagstone entryways; bearded fishermen in yellow oilskins heaving the day's catch into weatherbeaten boats, terns and seagulls wheeling in their wake. It's a way of life that feels deliciously exotic to the Frenchman and—like the ancient drone of the bagpipes—comfortably, delightfully, even primally familiar to the Anglo-Saxon.

This cozy regional charm extends inland to Rennes, at 200,000 inhabitants the largest city of Bretagne (to use the French name), as well as to Dinan, Vannes, Quimper, and seaside St-Malo. Though many towns

If you only have three days or so, concentrate on northeast Brittany. With five days you can explore the region in greater depth, including Rennes. With 10 days you can cover the entire region, if you don't dally too long in any one place. A car is necessary for getting to the small medieval towns and deserted coastline.

Numbers in the text correspond to numbers in the margin and on the Brittany and Nantes maps.

4

If you have 5 days

Choose either the medieval town of 🖾 **Dinan** ❹ ► or the fortified "pirates' city" port of 🖾 **St-Malo** ❽—surrounded on four sides by walls and on three by sea—as your base for exploring northeast Brittany. Dinan's obvious attractions are its medieval buildings. Lacking stoplights, the town built its Tour de l'Horloge to keep an eye on 16th-century traffic jams. For a small fee you can climb it and take a look at the pretty town yourself. Be sure to visit ancient **Dol-de-Bretagne** ❻—site of Mont Dol, where Satan and the Archangel Michael once did battle, and a great early Gothic cathedral—the Romantic writer and hero Vicomte Chateaubriand's boyhood home at **Combourg** ❺, or the 16th-century castle in La Bourbansais, all pleasant side trips from seaside **Dinard** ❾, the fashionable Edwardian-era resort. In addition, the magnificent rock island of **Mont-St-Michel** is only 50 km (30 mi) away to the north, within the confines of Normandy.

If you have 10 days

Make 🖾 **Rennes** ❷ ► your base for exploring the castles, châteaux, and fortresses in **Vitré** ❶ and **Montmuran** ❸, making an excursion to the Château de Caradeuc if you have time. On Day 3 stop in **Combourg** ❺ to see the Chateaubriand château or time-stained **Dol-de-Bretagne** ❻ on your way to the walled medieval town of 🖾 **Dinan** ❹ or the historic seaside port of 🖾 **St-Malo** ❽ for the night. Head west the following day on a scenic tour of the coast and spend the night in 🖾 **Trébeurden** ⓫, on the tip of the Corniche Bretonne. Start early the next day for quaint **Morlaix** ⓬, with its houses with richly sculpted facades. Continue west and briefly visit the splendid basilica at Le Folgoët. Stop for lunch in **Brest** ⓭, a huge, modern port town. By late afternoon plan on being in Locronan, where sails used to be made for French fleets. Try to reach picturesque 🖾 **Douarnenez** ⓯ by evening. On the sixth day head to earthenware-famous **Quimper** ⓰, with its lovely riverbank and cathedral. Stop briefly to see the offshore stronghold at **Concarneau** ⓱ and aim to reach Gauguin's getaway, 🖾 **Pont-Aven** ⓲ by the end of the day; then dine on oysters in nearby Riec-sur-Belon. On Day 7 drive down the Atlantic seaboard to the beaches of Quiberon and catch the ferry to the pretty island of 🖾 **Belle-Ile-en-Mer** ⓳. On Day 8 return to the mainland and meander along the coast through the beach resorts of **Carnac** ⓴ and La Trinité-sur-Mer, stopping in the medieval town of **Vannes** ㉒ and exploring the marshy parkland of La Grande Brière. Spend the night in Biarritz-like 🖾 **La Baule** ㉓. The following day head to tranquil, prosperous 🖾 **Nantes** ㉔–㉚ and take in its many sights.

took a beating during the course of the Nazi retreat in 1944, most have been gracefully restored, their sweet whitewashed cottages once again anchoring the soil. And the countryside retains the heather-and-emerald moorscape, framed in forests primeval and bordered by open sea, that first inspired wandering peoples to their pipes.

Exploring Brittany

Even the French may feel they are in a foreign land when they visit Brittany, the triangular patch of northwestern France that juts far out into the Atlantic. Cut off as they are from mainstream culture, the Bretons have closer cultural affinities with the Celts across the Channel than with Parisians. Attractions by the score are to be found here—village fêtes, prehistoric megaliths, and picturesque medieval towns among them. Little wonder Brittany remains a favorite vacation destination for Brits—but don't worry about overcrowding: its vast beaches offer space to spread out, and there are more than enough castles to go around.

Brittany can be divided into two basic areas. The first is the northeast, stretching from Rennes—the traditional capital of Brittany—to St-Malo and along the Channel coast. The **Côtes d'Armor**, the long stretch of Brittany's northern coast, recounts the dramatic struggle between sea and granite shore. The coastline is loosely divided into two parts: the **Côte d'Emeraude** (Emerald Coast), stretching westward from Cancale, where cliffs are punctuated by golden, curving beaches and chin-high forests of fern; and the peaceful **Côte de Granit Rose** (Pink Granite Coast), including the stupefying area around Trébeurden, where Brittany's granite glows an otherworldly pink. In northern Brittany mighty medieval castles survey the land and quaint resort towns line the seacoast. In addition to the cosmopolitan pleasures of Rennes and St-Malo, highlights include the splendid gabled wooden houses of Dinan; Chateaubriand's home at Combourg; and Dinard, the elegant Belle Epoque resort once favored by British aristocrats. Brittany's westernmost point is called **Le Finistère**, literally meaning "the end of the earth." Ties to ancient Celtic culture are strong here in Basse Bretagne (Lower Brittany); elders speak Breton, and Irish pubs replace French cafés. Heading southward you hit Brittany's second major area—the Atlantic coast between Brest and Nantes, where frenzied surf crashing against the cliffs alternates with sprawling beaches and bustling harbors. Between Lorient and Nantes is Brittany's breathtakingly beautiful **Le Morbihan** (Morbihan Coast), famed for its coast lined with sand, not rock. Hereabouts lies lively Quimper, with its fine cathedral and museum; Pont-Aven, a former artists' colony made famous by Gauguin; the pretty island of Belle-Ile; the prehistoric menhirs of Carnac; the 19th-century resort of La Baule; and the thriving city of Nantes.

Numbers in the text correspond to numbers in the margin and on the Brittany and Nantes maps.

About the Restaurants & Hotels

The region's two main cities, Rennes and Nantes, offer extensive dining options all year round, and serve dinner later than in smaller

4

Dining à l'armoricaine

Brittany is a land of the sea. Surrounded on three sides by water, it's a veritable mine of fish and shellfish. These aquatic delights, not surprisingly, dominate Breton cuisine, starting off with the famed *homard à l'armoricaine* (lobster with cream), a name derived from the ancient name for Brittany—Armorica—and not to be confused with Américaine. Other maritime headliners include *coquilles St-Jacques* (scallops); *cotriade*, a distinctive fish soup with potatoes, onions, garlic, and butter; and langoustines, which are something between a large shrimp and a lobster. Other popular meals include smoked ham and lamb, frequently served with green kidney beans. The lamb that hails from the farms on the little island of Ouessant, off the coast of Brest, are famed—called *pré-salé*, or "pre-salted," they feed on sea-salted grass, which marinates their meat while their hearts are still pumping, so to speak. Try the regional *ragout de mouton* and you can taste the difference. Fried eel is a traditional dish in Nantes.

Brittany is particularly famous for its crepes, served with sweet fillings, or as the heartier *galettes*—thicker, buckwheat crepes served as a main course and stuffed with meat, fish, or regional lobster. What's the difference between the two? The dark galette crepe has a deeper flavor best paired with savory fillings—like lobster and mushrooms, or the more traditional ham and cheese. A crepe plain and simple is wafer-thin and made with a lighter batter, reserved traditionally for the sweet—strawberries and cream, apples in brandy, or chocolate, for example. Accompanied by a glass of local cider, they are an ideal light, inexpensive meal; as *crêpes dentelles* (lace crepes) they make a delicious dessert. Incidentally, crepes are eaten from the triangular tails up to save the most flavorful buttery part for last. Folklore, however, permits older folks to eat the best part first in case some awful tragedy prevents them from enjoying *"la part de Dieu."* *Kouign* are delectable sugar cakes made from yeast dough, while *kouign-amann* are the same thing with butter or cream. A *far breton* is a warm or cold flanlike dessert made with prunes. If your sweet tooth is yearning for more, search for the kind of candy called *berlingot* and the region's very delicious macaroons. Of course, nothing is easier than to strike up a conversation with the Bretons than over a glass of Calvados.

Pardons & Festivals

It has been said that there are as many Breton saints as there are stones in the ground. One of the great attractions of Brittany, therefore, remains its many festivals, *pardons*, and folklore events—most occur in the months of June through September, but all year long you can attend special events, particularly village pardons held on various saints' days: banners and saintly statues are borne in colorful parades, accompanied by hymns, and the entire event is capped by a feast. In February, the great Pardon of Terre-Neuve takes place at St-Malo, and in March, Nantes celebrates with a pre-Lenten carnival procession. In mid-May there is the notable pardon of Saint-Yves, patron saint of lawyers, at Tréguier. Another of the great pardons takes place at Rumengol on Trinity Sunday, which usually comes at the end of May or early June. June is also the month of St. John, honored by the ceremonial Feux de Saint-Jean at Locronan and Nantes. July sees Quimper's Celtic Festival de Cornouaille and the famed pardon in Ste-Anne-d'Auray. August sees Lorient's Festival Interceltique, Pont Aven's Festival of the Golden Gorse, Brest's bagpipe festival, and a big pardon in Ste-Anne-la-Palud. Another pardon held in Le Folgoët during September is one of the most extraordinary. At the biggest and best of these celebrations, you may find yourself rubbing elbows with twenty bishops, numbers of Breton women in their traditional costumes, and thousands of pilgrims.

Water, Water, Everywhere

Brittany's best beaches will lure even the palest of sunbathers, especially those white-sand wonders that spangle the coastal waters along the southern Morbihan Coast. The best sandy beaches and a multitude of water sports are found in Dinard, Perros-Guirec, Trégastel-Plage (the latter two are near the town of Trébeurden), Douarnenez, Carnac, La Trinité-sur-Mer, and La Baule. As it turns out, wherever you go in Brittany, you will be near the coast and see the handiwork of the turbulent Atlantic Ocean, which gnaws at Brittany's peninsula, creating a seascape of wave-battered crags, isolated coves, and dozens of islands. Note that many "beaches" will comprise rock, not sand; exclusive beaches charge, as is the custom in Europe, a fee.

---

towns, where some restaurants close for some, if not all, of the off-season (November through March). Smaller towns around the coast may only have one or two restaurants, so don't be surprised if they're booked solid in July and August. Crêperies are the regional specialty, catering just as readily for those in quest of a quick snack as a three-course meal.

Brittany has plenty of small, appealing family-run hotels with friendly and personal service, as well as a growing number of luxury hotels and châteaux. Dinard, on the English Channel, and La Baule, on the Atlantic, are the area's two most expensive resorts. In summer expect crowds, so make reservations far in advance and confirm before arriving. Assume all hotel rooms have air-conditioning, TV, telephones, and private bath, unless otherwise noted. It's assumed that hotels operate on the European Plan (EP, with no meal provided) unless we note that they use the Breakfast Plan (BP), Modified American Plan (MAP, with breakfast and dinner daily, known as *demi-pension*), or Full American Plan (FAP, or *pension complète*, with three meals a day).

WHAT IT COSTS In euros				
	$$$$	**$$$**	**$$**	**$**	**¢**
RESTAURANTS	over €30	€23–€30	€17–€23	€11–€17	under €11
HOTELS	over €190	€120–€190	€80–€120	€50–€80	under €50

Restaurant prices are per person for a main course at dinner, including tax (19.6%) and service; note that if a restaurant offers only prix-fixe (set-price) meals, it has been given the price category that reflects the full prix-fixe price. Hotel prices are for a standard double room in high season, including tax (19.6%) and service charge; higher prices (inquire when booking) prevail for any board plans.

Timing

The tourist season is short in Brittany. Long, damp winters keep visitors away, and many hotels are closed until Eastertime. Brittany is particularly crowded in July and August, when most French people are on vacation, so choose crowd-free June or September, or early October, when autumnal colors and crisp evenings make for an invigorating visit. Late summer, however, is the most festive time in Brittany: the two biggest pardons take place on July 26 (Ste-Anne d'Auray) and the last Sunday in August (Ste-Anne-la-Palud); the Celtic Festival de Cornouaille is held in Quimper in late July; and the Festival Interceltique invades Lorient in early August.

NORTHEAST BRITTANY & THE CHANNEL COAST

Northeast Brittany extends from the city of Rennes to the coast. The rolling farmland around Rennes is strewn with mighty castles in Vitré, Fougères, and Dinan—remnants of Brittany's ceaseless efforts to repel invaders during the Middle Ages and a testimony to the wealth derived from pirate and merchant ships. The beautiful Côte d'Émeraude (Emerald Coast) stretches west from Cancale to St-Brieuc, and the dramatic Côte de Granit Rose (Pink Granite Coast) extends from Paimpol to Trébeurden and the Corniche Bretonne. Follow the coastal routes D786 and D34—winding, narrow roads that total less than 100 km (62 mi) but can take five hours to drive; the spectacular views that unfold en route make the journey worthwhile.

Vitré

❶ *32 km (20 mi) south of Fougères via D798 and D178.*

There's still a feel of the Middle Ages about the formidable castle, tightly packed half-timber houses, remaining ramparts, and dark alleyways of Vitré (pronounced vee-*tray*). Built high above the Vilaine Valley, the medieval walled town that spreads out from the castle's gates, though small, is the best preserved in Brittany, and utterly beguiling, though you'll have to put on extra-strong fantasy goggles to block out the many tourists who visit here. The castle stands at the west end of town, facing narrow, cobbled streets as picturesque as any in Brittany—rue Poterie, rue d'Embas, and rue Beaudrairie, originally the home of tanners (the name comes from *baudoyers,* or leather workers).

★ Rebuilt in the 14th and 15th centuries to protect Brittany from invasion, the 11th-century **Château de Vitré** (Silverware Tower)—shaped in an imposing triangle with fat, round towers—proved to be one of the province's most successful fortresses: during the Hundred Years' War (1337–1453), the English repeatedly failed to take it, even when they occupied the rest of the town. It's a splendid sight, especially from the vantage point of rue de Fougères across the river valley below. Time, not foreigners, came closest to ravaging the castle, which has been heavily though tastefully restored during the past century. The **Hôtel de Ville**

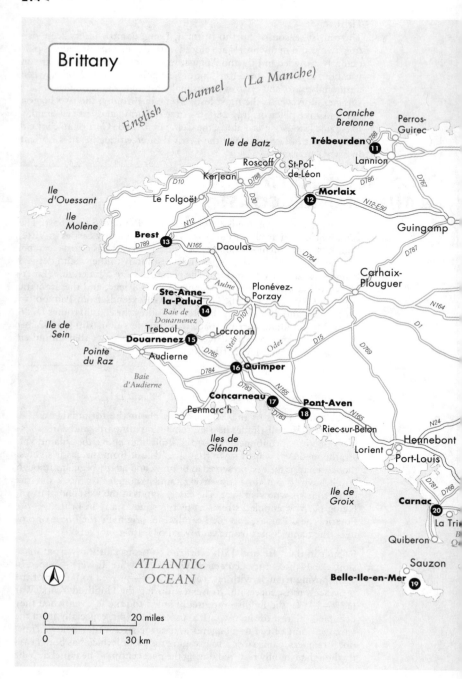

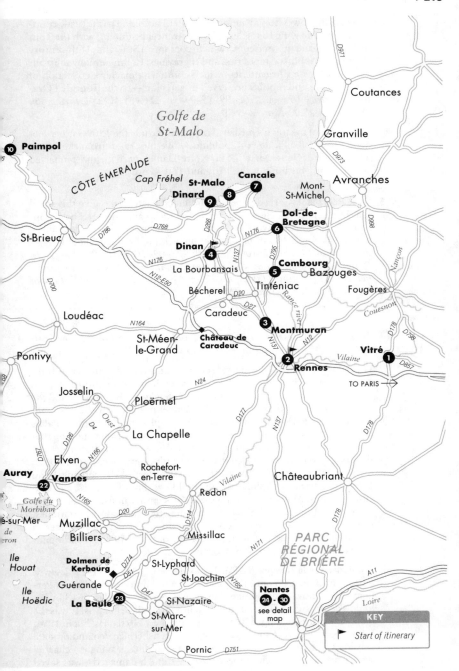

(town hall), however, is an unfortunate 1913 accretion to the castle court-yard. Visit the wing to the left of the entrance, beginning with the **Tour St-Laurent** and its museum, which contains 15th- and 16th-century sculptures, Aubusson tapestries, and engravings. Continue along the walls via the **Tour de l'Argenterie**—which contains a macabre collection of stuffed frogs and reptiles preserved in glass jars—to the **Tour de l'Ora-toire** (Oratory Tower). ☎ 02–99–75–04–54 ☞ €4 ☉ Wed.–Fri. 10–noon and 2–5:30, Sat.–Mon. 2–5:30.

Fragments of the town's medieval ramparts include the 15th-century **Tour de la Bridolle** (⊠ Pl. de la République), five blocks up from the castle. The church of **Notre-Dame** (⊠ Pl. Notre-Dame), with its fine, pinnacled south front, was built in the 15th and 16th centuries.

Where to Stay

¢–$ 🏨 **Le Petit Billot.** Carved paneling and faded pastel tones give this small family-run hotel a delightful French provincial air. The hotel has an in-formal relationship with Le Potager, the restaurant right next door, which serves reliable, though rather unexciting, Breton cuisine. ⊠ 5 pl. du Général-Leclerc, 35500 ☎ 02–99–75–02–10 🖷 02–99–74–72–96 ⊕ www.petit-billot.com ↩ 21 rooms, 5 with bath ☆ Cable TV, Inter-net, some pets allowed (fee); no a/c ⊟ AE, MC, V ☉ Closed last wk of Dec. and 1st wk of Jan. ¶◎¶ MAP.

Rennes

❷ 36 km (22 mi) west of Vitré via D857 and N157, 345 km (215 mi) west of Paris, 107 km (66 mi) north of Nantes.

Packed with students during the school year, studded with sterile 18th-century granite buildings, and yet graced with medieval houses, Rennes (pronounced *wren*) is the traditional gateway to Brittany. Since the province was joined to Paris in 1532, Rennes has been the site of squab-bles with the national capital, many taking place in the Rennes' Palais de Justice, long the political center of Brittany and the one building that survived a terrible fire in 1720 that lasted a week and destroyed half the city. The remaining cobbled streets and 15th-century half-timber houses form an interesting contrast to the Classical feel of the cathedral and Jacques Gabriel's disciplined granite buildings, broad avenues, and spa-cious squares. Many of the 15th- and 16th-century houses in the streets surrounding the cathedral have been converted into shops, boutiques, restaurants, and *crêperies* (crepe restaurants). The cavalier manner in which the French go about running a bar out of a 500-year-old build-ing can be disarming to New Worlders.

The **Parlement de Bretagne** (⊠ Rue Nationale ☎ 02–99–67–11–11 ⊕ www. parlement-bretagne.com), the palatial original home of the Breton Par-liament and now of the Rennes law courts, was designed in 1618 by Sa-lomon de Brosse, architect of the Luxembourg Palace in Paris. It was the most important building in Rennes to escape the 1720 flames, but in 1994, following a massive demonstration by Breton fishermen demanding state subsidies, a disastrous fire broke out at the building, leaving it a charred shell. Fortunately, much of the artwork—though damaged—was saved by firefighters, who arrived at the scene after the building was already engulfed in flames. It was a case of the alarm that cried "fire" once too often; a faulty bell, which rang regularly for no reason, had led the man on duty to ignore the signal. Restoration has now been completed. Call ahead for information on guided tours in English.

The **Musée de Bretagne** (Museum of Brittany) reopens in 2004 in its brand new headquarters, designed by architect Christian de Portzamparc, a vast three-part space that it shares with the Rennes municipal library and Espaces des Sciences. Portzamparc's layout harmonizes nicely with the organization of the museum's extensive ethnographic and archeological collection, which, chronologically ordered, depicts the everyday life of Bretons from prehistoric times up to the present. There is also a space devoted to the famous Dreyfus Affair; Alfred Dreyfus, an army captain who was wrongly accused of espionage and whose case was championed by Emile Zola, was tried a second time in Rennes in 1899. Service information was not available at press time; log on to the Web site for details. ✉ *20 quai Émile-Zola* ⊕ *www.musee-bretagne.fr.*

The **Musée des Beaux-Arts** (Fine Arts Museum) contains works by Georges de La Tour, Jean-Baptiste Chardin, Camille Corot, Paul Gauguin, and Maurice Utrillo, to name a few. The museum is particularly strong in French 17th-century paintings and drawings and has an interesting collection of modern French artists. ✉ *20 quai Émile-Zola* ☎ *02–99–28–55–85* ⊕ *www.mbar.org* ⊠ *€4* ◷ *Wed.–Mon. 10–noon and 2–6.*

---

need a break?

Thé au Fourneau (6 rue du Capitaine-Alfred-Dreyfus, near the Fine Arts Museum) is a cozy tearoom pleasantly cluttered with antiques, which serves chocolate cake, fruit crumble, excellent pastries, snacks, and salads. It's open weekdays 10–6:30.

A late-18th-century building in Classical style that took 57 years to construct, the **Cathédrale St-Pierre** looms above rue de la Monnaie at the west end of the *Vieille Ville* (Old Town), bordered by the Rance River. Stop in to admire its richly decorated interior and outstanding 16th-century Flemish altarpiece. ✉ *Pl. St-Pierre* ◷ *Mon.–Sat. 8:30–noon and 2–5, Sun. 8:30–noon.*

★ Take a stroll through the lovely **Parc du Thabor** (✉ Pl. St-Melaine), east of the Palais des Musées. It's a large, formal French garden with regimented rows of trees, shrubs, and flowers, and a notable view of the church of **Notre-Dame-en-St-Melaine.**

Where to Stay & Eat

$ ✕ **Piccadilly Tavern.** Around the corner from the Palais de Justice and next to the municipal theater is this oddly named brasserie that serves traditional Breton cuisine. Its huge, sunny terrace is the perfect place to people-watch while downing a half-dozen fresh oysters and an aperitif. The prix-fixe menu is €12. ✉ *15 Galeries du Théâtre* ☎ *02–99–78–17–17* ▭ *MC, V.*

★ $$$ ✕▯ **LeCoq-Gadby.** A 19th-century mansion with huge fireplaces and antiques sets the stage for this cozy retreat. Homey guest rooms have four-poster beds and floral covers, while hydrotherapy facilities, a *hammam* (steam room), a Jacuzzi, and a sauna are all available if you want to be pampered. Jean-Michel Boucault's cuisine must be good—French presidents have dined here on such delicacies as *pigeon fermier roti aux chataignes* (pigeon roasted with chestnuts). Book way in advance for this popular hotel and restaurant (which does not serve dinner Sunday). ⊠ *156 rue d'Antrain, 35700* ☎ *02–99–38–05–55* 🖷 *02–99–38–53–40* ⊕ *www.lecoq-gadby.com* ⇨ *11 rooms* ⚿ *Restaurant, minibars, cable TV, bar, Internet; no a/c* 🗖 *AE, DC, MC, V* ⦿ *MAP.*

$–$$$ ⊡ **Mercure Centre.** This stately 19th-century hotel is centrally located on a quiet, narrow back street close to the cathedral. Rooms overlook the street or a courtyard; all are modern and functional. ⊠ *6 rue Lanjuinais, 35000* ☎ *02–99–79–12–36* 🖷 *02–99–79–65–76* ⇨ *48 rooms* ⚿ *Cable TV, Internet, some pets allowed (fee)* 🗖 *AE, DC, MC, V* ⦿ *BP.*

★ ¢–$ ⊡ **Garden.** This picturesque, central hotel has an age-old wooden gallery overlooking a sunny inner courtyard where breakfast is served. Rooms are small but cheerful, with bright colors and antiques. ⊠ *3 rue Duhamel, 35000* ☎ *02–99–65–45–06* 🖷 *02–99–65–02–62* ⇨ *26 rooms, 8 with bath, 18 with shower* ⚿ *Some pets allowed; no a/c* 🗖 *AE, MC, V* ⦿ *EP.*

Nightlife & the Arts

The streets around place Ste-Anne are jammed with popular student bars, most of them housed in fantastic medieval buildings with character to spare. If you feel like dancing the night away, head to **L'Espace** (⊠ 45 bd. de la Tour d'Auvergne ☎ 02–99–30–21–95). For the night owl, the **Pym's Club** (⊠ 27 pl. du Colombier ☎ 02–99–67–30–00) stays open all night, every night.

Brittany's principal theater is the **Opéra de Rennes** (⊠ Pl. de la Mairie ☎ 02–99–78–48–78). All kinds of performances are staged at the **Théâtre National de Bretagne** (⊠ 1 rue St-Hélier ☎ 02–99–31–12–31). The famous annual international rock-and-roll festival, **Les Transmusicales** (☎ 02–99–31–12–10 for information), happens the second week of December in bars around town and at the Théâtre National de Bretagne.
★ The first week of July sees **Les Tombées de la Nuit** (☎ 02–99–67–11–11 for information), the "Nightfalls" Festival, featuring crowds, Celtic music, dance, and theater performances staged in old historic streets and churches around town.

Shopping

A lively **market** is held on Place des Lices on Saturday morning.

Montmuran

❸ *29 km (18 mi) northwest of Rennes via N137 and D221.*

The **Château de Montmuran** was once ground control to one of France's finest knights, Bertrand du Guesclin (1320–80). Commemorated in countless squares and hostelries across the province, du Guesclin sprang to prominence at the age of 17, when he entered a jousting tournament in disguise and successfully unseated several hoarier knights. He went on to lead the onslaught against the English during the Hundred Years' War. An alley of oak and beech trees leads up to the main 17th-century building, which is surrounded by a moat and flanked by four towers, two built in the 12th century, two in the 14th. You can visit the towers and a small museum devoted to the castle's history. The château also has two pleasant guest rooms that are open from May to October. Call to reserve. ⊠ *Les Iffs* ☎ *02–99–45–88–88* ⊕ *www.chateau-montmuran. com* 🎫 *€4* ⊙ *June–Sept., Sun.–Fri. 2–6.*

off the beaten path

CHÂTEAU DE CARADEUC – Ambitiously dubbed the Versailles of Brittany, this château, 8 km (5 mi) west of Montmuran just beyond Bécherel, is privately owned and not open to the public. But you can admire the statuary, flower beds, and leafy allées in the surrounding park—Brittany's largest. ⊠ *Rte. de Chateaubriand* ☎ *02–99–66–77–76* 🎫 *€3* ⊙ *Apr.–June, daily 2–6; July–Aug., daily noon–6; Sept., weekends 2–6; Oct., Sun. 2–6.*

Dinan

❹ Fodor'sChoice ★

29 km (18 mi) northwest of Montmuran via D27 and D68.

During the frequent wars that devastated other cities in the Middle Ages, the merchants who ruled Dinan got rich selling stuff to whichever camp had the upper hand, well aware that loyalty to any side, be it the French, the English, or the Breton, would eventually lead to the destruction of their homes. The strategy worked: Today, Dinan is one of the best-preserved medieval towns in Brittany. Although there is no escaping the crowds here in summer, in the off-season or early morning Dinan feels like a time-warped medieval playground.

Like Montmuran, Dinan has close links with warrior-hero Bertrand du Guesclin, who won a famous victory here in 1359 and promptly married a local girl, Tiphaine Raguenel. When he died in the siege of Châteauneuf-de-Randon in Auvergne (central France) in 1380, his body was dispatched home to Dinan. Owing to the great man's popularity, only his heart completed the journey (it rests in the basilica); the rest of him was confiscated by devoted followers along the way.

Along place des Merciers, rue de l'Apport, and rue de la Poissonnerie, take note of the splendid gabled wooden houses. Rue du Jerzual, which leads down to Dinan's harbor, is also a beautifully preserved medieval street, divided halfway down by the town walls and the massive Porte du Jerzual gateway and lined with boutiques and crafts shops in 15th- and 16th-century houses. A few restaurants brighten the area around the harbor, and boats sail up the Rance River in summer (€22 round-trip, call ☎ 02–23–18–01–80 for details), but the abandoned warehouses mostly bear witness to the town's vanished commercial activity. Above the harbor, near Porte St-Malo, is the leafy Promenade des Grands Fossés, the best-preserved section of the town walls, which leads to the castle.

For a superb view of town, climb to the top of the medieval **Tour de l'Horloge** (Clock Tower). ⊠ *Rue de l'Horloge* 🎫 *€2.50* ⊙ *Apr.–June, daily 2–6; July–Sept., daily 10–6:30* ⊙ *Closed Oct.–Mar.*

Du Guesclin's heart lies in the north transept of the **Basilique St-Sauveur** (⊠ Pl. St-Sauveur). The church's style ranges from the Romanesque south front to the Flamboyant Gothic facade and Renaissance side chapels. The old trees in the **Jardin Anglais** (English Garden) behind the church provide a nice frame. More spectacular views can be found at the bottom of the garden, which looks down the plummeting Rance Valley to the river below.

The **Château,** at the end of the Promenade des Petits Fossés, has a two-story tower, the **Tour du Coëtquen,** and a 100-foot, 14th-century **donjon** (keep) containing a museum with varied displays of medieval effigies and statues, Breton furniture, and locally made lace *coiffes* (head coverings). ⊠ *Porte de Guichet* ☎ *02–96–39–45–20* ⊡ *€3.90* ۞ *June–Oct., daily 10–6:30, Nov.–June, daily 1:30–5:30* ۞ *Closed Jan.*

Where to Stay & Eat

$$–$$$$ ✕ **Le Relais des Corsaires.** This riverbank spot is named for the old-time pirates who sporadically plundered Dinan and the Rance Valley. The mid-range prix-fixe menu provides an ample four-course meal of traditional French cuisine, with an emphasis on steak and fish. The welcoming proprietors, Sabine and Christian Boaumond, also have an informal, relaxed seafood restaurant, Au Petit Corsair, where you can compose your own seafood platter from the very fresh choices in the 15th-century building next door. ⊠ *7 rue du Port* ☎ *02–96–39–40–17* ⊟ *MC, V* ۞ *Closed mid-Nov.–mid-Feb.*

★ **$$–$$$** ▦ **L'Avaugour.** Set on the town ramparts, with pretty sash windows, mansard roofs, and a Breton stone facade, this hotel has a sunny flower garden, which the best rooms—all were renovated in 2002—overlook, and where breakfast and afternoon tea are served. Start the day with the full buffet breakfast and a chat with the charming owner, Nicolas Caron, who enjoys speaking English and helping everyone plan day trips. There's a colorful street market opposite the hotel every Thursday. ⊠ *1 pl. du Champ, 22100* ☎ *02–96–39–07–49* ⊟ *02–96–85–43–04* ⊕ *www. avaugourhotel.com/around.htm* ⤶ *21 rooms, 3 suites* ⴱ *Cable TV, Internet, some pets allowed (fee); no a/c* ⊟ *AE, DC, MC, V* ۞ *Closed mid-Nov.–Dec. 20 and Jan.* ▯◉▮ *BP.*

¢–$ ▦ **Arvor.** The cobbled streets of the *Vieille Ville* are visible from this comfortable 18th-century hotel directly across from the town theater. Now under new management, it offers clean and simple rooms with friendly service. ⊠ *5 rue Auguste-Pavie, 22100* ☎ *02–96–39–21–22* ⊟ *02–96–39–83–09* ⤶ *23 rooms* ⴱ *Cable TV, some pets allowed; no a/c* ⊟ *MC, V* ۞ *Closed Jan.* ▯◉▮ *EP.*

Nightlife & the Arts

In even years (the last was held in 2004), on the third weekend in July, medieval France is re-created with a market, parade, jousting tournament, and street music for **La Fête des Remparts** (Ramparts Festival), one of the largest medieval festivals in Europe.

Shopping

One of the leading craft havens in France, Dinan has attracted many wood-carvers, jewelers, leather workers, glass specialists, and silk painters, who have set up shop in the medieval houses that line the cobbled, sloping **rue de Jerzual.** Other delightful studios and artisan boutiques can be found on the nearby **rue de l'Apport, place des Merciers, and place des Cordeliers.**

en route

Between Dinan and Combourg is the château **La Bourbansais,** built in the 1580s. Most of the interior furnishings (guided tours only) date from the 18th century, including the fine collection of porcelain and tapestries. Its extensive gardens contain a small zoo, a playground for children, a picnic area (with an on-site restaurant that serves simple sandwiches, steaks, french fries, and salads), and a pack of hunting hounds who perform a popular 20-minute show called *La Meute* from April through September. ⊠ *Pleugueneuc* 🕿 *02–99–69–40–07* ⊕ *www.labourbansais.com* 🎟 *€14* ⊘ *Apr.–Sept., daily 10–7; Oct.–Mar., daily 2–6.*

Combourg

❺ *25 km (16 mi) southeast of Dinan via D794, 40 km (25 mi) north of Rennes.*

Fodor'sChoice
★

The pretty lakeside village of Combourg is dominated by the boyhood home of Romantic writer Viscount René de Chateaubriand (1768–1848), the thick-walled, four-tower **Château de Combourg** (Cat's Tower). Topped with "witches' cap" towers that the poet likened to Gothic crowns, the castle dates mainly from the 14th and 15th centuries. Here, quartered in the tower called "La Tour du Chat," accompanied by roosting birds, a sinister quiet, and the ghost of a wooden-legged Comte de Combourg—whose false leg would reputedly get up and walk by itself—the young René succumbed to the château's moody spell and, in turn, became a leading light of Romanticism. His novel *Atala and René,* about a tragic love affair between a French soldier and a Native American maiden, was an international sensation in the mid-19th century, while his multi-volume *History of Christianity* was required reading for half of Europe. The château grounds—ponds, woods, and cattle-strewn meadowland—are suitably mournful and can seem positively desolate when viewed under leaden skies. Its melancholy is best captured in Chateaubriand's famous *Mémoires d'outre-tombe* ("Memories from Beyond the Tomb"). Inside you can view neo-Gothic salons, the Chateaubriand archives, and the writer's severe bedroom up in the "Cat's Tower." 🕿 *02–99–73–22–95* ⊕ *www.combourg.net* 🎟 *€4, park only €1.50* ⊘ *Château open Apr.–Oct., Sun.–Fri. 2–5:30; park open Apr.–Oct., daily 9–noon and 2–6.*

off the beaten path

CHÂTEAU DE LA BALLUE – This château, 18 km (11 mi) east of Combourg and dating from 1620, has sophisticated gardens that feature modern sculpture, leafy groves, columns of yew, a fernery, a labyrinth, and a Temple of Diana. To visit the interior, with its gleaming wood paneling and huge granite staircase, you'll have to stay the night—in one of the five large, beautifully decorated, fabric-swathed guest rooms (each with a four-poster bed), and dine with the dynamic English-speaking owners Alain Schrotter and Marie-France

Barrère. Reserve well in advance and be sure to specify whether you'll be staying for dinner. Nineteenth-century writers Alfred de Musset, Honoré Balzac, and Victor Hugo all preceded you as guests. ⊠ *Bazouges-la-Pérouse* 🕾 *02–99–97–47–86* 🖷 *02–99–97–47–70* 🖃 *Gardens €8* ۩ *May–Sept., daily 10:30–5:30.*

Where to Eat

★ $ ✕ **L'Écrivain.** Gilles Menier's inventive, light cuisine showcases mussels in flaky pastry flavored with chervil, cod with cream of coriander and a red-berry sauce, and apple crepe with cider butter. Ask for a table in the intimate wood-panel dining room, with candles on the tables, rather than in the bustling larger hall, and take your *digestif* in the wood-panel bar with its oil paintings depicting scenes from Chateaubriand's life. Excellent fixed-price menus start at € 14. ⊠ *1 pl. St-Gilduin* 🕾 *02–99–73–01–61* 🖃 *MC, V* ۩ *Closed Thurs., 3 wks in Feb., and 2 wks in Oct. No dinner Wed. or Sun.*

Dol-de-Bretagne

❻ *17 km (11 mi) north of Combourg via D795.*

The ancient town of Dol-de-Bretagne, which still has its original ramparts, looks out over the Marais de Dol, a marshy plain stretching across to Mont-St-Michel, 21 km (13 mi) northeast. For extensive views of the Marais as well as Mont-Dol—a 200-foot windmill-topped mound 3 km (2 mi) north and the legendary scene of combat between St. Michael and the Devil—walk along the **Promenade des Douves,** on the northern part of the original ramparts. Dol's picturesque main street is **Grande-Rue des Stuarts,** lined with medieval houses; the oldest, the **Maison des Palets,** at No. 17, has a chunky row of Romanesque arches.

The **Cathédrale St-Samson** (⊠ Pl. de la Cathédrale) is a damp, soaring, fortresslike bulk of granite dating mainly from the 12th to the 14th centuries. This mighty building shows the influence wielded by the bishopric of Dol in bygone days. The richly sculpted great porch, carved-wood choir stalls, and stained glass in the chancel warrant scrutiny.

The **Cathédraloscope** (Cathedral Museum), opposite the cathedral, uses models, frescoes, ground plans, and special lighting effects to explain the construction of France's cathedrals, their feats of engineering, and the evolution of the soaring Gothic style that is their chief characteristic. There are also sections on church liturgy and stained glass. ⊠ *Pl. de la Cathédrale* 🕾 *02–99–48–35–30* 🖃 *€7.50* ۩ *Apr.–Nov., daily 10–7.*

Cancale

❼ *22 km (14 mi) northwest of Dol via D155 and D76.*

If you enjoy eating oysters, be sure to get to Cancale, a picturesque fishing village renowned for its offshore *bancs d'huîtres* (oyster beds). You can sample the little brutes at countless stalls or restaurants along the quay. The **Musée de l'Huître et du Coquillage** (Oyster and Shellfish Museum) explains everything you ever wanted to know about farming

NO MEAN CATCH!

TO THE GREAT SURPRISE OF MOST NORTH AMERICANS, *the humble canned sardine is a revered comestible—and justly so—among* French gourmands. *The best brands— Rodel, La Quibéronnaise, Gonidec and La Belle Illoise—are from Brittany, where the sardine industry was once the backbone of the Breton economy. The sardine tin, in fact, was invented by a Breton named Pierre-Joseph Colin (colin, incidentally, means hake; fish surnames are common in Brittany) in 1810. The preserved fish immediately made culinary history: Napoleon had thousands loaded into carts and brought to the Russian front where the tasty little fish, once extracted from their soldered cans with a hammer, must have helped soften the blow of France's defeat. The best cans of sardines, usually marked* première catégorie *or* extra, *are treated like bottles of fine wine, carefully dated (some cans are even stamped with the name of the fishing boat credited with the catch), laid away in cellars for up to a decade and lovingly turned every few months for proper aging. Even the vocabulary for aged sardines is borrowed from oenology: one speaks of* grands crus *and* millésimes. *With the current trend toward "limited-edition" canned sardines, the oily fish has acceded to an even more exalted status. Once caught, they are put in salt, rinsed, hand-sorted by size, grilled, deep-fried and hand-packed in peanut or extra virgin cold-pressed olive oil. Purists take them straight, crushed onto a slice of buttered bread with the back of a fork, with perhaps the tiniest squeeze of lemon to bring out the oily flavors. Whichever way you wolf them down, vintage sardines are tender, delicately flavored, and deeply satisfying as a snack or an entire meal*

oysters. ⊠ *Les Parcs St-Kerber, Plage de l'Aurore* ☎ 02–99–89–69–99 ⚏ €6.10 ⊙ *Guided 1-hr tours in English, mid-Feb.–Oct., daily 2.*

Where to Stay & Eat

★ **$$$–$$$$** ✕🏠 **Château Richeux.** One of three hotels owned by the famed Roellingers of Cancale's Relais Gourmand, the Château Richeux occupies an imposing turn-of-the-20th-century waterfront mansion built on the ruins of the du Guesclin family's 11th-century château, 4 mi (2½ km) south of Cancale. Request one of the rooms with large bay windows, which have stunning views of Mont-St-Michel. Le Coquillage, the hotel's small bistro (closed Monday, Tuesday, and Thursday lunch) specializes in local oysters and seafood platters served up in a relaxed, cozy atmosphere. ⊠ *Le Point du Jour, St-Méloir des Ondes, 35350* ☎ 02–99–89–64–76 🖨 02–99–89–18–49 ⊕ *www.maisons-de-bricourt.com* ⤵ *13 rooms* ♿ *Restaurant, cable TV, Internet; no a/c* ⊟ *AE, DC, MC, V* ⏐❙ *BP.*

$$$$ 🏠 **Le Relais Gourmand O. Roellinger.** The name of this place sounds the
FodorsChoice trumpet for chef Olivier Roellinger, who grew up in this grand 18th-
★ century, St-Malo-style stone house and, fittingly for a town named "Oysters," came to master the *cuisine marine* of this region to perfection. Even those land-locked lubbers, Parisians, don't think twice about

driving here just for dinner. Their 250-mi-long drive is worth it: Glowing murals, domed conservatory, stone fireplaces, spotlit trees, duck pond, and antique tiles all welcome them with a cozily imposing ambience. But the main attraction is Roellinger's way with seafood. He leaves *moules à la cancalaise* (mussels with butter)—the basic specialty of the region—in the dust with all sorts of culinary fireworks, such as the spiced consommé of cancalaises and foie gras, the John Dory steamed in seaweed and coconut milk, or the Saint-Pierre *"retour des Indes."* Luscious desserts all seduce, including farm raspberries with angelica, iced maingau, and "churned" milk. The restaurant is closed Tuesday and Wednesday. If you wish to stay the night, attractive rooms (with spectacular views across the oyster beds toward Mont-St-Michel) are available in the luxe **Les Rimains** cottage on rue des Rimains, a short walk away. ⊠ *1 rue Du-Guesclin, 35260* ☎ *02–99–89–64–76* 🖷 *02–99–89–88–47* 🌐 *www. maisons-de-bricourt.com* 🗗 *4 rooms* ⌂ *Restaurant, cable TV, Internet; no a/c* ▤ *AE, DC, MC, V* ⊘ *Closed mid-Dec.–mid-Mar.* ⦿**|** *BP.*

en route   Heading north from Cancale, past the attractive beach of Port-Mer, takes you to the jagged rock formations rising from the sea at the **Pointe de Grouin.**, a magical spot for catching a sunset. From here follow D201 along the coast to St-Malo.

Shopping

Sublime tastes of Brittany—salted butter caramels, fruity sorbets, rare honeys, and heirloom breads—are sold in upper Cancale at the Roellingers' **Grain de Vanille** (⊠ 12 pl. de la Victoire ☎ 02–23–15–12–70). Tables beckon so why not sit a spell and enjoy a cup of "Mariage" tea and—Brittany in a bite—some cinnamon-orange-flavor *malouine* cookies?

St-Malo

❽   *23 km (14 mi) west of Cancale via coastal D201.*

Fodor'sChoice
★

Thrust out into the sea, bound to the mainland only by tenuous manmade causeways, romantic St-Malo—"the pirates' city"—has built a reputation as a breeding ground for phenomenal sailors. Many were fishermen, but St-Malo's most famous sea dogs were corsairs, pirates paid by the French crown to harass the Limeys across the Channel. Robert Surcouf and Duguay-Trouin were just two of these privateers who helped make this town rich through piratical pillages. Facing Dinard across the Rance Estuary, the stone ramparts of St-Malo have withstood the pounding of the Atlantic since the 12th century, the founding date of the town's main church, the **Cathédrale St-Vincent** (on rue St-Benoît). The ramparts were considerably enlarged and modified in the 18th century and now extend from the castle for more than 1½ km (1 mi) around the Vieille Ville—known as *intra-muros* (within the walls). The views are stupendous, especially at high tide. The town itself has proved less resistant: a weeklong fire in 1944, kindled by retreating Nazis, wiped out nearly all the old buildings. Restoration work was more painstaking than brilliant, but the narrow streets and granite houses of the Vieille Ville were satisfactorily re-created, enabling St-Malo to regain its role as a busy fishing port, seaside resort, and tourist destination. The ramparts themselves are authentic and the flames also spared houses along the Vieille Ville's rue de Pelicot. Battalions of tourists invade this quaint part of town in summer, so if you want to avoid crowds, don't come then.

At the edge of the ramparts is the 15th-century **château**, whose great keep and watchtowers command an impressive view of the harbor and coastline. It houses the **Musée d'Histoire de la Ville** (Town History Museum), devoted to local history, and the **Galerie Quic-en-Grogne**, a museum in a tower, where various episodes and celebrities from St-Malo's past are recalled by way of waxworks. ⊠ *Hôtel de Ville* ☎ *02–99–40–71–57* ⊡ *€4.60* ⊗ *Tues.–Sun. 10–noon and 2–6.*

Five hundred yards offshore is the **Ile du Grand Bé**, a small island housing the somber military tomb of the great Romantic writer Viscount René de Chateaubriand, who was born in St-Malo. The islet can be reached by a causeway at low tide *only*.

The "Bastille of Brittany," the **Fort National**, also offshore and accessible by causeway at low tide only, is a massive fortress with a dungeon constructed in 1689 by that military-engineering genius Sébastien de Vauban. ☎ *02–99–85–34–33* ⊡ *€4* ⊗ *June–Sept., daily; call ahead at other times* ☞ *Times of ½-hr guided tours depend on tides.*

You can pay homage to Jacques Cartier, who set sail from St-Malo in 1535 on a voyage in which he would discover the St. Lawrence River and found Québec, at his tomb in the church of **St-Vincent** (⊠ Grand-Rue). His statue looks out over the town ramparts, four blocks away, along with that of swashbuckling corsair Robert Surcouf (hero of many daring 18th-century raids on the British navy), eternally wagging an angry finger over the waves at England.

Where to Stay & Eat

$$–$$$ ✕ **Chalut.** The reputation of this small restaurant with nautical decor has grown since chef Jean-Philippe Foucat decided to emphasize fresh seafood. The succinct menus change as frequently as the catch of the day. Try the sautéed John Dory in wild-mushroom broth or the fresh lobster in lime. ⊠ *8 rue de la Corne-de-Cerf* ☎ *02–99–56–71–58* ⊟ *AE, MC, V* ⊗ *Closed Mon. No lunch Tues.*

¢–$ ✕ **Café de la Bourse.** Prawns and oysters are downed by the shovelful in this bustling brasserie in the Vieille Ville. Replete with wooden seats, ships' wheels, and posters of grizzled old sea dogs, it's hardly high design. But the large L-shape dining room makes amends with friendly service and a seafood platter for two that includes tanklike crabs flanked by an army of cockles, snails, and periwinkles. ⊠ *1 rue de Dinan* ☎ *02–99–56–47–17* ⊟ *MC, V* ⊗ *Closed Wed. Nov.–Easter.*

★ $$$ ▦ **Elizabeth.** In a 16th-century town house built into the city wall, the Elizabeth, near the Porte St-Louis, is a little gem of sophistication in touristy St-Malo. North-facing rooms are modern, while the larger, recently renovated suites are tastefully furnished in period style. ⊠ *2 rue des Cordiers, 35400* ☎ *02–99–56–24–98* ▤ *02–99–56–39–24* ⊕ *www.st-malo-hotel-elizabeth.com* ⇥ *17 rooms* ⚬ *Some pets allowed (fee); no a/c* ⊟ *AE, DC, MC, V* ⎟◉⎟ *BP.*

$$ 🏨 **Bleu Marine-Atlantis.** The view of the sea is magnificent from the hotel's bar, terrace, and breakfast room. Rooms are airy, with modern furnishings; expect to pay around €10 extra for one with a sea view. ✉ *49 chaussée du Sillon, 35400* ☎ *02–99–56–09–26* 🖷 *02–99–56–41–65* ⊕ *www.bleumarine.fr* ⇝ *55 rooms, 14 with bath* ⚒ *Minibars, cable TV, gym, sauna, bar, some pets allowed (fee); no a/c* ☰ *AE, MC, V* ⅠOⅠ *BP.*

Nightlife & the Arts
Bar de l'Univers (✉ 12 pl. Chateaubriand) is a nice spot to enjoy sipping a drink in a pirate's-lair setting. **La Belle Époque** (✉ 11 rue de Dinan) is a popular hangout for all ages 'til the wee hours. **L'Escalier** (✉ La Buzardière, rue de la Tour-du-Bonheur) is the place for dancing the night away. In summer, performances are held at the **Théâtre Chateaubriand** (✉ 6 rue Groult-de-St-Georges ☎ 02–99–40–98–05). Bastille Day (July 14) sees the **Fête du Clos Poulet,** a town festival with traditional dancing. July and August bring a month-long religious music festival, the **Festival de la Musique Sacrée.**

Shopping
A lively outdoor **market** is held in the streets of Old St-Malo every Tuesday and Friday.

Dinard

❾ *13 km (8 mi) west of St-Malo via Rance Bridge.*

FodorśChoice
★

Dinard is the most elegant resort town on this stretch of the Brittany coast. Its picture-book perch on the Rance Estuary opposite the walled town of St-Malo lured the English aristocracy here in droves toward the end of the 19th century. What started out as a small fishing port soon became a seaside mecca of lavish Belle Epoque villas (more than 400 still dot the town and shoreline), grand hotels, and a bustling casino. A number of modern establishments punctuate the landscape, but the town still retains something of an Edwardian tone. To make the most of Dinard's beauty, head down to the Pointe de la Vicomté, at the town's southern tip, where the cliffs offer panoramic views across the Baie du Prieuré and Rance Estuary, or stroll along the narrow promenade.

The **Promenade Clair de Lune** hugs the seacoast on its way toward the English Channel and passes in front of the small jetty used by boats crossing to St-Malo. It really hits its stride as it rounds the **Pointe du Moulinet** and heads toward the sandy **Plage du Prieuré,** named after a priory that once stood here. River meets sea in a foaming mass of rock-pounding surf: use caution as you walk along the slippery path to the calm shelter of the **Plage de l'Écluse,** an inviting sandy beach bordered by the casino and numerous stylish hotels. The coastal path picks up on the west side of Plage de l'Écluse, ringing the Pointe de la Malouine and the Pointe des Étêtés before arriving at the **Plage de St-Énogat.**

☾ The 24 pools and aquariums at the **Musée de la Mer** (Marine Museum) contain almost every known species of Breton sea creature, and stuffed local birds are also on display. One room is devoted to the polar expeditions of explorer Jean Charcot, one of the first men to chart the

Antarctic. ⊠ *17 av. George-V* ☎ *02–99–46–13–90* ⊡ *€2.50* ⊙ *Mid-May–mid-Sept., daily 10:30–12:30 and 3:30–7:30.*

Where to Stay & Eat

$$–$$$ ✕ **La Salle à Manger.** Formerly of Paris's legendary Tour d'Argent, Chef Yannick Lalande serves up inventive Provençal cuisine, broadening its traditional olive oil–tomato-base repertoire to include balsamic vinegar reductions, sesame oil, even wasabi. The seasonal menu emphasizes market-fresh produce and, of course, local seafood. Chef Lalande also came up with the restaurant's home-sweet-home decor: lots of wood, forged iron, a cozy palette of Provençal red, orange, and yellow, and a fireplace. ⊠ *25 bd. Féart* ☎ *02–99–16–07–95* ▤ *MC, V* ⊙ *Mid-Oct.–Mid-March, Mon., and Sun. dinner.*

$–$$ ✕▦ **Printania.** This white-walled, family-run hotel is on the Clair de Lune Promenade. Rooms have regional furnishings and pictures of local scenes; the best ones have a balcony and sea view (ask for Room 101, 102, 211, or 311). Seafood and regional dishes are served in the paneled dining room. ⊠ *5 av. George-V, 35800* ☎ *02–99–46–13–07* ▦ *02–99–46–26–32* ⊕ *www.printaniahotel.com* ⇝ *56 rooms* ☾ *Restaurant, bar; no a/c* ▤ *AE, MC, V* ⊙ *Closed mid-Nov.–mid-Mar.* ⦿| *FAP.*

★ $$$–$$$$ ▦ **Villa Reine-Hortense.** All the aesthetical Napoléon-Trois glamor of 19th-century resort France is yours when you stay here at this "follie"—a villa built by the Russian Prince Vlassov in homage to his "queen," Hortense de Beauharnais (daughter of Napoléon's beloved Joséphine and mother to Emperor Napoléan III). A magical grand salon topped with a trompe l'oeil treillage, guest rooms with soaring, fairy-tale beds crowned with Empire-style canopies, and glamorous beach views are just some of the delights on tap here. The lucky guest who lands room No. 4 will even get to bathe in Queen Hortense's own silver-plated bathtub. ⊠ *19 rue de la Malouine, 35800* ☎ *02–99–46–54–31* ▦ *02–99–88–15–88* ⊕ *www.villa-reine-hortense.com* ⇝ *8 rooms* ☾ *Bar; no a/c* ▤ *AE, MC, V* ⦿| *EP.*

Nightlife

During July and August, stretches of the **Clair de Lune** promenade become a nighttime, *son-et-lumière* wonderland, thanks to spotlights and recorded music. The main nightlife activity in town is at the **casino** (⊠ 4 bd. du Président-Wilson ☎ 02–99–16–30–30).

Sports & the Outdoors

For windsurfing, wander over to the **Wishbone Club** (⊠ Digue de l'Écluse ☎ 02–99–88–15–20). Boats can be rented from the **Yacht Club** (⊠ Promenade Clair de Lune ☎ 02–99–46–14–32).

Paimpol

❿ *92 km (57 mi) west of Cap Fréhel via D786, 45 km (28 mi) northwest of St-Brieuc.*

Paimpol is one of the liveliest fishing ports in the area and a good base for exploring this part of the coast. The town is a maze of narrow streets lined with shops, restaurants, and souvenir boutiques. The harbor, where fishermen used to unload their catch from far-off seas, is its main focal point; today most fish are caught in the Channel. From the sharp cliffs you can see the coast's famous pink-granite rocks. For centuries, but no longer, Breton fishermen sailed to Newfoundland each spring to harvest cod—a long and perilous journey. The **Fête des Terres-Neuvas** is a celebration of the traditional return from Newfoundland of the Breton fishing fleets; it is held on the third Sunday in July.

Where to Stay

★ **$–$$** ⊞ **Repaire de Kerroc'h.** Built in the late 18th century by Corouge Kersau—one of the region's most notorious privateers—this delightful quayside hotel overlooks the harbor and yacht marina. Beyond elegant sash windows lie stone walls, fireplaces, a Neoclassical dining nook, while upstairs the spacious guest rooms use their artfully odd angles to best advantage. Most are decorated in an English style with flowered chintzes and wood accents; a favorite, Les Sept Isles, faces the street and has a view of the boats, while the Iles des Gizans double suite (with two bathrooms) is perfect for a large party traveling together. ⊠ *29 quai Morand, 22500* ☎ *02–96–20–50–13* 🖷 *02–96–22–07–46* 📶 *12 rooms, 1 duplex* ⅃ *No a/c* ⊟ *MC, V* ⑪ *MAP.*

Trébeurden

🕕 *46 km (27 mi) west of Paimpol via D786 and D65, 9 km (6 mi) north-*
Fodor'sChoice *west of Lannion.*
★

A small, pleasant fishing village that is now a summer resort town, Trébeurden makes a good base for exploring the pink-granite cliffs of the Corniche Bretonne, starting with the rocky point at nearby Le Castel. Take a look at the profile of the dramatic rocks off the coast near Trégastel and Perros-Guirec and use your imagination to see La Tête de Mort (Death's Head), La Tortoise, Le Sentinel, and Le Chapeau de Wellington (Wellington's Hat). The scene changes with the sunlight and the sweep and retreat of the tide, whose caprices can strand fishing boats among islands that were, only hours before, hidden beneath the sea. The famous footpath, the **Sentier des Douaniers,** starts up at the west end of the Trestraou beach in the town of Perros-Guirec, 3 km (2 mi) east of Trébeurden; from there it is a two-hour walk through fern forests and past cliffs and pink granite boulders to the pretty beach at Ploumanac'h. On a hillside perch above Ploumanac'h is the village of La Clarté, home to the little Chapelle Notre Dame de la Clarté (pl. de la Chapelle), built of local pink granite and decorated with 14 stations of the cross painted by the master of the Pont-Aven school, Maurice Denis. During the **Pardon of la Clarté** (August 15), a bishop preaches an outdoor mass for the Virgin Mary, village girls wear Trégor costumes, and the statue of the Virgin Mary wears a gold crown (she wears a fake one for the rest of the year).

Five kilometers (3 mi) east of Trébeurden is **Cosmopolis,** home to the Radôme: a giant white radar dome whose 340-ton antenna captured the first live TV satellite transmission from the U.S. to France in July 1962. Today the sphere houses one of Europe's largest planetariums, a museum retracing the history of telecommunications back to the first telegraph in 1792, and spectacular laser shows that employ 200 projectors to bring the history of satellite communication to life. ✉ *Pleumeur-Bodou* ☎ *02–96–46–63–80* ⊕ *www.telecom.museum* ✈ *€7* ☉ *Apr. and Sept., weekdays 11–6, weekends 2–6; May–June, daily 11–6; July and Aug., daily 11–7.*

Where to Stay & Eat

★ **$$$–$$$$** ✕▦ **Manoir de Lan-Kerellec.** The beauty of the Breton coastline is embraced by this Relais & Châteaux hotel, where guest rooms are far more than just comfortable. Set long and cruiseliner-low, this renovated 19th-century Breton manor house has now been outfitted with dramatic windows—plate-glass, round, panoramic—so as to frame stirring vistas of the endless sea and the cliffs of the Côte de Granit Rose. The restaurant, whose circular dining room has a delightful model of the *St-Yves* ship suspended from its ceiling, mostly serves seafood, but the roast lamb is also good; it does not serve lunch Tuesday and is closed Monday off-season. ✉ *11 allée Centrale, 22560* ☎ *02–96–15–47–47* ☎ *02–96–23–66–88* ➱ *18 rooms* ⚘ *Restaurant, cable TV, tennis court, Internet, some pets allowed (fee); no a/c* ▭ *AE, DC, MC, V* ☉ *Closed mid-Nov.–mid-Mar.* ❧ *MAP.*

Morlaix

⑫ *45 km (28 mi) southwest of Trébeurden via D65 and D786, 56 km (35 mi) northeast of Brest.*

An unforgettable sight is the 19th-century stone railroad viaduct of Morlaix (pronounced mor-*lay*). At 300 yards long and 200 feet high, it spans the entire town. The Vieille Ville's attractive mix of half-timber houses and shops deserves unhurried exploration. At its commercial heart is the pedestrian Grand'Rue, lined with quaint 15th-century houses. Look for the 16th-century, three-story Maison de la Reine Anne (Queen Anne House) on the adjacent rue du Mur—it's adorned with statuettes of saints. The town's museum, known as the **Musée des Jacobins** because it's in a former Jacobin church (note the early 15th-century rose window at one end), is just off rue d'Aiguillon, parallel to Grand'Rue; it has an eclectic collection ranging from religious statues to archaeological finds and modern paintings. ✉ *Pl. des Jacobins* ☎ *02–98–88–68–88* ✈ *€4* ☉ *Apr.–Oct., daily 10–12:30 and 2–6:30; Nov.–Mar., Mon. and Wed.–Fri. 10–noon and 2–5, Sat. 2–5.*

Beer at the **Brasserie des Deux Rivières** (Two Rivers Brewery—named for the two rivers, the Jarlo and the Queffleuth, that flow through Morlaix) is brewed according to traditional English methods. You complete your visit to the brewery—whose long, narrow building was originally a rope factory—with a glass of dark, cask-conditioned *Coreff* ale. ✉ *1 pl. de la Madeleine* ☎ *02–98–63–41–92* ✈ *Free* ☉ *July and Aug., tours weekdays 11 and 2. Call ahead at other times.*

Where to Stay & Eat

¢ ✕ **Tempo.** This relaxed, bustling brasserie by the marina on the northwest of town offers a good choice of quiches, salads and *plats du jour* in a glitzy modern decor. The outdoor terrace offers a front-row view

of the boats. ✉ *Bassin à Flot, Cours Beaumont* ☏ *02–98–63–29–11*
🖃 *MC, V* ✷ *Closed Sun. No lunch Sat.*

$–$$ 🏨 **L' Europe.** Rooms are spacious at this smartly renovated, centrally lo-
cated hotel. It has been in existence since 1800, although the building
itself is older, with some fine 17th-century wood paneling in the lobby
and stairwell; previous guests range from the Queen of Portugal to
General de Gaulle. ✉ *1 rue d'Aiguillon, 29600* ☏ *02–98–62–11–99*
🖨 *02–98–88–83–38* ↩ *60 rooms, 49 with bath* ⚬ *Cable TV, Internet,
some pets allowed (fee); no a/c* ✷ *Closed Christmas week* 🖃 *AE, DC,
MC, V* ❍▮ *BP.*

THE ATLANTIC COAST

What Brittany offers in the way of the sea handsomely makes up for its
shortage of mountain peaks and passes. Its hundreds of miles of saw-
tooth coastline reveal the Atlantic Ocean in its every mood and form—
from the peaceful cove where waders poke about hunting seashells to
the treacherous bay whose waters swirl over quicksands in unpredictable crosscurrents; from the majestic serenity of the breakers rolling
across La Baule's miles of golden-sand beaches to the savage fury of the
gigantic waves that fling their force against jagged rocks 340 dizzy feet
below the cliffs of Pointe du Raz. Brittany's Atlantic coast runs southeast from the down-to-earth port of Brest to the tony city of Nantes, at
the mouth of the Loire River. The wild, rugged creeks around the little-
visited northwestern tip of Finistère (Land's End) gradually give way to
sandy beaches south of Concarneau. Inland, the bent trees and craggy
rocks look like they've been bewitched by Merlin in a bad mood.

Brest

❸ *56 km (35 mi) southwest of Morlaix, 240 km (150 mi) west of Rennes.*

Brest's enormous, sheltered bay is strategically positioned close to the
Atlantic and the English Channel. You need not spend much time here:
World War II left the city in ruins. Postwar reconstruction, resulting in
long, straight streets of reinforced concrete, has given latter-day Brest
the unenviable reputation of being one of France's drabbest cities. Its
waterfront, however, offers dramatic views across the bay toward the
Plougastel Peninsula, and is worth visiting for its handful of old buildings, its castle, and the **Monument Américain,** a pink-granite tower commemorating the American troops who landed here in 1917. The Pont
de Recouvrance, which crosses the Penfeld River, is Europe's longest drawbridge at 95 yards. Boats leave from the Port du Commerce for the islands of Ouessant and Molène.

Begin your visit at one of the town's oldest monuments, the **Tour de la
Motte-Tanguy,** next to the bridge. This bulky, round 14th-century tower,
once used as a lookout post, contains a museum of local history with
scale models of scenes of the Brest of yore. ✉ *Square Pierre-Péron*
☏ *02–98–00–88–60* 🎟 *Free* ✷ *Oct.–May, Wed.–Sun. 2–6; June–Sept.,
daily 10–noon and 2–7.*

The medieval **château** across the bridge from the Tour Tanguy houses the **Musée de la Marine** (Naval Museum), containing boat models, sculpture, pictures, and naval instruments. One section is devoted to the castle's 700-year history. The dungeons can also be visited. ☎ 02–98–22–12–39 ⊕ *www.musee-marine.fr* ☒ €4.60 ☉ *Apr.–Sept., daily 10–6:30; Oct.–Mar., Wed.–Mon. 10–noon and 2–6.*

French, Flemish, and Italian paintings from the 17th to the 20th centuries and the regional Pont-Aven Postimpressionist school make up the collection at the **Musée des Beaux-Arts** (Fine Arts Museum). ☒ *24 rue Traverse* ☎ 02–98–00–87–96 ☒ €4 ☉ *Mon. and Wed.–Sat. 10–11:45 and 2–6, Sun. 2–6.*

The fauna and flora of the world's three ocean climates—temperate, polar, and tropical—are the themes of the exhibits at **Océanopolis,** one of the largest marine complexes in Europe, complete with a battery of pools and aquariums. Arrive at the park as early as you can, as it takes an entire day to do it justice. ☒ *Rue Alain-Colas* ☎ 02–98–34–40–40 ⊕ *www. oceanopolis.com* ☒ €13.50 ☉ *Apr.–mid-Sept., daily 9–7; mid-Sept.–Dec., Feb., and Mar., Tues.–Sun. 10–5.*

off the
beaten
path

LE FOLGOËT – In early September pilgrims come from afar to Le Folgoët, 24 km (15 mi) northeast of Brest, to attend the ceremonial religious procession known as the **pardon** and to drink from the Fontaine de Salaün, a fountain behind the church, whose water comes from a spring beneath the altar. The splendid church, known as the Basilique, has a sturdy north tower that serves as a beacon for miles around and, inside, a rare, intricately carved granite rood screen separating the choir and nave.

Where to Eat

$–$$$ ✕ **Maison de l'Océan.** This giant split-level brasserie by the waterfront mirrors the city of Brest: all earnest bustle with no frills. It serves the freshest seafood, or as they say here, the *top du top.* Try the delicious catch of the day or one of the traditional seafood platters. In the finest French tradition, the service remains hectically unflappable. ☒ *2 quai de la Douane* ☎ 02–98–80–44–84 ⌛ *Reservations essential* ☐ *MC, V.*

Ste-Anne-la-Palud

⑭ *68 km (42 mi) south of Brest via N165, D887, D7, D61.*

Fodor'sChoice
★

One of the great attractions of the Brittany calendar is the celebration of a religious festival known as a village *pardon,* replete with banners, saintly statues, a parade, bishops in attendance, women in folk costume, a feast, and hundred of attendees. The seaside village of Ste-Anne-la-Palud has one of the finest and most authentic age-old pardons in Brittany, held on the last Sunday in August.

Where to Stay & Eat

$$$–$$$$ ✕☐ **Hotel de la Plage.** This former private house sits nestled in a cove on a quiet strip of sandy beach around the bay—a remote retreat perfect for long, restorative walks. Some of the comfortably furnished

rooms face the sea. The hotel, however, has less of a feeling of Brittany than you might want. Alain Leduc's food is consistently good, especially the seafood dishes; reservations are essential, and a jacket is required. ⊠ *29550 Ste-Anne-la-Palud* ☎ *02–98–92–50–12* 🖷 *02–98–92–56–54* ⊕ *www.relaischateaux.com/laplage* ⤳ *26 rooms, 4 suites* 🛆 *Restaurant, minibars, cable TV, tennis court, pool, sauna, beach, Internet, some pets allowed (fee)* ▤ *AE, DC, MC, V* ⊗ *Closed Nov.–Apr.* ⏺⏺ *MAP.*

Douarnenez

⓯ *14 km (8 mi) south of Ste-Anne-la-Palud.*

Douarnenez is a quaint old fishing town of quayside paths and zigzagging narrow streets. Boats come in from the Atlantic to unload their catches of mackerel, sardines, and tuna. Just offshore is the Ile Tristan, accessible on foot at low tide (guided tours only, €5.50), and across the Port-Rhu channel is Tréboul, a seaside resort town favored by French families.

Ċ One of the three town harbors is fitted out with a unique **Port-Musée** (Port Museum). Along the wharves you can visit the workshops of boatwrights, sail makers, and other old-time craftspeople, then go aboard the historic trawlers, lobster boats, Thames barges, and a former lightship anchored alongside. On the first weekend in May you can sail on an antique fishing boat. ⊠ *Place de l'Enfer* ☎ *02–98–92–65–20* 🖾 *€3.20* ⊗ *June–Sept., daily 10–7; Oct., Apr., and May, Tues.–Sun. 10–12:30 and 2–6.*

Where to Stay & Eat

★ $$ ✕⏹ **Manoir de Moëllien.** Surrounded by extensive forested grounds, this textbook 17th-century stone Breton manor house, landmarked by a sturdy tower, and filled with precious antiques, makes an enviable choice. Another plus is the fine restaurant, famous for its local seafood dishes. Sample Bruno Garet's *terrine de poisson chaud* (warm seafood terrine) or the *duo de truites de mer* (poached sea trout). Rooms have terraces overlooking the garden, which makes for a peaceful country atmosphere. ⊠ *12 km (7 mi) northeast of Douarnenez, 29550 Plonévez-Porzay* ☎ *02–98–92–50–40* 🖷 *02–98–92–55–21* ⤳ *18 rooms* 🛆 *Restaurant, some minibars, cable TV, bar, Internet, some pets allowed (fee); no a/c* ▤ *AE, DC, MC, V* ⊗ *Closed mid-Nov.–mid-Mar.* ⏺⏺ *FAP.*

★ $$ ✕⏹ **Ty Mad.** In the 1920s artists and writers such as Picasso and Breton native Max Jacob frequented this small hotel in a quiet residential area near the beach in Tréboul. Rooms are not large, but the sea views are great. Michel Touchard's fishy menu, served in the glass-enclosed restaurant, includes skate pâté with mint sauce and monkfish flambéed with tarragon. ⊠ *Plage St-Jean, 29100* ☎ *02–98–74–00–53* 🖷 *02–98–74–15–16* ⤳ *19 rooms, 5 with bath, 14 with shower* 🛆 *Restaurant, bar, some pets allowed; no a/c, no room TVs* ▤ *MC, V* ⊗ *Closed Oct.–Easter* ⏺⏺ *MAP.*

Quimper

⓰ *22 km (14 mi) southeast of Douarnenez via D765.*

A traditional crowd-puller, the twisting streets and tottering medieval houses of Quimper furnish rich postcard material, but lovers of decorative arts head here because this is the home of Quimperware, one of the more famous variants of French hand-painted earthenware pottery. The techniques were brought to Quimper by Normands in the 17th century, but the Quimperois customized them by painting typical local Breton scenes on the pottery. This lively and commercial town began life as the ancient capital of the Cornouaille province, founded, it is said, by King Gradlon 1,500 years ago. Quimper (pronounced cam-*pair*) owes its strange name to its site at the confluence (*kemper* in Breton) of the Odet and Steir rivers. Stroll along the banks of the Odet and through the **Vieille Ville,** with its cathedral. Then walk along the lively shopping street, rue Kéréon, and down narrow medieval rue du Guéodet (note the house with caryatids), rue St-Mathieu, and rue du Sallé.

The **Cathédrale St-Corentin** (⊠ Pl. St-Corentin) is a masterpiece of Gothic architecture and the second-largest cathedral in Brittany (after Dol-de-Bretagne's). Legendary King Gradlon is represented on horseback just below the base of the spires, harmonious mid-19th-century additions to the medieval ensemble. The church interior remains very much in use by fervent quimperois, giving the candlelit vaults a meditative air. The 15th-century stained glass is luminous. Behind the cathedral is the stately **Jardin de l'Évêché** (Bishop's Garden).

More than 400 works by such masters as Rubens, Corot, and Picasso mingle with pretty landscapes from the local Gauguin-inspired Pont-Aven school in the **Musée des Beaux-Arts** (Fine Arts Museum), next to the cathedral. Of particular note is a fascinating series of paintings depicting traditional life in Breton villages. ⊠ *40 pl. St-Corentin* ☏ *02–98–95–45–20* ⊡ *€4* ☉ *July and Aug., daily 9–7; Sept.–June, Wed.–Mon. 10–noon and 2–6.*

In the mid-18th century Quimper sprang to nationwide attention as a pottery manufacturing center, when it began producing second-rate imitations of Rouen faïence, or ceramics with blue motifs. Today's more colorful designs, based on floral arrangements and marine fauna, are still often hand-painted. To understand Quimper's pottery past with the help of more than 500 examples of "style Quimper," take one of the guided tours at the **Musée de la Faïence** (Earthenware Museum). ⊠ *14 rue Jean-Baptiste-Bousquet* ☏ *02–98–90–12–72* ⊡ *€4* ☉ *Mid-Apr.–mid-Oct., Mon.–Sat. 10–6.*

Local furniture, ceramics, and folklore top the bill at the **Musée Départemental Breton** (Brittany Regional Museum). ⊠ *1 rue du Roi-Gradlon* ☏ *02–98–95–21–60* ⊡ *€4* ☉ *June–Sept., daily 9–6; Oct.–May, Tues.–Sun. 9–noon and 2–5.*

Where to Eat

$$$ ✕ **L'Ambroisie.** This cozy little restaurant has soft-yellow walls, huge contemporary paintings, and different settings at every table. Chef Gilbert Guyon's traditional yet nouvelle menu is seasonal; local products are chosen by hand. Try the buckwheat *galette* crepe stuffed with lobster or the pigeon roasted in apple liqueur with whipped potatoes and mushrooms. The homemade desserts, like the *omelette norvégienne* with warm chocolate and nougat ice cream in meringue, are delicious. ⊠ *49* *rue Élie-Fréron* ☎ *02–98–95–00–02* ⚑ *Reservations essential* ☰ *AE, MC, V* ☺ *Closed Mon. and early July, 2 wks in Feb. No dinner Sun.*

Nightlife & the Arts

In late July Quimper hosts the **Festival de Cornouaille** (☎02–98–55–53–53), a nine-day Celtic extravaganza. More than 250 artists, dancers, and musicians fill streets already packed with the 4,000 people who come each year to enjoy the traditional street fair.

Shopping

Keep an eye out for such typical Breton products as woven and embroidered cloth, woolen goods, brass and wood objects, puppets, dolls, and locally designed jewelry. When it comes to distinctive Breton folk costumes, Quimper is the best place to look. The streets around the cathedral, especially **rue du Parc**, are full of shops selling woolen goods (notably thick marine sweaters). Faïence and a wide selection of hand-painted pottery can be purchased at the **Faïencerie d'Art Breton** (⊠ 16 bis rue du Parc ☎ 02–98–95–34–13).

Concarneau

⓱ *22 km (14 mi) southeast of Quimper via D783.*

Concarneau is the third-largest fishing port in France. A busy industrial town, it has a grain of charm and an abundance of tacky souvenir shops. But it is worth visiting to see the fortified islet in the middle of the harbor. The **Ville Close**, which was regarded as impregnable from early medieval times on, is entered by way of a quaint drawbridge. The fortifications were further strengthened by the English under John de Montfort during the War of Succession (1341–64). Three hundred years later Sébastien de Vauban remodeled the ramparts into what you see today: 1 km (½ mi) long, with splendid views across the two harbors on either side. Held here during the second half of August is the **Fête des Filets Bleus** (Blue Net Festival), a weeklong folk celebration in which Bretons in costume swirl and dance to the wail of bagpipes. ⊠ *Ramparts* €1 ☺ *Easter–Sept., daily 10–7:30; Oct.–Easter, daily 10–noon and 2–5.*

The **Musée de la Pêche** (Fishing Museum), close to the island gateway, has aquariums and exhibits on fishing techniques from around the world. ⊠ *3 rue Vauban* ☎ *02–98–97–10–20* ⊠ *€6* ☺ *July–Aug., daily 9:30–7:30; Sept.–June, daily 10–noon and 2–6.*

Where to Eat

$$ ✕ Chez Armande. Rather than opting for one of the various tourist haunts in the Ville Clos, you might like to wander 300 yards down the waterfront for an excellent fish or seafood meal at Chez Armande. Specialties include *pot-au-feu de la mer au gingembre* (seafood in a clear ginger broth), *St-Pierre à la fricassée de champignons* (John Dory with fried mushrooms), and *homard rôti en beurre de corail* (roast lobster in coral butter). Try the *tarte de grand-mère aux pommes* (grandma's homemade apple pie) for dessert. ⊠ *15 bis av. du Dr-Nicolas* ☎ *02–98–97–00–76* ☰ *AE, MC, V* ☺ *Closed Tues. and Wed., mid-Dec.–early Jan., and 2 wks in Feb.*

Pont-Aven

⑱ *15 km (9 mi) east of Concarneau via D783.*

Long beloved by artists, this lovely village sits astride the Aven river as it descends from the Montagnes Noire to the sea, turning the town's windmills along the way (there were once 14; now just a handful remain). Surrounded by one of Brittany's most beautiful stretches of countryside, Pont-Aven is a former artists' colony where, most famously, Paul Gauguin lived before he headed off to the South Seas. Wanting to break with traditional Western culture and values, in 1888 the lawyer-turned-painter headed to Brittany, a destination almost as foreign to Parisians as Tahiti. Economy was another lure: the Paris stock market had just crashed and, with it, Gauguin's livelihood, so cheap lodgings were also at the top of his list. Before long, Gauguin took to wearing Breton sweaters, berets, and wooden clogs; in his art he began to leave dewy, sunlit Impressionism behind for a stronger, more linear style. The town museum captures some of the history of the Pont-Aven School, whose adherents painted Breton landscapes in a bold yet dreamy style called Syntheticism.

One glance at the **Bois d'Amour** forest, set just to the north of town (from the tourist office, go left and walk along the river for five minutes), will make you realize why artists continue to come here. Past some meadows, you'll find Gauguin's inspiration for his famous painting *The Yellow Christ*—a wooden crucifix inside the secluded **Chapelle de Trémalo** (usually open, per private owners, from 9 to 7) just outside the Bois d'Amour woods. While in Brittany, Gauguin painted many of his earliest masterpieces, now given pride of place in great museums around the world. The **Musée Municipal** (Town Museum) has a photography exhibition documenting the Pont-Aven School, and works by its participants, such as Paul Sérusier, Maurice Denis, and Emile Bernard. After Gauguin departed for Tahiti, a group of Americans came here to paint, attracted by the light, the landscape, and the reputation. If the spirit of Gauguin and his hangers-on inspires you, the Maison de la Presse, right next to the bridge at 5 place Paul Gauguin, has boxes of 12 colored pencils and sketchbooks for sale. ⊠ *Pl. de l'Hôtel-de-Ville* ☎ *02–98–06–14–43* ✐ €4 ☉ *July and Aug., daily 9:30–7:30; Feb.–June and Sept.–Dec., daily 10–12:30 and 2–6.*

The crêperies and pizzerias that surround **place de l'Hôtel-de-Ville** cater to the lazy visitor, just emerging from the tourist office at No. 5 (☎ 02–98–06–04–70); note the office's helpful list of chambres d'hôte accommodations offered by the residents in town. Instead, walk the few paces to **Le Moulin du Grand Poulguin** (⊠ 2 quai Théodore-Botrel ☎ 02–98–06–02–67), which provides a delightful setting in which to eat your crepe on a terrace directly on the flowing waters of the Aven River in view of the footbridge. Those of you with a sweet tooth can just fill up on the buttery Traou Mad cookies at the **Biscuiterie** (⊠ 10 pl. Gauguin ☎ 02–98–06–01–94); they're baked with the local wheat of the last running windmill in Pont-Aven. After exploring the village, cool off (in summer) with a boat trip down the estuary.

CloseUp
GAUGUIN & THE PONT-AVEN SCHOOL

SURROUNDED BY ONE OF BRITTANY'S most beautiful countrysides, Pont-Aven was a natural to become a "cité des artistes" in the heady days of Impressionism and Postimpressionism. It was actually the introduction of the railroad in the 19th century that put travel to Brittany in vogue, and it was here that Gauguin and other like-minded artists founded the noted Pont-Aven school. Inspired by the vibrant colors and lovely vistas to be found here, they created "synthétisme," a painting style characterized by broad patches of pure color and strong symbolism, in revolt against the dominant Impressionist school back in Paris. Gauguin arrived in the summer of 1886, happy to find a place "where you can live on nothing" (Paris's stock market had crashed and cost Gauguin his job). At Madame Gloanec's boarding house he welcomed a circle of painters to join him in his artistic quest for monumental simplicity and striking color.

Today Pont-Aven seems content to rest on its laurels. Although it's labeled a "city of artists," the galleries that line its streets display paintings that lack the unifying theme and common creative energy of the earlier works of art. The first Pont-Aven painters were American students who came here in the 1850s. The only one to gain recognition, Charles Fromuth, has some paintings on display in the town museum. Though Gauguin is not surprisingly absent (his paintings now go for millions), except for a few of his early zincographs, the exhibit Hommage à Gauguin is an interesting sketch of his turbulent life. Also on view in the museum are works by other near-great Pont-Aven artists: Maurice Denis, Emil Bernard, Emil Jordan, and Emmanuel Sérusier.

Where to Stay & Eat

$$$–$$$$ ╳ **La Taupinière.** On the road from Concarneau, 2 mi (3 km) west of Pont-Aven, is this roadside inn with an attractive garden. Chef Guy Guilloux's open kitchen (with the large hearth he uses to grill fish, langoustine, crab, and Breton ham specialties) turns out local delicacies such as galette crepes stuffed with spider crab. Splurge without guilt on the light homemade rhubarb and strawberry compote. ⊠ *Croissant St-André* ☎ 02–98–06–03–12 ⌂ *Reservations essential* ⌂ *Jacket required* ⊟ AE, MC, V ⊙ *Closed Mon., Tues., and mid-Sept.–mid-Oct.*

★ **$$–$$$** ╳⊡ **Hostellerie Le Moulin de Rosmadec.** You'll want to set up your easel in a second once you spot this pretty-as-a-picture, 15th-century, stone water mill. Set at the end of a quiet street, the Sébilleaus' beloved hostellerie sits in the middle of the rushing, rocky Aven River. Inside, atmospheric beamed ceilings, Breton stone fireplaces, and water views (you can hear the sound of water gently splashing over the stones beneath your window) cast their spell—but who can resist dining on the "island" terrace? Outside or inside, feast on the creations of a serious kitchen: the *sautée de langoustines,* duck in cassis, or lobster *grillé Rosmadec* are all winners. Reservations are essential; the restaurant does not serve dinner Sunday from September to June. If you're very lucky, you'll snag one of the four, gently priced guest rooms available. ✉ *Pl. Paul-Gauguin, 29930* ☎ *02–98–06–00–22* 🖨 *02–98–06–18–00* ⬦ *4 rooms* ☖ *Restaurant, some pets allowed; no a/c* ⊟ *MC, V* ⊗ *Closed Wed. and 2nd half Oct.* |◎| *EP.*

$–$$ ▣ **Roz Aven.** Built into a rock face on the bank of the Aven, this efficiently run hotel has simple, clean rooms. You can choose a room in one of three locations: the16th-century thatched cottage, the modern annex, or the *maison bourgeoise* with a river or garden view. Owner Yann Souffez speaks excellent English. He describes the furnishings as Louis XVI, but some might call them petit-bourgeois. ✉ *11 quai Théodore-Botrel, 29930* ☎ *02–98–06–13–06* 🖨 *02–98–06–03–89* ⊕ *www.hotelpontaven.online.fr* ⬦ *26 rooms, 2 suites* ☖ *Some minibars, bar, some pets allowed (fee); no a/c, no TV in some rooms* ⊟ *AE, MC, V* ⊗ *Closed Nov.–Feb.* |◎| *MAP.*

Belle-Ile-en-Mer

❶⑨ *45 mins by boat from Quiberon, 52 km (32 mi) southeast of Lorient.*

Fodor'sChoice ★

At 18 km (11 mi) long, Belle-Ile is the largest of Brittany's islands. It also lives up to its name: it's indeed beautiful, and less commercialized than its mainland harbor town, Quiberon. Because of the cost and inconvenience of reserving car berths on the ferry, cross over to the island as a pedestrian and rent a car—or, if you don't mind the hilly terrain, a bicycle.

Departing from Quiberon—a spa town with pearl-like beaches on the eastern side of the 16-km-long (10-mi-long) Presqu'île de Quiberon (Quiberon Peninsula), a stretch of coastal cliffs and beaches whose dramatic western coast, the Côte Sauvage (Wild Coast), is a mix of crevices and coves lashed by the sea—the ferry lands at **Le Palais,** crushed beneath a monumental Vauban citadel built in the 1680s. From Le Palais head northwest to **Sauzon,** the prettiest fishing harbor on the island; from here you can see across to the Quiberon Peninsula and the Gulf of Morbihan. Continue on to the **Grotte de l'Apothicairerie,** which derives its name from the local cormorants' nests, said to resemble apothecary bottles. At Port Goulphar is the **Grand Phare** (Great Lighthouse). Built in 1835, it rises 275 feet above sea level and has one of the most powerful beacons in Europe, visible from 120 km (75 mi) across the Atlantic. If the keeper is available and you are feeling well rested, you may be able to climb to the top.

Where to Stay & Eat

★ **$$$$** ✕▣ **Castel Clara.** Perched on a cliff overlooking the surf and the narrow Anse de Goulphar Bay, this '70s-era hotel was FranÁois Mitterrand's address when he vacationed on Belle-Ile. The hotel still retains its presidential glamour, with its renowned spa, salt-water pool, and spectacular room views. In the bright, airy restaurant, chef Christophe Hardouin specializes in seafood, caught just offshore. The John Dory baked in sea salt and the grilled sea bream are simple but delicious. Castel Clara's expansive wooden-decked terrace is the perfect lounging spot for cocktails at sundown. ✉ *Port-Goulphar, 56360* ☎ *02–97–31–84–21* 🖨 *02–97–31–51–69* ⬦ *33 rooms, 7 suites* ☖ *Restaurant, minibars, cable*

TV, tennis court, pool, spa, Internet; no a/c ☰ *AE, DC, MC, V* ⊘ *Closed mid-Nov.–mid-Feb.* ❢❶❘ *MAP.*

Nightlife & the Arts

Every year, from the end of July to mid-August, Belle Ile hosts **Lyrique-en-mer** (☎ 02–97–31–59–59 ⊕ www.belle-ile.net), an ambitious little festival whose heart is opera (the festival was founded by the American bass baritone, Richard Cowan) but which offers up a generous lyric menu of sacred music concerts, gospel, jazz, even the occasional sea shanty and Broadway musical number. Operas and concerts are performed by rising talents from around the world at various romantic locations around the island.

The Outdoors

The ideal way to get around to the island's 90 spectacular beaches is by bike. The best place to rent two-wheelers (and cars—this is also the island's Avis outlet) is at **Roue Libre** (⊠ Rue du Pont Orgo ☎ 02–97–31–49–81).

Carnac

❷⓪
FodorsChoice
★

19 km (12 mi) northeast of Quiberon via D768/D781.

At the north end of Quiberon Bay, Carnac is known for its expansive beaches and its ancient stone monuments. Dating from around 4500 BC, Carnac's **menhirs** remain as mysterious in origin as their English contemporary, Stonehenge, although religious beliefs and astronomy were doubtless an influence. The 2,395 megalithic monuments that make up the three *alignements*—Kermario, Kerlescan, and Ménec—form the largest megalithic site in the world and are positioned with astounding astronomical accuracy in semicircles and parallel lines over about 1 km (½ mi). The site, just north of the town, is fenced off for protection, and you can examine the menhirs up close only October through March; in summer you must join a guided tour (☎ 02–97–52–29–81), some in English, costing €4. More can be learned at the **Archéoscope**, a visitor center where a 30-minute presentation involving slides, a video, and models explains the menhirs' history and significance. ⊠ *Alignements du Ménec* ☎ 02–97–52–07–49 ⊡ €6 ⊘ *Mid-Feb.–mid-Nov., daily 10–5:30, English presentations at 10:30 and 2:30.*

Carnac also has smaller-scale dolmen ensembles and three *tumuli* (mounds or barrows), including the 130-yard-long, 38-foot-high **Tumulus de St-Michel,** topped by a small chapel with views of the rock-strewn countryside. ⊡ €2 ⊘ *Easter–Oct.; guided tours of tumulus Apr.–Sept., daily 10, 11, 2, and 3:30.*

Auray

❷①

16 km (10 mi) north of Carnac via D119/D768, 38 km (24 mi) southeast of Lorient.

The ancient town of Auray grew up along the banks of the Loch River, best admired from the Promenade du Loch overlooking the quayside. Cross the river to explore the old, cobbled streets of the St-Goustan neighborhood. Tied alongside the quay, across the bridge, is the **Goélette St-Sauveur,** an old topsail schooner that once ferried coal from Wales. Today it houses a sailing museum with many unusual nautical artifacts. ⊠ *Pl. St-Sauveur* ☎ *02–97–56–63–38* ⊠ *€3* ۞ *Easter–Sept., daily 10:30–12:30 and 2:30–7.*

Where to Eat

$$$$ ✕ **La Closerie de Kerdrain.** Ebullient chef Fernando Corfmat presides over the kitchen in this large 17th-century town-center manor draped in wisteria. His seasonal menus highlight fresh ingredients prepared in innovative ways: sea bass carpaccio with fresh green beans in Parmesan, scallops with hazelnuts, or breast of pigeon roasted in black pepper. The sweet-and-sour lemon pie with a "*salade*" of oranges in mango juice is the perfect way to end the meal. ⊠ *20 rue Louis-Billet* ☎ *02–97–56–61–27* 🖷 *02–97–24–15–79* ☰ *AE, DC, MC, V* ۞ *Closed Mon. and 3 wks in Dec. No dinner Sun.*

The Outdoors

Take a cruise down the Auray River on the **Navix-Vedettes du Golfe** (☎ 02–97–56–59–47); along the way you'll discover the lovely 16th-century Château du Plessis-Kaer and the tiny, tidal fishing port of Bono tucked between the steep banks and the oyster beds of the Pô estuary.

Vannes

★ **㉒** *18 km (11 mi) east of Auray via N165, 108 km (67 mi) southwest of Rennes.*

Scene of the declaration of unity between France and Brittany in 1532, historic Vannes is one of the few towns in Brittany to have been spared damage during World War II. Be sure to saunter through the Promenade de la Garenne, a colorful park, and admire the magnificent gardens nestled beneath the adjacent ramparts. Also visit the medieval wash houses and the cathedral; browse in the small boutiques and antiques shops in the pedestrian streets around pretty place Henri-IV; check out the Cohue, the medieval market hall now used as an exhibition center; and take a boat trip around the scenic Golfe du Morbihan.

The **Cathédrale St-Pierre** boasts a 1537 Renaissance chapel, a Flamboyant Gothic transept portal, and a treasury. ⊠ *Pl. de la Cathédrale* ۞ *Treasury mid-June–mid-Sept., Mon.–Sat. 2–6.*

Where to Stay & Eat

$$$–$$$$ ✕ **Richemont.** Step off the train and right into this popular spot, a haven of refinement where seafood reigns. Chef Régis Mahé prefers a small, seasonal menu with local hand-picked produce and fish so fresh they nearly swim to the plate. For a local specialty with a twist, try the buckwheat galette crepe filled with lobster and pigeon and served with caramelized leeks. Attention chocolate lovers: save room for the warm chocolate tart with homemade salty caramel ice cream. ⊠ *24 pl. de la Gare* ☎ *02–97–42–61–41* 🖷 *02–97–54–99–01* ☰ *MC, V* ۞ *Closed Sun. and Mon.*

★ **$$$–$$$$** ✕🖭 **Domaine de Rochevilaine.** *Respirer le mer*—it sounds so much more luxurious than "Breathe the sea." At this stunning hotel, you will be able to do that exquisitely and so much more. Set on a magical *presque'île* (peninsula) called the Pen Lan point, this enchanting collection of 15th- and 16th-century Breton stone buildings resembles a tiny village; one, however, that is surrounded by terraced gardens, has a spectacular spa, and offers grand vistas of the Bay of Vilaine. Once you step through the "Portail de la Verité"—a monumental 13th-century stone entryway—the interior allures with a mix of old and new, seen most elegantly in the restaurant, where Baroque ex-votos, Louis Treize chairs, rockface fireplaces, and plate-glass windows make a suitable backdrop for the delicious creations of chef Patrice Caillaut, late of Ledoyen and Troisgros. He is noted for his *coucou de Rennes* (a tender hen roasted whole and sliced steaming at the table), while the noted Breton dessert of caramelized apples in pastry layers with cinnamon ice cream is a real treat. Delights continue in the guest rooms, asparkle with checked fabrics, veneered woods, and modern furnishings, while some have four-poster beds and private terraces. Most rooms face the ocean, so be sure to specify, especially if you want to call the 270-degree view from the Admiral's Room your own. To get your toes in the water, head to the alluring spa, the Aqua Phénica, replete with a full spectrum of seawater hydrotherapy facilities and gigantic indoor pool. ⊠ *Pointe de Pen-Lan, 30 km (19 mi) southeast of Vannes, at tip of Pointe de Pen-Lan, 56190 Billiers* ☎ *02–97–41–61–61* 🖷 *02–97–41–44–85* ⊕ *www. domainerochevilaine.com* ⇨ *34 rooms, 3 suites* △ *Restaurant, minibars, cable TV, 3 pools (2 indoors), hot tub, sauna, Internet, some pets allowed (fee); no a/c* ⊟ *AE, DC, MC, V* ¶⊙¶ *FAP.*

$ ✕⊡ **Kyriad.** Set in an old, rustic building in town, this hotel attracts a varied foreign clientele, drawn by the homey guest rooms—clean, bright, and simple, with warm yellow walls—and the friendly and efficient staff. Claude Le Lausque serves a traditional menu in the rustic Image Sainte-Anne restaurant, with straightforward seasonal specialties like crab in milo pastry, grilled sole, and fisherman's stew. No dinner is served Sunday, November through March. ⊠ *8 pl. de la Libération, 56000* ☎ *02–97–63–27–36* 🖷 *02–97–40–97–02* ⊕ *www.kyriad.com* ⇨ *33 rooms* △ *Restaurant, minibars, cable TV, Internet; no a/c in some rooms* ⊟ *AE, DC, MC, V* ¶⊙¶ *BP.*

La Baule

㉓ *72 km (45 mi) southeast of Vannes via N165 and D774.*

Star of the Côte d'Amour coast and gifted with a breathtaking 5-km (3-mi) beach, La Baule is a fashionable resort town that can make you pay dearly for your coastal frolics. Though it once rivaled Biarrtiz, today tackiness has replaced sophistication, but you still can't beat that beach, or the lovely, miles-long seafront promenade lined with hotels. Like Le Touquet and Dinard, La Baule is a 19th-century creation, founded in 1879 to make the most of the excellent sandy beaches that extend around the broad, sheltered bay between Pornichet and Le Pouliguen. A pine forest, planted in 1840, keeps the shifting local sand dunes firmly at bay. All in all, this can offer an idyllic stay for those who will enjoy a day on the beach, an afternoon at the shops on avenue du Général-de-Gaulle and avenue Louis-Lajarrige, and an evening at the Casino.

Where to Stay & Eat

★ $ ✕ **La Ferme du Grand Clos.** At this lively restaurant in an old farmhouse, just 200 yards from the sea, you have to understand the difference between *crêpe* and *galette* to order correctly, since the menus showcase both in all their forms. Or you can opt for the simple, straightforward menu featuring food the owner likes to call *la cuisine de grand-mère* (grandmother's cooking). Come early for a table; it's a very friendly and popular place. ⊠ *52 av. du Maréchal-de-Lattre-de-Tassigny* ☎ *02–40–60–03–30* ⊟ *MC, V* ⊘ *Closed Oct. and Wed., Sept.–June.*

$$ ⌨ **Concorde.** This blue-shuttered, white-walled establishment numbers among the least expensive good hotels in pricey La Baule. It's calm, comfortable, modernized, and a short block from the beach (ask for a room with a sea view). ⊠ *1 bis av. de la Concorde, 44500* ☎ *02–40–60–23–09* 🖶 *02–40–42–72–14* ⊕ *www.hotel-la-concorde.com* ⌁ *47 rooms* ⌂ *Cable TV, Internet; no a/c* ⊟ *AE, DC, MC, V* ⊘ *Closed Oct.–mid-Apr.* ⦿ *EP.*

★ $–$$ ⌨ **Hôtel de la Plage.** One of the few hotels on the beach in St-Marc-sur-Mer, southeast of La Baule, this comfortable lodging was the setting for Jacques Tati's classic comedy *Mr. Hulot's Holiday*. It has been updated since and, *hélas,* the swinging door to the dining room is no longer there. But the view of the sea and the sound of the surf remain. The restaurant—reserve a beachfront table in advance—serves seasonal fish specialties like the *choucroute de la mer* (seafood sauerkraut stew). ⊠ *37 rue du Commandant-Charcot, 10 km (6 mi) southeast of La Baule, 44600 St-Marc-sur-Mer* ☎ *02–40–91–99–01* 🖶 *02–40–91–92–00* ⊕ *www. hotel-de-la-plage-44.com* ⌁ *30 rooms* ⌂ *Restaurant, cable TV, Internet; no a/c* ⊟ *MC, V* ⊘ *Closed Jan.* ⦿ *FAP.*

Nightlife

Occasionally you see high stakes on the tables at La Baule's **casino** (⊠ 6 av. Pierre-Loti ☎ 02–40–11–48–28).

Nantes

72 km (45 mi) east of La Baule via N171 and N165, 108 km (67 mi) south of Rennes.

The writer Stendhal remarked of 19th-century Nantes, "I hadn't taken twenty steps before I recognized a great city." Since then, the river that flowed around the upper-crust Ile Feydeau neighborhood has been filled in and replaced with a rushing torrent of traffic, and now major highways cut through the heart of town. Still, Nantes is more than the sum of its traffic jams. The 15th-century château is still in relatively good shape, despite having lost an entire tower during a gunpowder explosion in 1800. The 15th-century cathedral floats heavenward as well. Its white stones, immense height, and airy interior make it one of France's best. Across the broad boulevard, cours des 50-Otages, is the 19th-century city. The unlucky Ile Feydeau, surrounded and bisected by highways, still preserves the tottering 18th-century mansion built with wealth from Nantes's huge slave trade. The Loire River flows along the southern edge of the Vieille Ville, making Nantes officially part of the Loire region, although historically it belongs to Brittany. In town you'll see

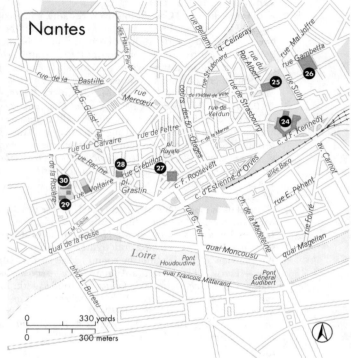

many references to Anne de Bretagne, the last independent ruler of Brittany, who married the region away to King Charles VIII of France in 1491. Bretons have never quite recovered from the shock.

Built by the dukes of Brittany, who had no doubt that Nantes belonged in their domain, the **Château des Ducs de Bretagne** is a massive, well-preserved 15th-century fortress with a moat. François II, the duke responsible for building most of it, led a hedonistic life here, surrounded by ministers, chamberlains, and an army of servants. Numerous monarchs later stayed in the castle, where in 1598 Henri IV signed the famous Edict of Nantes advocating religious tolerance. Reopened November 2003 after massive renovations, the castle interior can be visited during temporary exhibitions. ⊠ *4 pl. Marc-Elder* ☎ *02–40–41–56–56* 🔳 *€3.10* ☉ *Wed.–Sun. 10–6.*

The **Cathédrale St-Pierre–St-Paul** is one of France's last Gothic cathedrals, begun in 1434, well after most other medieval cathedrals had been completed. The facade is ponderous and austere, in contrast to the light, wide, limestone interior, whose vaults rise higher (120 feet) than those of Notre-Dame in Paris. ⊠ *Pl. St-Pierre* ☎ *02–51–88–95–47* 🔳 *Free* ☉ *Crypt Mon.–Sat. 10–12:30 and 2–6, Sun. 2–6:30.*

A fine collection of paintings from the Renaissance period onward, including works by Jacopo Tintoretto, Georges de La Tour, Jean-Auguste-Dominique Ingres, and Gustave Courbet, is at the **Musée des Beaux-Arts** (Museum of Fine Arts). ⊠ *10 rue Georges-Clemenceau* ☎ *02–40–41–65–65* ◻ *€3.10* ⊗ *Mon., Wed., and Thurs., and weekends 10–6, Fri. 10–8.*

㉖

Erected in 1843, the **Passage Pommeraye** (⊠ Rue Crébillon) is an elegant shopping gallery in the 19th-century part of town. The **Grand Théâtre** (⊠ Pl. Graslin), down the block from the Passage Pommeraye, was built in 1783.

㉗
㉘

The 15th-century **Manoir de la Touche** (⊠ Rue Voltaire) was once the abode of the bishops of Nantes. The mock-Romanesque **Musée Thomas-Dobrée** across the way was built by arts connoisseur Thomas Dobrée in the 19th century. Among the treasures within are miniatures, tapestries, medieval manuscripts, and enamels; one room is devoted to the Revolutionary War in Vendée. ⊠ *18 rue Voltaire* ☎ *02–40–71–03–50* ◻ *€3, free Sun.* ⊗ *Tues.–Fri. 9:45–5:30, weekends 2:30–5:30.*

㉙
㉚

Where to Stay & Eat

$–$$$ ✕ **La Cigale.** Miniature palm trees, gleaming woodwork, colorful enamel tiles, and painted ceilings have led to the official recognition of La Cigale brasserie (built in 1895) as a *monument historique*. You can savor its Belle Epoque blandishments without spending a fortune—the prix-fixe lunch menus are a good value. But the banks of fresh oysters and well-stacked dessert cart may tempt you to order à la carte. ⊠ *4 pl. Graslin* ☎ *02–51–84–94–94* ◿ *Reservations essential* ▤ *MC, V.*

★ $$ ✕ **Villa Mon Rêve.** This cozy, yellow-walled restaurant is in delightful parkland off the D751 east of Nantes. Chef Gérard Ryngel concocts elegantly inventive regional fare (the roast duck in caramel and Muscadet is a good choice), with which you can sample one of more than 50 varieties of Muscadet, the local white wine. Request a table on the terrace when you reserve. ⊠ *Levée Divatte, 506 bd. de la Loire, 8 km (5 mi) east of Nantes, Basse-Goulaine* ☎ *02–40–03–55–50* ⊕ *www.villa-mon-reve. com* ▤ *AE, DC, MC, V* ⊗ *Closed part of Feb. and Nov.*

$–$$ ✕ **L'Embellie.** Sweet and simple, this spot lures diners with its modern, inventive attitude and friendly service. Chef Yvonnick Briand's "creative regional" cuisine extends to his own smokehouse for salmon and duck, so the foie gras is homemade—he likes to serve it light, atop a mesclun salad. The menu is dependent on Briand's daily trips to markets, so don't hesitate to try any of the fresh fish specials, such as the sea bass steamed in rosemary or other briny delights laced with French West Indian spices. Pineapple *croquant* with rum-laced creole ice cream makes a fitting finale. ⊠ *14 rue Armand-Brossard* ☎ *02–40–48–20–02* ▤ *AE, MC, V* ⊗ *Closed Sun. and 2nd wk in Aug. No dinner Mon.*

$$ ▦ **Hotel Duchesse Anne.** Situated across from Nantes's Château des Ducs de Bretagne, this reasonably priced Art Deco hotel once played host to General Charles de Gaulle. The rooms are decorated in different styles, ranging from deco to contemporary, but all are comfortable. Some have stone balconies (overlooking the château), fireplace, and Jacuzzi. The hotel restaurant, run by chef Jean-François Corvaisier, is gastronomically conservative with emphasis, of course, on seafood. ⊠ *3 place de la Duchesse Anne, 44000* ☎ *02–51–86–78–78* 🖷 *02–40–74–60–20* ⊲ *69 rooms ⚖ Minibars, cable TV, some pets allowed (fee)* ☰ *AE, DC, MC, V* ⦾ *BP.*

Nightlife & the Arts

For live jazz, the informal **Pub Univers** (⊠ 16 rue Jean-Jacques Rousseau ☎ 02–40–73–49–55) is the spot. **Le Tie Break** (⊠ 1 rue des Petites-Écuries ☎ 02–40–47–77–00) is a popular piano bar. The **Théâtre Graslin** (⊠ 1 rue Molière ☎ 02–40–69–77–18) is Nantes's principal concert hall and opera house.

The Outdoors

You can take a 100-minute cruise along the pretty Erdre River, past a ⓒ string of gardens and châteaux, with the **Bateaux Nantais.** There are also four-course lunch and dinner cruises that last about 2½ hours (€40–€50). Call ahead to get the schedule for the special activities planned for children—treasure hunts, musical shows, or one of the Halloween dress-up cruises. ⊠ *Quai de la Motte Rouge* ☎ *02–40–14–51–14* 🖅 *€10* ⦾ *June–Aug., Mon., and Fri. at 3, weekends at 3 and 5; May, Sept., and Oct., weekends at 3.*

Shopping

The commercial quarter of Nantes stretches from place Royale to place Graslin. Various antiques shops can be found on rue Voltaire. The Devineau family has been selling wax fruit and vegetables at **Devineau** (⊠ 2 pl. Ste-Croix) since 1803; for €12, you can take home a basket of purple grapes or a cauliflower, as well as handmade candles and wildflower honey. For chocolate, head to **Gautier-Debotté** (⊠ 9 rue de la Fosse); try the local Muscadet grapes dipped in brandy and covered with chocolate.

BRITTANY A TO Z

To research prices, get advice from other travelers, and book travel arrangements, visit www.fodors.com.

AIRPORTS

Rennes, Brest, Nantes, Quimper, Dinard, and Lorient all have domestic airports. Air France (⇨ Air Travel *in* Smart Travel Tips A to Z) flies to them all, except Dinard.

BIKE TRAVEL

Bikes can be rented at most major train stations.

BUS TRAVEL

There are many bus routes linking Brittany, serviced by a bewildering number of bus companies. Buses connect the big city of Rennes (often via TIV and Cariane Atlantique Otages) with Nantes, St-Malo, Dinan (via CAT), Dinard (via CAT and TIV), Cancale (via TIV), Mont-St-Michel, Fougères, and Vitré (via TIV)—you can also bus to Mont-St-Michel from Fougères and (via Les Courriers Bretons) from St-Malo. Dinan is linked with Rennes (via TAE); Paimpol with St-Brieuc (via CAT); Morlaix with Roscoff (via Cars du Kreisker); Quimper with Brest (via CAT); Pont-

Aven with Brest, Quimper, and Concarneau (via Transports Caoudal); Vannes with Quiberon (via Cariane Atlantique); and Carnac (via Transports Le Bayon). There are many other links, so, as always, check in with the regional tourist office or information window at a big gateway rail or bus station to get printed bus schedules.

🚌 Bus Information **Cariane Atlantique** ☎ 02-97-47-29-64. **Cariane Atlantique Otages–Nantes** ☎ 02-40-20-46-99. **Cars du Kreisker** ☎ 02-98-69-00-93. **CAT** ☎ 02-96-39-21-05. **Les Courriers Bretons** ☎ 02-99-19-70-80. **TIV** ☎ 02-99-26-11-11. **Transports Caoudal** ☎ 02-98-90-88-89. **Transports Le Bayon** ☎ 02-97-24-26-20.

CAR RENTAL

🚗 Local Agencies **Avis** ☎ 08-20-05-05-05 national reservations number in Paris ✉ Pl. Rhin-et-Danube, La Baule ☎ 02-40-60-36-28 ✉ Aéroport, Dinard ☎ 02-99-46-25-20 ✉ 20 bis rue de Siam, Brest ☎ 02-98-44-63-02 ✉ Rue Lourmel, Nantes ☎ 02-40-89-25-50 ⊕ www.avis.fr. **Europcar** ✉ Pl. de la Gare, Rennes ☎ 02-23-44-02-73. **Hertz** ✉ Rte. de Trégastel, Lannion ☎ 02-96-05-82-82 ✉ 53 rue de la Gare, St-Brieuc ☎ 02-96-94-25-89.

CAR TRAVEL

Rennes, the gateway to Brittany, is 310 km (195 mi) west of Paris. It can be reached in about three hours via Le Mans and A81 and A11 (A11 continues southwest from Le Mans to Nantes). Rennes is linked by good roads to Morlaix and Brest (E50), Quimper (N24/N165), and Vannes (N24/N166). A car is a good idea if you want to see out-of-the-way places.

EMERGENCIES

🏥 Hospitals **Rennes** ✉ 2 rue Henri-Le-Guilloux, 35000 ☎ 02-99-28-43-21. **Brest** ✉ 5 av. Foch, 29200 ☎ 02-98-22-33-33. **Nantes** ✉ 1 pl. Alexis-Ricordeau, 44000 ☎ 02-40-08-33-33.

SPORTS & THE OUTDOORS

For information on various regional activities such as sailing, hiking, camping, fishing, and daily excursions, contact the Regional Tourist Boards.

🏄 **Comité Départemental du Tourisme des Côtes-d'Armor** ✉ 7 rue St-Benoît, St-Brieuc ☎ 02-96-62-72-00 🖨 02-96-33-59-10 ⊕ www.cotesdarmor.com. **Comité Départemental du Tourisme de Finistère** ✉ 11 rue Théodore-Le Hars, Quimper ☎ 02-98-76-20-70 🖨 02-98-52-19-19 ⊕ www.finisteretourisme.com.

TOURS

Information about organized tours of Brittany is available from the very helpful Maison de la Bretagne in Paris.

🚌 Fees & Schedules **Maison de la Bretagne** ✉ 203 bd. St-Germain, 75007 Paris ☎ 01-53-63-11-50 🖨 01-53-63-11-57.

TRAIN TRAVEL

The high-speed TGV (Train à Grande Vitesse) departs 15 times daily from Paris (Gare Montparnasse) for both Nantes and Rennes, making this region easily accessible. The trip to either city takes about 2¼ hours. There are 8 daily TGVs to Brest (4½ hours) and 10 regional trains to St-Malo. To find out about other regional timetables and fares or to reserve your seat, contact the SNCF Web site. Most towns in this region are accessible by train, though you need a car to get to some of the more secluded spots. Some trains from Paris stop in Vitré before forking at Rennes on their way to either Brest (via Morlaix) or Quimper (via Vannes). Change at Rennes for Dol-de-Bretagne and St-Malo; at Dol-de-Bretagne for Dinan and Dinard (bus link); at Morlaix for Roscoff; at Rosporden, 19 km (12 mi) south of Quimper, for Concarneau (bus link); and at Auray for Quiberon.

🚆 Train Information **SNCF** ☎ 08-36-35-35-35 ⊕ www.ter-sncf.com/UK/bretagne.

TRAVEL AGENCIES

🚆 Local Agent Referrals **Havas** ✉ 33 rue Jean-Macé, Brest ☎ 02-98-80-05-43 ⊕ www.havasvoyages.com ✉ 14 rue Ville-Pépin, St-Malo ☎ 02-99-19-79-90. **Carlson Wagons-lit** ✉ 1 impasse Joseph-Marie-Fourage, Nantes ☎ 02-51-89-39-00 ✉ 2 rue Jules-Simon, Rennes ☎ 08-26-82-56-20.

VISITOR INFORMATION

The principal regional tourist offices are in Brest, Nantes, and Rennes.

🚆 Tourist Information **Brest** ✉ 8 av. Georges-Clemenceau ☎ 02-98-44-24-96 🖨 02-98-44-53-73 ⊕ www.mairie-brest.fr. **Nantes** ✉ 2 allée Baco ☎ 02-51-72-95-30 🖨 02-40-20-44-54 ⊕ www.cdt44.com. **Rennes** ✉ 11 rue St-Yves ☎ 02-99-67-11-11 🖨 02-99-67-11-10 ⊕ www.ville-rennes.fr. **Carnac** ✉ 74 av. des Druides ☎ 02-97-52-13-52 🖨 02-97-52-86-10 ⊕ www.ot-carnac.fr. **Concarneau** ✉ Quai d'Aiguillon ☎ 02-98-97-01-44 🖨 02-98-50-88-81 ⊕ www.ville-concarneau.fr. **Dinan** ✉ 9 rue du Château ☎ 02-96-87-69-76 🖨 02-96-87-69-77 ⊕ www.dinan-tourisme. com. **Dinard** ✉ 2 bd. Féart ☎ 02-99-46-94-12 🖨 02-99-88-21-07 ⊕ www.ville-dinard. fr. **Dol-de-Bretagne** ✉ 3 Grande-Rue ☎ 02-99-48-15-37 ⊕ www.pays-de-dol.com. **Douarnenez** ✉ 2 rue du Dr-Mével ☎ 02-98-92-13-35 🖨 02-98-92-70-47 ⊕ www. douarnenez-tourisme.com. **La Baule** ✉ 8 pl. de la Victoire ☎ 02-40-24-34-44 🖨 02-40-11-08-10 ⊕ www.labaule.tm.fr. **Lorient** ✉ Maison de la Mer, quai de Rohan ☎ 02-97-21-07-84 🖨 02-97-21-99-44 ⊕ www.lorient-tourisme.com. **Morlaix** ✉ Pl. des Otages ☎ 02-98-62-14-94 ⊕ www.ville.morlaix.fr. **Quiberon** ✉ 14 rue de Verdun ☎ 02-97-50-07-84 🖨 02-97-30-58-22 ⊕ www.quiberon.com. **Quimper** ✉ 7 rue Déesse ☎ 02-98-53-04-05 🖨 02-98-53-31-33 ⊕ www.quimper-tourisme.com. **St-Malo** ✉ Esplanade St-Vincent ☎ 02-99-56-64-48 🖨 02-99-56-67-00 ⊕ www. saint-malo-tourisme.com. **Vannes** ✉ 1 rue Thiers ☎ 02-97-47-24-34 🖨 02-97-47-29-49 ⊕ www.mairie-vannes.fr. **Vitré** ✉ Pl. St-Yves ☎ 02-99-75-04-46 🖨 02-99-74-02-01 ⊕ www.ot-vitre.fr.

NORMANDY

5

Updated by
Simon Hewitt

Introduction by
Nancy Coons

SAY THE NAME "NORMANDY," and which Channel-side scenario comes to mind? Could it be long ships bristling with oars scudding into the darkness toward Hastings? Such ships were immortalized in the Bayeux Tapestry, which traces step-by-step the epic tale of William the Conqueror, who in 1066 sailed across the Channel to claim his right to England's throne. Or do you think of iron-gray convoys massing silently along the shore at dawn, lowering tailgates to pour troops of young Allied infantrymen into the line of German machine-gun fire? At Omaha Beach you may marvel at the odds faced by the handful of soldiers who in June 1944 were able to rise above the waterfront carnage to capture the cliff-top battery, paving the way for the Allies' reconquest of Europe.

Perhaps you think of Joan of Arc—imprisoned by the English yet burned at the Rouen stake by the Church she believed in? In a modern church you may light a candle on the very spot where, in 1431, the Maiden Warrior sizzled into history at the hands of panicky politicians and time-serving clerics: a dark deed that marked a turning point in the Hundred Years' War. Or are you reminded of the dramatic silhouette of Mont-St-Michel looming above the tidal flats, its cobbles echoing with the footfalls of medieval scholars? You may make a latter-day pilgrimage to the famous island-abbey, one of the most evocative monuments in Europe behind its crow's-nest ramparts.

The destinies of England and Normandie (as the French spell it) have been intertwined ever since William, duke of Normandy, insisted that King Edward the Confessor had promised him the succession to the English crown. When a royal council instead anointed the Anglo-Saxon Harold Godwinsson, the irate William stormed across the Channel with 7,000 well-equipped archers, well-mounted knights, and well-paid Frankish mercenaries. They landed at Pevensey Bay on September 28, 1066, and two weeks later, at Hastings, saw off a ragtag mix of battle-weary English troops hastily reinforced with peasant conscripts swinging stones tied to sticks. Harold met his maker, an arrow through his eye. William progressed to London and was crowned King of England on Christmas Day.

There followed nearly 400 years of Norman sovereignty in England. For generations England and Normandy vacillated and blurred, merged, and diverged. Today you'll still feel the strong flow of English culture over the Channel, from the Deauville horse races frequented by high-born ladies in gloves, to silver spoons mounded high with teatime cream; from the bowfront, slope-roof shops along the harbor at Honfleur to the black-and-white row houses of Rouen, which would seem just as much at home in the setting of *David Copperfield* as they would in *Madame Bovary*.

And just as in the British Isles, no matter how you concentrate on history and culture, sooner or later you'll find yourself beguiled by the countryside, by Normandy's rolling green hills dotted with dairy cows and half-timber farmhouses. Like the locals, you'll be tempted by seafood fresh off the boat, by sauces rich with crème fraîche, by cheeses

5

Named for the Norsemen who claimed this corner of Gaul and sent a famous conqueror over the Channel in 1066, and eternally tied in our memory to the D-Day landings, Normandy has always played shuttle diplomat in Anglo-French relations. From its half-timber houses to its green apple orchards to its rich dairy cream, it seems to mirror the culture of its English neighbor across the water. Treasures beckon: Mont-St-Michel, elegant Deauville, Rouen's great cathedral and museums, the legendary Bayeux Tapestry . . . and those warming glasses of calvados. With three days you can get a feel for the region. Five days gives you time to meander through the countryside and down the coast. And with nine days, if you don't spend much time in any one place, you can see most of Normandy.

Numbers in the text correspond to numbers in the margin and on the Normandy and Rouen maps.

If you have 3 days

Head straight to 🖼 **Rouen** ➎ ⌐ – ⓯ and spend a day and a half in the region's cultural capital. Then follow the Seine Valley past the abbey of **Jumièges** ⓰ and the sights of **Caudebec-en-Caux** ⓲ including the Abbaye de St-Wandrille, then head west to 🖼 **Honfleur** ㉓, the fishing port that caught the Impressionists' eyes.

If you have 9 days

Follow the Seine en route from Paris to 🖼 **Rouen** ➎ ⌐ – ⓯, visiting the gorgeous little villages of **Lyons-la-Forêt** ➋ and **Les Andelys** ➌. On the third day wind along the route des Abbayes to the abbeys of **Jumièges** ⓰ and St-Wandrille near **Caudebec-en-Caux** ⓲. Drive northwest to the fishing town of **Fécamp** ⓴, then head down the Côte d'Alabâtre to the spectacular cliffs of **Étretat** ㉑. Continue south, cross the Pont de Normandie, and spend the night in tony 🖼 **Honfleur** ㉓. On the next day travel along the Côte Fleurie to the fashionable seaside resorts of **Deauville-Trouville** ㉔ and Belle Epoque **Houlgate** ㉕, reaching 🖼 **Caen** ㉖, site of some of World War II's fiercest fighting and William the Conqueror's fortress, by mid-afternoon. The following day visit Gold, Juno, and Sword beaches and historic **Arromanches-les-Bains** ㉗, then party in 🖼 **Bayeux** ㉘ overnight. Visit the storied Bayeux Tapestry and continue your exploration of the **D-Day beaches** ㉙ – ㉜ before continuing up the Cotentin coast to 🖼 **Cherbourg** ㉞. On Day 7 ramble south to the cathedral town of **Coutances** ㊱ and on to seafaring **Granville** ㊲, then continue to the majestic abbey on a rock, 🖼 **Mont-St-Michel** ㊳. Next morning hurry east to the Suisse Normande's rocky expanse of hills, passing through Clécy before stopping for a picnic lunch at the Roche d'Oëtre, a rock with a spectacular view of the Orne Valley. If time allows, take in William the Conqueror's hilltop castle at **Falaise** ㊴.

redolent of farm and pasture. And perhaps with cheeks pink from the apple-scented country air, you'll eventually succumb to the local antidote to northern damp and chill: a mug of tangy hard cider sipped by a crackling fire, and the bracing tonic of Normandy's famous apple brandy, calvados.

Exploring Normandy

You won't want to miss medieval Rouen, seaside Honfleur, or magnificent Mont-St-Michel. But if you get away from these popular spots you can lose yourself along the cliff-lined coast and in the green spaces inland, where the closest thing to a crowd is a farmer with his herd of brown-and-white cows. From Rouen northeast to the coast—the area known as Upper Normandy—medieval castles and abbeys stand guard above rolling countryside, while resort and fishing towns line the white cliffs of the Côte d'Alabâtre. Popular seaside resorts and the D-Day landing sites occupy the sandy beaches along the Côte Fleurie; apple orchards and dairy farms sprinkle the countryside of the area known as Lower Normandy. The Cotentin Peninsula to the west juts out into the English Channel. Central Normandy encompasses the peaceful, hilly region of La Suisse Normande, along the scenic Orne River.

About the Restaurants & Hotels

With Normandy a mecca for weekending Parisians throughout the year, especially between March and November, it makes sense to book your table in advance Friday dinner through Sunday lunch. The plus side to this is that Normandy differs from other French coastal regions in that, buoyed by this Parisian clientele, few restaurants close for more than a month in winter. You can therefore expect a good choice of restaurants throughout the region at any time, most of all in the lively cities of Rouen and Caen (though July and August here are the quietest months). Note that from October through Easter Mont-St-Michel offers a limited number of options for weekday lunch, and even fewer for dinner; in summer, on the other hand, it's packed, making advance reservations—or a very early arrival—essential.

Accommodations to suit every taste can be found throughout Normandy. The beach-resort season is short—late June through early September only—but weekends are busy most of the year, and especially during school holidays. In much of June and September lodging is usually available on short notice, and good discounts are given off-season, particularly for stays of more than a single night. If you are traveling in the summer months, reserve your hotel well in advance, request a written confirmation, and inform your hotel of any possible late check-in, or they may give your room away. Assume all hotel rooms have air-conditioning, telephones, TV, and private bath, unless otherwise noted.

WHAT IT COSTS In euros					
	$$$$	$$$	$$	$	¢
RESTAURANTS	over €30	€23–€30	€17–€23	€11–€17	under €11
HOTELS	over €190	€120–€190	€80–€120	€50–€80	under €50

Restaurant prices are per person for a main course at dinner, including tax (19.6%) and service; note that if a restaurant offers only prix-fixe (set-price) meals, it has been given the price category that reflects the full prix-fixe price. Hotel prices are for a standard double room in high season, including tax (19.6%) and service charge; higher prices (inquire when booking) prevail for any meal plans.

Monet's Coast

Monet traveled to Normandy to immortalize on canvas the sea terraces at Le Havre and the ocean cliffs at Étretat—for good reason. Normandy has 600 km (375 mi) of some of the most striking coastline in France. Bordering the English Channel, there are major ports—Le Havre, Dieppe, and Cherbourg—plus coastal towns with seafaring pasts, like Honfleur (itself the subject of hundreds of canvases by Boudin, a noted Impressionist), and fishing villages, like Fécamp. Sandwiched between are beaches and fashionable resort towns such as Cabourg, Deauville, and Étretat. Though the waters are chilly, you might be tempted to take a dip on a hot, sunny day, but don't try this at Mont-St-Michel, where the tide rushes in at lightning speed.

5

Cuisine & Calvados

The Normans are notoriously heavy eaters. Between the warm-up and the main course traditionally comes the *trou normand* (Norman gap), a break for calvados—apple brandy (a typically Norman riddle asks, "Did the trou normand create calvados, or did calvados create the trou normand?"). Norman food isn't light; many dishes are prepared with cream sauces and apple flavoring—hence *à la normande* (with cream sauce or apples). Rich local milk makes excellent cheese: Pont-l'Évêque is made in the Pays d'Auge with milk still warm and creamy; Livarot uses milk that has stood a while—don't be put off by its pungent smell. Best known of them all is creamy Camembert, invented by a farmer's wife in the late 18th century. Although Normandy is not a wine-growing area, it produces excellent hard cider (the best comes from the Vallée d'Auge), calvados, and its lighter cousin *pommeau*, which is two-thirds apple juice and one-third calvados. Local specialties differ from place to place. Rouen is famous for its canard *à la rouennaise* (duck in blood sauce); Caen, for its *tripes à la mode de Caen* (tripe cooked with carrots in a seasoned cider stock); Mont-St-Michel, for omelettes *Mère Poulard* and *pré-salé* (salt-meadow lamb). Try *andouille de Vire*, a delicate, smoked chitterling sausage served in thin slices like salami. Fish and seafood lovers can feast on oysters, lobster, shrimp, and sole *dieppoise* (sole poached in a sauce with cream and mussels).

June 1944

One of the great events of modern history, the D-Day invasion of June 1944, was enacted on the beaches of Normandy—at Arromanches vestiges of the great artificial ports called "mulberries" still remain and in the town a diorama and description of the landings make those desperate days live again. Omaha Beach (site of an eye-opening museum), Utah Beach, as well as many sites on the Cotentin Peninsula, and the memorials to Allied dead, all bear witness to the furious fighting that once raged in this now-peaceful corner of France. Today, as seagulls sweep over the cliffs where American rangers scrambled desperately up ropes to silence murderous German batteries, visitors now wander through the blockhouses and peer into the bomb craters, the carnage of *Saving Private Ryan* thankfully now a distant, if still horrifying, memory. For further information on the 2004 60th anniversary of the D-Day Landings, log onto www.normandiememorie.com.

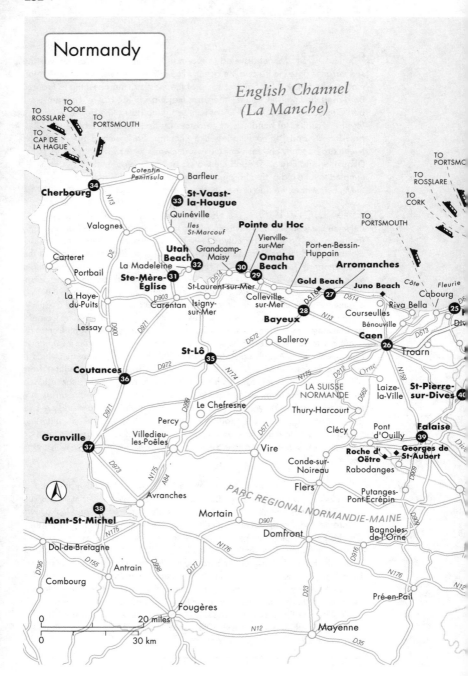

Normandy

English Channel
(La Manche)

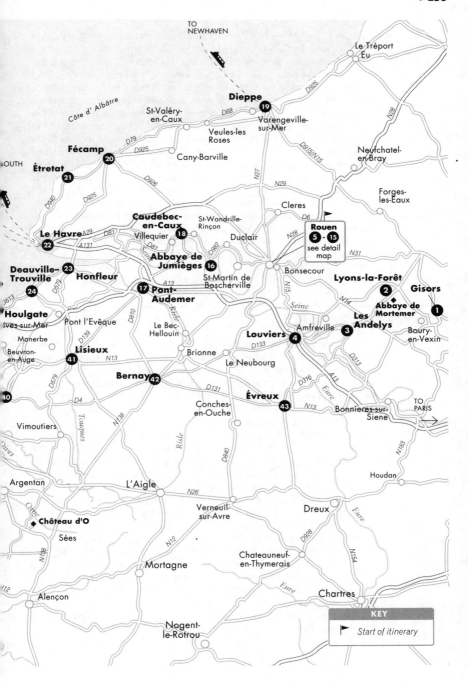

TO
NEWHAVEN

Le Tréport
Eu

Côte d' Albâtre

Dieppe **19**

St-Valéry-
en-Caux

Varengeville-
sur-Mer

D68

Veules-les
Roses

D925

D79

Cany-Barville

Neufchatel-
en-Bray

D915/N15

Fécamp **20**

D925

Étretat **21**

OUTH

D940

D925

D926

N27

N29

Cleres

Forges-
les-Eaux

D6

Caudebec-
en-Caux

St-Wandrille-
Rinçon

Villequier

18

D81

Duclair

Le Havre A29 D81

22

A131

D982

St-Martin de
Boscherville

Rouen
5 - **15**
see detail
map

N28

N31

Abbaye de
Jumièges **16**

Deauville–
Trouville

23 Honfleur

D579

D613

24

A131

Houlgate
ves-sur-Mer

Manerbe

Beuvron-
en-Auge

10

D579

Vimoutiers

Argentan

D4

Toutaines

Pont l'Evêque

D810

17 Pont-
Audemer

Le Bec-
Hellouin

Bonsecour

Lyons-la-Forêt

N15

Seine

2

N14

Abbaye de
Mortemer

Gisors

1

Boury-
en-Vexin

Les
Andelys

3

D313

Louviers

D133

4

Amfreville

Lisieux

41

N13

Brionne

Le Neubourg

Bernay **42**

D131

D316

Eure

A13

Conches-
en-Ouche

Évreux

43 N13

Bonnières-sur-
Siene

TO
PARIS

D840

Risle

N138

Houdan

N183

L'Aigle

N26

Verneuil-
sur-Avre

Dreux

Eure

Château d'O

Sées

N12

Mortagne

Chateauneuf-
en-Thymerais

D928

N154

Alençon

Eure

Chartres

12

Nogent-
le-Rotrou

Orne

N138

Dives

D579

Risle

Eure

KEY	
▶	*Start of itinerary*

Timing

July and August—when French families vacation—are the busiest months here, but also the most activity-filled: concerts are presented every evening at Mont-St-Michel, and the region's most important horse races are held in Deauville, culminating with the Gold Cup Polo Championship and the Grand Prix the last Sunday in August. June 6, the anniversary of the Allied invasion, is the most popular time to visit the D-Day beaches. If you're trying to avoid crowds, your best bet is late spring and early autumn, when it's still fairly temperate. May finds the apple trees in full bloom and miles of waving flaxseed fields spotted with tiny butter-yellow flowers. Some of the biggest events of the region take place during these seasons: at the end of May Joan of Arc is honored at a festival in Rouen, and there's jazz under the apple trees in Coutances; the first week of September in Deauville is the American Film Festival, and the last week sees the nationally acclaimed blues music festival in Lisieux. Winter offers quieter pleasures: the lush Normandy countryside rolling softly under a thick tent of clouds so low you can almost touch them; the strange desolate poetry of the empty D-Day beaches; intimate evenings in casinos with the fun-loving locals for company, or a good conversation with the less-harried hosts in a quiet country inn; and a last burning snifter of calvados in front of a roaring Norman hearth.

HAUTE NORMANDY

The French divide Normandy into two: Haute-Normandie and Basse-Normandie. Upper (Haute) Normandy is delineated by the Seine as it meanders northwest from Ile-de-France between chalky cliffs and verdant hills to Rouen—the region's cultural and commercial capital—and on to the port of Le Havre. Pebbly beaches and even more impressive chalk cliffs line the Côte d'Alabâtre from Le Havre to Dieppe. In the 19th century, the dramatic scenery and bathing resorts along the coast attracted and inspired writers and artists like Maupassant, Monet, and Braque. Lower (Basse) Normandy encompasses the sandy Côte Fleurie (Flowered Coast), stretching from the resort towns of Trouville and Deauville to the D-Day landing beaches and the Cotentin Peninsula, jutting out into the English Channel. Inland, lush green meadows and apple orchards form the heart of calvados country west of the pilgrim town of Lisieux. After the World War II D-Day landings, some of the fiercest fighting took place around Caen and Bayeux, as many monuments and memorials testify. To the south, in the prosperous Pays d'Auge, dairy farms produce the region's famous cheeses. The hilly Suisse Normande provides the region's most rugged scenery. Rising to the west is the fabled Mont-St-Michel. Our tour starts along the Seine Valley in Basse Normandie, then heads north to the Channel Coast, which we follow all the way from Dieppe to Mont-St-Michel. Here you can continue into Brittany or return east, cutting back inland to Falaise, Liseux, and Évreux.

Gisors

❶ *64 km (40 mi) northwest of Paris via A15 and D915, 35 km (24 mi) northeast of Vernon.*

Gisors, a peaceful market town in the Vexin region evoked by Impressionist painter Camille Pissarro (who lived just to the north in Eragny-sur-Epte), has several half-timber houses along the sloping rue de Vienne and a fine hilltop castle standing sentinel at the confines of Normandy. The town church, lovingly restored after being damaged in World War II, is a jumble of styles; the elaborate, two-towered 16th-century facade and florid vaulting in the side chapels clash with the sober choir, consecrated in 1249. The royal fleur-de-lis emblem keeps cropping up unexpectedly—carved on a spiral-patterned pillar, in a modern stained-glass window, or woven into the stone balustrade above the side chapels outside.

The **Château Fort** was begun in 1097 by the English king William Rufus, son of William the Conqueror, to defend Normandy's southeast frontier. The castle has two parts. One is the drumlike ring of curtain walls with a dozen towers, surrounded by a large ditch and enclosing a park of flowers and evergreens. The park is open daily without charge and offers a fine view of the church above the roofs of the *Vieille Ville* (Old Town). The other is the 70-foot artificial mound in the middle, the foursquare keep, with a staircase leading to the top—and also down to the dungeon. ⊠ *Pl. Blanmont* ☎ *02–32–55–59–36* 🕮 *€4* ☺ *Apr.–Sept., Wed.–Mon. 10–noon and 2–6; Oct.–Nov. and Feb.–Mar., weekends 10–noon and 2–5.*

In the pretty village of Boury-en-Vexin, 8 km (5 mi) southwest of Gisors, the steep-roofed **Château de Boury,** built in 1685 by Jules Hardouin-Mansart, displays the same monumental dignity as the architect's work at Versailles. The two-tiered facade, with arched ground-floor windows and Ionic pilasters above, surveys a trim lawn with cone-shape topiaries. The château has remained in the same family since it was built, which probably explains the prevailing homey, lived-in feel that complements its grand furniture, portraits, and crystal chandeliers. ⊠ *Boury-en-Vexin* ☎ *02–32–55–15–10* 🕮 *€5* ☺ *July and Aug., Wed.–Mon. 2:30–6:30; mid-Apr.–June, Sept. and Oct., weekends 2:30–6:30.*

Lyons-la-Forêt

❷ *34 km (21 mi) northwest of Gisors, 36 km (23 mi) east of Rouen.*

FodorśChoice
★

Few villages in France are as pretty as Lyons-la-Forêt, built in a verdant clearing surrounded by a noble beech forest. Lyons has entire streets of rickety half-timber houses and, on its main square, a venerable market hall built of robust, medieval oak. In fact, the square is more of a tumbling triangle—all bustle in summer, but come winter, when most hotels and restaurants are shut, as forlorn as the leafless beech trees all around. Lyons is built on two levels, and if you arrive from Gisors, take care not to miss the lower road—a quilt of medieval black-and-white frontages leading to the village church and its life-size wooden statues.

The scenic ruins of the Cistercian **Abbaye de Mortemer** are by a small lake in the heart of the forest, 5 km (3 mi) south of Lyons-la-Forêt. The 100-yard-long church was built at the start of the 13th century but destroyed during the Revolution. Some of the abbey buildings survive, including the large 15th-century pigeon loft that was also used as a prison. A small museum evokes aspects of monastic life. ⊠ *Rue de Mortemer, Lisors* ☎ *02–32–49–54–34* ⊠ *€6.10* ⊗ *Easter–Oct., daily 11–6:30; Nov.–Easter, weekends 2–5:30.*

Where to Stay

$–$$$ ⊞ **La Licorne.** This venerable 17th-century inn at the top of the village square has comfortable rooms with rustic wooden furniture. The smaller rooms, Nos. 2, 3, and 9, are also the most reasonably priced. The owners will kindly direct you to nearby restaurants and to the town square for its wonderful bakery (you won't soon forget those croisssants). ⊠ *27 pl. Isaac-Benserade, 27480* ☎ *02–32–49–62–02* 🖶 *02–32–49–80–09* ⇗ *19 rooms* ᗐ *Restaurant; no a/c* ⊟ *AE, DC, MC, V* ⊗ *Closed Dec. 20–Jan. 25* ⦿⧏ *MAP.*

Les Andelys

❸ *20 km (13 mi) southwest of Lyons-la-Forêt, 88 km (55 mi) northwest of Paris, 40 km (25 mi) southeast of Rouen.*

In one of the most picturesque loops of the Seine, the small town of Les Andelys, birthplace of France's leading classical painter, Nicolas Poussin, is set against magnificent chalky cliffs. The town is divided between riverside Petit Andely, with its 13th-century church of St-Sauveur and domed, 18th-century Hôpital St-Jacques, and bustling Grand Andely, whose Collégiale Notre-Dame gleams with a score of exquisite stained-glass windows created between 1540 and 1560. **Château Gaillard,** a formidable fortress built by England's King Richard the Lion-Hearted in 1196, overlooks Petit Andely from the cliff top, with spectacular views up- and down-river. Despite its solid defenses, the castle fell to French king Philippe-Auguste in 1204, after a lengthy siege during which it suffered considerable damage; further sections were torn down at the end of the 16th century, and only one of its five main towers remains intact. But the location and the history bring the ruins alive. ⊠ *Rue Richard-Coeur-de-Lion* ☎ *02–32–54–04–16* ⊠ *€3.50* ⊗ *Apr.–Oct., Thurs.–Mon. 9–noon and 2–5, Wed. 2–6.*

Where to Stay & Eat

$$–$$$ ✕⊞ **La Chaîne d'Or.** This charming inn in Le Petit Andely, founded in 1751 within sight of Château Gaillard, has a terrace that overlooks the banks of the Seine (just the place to enjoy your predinner aperitif on warmer days). Rooms are large and bright; for time-burnished charm, request one with a view of the church or courtyard. In the airy, flower-laden restaurant (no lunch Tuesday), Christophe Bouche's neoclassical Norman cuisine ranges from grilled lobster with truffles and olives to chicken with vanilla and cinnamon. ⊠ *27 rue Grande, 27700* ☎ *02–32–54–00–31* 🖶 *02–32–54–05–68* ⇗ *10 rooms* ᗐ *Restaurant; no a/c* ⊟ *AE, MC, V* ⊗ *Closed Mon. and Jan. No dinner Sun.* ⦿⧏ *BP.*

Louviers

❹ *22 km (14 mi) west of Les Andelys via D313, 104 km (65 mi) northwest of Paris.*

Picturesque Louviers owed its medieval prosperity to the weaving of woolen cloth, and a good illustration of this wealthy past is the elaborate stonework of the town church, the **Eglise Notre-Dame,** whose intricately sculpted porch and gables show just why the late Gothic style of the 15th century is known as *flamboyant.* The Eure River splits scenically into several branches in downtown Louviers, and the pretty valley can be explored just south of the town, with the quaint village of **Acquigny** and its château park (open Easter–September, weekends 2–6) well worth a detour.

Where to Stay & Eat

$$–$$$ ✕🏠 **L'Hostellerie St-Pierre.** This hotel, a few miles east of Louviers by the Seine, is a good place to stay when on your way to Rouen. Room 27 has French doors that open onto a terrace with the best view of the river; its size, like that of most others, is modest but all have comfortingly traditional decor. You have the choice of two prix-fixe menus, ranging from €38 to the epicurean seven-course menu at €53, complete with trou normand. ⊠ *6 chemin de la Digue, 6 km (4 mi) east of Louviers, 27430 St-Pierre-du-Vauvray* ☎ *02–32–59–93–29* 🖶 *02–32–59–41–93* 🔁 *14 rooms* ⚒ *Restaurant, some pets allowed (fee); no a/c* ⊟ *AE, MC, V* ⊗ *Closed mid-Nov.–mid-Mar.* †⊙| *MAP.*

en route From Louviers head east to cross the Seine at St-Pierre-du-Vauvray. Stay on the right bank of the Seine for 8 km (5 mi) to Amfreville; then turn right up steep D508 to what is known as the **Côte des Deux Amants** (Lovers' Mount) for a spectacular view of the Seine Valley and its chalky cliffs. Follow the road to Pont St-Pierre, then head northwest on D138 toward Rouen, pausing in the suburb of **Bonsecours** to check out its 1840s hilltop **Basilique Notre-Dame,** a fine neo-Gothic church overlooking the Seine.

Rouen

► *32 km (20 mi) north of Louviers, 130 km (80 mi) northwest of Paris,*
Fodor'sChoice *86 km (53 mi) east of Le Havre.*
★

"O Rouen, art thou then to be my final abode!" was the agonized cry of Joan of Arc as the English dragged her out to be burned alive on May 30, 1431. The exact spot of the pyre is marked by a concrete and metal cross in front of the Église Jeanne-d'Arc, an eye-catching modern church on place du Vieux-Marché, just one of the many landmarks that make Rouen a fascinating destination. Although much of the city was destroyed during World War II, a wealth of medieval half-timber houses still lines the cobblestone streets, many of which are pedestrian-only—most famously rue du Gros-Horloge between place du Vieux-Marché and the cathedral, suitably embellished halfway along with a giant Renaissance clock. Rouen is also a busy port—the fifth largest in France.

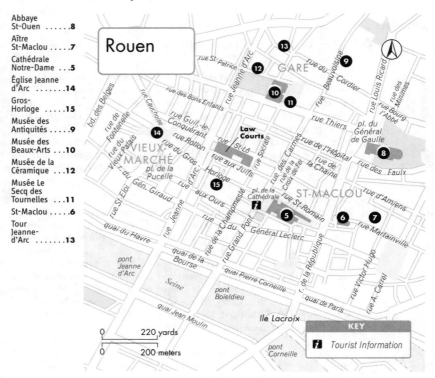

Rouen is known as the City of a Hundred Spires, because many of its important edifices are churches. Lording it over them all is the highest spire in France, erected in 1876, a cast-iron tour-de-force rising 490 feet **❺** above the crossing of the **Cathédrale Notre-Dame.** If you're familiar with the works of Impressionist artist Claude Monet, you will immediately recognize the cathedral's immense west facade, rendered in an increasingly hazy fashion in his series *Cathédrales de Rouen*—you can enjoy a ringside view and a coffee at the Brasserie Paul, just opposite. The original 12th-century construction was replaced after a devastating fire in 1200; only the left-hand spire, the **Tour St-Romain** (St. Romanus Tower), survived the flames. Construction on the imposing 250-foot steeple on the right, known as the **Tour de Beurre** (Butter Tower), was begun in the 15th century and completed in the 17th, when a group of wealthy citizens donated large sums of money for the privilege of continuing to eat butter during Lent. Interior highlights include the 13th-century choir, with its pointed arcades; vibrant stained glass depicting the crucified Christ (restored after heavy damage during World War II); and massive stone columns topped by some intriguing carved faces. The first flight of the famous **Escalier de la Librairie** (Library Stairway), attributed to Guillaume Pontifs (also responsible for most of the 15th-century work seen in the cathedral), rises from a tiny balcony just to the left of the transept. ⊠ *Pl. de la Cathédrale, St-Maclou* ☏ 02–32–08–32–40 ☉ *Tues.–Sun. 8–6, Mon. 2–6.*

❻ The late-Gothic church of **St-Maclou,** across rue de la République behind the cathedral, bears testimony to the wild excesses of Flamboyant architecture; take time to examine the central and left-hand portals of the main facade, covered with little bronze lion heads and pagan engravings. Inside, note the 16th-century organ, with its Renaissance wood carving, and the fine marble columns. ⊠ *Pl. St-Maclou, St-Maclou* ☏ 02–35–71–71–72 ☉ *Mon.–Sat. 10–noon and 2–6, Sun. 3–6.*

❼ A former ossuary (a charnel house used for the bodies of plague victims), the **Aître St-Maclou** (⊠ 186 rue Martainville, St-Maclou) is a reminder of the plague that devastated Europe during the Middle Ages; these days it holds Rouen's Fine Art Academy. French composer Camille Saint-Saëns (1835–1921) is said to have been inspired by the ossuary when he was working on his *Danse Macabre.* The half-timber courtyard, where you can wander at leisure and maybe visit a picture exhibition, contains graphic carvings of skulls, bones, and gravediggers' tools.

❽ A stupendous example of high Gothic architecture is the **Abbaye St-Ouen** next to the imposing Neoclassical City Hall. The abbey's stained-glass windows, dating from the 14th to 16th centuries, are the most spectacular grace notes of the spare interior, along with the 19th-century pipe organ, among the finest in France. ⊠ *Pl. du Général-de-Gaulle, Hôtel de Ville* ☏ 02–32–08–13–90 ☉ *Mid-Mar.–Oct., Wed.–Mon. 8–12:30 and 2–6; Nov.–mid-Dec. and mid-Jan.–mid-Mar., Wed. and weekends 10–12:30 and 2–4:30.*

❾ Gallo-Roman glassware and mosaics, medieval tapestries and enamels, and Moorish ceramics vie for attention at the **Musée des Antiquités,** an extensive antiquities museum housed in a former monastery dating from the 17th century. ⊠ *198 rue Beauvoisine, Gare* ☏ 02–35–98–55–10 🎫 €3 ☉ *Mon.–Sat. 10–12:15 and 1:30–5:30, Sun. 2–6.*

❿ One of Rouen's cultural mainstays is the **Musée des Beaux-Arts** (Fine Arts Museum), which has a scintillating collection of paintings and sculptures from the 16th to the 20th centuries, including works by native son Géricault as well as by David, Rubens, Caravaggio, Velasquez, Poussin, Delacroix, Chassériau, Degas, and Modigliani, not to mention the impressive Impressionist gallery, with Monet, Renoir, and Sisley, and the Postimpressionist School of Rouen headed by Albert Lebourg and Gustave Loiseau. ⊠ *Square Verdrel, Gare* ☏ 02–35–52–00–62 ⊕ *www. musees-rouen.org* 🎫 €3 ☉ *Wed.–Mon. 10–6.*

⓫ The **Musée Le Secq des Tournelles** (Wrought-Iron Museum), near the Musée des Beaux-Arts, claims to have the world's finest collection of wrought iron, with exhibits spanning from the 4th through 19th centuries. The displays, imaginatively housed in a converted medieval church, include many articles used in daily life, accessories, and professional instruments of surgeons, barbers, carpenters, clock-makers, and gardeners. ⊠ *2 rue Jacques-Villon, Gare* ☏ 02–35–88–42–92 🎫 €2.30 ☉ *Wed.–Mon. 10–1 and 2–6.*

A superb array of local pottery and European porcelain can be admired
⑫ at the **Musée de la Céramique** (Ceramics Museum), in an elegant mansion near the Musée des Beaux-Arts. ⊠ *1 rue Faucon, Gare* ☎ *02–35–07–31–74* ☞ *€2.30* ⊙ *Wed.–Mon. 10–1 and 2–6.*

Sole remnant of the early 13th-century castle built by French king
⑬ Philippe-Auguste, the beefy **Tour Jeanne-d'Arc,** a pointed-top circular tower, houses a small exhibit of documents and models charting the history of the castle where Joan of Arc was tried and held prisoner in 1430. ⊠ *Rue Bouvreuil, Gare* ☎ *02–35–98–55–10* ☞ *€1.50* ⊙ *Mon.–Sat. 10–12:30 and 2–6, Sun. 2–6.*

⑭ Dedicated to Joan of Arc, the **Église Jeanne d'Arc** (Joan of Arc Church) was built in the 1970s on the spot where she was burned to death in 1431. Not all is new, however: the church showcases some remarkable 16th-century stained-glass windows taken from the former Église St-Vincent, bombed out in 1944. The adjacent **Musée Jeanne-d'Arc** evokes Ste. Joan's history with waxworks and documents. ⊠ *Pl. du Vieux-Marché, Vieux-Marché* ⊕ *www.jeanne-darc.com.*

> **need a break?** The friendly **L'Adelshoffen** (⊠ Pl. du Vieux-Marché, Vieux-Marché ☎ 02–35–70–25–22) offers zestful service and a splendid view of the picturesque market-square, scene of the burning of Joan of Arc, whose story is retraced in colorful frescoes on the café wall.

The name of the pedestrian rue du Gros-Horloge, Rouen's most popu-
⑮ lar street, comes from the **Gros-Horloge** itself, a giant Renaissance clock. In 1527 the Rouennais had a splendid arch built especially for it, and today its golden face looks out over the street. You can see the clock's inner workings from the 15th-century belfry. Though the street is crammed with stores, a few old houses, dating from the 16th century, remain. Wander through the surrounding **Vieux Rouen** (Old Rouen), a warren of tiny streets lined with more than 700 half-timber houses, many artfully transformed into fashionable shops. ⊠ *Rue du Gros-Horloge, Vieux-Marché* ☎ *02–35–71–28–40* ☞ *€2* ⊙ *Wed.–Mon. 10–1 and 2–6.*

Where to Stay & Eat

$$$–$$$$ ✕ **L'Auberge de la Butte.** This 17th-century former post house, in the suburb of Bonsecours, is well worth seeking out (you'll need a car or taxi). Veteran chef Pierre Hervé's innovations include roasted *St-Pierre à la vanille* (John Dory with vanilla), whole lobster lasagna with West Indian spices, and *duck à la rouennaise.* The magnificent dining room has exposed beams and half-timber walls adorned with paintings and shining copper pots. ⊠ *69 rte. de Paris, 3 km (2 mi) east of city center, Bonsecours* ☎ *02–35–80–43–11* ▤ *AE, DC, MC, V* ⊙ *Closed Sun., Mon., and Aug.*

$$$ ✕ **La Couronne.** Behind a half-timber facade gushing geraniums, the "oldest inn in France," dating from 1345, is crammed with leather-upholstered chairs and a scattering of sculpture. The traditional Norman cuisine—lobster soufflé, sheep's feet, duck in blood sauce—makes few modern concessions. ⊠ *31 pl. du Vieux-Marché, Vieux-Marché* ☎ *02–35–71–40–90* ▤ *AE, DC, MC, V.*

$–$$ ✕ **La Toque d'Or.** Overlooking the Église Jeanne d'Arc, this large, bustling restaurant has been renowned since time immemorial for Jean-Jacques Baton's Normandy classics such as veal with Camembert flamed in calvados, breast of duck glazed in cider, or spicy braised turbot. Try the excellent home-smoked salmon (they'll give you a tour of the smokehouse if you wish) and the Norman apple *tarte soufflée*. Cheaper meals are available in the *grill* upstairs. ✉ *11 pl. du Vieux-Marché, Vieux-Marché* ☎ *02–35–71–46–29* ☰ *AE, DC, V.*

$$ ✕⌂ **Dieppe.** Established in 1880, the Dieppe remains up-to-date thanks to resolute management by five generations of the Guéret family. Staff members also are helpful, and they speak English. The compact rooms are cheerful and modern; street noise can be a problem, however, despite double-glazed windows. The restaurant, Les Quatre Saisons (no lunch Saturday), serves seasonal dishes with an emphasis on fish, such as the sole Michèle (poached in a light wine sauce), but is best known for its pressed duckling. ✉ *Pl. Bernard-Tissot, Gare, 76000* ☎ *02–35–71–96–00, 800/334–7234 for U.S. reservations* �🖨 *02–35–89–65–21* ⊕ *www.best.western.fr* ⌨ *41 rooms, 31 with bath, 10 with shower* ⚤ *Restaurant, cable TV, bar, some pets allowed; no a/c* ☰ *AE, DC, MC, V.* ⦿ *MAP.*

$ ✕⌂ **Vieux Carré.** In the heart of Old Rouen, this cute hotel has small, practical, and comfortable rooms simply furnished with a taste for the exotic: lamps from Egypt, tables from Morocco, and 1940s English armoires. Ask for one of the rooms on the third floor for a view of the cathedral. Breakfast and lunch (but not dinner) are served in the leafy courtyard, weather permitting, or in the cozy little bistro (closed Monday) off the reception area. Lunches are light and simple, based on creative tourtes—tomato, olive, and Camembert, for example. Brunch is served both Saturday and Sunday until 2 PM. ✉ *34 rue Ganterie, Gare, 76000* ☎ *02–35–71–67–70* 🖨 *02–35–71–19–17* ⌨ *14 rooms, 10 with bath, 4 with shower* ⚤ *Restaurant, cable TV, Internet, some pets allowed; no a/c* ☰ *AE, DC, MC, V* ⦿ *EP.*

$$–$$$ ⌂ **Mercure Centre.** In the jumble of streets near the cathedral—a navigational challenge if you arrive by car—this modern chain hotel has small, comfortable rooms done in breezy pastels. This hotel is handy for exploring the old streets of the city center. ✉ *7 rue de la Croix-de-Fer, St-Maclou, 76000* ☎ *02–35–52–69–52* 🖨 *02–35–89–41–46* ⌨ *139 rooms* ⚤ *Cable TV, bar, parking (fee)* ☰ *AE, DC, MC, V* ⦿ *BP.*

$ ⌂ **Cathédrale.** This hotel is in a medieval building on a narrow pedestrian street behind the cathedral. (You can sleep soundly, though: the cathedral bells do not boom out the hour at night.) Rooms are petite, but neat and comfortable. Breakfast is served in the beamed dining room. ✉ *12 rue St-Romain, St-Maclou, 76000* ☎ *02–35–71–57–95* 🖨 *02–35–70–15–54* ⊕ *www.hotel-de-la-cathedrale.fr* ⌨ *25 rooms, 8 with bath, 17 with shower* ⚤ *Cable TV, bar, Internet, parking (fee), some pets allowed (fee); no a/c* ☰ *MC, V* ⦿ *EP.*

Nightlife & the Arts

The **Fête Jeanne d'Arc** (Joan of Arc Festival) takes place on the Sunday nearest to May 30, with parades, street plays, concerts, exhibitions, and a medieval market. Evening **concerts** and organ recitals are held at St-

Maclou in August and at St-Ouen throughout the year; details are available from the Rouen tourist office. Operas, plays, and concerts are staged at the **Théâtre des Arts** (✉ 7 rue du Dr-Rambert, Vieux-Marché ☎ 02–35–71–41–36). Visit the popular local haunt **Bar de la Crosse** (✉ 53 rue de l'Hôpital, St-Maclou ☎ 02–35–70–16–68) for an aperitif and a good chat with some friendly Rouennais. At the **Big Ben Pub** (✉ 95 bis rue du Gros-Horloge, Vieux-Marché ☎ 02–35–88–44–50), relax with a glass of wine on the first floor, listen to music on the second, and on the third witness how the French do karaoke (not to be missed).

Abbaye de Jumièges

★ **⑯**   *24 km (15 mi) west of Rouen, head west on D982 through Duclair and then exit left onto D143.*

Imposing ruins are all that is left of the once mighty Benedictine Abbaye de Jumièges, founded in 654 by St-Philbert, plundered by Vikings in 841, then rebuilt by William Longswood, duke of Normandy, around 940, though not consecrated until 1067. The French Revolution forced the evacuation of the remaining 16 monks, whereupon the abbey was auctioned off to a timber merchant, who promptly demolished part of the building to sell the stone. What remains is impressive enough. ✉ *24 rue Guillaume-le-Conquérant* ☎ *02–35–37–24–02* ⊕ *www. monum.fr* ▨ *€4.60* ◯ *Apr.–Sept., daily 9:30–7; Oct.–Mar., daily 9:30–1 and 2:30–5:30.*

Pont-Audemer

⑰   *35 km (22 mi) southwest of Jumièges via ferry, D313 and N175; 53 km (33 mi) west of Rouen; 27 km (17 mi) southeast of Honfleur.*

Pont-Audemer, on the banks of the Risle River, luckily escaped destruction by warfare and bulldozers. Today many of its buildings are still as they were in the 16th century, when the town made its mark as an important trading center. Stroll along impasse St-Ouen and impasse de l'Épée, narrow streets by the church that are lined with timber-frame medieval houses. The pleasingly dilapidated church of **St-Ouen** has an unfinished single-tower facade and an entertaining clash of modern stained-glass windows and exuberant, late-medieval stonework. ✉ *Rue de la République* ☎ *02–32–41–12–88.*

Where to Stay & Eat

★ **$$$**   ✕▥ **Belle-Isle sur Risle.** It's hard not to feel like a personal guest of this private manor—an impression somehow heightened by a few rough edges. The newer, more modern rooms have wall-to-wall carpeting and department-store furniture, but the older ones have wooden floors with rugs and assorted traditional pieces; those on the first floor have balconies. In the restaurant, chef Loïc Rapper turns out foie gras with citrus fruit, honey-roast pigeon, and apple tart with mango. ✉ *112 rte. de Rouen, 27500* ☎ *02–32–56–96–22* ▤ *02–32–42–88–96* ⊕ *www. bellile.com* ⇌ *18 rooms, 2 suites* ♨ *Restaurant, minibars, tennis court, pool, sauna, some pets allowed (fee); no a/c* ⊟ *MC, V* ⑩ *MAP.*

Caudebec-en-Caux

⑱ *39 km (24 mi) northeast of Pont-Audemer via D139, 15 km (9 mi) north-west of Jumièges via D143/D982, 35 km (22 mi) northwest of Rouen.*

The riverside town of Caudebec-en-Caux is dominated by the spire of Notre-Dame-de-Caudebec, a wonderful medieval church with some of the most vivid 16th-century stained glass in Normandy. Don't miss the deep blood-reds of the window showing Pharaoh's army drowning in the Red Sea. The nearby **Musée de la Marine** charts the history of the Seine Valley with ship models, old photographs, and traditional costumes, and a section on the *mascaret,* the bore or tidal wave that used to power up the estuary during the equinox. ⊠ *Av. Winston-Churchill* ☎ *02–35–95–90–13* 🎫 *€3.20* ◷ *Wed.–Mon. 2–6:30.*

The **Musée Victor-Hugo** in the village of Villequier, 5 km (3 mi) west of Caudebec, occupies the prettily furnished riverside mansion where Hugo's daughter Léopoldine lived with her husband Charles Vacqueyrie. Pictures, letters, drawings, and documents evoke the great poet and his daughter, who, along with her husband, drowned when their boat was overturned by the Seine's notorious mascaret as they returned from Caude-bec in September 1843. Léopoldine, who is buried in the village church-yard up the hill, was just 19. ⊠ *Rue Ernest-Binet* ☎ *02–35–56–78–31* 🎫 *€3* ◷ *Daily 10–12:30 and 2–5.*

The Benedictine **Abbaye de St-Wandrille**, 3 km (2 mi) east of Caudebec, is still active today, with 40 monks in residence. Founded in the 7th cen-tury, the abbey was sacked by the Normans and rebuilt in the 10th cen-tury—although what you see today is an ensemble of styles from the 11th through the early 18th centuries (mainly the latter). You can hear the monks sing their Gregorian chants at morning mass if you arrive early (9:25 weekdays and 10 on Sunday and holidays), or wander at leisure in the gardens. Don't forget to visit the abbey shop down the hill; everything it sells—from floor polish to spiritual aids—is made by the monks. ☎ *02–35–96–23–11* ⊕ *www.st-wandrille.com* 🎫 *€3.50* ◷ *Guided tours Tues.–Sat. at 3:30, Sun. at 11:30 and 3:30.*

Dieppe

⑲ *67 km (44 mi) north of Caudebec, 64 km (40 mi) north of Rouen.*

Bustling Dieppe, beneath its clifftop castle, is part fishing and commercial port and part Norman seaside town—though its era in the fashionable spotlight is past, and the ramshackle church of St-Jacques, painted by Pissarro, has seen better days. Still, a year-round ferry service was re-introduced in 2001 to complement the summer-only jetfoil across the Channel to Newhaven, near Brighton. The seafront promenade, boule-vard du Maréchal-Foch, separates an immense lawn from an unspoiled pebble beach where in 1942 many Canadian soldiers were killed dur-ing the so-called Jubilee Raid.

The 15th-century **Château-Musée** (Castle-Museum), overlooking the Channel at the western end of the bay, contains a well-known collection of ivories. In the 17th century Dieppe imported vast quantities of elephant tusks from Africa and Asia, and as many as 350 craftsmen settled here to work the ivory; their efforts can be seen in the form of ship models, nautical accessories, religious artifacts, and everyday objects. The museum also has some fine French paintings and a room devoted to sketches by Georges Braque. ☒ *Rue de Chastes* ☎ *02–35–84–19–76* ☒ *€3* ⊕ *www.mairie-dieppe.fr* ☉ *Mon. and Wed.–Sat. 10–noon and 2–5, Sun. 10–noon and 2–6.*

Where to Stay & Eat

$–$$ ╳▦ **L'Auberge du Clos Normand.** This 15th-century inn in the tiny village of Martin-Église, 4 mi (6 km) southeast of Dieppe, is best known for its pretty garden, complete with a stream and flower-bedecked balconies. Even the bedrooms—which may seem a little chilly out of season—have flowery wallpaper, in the time-honored rural French tradition. The kitchen, all agleam with copper pots, is at one end of the restaurant, so you can glimpse the chef at work on his sturdy Norman dishes, with duck, sole, and chicken as specialties; round off your meal with a soufflé Grand-Marnier. ☒ *22 rue Henri-IV, 76370* ☎ *02–35–40–43–25* ☒ *02–35–04–48–49* ⇨ *8 rooms, 5 with bath, 3 with shower* ⚭ *Restaurant, cable TV; no a/c* ☰ *AE, MC, V* ☉ *Closed Tues. and mid-Nov.–mid-Dec. No dinner Mon.* ⧯ *MAP.*

Nightlife & the Arts

At night Dieppe's **casino** (☒ 3 bd. de Verdun ☎ 02–35–82–33–60) at the Grand Hotel comes alive with shows and gambling. If you love jazz, come for the **Festival Européen de Jazz Traditionnel** (European Traditional Jazz Festival), held in mid-June in Luneray, 8 km (5 mi) southwest of Dieppe. During the second week of September, the **International Kite Festival** fills the skies with the most amazing high-flying contraptions. For information contact the Dieppe tourist office.

The Outdoors

Bicycles can be rented at Dieppe's train station for around €10 a day. The rolling terrain around town makes for strenuous cycling. For information on routes, check with the tourist office.

Fécamp

⓴ *64 km (40 mi) southwest of Dieppe, 42 km (26 mi) northeast of Le Havre.*

★ The ancient cod-fishing port of Fécamp was once a major pilgrimage site. The magnificent abbey church, **Abbaye de La Trinité** (☒ Rue Leroux), bears witness to Fécamp's religious past. The Benedictine abbey was founded by the Duke of Normandy in the 11th century and became the home of the monastic order of the Précieux Sang de la Trinité (Precious Blood of the Trinity—referring to Christ's blood, which supposedly arrived here in the 7th century in a reliquary from the Holy Land).

Fécamp is also the home of Benedictine liqueur. The **Palais de la Bénédictine** (Benedictine Palace), across from the tourist office, is a florid building dating from 1892 that mixes neo-Gothic and Renaissance styles. Watery pastiche or taste-tingling architectural cocktail? Whether you're shaken or stirred, this remains one of Normandy's most popular attractions. The interior is just as exhausting as the facade. Paintings, sculptures, ivories, advertising posters, and fake bottles of Benedictine compete for attention with a display of the ingredients used for the liqueur, and a chance to sample it. There's also a shop selling Benedictine products and souvenirs. ⊠ *110 rue Alexandre-le-Grand* ☎ *02–35–10–26–10* ⊕ *www.benedictine. fr* ⊒ *€5, including tasting* ⊙ *Feb.–Dec., daily 10–11:15 and 2–5.*

Where to Stay & Eat

$ ✕ **L'Escalier.** This delightfully simple little restaurant overlooking the harbor serves traditional Norman cuisine, such as mussels in calvados and homemade fish soup. ⊠ *101 quai Bérigny* ☎ *02–35–28–26–79* ⌆ *Reservations essential* ▤ *DC, MC, V* ⊙ *Closed 2 wks in Nov.*

★ **$$–$$$** ✕▦ **Les Hêtres.** Top chef Bertrand Warin runs this restaurant in Ingouville, east of Fécamp. Reservations are essential—as are jacket and tie—for the elegant 17th-century dining room (closed Monday and Tuesday, January through Easter), where half-timber walls and Louis XIII chairs contrast with sleek, modern furnishings. The five pretty guest rooms, each with old wooden furniture and engravings, are for diners only; the largest has a terrace overlooking the garden. ⊠ *24 rue des Fleurs, 28 km (17 mi) east of Fécamp, 76460 Ingouville* ☎ *02–35–57–09–30* ⌸ *02–35–57–09–31* ⊕ *www.leshetres.com* ⌗ *5 rooms* ⌂ *Restaurant, cable TV, Internet, some pets allowed (fee); no a/c* ▤ *MC, V* ⊙ *Closed Jan.* ¶⊙ *MAP.*

$ ✕▦ **L'Auberge de la Rouge.** The Enderlins welcome you to this little inn just south of Fécamp. Rooms are actually good-size lofts that sleep four. The restaurant (closed Monday; no dinner Sunday) showcases modern classics (chef Thierry Enderlin trained under Ducasse) and local specialties such as roast turbot, veal and mushrooms in wine, or the duck with foie gras. Top it off, if you can, with a local favorite, soufflé *à la Bénédictine.* ⊠ *1 rue du Bois-de-Boclion, 1 km (½ mi) south of Fécamp, 76400 St-Léonard* ☎ *02–35–28–07–59* ⌸ *02–35–28–70–55* ⊕ *www. auberge-rouge.com* ⌗ *8 rooms* ⌂ *Restaurant, minibars; no a/c* ▤ *AE, DC, MC, V* ¶⊙ *BP.*

$ ✕▦ **La Ferme de la Chapelle.** The charm of this former priory lies neither in the simple, comfortable rooms around the courtyard, nor in its restaurant with its no-frills menu, but rather in its outstanding location high atop the cliffs overlooking Fécamp. There's a breathtaking, dramatic view over the entire coastline—explore it on an invigorating hike along the nearby coastal footpath. ⊠ *Côte de la Vierge, 76400* ☎ *02–35–10–12–12* ⌸ *02–35–10–12–13* ⊕ *www.fermedelachapelle.com* ⌗ *17 rooms, 5 studios* ⌂ *Restaurant, pool, some pets allowed (fee); no a/c* ¶⊙ *MAP.*

Étretat

㉑ *17 km (11 mi) southwest of Fécamp via D940, 88 km (55 mi) northwest of Rouen.*

This town, with its promenade running the length of the pebble beach, is renowned for the magnificent tall rock formations that extend out into the sea. The **Falaises d'Étretat** are white cliffs that are as famous in France as Dover's are in England—and have been painted by many artists, Claude Monet chief among them. At low tide it's possible to walk

Fodor'sChoice
★

through the huge archways formed by the rocks to neighboring beaches. The biggest arch is at the **Falaise d'Aval,** to the south. For a breathtaking view of the whole bay, take the path up to the top of the Falaise d'Aval. From here you can hike for miles across the Manneporte Hills . . . or play a round of golf on one of Europe's windiest and most scenic courses, overlooking **L'Aiguille** (The Needle), a 300-foot spike of rock jutting out of the sea just off the coast. To the north towers the **Falaise d'Amont,** topped by the chapel of Notre-Dame de la Garde.

Where to Stay & Eat

$ ✕ **Les Roches Blanches.** The exterior of this family-owned restaurant off the beach is a post–World War II concrete eyesore. But take a table by the window with a view of the cliffs, order Georges Trézeux's superb fresh seafood (try the sea bass roasted in calvados), and you'll be glad you came. Reservations are essential for Sunday lunch. ⊠ *Rue de l'Abbé-Cochet* ☎ *02–35–27–07–34* ▤ *MC, V* ☺ *Closed Tues. and Wed., mid-Nov.–mid-Jan.*

★ $$$–$$$$ ✕▦ **Donjon.** This charming ivy-covered château, built in 1862 in a park overlooking the town, has lovely sea views. Rooms are individually furnished, spacious, comfortable, and quiet. For a spectacular view, request the Oriental Suite or the Horizon or Marjorie room. Jean-Francois Toulain's flamboyant cuisine, ranging from warm hare terrine to scallops and salmon in cider, is dished up in a cozy, romantic restaurant. Rooms are reserved on a half-board basis on weekends. ⊠ *Chemin de St-Clair, 76790* ☎ *02–35–27–08–23* ◳ *02–35–29–92–24* ⊕ *www.ledonjon-etretat.fr* ↪ *21 rooms* ♻ *Restaurant, some minibars, cable TV, pool, bar, Internet, some pets allowed (fee); no a/c* ▤ *AE, DC, MC, V* ⅋○⅋ *MAP.*

$$ ✕▦ **Dormy House.** This unpretentious hotel is ideally located halfway up the Étretat cliffs. The rooms are simple and comfortable, but the real beauty is right out your bedroom window, thanks to views of *la mer,* so wonderful they would have Debussy humming in no time. The restaurant specializes in fresh fish and seafood platters, ranging from simple delights such as the sole stew to the full-scale *symphonie* of fish. Request a table near the window for a panoramic view of the coast. ⊠ *Rte. du Havre, 76790* ☎ *02–35–27–07–88* ◳ *02–35–29–86–19* ⊕ *www.dormy-house. com* ↪ *61 rooms* ♻ *Restaurant, Internet; no a/c* ▤ *AE, MC, V* ⅋○⅋ *MAP.*

¢–$ ✕▦ **Résidence.** The cheapest rooms in this gorgeous 16th-century house in the heart of Étretat are pretty basic—both the bathroom and the shower are in the hallway—but the more expensive have in-room bathrooms, and one (€110) even has a Jacuzzi. The service is friendly; staff are young and energetic. The brasserie-type restaurant on the ground floor, Le Salamandre, is rather cutting-edge for the region; all products are certified organic, farm-raised, and homemade, from the vegetable terrine to the nougat ice cream. In winter a fire crackles in the hearth. ⊠ *4 bd. du Président-René-Coty, 76790* ☎ *02–35–27–02–87* ◳ *02–35–27–17–07* ↪ *15 rooms* ♻ *Restaurant, minibars; no a/c, no TV in some rooms* ▤ *AE, MC, V* ⅋○⅋ *BP.*

Sports

Don't miss the chance to play at **Golf d'Étretat** (⊠ Rte. du Havre ☎ 02–35–27–04–89), where the breathtaking 6,580-yard, par-72 course drapes across the clifftops of the Falaise d'Aval; it's closed Tuesday.

NORMANDY ON CANVAS

ONG BEFORE CLAUDE MONET created his Giverny lily-pond by diverting the Epte River that marks the boundary with Ile-de-France, artists had been scudding into Normandy. For two watery reasons: the Seine and the sea. Just downstream from Vernon, where the Epte joins the Seine, Richard the Lionhearted's ruined castle at Les Andelys, immortalized by Paul Signac and Félix Vallotton, heralds the soft-lit, cliff-lined Seine Valley, impressionistically evoked by Albert Lebourg and Gustave Loiseau in the Arts Museum in Rouen—where Camille Corot once studied, and whose mighty cathedral Monet painted till he was pink, purple and blue in the face.

The Seine joins the Sea at Le Havre, where Monet grew up, a protégé of Eugène Boudin, often termed the precursor of Impressionism. Boudin would boat across the estuary from Honfleur, where he hobnobbed with Gustave Courbet,

Charles Daubigny, and Alfred Sisley at the Ferme St-Siméon. Le Havre in the 1860s was base-camp for Monet and his pals Frédéric Bazille and Johan Barthold Jongkind to explore the rugged coast up to Dieppe, with easels opened en route beneath the cliffs of Etretat.

The railroad from Gare St-Lazare (smokily evoked by Monet) put Dieppe within easy reach of Paris. Eugène Delacroix daubed seascapes here in 1852. Auguste Renoir visited Dieppe from 1878 to 1885; Paul Gauguin and Edgar Degas clinked glasses here in 1885; Camille Pissarro painted his way from Gisors to Dieppe in the 1890s. As the nearest port to Paris, Dieppe wowed the English too. Walter Sickert moved in from 1898 to 1905, and artists from the Camden Town Group he founded back in London often painted in Dieppe before World War I.

Le Havre

㉒ *28 km (18 mi) southwest of Étretat via D940, 88 km (55 mi) west of Rouen, 200 km (125 mi) northwest of Paris.*

Le Havre, France's second-largest port (after Marseille), was bombarded 146 times during World War II. You may find the rebuilt city, with its uncompromising recourse to reinforced concrete and open spaces, bleak and uninviting; on the other hand, you may admire Auguste Perret's rational planning and audacious modern architecture. The hilly suburb of **Ste-Adresse,** just west of town, is resplendent with Belle Epoque villas and an old fortress. It's also worth a visit for its beach, often painted by Raoul Dufy, and for its fine views of the sea and port, immortalized in a famous Monet masterpiece.

The **Musée André-Malraux,** the city art museum, is an innovative 1960s glass-and-metal structure surrounded by a moat, and includes an attractive sea-view café. Two local artists are showcased here—Raoul Dufy (1877–1953), through a remarkable collection of his brightly colored oils, watercolors, and sketches; and Eugène Boudin (1824–98), a forerunner of Impressionism, whose compelling beach scenes and landscapes tellingly evoke the Normandy coast and skyline. ☒ *2 bd. Clemenceau* ☎ *02–35–19–62–62* ☜ *€3.80* ◉ *Wed.–Mon. 11–6.*

★ The other outstanding building in Le Havre, and one of the most impressive 20th-century churches in France, is the **Église St-Joseph**, built to the plans of Auguste Perret in the 1950s. The 350-foot tower powers into the sky like a fat rocket. The interior is just as thrilling. No frills here: the 270-foot octagonal lantern soars above the crossing, filled almost to the top with abstract stained glass that hurls colored light over the bare concrete walls. ☒ *Bd. François-Ier* ☎ *02–35–42–20–03.*

Where to Stay & Eat

$$ ╳ **L'Odyssée.** With the port and fish market within netting distance, seafood is guaranteed to be fresh here. It's a no-frills place—the visual appeal is on your plate, in the pinks and greens of the smoked salmon and avocado sauce that accompany the chef's homemade fish terrine. Although it specializes in fresh fish, the Odyssée has its share of meat dishes—the breast of duck with three-pepper sauce is a winner. ☒ *41 rue du Général-Faidherbe* ☎ *02–35–21–32–42* ▭ *AE, MC, V* ◉ *Closed Mon. and mid-Aug.–early Sept. No dinner Sun., no lunch Sat.*

$ ▦ **Bordeaux.** The central location, overlooking the Bassin de Commerce, is this hotel's main plus—along with the welcoming owners. The light, airy rooms have modern furniture; the best have views of the port. As at all other hotels in Le Havre, prices are high for room size. ☒ *147 rue Louis-Brindeau, 76600* ☎ *02–35–22–69–44* 🖨 *02–35–42–09–27* ⤵ *30 rooms* ⚲ *Some minibars, cable TV, bar, Internet, parking (fee); no a/c* ▭ *AE, DC, MC, V* ⏏ *EP.*

HONFLEUR TO MONT-ST-MICHEL

Lower Normandy begins to the west of the Seine Estuary, near the Belle Epoque resort towns of Trouville and Deauville, extending out to the sandy Côte Fleurie (Flower Coast), stretching from the D-Day landing sites of Omaha and Utah beaches and continuing onward to the Cotentin Peninsula, which juts out into the English Channel. After the World War II D-Day landings, some of the fiercest fighting took place around Caen and Bayeux, as many monuments and memorials testify. 2004 saw the 60th anniversary of the landings and the subsequent 80-day Battle of Normandy. Leading the honorary June 5th celebrations, Prince Charles inaugurated the British Garden at the Caen Memorial museum, a massive parachuting display took place at Sante-Mère-Eglise (the site of the famous incident in The Longest Day), a replica of Philadelphia's Liberty Bell was set up at the landing beaches, and that night, L'Embrasement—fireworks set off simultaneously at 24 different sites along the coast—lit up the sky. Heading south, in the prosperous Pays d'Auge, dairy farms produce the region's famous cheeses. Rising to the west is the fabled Mont-St-Michel. Inland, heading back toward central France, lush green meadows and apple orchards cover the countryside starting west of the market town of Lisieux—the heart of calvados country.

Honfleur

㉓
Fodor'sChoice
★

24 km (15 mi) southeast of Le Havre via A131 and the Pont de Normandie, 27 km (17 mi) northwest of Pont-Audemer, 80 km (50 mi) west of Rouen.

The colorful port of Honfleur has become increasingly crowded since the elegant Pont de Normandie suspension bridge—providing a direct link with Le Havre and Upper Normandy—opened in 1995 across the Seine. It's the world's largest cable-stayed bridge, supported by two concrete pylons taller than the Eiffel Tower and designed to resist winds of 160 mph. The town of Honfleur, full of half-timber houses and cobbled streets, was once an important departure point for maritime expeditions, including the first voyages to Canada in the 15th and 16th centuries. The 17th-century harbor is fronted on one side by two-story stone houses with low, sloping roofs and on the other by tall, narrow houses whose wooden facades are topped by slate roofs.

★ Soak up the seafaring atmosphere by strolling around the old harbor and paying a visit to the ravishing wooden church of **Ste-Catherine**, which dominates a tumbling square. The church, and ramshackle belfry across the way, were built by townspeople to show their gratitude for the departure of the English at the end of the Hundred Years' War, in 1453. ⊠ *Rue des Logettes* ☎ *02–31–89–11–83.*

Where to Stay & Eat

$$-$$$ ✕ **La Terrasse de L'Assiette.** Gérard Bonnefoy, one of Honfleur's top chefs has opened this new place, offering seasonal delights such as succulent *noix de St-Jacques* (scallops with hazelnut risotto) and roast lamb from the salt marshes. ⊠ *8 pl. Ste-Catherine* ☎ *02–31–89–31–33* ▭ *AE, DC, MC, V* ☷ *Closed Mon. No dinner Sun. except July and Aug.*

¢-$ ✕ **L'Ancrage.** Massive seafood platters top the bill at this bustling restaurant in a two-story 17th-century building overlooking the harbor. The cuisine is authentically Norman—simple but good. If you want a change, try the succulent calf sweetbreads. ⊠ *16 rue Montpensier* ☎ *02–31–89–00–70* 🖷 *02–31–89–92–78* ▭ *MC, V* ☷ *Closed Wed. and last 2 wks in Mar. No dinner Tues. except July and Aug.*

★ $$$$ ✕▥ **La Ferme St-Siméon.** The story goes that this 19th-century manor house was the birthplace of Impressionism, and that its park inspired Monet and Sisley. Rooms are opulent, with pastel colors, floral wallpaper, antiques, and period accents. Those in the converted stables are quieter but have less character. Be aware, however, that the high prices have more to do with the hotel's reputation than with the amenities it offers (although thalassotherapy treatment is among them). The sophisticated restaurant specializes in fish; the cheese board does justice to the region. ⊠ *Rue Adolphe-Marais on D513 to Trouville, 14600* ☎ *02–31–81–78–00* 🖷 *02–31–89–48–48* ⊕ *www.saint-simeon.com* ⤵ *31 rooms, 3 suites* ⟡ *Restaurant, minibars, cable TV, tennis court, pool, sauna; no a/c* ▭ *AE, MC, V* ◯ *MAP.*

★ $$$-$$$$ ✕▥ **L'Absinthe.** A 16th-century presbytery with stone walls and beamed ceilings houses a small and charming hotel and the acclaimed restaurant of the same name. Rooms are comfortable but small, except for the attic suite, which has a private living room. Rooms are equipped with large modern bathrooms and Jacuzzis. The elegant and cozy reception area is adorned with an imposing stone fireplace. Chef Antoine Ceffrey is famous for his seasonal seafood and fish dishes such as turbot grilled with leeks. On sunny days request a table on the terrace; the restaurant is closed for dinner on Monday. ⊠ *10 quai de la Quarantaine* 🖀 *02–31–89–53–60* 🖷 *02–31–89–48–48* ⊕ *www.absinthe.fr* ➳ *7 rooms* ⚙ *Restaurant, in-room hot tubs, cable TV, some pets allowed (fee); no a/c* ▭ *DC, MC, V* ⊘ *Closed mid-Nov.–mid-Dec.* 🍽 *MAP.*

$$$ ✕🏠 **Le Manoir de Butin.** This scenic, ivy-covered Anglo-Norman manor is on top of a small wooded hill just 200 meters from the sea. All rooms have an appetizing view, are traditionally and tastefully furnished, and have modern marble bathrooms. The room on the first floor has a four-poster bed and its own balcony. The restaurant (closed Wednesday, no lunch Thursday or Friday) specializes in seasonal fish dishes such as a light lobster consommé and braised freshwater cod. ⊠ *Phare du Butin, 14600* 🖀 *02–31–81–63–00* 🖷 *02–31–89–59–23* ⊕ *www.hotel-lemanoir. fr* ➳ *10 rooms* ⚙ *Restaurant, cable TV, Internet, some pets allowed (fee); no a/c* ▭ *AE, MC, V* ⊘ *Closed Nov. and part of Jan.* 🍽 *MAP.*

$–$$ ✕🏠 **Le Clos St-Gatien.** This old Norman farmhouse with a modern annex, complete with outdoor swimming pool, is just outside Honfleur near the St-Gatien Forest. It's a perfect base for horseback riding (on-site facilities) or a round of golf at the nearby 18-hole course. Rooms in the main house are rustic, with exposed beams and traditional furniture; those in the annex lack character but have terraces that open out to the swimming pool. The restaurant serves simple Norman fare, such as blood sausage with roast apples, or grilled lamb with eggplant caviar. ⊠ *4 chemin des Bricoleurs, 14130* 🖀 *02–31–65–16–08* 🖷 *02–31–65–10–27* ⊕ *www.clos-st-gatien.fr* ➳ *58 rooms* ⚙ *Restaurant, 2 tennis courts, pool, gym, sauna, billiards* ▭ *AE, MC, V.*

Nightlife & the Arts

The two-day **Fête des Marins** (Marine Festival) is held on Pentecost Sunday and Monday. On Sunday all the boats in the harbor are decked out in flags and paper roses, and a priest bestows his blessing at high tide. The next day, model boats and local children head a musical procession.

Deauville-Trouville

㉔ *16 km (10 mi) southwest of Honfleur via D513, 92 km (57 mi) west*
Fodor's Choice *of Rouen.*
★

The twin seaside resorts of Deauville and Trouville are separated by the River Touques and joined by a bridge. The two towns have distinctly different atmospheres, but it's easy (and common) to shuttle between them. Trouville—whose beaches were immortalized in the 19th-century paintings of Eugène Boudin—is the oldest seaside resort in France. In the days of Louis-Philippe, it was discovered by artists and the upper crust; by the end of the Second Empire it was the beach à la mode. Then the Duc de Mornay, half-brother of Napoléon III, and other aristos who were looking for something more exclusive, built their villas along the deserted beach across the Touques. Thus was launched Deauville, a vigorous grande dame who started kicking up her heels during the Second Empire, kept swinging through the Belle Epoque, and is still frequented by a fair share of millionaires, princes, and French movie stars. Few of them ever actually get in the water here, since other attractions—casino, theater, music hall, polo, galas, racecourses, marina and regattas, palaces and gardens, and place Vendôme jewelry shops—compete. The Promenade des Planches—the boardwalk extending along the seafront and lined with deck chairs, bars, and striped cabanas—is the place for celebrity-spotting. With high-price hotels, designer boutiques, and one of the smartest gilt-edge casinos in Europe, Deauville's fashionable image still attracts the wealthy throughout the year.

Trouville—a short drive or five-minute boat trip across the Touques River from its more prestigious neighbor—remains more of a family resort, harboring few pretensions. If you'd like to see a typical French holiday spot rather than look for glamour, stay in Trouville. It, too, has a casino and boardwalk, an aquarium and bustling fishing port, plus a native population that makes it a livelier spot out of season than Deauville. ·

Where to Stay & Eat

$$$$ ✕⌂ **Normandy.** Well-heeled Parisians have been attracted to this imposing hotel, with its half-timber facade and underground passage to the casino, since it opened in 1912. Request a room with a sea view, and don't forget to ask about the special thalassotherapy rates with full or half-days of mud baths, salt massages, and soothing heated-seawater swims. Breakfast is served around the indoor pool. Creamy sauces are much in evidence in the mouthwatering Norman dishes served up in the restaurant. ✉ *38 rue Jean-Mermoz, 14800 Deauville* ☎ *02–31–98–66–22, 800/223–5652 for U.S. reservations* 🖷 *02–31–98–66–23* ⊕ *www. lucienbarriere.com* ⇱ *272 rooms, 25 suites* ⚴ *Restaurant, minibars, cable TV, pool, sauna, bar, Internet, some pets allowed (fee); no a/c* ⊟ *AE, DC, MC, V* ⦿ *BP.*

$ ⌂ **Continental.** One of Deauville's oldest buildings is now this provincial hotel, close to the train station yet within easy walking distance of the town center and downtown Trouville. Rooms are small but simple, pristine, and reasonably priced for Deauville. ✉ *1 rue Désiré-Le-Hoc, 14800 Deauville* ☎ *02–31–88–21–06* 🖷 *02–31–98–93–67* ⊕ *www. hotel-continental-deauville.com* ⇱ *42 rooms* ⚴ *Cable TV, Internet; no a/c* ⊟ *AE, DC, MC, V* ⊗ *Closed mid-Nov.–mid-Dec.* ⦿ *EP.*

Nightlife & the Arts

One of the biggest cultural events on the Norman calendar is the **American Film Festival,** held in Deauville during the first week of September. Formal attire is required at Deauville's **casino** (✉ 2 rue Edmond-Blanc ☎ 02–31–14–31–14). Trouville's **casino** (✉ Pl. du Maréchal-Foch ☎ 02–31–87–75–00) is slightly less highbrow than Deauville's. Night owls enjoy the smoky **Snake Pit Club** (✉ 13 rue Albert-Fracasse, Deauville); it's open until 5 AM. The **Y Club** (✉ 14 bis rue Désiré-le-Hoc, Deauville) is the place to go out dancing.

The Outdoors

At the **Club Nautique de Deauville** (✉ Quai de la Marine ☎ 02–31–88–38–19), hiring the smallest boat (16 feet) costs €25, although a day on an 80-foot yacht will set you back about €100 per person. Sailing boats large and small can also be rented from the **Club Nautique de Trouville** (✉ Digue des Roches Noires ☎ 02–31–88–13–59). Deauville becomes Europe's horse capital in August, when breeders jet in from around the world for its yearling auctions and the races at its two attractive **hippodromes** (racetracks). Head for the **Poney Club** (✉ Rue Reynolds-Mahn ☎ 02–31–98–56–24) for a wonderful horseback ride on the beach (the sunsets can be spectacular). They are open weekends and holidays, but be sure to call early to reserve your horse, or a pony for the little one.)

Houlgate

㉕   *14 km (9 mi) southwest of Deauville via D513, 27 km (17 mi) northeast of Caen.*

Cheerful Houlgate, bursting with wood-beam, striped-brick Belle Epoque villas and thatch-roof houses, paints a pretty picture, with the steep **Falaise des Vaches Noires** (Black Cow Cliffs) providing a rocky backdrop to the enormous sandy beach, which extends below the town casino. Leisure options include tennis, golf, and miniature golf, helping to make Houlgate a more personable alternative to neighboring **Cabourg**, evoked (as Balbec) by Marcel Proust in his epic *In Search of Lost Time*. Between the two resort towns is historic **Dives-sur-Mer,** with its oak-beam medieval market hall, rickety square, and chunky Gothic church. William the Conqueror set sail from Dives en route to England in 1066.

Where to Stay & Eat

★ $–$$ ✕▦ **1900.** Don't be misled by the tacky glass veranda: a wonderful dining room lurks within, with Art Nouveau lamps and a bronze and mahogany bar almost as old as the regiment of vari-sized calvados bottles that march across the top. Claire Lemarié is the good-humored *patronne*; her husband, André, is the deft cook with a penchant for fish and seafood (turbot, crayfish, and scallops); his pancake with orange-zest makes a distinctive dessert (you need to order it at the start of your meal). Service from the young trainees, impeccable in their black-and-white aprons, is discreet and helpful. The kitschy bedrooms are small but comfortable. ✉ *17 rue des Bains, 14510* ☎ *02–31–28–77–77* 🖷 *02–31–28–08–07* ⊕ *www.hotel-1900.fr* ⤶ *18 rooms* ⚹ *Restaurant, some pets allowed; no a/c* 🖃 *AE, MC, V* ⊙ *Closed Jan. and mid-Nov.–early Dec.* ¶◯❙ *MAP.*

$$$–$$$$ ▦ **Grand Hôtel.** This luxurious white-stucco hotel, on the seafront in Cabourg, has a lively piano bar in summer. Many rooms have balconies overlooking the sea; Proust used to stay in No. 147, which has been carefully refurnished following his descriptions. In the restaurant, Le Balbec (closed Monday and Tuesday from November through March), you can dine on traditional French cuisine of high quality but no great imagination. ✉ *Promenade Marcel-Proust, 14390 Cabourg* ☎ *02–31–91–01–79* 🖷 *02–31–24–03–20* ⊕ *www.cabourg-web.com/*

grandhotel ☞ *70 rooms* ♨ *Restaurant, minibars, cable TV, golf course,*
2 tennis courts, horseback riding, piano bar, Internet, some pets allowed
(fee); no a/c ▭ *AE, DC, MC, V* ⛄ *MAP.*

Caen

26 *26 km (16 mi) southwest of Houlgate, 120 km (75 mi) west of Rouen,*
Fodor'sChoice *150 km (94 mi) north of Le Mans.*
★

With its abbeys and castle, Caen, a busy administrative city and the capital of Lower Normandy, is very different from the coastal resorts.
William of Normandy ruled from Caen in the 11th century before he
conquered England. Nine hundred years later, the two-month Battle of
Caen in 1944 devastated much of the town in a fire that raged for 11
days. Today, the city is basically modern and commercial, with a vibrant
student scene. The Caen Memorial, an impressive museum devoted to
World War II, is considered a must-do by travelers interested in 20th-
century history (many avail themselves of the excellent bus tours the museum sponsors to the D-Day beaches). But Caen's former grandeur can
be seen in its extant historic monuments and along scenically restored
rue Ecuyère and place St-Sauveur. A good place to begin exploring Caen
is the **Hôtel d'Escoville,** a stately mansion in the city center built by
wealthy merchant Nicolas Le Valois d'Escoville in the 1530s. The building was badly damaged during the war but has since been restored; the
austere facade conceals an elaborate inner courtyard, reflecting the Italian influence on early Renaissance Norman architecture. The city **tourist
office** is housed here and is an excellent resource. ✉ *Pl. St-Pierre*
☎ *02–31–27–14–14* ⊕ *www.ville-caen.fr.*

Across the square, beneath a 240-foot spire, is the late-Gothic church
of **St-Pierre,** a riot of ornamental stonework. Looming on a mound
ahead of the church is the **château**—the ruins of William the Conqueror's fortress, built in 1060 and sensitively restored after the war.
The castle gardens are a perfect spot for strolling, and the ramparts afford good views of the city. The citadel also contains two museums and
the medieval church of **St-Georges,** used for exhibitions.

The **Musée des Beaux-Arts,** within the castle's walls, is a heavyweight among
France's provincial fine-arts museums. Its Old Masters collection includes
works by Poussin, Perugino, Rembrandt, Titian, Tintoretto, van der Wey-
den, and Paolo Veronese; there's also a wide range of 20th-century art.
✉ *Entrance by castle gateway* ☎ *02–31–30–47–70* ▭ *€3.90, free*
Wed. ☉ *Wed.–Mon. 9:30–6.*

The **Musée de Normandie** (Normandy Museum), in the mansion built
for the castle governor, is dedicated to regional arts, such as ceramics
and sculpture, plus some local archaeological finds. ✉ *Entrance by*
castle gateway ☎ *02–31–30–47–50* ⊕ *www.ville-caen.fr/mdn* ▭ *€1.50,*
free Wed. ☉ *Wed.–Mon. 9:30–12:30 and 2–6.*

Fodor'sChoice Caen's finest church, of cathedral proportions, is part of the **Abbaye aux**
★ **Hommes** (Men's Abbey), built by William the Conqueror from local Caen
stone (also used for Canterbury Cathedral, Westminster Abbey, and the

CloseUp

BILL CAME, SAW & CONQUERED

WHEN WILLIAM THE BASTARD, DUKE OF NORMANDY, got restless in 1066, he invaded England, and captured the English crown from King Harold in the Battle of Hastings. The Brits may still call him a bastard, but in France they changed his name to William the Conqueror. Ironically enough, the first town liberated by the British during the D-Day invasion was the town of Bayeux, where William's conquest of England is immortalized on the eponymous tapestry. Born in 1027, new Duke at eight, William survived an assassination attempt in Valognes and had to recapture Falaise Castle, where he was born, before ridding his duchy of feuding barons at the Battle of Val-ès-Dunes near Caen in 1047. In 1053 William snubbed a papal consanguinity ban to wed his distant cousin Matilda, daughter of the Count of Flanders. Alarmed by this new Norman-Flemish alliance, the King of France and Count of Anjou invaded Normandy. William defeated them at Mortemer in 1054. In 1059 new Pope Nicholas II gave William and Matilda his realpolitik blessing. Hoping to atone for having blown their chance at getting into heaven by their scandalous marriage, the lovebirds built the Abbaye aux Hommes and Abbays aux Dames in Caen. His severe salvation anxiety calmed a bit, William stormed west in 1062 to snare Dol, Dinan, and the Mont-St-Michel. Next stop England. When Edward the Confessor, cousin of William's father, died childless in London in 1066, William raised a fleet of 700 ships, sailed up the coast and crossed the Channel to Hastings, where he whupped usurper Harold on October 14. William returned home and died of wounds in Rouen in 1087 after laying siege to Mantes. He's buried in his manly abbey in Caen.

Tower of London). The abbey was begun in Romanesque style in 1066 and added to in the 18th century; its elegant buildings are now part of City Hall and some rooms are brightened by the town's fine collection of paintings. Note the magnificent yet spare facade of the abbey church of St-Étienne, enhanced by two 11th-century towers topped by octagonal spires. Inside, what had been William the Conqueror's tomb was destroyed by 16th-century Huguenots during the Wars of Religion. However, the choir still stands; it was the first to be built in Norman Gothic style, and many subsequent choirs were modeled after it. ⊠ Pl. Louis-Guillouard ☎ 02–31–30–42–81 ⊠ Church free, abbey tours €2 ☉ Tours daily at 9:30, 11, 2:30, and 4.

The **Abbaye aux Dames** (Ladies' Abbey) was founded by William the Conqueror's wife, Matilda, in 1063. Once a hospital, the abbey—rebuilt in the 18th century—was restored in the 1980s by the Regional Council, which then promptly requisitioned it for office space; however, its elegant arcaded courtyard and ground-floor reception rooms can be admired during a (free) guided tour. You can also visit the squat **Église de la Trinité** (Trinity Church), a fine example of 11th-century Romanesque architecture, though its original spires were replaced by timid balustrades in the early 18th century. Note the intricate carvings on columns and arches in the chapel; the 11th-century crypt; and, in the choir, the back marble slab commemorating Queen Matilda, buried here in 1083. ⊠ *Pl. de la Reine-Mathilde* ☎ *02–31–06–98–98* 🖼 *Free* ☉ *Guided tours daily at 2:30 and 4.*

★ The **Caen Mémorial,** an imaginative museum erected in 1988 in the north side of the city, is a must-see if you're interested in World War II history. The stark, flat facade, with a narrow doorway symbolizing the Allies' breach in the Nazi's supposedly impregnable Atlantic Wall, opens onto an immense foyer containing a café, brasserie, shop, and British Typhoon aircraft suspended overhead. The museum itself is down a spiral ramp, lined with photos and documents charting the Nazi's rise to power in the 1930s. The idea—hardly subtle but visually effective—is to suggest a descent into the hell of war. The extensive displays range from wartime plastic jewelry to scale models of battleships, with scholarly sections on how the Nazis tracked down radios used by the French Resistance and on the development of the atomic bomb. A room commemorating the Holocaust, with flickering candles and twinkling overhead lights, sounds a jarring, somewhat tacky note. The D-Day landings are evoked by a tabletop Allied map of the theater of war and by a split-screen presentation of the D-Day invasion from both the Allied and Nazi standpoints. Softening the effect of the modern 1988 museum structure are tranquil gardens; the newest is the British Garden, inaugurated by Prince Charles on June 5, 2004.

Readers rave about the Mémorial's four-hour minibus tours of the D-Day beaches, run daily April–September. You can book on their Web site (under "Guided Tours") and even make a day trip out of Paris for this by catching the 9 AM out of Gare St-Lazare to Caen and returning on the 8 PM train. The museum itself is fittingly set 10 minutes away from the Pegasus Bridge and 15 minutes from the D-Day beaches. ⊠ *Esplanade Dwight-D.-Eisenhower* ☎ *02–31–06–06–44* ⊕ *www.memorial. fr* 🖼 *€16.50* ☉ *Feb.–Oct., daily 9–7; Nov.–Dec. and late-Jan., daily 9–6.*

Where to Stay & Eat

$$$ ✕ **Le P'tit B.** On one of Caen's oldest pedestrian streets near the castle, this typically Norman 17th-century dining room—stone walls, beamed ceilings, and large fireplace—was home to Michel Bruneau, one of Normandy's top chefs, for nearly 30 years. Since 2003, and Bruneau's departure to the Mère Poulard on Mont-St-Michel, his former assistant, Cédric Mesnard, has taken over—offering a similar cuisine based on regional ingredients, at slightly more appetizing prices. ⊠ *15 rue de Vaugueux* ☎ *02–31–93–50–76* 🖼 *Reservations essential* 🖿 *MC, V* ☉ *Closed Mon.*

$$–$$$ ✕ **La Pommeraie.** Chef-owner José Aparicio's celebrated restaurant is in a former 17th-century priory in the village of Bénouville, close to Pegasus Bridge, northeast of Caen. Choose from seasonal dishes prepared in the classic Norman manner, such as the sole stuffed with wild autumn mushrooms or the pigeon stuffed with marinated cabbage and homemade foie gras. You can stay overnight in one of the 16 cozy rooms at the adjoining hotel, Le Manoir d'Hastings. ⊠ *18 av. de la Côte-de-Nacre,*

10 km (6 mi) northeast of Caen, 14970 Bénouville ☎ *02–31–44–62–43* ⏩ *Reservations essential* 🍽 *AE, DC, MC, V* ⊘ *Closed Mon., mid-Nov.–mid-Dec., and mid-Feb. No dinner Sun.*

$$–$$$ ✕🖼 **Dauphin.** Despite being in the heart of the city, this hotel, in a former 12th-century priory, is surprisingly quiet. Some of the smallish rooms have exposed beams; those overlooking the street are soundproof; the ones in back look out on the courtyard. Service is friendly and efficient in the hotel and in the excellent though expensive restaurant (dinner only in summer). ✉ *29 rue Gémare, 14000* ☎ *02–31–86–22–26* 🖨 *02–31–86–35–14* ⊕ *www.bestwestern.fr* 🛏 *37 rooms* 🍴 *Restaurant, minibars, cable TV, bar; no a/c* 🍽 *AE, DC, MC, V* ⊘ *Closed late July–early Aug. and part of Feb.* 🍽 *MAP.*

Shopping

A **marché aux puces** (flea market) is held on Friday morning on place St-Saveur and on Sunday morning on place Courtonne. In June, collectors and dealers flock to Caen's bric-a-brac and **antiques fair.**

The Outdoors

Take a barge trip along the canal that leads from Caen to the sea on the **Hastings** (✉ Quai Vendeuvre ☎ 02–31–34–00–00); there are four daily departures: 9 AM, noon, 3 PM, and 7 PM.

en route   Early on June 6, 1944, the British 6th Airborne Division landed by glider and captured the **Pegasus Bridge** (named for the division's emblem, showing Bellerophon astride his winged horse, Pegasus). This proved the first symbolic step toward the liberation of France from Nazi occupation. To see this symbol of the Allied invasion, from Caen take D514 north and turn right at Bénouville. The original bridge—erected in 1935—has been replaced by a similar but slightly wider bridge; but the original can still be seen at the adjacent **Mémorial Pegasus** visitor center (open daily February–November, €4). Café Gondrée by the bridge—the first building recaptured on French soil—is still standing, still serving coffee, and houses a small museum. A 40-minute son-et-lumière show lights up the bridge and the café at nightfall between June and September.

Five kilometers (3 mi) north of here, just beyond Ouistreham and its **Grand Bunker** museum recalling Hitler's Atlantic Wall, lie the easternmost D-Day landing beaches: **Sword Beach** extends to Luc-sur-Mer; **Juno Beach** to Courseulles; and **Gold Beach** to Arromanches. These flat, sandy beaches, stormed by British (Gold and Sword) and Canadian (Juno) troops, extend beneath pretty resort towns like Lion-sur-Mer, Langrune, and St-Aubin. Inland, slender church spires patrol the vast, flat horizon.

Arromanches-les-Bains

㉗ *31 km (19 mi) northwest of Caen, 10 km (6 mi) northeast of Bayeux.*

Little remains to mark the furious fighting waged hereabouts after D-Day. In the bay off Arromanches, however, some elements of the floating harbor are still visible. Head up to the terrace alongside Arromanches 360, high above the town on D65, to contemplate the seemingly insignificant hunks of concrete that form a broken offshore semicircle—and try to imagine the extraordinary technical feat involved in towing them across the Channel from England. General Eisenhower said that victory would have been impossible without this prefabricated harbor, which was nicknamed "Winston." The **Musée du Débarquement,** on the seafront, has models, mockups, and photographs depicting the creation of this technical marvel. ⊠ *Pl. du 6-Juin* ☎ *02–31–22–34–31* 🖃 *€6* ☽ *May–Sept., daily 9–7; Oct.–Dec. and Feb.–Apr., daily 10–12:30 and 1:30–5.*

Arromanches 360 is a striking modern movie theater with a circular screen—actually nine curved screens synchronized to show an 18-minute film (screenings at 10 past and 20 to the hour) titled *Le Prix de la Liberté* (*The Price of Freedom*). The film, which tells the story of the D-Day landings, is a mix of archival and more recent footage from major sites and cemeteries. Evocative music and sound effects serve as dramatic substitutes for spoken commentary. ⊠ *Chemin du Calvaire* ☎ *02–31–22–30–30* 🖃 *€3.70* ☽ *June–Aug., daily 9:10–6:40; May and Sept., 10:10–5:40; Oct.–Dec. and Feb.–Apr., daily 10:10–4:40.*

Where to Eat

$–$$ ✕ **Bistro d'Arromanches.** This brassy bistro has a warm and friendly aura and welcomes children—there is even a room upstairs with games and toys to keep them amused while Mommy and Daddy are enjoying the simple, classic fare. ⊠ *23 rue de Maréchal-Joffre* ☎ *02–31–22–31–32* 🖃 *MC, V* ☽ *Closed Tues., Wed., and Jan.*

Bayeux

28 *10 km (6 mi) southwest of Arromanches via D516, 28 km (17 mi) northwest of Caen.*

Bayeux, the first town to be liberated during the Battle of Normandy, was already steeped in history—as home to a Norman Gothic cathedral and the world's most celebrated piece of needlework: the Bayeux Tapestry. Bayeux's medieval backcloth makes it a popular base, especially among British travelers, for day trips to other towns in Normandy. The old-world mood is at its most boisterous during the Fêtes Médiévales, a market-cum-carnival held in the streets around the cathedral on the first weekend of July. Bayeux makes one of the best bases for visitors to the World War II sites.

Fodor'sChoice
★
Really a 225-foot-long embroidered scroll stitched in 1067, the **Bayeux Tapestry** (Tapestry Museum), known in French as the *Tapisserie de la Reine Mathilde* (Queen Matilda's Tapestry), depicts, in 58 comic-strip-type scenes, the epic story of William of Normandy's conquest of England in 1066. The tapestry was probably commissioned from Saxon embroiderers by the count of Kent—who was also the bishop of Bayeux—to be displayed in his newly built cathedral, the Cathédrale Notre-Dame. Despite its age, the tapestry is in remarkably good condition; the extremely detailed, often homey scenes provide an unequaled record of the clothes, weapons, ships, and lifestyles of the day. It's showcased in

the **Musée de la Tapisserie**; for €1 you can rent headphones and listen to an English commentary about the tapestry, scene by scene. ⊠ *Centre Guillaume-le-Conquérant, 13 bis rue de Nesmond* ☎ *02–31–51–25–50* ✉ *€7.40, joint ticket with Musée Baron-Gérard and the Hôtel du Doyen* ⊙ *May–Aug., daily 9–7; Sept.–Apr., daily 9:30–12:30 and 2–6.*

Housed in the Bishop's Palace beneath the cathedral, and fronted by a majestic plane tree planted in March 1797 and known as the Tree of Liberty, the **Musée Baron-Gérard** contains a fine collection of Bayeux porcelain and lace, ceramics from Rouen, a marvelous collection of pharmacy jars from the 17th and 18th centuries, and 16th- to 19th-century furniture and paintings by local artists. ⊠ *1 pl. de la Liberté* ☎ *02–31–92–14–21* ✉ *€7.40, joint ticket with Tapestry Museum and the Hôtel du Doyen* ⊙ *June–mid-Sept., daily 9–7; mid-Sept.–May, Wed.–Sun., 10–12:30 and 2–6.*

Bayeux's mightiest edifice, the **Cathédrale Notre-Dame,** is a harmonious mixture of Norman and Gothic architecture. Note the portal on the south side of the transept that depicts the assassination of English archbishop Thomas à Becket in Canterbury Cathedral in 1170, following his courageous opposition to King Henry II's attempts to control the church. ⊠ *Rue du Bienvenue* ☎ *02–31–92–01–85.*

Handmade lace is a specialty of Bayeux. The best place to learn about it and to buy some is the **Hôtel du Doyen,** which also houses a display of religious art. ⊠ *6 rue Lambert-Leforestier* ☎ *02–31–92–73–80* ✉ *€7.40, joint ticket with Tapestry Museum and Musée Baron-Gérard* ⊙ *Daily 9–12:30 and 2–6.*

At the **Musée de la Bataille de Normandie** (Battle of Normandy Museum) detailed exhibits trace the story of the struggle from June 7 to August 22, 1944. This modern museum near the British War Cemetery, sunk partly beneath the level of its surrounding lawns, contains some impressive war paraphernalia, including tanks, uniforms, weapons, and equipment. Waxworks and a film recount the invasion. ⊠ *Bd. du Général-Fabian-Ware* ☎ *02–31–51–46–90* ⊕ *www.mairie-bayeux.fr* ✉ *€5.50* ⊙ *May–mid-Sept., daily 9:30–6:30; mid-Sept.–Apr., daily 10–12:30 and 2–6.*

Fodor'sChoice
★ Sixteen kilometers (10 mi) southwest of Bayeux stands the **Château de Balleroy.** A connoisseur's favorite, it was built by architect François Mansart in 1626–36 and is a remarkably elegant 17th-century edifice. The *cour d'honneur* is marked by two stylish side pavilions—an architectural grace note adapted from Italian Renaissance models—which beautifully frame the small, but very seignorial, central mass of the house. Inside, the *salon d'honneur* is the very picture of Louis XIV decoration, while other rooms were recast in 19th-century chic by Malcolm Forbes, who bought the chateau in 1970. A gallery houses the fascinating **Musée des Ballons** (Balloon Museum), while the companion village was designed by Mansart in one of the first examples of town planning in France. ⊠ *Balleroy* ☎ *02–31–21–60–61* ⊕ *www.chateau-balleroy.com* ✉ *€7* ⊙ *Mid-Mar.–June and Sept.–mid-Oct., daily 9–noon and 2–6; July and Aug., daily 10–6.*

Where to Stay & Eat

$–$$$ ✕ **L'Amaryllis.** Pascal Marie's small restaurant has three prix-fixe menus, running €11–€28. The three-course dinner, with six selections per course, may include a half-dozen oysters, fillet of sole with a cider-based sauce, and pastries or chocolate gateau for dessert. Lobster and skate with shallots lurk *à la carte.* ⊠ *32 rue St-Patrice* ☎ *02–31–22–47–94* 🖿 *MC, V* ☺ *Closed Mon., Sun. evening in winter, and Jan.*

★ $$$$ ✕🏠 **Château d'Audrieu.** This family-owned château, with an elegant 18th-century facade, fulfills a Hollywood notion of a palatial property: princely opulence, wall sconces, overstuffed chairs, and antiques. Rooms 50 and 51 have peaked ceilings with exposed-wood beams. The restaurant (closed Monday, with lunch served weekends only) has an extensive wine list, and chef Alain Cornet keeps to a classic repertoire of dishes. ⊠ *13 km (8 mi) southeast of Bayeux off N13, 14250 Audrieu* ☎ *02–31–80–21–52* 🖨 *02–31–80–24–73* ⇔ *29 rooms* ⌂ *Restaurant, minibars, cable TV, pool, bar, helipad; no a/c* 🖿 *AE, MC, V* ☺ *Closed Dec.–mid-Feb.* ¶◎¶ *MAP.*

$$–$$$ ✕🏠 **Grand Hôtel du Luxembourg.** The Luxembourg has small but adequate rooms; all but two face a courtyard garden. It has one of the town's best restaurants, Les Quatre Saisons (closed January), with a seasonal menu. Depending on the time of year, choose the honey-roasted ham with melted apples, or braised turbot with sage. ⊠ *25 rue des Bouchers, 14400* ☎ *02–31–92–00–04, 800/528–1234 for U.S. reservations* 🖨 *02–31–92–54–26* ⇔ *23 rooms, 6 suites* ⌂ *Restaurant, cable TV, bar, dance club, Internet, some pets allowed (fee)* 🖿 *AE, DC, MC, V* ¶◎¶ *MAP.*

★ $$ 🏠 **Manoir du Carel.** The narrow slits serving as windows on the tower recall the origins of the 17th-century Manoir du Carel, set nicely halfway between Bayeux and the sea, which was originally constructed as a fortified manor during the Hundred Years' War. Current owner Jacques Aumond offers comfortable rooms with modern furnishings; public salons have 19th-century accents. The cottage on the grounds, ideal for families, has a kitchen plus a fireplace that masks a brick oven where villagers once had their bread baked. ⊠ *5 km (3 mi) northwest of Bayeux, 14400 Maisons* ☎ *02–31–22–37–00* 🖨 *02–31–21–57–00* ⇔ *3 rooms, 2 with bath, 1 with shower; 1 cottage* ⌂ *Tennis court; no a/c* 🖿 *MC, V* ¶◎¶ *BP.*

The Outdoors

Bicycles can be rented from **Family Home** (⊠ 39 rue Général-de-Dais ☎ 02–31–92–15–22) for about €8 a day. Ask the tourist office for in-

★ formation about trails. The **Rassemblement International de Ballons** (International Balloon Festival; ☎ 02–31–21–60–61 information) takes place every two years in mid-June, 16 km (10 mi) southwest of Bayeux at the early 17th-century **Château de Balleroy** (⇨ *see* above).

The D-Day Beaches

History focused its sights along the coasts of Normandy at 6:30 AM on June 6, 1944, as the 135,000 men and 20,000 vehicles of the Allied troops made land in their first incursion in Europe in World War II. The entire operation on this "Longest Day" was called Operation Overlord—the code name for the invasion of Normandy. Five beachheads (dubbed Utah,

Omaha, Gold, Juno, and Sword; they had previously had French names, such as St-Laurent and Colleville) were established along the coast to either side of Arromanches. Preparations started in mid-1943, and British shipyards worked furiously through the following winter and spring building two artificial harbors (called "mulberries"), boats, and landing equipment; the other harbor, moored off Omaha Beach, was destroyed on June 19, 1944, by a violent storm. The British and Canadian troops that landed on Sword, Juno, and Gold on June 6, 1944, quickly pushed inland and joined with parachute regiments previously dropped behind German lines, before encountering fierce resistance at Caen, which did not fall until July 9. Today, the best way to tour this region is by car. Public buses from Bayeux have fairly infrequent service, so opt instead for one of the guided bus tours leaving from Caen (*see* Tours *in* Normandy A to Z, *below*).

★ ❷ You won't be disappointed by the rugged terrain and windswept sand of **Omaha Beach**, 16 km (10 mi) northwest of Bayeux. Here you'll find the **Monument du Débarquement** (Monument to the Normandy Landings) and nearby, in Vierville-sur-Mer, the **U.S. National Guard Monument.** Throughout June 6th, Allied forces battled a hailstorm of German bullets and bombs, but by the end of the day they had taken the sector, although they had suffered grievous losses. In Colleville-sur-Mer is the hilltop **American Cemetery and Memorial,** designed by the landscape architect Markley Stevenson. It's a moving tribute to the fallen, with its Wall of the Missing (in the form of a semicircular colonnade), drumlike chapel, and avenues of holly oaks trimmed to resemble open parachutes. The crisply mowed lawns are studded with 9,386 marble tombstones; this is where Stephen Spielberg's fictional hero Captain John Miller was supposed to have been buried in *Saving Private Ryan.* You can look out to sea across the landing beach from a platform on the north side of the cemetery.

★ ❸ The most spectacular scenery along the coast is at the **Pointe du Hoc,** 13 km (8 mi) west of St-Laurent. Wildly undulating grassland leads past ruined blockhouses to a clifftop observatory and a German machine-gun post whose intimidating mass of reinforced concrete merits chilly exploration. Despite Spielberg's cinematic genius, it remains hard to imagine just how Colonel Rudder and his 225 men—only 90 survived—managed to scale the jagged cliffs with rope ladders and capture the German defenses in one of the most heroic and dramatic episodes of the war.

Head west around the coast on N13, pause in the town of **Carentan** to admire its modern marina and the mighty octagonal spire of the Église Notre-Dame, and continue northwest to **Sainte-Mère Église.** At 2:30 AM ❸ on June 6, 1944, the 82nd Airborne Division was dropped over Ste-Mère, heralding the start of D-Day operations. Famously, one parachutist—his name was John Steele—got stuck on the church tower (memorably recreated in the 1960 film *The Longest Day*); a dummy is strung up each summer to recall the event, and a stained-glass window inside the church honors American paratroopers. After securing their position at Ste-Mère, U.S. forces pushed north, then west, cutting off the Cotentin Peninsula on June 18 and taking Cherbourg on June 26. German defense proved fiercer farther south, and St-Lô was not liberated until July 19. Ste-Mère's symbolic importance as the first French village to be liberated from the Nazis is commemorated by the Borne 0 (Zero) outside the town hall—a large, domed milestone marking the start of the Voie de la Liberté (Freedom Way), charting the Allies' progress across France.

The **Musée des Troupes Aéroportées** (Airborne Troops Museum), built behind the church in 1964 in the form of an open parachute, houses documents, maps, mementos, and one of the Waco CG4A gliders used to drop troops. ⊠ *Pl. du 6-juin-1944* ☎ *02–33–41–41–35* 🖭 *€5* ⊙ *Feb.–mid-Nov., daily 10–noon and 2–6.*

★ ㉜ Head east on D67 from Ste-Mère to **Utah Beach**, which, being sheltered from the Atlantic winds by the Cotentin Peninsula and surveyed by lowly sand dunes rather than rocky cliffs, proved easier to attack than Omaha. Allied troops stormed the beach at dawn and just a few hours later had managed to conquer the German defenses, heading inland to then join up with the airborne troops. In **La Madeleine** (⊠ Plage de La Madeleine ☎ 02–33–71–53–35) inspect the glitteringly modern **Utah Beach Landing Museum** (⊠ Ste-Marie-du-Mont ☎ 02–33–71–53–35), whose exhibits include a W5 Utah scale model detailing the German defenses; it's open April–June and September–October, daily 9:30–noon and 2–6, and July and August, daily 9:30–6:30. Continue north to the **Dunes de Varreville**, set with a monument to French hero General Leclerc, who landed here. Offshore you can see the fortified **Iles St-Marcouf**. Continue to **Quinéville**, at the far end of Utah Beach, with its **museum** (⊠ Rue de la Plage ☎ 02–33–21–40–44) evoking life during the German Occupation; the museum is open April, May, and October, daily 10–noon and 2–6, and June–September, daily 9:30–6:30.

Where to Stay & Eat

$$$$ ✕🏨 **La Chenevière.** This grand 18th-century château, just inland from Port-en-Bessin, to the east of Omaha Beach, has rooms with modern furnishings, floor-to-ceiling windows, and flowered bedspreads. The restaurant (closed Monday, no lunch Tuesday) serves cuisine appropriate to its surroundings: chef Claude Esprabens specializes in scallops, while his roasted scampi with sesame seeds and fresh chanterelles is delicious. So is his warm sliced duck liver with raspberry sauce. ⊠ *Les Escures, 14520 Commes* ☎ *02–31–51–25–25* 🖷 *02–31–51–25–20* ⊕ *www.lacheneviere.fr* ⬐ *21 rooms* ⚭ *Restaurant, minibars, cable TV, bar, Internet, some pets allowed (fee); no a/c* ⊟ *AE, DC, MC, V* ⊙ *Closed Jan.–mid-Feb.* ⓧ *MAP.*

$ ✕🏨 **Casino.** You can't get closer to the action. This handsome, postwar, triangular-gabled stone hotel looks directly onto Omaha Beach. The bar is made from an old lifeboat, and it's no surprise that fish and regional cuisine with creamy sauces predominate in Bruno Clemençon's airy seaview restaurant. ⊠ *Rue de la Percée, 14710 Vierville-sur-Mer* ☎ *02–31–22–41–02* 🖷 *02–31–22–41–12* ⬐ *12 rooms, 4 with bath, 8 with shower* ⚭ *Restaurant, bar, some pets allowed; no a/c* ⊟ *MC, V* ⊙ *Closed mid-Nov.–mid-Mar.* ⓧ *MAP.*

St-Vaast-la-Hougue

㉝ *14 km (9 mi) north of Quineville D42/D14.*

The bustling harbor town of St-Vaast-la-Hougue has two waterfronts, one facing south toward its famous oyster beds, with Utah Beach beyond, the other to the west out toward the Channel. Between the two is a finger of land tipped by an imposing fort. Just offshore from St-Vaast is the **Ile de Tatihou,** a small island fortified by Vauban in 1692, along with the tiny Fort de l'Ilet, 200 yards to the south. Tatihou has a **Musée Maritime,** where you can admire objects salvaged from local shipwrecks and visit sprawling gardens where marine flora and exotic plants prosper in the temperate climate, along with thousands of seagulls and a hundred different species of migrating birds. ⊠ *Quai Vauban* ☏ *02–33–23–19–92* ⊕ *www.tatihou.com* ✑ *€7.60 round-trip boat ticket includes admission to museum and gardens.*

Cherbourg

㉞ *37 km (23 mi) northwest of St-Vaast-la-Hougue via N13.*

Perhaps best known for Michel Legrand's haunting theme from the 1960s film musical *Les Parapluies de Cherbourg* (*The Umbrellas of Cherbourg*), Cherbourg is no longer the thriving transatlantic port of a Belle Epoque heyday symbolized by the hyperelaborate facade of its 1882 **theater,** one of the few old monuments to survive World War II. Umbrellas are hardly the sunniest of city symbols, but the climate, though gusty, is generally mild, and it's fun to stroll around the grid of narrow lanes (many of them pedestrian-only) between the theater and the ramshackle **Église de la Trinité** (Holy Trinity Church) by the seafront—especially on Tuesday, Thursday, or Saturday, when the street market is in full swing.

It was back in 1686 that Vauban first spotted Cherbourg's potential as a defensive port beneath the rocky 360-foot Montagne du Roule, but it took the completion of a massive breakwater in 1853 before Cherbourg could harbor ocean-going ships. The first transatlantic liner docked in 1869; these days ferries ply the Channel to England (Portsmouth and Poole) and Ireland (Rosslare). You can take a short sea cruise around the bay from Port Chantereyne any afternoon from April through September (call 02–33–93–75–27 for details).

Cherbourg is also a major submarine base: more than 90 have been built here since 1899, and one, the *Redoutable,* is on display at the **Cité de La Mer** (Marine Center). You can tour the submarine with infrared commentary headsets; admire a barrage of designer fish-tanks; and plumb the depths of submarine history. There's also a salty seashop and a brasserie-type restaurant. The converted maritime rail station, a supremely elegant Art Deco edifice designed by René Levasseur, is spectacularly illuminated at night, when the restaurant stays open long after the museum has docked. ⊠ *Quai Lawton-Collins* ☏ *02–33–20–26–26* ⊕ *www.citedelamer.com* ✑ *€13* ♡ *June–mid-Sept., daily 9:30–7; mid-Sept.–Dec. and Feb.–May, daily 10–6.*

Uniforms, photographs, maps, flags, posters, and medals at the **Musée de la Libération** (Liberation Museum), on the hill above the town (excellent sea views), recall Cherbourg's pivotal role at the end of World War II, when it was the Allies' major bridgehead to France after the D-Day landings and the French terminus for the PLUTO sea-bed pipeline that pumped needed fuel under the Channel from the Isle of Wight. ✉ *Fort du Roule* ☎ *02–33–20–14–12* 🎟 *€3* ⏲ *May–Sept., daily 10–6; Oct.–Apr., Tues.–Sun. 9:30–noon and 2–5:30.*

Thirty works by local-born painter Jean-François Millet (of *Angélus* renown) can be seen at the **Musée Thomas-Henry,** the town art museum, along with works by Murillo, "Velvet" Brueghel, David, and such talented 19th-century regional artists as Guillaume Fouace and Félix Bahot. Sculpture and ceramics complete the collection. ✉ *Rue Vartel* ☎ *02–33–23–39–30* 🎟 *Free* ⏲ *Tues.–Sun. 10–noon and 2–6.*

5

Where to Stay & Eat

$$–$$$ ✕ **Vauban.** Warm, friendly, and family-owned, this spot is headed up by chef Daniel Imbert, who prefers to approach his cuisine with a light, modern touch, avoiding the cream that typifies classic Norman fare. The menu is seasonal, with set menus running €15–€38 and lots of fish and seafood temptations, such as the fresh *bar* (sea bass) with truffles or the coquilles St. Jacques with wild mushrooms. ✉ *22 quai de Caligny* ☎ *02–33–43–10–11* 📠 *02–33–43–15–18* 💳 *AE, MC, V* ⏲ *Closed Mon., 2 wks Feb., 2 wks Nov. No dinner Sun.*

¢ ✕ **Faitout.** This cozy, paneled bistro in the shopping district near the Church of the Trinity packs in locals with its friendly service and traditional French cuisine. Stews, steaks, duck, smoked salmon, and mussels are high on the menu. ✉ *25 rue de la Tour-Carree* ☎ *02–33–04–25–04* 💳 *MC, V* ⏲ *Closed Sun. No lunch Mon.*

¢–$ 🏨 **Ambassadeur.** This modernized quayside hotel offers good value, a central location, and an English-speaking staff. The better, and more expensive, rooms look out over the harbor. The Vauban restaurant, next door, is a calmer dinnertime alternative to the bustling Faitout. ✉ *22 quai de Caligny, 50100* ☎ *02–33–43–10–00* 📠 *02–33–43–10–01* 🌐 *www.ambassadeurhotel.com* *40 rooms, 35 with bath, 5 with shower* *Internet; no a/c* 💳 *AE, MC, V* ⏲ *Closed Dec. 24–Jan. 2* 🍽 *EP.*

St-Lô

35 *78 km (49 mi) southeast of Cherbourg, 36 km (22 mi) southwest of Bayeux.*

St-Lô, perched dramatically on a rocky spur above the Vire Valley, was a key communications center that suffered so badly in World War II that it became known as the "capital of ruins." The medieval **Église Notre-Dame** bears mournful witness to those dark days: its imposing, spire-topped west front was never rebuilt, merely shored up with a wall of greenish stone. Reconstruction elsewhere, though, was wholesale. Some of it was spectacular, like the slender, spiral-staircase tower outside Town Hall; the circular theater; or the openwork belfry of the church of Ste-Croix. The town was freed by American troops, and its rebuilding was financed with U.S. support, notably from the city of Baltimore.

The **Hôpital Mémorial France–États Unis** (France–United States Memorial Hospital), designed by Paul Nelson and featuring a giant mosaic by Fernand Léger, was named to honor those links.

St-Lô is capital of the Manche *département* (province) and, less prosaically, likes to consider itself France's horse capital. Hundreds of breeders are based in its environs, and the **Haras National** (National Stud) was established here in 1886. Call for details on how to visit on a summer afternoon. ✉ *Av. du Maréchal-Juin* ☎ *02-33-77-88-77* ⊕ *www. haras-nationaux.fr* ⌧ €4 ⊙ *June–Sept. 2:30 and 5:30, guided tours only.*

★ St-Lô's art museum, the **Musée des Beaux-Arts**, is the perfect French provincial museum. Its halls are airy, seldom busy, not too big, yet full of varied exhibits—including an unexpected masterpiece: *Gombault et Macée,* a set of nine silk-and-wool tapestries woven in Bruges around 1600 relating a tale about a shepherd couple, exquisitely showcased in a special circular room. Other highlights include brash modern tapestries by Jean Lurçat; paintings by Corot, Boudin, and Géricault; court miniatures by Daniel Saint (1778–1847); and the Art Deco pictures of Slovenian-born Jaro Hilbert (1897–1995), inspired by ancient Egypt. Photographs, models, and documents evoke St-Lô's wartime devastation. ✉ *Centre Culturel, pl. du Champ-de-Mars* ☎ *02-33-72-52-55* ⌧ €1.50 ⊙ *Wed.–Mon. 10–noon and 2–6.*

Coutances

36 *27 km (18 mi) southwest of St-Lô via D972.*

If you're interested in church architecture, you'll want to stop off in
★ Coutances. The largely 13th-century **Cathédrale Notre-Dame,** with its famous octagonal lantern rising 135 foot above the nave, is considered the most harmonious Gothic building in Normandy. On the outside, especially the facade, note the obsessive use of turrets, spires, slender shafts, and ultranarrow pointed arches squeezed senseless in their architectural pursuit of vertical takeoff. A further 200 yards down the street is the **Eglise St-Pierre,** topped by a chunky Renaissance pastiche of the cathedral lantern above a richly sculpted interior. The town's tumbling **Jardin des Plantes,** where an army of 12 gardeners tends 47,000 plants, is also worth a visit.

Where to Stay

★ ¢ ⊡ **Le Moulin Girard.** For English hospitality, cheerful conversation, and unusual, inexpensive accommodations, head to Brian and Pearl Mitchell's enchanting 200-year-old water mill. The main house has three small rooms, and there's also a miller's cottage with exposed beams and a two-bedroom suite—an ideal choice for a family or two couples. You can have your breakfast on the terrace overlooking the mill stream, or make arrangements for Pearl to whip up a regional specialty for lunch or dinner. ✉ *26 km (16 mi) southeast of Coutances; from Villedieu-les-Poêles take a right on D98 as you enter Percy in the direction of Tessy-sur-Vire and then go right on D452 for Le Chefresne, 50410 Le Chefresne* ☎ *02-33-61-62-06* ⮐ *3 rooms, 1 suite* ⚬ *No a/c* ⊟ *No credit cards* ⏏ *MAP.*

Granville

③⑦ *30 km (19 mi) south of Coutances via D971, 107 km (67 mi) south-west of Caen.*

Proud locals like to call Granville the "Monaco of the North." It perches on a rocky outcrop and does have a sea-water therapy center, but . . . the similarities end there. Free of casinos and sequins, Granville instead has a down-to-earth feel. Granite houses cluster around the church in the Vieille Ville, and the harbor below is full of working boats. From the ramparts there are fine views of the English Channel; catamarans breeze over to Jersey and the Iles Chausey daily in summer. Drive a few miles down the coast to find sandy beaches and a view of distant Mont-St-Michel.

¢ ✕ **Echaugette.** There is an excellent choice of grills and pancakes, both sweet and savory, at this quaint little crêperie on a narrow street in the upper town. Pancakes au gratin and with scallops are specialties. ⊠ *24 rue St-Jean* ☎ *02–33–50–51–87* ⊟ *No credit cards* ☉ *Closed Tues., Wed., and Nov.*

Nightlife & the Arts

The rambunctious **Carnaval de Granville** involves four days of parades and festivities, culminating each year on Shrove Tuesday. The **Grand Pardon des Corporations de la Mer,** a *pardon,* or religious festival, devoted to the sea, is celebrated on the last Sunday of July with a military parade, a regatta, and platefuls of shellfish.

The Outdoors

Granville is a center for aquatic sports; inquire about sailboat jaunts at the **Centre Régional de Nautisme** (⊠ Bd. des Amiraux ☎ 02–33–91–22–60). **Lepesqueux** (⊠ 3 rue Clément-Desmaisons ☎ 02–33–50–18–97) also rents boats and yachts.

Shopping

It's said that every French kitchen worth its salt buys its pans from **Villedieu-les-Poêles,** 28 km (18 mi) east of Granville. The town is famous for its copperware (and its bells), and shops line the main street, rue Carnot, but you can find smaller outlets, with better buys, on the parallel rue du Dr-Harvard. Note that Tuesday is market day, so parking can be a bit of a problem.

Mont-St-Michel

③⑧ *44 km (27 mi) south of Granville via D973, N175, and D43; 123 km*
Fodor'sChoice *(77 mi) southwest of Caen; 67 km (42 mi) north of Rennes; 325 km*
★ *(202 mi) west of Paris.*

Wrought by nature and centuries of tireless human toil, this sea-surrounded mass of granite adorned with the soul-lifting silhouette of the **Abbaye du Mont-St-Michel** may well be your most lasting image of Normandy. The abbey is perched on a 264-foot-high rock a few hundred yards off the coast: it's surrounded by water during the year's highest tides and by desolate sand flats the rest of the time. Be warned: tides in the bay are dangerously unpredictable. The sea can rise up to 45 feet at high tide and rushes in at incredible speed—more than a few ill-prepared tourists over the years have drowned. Also, be warned that there are patches of dangerous quicksand. A causeway—to be replaced in time by a bridge, allowing the bay waters to circulate freely—links Mont-St-Michel to the mainland. Leave your car in the parking lot (€2.50) along the causeway, outside the main gate. Just inside you'll find the tourist office, to the left, and a pair of old cannons (with cannonballs) to the right. If you're staying the night on Mont-St-Michel, take what you need in a small suitcase; you cannot gain access to your hotel by car. The Mont's tourist office is in the Corps de Garde des Bourgeois, just to the left of the island gates.

Legend has it that the Archangel Michael appeared in 709 to Aubert, Bishop of Avranches, inspiring him to build an oratory on what was then called Mont Tombe. The rock and its shrine were soon the goal of pilgrimages. The original church was completed in 1144, but further buildings were added in the 13th century to accommodate monks as well as the hordes of pilgrims who flocked here even during the Hundred Years' War, when the region was in English hands. During the period when Aquitaine was subjected to English rule, the abbey remained a symbol, both physical and emotional, of French independence. Because of its legendary origins and the sheer exploit of its centuries-long construction, the abbey became known as the *"Merveille de l'Occident"* (Wonder of the Western World). The granite used to build it was transported from the nearby Isles of Chausey and hauled up to the site. The abbey's construction took more than 500 years, from 1017 to 1521. The Romanesque choir was rebuilt in Gothic style during the 15th and 16th centuries and it was only thereabouts that the high Gothic spire was added—to step back several centuries, put your hand over your view of the spire and the abbey will, ipso facto, return to its original Romanesque squatness. The abbey's monastic independence was undermined during the 17th century, when the monks began to flout the strict rules and discipline of their order, drifting into a state of decadence that culminated in their dispersal and the abbey's conversion into a prison, well before the French Revolution. In 1874 the former abbey was handed over to a governmental agency responsible for the preservation of historic monuments. Emmanuel Frémiet's great gilt statute of St. Michael was added to the spire in 1897. Monks now live and work here again, as in medieval times: you can join them for daily mass at 12:15.

All year long, the hour-long guided tour in English (two a day and night in high season) and French (up to two an hour) takes you through the impressive Romanesque and Gothic abbey and the spectacular **Eglise Abbiatiale,** the abbey church which crowns the rock, as well as the **Merveille,** a 13th-century, three-story collection of rooms and passageways. La Merveille was built by King Philippe Auguste around and on top of the monastery; on its second floor is the Mont's grandest chamber, the **Salle des Chevaliers.** Another tour, which also includes the celebrated **Escalier de Dentelle** (Lace Staircase), and the pre-Roman and exquisitely evocative **Notre-Dame-sous-Terre** is longer, has a higher ticket price, and is only given in French. Invest in at least one tour while you are here—some of them get you on top of or into things you can't see alone. If you do go it alone, stop halfway up Grande-Rue at the medieval parish church of St-Pierre to admire the richly carved side chapel with its dramatic statue of St. Michael slaying the dragon. The **Grand Degré**, a steep, narrow staircase, leads to the abbey entrance, from which a wider flight of stone steps climbs to the **Saut Gautier Terrace** (named after a prisoner who jumped to his death from it) outside the sober, dignified church. After visiting the arcaded cloisters alongside, which offer vertiginous views of the bay, you can wander at leisure, and probably get lost, among the maze of rooms, staircases, and vaulted halls. Scattered through the Mont are four minimuseums, which share an admission ticket of €15. The **Maison Duguesclin** (⊠ Logis Tiphaine ☎ 02–33–60–14–09 ⊕ www.museesmontsaintmichel. com/) is the 15th-century home of Bertrand Duguesclin, a general fierce in his allegiance to the cause of French independence, and his wife, a noted astrologer. The **Musée Historique de Mont-St-Michel** (⊠ Chemin de la Ronde ☎ 02–33–60–07–01) traces the 1,000-year history of the Mont in one of its former prisons. The **Musée Maritime** (⊠ Grande Rue ☎ 02–33–60–14–09) explores the science of the Mont's tidal bay and has a vast collection of model ships. The **Archeoscope** (⊠ Chemin de la Ronde ☎ 02–33–60–14–09) explores the myths and legends of the Mont through a sound and light show. Some exhibits use wax figures fitted out in the most glamorous threads and costumes of the 15th century.

The island village, with its steep, narrow streets, is best visited out of season, from September to June. In summer the hordes of tourists and souvenir sellers can be stifling. Give yourself at least half a day here, and follow your nose. The mount is full of nooks, crannies, little gardens, and echoing views from the ramparts. When day-trippers depart, peace and quiet return to the Mont and you can appreciate its frightening grandeur. So make an overnight stay here, whatever the price. Time your visit a couple of days after the full moon to soak up sunsets over the Bay that touch lows of prestellar beauty. In past years, the Mont hosted a nighttime show, "**Les Imaginaires**"—the abbey was bathed in soft light and music and you could wander around without daytime crowds. Unfortunately, that has now been canceled but there are hopes to do a new light-show presentation, probably scheduled on weekends in May, then nightly during July and August. ☎ 02–33–89–80–00 ▣ *General admission: €7–11. Guided tours: 1 hour, €7; 2 hours, €11; audio-guide, €4.50. Museums: €15 ⊕ www.monum.fr ☉ May–Aug., daily 9–7; Sept.–Apr., daily 9:30–6.*

Where to Stay & Eat

$$–$$$ ✕▣ **La Mère Poulard.** This legendary hotel consists of adjoining houses with three steep flights of narrow stairs. The restaurant's reputation derives partly from Mère Poulard's famous soufflélike omelet, partly from its convenient location (right by the gateway, so don't expect views from atop the Mont), and partly from the talent of chef Michel Bruneau, who established his reputation with his own restaurant in Caen. Room prices start low but ratchet upward according to size; the smallest rooms are bearable for an overnight stay, not longer. Walls throughout are plastered with posters and photographs of illustrious guests. You are usually requested to book two meals with the room. Reservations are essential for the restaurant in summer. ⊠ *Grande-Rue, 50116*

☎ 02–33–89–68–68 🖷 02–33–89–68–69 ⊕ *www.mere-poulard.com* ⮑ *30 rooms ⚭ Restaurant, minibars, cable TV, piano bar; no a/c* ▭ *AE, DC, MC, V* ⦿| *MAP.*

★ **$–$$$** ✕▥ **Manoir de la Roche Torin.** Run by the Barraux family, this pretty, slate-roofed, stone-walled manor set in 4 acres of parkland is a delightful alternative to the high cost of staying on Mont-St-Michel. Rooms are pleasantly old-fashioned, and the bathrooms modern. With walls of Normand stonework and its open fireplace, the restaurant (closed Tuesday, Wednesday, and Saturday lunch) has superb seafood and char-grilled *pré-salé* (salt-meadow lamb), served by chef Patrice Soisnard. In summer, aperitifs are served in the garden, with a view of Mont-St-Michel. ✉ *34 rte. de la Roche-Torin, 9 km (5 mi) from Mont-St-Michel, 50220 Courtils* ☎ *02–33–70–96–55* 🖷 *02–33–48–35–20* ⊕ *www.manoir-rochetorin.com* ⮑ *15 rooms ⚭ Restaurant, minibars, bar, Internet, some pets allowed (fee); no a/c* ▭ *AE, DC, MC, V* ⊙ *Closed mid-Nov.–mid-Feb.* ⦿| *MAP.*

$$ ✕▥ **Les Terrasses Poulard.** Run by the folks who own the noted Mère Poulard hotel, this ensemble of buildings is clustered around a small garden in the middle of the Mount. Rooms at this hotel are some of the best—with views of the bay and rustic-style furnishings—and most spacious on the Mount, although many require you to negotiate a labyrinth of steep stairways. ✉ *Grande-Rue, opposite parish church, 50116* ☎ *02–33–89–02–02* 🖷 *02–33–60–37–31* ⊕ *www.terrasses-poulard.com* ⮑ *30 rooms ⚭ Restaurant, minibars, cable TV, billiards, library; no a/c* ▭ *AE, DC, MC, V* ⦿| *MAP.*

$ ✕▥ **Hôtel Du Guesclin.** The courtesy of the staff, the comfy and clean guest rooms, and a choice of two restaurants make this well-maintained hotel a pleasant option. Downstairs try the casual brasserie for salads and sandwiches; upstairs the panoramic full-service restaurant has a wonderful view of the bay. ✉ *Grande-Rue, 50116* ☎ *02–33–60–14–10* 🖷 *02–33–60–45–81* ⮑ *10 rooms ⚭ 2 restaurants; no a/c* ▭ *MC, V* ⊙ *Closed Wed. and Nov.–Mar.* ⦿| *MAP.*

$$–$$$ ▥ **L' Auberge St-Pierre.** You are not overwhelmed with choices on Mont-St-Michel when it comes to guest accommodations. However, this inn is a popular spot thanks to the fact that it's in a listed half-timber 15th-century building adjacent to the ramparts and has its own garden restaurant that offers seasonal specialties and interesting half-board rates. If you're lucky, you'll wind up in No. 16, which has a view of the abbey. The hotel annex, La Croix Blanche, has another nine rooms (shower only). ✉ *Grande-Rue, 50116* ☎ *02–33–60–14–03* 🖷 *02–33–48–59–82* ⊕ *www.auberge-saint-pierre.fr* ⮑ *21 rooms ⚭ Restaurant, cable TV, Internet; no a/c* ▭ *AE, MC, V* ⦿| *MAP.*

---

en route From Mont-St-Michel head east on N176/D977 to the attractive hilltop towns of Mortain and Domfront, then north on D962, through Flers and Condé-sur-Noireau, to Clécy, a cute hilltop town on the fringe of **La Suisse Normande** (Norman Switzerland), a rocky expanse of hills and gullies. Stop for a drink at La Potinière Café (closed October–April), on the bank of the Orne River beneath Clécy, then drive south along the bank to Pont d'Ouilly, whose Hôtel du

Commerce serves a good lunch. Take D167 to the Roche d'Oëtre, a rock with spectacular views of the craggy hills that give the region its name, and continue along D301 to the Gorges de St-Aubert, a dramatic river gorge, before taking D21 northeast to Falaise.

Falaise

39 *132 km (82 mi) northeast of Mont-St-Michel, 32 km (20 mi) south of Caen.*

The memory of William the Conqueror, born here in 1027 as the illegitimate child of Duke Robert of Normandy and a local girl called La Belle Arlette, haunts the lively town of Falaise. William can be admired on a rearing bronze steed in the main square, and you can see the fountain where Robert is said to have first laid eyes on the lovely Arlette as she washed her clothes. Although Falaise was badly mauled during the Battle of Normandy, parts of the original town walls remain, as do the impressive medieval churches of St-Gervais, La Trinité, and Notre-Dame de Guibray. The foursquare **Château Guillaume-le-Conquérant** (Conqueror's Castle) glowers down from a spur above the town. Little has survived from the original building where William was born—but what remains is old enough. ⊠ *Pl. Guillaume-le-Conquérant* ☎ *02-31-41-61-44* 🎫 *€5* 🕙 *Feb.–Dec., daily 10–6.*

☾ At **Automates Avenue,** 300 clockwork toys and automatons, from the turn of the 20th century to the 1950s, are artfully presented in display windows evoking the streets of Paris. ⊠ *Bd. de la Libération* ☎ *02-31-90-02-43* 🎫 *€4.60* 🕙 *Apr.–Sept., daily 10–12:30 and 1:30–6; Oct.–mid-Jan. and Feb.–Mar., weekends 10–12:30 and 1:30–6.*

Where to Eat

★ **$-$$** ✕ **La Fine Fourchette.** Chef Gilbert Costil attracts local devotees with dishes combining color, flavor, and quantity. Salmon and tuna gazpacho, foie gras with hazelnut dressing, grilled turbot with lemon, and chocolate cake with pistachio cream stand out among his specialties. Madame Costil provides a gracious welcome. ⊠ *52 rue Georges-Clemenceau* ☎ *02-31-90-08-59* ▤ *AE, MC, V* 🕙 *Closed Wed. and Feb. No dinner Tues.*

> **off the beaten path**
>
> **CHÂTEAU D'O –** This château's storybook turrets, checkerboard walls, and improbably steep slate roofs rise above a moat patrolled by regal swans near Mortrée, 35 km (22 mi) southeast of Falaise. Inside, look out for the sculpted ermine emblem of the O family, distinguished both as royal courtiers and for possessing the shortest family name in France. With old houses, a stately town hall, and a majestic bishop's palace, nearby **Sées** exudes faded charm. The 200-foot spires of the **Cathédrale St-Latrium** are visible for miles around; note the exquisite late-13th-century stained glass in the soaring choir and the two rose windows in the transepts. ☎ *02–33–35–34–69* 🎫 *€5* 🕙 *Mar.–Nov., Wed.–Mon. 2–5.*

Historic **Alençon,** 22 km (16 mi) south of Sées via N138, has been a lace-making center since 1665; by the end of the 17th-century *point d'Alençon* (Alençon needlepoint lace) was de rigueur on women's and men's clothing. The **Musée des Beaux-Arts et de la Dentelle** has a sophisticated collection of lace from Italy, Flanders, and France, along with paintings from the French school that span from the 17th to 20th centuries. ✉ *Rue du Capitaine-Charles-Aveline* ☎ *02–33–32–40–07* 🖭 *€2.90* 🕙 *Tues.–Sun. 10–noon and 2–6.*

St-Pierre-sur-Dives

40 *26 km (16 mi) northeast of Falaise on D511.*

St-Pierre-sur-Dives's main claim to fame is the finest medieval barn in Normandy; known as **Les Halles,** it was built in the 11th century, then enlarged in the 16th. It's best visited while the flower and food market is in full swing here on a Monday morning, when a lively cattle auction is held on the square outside. You can also admire the soaring medieval Eglise Abbatiale (abbey church), and visit its chapter house and cloisters; or explore the old tanners' district, with its washhouse and water mill.

> **en route** For apple brandy, make a detour through the **Pays d'Auge,** north of St-Pierre-sur-Dives. This is the heart of calvados country: you don't need a fixed itinerary, just follow your nose and the minor roads, keeping an eye out for local farmers selling calvados. When you are buying calvados, or any regional product for that matter, always request the AOC label, *appéllation d'origine contrôlée,* which assures that the product is made from the finest local ingredients. One good distillery to seek out is the Grandval Calvados Distillery in **Cambremer.**

Lisieux

41 *25 km (16 mi) northeast of St-Pierre-sur-Dives via D511, 82 km (51 mi) southwest of Rouen.*

Lisieux is the main market town of the prosperous and agriculturally bountiful Pays d'Auge region. Although the town emerged relatively unscathed from World War II, it has few historic monuments beyond the 12th- and 13th-century **Cathédrale St-Pierre.** (The tower to the left of the imposing facade is later than it looks—it's a rare example of 17th-century neo-Gothic reconstruction.) ✉ *Pl. François-Mitterrand* ☎ *02–31–62–09–82.*

Lisieux's fame stems from St. Theresa (1873–97), who came here as a child, joined a convent at 15, and spent the last 10 years of her life as a Carmelite nun. Theresa was canonized in 1925, and in 1954 the **Basilique Ste-Thérèse**—one of the world's largest 20th-century churches, with a huge dome and an interior of colored marble—was built in her honor. From the cathedral walk up avenue Victor-Hugo and branch left onto avenue Jean-XXIII. A **son-et-lumière** show, running through 2,000 years of history, is presented at the basilica Monday–Saturday nights at

9:45 from June to September. The **Procession de la Vierge** (Virgin's Procession) is held on August 15. The **Procession de la Fête Ste-Thérèse** (St. Theresa's Day Parade) is on the last Sunday in September. ✉ *Av. Jean-XXIII* ☎ *02–31–78–52–62* 🖱 *Son-et-lumière €6.*

$–$$ ✕🏨 **Espérance.** This imposing Art Deco hotel in the center of town has typically subdued Norman elegance with its exposed beams and small balconies. Rooms are clean, simple, and, despite the location, quiet. The Pays d'Auge restaurant, on the first floor, has a traditional menu with regional specialties like seafood terrine, leg of duck with apple, and sole flamed in calvados. ✉ *16 bd. St-Anne* ☎ *02–31–62–17–53* 🖶 *02–21–62–34–00* ⊕ *www.lisieux-hotel.com* 🛏 *100 rooms* ⌂ *Restaurant, cable TV, bar, Internet, some pets allowed (fee); no a/c* ▭ *AE, DC, MC, V* ⊙ *Closed Nov.–late Mar.* ⌾ *MAP.*

Bernay

⓬ *32 km (20 mi) southeast of Lisieux via N13/D138.*

It may be off some tourist tracks, but Bernay is well worth seeking out. Canals formed by the arms of the Cosnier and Charentonne rivers line its narrow, half-timbered streets. The avenues, liquid and solid, entwine the majestic Romanesque **Église Abbatiale** (abbey church), sparklingly restored for use as an exhibit center, and the lovably old-fashioned town museum with its earnest array of paintings and ceramics.

Thirteen kilometers (8 mi) southeast of Bernay lies the early 17th-century **Château de Beaumesnil,** one of the most grandiose constructions in Normandy: a stripey wedding cake of brick and stone whose ski-slope roofs soar above a moat with a Baroque boxwood maze, set within 100 acres of parkland designed by Jean-Baptiste de la Quintinye, Le Nôtre's assistant at Versailles. The interior is famed for its sumptuous library and permanent exhibit on the art of bookbinding. ☎ *02–32–44–40–09* 🖱 *€6* ⊙ *Apr.–June and Sept., Fri.–Mon. 2–6; July and Aug., Wed.–Mon. 10–noon and 2–6.*

Évreux

⓭ *59 km (37 mi) east of Bernay via D133/D31, 100 km (62 mi) northwest of Paris via A13 and N13.*

From the 5th century on, Évreux, capital of the Eure province, was ravaged and burned by a succession of armies—first the Vandals, followed by the Normans, the English, and various French kings. World War II played its part as well. But the town, crisscrossed by the Iton River and known as the City of 100 Bridges, has been embellished with gardens and placid, overgrown footpaths.

Évreux's principal historic site is the **Cathédrale Notre-Dame,** in the heart of town just off rue Corbeau. Unfortunately, it was an easy victim of the many fires and raids that took place over the centuries; all that's left of the original 12th-century construction are the nave arcades. The lower parts of the chancel date from 1260, the chapels from the 14th century. Yet it's an outstanding example of Flamboyant Gothic inside and out. Don't miss the choir triforium and transept or the 14th-century stained-glass windows in the apse. ⊠ *Pl. Notre-Dame* ☎ 02–32–33–06–57.

Where to Stay & Eat

★ ¢ ✕ **Biche.** This hotel restaurant, in a former coaching inn whose quaint, glass-roofed inner courtyard showcases racy Belle Epoque woodwork, offers startling value, with a choice of veal, coq au vin, skate, mussels and chips, or braised chicken with chives, all for €9 or less. For €10.50 you can have any of the above plus terrine, oysters, or mixed salad for starters. Try for a window seat overlooking the late Gothic church of St-Taurin, worth a post-prandial visit for its 13th-century, gilt-silver reliquary casket, shaped like a miniature Sainte-Chapelle. ⊠ *Pl. St-Taurin* ☎ *02–32–38–66–00* 🖨 *02–32–33–54–05* ▤ *MC, V* ⊘ *Closed Sun.*

NORMANDY A TO Z

To research prices, get advice from other travelers, and book travel arrangements, visit www.fodors.com.

AIR TRAVEL

CARRIERS Air France flies to Caen from Paris. Ryanair flies from Dinard in Brittany, 35 mi west of Mont-St-Michel, to London's Stansted airport.

🛂 **Airlines & Contacts Air France** ☎ 08-02-80-28-02 for information ⊕ www.airfrance.com. **Ryanair** ⊕ www.ryanair.com for information.

AIRPORTS

Paris's Charles de Gaulle (Roissy) and Orly airports are the closest intercontinental links with the region. From London there are regular flights to Caen and Deauville on Air France; and from Southampton and the Channel Islands to Cherbourg.

🛂 **Airport Information Caen** ☎ 02-31-71-20-10. **Cherbourg** ☎ 02-33-88-57-60. **Deauville** ☎ 02-31-65-65-65. **Rouen** ☎ 02-35-79-41-00.

BIKE & MOPED TRAVEL

You can rent bicycles at most major train stations for about €8 per day. Traveling with your bike is free on all regional trains and many national lines; be sure to ask the SNCF which ones when you're booking.

BOAT & FERRY TRAVEL

A number of ferry companies sail between the United Kingdom and ports in Normandy. Brittany Ferries travels between Caen (Ouistreham) and Portsmouth and between Poole and Cherbourg. The Dieppe-Newhaven route is covered both by boat, with a daily service from Transmanche, and by Hoverspeed, which runs daily in summer, weekends only in winter (and not at all January–mid-February). P&O goes between Le Havre and Portsmouth and between Cherbourg and Portsmouth.

FARES & 🛂 **Boat & Ferry Information Brittany Ferries** ☎ 08–03–82–88–28 ⊕ www.
SCHEDULES brittany-ferries.com. **Hoverspeed** ☎ 08-20-00-35-55 ⊕ www.hoverspeed. com. **P&O** ☎ 08-03-01-30-13 ⊕ www.poportsmouth.com. **Transmanche** ☎ 08-00-65-01-00 ⊕ www.transmancheferries.com.

BUS TRAVEL

Three main bus systems cover the towns not served by trains. **CNA** (Compagnie Normande Autobus) runs around Upper Normandy from Rouen to the towns along the Côte d'Alabâtre, including Le Havre. **Autos-Cars Gris** runs buses from Fécamp to Le Havre, stopping in Étretat along the way. **Bus Verts du Calvados** covers the coast from Honfleur to Bayeux; They also run, during July and August, the special D-Day Circuit 44, which allows you to see as many D-Day sights as you can squeeze into one day—these buses depart from the train stations in Bayeux and Caen.

Bus routes connect many towns, including Rouen, Dieppe, Fécamp, Étretat, Le Havre, Caen, Honfleur, Deauville, Trouville, Cabourg, and Arromanches. For Mont-St-Michel, hook up with buses from nearby Pontorson or from Rennes in adjacent Brittany. If you are traveling from Paris to the Mont, take the high-speed TGV train from Gare Montparnasse to Rennes (in high season, five departures a day), then a **Couriers Breton** bus transfer to the Mont. Tourist offices and train stations in Normandy will have printed schedules.

🔝 Bus Information **CNA** ☎ 02-35-52-92-92. **Autos-Cars Gris** ☎ 02-35-28-19-88. **Bus Verts du Calvados** ☎ 02-31-44-77-44. **Les Couriers Breton** ☎ 02-99-19-70-70.

CAR RENTAL

🔝 Local Agencies **Avis** ✉ 44 pl. de la Gare, Caen ☎ 02-31-84-73-80 ✉ 32 av. de Caen, Rouen ☎ 02-35-72-64-32. **Europcar** ✉ 6 rue du Dr-Piasecki, Le Havre ☎ 02-35-25-21-95.

CAR TRAVEL

From Paris A13 slices its way to Rouen in 1½ hours (toll €4.50) before forking to Caen (an additional hour, toll €6.70) or Le Havre (45 minutes on A131). N13 continues from Caen to Cherbourg via Bayeux in another two hours. From Paris, D915, the scenic route, will take you to Dieppe in about three hours.

The Pont de Normandie, between Le Havre and Honfleur, effectively unites Upper and Lower Normandy. A13/N13, linking Rouen to Caen, Bayeux, and Cherbourg, is the backbone of Normandy. At Caen the A84 forks off southwest toward Mont-St-Michel and Rennes.

EMERGENCIES

🔝 **Regional hospitals** ✉ Av. de la Côte-de-Nacre, Caen ☎ 02-31-06-31-06 ✉ 29 av. Pierre-Mendès-France, Montivilliers, Le Havre ☎ 02-32-73-32-32 ✉ 1 rue Germont, Rouen ☎ 02-32-88-89-90.

SPORTS & THE OUTDOORS

🔝 Canoeing & Kayaking **Fédération Française de Canoë-Kayak** ✉ 87 quai de la Marne BP 58, 94340 Joinville-le-Pont ☎ 01-48-89-39-89.

🔝 Fishing **Conseil Supérieur de la Pêche** ✉ 134 av. Malakoff, 75016 Paris ☎ 01-45-02-20-20.

🔝 Hiking **Comité Départemental de la Randonnée Pédestre de Seine-Maritime** ✉ 18 rue Henri-Ferric, 76210 Gruchet-le-Valasse ☎ 02-35-31-05-51.

🔝 Horseback Riding **Ligue de Normandie des Sports Équestres** ✉ 181 rue d'Auge, 14000 Caen ☎ 02-31-84-61-87.

TOURS

The firm Wellcome arranges personalized driving tours with an English-speaking driver. Viking Voyages specializes in two-day packages by car, with overnight stays in private châteaux, as well as bike trips around the region and the Normandy Antiques tour by car. They can also meet travelers at Orly or Roissy airports.

🔢 Fees & Schedules **Wellcome** ✉ 130 rue Martainville, 76000 Rouen ☎ 02-35-07-79-79. **Viking Voyages** ✉ 16 rue du Général-Giraud, 14000 Caen ☎ 02-31-48-58-52 ⊕ www.viking-voyages.com.

BUS TOURS Cityrama and Paris-Vision run full-day bus excursions from Paris to Mont-St-Michel for €140–€155, meals and admission included. This is definitely not for the faint of heart—buses leave Paris at 7:15 AM and return around 10:30 PM. In Caen, the Mémorial organizes four-hour English-language daily minibus tours of the D-Day landing beaches; the cost is €60, including entrance fees. Bus Fly runs a number of trips to the D-Day beaches and Mont-St-Michel; a full-day excursion to the D-Day beaches (8:30–6:00) runs about €55.

🔢 Fees & Schedules **Bus Fly** ✉ 25 rue des Cuisiniers, 14400 Bayeux ☎ 02-31-22-00-08. **Cityrama** ✉ 4 pl. des Pyramides, 75001 Paris ☎ 01-44-55-61-00. **Mémorial** ☎ 02-31-06-06-44. **Paris-Vision** ✉ 214 rue de Rivoli, 75001 Paris ☎ 08-00-03-02-14.

TRAIN TRAVEL

From Paris (Gare St-Lazare), separate train lines head to Upper Normandy (Rouen and Le Havre or Dieppe) and Lower Normandy (Caen, Bayeux, and Cherbourg, via Évreux and Lisieux). Taking the train from Paris to Mont-St-Michel is not easy—count on about 3½ hours to get to the closest station (Pontorson), with another 15-minute bus or taxi ride to take you to the foot of the abbey (buses are directly in front of the station, with departures every 20 minutes).

Unless you are content to stick to the major towns (Rouen, Le Havre, Dieppe, Caen, Bayeux, Cherbourg), visiting Normandy by train may prove frustrating. You can sometimes reach several smaller towns (Fécamp, Deauville, Houlgate) on snail-paced branch lines, but the irregular intricacies of what is said to be Europe's most complicated regional timetable will probably have driven you nuts by the time you get there.

🔢 Train Information **SNCF** ☎ 08-36-35-35-35 ⊕ www.ter-sncf.com/uk/haute-normandie.

TRAVEL AGENCIES

🔢 Local Agent Referrals **Havas** ✉ 57 quai George-V, Le Havre ☎ 02-32-74-75-76 ✉ 25 Grande-Rue, Alençon ☎ 02-33-82-59-00 ✉ 80 rue St-Jean, Caen ☎ 02-31-27-10-50.

VISITOR INFORMATION

The capital of each of Normandy's *départements*—Caen, Évreux, Rouen, St-Lô, and Alençon—has its own central tourist office. Other major Norman towns with tourist offices are listed below the département offices by name.

🔢 Tourist Information **Caen** ✉ Pl. du Canada ☎ 02-31-27-90-30 🖳 02-31-27-90-35 ⊕ www.ville-caen.fr for Calvados. **Évreux** ✉ Bd. Georges-Chauvin ☎ 02-32-31-51-51 🖳 02-32-31-05-98 ⊕ www.normandy-tourism.org for Eure. **Rouen** ✉ 6 rue de la

Couronne, B.P. 60 Bihorel Cedex ☎ 02-35-12-10-10 🖷 02-35-59-86-04 ⊕ www.mairie-rouen.fr for Seine-Maritime. **St-Lô** ✉ Maison du Département, rte. de Villedieu ☎ 02-33-05-98-70 ⊕ www.manchetourisme.com/gb/ for Manche.

Bayeux ✉ Pont St-Jean ☎ 02-31-51-28-28 ⊕ www.bayeux-tourism.com. **Cherbourg** ✉ 2 quai Alexandre-III ☎ 02-33-93-52-02 ⊕ www.cherbourg-channel.tm.fr. **Dieppe** ✉ Pont Jehan-An ☎ 02-35-84-11-77 ⊕ www.dieppe-tourisme.com. **Fécamp** ✉ 113 rue Alexandre-le-Grand ☎ 02-35-28-51-01 ⊕ www.fecamp.com. **Falaise** ✉ Le Forum, bd. de la Libération ☎ 02-31-90-17-26. **Le Havre** ✉ 186 bd. Clemenceau ☎ 02-32-74-04-04 ⊕ www.ville-lehavre.fr. **Honfleur** ✉ 9 rue de la Ville ☎ 02-31-89-23-30 ⊕ www.ville-honfleur.fr. **Lisieux** ✉ 11 rue d'Alençon ☎ 02-31-62-08-41 ⊕ www.ville-lisieux.fr. **Mont-St-Michel** ✉ Corps de Garde ☎ 02-33-60-14-30 ⊕ www.mont-saintmichel.com.

THE NORTH & CHAMPAGNE

6

Revised and
updated by
Simon Hewitt

Introduction by
Nancy Coons

FLAT AS A CREPE AS FAR AS THE EYE CAN SEE and shimmering with hoar-frost, magpies wheeling over gnarl-fingered trees, and white-brick cottages punctuating an otherwise uninterrupted sight line to the horizon: this is the landscape of the north of France, an evocative canvas that conjures up the great 16th-century paintings of Pieter Brueghel and reflects, as no history book can, how closely married this corner of France was—and is—to Flanders. Here, as in Belgium and the Netherlands, the iron grip of the Spanish Inquisition sent thinkers and threshers alike scrambling for cover. Here, also, numerous woolen mills spun the stuff of epic tapestries. And here, as well, the ill humors of the flatland air drove a people and a culture into golden, fire-lit Vermeer interiors to seek comfort, as did their brethren to the east, in steaming platters of *moules-frites* (mussels and french fries), a mug of amber beer, and a warming swallow of juniper gin.

The landscape recalls images relentlessly epic: medieval stoneworkers in fingerless gloves raised radically new Gothic arches to improbable heights, running for cover when the naves failed to stand, while in the region's industrial areas the hollow-eyed miners immortalized in Emile Zola's *Germinal* descended into hellish black-coal portals. In Compiègne, Joan of Arc languished in prison after suffering wounds in mounted battle with the English. At Agincourt, Henry V rallied the British to gory victory, temporarily reversing William the Norseman's 349-year-long conquest. And in the Somme, wave upon wave of doughboy infantry slogged through the bomb-torn countryside to gain, lose, and ultimately regain a scrap of land.

Most people give the north of France a wide berth, roaring through the Channel ports at Boulogne and Calais on a beeline for Paris, en route to the south for a sunshine cure. But this underappreciated region, with its chiaroscuro of bleak exteriors and interior warmth, conceals treasures of art, architecture, history, and natural beauty that reward slow and pleasurable study. Just an hour's trip from Paris on the TGV, Lille beckons with its Palais des Beaux-Arts, whose collections of Old Masters are worthy in scale of the capital's. There are no fewer than 10 cathedrals still standing (though you might want to hover near the exits at Beauvais, whose nave, the tallest in France, makes some engineers nervous) and worth a visit. You may choose to relax on the relatively uncrowded beaches that wrap the coast from Dunkerque to the Bay of the Somme, or to wander through World War I battlefields and cemeteries whose scale is imponderable.

And then you can recover with Champagne. Head southeast toward Reims, and the sky clears, the landscape loosens and undulates, and the hills tantalize with the vineyards that produce the world's antidote to gloom, *à la méthode champenoise*. Between tasting tours at Reims and Epernay, you can contemplate Reims Cathedral, where Clovis was baptized and to which St. Joan dragged a recalcitrant Dauphin to be crowned. No wonder more and more British are using the Channel Tunnel to visit northern France for day and weekend trips.

Exploring the North & Champagne

The region commonly referred to as northern France stretches from the Somme River up to the Channel Tunnel and includes the vibrant city of Lille, to the northeast. Champagne encompasses Reims and the surrounding vineyards and chalky plains. Picardy, to the south of the region, is traversed by the Aisne and Oise rivers. The hills and forests of the Ardennes lead northeast toward Belgium.

The north of France has a shared history with Flemish-speaking territories. Lille, France's northern metropolis, is the capital of what is known as French Flanders, which stretches northwest from the city to the coastal areas around Dunkerque and Gravelines. West of Lille extends the Côte d'Opale, the Channel coastline so named for the color of its sea and sky. To the southeast the grapes of champagne flourish on the steep slopes of the Marne Valley and the Montagne de Reims, really more of a mighty hill than a mountain. Reims is the only city in Champagne—and one of France's richest tourist sites.

About the Restaurants & Hotels

With the exception of a handful of resort towns along the Channel Coast, this region is less dependent on tourism than many in France, and most restaurants are open year-round—although in Lille and Amiens, the two liveliest cities, each with large student populations, many restaurants close for two to three weeks in July and August. Typical of northern France are *estaminets*: part-brasserie, part-pub, where locals gather for a meal or just a snack, to accompany a higher standard of beer than commonly found elsewhere in France. Another regional specialty, handy if you're in a hurry, is the ubiquitous wayside *frites* van selling French fries and hot dogs.

Northern France is overladen with old, rambling hotels, often simple rather than pretentious; there are also luxurious châteaux with fine restaurants. Top quality is hard to come by, except in major cities such as Lille and Reims. Assume all hotel rooms have air-conditioning, TV, telephones, and private bath, unless otherwise noted.

WHAT IT COSTS In euros					
	$$$$	**$$$**	**$$**	**$**	**¢**
RESTAURANTS	over €30	€23–€30	€17–€23	€11–€17	under €11
HOTELS	over €190	€120–€190	€80–€120	€50–€80	under €50

Restaurant prices are per person for a main course at dinner, including tax (19.6%) and service; note that if a restaurant offers only prix-fixe (set-price) meals, it has been given the price category that reflects the full prix-fixe price. Hotel prices are for a standard double room in high season, including tax (19.6%) and service charge; higher prices (inquire when booking) prevail for any meal plans.

Timing

Compared to many other regions of France, the north remains relatively uncrowded in July and August, and the huge Channel beaches have room for everyone. If you're lucky enough to visit the Champagne region in

France's northernmost out-thrust shows its Flemish roots in a Brueghelesque landscape, cozy Old Master interiors, and a violent history worthy of the images of Hieronymus Bosch. Add spectacular Gothic cathedrals, fine Flemish art in Lille, broad beaches, and Reims—the "Capital of Bubbly"—and you'll find that this overlooked region merits exploration. Count on a week to do justice to this vast treasury, starting at Beauvais, north of Paris. Five days will give you time to explore Lille and Arras before heading south to Reims. Only three days? Concentrate on the most scenic attractions of Picardy and Champagne.

6

Numbers in the text correspond to numbers in the margin and on the North and Champagne map.

If you have 3 days

Start in **Compiègne** 36 at its elegant Napoleonic palace, and then head to **Pierrefonds** 37 and its storybook castle. By dinnertime be in the hilltop cathedral town of **Laon** 31. After touring Laon the next morning, drive to the cathedral city of **Reims** 2–51 for the afternoon, the night, and maybe part of the third morning. Make the Champagne vineyards to the south—on the Montagne de Reims, along the Route du Vin, and in the Marne Valley west of **Épernay** 41—your final destination.

If you have 5 days

Begin with a day in the vibrant city of **Lille** 11–22, home to France's largest art museum outside Paris. The next morning take in stately **Arras** 26 and the moving war cemeteries nearby en route to princely **Compiègne** 36. Devote Day 3 to the medieval splendor of **Pierrefonds** 37 and **Laon** 31 and Day 4 to **Reims** 42–51. Spend your last day touring the Montagne de Reims and the Route du Vin, and then head east from **Épernay** 39 to the historic town of **Châlons-en-Champagne** 40.

If you have 8 days

Venture along the cliffs from the Channel Tunnel to the historic Upper Town of **Boulogne-sur-Mer** 9. If you want to go to the beach, head down the coast to the Victorian-era resort of **Le Touquet** 8 and rejoin the itinerary at Amiens. If you prefer history and culture, head inland from Boulogne to **Lille** 11–22 for the night and following morning. That afternoon go south to **Arras** 26. On Day 4 cross the **Somme battlefields,** ending the day in the cathedral city of **Amiens** 2. The next day visit **Beauvais** 1, home to France's tallest cathedral; then go east to **Compiègne** 36 and its famous palace. Spend Day 6 at the fairy-tale castle of **Pierrefonds** 37 and in **Laon** 31. On Day 7 head northeast into the Ardennes or explore historic **Reims** 42–51. On Day 8 head to the champagne vineyards south of Reims en route to **Châlons-en-Champagne** 40 and the fine hotel-restaurant by the basilica in nearby **L'Épine** 41.

the autumn, plan to drive along the Route du Vin through vineyards golden in the harvest sun. Champagne grapes are gathered in late September or early October (then pressed at once in *vendangeoirs* near the vineyards), and during this time you can even be hired as a grape-picker (according to law, the grapes that go into champagne must be picked by hand). But be sure to plan a visit to Reims and Champagne only between May and October; the region's ubiquitous vineyards are a dismal, leafless sight the rest of the year. The liveliest time in Lille is the first weekend in September, during its three-day street fair, La Grande Braderie. Other local fairs include the Dunkerque Carnival, in February, and the Giants' Carnival, in Douai in July. The wooded Ardennes, to the northeast, is attractive in fall, when local game highlights area menus.

THE NORTH

Starting with Beauvais and Amiens (both easily accessible by express-way from Paris) and two of France's most splendorous Gothic cathedrals, follow the Somme Valley to the Channel. Unfortunately, the ports of Calais and Dunkerque are among France's uglier towns, but the old sections of Boulogne-sur-Mer have scenic appeal, as do the narrow streets of ancient Montreuil and the posh avenues of fashionable Le Touquet. After wheeling inland to church-and-museum-rich Lille, head south to the World War I battlefields between Arras and Albert, continuing southeast into Picardy with its hilltop castles and cathedrals.

Beauvais

❶ *80 km (50 mi) north of Paris.*

Beauvais and its neighbor Amiens have been rivals since the 13th century, when they locked horns over who could build the bigger cathedral. Beauvais lost—gloriously.

Fodor'sChoice
★

A work-in-progress preserved for all time, soaring above the characterless modern blocks of the town center, is the tallest cathedral in France: the **Cathédrale St-Pierre.** You may have an attack of vertigo just gazing up at its vaults, 153 feet above the ground. It may be the tallest, but not the largest. Paid for by the riches of Beauvais's wool industry, the choir collapsed in 1284, shortly after completion, and was only rebuilt with the addition of extra pillars. This engineering fiasco proved so costly that the transept was not attempted until the 16th century. It was worth the wait: an outstanding example of Flamboyant Gothic, with ornate rose windows flanked by pinnacles and turrets. It's also still standing—which is more than can be said for the megalomaniacal 450-foot spire erected at the same time. This lasted precisely four years; when it came crashing down, all remaining funds were hurled at an emergency consolidation program, and Beauvais's dream of having the largest church in Christendom vanished forever. Now the cathedral is starting to lean, and cracks have appeared in the choir vaults because of shifting water levels in the soil. No such problems bedevil the **Basse Oeuvre** (Lower Edifice; closed to the public), which juts out impertinently where the

6

The Capital of Bubbly

An uplifting landscape tumbles about Reims and Epernay, perhaps because its inhabitants treat themselves to a regular infusion of the local, world-prized elixir we know and love as champagne. Each year, millions of bottles of bubbly mature in hundreds of kilometers of chalk tunnels carved under the towns' streets. Whether or not you choose to buy a bottle, you should be able to land yourself a complimentary glass of Champagne at the end of a tour. If you count yourself among the present-day crowds of case-toting bubblyphiles, you'll know that, unlike the great vineyards of Bordeaux and Burgundy, there are few country châteaux to go with the fabled names of this region—Mumm, Taittinger, Pommery, and Veuve-Clicquot. Most of the glory is to be found in *caves* and cellars.

Glorious Gothic

The hundreds of kilometers of chalk tunnels throughout the North, some dug by the ancient Romans as quarries, serve as the damp and moldy berth for millions of bottles of champagne, but they also gave up tons of blocks to create other treasures of the region: the magical and magnificent Gothic cathedrals of Northern France. Just a few are Amiens, the largest; Beauvais, the tallest; Noyon, the earliest; Abbeville, the last; Reims, the most regal; and Laon, with the most towers (and the most spectacular hilltop setting). Add in those at St-Omer, Soissons, St-Quentin, and Châlons-en-Champagne, along with the bijou churches in Rue, St-Riquier, and L'Épine, and fans of medieval architecture are in for a true feast.

Pigs & Potatoes

The cuisine of northern France is robust and hearty. In Flanders beer is often used as a base for sauces. French fries and mussels are featured on most menus; vans selling fries and hot dogs are a common sight; and large quantities of mussels and fish, notably herring, are consumed. Smoked ham and, in season, boar and venison are specialties of the eastern part of the region. Cheese aficionados will be keen to sample soft, square *Maroilles*, with its orange rind, and the spicy, pyramid-shape *boulette d'Avesnes*. To satisfy your sweet tooth, try macaroons and *bêtises de Cambrai* (minty lollipops). Ham, pigs' feet, gingerbread, and champagne-based mustard are specialties of the Reims area, as is ratafia, a sweet aperitif made from grape juice and brandy. To the north, a glass of *genièvre* (gin flavored with juniper berries, which is sometimes added to the dregs of a cup of black coffee to make a *bistouille*) is the classic way to finish a meal. In the old days champagne was treated as an aperitif or dessert wine, but it can be served throughout an entire meal, starting with the younger, lighter, and drier wines, and progressing gradually to the older, sweeter ones.

Beaches

Extending from Dunkerque to the Bay of the Somme is the Côte d'Opale, one long, sandy beach. It's sometimes short of sun, but not of space or beach sports, like *char à voile* (sand sailing). The climate is bracing, often windy, but there are wonderfully scenic spots along the cliffs south of Calais: Cap Gris Nez and Cap Blanc Nez. Le Touquet is one of France's fanciest coastal resort towns.

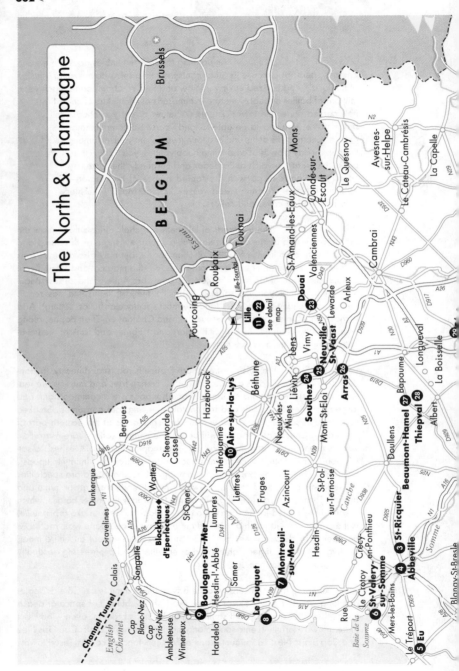

The North & Champagne

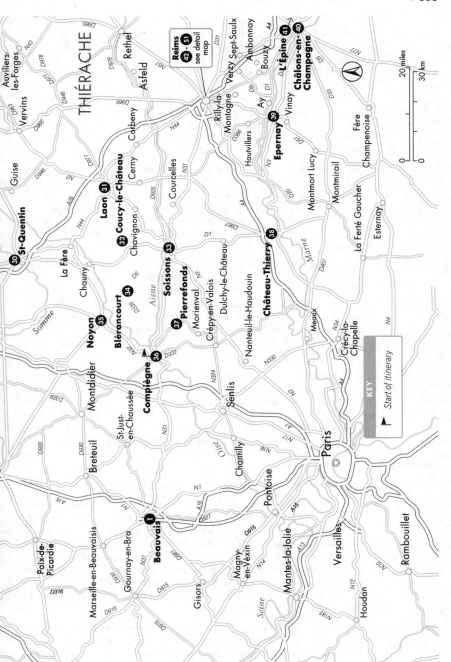

nave should have been. It has been there for 1,000 years. Fittingly donated to the cathedral by the canon Étienne Musique, the oldest surviving **chiming clock** in the world—a 1302 model with a 15th-century painted wooden face and most of its original clockwork—is built into the wall of the cathedral. Perhaps Auguste Vérité drew his inspiration from this humbler timepiece when, in 1868, he made a gift to his hometown of the gilded, templelike **astrological clock.** Animated religious figurines surrounded by all sorts of gears and dials emerge for their short program at erratic times, although there is a set schedule for visits with commentary. ⊠ *Rue St-Pierre* ⊙ *May–Oct., daily 9–12:15 and 2–6:15; Nov.–Apr., daily 9–12:15 and 2–5:30.*

From 1664 to 1939 Beauvais was one of France's leading tapestry centers; it reached its zenith in the mid-18th century under the gifted artist Jean-Baptiste Oudry, known for his hunting scenes. Examples from all periods are in the modern **Galerie Nationale de la Tapisserie** (National Tapestry Museum). ⊠ *1 rue St-Pierre* ☎ *03–44–15–39–10* ᙚ *€4* ⊙ *Apr.–Sept., Tues.–Sun. 9:30–noon and 2–6:30; Oct.–Mar., Tues.–Sun. 10–noon and 2:30–5.*

One of the few remaining testaments to Beauvais's glorious past, the old Bishop's Palace is now the **Musée Départemental de l'Oise** (Regional Museum). Don't miss the beautifully proportioned attic story, Thomas Couture's epic canvas of the French Revolution, the 14th-century frescoes of instrument-playing sirens on a section of the palace's vaults, or the 1st-century brass *Guerrier Gaulois* (Gallic Warrior). ⊠ *1 rue du Musée* ☎ *03–44–11–43–83* ᙚ *€2, free Wed.* ⊙ *Wed.–Mon. 10–noon and 2–6.*

Where to Eat

¢ ✕ **Le Marignan** This lively brasserie near Beauvais town hall (make for the cozy upstairs dining-room if you'd prefer some peace and quiet) offers a choice of fish, chicken, and savory flans, plus a three-course lunchtime menu at just €11. Succulent desserts range from crème brûlée to almond and raspberry tart. ⊠ *1 rue Malherbe* ☎ *03–44–48–15–15* ▤ *MC, V* ⊙ *Closed Mon., late July–mid-Aug. No dinner Sun.*

Amiens

❷ *58 km (36 mi) north of Beauvais via N1 or A16.*

Although Amiens showcases some pretty brazen postwar reconstruction, epitomized by Auguste Perret's 340-foot Tour Perret, a soaring concrete stump by the train station, the city is well worth exploring. It has lovely Art Deco buildings in its traffic-free city center, as well as elegant, older stone buildings like the 18th-century Beffroi (belfry) and Neoclassical prefecture. Crowning the city is its great Gothic cathedral, which has survived the ages intact. Nearby is the waterfront quarter of St-Leu—with its small, colorful houses—rivaling the old city center in Lille as the cutest city district north of Paris.

Fodor'sChoice ★ By far the largest church in France, the **Cathédrale Notre-Dame** could enclose Paris's Notre-Dame twice. It may lack the stained glass of Chartres or the sculpture of Reims, but for architectural harmony, engineering proficiency, and sheer size, it's without peer. The soaring, asymmetrical facade, bathed in colored spotlights on summer evenings, has a notable Flamboyant Gothic rose window. Inside, there is no stylistic disunity to mar the perspective, creating an overwhelming sensation of pure space. Construction took place between 1220 and 1264, a remarkably short period in cathedral-building spans. One of the highlights of a visit here is hidden from the eye, at least until you lift up some of the 110 choir-stall seats and admire the humorous, skillful misericord seat carvings executed between 1508 and 1518. ⊠ *Pl. Notre-Dame* ☎ *03–22–91–72–08* 🖾 *Free.*

The **Hôtel de Berny,** near the cathedral, is a steep-roof stone-and-brick mansion built in 1633. It's filled with 18th-century furniture, tapestries, and objets d'art. ⊠ *36 rue Victor-Hugo* ☎ *03–22–91–81–12* 🖾 *€1.50* ☉ *Oct.–Mar., Sun. 10–12:30 and 2–6; Apr.–Sept., Thurs.–Sun. 1–6.*

★ Behind an opulent columned facade, the **Musée de Picardie,** built 1855–67, looks like just another pompous offering from the Second Empire. Initial impressions are hardly challenged by its grand staircase lined with monumental frescoes by local-born Puvis de Chavannes, or its central hall with huge canvases, like Gérôme's 1855 *Siècle d'Auguste* and Maignon's 1892 *Mort de Carpeaux,* with flying muses wresting the dying sculptor from his earthly clay. One step beyond, though, and you're in a rotunda painted top to bottom in modern minimalist fashion by Sol LeWitt. The basement is filled with subtly lighted archaeological finds and Egyptian artifacts beneath masterly brick vaulting. On the top floor, El Greco leads the Old Masters, along with a humorous set of hunting scenes like Boucher's Rococo-framed *Crocodile Hunt,* from 1736. ⊠ *48 rue de la République* ☎ *03–22–97–14–00* 🖾 *€4, free Sun.* ☉ *Tues.–Sun. 10–12:30 and 2–6.*

Jules Verne (1828–1905) lived in Amiens for the last 35 years of his life, and his former home is now the **Centre International Jules-Verne** (⊠ 2 rue Charles-Dubois ☎ 03–22–45–37–84 ⊕ www.jules-verne.net). It contains some 15,000 documents about Verne's life as well as original furniture and a reconstruction of the writing studio where he created his science-fiction classics. If you're a true Verne fan, you might want to visit his last resting place in the **Cimetière de la Madeleine** (⊠ 2 rue de la Poudrière), where he is melodramatically portrayed pushing up his tombstone as if enacting his own sci-fi resurrection.

Where to Stay & Eat

★ **$$-$$$** ✕ **Les Marissons.** In the scenic St-Leu section of Amiens, beneath the cathedral, this picturesque waterside restaurant serves creative takes on foie gras and regional ingredients: burbot with apricots, rabbit with mint and goat cheese, and pigeon with black currants. To avoid pricey dining à la carte, order from the prix-fixe menus. ⊠ *68 rue des Marissons* ☎ *03–22–92–96–66* ⊕ *www.les-marissons.fr* ▱ *AE, DC, MC, V* ☉ *Closed Sun. and 3 wks in May. No lunch Sat.*

$-$$ ✕ **Joséphine.** Despite its unprepossessing facade and drab front room, this good-value restaurant in central Amiens is a reliable choice. It serves solid fare and has decent wines and a back room overlooking a garden courtyard. ⊠ *20 rue Sire-Firmin-Leroux* ☎ *03–22–91–47–38* ▤ *AE, MC, V* ⊘ *Closed Mon. and 3rd wk in Aug. No dinner Sun.*

$$ ⊡ **Carlton.** This hotel near the train station has a stylish Belle Epoque facade. In contrast, rooms are sober and functional, though light and airy, with spacious bathrooms. Foreign guests are common, and English is spoken. The brasserie-style restaurant, Le Baron, does not serve dinner Sunday. ⊠ *42 rue de Noyon, 80000* ☎ *03–22–97–72–22* ▦ *03–22–97–72–00* ⊕ *www.lecarlton.fr* ⇌ *24 rooms* ⸫ *Restaurant, some pets allowed (fee); no a/c* ▤ *AE, DC, MC, V* ⃝ *BP.*

The Arts

The **Théâtre de Marionnettes** (⊠ 31 rue Edouard-David ☎ 03–22–22–30–90) presents a rare glimpse of the traditional Picardy marionettes, known locally as Chès Cabotans d'Amiens. Shows are performed (in French), usually on Friday evening and Sunday afternoon (daily in August), with plot synopses printed in English.

St-Riquier

❸ *37 km (23 mi) northwest of Amiens via N1 and D32.*

★ The tumbling village of St-Riquier is dominated by its imposing abbey church. Magnificent **St-Riquier** has a majestic Flamboyant Gothic facade with a superbly sculpted 160-foot tower (illuminated on Friday and Saturday evenings), a 100-yard-long nave, and handsome 17th-century wrought-iron gates at the front of the choir.

Where to Stay & Eat

$$–$$$ ✕⊡ **Jean de Bruges.** The 1473 abbot's house next to the church has been transformed into a small, stylish hotel owned by the folks who run the neighboring Bernadette-Stubbe wine tavern. Gleaming marble floors, white stonework, cream-color curtains, designer lighting, old carved furniture, and impressive modern art throughout make for stylish accents. Ask for airy Room 2, or Room 8, with a small terrace; all are named for former abbots. The glass-roof breakfast room leads to a patio used for afternoon tea. ⊠ *18 pl. de l'Église, 80135* ☎ *03–22–28–30–30* ▦ *03–22–28–00–69* ⊕ *www.hotel-jean-de-bruges.com* ⇌ *11 rooms* ⸫ *Restaurant, minibars, some pets allowed (fee); no a/c in some rooms* ▤ *AE, MC, V* ⊘ *Closed Jan.* ⃝ *MAP.*

Abbeville

❹ *9 km (6 mi) southwest of St-Riquier via D925, 43 km (27 mi) northwest of Amiens.*

The historic town of Abbeville was heavily reconstructed after being reduced to rubble in 1944. Its most admirable building is its Gothic cathedral. Begun in 1488, **St-Vulfran** (⊠ Rue St-Vulfran) was the last cathedral-size church to be constructed in the Gothic style. According to 19th-century art historian John Ruskin, it was here that Gothic "lay down and died." After decades of restoration, the riotous tracery and ornament of its much-mauled facade have been revived. The tall, elegant nave retains fine medieval stained glass. Work is still in progress on the 17th-century choir. With typical Gallic flair, the derelict, war-ravaged Gothic church of **St-Sépulcre** was given a new lease on life in 1993, when local artist Alfred Manessier was commissioned to fit it out with 20 windows of stained glass of nearly psychedelic hue. The effect is glorious. ⊠ *Pl. St-Sépulcre* 🖾 *Free* ☉ *June–Sept., daily 2–6.*

The **Musée Boucher-de-Perthes,** housed in a beefy medieval belfry, contains an eclectic collection of Gallo-Roman artifacts, earthenware, Camille Claudel bronzes, ornithological displays, and Old Master altarpieces. ⊠ *24 rue Gontier-Patin* ☎ *03–22–24–08–49* 🖾 *Free* ☉ *Wed.–Mon. 2–6.*

Where to Eat

¢–$ ✕ **Étoile du Jour.** Abbeville is no great gastronomic shakes, so you might as well check out the town's prettiest restaurant, with its open beams and split-level floors. A hearty steak is your best bet, with the local delicacy, a béchamel-smothered pancake called *ficelle picarde,* served piping hot as an appetizer. ⊠ *2 chaussée Marcadé* ☎ *03–22–24–06–90* ⊕ *www.letoiledujour.com* ▭ *MC, V* ☉ *Closed Mon.*

Eu

5 *32 km (20 mi) west of Abbeville via D925.*

FodorsChoice
★

France's last royal residence graces hilltop Eu, set slightly inland from the English Channel. The stone-and-brick Renaissance **Château d'Eu,** built between 1578 and 1665, was used as a summer palace by France's last king, Louis-Philippe of Orléans, who ruled from 1830 to 1848. The château now houses the **Musée Louis-Philippe,** evoking Eu's regal heyday—including two visits by Queen Victoria. After extensive renovations, the museum reopened in 2004. Its lushly ornate dining room and other reception salons will be sure to please lovers of 19th-century decorative arts. ⊠ *Place d'Orléans* ☎ *02–35–86–44–00* ⊕ *www.ville-eu.fr* 🖾 *€3* ☉ *Wed.–Mon. 10–noon and 2–6. Closed Tues. and Fri. morning.*

On the old streets of town, clustered around the stately Gothic **Collé-giale** (Collegiate Church) are two outstanding 17th-century buildings, the **Chapelle des Jésuites** (Jesuit Chapel) and the **Hôtel-Dieu** (hospital).

St-Valery-sur-Somme

6 *22 km (14 mi) northeast of Eu via D940.*

St-Valery-sur-Somme is a pretty fishing harbor (squid and shellfish are specialties) on the Baie de Somme, with a shady seaside promenade, medieval fortifications, and the remains of St-Valery. The flint-and-sandstone-checkerboard 18th-century **Chapelle des Marins** (Mariners' Chapel), at the far end of the town's bayside promenade (where there are views of the Somme Estuary), houses the tomb of St-Valery. The wide sand flats of the **Baie de Somme** (Bay of the Somme) are a haven for wildlife—especially birds and sheep, which graze peacefully on the salt marshes.

☾ A good overview of the Baie de Somme is provided by the **Chemin de Fer de la Baie de Somme** (steam railway). It chugs around the bay between St-Valery and Le Crotoy on an hour-long trip powered by a 130T locomotive that was used during construction of the Panama Canal. ✉ *Departs from St-Valery-sur-Somme and Le Crotoy train stations* ☎ *03–22–26–96–96* ⊕ *www.chemin-fer-baie-somme.asso.fr* 🎫 *€7.20–€14.30* ⊙ *Apr.–June and Sept., Wed. and weekends departure 3:30 and return 5:30; July and Aug., Tues.–Sun. departure 3:30 and return 5:30; early Oct.–late Oct., Sun. departure 3:30 and return 5:30.*

⊙ The **Maison de l'Oiseau** (Bird Sanctuary), just west of St-Valery on D204 (in the direction of Cayeux-sur-Mer), has a collection of 400 stuffed birds, a video presentation about their local habitats, and occasional special appearances by live and happily obedient birds of prey. ✉ *Carrefour du Hourdel* ☎ *03–22–26–93–93* 🎫 *€9.25* ⊙ *Mar.–June and Sept.–mid-Nov., daily 10–6; July and Aug., daily 10–7.*

Where to Stay & Eat

¢–$ ✗ **Parc aux Huîtres.** This large-windowed restaurant in Le Hourdel, on the south side of the bay, is an honest, unpretentious place to have a lunch of fresh seafood, starring oysters (*huîtres*), scallops, turbot, and lobster. Service is brisk and matter of fact: you're treated like a local, and that's a compliment. ✉ *8 km (5 mi) northwest of St-Valery; Le Hourdel* ☎ *03–22–26–61–20* ⊕ *www.parc-aux-huitres.com* ▤ *MC, V* ⊙ *Closed Wed. No dinner Tues.*

$$–$$$ ✗▥ **Le Fiacre.** The Fiacre, an old coaching inn as its name suggests, exudes the unhurried charm of rural France with its whitewashed walls and steep, red-tiled roofs. Rooms are large and plainly furnished in light colors, and most overlook the garden with its pond and rose bushes. The restaurant, recalling an old farm kitchen with its giant hearth and massive oak furniture, has a wide choice of fish dishes (try the turbot with sorrel), game, and lamb from the Somme's salt-marshes. Breakfasts are pleasantly copious by French standards, with a ready supply of succulent homemade pastries. ✉ *Rue des Pommiers; Quend, 24 km (15 mi) north of St-Valery on D940, Routhiauville, 80120* ☎ *03–22–23–47–30* 🖷 *03–22–27–19–80* 🛏 *11 rooms* 🕭 *Restaurant; no a/c* ▤ *MC, V* ⊙ *Closed mid-Jan.–mid-Feb.* ꡘ *MAP.*

en route   The small town of **Rue,** 7 km (4½ mi) north of St-Valery, is famed for its extravagantly sculpted **Chapelle du St-Esprit,** with lacelike stonework and star-patterned vaulting.

Montreuil-sur-Mer

❼ *45 km (28 mi) north of St-Valery via D940 and D917.*

Despite its seaside-sounding name, Montreuil-sur-Mer is 18 km (11 mi) inland. It was once a port, but the Canche River silted up and left it high and dry. The ancient town has majestic walls and ramparts, as well as a faded charm to which various authors, notably Victor Hugo, succumbed; an episode of *Les Misérables* is set here. Wherever citadels and city walls loom in France, it's a fair bet that Vauban had a hand in their construction. Montreuil is no exception. First Errard de Bar-le-Duc and then Vauban supplemented the existing 16th-century towers of the **Citadelle.** ✉ *Rue*

Carnot ☎ *03–21–06–10–83* ✉ *€2.50* ⊙ *Nov.–Sept., Wed.–Mon. 9–11:30 and 2–5:30.*

off the
beaten
path

AZINCOURT – The Battle of Agincourt (Azincourt in French) took place 30 km (19 mi) east of Montreuil in October 1415, when Henry V's longbowmen defeated Charles VI's more numerous and heavily armored French troops. A museum, an orientation map, and a clearly marked 3-km (2-mi) trail recall the event.

Where to Stay & Eat

★ $$$–$$$$ ✕⌂ **Château de Montreuil.** At this manor house facing the citadel, rooms are furnished with 18th- and 19th-century antiques. The less expensive rooms in the converted stables are also pleasantly furnished but smaller. Owner Lindsay Germain is English. Her husband, Christian, is an excellent chef: his forte is bringing out the natural flavor in such dishes as lightly sautéed scallops served with *pompadour* potatoes, or lamb chops with a wine-sauce glaze. There's no lunch on Thursday or (October through April) on Tuesday. ✉ *4 chaussée des Capucins, 62170* ☎ *03–21–81–53–04* 🖷 *03–21–81–36–43* ➲ *14 rooms* ♦ *Restaurant, some minibars, cable TV, some pets allowed (fee); no a/c in some rooms* ▤ *AE, DC, MC, V* ⊙ *Closed Mon. and mid-Dec.–end Jan.* ⎨⊙⎬ *MAP.*

Le Touquet

8 *15 km (9 mi) northwest of Montreuil via N39.*

At the mouth of the Canche Estuary, Le Touquet is an elegant Victorian seaside resort town. First transformed into a sandy pine forest by Alphonse Daloz in the mid-19th century, the town was developed by Yorkshire businessman John White to attract English vacationers. Paris newspaper *Le Figaro* then baptized it "Paris-Plage" (Paris-Beach) and launched a huge advertising campaign to lure well-to-do Parisians. A cosmopolitan atmosphere remains, and many French retirees, attracted by the airy, elegant avenues and invigorating climate, have moved here for good. On one side is a fine sandy beach; on the other, a flourishing pine forest. There are also a casino, golf courses, and a racetrack.

Where to Stay & Eat

$$$–$$$$ ✕ **Flavio.** Fish and lobster (at whale-size prices) number among Guy Delmotte's specialties at this elegant spot. The two prix-fixe menus are more reasonable (wine is included in the €38 weekday menu). Cut glass and Oriental carpets add a colorful note of dated glamour. ✉ *1 av. du Verger* ☎ *03–21–05–10–22* ⌬ *Reservations essential* 🏛 *Jacket and tie* ▤ *AE, DC, MC, V* ⊙ *Closed Jan.–mid-Feb. and Mon. Sept.–June.*

$$$–$$$$ ✕⌂ **Westminster.** The Westminster's mammoth redbrick facade looks as if it had been built just a few years ago; in fact, it dates from the 1930s and, like the rest of the hotel, has been extensively restored. The enormous double rooms are a good value, and the bridal suite is the last word in thick-carpeted extravagance. The hotel's brasserie, Le Coffee-Shop, is modestly priced (lunch and dinner); the Pavillon restaurant serves inventive French cuisine (it's closed Tuesday and January–February). ✉ *Av. du Verger, 62520* ☎ *03–21–05–48–48* 🖷 *03–21–05–45–45*

～ *115 rooms △ Restaurant, minibars, cable TV, pool, hot tub, sauna, bar, some pets allowed (fee); no a/c* ⊟ *AE, DC, MC, V* ⌾ *BP.*

Sports & the Outdoors

The **Enduro** in February sees thousands of motorbikes converge on Le Touquet for an epic race through the dunes. **Aqualud,** a water park on the beachfront, has numerous water-sports facilities, half outdoors, half in, including a giant pool with wave machine. ⊠ *Bd. Thierry-Sabine* ☎ *03–21–90–07–07* 🖻 *€13 for 3 hrs, €15 all day* ⊗ *Apr.–June and Sept., Wed.–Sun. 10:15–5:45; July and Aug., daily 10:15–6:45; Oct., Nov., and mid-Feb.–Mar., weekends only 10:15–5:45.*

Boulogne-sur-Mer

▶ ❾ *24 km (15 mi) north of Le Touquet via D940.*

Boulogne-sur-Mer, famous for its smoked herring, is France's largest fishing port. The rebuilt concrete streets around the port are gruesome and ugly, but the Vieille Ville up the hill is on a different plane—pretty, well kept, and full of character. Perhaps this is why Napoléon chose Boulogne as his base in 1803 while making his fruitless plans to cross the Channel with 2,000 boats and 180,000 men. The four main streets of the **Ville Haute** (Upper Town) intersect at **place Godefroy-de-Bouillon.** The square is flanked by the 18th-century rose-brick **Hôtel de Ville,** the 12th- to 13th-century **belfry,** the cloistered **Annonciades** (a former convent, now a library), and the **Hôtel Desandrouins,** Napoléon's imperial palace. Dominating them all is the formidable **Basilique Notre-Dame,** its monstrous elongated dome visible from far out at sea.

Inside the 13th-century ramparts, studded with four gateways and 17 watchtowers, is the polygonal castle, today known as the **Château-Musée.** Built for the counts of Boulogne, the castle dates in part from the 13th-century and houses a fine collection of Egyptian artifacts donated by the celebrated Louvre Egyptologist Auguste Mariette, who was born in Boulogne in 1821. The museum's collection of Greek vases is considered second only to the Louvre's. ⊠ *Rue de Bernet* ☎ *03–21–10–02–20* 🖻 *€3.50* ⊗ *Wed.–Mon. 10–12:30 and 2–5, Sun. 10–12:30 and 2:30–5:30.*

★ ℭ **Nausicaä,** the Centre National de la Mer (National Sealife Center), has a battery of aquariums containing more than 4,000 creatures. Highlights include sharks, sea lions, a Plexiglas column of shimmering jellyfish, and playful rays. It also has a coral reef, 3-D films, a swimming pool, a weather center, a library, a large bookstore, and a classy restaurant. ⊠ *Bd. Ste-Beuve* ☎ *03–21–30–99–99* ⊕ *www.nausicaa.fr* 🖻 *€11* ⊗ *Sept.–June, daily 9:30–6:30; July and Aug., daily 9:30–8.*

The **Colonne de la Grande Armée,** a 175-foot marble column begun in 1804 to commemorate Napoléon's invasion of England, is high on a hill just north of town. The idea was shelved in 1805, and the column (due to reopen sometime in 2004 after renovation) was only finished 30 years later under Louis-Philippe. The 263 steps take you to the top and a wide-reaching panoramic view; if the weather is clear, and you're blessed with Napoleonic eyesight, you may be able to make out the distant Cliffs of Dover. ⊠ *Off D940, the road to Calais* ☎ *03–21–80–43–69* ⊡ *Free* ⊘ *Apr.–Sept., daily 9–noon and 2–7; Oct.–Mar., Thurs.–Mon. 9–noon and 2–5.*

Where to Stay & Eat

$$$ ✕ **Matelote.** The name of this hotel-restaurant, across the way from Nausicaä, means "the Sailor's Wife." Chef Tony Lestienne serves up asparagus with truffles and Serrano ham, and duck with peach and apricot. ⊠ *80 bd. Ste-Beuve, 62200* ☎ *03–21–30–33–33* ☏ *03–21–30–87–40* ⊲⊐ *20 rooms* ⚬ *Restaurant, cable TV, some pets allowed (fee); no a/c* ⊟ *AE, MC, V* ⊘ *Closed mid-Dec.–mid-Jan. No dinner Sun.* ⦿| *BP.*

★ **$$** ✕ **L'Epicure.** This intimate, 20-seat restaurant in neighboring Wimereux serves an outstanding three-course (€22) menu that might include duck terrine, salmon with parsley and horseradish butter, and hot pear and chocolate cake. There's a monumental cheese board and an imaginative wine list. Chef Philippe Carrée works alone in the kitchen and is entitled to foibles like refusing diners who turn up "too late"—after 9 PM. Claudette Carrée anxiously surveys the dining room. ⊠ *1 rue de la Gare, 6 km (4 mi) north of Boulogne, Wimereux* ☎ *03–21–83–21–83* ⊟ *AE, DC, V* ⊘ *Closed Sun. and late Dec.–mid-Jan. No dinner Wed.*

★ **$$–$$$** ✕⛉ **Cléry.** It was at this very hotel that Napoléon decided to abandon his plans to invade England. As you bask on the peaceful grounds of this 18th-century château you may understand why. Inside, the hotel has received more of a face-lift. While some ambience from its days as the Château d'Hesdin-L'abbé remain—the entry way has a beautiful Rococo staircase—most salons are retrofitted with modern-traditional furniture, new ceilings, and 1980s hues. Rooms vary in price and decor; those in the former stables have been converted into light and airy spaces. Restaurant Le Berthier is set in a lovely glass conservatory porch. ⊠ *Rue du Château, 8 km (5 mi) inland from Boulogne via N1, 62360 Hesdin-l'Abbé* ☎ *03–21–83–19–83* ☏ *03–21–87–52–59* ⊕ *www. hotelclery-hesdin-labbe.com* ⊲⊐ *22 rooms* ⚬ *Restaurant, tennis court; no a/c* ⊟ *AE, DC, MC, V* ⊘ *Closed 3 wks in Jan.* ⦿| *BP.*

$ ⛉ **Métropole.** This small hotel is handy for hovercraft passengers but, like most of the Ville Basse (Lower Town), no great architectural shakes (it's a rather faceless '50s building). The small garden is pleasant for breakfast in summer, however, and rooms are adequately furnished. ⊠ *51 rue Adolphe-Thiers, 62200* ☎ *03–21–31–54–30* ☏ *03–21–30–45–72* ⊕ *www.hotel-metropole-boulogne.com* ⊲⊐ *25 rooms* ⚬ *Minibars, cable TV, some pets allowed (fee)* ⊟ *AE, DC, MC, V* ⊘ *Closed late Dec.–early Jan.* ⦿| *EP.*

Aire-sur-la-Lys

❿ *90 km (42 mi) southeast of Boulogne-sur-Mer via D31.*

An unspoiled town center and the proximity of A26 have made Aire, once a busy market town and army base, a favored stopover for tourists arriving from England. The town center contains many 18th-century Neoclassical buildings—you can get details of a numbered trail from the tourist office, which is housed in a notable survivor from the 17th century: the arcaded stone-and-brick *bailliage* (guard house), on the corner of Grand'-Place. The Jesuit **Chapelle St-Jacques**, built in the 1680s, is another survivor from the 17th century. The grandiose **Hôtel de Ville** (Town Hall), with its sculpted pediment, giant pilasters, and 145-foot cupola-topped belfry, dominates the Grand'Place, the main square. It was built in 1717–21 as a symbol of the town's resurgence after being partially destroyed by the duke of Marlborough in 1710. The 210-foot stone tower of the **Collégiale St-Pierre** (✉ Pl. St-Pierre) dominates the land for miles around. Despite all the pinnacles at the top, this is not a strictly Gothic tower—it was completed only in 1634, and pilasters and rounded arches betray the stylistic influence of the Renaissance. At over 110 yards, the interior is impressively long but has suffered heavily down the ages—most recently from bombs in 1944—and its flaking 19th-century paintwork makes it look messy and disjointed. The highlight is the carved organ case made in 1633.

Where to Stay & Eat

$$–$$$ ✕⌂ **Les Trois Mousquetaires.** English travelers flock to this spacious, timber-frame-and-brick late-19th-century hotel on the outskirts of town (well back from N43 behind a large garden). It has the feel of a baronial Scottish mansion, especially when a log fire is blazing in the wood-paneled lobby. Rooms have heavy brass lamps, plush carpeting, and floral-patterned quilts. The restaurant looks out across the fields and serves regional dishes. ✉ *Château du Fort de la Redoute, Rte de Béthune, 62120* ☎ *03–21–39–01–11* 🖷 *03–21–39–50–10* ⊕ *www. hostelleriedes3mousquetaires.com* ⤵ *33 rooms* ⌂ *Restaurant, cable TV, bar; no a/c* ▭ *AE, DC, MC, V* ⊗ *Closed mid-Dec.–mid-Jan.* ⏀ *MAP.*

Lille

▶ *60 km (37 mi) east of Aire-sur-la-Lys, 220 km (137 mi) north of Paris, 100 km (62 mi) southeast of Calais, 100 km (62 mi) west of Brussels.*

For a city supposedly reeling from the problems of its main industry—textiles—Lille is remarkably dynamic; years of ultra-stylish renovation culminated in the title of European City of Culture for 2004. After experiencing Flemish, Austrian, and Spanish rule, Lille passed into French hands for good in 1668. Lille (the name comes from *l'isle,* the island, in the Deûle River, where the city began) is a European crossroads—one hour by train from Paris and Brussels, under two from London. The shiny glass towers of the Euralille complex, a high-tech commercial center of dubious aesthetic merit, greet travelers arriving at the TGV station, Lille-Europe.

⑪ The sumptuous church of **St-Maurice** (✉ Rue de Paris), just off place de la Gare, is a large, five-aisle structure built between the 14th and 19th
⑫ centuries. The majestic **Porte de Paris** (✉ Rue de Paris), overlooked by the 340-foot brick tower of the **Hôtel de Ville,** is a cross between a mansion and a triumphal arch. It was built by Simon Vollant in the 1680s in honor of Louis XIV and was originally part of the city walls.

★ ⑬ The **Palais des Beaux-Arts** is the country's largest fine arts museum outside Paris. It houses a noteworthy collection of Dutch and Flemish

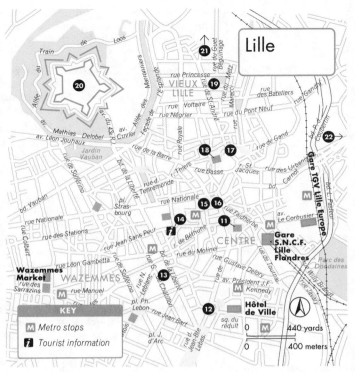

paintings (Anthony Van Dyck, Peter Paul Rubens, Flemish Primitives, and Dutch landscapists) as well as some charmingly understated still lifes by Chardin, works by the Impressionists, and dramatic canvases by El Greco, Tintoretto, Paolo Veronese, and Goya (including two of his most famous—*Les Jeunes* and the ghastly *Les Vieilles*). A ceramics section displays some fine examples of Lille faïence (earthenware), and there's a superbly lighted display of *plans reliefs* (18th-century scale models of French towns) in the basement, with binoculars provided to help you admire all the intricate detail. ⊠ *Pl. de la République* ☎ 03–20–06–78–00 🖀 €4.60 ⊙ *Wed.–Thurs. and weekends 10–6, Fri. 10–7, Mon. 2–6.*

⓮ The late-15th-century **Palais Rihour** (Rihour Palace; ⊠ Pl. Rihour), built for Philippe le Bon, duke of Burgundy, is famed for its octagonal turret and staircase with intricate swirling-pattern brickwork. The city **tourist office** is housed in the vaulted former guardroom on the ground floor.

⓯ Lille's most famous square, Grand'Place, is just one block from place Rihour and is now officially called **Place du Général-de-Gaulle.** The *Déesse* (goddess), atop the giant column clutching a linstock (used to fire a cannon), has dominated the square since 1845; she commemorates Lille's heroic resistance to an Austrian siege in 1792. Other landmarks include the handsome, gabled 1936 facade of *La Voix du Nord* (the main regional newspaper), topped by three gilded statues symbolizing the three historic regions of Flanders, Artois, and Hainaut; and the Furet du Nord, which immodestly claims to be the world's largest bookstore.

⑯ The elegant **Vieille Bourse** (Old Commercial Exchange), on one side of Grand'Place, was built in 1653 by Julien Destrées as a commercial exchange to rival those of the Low Countries. Note the bronze busts, sculpted medallions, and ornate stonework of its arcaded quadrangle.

The **Vieux Lille** (Old Lille) neighborhood dates mainly from the 17th and 18th centuries; most of its richly sculpted facades, often combining stone facings with pale pink brickwork, have been restored. Perhaps the most ornate building is the Maison de Gilles de La Boë on Place Louise-de-Bettignies, built in 1636 for a rich grocer.

⑰ The **Hospice Comtesse** (Countess Hospital), founded as a hospital in 1237 by Jeanne de Constantinople, countess of Flanders, was rebuilt in the 15th century after a fire destroyed most of the original structure. Local artifacts from the 17th and 18th centuries form the backbone of the museum now housed here, but its star attraction is the **Salle des Malades** (Sick Ward), featuring a majestic wooden ceiling. ⊠ *32 rue de la Monnaie* ☎ *03–28–36–84–00* ⌸ *€8* ⊘ *Wed.–Fri. 10–12:30 and 2–6, weekends 10–6, Mon. 2–6.*

⑱ The cathedral of **Notre-Dame de la Treille** (⊠ Rue des Trois-Mollettes) stands on the spot of a medieval church dismantled during the Revolution. The present building was begun—in a suitably neo-Gothic style—in 1854. Construction was halted from 1869 to 1893, and by World War I only the choir was complete. The roof vaults were only finished in 1973, and the west front, with its dismal expanses of gray concrete, remained despairingly incomplete until a translucent marble facade was added in 1999.

⑲ General Charles de Gaulle (1890–1970), the famous former President of France, was born in Lille. His birthplace, the **Maison Natale du Général de Gaulle,** is now a museum. ⊠ *9 rue Princesse* ☎ *03–28–38–12–05* ⊕ *www.charles-de-gaulle.org* ⌸ *€5.50* ⊘ *Wed.–Sun. 10–noon and 2–5.*

⑳ Lille's gigantic **Citadelle** patrols the northwest of the city from the enchanting Bois de Boulogne Gardens, whose leafy walkways alongside photogenic streams attract hordes of strollers, cyclists, and joggers. The colossal walls of the citadel are immaculately preserved, no doubt because the site is still inhabited by the French military (you can only visit the interior on Sunday afternoon). It was constructed rapidly between 1667 and 1670; of course, that genius of military engineering Sébastien de Vauban got the commission. Some 60 million bricks were baked in record time, and the result is a fortified town in its own right. ☎ *03–20–21–94–21 for tourist office to arrange tours* ⌸ *€6.50* ⊘ *Guided tours only, May–Sept. Sun. 3–5.*

★ ㉑ **La Piscine,** in the northeast suburb of Roubaix, is one of France's most unusual and visually exciting museums—it's housed in a converted swimming pool, opened 1932, closed 1985, transformed 2002, still complete with Art Deco mosaics, tile work, and giant half-moon stained-glass windows. The collection of 19th- and 20th-century art, sculpture, and textiles is imaginatively displayed along the waterside and in the former changing cubicles, while a subtle background soundtrack of swishing water and childlike yelps conjures up the public pool of yore. ⊠ *23 rue de l'Espérance* ☎ *03–20–69–23–60* ⬛ €*5* ◷ *Tues.–Fri. 11–6, weekends 1–6.*

㉒ The **Musée d'Art Moderne,** in the eastern suburb of Villeneuve d'Ascq, is a modern, sober brick building ringed by trim lawns alive with boxing bronze hares by Barry Flanagan and a giant Calder mobile. The picture collection ranges from the Cubists, Modigliani, and the Surrealists to Chaissac, Soulages, and postwar abstraction. ⊠ *1 allée du Musée* ☎ *03–20–19–68–68* ⊕ *www.nordnet.fr/mam* ⬛ €*6.50* ◷ *Wed.–Mon. 10–6.*

Where to Stay & Eat

$$$$ ✕ **A L'Huîtrière.** Behind a magnificent Art Deco fish store lined with local Desvres tiles, this elegant seafood restaurant serves fresh, local seafood, simply prepared in regional (Flemish) style—turbot hollandaise, *waterzoï* (a mild, creamy fish stew), braised eel, scallops, and oysters. The clientele is well heeled and the prices are justifiably high. ⊠ *3 rue des Chats-Bossus* ☎ *03–20–55–43–41* ⊕ *www.huitriere.fr* ▭ *AE, DC, MC, V* ◷ *Closed mid-July–late Aug. No dinner Sun.*

★ $ ✕ **Le Lion Bossu.** Old bricks and beams distinguish the 17th-century interior of this restaurant in the heart of Old Lille, a cozy, old-fashioned spot serving simple, homey regional food. ⊠ *1 rue St-Jacques* ☎ *03–20–06–06–88* ▭ *AE, V* ◷ *Closed Sun. No lunch Mon.*

¢ ✕ **Les Brasseurs.** This dark, wood-panel brasserie beside the Lille-Flandres station brews its own beer. Four types—blond (lager), amber, dark (stout), and white (wheat beer)—are available, and La Palette du Barman lets you sample all for €4. *Carbonnade flamande* (Flemish-style beef cooked in a sweet and sour sauce) and *flammekueches* (flattened bread dough topped with bacon and onions) are served. ⊠ *18 pl. de la Gare* ☎ *03–20–06–46–25* ▭ *MC, V.*

$$–$$$ ▦ **Grand Hôtel Bellevue.** The former Hôtel de Bourbon, home to Mozart in 1765, is now an elegant central lodging near Grand'Place. Large, comfortable Art Deco rooms and modern bathrooms are complemented by the sort of deferential service you can no longer take for granted. The leather-lined bar is a good spot in which to rendezvous. ⊠ *5 rue Jean-Roisin, 59800* ☎ *03–20–57–45–64* 📠 *03–20–40–07–93* ⊕ *www.grandhotelbellevue.com* ⇴ *60 rooms* ⚙ *Minibars, bar, some pets allowed (fee); no a/c* ▭ *AE, DC, MC, V* ⍰ *BP.*

★ $–$$ ▦ **Brueghel.** The Brueghel, named in honor of one of the most famous of Flemish painting dynasties, is a picture of revived Art Deco charm; antiques are scattered throughout the corridors and rooms, many of which retain their original interwar furniture. The mood in the wood-panel lobby is friendly and welcoming, and that has made the hotel a favorite among visiting performers at the nearby opera house. The hotel is also handily placed for the Vieille Bourse and Grand'Place, as well as Lille's two train stations, and looks onto the pedestrian piazza around the ven-

erable Gothic church of St-Maurice. ⊠ *3 parvis St-Maurice, 59000*
☎ *03–20–06–06–69* 🖷 *03–20–63–25–27* ⊕ *www.hotel-brueghel.com*
⌐➔*66 rooms* ᵭ *Bar, some Internet, some pets allowed (fee); no a/c* ▭ *AE,*
DC, MC, V ¶◎¶ *EP.*

Nightlife & the Arts

Jazz clubs, piano bars, nightclubs, and all kinds of performances are listed
in *Lille by Night,* available at the Lille tourist office. Lille is at its liveli-
★ est during the first weekend of September, when the **Grande Braderie** summons folk from across northern Europe to what is theoretically a street
market but is better described as one giant beer- and mussel-swilling party.

The Belle Epoque **Opéra de Lille** (⊠ Pl. du Théâtre ☎ 03–20–74–32–99
⊕ www.opera-lille.fr/) reopened in 2003 after extensive renovation. The
Orchestre National de Lille (⊠ 30 pl. Mendès-France ☎ 03–20–12–82–40
⊕ www.onlille.com) is a well-respected symphony orchestra. The **Théâtre
du Nord** (⊠ 4 pl. Général-de-Gaulle ☎ 03–20–14–24–24 ⊕ www.
theatredunord.com) is one of Lille's most prominent theaters.

Douai

㉓ *32 km (20 mi) west of Valenciennes, 35 km (22 mi) south of Lille.*

The industrial town of Douai is most noteworthy as the home of northern France's most famous *beffroi* (belfry), whose turrets and pinnacles
are immortalized in a painting, now in the Louvre, by Camille Corot.
The sturdy tower, completed in 1410, rises 210 feet and is topped by a
huge weather vane in the form of a Flanders Lion. The peal of bells—
62 of them!—sounds the quarter hour with a selection of tunes. Climb
the 193 steps to the top for a view of the town and the Scarpe River.
⊠ *Rue de la Mairie* ☉ *Sept.–June, Mon.–Sat. at 2, 3, 4, and 5, Sun. at*
10, 11, 3, 4, and 5; July and Aug., daily at 10, 11, 2, 3, 4, and 5.

The Artois Battlefields

The most poignant memories of World War I are evoked in the superbly
maintained war cemeteries in the countryside between Lens and Arras.
Take A1 south from Lille toward Douai, then A21 west to Lens, and
㉔ head through Liévin and Angres to **Souchez.** Standing on a windswept
hill 500 feet above the Artois plain is **Notre-Dame de Lorette,** a 30-acre
cemetery with endless rows of white crosses, a pseudo-Byzantine church,
an ossuary, and a huge tower with a small war museum. From the top
there are extensive views of the surrounding countryside.

From Souchez head south on D937, past the beautiful circular ceme-
㉕ tery of Cabaret Rouge, to **Neuville-St-Vaast,** whose Art Deco church is
a stately example of 1920s reconstruction. Just off D937 is gently sloping **La Targette,** one of the most serene and beautiful of all French war
cemeteries. At the nearby crossroads of D937 and D49, opposite a
stark war memorial in the form of a giant torch, is the small **Musée de
la Guerre 1914–18** (World War I Museum), with a musty collection of
posters, documents, costumes, and weapons. From Neuville take D55
east to **Vimy,** where there's a park commemorating the epic Canadian

victory during World War I, or D49 west to the mournful, ruined, hill-top towers of **Mont-St-Éloi.**

Arras

26 *9 km (5½ mi) south of Mont-St-Eloi via D341, 11 km (7 mi) south of Vimy via N17, 54 km (34 mi) southwest of Lille.*

At first glance you might not guess that Arras, the capital of the historic Artois region between Flanders and Picardy, was badly mauled during World War I. In the Middle Ages, Arras was an important trading and tapestry-weaving center, its wealth reflected in two of the finest squares in the country—now home to lively markets on Wednesday and Saturday mornings. Other landmarks include the 18th-century theater, the Palais des États (former regional parliament), the octagonal place Victor-Hugo, and the former home of revolutionary firebrand Maximilien Robespierre. An hour-long audio guided tour of the city is available from the tourist office for a small fee.

★ Start your visit at the arcaded **Place des Héros,** the smaller of the two main squares, dominated by the richly worked—and much restored— Hôtel de Ville (Town Hall). You can take an elevator to the top of its ornate 240-foot **belfry** (€2.30) for a view that stretches as far as the ruined towers of Mont-St-Eloi, 10 km (6 mi) northwest, and you can join a guided tour through the **boves** (€3.80), a maze of underground chalk galleries quarried out back in the 10th century and then transformed into an underground city by 10,000 British troops during World War I. The tunnels run for miles in all directions—even, it is said, as far as Mont-St-Eloi. The tour lasts about an hour, and you'll need sturdy footwear to negotiate all the steep, damp stairs. ⊠ *Pl. des Héros* ⊙ *May–Sept., Mon.–Sat. 9–6:30, Sun. 10–1 and 2–6:30; Oct.–Apr., Mon.–Sat. 9–noon and 2–6, Sun. 10–12:30 and 3–6:30.*

Fodor'sChoice
★ **Grand'Place,** linked to place des Héros by rue de la Taillerie, is a grand, harmonious showcase of 17th- and 18th-century Flemish architecture. The gabled facades recall those in Belgium and Holland and are a reminder of the unifying influence of the Spanish colonizers of the Low Countries during the 17th century—though the oldest house here, the Trois Luppars hotel, at No. 49, actually dates from 1467.

The 19th-century **Cathédrale St-Vaast** (⊠ Rue des Teinturiers) is a stately Classical building in cool white stone, every bit as vast as its name (pronounced *va*) almost suggests. It was built between 1775 and 1830 to the designs of Contant d'Ivry; it was half-razed during World War I, although restoration was so diligent you'd never guess.

The **Musée des Beaux-Arts** (Fine Arts Museum), in the massive, regimented 18th-century abbey next to the cathedral, has a rich collection of objects and pictures, including cobalt-blue Arras porcelain; 19th-century landscapes by Camille Dutilleux and other local artists inspired by Camille Corot (also represented), who frequently visited the region; and two smiling 13th-century gilded wooden angels, the *Anges de Saudémont.* ⊠ *20 rue Paul-Doumer* ☎ *03–21–71–26–43* ⊠ *€4* ⊙ *Wed.–Mon. 9:30–noon and 2–5:30.*

Where to Stay & Eat

★ $$$ ✕ **La Faisanderie.** In a former stable, this splendid restaurant serves memorable variations on international fare: *pied de veau* (calves' feet), pike baked with frogs' legs, and cod with local Arleux garlic. A loyal clientele supports its long-standing gastronomic reputation. ✉ *45 Grand'Place* ☎ *03–21–48–20–76* ⚖ *Reservations essential* 🏛 *Jacket and tie* ▭ *AE, DC, MC, V* ⊘ *Closed Aug. and Mon. No dinner Sun.*

$–$$ ✕ **La Rapière.** This lively, two-level bistro, with an airy ground-floor room and a more atmospheric, vaulted stone cellar, dishes up distinctly local cuisine, including andouillettes (a kind of chitterling sausage) and *poule à la bière* (chicken in beer), as well as specialties like *flan aux maroilles* (flan made with regional cheese) and homemade foie gras, all in a casual setting. ✉ *44 Grand'Place* ☎ *03–21–55–09–92* ⊕ *www.larapiere. com* ▭ *AE, MC, V* ⊘ *No dinner Sun.*

★ $$–$$$ 🏨 **Univers.** Once an 18th-century Jesuit monastery, this stylish hotel has a pretty garden, a charming restaurant (no dinner Sunday during January and February), and pale pink brickwork. Although centrally located, it's set well back from the main street and is an oasis of calm. The interior has been modernized but retains rustic provincial furniture. ✉ *3 pl. de la Croix-Rouge, 62000* ☎ *03–21–71–34–01* 🏨 *03–21–71–41–42* ⊕ *www.hotel-univers-arras.com* 🛏 *38 rooms* ⚘ *Restaurant, cable TV, bar, Internet, some pets allowed (fee); no a/c* ▭ *AE, MC, V* 🍴 *BP.*

The Somme Battlefields

32 km (20 mi) south of Arras near Albert.

The Battle of the Somme—a name forever etched into history as the site of one of the bloodiest battle campaigns of World War I—raged south of Arras, near Albert, from July through November 1916, leaving a million dead. During those five futile months, the Allies, including Irish, Canadian, Australian, and South African soldiers, progressed about 8 km (5 mi) along the hills above the Ancre River north of Albert. From Arras take D919 through gently rolling farmland, via Puisieux, and turn right on D415, through Beaumont, down to the north bank of the **27** Ancre River. Follow signs to the memorial of **Beaumont-Hamel,** where a bronze caribou—emblem of the Newfoundland regiments that fought here—gazes accusingly over trenches and undulating, still shell-shocked terrain. Across the Ancre and up the hill on the other side is the **Tour Ulster** (Ulster Tower), commemorating troops from Northern Ireland.

28 From the village of **Thiepval,** follow signs to the bombastic brick **British War Memorial,** a disjointed triumphal arch that looks as if it were made of giant Lego blocks. Take D73 then D20 to Longueval, site of the **Delville Wood Memorial,** set on a long lawn framed by a stately avenue of oaks.

Péronne

29 *17 km (11 mi) southeast of Longueval via D20 and N17.*

The small, brick town of Péronne was almost entirely razed in 1916. It ★ now contains, however, a fine World War I museum, the **Historial de la**

Grande Guerre. Integrated into a ruined brick castle, this spacious modern museum has a thought-provoking spectrum of exhibits, from TV monitors playing old newsreels, to soldiers' uniforms strung out on the floor surrounded by machine guns, and a dim roomful of nightmarish war lithographs by Otto Dix. It also has a good gift shop, with books in English, and a café with views of a leafy-banked lake. Walk around to the end, and you'll find the Somme River, strewn with islands, languidly colliding with its tributary, the Cologne. ⊠ *Pl. du Château* ☎ *03–22–83–14–18* ⊕ *www.historial.org* ⊞ *€6.20* ☉ *May–Sept., daily 10–6; Oct.–Apr., Tues.–Sun. 10–6.*

Where to Stay & Eat

$ ✕🏠 **Remparts.** Péronne makes a fine base for exploring the local battlefields and war cemeteries. This small hotel has long been an old-fashioned favorite among traveling salesmen, but redecorated rooms and increasingly inventive cuisine—snail ravioli with mushrooms or fish cooked with chicory and beetroot sauce—suggest the hotel is striving to broaden its appeal. A set menu at lunch runs €14.50, while complete dinners range from € 16 to € 40. ⊠ *23 rue Beaubois, 80200* ☎ *03–22–84–01–22* 🖷 *03–22–84–31–96* ⊕ *www.logis-de-france.fr/ uk* ⌂ *16 rooms* ♺ *Restaurant, cable TV, some pets allowed (fee); no a/c* ⊟ *AE, DC, MC, V* ⒑ *MAP.*

St-Quentin

㉚ *28 km (18 mi) southeast of Péronne via D44 and N29.*

Bustling St-Quentin, an industrial town rebuilt with considerable Art Deco panache after World War I (ask about a guided tour at the tourist office), is famed as the birthplace of 18th-century pastelist Maurice Quentin de La Tour—his work can be admired at the town museum. Appearing to survey the town's sloping, pedestrian-only main square is the riotously sculpted, early 16th-century facade of the **Hôtel de Ville** (Town Hall; ⊠ Pl. de l'Hôtel de Ville), complete with arcades and gables and topped by an 18th-century campanile with an attractive peal of bells. The town's hilltop cathedral, officially styled **La Basilique** (⊠ Pl. de la Basilique) at the top of rue St-André, is topped by a 270-foot flèche, reconstructed in 1976. Most of the building, however, is resolutely medieval: the elegant 13th-century choir retains some original stained glass; the soaring nave, rising 112 feet, was added 200 years later (note the black-and-white labyrinth pattern embedded in the floor); the ornate organ case was designed by Berain in 1690.

Where to Stay & Eat

$$ ✕🏠 **Château de Neuville.** If you're looking to escape the hustle and bustle of St-Quentin, one option is the 2-mi drive to the neighboring village of Neuville St-Amand, whose self-styled "château"—in fact a sturdy, century-old mansion with white walls, large windows, and dark green shutters, set deep in a tree-studded park—offers impersonal service and rooms decked out in cool pastel shades. Those in the modern annex lack character but are slightly larger than those in the main block. The workmanlike restaurant (soup and steak are staples) fails to

provide lunch on Saturday or Monday. ✉ *Rue du Midi, 3 km (2 mi) southwest of St-Quentin off N44, 02100 Neuville St-Amand* 🕿 *03–23–68–41–82* 🖷 *03–23–68–46–02* ⤳ *15 rooms* ⚘ *Restaurant, some minibars, bar, Internet; no a/c* ▤ *AE, DC, MC, V* ⊘ *Closed Sun. and Aug.* ⑩ *EP.*

off the beaten path

MUSÉE MATISSE – Artist Henri Matisse (1869–1954) was born in Le Cateau-Cambrésis, 35 km (21 mi) northeast of St-Quentin. The Matisse Museum, housed in the **Palais Fénelon,** a former bishop's palace, contains a number of early oil paintings and sculptures, plus a superb collection of 50 drawings selected by Matisse himself; and 25 psychedelic abstract paintings by Auguste Herbin, who also hailed from the region. The museum reopened in 2002 after a three-year extension and renovation program. ✉ *Palais Fénelon* 🕿 *03–27–84–13–15* ✉ *€7* ⊘ *Wed.–Mon. 10–6.*

Laon

③① *40 km (25 mi) southeast of St-Quentin via A26.*

Thanks to its awesome hilltop site and the forest of towers sprouting from its ancient cathedral, lofty Laon basks in the title of the "crowned mountain." The medieval ramparts, virtually undisturbed by passing traffic, provide a ready-made itinerary for a tour of old Laon. Panoramic views, sturdy gateways, and intriguing glimpses of the cathedral lurk around every bend. There's even a funicular, which makes frequent trips (except on Sunday in winter) up and down the hillside between the station and the Vieille Ville.

Fodor'sChoice
★

The **Cathédrale Notre-Dame,** constructed between 1150 and 1230, is a superb example of early Gothic. The light interior gives the impression of order and immense length, and the first flourishing of Gothic architecture is reflected in the harmony of the four-tiered nave: from the bottom up, observe the wide arcades, the double windows of the *tribune,* the squat windows of the *triforium,* and, finally, the upper windows of the clerestory. The majestic towers can be explored during the guided visits that leave from the tourist office, housed in a 12th-century hospital on the cathedral square. The filigreed elegance of the five towers is audacious and rare. Look for the 16 stone oxen protruding from the tops, a tribute to the stalwart 12th-century beasts that carted up blocks of stone from quarries far below. Medieval stained glass includes the rose window dedicated to the liberal arts in the left transept, and the windows in the flat east end, an unusual feature for France although common in England. ✉ *Pl. du Parvis* ✉ *Guided tours €6* ⊘ *Daily 8:30–6:30; guided tours Apr.–Sept., daily at 3 PM.*

The **Musée Muncipal** (town museum) has some fine antique pottery and work by the local-born Le Nain brothers. But its chief draw is the **Chapelle des Templiers** in the garden—a small, octagonal 12th-century chapel topped by a shallow dome. It houses fragments of the cathedral's gable and the chilling effigy of Guillaume de Harcigny, doctor to the insane king Charles VI, whose death from natural causes in 1393 did not prevent his memorializers from chiseling a skeletal portrait that recalls the Black Death. ☒ *32 rue Georges-Ermant* ☎ *03–23–20–19–87* 🎫 *€3.20* ⊘ *June–Sept., Tues.–Sun. 11–6; Oct.–May, Tues.–Sun. 2–6.*

Where to Stay & Eat

★ $ ✕🏨 **Bannière de France.** In business since 1685, this old-fashioned, uneven-floored hostelry is just five minutes from the cathedral. Lieselotte Lefèvre, the German patronne, speaks fluent English. Rooms are cozy and quaint. The restaurant's venerable dining room showcases sturdy cuisine (trout, lemon sole, guinea fowl) and good-value prix-fixe menus. ☒ *11 rue Franklin-Roosevelt, 02000* ☎ *03–23–23–21–44* 🖷 *03–23–23–31–56* ⊕ *www.hoteldelabannieredefrance.com* ⤶ *18 rooms, 17 with bath or shower* ⌕ *Restaurant, cable TV, bar; no a/c* 🖃*AE, DC, MC, V* ⊘ *Closed mid-Dec.–mid-Jan.* 🍽 *MAP.*

Coucy-le-Château

㉜ *28 km (18 mi) southwest of Laon via N2 and D5.*

Fodor'sChoice The majestic hilltop fortress, or **château,** in Coucy-le-Château is but a
★ glimmer of its former self—but it still casts a pretty intimidating shadow over the lush, rolling countryside of eastern Picardy. The 30-acre site, ringed with nearly 3 km (2 mi) of walls and no fewer than 31 towers, was developed by all-powerful warlords, the Enguerrands de Coucy, in the 12th century. They also erected the largest keep in Christendom, more than 210 feet high (Barbara Tuchman's *A Distant Mirror* provides fascinating background reading). The fortifications were partially dismantled by Mazarin in 1650 to prevent their use by rebels during the Fronde, later used as an open quarry after the Revolution, and then dynamited by retreating Germans in 1917. You can visit what's left of the keep and the vaulted cellars, and follow a path around the still-imposing town walls. ☎ *03–23–52–71–28* 🎫 *€4* ⊘ *Daily 10–12:30 and 2–6.*

Soissons

㉝ *19 km (12 mi) south of Coucy via D1.*

Although much damaged in World War I, Soissons commands attention for its two huge churches, one intact, one in ruins. The Gothic **Cathédrale Notre-Dame** was appreciated by Rodin, who famously declared that "there are no hours in this cathedral, but rather eternity." The interior, with its pure lines and restrained ornamentation, creates a more harmonious impression than the asymmetrical, one-towered facade. The most remarkable feature, however, is the rounded two-story transept, an element more frequently found in the German Rhineland than in France. Rubens's freshly restored *Adoration of the Shepherds* hangs on the other side of the transept. ☒ *Pl. Fernand-Marquigny* ⊘ *Daily 9:30–noon and 2:30–5:30.*

The twin-spire facade, arcaded cloister, and airy refectory, constructed from the 14th to the 16th centuries, are all that is left of the hilltop abbey church of **St-Jean-des-Vignes,** which was largely destroyed just after the Revolution. Its fallen stones were used to restore the cathedral and neighboring homes. But the church remains the most impressive sight in Soissons, its hollow rose window peering out over the town like the eye of some giant Cyclops. ⊠ *Cours St-Jean-des-Vignes* ☺ *Free* ⊙ *Mon.–Sat. 9–12:30 and 1:30–6, Sun. 10–12:30 and 1:30–7.*

Partly housed in the medieval abbey of St-Léger, the **Musée de Soissons,** the town museum, has a varied collection of local archaeological finds and paintings, with fine 19th-century works by Gustave Courbet and Eugène Boudin. ⊠ *2 rue de la Congrégation* ☎ *03–23–59–15–90* ☺ *Free* ⊙ *Wed.–Mon. 10–noon and 2–5.*

Where to Stay & Eat

★ $$$–$$$$ ╳⌂ **Château de Courcelles.** This refined château by the Vesle River is run by easygoing Frédéric Nouhaud. Its pure, classical Louis XIV facade harmonizes oddly with the sweeping brass main staircase attributed to Jean Cocteau. Rooms vary in size and grandeur; the former outbuildings have been converted into large family-size suites. Wind down in the cozy bar next to a roaring fire while anticipating excellent fare, including seasonal game, prepared by chef Joel Orceau and served up in the stately dining room. A formal garden and pool are the gateway to 40 acres of parkland and a tree-shaded canal. ⊠ *8 rue du Château, 20 km (12 mi) east of Soissons via N31, 02220 Courcelles-sur-Vesle* ☎ *03–23–74–13–53* ☒ *03–23–74–06–41* ⊕ *www.chateau-de-courcelles.fr* ↵ *11 rooms, 7 suites* ♣ *Restaurant, minibars, cable TV, tennis court, pool, sauna, bar, some pets allowed (fee); no a/c* ☰ *AE, DC, MC, V* ⦿ *MAP.*

★ ¢ ╳⌂ **Abbaye.** The shambling village of Longpont, on the northeast fringe of the Forest of Retz, boasts a ruined Cistercian abbey, a turreted 14th-century gateway, and this ivy-clad, foursquare hotel. The cavernous dining room welcomes all with massive wooden tables, a crackling fireplace, and generous portions of family cooking, much of it prepared over a charcoal grill, with mushrooms, game, and duck with cherries among the favorites. To work it all off, you can rent a bike from the hotel to explore the forest. Rooms are calm and look out over either the forest or the abbey ruins. ⊠ *8 rue des Tourelles, 14 km (9 mi) southwest of Soissons via N2/D17, 02600 Longpont* ☎ *03–23–96–10–60* ☒ *03–23–96–10–60* ↵ *11 rooms, 1 with bath, 10 with showers* ♣ *Restaurant, bar; no a/c, no TV in some rooms* ☰ *MC, V* ⦿ *EP.*

Blérancourt

③④ *23 km (14 mi) northwest of Soissons via D6.*

The village of Blérancourt is the home of the **Musée National de la Coopération Franco-Américaine** (Museum of Franco-American Cooperation). Two style-setting pavilions and monumental archways are all that remain of the original château, built in 1612–19 by the great architect Salomon de Brosse but largely demolished during the French Revolution. American Anne Morgan founded the museum in 1924. The airy, modern museum contains art and documents charting Franco-American relations, with a section on American involvement in World War I.

A beguiling female portrait by Missouri Postimpressionist Richard Miller stands out: an American Mona Lisa. The trim gardens (open 8–7) include a bronze casting of the statue of George Washington by Jean-Antoine Houdon and an arboretum. ⊠ *33 pl. du Gal-Leclerc* ☎ *03–23–39–60–16* 🔳 *€3* 🕓 *Wed.–Mon. 10–12:30 and 2–6.*

Noyon

⑤ *14 km (9 mi) northwest of Blérancourt via D934.*

Noyon is an often overlooked cathedral town that owed its medieval importance to the cult of 7th-century St. Eloi, patron of blacksmiths and a former town bishop. Its second famous son, the Protestant theologian John Calvin, was born here in 1509. The old streets around the cathedral are at their liveliest during the Saturday morning market.

Constructed between 1140 and 1290, the **Cathédrale St-Eloi** was one of the earliest attempts at building a full-fledged Gothic cathedral. This is evident in the four-story nave; the intermittent use of rounded as well as pointed arches; and the thin, pointed lancet (as opposed to rose) windows in the austere facade. Pause for a wry smile at the "piazza" in front of the cathedral, with its elegant town houses arranged in a semicircle in bashful imitation of St. Peter's in Rome; then head down the cobbled lane to the left of the facade to admire the timber-front 16th-century library behind the cathedral. ⊠ *Pl. du Parvis* 🕓 *Daily 8–noon and 2–6.*

Where to Stay & Eat

$–$$ ✕🖻 **St-Eloi.** Between the train station and the cathedral, this hotel charms with its provincial elegance. The redbrick and timber Victorian exterior, marble-lined reception area, and airy dining room are all staunchly French bourgeois. The spacious, pastel rooms have high ceilings; several have views of the interior courtyard. Avoid, however, the chain hotel–like annex. Several prix-fixe menus are available in the stylish restaurant, which does not serve Sunday dinner. ⊠ *81 bd. Carnot, 60400* ☎ *03–44–44–01–49* 🖨 *03–44–09–20–90* ⊕ *www.hotelsainteloi. fr* 🛏 *22 rooms* ♻ *Restaurant, cable TV, bar, Internet, some pets allowed (fee); no a/c* 🖃 *AE, DC, MC, V* 🕓 *Closed mid-July–mid-Aug.* ⊠⊙I *MAP.*

Compiègne

㊱ *24 km (15 mi) southwest of Noyon via N32.*

Compiègne, a bustling town of some 40,000 people, is at the northern limit of the Forêt de Compiègne, on the edge of the misty plains of Picardy; this being prime hunting country, you can be sure there's a former royal hunting lodge in the vicinity. The one here enjoyed its heyday in the mid-19th century under upstart emperor Napoléon III. But the town's history stretches farther back—to Joan of Arc, who was captured in battle and held prisoner here, and to its 15th-century Hôtel de Ville (Town Hall), with its exceptional Flamboyant Gothic facade; and farther forward—to the World War I armistice, signed in Compiègne Forest on November 11, 1918.

The 18th-century **Palais de Compiègne** was restored by Napoléon I and **FodorśChoice** favored for wild weekends by his nephew Napoléon III. The first ★ Napoléon's legacy is more keenly felt: his state apartments have been refurbished using the original designs for hangings and upholstery, and bright silks and damasks adorn every room. Much of the mahogany furniture gleams with ormolu, and the chairs sparkle with gold leaf. Napoléon III's furniture looks ponderous in comparison. Behind the palace is a gently rising 4-km (2½-mi) vista, inspired by the park at Schönbrunn, in Vienna, where Napoléon I's second wife, Empress Marie-Louise, grew up. Also here is the **Musée du Second Empire**, a collection of Napoléon III–era decorative arts, including works by the caricaturist Honoré Daumier. Make time for the **Musée de la Voiture** and its display of carriages, coaches, and old cars, including the *Jamais Contente* (*Never Satisfied*), the first car to reach 100 kph (62 mph). ⊠ *Pl. du Général-de-Gaulle* ☎ *03–44–38–47–00* ⌚ *€5.50* ⊙ *Wed.–Mon. 10–5.*

A collection of 85,000 miniature soldiers—fashioned of lead, cardboard, and other materials—depicting military uniforms through the ages is found in the **Musée de la Figurine Historique** (Toy Soldier Museum). ⊠ *28 pl. de l'Hôtel-de-Ville* ☎ *03–44–40–72–55* ⌚ *€2* ⊙ *Mar.–Oct., Tues.–Sat. 9–noon and 2–6, Sun. 2–6; Nov.–Feb., Tues.–Sat. 9–noon and 2–5, Sun. 2–5.*

Some 7 km (4 mi) east of Compiègne via N31 and D546, off the road to Rethondes, is the **Wagon de l'Armistice** (Armistice Railcar), a replica of the one in which the World War I armistice was signed in 1918. In 1940 the Nazis turned the tables and made the French sign their own surrender in the same place—accompanied by Hitler's infamous jig for joy—then tugged the original car off to Germany, where it was later destroyed. The replicated car is part of a small museum in a leafy clearing. ⊠ *Clairière de l'Armistice* ☎ *03–44–85–14–18* ⌚ *€3* ⊙ *Apr.–Oct., Wed.–Mon. 9–noon and 2–6:30; Nov.–Mar., Wed.–Mon. 10–noon and 2–5.*

Where to Stay & Eat

$–$$ ✕▦ **France.** A former 17th-century coaching inn, the hotel is central, cheap, and the epitome of French Provincial. Rooms have matching fruit-and-flower wallpaper and bedspreads and range in size from nook-and-cranny to family sleeper. The restaurant (no lunch Monday, no dinner Sunday) with its brass lights, plush curtains, and waiters in black tie, tries valiantly to be upper crust, while the brasserie serves a lighter, more casual fare. ⊠ *17 rue Eugène-Floquet, 60200* ☎ *03–44–40–02–74* 🖶 *03–44–40–48–37* ⊕ *www.logisdefrance.fr* ↪ *20 rooms* ⌂ *Restaurant, bar, some pets allowed (fee); no a/c* ⊟ *AE, DC, MC, V* ❍ *BP.*

Pierrefonds

③⑦ *14 km (9 mi) southeast of Compiègne via D973.*

Dominating the attractive lakeside village of Pierrefonds is its huge er**FodorśChoice** satz medieval castle. Built on a huge mound in the 15th century, the **Château** ★ **de Pierrefonds** was comprehensively restored and re-created in the 1860s to imagined former glory at the behest of upstart emperor Napoléon

III, then seeking to cash in on the craze for the Middle Ages. Architect Viollet-le-Duc left a crenelated fortress with a fairy-tale silhouette, although, like the fortified town of Carcassonne, which he also restored, Pierrefonds is more a construct of what Viollet-le-Duc thought it should have looked like than what it really was. A visit takes in the chapel, barracks, and the majestic keep holding the lord's bedchamber and reception hall, which is bordered by a spiral staircase whose lower and upper sections reveal clearly what is ancient and modern in this former fortress. Don't miss the plaster casts of tomb sculptures from all over France in the cellars, and the **Collection Monduit**—industrially produced, larger-than-life lead decorations made by the 19th-century firm that brought the Statue of Liberty to life. ☎ *03–44–42–72–72* 🖙 *€6.10* ☉ *Mon.–Sat. 9:30–12:30 and 2–5:30, Sun. 9:30–5:30.*

off the
beaten
path

MORIENVAL – This village, 6 km (4 mi) south of Pierrefonds via D335, is known for its modest 11th-century Romanesque church, one of the key buildings in architectural history. It was here, in the 1120s, that masons first hit on the idea of using stone vaults supported on "ribs" springing diagonally from column to column, an architectural breakthrough that formed the structural basis of the Gothic style. The trend was soon picked up at the great basilica of St-Denis near Paris and swept through northern France during the years that followed.

Where to Stay & Eat

$ ✕🏠 **Le Relais Brunehaut.** Just down the valley from Pierrefonds, in the hamlet of Chelles, is this quaint hotel-restaurant with a view of the abbey church next door. It's made up of a tiny ensemble of stucco buildings bordered by several acres of pleasant park and a small duck-populated river. An old wooden water mill in the dining room and the good, simple seasonal fare make eating here a pleasure. The dining room is closed Monday and Tuesday year-round, and on Wednesday and Thursday from mid-November through late April. ✉ *3 rue de l'Église, 5 km (3 mi) east of Pierrefonds on D85, 60350 Chelles* ☎ *03–44–42–85–05* 🖷 *03–44–42–83–30* 🛏 *7 rooms* ♨ *Restaurant; no a/c* 🖃 *MC, V* ⦿ *MAP.*

CHAMPAGNE

Champagne, a place name that has become a universal synonym for joy and festivity, is a word of humble origin. Like *campagna,* its Italian counterpart, it is derived from the Latin *campus,* which means "open field." In French campus became *champ,* with the old language extending this to *champaign,* for "battlefield," and *champaine,* for "district of plains." *Battlefield* and *plains* both accurately describe the province, as Champagne is crisscrossed by Roman roads along which defenders and invaders have clashed for two millennia.

Today, of course, the province is best known for its champagne vineyards, which start just beyond Château-Thierry, 96 km (60 mi) northeast of Paris, and continue along the towering Marne Valley to Epernay.

Cheerful villages line the Route du Vin (Wine Road), which twines north to Reims, the capital of bubbly. As you head farther northeast, rolling chalk hills give way to the rugged Ardennes Forest, straddling the Belgian border. For a handy Web source for many of the great Champagne *maisons* (houses) of the region, log on to www.umc.fr.

Château-Thierry

38 *96 km (60 mi) northeast of Paris via A4, 40 km (25 mi) south of Soissons.*

Built along the Marne River beneath the ruins of a hilltop castle that dates from the time of Joan of Arc, and within sight of the American **Belleau Wood** War Cemetery, Château-Thierry is best known as the birthplace of the French fabulist Jean de La Fontaine (1621–95). The 16th-century mansion where La Fontaine was born is now a museum, the **Musée Jean de La Fontaine,** furnished in the style of the 17th century. It contains La Fontaine's bust, portrait, and baptism certificate, plus editions of his fables magnificently illustrated by Jean-Baptiste Oudry (1755) and Gustave Doré (1868). ⊠ *12 rue Jean-de-La-Fontaine* ☎ *03–23–69–05–60* ✉ *€3.20* ⊙ *Wed.–Mon. 10–noon and 2–5.*

Épernay

39 *50 km (31 mi) east of Château-Thierry via D3/N3.*

Unlike Reims with its numerous treasures, the town of Épernay, on the south bank of the Marne, appears to live only for champagne. Unfortunately, no relation exists between the fabulous wealth of Épernay's illustrious wine houses and the drab, dreary appearance of the town as a whole. Most champagne firms are spaced out along the long, straight avenue de Champagne, and although their names may provoke sighs of wonder, their facades are either functional or overdressy. The attractions are underground.

Of the various champagne houses open to the public, **Mercier** offers the best deal; its sculpted, labyrinthine cellars contain one of the world's largest wooden barrels (with a capacity of more than 215,000 bottles). A tour of the cellars takes 45 minutes in the relative comfort of a small train. A glass of champagne is your post-visit reward. ⊠ *75 av. de Champagne* ☎ *03–26–51–22–22* 🖨 *03–26–51–22–23* ✉ *€6.50* ⊙ *Weekdays 9:30–11:30 and 2–4:30. Closed Tues., Wed. in Jan.–Mar.*

To understand how the region's still wine became sparkling champagne, head across the Marne to **Hautvillers.** Here the monk Dom Pérignon (1638–1715)—upon whom, legend has it, blindness conferred the gifts of exceptional taste buds and sense of smell—invented champagne as everyone knows it by using corks for stoppers and blending wines from different vineyards. Dom Pérignon's simple tomb, in a damp, dreary Benedictine abbey church (now owned by Moët et Chandon), is a forlorn memorial to the hero of one of the world's most lucrative drink industries.

Where to Stay & Eat

$$$–$$$$ ✕🏨 **La Briqueterie.** Épernay is short on good hotels, so it's worth driving south to Vinay to find this luxurious manor. The spacious rooms

"BROTHER, COME QUICKLY, I'M DRINKING STARS"

SO EXCLAIMED DOM PÉRIGNON *upon first sipping the bubbling beverage that he invented through luck and alchemy. The blind 17th-century Benedictine monk was the first to discover the secret of its production at the Abbey of Hautvillers by combining the still wines of the region and storing the mix in bottles. Today, the world's most famous sparkling wine comes from this region's vineyards, along the towering Marne Valley between Épernay and Château-Thierry and on the slopes of the Montagne de Reims between Épernay and Reims.*

Champagne firms—Veuve-Clicquot, Mumm, Pommery, Taittinger, and others—welcome you into their chalky, mazelike cellars. Most of the big houses give tours of their caves (cellars), accompanied by informative lectures on the champagne production process. The quality of the tours is inconsistent, ranging from hilarious to desparingly tedious, though a glass of champagne at the end makes even the most mediocre worth it (some would say). On the tours, you'll discover that champagne is not made so differently from the way the Dom did it three centuries ago. Chardonnay, pinot noir, and sometimes Pinot Meunier grapes ferment separately and are then mixed into each house's distinctive blend and bottled. The use of a bottle is key.

Previously, wines were only stored in large barrels and the effervescence caused by fermentation escaped. When bottles replaced barrels, the wines' natural sparkle was kept imprisoned until they were opened. Left tilted almost upside down in chilly underground tunnels, the heavy-walled bottles are frequently turned by "riddlers," men who spend three years learning exactly how to turn bottles in order to nudge the sediment down into the

neck. After a while the bottles are opened, the sediment shoots out, a small quantity of liqueur is added, and the corks are tied down for good with wire. It takes about three years of fermentation to produce the proper level of fizz, alcohol, and taste. Only wine from Champagne can properly be called champagne; otherwise, it's sparkling wine.

Irritatingly, champagne costs about as much in Champagne as it does in Chicago, but there are some wine stores in the region that can usually recommend excellent but unknown champagnes for half the price of the big names. Vin mousseux and Crémant are inferior products that don't conform to the champagne cartel's strict regulation. Remember that you can tell a lot about champagne just by looking at the label. The words brut, sec, demi-sec, and doux tell you how sweet the drink is; brut is driest and doux is sweetest. The words vintage or millésime mean you might wish to pick a cheaper bottle because this one was made entirely from grapes harvested during a single good year, and you're going to have to pay for it. Champagnes made from a mixture of grapes from different years are more common and less expensive. No matter if pricey or basic, brut or doux, the Champagne region fixates obsessively on the bubbly brew and you'll find the popping of champagne corks builds to quite a roar as you travel the Route du Vin, a road that leads to many local champagne houses and dégustations (tastings) as it threads through the countryside south of Reims. Remember to always ask for a coupe of champagne, never a verre (glass).

are modern; ask for one overlooking the extensive gardens. The chef has the Mediterranean on his mind, hence the lobster and prawns in citrus sauce. For more regional fare try the Champagne snails with herbed butter and, for dessert, the *crêpe soufflée au marc de champagne* (a crepe filled with pastry cream and flavored with brandy). ⊠ *4 rte. de Sézanne, 6 km (4 mi) south of Épernay, 51530 Vinay* ☎ *03–26–59–99–99* 🖷 *03–26–59–92–10* ⊕ *www.labriqueterie.com* ⟿ *40 rooms, 2 suites* ⚭ *Restaurant, minibars, cable TV, pool, gym, sauna, bar, Internet, some pets allowed (fee)* ⊟ *AE, MC, V* ⊗ *Closed late Dec.* ⊚| *BP.*

Nightlife & the Arts

The leading wine festival in the Champagne region is the **Fête St-Vincent** (named for the patron saint of vine growers), held on either January 22 or the following Saturday in Ambonnay, 24 km (15 mi) east of Épernay.

Châlons-en-Champagne

40 *34 km (21 mi) southeast of Épernay via N3.*

Strangely enough, the official administrative center of the champagne industry is not Reims or Épernay but Châlons-en-Champagne. Yet this large town is mainly of interest for its vast cathedral and smaller, early Gothic church.

★ With its twin spires, Romanesque nave, and early Gothic choir and vaults, the church of **Notre-Dame-en-Vaux** bears eloquent testimony to Châlons's medieval importance. The small **museum** beside the excavated cloister contains outstanding medieval statuary. ⊠ *Rue Nicolas-Durand* ☎ *03–26–64–03–87* 🖻 *€4.60* ⊗ *Apr.–Sept., Wed.–Mon. 10–noon and 2–6; Oct.–Mar., Wed.–Fri. 10–noon and 2–5, weekends 10–noon and 2–6.*

The 13th-century **Cathédrale St-Étienne** (⊠ Rue de la Marne) is a harmonious structure with large nave windows and tidy flying buttresses; the exterior effect is marred only by the bulky 17th-century Baroque west front.

Where to Stay & Eat

$$–$$$ ✕🖭 **Angleterre.** Rooms at this stylish spot in central Châlons have elaborate decor and marble bathrooms; those in the back are quietest. In the outstanding restaurant (closed Sunday; no lunch Monday or Saturday), chef Jacky Michel's creations include quail with foie gras and red mullet with artichoke, as well as the seasonal dessert *tout-pommes*, featuring five variations on the humble apple. Breakfast is a superb buffet. ⊠ *19 pl. Monseigneur-Tissier, 51000* ☎ *03–26–68–21–51* 🖷 *03–26–70–51–67* ⊕ *www.hotel-dangleterre.fr* ⟿ *25 rooms* ⚭ *Restaurant, minibars, bar, Internet, some pets allowed (fee)* ⊟ *AE, DC, MC, V* ⊗ *Closed mid-July–early Aug. and late Dec.–early Jan.* ⊚| *BP.*

en route The grapes of Champagne flourish on the steep slopes of the Montagne de Reims—more of a forest-topped plateau than a mountain—northwest of Châlons. Take D1 northwest, then turn right on D37 to Ambonnay to join the Route du Vin (Wine Road). This winds around the vine-entangled eastern slopes of the Montagne through such pretty wine villages as the aptly named **Bouzy** (known for its fashionable if overpriced red), **Verzy, Mailly-Champagne, Chigny-les-Roses,** and **Rilly-la-Montagne.**

L'Épine

41 *7 km (4½ mi) east of Châlons via N3.*

The tiny village of L'Épine is dominated by its church, the twin-towered Flamboyant Gothic **Basilique de Notre-Dame de l'Épine.** The church's facade is a magnificent creation of intricate patterns and spires, and the interior exudes elegance and restraint.

Where to Stay & Eat

★ **$$–$$$** ✕⊡ **Aux Armes de Champagne.** The highlight of this cozy former coaching inn (just opposite the town church, so ask for a table with a view) is the restaurant, with its renowned champagne list and imaginative, often spectacular cuisine by chef Gilles Blandin. Among his specialties are artichokes with local goat cheese, and red mullet prepared with juice from roast veal. (From November through March, the restaurant is closed Monday, and no dinner is served Sunday.) Rooms are furnished with solid, traditional reproductions, wall hangings, and thick carpets. No. 21, with wood beams, is the most atmospheric. ⊠ *31 av. du Luxembourg, 51460* ☎ *03–26–69–30–30* 🖶 *03–26–69–30–36* ⊕ *www.auxarmesdechampagne.com* ↪ *37 rooms, 2 suites* ⅏ *Restaurant, minibars, cable TV, tennis court, bar, Internet; no a/c* ⊟ *AE, DC, MC, V* ⊙ *Closed Jan.–mid-Feb.* ⦿⎮ *BP.*

Reims

44 km (27 mi) northwest of Châlons via N44, 144 km (90 mi) northeast of Paris.

Although most of its historic buildings were flattened in World War I and replaced by drab, modern architecture, those that do remain are of royal magnitude. Top of the list goes to the city's magnificent cathedral, in which the kings of France were crowned until 1825, while the Musée des Beaux-Arts has a stellar collection, including the famed Jacques-Louis David painting of Marat in his bath. Reims sparkles with some of the biggest names in champagne production, and the thriving industry has conferred wealth and sometimes an arrogant reserve on the region's inhabitants. Nevertheless, the maze of champagne cellars constitutes another fascinating sight of the city. Several champagne producers organize visits to their cellars, combining video presentations with guided tours of their cavernous, hewn-chalk underground warehouses. For a complete list of champagne cellars, head to the **tourist office** (⊠ 2 rue Guillaume-de-Machault ☎ 03–26–77–45–25) near the cathedral. A handy Web site that lists many of the leading houses is another way to plan your visits: www.umc.fr.

㊷ The tour of the cavernous **Taittinger** cellars is the most spectacular of the
FodorśChoice champagne producer visits. It includes a champagne *dégustation* (tast-
★ ing) afterward. ⊠ *9 pl. St-Nicaise* ☎ *03–26–85–84–33* 🖃 *€7*
☉ *Mar.–Nov., daily 9:30–noon and 2–4:30; Dec.–Feb., weekdays
9:30–noon and 2–4:30.*

㊸ **Piper-Heidsieck** offers the most amusing champagne tours, complete
FodorśChoice with zillions of bubbles, a "scene" from *Casablanca,* and even the ghost
★ of Monsieur Heidsieck. ⊠ *51 blvd. Henry-Vasnier* ☎ *03–26–84–43–44*
⊕ *www.piper-heidsieck.com* 🖃 *€7* ☉ *Thurs.–Mon, 9:30–11:45 and 2–5*
☉ *Closed Jan. and Feb.*

㊹ The 11th-century **Basilique St-Rémi** honors the 5th-century saint who gave
his name to the city. Its interior seems to stretch into the endless distance, an impression created by its relative murk and lowness. The airy
four-story Gothic choir contains some fine original 12th-century stained
glass. Like the cathedral, the basilica puts on indoor **son-et-lumière**
shows every Saturday evening at 9:30 from late June to early October.
They are preceded by a tour of the building and are free. ⊠ *53 rue St-
Rémi* ☎ *03–26–85–31–20* ☉ *Daily 8–6.*

★ ㊺ The **Palais du Tau** (formerly the Archbishop's Palace), alongside the
cathedral, houses an impressive display of tapestries and coronation robes,
as well as several statues rescued from the cathedral facade before they
fell off. The second-floor views of Notre-Dame are terrific. ⊠ *2 pl. du
Cardinal Luçon* ☎ *03–26–47–81–79* 🖃 *€4.10* ☉ *July and Aug., daily
9:30–6:30; Sept.–June, daily 9:30–12:30 and 2–5:30.*

㊻ The **Musée des Beaux-Arts** (Museum of Fine Arts), two blocks southwest
of the cathedral, has an outstanding collection of paintings: no fewer
than 27 Corots are here, as well as Jacques-Louis David's unforgettable
portrait of the revolutionary polemicist Jean-Paul Marat, stabbed to death
in his bath by Charlotte Corday in 1793. ⊠ *8 rue Chanzy*
☎ *03–26–47–28–44* 🖃 *€3, joint ticket with Salle de Reddition*
☉ *Wed.–Mon. 10–noon and 2–6.*

㊼ The **Cathédrale Notre-Dame** was the age-old setting for the coronations
FodorśChoice of the French kings. Clovis, king of the Franks in the 6th century, was
★ baptized in an early structure on this site; Joan of Arc led her recalcitrant Dauphin here to be crowned King Charles VII; Charles X's coronation, in 1825, was the last. The east-end windows have stained glass
by Marc Chagall. Admire the vista toward the west end, with an inter-
play of narrow pointed arches. The glory of Reims's cathedral is its facade: it's so skillfully proportioned that initially you have little idea of
its monumental size. Above the north (left) door hovers the *Laughing
Angel,* a delightful statue whose famous smile threatens to melt into an
acid-rain scowl; pollution has succeeded war as the ravager of the building's fabric. With the exception of the 15th-century towers, most of the
original building went up in the 100 years after 1211. A stroll around
the outside reinforces the impression of harmony, discipline, and decorative richness. The east end presents an idyllic sight across well-tended
lawns. Spectacular **son-et-lumière** shows are performed both inside (small

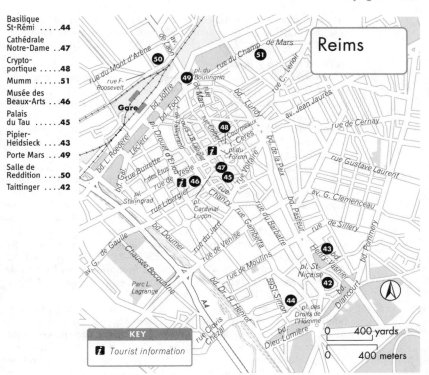

Reims

KEY

i *Tourist information*

0 — 400 yards
0 — 400 meters

---

charge) and outside (free) the cathedral on Friday and Saturday evenings from July to mid-September. ⊠ *Pl. du Cardinal-Luçon* ⊙ *Daily 7:30–7:30.*

48 The Gallo-Roman **Cryptoportique,** an underground gallery and crypt, now a semi-subterranean passageway, was constructed around AD 200 under the forum of what was Reim's predecessor, the Roman town of Duro-cortorum. ⊠ *Pl. du Forum* ☎ *03–26–85–23–36* ⊙ *Mid-June–mid-Sept., Tues.–Sun. 2–6.*

49 The **Porte Mars** (⊠ Rue de Mars), an unlikely but impressive 3rd-century Roman arch adorned by worn bas-reliefs depicting Jupiter, Romulus, and Remus, looms up across from the train station.

50 The **Salle de Reddition** (Surrender Room), near the train station, also known as the Salle du 8 mai 1945, is a well-preserved map-covered room used by General Eisenhower as Allied headquarters at the end of World War II. It was here that General Alfred Jodl signed the German surrender at 2:41 AM on May 7, 1945. Fighting officially ceased at midnight the next day. ⊠ *12 rue Franklin-Roosevelt* ☎*03–26–47–84–19* ⊠€*3, joint ticket with the Musée des Beaux-Arts* ⊙ *Wed.–Mon. 10–noon and 2–6.*

51 **Mumm** is the closest champagne house to the centre ville, about a 10-minute walk north from the cathedral. This is one of the few champagne houses to give out free samples after a tour, which is usually on the bland side (the tour, that is). ☎ *34 rue du Champ-de-Mars* ☎ *03–26–49–59–70* 🖃 *€6* ⊙ *Mar.–Oct., daily 9–11 and 2–5; Nov.–Feb., daily 2–5.*

Where to Stay & Eat

$–$$ ✕ **Vigneron.** This little brasserie in a 17th-century mansion is cozy and cheerful, with two tiny dining rooms displaying a jumble of champagne-related paraphernalia. The food is delightful as well: relatively cheap, distinctly hearty, and prepared with finesse. Try the pigs' feet or andouillettes slathered with delicious mustard made with champagne. ✉ *1 pl. Paul-Jamot* ☎ *03–26–79–86–86* ▤ *MC, V* ⊙ *Closed weekends, late Dec.–early Jan., and most of Aug.*

★ **$$$$** ✕▦ **Les Crayères.** The top attraction at this hotel—a late-19th-century château surrounded by a hilly park and with a gilt-trimmed interior—is Gérard Boyer, one of the country's most highly rated chefs, whose delectable dishes range from wild mushrooms in cream to scallops with endive confit. The extensive wine list pays homage to Reims's champagne heritage. The restaurant is closed Monday, and no luncheon is offered Tuesday; reservations and jacket and tie are all essential. ✉ *64 bd. Henry-Vasnier, 51100* ☎ *03–26–82–80–80* 🖷 *03–26–82–65–52* ⊕ *www.gerardboyer.com* ⤴ *19 rooms* ⚭ *Restaurant, minibars, cable TV, tennis court, bar, Internet, some pets allowed (fee)* ▤ *AE, DC, MC, V* ⊙ *Closed late Dec.–mid-Jan.* ⦿ *BP.*

$$ ✕▦ **Le Cheval Blanc.** This hotel, owned for five generations by the hospitable Robert family, is in the small village of Sept-Saulx, southeast of Reims. Guest rooms overlook a parklike glade on the Vesle River—some are quite small, but the newer suites are larger and have modern furnishings. Restaurant specialties include St-Pierre fish seasoned with Chinese pepper and pigeon with dried raisins. There's no lunch on Wednesdays. ✉ *Rue du Moulin, 24 km (15 mi) southeast of Reims via D8, 51400 Sept-Saulx* ☎ *03–26–03–90–27* 🖷 *03–26–03–97–09* ⊕ *www.chevalblanc-sept-saulx.com* ⤴ *25 rooms* ⚭ *Restaurant, minibars, cable TV, tennis court, fishing, Internet; no a/c* ▤ *AE, DC, MC, V* ⊙ *Closed Tues. in Oct.–Mar., and Feb.* ⦿ *MAP.*

$$ ✕▦ **La Paix.** A modern eight-story hotel, 10 minutes' walk from the cathedral, La Paix has stylish rooms with 18th- and 19th-century reproductions, a pretty garden, and an incongruous chapel. Its brasserie-style restaurant serves good, though not inexpensive, cuisine (mainly grilled meats and seafood). ✉ *9 rue Buirette, 51100* ☎ *03–26–40–04–08* 🖷 *03–26–47–75–04* ⊕ *www.bw-hotel-la-paix.com* ⤴ *91 rooms, 15 suites* ⚭ *Restaurant, minibars, cable TV, pool, bar, some pets allowed (fee)* ▤ *AE, DC, MC, V* ⦿ *BP.*

THE NORTH & CHAMPAGNE A TO Z

To research prices, get advice from other travelers, and book travel arrangements, visit www.fodors.com.

AIRPORTS

If you are coming from the United States and most other destinations, count on arriving at Paris's Charles de Gaulle or Orly airport. Charles de Gaulle offers easy access to the northbound A1 and the TGV line for Lille. If coming from the U.K., consider the occasional direct flights from Heathrow to Lille-Lesquin or from Lydd, near Folkestone, to Le Touquet.

BOAT & FERRY TRAVEL

Ferry and hovercraft companies travel between northern France and the United Kingdom. Companies traveling between Calais and Dover include Hoverspeed, P&O Stena, and Seafrance. The Norfolk Line operates between Dunkerque and Dover. For more information, *see* Boat and Ferry Travel *in* Smart Travel Tips A to Z.

BUS TRAVEL

The main bus operator in Picardy is **Courriers Automobiles Picards** (✉ Rue de la Vallée, Amiens ☎ 03–22–92–27–03); their main hub is the Gare Routière in Amiens. In the Champagne region, services are run by STDM Trans-Champagne; the main hub is Reims, where buses depart from the train station. Some sample bus links include Reims to Troyes (via STDM Trans-Champagne); Amiens to Arras (via Courriers Automobiles Picards); and Boulogne to Calais (via Cariane Littoral, the main operator for services along the Channel coast). There are many other links, so always check in with the regional tourist office or information window at a big gateway rail or bus station to get printed bus schedules.

🚌 Bus Information **Cariane Littoral** ✉ 10 rue d'Amsterdam, 62100 Calais ☎ 03-21-34-74-40 🖨 03-21-97-73-33. **Courriers Automobiles Picards** ✉ B.P. 59, ZAC La Haute Borne, 80136 Rivéry ☎ 03-22-91-46-82 🖨 03-22-70-70-71. **STDM Trans-Champagne** ✉ 86 rue des Fagnières, 51000 Châlons-en-Champagne ☎ 03-26-65-17-07.

CAR RENTAL

Be aware that the Avis offices at the Calais car ferry and Hoverport terminals may not always be staffed. Look for instructions on how to use the red phones provided in these offices to reach the central office in the town of Calais, which will handle your rental.

🚗 Local Agencies **Avis** ✉ 36 pl. d'Armes, Calais ☎ 03-21-34-66-50 ✉ Calais car ferry terminal ☎ 03-21-96-47-65 ✉ Calais Hoverport ☎ 03-21-96-66-52 ✉ Cour de la Gare, Reims ☎ 03-26-47-10-08. **Europcar** ✉ Gare Lille-Europe, av. Le Corbusier, Lille ☎ 03-20-06-01-46 ✉ Gare Lille-Flandre, rue de Tournai ☎ 03-20-06-10-04. **Hertz** ✉ 5 bd. d'Alsace-Lorraine, Amiens ☎ 03-22-91-26-24 ✉ 10 bd. Daunou, Boulogne-sur-Mer ☎ 03-21-31-53-14.

CAR TRAVEL

Two highways head north from Paris. Busy A1 passes close to Compiègne and Arras (where A26 branches off to Calais) before reaching Lille. Journey time is about 1 hour and 40 minutes to Arras and 2½ hours to Lille. The new, much quieter A16 leads from L'Isle-Adam, north of Paris, up to Beauvais and Amiens, before veering northwest to Abbeville and around the coast to Boulogne, Calais, and Dunkerque. Journey time is about 90 minutes to Amiens and 2½ hours to Boulogne. If you're arriving by car via the Channel Tunnel, you'll disembark at Coquelles, near Calais, and join A16 not far from its junction with A26, which heads to Arras

(75 minutes) and Reims (2½ hours). A4 heads east from Paris to Reims; allow 90 minutes to two hours, depending on traffic.

EMERGENCIES

🚹 **Ambulance** ☎ 15. **Regional hospitals** ✉ 1 pl. Victor-Pauchet, Amiens ☎ 03-22-66-80-00 ✉ 8 av. Henri-Adnot, Compiègne ☎ 03-44-23-60-00 ✉ 51 bd. de Belfort, Lille ☎ 03-20-87-48-48 ✉ American Hospital, 47 rue Cognac-Jay, Reims ☎ 03-26-78-78-78.

TOURS

Service des Visites Guidées in Boulogne's Château-Musée arranges trips to Boulogne's old town and port for groups of up to 30 people; the cost for two hours totals €60 for two or more.

🚹 **Fees & Schedules Service des Visites Guidées** ✉ Rue Bernet, Boulogne-sur-Mer ☎ 03-21-80-56-78.

BUS TOURS   The Lille Tourist Office is a mine of information about companies that operate bus tours through northern France. Loisirs-Accueil Nord organizes bus trips to Boulogne and Flanders and can arrange fishing, walking, and beer-tasting tours.

🚹 **Fees & Schedules Lille Tourist Office** ✉ 42 pl. Rihour ☎ 03-20-21-94-21 ⊕ www.lilletourism.com. **Loisirs-Accueil Nord** ✉ 6 rue Gauthier-de-Châtillon, Lille ☎ 03-20-57-59-59.

TRAIN TRAVEL

It's easy to get around the region by train. Most sites can be reached by regular train service, except for the war cemeteries and the castle in Pierrefonds. TGV (Trains à Grande Vitesse) trains speed from Paris (Gare du Nord) to Lille (255 km [165 mi]) in just one hour. A separate TGV service links Paris (Gare du Nord) to Arras (50 minutes) and Dunkerque (two hours). The Paris–Boulogne–Calais train chugs unhurriedly around the coast, taking nearly three hours to cover 300 km (185 mi) via Amiens, Abbeville, and Étaples (bus links to nearby Le Touquet and Montreuil). There are also frequent daily services from Paris (Gare du Nord) to Beauvais and to Compiègne, Noyon, and Laon (taking up to two leisurely hours to cover 140 km [87 mi]). Regular trains cover the 170 km (105 mi) from Paris (Gare de l'Est) to Reims, via Château-Thierry, in 1½ hours. Cross-country services connect Reims to Épernay, Châlons, and Amiens (via Laon). Eurostar trains, via the Channel Tunnel, link London to Lille in under two hours; some stop at Fréthun, just outside Calais.

🚹 Train Information **SNCF** ☎ 08-36-35-35-35 ⊕ www.ter-sncf.com/uk/nord-pas-de-calais.

TRAVEL AGENCIES

🚹 Local Agent Referrals **Carlson Wagons-lit** ✉ 1 rue Paul-Bert, Calais ☎ 03-21-34-79-25 ✉ 9 rue Faidherbe, Lille, ☎ 03-20-55-05-76.

VISITOR INFORMATION

The principal regional tourist offices in Amiens, Lille, and Reims are good sources of information about the region. Other, smaller towns also have their own tourist offices, listed below by town.

7 Tourist Information **Abbeville** ✉ 1 pl. de l'Amiral-Courbet ☎ 03-22-24-27-92 ⊕ www.ville-abbeville.fr. **Amiens** ✉ 6 bis rue Dusevel ☎ 03-22-71-60-50 ⊕ www. amiens.com/tourisme. **Arras** ✉ Hôtel de Ville, pl. des Héros ☎ 03-21-51-26-95 ⊕ www.ot-arras.fr. **Beauvais** ✉ 1 rue Beauregard ☎ 03-44-45-08-18 ⊕ www.cci-oise. fr. **Boulogne-sur-Mer** ✉ Forum Jean-Noël, quai de la Poste ☎ 03-21-31-68-38 ⊕ www.tourisme-boulognesurmer.com. **Calais** ✉ 12 bd. Clemenceau ☎ 03-21-96-62-40 ⊕ www.ot-calais.fr. **Compiègne** ✉ Pl. de l'Hôtel-de-Ville ☎ 03-44-40-01-00 ⊕ www. compiegne.fr. **Eu** ✉ 41 rue Paul-Bignon ☎ 02-35-86-04-68 ⊕ www.ville-eu.fr. **Laon** ✉ Pl. du Parvis ☎ 03-23-20-28-62 ⊕ www.ville-laon.fr. **Le Touquet** ✉ Palais de l'Europe, pl. de l'Hermitage ☎ 03-21-06-72-00 ⊕ www.letouquet.com. **Lille** ✉ 42 pl. Rihour ☎ 03-20-21-94-21 ⊕ www.lilletourism.com. **Montreuil-sur-Mer** ✉ 21 rue Carnot ☎ 03-21-06-04-27 ⊕ www.montreuil62.net. **Noyon** ✉ Pl. de l'Hôtel-de-Ville ☎ 03-44-44-21-88 ⊕ www.noyon.com/tourisme. **Pierrefonds** ✉ Rue Louis-d'Orléans ☎ 03-44-42-81-44. **Reims** ✉ 2 rue Guillaume-de-Machault ☎ 03-26-77-45-25 ⊕ www.tourism.fr-reims. **Soissons** ✉ 16 pl. Fernand-Marquigny ☎ 03-23-53-17-37 ⊕ www.ville-soissons.fr. **St-Omer** ✉ 4 rue du Lion-d'Or ☎ 03-21-98-08-51 ⊕ www. tourisme.fr/saint-omer.

ALSACE-LORRAINE

7

Updated by
Christopher
Mooney

Introduction by
Nancy Coons

WHO PUT THE HYPHEN IN ALSACE-LORRAINE? The two regions, long at odds physically and culturally, were bonded when Kaiser Wilhelm sliced off the Moselle chunk of Lorraine and sutured it, à la Dr. Frankenstein, to Alsace, claiming the unfortunate graft as German turf. Though their names to this day are often hyphenated, Alsace and Lorraine have always been two separate territories, with distinctly individual characters. It's only their recent German past that ties them together—it wasn't until 1879, as a concession after France's surrender in 1871, that the newly hyphenated "Alsace-Lorraine" became part of the enemy's spoils. At that point the region was systematically Teutonized—architecturally, linguistically, culinarily (" . . . ve haff our own vays of cookink sauerkraut!")—and the next two generations grew up culturally torn. Until 1918, that is, when France undid its defeat and reclaimed its turf. Until 1940, when Hitler snatched it back and reinstated German textbooks in the primary schools. Until 1945, when France once again triumphantly raised the *bleu-blanc-rouge* over Strasbourg.

But no matter how forcefully the French tout its hard-won Frenchness, Alsace's German roots go deeper than the late 19th century, as one look at its storybook medieval architecture will attest. In fact, this strip of vine-covered hills squeezed between the Rhine and the Vosges mountains was called Prima Germania by the Romans, and belonged to the fiercely Germanic Holy Roman Empire for more than 700 years. Yet west of the Vosges, Lorraine served under French and Burgundian lords as well as the Holy Roman Empire, coming into its own under the powerful and influential dukes of Lorraine in the Middle Ages and Renaissance. Stanislas, the duke of Lorraine who transformed Nancy into a cosmopolitan Paris of the East, was Louis XV's father-in-law. Thus Lorraine's culture evolved as decidedly less German than its neighbor to the southeast.

But that's why these days most travelers find Alsace more exotic than Lorraine: its gabled, half-timber houses, ornate wells and fountains, oriels (upstairs bay windows), storks' nests, and carved-wood balustrades would serve well as a stage set for the tale of William Tell and satisfy a visitor's deepest craving for well-preserved Old World atmosphere. Strasbourg, perhaps France's most fascinating city outside Paris, offers all this ambience, and urban sophistication as well. And throughout Alsace, hotels are well scrubbed, with tile bathrooms, good mattresses, and geraniums spilling from every windowsill. Although the cuisine leans toward wursts and sauerkraut, sophisticated spins on traditional fare have earned it a reputation—perhaps ironic, in some quarters—as one of the gastronomic centers of France. In fact, it has been crudely but vividly put that Alsace combines the best of both worlds: one dines in France but washes up, as it were, in Germany.

Lorraine, on the other hand, has suffered over the last 20 years, and a decline in its northern industry and the miseries of its small farmers have left much of it tarnished and neglected—or, as others might say, kept it unspoiled. Yet Lorraine's rich caches of verdure, its rolling countryside dotted with *mirabelle* (plum) orchards and crumbling-stucco villages, abbeys, fortresses, and historic cities (majestic Nancy, verdant Metz, war-ravaged Verdun) offer a truly French view of life in the north. Its borders flank Belgium, Luxembourg, and Germany's mellow Mosel (Moselle in French). Home of Baccarat and St-Louis crystal (thanks to limitless supplies of firewood from the Vosges Forest), the birthplace of Gregorian chant, Art Nouveau, and Joan of Arc, Lorraine-the-underdog has long had something of its own to contribute. Although it may lack the Teutonic comforts of Alsace—it subscribes to the more laissez-faire school of innkeeping (concave mattresses, dusty bolsters, creaky floors)—it serves its regional delicacies with flair: *tourte Lorraine* (a pork-and-beef pie), madeleines (shell-shape butter cakes), mirabelle plum tarts, and the famous local quiche.

Exploring Alsace & Lorraine

These two regions of eastern France border three countries. Alsace, the smallest region, occupies a narrow strip of territory between the Vosges mountains and Germany, across the Rhine river. The capital of Alsace, Strasbourg, is the largest city in the region and one of the most attractive in France. The large town holding down the southern stretch of the region is historic Colmar. To the west of Alsace, across the Vosges and sharing a northern frontier with Germany and Luxembourg, is Lorraine. The largest city here, Nancy, also has considerable charm. North of Nancy is Metz, a picturesque town, and to the west lies Verdun. Most visitors begin exploring this region to the west—nearest Paris—where the battlegrounds of Verdun provide a poignant introduction to Lorraine. Linger in the artistic city of Nancy and then head east to Strasbourg (145 km [90 mi]), a city of such historic and cultural importance that it's worth exploring in depth. From here, tour the rest of Alsace, following the photogenic Route du Vin (Wine Road) to Colmar.

About the Restaurants & Hotels

Strasbourg and Nancy may be known as two of France's more expensive cities, but you wouldn't know it by the eating scene: no matter where you are, you can find down-to-earth eating spots with down-to-earth prices. Most notably, the regional *winstubs* (pronounced *veen*-shtoob), cozier and more wine-oriented than the usual French brasserie, are to be found in most Alsace towns and villages. In Alsace's capital, Strasbourg, along with Nancy and Metz, the two cities of Lorraine, as well as the villages along Alsace's pretty wine road, you'll need to arrive early (soon after noon, before eight) to be sure of a restaurant table in July and August. Out of season is a different matter throughout. As for food, these regions are typically French in their appreciation of fine foods, breads, and outdoor cafés, but a love of beer and beer pubs betrays that strong German influence.

Accommodations are easier to find in Lorraine than in Alsace, where advance reservations are essential in summer. Alsace is rich in *gîtes,* coun-

7

Only the Rhine River separates Germany from Alsace-Lorraine, a region that often looks and even sounds German. But its heart—after all, its natives were the first to sing the "Marseillaise"—is passionately French. In Alsace, wind along the Route du Vin through vineyards and storybook villages, then explore Strasbourg, which for all its medieval charms rivals Paris in history and haute cuisine. In mellow Lorraine, trace Joan of Arc's childhood, then discover the elegant 18th-century town of Nancy. Great art treasures—the Grünewald altarpiece at Colmar is one—also entice, as do hikes in the forested wilds of Franche-Comté. You can cover most of Alsace-Lorraine and Franche-Comté in about nine days. With six days you can see the northern part of Lorraine, from Verdun to Nancy, and most of Alsace. Three days will give you just enough time to explore Alsace, including the cosmopolitan city of Strasbourg.

Numbers in the text correspond to numbers in the margin and on the Lorraine, Alsace, Nancy, and Strasbourg maps.

If you have
3 days

Explore Alsace, beginning with a day and night in the delightful city of 🗺 **Strasbourg** ㉗–㊵ ☞. The next day start out early, cruising south along the Route du Vin to pretty **Obernai** ㊶; the charming villages of **Barr** ㊸, **Andlau** ㊹, and **Dambach-la-Ville** ㊺; and the dramatic castle in **Haut-Koenigsbourg** ㊼. Spend the night in the wine town of 🗺 **Ribeauvillé** ㊽ or medieval 🗺 **Riquewihr** ㊾. On Day 3 soak up the art and atmosphere in **Colmar** ㊿, whose museum headlines the world-famous Grünewald altarpiece.

If you have
8 days

Begin in memory-haunted **Verdun** ⑲ ☞ and 🗺 **Metz** ⑳; then head south through Lorraine to the crumbling cathedral town of **Toul** ㉒ and to Joan of Arc's birthplace in 🗺 **Domrémy-la-Pucelle** ㉔. Spend Days 3 and 4 in 🗺 **Nancy** ①–⑱ and discover its dazzling treasures of 18th-century and Art Nouveau architecture. On Day 5 make 🗺 **Strasbourg** ㉗–㊵ your goal, with the Rohan Palace and Petite France perched at the top of your list. On the sixth day follow the Route du Vin to **Obernai** ㊶—perhaps choose lunch here at the famed L'Ami Fritz or opt instead for a once-in-a-lifetime dinner tonight in **Sélestat** ㊻ at the legendary L'Auberge de L'Ill. Overnight nearby in ravishing 🗺 **Ribeauvillé** ㊽. On the seventh day, tour the town, then spend the afternoon at the nearby castle of **Haut-Koenigsbourg** ㊼. Forge on to quaint 🗺 **Riquewihr** ㊾ and your hotel. On Day 8 head to 🗺 **Colmar** ㊿ to see its splendid Unterlinden Museum. Spend the night here, and why not take a last look at Grünewald's great altarpiece the next morning before you return home?

try houses that can be rented. Throughout Alsace, hotels are models of good housekeeping. Lorraine tends to lack the Teutonic comforts of Alsace but is coming around as renovations get under way. Assume that all hotel rooms have air-conditioning, TV, telephones, and private bath, unless otherwise noted.

WHAT IT COSTS In euros					
	$$$$	$$$	$$	$	¢
RESTAURANTS	over €30	€23–€30	€17–€23	€11–€17	under €11
HOTELS	over €190	€120–€190	€80–€120	€50–€80	under €50

Restaurant prices are per person for a main course at dinner, including tax (19.6%) and service; note that if a restaurant offers only prix-fixe (set-price) meals, it has been given the price category that reflects the full prix-fixe price. Hotel prices are for a standard double room in high season, including tax (19.6%) and service charge; higher prices (inquire when booking) prevail for any board plans.

Timing

Outside tourist-packed high summer, June and September are the warmest and sunniest months. Many of the region's towns and villages, especially the wine villages of Alsace, stage summer festivals, including the spectacular pagan-inspired burning of the three pine trees in Thann (late June), the Flower Carnival in Sélestat (mid-August), and the wine fair in Colmar (first half of August). Some of the region's top sights, however—notably Haut-Koenigsbourg—can be besieged by tourists in July and August, so if you're there then, try to visit early in the morning. Although Lorraine is a lusterless place in winter, the Vosges mountains make attempts at being ski venues—plentiful snow cannot always be guaranteed—while Strasbourg pays tribute to the Germanic tradition with a Christmas fair.

NANCY

For architectural variety, few French cities match Nancy, which is in the heart of Lorraine, 300 km (190 mi) east of Paris. Medieval ornamentation, 18th-century grandeur, and Belle Epoque fluidity rub shoulders in the town center, where the bustle of commerce mingles with stately elegance. Its majesty derives from a long history as domain to the powerful dukes of Lorraine, whose double-barred crosses figure prominently on local statues and buildings. Never having fallen under the rule of the Holy Roman Empire or the Germans, this Lorraine city retains an eminently Gallic charm.

The city is at its most sublimely French in its harmoniously constructed squares and buildings, which, as vestiges of the 18th century, have the quiet refinement associated with the best in French architecture. Curiously enough, it was a Pole, and not a Frenchman, who was responsible for much of what is beautiful in Nancy. Stanislas Leszczynski, ex-king of Poland and father of Marie Leczinska (who married Louis XV of France) was given the Duchy of Lorraine by his royal son-in-law on the understanding that on his death it would revert to France. Stanislas installed himself in Nancy and devoted himself to the glorious embellishment of the city. Today place Stanislas remains one of the loveliest and most perfectly proportioned squares in the world, with place de la Carrière—reached through Stanislas's Arc de Triomphe—with its elegant, homogeneous 18th-century houses, its close rival for this honor.

7

Beyond Quiche Lorraine

A bottle of sharp Savagnin, a pink slab of air-dried ham, a patty of silky Vacherin Mont d'Or melted over potatoes: You don't need pink linens to dine on this primal mountain food, just a hiker's appetite, perhaps whetted by exploring the forested ranges of the region. Alsace cooking tends to be hearty and influenced by its Germanic origins—*choucroute* (sauerkraut served with ham and sausages) and *baeckoffe* (a meat-and-potato casserole) are two mainstays—but there is sophistication, too: foie gras accompanied by a glass of *vendanges tardives* (late-harvested) Gewürztraminer, and trout and chicken cooked in Riesling, the classic wine of Alsace. Snails and seasonal game are other favorites, as are Muenster cheese, salty *bretzel* loaves, and briochelike *kouglof* bread. Geese are very popular, especially if they're stuffed with apples or chestnuts! Carp fried in bread crumbs is a specialty of southern Alsace. Another regional favorite is the *tarte flambée*, a thin-crusted, pizzalike thing, topped with everything from fresh cream and cheese to mushrooms and fish. Desserts are also rich, most notably the *Kougelhopf*, a buttery upside-down cake cooked in a round pan and commonly served with kirsch, the local liqueur made from cherries. Lorraine, renowned for quiches, is also famous for its madeleines, *dragées* (almond candies), macaroons, and the lovely little *mirabelle*, a small yellow plum juicy with heady, perfumed nectar. Lorraine shares the Alsatian love of pastry and fruit tarts, served as often at 4 in the afternoon, with coffee, as an after-dinner dessert.

A Glass of Gewürztraminer

Wine is an object of worship in Alsace, and any traveler down the region's Route du Vin will want to become part of the cult. Just because Alsatian vintners use German grapes, don't expect their wines to taste like their counterparts across the Rhine. German vintners aim for sweetness, creating wines that are best appreciated as an aperitif. Alsatian vintners, on the other hand, eschew sweetness in favor of strength, and their wines go wonderfully with knock-down, drag-out meals. The main wines you need to know about are Gewürztraminer, Riesling, muscat, pinot gris, and sylvaner, all white wines. The only red wine produced in the region is the light and delicious pinot noir.

Gewürztraminer, which in Germany is an ultrasweet dessert wine, has a much cleaner, drier taste in Alsace, despite its fragrant bouquet. It is best served with the richest of Alsace dishes, such as goose. Riesling is the premier wine of Alsace, balancing a hard flavor with a certain gentleness. Pinot gris, also called tokay, and muscat are known as the Noble Wines of Alsace. With a grapy bouquet and clean finish, the dry muscat does best as an aperitif. Tokay is probably the most full-bodied of Alsatian wines. Sylvaner falls below those grapes in general acclaim, tending to be lighter and a bit dull. You'll discover many of these wines as you drive along the Route du Vin as it makes its way between Mulhouse and Strasbourg.

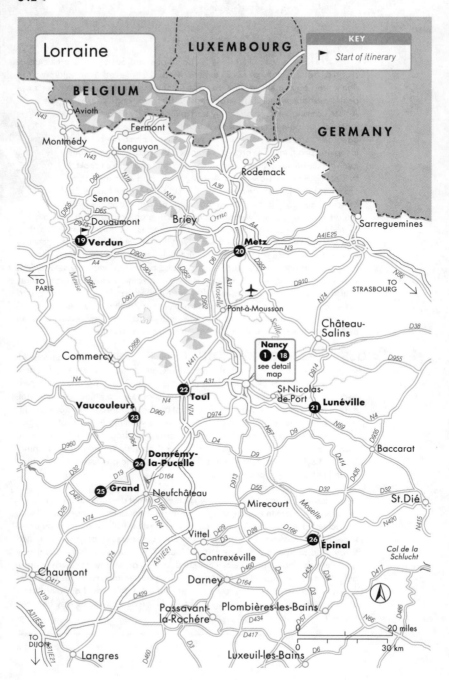

Lorraine

LUXEMBOURG

BELGIUM

GERMANY

KEY

▶ Start of itinerary

Avioth

Fermont

Montmédy

Longuyon

Rodemack

Senon

Douaumont

Briey

Orne

Sarreguemines

19 Verdun

Metz

20

TO PARIS

Pont-à-Mousson

TO STRASBOURG

Château-Salins

Commercy

Nancy

1 - **18**

see detail map

St-Nicolas-de-Port

22 Toul

21 Lunéville

Vaucouleurs

23

Baccarat

Domrémy-la-Pucelle

24

25 Grand

Neufchâteau

Mirecourt

St. Dié

Moselle

Vittel

26 Épinal

Col de la Schlucht

Chaumont

Contrexéville

Darney

Plombières-les-Bains

Passavant-la-Rochère

TO DIJON

Langres

Luxeuil-les-Bains

20 miles

0   30 km

The Historic Center

Concentrated northeast of the train station, this neighborhood—rich in architectural treasures as well as museums—includes classical place Stanislas and the shuttered, medieval *Vieille Ville* (Old Town).

a good walk

Begin your walk at the symbolic heart of Nancy, **place Stanislas ❶ ☞**, one of the grandest architectural set-pieces of the 18th century. The crown jewel of the city, enclosed by gold-and-black gates and Neoclassical buildings, the huge public square is bordered by many of the city's main institutions, including the art museum, the Hôtel de Ville (Town Hall), the Opéra, the tourist office, outdoor cafés, fountains, and a triumphal arch. On its western corner is the **Musée des Beaux-Arts ❷**, the Fine Arts Museum, fitted out with treasures from Rubens to great Daum glass. Cross place Stanislas diagonally and head south down rue Maurice Barrès to the Baroque **Cathédrale ❸**. On leaving, turn left on rue St-Georges and right up rue des Dominicains, stopping to admire the elegant stonework on No. 57, the Maison des Adams, named for the sculptors who lived in (and decorated) the edifice in the 18th century.

Recross place Stanislas and go through the monumental Arc de Triomphe, entering into peaceful **place de la Carrière ❹**, another square that is a triumph of elegant symmetry. At the colonnaded Palais du Gouvernement, former home of the governors of Lorraine, turn right into the vast, formal city park known as **La Pépinière ❺**. From the park's entrance at the foot of place de la Carrière, head straight under the arches and into the Vieille Ville. Dominating the square is the mighty basilica of **St-Epvre ❻**, which compensates for the absence of a Gothic cathedral in Nancy.

Head immediately right up picturesque Grande-Rue, with its antiques shops, bookstores, and artisanal bakeries behind brightly painted facades. On your right is the **Palais Ducal ❼**, one wing of which is a spectacular example of Flamboyant Gothic. Here's the main branch of the Musée Historique Lorraine, an ambitious complex that covers art—Georges de la Tour, Jacques Callot, Jacques de Bellange are the best known of Lorraine's great masters—as well as fascinating regional lore. The neighboring **Musée des Arts et Traditions Populaires ❽** occupies the Couvent des Cordeliers, combining a folk-arts museum and a Gothic chapel. At the end of Grande-Rue is the delightfully imposing **Porte de la Craffe ❾**, the last of Nancy's medieval fortifications.

TIMING   Depending on how much time you spend in the museums, this walk could take an hour or a whole day. Note that all the museums are closed on Tuesday.

Sights to See

❸ **Cathédrale.** This vast, frigid edifice was built in the 1740s in a ponderous Baroque style, eased in part by the florid ironwork of Jean Lamour. Its most notable interior feature is a murky 19th-century fresco in the dome. The **Trésor** (Treasury) contains minute 10th-century splendors carved in ivory and gold. ⊠ *Rue St-Georges, Ville Neuve.*

★ ❽ Just up the street from the Palais Ducal, the quirky, appealing **Musée des Arts et Traditions Populaires** (Museum of Folk Arts and Traditions) is housed

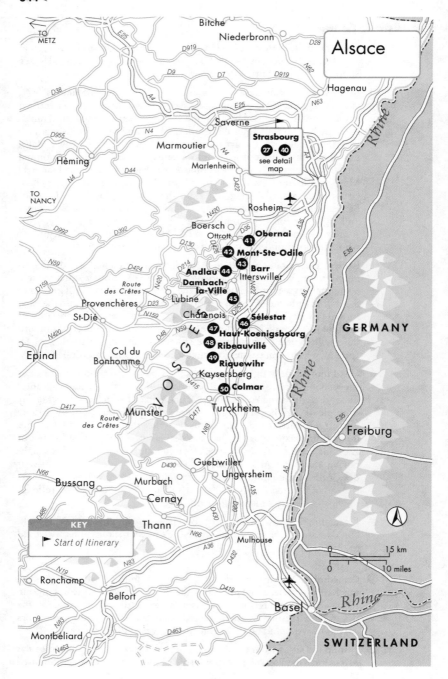

Alsace

Strasbourg
27 - **40**
see detail
map

41 Obernai
42 Mont-Ste-Odile
43 Barr
44 Andlau
Dambach-
la-Ville
45
46 Sélestat
47 Haut-Koenigsbourg
48 Ribeauvillé
49 Riquewihr
50 Colmar

GERMANY

SWITZERLAND

KEY
Start of Itinerary

0   15 km
0   10 miles

in the **Couvent des Cordeliers** (Convent of the Franciscans, who were known as Cordeliers until the Revolution). It re-creates how local people lived in pre-industrial times, using a series of evocative rural interiors. Craftsmen's tools, colorful crockery, somber stone fireplaces, and dark waxed-oak furniture accent the tableaulike settings. The dukes of Lorraine are buried in the crypt of the adjoining **Église des Cordeliers,** a Flamboyant Gothic church; the *gisant* (reclining statue) of Philippa de Gueldra, second wife of René II, executed in limestone in flowing detail, is a moving example of Renaissance portraiture. The octagonal Ducal Chapel was begun in 1607 in the Renaissance style, modeled on the Medici Chapel in Florence. ⊠ *66 Grande-Rue, Vieille Ville* ☎ *03–83–32–18–74* ☑ *€3.10; €4.60 joint ticket with Musée Lorrain* ✆ *Wed.–Mon. 10–12:30 and 2–6.*

② **Musée des Beaux-Arts** (Fine Arts Museum). In a splendid building that now spills over into a spectacular modern wing, a broad and varied collection of art treasures lives up to the noble white facade designed by Emmanuel Héré. Among the most striking are the freeze-the-moment realist tableaux painted by native son Emile Friant at the turn of the 20th century. A sizable collection of Lipschitz sculptures includes portrait busts of Gertrude Stein, Jean Cocteau, and Coco Chanel. You'll also find 19th- and 20th-century paintings by Monet, Manet, Utrillo, and Modigliani; a Caravaggio *Annunciation* and a wealth of Old Masters from the Italian, Dutch, Flemish, and French schools; and impressive glassworks by Nancy native Antonin Daum. The showpiece is Rubens's massive *Transfiguration.* Good commentary cards in English are available in every hall. ⊠ *Pl. Stanislas, Ville Royale* ☎ *03–83–85–30–72* ☑ *€4.57; €5.34 for joint ticket with Musée de l'École* ✆ *Wed.–Mon. 10:30–6.*

★ **⑦** **Palais Ducal** (Ducal Palace). This palace was built in the 13th century and completely restored at the end of the 15th century and again after a fire at the end of the 19th century. The main entrance to the palace, and the **Musée Lorrain** (Lorraine History Museum), which it now houses, is 80 yards down the street from the spectacularly flamboyant Renaissance portal. A spiral stone staircase leads up to the palace's most impressive room, the **Galerie des Cerfs** (Stags Gallery). Exhibits here (including pictures, armor, and books) recapture the Renaissance mood of the 16th century—one of elegance and merrymaking, with an undercurrent of stern morality: an elaborate series of huge tapestries, *La Condemnation du Banquet* (Condemnation of the Banquet), expounds on the evils of drunkenness and gluttony. Exhibits showcase Stanislas and his court, including "his" oft-portrayed dwarf; a section on Nancy in the revolutionary era; and works of Lorraine native sons, including a collection of Jacques Callot engravings and a handful of works by Georges de La Tour. ⊠ *64 Grande-Rue, Vieille Ville* ☎ *03–83–32–18–74* ☑ *€3.10; €4.60 joint ticket with Musée des Arts et Traditions* ✆ *Wed.–Mon. 10–12:30 and 2–6.*

🕲 **⑤** **La Pépinière.** This picturesque, landscaped city park has labeled ancient trees, a rose garden, playgrounds, a carousel, and a small zoo. ⊠ *Entrance off pl. de la Carrière, Vieille Ville.*

★ **④** **Place de la Carrière.** Spectacularly lined with pollarded trees and handsome 18th-century mansions (another successful collaboration between King

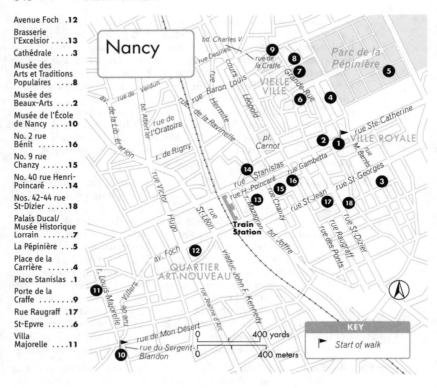

Stanislas and Emmanuel Héré), this elegant rectangle leads from place Stanislas to the colonnaded facade of the **Palais du Gouvernement** (Government Palace), former home of the governors of Lorraine. ⊠ *Vieille Ville.*

★ ▶ ❶ **Place Stanislas.** With its severe, gleaming-white Classical facades given a touch of Rococo jollity by fanciful wrought gilt-iron railings, this perfectly proportioned square will probably remind many of Versailles. The square is named for Stanislas Leszczynski, twice dethroned as king of Poland but offered the Duchy of Lorraine by Louis XV (his son-in-law) in 1736. Stanislas left a legacy of spectacular buildings, undertaken between 1751 and 1760 by architect Emmanuel Héré and ironwork genius Jean Lamour. The sculpture of Stanislas dominating the square went up in the 1830s, when the square was named after him. Framing the exit, and marking the divide between the Vieille Ville and the *Ville Neuve* (New Town), is the **Arc de Triomphe,** erected in the 1750s to honor Louis XV. The facade trumpets the gods of war and peace; Louis's portrait is here. Fitting showpiece of the southern flank of the square is the 18th-century **Hôtel de Ville,** Nancy's Town Hall, where the handiwork of Lamour can also be seen to stunning effect on the wrought-iron handrail of the *grand escalier* (grand staircase) leading off the lobby. You could get a closer view when the building was open to the public on summer evenings (July and

August, 10:30 to 11 PM) but it is now closed for renovations and will only reopen in 2005, the 250th anniversary of the place Stanislas. Hopefully, you will once again be allowed to mount the staircase and enter the Salle des Fêtes from whose windows the full beauty of the place Stanislas may truly be savored. ⊠ *Ville Royale.*

❾ **Porte de la Craffe.** A fairy-tale vision out of the late Middle Ages, this gate is the only remains of Nancy's medieval fortifications. With its twin *châtelet* towers looming at one end of the Grande-Rue, built in the 14th and 15th centuries, this arch served as a prison through the Revolution. Above the main portal is the Lorraine Cross, comprising a thistle and cross. ⊠ *Vieille Ville.*

❻ **St-Epvre.** A 275-foot spire towers over this splendid neo-Gothic church rebuilt in the 1860s. Most of the 2,800 square yards of stained glass were created by the Geyling workshop in Vienna; the chandeliers were made in Liège, Belgium; many carvings are the work of Margraff of Munich; the heaviest of the eight bells was cast in Budapest; and the organ, though manufactured by Merklin of Paris, was inaugurated in 1869 by Austrian composer Anton Bruckner. ⊠ *Pl. du Général-de-Gaulle, Vieille Ville.*

Art Nouveau Nancy

Fodor'sChoice ★ Think of *"l'Art Nouveau"* and many will conjure up the rich Parisian salons of Paris's Maxim's restaurant, the lavender-hue Prague posters of Alphonse Mucha, and the stained-glass dragonflies and opalescent vases that, to this day, remain the darlings of such collectors as Barbra Streisand. All of that beauty was born, to a great extent, in 19th-century Nancy. Inspired and coordinated by the glass master Émile Gallé, the local movement was formalized in 1901 as L'École de Nancy—from there, it spread like wildfire through Europe, from Naples to Monte-Carlo to Prague. The ensuing flourish encompassed the floral *pâte de verre* (literally, glass dough) works of Antonin Daum and Gallé; the Tiffany-esque stained-glass windows of Jacques Gruber; the fluidity of Louis Majorelle's furniture designs; and the sinuous architecture of Lucien Weissenburger, Émile André, and Eugène Vallin. Thanks to these artists, Nancy's downtown architecture gives the impression of a living garden suspended above the sidewalks.

a good walk

The magical **Musée de l'École de Nancy** ❿ ☛ is the best place to immerse yourself in the fanciful style that crept into interiors and exteriors throughout Nancy. To get to the museum from the busy shopping street rue St-Jean (just up rue des Dominicains from place Stanislas), take Bus 5 or 25 uphill and get off at place Painlevé. From the museum turn left down rue du Sergent-Blandan and walk about four blocks to **Villa Majorelle** ⓫. Cut east to place de la Commanderie and head up **avenue Foch** ⓬ to admire the colorful structures at Nos. 71, 69, and 41. Hike over the Viaduct Kennedy and the *gare* (train station), turn left past the department store Printemps, and follow rue Mazagran to the **Brasserie l'Excelsior** ⓭. Turn right toward **No. 40 rue Henri-Poincaré** ⓮. Turn right and walk past **No. 9 rue Chanzy** ⓯ (now the Banque Nationale de Paris). Head left to find **No. 2 rue Bénit** ⓰, with its ornate metal structure. Head south to rue St-Jean; at the corner of **rue Raugraff** ⓱ are two bay windows, remnants of stores that were once here. Continue down rue St-Jean and turn right to find **Nos. 42–44 rue St-Dizier** ⑱. Many more Art Nouveau addresses are scattered throughout the city; you can get a detailed map at the tourist office.

TIMING Allow a full morning to linger in the Musée de l'École de Nancy and then, during the course of about an hour and a half, wander back circuitously toward the Vieille Ville, stopping to admire Art Nouveau masterworks along the way.

Sights to See

⑫ **Avenue Foch.** This busy boulevard lined with mansions was built for Nancy's affluent 19th-century middle class. At No. 69, the occasional pinnacle suggests Gothic influence on a house built in 1902 by Émile André, who designed the neighboring No. 71 two years later. No. 41, built by Paul Charbonnier in 1905, bears ironwork by Majorelle. ⊠ *Quartier Art-Nouveau.*

⑬ **Brasserie l'Excelsior.** This bustling brasserie has a severely rhythmic facade that is invitingly illuminated at night. The popular restaurant continues to evoke the turn of the 20th century, both in its historic decor and its fin-de-siècle perfume. ⊠ *5 rue Mazagran, Quartier Art-Nouveau.*

★ ☞ ⑩ **Musée de l'École de Nancy** (School of Nancy Museum). The only museum in France devoted to Art Nouveau is housed in an airy turn-of-the-last-century garden–town house. It was built by Eugène Corbin, an early patron of the School of Nancy. There isn't a straight line in the house; pianos ooze, bedsteads undulate; the wood itself, hard and burnished as it is, seems to have melted and re-formed. Re-created rooms and original works of art by local Art Nouveau stars Gallé, Daum, Muller, and Walter all allure. Gallé (1846–1904) was the engine that drove the whole Art Nouveau movement. He called upon artists to resist the imperialism of Paris, follow examples in nature (not those of Greece or Rome), and use a variety of techniques and materials. Many of their gorgeous artifacts are on view here. ⊠ *36 rue du Sergent-Blandan, Quartier Art-Nouveau* ☎ *03–83–40–14–86* ⊕ *www.ecole-de-nancy.com* ☑ *€4.60; €6.10 for joint ticket with Musée des Beaux-Arts* ☉ *Mon. 2–6, Wed.–Sun. 10:30–6.*

⑯ **No. 2 rue Bénit.** This elaborately worked metal exoskeleton, the first in Nancy (1901), exudes functional beauty. The fluid decoration reminds you of the building's past as a seed supply store. Windows were worked by Gruber; the building was designed by Henry-Barthélemy Gutton, while Victor Schertzer conceived the metal frame. ⊠ *Quartier Art-Nouveau.*

⑮ **No. 9 rue Chanzy.** Designed by architect Émile André, this lovely structure—now a bank—can be visited during business hours. You can still see the cabinetry of Majorelle, the decor of Paul Charbonnier, and the stained-glass windows of Gruber. ⊠ *Quartier Art-Nouveau.*

⑭ **No. 40 rue Henri-Poincaré.** The Lorraine thistle and brewing hops weave through this undulating exterior, designed by architects Émile Toussaint and Louis Marchal. Victor Schertzer conceived this metal structure in 1908, after the success of No. 2 rue Bénit. Gruber's windows are enhanced by the curving metalwork of Majorelle. ⊠ *Quartier Art-Nouveau.*

⑱ Nos. 42–44 rue St-Dizier. Eugène Vallin and Georges Biet left their mark on this graceful 1903 bank. ✉ *Quartier Art-Nouveau* ☉ *Weekdays 8:30–5:30.*

⑰ Rue Raugraff. Once there were two stores here, both built in 1901. The bay windows are the last vestiges of the work of Charles Vallin, Émile André, and Eugène Vallin. ✉ *At corner of rue St-Jean, Quartier Art-Nouveau.*

★ ⑪ Villa Majorelle. This villa was built in 1902 by Paris architect Henri Sauvage for Majorelle himself. Sinuous metal supports seem to sneak up on the unsuspecting balcony like swaying cobras, and there are two grand windows by Gruber: one lighting the staircase (visible from the street) and the other set in the dining room on the south side of the villa (peek around from the garden side). ✉ *1 rue Louis-Majorelle Quartier Art-Nouveau.*

Where to Stay & Eat

★ $$–$$$ ✕ **Le Capucin Gourmand.** With a chic decor making the most of Nancy's Art Nouveau pâte de verre, including a giant chandelier and glowing mushroom lamps on the tables, this landmark puts its best foot forward under chef Hervé Fourrière. Soigné specialties include a light lobster lasagna with mushrooms, beef marrow served in the bone with truffles and white beans, and a trio of fresh mango desserts. The choice of Toul wines is extensive. ✉ *31 rue Gambetta, Ville Royale* ☎ *03-83-35-26-98* ⌕ *Reservations essential* ⊟ *AE, DC, MC, V* ☉ *Closed Mon., Aug., and end Feb.–early Mar. No dinner Sun.*

$$ ✕ **La Gastrolâtre.** Under the inspired direction of chef Patrick Tanesy, this stylish checked-cloth bistro off place Stanislas serves sophisticated regional cooking. Combinations include baeckoffe with foie gras, mullet with pigs' feet, and authentic *bouchée à la reine* (pastry shell with creamed meat), complete with cock's comb, sweetbreads, and morel mushrooms. Reserve ahead for summer terrace dining. ✉ *1 pl. de Vaudemont, Vieille Ville* ☎ *03-83-35-51-94* ⊟ *MC, V* ☉ *Closed Sun. and 2 wks Aug. No lunch Mon. No dinner Thurs.*

¢ ✕ **Le P'tit Cuny.** If you were inspired by the rustic exhibits of the Musée des Arts et Traditions Populaires, cross the street and sink your teeth into authentic Lorraine cuisine in the form of choucroute, *tête de veau* (calf's head), or tangy veal *tourte* (pie). ✉ *95 Grande-Rue, Vieille Ville* ☎ *03-83-32-85-94* ⊟ *MC, V* ☉ *Closed Sun. and Mon.*

★ $$$ ✕☐ **Grand Hôtel de la Reine.** This hotel is every bit as grand as place Stanislas, on which it stands; the magnificent 18th-century building is officially classified as a historic monument. Rooms are in a suitably regal Louis XV style; the most luxurious overlook the square. The restaurant, Le Stanislas (closed Sunday during November–March, no lunch Saturday), aglitter with chandeliers and carved-wood boiseries and run with elan by Olivier Hubert, has four- and five-course menus at €43 and €55. Showstoppers here include Lobster Bavaroise, duck in Vosges honey, and a supreme of melted chestnuts served with a morel mushroom caramel sauce. ✉ *2 pl. Stanislas, Ville Royale, 54000* ☎ *03-83-35-03-01* ⎙ *03-83-32-86-04* ⊕ *www.concorde-hotels.com* ⇄ *42 rooms* ⌕ *Restaurant, minibars, cable TV, bar, some pets allowed (fee)* ⊟ *AE, DC, MC, V* ☉❘ *BP.*

$–$$ ⌂ **Guise.** Deep in the shuttered Vieille Ville, this hotel is in an 18th-century nobleman's mansion with a magnificent stone-floor entry. Three and a half years of renovation were completed in 2002 and rooms are now furnished with period pieces. Breakfast on the once-grand main floor and an excellent location make this a good choice if you're a bargain-hunting romantic. ⊠ *18 rue de Guise, Vieille Ville, 54000* ☎ *03–83–32–24–68* 🖶 *03–83–35–75–63* ⊕ *www.hoteldeguise.com* ⌗ *42 rooms, 6 junior suites* ⌂ *Some pets allowed (fee); no a/c* ☰ *MC, V* ⵔ *BP.*

¢ ⌂ **Carnot.** This somewhat generic downtown hotel, with 1950s-style comforts and mostly tiny rooms, is handy to cours Léopold parking and backs up on the Vieille Ville. Corner rooms are sizable, rooms in the rear quiet. ⊠ *4 cours Léopold, Vieille Ville, 54000* ☎ *03–83–36–59–58* 🖶 *03–83–37–00–19* ⌗ *33 rooms* ⌂ *Bar, some pets allowed (fee); no a/c, no TV in some rooms* ☰ *MC, V* ⵔ *EP.*

Nightlife & the Arts

On summer evenings (June–September) at 10 PM, place Stanislas comes alive with a **sound-and-light show,** and the doors of the magnificent Hôtel de Ville are opened to the public (€2.30). Nancy's **Orchestre Symphonique & Lyrique** (⊠ 1 rue Ste-Catherine, Ville Royale ☎ 03–83–85–30–65) is a highly rated classical orchestra.

Le Chat Noir (⊠ 63 rue Jeanne-d'Arc, Ville Neuve ☎ 03–83–28–49–29) draws a thirtysomething crowd to retro-theme dance parties. **Métro** (⊠ 1 ter rue du Général-Hoche, Ville Neuve ☎ 03–83–40–25–13) is a popular dance club. **La Place** (⊠ 9 pl. Stanislas, Ville Royale ☎ 03–83–35–24–14) attracts a young upscale crowd that comes to dance.

Shopping

Daum (⊠ 17 rue des Cristalleries, Vieille Ville ☎ 03–83–30–80–20) sells deluxe crystal and examples of the city's traditional Art Nouveau pâte de verre. **Librairie Lorraine** (⊠ 93 Grande-Rue, Vieille Ville ☎ 03–83–36–79–52), across from the Musée des Arts et Traditions Populaires, is an excellent bookstore devoted entirely to Lorraine history and culture.

LORRAINE

In long-neglected Lorraine there are hidden treasures worth digging up. You can study the evolution of Gregorian chant in the municipal museum in Metz, where it was first codified. You can observe the luster of Baccarat crystal at its ancient factory, and the consummate artistry of Daum glassware in Nancy, where it sprang from the roots of Art Nouveau. You can stand on the unquiet earth of Verdun, and hear the church bells in which Joan of Arc discerned voices challenging her to save Orléans. Throughout Lorraine you'll find the statue of the region's patron saint, St. Nicholas—old St. Nick himself—with three children in a *saloir* (salting tub). Every December 6, Lorraine schoolchildren reenact the legend: a greedy butcher slaughters and salts down three children as hams, but when St. Nicholas drops by his place for a meal, he discovers the dastardly deed and brings them back to life.

Verdun

► ⑲ *96 km (60 mi) northwest of Nancy, 264 km (165 mi) east of Paris.*

A key strategic site along the Meuse Valley, Verdun is known, above all, for the 10-month battle between the French and the Germans in World War I that left more than 350,000 dead and nine villages wiped off the map. Both sides fought with suicidal fury, yet no significant ground was gained or lost. The French declared victory once they regained the 10 km (6 mi) the Germans had taken, but bloody scrapping continued until the Armistice, leaving a total of more than 700,000 dead. To this day, the scenes of battle are scarred by bomb craters, stunted vegetation, and thousands of unexploded mines and shells, rendering the area permanently uninhabitable.

The most shocking memorial of the carnage is the **Ossuaire de Douaumont**, 10 km (6 mi) north of the city. The bizarre, evocative structure—a little like a cross, a lot like a bomb—rears up over an endless sea of graves, its ground-level windows revealing undignified heaps of human bones harvested from the killing fields. Climb to the top of the tower (€1) for a view of the cemetery. In the basement a film is shown that dwells on the agony of the senseless butchery. ☎ *03–29–84–54–81* ⊕ *www.verdun-douaumont.com* ▦ *Slide show €3* ☉ *Mar. and Oct., daily 9–noon and 2–5:30; Apr., daily 9–6; May–Aug., daily 9–6:30; Sept., daily 9–noon and 2–6; Nov., daily 9–noon and 2–5.*

The square, modern **Mémorial de Verdun** (Verdun Memorial), in the town of Fleury-devant-Douaumont, is a World War I museum with emotionally charged texts and video commentary, as well as uniforms, weapons, and the artwork of soldiers (Art Nouveau vases hammered from artillery shells). ☎ *03–29–84–35–34* ▦ *€4.60* ☉ *Mid-Apr.–Dec., daily 9–6; Feb. and Mar., daily 9–noon and 2–6.*

Where to Stay & Eat

$$–$$$ ✕▦ **Le Coq Hardi.** This large, steep-roof, half-timber hotel, built in 1827 on the bank of the Meuse, is a Lorraine landmark, with comfy, unpretentious rooms and a familial welcome. Young chef Frédèric Engel has brought a breath of fresh air to the place. His training at Buerehiesel and Crocodile in Strasbourg shows, blending fashionable Mediterranean touches with Lorraine tradition: frothy pea-soup "cappuccino" with Spanish ham, pig's foot stuffed with foie gras, and raspberry-lemon gratin. The restaurant is closed Friday and Sunday dinner. ⊠ *8 av. de la Victoire, 55100* ☎ *03–29–86–36–36* 🖷 *03–29–86–09–21* ⊕ *www.coq-hardi.com* ➽ *35 rooms* ⚐ *Restaurant, minibars, cable TV, bar, some pets allowed (fee); no a/c* ⊟ *AE, DC, MC, V* �ŧOŧ *BP.*

Metz

★ ⑳ *64 km (40 mi) east of Verdun via D3, 56 km (35 mi) north of Nancy, 160 km (100 mi) northwest of Strasbourg.*

Despite its industrial background, Metz, the capital of the Moselle region, is one of France's greenest cities: parks, gardens, and leafy squares frame an imposing mix of military and classical architecture, all carved out of the region's yellow sandstone. At the Vieille Ville's heart is one of the finest Gothic cathedrals in France.

The **Musée de la Cour d'Or** (Museum of the Golden Courtyard), two blocks up from the cathedral in a 17th-century former convent, has a wide-ranging collection of French and German paintings from the 18th century on; military arms and uniforms; and religious works of art stored in the **Grenier de Chèvremont**, a granary built in 1457. Best by far are the stelae, statuary, jewelry, and arms evoking the city's Gallo-Roman and Merovingian past. Not to be missed: the ethereal reconstruction of the ancient chapel of St-Pierre-aux-Nonnains. Unfortunately, the museum's labyrinth of stairways excludes wheelchairs, strollers, and poor navigators. ⊠ *2 rue du Haut-Poirier* ☎ *03–87–68–25–00* ☑ *€4.60* ⊘ *Wed.–Mon. 10–5.*

★ At 137 feet from floor to roof, the **Cathédrale St-Étienne** is one of France's tallest; and thanks to nearly 1½ acres of window space, one of the most luminous. The narrow, sloping 13th- to 14th-century nave channels the eye toward the dramatically raised 16th-century choir, whose walls have given way to richly colored, gemlike glass created by masters old and modern, including artist Marc Chagall. The oldest windows—on the right rear wall of the transept above the modern organ—date from the 12th century, their dark, mosaiclike simplicity a stark contrast to the ethereal stained glass of modern times. A pair of symmetrical 290-foot towers flank the nave, marking the division between the two churches that were merged to form the cathedral. The **Grand Portal**, beneath the large rose window, was reconstructed by the Germans at the turn of the 20th century; the statues of the prophets include, on the right, *Daniel,* sculpted to resemble Kaiser Wilhelm II (his unmistakable upturned mustache was snapped off in 1940). ⊠ *Pl. des Armes.*

The lively **Marché Couvert** (Market Hall) was built as a bishop's palace at the end of the 18th century, but the Revolution saw it converted to its current, more practical use as a home to smelly, farm-cured cheeses and still-flopping seafood. At the bottom of the slope down rue d'Estrées from the market, veer left and cut right over the rushing river for picturesque views of bridges and flower-laden balconies. ⊠ *Pl. de la Cathédrale* ⊘ *Closed Sun. and Mon.*

Take in the broad perspective of grand Classical symmetry on the **place de la Comédie,** with its turn-of-the-last-century Protestant temple. The curving sandstone buildings date from the 18th century and include the opera and theater.

The small, heavily restored church of **St-Pierre-aux-Nonnains** has round stones and rows of red bricks thought to date from the 4th century, predating Attila the Hun's sacking of Metz and helping the city lay claim to the oldest church in France. But you may want to skip the church itself: the best of the rare Merovingian ornaments salvaged from the 6th-century version of the chapel are displayed in a full reproduction in the Musée de la Cour d'Or, demonstrating as chronologies never can how early Christian times mixed the cultures and tastes of Celts, Romans, and Gauls. ⊠ *Rue Poncelet* ⊘ *Weekends.*

Where to Stay & Eat

$$–$$$ ✕ **La Dinanderie.** Chef Claude Piergiorgi serves inventive cuisine—scallops with delicate bacon threads, farm pigeon in salt crust, and pear gratin with gingerbread ice cream—with dependable flair. The intimate restaurant is across the Moselle, a 10-minute hike from the cathedral. ⊠ *2 rue de Paris* ☎ *03–87–30–14–40* ⊟ *AE, MC, V* ⊙ *Closed Sun. and Mon. and 3 wks Aug.*

$ ✕ **Le Pont St-Marcel.** Murals, dirndl skirts, and rib-sticking old-style cuisine make this a culinary plunge into Lorraine culture. There's quiche, of course, but also stewed rabbit, *potée* (boiled pork and cabbage), and carp. The list of Lorraine wines (from Toul) is encyclopedic, with the oak-cured red from Laroppe worth the splurge. In summer reserve a spot on the tiny terrace on the river. ⊠ *1 rue du Pont St-Marcel* ☎ *03–87–30–12–29* ⊟ *AE, DC, MC, V.*

¢ ✕ **La Dauphiné.** Come to this unpretentious barrel-vaulted lunch spot for *tourte Lorraine* (meat pie), a plat du jour with delicious gratin potatoes, and a generous slice of fruit tart. Locals claim permanent lunch stations, but there's room upstairs, too. It's between the cathedral and the museum. ⊠ *8 rue du Chanoine-Collin* ☎ *03–87–36–03–04* ⊟ *MC, V* ⊙ *Closed Sun. No dinner Mon.–Thurs.*

★ $ ▦ **Cathédrale.** From its waxed plank floors, ironwork banister, beamed ceilings, and French windows to its views of the cathedral, this gem of a hotel is reason enough to spend the night in Metz. The country-chic bedspreads, linen drapes, and hand-painted furniture are the work of the friendly owner; she collected all the antiques, too. Breakfast is served in the Baraka, downstairs. ⊠ *25 pl. de Chambre, 57000* ☎ *03–87–75–00–02* ⊟ *03–87–75–40–75* ⊕ *www.hotelcathedrale-metz.fr* ⊅ *20 rooms* ♢ *Restaurant, cable TV, bar, Internet, some pets allowed (fee); no a/c* ⊟ *AE, DC, MC, V* ⊙ *Closed 2 wks Aug.* ⦿ *BP.*

Lunéville

㉑ *30 km (19 mi) southeast of Nancy via N4.*

Lunéville rose to prominence at the start of the 18th century when Duke Léopold of Lorraine had the château built by Mansart's pupil Germain Boffrand, who also designed the Baroque town church of St-Jacques (of note for its carved pulpit and choir stalls). The château's glory days, however, came under King Stanislas, who held court here from 1735 to 1760, treating Lunéville as his own (scaled-down) version of Versailles. After Stanislas died, Lorraine reverted to the French crown, and Lunéville lost its luster. The château gardens have been painstakingly restored but, tragically, the château itself was devastated by fire at the start of 2003 and is likely to be closed to the public for several years.

The small industrial town of St-Nicolas-de-Port, 18 km (11 mi) northwest of Lunéville, is saved from mediocrity by its colossal basilica. Legend has it that a finger of St. Nicholas was brought to the town during the 11th-century Crusades. Sheltering such a priceless relic, the **Basilique de St-Nicolas-de-Port** (1495–1555) was rapidly besieged by pilgrims (including Joan of Arc, who came to ask St. Nicholas's blessing on her famous journey to Orléans). The simplified column capitals and elaborate rib vaulting are shining examples of Flamboyant Gothic enjoying a final fling before the gathering impetus of the Renaissance, as are the 280-foot onion-dome towers, almost symmetrical but, as was the Gothic wont, not quite. Inside, the slender, freestanding 90-foot pillars in the transept are the highest in France.

Where to Stay & Eat

★ $$$ ╳▦ **Château d'Adoménil.** Quite a magnificent sight, this steep-roofed, pink-walled, ivy-covered 18th-century château makes a super-stylish base for visiting Nancy, Baccarat, and St-Nicolas-de-Port. Flamboyant owner Michel Million is a skilled chef and his elegant dining room showcases his specialties, which range from roast pike-perch with wild mushrooms to grilled foie gras and frogs'-leg omelet, perfect with a bottle of Côtes de Toul, the tangy local wine. Rooms in the château have weighty regional furniture; those in the annex—the converted stable—offer a mix of modern and Neoclassical designs. Outside, a gentle parkland and lake await your contemplative strolls. ✉ *54300 Rehainviller, 5 km (3 mi) southwest of Lunéville* ☎ *03–83–74–04–81* 🖷 *03–83–74–21–78* ⊕ *www. relaischateaux.com/adomenil* ⇨ *14 rooms* ♨ *Restaurant, pool, Internet* ▤ *AE, DC, MC, V* ⊘ *Closed Jan.–mid-Feb., Sun. and Mon. in Nov.–Apr. No dinner Sun., no lunch Tues.* ⧖| *MAP.*

Toul

㉒ *21 km (13 mi) west of Nancy via A31.*

The Vieille Ville of Toul, behind mossy, star-shape ramparts, has been a bishopric since AD 365 and merited visits from the Frankish king Clovis to study the Christian faith; from Charlemagne in passing; and from a young, premilitary Joan of Arc, who was sued in the Toul court for breach of promise when she tossed aside a beau for the voice of God. In 1700, under Louis XIV, the military engineer Vauban built the thrusting ramparts around the town.

The ramshackle streets of central Toul haven't changed much for centuries—not since the embroidered twin-tower facade, a Flamboyant Gothic masterpiece, was woven onto the **Cathédrale St-Étienne** in the second half of the 15th century. The cathedral's interior, begun in 1204, is long (321 feet), airy (105 feet high), and more restrained than its exuberant facade. On one side of the cathedral are the 14th-century **cloisters,** and on the other is a pleasant **garden** behind the **Hôtel de Ville** (Town Hall), built in 1740 as the Bishop's Palace. ✉ *Pl. d'Armes* ⊘ *Mon.–Fri. 9:30–noon, 2:30–6; weekends 10–noon, 2–4.*

The **Musée Municipal** (Town Museum), in a former medieval hospital, has a well-preserved Salle des Malades (Patients' Ward) dating from the 13th century. Archaeological finds, ceramics, tapestries, and medieval sculpture are on display. ✉ *25 rue Gouvion-St-Cyr* ☎ *03–83–64–13–38* 🖾 *€2.60* ⊘ *Mar.–Oct., Wed.–Mon. 10–noon and 2–6; Nov.–Feb., Wed.–Mon. 2–6.*

Where to Eat

$$$ ╳ **Le Dauphin.** In a bleak industrial neighborhood and with a dated decor, this grand restaurant seems out of place in humble Toul. But the

modern and imaginative cooking of Christophe Vohmann draws kudos for its exotic touches and balance of flavor—opt for the langoustines with ginger and radishes or the local foie gras with artichokes. ✉ *65 allée Gaumiron* ☎ *03–83–43–13–46* ▤ *AE, DC, MC, V* ✹ *Closed Mon. and mid-July–mid-Aug. No dinner Sun. and Wed.*

Vaucouleurs

❷❸ *24 km (15 mi) southwest of Toul on D960.*

Above the modest main street in the market town of Vaucouleurs, you can see ruins of Robert de Baudricourt's ancient medieval castle and the Porte de France, through which Joan of Arc led her armed soldiers to Orléans. The barefoot Maid of Orléans spent a year within these walls, first wheedling an audience with Baudricourt and then, having convinced him of the necessity of her mission, learning to ride and to sword-fight.

Where to Stay & Eat

¢ ✕▦ **Relais de la Poste.** On the main street, this simple hotel has quiet rooms and a pleasant, intimate restaurant (closed Friday–Sunday in November–May). The good regional menu is served noon and night. A friendly family cooks, serves the meals, and checks you in. ✉ *12 av. André-Maginot, 55140* ☎ *03–29–89–40–01* 🖷 *03–29–89–40–93* ➮ *9 rooms* ⚭ *Restaurant, bar, Internet; no a/c* ▤ *AE, MC, V* ✹ *Closed last 2 wks Dec.* ❑ *EP.*

Domrémy-la-Pucelle

❷❹ *19 km (12 mi) south of Vaucouleurs on D964.*

Joan of Arc was born in Domrémy-la-Pucelle in a stone hut in either 1411 or 1412. You can see it as well as the church where she was baptized, the actual statue of St. Marguerite before which she prayed, and the hillside where she tended sheep and first heard voices telling her to take up arms and save France from the English. The humble stone-and-stucco **Maison Natale Jeanne d'Arc** (Joan of Arc's Birthplace)—an irregular, slope-roof, two-story cottage—has been preserved with style and reverence. The modern museum alongside, the **Centre Johannique**, shows a film (French only) while mannequins in period costume present Joan of Arc's amazing story. After she heard mystical voices, Joan walked 19 km (12 mi) to Vaucouleurs. Dressed and mounted like a man, she led her forces to lift the siege of Orléans, defeated the English, and escorted the unseated Charles VII to Reims, to be crowned king of France. Military missions after Orléans failed—including an attempt to retake Paris—and she was captured at Compiègne. The English turned her over to the Church, which sent her to be tried by the Inquisition for witchcraft and heresy. She was convicted and burned at the stake in Rouen. No matter: as a figure she remains pivotal to her "époque de transformation." Thanks to her and other leaders, civilization began to evolve from the medieval to the modern. ✉ *2 rue de la Basilique* ☎ *03–29–06–95–86* ▦ *€3* ✹ *Apr.–Sept., daily 9–noon and 1:30–6:30; Oct.–Mar., Wed.–Mon. 9:30–noon and 2–5.*

FodorsChoice
★

The ornate late-19th-century **Basilique du Bois-Chenu** (Bois Chenu Basilica), high up the hillside above Domrémy, boasts enormous painted and mosaic panels expounding on her legend in glowing Pre-Raphaelite tones. Outside lurk serene panoramic views over the emerald, gently rolling Meuse Valley. If you are traveling to Domrémy without a car, you need to train it to either Nancy or Toul, then bus it to Neufchâteau to catch one of the two daily buses to Domrémy.

Where to Stay

¢ ⊡ **Jeanne d'Arc.** Stay next door to Joan of Arc's childhood church and wake to the bells that accompanied her voices. Accommodations are considerably less evocative, in jazzy '60s tile and paneling, but bathrooms are spotless and breakfasts (in-room only) generous. ⊠ *1 rue Principale, 88630* ☎ *03–29–06–96–06* ⇝ *12 rooms* ⚬ *No a/c, no room TVs* ⊟ *MC, V* ☉ *Closed mid-Nov.–Mar.* ⦿ *EP.*

Grand

㉕ *20 km (12 mi) southwest of Domrémy; from Bois-Chenu follow signs down country roads.*

In the tiny, enigmatic hamlet of Grand, a natural spring developed into a center for the worship of the Gallo-Roman sun god Apollo-Grannus. It was important enough to draw the Roman emperors Caracalla and Constantine. Thus Grand today is a treasure trove of classical ruins. At the edge of the village the remains of a giant **amphitheater** that once seated 20,000 have been reconstructed as an imposing outdoor theater; displays illustrate its history. In a tiny museum in the centre of the village there is an expressive floor **mosaïque** with marvelously realistic animal details. Surrounding this mosaic are scraps of exotic stone and relics transported from across two continents, bearing witness to this isolated village's opulent past. ☎ *03–29–06–63–43* ⊡ *Amphitheater and mosaic* €3 ☉ *Apr.–Sept., daily 9–noon and 2–7; Oct.–mid-Dec. and mid-Jan.–Mar., daily 10–noon and 2–5.*

Épinal

㉖ *96 km (60 mi) southeast of Grand via Neufchâteau and Mirecourt, 72 km (45 mi) south of Nancy.*

On the Moselle River at the feet of the Vosges, Épinal, a printing center since 1735, is famous throughout France for boldly colored prints, popular illustrations, and hand-colored stencils. **Cité de l'image,** opened in 2003, combines a new public exhibition space with the private museum of the town's most famous printing workshop, l'Imagerie d'Epinal. ⊠ *42 quai de Dogneville* ☎ *03–29–81–48–30* ⊡ €7 ☉ *Sept.–June, Mon.–Sat. 9:30–noon and 2–6, Sun. 10–noon and 2–6; July–Sept., Mon.–Sat. 9:30–12:30 and 1:30–6:30, Sun. 10–12:30 and 1:30–6.*

★ On an island in the Moselle in the center of Épinal, the spectacular **Musée Départemental d'Art Ancien et Contemporain** (Museum of Antiquities and Contemporary Art) is in a renovated 17th-century hospital, whose ancient classical traces are still visible under a dramatic barrel-vaulted skylight. The crowning jewel here is *Job Lectured by His Wife,* one of the greatest works of Georges de la Tour, the painter whose candelit scenes constitute Lorraine's most memorable artistic legacy. Other Old Masters, including works by Fragonard and Boucher, are on view, once part of the famous collection of the Princes of Salm. The museum also contains one of France's largest collections of contemporary art, as well as Gallo-Roman artifacts, rural tools, and local faïence. ⊠ *1 pl. Lagarde* ☎ *03–29–82–20–33* ✇ *€4.60* ✆ *Wed.–Mon. 10–6.*

The small but bustling Vieille Ville is anchored by the lovely old **Basilique St-Maurice,** a low gray-stone basilica blending Romanesque and Gothic styles. Its deep 15th-century entry porch prepares you for passing into dark, sacred space. ⊠ *Pl. St-Goëry* ☎ *03–29–82–58–36.*

STRASBOURG

Though centered in the heart of Alsace 490 km (304 mi) east of Paris, and drawing appealingly on Alsatian Gemütlichkeit (coziness), the city of Strasbourg is a cosmopolitan French cultural center and, in many ways, the unofficial capital of Europe. Against an irresistible backdrop of old half-timber houses, waterways, and the colossal single spire of its red-sandstone cathedral, which seems to insist imperiously that you pay homage to its majestic beauty, Strasbourg is an incongruously sophisticated mix of museums, charming neighborhoods like La Petite France, elite schools (including that notorious hothouse for blooming politicos, the École Nationale d'Administration, or National Administration School), international think tanks, and the European Parliament. The *strasbourgeoisie* have a lot to be proud of.

The Romans knew Strasbourg as Argentoratum before it came to be known as Strateburgum, or City of (Cross) Roads. After centuries as part of the Germanic Holy Roman Empire, the city was united with France in 1681, but retained independence regarding legislation, education, and religion under the honorific title Free Royal City. Since World War II Strasbourg has become a symbolic city, embodying Franco-German reconciliation and the wider idea of a united Europe. The city center is effectively an island within two arms of the River Ill; most major sites are found here, but the northern districts also contain some fine buildings erected over the last 100 years, culminating in the Palais de l'Europe.

Note to drivers: the configuration of downtown streets makes it difficult to approach the center via the autoroute exit marked STRASBOURG CENTRE. Instead, hold out for the exit marked PLACE DE L'ÉTOILE and follow signs to CATHÉDRALE/CENTRE VILLE. At place du Corbeau, veer left across the Ill, and go straight to the place Gutenberg parking garage, a block from the cathedral.

The Historic Heart

This central area, from the cathedral to picturesque Petite France, concentrates the best of Old Strasbourg, with its twisting backstreets, flower-lined courts, tempting shops, and inviting winstubs (wine taverns).

a good
walk

Begin at place Gutenberg and head up rue des Hallebardes. To see a bit of Strasbourg's appealing combination of cozy winstubs, medieval alleys, and chic shops, turn left up rue des Orfevres (marked RUE PITTORESQUE); then circle right down rue Chaudron and again down rue du Sanglier. Head back right down rue des Hallebardes and onto place de la Cathédrale, passing the landmark Maison Kammerzell. Emerging from this close-packed warren of dark-timber buildings and narrow streets, you'll confront the magnificent **Cathédrale Notre-Dame** ㉗ ☞. Continue across the square to the **Musée de l'Oeuvre Notre-Dame** ㉘, with its collection of statuary. Leaving the museum, turn right and approach the vast neighboring palace, the **Palais Rohan** ㉙. Once the headquarters of the powerful prince-bishops, the Rohans, it now houses the art and archaeology museums.

Once out of the château's entry court, double back left and turn left again, following rue des Rohan to the river. From here you can take a boat tour of the Vieille Ville. Veer right away from the water and cross place du Marché aux Cochons-de-Lait (Suckling Pig Market Square) and place de la Grande Boucherie (Grand Slaughterhouse Square) to reach the **Musée Historique** ㉚, with its collection of paintings, weapons, and furniture from Strasbourg (reopening 2006 after renovations). Across the street is the modern glass entrance to the **Ancienne Douane** ㉛, the former customs house, now a vast venue for temporary exhibitions. Over the Ill, cross Pont du Corbeau and veer right to the **Musée Alsacien** ㉜, where you can get a glimpse of how Alsatian families used to live.

Now cross back over the river on the Pont St-Nicolas and follow the riverside promenade west to the picturesque quarter of **Petite France** ㉝. At Pont St-Martin, take rue des Dentelles to rue du Bain aux Plantes. Explore the alleys, courtyards, cafés, and shop windows as you work your way west. Eventually you'll reach the four monumental **Ponts Couverts** ㉞. Just beyond the bridges lies the grass-roof dam, the **Barrage Vauban** ㉟. Climb to the top; from here you'll see a gleaming glass-frame building, the **Musée d'Art Moderne et Contemporain** ㊱.

TIMING Allow at least a full day to see Strasbourg—perhaps visiting the Vieille Ville and cathedral in the morning, ending at 12:30 with the astronomical clock, and then lunch on a nearby backstreet. The afternoon might allow a museum stop and time to wander through Petite France. Two days would allow more museum time; a third day would allow you to take in the monumental sights on place de la République and the Palais de l'Europe.

Sights to See

㉛ **Ancienne Douane** (Old Customs House). In 2000, a terrible fire ravaged this old customs house set on the Ill River; extensive repairs are expected to continue until 2004. When operational, the airport-hangar scale and flexible walls here lend themselves to enormous expositions of Old Master paintings as well as archaeology and history. ⊠ *1 rue de Vieux-Marché-aux-Poissons* ☎ *03–88–52–50–00* 🖼 *Call ahead.*

㉟ **Barrage Vauban** (Vauban Dam). Just beyond the Ponts Couverts is the grass-roof Vauban Dam, built by its namesake in 1682. Climb to the top for wide-angle views of the Ponts Couverts and, on the other side,

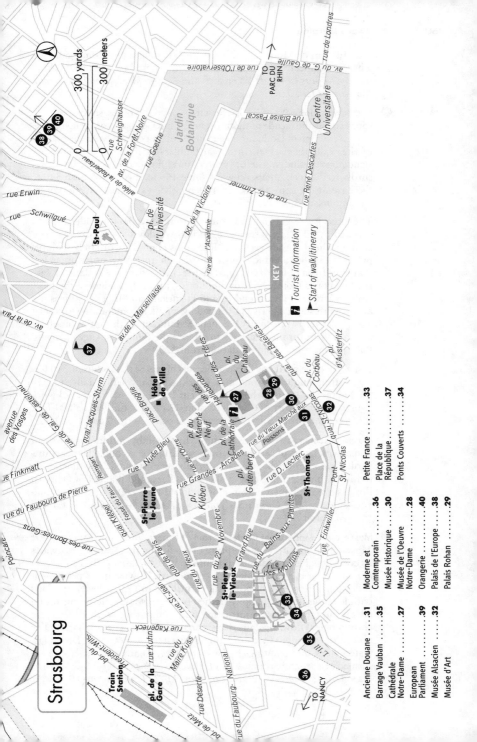

Strasbourg

KEY

🛈 Tourist information

▲ Start of walk/itinerary

300 yards
300 meters

Train Station

Jardin Botanique

Centre Universitaire

Hôtel de Ville

St-Paul

St-Pierre-le-Jeune

St-Pierre-le-Vieux

St-Thomas

PETITE FRANCE

TO PARC DU RHIN

TO NANCY

the Museum of Modern Art. Then stroll through its echoing galleries, where magnificent cathedral statuary lies scattered among pigeon droppings. ⊠ *Ponts Couverts* ▨ *Free* ☯ *Mid-Oct.–mid-Mar., daily 9–7; mid-Mar.–mid-Oct., daily 9–8.*

★ ☾ ⌐ ❷ **Cathédrale Notre-Dame.** Rosy, ornately carved Vosges sandstone masonry covers the facade of this most novel and Germanic of French cathedrals, a triumph of Gothic art begun in 1176. Not content with the outlines of the walls themselves, medieval builders lacily encased them with slender stone shafts. The off-center **spire,** finished in 1439, looks absurdly fragile as it tapers skyward some 466 feet; you can climb 330 to the base of the spire to take in sweeping views of the city, the Vosges Mountains, and the Black Forest.

The interior presents a stark contrast to the facade: it is older (mostly finished by 1275), and the nave's broad windows emphasize the horizontal rather than the vertical. Note Hans Hammer's ornately sculpted pulpit (1484–86) and the richly painted 14th- to 15th-century organ loft that rises from pillar to ceiling. The left side of the nave is flanked with richly colored Gothic windows honoring the early leaders of the Holy Roman Empire—Otto I and II, and Heinrich I and II. The **choir** is not ablaze with stained glass but framed by chunky Romanesque masonry. The elaborate 16th-century **Chapelle St-Laurent,** to the left of the choir, merits a visit; turn to the right to admire the **Pilier des Anges** (Angels' Pillar), an intricate column dating from 1230.

Just beyond the pillar, the Renaissance machinery of the 16th-century **Horloge Astronomique** (Astronomical Clock) whirs into action daily at 12:30 PM (but the line starts at the south door at 11:45 AM): macabre clockwork figures enact the story of Christ's Passion. ⊠ *Pl. de la Cathédrale* ▨ *Clock €1, spire platform €3* ☯ *Cathedral open daily 7–11:30 and 12:40–7.*

❸❷ **Musée Alsacien** (Alsatian Museum). In this labyrinthine half-timber home, with layers of carved balconies sagging over a cobbled inner courtyard, local interiors have been faithfully reconstituted. The diverse activities of blacksmiths, clog makers, saddlers, and makers of artificial flowers are explained with the help of old-time craftsmen's tools and equipment. ⊠ *23 quai St-Nicolas* ☏ *03–88–52–50–00* ▨ *€3* ☯ *Wed.–Mon. 10–6.*

❸❻ **Musée d'Art Moderne et Contemporain** (Modern and Contemporary Art Museum). A magnificent sculpture of a building that sometimes dwarfs its contents, this spectacular museum frames a relatively thin collection of new, esoteric, and unsung 20th-century art. Downstairs, a permanent collection of Impressionists and modernists up to 1950 is heavily padded with local heroes but happily fleshed out with some striking furniture; all are juxtaposed for contrasting and comparing, with little to no chronological flow. Upstairs, harsh, spare works must work hard to live up to their setting; few contemporary masters are featured. Drawings, watercolors, and paintings by Gustave Doré, a native of Alsace, are enshrined in a separate room. ⊠ *1 pl. Hans-Jean Arp* ☏ *03–88–23–31–31* ▨ *€4.50* ☯ *Tues.–Wed. and Fri.–Sun. 11–7, Thurs. noon–10.*

③⓪ Musée Historique (Local History Museum). This museum, in a step-gabled slaughterhouse dating from 1588, is closed for extensive renovation and not expected to reopen before 2006. It contains a collection of maps, armor, arms, bells, uniforms, traditional dress, printing paraphernalia, and two huge relief models of Strasbourg. ⊠ *2 rue du Vieux-Marché-aux-Poissons.*

★ **㉘ Musée de l'Oeuvre Notre-Dame** (Cathedral Museum). There's more to this museum than the usual assembly of dilapidated statues rescued from the cathedral before they fell off (you'll find *those* rotting in the Barrage Vauban). Sacred sculptures stand in churchlike settings, and secular exhibits are enhanced by the building's fine old architecture. Subjects include a wealth of Flemish and Upper Rhine paintings, stained glass, gold objects, and massive, heavily carved furniture. ⊠ *3 pl. du Château* ☎ *03–88–32–88–17* ⌛ *€3* ⊙ *Tues.–Sun. 10–6.*

★ **㉙ Palais Rohan** (Rohan Palace). The exterior of Robert de Cotte's massive Neoclassical palace (1732–42) may be starkly austere, but there's plenty of glamour inside. Decorator Robert le Lorrain's magnificent ground-floor rooms are led by the great **Salon d'Assemblée** (Assembly Room) and the book- and tapestry-lined **Bibliothèque des Cardinaux** (Cardinals' Library). The library leads to a series of less august rooms that house the **Musée des Arts Décoratifs** (Decorative Arts Museum) and its elaborate display of ceramics. This is a comprehensive presentation of works by Hannong, a porcelain manufacturer active in Strasbourg from 1721 to 1782; dinner services by other local kilns reveal the influence of Chinese porcelain. The **Musée des Beaux-Arts** (Fine Arts Museum), also in the château, includes masterworks of European painting from Giotto and Memling to El Greco, Rubens, and Goya. Downstairs, the **Musée Archéologique** (Archaeology Museum) displays regional archaeological finds, including gorgeous Merovingian treasures. ⊠ *2 pl. du Château* ☎ *03–88–52–50–00* ⌛ *€3 each museum* ⊙ *Wed.–Mon. 10–6.*

㉝ Petite France. With its gingerbread half-timber houses that seem to lean precariously over the canals of the Ill, its shops, and inviting little restaurants, this is the most magical neighborhood in Strasbourg. Historically Alsatian in style, "Little France"—the district is just southwest of the center ville—is filled with Renaissance buildings that have survived plenty of wars. Wander up and down the tiny streets that connect rue du Bain-aux-Plantes and rue des Dentelles to Grand-Rue, and stroll the waterfront promenade.

Fodor'sChoice
★

㉞ Ponts Couverts (Covered Bridges). These three bridges, distinguished by their four stone towers, were once covered with wooden shelters. Part of the 14th-century ramparts that framed Old Strasbourg, they span the Ill as it branches into four fingerlike canals.

Beyond the Ill

If you've seen the center and have time to strike out in new directions, head across the Ill to view two architectural landmarks unrelated to Strasbourg's famous medieval past: place de la République and the Palais de l'Europe.

a good walk

North of the cathedral, walk up rue des Hallebardes and turn left on rue du Dôme. Take a right onto place Broglie (pronounced "broiye") and continue up this main thoroughfare across the river to the striking circle of red-sandstone buildings on **place de la République** ③ ➤. Back at the river, head for a bus stop on avenue de la Marseillaise and take Bus no. 23 to the **Palais de l'Europe** ③ for a guided tour (by appointment, arranged in advance). You may also want to visit the sleek **European Parliament** ③, just across the river. From here, plunge into the greenery of the **Orangerie** ④. Indulge in a three-hour lunch at the stellar Buerehiesel or have a picnic on a bench.

TIMING Basing your schedule on your tour appointment at the Palais de l'Europe, allow about a half day for this walk; if need be, you can while away the wait in the Orangerie.

Sights to See

③ **European Parliament.** This sleek building testifies to the growing importance of the governing body of the European Union, which used to make do with rental offices in the Palais de l'Europe. Eurocrats continue to commute between Brussels, Luxembourg, and Strasbourg, hauling their staff and files with them. One week per month, visitors can slip into the hemicycle and witness the tribune in debate, complete with simultaneous translation. ⊠ *Behind the Palais de l'Europe* 🕾 *03–88–17–52–85* ☜ *Free* ☉ *Call ahead to verify Parliament in session.*

④ **Orangerie.** Like a private backyard for the Eurocrats in the Palais de l'Europe, this delightful park is laden with flowers and punctuated by noble copper beeches. It contains a lake and, close by, a small reserve of rare birds, including flamingos and noisy local storks. ⊠ *Av. de l'Europe.*

③ **Palais de l'Europe.** Designed by Paris architect Henri Bernard in 1977, this Continental landmark is headquarters to the Council of Europe, founded in 1949 and independent of the European Union. A guided tour introduces you to the intricacies of its workings and may allow you to eavesdrop on a session. Arrange your tour by telephone in advance; appointments are fixed according to language demands and usually take place in the afternoon. Note: You must provide a *pièce d'identité* (I.D.) before entering. ⊠ *Av. de l'Europe* 🕾 *03–90–21–49–40 for appointments* ☜ *Free* ☉ *Guided tours by appointment weekdays.*

➤ ③ **Place de la République.** The spacious layout and ponderous architecture of this monumental *cirque* (circle) have nothing in common with the Vieille Ville except for the local red sandstone. A different hand was at work here—that of occupying Germans, who erected the former Ministry (1902); the Academy of Music (1882–92); and the Palais du Rhin (1883–88). The handsome neo-Gothic church of **St-Paul** and the pseudo-Renaissance **Palais de l'Université** (University Palace), constructed between 1875 and 1885, also bear the German stamp. Heavy turn-of-the-20th-century houses, some reflecting the whimsical curves of the Art Nouveau style, frame **allée de la Robertsau**, a tree-lined boulevard that would not look out of place in Berlin.

Where to Stay & Eat

★ **$$$$** ✕ **Le Buerehiesel.** This lovely Alsatian farmhouse, reconstructed in the lovely Orangerie park, warrants a pilgrimage if you are willing to pay for the finest cooking in Alsace. Antoine Westermann stands in the upper echelon of chefs while remaining true to the ingredients and specialties of his native Alsace: *schniederspaetzle* (onion-perfumed ravioli) with frogs' legs, duck braised and caramelized in Asian spices, and plum tart Tatin with vanilla ice cream. Two smaller salons are cozy, but most tables are set in a modern annex that is mostly glass and steel. In any event, plump European *parlementaires* come on foot; others might come on their knees. ⊠ *4 parc de l'Orangerie* ☎ *03–88–45–56–65* ⌁ *Reservations essential* ☰ *AE, DC, MC, V* ⊘ *Closed Tues. and Wed., 3 wks Jan., and 1st half Aug.*

★ **$$$$** ✕ **Au Crocodile.** As one of the temples of Alsatian-French haute cuisine, this has the expected grand salon—asparkle with skylights and a spectacular 19th-century mural showing the *strasbourgeoisie* at a country fair—an exhaustive wine list, and some of the most dazzling dishes around, courtesy of master chef Émile Jung. Fittingly for a restaurant founded in the early 1800s, you'll get a real taste of the-way-Alsace-was here but given a nouvelle spin. Delights include truffle turnover, warmed goose liver with rhubarb, lobster with vermicelli and pink pepper, bitter-chocolate cherry cake, and grapefruit sorbet with a green tea "cigarette." Even more urban finesse is given to the theme menus that are occasionally offered (recent homages include those to the Brothers Goncourt, Goethe, and Gutenberg). As for the crocodile, it refers to a stuffed specimen brought back by a Strasbourg general from Napoléon's Egyptian campaign which took pride of place in a tavern that centuries later became this luxe outpost, today more central than the Buerehiesel and nearly as revered. The wine cellar is vast and has plenty Tokay Pinot Gris, Riesling, and other luscious Alsatian vintages to choose from. ⊠ *10 rue de l'Outre* ☎ *03–88–32–13–02* ⊕ *www.au-crocodile.com* ⌁ *Reservations essential* ⛉ *Jacket and tie* ☰ *AE, DC, MC, V* ⊘ *Closed Sun. and Mon., late Dec.–early Jan., and 3 wks in July.*

$$ ✕ **Maison Kammerzell.** This restaurant glories in its richly carved, half-timber 16th-century building—probably the most familiar house in Strasbourg. Fight your way through the tourist hordes on the terrace and ground floor to one of the atmospheric rooms above, with their gleaming wooden furniture and stained-glass windows. Foie gras and choucroute are best bets, though you may want to try the chef's pet discovery, choucroute with freshwater fish. ⊠ *16 pl. de la Cathédrale* ☎ *03–88–32–42–14* ☰ *AE, DC, MC, V* ⊘ *Closed Feb.*

★ **$** ✕ **Chez Yvonne.** Behind red-checked curtains you'll find artists, tourists, lovers, and heads of state sitting elbow-to-elbow in this classic winstub. All come to savor steaming platters of local specialties: watch for duck confit on choucroute, and *tête de veau* (calf's head) in white wine. Warm Alsatian fabrics dress tables and lamps, the china is regional, the photos historic, and the ambience chic—and no kitsch. ⊠ *10 rue du Sanglier* ☎ *03–88–32–84–15* ⌁ *Reservations essential* ☰ *AE, MC, V* ⊘ *Closed Sun. and 1st half Aug. No lunch Mon.*

$ ✕ **St-Sépulcre.** Shared plank tables, a jovial red-vested patron (with a nose to match), and a wisecracking waitstaff enhance the convivial welcome at this no-frills, down-home winstub. A massive ham sits casually on the counter, and slabs of it find their way onto every platter—even the salads. A crock of crunchy pickles, chewy bread, and a cereal bowl heaped with fresh horseradish accompany every order except dessert. ✉ *15 rue des Orfèvres* ☎ *03–88–32–39–97* ▤ *MC, V* ☉ *Closed Sun. and Mon., last wk Jan., 1st half Feb., 2nd half July.*

★ ¢ ✕ **Suzel.** This cozy little tearoom, just off rue Bain-aux-Plantes in Petite France, mixes rustic-chic blandishments (blue gingham, artfully arranged bric-a-brac, rows of potted boxwood) with excellent and unpretentious regional food. There's rabbit stew with dumplings, fresh trout, baeckoffe, fruit tarts, and good wines. It's also marvelous for an atmospheric afternoon tea break. Too bad it's closed nights. ✉ *2 rue des Moulins* ☎ *03–88–23–10–46* ▤ *MC, V* ☉ *Closed Mon. No dinner.*

★ **$$$$** ▥ **Régent-Petite France.** Opposite the Ponts Couverts and surrounded by rushing canals, this centuries-old former ice factory—replete with noble pediment and mansard roofs—has been transformed into a boldly modern luxury hotel. Delightfully set in the heart of Strasbourg's quaintest quarter, La Petite France, the hotel welcomes you with a spacious marble vestibule, vivid graffiti art, and Le Pont Tournant, a eye-popping modernistic restaurant done up in white, pinks, and reds (enjoy its summer tables over the torrent). Upstairs, sculptural room furnishings by Philippe Starck contrast sharply with the half-timber houses and roaring river viewed from nearly every room. There's no skimping on the amenities— both the beds and the bathrooms are divine. ✉ *5 rue des Moulins, 67000* ☎ *03–88–76–43–43* ☒ *03–88–76–43–76* ⊕ *www.regent-hotels.com* ⤳ *72 rooms* ఉ *Restaurant, minibars, cable TV, bar, Internet, some pets allowed (fee)* ▤ *AE, DC, MC, V* ▯◎▮ *MAP.*

$–$$$ ▥ **Cathédrale.** Expansion and renovation have brought this superbly positioned hotel more than up to par. A sleek marble lobby abuts lounges, a bar, and breakfast room that are rich with ancient beams and sandstone. Rooms feature dark timbers, and most have windows framing a view of the 16th-century half-timbered Maison Kammerzell or the cathedral. For summer drinks and breakfast, there's a garden courtyard cloistered from the outside world. ✉ *12 pl. de la Cathédrale, 67000* ☎ *03–88–22–12–12* ☒ *03–88–23–28–00* ⊕ *www.hotel-cathedrale.fr* ⤳ *47 rooms* ఉ *Minibars, cable TV, bar, some Internet, some pets allowed (fee)* ▤ *AE, DC, MC, V* ▯◎▮ *BP.*

$$–$$$ ▥ **Rohan.** Across from the cathedral on a picturesque pedestrian street, this modest little hotel has a welcoming air and a marvelous sense of French style, from the Louis XV furniture to the gilt mirrors. Though swagged in rich fabrics, rooms are fully modern, with impeccable all-tile baths. ✉ *17 rue Maroquin, 67000* ☎ *03–88–32–85–11* ☒ *03–88–75–65–37* ⊕ *www.hotel-rohan.com* ⤳ *36 rooms* ఉ *Minibars, cable TV, Internet, parking (fee), some pets allowed (fee)* ▤ *AE, DC, MC, V* ▯◎▮ *EP.*

$–$$ ▥ **Gutenberg.** In a 200-year-old mansion just off place Gutenberg, this sturdy urban hotel has rooms with fresh, old-fashioned wallpaper and built-in wood cabinetry. Charming little fifth-floor lofts reveal roof timbers. The skylit breakfast room is a charmer. The location is sweet and just a few blocks from the cathedral. ⊠ *31 rue des Serruriers, 67000* ☎ *03–88–32–17–15* 🖷 *03–88–75–76–67* ⊕ *www.hotel-gutenberg.com* 🖙 *42 rooms* ⚒ *Internet; no a/c in some rooms* ⊟ *MC, V* ⊘ *Closed 1st 2 wks in Jan.* ⏇ *BP.*

Nightlife & the Arts

The annual **Festival de Musique** (Music Festival; ⊠ 1 av. de la Marseillaise ☎ 03–88–39–64–10) is held from June to early July at the Palais des Congrès and the cathedral; contact the Amis de la Musique for information (☎ 03–88–15–44–66). The **Opéra du Rhin** (⊠ 19 pl. Broglie ☎ 03–88–75–48–23) has a sizable repertoire. Classical concerts are staged by the **Orchestre Philharmonique** (⊠ Palais des Congrès ☎ 03–88–15–09–09).

The Vieille Ville neighborhood east of the cathedral, along rue des Frères, is the nightlife hangout for university students and twentysomethings; among its handful of heavily frequented bars is **Le Velvet** (⊠ 6 rue Tonnelet Rouge ☎ 03–88–37–95–84). **Le Chalet** (⊠ 376 rte. de la Wantzenau ☎ 03–88–31–18–31) is the biggest and most popular disco, but it's some 10 km (6 mi) northeast of the city center.

The Outdoors

The **Port Autonome de Strasbourg** (☎ 03–88–84–13–13) organizes 75-minute boat tours along the Ill four times a day in winter and up to every half hour from 9:30 to 9, April–October. Boats leave from behind the Palais Rohan; the cost is €6.30.

Shopping

The lively city center is full of boutiques, including chocolate shops and delicatessens selling locally made foie gras. Look for warm paisley linens and rustic homespun fabrics, Alsatian pottery, and local wines. Forming the city's commercial heart are **rue des Hallebardes,** next to the cathedral; **rue des Grandes Arcades,** with its shopping mall; and **place Kléber.** An **antiques market** takes place behind the cathedral on rue du Vieil-Hôpital, rue des Bouchers, and place de la Grande Boucherie every Wednesday and Saturday morning.

ALSACE

The Rhine River forms the eastern boundary of both Alsace and France. But the best of Alsace is not found along the Rhine's industrial waterfront. Instead it's in the Ill Valley at the base of the Vosges, southwest of cosmopolitan Strasbourg. Northwest is Saverne and the beginning of the **Route du Vin,** the great Alsace Wine Road, which winds its way south through the Vosges foothills, fruitful vineyards, and medieval villages that would serve well as stage-sets for Rossini's *William Tell.* Signs for the road help you keep your bearings on the twisting way south, and you'll find limitless opportunities to stop at wineries and sample the local wares. The Wine Road stretches 170 km (100 mi) between Thann and Marienheim and is easily accessible from Strasbourg or Colmar. Many of the towns and villages have designated "vineyard trails" winding between towns (a bicycle will help you cover a lot of territory). Riquewihr and Ribeauville—accessible by bus from Colmar—are connected by an especially picturesque route. Along the way, stop at any *"Dégustation"* sign for a free tasting and pick up brochures on the "Alsace Wine Route" at any tourist office.

Obernai

❹ *30 km (19 mi) southwest of Strasbourg via A35/ N422.*

Many visitors begin their saunter down the Route du Vin at Obernai, a thriving, colorful Renaissance market town named for the patron saint of Alsace. Head to the central town enclosed by the ramparts to find some particularly Nikon-friendly sites, including a medieval belfry, Renaissance well, and late-19th-century church. Place du Marché, in the heart of town, is dominated by the stout, square 13th-century **Kapelturm Beffroi** (Chapel Tower Belfry), topped by a pointed steeple flanked at each corner by frilly openwork turrets added in 1597. An elaborate Renaissance well near the belfry, the **Puits à Six-Seaux** (Well of Six Buckets), was constructed in 1579; its name recalls the six buckets suspended from its metal chains. The twin spires of the parish church of **St-Pierre–St-Paul** compete with the belfry for skyline preeminence. They date, like the rest of the church, from the 1860s, although the 1504 Holy Sepulchre altarpiece in the north transept is a survivor from the previous church. Other points of interest include the flower-bedecked **place de l'Etoile** and the **Hôtel de Ville**, whose council chamber and historic balcony can be viewed.

Where to Stay & Eat

★ $–$$ ✕▦ **L'Ami Fritz.** White-shuttered, flower-bedecked, with sunny yellow walls, this welcoming inn combines style, rustic warmth, and three generations of family tradition. Set several miles west of Obernai, this picture-perfect freestone residence of the 17th century continues its allurements inside, thanks to pretty, impeccable guest rooms decked in toile de Jouy and homespun checks (opt for rooms in the main hotel, not in the adjacent annex). Top attraction here is the fine restaurant, where you can feast on Patrick Fritz's sophisticated twists on regional specialties, including feather-light blood sausage in flaky pastry, a delicate choucroute of grated turnips, strudel of black pudding, fillet of zander with beer-flavored choucroute, or the gratinéd freshwater fish braised in Sylvaner. Don't miss the fruity red wine, an Ottrott exclusive, or taking a gander at the town's two medieval castles. The restaurant is closed Wednesday. ✉ *8 rue des Châteaux, 5 km (3 mi) west of Obernai, 67530 Ottrott* ☎ *03–88–95–80–81* ᗩ *03–88–95–84–85* ⊕ *www.amifritz. com* ⟳ *22 rooms* ♿ *Restaurant, minibars, pool, Internet, some pets allowed (fee); no a/c in some rooms* ▭ *AE, DC, MC, V* ⦿ *MAP.*

¢ ✕▦ **Cloche.** Leaded glass, dark oak, and Hansi-like murals set the tone in this sturdy half-timber 14th-century landmark on Obernai's market square. Standard local dishes and blackboard specials draw locals on market days. Rooms are well equipped and country-pretty; two double-decker duplex rooms accommodate four. ✉ *90 rue Général-Gouraud,*

67210 ☎ *03–88–95–52–89* 🖷 *03–88–95–07–63* ⊕ *www.la-cloche.
com* 🖘 *20 rooms* ⌂ *Restaurant, bar, Internet; no a/c* ⊟ *AE, DC, MC,
V* ⊘ *Closed 2 wks in Jan.* †◉| *MAP.*

Shopping

Dietrich (⊠ 58 and 74 rue du Général-Gouraud ☎ 03–88–95–57–58)
has a varied selection of Beauvillé linens, locally hand-blown Alsatian
wine glasses, and Obernai-patterned china.

Mont-Ste-Odile

★ ❷ *12 km (8 mi) southwest of Obernai via Ottrott.*

Mont-Ste-Odile, a 2,500-foot hill, has been an important religious and
military site for 3,000 years. The eerie 9½-km-long (6-mi-long) **Mur Païen,**
up to 12 feet high and, in parts, several feet thick, rings the summit; its
mysterious origins and purpose still baffle archaeologists. The Romans
established a settlement here and, at the start of the 8th century Odile,
daughter of Duke Etichon of Obernai, who had been born blind, founded
a convent on the same spot after receiving her sight while being baptized.
The relatively modern convent is now a workaday hostelry for modern
pilgrims on group retreats. Odile—the patron saint of Alsace—died here
in AD 720; her sarcophagus rests in the 12th-century **Chapelle Ste-Odile.**
The spare, Romanesque **Chapelle de la Croix** adjoins St-Odile.

Barr

❸ *11 km (7 mi) southeast of Mont-Ste-Odile, 8 km (5 mi) south of Obernai.*

Surrounded by vineyards that harvest some of the finest vintages of Sylvaner and Gewürztraminer wines, Barr is a thriving, semi-industrial town
surrounded by vines, with some charming narrow streets lined with half-
timbered houses (notably rue des Cigognes, rue Neuve, and the tiny rue
de l'Essieu), a cheerful 17th-century Hôtel de Ville, and a decorative arts
museum. Most buildings date from after a catastrophic fire in 1678; the
only medieval survivor is the Romanesque tower of St-Martin, the Protestant church. Admire original furniture, local porcelain, earthenware, and
pewter at the **Musée de la Folie Marco,** in a mansion built by local magis-
trate Félix Marco in 1763. One section of the museum explains the traditional process of *schlittage*: sleds, bearing bundles of freshly sawed tree
trunks, once slid down the forest slopes over a "corduroy road" made of
logs. ⊠ *30 rue du Dr-Sultzer* ☎ *03–88–08–94–72, 03–88–08–66–65
winter* 🎟 €*3.10* ⊘ *July–Sept., Wed.–Mon. 10–noon and 2–6; May–June,
Oct.–Jan., weekends 10–noon and 2–6; closed Feb.–Apr.*

Andlau

❹ *3 km (2 mi) southwest of Barr on the Route du Vin.*

Andlau has long been known for its magnificent abbey. Built in the 12th
century, the **Abbaye d'Andlau** has the richest ensemble of Romanesque sculpture in Alsace. Sculpted vines wind their way around the doorway as a
reminder of wine's time-honored importance to the local economy. A statue
of a female bear, the abbey mascot—bears used to roam local forests and

were bred at the abbey until the 16th century—can be seen in the north transept. Legend has it that Queen Richarde, spurned by her husband, Charles the Fat, founded the abbey in AD 887 when an angel enjoined her to construct a church on a site to be shown to her by a female bear.

Where to Stay & Eat

$$ ✕▣ **Arnold.** This yellow-wall, half-timber hillside hotel overlooks the cute wine village of Itterswiller; most rooms have views across the vines. The cheapest rooms, on the top floor, have a shower and no balcony; the priciest have a bath and a balcony facing south. The wood-beam lobby with its wrought-iron staircase has the same quaint charm as the hotel restaurant across the street, with its old winepress and local Alsace wines served by the jug; homemade foie gras and venison in cranberry sauce top the menu, along with sauerkraut and baeckoffe. ✉ *98 rte. des Vins, 3 km (2 mi) south of Andlau on D253, 67140 Itterswiller* ☎ *03–88–85–50–58* 🖷 *03–88–85–55–54* ⊕ *www.hotel-arnold.com* ➴ *30 rooms* ♿ *Restaurant, minibars, cable TV, Internet, some pets allowed (fee); no a/c* ▤ *AE, MC, V* ☺ *Closed 2 wks Feb. No dinner Sun., during May–Nov.* ❖◎ *MAP.*

Dambach-la-Ville

㊺ *8 km (5 mi) southeast of Andlau via Itterswiller.*

One of the prettiest villages along the Alsace Wine Road, Dambach-la-Ville is a fortified medieval town protected by ramparts and three powerful 13th-century gateways. It is particularly rich in half-timber, high-roof houses from the 17th and 18th centuries, clustered mainly around **place du Marché** (Market Square). Also on the square is the 16th-century **Hôtel de Ville** (Town Hall). As you walk the charming streets, notice the wrought-iron signs and roof-top oriels.

Where to Stay & Eat

¢ ✕▣ **Le Raisin d'Or.** Set around the corner from the village church and halfway up the street that climbs straight into the vineyards, this unpretentious hotel is where you'll get a down-to-earth welcome and a hearty meal in a typical Alsace dining room (closed Monday and Tuesday) with heavy wooden tables and checked tablecloths. Hearty fare like sauerkraut, sausage meat, and potatoes will make you feel like the cook is one of those geese-stuffers. Rooms are on the small side, with functional dark-wood furnishings, but the best have balconies overlooking the street. ✉ *28 bis rue Clemenceau, 67650* ☎ *03–88–92–48–66* 🖷 *03–88–92–61–42* ⊕ *www.au-raisin-dor.com* ➴ *8 rooms* ♿ *Restaurant, minibars, bar; no a/c* ▤ *DC, MC, V* ☺ *Closed Jan.* ❖◎ *MAP.*

Sélestat

㊻ *9 km (5½ mi) southeast of Dambach via D210 and N422, 47 km (29 mi) southwest of Strasbourg.*

Sélestat, midway between Strasbourg and Colmar, is a lively, historic town with a Romanesque church and a library of medieval manuscripts (and, important to note, a railway station with trains to and from Strasbourg). Head directly to the Vieille Ville and explore the quarter on foot.

The church of **St-Foy** (⊠ Pl. du Marché-Vert) dates from between 1155 and 1190; its Romanesque facade remains largely intact (the spires were added in the 19th century), as does the 140-foot octagonal tower over the crossing. Sadly, the interior was mangled over the centuries, chiefly by the Jesuits; their most inspired legacy is the Baroque pulpit of 1733 depicting the life of St. Francis Xavier. Note the Romanesque bas-relief next to the baptistery, originally the lid of a sarcophagus. Among the precious medieval and Renaissance manuscripts on display at the **Bibliothèque Humaniste** (Humanist Library), a major library founded in 1452 and installed in the former Halle aux Blés, are a 7th-century lectionary and a 12th-century Book of Miracles. ⊠ *1 rue de la Bibliothèque* 🕾 *03–88–58–07–20* 🖾 *€3.50* ☉ *Sept.–June, Mon. and Wed.–Fri. 9–noon and 2–6, Sat. 9–noon; July and Aug., Mon. and Wed.–Fri. 9–noon and 2–6, weekends 9–noon and 2–5.*

Nightlife & the Arts

The colorful **Corso Fleuri** (Flower Carnival) takes place on the second Sunday in August, when the town decks itself—and the floats in its vivid parade—with a magnificent display of dahlias.

Haut-Koenigsbourg

47 *11 km (7 mi) west of Sélestat via D159.*

One of the most popular spots in Alsace is the romantic, crag-top castle of Haut-Koenigsbourg, originally built as a fortress in the 12th century. The ruins of the **Château du Haut-Koenigsbourg** were presented by the town of Sélestat to German emperor Wilhelm II in 1901. The château looked just as a kaiser thought one should, and he restored it with some diligence and no lack of imagination—squaring the main tower's original circle, for instance. The site, panorama, drawbridge, and amply furnished imperial chambers may lack authenticity, but they are undeniably dramatic. 🕾 *03–88–92–11–46* 🖾 *Château €6.20* ☉ *Nov.–Feb., daily 9:30–noon and 1–4:30; Mar., Apr., and Oct., daily 9–noon and 1–5:30; May, June, and Sept., daily 9–6; July and Aug., daily 9–6:30.*

FodorsChoice ★
🕙

Ribeauvillé

48 *13 km (8 mi) south of Haut-Koenigsbourg via St-Hippolyte, 16 km (10 mi) southwest of Sélestat.*

FodorsChoice ★

The beautiful half-timber town of Ribeauvillé, surrounded by rolling vineyards and three imposing châteaux, produces some of the best wines in Alsace. (The Trimbach family has made Riesling and superb Gewürztraminer here since 1626.) The town's narrow main street, crowded with winstubs, pottery shops, bakeries, and wine sellers, is bisected by the 13th-century **Tour des Bouchers,** a clock-belfry completed (gargoyles and all) in the 15th century. Storks' nests crown several towers in the village, while streets are adorned with quaint shop signs, fairy-tale turrets, and tour guides herding the crowds with directions in French and German. Make for the place de la Marie and its Hôtel de Ville to see its famous collection of silver-gilt 16th-century tankards and chalices. The place is also a good place to perch come every first Sunday in September, when the town hosts a grand parade to celebrate the **Jour des Menetriers** (Fete of the Minstrels), a day when at least one fountain here spouts free Riesling.

Where to Stay & Eat

$ ✕ **Zum Pfifferhüs.** This is a true-blue winstub, with yellowed murals, glowing lighting, and great local wines available by the glass. The cooking is pure Alsace, with German-scale portions of choucroute, ham hock, and fruit tarts. No smoking here. ✉ *14 Grand-Rue* 🕾 *03–89–73–62–28* ⌨ *Reservations essential* ▤ *MC, V* ⊗ *Closed Wed. and Thurs., Feb., and 2 wks in July.*

$$$$ ✕▦ **L'Auberge de l'Ill.** England's late Queen Mother, Marlene Dietrich, and Montserrat Caballé are just a few of the famous who have feasted at this culinary temple, but, oddly, this place has never been as famous as it should be, the long trek from Paris to the half-timbered village of Illhaeusern perhaps the reason. Still, you need to book weeks in advance to snare a table in this classic yet casual dining room. Master chef Paul Haeberlin marries grand and Alsatian cuisine, with the emphasis on proper marriage, not passionate love. The results are wonderful enough: Salmon soufflé, lamb chops in dainty strudel, and showstoppers like *le homard Prince Wladimir,* or lobster with shallots braised in champagne and crème fraîche. Germanic-Alsatian flair is particularly apparent in such dishes as the truffled *baeckoffa* (baker's oven), a casserole-terrine of lamb and pork with leeks. The kitchen's touch is incredibly light (though not nouvelle, thank you), so you can even enjoy such master desserts as white peaches in vanilla syrup served in a chocolate "butterfly" with champagne sabayon sauce. If you want to enjoy the pleasant surroundings of the auberge, with its terraced lawns, romantic trees, and famous flowing brook, opt for an overnight in one of the guest rooms in the new **Hôtel des Berges,** set behind the restaurant and designed to evoke an Alsatian tobacco barn, replete with Havenese woods, rooms named after famous cigars, and a lulling and lovely country-luxe decor. ✉ *2 rue de Collonges, 10 km (6 mi) east of Ribeauville, Illhaeusern* 🕾 *03–89–71–89–00* 🖶 *03–89–71–82–83* ⊕ *www.auberge-de-l-ill.com* ⌨ *Reservations essential* ⇌ *6 rooms* ⌂ *Restaurant, minibars, cable TV, some pets allowed (fee)* ▤ *AE, DC, MC, V* ⊗ *Closed Mon. and Tues., 1st wk Jan. and Feb.*

*Fodor's*Choice
★

$$ ▦ **Seigneurs de Ribeaupierre.** On the edge of Ribeauvillé's old quarter, this gracious half-timber inn offers a warm regional welcome with a touch of flair. It has exposed timbers in pastel tones, sumptuous fabrics, and slick bathrooms upstairs, as well as a fire crackling downstairs on your way to the generous breakfast. ✉ *11 rue du Château, 68150* 🕾 *03–89–73–70–31* 🖶 *03–89–73–71–21* ⇌ *10 rooms* ⌂ *Bar; no a/c, no room TVs* ▤ *AE, MC, V* ⊗ *Closed Jan. and Feb.* � *BP.*

$ ▦ **Tour.** In the center of Ribeauvillé and across from the Tour des Bouchers, this hotel, with an ornate Renaissance fountain outside its front door, is a good choice for experiencing the atmospheric town by night. Rooms and amenities are modern; those on the top floor have exposed timbers and wonderful views of ramshackle rooftops. ✉ *1 rue de la Mairie, 68150* 🕾 *03–89–73–72–73* 🖶 *03–89–73–38–74* ⊕ *www.hotel-la-tour.com* ⇌ *33 rooms* ⌂ *Hot tub, sauna, bar, some Internet; no a/c* ▤ *AE, DC, MC, V* ⊗ *Closed mid-Feb.–mid-Mar.* � O *EP.*

Shopping

Find rich paisley Alsatian tablecloths discounted at the factory outlet for **Beauvillé** (⊠ 19 rte. de Ste-Marie-aux-Mines ☎ 03–89–73–74–74), at the foot of forested hills just past the town center.

Riquewihr

🅐 *5 km (3 mi) south of Ribeauvillé.*

Fodor'sChoice
★

With its dormer windows fit for a Rapunzel, hidden cul-de-sacs home to Rumpelstiltskins, and unique once-upon-a-time spell, Riquewihr is the showpiece of the Wine Route and a living museum of the quaint architecture of old Alsace. Its steep main street, ramparts, and winding back alleys have scarcely changed since the 16th century, and could easily serve as a film set. Merchants cater to the sizable influx of tourists with a plethora of kitschy souvenir shops; bypass them to peep into courtyards with massive wine presses, to study the woodwork and ornately decorated houses, to stand in the narrow old courtyard that was once the Jewish quarter, or to climb up a narrow wooden stair to the ramparts. You would also do well to settle into a winstub to sample some of Riquewihr's famous wines. Just following your nose down the heavenly romantic streets will reward your eye with bright blue, half-timbered houses, storybook gables, and storks'-nest towers. The facades of certain houses dating from the late Gothic period take pride of place, including the Maison Kiener (1574), the Maison Priess (1686), and the Maison Liebrich (1535), but the Tower of Thieves and the Postal Museum, ensconced in the château of the duke of Württemberg, are also fascinating.

Where to Stay & Eat

★ ¢–$$ ✕ **Au Tire-Bouchon.** "The Corkscrew" is the best winstub in town to feast on Alsatian varieties of choucroute garni, including some rare delights like the *verte* (or green, flavored with parsley) version and the blow-out "Choucroute Royale." This extravaganza is garnished with seven different kinds of wursts and meats and served with a half-bottle of mulled champagne plopped in the center of a mound of sauerkraut. The bottle is then poured by the waitress, with great flourish, over the entire dish. There are also fine Muscats, great breads, and fragrant onion tarts to savor. With communal tables and kind service, this is heartily recommended. If booked up, try the nearby Auberge du Schoenebourg. ⊠ *29 rue du Génèral-de-Gaulle* ☎ 03–89–47–91–61 ⊟ *AE, MC, V.*

$–$$ ✕▦ **Sarment d'Or.** This cozy little hotel stands apart for its irreproachable modern comforts tactfully dovetailed with stone, dark timbers, and thick walls. The restaurant downstairs offers firelight romance and delicious cuisine—foie gras, frogs' legs in garlic cream, and breast of duck in pinot noir; it's closed Monday and does not serve dinner Sunday or lunch Tuesday. ⊠ *4 rue du Cerf, 68340* ☎ 03–89–86–02–86 🖷 03–89–47–99–23 ⇝ *9 rooms* ⚘ *Restaurant; no a/c* ⊟ *MC, V* ⊙ *Closed Jan.–mid-Feb.* ⌾ *MAP.*

★ $–$$ ▦ **Hôtel de la Couronne.** Like an illustration out of the Brothers Grimm, this hotel is set in a 17th-century house with central tower and side wings. Its steep mansard roof, country shutters, and rusticated stone trim beautifully blend into the heart of medieval Riquewihr—the only modern note

CloseUp

SAUERKRAUT & CHOUCROUTE

TO EMBARK ON A FULL GASTRONOMIC excursion into the hearty, artery-clogging terrain of Alsatian cuisine, your tour should probably start with flammekueche—a flat tart stuffed with bacon, onions, cream cheese, and heavy cream. The next stop is baeckaoffa, marinated pork, mutton, and beef simmered in wine with potatoes and onions, sometimes with a round of creamy Munster cheese melted on top. And to finish up, land with a thud on a hefty slice of Kougelhopf, a butter-rich ring-shaped brioche cake with almonds and raisins. If, however, you have neither the constitution nor the inclination for such culinary heft, there is one dish that sums up the whole of Alsatian cuisine: choucroute garnie. Borrowed from the Germans, who call it sauerkraut, the base definition of choucroute is cabbage pickled in brine. In more elaborate terms, this means quintal d'Alsace, a substantial variety of local white cabbage, shredded and packed into crockery and left to ferment with salt and juniper berries for at least two months. Beyond this, any unanimity regarding the composition of choucroute garnie breaks down. The essential ingredients, however, seem to be sauerkraut, salted bacon, pork sausages, juniper berries, white wine, onions, cloves, black peppercorns, garlic, lard or goose fat, potatoes, and salt pork—pig's knuckles, cheeks, loin, shanks, feet, shoulder, and who knows what else? No matter—the taste is unforgettable, especially if you have the version served up at Au Tire-Bouchon in Riquewihr. There, the "Choucroute Royale" is lavished with seven different kinds of meat, served with a half bottle of mulled champagne set in the center, which is then poured by the waitress over the entire dish.

will be your car (allowed to drive to the hotel even though the town center is pedestrianized). Inside, several rooms have grand timber beams and folkloric wall stencils, making this a truly charming base to tour a truly charming town. ⊠ *5 rue de la Couronne, 68340* ☎ *03–89–49–03–03* 🖷 *03–89–49–01–01* ⊕ *www.hoteldelacouronne.com* ⇝ *40 rooms* ⌂ *No a/c* ▤ *AE, MC, V* ⦿ *EP.*

Colmar

 13 km (8 mi) southeast of Riquewihr via D3/ D10, 71 km (44 mi) southwest of Strasbourg.

Forget that much of Colmar's architecture is modern (because of the destruction wrought by World Wars I and II): the heart of this proud merchant town—an atmospheric maze of narrow streets lined with Renaissance houses restored to the last detail—outcharms Strasbourg. Especially as you wander along the calm canals that wind through **La Petite Venise** (Little Venice), an area of bright Alsatian houses with colorful shutters and window boxes that's south of the center of town. Here, amid weeping willow trees that shed their tears into the eddies of the Lauch River and half-timbered houses gaily bedecked with geraniums and carnations, you have the sense of being in a tiny village. Elsewhere, the Vieille Ville streets fan out from the beefy towered church of **St-Martin.** Each shop-lined backstreet winds its way to the 15th-century customs house, the **Ancienne Douane,** and the square and canals that surround it. The **Maison Pfister** (Pfister House; ✉ 11 rue Mercière), built in 1537, is the most striking of Colmar's many old dwellings. Note its decorative frescoes and medallions, carved balcony, and ground-floor arcades. Up the street from the Ancienne Douane on the Grand'Rue, the **Maison aux Arcades** (Arcades House) was built in 1609 in High Renaissance style with a series of arched porches (arcades) anchored by two octagonal towers.

The cultural highpoint of Colmar is the **Musée d'Unterlinden,** once a medieval Dominican convent and hotbed of Rhenish mysticism, and now an important museum. "Under the Linden Tree"'s star attraction is one

Fodor'sChoice of the greatest art works of the 16th century, the *Issenheim Altarpiece*
★ (1512–16), by Matthias Grünewald, majestically displayed in the convent's Gothic chapel. Originally painted for the convent at Issenheim, 22 km (14 mi) south of Colmar near Guebwiller, the multipanel *retable* (altarpiece) is framed with two-sided wings, which unfold to show the Crucifixion and Incarnation, with side panels illustrating the Annunciation and the Resurrection. Other panels depict the life of St. Anthony, notably the Temptation. Grünewald's altarpiece, replete with its raw realism (note the chamber pots, boil-covered bellies, and dirty linen), was believed to have miraculous healing powers over ergotism, a widespread disease in the Middle Ages. Produced by the ingestion of fungus-ridden grains, the malady caused its victims to experience delusional fantasies. Hallucinogenic, indeed, is the word to describe the proto-Expressionist power of Grünewald's tortured faces and poses, whose emotional power made a direct appeal to the pain-racked victims living out their last days at the convent. Arms and armor, stone sculpture, ancient wine presses and barrels, and antique toys cluster around the enchanting 13th-century cloister. Upstairs are fine regional furnishings and a collection of Rhine Valley paintings from the Renaissance, including Martin Schongauer's opulent 1470 altarpiece painted for Jean d'Orlier. ✉ *1 rue Unterlinden* ☎ *03–89–20–15–50* 🖼 €7 ✪ *May–Oct., daily 9–6; Nov.–Apr., Wed.–Mon. 9–noon and 2–5.*

★ The **Église des Dominicains** (Dominican Church) houses the Flemish-influenced *Madonna of the Rosebush* (1473), by Martin Schongauer (1445–91), the most celebrated painting by the noted 15th-century German artist. This work, stolen from St-Martin's in 1972 and later recovered and hung here, has almost certainly been reduced in size from its original state but retains enormous impact. The grace and intensity of the Virgin match that of the Christ child; yet her slender fingers dent the child's soft flesh (and his fingers entwine her curls) with immediate intimacy. Schongauer's text for her crown is: ME CARPES GENITO TUO O SANTISSIMA VIRGO ("Choose me also for your child, o holiest Virgin"). ✉ *Pl. des Dominicains* ☎ *03–89–24–46–57* 🖼 €1.30 ✪ *Apr.–Dec., daily 10–1 and 3–6.*

The **Musée Bartholdi** (Bartholdi Museum) is the birthplace of Frédéric-Auguste Bartholdi (1834–1904), the local sculptor who designed the Statue of Liberty. Exhibits of Bartholdi's works claim the ground floor; a reconstruction of the artist's Paris apartments and furniture are upstairs;

and, in adjoining rooms, the creation of Lady Liberty is explored. ✉ *30 rue des Marchands* ☎ *03–89–41–90–60* 🖅 €4 ⊗ *Mar.–Dec., Wed.–Mon. 10–noon and 2–6.*

Where to Stay & Eat

★ **$$$–$$$$** ✕ **Au Fer Rouge.** If you want a delicious feast of Old Colmar, head to this cobblestone square to find an adorable 17th-century Alsatian *colombage* (dovecote) mansion, replete with carved timber beams, oil paintings, stained glass, leaded windows, copper tankards, and flower window boxes. Even better, the kitchen is manned by a chef happy to leapfrog from yesteryear to tomorrow by offering nouvelle versions of classic standards. Patrick Fulgraff's salads are *"gourmandise d'oie"* (garnished with goose), his *croustillant au camembert* is topped with aspics and creams, his rabbit sausage comes with grilled polenta, and his wine list has one foot in Alsace and the other in France. Be sure to sit in the main floor salon and avoid the lackluster basement room. All in all, very much the best restaurant in Colmar. ✉ *52 Grand'rue* ☎ *03–89–41–37–24* 🖃 *AE, MC, V* ⊗ *Closed Sun.*

$$ ✕ **Chez Hansi.** Named for the Rockwell-like illustrator whose beclogged folk children adorn most of the souvenirs of Alsace, this hypertraditional beamed tavern in the Vieille Ville serves excellent down-home classics such as choucroute and pot-au-feu, prepared and served with a sophisticated touch despite the waitresses' dirndls. ✉ *23 rue des Marchands* ☎ *03–89–41–37–84* 🖃 *MC, V* ⊗ *Closed Wed., Thurs., and Jan.*

¢–$ ✕ **Au Koïfhus.** Not to be confused with the shabby little Koïfhus on rue des Marchands, this popular landmark serves huge portions of regional standards, plus changing specialties: roast quail and foie gras on salad, game stews with spaetzle (dumplings), and freshwater fish. Choose between the big, open dining room, glowing with wood and warm fabric, and a shaded table on the broad, lovely square. ✉ *2 pl. de l'Ancienne-Douane* ☎ *03–89–23–04–90* 🖃 *DC, MC, V* ⊗ *Closed Thurs. and Jan.*

★ **$$–$$$$** ✕🖼 **Hostellerie le Maréchal.** A maze of narrow, creaky corridors connects the series of Renaissance houses that make up this romantic riverside inn. Built in 1565 in the fortified walls that encircle the Vieille Ville, the Maréchal has rooms that are small but lavished with extravagant detail, from glossy rafters to rich brocades to four-poster beds. A vivid color scheme—scarlet, sapphire, candy pink—adds to the Vermeer atmosphere. This is not a high-tech luxury hotel: it's an endearing, quirky, lovely old place hanging over a Petite Venise canal. The gastronomic restaurant, A l'Echevin, offers such dishes as terrine of rouget, leeks, truffles, and pigeon breast and foie gras crisped in pastry, in salons and on a terrace that perch over the river. ✉ *4 pl. des Six-Montagnes-Noires, 68000* ☎ *03–89–41–60–32* 🖷 *03–89–24–59–40* ⊕ *www.hotel-le-marechal.com* 🛏 *30 rooms* ⅄ *Restaurant, minibars, cable TV, some Internet, some pets allowed (fee)* 🖃 *AE, DC, MC, V* 🍽 *MAP.*

$ ✕🖼 **Rapp.** In the Vieille Ville, just off the Champ de Mars, this solid, modern hotel has business-class comforts, a professional and welcoming staff, and a good German-scale breakfast. There's even an extensive indoor-pool complex, including sauna, steam bath, and workout equipment—all included in the low price. The restaurant is closed on Friday and does not serve lunch Saturday. ✉ *1 rue Weinemer, 68000* ☎ *03–89–41–62–10* 🖶 *03–89–24–13–58* 🌐 *www.rapp-hotel.com* 🛏*42 rooms* ⚙*Restaurant, cable TV, pool, gym, sauna, bar; no a/c* 🖃*AE, DC, MC, V* ⊘ *Closed July and 2 wks in Jan.* ⧧ *EP.*

The Arts
During the first half of August, Colmar celebrates with its annual **Foire Régionale des Vins d'Alsace,** an Alsatian wine fair in the Parc des Expositions. Events include folk music and theater performances and, above all, the tasting and selling of wine.

> ### off the beaten path

ECOMUSÉE DE HAUTE-ALSACE – Great for kids, this open-air museum near Ungersheim, southeast of Guebwiller (via D430), is really a small village created from scratch in 1980, including 70 historic peasant houses and buildings typical of the region. The village is crisscrossed by donkey carts and wagons, and behind every door lie entertaining demonstrations of the old ways. An off-season visit is a study in local architecture; in high season the place comes alive. Small restaurants, snack bars, a playground, and a few amusement rides are scattered about for breaks. Inexpensive lodging is available on-site. ☎ *03–89–74–44–74* 🖶 *€15* 🌐 *www.ecomusee-alsace.com* ⊘ *July and Aug., daily 9–7; Apr.–June and Sept., daily 9:30–6; Mar. and Oct., daily 10–5; Nov.–Feb., daily 10:30–5.*

ALSACE-LORRAINE A TO Z

To research prices, get advice from other travelers, and book travel arrangements, visit www.fodors.com.

AIRPORTS
Most international flights to Alsace land at Mulhouse-Basel Airport, on the Franco-Swiss border; some others at Entzheim, near Strasbourg. Metz-Nancy and Mirecourt (Vittel/Épinal) also have tiny airports for charter- and private-plane landings.

BUS TRAVEL
The two main bus companies are Les Rapides de Lorraine, based in Nancy, and Compagnie des Transports Strasbourgeois, based in Strasbourg. Various regional bus lines can connect you with towns and villages such as Mont-St-Odile, and those departing from Colmar for the towns along the Route du Vin, such as Riquewihr and Ribeauvillé; getting there when you want is another problem entirely. Bus routes run to Metz and Verdun from Nancy; Nancy, Strasbourg, and Colmar all have city buses. There are many other routes throughout Alsace and Lorraine, so always check in with the regional tourist office or information window at a gateway rail or bus station to get printed bus schedules.

🚌 Bus Information **Les Rapides de Lorraine** ✉ 52 bd. d'Austrasie, 54000 Nancy ☎ 03–83–32–34–20. **Compagnie des Transports Strasbourgeois** ✉ 14 rue de la Gare-aux-Marchandises, 67200 Strasbourg ☎ 03–88–77–70–70.

CAR RENTAL

Local Agencies Avis ✉ 7 pl. Flore, Besançon ☎ 03-81-80-91-08 ✉ Pl. de la Gare, Strasbourg ☎ 03-88-32-30-44. **Europcar** ✉ 18 rue de Serre, Nancy ☎ 03-83-37-57-24. **Hertz** ✉ 7 pl. Thiers, Nancy ☎ 03-83-32-13-14 ✉ Pl. Flore, Besançon ☎ 03-81-47-43-23.

CAR TRAVEL

A4 heads east from Paris to Strasbourg, via Verdun, Metz, and Saverne. It is met by A26, descending from the English Channel, at Reims. A31 links Metz to Nancy, continuing south to Burgundy and Lyon.

N83/A35 connects Strasbourg, Colmar, and Mulhouse. A36 continues to Belfort and Besançon. A4, linking Paris to Strasbourg, passes through Lorraine via Metz, linking Lorraine and Alsace. Picturesque secondary roads lead from Nancy and Toul through Joan of Arc country and on to Épinal. Several scenic roads climb switchbacks over forested mountain passes through the Vosges, connecting Lorraine to Alsace and Alsace to Belfort; a quicker alternative is the tunnel *under* the Vosges at Ste-Marie-aux-Mines, linking Sélestat to Lunéville and Épinal. Alsace's Route du Vin, winding from Marlenheim, in the north, all the way south to Thann, is the ultimate in scenic driving.

EMERGENCIES

Ambulance ☎ 15. **Hôpital Central** ✉ 29 av. du Mal-de-Lattre-de-Tassigny, 54000 Nancy ☎ 03-83-85-85-85. **Hôpital Civil** ✉ 1 pl. de l'Hôpital, 67000 Strasbourg ☎ 03-88-11-67-68.

LODGING

APARTMENT-VILLA RENTALS Contact Gîtes de France for its brochure on "Gîtes de France" in the Jura. The list includes both bed-and-breakfasts and houses for rent.
Local Agents Gîtes de France ✉ 8 rue Louis Rousseau, 39016 Lons-le-Saunier ☎ 03-84-87-08-88 ⊕ www.gitesdefrance.com.

SPORTS & THE OUTDOORS

A guide to bicycling in the Lorraine is available from the Comité Départemental de Cyclisme. For a list of signposted trails in the Vosges foothills, contact the Sélestat Tourist Office (*see* Visitor Information, *below*).
Bicycling Comité Départemental de Cyclotourisme de Meurthe et Moselle ✉ 2 rue des Marguerites, 54700 Blénod-lés-Pont-à-Mousson ☎ 03-83-82-26-58 ⊕ http://cd54ffct.chez.tiscali.fr/
Horseback Riding Délégation Départementale de Tourisme Équestre ✉ 4 rue des Violettes, 67201 Eckbolsheim ☎ 03-88-77-39-64.

TOURS

Walking tours of Strasbourg's Vieille Ville are directed by the tourist office (*see* Visitor Information, *below*) for €6 and depart at 2:30 every Saturday afternoon in low season, daily at 10:30 in July and August. For Colmar and its enchanting environs, take a highly recommended van tour with Les Circuits d'Alsace—castles, villages, and vineyards make for an exhilarating itinerary.
Les Circuits d'Alsace ✉ 6 pl. de la Gare, 68000 Colmar ☎ 03-89-41-90-88 ⊕ www.alsace-travel.com. **Strasbourg minitrain tours** ☎ 03-88-77-70-03.

TRAIN TRAVEL

Mainline trains leave Paris (Gare de l'Est) every couple of hours for the four-hour, 500-km (315-mi) journey to Strasbourg. Some stop in Toul, and all stop in Nancy, where there are connections for Épinal. Trains run three times daily from Paris to Verdun and more often to Metz (around three hours to each). Mainline trains stop in Mulhouse (four to five hours) en route to Basel.

Several local trains a day run between Strasbourg and Mulhouse, stopping in Sélestat and Colmar; some continue to Belfort and Besançon. Local trains occasionally link Besançon to Arbois. Other towns, such as Obernai and Montbenoît are accessible, with planning, by train. But without any bus connection you'll need a car to visit smaller villages and the region's spectacular natural sights.

🚉 Train Information **SNCF** ☎ 08-36-35-35-35 ⊕ www.ter-sncf.com/uk/alsace/default.htm.

TRAVEL AGENCIES

🚉 Local Agent Referrals **Havas Voyages** ✉ 23 rue de la Haute-Montée, Strasbourg ☎03-88-32-99-77. **Carlson Wagons-lit** ✉30 pl. Kléber, Strasbourg ☎03-88-32-16-34 ✉ 2 rue Raymond-Poincaré, Nancy ☎ 03-83-35-06-97.

VISITOR INFORMATION

The principal regional tourist offices are in Nancy and Strasbourg. Other tourist offices are listed by town below the principal offices.

🚉 Tourist Information **Nancy** ✉14 pl. Stanislas ☎03-83-35-22-41 ⊕www.ot-nancy.fr. **Strasbourg** ✉17 pl. de la Cathédrale ☎03-88-52-28-28 ⊕www.strasbourg.com ✉Pl. de la Gare ☎ 03-88-32-51-49; there's also a city tourist office at the train station.

Colmar ✉4 rue Unterlinden ☎ 03-89-20-68-95 ⊕ www.ville-colmar.fr. **Guebwiller** ✉ 73 rue de la République ☎ 03-89-76-10-63. **Lons-le-Saunier** ✉1 rue Louis-Pasteur ☎ 03-84-24-65-01. **Lunéville** ✉ Pl. du Château ☎03-83-74-06-55 ⊕ www.ville-luneville.fr. **Metz** ✉ Pl. d'Armes ☎03-87-55-53-76 ⊕ www.mairie-metz.fr. **Obernai** ✉ 59 rue du Général-Gouraud ☎ 03-88-95-64-13 ⊕ www.obernai.fr. **Saverne** ✉37 Grand'Rue ☎03-88-91-80-47. **Sélestat** ✉10 bd. Leclerc ☎03-88-58-87-20. **Toul** ✉ Parvis de la Cathédrale ☎ 03-83-64-11-69 ⊕ www.ot-toul.fr. **Verdun** ✉ Pl. de la Nation ☎ 03-29-86-14-18 ⊕ www.verdun-tourisme.com.

BURGUNDY

8

Updated by
Simon Hewitt

Introduction by
Nancy Coons

DRAIN TO THE DREGS BURGUNDY'S FULL-BODIED VISTAS: rolling hillsides carpeted in emerald green, each pasture cross-hatched with hedgerows, patterned with cows, quilted with vineyards. Behind a massive quarried-stone wall, a château looms, seemingly untouched by time, the only signs of human habitation the featherbeds airing from casement windows and a flock of sheep mowing the grounds. In the villages, tightly clustered houses—with roofs of slate from the days when they protected against brigands—circle the local church, its spire a lightning rod for the faithful. On a hilltop high over the patchwork of green rises a patrician edifice of white rock, a Romanesque church whose austerity and architectural purity hark back to the early Roman temples on which it was modeled. And deep inside a musty *cave* or perhaps a wine cellar redolent of cork and soured grapes, a row of glasses gleams like a treasured necklace, their garnet contents waiting to be swirled, sniffed, and savored.

Although you may often fall under the influence of extraordinary wine during a sojourn in Burgundy—in French, Bourgogne—the beauty surrounding you will be no boozy illusion. Passed over by revolutions, both political and industrial, left unscarred by world wars, and relatively inaccessible thanks to necessarily circuitous country roads, the region still reflects the pastoral prosperity it enjoyed under the Capetian dukes and kings.

Those were the glory days—when self-sufficient Burgundy held its own against the creeping spread of France and the mighty Holy Roman Empire—a period characterized by the expanding role of the dukes of Bourgogne. Consider the Capetians, history-book celebrities all: there was Philippe le Hardi (the Bold), with his power-brokered marriage to Marguerite of Flanders. There was Jean sans Peur (the Fearless), who murdered Louis d'Orléans in a cloak-and-dagger affair in 1407 and was in turn murdered, in 1419, on a dark bridge while negotiating a secret treaty with the future Charles VII. There was Philippe le Bon (the Good), who threw in with the English against Joan of Arc, and then Charles le Téméraire, whose temerity stretched the boundaries of Burgundy—already bulging with Flanders, Luxembourg, and Picardy—to include most of Holland, Lorraine, Alsace, and even parts of French-speaking Switzerland. He met his match in 1477 at the Battle of Nancy, where he and his boldness were permanently parted. Nonetheless, you can still see Burgundian candy-tile roofs in Fribourg, Switzerland, his easternmost conquest.

Yet the Capetians in their acquisitions couldn't hold a candle to the "light of the world": the great Abbaye de Cluny, founded in 910, grew to such overweening ecclesiastical power that it dominated the European Church on a papal scale for some four centuries. It was Urban II himself who dubbed it *"la Lumière du Monde."* And like the Italian popes, Cluny, too, indulged a weakness for worldly luxury and knowledge, both sacred and profane. In nearby Clairvaux, St-Bernard himself vented his outrage, chiding the monks who, although sworn to chastity and poverty, kept mistresses, teams of horses, and a library of unfathomable depth that codified classical and Eastern lore for all posterity—that is, until it was destroyed in the Wars of Religion, its wisdom lost for all time. The abbey itself met a similar fate, its wealth of quarry stone ransacked after the French Revolution.

Neighboring abbeys, perhaps less glorious than Cluny but with more humility than hubris, fared better. The stark geometry of the Cistercian abbeys—Clairvaux, Cîteaux—stand in silent rebuke to Cluny's excess. The basilicas at Autun, Vézelay, and Paray le Monial remain today in all their noble simplicity, yet manifest some of the finest Romanesque sculpture ever created; the tympanum at Autun rejects all time frames in its visionary daring. Anchored between Autun and Vézelay rises the broad massif of the Morvan, its dewy green flanks densely wooded in oak and beech. Hidden streams, rocky escarpments, dark forests, and meadows alive with falcons and hoopoes—a hiker's dream—are protected today by the Parc Naturel Régional du Morvan.

It's almost unfair to the rest of France that all this history, all this art, all this natural beauty comes with delicious refreshments. As if to live up to the extraordinary quality of its Chablis, its Chassagne-Montrachet, its Nuits-St-Georges, its Gevrey-Chambertin, Burgundy flaunts some of the best good, plain food in the world. Two poached eggs in savory wine sauce, a slab of ham in aspic, a platter of beef stew, a half-dozen earthy snails—no frills needed—just the pleasure of discovering that such homely material could resonate on the tongue, and harmonize so brilliantly with the local wine. This is simplicity raised to Gallic heights, embellished by the poetry of one perfect glass of pinot noir paired with a licensed and diploma'd *poulet de Bresse* (Bresse chicken), sputtering in unvarnished perfection on your white-china plate. Thus you may find that food and drink entries take up as much space in your travel diary as the sights you see. And that's as it should be in such well-rounded, full-bodied terrain.

Exploring Burgundy

The best way to enter Burgundy is southeast from Paris by car. As you enter the region, you'll first hit the northwest part of Burgundy, so grand-tour it from Sens to Autun, with a rewarding detour to the town of Troyes, in Champagne, and also the hilly forests in the west around the Parc du Morvan. In Northern Burgundy the accents are thinner than around Dijon, and sunflowers cover the countryside instead of vineyards. Near Auxerre, many small, unheard-of villages boast a château or a once-famous abbey; they happily see few tourists, partly because public transportation is more than a bit spotty. Highlights of Northern Burgundy include Sens's great medieval cathedral, Troyes's Vieux Troyes historic quarter, Auxerre's Flamboyant Gothic cathedral, the great Romanesque sculptures of the basilica at Vézelay and church at Autun, and the lakes of the Morvan Regional Park.

Go next to Burgundy's wine country, in the southeast region of Burgundy, which begins at Dijon, home to three noted churches and some fine museums, including the Chartreuse de Champmol and its great *Well of Moses*

Having done its duty by producing a wealth of what many consider the world's greatest wines and harboring an abundance of magnificent Romanesque abbeys, Burgundy hardly needs to be beautiful—but it is. Its green-hedgerowed countryside and densely forested Morvan, its manor houses and scattered villages, its numerous vineyards, all deserve to be rolled on the palate and savored. Like glasses filled with Clos de Vougeot, the sights here— from the stately hub of Dijon to the medieval sanctuaries of Cluny and Clairvaux—invite the wanderer to tarry and partake of their mellow splendor. If you have only three days, take in two of Burgundy's most interesting cities—Dijon and Beaune. With five days you can explore the northwest part of the region, from Sens to Beaune. Eight days will give you time to get to trawl the Morvan and Burgundy's finest vineyards.

8

Numbers in the text correspond to numbers in the margin and on the Burgundy, Troyes, and Dijon maps.

**If you have
3 days**

Start with Burgundy's two most interesting cities: first, the age-old capital of Burgundy, 🖼 **Dijon** ㉗– ㊳ ▶—one-time haunt of the dukes of Burgundy, who were among the richest people in the late Middle Ages and who bequeathed to the city a dazzling legacy of art, goldsmithery, and tapestry; and then on to medieval 🖼 **Beaune** ㊶ to view its majestic Hospice, founded by Chancellor Rolin, the great patron of Jan van Eyck and Rogier van der Weyden, whose *Last Judgment* altarpiece takes pride of place here. Between touring the two towns, visit the famous Burgundy vineyards around **Clos de Vougeot** ㊴—if you're here in September or October, you may be in time for the *vendanges* (grape harvests).

**If you have
5 days**

Coming from Paris, stop first in the small town of **Sens** ❶ ▶, with its vast cathedral and 13th-century Palais Synodal. Then head for the serene abbey in **Pontigny** ⑮ and the Ancien Hôpital in **Tonnerre** ⑱. End the day tasting the famous white wine in 🖼 **Chablis** ⑰ and spend the night there. Begin Day 2 with a visit to **Auxerre** ⑯ and its cathedral before going on to the famous basilica in **Vézelay** ㉓. Stay overnight in pretty 🖼 **Avallon** ㉒, with its medieval church of St-Lazare. Get to 🖼 **Dijon** ㉗–㊳ on Day 3 and stay two nights. On Day 5 take a short run along the wine-producing Côte d'Or to 🖼 **Beaune** ㊶.

**If you have
9 days**

Make 🖼 **Troyes** ❷ ▶ –⑭, with its medieval pedestrian streets, your first stop. On Day 2 head south to see the Renaissance château of **Ancy-le-Franc** ⑳ and the Cistercian **Abbaye de Fontenay** ㉑. End the day in 🖼 **Dijon** ㉗–㊳. Give yourself two nights in Dijon, then head to 🖼 **Beaune** ㊶ and spend the night there before driving south along the Saône Valley to medieval **Tournus** ㊺ and the abbey of St-Philibert, then across to 🖼 **Cluny** ㊻ and its ruined abbey. The next day drive north to see the cathedral and Roman remains in **Autun** ㊸, the **Château de Sully** ㊷, and end the day with a feast in 🖼 **Saulieu** ㉕. On Day 7 drive through the wooded hills of the **Morvan** ㉔ before spending the night in 🖼 **Vézelay** ㉓. Stop off in **Avallon** ㉒ before reaching 🖼 **Auxerre** ⑯—a good base for exploring **Chablis** ⑰ and its towering vineyards on your final day, before heading up to **Sens** ❶ sculpture, and stretches south down the Saône Valley through charming Beaune to Mâcon. The area includes the prestigious Côte de Nuits and Côte de Beaune, while southward in the region of Mercurey's Côte Chalonnaise, great red and white wines are produced from the pinot noir and chardonnay grapes that thrive here. Still farther south, around Mâcon, more chardonnay grapes are grown for whites like Pouilly-Fuissé. Throughout this killer countryside, small towns with big wine names draw tourists to their cellars. Farther south, where the Aligoté and pinot blanc are also grown (for whites), and the fruity gamay (red) heralds neighboring Beaujolais, Cluny and Tournus add more spice to Burgundy's reputation for tasty church architecture.

About the Restaurants & Hotels

Welcome to the land of the Appellation d'Origine Contrôlée (AOC), an organization that slaps its mark onto quality products according to sacred rules of food and wine cultivation. In Burgundy this means that the *poulet de Bresse* (Bresse chicken), *boeuf Bourguignon* (beef stew with vegetables, braised in red Burgundy wine), *coq au vin* (chicken stewed in red wine), or escargots (snails) you ordered came from a pure lineage and were raised on natural ingredients before landing on your dinner table. And don't forget to down your victuals with a drink invented by a monk from Dijon—the kir, a mix of local crème de cassis (blackcurrant liqueur) and white Aligoté wine. Keep in mind some restaurants close the last two weeks in August and go into winter hibernation for January.

Burgundy is seldom overrun by tourists, so finding accommodations is not usually a problem. But it's still wise to make advance reservations, especially in the wine country (from Dijon to Beaune). Note that nearly all country hotels have restaurants, and you are usually expected to eat at them. Some towns have a large number of inexpensive hotels. In Dijon you can find them around place Émile Zola; in Beaune look around place Madeleine; in Auxerre they're tucked away in the streets heading down from Cathédrale St-Étienne; in Tournus and Avallon check out the *Vieille Ville* (Old Town) sections. Assume all hotel rooms have air-conditioning, TV, telephones, and private bath, except when noted.

WHAT IT COSTS In euros				
$$$$	**$$$**	**$$**	**$**	**¢**
RESTAURANTS over €30	€23–€30	€17–€23	€11–€17	under €11
HOTELS over €190	€120–€190	€80–€120	€50–€80	under €50

Restaurant prices are per person for a main course at dinner, including tax (19.6%) and service; note that if a restaurant offers only prix-fixe (set-price) meals, it has been given the price category that reflects the full prix-fixe price. Hotel prices are for a standard double room in high season, including tax (19.6%) and service charge; higher prices (inquire when booking) prevail for any board plans.

Timing

May in Burgundy is especially lovely, as are September and October, when the sun is still warm on the shimmering golden trees and the grapes, now

8

Beyond Boeuf Bourguignon
"Tonton Moutarde" (Uncle Mustard) is what one young Parisian sophisticate affectionately used to call her Dijon relative, who was actually in the mustard business. For many French people, mention of Burgundy's capital conjures up images of round, rosy, merry men enjoying large suppers of boeuf à la Bourguignonne and red wine. And admittedly, chances are that in any decent restaurant you'll find at least one *Dijonnais* true to the stereotype. These days, however, Dijon is not quite the wine-mustard capital of the world it used to be as mustard production has been displaced by the more profitable colza plant, from which cooking oil is made. You'll find several people continue to make it by hand (importing the seed from Canada) in Dijon, but the happy fact remains that mustard finds its way into many regional specialties, including the sauce that usually accompanies andouillettes (chitterling sausages). Dijon ranks with Lyon as the gastronomic capital of France and Burgundy's hearty traditions help explain why. It all began in the early 15th century when Jean, Duc de Berry, arrived here, built many castles, and proceeded to make food, wine, and art top priorities for his courtiers. Today, Parisian gourmands consider a three-hour drive a small price to pay for the cuisine of Beaune's Jean Crotet or Vézelay's Marc Meneau.

Game, freshwater trout, coq au vin, *poulet au Meursault* (chicken in white wine sauce), snails, and, of course, beef *à la Bourguignonne* (incidentally, this dish is only called boeuf bourguignon when you are *not* in Burgundy) number among the region's specialties. The queen of chickens is the *poulet de Bresse*, which hails from east of the Côte d'Or and can be as pricey as a bottle of fine wine. Sausages—notably the *rosette du Morvan* and others served with a potato puree—are great favorites. Ham is a big item, especially around Easter, when garlicky *jambon persillé*—ham boiled with pig's trotters and served cold in jellied white wine and parsley (no wonder it is now found throughout the summer months) often tops the menu. Also look for *saupiquet des Amognes*— a Moravian delight of hot braised ham served with a spicy cream sauce. *Pain d'épices* (gingerbread) is the dessert staple of the region. Like every other part of France, Burgundy has its own cheeses. The Abbaye de Cîteaux, birthplace of Cistercian monasticism, has produced its mild cheese for centuries. Chaource and hearty Époisses also melt in your mouth—as do Bleu de Bresse and Meursault. Meat and poultry are often served in rich, wine-base sauces.

Heavenly Mansions
From the sober splendor of well-preserved Fontenay to the majestic ruins of Cluny and the isolated remains of Pontigny and Clairvaux, the abbeys, basilicas, and cathedrals of Burgundy evoke the region's storied past. Reminders of medieval religious luminaries—notably Thomas à Becket and Bernard of Clairvaux—are everywhere, laying a mantle of history over the region. Many of the region's greatest structures were built in the Romanesque style (11th–12th centuries) rather than the Gothic (13th–15th centuries) often prevalent elsewhere in France.

Rich Wines, Rich Past Some prefer Bordeaux, others insist that Burgundy is an oenophile's nirvana, to be accorded religious reverence. Indeed, this used to be literally the case, for the region's wine husbandry was perfected in large part by the great monasteries of the region, including Cluny and Cîteaux; the Cistercians founded the Clos de Vougeot, a great favorite of the 17th-century writer and gourmand Rabelais. The first evidence of vineyards in Cluny dates from 330 BC. Centuries later, during the Holy Roman Empire, nobility often gave vineyards to the church. The monks tasted and analyzed the wines and recorded the nuances of the different plots of land. Detailed maps were drawn, indicating the temperatures and miniclimates of the plots. The term *clos* (an ancient word for climate) comes from the names given these climates by the monks.

Each part of Burgundy produces wine of distinctive quality: Chablis (steely white wine), Côte de Nuits (rich and full-flavored red wine), Côte de Beaune (delicately flavored red and white wines), Côte Chalonnaise (whites and full-flavored reds), Irancy (earthy reds), St-Bris (flinty whites), Pouilly-Fuissé (fruity whites). The famous vineyards south of Dijon—the Côte de Nuits and Côte de Beaune—are among the world's most distinguished and picturesque. Don't expect to unearth many bargains in the vineyards themselves, however. The best place to sample a goodly selection is in the Marché aux Vins in Beaune, a Vieille Ville clustered around the patterned-tile roofs of its medieval Hôtel-Dieu (hospital).

---

ready for harvesting, are scenting the air with anticipation. This is when the grapevines are colorful and the *caves* (wine cellars) are open for business. Many festivals also take place around this time. Note that some restaurants and hotels close down for a month or more in winter.

NORTHWEST BURGUNDY

In the Middle Ages, Sens, Auxerre, and Troyes (officially in the neighboring Champagne region), came under the sway of the Paris-based Capetian kings, who erected mighty Gothic cathedrals in those towns. Outside these major centers of northwest Burgundy, countryside villages are largely preserved and the surprisingly rural landscape seems to have remained the same for centuries. Here "life in the fast lane" is considered a reference to the Paris-bound A6 expressway. Arriving from Paris, most travelers drive southeast into Burgundy on A6 (or, as an alternative, on A5 direct to Troyes) before making a scenic clockwise loop around the Parc du Morvan.

Sens

▶ ❶ *112 km (70 mi) southeast of Paris on N6.*

It makes sense for Sens to be your first stop in Burgundy, since it's only 90 minutes by car from Paris on N6, a fast road that hugs the pretty Yonne Valley south of Fontainebleau. Historically linked more with Paris than with Burgundy, Sens was for centuries the ecclesiastical center of France and is still dominated by its **Cathédrale St-Étienne,** once the French sanctuary for Thomas à Becket and a model for England's Canterbury

Fodor'sChoice
★

Cathedral. You can see the cathedral's 240-foot south tower from a considerable distance; the highway forges straight past it. The pompous 19th-century buildings lining the narrow main street—notably the meringue-like Hôtel de Ville—can give you a false impression if you're in a hurry: the streets leading off it near the cathedral (notably rue Abelard and rue Jean-Cousin) are full of half-timber medieval houses. On Monday the cathedral square is crowded with merchants' stalls, and the beautiful late-19th-century Baltard-style market—a distant cousin of Baltard's former iron-and-glass Halles in Paris—throbs with people buying meat and produce. A smaller market is held on Friday morning.

Begun around 1140, the cathedral once had two towers; one was topped in 1532 by an elegant though somewhat incongruous Renaissance campanile that contains two monster-class bells; the other collapsed in the 19th century. Note the trefoil arches decorating the exterior of the remaining tower. The gallery, with statues of former archbishops of Sens, is a 19th-century addition, but the statue of St. Stephen, between the doors of the central portal, is thought to date from late in the 12th century. The vast, harmonious interior is justly renowned for its stained-glass windows; the oldest (circa 1200) are in the north transept and include the stories of the Samaritans and the Prodigal Son; those in the south transept were manufactured in 1500 in Troyes and include a much-admired *Tree of Jesse.* Stained-glass windows in the north of the chancel retrace the story of Thomas à Becket: Becket fled to Sens from England to escape the wrath of Henry II before returning to his cathedral in Canterbury, where he was murdered in 1170. Below the window (which shows him embarking on his journey in a boat, and also at the moment of his death) is a medieval statue of an archbishop said to have come from the site of Becket's home in Sens. Years of restoration work have permitted the display of his *aube* (vestment) in the annex to the Palais Synodal. ✉ *Pl. de la République* ☎ *03–86–64–15–27.*

The roof of the 13th-century **Palais Synodal** (Synodal Palace), alongside Sens's cathedral, is notable for its Burgundian yellow, green, and red diamond-tile motif—incongruously (and misleadingly) added in the mid-19th century by medieval monument restorer Viollet-le-Duc. Its six grand windows and vaulted Synodal Hall are outstanding architectural features; the building now functions as an exhibition space. Annexed to the Palais Synodal is an ensemble of Renaissance buildings from whose courtyard there is a fine view of the cathedral's Flamboyant Gothic south transept, constructed by master stonemason Martin Chambiges at the start of the 16th century (rose windows were his specialty, as you can appreciate here). Inside is a museum with archaeological finds from the Gallo-Roman period, including the *trésor de Villethierry,* a cache of bronze popular jewelry unearthed during the construction of the A5 highway; exceptional stelae depicting various trades; and the remains of Roman baths discovered in situ 20 years ago. The cathedral treasury, now on the museum's second floor, is one of the richest in France, comparable to that of Conques. It contains a collection of miters, ivories, the shrouds of St. Sivard and St. Loup, and sumptuous reliquaries. But

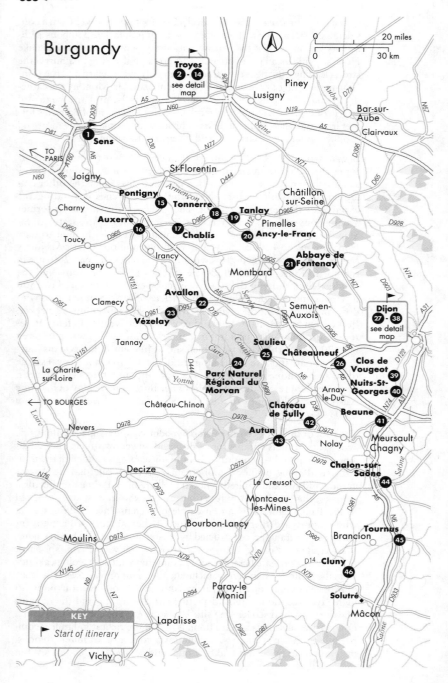

the star of the collection is Thomas à Becket's restored brown- and silver-edged linen robe. His chasuble, stole, and sandals are too fragile to display. ☎ *03–86–64–30–85* ✉ *€3* ⊙ *June–Sept., daily 10–noon and 2–6; Oct.–May, Wed. and weekends 10–noon and 2–6, Mon. and Thurs.–Fri. 2–6.*

Where to Stay & Eat

$$-$$$ ✗ **Clos des Jacobins.** With its pale orange walls and exceptional fish specialties, this restaurant in the center of town strikes a happy balance between elegant and casual. Try the €17 lunch *menu du marché,* which may include *matelotte d'oeufs pochés à l'Irancy* (poached eggs in Irancy wine sauce), and *blanc de turbot au Noilly-Prat* (turbot with dry vermouth). ⊠ *49 Grande-Rue* ☎ *03–86–95–29–70* 🖃 *AE, MC, V.*

★ $$$ ✗🖾 **La Lucarne aux Chouettes.** There's nothing Hollywoodesque about actress Leslie Caron's charmingly rustic riverside hotel and restaurant, the "Owl's Nest," set in four 17th-century buildings. The lovely whitewash-brick dining room, with its ingenious twisted rope chandeliers, has a homey-meets-elegant feel, as do the rooms: "The Loft" is an enormous wood-beamed aerie atop the house (the bathroom is in the room itself, just as it was in the rip-roaring days of the 1680s), while "The Suite" glows with a portrait of Sarah Bernhardt. The legendary hostess (the beloved Lili-Gigi-Fanny of everyone's memories) is often on hand to extend a warm greeting, although she does still depart for rare film shoots. In summer enjoy the terrace over the Yonne. The town itself, a *bastide* (fortified town, built on a grid pattern), is entered and exited via sturdy, angular 13th- and 14th-century gateways. ⊠ *7 quai Bretoche, 12 km (7 mi) south of Sens on N6, 89500 Villeneuve-sur-Yonne* ☎ *03–86–87–18–26* 🖹 *03–86–87–22–63* ⊕ *www.lesliecaron-auberge.com* ⇌ *4 rooms* ᘒ *Restaurant, cable TV; no a/c* 🖃 *AE, MC, V* ⅇ *EP.*

$$ ✗🖾 **Hôtel de Paris et de la Poste.** Owned for the last several decades by the Godart family, the modernized Paris & Poste, which began life as a posthouse in the 1700s, is a convenient and pleasant stopping point. Rooms are clean, spacious and well equipped; most open onto a patio (No. 42 is especially nice). But it's the traditional red-and-gold restaurant (with great home-smoked salmon), padded, green leather armchairs in the lounge, and the little curved wooden bar that give this place its comfy charm. Better, the dishes of chef-owner Phillipe Godard exhibit real flair. ⊠ *97 rue de la République, 89100* ☎ *03–86–65–17–43* 🖹 *03–86–64–48–45* ⊕ *www.hotel-paris-poste.com* ⇌ *25 rooms* ᘒ *Restaurant, cable TV, free parking; no a/c in some rooms* 🖃 *AE, DC, MC, V* ⅇ *EP.*

★ $$$ 🖾 **Château de Prunoy.** Though it's a little out of the way, this château and park—built by one of Louix XVI's finance ministers—is spectacular enough to be worth the trip. Grand public rooms are a stylish blend of Louis Seize gilt-trimmed antiques and grandmother's knick-knackery, although many of the guest rooms seem to be the suave result of an elegant decorator (but do avoid the one designed as a Japanese teahouse). Quirky flea-market finds help make it all very *chez soi,* right down to the presence of the owner's friendly Labradors. Dinner is not especially grand but the dining salon itself is country-adorable. ⊠ *40* *km (25 mi) southwest of Sens, 40 km (25 mi) northwest of Auxerre on N6 to D943 to D18, 89120 Prunoy* ☎ *03–86–63–66–91* 🖨 *03–86–63–77–79* ⊕ *www.chateaudeprunoy.com* ⇲ *19 rooms, 4 suites* ⅄ *Restaurant, tennis court, pool, gym, sauna; no a/c* ▤ *AE, DC, MC, V* ❴◑ *EP.*

Nightlife & the Arts

Sens is known throughout France for **Les Synodales,** an annual dance festival held in late June and July, which headlines distinguished dancers and other artists from around the world. Events are held in front of the cathedral and in surrounding streets; contact the tourist office for information.

Troyes

★ ☞   *64 km (40 mi) east of Sens, 150 km (95 mi) southeast of Paris.*

The inhabitants of Troyes would be dismayed if you mistook them for Burgundians. Troyes is the historic capital of the counts of Champagne; as if to prove the point, its historic town center is shaped like a champagne cork, the part corresponding to the rounded top enclosed by a loop of the Seine. It was also the home of the late-12th-century writer Chrétien (or Chrestien) de Troyes, who, in seeking to please his patrons Count Henry the Liberal and Marie de Champagne, penned the first Arthurian legends. Few, if any, other French town centers contain so much to see. A web of enchanting pedestrian streets with timber-frame houses, magnificent churches, fine museums, and a wide choice of restaurants make the Old Town—Vieux Troyes—especially appealing. The center of Troyes is divided by the boulevard Dampierre, a broad, busy thoroughfare. On one side is the quiet cathedral quarter, on the other the more upbeat commercial part. Modern development and several major fires have removed large chunks of this area of Troyes—so brace yourself for the '70s concrete of the Quartier du 14 Juillet, intersected by the boulevard of the same name.

Keep your eyes peeled, instead, for the delightful architectural accents that make Troyes unique: *essentes,* geometric chestnut tiles that keep out humidity and are fire resistant; and sculpted *poteaux* (in Troyes they are called *montjoies*), carvings at the joint of corner structural beams. There's a lovely one of Adam and Eve next door to the Comtes de Champagne hotel. Along with its neighbors Provins and Bar-sur-Aube, Troyes was one of Champagne's major fair towns in the Middle Ages. The wool trade gave way to cotton in the 18th century, and today Troyes draws busloads of shoppers from all over Europe to scour for bargains at its outlet clothing stores.

The **tourist office** (✉ 16 bd. Carnot ☎ 03–25–82–62–70 ⊕ www.ot-troyes. fr) has information and sells museum passes that admit you to the four major museums for €12.

Although Troyes is on the Seine, it's the capital of the Aube *département* (province) administered from the elegant **Préfecture** behind its gleaming gilt-iron railings.

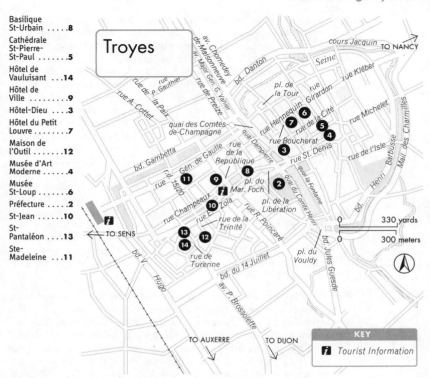

3 Across the Bassin de la Préfecture, an arm of the Seine, is the **Hôtel-Dieu** (hospital), fronted by superb 18th-century wrought-iron gates topped with the blue-and-gold fleurs-de-lis emblems of the French monarchy. Around the corner is the entrance to the **Apothicairie de l'Hôtel-Dieu,** a former medical laboratory, the only part of the Hôtel-Dieu open to visitors. Inside, time has been suspended: floral-painted boxes and ceramic jars containing medicinal plants line the antique shelves. ⊠ *Quai des Comtes-de-Champagne* ☎ *03–25–80–98–97* ⊑ *€2* ☉ *July and Aug., Wed.–Mon. 10–6; Sept.–June, Wed. and weekends 10–noon and 1:30–5:45.*

4 The **Musée d'Art Moderne** (Modern Art Museum) is housed in the 16th- to 17th-century former bishop's palace. Its magnificent interior, with a wreath-and-cornucopia carved oak fireplace, ceilings with carved wood beams, and a Renaissance staircase, now contains the Lévy Collection of modern art—including an important group of works by André Derain and other Fauves. In the back are formal gardens. ⊠ *Palais Épiscopal, pl. St-Pierre* ☎ *03–25–76–26–80* ⊑ *€5* ☉ *Tues.–Sun. 11–6.*

Noted monument of Flamboyant Gothic—a style now regarded as the **5** last gasp of the Middle Ages—the **Cathédrale St-Pierre–St-Paul** dominates the heart of Troyes; note the incomplete single-tower west front, the small

Renaissance campaniles on top of the tower, and the artistry of Martin Chambiges, who worked on Troyes's facade (with its characteristic large rose window) around the same time as he did the transept of Sens. At night the floodlit features burst into dramatic relief. The cathedral's vast five-aisle interior, refreshingly light thanks to large windows and the near-whiteness of the local stone, dates mainly from the 13th century. It has fine examples of 13th-century stained glass in the choir, such as the *Tree of Jesse* (a popular regional theme), and richly colored 16th-century glass in the nave and west front rose window. The choir stalls and organ were requisitioned from Clairvaux Abbey. One of the chapels contains black-basalt tombstones marking the remains of Count Henry I of Champagne, carved in 1792 after the count's palace was destroyed, and the cathedral treasury displays such curiosities as a piece of St. Bernard of Clairvaux's skull. The arcaded triforium above the pillars of the choir was one of the first in France to be glazed rather than filled with stone. Across the street from the cathedral, behind an iron fence, is an unusual, lopsided, late-medieval **grange aux dîmes** (tithe barn) with a peaked roof. It is used as a warehouse by the wine maker next door. ✉ *Pl. St-Pierre* ☎ *03–25–76–98–18* 🎟 *Free* ☉ *July–mid-Sept., daily 9–1 and 2–7; mid-Sept.–Feb., daily 10–noon and 2–4; Mar.–June, daily 10–noon and 2–5.*

⑥ Facing the cathedral square, the buildings of the former Abbaye St-Loup now house the **Musée St-Loup,** an arts and antiquities museum. Exhibits are devoted to natural history, with impressive collections of birds and meteorites; local archaeological finds, especially gold-mounted 5th-century jewelry and a Gallo-Roman bronze statue of Apollo; medieval statuary and gargoyles; and paintings from the 15th to 19th centuries, including works by Rubens, Anthony Van Dyck, Antoine Watteau, François Boucher, and Jacques-Louis David. ✉ *1 rue Chrestien-de-Troyes* ☎ *03–25–76–21–68* 🎟 *€4* ☉ *Sept.–June, Wed.–Mon. 10–noon and 2–6; July and Aug., Wed.–Mon. 10–noon and 2–7.*

⑦ The **Hôtel du Petit Louvre** (✉ Rue Boucherat) is a handsome, 16th-century former coaching inn.

★ ⑧ The **Basilique St-Urbain** was built between 1262 and 1286 by Pope Urban IV, who was born in Troyes. St-Urbain is one of the most remarkable churches in France, a perfect culmination of the Gothic quest to replace stone walls with stained glass. Its narrow porch frames a 13th-century *Last Judgment* tympanum, whose highly worked elements include a frieze of the dead rising out of their coffins (note the grimacing skeleton) and an enormous crayfish, a testament to the local river culture. Inside, a chapel on the south side houses the *Vièrge au Raisin* (*Virgin with Grapes*), clutching Jesus with one hand and a bunch of Champagne grapes in the other. ✉ *Pl. Vernier* ☎ *03–25–73–37–13* 🎟 *Free* ☉ *July and Aug., daily 10:30–7; 1st 2 wks in Sept., daily 10:30–5; mid-Sept.–June, daily 10–noon and 2–4.*

⑨ Place du Maréchal-Foch, the main square of central Troyes, is flanked by cafés, shops, and the delightful facade of the **Hôtel de Ville** (Town Hall). In summer the square is filled with people from morning to night.

⑩ The clock tower of the church of **St-Jean** is an unmistakable landmark. England's warrior king Henry V married Catherine of France here in 1420. The church's tall 16th-century choir contrasts with the low nave, constructed earlier. ⊠ *Pl. du Marché au Pain* ☎ *03–25–73–06–96* ▨ *Free* ⊙ *July and Aug., daily 10:30–7; 1st 2 wks in Sept., daily 10:30–5; mid-Sept.–June, daily 10–noon and 2–4.*

⑪ **Ste-Madeleine,** the oldest church in Troyes, is best known for its elaborate triple-arched stone rood screen separating the nave and the choir. Only six other such screens still remain in France—most were dismantled during the French Revolution. This filigreed Flamboyant Gothic beauty was carved with panache by Jean Gailde between 1508 and 1517. ⊠ *Rue de la Madeleine* ☎ *03–25–73–82–90* ▨ *Free* ⊙ *July and Aug., daily 10:30–7; 1st 2 wks in Sept., daily 10:30–5; mid-Sept.–June, daily 10–noon and 2–4.*

⟳ ⑫ There's a practical reason why the windows of the **Maison de l'Outil** (Tool and Craft Museum) are filled with bizarre and beautiful outsize models—like a winding staircase and a globe on a swivel. It's the display venue for the "final projects" created by apprentice Compagnons de Devoir, members of the national craftsmen's guild whose school is in Troyes. The museum, in the 16th-century Hôtel de Mauroy, also contains a collection of paintings, models, and tools relevant to such traditional wood-related trades as carpentry, clog making, and barrel making—including a medieval anvil, called a *bigorne.* ⊠ *7 rue de la Trinité* ☎ *03–25–73–28–26* ▨ *€6.50* ⊙ *Daily 10–6.*

⑬ The 16th- to 18th-century church of **St-Pantaléon** primarily serves the local Polish community. A number of fine canopied stone statues, many of them the work of the Troyen Dominique le Florentin, decorator to François I, are clustered around its pillars. ⊠ *Rue de Turenne* ☎ *03–25–73–06–99* ▨ *Free* ⊙ *July and Aug., daily 10:30–12:30 and 2:30–6:30; 1st 2 wks in Sept., daily 10:30–12:30 and 2:30–5:30; mid-Sept.–June, daily 10–noon and 2–4.*

⟳ ⑭ The 16th- to 17th-century **Hôtel de Vauluisant** houses two museums: the **Musée Historique** (History Museum) and the **Musée de la Bonneterie** (Textile Museum). The former traces the development of Troyes and southern Champagne, with a section devoted to religious art; the latter outlines the history and manufacturing procedures of the town's 18th- to 19th-century textile industry. ⊠ *4 rue Vauluisant* ☎ *03–25–42–33–33* ▨ *Joint ticket for both museums €5* ⊙ *Sept.–June, Wed.–Sun. 10–noon and 2–6; July and Aug., Wed.–Mon. 10–6.*

Where to Stay & Eat

The pleasure of Troyes is its Vieille Ville, Vieux Troyes. This is where you want your hotel to be—or at least within walking distance of it. If you want to dine informally, it's also the area to find a restaurant, especially along rue Champeaux.

$$–$$$ ✕ **Vivien.** Despite the subdued elegance of the airy modern dining-room, with its padded wooden chairs and crisp white tablecloths, many diners at this friendly restaurant prefer to eat outside, on the terrace overlooking the leafy pedestrian square beside St-Rémy's church. Although chef Jean-Michel Jadot counts venison in grape juice, and bacon, pea and potato flan among his specialties, he is best known for his fish and seafood dishes, like fried pike-perch, or prawns and scallops flambéed in brandy. Prix-fixe menus at €18, €28, and €38 offer three, four, or five delicious courses respectively. ☒ *7 pl. St-Rémy* ☎ *03–25–73–70–70* ⌕ *Reservations essential* ▤ *AE, MC, V* ☯ *Closed Mon. and second half Sept. No dinner Sun.*

¢–$ ✕ **La Taverne de l'Ours.** This popular, convivial brasserie has faux Art Nouveau and neo-Gothic furbelows, brass globe lamps, and plushy seating alcoves. It also has delicious, hearty cuisine, such as roast *cochon de lait* (suckling pig) straight off the spit. The €11 lunch menu is a real bargain, and even tastier when accompanied with the grapey, dark pink rosé *des Riceys* from the Champagne–Burgundy border. Happily, this place is open year-round. ☒ *2 rue Champeaux* ☎ *03–25–73–22–18* ▤ *AE, MC, V.*

★ $$–$$$ ▦ **Le Champ des Oiseaux.** "There are places like moments; those which permanently imprint memories," lyrically declaims the Web site for this *chic et charmant* treasure. Le Champ delightfully comes through on that promise. Idyllically situated in ancient Troyes and named after the city's centuries-old roosting haunts of storks, this ensemble of three vine-clad pink-and-yellow 15th- and 16th-century houses (their bright colors are part of a town campaign to "medievalize" half-timber facades) seem ready to receive Manon Lescaut on the run. A daub-and-wattle facade abuzz with the pattern of timbered logs and a storybook courtyard, graced with a fairy-tale staircase, overhanging porch, and cobblestone patio, all set the scene for the charm within. Tin chandeliers, Nantes silks and calico hangings, 15th-century scrollwork panels, beamed roofs right out of the *Return of Martin Guerre,* and more traditional luxe touches make the interiors a joy. The guest salon is set in a vaulted cave-wine cellar fitted out with the latest in soigné furniture. The biggest guest room, the Suite Médiévale, is under the oak-beam eaves, while the Salle Bleu (Blue Room) looks worthy of the cover of *Maison Française.* Downstairs is a lovely breakfast room with a stone fireplace. ☒ *20 rue Linard Gonthier, 10000* ☎ *03–25–80–58–50* 🖷 *03–25–80–98–34* ⊕ *www. champdesoiseaux.com* ⤳ *9 rooms, 3 suites* ⌕ *Cable TV, Internet; no a/c* ▤ *AE, MC, V* ☯ *EP.*

$$ ▦ **Relais St-Jean.** This calm half-timber hotel, in the pedestrian zone near the church of St-Jean, has fully equipped, good-size rooms—some connected by a path running through the second floor's tree-filled atrium. Black-leather chairs and mirrored walls in the bar contrast rudely with the wicker and plants of an adjoining room. But have a drink here, and good-natured owner Monsieur Rinaldi will gladly stop to chat. The hotel has no restaurant, but just along the street is the friendly **Valentino** (☒ *35 rue Paillot-de-Montabert* ☎ *03–25–73–14–14*), which has dining in its courtyard. ☒ *49 rue Paillot-de-Montabert, 10000* ☎ *03–25–73–89–90* 🖷 *03–25–73–88–60* ⤳ *25 rooms* ⌕ *Minibars, bar, Internet* ▤ *AE, DC, MC, V* ☯ *Closed mid-Dec.–early Jan.* ▥ *EP.*

¢ ▦ **Comtes de Champagne.** In Vieux Troyes's former mint is this bargain hotel. The topsy-turvy 12th-century building, with its solid, squat staircase and faded floral wallpaper, has a quaint inner courtyard with large vines and a philodendron. The two couples who co-manage, the Gribourets and the Picards, are friendly folk. ☒ *56 rue de la Monnaie, 10000* ☎ *03–25–73–11–70* ⌂ *03–25–73–06–02* ⇆ *35 rooms, 5 with bath* ⊟ *MC, V* ⏍ *EP.*

Shopping

If there's an ideal place for a shopping spree, it's Troyes. Many clothing manufacturers are just outside town, clustered together in two large suburban malls: **Marques Avenue,** in St-Julien-les-Villas (take N71 toward Dijon); and **Marques City** and the American outlet store **McArthur Glen,** in Pont-Ste-Marie (take N77 toward Chalons-sur-Marne). Ralph Lauren and Calvin Klein at McArthur Glen face off with Laura Ashley at Marques Avenue and Doc Martens at Marques City, to name a few of the shops. The malls are open Monday 2–7, Tuesday–Friday 10–7, and Saturday 9:30–7.

off the beaten path

CLAIRVAUX – Although much of it has been replaced by a sprawling 19th-century prison, the Abbaye de Clairvaux, 64 km (40 mi) east of Troyes via N19, was once the Cistercian mother abbey of Champagne and northern Burgundy. St. Bernard, a native of Fontaine-les-Dijon, founded Clairvaux (meaning "bright valley") only two years after his entry into Cîteaux, in 1115, and three years before establishing the community of Fontenay, in 1118. Subsequently known as Bernard of Clairvaux, he went on to condemn the behavior of Pierre Abélard, preach the Second Crusade in Vézelay, and decry the lavish pomp of Cluny. The 12th-century vaulted halls of the lay brothers' dormitory remain, as do parts of the once-flourishing 18th-century abbey. ☒ *Off N19, watch for signs* ☎ *03–25–27–88–17* ☉ *May–Oct., Sat. only. Guided tours at 2, 3, 4, and 5* ☞ *Bring I.D.*

Pontigny

🔟 *60 km (37 mi) south of Troyes, 56 km (35 mi) southeast of Sens.*

The town of Pontigny can easily be mistaken for another drowsy, dusty village, but its once proud **Abbaye de Pontigny** is as large as many cathedrals. In the 12th and 13th centuries it sheltered three archbishops of Canterbury, including St. Thomas à Becket (from 1164 to 1166). His path to refuge from the king of England was followed by his successor, Stephen Langton (here from 1207 to 1215), and, lastly, Edmund of Abingdon—whose body, naturally mummified in the years following his death in 1240, has been venerated (as St. Edmund) by centuries of English pilgrims to Pontigny. His Baroque tomb, whose occupant is supposedly very much intact, can be seen at the rear of the church, although peeking through one of the openings is now strictly forbidden. The abbey was founded in 1114, and the current church finished around 1150. By Burgundian standards the church and lay brothers' quarters (all that remain) were precociously Gothic—the first buildings in the region to have rib vaults. Inside, note the beautiful, late-17th-century Baroque choir stalls, carved with garlands and angels. On the grassy lawn next to the church is a large, plate-shape 12th-century **fountain** with 31 spigots and sculpted Gothic feet—one of the few functioning medieval abbey fountains remaining in Europe. ☎ *03–86–47–54–99* ⛛ *Free, €3.50 for guided tour* ☉ *June–Oct., daily 9–7; Nov.–May, daily 10–5, except during services.*

Auxerre

⑯

21 km (13 mi) southwest of Pontigny, 58 km (36 mi) southeast of Sens.

Auxerre is a beautifully laid-out town with three imposing and elegant churches perched above the Yonne River. Its steep, undulating streets are full of massively photogenic, half-timber houses in every imaginable style and shape and, as late-medieval towns go, it is much more harmonious and architecturally interesting than most. Yet Auxerre is underappreciated, perhaps because of its location, midway between Paris and Dijon.

Fanning out from Auxerre's main square, **place des Cordeliers** (just up from the cathedral), are a number of venerable, crooked, steep streets lined with half-timber and stone houses. The best way to see them is to start from the riverside on the quai de la République, where you find the tourist office (and can pick up a handy local map), and continue along the quai de la Marine. The medieval arcaded gallery of the **Ancien Evêché** (Old Bishop's Palace), now an administrative building, is just visible on the hillside beside the tourist office. At **9 rue de la Marine** (which leads off one of several riverside squares) are the two oldest houses in Auxerre, dating from the end of the 14th century. Continue up the hill to rue de l'Yonne, which leads into the **rue Cochois.** Here, at No. 23, is the appropriately topsy-turvy home and shop of a *maître verrier* (lead-glass maker). Closer to the center of town, the most beautiful of Auxerre's many *poteaux* (the carved tops of wooden corner posts) can be seen at **8 rue Joubert:** the building dates from the late 15th century and its Gothic tracery windows, acorns, and oak leaves are an open-air masterpiece.

The town's dominant feature is the ascending line of three magnificent churches—St-Pierre, St-Étienne, and St-Germain—and the **Cathédrale St-Étienne,** in the middle, rising majestically above the squat houses around it. The 13th-century choir, the oldest part of the edifice, contains its original stained glass, dominated by brilliant reds and blues. Beneath the choir, the frescoed 11th-century Romanesque crypt keeps company with the treasury, which has a panoply of medieval enamels, manuscripts, and miniatures. A 75-minute son-et-lumière show focusing on Roman Gaul is presented every evening from June to September. ⛛ *Pl. St-Étienne* ☎ *03–86–52–31–68* ⛛ *Crypt and treasury €2 each; €4 Passport ticket allows entry to crypt and treasury plus St-Germain* ☉ *Easter–Nov., Mon.–Sat. 9–noon and 2–6, Sun. 2–6.*

North of place des Cordeliers is the former **Abbaye de St-Germain,** which stands parallel to the cathedral some 300 yards away. The church's earliest aboveground section is the 12th-century Romanesque bell tower, but the extensive underground crypt was inaugurated by Charles the Bald in 859 and contains its original Carolingian frescoes and Ionic capitals. It's the only monument of its kind in Europe—a labyrinth retaining the plan of the long-gone church built above it—and was a place of pilgrimage until Huguenots burned the remains of its namesake, a Gallo-Roman governor and bishop of Auxerre, in the 16th century. Several hundred years of veneration had already seen the burial of 33 bishops of Auxerre as close to the central tomb of St-Germain as they could physically get. The frescoes are a testimony to the brief artistic sophistication of the Carolingian Renaissance: witness St. Stephen running from a stone-hurling crowd toward the disembodied hand of God, a date-bearing palm tree, and the reversed images of a young bishop and an old one teaching each other. ⊠ *Pl. St-Germain* 🕾 *03–86–51–09–74* 🖭 €*4* 🕙 *Guided tours of crypt Oct.–Apr., daily 10, 11, and 2–5; May–Sept., daily every ½ hr between 10 and 5:30.*

Where to Stay & Eat

$$–$$$ ✕ **La Chamaille.** This restaurant is remarkably low-key for its culinary aspirations. The mood is set by a babbling brook running through the garden and the exposed brick walls in the dining room. Try the rabbit in a rich brown sauce and pastry. You'll be hard-pressed to find room for the apple flan, but you must—it's delectable. Prices are reasonable, especially for the four-course menu, which includes a half bottle of regional wine, for €32. ⊠ *4 rte. de Boiloup, 10 km (6 mi) south of Auxerre, Chevannes* 🕾 *03–86–41–24–80* 🍽 *Reservations essential* 🖃 *AE, MC, V* 🕙 *Closed Mon. and Tues.*

$$–$$$ ✕ **Le Jardin Gourmand.** As its name implies, this restaurant in a former manor house has a pretty garden (*jardin*) where you can eat in summer. The interior is accented by sea-green and yellow panels and is equally congenial and elegant. Terrine of pheasant breast is a specialty, and hope that the superb snails with barley and chanterelles is available. The staff is discreet and friendly. ⊠ *56 bd. Vauban* 🕾 *03–86–51–53–52* 🖃 *AE, MC, V* 🕙 *Closed Mon.*

★ $ 🏨 **Château de Ribourdin.** Retired farmer Claude Brodard began building his *chambres d'hôtes* (bed-and-breakfast) in an old stable six years ago, and the result is cozy, comfortable, and reasonably priced. Château de la Borde is the smallest, sunniest, and most intimate room; all overlook Monsieur Brodard's fields. Homemade preserves—cassis, quince, and carrot—are served at breakfast. ⊠ *8 rte. de Ribourdin, 8 km (5 mi) southwest of Auxerre on D1, 89240 Chevannes* 🕾 *03–86–41–23–16* 🛏 *5 rooms* 🏊 *Pool; no a/c, no room phones, no room TVs* 🖃 *No credit cards* 🍽 *BP.*

$ 🏨 **Normandie.** Set in a rather grand 19th-century mansion, the vine-covered Normandie is in the center of Auxerre, just a short walk from the cathedral. Rooms are unpretentious and clean. There's a billiard room, and the terrace is a nice place to relax after a long day of sightseeing. ⊠ *41 bd. Vauban, 89000* 🕾 *03–86–52–57–80* 🖷 *03–86–51–54–33* 🌐 *www.hotelnormandie.fr* 🛏 *47 rooms* 🏋 *Gym, sauna, bar; no a/c, no room phones, no room TVs* 🖃 *AE, DC, MC, V* 🍽 *EP.*

Chablis

⑰   *16 km (10 mi) east of Auxerre.*

The pretty village of Chablis nestles amid the towering vineyards that produce its famous white wine on the banks of the River Serein and is protected, perhaps from an ill wind, by the massive, round, turreted towers of the Porte Noël gateway. Although in America Chablis has become a generic name for cheap white wine, it's not so in France: there it's a sharp, slightly acacia-tasting wine of tremendous character, with the Premier Cru and Grand Cru wines standing head to head with the best French whites. Prices in the local shops tend to be inflated, so your best bet is to buy directly from a vineyard; keep in mind that most are closed Sunday. The town's **Maison de la Vigne et du Vin** can provide information on nearby cellars where you can take tours and taste wine. ⊠ *28 rue Auxerroise* ☎ *03–86–42–42–22.*

Where to Stay & Eat

★ **$–$$**   ✕▦ **L'Hostellerie des Clos.** The moderately priced, simple yet comfortable rooms at this inn have floral curtains and wicker tables with chairs. But most of all, come here for chef Michel Vignaud's cooking, some of the best in the region. ⊠ *18 rue Jules-Rathier, 89800* ☎ *03–86–42–10–63* 🖷 *03–86–42–17–11* ⊕ *www.hostellerie-des-clos.fr* ↩ *26 rooms, 10 suites* ⚘ *Restaurant, minibars, cable TV, sauna, Internet* ⊟ *AE, MC, V* ⊘ *Closed late Dec.–mid-Jan.* ¶⊙¶ *MAP.*

Tonnerre

⑱   *16 km (10 mi) northeast of Chablis.*

Although its name means "thunder," the tiny town of Tonnerre is better known for its quiet streets and views. It was mostly rebuilt after a devastating fire in 1556. A good spot from which to survey the 16th-century reconstruction and the Armançon Valley is the terrace of the church of **St-Pierre.** The town's chief attraction, the high-roof **Ancien Hôpital,** or Hôtel-Dieu (hospital), was built in 1293 and has survived the passing centuries—flames and all—largely intact. The main room, the **Grande Salle,** is 280 feet long and retains its oak ceiling; it was designed as the hospital ward and after 1650 served as the parish church. The original hospital church leads off from the Grande Salle; in the adjoining **Chapelle du Revestière,** a dramatic 15th-century stone group represents the *Entombment of Christ.* ⊠ *Rue du Prieuré* ☎ *03–86–55–15–54* ▦ *€4* ⊙ *June–Sept., Wed.–Mon. 10–noon and 1:30–6:30; Apr., May, Oct., and Nov., weekends 1:30–6:30.*

Tanlay

⑲   *10 km (6 mi) east of Tonnerre.*

Fodor's Choice   A masterpiece of the French Early Baroque, the **Château de Tanlay,** built
★   around 1550, is a miraculous survivor due to the fact, unlike most aristos who fled the countryside to take up the royal summons to live at Versailles, the Marquis and Marquise de Tanlay opted to live here among their village retainers. Spectacularly adorned with rusticated obelisks, pago-

dalike towers, the finest in French Classicist ornament, and a "grand canal," the château is centered around a typical *cour d'honneur*. Inside, the Hall of Caesars vestibule, framed by wrought-iron railings, leads to a wood-panel salon and dining room filled with period furniture. A graceful staircase climbs to the second floor, which has the showstopper—a gigantic gallery frescoed in Italianate trompe l'oeil. A small room in the tower above was used as a secret meeting-place by Huguenot Protestants during the 1562–98 Wars of Religion; note the cupola with its fresco of scantily clad 16th-century religious personalities. ☎ 03–86–75–70–61 ⊕ *www. chateaudetanlay.com* ✉ *Guided tours €7; grounds only €2* ◷ *Apr.–Nov. 15, Wed.–Mon. 9:30–11:30 and 2:15–5:15.*

Where to Stay

¢ ▦ **Hôtel Poste.** Set in the lovely hilltop farming village of Cruzy-le-Chatel, 12 km (7 mi) from Tanlay, this inn comes with its own walled garden. Rooms are large and filled with family furnishings; beds sag a little. Nonetheless, the rooms are good value for the money, especially the one at the end of the hall, whose exposed timbers and cross beams form a sort of loft. ✉ *30 rue de la Ville, 89740 Cruzy-le-Chatel* ☎ *03–86–75–23–27* ⌨ *4 rooms, 2 with bath* ▭ *No credit cards* ⍾ *BP.*

Ancy-le-Franc

㉑ *14 km (9 mi) southeast of Tanlay.*

It may be strange to find a textbook example of the Italian Renaissance in Ancy-le-Franc but in mid-16th-century France the court had taken up this import as the latest rage. So, quick to follow the fashion and gain kingly favor, the Comte de Tonnerre decided to create a family seat using all the artists François I (1515–47) had imported from Italy to his court at Fontainebleau. Built from Sebastiano Serlio's designs, with interior blandishments by Primaticcio, the **Château d'Ancy-le-Franc** is an important example of Italianism, with a plain, majestic exterior heavy with a sense of horizontality. Inside are sumptuous rooms and apartments, many—particularly the magnificent Chambre des Arts (Art Gallery)—with carved or painted walls and ceilings and original furnishings. Here, Niccolo dell'Abate and other court artists created rooms filled with murals, depicting the signs of the zodiac, the Battle of Pharsala, and the motif of Diana in Her Bath (much favored by Diane de Potiers, sister of the Comtesse de Tonnerre)—some of the finest examples of French Mannerism. Such grandeur won the approval of the Sun King, Louis XIV, no less, who once stayed in the Salon Bleu (Blue Room). Adjoining the château is a small **Musée de l'Automobile** (automobile museum). ✉ *Pl. Clermont-Tonnerre* ☎ *03–86–75–00–25* ⊕ *www.chateau-ancy.com* ✉ *Château and museum €7; museum only €3* ◷ *Early Apr.–mid-Nov., guided château tours at 10, 11, 2, 3, 4, 5, and 6; last one at 5 mid-Sept.–mid-Nov.*

FodorśChoice
★

Abbaye de Fontenay

㉑ *32 km (20 mi) southeast of Ancy-le-Franc.*

FodorśChoice
★

The best-preserved of the Cistercian abbeys, the Abbaye de Fontenay, was founded in 1118 by St. Bernard. The same Cistercian criteria applied to Fontenay as to Pontigny: no-frills architecture and an isolated site—the spot was especially remote, for it had been decreed that these monasteries could not be established anywhere near "cities, feudal manors, or villages." The monks were required to live a completely self-sufficient existence, with no contact whatsoever with the outside world. By the end of the 12th century the buildings were finished, and the abbey's community grew to some 300 monks. Under the protection of Pope Gregory IX and Hughes IV, duke of Burgundy, the monastery soon controlled huge land holdings, vineyards, and timberlands. It prospered until the 16th century, when religious wars and administrative mayhem hastened its decline. Dissolved during the French Revolution, the abbey was used as a paper factory until 1906. Fortunately, the historic buildings emerged unscathed. The abbey is surrounded by extensive gardens dotted with the fountains that gave it its name. The church's solemn interior is lightened by windows in the facade and by a double row of three narrow windows, representing the Trinity, in the choir. A staircase in the south transept leads to the wood-roofed dormitory (spare a thought for the bleary-eyed monks, obliged to stagger down for services in the dead of night). The chapter house, flanked by a majestic arcade, and the scriptorium, where monks worked on their manuscripts, lead off from the adjoining cloisters. ⊠ *Marmagne* ☎ *03–80–92–15–00* ⊕ *www.abbayedefontenay.com* ⊠ *€8.50* ⊘ *Daily 10–noon and 2–5.*

Avallon

㉒ *44 km (28 mi) southwest of the Abbaye de Fontenay.*

Avallon is on a spectacular promontory jutting over the Vallée du Cousin. Its old streets and ramparts are pleasant places to stroll, and its medieval market-town ambience is appealing. It has enough cafés, bars, and shops to seem lively, yet it's small enough that you can quickly become familiar with it and turn it into your base for exploring the rest of the region. The main sight to see in town is the work of Romanesque stone carvers whose imaginations ran riot on the portals and 15th-century belfry of the venerable church of **St-Lazare**.

Where to Stay & Eat

★ ¢–$ ✕ **Relais des Gourmets.** You can no longer stay at the former Hôtel de Paris, which dates from the days when Avallon was a stopping-off point for stagecoaches, but you can still get a great meal at a reasonable price. This is the liveliest restaurant in Avallon, with excellent regionally inspired cuisine and an especially attractive patio in summer. The €16 menu, with wine, is a sumptuous steal. ⊠ *47 rue de Paris* ☎ *03–86–34–18–90* ⊟ *AE, MC, V* ⊘ *Closed Sun. night and Mon.*

$–$$ ✕▦ **Moulin des Ruats.** Once an old flour mill, the Moulin des Ruats became a family hotel in 1924 and is now a comfortable country inn run by twinkle-toe Claude-François Rossi. Guest rooms are pretty country-French in style; some have balconies overlooking the Cousin River. Ask for one that has been renovated; No. 11, for instance, with its exposed beams and a cozy alcove. The restaurant, fronting the river, serves traditional Burgundian fare with a strong Provençal accent. Be forewarned that dishes can be uneven: you're better off choosing simple rather than complex preparations, although you can't go wrong with the distinctive foie gras salad. ☒ *4 km (2½ mi) southwest of Avallon, 89200 Vallée du Cousin* ☎ *03–86–34–97–00* 🖨 *03–86–31–65–47* ⊕ *www.hostellerie-moulin-ruats.fr* ⌨ *24 rooms, 1 suite* ⚒ *Restaurant; no a/c* ☰ *AE, DC, MC, V* ⊗ *Closed Dec. and Jan.* †◎† *MAP.*

★ $ ✕⊞ **Les Capucins.** On a peaceful square 10 minutes from the town center, this intimate hotel has rooms in a range of prices. It's better known for its lovely restaurant, however, whose mirrored walls set off the hosts' collection of painted-glass cookie jars, *seaux à biscuits,* dating from the early part of the century. The prix-fixe menus are dominated by regional fare—pike perch, snails, and the *oeufs en meurette* (eggs poached in broth and red wine). A garden makes a pleasant spot for breakfast and aperitifs, and there are small, cozy rooms for a postprandial drink. ☒ *6 av. Paul-Doumer, 89200* ☎ *03–86–34–06–52* 🖨 *03–86–34–58–47* ⌨ *8 rooms, 7 with bath* ⚒ *Restaurant; no a/c* ☰ *AE, MC, V* ⊗ *Closed Dec. and Jan.* †◎† *EP.*

Vézelay

㉓ *16 km (10 mi) west of Avallon.*

In the 11th and 12th centuries one of the most important places of pilgrimage in the Christian world, Vézelay today is a somewhat isolated, picturesque village set on a peak. Its one main street, rue St-Étienne, climbs steeply to the summit and its medieval basilica, world-famous for its Romanesque sculpture. In summer you have to leave your car at the bottom and walk up. Off-season you can drive up and look for a spot to park in the square.

It's easy to ignore this tiny village, but don't: hidden under its narrow *ruelles* (small streets) are Romanesque cellars that once sheltered pilgrims and are now opened to visitors by homeowners in summer. Sections of several houses have arches and columns dating from the 12th and 13th centuries: don't miss the hostelry across from the tourist office and, next to it, the house where Louis VII, Eleanor of Aquitaine, and the king's religious supremo Abbé Suger stayed when they came to hear St. Bernard preach the Second Crusade in 1146.

FodorśChoice ★ In the 11th and 12th centuries the celebrated **Basilique Ste-Madeleine** was one of the focal points of Christendom. Pilgrims poured in to see the relics of St. Mary Magdalene (in the crypt) before setting off on the great trek to the shrine of St. James at Santiago de Compostela, in northwest Spain. Several pivotal church declarations of the Middle Ages were made from here, including St. Bernard's preaching of the Second Crusade (which attracted a huge French following) and Thomas à Becket's excommunication of English king Henry II. By the mid-13th century the authenticity of St. Mary's relics was in doubt; others had been discovered in Provence. The basilica's decline continued until the French Revolution, when the basilica and adjoining monastery buildings were sold by the state. Only the basilica, cloister, and dormitory escaped demolition, and were falling into ruin when ace restorer Viollet-le-Duc, sent by his mentor Prosper Merimée, rode to the rescue in 1840 (he also restored the cathedrals of Laon and Amiens and Paris's Notre-Dame).

Today the UNESCO-listed basilica has recaptured much of its glory and is considered to be one of France's most prestigious Romanesque showcases. The exterior tympanum was redone by Viollet-le-Duc (have a look at the eroded original as you exit the cloister), but the narthex (circa 1150) is a Romanesque masterpiece. Note the interwoven zodiac signs and depictions of seasonal crafts along its rim, similar to those at both Troyes and Autun. The pilgrims' route around the building is indicated by the majestic flowers over the left-hand entrance, which metamorphose into full-blown blooms on the right; an annual procession is still held on July 22. Among the most beautiful scenes on the nave capitals is one of Moses grinding grain (symbolizing the Old Testament) into flour (the New Testament), which St. Paul collects in a sack.

The basilica's exterior is best seen from the leafy terrace to the right of the facade. Opposite, a vast, verdant panorama encompasses vines, lush valleys and rolling hills. In the foreground is the Flamboyant Gothic spire of St-Père-sous-Vézelay, a tiny village 3 km (2 mi) away that is the site of Marc Meneau's famed restaurant. ⊠ *Pl. de la Basilique* ☎ *03-86-33-39-50* 🖭 *Free, donation of €3 for guided visit* ⊘ *Daily 8–8, except during offices Mon.–Sat. 12:30–1:15 and 6–7, Sun. 11–12:15.*

Just 10 km (6 mi) out of Vézelay in the small town of Bazoches-du-Morvan is the **Château de Bazoches,** the former home of Maréchal de Vauban. Built in the 12th century in the form of a trapezium with four towers and a keep, the building was bought by Vauban in 1675 with the money Louis XIV awarded him for devising the parallel trenches successfully used in the siege of Maastricht. Vauban transformed the building into a fortress and created many of his military engineering designs here. These and furnishings of his day are on display. ⊠ *Bazoches-du-Morvan* ☎ *03-86-22-10-22* 🖭 *Free* ⊘ *Late Mar.–early Nov., daily 9:30–noon and 2:15–6.*

Where to Stay & Eat

¢–$ ✕ **Bougainville.** One of the few affordable restaurants in this well-heeled town is in an old house with a fireplace in the dining room and the requisite Burgundian color scheme of brown, yellow, and ocher. Philippe Guillemard presides in the kitchen, turning out such regional favorites as hare stew, crayfish, escargot ragout in chardonnay sauce, and venison with chestnuts. He has also devised a vegetarian menu—a rarity in Burgundy—with deeply satisfying dishes like terrine of Époisses cheese and artichokes. ⊠ *26 rue St-Etienne* ☎ *03–86–33–27–57* 🖃 *MC, V* ⊘ *Closed Wed. and Dec. and Jan. No dinner Tues.*

★ $$$–$$$$ ✕🖭 **L'Espérance.** Heading one of the greatest kitchens in Burgundy, chef Marc Meneau is justly renowned for his original creations, such as roast veal in a bitter caramel-based sauce and turbot in a salt-crust *croûte*. The setting—by a stream and a large, statue-filled garden with Vézelay in the background—is exquisite. Note that the restaurant is closed Tuesday mid-September through mid-June and there is no lunch Wednesday.

Accommodations, which vary in price, come in a trinity of delights: charming rooms overlooking the garden; full suites in a renovated mill by the trout stream; and rooms in the annex, the Pré des Marguerites, where rooms are done up in a cozy *style anglais*. ⊠ *St-Père-en-Vézelay 89450 St-Père* ☎ *03–86–33–39–10* 🖷 *03–86–33–26–15* ⊕ *www.marc-meneau-esperance.com* 🖎 *Reservations essential* 🗪 *44 rooms* 🕭 *Restaurant, minibars, cable TV, pool, Internet; no a/c in some rooms* 🟰 *AE, DC, MC, V* ☉ *Closed Feb.* ⌁⃝| *MAP.*

$–$$ ✕⌖ **Poste & Lion d'Or.** On a small square in the lower part of town is this old-fashioned, rambling hotel. A terrace out front welcomes you; the good-size rooms have traditional chintzes. The comfortable restaurant is a popular spot with locals, who come for the regional fare, such as roast partridge in black-currant sauce and rabbit casserole. ⊠ *Pl. du Champ de Foire, 89450* ☎ *03–86–33–21–23* 🖷 *03–86–32–30–92* 🗪 *39 rooms* 🕭 *Restaurant, bar; no a/c* 🟰 *AE, MC, V* ☉ *Closed mid-Nov.–mid-Mar.* ⌁⃝| *MAP.*

$$–$$$ ⌖ **Pontot.** With Vézelay's limited lodging you would do well to book ahead, especially for this historic fortified house with sumptuous little rooms and a lovely garden. Another advantage is the hotel's location in the center of the village halfway up the hill. ⊠ *Pl. du Pontot, 89450* ☎ *03–86–33–24–40* 🖷 *03–86–33–30–05* 🗪 *10 rooms* 🕭 *No a/c, no room TVs* 🟰 *DC, MC, V* ☉ *Closed mid-Nov.–mid-Apr.* ⌁⃝| *EP.*

The Morvan

㉔ *South of Vézelay.*

The vast **Parc du Morvan** encompasses a 3,500-square-km (1,350-square-mi) chunk of Burgundy. A network of roads and **Grandes Randonnées** (GRs, or Long Trails) winds around the park's lush forests, granite outcrops, photogenic lakes, idyllic farms, and tiny villages. Hiking in the Morvan is not strenuous, but it is enchanting: every turn down a trail provides a new idyllic scene. Numerous itineraries through the park are mapped and marked (maps for specific trails are available from local tourist offices). About 50 5- to 15-km (3- to 9-mi) routes are good for day hikes; another 10 or so trails of around 110 km (68 mi) each are good for much longer walks.

Quarré-les-Tombes, one of the prettiest villages peppering the park, is so named because of the empty prehistoric stone tombs eerily arrayed in a ring around its church. Eight kilometers (5 mi) south of Quarré-les-Tombes is the **Rocher de la Pérouse,** a mighty rocky outcrop worth scrambling up for a view of the park and the Cure and Cousin valleys.

Some 25 **gîtes d'étapes** (☎ 03–86–78–74–93 reservations) (simple bed-and-breakfasts, also known as *chambres d'hôtes*) en route provide for overnight stays. Twenty-one gîtes have facilities for you and your horse to stay overnight. For the pamphlet "Le Morvan à Cheval," which lists stables and gîtes for overnight accommodations, contact the **Parc Naturel Régional du Morvan** (⊠ Maison du Parc, St-Brisson ☎ 03–86–78–79–00 🖷 03–86–78–74–22). Horses can be rented from several stables: **La Ferme des Ruats** (⊠ Off N6, between St-Emilion and

Bussières ☏03–86–33–16–57); **Le Triangle** (✉Usy ☏03–86–33–32–78); and **La Vieille Diligence** (✉ Rive Droite, Lac des Settons, 58230 Montsauche ☏03–86–84–55–22).

Saulieu

㉕ *29 km (17 mi) southeast of Quarré-les-Tombes.*

Saulieu's reputation belies its size: it is renowned for good food (Rabelais, that roly-poly 16th-century man of letters, extolled its gargantuan hospitality) and Christmas trees (a staggering million are packed and sent off from the area each year). The town's **Basilique de St-Andoche** (✉ Pl. du Docteur Roclore) is almost as old as that of Vézelay, though less imposing and much restored. Note the Romanesque capitals. The **Musée François-Pompon,** adjoining the basilica, is a museum partly devoted to the work of animal-bronze sculptor Pompon (1855–1933), whose smooth, stylized creations seem contemporary but predate World War II. The museum also contains Gallo-Roman funeral stones, sacred art, and a room devoted to local gastronomic lore. ✉ *Rue Sallier* ☏ *03–80–64–00–21* 💷 *€4* 🕙 *Apr.–Sept., Wed.–Mon. 10–12:30 and 2–6; Oct.–Mar., Wed.–Mon. 10–12:30 and 2–5:30.*

Where to Stay & Eat

★ **$$$$** ✕🏨 **Le Relais Bernard Loiseau.** Originally a historic coaching auberge, this is now one of the region's finest hotels and restaurants, celebrated as the home base for chef Bernard Loiseau, one of France's culinary superstars, who took his life in early 2003. Loiseau made his mark by offering up a feather-light nouvelle version of rich Burgundian fare, and he is sorely missed. Despite this tragedy, the restaurant and hotel continue to receive guests under the direction of Dominique Loiseau and her devoted staff. The setting is exquisite: a chapel-like wood-beam dining room with a lush flower garden radiating around it. Guest rooms combine exposed beams and glass panels with cheerful traditional furnishings; a newer annex has the most comfortable (and air-conditioned) rooms, while the more stylish accommodations (styles range from Louis XVI to Empire) are in the main house. Some are tiny (one is complete with porthole window), some are luxurious (one has a comfy balcony overlooking the countryside)—no matter which you book, try to get a room facing the garden courtyard. ✉ *2 rue d'Argentine, off N6, 21210 Saulieu* ☏ *03–80–90–53–53* 📠 *03–80–64–08–92* ⊕ *www.bernard-loiseau.com* ⇄ *33 rooms* ♿ *Restaurant, cable TV, health club, Internet, meeting room; no a/c in some rooms* ⊟ *AE, DC, MC, V* ⦿ *BP.*

$$ ✕🏨 **Chez Camille.** Small, quiet, and friendly sum up this hotel in a 16th-century house with an exterior so ordinary you might easily pass it by. But within, rooms have period furniture and original wooden beams; ask for No. 22 or No. 23, the most dramatic, with a beamed ceiling that looks like spokes in a wheel. Traditional Burgundian fare—duck and boar are specialties—makes up the menu in the glass-roof restaurant. ✉ *1 pl. Édouard-Herriot, on N6 between Saulieu and Beaune, 21230 Arnay-le-Duc* ☏ *03–80–90–01–38* 📠 *03–80–90–04–64* ⇄ *11 rooms* ♿ *Restaurant, cable TV, Internet; no a/c* ⊟ *AE, DC, MC, V* ⦿ *MAP.*

Châteauneuf

㉖ *36 km (23 mi) east of Saulieu.*

The hilltop village of Châteauneuf catches your eye from A6. Turn off at Pouilly-en-Auxois and take any one of the three narrow, winding roads up, and you'll suddenly feel you've entered the Middle Ages. The town's modest 15th-century church ministered to as many as 500 souls when the village was at its zenith. In the last few years tourists have discovered the charm of this village, so try to avoid it on weekends. The **château**, built in the 12th and 15th centuries (with some later modifications), commands a broad view over rolling farmland as far as the eye can see. Clustered behind the château are houses for ordinary folk, at least a score of them notable for their 14th- and 15th-century charm, where today only about 80 people live. One of these, the charming **Monsieur Simon** (☎ 03–80–49–21–59), is so proud of his village that he gladly takes small groups on tours of the sights. ☎ *03–80–49–21–89* ☑ *€4.60* ◯ *Apr.–Sept., Tues.–Sun. 9:30–12:30 and 2–6; Oct.–Mar., Tues.–Sun. 10–noon and 2–6.*

Where to Stay & Eat

$$$–$$$$ ✕⌂ **Château la Chassagne.** Feel like a king or a queen for a night at this stylish domain 12 km (7 mi) from Châteauneuf, close to the junction of A38 and A6; you can even arrive by private plane or helicopter and be picked up in a Rolls-Royce. Rooms have high ceilings and are spacious; the modern iron-and-cane furnishings are obviously expensive, but of somewhat questionable taste. The grounds include a golf range, tennis court, and swimming pool. Nouvelle cuisine is served in the restaurant, but the chef seems to focus more on artistic presentation than creative flavoring; still, it's enjoyable. ✉ *900 chemin de Chassagne, 21410 Pont-de-Pany* ☎ *03–80–49–76–00* ⌂ *03–80–49–76–19* ⬚ *11 rooms* ⏃ *Restaurant, cable TV, driving range, 2 tennis courts, pool; no a/c* ▤ *AE, DC, MC, V* ◯ *Closed Nov.–Mar.* ⍾ *EP, MAP.*

$ ✕⌂ **Hostellerie du Château.** This hotel is in an ancient timbered building in the shadow of the town castle. The restaurant serves classical Bourgogne fare—roasted Époisses (local cow's-milk cheese) on a salad bed with walnuts, noisettes of lamb with thyme, and coq au vin; it's closed Tuesday and doesn't serve dinner Monday, except in July and August. Rooms vary considerably—from small to commodious; the best have a view of the castle. ✉ *Rue du Centre, 21320* ☎ *03–80–49–22–00* ⌂ *03–80–49–21–27* ⬚ *17 rooms* ⏃ *Restaurant; no a/c, no room phones, no room TVs* ▤ *AE, DC, MC, V* ◯ *Closed late Nov.–early Feb.* ⍾ *EP.*

DIJON

38 km (23 mi) northeast of Châteauneuf, 315 km (195 mi) southeast of Paris.

The erstwhile wine-mustard center of the world, site of an important university, and studded with medieval art treasures, Dijon—linked to Paris by expressway (A6/A38) and the high-speed TGV (Train à Grande

Vitesse)—is the age-old capital of Burgundy. Throughout the Middle Ages, Burgundy was a duchy that led a separate existence from the rest of France, culminating in the rule of the four "Grand Dukes of the West" between 1364 and 1477—Philippe le Hardi (the Bold), Jean Sans Peur (the Fearless), Philippe le Bon (the Good), and the unfortunate Charles le Téméraire (the Foolhardy, whose defeat by French king Louis XI at Nancy spelled the end of Burgundian independence). A number of monuments date from this period, including the Palais des Ducs (Ducal Palace), now largely converted into an art museum. The city has magnificent half-timber houses and *hôtels particuliers,* some rivaling those in Paris. But the most striking ensemble of buildings is its three central churches, built one following the other for three distinct parishes—St-Bénigne, its facade distinguished by Gothic galleries; St-Philibert, Dijon's only Romanesque church (with Merovingian vestiges); and St-Jean, an asymmetrical building now used as a theater.

Dijon's fame and fortune outlasted its dukes, and the city continued to flourish under French rule from the 17th century on. It has remained the major city of Burgundy—and the only one with more than 150,000 inhabitants. Its site, on the major European north–south trade route and within striking distance of the Swiss and German borders, has helped maintain its economic importance. It's also a cultural center—just a portion of its museums are mentioned below. And many of the gastronomic specialties that originated here are known worldwide, although unfortunately the Dijon traditions have largely passed into legend. They include snails (now, shockingly, mainly imported from the Czech Republic), mustard (the handmade variety is a lost art), and cassis (a black-currant liqueur often mixed with white wine—preferably Burgundy Aligoté—to make *kir,* the popular aperitif).

The Historic Center

a good
walk

Begin at the **Palais des Ducs** ㉗ ▶, Dijon's leading testimony to bygone splendor; these days it contains a major art museum. Cross to the left side of place de la Libération and take rue des Bons-Enfants, where you'll find the **Musée Magnin** ㉘, with exhibits of furniture and paintings. Continue on to rue Philippe Pot to see the elegant **Chambre des Métiers** ㉙. Just south of here is the **Palais de Justice** ㉚, with its elaborate Baroque facade. Turn onto rue Jean-Baptiste-Liégeard, where the imposing pink-and-yellow limestone Hôtel Legouz de Gerland watches over the street from its distinctive *échauguettes* (watchtowers). Return to rue de la Liberté to get to the church of **St-Michel** ㉛. West of here, behind the palace, is **Notre-Dame** ㉜, one of the city's oldest churches. The rue Verrerie, behind Notre-Dame and the Palais des Ducs, is lined with half-timber houses. Facing the church on rue de la Chouette is the elegant **Hôtel de Vogüé** ㉝. Walk from here to the somewhat plain **Cathédrale St-Bénigne** ㉞. In the former abbey of St-Bénigne is the **Musée Archéologique** ㉟. The former Cistercian convent houses the **Musée de la Vie Bourguignonne & d'Art Sacré** ㊱. Behind the train station is the **Musée d'Histoire Naturelle** ㊲, in the lovely Jardin de l'Arquebuse, the

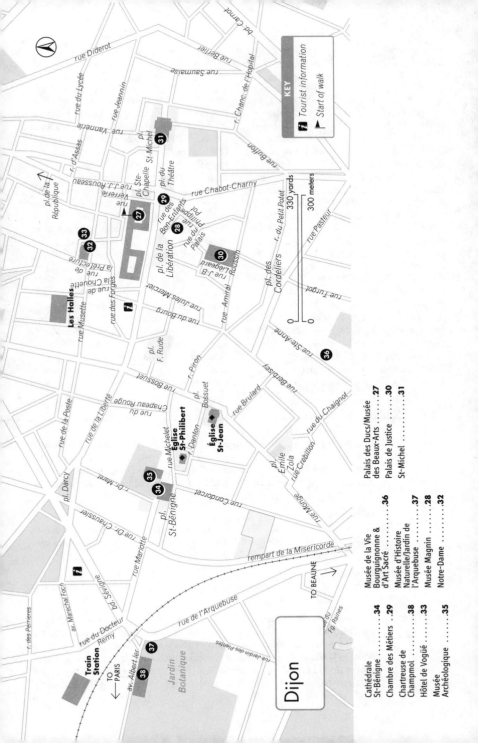

Dijon

KEY
- 🛈 Tourist information
- ▲ Start of walk

Cathédrale St-Bénigne **34**
Chambre des Métiers .. **29**
Chartreuse de Champmol **38**
Hôtel de Vogüé **33**
Musée Archéologique **35**

Musée de la Vie Bourguignonne & d'Art Sacré **36**
Musée d'Histoire Naturelle/Jardin de l'Arquebuse **37**
Musée Magnin **28**
Notre-Dame **32**

Palais des Ducs/Musée des Beaux-Arts **27**
Palais de Justice **30**
St-Michel **31**

330 yards
300 meters

CloseUp

BURGUNDY BIGTIME

WITH NO CITY larger than the capital Dijon (population 150,000), Burgundy seems the sleepy epitome of La France Profonde. Yet Dijon is one of the richest cities in France, and top European medieval painter Rogier van der Weyden stars down the road in Beaune. How come? Because, from 1369 to 1477, Burgundy hit the bigtime as an independent European power. In 1369, Philip II of Burgundy, then a minor duchy smaller than today's administrative region, married Marguerite de Flandre. She brought Nevers, Franche-Comté, and French Flanders with her as dowry. Burgundy prospered. In 1435, the Peace of Arras, signed with France, recognized Burgundy's further claims to Belgium, Picardy, and the Netherlands. The Duchy now extended up past Amsterdam to the Friesian Islands—the nearest the Burgundians ever came to regaining their Viking roots. Burgundy's capital moved from Dijon to Brussels where, in 1436, Van der Weyden was appointed official city painter. In 1443 the art-loving Burgundian Chancellor Nicolas Rolin commissioned the Last Judgment from Van der Weyden that still hangs in Beaune's Hôtel Dieu. Burgundy bought Luxembourg off the Habsburgs the same year. Everything in the vineyard looked rosy, but there was just one problem: the northern and southern ends of Burgundy remained asunder, with Lorraine in between. When Charles the Bold succeeded Philip the Good in 1467, conquering Lorraine was top priority. Charles snatched part of Lorraine in 1475, but was slain two years later laying siege to Nancy. French King Louis XI seized the chance to invade Burgundy to annex it for the French crown. Charles' daughter Mary married Maximilian of Habsburg, taking Flanders and Holland with her. The Duchy of Burgundy had passed into the wine-vat of history.

botanical garden. More links with Dijon's medieval past can be found west of the town center, beyond the train station, just off avenue Albert-1er, including the gateway to the celebrated **Chartreuse de Champmol ㊳**, where the spotlight is held by the Claus Sluter masterpiece, the *Puits de Moïse (Well of Moses)*.

What to See

㉞ Cathédrale St-Bénigne. The chief glory of this comparatively austere cathedral is its atmospheric 11th-century crypt—a forest of pillars surmounted by a rotunda. ⊠ *Pl. St-Bénigne.*

㉙ Chambre des Métiers. This stately mansion with Gallo-Roman *stelae* incorporated into the walls (a quirky touch) was built in the 19th century. ⊠ *Rue Philippe Pot.*

★ **㊳ Chartreuse de Champmol.** All that remains of this former charterhouse— a half-hour walk from Dijon's center and now surrounded by a psychiatric hospital—are the exuberant 15th-century gateway and the *Puits de Moïse (Well of Moses)*, one of the greatest examples of late-medieval sculpture. The well was designed by Flemish master Claus Sluter, who also created several other masterpieces during the late 14th and early

15th centuries, including the tombs of the dukes of Burgundy. If you closely study Sluter's six large sculptures, you will discover the Middle Ages becoming the Renaissance right before your eyes. Representing Moses and five other prophets, they are set on a hexagonal base in the center of a basin and remain the most compellingly realistic figures ever crafted by a medieval sculptor.

33 **Hôtel de Vogüé.** This stately 17th-century mansion has a characteristic red, yellow, and green Burgundian tile roof—a tradition whose disputed origins lie either with the Crusades and the adoption of Arabic tiles or with Philip the Bold's wife, Marguerite of Flanders. ⊠ *Rue de la Chouette.*

35 **Musée Archéologique** (Antiquities Museum). This museum, in the former abbey buildings of the church of St-Bénigne, traces the history of the region through archaeological finds. ⊠ *5 rue du Dr-Maret* ☎ *03–80–30–88–54* ⌨ *€2.20* ☉ *June–Sept., Wed.–Mon. 9:30–6; Oct.–May, Wed.–Sun. 9–12:30 and 1:35–6.*

37 **Musée de la Vie Bourguignonne & d'Art Sacré** (Museum of Burgundian Traditions & Religious Art). Housed in the former Cistercian convent, one museum contains religious art and sculpture; the other has crafts and artifacts from Burgundy, including old storefronts saved from the streets of Dijon that have been reconstituted, Hollywood moviemaking style, to form an imaginary street. ⊠ *17 rue Ste-Anne* ☎ *03–80–44–12–69* ⌨ *€2.80* ☉ *May–Sept., Wed.–Mon. 9–6; Oct.–Apr., Wed.–Mon. 9–noon and 2–6.*

37 **Musée d'Histoire Naturelle** (Natural History Museum). The museum is in the impressive botanical garden, the **Jardin de l'Arquebuse,** a pleasant place to stroll amid the wide variety of trees and tropical flowers. ⊠ *1 av. Albert-Ier* ☎ *03–80–76–82–76 museum, 03–80–76–82–84 garden* ⌨ *Museum €2.20, garden free* ☉ *Museum Wed.–Fri. and Mon. 9–noon and 2–6; weekends, 2–6; garden daily 7:30–6; until 8 PM in summer.*

28 **Musée Magnin.** In a 17th-century mansion, this museum showcases a private collection of original furnishings and paintings from the 16th to the 19th centuries. ⊠ *4 rue des Bons-Enfants* ☎ *03–80–67–11–10* ⌨ *€3* ☉ *Tues.–Sun. 10–noon and 2–6.*

32 **Notre-Dame.** One of the city's oldest churches, Notre-Dame stands out with its spindlelike towers, delicate arches gracing its facade, and 13th-century stained glass. Note the windows in the north transept tracing the lives of five saints, as well as the 11th-century Byzantine cedar Black Virgin. ⊠ *Rue de la Préfecture.*

need a break?

A pieman in Burgundy? Come taste his wares! For a quick *grignotage* (nibble) between meals or full-on Sunday brunch, **Simple Simon** (⊠ 4 rue de la Chouette) is the best address in town, and the only one in the entire region to offer such non-Burgundian delicacies as cheese and onion pie and buttered scones. Run by expat Brits, this is the ideal spot for a break or breakfast.

▶ ㉗ **Palais des Ducs** (Ducal Palace). The elegant, classical exterior of the for-
Fodor'sChoice mer palace can best be admired from the half-moon place de la Libéra-
★ tion and the Cour d'Honneur. The **kitchens** (circa 1450), with their six
huge fireplaces and (for its time) state-of-the-art aeration funnel in the
ceiling, and the 14th-century **chapter house** catch the eye, as does the
15th-century **Salle des Gardes** (Guard Room), with its richly carved and
colored tombs and late-14th-century altarpieces. The palace now houses
one of France's major art museums, the **Musée des Beaux-Arts** (Fine Arts
Museum). Here are displayed the magnificent tombs sculpted by celebrated artist Claus Sluter for dukes Philip the Bold and his son John the
Fearless—note their dramatically moving mourners, hidden in shrouds.
These are just two of the highlights of a rich collection of medieval objects and Renaissance furniture gathered here as testimony to Marguerite of Flanders, wife of Philip the Bold, who brought to Burgundy
not only her dowry, the rich province of Flanders (modern-day Belgium),
but also a host of distinguished artists—including Rogier van der Weyden, Jan van Eyck, and Claus Sluter. Their artistic legacy can be seen in
this collection, as well as at several of Burgundy's other museums and
monuments. Among the paintings are works by Italian Old Masters and
French 19th-century artists, such as Théodore Géricault and Gustave
Courbet, and their Impressionist successors, notably Édouard Manet and
Claude Monet. ⊠ *Rue Rameau* ☎ *03–80–74–52–70* 🖭 *€3.40*
⊙ *Wed.–Mon. 10–5.*

㉚ **Palais de Justice.** The meeting place for the old regional Parliament of
Burgundy serves as a reminder that Louis XI incorporated the province
into France in the late 15th century. ⊠ *Rue du Palais.*

㉛ **St-Michel.** This church, with its chunky Renaissance facade, fast-forwards
300 years from Notre-Dame. ⊠ *Pl. St-Michel.*

Where to Stay & Eat

As a culinary capital of France, Dijon has many superb restaurants, with
three areas popular for casual dining. One is around place Darcy, a square
catering to all tastes and budgets: choose from the bustling Concorde
brasserie, the quiet bar of the Hôtel de la Cloche, the underground Caveau
de la Porte Guillaume wine-and-snack bar, or—for your sweet tooth—
the Pâtisserie Darcy. For a really inexpensive meal, try the cafeteria Le
Flunch on boulevard de Brosses (near place Darcy). Two other areas for
casual dining in the evening are place Émile-Zola and the old market
(Les Halles), along rue Bannelier.

★ $$$–$$$$ ✗ **Le Pré aux Clercs.** This bright and beautiful Napoléon III–style restau-
rant is the perfect showcase for chef Jean-Pierre Billoux's golden touch,
which can turn the lowliest farmyard chicken into a palate-plucking pièce
de résistance. Most house specialties are inventive, the welcome is al-
ways convivial, and the wine list reads like a who's who of the region's
best—but not necessarily best-known—wine makers. The €35 lunch menu
(including wine) is a startling introduction to modern Burgundian cui-
sine. ⊠ *13 pl. de la Libération* ☎ *03–80–38–05–05* ⚏ *Reservations es-
sential* 🖃 *AE, DC, MC, V* ⊙ *Closed Mon. No dinner Sun.*

★ $$$–$$$$ ✕ **Stéphane Derbord.** From starters like crawfish tails with anise or duck foie gras with gingerbread, to entrées like sizzling Charolais beef with ham and onions, and to desserts such as rice pudding topped with caramelized spices, the talented Derbord, the city's rising gastronomic star, ensures dinner in this Art Deco restaurant is an elegantly refined affair. ✉ *10 pl. Wilson* ☎ *03–80–67–74–64* ⊕ *www.restaurantstephanederbord.fr* ⌂ *Reservations essential* ⋔ *Jacket and tie* ⊟ *MC, V* ☉ *Closed Sun., early Jan., and Aug. No lunch Mon. and Tues.*

★ $$$ ✕ **La Dame d'Aquitaine.** In a happy marriage between two of France's greatest gastronomic regions, chef Monique Saléra, from Pau, and her Dijonnais husband create a wonderful blend of regional cuisines. The foie gras and duck, in confit or with cèpes, come from Saléra's native region; the coq au vin, snails, and *lapin à la moutarde* (rabbit with mustard) from her husband's Burgundy; the *magret de canard aux baies de cassis* (duck breast with cassis berries) is a hybrid. The moderate prix-fixe menus are an extremely good value. ✉ *23 pl. Bossuet* ☎ *03–80–30–45–65* ⌂ *Reservations essential* ⊟ *AE, DC, MC, V* ☉ *Closed Sun. No lunch Mon.*

$$$ ✕ **Les Oenophiles.** A collection of superbly restored 16th-century buildings belonging to the Burgundian Company of Wine Tasters forms the backdrop to this pleasant restaurant. It is lavishly furnished but also quaint (candlelight in the evening). The food is good, especially the langoustines with ginger and the nougat-and-honey dessert. After dinner you can visit the small wine museum in the cellar. ✉ *18 rue Ste-Anne* ☎ *03–80–30–73–52* ⌂ *Reservations essential* ⋔ *Jacket required* ⊟ *AE, DC, MC, V* ☉ *No dinner Sun.*

$$ ✕ **Le Bistrot des Halles.** Of the many restaurants in the area, this one is the best value. Well-prepared dishes range from escargots to boeuf Bourguignon with braised endive. Dine either at the sidewalk tables or inside, where traditional French decor—mirrors and polished wood—predominates. ✉ *10 rue Bannelier* ☎ *03–80–49–94–15* ⊟ *MC, V* ☉ *No dinner Sun.*

$$$–$$$$ ✕▣ **L'Hostellerie du Chapeau Rouge.** A player piano in the bar and an elegant staircase give this hotel a degree of charm that the rooms, though clean and well appointed, lack. The restaurant, renowned as a haven of classic regional cuisine, serves snails cooked in basil and stuffed pigeon. The staff and owner Patrick Lagrange are attentive. ✉ *5 rue Michelet, 21000* ☎ *03–80–50–88–88* 🖷 *03–80–50–88–89* ⊕ *www.bourgogne. net/chapeaurouge* ⇌ *30 rooms* ⌂ *Restaurant, bar, Internet* ⊟ *AE, DC, MC, V* ⑩ *EP.*

$$$–$$$$ ▣ **La Cloche.** In use since the 19th century, La Cloche is a successful cross between a luxury chain and a grand hotel. The entry hall is imposing, and the gleaming bar has stylish leather-covered chairs. Rooms are large and plush; try to get one overlooking the tiny, tranquil back garden with its reflecting pool. The garden is also the backdrop for La Rotonde restaurant, but opt for the more relaxed Les Caves de la Cloche, in the cellar, which offers French sing-alongs with dinner and a choice of burgundies. ✉ *14 pl. Darcy, 21000* ☎ *03–80–30–12–32* 🖷 *03–80–30–04–15* ⊕ *www.hotel-lacloche.com* ⇌ *53 rooms, 15 suites* ⌂ *2 restaurants, minibars, cable TV, gym, sauna, bar, Internet, no-smoking floor* ⊟ *AE, DC, MC, V* ⑩ *EP.*

$ ⊞ Wilson. This hotel's "bones" are 17th century, set as it is in a fetching timber-frame post house, but inside rooms are modern, airy, light, and accented with wooden beams and Louis Treize chairs. Another plus— the hotel is connected by a walkway to Stéphane Derbord's noted restaurant. ⊠ *Pl. Wilson, 21000* ☎ *03–80–66–82–50* 🖷 *03–80–36–41–54* ⊕ *www.wilson-hotel.com* ↷ *27 rooms* ♿ *Internet, parking (fee); no a/c* ⊟ *AE, MC, V* ⦿❘ *EP.*

¢–$ ⊞ Jacquemart. In old Dijon, in a neighborhood known for its antiques shops, Le Jacquemart is housed in an 18th-century building with high-ceilinged rooms and warm, rustic furniture. It's a quiet, restful spot and thus very popular, so make sure you book well in advance. ⊠ *32 Rue Verrerie, 21000* ☎ *03–80–60–09–60* 🖷 *03–80–60–09–69* ⊕ *www. hotel-lejacquemart.fr* ↷ *30 rooms, 2 suites* ♿ *Internet, cable TV, parking (fee); no a/c* ⊟ *MC, V* ⦿❘ *EP.*

Nightlife & the Arts

Dijon stages **L'Été Musical** (Musical Summer), a predominantly classical music festival in June; the tourist office can supply the details. For three days in June the city hosts **Arts in the Streets** (☎ 03–80–65–91–00 for information), an event at which dozens of painters exhibit their works. During the **Bell-Ringing Festival,** in mid-August, St-Bénigne's bells chime and chime. In September Dijon puts on the **Festival International de Folklore.** November in Dijon is the time for the **International Gastronomy Fair.**

New Galaxy (⊠ 8 bis rue Marceau ☎ 03–80–70–03–69) caters to a slightly youngish clientele. **Cinquiéme Avenue** (⊠ Centre Dauphine ☎ 03–80–30–60–63 ⊘ Wed.–Sat.) is a popular Dijon disco. The **Bar Messire** (⊠ 3 rue Jules-Mercier ☎ 03–80–30–16–40) attracts an older crowd.

Shopping

The auction houses in Dijon are good places to prospect for antiques and works of art. Tempting food items—mustard, snails, and candy (including snail-shape chocolates–*les escargots de Bourgogne*) can easily be found in the pedestrian streets in the heart of Dijon.

> **en route**   A31 connects Dijon to Beaune, 40 km (25 mi) south. But if you prefer a leisurely route through the vineyards, chug along D122, the **route des Grands Crus,** past venerable properties such as Gevrey-Chambertin, Chambolle-Musigny, and Morey-St-Denis, to Clos de Vougeot.

THE WINE COUNTRY

Burgundy—Bourgogne to the French—has given its name to one of the world's great wines. Although many people will allow a preference for Bordeaux, Alsace, Loire, or Rhône wines, some French gourmets insist that the precious red nectars of Burgundy have no rivals, and treat them with reverence. So for some travelers a trip to Burgundy's Wine Country takes on the feel of a spiritual pilgrimage. East of the Parc du Morvan, the low hills and woodland gradually open up, and vineyards, clothing the contour of the land in orderly beauty, appear on all sides. The vineyards' steeply banked hills stand in contrast to the region's characteristic gentle slopes. Burgundy's most famous vineyards run south from Dijon through Beaune to Mâcon along what has become known as the Côte d'Or (*or* doesn't mean gold here, but is an abbreviation of *orient*, or east). Here you can go from vineyard to vineyard tasting the various samples (both the powerfully tannic young reds and the mellower older ones). Purists will remind you that you're not supposed to drink them but simply taste them, then spit them into the little buckets discreetly provided. But who wants to be a purist?

The Côte d'Or is truly a golden slope for wine lovers, branching out over the countryside in four great vineyard-*côtes* (slopes or hillsides) in southern Burgundy. The northernmost, the Côte de Nuites, often called the "Champs-Élysées of Burgundy," is the land of the unparalleled Grand Cru reds from the Pinot Noir grape. The Côte de Beaune, just to the south, is known for both full-bodied reds and some of the best dry whites in the world. Even farther south is the Côte Chalonnaise, while not as famous, produces bottle after bottle no less rich than its northern vineyard-kin of the same Chardonnay grape. Finally, the Côte Mâconnaise, the largest of the four côtes, brings its own quality whites to the market. There are more than a hundred vintners in this region, many of them producing top wines from surprisingly small parcels of land. To connect these dots, consult the regional tourist offices for full information of the noted wine routes of the region. The 50-mi Route des Grands Crus ranges from Dijon to Beaune and Santenay. You can extend this route southward by the Route Touristique des Grands Vins, which travels some 60 mi in and around Chalon-sur-Saône. Coming from the north, you can tour the areas (covered above) around Auxerre and Chablis on the route des Vignobles de l'Yonne. Whether touring by car, bike, or barge (several outfitters offer luxe barge cruises through the vineyard region waterways), you may wish to learn how to tell a Meursault from a Puligny-Montrachet by signing up with one of the English-language wine classes offered at L'Ecole des Vins de Bourgogne in Beaune.

Clos de Vougeot

㊴ *16 km (10 mi) south of Dijon.*

FodorśChoice
★

The reason to come to Vougeot is to see its *grange viticole* (wine-making barn) surrounded by its famous vineyard—a symbolic spot for all Burgundy aficionados. The **Château du Clos de Vougeot** was constructed in the 12th century by Cistercian monks from neighboring Cîteaux—who were in need of wine for mass and also wanted to make a diplomatic offering—and completed during the Renaissance. It's best known as the seat of Burgundy's elite company of wine lovers, the Confrérie des Chevaliers du Tastevin, who gather here in November at the start of an annual three-day festival, Les Trois Glorieuses. Josephine Baker slurped here once. You can admire the château's cellars, where ceremonies are held, and ogle the huge 13th-century grape presses, true marvels of medieval engineering. ☎ *03–80–62–86–09* ⊕ *www.closdevougeot.com/uk* 🎫 *€3.40* ⊙ *Apr.–Sept., daily 9–6:30; Oct.–Mar., weekdays and Sun. 9–11:30 and 2–5:30, Sat. 9–5.*

Near Clos de Vougeot at St-Nicolas-lès-Cîteaux is the **Abbaye de Cîteaux,** where the austere Cistercian order was founded in 1098 by Robert de Molesmes. The abbey has housed monks for more than 900 years. ✉ *Off D996, signs point the way along a short country road that breaks off from the entry road to Château de Gilly* ☎ *03–80–61–32–58* 🎫 *€7* ⊙ *May–early Oct., Tues.–Sat. 9:15–noon and 1:45–4:45; Sun. after 10:30 mass* ☞ *Guided tours available.*

Where to Stay & Eat

$$$$ ✕🏨 **Château de Gilly.** Considered by some an obligatory stop on their tour of Burgundy's vineyards, this château, just 2 mi from Vougeot, has almost become too popular for its own good (a conference center on-site doesn't help things). Formerly an abbey and a government-run avant-garde theater, the château does show some glorious vestiges worthy of its Relais & Châteaux parentage: painted ceilings, a gigantic vaulted crypt-cellar (now the dining room), suits of armor. Guest rooms have magnificent beamed ceilings and lovely views, but standard-issue fabrics, reproduction furniture, and ordinary bathrooms will greatly benefit from planned renovations. The restaurant's menu includes pastries made with Cîteaux's famous handmade cheese and pike perch with a *pain d'épices* (gingerbread) crust. An "elegant form of dress" is requested for dinner. ✉ *Gilly-lès-Cîteaux, 21640* ☎ *03–80–62–89–98* 🖨 *03–80–62–82–34* ⊕ *www.chateau-gilly.com* ⬌ *37 rooms, 11 suites* ♨ *Restaurant, cable TV, tennis court, pool, Internet, meeting room; no a/c* ☰ *AE, DC, MC, V* ⊙ *Closed in Feb.* ⦿l *MAP.*

Nuits-St-Georges

40 *21 km (13 mi) south of Dijon, 5 km (3 mi) south of Clos de Vougeot.*

Wine has been made in Nuits-St-Georges since Roman times; its "dry, tonic, and generous qualities" were recommended to Louis XIV for medicinal use. There isn't much to see or do here—it mostly serves as a good stop while visiting the surrounding area.

Where to Stay & Eat

¢–$ ✕ **Au Bois de Charmois.** Three kilometers (2 mi) out of Nuits-St-Georges, on the way toward Meuilley, is this marvelous little inn serving local fare at great prices—a three-course lunch (sample the huge plate of garlicky frogs' legs) is only €12. An even less-expensive menu is available at lunch on weekdays. It's especially pleasant to sit in the courtyard under the ancient trees, though even on chilly, gray days the small dining room is full of good cheer. ✉ *Rte. de la Serrée* ☎ *03–80–61–04–79* ☰ *MC, V* ⊙ *Closed Mon.*

$ ✕ **La Toute Petite Auberge.** Vosne-Romanée, the greatest vine village on the Côte, also entices with one of the most charming restaurants in Burgundy. No surprises on the menu (jambon persillé, coq au vin, crème brûlée), but everything is excellent and prices are more than reasonable.

As you would expect, the wine list is top-notch. ✉ *Vosne-Romanée, on the N74, 2 km (1 mi) north of Nuits-St-George* ☎ *03–80–61–02–03* ⏃ *Reservations essential* ▤ *MC, V* ⊗ *Closed Aug. No lunch Mon.*

★ **\$\$–\$\$\$** ▦ **Domaine Comtesse Michel de Loisy.** Comtesse Christine de Loisy is an institution unto herself in the Nuits-St-Georges area: an internationally traveled, erudite *dame d'un certain âge*, who is also a well-known oenologist and local historian. Rooms in her eclectic *hôtel particulier* are furnished with fine antiques, tapestries, chintz-covered walls, and Oriental carpets, and memorably temper grandeur with old-fashioned charm. Four of the five have a view of the flower-filled courtyard or the magnificent winter garden. Happily, the domain offers an optional two-day program of wine tastings, Burgundy-focused meals, and vineyard excursions. ✉ *28 rue du Général-de-Gaulle, 21700* ☎ *03–80–61–02–72* ▦ *03–80–61–36–14* ⛱ *5 rooms* ⚱ *No a/c, no room TVs* ▤ *AE, MC, V* ⊗ *Closed mid-Nov.–mid-Mar.* ❐ *BP.*

\$ ▦ **Albizzia.** The Dufouleur family, Burgundian wine growers since the sixteenth century, run this charming *chambre d'hôte* in the small village of Quincey, just outside Nuits-St-George. Facing the night-lit church in the village square, the B&B is in an old stone farmhouse, entirely renovated, with two very cozy double rooms. Breakfast in summer is served in the beautiful garden, and wine tastings (with local cheeses) are held year-round in the Dufouleur cellar. ✉ *Place de l'Eglise, Quincey, 4 km (2½ mi) south of Nuits-St-George, 21700* ☎ *03–80–61–13–23* ▦ *03–80–61–13–23* ⛱ *2 rooms* ⚱ *No a/c, no room TVs* ▤ *AE, MC, V* ❐ *BP.*

Beaune

❹❶ 19 km (12 mi) south of Nuits-St-Georges, 40 km (25 mi) south of
Fodor'sChoice Dijon, 315 km (197 mi) southeast of Paris.
★

Beaune is sometimes considered the wine capital of Burgundy because it's at the heart of the region's vineyards, with the Côte de Nuits to the north and the Côte de Beaune to the south. In late November, Les Trois Glorieuses, a three-day wine auction and fête at the Hospices de Beaune, pulls in connoisseurs and the curious from France and abroad. Despite the hordes, Beaune remains one of France's most attractive provincial towns, teeming with art above ground and wine barrels down below.

Some of the region's finest vineyards are owned by the **Hospices de Beaune** (better known to some as the **Hôtel-Dieu**), founded in 1443 as a hospital to provide free care for men who had fought in the Hundred Years' War. A visit to the Hospices (across from the tourist office) is one of the highlights of a stay in Beaune; its tiled roofs and Flemish architecture have become icons of Burgundy, and the same glowing colors and intricate patterns are seen throughout the region. Misleadingly appearing to be medieval, the interior was repainted by 19th-century Gothic restorer Viollet-le-Duc. Of special note are the **Grand' Salle,** more than 160 feet long, with the original furniture, a great wooden roof, and the picture-postcard **Cour d'Honneur.** The Hospices carried on its medical activities until 1971—its nurses still wearing their habit-

CloseUp

THROUGH THE GRAPEVINE

THROUGHOUT THE VILLAGES *of the different côtes, wine tastings abound. Some we've imbibed at include Caveau Napoléon (✉ 12 rue Noisot ☎ 03–80–52–45–48) in Fixin, which specializes in the Côte de Nuites-Villages and a Fixin Premier Cru. Only 2 km (1 mi) south is Gevrey-Chambertin, where you can sample one of ten wines— including the unusual Crémant de Bourgogne sparkling white—at Caveau du Chapître (✉ 1 rue de Paris ☎ 03–80–51–82–82). Still a couple of miles farther south in the celebrated village of Vougeot, you will come upon the Grand Cave (✉ R.N. 74 ☎ 03–80–62–87–13), which offers a trip through the cellars of the old castle of Vougeot as well as a chance to try a drop of wine from the barrels of the nearby Maison l'Hériter (✉ Rue des Clos Prieurs ☎ 03–80–62–86–58), one of the most distinguished wine houses in the Côte de*

Nuits. Most vineyards here are separated into patches of land called "clos"—a word redolent of Burgundian history. The first evidence of vineyards in the region dates from 300 BC in Cluny. Centuries later, during the Holy Roman Empire, nobility often gave vineyards to the church, giving control of fairly large properties to the monks at this holy center of Christendom. The monks made a life of recording everything, and so they did with the vineyards. They tasted and analyzed the wines and recorded the nuances of the different plots of land. Detailed maps were drawn, indicated the temperatures and miniclimates of the plots. The term "clos" (an ancient word for climate) comes from the name given these climates by the monks. Here's hoping you'll enjoy quite a few clos calls yourself on your trip through Bourgogne.

like uniforms—and the hospital's history is retraced in the museum, whose wide-ranging collections contain some weird and wonderful medical instruments from the 15th century. You can also see a collection of tapestries that belonged to the repentant founder of the Hospices, ducal chancellor Nicolas Rolin, who hoped charity would relieve him of his sins—one of which was collecting wives. Outstanding are both the tapestry he had made for Madame Rolin III, with its repeated motif of "my only star," and one relating the legend of St. Eloi and his miraculous restoration of a horse's leg. But the star of the collection is Rogier Van der Weyden's stirring, gigantic 15th-century masterpiece *The Last Judgment*, commissioned for the hospital by Rolin and a superb example of *l'art primitif*, a style popular right before the Renaissance. The intense colors and mind-tripping imagery were meant to scare the illiterate patients into religious submission. Notice the touch of misogyny; more women are going to hell than to heaven, while Christ, the judge, remains completely unmoved. A son-et-lumière show is presented every evening April through October. ✉ *Rue de l'Hôtel-Dieu* ☎ *03–80–24–45–00* ⊕ *www.hospices-de-beaune.com* ✉ *€5.40* ☉ *Late Mar.–mid-Nov., daily 9–6:30; mid-Nov.–Mar., daily 9–11:30 and 2–5:30.*

A series of tapestries relating the life of the Virgin hangs in Beaune's main church, the 12th-century **Collégiale Notre-Dame.** ⊠ *Just off av. de la République.*

★ To many, the liquid highlight of a visit to Burgundy is a visit to the **Marché aux Vins** (Wine Market) where, in flickering candlelight, and armed with your own tastevin (which you get to keep as a souvenir), you can taste a tongue-tingling, mind-spinning array of regional wines in the atmospheric setting of barrel-strewn cellars and vaulted passages. The selection runs from young Beaujolais to famous old Burgundies and there's no limit on how much you drink. Other Beaune tasting houses include Cordelier on the rue de l'Hôtel-Dieu and the Caves Patriarche on the rue du Collège. ⊠ *Rue Nicolas-Rolin* ☎ *03–80–25–08–20* ⊠ *€9* ⊙ *Daily 9:30–noon and 2–5:45.*

If you're going to spend a fortune on a bottle of Romanée-Conti and want to know how to properly savor it, sign up for one of the wine classes offered by the **L'Ecole des Vins de Bourgogne,** sponsored by the Bureau Interprofessionel des Vins de Bourgogne (B.I.V.B.) They offer several choices, ranging from a two-hour intro to a full weekend jammed with trips to vineyards and cellars in Macon and Chablis. ⊠ *6 rue du 16éme Chasseurs* ☎ *03–80–26–35–10* ⊠ *03–80–26–35–11* ⊕ *www.bivb.com.*

need a break? For a break and a snack of handmade pain d'épices (gingerbread) in all shapes and incarnations, stop by **Mulot & Petitjean** (⊠ Pl. Carnot). This famed pastry shop has a 200-year-old history; the firm is headquartered in Dijon.

Where to Stay & Eat

★ **$$$$** ✕ **Bernard Morillon.** This famous restaurant, in a stylish 18th-century town house that shares a courtyard (where you can dine in summer) with the neighboring Cep hotel, is embellished with old furniture and works of art, and considered by many top critics to be the best table in Beaune. Quiet-spoken chef Bernard Morillon lets his cooking—and his radiant wife Régine, who welcomes guests as if they were old family friends—do the talking. Warm oyster soup with poached quail eggs, fillet of local Charolais beef with foie gras, and Poulet de Bresse (that famous succulent regional chicken) simmered in red wine, are among Bernard's mouthwatering delights. Service is as polished as the gleaming silverware, and as warm-hearted as the Burgundy wine-list. ⊠ *31 rue Maufoux* ☎ *03–80–24–12–06* ⌂ *Reservations essential* ▤ *AE, DC, MC, V* ⊙ *Closed Jan. and Mon.–Sun. No lunch Tues.-Wed.*

$$$–$$$$ ✕ **L'Écusson.** Don't be put off by its unprepossessing exterior: this is a comfortable, friendly, thick-carpeted restaurant with good-value prix-fixe menus. Showcased is chef Jean-Pierre Senelet's sure-footed culinary mastery with dishes like boar terrine with dried apricot and juniper berries, and roast crayfish with curried semolina and ratatouille. ⊠ *2 rue du Lieutenant-Dupuis* ☎ *03–80–24–03–82* ⌂ *Reservations essential* ▤ *AE, DC, MC, V* ⊙ *Closed Sun. No lunch Mon.*

$–$$ ✕ **La Grilladine.** Chef Jean-Marc Jacquel's cuisine, though not elaborate, is good, hearty Burgundy fare: boeuf Bourguignon and oeufs en meurette.

The prix-fixe menus are extremely reasonable. Warm and cheerful, the room allures with rose-pink tablecloths, exposed stone walls, and an ancient beam supporting the ceiling. ⊠ *17 rue Maufoux* ☎ *03–80–22–22–36* ⌂ *Reservations essential* ▤ *MC, V* ⊗ *Closed Mon. and late Nov.–mid-Dec.*

★ **$$$–$$$$** ✕▦ **Hostellerie de Levernois.** The Crotets' hotel-restaurant, a Relais & Châteaux property, gleams with light from its large picture windows. The cuisine is still of the highest standard but the stylishly decorated lodgings are looking just a tad shopworn; those in the modern building in the landscaped garden are more up-to-date. In the kitchen Jean works with his sons, Christophe and Guillaume, who have a more nouvelle approach. Meals are occasions to be savored, but they are also expensive; menus begin at €53 (€30 at lunch) and may spotlight pigeon with foie gras and truffles or smoked salmon with vine shoots. ⊠ *Rte. de Combertault, 3 km (2 mi) east of Beaune, 21200 Levernois* ☎ *03–80–24–73–58* ▤*03–80–22–78–00* ⊕*www.levernois.com* ⟿*15 rooms, 1 suite* ⌂*Restaurant, minibars, cable TV, Internet* ▤ *AE, DC, MC, V* ⦿ *MAP.*

★ **$$$** ▦ **Hôtel Le Cep.** This venerable city-center hotel might be considered the shining showpiece among Beaune's myriad hostelries. It's actually an ensemble of buildings spanning the 14th–16th centuries, oozing history from every arcade of its Renaissance courtyard, yet all rooms—named for different Burgundy wines—have been luxuriously modernized, and decorated with crystal chandeliers and individual panache; some have wood beams, others canopied or four-poster beds. Those on the top story offer views over Beaune's famed multicolored tile roofs. Breakfast is served in a vaulted cellar; there's no hotel restaurant as such, but the lip-smackerous Bernard Morillon operates right next door. ⊠ *27 rue Maufoux, 21200* ☎ *03–80–22–35–48* ▤ *03–80–22–76–80* ⊕ *www. hotel-cep-beaune.com* ⟿ *46 rooms, 11 suites* ⌂ *Bar, minibars, cable TV* ▤ *AE, DC, MC, V* ⦿ *EP.*

$$–$$$ ✕▦ **Central.** This well-run establishment with modernized rooms, just 100 yards from the Hospices, lives up to its name. The stone-walled restaurant is cozy—some might say cramped—and the consistently good cuisine is popular with locals, who come to enjoy oeufs en meurette and coq au vin. Service is efficient, if a little hurried. ⊠ *2 rue Victor-Millot, 21200* ☎*03–80–24–77–24* ▤*03–80–22–30–40* ⟿*20 rooms* ⌂*Restaurant, minibars, cable TV; no a/c in some rooms* ▤ *MC, V* ⊗ *Closed late Nov.–mid-Dec.* ⦿ *EP.*

$$$ ▦ **Château de Chorey.** To really soak up the flavor of the vineyards, stay at the Germain family's winery and B&B a mile north of Beaune. Guest rooms are up a circular stone staircase; furnishings are from the attic. Though it's a bit rustic and casual, it's the kind of place where you can open the windows and let the country air, perfumed by grapes, waft in. A good breakfast is served but no dinner; you may have a chance to try their wine before going out to eat in Beaune. ⊠ *2 rue Jacques-Germain, 21200 Chorey-les-Beaune* ☎ *03–80–22–06–05* ▤ *03–80–24–03–93* ⟿ *7 rooms* ⌂ *Some minibars, parking (fee); no a/c* ▤ *MC, V* ⊗ *Closed Dec.–Apr.* ⦿ *BP.*

$ ▦ **Hôtel de la Cloche.** In a 15th-century residence in the heart of town, this hotel has rooms furnished with care by owners Monsieur and

Madame Lamy, both of whom are always on hand to assist. The best rooms, those with a full bath, are more expensive; the smaller yet delightful attic rooms, each with a shower and separate toilet, are less. Breakfast is served on the garden terrace in summer. Note that some readers raise alarms that La Cloche has become a bit shopworn—but the price is certainly right. ✉ 42 pl. Madeleine, 21200 ☎ 03–80–24–66–33 🖷 03–80–24–04–24 ☞ 22 rooms ↻ Restaurant, minibars, cable TV, Internet, parking (fee) ☰ AE, MC, V ⊙ Closed late Dec.–mid-Jan. ⵔ◯ǀ MAP.

The Arts

In July Beaune celebrates its annual **International Festival of Baroque Music,** which draws big stars of the music world. On the third Sunday in November at the Hospices is Beaune's famous wine festival, **Les Trois Glorieuses** (⊕ www.bourgogne.net/vente/1vente.html). For both festivals, contact **Beaune's Office de Tourisme** (✉ 1 rue de l'Hôtel-Dieu ☎ 03–80–26–21–35 🖷 03–80–25–04–81).

Château de Sully

42 35 km (19 mi) west of Beaune.

"The Fontainebleau of Burgundy" was how Madame de Sévigné described this turreted Renaissance château, continuing on to proclaim the inner court, whose Italianate design was inspired by Sebastiano Serlio, as the latest in chic. The building is magnificent, landmarked by four lantern-topped corner towers that loom over a romantic moat filled with the waters of the River Drée. Originally constructed by the de Rabutin family and once owned by Gaspard de Saulx-Tavannes—an instigator of the St. Bartholomew's Day Massacre, August 24, 1572, he reputedly ran through Paris's streets yelling, "Blood, blood! The doctors say that bleeding is as good for the health in August as in May!"—the château was partly reconstructed in elegant Régence style in the 18th century. Marshal MacMahon, president of France from 1873 to 1879, was born here in 1808. ☎ 03–85–82–10–27 ⊠ Guided tours €6, grounds €3 ⊙ Château 45-min guided tours June–Sept., call for times. Grounds daily 10–noon and 2–6.

Autun

43 20 km (12 mi) southwest of Sully, 48 km (30 mi) west of Beaune.

FodorśChoice
★

One of the most richly endowed villes d'art in Burgundy, Autun is a great draw for fans of both Gallo-Roman and Romanesque art. The name derives from Augustodonum—city of Augustus—and it was Augustus Caesar who called it "the sister and rival of Rome itself." You may still see traces of the Roman occupation—dating from when Autun was much larger and more important than it is today—in its well-preserved archways, Porte St-André and Porte d'Arroux, and the Théâtre Romain, once the largest arena in Gaul. Parts of the Roman walls surrounding the town also remain and give a fair indication of its size in those days. The curious Pierre de Couhard, a pyramidlike Roman construction, has so far baffled archaeologists, who are undecided as to its significance. Perhaps not unsurprisingly, this Roman outpost became a center for the new 11th-century style based on Roman precedent, the Romanesque, and its greatest sculptor, Gislebertus, left his precocious mark on the town cathedral. Several centuries later, Napoléon and his brother Joseph studied here at the military academy.

★ Autun's principal monument is the **Cathédrale St-Lazare,** a Gothic cathedral in Classical clothing. It was built between 1120 and 1146 to house the relics of St. Lazarus; the main tower, spire, and upper reaches of the chancel were added in the late 15th century. Lazarus's tricolor tomb was dismantled in 1766 by canons: vestiges of exquisite workmanship can be seen in the neighboring Musée Rolin. The same canons also did their best to transform the Romanesque-Gothic cathedral into a Classical temple, adding pilasters and other ornaments willy-nilly. Fortunately, the lacy Flamboyant Gothic organ tribune and some of the best Romanesque stonework, including the inspired nave capitals and the tympanum above the main door, emerged unscathed. Jean Ingres's painting *The Martyrdom of St. Symphorien* has been relegated to a dingy chapel in the north aisle of the nave. The *Last Judgment,* above the main door, was plastered over in the 18th century, which preserved not only the stylized Christ and elongated apostles but also the inscription GISLEBERTUS HOC FECIT (Gislebertus did this). Christ's head, which had disappeared, was found by a local canon shortly after World War II. Make sure to visit the cathedral's **Salle Capitulaire,** which houses Gislebertus's original capitals, distinguished by their relief carvings. The cathedral provides a stunning setting for **Musique en Morvan,** a festival of classical music held in July. ⊠ *Pl. St-Louis.*

The **Musée Rolin,** across from the cathedral, was built by Chancellor Nicholas Rolin, an important Burgundian administrator and famous art patron (he's immortalized in one of the Louvre's greatest paintings, Jan van Eyck's *Madonna and the Chancellor Rolin*). The museum is noteworthy for its early Flemish paintings and sculpture, including the magisterial *Nativity* painted by the Maître de Moulins in the 15th century. But the collection's star is a Gislebertus masterpiece, the *Temptation of Eve,* which originally topped one of the side doors of the cathedral. Try to imagine the missing elements of the scene: Adam on the left and the devil on the right. ⊠ *3 rue des Bancs* ☎ *03–85–52–09–76* 🎫 *€3.20* ☉ *Oct.–Mar., Wed.–Sat. 10–noon and 2–5, Sun. 10–noon and 2:30–5; Apr.–Sept., Wed.–Mon. 9:30–noon and 1:30–6.*

The **Théâtre Romain,** at the edge of town on the road to Chalon-sur-Saône, is a historic spot for lunch. Pick up the makings for a picnic in town and eat it on the stepped seats, where as many as 15,000 Gallo-Roman spectators perched during performances two millennia ago. In August a Gallo-Roman performance—the only one of its kind—is put on by locals wearing period costumes. The peak of a Gallo-Roman pyramid can be seen in the foreground. Elsewhere on the outskirts of town are the remains of an ancient Roman Temple of Janus.

Where to Stay & Eat

$$ ✕🏠 **St-Louis & Poste.** This Best Western hotel, in a former post house, is noteworthy more for its history than its pretensions to elegance. It has Mex-

ican wrought-iron furnishings and a remarkable family-size suite—it was while making a speech from this room's balcony in 1815 on his way back to Paris that Napoléon was rebuffed by crowds; George Sand also stayed here. The staff is friendly and helpful, and the restaurant, La Rotonde, is one of Autun's best. ☒ 6 *rue de l'Arbalète, 71400* ☎ *03–85–52–01–01* 🖶 *03–85–86–32–54* 📞 *38 rooms ⚱ Restaurant, minibars, cable TV, Internet, no-smoking rooms; no a/c* ☰ *AE, DC, MC, V* ⦿ *EP.*

$–$$ ✕▦ **Les Ursulines.** Placed above the Roman ramparts of the old city, this converted 17th-century convent offers spacious, well-kept rooms overlooking a geometric, French-style garden. The restaurant, adorned with red-velvet flocking and run by Paul Bocuse protégé Bruno Schlewitz, is worth a trip in itself, especially for the escargots with dried tomatoes and garlic *confit.* Some guest rooms have fine views of the surrounding Morvan hills, and breakfast is served in the historic chapel area. ☒ *14 rue Rivault,* ☎ *03–85–86–58–58* 🖶 *03–85–86–23–07* ⊕ *www. hotelursulines.fr* 📞 *40 rooms, 3 apartments ⚱ Minibars, cable TV, Internet, no-smoking rooms; no a/c* ☰ *AE, DC, MC, V* ⦿ *EP.*

Chalon-sur-Saône

❹❹ *42 km (25 mi) southeast of Autun, 29 km (18 mi) south of Beaune.*

Chalon-sur-Saône's medieval heart is close to the bank of the Saône River, around the former Cathédrale St-Vincent (now a parish church), which displays a jumble of styles. This area was reconstructed to have an old-world charm, but the rest of Chalon is modern and commercial—the cultural and shopping center of southern Burgundy. Chalon is best known as the birthplace of Nicéphore Niepce (1765–1833), whose early experiments, developed further by Jacques Daguerre, qualify him as the father of photography. The **Musée Nicéphore Niepce,** occupying an 18th-century house overlooking the Saône, retraces the early history of photography and motion pictures with the help of some pioneering equipment. It also includes a selection of contemporary photographic work and a lunar camera used during the U.S. Apollo program. But the star of the museum is the primitive camera used to take the very first photograph in 1816. ☒ *28 quai des Messageries* ☎ *03–85–48–41–98* 🎟 *€3.10.* ☉ *Sept.–June, Wed.–Mon. 9:30–11:45 and 2:30–5:45; July and Aug., Wed.–Mon. 10–5:45.*

Where to Stay & Eat

$ ✕▦ **St-Georges.** Close to the train station and town center, this friendly, white-walled hotel is tastefully modernized and has many spacious rooms. Its cozy restaurant is known locally for its efficient service and menus of outstanding value, with such specialties as veal kidney with mustard; it's closed in early August and does not serve lunch Saturday. ☒ *32 av. Jean-Jaurès, 71100* ☎ *03–85–90–80–50* 🖶 *03–85–90–80–55* ⊕ *www.lesaintgeorges71.fr* 📞 *48 rooms ⚱ Restaurant, minibars, cable TV, Internet* ☰ *AE, DC, MC, V* ⦿ *MAP.*

The Arts

For two weeks in July all of Chalon becomes a stage as street-theater groups from around the world come to perform in the annual **Chalon dans la Rue** (Chalon in the Street) festival.

Tournus

★ ㊺ *27 km (17 mi) south of Chalon-sur-Saône.*

Tournus, which retains much of the charm of the Middle Ages and the Renaissance and has one of Burgundy's most spectacular and best-preserved Romanesque buildings, has long been overshadowed as a tourist attraction by other medieval Burgundian towns. But it's worth a stop, and it's also a great spot for a picnic, especially along the left bank (*rive gauche*) of the Saône River. The **tourist office** (⊠ 2 pl. Carnot ☎ 03–85–51–13–10) has a map of the town's many *traboules*—its hidden covered walkways—which are fun to explore.

The 17th-century **Hôtel-Dieu** (hospital) reopened in 1999 after extensive renovation. Particularly noteworthy is its pharmacy. In one wing is the **Musée de Greuze,** displaying the work of painter Jean-Baptiste Greuze (1725–1805), a native of Tournus, as well as pieces by other painters past and present, sculpture, and archaeological finds. ⊠ *Rue de l'Hôpital* ☎ *03–85–51–23–50* 🔲 *€5* ☉ *Apr.–Nov., Wed.–Mon. 10–6.*

The abbey church of **St-Philibert,** despite its massiveness—unadorned cylindrical pillars more than 4 feet thick support the nave—is spacious and light. No effort was made to decorate or embellish the interior, whose sole hint of frivolity is the alternating red-and-white stones in the nave arches. The crypt—with its chapels containing 12th-century frescoes of *Christ in Majesty* and the *Virgin with Child*—and former abbey buildings, including the cloister and magnificent 12th-century refectory, can also be visited. ⊠ *Pl. de l'Abbaye.*

Where to Stay & Eat

★ $ ✕🔲 **Aux Terrasses.** For an enjoyable meal of the region's products at reasonable prices—such as chef Michel Carrette's fricassee of rabbit with pepper—this is the place. (The restaurant is closed Sunday dinner and Monday.) Many French, German, and Dutch travelers stop here for dinner and a night's rest. Rooms are reasonably large and comfortable, with standard floral decor. ⊠ *18 av. du 23-Janvier, 71700* ☎ *03–85–51–01–74* 🖨 *03–85–51–09–99* ➳ *18 rooms* ⌂ *Restaurant* ☰ *MC, V* ☉ *Closed early Jan.–early Feb.* ⍩ *MAP.*

$$ ✕🔲 **Rempart.** This hotel, originally a 15th-century guardhouse built on the town ramparts, has an elegant foyer and dining room incorporating Romanesque pillars. Rooms are modern, functional, and kept up. Double-glazed windows keep out traffic noise. At the restaurant, prix-fixe dinners begin at €28; in the bistrot, menus start at €20. The cooking in both establishments, though competently prepared by chef Daniel Rogie, doesn't live up to its reputation; you may wish to dine elsewhere. ⊠ *2 av. Gambetta, 71700* ☎ *03–85–51–10–56* 🖨 *03–85–40–77–22* ⊕ *www.lerempart.com* ➳ *32 rooms, 6 suites* ⌂ *Restaurant, minibars, bar* ☰ *AE, DC, MC, V* ⍩ *MAP.*

---

en route

The best way to reach Cluny from Tournus is to use picturesque D14. Along the way you pass the fortified hilltop town of **Brancion,** with its old castle and soaring keep, before turning left at Cormatin.

Cluny

⑥ *36 km (22 mi) southwest of Tournus, 24 km (15 mi) northwest of Mâcon.*

The village of Cluny is legendary for its medieval abbey, once the center of a vast Christian empire and today one of the most towering of medieval ruins. Unfortunately, only one transept of this mammoth church remains standing, thanks to the mobs of the French Revolution—one reason art historians have written themselves into knots tracing the fundamental influence of its architecture in the development of early Gothic style. Founded in the 10th century, the **Ancienne Abbaye** was the largest church in Europe until the 16th century, when Michelangelo built St. Peter's in Rome. Cluny's medieval abbots were as powerful as popes; in 1098 Pope Urban II (himself a Cluniac) assured the head of his old abbey that Cluny was the "light of the world." That assertion, of dubious religious validity, has not stood the test of time—after the Revolution the abbey was sold as national property and much of it used as a stone quarry. Today Cluny stands in ruins, a reminder of the limits of human grandeur. The ruins, however, suggest the size and glory of the abbey at its zenith, and piecing it back together in your mind is part of the attraction.

Fodor'sChoice ★

In order to get a clear sense of what you are looking at, start at the **Porte d'Honneur,** the entrance to the abbey from the village, whose classical architecture is reflected in the pilasters and Corinthian columns of the **Clocher de l'Eau-Bénite** (a majestic bell tower), crowning the only remaining part of the abbey church, the south transept. Between the two are the reconstructed monumental staircase, which led to the portal of the abbey church, and the excavated column bases of the vast narthex. The entire nave is gone. On one side of the transept is a national horse-breeding center (*haras*) founded in 1806 by Napoléon and constructed with materials from the destroyed abbey; on the other is an elegant pavilion built as new monks' lodgings in the 18th century. The gardens in front of it once contained an ancient lime tree (destroyed by a 1982 storm) named after Abélard, the controversial philosopher who sought shelter at the abbey in 1142. Off to the right is the 13th-century *farinier* (flour mill), with its fine oak-and-chestnut roof and collection of exquisite Romanesque capitals from the vanished choir. The **Musée Ochier,** in the abbatial palace, contains Europe's foremost Romanesque lapidary museum. Vestiges of both the abbey and the village constructed around it are conserved here, as well as part of the Bibliothèque des Moines (Monks' Library). ☎ *03–85–59–15–93* ⊕ *www.monum.fr* ▦ *€6.10* ☉ *Sept.–Apr., daily 9:30–noon and 1:30–5; May–Aug., daily 9:30–6:30.*

The village of Cluny was built to serve the abbey's more practical needs, and several fine Romanesque houses around the rue d'Avril and the rue de la République, including the so-called **Hôtel de la Monnaie** (Abbey Mint; ⊠ 6 rue d'Avril ☎ 03–85–59–25–66), are prime examples of the period's different architectural styles. Parts of the town ramparts, the much-restored 11th-century defensive **Tour des Fromages** (⊠ 6 rue Mercière (☎ 03–85–59–05–34), now home to the tourist office, and several noteworthy medieval churches also remain.

Where to Stay & Eat

$$ ✕▥ **Bourgogne.** Get into Cluny's medieval mood at this old-fashioned hotel dating from 1817, where parts of the abbey used to be. It has a small garden and an atmospheric restaurant with sober pink palette and comfort cuisine, such as *volaille de Bresse au Noilly et morilles* (Bresse chicken with Noilly Prat and morels). The evening meal is mandatory in July and August, and lunch is not served on Tuesday or Wednesday. ✉ *Pl. de l'Abbaye, 71250* ☎ *03–85–59–00–58* 🖷 *03–85–59–03–73* ⇌ *13 rooms* ⚅ *Restaurant, bar; no a/c in some rooms* ▤ *AE, DC, MC, V* ⊘ *Closed mid-Nov.–early Mar.* ⍿ *MAP.*

$ ✕▥ **Abbaye.** This modest hotel is a five-minute walk from the center. The three rooms to the right of the dining room are the best value. The restaurant serves rich, hearty local fare that's less elaborate than at the Bourgogne but better; if you're feeling adventurous, try the *pâté en croûte de grenouilles au Bleu de Bresse* (frog and Bresse blue-cheese pie). The prix-fixe menus are very reasonable, and the restaurant is closed Monday and doesn't serve dinner Sunday. ✉ *Av. Charles-de-Gaulle, 71250* ☎ *03–85–59–11–14* 🖷 *03–85–59–09–76* ⇌ *12 rooms* ⚅ *Restaurant; no a/c* ▤ *AE, MC, V* ⊘ *Closed mid-Jan.–mid-Feb.* ⍿ *MAP.*

The Arts

The ruined abbey of Cluny forms the backdrop of the **Grandes Heures de Cluny** (☎ 03–85–59–05–34 for details), a classical music festival held in August.

BURGUNDY A TO Z

To research prices, get advice from other travelers, and book travel arrangements, visit www.fodors.com.

AIRPORTS

Dijon Airport serves domestic flights between Paris and Lyon.

🛈 Airport Information **Dijon Airport** ☎ 03-80-67-67-67.

BIKE & MOPED TRAVEL

Details about recommended bike routes and where to rent bicycles (train stations are a good bet) can be found at most tourist offices. La Peurtantaine arranges bicycle tours of Burgundy.

🛈 Bike Tours **La Peurtantaine** ✉ Morvan Découverte, Le Bourg, 71550 Anost ☎ 03-85-82-77-74.

BUS TRAVEL

Local bus services are extensive; where the biggest private companies, Les Rapides de Bourgogne and TRANSCO, do not venture, the national SNCF routes often do. TRANSCO's No. 44 bus travels through the Côte d'Or wine region, connecting Dijon to Beaune via Vougeot and Nuits-St-Georges. The buses of Les Rapides des Bourgogne connect Auxerre to Chablis, Avallon, and Vézelay, and run between Autun, Beaune,

Dijon, and Chalon-sur-Saône's train station, where you can take an SNCF bus over to Cluny. Another SNCF route connects Saulieu, Montbard (near Fontenay), Autun, and Avallon. Cars Taboreau operate in the Parc du Morvan. Always inquire at the local tourist office for timetables and ask your hotel concierge for information.

🚍 Bus Information **Les Rapides de Bourgogne** ✉ 3 rue des Fontenottes, Auxerre 🕾 03-86-94-95-00. **TRANSCO** ✉ Rue des Perrières, Dijon 🕾 03-80-42-11-00. For SNCF, see Train Information, *below*.

CAR RENTAL

🚍 Local Agencies **Avis** ✉ 5 av. du Maréchal-Foch, Dijon 🕾 03-80-43-60-76. **Europcar** ✉ 47 rue Guillaume-Tell, Dijon 🕾 03-80-43-28-44. **Hertz** ✉ 78 cours de la Gare, Dijon 🕾 03-80-53-14-00.

CAR TRAVEL

Although bus lines do service smaller towns and scenic byways, traveling through Burgundy by car allows you to explore its meandering country roads at leisure. A6 is the main route through the region; A6 heads southeast from Paris through Burgundy, past Sens, Auxerre, Chablis, Avallon, Saulieu, and Beaune, continuing on to Mâcon, Lyon, and the south. A38 links A6 to Dijon, 290 km (180 mi) from Paris; the trip takes around three hours, depending on traffic. A31 heads down from Dijon to Beaune, a distance of 45 km (27 mi). The uncluttered A5 links Paris to Troyes, where the A31 segues south to Dijon.

SPORTS & THE OUTDOORS

From April to November, Air Escargot arranges hot-air balloon rides over the countryside.

🚍 Hot-Air Ballooning **Air Escargot** ✉ Chemin du 6-septembre, 71150 Remigny 🕾 03-85-87-12-30 ⊕ www.air-escargot.com.

TOURS

For general information on tours in Burgundy, contact the regional tourist office, the Comité Régional du Tourisme. Tours of Beaune with a guide and a wine tasting can be arranged in advance through the Beaune tourist office. Gastronomic weekends, including wine tastings, are organized by Bourgogne Tour.

🚍 **Beaune tourist office** ✉ Rue de l'Hôtel-Dieu 🕾 03-80-26-21-30. **Bourgogne Tour** ✉ 11 rue de la Liberté, 21000 Dijon 🕾 03-80-30-49-49. **Comité Régional du Tourisme** ☎ B.P. 1602, 21035 Dijon Cedex 🕾 03-80-50-90-00.

TRAIN TRAVEL

The TGV zips out of Paris (Gare de Lyon) to Dijon (75 minutes), Mâcon (100 minutes), and on to Lyon (two hours). Trains run frequently, though the fastest Paris–Lyon trains do not stop at Dijon or go anywhere near it. Some TGVs stop at Le Creusot, between Chalon and Autun, 90 minutes from Paris. There is also TGV service directly from Roissy Airport to Dijon (1 hour 50 minutes). Sens is on a mainline route from Paris (45 minutes). The region has two local train routes: one linking Sens, Joigny, Montbard, Dijon, Beaune, Chalon, Tournus, and Mâcon and the other connecting Auxerre, Avallon, Saulieu, and Autun. If you want to get to smaller towns or to vineyards, use bus routes or opt for the convenience of renting a car.

🚆 Train Information **SNCF** ☎ 08-36-35-35-35 ⊕ www.ter-sncf.com/uk/bourgogne.

TRAVEL AGENCIES

🚆 Local Agent Referrals **Air France** ✉ 29 pl. Darcy, Dijon ☎ 03-80-42-89-90. **Carlson-Wagonlit** ✉ 8 av. du Maréchal-Foch, Dijon ☎ 03-80-45-26-26.

VISITOR INFORMATION

Following are principal regional tourist offices, listed by town, as well as addresses of other tourist offices in towns mentioned in this chapter.

🚆 Tourist Information **Autun** ✉ 2 av. Charles-de-Gaulle ☎ 03-85-86-80-38 ⊕ www.autun.com. **Auxerre** ✉ 1 quai de la République ☎ 03-86-52-06-19 ⊕ www.ot-auxerre.fr. **Avallon** ✉ 4 rue Bocquillot ☎ 03-86-34-14-19. **Beaune** ✉ Rue de l'Hôtel-Dieu ☎ 03-80-26-21-30 ⊕ www.beaune-burgundy.com. **Clamecy** ✉ Rue du Grand-Marché ☎ 03-86-27-02-51. **Cluny** ✉ 6 rue Mercière ☎ 03-85-59-05-34 ⊕ www.perso.wanadoo.fr/otcluny. **Dijon** Principal regional tourist office ✉ 29 pl. Darcy, close to cathedral ☎ 03-80-44-11-44 ⊕ www.ot-dijon.fr. **Mâcon** Principal regional tourist office ✉ 1 pl. St-Pierre ☎ 03-85-21-07-07. **Sens** ✉ Pl. Jean-Jaurès ☎ 03-86-65-19-49. **Tournus** ✉ 2 pl. Carnot ☎ 03-85-51-13-10. **Troyes** ✉ 16 bd. Carnot ☎ 03-25-82-62-70 ⊕ www.ot-troyes.fr ✉ Rue Mignard ☎ 03-25-73-36-88. **Vézelay** ✉ Rue St-Pierre ☎ 03-86-33-23-69.

LYON & THE ALPS

9

Updated by
George Semler

Introduction by
Nancy Coons

AS THE NOBLE RHÔNE COURSES DOWN from Switzerland, flowing out of Lake Geneva and being nudged west and south by the flanking Jura Mountains and the Alps, it meanders through France at its bracing best. Here you'll find the pretty towns and fruity purple wines of Beaujolais, the brawny, broad-shoulder cuisine of Lyon, the extraordinary beauty of the Alps, and friendly wine villages sitting high on the steep hills bordering the Rhône as it flows to the Mediterranean. To the west, deep gorges cut grooves through a no-man's-land of ragged stone and pine: the Ardèche. History is to be found here, but the kind that treads lightly: the ruins at Vienne mark, with more grace than pomp, the region's Gallo-Roman roots, while Lyon's gigantic amphitheater and intimate Odéon confirm Roman Lugdunum's 2,000 years of bright cultural history.

So relax and dig into the *terroir,* the earth. Strike up a flirtation with saucy Beaujolais, the region's pink-cheeked country lass-in-a-glass, blushing modestly next to Burgundy, its high-toned neighbor. The very names of Beaujolais's robust wines conjure up a wildflower bouquet: Fleurie, Chiroubles, Juliénas, St-Amour. Glinting purple against red-checked linens in a Lyonnais *bouchon,* they flatter every delight listed on the blackboard menu: a salty chew of sausage, a crunch of bacon, a fat boudin noir bursting from its casing, a tangle of country greens in a tangy mustard vinaigrette, or a taste of crackling roast chicken.

If you are what you eat, then Lyon itself is real and hearty, as straightforward and unabashedly simple as a *poulet de Bresse.* Yet the refinements of world-class opera, theater, and classical music also happily thrive in Lyon's gently patinated urban milieu, one strangely reminiscent of 1930s Paris—lace curtains in painted-over storefronts, elegant bourgeois town houses, deep-shaded parks, and low-slung bridges lacing back and forth over the broad, lazy Saône and Rhône rivers. Far from the madding immensity of Paris, immerse yourself in what feels, tastes, and smells like the France of yore.

When you've had your fill of this, pack a picnic of victuals to tide you over and take to the hills. If you head west, the Gorges de l'Ardèche will land you in a craggy world of stone villages; if you head northeast, you'll ease into the Alps, a land of green-velvet slopes and icy mists, ranging from the modern urban hub of Grenoble and the crystalline lake of Annecy to the state-of-the-art ski resorts of Chamonix and Megève. The grand finale: awe-inspiring Mont-Blanc, at 15,700 feet Western Europe's highest peak. End your day's exertions on the piste or the trail with a bottle of gentian-perfumed Suze, repair to your fir tree–enclosed chalet, and dress down for a hearty mountain-peasant supper of raclette, fondue, or cheesy *ravioles,* all in the company of a crackling fire.

Grouped together in this guide solely for geographic convenience, Lyon and the Alps are as alike as chocolate and broccoli. Lyon is fast, congested, and saturated with culture (and smog). Lyon may be the gateway to the Alps, but otherwise the two halves of the region could be on different continents. While in the bustling city, it's hard to believe the pristine Alps are only an hour's train ride away from this rich metropolis. Likewise, while in a small Alpine village you could almost forget that

9

In this diverse region you can ski in the shadow of Mont Blanc, hike the trails over Alpine slopes, sail across idyllic Lake Annecy, and enjoy a broad palette of Lyon's cultural offerings. You can visit the Roman sites and medieval towns— evocative reminders of pre-modern eras—or take a heady trip along the Beaujolais Wine Road to discover the region's refreshingly unaffected vintages. As you plan your trip, remember that although you can make good time along the highways, you'll have to slow down on lesser roads and in the Alps. In more rural and mountainous regions avoid making your daily itineraries too ambitious.

Numbers in the text correspond to numbers in the margin and on the Lyon & the Alps map, the Lyon map, and the Grenoble map.

If you have
3 days

To enjoy some of France's best cooking, best museums, and theater, concentrate on ⊡ **Lyon** ❶–❸⓿ ▶, but also spend a day heading down the Rhône to see a vineyard in Côte Rôtie or the Roman ruins in **Vienne** ❸❻. For mountains and the wide open spaces, spend your second two days around the gorgeous lake in ⊡ **Annecy** ❹❽ or in the Alps, using ⊡ **Megève** ❺❺—where off-piste action outpaces the skiing—as your base. Of course, you'll want to save your euros for a blow-out at either one of Marc Veyrat's restaurants in Annecy and Megève.

If you have
7 days

Stay in ⊡ **Lyon** ❶–❸⓿ ▶ for at least two days. If you love wine, travel up the Saône Valley, through the villages along the **Beaujolais Wine Road,** and then, for your third night, head to ⊡ **Bourg-en-Bresse** ❸❸, landmarked by its Flamboyant Gothic church, or medieval ⊡ **Pérouges** ❸❺. On Day 4 make ⊡ **Annecy** ❺❸, with its medieval Vieille Ville, your destination; be sure to drive around the lake to lovely Talloires; stay the night in either one. The next day travel along the narrow roads connecting small villages via mountain passes in the Alps. Stop in the fashionable mountain resort town of **Megève** ❺❺—home to Marc Veyrat's culinary shrine, La Ferme de Mon Père—before driving on to elegant ⊡ **Chambéry** ❺❶. On Day 6 visit the abbey of **Grande Chartreuse** ❺❶; then either go to **Grenoble** ❹❸–❹❾ to see the Grenoble Museum's fabulous collection or zip via the autoroute to ⊡ **Valence** ❹❶ to view its Vieille Ville's cathedral and art museum. On the final day, drive through the spectacular Ardèche Gorge if you're heading for Provence. Or return to Lyon via **Vienne** ❸❻ to see the Roman sites or Côte du Rhône vineyards.

France has any large cities at all—much less one of the biggest and noisiest just on the other side of the mountains. When leaving Lyon, few travelers can resist paying a call on the Alps. Everything you imagine when you hear their name—soaring snowcaps, jagged ridges, crystalline lakes— is true. Their major outpost—Grenoble—buzzes with Alpine talk, propelling visitors away from city life and into the great Alpine high.

Exploring Lyon & the Alps

East-central France can be divided into two areas: the Alps and "not the Alps." The second area includes Lyon—a magnet for the surrounding region, including the vineyards of Beaujolais—and the area south of Lyon, dominated by the mighty Rhône as it flows toward the Mediterranean. This chapter is divided into four chunks: Lyon, France's "second city"; Beaujolais and La Dombes—where hundreds of wine *caves* alternate with glacier-created lakes and towns built of *pierres dorées,* soft, golden-tone stones that come from the local hillsides; the Rhône Valley, studded with quaint villages and hilltop castles; and Grenoble and the Alps, where you'll often find down-home friendliness on tap at sky-high ski resorts.

About the Restaurants & Hotels

Lyon's famous bouchons are, of course, irresistible in their checkered-tablecloth cozy atmosphere. The fare, however, is notoriously heavy, featuring creamy pike dumplings and pork and the like. The answer? Stick to soups and salads and other heretical bouchon specialties and live to dine again that day, or the next. Of course, you're also here to enjoy the region's famous restaurants, which rank right up there with Paris's—after all, the area has not one but two culinary shrines: Lyon's Paul Bocuse and Megève's La Ferme de Mon Père, the latter masterminded by Marc Veyrat. Since the luxe here can get very luxe, remember that prix-fixe menus are usually a fine way to keep tabs from soaring into the empyrean. House wines in Lyon are served in the traditional pot-de-Lyon, thick-bottomed bottles designed not to fool the customer, but to mock the government functionaries that (unsuccessfully) tried to limit the wine intake of the 19th-century silkworkers. The pot-de-Lyon wine is unbeatable for price-value, but otherwise undistinguished.

Hotels, inns, bed-and-breakfasts, *gîtes d'étapes* (hikers' way stations), and *tables d'hôte* run the gamut from grande luxe to spartanly rustic in this ample region. Many hotels come complete with dining rooms and they expect you to have at least your evening meal there, especially in summer; in winter they up the ante and hope travelers will take all three meals. However, it is assumed that hotels operate on the European Plan (EP, with no meal provided) unless we note that they use the Breakfast Plan (BP), Modified American Plan (MAP, with breakfast and dinner daily, known as *demi-pension*), or Full American Plan (FAP, or *pension complète,* with three meals a day); note the latter two plans are often only offered with a minimum three-night stay. Assume all hotel rooms have air-conditioning, TV, telephones, and private bath, unless otherwise noted.

WHAT IT COSTS In euros					
	$$$$	**$$$**	**$$**	**$**	**¢**
RESTAURANTS	over €30	€23–€30	€17–€23	€11–€17	under €11
HOTELS	over €190	€120–€190	€80–€120	€50–€80	under €50

Restaurant prices are per person for a main course at dinner, including tax (19.6%) and service; note that if a restaurant offers only prix-fixe (set-price) meals, it has been given the price category that reflects the full prix-fixe price. Hotel prices are for a standard double room in high season, including tax (19.6%) and service charge; higher prices (inquire when booking) prevail for any meal plans.

Dining with Bocuse & Veyrat

Haute cuisine today owes a great deal to the renovations of Lyonnais master chef Paul Bocuse. Back in the mid-1970s he unleashed his revolutionary dishes on an unsuspecting world, taking a stodgy, mortified tradition and creating fireworks by fusing unlikely ingredients, lighting up sauces, and putting the grand classics of Escoffier into jogging shoes. The amazing thing is that he did it all in traditional Lyon. For centuries, dining here has not been for the fainthearted. Indeed, most people throw out the dieter's notebook and roll up their sleeves in this city—everyone knows it's time to *eat!* Food lovers have long celebrated Lyon's cuisine and still rank it among the most complete and diverse in the world. The flavors are strong and cholesterol-heavy, the portions are trencherman-huge (oddly enough, many of these time-honored dishes were created by women, one reason so many Lyon dining establishments are affectionately called La Mère). Typical dishes are *sabodet,* a sausage made of pig's head; *gâteau de foie de volaille* (chicken liver pudding); *museau vinaigrette* (pickled beef muzzle); and the daunting *tête de veau* (calf's head). There are also such exquisitely light delicacies as *quenelles* (poached fish dumplings, often in sauce Nantua), which appear on tables in restaurants from the truly elegant to the truly simple. Lyon is most famous for its traditional *bouchons* (taverns), with homey wooden benches, zinc counters, and paper table coverings, that serve salads, pork products like garlicky *rosette* sausage, and sturdy main courses such as tripe, veal stew, and *andouillette* (chitterling sausage). Also the word for cork, *bouchon* in this case refers to the handfuls of straw used by grooms to *bouchonner* (rub down) horses after a day's ride. Taverns supplied piles of straw at the door and sold simple fare to horsemen. Unfortunately, the bouchon tradition has led to a host of modern-day fakes, so look for the little plaque at the door showing Gnafron, a Grand Guignol character, raising a glass of the grape, signifying a seal of approval from the town's historical association.

If you're not enthralled by traditional Lyonnais fare (only so much pork tripe and pike dumpling can be consumed in a day), turn to the full rainbow of Lyon's vast modern and postmodern culinary wealth, best seen in the absolutely extraordinary creations of Megève's poet-chef, Marc Veyrat: butter and creams from the north, Charolais beef to the west, olive oil, seafood from the Rhône estuary and the Mediterranean to the south, and game and highland delicacies from the Alps to the east. For a full account of this chef's fireworks, see our reviews of his La Maison de Marc Veyrat in Annecy and his La Ferme de Mon Père in Mègeve. The Dombes is rich in game and fowl; the chicken is famous, especially *poulet de Bresse,* traditionally cooked with cream. Thrush, partridge, and hare star along the Rhône. Local cheeses include St-Marcellin, Roquefort, Beaufort, Tomme, and goat's-milk Cabecou. Privas has its *marrons glacés* (candied chestnuts), Montélimar its nougats. Alpine rivers and lakes supply abundant pike and trout. When in the Alps don't forget to try a raclette, cheese melted over potatoes. Mountain herbs yield liqueurs and aperitifs such as tangy, dark Suédois; the sweet, green Chartreuse; and bittersweet Suze (made from gentian).

Le Beaujolais Nouveau

Many of France's most accessible and friendly wines hail from the 40-km (25-mi) north–south stretch of land known as the "Vignobles de Beaujolais" found about 30 km (20 mi) north of Lyon. Beaujolais wine is made exclusively from the *gamay noir à jus blanc* grape. The region's 10 best wines—Brouilly, Côte-de-Brouilly, Chénas, Chiroubles, Fleurie, Julienas, Morgon, St-Amour, Moulin-à-Vent, and Régine—are all labeled "Grands Crus," a more complex version of the otherwise light, fruity Beaujolais. Although the region's wines get better with age, many Beaujolais wines are drunk nearly fresh off the vine; every third Thursday in November marks the arrival of the Beaujolais Nouveau, a bacchanalian festival that also showcases regional cuisine.

Powder-Perfect Skiing

If you're going to work off all the highly calorific Lyonnais cuisine, there's no better way than by taking to the fabled ski runs of the region. Skiing can be a costly pastime, but if you're committed to the sport, the Alps are unbeatable, with verticals up to 9,240 feet and seemingly endless networks of *pistes* (runs), most above the tree line. While some resorts (Tignes, Les Arcs) have year-round skiing, skiers seeking the true Alpine experience will head straight for the better-known resorts in Chamonix and Megève. These places are so big you can stay in them for one week and never cross your own tracks. One ideal situation is to gather a few friends together and rent an apartment for a week; contact the local tourist office for rental information. The longer you stay, the better chance you can get a cut in prices on lift tickets, equipment, even lodging. But if time is of the essence, you can always enjoy a short ski stint with one-day packages leaving from Grenoble for Chamrouse and Les Deux Alps. For most resorts, the ski season lasts from December through April. Which only leads us to remind you that these regions make almost more delightful destinations in summer.

Timing

Midsummer can be hot and sticky. The best time of year in Lyon and the Rhône Valley is autumn, when the lakes are still warm, the grape harvest is under way, and festivals are all over the place. Note, however, that many of Lyon's hotels book early for September and October, when masses of delegates arrive for conventions. Winter tends to be dreary, though the crystal mist hovering over the Rhône can be beautiful. In the Alps summer is the time to hike, explore isolated villages, and admire the vistas; in winter the focus is on snow and skiing. Many hotels in the Alps are closed in early spring and late autumn.

LYON

Lyon and Marseille each claim to be France's "second city." In terms of size and industrial importance, Marseille probably deserves that title. But for tourist appeal, Lyon, 462 km (287 mi) southeast of Paris, is the clear winner. Easily accessible by car or by train, Lyon's speed and scale are human in ways that Paris may have lost forever. Lyon has its share of historic buildings and quaint *traboules* (from the Latin *trans-ambulare*, or walk-through), which are the passageways under and through town houses dating from the Renaissance (in Vieux Lyon) and the 19th century (in La Croix Rousse). Originally designed as dry, high-speed shortcuts for silk weavers delivering their wares, these passageways were used by the French Resistance during World War II to elude German street patrols. The city's setting at the confluence of the Saône and the Rhône is a spectacular riverine landscape overlooked from the heights to the west by the imposing Notre-Dame de Fourvière church and from the north by the hilltop neighborhood of La Croix Rousse. And when it comes to dining, you will be spoiled for choice—Lyon has more good restaurants per square mile than any other European city except Paris.

Lyon's development owes much to its riverside site halfway between Paris and the Mediterranean, and within striking distance of Switzerland, Italy, and the Alps. Lyonnais are proud that their city has been important for more than 2,000 years: Romans made their Lugdunum (the name means "hill of the crow"), the second largest Roman city after Rome itself, capital of Gaul around 43 BC. The remains of the Roman theater and the Odéon, the Gallo-Roman music hall, are among the most spectacular Roman ruins in the world. In the middle of the city is the Presqu'île, a fingerlike peninsula between the rivers, only half a dozen blocks wide and about 10 km (6 mi) long, where modern Lyon throbs with shops, restaurants, museums, theaters, and a postmodern Jean Nouvel–designed opera house. West of the Saône is Vieux Lyon (Old Lyon), with its peaceful Renaissance charm and lovely traboules and patios; above it is the old Roman district of Fourvière. To the north is the hilltop Croix Rousse District, where Lyon's silk weavers once operated their looms in lofts designed as workshop dwellings, while across the Rhône to the east is a mix of older residential areas, the famous Halles de Lyon market, and the ultramodern Part-Dieu business and office district with its landmark *gratte-ciel* (skyscraper) beyond.

All in all, Lyon is a city of ups and downs: from the Presqu'île to the top of the Croix Rousse or from Vieux Lyon to the top of the Roman Fourvière, from a simple bouchon with checked tablecloths to a stunningly haute-cuisine establishment such as Paul Bocuse (this is where the superstar chef became world famous) or Leon de Lyon. Consider taking advantage of the Clés de Lyon (Keys to Lyon), a three-day museum pass costing €14.

Vieux Lyon & Fourvière

Vieux Lyon—one of the richest groups of urban Renaissance dwellings in Europe—has narrow cobblestone streets, 15th- and 16th-century mansions, lovely *traboules* (passageways) and patios, small museums, and the cathedral. When Lyon became an important silk weaving town in the 15th century, Italian merchants and bankers built dozens of Renaissance-style town houses. Officially catalogued as national monuments, the courtyards and passageways are open to the public during the morning. The excellent Renaissance Quarter map of the traboules and courtyards of Vieux Lyon, available at the tourist office and in most hotel lobbies, offers the city's most gratifying exploring (use the silver buttons at the top of entryway door-buzzer panels to gain access). Above

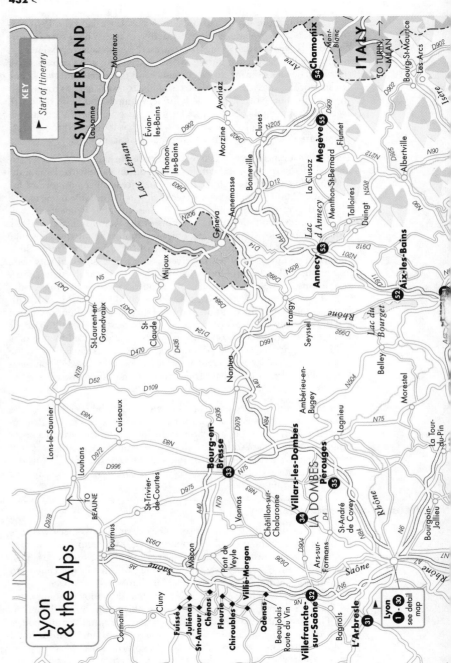

Lyon
& the Alps

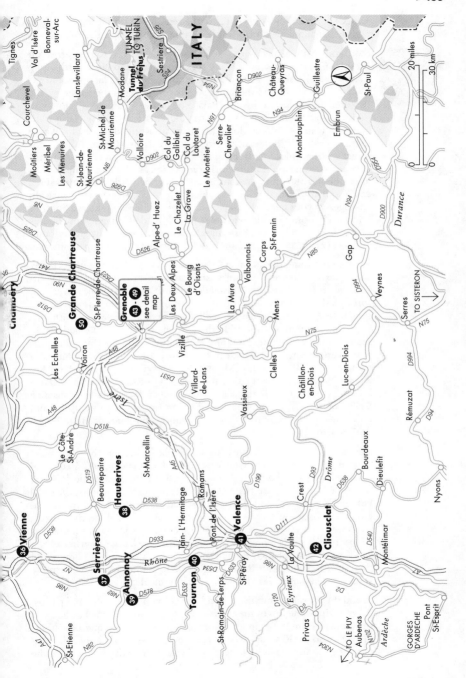

Vieux Lyon, in hilly Fourvière, are the remains of two Roman theaters and the Basilique de Notre-Dame, visible from all over the city.

Start your walk armed with free maps from the Lyon tourist office on Presqu'île's **place Bellecour ❶** ▶. Cross the square and head north along lively rue du Président-Herriot; turn left onto place des Jacobins and explore rue Mercière and the small streets off it. Cross the Saône on the Passerelle du Palais de Justice (Palace of Justice Footbridge); now you are in Vieux Lyon. Facing you is the old Palais de Justice. Turn right and then walk 200 yards along quai Romain Rolland to No. 17, where there's a traboule that leads to No. 9 rue des Trois Maries. Take a right to get to small place de la Baleine. Exit the square on the left (north) side and then go right on historic **rue St-Jean ❷**. All along rue St-Jean are traboules and patios leading into lovely courtyards with spiral staircases and mullioned windows. Head up to cobblestoned place du Change; on your left is the **Loge du Change ❸** church. Take rue Soufflot and turn left onto rue de Gadagne. The Hôtel de Gadagne now houses two museums: the **Musée Historique de Lyon ❹**, with medieval sculpture and local artifacts, and the Musée de la Marionnette, a puppet museum.

Walk south along **rue du Boeuf ❺**, parallel to rue St-Jean, with its many traboules, courtyards, and spiral staircases. Just off tiny place du Petit-Collège, at No. 16, is the **Maison du Crible ❻**, with its pink tower. Cut through the traboule at 31 rue du Boeuf into rue de la Bombarde and go left to get to the **Jardin Archéologique ❼**, a small garden with two excavated churches. Alongside the gardens is the solid **Cathédrale St-Jean ❽**, itself an architectural history lesson. The *ficelle* (funicular railway) runs from the cathedral to the top of Colline de Fourvière (Fourvière Hill). Take the Montée de Fourvière to the **Théâtres Romains ❾**, the well-preserved remnants of two Roman theaters. Overlooking the theaters is the semi-subterranean **Musée de la Civilisation Gallo-Romaine ❿**, a repository for Roman finds. Continue up the hill and take the first right to the mock-Byzantine **Basilique de Notre-Dame-de-Fourvière ⓫**.

Return to Vieux Lyon via the Montée Nicolas-de-Lange, the stone stairway at the foot of the metal tower, the **Tour Métallique ⓬**. You will emerge alongside the St-Paul train station. Venture onto rue Juiverie, off place St-Paul, to see two splendid Renaissance mansions, the **Hôtel Paterin ⓭**, at No. 4, and the **Hôtel Bullioud ⓮**, at No. 8. On the northeast side of place St-Paul is the church of **St-Paul ⓯**. Behind the church, cross the river on the Passarelle St-Vincent and take a left on quai St-Vincent; 200 yards along on the right is the **Jardin des Chartreux ⓰**, a small park. Cut through the park up to cours du Général Giraud and then turn right to place Rouville. Rue de l'Annonciade leads from the square to the **Jardin des Plantes ⓱**, the botanical gardens.

TIMING   Spend the morning ambling around Vieux Lyon's traboules and patios. After a trip to the top of the Fourvière hill for a look at the basilica and the Roman ruins, have lunch in one of Vieux Lyon's many bouchons. (There's also the Restaurant de Fourvière [☎ 04–78–25–21–15], a spectacular restaurant overlooking all of Lyon next to the basilica.) In the

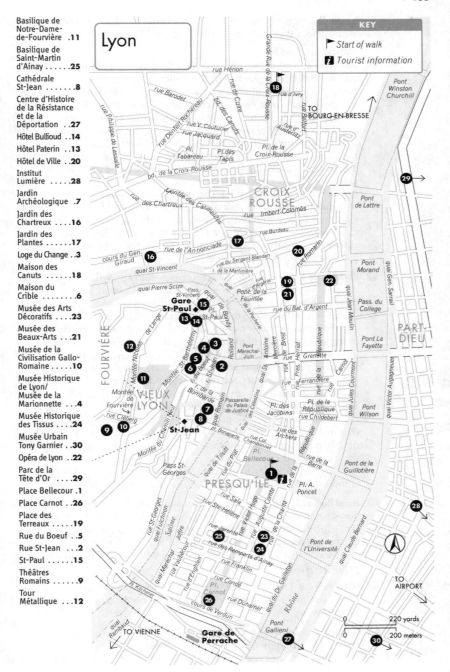

afternoon explore the Croix Rousse District and its traboules and museums. Note that most museums are closed Monday.

What to See

⓫ **Basilique de Notre-Dame-de-Fourvière.** The rather pompous late-19th-century basilica, at the top of the ficelle, is—for better or worse—the symbol of Lyon. Its mock-Byzantine architecture and hilltop site make it a close relative of Paris's Sacré-Coeur. Both were built to underline the might of the Roman Catholic Church after the Prussian defeat of France in 1870 gave rise to the birth of the anticlerical Third Republic. The excessive gilt, marble, and mosaics in the interior underscore the Church's wealth, although they masked its lack of political clout at that time. One of the few places in Lyon where you can't see the basilica is the adjacent terrace, whose panorama reveals the city—with the cathedral of St-Jean in the foreground and the glass towers of the reconstructed Part-Dieu business complex glistening behind. For a yet more sweeping view, climb the 287 steps to the basilica observatory. ⊠ *Pl. de Fourvière, Fourvière* ⌨ *Observatory* €1.53 ⊙ *Observatory Easter–Oct., daily 10–noon and 2–6; Nov.–Easter, weekends 2–6. Basilica daily 8–noon and 2–6.*

❽ **Cathédrale St-Jean.** Solid and determined—having withstood the sieges of time, revolution, and war—the cathedral's stumpy facade is stuck almost bashfully onto the nave. Although the mishmash inside has its moments—the fabulous 13th-century stained-glass windows in the choir and the varied window tracery and vaulting in the side chapels—the interior lacks drama and harmony. Still, it is an architectural history lesson. The cathedral dates from the 12th century, and the chancel is Romanesque, but construction on the whole continued over three centuries. The 14th-century astronomical clock, in the north transept, is a marvel of technology very much worth seeing. It chimes a hymn to St. John on the hour at noon, 2, 3, and 4 as a screeching rooster and other automatons enact the Annunciation. History majors will want to know that in 1600 Henri IV came to Lyon to meet his Italian fiancée, Marie de' Medici, en route from Marseille; he took one look at her, gave her the okay, and they were married immediately in this cathedral. To the right of the Cathédrale St-Jean stands the 12th-century **Manécanterie** (choir school). ⊠ *70 rue St-Jean, Vieux Lyon* ☎ *04–78–92–82–29.*

⓮ **Hôtel Bullioud.** This Renaissance mansion, close to the Hôtel Paterin, is noted for its courtyard, with an ingenious gallery (1536) built by Philibert Delorme, one of France's earliest and most accomplished exponents of Classical architecture. He also worked on several spectacular châteaux in central France, including those at Fontainebleau and Chenonceau. ⊠ *8 rue Juiverie, off pl. St-Paul, Vieux Lyon.*

⓭ **Hôtel Paterin.** This is a particularly fine example of the type of splendid Renaissance mansion found in the area. ⊠ *4 rue Juiverie, off pl. St-Paul, Vieux Lyon.*

❼ **Jardin Archéologique** (Archaeological Garden). This garden contains the excavated ruins of two churches that succeeded one another on this site. The foundations of the churches were unearthed during a time when apartment buildings—constructed here after churches had been destroyed during the Revolution—were being demolished. One arch still remains and forms part of the ornamentation in the garden. ⊠ *Entrance on rue de la Bombarde, Vieux Lyon.*

⑯ Jardin des Chartreux. This garden is just one of several small, leafy parks in Lyon. It's a peaceful place to take a break while admiring the splendid view of the river and Fourvière Hill. ⊠ *Entrance on quai St-Vincent, Presqu'île.*

⑰ Jardin des Plantes (Botanical Garden). In the peaceful, luxurious Botanical Garden are remnants of the once-huge **Amphithéâtre des Trois Gauls** (Three Gauls Amphitheater), built in AD 19. ⊠ *Entrance on rue de la Tourette, Vieux Lyon* ۞ *Dawn–dusk.*

❸ Loge du Change. Originally a center for the money-changing activities that took place here in the late 15th and 16th centuries, the building was constructed by Simon Gourdet in the mid-16th century and completely redesigned in 1747 by Jean-Baptiste Roche, using plans supplied by his famous colleague Jacques-Germain Soufflot, the architect of Paris's Panthéon. After serving as an inn during the French Revolution, the Loge became a Protestant church in 1803, and is now one of Vieux Lyon's prime concert venues. ⊠ *Pl. du Change, Vieux Lyon.*

❻ Maison du Crible. This 17th-century mansion is one of Lyon's oldest. In the courtyard you can glimpse a charming garden and the original Tour Rose—an elegant pink tower. The higher the tower in those days, the greater the prestige—this one was owned by the tax collector—and it's not so different today. ⊠ *16 rue du Boeuf, off pl. du Petit-Collège, Vieux Lyon* ☜ *Free* ۞ *Daily 10–noon and 2–6.*

❿ Musée de la Civilisation Gallo-Romaine (Gallo-Roman Civilization Museum). Since 1933, systematic excavations have unearthed vestiges of Lyon's opulent Roman precursor. The statues, mosaics, vases, coins, and tombstones are excellently displayed in this semisubterranean museum next to the Roman theaters. The large, bronze Table Claudienne is inscribed with part of Emperor Claudius's address to the Roman Senate in AD 48, conferring senatorial rights on the Roman citizens of Gaul. ⊠ *17 rue Clébert, Fourvière* ☎ *04–72–38–81–90* ☜ *€4* ۞ *Tues.–Sun. 10–5.*

⚘ ❹ Musée Historique de Lyon (Lyon Historical Museum). This museum is housed in the city's largest ensemble of Renaissance buildings, the Hôtel de Gadagne, built between the 14th and 16th centuries. Medieval sculpture, furniture, pottery, paintings, and engravings are on display. Also housed here is the **Musée de la Marionnette** (Puppet Museum), tracing the history of marionettes, beginning with Guignol and Madelon (Lyon's Punch and Judy, created by Laurent Mourguet in 1795). ⊠ *1 pl. du Petit-Collège, Vieux Lyon* ☎ *04–78–42–03–61* ☜ *€4* ۞ *Daily 10:45–6* ۞ *Closed Tues.*

➤ ❶ Place Bellecour. Shady, imposing place Bellecour is one of the largest squares in France and is Lyon's fashionable center, midway between the Saône and the Rhône. Classical facades erected along its narrower sides in 1800 lend architectural interest. The large, bronze equestrian statue of Louis XIV, installed in 1828, is the work of local sculptor Jean Lemot. On the south side of the square is the **tourist office** (☎ 04–72–77–69–69). ⊠ *Presqu'île.*

❺ Rue du Boeuf. Like the parallel rue St-Jean, rue du Boeuf has lovely tra-
Fodor'sChoice boules, courtyards, spiral staircases, towers, and facades. The traboule
★ at No. 31 rue du Boeuf hooks through and out on to rue de la Bombarde. No. 36 has a notable courtyard. At No. 19 is the standout Maison de l'Outarde d'Or, so named for the great bustard, a goose-like game bird, depicted in the coat of arms over the door. The late-15th-century house and courtyard inside have spiral staircases in the towers, which were built as symbols of wealth and power. The Hotel Tour Rose at No. 22 has, indeed, a beautiful *tour rose* (pink tower) in the inner courtyard. At the corner of place Neuve St-Jean and rue du Boeuf is the famous sign portraying the bull for which rue du Boeuf is named, the work of the Renaissance Italy–trained French sculptor Jean de Bologne. No. 18 contains Antic Wine, the emporium of English-speaking Georges Dos Santos, "the flying sommelier," who is a wealth of information (throw away this book and just ask Georges). No. 20 conceals one of the rare open-shaft spiral staircases allowing for a view all the way up the core. At No. 16 is the Maison du Crible, and No. 14 has another splendid patio. ⊠ *Vieux Lyon.*

❷ Rue St-Jean. Once Vieux Lyon's major thoroughfare, this street leads north from place St-Jean to place du Change, where moneychangers operated during medieval trade fairs. Many area streets were named for their shops, still heralded by intricate iron signs. The elegant houses along the street were built for illustrious Lyonnais bankers and Italian silk merchants during the French Renaissance. The traboule at No. 54 leads all the way through to rue du Boeuf No. 27. Beautiful Renaissance courtyards can be visited at No. 50, No. 52, and No. 42. At No. 27 rue St-Jean an especially lovely traboule winds through to No. 6 rue des 3 Maries. No. 28 has a pretty courtyard; No. 24, the Maison Laurencin, has another; Maison Le Viste at No. 21 has a splendid facade. The courtyard at No. 18 merits a close look. The houses at No. 5 place du Gouvernment and No. 7 and No. 1 rue St-Jean also have facades you won't want to miss. ⊠ *Vieux Lyon.*

⓯ St-Paul. The 12th-century church of St-Paul is noted for its octagonal lantern, its frieze of animal heads in the chancel, and its Flamboyant Gothic chapel. ⊠ *Pl. St-Paul, Vieux Lyon.*

❾ Théâtres Romains (Roman Theaters). Two ruined, semicircular Roman-built theaters are tucked into the hillside, just down from the summit of Fourvière. The **Grand Théâtre**, the oldest Roman theater in France, was built in 15 BC to seat 10,000. The smaller **Odéon**, with its geometric flooring, was designed for music and poetry performances. Lyon International Arts Festival performances are held here each September. ⊠ *Colline Fourvière, Fourvière* 🎟 *Free* ⊙ *Daily 9–dusk.*

⓬ Tour Métallique (Metal Tower). Beyond Fourvière Basilica is this skeletal metal tower built in 1893 and now a television transmitter. The stone staircase, the **Montée Nicolas-de-Lange,** at the foot of the tower, is a direct but steep route from the basilica to the St-Paul train station. ⊠ *Colline Fourvière, Fourvière.*

Presqu'île & the Croix Rousse District

Presqu'île, the peninsula flanked by the Saône and the Rhône, is Lyon's modern center, with fashionable shops, a trove of restaurants and museums, and squares graced by fountains and 19th-century buildings. This is the core of Lyon, where you'll be tempted to wander the streets from one riverbank to the other and to explore the entire stretch from the Gare de Perrache railroad station to the place Bellecour and up to place des Terreaux.

The hillside and hilltop district north of place des Terreaux, the Croix Rousse District, is flanked by the Jardins des Plantes on the west and the Rhône on the east. It once resounded to the clanking of looms churning out the exquisite silks and other cloth that made Lyon famous. By the 19th century more than 30,000 *canuts* (weavers) worked on looms on the upper floors of the houses. So tightly packed were the buildings that the only way to transport fabrics was through the traboules, which had the additional advantage of protecting the fine cloth in poor weather.

a good walk

Armed with a detailed map, available from the Lyon Tourist Office, you could spend hours "trabouling" on the Croix Rousse hillside, which is still busy with textile merchants despite the demise of the old-style cottage industry of silk weaving. In the very northern part of the Croix Rousse District you can see ancient looms at the **Maison des Canuts** ⑱ ☞. For an impromptu tour of the area, walk along rue Imbert-Colomès. At No. 20, turn right through the traboule that leads to rue des Tables Claudiennes and right again across place Chardonnet. Take the Passage Mermet alongside the church of St-Polycarpe; then turn left onto rue Leynaud. A traboule at No. 32 leads to the Montée St-Sébastien. Here's a transfixing trompe l'oeil on the Mur des Canuts, a large wall painted with depictions of local citizens both seated and walking up a passageway of steps. Exit the Croix Rousse District by taking rue Romarin down to **place des Terreaux** ⑲.

The sizable place des Terreaux has two notable buildings: on the north side is the **Hôtel de Ville** ⑳, the Town Hall; on the south side is the elegant **Musée des Beaux-Arts** ㉑, the art museum. To reach the barrel-vaulted **Opéra de Lyon** ㉒, walk east across place des Terreaux and through the ground floor of the Hôtel de Ville (go around if it's closed). For a culinary delight, detour to the east over the Rhône by walking south along the boulevard de la République; at place Regaud turn left and head over the Pont Lafayette for a 2 km (1½ mi) walk to **Les Halles de Lyon,** the city's main produce market—in a city where food is worshipped, this is one of its many temples. Backtrack over the river and check out Lyon's fashionable shops by walking down the pedestrian-only rue de la République and cross place Bellecour. Continue 300 yards farther (now rue de la Charité) to the **Musée des Arts Décoratifs** ㉓, a decorative arts museum. Next door is the **Musée Historique des Tissus** ㉔, a textile museum.

Now cut west across rue des Remparts d'Ainay to the **Basilique de Saint-Martin d'Ainay** ㉕, the abbey church of one of the oldest monasteries in the Lyon region. The lovely, archaic **Voûte d'Ainay** just past the church was the former gateway to the abbey. Just outside to the left is the much-filmed and -photographed restaurant Comptoir Abel Bar, also known as À La Voûte d'Ainay. Continue south to **place Carnot** ㉖ and the Gare de Perrache railway and subway station.

After crossing the Rhône on Pont Galliéni and going up avenue Berthelot, visit the **Centre d'Histoire de la Résistance et de la Déportation** ㉗, which focuses on Lyon's Resistance movement during World War II. If you're a film buff, head to the **Institut Lumière** ㉘. From the center walk east along avenue Berthelot to avenue Jean-Jaurès; take a right and then a left on grande rue de Guillotière, then another right on rue Premier-Film. To return to Presqu'île, walk west to Pont de la Guillotière.

If you've seen all of Lyon's main cultural sights and want to indulge your children, take the métro from Perrache train station to Masséna and the **Parc de la Tête d'Or** ㉙, which has a small zoo and pony rides. If you're an architecture buff, take the métro from place Bellecour to Monplaisir-Lumière (it's a bit of a long trip) and walk 10 minutes south along rue Antoine to the **Musée Urbain Tony Garnier** ㉚, usually referred to as the Cité de la Création.

TIMING It will take you at least five hours to explore Presqu'île and the Croix Rousse District. A full day would be even better. The Musée des Beaux-Arts deserves at least two hours, the Musée des Arts Décoratifs and the Musée Historique des Tissus another 45 minutes each. The explorations east of the Rhône might entail another half day. Note that most museums are closed Monday; the Musée des Beaux-Arts is open Monday but closed Tuesday.

What to See

㉕ **Basilique de Saint-Martin d'Ainay.** The abbey church of one of Lyon's most ancient monasteries, this fortified church dates back to a 10th-century Benedictine abbey and a 9th-century sanctuary before that. The millenary, circa1000 energy field is palpable around this hulking structure, especially near the rear of the apse where the stained-glass windows glow richly in the twilight. One of the earliest buildings in France to be classified a national monument, in 1844, its interior murals and frescoes are disappointingly severe compared to the quirky, rough exterior. ⊠ *Place de l'Abbaye d'Ainay, Presqu'île* ☎ *04–78–72–10–03* ☜ *Free* ☉ *Daily 9–1 and 4–7.*

㉗ **Centre d'Histoire de la Résistance et de la Déportation** (Museum of the History of the Resistance and the Deportation). During World War II, especially after 1942, Lyon played an important role in the Resistance movement against the German occupation of France. Displays include equipment, such as radios and printing presses, photographs, and exhibits recreating the clandestine lives and heroic exploits of Resistance fighters. ⊠ *14 av. Berthelot, Part-Dieu* ☎ *04–78–72–23–11* ☜ *€4* ☉ *Wed.–Sun. 9–5:30.*

⓴ **Hôtel de Ville** (Town Hall). Architects Jules Hardouin-Mansart and Robert de Cotte redesigned the very impressive facade of the Town Hall after a 1674 fire. The rest of the building dates from the early 17th century. ✉ *Pl. des Terreaux, Presqu'île.*

---

off the beaten path

LES HALLES DE LYON – For a sensory feast you won't soon forget, walk over west of the Rhône to Les Halles de Lyon, the city's main produce market, especially on Saturday, Sunday, or a holiday morning when the place crackles with excitement. On the left bank of the Rhône on Part-Dieu's Cours Lafayette, the market offers everything from pristine lettuce to wild mushrooms to poulet de Bresse to caviar, from 150 kinds of cheese at the Alain Martinet stand to the *"Rolls de l'huitre"* (Rolls-Royce of oysters) at Chez Georges. The *salons de dégustation* (tasting rooms) are in fact raging restaurants with a joie de vivre hard to surpass in Lyon, or anywhere else. Maison Monestir, le Jardin des Halles, Chez Léon, Au Patio are all good, but Maison Rousseau, with its raised platforms amid the produce for serving oysters and snails with marvelous bread, St-Marcellin cheese, and a white Côtes du Rhône, stands out.

㉘ **Institut Lumière.** On the site where the Lumière brothers invented the first cinematographic apparatus, this museum has daily showings of early films and contemporary movies as well as a permanent exhibit about the Lumières. Researchers may access the archives, which contain numerous films, books, periodicals, director and actor information, photo files, posters, and more. ✉ *25 rue Premier-Film, Part-Dieu* ☎ *04–78–78–18–95* 🖼 *€4* ☉ *Tues.–Fri. 9–12:30 and 2–6, weekends 2–6.*

▶ ☾ ⓲ **Maison des Canuts** (Silk Weavers' Museum). Despite the industrialization of silk and textile production, old-time Jacquard looms are still in action at this historical house in the Croix Rousse. The weavers are happy to show children how to operate a miniature loom. ✉ *12 rue d'Ivry, La Croix Rousse* ☎ *04–78–28–62–04* 🖼 *€3* ☉ *Sept.–July, weekdays 8:30–noon and 2–6:30, Sat. 9–noon and 2–6; Aug., Tues.–Fri. 8:30–noon and 2–6:30, Sat. 9–noon and 2–6.*

★ ㉓ **Musée des Arts Décoratifs** (Decorative Arts Museum). Housed in an 18th-century mansion, this museum has fine collections of silverware, furniture, objets d'art, porcelain, and tapestries. ✉ *34 rue de la Charité, Presqu'île* ☎ *04–78–38–42–00* 🖼 *€6, joint ticket with the nearby Musée Historique des Tissus* ☉ *Tues.–Sun. 10–5:30.*

★ ㉑ **Musée des Beaux-Arts** (Fine Arts Museum). In the elegant 17th-century Palais St-Pierre, once a Benedictine abbey, this museum has one of France's largest collections of art after that of the Louvre, including Rodin's *Walker,* Byzantine ivories, Etruscan statues, and Egyptian artifacts. Amid Old Master, Impressionist, and modern paintings are works by the tight-knit Lyon School, characterized by exquisitely rendered flowers and overbearing religious sentimentality. Note Louis Janmot's *Poem of the Soul,* immaculately painted visions that are by turns heavenly, hellish, and downright spooky. ✉ *Palais St-Pierre, 20 pl. des Terreaux, Presqu'île* ☎ *04–72–10–17–40* 🖼 *€4* ☉ *Wed.–Mon. 10:30–6.*

need a
break? For an adorable perch over the Rhône and a perfect sunset observation point, **Pieds Humides** (✉ 15 Quai Victor Augagneur, Part-Dieu)—literally, "wet feet"—is a nonpareil little kiosk for a coffee, a *pot de vin,* or a passable *plat du jour.*

㉔ Musée Historique des Tissus (Textile History Museum). On display is a fascinating exhibit of intricate carpets, tapestries, and silks, including Asian tapestries from as early as the 4th century, Turkish and Persian carpets from the 16th to the 18th centuries, and 18th-century Lyon silks, so lovingly depicted in many portraits of the time and still the star of many costume exhibits mounted throughout the world today. ✉ *34 rue de la Charité, Presqu'île* ☎ *04–78–38–42–00* 💲 *€6, joint ticket with Musée des Arts Décoratifs* ⊙ *Tues.–Sun. 10–5:30.*

㉚ Musée Urbain Tony Garnier (Tony Garnier Urban Museum). Known also as the Cité de la Création (City of Creation), this project was France's first attempt at low-income housing. Over the years, tenants have tried to bring some art and cheerfulness to their environment: 22 giant murals depicting the work of Tony Garnier, the turn-of-the-20th-century Lyon architect, were painted on the walls of these huge housing projects, built in 1920 and 1933. Artists from around the world, with the support of UNESCO, have added their vision to the creation of the ideal housing project. To get there, take the métro from place Bellecour to Monplaisir-Lumière and walk 10 minutes south along rue Antoine. ✉ *4 rue Serpollières, Part-Dieu* ☎ *04–78–75–16–75* 💲 *€4* ⊙ *Daily 2–6.*

㉒ Opéra de Lyon. The barrel-vaulted Lyon Opera, a reincarnation of a moribund 1831 building, was designed by star French architect Jean Nouvel and built in the early 1990s. It incorporates a columned exterior, soaring glass vaulting, Neoclassical public spaces, an all-black interior down to and including the bathrooms and toilets, and the latest backstage magic. High above, looking out between the heroic statues lined up along the parapet, is a small restaurant, Les Muses. ✉ *Pl. de la Comédie, Presqu'île* ☎ *04–72–00–45–00, 04–72–00–45–45 for tickets.*

㉙ Parc de la Tête d'Or (Golden Head Park). On the bank of the Rhône, this 300-acre park encompasses a lake, pony rides, and a small zoo. It's ideal for an afternoon's outing with children. Take the métro from Perrache train station to Masséna. ✉ *Pl. du Général-Leclerc, quai Charles-de-Gaulle, Cité Internationale* 💲 *Free* ⊙ *Dawn–dusk.*

㉖ Place Carnot. Spread out in front of the Perrache train station built in 1857, this bustling square holds an excellent Christmas market from early December through New Year's. The two main monuments represent La République and (the seated figure) the City of Lyon. The Brasserie Georges, dating from 1836, has hosted legendary personalities from Mistinguet to Jacques Brel and Johnny Halliday. ✉ *Presqu'île.*

⑲ Place des Terreaux. The four majestic horses rearing up from a monumental 19th-century fountain in the middle of this large square are by Frédéric-Auguste Bartholdi, who sculpted New York Harbor's Statue of Liberty. The 69 fountains embedded in the wide expanse of the square are illuminated by fiber-optic technology at night. The notable buildings on either side are the Hôtel de Ville and the Musée des Beaux-Arts. ⊠ *Presqu'île.*

Where to Stay & Eat

★ **$$$$** ✕ **Léon de Lyon.** Chef Jean-Paul Lacombe's innovative uses of the region's butter, cream, and foie gras put this restaurant at the forefront of the city's gastronomic scene. Dishes such as fillet of veal with celery and leg of lamb with fava beans are memorable; suckling pig comes with foie gras, onions, and a truffle salad. Alcoves and wood paneling in this 19th-century house add charm to the mix. Prix-fixe menus are €91 and €115. ⊠ *1 rue Pléney, Presqu'île* ☎ *04–72–10–11–12* ⚹ *Reservations essential* ⚏ *Jacket required* ⊟ *AE, DC, MC, V* ⊗ *Closed Sun. and Mon. and 1st 3 wks Aug.*

★ **$$$$** ✕ **Les Loges.** With dazzlers like roast wild boar with rosemary raisins and poached red pears or cinnamon chicken with Swiss chard on his bill of fare, it's little wonder their creator, Nicolas Le Bec, was named Gault-Millau Chef of the Year 2002. Vegetables triumph here, so much so that this young Breton chef lists them first on the menu for each entrée. To top it all off, mahogany chairs, modern art, and a giant medieval hearth make for a stunning setting. ⊠ *6 rue du Boeuf, Vieux Lyon* ☎ *04–72–77–44–44* ⊟ *AE, DC, MC, V* ⊗ *Sun., Mon., and Aug. 4–26.*

$$$$ ✕ **Paul Bocuse.** Parisians hop the TGV to dine at this culinary shrine north
Fodor'sChoice of Lyon in Collonges-au-Mont-d'Or, then snooze back to the capital.
★ Whether Bocuse—who kickstarted the "new" French cooking back in the 1970s and became a superstar in the process—is here or not, the legendary black-truffle soup in pastry crust he created to honor President Giscard d'Estaing will be. So will the frogs'-leg soup with watercress, the green bean–and–artichoke salad with foie gras, or the Bresse chicken cooked *en vessie* (in a bladder). Like the desserts, the grand dining room is done in traditional style. Call ahead if you want to find out whether Bocuse will be cooking, and book far in advance. ⊠ *50 quai de la Plage, Collonges-au-Mont-d'Or, Pont de Collonges Nord* ☎ *04–72–42–90–90* ⚹ *Reservations essential* ⚏ *Jacket required* ⊟ *AE, DC, MC, V.*

$$$$ ✕ **Pierre Orsi.** Pierre Orsi's lavish restaurant, a pink-stucco wonder, is alongside a tiny tree-lined square. Marble floors, brocade draperies, bronze nudes, and gilt-frame paintings make it glamorously festive. The foie gras ravioli with truffles and the mesclun with goat cheese are hard acts to follow, though the dessert of sliced figs with pistachio ice cream holds its own. ⊠ *3 pl. Kléber, Presqu'île* ☎ *04–78–89–57–68* ⚹ *Reservations essential* ⚏ *Jacket required* ⊟ *AE, MC, V* ⊗ *Closed Sun. except holidays.*

$$–$$$$ ✕ **L'Alexandrin.** Chef Alex Alexanian's take on nouvelle cuisine is everything to every mouth. If succulent game is your weakness, this is the place, especially during hunting season. If you're tired of oversaturated Lyonnaise cuisine, try the special "*fruits et légumes*" menu, a creative feast of fresh goodies selected each morning from Les Halles market, just around the corner. Whether a dish is based on veal, rabbit, or sole, Alexanian's touch is always light on calories and heavy on flavor. ⊠ *83 rue Moncey, Part-Dieu* ☎ *04–72–61–15–69* ⊟ *MC, V* ⊗ *Closed Sun. and Mon. and July 29–Aug. 20.*

★ **$$–$$$** ✕ **L'Étage.** Hidden over place des Terreaux, this semi-secret upstairs dining room prepares some of Lyon's finest new cuisine. A place at the window (admittedly hard to come by), overlooking the facade of the Beaux Arts academy across the square, is a moment to remember, especially if it's during the December 8th Festival of Lights. ✉ *4 pl. des Terreaux, Presqu'île* ☎ *04–78–28–19–59* ▬ *AE, DC, MC, V* ☯ *Closed Feb., July 22–Aug. 22, Sun., and Mon.*

$$–$$$ ✕ **Le Nord.** Should you want to keep some change in your pocket and still sample cooking by Paul Bocuse–trained chefs, lunch at one of his four bistros distributed around Lyon's cardinal points. Specialties include dishes from the *rotissoire* and excellent fish and seafood. Bocuse's other spots are **Le Sud** (✉ 11 pl. Antonin-Poncet, Presqu'île ☎ 04–72–77–80–00), the rollicking **L'Est** (✉ Gare des Brotteaux 14, Les Brotteaux ☎ 04–37–24–25–26) in the old 19th-century Brotteaux train station, and **L'Ouest** (✉ Quai du Commerce 1, Villefranche ☎ 04–78–35–63–13). ✉ *18 rue Neuve, Presqu'île* ☎ *04–72–10–69–69* ▬ *AE, DC, MC, V.*

★ **$$–$$$** ✕ **Les Muses.** High up under the glass vault of the Opéra de Lyon designed by Jean Nouvel, this small restaurant run by Philippe Chavent looks out between statues of the Muses to the Hôtel de Ville. The quality of the nouvelle cuisine makes it hard to choose between the choices offered, but the salmon in butter sauce with watercress mousse is a winner. ✉ *Opéra de Lyon, Presqu'île* ☎ *04–72–00–45–58* ⚖ *Reservations essential* ▬ *AE, MC, V* ☯ *Closed Sun.*

$–$$ ✕ **Anticipation.** Light, creative dishes using the region's famed specialties (such as poulet de Bresse) are carefully prepared here by John Rosiak, a former cook at Georges Blanc. The homey feel makes it a place where you can settle in for an evening of good fare and fun. ✉ *8 rue Chavanne, Presqu'île* ☎ *04–78–30–91–92* ▬ *AE, MC, V* ☯ *Closed Mon. No dinner Sun.*

$–$$ ✕ **Café des Fédérations.** For 80 years this sawdust-strewn café with homey red-check tablecloths has reigned as one of the city's leading *bouchons* (historic taverns). It may have overextended its stay, however, by trading on past glory. Some readers report a desultory hand in the kitchen, and native Lyonnais seem to head elsewhere. Others say Raymond Fulchiron not only serves deftly prepared local classics like *boudin blanc* (white-meat sausage) but also stops by to chat with you, making you feel at home. ✉ *8 rue du Major-Martin, Presqu'île* ☎ *04–78–28–26–00* ▬ *AE, DC, MC, V* ☯ *Closed weekends and Aug.*

★ **¢–$** ✕ **Café 203/Café 100 Tabac.** These two clever sister bistros near the opera are young, hot, and happening. One is named for the Peugeot 203 (an antique model of which is parked outside), and the other is a play on "100/sans" (100 percent–without) tobacco—yes, you read it here: a smoke-free restaurant in Europe. The Italianate cuisine is fresh and original, fast, inexpensive, and delicious. For a quick pre- or post-opera meal, this is the spot. ✉ *9 rue du Garet Presqu'île* ✉ *23 rue de l'Arbre Sec, Presqu'île* ☎ *04–78–42–24–62* ▬ *AE, DC, MC, V* ☯ *Closed Sun., no lunch except Sat. from Sept. to Easter.*

$–$$ ✕ **Chez Hugon.** This typical bouchon-tavern with red-check tablecloths is behind the Musée des Beaux-Arts and is one of the city's top-rated insider spots. Practically a club, it's crowded with regulars, who keep busy trading quips with the owner while Madame prepares the best *tablier de sapeur* (tripe marinated in wine and fried in breadcrumbs) in town. Whether you order the hunks of homemade pâté, the stewed chicken in wine vinegar sauce, or the plate of *ris de veau* (sweetbreads), your dinner will add up to good, inexpensive food and plenty of it. ⊠ *12 rue Pizay, Presqu'île* ☎ *04–78–28–10–94* ⊟ *MC, V* ⊘ *Closed weekends and Aug.*

★ **$–$$** ✕ **Comptoir Abel.** This charming 400-year-old house is one of Lyon's most frequently filmed and photographed taverns. Simple wooden tables in wood-paneled dining rooms, quirky art on every wall, heavy-bottomed *pot lyonnais* wine bottles: every detail is obviously pampered and lovingly produced. The *salade lyonnaise* (green salad with homemade croutons and sautéed bacon, topped with a poached egg) or the *rognons madère* (kidneys in a madeira sauce) are standouts. ⊠ *25 rue Guynemer, Presqu'île* ☎ *04–78–37–46–18* ⊟ *AE, DC, MC, V* ⊘ *Closed Sat., Sun., and Dec. 22–Jan. 2.*

$ ✕ **Jura.** The rows of tables, the 1934 mosaic-tile floor, and the absence of anything pretty gives this place the feel of a men's club. The mustachioed owner, looking as if he stepped out of the turn-of-the-20th-century prints on the walls, acts gruffly but with a smile, as his wife rushes around. The game and steak dishes are robust, as is the *cassoulet des escargots* (stew of beans, mutton, and snails). For dessert, stick with the fine cheese selection. ⊠ *25 rue Tupin, Presqu'île* ☎ *04–78–42–20–57* ⊟ *MC, V* ⊘ *Closed Sun., weekends May–Sept., Mon. Sept.–Apr.*

$ ✕ **Le Vivarais.** Robert Duffaud's simple, tidy restaurant is an outstanding culinary value. Don't expect napkins folded into flower shapes— the excitement is on your plate, with dishes like *lièvre royale* (hare rolled and stuffed with foie gras and a hint of truffles). ⊠ *1 pl. du Dr-Gailleton, Presqu'île* ☎ *04–78–37–85–15* ⚎ *Reservations essential* ⊟ *AE, MC, V* ⊘ *Closed Sun. and July 27–Aug. 19; Dec. 25–Jan. 1.*

$ ✕ **Les Lyonnais.** This popular brasserie, decorated with photographs of local celebrities, is particularly animated. The simple food—chicken simmered for hours in wine, meat stews, and grilled fish—is served on bare wood tables. A blackboard announces plats du jour, which are less expensive than items on the printed menu. Try the *caille aux petits legumes* (quail with vegetables) for a change from heavier bouchon fare such as *la quenelle* (pike dumpling) or *l'andouillette* (sausage). ⊠ *1 rue Tramassac, Vieux Lyon* ☎ *04–78–37–64–82* ⊟ *MC, V* ⊘ *Closed Aug. and 1st wk Jan.*

★ **$** ✕ **Mâchonnerie.** The word *mâchon* comes from the morning snack of the silkweaver or *canut,* and has come to mean the typical food of the Lyon region. This is one of Lyon's most respected popular bistros, under the *ficelle,* the funicular up to the Fourvière hill. Try the *andouillettes* (sausage). ⊠ *36 rue Tramassac, Vieux Lyon* ☎ *04–78–42–24–62* ⊟ *AE, DC, MC, V* ⊘ *Closed Sun. and lunch except Sat. from Sept. to Easter.*

¢ ✕ **Brasserie Georges.** This inexpensive brasserie at the south end of rue de la Charité next to the Perrache train station is one of the city's largest and oldest, founded in 1836 but now in a palatial Art Deco building. Meals range from hearty veal stew or sauerkraut and sausage to more refined fare. The kitchen could be better—stick with the great standards, such as *saucisson brioché* (sausage in brioche stuffed with truffled foie gras)—but the ambience is as delicious as it comes. ⊠ *30 cours Verdun, Perrache* ☎ *04–72–56–54–54* ☐ *AE, DC, MC, V.*

★ **$$$$** ✕⊡ **La Cour des Loges.** King Juan Carlos of Spain, Celine Dion, and the Rolling Stones have all graced this most eye-popping of Lyon hotels. Spectacularly renovated around a glassed-in Renaissance courtyard, this former Jesuit convent is now an extravaganza of glowing fireplaces, Florentine crystal chandeliers, Baroque credenzas, high beamed ceilings, mullioned windows, guest rooms swathed in Venetian red and antique Lyon silks, suites that are like artist ateliers, and Phillipe Starck bathrooms. The restaurant, **Les Loges,** is one of Lyon's most talked-about, since it is run by Nicolas Le Bec, a young Breton who was named Gault-Millau Chef of the Year 2002. In addition, there is a cellar-level wine bar and a tapas bar with a lovely vaulted ceiling. ⊠ *6 rue du Boeuf, Vieux Lyon, 69005* ☎ *04–72–77–44–44* 🖷 *04–72–40–93–61* ⊕ *www. courdesloges.com* ◁ *52 rooms* ᗉ *Restaurant, tapas bar, minibars, cable TV, pool, health club, sauna, bar, meeting rooms, parking (fee)* ☐ *AE, DC, MC, V* ᵀᴼᵀ *EP.*

★ **$$$$** ✕⊡ **La Tour Rose.** Philippe Chavent's silk-swathed Vieux Lyon hotel occupies a Renaissance-period convent set around a gorgeous Florentine-style courtyard under a rose-washed tower. The glass-roof restaurant occupies a former chapel and offers views of the hanging garden overhead. Each guest room is named for a famous silkweaving concern and decorated in its goods; taffetas, plissés, and velvets cover walls, windows, and beds in daring, even startling styles. The signature specials here—smoked-duck soup, skate in oyster coulis, hibiscus sorbet—are well worth all the extra *louis d'or.* Six apartments with kitchenettes in an adjacent annex provide excellent value for longer stays. ⊠ *22 rue du Boeuf, Vieux Lyon, 69005* ☎ *04–78–92–69–10* 🖷 *04–78–42–26–02* ⊕ *www.tour-rose.com* ◁ *12 rooms, 6 apartments* ᗉ *Restaurant, minibars, cable TV, bar, meeting rooms, parking (fee), some pets allowed* ☐ *AE, DC, MC, V* ᵀᴼᵀ *EP.*

★ **$$$$** ⊡ **Villa Florentine.** High above the *Vieille Ville* (Old Town), near the Roman theaters and the basilica, this pristine hotel was once a 17th-century convent—and everyone knows the sisters always enjoyed the best real estate in town. It has beamed and vaulted ceilings, terraces, and particularly marvelous views, which are seen to best advantage from the pool and the excellent restaurant, Les Terrasses de Lyon. In time-warp fashion, 17th-century Italianate architectural details are contrasted with the latest in bright postmodern Italian furnishings. ⊠ *25–27 Montée St-Barthélémy, Fourvière, 69005* ☎ *04–72–56–56–56* 🖷 *04–72–40–90–56* ⊕ *www.villaflorentine.com* ◁ *11 rooms, 8 suites* ᗉ *Restaurant, café, minibars, cable TV, pool, bar, Internet, meeting rooms, parking (fee), some pets allowed (fee)* ☐ *AE, DC, MC, V* ᵀᴼᵀ *EP.*

$$$–$$$$ ⊡ **Boscolo Grand Hôtel.** This Belle Epoque hotel off place de la République has a courteous and efficient staff. Rooms have high ceilings, mostly modern furnishings, and one special piece such as an armoire or writing desk. Erté prints try hard to set a stylish tone in the guest rooms, the Rhône is just across the street, and tour groups are kept happy and content. ⊠ *11 rue Grôlée, Presqu'île, 69002* ☎ *04–72–40–45–45*

🖦 *04-78-37-52-55* ⊕ *www.boscolohotels.com* ⤶ *140 rooms* ⟨ *Restaurant, cable TV, bar, meeting rooms, parking (fee), some pets allowed (fee)* ⊟ *AE, DC, MC, V* |◎| *BP.*

$$$ ▦ **Globe et Cécil.** This impeccably bright and clean hotel tucked in just one block north of place Bellecour is in the very heart of Lyon. The rooms are as cheery and fresh as the lobby; the staff is effervescent and pleasant, and the cost-value ratio is a definite boon to the soul (and wallet). What this place may lack in time-varnished charm it compensates for with crisp, polite efficiency and comfort. ⊠ *21 rue Gasparin, Presqu'île, 69002* ☎ *04-78-42-58-95* 🖦 *04-72-41-99-06* ⊕ *www. globeetcecilhotel.com* ⤶ *60 rooms* ⟨ *Cable TV, bar, parking (fee), some pets allowed* ⊟ *AE, DC, MC, V* |◎| *BP.*

$-$$ ▦ **Hôtel des Artistes.** This intimate hotel on an elegant square opposite the Théâtre des Célestins has long been popular among stage and screen artists; black-and-white photographs of actors and actresses adorn lobby walls. Rooms are smallish but modern and comfortable, and the friendly reception and great location appeal to all comers. ⊠ *8 rue Gaspard-André, Presqu'île, 69002* ☎ *04-78-42-04-88* 🖦 *04-78-42-93-76* ⤶ *45 rooms* ⟨ *Minibars; no a/c* ⊟ *AE, DC, MC, V* |◎| *EP.*

$ ▦ **Hôtel Bayard.** Rooms at this hotel in the heart of town each have a distinctive look. One favorite, No. 2, overlooks the large square and has a canopy bed. For a group, opt for No. 15, which sleeps four. Only breakfast is served, but there are dozens of restaurants nearby. ⊠ *23 pl. Bellecour, Presqu'île, 69002* ☎ *04-78-37-39-64* 🖦 *04-72-40-95-51* ⊕ *www.hotelbayard.com* ⤶ *22 rooms* ⟨ *Cable TV, bar, parking (fee); no a/c* ⊟ *MC, V* |◎| *EP.*

★ $ ▦ **Hôtel du Théâtre.** The friendly and enthusiastic owner is sufficient reason to recommend this small hotel. But its location and reasonable prices make it even more commendable. Rooms are simple but clean; those overlooking place des Célestins not only have a theatrical view but also a bathroom with a tub. Those facing the side have a shower only. Breakfast is included. ⊠ *10 rue de Savoie, Presqu'île, 69002* ☎ *04-78-42-33-32* 🖦 *04-72-40-00-61* ⤶ *21 rooms* ⟨ *Bar, parking (fee); no a/c* ⊟ *AE, DC, MC, V* |◎| *EP.*

¢ ▦ **Citôtel Dubost.** This little gem is a lot better than a first glance might indicate. Rooms are small but impeccable; the art hanging around the walls is generic but good; the breakfast bread, croissant, and coffee is uniformly excellent; and the staff is friendly and helpful. The one-minute walk to Lyon's slick subway line at Gare Perrache can be handy in rain or in haste, though the walk to the other end of Presqu'île is an entertaining 45-minute gallop not to miss. ⊠ *19 pl. Carnot, Presqu'île, 69002* ☎ *04-78-42-00-46* 🖦 *04-72-40-96-66* ⤶ *56 rooms* ⟨ *Some pets allowed* ⊟ *AE, DC, MC, V* |◎| *EP.*

Nightlife & the Arts

Lyon is the region's liveliest arts center; check the weekly *Lyon-Poche*, published on Wednesday and sold at newsstands, for cultural events and goings-on at the dozens of discos, bars, and clubs.

CloseUp

LYON'S DANCE BLOW-OUT

LYON'S BIENNALE DE LA DANCE *throws France's second city into perpetual motion for nearly three weeks every other September (on even-numbered years). Brainchild of Lyon choreographer Guy Darmet, 2002's tenth edition, entitled "Terra Latina—From the Rio Grande to Tierra del Fuego," brought together some 600 dancers and choreographers from 11 Latin American countries with another eight contemporary dance troupes invited from France. The 2004 chapter of the biennale featured dance companies from all over Europe, with an emphasis on new members of the European Union such as Poland, Hungary, Bulgaria, Slovakia, and the Czech Republic. The result, no matter which even year you choose, is a nonpareil dance blow-out at the confluence of the Saône and Rhône rivers. At each biennale, in addition to the more than 100 performances scheduled in the city's finest venues such as the Jean*

Nouvel opera house, the Maison de la Danse, and the cookie box-like Théâtre des Célestins, popular highlights include the tumultuous 4,500-dancer street parade that roars down the left bank of the Rhône on the festival's first Sunday, and the three Saturday night dance galas held in the graceful Brotteaux train station, the Halle Tony Garnier, or the Place des Terreaux. Collective dance classes for thousands and spontaneous outbursts of tango, salsa, or nearly any other genre of rhythmic movement ever devised, pop up all over town, while newspaper front pages feature little else. With the world's largest dance festival budget ($5,000,000) and two decades of solid success under his belt, Darmet's spectacular celebration of modern and contemporary dance in one of Europe's most exciting cities is still gaining momentum. The Web site (⊕ www.biennale-de-lyon.org) has all the exciting details.

For darts and pints and jazz on weekends, head to the **Albion Public House** (✉ 12 rue Ste-Catherine, Presqu'île ☎ 04–78–28–33–00), where they even accept British pounds. The low-key, chic **L'Alibi** (✉ 13 quai Romain-Roland, Vieux Lyon ☎ 04–78–42–04–66) has a laser show along with the music. **Bar Live** (✉ 13 pl. Jules Ferry, Vieux Lyon ☎ 04–72–74–04–41) is in the old Brotteaux train station and is the current drinking haunt. Romantics rendezvous at the **Bar de la Tour Rose** (✉ 22 rue du Boeuf, Vieux Lyon ☎ 04–78–37–25–90).

Bouchon aux Vin (✉ 64 rue Mercière, Presqu'île ☎ 04–78–42–88–90) is a wine bar with 30-plus vintages. Computer jocks head into cyberspace at **Le Chantier** (✉ 18–20 rue Ste-Catherine, Presqu'île ☎ 04–78–39–05–56), while their friends listen to jazz and nibble on tapas. Caribbean and African music pulses at **Le Club des Iles** (✉ 1 Grande-Rue des Feuillants, Presqu'île ☎ 04–78–39–16–35). Live jazz is played in the stone-vaulted basement of **Hot Club** (✉ 26 rue Lanterne, Presqu'île ☎ 04–78–39–54–74). A gay crowd is found among the 1930s blandishments at **La Ruche** (✉ 22 rue Gentil, Presqu'île ☎ 04–78–39–03–82). **Villa Florentine** (✉ 25 Montée St-Barthélémy, Fourvière ☎ 04–72–56–56–56) is a quiet spot for sipping a drink to the strains of a harpist, who plays on Friday and Saturday. **La**

Cave des Voyageurs (✉ 7 pl. St-Paul–St-Barthélémy, Vieux Lyon ☎ 04–78–28–92–28), just below the St-Paul train station, is a cozy place to try some top wines.

Café-Théâtre de L'Accessoire (✉ 26 rue de l'Annonciade, Presqu'île ☎ 04–78–27–84–84) is a leading café-theater where you can eat and drink while watching a review. **Le Complexe du Rire** (✉ 7 rue des Capucins, Presqu'île ☎ 04–78–27–23–59) is a lively satirical and comic review above place des Terreaux. The café-theater **Espace Gerson** (✉ 1 pl. Gerson, Vieux Lyon ☎ 04–78–27–96–99) presents revues in conjunction with dinner. The **Opéra de Lyon** (✉ 1 pl. de la Comédie, Presqu'île ☎ 04–72–00–45–45) presents plays, concerts, ballets, and opera from October to June. Lyon's Société de Musique de Chambre performs at **Salle Molière** (✉ 18 quai Bondy, Vieux Lyon ☎ 04–78–28–03–11).

Early fall sees the unforgettably spectacular **Biennale de la Danse** (Dance Biennial), which occurs every other year in even-numbered years. See our CloseUp Box, "Lyon's Dance Blow-Out" (⊕ www.biennale-de-lyon.org/) for the full scoop. September is the time for the **Foire aux Tupiniers** (☎ 04–78–37–00–68), a pottery fair. October brings the **Festival Bach** (☎ 04–78–72–75–31). The **Biennale d'Art Contemporain** (Contemporary Art Biennial; ☎ 04–78–30–50–66) is held in odd-numbered years in October. The **Festival du Vieux Lyon** (☎ 04–78–42–39–04) is a music festival in November and December. On December 8, the Fête de La Immaculée Conception (Feast of the Immaculate Conception), startling lighting creations transform the city into a fantasy for the marvelous **Fête de Lumière,** Lyon's Festival of Lights.

Shopping

Lyon has the region's best shopping; it's still the nation's silk-and-textile capital, and all big-name designers have shops here—for their chic clothing emporia try the stores on rue du Président Édouard-Herriot and rue de la République in the center of town. Lyon's biggest shopping mall is the **Part-Dieu Shopping Center** (✉ Rue du Dr-Bouchut, Part-Dieu ☎ 04–72–60–60–62), where there are 14 movie theaters and 250 shops. France's major department stores are well represented in Lyon. **Galeries Lafayette** (✉ in Part-Dieu Shopping Center, Part-Dieu ☎ 04–72–61–44–44 ✉ 6 pl. des Cordeliers, Presqu'île ☎ 04–72–40–48–00 ✉ 200 bd. Pinel, Villeurbanne ☎ 04–78–77–82–12) has always brought Parisian flair to its outlying branches. **Printemps** (✉ 42 rue de la République, Presqu'île ☎ 04–72–41–29–29) is the Lyon outpost of the big Paris store.

Captiva (✉ 10 rue de la Charité, Perrache ☎ 04–78–37–96–15) is the boutique of a young designer who works mainly in silk. **Les Gones** (✉ 33 rue Leynaud, La Croix Rousse ☎ 04–78–28–40–78), in the Croix Rousse, is a boutique carrying the work of several young designers. The workshop of **Monsieur Georges Mattelon** (✉ Rue d'Ivry, Presqu'île ☎ 04–78–28–62–04) is one of the oldest silk-weaving shops in Lyon. Lyonnais designer **Clémentine** (✉ 18 rue Émile-Zola, Presqu'île) is good for well-cut, tailored clothing. **Étincelle** (✉ 34 rue St-Jean, Vieux Lyon) has trendy outfits for youngsters.

For antiques, wander down **rue Auguste-Comte** (✉ From pl. Bellecour to Perrache). **Image en Cours** (✉ 26 rue du Boeuf, Vieux Lyon) sells superb engravings. **La Maison des Canuts** (✉ 10–12 rue d'Ivry, Croix Rousse) carries local textiles. Fabrics can also be found at the **Boutique des Soyeux Lyonnais** (✉ 3 rue du Boeuf, Vieux Lyon).

For arts and crafts there are several places where you can find irresistible objects. Look for Lyonnais puppets on **place du Change**. For new art, try the **Marché des Artistes** (Artists' Market; ✉ Quai Romain-Rolland, 5ᵉ, Vieux Lyon) every Sunday morning from 7 to 1. Held on Sunday morning is another **Marché des Artisans** (Crafts Market; ✉ Quai Fulchiron, 5ᵉ, Vieux Lyon). A **Marché aux Puces** (Flea Market; ✉ Take Bus 37; 1 rue du Canal, Villeurbanne) takes place on Thursday and Saturday mornings 8–noon and on Sunday 6–1. For **secondhand books** try the market along quai de la Pêcherie (2ᵉ) near place Bellecour, held every Saturday and Sunday 10–6.

Food markets are held from Tuesday through Sunday on boulevard de la Croix-Rousse (4ᵉ), at Les Halles on cours Lafayette (3ᵉ), on quai Victor Augagneur (3ᵉ), and on quai St-Antoine (2ᵉ). For up-to-the-minute information on food, restaurants, and great wines, don't miss the (English speaking) "flying sommelier," Georges Dos Santos at **Antic Wine** (✉ 18 rue du Boeuf, Vieux Lyon ☎ 04–78–37–08–96). A wine shop with an excellent selection is **À Ma Vigne** (✉ 18 rue Vaubecour, Presqu'île ☎ 04–78–37–05–29). **La Compagnie Beaujolaise 3è Fleuve** (✉ 7 rue Colonel Chambonnet, Presqu'île ☎ 04–78–42–70–96) offers excellent *3ème fleuve* (Lyon's third river: Beaujolais) products, from wines to pots lyonnais to olive oils. **Cave de la Côte** (✉ 5 rue Pleney, Presqu'île ☎ 04–78–42–93–20) also has good wines. For chocolates head to **Bernachon** (✉ 42 cours Franklin-Roosevelt, Les Brotteaux); some say it's the best *chocolaterie* in France. For fragrances, photos, furniture, philosophy, and comprehensive Oriental tea culture, **Cha Yuan** (✉ 7–9 rue des Remparts d'Ainay, Presqu'île) is the best boutique in Lyon, with more than 300 varieties of tea on sale from all over the world. **Eléphant des Montagnes** (✉ 43 rue Auguste Comte, Presqu'île), not far from Perrache station, has treasures from Nepal, Afghanistan, India, and the Himalayas, lovingly retrieved by Pierre Chavanne. **La Boîte à Dessert** (✉ 1 rue de l'Ancienne-Préfecture, Presqu'île) makes luscious peach turnovers. For culinary variety, shop **Les Halles** (✉ 102 cours Lafayette, Part-Dieu). **Pignol** (✉ 17 rue Émile-Zola, Presqu'île) is good for meats and sandwich-makings. **Reynon** (✉ 13 rue des Archers, Presqu'île) is the place for charcuterie.

BEAUJOLAIS & LA DOMBES

North of Lyon along the Saône are the vineyards of Beaujolais, a thrill for any oenophile. In the area around Villefranche, small villages—perhaps comprising a church, a bar, and a boulangerie—pop up here and there out of the rolling vine-covered hillsides. Lyon's tourist office has a decent map of the Beaujolais region; even better is the "Vignobles de Beaujolais" map, available in Villefranche's tourist office. Beaujolais wine is made exclusively from the *gamay noir à jus blanc* grape. The region's best wines are all labeled "Grand Cru," a more complex version of the otherwise light, fruity Beaujolais. For the price of one bottle, you can spend an afternoon getting a wealth of knowledge (and a little buzz) by visiting one of the village *caves* (cellars where wine is made, stored, and sold), from big-time tourist operators to mom-and-pop stops. Make sure the ones you pick have DÉGUSTATION signs out front. Signs that say VENTE EN DIRECT (sold directly from the property) and VENTE AU DÉTAIL (sold by the bottle) are also good indicators.

East of the Saône is the fertile land of La Dombes, where ornithologists flock to see migratory bird life. North of La Dombes and east of the Beaujolais wine villages is Bourg-en-Bresse, famous for its marvelous church and a breed of poultry that delights gourmands; it makes a good base after Lyon. South toward the Rhône, the great river of southern France, is the well-preserved medieval village of Pérouges.

L'Arbresle

③ *16 km (10 mi) northwest of Lyon.*

If you love modern architecture, don't miss Éveux, outside L'Arbresle. Here the stark, blocky Dominican convent of **Ste-Marie de la Tourette** protrudes over the hillside, resting on slender pillars that look like stilts and revealing the minimalist sensibilities of architect Le Corbusier, who designed it in 1957–59. ☏ *04–74–01–01–03* ☒*€5* ☉ *July and Aug., daily 9–noon and 2–6; Sept.–June, weekends 2–6.*

Villefranche-sur-Saône

㉜ *6 km (4 mi) east of Ars-sur-Formans, 31 km (19 mi) north of Lyon.*

The lively industrial town of Villefranche-sur-Saône is the capital of the Beaujolais region and is known for its *vin nouveau* (new wine). Thanks to marketing hype, this youthful, fruity red wine is eagerly gulped down around the world every year on the third Thursday of November.

Where to Stay & Eat

$$–$$$ ✕ **Juliénas.** This simple little restaurant delivers what other, pricier restaurants in town don't, won't, or can't: bistro fare that does honor to traditional Beaujolais cookery. All the all-stars are here: andouillette, hot sausage, pork with tarragon, and, for dessert, a luscious *île flottante*. The €17 prix-fixe menu, served lunch and dinner, is one of the best deals in the region. ☒ *236 rue d'Anse* ☏ *04–74–09–16–55* ⊟ *AE, MC, V* ☉ *Closed Mon. No dinner Sun.*

★ $$$$ ✕⌂ **Château de Bagnols.** This intimate and exquisite 13th-century castle southwest of Villefranche is filled with period glassware, fabrics, and porcelain to go with the antique furniture. The 17th- and 18th-century murals were inspired by Lyon's textile industry. Rooms are huge, as are the baronial bathrooms. Those in the main château evoke the 18th century, while the ones in La Résidence, converted stables, and carriage houses, are rustic-contemporary. Wine tastings are held in the beautiful stone *cuvage* (wine-pressing room). ☒ *15 km (9 mi) southwest of Villefranche on D38 to Tarare, 69620 Bagnols* ☏ *04–74–71–40–00*

⌂ *04–74–71–40–49* ⊕ *www.bagnols.com* ⊷ *12 rooms, 4 apartments* ♨ *Restaurant, minibars, cable TV, pool, bar, library, some pets allowed* ▭ *AE, DC, MC, V* ⊗ *Closed Jan.–Mar.* ⏍ *EP.*

Beaujolais Route du Vin

Fodor's Choice
★ *16 km (10 mi) north of Villefranche-sur-Saône, 49 km (30 mi) north of Lyon.*

Not all Beaujolais wine is promoted as *vin nouveau*—that's just a marketing gimmick celebrated in full force on the third Thursday of November annually, both here in this region and around the world. Wine classed as "Beaujolais Villages" is higher in alcohol and produced from a clearly defined region northwest of Villefranche. Beaujolais is made from one single variety of grape, the *gamay noir à jus blanc*. However, there are 12 different appellations: Beaujolais, Beaujolais Villages, Brouilly, Chénas, Chiroubles, Côte de Brouilly, Fleurie, Juliénas, Morgon, Moulin à Vent, Régnié, and St-Amour. The Beaujolais Route du Vin (Wine Road), a narrow strip 23 km (14 mi) long, is home to nine of these deluxe Beaujolais wines, also known as *grands crus*. Most villages have a *cave* (communal cellar) or *coopérative* where you can taste and buy. The **École Beaujolaise des Vins** (Beaujolais School of Wine; ✉ Villefranche ☎ 04–74–02–22–18 ⌂ 04–74–02–22–19 ⊕ www.beaujolais.com) organizes lessons in wine tasting and on creating your own cellar.

In the southernmost and largest *vignoble* (vineyard) of the Beaujolais crus is **Odenas,** producing Brouilly, a soft, fruity wine best consumed young. In the vineyard's center is towering Mont Brouilly, a hill whose vines produce a tougher, firmer wine classified as Côte de Brouilly. From Odenas take D68 via St-Lager to **Villié-Morgon,** in the heart of the Morgon vineyard; robust wines that age well are produced here. At Monternot, east of Villié-Morgon, you will find the 15th-century **Château de Corcelles,** noted for its Renaissance galleries, canopied courtyard well, and medieval carvings in its chapel. The guardroom is now an atmospheric tasting cellar. ✉ *Off D9 from Villié-Morgon* ☎ *04–74–66–72–42* ⊗ *Mon.–Sat. 10–noon and 2:30–6:30.*

From Villié-Morgon D68 wiggles north through several more wine villages, including **Chiroubles,** where a rare, light wine best drunk young is produced. The wines from **Fleurie** are elegant and flowery. Well-known **Chénas** is favored for its two crus: the robust, velvety, and expensive Moulin à Vent and the fruity and underestimated Chénas. The wines of **Juliénas** are sturdy and a deep color; sample them in the cellar of the town church (closed Tuesday and lunchtime), amid bacchanalian decor. **St-Amour,** west of Juliénas, produces light but firm reds and a limited quantity of whites. The famous white Pouilly-Fuissé comes from the area around **Fuissé.**

Bourg-en-Bresse

❸❸ *43 km (27 mi) east of St-Amour on N79, 65 km (40 mi) northeast of Lyon.*

Cheerful Bourg-en-Bresse is esteemed among gastronomes for its fowl—striking-looking chickens, the *poulet de Bresse,* with plump white bodies, bright blue feet and red combs (adding up to France's *tricolore,* or national colors). The town's southeasternmost district, Brou, is its most interesting and the site of a singular church. This is a good place to stay before or after a trip along the Beaujolais Wine Road.

The **Église de Brou,** a marvel of the Flamboyant Gothic style, is no longer in religious use. The church was built between 1506 and 1532 by Margaret of Austria in memory of her husband, Philibert le Beau, Duke of Savoy, and their finely sculpted tombs highlight the rich interior. **Son-et-lumière** shows—on Easter and Pentecost Sunday and Monday, and on Thursday, Saturday, and Sunday from May through September—are magical. A massive restoration of the roof has brought it back to its 16th-century state with the same gorgeous, multicolor, intricate patterns found throughout Burgundy. The museum in the nearby **cloister** stands out for its paintings: 16th- and 17th-century Flemish and Dutch artists keep company with 17th- and 18th-century French and Italian masters, 19th-century artists of the Lyon School, Gustave Doré, and contemporary local painters. ⊠ *63 bd. de Brou* ☎ *04–74–22–83–83* ✉ €*5* ⊘ *Apr.–Sept., daily 9–12:30 and 2–6:30; Oct.–Mar., daily 9–noon and 2–5.*

Where to Stay & Eat

★ **$$–$$$** ✕ **L'Auberge Bressane.** Overlooking the Brou church, the modern, polished dining room and chef Jean-Pierre Vullin's cuisine are a good combination. Frogs' legs and Bresse chicken with wild morel cream sauce are specialties; also try the *quenelles de brochet* (poached fish dumplings). Jean-Pierre wanders through the dining room ready for a chat while his staff provides excellent service. Don't miss the house aperitif, a champagne cocktail with fresh strawberry puree. The wine list has 300 vintages. ⊠ *166 bd. de Brou* ☎ *04–74–22–22–68* ⚠ *Reservations essential* ▭ *AE, DC, MC, V* ⊘ *Closed Tues. except holidays.*

$$–$$$ ✕ **La Petite Auberge.** This cozy flower-decked inn is in the countryside on the outskirts of town. Madame Bertrand provides games for children. Chef Philippe Garnier has a subtle way with mullet (he grills it in saffron butter) and Bresse chicken (browned in tangy cider vinegar). ⊠ *St-Just, rte. de Ceyzeriat* ☎ *04–74–22–30–04* ▭ *MC, V* ⊘ *Closed Jan. and Tues. No dinner Mon.*

★ **$$$–$$$$** ✕▫ **Georges Blanc.** Set in the village of Vonnas and one of the great culinary addresses in all Gaul, this simple 19th-century inn full of antique country furniture makes a fine setting for poulet de Bresse, truffles, and lobster, all featured on this legendary menu. The wizard here is Monsieur Blanc, whose culinary DNA extends back to innkeepers dating from the French Revolution. He made his mark in the 1980s with a series of cookbooks, notably *The Natural Cuisine of Georges Blanc.* Today, he serves up his traditional-yet-nouvelle delights in a vast dining room, renovated (overly so, some might say) in a stately style replete with Louis Treize–style chairs, fireplace, and floral tapestries. Wine connoisseurs will go weak in the knees at the cellar here, overflowing with 130,000 bottles. The 30 guest rooms range from (relatively) simple to luxurious. It's worth the trip from Bourg-en-Bresse, but be sure you bring deep pockets. However, a block south you can also repair to Blanc's cheaper and more casual restaurant, **L'Ancienne Auberge,** most delightfully set in a

1900s "Fabrique de Limonade" soda-water plant and now festooned with antique bicycles and daguerrotypes. ✉ *Pl. du Marché, 19 km (12 mi) from Bourg-en-Bresse, 01540 Vonnas* ☎ *04–74–50–90–90* 🖷 *04–74–50–08–80* ⊕ *www.georgesblanc.com* ♨ *Reservations essential* ⇌ *48 rooms* ♨ *Restaurant, minibars, cable TV, tennis court, pool, meeting rooms, helipad, some pets allowed* ▤ *AE, DC, MC, V* ⊘ *Closed Mon.–Tues. and Jan. No lunch Wed.* ❙◯❙ *EP.*

Villars-les-Dombes

㉞ *29 km (18 mi) south of Bourg-en-Bresse, 37 km (23 mi) north of Lyon.*

Villars-les-Dombes is the unofficial capital of La Dombes, an area once covered by a glacier. When the ice retreated, it left a network of lakes and ponds that draws anglers and bird-watchers today. The 56-acre **Parc des Oiseaux,** one of Europe's finest bird sanctuaries, is home-sweet-home to 400 species of birds (some 2,000 individuals from five continents); 435 aviaries house species from waders to birds of prey; and tropical birds in vivid hues fill the indoor birdhouse. Allow two hours. ✉ *Off N83* ☎ *04–74–98–05–54* ⊕ *www.parc-des-oiseaux.com* 🖾 *€7* ⊘ *Daily 9:30–dusk.*

Pérouges

★ **㉟** *21 km (13 mi) southeast of Villars-les-Dombes, 36 km (22 mi) northeast of Lyon.*

Wonderfully preserved (though a little too precious), hilltop Pérouges, with its medieval houses and narrow cobbled streets surrounded by ramparts, is just 200 yards across. Hand-weavers first brought it prosperity; the industrial revolution meant their downfall, and by the late 19th century the population had dwindled from 1,500 to 12. Now the government has restored the most interesting houses, and a potter, bookbinder, cabinetmaker, and weaver have given the town a new lease on life. A number of restaurants make Pérouges a good lunch stop.

Encircling the town is **rue des Rondes;** from this road you can get fine views of the countryside and, on clear days, the Alps. Park your car by the main gateway, **Porte d'En-Haut,** alongside the 15th-century fortress-church. Rue du Prince, the town's main street, leads to the **Maison des Princes de Savoie** (Palace of the Princes of Savoie), formerly the home of the influential Savoie family that once controlled the eastern part of France. Note the fine watchtower. **Place de la Halle,** a pretty square with great charm, around the corner from the Maison des Princes de Savoie, is the site of a lime tree planted in 1792. The **Musée du Vieux Pérouges** (Old Pérouges Museum), to one side of the place de la Halle, contains local artifacts and a reconstructed weaver's workshop. The medieval **garden** is noted for its array of rare medicinal plants. ✉ *Pl. du Tilleul* ☎ *04–74–61–00–88* 🖾 *€5* ⊘ *May–Sept., daily 10–noon and 2–6.*

Where to Stay & Eat

★ **$$–$$$** ✕▥ **L'Ostellerie du Vieux Pérouges.** "The Old Man of Pérouges" is uniquely comprised of four medieval stone residences set around its main showpiece—an extraordinary corbelled, 14th-century timber-frame house now home to the inn's restaurant. Here, regional delights are served up on pewter plates by waitresses in folk costumes, recipes handed down from the days of Charles VII inspire the cook, and everybody partakes of the famous "pancake of Pérouges" dessert. The sweet taste will linger in your guest room, thanks to some time-burnished accents, such as antiques, gigantic stone hearths, and glossy wood floors and tables. Rooms in the geranium-decked 15th-century Au St-Georges et Manoir manor are more spacious—but also nearly twice the cost—than those in L'Annexe and have marble bathrooms and period furniture (one or two rooms even have their own garden). At the lower end of the scale, however, the rooms are fairly simple and threadbare. ⊠ *Pl. du Tilleul, 01800 Pérouges* 🖀 *04–74–61–00–88* 🖷 *04–74–34–77–90* ⊕ *www.ostellerie.com* ↩ *28 rooms* ♨ *Restaurant, minibars, cable TV, bar, meeting rooms, some pets allowed; no a/c* ⊟ *AE, DC, MC, V* 🍽 *EP.*

THE RHÔNE VALLEY

At Lyon, the Rhône, joined by the Saône, truly comes into its own, plummeting south in search of the Mediterranean. The river's progress is often spectacular, as steep vineyards conjure up vistas that are more readily associated with the river's Germanic cousin, the Rhine. All along the way, small-town vintners invite you to sample their wines. Early Roman towns like Vienne and Valence reflect the Rhône's importance as a trading route. To the west is the rugged, rustic Ardèche *département* (province), where time seems to have slowed to a standstill.

Vienne

36 *27 km (17 mi) south of Lyon via A7.*

One of Roman Gaul's most important towns, Vienne became a religious and cultural center under its count-archbishops in the Middle Ages and retains considerable historic charm despite being a major road and train junction. The tourist office anchors cours Brillier in the leafy shadow of the Jardin Public (Public Garden). The €7 Passport admits you to most local monuments and museums; it's available at the tourist office or at the first site that you visit.

On quai Jean-Jaurès, beside the Rhône, is the church of **St-Pierre.** Note the rectangular 12th-century Romanesque bell tower with its arcaded tiers. The lower church walls date from the 6th century. Although religious wars deprived the cathedral of **St-Maurice** of many of its statues, much original decoration is intact; the portals on the 15th-century facade are carved with Old Testament scenes. The cathedral was built between the 12th and 16th centuries, with later additions, such as the splendid 18th-century mausoleum to the right of the altar. A frieze of the zodiac adorns the entrance to the vaulted passage that once led to the cloisters but now opens onto place St-Paul.

★ Place du Palais is the site of the remains of the **Temple d'Auguste et de Livie** (Temple of Augustus and Livia), accessible via place St-Paul and rue Clémentine; they probably date in part from Vienne's earliest Roman settlements (1st century BC). The Corinthian columns were walled in during the 11th century, when the temple was used as a church; in 1833 Prosper Mérimée intervened to have the temple restored. The last vestige of the city's sizable Roman baths is a **Roman gateway** (⊠ Rue Chantelouve) decorated with delicate friezes.

★ The **Théâtre Romain** (Roman Theater), on rue de la Charité, is one of the largest in Gaul (143 yards across). It held 13,000 spectators and is only slightly smaller than Rome's Theater of Marcellus. Rubble buried Vienne's theater until 1922; excavation has uncovered 46 rows of seats, some marble flooring, and the frieze on the stage. Concerts take place here in summer. ⊠ *7 rue du Cirque* ☎ *04–74–85–39–23* 🖅 *€5* ☉ *Apr.–Aug., daily 9–12:30 and 2–6; Sept.–mid-Oct., Tues.–Sun. 9–12:30 and 2–6; mid-Oct.–Mar., Tues.–Sat. 9:30–12:30 and 2–5, Sun. 1:30–5:30.*

Rue des Orfèvres (off rue de la Charité) is lined with Renaissance facades and distinguished by the church of **St-André-le-Bas,** once part of a powerful abbey. If possible, venture past the restoration now in progress to see the finely sculpted 12th-century capitals (made of Roman stone) and the 17th-century wood statue of St. Andrew. It's best to see the cloisters during the music festival held here and at the cathedral from June to August. ⊠ *Cour St-André* ☎ *04–74–85–18–49* 🖅 *€3* ☉ *Apr.–mid-Oct., Tues.–Sun. 9:30–1 and 2–6; mid-Oct.–Mar., Tues.–Sat. 9:30–12:30 and 2–5, Sun. 2–6.*

Across the Rhône from the town center is the excavated **Cité Gallo-Romaine** (Gallo-Roman City), covering several acres. Here you can find villas, houses, workshops, public baths, and roads, all built by the Romans. 🖅 *€5* ☉ *Daily 9–6.*

Where to Stay & Eat

$$–$$$ ✕ **Le Bec Fin.** With its understatedly elegant dining room and an inexpensive weekday menu, this unpretentious enclave opposite the cathedral is a good choice for lunch or dinner. Red meat, seafood, and freshwater fish are well prepared here. Try the turbot cooked with saffron. ⊠ *7 pl. St-Maurice* ☎ *04–74–85–76–72* 🍴 *Reservations essential* ☐ *AE, DC, MC, V* ☉ *Closed July 1–17, Dec. 23–Jan 2. Closed Mon. No dinner Sun. or Wed.*

★ **$$$–$$$$** ✕🖼 **La Pyramide.** Back when your grandmother's grandmother was making the grand tour, La Pyramide was *le must*—Fernand Point had perfected haute cuisine for a generation and became the first superstar chef, teaching a regiment of students who went on to glamorize dining the world over. Many decades later, La Pyramide has dropped its museum status and now offers contemporary classics by acclaimed chef Patrick Henriroux, accompanied by a peerless selection of wines featuring local stars from the nearby Côte Rôtie and Condrieu vineyards. Both classical and avant-garde dishes triumph here, from *crème soufflée de crabe au croquant d'artichaut* (cream crab soufflé with crunchy artichoke) to the *veau de lait aux légumes de la vallée* (suckling veal with vegetables from the Drôme valley). Rooms are graceful and comfortable in this relaxed setting. ⊠ *14 bd. Fernand-Point, 38200 Vienne* 🕾 *04-74-53-01-96* 🖷 *04-74-85-69-73* ⊕ *www.relaischateaux.com/ pyramide* 🛏 *21 rooms* ♨ *Restaurant, minibars, cable TV, bar, meeting rooms, some pets allowed* ⊟ *AE, DC, MC, V* ¶⊙I *EP.*

Serrières

㊲ *32 km (20 mi) south of Vienne, 59 km (37 mi) south of Lyon.*

Riverboats traditionally stop at little Serrières, on the Rhône's west bank. Life on the water is depicted at the **Musée des Mariniers du Rhône** (Boatmen's Museum), in the wooden-roof Gothic chapel of St-Sornin. 🕾 *04-75-34-01-26* 🖾 *€5* ⊙ *Apr.–Oct., weekends 3–6.*

Where to Stay & Eat

$$$-$$$$ ✕⊡ **Schaeffer.** Guest rooms here are decorated in contemporary style, but the real draw is the dining room, where chef Bernard Mathé invents variations on traditional French dishes: smoked duck cutlet in lentil stew or lamb with eggplant in anchovy butter. The number of desserts is overwhelming, but pistachio cake with bitter chocolate is the clear winner. Reservations are essential for the restaurant. Menus run from €40 to €60. ⊠ *Quai Jules Roche, 07340* 🕾 *04-75-34-00-07* 🖷 *04-75-34-08-79* ⊕ *www.hotel-schaeffer.com* 🛏 *11 rooms* ♨ *Restaurant, minibars, cable TV, bar, meeting rooms, some pets allowed* ⊟ *AE, DC, MC, V* ⊙ *Closed Mon. and 1st 3 wks Jan. No dinner Sun.* ¶⊙I *EP.*

Hauterives

㊳ *28 km (17 mi) east of Serrières, 40 km (25 mi) south of Vienne.*

Hauterives would be just another quaint village on the eastern side of the Rhône if not for the **Palais Idéal,** one of Western Europe's weirdest constructions. A fantasy constructed entirely of stones (called *galets*) from the nearby Galaure River, it was the life's work of a local postman, Ferdinand Cheval (1836–1924), who was haunted by visions of faraway mosques and temples. One of many wall inscriptions reads "1879–1912: 10,000 days, 93,000 hours, 33 years of toil." 🕾 *04-75-68-81-19* 🖷 *04-75-68-88-15* 🖾 *€5* ⊙ *Mid-Apr.–mid-Sept., daily 9–7; mid-Sept.–mid-Apr., daily 9:30–5:30.*

Where to Stay & Eat

¢-$ ✕⊡ **Le Relais.** A stone's throw from the Palais Idéal, this rustic inn is a good place for a meal—and a night's stay, if desirable. Rooms are small and could use refurbishing in the not-too-distant future. Owner Roland Graillat is better as a chef—roast partridge and delicately seasoned frogs' legs are good bets. From September to June the restaurant is closed Monday and does not serve dinner Sunday. ⊠ *Pl. de l'Église, 26390* 🕾 *04-75-68-81-12* 🖷 *04-75-68-92-42* 🛏 *17 rooms* ♨ *Restaurant, café, minibars, cable TV, bar; no a/c* ⊟ *AE, DC, MC, V* ⊙ *Closed Jan. and Feb.* ¶⊙I *MAP.*

Annonay

39 *44 km (27 mi) south of Vienne, 43 km (27 mi) southeast of St-Étienne.*

The narrow streets and passageways of central Annonay are full of character. The town, which grew up around the leather industry, is best known as the home of Joseph and Étienne Montgolfier, who, in 1783, invented the hot-air balloon (known in French as a *montgolfière*). The first flight was on June 4, 1783, from place des Cordeliers (although a commemorating obelisk is on avenue Marc-Seguin); the flight lasted a half hour and reached 6,500 feet.

Local history and folklore are evoked at the **Musée Vivarais César Filhol,** between the Mairie (Town Hall) and the church of Notre-Dame. ⊠ *15 rue Béchetoille* ☎ *04–75–33–24–51* ⌨ *€5* ⊙ *July and Aug., Tues.–Fri. 3–6, weekends 3–6; Sept.–June, Wed. and weekends 3–6.*

Tournon

40 *37 km (23 mi) southeast of Annonay, 59 km (37 mi) south of Vienne.*

Tournon is on the Rhône at the foot of granite hills. Its hefty **Château,** dating from the 15th and 16th centuries, is the chief attraction. The castle's twin terraces have wonderful views of the Vieille Ville, the river, and—towering above Tain-l'Hermitage across the Rhône—the steep vineyards that produce Hermitage wine, one of the region's most refined—and costly—reds. In the château is a museum of local history, the **Musée Rhodanien** (or du Rhône). ⊠ *Pl. Auguste-Faure* ☎ *04–75–08–10–23* ⌨ *€5* ⊙ *June–Aug., Wed.–Mon. 10–noon and 2–6; Apr., May, Sept., and Oct., Wed.–Mon. 2–6.*

℃ A ride on one of France's last steam trains, the **Chemin de Fer du Vivarais,** makes an adventurous two-hour trip 33 km (21 mi) along the narrow, rocky Doux Valley to Lamastre and back to Tournon. ⊠ *Departs from Tournon station* ☎ *04–78–28–83–34* ⌨ *Round-trip €20* ⊙ *June–Aug., daily 10 AM; May and Sept., weekends 10 AM.*

Where to Stay & Eat

$$$–$$$$ ✕⌘ **Michel Chabran.** This modern interpretation of Drôme-style stone-and-wood design has floral displays, airy picture windows over the garden, and guest rooms with a touch of contemporary Danish influence. Next to the main road, sleeping with the windows open can make for a noisy night (though the air-conditioning largely solves that). The restaurant serves a truffle menu from December to March and imaginative and light fare such as mille-feuille de foie gras with artichokes and lamb from Rémuzat. ⊠ *29 av. du 45ᵉ Parallèle, on left (east) bank of the Rhône, 10 km (6 mi) south of Tournon via N7 and 7 km (4½ mi) north of Valence, 26600 Pont de l'Isère* ☎ *04–75–84–60–09* 🖷 *04–75–84–59–65* ⊕ *www.chateauxhotels.com/chabran* ⌨ *12 rooms* ₯ *Restaurant, café, minibars, cable TV, pool, meeting room, some pets allowed* ⊟ *AE, DC, MC, V* ⊙ *Closed Mon. from Jan. through Apr. No dinner Sun.* ⏀ *EP, MAP.*

$–$$ ✕⊡ **Reynaud.** Tain-l'Hermitage, across the Rhône from Tournon, entices with this fine inn and restaurant. The dining room is comfortable and traditional, the river magnificent. Rooms are on the small side but cozy and tastefully furnished. The classic cuisine is excellent, with specialties from poached egg with foie gras to pigeon fillet in black-currant sauce. ⊠ 82 av. du Président-Roosevelt, Tain-l'Hermitage, 07300 ☎ 04–75–07–22–10 ⊟ 04–75–08–03–53 ⇆ 13 rooms ⚭ Restaurant, minibars, cable TV, pool, bar ⊟ AE, DC, MC, V ⊗ Closed Mon., Jan., and 1 wk in Aug. No dinner Sun. ⦙⊙⦙ EP.

| en route | From Tournon's place Jean-Jaurès, slightly inland from the château, follow signs to the narrow, twisting **Route Panoramique**; the views en route to the old village of **St-Romain-de-Lerps** are breathtaking. In good weather the panorama at St-Romain includes 13 départements, Mont Blanc to the east, and arid Mont Ventoux to the south. D287 winds down to St-Péray and Valence; topping the **Montagne de Crussol,** 650 feet above the plain, is the ruined 12th-century **Château de Crussol.** |

Valence

④ 17 km (11 mi) south of Tournon, 92 km (57 mi) west of Grenoble, 127 km (79 mi) north of Avignon.

Largish Valence, the Drôme département capital, is the region's market center. Steep-curbed alleyways called côtes extend into the Vieille Ville from the Rhône. At the center of the Vieille Ville is the cathedral of **St-Apollinaire.** Although begun in the 12th century in the Romanesque style, it's not as old as it looks: parts of it were rebuilt in the 17th century, with the belfry rebuilt in the 19th. The **Musée des Beaux-Arts** (Fine Arts Museum), next to the cathedral of St-Apollinaire, in the former 18th-century bishops' palace, displays archaeological finds as well as sculpture and furniture and drawings by landscapist Hubert Robert (1733–1808). ⊠ Pl. des Ormeaux ☎ 04–75–79–20–80 ⊠ €5 ⊗ Mon., Tues., Thurs., and Fri. 2–6, Wed. and weekends 9–noon and 2–6.

Where to Stay & Eat

$$$–$$$$ ✕⊡ **Pic.** Kubla Khan would have decamped from Xanadu in a minute
Fodor'sChoice for this Drôme pleasure palace. The Maison Pic has been a culinary land-
★ mark for decades, although its (too?) glossy Relais & Château makeover into a full-scale hotel has nearly obliterated any traces of its time-stained past. Not that you will complain—much of the decor is to die for: vaulted white salons, red-velvet sofas, 18th-century billiard tables, gigantic Provençal (that's where the Pic family came from) armoires, lovely gardens, and an eye-popping pool make this a destination in itself. The famous restaurant is going stronger than ever—try the truffle-flavored galettes (pancakes) with asparagus or bass with caviar (served either "avec modération" or "passionnément") to see how Anne-Sophie, great-granddaughter of the founding matriarch, is continuing the family legacy. Dine in the cardinal-red dining room seated on Louis Seize–style bergères or, in summer, on the shaded terrace, then retire upstairs to the

guest rooms, done in a mix of rustic antiques and high-style fabrics. A café, the Auberge du Pin, also entices (with much lower prices). ⊠ *285 av. Victor-Hugo, 26000* ☎ *04–75–44–15–32* 🖷 *04–75–40–96–03* ⊕ *www.pic-valence.com* ↩ *12 rooms, 3 apartments* ♨ *Restaurant, café, minibars, cable TV, pool, bar, meeting rooms, some pets allowed* ➟ *AE, DC, MC, V* ⊘ *Closed Mon. No dinner Sun.* ⫟ *EP.*

Shopping

In the small town of Romans, 15 minutes northeast of Valence via D532, is a score of retail outlets for designer shoes. Romans, with its tradition of leather making, has become the major factory center for the production of high-quality shoes. Many of the top European designers are represented, and their products may be had at bargain prices from any number of stores. **Charles Jourdan** (⊠ Galerie Fan Halles ☎ 04–75–02–32–36) is perhaps the highest-quality brand name represented in Romans. **Chaussures Tchlin** (⊠ Quai Chopin ☎ 04–75–72–51–41) is a longtime mainstay for French shoes. **Stephane Kelian** (⊠ 11 pl. Charles-de-Gaulle ☎ 04–75–05–23–26) is a name that speaks hip and high style.

> **en route** The prettiest route between Valence and Privas is N86, on the right bank of the Rhône; after 16 km (10 mi) and just before La Voulte, turn onto the scenic D120, which follows the Eyrieux Valley as far as Les Ollières-sur-Eyrieux; then turn south along D2, under the thick canopy of horse-chestnut trees.

Cliousclat

㊷ *21 km (13 mi) south of Valence, 27 km (17 mi) north of Montélimar.*

Less than 10 km (6 mi) off A7 and N7, the roads running south from Valence to Montélimar and on to Provence, is the delightful, tiny village of Cliousclat. It's built on a hillside, with room for just one narrow street running through it. There's not much to do or see, but its charming atmosphere and its gorgeous views make it very appealing. While you're here, however, drop in at the small **Histoires de Poteries** (Pottery History Museum) to see the work of local potters. You might want to buy some of the lovely wares, too. ☎ *04–75–63–15–60* ☜ *€5* ⊘ *Apr.–June, Tues.–Sun. 2–7; July and Aug., daily 10–1 and 2–8; Sept., Tues.–Sun. 10–noon and 2–7; Oct., Tues.–Sun. 2–6.*

Where to Stay & Eat

★ **$–$$** ✕🏠 **La Treille Muscate.** Between Lyon and Avignon there's no better place to spend a night than at this gem of a hotel, a symphony of muted 18th-century pastels, Provençal furnishings, and a decidedly rustic-luxe air. Lovingly collected antiques and clay-tile floors with throw rugs make each room different. Room No. 11 has a huge terrace overlooking fields to the Rhône. The restaurant gets kudos from all the critics, and you can't lose with the Sisteron lamb, Mediterranean fish, or homemade foie gras. The friendly owner, Madame de Laître, speaks English fluently but politely refrains from doing so until you have exhausted your French. ⊠ *26270 Cliousclat* ☎ *04–75–63–13–10* 🖷 *04–75–63–10–79*

⊕ *www.latreillemuscate.com* ⤴ *12 rooms* ⟁ *Restaurant, café, mini-bars, cable TV* ▭ *AE, DC, MC, V* ⊘ *Closed Wed. and mid-Dec.–Feb.* ⦿ *BP, MAP.*

GRENOBLE & THE ALPS

This is double-treat vacationland: in winter some of the world's best skiing is found in the Alps; in summer chic spas, shimmering lakes, and hilltop trails offer additional delights. The Savoie and Haute-Savoie départements occupy the most impressive territory; Grenoble, in the Dauphiné, is the Alps' gateway and the area's only city. It's all at the nexus of highways from Marseille, Valence, Lyon, Geneva, and Turin.

The skiing season for most French resorts runs from December 15 to April 15. By late December resorts above 3,000 feet usually have sufficient snow. January is apt to be the coldest—and therefore the least popular—month; in Chamonix and Megève, this is the time to find hotel bargains. At the high-altitude resorts the skiing season lasts until May. In summer the lake resorts, as well as the regions favored by hikers and climbers, come into their own. Let's not forget that this is the region where Stendhal was born, and where the great 18th-century philosopher Jean-Jacques Rousseau lived out his old age. Worldly pleasures also await: incredibly charming Annecy, set with arcaded lanes and quiet canals in the old quarter around the lovely 16th-century Palais de l'Isle; the Old Master treasures on view at Grenoble's Musée; and the fashionable lakeside promenades of spa towns like Aix-les-Bains are just some of the civilized enjoyments to be discovered here.

Grenoble

104 km (65 mi) southeast of Lyon, 138 km (86 mi) northeast of Montélimar.

Capital of the Dauphiné (Lower Alps) region, Grenoble sits at the confluence of the Isère and Drac rivers and lies within three *massifs* (mountain ranges): La Chartreuse, Le Vercors, and Belledonne. This cosmopolitan city's skyscrapers seem intimidating by homey French standards. But along with the city's nuclear research plant, they bear witness to the fierce local desire to move ahead with the times, and it's not surprising to find one of France's most noted universities here. Grenoble's main claim to fame is as the birthplace of the great French novelist Henri Beyle (1783–1842), better known as Stendhal, author of *The Red and the Black* and *The Charterhouse of Parma*. The heart of the city forms a crescent around a bend of the Isère, with the train station at the western end and the university all the way at the eastern tip. As it fans out from the river toward the south, the crescent seems to develop a more modern flavor. The hub of the city is **place Victor Hugo**, with its flowers, fountains, and cafés, though most sights and nightlife are near the Isère in place St-André, place de Gordes, and place Notre-Dame; avenue Alsace-Lorraine, a major pedestrian street lined with modern shops, cuts right through it. The layout of the city is very tricky, so it is best to stop into the city tourist office for detailed maps and directions.

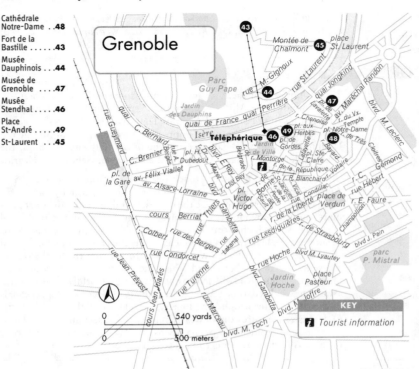

Near the center curve of the River Isère is a **Téléphérique** (cable car), starting at quai St-Stéphane-Jay, which whisks you over the River Isère and up to the hilltop and its **Fort de la Bastille**, where there are splendid views. Walk back down via the footpath through the Jardin Dauphinoise. ⌑ €7 *round-trip* ⊘ *Apr.–Oct., daily 9 AM–midnight; Nov., Dec., Feb., and Mar., daily 10–6.*

On the north side of the River Isère is rue Maurice-Gignoux, lined with gardens, cafés, mansions, and a 17th-century convent that contains the **Musée Dauphinois**, featuring the history of mountaineering and skiing. The Premiers Alpins section explores the evolution of the Alps and its inhabitants. ⊠ *30 rue Maurice-Gignoux* ☎ *04-76-85-19-01* ⌑ €4 ⊘ *Nov.–Apr., Wed.–Mon. 10–6; May–Oct., Wed.–Mon. 10–7.*

The church of **St-Laurent**, near the Musée Dauphinois, has a hauntingly ancient 6th-century crypt—one of the country's oldest Christian monuments—supported by a row of formidable marble pillars. ⊠ *2 pl. St-Laurent* ☎ *04-76-44-78-68* ⌑ €3 ⊘ *Wed.–Mon. 8–noon and 2–6.*

On the south side of the River Isère and nearly opposite the cable-car stop is the Jardin de Ville—an open space filled with immense plane trees—where a handsome conical tower with slate roof marks the **Palais Lesdiguières**. This was built by the right hand of King Henri IV, the Duc de

Lesdiguières (1543–1626), and possibly the prototype for Stendhal's voraciously egoistic protagonists (as Constable of France, the duke had a reign of terror, marrying his young lover Marie Vignon—31 years his junior—after having her husband assassinated). A master urbanist, Lesdiguières did much to establish the Grenoble you see today, so it may

46 only be apt his palace is now the **Musée Stendhal,** where family portraits trace the life of Grenoble's greatest writer amidst elegant wooden furniture turned out by the Hache family dynasty of famous woodworkers. Although some of the city's residents will be surprised that non-natives know who Stendhal (much less Henri Beyle) is, there is no denying that this great author remains Grenoble's most famous native son. Copies of original manuscripts and major memorabilia will please fans, who will wish to then pay a call to the **Maison Stendhal,** at 20 Grande Rue, Stendhal's grandfather's house and the place where the author spent the "happiest days of his life"; you can also take a stroll back over to the **Jardin de Ville,** where the author met his first "love" (basically unrequited), the

FodorśChoice actress Virginie Kubly. The city tourist office distributes a *"Stendhal*
★ *Itinerary"* that also includes the author's birthplace, at 14 rue Hébert, now a repository for memorabilia on the Resistance and deportations of World War II. ⊠ *1 rue Hector-Berlioz* ☎ *04–76–42–02–62* 🖅 *Free* ☉ *Oct.–June, Tues.–Sun. 2–6; July–Sept., Tues.–Sun. 9–noon and 2–6.*

Several blocks east of the Musée Stendhal is place de Lavalette, on the south side of the river where most of Grenoble is concentrated, and site

★ **47** of the **Musée de Grenoble,** formerly the Musée de Peinture et de Sculpture (Painting and Sculpture Museum). Founded in 1796 and since enlarged, it's one of France's oldest museums and the first to concentrate on modern art (Picasso donated his *Femme Lisant* in 1921); a modern addition incorporates the medieval Tour de l'Isle (Island Tower), a Grenoble landmark. The collection includes 4,000 paintings and 5,500 drawings, among them works from the Italian Renaissance, Rubens, Flemish still lifes, Zurbaran, and Canaletto; Impressionists such as Renoir and Monet; and 20th-century works by Matisse (*Intérieur aux Aubergines*), Signac, Derain, Vlaminck, Magritte, Ernst, Miró, and Dubuffet. Modern-art lovers should also check out the **Centre National d'Art Contemporain** (⊠ 155 cours Berriat ☎ 04–76–21–95–84). Behind the train station in an out-of-the-way district, it is noted for its distinctive warehouse museum and cutting-edge collection. ⊠ *5 pl. de Lavalette* ☎ *04–76–63–44–44* 🖅 *€4* ☉ *Wed. 11–10, Thurs.–Mon. 11–7.*

48 Despite its 12th-century exterior, the 19th-century interior of the **Cathédrale Notre-Dame** is somewhat bland. But don't miss the adjoining bishop's house, now a museum on the history of Grenoble; the main treasure is a noted 4th-century baptistery. ⊠ *Pl. Notre-Dame* 🖅 *€4* ☉ *Museum: Wed.–Mon. 10–noon and 2–5.*

49 **Place St-André** is a medieval square, now filled with umbrella-shaded tables and graced with the **Palais de Justice** on one side and the **Église St-André** on the other. For a tour of Grenoble's oldest and most beautiful streets, head to the area around **La Halle Sainte-Claire,** the splendid glass-and-steel-covered market in place Sainte-Claire, several blocks southeast of the Jardin de Ville. Facing the market's spouting fish fountain on the facade, to your right at the end of the street you will see the Baroque entryway to the Lyçee et College Stendhal.

Where to Stay & Eat

★ **$$$–$$$$**   ✕ **L'Auberge Napoléon.** Frédéric Caby's culinary haven in a meticulously restored town house is where chef Agnès Chotin, one of France's top *cuisinères* (lady chefs) puts together the best table in Grenoble. Specializing in *terroir* creations ranging from *daube de sanglier en aumonière croustillante* (wild boar stewed in port wine with lemon crust) or *crème de potiron* (cream of squash soup), Mlle. Chotin proposes a foie menu that is nearly as wicked and wonderful as her "*cru*" chocolate dessert offering. ✉ *7 rue Montorge* ☎ *04–76–87–53–64* ⊕ *www.auberge-napoleon. fr* ▤ *AE, DC, MC, V* ⊘ *No lunch except Sat. Closed Sun., May 1–8, Aug. 25–Sept. 7, Jan. 2–7.*

¢–$ ✕ **Café de la Table Ronde.** The second-oldest café in France, junior only to the Procope in Paris, this was a favorite haunt of Henri Beyle as well as the spot where Choderlos de Laclos sought inspiration for his 1784 *Liaisons Dangereuses.* Traditionally known for gatherings of "*les mordus*" (literally the "bitten," or passionate ones), the café still hosts poetry readings and concerts and serves dinner until nearly midnight. ✉ *7 pl. St-André* ☎ *04–76–44–51–41* ▤ *AE, DC, MC, V.*

★ **$$$–$$$$**   ✕▥ **Park Hôtel Grenoble.** Grenoble's finest hotel, with spacious corner rooms over the leafy Parc Paul Mistral, is more than comfortable. This smoothly run establishment attends to your every need with skill and good cheer, from recommendations around town to dinner in front of a roaring fire in Le Parc, the excellent restaurant. Try the sumptuous *foie gras de canard poelé aux figues* (duck liver sautéed with figs) and the *tournedos de charolais aux morilles* (Charolais beef with morels) with a Château Fombrauge, Saint Emilion '95 grand cru. ✉ *10 pl. Paul Mistral, 38000* ☎ *04–76–85–81–23* 🖶 *04–76–46–49–88* ⊕ *www.parkaffaires.com* ➦ *40 rooms, 12 apartments* ⚲ *Restaurant, minibars, cable TV, hot tubs, bar, meeting rooms, parking (fee), some pets allowed (fee)* ▤ *AE, DC, MC, V* ⦿ *EP.*

★ **$$$**   ✕▥ **Chavant.** Dining under the watchful eye of the charming Danièle Chavant is a pleasure at this ivy-covered mansion. The lobster smothered in truffles is wonderfully wicked and wholly delicious, while the *civet de biche en robe d'automne* (venison with apples, potatoes, and turnips in a daube sauce) is unforgettable. Rooms are elegant and spacious, overlooking meadows and forests beyond the lush garden and pool. ✉ *Rue Bresson, 8 km (5 mi) south of Grenoble, 38320 Bresson* ☎ *04–76–25–25–38* 🖶 *04–76–62–06–55* ⊕ *www.chavant.fr* ➦ *7 rooms* ⚲ *Restaurant, minibars, cable TV, pool, meeting rooms, some pets allowed (fee); no a/c* ▤ *AE, DC, MC, V* ⊘ *Closed Dec. 25–31. Restaurant closed Sat. lunch, Sun. dinner, Mon.* ⦿ *EP.*

$–$$ ▥ **Europe.** This modest hotel at the edge of old Grenoble on a corner of Place Grenette is handy for its central location. As it is an easy walk from the river, the Jardin de Ville, and the city museums, once you're ensconced here, you're set to explore the town. Rooms are adequate and the staff is helpful. ✉ *22 pl. Grenette* ☎🖶 *04–76–46–16–94* ➦ *45 rooms* ⚲ *Minibars, cable TV, health club, parking (fee)* ▤ *AE, DC, MC, V* ⦿ *EP.*

Nightlife & the Arts

Look for the monthly *Grenoble-Spectacles* for a list of events around town. **La Soupe aux Choux** (⊠ 7 rte. de Lyon) is the spot for jazz. **Cinq Jours de Jazz** is just that—five days of jazz—in February or March. In summer, classical music characterizes the **Session Internationale de Grenoble-Isère.**

Sports & the Outdoors

The **Maison de la Randonnée** (⊠ 7 rue Voltaire ☎ 04–76–51–76–00) can provide you with information on places to hike around Grenoble.

en route   If you have time only for a brief glimpse of the Alps, take N91 out of Grenoble toward Briançon, past the spectacular mountain scenery of **L'Alpe d'Huez, Les Deux Alpes,** and the **Col du Galibier.** Or take D512 north from Grenoble for 17 km (11 mi), fork left, and follow small D57-D as far as you can (only a few miles) before leaving your car for the 30-minute climb to the top of the 6,000-foot **Charmant Som peak.** Your reward will be a stunning view of the Grande Chartreuse Monastery to the north. If you're heading to Provence and using Grenoble as your gateway through the Alps, be sure to take N76, which cuts through the mountains and presents some majestic scenery. From spring through fall the valleys are lush with greenery; in winter they are snow-covered bowls attracting skiers. Along the way you'll pass many small villages tucked inside mountain ridges, which guard them from winter winds.

Grande Chartreuse

50 *23 km (14 mi) north of Grenoble; head north on D512 and fork left 8 km (5 mi) on D520-B just before St-Pierre-de-Chartreuse.*

St. Bruno founded this 12-acre monastery in 1084; it later spawned 24 other charterhouses in Europe. Burned and rebuilt several times, it was stripped of possessions during the French Revolution, when the monks were expelled. On their return they resumed making their sweet liqueur, Chartreuse, the 132-plant–based formula that is today known to only a few monks. Sold worldwide, Chartreuse is a main source of income for the monastery. Enclosed by wooded heights and limestone crags, the monastery is austere and serene. Although it is not open to visitors, you can see the road that goes to it. The **Musée de la Correrie,** near the road to the monastery, has exhibits on monastic life and sells the monks' distillation. ☎ 04–76–88–60–45 ⊠ €5 ☉ Easter–Oct., daily 10–noon and 2–6.

Chambéry

51 *44 km (27 mi) northeast of Voiron, 40 km (25 mi) north of St-Pierre-de-Chartreuse, 55 km (34 mi) north of Grenoble.*

Elegant old Chambéry is the region's shopping hub. Townspeople congregate for coffee and people-watching on pedestrians-only **place St-Léger.** The town's highlight is the 14th-century **Château des Ducs de Savoie.** Its Gothic **Ste-Chapelle** has good stained glass and houses a replica of the

MONK-EYING AROUND

The formula for the green, 110-proof liqueur Chartreuse is a secret, entrusted to three monks at the **Chartreuse Distillery** (✉ 10 blvd. Edgar Kofler ☎ 04–76–05–81–77), located in Voiron, set 26 km (16 mi) west of St-Pierre-de-Chartreuse and 27 km (17 mi) northwest of Grenoble (making for a 20-minute bus ride from Grenoble). The liqueur was originally presented to the monastery in 1605 as a health elixir by Marshall d'Estrées and is known to use a combination of plants and herbs. You can visit the distillery and its museum at the original site of the monastery, founded by St. Bruno in 1084. Free tours (in French) are given June through September, daily 8:30 to 11:30 and 2 to 5:30. From October to May, tours are held weekdays 8:30–11:30 and 2–5:30. Happily, tastings are always free and offer a perfect time to contemplate the soberer meanings of the maxim, "Eat, drink, and be merry."

Turin Shroud. ✉ *Rue Basse du Château* ☎ *No phone* 🎟 €4 ⊙ *Guided tours May, June, and Sept., daily at 10:30 and 2:30; July and Aug., daily at 10:30, 2:30, 3:30, 4:30, and 5:30; Mar., Apr., Oct., and Nov., Sat. at 2:15, Sun. at 3:30.*

Where to Stay & Eat

★ $$$–$$$$ ✕🏠 **Château de Candie.** If you wish to experience "la vie Savoyarde" in all its pastel-hue, François Boucher–charm, head to this towering centuries-old manor on a hill east of Chambéry. Its large restaurant is famous for its wedding feasts but anyone can delight in its special treats, such as the rabbit terrine with shallot compote and an *escalope de fruits de mer,* where the copious seafood is arranged in the shape of a lobster. Even more delicious are the guest rooms, which range from blow-out magnificent—the chandeliered nuptial chamber has a canopied red-velvet bed—to rooms done up in a sweet peasant-luxe decor. Owner Lhostis Didier, an avid antiques collector, spent four years renovating, so rooms feature an array of delights—antique panels of boiserie, honey-gold beams, a grandfather clock, carved armoires, a 19th-century "psyché" mirror, and glorious regional fabrics. Better yet are views ranging over the neighboring chartreuse monastery and villages. So who can blame you for lingering over the lavish breakfast? ✉ *Rue du Bois de Candie, 6 km (4 mi) east of Chambéry, 73000 Chambéry-le-Vieux* ☎ 04–79–96–63–00 🖷 04–79–96–63–10 ⊕ *www.chateaudecandie.com* ⇆ 17 rooms, 3 apartments ⚒ *Restaurant, minibars, cable TV, pool, bar, meeting rooms, some pets allowed (fee); no a/c* ▤ AE, MC, V ⚍ EP, MAP.

Aix-les-Bains

52 *14 km (9 mi) north of Chambéry, 106 km (65 mi) east of Lyon.*

The family resort and spa town of Aix-les-Bains takes advantage of its position on the eastern side of **Lac du Bourget,** the largest natural freshwater lake in France, with a fashionable lakeshore esplanade. Although the lake is icy cold, you can sail, fish, play golf and tennis, or picnic on the 25 acres of parkland at the water's edge. (Try to avoid it on weekends, when it gets really crowded.) The main town of Aix is 3 km (2 mi) inland from the lake itself. Its sole reason for being is its thermal waters. Many small hotels line the streets, and streams of the weary take to the baths each day; in the evening, for a change of pace, they play the slot machines at the casino or attend tea dances. The Roman Temple of Diana (2nd to 3rd centuries AD) now houses the **Musée Archéologique** (Archaeology Museum); enter via the tourist office on place Mollard. The ruins of the original Roman baths are underneath the present **Thermes Nationaux** (National Thermal Baths), built in 1934. ☉ *Guided tours only Apr.–Oct., Mon.–Sat. at 3; Nov.–Mar., Wed. at 3.*

off the beaten path

ABBAYE DE HAUTECOMBE – You can tour this picturesque spot, a half-hour boat ride from Aix-les-Bains, every day but Tuesday; mass is celebrated in French at noon and at 6 PM. ☎ *04–79–54–26–12 ⊠ €10 ☉ Departures from Grand Pont, Mar.–June, Sept. and Oct., daily at 2:30; July and Aug., daily at 9:30, 2, 2:30, 3, 3:30, and 4:30.*

Annecy

🔢 *33 km (20 mi) north of Aix-les-Bains, 137 km (85 mi) east of Lyon, 43*
FodorśChoice *km (27 mi) southwest of Geneva.*
★

Jewel-like Annecy is on crystal-clear **Lac d'Annecy** (Annecy Lake), surrounded by snow-tipped peaks. Though the canals, flower-decked bridges, and cobbled pedestrian streets are filled on market days—Tuesday and Friday—with shoppers and tourists, the town is still tranquil. Does it seem to you that the River Thiou flows backward, that is, out of the lake? You're right: it drains the lake, feeding the town's canals. Most of the Vieille Ville is now a pedestrian zone lined with half-timber houses. Here is where the best restaurants are, so you'll probably be back in the evening.

Meander through the Vieille Ville, starting on the small island in the River Thiou, at the 12th-century **Palais de l'Isle** (Island Palace), once site of courts of law and a prison, now a landmark and one of France's most photographed sites. It houses the **Musée d'Histoire d'Annecy** and is where tours of the old prisons and cultural exhibitions begin. ☎ *04–50–33–87–30 ⊠ €5 ☉ June–Sept., daily 10–6; Oct.–May, Wed.–Mon. 10–noon and 2–6.*

★ Crowning the city is one of the most picturesque castles in France, the medieval **Château d'Annecy.** Set high on a hill opposite the Palais and bristling with stolid towers, the complex is landmarked by the Tour Perrière, which dominates the lake, and the Tour St-Paul, Tour St-Pierre, and Tour de la Reine (the oldest, dating from the 12th century), which overlook the town. All give storybook views over the town and countryside. Dwellings of several eras line the castle courtyard, one of which contains a small museum on Annecy history and how it was shaped by the Nemeurs and Savoie dynasties. ☎ 04–50–33–87–31 🖾 €5 ⊙ June–Sept., daily 10–6; Oct.–May, Wed.–Mon. 10–noon and 2–6.

A drive around Lake Annecy—or at least along its eastern shore, which is the most attractive—is a must; set aside a half day for the 40-km (25-mi) trip. Picturesque **Talloires,** on the eastern side, has many hotels and restaurants. Just after Veyrier-du-Lac, keep your eyes open for the privately owned medieval **Château de Duingt.** Continue around the eastern shore to get to the magnificently picturesque **Château de Menthon-St-Bernard.** The exterior is the stuff of fairy tales; the interior is even better. The castle's medieval rooms—many adorned with tapestries, Romanesque frescoes, Netherlandish sideboards, and heraldic motifs—have been lovingly restored by the owner, who can actually trace his ancestry directly back to St. Bernard. All in all, this is one of the loveliest dips into the Middle Ages you can make in eastern France. You can get a good view of the castle by turning onto the Thones road out of Veyrier. ☎ 04–50–60–12–05 🖾 €5 ⊙ July and Aug., daily 2–4:30; May, June, and Sept., Tues., Thurs., and weekends 2–4:30; Oct.–Apr., Thurs. and weekends 2–4:30.

FodorsChoice ★

Where to Stay & Eat

$–$$ ✕ **L'Étage.** This small second-floor restaurant serves inexpensive local fare—from cheese and beef fondue to grilled freshwater fish from Lake Annecy, and raclette made from the local Reblochon cheese. Minimal furnishings and plain wooden tables give it a rather austere look, but the often lively crowd makes up for it by creating true bonhomie. ✉ 13 rue Paquier ☎ 04–50–51–03–28 ⊟ AE, DC, MC, V.

$ ✕ **L'Estamille.** The decor is always changing at this restaurant, as it sells its furnishings and decorations in addition to the food. So it's no surprise that it feels like an antiques store—albeit one serving modern, inexpensive cuisine such as grilled river perch and raclette (a round of cheese baked with potatoes). ✉ 4 quai E. Chappuis ☎ 04–50–45–21–16 ⊟ MC, V.

★ **$$$$** ✕🖾 **La Maison de Marc Veyrat.** Once known as "l'Auberge de l'Eridan," this elegant Third Empire mansion offers guest rooms with spectacular views of Lake Annecy, but most everyone will be too knocked out by what's going on in the dining room to even notice. Veyrat, the only six-starred Michelin chef on the planet—three here and three for his restaurant in Megève (see below for a perspective on his house style)—performs miracles with local Alpine produce, most of which the self-taught shepherd handpicks himself during daily treks through the idyllic mountain pastures that surround the hotel. The hikes are part of the Veyrat myth, as is the signature black hat he wears 24 hours a day. The menu changes according to the seasons, the chef's whims, and what the mountain hikes bring in. The results are once-in-a-lifetime events. To wit: his hot and cold Foie Gras with Fig Purée, Bitter Chocolate, and Bitter Orange Juice; or his Crayfish and Roquefort Sabayon with Queen of the Meadow Froth; or his Roasted Langoustines with Hogweed Semolina; or his amazing desserts—"The Dish of Our Adolescence"—such as his oven-baked cream-pots of Chicory, Wild Fern, Verbena, and Pansy, or his sublime molasses sorbet. At these prices, it had better be sublime. The sorbet is €60 while his Degreased Kidneys with Goutweed and Wild Lovage flavored with Coffee Bonbons is €106, the average rate for many of his entreés. The restaurant is closed Monday and Tuesday (but open Tuesday for dinner in July and August); there is no lunch served Monday to Friday. Upstairs, super-expensive guest rooms and suites—many done in a luxe-châlet style—await those who just want to retire and digest the feast. Note Veyrat closes up shop here November to May 15 to move to his Megève outpost, La Ferme de Mon Père. ⊠ *13 Vieille route des Pensières, 5½ km (3½ mi) from Annecy on D909, Veyrier-du-Lac 74290* ☎ *04–50–60–24–00* 📠 *04–50–60–23–00* ⊕ *www.marc-veyrat.com* ⤙ *9 rooms, 3 suites* ⌕ *Restaurant, minibars, cable TV, bar, some pets allowed (fee)* ▤ *AE, DC, MC, V* ⊙ *Closed Nov. 1–May 15* ⎟⊙⎟ *EP.*

$$$$ ✕⌕ **L'Impérial Palace.** Though the Palace, across the lake from the town center, is Annecy's leading hotel, it lacks depth of character. In contrast to its Belle Epoque exterior, the spacious, high-ceiling guest rooms are done in the subdued colors so loved by contemporary designers. The better rooms face the public gardens on the lake; waking up to breakfast on the terrace is a great way to start the day. Service is professional, but you pay for it. Fine cuisine is served in the stylish La Voile; the food in Le Jackpot Café, in the casino, is acceptable and less costly. ⊠ *32 av. Albigny, 74000* ☎ *04–50–09–30–00* 📠 *04–50–09–33–33* ⊕ *www.lac-annecy.com* ⤙ *91 rooms, 7 suites* ⌕ *2 restaurants, minibars, cable TV, health club, bar, casino* ▤ *AE, DC, MC, V* ⎟⊙⎟ *EP, MAP.*

★ **$$** ⌕ **Hôtel du Palais de l'Isle.** Steps away from the lake, in the heart of Old Annecy, is this delightful small hotel. Without destroying the building's ancient feel, rooms have a cheery, contemporary look and Philippe Starck furnishings; some have a view of the Palais de l'Isle. Rates reflect the size of the room. Breakfast is served. Though the area is pedestrian-only, you can drive up to unload luggage. ⊠ *13 rue Perrière, 74000* ☎ *04–50–45–86–87* 📠 *04–50–51–87–15* ⤙ *26 rooms* ⌕ *Cable TV, some pets allowed (fee); no a/c* ▤ *AE, MC, V* ⎟⊙⎟ *EP.*

Sports & the Outdoors

Bikes can be rented at the **train station** (⊠ Pl. de la Gare). Mountain bikes are available from **Loca Sports** (⊠37 av. de Loverchy ☎04–50–45–44–33). **Sports Passion** (⊠ 3 av. du Parmelan ☎ 04–50–51–46–28) is a convenient source for cyclists. From April through October you can take an hour-long cruise around Lake Annecy on the **M.S. Libellule** (⊠ Compagnie des Bateaux du Lac d'Annecy, 2 pl. aux Bois ☎ 04–50–51–08–40) for €9.

Chamonix

🟢 *94 km (58 mi) east of Annecy, 83 km (51 mi) southeast of Geneva.*

Chamonix is the oldest and biggest of the French winter-sports resort towns. It was the site of the first Winter Olympics, held in 1924. As a ski resort, however, it has its limitations: The ski areas are spread out, none is very large, and the lower slopes often suffer from poor snow conditions. On the other hand, some runs are extremely memorable, such as the 20-km (12-mi) run through the **Vallée Blanche** or the off-trail area of **Les Grands Montets**. And the situation is getting better: many lifts have been added, improving access to the slopes as well as lessening lift lines. In summer it's a great place for hiking, climbing, and enjoying outstanding views.

If you're heading to Italy via the Mont Blanc Tunnel, Chamonix will be your gateway. The world's highest **cable car** soars 12,000 feet up the Aiguille du Midi, providing positively staggering views of 15,700-foot **Mont Blanc**, Europe's loftiest peak. Be prepared for a lengthy wait, both going up and coming down—and wear warm clothing. ⊠ €35 round-trip ☉ May–Sept., daily 8–4:45; Oct.–Apr., daily 8–3:45.

Where to Stay & Eat

$$$$ ✕⊡ **Hameau Albert 1ᵉʳ.** At Chamonix's most desirable hotel, rooms are furnished with elegant reproductions, and most have balconies. Many, such as No. 33, have unsurpassed views of Mont Blanc. Choose between rooms in the original building or Alpine lodge–style accommodations— with touches of contemporary rustic elegance—in the complex known as le Hameau. The dining room also has stupendous Mont Blanc views. Pierre Carrier's cuisine is best characterized as perfectly prepared and presented, though sometimes not so interesting or original. ⊠ 119 impasse du Montenvers, 74400 ☎ 04–50–53–05–09 ᕲ 04–50–55–95–48 ⊕ www.hameaualbert.fr ⇆ 17 rooms, 12 suites, 3 chalets, 12 rooms in farmhouse ♨ 2 restaurants, minibars, cable TV, pool, health club, hot tub, bar, meeting rooms, parking (fee), some pets allowed (fee) ▤ AE, DC, MC, V ☉ Closed 2 wks in May, 3 wks in Nov. ¶O¶ EP, FAP.

$$$–$$$$ ✕⊡ **Mont-Blanc.** In the center of town, this Belle Epoque hotel has catered to the rich and famous since 1878. Family owned, it is permeated by a sense of well-being; the staff is warm and efficient. High ceilings give guest rooms a majestic feel, accentuated by warm, pale colors, and period pieces. Most rooms look onto Mont Blanc or Mont Brevant. Dining on chef Morand's creations in the restaurant, Le Matafan, is a refined pleasure. Besides classic French dishes (try the succulent crayfish with shallots and chanterelle mushrooms), many foods available only locally are served, such as a delicious lake fish known as fera. ⊠ 62 allée Majestic, 74400 ☎ 04–50–53–05–64 ᕲ 04–50–55–89–44 ⊕ www. chamonixhotels.com ⇆ 34 rooms, 8 suites ♨ Restaurant, minibars, cable TV, 2 tennis courts, pool, bar, parking (fee), some pets allowed (fee) ▤ AE, DC, MC, V ☉ Closed Nov. ¶O¶ EP, MAP.

$$–$$$ ✕⊡ **L'Auberge Croix-Blanche.** In the heart of Chamonix, this small inn has modest and tidy rooms, each with a good-size bathroom—from one you can even lie in the tub and look out the window at Mont Blanc. Make sure you ask for one of the newly renovated rooms. The hotel has no restaurant, but right next door is the Brasserie de L'M, where reasonably priced Savoie specialties are served. The hotel shuttle bus can take you to the slopes. ⊠ 87 rue Vallot, 74404 ☎ 04–50–53–00–11 ᕲ 04–50–53–48–83 ⇆ 35 rooms ♨ Restaurant, minibars, cable TV, bar; no a/c ▤ AE, DC, MC, V ☉ Closed May 2–June 29 ¶O¶ EP.

Nightlife

Chamonix is a lively place at night with its discos and late-night bars. A popular place to start or end the evening is at the **Casino** (⊠ Pl. de Saussure ☎ 04–50–53–07–65), which has a bar, a restaurant, roulette, and blackjack. Entrance to the casino is €12, though entry is free to the slot machine rooms.

Sports & the Outdoors

Contact the **Chamonix Tourist Office** for information on skiing in the area. Want to try bobsledding? Two approximately 3,000-foot-long runs are open winter and summer at **Parc de Loisirs des Planards** (☎ 04–50–53–08–07). Chamonix's indoor **skating rink** (☎ 04–50–53–12–36) is open year-round, Thursday–Tuesday 3–6 and Wednesday 3–11. Admission is €4, and skates are €3. The **Sports Centre Olympide** (☎ 04–50–53–09–07) has an indoor-outdoor Olympic-size pool.

Megève

55 *35 km (22 mi) west of Chamonix, 69 km (43 mi) southeast of Geneva.*

The smartest of the Mont Blanc stations, idyllic Alpine Megève is not only a major ski resort but also a chic winter watering hole that draws royalty, celebrities, and fat wallets from all over the world (many will fondly recall Cary Grant bumping into Audrey Hepburn here in the opening scenes of the 1963 thriller *Charade*). The aprés-ski amusements tend to submerge the skiing here because the slopes are comparatively easy, and beginners and skiers of only modest ability will find Megève more to their liking than Chamonix. This may account for Megève's having one of France's largest ski schools. Ski passes purchased here cover the slopes not only around Megève but also in Chamonix. In summer the town is a popular spot for golfing and hiking. From Megève the drive along N212 to Albertville goes along one of the prettiest little gorges in the Alps.

Where to Stay & Eat

$$$$ ✕🏠 **La Ferme de Mon Père.** "Environmental cuisine conveys a real message; the message of well-being." So proclaims the new culinary messiah and wunderkind, Marc Veyrat. Little wonder that this superb Savoyard inn has become one of Europe's latter-day culinary shrines, packed with critics and millionaires fighting to pay top dollar to taste the creations of this mega-talented chef. Past and future collide in the dazzling surroundings—a Savoyard farmhouse that looks like it was put together by a Ralph Lauren on mushrooms. Farm implements, drying hams, old pots, and even moss growing out of the rough-hewn floorboards all add up to Farmhouse Chic with an edge. Amusing is the bread cart—an antique crib. Not amusing, however, are the stables that Veyrat has concocted for resident cows, goats, sheep, and chickens—they can be seen through glass panels in the floor, allowing animals and humans to eye each other as one devours the other. Foodies insist that Veyrat's creations—fir-sap soup, bass cooked on slate, eggs infused with lichen and nutmeg, coquilles St-Jacques served up with a puree of dates in an essence of pink grapefruit, lobster with lovage and licorice root—hurtle the lessons of Escoffier far into the 21st century. There are those, however, who will carp that Alpine haute cuisine is at best merely a question of distance above sea level, and at worst an oxymoron. Still, his creations are extraordinary events—who can resist his Jar of Forgotten Vegetables, with Savoie Truffles and Master Dalí's Preferred Juice, or his Pan Fried Langoustine, with Sour Passion Fruit and Virtual Lichen Semolina from Megève (other signature dishes are found in our review for his

Fodor's Choice ★

Auberge de l'Éridan in Annecy)? Extraordinary, too, are his house-mortgaging prices: appetizers go for around €70, main courses, €110, and desserts, €60, while his special tasting menus run €270 and €360. The restaurant is closed Monday; there is no lunch served Monday to Friday. Upstairs are guest rooms that are the last word in Alpine luxe. Note that from mid-April to mid-December, Veyrat and his chefs close this hotel and move to La Maison in Annecy. ✉ *367 rte. du Crêt* ☎ *04–50–21–01–01* 🖷 *04–50–21–43–43* ⊕ *www.marc-veyrat.com* 🛏 *6 rooms, 3 apts.* � *Minibars, cable TV, bar, some pets allowed (fee); no a/c* ⊟ *AE, DC, MC, V* ⊙ *Closed Apr. 16–Dec. 15.*

$$$$ ✕⌑ **Les Fermes de Marie.** By reassembling four Alpine chalets brought down from the mountains and decorating rooms with old Savoie furniture (shepherds' tables, sculptured chests, credenzas), Jocelyne and Jean-Louis Sibuet have created a luxury hotel with a delightfully rustic feel. Both a summer and winter resort, it has shuttle-bus service to ski lifts in season and a spa providing a wide range of services in this most tranquil of settings. In the kitchen, chef Christophe Cote creates fine cuisine based on local products. ✉ *Chemin de Riante Colline, 74120* ☎ *04–50–93–03–10* 🖷 *04–50–93–09–84* ⊕ *www.c-h-m.com* 🛏 *69 rooms* ⚙ *3 restaurants, minibars, cable TV, pool, gym, spa, bar, some pets allowed (fee); no a/c* ⊟ *AE, DC, MC, V* ⊙ *Closed Apr. and May, Oct. and Nov.* ⍓ *EP, MAP.*

$$ ⌑ **Les Cîmes.** Friendly owners Monsieur and Madame Bourdin put their hearts into running this tiny, reasonably priced hotel with small, neat rooms and a pleasant little restaurant. Simple food is served, such as roast lamb or grilled fish. Breakfast is included in room rates. The hotel's only drawback is its location on a main street entering Megève, which can be a little noisy. ✉ *341 av. Charles Feige, 74120* ☎*04–50–21–01–71* 🖷*04–50–58–70–95* ⊕*www.hotellescimes.com* 🛏*8 rooms* ⚙ *Restaurant, minibars, cable TV, parking (fee); no a/c* ⊟ *AE, DC, MC, V* ⍓ *BP, FAP, MAP.*

Sports & the Outdoors

For information about skiing in the area, contact the **Megève Tourist Office**. In summer you can play at the 18-hole **Megève Golf Course** (✉ Golf du Mont d'Arbois ☎ 04–50–21–29–79); it costs about €5 per round.

LYON & THE ALPS A TO Z

To research prices, get advice from other travelers, and book travel arrangements, visit www.fodors.com.

AIR TRAVEL

CARRIERS   Air France, British Airways, and many other major carriers have connecting services from Paris into Aéroport-Lyon-Saint-Exupéry in Satolas. Only domestic airlines, such as Air France, fly into Grenoble Airport.

AIRPORTS

The region's international gateway airport is Aéroport-Lyon-Saint-Exupéry, 26 km (16 mi) east of Lyon, in Satolas. There are domestic airports at Grenoble, Valence, Annecy, Chambéry, and Aix-les-Bains.

To get between the Aéroport-Lyon-Saint-Exupéry and downtown Lyon take the Satobus, a shuttle bus that goes to the city center between 5 AM and 9 PM and to the train station between 6 AM and 11 PM; journey time is 35–45 minutes, and the fare is €6.92. There's also a bus from Satolas to Grenoble; journey time is just over an hour, and the fare is €18. A taxi into Lyon costs about €30. Taking a taxi from the small Grenoble airport to downtown Grenoble is expensive, but it may be your only option.

🚇 Airport Information **Aéroport-Lyon-Saint-Exupéry** ☎ 04-72-22-72-21 for information. **Satobus** ☎ 04-72-22-71-28.

BUS TRAVEL

Where there's no train service, SNCF often provides bus transport. Buses cover the entire region, but Lyon and Grenoble are the two main bus hubs for long-distance (national and international) routes. From these towns, buses go to the smaller towns. Many ski centers, such as Chamonix, have shuttle buses connecting them with surrounding villages. Tourist destinations, such as Annecy, have convenient bus links with Grenoble. There are many other routes, so always check in with the regional tourist office or information window at a gateway rail or bus station to get printed bus schedules.

🚍 Bus Information **SNCF** ☎ 02-38-53-94-75 ⊕ www.sncf.com.

CAR RENTAL

🚗 Local Agencies **Avis** ✉ 1 av. du Dr-Desfrançois, Chambéry ☎ 04-79-33-58-54 🖨 04-79-15-13-63 ✉ In Aéroport-Lyon-Saint-Exupéry. **Hertz** ✉ 16 rue Émile-Gueymard, Grenoble ☎ 04-76-43-12-92 🖨 04-76-47-97-26 ✉ 11 rue Pasteur, Valence ☎ 04-75-44-39-45 🖨 04-75-44-76-88.

CAR TRAVEL

A6 speeds south from Paris to Lyon (463 km [287 mi]). The Tunnel de Fourvière, which cuts through Lyon, is a classic hazard, and at peak times you may sit idling for hours. Lyon is 313 km (194 mi) north of Marseille on A7. To get to Grenoble (568 km [352 mi] from Paris) from Lyon, take A43. Coming from the south, take A7 to Valence and then swing east on A49 to Grenoble. Access to the Alps is easy from Geneva or Italy (via the Tunnel du Mont Blanc at Chamonix or the Tunnel du Fréjus from Turin). Another popular route into the Alps, especially coming north from Provence, is from Sisteron via N85.

ROAD CONDITIONS Regional roads are fast and well maintained, though smaller mountainous routes can be difficult to navigate and high passes may be closed in winter.

EMERGENCIES

In case of an emergency, call the fire department or the police. Samu, in Lyon, provides emergency medical aid and ambulance service. Lyon has several all-night pharmacies. One of the largest, with an equivalence chart of foreign medicines, is Pharmacie Blanchet. In Grenoble contact Europ'ambulance.

🚓 **Police** ☎ 17. **Fire department** ☎ 18. **Europ'ambulance** ☎ 04-76-33-10-03 Grenoble. **Pharmacie Blanchet** ✉ 5 pl. des Cordeliers, ☎ 04-78-37-81-31 Lyon. **Samu** ☎ 04-72-33-15-15 Lyon.

TOURS

BOAT TOURS Navig-Inter arranges daily boat trips from Lyon along the Saône and Rhône rivers.

🛈 Fees & Schedules **Navig-Inter** ✉ 13 bis quai Rambaud, 69002 Lyon ☎ 04-78-42-96-81.

BUS TOURS Philibert runs bus tours of the region from April to October starting in Lyon.

🛈 Fees & Schedules **Philibert** ✉ 24 av. Barthélémy-Thimonier, B.P. 16, 69300 Caluire ☎ 04-72-23-10-56 🖷 04-72-27-00-97.

WALKING TOURS The Lyon tourist office organizes walking tours of the city in English, as well as minibus tours.

🛈 Fees & Schedules **Lyon Tourist Office** ✉ Pl. Bellecour ☎ 04-72-77-69-69.

TRAIN TRAVEL

The high-speed TGV (Train à Grande Vitesse) to Lyon leaves Paris (from Gare de Lyon) hourly and arrives in just two hours. There are also six TGVs daily between Paris's Charles de Gaulle Airport and Lyon. The TGV also has less frequent service to Grenoble, where you can connect to local SNCF trains headed for villages in the Alps. South of Lyon the TGV goes to Avignon and then splits and goes either to Marseille or Montpellier. The trips from Lyon to Marseille and Lyon to Montpellier take about 1½ hours. Major rail junctions include Grenoble, Annecy, Valence, Chambéry, and Lyon, with frequent train service to other points.

🛈 Train Information **SNCF** ☎ 08-36-35-35-35 ⊕ www.ter-sncf.com/uk/rhone-alpes/default.htm.

TRANSPORTATION AROUND LYON

Lyon's good subway system serves both of the city's train stations. A single ticket costs €1.23, and a 10-ticket book is €10.46. A day pass for bus and métro is €3.69 (available from bus drivers and the automated machines in the métro). Lyon Espace Affaires runs a fleet of well-kept taxi-vans in the city.

🛈 **Lyon Espace Affaires** ☎ 04-78-39-26-11.

TRAVEL AGENCIES

🛈 Local Agent Referrals **American Express** ✉ 6 rue Childebert, 69002 Lyon ☎ 04-72-77-74-50. **Carlson Wagons-lit** ✉ 2 bd. des Alpes, 38240 Melan ☎ 04-76-04-24-00 🖷 04-76-04-24-02.

VISITOR INFORMATION

Contact the Comité Régional du Tourisme Rhône-Alpes for information on Lyon and the Alps. The Maison du Tourisme deals with the Isère département and the area around Grenoble. Local tourist offices for towns mentioned in this chapter are listed by town below.

🛈 Tourist Information **Comité Régional du Tourisme Rhône-Alpes** ✉ 78 rte. de Paris, 69260 Charbonnières-les-Bains ☎ 04-72-59-21-59 🖷 04-72-59-21-60 ⊕ www.rhonealpes-tourisme.com. **Maison du Tourisme** ✉ 14 rue de la République, B.P. 227, 38019 Grenoble ☎ 04-76-42-41-41 🖷 04-76-00-18-98 ⊕ www.grenoble-isere-tourisme.com. **Annecy** ✉ Centre Bonlieu, 1 rue Jean-Jaurès ☎ 04-50-45-00-33 ⊕ www.lac-annecy.com/. **Aubenas** ✉ Centre Ville ☎ 04-75-89-02-03 ⊕ www.aubenas-tourisme.com/. **Bourg-**

en-Bresse ✉6 av. d'Alsace-Lorraine ☎04-74-22-49-40 ⊕ www.bourg-en-bresse. org/. **Chambéry** ✉24 bd. de la Colonne ☎04-79-33-42-47 ⊕www.chambery-tourisme. com/. **Chamonix** ✉85 pl. du Triangle de l'Amitié ☎04-50-53-00-24 ⊕www.chamonix. com/. **Courchevel** ✉La Croisette ☎04-79-08-00-29 ⊕ www.courchevel.com/. **Évian-les-Bains** ✉Pl. d'Allinges ☎04-50-75-04-26 ⊕ www.evian.fr/. **Grenoble** ✉14 rue de la République ☎04-76-42-41-41 ⊕ www.ville-grenoble.fr/ ✉ Train station ☎04-76-54-34-36. **Lyon** ✉Pl. Bellecour ☎04-72-77-69-69 ⊕www.lyon-france. com/ ✉Av. Adolphe Max near cathedral ☎04-72-77-69-69 ✉Perrache train station. **Megève** ✉Rue Monseigneur Conseil ☎04-50-21-27-28 ⊕ www.megeve.com/. **Montélimar** ✉Allées Provençales ☎04-75-01-00-20 ⊕ www.montelimar-tourisme.com/. **Privas** ✉3 rue Elie-Reynier ☎04-75-64-33-35 ⊕ www.paysdeprivas.com/. **Tournon** ✉Mairie de Tournon ☎04-75-08-10-23 ⊕ www.ville-tournon.com/. **Valence** ✉Parvis de la Gare ☎04-75-44-90-40 ⊕ www.tourisme-valence.com/. **Vienne** ✉ Cours Brillier ☎04-74-53-80-30 ⊕www.vienne-tourisme.fr/.

THE MASSIF CENTRAL

10

INDULGE YOUR SWEETEST TOOTH
with Troisgros's dessert trolley ⇨*p.488*

LOVE THAT LAVA
in the volcanic-rock churches
atop Le Puy-en-Velay ⇨*p.492*

PICK UP THE PACE
on a hike of the Gorges du Tarn ⇨*p.500*

SIZE UP 15TH-CENTURY LUXE
at Bourges' Palais Jacques Coeur ⇨*p.481*

GET FULL OF HOT AIR
on a balloon ride over
volcano-perched Puy-de-Dome ⇨*p.490*

BE BLINDED BY THE GOLD
of the medieval reliquary of Ste-Foy ⇨*p.498*

SCALE THE HIGHEST HEIGHTS
of the bluff-top town of Salers ⇨*p.494*

Updated by
Simon Hewitt

Introduction by
Nancy Coons

NOT FOR NOTHING IS THIS REGION termed *massif*. Stretching over a vast landscape that manages to border both Beaune and Avignon as well as Toulouse and Tours, it covers a truly massive portion of the nation. But what's here? The answer to that question is: very little you've ever heard of. If the points of France's topographic star are its outthrust limbs—Alsace, Provence, the Basque Country, Bretagne—then this is the country's underbelly: raw, unprotected, and unrevealed. Its biggest city? Clermont-Ferrand, best known as the home of the Michelin Tire Man. Its most (in)famous city? Vichy, whose dubious distinction it is to bear the name of the Nazi puppet government Pétain established there.

It's a pity that the Massif Central doesn't automatically bring to mind French culture or civilization, as it is also the setting for Bourges, which is graced with a fabulous Gothic cathedral and the medieval mansion of Jacques Coeur, and for Roanne, site of that culinary shrine La Maison Troisgros. Yet this region is home to another side of France—usually the last one you might choose to explore. For aside from the occasional bicycle-with-baguette ride, few outsiders know natural France, the nation of rugged country carved deep with torrential rivers and sculpted with barren and beautiful landscapes just begging to be hiked, climbed, or surveyed from horseback. Windswept plains are punctuated with tiny villages cut into time-ravaged stone. Here and there, the silhouettes of volcanic cones pierce the horizon and speak of a landscape still forming, even as the rivers continue their work of gouging out canyons of dizzying depth. The Gorges du Tarn is one of France's most famous natural landmarks, and the extinct volcano of Puy de Dôme one of its most admired phenomena.

Battles have raged across this rugged land since the dawn of history: Romans versus Arvernes (the original Celtic settlers), Gauls versus Visigoths, Charlemagne versus Saracens, the dukes of Bourbon versus François I, and Huguenots versus Catholics in the Wars of Religion. Small wonder, then, that the Auvergnois kept to themselves during the French Revolution, thereby managing to escape much of its mayhem. Collaborating with Hitler under Pétain's Vichy-based government spared the region from the destructive forces of World War II. Thus little was lost—though, some might add, little was there in the first place.

This is truly *La France profonde,* or deepest France, sought by lovers of natural beauty, overlooked for the most part by seekers of art museums and grand châteaux. But before you turn the page in search of a more tourist-intensive region, take note of a simple truth: the more rural the region, the better the cheese. And any area that proffers crusty yellow Cantal, redolent of volcanic ash; nutty-smooth St-Nectaire; mild and tangy Bleu d'Auvergne; and the world-famous Roquefort, salty-sharp and sheepy . . . well, perhaps the landscape hasn't gone to waste after all. As the lucky travelers who venture to discover the Massif Central realize, there are few greater pleasures than a day's hard hiking in France's deepest backcountry, then sitting down at night to a local roadhouse feast. After all, the way to France's heart is almost always through its stomach, and the Massif Central is indeed the nation's heartland.

Exploring the Massif Central

The Massif Central is roughly demarcated by Burgundy, the Rhône River, Languedoc-Roussillon, and the Dordogne. France's central highlands offer dramatic, untouched terrain, quiet medieval villages, imposing castles, and few large towns. Clermont-Ferrand (population 150,000), the capital of the Auvergne region, is the only major metropolis, hemmed in by the extinct volcanoes that form the Parc National des Volcans. Farther south lies canyon country, with the intimidating Gorges du Tarn, and the magnificent Cévennes Mountains, favorite destinations for nature lovers.

About the Restaurants & Hotels

Although Troisgros in Roanne has long been one of the finest restaurants in France, and the region's major towns and cities (such as Bourges, Vichy, and Clermont-Ferrand) more than hold their own gastronomically, you'll discover that once you get out into mountainside villages, all you really need is a tasty wood-stove pizza, fragrant melting Bleu d'Auvergne cheese, and a warm fire. And perhaps a taste of some *verveine du Puy,* a local green liquor, to accompany your picnic. Keep in mind many restaurants in the smaller villages start their annual hibernation in November.

Because the region was difficult to reach for so long, you will not find a broad selection of accommodations. The larger towns generally have modest hotels, the villages have small inns, and a few châteaux dot the countryside. In July and August rates are higher and rooms are at a premium, so be sure to make reservations in advance. Many hotels are closed from November to March. Assume all rooms have air-conditioning, TV, telephones, and private bath, unless otherwise noted.

WHAT IT COSTS In euros				
	$$$$	**$$$**	**$$**	**$**	**¢**
RESTAURANTS	over €30	€23–€30	€17–€23	€11–€17	under €11
HOTELS	over €190	€120–€190	€80–€120	€50–€80	under €50

Restaurant prices are per person for a main course at dinner, including tax (19.6%) and service; note that if a restaurant offers only prix-fixe (set-price) meals, it has been given the price category that reflects the full prix-fixe price. Hotel prices are for a standard double room in high season, including tax (19.6%) and service charge; higher prices (inquire when booking) prevail for any meal plans.

Timing

Autumn, when the sun is still warming the shimmering, golden trees, and early spring, May particularly, when the wildflowers are in bloom, are the best times to visit central France. In summer the *canicule* (literally, dog days) can be oppressive, and the sky is often cloudy; in winter it's cold, and a snowstorm can make a catastrophic intrusion, unless the thought of getting snowed in by a cozy fire somewhere in France's central highlands appeals to you.

10

Continental France's wildest region, the Massif Central, offers a top 10 medley of land masses, including windswept plains, snowcapped mountains, volcanic plateaus, and romantic forests. This is a country of early-to-bed and early-to-rise, the better to take delight in the great outdoors, where unblemished landscapes and spectacular panoramas seem to appear around nearly every turn. Because the Massif Central is so large, it's almost impossible to see everything in a short trip. But with 3–10 days you can get a fair sense of the region.

Numbers in the text correspond to numbers in the margin and on the Massif Central map.

If you have
4 days

Begin your first day in the former, short-lived capital of France, ⊠ **Bourges** ❶ ☞, a medieval city adorned with one of the tallest Gothic cathedrals in the country, and one of its most beautiful medieval town-houses; spend the night there or in nearby ⊠ **St-Amand-Montrond** ❷ at the Château de la Commanderie. On Day 2 explore Bourbonnais country, with stops in **Bourbon-l'Archambault** ❸ for its weathered mansions. Head to medieval ⊠ **Moulins** ❹ to gape at its Flamboyant Gothic cathedral and overnight at one of the hotels here. On Day 3 drive through the Parc National des Volcans to see its natural marvel, the extinct volcano of **Puy de Dôme** ❿; then visit the Romanesque church in **Orcival** ⓫. Backtrack north on the fourth day to enjoy a *grande bouffe* (feast) at the famed restaurant Troisgros in **Roanne** ❼.

If you have
9 days

You can cover much of the region by car if you don't mind a lot of driving. Begin with lunch in **Bourges** ❶ ☞ and then head to the Château de la Commanderie, near ⊠ **St-Amand-Montrond** ❷, to stay the night. The second day explore **Bourbon-l'Archambault** ❸ and ⊠ **Moulins** ❹, home of the Bourbons and another good place to spend a night. On Day 3 pass through the spa town of **Vichy** ❼ on your way to **Thiers** ❽ to ponder its House of the Seven Deadly Sins; stop in ⊠ **Roanne** ❼ for the night and try to dine at the superb Troisgros restaurant. On the fourth day drive south to the most spectacular of the lava peak towns, **Le Puy** ⓮, and then on to overnight near the ⊠ **Gorges du Tarn** ㉓ and its natural chasms that do their best to conjure up a mini Grand Canyon. On Day 5 explore the gorge, then head for the **Gorges de la Jonte** ㉕ on your way back westward toward **Millau** ㉒. If you want to really get off the beaten track, continue east through the Canyon de la Dourbie to two tiny villages evocative of Shangri-la, Cantobre and La Couvertoirade. On Day 6 head over to **Rodez** ㉑ to see its pink-sandstone cathedral en route to the famed medieval basilica in **Conques** ⓴. By nightfall get to ⊠ **Aurillac** ⓱ or enchanting ⊠ **Salers** ⓰. Spend Day 7 exploring the *cols* (passes) and valleys in this area and the sparse lands around **Laguiole** ⓲—home to the famous auberge of Michel Bras—and the perched village of **St-Flour** ⓯. On Day 8 travel through the **Parc National des Volcans** around the celebrated **Puy de Dôme** ❿, perhaps spending the night in ⊠ **St-Nectaire** ⓬ or ⊠ **Montpeyroux** ⓭. On your last day make your way to the region's urban center, ⊠ **Clermont-Ferrand** ❾.

BOURGES & AUVERGNE

Historic Bourges, capital of the Berry region, is the gateway to Auvergne as you arrive from Paris. The northern part of Auvergne is known as the Bourbonnais, after the dynasty of French kings that it spawned. The heart of Auvergne—if not of France—is the Parc National des Volcans around Clermont-Ferrand, with its *puys* (craggy lava outcrops) and extinct volcanoes resembling giant grassy cones. Medieval villages perch on the hilltops, and outdoor markets bring the narrow streets to life. Good restaurants, informative museums, and venerable churches are to be found throughout the area. Everywhere you go, religious architecture harmonizes with the terrain, be it a mountain crest, as at St-Nectaire, or the hollow of a green valley nestling its church, as at Orcival.

Bourges

► ❶ *240 km (150 mi) south of Paris, 70 km (42 mi) west of Nevers, 150 km*
Fodor'sChoice *(95 mi) east of Tours.*
★

Find your way to Bourges, and you'll find yourself at the center of France. Or rather, medieval France. Modern times have largely passed by this neck of the woods and the result is this preserved market town with a spectacularly high cathedral and streets lined with timber-frame houses right out of the Middle Ages. Pedestrians-only rue Mirabeau and rue Coursarlon are particularly appealing places to stroll and shop. In the early 15th century the town was home-base for France's most flamboyant art patron and fashion plate, Jean, Duc de Berry, who spent lavishly on castles, jewels, and art. Later in the 15th century, Bourges served as temporary capital for Charles VII, who had been forced to flee invading English forces. The town hero at that time was Jacques Coeur, the son of a local fur trader, who amassed a fortune as the king's finance minister. His lavish early-Renaissance mansion still stands as one of central France's foremost sights.

Approaching the town, you'll see the soaring towers of the 13th-century
★ **Cathédrale St-Étienne.** For connoisseurs of Gothic architecture, this cathedral is one of the skyscrapers of the Middle Ages. The architects who completed the nave in 1280 really pushed the envelope, as shown by the side aisles flanking the nave, which rise to an astonishing 65 feet—high enough to allow windows to be placed above the level of the second side aisles. The nave of the cathedral of Senlis is shorter than the aisles here. The central portal is a sculpted masterpiece: cherubim, angels, saints, and prophets cluster mightily in the archway. The interior is sleek, elegant, and entirely given over to heaven-seeking vertical forces, particularly as there are no transepts, crossings, or lanterns here. Study the stained-glass windows in the aisles, which are relatively close to the ground. Note the pillars painted in royal blue and gold—testimony to the great wealth and power this church once enjoyed, also seen in the massive crypt, one of the last to be built in France. ⊠ *Off rue Porte Jaune.*

10

The Rocky Road

"The countryside here alone would cure me," wrote the Marquise de Sévigné when she came to this region in the 17th century to enjoy its famed medicinal waters and mountainside spas. France's great woman of letters was on to something—travelers since the days of ancient Rome have marveled at this land of exotic volcanic peaks and impressive gorges. Today, for those who would not do battle with glaciers and crevasses, there are peaceful excursions across pastures and along the grassy tops of volcanic mountains. Since there is more oxygen here than in the Alps—the highest peak measures in at 6,561 feet here, compared to a maximum height of more than 15,000 feet in the Alps—biking, mountain biking (mountain bikes are known as *vélos tout terrain*, or VTT; bikes can be rented at train stations in most towns), and mountain climbing are popular. For serious hiking, strike out along the extensive network of trails that crisscrosses the Parc National des Volcans, centered around Puy de-Dôme. For gentler walking from village to village and valley to valley, follow the Monts du Cantal. During winter there's limited skiing around Le Mont-Dore and Mt. Aigoual in the Causses, a desolate, windy limestone plateau scattered with dormant cone-shaped craters, lakes, and "plugs" (enormous stone outcrops). Mountains loom to the east of Clermont-Ferrand (the Massif Central's only large city), beyond giant granite rocks and heather-clad hills. Wide "fallaway" panoramic views are plentiful over russet valleys sprinkled with spare vegetation. The landscape here suggests an ancient Chinese painting, with broad plateaus broken by humped domes or *puys*. Down in the fertile valleys, cultivated yellow and tan squares lie like carpets spread over emerald hills. Here, the ultimate destination is the town of Le Puy-en-Velay—a rocky needle and two big volcanic trays springing up from the plain, crowned by a church built of polychrome lava.

The Hearty Kitchen

Food in the Massif Central is fuel for the body; fine dining it is often not. But there are many regional specialties to savor: *aligot* (puree of potatoes with Tomme de Cantal cheese and garlic), *cousinat* (chestnut soup), *sanflorin* (fried pork and herbs in pastry), and *salmis de colvert cévenol* (wild duck sautéed in red wine and onions). Auvergne is an area where the rivers teem with trout and the natives love serving it up swimming in butter. Regional produce can be transmogrified into glorious haute cuisine, as you will discover dining on Aubrac beef and wild boar at the famed hostelry of Michel Bras in Laguiole. This is also a land of cheeses famous throughout the world—Roquefort, creamy Bleu d'Auvergne, Gaperon with garlic, and nutty St-Nectaire. In summer, bakers turn *myrtilles* (blueberries) into tangy pies and tarts. And, if you have a sweet tooth, search out the barley sugar of Vichy.

★ Once showplace for the staggeringly wealthy Jacques Coeur, the **Palais Jacques-Coeur** is one of the most important late-Gothic dwellings in France, as you can tell from its vaulted chapel, the wooden ceilings covered with original paintings, and the dining room with its tapestries and massive fireplace. There are few furnishings to be seen, but the Gothic building

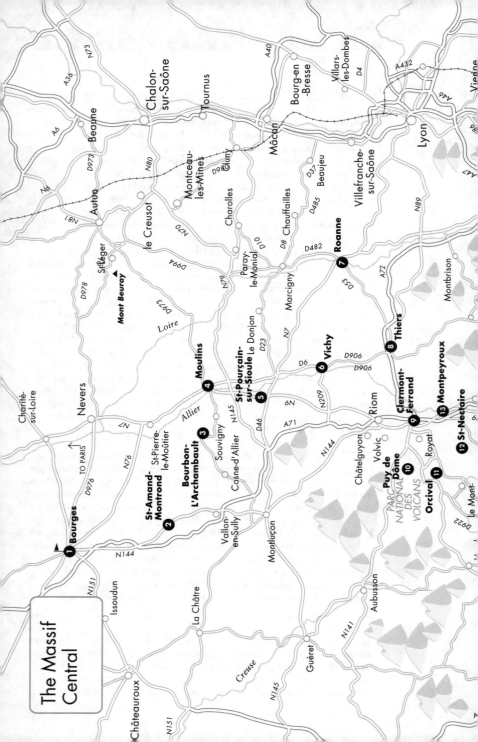

The Massif Central

itself is beautiful, from the carved and frescoed walls to the sculpture-covered facade (spot the celebrated stone carvings of courtiers staring out of "windows"). As well as being Charles VII's finance minister, Coeur was a great art patron (along with Jean, Duc de Berry, he sponsored some of the finest 15th-century illuminated books of hours) and helped spread a taste for the Italian Renaissance. ⊠ *Rue Jacques-Coeur* ☎ *02–48–24–06–87* ⌕ *€6.10* ☉ *Apr.–June, Sept. and Oct., daily 9–noon and 2–6; Nov.–Mar., daily 9:30–12:15 and 2–5:15; July and Aug., daily 9–noon and 2–7; 45-min guided tours only.*

Where to Stay & Eat

★ ¢ ✕ **Le Comptoir de Paris.** The red exterior of this cozy bar-restaurant beckons from afar; inside, the all-wood interior is warm and welcoming. On the prettiest square in Bourges, surrounded by magnificent medieval houses, this is a very popular and lively spot, especially in the bar area, where dinner is served until 10:30 every night but Sunday. Menus run from €11 to €15. The food is creative and tasty and the portions generous. If you're feeling adventurous, try the *andouillette* (grilled pork chitterlings). ⊠ *1 rue Jean-Girard* ☎ *02–48–24–17–16* ☐ *AE, MC, V* ☉ *Closed Sun.*

$$–$$$ ✕⌂ **Bourbon.** Set on beautiful grounds close to Bourges's medieval quarter, this former 17th-century abbey combines the grandeur of vaulted ceilings with the modern comfort of contemporary furnishings, a conference center, and an Internet connection in every room. Adjacent to the hotel is its restaurant, L'Abbaye Saint-Ambroix. Chef Pascale Auger has a light, innovative touch with fish and does playful desserts such as strawberries with rosemary. The restaurant also has an extensive wine cellar for intrepid tipplers. ⊠ *60 rue Jean Jaurès, 18000* ☎ *02–48–70–80–00* ⎙ *02–48–70–21–22* ⇆ *60 rooms* ⟓ *Restaurant, minibars, cable TV, bar, Internet, meeting room, parking (fee); no a/c* ☐ *AE, DC, MC, V* ⦿❘ *MAP.*

$–$$ ⌂ **Angleterre.** This foursquare hotel in the center of town near the palace is popular with business travelers. As it is part of the Best Western chain, its rooms compensate for their lack of character with soothing modern conveniences. ⊠ *1 pl. des Quatre-Piliers, 18000 Bourges* ☎ *02–48–24–68–51* ⎙ *02–48–65–21–41* ⊕ *www.bestwestern.fr* ⇆ *31 rooms* ⟓ *Restaurant, minibars, cable TV, bar; no a/c* ☐ *AE, DC, MC, V* ⦿❘ *EP.*

St-Amand-Montrond

❷ *44 km (27 mi) south of Bourges.*

The small market town of St-Amand-Montrond is a convenient stopping point as you head south into the Massif Central. If time permits, visit the **town museum,** housed in a 16th-century mansion, for an account of the region's history from the Stone Age to the present. ⊠ *Off pl. du Marché* ☎ *02–48–96–55–20* ⌕ *€2.10* ☉ *Mon. and Wed.–Sat. 10–noon and 2–6, Sun. 2–6.*

Also worth exploring is the town park with its ruined **Château,** once a residence of Louis II.

off the beaten path

ABBAYE DE NOIRLAC – Twenty kilometers (12 mi) northwest of St-Amand, this abbey, constructed in 1150, remains one of the finest examples of medieval monastic architecture in France. The abbey church, with its 13th- and 14th-century arcades flanking the south cloister, is still intact, as are the monastery, the chapter house, and the monks' hall. ⊠ *18200 Bruère-Allichamps* ☎ *02–48–62–01–01* ☞ *€5.50* ⊙ *Feb.–Sept., daily 9:45–12:30 and 2–5; Oct.–Dec., Wed.–Mon. 9:45–noon and 2–5.*

Where to Stay & Eat

★ $$$ ✕⊞ **Château de la Commanderie.** You won't regret going out of your way to reach this impressive medieval château, 11 km (7 mi) northwest of St-Amand-Montrond. The storybook main building, built of gleaming white stone, has large, elegant bedrooms, a mansard roof, turrets, and towers. Dinner can be arranged with the owners, Laura and Umberto Ronsisvalle, in the paneled dining room. Expect well-prepared family fare, often including perfectly aged Charolais beef. ⊠ *18200 Farges-Allichamps* ☎ *02–48–61–04–19* 🖨 *02–48–61–01–84* ⊕ *ila-chateau.com/command* ☞ *6 rooms, 2 suites* ⚐ *No a/c; no room phones, no room TVs* ⊟ *AE, MC, V* ⦿ *MAP.*

¢ ✕⊞ **Poste.** The main draw of this 16th-century hostelry is the restaurant—where reasonably priced, delicious food is prepared with loving care and fresh ingredients from imaginative recipes (note that it's closed Sunday and does not serve dinner Monday). Rooms are small and plainly furnished, but perfectly adequate. ⊠ *9 rue du Dr-Vallet, 18200* ☎ *02–48–96–27–14* 🖨 *02–48–96–97–74* ☞ *18 rooms* ⚐ *Restaurant; no a/c* ⊟ *AE, MC, V* ⊙ *Closed Nov.–Mar.* ⦿ *MAP.*

Bourbon-L'Archambault

❸ *54 km (34 mi) southeast of St-Amand-Montrond.*

Since Roman days, Bourbon-L'Archambault has been renowned for its healing waters: during the 17th–19th centuries it became a ritzy thermal spa-town, welcoming such glitterati as Talleyrand, France's powerful foreign minister. The weathered buildings and the ruined 14th-century **Château**—once quarters for visiting nobility, with three towers still standing—retain faded appeal and invite you to ruminate on long-gone glories. ⊠ *Rue du Château* ⊙ *Mid-Apr.–mid-Oct., daily 2–6.*

Where to Stay & Eat

★ $ ✕⊞ **Grand Hôtel Montespan-Talleyrand.** Napoléon's foreign minister, Charles-Maurice de Talleyrand, used to stay here every August when he came to take the waters—just one member of an A-list 19th-century clientele. The hotel is actually a converted trio of houses with a sumptuous (tapestries and antiques) reading room, covered passageway to the bathhouse, and a swimming pool set amid formal French gardens. The rooms are large, but for true grandeur spring for one of the apartment-size suites. The service is very accommodating, one reason many of the guests here become habitués. The restaurant's food is heavy, but consistently good. ⊠ *1 pl. des Thermes, 03160*

☎ *04–70–67–00–24* 🖭 *04–70–67–12–00* ⊕ *www.hotel-montespan. com* ⇌ *45 rooms, 4 suites* ⚭ *Restaurant, pool, gym; no a/c* ⊟ *AE, MC, V* ⊗ *Closed Nov.–Apr.* ⑩| *MAP.*

¢ ⊡ **Les Trois Puits.** Like any good French inn, Les Trois Puits (*puits* is regional jargon for "welcome") offers no-frills lodgings and warm, friendly service. Rooms are comfortable, the bathrooms unusually spacious, and the restaurant serves honest and hearty fare. ⊠ *Rue des Trois-Puits, 03160* ☎ *04–70–67–08–35* ⇌ *10 rooms* ⚭ *Restaurant; no a/c* ⊟ *AE, MC, V* ⑩| *EP.*

Moulins

❹ *24 km (15 mi) east of Bourbon-L'Archambault.*

★ Once the capital of the dukes of Bourbon, Moulins has a compact medieval center dominated by its cathedral. The oldest part of the **Cathédrale Notre-Dame** (⊠ Rue de Paris) is the Flamboyant Gothic, late 15th-century choir, famed for its stained-glass windows, designed as picture books for illiterate peasants, enabling them to follow the story of Louis IX (St-Louis) and the Crusades. The cathedral's other medieval treasure is the triptych by the Maître de Moulins—one of the greatest, although anonymous, artists of early Renaissance France—painted toward the end of the 15th century. The painter mixed classicizing style with realistic detail—notice the Virgin is not as richly clothed as the duke and duchess of Bourbon, the nobles who commissioned the painting. The town's belfry, known as the **Jacquemart** (⊠ Pl. de l'Hôtel-de-Ville), was built in 1232 and rebuilt in 1946 after it ignited during a fireworks display. The **Musée du Bourbonnais** (Regional Folklore Museum), in a 15th-century mansion next door to the Jacquemart, is filled with costumes, farming implements, and old-time household utensils. ⊠ *4 pl. de l'Ancien Palais* ☎ *04–70–44–39–03* ⬛ *€4* ⊗ *Apr.–Sept., Mon. and Tues. 9:30–11:30 and 3–6:30, Fri.–Sun. 3–6:30; Oct.–Mar., Mon. and Tues. 9:30–11:30 and 2–5:30, Fri.–Sun. 2–5:30; 60-min guided tours only.*

Where to Stay & Eat

$$ ✕ **Cours.** Easily the best in town, this chic brasserie-style restaurant in a lovely vine-covered building serves classic dishes with creative twists, perfectly turned out. Service is impeccable, and the wine list is balanced and sanely priced. The €15 menu fixe is outstanding. ⊠ *36 cours Jean-Jaurès* ☎ *04–70–44–25–66* ⊟ *MC, V* ⊗ *Closed Wed. and 1st 2 wks July.*

★ $-$$ ✕⊡ **Paris-Jacquemart.** This family-owned hotel, just a block from the town's medieval quarter, is a genuine delight—traditional France at its very best. Service is welcoming and efficient. Rooms are suitably large, with high ceilings and 19th-century antiques. The menus range from a weekday special at €24 to a €70 deal for a three-course combination meal, usually including a hearty portion of Charolais beef. ⊠ *21 rue de Paris, 03000 Moulins* ☎ *04–70–44–00–58* 🖭 *04–70–34–05–39* ⇌ *22 rooms, 5 suites* ⚭ *Restaurant, minibars, cable TV, pool* ⊟ *AE, DC, MC, V* ⊗ *Closed 1st 3 wks Jan. and last 2 wks June* ⑩| *MAP.*

St-Pourçain-sur-Sioule

⑤ *32 km (20 mi) south of Moulins.*

The attractive village of St-Pourçain-sur-Sioule, with its medieval abbey church nestling snugly among old houses at the top of the hill, is best known for its wines—mainly fruity reds and rosés, made from the gamay grape. Vines were first planted here 2,000 years ago, making this one of the oldest vine-growing centers in France.

Where to Stay & Eat

¢–$ ✕⌂ **Le Chêne Vert.** This traditional hotel is clean, comfortable, and well-serviced. Rooms are large and nicely decorated; many have been recently renovated. Tasty, uncomplicated fare is served in the two dining rooms—veal kidneys in mustard, superb Charolais beef, rabbit in aspic—all to be washed down with excellent St-Pourçain. ✉ *35 bd. Ledru-Rollin, 03500* ☎ *04-70-47-77-00* ☐ *04-70-47-77-39* ⚊ *29 rooms* ☖ *Restaurant; no a/c* ⊟ *AE, MC, V* ⊘ *Closed 2 wks Jan. and Sun. in winter* |◯| *EP.*

$$–$$$ ✕⌂ **Château de Boussac.** Although the beefy turrets and gigantic moat reflect its defensive origins, this château-inn, 10 km (6 mi) southwest of St-Pourçain on D987, is fully modernized and, despite doubling as a working Charolais cattle-ranch, surprisingly quiet. Copious breakfasts are served in guest rooms, which are furnished with antiques. In the evening you can sometimes enjoy an aperitif with the Marquis and Marquise de Longueil before tucking into an extensive €41 table d'hôte feast (advance arrangements required). ✉ *03140 Target* ☎ *04-70-40-63-20* ☐ *04-70-40-60-03* ⊕ *www.chateau-de-boussac. com* ⚊ *3 rooms* ☖ *Restaurant; no a/c, no room TVs* ⊟ *AE, MC, V* ⊘ *Closed Dec.–Mar.* |◯| *MAP.*

Vichy

⑥ *30 km (19 mi) south of St-Pourçain, 350 km (215 mi) south of Paris.*

Vichy, one of the few large towns in the region, does not have the depth of character you'd expect from a place whose mineral waters attracted the Romans and, later, Paris haute society. Nobles such as Madame de Sévigné and her friend, the Duchess of Angoulême, started the trend in the 17th century; Napoléon III graced the scene in the mid-19th century, then the arrival of the railroad attracted the middle classes. When France fell to the Germans in 1940 and was divided under direct and indirect German control, the country's collaborationist government, under Marshal Pétain, moved to Vichy, using its hotels as embassies and ministries. After the war the puppet government left a stain of infamy on the town. Today Vichy is trying to overcome its past, as well as the perception that it's only a place for retirement. A stretch of the River Allier is being transformed into a lake, and large conference facilities and thermal baths have been built. Although there are no old, famous buildings to admire, you'll want to pay a visit, and drink a cup of spa water, at the Art Nouveau **Hall des Sources** (Pump Room) at one end of the leafy Parc des Sources. Across the park is the ornate **Grand**

Casino, which contains an opera house. Shops and stately mansions ring the park, along with the **Office de Toursime** (⊠ 19 rue du Parc ☎ 04–70–98–71–94) where you can pick up a map showing the buildings used by the Pétain government.

Where to Stay & Eat

$–$$　✕ **Alambic.** A master with local produce, chef-owner Jean-Jacques Barbot creates such dishes as fish, caught fresh from nearby streams, grilled with endives, and lentil salad using the famous tiny *lentilles du Puy.* Menus start at €25. ⊠ *8 rue Nicolas-Larbaud* ☎ *04–70–59–12–71* ⚖ *Reservations essential* ⊟ *MC, V* ☉ *Closed late Feb.–early Mar., late Aug.–early Sept., and Mon. No lunch Tues.*

¢–$　🏨 **Arverna.** This hotel in an 18th-century building in the center of town is an excellent value for the money. The owner, who has traveled the world extensively, provides a friendly welcome. Rooms are modest but functional (Nos. 101 and 102 are the best); bathrooms are clean. ⊠ *12 rue Desbrest, 03200* ☎ *04–70–31–31–19* 🖷 *04–70–97–86–43* 🖙 *22 rooms, 4 suites* ᗘ *Cable TV, parking (fee); no a/c* ⊟ *AE, DC, MC, V* ☉ *Closed Dec. 15–Jan. 5* ❙⊘❙ *EP.*

Roanne

❼　*64 km (40 mi) east of Vichy, 87 km (54 mi) west of Lyon, 390 km (245 mi) south of Paris.*

Industrial Roanne, a textiles center that grew up as a hub for river transportation, will probably be on your itinerary for only one reason—the world-famous Troisgros restaurant.

Where to Stay & Eat

$$$$　✕🏨 **Troisgros.** Since the 1950s one of the most revered restaurants in France, Troisgros is an obligatory pilgrimage stop for foodies (book weekends two months in advance) interested in the mainstays of haute cuisine. Happily, you'll find the old magic is still here—quite a feat for a place that first set up shop in Roanne's station hotel in 1930. The third generation is now at the helm, and they have learned their lessons well: lightly sautéed foie gras with grilled groundnuts, frogs'-legs lasagna, regional cheeses, and the most celebrated dessert trolley in France are just a few highlights. Service is impeccable, with a waiter-to-diner ratio of three to one. You don't have to deprive your heirs to dine here, however: you can also enjoy the Troisgros's buffet breakfast—a dazzling spread—and the Grand Dessert, a high tea served in mid-afternoon. The restaurant is closed Tuesday and Wednesday, and reservations are essential. This is now officially La Maison Troisgros, for the family now owns the adjacent hotel as well. As in the restaurant, decor here is modern, so if you're out for charm, escape to the hotel's lovely garden-courtyard. ⊠ *Pl. Jean-Troisgros, across from train station, 42300* ☎ *04–77–71–66–97* 🖷 *04–77–70–39–77* ⊕ *www.troisgros.fr* 🖙 *18 rooms* ᗘ *Restaurant, minibars, cable TV* ⊟ *AE, DC, MC, V* ☉ *Closed 1st 3 wks Feb. and 1st 2 wks Aug.* ❙⊘❙ *EP.*

Fodor'sChoice
★

Thiers

❽ *60 km (38 mi) southwest of Roanne, 47 km (29 mi) northeast of Clermont-Ferrand.*

Built on a steep hill, Thiers is a slightly grimy yet intriguing 18th- and 19th-century town famous for its cutlery. It supplies 70% of France's carving and cutting needs, producing everything from table knives to daggers. In the old days, while the River Durolle turned the massive grindstones, craftsmen would lie on planks over the icy water to hone their blades on the stone. Today's factories use less exotic methods, but the tourist office gives demonstrations of the old way (as well as maps and information). Be prepared for stiff walking—the streets run only up and down! Follow rue Conchette, then rue Bourg to appealing place du Pirou, where there's a wonderful example of ancient half-timber architecture, the 15th-century **Maison du Pirou** (Pirou House). At 11 rue de Pirou is the **Maison des Sept Péchés Capitaux** (House of the Seven Deadly Sins)—look at the carvings on the ends of the beams, and you'll know why it is so named). On rue de la Coutellerie are old knife-making workshops and the 15th-century **Maison de la Coutellerie** (Cutlery House), a small museum and workshop with demonstrations covering five centuries of knife making. ⊠ *58 rue de la Coutellerie* ☏ *04–73–80–58–86* 🖭 *€4.75* ⊙ *Oct.–May, Tues.–Sun. 10–noon and 2–6; June and Sept., daily 10–noon and 2–6:30; July and Aug., daily 10–6:30.*

Where to Eat

$ ✕ **Le Coutelier.** Housed in a former *coutelier*'s (cutler's) shop, this restaurant is filled with old Thiers cutlery. The fare is traditional Auvergne style—dishes such as lentils with bacon and sausage, chicken cooked in wine, and, most traditional of all, *truffade* (a potato dish with ham, cheese, and green salad). ⊠ *4 pl. du Palais* ☏ *04–73–80–79–59* 🖃 *MC, V* ⊙ *Closed June. No dinner Mon.–Thurs. in winter, no dinner Mon. in summer.*

Clermont-Ferrand

❾ *40 km (24 mi) southwest of Thiers, 400 km (250 mi) south of Paris.*

Known to historians as the hometown of Vercingétorix, who rallied the Arvernes to defeat Julius Caesar in 52 BC (and who is immortalized in Astérix comic books), Clermont-Ferrand is the only large city in Auvergne. A bustling, modern commercial center that is home to the Michelin tire company's headquarters, Clermont-Ferrand probably won't draw you for more than a few hours. But the city serves as an ideal transfer point to the rest of Auvergne. It has some good museums and a small Old Quarter dominated by its cathedral. The Gothic **Cathédrale Notre-Dame-de-l'Assomption** (⊠ Pl. de la Victoire) was constructed of especially durable black volcanic stone that enabled the pillars to be unusually slender. It's famed for its stained glass and its two spires, added in the 19th-century to the design of ace restorer Eugène Viollet le Duc, who also lengthened the nave while he was at it.

The older **Notre-Dame-du-Port** (⊠ Rue du Port) was built of sandstone and has an entirely different feel from the cathedral. Though founded in the 6th century, it dates mainly from the 11th and 12th centuries and is Romanesque in style. Note the raised choir with its carved capitals illustrating The Fall and the struggle between Good and Evil.

Housed in a former Ursuline convent, the **Musée d'Art Roger-Quillet** (Arts Museum) has a beautifully designed exhibit on the history of painting and sculpture. ⊠ *Pl. Louis-Deteix* ☎ *04–73–16–11–30* ☞ *€4* ⊙ *Tues.–Sun. 10–6.*

Where to Stay & Eat

★ $$$–$$$$ ✕**Bernard Andrieux.** Chef Bernard Andrieux cooks deceptively simple dishes such as salmon with truffle sauce and *escalope de foie chaud de canard* (hot scalloped duck liver). The restaurant's elegance—cream-color walls, white linens, and well-spaced tables—reflects the prices (the least expensive prix-fixe menu is €28), but not the suburban location. ⊠ *Rte. de la Baraque, Durtel, 3 km (2 mi) northwest of Clermont-Ferrand on D141A* ☎ *04–73–19–25–00* 🖶 *04–73–19–25–04* ▭ *AE, DC, MC, V* ⊙ *Closed Sun. mid-Aug.–mid-July, 1st wk in May, school holidays in Feb., and Mon.*

★ $$$–$$$$ ✕**Clavé.** The finest restaurant in the *centre ville* is tucked away on a little street near the law courts. The decor—plain walls, good modern paintings, subtle lighting—has as much understated style as the chic waiters. Chef Jean-Claude Leclerc numbers ravioli of foie gras and pigeon with chanterelles among his specialties, but his touch is at its deftest with vegetables. Just taste the salad of green beans and candied tomatoes that he drapes alongside roast langoustines to form a culinary still life that looks almost too good to eat. ⊠ *12 rue St-Adjutor* ☎ *04–73–36–46–30* 🖶 *04–73–31–30–74* ▭ *AE, MC, V* ⊙ *Closed Sun. and 2nd half Aug.*

$ ▤ **Lyon.** With its exposed timbers, this centrally located hotel stands out in contrast to the surrounding buildings made of volcanic stone and concrete, but don't expect much more than clean rooms and perfunctorily efficient service. ⊠ *16 pl. de Jaude, 63000* ☎ *04–73–17–60–80* 🖶 *04–73–17–60–81* 🖘 *32 rooms* ⚐ *Restaurant; no a/c* ▭ *AE, DC, MC, V* ⭕I *MAP.*

Parc National des Volcans

★   *The Puy de Dôme is 15 km (9 mi) west of Clermont-Ferrand.*

Stretching 150 km (90 mi) from north to south, the **Parc National des Volcans** (National Volcano Park) contains 80 or so dormant volcanoes, with all kinds of craters, dikes, domes, prismatic lava flows, caldera cones, and basaltic plateaus dotting the terrain. The volcanoes are (relatively) young; the most recent is only 6,000 to 8,000 years old, which explains why their shapes are so well preserved.

The most famous *puy* (peak) of all is also the most convenient to visit from Clermont-Ferrand, 15 km (9 mi) to the east. At 4,800 feet, the **Puy de Dôme,** is the highest volcano in the Mont-Dôme range, and one heck of a 6 km (4 mi) climb—just ask the Tour de France bike riders, who are relieved they only have to visit every few years. If you're not up for the hike to the top, take an excursion bus from Clermont-Ferrand (such as those run by Voyages Maisonneuve). The road to the peak is mostly paved, so if you want hardcore nature, you're out of luck. Luckily, once you are at the top there are trails in every direction—one two-hour hike takes you to a cone-shape crater. The Romans built a temple to Mercury here; its ruins were uncovered in 1872. The number of tourists, especially in July and August, is tremendous—the Puy de Dôme is one of the most visited sights in France. Count on spending most of the day here, and bring your walking shoes so that you can follow the trails up to magnificent panoramas. If you're set on a bird's-eye view, parasailing, hot-air ballooning, and hang gliding can be arranged. 🎫 €4.50 per car except July and Aug., when access is by shuttle bus only, €3 ⊙ Mar. and Nov., daily 8–6; Apr. and Oct., daily 8–8; May–Sept., daily 7 AM–10 PM; Dec., weekends 7–5:30.

A new volcano visitor center called **Vulcania** opened 16 km (10 mi) northwest of Clermont-Ferrand in 2002. Occupying the site of an extinct volcano, the center consists of an artificial volcanic cone, 90 feet high, and a crater dug into lava rock to a depth of 125 feet, lined with shimmering, stainless-steel scales designed to evoke the interior of a volcano. Video displays and spectacular lighting effects provide a razzmatazz introduction to fiery geology. ⊠ Rte. de Mazaye, St-Ours-les-Roches ☎ 08–20–82–78–28 ⊕ www.vulcania.com 🎫 €19 ⊙ July and Aug., daily 9–7; Apr.–June, daily 9–6; Feb., Mar., and Sept.–mid-Nov., Wed.–Sun. 9–6.

Orcival

⑪ 13 km (8 mi) southwest of Puy de Dôme, 22 km (14 mi) southwest of Clermont-Ferrand.

To house pilgrims making the long trek from Le Puy to Santiago de Compostela in Spain, five Romanesque hospices—St-Austremoine d'Issoire, Notre-Dame-du-Port, Notre-Dame d'Orcival, St-Nectaire, and St-Saturnin—were erected in Auvergne in the 12th century. Of these, ★ **Notre-Dame d'Orcival** (1146–78) was and remains the most famous. Step inside to inspect a most unusual statue of the Virgin carrying an adult-looking Child.

en route From Orcival take D27 south, which joins D983, for a beautiful ride over the **Col de Guéry** pass, at 4,800 feet.

St-Nectaire

⑫ 16 km (10 mi) southwest of Orcival, 44 km (27 mi) southwest of Clermont-Ferrand.

Dominating the upper part of the former spa town of St-Nectaire is its 12th-century Romanesque church—you may want to give thanks here after surviving the challenge of driving over the passes, and admire the superb carved and gilded 12th-century bust of St-Baudime. Another reward is St-Nectaire's superb, soft, nutty-tasting cheese, made locally since the 3rd century.

Where to Stay

$ ▦ **Le Relais Mercure.** On the site of the former Roman baths, in a dignified 19th-century building, is this attractive, modern hotel in the lower town. Soaring ceilings in the palatial public areas and picture windows in the restaurant and bar give the place a light, airy feel. Part of the reliable Mercure chain, the hotel has all the amenities, from cable TV to direct-dial phones and in-room modem lines. The grounds in back, rising protectively from the hotel, include a tranquil arboretum. ⊠ *Les Bains Romains 63710* ☎ *04–73–88–57–00* 🖳 *04–73–88–57–02* 🗗 *71 rooms* ⚘ *Restaurant, minibars, cable TV, pool, health club, hot tub, bar, Internet; no a/c* ▤ *AE, DC, MC, V* ⦿| *MAP.*

Montpeyroux

⑬   *20 km (12 mi) east of St-Nectaire, 23 km (13 mi) south of Clermont-Ferrand.*

Well into the 19th century, this granite-walled, hilltop village—perched on a knoll just 8 km (5 mi) off A75 Exit 7—boasted 450 inhabitants, most of whom tended the surrounding vineyards. Then came phylloxera. The vines were destroyed and the population dwindled to 125. The village's once-proud medieval homes fell into disrepair. It was not until the 1970s that Montpeyroux's scenic potential was recognized and a revival began. Now the village has 360 residents, restored houses, and an annual flower festival in the third week in May. There isn't actually that much to see here, except for the circular 13th-century keep and a restaurant or two. But the sense of history, and the panoramic views across to the distant volcanic mountains, combine to create a sense of serenity.

Where to Stay

$ ▦ **Chez Astruc.** Owner M. Astruc's enthusiasm for the village—he is its mayor—and his knowledge of the area make staying at this charming four-story inn a pleasure. The Astrucs live on the top floor; guest rooms—not large but pleasant if a bit fussy—are on the lower three floors. Ask to stay on the second floor, where two rooms have balconies and views of the countryside. ⊠ *Rue du Donjon, 63114* ☎ *04–73–96–69–42* 🗗 *5 rooms* ⚘ *No a/c, no room TVs* ▤ *No credit cards* ⦿| *EP.*

Le Puy-en-Velay

⑭   *108 km (68 mi) southeast of Montpeyroux.*

FodorśChoice
★

★   Built around three *puys* (lava outcrops) that rise from the fertile valley like elongated pyramids, Le Puy-en-Velay presents the most astonishing **cityscape** in France. The monuments perched daringly atop these oversize pumice stones are the not-so-subtle beacons of power and religion that has made Le Puy a major pilgrimage destination since the days of Charlemagne, and one of the four principal departure points for the great medieval pilgrim road to Santiago de Compostela in Spain. The lowest of the peaks is crowned with a statue of St. Joseph and the Infant Jesus; the highest with an 11th-century chapel dedicated to St-Michel. The third hosts a huge red statue of the Virgin that strikes some as a tacky Biblical cousin of the Statue of Liberty.

The city's sturdiest religious monument is the hilltop Romanesque cathedral of **Notre-Dame-du-Puy,** begun in the early 5th century by Bishop Scutarious on the site of a Gallo-Roman temple. The cathedral was enlarged continuously until the end of the 12th century to accommodate pilgrim crowds. Admire the crazy, black-and-white banded stonework of the Byzantine facade; inside, note the Black Madonna on the high altar, a copy of the figure burned by revolutionaries in 1794. The origin of this first statue—perhaps a figure of Isis transformed into a Madonna, perhaps a statue carved by an Arab craftsman in Le Puy—remains a mystery. The cathedral sits squarely between the adjoining 11th-century cloisters and the baptistery, at the top of a long flight of steps rising from the steep streets of the medieval *haute ville* (upper town), which ooze history. The rest of Le Puy seems shabbily provincial in comparison, overrun with overpriced boutiques selling the last remains of the town's oncegreat *dentelle-* (lace-) making tradition. ⌨ €2 *for cloister* ☉ *Cathedral daily 9:30–noon and 2–7; cloister daily 9:30–noon and 2–4.*

Just to the north of the cathedral you'll see the huge red statue of Notre-Dame de France (Our Lady of France) atop the **Rocher Corneille.** The hollow statue (you can venture inside) was built in 1860 using Russian cannons captured during the Crimean War, and melted down on their return to France. The view from the base of the 75-foot statue extends beyond the red roofs of the town to the castle of Polignac, 4 mi distant. ⌨ €3 ☉ *Mid-Mar.–early Sept., daily 9–6; Oct.–mid-Mar., daily 10–5.*

The 10th-century **Chapelle de St-Michel d'Aiguilhe,** perched on what was once the vent of an old volcano, also has a view that justifies a stiff climb. Notice the white, black, and red tiles on the facade, reflecting a blend of Romanesque and Islamic traditions. Come early to beat the backup along the winding staircase. ⌨ €1 ☉ *Mid-June–mid-Sept., daily 9–7; mid-Sept.–mid-June, daily 10–noon and 2–5; closed mornings mid-Dec.–mid-Mar.*

Where to Stay & Eat

$–$$ ✕▥ **Régina.** In the town center (ask for a room at the rear), the hotel's building dates from the late 19th century, but renovations made in the 1990s, including updates like Internet connections and Jacuzzis, have kept clientele equipped with all the modern essentials. A big selling point of the hotel is the restaurant, with its cozy interior and veranda, which makes it one of the prettiest addresses in town year-round—and one of the most delicious: desserts are to die for, and the bread is *fait maison* (homemade). ✉ *34 bd. du Mal-Fayolle, 43000* ☎ *04–71–09–14–71* 🖷 *04–71–09–18–57* ⌕ *27 rooms* ⚬ *Restaurant, some in-room hot tubs, minibars, cable TV, Internet* ▭ *AE, MC, V* ▯ *EP.*

St-Flour

⓯ *96 km (60 mi) west of Le Puy.*

St-Flour is a medieval enclave perched on the edge of an escarpment 2,800 feet above sea-level, with cliffs dropping down on three sides toward the more recent *ville basse* (lower town). Narrow cobblestone streets meander between 16th- and 17th-century buildings in the ancient *ville haute* (upper town). The **Musée de la Haute-Auvergne** (Auvergne Museum), in the former bishop's palace, presents some local archaeological finds but is mostly filled with artifacts and furnishings used by residents over the last 300 years. ⊠ *1 pl. d'Armes* ☎ *04–71–60–61–34* ☑ *€4* ☉ *Mid-Oct.–mid-Apr., Mon.–Sat. 10–noon and 2–6; mid-Apr.–July and Sept.–mid-Oct., daily 10–noon and 2–6; July and Aug., daily 10–noon and 2–7.*

Across the square from the Musée de la Haute-Auvergne is the **Musée Alfred-Douet**. The 13th-century building, renovated in the 16th century, has on display tapestries and furnishings from the 16th, 17th, and 18th centuries. The objects are laid out just as they might have been when the building was occupied by the consul-general. ⊠ *Pl. d'Armes* ☎ *04–71–60–44–99* ☑ *€3.40* ☉ *Mid-Apr.–mid-Oct., daily 9–noon and 2–6; mid-Oct.–mid-Apr., weekdays 9–noon and 2–6, Sat. 10–noon and 2–6.*

Where to Stay

¢–$ 🏨 **Europe.** The choice of hotels in St-Flour's ville haute is limited; the family-run Europe is the best. A long, horizontal building on the edge of town, it overlooks the valley below and the hills beyond—this view being a large part of the hotel's appeal. Ask for a room—and in the restaurant, a table—with a view of the valley. Rooms, though not large, are old-fashioned, homey, and comfortable. ⊠ *12 cours Ternes, 15100* ☎ *04–71–60–03–64* 🖷 *04–71–60–03–45* ⇨ *44 rooms* ⚘ *Restaurant, cable TV, bar; no a/c* ☰ *AE, DC, MC, V* ⏸ *MAP.*

en route   Take D926 northwest from St-Flour to Murat, then D680 toward Salers via the **Pas de Peyrol,** at nearly 5,200 feet Auvergne's highest pass. Leave your car in the parking lot and make the 30-minute climb ★ to the summit of the **Puy Mary,** 5,800 feet above sea-level. The views of 13 valleys radiating from the mountain are stupendous.

Salers

16   *20 km (13 mi) west of the Pas de Peyrol, 68 km (43 mi) west of St-Flour.*

Fodor'sChoice   Medieval Salers, perched on a bluff above the Maronne Valley, is filled
★   with visitors—little wonder, since the town casts a spell on most travelers. In the 15th century the people of Salers, feeling isolated in the country, began building protective ramparts and the town subsequently won the right to govern itself. Many 15th- and 16th-century houses of black lava stone remain, given over to boutiques and small restaurants. Although this was once an important cattle-market town, farming today plays a smaller role than tourism—though you may wake to the sound of cowbells and hooves clattering over **Grande-Place** on market days.

About 15 km (9 mi) south of Salers, the valley ridges are so fetching that you could spend a day or two exploring the region's tiny, winding roads. The *cols* (mountain passes) are high enough (plus or minus 3,000 feet) to have snow in the winter, but they are really quite gentle, and they provide a good view of the comely valleys below. Wend your way down D35 to **Fontanges,** with its tiny chapel hollowed out of a limestone bluff topped by a white Madonna, then on to St-Projet and, via D43 and D60, to the pretty hillside village of Tournemire. The **Château d'Anjony** here is worth a visit. ☎ *04–71–47–61–67* ✆ *€5.20* ☉ *Mid-Feb.–mid-Nov., daily 2–6:30.*

Where to Stay

★ $$ ⌂ **Château de la Vigne.** Monsieur and Madame du Fayet de la Tour's château-inn retains elements of its past roles as an 8th-century Merovingian castle and medieval fortress, though it was rebuilt in the 15th century. Family coats of arms and stained-glass windows decorate the best guest room, where Jean-Jacques Rousseau is said to have stayed in 1767. Elsewhere furnishings are sparse and bathrooms makeshift. A table d'hôte dinner of regional dishes is served in the splendid dining room. ⌂ *16 km (10 mi) from Salers, 15700 Ally* ☎☎ *04–71–69–00–20* ⇨ *4 rooms* ⌂ *No a/c; no room TVs* ⊟ *No credit cards* ☉ *Closed mid-Oct.–late Mar.* ¶⊙¶ *MAP.*

★ $ ✕⌂ **Hôtel des Remparts.** From its position atop the ramparts, this hotel has spectacular panoramic views. Rooms are simple and functional. The management likes to quote half-pension rates, which you should resist if you are staying for more than one night. ⌂ *Esplanade de Barrouze, 15140* ☎ *04–71–40–70–33* 🖶 *04–71–40–75–32* ⇨ *18 rooms* ⌂ *Restaurant; no a/c* ⊟ *MC, V* ☉ *Closed late Oct.–late Dec.* ¶⊙¶ *FAP.*

Aurillac

⑰ *44 km (27 mi) south of Salers, 160 km (100 mi) southwest of Clermont-Ferrand.*

The administrative center and market town of Aurillac, on the edge of the Monts du Cantal, bustles by day and becomes a sleepy country village at night. The dinky town center has an old cheese market, ancient houses, and narrow streets that twist along the banks of the River Jordanne. Locals and tourists spend their days at the cafés on place du Palais-de-Justice, the leafy main square. Stop by the tourist office here for a free walking-tour map—well worth following.

At the **Musée d'Art et d'Archéologie** (Art & Antiquities Museum), remains of a Gallo-Roman temple and various religious objects are on display. A unique collection of umbrellas from the past three centuries—about half of all French umbrellas are made in Aurillac—is also housed here. ⌂ *Centre Pierre-Mendès-France, 1 pl. des Carmes* ☎ *04–71–45–46–10* ✆ *€3* ☉ *Apr.–Oct., Tues.–Sat. 10–noon and 2–6; July and Aug., Sun. 2–6.*

Where to Stay & Eat

$–$$ ✕ **Poivre et Sel.** This intimate, friendly bistro serves a refined version of Auvergne fare. It is a good place to try Salers beef, as well as other regional dishes such as *salmis de colvert cévenol* (ragout of duck). Two menus are offered, for €11 and €27. ⌂ *4 rue du XIV Juillet* ☎ *04–71–64–20–20* ⊟ *MC, V* ☉ *Closed Sun. and Mon.*

$–$$ ⌂ **Bordeaux.** There are advantages to this Best Western hotel—its central location, its private garage, and its professional staff. Otherwise, rooms are what you'd expect from this chain—compact but clean, functional, and adequate, though some have views of the gardens of the Palais de Justice. ⌂ *2 av. de la République, 15000* ☎ *04–71–48–01–84* 🖶 *04–71–48–49–93*

⊕ *www.hotel-de-bordeaux.fr* ⤳ *30 rooms, 3 suites* ☌ *Cable TV, bar, Internet; no a/c in some rooms* ☰ *AE, DC, MC, V* ⊙ *Closed late Dec.–early Jan.* ⓸⎸ *EP.*

CANYON COUNTRY

Breathtaking gorges carved into the limestone plateaus known as the Causses mark the landscape here. Millennia ago, pressure caused fractures and cleavages that trapped torrential rains. Through thousands of years the swirling waters ate into the mass of stone, gouging out the canyons and caves and the underground rivers and lakes that are today such wonders to the tourist, boatman, and geologist. The most famous of these are the Gorges du Tarn, a wilderness filled with sudden views of dramatic silhouettes of red and yellow cliffs. The lovely, old, rural towns make perfect bases for exploring the area, which also headlines some great medieval churches.

Laguiole

⑱ *80 km (50 mi) southeast of Aurillac.*

On the high basalt plateau, Laguiole is more than 3,000 feet above sea level. In winter the wind roars across the land, piling up snow on ski trails; in summer the sun scorches it; in spring and fall the angled sunlight dances on the granite outcroppings. The town is known for its hardy breed of Aubrac cattle; for its distinctive cheese made from unpasteurized cows' milk, flavored by the varied local flora; and for its spring-hinged pocket knife. You can visit the factory, the **Société Forge de Laguiole** (☎ 05–65–48–43–34), where they make these knives, which have a slightly curved handle and a long blade; buy one here or in town (but don't carry it home on the plane).

Where to Stay & Eat

★ **$$$$** ✕⎁ **Michel Bras.** Despite the flowery prose used by Monsieur Bras to describe his contemporary hotel-restaurant, it does not really "mold itself perfectly to the countryside," but stands on a promontory like a spaceship about to be launched. To be fair, the rooms are bright and comfortable and the views of the granite outcrops are haunting. But the main draw is Michel Bras's unique creations—foie gras with apricots and honey vinegar and asparagus with truffle vinaigrette—as well as his more classic Aubrac beef and wild boar dishes. The €42 lunch menu alone is worth a visit. ✉ *Rte. de l'Aubrac, 12210* ☎ *05–65–51–18–20* 🖶 *05–65–48–47–02* ⊕ *www.michel-bras.com* ⤳ *15 rooms* ☌ *Restaurant, minibars, cable TV, Internet* ☰ *AE, DC, MC, V* ⊙ *Closed Nov.–Easter and Mon. No lunch Tues., except July and Aug.* ⓸⎸ *EP.*

$ ✕⎁ **Auguy.** A good alternative to the high-price Michel Bras, the Auguy has basic, standard-issue rooms. Ask for one of the quieter ones away from the street. Owner Isabelle Auguy is a creative cook who uses her grandparents' rustic recipes, but gives them a lighter touch. The foie gras salad is a delight, as are the Aubrac beef and the fresh trout. The restaurant is closed Monday and does not serve dinner Sunday. ✉ *2 allée de l'Amicale, 12210* ☎ *05–65–44–31–11* 🖶 *05–65–51–50–81* ⤳ *20* *rooms* ⚭ *Restaurant, minibars, cable TV, bar, Internet; no a/c* ▤ *AE, DC, MC, V* ⊘ *Closed Dec. and Jan.* ⦿ *MAP.*

Figeac

⑲ *64 km (40 mi) southwest of Aurillac, 100 km (62 mi) west of Laguiole.*

The Vieille Ville of Figeac, which has a lively Saturday-morning market, was once a major stopping point for pilgrims heading toward Santiago de Compostela in Spain. Many of the 13th-, 14th-, and 15th-century houses in the old part of town have been carefully restored; note their octagonal chimneys and *soleilhos* (open attics used for drying flowers and wood). The elegant 13th-century **Hôtel de la Monnaie**, a block from the Célé River, is a characteristic old Figeac house. Probably used as a money-changing office in the Middle Ages, today it houses the tourist office and a museum of sculpture, coins, and antiquities. ⊠ *Pl. Vival* ☎ *05–65–34–06–25* ▱ *€2* ⊘ *July and Aug., daily 10–1 and 2–7; Sept.–June, daily 10–noon and 2:30–6.*

★ Jean-François Champollion (1790–1830), the first man to decipher Egyptian hieroglyphics, was born in Figeac. The **Musée Champollion** (leave place Vival on rue 11-Novembre, take the first left, and follow it as it veers right) contains a copy of the Rosetta stone, discovered in the Nile Delta in 1799, whose twin texts in Egyptian and Ancient Greek enabled Champollion to decode Pharaonic writing in 1821. A varied collection of Egyptian antiquities is also on display. ⊠ *5 impasse Champollion* ☎ *05–65–50–31–08* ▱ *€3.10* ⊘ *July and Aug., daily 10–noon and 2:30–6:30; Mar.–June, Sept. and Oct., Tues.–Sun. 10–noon and 2:30–6:30; Nov.–Feb., Tues.–Sun. 2–6.*

Where to Stay & Eat

$$$–$$$$ ✕⊡ **Château du Viguier du Roy.** Everything—the tower, the cloister, the gardens, the wood beams, the tapestries, and the canopy beds—in this 14th-century palace, once the residence of the king's *viguier* (representative), has been painstakingly restored. Rooms throughout are regal. The restaurant, La Dinée du Viguier, serves excellent prix-fixe meals. ⊠ *52 rue Emile-Zola, 46100* ☎ *05–65–50–05–05* 🖷 *05–65–50–06–06* ⊕ *www.chateau-viguier-figeac.com* ⤴ *18 rooms, 3 suites* ⚭ *Restaurant, minibars, cable TV, pool, Internet, no-smoking rooms* ▤ *AE, DC, MC, V* ⊘ *Closed Dec.* ⦿ *MAP.*

$$ ⊡ **Domaine des Villedieu.** This lovely farmhouse 10 km (6 mi) from Figeac on D13, dates partly from the 16th century and is lovingly run by the Villedieu family. Not only are there cozy rooms in ancient (restored) outbuildings such as the former bakery, but you can also look forward to a fireside dinner of cassoulet in a bubbling earthenware casserole accompanied by homemade foie gras and a local Cahors wine. ⊠ *Les Olives, Vallée du Célé, 46100 Boussac* ☎ *05–65–40–06–63* 🖷 *05–65–40–09–22* ⊕ *www.villedieu.com* ⤴ *5 rooms* ⚭ *Dining room, pool; no a/c, no room TVs* ▤ *DC, MC, V* ⦿ *MAP.*

en route Leave Figeac on the road to Rodez and head left on narrow D52, which leads through the beautiful Lot Valley to D901, and hence to Conques.

Conques

20 *44 km (27 mi) east of Figeac.*

Fodor's Choice
★

The pretty ochre houses of Conques harmonize perfectly with the surrounding rocky gorge. The village was put on the map by its Benedictine abbey, whose outstanding Romanesque church was one of the principal stopping points on the pilgrimage route between Le Puy and Santiago de Compostela. Outside town are several destinations that can make for delightful side trips. You can travel through the Lot Valley to **Entraygues** with its 13th-century bridge and 16th-century houses; to the old medieval town of **Estaing**, hugging the banks of the Lot River, with its picturesque bridge and old castle; to nearby Espalion,

beloved by fishermen and artists for its red stone bridge and Renaissance riverside château; to the tiny fortified village of **St-Côme d'Olt**, with its tortuous cobbled streets; or to **Bozouls**, precariously clinging to the edge of a deep canyon.

★ Begun in the early 11th century, the leading monument in Conques, the abbey church of **Ste-Foy**, had its heyday in the 12th and 13th centuries, whereafter the torrent of pilgrims, and their revenue, ran dry. The two centuries of success were due to the purloined relics of Sainte-Foy (St. Faith), a 13-year-old Christian girl who was martyred in 303 in Agen, where her remains were jealously guarded. A monk from Conques revered them so highly that he traveled to Agen, joined the community of St. Faith, and won their trust. After 10 years they put him in charge of guarding the saint's relics, whereupon he stole them and brought them back to Conques. Devastated by Huguenot hordes, the church languished until the mid-19th century, when the writer and government conservationist Prosper Mérimée stepped in to salvage it. Ste-Foy clings to a hill so steep that even driving and walking—let alone building—are still precarious activities. The church's interior is high and dignified; the ambulatory was given a lot of wear by medieval pilgrims, who admired the church's most precious relic, a 10th-century wooden statue of Ste-Foy encrusted with gold and precious stones. You can see this statue—prized by connoisseurs of medieval art the world over—in the treasury, off the recently restored cloister.

The **Musée Joseph-Fau** (Trésor II), opposite the pilgrims' fountain near Ste-Foy, houses a collection of 17th-century furniture, neo-Gothic reliquaries, and tapestries from Ste-Foy Abbey. 🖭 €4 🕾 05–65–72–92–28 ◷ *Sept.–June, Mon.–Sat. 9–noon and 2–6, Sun. 2–6; July and Aug., Mon.–Sat. 9–noon and 2–7, Sun. 2–7.*

Rodez

21 *40 km (25 mi) southeast of Conques.*

Rodez, capital of the Aveyron, stands on a windswept hill. At its center is the pink-sandstone **Cathédrale Notre-Dame** (13th–15th centuries). Its sober bulk is lightened by decorative upper stories, completed in the 17th century, and by the magnificent 285-foot bell tower. The renovated

Cité district, once ruled by medieval bishops, lies behind the cathedral. On tiny place de l'Olmet, just off place du Bourg, is the 16th-century **Maison d'Armagnac**, a fine Renaissance mansion with a courtyard and an ornate facade covered with medallion emblems of the counts of Rodez. The extensively modernized **Musée Denys-Puech**, an art museum named for a local painter, is just east of the wide boulevard that circles the Vieille Ville. ⊠ *Pl. Clemenceau* ☎ *05–65–77–89–60* ⛱ *€2.50* ⊘ *Wed.–Sat. 10–noon and 2–6, Sun. and Tues. 2–6.*

Where to Stay & Eat

$$ ✕ **Goûts & Couleurs.** In an intimate, pastel-color atmosphere, enjoy the à la carte selections or the prix-fixe seasonal menus (€28 and €58), which have such selections as pan-fried calf's liver stuffed with cabbage, or rabbit with fresh herbs. In summer lunch and dinner are served on the beautiful terrace. ⊠ *38 rue de Bonald* ☎ *05–65–42–75–10* ▭ *MC, V* ⊘ *Closed Sun. and Mon. and mid-Jan.–mid-Feb.* ⑩ *EP.*

★ ¢ ✕⊞ **La Diligence.** It's worth seeking out this hotel-restaurant, 10 km (6 mi) northwest of Rodez via N140, to savor the talents of chef Joël Delmas, whose specialties include succulent mille-feuille of lamb kidneys and a superb banana and coconut tart. Equally impressive are the prices: prix-fixe lunches start at €14. Rooms, furnished in modern style, are not luxurious, but they are adequate and modestly priced. ⊠ *Rte. de Rodez, 12330 Nuces* ☎ *05–65–72–60–20* ⬦ *6 rooms* ⌂ *Restaurant; no a/c* ▭ *MC, V* ⊘ *Closed 1st 2 wks Jan., Sun. night and Mon.* ⑩ *EP.*

Millau

㉒ *66 km (41 mi) southeast of Rodez.*

Millau is primarily a jumping-off point for exploring the magnificent gorges that cut through the limestone *causses* (plateaus). Give yourself time to wander through the Old Quarter, especially around place du Maréchal-Foch, with its medieval arcades. Browse through the shops on place du Mandarous and place de la Tine for leather goods, by-products of all those sheep producing the milk for Roquefort cheese. In Roman times Millau produced pottery and sent its vases as far afield as Scotland. Some of these artifacts, collected from the nearby archaeological site, are in the **Musée de Millau**. ⊠ *Hôtel de Pégayrolles, pl. du Mal-Foch* ☎ *05–65–59–01–08* ⛱ *€5* ⊘ *Apr.–Sept., daily 10–noon and 2–6; Oct.–Mar., Mon.–Sat. 10–noon and 2–6.*

Where to Stay & Eat

$ ✕⊞ **Château de Creissels.** This hotel in an ancient 12th-century fort, 3 km (2 mi) outside town on D992, has rooms furnished in simple country style with modern accents. A few have a terrace overlooking the small village of Creissels. Dinner is served in the medieval allure of the vaulted cellar. ⊠ *Pl. du Prieur, 12100 Creissels* ☎ *05–65–60–31–79* 🖷 *05–65–61–24–63* ⬦ *30 rooms* ⌂ *Restaurant; no a/c* ▭ *AE, DC, MC, V* ⊘ *Closed mid-Dec.–mid-Feb.* ⑩ *MAP.*

The Outdoors

Mountain bikes, a good way to explore the gorges, can be rented from **William Orts** (⊠ 21 bd. de l'Ayrolle ☎ 05–65–61–14–29).

> **off the beaten path**

THE GORGES DE LA DOURBIE – Southeast from Millau is one of the region's most peaceful river canyons, the verdant, meadow-covered **Gorges de la Dourbie**, extending from Millau 40 km (25 mi) to Nant. Follow the gorge to the hilltop hamlet of **St-Véron** and the ruined castle once owned by the Marquis de Montcalm. Father on, where the Trévezel joins the Dourbie, beautiful **Cantobre** clings as if by magic to the cliff. Its tiny houses are prized and even its name says it is extraordinary, as it derives from *quant obra:* "some masterpiece." Past Cantobre is a fertile valley and the pleasant town of **Nant**, with its arcaded 14th-century market and impressively austere church of St-Pierre, built in 1135. Another 16 km (10 mi) south of Nant is the intact medieval village of **La Couvertoirade**, home to the Knights Templar in the 12th century and later the Knights of St. John, who built the encircling ramparts about 1450. Now classified as one of France's most beautiful villages, it is home to craftsmen and pretty stone houses; you can visit the fortress, the church, and a small historical museum, all of which are usually open daily (10 to noon and 2 to 4), for a small fee.

Gorges du Tarn

❷❸
Fodor'sChoice
★

Extends from Le Rozier (21 km [13 mi] northeast of Millau) to Florac, 83 km (52 mi) to the northeast.

Though not quite as awesome as the Grand Canyon, the Gorges du Tarn (Tarn River Gorge) is both beautiful and dramatic. The D907 runs along the foot of the gorge, 2,000 feet below the clifftop, from **Le Rozier,** where the Tarn River is joined by the swirling waters of the Jonte. Follow the road to **Les Vignes,** where the gorge opens into a little valley, and detour up D995, along some challenging switchbacks, and follow signs along the clifftop to the **Point Sublime,** where the views justify the name. Return to Les Vignes and follow the gorge as it grows ever more dramatic, with sheer cliffs and rock faces dappled with grays, whites, and blues.

At the **Cirque des Baumes** the cliffs form a natural amphitheater. Soon after, though, come **Les Détroits** (the straits), the gorge's narrowest and fastest-flowing section. Just past **La Malène,** note the 15th-century **Château de la Caze,** with its imposing parade of turrets. Beyond the castle, just before the village of St-Chély-du-Tarn, is the **Cirque de Pournadoires,** and catercorner to it is another, larger natural amphitheater. On summer nights it's the site of a son-et-lumière show. You may feel the gorge looks even more impressive in the light of day.

Ste-Énimie, the gorge's only town, is mired under a flood of tourists in summer. In its little church, ceramic tiles tell the 7th-century legend of Ste-Énimie, the beautiful sister of King Dagobert. When she was about to marry, she fell ill with leprosy and was scorned by her suitor. On the advice of an angel she was cured at the Fountain of Burle, where she then founded a convent. Its ruins can still be seen, as can the fountain. From Ste-Énimie, the road winds through the valley, opening out just before the small market town of **Florac.**

Where to Stay & Eat

¢ ✕⌂ **Le Vallon.** Locals are drawn year-round by the simple yet good fare at this restaurant-inn in the touristy village of Ispagnac, between Florac and Ste-Enimie. Prix-fixe menus range from €10 to €25; €15 buys you a very respectable four-course repast, which might include an omelet, a salad, a casserole, and some cheese. Rooms are simple, clean, and inexpensive. ⌂ *Rte. D907B, 48320 Ispagnac* ☎ *04–66–44–21–24* 🖷 *04–66–44–26–05* ⊕ *www.camping-cerisiers.com* ⇥ *24 rooms* ⚴ *Restaurant, bar; no a/c* ⊟ *AE, MC, V* ⊙ *Closed late Dec. and Jan.* ⊙| *MAP.*

Sports & the Outdoors

For kayaking down through the Gorges du Tarn, try **Canöe Canyon** (⌂ Rte. de Millau, Ste-Énimie ☎04–66–48–50–52). Trips can be as short as 9 km (5½ mi) and as long as 72 km (50 mi). **FREMYC** (⌂ Pl. Sully, Meyrueis ☎ 04–66–45–61–54) is another outfit for kayaking the Gorges du Tarn, which also organizes horseback riding, rents mountain bikes, and sends you riding the winds in a hang glider (*parapente*).

en route   Between Florac and St-Jean-du-Gard, the **Corniche des Cévennes** road winds its way through spectacular scenery. Follow D907 from Florac; then take a left on D983 toward St-Laurent-de-Trèves. From here the road ascends the **Col du Rey,** high above the valley.

Meyrueis

㉔ *35 km (22 mi) southwest of Florac.*

The Jonte and Bétuzon rivers join at the village of Meyrueis (2,300 feet), whose warm days and cool nights make it a perfect base for exploring the Gorges du Tarn, Gorges de la Jonte, and other nearby caves, causses, and cirques. Meyrueis itself has a medieval tower, some ancient fortifications, which house the tourist office, as well as a ruined château high above. The narrow streets of the oldest part of town, once within the walls, conceal a minuscule Jewish quarter and a noble house you can stay in.

Where to Stay & Eat

★ $$–$$$ ✕⌂ **Château d'Ayres.** A Benedictine monastery before the Wars of Religion, this aristocratic manor house has been transformed into a marvelous country retreat. A serene pool reflects the vine-covered building, and spacious grounds include a tennis court and pool. Inside are comfortable public spaces and two dining rooms where delightful Auvergne meals are served: Aubrac beef and Mt. Aigoual mushrooms are just some of the regional riches. Up the broad stone staircase are spacious, high-ceiling guest rooms. ⌂ *Rte. d'Ayres, 1½ km (1 mi) east of Meyrueis by D57, 48150* ☎ *04–66–45–60–10* 🖷 *04–66–45–62–26* ⊕ *www.chateau-d-ayres.com* ⇥ *20 rooms, 7 suites* ⚴ *Restaurant, minibars, cable TV, tennis court, pool, horseback riding; no a/c* ⊟ *AE, DC, MC, V* ⊙ *Closed mid-Nov.–late Mar.* ⊙| *MAP.*

¢–$ ⌂ **St-Sauveur.** This sturdy 18th-century mansion, with stone arches and parquet floors, is tastefully furnished with antiques and offers excellent value for the money. The guest rooms are on the small side; the best look out over the courtyard, where you can dine in some style beneath the fanning branches of a giant, century-old sycamore. Otherwise, repair to the charming dining room lined with floral wallpapers and lit with a chandelier to dine on regional specialties. ⊠ *2 pl. Jean-Sêquier, 48150* ☎ *04–66–45–62–12* 🖶 *04–66–45–65–94* ⊕ *www.hotelstsauveur.com* 🍽 *10 rooms* ♨ *Restaurant, cable TV; no a/c* ⊟ *AE, DC, MC, V* ☉ *Closed Nov.–mid-Mar.* ᵀᴼᴵ *MAP.*

Gorges de la Jonte

㉕ *Runs from Meyrueis 21 km (13 mi) west to Le Rozier, 21 km (13 mi) northeast of Millau.*

The splendid Gorges de la Jonte (Jonte River Gorge) is narrower than the Gorges du Tarn. Start from the village of **Meyrueis,** where the gorge is at its broadest. It soon narrows, and the eroded limestone cliffs form strange pinnacles. A good spot to stop for a snack is **Les Douzes** halfway along. Soon after comes the deepest part of the gorge; past **Truel,** a cluster of houses clinging to the cliff face forms a lookout, where the view opens to reveal two levels of cliffs—**Les Terrasses de Truel**—then closes again before Le Rozier. Four kilometers (2½ mi) from Rozier a sign to the right directs you up to the **Belvédère des Vautours,** a natural reserve for birds of prey. Since the 1980s these birds have been reestablished on the causse, offering you a rare chance to see them in their proper habitat—as well as marvel at the cliff-hanging views. ☎ *05–65–62–69–69 for information about bird reserve* 🎫 *€5.5* ☉ *Mid-Mar.–Nov., daily 10–7.*

THE MASSIF CENTRAL A TO Z

To research prices, get advice from other travelers, and book travel arrangements, visit www.fodors.com.

AIR TRAVEL

The major airport for the region, at Clermont-Ferrand, has regularly scheduled Air France flights to Paris (Orly and CDG), Bordeaux, Biarritz, Dijon, La Rochelle, Lille, Lyon, Marseille, Metz, Montpellier, Nantes, Nice, Strasbourg, and Toulouse, and direct international flights to Amsterdam, Basle, Brussels, Geneva, and Milan. Air France also flies from Paris's Orly Airport to Rodez, and Ryanair flies to Rodez from London.

🛈 Airlines & Contacts **Air France** ☎ 08-20-82-08-20; **Ryanair** ☎ 08-92-55-56-66.

AIRPORTS

Clermont-Ferrand has the major regional airport; there's also a small airport in Rodez.

🛈 Airport Information **Clermont-Ferrand** ☎ 04-73-62-71-00; **Rodez** ☎ 05-65-76-02-09.

BUS TRAVEL

Where there's no train service, the SNCF will often provide bus transports. Contact local tourist offices for schedules and advice for this national service plus the two main regional outfits, T2C Transports Urbains and Voyages Coudert.

🔃 Bus Information **SNCF** ☎ 08-36-35-35-35 ⊕ www.sncf.com. **T2C Transports Urbains** ✉ 17 bd. R. Schumann, 63000 Clermont-Ferrand ☎ 04-73-28-56-56. **Voyages Coudert** ✉ 7 pl. Renoux, 63013 Clermont-Ferrand ☎ 04-73-92-00-40.

CAR RENTAL

🔃Local Agencies **Avis** ✉22 bd. Etienne-Clémentel, Clermont-Ferrand ☎04-73-25-72-06 🖨04-73-25-86-34 ✉Clermont-Ferrand Airport ☎04-73-91-18-08 🖨04-73-61-06-93 ✉ Clermont-Ferrand train station ☎ 04-73-91-72-94 🖨 04-73-90-74-11. **Europcar** ✉ Rue Émile-Loubet ☎ 04-73-92-70-26 🖨 04-73-90-28-10 ✉ Clermont-Ferrand Airport ☎ 04-73-92-70-26. **Hertz** ✉ 71 av. de l'Union Soviétique, Clermont-Ferrand ☎04-73-92-36-10 🖨04-73-90-46-47 ✉Clermont-Ferrand Airport ☎04-73-62-71-93 🖨 04-73-62-71-96.

CAR TRAVEL

There's only one way fully to explore the region, and that is by car. The region's beauty is best discovered on the small roads that twist through the mountains and along the gorges. Take A10 from Paris to Orléans, then A71 into the center of France. From Paris, Bourges is 230 km (137 mi), and Clermont-Ferrand is 380 km (243 mi). Coming from Lyon it takes less than 90 minutes to drive the 180 km (111 mi) on A72 to Clermont-Ferrand. Entry into Auvergne from the south is mostly on small curving national roads, or by the new A75, which links Montpellier with Clermont-Ferrand through Millau.

SPORTS & THE OUTDOORS

Rafting trips of the Gorges du Tarn can be arranged through Association Le Merlet.

🔃 Canoeing, Kayaking & Rafting **Association Le Merlet** ✉ Rte. de Nîmes, St-Jean du Gard ☎ 04-66-85-18-19.

TRAIN TRAVEL

The fastest way from Paris to Clermont-Ferrand, the capital of Auvergne, is on the direct train from Gare de Lyon; the journey takes 3 ½ hours. Regular SNCF trains also go from Paris to Bourges and from Nantes, Limoges, Toulouse, Brive, Bordeaux, and Nîmes to Clermont-Ferrand.

🔃 Train Information **SNCF** ☎ 08-36-35-35-35 ⊕ www.ter-sncf.com/uk/auvergne/default.htm.

TRAVEL AGENCIES

🔃 Local Agent Referrals **Centre Auvergne Tourisme** ✉ 9 rue Ballainvilliers, 63000 Clermont-Ferrand ☎ 04-73-90-10-20. **Voyagers Maisonneuve** ✉ 24 rue Georges-Clemenceau, 63000 Clermont-Ferrand ☎ 04-73-93-16-72.

VISITOR INFORMATION

The main tourist office for the region is the Comité Régional du Tourisme d'Auvergne. Other departmental and regional tourist offices are listed below by town.

🔃 Departmental tourist offices **Comité Régional du Tourisme d'Auvergne** ✉ 43 av. Julien, 63011 Clermont-Ferrand ☎ 04-73-29-49-49 🖨 04-73-34-11-11 ⊕ www. crt-auvergne.fr/uk.htm. **Allier** ✉ 11 rue François-Péron, 03000 Moulins

☎ 04-70-44-14-14. **Aveyron** ✉ Pl. Maréchal-Foch, 12000 Rodez ☎ 05-65-68-02-27. **Cantal** ✉ Pl. du Square, 15000 Aurillac ☎ 04-71-48-46-58. **Cher** ✉ 5 rue de Séaucourt, 18000 Bourges ☎ 02-48-67-00-18. **Haute-Loire** ✉ Pl. du Breuil, 43000 Le Puy-en-Velay ☎ 04-71-09-38-41. **Lot** ✉ Pl. François-Mitterrand, 46000 Cahors ☎ 05-65-53-20-65 ⊕ www.tourisme-lot.com. **Lozère** ✉ 14 bd. Henri-Bourrillon, 48000 Mende ☎ 04-66-65-60-00. **Puy-de-Dôme** ✉ 26 rue St-Esprit, 63000 Clermont-Ferrand ☎ 04-73-42-21-21.

🚹 Local tourist offices **Bourbon-l'Archambault** ✉ 1 pl. de Thermes, 03160 ☎ 04-70-67-09-79 ⊕ www.bourbon-archambault.auvergne.net. **Montluçon** ✉ 5 pl. Piquand, 03100 ☎ 04-70-05-11-44 ⊕ www.montlucon.auvergne.net. **Montpeyroux** ✉ Les Pradets-Lebourg, 63114 ☎ 04-73-96-68-80. **Moulins** ✉ 11 rue François-Péron, 03006 ☎ 04-70-44-14-14 ⊕ www.moulins.auvergne.net. **Orcival** ✉ Le Bourg, 63210 ☎ 04-73-65-92-25. **St-Amand-Montrond** ✉ Pl. de la République, 18200 ☎ 02-48-96-16-86. **St-Nectaire** ✉ Les Grands Thermes, 63710 ☎ 04-73-88-50-86. **St-Pourçain-sur-Sioule** ✉ 13 pl. du Maréchal-Foch, 03500 ☎ 04-70-45-32-73. **Thiers** ✉ Pl. du Pirou, 63300 ☎ 04-73-80-10-74.

PROVENCE

11

Updated by
Sarah Fraser

Introduction by
Nancy Coons

AS YOU APPROACH PROVENCE there's a magical moment when you finally leave the north behind: cypresses and red-tile roofs appear; you hear the screech of cicadas and breathe the scent of wild thyme and lavender. Along the highway, oleanders bloom on the center strip against a backdrop of austere, sun-filled landscapes, the very same that inspired the Postimpressionists.

Then you notice a hill town whose red roofs skew downhill at Cubist angles, sun-bleached and mottled with age. Your eye catches the rhythm of Romanesque tiles overlapping in sensual, snaking rows, as alike and yet as varied as the reeds in a pan pipe, their broad horizontal flow forming a foil for the contrasting verticals of the cypresses, and the willowy puffs of the silvery olive. Overhead, the sky is an azure prism thanks to the path of the famous mistral—a fierce, cold wind that razors through the Rhône Valley. Sheep bells *tonk* behind dry rock walls, while your ear picks up from the distance the roar of the sea. The Phoenicians, the Greeks, and the Romans recognized a new Fertile Crescent and founded vital civilizations here, whose traces seem to have been untouched by millennia of clean, dry air. Nowhere else in France, and rarely in the Western world, can you touch antiquity with this intimacy—its exoticism, its purity. This is Provence the primordial, eternal and alive.

But there's another Provence in evidence today, a disarming culture of *pastis* (an anise-based aperitif), *pétanque* (lawn bowling), and shady plane trees, where dawdling is a way of life, where you may plant yourself in a sidewalk café and listen to the trickling fountain, putter aimlessly down narrow cobbled alleyways, heft melons in the morning marketplace and, after a three-hour lunch, take an afternoon snooze in the cool shade of a 500-year-old olive tree.

Until the cell phone rings, that is. Because ever since Peter Mayle abandoned the London fog and described with sensual relish a life of unbuttoned collars and espadrilles in his best-selling *A Year in Provence,* the world has beaten a path here. Now Parisians are heard in the local marketplaces passing the word on the best free-range rabbit, the purest olive oil, the lowest price on a five-bedroom *mas* (farmhouse) with vineyard and pool. And a chic *bon-chic-bon-genre* city crowd languishes stylishly at the latest country inn and makes an appearance at the most fashionable restaurant. Ask them, and they'll agree: ever since Princess Caroline of Monaco moved to St-Rémy, Provence has become the new Côte d'Azur.

But chic Provence hasn't eclipsed idyllic Provence, and it's still possible to melt into a Monday-morning market crowd, where blue-aproned *paysannes* scoop fistfuls of mesclun into willow baskets, matron-connoisseurs paw through bins containing the first Cavaillon asparagus, a knot of *pépés* in workers' blues takes a pétanque break . . . welcoming all into the game.

Relax and join them—and plan to stay around a while. There are plenty of sights to see: some of the finest Roman ruins in Europe, from the Pont du Gard to the arenas at Arles and Nîmes; the pristine Romanesque abbeys

Peter Mayle's book *A Year in Provence* prescribes just that, but even a year might not be long enough to soak up all the charm of this captivating region. In three days you can see three representative (and very different) towns: Arles, Avignon, and St-Rémy; with seven days you can easily add the Camargue, the Luberon, and Aix-en-Provence; with 10 days you can add Vaison-la-Romaine and Marseille. The following are suggested itineraries for touring the area; another option is to base yourself in one place and take day trips from there.

To make the most of your time in the region, plan to divide your days between big-city culture, backcountry tours, and waterfront leisure. If you must, you can "do" Provence at an if-this-is-Tuesday breakneck pace, but its rural roads and tiny villages will amply reward a more leisurely approach. Provence is as much a way of life as a region charged with tourist must-sees, so you should allow time to enjoy its old-fashioned pace.

Numbers in the text correspond to numbers in the margin and on the Provence, Nîmes, Arles, Avignon, and Marseille maps.

If you have 3 days

The best gateway to the region is **Avignon** ㉗– ㉞ ►, where tiny, narrow streets cluster around the 14th-century Palais des Papes, as if still seeking the protection afforded them when this massive structure represented the supreme Christian authority of the world, back in the 14th century. Then make an afternoon outing west to the **Pont du Gard** ㉟ aqueduct, a majestic relic from the ancient Romans that strikes all as more a work of art than a practical construction. On Day 2 stop briefly in **Nîmes** ⑭– ㉒ to see the antiquities of the Arènes and the Maison Carrée—a striking contrast to this busy commercial center—then head into atmospheric old 🖾 **Arles** ①– ⑩, inspiration to van Gogh, who captured the delicate, pointed features of the Arlésienne in some of his finest portraits. On Day 3 drive through the countryside, stopping at the **Abbaye de Montmajour** ㉓—whose cloisters are a particularly charming spot when the oleander trees are in bloom—and the medieval hill town of **Les Baux-de-Provence** ㉔; stay overnight in 🖾 **St-Rémy-de-Provence** ㉕, with its Roman ruins and recognizable van Gogh landmarks.

If you have 7 days

Visit **Orange** ㊲ ► on your first day before stopping to see the **Pont du Gard** ㉟— both the ancient Roman theater in Orange and the famous aqueduct will allow you to travel back two millennia in time. Spend two nights in 🖾 **Avignon** ㉗–㉞ and don't forget to visit the Bridge of St-Bénézet (made famous in the old song "Sur le pont d'Avignon"). In the morning stop briefly in **Nîmes** ⑭–㉒ on your way to the fortified town of **Aigues-Mortes** ⑬ and make a slight detour through the Camargue to 🖾 **Arles** ①–⑩. The next morning explore Arles's Roman remains. Try to get to the rocky perch of **Les Baux-de-Provence** ㉔ by lunchtime and then continue to 🖾 **St-Rémy-de-Provence** ㉕ to see where van Gogh set up his easel. On day five wend your way through **L'Isle-sur-la-Sorgue** ㊶ to **Gordes** ㊸, in the Luberon Mountains, one of Provence's most famous *villages perchés* (perched villages). Spend the night in the hilltop village of **Bonnieux** ㊼ and drive over the windswept spine of the Luberon on your way south to ⊞ **Aix-en-Provence** ㊽–㊾; spend two days there visiting the marvelous 18th-century mansions, the museums, and its cours Mirabeau, which is to Aix what the Champs-Élysées is to Paris.

If you have
10
days

To the seven-day itinerary, add a day visiting ruins in the Rhône-side Roman market town of **Vaison-la-Romaine** ㉟ ☛ and drive the winding back roads of the neighboring Mont Ventoux region, whose fruited plains lead to forested heights. Or make a broader sweep through the Camargue to include the eccentric seaside town of **Stes-Maries-de-la-Mer** ⑫, its gloomy Romanesque church (full of Gypsy tributes to the two St. Marys and their servant girl Sarah). Then take the time to experience the urban vitality of **Marseille** ㊶–㊸, or cool your heels at the gentrified seaside retreat of ⊞ **Cassis** ㊾.

of Senanque and de Montmajour; bijoux chapels and weathered *mas* (farmhouses); the feudal châteaux at Tarascon and Beaucaire; the monolithic Papal Palace in old Avignon; and everywhere vineyards, pleasure ports, and sophisticated city museums. But allow yourself time to feel the rhythm of modern Provençal life, to listen to the pulsing *breet* of the insects, smell the *parfum* of a tiny country path, and feel the air of a summer night on your skin. . . .

Exploring Provence

Bordered to the west by the Languedoc and melting to the south and east into the blue waters of the Mediterranean, Provence falls easily into four areas. The Camargue is at the heart of the first, flanked by Nîmes and Van Gogh's picturesque Arles to the east. Here, the Camargue's hypnotic plane of marsh grass stretching to the sea is interrupted only by an explosion of flying flamingos or a modest stampede of stocky bulls led by latter-day cowboys. Northeast of Arles, the rude and rocky Alpilles jut upward, their hillsides green with orchards and olive groves; here you'll find feudal Les Baux and the Greco-Roman enclave of St-Rémy, now fashionable with the Summer People. The third area, which falls within the boundaries of the Vaucluse, begins at Avignon and extends north to Orange and Vaison-la-Romaine, then east to the forested slopes of the Luberon, where you'll find the countryside made famous by Peter Mayle—hilltop towns like Ménerbes, Roussillon, and Gordes are the jewels in a landscape studded with blue-black forests, sun-bleached rocks, and golden perched villages. The fourth area encompasses Cézanne country, east of the Rhône, starting in Aix-en-Provence, then winding southward to big-city Marseille—tough, gorgeous, and larger than life—and east along the Mediterranean coast to the idyllic Iles d'Hyères. Note: a very handy Web resource to all the villages of Provence is ⊕ www.provencebeyond.com/villages.

About the Restaurants & Hotels
You'll eat late in the south, rarely before 1 for lunch, usually after 9 at night. In summer, shops and museums may shut down until 3 or

4, as much to accommodate lazy lunches as for the crowds taking sun on the beach. But a late lunch works nicely with a late breakfast—and that's another southern luxury. As morning here is the coolest part of the day and the light is at its sweetest, hotels and cafés of every class take pains to make breakfast memorable and whenever possible served outdoors. Complete with tables in the garden with sunny-print cloths and a nosegay of flowers, accompanied by birdsong, and warmed by the cool morning sun, it's one of the three loveliest meals of the day.

Accommodations in Provence range from luxurious villas to elegantly converted *mas* to modest city-center hotels. Reservations are essential for much of the year, and many hotels are closed in winter. Assume all hotel rooms have air-conditioning, TV, telephones, and private bath, unless otherwise noted.

WHAT IT COSTS In euros					
	$$$$	$$$	$$	$	¢
RESTAURANTS	over €30	€23–€30	€17–€23	€11–€17	under €11
HOTELS	over €190	€120–€190	€80–€120	€50–€80	under €50

Restaurant prices are per person for a main course at dinner, including tax (19.6%) and service; note that if a restaurant offers only prix-fixe (set-price) meals, it has been given the price category that reflects the full prix-fixe price. Hotel prices are for a standard double room in high season, including tax (19.6%) and service charge; higher prices (inquire when booking) prevail for any meal plans.

Timing
Spring and fall are the best months to experience the dazzling light, rugged rocky countryside, and fruited vineyards of Provence. Though the lavender fields show peak color in mid-July, summertime here is beastly hot; worse, it's always crowded on the beaches and connecting roads. Winter has some nice days, when the locals are able to enjoy their cafés and their town squares tourist-free, but it often rains, and the razor-sharp mistral wind can cut to the bone.

ARLES & THE CAMARGUE

Sitting on the banks of the Rhône River, with a *Vieille Ville* (Old Town) where time seems to have stood still since 1888—the year Vincent van Gogh immortalized the city in his paintings—Arles remains both a vibrant example of Provençal culture and the gateway to the Camargue, a wild and marshy region that extends south to the Mediterranean. Arles, in fact, once outshone Marseille as the major port of the area before sea gave way to sand. Today it competes with nearby Nîmes for the title "Rome of France," thanks to its magnificent Roman theater and Arènes (amphitheater). Just west and south of these landmarks, the Camargue is a vast watery plain formed by the sprawling Rhône delta and extending over 800 square km (300 square mi)—its landscape remains one of the most extraordinary in France.

Arles

36 km (22 mi) south of Avignon, 31 km (19 mi) east of Nîmes, 92 km (57 mi) northwest of Marseille, 720 km (430 mi) south of Paris.

If you were obliged to choose just one city to visit in Provence, lovely little Arles would give Avignon and Aix a run for their money. It's too chic to become museumlike yet has a wealth of classical antiquities and Romanesque stonework, quarried-stone edifices and shuttered town houses, and graceful, shady Vieille Ville streets and squares. Throughout the year there are pageantry, festivals, and cutting-edge arts events. Its panoply of atmospheric restaurants and picturesque small hotels makes it the ideal headquarters for forays into the Alpilles and the Camargue.

A Greek colony since the 6th century BC, little Arles took a giant step forward when Julius Caesar defeated Marseille in the 1st century BC. The emperor-to-be designated Arles a Roman colony and lavished funds and engineering know-how on it. It became an international crossroads by sea and land and a market to the world, with goods from Africa, Arabia, and the Far East. The emperor Constantine himself moved to Arles and brought with him Christianity.

The remains of this golden age are reason enough to visit Arles today, yet its character nowadays is as gracious and low-key as it once was cutting-edge. Seated in the shade of the plane trees on place du Forum or strolling the rampart walkway along the sparkling Rhône, you'll see what enchanted Gauguin and drove van Gogh frantic with inspiration.

Note: If you plan to visit many of the monuments and museums in Arles, buy a *visite generale* ticket for €12. This covers the entry fee to the Musée de l'Arles Antique and any and all of the other museums and monuments (except the independent Museon Arlaten, which charges €4 each). The ticket is good for the length of your stay.

★ ❶ Though it's a hike from the center, a good place to set the tone and context for your exploration of Arles is at the state-of-the-art **Musée de l'Arles Antique** (Museum of Ancient Arles). The bold, modern triangular structure (designed by Henri Ciriani) lies on the site of an enormous Roman *cirque* (chariot-racing stadium). The permanent collection includes jewelry, mosaics, town plans, and 4th-century carved sacophagi from *Les Alyscamps*. You'll learn all about Arles in its heyday, from the development of its monuments to details of daily life in Roman times. Ask for the English-language guidebook. ⊠ *Presqu'île du Cirque Romain* ☎ *04–90–18–88–88* ⌨ *€5.50* ☉ *Mar.–Oct., daily 9–7; Nov.–Feb., daily 10–5.*

❷ A good way to plunge into post-Roman Arles is through the quirky old **Museon Arlaten** (Museum of Arles). Created by the father of the Provençal revival, turn-of-the-20th-century poet Frédéric Mistral, it enshrines a seemingly bottomless collection of regional treasures ranging from 18th-century furniture and ceramics to a mixed-bag collection of toothache-prevention cures. Following Mistral's wishes, women in full Arlésienne costume oversee the labyrinth of lovely 16th-century halls.

11

Shopping à la Folklorique
Some of the smallest villages have their predatory claws unfurled these days, with every house a storefront overflowing with doodads and gewgaws on Provençal themes. Pottery mugs with good-luck cicadas and coasters of the famous sunflowers are the bastard children of legitimate crafts and products that are intrinsically Provence—*boutis,* intricately quilted cotton throws; richly textured Provençal fabrics in 18th-century reproduction paisley prints, put to legitimate use as skirts, curtains, and tablecloths; marvelously mild and natural *savon de Marseille* (Marseille soap); artisanal olive oils from the Alpilles; and if you acquire the taste, the sometimes exquisitely rendered *santons,* tiny terra-cotta figurines first made for Provençal Christmas crèches. The best *santonniers* have studios in Aubagne.

Roman to Romanesque
This isn't Gothic cathedral country, but a treasure trove of smaller church gems offers a moving, more intimate alternative. Provence is peppered with churches, châteaux, and abbeys, a surprising concentration of them pure Romanesque of the 12th and 13th centuries. Signs point to ÉGLISE ROMANE XIIÈME—meaning Romanesque. *Romain* refers to Roman remains, which you'll also find throughout Provence (in fact, its name comes from the Roman *provincia,* or "the province"). The most beautifully preserved are concentrated around the Rhône, their main shipping artery. There are two arenas (in Arles and Nîmes), the ancient Hellenistic settlement outside St-Rémy (Glanum), the miraculously preserved temple in Nîmes (Maison Carrée), a theater in Orange, and two villages in Vaison-la-Romaine. The granddaddy of all Roman treasures is the Pont du Gard, the magnificent multi-tier aqueduct straddling the Gardon River west of Avignon.

La Cuisine de Soleil
Universally emulated for its winning combination of simplicity, healthy ingredients, and vivid sun-kissed flavors, Provençal cooking glories in olive oil, garlic, tomatoes, olives, and the ubiquitous wild herbs that crunch underfoot. France's greatest chefs scour lively markets for melons still warm from the morning sun, and buy glistening olives by the pailful. You can't lose when you start with an icy pastis, the pale yellow, anise-based aperitif; smear your toast with *tapenade,* a delicious paste of olives, capers, and anchovies; heap aioli, a garlicky mayonnaise, on your fresh fish; and rub thyme and garlic on your lamb. No meal is complete without a round of goat cheese, sun-ripened fruit, and a chilled bottle of rosé from the surrounding hills.

Markets
Browsing through the *marché couvert* (covered food market) in Avignon is enough to make you regret all the tempting restaurants around. At nearly all Provençal markets, seafood, poultry, olives, melons, and asparagus cry out to be gathered in a basket, arranged lovingly in pottery bowls, and later cooked in their purest form. For picnics, stock up on tubs of tapenade and *anchoïade* (anchovy spread), dried game sausage, tangy marinated seafood, and tiny pucks of withered goat cheese. And antiques and *brocantes* (collectibles) are never far away, sometimes providing the most authentic local souvenirs. Many antique stores are located in L'Isle-sur-la-Sorgue, also home to the finest Sunday morning flea market.

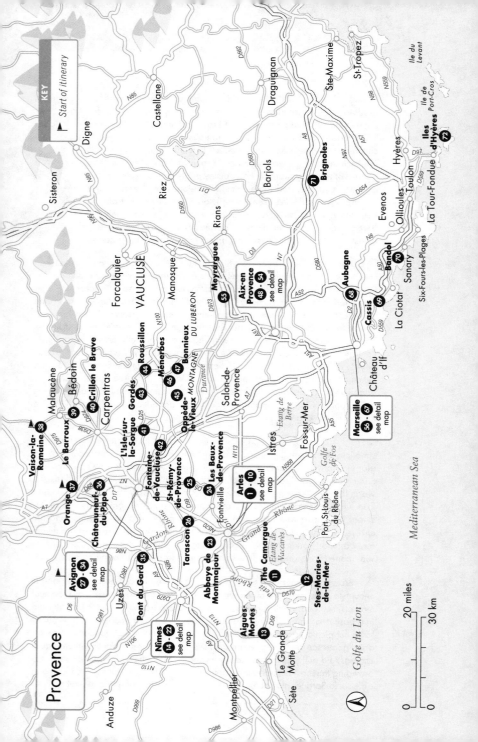

Provence

KEY

▲ Start of itinerary

Mediterranean Sea

Golfe du Lion

VAUCLUSE

MONTAGNE DU LUBERON

Arles **1 - 10** see detail map

Nîmes **14 - 22** see detail map

Avignon **27 - 34** see detail map

Aix-en-Provence **48 - 54** see detail map

Marseille **56 - 67** see detail map

38 Vaison-la-Romaine
37 Orange
39 Le Barroux
40 Crillon le Brave
41 L'Isle-sur-la-Sorgue
42 Fontaine-de-Vaucluse
43 Gordes
44 Roussillon
45 Oppède-le-Vieux
46 Ménerbes
47 Bonnieux
55 Meyrargues
36 Châteauneuf-du-Pape
35 Pont du Gard
25 St-Rémy-de-Provence
24 Les Baux-de-Provence
26 Tarascon
23 Abbaye de Montmajour
11 The Camargue
12 Stes-Maries-de-la-Mer
13 Aigues-Mortes
68 Cassis
69
70 Bandel
71 Brignoles
72 Iles d'Hyères
56 - 67

Sète
Montpellier
Le Grande Motte
Anduze
Uzès
Port St-Louis du Rhône
Fos-sur-Mer
Istres
Salon-de-Provence
Etang de Berre
Golfe de Fos
Château d'If
Marseille
Aubagne
Cassis
La Ciotat
Sanary
Six-Fours-les-Plages
Toulon
Ollioules
Evenos
La Tour-Fondue
Hyères
St-Tropez
Ste-Maxime
Draguignan
Barjols
Rians
Meyrargues
Manosque
Forcalquier
Riez
Castellane
Digne
Sisteron
Malaucène
Bédoin
Carpentras
Orange
Tarascon
Salon-de-Provence
Port-Cros
Ile de Port-Cros
Ile du Levant
Golfe du Lion

0 — 20 miles
0 — 30 km

⊠ 29 *rue de la République* 🏛 *04–90–93–58–11* 🎫 *€4, free 1st Sun. of every month* ☉ *Apr., May, Sept., daily 9:30–12:30 and 2–6; June–Aug., daily 9–1 and 2–6:30; Oct.–Mar., Tues.–Sun. 9:30–12:30 and 2–5.*

❸ At the entrance to a 17th-century Jesuit college you can access the ancient underground galleries called the **Cryptoportiques.** Dating from 30 BC to 20 BC, this horseshoe of vaults and pillars buttressed the ancient forum from below ground. Used as a refuge for Resistance members in WWII, these galleries still have a rather ominous atmosphere. Yet openings let in natural daylight, and artworks of considerable merit and worth were unearthed here, adding to the mystery of the original function of these passages. ⊠ *Rue Balze* 🏛 *04–90–49–36–74* 🎫 *€3.50* ☉ *May–Sept., daily 9–noon and 2–7; Oct., daily 9–noon and 2–6; Nov.–Feb., daily 10–noon and 2–5; Mar. and Apr., 9–noon and 2–6.*

★ ❹ Classed as a world treasure by UNESCO, the extraordinary Romanesque **Église St-Trophime** (⊠ Pl. de la République) alone would justify a visit to Arles, though it's continually upstaged by the antiquities around it. Its transepts date from the 11th century and its nave from the 12th; the church's austere symmetry and ancient artworks (including a stunning Roman-style 4th-century sarcophagus) are fascinating in themselves. But it's the church's superbly preserved Romanesque sculpture on the 12th-century **portal**—its entry facade—that earns international respect. Recent restorations have made it even more vivid. Particularly noteworthy is the frieze of the Last Judgment with chain-bound souls being dragged off to Hell or, on the contrary, being lovingly delivered into the hands of the Saints.

❺ Tucked discreetly behind St-Trophime is a peaceful haven, the **Cloître St-Trophime** (St-Trophime Cloister). A Romanesque treasure worthy of the church, it's one of the loveliest cloisters in Provence. A sturdy walkway above offers up good views of the town. 🏛 *04–90–49–36–74* 🎫 *€3.50* ☉ *May–Sept., daily 9–7; Oct., daily 9–6; Nov.–Feb., daily 10–5; Mar. and Apr., daily 9–6.*

❻ Directly up rue de la Calade from place de la République are the picturesque ruins of the **Théâtre Antique** (Ancient Theater), built by the Romans under Augustus in the 1st century BC. Now overgrown and a pleasant, parklike retreat, it once served as an entertainment venue to some 20,000 spectators. Today it serves as a concert stage for the Festival d'Arles (in July and August) and site of the Recontres Internationales de la Photographie (Photography Festival). ⊠ *Rue de la Calade* 🏛 *04–90–49–36–74* 🎫 *€3* ☉ *May–Sept., daily 9–noon and 2–7; Oct., daily 9–noon and 2–6; Nov.–Dec., daily 10–noon and 2–5; Mar. and Apr., 9–noon and 2–5.*

❼ Rivaled only by the even better-preserved version in Nîmes, the **Arènes** (Arena) dominates old Arles. Its four medieval towers are testimony to its transformation from classical sports arena to feudal fortification in the middle ages. Younger than Arles's theater, it dates from the 1st century AD, and unlike the theater, seats 20,000 to this day. Its primary function is as a venue for the traditional spectacle of the corridas, or bullfights, which take place annually during the *féria pascale,* or Easter festival.

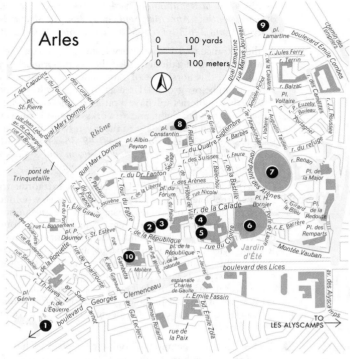

Nearby is the **Fondation Van Gogh** (✉ 24 bis rond point des Arènes
☎ 04–90–93–08–08 ⊙ Daily 10–7 ☞ €5), where you can savor works
by various modern and contemporary artists, including Francis Bacon
and Doisneau, inspired by van Gogh. ✉ *Rond Point des Arènes*
☎ *04–90–49–36–74 ☞ €4 ⊙ May.–Sept., daily 9–7; Oct., daily 9–noon
and 2–6; Nov. and Dec., daily 10–noon and 2–5; Mar. and Apr., daily
9–noon and 2–5.*

Though it makes every effort today to make up for its past misjudgment
of him, Arles treated Vincent van Gogh very badly during the time he
passed here near the end of his life. It was 1888 when he settled in to
work in Arles with an intensity and tempestuousness that drove away
his colleague and companion Paul Gauguin and alienated his neighbors.
In 1889 the people of Arles circulated a petition to have him evicted, a
shock that left him more and more at a loss to cope with life and led to
his voluntary commitment to an insane asylum in nearby St-Rémy. Thus
Arles can't boast a single van Gogh painting—even so, did they have to
name their art museum after Jacques Réattu, a local painter of confirmed
mediocrity? The **Musée Réattu** lavishes three rooms on his turn-of-the-
19th-century ephemera but redeems itself with a decent collection of 20th-
century art including some daubs by Dufy and Gauguin. There's also

VAN GOGH'S ARLES & ST-RÉMY

I T WAS THE LIGHT that drew Vincent van Gogh to Arles. For a man raised under the iron-gray skies of the Netherlands and the gaslight pall of Paris, Provence's clean, clear sun was a revelation. In his last years he turned his frenzied efforts toward capturing the resonance of ". . . golden tones of every hue: green gold, yellow gold, pink gold, bronze or copper colored gold, and even from the yellow of lemons to the matte, lusterless yellow of threshed grain." Arles, however, was not drawn to van Gogh. Though it makes every effort today to make up for its misjudgment, Arles treated the artist very badly during the time he passed here near the end of his life—a time when his creativity, productivity, and madness all reached a climax.

It was in 1888 that he settled in to work in Arles with an intensity and tempestuousness that first drew, then drove away his companion Paul Gauguin, with whom he had dreamed of founding an artists' colony. Astonishingly productive— he applied a pigment-loaded palette knife to some 200 canvases in that year alone—he nonetheless lived within intense isolation, counting his sous, and writing his visions in lengthy letters to his long-suffering, infinitely patient brother Theo. Often heavy-drinking, occasionally whoring, Vincent alienated his neighbors, driving them to distraction and ultimately goading them to action.

In 1889 the people of Arles circulated a petition to have him evicted, a shock that left him more and more at a loss to cope with life and led to his eventual self-commitment to an asylum in nearby St-Rémy. The houses he lived in are no longer standing, though many of his subjects remain as he saw them (or are restored to a similar condition). But with a little imagination you can glean something of van Gogh's Arles from a tour of the modern town. In fact, the city has provided helpful markers and a numbered itinerary to guide you between landmarks. You can stand on the place Lamartine, where his famous Maison Jaune stood until it was destroyed by World War II bombs. Starry Night may have been painted from the quai du Rhône just off place Lamartine, though another was completed at St-Rémy. The Café La Nuit on place Forum is an exact match for the terrace platform, scattered with tables and bathed in gaslight under the stars, from the painting Terrace de café le Soir; Gauguin and van Gogh used to drink here.

Both the Arènes and Les Alyscamps were featured in paintings, and the hospital where he broke down and cut off his ear lobe is now a kind of shrine, its garden reconstructed exactly as it figured in Le Jardin de l'Hôtel-Dieu. The drawbridge in Le pont de Langlois aux Lavandières has been reconstructed outside of town, at Port-de-Bouc, 3 km (2 mi) south on D35.

About 25 km (16 mi) away is St-Rémy-de-Provence, where van Gogh retreated to the asylum St-Paul-de-Mausolée. Here he spent hours in silence, painting the cloisters. On his ventures into town he painted the dappled lime trees at the intersection of boulevard Mirabeau and boulevard Gambetta.

And on the route between the towns and, in fact, in traveling anywhere nearby, you'll see the orchards whose spring blooms ignite joyous explosions of yellow and cream, olive groves twisting like dancers in silver and green, ocher houses and red roofs, star-spangled crystalline skies—the stuff of inspiration.

an impressive collection of 57 drawings done by Picasso in 1971, including one delightfully tongue-in-cheek depiction of noted muse and writer Lee Miller in full Arles dress. The best thing about the Réattu may be the building itself, a Knights of Malta priory dating from the 15th century. ✉ *Rue Grand Prieuré* ☎ *04–90–49–38–34* 🖅 *€4* ☉ *Apr.–Sept., daily 10–12:30 and 2–7:30; Oct.–Mar., daily 1–5.*

You'll have to go to Amsterdam to view van Goghs. But the city has provided helpful markers and a numbered itinerary to guide you from one landmark to another—many of them recognizable from his beloved canvases. You can stand on **Place Lamartine** (between the rail station and the ramparts), which is the site of his residence here, the now-famous Maison Jaune (Yellow House); it was destroyed by bombs in 1944. The artist may have set up his easel on the quai du Rhône, just off place Lamartine, to capture the view that he transformed into his legendary *Starry Night.*

The most strikingly resonant site, impeccably restored and landscaped to match one of van Gogh's paintings, is the courtyard garden of what is now the **Espace van Gogh** (✉ Pl. Dr. Félix Rey), featured in *Le Jardin de l'Hôtel-Dieu.* This was the hospital to which the tortured artist repaired after cutting off his earlobe—contrary to myth, he didn't cut off his entire ear and, in fact, made the desperate gesture in homage to Gauguin, whom he had come to idolize, following the fashion in Provençal bullrings for a matador to present his lady love with an ear from a dispatched bull—and its cloistered grounds have become something of a shrine for visitors. For more information about van Gogh, see the Close-Up Box, "Van Gogh in Arles and St-Rémy," *below.*

off the beaten path

LES ALYSCAMPS – Though this romantically melancholy Roman cemetery lies away from the Vieille Ville, it's worth the hike—certainly, van Gogh thought so, as several of his famous canvases prove. This long necropolis amassed the remains of the dead from antiquity to the Middle Ages. Greek, Roman, and Christian tombs line the long shady road that was once the entry to Arles—the Aurelian Way. ☎ *04–90–49–36–74* 🖅 *€3.50* ☉ *May–Sept., daily 9–noon and 2–7; Oct., daily 9–noon and 2–6; Nov.–Feb., daily 10–noon and 2–5; Mar. and Apr., 9–noon and 2–6.*

Where to Stay & Eat

★ **$$$$** ✕ **La Chassagnette.** Sophisticated yet down-home comfortable, this restaurant is the latest fashionable address in the area (8 mi south of Arles). Stone walls, a stunning wood and green-marble bar, burnt-sienna tiles, Provençal chairs, and comfortable settees brightened by colorful pillows make for a fetching setting. Better, the dining area extends outdoors, where large family-style picnic tables can be found under a wooden slate canopy overlooking extensive gardens. Using ingredients that are certified organic and grown right on the property, innovative master chef Luc Rabanel serves up open-rotisserie style prix-fixe menus that are a refreshing mix of modern and classic French-country cuisine. ✉ *Route du Sambuc, 13 km (8 mi) south of Arles on the D36*

☎ 04–90–97–26–96 ⚑ *Reservations essential* ▤ *MC, V* ⊘ *Closed Tues. and Nov.–mid-Dec. No lunch Wed.*

$$$–$$$$ ✕ **Brasserie Nord-Pinus.** With its tile-and-ironwork interior, tastefully framed black-and-white photos, crisp white tablecloths, and its terrace packed with all the right people, this cozy-chic retro brasserie showcases the light, stylish and unpretentious cooking of chef Eric Griés: zucchini-flower risotto with fresh goat cheese, oven-cooked bass, or wild king prawns sautéed with pepper and cognac are some signature dishes. Immaculate service and a nicely balanced wine list only add to its charm. ⊠ *Pl. du Forum* ☎ 04–90–93–44–44 ⚑ *Reservations essential* ▤ *AE, DC, MC, V* ⊘ *Closed Feb. and Wed. in Nov.–Mar.*

$$–$$$ ✕ **L'Affenage.** A vast smorgasbord of Provençal hors d'oeuvres draws loyal locals to this former fire-horse shed. They come here for heaping plates of grilled vegetables, tapenade, chickpeas in cumin, and a slab of ham carved off the bone. In summer you can opt for just the first-course buffet and go back for thirds; reserve a terrace table out front. ⊠ *4 rue Molière* ☎ 04–90–96–07–67 ⚑ *Reservations essential* ▤ *AE, MC, V* ⊘ *Closed Sun., Mon. night, and 3 wks in Aug.*

$–$$$ ✕ **La Gueule du Loup.** Serving as hosts, waiters, and chefs, the ambitious couple that owns this restaurant tackles serious cooking—lamb with eggplant and red-pepper puree, monkfish and squid in saffron, or chestnut mousse perfumed with almond milk top the delights here. Jazz music and vintage magic-act posters add color and warmth to the old Arles stone-and-beam rooms. ⊠ *39 rue des Arènes* ☎ 04–90–96–96–69 ⚑ *Reservations essential* ▤ *MC, V* ⊘ *Closed Sun. and Mon., Oct.–Mar.; closed Sun. in Apr.–Sept. No lunch Mon.*

$$$–$$$$ ▦ **L'Hôtel Particulier.** Once owned by the Baron of Chartrouse, this extraordinary 18th-century *hôtel particulier* (mansion) is delightfully intimate and carefully discreet behind a wrought-iron gate. Decor is sophisticated yet charmingly simple: stunning gold-framed mirrors, white-brocaded chairs, marble writing desks, artfully hung curtains, and hand-painted wallpaper. Rooms look out onto a beautifully landscaped garden; even if you take the five-minute walk into the center of town you can come back, stretch out by the pool, and listen to the birds chirp. ⊠ *4 rue de la Monnaie, 13200* ☎ 04–90–52–51–40 🖷 04–90–96–16–70 ⊕ *www.hotel-particulier.com* ⇗ *8 rooms* ♿ *Minibars, cable TV, pool, Internet, some pets allowed (fee)* ▤ *AE, DC, MC, V* ❙◯❙ *EP.*

$$$–$$$$ ▦ **Jules César.** Once a Carmelite convent but styled like a Roman palace, this pleasant landmark anchors the lively (sometimes noisy) boulevard des Lices. Don't be misled by the rather imposing lobby as this place turns out to be a friendly, traditional hotel. Rooms have high arched ceilings and massive Provençal armoires softened by plush carpets and burnished reds and oranges. Some windows look over the pool; others over the pretty cloister, where breakfast is served under a vaulted stone arcade. The restaurant, unexpectedly intimate for its size, has nice, simply prepared dishes—try the lobster risotto or the grilled steak. A meal plan is available with a minimum stay of three nights. ⊠ *Bd. des Lices, 13200* ☎ 04–90–52–52–52 🖷 04–90–52–52–53 ⊕ *www.hotel-julescesar. fr* ⇗ *53 rooms, 5 suites* ♿ *2 restaurants, minibars, cable TV, pool, In-*

ternet, parking (fee), some pets allowed (fee) ☰ *AE, DC, MC, V*
⊘ *Closed mid-Nov.–late Dec.* ‖○‖ *BP, MAP.*

★ **$$$–$$$$** ⊞ **Nord-Pinus.** The adventurer and mail-order genius J. Peterman would
feel right at home in this eclectic and quintessentially Mediterranean hotel
on place du Forum; Picasso certainly did. Richly atmospheric, the salon
is dramatic with angular wrought iron, heavy furniture, colorful ceramics,
and a standing collection of Peter Beard's black-and-white photographs.
Rooms are individually decorated: wood or tiled floors, large bathrooms,
hand-woven rugs, and tasteful (if somewhat exotic) artwork are clev-
erly set off to stylish art director–chic advantage. Although it's hard to
beat the low-key and accommodating service, this hotel may not be for
everyone: traditionalists should head for the more mainstream luxuries
of the Jules César. ⊠ *Pl. du Forum, 13200* ☎ *04–90–93–44–44*
🖶 *04–90–93–34–00* ⊕ *www.nord-pinus.com* ⇨ *25 rooms* ⚬ *Some
minibars, cable TV, parking (fee), some pets allowed* ☰ *AE, DC, MC,
V* ‖○‖ *EP.*

$ ⊞ **Le Cloître.** Built as a private home, this grand old medieval building
has luckily fallen into the hands of a couple devoted to making the most
of its historic details—with their own bare hands. They've chipped
away plaster from pristine quarry-stone walls, cleaned massive beams,
restored tile stairs, and mixed natural chalk and ocher to plaster the walls.
⊠ *16 rue du Cloître, 13200* ☎ *04–90–96–29–50* 🖶 *04–90–96–02–88*
⊕ *www.members.aol.com/hotelcloitre* ⇨ *30 rooms* ⚬ *Parking (fee), some
pets allowed (fee); no TV in some rooms, no A/C in some rooms* ☰ *AE,
MC, V* ⊘ *Closed Nov.–mid-Mar.* ‖○‖ *EP.*

★ $ ⊞ **Muette.** With 12th-century exposed stone walls, a 15th-century spi-
ral stair, weathered wood, and an Old Town setting, a hotelier would-
n't have to try very hard to please. But the couple that owns this place
does: hand-stripped doors, antiques, sparkling blue-and-white-tile baths,
hair dryers, good mattresses, Provençal prints, and fresh sunflowers in
every room show they care. ⊠ *15 rue des Suisses, 13200*
☎ *04–90–96–15–39* 🖶 *04–90–49–73–16* ⊕ *www.logisdefrance.com/arles*
⇨ *18 rooms* ⚬ *Cable TV, parking (fee), some pets allowed* ☰ *AE, MC,
V* ⊘ *Closed last 2 wks of Feb.* ‖○‖ *EP.*

Nightlife & the Arts

To find out what's happening in and around Arles (even as far away as
Nîmes and Avignon), the free weekly **Le César** lists films, plays, cabarets,
and jazz and rock events. It's distributed at the tourist office and in bars,
clubs, and cinemas. In high season the cafés stay lively 'til the wee
hours; in winter the streets empty out by 11. **Le Cargo de Nuit** (⊠ 7 av.
Sadi-Carnot ☎ 04–90–49–55–99) is the main venue for live jazz, reg-
gae, and rock, with a dance floor next to the stage. Though Arles seems
to be one big sidewalk café in warm weather, the place to tipple is the
hip bar **Le Cintra,** in the Hôtel Nord-Pinus.

The Camargue

 19 km (12 mi) east of Aigues-Mortes, 15 km (9 mi) south of Arles.

Fodor's Choice
★

Stretching to the horizon for about 800 square km (309 square mi), the
vast alluvial delta of the Rhône known as the Camargue is an austere,

unrelievedly flat marshland, scoured by the mistral and swarmed over by mosquitoes. Between the endless flow of sediment from the Rhône and the erosive force of the sea, its shape is constantly changing. Even the Provençal poet Frederic Mistral described it in bleak terms: "*Ni arbre, ni ombre, ni âme*" ("Neither tree, nor shade, nor a soul").

Yet its harsh landscape harbors a concentration of exotic wildlife unique in Europe, and its isolation has given birth to an ascetic and ancient way of life that transcends national stereotype. This strange region is worth discovering, slowly, either on foot or on horseback—especially as its wildest reaches are inaccessible by car. People find the Camargue intriguing, birds find it irresistible. Its protected marshes lure some 400 species, including more than 160 in migration. As you drive the scarce roads that barely crisscross the Camargue, you'll usually be within the boundaries of the **Parc Regional de Camargue**. Unlike state and national parks in the United States, this area is privately owned and utilized following regulations imposed by the French government. The principal owners are the *manadiers* (the Camargue equivalent of small-scale ranchers) and their *gardians* (a kind of open-range cowboy), who keep it for grazing their wide-horn bulls and their dappled-white horses. When it's not participating in a bloodless bullfight (mounted players try to hook a red ribbon from its horns), a bull may well end up in the wine-rich regional stew called *gardianne de taureau*. Riding through the marshlands in leather pants and wide-rimmed black hats and wielding long prongs to prod their cattle, the gardians themselves are as fascinating as the wildlife. Their homes—tiny and whitewashed—dot the countryside.

The easiest place to view bird life is in a private reserve just outside the regional park called the **Parc Ornithologique du Pont de Gau** (Pont du Gau Ornithological Park). On some 150 acres of marsh and salt lands, birds are welcomed and protected (but in no way confined); injured birds are treated and kept in large pens, to be released if and when able to survive. A series of boardwalks (including a short, child-friendly inner loop) snakes over the wetlands, the longest leading to an observation blind, where a half hour of silence, binoculars in hand, can reveal unsuspected satisfactions. ☎ 04–90–97–82–62 ⊕ *www.parc-ornitho.com* ▧ €6 ☉ *Oct.–Mar., daily 10–sunset; Apr.–Sept., daily 9–sunset.*

Where to Stay & Eat

★ **$$$$**   ✕▦ **Le Mas de Peint.** In a 17th-century farmhouse on some 1,250 acres of Camargue ranch land, this quietly sophisticated jewel of a hotel may just be the ultimate *mas* experience. A study in country elegance, rooms showcase beautifully preserved 400-year-old wood beams, carefully polished stone floors, and creamy linen fabrics all tastefully complemented by brass beds, claw-foot bathtubs, and natural, soft Provençal colors. The small restaurant (reservations essential), charmingly decorated with checked curtains, paysan chairs, and fresh roses on every table, is worth the trip even if you can't stay the night. The prix-fixe menu €34–€43, changing daily, features sophisticated specialties often using home-grown products—roasted tuna flank with escargots *à la provençale,* or grilled game hen with roasted baby potatoes and exquisite cinnamon-flavored beets. A meal plan is available with a minimum stay of three nights. ✉ *Le Sambuc, 20 km (12 mi) south of town, 13200 Arles* ☎ *04–90–97–20–62* 🖷 *04–90–97–22–20* ⊕ *www.masdepeint.com* 🛏 *8 rooms, 3 apartments* ⚭ *Restaurant, minibars, cable TV, pool, horseback riding, some pets allowed (fee)* 🖃 *AE, DC, MC, V* ☯ *Closed mid-Jan.–mid-Mar., mid-Nov.–mid-Dec.* ⵀ *MAP.*

Stes-Maries-de-la-Mer

⑫   *18 km (10 mi) south of the Camargue, 129 km (80 mi) west of Marseille, 39 km (24 mi) south of Arles.*

The principal town within the confines of the Parc Régional de Camargue, Stes-Maries is a beach resort with a fascinating history. Provençal legend has it that around AD 45 a band of the very first Christians were rounded up and set adrift at sea without provisions in a boat without a sail. Their stellar ranks included Mary Magdalene, Martha, and Mary Salome, mother of apostles James and John; Mary Jacoby, sister of the Virgin; and Lazarus, not necessarily the one risen from the dead. Joining them in their fate was a dark-skinned servant girl named Sarah. Miraculously, their boat washed ashore at this ancient site, and the grateful Marys built a chapel in thanks. The pilgrims attracted to Stes-Maries aren't all lighting candles to the two St. Marys: Sarah has been adopted as an honorary saint by the Gypsies of the world. Two extraordinary festivals celebrating the Marys take place every year in Stes-Maries, one on May 24–25 and the other on the Sunday nearest October 22.

★   What is most striking to a visitor entering the damp, dark, and forbidding fortress-church, **Église des Stes-Maries,** is its novel character. Almost devoid of windows, its tall, barren single nave is cluttered with florid and sentimental ex-votos (tokens of blessings, prayers, and thanks) and primitive and sentimental artworks depicting the famous trio. Another oddity brings you back to the 20th century: a sign on the door forbids visitors from entering *torso nu* (topless). For outside its otherworldly role Stes-Maries is first and foremost a beach resort: dead flat, whitewashed, and more than a little tacky. Unless you've made a pilgrimage here for the sun and sand, don't spend much time in the town center; if you've chosen Stes-Maries as a base for viewing the Camargue, stay in one of the discreet *mas* (country inns) outside its city limits.

Where to Stay

★ $$$ 🏨 **Mas de Cacharel.** A haven for nature lovers, this quiet, laid-back retreat is nestled in the middle of 170 acres of private marshland. The Wild West–like ranch setting is enhanced by simple whitewashed buildings and rather sparse decor; rooms are furnished with terra-cotta tiles, jute rugs, and white cotton throws while large picture windows gaze out over hauntingly beautiful stretches of rose-colored reeds. A rather cavernous dining hall—complete with Provençal chairs and an enormous hand-carved fireplace—is really just a gathering place for sharing stories, local wine, and a hearty plate of selected meats, fresh tomato, and regional goat cheese. ✉ *4 km (2½ mi) north of town on D85, 13460 Stes-Maries-de-la-Mer* ☎ *04–90–97–95–44* 🖷 *04–90–97–87–97* ⊕ *www. hotel-cacharel.com* 🛏 *16 rooms* ⚭ *Pool, horseback riding, bar, some pets allowed; no a/c, no room TVs* 🖃 *MC, V* ⵀ *EP.*

Aigues-Mortes

⑬ *16 km (10 mi) northwest of Stes-Maries-de-la-Mer, 41 km (25 mi) south of Nîmes, 48 km (30 mi) southwest of Arles.*

Like a tiny illumination in a medieval manuscript, Aigues-Mortes is a precise and perfect miniature fortress-town contained within symmetrical crenellated walls, its streets laid out in geometric grids. Now awash in a flat wasteland of sand, salt, and monotonous marsh, it was once a major port town from which no less than St-Louis himself (Louis IX) set sail in the 13th century to conquer Jerusalem. In 1248 some 35,000 zealous men launched 1,500 ships toward Cyprus, engaging the infidel on his own turf and suffering swift defeat; Louis himself was briefly taken prisoner. A second launching in 1270 led to more crushing loss, and Louis succumbed to the plague.

Louis's state-of-the-art **fortress-port** remains astonishingly well preserved. Its stout walls now contain a small Provençal village milling with tourists, but the visit is more than justified by the impressive scale of the original structure. ⊠ *Porte de la Gardette* ☎ *04-66-53-61-55* 🖃 *€6.10* ☉ *Easter–late May, daily 10–6; late May–mid-Sept., daily 9:30–7; mid-Sept.–Easter, daily 10–5.*

It's not surprising that the town within the rampart walls has become tourist oriented, with the usual plethora of gift shops and postcard stands. But **place St-Louis,** where a 19th-century statue of the father of the fleur-de-lis reigns under shady pollards, has a mellow village feel. The pretty, bare-bones **Église Notre-Dame des Sablons,** on one corner of the square, has a timeless air (the church dates from the 13th century, but the stained glass is ultramodern).

Where to Stay & Eat

★ **$$–$$$** ✕🖵 **Les Arcades.** Long a success as an upscale seafood restaurant, this beautifully preserved 16th-century house now has large, airy rooms, some with tall windows overlooking a green courtyard. Pristine white-stone walls, color-stained woodwork, and rubbed-ocher walls frame antiques and lush fabrics. Classic cooking includes lotte (monkfish) in saffron and poached turbot in hollandaise and the house specialty: hot oysters in a creamy herbed butter sauce. Breakfast is included in the hotel price. ⊠ *23 bd. Gambetta, 30220* ☎ *04-66-53-81-13* 🖷 *04-66-53-97-12* ⊕ *www.les-arcades.fr* ➷ *9 rooms* ⚘ *Restaurant, pool, Internet, some pets allowed (fee)* ▭ *AE, MC, V* ☉ *Closed 1st 2 wks of Mar., 1st 2 wks of Oct.* ⑩ *BP.*

$$ 🖵 **Les Templiers.** In a 17th-century residence within the ramparts, this delightful hotel sets an atmospheric stage with stone, stucco, and terracotta floors. Two lovely suites in the building next door look out over the garden and pool. Furnishings are elegant, classically simple and softened with antiques. On the ground floor are two small cozy sitting areas; breakfast, weather permitting, is served in the quiet oasis of a flower-filled garden courtyard. ⊠ *23 rue de la République, 30220* ☎ *04-66-53-66-56* 🖷 *04-66-53-69-61* ➷ *14 rooms, 2 suites* ⚘ *Pool, Internet, parking (fee), some pets allowed (fee)* ▭ *AE, MC, V* ⑩ *EP.*

Nîmes

35 km (20 mi) north of Aigues-Mortes, 43 km (26 mi) south of Avignon, 121 km (74 mi) west of Marseille.

If you've come to the south seeking Roman treasures, you need look no further than Nîmes (pronounced *neem*): The Arènes and Maison Carrée are among continental Europe's best-preserved antiquities. But if you've come seeking a more modern mythology—of lazy, graceful Provence—give Nîmes a wide berth. It's a feisty, rundown rat race of a town, with jalopies and Vespas roaring irreverently around the ancient temple. Its medieval Vieille Ville has none of the gentrified grace of those in Arles or St-Rémy. Yet its rumpled and rebellious ways trace directly back to its Roman incarnation, when its population swelled with newly victorious soldiers, flaunting arrogant behavior after their conquest of Egypt in 31 BC.

Already anchoring a fiefdom of pre-Roman *oppida* (elevated fortresses) before ceding to the empire in the 1st century BC, this ancient city grew to formidable proportions under the Pax Romana. Its next golden age bloomed under the Protestants, who established an anti-Catholic stronghold here and wreaked havoc on iconic architectural treasures—not to mention the papist minority. Their massacre of some 200 Catholic citizens is remembered as the Michelade; many of those murdered were priests sheltered in the *évêché* (bishop's house), now the Museum of Old Nîmes.

★ ⑭ The **Arènes** (Arena) is considered the best-preserved Roman amphitheater in the world. A miniature of the Colosseum in Rome (note the small carvings of Romulus and Remus—the wrestling gladiators—on the exterior and the intricate bulls' heads etched into the stone over the entrance on the north side), it stands more than 520 feet long and 330 feet wide, and has a seating capacity of 24,000. Bloody gladiator battles and theatrical wild-boar chases drew crowds to its bleachers. Nowadays its most colorful use is the *corrida,* the bullfight that transforms the arena (and all of Nîmes) into a sangria-flushed homage to Spain. ⊠ *Bd. Victor-Hugo* ☎ *04–66–76–72–77* ✆ *€4.55; joint ticket to Arènes and Tour Magne €5.55* ۞ *May–Sept., daily 9–6:30; Oct.–Apr., daily 9–noon and 2–5.*

⑮ The **Musée des Beaux-Arts** (Fine Arts Museum) has now been beautifully restored by architect Jean-Michel Wilmotte. Centerpiece of this early 20th-century building remains a vast ancient Roman mosaic of a marriage ceremony that provides intriguing insights into the Roman aristocratic lifestyle. Temporary exhibitions (such as one devoted to Cleopatra) offer fascinating glimpses into history, but it is the varied collection of Italian, Flemish, and French paintings (notably Rubens's *Portrait of a Monk*) that is the particularly interesting mainstay of the collection. ⊠ *Rue de la Cité-Foulc* ☎ *04–66–67–38–21* ✆ *€4.55* ۞ *Tues.–Sun. 10–6.*

⑯ The **Musée Archéologique et d'Histoire Naturelle** (Museum of Archaeology and Natural History) is rich in local archaeological finds, mainly statues, busts, friezes, tools, coins, and pottery. ⊠ *Bd. de l'Admiral-Courbet* ☎ *04–66–76–74–80* ✆ *Free* ۞ *Tues.–Sun. 10–6.*

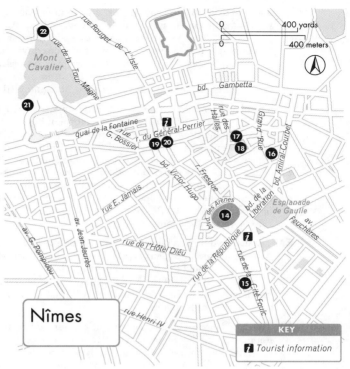

Nîmes

KEY

i Tourist information

Destroyed and rebuilt in several stages, with particular damage by rampaging Protestants who slaughtered eight priests from the neighboring *évêché* (bishop's house), the **Cathédrale Notre-Dame et St-Castor** (✉ Pl. aux Herbes) still shows traces of its original construction in 1096. A remarkably preserved Romanesque frieze portrays Adam and Eve cowering in shame, the gory slaughter of Abel, and a flood-wearied Noah. Inside, look for the 4th-century sarcophagus (third chapel on the right) and a magnificent 17th-century chapel (in the apse).

The **Musée du Vieux Nîmes** (Museum of Old Nîmes), in the 17th-century bishop's palace opposite the cathedral, has embroidered garments in exotic and vibrant displays. Look for the 14th-century jacket made of blue-serge de Nîmes, the famous fabric from which Levi-Strauss first fashioned blue jeans. ✉ *Pl. aux Herbes* ☎ *04–66–76–73–70* 🎫 *Free* ☺ *Tues.–Sun. 10–6.*

★ Lovely and forlorn in the middle of a busy downtown square, the exquisitely preserved **Maison Carrée** (Square House) strikes a timeless balance between symmetry and whimsy, purity of line and richness of decor. Modeled on the Temple to Apollo in Rome, adorned with magnificent marble columns and elegant pediment, it remains one of the most noble surviving structures of ancient Roman civilization anywhere. Built around

5 BC and dedicated to Caius Caesar and his grandson Lucius, it has survived subsequent use as a medieval meeting hall, an Augustine church, a storehouse for Revolutionary archives, and a horse shed. The interior of the great structure serves as a venue for temporary exhibitions as well as a display for photos and drawings of current archeological work. ⊠ *Bd. Victor-Hugo* ☎ *04–66–36–26–76* ⊕ *www.ot-nimes.fr* ⊠ *Free* ☉ *Mid-Mar.–mid-Oct., daily 9–7; mid-Oct.–mid-Mar., daily 10–5.*

The glass-fronted Carré d'Art (directly opposite the Maison Carrée) was designed by British architect Sir Norman Foster as its neighbor's stark contemporary mirror: it literally reflects the Maison Carrée's creamy symmetry and figuratively answers it with a feather-light deconstructed colonnade. Homages aside, it resembles an airport terminal.

㉕ It now houses the **Musée d'Art Contemporain** (Contemporary Art Museum), featuring art dating from 1960 onward from artists such as Arman and Ben, and temporary exhibitions of newer works by artists like Javier Perez. ⊠ *Pl. de la Maison Carrée* ☎ *04–66–76–35–70* ⊠ *€4.45* ☉ *Tues.–Sun. 10–6.*

㉑ The shattered Roman ruin known as the **Temple de Diane** (Temple of Diana) dates from the 2nd century BC. The temple's function is unknown, though it is thought to have been part of a larger Roman complex that is still unexcavated. In the Middle Ages Benedictine nuns occupied the building before it was converted into a church. Destruction came during the Wars of Religion.

㉒ The **Tour Magne** (Magne Tower), at the far end of the Jardin de la Fontaine, is all that remains of a tower the emperor Augustus had built on Gallic foundations; it was probably used as a lookout post. Despite a loss of 30 feet in height over the course of time, it still provides fine views of Nîmes for anyone energetic enough to climb the 140 steps. ⊠ *Quai de la Fontaine* ☎ *04–66–67–65–56* ⊠ *Tour Magne €2.45, joint ticket with Arènes €5.55* ☉ *Mid-Mar.–mid-Oct., daily 9–7; mid-Oct.–mid-Mar., daily 10–4:45.*

Where to Stay & Eat

★ **$$–$$$** ✕ **Chez Jacotte.** Duck into a Vieille Ville back alley and into this cross-vaulted grotto that embodies Nîmes's Spanish-bohemian flair. Candlelight flickering on rich tones of oxblood, ocher, and cobalt enhances the warm welcome from the staff. Mouthwatering goat-cheese-and-fig gratin, mullet crisped in olive oil and basil, herb-crusted oven-roasted lamb, and seasonal fruit crumbles show off a flair with local ingredients. ⊠ *15 rue Fresque, impasse* ☎ *04–66–21–64–59* ⚠ *Reservations essential* ▭ *MC, V* ☉ *Closed Sun. and Mon. No lunch Sat.*

$$–$$$ ✕ **Le Jardin d'Hadrien.** This chic enclave, with its quarried white stone, ancient plank-and-beam ceiling, and open fireplace, would be a culinary haven even without its lovely hidden garden, a shady retreat for summer meals. Fresh cod crisped in salt and olive oil, zucchini flowers filled with *brandade* (the creamy, light paste of salt cod and olive oil), and a frozen parfait perfumed with licorice all show chef Alain Vinouze's subtle skills. Prix-fixe menus are €17 and €26. ⊠ *11 rue Enclos Rey* ☎ *04–66–21–86–65* ⚠ *Reservations essential* ▭ *AE, MC,*

V ⊙ *Closed Wed. No dinner Tues.; July and Aug. closed Sun., no lunch Mon. and Wed.*

$–$$ ✕ **Vintage Café.** This popular Vieille Ville wine bar draws a loyal crowd of oenophiles for serious tastings and compatible regional viands using fresh ingredients straight from the marketplace—traditional fois gras, hot lentil salad with smoked haddock, and pan-fried bull steak. Exhibitions by local painters, bright ceramics, and warm-color lamplight enhance the artful Mediterranean decor. Summer nights on the terrace are idyllic. Better to make reservations on the weekend. ⊠ *7 rue de Bernis* ☎ *04–66–21–04–45* ▤ *DC, MC, V* ⊙ *Closed Sun. and Mon. No lunch Sat.*

$$ ▦ **La Baume.** In the heart of scruffy Vieux Nîmes, this noble 17th-century *hôtel particulier* (mansion) has been reincarnated as a stylish hotel with an architect's eye for mixing ancient detail with modern design. The balustraded stone staircase is a protected historic monument, and stenciled beamed ceilings, cross vaults, and archways counterbalance hot ocher tones, swags of raw cotton, leather, and halogen lighting. ⊠ *21 rue Nationale, 30000* ☎ *04–66–76–28–42* 🖷 *04–66–76–28–45* ⊕ *www. new-hotel.com* ⇱ *34 rooms* ⌂ *Minibars, cable TV, bar, parking (fee), some pets allowed (fee)* ▤ *AE, DC, MC, V* ¶❶ *EP.*

Shopping

The only commercial maker of authentic brandade, Nîmes's signature salt-cod-and-olive-oil paste, is **Raymond** (⊠ 24 rue Nationale ☎ 04–66–67–20–47). It's paddled fresh into a plastic carton or sold in sealed jars so you can take it home. **L'Huilerie** (⊠ 10 rue des Marchands ☎ 04–66–67–37–24) is a delightful treasure house of teas and spices that shows off great gift ideas, including smartly packaged mustards, honeys, and olive oils.

THE ALPILLES & THE RHÔNE FORTRESSES

The low mountain range called the Alpilles (pronounced ahl-*pee*-yuh) forms a rough-hewn, rocky landscape that rises into nearly barren limestone hills, the flanking fields silvered with ranks of twisted olive trees and alleys of gnarled *amandiers* (almond trees). There are superb antiquities in St-Rémy and feudal ruins in Les Baux. West of the Alpilles, the fortresses of Tarascon and Beaucaire guard the Rhône between Avignon and the sea.

Abbaye de Montmajour

㉓ *35 km (20 mi) southeast of Nîmes, 5 km (3 mi) northeast of Arles, 17 km (11 mi) south of Tarascon.*

An extraordinary structure looming over the marshlands north of Arles, this magnificent Romanesque abbey stands in partial ruin. Begun in the 12th century by a handful of Benedictine monks, it grew according to an ambitious plan of church, crypt, and cloister. Under the management of corrupt lay monks in the 17th century, it grew more sumptuous; when those lay monks were ejected by the Church, they sacked the place. After the Revolution it was sold to a junkman, and he tried to pay the mortgage by stripping off and selling its goods. A 19th-century medieval revival spurred its partial restoration, but its 18th-century portions remain in ruins. Ironically, because of this mercenary history, what remains is a spare and beautiful piece of Romanesque architecture. The **cloister** rivals that of St-Trophime in Arles for its balance, elegance, and air of mystical peace: van Gogh was drawn to its womblike isolation and came often to the abbey to paint and reflect. ☎ *04–90–54–64–17* 🖼 *€6.10* 🕑 *Apr.–Sept., daily 9–7; Oct.–Mar., Wed.–Mon. 10–1 and 2–5.*

Les Baux-de-Provence

★ ㉔ *17 km (10 mi) west of Montmajour, 18 km (11 mi) northeast of Arles, 29 km (18 mi) south of Avignon.*

When you first search the craggy hilltops for signs of Les Baux-de-Provence (pronounced lay-*bo*), you may not quite be able to distinguish between bedrock and building, so naturally do the ragged skyline of towers and crenellation blend into the sawtooth jags of stone. This tiny château-village ranks as one of the most visited tourist sites in France, a tour-de-force blend of natural scenery and medieval ambience of astonishing beauty. From this intimidating vantage point, the lords of Les Baux ruled throughout the 11th and 12th centuries over one of the largest fiefdoms in the south. Only in the 19th century did Les Baux find new purpose: the mineral bauxite, valued as an alloy in aluminum production, was discovered in its hills and named for its source. A profitable industry sprang up that lasted into the 20th century before fading into history.

Today Les Baux offers two faces to the world: its beautifully preserved medieval village and the ghostly ruins of its fortress, once referred to as the *ville morte* (dead town). In the village, lovely 12th-century stone houses, even their window frames still intact, shelter the shops, cafés, and galleries that line the steep cobbled streets. The 17-acre clifftop sprawl of ruins is contained under the umbrella name the **Château des Baux**. At the entry, the Tour du Brau contains the **Musée d'Histoire des Baux**, a small collection of relics and models. Its exit gives access to the wide and varied grounds, where Romanesque chapels and towers mingle with skeletal ruins. The tiny **Chapelle St-Blaise** shelters a permanent music-and-slide show called *Van Gogh, Gauguin, Cézanne au Pays de l'Olivier,* of artworks depicting olive orchards in their infinite variety. In July and August there are fascinating medieval exhibitions: people dressed up in authentic costumes, displays of medieval crafts, and even a few jousting tournaments complete with handsome knights carrying fluttering silk tokens of their beloved ladies. ☎ *04–90–54–55–56* 🖼 *€7 with audio guide* 🕑 *Mar., May, Sept., and Oct., daily 9–6:30; June–Aug., daily 9–8; Nov. and Feb., daily 9–6; Dec. and Jan., daily 9–5.*

Where to Stay & Eat

$$$$ ✕🏨 **L'Oustau de la Baumanière.** Sheltered by rocky cliffs below the vil-
FodorsChoice lage of Les Baux, this long-famous hotel, with its formal landscaped ter-
★ race and broad swimming pool, has a guest book studded with names like Winston Churchill, Elizabeth Taylor, and Picasso. The interior is luxe-Provençal, thanks to tile floors, arched stone ceilings, and brocaded

settees done up in Canovas and Halard fabrics. Guest rooms—breezy, private, and beautifully furnished with antiques—were renovated in 1999 and brought up to snuff with contemporary flair, but the basic style remains archetypal Baux. These rooms are set in three buildings on broad landscaped grounds, the best of which are in the enchanting Le Manoir. As for the famed Baumanière restaurant (reservations essential), chef Jean-André Charial's hallowed reputation continues to attract culinary pilgrims (too many, it would appear from the noisy crowds that drive up the nearby road to the hotel). You can't blame them: the Oustau tradition is a veritable museum of Provençal tradition, but one that has been given a nouvelle face-lift—lobster cooked in Châteauneuf-du-Pape and set on a bed of polenta is a typical dazzler. If you're only dining here, be sure to make reservations. Note that from November to December and in March the restaurant is closed Wednesday and doesn't serve lunch Thursday; during January and February both the hotel and restaurant are closed. You can try a less expensive Oustau experience a kilometer (half mile) away at **La Cabro d'Or** (☎ 04–90–54–33–21 🖷 04–90–54–45–98 ⊕ www.cabrodor.com). Run by the same owners, it's cheaper (€200–€270), more rustic, more private, and don't be surprised to see a billy-goat wander by your guest-room window. Meal plans for both hotels are available with a two-night minimum stay. ✉ *Val d'Enfer, 13520* ☎ *04–90–54–33–07* 🖷 *04–90–54–40–46* ⊕ *www.oustaudebaumaniere.com* 🛏 *18 rooms, 9 suites, 3 apts.; 30 rooms in La Cabro* ⚐ *Restaurant, minibars, cable TV, 2 tennis courts, pool, horseback riding, some pets allowed (fee)* ▤ *AE, DC, MC, V* ☉ *Closed Jan. and Feb.; La Cabro Nov.–mid-Dec.* ⦿ *MAP.*

$ ✕▥ **La Reine Jeanne.** At this modest inn majestically placed right at the entrance to the village, you can stand on balconies and look over rugged views worthy of the châteaux up the street. Rooms are small, simple, and—despite the white vinyl–padded furniture—lovingly decorated. Reserve in advance for one of the two rooms with a balcony, though even one of the tiny interior rooms gives you the chance to spend an evening in Les Baux after the tourists have drained away. Good homestyle cooking is served in the restaurant, which has views both from inside and outside on the pretty terrace. ✉ *Grande Rue Baux 13520* ☎ *04–90–54–32–06* 🖷 *04–90–54–32–33* ⊕ *www.la-reinejeanne.com* 🛏 *10 rooms* ⚐ *Restaurant, cable TV, some pets allowed (fee)* ▤ *MC, V* ☉ *Closed Jan.* ⦿ *EP.*

$$$ ▥ **Mas de L'Oulivié.** Built to look ancient, with recycled roof tiles and hand-waxed chalk walls, this mas is clarity itself, with a cool, clean look and a low-key aura. There's no upscale restaurant—just easy and unpretentious lunches by the pool (grilled meats, salads, and goat cheese). Eight rooms on the upper floor of the main house are pretty enough, with floral-print curtains and rich carpets, but ask for one with doors opening onto the lavender gardens and olive groves. ✉ *2 km (1 mi) after the exit Les Baux, D278F direction Fontvieille-Arles, 13520* ☎ *04–90–54–35–78* 🖷 *04–90–54–44–31* ⊕ *www.masdeloulivie.com* 🛏 *25 rooms, 2 suites* ⚐ *Restaurant, minibars, cable TV, tennis court, pool, bar, Internet, some pets allowed (fee)* ▤ *AE, DC, MC, V* ☉ *Closed mid-Mar.–mid-Nov.* ⦿ *EP.*

St-Rémy-de-Provence

㉕ *8 km (5 mi) north of Les Baux, 24 km (15 mi) east of Arles, 19 km (12*
Fodor'sChoice *mi) south of Avignon.*

★ Something felicitous has happened in this market town in the heart of
the Alpilles—a steady infusion of style, of art, of imagination—all
brought by people with a respect for local traditions and a love of
Provençal ways. Here more than anywhere you can meditate quietly on
antiquity, browse redolent markets with basket in hand, and enjoy ur-
bane galleries, cosmopolitan shops, and specialty food boutiques. An
abundance of choices in restaurants, mas, and even châteaux awaits you;
the almond and olive groves conceal dozens of stone-and-terra-cotta gîtes,
many with pools.

First established by an indigenous Celtic-Ligurian people who worshiped
the god Glan, the village Glanum was adopted and gentrified by the Greeks
of Marseille in the 2nd and 3rd centuries before Christ. Rome moved in
to help ward off Hannibal, and by the 1st century BC Caesar had taken
full control. The Via Domitia, linking Italy to Spain, passed by its doors,
and the main trans-Alpine pass emptied into its entrance gate. Under the
Pax Romana there developed a veritable city, complete with temples and
forum, luxurious villas, and baths. The Romans eventually fell, but a town
grew up next to their ruins, taking its name from their protectorate
Abbey St-Remi, in Reims. It grew to be an important market town, and
wealthy families built fine mansions in its center—among them the family de Sade (whose black-sheep relation held forth in the Lubéron at Lacoste). Another famous native son was the eccentric doctor, scholar, and
astrologer Michel Nostradamus (1503–66), who is credited by some as
having predicted much of the modern age. Perhaps the best known of
St-Rémy's residents was the ill-fated Vincent van Gogh. Shipped unceremoniously out of Arles at the height of his madness (and creativity), he
committed himself to the asylum St-Paul-de-Mausolé.

To approach Glanum, you must park in a dusty roadside lot on D5 south
of town (toward Les Baux). But before crossing, you'll be confronted
with two of the most miraculously preserved classical monuments in
France, simply called **Les Antiques**. Dating from 30 BC, the **Mausolée** (mausoleum), a wedding-cake stack of arches and columns, lacks nothing but
its finial on top, yet it is dedicated to a Julian (as in Julius Caesar), probably Caesar Augustus. A few yards away stands another marvel: the **Arc
Triomphal**, dating from AD 20.

Across the street from Les Antiques and set back from D5, a slick visitor center prepares you for entry into the ancient village of **Glanum** with
scale models of the site in its various heydays. A good map and an English brochure guide you stone by stone through the maze of foundations, walls, towers, and columns that spread across a broad field;
helpfully, Greek sites are noted by numbers, Roman ones by letters. ⊠ *Off
D5, direction Les Baux, info phone at Hôtel de Sade* ☎ *04–90–92–64–04*
🖼 *€5; €6.50 includes entry to Hôtel de Sade* ☉ *Apr.–Sept., daily 9–7;
Oct.–Mar., daily 9–noon and 2–5.*

★ You can cut across the fields from Glanum to **St-Paul-de-Mausolée,** the lovely, isolated asylum where van Gogh spent the last year of his life (1889–90). But enter it quietly: it shelters psychiatric patients to this day— all of them women. You're free to walk up the beautifully manicured garden path to the church and its jewel-box Romanesque **cloister,** where the artist found womblike peace. ⊠ *Route des Baux; next to Glanum, off D5, direction Les Baux* ☎ *04–90–92–77–00* 🖂 *€3.40* ⊙ *May–Sept., daily 9:30–7; Oct.–Apr., daily 10:45–4:45.*

Within St-Rémy's fast-moving traffic loop, a labyrinth of narrow streets leads you away from the action and into the slow-moving inner sanctum of the **Vieille Ville.** Here trendy, high-end shops mingle pleasantly with local life, and the buildings, if gentrified, blend in unobtrusively.

Make your way to the **Hôtel de Sade,** a 15th- and 16th-century private manor now housing the treasures unearthed from the ruins of Glanum. The de Sade family built the house around remains of 4th-century baths and a 5th-century baptistery, now nestled in its courtyard. ⊠ *Rue du Parage* ☎ *04–90–92–64–04* 🖂 *€2.50; €6.50 includes Glanum entry* ⊙*Feb.–Mar. and Oct., Tues.–Sun. 10–noon and 2–5; Apr.–Sept., Tues.–Sun. 10–noon and 2–6; Nov. and Dec., Wed. and weekends 10–noon and 2–5.*

Where to Stay & Eat

$$$ ✕ **La Maison Jaune.** This modern retreat in the Vieille Ville draws crowds of summer people to its pretty roof terrace, with accents of sober stone and lively contemporary furniture both indoors and out. The look reflects the cuisine: with vivid flavors and a cool, contained touch, chef François Perraud prepares grilled sardines with crunchy fennel and lemon confit, and veal lightly flavored with olives, capers, and celery. ⊠ *15 rue Carnot* ☎ *04–90–92–56–14* ⚲ *Reservations essential* ▭ *MC, V* ⊙ *Closed Mon. No dinner Sun. or lunch Tues.*

★ **$–$$** ✕ **L'Assiette de Marie.** Marie Ricco is a collector, and she's turned her tiny restaurant into a bower of attic treasures. Seated at an old school desk, you choose from the day's specials, all made with Marie's Corsican-Italian touch—marinated vegetables with tapenade, a cast-iron casserole of superb pasta, satiny *panetone* (flan). ⊠ *1 rue Jaume Roux* ☎ *04–90–92–32–14* ⚲ *Reservations essential* ▭ *MC, V* ⊙ *Nov.–Mar., closed Thurs.*

$–$$ ✕ **La Gousse d'Ail.** Another intimate, indoor Vieille Ville hideaway, this family-run bistro lives up to its name (the Garlic Clove), serving robust, highly flavored southern dishes in hearty portions. Try the house specialties: grilled bull steak with creamed garlic or a powerful garlic-almond pesto. Aim for Thursday night, when there's Gypsy music and jazz. ⊠ *25 rue Carnot* ☎ *04–90–92–16–87* ▭ *AE, DC, MC, V* ⊙ *Closed mid-Nov.–mid-Mar.; no lunch Thurs. and Sat.*

$$$–$$$$ ✕🏠 **Domaine de Valmouriane.** In this genteel mas-cum-resort, peacefully isolated within a broad park, overstuffed English-country decor mixes cozily with cool Provençal stone and timber. The grounds are impressive and are dotted with some picture-perfect cypress trees; inside, much has been restored, so all is comfort and ease, if not the height of authenticity. The restaurant is masterminded by chef Pascal Volle, who is determined to please with fresh game, seafood, local oils, and truffles; his ravioli fois gras is sheer decadence. But it's the personal welcome from Philippe and Martin Capel that makes you feel like an honored guest. The pool, surrounded by a slate walk and delightful gardens, is most inviting. ⊠ *Petite rte. des Baux (D27), 13210* ☎ *04–90–92–44–62* 🖷 *04–90–92–37–32* ⊕ *www.valmouriane.com* ⤵ *14 rooms* & *Restaurant, minibars, cable TV, tennis court, pool, hot tub, steam room, billiards* ⊟ *AE, DC, MC, V* ⑂ *FAP, MAP.*

★ **$$$** ✕⬚ **Bistrot d'Eygalières.** Belgian chef Wout Bru's understated restaurant in nearby Eygalières is quickly gaining a reputation (and stars) for its elegant, light, and subtly balanced cuisine, like sole with goat cheese, lobster salad with candied tomatoes, and foie gras carpaccio with summer truffles. The wine list is both eclectic and thorough, though prices are a bit on the high side. Guest rooms are very chic, very comfortable; Wout's wife, Suzy, has a wonderful eye and a welcoming disposition. ⊠ *Rue de la République, Eygalières, 10 km (6 mi) southeast of St-Rémy-de-Provence on the D99 and then the D24, 13810* ☎ *04–90–90–60–34* 🖷 *04–90–90–60–37* ⊕ *www.chezbru.com* ⤵ *Reservations essential* ⤵ *2 rooms, 2 suites* & *Restaurant, minibars, parking, some pets allowed (no fee)* ⊟ *AE, MC, V* ⑂ *EP.*

$$$–$$$$ ⬚ **Mas de Cornud.** An American stewards the wine cellar and an Egyptian runs the kitchen, but the attitude is pure Provence: David and Nito Carpita have turned their fairly severe, stone, black-shuttered farmhouse, just outside St-Rémy, into a bed-and-breakfast filled with French country furniture and objects from around the world. The welcome is so sincere you'll feel like one of the family in no time. Table d'hôte dinners, cooking classes, and tours can be arranged. Breakfast is included and the minimum stay is two nights. ⊠ *Rte. de Mas-Blanc, 13210* ☎ *04–90–92–39–32* 🖷 *04–90–92–55–99* ⊕ *www.mascornud.com* ⤵ *5 rooms, 1 suite* & *Dining room, pool, free parking, some pets allowed (fee); no a/c* ⊟ *No credit cards* ⊙ *Closed Jan. and Feb.* ⑂ *BP, MAP.*

★ **$$–$$$** ⬚ **Château de Roussan.** In a majestic park shaded by ancient plane trees, this yellow-stone 18th-century château is a helter-skelter of brocantes and bric-a-brac, and the bathrooms have an afterthought air about them. Cats outnumber the staff. Yet if you're the right sort for this place—backpackers, romantic couples on a budget, lovers of atmosphere over luxury—you'll blossom in this three-dimensional costume-drama scene. Meal plans are available with a two-night minimum stay. ⊠ *D99, rte. de Tarascon, 13210* ☎ *04–90–92–11–63* 🖷 *04–90–92–50–59* ⊕ *www. chateau-de-roussan.com* ⤵ *22 rooms* & *Restaurant, cable TV, babysitting, some pets allowed (fee)* ⊟ *AE, DC, MC, V* ⑂ *MAP.*

★ **$$** ⬚ **Mas des Carassins.** A textbook example of a Provençal mas, this rambling 19th-century farmhouse is done with an impressive amount of style. Guest rooms come with stonework walls and wrought-iron canopy beds but you may wish to sleep under the stars since the mas is beautifully surrounded with thyme bushes, pots of lemon and orange trees, fountains, pools, and centuries-old olive trees. *Bien sûr,* you'll want to enjoy the copious lunch outside at a shady and intimate table. ⊠ *1 chemin Gaulois, 13810* ☎ *04–90–92–15–48* 🖷 *04–90–92–49–65* ⊕ *www. hoteldescarassins.com* ⤵ *14 rooms* & *Restaurant, minibars, cable TV, pool, pets allowed (fee)* ⊟ *AE, MC, V* ⑂ *EP.*

Shopping

Every Wednesday morning St-Rémy hosts one of the most popular and picturesque **markets** in Provence, during which place de la République and narrow Vieille Ville streets overflow with fresh produce, herbs, and olive oil by the vat, as well as fabrics and brocantes (antiques).

Tarascon

26 *16 km (10 mi) west of St-Rémy, 17 km (11 mi) north of Arles, 25 km (15 mi) east of Nîmes.*

Tarascon's claim to fame is as the haunt of the mythical Tarasque, a monster that was said to emerge from the Rhône to gobble up children and cattle. Luckily, St. Marthe, who washed up at Stes-Maries-de-la-Mer, tamed the beast with a sprinkle of holy water, after which the inhabitants slashed it to pieces. This dramatic event is celebrated on the last weekend in June with a parade, and was immortalized by Alphonse Daudet, who lived in nearby Fontvieille, in his tales of a folk hero known to all French schoolchildren as *Tartarin de Tarascon.* Unfortunately, a saint has not yet been born who can vanquish the fumes that emanate from Tarascon's enormous paper mill, and the hotel industry

★ is suffering for it. Nonetheless, with the walls of its formidable **Château** plunging straight into the roaring Rhône, this ancient city on the river presents a daunting challenge to Beaucaire, its traditional enemy across the water. Begun in the 13th century by the noble Anjou family on the site of a Roman *castellum,* it grew through the generations into a splendid structure, crowned with both round and square towers and elegantly furnished. Complete with a moat, a drawbridge, and a lovely faceted spiral staircase, it retains its beautiful decorative stonework and original window frames. ☎ 04–90–91–01–93 ✉ Bd. de Roi Réné ⛴ €6.10 ⊙ Apr.–Sept., daily 9–7; Oct.–Mar., daily 10:30–5.

AVIGNON & THE VAUCLUSE

Anchored by the magnificent papal stronghold of Avignon, the Vaucluse spreads luxuriantly east of the Rhône. Its famous vineyards—Châteauneuf-du-Pape, Gigondas, Vacqueyras, Beaumes-de-Venise—seduce connoisseurs, and its Roman ruins in Orange and Vaison-la-Romaine draw scholars and arts lovers. Arid lowlands dotted with orchards of olives, apricots, and almonds give way to a rich and wild mountain terrain around the formidable Mont Ventoux and flow into the primeval Luberon, made a household name by Peter Mayle. The hill villages around the Luberon—Gordes, Roussillon, Oppède, Bonnieux—are as lovely as any you'll find in the south of France.

Avignon

24 km (15 mi) northeast of Tarascon, 82 km (51 mi) northwest of Aix-en-Provence, 95 km (59 mi) northwest of Marseille, 224 km (140 mi) south of Lyon.

From its famous Palais des Papes (Papal Palace), where seven exiled popes camped between 1309 and 1377 after fleeing from the corruption and civil strife of Rome, to the long, low bridge of childhood song fame stretching over the river, you can beam yourself briefly into 14th-century Avignon, so complete is the context, so evocative the setting. Yet the town is anything but a museum; it surges with modern ideas and energy and thrives within its ramparts as it did in the heyday of the popes—and, like those radical church lords, is sensual, cultivated, and cosmopolitan, with a taste for laic pleasures. Avignon remained papal property until 1791, and elegant mansions bear witness to the town's 18th-century prosperity.

★ ㉗ The colossal **Palais des Papes** creates a disconcertingly fortresslike impression, underlined by the austerity of its interior. Most of the original furnishings were returned to Rome with the papacy, others were lost during the French Revolution. Some imagination is required to picture its earlier medieval splendor, awash with color and with worldly clerics enjoying what the 14th-century Italian poet Petrarch called "licentious banquets." On close inspection, two different styles of building emerge at the palace: the severe **Palais Vieux** (Old Palace), built between 1334 and 1342 by Pope Benedict XII, a member of the Cistercian order, which frowned on frivolity, and the more decorative **Palais Nouveau** (New Palace), built in the following decade by the artsy, lavish-living Pope Clement VI. The Great Court, entryway to the complex, links the two.

The main rooms of the Palais Vieux are the **Consistory** (Council Hall), decorated with some excellent 14th-century frescoes by Simone Martini; the **Chapelle St-Jean** (original frescoes by Matteo Giovanetti); the **Grand Tinel**, or Salle des Festins (Feast Hall), with a majestic vaulted roof and a series of 18th-century Gobelin tapestries; the **Chapelle St-Martial** (more Giovanetti frescoes); and the **Chambre du Cerf,** with a richly decorated ceiling, murals featuring a stag hunt, and a delightful view of Avignon. The principal attractions of the Palais Nouveau are the **Grande Audience,** a magnificent two-nave hall on the ground floor, and, upstairs, the **Chapelle Clémentine,** where the college of cardinals once gathered to elect the new pope. ⊠ *Pl. du Palais* ☎ *04–90–27–50–00* ⊕ *www.palais-des-papes.com* ⊠ *€7.50 entry includes choice of guided tour or individual audio guide; €8.50 includes audio guided tour to pont St-Bénézet* ☉ *Oct.–Mar., daily 9:30–5:45; Apr.–Nov., daily 9–7; July, during theater festival, daily 9–9.*

㉘ The **Cathédrale Notre-Dame-des-Doms,** first built in a pure Provençal Romanesque style in the 12th century, was quickly dwarfed by the extravagant palace that rose beside it. It rallied in the 14th century with the addition of a cupola—which promptly collapsed. As rebuilt in 1425, it's a marvel of stacked arches with a strong Byzantine flavor and is topped nowadays with a gargantuan Virgin Mary lantern—a 19th-century afterthought—whose glow can be seen for miles around. ⊠ *Pl. du Palais* ☎ *04–90–86–81–01* ☉ *Mon.–Sat. 7–7, Sun. 9–7.*

㉙ The **Petit Palais**—the former residence of bishops and cardinals before Pope Benedict built his majestic palace—houses a large collection of Old Master paintings. The majority are Italian works from the Early Renaissance schools of Siena, Florence, and Venice—styles with which the

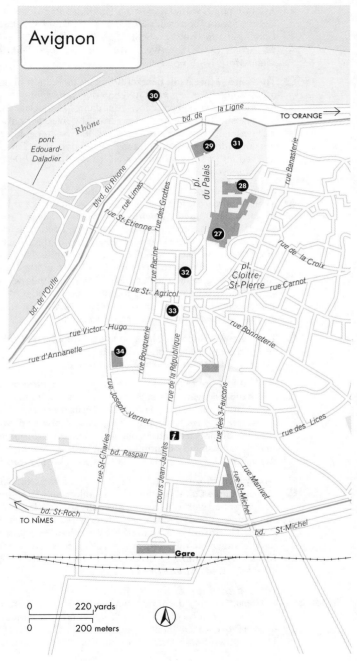

Avignon

Avignon popes would have been familiar. Later key works to seek out include Sandro Botticelli's *Virgin and Child* and Venetian paintings by Carpaccio and Giovanni Bellini. ⊠ *Pl. du Palais* ☎ *04–90–86–44–58* ▦ *€6* ⊘ *Oct.–May, Wed.–Mon. 9:30–1 and 2–5:30; June–Sept., Wed.–Mon. 10–1 and 2–6.*

★ ③⓪ The **Pont St-Bénézet** (St. Bénézet Bridge) is the subject of the famous children's song: *"Sur le pont d'Avignon on y danse, on y danse . . ."* ("On the bridge of Avignon one dances, one dances . . ."). Unlike London Bridge, this one still stretches its arches across the river, but only partway: half was washed away in the 17th century. Its first stones allegedly laid with the miraculous strength granted St-Bénézet in the 12th century, it once reached all the way to Villeneuve. ⊠ *Port du Rochre* ⊕ *www.palais-des-papes.com.*

③① From the entrance to the Pont St-Bénézet, walk along the ramparts to a spiral staircase leading to the hilltop garden known as **Rocher des Doms** (Rock of the Domes). Set with grand Mediterranean pines, this park on a bluff above town is dotted with statuary, lined with an elegant stone balustrade, and offers extraordinary views of the palace, the rooftops of Old Avignon, the Pont St-Bénézet, and formidable Villeneuve across the Rhône. On the horizon loom Mont Ventoux, the Luberon, and Les Alpilles. Often called the "cradle of Avignon," the rock's grottos were among the first human habitations in the area. Today, the park also has a fairly fake lake, home to some swans. ⊠ *Montée du Moulin off pl. du Palais* ⊕ *www.avignon-et-provence.com.*

Fodor'sChoice
★

③② The **Place de l'Horloge** (Clock Square) is the social nerve center of Avignon, where the concentration of bistros, brasseries, and restaurants draws swarms of locals to the shade of its plane trees.

③③ Housed in a pretty little Jesuit chapel on the main shopping street, the **Musée Lapidaire** gathers a collection of classical sculpture and stonework from Gallo-Roman times (1st and 2nd centuries), as well as pieces from the Musée Calvet's collection of Greek and Etruscan works. They are haphazardly labeled and insouciantly scattered throughout the noble chapel, itself slightly crumbling but awash with light. ⊠ *27 rue de la République* ☎ *04–90–85–75–38* ▦ *€2* ⊘ *Wed.–Mon. 10–1 and 2–6.*

③④ Worth a visit for the beauty and balance of its architecture alone, the fine old **Musée Calvet** contains a rich collection of antiquities and classically inspired works. Recent acquisitions are Neoclassical and Romantic and almost entirely French, including works by Manet, Daumier, and David. The main building itself is a Palladian-style jewel in pale Gard stone dating from the 1740s; the garden is so lovely that it may distract you from the paintings. ⊠ *65 rue Joseph-Vernet* ☎ *04–90–86–33–84* ▦ *€6* ⊘ *Wed.–Mon. 10–1 and 2–6.*

Where to Stay & Eat

$$–$$$$ ✕ **Brunel.** Stylishly decorated in a hip, contemporary retro-bistro style with urbane shades of gray, this Avignon favorite entices with the passionate Provençal cooking of Avignon-born and -bred chef Roger Brunel. This is down-home bistro cooking based on a sophisticated larder:

parchment-wrapped mullet with eggplant, peppers, and tomatoes, pigeon roasted with basil, and caramelized apples in tender pastry. The prix-fixe menu is €38. ⊠ *46 rue de la Balance* 🕾 *04–90–85–24–83* ⌕ *Reservations essential* ⊟ *MC, V* ⊗ *Closed Sun. and Mon.*

$$–$$$ ✕ **La Compagnie des Comptoirs.** Glassed into the white stone cloister of the trendy complex called Les Cloître des Arts is the culinary haven of celebrated Porcel twins of the Le Jardin de Sens fame (in Montpellier). Contemporary decorator Imaad Rahmouni did the interior, bringing together classic simplicity with modern elegance: in summer the 15th-century walls are artfully draped with Indian fabrics. Menu selections are beautifully presented and offer flavor mixtures from India, Italy, and Morocco: who can resist chicken breast wrapped in hazelnuts baked with prunes and *trompette des morts* mushrooms, or the dessert of cubed banana and pineapple served on softened fresh vanilla? ⊠ *83 rue Joseph-Vernet* 🕾 *04–90–85–99–04* ⌕ *Reservations essential* ⊟ *AE, MC, V* ⊗ *Closed Mon. in Oct.–Apr.*

★ **$$–$$$** ✕ **Le Grand Café.** Behind the Papal Palace and set in a massive former army supply depot—note the carefully preserved industrial decay—this urban-chic entertainment complex combines an international cinema, a bar, and this popular bistro. Gigantic 18th-century mirrors and dance-festival posters hang on crumbling plaster and brick, and votive candles half-light the raw metal framework—an inspiring environment for intense film talk and a late supper of apricot lamb on a bed of semoule, goat cheese, or marinated artichokes. The prix-fixe dinner menu is €30. ⊠ *La Manutention, cours Maria Casares* 🕾 *04–90–86–86–77* ⊟ *MC, V* ⊗ *Closed Jan. and Sun.–Mon.*

¢–$ ✕ **Maison Nani.** Crowded inside and out with trendy young professionals, this pretty lunch spot serves stylish home cooking in generous portions without the fuss of multiple courses. Choose from heaping salads sizzling with fresh meat, enormous kebabs, and a creative quiche du jour. It's just off rue de la République. ⊠ *29 rue Théodore Aubanel* 🕾 *04–90–82–60–90* ⊟ *No credit cards* ⊗ *Closed Sun. No dinner Mon.–Thurs.*

★ **$$$$** ✕🖃 **Hôtel de la Mirande.** A designer's dream of a hotel, this *petit palais* permits you to step into 18th-century Avignon, thanks to painted coffered ceilings, sumptuous antiques, and other superb *grand siècle* touches (those rough sisal mats on the floors were the height of chic back in the Baroque era). The central lounge is a skylit and jazz-warmed haven. Upstairs, guest rooms are both gorgeous and comfy, with extraordinary baths and even more extraordinary handmade wall coverings. The costume-drama dining room provides an idyllic setting for the restaurant's sophisticated cuisine. Look for friendly Friday-night cooking classes from chef Jerome Verrière in the massive downstairs "country" kitchen. ⊠ *Pl. de la Mirande, 84000* 🕾 *04–90–85–93–93* 🖷 *04–90–86–26–85* ⊕ *www.la-mirande.fr* ↩ *19 rooms, 1 suite* ⌕ *Restaurant, minibars, cable TV, bar, Internet, meeting room, parking (fee), some pets allowed (fee)* ⊟ *AE, DC, MC, V* ⦿| *EP.*

$$$–$$$$ ✕🖃 **Hôtel d'Europe.** Once host to guests like Napoléon and Emperor Maximilian, this vine-covered 16th-century home is regally discreet and classic. In a walled court shaded by trees, the splendor continues inside with Aubusson tapestries, porcelains, and Provençal antiques. Guest rooms are mostly emperor-size, with two suites overlooking the Papal Palace. The highly acclaimed restaurant, La Vieille Fontaine, is certainly one of Avignon's finest; during the festival period, tables in the courtyard are highly coveted and are top places to preen while enjoying such delights as hot duck foie gras with peaches. ☒ *12 pl. Crillon, 84000* ☎ *04–90–14–76–76* 🖶 *04–90–14–76–71* ⊕ *www.hotel-d-europe.fr* ↩ *44 rooms* ⚭ *Restaurant, minibars, cable TV, Internet, meeting room, parking (fee), some pets allowed (fee)* ▭ *AE, DC, MC, V* �|⊙| *EP.*

$$–$$$ ▦ **Du Palais des Papes.** Despite its mere two-star rating, this is a remarkably solid, comfortable hotel, just off the place de Palais. With chic ironwork furniture and rich fabrics, the exposed-stone-and-beam decor fulfills fantasies of a medieval city—but one with good tile baths (top rooms include Nos. 10, 11, 12, 20, and 21). ☒ *1 rue Gérard-Philippe, 84000* ☎ *04–90–86–04–13* 🖶 *04–90–27–91–17* ⊕ *www.hotel-avignon.com* ↩ *26 rooms, 1 suite* ⚭ *Restaurant, minibars, cable TV, bar; no a/c in some rooms* ▭ *AE, DC, MC, V* �|⊙| *EP.*

★ $ ▦ **Hôtel du Blauvac.** Just off rue de la République and place de l'Horloge, this 17th-century nobleman's home has been lovingly decorated while keeping much of the original structures intact. Rooms have pristine exposed stonework, aged-oak details, and lovely tall windows; many of which, alas, look onto backstreet walls. Pretty fabrics and a warm, familial welcome more than compensate, however. ☒ *11 rue de la Bancasse, 84000* ☎ *04–90–86–34–11* 🖶 *04–90–86–27–41* ⊕ *www. hotel-blauvac.com* ↩ *16 rooms* ⚭ *Cable TV, Internet, free parking; no a/c* ▭ *AE, DC, MC, V* �|⊙| *EP.*

$ ▦ **Hôtel de Mons.** Tatty and almost intolerably eccentric, this is a neo-Gothic budget flophouse after Edward Gorey's own heart, first built as a 13th-century chapel. Transformation took some maneuvering, but guest rooms with baths (with '70s-style decor) have been fitted into crooked nooks and crannies, while retaining some period detail (slanting spiral stairs, quarried stone). Breakfast is served in a groin-vaulted crypt. Location is everything: it's two steps off place de l'Horloge. And it's dirt cheap. ☒ *5 rue de Mons, 84000* ☎ *04–90–82–57–16* 🖶 *04–90–85–19–15* ⊕ *www.hoteldemons.com* ↩ *11 rooms* ⚭ *Cable TV, some pets allowed; no a/c* ▭ *AE, MC, V* �|⊙| *EP.*

Nightlife & the Arts

Held annually in July, the Avignon festival, known officially as the **Festival Annuel d'Art Dramatique** (Annual Festival of Dramatic Art; ☎ 04–90–27–66–50 tickets and information) has brought the best of world theater to this ancient city since 1947. Some 300 productions take place every year; the main performances are at the Palais des Papes.

Within its fusty old medieval walls, Avignon teems with modern nightlife well into the wee hours. Having recently joined the masses near place Pie, **The Red Lion** (☒ 21 rue St-Jean-les-Vieux ☎ 04–90–86–40–25) serves Guinness, Stella, and Beck on tap and is hugely popular with students and the English-speaking crowd. At **AJMI** (Association Pour le Jazz et la Musique Improvisée; ☒ 4 rue Escaliers Ste-Anne ☎ 04–90–86–08–61), in La Manutention, you can hear live jazz acts of some renown. At the cabaret **Dolphin Blues** (✉ Chemin de L'île Piot ☎ 04–90–82–46–96), a hip mix of comedy and music dominates the repertoire, and there's children's theater as well. **Le Rouge Gorge** (✉ 10 bis rue Peyrollerie, behind palace ☎ 04–90–14–02–54) presents a dinner show and after-dinner dancing every Friday and Saturday night.

Shopping

Avignon has a cosmopolitan mix of French chains, youthful clothing shops (it's a college town), and a few plummy shops. **Rue St. Agricole** is where to find Parisian designers Lacroix and Hermès, and **rue des Marchands** off place Carnot is another, more mainstream shopping stretch. But **rue de la République** is the main artery, with chic street fashion names like Zara.

Pont du Gard

③⑤ *22 km (13 mi) southwest of Avignon, 37 km (23 mi) southwest of* Fodor'sChoice *Orange, 48 km (30 mi) north of Arles.*
★

No other architectural sight in Provence rivals the Pont du Gard, a mighty, three-tiered aqueduct nearly midway between Nîmes and Avignon. Erected some 2,000 years ago as part of a 48-km (30-mi) canal supplying water to the Roman settlement of Nîmes, it is astonishingly well preserved. In the early morning the site offers an amazing blend of natural and classical beauty—the rhythmic repetition of arches resonates with strength, bearing testimony to an engineering concept relatively new in the 1st century AD, when it was built under Emperor Claudius. Later in the day crowds become a problem, even off-season. At the visitor center, a film and a multimedia display detail the history of the aqueduct; in addition, there is a nifty children's area and an interactive exhibition about life in Roman times, archaeology, nature, and water. You can approach the aqueduct from either side of the Gardon River. If you choose the north side (Rive Gauche), the walk to the *pont* (bridge) is shorter and the views arguably better from here (and the tour buses seem to stay on the Rive Droite). Note there have been reports of break-ins in the parking area, so get a spot close to the booth. Although access to the spectacular walkway along the top of the aqueduct is now off-limits, the bridge itself is still a breathtaking experience. ✉ *Concession Pont-du-Gard* ☎ *04–66–37–50–99* 🏷 *€10, including parking* ☉ *Oct.–Apr., daily 10–6; May–Sept., daily 9:30–7.*

Châteauneuf-du-Pape

③⑥ *18 km (11 mi) north of Avignon, 23 km (14 mi) west of Carpentras.*

The countryside around this very famous wine center is a patchwork of rolling vineyards. Imposing gates and grand houses punctuate the scene, as symmetrical and finely detailed as the etching on a wine label, and signs beckon you to follow the omnipresent smell of fermenting grapes to its source.

Once the table wine of the Avignon popes, who kept a fortified summer house here (hence the name of the town, which means "new castle of the pope"), the vineyards of Châteauneuf-du-Pape had the good fortune to be wiped out by phylloxera in the 19th century—good in that its revival as a muscular and resilient mix of up to 13 varietals has moved it to the forefront of French wines. To learn more, stop in at the **Musée des Outils de Vignerons Père Anselme,** a private collection of tools and equipment displayed in the *caveau* (wine cellar) of the Brotte family. ⊠ *Rte. d'Avignon* ☎ *04–90–83-70–07* ⌕ *Free* ⊙ *Daily 9–noon and 2–6.*

If you're disinclined to spend your holiday sniffing and sipping in a dark basement, climb the hill to the ruins of the **Château.** Though it was destroyed in the Wars of Religion and its remaining donjon blasted by the Germans in World War II, it still commands magnificent views.

Where to Stay & Eat

$–$$ ✕ **Le Pistou.** This friendly little restaurant serves sophisticated cooking by a chef in love with things Provençal, from marketing to cooking all day to cheerfully writing his whims on the menu-cum-blackboard. A regular feature? The mouthwateringly delicious *soup au pistou.* The welcome is warm, and the fixed-price menus start at the low end of our price level. ⊠ *15 rue Joseph-Ducos* ☎ *04–90–83–71–75* ⌕ *Reservations essential* ▤ *MC, V* ⊙ *Apr.—Sept., closed Mon., no dinner Sun., no lunch Tues.; Oct.–Mar. closed Mon., no dinner weekends, no lunch Tues.*

$$ ✕▨ **La Garbure.** With eight rooms decked out in soft pastel ruffles and a low-price *menu terroir* (prix-fixe menu of regional specialties), this pretty inn aims to please. Look for potted quail in Carpentras truffles and stuffed rabbit with subtle thyme sauce (the restaurant is closed Sunday, October through June, and does not serve Sunday lunch in season, July–September). ⊠ *3 rue Joseph-Ducos, 84230* ☎ *04–90–83–75–08* 🖶 *04–90–83–52–34* ⊕ *www.la-garbure.com* ➪ *8 rooms* ⚬ *Restaurant, minibars, cable TV, some pets allowed* ▤ *MC, V* ⦿ *MAP.*

Orange

㊲ *10 km (6 mi) north of Châteauneuf-du-Pape, 31 km (19 mi) north of Avignon, 193 km (121 mi) south of Lyon.*

Even less touristy than Nîmes and just as eccentric, the city of Orange (pronounced oh-*rawnzh*) nonetheless draws thousands every year to its
★ spectacular **Théâtre Antique,** a colossal Roman theater built in the time of Caesar Augustus. Its vast stone stage wall, bouncing sound off the facing hillside, climbs four stories high, and the niche at center stage contains the original statue of Augustus, just as it reigned over centuries of productions of classical plays. Today this theater provides a backdrop for world-class theater and opera. ⊠ *Pl. des Frères-Mounet* ☎ *04–90–51–17–60* ⌕ *€7 with audio guide, includes entry to museum* ⊙ *Apr.–Sept., daily 9:30–6; Oct.–Mar., daily 9:30–noon and 1:30–5.*

Privitization required that the small Musée Municipal (Town Museum) change its name. As the **Espace Culturel** (Cultural Space), it is now a joint venture with the Théâtre Antique. A touristy boutique offers theatre figurines and books; the displays include antiquities unearthed around Orange, including three detailed marble *cadastres* (land survey maps) dating from the 1st century. Upstairs are Provençal fabrics manufactured in local mills in the 18th century and a collection of faïence pharmacy jars.

✉ *Pl. des Frères-Mounet* ☎ *04–90–51–18–24* ✆ *€7, joint ticket with theater* ☼ *Apr.–Sept., daily 9:30–6; Oct.–Mar., daily 9:30-noon and 1:30–5.*

North of the city center is the **Arc de Triomphe,** which once straddled the Via Agrippa between Lyon and Arles. Three arches support a heavy double attic (horizontal top) floridly decorated with battle scenes and marine symbols, references to Augustus's victories at Actium. The arch, which dates from about 20 BC, is superbly preserved, particularly the north side, but to view it on foot, you'll have to cross a roundabout seething with traffic. ✉ *North of center on av. de l'Arc, in direction of Gap.*

Where to Stay & Eat

$–$$ ✕ **La Yaka.** At this intimate, unpretentious bistro you are greeted by the beaming owner, who is also your host and waiter, then pampered with specialties that are emphatically *style grandmère* (like Grandma used to make: rabbit stew, *caillette,* or pork-liver meat loaf, and even canned peas with bacon). It's all served up in charming stone-and-beam rooms. ✉ *24 pl. Sylvain* ☎ *04–90–34–70–03* ▭ *MC, V* ☼ *Closed Wed. and Nov. No dinner Tues.*

$–$$$ ▦ **Arène.** On a quiet square in the Vieille Ville center, this comfortable old hotel has attentive owners and a labyrinth of rooms done in rich colors and heavy fabrics. The nicest ones look out over the square. As it's built of several fine old houses strung together, there's no elevator, but a multitude of stairways compensates. ✉ *Pl. de Langues, 84100* ☎ *04–90–11–40–40* ✆ *04–90–11–40–45* ⊕ *www.avignon-et-provence. com/hotel-arene* ⇖ *30 rooms* ⚙ *Minibars, cable TV, Internet, parking (fee), some pets allowed (no fee)* ▭ *AE, DC, MC* ✸ *EP.*

The Arts

Every July **Les Chorégies d'Orange** (☎ 04–90–34–24–24 ✆ 04–90–11–04–04 ♫ Chorégies, B.P. 205, Cedex, 84107 Orange) echo tradition and present operatic and classical music spectacles under the summer stars. Write for information well in advance.

Vaison-la-Romaine

㊳ *27 km (17 mi) northeast of Orange, 30 km (19 mi) northeast of Avignon.*

This ancient town thrives as a modern market center yet retains an irresistible Provençal charm, with medieval backstreets, lively squares lined with cafés, and, as its name implies, the remains of its Roman past. Vaison's well-established Celtic colony joined forces with Rome in the 2nd century BC and grew to powerful status in the empire's glory days. No gargantuan monuments were raised, yet the luxurious villas surpassed even those of Pompeii.

There are two broad fields of **Roman ruins,** both in the center of town: before you pay entry at either of the ticket booths, pick up a map (with English explanations) at the **Maison du Tourisme et des Vins** (☎ 04–90–36–02–11), which sits between them; it's open July and August, daily 9–12:30 and 2–6:45; September–June, Monday–Saturday 9–noon and 2–5:45. Like a tiny Roman forum, the **Maison des Messii** (Messii House) spreads over the field and hillside in the heart of town.

Its skeletal ruins of villas, landscaped gardens, and museum lie below the ancient theater, all of which are accessed next to the booth across from the tourist office. Closest to the entrance, the foundations of the Maison des Messii retain the outlines of its sumptuous design. A formal garden echoes a similar landscape of the time; wander under its cypresses and flowering shrubs to the **Musée Archéologique Théo-Desplans** (Théo-Desplans Archaeology Museum). In this streamlined venue the accoutrements of Roman life have been amassed and displayed by theme: pottery, weapons, representations of gods and goddesses, jewelry, and sculpture. Cross the park behind the museum to climb into the bleachers of the 1st-century **theater**, which is smaller than Orange's but is still used today for concerts and plays. Across the parking lot is the **Quartier de la Villasse,** where the remains of a lively market town evoke images of main-street shops, public gardens, and grand private homes, complete with floor mosaics. The most evocative image of all is in the area of the *thermes* (baths): a neat row of marble-seat toilets. In July and August guided nocturnal visits (€5, start 10 PM) are a must and come replete with eerie backlighting and clever narration. ⊠ *Av. Général-de-Gaulle at pl. du 11 Novembre* ☎ *04–90–36–02–11* ⊠ *Ruins, museum, and cloister €7; €5 each* ☉ *Museum June–Sept., daily 9:30–6; Mar.–May and Oct., daily 10–12:30 and 2:30–6; Nov.–Feb., daily 10–11:30 and 2–4. Villasse June–Sept., daily 9:30–noon and 2–6; Mar.–May and Oct., daily 10–12:30 and 2–6; Nov.–Feb., daily 10–noon and 2–4:30.*

Take the time to climb up into the **Haute Ville,** a medieval neighborhood perched high above the river valley. Its 13th- and 14th-century houses owe some of their beauty to stone pillaged from the Roman ruins below, but their charm is from the Middle Ages.

If you're in a medieval mood, stop into the sober Romanesque **Cathédrale Notre-Dame-de-Nazareth,** based on recycled fragments and foundations of a Gallo-Roman basilica. Its richly sculpted **cloister** is the key attraction. ⊠ *Av. Jules-Ferry* ☉ *June–Sept., daily 9:30–noon and 2–5:30; Mar.–May and Oct., daily 10–noon and 2–5:30; Nov.–Feb., daily 10–noon and 2–4.*

One last highlight: the remarkable single-arch **Pont Romain** (Roman Bridge), built in the 1st century, stands firm across the Ouvèze River.

While Vaison has centuries-old attractions, the most popular for Americans may well now be **Patricia Wells's Cooking Classes.** A living monument of Provence, the celebrated food critic first made her name known through posh food columns and *The Food Lover's Guide to France.* Firsthand, she now introduces people to the splendors of French cooking in her lovely farmhouse near Vaison through week-long cooking seminars—luxe ($3,000 a student), eight students only, and set over Madame Wells's own Chanteduc vineyards. The truffle workshop is usually sold out, so book early. ⊕ *www.patriciawells.com.*

Where to Stay & Eat

$$$$ ✕ **Le Moulin à Huile.** Innovative chef Robert Bardot shows off his superb culinary talents by mixing creative regional cuisine with a touch of the exotic—top creations include the veal marinated in spiced milk, ginger, and cloves, or the unusual roasted peach with strawberry coulis. His impressive prix-fixe menus are served in an old, beautifully restored *moulin* (mill) by the Pont Romain, with a lovely garden terrace and a fairly spectacular view over the old city. ✉ *Rte. de Malaucene* ☎ *04–90–36–20–67* ⊟ *AE, MC, V* ⊗ *Closed Mon. No dinner Sun.*

★ **$$–$$$$** ✕⌂ **Le Beffroi.** Crowned with a centuries-old stone clock tower and set on a clifftop in the Vieille Ville, this elegant grouping of 16th-century homes makes a fine little hotel. The extravagant salon decked out in period style leads to the sizable rooms with beams and antiques; the big corner rooms have breathtaking views. From April through October, dine on local specialties under the fig tree in the intimate enclosed garden court. The hotel restaurant, La Fontaine, has real flair—as one taste of their fois gras ravioli or duck filled in lavender honey will prove. By day you can enjoy a simple salad on the garden terrace or take a dip in the rooftop pool. Meal plans are available only with a two-night minimum stay. ✉ *Rue de l'Évêché, 84110* ☎ *04–90–36–04–71* 🖨 *04–90–36–24–78* ⊕ *www.le-beffroi.com* ⇌ *22 rooms* ⚘ *Restaurant, minibars, cable TV, pool, some pets allowed (fee); no a/c* ⊟ *AE, DC, MC, V* ⊗ *Closed mid-Feb.–mid-Mar.* ⧖ *MAP.*

$–$$ ⌂ **Évêché.** In the medieval part of town, this turreted 16th-century former bishop's palace has just four small rooms. The warm welcome and rustic charm—delicate fabrics, exposed beams, wooden bedsteads—have garnered a loyal following among travelers who prefer B&B character over modern luxury. Room rates include breakfast. ✉ *Rue de l'Évêché, 84110* ☎ *04–90–36–13–46* 🖨 *04–90–36–32–43* ⊕ *eveche.free.fr* ⇌ *4 rooms, 1 suite* ⚘ *Some pets allowed (no fee)* ⊟ *No credit cards* ⧖ *BP.*

Le Barroux

❸9 16 km (10 mi) south of Vaison-la-Romaine, 34 km (21 mi) northeast
Fodor'sChoice of Avignon.
★

Of all the marvelous hilltop villages stretching across the south of France, this tiny ziggurat of a town may be unique: it's 100% boutique-and-gallery-free and has only one tiny old *épicerie* (small grocery) selling canned goods, yellowed postcards, and today's *Le Provençal*. You are forced, therefore, to look around you and listen to the trickle of the ancient fountains at every labyrinthine turn. The **château** is its main draw, though its perfect condition reflects a complete restoration after a World War II fire. Grand vaulted rooms and a chapel date from the 12th century, and other halls serve as venues for contemporary art exhibits. ☎ *04–90–62–35–21* ⛁ *€3.50* ⊗ *Apr.–June, weekends 10–7; July–Sept., daily 10–7; Oct., daily 2–6.*

Where to Stay & Eat

¢–$ ✕⌂ **Les Géraniums.** Though it has simple, pretty rooms, many with views sweeping down to the valley, this family-run auberge emphasizes its restaurant. A broad garden terrace stretches along the cliffside, where you can sample herb-roasted rabbit, a truffle omelet, and local cheeses. New rooms in the annex across the street take in panoramic views, and half-pension is strongly encouraged. ✉ *Pl. de la Croix, 84330* ☎ *04–90–62–41–08* 🖨 *04–90–62–56–48* ⇌ *22 rooms* ⚘ *Restaurant, bar, some pets allowed (fee)* ⊟ *AE, DC, MC, V* ⊗ *Closed mid-Nov.–mid-Mar.* ⧖ *MAP.*

Crillon le Brave

40 *12 km (7 mi) south of Malaucène (via Caromb), 21 km (13 mi) south-east of Vaison-la-Romaine.*

The main reason to come to this tiny village, named after France's most notable soldier-hero of the 16th century, is to stay or dine at its hotel, the Hostellerie de Crillon le Brave. But it's also pleasant—perched on a knoll in a valley shielded by Mont Ventoux, with the craggy hills of the Dentelles in one direction and the hills of the Luberon in another. Today the village still doesn't have even a *boulangerie* (bakery), let alone a souvenir boutique.

Where to Stay & Eat

$$$–$$$$ ✕⊡ **Hostellerie de Crillon le Brave.** The views from the interconnected hilltop houses of this Relais & Châteaux property are as elevated as its prices, but for this you get a rarefied stage-set of medieval luxury. A cozy-chic southern touch informs book-filled salons and brocante-trimmed guest rooms, some with terraces looking out onto infinity. In the stone-vaulted dining room, stylish French cuisine is served. Wine tastings and regional discovery packages encourage longer stays. ⊠ *Pl. de l'Église, 84410* ☎ *04–90–65–61–61* 🖶 *04–90–65–62–86* ⊕ *www.crillonlebrave. com* ⤳ *31 rooms* ⚭ *Restaurant, minibars, cable TV, tennis court, pool, massage, baby-sitting, Internet, parking (no fee), pets (fee); no a/c in some rooms* ▤ *AE, DC, MC, V* ☉ *Closed Jan.–mid-Mar.* ⑩ *EP.*

L'Isle-sur-la-Sorgue

41 *18 km (11 mi) south of Malaucène, 41 km (25 mi) southeast of Orange,*
Fodor'sChoice
★ *26 km (16 mi) east of Avignon.*

Crisscrossed with lazy canals and alive with moss-covered waterwheels that once drove its silk, wool, and paper mills, this old valley town retains a gentle appeal—except, that is, on Sunday, when it transforms itself into a Marrakech of marketeers, its streets crammed with antiques and brocantes, its cafés swelling with crowds of bargain seekers making a day of it. There are also street musicians, food stands groaning under mounds of rustic breads, vats of tapenade, and cloth-lined baskets of spices, and miles of café tables offering ringside seats to the spectacle. On a non-market day life returns to its mellow pace, with plenty of antiques dealers open year-round, as well as fabric and interior design shops, bookstores, and food stores for you to explore. The token sight to see is L'Isle's 17th-century church, the **Collégiale Notre-Dame-des-Anges,** extravagantly decorated with gilt, faux marble, and sentimental frescoes. Its double-colonnaded facade commands the center of the Vieille Ville.

Where to Stay & Eat

$$$–$$$$ ✕ **La Prévôté.** With all the money you saved bargaining on that chipped Quimper vase, splurge on lunch at this discreet, pristine spot hidden off a backstreet courtyard. The cuisine has won top awards for chef Roland Mercier—try his cannelloni stuffed with salmon and goat cheese, or tender duckling with lavender honey. The prix-fixe menus start at €25 and top out at €60. ⊠ *4 bis rue Jean-Jacques-Rousseau* ☎ *04–90–38–57–29*

⚛ *Reservations essential* ▤ *MC, V* ☉ *Closed Tues. and Wed. in Dec.–June. No dinner Wed. in July and Aug.*

$$ ✕ **Lou Nego Chin.** In winter you sit shoulder to shoulder in the cramped but atmospheric dining room (chinoiserie linens, brightly hued tiles), but in summer tables are strewn across the quiet street, on a wooden deck along the river. Ask for a spot at the edge so you can watch the ducks play, then order the inexpensive house wine and the menu du jour, often a hearty omelette Provençal, goat-cheese salad, or a good, garlicky stew. ⊠ *12 quai Jean Jaurès* ☎ *04–90–20–88–03* ⚛ *Reservations essential* ▤ *DC, MC, V* ☉ *Closed Wed. No dinner Tues. in Oct.–Apr.*

★ **$$** ✕⊡ **Le Mas de Cure-Bourse.** This graceful old 18th-century post-coach stop is well outside the fray, snugly hedge-bound in the countryside amid 6 acres of fruit trees and fields. Rooms are freshly decked out in Provençal prints and painted country furniture. You can be served sophisticated home cooking with a local touch. Half-pension is strongly encouraged, although the restaurant is closed Monday, and lunch is not served Tuesday. ⊠ *Rte. de Caumont, 84800* ☎ *04–90–38–16–58* 🖷 *04–90–38–52–31* ↩ *13 rooms* ⚙ *Restaurant, pool, free parking; no a/c* ▤ *MC, V* ☉ *Closed 1st 3 wks in Nov., 1st 2 wks in Jan.* ⎚❙ *MAP.*

$ ✕⊡ **La Gueulardière.** After a Sunday glut of antiquing along the canals, you can dine and sleep just up the street in a hotel full of collectible finds, from the school posters in the restaurant to the oak armoires and brass beds that furnish the simple lodgings. Each room has French windows that open onto the enclosed garden courtyard, where you can enjoy a private breakfast in the shade. ⊠ *1 cours René Char, 84800* ☎ *04–90–38–10–52* 🖷 *04–90–20–83–70* ↩ *5 rooms* ⚙ *Restaurant, parking (no fee), pets (no fee); no a/c* ▤ *AE, MC, V* ☉ *Closed mid-Dec.–mid-Jan.* ⎚❙ *EP.*

Shopping

Of the dozens of antiques shops in L'Isle, one conglomerate concentrates some 40 dealers under the same roof: **L'Isle aux Brocantes** (⊠ 7 av. des Quatre Otages ☎ 04–90–20–69–93); it's open Saturday–Monday. Higher-end antiques are concentrated next door at the twin shops of **Xavier Nicod et Gérard Nicod** (⊠ 9 av. des Quatre Otages ☎ 04–90–38–35–50 or 04–90–38–07–20). **Maria Giancatarina** (⊠ 4 av. Julien Guigue, across from train station ☎ 04–90–38–58–02) showcases beautifully restored linens, including *boutis* (Provençal quilts). The famous **L'Isle-sur-la-Sorgue Sunday morning flea market** takes place from the Place Gambetta up the length of Avenue des Quatre Otages.

Fontaine-de-Vaucluse

㊷ *8 km (5 mi) east of L'Isle-sur-la-Sorgue, 33 km (20 mi) east of Avignon.*

★ The **Fontaine de Vaucluse,** for which the town is named, is a strange and beautiful natural phenomenon that has been turned into a charming, albeit slightly tacky, tourist center—like a tiny Niagara Falls—and should not be missed if you're either a connoisseur of rushing water or a fan of foreign kitsch. There's no exaggerating the magnificence of the *fontaine* itself, a mysterious spring that gushes from a deep underground source that has been explored to a depth of 1,010 feet . . . so far. Framed by towering cliffs, a broad, pure pool wells up and spews dramatically over massive rocks down a gorge to the village, where its roar soothes and cools the tourists who crowd the riverfront cafés. You must pay to park and then run a gauntlet of souvenir shops and tourist traps on your way to the top. But even if you plan to make a beeline past the kitsch, do stop in at the legitimate and informative **Moulin Vallis-Clausa**. A working paper mill, it demonstrates a reconstructed 15th-century waterwheel that drives timber crankshafts to mix rag pulp, while artisans roll and dry thick paper *à l'ancienne* (in the old manner). ☎ *04–90–20–34–14* ✆ *Sept.–June, daily 9–noon and 2–5:30; July and Aug., daily 9–7:30.*

Fontaine has its own ruined **château,** perched romantically on a forested hilltop over the town and illuminated at night. First built around the year 1000 and embellished in the 13th century by the bishops of Cavaillon, it was destroyed in the 15th century and now forms little more than a saw-tooth silhouette against the sky.

The Renaissance poet Petrarch, driven mad with unrequited love for a beautiful married woman named Laura, retreated to this valley to nurse his passion in a cabin with "one dog and only two servants." Sixteen years in this wild isolation didn't ease the pain, but the serene landscape inspired him to poetry. The small **Musée de Fontaine de Vaucluse Pétrarch,** built on the site of his stay, displays prints and engravings of the virtuous lovers. ☎ *04–90–20–37–20* 🎫 *€3.50* ✆ *Apr. and May, Wed.–Mon. 10–noon and 2–6; June–Sept., Wed.–Mon. 10–12:30 and 1:30–6; Oct., weekends 10–noon and 2–5.*

Where to Stay & Eat

$ ✕🏨 **Le Parc.** In a spectacular riverside locale in the shadow of the ruined château, this solid old hotel has basic, comfortable rooms (whitewashed stucco, all-weather carpet) with clean bathrooms and no creaks; five of them offer river views. The restaurant (closed Wednesday) spreads along the river in a pretty park, with tables shaded by trellises heavy with grapes and trumpet vine. Moderately priced daily menus include river-fresh salmon. ⊠ *Rue de Bourgades, 84800* ☎ *04–90–20–31–57* 📠 *04–90–20–27–03* ➾ *12 rooms* ⚭ *Restaurant, some pets allowed (fee); no a/c* ☰ *AE, DC, MC, V* ✆ *Nov.–mid-Feb.* ¶◎¶ *MAP.*

en route Gordes is only a short distance from Fontaine de Vaucluse, but you need to wind your way south, east, and then north on D100A, D100, D2, and D15 to skirt the impassable hillside. It's a lovely drive through dry, rocky country covered with wild lavender and scrub oak and may tempt you to a picnic or a walk.

Gordes

43

Fodor'sChoice
★

16 km (10 mi) southeast of Fontaine-de-Vaucluse, 35 km (22 mi) east of Avignon.

Gordes was once merely an unspoiled hilltop village; it's now a famous unspoiled hilltop village surrounded by luxury vacation homes, modern hotels, restaurants, and B&Bs. No matter: the ancient stone village still rises above the valley in painterly hues of honey gold, and its mosaiclike cobbled streets—lined with boutiques, galleries, and real-estate offices—still wind steep and narrow to its Renaissance château—making this certainly one of the most beautiful and picturesque towns in Provence. The only way to see the interior of the **château** is to view its ghastly collection of photo paintings by pop artist Pol Mara, who lived in Gordes. It's worth the price of admission to look at the fabulously decorated stone fireplace, created in 1541. ☎ *04–90–72–02–75* ☜ *€4.00* ☉ *Daily 10–noon and 2–6.*

Just outside Gordes, on a lane heading north from D2, follow signs to the **Village des Bories.** Found throughout this region of Provence, the bizarre and fascinating little stone hovels called *bories* are concentrated some 20 strong in an ancient community. Their origins are provocatively vague: built as shepherds' shelters with tight-fitting, mortarless stone in a hivelike form, they may date to the Celts, the Ligurians, even the Iron Age—and were inhabited or used for sheep through the 18th century. ☎ *04–90–72–03–48* ☜ *€5.50* ☉ *Daily 9–sunset or 8, whichever comes 1st.*

If you've dreamed of Provence's famed lavender fields, head to a wild valley some 4 km (2½ mi) north of Gordes (via D177) to find the beau-
★ tiful 12th-century Romanesque **Abbaye de Sénanque,** which floats above a redolent sea of lavender (in full bloom in July and August). Begun in 1150 and completed at the dawn of the 13th century, the **church** and adjoining **cloister** are without decoration, but still touch the soul with their chaste beauty. In this orbit, the graystone buildings seem to have special resonance—ancient, organic, with a bit of the borie about it. Next door, the enormous vaulted **dormitory** contains an exhibition on the abbey's construction, and the **refectory** shelters a display on the history of Cistercian abbeys. ☎ *04–90–72–05–72* ☜ *€4.75* ☉ *Mar.–Oct., Mon.–Sat. 10–noon and 2–6, Sun. 2–6; Nov.–Feb., weekdays 2–5, weekends 2–6.*

Where to Stay & Eat

$$–$$$ ✕ **Le Comptoir du Victuailler.** Across from the château, this tiny but deluxe bistro entices with daily *aioli,* a smorgasbord of fresh cod and lightly steamed vegetables crowned with the garlic mayonnaise. Evenings are reserved for intimate, formal indoor meals à la carte—roast Luberon lamb, beef with truffle sauce. The '30s-style bistro tables and architectural lines are a relief from Gordes's ubiquitous rustic-chic. ⊠ *Pl. du Château* ☎ *04–90–72–01–31* ⌑ *Reservations essential* ▤ *MC, V* ☉ *Closed Wed., Sept.–May. No dinner Tues., mid-Jan.–Easter. Closed mid-Nov.–mid-Dec.*

$$$ ✕⌑ **Le Ferme de la Huppe.** This 17th-century stone farmhouse with a well in the courtyard, a swimming pool in the garden, and rooms with pretty prints and secondhand finds is in the countryside outside Gordes. Dine poolside on three styles of roast lamb, prepared by the proprietors' son, Gerald Konings, but reserve ahead: the restaurant (closed Thursday) is as popular as the hotel. Meal plans are available with a minimum stay of three nights. ⊠ *Les Pourquiers, 3 km (2 mi) east of Gordes, R.D.156, 84220* ☎ *04–90–72–12–25* 🖷 *04–90–72–01–83* ⊕ *www.*

laprovence.com/lahuppe ⇨ *9 rooms* ♂ *Restaurant, pool, pets (fee); no a/c in some rooms* ▭ *MC, V* ⊙ *Closed end Nov.–mid-Mar.* 🍽 *MAP.*

$$$–$$$$ 🏨 **Domaine de l'Enclos.** This cluster of private stone cottages has newly laid antique tiles and fresh faux-patinas that keep it looking fashionably old. There are panoramic views and a pool, baby-sitting services and swing sets, and an aura that is surprisingly warm and familial for an inn of this sophistication. ✉ *Rte. de Sénanque, 84220* ☎ *04–90–72–71–00* 🖷 *04–90–72–03–03* 🌐 *www.domaine-enclos.com* ⇨ *12 rooms, 5 apartments* ♂ *Restaurant, minibars, cable TV, tennis court, pool, some pets allowed (fee)* ▭ *AE, MC, V* 🍽 *MAP.*

$$$–$$$$ 🏨 **Les Romarins.** At this small hilltop inn on the outskirts of Gordes you can gaze at the town across the valley while having breakfast on a sheltered terrace in the morning sun. Rooms are clean, well lighted, and feel spacious—ask for either No. 1, in the main building, from whose white-curtained windows you can see forever, or the room with a terrace in the atelier. Oriental rugs, antique furniture, and a pool add to your contentment. ✉ *Rte. de Sénanque, 84220* ☎ *04–90–72–12–13* 🖷 *04–90–72–13–13* 🌐 *www.hoteldesromarins.com* ⇨ *13 rooms* ♂ *Minibars, cable TV, pool, some pets allowed (fee)* ▭ *AE, MC, V* 🍽 *EP.*

Roussillon

㊹ *10 km (6 mi) east of Gordes, 45 km (28 mi) east of Avignon.*

Fodor's Choice ★

In shades of deep rose and russet, this quintessential and gorgeous hilltop cluster of houses blends into the red-ocher cliffs from which its stone was quarried. The ensemble of buildings and jagged, hand-cut slopes is equally dramatic, and views from the top look out over a landscape of artfully eroded bluffs that Georgia O'Keeffe would have loved. Unlike neighboring hill villages, there's little of historic architectural detail here; the pleasure of a visit lies in the richly varied colors that change with the light of day, and in the views of the contrasting countryside, where dense-shadowed greenery sets off the red stone with Cézanne-esque severity. There are pleasant *placettes* (tiny squares) to linger in nonetheless, and a Renaissance fortress tower crowned with a clock in the 19th century; just past it, you can take in expansive panoramas of forest and ocher cliffs.

The area's famous vein of natural ocher, which spreads some 25 km (15 mi) along the foot of the Vaucluse plateau, has been mined for centuries, beginning with the ancient Romans, who used it for their pottery. You can visit the old **Usine Mathieu de Roussillon** (Roussillon's Mathieu Ochre Works) to learn more about ocher's extraction and its modern uses. There are explanatory exhibits, ocher powders for sale, and guided tours in English on advance request. ✉ *On D104 southeast of town* ☎ *04–90–05–66–69* ⊙ *Mar.–Nov., daily 10–7.*

From Rousillon's reds it is a drive of some 40 km (25 mi) west to discover the epicenter of Haute-Provence's fabled lavender in the sleepy, dusty town of Forcalquier. In the 12th century, this was known as the capital city of Haute-Provence and was called the *Cité des Quatre Reines* ("the City of the Four Queens") since the four daughters of the ruler of this region, Raimond Béranger V (Eleanor of Aquitaine among

THE LAVENDER ROUTE

UNPREPOSSESSING, FRAGRANT, AND **TINY**, this flower not only enchants all who behold it but manages to bring in big tourist dollars along la "Route de la Lavande" (the Lavender Route), a wide blue-purple swath that connects over 2,000 producers across the Drôme, the plateau du Vaucluse, and the Alpes-de-Haute-Provence.

Once described as the "soul of Haute-Provence," lavender has colored the high plains and brought prosperity and clean smells to village life since the Middle Ages. The word itself comes from Latin lavare, which means "to wash"; since its discovery in ancient, unrecorded times, it has been indiscriminately used for anything from perfume to cleansers to tonics for the prevention of freckles.

And for good reason: today's trend for natural remedies has proven its innate properties and given it well-deserved recognition. Not only a disinfectant, a calmative against stress, preventative for migraines and sunburn, and effective in treating rheumatism and vertigo, lavender also smells good. Stylish body care product producers like the Body Shop and Occitane were quick to catch on and perfumers Dior and Gautier soon followed suit.

Today, there are literally hundreds of beauty products that use some form of lavender or lavender essence, and consumers are madly buying. They are also—when visiting the Côte d'Azur and Provence—madly frolicking through the fields.

To do so yourself, go in season, June to early September (although the harvest doesn't start until July). **L'Association des Routes de la Lavande** (☎ 04–75–26–65–91 ⊕ www.routes-lavande.com) has itineraries that zigzag across the range. And the range is quite

large: broken up into six main regions, they comprise the Vallée de la Drôme et Diois; the Drôme Provençal; the Pays de Sault, Mont Ventoux, and Luberon; the Pays du Buëch; the Pays de Forcalquier and Montagne de Lure; and the Pays de Digne, from the Plateau de Valensole to Verdon. All through this area there are countless events, hikes, and workshops, featuring everything from touring with a donkey to seminars on "blue gold" and lavender honey.

The very popular **Moulin de Savoirs** (☎ 04–75–28–15–94) has guided walks through the fields in the Drôme Provençal and runs workshops about lavender, its properties, and its essential oil. You can buy wine and lavender products at the famed **Ferme Lavanicole Chateau du Bois** (✉ Les Espagnols, Largarde d'Apt ☎ 04–90–76–91–23). Finally, see lavender distilled at the **Distillerie "Lavande 1100"** (✉ D34 between Sault and Apt ☎ 04–90–75–01–42).

The most generous patches of color are along the edge of Mont Ventoux, near Forcalquier, and the plateau de Valensole. Here, the fields are simply glorious. Arranged in nodding little rows, the lavender seems to stripe the landscape, maturing from baby blue to deep mauve amidst a haze of bees. A walk or a bicycle ride—in season—is like being transported into a magical world, one usually only found on a picture-perfect postcard.

them), all married royals. Relics of this former glory can be glimpsed in the Vieille Ville of Forcalquier, notably its Cathdédrale Notre-Dame and the Couvent des Cordeliers. However, everyone heads here to marvel at

Fodor's Choice
★ the **lavender fields of Forcalquier,** which burst into bloom with *Lavandula vera,* true wild lavender, during the last two weeks of July only. Contact the Forcalquier's tourist office (⊠ 13 place Bourguet ☎ 04–92–75–25–30 ⊕ www.forcalquier.com) for information on all things lavender, then get saddled up on a bicycle for a trip into the countryside at the town's Moulin de Sarret. If you wish to enjoy a fine meal and reserve (way in advance) a room, contact the town's most historic inn, the **Hostellerie des Deux Lions** (⊠ 11 pl. du Bourguet ☎ 04–92–75–25–30). For a workshop on lavender, meet **Monique Claessens** (☎ 04–92–73–06–76), located in the village of Mane, but found often at her stand in the vibrant Monday market (8 AM–noon) in Forcalquier. For routes through the fields, contact **Les Routes de la Lavande** ⊠ *2 av. de Venterol, 26111 Nyons* ☎ *04–75–26–65–91* 🖷 *04–75–26–32–67.*

Where to Stay & Eat

★ **\$\$\$** ✕⌑ **Mas de Garrigon.** An exquisite hotel, tastefully decorated in classic Provençal style, the Garrigon has spacious rooms, a cozy library, and views of the surrounding ocher cliffs. It also showcases the best restaurant (by far) in Roussillon—which is a good thing, as the management takes it very personally if you pass on their demi-pension offer. So don't: the food is superb—monkfish in salt crust, straw-baked lamb with rosemary jus, inventive vegetable courses, plus wonderful desserts—and the family welcome is warm and genuine. ⊠ *Rte. de St-Saturnin-d'Apt, 3 km (2 mi) north on the D2, 84220* ☎ *04–90–05–63–92* 🖷 *04–90–05–70–01* ⊕ *www.masdegarrigon-provence.com* ⇆ *8 rooms, 1 suite* △ *Cable TV, pool, free parking; no pets* ⊟ *AE, DC, MC, V* ⃝I *MAP.*

\$\$ ⌑ **Ma Maison.** In the valley 4 km (2½ mi) below Roussillon, this isolated 1850 mas has been infused with a laid-back, cosmopolitan style by its artist-owners. Wicker-backed chairs mix with oriental rugs, wrought iron, and fluffy white bedspreads. There's a big saltwater pool, a massive country kitchen, and an idyllic garden complete with lovely breakfast tables romantically set under sprawling, shady branches. Breakfast is included. ⊠ *Quartier Les Devens, 84220* ☎ *04–90–05–74–17* 🖷 *04–90–05–74–63* ⊕ *www.mamaison-provence.com* ⇆ *3 rooms, 2 suites* △ *Pool, some pets allowed (fee); no a/c* ⊟ *MC, V* ⊘ *Closed mid-Oct.–mid-Mar.* ⃝I *BP.*

Oppède-le-Vieux

❹ *25 km (15 mi) southeast of Avignon, 15 km (9 mi) southwest of Gordes.*

Follow signs toward Oppède; you'll occasionally be required to follow signs for Oppède-le-Village, but your goal will be marked with the symbol of *monuments historiques:* Oppède-le-Vieux. A Byronesque tumble of ruins arranged against an overgrown rocky hillside, Oppède's charm—or part of it—lies in its preservation. Taken over by writers and artists who have chosen to live here and restore but not develop it, the village has a café or two but little else. Bring a lunch, wander, and contemplate. Cross the village square, pass through the old city gate, and climb up steep trails past restored houses to the church known as **Notre-Dame-d'Alydon**. First built in the 13th century, its blunt buttresses were framed into side chapels in the 16th century; you can still see the points of stoned-in Gothic windows above. The marvelous hexagonal bell tower sprouts a lean, mean gargoyle from each angle. It once served as part of the village's fortifications. Head left past the cliff-edge wall, plunge into the rock tunnel, and clamber up to the ruins of the **château**, built in the 13th century and then transformed in the 15th century. From the left side of its great square tower, look down into the dense fir forests of the Luberon's north face.

Ménerbes

46 *5 km (3 mi) east of Oppède-le-Vieux, 30 km (19 mi) southeast of Avignon.*

The town of Ménerbes clings to a long, thin hilltop over this sought-after valley, looming over the surrounding forests like a great stone ship. At its prow juts the **Castellet,** a 15th-century fortress. At its stern looms the 13th-century **Citadelle.** These redoubtable fortifications served the Protestants well during the Wars of Religion—until the Catholics wore them down with a 15-month siege. A campanile tops the Hôtel de Ville (Town Hall) on pretty **place de l'Horloge** (Clock Square), where you can admire the delicate stonework on the arched portal and mullioned windows of a Renaissance house. Just past the tower on the right is an overlook taking in views toward Gordes, Roussillon, and Mont Ventoux.

But what you really came to see is **Peter Mayle's house,** right? Do its current owners a favor and give it a wide berth: after years of tour buses spilling the curious into the private driveway to crane their necks and snap pictures, the heirs to the stone picnic table, the pool, and Faustin's grapevines wish the books had never been written. And besides, Peter Mayle has moved to Lourmarin now, on the other side of the mountain. Do leave these folk in peace.

Seven kilometers (4 mi) east of Ménerbes is the eagle's-nest village of Lacoste, presided over by the once magnificent Château de Sade, erstwhile retreat to the notorious Marquis de Sade (1740–1814) when he wasn't on the run from authorities. For some years, the wealthy Paris couturier Pierre Cardin has been restoring the castle wall by wall and under his generous patronage the **Festival Lacoste** takes place here throughout the months of July and August. A lyric, musical, and theatrical extravaganza, events (and their dates) change yearly, ranging from outdoor poetry recitals to ballet to colorful operettas. ⊠ *Carrières du Château, Lacoste* ☎ *04–90–75–93–12* ⊕ *www.lacoste.easyclassic.com* 🎫 *€20–€140.*

Where to Stay

★ $$$ 🏨 **Hostellerie Le Roy Soleil.** In the imposing shadow of the Luberon, this luxurious country inn has pulled out all stops on comfort and decor: marble and granite bathrooms, wrought-iron beds, and coordinated fabrics. But the integrity of its 17th-century building, with thick stone walls and groin vaults and beams, redeems it just short of pretentiousness and makes it a lovely place to escape to. ⊠ *Rte. des Beaumettes, 84560* ☎ *04–90–72–25–61* 🖶 *04–90–72–36–55* ⊕ *www.roy-soleil.*

com ✑ *10 rooms, 9 suites* ⚭ *Restaurant, minibars, cable TV, tennis court, pool, bar, free parking, pets (fee)* ⊟ *AE, MC, V* ⊘ *Closed Nov.–mid-Mar.* ⦿ *FAP.*

Bonnieux

★ ❹ *11 km (7 mi) south of Roussillon, 45 km (28 mi) north of Aix-en-Provence.*

The most impressive of the Luberon's hilltop villages, Bonnieux rises out of the arid hills in a jumble of honey-color cubes that change color subtly as the day progresses. The village is wrapped in crumbling ramparts and dug into bedrock and cliff. Most of its sharply raked streets take in wide-angle valley views, though you'll get the best view from the pine-shaded grounds of the 12th-century church, reached by stone steps that wind past tiny niche houses.

Where to Stay & Eat

★ **$$–$$$** ✕ **Auberge de la Loube.** The chef's inclusion in a Peter Mayle book hasn't gone to his toque: for simple, unpretentious Provençal food perfectly prepared, nothing beats this idyllic little restaurant in the neighboring hamlet of Buoux. Meals are served on a covered terrace out back. The gargantuan starters are famous and fabulous, as are house specialties like scrambled eggs with truffles and roasted leg of lamb. Sunday lunch is a feast worthy of Pagnol. ⊠ *Quartier la Loube–Buoux* ☎ *04–90–74–19–58* 🖷 *04–90–74–19–58* ⚭ *Reservations essential* ⊟ *No credit cards* ⊘ *Closed Wed. and Thurs.; Jan.*

$$–$$$$ ✕ **Le Fournil.** In an old bakery in a natural grotto deep in stone, lighted by candles and arty torchères, this restaurant would be memorable even without its trendy look and stylishly presented Provençal cuisine. Try the adventurous dishes such as the crisped pigs'-feet *galette* (patty) and check out the informed wine list. ⊠ *5 pl. Carnot* ☎ *04–90–75–83–62* 🖷 *04–90–75–96–19* ⚭ *Reservations essential* ⊟ *MC, V* ⊘ *Closed Mon. and Tues.; Dec. and Jan.*

★ **$$–$$$** ▦ **Hostellerie du Prieuré.** Not every hotel has its own private chapel, but this gracious inn occupies an 18th-century abbey, right in the village center. A pleasantly warm glow quietly surrounds you from the firelit salon to the dining room burnished with Roussillon ocher. Summer meals and breakfasts are served in the enclosed garden oasis. Rooms have plush carpets and antiques. The Coutaz family has been in the hotel business since Napoléon III, and it shows. ⊠ *In center of village, 84480* ☎ *04–90–75–80–78* 🖷 *04–90–75–96–00* ⊕ *www.esprit-de-france.com* ✑ *10 rooms* ⚭ *Restaurant, tennis court, free parking, some pets allowed (fee); no a/c* ⊟ *MC, V* ⊘ *Closed Nov.–Feb.* ⦿ *FAP, MAP.*

★ **$$** ▦ **Le Clos du Buis.** At this B&B, whitewash and quarry tiles, lovely tiled baths, and carefully juxtaposed antiques create a regional look in the guest rooms. Public spaces, with scrubbed floorboards, a fireplace, and exposed stone, are free for your use around the clock. It even has a pool and a pretty garden, and it's all overlooking the valley from the village center. ⊠ *Rue Victor Hugo, 84480* ☎ *04–90–75–88–48* 🖷 *04–90–75–88–57* ⊕ *www.leclosdubuis.com* ✑ *7 rooms* ⚭ *Pool, free parking, some pets allowed (fee); no a/c* ⊟ *MC, V* ⊘ *Closed mid-Nov.–mid-Dec. and mid-Jan.–mid-Feb.* ⦿ *BP.*

AIX-EN-PROVENCE & THE MEDITERRANEAN COAST

The southeastern part of this area of Provence, on the edge of the Côte d'Azur, is dominated by two major towns: Aix-en-Provence, considered the main hub of Provence and the most cultural town in the region; and Marseille, a vibrant port town that combines seediness with fashion and metropolitan feistiness with classical grace. For a breathtaking experience of the dramatic contrast between the azure Mediterranean sea and the rocky, olive tree–filled hills, take a trip along the coast east of Marseille and make an excursion to the Iles d'Hyères.

Aix-en-Provence

★ *48 km (29 mi) southeast of Bonnieux, 82 km (51 mi) southeast of Avignon, 176 km (109 mi) west of Nice, 759 km (474 mi) south of Paris.*

Gracious, cultivated, and made all the more cosmopolitan by the presence of some 30,000 international university students, the lovely old town of Aix (pronounced *ex*) was once the capital of Provence. The vestiges of that influence and power—fine art, noble architecture, and graceful urban design—remain beautifully preserved today. That and its thriving market, vibrant café life, and world-class music festival make Aix vie with Arles and Avignon as one of the towns in Provence that shouldn't be missed.

The Romans were first drawn here by mild thermal baths, naming the town Aquae Sextiae (Waters of Sextius) in honor of the consul who founded a camp near the source in 123 BC. Just 20 years later some 200,000 Germanic invaders besieged Aix, but the great Roman general Marius flanked them and pinned them against the mountain known ever since as Ste-Victoire. Marius remains a popular local first name to this day.

Under the wise and generous guidance of Roi René (King René) in the 15th century, Aix became a center of Renaissance arts and letters. At the height of its political, judicial, and ecclesiastic power in the 17th and 18th centuries, Aix profited from a surge of private building, each grand *hôtel particulier* (mansion) vying to outdo its neighbor. Its signature *cours* (courtyards) and *places* (squares), punctuated by grand fountains and intriguing passageways, date from this time.

It was into this exalting elegance that artist Paul Cézanne (1839–1906) was born, though he drew much of his inspiration from the raw countryside around the city and often painted Ste-Victoire. A schoolmate of Cézanne's made equal inroads: the journalist and novelist Émile Zola (1840–1902) attended the Collège Bourbon with Cézanne and described their friendship as well as Aix itself in several of his works. You can still sense something of the ambience that nurtured these two geniuses in the streets of modern Aix.

48 Under the deep shade of tall plane trees whose branches interlace over the street, **Cours Mirabeau** prevails as the city's social nerve center. One side of the street is lined with dignified 18th-century hôtels particuliers;

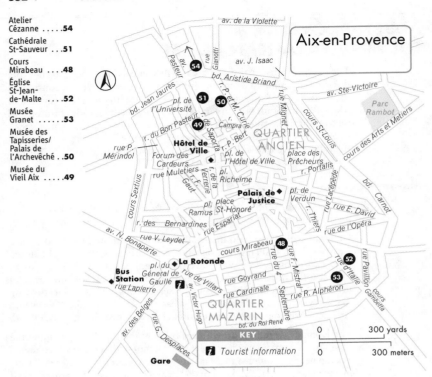

Aix-en-Provence

you can view them from a comfortable seat in one of the dozen or so cafés and restaurants that spill onto the sidewalk on the other side.

49 In the **Musée du Vieil Aix** (Museum of Old Aix), an eclectic assortment of local treasures resides in a 17th-century mansion, from faïence to *santons* (terra-cotta figurines) to ornately painted furniture. The building itself is lovely, too. ⊠ *17 rue Gaston-de-Saporta* ☎ *04–42–21–43–55* 💷 *€4* ⊙ *Apr.–Oct., Tues.–Sun. 10–noon and 2:30–6; Nov.–Mar., Tues.–Sun. 10–noon and 2–5.*

50 The **Musée des Tapisseries** is housed in the 17th-century **Palais de l'Archevêché** (Archbishop's Palace) and showcases a sumptuous collection of tapestries that once decorated the walls of the bishops' quarters. Their taste was excellent: there are 17 magnificent hangings from Beauvais and a series on the life of Don Quixote from Compiègne. In the broad courtyard, the main opera productions of the Festival International d'Art Lyrique take place. ⊠ *Pl. de l'Ancien-Archevêché* ☎ *04–42–23–09–91* 💷 *€2* ⊙ *Wed.–Mon. 10–5.*

★ **51** The **Cathédrale St-Sauveur** (⊠ Rue Gaston de Saporta) juxtaposes so many eras of architectural history, all clearly delineated and preserved, it's like a survey course in itself. It has a double nave, Romanesque and Gothic side by side, and a Merovingian (5th-century) **baptistery,** its colonnade mostly recovered from Roman temples built to honor pagan deities. Shutters hide the ornate 16th-century carvings on the **portals,** opened by a guide on request. The guide can also lead you into the tranquil Romanesque **cloister** next door, so that you can admire its carved pillars and slender columns. As if these treasures weren't enough, the cathedral also houses an extraordinary 15th-century triptych painted by Nicolas Froment in the heat of inspiration following his travels in Italy and Flanders. Called the *Triptyque du Buisson Ardent* (*Burning Bush Triptych*), it depicts the generous art patrons King René and Queen Jeanne kneeling on either side of the Virgin, who is poised above a burning bush. These days, to avoid light damage, it's only opened for viewing on Tuesday from 3 to 4.

52 The 12th-century **Église St-Jean-de-Malte** (⊠ Intersection of rue Cardinale and rue d'Italie) served as a chapel of the Knights of Malta, a medieval order of friars devoted to hospital care. It was Aix's first attempt at the Gothic style. It was here that the counts of Provence were buried throughout the 18th century; their tombs (in the upper left) were attacked during the Revolution and have been only partially repaired.

need a break? Just behind the Palais de la Justice is the colorful world of bric-a-brac collectibles and bookstands of place Verdun (stalls open Tuesday, Thursday, and Saturday). The best place to people-watch is from the sunny terrace of **Le Verdun** (⊠ 20 pl. St-de Verdun ☎ 04–42–27–03–24). Light snacks are served all day.

53 In the graceful Quartier Mazarin, the **Musée Granet** is set below the cours Mirabeau. Once the Ecole de Dessin (Art School) that granted Cézanne a second prize in 1856, this former priory of the Eglise St-Jean-de-Malte is now an art museum. There are eight of Cézanne's paintings upstairs as well as a nice collection of his watercolors and drawings. You'll also find works by Rubens, David, and a group of sentimental works by the museum's founder, François Granet. A renovation project which should eventually double the exhibition area is planned for mid-2004 until mid-2005, during which time the museum will be closed. ⊠ *13 rue Cardinale* ☎ *04–42–26–84–55* ☜ *€2* ☉ *Wed.–Mon., 10–noon and 2–6.*

★ **54** Just north of the Vieille Ville loop is the **Atelier Cézanne** (Cézanne Studio). After the death of his mother forced the sale of the painter's beloved country retreat, known as Jas de Bouffan, he had this studio built just above the town center. In the upstairs work space Cézanne created some of his finest paintings, including *Les Grandes Baigneuses* (*The Large Bathers*). But what is most striking is its collection of simple objects that once featured prominently in the portraits and still-lifes he created—redingote, bowler hat, ginger jar, and all—displayed as if awaiting his return. ⊠ *9 av. Paul-Cézanne* ☎ *04–42–21–06–53* ☜ *€5.50* ☉ *Apr.–Sept., daily 10–noon and 2:30–6; Oct.–Mar., daily 10–noon and 2–5.*

Where to Stay & Eat

★ **$$$$** ✕ **Le Clos de la Violette.** Whether you dine under the chestnut trees or in the airy, pastel dining room, you'll get to experience the cuisine of one of the south's top chefs, Jean-Marc Banzo. He spins tradition into gold, from poached crab set atop a humble white-bean-and-shrimp salad to grilled smoked pork ribs with hazelnuts and mashed potatoes. The restaurant isn't far from the Atelier Cézanne, outside the Vieille Ville ring. ✉ *10 av. de la Violette* ☎ *04–42–23–30–71* ⊕ *www.closdelaviolette. fr* ⌂ *Reservations essential* 🏛 *Jacket required* ▭ *AE, MC, V* ☯ *Closed Sun. No lunch Mon. and Wed.*

$$–$$$ ✕ **Les Bacchanales.** Despite being positioned on a tourist-trap street off cours Mirabeau, this is a pleasant, intimate restaurant with inviting decor of daub-filled beams, yellow-ocher stucco, and Louis XIII chairs. The broad range of fixed-price menus may include smoked salmon with rosemary and green onion cream, *rouget* (red mullet) perfumed with sage and fennel, and crushed almonds flavored with marinated cherries. As the name implies, wine figures large here, and the list is extensive. ✉ *10 rue de la Couronne* ☎ *04–42–27–21–06* ▭ *AE, MC, V* ☯ *Closed Tues. No lunch Wed. and Sat.*

★ $$–$$$ ✕ **Brasserie Les Deux Garcons.** Cézanne and Emile Zola used to chow down here back when, so who cares if the food is rather ordinary. Eating isn't what you came for. Instead, revel in the exquisite gold-ivory *style Consulate* decor, which dates from the restaurant's founding in 1792. It is not so hard to picture the greats—Mistinguett, Churchill, Sartre, Picasso, Delon, Belmondo, and Cocteau—enjoying their demi-tasse under these mirrors. Better, savor the linen-decked sidewalk tables that look out to the cours Mirabeau, the fresh flowers, and the white-swathed waiters serving espressos in tiny gilt-edge cups. At night, the upstairs turns into a cozy, dimly lit piano bar buzzing with an interesting mix of local jazz lovers, tourists, and students. ✉ *53 cours Mirabeau* ☎ *04–42–26–00–51* ▭ *AE, MC, V.*

¢–$$ ✕ **Antoine Coté Cour.** Filled with trendy insiders and fashion conscious Aixois, this lively Italian restaurant has floor-to-ceiling windows that give almost every table a view of the plant-filled courtyard. Delicious smells wafting out from the open kitchen make the restaurant literally hum in hungry anticipation. Pastas are superb; try the mushroom and prosciutto ham fettucini or the gnocci à la Provençal. ✉ *19 cours Mirabeau* ☎ *04–42–93–12–51* ▭ *DC, MC, V* ☯ *Closed Sun. No lunch Mon.*

★ $$$$ 🏨 **Villa Gallici.** Perhaps the most beautiful hotel in Provence, this high-style retreat made the editors of decorating magazines mad with joy when it opened its doors in 1994. A former archbishop's palace perched on a hill overlooking the pink roofs of Aix, the Gallici was transformed into a homage to *le style Provençal* thanks to the wizardry of three designers, Gilles Dez, Charles de Montemarco, and Daniel Jouvre. But don't come here for sunbaked walls, white tiles, and urns with cactus—this is the Provence that Parisian aristocrats enjoyed back in the 19th-century. Hued in the lavenders and blues, ochres and oranges of Aix, rooms swim in the most gorgeous Souleiado and Rubelli fabrics and trim. If a Louis Seize chair covered in gingham check gets to be a bit much, just step outside to the Florentine-style garden, shaded by ancient cypress and plane trees and landscaped with jars of laurel and topiary boxwood. A pool beckons, as does Marcel, the cat. Happily, this luxurious hilltop garden retreat stands serenely apart from the city center on the outskirts of town (offering great views), but the shops of cours Mirabeau are only a 15-minute walk away. But who will want to leave?—After all, you have to choose between tea by the pool or luncheon on the terrace. That noted, some readers say the food needs work. ⊠ *Av. de la Violette, 13100* ☎ *04–42–23–29–23* 🖶 *04–42–96–30–45* ⊕ *www.villagallici.com* 📑 *18 rooms, 4 suites, 3 duplexes* ⚎ *Restaurant, cable TV, pool, Internet, parking (no fee), some pets allowed (fee)* ☰ *AE, DC, MC, V* ⦿ *EP.*

★ **$$$–$$$$** 🖼 **Le Pigonnet.** Cézanne painted Ste-Victoire from what is now the large flower-filled garden terrace of this abode, and the likes of Princess Caroline, Iggy Pop, and Clint Eastwood have spent a few nights under the luxurious roof of this family-owned, Old World, country-style hotel. Spacious and filled with light, each room is a marvel of decoration: baby-soft plush rugs, beautifully preserved antique furniture, rich colors of burnt reds, autumn yellows, and delicate oranges. The restaurant's terrace spills out onto a sculpted green, but the inside dining salon is equally pleasant on a rainy day, thanks to its softly draped yellow curtains and large picture windows. ⊠ *5 av. du Pigonnet, 13100* ☎ *04–42–59–02–90* 🖶 *04–42–59–47–77* ⊕ *www.hotelpigonnet.com* 📑 *52 rooms, 1 apartment* ⚎ *Restaurant, minibars, cable TV, pool, some pets allowed (fee)* ☰ *AE, MC, V* ⦿ *EP.*

$–$$$ 🖼 **Nègre-Coste.** Its prominent cours Mirabeau position and its lavish public areas make this 18th-century town house a popular hotel. Provençal decor and newly tiled bathrooms live up to the lovely ground-floor salons. Large windows open up to the cours Mirabeau, perfect for people-watching with a morning cup of coffee; quieter ones at the back look over the rooftops to the cathedral. ⊠ *33 cours Mirabeau, 13100* ☎ *04–42–27–74–22* 🖶 *04–42–26–80–93* ⊕ *www.hotelnegrecoste.com* 📑 *36 rooms, 1 suite* ⚎ *Minibars, cable TV, parking (fee)* ☰ *AE, MC, V* ⦿ *EP.*

$$ 🖼 **St-Christophe.** With so few midprice *hôtels de charme* in Aix and a distinct shortage of regional style, you might as well opt for this glossy art deco–style hotel, where the comfort and services are remarkable for the price. Rooms are slickly done in deep jewel tones, and the top-floor rooms have artisanal tiles in the bathrooms. Meal plans are available with a three-night minimum stay. ⊠ *2 av. Victor-Hugo, 13100* ☎ *04–42–26–01–24* 🖶 *04–42–38–53–17* ⊕ *www.hotel-saintchristophe.com* 📑 *58 rooms, 7 suites* ⚎ *Restaurant, cable TV, parking (fee), some pets allowed (fee)* ☰ *AE, MC, V* ⦿ *BP, MAP.*

★ **$–$$** 🖼 **Quatre Dauphins.** In the quiet Mazarin quarter, this modest but impeccable lodging inhabits a noble hôtel particulier. Its pretty, comfortable little rooms have been spruced up with *boutis* (Provençal quilts), Les Olivades fabrics, quarry tiles, jute carpets, and hand-painted furniture. The house-proud but unassuming owner-host bends over backward to please. ⊠ *55 rue Roux-Alphéran, 13100* ☎ *04–42–38–16–39* 🖶 *04–42–38–60–19* 📑 *13 rooms* ⚎ *Some pets allowed (fee)* ☰ *MC, V* ⦿ *EP.*

Nightlife & the Arts

To find out what's going on in town, pick up a copy of the events calendar *Le Mois à Aix* or the bilingual city guide *Aix la Vivante* at the tourist office. **Le Scat Club** (⊠ 11 rue de la Verrerie ☎ 04–42–23–00–23) is the place for live soul, funk, reggae, rock, blues, and jazz. **The Bistrot**

Aixois (✉ 37 cours Sextius ☎ 04–42–27–50–10) is the hottest student night spot, with young BCBGs lining up to get in. For a night of playing roulette and the slot machines, head for the **Casino Municipal** (✉ 2 bis av. N.-Bonaparte ☎ 04–42–26–30–33).

Every July during the **Festival International d'Art Lyrique** (International Opera Festival; ☎ 04–42–17–34–00 for information), you can see world-class opera productions in the courtyard of the Palais de l'Archevêché.

Shopping

Aix is a market town, and a sophisticated **food and produce market** sets up every morning on place Richelme; just up the street, on place Verdun, is a good high-end *brocante* (collectibles market) Tuesday, Thursday, and Saturday mornings. A famous Aixois delicacy is *calissons,* a blend of almond paste and glazed melon in almond shapes. The most picturesque shop specializing in calissons is **Bechard** (✉ 12 cours Mirabeau). **Leonard Parli** (✉ 35 av. Victor-Hugo), near the train station, also offers a lovely selection of calissons.

In addition to its old-style markets and jewel-box candy shops, Aix is a modern shopping town—perhaps the best in Provence. The winding streets of the Vieille Ville above cours Mirabeau—centered around **rue Clemenceau, rue Marius Reinaud, rue Espariat, rue Aude,** and **rue Maréchal Foch**—have a head-turning parade of goods.

Meyrargues

❸ *12 km (7 mi) northwest of Aix-en-Provence on the N96.*

A picturesque village dominated by a feudal fortress, Meyrargues has been a pilgrimage stop for more than nine centuries. The fortress, transformed into a chateau in the 17th century and into a four-star hotel in 1952, remains the chief attraction, but the little town nestled beneath the chateau's monumental flight of steps is perfectly charming in itself. The clay santons, or terra-cotta figurines, from the village factory are much coveted, the surrounding woods are great for horseback riding, and Monsieur Sallier's wines (Château de Vauclaire, Coteaux d'Aix) are among the most *buvable* (drinkable) in the region. There are two ancient chapels in the village, and three arches of a Roman aqueduct that once fed Aix-en-Provence still stand in a valley just behind the chateau's cemetery.

Where to Stay & Eat

★ **$$$–$$$$** ✕🏨 **Château de Meyrargues.** A Celtic outpost in 600 BC, a military fortress in AD 900: few places, even in France, have as much history as the Château de Meyrargues. Fewer still take paying guests. Constructed over six centuries, the imposing chateau, with its massive stone walls and staircase, is a truly formidable sight, perched high above the Durance Valley, lording over the medieval village from the top of a rocky outcrop, surrounded by hills of pine. The views are breathtaking, as are the spacious, Provençal-decorated rooms and luxurious baths. If you can't stay the night, at least try to fit in lunch or dinner in the excellent restaurant. (✉ 13650 Traverse St-Pierre, Meyrargues ☎ 04–42–63–49–90

🛏 *04–42–63–49–92* ⊕ *www.chateau-de-meyrargues.com* ☎ *8 rooms, 3 suites △ Restaurant, minibars, 2 tennis courts, pool; no pets ▭ AE, MC, V ⊙ Closed Nov.* ⧸⦶ *FAP, MAP.*

Marseille

31 km (19 mi) south of Aix-en-Provence, 188 km (117 mi) west of Nice, 772 km (483 mi) south of Paris.

Marseille may sometimes be given a wide berth by travelers in search of a Provençal idyll, but it's their loss. Miss it and you miss one of the vibrant, exciting cities in France. With its Cubist jumbles of white stone rising up over a picture-book seaport, bathed in light of blinding clarity and crowned by larger-than-life neo-Byzantine churches, the city's neighborhoods teem with multiethnic life, its souklike African markets reek deliciously of spices and coffees, and its labyrinthine Vieille Ville is painted in broad strokes of saffron, cinnamon, and robin's-egg blue. Feisty and fond of broad gestures, Marseille is a dynamic city, as cosmopolitan now as when the Phoenicians first founded it, and with all the exoticism of the international shipping port it has been for 2,600 years. Vital to the Crusades in the Middle Ages and crucial to Louis XIV as a military port, Marseille flourished as France's market to the world— and still does today.

The heart of Marseille is clustered around the Vieux Port—immortalized in all its briny charm in the 1961 Leslie Caron film version of *Fanny.* The hills to the south of the port are crowned with mega-monuments, such as Notre-Dame de la Garde and Fort St-Jean. To the north lies the ramshackle hilltop Vieille Ville known as Le Panier. East of the port you'll find the North African neighborhood and, to its left, the famous thoroughfare called La Canebière. South of the city, the clifftop waterfront highway leads to obscure and colorful ports and coves.

Note: If you plan on visiting many of the museums in Marseille buy a museum *passport* for €8 at the tourism office. It covers the entry fee into all the museums in Marseille.

56 One of many museums devoted to Marseille's history as a shipping port, is the **Musée de la Marine et de l'Economie de Marseille** (Marine and Economy Museum). Inaugurated by Napoléon III in 1860, this impressive building houses both the museum and the city's Chamber of Commerce. The front entrance and hallway are lined with medallions celebrating the ports of the world with which the city has traded, or trades still. The museum charts the maritime history of Marseille from the 17th-century onward with paintings and engravings. It's a model-lover's dream with hundreds of steamboats and schooners, all in miniature. ✉ *Palais de la Bourse, 7 La Canebière, La Canebière* ☎ *04–91–39–33–33* 🎫 *€2* ⊙ *Daily 10–6.*

★ **57** The modern, open-space **Musée d'Histoire de Marseille** (Marseille History Museum) illuminates Massalia's history by mounting its treasure of archaeological finds in didactic displays. There's a real Greek-era wooden boat in a hermetically sealed display case. ✉ *Centre Bourse, entrance*

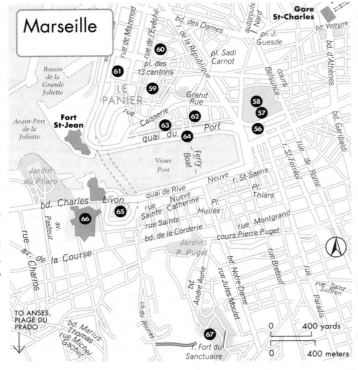

on rue de Bir-Hakeim, Vieux Port ☎ *04–91–90–42–22* ✉ *€2 includes entry into Jardin des Vestiges* ☉ *Mon.–Sat. noon–7.*

58 The **Jardin des Vestiges** (Garden of Remains), just behind the Marseille History Museum, stands on the site of Marseille's classical waterfront and includes remains of the Greek fortifications and loading docks. It was discovered in 1967 when roadwork was being done next to the Bourse (Stock Exchange). ✉ *Centre Bourse, Vieux Port* ☎ *04–91–90–42–22* ✉ *€2 includes entry to Museum of History* ☉ *Mon.–Sat. noon–7.*

★ **59** **Le Panier** is the old heart of Marseille, a maze of high shuttered houses looming over narrow cobbled streets, *montées* (stone stairways), and tiny squares. Long decayed and neglected, it is the principal focus of the city's efforts at urban renewal. Wander this atmospheric neighborhood at will, making sure to stroll along rue du Panier, the montée des Accoules, rue du Petit-Puits, and rue des Muettes.

★ **60** At the top of the Panier district, the **Centre de la Vieille Charité** (Center of the Old Charity) is a superb ensemble of 17th- and 18th-century architecture designed as a hospice for the homeless by Marseillais artist-architects Pierre and Jean Puget. Even if you don't enter the museums, walk around the inner court, studying the retreating perspective of triple arcades and admiring the Baroque chapel with its novel egg-peaked dome. Of the complex's two museums, the larger is the **Musée d'Archéologie Méditerranée** (Museum of Mediterranean Archaeology), with a sizable collection of pottery and statuary from classical Mediterranean civilization, elementally labeled (for example, "pot"). There's also a display on the mysterious Celt-like Ligurians who first peopled the coast, cryptically presented with emphasis on the digs instead of the finds themselves. The best of the lot is the evocatively mounted Egyptian collection, the second largest in France after the Louvre's. There are mummies, hieroglyphs, and gorgeous sarcophagi in a tomblike setting. Upstairs, the **Musée d'Arts Africains, Océaniens, et Amérindiens** (Museum of African, Oceanic, and American Indian Art) creates a theatrical foil for the works' intrinsic drama: the spectacular masks and sculptures are mounted along a pure black wall, lighted indirectly, with labels across the aisle. ⊠ *2 rue de la Charité, le Panier* ☎ *04–91–14–58–80* ☜ *€2 per museum* ☉ *May–Sept., Tues.–Sun. 11–6; Oct.–Apr., Tues.–Sun. 10–5.*

need a break?

With handsome decor and pale green walls, the pretty 1901 **Café Parisian** (⊠ 1 pl. Sadi Carnot, Le Panier ☎ 04–91–90–05–77) is always buzzing. It's where the club scene comes for breakfast while locals and tourists stop by later in the day. It opens at 4:30 AM and serves until around midnight.

61 A gargantuan, neo-Byzantine 19th-century fantasy, the **Cathédrale de la Nouvelle Major** (⊠ Pl. de la Major, Le Panier) was built under Napoléon III—but not before he'd ordered the partial destruction of the lovely 11th-century original, once a perfect example of the Provençal Romanesque style. You can view the flashy decor—marble and rich red porphyry inlay—in the newer of the two churches; the medieval one is being restored.

62 The **Musée du Vieux Marseille** (Museum of Old Marseille) is set in the 16th-century **Maison Diamantée** (Diamond House)—so named for its diamond-faceted Renaissance facade—and built in 1570 by a rich merchant. Focusing on the history of Marseille, the museum normally features santons, crèches, and furniture, but at press time was closed indefinitely. ⊠*Rue de la Prison, Vieux Port* ☎ *04–91–13–89–00 for information.*

63 In 1943 Hitler destroyed the neighborhood along the quai du Port—some 2,000 houses—displacing some 20,000 citizens. This act of brutal urban renewal, ironically, laid the ground open for new discoveries. When Marseille began to rebuild in 1947, they dug up remains of a Roman shipping warehouse full of the terra-cotta jars and amphorae that once lay in the bellies of low-slung ships. The **Musée des Docks Romains** (Roman Docks Museum) created around it demonstrates the scale of Massalia's shipping prowess. ⊠ *2 pl. de Vivaux, Vieux Port* ☎ *04–91–91–24–62* ☜ *€2* ☉ *Oct.–May, Tues.–Sun. 10–5; June–mid-Sept., Tues.–Sun. 11–6.*

64 Departing from the quai below the Hôtel de Ville, the **Ferry Boat** is a Marseille treasure. To hear the natives pronounce "fer-ry bo-at" (they've adopted the English) is one of the joys of a visit here. For a pittance you can file onto this little wooden barge and chug across the Vieux Port.

Fodor'sChoice
★

✉ *Travels between pl. des Huiles on quai de Rive Neuve side and Hôtel de Ville on quai du Port, Vieux Port* ☎ €1.

Founded in the 4th century by St-Cassien, who sailed into Marseille's port full of fresh ideas on monasticism acquired in Palestine and Egypt, the ★ ⑥⑤ **Abbaye St-Victor** grew to formidable proportions. With its severe exterior of crenellated stone and the spare geometry of its Romanesque church, the structure would be as much at home in the Middle East as its founder had been. The Saracens destroyed the first structure, so the abbey was rebuilt in the 11th century and fortified against further onslaught in the 14th. By far the best reason to come is the **crypt**, St-Cassien's original, which lay buried under the medieval church's new structure. In evocative nooks and crannies you'll find the 5th-century sarcophagus that allegedly holds the martyr's remains. Upstairs look for the reliquary containing what's left of St. Victor himself, who was ground to death between millstones, probably by Romans. ☎ *Crypt entry €2* ⊙ *Daily 8:30–6:30.*

⑥⑥ The twin structures of **Fort St-Nicolas and Fort St-Jean** flank the entrance to the Vieux Port. In order to keep the feisty, rebellious Marseillais under his thumb, Louis XIV had the fortresses built with the guns pointing *toward* the city. The Marseillais, whose local identity has always been mixed with a healthy dose of irony, are quite proud of this display of the king's (later justified) doubts about their allegiance. To view them, climb up to the Jardin du Pharo.

Towering above the city and visible for miles around, the preposterously ⑥⑦ overscaled neo-Byzantine monument called **Notre-Dame-de-la-Garde** was erected in 1853 by the ever-tasteful Napoléon III. Its interior is a Technicolor bonanza of red-and-beige stripes and glittering mosaics. The gargantuan *Madonna and Child,* on the steeple (almost 30 feet high), is covered in real gold leaf. The boggling panoply of naive ex-votos, mostly thanking the Virgin for death-bed interventions and shipwreck survivals, makes the pilgrimage worth it. ✛ *On foot, climb up cours Pierre Puget, cross Jardin Pierre Puget, cross bridge to rue Vauvenargues, and hike up to pl. Edon. Or catch Bus 60 from cours Jean-Ballard,* ☎ *04–91–13–40–80* ⊙ *May–Sept., daily 7 AM–8 PM; Oct.–Apr., daily 7–7.*

off the
beaten
path

★

CHÂTEAU D'IF – François I, in the 16th century, recognized the strategic advantage of an island fortress surveying the mouth of Marseille's vast harbor, so he had one built. Its effect as a deterrent was so successful that it never saw combat, and was eventually converted into a prison. It was here that Alexandre Dumas locked up his most famous character, the Count of Monte Cristo. Though he was fictional, the hole Dumas had him escape through is real enough, and is visible in the cells today. Video monitors playing relevant scenes from dozens of Monte Cristo films bring each tower and cell to life. On the other hand, the real-life Man in the Iron Mask, whose cell is still being shown, was not actually imprisoned here. The boat ride (from the quai des Belges, €10) and the views from the broad terrace alone are worth the trip. ☎ *04–91–59–02–30* ⊕ *www. monuments-france.fr* ☎ *Château €4.60* ⊙ *Apr.–Sept., daily 9–7; Oct.–Mar., Tues.–Sun. 9–5:30.*

Where to Stay & Eat

$$$–$$$$ ✕ **Chez Fonfon.** Tucked into a filmlike setting of the tiny fishing port Vallon des Auffes, this Marseillais landmark has one of the loveliest settings in greater Marseille. A variety of fresh seafood, impeccably grilled, steamed, or roasted in salt crust are served in two pretty dining rooms with picture windows overlooking the fishing boats that supply your dinner. Try classic bouillabaisse served with all the bells and whistles—broth, hot-chili rouille, and flamboyant table-side filleting. ⊠ *140 rue du Vallon des Auffes, Vallon des Auffes* ☎ *04–91–52–14–38* ⊕ *www. chezfonfon.com* ⌂ *Reservations essential* ▤ *AE, DC, MC, V* ⊘ *Closed Sun. No lunch Mon. Closed 1st 2 wks in Jan.*

★ $$$–$$$$ ✕ **L'Epuisette.** Artfully placed on a rocky, fingerlike cliff surrounded by the sea, this seafood restaurant offers gorgeous views of crashing surf on one side and the port of Vallon des Auffes on the other. Chef Guillaume Sourrieu is acquiring a big reputation (and Michelin stars) for sophisticated cooking—mullet fillets on a bed of peppers and eggplant, sauced with peppery rouille, or sea bass baked in a salt crust, are some top delights—all matched with a superb wine list. Save room for dessert. ⊠ *Anse du Vallon des Auffes, Vallon des Auffes* ☎ *04–91–52–17–82* ▤ *AE, DC, MC, V* ⊘ *Closed Mon. No lunch Sat. No dinner Sun.*

$$$$ ✕ **Mets de Provence.** Climb the oddly slanted wharf-side stairs and enter a cosseted Provençal world. With boats bobbing out the window and a landlubbing country decor, this romantic restaurant makes the most of Marseille's split personality. Classic Provençal hors d'oeuvres—tapenade, brandade, aioli—lead into seafood (dorade roasted with fennel and licorice) and meats (rack of lamb in herb pastry). The four-course lunch (€35, including wine) is marvelous. ⊠ *18 quai de Rive-Neuve, Vieux Port* ☎ *04–91–33–35–38* ▤ *MC, V* ⊘ *Closed Sun. No lunch Sat., no dinner Mon.*

$$$$ ✕ **Le Peron.** Chic and stylishly modern with its dark-wood interior and large windows overlooking the sea, this restaurant is the latest magnet for hip, young professionals. The staff are efficient and friendly; meals are well-presented and tasty—try grilled garlic scallops in a puree of purple potatoes or the lobster risotto—and the prix-fixe lunch menu at €41 is worth the splurge. The view is one of the best in the city. ⊠ *56 Corniche J.-F.-Kennedy, Endoume* ☎ *04–91–52–15–22* ▤ *AE, DC, MC, V.*

$$$–$$$$ ✕ **Les Arcenaulx.** At this book-lined, red-walled haven in the stylish book-and-boutique complex of a renovated arsenal, you can have a sophisticated regional lunch—and read while you're waiting. Look for mussels in saffron with buckwheat crêpes, carpaccio of cod with crushed olives, or rabbit with garlic confit. The terrace (on the Italian-scale cours d'Estienne d'Orves) is as pleasant as the interior. ⊠ *25 cours d'Estienne d'Orves, Vieux Port* ☎ *04–91–59–80–30* ▤ *AE, DC, MC, V* ⊘ *Closed Sun.*

$$–$$$$ ✕ **Baie des Singes.** On a tiny rock-ringed lagoon as isolated from the nearby city as if it were a desert island, this cinematic corner of paradise was once a customs house under Napoléon III. You can rent a mattress and lounge chair, dive into the turquoise water, and shower off for the only kind of food worthy of such a locale: fresh fish. It's all served at terrace tables overlooking the water. ⊠ *Anse des Croisettes, Les Goudes* ☎ *04–91–73–68–87* ▤ *MC, V* ⊘ *Closed Oct.–Mar.*

★ ¢-$ ✕ **Etienne.** This historic Le Panier hole-in-the-wall has more than just good fresh-anchovy pizza from a wood-burning oven. There are also fried squid, eggplant gratin, a slab of rare-grilled beef big enough for two, and the quintessential *pieds et paquets*, Marseille's earthy classic of sheeps' feet and stuffed tripe. Be warned: pizza is considered an appetizer here and main courses are huge. ⊠ *43 rue de la Lorette, Le Panier* 🕾 *No phone* ▭ *No credit cards.*

¢-$ ✕ **Au Petit Naples.** With huge portions, a convivial atmosphere, and a small, busy beachfront location, this restaurant is jammed with locals and savvy tourists from every walk of life. Some connoisseurs say that the pizza here is even better than at Marseille's noted Etienne. ⊠ *14 plage de l'Estaque, l'Estaque* 🕾 *04–91–46–05–11* ▭ *No credit cards* ☉ *Closed Sun. No lunch Sat.*

★ $$$$ ✕▥ **Le Petit Nice.** On a rocky promontory overlooking the sea, this fantasy villa was bought from a countess in 1917 and converted to a hotel–restaurant. The Passédat family has been getting it right ever since, with father and son manning the exceptional kitchen (one of the coast's best), creating truffled brandade, sea-anemone beignets, fresh fish roasted whole, and licorice soufflé (the restaurant is closed Sunday and Monday for lunch in summer, and Sunday and Monday for lunch and dinner in winter; prix-fixe menus are €110 and €139). Most rooms are sleek and minimalist, with some art deco–cum–postmodern touches, while outside the fetching pool is illuminated at night by antique gaslight fixtures. ⊠ *Anse de la Maldormé, Corniche J.-F.-Kennedy, Endoume, 13007* 🕾 *04–91–59–25–92* 📠 *04–91–59–28–08* ⊕ *www.petitnice-passedat.com* ⇨ *13 rooms, 3 suites* ♿ *Restaurant, minibars, cable TV, pool, Internet, free parking, some pets allowed (fee)* ▭ *AE, DC, MC, V* ¶◎¶ *MAP.*

★ $$$ ▥ **Mercure Beauvau Vieux Port.** Chopin has spent the night and George Sand kept a suite in this historic hotel overlooking the Vieux Port. Public rooms have real antiques, burnished woodwork, Provençal-style decor, and plush carpets, all comprising a convincing part of this intimate urban hotel's genuine Old World charm. Port-view rooms with balconies high over the fish market more than justify the splurge. Undergoing extensive renovations, this beloved landmark will probably see a price jump to the top level when it reopens in mid-2004. ⊠ *4 rue Beauvau, Vieux Port, 13001* 🕾 *04–91–54–91–00, 800/637–2873 for U.S. reservations* 📠 *04–91–54–15–76* ⊕ *www.mercure.com* ⇨ *72 rooms* ♿ *Minibars, cable TV, bar, Internet, some pets allowed (fee)* ▭ *AE, DC, MC, V* ¶◎¶ *EP.*

$ ▥ **Alizé.** On the Vieux Port, its front rooms taking in postcard views, this straightforward lodging has been modernized to include tight double-pane windows, slick modular baths, and a laminate-and-all-weather carpeted look. Public spaces have exposed stone and preserved details, and a glass elevator whisks you to your floor. It's an excellent value and location for the price. ⊠ *35 quai des Belges, Vieux Port, 13001* 🕾 *04–91–33–66–97* 📠 *04–91–54–80–06* ⊕ *www.alize-hotel.com* ⇨ *39 rooms* ♿ *Cable TV, some pets allowed (fee)* ▭ *AE, DC, MC, V* ¶◎¶ *EP.*

Nightlife & the Arts
With a population of more than 800,000, Marseille is a big city by French standards, with all the nightlife that entails. Arm yourself with *Marseille*

Poche, a glossy monthly events minimagazine; the monthly *In Situ,* a free guide to music, theater, and galleries; *Sortir,* a weekly about film, art, and concerts in southern Provence; or *TakTik,* a hip weekly on theater and art. They're all in French. Rock, jazz, and reggae concerts are held at the **Espace Julien** (⊠ 39 cours Julien, Préfecture ☎ 04–91–24–34–10). **Le Trolleybus** (⊠ 24 quai de Rive Neuve, Bompard ☎ 04–91–54–30–45) is the most popular disco in town, with a young, *branché* (hip) crowd. Classical music concerts are given in the **Abbaye St-Victor** (☎ 04–91–05–84–48 for information). Operas and orchestral concerts are held at the **Opéra Municipal** (⊠ 2 rue Molière, Vieux Port ☎ 04–91–55–21–24).

Sports & the Outdoors

Marseille's waterfront position makes it easy to swim and sunbathe within the city sprawl. From the Vieux Port, Bus 83 or Bus 19 will take you to the vast green spread of reclaimed land called the **Parc Balnéaire du Prado.** Its waterfront is divided into beaches, all of them public and well equipped. The beach surface varies between sand and gravel. Marseille is a mecca for diving (*plongée*), with several organizations offering *baptêmes* (baptisms, or first dives) to beginners. The coast is lined with rocky inlets, grottos, and ancient shipwrecks, not to mention thronging with aquatic life. For general information contact the **Centre de Loisirs des Goudes** (⊠ 2 bd. Alexandre Dumas, Saint-Giniez, 13008 ☎☎ 04–91–25–13–16).

Shopping

Savon de Marseille (Marseille soap) is a household standard in France, often sold as a satisfyingly crude and hefty block in odorless olive-oil green. But its chichi offspring are dainty pastel guest soaps in almond, lemon, vanilla, and other scents.

The locally famous bakery **Four des Navettes** (⊠ 136 rue Sainte, Garde Hill ☎ 04–91–33–32–12), up the street from Notre-Dame-de-la-Garde, makes orange-spice, shuttle-shape *navettes.* These cookies are modeled on the little boat in which Mary Magdalene and Lazarus washed up onto Europe's shores.

Aubagne

 16 km (10 mi) east of Marseille, 36 km (22 mi) south of Aix-en-Provence.

You can spend a delightful morning browsing through Aubagne's Vieille Ville or basking on its broad plane tree–shaded squares. Aubagne claims the title of *santon*-making capital of Provence. The craft, originally from Marseille, was focused here at the turn of the 20th century, when artisans moved inland to make the most of local clay. The more than a dozen studios in town are set up for you to observe the production process. Make sure you visit Aubagne on a market day, when the sleepy center is transformed into a tableau of Provençal life. The Tuesday market is the biggest.

The town is proud of its native son, the dramatist, filmmaker, and chronicler of all things Provençal, Marcel Pagnol, best known as the author of *Jean de Florette* and *Manon des Sources* (*Manon of the Springs*) and the stories that comprise the Fanny trilogy. You can study miniature dioramas of scenes from Pagnol stories at **Le Petit Monde de Marcel Pagnol** (The Small World of Marcel Pagnol). ⊠ *Esplanade de Gaulle* 🖭 *Free* ⊙ *Daily 9–noon and 2–6.*

Even if you haven't read Pagnol's works or seen his films, you can enjoy the **Circuit Pagnol,** a hike in the rough-hewn, arid *garrigues* (scrublands) behind Marseille and Aubagne. Here Pagnol spent his idyllic summers, described in his *Souvenirs d'un Enfance* (*Memories of a Childhood*). When he grew up to be a famous playwright and filmmaker, he shot some of his best work in these hills. After Pagnol's death, Claude Berri came back to find a location for his remake of *Manon des Sources,* but found it so altered by brush fires and power cables that he chose to shoot in the Luberon instead. Although the trail may no longer shelter the pine-shaded olive orchards of its past, it still gives you the chance to walk through primeval Provençal countryside and rewards you with spectacular views of Marseille and the sea. For an accompanied tour with literary commentary, contact the tourist office. ⊠ *To access marked trail by yourself, drive to La Treille, northeast of Aubagne, and follow signs* ☎ *04–42–03–49–98 tourist office.*

Where to Eat

$–$$ ✕ **La Farandole.** Cosseted here by rustic Provençal lemon-print cloths, lace curtains, and the region's typical bow-legged chairs, you can enjoy good home cooking with local regulars who claim the same table every day. The inexpensive daily menu may feature crisp green salad with fois gras in a raspberry vinaigrette, garlicky steak and *frites* (fries), or baked goat cheese; wine is included. ⊠ *6 rue Martino, off cours Maréchal, on a narrow street leading into Vieille Ville* ☎ *04–42–03–26–36* 🖃 *MC, V* ⊙ *No dinner Sun. and Mon.*

Cassis

69 *11 km (7 mi) south of Aubagne, 30 km (19 mi) east of Marseille, 42 km (26 mi) west of Toulon.*

Surrounded by vineyards, flanked by monumental cliffs, guarded by the ruins of a medieval castle, and nestled around a picture-perfect fishing port, Cassis is the prettiest coastal town in Provence. Stylish without being too recherché, it provides shelter to numerous pleasure-boaters, who restock their galleys at its market, replenish their nautical duds in its boutiques, and relax with a bottle of Cassis and a platter of sea urchins in one of its numerous waterfront cafés. Pastel houses set at Cubist angles frame the port, and the mild rash of parking-garage architecture that scars its outer neighborhoods doesn't spoil the general effect, one of pure and unadulterated charm. The **Château de Cassis** has loomed over the harbor since the invasions of the Saracens in the 7th century, evolving over the centuries into a walled enclosure crowned with stout watchtowers. It's private property today and best viewed from a port-side café.

You can't visit Cassis without touring the **calanques,** the fjordlike finger bays that probe the rocky coastline. Either take a sightseeing cruise or hike across the clifftops, clambering down the steep sides to these barely accessible retreats. Or you can combine the two, going in by boat and hiking back; make arrangements at the port. The calanque closest to Cassis is the least attractive: **Port Miou** was a stone quarry until 1982, when the calanques became protected sites. Now this calanque is an active leisure and fishing port. **Calanque Port Pin** is prettier, with wind-twisted pines growing at angles from the white-rock cliffs. But it's the

★ third calanque that's the showstopper: the **Calanque En Vau** is a castaway's dream, with a tiny beach at its root and jagged cliffs looming overhead. The series of massive cliffs and calanques stretches all the way to Marseille. Note that boats make round-trips several times a day to the Calanques de Cassis from Marseille's Quai des Belges.

Where to Stay & Eat

$$$ ✕ **Chez Nino.** This is the best of the many restaurants lining the harbor, with top-notch Provençal food and wine and a spectacular terrace view. The owners, Claudie and Bruno, are extremely hospitable as long as you stick to the menu—don't ask for sauce on the side—and you are as passionate about fish and seafood as they are. The sardines in *escabeche* are textbook perfect, as are the grilled fish and the bouillabaisse. ☒ *Quai Barthélémy* ☎ *04–42–01–74–32* ⊟ *AE, DC, MC, V* ⊘ *Closed Mon. No dinner Sun. off-season. Closed mid-Dec.–mid-Feb.*

$$–$$$ ✕ **Monsieur Brun.** One of the most authentic meals you can have in Cassis is a platter of raw shellfish. At this terrace bar-brasserie on the west side of the port, a multitiered tower of shellfish on a bed of kelp is served with nothing but bread, butter, and a finger towelette. Have the nutty little *bleues,* the local oyster, but *oursins* (sea urchins) are a Cassis specialty, and these are brought in daily by the chef's fisherman friend. Omelets and salads are other alternatives. ☒ *2 quai Calendal* ☎ *04–42–01–82–66* ⊟ *No credit cards* ⊘ *Closed mid-Nov.–mid-Jan.*

★ **$$–$$$** ✕◻ **Jardin d'Émile.** Tucked back from the waterfront under quarried cliffs and massive parasol pines, this stylish, cozy inn takes in views of the cape. Rooms are intimate, with rubbed-chalk walls, scrubbed pine, and weathered stone. The restaurant (closed Wednesday) is atmospheric, on a sheltered terrace surrounded by greenery and, by night, the illuminated cliffs. Regional specialties with a cosmopolitan twist—such as snapper filled with goat cheese and wrapped in eggplant—are served on locally made pottery. ☒ *Plage du Bestouan, 13260* ☎ *04–42–01–80–55* ☐ *04–42–01–80–70* ⊕ *www.lejardindemile.fr* ↙ *7 rooms* ♧ *Minibars, cable TV* ⊟ *AE, DC, MC, V* ⊘ *Closed mid-Nov.–mid-Dec.* ⦿❘ *EP.*

$$–$$$ ◻ **Les Roches Blanches.** First built as a private home in 1887, this cliffside villa takes in smashing views of the port and the Cap Canaille, both from the best rooms and from the panoramic dining hall. The beautifully landscaped terrace is shaded by massive pines, and the horizon pool appears to spill into the sea. Yet the aura is far from snooty or deluxe; it's friendly, low-key, and pleasantly mainstream. ☒ *Rte. des Calanques, 13260* ☎ *04–42–01–09–30* ☐ *04–42–01–94–23* ⊕ *www.roches-blanches-cassis.com* ↙ *19 rooms, 5 suites* ♧ *2 restaurants, pool, bar, some pets allowed (fee); no a/c* ⊟ *AE, MC, V* ⦿❘ *MAP.*

The Outdoors

To go on a **boat ride** to Les Calanques, get to the port around 10 AM or 2 PM and look for a boat that's loading passengers. Round-trips should include visits to at least three calanques and average €10. To **hike** the calanques, gauge your skills: the GR98 (marked with red-and-white bands) is the most scenic, but requires scrambling to get down the sheer walls of En Vau. The alternative is to follow the green markers and approach En Vau from behind. If you're ambitious, you can hike the length of the GR98 between Marseille and Cassis, following the coastline.

en route   From Cassis head east out of town and cut sharply right up the **route des Crêtes.** This road takes you along a magnificent crest over the water and up to the very top of **Cap Canaille.** Venture out on the vertiginous trails to the edge, where the whole coast stretches below.

Bandol

⑦ *25 km (16 mi) southeast of Cassis, 15 km (9 mi) west of Toulon.*

Although its name means wine to most of the world, Bandol is also a popular and highly developed seaside resort town. It has seafood snack shacks, generic brasseries, a harbor packed with yachts, and a waterfront promenade. Yet the east end of town conceals lovely old villas framed in mimosas, bougainvillea, and pine. And a port-side stroll up the palm-lined allée Jean-Moulin feels downright Côte d'Azur. But be warned: the sheer concentration of high-summer crowds cannot be exaggerated. If you're not a beach lover, pick up an itinerary from the tourist office and visit a few Bandol vineyards just outside town.

Where to Eat

$$$–$$$$ ✕ **Auberge du Port.** This is a fish-first-and-foremost establishment, with a terrace packed night and day—and not because of the splendid view it offers of Ile Bandor. Going off menu for a daily catch special can be costly, but worth it if a memorable fish-dish experience has so far eluded you on the trip. Otherwise, try the excellent *friture* of small fish fried with lemon or the classic fish stew *bourride.* Get here early for something especially fresh and savory. And book ahead. ⊠ *9 allée Jean-Moulin* ☎ *04–94–29–42–63* ⌂ *Reservations essential* ▭ *AE, DC, MC, V.*

Brignoles

⑦ *86 km (47 mi) northwest of Bandol, 70 km (39 mi) north of Toulon.*

This rambling backcountry hill town, crowned with a medieval chateau, is the market center for the wines of the Var and the crossroads of this green, ungentrified region—until now, that is. With a Ducasse restaurant now in the region, real estate has rocketed, and le tout Paris whispers that this little corner of nowheresville is *the* next Luberon. The main point of interest in the region is the **Abbaye de La Celle,** a 12th-century Benedictine abbey that served as a convent until the 17th century, when it was closed because its young nuns had begun to run wild and were known less for their chastity than "the color of their petticoats and the name of their lover." There's a refectory and a ruined cloister; the simple Romanesque chapel still serves as the parish church.

Where to Stay & Eat

★ $$$$ ✕⌂ **Hostellerie de l'Abbaye de La Celle.** Superchef Alain Ducasse put this country inn—buried in the unspoiled backcountry north of Toulon and just south of Brignoles—back on the map a decade ago. Up the road from the town's royal abbey, this beautifully restored 18th-century *bastide* (country house)—a dream in ocher-yellow walls, Arles green shutters, and white stone trim—was once part of the convent where future queens of Provence were raised. Guest rooms mix Louis XVI and regional accents; half are split-level with their own gardens, some with views of vineyards, others of a park thick with chestnut and mulberry tress. Beds are enormous—none more so than those of the Charles de Gaulle suite (where the great man once stayed). Wherever you bed down, the scent of fresh thyme and lemon basil waft through the windows from the gardens. Today, the formidable kitchen is headed up by Chef Benoît Witz, whose seemingly magical creations find a superb balance between taste and texture: velouté of crawfish gently covering a bruschetta topped with tomatoes and garden herbs, or duck breast with polenta and cherries. ✉ *Pl. du Général-de-Gaulle, 83170 La Celle* ☎ *04–98–05–14–14* 🖷 *04–98–05–14–15* ⊕ *www.abbaye-celle.com* ➷ *9 rooms, 1 suite, 3 duplexes* ⚭ *Restaurant, minibars, cable TV, pool, Internet, meeting room* ▭ *AE, DC, MC, V* ⎜⊘⎜ *EP.*

Iles d'Hyères

⑰ *32 km (20 mi) off the coast south of Hyères. To get to the islands, follow the narrow Giens Peninsula to La Tour-Fondue, at its tip. Boats (leaving every half hour in summer, every 60 or 90 minutes rest of year, for €12 round-trip) make a 20-minute beeline to Porquerolles. For Port-Cros and Levant, you'll depart from Port d'Hyères at Hyères-Plages.*

Off the southeastern point of France's star and spanning some 32 km (20 mi), this archipelago of islands could be a set for a pirate movie; in fact, it has featured in several, thanks to a soothing microclimate and a wild and rocky coastline dotted with palms. And not only film pirates made their appearance: in the 16th century the islands were seeded with convicts to work the land. They soon ran amok and used their adopted base to ambush ships heading into Toulon. A more wholesome population claims the islands today. They are made up of three main areas. **Port-Cros** is a national park, with both its surface and underwater environs protected. **Levant** has been taken over, for the most part, ★ by nudists. **Porquerolles** is the largest and best of the lot—and a popular escape from the modern world. Off-season, it's a castaway delight of pine forests, sandy beaches, and vertiginous cliffs above rocky coastline. Inland, its preserved pine forests and orchards of olives and figs are crisscrossed with dirt roads to be explored on foot or on bikes; except for the occasional jeep or work truck, the island is car-free. In high season (April to October), day-trippers pour off the ferries and surge to the beaches.

Where to Stay & Eat

★ $$$$ ✕▣ **Mas du Langoustier.** A fabled forgetaway, the Langoustier comes with a lobster-orange building, pink bougainvillea, and a secluded spot at the westernmost point of the Ile de Porquerolles, 3 km (2 mi) from the harbor. Manager Madame Richard—who may pick you up at the port in her Dodge—knows a thing or two about the island: her grandmother was given the island as a wedding gift. Choose between big California-modern rooms and charming old-style Provençal. Chef Joël Guillet creates inspired spectacular southern French cuisine, to be accompanied by the rare island rosé (note that prices include breakfast and dinner). ✉ *Pointe du Langoustier, 83400 Ile de Porquerolles* ☎ *04-94-58-30-09* 🖶 *04-94-58-36-02* ⊕ *www.langoustier.com* 🛏 *50 rooms* ⚘ *Restaurant, minibars, cable TV, tennis court, beach, billiards, Internet* ⊟ *AE, DC, MC, V* ⊙ *Closed Nov.–Apr.* ❤❘ *MAP.*

$$$ ✕▣ **Les Glycines.** In soft shades of yellow-ocher and sky-blue, this sleekly modernized little bastide has an idyllic enclosed courtyard. Back rooms look over a jungle of mimosa and eucalyptus. Public salons have Provençal chairs and fabrics. The restaurant, where food is served on the terrace or in the garden, proffers port-fresh tuna and sardines. The inn is just back from the port in the village center. Prices include breakfast and dinner. ✉ *Pl. d'Armes, 83400 Ile de Porquerolles* ☎ *04-94-58-30-36* 🖶 *04-94-58-35-22* ⊕ *www.porquerolles.net* 🛏 *8 rooms, 3 suites* ⚘ *Restaurant, cable TV, bar, Internet; no a/c* ⊟ *AE, MC, V* ❤❘ *MAP.*

$$$ ✕▣ **Le Manoir.** A mix of southern-coast bourgeois and Provençal decor adds a splash of color to the sunlit airy rooms of this family owned colonial-style hotel. Private patios overlook a large secluded park bordered by eucalyptus, pink oleanders, and palm trees. Thoughtful service and absolute calm firmly encourage relaxation. After a day of hiking through forests, swimming in the pool, or simply sitting on the flower filled terrace, you can partake of chef Vincent Cordier's delicious hearty Provençal fare in the rather plainly decorated restaurant. With a price that includes both your meals and your accommodation, this is a gentle touch of civilization in the isolated wilderness. ✉ *Ile de Port Cros, 83400* ☎ *04-94-05-90-52* 🖶 *04-94-05-90-89* 🛏 *23 rooms* ⚘ *Restaurant, bar; no a/c in some rooms, no room TVs* ⊟ *MC, V* ⊙ *Closed end of Oct.–mid-Apr.* ❤❘ *MAP.*

The Outdoors

You can rent a mountain bike (*velo tout-terrain*, or VTT) for a day to pedal the paths and clifftop trails of Porquerolles at **Cycle Porquerol** (✉ Rue de la Ferme ☎ 04-94-58-30-32). **L'Indien** (✉ Pl. d'Armes ☎ 04-94-58-30-39) offers a wide variety of bikes. **Locamarine 75** (✉ On port ☎ 04-94-58-35-84) rents motorboats to amateurs with or without license.

PROVENCE A TO Z

To research prices, get advice from other travelers, and book travel arrangements, visit www.fodors.com.

AIR TRAVEL

Marseille is served by frequent flights from Paris and London, and daily flights from Paris arrive at the smaller airport at Nîmes, which serves Arles and the Camargue (the trip takes about an hour). There are direct flights in summer from the United States to Nice, 160 km (100 mi) from Aix-en-Provence.

BIKE & MOPED TRAVEL

Bikes can be rented from the train stations in Aix-en-Provence, Arles, Avignon, Marseille, Nîmes, and Orange at a cost of about €10 per day. Contact the Comité Départemental de Cyclotourisme for a list of scenic bike routes in Provence.

🚲 Bike Maps **Comité Départemental de Cyclotourisme** ⊠ Les Passadoires, 84420 Piolenc ☎ 04-90-29-64-80.

BUS TRAVEL

A moderately good network of bus services—run by a perplexing number of independent bus companies (for best advice on schedules, consult the town tourist office or your hotel concierge)—links places not served, or poorly served, by train. If you plan to explore Provence by bus, Avignon, Marseille, Aix-en-Provence, and Arles are good bases. Avignon is also the starting point for excursion-bus tours and boat trips down the Rhône. In most cases, you can buy bus tickets on the bus itself.

Aix-en-Provence: One block west of La Rotonde, the station (rue Lapierre) is crowded with many bus companies, which offer numerous regional connections, the farthest links being Orange, Nice, Marseille, Avignon, and Arles. **Arles:** The gare routière (av. Paulin Talabot) is adjacent to the train station. Five buses leave daily for Aix-en-Provence and Marseille (only two run on weekends); others travel daily to Avignon and Nîmes. **Avignon:** The bus station is right by the rail station on boulevard St-Roch; lines connect to nearby towns such as Châteauneuf-du-Pape and Fontaine-de-Vaucluse. **Les Baux:** Buses here head for Avignon or Arles. **Nîmes:** The bus station (rue Ste-Félicité) connects with Montpellier, Pont du Gard, and many other places. **Marseille:** The station (3 pl. Victor Hugo) is next to the train station and offers myriad connections to cities and small towns. **St-Remy-de-Provence** is 40 minutes from Avignon by bus. **Orange:** The station is on cours Pourtoules, on the eastern edge of the city, and offers links to Avignon, Vaison-la-Romaine, and Marseille. **Pont du Gard:** This is a 40-minute ride from Nîmes; you are dropped off 1 km (½ mi) from the bridge at the Auberge Blanche. **Stes-Maries-de-la-Mer:** As the gateway to the Camargue region (in which there is little or no public transportation), buses head here from Arles, Nîmes, and Aigues-Mortes. For a complete list of bus Web sites for the region, log on to www.provence-jouques.com/fr/venir/venir15.html.

🚌 Bus Information **Les Cars Lieutaud** ☎ 04-90-36-05-22 ⊕ www.cars-lieutaud.fr. **Ceyte Tourisme Méditerranée** ☎ 04-90-93-74-90.

CAR RENTAL

🚗 Local Agencies **Avis** ⊠ 11 bd. Gambetta, Aix ☎ 04-42-21-64-16 ⊠ At train station, Avignon ☎ 04-90-27-96-10 ⊠ At train station, Marseille ☎ 04-91-64-71-00 ⊠ 19 av. Charles de Gaulle, Orange ☎ 04-90-34-11-00.

Budget ⊠ Bd. St-Roch, Avignon ☎ 04-90-27-94-95 ⊠ 42 bd. Edouard Daladier, Orange ☎ 04-90-34-00-34.

Hertz ⊠ 43 av. Victor Hugo, Aix ☎ 04-42-27-91-32 ⊠ 2A av. Monclar, Avignon ☎ 04-90-14-26-90 ⊠ Train station, Marseille ☎ 04-91-90-14-03.

CAR TRAVEL

A6–A7 (a toll road) from Paris, known as the Autoroute du Soleil—the Highway of the Sun—takes you straight to Provence, where it divides at Orange, 659 km (412 mi) from Paris; the trip can be done in a fast five or so hours.

After route A7 divides at Orange, A9 heads west to Nîmes (723 km [448 mi] from Paris) and continues into the Pyrénées and across the Spanish border. Route A7 continues southeast from Orange to Marseille, on the coast (1,100 km [680 mi] from Paris), while A8 goes to Aix-en-Provence (with a spur to Toulon) and then to the Côte d'Azur and Italy.

LODGING

APARTMENT-VILLA RENTALS Properties for rent in Provence are listed by the national house-rental agency, Gîtes de France. Regional offices are in Bouches-du-Rhône, Gard, Var, and Vaucluse. In addition, each of the tourist offices in towns in the region usually publishes lists of independent rentals (*locations meublés*), many of them inspected and classified by the tourist office itself.

🖪 **Local Agents Bouches-du-Rhône** ⊠ Domaine du Vergon, B.P. 26, 13370 Mallemort ☎ 04-90-59-49-40 🖶 04-90-59-16-75. **Gard** ⊠ 3 pl. des Arènes, B.P. 59, 30007 Nîmes, Cedex 4 ☎ 04-66-27-94-94 🖶 04-66-27-94-95. **Var** ⊠ 1 bd. Maréchal Foch, Draguignan ☎ 04-94-50-93-93 🖶 04-94-50-93-90. **Vaucluse** ⊠ Pl. Campana, B.P. 164, Cedex 1, 84008 Avignon ☎ 04-90-85-45-00.

B&BS Gîtes de France, the French national network of vacation lodging, rates participating B&Bs for comfort and lists them in a catalog. For chambres d'hôtes regulated by this national network, contact the local branches, divided by *départements* (administrative regions).

TOURS

PRIVATE GUIDES Bus tours through the Camargue, departing from Avignon with a passenger pick-up in Arles (behind the tourism office, in front of the Atrium hotel, 9:45 AM) are offered by Self-Voyages Provence for about €45. Ask about the optional riverboat trip down the Rhone. Taxis T.R.A.N. can take you round-trip from Nîmes to the Pont du Gard (ask the taxi to wait while you explore for 30 minutes).

🖪 **Self Voyages Provence** ⊠ 42 bd. Raspail, 84000 Avignon ☎ 04-90-14-70-00 ⊕ www. self-voyages.fr. **Taxis T.R.A.N** ☎ 04-66-29-40-11.

WALKING TOURS The tourist offices in Arles, Nîmes, Avignon, Aix-en-Provence, and Marseille all organize a full calendar of walking tours (some in summer only).

TRAIN TRAVEL

The high-speed TGV *Méditerranée* line ushered in a new era in Trains à Grande Vitesse travel in France; the route (lengthened last year from the old terminus, Valence, in Haute Provence) means that you can travel from Paris's Gare de Lyon to Avignon in two hours and 40 minutes, with a mere three-hour trip to Nîmes, Aix-en-Provence, and Marseille. Not only is the idea of Provence as a day-trip now possible (though, of course, not advisable), you can even whisk yourself there directly upon arrival at Paris's Charles de Gaulle airport.

After the main line of the TGV divides at Avignon, the westbound link heads to Nîmes and points west; heading east, the line connects with Orange. The southeast-bound link takes in Marseille, Toulon, and the Côte d'Azur. Montpellier is the stop after Nîmes, with other links at Béziers and Narbonne. There is also frequent service by daily local trains to other towns in the region from these main TGV stops. With high-speed service now connecting Nîmes, Avignon, and Marseille, travelers without cars will find a Provence itinerary much easier to pull off. For full information on the TGV *Méditerranée,* log onto the TGV Web site; you can purchase tickets on this Web site or through RailEurope, and you should always buy your TGV tickets in advance.

Aix-en-Provence: The station (pl. Victor Hugo) is a five-minute walk from place du Général-de-Gaulle and offers many connections, with hourly departures to Marseille. **Arles:** The train station (av. Paulin Talabot) has frequent trains to Avignon, Nîmes, Marseille, and other stops. **Avignon:** The Gare d'Avignon (bd. St-Roch) is across from the entrance to the walled city—easy connections here include Arles, Nîmes, Marseille, and Aix-en-Provence. **Marseille:** The station (esplanade St-Charles) serves all regions of France and is at the northern end of center city, a 20-minute walk from the Vieille Ville. Trains run almost hourly to Arles, Aix-en-Provence, Avignon, and Nice. **Nîmes:** Frequent trains connect with Arles, Avignon, Montpellier, and Marseille; to reach the Vieille Ville from the station, walk north on av. Fauchères. **Orange:** The center city is a 15-minute walk from the train station—walk from av. Frédéric Mistral to rue de la République, then follow signs.
🚆 Train Information **SNCF** ☎ 08-36-35-35-35 ⊕ www.ter-sncf.com/uk/paca. **TGV** ⊕ www.tgv.com.

TRAVEL AGENCIES
🚆 Local Agent Referrals **Havas** ✉ 4 bd. des Lices, Arles ☎ 04-90-18-31-31 ✉ 35 rue de la République, Avignon ☎ 04-90-80-66-80 ✉ 44 bd. Victor Hugo, Nîmes ☎ 04-66-36-99-99 ✉ 34 rue de la République, Orange ☎ 04-90-11-44-44. **Nouvelle Frontières** ✉ 14 rue Carnot, Avignon ☎ 04-90-82-31-32. **Provence-Camargue Tours** ✉ 1 rue Émile Fassin, Arles ☎ 04-90-49-85-58.

VISITOR INFORMATION
Regional tourist offices prefer written queries only. The mother lode of general information is the Comité Regional du Tourisme de Provence-Alpes-Côte d'Azur. For information specific to one département, contact the following: Comité Départemental du Tourisme des Bouches-du-Rhône, Comité Départemental du Tourisme du Var, Comité Départemental du Tourisme de Vaucluse. Local tourist offices for major towns covered in this chapter can be phoned, faxed, or addressed by mail.
🚆 Regional Tourist Offices **Comité Regional du Tourisme de Provence-Alpes-Côte d'Azur** ✉ 12 pl. Joliette, 13002 Marseille ☎ 04-91-56-47-00 🖷 04-91-56-47-01 ⊕ www.crt-paca.fr/fre/accueil_flash.jsp. **Comité Départemental du Tourisme des**

Bouches-du-Rhône ✉ 13 rue Roux de Brignole, 13006 Marseille ☏ 04-91-13-84-13 🖷 04-91-33-01-82 ⊕ www.visitprovence.com. **Comité Départemental du Tourisme du Var** ✉ 1 bd. Maréchal Foch, 83300 Draguignan ☏ 04-94-50-55-50 🖷 04-94-50-55-51 ⊕ www.tourismevar.com. **Comité Départemental du Tourisme de Vaucluse** 🖸 B.P. 147, Cedex 1, 84008 Avignon ☏ 04-90-80-47-00 🖷 04-90-86-86-08.

🔳 Local Tourist Offices **Aix** ✉ 2 pl. du Général-de-Gaulle, B.P. 160, Cedex 1, 13605 ☏ 04-42-16-11-61 🖷 04-42-16-11-62 ⊕ www.aixenprovencetourism.com. **Arles** ✉ 35 pl. de la République, 13200 ☏ 04-90-18-41-21 🖷 04-90-93-17-17 ⊕ www.ville-arles. fr. **Avignon** ✉ 41 cours Jean-Jaurès, 84000 ☏ 04-90-82-65-11 🖷 04-90-82-95-03 ⊕ www.ot-avignon.fr. **Marseille** ✉ 4 la Canebière, 13001 ☏ 04-91-13-89-00 🖷 03-91-13-89-20 ⊕ www.destination-marseille.com. **Nîmes** ✉ 6 rue Auguste, 3000 ☏ 04-66-67-29-11 🖷 04-66-21-81-04 ⊕ www.ot-nimes.fr. **Orange** ✉ 5 cours A. Briand, 84100 ☏ 04-90-34-70-88 🖷 04-90-34-99-62 ⊕ www.provence-orange. com. **St-Rémy** ✉ Pl. Jean-Jaurès, 13210 ☏ 04-90-92-05-22 🖷 04-90-92-38-52 ⊕ www.saintremy-de-provence.com.

THE CÔTE D'AZUR

12

Revised and
updated by
Sarah Fraser

Introduction by
Nancy Coons

WITH THE ALPS AND PRE-ALPS PLAYING bodyguard against inland winds and the sultry Mediterranean warming the breezes, the Côte d'Azur is pampered by a nearly tropical climate. This is where the dreamland of azure waters and indigo sky begins, where balustraded white villas edge the blue horizon, evening air is perfumed with jasmine and mimosa, and parasol pines silhouette against sunsets of ripe apricot and gold. As emblematic as the sheet-music cover for a Jazz Age tune, the Côte d'Azur seems to epitomize happiness, a state of being the world pursues with a vengeance.

But the Jazz Age dream confronts modern reality: on the hills that undulate along the blue water, every cliff, cranny, gully, and plain bristles with cubes of hot-pink cement and iron balconies, each skewed to catch a glimpse of the sea and the sun. Like a rosy rash, these crawl and spread, outnumbering the trees and blocking each other's views. Their owners and renters, who arrive on every vacation and at every holiday—Easter, Christmas, Carnival, All Saints' Day—choke the tiered highways with bumper-to-bumper cars, and on a hot day in high summer the traffic to the beach—slow-flowing at any time—coagulates and blisters in the sun.

There has always been a rush to the Côte d'Azur (or Azure Coast), starting with the ancient Greeks, who were drawn eastward from Marseille to market their goods to the natives. From the 18th-century English aristocrats who claimed it as one vast spa to the 19th-century Russian nobles who transformed Nice into a tropical St. Petersburg to the 20th-century American tycoons who cast themselves as romantic sheiks, the beckoning coast became a blank slate for their whims. Like the modern vacationers who followed, they all left their mark—villas, shrines, Moroccan-fantasy castles-in-the-air—temples all to the sensual pleasures of the sun and sultry sea breezes. Artists, too, made the Côte d'Azur their own, as museum goers who have studied the sunny legacy of Picasso, Renoir, Matisse, and Chagall will attest. Today's admirers can take this all in, along with the Riviera's textbook points of interest: animated St-Tropez; the Belle Epoque aura of Cannes; the towns made famous by Picasso—Antibes, Vallauris, Mougins; the urban charms of Nice; and several spots where the per-capita population of billionaires must be among the highest on the planet: Cap d'Antibes, Villefranche-sur-Mer, and Monaco. The latter, once a Belle Epoque fairyland, has for some time been known as the Hong Kong of the Riviera, a bustling community where the sounds of drills tearing up the ground for new construction has mostly replaced the clip-clop of the horse-drawn fiacres. The ghosts of Grace Kelly and Cary Grant must have long since gone elsewhere.

Veterans know that the beauty of the Côte d'Azur coastline is only skin deep, a thin veneer of coddled glamour that hugs the water and hides a much more ascetic region up in the hills. These low-lying mountains and deep gorges are known as the *arriére-pays* (backcountry) for good cause: they are as aloof and isolated as the waterfront resorts are in the swim. Medieval stone villages cap rocky hills and play out scenes of Provençal life—the game of boules, the slowly savored *pastis* (the anise-and-licorice-flavored spirit mixed slowly with water), the farmers' market—as if the ocean were a hundred miles away. Some of them—Èze,

This is the Riviera of Hollywood lore, a land of sunglasses, convertibles, and palm trees lording it over indigo surf. From glamorous St-Tropez and Cannes through picturesque Antibes to sophisticated Nice, this sprawl of pebble beaches and ocher villas has captivated sun lovers and socialites since the days of the Grand Tour. Artists, too: Renoir, Matisse, Picasso, and Cocteau all reveled in its light and adored the golden hill towns of Old Provence: St-Paul, Vence, and Grasse.

Numbers in the text correspond to numbers in the margin and on the Côte d'Azur: St-Tropez to Cannes; the Côte d'Azur: Cannes to Menton; Nice; and Monaco maps.

12

If you have 3 days

Base yourself for the first two days in 🖼 **Antibes** ⑩ ▶, exploring the **Cap d'Antibes** ⑫—one of the few places in the region where the legend lingers; rich and residential, this 3-km-long (2-mi-long) peninsula is studded with private delights (great villas) and public wonders (the Jardin Thuret). Make a daytrip westward to **Cannes** ⑧, a town that maintains its grand-tour grace and glamour even after the film stars head home from its famous film festival; then stop in Picasso country at **Vallauris** ⑬; or head inland for **Vence** ⑯ and 🖼 **St-Paul-de-Vence** ⑰, two gorgeous hill towns famous for their modern art treasures (Matisse's Chapelle du Rosaire among them). After your St-Paul overnight, on Day 3 explore the museums and the Vieille Ville of **Nice** ⑲–㊱, where buildings are sumptuously adorned with wedding-cake half-domes and cupolas.

If you have 5 days

Spend your first day and night in 🖼 **St-Tropez** ❶ ▶, whose fishing-village cachet translates into port-front cafés thick with young gentry affecting nonchalance but peeping furtively over their sunglasses in hope of sighting a film star, then make an excursion up to the hill villages of **Ramatuelle** ❷ and **Gassin** ❸— the latter has a fetching medieval ambience. The next day cruise (or, in high summer, crawl along) the coastal highway N98, stopping to visit **Fréjus** ❺, home to Roman ruins and a fine cathedral. Still on N98, wind around the dramatic Corniche de l'Estérel and make a triumphant entry into 🖼 **Cannes** ⑧, straight down La Croisette. Spend your third morning in **Antibes** ⑩—be sure to visit the famous Château Grimaldi and Picasso museum—then head inland for an afternoon in 🖼 **Vence** ⑯ or 🖼 **St-Paul-de-Vence** ⑰, both good stopovers (and where hotel dining rooms are often hung with Braque sketches). Day 4 could be spent in dazzling **Nice** ⑲–㊱. Then escape for a quiet night in 🖼 **St-Jean-Cap-Ferrat** ㊴, a lush peninsula that shelters the lovely gardens of the Musée Ephrussi de Rothschild. On your last day bet your return ticket on the baccarat tables in **Monaco** ㊷–㊿.

If you have 8 days

Expand the five-day itinerary with a second night in Cannes so you can make a boat trip to one of the idyllic **Iles de Lérins** ❾. Spend two nights in Nice so you can take in the Matisse and Chagall museums and see the Baroque churches in the Vieille Ville. Then spend two nights in 🖼 **Menton** ㊼ to visit its heavenly gardens and then make an excursion to **Roquebrune** ㊶ to see its château and walk the length of the cape.

St-Paul, Vence—have become virtual Provençal theme parks, catering to busloads of tourists day-tripping from the coast. But just behind them, dozens of hill towns stand virtually untouched, and you can lose yourself in a cobblestone maze.

You could drive from St-Tropez to the border of Italy in three hours and take in the entire Riviera, so small is this renowned stretch of Mediterranean coast. Along the way you'll undoubtedly encounter the downside: jammed beaches, insolent waiters serving frozen seafood, traffic gridlock. But once you dabble your feet off the docks in a picturesque port full of brightly painted boats, or drink a Lillet in a hilltop village high above the coast, or tip your face up to the sun from a boardwalk park bench and doze off to the rhythm of the waves, you—like the artists and nobles who paved the way before you—will very likely be seduced to linger.

Exploring the Côte d'Azur

You can visit any spot between St-Tropez and Menton in a day trip; the hilltop villages and towns on the coastal plateau are just as accessible. Thanks to the efficient raceway, A8, you can whisk at high speeds to the exit nearest your destination up or down the coast; thus, even if you like leisurely exploration, you can zoom back to your home base at day's end. The lay of the land east of Nice is nearly vertical, as the coastline is one great cliff, a corniche terraced by three parallel highways—the **Basse Corniche**, the **Moyenne Corniche**, and the **Grande Corniche**—that snake along its graduated crests. The lowest (*basse*) is the slowest, following the coast and crawling through the main streets of resorts—including downtown Monte Carlo, Cap-Martin, Beaulieu, and Villefranche-sur-Mer. The highest (*grande*) is the fastest, but its panoramic views are blocked by villas, and there are few safe overlooks. The middle (*moyenne*) runs from Nice to Menton and offers views down over the shoreline and villages—it passes through a few picturesque towns, most notably Èze. Above the autoroutes, things slow down considerably, but you'll find exploring the winding roads and overlooks between villages an experience in itself.

About the Restaurants & Hotels

Even in tiny villages some haute cuisine places can be as dressy, if not more so, than Monaco, but in general, restaurants on the Côte D'Azur are quite relaxed. At lunchtime, a T-shirt and shorts are just fine in all but the fanciest places; bathing suits, however, should be kept for the beach. Nighttime wear is casual, too—but be aware that for after-dinner drinks, many clubs and discos draw the line at running shoes and jeans.

If you've come from other regions in France—even western Provence—you'll notice a sharp hike in hotel prices, costly by any measure, but actually vertiginous in summer. In Cannes and Nice the grand hotels are big on prestige and weak on swimming pools, which are usually just big enough to dip in; their private beaches are on the opposite side of the busy street, and you pay for access, just as nonguests do. It's up in the hills above the coast that you'll find the charm you expect from France,

12

Relishing the Riviera

The Côte d'Azur is home to such posh villages as Mougins, a medieval township filled with restaurants that showcase the "new Mediterranean cuisine" in all its costly splendor: "scrambled" sea urchins; herb sausages with chopped truffles and lobster; frogs' legs soup with fresh mint; Sisteron lamb with Madeira sauce; and poached sea bass flan with crayfish sauce. Grand names like Alain Ducasse still present such delights at showplaces like Le Louis XV, but there are any number of young stars on the make—Jean-Paul Battaglia at Mougins's Le Feu Follet, to name one. But you can also go the less-than-*haute* route and simply stock up with fixings for a country picnic at any of the village food markets, such as the great one in Valbonne. In between the high and the low, you'll want to get to know the main regional delights. Typical throughout the Côte d' Azur, but especially at home with a slab of fresh coastal fish, the garlicky mayonnaise called aioli is a staple condiment—in many areas of the region this delight is called *la rouille*. Even more pungent is the powerful paste called *anchoiade*, made of strong, salty anchovies. Fresh Mediterranean fish, such as *rouget* (mullet) and *loup* (sea bass), are often served grilled with a crunch of fennel. Niçois specialties include the *pissaladière*, the father of modern pizza, topped with a heap of caramelized onions. Try *socca*, a paste of ground chickpeas smeared on a griddle and scraped up like a gritty pancake; *petits farcis*, a selection of red peppers, zucchini, and eggplant stuffed with spicy sausage paste and roasted; and sardine beignets, fresh, whole sardines fried in a thick puff of spicy batter. Down it all with a glass of one of the great regional rosé wines.

Picasso & Company

Because the Côte d'Azur has long nurtured a relationship among artists, art lovers, and wealthy patrons, this region is blessed with superb art museums. Renoir, Picasso, Matisse, Chagall, Cocteau, Léger, and Dufy all left their mark here; museums devoted to their work are scattered along the coast, most notably the Musée Picasso at Antibes's Château Grimaldi, the smaller Picasso museum in Vallauris, Renoir's house in Cagnes, and the Matisse museum in Nice (not forgetting Matisse's sublime Chapelle de Rosaire in Vence). Formidable collections of modern masters and contemporary works can be seen in the museums of Nice and at the Fondation Maeght above St-Paul, while St-Tropez has a good collection of Impressionist paintings of its port at the Musée de l'Annonciade.

Sunbelievable Beaches

With their worldwide fame as the earth's most glamorous beaches, the real thing often comes as a shock to first-timers: much of the Côte d'Azur is lined with rock and pebble, and the beaches are narrow swaths backed by city streets or roaring highways. Only St-Tropez, Cannes, and isolated bits around Fréjus and Antibes have sandy waterfronts, hence their legendary popularity. Many beaches are privately operated, renting parasols and mattresses to anyone who pays; if you're a guest at one of the local hotels, you'll get a discount. Fees for private beaches average €6–€10 for a dressing room and mattress, between €2 and €4 for a parasol, and between €4 and €5 for a cabana to call your own. Private beaches alternate with open stretches of public frontage.

both in sophisticated hotels with gastronomic restaurants and in friendly mom-and-pop auberges (inns); the farther north you drive, the lower the prices. Assume all hotel rooms have air-conditioning, TV, telephones, and private bath, unless otherwise noted. Internet, when listed in facilities, means in-room data ports and/or public-area computer provides computer access.

WHAT IT COSTS In euros				
	$$$$	$$$	$$	$	¢
RESTAURANTS	over €30	€23–€30	€17–€23	€11–€17	under €11
HOTELS	over €190	€120–€190	€80–€120	€50–€80	under €50

Restaurant prices are per person for a main course at dinner only, including tax (19.6%) and service; note that if a restaurant offers only prix-fixe (set-price) meals, it has been given the price category that reflects the full prix-fixe price. Hotel prices are for a standard double room in high season, including tax (19.6%) and service charge; higher prices (inquire when booking) prevail for any meal plans.

Timing

Unless you enjoy jacked-up prices, traffic jams, and sardine-style beach crowds, avoid the coast like the plague in July and August. Many of the better restaurants simply shut down to avoid the coconut-oil crowd, and the Estérel is closed to hikers during this flash-fire season. Cannes books up early for the film festival in May, so aim for another month (April, June, September, or October). Between Cannes and Menton, the Côte d'Azur's gentle microclimate usually provides moderate winters; it's protected by the Estérel from the mistral wind that razors through Fréjus and St-Raphaël.

ST-TROPEZ TO ANTIBES

Flanked at each end by subtropical capes and crowned by the red-rock Estérel, this stretch of the coast has a variety of waterfront landmarks. St-Tropez first blazed into fame when it was discovered by painters like Paul Signac and writers like Colette. Since then it has never looked back, and remains one of the most animated little stretches of territory on the Côte d'Azur, flooded at high season with people who like to roost at waterfront cafés and watch the passing parade. St-Tropez vies with Cannes for name recognition and glamour, but the more modest resorts— Ste-Maxime, Fréjus, and St-Raphaël—offer a more affordable Riviera experience. Historic Antibes and jazzy Juan-les-Pins straddle the subtropical peninsula of Cap d'Antibes.

St-Tropez

 35 km (22 mi) southwest of Fréjus, 66 km (41 mi) northeast of Toulon.

At first glance, it really doesn't look all that lovely: there's a moderately pretty port full of bobbing boats, a picturesque *Vieille Ville* (Old Town) in candied-almond hues, sandy beaches, and old-fashioned squares with plane trees and *pétanque* (lawn bowling) players. So what made St-Tropez

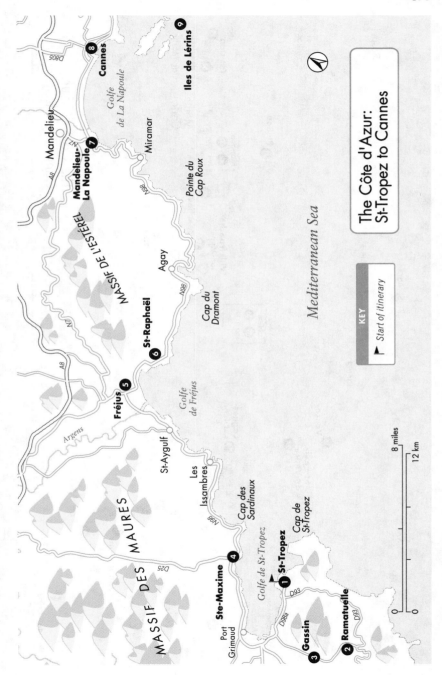

The Côte d'Azur: St-Tropez to Cannes

KEY

▲ Start of itinerary

Mediterranean Sea

8 miles

12 km

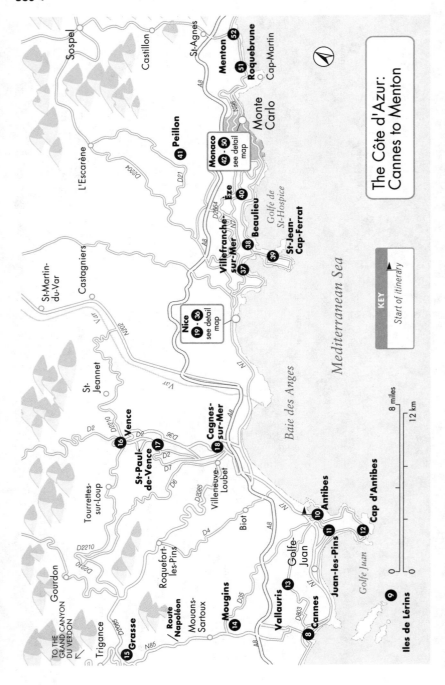

The Côte d'Azur:
Cannes to Menton

KEY

Start of itinerary

Mediterranean Sea

Baie des Anges

Golfe Juan

Golfe de St-Hospice

Iles de Lérins

a household word? In two words: Brigitte Bardot. When this *pulpeuse* (voluptuous) teenager showed up in St-Tropez on the arm of the late Roger Vadim in 1956 to film *And God Created Woman,* the heads of the world snapped to attention. Neither the gentle descriptions of writer Guy de Maupassant (1850–93) nor the watercolor tones of Impressionist Paul Signac (1863–1935) nor the stream of painters who followed him (including Matisse and Bonnard) could focus the world's attention on this seaside hamlet as could this one luscious female, in head scarf, Ray-Bans, and capri pants. With the film world following in her steps, St-Tropez became the hot spot it to some extent remains. What makes it worthwhile is if you get up early (before the 11 o'clock breakfast rush at Le Gorille Café and other port-side spots lining quai Suffern and quai Jean-Jaurès) and wander the medieval backstreets and waterfront by yourself, you'll experience what the artists first found to love and what remains of the village's real charms: its soft light, warm pastels, and the scent of the sea wafting in from the waterfront.

Anything associated with the distant past almost seems absurd in St-Tropez. Still, the place has a history that predates the invention of the string bikini, and people have been finding reasons to come here since AD 68, when a Roman soldier from Pisa named Torpes was beheaded for professing his Christian faith in front of Emperor Nero, transforming this spot into a place of pilgrimage. Since then people have come for the sun, the sea, and, much more recently, the celebrities. The latter—ever since St-Tropez became "hot" again, there have been Elton, Barbra, Oprah, and Jack sightings—stay hidden in villas, so the people you'll see are mere mortals, lots of them, many intent on displaying the best (or at least the most) of their youth, beauty, and wealth. Still, if you take an early morning stroll along the harbor or down the narrow medieval streets—the rest of the town will still be sleeping off the Night Before—you'll see just how charming St-Tropez is. There's a weekend's worth of boutiques to explore and many cute cafés where you can sit under colored awnings and watch the spectacle that is St-Trop (*trop* in French means too much) saunter by. Along medieval streets lined with walled gardens and little squares set with dripping fountains you'll be able to discover historic delights like the Chapelle de la Misericorde, topped by its wrought-iron campanile, and Rue Allard, lined with picturesque houses like the "Maison du Maure." In the evening, everyone moves from the cafés on the quais to the cafés on the squares, particularly place des Lices, where a seat at the Café des Arts allows you to watch the boule players under the glow of hundreds of electric bulbs. Paging Deborah Kerr and David Niven in *Bonjour Tristesse.*

★ Happily, the legacy of the artists who loved St-Tropez has been preserved in the extraordinary **Musée de l'Annonciade** (Annunciation Museum), a 14th-century chapel converted to an art museum that alone merits a visit to St-Tropez. Works by Signac, Matisse, Signard, Braque, Dufy, Vuillard, and Rouault, many of them painted in (and about) St-Tropez, trace the evolution of painting from Impressionism to Expressionism. ⊠ *Quai de l'Épi/pl. Georges Grammont* ☎ *04-94-97-04-01* ☜ *€4.50* ⊙ *June–Sept., Wed.–Mon. 10–noon and 3–7; Oct.–May, Wed.–Mon. 10–noon and 2–6* ⊙ *Closed Nov.*

CloseUp

THE DOGS OF ST-TROPEZ

N AD 68 the Roman emperor Nero *had a centurion from Pisa decapitated for his Christian tendencies; to drive the lesson home for witnesses, he had the headless body placed in a boat with a cock and a dog, then set adrift at sea. When the boat washed ashore on St-Tropez's beach, the starving animals still kept their loyal vigil, refusing to touch the holy flesh.*

Perhaps it's because of this heroic act of self-discipline that dogs are held in such high esteem in modern St-Tropez. They are clearly the companion (and accessory) of choice, as prevalent as mobile phones in the Vieux Port cafés.

Whether tucked into handbags, strutted in pairs as beautifully matched as coach horses, dyed to match their mistress's hair, bounding nobly out of yachts, snarling at each other from under café tables, or lapping out of the ice bucket that chilled the champagne, they provide a spectacle almost as intriguing as their owners.

If you want to get the right port-front table at Le Gorille, consider borrowing a dog and accessorizing appropriately. Want to look like your yacht's being swabbed down for that lunch-run to Monte Carlo? A Lhasa Apso to match your ascot. Showing those canvases you daubed in the Alps last winter? Hot pants, hip-length hair, Timberlands, and an Afghan hound.

Your bistro courting the Festival crowd out of Cannes? Green Lacoste sweater, red toupée, red German shepherd. Just drawn up a marriage contract to cover the London flat and Daddy's domain in Burgundy? Matching buckskin jackets, separate phones, and a twinned team of golden retrievers.

From the quai, head up rue Laugier and rue de la Citadelle to the 16th-century **Citadelle,** which stands in a lovely hilltop park; its ramparts offer up a fantastic view over the town and the sea. Inside its donjon the **Musée Naval** (Naval Museum) displays ship models, cannons, and pictures of St-Tropez from its days as a naval port. Right on the coast is the lovely **Cimetière Marin,** where some noted natives are buried, including film director Roger Vadim. In places, the waves lap up just a few feet from the graves. ⊠ *Rue de la Citadelle* ☎ *04-94-97-59-43* ☞ *€4* ☉ *Dec.–Easter, Wed.–Mon. 10–12:30 and 1:30–5:30; Easter–Oct., daily 9–12:30 and 1:30–6:30.*

From the citadel head back down and lose yourself in the **Quartier de la Ponche,** the Vieille Ville maze of backstreets and old ramparts daubed in shades of gold, pink, ocher, and sky-blue. Trellised jasmine and wrought-iron birdcages hang from shuttered windows, and many of the tiny streets dead-end at the sea. Wander back across rue Citadelle to the medieval rue Miséricorde, which leads to the 17th-century Chapelle de la Miséricorde, and on to rue Gambetta. Chances are you won't bump into La Bardot—she spends most of her time at her villa, La Madrague, which overlooks the Plage des Canebiers.

Where to Stay & Eat

$$$$ ✕ **Lei Mouscardins.** Breton-born chef Laurent Tarridec has left the Bistrot des Lices for a spectacular seaside locale offering 180-degree sea views, just on the edge of St-Tropez's Vieille Ville. His cooking, however, maintains the sophisticated tradition of upscale Provençal cuisine: opt for a frothy mullet soup, roast pigeon with caramelized garlic and prunes, the house bourride, or the tender, long-simmered veal. Fixed-price menus are €58 and €130. ⊠ *Tour du Portalet* ☎ *04-94-97-29-00* ⊕ *www. leimouscardins.com* ⊟ *AE, DC, MC, V* ☻ *Closed Tues.; mid-Nov.–mid-Dec. and mid-Jan.–mid-Feb.*

$$-$$$ ✕ **La Table du Marché.** With an afternoon tearoom and a summer sushi bar, this charming bistro, masterminded by celebrity chef Christophe Leroy, offers up a mouthwatering spread of regional specialties. For something light, try the tomato pistou tart or dive into an €18 or €25 set menu and sink into one of the overstuffed armchairs in the upstairs dining room, cozy with warm colors, chic Provençal accents, and antique bookshelves. ⊠ *38 rue Georges Clemanceau* ☎ *04-94-97-85-20* ⊟ *AE, MC, V.*

$-$$ ✕ **Le Girelier.** Like his father before him, chef Yves Rouet makes an effort to prepare Mediterranean-only fish for his buffed and bronzed clientele, who enjoy the casual sea-shanty decor and the highly visible Vieux Port terrace tables. Grilling is the order of the day, with most fish sold by weight, but this is also a stronghold of bouillabaisse. ⊠ *Quai Jean-Jaurès* ☎ *04-94-97-03-87* ⊕ *www.legirelier. com* ⊟ *AE, DC, MC, V* ☻ *Closed Nov.–Mar., Mon., and closed for lunch July and Aug.*

$$$$ ✕⊡ **Le Byblos.** Arranged like a toy Provençal village, fronted with stunning red, rust, and yellow facades, and complete with ocher-stucco cottagelike suites grouped around courtyards landscaped with palms, olive trees, and lavender, this landmark stresses fitness and beauty treatment. Guest rooms are *à la provençale,* but modern in comfort. Chef Georges Pelissier creates artful classics with a Mediterranean touch: sea bass roasted with salsify and garlic chips or rib-sticking beef tournedos with foie gras. Opt for more nouvelle Med fireworks on offer at **Spoon Byblos** (⊠ Entrance on av. du Maréchal-Foch ☎ 04-94-56-68-20) the latest outpost of superstar chef Alain Ducasse. At evening, all head to the hotel's Caves du Roy—a gigantic disco extravaganza. ⊠ *Av. Paul-Signac, 83990* ☎ *04-94-56-68-00* ⊟ *04-94-56-68-01* ⊕ *www.byblos.com* ⇱ *52 rooms, 43 suites* ⚲ *2 restaurants, minibars, cable TV, pool, gym, health club, spa, nightclub, baby-sitting, Internet, meeting room, free parking, some pets allowed (fee)* ⊟ *AE, DC, MC, V* ☻ *Closed mid-Oct.–Easter* ⊖l *EP.*

$$$$ ✕⊡ **La Résidence de la Pinède.** Perhaps the most opulent of St-Tropez's luxe hangouts, this balustraded white villa and its broad annex sprawl elegantly along a private waterfront, wrapped around an isolated courtyard and a pool shaded by parasol pines. Louis XVI bérgères, a beam here and there, gilt frames, indirect spots, and oh-so-comfy beds make for an alluring if overly homogenized interior. Pay extra for a seaside room, where you can lean over the balcony and take in broad views of the coast and the large seafront restaurant; the chef has a celebrated reputation, and you'll understand why after one taste of his truffled ravioli. Rates including half-board are available. ✉ *Plage de la Bouillabaisse, 83991* ☎ *04-94-55-91-00* 🖶 *04-94-97-73-64* ⊕ *www. residencepinede.com* ↪ *35 rooms, 4 suites* ♿ *Restaurant, minibars, cable TV, pool, bar, Internet, meeting room, some pets allowed (fee), free parking* ▭ *AE, DC, MC, V* ⊘ *Closed mid-Oct.–mid-Apr.* ⦿ *MAP.*

$$-$$$ 🏨 **Ermitage.** Surrounded by mimosas and lemon trees, this big, old-fashioned, tangerine-hue hotel is on a hill above town and, from its back rooms and garden, commands striking sea views. The fireplace and colonial rattan in the bar; the solid, light-bathed rooms in soft pastels; and owner Annie Bolloreis's friendly welcome make this a real charmer. ✉ *Av. Paul-Signac, 83990* ☎ *04-94-97-52-33* 🖶 *04-94-97-10-43* ↪ *27 rooms* ♿ *Bar, some pets allowed (fee), free parking; no a/c* ▭ *MC, V* ⦿ *EP.*

★ $-$$ 🏨 **Lou Cagnard.** Inside an enclosed garden courtyard, this pretty little hotel is owned by an enthusiastic young couple that is fixing it up room by room. Five ground-floor rooms open onto the lovely manicured garden, where breakfast is served in the shade of a fig tree. Freshly decorated rooms have regional tiles and Provençal fabrics. ✉ *18 av. Paul Roussel, 83900* ☎ *04-94-97-04-24* 🖶 *04-94-97-09-44* ⊕ *www. hotel-lou-cagnard.com* ↪ *19 rooms* ♿ *No a/c* ▭ *MC, V* ⊘ *Closed Nov.–late Dec.* ⦿ *EP.*

Nightlife & the Arts

The most elite and sought-after nightspot in St-Tropez is the evergreen **Les Caves du Roy** (✉ Byblos Hotel, av. Paul-Signac ☎ 04-94-97-16-02). **Le Papagayo** (✉ Résidence du Port ☎ 04-94-54-88-18), a vast disco, caters to a crowd of young teens and twentysomethings. The **VIP Room** (✉ Residence du nouveau Port ☎ 04-94-97-14-70) draws a chic mix of young professionals and baby boomers. Every July and August, **classical music concerts** (✉ Rte. des Salins ☎ 04-94-97-45-21 information) are given in the gardens of the Château de la Moutte. For ticket information inquire at the tourist office.

The Outdoors

The best *plages* (beaches) are scattered along a 5-km (3-mi) stretch reached by the Route des Plages (Beach Road); the most fashionable are **Moorea** and **Club 55**; the most daring is the mostly topless **Tahiti.** Those beaches close to town—**Plage des Greniers** and the **Bouillabaisse**—are accessible on foot, but many prefer the 10-km (6-mi) sandy crescent at **Les Salins** and the long, sandy stretch of the **Plage de Pampelonne**, 4 km (3 mi) from town. Bicycles are an ideal way to get to the beach, and **Espace 83** (✉ 2 av. Général-Leclerc ☎ 04-94-55-80-00) is a popular place for rentals. **Holiday Bikes** (✉ 14 av. Général-Leclerc ☎ 04-94-97-09-39) offers a wide variety of bikes for hire.

Shopping

Rue Sibilli, behind the quai Suffren, is lined with all kinds of trendy boutiques. The **place des Lices** overflows with produce, regional foods, clothing, and *brocantes* (collectibles) on Tuesday and Saturday mornings. The picturesque little fish market fills up **place aux Herbes** every morning.

Ramatuelle

❷ *12 km (7 mi) southwest of St-Tropez.*

A typical hilltop whorl of red-clay roofs and dense inner streets topped with arches and lined with arcades, this ancient market town was destroyed in the Wars of Religion and rebuilt as a harmonious whole in 1620, complete with venerable archways and vaulted passages. Now its souvenir shops and galleries attract day-trippers out of St-Tropez, who enjoy the pretty drive through the vineyards as much as the village itself. The town cemetery is the final resting place of Gérard Phillipe, an aristocratic heartthrob who died in 1959 after making his mark in such films as *Le Diable au Corps.*

en route From Ramatuelle the lovely ride to the hilltop village of Gassin takes you through vineyards and woods full of twisted cork oaks over the highest point of the peninsula (1,070 feet).

Where to Stay & Eat

$$$$ ✕▦ **Les Moulins.** A satellite of planet St-Tropez, this outpost of showbiz chef Christophe Leroy lures off-duty celebrities and the swank to its lovely perch near Pampelonne beach. Ceiling fans, rattan chairs, and blonde-wood accents heighten the pleasure of the scrumptious dishes served here—don't miss out on the vichyssoise with truffles. Upstairs are five cozy, rustic guest rooms. ⊠ *Route des Plages, 83350* ☎ *04–94–97–17–22* ⊕ *04–94–79–72–70* ⊕ *www.christophe-leroy. com* ⌨ *5 rooms* ⚐ *Restaurant, cable TV, some pets allowed* ⊟ *AE, MC, V* ⊗ *Closed Nov.–Mar.* ⍩ *MAP.*

$–$$ ✕▦ **Ferme Ladouceur.** Not far from the talcum-powder beach of Pampelonne and surrounded by vineyards is this *naïf* farmhouse, domain of Constance Ladouceur, whose paintings adorn the hallways and whose restaurant is a draw for budget-minded locals. Quirky, simple, affordable, with breakfast included in the price—little wonder you need to book here far in advance. ⊠ *Quartier la Rouillère, 83350* ☎ *04–94–79–24–95* ⊕ *04–94–79–12–14* ⍩ *7 rooms* ⚐ *Restaurant, some pets allowed; no a/c, no room phones, no room TVs* ⊟ *AE, MC, V* ⊗ *Closed Nov.–Mar.* ⍩ *BP.*

Gassin

❸ *7 km (4½ mi) north of Ramatuelle.*

Though not as picturesque as Ramatuelle, this hilltop village gives you spectacular views over the surrounding vineyards and St-Tropez's bay. In winter, before the summer haze drifts in and after the mistral has given the sky a good scrub, you may be able to make out a brilliant white chain of Alps looming on the horizon. There's less commerce here to keep you distracted; for shops, head to Ramatuelle.

Where to Stay & Eat

$$$$ ✕▦ **Villa Belrose.** Done up in a glitzy Côte d'Azur Louis Seize, this Hollywoodesque palace perched on the highest point of the peninsula has unrivaled views of the Gulf of St-Tropez and the kind of decadently rich élan that would make Scott and Zelda feel right at home. This hotel was opened in the late 1990s so don't come here for any real historic ambience. Public salons have Louis XVI and Florentine accents, while guest rooms are spacious yet cozy, with marble bathrooms and romantic balconies. Besides the 180-degree views, the restaurant, run by Alain Ducasse disciple Thierry Thiercelin, supplies first-rate Mediterranean cuisine, pleasant service, and a top-drawer wine list. Rates including half-board are available. ⊠ *Bd. Crète, 83580* ☎ *04–94–55–97–97* 🖷 *04–94–55–97–98* ⊕ *www.relaischateaux.fr* ⇆ *34 rooms, 2 suites, 2 apartments* ⟑ *Restaurant, minibars, cable TV, pool, spa, bar, Internet, some pets allowed (fee)* ⊟ *AE, DC, MC, V* ⊘ *Closed Nov.–mid Mar.* ⟲ *MAP.*

Ste-Maxime

❹ *8 km (5 mi) east of Port-Grimaud, 33 km (20 mi) east of St-Tropez.*

You may be put off by the heavily built-up waterfront bristling with parking-garage-style apartments and hotels, and its position directly on the waterfront highway, but Ste-Maxime is an affordable family resort with fine sandy beaches. It even has a sliver of car-free Vieille Ville and a stand of majestic plane trees sheltering central place Victor-Hugo. The main beach, north of town, is the wide and sandy La Nartelle.

Fréjus

❺ *19 km (12 mi) northeast of Ste-Maxime, 37 km (23 mi) northeast of St-Tropez.*

After a stroll on the sandy curve along the tacky, overcommercial Fréjus-Plage (Fréjus Beach), turn your back on modern times and head uphill to Fréjus-Centre. Here you'll enter a maze of narrow streets lined with small shops barely touched by the cult of the lavender sachet. The farmers' market (Monday, Wednesday, and Saturday mornings) is as real and lively as any in Provence, and the cafés encircling the fountains and squares nourish an easygoing social scene.

Yet Fréjus has the honor of owning some of the most important historic monuments on the coast. Founded in 49 BC by Julius Caesar himself and named Forum Julii, this quiet town was once a thriving Roman city of 40,000 citizens. Today you can see the remains. Just outside the Vieille Ville is the Roman **Théâtre Antique**; its remaining rows of arches are mostly intact, and much of its stage works are still visible at its center. The **Arènes** (often called the Amphithéâtre) is still used today for concerts and bullfights. Back down on the coast, a big French naval base occupies the spot where ancient Roman galleys once set out to defeat Cleopatra and Mark Anthony at the Battle of Actium.

★ Fréjus is also graced with one of the most impressive religious monuments in Provence: called the **Groupe Épiscopal**, it's made up of an early Gothic **cathedral**, a 5th-century Roman-style **baptistery**, and an early Gothic **cloister**, its gallery painted in sepia and earth tones with a phantasmagoric assortment of animals and biblical characters. Off the entrance and gift shop is a small museum of finds from Roman Fréjus, including a complete mosaic and a sculpture of a two-headed Hermès. ⌧ *58 rue de Fleury* ☎ *04–94–51–26–30* ✆ *Cathedral free; cloister, museum, and baptistery* €*4.60* ☉ *Cathedral daily 8:30–noon and 2–6. Cloister, museum, and baptistery Apr.–Sept., daily 9–6; Oct.–Mar., Tues.–Sun. 9–noon and 2–5.*

St-Raphaël

❻ *1 km (½ mi) southeast of Fréjus, 41 km (25½ mi) southwest of Cannes.*

Right next door to Fréjus, with almost no division between, is St-Raphaël, a sprawling resort town with a busy downtown anchored by a casino. It's also a major sailing center, has five golf courses nearby, and draws the weary and indulgent to its seawater-based thalassotherapy. It serves as a major rail crossroads, the closest stop to St-Tropez. The port has a rich history: Napoléon landed at St-Raphaël on his triumphant return from Egypt in 1799; it was also from here in 1814 that he cast off for Elba in disgrace. And it was here, too, that the Allied forces landed in their August 1944 offensive against the Germans.

Where to Stay & Eat

$$$–$$$$ ✕ **La Bouillabaisse.** Enter through the beaded curtain covering the open doorway to a wood-panel room decked out with starfish and the mounted head of a swordfish: this classic hole-in-the-wall has a brief, straightforward menu inspired by the fish markets. You might have the half lobster with spicy *rouille* (peppers and garlic whipped with olive oil), the seafood-stuffed paella, or the generous house bouillabaisse. ⌧ *50 pl. Victor-Hugo* ☎ *04–94–95–03–57* ▭ *AE, MC, V* ☉ *Closed Mon.*

★ $ ▦ **Le Thimothée.** The owners of this bargain lodging are throwing themselves wholeheartedly into improving an already attractive 19th-century villa. They've also restored the garden, with its grand palms and pines shading the walk to the pretty little swimming pool. Though it's tucked away in a neighborhood far from the waterfront, top-floor rooms have poster-perfect sea views. ⌧ *375 bd. Christian-Lafon, 83700* ☎ *04–94–40–49–49* ▤ *04–94–19–41–92* ⊕ *www.thimothee. com* ⇌ *12 rooms* ⚴ *Minibars, cable TV, pool; no a/c in some rooms* ▭ *AE, MC, V* ⍭ *EP.*

en route The rugged **Massif de l'Estérel,** between St-Raphaël and Cannes, is a hiker's dream. Made up of rust-red volcanic rocks (porphyry) carved by the sea into dreamlike shapes, the harsh landscape (now made even harsher due to the ravages of forest fires set by greedy developers) is softened by patches of lavender, scrub pine, and gorse. By car, take N7, the mountain route to the north, and lose yourself in the desert landscape far from the sea. Or keep on N98, the **Corniche de l'Estérel** (the coastal road along the dramatic corniche), and drive past little coves dotted with sunbathers, tiny calanques and sheer rock faces plunging down to the waves. Try to leave early in the morning, as tempers fray when the route gets congested with afternoon traffic.

Mandelieu–La Napoule

7 *32 km (20 mi) northeast of St-Raphaël, 8 km (5 mi) southwest of Cannes.*

La Napoule is the small, old-fashioned port village devoured by the big-fish resort town of Mandelieu. You can visit Mandelieu for a golf-and-sailing retreat—the town is replete with many sporting facilities and hosts a bevy of sporting events, including sailing regattas, windsurfing contests, golf championships (there are two major golf courses in Mandelieu right in the center of town by the sea), and, every August, the Kelly Challenge, a rowing regatta named after Grace Kelly's father, who was a keen oarsman—and La Napoule for a port-side stroll, a meal, or a tour of its peculiar castle.

★ Set on Pointe des Pendus (Hanged Man's Point), the **Château de la Napoule,** looming over the sea and the port, is a bizarre hybrid of Romanesque, Gothic, Moroccan, and Hollywood cooked up by the eccentric American sculptor Henry Clews (1876–1937). Working with his architect wife, he transformed the 14th-century bastion into something that suited his own expectations and then filled the place with his fantastical sculptures. Fond of spouting Nietzsche to his titled dinner guests, surrounding himself with footmen and lackeys, and dedicating his house to Don Quixote (its name is actually "Mancha"), Clewes may have had a dubious artistic vision but he certainly enjoyed a vibrant sense of fantasy. The couple resides in their tombs in the tower crypt, its windows left slightly ajar to permit their souls to escape and allow them to "return at eventide as sprites and dance upon the windowsill." Today the château's foundation hosts visiting writers and artists, who set to work surrounded by Clews's gargoyle-ish sculptures. ✉ *Av. Henry Clews* ☎ *04–93–49–95–05* 🎟 *€6* ⏲ *Guided visits daily at 11:30, 2:30 and 3:30.*

Where to Stay & Eat

$$$–$$$$ ✕ **L'Oasis.** This Gothic villa by the sea is home to Stéphane Raimbault, a master of Provençal cuisine and a great connoisseur of Asian techniques and flavorings. The combination creates unexpected delights—Jabugo ham with anise, lobster, and ginger, or Thai-spiced crayfish with squid-ink ravioli—all exceedingly delicious *and* beautifully presented on a garden terrace filled with plants. ✉ *Rue J. H. Carle* ☎ *04–93–49–95–52* 💳 *AE, MC, V* ⏲ *No dinner Sun., no lunch Mon. May–Sept.; closed mid-Jan.–mid-Feb.*

★ **$$$** ✕ **Le Boucanier.** The drab, low-ceiling dining room is upstaged by wraparound plate-glass views of the marina and château at this waterfront favorite. Locals gather here for mountains of oysters and whole fish, simply grilled and served with a drizzle of fruity olive oil, a pinch of rock salt, or a brief flambé in pastis. ✉ *Port de La Napoule* ☎ *04–93–49–80–51* 💳 *AE, DC, MC, V.*

$$$–$$$$ 🏨 **Le Domaine d'Olival.** Set back from the coast on its own vast landscaped grounds along the Siagne River, this inn has a Provençal feel that belies its waterfront-resort situation. Bright rooms with country-fresh fabrics have built-in furniture and small kitchenettes. Balconies, ideal for breakfast, overlook the semitropical garden. ✉ *778 av. de la Mer, 06210* ☎ *04–93–49–31–00* 📠 *04–92–97–69–28* *7 rooms, 11 suites*

♻ *Minibars, cable TV, tennis court, pool, Internet, some pets allowed, free parking* ⊟ *AE, DC, MC, V* ⊘ *Closed Nov.–mid-Jan.* ⏹ *EP.*

Sports
The **Golf Club de Cannes-Mandelieu** (⊠ Rte. du Golf ☎ 04–92–97–32–00) is one of the most beautiful in the south of France; it is bliss to play on English turf, under Mediterranean pines with mimosa blooming here and there in the spring. The club has two courses—one with 18 holes (par 71) and one with 9 (par 33).

Cannes

❽ *73 km (45 mi) northeast of St-Tropez, 33 km (20 mi) southwest of Nice, 908 km (563 mi) southeast of Paris.*

A tasteful and expensive breeding ground for the upscale (and those who are already "up"), Cannes is a sybaritic heaven for those who believe that life is short and sin has something to do with the absence of a tan. Backed by gentle hills and flanked to the southwest by the Estérel, warmed by dependable sun but kept bearable in summer by the cool Mediterranean breeze, Cannes is pampered with the luxurious climate that has made it one of the most popular and glamorous resorts in Europe. Ever since the 1860s, the cynosure of sun worshipers, it has been further glamorized by the success of its film festival.

Its bay served as nothing more than a fishing port until 1834, when an English aristocrat, Lord Brougham, made an emergency stopover with his sick daughter and fell in love with the site. He had a home built here and returned every winter for a sun cure—a ritual quickly picked up by his peers. With the democratization of modern travel, Cannes has become a tourist and convention town; there are now 20 compact Twingos for every Rolls-Royce. But glamour—and the perception of glamour—is self-perpetuating, and as long as Cannes enjoys its ravishing climate and setting, it will maintain its incomparable panache. If you're a culture-lover into art of the noncelluloid type, however, you should look elsewhere—there are only two museums here: one is devoted to history, the other to a collection of dolls. Still, as his lordship understood, this is a great place to pass the winter.

Pick up a map at the tourist office in the **Palais des Festivals,** the scene of the famous Festival International du Film, known as the Cannes Film Festival. As you leave the information center, follow the Palais to your right to see the red-carpeted stairs where the stars ascend every year. Set into the surrounding pavement, the **Allée des Etoiles** (Stars' Walk) enshrines some 300 autographed imprints of film stars' hands—of Dépardieu, Streep, and Stallone, among others.

The most delightful thing to do is to head to the famous mile-long waterfront promenade, **La Croisette,** which starts at the western end by the Palais des Festivals, and let the *esprit de Cannes* take control. This is precisely the sort of place for which the verb *flâner* (to dawdle, saunter) was invented, so stroll among the palm trees and flowers and crowds of strolling poseurs (fur coats in tropical weather, cell phones on

Rollerblades, and sunglasses at night). Head east past the broad expanse of private beaches, glamorous shops, and luxurious hotels (such as the wedding-cake Carlton, famed for its see-and-be-seen terrace-level brasserie). The beaches along here are almost all private, though open for a fee—each beach is marked with between one and four little life buoys, rating their quality and expense. If you need a culture fix, check out the modern art and photography exhibitions (varying admission prices) held at the **Malmaison**, a 19th-century mansion that was once part of the Grand Hotel. ⊠ *47 La Croisette, La Croisette* ☎ *04–93–06–44–90* ⊘ *Sept.–June, daily 10:30–12:30 and 2–6:30; July–Aug., daily 10:30–12:30 and 2–7:30.*

need a break? Head down the Croisette and fight for a spot at **Le 72 Croisette** (⊠ 72 La Croisette, 04–93–94–18–30)—the most feistily French of all the Croisette bars and open 24 hours a day, it offers great ringside seats for watching the rich and famous enter the Martinez hotel next door.

Two blocks behind La Croisette lies **rue d'Antibes**, Cannes's main high-end shopping street. At its western end is **rue Meynadier**, packed tight with trendy clothing boutiques and fine food shops. Not far away is the covered **Marché Forville**, the scene of the animated morning food market. Hidden away in this section of town is the tiny, eccentric, and unfortunately easy to miss **Musée de l'Enfance** (Museum of Childhood), where collector Madame Nicod gives an intimate version of 19th-century French history through a display of antique dolls and accessories. ⊠ *2 rue Venizelos, Le Suquet* ☎ *04–93–68–29–28* ⊠ *€5.50* ⊘ *By appointment only.*

Climb up rue St-Antoine into the picturesque Vieille Ville neighborhood known as **Le Suquet,** on the site of the original Roman *castrum.* Shops proffer Provençal goods, and the atmospheric theme restaurants give you a chance to catch your breath; the pretty pastel shutters, Gothic stonework, and narrow passageways are lovely distractions. The hill is crowned by the 11th-century château, housing the **Musée de la Castre,** and the imposing four-sided **Tour du Suquet** (Suquet Tower), built in 1385 as a lookout against Saracen-led invasions. ⊠ *Pl. de la Castre, Le Suquet* ☎ *04–93–38–55–26* ⊠ *€3* ⊘ *Apr.–June, Wed.–Mon. 10–noon and 2–6; July–Sept., Wed.–Mon. 10–noon and 2–7; Oct.–Dec. and Feb.–Mar., Wed.–Mon. 10–noon and 2–5.*

Where to Stay & Eat

★ **$$$$** ✕**La Villa des Lys.** Superstar decorator Jacques Garcia only works for art-collecting billionaires, high-style industrialists, and the most-talked-about restaurants. Into that latter category falls the Villa de Lys, home to the culinary wizard Bruno Oiger, who produces stunning menus that leave discerning palettes craving more. Inspired by the Belle-Epoque-meets-the-Parthenon style of the Villa Kerylos (up the coast in Beaulieu), Garcia has garnished these luxe rooms with Homeric chandeliers, Mycenean doorways, egg-and-dart moldings, a retractable ceiling, and fabrics that smolder with ancient terra-cotta hues. No matter: Oiger's creations take center stage. How can they not with such delights as warm duck foie gras with truffle and peanut tapenade in a braised Jerusalem artichoke (€38, yes for an appetizer); or purple urchin soup with crab meat, accompanied by a mincemeat crêpe with coral (€32), or turbot marineìre with lemon breadcrumbs, confit shallots, and creamy Arborio risotto (€59), or Breton lobster with black truffles and creamed macaroni (€115)? Save room for dessert: the stuffed orange au supréme caramélisé is a little slice of heaven. ⊠ *10 La Croisette, La Croisette* ☎ *04–92–98–77–41* ⌛ *Reservations essential* ☐ *AE, DC, MC, V* ⊙ *Closed Sun. and Mon.; mid-Nov.–mid-Dec.*

$$–$$$ ✕ **Astoux et Brun.** Deserving of its reputation for impeccably fresh *fruits de mer,* this restaurant is a beacon to all fish lovers. Well-trained staff negotiate cramped quarters to lay down heaping seafood platters, shrimp casseroles, or piles of oysters shucked to order. Astoux is noisy, cheerful, and always busy, so get there early to get a table and avoid the line. ⊠ *27 rue Felix Faure, La Croisette* ☎ *04–93–39–21–87* ☐ *AE, MC, V.*

$–$$ ✕ **Le Bouchon d'Objectif.** Popular and unpretentious, this tiny bistro serves inexpensive Provençal menus prepared with a sophisticated twist. Watch for terrine of hare with sultanas and Armagnac, stuffed sardines, or a trio of fresh fish with aioli. An ever-changing gallery display of photography adds a hip touch to the simple ocher-and-aqua room. ⊠ *10 rue Constantine, La Croisette* ☎ *04–93–99–21–76* ☐ *AE, MC, V* ⊙ *Closed Mon.; mid-Nov.–mid-Dec.*

$–$$ ✕ **La Mère Besson.** This long-standing favorite continues to please a largely foreign clientele with its regional specialties such as sweet-and-sour sardines *à l'escabèche* (marinated), monkfish Provençal (with tomatoes, fennel, and onion), and roast lamb with garlic puree. The formality of the damask linens and still-life paintings is moderated by clatter from the open kitchen. Dinner menus are €27 and €32. ⊠ *13 rue des Frères-Pradignac, La Croisette* ☎ *04–93–39–59–24* ☐ *AE, DC, MC, V* ⊙ *Closed Sun. Sept.–June. No lunch except during festivals.*

¢–$ ✕ **La Pizza.** Sprawling up over two floors and right in front of the old port, this busy Italian restaurant serves steaks, fish, and salads, but go there for what they're famous for: gloriously good right-out-of-the-woodfire-oven pizza in hungry-man size portions. ⊠ *3 quai St-Pierre, La Croisette* ☎ *04–93–39–22–56* ☐ *AE, MC, V.*

★ $$$$ ⌂ **Carlton Inter-Continental.** As one of the turn-of-the-19th-century pioneers of this resort town, this deliciously pompous Neoclassical landmark quickly staked out the best position: La Croisette seems to radiate symmetrically from its figurehead waterfront site. Seafront rooms are deluxe; those on the back compensate for the lack of a sea view with cheery Provençal prints. The restaurant is good, the brasserie swank, and the Bar des Célébrités lives up to its name during the film festival. ⊠ *58 bd. de la Croisette, La Croisette 06414* ☎ *04–93–06–40–06* 🖶 *04–93–06–40–25* ⊕ *www.interconti.com* ➘ *298 rooms, 28 suites* ⌂ *3 restaurants, minibars, cable TV, 2 bars, Internet, meeting rooms, parking (fee), some pets allowed, no-smoking rooms* ☐ *AE, DC, MC, V* ⦿*EP.*

★ $$$$ ⌂ **Martinez.** Built at the end of the Roaring '20s—a time when excess and glamour were key—this hotel has been lovingly preserved by the champagne-making Tattinger family. Perhaps the most casual of the big hotels on the Croisette, the Martinez revels in a history that is unquestionable. However, it has had such a sleek renovation most of its guest rooms are more contempo than authentic Art Deco. No matter—the views out over the sea are delicious. Recent additions have added on top-level new suites in 1930s decor with teak terraces and a grand Givenchy spa. Don't be surprised to see tuxedo-clad stars at the Palme d'Or restaurant where chef Christian Willer draws lavish praise for his cuisine, served in an extravagantly "moderne" burled-wood and ebony setting. ⊠ *73 bd. de la Croisette, La Croisette 06400* 🕾 *04-92-98-73-00* 🖶 *04-93-39-67-82* ⊕ *www.hotel-martinez.com* ⟿ *369 rooms, 24 apartments ₺ 3 restaurants, cable TV, pool, spa, beach, bar, free parking, some pets allowed (fee)* ⊟ *AE, DC, MC, V* ❍❙ *EP.*

★ **$$$–$$$$** 🖼 **Le Cavendish Boutique Hotel.** Lovingly restored by friendly owners Christine and Guy Welter, this former residence of English Lord Cavendish is a true delight. Rooms—designed by Christopher Tollemar of JoJo Bistro in New York fame—are done in bright swaths of color ("wintergarden" greens, "incensed" reds) that play up both contemporary decor and 19th-century elegance. Beauty, conviviality, even smells—sheets are scented with lavender water and fresh flowers line the entryway—all work together in genuine harmony. The downstairs bar is cozy for a nightcap and the copious breakfast is simply excellent. ⊠ *11 bd. Carnot, St. Nicolas, 06400* 🕾 *04-97-06-26-00* 🖶 *04-97-06-26-01* ⊕ *www.cavendish-cannes.com* ⟿ *34 rooms ₺ Bar, minibars, cable TV, parking (fee), some pets allowed (fee)* ⊟ *AE, MC, V* ❍❙ *EP.*

$–$$ 🖼 **Molière.** Plush, intimate, and low-key, this hotel, a short stroll from the Croisette, has pretty tile baths and small rooms in cool shades of peach, indigo, and white-waxed oak. Nearly all overlook the vast, enclosed front garden, where palms and cypresses shade terrace tables, and breakfast, included in the price, is served most of the year. ⊠ *5 rue Molière, La Croisette 06400* 🕾 *04-93-38-16-16* 🖶 *04-93-68-29-57* ⟿ *24 rooms ₺ Cable TV, bar, some pets allowed (fee)* ⊟ *AE, MC, V* ☉ *Closed mid-Nov.–late Dec.* ❍❙ *BP.*

$ 🖼 **Albert I**er**.** In a quiet residential area above the Forville market—a 10-minute walk uphill from La Croisette and the beach—this neo-Deco mansion has pretty rooms in pastels, as well as tidy tile baths and an enclosed garden. You can have breakfast on the flowered, shady terrace or in the family-style salon. ⊠ *68 av. de Grasse, Le Suquet 06400* 🕾 *04-93-39-24-04* 🖶 *04-93-38-83-75* ⟿ *11 rooms ₺ Minibars, cable TV, free parking, some pets allowed; no a/c* ⊟ *MC, V* ❍❙ *EP.*

Nightlife & the Arts

The Riviera's cultural calendar is splashy and star-studded, and never more so than during the **International Film Festival** in May. The film screenings are not open to the public, so unless you have a pass, your star-studded glimpses will be on the streets or in restaurants (though if you hang around in a tux, a stray ticket might come your way).

As befits a glamorous seaside resort, Cannes has two casinos. The famous **Casino Croisette** (⊠ In Palais des Festivals, La Croisette 🕾 04-92-98-78-00) draws more crowds to its slot machines than any other casino in France. The **Palm Beach Casino Club** (⊠ Pl. Franklin Roosevelt, point de la Croisette, La Croisette 🕾 04-97-06-36-90) manages to retain an exclusive atmosphere even though you can show up in jeans. To make the correct entrance at the popular **Le Cat Corner** (✉ 22 rue Macé, La Croisette ☎ 04–93–39–31–31), have yourself whisked by limo from the steak house Le Farfalla. At **Jimmy'z** (✉ Palais des Festivals, La Croisette ☎ 04–93–68–00–07) the cabaret shows are legendary. The stylish and the beautiful flock to **Les Coulisses** (✉ 29 rue de Commandant André, La Croisette ☎ 04–92–99–17–17). The hip Latin bar **Caliente** (✉ 84 bd. de la Croisette, La Croisette ☎ 04–93–94–49–59) is jammed in summer until dawn with salsa dancing regulars.

The Outdoors

Most of the **beaches** along La Croisette are owned by hotels and/or restaurants, though this doesn't necessarily mean the hotels or restaurants front the beach. It does mean they own a patch of beachfront bearing their name, where they rent out chaise longues, mats, and umbrellas to the public and hotel guests (who also have to pay). Public beaches are between the color-coordinated private beach umbrellas and offer simple open showers and basic toilets. Sailboats can be rented at either port or with some of the beachfront hotels.

Iles de Lérins

❾ *15–20 minutes by ferry off the coast of Cannes.*

When you're glutted on glamour, you may want to make a day trip to the peaceful Iles de Lérins (Lérins Islands); boats depart from Cannes's Vieux Port. Allow at least a half day to enjoy either of the islands; you can see both only if you get an early start. You have two options: **Horizon/Caribes Company** (✉ Jetée Edouard, La Croisette ☎ 04–92–98–71–36) or the less comfortable **Estérel Chanteclair** (✉ Promenade La Pantiéro, La Croisette ☎ 04–93–39–11–82).

It's a 15-minute, €10 round-trip to **Ile Ste-Marguerite**. Its **Fort Royal**, built by Richelieu and improved by Vauban, offers views over the ramparts to the rocky island coast and the open sea.

Behind the prison buildings is the **Musée de la Mer** (Marine Museum), with its Roman boat dating from the 1st century BC and its collection of amphorae and pottery recovered from ancient shipwrecks. ☎ 04–93–43–18–17 📷 €3 ⊙ *Oct.–Dec., Feb., and Mar., Wed.–Mon. 10:30–12:15 and 2:15–4:30; Apr.–June and Sept., Wed.–Mon. 10:30–12:15 and 2:15–5:30; July and Aug., Wed.–Mon. 10:30–12:15 and 2:15–6:30.*

Ile St-Honorat can be reached in 20 minutes (€8 round-trip) from the Vieux Port. Smaller and wilder than Ste-Marguerite, it is home to an active monastery and the ruins of its 11th-century predecessor.

Antibes

▶ ❿ *11 km (7 mi) northeast of Cannes, 15 km (9 mi) southeast of Nice.*

With its broad stone ramparts scalloping in and out over the waves and backed by blunt medieval towers and a skew of tile roofs, Antibes is one of the most romantic old towns on the Mediterranean coast. As gateway to the Cap d'Antibes, Antibes's Port Vauban Harbor has some of the largest yachts in the world tied up at its berths—their millionaire owners won't find a more dramatic spot to anchor, with the tableau of the snowy Alps looming behind and the formidable medieval block towers of the Fort Carré guarding entry to the port. Stroll Promenade Amiral-de-Grasse along the crest of Vauban's sea walls, and you'll understand why Picasso was inspired here to paint on a panoramic scale. Yet a few steps inland you'll enter a souklike maze of atmospheric old streets.

To visit Old Antibes, pass through the **Porte Marine**, an arched gateway in the rampart wall. Follow rue Aubernon to **cours Masséna**, where the little sheltered market sells lemons, olives, and hand-stuffed sausages, and the vendors take breaks in the shoebox cafés flanking one side. From cours Masséna head up to the **Église de l'Immaculée-Conception** (⊠ Pl. de la Cathédrale), which served as the region's cathedral until the bishopric was transferred to Grasse in 1244. Its stout medieval watchtower was built in the 11th century with stones "mined" from Roman structures. Inside is a Baroque altarpiece painted by the Niçois artist Louis Bréa in 1515.

FodorśChoice Next door to the cathedral, the medieval **Château Grimaldi** rises high over
★ the water on a Roman foundation. The Grimaldi family—which still rules Monaco today in the person of Prince Rainier—lived here until the Revolution, but this fine old castle was little more than a monument until in 1946 its curator offered use of its vast chambers to Picasso, and at a time when that extraordinary genius was enjoying a period of intense creative energy. The result is now housed in the **Musée Picasso,** a bounty of exhilarating paintings, ceramics, and lithographs inspired by the sea and by Greek mythology—all very Mediterranean. Even those who are not great Picasso fans should enjoy his vast paintings on wood, canvas, paper, and walls, alive with nymphs, fauns, and centaurs. The museum houses more than 300 works by the artist, as well as pieces by Miró, Calder, and Léger. ⊠ *Pl. du Château* ☎ *04–92–90–54–20* ⊠ *€5* ☉ *June–Sept., Tues.–Sun. 10–6; Oct.–May, Tues.–Sun. 10–noon and 2–6.*

The Bastion St-André, a squat Vauban fortress, now contains the **Musée Archéologique** (Archaeology Museum). Its collection focuses on Antibes's classical history, displaying amphorae and sculptures found in local digs as well as in shipwrecks from the harbor. ⊠ *Av. Général-Maizières* ☎ *04–93–34–00–39* ⊠ *€3* ☉ *Oct.–May, Tues.–Sun. 10–noon and 2–6; June–Sept., Tues.–Sun. 10–6.*

Where to Stay & Eat

$$$–$$$$ ✕ **La Jarre.** You can dine under the beams or the ancient fig tree at this lovely little garden hideaway, just off the ramparts and behind the cathedral. It has an ambitious menu of Provençal specialties filtered through an international lens: lobster sushi with butter and basil, roasted sea bass with creamed soya and green asparagus, grilled pepper steak, sweet-and-sour duck breast, and coconut crème brûlée are the headliners here. ⊠ *14 rue St-Esprit* ☎ *04–93–34–50–12* ▤ *AE, MC, V* ☉ *Closed Wed.*

★ $$–$$$$ ✕ **Le Brûlot.** One street back from the market, this bistro remains one of the most popular in Antibes. Burly chef Christian Blancheri hoists anything from pigs to apple pies in and out of his roaring wood oven, and it's all delicious. Watch for the sardines *à l'escabèche* (in a tangy sweet-sour marinade), sizzling lamb chops, or grilled fresh fish. ☒ *3 rue Frédéric Isnard* ☏ *04–93–34–17–76* ▤ *MC, V* ☉ *Closed Sun. No lunch Mon.–Wed.*

$$ ▦ **Le Mas Djoliba.** Tucked into a residential neighborhood on the crest between Antibes and Juan, this converted Provençal farmhouse is surrounded by greenery and well protected from traffic noise. Rooms decked out in bright colors and floral prints have views of the garden or the sea. Note that in winter prices include breakfast and in summer the restaurant serves half board only. ☒ *29 av. de Provence, 06600* ☏ *04–93–34–02–48* 🖶 *04–93–34–05–81* ⊕ *www.hotel-djoliba.com* 🛏 *13 rooms* ⚭ *Restaurant, minibars, cable TV, pool, Internet; no a/c* ▤ *AE, DC, MC, V* ☉ *Closed Nov.–Jan.* ⟨○⟩ *BP, MAP.*

$–$$ ▦ **L'Auberge Provençale.** The six rooms in this onetime abbey come complete with exposed beams, canopy beds, and lovely antique furniture. The dining room and the arbored garden are informed with the same impeccable taste; the menu allures with fresh seafood inventions such as rascasse (rock fish) sausage with mint, as well as bouillabaisse and duck grilled over wood coals. The restaurant is closed Monday and for Tuesday lunch. ☒ *61 pl. Nationale, 06600* ☏ *04–93–34–13–24* 🖶 *04–93–34–89–88* 🛏 *7 rooms* ⚭ *Restaurant, cable TV, some pets allowed (fee)* ▤ *MC, V* ⟨○⟩ *EP.*

Nightlife

La Siesta (☒ Rte. du Bord de Mer, Antibes ☏ 04–93–33–31–31) is an enormous summer entertainment center with seven dance floors (some on the beach), bars, slot machines, and roulette.

The Outdoors

Antibes and Juan together claim 25 km (15½ mi) of coastline and 48 **beaches** (including Cap d'Antibes). In Antibes you can choose between small sandy inlets—such as **La Gravette,** below the port; the central **place de Ponteil;** and **Plage de la Salis,** toward the Cap—rocky escarpments around the Vieille Ville; or the vast stretch of sand above the Fort Carré.

Juan-les-Pins

⑪ *5 km (3 mi) southwest of Antibes.*

If Antibes is the elderly, historic parent, then Juan-les-Pins is the jazzy younger-sister resort town that, with Antibes, bracelets the wrist of the Cap d'Antibes. The scene along Juan's waterfront is something to behold, with thousands of international sunseekers flowing up and down the promenade or lying flank to flank on its endless stretch of sand. The **Plage de Juan-les-Pins** is made up of sand, not pebbles, and ranks among the Riviera's best (rent a beach chair from the nearby hotel concessions, the best of which is Les Belles Rives). Along with these white powder wonders, Juan is famous for the quality—some pundits say quantity—of its nightlife. There are numerous nightclubs where you can do everything but sleep, ranging from casinos to discos to strip clubs. If all this sounds like too much hard work, wait for July's jazz festival—one of

Europe's most prestigious—or simply repair to the Juana or Les Belles
Rives; if you're lucky enough to be a guest at either hotel, you'll understand why F. Scott Fitzgerald set his *Tender is the Night* in Juantibes,
as both places retain the golden glamour of the Riviera of yore. These
hotels are surrounded by the last remnants of the pine forests that gave
Juan its name. Elsewhere, Juan-les-Pins suffers from a plastic feel and
you might get more out of Antibes.

Where to Stay & Eat

★ $$$$ ✕ **La Terrasse.** The renowned restaurant of the historic Hotel Juana, this
was where superstar chef Alain Ducasse first earned his toque. After he
left, all Juan-les-Pins heaved a high-octane sigh of relief when he was
replaced by the equally superlative Christian Morisset, who maintains
top honors with such dishes as sea bass steamed with Menton lemon,
lamb roasted in Vallauris clay, and Tour d'Argent–style roasted duck.
Menus run from €92 to €135. Unfortunately, some carp that the decor
is a bit too nouveau for its own good. ⊠ *Av. Georges-Gallice*
☎ *04–93–61–08–70* ⊕ *www.laterrasse-restaurant.com* 🖃 *AE, MC, V*
☉ *Closed Nov.–Mar.*

★ $$$$ ✕🖭 **Les Belles Rives.** If "living well is the best revenge," then vacationers at this landmark hotel should know. Not far from the one-time villa
of Gerald and Sara Murphy—those Roaring Twenties millionaires who
devoted their life to proving this maxim—the Belles Rives became the
home-away-from-home for literary giant F. Scott Fitzgerald and his
wife Zelda (chums of the Murphys). Lovingly restored to 1930's glamour, the public salons prove that what's old is new again: France's
stylish young set now make this endearingly *neoclassique* place one of
their favorites. The restaurant's classic cuisine is impeccably served; dine
on the terrace on a fine summer night, with the sea lapping below and
stars twinkling in the velvety Mediterranean sky. No pool, but happily
the beach is nearby. ⊠ *Bd. Baudoin, 06160* ☎ *04–93–61–02–79*
🖷 *03–93–67–43–51* ⊕ *www.bellesrives.com* 🛏 *45 rooms* ⟐ *2 restaurants, minibars, cable TV, beach, bar, Internet, free parking, some pets
allowed (fee)* 🖃 *AE, V* ☉ *Closed late Oct.–mid-Apr.* ⑩ *EP.*

★ $$$$ ✕🖭 **Juana.** The luxuriously renovated Juana is one of the defining monuments of 1930s Côte d'Azur architectural style. Run by the Barrache
family since it opened in 1931, the hotel retains a wonderful Gatsby feel,
with striped awnings and white balustrades. Pine trees tower over the
grounds and the white-marble pool, balconies offer sunset views of the
Esterel red-cliff mountains, while rooms are cool and plain-pastel, with
marble and acajou accents. Though two blocks from the waterfront, the
Juana has its own private sand beach. The excellent restaurant is La Terrasse. ⊠ *Av. Georges-Gallice, 06160* ☎ *04–93–61–08–70*
🖷 *04–93–61–76–60* ⊕ *www.hotel-juana.com* 🛏 *45 rooms, 5 suites*
⟐ *Restaurant, minibars, cable TV, pool, bar, Internet, meeting room,
parking (fee)* 🖃 *AE, MC, V* ☉ *Closed late Nov.–late Dec.* ⑩ *EP.*

$$ 🖭 **Le Mimosa.** The fabulous setting, in an enclosed hilltop garden stud-
ded with tall palms, mimosas, and tropical greenery, makes up for the
hike down to the beach. Rooms are small and modestly decorated in
Victorian florals, but ask for one with a balcony: many look over the
garden and sizable pool. Rates can include half-board. ⊠ *Rue Pauline,*

06160 📠 04–93–61–04–16 🖳 04–92–93–06–46 ⊕ *www.hotelmimosa. com* ⇥ *34 rooms* ⚭ *Cable TV, pool, free parking; no a/c* ⊟ *MC, V* ⊘ *Closed Oct.–Apr.* ⑩ *MAP.*

Nightlife & the Arts

The glassed-in complex of the **Eden Casino** (⊠ Bd. Baudoin, Juan-les-Pins 📠 04–92–93–71–71) houses restaurants, bars, dance clubs, and a casino. Every July the **Festival International Jazz à Juan** (📠 04–92–90–50–00 information) challenges Montreux for its stellar lineup and romantic venue under ancient pines. This place hosted the European debut performances of such stars as Meels Dah-*vees* (Miles Davis) and Ray Charles. It can only be hoped that by now they've changed the tacky stage decor—a gigantic "rendition" of a Picasso dove.

Cap d'Antibes

⑫ *2 km (1 mi) south of Antibes.*

This extravagantly beautiful peninsula, protected from the concrete plague infecting the mainland coast, has been carved up into luxurious estates shaded by thick, tall pines. Since the 19th century its wild greenery and isolation have drawn a glittering guest list of aristocrats, artists, literati, and the merely fabulously wealthy: Guy de Maupassant, Anatole France, Claude Monet, the Duke and Duchess of Windsor, the Greek shipping tycoon Stavros Niarchos, and the cream of the Lost Generation, including Ernest Hemingway, Gertrude Stein, and Scottie and Zelda Fitzgerald. Now the most publicized focal point is the Hotel Eden Roc, rendezvous and weekend getaway of film stars. You can sample a little of what draws famous people to the site by walking up the chemin de Calvaire from the Plage de la Salis in Antibes (about 1 km [½ mi]) and taking in the extraordinary views (spectacular at night) from the hill that supports the old lighthouse, the **Phare de la Garoupe** (Garoupe Lighthouse). Next to the lighthouse, the 16th-century double chapel of **Notre-Dame-de-la-Garoupe** contains ex-votos and statues of the Virgin, all in memory of and for the protection of sailors. 📠 04–93–67–36–01 ⊘ *Easter–Sept., daily 9:30–noon and 2:30–7; Oct.–Easter, daily 10–noon and 2:30–5.*

Another lovely walk (about 1½ km [1 mi]), along the **Sentier Tirepoil**, begins at the cape's pretty Plage de la Garoupe and winds along dramatic rocky shores, magnificent at sunset. The final destination of the Sentier Tirepoil is the **Villa Eilenroc**, designed by Charles Garnier, who created the Paris Opera—which should give you some idea of its style. It commands the tip of the peninsula from a grand and glamorous garden. You may tour the grounds freely, but, during high season, the house remains closed (unless the owners, on a good day, choose to open the first floor to visitors). But from September to June visitors are allowed to wander through the reception salons, which retain the Louis Seize–Trianon feel of the noble facade. The Winter Salon still has its "1,001 Nights" ceiling mural painted by Jean Dunand, the famed Art Deco designer; display cases are filled with memorabilia donated by Caroline Groult-Flaubert (Antibes resident and god-daughter of the great author); while the boudoir has boiseries from the Marquis de Sévigné's Paris man-

FodorsChoice
★

sion. Today, the estate is maintained by the Mrs. L. D. Beaumont Foundation, which continues to manicure every blade of grass in the gardens to gorgeous effect. Whether or not the estate is haunted by Helene Beaumont, the rich singer who built it, or King Leopold II of Belgium, King Farouk of Egypt, Aristotle Onassis, and Greta Garbo—who all rented here—only you will be able to tell. ⊠ *At peninsula's tip* ☎ *04–93–67–74–33* ⊕ *www.antibes-juanlespins.com* ⧑ *Free* ۞ *House: mid-Sept.–June, Wed. 9–noon and 1:30—5; Gardens: mid-Sept.–June, Tues. and Wed. 9–5.*

★ To fully experience the Riviera's heady hothouse exoticism, visit the glorious **Jardin Thuret** (Thuret Garden), established by botanist Gustave Thuret in 1856 as a testing ground for subtropical plants and trees. Thuret was responsible for the introduction of the palm tree, forever changing the profile of the Côte d'Azur. On his death the property was left to the Ministry of Agriculture, which continues to dabble in the introduction of exotic species. From the Port du Croûton head up chemin de l'Aureto, then chemin du Tamisier, and turn right on the boulevard du Cap. ⊠ *Bd. du Cap* ☎ *04–93–67–88–00* ⊕ *jardin-thuret.antibes.inra.fr* ⧑ *Free* ۞ *Weekdays 8:30–5:30.*

At the southwest tip of the peninsula, an ancient battery contains the **Musée Naval et Napoléonien** (Naval and Napoleonic Museum), where you can peruse a collection of watercolors of Antibes, platoons of lead soldiers, and scale models of military ships. ⊠ *Batterie du Grillon, av. Kennedy* ☎ *04–93–61–45–32* ⧑ *€3* ۞ *Tues.–Sat. 9–12:30 and 2–5:45.*

Where to Stay & Eat

★ **$$$$** ✕ **Restaurant de Bacon.** Since 1948, under the careful watch of the Sordello brothers, this has been *the* spot for seafood on the Côte d'Azur. The catch of the day may be minced in lemon ceviche, floating in a top-of-the-line bouillabaisse, or simply grilled with fennel, crisped with hillside herbs. The warm welcome, discreet service, sunny dining room, and dreamy terrace over the Baie des Anges, with views of the Antibes ramparts, justify extravagance. Fixed menu prices are €45 and €75. ⊠ *Bd. de Bacon* ☎ *04–93–61–50–02* ⧓ *Reservations essential* ⊟ *AE, DC, MC, V* ۞ *Closed Mon. and Tues. lunch and Nov.–Jan.*

$$$$ ✕⊞ **Imperial Garoupe.** The newest Provençal palace in the Cap is a terra-cotta oasis of Mediterranean comfort and glitz. Fronted by grand gates, surrounded by gardens and spotlit palm trees, and framed by an Andalusian-design patio, the main structure is lined with balconies and filled with posh Louis XVI and Provençal furnishings, all brand new and aglitter. Add in superequipped bathrooms, floor-to-ceiling chintz, thick towels, daily deliveries of fresh fruit, and you have all the fixings for a luxe blow-out stay. Many guests here spend the days relaxing at the adorable private beach or swimming pool, only moving in to L'Anse, the serious restaurant, to dine on soigné offerings such as Bresse chicken with Mediterranean lemon rind or lobster with Niçoise olives. The sweet life, indeed. ⊠ *770 chemin Garoupe, 06160* ☎ *04–92–93–31–61* 🖷 *04–92–93–31–62* ⊕ *www.imperial-garoupe.com* ⇝ *30 rooms, 4 suites ᗜ Restaurant, minibars, cable TV, pool, bar, some pets allowed (fee)* ⊟ *AE, DC, MC, V* ۞ *Closed Nov.–mid-Apr.* ⏀ *EP.*

★ **$$$$** ⊞ **La Baie Dorée.** Clinging to the waterfront and skewed toward the open sea, this elegant little inn provides private sea-view terraces off every room. Guest rooms are plush and subdued, yet even the small standard doubles feel deluxe when you look out the window. The public grounds and terraces fall in tiers down to the water, from the shaded restaurant to the private beach on the Baie de la Garoupe. ⊠ *579 bd. de la Garoupe, 06160* ☎ *04–93–67–30–67* 🖷 *04–92–93–76–39* ⊕ *www.baiedoree. com* ⮩ *17 rooms* ⚹ *Restaurant, minibars, cable TV, beach, some pets allowed (fee)* ⊟ *AE, MC, V* ⦿⎮ *FAP.*

THE HILL TOWNS: ON THE TRAIL OF PICASSO & MATISSE

The hills that back the Côte d'Azur are often called the *arrière-pays,* or backcountry. This particular wedge of backcountry—behind the coast between Cannes and Antibes—has a character all its own: deeply, unselfconsciously Provençal, with undulating fields of lavender watched over by villages perched in golden stone. Many of these villages look as if they do not belong to the last century—but they do, since they played the muse to some of modern art's most famous exemplars, notably Pablo Picasso and Henri Matisse. A highlight here is the Maeght Foundation, in St-Paul de Vence, one of France's leading museums of modern art. Its neighbor, Vence, has the Chapelle du Rosaire, entirely designed and decorated by Matisse. It's possible to get a small taste of this backcountry on a day trip out of Fréjus, Cannes, or Antibes; even if you're vacationing on the coast, you may want to settle in for a night or two. Of course, you'll soon discover the stooped, stone row houses that are now galleries and boutiques offering everything from neo–Van Gogh sofa art to assembly-line lavender sachets, and everywhere you'll hear the gentle *breet-breet* of mechanical souvenir *cigales* (cicadas). So if you're at all allergic to souvenir shops and middlebrow art galleries, aim to visit off-season or after hours, when the stone-paved alleys empty of tourists and the scent of strawberry potpourri is washed away by the natural perfume of bougainvillea and jasmine wafting from terra-cotta jars.

Vallauris

🔞 *6 km (4 mi) northeast of Cannes, 6 km (4 mi) west of Antibes.*

In the low hills over the coast, dominated by a blocky Renaissance château, this ancient village was ravaged by waves of the plague in the 14th century, then rebuilt in the 16th century by 70 Genoese families imported to repopulate the abandoned site. They brought with them a taste for Roman planning—hence the grid format in the Old Town—but, more important in the long run, a knack for pottery making. Their skills and the fine clay of Vallauris proved to be a marriage made in heaven, and the village thrived as a pottery center for hundreds of years. In the 1940s Picasso found inspiration in the malleable soil and settled here in a simple stone house, creating pottery art with a single-minded passion. But he returned to painting in 1952 to create one of his master works in the château's Romanesque chapel, the vast multipanel oil-on-wood composition called *La Guerre et la Paix (War and Peace)*. The ★ chapel is part of the **Musée National Picasso** today, where several of Picasso's ceramic pieces are displayed. There's also a group of paintings by a contemporary of Picasso's, Italian artist Alberto Magnelli. ✉ *Pl. de la Libération* ☎ 04–93–64–16–05 ☝ €3 ⊙ *June–Sept., Wed.–Mon. 10–noon and 2–6; Oct.–May, Wed.–Mon. 10–noon and 2–5.*

Mougins

⑭ *6 km (4 mi) north of Vallauris, 8 km (5 mi) north of Cannes, 11 km (7 mi) northwest of Antibes.*

Passing through Mougins, a popular summer-house community convenient to Cannes and Nice and famously home to a group of excellent restaurants, you may perceive little more than suburban sprawl. But in 1961 Picasso found much to admire and settled into a *mas* (farmhouse) that verily became a pilgrimage spot for artists and art lovers; he died here in 1973. You can find Picasso's final home and see why, of all spots in the world, he chose this one, by following D35 1 mi south of Mougins to the ancient ecclesiastical site of **Notre-Dame-de-Vie** (✉ Chemin de la Chapelle). This was the hermitage, or monastic retreat, of the Abbey of Lérins, and its 13th-century bell tower and arcaded chapel form a pretty ensemble. Approached through an allée of ancient cypresses, the house Picasso shared with his wife, Jacqueline, overlooks the broad bowl of the countryside (now blighted with modern construction). Unfortunately, the residence—the former priory—is closed to the public. The chapel is only open during Sunday Mass at 9 AM. Elsewhere in town are a small **Musée Municipal**, set in the 17th-century St.-Bernardin Chapel, and a huge **Musée de l'Automobiliste**, with 100 vintage cars, in a modern structure on the aire des Bréguières.

Where to Stay & Eat

$$–$$$ ✕ **Le Bistrot de Mougins.** Set in an old 15th-century stable with high, curved brick ceilings this is a restaurant that plays up to its historical past. Rustic chairs and flowered tablecloths offer a real picnic-in-the-country feel. Simple, Provençal-style dishes are hard to beat: escargots in butter and herbs, steak with a green peppercorn sauce, or sea bass grilled with fennel are top choices. ✉ *Place du Village* ☎ 04–93–75–78–34 ☰ AE, MC, V ⊙ *No lunch Wed. and Sat.*

★ **$$–$$$** ✕ **Le Feu Follet.** In a beautiful period-house setting right in the center of the village, reputed chef Jean-Paul Battaglia heads up a battalion of young chefs in an open-plan kitchen. Why so many? Because everything is homemade, from the fois gras to the hand-smoked salmon to mouth-watering basics like roasted scampi with lemon and basil. The best seats are on the enclosed terrace by the quietly tinkling fountain looking out into the mayor's flower garden, but the cozy rooms inside are atmospheric too. Save room for desert—the lavender-infused crème brulée is truly outstanding. ✉ *Pl. du Commandant Lamy* ☎ 04–93–90–15–78 ☰ AE, MC, V ⊙ *Closed Mon. No dinner Sun.*

$$$$ ✕▦ **Le Mas Candille.** Nestled in a huge private park, this 19th-century *mas* has been cleverly transformed into an ultraluxurious hotel. Rooms—

all cool colors and country chic—are very refined: a profusion of pillows, heated towels, and all the hidden electrical hook-ups you could possibly need. Antique wallpapers, "re-issued" vintage furniture, and too many other high-gloss touches make this place *Elle Decor*–worthy, if not really authentic to the locale. The opulent, saffron-hue restaurant is the well-ordered domain of chef Serge Gouloumes whose impressive resume includes stints at Ma Maison in Beverly Hills and the Poisson d'Or in Saint Martin. His succulent menus are causing quite a stir in gastronomic circles; watch for items like wild bass in a rosemary tempura clay crust or fois gras tartin with Armagnac. In addition to the main house and the gourmet restaurant, there's a bastide and a Shiseido spa. ⊠ *Bd. Clément-Rebuffel, 06250* ☎ *04–92–28–43–43* 🖷 *04–92–28–43–40* ⊕ *www.lemascandille.com* 🛏 *39 rooms, 1 suite* ⌁ *2 restaurants, minibars, cable TV, 2 pools, spa, golf course, some pets allowed (fee)* 🖃 *AE, DC, MC, V* ⏺ *EP.*

$$$–$$$$ ╳🏠 **Le Moulin de Mougins.** Housed in a 16th-century olive mill on a hill above the coastal fray, this sophisticated inn houses one of the most famous restaurants in the region and has been a de rigueur lunch trip out of Cannes for years. When celebrity chef Roger Vergé relocated to the Roger Vergé Ecole de Cuisine at Mougins's Restaurant L'Amandier and set Serge Chollet at the helm, the loyal clientele, skeptical at first, were soon reassured. The sun-drenched Mediterranean cuisine is still excellent—if a shade less inventive—using the freshest fish and whitest asparagus. Inside are intimate, beamed dining rooms; in summer dine outside under the awnings. Guest rooms are elegantly rustic; the apartments small but deluxe. ⊠ *Notre-Dame-de-Vie, 06250* ☎ *04–93–75–78–24* 🖷 *04–93–90–18–55* ⊕ *www.moulin-mougins. com* 🛏 *3 rooms, 4 apartments* ⌁ *Restaurant, minibars, cable TV, some pets allowed (fee)* ⌁ *Reservations essential* 🖃 *AE, DC, MC, V* ⊗ *Closed mid-Nov.–mid-Jan. Restaurant closed Mon.* ⏺ *EP.*

$$–$$$ ╳🏠 **La Terrasse à Mougins.** Perfectly situated, this friendly little hotel offers a decor that is casual, country, and chic. The dapper yellow, white, and pastel blues walls fade into insignificance before the panoramic views that look out on the edge of the Vieille Ville. Guest rooms sparkle in a stripped-down country version of Louis Seize. The service is excellent, the restaurant menu varied, although its decor is nothing to write home about and its windows are plate-glass (we are in rural France, are we not?). In any event, an after-dinner drink on the terrace looking out over the valley should constitute a moment of sheer, unadulterated pleasure. ⊠ *1 Bd. Courteline, 06250* ☎ *04–92–28–36–20* 🖷 *04–92–28–36–21* ⊕ *www.la-terrasse-a-mougins.com* 🛏 *2 rooms, 2 suites* ⌁ *Restaurant, minibars, cable TV, some pets allowed (fee)* 🖃 *AE, DC, MC, V* ⏺ *EP.*

$$ ╳🏠 **Le Manoir de l'Etang.** In keeping with the charm of a family country home, guests are welcomed here with genuine warmth and friendly, eager-to-please service. The views of the surrounding countryside are lovely, as is the simple decor, and you simply can't beat the price. Reserve early. ⊠ *Route d'Antibes, allée de Manoir, 06250* ☎ *04–92–28–36–00* 🖷 *04–92–28–36–10* ⊕ *www.manoir.de.letange.com* 🛏 *17 rooms, 3 suites* ⌁ *Restaurant, minibars, cable TV, pool, some pets allowed (fee)* 🖃 *AE, DC, MC, V* ⊗ *Closed Nov.–Feb.* ⏺ *EP.*

Grasse

⑮ *10 km (6 mi) northwest of Mougins, 17 km (10½ mi) northwest of Cannes, 22 km (14 mi) northwest of Antibes, 42 km (26 mi) southwest of Nice.*

High on a plateau over the coast, this busy, modern town is usually given a wide berth by anyone who isn't interested in its prime tourist industry, the making of perfume. But its unusual art museum featuring works of the 18th-century artist Fragonard and the picturesque backstreets of its very Mediterranean Vieille Ville round out a pleasant day trip from the coast. You can't visit the laboratories where the great blends of Chanel, Dior, and Guerlain are produced. But to accommodate the crowds of tourists who come here wanting to know more, Grasse has three functioning perfume factories that create simple blends and demonstrate production techniques for free. **Fragonard** (⊠ Rte. de Cannes Les 4-Chemins ☎ 04–93–77–94–30) operates in a factory built in 1782. **Galimard** (⊠ 73 rte. de Cannes) traces its pedigree back to 1747. **Molinard** (⊠ 60 bd. Victor-Hugo ☎ 04–93–36–01–62) was established in 1849.

The **Musée International de la Parfumerie** (International Museum of Perfume), not to be confused with the museum in the Fragonard factory, traces the 3,000-year history of perfume-making. ⊠ *8 pl. du Cours* ☎ *04–93–36–80–20* ⊡ *€3* ◷ *June–Sept., daily 10–7; Oct.–May, Wed.–Sun. 10–12:30 and 2–5:30.*

The **Musée Fragonard** headlines the work of Grasse's most famous son, Jean-Honoré Fragonard (1732–1806), one of the great French artists of his day. The lovely villa contains a collection of drawings, engravings, and paintings by the artist. Other rooms in the mansion display works by Fragonard's son Alexandre-Evariste and his grandson Théophile. ⊠ *23 bd. Fragonard* ☎ *04–93–36–02–71* ⊡ *€3* ◷ *June–Sept., daily 10–7; Oct.–May, Wed.–Sun. 10–12:30 and 2–5:30.*

The **Musée d'Art et d'Histoire de Provence** (Museum of the Art and History of Provence), just down from the Fragonard perfumery, has a large collection of faïence from the region, including works from Moustiers, Biot, and Vallauris. ⊠ *2 rue Mirabeau* ☎ *04–93–36–01–61* ⊡ *€3* ◷ *June–Sept., daily 10–7; Oct.–May, Wed.–Sun. 10–12:30 and 2–5:30.*

Continue down rue Mirabeau and lose yourself in the dense labyrinth of the **Vieille Ville** (Old Town), its steep, narrow streets thrown into shadow by shuttered houses five and six stories tall.

Where to Stay & Eat

$$–$$$ ✗ **Arnaud.** Just off place aux Aires, this easygoing corner bistro serves up inventive home cooking under a vaulted ceiling decorated with stenciled grapevines. Choose from an ambitious and sophisticated menu of à la carte specialties—three kinds of fish in garlic sauce, *pieds et paquets* (pigs' feet and tripe), or a hearty *confit de canard* (preserved duck). ⊠ *10 pl. de la Foux* ☎ *04–93–36–44–88* ⊟ *AE, DC, MC, V.*

★ $$$$ ✗⌨ **La Bastide Saint-Antoine.** The cicadas live better than most humans at this picture-perfect 18th-century estate overlooking the Estéval and once home of an industrialist who hosted Kennedys and Rolling Stones.

Now the domain of celebrated chef Jacques Chibois, it welcomes you with old stone walls, shaded walkways, an enormous pool, and a mouth-watering ocher-hue and blue-shutter mansion draped with red trumpet-flower bignonia and purple bougainvillea. The guest rooms glossily mix Louis Seize–style chairs, Provençal embroidered bedspreads, and high-tech delights (massaging showers). Although the restaurant is exceedingly excellent and expensive (lobster with a black-olive fondue and beet juice will run you €60), lunch is a bargain €47. Prices are in our top price category, but some rooms hover close to $$$ level. ⊠ *48 av. Henri-Dunant, 06130* ☎*04–93–70–94–94* 🖷*04–93–70–94–95* ⊕*www. jacques-chibois.com* ↩ *8 rooms, 3 suites* ⚴ *Restaurant, minibars, cable TV, pool, shop; no a/c* ⊟ *AE, DC, MC, V* ¶⨀| *EP.*

Route Napoléon

Extends 176 km (109 mi) from Grasse to Sisteron.

One of the most famous and panoramic roads in France is the Route Napoléon, taken by Napoléon Bonaparte in 1815 after his escape from imprisonment on the Mediterranean island of Elba. Napoléon landed at Golfe-Juan, near Cannes, on March 1 and forged northwest to Grasse, then through dramatic, hilly countryside to Castellane, Digne, and Sisteron. Commemorative plaques bearing the imperial eagle stud the route, inspired by Napoléon's remark, "The eagle will fly from steeple to steeple until it reaches the towers of Notre-Dame." Nowadays there are some lavender-honey stands and souvenir shacks, but they are few and far between. It's the panoramic views as the road winds its way up into the Alps that make this a route worth taking. Roads are curvy but well maintained. The whole route takes about fourteen hours but you can just do part of it and still take in the lovely scenery. In fact, if you like scenic drives, follow the Route Napoléon to Trigance and on to the spectacular gorge called the **Grand Canyon du Verdon.** You can then continue on to the heart of the Var and in a mere 30 minutes be swallowed up in the beauty of the spectacular Gorges Country.

Vence

⑯ *20 km (12 mi) west of Grasse, 4 km (2½ mi) north of St-Paul, 22 km (14 mi) north of Nice.*

Encased behind stone walls inside a thriving modern market town is **la Vieille Ville,** the historic part of Vence, which dates from the 15th century. Though crowded with boutiques and souvenir shops, it's slightly more conscious of its history than St-Paul—plaques guide you through its historic squares and *portes* (gates). Leave your car on place du grand Jardin and head to the gate to the Vieille Ville, passing place du Frêne, with its ancient ash tree planted in the 16th century, and then through the Portail du Peyra to the place du Peyra, with its fountains. Ahead lies the former cathedral on place Clemenceau, also address to the ocher-color Hôtel de Ville (town hall). A flea market is held on the square on Wednesdays; back streets and alleys hereabouts have been colonized by craft stores and "art galleries." In the center of the Vieille Ville, the **Cathédrale de la**

Nativité de la Vierge (Cathedral of the Birth of the Virgin, on place Godeau) was built on the Romans' military drilling field and traces bits and pieces to Carolingian and even Roman times. It's a hybrid of Romanesque and Baroque styles, expanded and altered over the centuries. Note the rostrum added in 1499—its choir stalls are carved with particularly vibrant and amusing scenes of daily life back when. In the baptistery is a ceramic mosaic of Moses in the bulrushes by Chagall.

★ On the outskirts of "new" Vence, toward St-Jeannet, the **Chapelle du Rosaire** (Chapel of the Rosary) was decorated with beguiling simplicity and clarity by Matisse between 1947 and 1951—the chapel was the artist's gift to nuns who had nursed him through illness. It reflects the reductivist style of the era: walls, floor, and ceiling are gleaming white, and the small stained-glass windows are cool greens and blues. "Despite its imperfections I think it is my masterpiece . . . the result of a lifetime devoted to the search for truth," wrote Matisse, who designed and dedicated the chapel when he was in his eighties and nearly blind. ☒ *Av. Henri-Matisse* ☎ *04–93–58–03–26* ▨ *€2.50* ☉ *Tues. and Thurs. 10–11:30 and 2–5:30; Mon., Wed., and Sat. 2–5:30.*

Where to Stay & Eat

★ **$$$$** ✕ **Jacques Maximin.** This temperamental legend and superchef has found peace of mind in a gray-stone farmhouse covered with wisteria—his home and his own country restaurant. Here he devotes himself to creative country cooking superbly prepared and unpretentiously priced—white beans in rich squid ink, Mediterranean fish grilled in rock salt and olive oil, and candied-eggplant sorbet. The yellow dining room is airy and uncluttered; the garden is a palm-shaded delight. Reserve way in advance. ☒ *689 chemin de la Gaude* ☎ *04–93–58–90–75* ⌖ *Reservations essential* ▭ *AE, MC, V* ☉ *Closed Sun. dinner. No lunch Mon.–Tues. during mid-Dec.–May or Sat.–Fri. Oct.–June; closed mid-Nov.–mid-Dec.*

$$–$$$$ ✕ **La Farigoule.** A long, beamed dining room that opens onto a shady terrace casts an easygoing spell and serves as an hors d'oeuvre for some sophisticated Provençal cooking. Watch for tangy pissaladières with sardines marinated in ginger and lemon, salt-cod ravioli, lamb with olive polenta, and a crunchy parfait of honey and hazelnuts. Fixed-menu dinners are €28 and €43. ☒ *15 rue Henri-Isnard* ☎ *04–93–58–01–27* ▭ *MC, V* ☉ *Closed Tues. and Wed. in winter; closed Tues., no lunch Wed. or Sat. in summer.*

★ **$$$$** ✕▣ **Château du Domaine St. Martin.** Exuding an expensive charm, this famous domain occupies the ancient site of a fortress of the Knights Templars. Sitting on a hilltop perch and surrounded by acres of greenery designed by Jean Mus, the mansion welcomes you with public salons that are light and airy—perhaps too much, as they seem to be overly renovated. All guest rooms are, in fact, junior suites, except for six *bastides* (two- and three-bedroom villas) accented with beautiful antiques. **La Commanderie** restaurant is perhaps the best reason to come here, thanks to its stunning walls adorned with china, chef Philippe Guéin's superb creations, and one of the most panoramic terraces around—the views over Old Vence to the Baie des Anges are eye-popping. ☒ *Av. des Templiers* ☎ *04–93–58–02–02* ⎙ *04–93–24–08–91* ⊕ *www.chateau-st-martin.com*

$\Large\leftrightharpoons$ *38 rooms & 2 restaurants, minibars, cable TV, 2 tennis courts, pool, bar, Internet, free parking, some pets allowed (fee)* $\boxminus$ *AE, MC, V* $\odot$ *Closed mid-Oct.–mid-Feb.* ¶◯¶ *MAP.*

★ **$–$$$** ⊞ **Villa Roseraie.** This quiet little inn outside the center is a pet project of the enthusiastic owners, Monsieur and Mme. Martefon, who have scoured antiques shops for regional details and invested in fine local tiles and fabrics. There's a generous breakfast served until 11:30 AM on the terrace by the pool much of the year, and it's a quick walk down to Old Vence. ⊠ *51 av. Henri-Giraud, 06140* ☏ *04–93–58–02–20* 🖶 *04–93–58–99–31* $\leftrightharpoons$ *14 rooms & Minibars, cable TV, pool, free parking, some pets allowed (fee); no a/c* $\boxminus$ *AE, MC, V* $\odot$ *Closed mid-Nov.–mid-Feb.* ¶◯¶ *EP.*

$–$$ ⊞ **L'Auberge des Seigneurs.** Although the entrance is dim and has a certain rustic medieval charm, rooms are surprisingly airy and bright with provençal fabrics. The small restaurant specializes in roast meats and hearty cheeses and is very convivial. It's also very busy, so be sure to book well in advance. ⊠ *Place du Frêne* ☏ *04–93–58–04–24* 🖶 *04–93–24–08–01* $\leftrightharpoons$ *6 rooms & Restaurants, minibars, cable TV, some pets allowed (fee)* $\boxminus$ *AE, MC, V* $\odot$ *Closed mid-Jan.–mid-Feb.* ¶◯¶ *EP.*

St-Paul-de-Vence

⑰ *18 km (11 mi) north of Nice, 4 km (2½ mi) south of Vence.*

Fodor'sChoice
★

The medieval village of St-Paul-de-Vence can be seen from afar, standing out like its companion, Vence, against the skyline. In the Middle Ages St-Paul was basically a city-state, and it controlled its own political destiny for centuries. But by the early 20th century St-Paul had faded to oblivion, overshadowed by the growth of Vence and Cagnes—until it was rediscovered in the 1920s when a few penniless artists began paying for their drinks at the local auberge with paintings. Those artists turned out to be Signac, Modigliani, and Bonnard, who met at the Auberge de la Colombe d'Or, now a sumptuous inn, where the walls are still covered with their ink sketches and daubs. Nowadays art of a sort still dominates in the myriad tourist traps that take your eyes off the beauty of St-Paul's old stone houses and its rampart views. The most commercially developed of Provence's hilltop villages, St-Paul is nonetheless a magical place when the tourist crowds thin. Artists are still drawn to its light, its pure air, its wraparound views, and its honey-color stone walls, soothingly cool on a hot Provençal afternoon. Film stars continue to love its lazy yet genteel ways, lingering on the garden-bower terrace of the Colombe d'Or and challenging the locals to a game of pétanque under the shade of the plane trees. Even so, you have to work hard to find the timeless aura of St-Paul; get here early in the day to get a jump on the cars and tour buses, which can clog the main D36 highway here by noon, or plan on a stay-over. Either way, do consider a luncheon or dinner beneath the Picassos at the Colombe d'Or, even if the menu prices seem almost as fabulous as the collection.

★ Many people come to St-Paul just to visit the **Fondation Maeght,** founded in 1964 by art dealer Aimé Maeght and set on a wooded clifftop high above the medieval town. It's not just a small modern art museum but an extraordinary marriage of the arc-and-plane architecture of José Sert; the looming sculptures of Miró, Moore, and Giacometti; and a humbling hilltop perch of pines, vines, and flowing planes of water. On display is an intriguing and ever-varying parade of the work of modern masters, including the wise and funny late-life masterwork *La Vie* (*Life*), by Chagall. ☎ 04–93–32–81–63 ☒ €10 ☉ *July–Sept., daily 10–7; Oct.–June, daily 10–12:30 and 2:30–6.*

Where to Stay & Eat

★ **$$$$** ✕☒ **La Colombe d'Or.** The art display here may cause a double-take—are those really Mirós, Bonnards, Picassos, Légers, and Braques hanging on the rustic walls? Yes, they were indeed given in payment by the artists in hungrier days when this auberge was known as the "Café-Restaurant Robinson" and run by the Roux family. It soon became the heart and soul of St-Paul's artistic revival, and the cream of 20th-century France lounged together under its fig trees—Picasso and Chagall, Maeterlinck and Kipling, Yves Montand and Simone Signoret (who met and married here). Today, the inn's *pastorale* history is the lure, not the food, which is unambitious bordering on fine, but high-priced nonetheless. (Note you can enjoy a dinner or drink here without being a hotel guest.) Give in to the green-shaded loveliness of the terrace and the creamy manners of the waitstaff. A dinner table here is lorded over by a ceramic Léger mural, while the pool is an idyllic garden bower, complete with a Calder, and there's even a Braque by the fireplace in the bar. The auberge's stone entry portal is a grand Renaissance set piece, the public salons are most alluring, and the guest rooms possess a certain understated charm, thanks to some Provençal painted borders and murals. This is a guarded star—there are minuses here, but where else can you enjoy your Campari sitting under a Dubuffet? Reserve well in advance for guest rooms. ☒ *Pl. Général-de-Gaulle, 06570* ☎ *04–93–32–80–02* 📠 *04–93–32–77–78* ⊕ *www.lacolombe-dor.com* ⤴ *15 rooms, 11 suites* ♿ *Restaurant, minibars, cable TV, pool, bar, Internet, some pets allowed; no a/c in some rooms* ☰ *AE, DC, MC, V* ☉ *Closed Nov.–late Dec.* ▯◯▯ *MAP.*

★ **$$$$** ✕☒ **Le Saint-Paul.** Right in the center of the labyrinth of stone alleys, with views over the ancient ramparts, this luxurious inn fills a noble 15th-century house with splendid comfort and charm. Provençal furniture, golden quarried stone, and lush reproduction fabrics warm the salons; rooms are decked in sleek pastels and botanical prints, and some have balconies looking out over the valley. The restaurant, serving sophisticated regional specialties like pigeon roasted with Corsican pancetta, or sea bass and lemon cooked in a clay crust, is fast acquiring a big reputation. And a candlelit meal on the terrace, where flowers spill from every niche, is a romantic's dream. Rates including half or full board are available with a three-night minimum stay. ☒ *86 rue Grande, 06570* ☎ *04–93–32–65–25* 📠 *04–93–32–52–94* ⊕ *www.lesaintpaul.com* ⤴ *15 rooms, 3 suites* ♿ *Restaurant, minibars, cable TV, bar, Internet, some pets allowed (fee)* ☰ *AE, DC, MC, V* ▯◯▯ *FAP, MAP.*

$$–$$$ ☒ **Le Hameau.** Less than 1½ km (1 mi) outside St-Paul, with views of the valley and the village, this lovely little inn is a jumble of terraces, trellises, archways, and honeysuckle vines. The main hotel, built in 1920, has good-size rooms and old Provençal furniture; or you can opt for the 18th-century farmhouse, with smaller, more modern rooms but wonderful views. The friendly owners make for a comfortable welcome and there is a sizable pool. ✉ *528 rte. de La Colle, 06570* ☎ *04–93–32–80–24* 🖷 *04–93–32–55–75* 🌐 *www.le-hameau.com* *17 rooms* *Minibars, cable TV, pool, Internet, some pets allowed* 💳 *MC, V* ⏲ *Closed mid-Nov.–mid-Dec. and mid-Jan.–mid-Feb.* 🍽 *EP.*

$–$$ **Hostellerie les Remparts.** With original stone walls, coved ceilings, light-color fabrics, and a warm welcome, this small medieval hotel in the center of town is a real gem. Its restaurant serves good regional specialties, too. ✉ *72 rue Grande, 06570* ☎ *04–93–32–09–88* 🖷 *04–93–32–09–88* *9 rooms* *Restaurant, minibars, some pets allowed; no a/c, no room TVs* 💳 *AE, MC, V* 🍽 *EP.*

Cagnes-sur-Mer

18 *6 km (4 mi) south of St-Paul-de-Vence, 21 km (13 mi) northeast of Cannes, 10 km (6 mi) north of Antibes, 14 km (9 mi) southwest of Nice.*

Although from N7 you may be tempted to give wide berth to the congested and modern sprawl of Cagnes-sur-Mer, follow the signs inland and up into **Haut Cagnes.** Its steep-cobbled Vieille Ville is crowned by the fat, crenelated **Château de Cagne,** built in 1310 by the Grimaldis and reinforced over the centuries. Within are vaulted medieval chambers, a vast Renaissance fireplace, a splendid 17th-century trompe-l'oeil fresco of the fall of Phaëthon from his sun-chariot, and three small specialized collections dealing with the history of the olive; memorabilia of the cabaret star Suzy Solidor; and a collection of modern Mediterranean artists, including Cocteau and Dufy. ✉ *Pl. Grimaldi* ☎ *04–93–02–47–35* 🎫 *€3, €4.50 joint ticket with Musée Renoir* ⏲ *Oct.–Apr., Wed.–Mon. 10–11:30 and 2–5; May–Sept., Wed.–Mon. 10–11:30 and 2–6.*

After staying up and down the coast, Auguste Renoir (1841–1919) settled in a house in Les Collettes, just east of the Vieille Ville, now the **Musée Renoir.** Here he passed the last 12 years of his life, painting the landscape around him, working in bronze, and rolling his wheelchair through the luxuriant garden, tiered with roses, citrus groves, and some of the most spectacular olive trees along the coast. You can view his home as it has been preserved by his children, as well as 11 of his last paintings. ✉ *Av. des Collettes* ☎ *04–93–20–61–07* 🎫 *€3, €4.50 joint ticket with the Château de Cagne* ⏲ *Oct.–Apr., Wed.–Mon. 10–11:30 and 2–5; May–Sept, Wed.–Mon. 10–11:30 and 2–6. Guided tours in English, Thurs. July and Aug.*

Where to Stay & Eat

★ **$$$$** **Le Cagnard.** Housed in a 14th-century residence built on the outer walls of the Grimaldi castle, this lovely hideaway is a modern escape to a medieval world. Faithful to old-world style in antique-abounding decor, the rooms are very elegant but it's the ceiling of the restaurant that is truly remarkable: covered in Renaissance-style murals, it can be retracted to show off the night sky. The lavish menu (no lunch Tuesday and closed Thursday; reservations essential) lives up to the surrounding splendor with dishes like fois gras cooked with figs, peaches, apricots, and rosemary, or black truffle lasagna. Portions are generous, but try to resist and wait for dessert—the caramelized apple pie is amazing. ⊠ *54 rue Sous Barri, Haute Cagnes* ☎ *04–93–20–73–21* 🖶 *04–93–22–06–39* ⊕ *www.le-cagnard.com* ⇝ *15 rooms, 11 suites* ⚮ *Restaurant, minibars, cable TV, bar, Internet, some pets allowed (fee), free parking* ⊟ *AE, MC, V* ⊘ *Closed Nov.–mid-Dec.* †⊙† *EP.*

NICE

As the fifth-largest city in France, this distended urban tangle is often avoided, but that decision is one to be rued: Nice's waterfront, paralleled by the famous Promenade des Anglais and lined by grand hotels, is one of the noblest in France. It is capped by a dramatic hilltop château, below which the slopes plunge almost into the sea and at whose base a bewitching warren of ancient Mediterranean streets unfold.

It was in this old quarter, now Vieux Nice, that the Greeks established a market-port in the 4th century BC and named it Nikaia. After falling to the Saracen invasions, Nice regained power and developed into an important port in the early Middle Ages. In 1388, under Louis d'Anjou, Nice, along with the hill towns behind, effectively seceded from the county of Provence and allied itself with Savoie as the Comté de Nice (Nice County). It was a relationship that lasted some 500 years and added rich Italian flavor to the city's culture, architecture, and dialect.

Nowadays Nice strikes an engaging balance between historic Provençal grace, port-town exotica, urban energy, whimsy, and high culture. You could easily spend your vacation here, attuned to Nice's quirks, its rhythms, its very multicultural population, and its Mediterranean tides. The high point of the year falls in mid-February when the city hosts one of the most spectacular Carnival celebrations in France (⊕ www.nicecarnival.com).

Vieux Nice

Framed by the "château"—really a rocky promontory—and cours Saleya, Nice's Vieille Ville is its strongest drawing point and, should you only be passing through, the best place to capture the city's historic atmosphere. Its grid of narrow streets, darkened by houses five and six stories high with bright splashes of laundry fluttering overhead and jewel-box Baroque churches on every other corner, creates a magic that seems utterly removed from the Côte d'Azur fast lane.

a good walk

First, head for the morning flower market on the **cours Saleya** ⑲ ▶. At the center of cours Saleya is the florid, Baroque **Chapelle de la Miséricorde** ⑳. Thread your way into the Vieille Ville maze to the extravagant **Chapelle de l'Annonciation** ㉑. Continue up Poissonerie to rue de la Place Vieille, then head right to rue Droite; the **Chapelle St-Jacques-Jesu** ㉒ looms large and spare. Turn left on rue Rossetti and cross the square to the **Cathédrale Ste-Réparate** ㉓. Now take a break from the sacred, doubling back up rue Rossetti and continuing left up narrow rue Droite to the magnificent **Palais Lascaris** ㉔. Head next to boulevard Jean-Jaurès,

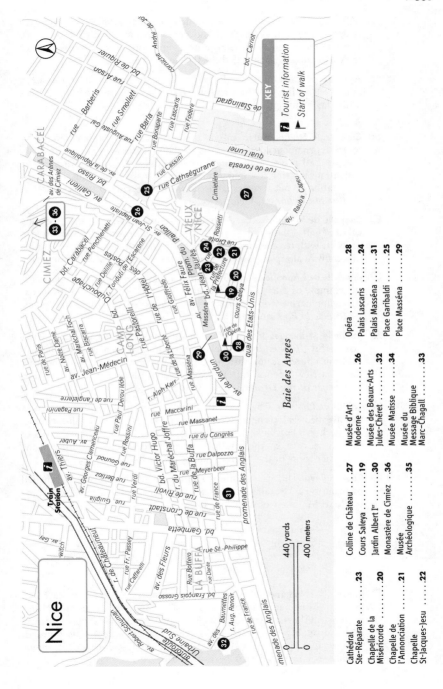

Nice

Train Station

Baie des Anges

KEY

i Tourist information

▲ Start of walk

440 yards

400 meters

which empties onto the grand, arcaded **place Garibaldi** ㉓; one of its five street spokes points straight to the **Musée d'Art Moderne** ㉖. From place Garibaldi and boulevard Jean-Jaurès, wind your way up to the ruins of the castle, now a park called the **Colline de Château** ㉗.

TIMING Aim for morning on this walk, so you'll see the market on cours Saleya at its liveliest. If you include a visit to the Palais Lascaris, this could make a full day's outing.

Sights to See

㉓ **Cathédrale Ste-Réparate.** An ensemble of columns, cupolas, and symmetrical ornaments dominates the Vieille Ville, flanked by its own 18th-century bell tower and capped by its glossy ceramic-tile dome. The cathedral's interior, restored to a bright palette of ocher, golds, and rusts, has elaborate plasterwork and decorative frescoes on every surface. ✉ *Rue Ste-Réparate, Vieux-Nice.*

㉔ **Chapelle de la Miséricorde.** A superbly balanced *pièce-montée* (wedding cake) of half-domes and cupolas, this chapel is decorated within an inch of its life with frescoes, faux marble, gilt, and crystal chandeliers. A magnificent Bréa altarpiece crowns the ensemble. ✉ *Cours Saleya, Vieux-Nice.*

㉑ **Chapelle de l'Annonciation.** This 17th-century Carmelite chapel is a classic example of pure Niçoise Baroque, from its sculpted door to its extravagant marble work and the florid symmetry of its arches and cupolas. ✉ *Rue de la Poissonerie, Vieux-Nice.*

㉒ **Chapelle St-Jacques-Jesu.** If the Vieille Ville's other chapels are jewel boxes, this 17th-century chapel is a barn: broad, open, and ringing hollow, this church seems austere by comparison, but that's only because the theatrical decoration is spread over a more expansive surface. ✉ *Corner of rue Droite and rue Gesu, Vieux-Nice.*

㉗ **Colline de Château** (Château Hill). Though nothing remains of the once-massive medieval stronghold but a few ruins left after its 1706 dismantling, this park still bears its name. From here take in extraordinary views of the Baie des Anges, the length of the Promenade des Anglais, and the red-ocher roofs of the Vieille Ville. ⊙ *Daily 7–7.*

㉙ **Cours Saleya.** This street is framed with 18th-century houses and shaded by plane trees. The tall yellow-stone building at the far-east end was home to Henri Matisse from 1921 to 1938.

need a break? Choose from a fantastic array of colorful sorbets, gelati, and ice creams and settle in to do some serious people-watching at one of the patio tables overlooking the fountain at **Fennocchio** (✉ 2 pl. Rossetti, Vieux-Nice ☎ 04–93–80–72–25).

㉖ **Musée d'Art Moderne.** The assertive contemporary architecture of the Modern Art Museum makes a bold and emphatic statement regarding Nice's presence in the modern world. The art collection inside focuses intently and thoroughly on contemporary art from the late 1950s onward. ✉ *Promenade des Arts, Vieux-Nice* ☎ *04–93–62–61–62* ⊕ *www.mamac-nice.org* ▣ €4 ⊙ *Tues.–Sun. 10–6.*

㉔ **Palais Lascaris.** The aristocratic Lascaris Palace was built in 1648 for Jean-Baptiste Lascaris-Vintimille, *marechal* to the duke of Savoy. The magnificent vaulted staircase, with its massive stone balustrade and niches filled with classical gods, is surpassed in grandeur only by the Flemish tapestries (after Rubens) and the extraordinary trompe-l'oeil fresco depicting the fall of Phaëthon. ⊠ *15 rue Droite, Vieux-Nice* ☎ *04-93-62-05-54* ⛬ *Free entry or €3 for the guided tour, including the Vieille Ville* ⊘ *Wed.–Mon. 10–6.*

㉕ **Place Garibaldi.** Encircled by grand vaulted arcades stuccoed in rich yellow, the broad pentagon of this square could have been airlifted out of Turin. In the center, the shrinelike fountain sculpture of Garibaldi seems to be surveying you as you stroll under the arcades and lounge in its cafés.

Along the Promenade des Anglais

Nice takes on a completely different character west of cours Saleya, with broad city blocks, vast Neoclassical hotels and apartment houses, and a series of inviting parks dense with palm trees, greenery, and splashing fountains. From the Jardin Albert Ier, once the delta of the Paillon River, the famous promenade des Anglais stretches the length of the city's waterfront. The original promenade was the brainchild of Lewis Way, an English minister in the then-growing community of British refugees drawn to Nice's climate. Nowadays it's a wide multilane boulevard thick with traffic—in fact, it's the last gasp of the N98 coastal highway. Beside it runs its charming parallel, a wide, sun-washed pedestrian walkway with intermittent steps leading down to the smooth-rock beach. A daily parade of *promeneurs,* rollerbladers, joggers, and sun baskers strolls its broad pavement, looking out over the hypnotic blue expanse of the sea. Only in the wee hours is it possible to enjoy the waterfront stroll as the cream of Nice's international society once did, when there was nothing more than hoofbeats to compete with the roar of the waves.

a good walk

From the west end of cours Saleya, walk down rue St-François-de-Paule past the Belle Epoque **Opéra** ㉘ ☞. Continue up the street, then head right up rue de l'Opéra to **Place Masséna** ㉙, framed in broad arcades and opening onto the vast, green **Jardin Albert 1er**㉚. Three long blocks past the Casino Ruhl, you'll reach the gates and park of the imposing **Palais Masséna** ㉛. Walk along the waterfront for a few blocks, past busy boulevard Gambetta, then head inland up tiny rue Sauvan. Cross boulevard Grosso and head diagonally up the hill on avenue des Baumettes. In this quiet, once luxurious neighborhood is the **Musée des Beaux-Arts Jules-Chéret** ㉜, built in extravagant Italianate style.

TIMING This walk covers a long stretch of waterfront, so it may take up to an hour to stroll the length of it. Allow a half day if you intend to explore the Palais Massena or the Musée des Beaux Arts.

Sights to See

㉚ **Jardin Albert Ier** (Albert I Garden). Along the Promenade des Anglais, this luxurious garden stands over the delta of the River Paillon, underground since 1882. Every kind of flower and palm tree grows here, thrown into exotic relief by night illumination.

★ ㉜ **Musée des Beaux-Arts Jules-Chéret** (Jules-Chéret Fine Arts Museum). While the collection here is impressive, it is the 19th-century Italianate mansion that houses it that remains the showstopper. Originally built for a member of Nice's Old Russian community, the Princess Kotschoubey, this was a Belle Epoque wedding cake, replete with one of the grandest staircases on the coast, salons decorated with Neo-Pompiénne frescoes, an English-style garden, and white columns and balustrades by the dozen. After the *richessime* American James Thompson took over and the last glittering ball was held here, the villa was bought by the municipality as a museum in the 1920s. Unfortunately, much of the period decor was sold but, in its place, now hang paintings by Degas, Boudin, Monet, Sisley, Dufy, and Jules Chéret, whose posters of winking *damselles* distill all the *joie* of the Belle Epoque. ⊠ *33 av. des Baumettes, Centre-Ville* ☎ *04–92–15–28–28* ⊕ *www.musee-beaux-arts-nice.org* ⊠ €4 ☼ *Tues.–Sun. 10–6.*

㉘ **Opéra.** A half block west of the cours Saleya stands a flamboyant Italian-style theater designed by Charles Garnier, architect of the Paris Opéra. It's home today to the Opéra de Nice, with a permanent chorus, orchestra, and ballet corps. ⊠ *4 rue St-François-de-Paule, Vieux-Nice–Port* ☎ *04–92–17–40–40.*

㉛ **Palais Masséna** (Masséna Palace). This handsome Belle Epoque building, housing the **Musée d'Art et d'Histoire** (Museum of Art and History), is undergoing a complete renovation and is scheduled to reopen sometime in 2006. ⊠ *Entrance at 65 rue de France, Centre-Ville* ☎ *04–93–88–11–34.*

㉙ **Place Masséna.** As cours Saleya is the heart of the Vieille Ville, so this broad square is the heart of the city as a whole. It's framed by an ensemble of Italian-style arcaded buildings first built in 1815, their facades stuccoed in rich red ocher.

Cimiez

Once the site of the powerful Roman settlement Cemenelum, the hilltop neighborhood of Cimiez—4 km (2½ mi) north of cours Saleya—is Nice's most luxurious quarter (use Bus 15 from place Massena or avenue Jean-Médecin to visit its sights).

Begin at the **Musée du Message Biblique Marc-Chagall** ㉝, which houses one of the finest collections of Chagall's works based on biblical themes. Then make the pilgrimage to the center of Cimiez and the **Musée Matisse** ㉞, where an important collection of Matisse's life work is amassed in an Italianate villa. Just behind, the **Musée Archéologique** ㉟ displays a wealth of Roman treasures. Slightly east of the museum is the thriving **Monastère de Cimiez** ㊱, a Franciscan monastery.

TIMING Between bus connections and long walks from sight to sight, this walk is a half-day commitment at minimum. Or if you plan to really spend time in the Matisse Museum and the Chagall Museum, it could easily become a day's outing.

Sights to See

㊱ Monastère de Cimiez. This fully functioning monastery is worth the pilgrimage. You'll find a lovely **garden,** replanted along the lines of the original 16th-century layout; the **Musée Franciscain,** a didactic museum tracing the history of the Franciscan order; and a 15th-century **church** containing three works of remarkable power and elegance by Bréa. ✉ *Pl. du Monastère, Cimiez* ☎ *04–93–81–00–04* 🔓 *Free* ⊙ *Mon.–Sat. 10–noon and 3–6.*

㉟ Musée Archéologique (Archaeology Museum). This museum, next to the Matisse Museum, has a dense and intriguing collection of objects extracted from the digs around the Roman city of Cemenelum, which flourished from the 1st to 5th centuries. ✉ *160 av. des Arènes-de-Cimiez, Cimiez* ☎ *04–93–81–59–57* ☎ *€4* ⊙ *Wed.–Mon. 10–6.*

㉞ Musée Matisse. In the '60s the city of Nice bought this lovely, light-bathed 17th-century villa, surrounded by the ruins of Roman civilization, and restored it to house a large collection of Henri Matisse's works. Matisse settled in Nice in 1917, seeking a sun cure after a bout with pneumonia, and remained here until his death in 1954. During his years on the Côte d'Azur, Matisse maintained intense friendships and artistic liaisons with Renoir, who lived in Cagnes, and with Picasso, who lived in Mougins and Antibes. Settling first along the waterfront, he eventually moved up to the rarified isolation of Cimiez and took an apartment in the Hôtel Regina (now an apartment building), where he lived out the rest of his life. Matisse walked often in the parklands around the Roman remains and was buried in an olive grove outside the Cimiez cemetery. The collection of artworks includes several pieces the artist donated to the city before his death; the rest were donated by his family. In every medium and context—paintings, gouache cutouts, engravings, and book illustrations—it represents the evolution of his art, from Cézanne-like still lifes to exuberant dancing paper dolls. Even the furniture and accessories speak of Matisse, from the Chinese vases to the bold-printed fabrics with which he surrounded himself. A series of black-and-white photographs captures the artist at work, surrounded by personal—and telling—details. ✉ *164 av. des Arènes-de-Cimiez, Cimiez* ☎ *04–93–81–08–08* ☎ *€4* ⊙ *Wed.–Mon. 10–6.*

★ **㉝ Musée du Message Biblique Marc-Chagall** (Marc Chagall Museum of Biblical Themes). This museum has one of the finest permanent collections of Chagall's (1887–1985) late works. Superbly displayed, 17 vast canvases depict biblical themes, each in emphatic, joyous colors. ✉ *Av. du Dr-Ménard, head up av. Thiers, then take a left onto av. Malausséna, cross railway tracks, and take first right up av. de l'Olivetto, Cimiez* ☎ *04–93–53–87–20* ☎ *€5.50, in summer €6.50* ⊙ *Wed.–Mon. 10–6.*

FodorsChoice
★

Where to Stay & Eat

★ **$$$$** ✕ **Le Parcours.** In May 2003 chef Marc Delacourt left the prestigious kitchens of the Château Chevre d'Or hotel to set up this sleek, streamlined restaurant in Falicon, a small perched village on the outskirts of Nice. Decor tends to Zen with a modern twist; there are even TV screens showing what's happening in the kitchen if you can drag your eyes away from the spectacular window views for long enough to watch. Most main courses are delicious, the wine list is short but well thought out, and the €30 lunch menu is a bargain. ⊠ *1 pl. Marcel Eusebi, Falicon village: 15 mins outside Nice direction Sospel* ☎ *04–93–84–94–57* ⌾ *Reservations essential* ▭ *MC, V.*

$$–$$$$ ✗ **Indyana.** Targeting hip twenty- to thirtysomethings, enterprising brothers Christophe and Pascal Ciamos have come up with a stylish, swanky place that fills nightly with an intriguing mix of young entrepreneurs, artsy types, and the fashion-forward. Intimate lighting and an eclectic combination of loft-meets-art-deco-Moroccan decor is matched by a fusion cuisine menu that ranges from sushi to traditional beef platters with potato zucchini gratin. ⊠ *11 rue Gustave Deloye, Vieux-Nice* ☎ *04–93–80–67–69* ⌾ *Reservations essential* ▭ *AE, DC, MC, V* ⊗ *Closed Sun.*

$$–$$$$ ✗ **L'Olivier.** In this hole-in-the-wall bistro on place Garibaldi, two brothers have gone back to their roots, and all of Nice has followed. Frank Musso, trained at the Tour d'Argent in Paris, concentrates his sophisticated gifts on simple dishes: tripe simmered in tomatoes, daubes and pork confits, and crepes with homemade bitter-orange marmalade. His brother Christian provides the cheery welcome. Dinner menus are €20 to €35. ⊠ *2 pl. Garibaldi, Vieux-Nice* ☎ *04–93–26–89–09* ⌾ *Reservations essential* ▭ *AE, DC, MC, V* ⊗ *Closed Sun. and Aug. No dinner Wed.*

$$–$$$ ✗ **Grand Café de Turin.** Whether you squeeze onto a banquette in the dark, low-ceiling bar or win a coveted table under the arcaded porticoes on place Garibaldi, this is *the* place to go for shellfish in Nice: sea snails, clams, plump *fines de claires,* and salty *bleues* oysters, and urchins by the dozen. It's packed noon and night. ⊠ *5 pl. Garibaldi, Vieux-Nice* ☎ *04–93–62–29–52* ▭ *AE, DC, MC, V* ⊗ *Closed June.*

★ $$ ✗ **La Mérenda.** The back-to-bistro boom climaxed here when Dominique Le Stanc retired his crown at the Negresco to take over this tiny, unpretentious landmark of Provençal cuisine. Now he and his wife work in the miniature open kitchen, creating the ultimate versions of stuffed sardines, pistou, and slow-simmered *daubes* (beef stews). To reserve entry to the inner sanctum, you must stop by in person (there's no telephone). The dinner menu is €25 to €30. ⊠ *4 rue de la Terrasse, Vieux-Nice* ☎ *No phone* ▭ *No credit cards* ⊗ *Closed weekends, last wk July, and 1st 2 wks Aug.*

¢ ✗ **Chez René/Socca.** This back-alley landmark is the most popular dive in town for socca, the chickpea-pancake snack food unique to Nice. Rustic olive-wood tables line the street, and curt waiters splash down your drink order. For the food, you get in line at the Socca, choose your €3 plate (or plates), and carry it steaming to the table yourself. It's off place Garibaldi on the edge of the Vieille Ville, across from the *gare routière* (bus station). ⊠ *2 rue Miralheti, Vieux-Nice* ☎ *04–93–92–05–73* ▭ *No credit cards* ⊗ *Closed Mon.*

★ $$$–$$$$ ✗▥ **La Perouse.** Just past the Vieille Ville, at the foot of the château, this hotel is a secret treasure cut into the cliff (an elevator takes you up to reception). Some of the best rooms (including Raoul Dufy's favorite) not only have views of the azure sea but also look down into an intimate garden with lemon trees and a cliffside pool. The restaurant serves meals in the candlelit garden May–September. ✉ *11 quai Rauba-Capeau, Le Château 06300* ☎ *04–93–62–34–63* 🖷 *04–93–62–59–41* ⊕ *www.hroy.com/la-perouse* ⌁ *63 rooms* ⅋ *Restaurant, minibars, cable TV, pool, health club, sauna, Internet, meeting room, some pets allowed* ⊟ *AE, DC, MC, V* ⏀*EP.*

$$$–$$$$ ✕⏚ **Beau Rivage.** Occupying an imposing late-19th-century town house near cours Saleya, this hotel (guests have included Chekhov, Matisse, and Nietzsche) is just a few steps from the best parts of Old Nice and the beach, though other buildings have long since blocked its sea views. With great hoopla, Jean-Michel Wilmotte—one of France's most cutting-edge designers—was brought in 2003 to redo the interiors, so all is now *Wallpaper*-perfect: beige, minimalist, hard-edge, and just the antidote to all the froufrou found in Nice. What Chekhov would think is another matter, however. ✉ *24 rue St-François-de-Paule, Vieux-Nice, 06000* ☎*04–92–47–82–82* 🖷*04–92–47–82–83* ⊕*www.nicebeaurivage. com* ⌁ *106 rooms, 12 suites* ⅋ *Restaurant, minibars, cable TV, beach, bar, some pets allowed, no-smoking rooms* ⊟ *AE, DC, MC, V* ⏀*EP.*

★ $$–$$$ ⏚ **Windsor.** This is a memorably eccentric hotel with a vision: most of its white-on-white rooms either have frescoes of mythological themes or are works of artists' whimsy. But the real draw of this otherworldly place is its astonishing city-center garden—a tropical oasis of lemon, magnolia, and palm trees. You can breakfast or dine here by candlelight (guests only) and dip into the small, shrubbery-screened pool. ✉*11 rue Dalpozzo, Vieux-Nice, 06000* ☎ *04–93–88–59–35* 🖷 *04–93–88–94–57* ⊕ *www. hotelwindsor.com* ⌁ *57 rooms* ⅋ *Restaurant, minibars, cable TV, pool, bar, parking (fee); no a/c in some rooms* ⊟ *AE, DC, MC, V* ⏀*MAP.*

$ ⏚ **Felix.** On popular, pedestrian rue Masséna and a block from the beach, this tiny hotel owned by a hard-working couple (both fluent in English) that make you feel welcome. Rooms are compact but neat and bright, so they don't feel as small, and four have tiny balconies providing a ringside seat over the pedestrian thoroughfare. ✉ *41 rue Masséna, Vieux-Nice, 06000* ☎ *04–93–88–67–73* 🖷 *04–93–16–15–78* ⌁ *14 rooms* ⅋ *Minibars, cable TV, Internet* ⊟ *AE, DC, MC, V* ⏀*EP.*

Nightlife & the Arts

The **Casino Ruhl** (✉ 1 Promenade des Anglais, Vieux-Nice ☎ 04–93–87–95–87), gleaming neon-bright and modern, is a sophisticated Riviera landmark. With sleek decor, a piano bar, and live bands, the **Dizzy Club** (✉ 26 quai Lunel, Vieux-Nice ☎ 04–93–26–54–79) is consistently popular. If you're all dressed up and have just won big, invest in a drink in the intimate walnut-and-velour **Bar Anglais** (✉ 37 Promenade des Anglais, Vieux-Nice ☎ 04–93–88–39–51), in the landmark Hôtel Negresco.

In July the **Nice Jazz Festival** (☎ 04–92–17–77–77 information) draws performers from around the world. Classical music and ballet performances take place at Nice's convention center, the **Acropolis** (✉ Palais des Congrès, Esplanade John F. Kennedy, Centre-Ville ☎ 04–93–92–83–00). The season at the **Opéra de Nice** (✉ 4 rue St-François-de-Paul, Vieux-Nice ☎ 04–92–17–40–40) runs from September to June.

The Outdoors

Nice's **beaches** extend all along the Baie des Anges, backed full-length by the Promenade des Anglais. Public stretches alternate with posh private beaches that have restaurants—and bar service, mattresses and parasols, waterskiing, parasailing, windsurfing, and jet-skiing. One of the handiest private beaches is the **Beau Rivage** (☎ 04–92–47–82–82), set across from the Opera. The sun can also be yours for the basking at **Ruhl** (☎ 04–93–87–09–70), across from the casino.

Shopping

Olive oil by the gallon in cans with colorful, old-fashioned labels is sold at tiny **Alziari** (⊠ 14 rue St-François-de-Paule, Vieux-Nice). A good source for crystallized fruit, a Nice specialty, is the **Confiserie du Vieux Nice** (⊠ 14 quai Papacino, Vieux-Nice), on the west side of the port. The venerable **Henri Auer** (⊠ 7 rue St-François-de-Paule, Vieux-Nice) has sold crystallized fruit since 1820. For fragrances, linens, and pickled-wood furniture, head to **Boutique 3** (⊠ 3 rue Longchamp, Vieux-Nice), run by three Niçoise women of rare talent and taste.

Seafood of all kinds is sold at the **fish market** (⊠ Pl. St-François, Vieux-Nice) every morning except Monday. At the daily **flower market** (⊠ Cours Saleya, Vieux-Nice) you can find all kinds of plants and fruits and vegetables. The **antiques and brocante market** (⊠ Pl. Robilante, Vieux-Nice), by the old port, is held Tuesday through Saturday.

> **en route** The lay of the land east of Nice is nearly vertical, as the coastline is one great cliff, a corniche terraced by three parallel highways—the **Corniche Inférieure,** the **Moyenne Corniche,** and the **Grande Corniche**—that snake along its graduated crests. The lowest (*inférieure*) is the slowest, following the coast and crawling through the main streets of resorts—including downtown Monte Carlo. Villefranche, Cap-Ferrat, and Beaulieu are some of the towns located along this 20-mi-long highway (also called the Basse Corniche). The highest (*grande*) is the fastest, but its panoramic views are blocked by villas, and there are few safe overlooks. The middle (*moyenne*) offers views down over the shoreline and villages and passes through a few picturesque towns, including Èze.

THE EASTERN CÔTE D'AZUR

You may build castles in Spain or picture yourself on a South Sea island, but when it comes to serious speculation about how to spend that first $10 million and slip easily into the life of the idle rich, most people head for France and the stretch of coast that covers the eastern Côte d'Azur. Here, backed by the mistral-proof Alps and coddled by mild Mediterranean breezes, waterfront resorts—Villefranche and Menton—draw energy from the thriving city of Nice, while jutting tropical peninsulas—Cap Ferrat, Cap Martin—frame the tiny principality of Monaco. Here the corniche highways snake above sparkling waters, their pink-and-white villas turning faces toward the sun. Cliffs bristle with palm trees and parasol pines, and a riot of mimosa, bougainvillea, jasmine, and even cactus blooms in the hothouse climate. Crowded with sunseekers, the Riviera still reveals quiet corners with heart-stopping views of sea, sun, and mountains—all within one memorable frame.

Villefranche-sur-Mer

37 *10 km (6 mi) east of Nice.*

Fodor'sChoice
★

Nestled discreetly along the deep scoop of harbor between Nice and Cap Ferrat, this pretty watercolor of a fishing port seems surreal, flanked as it is by the big city of Nice and the assertive wealth of Monaco. The town is a stage-set of brightly colored houses—the sort of place where Pagnol's *Fanny* could have been filmed. Genuine fishermen actually skim up to the docks here in weathered-blue *barques,* and the streets of the Vieille Ville flow directly to the waterfront, much as they did in the 13th century. Some of the prettiest spots in town are around place de la Paix, rue du Poilu, and place du Conseil, which looks out over the water. The deep harbor, in the caldera of a volcano, was once preferred by the likes of Onassis and Niarchos and royals on their yachts (today, unfortunately, these are usually replaced by warships as a result of the presence of a nearby naval base). The character of Villefranche was subtly shaped by the artists and authors who gathered at the Hôtel Welcome—Diaghilev and Stravinsky, taking a break from the Ballet Russe in Monaco; Somerset Maugham and Evelyn Waugh; and, above all, Jean Cocteau, who came here to recover from the excesses of Paris life. Behind towering gates and secluded groves are the private vacation villas of some of the wealthiest people on earth. The most celebrated is La Leopolda, built in the early 20th century by King Leopold of Belgium for his mistress; the villa is private but has a famous garden staircase, immortalized in the film *The Red Shoes,* whose endless stairs may be glimpsed through gates on the road below the villa.

So enamored was Jean Cocteau of this painterly fishing port that he decorated the 14th-century **Chapelle St-Pierre** with images from the life of St. Peter and dedicated it to the village's fishermen. ⊠ *Pl. Pollanais* ☎ *04–93–76–90–70* 🖾 *€2* ☺ *Mid-June–mid-Sept., Tues.–Sun. 10–noon and 4–8:30; mid-Sept.–mid-Nov., Tues.–Sun. 9:30–noon and 2–6; end Dec.–Mar., Tues.–Sun. 9:30–noon and 2–5:30; Apr.–mid-June, Tues.–Sun. 9:30–noon and 3–7.*

Running parallel to the waterfront, the extraordinary 13th-century **rue Obscure** (literally, Dark Street) is entirely covered by vaulted arcades; it sheltered the people of Villefranche when the Germans fired their parting shots—an artillery bombardment—near the end of World War II. The stalwart 16th-century **Citadelle St-Elme,** restored to perfect condition, anchors the harbor with its broad, sloping stone walls. Beyond its drawbridge lie the city's administrative offices and a group of minor gallery-museums, with a scattering of works by Picasso and Miró. Whether or not you stop into these private collections of local art (all free of charge), you are welcome to stroll around the inner grounds and to circle the imposing exterior.

Where to Stay & Eat

¢–$ ✕ **La Grignotière.** Tucked down a narrow side street just a few steps away from the marketplace, this small and friendly local restaurant offers up top quality, inexpensive dishes. The homemade lasagna is excellent, as is the spaghetti pistou. ⊠ *3 rue du Poilu* ☎ *04–93–76–79–83* ▤ *MC, V* ⊘ *No lunch.*

$–$$ ✕▤ **Hôtel de Versailles.** Comfortable, welcoming, and family-owned, this hotel is perched up above the town and boasts splendid views over scattered rooftops to the bay. Rooms are basic: wicker chairs, thick carpets, and brightly matching bedspreads and curtains (some with an unfortunate bent for floral). The balconies are large, however, as are the newly tiled bathrooms. Half-board is available and straightforward meals are served in the panoramic-view restaurant. ⊠ *7 av Princess Grace Blvd., 06230* ☎ *04–93–76–52–52* 🖳 *04–93–01–97–48* ⊕ *www.hotelversailles. com* ⌖ *50 rooms* ☖ *Restaurant, minibars, cable TV, pool, bar, some pets allowed (fee), free parking* ▤ *AE, MC, V* ⊘ *Closed Nov.–Jan.* ⦿| *MAP.*

$–$$ ✕▤ **Hôtel Provençal.** Within walking distance of the port, this delightful hotel is friendly and accommodating. The rooms are large and comfortably decorated with deep blue carpets, plush velvet green chairs, and sparkling white bedspreads. About half of the rooms have a sea view; the other half look out over colorful rooftops. The Provençal-style restaurant serves up tasty items ranging from freshly grilled fish to hearty soups on a large terrace overflowing with flowers. ⊠ *Av. Maréchal Joffre, 06360* ☎ *04–93–76–53–53* 🖳 *04–93–76–96–00* ⊕ *www. hotelprovencal.com* ⌖ *45 rooms* ☖ *Restaurant, minibars, cable TV, bar, some pets allowed* ▤ *MC, V* ⊘ *Closed Nov.–Dec 24* ⦿| *EP.*

★ $$$ ▤ **Hôtel Welcome.** When Villefranche harbored a community of artists and writers, this waterfront landmark was their adopted headquarters. Somerset Maugham holed up in one of the tiny crow's-nest rooms at the top, and Jean Cocteau lived here while writing *Orphée* and much of *Oediphus Rex.* Elizabeth Taylor and Richard Burton used to tie one on in the bar (now nicely renovated). It's comfortable and modern, with the best rooms brightened with vivid colors and stenciled quotes from Cocteau, and some of the guest rooms have spectacular views. ⊠ *Quai Courbet, 06230* ☎ *04–93–76–27–62* 🖳 *04–93–76–27–66* ⊕ *www. welcomehotel.com* ⌖ *36 rooms, 1 apartment* ☖ *Minibars, cable TV, bar, Internet, some pets allowed (fee)* ▤ *AE, DC, MC, V* ⊘ *Closed mid-Nov.–mid-Dec.* ⦿| *EP.*

Beaulieu

㊳ *4 km (2½ mi) east of Villefranche, 14 km (9 mi) east of Nice.*

With its back pressed hard against the cliffs of the corniche and sheltered between the peninsulas of Cap Ferrat and Cap Roux, this once-grand resort basks in a tropical microclimate that earned its central neighborhood the name *Petite Afrique.* The town was the pet of 19th-century society, and its grand hotels welcomed Empress Eugénie, the Prince of Wales, and Russian nobility. It's still home to some of the poshest hotels and grandest villas (most still private and some still occupied by the British, who particularly favored this town) along the coast.

One manifestation of Beaulieu's Belle Epoque excess is the eye-knocking
FodorsChoice **Villa Kerylos,** a mansion built in 1902 in the style of classical Greece (to
★ be exact, of the villas that existed on the island of Delos in the 2nd century [BC]). It was the dream house of the amateur archaeologist Théodore
Reinach, who originally hailed from a super-rich family from Frankfurt,
helped the French in their excavations at Delphi, and became an authority on ancient Greek music. He commissioned an Italian architect from
Nice, Emmanuel Pontremoli, to surround him with Grecian delights: cool
Carrara marble, rare fruitwoods, and a dining salon where guests reclined
to eat *à la Greque.* Don't miss this—it's one of the most unusual houses
in the south of France. Not far from the house is the **Promenade Maurice Rouvier,** an enchanting coastal path which leads to St-Jean-Cap-Ferrat. ✉ *Rue Gustave-Eiffel* ☎ *04–93–01–01–44* ☑ *€7.50, €13.50 to
visit both Villa Kerylos and Villa Ephrussi de Rothschild in same wk* ☉ *Mid-
Feb.–June and Sept.–mid–Nov., daily 10–6; July–Aug., daily 10–7; mid-
Dec.–mid-Feb., weekdays 2–6, weekends 10–6.*

Where to Stay & Eat

★ **$$$$** ✕▦ **Métropole.** Affluent travelers have been coming to this palace for
more than 100 years, attracted by the heated saltwater pool and beautiful seaside terrace. The Restoration-style furniture and subdued beige
and blue-gray tones in the guest rooms offer a welcome change from
the Provençal patterns that tyrannize the region. Excellent new chef
François Blanchet offers up mouthwatering Mediterranean-style cuisine:
grilled scallops on balsamic-infused barely, creamed lentil and stuffed
ravioli soup, or slow-roasted venison are some best bets. ✉ *16 bd.
Mar. Leclerc, 06160* ☎ *04–93–01–00–08* 🖷 *04–93–01–18–51* ⊕ *www.
le-metropole.com* ↪ *35 rooms, 5 suites* ⌂ *Restaurant, minibars, cable
TV, pool, beach, bar, some pets allowed (fee)* ▤ *AE, DC, MC, V*
☉ *Closed mid-Oct.–mid-Dec.* ﾟﾟ *FAP, MAP.*

St-Jean-Cap-Ferrat

★ ➌➒ *2 km (1 mi) south of Beaulieu on D25.*

This luxuriously sited pleasure port moors the peninsula of Cap Ferrat;
from its port-side walkways and crescent of beach you can look over
the sparkling blue harbor to the graceful green bulk of the corniches.
Yachts purr in and out of port, and their passengers scuttle into cafés
for take-out drinks to enjoy on their private decks.

FodorsChoice Between the port and the mainland, the floridly beautiful **Villa Ephrussi de
★ Rothschild** stands as witness to the wealth and worldly flair of the baroness
who had it built. Constructed in 1905 in neo-Venetian style (its flamingo-
pink facade was thought not to be in the best of taste by the local gentry), the house was baptized "Ile-de-France" in homage to the Baroness
Bétrice de Rothschild's favorite ocean liner (her staff used to wear sailing
costumes and her ship travel-kit is on view in her bedroom). Precious artworks, tapestries, and furniture adorn the salons—in typical Rothschildian
fashion, each room is given over to a different 18th-century "époque."
Upstairs are the private apartments of Madame la Baronne, which can
only be seen on a guided tour offered around noon. The grounds are land-

scaped with no fewer than seven theme gardens and topped off with a Temple of Diana (no less); be sure to allow yourself time to wander here, as this is one of the few places on the coast where you'll be allowed to experience the lavish pleasures characteristic of the Belle Epoque Côte d'Azur. Tea and light lunches are served in a glassed-in porch overlooking the grounds and spectacular views of the coastline. ✉ *Av. Ephrussi* ☎ *04–93–01–33–09* ♿ *Access to ground floor and gardens €8.50, €13.50 joint ticket for Villa Kerylos to be used in same wk, guided tour upstairs €2 extra* ⊙ *Feb.–June and Sept.–Nov., daily 10–6; July and Aug., daily 10–7; Nov.–Jan., weekdays 2–6, weekends 10–6.*

The residents of Cap Ferrat fiercely protect it from curious tourists; its grand old villas are hidden for the most part in the depths of tropical gardens. You can nonetheless walk its entire **coastline promenade** if you strike out from the port; from the restaurant Capitaine Cook, cut right up avenue des Fossés, turn right on avenue Vignon, and follow the chemin de la Carrière. The 11-km (7-mi) walk passes through rich tropical flora and, on the west side, over white cliffs buffeted by waves. When you've traced the full outline of the peninsula, veer up the chemin du Roy past the fabulous gardens of the **Villa des Cèdres,** once owned by King Leopold II of Belgium at the turn of the last century. The king owned several opulent estates along the Côte d'Azur, undoubtedly paid for by his enslavement of the Belgian Congo. His African plunder also stocked the private zoo on his villa grounds, today the town's **Parc Zoologique** (✉ Bd. du Général-de-Gaulle). Past the gardens, you'll reach the **Plage de Passable,** from which you cut back across the peninsula's wrist. A shorter loop takes you from town out to the **Pointe de St-Hospice,** much of the walk shaded by wind-twisted pines. From the port climb avenue Jean Mermoz to place Paloma and follow the path closest to the waterfront. At the point are an 18th-century prison tower, a 19th-century chapel, and unobstructed views of Cap Martin.

Where to Stay & Eat

$$–$$$ ✕ **Le Sloop.** This sleek port-side restaurant caters to the yachting crowd and sailors who cruise into dock for lunch. The focus is fish, of course: *soupe de poisson* (fish soup), *St-Pierre* (John Dory) steamed with asparagus, roasted whole sea bass. Its outdoor tables surround a tiny "garden" of potted palms. The menu is €26. ✉ *Port de Plaisance* ☎ *04–93–01–48–63* ▤ *MC, V* ⊙ *Closed Wed. mid-Sept.–mid-Apr. No lunch Tues. and Wed. mid-Apr.–mid-Sept.*

★ $$$$ ✕▨ **Royal Riviera.** Completely revamped by Parisian designer guru Grace Leo Andrieu, this former *residence hôtelière* for British aristos now invites visitors on an intimate voyage into neo-Hellenic style, complete with an admiring wink at the nearby Villa Kerylos museum. Beyond the jaw-droppingly spectacular reception area, guest rooms are sun-drenched; bleached-wood furniture and shades of lavender, cream and orange sherbet abound. Landscape genius Jean Mus designed the extensive gardens favoring lime-verbena and olive trees, and there's a splendid pool and fitness center. If you can't afford to stay the night, stop for lunch at the poolside restaurant La Pergola—the buffet is worth every euro. ✉ *3 av. Monnet, 06360* ☎ *04–93–76–31–00* 🖶 *04–93–01–23–07*

⊕ *www.royal-riviera.com/history.html* ⤲ *70 rooms, 7 suites ⅄ Restaurant, minibars, cable TV, pool, exercise equipment, beach, bar, some pets allowed (fee), free parking* ⊟ *AE, MC, V* ⦿I *EP.*

★ $$$ 🖼 **Brise Marine.** With a glowing Provençal-yellow facade, bright blue shutters, and balustraded sea terrace, this lovely vision fulfills most desires for that perfect, picturesque Cap Ferrat hotel. Pretty pastel guest rooms feel like bedrooms in a private home—many offer window views of the gorgeous peninsula stunningly framed by statuesque palms. ⊠ *58 av. Jean Mermoz, 06230* ☎ *04–93–76–04–36* 🖨 *04–93–76–11–49* ⊕ *www. hotel-brisemarine.com* ⤲ *18 rooms ⅄ Minibars, bar, parking (fee), some pets allowed* ⊟*AE, DC, MC, V* ⊘ *Closed Nov.–Jan.* ⦿I*EP.*

$–$$$ 🖼 **Clair Logis.** With soft pastels, antique furniture, and large picture windows, this converted villa is perfectly framed by a sprawling garden park. The main house offers up subtle bourgeois elegance; for the budget-conscious there are other simpler, airy rooms scattered over several small buildings. Most have charming balconies looking out over gently swaying palms. There's no pool, but breakfast on the cobblestone terrace is lovely, and it's a good way to gear up for the 15-minute walk down to the beach. ⊠ *12 av. Centrale, point de St-Jean, 06230* ☎*04–93–76–51–81* 🖨 *04–93–76–51–82* ⊕ *www.hotel-clair-logis.fr* ⤲ *18 rooms ⅄ Minibars, cable TV, some pets allowed (fee), free parking* ⊟*AE, MC, V* ⦿I*EP.*

Èze

❹⓪ *2 km (1 mi) east of Beaulieu, 12 km (7 mi) east of Nice, 7 km (4½ mi)*
Fodor's Choice *west of Monte Carlo.*
★

Towering like an eagle's nest above the coast and crowned with ramparts and the ruins of a medieval château, Èze (pronounced *ehz*) is unfortunately the most accessible of all the perched villages. Consequently, it's by far the most commercialized, surpassing St-Paul-de-Vence for the tackiness of its souvenir shops (some carved out of the rock face) and the indifference of its waiters. It is, nonetheless, the most spectacularly sited; if you can manage to shake the crowds and duck off to a quiet overlook, the village commands splendid views up and down the coast, one of the draws that once lured fabled visitors—lots of crowned heads, Georges Sand, Friedrich Nietzsche—and residents: Consuelo Vanderbilt, when she was tired of being duchess of Marlborough, traded in Blenheim Palace for a custom-built house here.

From the crest-top **Jardin Exotique** (Tropical Garden), full of rare succulents, you can pan your videocam all the way around the hills and waterfront. But if you want a prayer of a chance of enjoying the magnificence of the village's arched passages, stone alleyways, and ancient fountains, come at dawn or after sunset—or (if you have the means) stay the night—but spend the midday elsewhere. The church of **Notre-Dame,** consecrated in 1772, glitters inside with Baroque retables and altarpieces. Èze's tourist office, on place du Général-de-Gaulle, can direct you to the numerous footpaths—the most famous being the **Sentier Friedrich Nietzsche**—that thread Èze with the coast's three corniche highways. Èze extends from hilltop down to the coastal beach; on either side a vast **Grande Corniche Parc** keeps things green and verdant.

Where to Stay & Eat

$$$-$$$$ ✕ **Troubadour.** Amid the clutter and clatter, this is a wonderful find: comfortably relaxed, this old family house proffers pleasant service and excellent dishes like roasted scallops with chicken broth and squab with citrus zest and beef broth. Full-course menus range from €28 to €48. ⊠ *4 rue du Brec* ☎ *04–93–41–19–03* ▭ *AE, MC, V* ⊘ *Closed Sun. and mid-Nov.–mid-Dec., late Feb.–mid-Mar. No lunch Mon.*

¢–$ ✕ **Loumiri.** Classic Provençal and regional seafood dishes are tastily prepared and married with decent, inexpensive wines at this cute little bistro near the entrance to the Vieille Ville. The best bet is to order *à l'ardoise*—that is, from the blackboard listing of daily specials. The lunch menu prix-fixe (€15) is the best deal in town. Dinner menus start at €21. ⊠ *Av. Jardin Exotique* ☎ *04–93–41–16–42* ▭ *MC, V* ⊘ *Closed Mon. and mid-Dec.–mid-Jan. No dinner Wed.*

★ $$$$ ✕▦ **Château de la Chèvre d'Or.** Though on the main tourist thoroughfare, these weathered stone houses allow you to turn your back on the world and drink in unsurpassed sea views. More than half the creamy white rooms look over the water, and the others compensate with exposed stone, beams, and burnished antiques. The three restaurants all take in the views, too, as does the Louis XIII–style bar. It's the luxurious if occasionally precious main restaurant that draws kudos for its delicate stuffed pastas and near-crunchy risotto, its buttery mullet fillets, and its gingerbread soufflés. The swimming pool alone, clinging like a swallow's nest to the hillside, may justify the investment, as do the liveried footmen who greet you at the village entrance to wave you VIP-style past the cattle-drive of tourists. ⊠ *Rue du Barri, 06360* ☎ *04–92–10–66–66* 🖷 *04–93–41–06–72* ⊕ *www.chevredor.com* ⇨ *23 rooms, 9 suites* ⚙ *4 restaurants, minibars, cable TV, tennis court, pool, bar, Internet, some pets allowed* ▭ *AE, DC, MC, V* ⊘ *Closed Dec.–Feb.* ▮❍▮ *EP.*

★ $$$$ ✕▦ **Château Eza.** Vertiginously perched on the edge of a cliff 3,000 feet above the crouching tiger of St-Jean-Cap-Ferrat, this former residence of Prince William of Sweden is one of the most dramatic, romantic, and expensive inns on the entire Mediterranean coast. Rooms are spread among a cluster of 13th-century buildings on cobblestone streets too narrow for cars. Most have private entrances and all are luxed out to the max: canopy beds, costly objets d'art and antiques, exquisite carpets and tapestries, wood-burning fireplaces and unbelievable views. If you're not staying the night, the views from the panoramic restaurant and outdoor terrace are just as good. The wine list is one of the best on the Côte, though the food has slipped a notch and service can be haughty. Still, for fairy-tale experiences, the surroundings are impossible to beat. ⊠ *Rue de la Pise 06360* ☎ *04–93–41–12–24* 🖷 *04–93–41–16–64* ⊕ *www.chateaueza.com* ⇨ *7 rooms, 3 suites* ⚙ *Restaurant, minibars* ▭ *AE, DC, MC, V* ⊘ *Closed Oct.–Mar.* ▮❍▮ *EP.*

★ $$ ▦ **La Bastide aux Camelias.** There are only three bedrooms in this lovely B&B, each individually decorated with softly draped fabrics and polished antiques. Close to Èze village, set in the nearby Grande Corniche Park, it offers up the usual run of breathtaking views, but also has inviting, less precipitous ones of garden greenery. Have the complimentary breakfast on the picture-perfect veranda, indulge in a cooling drink by the gorgeous pool, or stretch out on the manicured lawn. It's a gentle hospitality that's much in demand, however, so reserve well in advance. ✉ *Route de l'Adret, 06360* ☎ *04–93–41–13–68* 📠 *04–93–41–13–68* ⊕ *www.bastide-aux-camelias.fr.st* ⇨ *3 rooms* ₺ *Minibars, cable TV, pool, hot tubs, some pets allowed (fee), free parking* ◎| *BP.*

Peillon

★ ❹ 15 km (9 mi) northeast of Nice via D2204 and D21.

Perhaps because it's difficult to reach and not on the way to or from anything else, this idyllic village has maintained the magical ambience of its medieval origins. You can hear the bell toll here, walk in silence along its weathered cobblestones, and smell the thyme crunching underfoot if you step past its minuscule boundaries onto the unspoiled hillsides. And its streets are utterly and completely commerce-free; the citizens have voted to vaccinate themselves against the plague of boutiques, galleries, and cafés that have afflicted its peers along the coast.

Where to Stay & Eat

★ $$–$$$ ✕🖫 **L'Auberge de la Madone.** With its shaded garden terrace and its impeccable, bright-color rooms, this inn is a charming oasis. A lunch of sea bass, pigeon, and goat cheese on the flowery veranda is everything the south of France should be. The inn has a tennis court on the slope above it and, in the village annex Lou Pourtail, six little rooms offering shelter at bargain rates. ✉ *06440 Peillon Village* ☎ *04–93–79–91–17* 📠 *04–93–79–99–36* ⊕ *www.chateauxhotels.com* ⇨ *20 rooms* ₺ *Restaurant, minibars, tennis court, Internet, no-smoking rooms; no a/c* ▭ *MC, V* ⊗ *Closed late Oct.–late Dec. and Jan.* ◎| *MAP.*

Monaco

7 km (4½ mi) east of Èze, 21 km (13 mi) east of Nice.

It's positively feudal, the idea that an ancient dynasty of aristocrats could still hold fast to its patch of coastline, the last scrap of a once-vast domain. But that's just what the Grimaldi family did, clinging to a few acres of glory and maintaining their own license plates, their own telephone area code (377—don't forget to dial this when calling Monaco from France or other countries), and their own highly forgiving tax system. Yet the Principality of Monaco covers just 473 acres and would fit comfortably inside New York's Central Park or a family farm in Iowa. And its 5,000 pampered citizens would fill only a small fraction of the seats in Yankee Stadium. The harbor district, known as **La Condamine,** connects the new quarter, officially known as **Monte Carlo,** with the Vieille Ville, officially known as **Monaco-Ville** (or Le Rocher). Have no fear that you'll need to climb countless steps to get to the Vieille Ville, as there are plenty of elevators and escalators climbing the steep cliffs.

The present ruler, Prince Rainier III, traces his ancestry to Otto Canella, who was born in 1070. The Grimaldi dynasty began with Otto's great-great-great-grandson, Francesco Grimaldi, also known as Frank the Rogue. Expelled from Genoa, Frank and his cronies disguised themselves

CloseUp

CRASHING THE GRAND PRIX?

In late May, the entire racing world speeds to Monaco to see the best Formula One drivers compete in the Grand Prix. During the event, the streets are roped off, the liquor is iced, the brass is polished, and the super rich alight on rented balconies (some cost e10,000 for the two-day stint). Monaco on the day of the race is one big human sardine can, so buy your train ticket ahead of time. Though reserved bleacher seats start at e516 and are sold months in advance, tickets for the

section along the cliff under the palace, called "Secteur rocher," cost a mere €93. Come before 10 AM to stake out a place where thousands of people won't block your view. You can buy a ticket at box offices all around town until the race starts at 3:30 PM. Unfortunately, there are no other blocks where you can view the race up close, and police are everywhere to make sure you don't crash the party if you don't have a ticket.

as monks and in 1297 seized the fortified medieval town known today as Le Rocher (the Rock). Except for a short break under Napoléon, the Grimaldis have been here ever since, which makes them the oldest reigning family in Europe (they also seem to be the tackiest, considering all the lurid tabloid coverage of princesses Caroline and Stephanie).

It's the tax system, not the gambling (actually, the latter helps pay for the former), that has made Monaco one of the most sought-after addresses in the world. It bristles with gleaming glass-and-concrete corncob-towers 20 and 30 stories high and with vast apartment complexes, their terraces, landscaped like miniature gardens, jutting over the sea. You now have to look hard to find the Belle Epoque grace of yesteryear. But if you repair to the town's great 1864 landmark Hôtel de Paris—still a veritable crossroads of the buffed and befurred Euro-gentry—or enjoy a grand bouffe at its famous Louis XV restaurant, or attend the Opéra, or visit the ballrooms of the Casino (avert your eyes at the flashy gambling machines), you may still be able to conjure up Monaco's elegant past and the much-missed spirit of Princess Grace.

★ ❷ Place du Casino is the center of Monte Carlo, and the **Casino** is a must-see, even if you don't bet a sou. Into the gold-leaf splendor of the Casino, the hopeful traipse from tour buses to tempt fate beneath the gilt-edge Rococo ceiling (but do remember the fate of Sarah Bernhardt, who lost her last 100,000 francs here). Jacket and tie are required in the back rooms, which open at 3 PM. Bring your passport (under-21s not admitted). Note that there are special admission fees to get into many of the period gaming rooms—only the Salle des Jeux Americains is free. ✉ *Pl. du Casino* ☎ *377/92–16–20–00* ⊕ *www.sbm.mc* ⊙ *Daily noon–4 AM.*

❸ In the true spirit of the town, it seems that the **Opéra de Monte-Carlo** (✉ Pl. du Casino ☎ 377/92–16–22–99), with its 18-ton gilt-bronze chandelier and extravagant frescoes, is part of the Casino complex. The grand

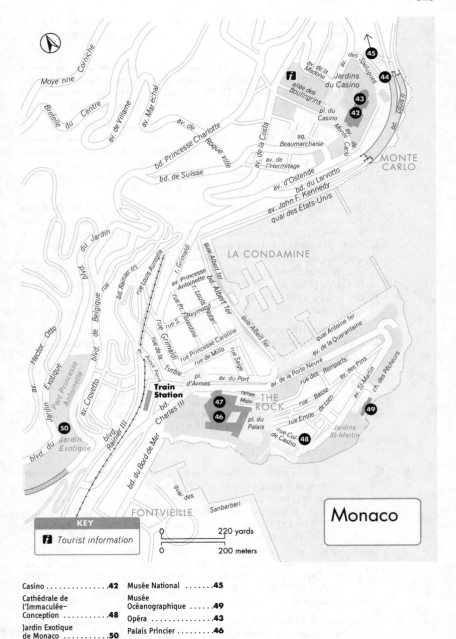

Monaco

theater was designed by Charles Garnier, who also built the Paris Opéra. Its main auditorium, the Salle Garnier, was inaugurated by Sarah Bernhardt in 1879.

④④ Some say the most serious gamblers play at **Sun Casino,** in the Monte Carlo Grand Hotel, by the vast convention center that juts over the water. ⊠ *12 av. des Spélugues* ☎ *377/92–16–21–23* ☉ *Tables open weekdays at 5 PM and weekends at 4 PM; slot machines open daily at 11 AM.*

④⑤ From place des Moulins an elevator descends to the Larvotto Beach complex, artfully created with imported sand, and the **Musée National,** housed in a Garnier villa within a rose garden. It has a beguiling collection of 18th- and 19th-century dolls and automatons. ⊠ *17 av. Princesse Grace* ☎ *377/93–30–91–26* ⊡ *€6* ☉ *Easter–Aug., daily 10–6:30; Sept.–Easter, daily 10–12:15 and 2:30–6:30.*

④⑥ West of Monte Carlo stands the famous Rock, crowned by the **Palais Princier,** where the royal family resides. A 40-minute guided tour (summer only) of this sumptuous chunk of history, first built in the 13th century and expanded and enhanced over the centuries, reveals an extravagance of 16th- and 17th-century frescoes, as well as tapestries, gilt furniture, and paintings on a grand scale. Note that the **Relève de la Garde** (Changing of the Guard) is held outside the front entrance of the palace most days at 11:45. ⊠ *Pl. du Palais* ☎ *377/93–25–18–31* ⊡ *€6, joint ticket with Musée Napoléon €8* ☉ *June–Oct., daily 9:30–5.*

④⑦ One wing of the Palais Princier, open throughout the year, is taken up by the **Musée Napoléon,** filled with Napoléonic souvenirs—including that hat and a tricolor scarf—and genealogical charts. ⊠ *In Palais Princier* ☎ *377/93–25–18–31* ⊡ *€4, joint ticket with palace apartments €8* ☉ *June–Sept., daily 9:30–6:30; Oct.–May, Tues.–Sun. 10:30–12:30 and 2–5.*

④⑧ Follow the flow of crowds down the last remaining streets of medieval Monaco to the **Cathédrale de l'Immaculée-Conception** (⊠ Av. St-Martin), an uninspired 19th-century version of the Romanesque style. Nonetheless, it harbors a magnificent altarpiece, painted in 1500 by Bréa, and the tomb of Princess Grace.

★ ⊙ **④⑨** At the prow of the Rock, the grand **Musée Océanographique** (Oceanography Museum) perches dramatically on a cliff. It's a splendid Edwardian structure, built under Prince Albert I to house specimens collected on amateur explorations. Jacques Cousteau (1910–97) led its missions from 1957 to 1988. The main floor displays skeletons and taxidermy of enormous sea creatures; early submarines and diving gear dating from the Middle Ages; and a few interactive science displays. The main draw is the famous **aquarium,** a vast complex of backlighted tanks containing every imaginable species of fish, crab, and eel. ⊠ *Av. St-Martin* ☎ *377/93–15–36–00* ⊡ *€11* ☉ *July and Aug., daily 9–7:30; Sept., May, and June, daily 9–7; Oct.–Apr., daily 10–6.*

⑤⓪ Carved out of the rock face and one of Monte Carlo's most stunning escape hatches, the **Jardin Exotique de Monaco** (Monaco Exotic Garden) is studded with thousands of succulents and cacti, all set along promenades, belvederes over the sea, and even framing faux boulders (actually hollow sculptures). There are rare plants from Mexico and Africa, and the hillside plot, threaded with bridges and grottoes, can't be beat for coastal splendor. Thanks go to Prince Albert I, who started it all. Also on the grounds, or actually under them, are the **Grottes de l'Observatoire**—spectacular grottoes and caves a-drip with stalagmites and spotlit with fairy lights. The largest cavern is called "La Grande Salle" and looks like a Romanesque rock cathedral. Traces of Cro-Magnon civilization have been found here so the grottoes now bear the official name of the **Musé d'Anthropologie Préhistorique.** ✉ *Bd. du Jardin Exotique* ☎ *377/93–30–33–65* 🎫 *€6.60* ⊙ *May–Aug., daily 9–7; Sept.–Apr., daily 9–6.*

Where to Stay & Eat

★ **$$$$** ✕ **Le Louis XV.** This sumptuous neo-Baroque restaurant, in the Hôtel de Paris, stuns with royal pomp that is nonetheless upstaged by its product: the superb cuisine of Alain Ducasse, one of Europe's most celebrated chefs. Ducasse often refers to his deceptively simple style as "country cooking," where caviar and truffles slum happily with stockfish (stewed salt cod) and tripe. In short, it's a panoply of Mediterranean delights. If your wallet is a fat one, this is a must. Menus run from €160 to €270 (includes drinks). ✉ *Hôtel de Paris, pl. du Casino* ☎ *377/92–16–30–01* ⊕ *www.alain-ducasse.com* ▤ *AE, DC, MC, V* ⊙ *Closed Tues., Wed. (Sept.–mid-June only), and late Nov.–late Dec.*

$$$–$$$$ ✕ **Café de Paris.** This landmark Belle Epoque brasserie, across from the Casino, offers the usual classics (shellfish, steak tartare, matchstick frites, and fish boned table-side). Supercilious, super-pro waiters fawn gracefully over titled preeners, gentlemen, jet-setters, and tourists alike. Happily, there's good hot food until 2 AM. ✉ *Pl. du Casino* ☎ *377/92–16–20–20* ▤ *AE, DC, MC, V.*

$$–$$$$ ✕ **Castelroc.** With its tempting pine-shaded terrace just across from the entrance to the palace, this popular local lunch spot serves up specialties of cuisine Monegasque, ranging from anchoiade to stockfish. There are only fixed-price menus, at lunch €20 and at dinner €39. ✉ *Pl. du Palais* ☎ *377/93–30–36–68* ▤ *AE, MC, V* ⊙ *Closed Sat. and Dec. and Jan.*

$$$$ ▦ **Hermitage.** A riot of frescoes and plaster flourishes embellished with gleaming brass, this landmark 1900 hotel, set back a block from the Casino scene, nonetheless maintains a relatively low profile. Even if you're not staying, come to see the glass-dome Art Nouveau vestibule, designed by Gustav Eiffel. The best rooms face the sea or angle toward the port. ✉ *Square Beaumarchais, 98005* ☎ *377/92–16–40–00* 🖷 *377/ 92–16–38–52* ⊕ *www.montecarloresort.com* ⇗ *195 rooms, 14 junior suites, 18 suites* ♨ *Restaurant, minibars, cable TV, pool, health club, bar, Internet, parking (fee), some pets allowed* ▤ *AE, DC, MC, V* ⊙⏀ *EP.*

$$$$ ▦ **Monte Carlo Grand Hotel.** Sprawling long and low along the waterfront at Monte Carlo's base, this ultramodern airport-scale complex is so vast it commands a full-time staff of upholsterers. Bright rooms decked in vivid hues angle onto the open sea. The bars, casino, boutiques, and mall-size lobby easily contain megaconventions, but vacationers will feel at home, too. ✉ *12 av. des Spélugues, 98000* ☎ *377/93–50–65–00* 🖷 *377/93–30–01–57* ⊕ *www.montecarlograndhotel.com* ⇗ *619 rooms,*

69 apartments ♁ *3 restaurants, minibars, cable TV, pool, health club, hot tub, bar, cabaret, casino, Internet, meeting room, parking (fee), some pets allowed (fee)* ▭ *AE, DC, MC, V* ¶ *MAP.*

$$–$$$ **Alexandra.** The friendly proprietress, Madame Larouquie, makes you feel right at home at this central, comfortable spot just north of the Casino. Though the color schemes clash and the bedrooms are spare, bathrooms are spacious and up to date, and insulated windows keep traffic noise out. Breakfast is included in the price. ✉ *35 bd. Princesse-Charlotte, 98000* ☎ *377/93–50–63–13* ⎙ *377/92–16–06–48* ⇨ *56 rooms* ♁ *Minibars, cable TV* ▭ *AE, DC, MC, V* ¶ *BP.*

Nightlife & the Arts

There's no need to go to bed before dawn in Monte Carlo when you can go to the **casinos.** Monte Carlo's spring arts festival, **Printemps des Arts,** takes place from early April to mid-May and includes the world's top ballet, operatic, symphonic, and chamber-music performers. Year-round, opera, ballet, and classical music can be enjoyed at the magnificently sumptuous Salle Garnier auditorium of the **Opéra de Monte-Carlo** (✉ Pl. du Casino ☎ 337/92–16–22–99 ⊕ www.opera.mc), the main venue of the Opéra de Monte-Carlo and the Orchestre Philharmonique de Monte-Carlo, both worthy of the magnificent hall.

Sports

Held at the beautiful Monte Carlo Country Club, the **Monte Carlo Open Tennis Masters Series** (⊕ www.masters-series.com/montecarlo) is held during the last two weeks of April every year. When the tennis stops, the auto racing begins: the **Grand Prix de Monaco** (☎ 377/93–15–26–00 for information ⊕ www.monaco.mc/monaco/gprix) takes place in mid-May.

Roquebrune–Cap-Martin

(51) *5 km (3 mi) east of Monaco.*

In the midst of the frenzy of overbuilding that defines this last gasp of the coast before Italy, two twinned havens have survived, each in its own way: the perched Vieille Ville of Roquebrune, which gives its name to the greater area, and Cap-Martin—luxurious, isolated, exclusive, and the once favored retreat of the Empress Eugénie and Winston Churchill. With its lovely tumble of raked tile roofs and twisting streets, fountains, archways, and quiet squares, Roquebrune retains many of the charms of a hilltop village, although it has become heavily gentrified and commercialized. Rue Moncollet is lined with arcaded passageways and a number of medieval houses. Somerset Maugham—who once memorably described these environs as a "sunny place for shady people"—resided in the town's famous Villa Mauresque (still private) for many years. Roquebrune's main attraction is its **Château Féodal** (Feudal Castle). Around the remains of a 10th-century tower, the Grimaldis erected an impregnable fortress that was state-of-the-art in the 16th century, with crenellation, watchtowers, and a broad moat. 🎟 *€4* ⏲ *Oct.–Jan., daily 10–12:30 and 2–5; Feb.–May, daily 10–12:30 and 2–6; June–Sept., daily 10–12:30 and 3–7:30.*

In the **cemetery,** Swiss-French architect Le Corbusier lies buried with his wife in a tomb of his own design. He kept a humble *cabanot* (beach bungalow) on the rocky shore of the Cap-Martin, where he drowned while swimming in 1965. You can see the glorious flora of the cape by walking the **Promenade Le Corbusier.** It leads over chalk cliffs and through dense Mediterranean flora to the famed modernist architect's "Cabanon" bungalow (plans are in the works to open this as a museum—check with local tourist office)—a tiny retreat, as much outdoors as in and designed along the rigorous lines he preferred. Park at the base of the cape on avenue Winston-Churchill and follow the signs.

Menton

52 *1 km (½ mi) east of Roquebrune, 9 km (5½ mi) east of Monaco.*

Fodor's Choice

Menton, the most Mediterranean of the French resort towns, rubs shoulders with the Italian border and owes its balmy climate to the protective curve of the Ligurian shore. Its picturesque harbor skyline seems to beg artists to immortalize it, while its Cubist skew of terra-cotta roofs and yellow-ocher houses, Baroque arabesques capping the church facades, and ceramic tiles glistening on their steeples all evoke the villages of the Italian coast. Also worth a visit are the many exotic gardens set in the hills around the town. Menton is the least pretentious of the Côte d'Azur resorts and all the more alluring for its modesty. The **Basilique St-Michel** (☒ Parvis St-Michel), a majestic Baroque church, dominates the skyline of Menton with its bell tower. Beyond the beautifully proportioned facade—a 19th-century addition—the richly frescoed nave and chapels contain several works by Genovese artists and a splendid 17th-century organ.

Just above the main church, the smaller **Chapelle de l'Immaculée-Conception** answers St-Michel's grand gesture with its own pure Baroque beauty, dating from 1687. Between 3 and 5 you can slip in to see the graceful trompe l'oeil over the altar and the ornate gilt lanterns early penitents carried in processions.

Two blocks below the square, **rue St-Michel** serves as the main commercial artery of the Vieille Ville, lined with shops, cafés, and orange trees. Between the lively pedestrian rue St-Michel and the waterfront, the marvelous **Marché Couvert** (Covered Market) sums up Menton style with its Belle Epoque facade decorated in jewel-tone ceramics. Inside, it's just as appealing, with merchants selling chewy bread, mountain cheeses, oils, fruit, and Italian delicacies in Caravaggio-esque disarray.

On the waterfront opposite the market, a squat medieval bastion crowned with four tiny watchtowers houses the **Musée Jean-Cocteau.** Built in 1636 to defend the port, it was spotted by the artist-poet-filmmaker Jean Cocteau (1889–1963) as the perfect site for a group of his works. There are bright, cartoonish pastels of fishermen and wenches in love, and a fantastical assortment of ceramic animals in the wrought-iron windows he designed. ☒ *Vieux Port* ☎ *04–93–57–72–30* ☒ €3 ☺ *Wed.–Mon. 10–noon and 2–6.*

The 19th-century Italianate **Hôtel de Ville** conceals another Cocteau treasure: it was he who decorated the **Salle des Mariages** (Marriage Room), the room in which civil marriages take place, with vibrant allegorical scenes. ⊠ *17 av. de la République* ☒ *€2* ⊙ *Weekdays 8:30–12:30 and 1:30–5.*

At the far west end of town stands the 18th-century **Palais Carnolès** (Carnolès Palace) in vast gardens luxuriant with orange, lemon, and grapefruit trees. It was once the summer retreat of the princes of Monaco; nowadays it contains a sizable collection of European paintings from the Renaissance to the present day. ⊠ *3 av. de la Madone* ☎ *04–93–35–49–71* ☒ *Free* ⊙ *Wed.–Mon. 10–noon and 2–6.*

The Cote d'Azur was famed for its panoply of grand villas and even grander gardens built by Victorian dukes, Spanish exiles, Belgian royals, and American bluebloods. With its temperate microclimate created by its southeastern and sunny exposure (the Alps were a natural buffer against cold winds), Menton attracted a great share of these wealthy hobbyists, including Major Lawrence Johnston, a gentleman gardener best known for his Cotswolds wonderland, Hidcote Manor. Fair-haired and blue-eyed, this gentle American wound up buying a choice estate in the village of Gorbio—one of the loveliest of all perched seaside villages, set 10 km (6 mi) west of Menton—and spent the 1920s and

★ 1930s making the **Serre de la Madone** one of the horticultural masterpieces of the coast. He brought back exotica from his many trips to South Africa, Mexico, and China, and planted them in a series of terraces, accented by little pools, vistas, and stone steps. While most of his creeping plumbago, pink belladona, and night-flowering cacti are now gone, his garden has been reopened by the municipality. It is best to call for a reservation at the Serre de la Madone; car facilities are very limited but the garden can also be reached from Menton via bus No. 7 (get off at Mers et Monts' stop). Back in Menton, green-thumbers will also want to visit the town's Jardin Botanique, the **Val Rahmeh Botanical Garden** (Av. St-Jacques), planted by Maybud Campbell in the 1910s, much prized by connoisseurs, bursting with rare ornamentals and subtropical plants, and adorned with water-lily pools and fountains. The tourist office can also give you directions to other gardens around Menton, including the Fontana Rosa and the Villa Maria Serena, as well as issue Heritage Passports for select garden visits; log onto (⊕ www.menton. com). ⊠ *74 route de Gorbio* ☎ *04–93–57–73–90* ⊕ *www. serredelamadone.com/* ☒ *€8* ⊙ *Mid-Feb.–end of Oct., tours only: Tues.–Sun., 3; Feb. 20–Apr. 30, Fri. 9:30; May 1–Oct. 30, Tues.–Sun. 9:30.*

Where to Stay & Eat

★ **$$–$$$** ✕▦ **Aiglon.** Sweep down the curving stone stair to the terrazzo mosaic lobby of this lovely 1880 garden villa and wander out for a drink or a meal by the pool. Or settle onto your little balcony overlooking the grounds and a tiny wedge of sea. The poolside restaurant, Le Riaumont, serves classic seafood by candlelight; breakfast, included in the price, is served in a shady garden shelter. From here it's a three-minute walk to the beach. ⊠ *7 av. de la Madone, 06502* ☎ *04–93–57–55–55* ☒ *04–93–35–92–39* ⊕ *www.hotelaiglon.com* ⇆ *28 rooms, 2 apartments*

☆ *Restaurant, pool, bar, Internet, some pets allowed (fee); no room TVs* ☰ *AE, DC, MC, V* ⓘⓞⓘ *MAP.*

Nightlife & the Arts
In August the **Festival de Musique de Chambre** (Chamber Music Festival) takes place on the stone-paved plaza outside the church of St-Michel. The **Fête du Citron** (Lemon Festival), at the end of February, celebrates the lemon with floats and sculptures like those of the Rose Bowl Parade, all made of real fruit.

THE CÔTE D'AZUR A TO Z

To research prices, get advice from other travelers, and book travel arrangements, visit www.fodors.com.

AIR TRAVEL
There are frequent flights between Paris and Nice on Easy Jet, AOM, and Air France, as well as direct flights on Delta Airlines from New York. The flight time between Paris and Nice is about one hour.

AIRPORTS
The Nice–Côte d'Azur Airport sits on a peninsula between Antibes and Nice.

🖪 Airport Information **Nice–Côte d'Azur Airport** ✉ 7 km (4½ mi) from Nice 🕾 04-93-21-30-30.

BUS TRAVEL
Buses allow you to penetrate deeper into villages and backcountry spots not on the rail line; pick up a schedule for local and commercial excursion buses at the train station, at tourist offices, and at the local *gare routière* (bus station). Phocéens Santa Azur (Voyages) is the best bus service covering the Côte d'Azur region, with buses departing from Nice, Antibes, Cannes, Menton, and Mandelieu and regular minibus service between Nice, Marseille, Toulon, and some towns inland of Nice. Alpes-Maritimes Bus Services—RCA Transport (Rapides Côte d'Azur) covers the coastal area, from Menton to Villeneuve Loubet, and inland, to Peille and Aspremont; routes run between Nice and Cannes, with stops at Cagnes-sur-Mer and Juan-les-Pins and they also service Menton, Villefranche, St-Jean-Cap-Ferrat, Èze, and Monaco (plus a "rapid" airport service from Menton and/or Monaco to Nice International). SAP offers buses serving Vence, St-Paul, La Colle-sur-Loup, St-Laurent-du-Var, and Nice. Compagnie des Autobus de Monaco covers that principality. Rapides Côte d'Azur traffics the routes in and around Cannes, while SODETRAV buses head to and from St-Tropez and St-Raphael. In addition, the national SNCF service covers more distant locales.

🖪 Bus Information **Alpes-Maritimes Bus Services—RCA Transport (Rapides Côte d'Azur)** ✉ 5 bd. Jean Jaures, Nice 🕾 04-93-85-64-44 ⊕ www.rca.tm.fr. **Compagnie des Autobus de Monaco** ✉ 2 av. du pdt J. F. Kennedy, Monaco 🕾 377/97-70-22-22 ⊕ www. cam.mc. **Phocéens Santa Azur (Voyages)** ✉ 4 pl. Massena, Nice 🕾 04-93-13-18-20 ✉ 5 sq. Mérimée, Cannes 🕾 04-93-39-79-40 ✉ 8 pl. de Gaul, Antibes 🕾 04-93-34-15-98. **SAP (Société Automobile de Provence)** 🕾 04-93-58-37-60. SNCF

🕾 08-36-35-35-35 ⊕ www.ter-sncf.com/uk/paca. **SODETRAV (Société départemen-tale de transports du Var** 🕾 0825/000650 ⊕ www.sodetrav.fr.

CAR RENTAL

Most likely you'll want to rent your car at one of the main rail stops, either St-Raphäel, Nice, Monaco, or Menton, or at the airport in Nice, where all major companies are represented.

🔠 **Local Agencies Avis** ✉ 2 av. des Phocéens, Nice 🕾 04-93-80-63-52 ✉ Nice Airport 🕾 04-93-21-42-80 ✉ 190 pl. Pierre Coullet, St-Raphaël 🕾 04-94-95-60-42. **Budget** ✉ 23 rue de Belgique, Nice 🕾 04-93-16-24-16 ✉ Nice Airport 🕾 04-93-21-36-50 ✉ 40 rue Waldeck-Rousseau, St-Raphaël 🕾 04-94-82-24-44. **Europcar** ✉ 3 av. Gustave V, Nice 🕾 04-92-14-44-50 ✉ Nice Airport 🕾 04-93-21-43-54 ✉ 47 av. de Grande-Bretagne, Monaco 🕾 377/93-50-74-95 ✉ 54 pl. Pierre Coullet, St-Raphaël, 🕾 04-94-95-56-87. **Hertz** ✉ 1 Promenade des Anglais, Nice 🕾 04-93-87-11-87 ✉ Nice airport 🕾 04-93-21-36-72 ✉ 32 rue Waldeck-Rousseau, St-Raphaël 🕾 04-94-95-48-68 ✉ 27 bd. Albert I, Monaco 🕾 377/93-50-79-60.

CAR TRAVEL

The best way to explore the secondary sights in this region, especially the backcountry hill towns, is by car. It also allows you the freedom to zip along A8 between the coastal resorts and to enjoy the tremendous views from the three corniches that trace the coast from Nice to the Italian border. N98, which connects you to coastal resorts in between, can be extremely slow, though scenic. A8 parallels the coast from above St-Tropez to Nice to the resorts on the Grand Corniche; N98 follows the coast more closely. From Paris the main southbound artery is A6/A7, known as the Autoroute du Soleil; it passes through Provence and joins the eastbound A8 at Aix-en-Provence.

LODGING

APARTMENT & VILLA RENTALS

The tourist offices of individual towns often publish lists of *locations meublés* (furnished rentals), sometimes vouched for by the tourist office and rated for comfort. Gîtes de France is a nationwide organization that rents *gîtes ruraux* (rural vacation lodgings) by the week, usually outstanding examples of a region's character. The headquarters for the regions covered in this chapter are listed below. Write or call for a catalog, then make a selection and reservation.

🔠 **Local Agents Gîtes de France Var** ✉ Rond-Point du 4 Décembre 1974, B.P. 215, 83006 Draguignan Cedex 🕾 04-94-50-93-93 🔒 04-94-50-93-90. **Gîtes de France des Alpes-Maritimes** ✉ 55 Promenade des Anglais, B.P. 1602, Cedex 01, 06011 Nice 🕾 04-92-15-21-30 🔒 04-93-86-01-06 ⊕ www.crt-riviera.fr/gites06.

SPORTS & THE OUTDOORS

This is golf country, and you can pick up the brochure and map *Les Golfs du Soleil* (*Golf Courses of the Sun*) and *Destination Golf* at local tourist offices to get a complete listing of golf courses and facilities from St-Tropez to Monaco.

TOURS

BUS TOURS

Santa Azur organizes all-day or half-day bus excursions to sights near Nice, including Monaco, Cannes, and nearby hill towns, either leaving from its offices or from several stops along the Promenade des Anglais, mainly in front of the big hotels. In Antibes, Phocéens Voyages organizes similar bus explorations of the region.

🚩 Fees & Schedules **Phocéens Voyages** ✉ 8 pl. de Gaulle, Antibes ☎ 04-93-34-15-98. **Santa Azur** ✉ 11 av. Jean-Médecin, Nice ☎ 04-93-85-46-81.

TOUR GUIDES The city of Nice arranges individual guided tours on an à la carte basis according to your needs. For information contact the Bureau d'Accueil and specify your dates and language preferences.

🚩 **Bureau d'Accueil** ☎ 04-93-14-48-00.

TRAIN TOURS A small tourist train goes along the Nice waterfront from in front of the Casino Ruhl, along cours Saleya, and up to the Château.

🚩 Fees & Schedules **Tourist train** ☎ 04-93-92-45-59.

TRAIN TRAVEL

Nice is the major rail crossroads for trains arriving from Paris and other northern cities, as well as from Italy. This coastal line, working eastward from Marseille and west from Ventimiglia, stops at Fréjus, Antibes, Monaco, and Menton. There is no rail access to St-Tropez; St-Raphaël is the nearest stop. To get from Paris to Nice, you can take the TGV, though it only maintains high speeds to Valence before returning to conventional rails and rates.

You can easily move along the coast by train on the Côte d'Azur line, a dramatic and highly tourist-pleasing route that offers panoramic views as it rolls from one famous resort to the next. But train travelers will have difficulty getting up to St-Paul, Vence, Peillon, and other backcountry villages; that you must accomplish by bus or car.

🚩 Train Information **SNCF** ☎ 08-36-35-35-35 ⊕ www.ter-sncf.com/uk/paca.

TRAVEL AGENCIES

🚩 Local Agent Referrals **American Express Voyages** ✉ 11 Promenade des Anglais, Nice ☎ 04-93-16-53-51 ✉ 35 bd. Princess Charlotte, Monte Carlo ☎ 377/93-25-74-45 ✉ 8 rue des Belges, Cannes ☎ 04-93-38-15-87. **Havas Voyages** ✉ 12 av. Félix Faure, Nice ☎ 04-93-62-76-30 ✉ 64 av. Commandant Guilbaud, St-Raphael ☎ 04-94-19-82-20 ✉ 17 bd. Louis Blanc, St-Tropez ☎ 04-94-56-64-64.

VISITOR INFORMATION

For information on travel within the department of Var (St-Tropez to La Napoule), write to the Comité Départemental du Tourisme du Var. The Comité Régional du Tourisme Riviera Côte d'Azur provides information on tourism throughout the department of Alpes-Maritimes, from Cannes to the Italian border. For information on the Belle Epoque splendors of the region, log on to a helpful Comite Régionale Web site (⊕ www.guideriviera.com/belle-epoque/en). Local tourist offices (*Office du Tourisme*) in major towns discussed in this chapter are listed below by town.

🚩 Tourist Information **Antibes/Juan-les-Pins** ✉ 11 pl. de Gaulle, 06600 Antibes ☎ 04-92-90-53-00 🖶 04-92-90-53-01. **Cannes** ✉ Palais des Festivals, Esplanade G. Pompidou, B.P. 272 ☎ 04-93-39-24-53 🖶 04-92-99-84-23 ⊕ www.cannes-on-line.com. **Comité Départmental du Tourisme du Var** ✉ 1 bd. Maréchal Foch, 83300 Draguignan ☎ 03-94-50-55-50 🖶 04-94-50-55-51. **Comité Régional du Tourisme Riviera Côte d'Azur** ✉ 55 Promenade des Anglais, B.P. 1602, Cedex 1, 06011 Nice ☎ 04-93-37-78-78 ⊕ www.crt-riviera.fr. **Èze** ✉ Place du Gl. de Gaulle, 06360 Èze

☎ 04-93-41-26-00 🖶 04-93-41-04-80 🌐 www.eze-riviera.com. **Fréjus** ✉ 325 rue Jean-Jaurès, B.P. 8, 83601 ☎ 04-94-51-83-83 🖶 04-94-51-00-26. **Grasse** ✉ Palais des Congrés, 22 Cours Honoré Cresp ☎ 04-93-36-66-66 🖶 04-93-36-86-36 🌐 www.ville-frejus.fr. **Menton** ✉ Palais de l'Europe, av. Boyer, 06500 ☎ 04-92-41-76-76 🖶 04-92-41-76-78 🌐 www.villedementon.com. **Monaco** ✉ 2a bd. des Moulins, 98000 Monte Carlo ☎ 377/92-16-61-66 🖶 377/92-16-60-00 🌐 www.monaco-tourism.com. **Nice** ✉ 5 Promenade des Anglais, 06000 ☎ 04-92-14-48-00 🖶 04-92-14-48-03 🌐 www.nicetourism.com or in person at the train station or airport. **St-Jean-Cap-Ferrat** ✉ 59 avenue Denis Semeria, 06230 St-Jean-Cap-Ferrat ☎ 04-93-76-08-90 🖶 04-93-76-16-67 🌐 www.ville-saint-jean-cap-ferrat.fr/.**St-Paul-de-Vence** ✉ 2 rue Grande, 06570 ☎ 04-93-32-86-95 🖶 04-93-32-60-27. **St-Raphaël** ✉ Rue Waldeck-Rousseau, 83700 ☎ 04-94-19-52-52 🖶 04-94-83-85-40 🌐 www.saint-raphael.com. **St-Tropez** ✉ Quai Jean-Jaurès, B.P. 183, 83992 ☎ 04-94-97-45-21 🖶 04-94-97-82-66 🌐 www.ot-saint-tropez.com. **Vence** ✉ Pl. du Grand Jardin, 06140 ☎ 04-93-58-06-38 🖶 04-93-58-91-81.

CORSICA

13

Updated by
George Semler

Introduction by
George Semler

"THE BEST WAY OF KNOWING CORSICA," according to Napoléon, "is to be born there." Not everyone has had his luck, so chances are you'll be arriving on the overnight ferry from Marseille to discover "the mountain in the sea." This vertical granite world of its own, plopped down in the Mediterranean between Provence and Tuscany, remains France's very own Wild West: a powerful natural setting and, literally, a breath of fresh air. Corsica is where you go to get away from it all, to clear your head, to find your magnetic north; a microcosm of mountains, beaches, fishing ports, wilderness, and the purest strain of proto-Mediterranean culture. Mountain people born and bred, Corsicans have historically distrusted the sea and the cosmopolitan coastal landing points, open to invading forces. The true Corsican is a highland spirit, at home in the dense undergrowth of the *maquis*—the all-sustaining chestnut forest—or the Laricio pines that climb the upper reaches of what Guy de Maupassant christened his "mountain in the sea."

Corsica's gifts of artistic and archaeological treasures, crystalline waters, granite peaks, and pine forests add up to one of France's most unspoiled sanctuaries—a logical crucible for the emergence of a force such as Napoléon Bonaparte. Its strategic location 168 km (105 mi) south of Monaco and 81 km (50 mi) west of Italy made Corsica a prize hotly contested by a succession of Mediterranean powers, notably Genoa, Pisa, and France. Their vestiges remain: the city-state of Genoa ruled Corsica for more than 200 years, leaving impressive citadels, churches, bridges, and nearly 100 medieval watchtowers around the island's coastline. The Italian influence is also apparent in village architecture and in the Corsican language, which is a combination of Italian, Tuscan dialect, and Latin.

Corsica gives an impression of immensity, seeming far larger than its 215 km (133 mi) length and 81 km (50 mi) width, partly because its rugged, mountainous terrain makes for slow traveling and partly because the landscape and the culture vary greatly from one microregion to another. Much of the terrain of Corsica that is not wooded or cultivated is covered with a dense thicket of undergrowth, called the maquis, a variety of wild and aromatic plants including lavender, myrtle, and heather that gave Corsica one of its sobriquets, "the perfumed isle." The maquis, famous for harboring fugitives, became the term used for the French Resistance movement during World War II. In Corsica "going underground" meant taking to the maquis.

Along with the word *maquis*, the term *vendetta* is one of Corsica's contributions to world lexicography. The rough-and-ready legend associated with the island comes from a long tradition of apparent lawlessness and deeply entrenched clannishness. As justice from "the Continent," whether France or Italy, was usually slow and often unsatisfying, Corsican clans frequently fought each other in blood feuds of honor and revenge.

Although famous as the birthplace of Napoléon Bonaparte (who never returned to the island after beginning his military career), Corsica's real national hero is Pasquale Paoli, who framed the world's first republi-

Four days is barely sufficient time to visit Corsica. In five days you can cover most of Haute Corse, and in 10 days it's possible, though not necessarily advisable, to see the whole island. The danger is spending too much time carbound. One approach is to settle in Corte, near the island's center, setting out each day on a quest to see different attractions.

Numbers in the text correspond to numbers in the margin and on the Corsica and Ajaccio maps.

13

**If you have
4 days**

Start out in Napoléon's hometown, ⊠ **Ajaccio** ❶ ▶ – ❽ for a walk through the market, the port and Vieille Ville, and the Musée Fesch. On your second day, head up into the highlands by train or automobile to Corsica's spiritual capital at ⊠ **Corte** ⑰. On the third day, drive through the Castagniccia to ⊠ **Piedicroce** ⑳ for a night in the chestnut forest. On your final day, find your way out of the Castagniccia to ⊠ **Bastia** ㊱ with a stop at **Murato** ㉙ for lunch and a look at the San Michele church. From Bastia choose between Livorno, Italy, or Marseille or Nice for a return to the continent.

**If you have
10
days**

Start in **Ajaccio** ❶ ▶ – ❽, visiting the market and the Musée Fesch and reaching the megalithic site at **Filitosa** ⑩ by midday. Have a look through **Sartène** ⑪ and drive into ⊠ **Bonifacio** ⑭ as the sun sets into the sea. The next day get to the Laricio pine forest, near the **Col de Bavella** ⑮, to see or even walk to the famous granite peaks. Tiny D268 comes out on the east coast at N198, which will take you up to **Aléria** ⑯ and into ⊠ **Corte** ⑰ on N200. Make Corte your base: devote day three to Corte and the Restonica Gorge, day four to **Haut-Asco** ㉑, Day 5 to the small villages in **La Castagniccia.** On day six take the **Scala di Santa Regina** drive through the Aitone Forest. Spend the night in ⊠ **Ota** ㉒. Pass through the Scandola Natural Reserve on day seven, reaching the Riviera-like ⊠ **Calvi** ㉔ by evening. Tour its citadel, then dally at the beach in Calvi on day eight for a needed time-out. Check out **Patrimonio** ㉛ and the Orenga de Gaffory vineyards before driving through ⊠ **Nonza** ㉜ and **Centuri** ㉝ to ⊠ **Erbalunga** ㉞ or ⊠ **San Martino di Lota** ㉟ on your ninth day, and check into ⊠ **Bastia** ㊱ for your last and tenth day.

can constitution for his independent Corsican nation in 1755. Paoli's ideas significantly influenced the French Revolution, as well as the founding fathers of the United States. Inspiration for generations of literati, from Homer to Mérimée, Boswell, Dumas, and Balzac, Corsica has always been, in Greek, *Kallisté,* "the most beautiful," a sylvan land and repository for romantic characters from Mérimée's Robin Hood–like *bandit d'honneur* Colomba to comic-book Asterix's pal Aucatarinabellachichix. In the end you'll find Corsica composed of equal parts vendetta, witchcraft, dream hunters, shepherds improvising the rough and haunting Corsican polyphony, megalithic menhirs, chestnuts, free-range livestock, powerful cheeses, and—always—the bittersweet, lemon-pepper fragrance of the maquis, an aroma like no other, described by Dorothy Carrington in her *Granite Island* as "akin to incense," and the only fitting perfume for Balzac's "back of beyond."

Exploring Corsica

Leaving Marseille on the excellent SNCM *Ferryterranée* (which also departs from Toulon and Nice) at sunset and arriving in Ajaccio at sunrise are among the finest moments of any trip to Corsica. Inasmuch as Napoléon claimed he could identify the fragrance of the Corsican maquis from many miles out at sea, approaching the island by some means other than a boat seems like heresy. The northern half of the island (Haute Corse) is generally wilder than the southern half (Corse du Sud), which is hotter and more barren. On the other hand, southern Corsica's archaeological sites at Filitosa and Pianu de Levie, the Col de Bavella and its majestic Laricio pine forest, and the towns of Sartène and Bonifacio all rank indisputably among the island's finest treasures. The least interesting part of the island is the coast road between Porto-Vecchio and Bastia, although one of the prettiest drives is the tour around the northward-pointing finger of Cap Corse. Don't hesitate to drive into the interior highlands, the true Corsica; if you spend too much time at sea level you'll be missing the remote villages and dramatic heights for which the island is famous.

About the Restaurants & Hotels

While entire geopolitical campaigns have been waged over warm-water harborage, this mountain in the Mediterranean has traditionally fled to its highest crags and crannies for defensive reasons, taking its best cooking along with it. The Corsican maquis grows some of Europe's wildest flora and fauna, ranging from free-range pigs to woodcock and pigeon. Chestnuts are a Corsican staple not to miss, whether in pastries, *pulenta,* or beer, while cheeses, especially the characteristic *brocciu* fresh cheese, are omnipresent upland delicacies. Dorothy Carrington accurately described Corsican cuisine as "winter cuisine," better between October and May, when game as well as brocciu are well represented on all menus.

The quantity of construction around Porto-Vecchio in the 1950s was so burdensome to Corsicans that, with some extra unwanted encouragement from separatist bombers, they resolved to avoid excessive, tourist-driven development. Instead, *fermes-auberges* (farmhouse-inns) are being restored at a rapid clip, and tastefully designed hotels are being built. During the peak season (from July to mid-September) prices are higher, and some hotels insist that breakfast and dinner be included as part of the price. The best seaside hotels are priced only marginally lower than on the Riviera, but lodgings in the interior villages remain substantially cheaper. Off-season, good prices can be found all over. Assume all rooms have air-conditioning, TV, telephones, and private bath unless otherwise noted.

13

La Cuisine Sauvage Authentic Corsican fare is based on free-range live-stock, game (especially *sanglier*, or wild boar), herbs, and wild mushrooms best found between October and May in the villages of the mountainous interior. *Civets* (meaty stews) headline menus as do the many versions of the prototypical, hearty Corsican soup (*soupe paysanne, soupe corse,* or *soupe de montagne*) made from herbs and vegetables simmered for hours with a ham bone. Seafood dishes available on the coast include *aziminu,* a rich bouillabaisse. Excellent *charcuterie* (pork products) include *lonzu* (shoulder), *coppa* (fillet), and *figatelli* (liver sausage), along with *prisuttu* (cured ham). Corsica's most emblematic cheese is really not a cheese at all: *brocciu* (pronounced broach), similar to ricotta, is used in omelets, *fiadone* (cheesecake), *fritelli* (chestnut-flour doughnuts), and as stuffing for trout or rabbit. Cheeses from Corsica's microregions include *bastelicaccia,* a soft, creamy sheep cheese, and the harder and sharper *sartenais.* Many of the most powerful cheeses are simply designated as *brebis* (sheep) or *chèvre* (goat). Chestnuts and chestnut flour, major players in Corsican gastronomy, are found in *castagna* (Corsican for chestnut), a cake; *panetta,* a kind of bread; *canistrelli,* dry cookies; beignets (fried dough), often made of chestnut flour; *pulenta,* a doughy chestnut-flour bread; and *Pietra,* chestnut beer. Corsica's best wines include the Arenas, Orenga de Gaffory, and Gentile cellars from the Patrimonio vineyards; Domaine Peraldi, Clos de Capitoro, or Clos Alzeto, from Ajaccio; Fiumicicoli, from Sartène; or Domaine de Torracia, from Porto-Vecchio.

Hiking Heaven Corsica is really just one big mountain, and if you come here without your hiking boots you may feel sorely out of place. From the wild, un-developed strands of the northern Cap Corse (Cape Corsica) to the Riviera-like tourist beaches near Calvi and Propriano, the island's scenery is astonishingly varied and rugged. In summer, during the *canicule* (literally, dog days), Corsi-cans take to the rivers, always cooler than the Mediterranean. Others take on the rugged GR 20 (Grande Randonnée 20); considered one of Europe's great-est hiking trails, it requires from 70 to 100 hours to complete and cuts a 160-km (100-mi) path from Calenzana (accessible by bus from Calvi) to Conca, near Porto-Vecchio. Planned in stages from one mountain refuge to another, the well-marked GR 20 is the ultimate way to see Corsica. Reaching altitudes of over 6,000 feet, it remains one of the most difficult hiking trails in Europe, taking 17 days to com-plete and open from May to October (stormy weather takes over the other months). If you are traveling by car, short probes along the GR 20 are easily fea-sible. In addition to the GR 20 there are shorter cross-island, coast to coast ("*Tra mare a mare*") hikes with villages and refuges at convenient intervals. If the GR20 is your idea of hell, you can go for short hikes on some of the other numerous trails in the Parc Naturel Régional de Corse. Pick up area-specific leaflets at most tourist offices. Everywhere, of course, the reward for the blistered feet of all hike-a-holics is Corsica's marvelous scenery. Old Genoese watchtowers, villas, lime trees, meaglithic dolmens, menhirs, and stone circles, ancient citadels, and olive groves contrast with rocky fjords and mountain peaks, the latter all *maquis*-stunted and warped by the force of the northeast wind called the *libeccio*. This, after all, was the land that fashioned and tempered Napoléon.

WHAT IT COSTS In euros				
	$$$$	**$$$**	**$$**	**$**	**¢**
RESTAURANTS	over €25	€17–€25	€12–€17	€8–€12	under €8
HOTELS	over €175	€120–€175	€70–€120	€40–€70	under €40

Restaurant prices are per person for a main course at dinner, including tax (19.6%) and service; note that if a restaurant offers only prix-fixe (set-price) meals, it has been given the price category that reflects the full prix-fixe price. Hotel prices are for a standard double room in high season, including tax (19.6%) and service charge; higher prices (inquire when booking) prevail for any meal plans.

Timing

The best time to visit Corsica is fall or spring, when the weather is cool. Most Corsican culinary specialties are at their best between October and June. Try to avoid July and August, when French and Italian vacationers fill hotels. Prices soar and the Corsican temperament is at its most volatile. In winter the island has the best weather in France, but a majority of the hotels and restaurants are closed.

CORSE DU SUD

Corse du Sud includes the French administrative capital of Ajaccio, the mountainous zones of the Cinarca and Alta Rocca, megalithic treasures at Filitosa and Levie, and the fortresslike towns of Sartène, Bonifacio, and Porto-Vecchio. Perhaps because southern Corsica is on the French side of the island, it seems more Continentalized. Forest fires and the resulting flooding scarred much of the southern part of the island in the mid-'90s, though the irrepressible maquis has quickly rebounded.

Ajaccio

40 mins by plane, 5–10 hrs by ferry from Marseille, Nice, or Toulon.

Ajaccio, Napoléon's birthplace and Corsica's modern capital, is a busy, French-flavored town with a bustling port, beautiful beaches, ancient streets, and, in the Musée Fesch, five centuries of Italian masterpieces. ❶ Start at the spectacular **food market** held every morning except Monday in place Campinchi, across the quai from the ferry port, an opportunity to admire an enticing parade of Corsican cheeses, pastries, sausages, and everything from traditional chestnut-flour beignets to prehistoric *rascasse* (red scorpion fish), at the fish market tucked in under the Hôtel de Ville.

❷ ❸ Rows of stately palm trees lead up to a marble statue of Napoléon on **Place Maréchal-Foch,** the city's main square. The **Hôtel de Ville** (town hall) has an Empire-style grand salon hung with portraits of a long line of Bonapartes. You'll find a fine bust of Letizia, Napoléon's formidable mother; a bronze death mask of the emperor himself; and a frescoed ceiling depicting Napoléon's meteoric rise. ⊠ *Pl. Maréchal-Foch* ☎ *04–95–21–90–15* 🖾 *€2.50* ☾ *Weekdays 9–noon and 2:30–5:30.*

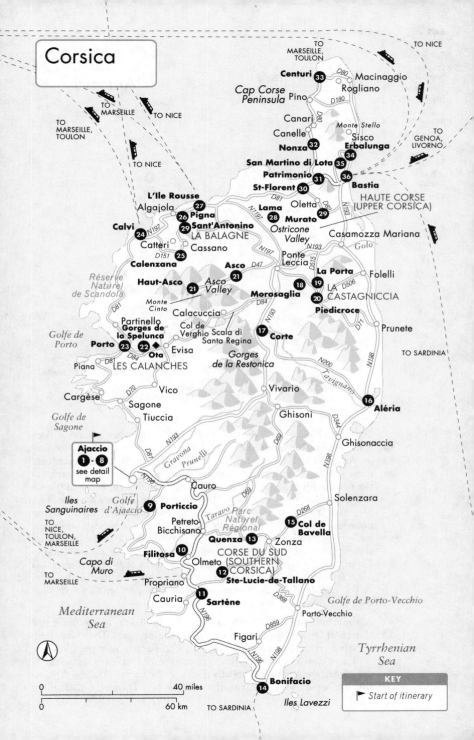

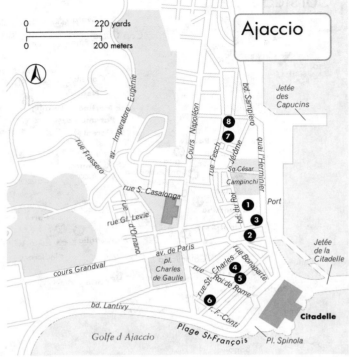

Ajaccio

Jetée
des
Capucins

Port

Jetée
de la
Citadelle

Citadelle

Golfe d Ajaccio

Pl. Spinola

❹ Two short blocks left of the statue of Napoléon on place Maréchal-Foch is the **Maison Bonaparte** (Bonaparte House). Here Napoléon was born on August 15, 1769. Today this large (once middle-class) house contains a museum with portraits of the entire Bonaparte clan. Search out the two family trees woven out of actual human hair. Most of the salons are 20th-century redos and hommages to the emperor's favored Empire neoclassical style. Several are distressingly bare, others flaunt antiques created under King Louis-Phillipe (his sworn enemy), while only one—the Chambre à Alcóve—seems to evince the life of the little giant, since legend has it he spent his nights here when after his conquest of Egypt. Still, fans of the man—and connoisseurs of *le style empire à la ajaccienne*—will find this very worth while ✉ *Rue St-Charles* 📞 *04–95–21–43–89* 🌐 *www.musee-maisonbonaparte.fr* 🎟 *€4* 🕐 *Mon. 2–5, Tues.–Sun. 10–noon and 2–5.*

FodorśChoice
★

❺ At the corner of rue St-Charles and rue Roi-de-Rome, opposite the tiny church of **St-Jean Baptiste**, are the city's oldest houses. They were built shortly after the town was founded in 1492. For a look at the Citadelle, walk east down rue Roi-de-Rome to boulevard Danielle Casanova. At the corner, the **Musée du Capitellu** traces the history of Ajaccio through the career of a single family. ✉ *18 bd. Danielle Casanova*

☎ *04–95–21–50–57* 🖾 *€4* ☉ *Mon.–Sat. 10–noon and 2–6, Sun. 10–noon.*

❻ The 16th-century Baroque **Cathédrale** where Napoléon was baptized is at the end of rue St-Charles. The interior is covered with trompe-l'oeil frescoes, and the high altar, from a church in Lucca, Italy, was donated by Napoléon's sister Eliza after he made her princess of Tuscany. Eugène Delacroix's *Virgin of Sacré Coeur* hangs above the altar. ⊠ *Rue F.-Conti.*

❼ The Renaissance-style **Chapelle Impérial** (Imperial Chapel) was built in 1857 by Napoléon's nephew, Napoléon III, to accommodate the tombs of the Bonaparte family (Napoléon Bonaparte himself is buried in the Hôtel des Invalides in Paris). The Coptic crucifix over the altar was taken from Egypt during the general's 1798 campaign. ⊠ *50 rue Fesch* 🖾 *€1.50* ☉ *Tues.–Sat. 10–12:30 and 3–7.*

★ **❽** Adjacent to the Chapelle Impérial, the **Musée Fesch** houses a fine collection of Italian masters, ranging from Botticelli and Canaletto to De Tura—part of a massive collection of 30,000 paintings bought at bargain prices by Napoléon's uncle, Cardinal Fesch, archbishop of Lyon, following the French Revolution. Thanks to his nephew's military conquests, the cardinal was able to amass (steal, some would say) many celebrated Old Master paintings, the most famous of which are now in the Louvre. ⊠ *50 rue Fesch* ☎ *04–95–21–48–17* ⊕ *www.musee-fesch.com/* 🖾*€5.50* ☉*Apr., June, Sept., and Oct., Wed.–Mon. 9:30–noon and 3–6:30; July and Aug., Tues.–Sat. 9–midnight, Sun. and Mon. 9:30–noon and 3–6:30; Nov.–Mar., Wed.–Mon. 9:30–noon and 2:30–6.*

Where to Stay & Eat

$$–$$$ ✕ **Le Floride.** This port restaurant overlooking the docks serves simple but sound combinations of maritime and upland products. Fresh fish and shellfish are the specialty, with spaghetti *au langouste* (with lobster) one of the stars in chef Nicolas Baubé's firmament of seafood creations. ⊠ *Rue Charles Ornano s/n, Port* ☎ *04–95–22–67–48* 🖃 *AE, DC, MC, V* ☉ *Closed Sun. No lunch Sat.*

$$–$$$ ✕ **A La Funtana.** A fountain greets diners at the door of this noted restaurant, named for a popular Corsican folk song. Fresh flowers and Oriental carpets are the only touches of decoration in the simple white dining room. The house specialty is homemade foie gras; other items worth sampling include *morilles* (morels) in foie gras and homemade sorbets. ⊠ *9 rue Notre-Dame* ☎*04–95–21–78–04* 🖃 *AE, DC, MC, V* ☉ *Closed Sun. No lunch Mon.*

$–$$$ ✕ **20123.** This well-loved Ajaccio favorite is known for its traditional cuisine, fresh fish from the nearby market and, in season, game specials such as *civet de sanglier* (wild boar stew) with *trompettes de la mort* (wild mushrooms) served in a bubbling earthenware casserole. ⊠ *2 rue Roi-de-Rome* ☎ *04–95–21–50–05* 🖃 *MC, V* ☉ *Closed Mon., Tues., and Jan. 15–Feb. 15. No lunch June 15–Sept. 15.*

$$$–$$$$ ✕🖾 **La Dolce Vita.** Spread out over flower-filled terraces at the edge of the Golfe d'Ajaccio, this hotel-restaurant is lavishly Italianate. The spectacular swimming pool overlooks the sea, and the restaurant ranks as one of the island's best for stylish interpretations of traditional Corsican dishes. ⊠ *Rte. des Iles Sanguinaires, 8 km (5 mi) from center of town, 20000* ☎ *04–95–52–42–42* ☎ *04–95–52–07–15* ☞ *32 rooms* ⚐ *Restaurant, minibars, cable TV, pool, beach, bar, free parking, some pets allowed (fee)* ☰ *AE, DC, MC, V* ☉ *Closed Nov. 1–Mar. 31* ⏐○⏐ *EP, MAP.*

★ **$$** ▦ **Hôtel San Carlu.** On the edge of the *Vieille Ville* (Old Town), this friendly hotel overlooking the ramparts and the sea makes an ideal base for exploring Ajaccio. Rooms are clean and comfortable; those on the Golfe d'Ajaccio side (east) on the third floor get an abundance of morning sunshine streaming across the beds and into the bathtubs, not a bad way to greet a new day on the Isle de la Beauté. ⊠ *8 bd. Danielle Casanova, 20000* ☎ *04–95–21–13–84* ☎ *04–95–21–09–99* ☞ *40 rooms* ⚐ *Minibars; no a/c* ☰ *AE, DC, MC, V* ☉ *Closed Dec. 20–Feb. 6* ⏐○⏐ *EP.*

Nightlife & the Arts

Many of Ajaccio's top nightspots are 4 km (2½ mi) north of town, in the Santa-Lina District along route des Iles Sanguinaires. For in-town action, **Le Pigalle** (⊠ Pl. Charles de Gaulle) is a spot to check. **L'Entreacte** (⊠ Bd. Lantivy, next to casino) is a popular stop on the night-owl circuit. A continuing success in Ajaccio's night scene is **Le Privilège** (⊠ Rue Macchini, pl. Charles-de-Gaulle). **Le Cohiba** (⊠ Bd. Lantivy, 1 Résidence Diamant) is a vibrant music bar. **La Place** (⊠ Bd. Lantivy) is another well-known boîte and piano bar. On the road to the airport, **Le Duplex** (⊠ Av. Campo dell'Oro) is a brash young addition to the disco scene in the Corsican capital.

The **Fête de la Miséricorde** (Feast of Our Lady of Mercy), on March 18, spotlights the Procession de la Madunnuccia (Procession of the Madonna), Ajaccio's patron saint. In May all Ajaccio celebrates during its festive ★ **Carnival.** A major festival, the **Fêtes Napoléoniennes,** is held on August 15, Napoléon's birthday.

Sports & the Outdoors

NAVE VA (⊠ 2 rue J. B. Marcaggi ☎ 04–95–21–83–98) operates boating excursions to the Îles Sanguinaires, Reserve Naturelle de Scandola, Girolata, Calanches de Piana, and the chalk cliffs of Bonifacio. **BMS** (⊠ Quai de la Citadelle ☎ 04–95–21–33–75) rents bicycles year-round. **Locacorse** (⊠ 10 av. Bévérini-Vico ☎ 04–95–20–71–20) has bike rentals April–September. **Les Dauphins** (⊠ Rte. des Sanguinaires, Plage de Barbicaja ☎ 04–95–52–07–78) has water-sports gear among other offerings. For information about sailing, contact the **Ligue Corse de Voile** (⊠ Port de la Citadelle ☎ 04–95–21–07–79). A popular spot to rent a sailboat is the **Tahiti Nautic Club d'Ajaccio** (⊠ Plage du Ricanto ☎ 04–95–20–05–95).

Shopping

Much more than just a bookstore specializing in books about Corsica, **Librairie la Marge** (⊠ 7 rue Emmanuelle-Arène) is a hub of Corsican culture, where you can also buy music and attend poetry readings. **Paese Nostru** (⊠ Passage Guinguetta) sells Corsican crafts of all kinds. **U Tilaghju** (⊠ Rue Forcioli Conti), one of several artisanal shops near the cathedral, has an impressive collection of ceramics.

Porticcio

❾ *17 km (11 mi) south of Ajaccio on N196.*

Across the Prunelli River south of Ajaccio, Porticcio is the capital's upscale suburb and luxurious beach resort town. It's primarily notable for its seawater cures at the **Institut de Thalassothérapie** (Institute of Thalassotherapy), on the Punta di Porticcio, and the *grand luxe* Le Maquis hotel.

Where to Stay & Eat

$$$$ ✗▦ **Le Maquis.** Ranking as one of the island's (and even France's) finest
Fodor'sChoice *hôtels de charme,* this graceful ivy-covered Genoese-style retreat ram-
★ bles down through terraced gardens to a quiet private beach overlooking the Golfe d'Ajaccio. The best rooms have ample views of the sea while some overlook the hills as well. At the candlelight restaurant L'Arbousier, its ancient beams recycled from what was once the Ajaccio prison, a blend of traditional and nouvelle cuisine is served: fish tartare, scrambled eggs with truffles, and fresh tagliatelle. Supreme comfort, taste, service, and discretion are guaranteed at this exquisite hideaway 19 km (11 mi) south of Ajaccio. ⊠ *D55, 20166 Porticcio* ☎ *04-95-25-05-55* 🖷 *04-95-25-11-70* ⊕ *www.lemaquis.com* 🛏 *19 rooms, 6 apartments* ⚹ *Restaurant, minibars, cable TV, tennis court, pool, beach, bar, meeting rooms, some pets allowed (fee)* ☰ *AE, DC, MC, V* ⦿ *EP, MAP.*

Filitosa

★ **❿** *71 km (43 mi) southeast of Ajaccio off N196.*

Filitosa is the site of Corsica's largest grouping of megalithic menhir statues. Bizarre, life-size stone figures of ancient warriors rise up mysteriously from the undulating terrain, many with human faces whose features have been flattened over time by erosion. A small museum on the site houses archaeological finds, including the menhir known as *Scalsa Murta,* whose delicately carved spine and rib cage are surprisingly contemporary for a work dating from some 5,000 years ago. The guidebook in English (€5) by experts Cesari and Acquaviva is supplemented by information in English at each site. ⊠ *Contact Centre Préhistorique Filitosa* ☎ *04-95-74-00-91 for information* 🖾 *Guided tours in English €5* ⊙ *June–Aug., daily 8–7.*

Sartène

⓫ *27 km (16 mi) southeast of Filitosa on N196.*

Described as the "most Corsican of all Corsican towns" by French novelist Prosper Mérimée, Sartène, first founded in the 16th century, has survived pirate raids and bloody feuding among the town's families. The word "vendetta" is believed to have originated here as the result of a 19th-century family feud so serious that French troops were brought in to serve as a peacekeeping buffer force. Centuries of fighting have left the town with a somewhat eerie and menacing atmosphere. Perhaps adding to this is the annual Good Friday *catenacciu* (enchaining) procession in which an anonymous penitent, dragging ankle chains, lugs a heavy cross through the village streets.

Vieux Sartène (Old Sartène), surrounded by ancient ramparts, begins at place de la Libération, the main square. To one side is the **Hôtel de Ville** (town hall), in the former Genoese governor's palace. Slip into the Middle Ages through the tunnel under the Town Hall to place du Maggiu and the ancient **Santa Anna** quarter, a warren of narrow, cobbled streets lined with granite houses. Scarcely 100 yards from the Hôtel de Ville, down a steep and winding street, is a 12th-century *tour de guet* (watchtower).

Sartène is a key link to Corsica's prehistory, thanks to its proximity to Pianu de Levie's dolmens and megalithic statues. Some of the island's best prehistoric relics are at the **Musée Départemental de Préhistoire Corse** (Regional Museum of Corsican Prehistory), in the town's former prison. ⊠ *Rue Croce* ☎ *04–95–77–01–09* ⬚ *€4* ⊘ *Mon.–Sat. 10–noon and 2–6.*

Where to Eat

$$ ✕ **Auberge de Santa Barbara.** This excellent restaurant is just 1 km (½ mi) north of Sartène. Known as one of the top specialists in authentic Corsican cuisine, chef Giselle Lovighi also serves innovative seafood specialties such as shrimp soufflé and crayfish salad. ⊠ *Rte. de Propriano, Alzone, Sartène* ☎ *04–95–77–09–06* ⊟ *MC, V* ⊘ *Closed Oct. 15–Mar. 15. No lunch Mon.*

Ste-Lucie-de-Tallano

⑫ *15 km (9 mi) northeast of Sartène, 12 km (7 mi) southeast of Levie*
Fodor'sChoice *on D268.*
★

The pretty little village of Ste-Lucie-de-Tallano is in the heart of Mérimée country, the setting for *Colomba,* the tale of a beautiful young Corsican woman caught in an Andromaque-like web of love, honor, vendetta, and death. Driving up the Rizzanese Valley, the Spin' a Cavallu (Horse's Back) Bridge, one of the oldest and loveliest Genoese bridges on the island, is the first important sight. The St-François convent and the church of Ste-Lucie are the main religious buildings in town.

Where to Eat

$$ ✕ **Vecchiu Mulinu.** This restored mill serves simple but delicious *cuisine du terroir* (regional country cooking). The local Fiumicicoli red is the perfect match. ⊠ *Bains de Caldanes* ☎ *04–95–77–00–54* ⬚ *Reservations essential* ⊟ *MC, V* ⊘ *Closed Mon. in Oct.–Easter.*

Quenza

⑬ *8 km (5 mi) west of Zonza on D420.*

Quenza is known for its 10th-century chapel of **Santa Maria.** It's also the headquarters of **I Muntagnoli Corsi** (☎ *04–95–78–64–05*), which organizes guided hikes into the Coscione Forest.

Where to Stay & Eat

★ $$–$$$ ✕⬚ **Auberge Sole e Monti.** One of southern Corsica's best options for authentic Corsican cooking and a standout as a hotel as well, this place is definitely worth a detour. Rooms are modern and well kept, and the staff is friendly. Try the local version of *soupe corse* (Corsican soup) and, in summer, trout with wild mint and brocciu. Be sure to reserve in advance. ✉ *1 km (½ mi) east of town on the Zonza road, 20122, Quenza* ☏ *04–95–78–62–53* 🖳 *04–95–78–63–88* 🛏 *20 rooms* 🍴 *Restaurant, bar, some pets allowed (fee); no a/c* ▤ *AE, DC, MC, V* ◐ *Closed Dec.–Mar.* ⅋ *EP, MAP.*

Bonifacio

❶❹ *52 km (31 mi) southeast of Sartène via N196.*

Fodor'sChoice
★

The ancient fortress town of Bonifacio occupies a spectacular clifftop aerie above a harbor carved from limestone cliffs. It's just 13 km (8 mi) from Sardinia, and the local speech is heavily influenced by the accent and idiom of that nearby Italian island. Established in the 12th century as Genoa's first Corsican stronghold, Bonifacio remained Genoese through centuries of battles and sieges. As you wander the narrow streets of the **Haute Ville** (Upper Village), inside the walls of the citadel, think of Homer's *Odyssey.* It's here, in the harbor, that scholars place the catastrophic encounter (Chapter X) between Ulysses's fleet and the Laestrygonians, who hurled lethal boulders down from the cliffs.

From place d'Armes at the city gate, enter the **Bastion de l'Étendard** (Bastion of the Standard); you can still see the system of weights and levers used to pull up the drawbridge. The former garrison now houses life-size dioramas of Bonifacio's history. 🎫 €2 ◐ *Mid-June–mid-Sept., daily 9–7.*

In the center of the maze of cobbled streets that makes up the citadel is the 12th-century church of **Ste-Marie-Majeure,** with buttresses attaching it to surrounding houses. Inside the church, note the Renaissance baptismal font, carved in bas-relief, and the 3rd-century white-marble Roman sarcophagus. Walk around the back to see the loggia, which is built above a huge cistern that stored water for use in times of siege, as did the circular stone silos seen throughout the town.

★ From Bonifacio you can take a boat trip to the **Dragon Grottoes** (✉ Boats leave from outside Hôtel La Caravelle ☏ 04–95–75–05–93 for information) and **Venus's Bath** (the trip takes one hour on boats that set out every 15 minutes during July and August) or the **Lavezzi Islands.**

Where to Stay & Eat

$$$ ✕ **La Rascasse.** In prime position to haul the freshest seafood from the boat to your table, this portside spot is an old favorite in Bonifacio. Try the fish for which the restaurant is named, the prehistorically spiny (and light) *rascasse* (red scorpion fish). ✉ *Quai Comparetti* ☏ *04–95–73–01–26* ▤ *AE, DC, MC, V* ◐ *Closed Nov.–Easter.*

★ **$$–$$$** ✕ **Le Voilier.** This popular year-round restaurant in the port serves carefully selected and prepared fish and seafood, along with fine Corsican sausage and traditional cuisine from *soupe corse* to *fiadone* (cheesecake). ✉ *Quai Comparetti* ☏ *04–95–73–07–06* ▤ *AE, DC, MC, V* ◐ *Closed Mon. No dinner Sun.*

$$ ✕ **Les 4 Vents.** This friendly restaurant near the Sardinia boat terminal is popular with the yachting crowd and family groups. In winter the kitchen serves up such Alsatian specialties as sauerkraut and sausages. In summer the focus is on barbecued fish and meats, as well as typical Corsican dishes. ⊠ *29 quai Bando di Ferro* ☎ *04–95–73–07–50* ⊟ *MC, V* ⊗ *Closed mid- to late Nov. and Tues. in Nov.–June.*

$$$$ ⌑ **Hôtel le Genovese.** This small, intimate hotel is built into the ramparts of the upper town's citadel. Peach fabric wallcoverings set the rooms aglow. Upstairs rooms have superb views over the cliffs and out to Sardinia. ⊠ *Quartier de Citadelle, Haute Ville, 20169* ☎ *04–95–73–12–34* ⌂ *04–95–73–09–03* ⊕ *www.woda.fr-aa-genovese* ⤳ *15 rooms* ⚭ *Minibars, cable TV, pool, bar* ⊟ *AE, DC, MC, V* ▯⊙▯ *EP, MAP.*

Nightlife & the Arts

Party early at the *avant-boîte* ("before club," until 2) at **B–52** (⊠ Quai Comparetti ☎ 04–95–73–57–52), in the port. Raging until sunrise is the happening **Lollapalooza** (⊠ Quai Comparetti ☎ 04–95–73–04–54), open around the clock in summer.

Sports & the Outdoors

The area around Bonifacio is ideal for water sports. Contact **Club Atoll** (⊠ Rte. de Porto-Vecchio ☎ 04–95–73–02–83). The best golf course on Corsica (and one of the best in the Mediterranean), a 20,106-foot, par-72 gem designed by Robert Trent Jones, is at **Sperone** (⊠ Domaine de Sperone ☎ 04–95–73–17–13), just east of Bonifacio.

Col de Bavella

⑮ *50 km (31 mi) northeast of Porto-Vecchio on D368 and D268.*

Fodor'sChoice
★

The granite peaks known as the **Aiguilles de Bavella** (Needles of Bavella) tower some 6,562 feet overhead as you reach the Col de Bavella (Bavella Pass). Hiking trails are well marked. The narrow but mostly well-paved roadway over the pass will take you back to the coast along the Solenzara River.

Where to Stay & Eat

¢ ✕⌑ **Auberge du Col.** Near the top of the spectacular drive from Porto-Vecchio to Col de Bavella, this little *gîte d'étape* (hikers' inn) offers Corsican mountain fare and a night in simple but adequate accommodations under immense laricio pines. Each room has six beds. ⊠ *Col de Bavella* ☎ *04–95–72–09–87* ⌂ *04–95–72–16–48* ⤳ *4 rooms* ⊟ *MC, V* ⊗ *Closed Nov.–Mar.* ▯⊙▯ *EP.*

Aléria

⑯ *32 km (20 mi) north of Solenzara on N198, 48 km (29 mi) southeast of Corte.*

Just before the village of Aléria are the ruins of the Roman city of the same name. On a pine-studded plateau is the carefully restored 16th-century **Fort de Matra,** which houses the **Musée Jérôme Carcopino.** On display are pottery and tools found on the site, as well as Etruscan, Greek, and Roman artifacts dating from as far back as 500 BC. ⌑ €4 ⊗ *Apr.–Oct., daily 8–noon and 2–7; Nov.–Mar., Mon.–Sat. 8–noon and 2–5.*

HAUTE CORSE

Haute Corse (Upper Corsica) is the northeastern end of the island and is, indeed, higher in mean altitude than Corse du Sud, topped by the 8,876-foot Monte Cinto. Most Corsica enthusiasts agree that Haute Corse is the island's finest trove of highland forests, remote villages, hidden cultural gems, vineyards, beaches, alpine lakes and streams. In the center of Haute Corse is the city of Corte, Corsica's historic heart. To the east is the forested region of La Castagniccia, named for its *châtaigniers* (chestnut trees), one of Corsica's treasures, especially in the fall, when fallen leaves and chestnuts blanket the ground. The forest's tiny roadways go through villages with stunning Baroque churches and houses still roofed in traditional blue-gray slate. To the northwest is Calvi, Corsica's Riviera-like beach resort, while farther north the island's finger pointing to the continent is Cap Corse, with the port city of Bastia, Corsica's largest and most Italianate city, at its base.

Corte

⑰
Fodor'sChoice
★

48 km (30 mi) northwest of Aléria on N200, 83 km (51 mi) northeast of Ajaccio, 70 km (43 mi) southwest of Bastia.

Set amid spectacular cliffs and gorges at the confluence of the Tavignano, Restonica, and Orta rivers, Corte is the spiritual heart and soul of Corsica. Capital of Pasquale Paoli's government from 1755 to 1769, it was also where Paoli established the Corsican University in 1765. Closed by the victorious French in 1769, the university, always a symbol of Corsican identity, was reopened in 1981. To reach the upper town and the 15th-century château overlooking the rivers, walk up the cobblestone ramp from place Pasquale-Paoli. Stop in lovely **place Gaffori** at one of the cafés or restaurants. Note the bullet-pocked house where the Corsican hero Gian Pietro Gaffori and his wife, Faustina, held off the Genoese in 1750.

★ The **Citadelle,** a Vauban-style fortress (1769–78), is built around the original 15th-century fortification at the highest point of the cliff, with the river below. It contains the **Musée de la Corse** (Corsica Museum), dedicated to the island's history and ethnography. ☎ 04–95–45–25–45 ☑ €5.50 ☉ *Nov.–Apr., Tues.–Sat. 10–5; May–Oct., daily 10–8.*

The **Palais National** (National Palace), just outside the citadel and above place Gaffori, is the ancient residence of Genoa's representatives in Corsica and was the seat of the Corsican parliament from 1755 to 1769. The building is now part of the Corsican University. ☒ *Pl. du Poilu* ☉ *Weekdays 2–6.*

★ For an unforgettable view of the river junction and the Genoese bridge below and the citadel's tiny watchtower above, walk left along the citadel wall to the **Belvédère.**

Leave the Haute Ville and go through the tiny alleys of the **Quartier de Chiostra.** Follow the cobblestone path (as you look down) to the right from the Belvédère, bearing right and across at the **Chapelle St-Théophile.**

Coming into the tiny square on your left, don't miss the open stone staircase on the opposite wall, or the prehistoric fertility goddess carved into the wall to the left. Farther downhill you will rejoin the ramp leading into place Pasquale-Paoli.

The **Gorges de la Restonica** (Restonica Gorges) make a spectacular day hike. At the top of the Restonica Valley, leave your car in the parking area at the end of the road. A two-hour climb will take you to **Lac de Mélo**, a trout-filled mountain lake 6,528 feet above sea level. Another hour up is the usually snow-bordered **Lac de Capitello**. Information on trails is available from the tourist office or the Parc Naturel Régional. Light meals are served in the stone shepherds' huts at the **Bergeries de Grotelle**.

Where to Stay & Eat

$$–$$$ 🏨 **Hôtel Dominique Colonna.** The modern hotel across from the **Auberge de la Restonica** has sliding doors leading directly out to breakfast nooks by the stream. Owner Dominique "Dumé" Colonna, one of France's (and certainly Corsica's) greatest soccer stars, drops by from time to time. The Auberge serves fine Corsican fare and offers seven more traditional rooms. ⊠ *Vallée de la Restonica, 20250* ☎*04–95–45–25–65* 🖷*04–95–61–03–91* ⇨ *28 rooms* ৬ *Restaurant, minibars, pool, some pets allowed (fee); no a/c* ☰ *AE, DC, MC, V* ☉ *Closed Nov. 5–Mar. 14* ¶◯¶ *EP, MAP.*

Morosaglia

⑱ *14 km (9 mi) southeast of Ponte Leccia, 9 km (5 mi) east of La Porta.*

The town of Morosaglia is the birthplace of Pasquale Paoli, Corsica's most celebrated national hero and author of the first republican constitution, drafted for Corsica in 1755 (with reverberations extending to the founding fathers of the United States). Letters, portraits, and memorabilia from Paoli's life are on display at the **Maison de Pasquale Paoli** (Pasquale Paoli House). ☎ *04–95–61–04–97* 🖃 *€4* ☉ *Spring–fall, daily 9–noon and 2:30–7:30; winter, daily 1–5.*

La Porta

⑲ *9 km (5 mi) west of Morosaglia, 14½ km (9 mi) north of Piedicroce on D515.*

As the name of the village suggests, La Porta (the Door) is an entranceway to La Castagniccia. The **St-Jean-Baptiste** church here is widely accepted as the crowning glory of Corsican Baroque art. The bright ocher facade and the five-story bell tower are feasts for the eyes, as are the paintings inside. Look for the *Martyrdom of St. Eulalie of Barcelona* (1848), by Louis Destouches (1819–81), just inside on the left.

Where to Eat

★ $$ ✕ **L'Ampugnani–Chez Elisabeth.** This excellent restaurant is known throughout Corsica as a treasury of fine local cooking. Specializing in *cuisine du terroir* (local country cooking), it offers such dishes as a superb leg of lamb with herbs and *figatellu* (liver sausage). ⊠ *La Porta* ☎ *04–95–39–22–00* ৬ *Reservations essential* ☰ *MC, V* ☉ *Closed Mon. from Sept. 15 to Easter and closed altogether Jan.–Feb.*

Piedicroce

★ ⑳ *14 km (9 mi) south of La Porta on D515, 66 km (40 mi) south of Bastia.*

Piedicroce's panoramic view of La Castagniccia is superb. Be sure to stop in to visit the vividly painted Baroque church of **St-Pierre-et-St-Paul,** one of the finest of its type in the area. The nearby mineral springs of **Orezza** are reputed to have miraculous powers. The **Fium Alto,** running along the road that goes northeast to Folelli, is one of Corsica's best trout streams. To exit La Castagniccia, follow signs for **Folelli** (37 km [22 mi] north) or **Bastia** (66 km [40 mi] north).

Where to Stay & Eat

★ **$$** ✕ Le Refuge. A handy midway point in the labyrinthine La Castagniccia, this hotel-restaurant is a good place for a delicious meal based on the Rafalli family's home-processed charcuterie and a night's sleep in the small but cozy quarters overlooking the Castagniccia and the valley of the Fium Alto. ✉ *20229 Piedicroce* ☎ *04–95–35–82–65* 🖷 *04–95–35–84–42* 🛏 *20 rooms* ⌂ *Restaurant, bar; no a/c, no room TVs* ▤ *MC, V* ☉ *Closed Nov.* ⦿ *EP, MAP.*

Asco & Haut-Asco

㉑ *22 km (13 mi) west of Ponte Leccia: 2 km (1 mi) north of Ponte Leccia, D147 turns off N197 toward the village of Asco, 16 km (10 mi) away.*

Studded with beehives, the Asco Valley is a honey and cheese haven. The Genoese bridge below Asco is a perfect spot for a swim in the river. Above Asco the granite gorge becomes a cool pine forest for hiking. Follow the road for another 12 km (7 mi) past the village, ending at the top against a wall of mountains. The Asco Valley runs west to an awe-inspiring barrier of mountains crowned by **Monte Cinto,** the highest point in Corsica. As you travel up the valley, the maquis-covered slopes give way to a sheer granite gorge hung with sweet-smelling juniper. Thirteen km (8 mi) above is **Haut Asco,** starting point for the eight- to nine-hour (round-trip) walk up Monte Cinto. From the top, on a clear day, you can see the entire island and even the Apennines on the Italian mainland. Clouds and mist gather after about 10 AM, however, particularly in summer. For this reason a 4 AM start is recommended. Questions can be answered at Le Chalet.

Where to Stay & Eat

$ ✕ Le Chalet. This tidy hideaway at the very top of the island has a simple, no-frills restaurant serving Corsican cuisine. Walls are covered with photographs of famous mountaineers. Along with the 22 private rooms there are also a hikers' dormitory, a bar, and a store selling supplies to trekkers, who use the chalet as a way station from the GR 20. ✉ *20276 Haut-Asco* ☎🖷 *04–95–47–81–08* 🛏 *22 rooms, plus dormitory without bath* ⌂ *Restaurant, bar, some pets allowed (fee); no a/c, no room TVs* ▤ *MC, V* ☉ *Closed early Nov.–early May* ⦿ *EP.*

Sports & the Outdoors

From at least December to April, Corsica's upper reaches are snowed in, creating options for both alpine and cross-country skiing; consult the **Club Alpin Français** (☎ 04–95–22–73–81) in Ajaccio. For information about hiking up Monte Cinto, in Bastia contact the **Office National des Forêts** (☎ 04–95–32–81–90).

La Scala di Santa Regina

Fodor's Choice
★

9 km (5 mi) south of Ponte Leccia, D84 leaves N193, starts up the Golo River, and turns into La Scala di Santa Regina.

This road, known as La Scala di Santa Regina (Stairway of the Holy Queen), is one of Corsica's most spectacular, and one of the most difficult to navigate, especially in winter. The route follows the twisty path of the Golo River, which has carved its way through layers of red granite, forming dramatic gorges and waterfalls. Be prepared to stop for herds of animals crossing the road. Follow the road to the **Col de Verghio** (Verghio Pass) for superb views of Tafunatu, the legendary perforated mountain, and Monte Cinto. On the way up you'll pass through the **Valdo Niello Forest**, Corsica's most important woodlands, filled with pines and beeches. The col is considered the border between Haute Corse and Corse du Sud. As you descend from the Verghio Pass through the **Forêt d'Aitone** (Aitone Forest), note how well manicured it is—the pigs, goats, and sheep running rampant through the tall Laricio pines keep it this way. As you pass the village of Evisa, with its orange roofs, look across the impressive **Gorges de Spelunca** (Spelunca Gorge) to see the hill village of Ota. A small road on the right will take you across the gorge, where there's an ancient Genoese-built bridge.

Ota

㉒ *16 km (10 mi) northwest of Evisa on La Scala di Santa Regina.*

The tiny village of Ota, overlooking the **Gorges de Spelunca,** has traditional stone houses that seem to be suspended on the mountainside, an amazing view of the surrounding mountains, and a number of trailheads. It's an excellent base for hiking in the area.

Where to Stay & Eat

¢   ✕🔲 **Chez Félix.** This homey place serves as dining room, taxi stand, and town hall. Cheerful owner Marinette Ceccaldi cooks up heaping portions of Corsican specialties ranging from wild boar to chestnut-flour beignets. Suites are decorated with curios and antiques, each with a balcony overlooking the gorge. Rooms are comfortable and rustic; some have private bathrooms, others share. The hotel has a van that will transport you out to hiking routes. ⊠ *Pl. de la Fontaine, 20150* 🖀🖀 *04–95–26–12–92* ⋈ *4 2-bedroom apartments, 36 beds in 4- and 6-bed rooms with shared bath* ♤ *Restaurant, bar, some pets allowed (fee); no a/c, no room TVs* ▤ *AE, DC, MC, V* ◯ *EP.*

Porto–Les Calanches

㉓ *5 km (3 mi) west of Ota, 30 km (19 mi) south of Calvi.*

The flashy resort town of Porto doesn't have much character, but its setting on the crystalline **Golfe de Porto** (Gulf of Porto), surrounded by massive pink-granite mountains, is superb. Activity focuses on the small port, where there is a boardwalk with restaurants and hotels. A short hike from the boardwalk will bring you to a 16th-century Genoese tower that overlooks the bay. Boat excursions leave daily for the **Réserve Naturel de Scandola.** Detour south of Porto on D81 to get to **Les Calanches,** jagged outcroppings of red rock considered among the most extraordinary natural sites in France. Look for arches and stelae, standing rock formations shaped like animals and phantasmagoric human faces.

Calvi

24 *92 km (58 mi) north of Piana, 159 km (100 mi) north of Ajaccio.*

Calvi, Corsica's slice of the Riviera, has been described by author Dorothy Carrington as "an oasis of pleasure on an otherwise austere island." Calvi grew rich by supplying products to Genoa; its citizens remained loyal supporters of Genoa long after the rest of the island declared independence. Calvi also claims to be the birthplace of Christopher Columbus. During the 18th century the town endured assaults from Corsican nationalists, including celebrated patriot Pasquale Paoli. Today Calvi sees a summertime invasion of tourists, drawn to the 6-km (4-mi) stretch of sandy white beach, the citadel, and the buzzing nightlife.

The Genoese **Citadelle,** perched on a rocky promontory at the tip of the bay, competes with the beach as a major attraction. An inscription above the drawbridge—CIVITAS CALVI SEMPER FIDELIS (The citizens of Calvi always faithful)—reflects the town's unswerving allegiance to Genoa. At the welcome center, just inside the gates, you can see a video on the city's history and arrange to take a guided tour given in English (three times a day) or a self-guided walking tour. ⊠ *Up the hill off av. de l'Uruguay* ☎ *04–95–65–36–74* ⊠ *Guided tour and video show* €9 ☉ *Tours Easter–early Oct., daily at 10, 4:30, and 6:30.*

Stop in at the 13th-century church of **St-Jean-Baptiste** (⊠ Pl. d'Armes); it contains an interesting Renaissance baptismal font. Look up to see the rows of pews screened by grillwork: the chaste young women of Calvi's upper classes sat here.

Where to Stay & Eat

★ $$$–$$$$ ✕ **Chez Tao.** At Chez Tao, a mandatory stop on almost everyone's itinerary, you can rub elbows with the town's glitterati on the ocher-color 16th-century terraces that look out over the bay. Seafood is what everyone eats, but food plays second fiddle to the atmosphere, which includes Corsican folk singing and a tinkling piano until the wee hours. ⊠ *Pl. de la Citadelle* ☎ *04–95–65–00–73* ⊟ *AE, DC, MC, V* ☉ *Closed mid-Sept.–Easter.*

$$$ ✕ **Emile's.** With panoramic views of the port, this is a lucky place to find a table in summer. Classic French cuisine with *terroir* (local Corsican) touches is available, but fish and seafood hold center stage. ⊠ *Quai Landry* ☎ *04–95–65–09–60* ⊟ *AE, DC, MC, V* ☉ *Closed Dec. 1–Jan. 15, Mon. in winter, and Tues. year-round.*

★ $$$–$$$$ ✕▦ **Le Signoria.** This 17th-century country manor (and annex) has homey bedrooms and large bathrooms. From the pool and patio there

The Outdoors

Two of the best **beaches** in the area are the **Plage d'Ostriconi**, at the mouth of the Ostriconi River (20 km [13 mi] north of town), and the wilder and much-frequented-by-nudists **Plage Saleccia**, used in the 1960s filming of *The Longest Day*.

Lama

28   *15 km (9 mi) southeast of L'Ile Rousse, 57 km (24 mi) north of Corte.*

The charmingly restored medieval village of Lama is only 10 minutes up the Ostriconi Valley. Everyone from the mayor to local children accommodates visitors; people say hello in the streets and seem to know where you are staying. Once a prosperous olive-growing town, the village was nearly deserted after a 1971 fire destroyed 35,000 olive trees in a single afternoon.

Where to Stay & Eat

$$ ✕⌨ **Auberge de Lama.** Lodgings are scattered throughout the village in small stone cottages that sleep from two to eight. The lively restaurant, open year-round, is the town's informal nerve center. Excellent Corsican specialties are served, such as a mint-and-brocciu omelet or roast kid. ✉ *20218 Lama* ☎ *04–95–48–22–99* 📠 *04–95–48–23–77* ⊕ *www. corse-escapades.com* ↯ *50 cottages* ⟟ *EP, MAP.*

The Outdoors

Riding along the old mule trails on horseback is an excellent way to see the countryside; for this and nearly any other outdoor activity you can imagine, from hang-gliding to canyoning contact Pierre-Jean Costa at **Corse Escapades** (✉ Village de Lama, 20218 Lama ☎ 04–95–48–22–99 📠 04–95–48–23–77 ⊕ www.corse-escapades.com).

Murato

29   *15 km (9 mi) west of Lama, 12 km (7 mi) south of Bastia: take N193 to D82 to D305 at Rutalli.*

The village of Murato has two excellent restaurants and a remarkable 12th-century Pisan church, one of Corsica's finest architectural treasures. The polychrome, green-marble, and white-limestone **Église Mosaïque de San Michele de Murato** (Mosaic Church of San Michele of Murato) suggests many interpretations. Look for the relief depicting Eve tempted by a serpent, covering her nakedness with an oversized hand. The site overlooks the Golfe de St-Florent. When the *libecciu* (a powerful and persistent west wind) is blowing full force, the Continent is often visible.

Where to Eat

★ **$$–$$$**   ✕ **Le Ferme Campo di Monte.** The Julliard sisters prepare what is widely regarded as Corsica's most authentic cuisine at this lovely 350-year-old stone farmhouse. Especially good are the *storzapreti* (brocciu croquettes). ✉ *D305 Rutali-Murato* ☎ *04–95–37–64–39* ✍ *Reservations essential* 🖃 *AE, DC, MC, V* ☼ *No lunch Mon.–Sat. Closed Mon.–Wed in Sept.–June.*

★ **$$–$$$** ✕ **U Fragnu.** While this noted spot may be 33 km (20 mi) southwest of Murato, the detour is well worth it. Turn off the N 198 road 22 km (13 mi) south of Bastia and take the drive up to Vescovato and Venzolasca to be rewarded with one of Corsica's finest culinary experiences at U Fragnu. After you've exited La Castagniccia near La Porta, head north to this restaurant for some exquisite local country cooking. Madame Garelli is a specialist in *soupe de berger* (shepherd's soup)—made from a restored original recipe recovered after painstaking research. ⊠ *Rte. de Vescovato, Venzolasca, 7 km (4 mi) north of Folelli on N198, then 2 km (1 mi) up D37* ☎ *04–95–36–62–33* ♠ *Reservations essential* ▤ *No credit cards* ⊘ *No lunch Thurs.–Sat. in Nov.–Mar.*

St-Florent

③⓪ *28 km (17 mi) northeast of the exit for Lama on D81, 46 km (28 mi) northeast of L'Ile Rousse.*

St-Florent is a postcard-perfect village nestled into the crook of the Golfe de St-Florent between the rich Nebbio Valley and the desert of Agriates. The town has a crumbling citadel and a yacht basin ringed by shops and restaurants. Look for the exceptional Romanesque **Santa Maria Assunta** (⊠ Rue Agostino Giustiniani), just outside the village. Standing in isolated splendor among the vineyards, this 12th-century white-limestone church is one of only three Pisan churches remaining on the island. The facade and interior columns are sculpted with human faces, snakes, snails, and mythical animals.

Patrimonio

③① *5 km (3 mi) northeast of St-Florent, 18 km (11 mi) west of Bastia.*

Patrimonio lies at the base of the Cap Corse Peninsula, among vineyards that produce most of Corsica's best wines. The most prestigious of the Patrimonio vineyards is the **Orenga de Gaffory** (☎ 04–95–30–11–38) operation, a hard-to-beat combination of wine brewery and art gallery. Tours of the vineyards and of the Orenga de Gaffory gallery can be arranged; open weekdays 9–noon and 3–6. **Antoine Arena** (☎ 04–95–37–08–27) is one of the leading young vintners. **Dominique Gentile** (☎ 04–95–37–01–54) is a leading Patrimonio wine maker who combines old techniques and modern technology.

Nightlife & the Arts

The **Nuits de la Guitare** music festival during the third week of July is one of Corsica's top musical events, featuring blues, jazz, and flamenco guitarists from all over the world.

The Outdoors

One of the most beautiful mountain **hiking** routes in Corsica follows the crest of Cap Corse over the 4,287-foot Monte Stello, from which you can see the hills of Tuscany and Provence. Contact the Parc Naturel Régional de la Corse for details.

Nonza

32 *14 km (9 mi) north of Patrimonio, 8 km (5 mi) south of Canelle.*

On your way around Cap Corse, be sure to stop in Nonza. This vertiginous crag seems impossibly high over its famous black beach, the legacy of a former asbestos mine down the coast at Canari. The beach is accessible only by trudging down the 600 steps from Nonza, and no doubt this is the reason why it's usually deserted. The chapel is dedicated to the martyred St. Julie, whose severed breasts, it's said, became the double fountain known as the *Fontaine aux Mamelles* (Fountain of Mammaries) on the way down to the beach. The spectacular gravity-defying tower was constructed by Pasquale Paoli in 1760. Its squared corners made it easier to defend, as famed Captain Casella proved in 1768 when he stood off 1,200 French troops.

Where to Stay & Eat

$–$$ ✕🖼 **Auberge Patrizi.** On a shady terrace in the center of town, this place serves excellent Corsican cuisine in a lively setting. It also has rooms—small and a little too close to the road—with spectacular views. ⊠ *Pl. du Village, 20217* ☎ *04-95-37-82-16* 🖶 *04-95-37-86-40* 🛏 *13 rooms* ☼ *Restaurant, bar, pets (fee); no a/c* ⊟ *AE, MC, V* ⊙ *Closed Nov.–Mar.* ⃝ *EP.*

Centuri

33 *55 km (34 mi) north of Patrimonio, 41 km (25 mi) north of Nonza.*

Centuri (pronounced *chen*-toori), Cap Corse's top fishing port, is a good place for lunch on your way around the cape. The late afternoon arrival and unloading of the fishing boats is also a major event.

Where to Stay & Eat

★ **$$–$$$** ✕🖼 **Le Vieux Moulin.** Old World charm and authentic Corsican flavor characterize this place. The main house was built in 1870 as a private residence; the eight-room annex is less antique but no less inviting, with bougainvillea cascading from its balconies. The restaurant specializes in Centuri's famous seafood. ⊠ *Rte. de Cap Corse, 20238 Centuri Port* ☎ *04-95-35-60-15* 🖶 *04-95-35-60-24* 🛏 *14 rooms* ☼ *Restaurant, 2 tennis courts, pool, bar, pets (fee); no a/c* ⊟ *AE, DC, MC, V* ⊙ *Closed Nov.–Mar.* ⃝ *EP.*

Erbalunga

34 *40 km (25 mi) southeast of Centuri, 10 km (6 mi) north of Bastia.*

Erbalunga is one of the most charming villages on Cap Corse's east coast, with stone houses sloping gently down to a Genoese tower built into a rock ledge. Possibly because it was French poet Paul Valéry's ancestral home, a famous colony of artists settled here in the 1920s.

Where to Stay

★ **$$$–$$$$** 🖼 **Castel' Brando.** This 19th-century mansion has dark-green shutters and terra-cotta tiles. The spacious rooms are furnished with country-style antiques. Breakfast is served in the garden next to the swimming pool. ⊠ *Off D80, 20222 Erbalunga* ✆ *B.P. 20* ☎ *04–95–30–10–30* 🖷 *04–95–33–98–18* ⊕ *www.castelbrando.corsica-net.com* ⇆ *27 rooms* ⚭ *Kitchenettes, cable TV, pool, pets (fee)* ⊟ *AE, MC, V* ⊘ *Closed Nov. 1–Mar. 15* ❧ *EP.*

San Martino di Lota

❸❺ *12 km (7 mi) north of Bastia.*

Just 20 minutes from downtown Bastia, the turnoff to the perched village of San Martino di Lota winds through thick vegetation as the flat blue expanse of the Tyrrhenian Sea spreads out below. A hike up to the mountain pass, **Bocca di Santo Lunardo,** above the village, is a perfect way to develop a ravenous appetite: the trek takes between six and eight hours round-trip and provides fantastic views of Cap Corse, the Tyrrhenian Sea, and the Tuscan hills.

Where to Stay & Eat

$$ ✕🖾 **La Corniche.** The Anziani family runs this excellent hotel-restaurant serving innovative Corsican fare that changes with the seasons. The *cabri aux herbes du maquis* (roast kid in maquis herbs) is a winter favorite. Rooms are decorated in light pastels and have panoramic sea views. ⊠ *20200 San Martino di Lota* ☎ *04–95–31–40–98* 🖷 *04–95–32–37–69* ⇆ *18 rooms* ⚭ *Restaurant, minibars, pool, bar, pets (fee); no a/c* ⊟ *AE, DC, MC, V* ⊘ *Closed Dec. and Jan.* ❧ *EP, MAP.*

Bastia

★ ❸❻ *13 km (7 mi) south of San Martino di Lota, 10 km (6 mi) south of Erbalunga, 23 km (14 mi) east of St-Florent, 93 km (58 mi) northeast of Calvi, 170 km (105 mi) north of Bonifacio, 153 km (95 mi) northeast of Ajaccio.*

Notably more Italianate than the "continental" French capital at Ajaccio, Bastia is, along with Corte, quintessentially Corsican. Despite sprawling suburbs, it has an historic center that retains the timeless, salty flavor of an ancient Mediterranean port, so approaching and departing by sea are particularly dramatic while rounding the Cap Corse peninsula. With its four churches, its ethnographical museum, many picturesque corners, and a number of fine dining options overlooking the comings and goings of boat traffic to the tune of foghorn blasts, Bastia has a full bouquet of sights to savor. Its name is derived from the word bastion, in reference to the fortress the Genoese built here in the 14th century as a stronghold against rebellious islanders and potential invaders. Today the city is Corsica's business center and largest town. The **Terra Vecchia** (Old Town) is best explored on foot. Start at the wide, palm-filled **place St-Nicolas,** bordered on one side by docked ships looming large in the port and on the other by two blocks of popular cafés along boulevard Général-de-Gaulle. From place St-Nicolas head south on boulevard Général-de-Gaulle, which becomes rue Napoléon, for two blocks to the **Église de la Conception** (Church of the Conception; ⊠ Rue Napoléon), occupying a pebble-studded square. Step inside to admire the church's ornate 18th-century interior, although the lighting is poor, requiring a bright day to see much detail. The walls are covered with a riot of wood carvings, gold, and marble, and the ceiling is painted with vibrant frescoes. **Place du Marché,** the market square behind the church, buzzes with activity every morning except Monday. The warren of tiny streets that make up the old fishermen's quarter begins at the far side of the square.

To the south is the picturesque **Vieux Port** (Old Port), along quai des Martyrs de la Libération, dominated by the hilltop citadel. The harbor, lined with excellent seafood restaurants, is berthed by several million-dollar yachts, but you can still find many bright red-and-blue fishing boats and tangles of old nets and lines. A walk around the port takes you to **Terra Nova** (New Town), a maze of not-so-new streets and houses at the base of the 15th-century fortress. Climb the Escalier Romieu steps beside the leafy Jardins Romieu for a sweeping view of the Italian islands of Capraia, Elba, and Montecristo.

The vaulted, colonnaded galleries of the **Palais des Nobles Douzes** (also known as the Palais des Gouverneurs Genois, or Genoese Governors' Palace) hold the **Musée d'Ethnographie Corse** (Corsican Ethnographic Museum). Don't miss the *Casablanca,* a French submarine used by the Resistance with swastikas on the turret representing downed Nazi aircraft. ⊠ *Pl. du Donjon* 🕾 *04–95–31–09–12.*

A network of cobbled alleyways rambles across the citadel to the 15th-century **Cathédrale Ste-Marie** (⊠ Rue Notre-Dame). Inside, classic Baroque abounds in an explosion of gilt decoration. The 18th-century silver statue of the Assumption is paraded at the head of a religious procession every August 15. The sumptuous Baroque style of the **Chapelle Ste-Croix** (Chapel of the Holy Cross), behind the cathedral, makes it look more like a theater than a church. The chapel owes its name to a blackened oak crucifix, dubbed "Christ of the Miracles," discovered by fishermen at sea in 1428 and venerated to this day by Bastia's fishing community.

Where to Stay & Eat

$$–$$$ ✕ **La Citadelle.** This rustic and intimate spot, arranged around an ancient oil press, is near the Governor's Palace on the heights of the Terra Nova. Dishes are carefully and elegantly prepared and presented; especially tasty is the rockfish soup, a delicious dark and thick potage. ⊠ *5 rue du Dragon* 🕾 *04–95–31–44–70* 🖃 *AE, MC, V* ⊘ *Closed Sun. and Dec. 20–Jan. 14. No lunch Sat.*

★ ¢ ✕ **A Scaletta.** Enjoy the view of the Vieux Port as you choose from a host of fish and seafood specials at this popular spot. (Lavezzi, next door, has the same view, fine cuisine, and higher prices.) The cuisine in this rollicking little bistro is traditional Corsican with maritime leanings. ⊠ *4 rue St-Jean* 🕾 *04–95–32–28–70* 🖃 *AE, DC, MC, V* ⊘ *Closed Sun.*

$–$$ 🖽 **Posta Vecchia.** The top selling point of this hotel in an old building not far from place St-Nicolas is its quai-side location. The unpretentious rooms have floral wallpaper and wood-beam ceilings; some are quite small. Ask for one in the main house facing the port. ⊠ *Quai des Martyrs-de-la-Libération, 20200* 🕾 *04–95–32–32–38* 🖶 *04–95–32–14–05* 🛏 *49 rooms* ⚐ *Pets (fee); no a/c* 🖃 *AE, DC, MC, V* ⭗ *EP.*

Nightlife & the Arts

L'Alba (⊠ 22 quai des Martyrs-de-la-Libération ☎ 04–95–31–13–25) is a piano bar with occasional cabaret and floor shows. Musicians fill the lively patio of the **Pub Chez Assunta** (⊠ Pl. Fontaine Nueve 4 ☎ 04–95–34–11–40) on most summer nights. For a night of traditional Corsican music, head to **U-Fanale** (⊠ Vieux Port ☎ 04–95–32–68–38).

★ One of Corsica's major carnivals, the **Fête du Christ Noir** (Feast of the Black Christ), dedicated to Bastia's most important religious icon, is on May 3. The **Fête de St-Jean,** on Midsummer's Eve (June 23), means concerts in all of Bastia's Baroque spaces. A **Film Festival of Mediterranean Cultures** is held every November. An **International Music Festival** is in early December.

Shopping

Casa di l'Artigiani (⊠ 5 rue des Terrasses) has a wide selection of local crafts. **Mattei Cap Corse** (⊠ Pl. St-Nicolas) sells the Mattei family's special Cap Corse liqueur (made from grapes). At the **market** (⊠ Pl. du Marché, behind St-Jean-Baptiste), everything from local cheeses to charcuterie to myrtle liqueur is sold on weekday mornings.

CORSICA A TO Z

To research prices, get advice from other travelers, and book travel arrangements, visit www.fodors.com.

AIR TRAVEL

CARRIERS Air France has daily service connecting Paris and Lyon with Ajaccio, Bastia, and Calvi. Compagnie Corse Méditérranée connects Ajaccio and Bastia to Nice and Marseille, with several flights a day. Delta connects with Air France for flights from the United States to Corsica from May to October. TAT (Transport Aérien Transrégional) flies to Figari from Paris. Air Balagne, ATM (Air Transport Méditérranée), and Kyrnair are airlines with intra-island flights.

🚺 Airlines & Contacts **Air Balagne** ☎ 04-95-65-02-97. **Air France** ☎ 04-95-29-45-45 Ajaccio, 01-45-46-90-00 Paris. **ATM** ☎ 04-95-76-04-99. **Compagnie Corse Méditérranée** ☎ 04-95-29-05-00 Ajaccio. **Delta** ☎ 800/241-4141. **Kyrnair** ☎ 04-95-20-52-29. **TAT** ☎ 04-95-71-01-20.

AIRPORTS

Corsica has four major airports: Ajaccio, Bastia, Calvi, and Figari. The airports at Ajaccio and Bastia run regular shuttle-bus services to and from town. At Figari a bus meets all incoming flights and will take passengers as far as Bonifacio and Porto-Vecchio for about €15.38. From Calvi the best way to get into town is to take a taxi for about €15.38.

🚺 Airport Information **Bastia-Poretta** ☎ 04-95-55-96-96. **Figari-Sud Corse** ☎ 04-95-71-10-10. **Ajaccio-Campo dell'Oro** ☎ 04-95-23-56-56. **Calvi-Ste Catherine** ☎ 04-95-65-88-88.

BOAT & FERRY TRAVEL

Regular car ferries run from Marseille, Nice, and Toulon to Ajaccio, Bastia, Calvi, L'Ile Rousse, and Propriano. These crossings take from 5 to 10 hours, with sleeping cabins available. The high-speed ferry from Nice to either Calvi or Bastia takes about three hours. Package deals, which include making the crossing with a car, an onboard cabin, and a hotel in Corsica, are available from SNCM, the Société Nationale Maritime Corse-Méditérranée. Connections from the Italian mainland are run by Corsica Ferries. Moby Lines also runs Italian mainland connections. Sardinia can be reached by ferry from Bastia or Bonifacio on Navarma Lines. Saremar also runs ferries to Sardinia.

🚢 Boat & Ferry Information **CMN** ✉ Compagnie Méridionale de Navigation, Ajaccio ☎ 04-95-21-20-34 ✉ Bastia ☎ 04-95-31-63-38. **Corsica Ferries** ✉ Bastia ☎ 04-95-32-95-95 ✉ Genoa, Italy ☎ 010-59-33-01. **Moby Lines** ✉ Bastia ☎04-95-31-46-29 ✉Bonifacio ☎04-95-73-00-29 ✉Genoa, Italy ☎010-20-56-51. **Navarma Lines** ✉ 4 rue Luce-de-Casablanca, Bastia ☎ 04-95-31-46-29. **Saremar** ✉ Gare Maritime, Bonifacio ☎ 04-95-73-06-75. **SNCM** ✉ Paris ☎ 01-49-24-24-24 ✉ Marseille ☎ 04-91-56-30-30 ✉ Nice ☎ 04-93-13-66-99 ✉ Toulon ☎ 04-94-16-66-66 ✉ Ajaccio ☎ 04-95-29-66-99 ✉ Bastia ☎ 04-95-54-66-88 ✉ Calvi ☎ 04-95-65-01-38 ✉ L'Ile Rousse ☎ 04-95-60-09-56.

BUS TRAVEL

The local bus network is geared to residents who take it to school and work. At least two buses a day connect all the southern towns with Ajaccio, while northern towns are connected by bus to Bastia.

🚌 Bus Information **Autocars Eurocorse** ☎ 04-95-31-03-79. **Autocars "Les Beaux Voyages"** ☎ 04-95-65-11-35. **Autocars Les Rapides Bleus** ☎ 04-95-31-03-79. **Autocars Santini** ☎ 04-95-37-02-98.

CAR RENTAL

Hertz serves the entire island; its 18 offices are at all airports and harbors and in the major towns. Be sure to reserve at least two weeks in advance in July and August.

🚗 Local Agencies **Avis Ollandini** ✉ Ajaccio Airport ☎ 04-95-23-25-14. **Europcar** ✉ 1 rue du Nouveau Port, Bastia ☎ 04-95-31-59-29. **Hertz** ✉ Ajaccio Airport ☎ 04-95-22-14-84 ✉ 8 cours Grandval, Ajaccio ☎ 04-95-21-70-94 ✉ Sq. St-Victor, Bastia ☎ 04-95-31-14-24 ✉ Quai du Commerce, Bonifacio ☎ 04-95-73-02-47 ✉ 2 rue Maréchal-Joffre, Calvi ☎ 04-95-65-06-64.

CAR TRAVEL

Though driving is undoubtedly the best way to explore the island's scenic stretches, note that winding, mountainous roads and uneven surfaces can actually double or triple your expected travel time. The Michelin 1/200,000 map No. 90 is essential. Be prepared for spelling anomalies, many of which are Corsican, not French. Drive defensively: you'll find that others on the road tend to move at terrifying speeds.

SPORTS & THE OUTDOORS

Canoeing, kayaking, and rafting are popular pastimes on the mountain rivers; for details write the Association Municipale de Ponte-Leccia.

🚣 Canoeing, Kayaking & Rafting **Association Municipale de Ponte-Leccia** ✉ 20218 Ponte Leccia.

TOURS

AIRPLANE TOURS   ATM and Kyrnair arrange sightseeing tours by plane.

🛩 Fees & Schedules **ATM** ☎ 04-95-76-04-99. **Kyrnair** ☎ 04-95-20-52-29.

BOAT TOURS Most of Corsica's spectacular scenery is best viewed from the water. Colombo Line and Promenades en Mer, in Calvi, organize whole-day glass-bottom boat tours of Girolata, the Scandola Nature Reserve, and the Golfe de Porto. The Promenades en Mer, in Ajaccio, organizes daily trips (at 9 and 2) to the Iles Sanguinaires. Vedettes Christina and Vedettes Méditérranée arrange outings from Bonifacio to the Iles Lavezzi, Les Calanches, and Les Grottes.

🔁 Fees & Schedules **Colombo Line** ✉ Quai Landry, Calvi ☎ 04-95-65-32-10. **Promenades en Mer** ✉ Port de l'Amirauté, 20000 Ajaccio ☎ 04-95-23-23-38 ✉ Porto Marine, Calvi ☎ 04-95-26-15-16. **Vedettes Christina** ☎ 04-95-73-14-69. **Vedettes Méditérranée** ☎ 04-95-73-07-71.

BUS TOURS Ollandini arranges whole- and half-day bus tours of the island, leaving from Ajaccio.

🔁 Fees & Schedules **Ollandini** ✉ 1 rte. d'Alata, Ajaccio ☎ 04-95-21-10-12.

WALKING TOURS Two- and three-day guided hikes through the mountains and lake region are organized by several walking and hiking associations.

🔁 Fees & Schedules **Associu di Muntagnoli Corsi** ✉ Quartier Pentaniedda, 20122 Quenza ☎ 04-95-78-64-05. **Association Sportive du Niollu** ✉ Centre Ville, 20224 Calacuccia ☎ 04-95-48-05-22. **La Compagnie Régionale de Guides** ✉ Centre Ville, 20224 Calacuccia ☎ 04-95-48-10-43. **In Terra Corsa** ✉ Centre Ville, 20249 Ponte Leccia ☎ 04-95-47-64-48. **Objectif Nature** ✉ Quartier Terra Vecchia, 20200 Bastia ☎ 04-95-54-20-42. **La Trace** ✉ Quartier Terra Vecchia, 20200 Bastia ☎ 04-95-35-86-37.

TRAIN TRAVEL

The main line of Corsica's simple rail network runs from Ajaccio, in the west, to Corte, in the central valley, then divides at Ponte Leccia. From here one line continues to L'Ile Rousse and Calvi, in the north, and the other to Bastia, in the northeast. Another service runs four times daily between Ajaccio and Bastia. In summer a small train connects Calvi and L'Ile Rousse, stopping at numerous beaches and resorts. Telephone numbers for local train stations are listed below by town.

🔁 Train Information **SNCF Ajaccio** ☎ 04-95-23-11-03. **SNCF Bastia** ☎ 04-95-32-60-06. **SNCF Calvi** ☎ 04-95-65-00-61. **SNCF Ponte Leccia** ☎ 04-95-47-61-29.

TRAVEL AGENCIES

🔁 Local Agent Referrals **Corse Itineraries** ✉ 32 cours Napoléon, Ajaccio ☎ 04-95-51-01-10 🖨 04-45-21-52-30. **Corse Voyages** ✉ Immeuble Les Remparts, bd. Wilson, Calvi ☎ 04-95-65-26-71. **Cyrnea Tourisme** ✉ 9 av. Xavier-Luciani, Corte ☎ 04-95-46-24-62 🖨 04-95-46-11-22. **Kallistour** ✉ 6 av. Maréchal-Sebastiani, Bastia ☎ 04-95-31-71-49 🖨 04-95-32-35-73.

VISITOR INFORMATION

The Agence du Tourisme de la Corse can provide information about the whole island. The Parc Naturel Régional de la Corse, Corsica's wildlife and natural-resource management authority, controlling well over a third of the island, can provide trail maps, booklets, and a wide variety of information. Local tourist offices are listed below by town.

🔁 Tourist Information **Agence du Tourisme de la Corse** ✉ 17 bd. Roi-Jérôme, 20000

Ajaccio ☎ 04-95-51-77-77 🖷 04-95-51-14-40. **Ajaccio** ✉ Hôtel de Ville, pl. Foch ☎ 04-95-51-53-03 ⊕ www.tourisme.fr/ajaccio/. **Bastia** ✉ Pl. St-Nicolas ☎ 04-95-54-20-40 ⊕ www.bastia-tourisme.com/. **Bonifacio** ✉ Rue des Deux Moulins ☎ 04-95-73-11-88 ⊕ www.bonifacio.com. **Calvi** ✉ Port de Plaisance ☎04-95-65-16-67 ⊕www.tourisme.fr/calvi/. **Corte** ✉La Citadelle ☎04-95-46-26-70 ⊕ www.tourisme.fr/corte/. **L'Ile Rousse** ✉ Pl. Paoli ☎ 04-95-60-04-35. **Levie-Alta Rocca** ✉ Rue Sorba ☎ 04-95-78-41-95. **Parc Naturel Régional de la Corse** ✉ Rue du Général-Fiorella ☎ 04-95-21-56-54 🖷 Mailing address: B.P. 417, 20100 Ajaccio. **Piana** ✉ Hôtel de Ville ☎ 04-95-27-84-42. **Piedicroce-Castagniccia** ✉ Piedicroce ☎ 04-95-35-82-54. **Porticcio** ✉ 428 bd. Rive Sud ☎ 04-95-25-01-00. **Porto-Vecchio** ✉ Rue du Député de Rocca Serra ☎ 04-95-70-09-58. **Propriano** ✉ Port de Plaisance ☎04-95-76-01-49. **Sartène** ✉Rue Borgo ☎04-95-77-15-40. **Sollacaro-Filitosa** ✉ Filitosa ☎ 04-95-74-07-64. **St-Florent** ☎ 04-95-37-06-04.

THE MIDI-PYRÉNÉES & THE LANGUEDOC-ROUSSILLON

14

Revised and
updated by
George Semler

Introduction by
George Semler

LIKE THE MOST CELEBRATED DISH OF THIS AREA, cassoulet, the south-western region of France is a feast of diverse ingredients. Just as it would be a gross oversimplification to refer to cassoulet as a dish of baked beans, southwestern France is more than just Toulouse, the peaks of the Pyrénées, and the fairy-tale ramparts of Carcassonne. Rolling, sun-baked plains and rock- and shrub-covered hills dotted with ruins of ancient civilizations parallel the burning coastline; the fortifications and cathedrals of once-great cities like Béziers and Narbonne rise mirage-like out of the Mediterranean haze; and Collioure and the famed Côte Vermeille, immortalized by Picasso and Matisse, nestle colorfully just north of the border with Spain. Nevertheless, just as cassoulet *toulousain* (made with goose) is the variety you are most apt to find all over France, so the city of Toulouse tops the tourist "bill of fare" here. Serving as gateway to the region, alive with music, sculpture, and architectural gems, and vibrant with students, Toulouse is all that more famous regional capitals would like to have remained, or to become. Sinuously spread along the romantic banks of the Garonne as it meanders north and west from the Catalan Pyrénées on its way to the Atlantic, "La Ville Rose"—so-called for its redbrick buildings—has a Spanish sensuality unique in all Gaul, a feast for eyes and ears alike. Toulouse was the ancient capital of the province called Languedoc, so christened when it became royal property in 1270, meaning the country where *oc*—instead of the *oil* or *oui* of northeastern France—meant yes.

Outside Toulouse, the terrain of the Midi-Pyrénées and Languedoc-Roussillon is studded with highlights, like so many raisins sweetening up a spicy stew. Albi, with its Toulouse-Lautrec legacy, is a star attraction, while each outlying town—from Montauban to Moissac to Auch, Mirepoix, or Cordes-sur-Ciel—has artistic and architectural treasures waiting to be uncovered. Besides Albi's Toulouse-Lautrec Museum, other art museums not to miss here are Montauban's Musée Ingres, devoted to France's most accomplished Neoclassical painter, and Ceret's Musée d'Art Moderne, which is packed with Picassos, Braques, and Chagalls.

There's also an "open-air museum" prized by artists and poets: the Côte Vermeille, or Vermilion Coast, centered around the fishing village of Collioure, where Matisse, Derain, and the Fauvists committed chromatic mayhem in the early years of the 20th century. The view of the Côte Vermeille from the Alberes mountain range reveals a bright-yellow strand of beach curving north and east toward the Camargue wetlands. From the vineyards above Banyuls-sur-Mer to the hills once traversed by Hannibal and his regiment of elephants, this storied coast has been irresistible to everyone from Pompey to Louis XIV. The Mediterranean smooth and opalescent at dawn; villagers dancing sardanas to the music of the raucous and ancient woodwind *flavioles* and *tenores*; the flood of golden light so peculiar to the Mediterranean . . . everything about it seems to be asking to be immortalized in oil on canvas. The heart of the region is Collioure, with its narrow, cobbled streets and pink-and-mauve houses. A town of espadrille merchants, anchovy packers, and lateen-rigged fishing boats in the shadow

The Midi-Pyrénées and the Languedoc-Roussillon form the main body of France's traditional southwestern region. Sports- and nature-lovers flock here to enjoy the natural attributes of the area, of which Toulouse—a university town of rosy pink brick—is the cultural star. Here, too, are Albi and its wonderful Toulouse-Lautrec Museum; Moissac and its famous Romanesque cloister; the once-upon-a-timeliness of Carcassonne; the spa towns that enliven the Pyrénées; and the relatively undiscovered city of Montpellier. And when you see picturesque Collioure's stunning Mediterranean setting, you can understand why Fauvist painters Matisse and Derain went color-berserk while there. Getting to know this vast region would take several weeks, or even years. But it's possible to sample its finest offerings in three to seven days, if that's all the time you have.

14

Numbers in the text correspond to numbers in the margin and on the Midi-Pyrénées & the Languedoc-Roussillon and Toulouse maps.

If you have 3 days

Bask in the rich rose color of 🖾 **Toulouse ❶ ☛ – ㉔** for a day and then head to **Cordes-sur-Ciel ㉖**, a fortified medieval village. Make Toulouse-Lautrec's home town, 🖾 **Albi ㉕**, your home for the night. On Day 3 explore the medieval citadel at 🖾 **Carcassonne ㉜**.

If you have 7 to 11 days

Spend the first day and a half in 🖾 **Toulouse ❶ ☛ – ㉔**; then drive west to 🖾 **Auch ㉛**, the capital of the Gers département. Next, head north to the old Roman town of **Lectoure ㉚**. Next up is a true high point of the trip: the famous Romanesque sculptures of the abbey church at 🖾 **Moissac ㉘**. On Day 3 study up on the university town of **Montauban ㉗** before visiting the medieval age in **Cordes-sur-Ciel ㉖**. Spend the night in 🖾 **Albi ㉕**. On the fourth day head some 70 mi south to storybook 🖾 **Carcassonne ㉜** for a day filled with medieval history and glamour. On your fifth day drive into the Pyrénées, passing through **Tarascon-sur-Ariège ㉟** to see the Grotte de Niaux, the mountain resorts of **Ax-les-Thermes ㊱**, and **Font-Romeu ㊲**. Spend the fifth night in nearby 🖾 **Eyne ㊳** before continuing east out of the Pyrénées toward the Mediterranean. On your sixth day, stop in the fortified town of **Villefranche-de-Conflent ㊵** to hike up to the amazing Abbaye de St-Martin-de-Canigou. Pass through the spa town of **Vernet-les-Bains ㊶** on your way to 🖾 **Prades ㊷**, famed for its music festival and the Abbaye de St-Michel-de-Cuxa. After spending your sixth night here, head out to 🖾 **Céret ㊸**, immortalized by Picasso. After your seventh night here, set out on your eighth day to Roussillon's most picturesque coastal town, 🖾 **Collioure ㊹** and channel the spirits of Matisse and Dufy. Then on the morn of your ninth day, drive north to **Perpignan ㊺**, the historic hub city of the Roussillon, then head out of the region to discover the sights of 🖾 **Narbonne ㊼**. On your tenth day, make a detour to **Minerve ㊾**, a sublime medieval hilltop village, then head back northeast past the Languedoc frontier to spend your last night in 🖾 **Montpellier ㊿ – ㊽**; on your eleventh day tour this city's fascinating *Vieille Ville*, steeped in culture, history, and young blood (a famous university is based here).

of its 13th-century Château Royal, Collioure, home of the late novelist Patrick O'Brian, is now as much a magnet for tourists as it once was and still is a lure for artists. Although nearby villages are apparently only rich in quaintness, Collioure is surprisingly prosperous, thanks to the cultivation of *primeurs,* early ripe fruit and vegetables, shipped to the markets of northern France.

The abundant mountains, lakes, rivers, wide green valleys, and arid limestone plateaus make many of the areas in this chapter ideal for outdoor activities. The Ariège Valley and the Pyrénées Orientales provide a dramatic route through Cathar country and the Cerdagne Valley on the way to the Mediterranean. For the *sportif,* options run from kayaking and windsurfing to climbing to high Pyrenean lakes and peaks, exploring mountain monasteries such as St-Martin de Canigou, fly-fishing the upper Aude and Ariège rivers, or walking up to the Spanish border at the Gorges de Carança above Thuès-entre-Valls or the Col de Nuria above Eyne. To finish off on a cultural high note, take in the famous Romanesque cloister of St-Guilhem-le-Désert and the nearby student mecca of Montpellier, home to a fine university, museum, and the Ricardo Bofill–designed Quartier Antigone, the old city's nod to the future.

Exploring the Midi-Pyrénées & the Languedoc-Roussillon

France's largest region, Midi-Pyrénées spreads from the Dordogne in the north to the Spanish border along the Pyrénées. Radiating out from Toulouse to the surrounding towns of Albi, Carcassonne, Montauban, and Auch, and up through the Ariège Valley into the Pyrénées Orientales, the central and southern parts of the Midi-Pyrénées are rich in history, natural resources, art, and architecture. Languedoc-Roussillon fits in along the Mediterranean from Collioure north through Perpignan, Narbonne, Beziers, and Montpellier, all once part of Catalonia and the crown of Aragon's medieval Mediterranean empire. Montpellier is at the dead center of the Mediterranean coastline, a five-hour train ride from Paris and Nice, as well as from Barcelona.

This chapter divides the region into three sections. The first covers the lively city of Toulouse. The second encompasses the area to the north and west of Toulouse, including the Gers *département,* Albi, the Lot Valley, Montauban, and verdant Gascony. The third extends southeast into the Languedoc-Roussillon and up the Mediterranean coast to the now-inland crossroads of Narbonne.

About the Restaurants & Hotels

As a rule, the closer you get to the Mediterranean coast, the later you dine and the more you pay for your seafood platter and that bottle of iced rosé. The farther you travel from the coast, the higher the altitude, the more rustic the setting you'll find yourself in, and the more reasonable the prices will be. During the scorching summer months in sleepy mountain villages, lunches are light, interminable, and *bien arrosé* (French for "with lots of wine"). Here you will also find that small personal restaurant where the chickens roasting on spits above the open fire have first names and the cheese comes from the hippie couple down

14

Matisse Country

Toulouse, the regional capital, may be nicknamed "La Ville Rose" (the Pink City) because of the color of its brick buildings but head southeast over to the Roussillon—so called for the red color of its earth—and watch the palette get notched up to deep vermilions, breathtaking aquamarines, and shocking magentas (those bougainvilleas). Little wonder, then, that the famous group of painters known as the Fauves were seduced in the early 1900s by La Côte Vermeille and its ochre-color coastal villages. These painters were called Fauves, or "wild beasts," partly because their colors were taken from the savage tones found in Mother Nature, not those of the masters of the Louvre. Where Matisse, Derain, Picasso, Gris, and Braque first vacationed and painted, thousands followed and discovered Collioure and Céret (whose name derives from *cerise*, or "cherry"). Today, Collioure is a living museum, as you can discover by touring its Chemin du Fauvisme, where 20 points along a route through town compare reproductions of noted Fauvist canvases with the actual scenes that were depicted in them (view-finder picture-frames let you see how little has changed in eight decades). After studying some of the paintings created by these masters in Céret's Musée de l'Art Moderne, you can set off through the streets of Collioure's old quarter of Le Mouré to discover numerous studios of contemporary artists. And if their prices are too steep, you can always step outside to the awe-inspiring view from the town beach of Plage Boramar and exult in your own free "3-D" Matisse. If your tastes incline more to Picasso, your place will be Céret, whose rocky landscape is said to have inspired the artist's invention of Cubism.

Cassoulet Cuisine

Dining in the southwest is a rougher, heartier, and more rustic version of classic Mediterranean cooking—the peppers are sliced thick, the garlic and olive oil used with a heavier hand, the herbs crushed or coarsely chopped and served au naturel. Expect *cuisine de marché*, market-based cooking, savory seasonal dishes based on the culinary trinity of the south—garlic, onion, and tomato—straight from the village market. Languedoc is known for powerful and strongly seasoned cooking. Garlic and goose fat are generously used in traditional recipes. Be sure to try some of the renowned *foie gras* (goose or duck liver) and *confit de canard* (preserved duck). The most famous regional dish is *cassoulet,* a succulent white-bean stew with *confit d'oie* (preserved goose). Keep your eyes open for festive *cargolades*—huge communal barbecues starting off with thousands of buttery-garlic snails roasted on open grills and eaten by hand, followed by cured bacon and lamb cutlets and vats (and vats) of local wine. Mountain restaurants and inns serve rugged highland fare—be sure to try a bowl of *ollada*, a thick hearty soup made with sausage and lamb, cabbage and onion, thrown into black cauldrons and left to simmer at least 24 hours. In the Gers *département* (province) finish your meal with a glass of Armagnac, the local brandy distilled throughout the province. In the Pyrénées look for rich, dark *civet d'isard* (stewed mountain goat) or *trinxat,* a Cerdagne Valley specialty of mashed half-frozen cabbage, potato, and bacon.

In the Roussillon and along the Mediterranean coast from Collioure up through Perpignan to Narbonne, the prevalent Catalan cuisine features olive oil–based cooking and sauces such as the classic aioli (crushed and emulsified garlic and olive oil). When you're on the coast, it's fish of course, often cooked over wood coals.

---

the road who came here in the sixties and love their mountains, their goats, and the universe in general.

Hotels range from Mediterranean modern to medieval baronial to Pyrenean chalet; most are small and cozy rather than luxurious and sophisticated. Toulouse has the usual range of big-city hotels; make reservations well in advance if you plan to visit in spring or fall. Look for *gîtes d'étape* (hikers' waystations) and table d'hôtes (bed-and-breakfasts), which offer excellent value and a chance to meet local and international travelers and sample life on the farm, as well as the delights of *cuisine du terroir* (country cooking). Assume all hotel rooms have air-conditioning, TV, telephones, and private bath, unless otherwise noted.

WHAT IT COSTS In euros				
$$$$	**$$$**	**$$**	**$**	**¢**
RESTAURANTS over €30	€23–€30	€17–€23	€11–€17	under €11
HOTELS over €190	€120–€190	€80–€120	€50–€80	under €50

Restaurant prices are per person for a main course at dinner, including tax (19.6%) and service; note that if a restaurant offers only prix-fixe (set-price) meals, it has been given the price category that reflects the full prix-fixe price. Hotel prices are for a standard double room in high season, including tax (19.6%) and service charge; higher prices (inquire when booking) prevail for any meal plans.

Timing

Although spring in this mountainous region is inclined to be rainy, it's also the time when the Pyrenean flowers are at their best. April and May are delightful months on the Côte Vermeille, and June and September are equally good for the inland points. As for "off-season"—if there is such a thing, since chic Parisians often arrive in November in their SUVs with a hunger for the authentic—call ahead and double-check when restaurants and hotels close for their annual hibernation (which usually starts sometime in winter, either before, or right after, the Christmas holidays).

TOULOUSE

The ebullient city of Toulouse is the capital of the Midi-Pyrénées and the fourth-largest city in France. Just 96 km (60 mi) from the border with Spain, Toulouse's flavor is in many ways closer to southern European Spanish than to northern European French. Weathered redbrick buildings line sidewalks, giving the city its nickname, "La Ville Rose" (the Pink City). Downtown, the sidewalks and restaurants pulse late into the night with tourists, workers, college students, and technicians from the giant Airbus aviation complex headquartered outside the city.

Toulouse was founded in the 4th century BC and quickly became an important part of Roman Gaul. In turn, it was made into a Visigothic and Carolingian capital before becoming a separate county in 843. Ruling from this Pyrenean hub that was one of the great artistic and literary capitals of medieval Europe, the counts of Toulouse held sovereignty over nearly all of the Languedoc and maintained a brilliant court known for its fine troubadours and literature. In the early 13th century Toulouse was attacked and plundered by troops representing an alliance between the northern French nobility and the papacy, ostensibly to wipe out the Albigensian heresy (Catharism), but more realistically as an expansionist move against the power of Occitania, the French southwest. The counts toppled, but Toulouse experienced a cultural and economic rebirth thanks to the *woad* (dye) trade; consequently, wealthy merchants' homes constitute a major portion of Toulouse's architectural patrimony.

In 1659 the Roussillon region was officially ceded to France by Spain in the Treaty of the Pyrénées, 17 years after Louis XIII conquered the area from Spain. Toulouse, at the intersection of the Garonne and the Canal du Midi, midway between the Massif Central and the Pyrénées, became an important nexus between Aquitania, Languedoc, and the Roussillon. Today Toulouse is France's second-largest university town after Paris and the center of France's aeronautical industry.

Old Toulouse

The area between the boulevards and the Garonne forms the historic nucleus of Toulouse. Originally part of Roman Gaul and later the capital for the Visigoths and then the Carolingians, by AD 1000 Toulouse was one of the artistic and literary centers of medieval Europe. Despite its 13th-century defeat by the lords of northern France, Toulouse quickly reemerged as a cultural and commercial power and has remained so ever since. Religious and civil structures bear witness to this illustrious past, even as the city's booming student life mirrors a dynamic present. This is the heart of Toulouse, with place du Capitole at its center.

The huge garage beneath place du Capitole is a good place to park, and offers easy walking distance to all the major sites. If you leave your car in another garage, you can take the subway that runs east–west to central Toulouse; it costs €1.20 for one zone, €1.50 for two.

a good walk

Start on **place du Capitole** ❶ ➣, stopping at the donjon (dungeon or tower) next to the **Capitole/Hôtel de Ville** ❷, where there's a tourist office with maps. Rue du Taur, off the square, leads to **Notre-Dame du Taur** ❸. Continue along rue du Taur to the **Ancien Collège de Périgord** ❹ to see the oldest part of the medieval university. Toulouse's most emblematic church, **St-Sernin** ❺, is at the end of rue du Taur on place St-Sernin. Next door is the **Musée St-Raymond** ❻, the city's archaeological museum.

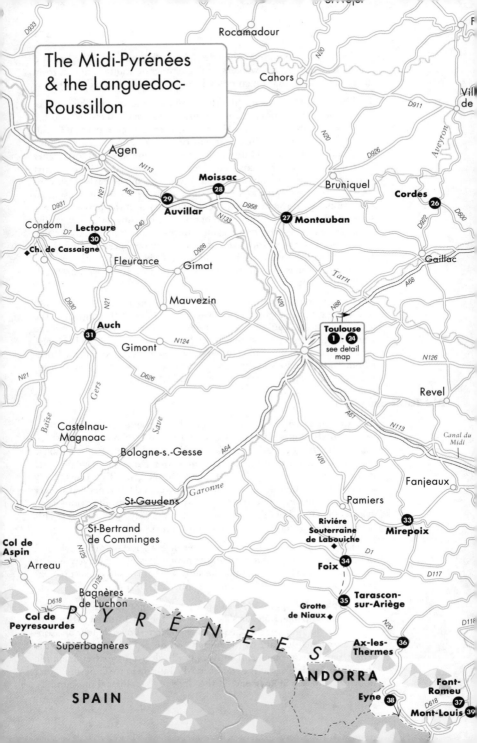

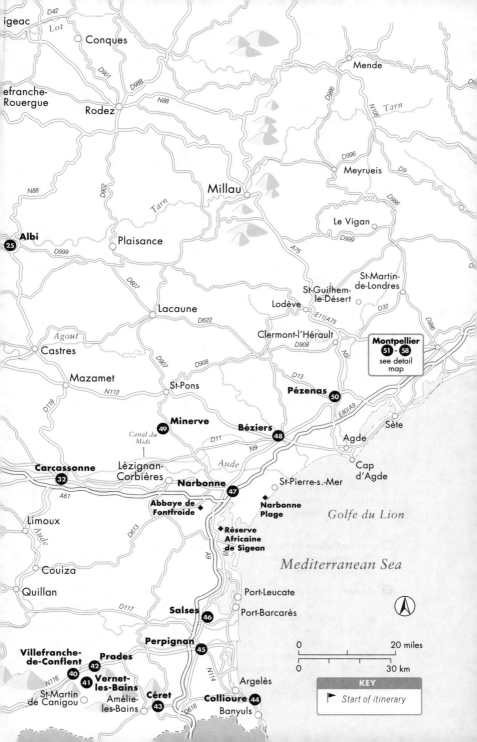

Leave place St-Sernin and cut out along rue Bellegarde to the boulevard de Strasbourg, site of the vegetable and produce market. Take the boulevard to rue Victor-Hugo and the **Marché Victor Hugo** ⑦, the large market hall. Find your way back to place du Capitole, cross the square, and take rue Gambetta past the colorfully restored Art Nouveau facade on the left to rue Lakanal. To the right is the **Église des Jacobins** ⑧ with its famous palm vault, one of the city's most important architectural sites.

Back on rue Gambetta is the opulent **Hôtel de Bernuy** ⑨. Cut through rue Jean Suau to **place de la Daurade** ⑩. **Notre-Dame de la Daurade** ⑪ is the nonsteepled and domeless church on your left; the Café des Artistes is to the right. After a pause here, continue up quai de La Daurade past the sculpted goddesses on the facade of the École des Beaux-Arts to the **Pont Neuf** ⑫. Here you can cross the Garonne to the **Château d'Eau** ⑬, the water tower once used to store and pressurize the city's water system, now an excellent photographic gallery-museum. Or you can turn left on rue de Metz to the **Hôtel d'Assézat** ⑭, home of the Fondation Bemberg and its excellent collection of paintings. The nearby **Musée des Augustins** ⑮ has one of the world's finest collections of Romanesque sculpture and is a de rigueur visit, especially on a rainy day.

Take a left on rue des Changes, once part of the Roman road that sliced through Toulouse from north to south; now it's a chic pedestrian-only shopping area. Stop to admire the **Hôtel d'Astorg** ⑯, the **Hôtel d'Arnault Brucelles** ⑰, and the **Hôtel Delpech** ⑱. Continue along rue des Changes to the intersection with rue de Temponières. Note the handsome woodbeam and brick building on the far right corner and the faux granite one at the near left, complete with painted lines between the "stones" and trompe-l'oeil windows (one of the clever ways the good citizens struggled to avoid paying the legendary window tax). The next street to the left, rue Tripière, loops through place du May onto rue du May, which leads to the **Musée du Vieux Toulouse** ⑲, housed in the Hôtel Dumay.

TIMING   This walk covers some 3 km (2 mi) and should take three–four hours, depending on how long you spend at each site. Most sites close punctually at noon, so it's essential that you get an early start. Or better yet, take a long lunch at some lovely spot and continue on again after 1 or 2, when places reopen.

What to See

❹ **Ancien Collège de Périgord** (Old Périgord College). The wooden gallery-like structure on the street side of the courtyard is the oldest remnant of the 14th-century residential college. ⊠ *56–58 rue du Taur.*

❷ **Capitole/Hôtel de Ville** (Capitol/Town Hall). The 18th-century Capitole is home to the Hôtel de Ville and the city's highly regarded opera company. The reception rooms are open to the public when not in use for official functions or weddings. Halfway up the **Grand Escalier** (Grand Staircase) hangs a large painting of the *Jeux Floraux* (*Floral Games*), organized by a literary society created in 1324 to promote the local Occitanian language, Langue d'Oc. The festival continues to this day: poets give public readings here each May, and the best are awarded silver- and gold-plated violets, one of the emblems of Toulouse. At the top

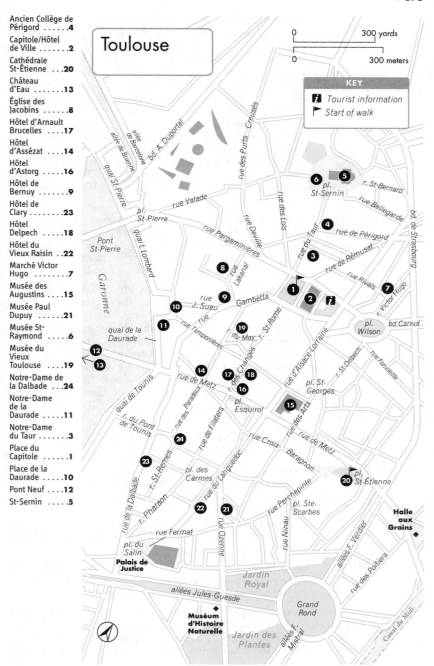

Toulouse

| 0 | | 300 yards |
| 0 | | 300 meters |

KEY

i *Tourist information*

▶ *Start of walk*

of the stairs is the **Salle Gervaise,** a hall used for weddings, over which hangs a series of paintings inspired by the themes of love and marriage. The mural at the far end of the room portrays the Isle of Cythères, where Venus received her lovers, alluding to a French euphemism for getting married: *embarquer pour Cythères* (to embark for Cythères). More giant paintings in the **Salle Henri-Martin,** named for the artist (1860–1943), show the passing seasons set against the eternal Garonne. Look for Jean Jaurès (1859–1914), one of France's greatest socialist martyrs, in *Les Rêveurs* (*The Dreamers*); he's wearing a boater-style hat and a beige coat. At the far left end of the elegant **Salle des Illustres** (Hall of the Illustrious) is a large painting of a fortress under siege, portraying the women of Toulouse slaying Simon de Montfort, leader of the Albigensian crusade against the Cathars, during the siege of Toulouse in 1218. ⊠ *Pl. du Capitole* ☎ *05–61–11–34–12* ⊠ *Free* ☉ *Weekdays 8:30–5, weekends 10–6.*

⓫ Château d'Eau. This 19th-century water tower at the far end of the Pont Neuf, once used to store water and build water pressure, is now used for photography exhibits (it was built in 1823, the same year Nicéphore Nièpce created the first permanent photographic images). ⊠ *1 pl. Laganne* ☎ *05–61–77–09–40* ⊠ *€2.30* ☉ *Tues.–Sun. 1–7.*

★ ⓭ Église des Jacobins. An extraordinary structure built in the 1230s for the Dominicans (renamed Jacobins in 1217 for their Parisian base in rue St-Jacques), the church is dominated by a single row of seven columns running the length of the nave. The easternmost column (on the far right) is one of the finest examples of palm-tree vaulting ever erected, the much-celebrated *Palmier des Jacobins,* a major masterpiece of Gothic art. Fanning out overhead, its 22 ribs support the entire apse. The original refectory site is used for temporary art exhibitions. The cloister is one of the city's aesthetic and acoustical gems and in summer hosts piano and early music concerts. ⊠ *Rue Lakanal s/n* ☎ *05–61–22–21–92* ⊠ *Church free, cloister €2.30* ☉ *Daily 10–7.*

⓱ Hôtel d'Arnault Brucelles. One of the tallest and best of Toulouse's 49 towers can be found at this 16th-century mansion. ⊠ *19 rue des Changes.*

⓮ Hôtel d'Assézat. Built in 1555 by Toulouse's top Renaissance architect, Nicolas Bachelier, this mansion, considered the city's most elegant, has arcades and ornately carved doorways. It's now home to the **Fondation Bemberg,** an exceptional collection of paintings ranging from Tiepolo to Toulouse-Lautrec, Manet, Monet, and Bonnard. Climb to the top of the tower for splendid views over the city's rooftops. ⊠ *Rue de Metz* ⊠ *€4* ☉ *Daily 10–noon and 2–6.*

⓰ Hôtel d'Astorg. This 16th-century mansion is notable for its lovely wooden stairways and galleries and for its top-floor *mirande,* a wooden balcony. ⊠ *16 rue des Changes.*

⓭ Hôtel de Bernuy. Now part of a school, this mansion, around the corner from the Église des Jacobins, was built for Jean de Bernuy in the 16th century, the period when Toulouse was at its most prosperous. De Bernuy made his fortune exporting woad, the dark-blue dye that brought unprecedented wealth to 18th-century Toulouse. De Bernuy's success is reflected in the use of stone, a costly material in this region of brick, and by the octagonal stair tower, the highest in the city. You may wander freely around the courtyard. ⊠ *Rue Gambetta.*

⑱ Hôtel Delpech. Look for the biblical inscriptions carved in Latin in the stone under the windows. ⊠ *20 rue des Changes.*

❼ Marché Victor Hugo (Victor Hugo Market). This hangarlike indoor market is always a refreshing stop. Consider eating lunch at one of the seven upstairs restaurants. **Chez Attila,** just to the left at the top of the stairs, is the best of them. ⊠ *Pl. Victor-Hugo.*

★ **⑮ Musée des Augustins** (Augustinian Museum). In this former medieval Augustinian convent, the museum uses the sacristy, chapter house, and cloisters for displaying an outstanding array of Romanesque sculpture and religious paintings. Built in the Mediterranean Gothic style, the architectural complex is vast and holds a collection rich with treasures and discoveries. ⊠ *Rue de Metz* 🕾 *05–61–22–21–82* 🖃 *Museum €2.20, museum and exhibit €4; free Sun.* ☉ *Wed.–Mon. 10–6.*

❻ Musée St-Raymond. The city's archaeological museum, next to the basilica of St-Sernin, has an extensive collection of imperial Roman busts, as well as ancient coins, vases, and jewelry. ⊠ *Pl. St-Sernin* 🕾 *05–61–22–21–85* 🖃 *€2* ☉ *Mon. and Wed.–Sat. 8–noon and 2–6, Sun. noon–6.*

⑲ Musée du Vieux Toulouse (Museum of Old Toulouse). This museum is worthwhile for the building itself as much as for its collection of Toulouse memorabilia, paintings, sculptures, and documents. Be sure to note the ground-floor fireplace and wooden ceiling. ⊠ *7 rue du May* 🕾 *05–61–13–97–24* 🖃 *€3* ☉ *June–Sept., Mon.–Sat. 3–6.*

⑪ Notre-Dame de la Daurade. Overlooking the Garonne is this 18th-century church. The name *Daurade* comes from *doré* (gilt), referring to the golden reflection given off by the mosaics decorating the 5th-century temple to the Virgin Mary that once stood on this site. ⊠ *Pl. de la Daurade.*

❸ Notre-Dame du Taur. Built on the spot where St. Saturnin (or Sernin), the martyred bishop of Toulouse, was dragged to his death in AD 257 by a rampaging bull, this church is famous for its *cloche-mur,* or wall tower. The wall looks like an extension of the facade and has inspired many similar versions throughout the region. ⊠ *Rue du Taur.*

▶ **❶ Place du Capitole.** This vast, open square in the city center, lined with shops and cafés, is a good spot for getting your bearings or for soaking up some spring or winter sun. A parking lot is conveniently underneath.

❿ Place de la Daurade. On the Garonne, this is one of Toulouse's nicest squares. A stop at the Café des Artistes is almost obligatory. The corner of the quai offers a romantic view of the Garonne, the Hôtel Dieu across the river, and the Pont Neuf.

⑫ Pont Neuf (New Bridge). Despite its name, the graceful span of the Pont Neuf opened to traffic in 1632. The remains of the old bridge—one arch and the lighter-color outline on the brick wall of the **Hôtel-Dieu** (hospital)—are visible across the river. The 16th-century hospital was used for pilgrims on their way to Santiago de Compostela. Just over the bridge, on a clear day in winter, the snowcapped peaks of the Pyrénées are often visible in the distance, said to be a sign of imminent rain.

⑤ St-Sernin. Toulouse's most famous landmark and the world's largest Romanesque church once belonged to a Benedictine abbey, built in the 11th century to house pilgrims on their way to Santiago de Compostela in Spain. Inside, the aesthetic highpoint is the magnificent central apse, begun in 1080, glittering with gilded ceiling frescoes which date from the 19th century. When illuminated at night, St-Sernin's five-tier octagonal tower glows red against the sky. Not all the tiers are the same: The first three, with their rounded windows, are Romanesque; the upper two, with pointed Gothic windows, were added around 1300. ⊠ *Rue du Taur* 🕿 *05–61–21–70–18* 🖭 *Crypt €3* ☉ *Daily 10–11:30 and 2:30–5:30.*

FodorśChoice
★

need a break? Just a 10-minute walk from the Basilique St-Sernin, you will find one of the oldest cafés in Toulouse, **Le Concorde** (⊠ 17 rue de la Concorde). This is the perfect place to sip a glass of Banyuls and listen to a wonderful live accordion concert of some classic French cabaret tunes in the evenings.

South of rue de Metz

South of rue de Metz you'll discover the cathedral of St-Étienne, the antiques district along rue Perchepinte, and town houses and palaces along the way on rue Ninau, rue Ozenne, and rue de la Dalbade—all among the top sights in Toulouse.

a good walk From the **Cathédrale St-Étienne** ㉜ ⌐ walk down rue Fermat to place Stes-Scarbes and the 17th-century Hôtel du Bourg, at 6 rue Perchepinte, where you'll find the old antiques district, lined with noble 16th- to 18th-century houses all the way down to place du Salin. Take a left on rue Ninau; at No. 15 is the 16th-century Hôtel d'Ulmo, with its graceful tower, front stairs, courtyard, and interior garden; at No. 19 is the 18th-century Hôtel Castagnier. Place Montoulieu opens into rue Vélane, passing brick and timber-frame houses and the narrow 14th-century rue Neuve. At 16 rue Vélane is the 17th-century Hôtel Penautier, with an elegant courtyard, stairway, and garden through the entryway next to the Laure Bandet antiques shop. Rue Vélane emerges back out on rue Perchepinte. Take a left on Perchepinte and a quick right onto rue de la Pléau to get to the **Musée Paul Dupuy** ㉑, a museum of medieval arts. Head right on rue Ozenne to No. 9, the 15th-century Hôtel de Dahus. Go left on rue du Languedoc; at No. 36 is the 15th- and 16th-century mansion **Hôtel du Vieux Raisin** ㉒, crowned by an unusual octagonal tower. Continue back down rue du Languedoc to place du Salin, where farmers sell homemade foie gras on market mornings. Rue de la Dalbade, parallel to the Garonne, leads past one stately facade after another. The finest is No. 25, the **Hôtel de Clary** ㉓, also known as the Hôtel de Pierre (not for Peter but for the stone [*pierre*] used in its construction). Continue up the street to the church of **Notre-Dame de la Dalbade** ❷. From here cut through rue Pont de Tounis, go past the doorway on the left with the sculpted Gambrinus—legendary Flemish inventor of beer—then over the bridge (which used to span a branch of the Garonne) and out to quai de Tounis. The Pont Neuf is just up to the right.

TIMING This walk will take you about three hours.

Sights to See

▶ ❷⓿ **Cathédrale St-Étienne.** The cathedral was erected in stages between the 13th and 17th centuries, though the nave and choir languished unfinished because of a lack of funds. A fine collection of 16th- and 17th-century tapestries traces the life of St. Stephen. In front of the cathedral is the city's oldest fountain, dating from the 16th century. ⊠ *Pl. St-Étienne.*

❷❸ **Hôtel de Clary.** This mansion, known as the Hôtel de Pierre because of its unusually solid *pierre* (stone) construction—at the time considered a sign of great wealth—is one of the finest 17th- and 18th-century mansions on the street. The ornately sculpted stone facade was built in 1608 by parliamentary president François de Clary. ⊠ *25 rue de la Daurade.*

❷❷ **Hôtel du Vieux Raisin.** Officially the Hôtel Maynier, named for the original owner, the house became the Vieux Raisin (Old Grape) after the early name of the street and even earlier inn. Built in 1550, the mansion has an octagonal tower, male and female figures on the facade, and allegorical sculptures of the three stages of life—infancy, maturity, and old age—over the windows to the left. ⊠ *36 rue de Languedoc.*

❷❶ **Musée Paul Dupuy.** This museum, dedicated to medieval applied arts, is housed in the Hôtel Pierre Besson, a 16th-century mansion. ⊠ *13 rue de la Pleau* ☎ *05–61–14–65–50* 💴 €2.30 ◷ *Wed.–Mon. 10–5.*

❷❹ **Notre-Dame de la Dalbade.** Originally Sancta Maria de Ecclesia Alba, in Langue d'Oc (Ste-Marie de l'Église Blanche, in French, or St. Mary of the White Church—*alba* meaning "white"), the name of the church evolved into "de Albata" and later "Dalbade." Ironically, one of its outstanding features today is the colorful 19th-century ceramic tympanum over the Renaissance door. ⊠ *Pl. de la Dalbade.*

Where to Stay & Eat

$$$$ ✕ **Toulousy–Jardins de l'Opéra.** Dominique Toulousy's elegant restaurant next to the Grand Hôtel de l'Opéra is a perennial favorite. Intimate rooms and a covered terrace around a little pond make for undeniable charm, though some will find the grand flourishes—glass ceilings, *echt* statuary, and mammoth chandeliers—a little too, well, operatic, and might prefer the adjacent brasserie, Grand Café de l'Opéra. The food is an innovative departure from local fare, with seductive nouvelle or Gascon touches such as the ravioli stuffed with foie gras and truffle sauce. ⊠ *1 pl. du Capitole* ☎ *05–61–23–07–76* ⌦ *Reservations essential* ▤ *AE, DC, MC, V* ◷ *Closed Sun. and Mon.*

★ $$–$$$ ✕ **Michel Sarran.** This clean-lined post-nouvelle haven for what is arguably Toulouse's finest dining departs radically from traditional stick-to-your-ribs southwest France cuisine in favor of Mediterranean formulas suited to the rhythms and reasons of modern living. Foie-gras soup with belon oysters, and *loup cuit et cru au chorizo* (sea-bass, cooked and raw, with chorizo sausage) are two examples of Michel Sarran's light but flavorful cuisine. ⊠ *21 bd. A. Duportal* ☎ *05–61–12–32–32* ⌕ *Reservations essential* ▤ *AE, DC, MC, V* ☉ *Closed weekends, July 27–Aug. 29, and Dec. 23–31.*

$–$$$ ✕ **Brasserie des Beaux-Arts.** Overlooking the Pont Neuf, this elegant brasserie is the place to be at sunset. Watch the colors change over the Garonne from a quayside window or a sidewalk table while enjoying delicious seafood, including a dozen varieties of oysters. The house white wine, a local St-Lannes from the nearby Gers region, is fresh and fruity yet dry, and the service is impeccable. ⊠ *1 quai de la Daurade* ☎ *05–61–21–12–12* ▤ *AE, DC, MC, V.*

$$ ✕ **Le 19.** Centrally placed across the street from the Hôtel des Capitouls and next to the Pont Neuf, this lovely former 16th-century fish market has vaulted ceilings that will take your breath (but not your appetite) away. Sleek contemporary design and international cuisine combine happily and economically here. ⊠ *19 descente de la Halle aux Poissons* ☎ *05–34–31–94–84* ▤ *AE, DC, MC, V* ☉ *Closed Jan. 1–13, Aug. 13–30, and Sun. No lunch Sat. and Mon.*

$–$$ ✕ **Au Bon Vivre.** This intimate bistro lined with tables with red-check tablecloths fills up at lunch and dinner every day. Quick, unpretentious, and always good, the house specialties include such dishes as roast monkfish in garlic, venison, and cassoulet. ⊠ *15 pl. Wilson* ☎ *05–61–23–07–17* ▤ *AE, DC, MC, V.*

★ ¢–$$ ✕ **La Corde.** This little hideaway is worth taking the time to find. Built into a lovely 15th-century corner tower hidden in the courtyard of the 16th-century Hôtel Bolé, La Corde claims the distinction of being the oldest restaurant in Toulouse. Try the *effiloché de canard aux pêches* (shredded duck with caramelized peach). ⊠ *4 rue Jules-Chalande* ☎ *05–61–29–09–43* ▤ *AE, DC, MC, V* ☉ *Closed Sun. No lunch Mon.*

¢–$ ✕ **Chez Paloma.** Go ahead and order the foie gras, the sole *meuniére,* the grilled pigeon, or the delicious duck *à l'orange*—this is the spot for classic *cuisine du terroir,* but that doesn't mean they don't do a mean vegetable, lushly roasted in garlic, steamed still crisp, or fresh with a side of tangy sauce. Everything is homemade including the bread and the pastries, *and* the prices are delicious, too. ⊠ *54 rue Peyroliers* ☎ *05–61–21–76–50* ▤ *AE, DC, MC, V* ☉ *Closed Sat. and Sun.*

★ $$$–$$$$ ▦ **Grand Hôtel de l'Opéra.** In a former 17th-century convent, this downtown doyen has an old-world feel with 21st-century amenities. Grandeur is the keynote in the lobby, complete with marble columns and Second Empire bergeres and sofas of tasseled velvet. Guest rooms are plush, with rich fabrics and painted headboards in many, while three restaurants range from provincial bistro to international gourmet (⇨ Jardins de l'-Opera, *above*). Even though you're on busy place du Capitole, this hotel is a tranquil oasis. ⊠ *1 pl. du Capitole, 31000* ☎ *05–61–21–82–66* 📠 *05–61–23–41–04* ⊕ *www.grand-hotel-opera.com* ➷ *57 rooms* ♿ *Café, minibars, cable TV, pool, health club, bar, meeting rooms, parking (fee)* ▤ *AE, DC, MC, V* ❙◯❙ *EP.*

★ **$$$–$$$$** 🖭 **Hôtel des Capitouls.** In the thick of the most Toulousain part of town, next to the Pont Neuf and the former fish market, this cozy place has small but tasteful rooms; the best suite has a view of the Garonne. The staff is cheery and helpful. ⊠ *22 descente de la Halle aux Poissons, 31000* 🕾*05–34–31–94–80* 🖶*05–34–31–94–81* ⊕*www.hotelsdecharmetoulouse. com* 🛏️ *14 rooms* ⚷ *Minibars, cable TV, parking (fee)* ⊟ *AE, DC, MC, V* ⍩⊙⍵ *EP.*

$ 🖭 **Hôtel Albert I.** The building may seem undistinguished and the reception hall is no Versailles, but the rooms are cheerful and spacious (especially the older ones with giant fireplaces and mirrors). The extremely warm and personable owner, Madame Hilaire, is on hand to give suggestions of all kinds. A Continental breakfast is served, and nearby parking can be arranged by the hotel. ⊠ *8 rue Rivals, 31000* 🕾 *05–61–21–17–91* 🖶 *05–61–21–09–64* 🛏️ *50 rooms* ⚷ *Cable TV, parking (fee), some pets allowed (fee)* ⊟ *AE, DC, MC, V* ⍩⊙⍵ *EP.*

¢–$ 🖭 **Grand Hôtel d'Orléans.** This picturesque former stagecoach relay station was built in 1867 and still retains a certain 19th-century charm. Four floors of wooden balustrades overhung with plants look down over a central patio. Guest rooms are small but cozy. ⊠ *72 rue Bayard, near Matabiau railroad station, 31000* 🕾 *05–61–62–98–47* 🖶 *05–61–62–78–24* 🛏️ *56 rooms* ⚷ *Restaurant, cable TV, parking (fee), some pets allowed (fee)* ⊟ *AE, DC, MC, V* ⍩⊙⍵ *EP.*

Nightlife & the Arts

For a schedule of events, contact the city tourist office. If you want to stay up late—as many do in Toulouse—a complete list of clubs and discos can be found in the weekly *Toulouse Pratique,* available at any newsstand. As for cultural highlights, so many opera singers perform at the **Théâtre du Capitole** and the **Halle aux Grains** that the city is known as the *capitale du bel canto.* The opera season lasts from October until late May, with occasional summer presentations as well. A wide variety of dance companies perform in Toulouse: the **Ballet du Capitole** stages classical ballets; **Ballet-Théâtre Joseph Russilo** and **Compagnie Jean-Marc Matos** put on modern-dance performances. The **Centre National Chorégraphique de Toulouse** welcomes international companies each year in the St-Cyprien quarter.

The most exciting music venue in Toulouse is the auditorium-in-the-round **Halle Aux Grains** (⊠ Pl. Dupuy 🕾 05–61–63–18–65). **Théâtre du Capitole** (⊠ Pl. du Capitole 🕾 05–61–23–21–35) is the orchestra, opera, and ballet specialist. **Théâtre Daniel Sorano** (⊠ 35 allée Jules-Guesde 🕾 05–61–25–66–87) stages dramatic productions and concerts. **Théâtre de la Digue** (⊠ 3 rue de la Digue 🕾 05–61–42–97–79) is a theater and dance venue. **Théâtre du Taur** (⊠ 69 rue du Taur 🕾 05–61–21–77–13) puts on theatrical productions of every stripe and spot.

For general carousing and carrying on, the **Bagamoyo** (⊠27 rue des Couteliers 🕾 05–62–26–11–36) is a lively spot for nocturnal snacks of simple but delicious African fare. **Bar Basque** (⊠ 7 pl. St-Pierre 🕾 05–61–21–55–64) is one of the many good watering holes around place St-Pierre. **Le Bistro à Vins** (⊠ 5 rue Riguepels 🕾 05–61–25–20–41), near the Cathedral of St-Étienne, is a hot spot for the third-Thursday-in-November Beaujolais Nouveau blowout. Brazilian guitarists perform at **La Bonita** (✉ 112 Grand-Rue St-Michel ☎ 05–62–26–36–45). For jazz, try **Le Café des Allées** (✉ 64 allée Charles-de-Fitte ☎ 05–62–27–14–46), a hothouse for local musicians. Be sure to stop by the top jazz spot **Le Mandela** (✉ 23 rue des Aminodiers ☎ 05–61–21–10–05) for a bit of the bubbly and some of the best jazz in town. **Café Le Griot** (✉ 34 rue des Blanchers ☎ 05–62–36–41–56) features a number of American duos and trios.

At **El Mexicano** (✉ 37 rue de l'Industrie ☎ 05–61–63–17–36) a crush of people inhales tequila and 3-inch-thick steaks. **La Péniche** (✉ Canal de Brienne, 90 allée de Barcelone ☎ 05–61–21–13–40) is a local gay bar. Begin your night on the town at **Père Louis** (✉ 45 rue des Tourneurs ☎ 05–61–21–33–45), an old-fashioned winery (and restaurant), with barrels used as tables plus vintage photographs. **Puerto Habana** (✉ 12 port St-Étienne ☎ 05–61–54–45–61) is the place for salsa music. If you're looking for onion soup and other treats in the wee hours, head for **St-André** (✉ 39 rue St-Rome ☎ 05–61–22–56–37), open from 7 PM to dawn (closed Sunday). Local glitterati and theater stars go to **L'Ubu** (✉ 16 rue St-Rome ☎ 05–61–23–97–80), the city's top nightspot for 20 years.

Shopping

Toulouse is a chic design outlet for clothing and artifacts of all kinds. **Rue St-Rome, rue Croix Baragnon, rue des Changes,** and **rue d'Alsace-Lorraine** are all good shopping streets.

ALBI & THE GERS

Along the banks of the Tarn to the northeast of Toulouse is Albi, Toulouse's rival in rose colors. West from Albi, along the river, the land opens up to the rural Gers *département,* home of the heady brandy Armagnac and heart of the former dukedom of Gascony. Studded with châteaux—from simple medieval fortresses to ambitious classical residences—and with tiny, isolated villages, the Gers is an easy place to fall in love with, or in.

Albi

★ ㉕ *75 km (47 mi) northeast of Toulouse.*

Toulouse-Lautrec's native Albi is a well-preserved and busy provincial market town. In its heyday, Albi was a major center for the Cathars, members of a dualistic and ascetic religious movement critical of the hierarchical and worldly ways of the Catholic Church. Pick up a copy of the excellent visitor booklet (in English) from the **tourist office** (✉ Pl. Ste-Cécile ☎ 05–63–49–48–80 ⊕ www.mairie-albi.fr), and follow the walking tours—of the *Vieille Ville* (Old City), the old ramparts, and the banks of the River Tarn.

Fodor'sChoice   One of the most unusual and dazzling churches in France, the huge **Cathé-
★   drale Ste-Cécile,** with its intimidating clifflike walls, resembles a cross

between a castle and an ocean liner. It was constructed as a symbol of the Church's return to power after the 13th-century crusade that wiped out the Cathars. The interior is an astonishingly ornate contrast to the massive austerity of the outer walls. Maestro Donnelli and a team of 16th-century Italian artists (most of the Emilian school) covered every possible surface with religious scenes and brightly colored patterns—it remains the largest group of Italian Renaissance paintings in a French church. The most striking fresco is a 15th-century depiction of the Last Judgment, on the west wall, just below one of the most splendid organs in the world, built in 1734 and outfitted with 3,500 pipes. ⊠ *Pl. Ste-Cécile* ☎ *05–63–43–23–43* ◷ *June–Sept., daily 9–6:30; Oct.–May, daily 9–noon and 2–6.*

Fodor'sChoice The **Musée Toulouse-Lautrec** occupies the **Palais de la Berbie** (Berbie ★ Palace), set between the cathedral and the Pont Vieux (Old Bridge) in a garden designed by the famed André Le Nôtre (creator of the famous "green geometries" at Versailles). Built in 1265, the fortress was transformed in 1905 into a museum to honor Albi's most famous son, Belle Epoque painter Henri de Toulouse-Lautrec (1864–1901). Toulouse-Lautrec left Albi for Paris in 1882, and soon became famous for his colorful and tumultuous evocations of the lifestyle of bohemian glamour found in and around Montmartre. Son of a wealthy and aristocratic family (Lautrec is a town not far from Toulouse), the young Henri suffered from a genetic bone deficiency and broke both legs as a child, which stunted his growth. The artist's fascination with the decadent side of life led to an early grave at the age of 37 and Hollywood immortalization in the 1954 John Huston film *Moulin Rouge.* With more than 1,000 of the artist's works, the Albi exhibit is the country's largest Toulouse-Lautrec collection. There are other masterworks here, including paintings by Georges de la Tour and Francesco Guardi. ⊠ *Just off pl. Ste-Cécile* ☎ *05–63–49–48–70* ⊠ *€4.50, guided tour €8.50, gardens free* ◷ *June, daily 9–noon and 2–6; July and Aug., daily 9–6; Sept., daily 9–noon and 2–6; Oct.–Mar., daily 10–noon and 2–5; Apr. and May, daily 10–noon and 2–6.*

From the central square and parking area in front of the Palais de la Berbie, walk to the 11th- to 15th-century college and **Cloître de St-Salvy** (⊠ Rue Ste-Cécile). Next, visit Albi's finest restored traditional house, the **Maison du Vieil Albi** (Old Albi House; ⊠ Corner of Rue de la Croix-Blanche and Puech-Bérenguer). If you're a real fan of Toulouse-Lautrec, you might view his birthplace, the **Maison Natale de Toulouse-Lautrec** (⊠ 14 rue Henri de Toulouse-Lautrec), although there are no visits to the house, the Hôtel Bosc, which remains a private residence. Rue de l'Hôtel de Ville, two streets west of the Maison Natale, leads past the Mairie (City Hall), with its hanging globes of flowers, to Albi's main square, **place du Vigan.** Take a break in one of the two main cafés, Le Pontie or Le Vigan.

Where to Stay & Eat

$–$$$ ✕ **Le Jardin des Quatre Saisons.** A good-value menu and superb fish dishes are the reasons for this restaurant's excellent reputation. Chef-owner Georges Bermond's house specialties include mussels baked with leeks and *suprême de sandre* (a freshwater fish cooked in wine), and change with *les saisons.* ✉ *19 bd. de Strasbourg* ☎ *05–63–60–77–76* ⊟ *AE, MC, V* ☺ *Closed Mon. No dinner Sun.*

$–$$$ ✕ **Le Moulin de la Mothe.** Set at the foot of Albi Cathedral, this onetime mill on the bank of the Tarn is consequently surrounded by lush vegetation. Chef-owner Michel Pellaprat specializes in inventive cooking *à l'albigeoise*—his hare sausage in beetroot vinaigrette is sublime—based on high-quality products of the Tarn region. ✉ *Rue de la Mothe* ☎ *05–63–60–38–15* ⊟ *AE, MC, V* ☺ *Closed Feb. No dinner Sun. (except July–Aug.) or Tues. Sept. 15–Apr. 30.*

$$–$$$ ✕⊡ **Hostellerie St-Antoine.** Founded in 1734, this hotel in the center of town is one of the oldest in France. Run by the same family for five generations, this lineage is attested to by the presence of some Toulouse-Lautrec sketches given to the owner's great-grandfather, a friend of the painter. Modern renovations have made it eminently comfortable. Room 30 has a pleasing view of the garden; pristine white furnishings give it a spacious feel. The superb restaurant serves classic Gallic cuisine, such as *foie gras de canard* (duck liver) and saddle of hare with a foie gras–based sauce. ✉ *15 rue St-Antoine, 81000* ☎ *05–63–54–04–04* 🖶 *05–63–47–10–47* ⊕ *www.saint-antoine-albi.com* ⬎ *43 rooms* ☖ *Restaurant, minibars, cable TV, meeting rooms, parking (fee)* ⊟ *AE, DC, MC, V* ¶⊙¶ *EP.*

$–$$ ✕⊡ **Hôtel Chiffre.** A former stagecoach inn, this centrally located town house has impeccable rooms overlooking a cozy garden. The restaurant serves hearty regional cuisine such as pigeon stuffed with mushrooms or trout with spicy cabbage. ✉ *50 rue Séré-de-Rivières, 81000* ☎ *05–63–48–58–48* 🖶 *05–63–47–20–61* ⊕ *www.hotelchiffre.com* ⬎ *36 rooms* ☖ *Restaurant, minibars, cable TV, meeting rooms, parking (fee)* ⊟ *AE, DC, MC, V* ¶⊙¶ *EP.*

¢ ⊡ **Le George V.** This little in-town B&B is near the cathedral and the train station. Each room is unique, and the garden makes for a pleasant retreat in summer. ✉ *29 av. Maréchal-Joffre, 81000* ☎ *05–63–54–24–16* 🖶 *05–63–49–90–78* ⬎ *9 rooms* ☖ *Café, some pets allowed (fee); no a/c* ⊟ *AE, DC, MC, V* ¶⊙¶ *EP.*

Shopping

Around **place Ste-Cécile** are numerous clothing, book, music, and antiques shops. The finest foie gras in town is found at **Albi Foie Gras** (✉ 29 rue Mariès ☎ 05–63–38–21–23). **L'Artisan Chocolatier** (✉ 4 rue Dr-Camboulives, on pl. du Vigan ☎ 05–63–38–95–33) is famous for its chocolate.

Albi has many **produce markets:** one takes place Tuesday through Sunday in the market halls near the cathedral; another is held on Sunday morning on place Ste-Cécile. A Saturday-morning **flea and antiques market** (✉ Pl. du Castelviel) is held in the Halle du Castelviel.

Cordes-sur-Ciel

26 *25 km (15 mi) northwest of Albi, 80 km (50 mi) northeast of Toulouse.*

Fodor'sChoice
★ A must stop for all travelers, the picture-book hilltop village of Cordes-sur-Ciel, built in 1222 by Count Raymond VII of Toulouse, is one of

SEX, DEATH & THE CATHARS

SCORCHED BY THE SOUTHERN HEAT, the dusty ruins perched high atop cliffs in southern Laengeudoc were once the refuges of the Cathars, the notoriously ascetic religious group persecuted out of existence by the Catholic church in the 12th and 13th centuries. The Cathars inhabited the area from present-day Germany all the way to the Atlantic Ocean. Adherents to this dualistic doctrine of material abnegation and spiritual revelation abstained from fleshly pleasures in all forms—forgoing even procreation and the consumption of animal products. In some cases, they committed suicide by starvation; diminishing the amount of flesh in the world was the ultimate way to foil the forces of evil. However, not thrilled by a religion that did not "go forth and multiply" (and that saw no need to pay taxes to the church), Pope Innocent III launched the Albigensian Crusade (Albi was one of the major Cathar strongholds), and Pope Gregory IX rounded up the stragglers during a period of inquisition starting in 1233. These forces had been given scandalously free reign by the French court, who allowed dukes and counts from northern France to build fortified bastide towns through the area to subdue and entrap the peasantry. These counts were more than happy to oblige the pope with a little hounding, an inquisition or two, and some burnings at the stake—as long as forfeiture laws worked in favor of the inquisitor, not the inquisitee. Forthwith, entire towns were judged to be guilty of heresy and inhabitants were thrown by the dozens to their deaths from the high town walls. The persecuted "pure" soon took refuge in the Pyrénées mountains, where they survived for 100 years. Now that all that remains of this unhappy sect are their former hideouts, tour groups visit the vacant stone staircases and roofless chapels of places like Peyrepertuse and Quéribus. For more information (in French), log on to (⊕ www.cathares.org).

the most impressively preserved *bastides* (fortified medieval towns built along a strict grid plan) in France. When mists steal up from the Cérou Valley and enshroud the hillside, Cordes appears to hover in midair, hence its nickname, Cordes-sur-Ciel (Cordes-in-the-Sky/Heaven). Many of the restored medieval houses are occupied by artisans and craftspeople; the best crafts shops are found along the main street, Grande-Rue. The village's venerable covered market, supported by 24 octagonal stone pillars, is also noteworthy, as is the nearby well, which is more than 300 feet deep.

Where to Stay & Eat

★ $$$–$$$$ ✕⌨ **Le Grand Écuyer.** The dramatic hilltop setting of this hotel suits it well—it's a perfectly preserved Gothic mansion. Rooms have period furnishings; the best, Planol, Horizon, and Ciel, have grand views of the rolling countryside. Yves Thuriès is one of the region's best chefs and chocolatiers; sample his salmon and sole twist in vanilla or the guinea fowl supreme in pastry. Menus begin around €38 and culminate in a seven-course gourmet extravaganza that costs more than €72. ⊠ *Rue Voltaire, 81170* ☎ *05–63–53–79–50* 🖨 *05–63–53–79–51* ⊕ *www. thuries.fr* ⌨ *13 rooms* ♻ *Restaurant, minibars, cable TV, bar, some pets allowed (fee)* ▤ *AE, DC, MC, V* ☺ *Closed mid-Oct.–early Apr.* ⍾⌨ MAP.

¢–$ ✕⊡ **L'Hostellerie du Vieux Cordes.** This magnificent 13th-century house is built around a lovely courtyard dotted with tiny white tables and shaded by a 200-year-old wisteria. Guest rooms are richly decorated but not nearly as opulent as the vast crimson dining rooms (the restaurant is closed Monday from November to Easter and also the month of January). ⊠ *Rue St-Michel, 81170* ☎ *05–63–53–79–20* 🖷 *05–63–56–02–47* ⊕ *www.thuries.fr* ⇗ *21 rooms* ⚲ *Restaurant, minibars, cable TV; no a/c* ⊟ *AE, DC, MC, V* ⊗ *Closed Jan. 1–mid-Feb* ⦿ *EP.*

Montauban

🟤 *59 km (37 mi) west of Cordes-sur-Ciel, 55 km (33 mi) north of Toulouse.*

Montauban, built in 1144, was one of the first bastides in France. The town is best known as the birthplace of the great painter Jean-Auguste-Dominique Ingres (1780–1867), and is home to a superb collection of his works. The **Musée Ingres**, overlooking the Tarn River, is housed in what was originally the château of Edward the Black Prince (1330–76), who was briefly ruler of the English principality of Aquitaine. The château was later converted into a bishop's palace in the 17th century. Ingres has the second floor to himself; note the contrast between his love of myth (*Ossian's Dream*) and his deadpan, uncompromising portraiture (*Madame Gonse*). Ingres was the last of the great French Classicists, who favored line over color and used classical antiquity as a source for subject matter. However, Ingres fell out of favor with the strict Neoclassicists of his day as a result of his unusual combination of superb draftsmanship and sensuality. Later, artists such as Degas, Renoir, and Picasso acknowledged their debt to Ingres. Most paintings here are from Ingres's excellent private collection, ranging from his followers (Théodore Chassériau) and precursors (Jacques-Louis David) to Old Masters. ⊠ *19 rue de l'Hôtel de Ville* ☎ *05–63–22–12–92* ▦ *€4* ⊗ *July and Aug., Mon.–Sat. 9:30–noon and 1:30–6, Sun. 1:30–6; Sept.–June, Tues.–Sat. 10–noon and 2–6.*

FodorśChoice
★

Beyond the Musée Ingres, there are several other notable sights in town. The 14th-century **Pont Vieux** (Old Bridge), with its seven pointed arches, is another of Montauban's attractions. A chapel dedicated to St. Catherine, protector of mariners (Montauban had some 3,000 river men during the 18th century), used to stand on the fourth piling until it was uprooted and washed away by a flood in 1766. In the 12th-century arcaded and brick-vaulted **place National,** in the center of Montauban, look for the simple wooden cross marking the medieval execution and pillory site (it's in front of the Brasserie des Arts, a good spot for lunch or coffee). Note the sundial on the north side of the square with its carpe diem inscription UNA TIBI ("one for you"—meaning, your hour will come). Markets are held on the square almost every day; Wednesday markets are held across the river on place Lalaque. The **Hôtel Lefranc-de-Pompignon** is a classic 17th- to 18th-century *portail monumentale* (monumental entryway) just north of the Église St-Jacques. One of Montauban's architectural gems, this redbrick portico with its wrought-iron grille announced the residence of M. Lefranc-de-Pompignon (whose unsuccessful tenure at Paris's Royal Academy was once mocked by Voltaire). ⊠ *Rue Armand Cambon s/n.*

The mid-13th-century **Église St-Jacques** (⊠ Pl. Victor Hugo), with its Toulouse-style steeple, is a dark, single-nave church of austere dignity. The 17th- to 18th-century **Notre-Dame Cathedral** (⊠ Pl. Franklin Roosevelt) was built of white stone to contrast with the city's predominant redbrick architecture and to proclaim Catholicism's triumph over Protestantism. On display here is an Ingres masterpiece, poorly illuminated. *The Vow of Louis XIII.*

Where to Stay & Eat

$$-$$$ ✕ **Les Saveurs d'Ingres.** Cyril Paysserand's *cuisine d'auteur* is some of the best fare in the area, served in a graceful vaulted dining room in midtown Montauban, just a few doors up from the Ingres Museum. Not unlike Ingres himself, Paysserand sticks with the classical canons prepared in novel and sensual ways. If you've maxed out on cassoulet and web-footed fare in general, try the frogs' legs here or the *bécasse* (woodcock) in season for a welcome change of pace. ⊠ *13 rue de l'Hôtel de Ville* ☎ *05–63–91–26–42* ⊟ *AE, DC, MC, V* ☺ *Closed Sun. and Mon.*

$$ ⌨ **Hôtel du Midi–Mercure.** The Hôtel du Midi combines old-world elegance with modern comforts. A plaque on the hotel's facade attests that Manuel Azaña, last president of the Spanish Republic, died here in exile in 1940. ⊠ *12 rue Notre-Dame, 82000* ☎ *05–63–63–17–23* 🖷 *05–63–66–43–66* ⊕ *www.accor.hotel.fr* ⤳ *44 rooms* ⌂ *Restaurant, minibars, cable TV, bar, parking (fee), some pets allowed (fee)* ⊟ *AE, DC, MC, V* ⑩ *EP.*

Moissac

❷⓼ *29 km (18 mi) west of Montauban, 72 km (45 mi) northwest of Toulouse.*

Moissac has both the region's largest (and most beautiful) Romanesque cloisters and one of its most remarkable abbey churches. The port—at the confluence of the Tarn, Aveyron, and Garonne rivers, and the lateral canal—is a surprising sight so far from the sea. For a spectacular view over this Mississippi-like riverine expanse, France's widest, head to the lookout point at Boudou, 2 km (1 mi) west of Moissac off route N113.

★ Fronted by a magnificent Romanesque sculpted portal that depicts in stone Book 4 of the Apocalypse, the **Abbaye St-Pierre** was founded in the 7th century by Saint Didier, bishop of Cahors, and bears traces of many settlers of the region, Arabs to Normans to Magyars. Little is left of the original abbey, and subsequent religious wars laid waste to its 11th-century replacement. Today's abbey, dating mostly from the 15th century, narrowly escaped demolition early in the 20th century when the Bordeaux-Sète railroad was rerouted within feet of the cloisters. Each of the 76 capitals has a unique pattern of animals, geometric motifs, and religious or historical scenes. Look for the Cain and Abel story on the 19th column to the right of the entry point. The 63rd column (fourth back from the northeast corner) shows St-Sernin being dragged to his death by a bull. On the famed Apocalypse south portal, carved in the

12th century, the representation of a sweetly mournful Jeremiah (author of the Old Testament Book of Lamentations), on the lower part of the door, is especially noteworthy. The **Musée des Arts et Traditions Populaires** (Folk Art Museum), in the abbey, contains regional treasures and a room of local costumes. ⊠ *6 bis rue de l'Abbaye* ☎ *05–63–04–05–73* 🖾 *Cloisters and museum €5* ⊘ *Oct.–Mar., Tues.–Sun. 9–noon and 2–5; Apr.–June and Sept., Tues.–Sun. 9–noon and 2–6; July and Aug., Tues.–Sun. 9–noon and 2–7.*

Where to Stay & Eat

★ ¢–$$ ✕🖾 **Le Pont Napoléon.** One of France's rising culinary stars, Michel Dussau, who trained with Alain Ducasse (and others), is a master of refined simplicity and innovative combinations of regional products. Try such dishes as scallops with chestnut-flour pasta or foie gras *pôelé* (sautéed goose liver), and anything made with Moissac's *chasselas* grape (the restaurant is closed Sunday dinner, Monday lunch, and Wednesday). Guest rooms are furnished with elegant, authentic amenities; some have lovely views of the Tarn and the bridge. ⊠ *2 allées Montebello, 82200* ☎ *05–63–04–01–55* 🖨 *05–63–04–34–44* ⊕ *www.canalalaune.fr* 🛏 *12 rooms ⚭ Restaurant, cable TV, bar* ⊟ *AE, DC, MC, V* ⊘ *Closed Jan. 5–20* ⍿⊘ *EP.*

Auvillar

㉙ *23 km (14 mi) west of Moissac.*

Officially classified as one of France's most beautiful villages, Auvillar is centered on its gorgeous, covered **Halle aux Grains** (Grain Market), a circular structure built in 1825. Most other buildings in the town are equally lovely, including the stone-and-brick **Tour de l'Horloge** (Clock Tower), now connected to the town's only hotel, the 18th-century brick-and-beam **Maison des Consuls** (Consuls' House), once the local magistrate's home.

Where to Stay & Eat

¢–$ ✕🖾 **L'Horloge.** This cozy spot next to (and named for) Auvillar's trademark clock tower is the town's de facto hub and nerve center. The restaurant is a combination brasserie, le Bouchon, and full-scale dining establishment all in one, with menus and *formules* for all tastes and tendencies. The rooms are modest and intimate, and Madame Martigue and her staff are warm and welcoming. ⊠ *Pl. de l'Horloge, 82340* ☎ *05–63–39–91–61* 🖨 *05–63–39–75–20* 🛏 *10 rooms ⚭ Restaurant, café, bar; no a/c* ⊘ *Closed Dec. 16–Jan. 19. No lunch Fri. and Sat. mid-Oct.–mid-Apr.* ⊟ *AE, DC, MC, V* ⍿⊘ *MAP.*

Lectoure

㉚ *57 km (35 mi) southwest of Moissac, 94 km (58 mi) northwest of Toulouse.*

Once a Roman city and a fortified Gallic town, Lectoure stands on a promontory above the Gers Valley in the heart of the former dukedom of Gascony. Lectoure was ravaged in 1473 when Louis XI attacked its fortress and established direct royal rule by killing the last count of Armagnac, but there's still plenty to see in its old arched streets. The 13th-century **Fontaine Diane** (Diana Fountain; ⊠ Rue Fontélie) is the town's most interesting monument, as well as a visual feast. The 15th- to 16th-century **Cathédrale St-Gervais et St-Protais** (⊠ Pl. de la Cathédrale) is an enormous structure for a town of this size and an immense trove of art and architecture.

The **Musée Municipal** (Town Museum), near the cathedral, is in the vaulted cellars of the former **Palais Épiscopal** (Bishop's Palace), now the Town Hall. It contains an array of 2,000-year-old Gallo-Roman arti-facts ranging from tweezers and hairbrushes to Latin-engraved pre-Christian altars and heads of sacrificial bulls. Ask about the sculpture of Priapus, god of fertility, and what happened to his allegedly heroic virility. ⊠ *Pl. de la Cathédrale, in the Hôtel de Ville* ☎ *05–62–68–70–22* ▨ *€3* ☉ *Wed.–Mon., 10–noon and 2–6.*

Where to Stay & Eat

★ **$–$$** ✕▦ **Hôtel de Bastard.** This elegant hotel and restaurant on an 18th-century estate is the creation of chef Jean-Luc Arnaud and his wife, Anne (who speaks excellent English). The rooms, although not spacious, are modern and comfortable and have fine views over the fields. The in-novative cuisine is prepared with fresh local produce; try *il était trois foies,* foie gras prepared three ways—raw, steamed, and grilled—all with herbs and vegetables. ⊠ *Rue Lagrange, 32700* ☎ *05–62–68–82–44* 🖷 *05–62–68–76–81* ⊕ *www.hotel-de-bastard.com* ⤴ *29 rooms* ⚘ *Restaurant, cable TV, pool, bar, some pets allowed (fee); no a/c* ▤ *AE, DC, MC, V* ☉ *Closed Dec. 18–Feb. 1* ⎮◯⎮ *EP.*

Auch

❸❶ *24 km (14 mi) south of Fleurance, 77 km (46 mi) west of Toulouse, 73 km (44 mi) northeast of Tarbes.*

Auch, the capital of the Gers département, is best known for its stun-ning Gothic **Cathédrale de Ste-Marie.** Most of the stained-glass windows in the choir were done by Arnaud de Moles; vividly colorful, they por-tray biblical figures and handsome pre-Christian sibyls, or prophetesses. The oak choir stalls are intricately carved with more than 1,500 bibli-cal and mythological figures that took 50 years and three generations of artisans to complete. In June, classical music concerts are held here. ⊠ *Pl. Salinis* ▨ *€4* ☉ *Daily 8–noon and 2–6.*

On the first floor of the 15th-century brick and wood-beam Maison Fedel, on the other side of the cathedral, is the **tourist office** (⊠ 1 rue Dessoles), where you can obtain maps and information.

Across place Salinis is a terrace overlooking the Gers River. A monu-mental flight of 370 steps leads down to the riverbank. Halfway down is the **Statue of D'Artagnan,** the musketeer immortalized by Alexandre Dumas. Although Dumas set the action of his historical novel *The Three Musketeers* in the 1620s, the true D'Artagnan—Charles de Batz—was born in 1620, probably in Castlemore, near Lupiac, and did not become a musketeer until 1645.

Off place Salinis, in a wood-beam and brick house known as the **Maison d'Henri IV** (⊠ 32 rue d'Espagne), the French and Navarran monarch is said to have cavorted with several of his 57 mistresses. A left at the end of rue d'Espagne will take you through one of the *pousterles*, steep and narrow alleys leading up from the river.

The **Musée des Jacobins,** behind the former Archbishop's Palace (now the Préfecture), has a fine collection of Latin-American art, pre-Columbian pottery, and Gallo-Roman relics. Look for the white-marble epitaph dedicated by a grief-stricken Roman mistress to her dog Myia, for whose *"douces morcures"* ("sweet love bites") she mourned. ⊠ *Rue Daumesnil* ☎ *05–62–05–74–79* ⛉ *€4* ☙ *May–Oct., Tues.–Sun. 10–noon and 2–6; Nov.–Apr., Tues.–Sat. 10–noon and 2–5.*

Where to Stay & Eat

★ ¢–$ ✕ **Café Gascon.** This ramshackle and romantic little spot is right over the Halles aux Herbes. The fare is typical country Gascon with innovative personal touches such as the *salade folle* (duck prepared three different ways, with apples, tomatoes, and raspberries on lettuce). Chef, poet, and painter Georges Nosella is likely to come out to your table and serve your *café gascon* (coffee, whipped cream, and flaming Armagnac) with grace and humor. ⊠ *5 rue Lamartine* ☎ *05–62–61–88–08* ⊟ *MC, V* ☙ *Closed Sun. during Sept.–June, closed Mon. during July–Aug.*

★ $$–$$$ ✕🏨 **Hôtel de France.** Roland Garreau's gourmet restaurant, Le Jardin des Saveurs, is an institution at this classic central Auch hotel; his specialty is the reduction or lighter interpretation of traditional country cooking. The duplex suite behind the circular dormer window on the facade facing the square is worth a look, if not occupied, even if you resist the temptation to spend the €350 it costs to sleep there. Other rooms are cozy, if a bit small and overly fabric-filled. ⊠ *Pl. de la Libération, 32000* ☎ *05–62–61–71–71* 🖶 *05–62–61–71–81* ⊕ *www.auchgarreau. com* ⥯ *29 rooms* ⚭ *Restaurant, cable TV, bar, shop, parking (fee)* ⊟ *AE, DC, MC, V* ⛿ *MAP.*

Shopping

Caves de l'Hôtel de France (⊠ Rue d'Étigny) sells a wide selection of Armagnac.

LANGUEDOC-ROUSSILLON

A region immortalized by Matisse and Picasso, Languedoc-Roussillon extends along the southern Mediterranean coast of France to the Pyrénées. Draw a line between Toulouse and Narbonne: the area to the south down to the Pyrénées, long dominated by the House of Aragón, the ruling family of adjacent Catalonia, is known as the Roussillon. Inland, the area, with its dry climate, is virtually one huge vineyard. The Canal du Midi flows through the region to **Le Littoral Languedocien** (the Languedoc Coast). Beaches stretch down the coast to Cerebère at the Spanish border. This strip is known as the Côte Vermeille (Vermilion Coast) and attracts droves of European sunworshippers even though the beaches are rocky. The farther south you go, the stronger the Spanish influence. Heading northward, the Languedoc region begins around Narbonne and extends to the region's hub, the elegant city of Montpellier. All in all, the Languedoc-Roussillon is one of the most idyllic regions in France. Life here—even in such cities as Béziers or Perpignan, the urban heart of the region—is distinctly relaxed and friendly. You'll probably be taking afternoon *siestes* (naps) before you know it.

Carcassonne

③② *88 km (55 mi) southeast of Toulouse, 105 km (65 mi) south of Albi.*

★ Set atop a hill overlooking lush green countryside and the Aude River, Carcassonne is a medieval town that looks lifted from the pages of a storybook—literally, perhaps, as its circle of towers and battlements (comprising the longest city walls in Europe) is said to be the setting for Charles Perrault's classic tale *Puss in Boots.* The oldest sections of the walls, built by the Romans in the 1st century AD, were later enlarged, in the 5th century, by the Visigoths. Charlemagne once set siege to the settlement in the 9th century, only to be outdone by one Dame Carcas, a clever woman who boldly fed the last of the city's wheat to a pig in full view of the conqueror; Charlemagne, thinking this indicated endless food supplies, promptly decamped, and the exuberant townsfolk named their city after her. During the 13th century, Louis IX (St. Louis) and his son Philip the Bold strengthened Carcassonne's fortifications—so much so that the town became considered inviolable by marauding armies and was duly nicknamed "the virgin of Languedoc." A town that can never be taken in battle is often abandoned, however, and for centuries thereafter Carcassonne remained under a Sleeping Beauty spell. It was only awakened during the mid-19th-century craze for chivalry and the Gothic style, when, in 1835, the historic-monument inspector (and poet) Prosper Mérimée arrived. He was so appalled by the dilapidated state of the walls he commissioned the painter and historian Viollet-le-Duc (who found his greatest fame restoring Paris's Notre-Dame) to restore the town. Today the 1844 renovation is considered almost as much a work of art as the medieval town itself. No matter if the town is more Viollet than authentic medieval, it still remains one of the most romantic sights in France.

The town is divided by the river into two parts—La Cité, the fortified upper town, and the lower, newer city (the *ville basse*), known simply as Carcassonne. Unless you are staying at a hotel in the upper town, you are not allowed to enter it with your car; you must park in the lot (€2) across the road from the drawbridge. Be aware that the train station is in the lower town, which means either a cab ride, a 45-minute walk up to La Cité, or a ride on the *navette* shuttle bus. Plan on spending at least a couple of hours exploring the walls and peering over the battlements across sun-drenched plains toward the distant Pyrénées. Once inside the walls of the upper town, a florid carousel announces that 21st-century tourism is about to take over. The streets are lined with souvenir shops, crafts boutiques, restaurants, and tiny "museums" (i.e., a Cathars Museum, a Hat Museum), all out to make a buck and rarely worth that. Staying overnight within the ancient walls lets you savor the timeless atmosphere after the daytime hordes are gone.

The 12th-century **Château Comtal** is the last inner bastion of Carcassonne. It has a drawbridge and a museum, the **Musée Lapidaire,** where stone sculptures found in the area are on display. ☎ *04–68–11–70–77* ✉ €5 ⊙ *June–Sept., daily 9–6; Oct.–May, daily 9–noon and 2–5.*

The best part about the ville basse, built between the Aude and the Canal du Midi, is the **Musée des Beaux-Arts** (Fine Arts Museum). It houses a nice collection of porcelain, 17th- and 18th-century Flemish paintings, and works by local artists—including some stirring battle scenes by Jacques Gamelin (1738–1803). ✉ *Rue Verdun* ☎ *04–68–77–73–70* ✉ *Free* ⊙ *Nov.–June, Mon.–Sat. 10–noon and 2–6; July and Aug., daily 9–6.*

Where to Stay & Eat

$–$$ ✕ **Le Languedoc.** This restaurant in the ville basse serves up light versions of the region's specialties, from confit to game. In summer the flowery patio is a perfect spot for a long evening dinner. Be sure to try the quail with foie gras, if available. ✉ *32 allée d'Iéna* ☎ *04–68–25–22–17* ▤ *MC, V* ⊙ *Closed mid-Dec.–mid-Jan. and Mon. No dinner Sun. July–Oct.*

$$$$ ✕▦ **Hôtel de la Cité.** Set within the walled upper town, this is *the* spot for celebrities in Carcassonne. This ivy-covered former episcopal palace offers creature comforts the ascetic Cathars would have hated. Afternoon tea is in the library or rotunda lounge with its antique-tile floors, detailed woodwork, and leaded windows (with storybook views). Dining in the sumptuous La Barbacane restaurant—all double-vaulted ceiling, ogival windows, and agate-green walls—is an event. For more casual fare, try the brasserie Chez Saskia or, in summer, the bistro outside on a charmingly cobbled square. A pool, set like a sapphire in the garden, beckons on hot days. ✉ *Pl. de l'Église, 11000 La Cité de Carcassonne* ☎ *04–68–71–98–71* 🖷 *04–68–71–50–15* ⊕ *www.hoteldelacite.orient-express.com* ⇆ *66 rooms* ♨ *2 restaurants, minibars, cable TV, pool, meeting rooms, parking (fee)* ▤ *AE, DC, MC, V* ⊙ *Closed Dec.–mid-Jan.* ⦿ *EP.*

★ **$$–$$$$** ✕▦ **Domaine d'Auriac.** Former rugby star and present star-chef Bernard Rigaudis and his family maintain a countrified atmosphere in this elegant 19th-century manor house southwest of Carcassonne. Room prices vary according to size and view; the largest look out onto a magnificent park and vineyards. Next to a terrace planted with mulberry trees, the restaurant, famed as one of the best in the area, offers superlative Languedoc cuisine; enjoy the Provençal-style salon festooned with copper pots while savoring truffled pigeon, John Dory in blueberry wine, and game dishes, in season, accompanied by rare regional vintages. ✉ *Rte. de St-Hilaire 4 km (2½ mi) southwest of Carcassonne, 11330 Auriac* ☎ *04–68–25–72–22* 🖷 *04–68–47–35–54* ⊕ *www.relaischateaux.fr* ⇆ *26 rooms* ♨ *Restaurant, golf course, tennis court, pool, bar* ▤ *AE, MC, V* ⊙ *Closed Jan., Apr. 27–May 5, Nov. 16–25* ⦿ *MAP.*

$$$ ▦ **Château de Garrevaques.** With a florid Roussillon-ochre facade and set equidistant (50 km [31 mi]) from Toulouse, Carcassonne, and Albi, this retreat makes a particularly apt base camp for exploring the region, the more so since the current châtelaines are the 15th generation to call this home. Marie-Christine and Claude Combes receive guests with a friendly welcome amid family heirlooms. The only salon in truly baronial style is the main living room graced with a dazzling Zuber suite of *grisaille* (grey-and-white) hand-painted wallpaper panels depicting scenes of the Psyché and Cupid legend. Guest rooms are graced with period accents, stolid antiques, paisley fabrics, and some fetching 19th-century color schemes. The table d'hôte dinner is a good chance to sample the local country cooking. Since they have acres of private parkland to play with, the Combes opened (June 2004) a new section called the **Pavillon du Château,** with 15 rooms, two restaurants, and a spa, not reviewed yet at press time. ⊠ *5 km (3 mi) northwest of Revel, 81700 Garrevaques* ☏ *05–63–75–04–54* ⌂ *05–63–70–26–44* ⊕ *www.garrevaques. com* ⤶ *23 rooms, 1 suite* ⋄ *2 Restaurants, tennis court, pool, spa, billiards* ⊟ *AE, DC, MC, V* ⍝ *BP.*

$–$$ ⊞ **Hôtel Montségur.** With its ville basse location, this hotel is especially convenient. Rooms on the first two floors have Louis XV and Louis XVI furniture, some of it genuine; those above are more romantic, with gilt-iron bedsteads under sloping oak beams. ⊠ *27 allée d'Iéna, 11000* ☏ *04–68–25–31–41* ⌂ *04–68–47–13–22* ⤶ *21 rooms* ⋄ *Cable TV, bar, parking (fee), some pets allowed (fee)* ⊟ *AE, DC, MC, V* ⊙ *Closed mid-Dec.–mid-Jan.* ⍝ *EP.*

The Arts

Carcassonne hosts a major arts festival in July, with dance, theater, classical music, and jazz; for details, contact the **Théâtre Municipal** (⌕ B.P. 236, rue Courtejaire, 11005 ☏ 04–68–25–33–13, 04–68–77–71–26 reservations). The city usually goes medieval in mid-August with **Les Médiévales,** a festival of troubadour song, rich costumes, and jousting performances (some years the event isn't held; check with tourist office). The Bastille Day fireworks over La Cité are spectacular.

Mirepoix

㉝ *48 km (29 mi) southwest of Carcassonne, 88 km (53 mi) southeast of Toulouse, 35 km (22 mi) northeast of Foix.*

The 13th-century walled town of Mirepoix is in the heart of Cathar country. A good time to come here is during Mirepoix's Medieval Festival, always in July, when a historical procession is held on the third Sunday of the month. The town is built around the lovely, medieval main square, **place Général-Leclerc,** surrounded by 13th- to 15th-century houses with intricately carved timbers forming arcades or porticoes called *couverts.*

Where to Stay

★ $$ ⊞ **La Maison des Consuls.** This extraordinary 14th-century town-house hotel on the central square is a classified historic site. The 500-year-old carved timber gargoyles concentrated around the hotel facade make the exquisitely restored interior even more surprising. Each room is decorated in a different color, most with exposed beams. The Chambre de Dame Louise and the Chambre du Maréchal, both overlooking the square, are the best. ⊠ *Pl. des Couverts, 09500 Mirepoix* ☏ *05–61–68–81–81* ⌂ *05–61–68–81–15* ⊕ *www.pyrenevoyages.com*

⚡7 *rooms, 1 suite* ♿ *Parking (fee), some pets allowed (fee); no a/c* ▭*AE, DC, MC, V* ⦿ *EP.*

Foix

③④ *16 km (10 mi) north of Tarascon-sur-Ariège, 84 km (52 mi) south of Toulouse, 35 km (22 mi) southwest of Mirepoix, 138 km (86 mi) west of Perpignan.*

Nestled in the Ariège Valley, Foix is the capital of the Ariège département. Notice the fancy 19th-century administrative buildings south of avenue Fauré, the town's major thoroughfare. Now that you're in the thick of the Midi-Pyrénées, try to do some hiking. East of Foix is one of the best routes, the **Sentier Cathare** (Path of the Cathars)—a tough, 100-mi trail that takes you through a chain of cliff-side châteaux all the way to the Mediterranean. Pick up maps in Toulouse.

★ One of the leading postcard images of the area, the gigantic 12th-century **Château de Foix**, sitting impregnably on a promontory above the town and river, has three enormous towers reaching skyward like sentinels. The castle **museum** features archaeological finds and regional history, including the castle's earliest history as a Benedictine monastery, its later starring role in the Cathar wars, and its function as a redoubt for figures ranging from Saint Augustine to the blond and bold Count of Foix, Gaston Phoebus. Tours in French are offered on the hour, while there is one English tour scheduled daily at 1. ✉ *Rue Mercadal* ☎ *05–34–09–83–83* ⛁ €*4* ⊙ *July–Aug. daily 9:45–6:30; June and Sept. 9:45–noon and 2–6; Oct.–May Wed.-Sun. 10:30–noon and 2–5:30.*

A 5-km (3-mi) drive northwest from Foix along D1 leads to the **Rivière Souterraine de Labouiche** (Labouiche Subterranean River), a mysterious underground stream whose waters have tunneled a 5-km (3-mi) gallery through the limestone. The 75-minute boat trip covers a 1½-km (1-mi) stretch, past weirdly shaped, subtly lighted stalactites and stalagmites, ending at a subterranean waterfall. Dry land is 230 feet overhead. ☎ *05–61–65–04–11* ⛁ €*8* ⊙ *Apr.–mid-June and mid-Sept.–mid-Nov., daily 2–5; mid-June–mid-Sept., daily 10–noon and 2–5.*

Where to Stay & Eat

$ ✕ **Le Phoebus.** The views across the Ariège and over the Château de Foix, which once belonged to the illustrious Gaston Phoebus himself, the most famous of the counts of Foix, are superb. The Phoebus is known for game specialties in season and cuisine du terroir, such as *foie de canard mi-cuit* (half-cooked duck liver) and *rable de lièvre au poivrade* (hare in pepper sauce). ✉ *3 cours Irénée Cros* ☎ *05–61–65–10–42* ▭ *AE, DC, MC, V* ⊙ *Closed Mon. and mid-Feb.–mid-Mar. No lunch Sat.*

$ ✕⊡ **Audoye-Lons.** This former post house in the town center has comfortable, modernized rooms that vary in size. The restaurant is reasonably priced and overlooks the Ariège; it's closed Saturday in winter. ✉ *6 pl. Georges-Duthil, 09000* ☎ *05–61–65–52–44* ⊟ *05–61–02–68–18* ⚡ *39 rooms, 24 with bath or shower* ♿ *Restaurant, parking (fee)* ▭ *AE, DC, MC, V* ⊙ *Closed Dec. 20–Jan. 20* ⦿ *MAP.*

Tarascon-sur-Ariège

㉟ *16 km (10 mi) south of Foix.*

★ Tarascon is best known for its superb grotto and its collection of prehistoric art second only to that of Lascaux. As you enter Tarascon, veer left along D8 to the **Grotte de Niaux**, which contains scores of red-and-black Magdalenian rock paintings done in charcoal and iron oxide. Stylized horses, goats, deer, and bison, dating from about 20,000 BC, gallop around a naturally circular underground gallery (known as the Salon Noir, or Black Room) 1 km (½ mi) inside the entrance. Now that the famous caves at Lascaux in the Dordogne can be seen only in reproduction, this is the finest assembly of prehistoric art open to the public anywhere in France. Guided tours only; call ahead for reservations and to check schedule. ☎ *05–61–05–88–37* ✉ €9.60 ☉ *July–Sept., tours daily every 45 mins 8:30–11:30 and 1:30–5:15; Oct.–June, tours daily at 11, 3, and 4:30.*

Ax-les-Thermes

㊱ *26 km (15 mi) southeast of Tarascon-sur-Ariège, 104 km (64 mi) southwest of Carcassonne.*

A summer and winter resort town, Ax-les-Thermes has more than 80 mineral springs—at one, in the middle of town, you can often see local merchants on a coffee break or lunch hour reading the newspaper with trousers rolled to the knees and legs immersed. There are ski stations in Ax-Bonascre and Ascou-Pailhères, 5 km (3 mi) from town, and cross-country skiing is available at the Plateau de Beille and Domaine de Chioula, 10 km (6 mi) from town; for complete information, contact the **tourist office** (☎ 05–61–64–60–60). After a day of skiing, come back to Ax for a thermal hot bath—an unbeatable winter combination. Crisscrossing the surrounding heights are 400 km (248 mi) of hiking trails.

Font-Romeu

㊲ *75 km (45 mi) southeast of Ax-les-Thermes, 87 km (54 mi) southeast of Tarascon-sur-Ariège, 88 km (55 mi) southwest of Perpignan.*

In this high-altitude vacation spot, French Olympians trained for the Mexico City games of 1968. The views over the Cerdagne Valley from the balcony across from the tourist office should not be missed. Sports facilities include various ski lifts (one operates from the center of town), an ice rink, a riding school, a swimming pool, tennis courts, and a 9-hole golf course. As it is known for the sunniest slopes and best snow-making machines in the area, the skiing can get very crowded during peak Christmas and Easter vacation weekends. The **École de Ski Français** (☎ 04–68–30–03–74) is a local resource for sport fans.

Where to Stay & Eat

¢–$ ✕🏨 **Pyrénées.** This modern hotel perched above the Cerdagne Valley offers stunning views over the sunniest and widest highland space in the Pyrénées. A five-minute walk from the gondola ski lift up to the snow (or to hiking trails in summer), rooms are small but command unforgettable panoramas, and the hotel pool seems all but suspended over the valley. ✉ *Pl. des Pyrénées, 66120* ☎ *04–68–30–01–49* 🖷 *04–68–30–35–98* ⇔ *37 rooms* ⚹ *Restaurant, pool, sauna, bar; no a/c* ☰ *AE, DC, MC, V* ⊘ *Closed Apr. 21–May 30 and Oct.19–Dec.1* ⊠ *MAP.*

Sports & the Outdoors
For general advice and ski equipment in Font-Romeu, look for the knowledgeable and English-speaking Roy van der Groen at **Sport 2000** (✉ 102 av. Emmanuel Brousse ☎04–68–30–15–99 🖷04–68–30–09–34). For fly-fishing, contact **Marc Ribot** (✉ 6 impasse des Lutins ☎ 04–68–30–30–93 🖷 04–68–30–06–75), who can arrange for guides, equipment, and fly-fishing courses.

Eyne

❸❽ *12 km (7 mi) southeast of Font-Romeu, 5 km (3 mi) southwest of Mont-Louis.*

Eyne Village, with a grand total of zero in-town commercial establishments—not even a café or a bakery—is one of the purest and best-preserved villages remaining in the broad Pyrenean valley of the Cerdagne. There are archaeological walks to megalithic menhirs and dolmens, a ski station uphill (2 km [1 mi] away), and hiking trails to neighboring villages and thermal springs. Set below a nationally classified botanical park, the **Réserve Naturelle d'Eyne,** the town has been famous since the 17th century as the point where Atlantic and Mediterranean weather systems and vegetation converge. Information about the park can be obtained at the park headquarters and museum in Eyne Village. ☎ *04–68–04–08–05.*

Where to Stay & Eat
★ **$–$$** ✕⊡ **Cal Pai.** In a lovely old farmhouse filled with heavy wooden beams and massive granite pillars, this *gîte d'étape* (way station for hikers and skiers) has a variety of accommodations (doubles, dormitory-style beds, with bathrooms and without) and table d'hôte (communal prix-fixe dinners) of uncommon quality—note that the room rate includes breakfast and dinner (confirm when booking, as rate schedule may change). Manager and chef Françoise Massot knows every wild mushroom and raspberry in the valley and puts them to delicious use in memorable breakfasts and dinners. ✉ *Eyne Village* ☎ *04–68–04–06–96* 🖷 *04–68–04–10–60* ⊘ *calpai@libertysurf.fr* ⇔ *9 rooms, 5 with bath* ⚹ *Dining room; no a/c, no room TVs* ☰ *No credit cards* ⊠ *MAP.*

Mont-Louis

❸❾ *30 km (18 mi) west of Villefranche-de-Conflent, 5 km (3 mi) east of Eyne, 118 km (73 mi) south of Carcassonne.*

This fortified village, at 5,200 feet France's highest, was set up as a border stronghold by Vauban in 1679, and commands views over the Cerdagne Valley to the west, the Capcir to the north, and the Conflent to the east. The ramparts and the citadel, never attacked, are perfectly preserved. A solar oven—over the bridge and inside the portal in the town—is the only one in France in commercial use and is a key attraction.

$$ ✕⊡ **Lou Rouballou.** Famed as the best value and top cuisine in Mont-Louis, mother and daughter Christiane and Christine Bigorre's tiny flower-covered hideaway is the place to go (closed for lunch). Rooms are simple, small, and cozy. The cuisine is rich in sauces based on Pyrenean herbs, wild mushrooms, and game; try the *chartreuse de perdreaux* (partridge with winter cabbage) or the *ouillade* (a soup of potatoes, pork, and cabbage). ⊠ *Rue des Écoles Laïques, 66210* ☎ *04–68–04–23–26* 🖷 *04–68–04–14–09* ⌂ *Reservations essential* ⇥ *7 rooms* ⚭ *Restaurant; no a/c* ▭ *AE, DC, MC, V* ⊘ *Closed May and Nov. No lunch* ¶◐ *EP.*

Villefranche-de-Conflent

➍⓿ *6 km (4 mi) west of Prades, 30 km (18 mi) east of Mont-Louis, 49 km (30 mi) southwest of Perpignan.*

If you spent your childhood poring over *Quentin Durward* and *The Three Musketeers,* you'll delight over the ramparts and *donjons* of the villages in this region. Named for its location at the confluence of the Têt and Cady rivers, Villefranche-de-Conflent has remnants of an 11th-century fortress, with Vauban improvements from the 17th century. Cross the tiny St-Pierre Bridge over the Têt and use the pink-marble "stairway of a thousand steps" to climb up to Fort Liberia for views of the village, the Canigou, and the valleys east to Prades. A guided tour of the ramparts and the town can be arranged in advance by calling the **Villefranche tourist office** (☎ 04–68–96–22–96).

Le petit train jaune ("Little Yellow Train") is a fun way to see some of the most spectacular countryside in the Pyrénées. This life-size toy train makes the 63-km (40-mi) three-hour trip from Villefranche to La Tour de Carol about five times a day. When the weather is nice, ride in one of the open-air cars. For information about hours and prices, contact the Villefranche tourist office.

Where to Stay & Eat

$$–$$$ ✕ **Auberge Saint-Paul.** One of the best-known tables in the area, this warm stone-surrounded refuge is known for its fine Catalan and Roussillon cuisine, such as *truite à la llosa* (trout on slate slabs) and *civet d'isard* (stewed mountain goat). It also has one of the best wine selections in the area—opt for one of the delicious local wines from Collioure. Dining al fresco is recommended in summer, but bring along a light jacket—it gets chilly at night. ⊠ *7 pl. de l'Église* ☎ *04–68–96–30–95* ⌂ *Reservations essential* ▭ *MC, V* ⊘ *Closed Mon.*

Vernet-les-Bains

➍❶ *12 km (7 mi) southwest of Prades, 55 km (34 mi) west of Perpignan.*

English writer Rudyard Kipling came to take the waters in Vernet-les-Bains, a long-established spa town that is dwarfed by imposing Mont

Canigou; even higher up is its medieval abbey, which you can trek to by leaving your car first in Casteil, 2 km (1 mi) farther on, and completing the journey to the **Abbaye St-Martin du Canigou** on foot. Brace yourself for the steep half-hour climb but the blisters will be worth it—as removed from time and space as a dream, this is one of the most photographed abbeys in Europe, thanks to its sky-kissing perch atop a triangular promontory at an altitude of nearly 3,600 feet. It was constructed in 1007 by Count Guifred of Cerdagne in expiation for murdering his son. Although the abbey was perhaps too diligently restored by the bishop of Perpignan early in the 20th century, part of the cloisters, along with the higher (and larger) of the two churches, dates from the 11th century. The lower church, dedicated to Notre-Dame-sous-Terre, is even older. Rising above is a stocky, fortified bell tower. Although the hours vary, masses are sung daily; call ahead to confirm. ☎ 04–68–05–50–03 ☞ €3 ⊙ *Mid-June–mid-Sept., visits daily at 10, noon, 2, 3, 4, and 5; mid-Sept.–mid-June, Mon.–Sat. at 10, 12:30, 2:30, 3:30, and 4:30, Sun. 11 and 12:30.*

Prades

❹❷ *6 km (4 mi) east of Villefranche-de-Conflent, 43 km (27 mi) west of Perpignan.*

Once home to Catalan cellist Pablo Casals, the market town of Prades is famous for its annual summer music festival (from late July to mid-August), the **Festival Pablo Casals**. Founded by Casals in 1950, the music festival is primarily held at the medieval **Abbaye de St-Michel de Cuxa** (⊠ 3 km [2 mi] on D7 south of Prades and Codalet ☎ 04–68–96–15–35 ☞ €3 ⊙ Daily 9:30–11:30 and 2–5). One of the gems of the Pyrénées, the abbey's sturdy, crenellated four-story bell tower is visible from afar. If the remains of the cloisters here seem familiar, it may be because you have seen the missing pieces in New York City's Cloisters Museum. The 10th-century pre-Romanesque church is a superb aesthetic and acoustical venue for the summer cello concerts. The six-voice Gregorian vespers service held (somewhat sporadically—call to confirm) at 7 PM in the monastery next door is hauntingly simple, and medieval in tone and texture.

Where to Stay & Eat

¢–$$ ☒ **Les Glycines.** This flower-covered, traditional hotel in the middle of Prades offers small but charming rooms of impeccable cleanliness and simplicity. A healthy hike from Saint-Michel-de-Cuxa, this cozy spot has a rambling restaurant of its own as well, Le Jardin d'Aymeric (closed Monday, and no dinner Sunday; reservations essential), a charming little place that serves excellent *cuisine du terroir* in a relaxed and rustic setting. Offerings change seasonally and the market rules supreme in this slightly Bohemian refuge where local artists show their work. ⊠ 129 av. Gén de Gaulle, 66500 ☎ 04–68–96–51–65 📠 04–68–96–45–57 ☞ 19 rooms ⚙ Restaurant, cable TV, parking (fee); no a/c ⊟ MC, V ❢◉❢ EP.

Céret

43 *68 km (41 mi) southeast of Prades, 35 km (21 mi) west of Collioure, 31 km (19 mi) southwest of Perpignan.*

Fodor's Choice ★

The "Barbizon of Cubism," Céret achieved immortality when leading 20th-century artists found this small Pyrenean town irresistible at the beginning of this century. Here in this medieval enclave set on the banks of the Tech River, Picasso and Gris developed a vigorous new way of seeing that would result in the fragmented forms of Cubism, a thousand years removed from the Romanesque sculptures of the Roussillon chapels and cloisters. Adorned by cherry orchards—the town famously grows the first and finest crop in France—the town landscapes have been captured in paintings by Picasso, Gris, Dufy, Braque, Chagall, Kisling, and others. Some of these are on view in the fine collection of the ★ **Musée d'Art Moderne** (Modern Art Museum). ✉ *8 bis Maréchal-Joffre* ☎ *04–68–87–27–76* 🎫 *€6* ⏲ *May–Sept., Wed.–Mon. 10–6.*

The heart of town is, not surprisingly, the place Pablo Picasso. Like the Spanish roots of this artist, Céret is proud of its Catalan heritage and it often hosts Sardana dances. Be sure to stroll through pretty **Vieux Céret** (Old Céret): find your way through **place des Neufs Jets** (Nine Fountains Square), around the church, and out to the lovely fortified **Porte de France** gateway. Then walk over the single-arched **Vieux Pont** (Old Bridge).

Where to Stay & Eat

★ $$–$$$ ✕🏨 **Les Feuillants.** One of the top restaurants in the area, this elegant address offers refined Mediterranean and international cuisine, a good wine list, traditional-contemporary design, and paintings by Michel Becker. Dishes, such as pan-fried cuttlefish, are showpieces of the region and often come with flowers, herbs, cherries (the town emblem), and a hint of Catalonian *cuisine d'auteur* thrown in. Touches of creativity—seared foie gras with cherry and raison chutney, a violet artichoke heart cooked tempura style—are often in evidence. Guest rooms, though few, are gems. ✉ *1 bd. La Fayette* ☎ *04–68–87–37–88* 📠 *04–68–87–44–68* 🌐 *www.feuillants.com/* *3 rooms, 3 apartments* *Restaurant, cable TV* 💳 *AE, DC, MC, V* ⏲ *Closed Mon., 2 wks in Feb., and 2 wks in Nov. No dinner Sun.* 🍽 *MAP.*

★ ¢–$ 🏨 **Les Arcades.** This comfortable spot in mid-Céret looks, smells, and feels exactly the way an inn ensconced in the heart of a provincial French town should. That the world-class collection of paintings of the Musée d'Art Moderne and the top-rated Les Feuillants restaurant (⇨ *above*) are both just across the street puts it over the top. ✉ *1 pl. Picasso, 66400 Céret* ☎ *04–68–87–12–30* 📠 *04–68–87–49–44* *31 rooms* *Cable TV, parking (fee); no a/c* 💳 *MC, V* 🍽 *EP.*

Collioure

44 *35 km (21 mi) east of Céret, 27 km (17 mi) southeast of Perpignan.*

Fodor's Choice ★

The heart of Matisse Country, this pretty seaside fishing village with a sheltered natural harbor has become a summer magnet for tourists (beware the crowds in July and August). Painters such as Henri Matisse, André Derain, Henri Martin, and Georges Braque—who were dubbed Fauves for their "savage" (*fauve* means "wild animal") approach to color and form—were among the early discoverers of Collioure. The view they admired remains largely unchanged today: to the north, the rocky Îlot St-Vincent juts out into the sea, a modern lighthouse at its tip, while inland the Albères mountain range rises to connect the Pyrénées with the Mediterranean. The town harbor is a painting unto itself, framed by a 12th-century royal castle and a 17th-century church fortified with a tower. Collioure continues to play the muse to the entire Côte Vermeille—after all, it gave rise to the name of the Vermilion Coast because Matisse daringly painted Collioure's yellow-sand beach using a bright red terra-cotta hue. Matisse set up shop in the summer of 1905 and was greatly inspired by the colors of the town's terra-cotta roofs. The town's information center, behind the Plage Boramar, has an excellent map that points out the main locales once favored by the Fauve painters. In the streets behind the Vieux Port you'll see former fishermen's stores now occupied by smart boutiques and restaurants. To find tomorrow's Matisses and Derains, head to the streets behind the place du 18-Juin and to the old quarter of Le Mouré, set under Fort Miradou, to find studios filled with contemporary artists at work. Today, the most prized locales are—well, everyone can't be a Picasso—the café-terraces overlooking the main beach. Here you can feast on Collioure's tender, practically boneless anchovies and incredible wine (note the perfectly cultivated vineyards surrounding the town).

Near the old Quartier du Mouré is the 17th-century church of **Notre-Dame-des-Anges** (⊠ Pl. de l'Église). It has exuberantly carved, gilded Churrigueresque altarpieces by celebrated Catalan master Josep Sunyer and a pink-dome bell tower that doubled as the original lighthouse.

A slender jetty divides the Boramar Beach, beneath the church, from the small landing area at the foot of the **Château Royal,** a 13th-century castle, once the summer residence of the kings of Majorca (from 1276 to 1344), remodeled by Vauban 500 years later. ☎ 04–68–82–06–43 ⌦ €3 ۞ Mar.–Oct., daily 10–noon and 2–5.

If you're around the first Sunday of September, the **Concours de Sardanes** (⊠ Place du 18-Juin ☎ 04–68–82–15–47) is a festival of Catalan dance and music. Contact the town tourist office for full information. Throughout the region, in neighboring towns like Céret, other Sardane events are also held during this time of year.

Where to Stay & Eat

$$$–$$$$ ✕📷 **Relais des Trois Mas.** The vistas are priceless, but are they worth the very pricey room rates? Overlooking the harbor from the cliffs south of town, this hotel enjoys a perfect perch. Inside are small but interestingly furnished rooms—headboards, for example, are made from antique Spanish doors. Rooms are named for painters whose work appears on the bathroom tiles. Below is a pebbled beach, though you may prefer the small pool (hewn from rock) or the huge Jacuzzi. Dine at the restaurant, La Balette, on the terrace or in one of the two small dining rooms looking over the harbor. ⊠ *Rte. de Port-Vendres, 66190*

☎ *04–68–82–05–07* 🖶 *04–68–82–38–08* ⊷ *19 rooms, 4 suites* ⟁ *Restaurant, 2 dining rooms, minibars, cable TV, pool, gym, hot tub, beach* ▤ *MC, V* ⊘ *Closed Jan.* ⵙ *FAP.*

★ **$–$$** ✕⊡ **Les Templiers.** Universally considered the "soul" of Collioure, this place merits a visit on every itinerary. Way back when, Matisse, Maillol, Dalí, Picasso, and Dufy used to hang out here (occasionally paying for a meal or room with a watercolor). Today, owner Jojo Pous, son of the force behind Collioure's art colony, is proud to show off the more than 2,500 original works hanging from every nook and cranny (including the ceiling and stairs)—one of the most glorious sights in Languedorc-Roussillon. The bar itself is a work of art, curved like the hull of a skiff and ending with a wood sculpture of a mermaid suckling an infant sailor. Collioure is Catalan in all senses but cartographically, so the food here is mostly Catalan and usually excellent; be sure to try dishes that feature the town's fabled anchovies. The rooms overlooking the château are cozy, but be sure yours is not in the annex. ⊠ *Quai de l'Amirauté, 66190* ☎*04–68–98–31–10* 🖶*04–68–98–01–24* ⊕*www.hotel-templiers. com* ⊷ *43 rooms* ⟁ *Restaurant, café, cable TV, bar; no a/c* ▤ *AE, DC, MC, V* ⊘ *Closed Jan.* ⵙ *FAP.*

$$ ⊡ **Casa Pairal.** An idyllic, palm-shaded 19th-century townhouse surrounded by a leafy garden, this small oasis is a handy address in often tumultuous (for all its idyllic reputation) Collioure. The main house is more charming than the annex but all rooms are comfortable and tastefully appointed. A two-minute walk to the water's edge, the hotel decor is comfortingly traditional, while the alluring courtyard, garden, and pool are relaxing and intimate. ⊠ *Impasse des Palmiers, 66190 Collioure* ☎ *04–68–82–05–81* 🖶 *04–68–82–52–10* ⊕ *www.hotel-casa-pairal.com* ⊷ *28 rooms* ⟁ *Cable TV, pool, parking (fee)* ▤ *AE, DC, MC, V* ⵙ *EP.*

Perpignan

㊺ *27 km (17 mi) northwest of Collioure, 64 km (40 mi) south of Narbonne, 204 km (126 mi) southeast of Toulouse.*

Salvador Dalí once called Perpignan's train station "the center of the world." That may not be true but the city is certainly the capital hub of the Roussillon. Although it's big, the few squares of the *centre ville*, grouped near the quays of the Basse River, are the places to be for evening concerts and casual tapas sessions—you might even succumb to the "cosmological ecstasy" Dalí said he experienced here. In medieval times Perpignan was the second city of Catalonia (after Barcelona), before falling to Louis XIII's French army in 1642. The Spanish influence is evident in Perpignan's leading monument, the fortified **Palais des Rois de Majorque** (Kings of Majorca Palace), begun in the 14th century by James II of Majorca. Highlights here are the majestic **cour d'Honneur** (Courtyard of Honor), the two-tier Flamboyant Gothic chapel of **Ste-Croix**, and the **Grande Salle** (Great Hall) with its monumental fireplaces. ⊠ *Rue des Archers* ☎ *04–68–34–48–29* ▨ *€2* ⊘ *Daily 9–5.*

Perpignan's centre ville is sweet and alluring, lined in blooming rosemary bushes and landmarked by a medieval monument, the 14th-century **Le Castillet,** with its tall, crenellated twin towers. Originally this hulking brick building was the main gate to the city; later it was used as a prison. Now the **Casa Pairal**, a museum devoted to Catalan art and traditions, is housed here. ⊠ *Pl. de Verdun* ☎ *04–68–35–42–05* 🔳 *Free* ☻ *Wed.–Mon. 9–noon and 2–6.*

The **Promenade des Plantanes,** across boulevard Wilson from Le Castillet, is a cheerful place to stroll among flowers, plane trees, and fountains. To see other interesting medieval buildings, walk along the streets—the **Petite Rue des Fabriques d'En Nabot** is the best—near Le Castillet and the adjacent place de la Loge, the town's nerve center. Note the frilly wrought-iron campanile and dramatic medieval crucifix on the **Cathédrale St-Jean** (⊠ Pl. Gambetta).

Where to Stay & Eat

★ **$–$$** ✕ **Banyols et Banyols.** Highly acclaimed chef Didier Banyols has made this semi-clandestine oasis just a block in from the River Têt on a tiny and ancient alley one of Perpignan's best bistros. A popular hideaway, intimate and cozy, this spot serves up nouvelle market cuisine in a contemporary setting. ⊠ *7 rue Cardeurs* ☎ *04–68–34–48–40* ▭ *AE, DC, MC, V* ☻ *Closed Sun. and Mon.*

$–$$ ✕ **Le France.** In the center of Perpignan in an amazing 15th-century monument (it used to be the stock market), this café-restaurant is a wonderful place to have a light meal or a glass of iced champagne under the parasols as you watch the world go by. There is a great choice of light appetizers—scallops marinated in orange, two different types of oysters, or a Nordic salad with smoked fish and steamed potatoes—or a simple main course, such as the grilled duck with prunes or salmon filet with fresh vegetable spaghetti. ⊠ *1 pl. de la Loge* ☎ *04–68–51–61–71* ▭ *MC, V* ☻ *No dinner Sun.*

$$–$$$ ✕▥ **La Villa Duflot.** In a large park filled with olive and cypress trees, this hotel-restaurant complex serves some of the best meals in one of the calmest, prettiest settings in the city. Request a room with a view over the park—they're airy and comfortable with warm creamy colors— the rooms with the view of the patio aren't nearly as nice although they are a bit more economical. The ambience here is relaxed, all the finesse is saved for the food and the food is *good.* The gastronomic restaurant popular with haute Perpignan serves light Mediterranean specialties around the pool—try the *parillade,* an assortment of the freshest catch of the day grilled to perfection and served with tangy aioli. ⊠ *Rond Pont Albert Donnezan* ☎ *04–68–56–67–67* 📮 *32 rooms* ♿ *Restaurant, minibars, cable TV, bar, some pets allowed* ▭ *AE, DC, MC, V* ▥ *EP.*

¢ ▥ **Hôtel de la Poste et de la Perdrix.** If you're looking for an inexpensive place with Old French charm in the center of town next to Le Castillet, don't miss this little spot. Rooms, like the hotel, are simple and poetic, as opposed to pampering and prosaic. The cuisine is Catalan. ⊠ *6 rue Fabriques Nabot, 66000* ☎ *04–68–34–42–53* 🖶 *04–68–34–58–20* 📮 *38 rooms* ♿ *Restaurant, parking (fee); no a/c, no room TVs* ▭ *AE, DC, MC, V* ☻ *Closed Feb.* ▥ *FAP.*

Shopping

Rue des Marchands, near Le Castillet, is thick with chic shops. **Maison Quinta** (⊠ Rue Louis Blanc) is a top design and architectural artifacts store. Excellent local ceramics can be found at the picturesque **Sant Vicens Crafts Center** (⊠ Rue Sant Vicens, off D22 east of town center).

Salses

㊻ *16 km (10 mi) north of Perpignan, 48 km (30 mi) south of Narbonne.*

Salses has a history of sieges. History relates that Hannibal stormed through the town with his elephants on his way to the Alps in 218 BC, though no trace of his passage remains. The colossal and well-preserved **Fort de Salses,** built by Ferdinand of Aragon in 1497 and equipped for 300 horses and 1,000 soldiers, fell to the French under Cardinal Richelieu in 1642 after a three-year siege. Bulky round towers ring the rectangular inner fort, and the five-story keep, with its narrow corridors and small-scale drawbridges, was designed to keep the fort's governor safe to the last. ☎ *04–68–38–60–13* ⌨ *€6.10* ☉ *July and Aug., daily 9–6; Sept. and Oct. and Easter–June, daily 9:30–11:30 and 2–5:30; Nov.–Easter, 9:30–11:30 and 2–4.*

Narbonne

㊼ *64 km (40 mi) north of Perpignan, 60 km (37 mi) east of Carcassonne, 94 km (58 mi) south of Montpellier.*

In Roman times, bustling, industrial Narbonne was the second-largest town in Gaul (after Lyon) and an important port, though today little remains of its Roman past. Until the sea receded during the Middle Ages, Narbonne prospered. The town's former wealth is evinced by the 14th-century **Cathédral St-Just** (⊠ Rue Armand-Gauthier); its vaults rise 133 feet from the floor, making it the tallest cathedral in southern France. Only Beauvais and Amiens, in Picardy, are taller, and as at Beauvais, the nave at Narbonne was never built.

Richly sculpted cloisters link the cathedral to the former **Palais des Archevêques** (Archbishops' Palace), now home to **museums** of archaeology, art, and history. Note the enormous palace kitchen and the late-13th-century keep, the Donjon Gilles-Aycelin; climb the 180 steps to the top for a view of the region and the town. ⊠ *Palais des Archevêques* ☎ *04–68–90–30–30* ⌨ *€7.50, includes all town museums* ☉ *May–Sept., daily 9–noon and 2–6; Oct.–Apr., Tues.–Sun. 10–noon and 2–5:30.*

On the south side of the Canal de la Robine is the **Musée Lapidaire** (Sculpture Museum), in the handsome 13th-century former church of **Notre-Dame de la Mourguié.** Classical busts, ancient sarcophagi, lintels, and Gallo-Roman inscriptions await you. ⊠ *Pl. Lamourguier* ☎ *04–68–65–53–58* ⌨ *€7.50, includes all town museums* ☉ *May–Sept., daily 9–noon and 2–6; Oct.–Apr., Tues.–Sun. 10–noon and 2–5:30.*

Where to Stay & Eat

¢–$ ╳▨ **Languedoc.** In this old-fashioned, early-20th-century hotel downtown, the smallish rooms vary in style and comfort; a full bath is an extra €15. La Petite Cour restaurant (closed Monday, no dinner Sunday) serves inexpensive regional dishes, with menus starting at €18. ⊠ *22 bd. Gambetta, 11100* ☎ *04–68–65–14–74* 🖶 *04–68–65–81–48* ⇨ *38* rooms, 34 with bath or shower; 2 suites ♿ Restaurant, piano bar, parking (fee); no a/c ▭ AE, DC, MC, V ⦿ FAP.

Béziers

48 20 km (12 mi) northeast of Narbonne, 54 km (33 mi) southwest of Montpellier.

The Languedoc's *capital du vin* (wine capital)—crowds head here for *dègustation* tastings during the October wine harvest festival—and centerpiece of the Canal du Midi, Béziers owes its reputation to the genius of native son and royal salt-tax collector Pierre-Paul Riquet (that's his statue presiding over the allées Paul Riquet). He was a visionary at a time when roads were in deplorable shape and grain was transported on the backs of mules. Yet he died a pauper in 1680, a year before the canal's completion (it was begun by the ancient Romans) and the revolutionizing of commerce in the south of France. Few would have predicted much of a future for Béziers in July of 1209, after Simon de Montfort, leader of the crusade against the Cathars, scored his first major victory here, massacring 20,000. Today the Canal du Midi hosts mainly pleasure cruisers, and Béziers sits serenely on its perch overlooking the distant Mediterranean and the foothills of the Cévennes Mountains. Early August sees the four-day *féria*—a festival with roots in Spain and replete with gory bullfighting (you've been warned).

The heavily restored **Église de la Madeleine** (✉ Off rue de la République), with its distinctive octagonal tower, was the site of the beginning of the 1209 massacre. About 7,000 townspeople who had sought refuge from Simon de Montfort in the church were burned alive before he turned his attention to sacking the town; the event is known as "*le grand mazel*" ("the great bonfire"). Restoration work means that you may only be able to admire the crenellations, gargoyles, floral frieze, and crooked arches of the late 11th-century pentagonal apse.

Béziers's late-19th-century **Halles** (Market Hall) was done in the style of the architect Baltard, who built the original Les Halles in Paris. This is a particularly beautiful example, with large stone cabbages gracing the entrance like urns. ✉ *Entrances on rue Paul Riquet, pl. Pierre Sémard* ☉ *Daily 6:30–12:30.*

The **Ancienne Cathédrale St-Nazaire** (✉ Pl. des Albigeois) was rebuilt over several centuries after the sack of Béziers. Note the medieval wall along rue de Juiverie, which formed the limit between the cathedral precincts and the Jewish quarter of town. The western facade resembles a fortress for good reason: it served as a warning to would-be invaders. Look for the magnificent 17th-century walnut organ and the frescoes about the lives of St. Stephen and others. Adjoining the cathedral are a 14th-century cloister and the **Jardin des Evêques** (Bishops' Garden), conceived of as a terraced garden descending to the banks of the Orb. The views from here, which take in Béziers's five bridges, are magnificent. ✉ *Pl. des Albigeois* ☉ *Oct.–Apr., daily 10–noon and 2–5:30; May–Sept., daily 10–7.*

Where to Stay & Eat

$–$$ ✕🔲 **Château de Lignan.** Set in its own park, this elegant estate northwest of Béziers has four slender roof-tiled towers, lending a vaguely Italianate feel to go with the austere stucco facade. Pity that rooms have little to distinguish them from standard chain hotels except their size and louvered windows, but the restaurant is exceptional. The octagonal sprawl of the skylit dining room is cheery and welcoming. Simple, streamlined fare such as strongly flavored *loup en papillote* (sea perch cooked in foil) makes a perfect prelude to the vanilla ice cream–filled baked pears. ⊠ *Pl. de l'Église, 6 km (4 mi) northwest of Béziers, 34490 Lignan-sur-Orb* 🕾 *04–67–37–91–47* 🖷 *04–67–37–99–25* ⊕ *www. chateauxhotels.com* ⤳ *50 rooms* ⌂ *Restaurant, minibars, cable TV, pool* ▭ *AE, MC, V* ⦿❙ *MAP.*

The Outdoors

Daylong excursions on the Canal du Midi include passage over the canal bridge spanning the Orb and through the nine locks. Some companies working the Canal de Midi have extensive routes, some as far as the Mediterranean resort town of Agde, 21 km (14 mi) away. **Les Bâteaux du Soleil** (⊠ 6 rue Chassefière, 34300 Agde 🕾 04–67–94–08–79 🖷 04–67–21–28–38) includes some wide-ranging excursions.

Minerve

49 *40 km (25 mi) west of Béziers, 30 km (19 mi) northwest of Narbonne.*

Fodor'sChoice
★

Surrounded by the meandering, juniper-covered limestone gorges of the Vallée de la Cesse, Minerve is the quintessential medieval hilltop village. The town sheltered a large number of heretics at the start of the Albigensian Crusade. But its defensive position was no match for Simon de Montfort's army in July 1210, when after a seven-week siege the dehydrated citizens capitulated and 180 Cathar *Perfecti* (elite Cathari) were burned. De Montfort's army had blocked the village well with the aid of a catapult called La Malvoisine (the Evil Neighbor), which has been reconstructed on its original strategic site. Stroll around the remaining fortifications and try to imagine the assault. Around Minerve are a number of geological and archaeological curiosities, including *ponts naturels* (natural bridges), enormous tunnels in the rock cut by the path of the Cesse River, prehistoric grottoes, and dolmens.

Maps and information are available from the somewhat hidden **Syndicat d'Initiative** (⊠ Pl. du Monument aux Morts 🕾 04–68–91–81–43), the tourist office in the center of the village. You can also get addresses of local winemakers who produce the classed wine Minervois (a rough, fruity red) from grapes grown in arid, pebbly soil.

The austere, Romanesque **Église St-Etienne** has one of the oldest altar tables in Europe, dating from AD 456. Next to the church is a carving of a dove, a monument to the village's resistance during the Crusades. The château was destroyed by Simon de Montfort. Only the curious, candlelike **Tour du Guet** (Watchtower) remains on a ledge at the far end of the village.

The **Musée Hurepel** re-creates the events of the Albigensian Crusade in a series of figurine-populated dioramas and does a good job of explaining how villagers would have interacted with the Cathars they sheltered. ⊠ *5 rue des Martyrs* ☎ *04-68-91-12-26* ⊠ *€2.50* ⊙ *Daily 10:30–12:30 and 2–6:30; Closed mid-Nov.–Mar.*

Where to Stay & Eat

¢–$ ╳⊡ **Le Relais Chantovent.** Overlooking the gorges of the Brian River, this oak-beamed, terra-cotta-tile restaurant and inn is decorated with exceptional paintings by local artists. Rooms are basic but quaint, with old lamps, framed prints, and wooden furniture. Owners Maïté and Loulou Evenou serve up elegantly garnished local fare, including strong, salty *jambon de la Montagne Noire* (Black Mountain ham) and trout in a cream and red-pepper sauce. The restaurant (prix-fixe menu only) is closed Monday, and there is no dinner Sunday. ⊠ *17 Grande-Rue, 34210 Minerve* ☎ *04-68-91-14-18* 🖶 *04-68-91-81-99* ⇗ *10 rooms* ⚐ *Restaurant; no a/c, no room TVs* ⊟ *MC, V* ⊙ *Closed mid-Dec.–mid-Mar.* ⍓⚏ *MAP.*

★ $$–$$$ ⊡ **Les Aliberts.** Ensconced among the vine- and asphodel-covered hills outside Minerve, with stunning views of the Pyrénées and the Montagne Noire, this *gîte* (hiker's way-station) is in a restored and renovated set of 12th- to 17th-century farm buildings. Cosmopolitan owners Pascal and Monique Bourgogne treat guests like friends. The majestic main farmhouse has common rooms with an enormous fireplace, library, and piano. The five cozy houses (€540 to €1,950 per week, with accommodations for from 4 to 10 persons), range in style from Scandinavian to Asian to French contemporary; all have full kitchens and fireplaces. Meals and breakfasts can be ordered in advance. ⊠ *Les Aliberts, off D10 south toward Olonzac, 34210 Minerve* ☎ *04-68-91-81-72* 🖶 *04-68-91-22-95* ⊕ *www.gite.com/aliberts* ⇗ *5 houses, with 13 rooms total* ⚐ *Pool, library, laundry facilities, Internet; no room TVs* ⊟ *No credit cards* ⍓⚏ *FAP.*

Pézenas

㊿ *23 km (14 mi) northeast of Béziers, 52 km (32 mi) southwest of Montpellier.*

Pézenas retains the courtly appearance and feel it acquired in the 16th century, when the Estates General of the Languedoc, the regional administrative body, governed from here. The town made its fortune with 16th- to 18th-century textile fairs, at which denim was sold. Hence you have Pézenas's architectural richness: around every picturesque corner is another *hôtel particulier* (town-house mansion)—and because of architectural competition among the wealthy, they are all unique. Some notable streets are rue Triperie Vieille; rue de la Foire, where you'll find the Maison Carrion de Nizas and the Hôtel de Wicque; cour Jean-Jaurès, famous for its Maison Émile Mâzuc, at No. 10; place du 14 Juillet and its outstanding Hôtel des Barons de Lacoste; and rue Émile Zola, home to the Maison de Jacques Coeur. At the end of rue Émile Zola is a rounded archway leading into the rue Juiverie, also called La Carriera, which in the Occitan language denotes a Jewish ghetto.

The tourist office, which organizes a variety of tours of Pézenas, is in the **Maison du Barbier Gély** (⊠ 1 pl. Gambetta), once home to Molière's barber and friend, Monsieur Gély. Pézenas's most impressive hôtel particulier is the **Hôtel d'Alfonce,** with its twisted Baroque columns, three-tiered balustraded loggia overlooking the garden, and vinelike corner staircase. This was the residence of the Prince de Conti, who sponsored visits by Molière and his acting troupe in 1650, 1653, and 1655. *Le Médecin Volant* (*The Flying Doctor*) may have premiered here shortly before Conti, mad from syphilis, purged his illustrious court. The owners, Monsieur Aubert and his daughter, give private tours of their family home and rent out two double rooms with bath. (€100 with breakfast). ⊠ *Rue Conti 32* ☎ *04–67–90–71–89* ⊠ *€2* ⊘ *June–Sept., Mon.–Sat. 10–noon and 2–6.*

Nightlife & the Arts

As part of **La Mirondela Del Arts** festival in July and August, Molière's spirit comes alive with performances by comedy troupes; there are also Occitan-language music and poetry events. In February the town's medieval mascot, **Le Poulain** (a giant horse made out of chestnut and cloth), gets toted around in honor of Carnival.

Montpellier

40 km (25 mi) southeast of St-Guilhem-le-Désert, 42 km (26 mi) southwest of Nîmes.

Vibrant Montpellier (pronounced monh-pell-*yay*), capital of the Languedoc-Roussillon region, has been a center of commerce and learning since the Middle Ages, when it was a crossroads for pilgrims on their way to Santiago de Compostela, in Spain, and an active shipping center trading in spices from the East. With its cargo of exotic luxuries, it also imported Renaissance learning, and its university—founded in the 14th century—has nurtured a steady influx of ideas through the centuries. Though the port silted up by the 16th century, Montpellier never became a backwater, and as a center of commerce and conferences it keeps its focus on the future. An imaginative urban planning program has streamlined the 17th-century Vieille Ville, and monumental perspectives dwarf passersby on the 17th-century Promenade du Peyrou. An even more utopian venture in urban planning is the Antigone district: a vast, harmonious 100-acre complex designed in 1984 by Barcelona architect Ricardo Bofill. A student population of some 65,000 keeps things lively, especially on the place de la Comédie, the city's social nerve center. The Old Town is a pedestrian paradise; you can travel around the entire city on the excellent bus system (the gare routière station is by the train terminal on rue Jules Ferry).

★ ⑤ Montpellier's grandest avenue is the **Promenade du Peyrou,** built at the end of the 17th century and dedicated to Louis XIV. The Peyrou's centerpiece is the enormous **Arc de Triomphe,** designed by d'Aviler in 1689 and finished by Giral in 1776; it looms majestically over the peripheral highway that loops around the city center. Together, the noble scale of these harmonious stone constructions and the sweeping perspectives they frame make for an inspiring stroll through this posh stretch of town.

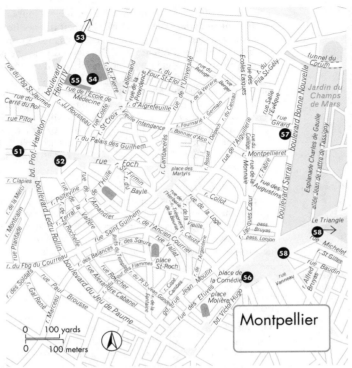

Montpellier

At the end of the park is the **Château d'Eau,** a Corinthian temple and the terminal for **les Arceaux,** an 18th-century aqueduct; on a clear day the view from here is spectacular, taking in the Cévennes Mountains, the sea, and an ocean of red-tile roofs (it's worth it to come back here at night to see the entire promenade lit up).

53 Boulevard Henri IV runs north from the Promenade du Peyrou to France's oldest botanical garden, the **Jardin des Plantes,** planted on order of Henri IV in 1593. An exceptional range of plants, flowers, and trees grows here. *Free ⊙ Gardens Mon.–Sat. 9–noon and 2–5. Greenhouses weekdays 9–noon and 2–5, Sat. 9–noon.*

After taking in the broad vistas of the Promenade de Peyrou, cross over into the Vieille Ville and wander its maze of narrow streets full of pretty shops and intimate restaurants. At the northern edge of the Vieille Ville, **54** visit the imposing **Cathédrale St-Pierre** (⊠ Pl. St-Pierre), its fantastical and unique 14th-century entry porch alone worth the detour: two cone-topped towers—some five stories high—flank the main portal and support a groin-vaulted shelter. The interior, despite 18th-century reconstruction, maintains the formal simplicity of its 14th-century origins.

55 Next door to the cathedral, peek into the noble **Faculté de Médecine,** on rue de l'École de Médecine, one of France's most respected medical schools, founded in the 14th century and infused with generations of international learning—especially Arab and Jewish scholarship.

From the medical school follow rue Foch, which slices straight east. The number of bistros and brasseries increases as you leave the Vieille Ville to cross place des Martyrs; veering right down rue de la Loge, you spill

56 out onto the festive gathering spot known as **Place de la Comédie.** Anchored by the Neoclassical 19th-century **Opéra-Comédie**, this broad square is a beehive of leisurely activity, a cross between Barcelona's Ramblas and a Roman *passagiata* (afternoon stroll, en masse). Brasseries, bistros, fast-food joints, and cinemas draw crowds, but the pleasure is getting there and seeing who came before, in which shoes, and with whom.

★ **57** From place de la Comédie, boulevard Sarrail leads north past the shady esplanade Charles de Gaulle to the **Musée Fabre.** A mixed bag of architectural styles (a 17th-century *hôtel,* a vast Victorian wing with superb natural light, and a remnant of a Baroque Jesuit college), this rich art museum has a surprisingly big collection, thanks to its namesake. François-Xavier Fabre, a native of Montpellier, was a student of the great 18th-century French artist David, who established roots in Italy and acquired a formidable collection of masterworks—which he then donated to his hometown, supervising the development of this fine museum. Among his gifts were the *Mariage Mystique de Sainte Catherine,* by Veronese, and Poussin's coquettish *Venus et Adonis.* Later contributions include a superb group of 17th-century Flemish works (Rubens, Steen), a collection of 19th-century French canvases (Géricault, Delacroix, Corot, Millet) that inspired Gauguin and Van Gogh, and a growing group of 20th-century acquisitions that buttress a legacy of paintings by early Impressionist Frédéric Bazille. ⊠ *3 bd. Bonne Nouvelle* ☎ *04–67–14–83–00* ✒ *€5.50* ☉ *Tues.–Fri. 9–5:30, weekends 9:30–5.*

need a break? Enjoy a 15-minute stroll from the Musée Fabre to the very chic café-bar **Les Planches** (⊠ 5 pl Jean Jaurés, ☎ 04–67–66–43–60). Pop in for an aperitif, a look at the ever-changing exhibit of local artists and trendy Montpellierains nibbling olives.

58 At the far-east end of the city loop, Montpellier seems to transform itself into a futuristic ideal city, all in one smooth, low-slung postmodern style. This is the **Antigone** district, the result of city planners' efforts (and local industries' commitment) to pull Montpellier up out of its economic doldrums. It worked. This ideal neighborhood, designed by the Catalan architect Ricardo Bofill, covers 100-plus acres with plazas, esplanades, shops, restaurants, and low-income housing, all constructed out of stone-color, prestressed concrete. Be sure to visit place du Nombre d'Or—symmetrically composed of curves—and the 1-km-long (½-mi-long) vista that stretches down a mall of cypress trees to the glass-fronted **Hôtel de Region** (⊠ Av. du Pirée).

Where to Stay & Eat

★ **$$$$** ✕ **Le Jardin des Sens.** Blink and look again: twins Laurent and Jacques Pourcel, trained under separate masters, combine forces here to achieve a quiet, almost cerebral cuisine based on southern French traditions. At every turn are happy surprises: foie gras crisps, dried-fruit risotto, and lamb sweetbreads with *gambas* (prawns). A modest lunch menu (in the $$ category) lets you indulge on a budget. Decor is minimal stylish, with steel beams and tables on three tiers. Truth is, this is in a rather *delabré* working-class neighborhood and from the outside looks like an anonymous warehouse. ⊠ *11 av. St-Lazare* ☎ *04-99-58-38-38* 🖷 *04-99-58-38-39* ⊕ *www.jardindessens.com* ⊟ *AE, DC, MC, V* ⊘ *Closed Jan. and Sun. No lunch Mon.*

$$-$$$$ ✕ **Le Chandelier.** On the sixth and seventh floors of a building in the Antigone district, this restaurant has dramatic views, impeccable service, and bold blue-and-yellow Mediterranean decor. Chef Gilbert Furlan's inventive cuisine takes Provençal ingredients to sophisticated levels: sample his squid sautéed in fresh thyme, dried mullet eggs with brandade mousse, and pigeon roasted with cinnamon and nutmeg, all with a good range of Languedoc wines. ⊠ *Pl. Zeus 39* ☎ *04-67-15-34-38* ⊟ *AE, DC, MC, V* ⊘ *Closed Sun. No lunch Mon.*

★ $-$$ ✕ **Le Petit Jardin.** On a quiet Vieille Ville backstreet, this simple restaurant lives up to its name: you dine looking over (or seated in) a lovely, deep-shaded garden with views of the cathedral. A simple omelet with pepper sauce, spicy bourride, or hearty *osso buco* (veal shanks in saffron-tomato sauce) mirrors the welcome, which is warm and unpretentious. ⊠ *20 rue Jean-Jacques Rousseau* ☎ *04-67-60-78-78* ⊟ *AE, DC, MC, V* ⊘ *Closed Jan. and Mon.*

¢ ✕ **Chez Mémé.** This ever popular restaurant is the perfect spot for a traditional dinner reminiscent of *Mémé* (Grandma's) cooking, serving grilled trout with almonds, ratatouille, and warm apple tarte with a dollop of cream. The portions are ample, the atmosphere is fast, fun, and friendly with local musicians playing for their soupe, *and* it's ever so light on the pocket. *Yippee!* ⊠ *18 rue Ecoles Laïques* ☎ *04-67-02-43-26* ⊟ *MC, V* ⊘ *Closed Sun. No lunch.*

★ $$-$$$ ▦ **Le Guilhem.** On the same quiet backstreet as the restaurant Le Petit Jardin, this jewel of a *hôtel de charme* is actually a series of 16th-century houses. Rebuilt from ruins to include an elevator and state-of-the-art white-tile baths, it nonetheless retains original casement windows (many overlooking the extraordinary old garden), slanting floors, and views toward the cathedral. Soft yellows and powder blues add to its gentle, *temps perdu* atmosphere. Tiny garret-style rooms at the top are great if you're traveling alone; if not, ask for the largest available. ⊠ *18 rue Jean-Jacques-Rousseau, 34000* ☎ *04-67-52-90-90* 🖷 *04-67-60-67-67* ⊕ *www.hotel-guilhem.fr* ⇴ *36 rooms* ♿ *Cable TV, parking (fee)* ⊟ *AE, DC, MC, V* ⊘I *EP.*

Nightlife & the Arts

Concerts are performed in the 19th-century **Théâtre des Treize Vents** (⊠ 11 bd. Victor Hugo ☎ 04-67-60-05-45). The **Orchestre National de Montpellier** (☎ 04-67-61-66-16) is a young and energetic group of some reputation, performing regularly in the Opéra Berlioz in the Corum conference complex. The resident **Opera Comédie de Montpellier** (☎ 04-67-60-19-99) performs in the very imposing Opéra-Comédie on place de la Comédie. For rousing student hangouts, head to **place Jean-Jaurès.**

THE MIDI-PYRÉNÉES & THE LANGUEDOC-ROUSSILLON A TO Z

To research prices, get advice from other travelers, and book travel arrangements, visit www.fodors.com.

AIR TRAVEL

CARRIERS Air France has regular flights between Paris and Toulouse; Montpellier is served by frequent flights from Paris and London. Be sure to check out Ryan Air, Easyjet, and Buzz, who offer incredibly cheap flights to Perpignan, Montpellier, or Toulouse—often as low as €30 one way.

🔊 Airlines & Contacts **Air France** ☎ 08-20-82-08-20 ⊕ www.airfrance.com. **Ryan Air** ☎ 08-92-55-56-66 ⊕ www.ryanair.com. **Easyjet** ☎ 08-25-08-25-08 ⊕ www. easyjet.com. **Buzz** ☎ 01-55-17-42-42 ⊕ www.buzzaway.com.

AIRPORTS

All international flights arrive at Toulouse's Blagnac Airport, a 20-minute drive from the center of the city. Airport shuttles run regularly (every half hour between 8:15 AM and 8:45 PM) from the airport to the bus station in Toulouse (at the train station; fare €4) and also at 9:20 PM, 10 PM, and 10:45 PM. From the Toulouse bus station to the airport, buses leave every half hour 5:30 AM–8:30 PM.

🔊 Airport Information **Blagnac Airport** ☎ 05-61-42-44-65. **Airport Montpellier-Méditerranée** ☎ 04-67-20-85-00.

BUS TRAVEL

As in most rural regions in France, there's an array of bus companies (in addition to SNCF buses, Intercars, Semvat, Courriers du Midi, Salt Autocars, among others) threading the Midi-Pyrénées countryside; be sure to stop in the bigger tourist offices on your route to inquire in advance for detailed bus schedules and advice on which bus routes to use for your sightseeing itinerary. Toulouse's bus links include Albi, Auch, Castres, Foix, and Montauban; Albi connects with Cordes-sur-Ciel (summer only) and Montauban; Montauban with Moissac and Auch; Montpellier with Béziers. For Courriers Catalans and Car Inter 66 buses to the Côte Vermeille, Collioure, Céret, and Prades, depart from Perpignan. Everyone says you should take the train to Carcassonne, although buses do head there.

🔊 Bus Information **Montpellier Gare Routière** ☎ 04-67-92-01-43. **Toulouse Gare Routière** ☎ 05-61-61-67-67.

CAR RENTAL

🔊 Local Agencies **Avis** ✉ 13 bd. Conflent, Perpignan ☎ 04-68-34-26-71 ✉ Blagnac Airport, Toulouse ☎ 05-61-30-04-94. **Budget** ✉ Montpellier train station ☎ 04-67-92-69-00. **Hertz** ✉ Pl. Lagarrasic, Auch ☎ 05-62-05-26-26 ✉ 5 av. Chamier, Montauban ☎ 05-63-20-29-00 ✉ 18 rue Jules Ferry, Montpellier ☎ 04-67-58-65-18.

CAR TRAVEL

The fastest route from Paris to Toulouse (700 km [435 mi] southwest) is via Bordeaux on A10, then A62; the journey time is about nine hours.

If you choose to head south over the Pyrénées to Barcelona, the Tunnel du Puymorens saves half an hour of switchbacks between Hospitalet and Porta, but in good weather and with time to spare the drive over the Puymorens Pass is spectacular. Plan on taking three hours between Toulouse and Font-Romeu and another three to Barcelona. The fastest route from Toulouse to Barcelona is the four-hour, 421-km (253-mi) drive via Carcassonne and Perpignan on A61 and A9, which becomes A7 at Le Perthus.

A62/A61 slices through the region on its way through Carcassonne to the coast at Narbonne, where A9 heads south to Perpignan. At Toulouse, where A62 becomes A61, various highways fan out in all directions: N124 to Auch; N117/E80 to St-Gaudens, Tarbes, and Pau; A62/N20 to Montauban and Cahors; N20 south to Foix and the Ariège Valley; N88 to Albi and Rodez. A9 (La Languedocienne) is the main highway artery that connects Montpellier with Beziers to the south and Nîmes to the north.

MUSIC FESTIVALS

Fifty music festivals a year take place in the smaller towns throughout the region; the Comité Régional du Tourisme (CRT) and larger tourist offices can provide a list of dates and addresses. For complete musical information contact the Délégation Musicale Régionale.

🎵 **Délégation Musicale Régionale** ✉ 56 rue du Taur, 31080 Toulouse ☎ 05-61-29-21-00.

SPORTS & THE OUTDOORS

For information on canoeing or kayaking, contact the Ligue de Canoë-Kayak. For information on hiking or horseback riding, contact the Comité de Randonnées Midi-Pyrénées. Local tourist offices also have detailed maps of more than 3,220 km (2,000 mi) of marked trails. The Comité Regional du Tourisme du Languedoc-Roussillon publishes a brochure on golf courses in the area and sells a pass honored at 14 courses.

🎵 Canoeing, Kayaking & Rafting **Canoë-Kayak Toulousain** ✉ Ile du Ramier, 18 Chemin des Loges, 31000 Toulouse ☎ 05-61-55-30-80.

🎵 Hiking **Comité de Randonnées Midi-Pyrénées (CORAMIP)** ✉ 4 rue Berry, 31000 Toulouse ☎ 05-61-40-81-59.

TOURS

Contact the Toulouse tourist office for information about walking tours and bus tours in and around Toulouse. Ask for the English-speaking, encyclopedic, and superbly entertaining Gilbert Casagrande for a non-pareil tour of Toulouse. The Comité Régional du Tourisme has a brochure, "1,001 Escapes in the Midi-Pyrénées," with descriptions of weekends and short organized package vacations.

In addition to publishing map itineraries that you can follow yourself, the **Montpellier tourist office** (☎ 04–67–60–60–60) provides guided walking tours of the city's neighborhoods and monuments daily in summer and on Wednesday and Saturday during the school year (roughly, September–June). They leave from the place de la Comédie. There are also **horse-drawn carriage tours** (☎ 04–67–60–60–60 information) between the square and the Esplanade Charles de Gaulle; you can go for

15 minutes up to an hour and a half. A small **tourist train** (☎ 04–67–60–60–60 information) with broadcast commentary leaves from the Esplanade between 2 and 9, Monday through Saturday.

🖪 **Comité Régional du Tourisme (CRT)** ✉ 54 bd. de l'Embouchure, 31200 Toulouse ☎ 05-61-13-55-55. **Montpellier** ✉ 30 allée Jean de Lattre de Tassigny, Esplanade Comédie ☎ 04-67-60-60-60. **Toulouse tourist office** ✉ Donjon du Capitole ☎ 05-61-11-02-22 ⊕ www.ot-toulouse.fr.

TRAIN TRAVEL

The regional French rail network in the southwest provides regular service to many towns, though not all. Béziers is linked by train to Carcassonne, Perpignan, Narbonne, and Montpellier, as well as Paris (but via slow trains that take hours, not via TGVs). There's no train service to Pézenas, Minerve, and St-Guilhem. Most trains for the southwest leave from Paris's Gare d'Austerlitz. There are direct trains to Toulouse, Carcassonne, and Montauban. For Rodez, change in Brive, and for Auch, in Toulouse. Seven trains leave Paris (Gare de Lyon) daily for Narbonne and Perpignan; a change at Montpellier is often necessary. Most of these trips take between six or seven hours. Note that at least three high-speed TGV (Trains à Grande Vitesse) per day leave Paris (Gare Montparnasse) for Toulouse; the journey time is five hours. A TGV line also serves Montpellier.

Within the Midi-Pyrénées region, Toulouse is the biggest hub, with a major line linking Carcassonne, Béziers, Narbonne (change here for Perpignan), and Montpellier; trains also link up with Albi and Montauban; the latter connects with Moissac. Montpellier connects with Carcassonne, Perpignan, Narbonne, Béziers, and other towns.

🖪 Train Information **SNCF** ☎ 08-36-35-35-35 ⊕ www.ter-sncf.com/languedoc/default.htm.

TRAVEL AGENCIES

🖪 Local Agent Referrals **Havas** ✉ 2 pl. de la Comédie, Montpellier ☎ 04-67-91-31-70 ✉ 73 rue d'Alsace-Lorraine, Toulouse ☎ 05-61-23-16-35. **Carlson Wagons-lit** ✉ Voyages Dépêche, 42 bis rue d'Alsace-Lorraine, Toulouse ☎ 05-62-15-42-70.

VISITOR INFORMATION

The regional tourist office for the Midi-Pyrénées is the Comité Régional du Tourisme. For Pyrénées-Roussillon information, contact the Comité Départemental de Tourisme. For the Languedoc-Roussillon contact the Comité Régional du Tourisme du Languedoc-Roussillon. Local tourist offices are listed by town below. Other handy Web sites for the regions in this chapter include (⊕ www.audetourisme.com) and (⊕ www.tourisme-tarn.com).

🖪 Tourist Information **Comité Régional du Tourisme (CRT)** ✉ 54 bd. de l'Embouchure, 31200 Toulouse ☎ 05-61-13-55-55. **Comité Départemental de Tourisme** ✉ Quai de Lattre de Tassigny, B.P. 540, 66005 Perpignan ☎ 04-68-34-29-94. **Comité Régional du Tourisme du Languedoc-Roussillon** ✉ 20 rue de la République, 34000 Montpellier ☎ 04-67-22-81-00 🖷 04-67-58-06-10 ⊕ www.cr-languedocroussillon.fr/tourisme/. **Albi** ✉ Pl. Ste-Cécile ☎ 05-63-49-48-80 ⊕ www.mairie-albi.fr. **Auch** ✉ 1 rue Dessoles ☎ 05-62-05-22-89. **Béziers** ✉ Palais des Congrès, 29 av. St-Saëns ☎ 04-67-76-47-00. **Carcassonne** ✉ 15 bd. Camille-Pelletan ☎ 04-68-25-07-04

⊕ www.carcassonne-tourisme.org. **Céret** ⊠ 1 bd. Clemenceau ☎ 04-68-87-00-53 ⊕ www.ot-ceret.fr. **Collioure** ⊠ Pl. 18-juin ☎ 04-68-82-15-47 ⊕ www.collioure. com. **Cordes-sur-Ciel** ⊠ Maison Fonpeyrouse ☎ 05-63-56-00-52. **Eyne** ⊠ Eyne Station ☎ 04-68-04-08-01. **Fleurance** ⊠ Pl. de la République 2 ☎ 05-62-64-00-00. **Foix** ⊠ 45 Cours G.-Fauré ☎ 05-61-65-12-12. **Font-Romeu** ⊠ Av. E. Brousse ☎ 05-68-30-68-30. **Larressingle** ⊠ Syndicat D'Initiative ☎ 05-62-28-37-02. **Lectoure** ⊠ Pl. de l'Église ☎ 05-62-68-76-98. **Minerve** ⊠ Pl. du Monument aux Morts ☎ 04-68-91-81-43. **Mirepoix** ⊠ Pl. Mar.-Leclerc ☎ 05-61-68-83-76. **Montauban** ⊠ Ancien College, B.P. 201 ☎ 05-63-63-60-60 ⊕ www.officetourisme.montauban.com. **Moissac** ⊠ 6 pl. Durand de Bredon ☎ 05-63-04-01-85. **Mont-Louis** ⊠ Rue Vauban ☎ 04-68-04-21-97. **Montpellier** ⊠ 30 allée Jean de Lattre de Tassigny, Esplanade Comédie ☎ 04-67-60-60-60 ⊕ www.ot-montpellier.fr. **Narbonne** ⊠ Pl. Roger-Salengro ☎ 04-68-65-15-60. **Perpignan** ⊠ Quai de Lattre de Tassigny ☎ 04-68-66-30-30. **Pézenas** ⊠ 1 pl. Gambetta ☎ 04-67-98-36-40 ⊕ www. perpignantourisme.com. **Prades** ⊠ 4 rue Victor-Hugo ☎ 04-68-05-41-02. **St-Guilhem-le-Désert** ⊠ 2 rue de la Font du Portal ☎ 04-67-57-44-33. **Toulouse** ⊠ Donjon du Capitole ☎ 05-61-11-02-22 ⊕ www.ot-toulouse.fr. **Villefranche-de-Conflent** ⊠ Pl. de l'Eglise ☎ 05-62-64-00-00.

THE BASQUE COUNTRY, GASCONY & HAUTES-PYRÉNÉES

15

Revised and
updated by
George Semler

Introduction by
George Semler

A PELOTA-PLAYING MAYOR IN THE PROVINCE OF SOULE recently welcomed a group of travelers with the following announcements: that the Basque Country is the most beautiful place in the world; that the Basque people were very likely direct descendants of Adam and Eve via the lost city of Atlantis; that his own ancestors fought in the Crusades; and that Christopher Columbus was almost certainly a Basque. There, in brief, was a composite picture of the pride, dignity, and humor of the Basques. And if Columbus was not a Basque (a claim very much in doubt), at least historians know that whalers from the regional village of St-Jean-de-Luz sailed as far as America in their three-masted ships and that Juan Sebastián Elkano, from the Spanish Basque village of Guetaria, was one of those intrepid adventurers who accompanied Magellan on his voyage around the world.

The distinctive culture—from berets and pelota matches to Basque cooking—of this little "country" straddling the French and Spanish Pyrénées has cast its spell over the corners of the earth. And continues to do so—just witness the best-seller status of Mark Kurlansky's *The Basque History of the World* several years ago. Today travelers bruised by the crowding and commerce of more frequented parts of France are increasingly heading to this southwest region to enjoy its relatively undiscovered panoply of rich cultures and landscapes. In an easy stretch, a midsummer's day begun surfing in Biarritz could end at sunset glacier skiing at the Brèche de Roland above Gavarnie. The ocher sands along the Bay of Biscay and the bright reds and blues of the St-Jean-de-Luz fishing fleet are less than an hour from the emerald hills of St-Jean-Pied-de-Port in the Basque Pyrénées. Atlantic salmon and native Pyrenean trout still thrive in the River Nive, while puffball sheep tumble about in the moist highland pastures.

Center stage is held by the three Pays Basque provinces—Labourd, Soule, and Basse Navarre—which share with their four cousin Basque provinces in Spain a singular culture including: jai alai, whaleboat regattas, stone lifting, world-famous cuisine, as well as a mysterious and ancient non-Indo-European language. The origins of this culture remain obscure. The purported resemblance of the Basque evening (or war) call, the *irrinzina,* to that of the Upper Amazon Indians only adds to the mystery, as does the common use by both the Basques and the ancient Mayans of base 20 to reckon math. Some trace Basque origins back to the Berbers of North Africa, though the most tenable theory is that they are descended from aboriginal Iberian peoples who successfully defended their unique language and cultural identity from the influences of Roman and Moorish domination felt elsewhere on the peninsula.

At the eastern edge of the Basque Country, the ski and spelunking town of Pierre-St-Martin marks the start of the Béarn, with its splendid capital city of Pau and the pristine valleys of Aspe, Ossau, and Barétous descending from the Pyrénées. Sauveterre-de-Béarn's medieval drawbridge, Navarrenx and its *bastide* over the rushing Gave d'Oloron, and the Romanesque and Mudejar Ste-Croix church at Oloron-Ste-Marie provide stepping-stones into the limestone heights surrounding the 8,263-foot Pic d'Anie, the highest point in the Béarn.

15

The Basque Country boasts some of France's most dramatic natural extremes: from Atlantic beaches and lush, green pre-Pyrenean hills to the Béarn's rolling meadows and rushing trout and salmon streams, to the lofty heights of the Hautes-Pyrénées and their greatest marvel—the sheer granite walls of La Cirque de Gavarnie. Whether you head for Bay of Biscay resorts like Biarritz, picturesque villages like St-Jean-de-Luz, or the towering peaks of the central Pyrenean cordillera, you will discover some of France's most fascinating man-made and natural wonders in these parts. Consider Dax and Eugénie-les-Bains as excellent side trips to the basic itinerary outlined here. Begin in Bayonne, exploring the Basque coast, and then head east into the Atlantic Pyrénées.

Numbers in the text correspond to numbers in the margin and on the Basque Country & the Hautes-Pyrénées maps.

If you have 3 days

There is nothing leisurely about this three-day tour, nor is there time to do much walking, which is why it is recommended only if your time is limited and your curiosity unlimited. Begin in **Bayonne** ❶ ▶, spending a morning exploring the town. See the cathedral and the Bonnat Museum before hitting **Biarritz** ❷— still redolent with Belle Epoque *parfum*—in time for afternoon tea. Spend the night in ⊡ **St-Jean-de-Luz** ❸, famed for its picturesque fishing port. On Day 2 drive through **Sare** ❹, studded with Basque architecture, and relentlessly pretty **Ainhoa** ❺ and past **Pas de Roland** ❻ on the way up the Nive River to the fortified town of **St-Jean-Pied-de-Port** ❼ for lunch. Explore the Haute Soule during the afternoon: drive through the Irati Forest to the hiker's paradise of **Larrau** ❽ and **Ste-Engrâce** ❿, noted for its Basque-style church, on the way through **Oloron-Ste-Marie** ⓬ to the Béarn's capital, ⊡ **Pau** ⓯, where you should overnight. On Day 3 have a look around Pau, see the great shrine-church of **Lourdes** ⓲ at midday, and get up to ⊡ **Gavarnie** ⓴ in time to see the sun set from the legendary Hôtel du Cirque et de la Cascade.

If you have 8 days

Begin in ⊡ **Bayonne** ❶ ▶, spending a morning exploring the town. See the cathedral and the Bonnat Museum. The second day head back to the coast at soigné **Biarritz** ❷ for some time at the beach. Spend the night in the fetching harbor town of ⊡ **St-Jean-de-Luz** ❸. On Day 3 climb La Rhune (or take the little train to the top) for a stunning view over the entire Basque coast. Drive through **Sare** ❹ and **Ainhoa** ❺ and past **Pas de Roland** ❻ on the way up the Nive River to spend the night at ⊡ **St-Jean-Pied-de-Port** ❼. Explore the town and the Haute Soule on your fourth morning: drive through the Irati Forest to ⊡ **Larrau** ❽ and do the Holçarté Gorges walk to ⊡ **Ste-Engrâce** ❿ if there is time; return to Larrau if not. On Day 5 explore the lower Soule, **Oloron-Ste-Marie** ⓬, and ⊡ **Pau** ⓯. On Day 6 walk around Pau, tour the château, then head up to ⊡ **Eugénie-les-Bains** ⓰ and the fabulous domains created by superstar restaurateur-hotelier Michel Guéard. After a day and night of blissful *luxe, calme, et volupté*, it will be time, on the seventh day, to check out your more spiritual side in **Lourdes** ⓲. Then make the ascent to ⊡ **Gavarnie** ⓴ in time to see the sun set from the Hôtel du Cirque et de la Cascade. On Day 8 explore the area around Gavarnie.

East through the Aubisque Pass, at the Béarn's eastern limit, is the heart of the Hautes-Pyrénées, where France's highest Pyrenean peaks—Vignemale (10,820 feet) and Balaïtous (10,321 feet)—compete with other legendary natural treasures. The Cirque de Gavarnie, the world's most spectacular cirque (or natural amphitheater), is centered around a 1,400-foot waterfall. The nearby Brèche de Roland is a dramatic breach, or cleft, in the rock wall between France and Spain, while to the east, the Cirque de Troumouse is the largest of its kind in all the Pyrénées. When you get your fill of mountaintop vistas and Basque peaks, you can head to the regional spa towns and coastal cities, whose tony refinements once lured the crowned heads of Europe. It was Empress Eugènie who gave Biarritz its coming-out party, transforming it, in the era of Napoléon III, from a simple bourgeois town into an international favorite. Today, after a round of sightseeing, you can still enjoy the Second Empire trimmings from a perch at the roulette table in the town's casino.

Exploring the Basque Country, Gascony & Hautes-Pyrénées

From the lazy, sandy sea level around Bayonne, Biarritz, and St. Jean-de-Luz, this southwest tag end of the Pyrenees hops suddenly up to La Rhune (3,000 feet) and from there it's ever higher, through lush green hills of the inland Basque and Béarn countries past the 6,617-foot Pic d'Orhy to the 6,700-foot Vignemale peak just west of Gavarnie and its historically famous Cirque. Bayonne and Pau are the urban and cultural centers anchoring and connecting these lofty highlands to the rest of France, while the Basque, Béarn, Gascon, and Bigorre cultures offer linguistic as well as culinary variety as you meander eastward and upward from the Basque coast. Gascony is the realm bordered by the Bay of Biscay to the west, the Pyrénées to the south, and the Garonne River to the north and east—pretty Pau is the main city in the region, which sweeps south past Lourdes to Cauterets. Whether you approach from the Atlantic or the Mediterranean, you won't want to miss these beauty spots: Gavarnie, Ste-Engrâce, St-Jean-Pied-de-Port, Sauveterre-de-Béarn, Ainhoa, or St-Jean-de-Luz. Trans-Pyrenean hikers (and drivers) generally prefer moving from west to east for a number of reasons, especially the excellent light prevailing in the late afternoon and evening during the prime months of May to October.

About the Restaurants & Hotels

As with expensive bottles of wine, the point of diminishing returns in Basque dining arrives in a hurry, the local cuisine nearly always more satisfying in simple environments where the fare always seems better than it has any right to be. Once described as "essentially the art of cooking fish," the Basque coast's traditional fresh seafood is unsurpassable every day of the week except Monday, the fleet having stayed in port on Sunday. The inland Basque country and upland Béarn is famous for game in fall and winter and lambs in spring. In the Haute Pyrenees, the higher altitude makes power dining attractive and thick bean soups and wild boar stews come into their own.

From palatial beachside splendor in Biarritz to simple mountain auberges in the Basque Country to Pyrenean refuges in the Hautes-Pyrénées, the

La Cuisine de Pays Basque

Dining in the regions of the Basque country is invariably a feast, whether it's on seafood or upland dishes ranging from beef to lamb to game birds such as the famous migratory *palombes* (wood pigeons). Dishes to keep in mind include *ttoro* (hake stew), *pipérade* (tomatoes and green peppers cooked in olive oil, and often scrambled eggs), *bakalao al pil-pil* (cod cooked in oil "*al pil-pil*"—the bubbling sound the fish makes as it creates its own sauce), *marmitako* (tuna and potato stew), and *zikiro* (roast lamb). Home of the famous *sauce bérnaise*, Béarn is famous for its *garbure*, thick vegetable soup with *confit de canard* (preserved duck) and *fèves* (broad beans). *Civets* (stews) made with *isard* (wild goat) or wild boar are other specialties. La Bigorre and the Hautes-Pyrénées are equally dedicated to garbure, though they may call their version *soupe paysanne bigourdane* (Bigorran peasant soup) to distinguish it from that of their neighbors.

15

Attention Hike-a-holics

Supping on the hearty regional cuisine makes perfect sense after a day of hiking along the gorges and into the mountains of the Pyrénées, which are best explored on foot. The lengthy GR (Grande Randonnée) 10, a trail signed by discreet red-and-white paint markings, runs all the way from the Atlantic at Hendaye to Banyuls-sur-Mer on the Mediterranean, through villages and up and down mountains. Placed along the way are mountain refuges. The HRP (Haute Randonnée Pyrénéenne, or High Pyrenean Hike) stays closer to the border crest, following the terrain of both France and Spain irrespective of national borders. Local trails are also well indicated, usually with blue or yellow markings. Some of the classic walks in the Basque Pyrénées include the Iparla Ridge walk between Bidarrai and St-Étienne-de-Baïgorry, the Santiago de Compostela Trail's dramatic St-Jean-Pied-de-Port to Roncesvalles walk over the Pyrénées, and the Holçarté Gorge walk between Larrau and Ste-Engrâce. Trail maps are available from local tourist offices.

Gonzo over Games

Perhaps the best-known and most spectacular of Basque sports is the ancestral ball game of pelota, a descendant of the medieval *jeux de paume* (literally, palm games), a fundamental element of rural Basque culture. A Basque village without a fronton (backboard and pelota court) is as unimaginable as an American town lacking a baseball diamond. There are many versions and variations on this graceful, fast-paced sport, played with the bare hand, with wooden bats, or with curved basketlike gloves; a real wicker *chistera*—the wicker bat used in the game—is an interesting souvenir to buy (and makes a very pretty fruit basket, but let no Basque hear that bit of heresy). Other rural Basque sports include scything, wood-chopping and -sawing, sack hauling, stone lifting, long-distance racing, tug-of-war, competitive whaleboat rowing, and, for those who really want to take the weight of the world on their shoulders, *orga yoko*, or cart lifting—hefting and moving a 346-kilo (761-pound) hay wagon (you read it here).

gamut of lodging in southwest France is conveniently broad. For top value and camaraderie, look for *gîtes* or *tables d'hôtes* (rustic bed-and-breakfasts and way stations for hikers and skiers), where all guests dine together. Be sure to book summertime lodging on the Basque coast well in advance, particularly for August. In the Hautes-Pyrénées only Gavarnie during its third-week-of-July music festival presents a potential booking problem. An even better approach is to make it up as you go: the surprises that come along are usually very pleasant. Assume all hotel rooms have air-conditioning, TV, telephones, and private bath, unless otherwise noted.

WHAT IT COSTS In euros					
	$$$$	**$$$**	**$$**	**$**	**¢**
RESTAURANTS	over €25	€17–€25	€12–€17	€8–€12	under €8
HOTELS	over €175	€120–€175	€70–€120	€40–€70	under €40

Restaurant prices are per person for a main course at dinner, including tax (19.6%) and service; note that if a restaurant offers only prix-fixe (set-price) meals, it has been given the price category that reflects the full prix-fixe price. Hotel prices are for a standard double room in high season, including tax (19.6%) and service charge; higher prices (inquire when booking) prevail for any meal plans.

Timing

From early May through late October is the best time to explore this region. June and September are the height of the season. July is the only month you can be nearly 100% sure of being to able to, say, walk safely over the glacier to the Brèche de Roland. In winter, beach life is over and the Pyrénées are snowed in; many hotels and restaurants close. Only for skiing and the pleasure of the nearly total absence of tourists is the winter season recommended.

THE BASQUE COAST

La Côte Basque—a world unto itself with its own language, sports, and folklore—occupies France's southwesternmost corner along the Spanish border. Inland, the area is laced with rivers: the Bidasoa River border with Spain marks the southern edge of the region, and the Adour River, on its northern edge, separates the Basque country from the neighboring Les Landes. The Nive River flows through the heart of the verdant Basque littoral to join the Adour at Bayonne, and the smaller Nivelle River flows into the Bay of Biscay at St-Jean-de-Luz. Bayonne, Biarritz, and St-Jean-de-Luz are the main towns along the coast, all less than 40 km (25 mi) from the first peak of the Pyrénées.

Bayonne

▶ ❶ *48 km (30 mi) southwest of Dax, 184 km (114 mi) south of Bordeaux, 295 km (183 mi) west of Toulouse.*

At the confluence of the Adour and Nive rivers, Bayonne, France's most indelibly Basque city, was in the 4th century a Roman fort, or *castrum,* and for 300 years (1151–1451) a British colony. Source of the name of

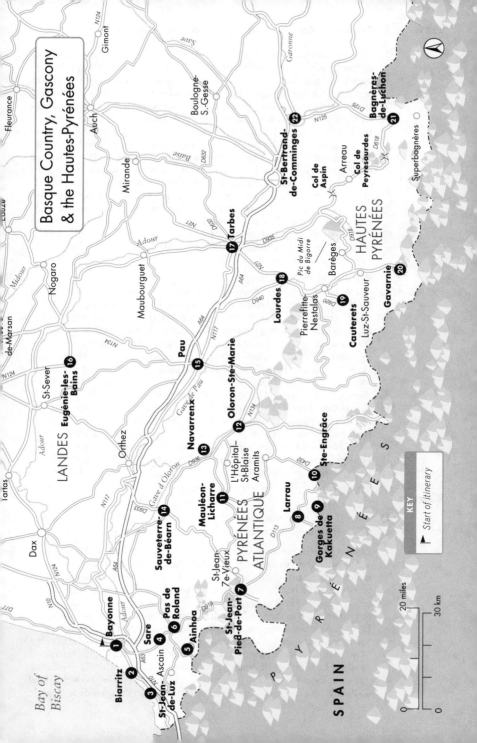

the bayonet blade (from the French *baïonnette*), invented here in the 17th century, today's Bayonne is more famous for its ham (*jambon de Bayonne*) and for the annual Basque pelota world championships held in September. Even though the port is spread out along the Adour estuary some 5 km (3 mi) from the sea, the two rivers and five bridges lend this small gem of a city a definite maritime feel. The houses fronting the quai, the intimate place Pasteur, the Château-Vieux, the elegant 18th-century homes along rue des Prébendés, the 17th-century ramparts, and the cathedral are some of the town's not-to-be-missed sights. The **Cathédrale** (called both Ste-Marie and Notre-Dame) was built mainly in the 13th century, and is one of France's southernmost examples of Gothic architecture. Its 13th- to 14th-century cloisters are among its best features. The airy, modernized **Musée Bonnat**, in itself reason enough to visit Bayonne, has a notable treasury of 19th-century paintings collected by French portraitist and historical painter Léon Bonnat (1833–1922). ⊠ *5 rue Jacques-Lafitte* ☎ *05–59–59–08–52* ⊞ *€3* ☉ *Wed.–Mon. 10–noon and 2:30–6:30.*

Where to Stay & Eat

★ **$$$–$$$$** ✕ **L'Auberge du Cheval Blanc.** This innovative Basque establishment in the Petit Bayonne quarter near the Bonnat Museum serves a combination of *cuisine du terroir* (home-style regional cooking) and original concoctions in contemporary surroundings. Jean-Claude Tellechea showcases fresh fish as well as upland specialties from the Basque hills, sometimes joining the two in ground-breaking dishes such as the *merlu rôti aux oignons et jus de volaille* (hake roasted in onions with essence of poultry). ⊠ *68 rue Bourgneuf* ☎ *05–59–59–01–33* ⊟ *MC, V* ☉ *Closed Sun. dinner, Mon. except Aug., June 25–July 2, Feb. 10–Mar. 8.*

$$–$$$ ✕⊡ **Le Grand Hôtel.** Just down the street from the Château-Vieux, this central spot has pleasant, comfortable rooms with an old-world feel. The restaurant, Les Carmes, built in a former Carmelite convent, is excellent. ⊠ *21 rue Thiers, 64100* ☎ *05–59–59–62–00* ☎ *05–59–59–62–01* ⊕ *www. bw-legrandhotel.com* ↬ *54 rooms* ⊙ *Restaurant, minibars, cable TV, bar, parking (fee), some pets allowed (fee)* ⊟ *AE, DC, MC, V* ⊙❘ *EP, MAP.*

Biarritz

❷ 8 km (5 mi) south of Bayonne, 190 km (118 mi) southwest of Bordeaux,
Fodor'sChoice 50 km (31 mi) north of San Sebastián, 115 km (69 mi) west of Pau.
★

Once a favorite resort of Charlie Chaplin, Coco Chanel, and exiled Russian royals, Biarritz first rose to prominence when rich and royal Carlist exiles from Spain set up shop here in 1838. Unable to visit San Sebastián just across the border on the Basque coast, they sought a summer watering spot as close as possible to their old stomping ground. Among the exiles was Eugénie de Montijo, soon destined to become empress of France. As a child, she vacationed here with her family, fell in love with the place, and then set about building her own palace once she married Napoléon III. During the 14 summers she spent here, half the crowned heads of Europe—including Queen Victoria and Edward VII—were her guests in Eugénie's villa, a gigantic wedding-cake edifice, now the **Hôtel du Palais,** set on the main sea promenade of town, the **quai de la Grande**

Plage, where the fashionable set used to stroll in Worth gowns and picture hats. Whether you consider Napoléon III's bombastic architectural legacies an eyesore or an eyeful—they at least have the courage of their convictions. Biarritz no longer lays claim to the title "the resort of kings and the king of resorts"—but there is no shortage of deluxe hotel rooms or bow-tie gamblers ambling over to the casino. Unfortunately, the old, down-to-earth charm of the former fishing village has been thoroughly trumped by Biarritz's glitzy Second Empire aura—but you won't find the bathing beauties and high-rollers here complaining.

Although far from as drop-dead stylish as it once was, the town is making a comeback as a swank surfing capital with its new casino and convention center. Explore the narrow streets around the cozy 16th-century church of **St-Martin.** Adjacent to the Grand Plage are the set-pieces of the Hôtel du Palais and the **Eglise Orthodoxe Russe,** a Byzantine-style church built by the White Russian community that considered Biarritz their 19th-century Yalta-by-the-Atlantic. The duchesses often repaired to the terraced restaurants of the festive **place Ste-Eugénie,** still considered the social center of town. A lorgnette view away is the harbor of the **Port des Pêcheurs** (Fishing Port), which provides a tantalizing glimpse of the Biarritz of old. Leading off the port is the plateau de l'Atalaye, where you can head through a tunnel to a Gustave Eiffel–designed footbridge and the **Rocher de la Vierge** (Rock of the Virgin). Her sculpted figure has blessed sailors in the Bay of Biscay since 1865. Enjoy the spectacular vista of the coast from the Rocher, then return to town. Biarritz's beaches attract crowds—particularly the fine, sandy beaches of **La Grande Plage** and the neighboring **Plage Miramar,** both set amid craggy natural beauty. A walk along the beach promenades gives a view of the foaming breakers that beat constantly upon the sands, giving the name Côte d'Argent (Silver Coast) to the length of this part of the French Basque coast.

★ If you wish to pay your respects to the Empress Eugénie, visit **La Chapelle Impérriale,** which she had built in 1864 to venerate a figure of a Mexican Black Virgin from Guadelupe (and perhaps to expiate her sins for furthering her husband's tragic folly of putting Emperor Maximilian and Empress Carlotta on the "throne" of Mexico). The style is a charming hybrid of Roman-Byzantine and Hispano-Mauresque. ⊠ *Rue Pellot* ☉ *Apr. 15–July 15, Sept. 16–Oct. 15, Mon., Tues., Sat. 3–7; July 16–Sept. 15, Mon.–Sat. 3–5; Oct. 15–Dec. 31 3–5.*

Where to Stay & Eat

$$–$$$$ ✕ **Chez Albert.** In summer it's nearly impossible to find a place on the terrace of this easygoing and popular seafood restaurant. Views of the fishing port and the salty harborside aromas of things maritime make the hearty fish and seafood offerings all the more irresistible here. ⊠ *Port des Pecheurs s/n* ☎ *05–59–24–43–84* ▭ *AE, DC, MC, V* ☉ *Closed Dec. 1–15, Jan. 5–10, Feb., and Wed. except in July and Aug.*

★ **$$$$** ✕▥ **Château de Brindos.** Take Jazz Age glamour, Spanish Gothic and Renaissance stonework, and the luxest of guest rooms and you have this Pays Basque Xanadu—a large, rambling, white-stone manor topped with a Spanish belvedere tower set 4 km (2½ mi) east of Biarritz in Anglet. This was originally the home of Sir Reginald Wright, whose great soirées held here in the 1920s and '30s are conjured up in the saloon, now presided over by that premier mixologist, barman Marc Pony. In recent years, interiors have been lovingly restored by Serge Blanco, who has managed to honor the mansion's history while installing state-of-the-art technology and comfort. Tapestries, wrought-iron Spanish wall sconces, Louis Quatorze–style armchairs, and dramatic stone fireplace all allure, while views of the estate lake also can be enjoyed from some guest rooms, which offer a bouquet of quilted fabrics, overstuffed chaise-longues, and a general air of *volupté*. In summer dine out under the willows at the edge of the water at the grand restaurant. Chef Antoine Antunès has trained with the best, from Guerard to Arrambide, and offers a guarantee of creative dining. ✉ *1 allée du Château, 64600* ☎ *05–59–23–17–68* 📠 *05–59–23–48–47* 🌐 *www.chateaudebrindos.com* *25 rooms* *Restaurant, minibars, cable TV, pool, bar, meeting rooms, parking (fee), some pets allowed (fee)* 💳 *AE, DC, MC, V* ⏲ *Closed 2 wks in winter, dates vary* 🍽 *EP.*

★ **$$$$** **Hôtel du Palais.** Set on the beach, this majestic, colonnaded redbrick hotel with an immense driveway, lawns, and a grand semicircular dining room, still exudes an opulent, aristocratic air, no doubt imparted by Empress Eugénie when she built it in 1855 as her Biarritz palace. Napoléonic frippery is everywhere in the public areas, but don't go looking for it in the more standard guest rooms, none of which have sea views. Still, the lobby alone may be worth the price of admission. The three restaurants—Hippocampe (where lunch is served beside the curved pool above the Atlantic), the regal dinner spot Villa Eugénie, and the La Rotonde (with its spectacular soaring columns, gilt trim, and sea views)—are all creatively directed by star chef Jean-Marie Gautier. Don't miss out on his lobster gazpacho. ✉ *1 av. de l'Impératrice, 64200* ☎ *05–59–41–64–00* 📠 *05–59–41–67–99* 🌐 *www.hotel-du-palais.com* *134 rooms, 22 suites* *Restaurant, minibars, cable TV, pool, bar, parking (fee), some pets allowed (fee)* 💳 *AE, DC, MC, V* ⏲ *Closed 2 wks in winter, dates vary* 🍽 *EP, MAP.*

★ **$$$–$$$$** **Café de Paris.** This hotel is known for its popular restaurants. One is an elegant (and expensive) spot featuring such dishes as *ris de veau* (veal sweetbreads) and fish served with an imaginative nouvelle touch. The other is a less formal brasserie (with the same chefs). The haute-cuisine restaurant is closed for lunch, as well as for dinner on Sunday; the brasserie is always open. Rooms are luxurious and many have ocean views. ✉ *5 pl. Bellevue, 64200* ☎ *05–59–24–19–53* 📠 *05–59–24–18–20* 🌐 *www.cafedeparis-biarritz.com* *18 rooms* *Restaurant, minibars, cable TV, pool, bar, some pets allowed (fee)* 💳 *AE, DC, MC, V* ⏲ *Closed mid-Nov.–mid-Mar.* 🍽 *EP.*

$$–$$$ **Windsor.** This hotel, built in the 1920s, is close to the casino and the beach. Rooms are modern and cozy; those with sea views cost about twice as much as the ones facing the inner courtyard and street. The restaurant serves up a fine terrine de foie gras with Armagnac, and ravioli stuffed with crab. ✉ *19 bd. du Général-de-Gaulle, 64200* ☎ *05–59–24–08–52* 📠 *05–59–24–98–90* *49 rooms* *Restaurant, bar, parking (fee), some pets allowed (fee); no a/c* 💳 *AE, MC, V* ⏲ *Closed Jan.–mid-Mar.* 🍽 *EP.*

$–$$ **Hôtel de Romance.** This tiny, early-19th-century villa on a quiet alley near the Hippodrome des Fleurs race track is an intimate refuge 10 minutes from downtown Biarritz. Madame Subra takes patient care of everyone here, while the minuscule garden becomes a dappled oasis of serenity during the midsummer Biarritz maelstrom. Quarters are tight but homey. ✉ *6 allée des Acacias, 64200* ☎ *05–59–41–25–65* 🖷 *05–59–41–25–65* ⤴ *10 rooms* ⚬ *No a/c* ☰ *AE, MC, V* ⊙ *Closed mid-Jan.–Mar. 1* ⦶ *EP.*

¢ 🖾 **Hotel Palym.** This excellent budget choice is stationed over a restaurant with a terrace five minutes from the Plage du Port-Vieux. Rooms range from low-end without bath to slightly more expensive with complete in-room bath facilities. The restaurant serves all-you-can-eat paellas in summer, as well as acceptable prix-fixe menus and à la carte selections. ✉ *7 rue du Port-Vieux, 64200* ☎ *05–59–24–16–56* 🖷 *05–59–24–96–12* ⊕ *www.le-palmarium.com* ⤴ *28 rooms, 16 without bath* ⚬ *Restaurant, cable TV, bar, some pets allowed (fee); no a/c* ☰ *AE, MC, V* ⊙ *Closed Jan.–mid-Mar.* ⦶ *EP.*

Nightlife & the Arts

During September, the three-week **Le Temps d'Aimer** festival presents dance performances, from classical to hip hop, in a range of venues throughout the city. They are often at the Théâtre Gare du Midi, a renovated railway station. Troupes such as the Ballets Biarritz, Les Ballets de Monte-Carlo, and leading etoiles from other companies take to the stage in an ambitious schedule of events. At the **Casino de Biarritz** (✉ 1 av. Edouard-VII ☎ 05–59–22–77–77) you can play the slots or blackjack, or go dancing at the Flamingo. **Le Queen's Bar** (✉ 25 pl. Clemenceau ☎ 05–59–24–70–65) is a comfortable hangout both day and night. **Le Caveau** (✉ 4 rue Gambetta ☎ 05–59–24–16–17) is a mythical Biarritz dance club with guaranteed action every night.

Sports & the Outdoors

France's Atlantic Coast has become one of the hottest surfing destinations in the world. The "Endless Summer" arrives in Biarritz every year in late July for a **Biarritz Surf Festival. Désertours Aventure** (✉ 65 av. Maréchal-Juin ☎ 05–59–41–22–02) organizes rafting trips on the Nive River and four-wheel-drive-vehicle tours through the Atlantic Pyrénées. **Golf de Biarritz** (✉ 2 av. Edith-Cavell ☎ 05–59–03–71–80) has an 18-hole, par-69 course. **Pelote Basque: Biarritz Athletic-club** (✉ Parc des Sports d'Aguilera ☎ 05–59–23–91–09) offers instruction in every type of Basque pelota including *main nue* (barehanded), *pala* (paddle), *chistera* (with a basketlike racquet) and *cesta punta* (another game played with the same curved basket). On Wednesday and Saturday at 9 PM in July, August, and September, you can watch pelota games at the **Parc des Sports d'Aguilera** (☎ 05–59–23–91–09).

St-Jean-de-Luz

❸ 23 km (16 mi) southwest of Bayonne, 24 km (18 mi) northeast of San
Fodor'sChoice   Sebastián, 54 km (32 mi) west of St-Jean-Pied-de-Port, 128 km (77 mi)
★   west of Pau.

Back in 1660, Louis XIV chose this tiny fishing village as the place to marry the Infanta Maria Teresa of Spain. Ever since, travelers have journeyed here to enjoy the unique coastal charms of St-Jean. Situated along the coast between Biarritz and the Spanish border, it remains memorable for its colorful harbor, old streets, curious church, and elegant beach. Its iconic port shares a harbor with its sister town Ciboure, on the other side of the Nivelle River. The glorious days of whaling and cod fishing are long gone, but some historic multihue houses around the docks are evocative enough. The tree-lined **place Louis-XIV**, alongside the Hôtel de Ville (Town Hall), with its narrow courtyard and dainty statue of Louis XIV on horseback, is the hub of the town. In summer, concerts are offered on the square, as well as the famous "Toro de fuego" festival, which honors the bull with a parade and a papier-mâché beast. Take a tour of the twin-towered **Maison Louis-XIV**. Built as the Château Lohobiague, it housed the French king during his nuptials and is austerely decorated in 17th-century Basque fashion. ⊠ *Pl. Louis XIV* 🕾 *05–59–26–01–56* ☜ *€6* ⊘ *July–Aug., 10–10; Apr.–June, Sept. and Oct., daily 10:30–noon and 2–6:30; Nov.–Mar., by appointment.*

The marriage of the Sun King and the Infanta took place in 1660 in the church of **St-Jean-Baptiste** (⊠ Pl. des Corsaires). The marriage tied the knot, so to speak, on the Pyrénées Treaty signed by Mazarin on November 7, 1659, ending Spanish hegemony in Europe. Note the church's unusual wooden galleries lining the walls, creating a theaterlike effect. Fittingly, St-Jean-Baptiste hosts a "Musique en Côte Basque" festival of early and Baroque music during the first two weeks of September. The church is open daily from 9 to 6, with a three hour closure for lunch.

Of particular note is the Louis XIII–style **Maison de l'Infante** (Princess's House), between the harbor and the bay, where Maria Teresa of Spain stayed prior to her marriage to Louis XIV. She was accompanied by her mother, Queen Anne of Austria, who brought a goodly number of her royal court. The foursquare mansion now houses the **Musée Grévin,** which contains wax figures and period costumes. ⊠ *Quai de l'Infante* 🕾 *05–59–51–24–88* ☜ *€6* ⊘ *July and Aug., daily 10–10; Apr.–June, Sept. and Oct., daily 10:30–noon and 2–6:30; Nov.–Mar., by appointment.*

Where to Stay & Eat

$$–$$$$ ✕ **Chez Pablo.** The catch of the day determines the daily offering here. Long tables covered with red-and-white tablecloths, benches, and plaster walls give off a casual vibe but the dishes are often excellent. ⊠ *Rue Mme. Etxeto* 🕾 *05–56–26–37–81* ⊟ *No credit cards* ⊘ *Closed Sun.*

$$–$$$ ✕ **Chez Dominique.** A walk around the picturesque fishing port to the Ciboure side of the harbor will take you past the house where Maurice Ravel was born (No. 27) to this rustic maritime eatery. The simple, home-style menu here is based on what the fishing fleet caught that morning; try the *marmitako* (tuna stew). The views over the harbor are unbeatable. ⊠ *15 quai M. Ravel* 🕾 *05–59–47–29–16* ⊟ *AE, DC, MC, V* ⊘ *Closed Mon. except mid-June–end of Aug. Closed mid-Feb.–mid-Mar. No dinner Sun.*

$$–$$$ ✕ **La Taverne Basque.** This well-known midtown standard is one of the old-faithful local dining emporiums, specializing in Basque cuisine with a pronounced maritime emphasis. Try the *ttoro* (a rich fish, crustacean, potato, and vegetable soup). ⊠ *5 rue République* 🕾 *05–59–26–01–26* ⊟ *AE, DC, MC, V* ⊘ *Closed Mon. and Tues. except in July and Aug.; month of Mar.*

$$ ✕ **Txalupa.** The name is Basque for "skiff" or "small boat," and you'll feel like you're in one when you're this close to the bay—yachts and fishing vessels go about their business just a few yards away. This well-known haunt with a terrace over the port serves the famous *jambon de Bayonne* (Bayonne ham) in vinegar and garlic sauce, as well as fresh fish and natural produce such as wild mushrooms. ⊠ *Pl. Louis-XIV* ☎ *05–59–51–85–52* ☰ *AE, DC, MC, V.*

$$$–$$$$ ✕▨ **Le Grand Hôtel.** Completely overhauled and refitted in 2001, the Grand Hôtel has resumed its long-standing place as St-Jean-de-Luz's premier hotel. Don't miss a meal at Le Rosewood, its top-rated restaurant overlooking the beach. The rooms are decorated in colorful pastels, wood, and marble, and the unbeatable location at the northern end of the St-Jean-de-Luz beach will make you feel like the Sun King himself. ⊠ *43 bd. Thiers, 64500* ☎ *05–59–26–35–36* ☒ *05–59–51–99–84* ⊕ *www. luzgrandhotel.fr* ↳*48 rooms, 2 suites, 2 apartments* ⚖ *Restaurant, minibars, cable TV, pool, bar, some pets allowed (fee)* ☰ *AE, DC, MC, V* ☽ *Closed Dec.–early Apr.* ⍾ *EP.*

THE ATLANTIC PYRÉNÉES

The Atlantic Pyrénées extend eastward from the Atlantic to the Col du Pourtalet, and encompass Béarn and the mountainous part of the Basque Country. Watching the Pyrénées grow from rolling green foothills in the west to jagged limestone peaks to glacier-studded granite massifs in the Hautes-Pyrénées makes for an exciting experience. The Atlantic Pyrénées' first major height is at La Rhune (2,969 feet), known as the Balcon du Côte Basque (Balcony of the Basque Coast). The highest Basque peak is at Orhi (6,617 feet); the Béarn's highest is Pic d'Anie (8,510 feet). Not until Balaïtous (10,381 feet) and Vignemale (10,820 feet), in the Hautes-Pyrénées, does the altitude surpass the 10,000-foot mark. Starting east from St-Jean-de-Luz up the Nivelle River, a series of picturesque villages that includes Ascain, Sare, Ainhoa, and Bidarrai leads up to St-Jean-Pied-de-Port and the Pyrénées.

This journey ends in Pau, far from the Pays Basque and set in the Béarn, akin in temperament to the larger region of which it is an enclave, Gascony. Gascony may be purse-poor, but is certainly rich in scenery and lore. Its proud and touchy temperament is typified in literature by the character d'Artagnan in Dumas's *Three Musketeers* and in history by the lords of the château of Pau. An inscription over its entrance, TOUCHEZ-Y, SI TU L'OSES— "Touch this if you dare"—was that of Gaston Phoebus, a golden-haired and volatile count of Foix. For an arts lover, he had a nasty temper, which led him to murder his own brother and his only son.

Sare

❹ *14 km (8 mi) southeast of St-Jean-de-Luz, 9 km (5½ mi) southwest of Ainhoa on D118: take the first left.*

The gemlike village of Sare is built around a large fronton, or backboard, where a permanent pelota game rages around the clock. Not surprisingly, the Hôtel de Ville (town hall) offers a permanent exhibition on Pelote Basque (open July and August, daily 9–1 and 2–6:30; September–June, daily 3–6). Sare was a busy smuggling hub throughout the 19th century. Its chief attractions are colorful wood-beam and whitewashed Basque architecture, the 16th-century late-Romanesque church with its lovely triple-decker interior, and the **Ospitale Zaharra** pilgrim's hospice behind the church. More than a dozen tiny chapels sprinkled around Sare were built as ex-votos by seamen who survived Atlantic storms. Up the Sare Valley are the panoramic Col de Lizarrieta and the **Grottes de Sare,** where you can study up on Basque culture and history at a **Musée Ethnographique** (Ethnographical Museum) and take a guided tour (in five languages) for 1 km (½ mi) underground and see a *son-et-lumière* (sound and light) show. ☎ *05–59–54–21–88* ✆ *€5* ⊙ *Mid-Feb.–Dec., Tues.–Sun. 11–7.*

West of Sare on D4, at the Col de St-Ignace, take the **Petit Train de la Rhune,** a tiny wood-panel cogwheel train that reaches the less-than-dizzying speed of 5 mph while climbing up La Rhune peak. The views of the Bay of Biscay, the Pyrénées, and the grassy hills of the Basque farmland are wonderful. ☎ *05–59–54–20–26* ✆ *€7* ⊙ *Round-trip (1 hr): Easter vacation and May and June, daily 10 and 3; July–Sept., daily every 35 mins.*

FodorśChoice ★

Where to Stay & Eat

★ $ ✕▣ **Baratxartea.** This little inn 1 km (½ mi) from the center of Sare in one of the town's prettiest and most ancient *quartiers* is a find. Monsieur Fagoaga's family-run hotel and restaurant occupy a 16th-century town house complete with *colombiers* (pigeon roosts), and are surrounded by some of the finest rural Basque architecture in Labourd. ⊠ *Quartier Ihalar, 64310* ☎ *05–59–54–20–48* 🖶 *05–59–47–50–84* ⊐ *22 rooms* ⚖ *Restaurant, cable TV, some pets allowed (fee); no a/c* ▤ *AE, DC, MC, V* ⊙ *Closed Jan.–mid-Mar.* ❑ *EP.*

Ainhoa

❺   *9 km (5½ mi) east of Sare, 23 km (14 mi) southeast of St-Jean-de-Luz,*
FodorśChoice   *31 km (19 mi) northwest of St-Jean-Pied-de-Port.*
★

The Basque village of Ainhoa is officially registered among the villages selected by the national tourist ministry as the prettiest in France. A town that best represents the Labourd region, it was established in the 13th century by Juan Perex de Bastan. Today, the streets are lined with lovely 16th- to 18th-century houses graced with whitewashed walls, flower-filled balconies, brightly painted shutters, and carved master beams. The Romanesque church of **Notre-Dame de l'Assomption** has a traditional Basque three-tier wooden interior with carved railings and ancient oak stairs. Explore Ainhoa's little streets, dotted with artisanal ateliers and art galleries. Unfortunately, you'll need your own wheels to get to Ainhoa.

Where to Stay & Eat

★ $$$ ✕▣ **Ithurria.** This is a registered historic monument, once a staging post on the fabled medieval pilgrims' route to Santiago de Compostela. If you are doing a modern version of the pilgrims' journey or just need a stopover on the way deeper into the mountains, the Ithurria—set in a 17th-century building in the prevailing Basque style and surrounded

PARLEZ-VOUS EUSKERA?

ALTHOUGH THE BASQUE PEOPLE speak French on their side of the Spanish border, they consider Euskera their first language and identify themselves as the "Euskaldunak" (the "Basque speakers"), not French. Euskera remains one of the great enigmas of linguistic scholarship. A bewildering range of theories connects it with everything from Sanskrit to Japanese to Finnish, even to the language of the mythical island of Atlantis or the language spoken by Adam and Eve. What is certain is where Euskera did not come from, namely the Indo-European family of languages that includes the Germanic, Italic, and Hellenic language groups. Attempts to link the Basque language to Iberian, Berber, and Etruscan languages have also proved inconclusive, though philologist Ramón Menéndez Pidal's *En torno a la lengua Vasca (On the Basque Language)* makes a convincing case, based on toponyms, that the language was spoken by aboriginals from the Iberian Peninsula, especially across the Pyrénées, and only endured in corners farthest from the reach of Roman and Moorish colonization. Presently spoken by about a million people in northern Spain and southwestern France, Euskera sounds like a consonant-ridden version of Spanish, with its five pure vowels, rolled "r" and palatal "n" and "l." Uniquely, Euskera uses suffixes to denote case and number and to form new words. Despite numerous Latinate loanwords, Basque has survived two millennia of cultural and political pressure and is the only remaining language of those spoken in southwestern Europe before the Roman conquest. Since the 10th century, Euskera has gradually been supplanted by Castilian Spanish, but under the present constitutional monarchy, Euskera has flourished through normalized academic instruction, radio and television broadcasts, newspapers, and literary publications.

by a garden—will give you a fine atmospheric night. The rustic dining room is the gemstone here, with fare to match, combining inland game and fresh seafood from the Basque coast in creative ways. Guest rooms are modern, comfortable, and tastefully decorated. ⊠ *Rue Principale, 64250* ☎ *05–59–29–92–11* 🖳 *05–59–29–81–28* ⊕ *www.ithuria.com* 🗪 *27 rooms* ⚲ *Restaurant, minibars, pool, gym, bar, some pets allowed (fee); no a/c* ⊟ *AE, DC, MC, V* ⊘ *Closed Nov.–Apr. 1, Wed. except in July and Aug.* ⑩ *EP.*

$ 🏠 **Oppoca.** This 17th-century *relais*, or stagecoach relay station, on Ainhoa's main square and pelota court remains one of the loveliest Basque houses in town. Rooms are small but adequate and the owners are a jolly group, always ready to share their knowledge about the locals and the locale. ⊠ *Place du Fronton, s/n, 64250* ☎ *05–59–29–90–72* 🖳 *05–59–29–81–03* 🗪 *12 rooms* ⚲ *Restaurant, minibars, bar, some pets allowed (fee); no a/c* ⊟ *AE, DC, MC, V* ⊘ *Closed Dec. and Jan.* ⑩ *EP.*

Pas de Roland

❻ *15 km (9 mi) east of Ainhoa, 30 km (18 mi) northwest of St-Jean-Pied-de-Port; follow signs for Itxassou and proceed past the town up to the pass.*

Legend has it that the Pas de Roland (Roland's Footprint) was where the legendary medieval French hero Roland enabled Charlemagne's troops to move forward by cutting a passageway through an impeding boulder with his mystical sword, Durandal. In the process he purportedly left his footprint in the rock, where the "evidence" may be seen to this day. The drive along this bend in the Nive River is a scenic detour off the D918 road up to St-Jean-Pied-de-Port.

Where to Stay & Eat

¢–$ ✕⊡ **Hôtel du Pas du Roland.** Just upstream from the Pas de Roland, this rustic little inn is a good place for a meal or a night. Native trout is available from the nearby Nive River, if you're skillful enough to capture one; otherwise, try the *pipérade basquaise au jambon* (an egg dish with tomatoes, green peppers, onions, and ham). Rooms are simple but clean and cozy. ✉ *Laxîa, 64250 Itxassou* ☎ *05–59–29–75–23* 🖷 *05–59–29–85–86* ⇱ *9 rooms with showers and sinks, toilet in hall* ⚹ *Restaurant, cable TV, bar, some pets allowed (fee); no a/c* ▤ *AE, DC, MC, V* ☉ *Closed Dec.–Mar.* ⍾ *EP, MAP.*

St-Jean-Pied-de-Port

❼ *54 km (33 mi) east of Biarritz, 46 km (28 mi) west of Larrau.*

St-Jean-Pied-de-Port, a fortified town on the Nive River, got its name from its position at the foot (*pied*) of the mountain pass (*port*) of Roncevaux (Roncesvalles). The pass was the setting for *La Chanson de Roland* (*The Song of Roland*), the 11th-century epic poem considered the true beginning of French literature. The bustling town center, a major stop for pilgrims en route to Santiago de Compostela, seems, after a tour through the Soule, like a frenzied metropolitan center—even in winter. In summer, especially around the time of Pamplona's San Fermin blowout (the running of the bulls, July 7–14), the place is filled to the gills and is somewhere between exciting and unbearable.

Walk into the old section through the Porte de France, just behind and to the left of the tourist office, climb the steps on the left up to the walkway circling the ramparts, and walk around to the stone stairway down to the rue de l'Église. The church of **Notre-Dame-du-Bout-du-Pont** (Our Lady of the End of the Bridge), known for its magnificent doorway, is at the bottom of this cobbled street. The church is a characteristically Basque three-tier structure, designed for women to sit on the ground floor, men to be in the first balcony, and the choir in the loft above. From the **Pont Notre-Dame** (Notre-Dame Bridge) you can watch the wild trout in the Nive (also an Atlantic salmon stream) as they pluck mayflies off the surface. Note that fishing is *défendu* (forbidden) in town. Upstream, along the left bank, is another wooden bridge. Cross it and then walk around and back through town, crossing back to the left bank on the main road.

The **Relais de la Nive** bar and café—hanging over the river at the north end of the bridge in the center of town—is the perfect spot to have a coffee while admiring the reflection of the pont de Notre-Dame upstream and watching the trout working in the current.

On **rue de la Citadelle** are a number of sights of interest: the **Maison Arcanzola** (Arcanzola House), at No. 32 (1510); the **Maison des Évêques** (Bishops' House), at No. 39; and the famous **Prison des Évêques** (Bishops' Prison), next door to it. Continue up along rue de la Citadelle to get to the **Citadelle**, a classic Vauban fortress, now occupied by a school. The views from the Citadelle, complete with maps identifying the surrounding heights and valleys, are panoramic.

Where to Stay & Eat

$$–$$$ ✕ **Chez Arbillaga.** Tucked inside the citadel ramparts, this lively bistro is a sound choice for lunch or dinner. The food represents what the Basques do best: simple cooking of excellent quality, such as *agneau de lait à la broche* (roast lamb), in winter, or *coquilles St-Jacques au lard fumé* (scallops with bacon), in summer. ⊠ *8 rue de l'Église* ☎ *05–59–37–06–44* ▤ *MC, V* ⊗ *Closed 1st 2 wks of June and Oct. and Wed. during Jan.–May.*

★ **$$–$$$** ✕▥ **Les Pyrénées.** This inn has the best restaurant in town, specializing in nouvelle Basque cuisine such as ravioli and prawns with caviar sauce and hot wild-mushroom terrine. Rooms are modern and vary in size; four have balconies. ⊠ *19 pl. Charles de Gaulle, 64220* ☎ *05–59–37–01–01* ⊟ *05–59–37–18–97* ⊕ *www.relais-chateaux.com/pyrenees* ⇛ *18 rooms, 2 apartments* ⟂ *Restaurant, minibars, cable TV, pool, bar, some pets allowed (fee)* ▤ *AE, DC, MC, V* ⊗ *Closed last 3 wks Jan. and late Nov.–late Dec.* ⼁⊙⼁ *EP, MAP.*

$$ ✕▥ **Central Hôtel.** Get the best quality for price in town at this family-run hotel and restaurant over the Nive, where trout could be literally (though illegally) caught from certain rooms. The wonderfully musical 200-year-old oak staircase is another memorable detail. The owners speak Basque, Spanish, French, English, and some German, so communicating is rarely a problem. The cuisine is superb, especially the lamb and *magret de canard* (duck breast). ⊠ *1 pl. Charles de Gaulle, 64220* ☎ *05–59–37–00–22* ⊟ *05–59–37–27–79* ⇛ *14 rooms* ⟂ *Restaurant, cable TV; no a/c* ▤ *AE, DC, MC, V* ⊗ *Closed mid-Dec.–early Mar.* ⼁⊙⼁ *EP, MAP.*

Larrau

❽ *46 km (28 mi) east of St-Jean-Pied-de-Port, 20 km (12 mi) west of Ste-Engrâce, 42 km (26 mi) southwest of Oloron-Ste-Marie.*

Larrau is a cozy way station on the road over the pass into Spain. The town has several hotels of distinction and a number of extraordinarily ancient, rustic mountain houses. Once known for its 19th-century forges, Larrau is now a winter base camp for hunters and a summer center for hikers. It's a good departure point for the **Holçarté Gorges walk.** This classic trek is a 90-minute round-trip hike, including a spectacular bridge that hangs 561 feet above the rocky stream bed. The full tour looping back around to the Logibar is a four-hour walk, although the hike over to Ste-Engrâce is a seven-hour trip each way, a good two-day project over and back. The well-marked trail begins at the Logibar Inn, 3 km (2 mi) east of Larrau.

Where to Stay & Eat

★ **$–$$$** ✕▥ **Hôtel Etxemaïté.** This sophisticated country inn has spectacular views and is one of the area's top dining spots (closed Monday and no dinner Sunday from mid-November to mid-May). The dining room seems suspended over the garden and often fills up in summer. The inn is well furnished with Basque antiques, including several unusual *susulia* chair-and-table combinations. The Basque cooking is excellent: terrine *de poule au foie gras* (hen with duck liver) is just one good choice. Rooms are done in light woods and cheery colors. ⊠ *Rte. D26, 64560 Larrau* 🕾 *05–59–28–61–45* 🖷 *05–59–28–72–71* 🛏 *16 rooms* ⚐ *Restaurant, cable TV, bar; no a/c* ☰ *AE, DC, MC, V* ⊗ *Closed Sun. night, Mon., and Sept. 15–June 15* 🍽 *EP, MAP.*

¢ ✕🖾 **Logibar.** This simple inn with a *gîte d'étape* (way station) for hikers serves nonpareil garbure and an even better *omelette aux cèpes* (wild mushroom omelet). Rooms are tiny but cozy, and the Quihilliry family, in its fourth generation running this well-known spot, has a knack for making you feel at home. ⊠ *Rte. D26, 64560 Larrau* 🕾 *05–59–28–61–14* 🖷 *05–59–28–61–14* 🛏 *12 rooms* ⚐ *Restaurant, bar; no a/c, no room TVs* ☰ *MC, V* ⊗ *Closed early Dec.–early Mar.* 🍽 *EP.*

Gorges de Kakuetta

❾ *13 km (8 mi) east of Larrau, 3 km (2 mi) west of Ste-Engrâe.*

FodorśChoice
★

A right turn onto D113 at the confluence of the Uhaitxa and Larrau rivers will take you toward Ste-Engrâce and past one of the area's great natural phenomena, the Gorges de Kakuetta (the Basque spelling). A famous canyon cut through the limestone cliffs by the Uhaitxa River, the gorge is at times as narrow as 12 feet across while reaching depths of more than 1,155 feet. Stairways are cut into the rock, and hanging bridges span the watercourse. A waterfall and a grotto mark the end of the climb, a two-hour walk round-trip. This hike is recommended only during low-water conditions, normally between June and October. Good hiking shoes are indispensable. 🕾 *05–59–28–73–44* 🖾 *€4* ⊗ *Mid-Mar.–mid-Nov., daily 8 AM–dark.*

Ste-Engrâce

❿ *66 km (40 mi) east of St-Jean-Pied-de-Port, 37 km (23 mi) southwest of Oloron-Ste-Marie, 100 km (62 mi) southwest of Pau.*

Ste-Engrâce is at the eastern edge of the Basque Country in the Haute Soule (Upper Soule). Soule is the smallest of the three French Basque provinces. Nearly all the inhabitants speak Euskera (Basque), a non-Indo-European language of uncertain (though probably native Pyrenean and Iberian) origins.

Medieval pilgrims on the way to Santiago de Compostela in northwest Spain once flocked to the village's lovely 11th-century church of **Ste-Engrâce** to venerate the arm of Sancta Gracia, a young Portuguese noblewoman martyred around the year 300. When pillaging Calvinists removed the cherished relic in 1569, a ring finger was sent from the scene of her martyrdom in Zaragoza to replace the stolen arm. The church has an asymmetrical, slanting roof, typical of the *maison Basque* (Basque house) design. Its gray stone contrasts eerily with the green hills and fields behind. The ornate interior is a surprising contrast to the church's stark exterior. The town remains a key crossroads for pilgrims traveling to Santiago and trans-Pyrenean trekkers going east across the "dragon's back," as generations of Pyreneists have respectfully dubbed the mountain range's jagged profile.

Where to Stay

¢ ⊞ **Auberge Elichalt.** This cozy *gîte d'étape* (hikers' way station) and table d'hôte (bed and breakfast) has 50 beds in varying situations. There are double rooms, dormitory beds, and an apartment for rent, all in the shadow of the church. Monsieur and Madame Burguburu (Euskera for "head of town") can recommend hikes into the mountains. ⊠ *64560 Ste-Engrâce* ☎ *05–59–28–61–63* 🖶 *05–59–28–75–54* 🛏 *5 double rooms, 1 apartment for 5, 40 dormitory beds without bath* ⊟ *MC, V* ⊚ *EP, MAP.*

Sports & the Outdoors

The nearby ski station, 10 km (6 mi) away in **Pierre-St-Martin,** has Alpine and Nordic skiing. If you're interested in fly-fishing, the **Gave d'Oloron** (*gave* is the word for river in the language of the Béarn), flowing through Sauveterre-de-Béarn, is a trout and Atlantic salmon fishery. On D919 between Aramits and Oloron-Ste-Marie, look for the Vert River and the nearby town of **Féas.** The gently flowing Vert is well populated with trout.

⎧ en route ⎫ The **Basse Soule** (Lower Soule), also known as the Barétous region, is a transition zone between the Basque Country and Béarn characterized by rolling green hills and cornfields. To explore the Basse Soule, take D132 from Pierre-St-Martin down to Arette. Drive the loop beginning west toward the hometown of the legendary Aramis of *The Three Musketeers* at **Aramits,** continuing through **Lannes, Trois-Villes, and Gotein,** with its characteristic *clocher-calvaire,* a three-peak bell tower designed as an evocation of Calvary. Just short of Mauléon-Licharre on D918 is the rustic 11th-century **Chapelle St-Jean-de-Berraute,** built by the Order of Malta for pilgrims heading to Santiago de Compostela.

Mauléon-Licharre

❶ *16 km (10 mi) southwest of Navarrenx, 40 km (24 mi) northeast of St-Jean-Pied-de-Port.*

Mauléon-Licharre, capital of the Soule, is the upland Basque Country's only industrial city, manufacturing rope-soled espadrilles. Spread along the banks of the Saison River, the 16th-century **Hôtel de Maytie** (also known as the Château d'Andurain), the 17th-century **Hôtel de Montréal,** and the remains of the 12th-century **château fort** fortress are the main spots to seek out.

Where to Stay & Eat

$ ✕⊞ **Bidegain.** This classic 18th-century Basque town house is filled with heavy oak beams and creaky wooden stairs and floorboards. Just off the trout-filled Gave du Saison, this onetime stagecoach and pony-express relay station serves excellent Basque country cooking in a four-course, prix-fixe *formule* with a choice of four desserts. The shady garden out back is a cool and quiet summer retreat. ✉ *13 rue de Navarre, 64560 Mauléon-Licharre* ☎*05–59–28–16–05* 🖷*05–59–19–10–26* ✍*bidegain-hotel@wanadoo.fr* ⟿ *20 rooms* ⚭ *Restaurant, cable TV; no a/c* ▭ *AE, DC, MC, V* ⟨◯⟩ *EP, MAP.*

en route   From L'Hôpital-St-Blaise, a right on D936 will take you into Oloron-Ste-Marie. A left on D936 will take you to **Navarrenx** and **Sauveterre-de-Béarn,** both of them spectacular towns in the Soule region.

Oloron-Ste-Marie

⑫ *33 km (20½ mi) southwest of Pau on N134.*

Oloron-Ste-Marie straddles the confluence of two rivers, the Gave d'Aspe and the Gave d'Ossau. Trout and even the occasional Atlantic salmon can (with luck) be spotted when the sun is out. Originally an Iberian and later a Roman military outpost, the town was made a stronghold by the viscounts of Béarn in the 11th century. The **Quartier Ste-Croix** occupies the once fortified point between the two rivers and is the most interesting part of town. The fortresslike church of **Ste-Croix,** with its Moorish-influenced cupola inspired by the mosque at Cordoba; the two Renaissance buildings nearby; and the 14th-century **Tour Grède** (Grède Tower) are the main attractions. A walk around the **Promenade Bellevue** along the ramparts below the west side of the church will give you a view down the Aspe Valley and into the mountains behind. The 12th- and 13th-century **Église Ste-Marie,** in the **bourg de Ste-Marie** across the river on the left bank of the Gave d'Aspe, is famous for its surprisingly well-preserved Romanesque doorway of Pyrenean marble.

Where to Stay & Eat

$–$$ ✕ **Le Biscondau.** Come here to sample some of the finest garbure, the hearty peasant vegetable soup, in Oloron. The view over the Gave d'Ossau is at its best from the terrace in summer. ✉ *7 rue de la Filature* ☎ *05–59–39–06–15* ▭ *DC, MC, V* ⊙ *Closed Mon.*

$$–$$$ ✕▣ **Alysson.** This modern building in the middle of town is a safe-and-sound, if charmless, place to spend a night in Oloron-Ste-Marie. The rooms are small but newly furnished and equipped. The restaurant serves excellent garbures (mountain soups with beans, vegetables, and duck confit) and *piperades* (red peppers, tomatoes, and eggs sautéed in goose fat and served with fatback or bacon). ✉ *Bd. Pyrénées, 64400* ☎ *05–59–39–70–70* 🖷 *05–59–39–24–47* ⟿ *34 rooms* ⚭ *Restaurant, cable TV, pool, some pets allowed (fee); no a/c* ▭ *AE, DC, MC, V* ⟨◯⟩ *EP.*

¢–$ ▣ **Chambre d'Hôtes Paris.** This B&B in Féas, run by Christian and Marie-France Paris, is a great deal, especially if you like fly-fishing. Christian, a registered guide, knows every trout in the Barétous by name. ✉ *7½ km (5 mi) past Oloron-Ste-Marie, 64570 Féas* ☎ *05–59–39–01–10* ⊕ *www.bwo.fr/destination-mouche/cparis* ⟿ *3 rooms* ⚭ *No a/c* ▭ *No credit cards* ⊙ *Closed late Dec.–early Jan.* ⟨◯⟩ *EP, MAP.*

Navarrenx

⑬ *19 km (11 mi) northwest of Oloron-Ste-Marie.*

Perched over the Gave d'Oloron, Navarrenx was built in 1316 as a *bastide* (fortified town) at an important crossroads on the Santiago de Compostela pilgrimage route. Henri d'Albret, king of Navarre, constructed the present ramparts in 1540. The bastion of Porte St-Antoine, with its miniature turret, is one of the Soule's best-known sights. The town motto, *Si You Ti Baou* (Béarnais for "If I should see you"), refers to the cannon guarding the approach to the town across the bridge. The Gave d'Oloron is an excellent trout and salmon river. Salmon angling is an important part of Navarrenx tradition: every year a salmon-fishing championship takes place, during which spectators line the banks of the legendary salmon pool about 300 yards upstream from the bridge.

Where to Stay & Eat

$–$$$ ✕⊞ **Hôtel du Commerce.** As the best restaurant and most traditional lodging in Navarrenx, the Commerce is an easy choice. Rooms are old-fashioned and cozy and have renovated, spacious bathrooms. The exquisite menu spotlights such items as *pigeonneau au style bécasse* (woodcock-style squab served up in a fragrant Madeira sauce), or *foie gras frais au myrtille* (fresh duck liver in a berry sauce). ⊠ *Pl. des Casernes, 64190* ☎ *05–59–66–50–16* ⊟ *05–59–66–52–67* ⊕ *www.hotel-commmerce. fr* ⤴ *28 rooms* ⚲ *Restaurant, cable TV, bar, some pets allowed (fee); no a/c* ⊟ *AE, DC, MC, V* ⦾ *EP, MAP.*

Sauveterre-de-Béarn

⑭ *19 km (11 mi) northwest of Navarrenx, 39 km (23 mi) northwest of Oloron-Ste-Marie, 39 km (23 mi) northeast of St-Jean-Pied-de-Port.*

Fodor's Choice
★

Make your first stop the terrace next to the church: the view from here takes in the Gave d'Oloron, the fortified 12th-century drawbridge, the lovely Montréal Tower, and the Pyrénées rising in the distance, and is among the finest in the region. The bridge, known both as the **Vieux Pont** (Old Bridge) and the Pont de la Légende (Bridge of the Legend), was named after the legend of Sancie, widow of Gaston V de Béarn. Accused of murdering a child after her husband's death in 1170, Sancie was subjected to the "Judgment of God" and thrown, bound hand and foot, from the bridge by order of her brother, the king of Navarre. When the river carried her safely to the bank, she was deemed exonerated of all charges.

Where to Stay

★ **$–$$** ⊞ **Hôtel de la Reine Sancie.** Enjoying a picture-perfect spot, this medieval manor house is built into the town's fortified 12th-century drawbridge, the Pont de la Légende, and sits atop the old foundations of the medieval Maison du Sénéchal. The views over the river and up to the ramparts of Sauveterre are superb. Rooms range from cozy and comfortable to grand and baronial (ask for the one in the corner, which has two views of the river and an immense bathroom). The owners, Tony and Brian Moore (from Dublin), will direct you to the best area restaurants. ⊠ *Rue du Pont de la Légende, 64390 Sauveterre-de-*

Béarn ☎ *05–59–38–95–11* 🖶 *05–59–38–99–10* 🛏 *6 rooms* ⚭ *Restaurant, bar, some pets allowed (fee); no a/c* 🗖 *AE, DC, MC, V* ⊘ *Closed mid-Dec.–mid-Apr.* ⦅◎⦆ *EP, MAP.*

Pau

⑮ *106 km (63 mi) east of Bayonne and Biarritz.*

The stunning views, mild climate, and elegance of Pau—the historic capital of Béarn, a state annexed to France in 1620—make it a lovely place to visit and a convenient gateway to the Pyrénées. The birthplace of King Henri IV, Pau was "discovered" in 1815 by British officers returning from the Peninsular War in Spain, and it soon became a prominent winter resort town. Fifty years later English-speaking inhabitants made up one-third of Pau's population, many believing in the medicinal benefits of mountain air (later shifting their loyalties to Biarritz for the sea air). They started the Pont-Long Steeplechase, still one of the most challenging in Europe, in 1841; created France's first golf course here in 1856; introduced fox hunting to the region; and founded a famous British tea shop where students now smoke strong cigarettes while drinking black coffee.

FodorśChoice Pau's regal past is commemorated at its **Musée National du Château de**
★ **Pau,** begun in the 14th century by Gaston Phoebus, the flamboyant count of Béarn. The building was transformed into a Renaissance palace in the 16th century by Marguerite d'Angoulême, sister of François I. A woman of diverse gifts, her pastorales were performed in the château's sumptuous gardens. Her bawdy *Heptameron*—written at age 60—furnishes as much sly merriment today as it did when read by her doting kingly brother. Marguerite's grandson, the future king of France Henri IV, was born in the château in 1553. Exhibits connected to Henri's life and times are displayed regularly, along with portraits of the most significant of his alleged 57 lovers and mistresses. His cradle, a giant turtle shell, is on exhibit in his bedroom, one of the sumptuous, tapestry-lined royal apartments. ⊠ *Rue du Château* ☎ *05–59–82–38–00* 🎫 *€5, free 1st Sun. of month* ⊙ *Apr.–Oct., daily 9:30–11:30 and 2–5:45; Nov.–Mar., daily 9:30–11:30 and 2–4:30.*

To continue on your royal path, follow the **Sentiers du Roy** (King's Paths), a marked trail just below the Boulevard des Pyrénées. When you reach the top, walk along until the sights line up with the mountain peaks you see. For some man-made splendors instead, head to the **Musée des Beaux-Arts** and feast on works by El Greco, Degas, and Rodin. ⊠ *Rue Mathieu-Lalanne* ☎ *05–59–27–33–02* ⊕ *musee.ville-pau.fr* 🎫 *€2* ⊙ *Tues.–Sun. 10–noon and 2–6.*

While in Pau, enjoy some of life's sweetest pleasures with a visit to the **Confiserie Francis Miot** (⊠ *48 rue Joffre* ☎ *05–59–27–69–51*) and enjoy his signature delicacies, "Les Coucougnettes du Vert Galant"—small, red, tender bon-bons made from almond paste. Their name is echoic of the Occitanian argot for testicles (in Spanish, *cojones*) and why not? Henri IV—a.k.a. le Vert Galant ("the dirty old man" or "the swordsman")—was famed for his 57 lovers. At the gates of Pau, in the village of Uzos, Miot has his own **Musée des Arts Sucré** (⊕ www.feerie-gourmande.com).

Where to Stay & Eat

$–$$$ ╳ **Gousse d'Ail.** In the Hédas district, the deep mid-city canyon in the oldest part of Pau, this lovely hideaway is tucked under the stairway at the end of the street. Traditional Béarn cooking and international cuisine are served; try the magret de canard cooked over coals. ⊠ *12 rue du Hédas* ☎ *05–59–27–31–55* 🖷 *05–59–06–10–53* ▤ *AE, DC, MC, V* ◷ *Closed Sun. No lunch Sat.*

$–$$ ▥ **Hôtel de Gramont.** Five minutes from the château, the Gramont is a cozy and convenient base for exploring Pau. Ask for one of the *chambres mansardées* (dormered bedrooms) under the eaves overlooking the Hédas. ⊠ *3 pl. de Gramont, 64000* ☎ *05–59–27–84–04* 🖷 *05–59–27–62–23* ⇆ *36 rooms* ⚙ *Cable TV; no a/c* ▤ *AE, DC, MC, V* ⑩ *EP.*

Nightlife & the Arts

During the music and arts **Festival de Pau,** theatrical and musical events take place almost every evening from mid-July to late-August, nearly all of them gratis. Nightlife in Pau revolves around the Hédas district, where bars and restaurants line the alleys heading down into this one-time river gorge. The streets around Pau's imposing château are sprinkled with cozy pubs and dining spots, although the **casino** (⊠ Parc Beaumont ☎ 05–59–27–06–92) offers racier entertainment.

Eugénie-les-Bains

⑯ *45 km (30 mi) north of Pau, 140 km (87 mi) south of Bordeaux.*

Empress Eugénie popularized Eugénie-les-Bains at the end of the 19th century, and in return the villagers renamed the town after her. Michel and Christine Guérard brought the village back to life in 1973 by putting together one of France's most fashionable thermal retreats, which became the birthplace of nouvelle cuisine, thanks to the great talents of chef Michel. Their little kingdom now includes two restaurants, two hotels, a cooking school, and a spa. The 13 therapeutic treatments address everything from weight loss to rheumatism. Two springs are certified by the French Ministry of Health: L'Impératrice and Christine-Marie, whose 39°C (102°F) waters come from nearly 1,300 feet below the surface.

Where to Stay & Eat

★ $$$$ ╳▥ **La Ferme aux Grives.** With four superb rooms for the lucky first-comers, Michel Guérard's delightfully re-created old coaching inn, set at one end of their Prés d'Eugénie fiefdom (⇨ *below*), is meant to be a more rustic alternative to their main flagship restaurant. Nature's bounty is the theme: a banquet table is laid out with vegetables and breads, darkened beams cast romantic shadows, and hunting paintings cover the walls. Grandmother's food is given a nouvelle spin, and nearly everything is *authentique*: even the suckling pig turns on a spit in the fireplace. ⊠ *Eugénie-les-Bains* ☎ *05–58–05–05–06* 🖷 *05–58–51–10–10* ⇆ *4 rooms* ⚙ *Restaurant, minibars, cable TV, bar, some pets allowed (fee); no a/c* ▤ *AE, DC, MC, V* ◷ *Closed Jan. 4–Feb. 12* ⑩ *EP, MAP.*

$$$$ ╳▥ **Les Prés d'Eugénie.** Ever since Michel Guérard's eponymously named **Fodor's**Choice restaurant fired the first shots of the nouvelle revolution of the late 1970s, ★ the excellence of this suave culinary landmark has been a given (so much so that the breakfast here outdoes dinner at most other places). Thanks to Guérard's signature flair, *cuisine minceur*—the slimmer's dream—collides with the lusty fare of the Landes region (langoustines garnished with foie gras and mesclun greens, lobster with confetti-ed calf's head). In the lovely Second Empire–style hotel, set in a fine garden, grandeur prevails and rooms are formal. However, those in the "annex"—the former 18th-century **Couvent des Herbes**—have an understated luxe and look out over the herb garden. To top it all off, the complex includes an excellent spa, dance studio, two pools, and a 9-hole golf course, and "theme" weeks are devoted to cooking, perfumes, wines, or gardening. ⊠ *40320 Eugénie-les-Bains* ☎ *05–58–05–06–07, 05–58–05–05–05 restaurant reservations* 🖶 *05–58–51–10–10* ⊕ *www.michelguerard. com* 🖘 *22 rooms, 6 apartments* ⏷ *Restaurant, minibars, cable TV, golf course, 2 tennis courts, indoor pool, outdoor pool, gym, bar, some pets allowed (fee); no a/c* ▭ *AE, DC, MC, V* ⭾⃠ *EP, MAP.*

★ **$$–$$$** ✕⊡ **La Maison Rose.** A low-cost, low-calorie alternative to Les Prés d'Eugénie (⇨ *above*), Michel and Christine Guérard's newest hotel beckons with a sybaritically simple spa approach. Set in a renovated, super-stylish 18th-century farmhouse adorned with old paintings hung with ribbons, rustic antiques, and Pays Basque handicrafts, this is a retreat that would have delighted the sober Madame de Maintenon—if she had wanted to lose weight, that is. This is a serious spa, complete with slimming cures and the most stylish relaxation room in France (oh, those Provençal-style chaises longues). No room service—everyone eats in the main dining room, a two-story, beam-ceiling delight. The kitchen's touch remains an inventive benediction to local produce. ⊠ *40320 Eugénie-les-Bains* ☎ *05–58–05–06–07* 🖶 *05–58–51–10–10* ⊕ *www. michelguerard.com* 🖘 *26 rooms, 5 studios* ⏷ *Restaurant, kitchenette, minibars, cable TV, pool, gym, some pets allowed (fee); no a/c* ▭ *AE, DC, MC, V* ⭾⃠ *EP, MAP.*

THE HAUTES-PYRÉNÉES

The Hautes-Pyrénées include the highest and most spectacular natural wonders in the cordillera. Although mountain peaks soar in this region, there are also centers of more civilized charms—notably, the towns of Cauterets and Bagnères-de-Luchon, set in a spa region that once attracted such formidable luminaries as Montaigne, Madame de Maintenon, Henri IV, and the composer Rossini. Traditionally known as La Bigorre, the border with the Béarn is at the Col d'Aubisque southeast of Oloron-Ste-Marie, and the eastern border with the Haute Garonne is at the Col de Peyresourde just west of Bagnères-de-Luchon. The legendary Cirque de Gavarnie (natural mountain amphitheater), the Vignemale peak (10,817 feet) and glacier, the Balaïtous peak (10,312 feet), the Brèche de Roland, and the Cirque de Troumouse are the star attractions in the Hautes-Pyrénées.

Tarbes

⓱ *40 km (24 mi) east of Pau, 152 km (94 mi) southwest of Toulouse, 214 km (133 mi) southeast of Bordeaux.*

Tarbes is the commercial and administrative center of the Bigorre region and the Hautes-Pyrénées Département. If Tarbes is your point of entry into the Hautes-Pyrénées, stop by the **tourist office** (⊠ 3 cours Gambetta ☏ 05–62–51–30–31) for information, brochures, and maps of the region. The **Halle Marcadieu** is the commercial center. The Thursday market offers a chance to check out widely acclaimed local products ranging from the *choux-fleurs* (cauliflower) of Arros to the carrots of Asté, from the onions of Trébons to the famed *haricot tarbais,* a delicate-skinned kidney bean essential in any authentic garbure.

Tarbes was the **birthplace of Maréchal Ferdinand Foch** (⊠ 2 rue de la Victoire ☏ 05–62–93–19–02), the general most responsible for the 1918 Allied victory. The town is also home to the **Haras National** (⊠ 70 av. du Régiment-de-Bigorre ☏ 05–62–34–44–59), a stud farm and dressage academy. A nice place for a walk on a warm day is the **Jardin Massey** (Massey Garden), a luxuriant park that is home to ducks and an abundance of flowers in summer.

Where to Stay & Eat

$ ▦ **Henri IV.** This comfortable spot in midtown Tarbes, near the Massey Garden and three blocks from the train station, is a safe if unspectacular choice for a night in town. The staff will direct you to the gastronomical star of Tarbes, L'Ambroisie, just two blocks toward the cathedral. ⊠ 7 *av. B. Barère, 65000* ☏05–62–34–01–68 ☏05–62–93–71–32 ↻*25 rooms* ⧖ *Cable TV, some pets allowed (fee); no a/c* ▭ *AE, DC, MC, V* ⎮⊙⎮ *EP.*

Lourdes

⑱ *41 km (27 mi) southeast of Pau, 19 km (12 mi) southwest of Tarbes.*

Five million pilgrims flock to Lourdes annually, many in quest of a miraculous cure for sickness or disability. A religious pilgrimage is one thing, but a sightseeing expedition has other requirements. The famous churches and grotto and the area around them are woefully lacking in beauty. Off-season, acres of empty parking lots echo. Shops are shuttered, restaurants closed. In season a mob jostles to see the grotto behind a forest of votive candles. Some pundits might say that Lourdes ingeniously combines the worst of both worlds.

It all started in February 1858 when Bernadette Soubirous, a 14-year-old miller's daughter, claimed she saw the Virgin Mary in the **Grotte de Massabielle,** near the Gave de Pau (in all, she had 18 visions). Bernadette dug in the grotto, releasing a gush of water from a spot where no spring had flowed before. From then on, pilgrims thronged the Massabielle rock for the water's supposed healing powers, though church authorities reacted skeptically. It took four years for the miracle to be authenticated by Rome and a sanctuary erected over the grotto. In 1864 the first organized procession was held. Today there are six official annual pilgrimages between Easter and All Saints' Day, the most important on August 15.

Lourdes celebrated the centenary of Bernadette Soubirous's visions by building the world's largest underground church, the **Basilique Souterraine St-Pie X,** with space for 20,000 people—more than the town's permanent population. Above St-Pie X stands the unprepossessing neo-Byzantine **Basilique du Rosaire** (1889). The **Basilique Supérieure** (1871), tall and white, hulks nearby.

The **Pavillon Notre-Dame,** across from St-Pie X, houses the **Musée Bernadette** (Museum of Stained-Glass Mosaic Religious Art), with mementos of Bernadette's life and an illustrated history of the pilgrimages. In the basement is the **Musée d'Art Sacré du Gemmail.** ⊠ *72 rue de la Grotte* 🕾 *05–62–94–13–15* ⬚ *Free* ⊙ *July–Nov., daily 9:30–11:45 and 2:30–6:15; Dec.–June, Wed.–Mon. 9:30–11:45 and 2:30–5:45.*

Across the river is the **Moulin de Boly** (Boly Mill), where Bernadette was born on January 7, 1844. ⊠ *12 rue Bernadette-Soubirous* ⬚ *Free* ⊙ *Easter–mid-Oct., daily 9:30–11:45 and 2:30–5:45.*

The **cachot,** a tiny room where, in extreme poverty, Bernadette and her family took refuge in 1856, can also be visited. ⊠ *15 rue des Petits-Fossés* 🕾 *05–62–94–51–30* ⬚ *Free* ⊙ *Easter–mid-Oct., daily 9:30–11:45 and 2:30–5:30; mid-Oct.–Easter, daily 2:30–5:30.*

The **château** on the hill above town can be reached by escalator, by 131 steps, or by the ramp up from rue du Bourg (from which a small Basque cemetery with ancient discoidal stones can be seen). Once a prison, the castle now contains the **Musée Pyrénéen,** one of France's best provincial museums, devoted to the popular customs, arts, and history of the Pyrénées. ⊠ *25 rue du Fort* 🕾 *05–62–94–02–04* ⬚ *€5* ⊙ *Easter–mid-Oct., daily 9–noon and 2–7, last admission at 6; mid-Oct.–Easter, Wed.–Mon. 9–noon and 2–7, last admission at 6.*

Fodor'sChoice
★

Where to Stay & Eat

$–$$ ✕⬚ **Hôtel Albret/La Taverne de Bigorre.** The Moreau family's popular establishment serves traditional French mountain cooking such as hearty garbure. Rooms are clean and comfortable, with a personal touch that is very welcome in Lourdes. ⊠ *21 pl. du Champ Commun, 65100* 🕾 *05–62–94–75–00* 🖷 *05–62–94–78–45* ⬚ *27 rooms* ⚹ *Restaurant, bar, parking (fee); no a/c* ⊟ *AE, DC, MC, V* ⊙ *Closed mid-Nov.–mid-Dec. and Jan.* ⦿ *EP.*

Cauterets

⑲ *30 km (19 mi) south of Lourdes, 49 km (30 mi) south of Tarbes.*

Cauterets (which derives from the word for hot springs in the local *bigourdan* dialect) is a spa and resort town (for long-term treatments) high in the Pyrénées. It has been revered since Roman times for thermal baths thought to cure maladies ranging from back pain to female sterility. Novelist Victor Hugo (1802–85) womanized here; Lady Aurore Dudevant— better known as the writer George Sand (1804–76)—is said to have discovered her feminism here. Other famous visitors include Gastón Fébus, Chateaubriand, Sarah Bernhardt, King Edward VII of England, and Spain's King Alfonso XIII.

en route Two kilometers (1 mi) south of Cauterets is the parking lot for the thermal baths, where the red-and-white-marked GR10 *Sentier des Cascades* (Path of the Waterfalls) departs for Pont d'Espagne. This famous walk (three hours round-trip) features stunning views of the waterfalls and abundant *marmottes* (Pyrenean groundhogs). From **Pont d'Espagne,** to which you can also drive, continue on foot or by chairlift to the plateau and a view over the bright blue **Lac de Gaube,** fed by the river of the same name. Above is **Le Vignemale** (10,817 feet), France's highest Pyrenean peak. Return via Cauterets to Pierrefitte-Nestalas and turn right on D921 up Luz-St-Saveur and Gavarnie.

Gavarnie

⓴ *30 km (19 mi) south of Cauterets on D921, 50 km (31 mi) south of Lourdes.*

The village of Gavarnie is a good base for exploring the mountains in the region. For starters, it's at the foot of **Le Cirque de Gavarnie,** one of the world's most remarkable examples of glacial erosion and a daunting challenge to mountaineers. Horses and donkeys, rented in the village, are the traditional way to reach the head of the valley (though walking is preferable), where the Hôtel du Cirque has hosted six generations of visitors. When the upper snows melt, numerous streams tumble down from the cliffs to form spectacular waterfalls; the greatest of them, Europe's largest, is the **Grande Cascade,** dropping nearly 1,400 feet.

FodorśChoice
★

Another dramatic sight is 12 km (7 mi) west of the village of Gavarnie. Take D921 up to the Col de Boucharo, where you can park and walk five hours up to the **Brèche de Roland** glacier (you cross it during the last two hours of the hike). For a taste of mountain life, have lunch high up at the Club Alpin Français's **Refuge de Sarradets ou de la Brèche.** This is a serious climb, only feasible from mid-June to mid-September, for which you need (at least) good hiking shoes and sound physical conditioning. Crampons and ice axes are available for rent in Gavarnie; check with the Gavarnie tourist office for weather reports and for information about guided tours.

Where to Stay & Eat

★ $–$$ ✕ **Hôtel du Cirque.** With its legendary views of the Cirque de Gavarnie, this spot is magical at sunset. Despite its name it's just a restaurant, but not just any old eating establishment: the garbure here is as delicious as the sunset is grand. Seventh-generation owner Pierre Vergez claims his recipe using water from the Cirque and *cocos de Tarbes,* or *haricots tarbais* (Tarbes broad beans) is unique. ⊠ *1-hr walk above the village of Gavarnie* ☎ *05–62–92–48–02* ☐ *MC, V* ☺ *Closed mid-Sept.–mid-June.*

$–$$ ✕▥ **Hôtel Marboré.** This multigabled house over a rushing mountain brook offers all the history and tradition of Gavarnie along with delightful creature comforts. Rooms are bright and pleasant and look out onto lush hillside meadows. The kind and lively owner-manager Roselyne Fillastre attends to all with great warmth and vivacity. The restaurant, too, is excellent: look forward to fine cuisine prepared with the freshest ingredients. ⊠ *Village de Gavarnie, 65120* ☎ *05–62–92–40–40* ▦ *05–62–92–40–30* ➶ *13 rooms* ⚭ *Restaurant, cable TV, bar; no a/c* ☐ *MC, V* ☺ *Closed Nov.–Dec. 20* ⦿ *EP, MAP.*

Nightlife & the Arts

Every July Gavarnie holds an outdoor ballet and music performance, **La Fête des Pyrénées** (☎ 05–62–92–49–10 information), using the Cirque de Gavarnie as a backdrop; show time is at sunset. For information contact the tourist office.

en route

The dramatic mountain scenery is impressive all along D921 between Gavarnie and **Luz-St-Sauveur**. Continuing east from Luz-St-Sauveur along D918 toward Arreau, the road passes through the lively little spa town of **Barèges** and under the brow of the mighty **Pic du Midi de Bigorre**, a mountain peak towering nearly 10,000 feet above the Col du Tourmalet pass. The finest views—and the sharpest curves—are found toward the Col d'Aspin pass. Another spectacular road is D618 from Arreau over the **Col de Peyresourde** to Bagnères de Luchon.

Bagnères-de-Luchon

㉑ *150 km (93 mi) east of Gavarnie.*

The largest and most fashionable Pyrenean spa is Bagnères de Luchon (generally known simply as Luchon), at the head of a lush valley. Dubbed the "Reine des Pyrénées" (Queen of the Pyrénées), Luchon was considered by the Romans to rank second as a spa only to Naples. Thermal waters here cater to the vocal cords: opera singers, lawyers, and politicians hoarse from spurious electoral promises all pile in to breathe the healing vapors. The **Parc des Quinconces** is a pretty stroll in summer. Look for the beautiful Couteillas sculpture *Le Baiser à la Source* (*The Kiss at the Spring*), hidden under a pine tree.

On display at the **Musée du Pays de Luchon** (⊠ 18 allée d'Étigny ☎ 05–61–79–29–87 ⌨ €1.70 ☉ Daily 9–noon and 2–6) are exhibits about Pyrenean history and lore and artifacts such as a curious sculpture portraying a woman and a serpent.

Where to Stay & Eat

$$–$$$ ✕▦ **Hôtel Corneille.** This elegant spot with a lovely terrace and park has all the comforts you could want and then some. Most of the furnishings are original Napoléon III. The staff is very helpful and pleasant. ⊠ *5 av. A. Dumas, 31110* ☎ *05–61–79–36–22* 🖶 *05–61–79–81–11* ⇨ *56 rooms* ⌂ *Restaurant, bar, meeting rooms, some pets allowed (fee); no a/c* ⊟ *AE, DC, MC, V* ☉ *Closed end Nov.–mid-Dec.* ⏀ *EP, MAP.*

$–$$ ✕▦ **L'Esquerade.** This little inn and restaurant, 6 km (4 mi) west of Bagnères, offers elegance, friendly service, intimacy, and excellent value. Rooms are comfortable, if small, and the cuisine has won deserved local fame for its classic Pyrenean fare. ⊠ *Rte. D618, 31110 Castillon-de-Larboust* ☎ *05–61–79–19–64* 🖶 *05–61–79–26–29* ⇨ *15 rooms* ⌂ *Restaurant, some pets allowed (fee); no a/c* ⊟ *AE, DC, MC, V* ☉ *Closed mid-Nov.–mid-Dec.* ⏀ *MAP.*

St-Bertrand-de-Comminges

㉒ *32 km (20 mi) north of Bagnères-de-Luchon, 57 km (35 mi) southeast*
Fodor'sChoice *of Tarbes, 107 km (66 mi) southwest of Toulouse.*
★

A Roman road once led directly from Luchon to St-Bertrand-de-Comminges (then a huge town of 60,000). This delightful village, whose inhabitants today number just over 200, is dwarfed beneath the imposing (mostly) 12th-century **Cathédrale Ste-Marie-de-Comminges** (✉ Rue des Gouverneurs); don't miss the cloisters and the intricately and playfully carved wood choir stalls. Described as a land-bound Mont-St-Michel, St-Bertrand numbers old houses, sloping alleyways, and crafts shops that add to its charm. The summer music festival held here and in neighboring villages in July and August is excellent.

Where to Stay & Eat

$ ✕🏨 **Moulin d'Aveux.** Four kilometers (2½ mi) west of St-Bertrand, this onetime cereal mill next to the trout-infested Ourse river is a restored barn. Specialties range from garbure to fresh trout. Rooms are cheery and rustic. ✉ *Rte. D925, 65370 Aveux* ☎ *05–62–99–20–68* 📠 *05–62–99–22–27* *10 rooms* *Restaurant, some pets allowed (fee); no a/c* 💳 *AE, DC, MC, V* ⏲ *Closed Oct. 8–17, Jan. 1–13; Mon. and Tues. Oct.–May* 🍽 *MAP.*

THE BASQUE COUNTRY, GASCONY, & THE HAUTES-PYRÉNÉES A TO Z

To research prices, get advice from other travelers, and book travel arrangements, visit www.fodors.com.

AIR TRAVEL

CARRIERS Air France flies to Pau, Bayonne, and Biarritz from Paris and from other major European destinations. Air Littoral flies between Biarritz, Pau, Toulouse, Nice, and Marseille.

Airlines & Contacts **Air France** ☎ 05-59-33-34-35. **Air Littoral** ☎ 05-59-33-26-64.

AIRPORTS

Biarritz-Parme Airport serves Bayonne and Biarritz and has several daily flights to and from Paris and several weekly to London, Marseille, Geneva, Lyon, Nice, and Pau. Pau-Pyrénées International Airport has 10 flights daily to and from Paris as well as flights to Nantes, Lyon, Marseille, Nice, Biarritz, Madrid, Rome, Venice, Milan, and Geneva.

Airport Information **Biarritz-Parme Airport** ☎ 05-59-43-83-20. **Pau-Pyrénées International Airport** ☎ 05-59-33-33-00.

BUS TRAVEL

Various private bus concerns—STAB (serving the Bayonne–Anglet–Biarritz metropolitan areas) and ATCRB (up and down the coast and inland to many Basque towns)—service the region. Where they don't, the trusty SNCF national bus lines can occasionally come to the rescue. Beware of peak-hour traffic on roads in the summer, which can mean both delays in transport time and few seats on buses. Check in with the local tourist office for handy schedules or ask your hotel concierge for the best advice.

Bus Information **STAB-Biarritz** ✉ Rue Louis Barthou, Biarritz ☎ 05-59-24-26-53. **ATCRB** ☎ 05-59-26-06-99.

CAR RENTAL

🔲 **Local Agencies Avis** ✉ Biarritz-Parme Airport, Biarritz ☎ 05-59-23-67-92 ✉ 107 bd. Général-de-Gaulle, Hendaye ☎ 05-59-20-79-04 ✉ Pau-Pyrénées International Airport, Pau ☎ 05-59-33-27-13 ✉ Train station, St-Jean-de-Luz ☎ 05-59-26-76-66. **Budget** ✉ Biarritz-Parme Airport, Biarritz ☎ 05-59-23-58-62 ✉ Pau-Pyrénées International Airport, Pau ☎ 05-59-33-77-45. **Eurodollar** ✉ Biarritz-Parme Airport, Biarritz ☎ 05-59-41-21-12. **Europcar** ✉ Train station, Bayonne ☎ 05-59-55-38-20 ✉ Biarritz-Parme Airport, Biarritz ☎ 05-59-23-90-68 ✉ Pau-Pyrénées International Airport, Pau ☎ 05-59-33-24-31. **Hertz** ✉ Biarritz-Parme Airport, Biarritz ☎ 05-59-43-92-92 ✉ Pau-Pyrénées International Airport, Pau ☎ 05-59-33-16-38.

CAR TRAVEL

A64 connects Pau and Bayonne in less than an hour, and A63 runs up and down the Atlantic coast. N117 connects Hendaye with Toulouse via Pau and Tarbes. N134 connects Bordeaux, Pau, Oloron-Ste-Marie, and Spain via the Col de Somport and Jaca. The D918 from Bayonne through Cambo and along the Nive river to St-Jean-Pied-de-Port is a pretty drive, continuing on (as D919 and D920) through the Béarn country to Oloron-Ste-Marie and Pau.

ROAD CONDITIONS   Roads are occasionally slow and tortuous in the more mountainous areas, but valley and riverside roads are generally quite smooth and fast. D132, which goes between Arette and Pierre-St-Martin, can be snowed in between mid-November and mid-May, as can N134 through the Valley d'Aspe and the Col de Somport into Spain.

TOURS

In Biarritz, Aitzin organizes tours of Bayonne, Biarritz, the Basque coast, and the Basque Pyrénées. The Association des Guides, in Pau, arranges tours with guides of the city, the Pyrénées, and Béarn and Basque Country. The Bayonne tourist office gives guided tours of the city. La Guild du Tourisme des Pyrénées-Atlantiques offers information on and organizes visits and tours of the Basque Country and the Pyrénées. Guides Culturels Pyrénéens, in Tarbes, arranges many tours, including explorations on such themes as cave painting, art and architecture, Basque sports, hiking, and horseback riding.

🔲 **Aitzin** ☎ 05-59-24-36-05. **Association des Guides** ☎ 05-59-30-44-01. **Bayonne tourist office** ☎ 05-59-46-01-46. **Guides Culturels Pyrénéens** ☎ 05-62-44-15-44. **La Guild du Tourisme des Pyrénées-Atlantiques** ☎ 05-59-46-37-05.

TRAIN TRAVEL

High-speed trains (TGVs, Trains à Grande Vitesse) cover the 800 km (500 mi) from Paris to Bayonne in 4½ hours. To get to Pau, take the TGV to Bordeaux (three hours) and connect to Pau (two hours). Bayonne and Toulouse are connected by local SNCF trains via Pau, Tarbes, Lourdes, Lannemezan, and St-Gaudens. A local train runs along the Nive from Bayonne to St-Jean-Pied-de-Port. Local trains go between Bayonne and Biarritz and from Bayonne into the Atlantic Pyrénées, a slow but picturesque trip. Hendaye is connected to Bayonne and to San Sebastián via the famous *topo* (mole) train, so-called for the number of tunnels it passes through.

🔲 **Train Information SNCF** ☎ 08-36-35-35-35 ⊕ www.ter-sncf.com/uk/aquitaine/default.htm.

TRAVEL AGENCIES

Note that the American Express agencies receive mail, but don't do any banking transactions.

🖪 Local Agent Referrals **Adour Voyages** ✉ 3 rue Gardères, Biarritz ☎ 05-59-24-14-25. **Agence Garrouste** ✉ 10 rue Thiers, Bayonne ☎ 05-59-59-02-35. **American Express** ✉ 14 Chausée du Bourg, Lourdes ☎ 05-62-94-40-84. **Havas Voyages** ✉ 5 rue Lormand, Bayonne ☎ 05-59-46-29-26. **L'Accueil Pyrénéen** ✉ 26 av. Maransin, Lourdes ☎ 05-62-94-15-62. **Maison du Pélérin** ✉ 12 av. Maransin, Lourdes ☎ 05-62-94-70-05. **Saga Tours** ✉ 4 av. du Maréchal-Foch, Biarritz ☎ 05-59-24-39-39.

VISITOR INFORMATION

🖪 Tourist Information **Ainhoa** ✉ Mairie ☎ 05-59-29-92-60. **Bagnères-de-Luchon** ✉ 18 allée d'Etigny ☎ 05-61-79-21-21. **Bayonne** ✉ Pl. des Basques ☎ 05-59-46-01-46 ⊕ www.ville-bayonne.fr/. **Biarritz** ✉ 1 sq. Ixelles ☎ 05-59-22-37-10 ⊕ www.biarritz. fr/. **Cauterets** ✉ 15 Cauterets ☎ 05-62-92-50-27. **Gavarnie** ✉ In center of village ☎ 05-62-92-49-10 ⊕ www.gavarnie.com/. **Hendaye** ✉ 12 rue des Aubépines ☎ 05-59-20-00-34 ⊕ www.hendaye.com/. **Lourdes** ✉ Pl. Beyramalu ☎ 05-62-42-77-40 ⊕ www.lourdes-france.com/. **Navarrenx** ✉ Mairie ☎ 05-59-66-10-22. **Oloron-Ste-Marie** ✉ Pl. de la Résistance ☎ 05-59-39-98-00 ⊕ www.oloron-ste-marie.fr/. **Pau** ✉ Pl. Royale ☎ 05-59-27-27-08 ⊕ www.ville-pau.fr/. **St-Bertrand-de-Comminges** ✉ Mairie ☎ 05-61-88-33-12. **St-Jean-de-Luz** ✉ Pl. Foch ☎ 05-59-26-03-16 ⊕ www.saint-jean-de-luz.com/. **St-Jean-Pied-de-Port** ✉ 14 pl. Charles-de-Gaulle ☎ 05-59-37-03-57. **Sare** ✉ Mairie ☎ 05-59-54-20-14. **Sauveterre-de-Béarn** ✉ Mairie ☎ 05-59-38-50-17 ⊕ www.tourisme.fr/office-de-tourisme/ sauveterre-de-bearn.htm.

BORDEAUX, DORDOGNE & POITOU-CHARENTES

16

Revised and
updated by
Thomas
Cussans

Introduction by
Nancy Coons

IF YOU'RE LOOKING FOR THE GOOD LIFE, your search may be ended. No other region of France packs such a concentration of fine wine, extraordinary spirits, and gustatory delights ranging from exquisite cuisine to the most rib-sticking of country cooking. It's almost too much to ask that it be lovely, too—but it is. Viewed by generations of British as the quintessential French escape and now enjoying a new vogue with American travelers, Dordogne is a picture-postcard fantasy of green countryside, stone cottages, and cliff-top châteaux, crowned by the enchanting medieval wine town of St-Émilion. The Atlantic coast north of Bordeaux offers elite enclaves of white-sand beach. The vineyards of Médoc extend their lush green rows to the south. And beyond the fertile outreaches of Charente, the canal-laced Marais Poitevin—France's "Green Venice"—is a luxuriant, watery bower.

It's no wonder the English fought for it so determinedly throughout the Hundred Years' War. This coveted corner of France was home to Eleanor of Aquitaine, and when she left her first husband, France's Louis VII, to marry Henry II of England, both she and the land came under English rule. Henry Plantagenet was, after all, a great-grandson of William the Conqueror, and the Franco-English ambiguity of the age exploded in a war that defined much of modern France and changed its face forever. Southwestern France was the stage upon which much of the war was conducted. Hence the region's defensive châteaux-forts; hence no end of sturdy churches dedicated to the noble families' cause; and hence the steady flow of Bordeaux wines to England, where it is still dubbed "claret," after *clairet,* a light red version from earlier days.

What they sought, the world still seeks. The wines of Bordeaux set the standard against which other wines are measured, especially the burgeoning worldwide parade of Cabernets. From the grandest *premiers grands crus*—the Lafite-Rothschilds, the Margaux—to the modest *supérieur* in your picnic basket, the rigorously controlled Bordeaux commands respect. Fans and oenophiles come from around the world to pay homage; to gaze at the noble symmetries of estate châteaux, whose rows of green-and-black vineyards radiate in every direction; to lower a nose deep into a well-swirled glass to inhale the heady vapors of oak and almond and leather; and, finally, to reverently pack a few bloodline labels into a trunk or a suitcase for home.

The rest you will drink on site, from the mouthful of golden Graves that eases the oysters down to the syrupy sip of Sauternes that civilizes the smooth gaminess of the foie gras to the last glass of Médoc paired with the salt-marsh lamb that leads to pulling the cork on a Pauillac—because there is, still to come, the cheese tray. . . .

But brace yourself: you've barely scratched the culinary surface. Take a deep breath and head inland, following the winding sprawl of the Dordogne River into duck country. This is the land of the *gavée* goose, force-fed extravagantly to plump its liver into one of the world's most renowned delicacies. Duck or goose fat glistens on potatoes, on salty confits, on *rillettes d'oie,* a spread of potted duck that melts on the tongue as no mere butter ever could. Wild mushrooms and truffles weave their musky perfume through dense game pâtés. The wines, such as Bergerac and Cahors, are coarser here, as if to stand up to such an onslaught of earthy textures and flavors. And a snifter of amber cognac is de rigueur for the digestion.

Dining thus, in a vine-covered stone *ferme auberge* deep in the green wilds of Dordogne, the day's parade of châteaux and chapel tours blurring pleasantly into a reverie of picturesque history, you'll begin to understand what the Plantagenets were fighting for.

Exploring Bordeaux, Dordogne & Poitou-Charentes

For three centuries during the Middle Ages, this region was a battlefield in the wars between the French and the English. Of the castles and châteaux dotting the area, those at Biron, Hautefort, and Beynac are among the most spectacular. Robust Romanesque architecture is more characteristically found in this area than the airy Gothic style in view elsewhere in France: Poitiers showcases the best examples, notably Notre-Dame-la-Grande, with its richly worked facade. The Romanesque style can also be admired in Angoulême and Périgueux, and in countless village churches.

If there is a formula for enjoying this region, it would include cultural highlights, relaxing by the sea, tasting wine, and indulging in oysters, truffles, and foie gras. Swaths of sandy beaches line the Atlantic coast: well-heeled resorts like Royan and Arcachon are packed with glistening bodies baking in the sun. The world-famous vineyards of Médoc, Sauternes, Graves, Entre-Deux-Mers, Pomerol, and St-Émilion surround the elegant 18th-century city of Bordeaux, set on the southwest edge of the region near the foot of the Gironde Estuary.

If you prefer solitude, you won't have any trouble finding it in the vast, underpopulated spaces stretching inland and eastward in the rolling countryside of Dordogne, chock full of storybook villages, riverside châteaux, medieval chapels, and prehistoric sites. To the north, the rural region of Poitou-Charentes reaches from Angoulême through Cognac country to the Atlantic coast, and back inland through the canals around Niort to Poitiers. Between La Rochelle and Poitiers lies the Marais Poitevin, a marshy area known as "Green Venice" for its network of crisscrossing waterways.

About the Restaurants & Hotels

Apart from cosmopolitan Bordeaux and the university towns of Poitiers and La Rochelle, this region of southwest France can seem pretty sleepy outside the summer months. You'll never have too much trouble finding a good place to eat in the larger coastal resorts like Royan and Arcachon, but if you're traveling in the Dordogne or the Marais Poitevin between October and March it's essential to call ahead to avoid disappointment.

Vacationers flock to the coast and islands, and for miles around hotels are booked solid for months in advance. Farther inland—except for the Dordogne Valley—the situation eases up, but there aren't as many places to choose from. Advance booking is particularly desirable in Bor-

From the grand châteaux of Bordeaux country to the stone-cottage pastorale of Dordogne, from the broad, sandy beaches of Royan to the watery bower of the Marais Poitevin, this region offers a wondrous mix of high culture and elemental nature. And in the land of foie gras and cognac you'll eat (and quaff) like the kings (and queens) who once disputed this coveted southwest corner, staking it out with châteaux-forts and blessing it with Romanesque churches. But to try to see all of the region in one trip would be overambitious, so you need to be selective. If you love the beach and the outdoors, head to the Royan Peninsula or the islands of Ré and Oléron. If you're a gourmand, go straight to Dordogne; if wine is your passion, use Bordeaux as your base. For nature, seek out the Marais-Poitevin. Following are two suggested itineraries.

16

Numbers in the text correspond to numbers in the margin and on the Bordeaux, Dordogne & Poitou-Charentes map.

If you have 3 days

Have a morning tour and lunch in vibrant **Bordeaux** ❶ ☞ –❾ before heading on to medieval 🚩 **St-Émilion** ⓬, showplace of the Bordeaux wine region, during the afternoon. On the second day head east to the heart of the storybook Dordogne region, 🚩 **Sarlat-la-Canada** ㉓ and enjoy its golden-stone houses, narrow, twisty streets, and lovely Renaissance ambience. If you are up for France's second most visited tourist site, keep heading east to 🚩 **Rocamadour** ⓳, whose medieval Cité Réligieuse famously clusters its way up a towering rock bluff. If, on the other hand, maddening crowds are not for you, spend a day touring fairy-tale sights in the Dordogne, such as the hilltop castle at **Beynac** ㉒, the enchanting cliffside village of **La Roque-Gageac** ㉑, and the château at **Biron** ⓰, before heading back east to Bordeaux and dinner.

If you have 7 days

Finish off your morning tour with lunch in **Bordeaux** ❶ ☞ –❾ before whizzing back to the Middle Ages in 🚩 **St-Émilion** ⓬ during the afternoon. On the second day visit the fortified medieval village of **Monpazier** ⓯ and the mighty château at **Biron** ⓰, before veering north to overnight at 🚩 **La Roque-Gageac** ㉑, huddled beneath a towering cliff. On Day 3 head along the Dordogne River to the castle at **Beynac** ㉒, lunch on foie gras and truffles in the medieval market town of 🚩 **Sarlat-la-Canéda** ㉓, then check out the cave paintings at the **Lascaux II** ㉕ or the archaeological finds at the Musée Nationale de Préhistoire in **Les Eyzies-de-Tayac** ㉔. Rest up near 🚩 **Hautefort** ㉖. On Day 4 leave Dordogne via quaint **Brantôme** ㉘ en route to hilltop **Angoulême** ㉙. Try to get to **Cognac** ㉚ by afternoon to pay a call on a *chai*, then continue along the Charente Valley before spending the night in 🚩 **Saintes** ㉛. On Day 5 drive up to the lovely 🚩 **Ile de Ré** ㉝. After an overnight, head to 🚩 **La Rochelle** ㉜ where you can explore the Vieille Ville and picturesque harbor, then enjoy your last overnight. On your final day head east to the Marais Poitevin, lunching in the pretty village of **Coulon** ㉞, and continuing to **Poitiers** ㉟ to end your tour.

deaux, at any time, and in Dordogne, where hotels fill up quickly, in midsummer. Many country or small-town hotels expect you to have at least one dinner with them, and if you have two meals a day with your lodging and stay several nights, you will save money. Prices off-season (October–May) often drop as much as 20%. Assume all hotel rooms have air-conditioning, TV, telephones, and private bath, unless otherwise noted.

WHAT IT COSTS In euros					
	$$$$	**$$$**	**$$**	**$**	**¢**
RESTAURANTS	over €30	€23–€30	€17–€23	€11–€17	under €11
HOTELS	over €180	€120–€180	€80–€120	€50–€80	under €50

Restaurant prices are per person for a main course at dinner, including tax (19.6%) and service; note that if a restaurant offers only prix-fixe (set-price) meals, it has been given the price category that reflects the full prix-fixe price. Hotel prices are for a standard double room in high season, including tax (19.6%) and service charge; higher prices (inquire when booking) prevail for any board plans.

Timing

Spring and fall are the best times to visit—there aren't as many tourists around, and the weather is still pleasant. The *vendanges* (grape harvests) usually begin about mid-September in the Bordeaux region (though you can't visit the wineries at this time), and two weeks later in the Cognac region, to the north. A number of hotels are closed from the end of October through March.

THE BORDEAUX REGION

As the capital of the Gironde *département* (province), Bordeaux is both the commercial and cultural center of southwest France and an important transportation hub for the entire region. And if you're a wine connoisseur, it is still the doorway to paradise: pretty Sauternes and Graves lie to the south; Pomerol and St-Émilion to the east; the flat and dusty Médoc peninsula to the northwest, looking across the Gironde Estuary at the vineyards of Bourg and Blaye.

Bordeaux

Fodor'sChoice ★ *580 km (360 mi) southwest of Paris, 240 km (150 mi) northwest of Toulouse, 190 km (118 mi) north of Biarritz.*

Bordeaux as a whole, rather than any particular points within it, is what you'll want to visit in order to understand why Victor Hugo described it as Versailles plus Antwerp, and why, when he was exiled from his native Spain, the painter Francisco de Goya chose it as his last home (he died here in 1828). The capital of southwest France and the region's largest city, Bordeaux remains synonymous with the wine trade: wine shippers have long maintained their headquarters along the banks of the Garonne, while buyers from around the world arrive for the huge biannual Vinexpo show. An aura of 18th-century elegance permeates downtown Bor-

Grape Expectations Everyone in Bordeaux is celebrating because the
2000 vintage was acclaimed as the "crop of the century," a vintage that
comes along once in a lifetime. But bringing everything down to earth are the
increasingly loud whispers that Bordeaux may be "over." Some critics feel
the world has moved away from pricey, rich, red wines and more people are opting for lighter choices from other lands. Be that as it may,
if you have any aspirations to being a wine connoisseur, Bordeaux
will always remain the top of the pyramid. It has been considered
so ever since the credentials of Bordeaux wines were traditionally
established in 1787. That year, Thomas Jefferson went down to the
region from Paris and splurged on bottles of 1784 Château d'Yquem
and Château Margaux, for prices that were, he reported, "indeed dear."
Jefferson knew his wines: In 1855, both Yquem and Margaux were officially classified among Bordeaux's top five. And two centuries later, some of
his very bottles fetched upward of $50,000 when offered in a high-flying auc-
tion in New York City. His Margaux—of which Jefferson boasted "there cannot be a better bottle of Bordeaux" (in fact, it was a half-bottle) was sold in the
late 1980s for $30,000. As it turns out, Bordeaux's reputation dates from the
Middle Ages. From 1152 to 1453, along with much of what is now western
France, Bordeaux belonged to England. The light red wine then produced was
known as *clairet,* the origin of our word "claret."

16

Today no other part of France has such a concentrated wealth of top-class vineyards. The versatile Bordeaux region yields sweet and dry whites and fruity or
full-bodied reds from a huge domain extending on either side of the Gironde (Blaye
and Bourg to the north, Médoc and Graves to the south) and inland along the
Garonne (Sauternes) and Dordogne (St-Émilion, Fronsac, Pomerol) or in between
these two rivers (Entre-Deux-Mers). Farther north, the verdant hills of Cognac produce the world's finest brandy. Less familiar appellations are also worth seeking
out, including Bergerac, Pécharmant, and Monbazillac, along the Dordogne River,
and the lighter whites and reds of the Fiefs Vendéens, north of La Rochelle.

At the top of the government-supervised scale—which ranks, from highest to
lowest, as Appelation d'Origine Contrôlée (often abbreviated AC); Vin Délim-
ité de Qualité Supérieur (VDQS—a level that represents about 10 percent of
French wines); Vins de Pays, and Vin de Table—are the fabled vintages of Bordeaux, leading off with Margaux. The vineyards of Margaux are among the
ugliest in France, lost amid the flat, dusty plains of Médoc. Bordeaux is better
represented at historic St-Émilion, with its cascading cobbled streets, or at Sauternes,
where the noble rot (a fungus that sucks water from the grapes, leaving them
sweeter) steals up the riverbanks as autumn mists vanish in the summer skies.
At this time, the harvests, or *vendanges,* begin in September and can last into
December. In Sauternes, at Château d'Yquem, up to seven successive manual
harvests may be required, with each grape inspected individually and picked
only after achieving the right degree of maturity. It is one of the miracles of
Bordeaux that these grapes—which often look like foul, shriveled messes—are
transformed into one of the most sublime wines in the world.

But there are also sour grapes in Bordeaux—there has been talk in the trade that Bordeaux is passé. In this world of nouvelle cuisine and uncellared wines, such heavy, expensive vintages are *démodé* and lack "relevance." Still, Bordeaux—whose 2000 crop was one of the all-time bests—remains one of the bedrocks of French viticulture. Unfortunately, many vineyards, especially those of the Médoc, have nothing to show except bottles of their product, and dusty hillsides covered with vines. Many are inaccessible without a car or bike. This is why a tour group might be best—the Bordeaux tourist office arranges such trips. If you're determined to go it alone, the Maison du Vin can tell you how to get to many of the vineyards by bus.

Along the Shore

Although the region's two main islands, Ile de Ré and Ile d'Oléron, are linked to the mainland by bridges, boats still ply the Atlantic waters south of La Rochelle, visiting Fort Boyard and docking at Ile d'Aix. Explore the oyster beds of the Baie de Seudre or make an excursion across the Gironde to the Cordouan Lighthouse, stranded on a sandbank in mid-estuary. Ferries ply the Gironde from Royan and Blaye; punts, steered with long poles, glide peacefully along the canals of the Marais Poitevin; and the Dordogne River is a favorite with canoers. French families concentrate on resort towns like Royan, but there are plenty of other spacious beaches where you can escape the crowds: along the forest-girdled Côte Sauvage (Wild Coast) north of Royan; along the shores of the islands of Ré, Aix, and Oléron; and beneath the huge dunes south of Arcachon.

On the Menu

Truffles, foie gras, walnuts, plums, trout, eel, oysters, and myriad species of mushrooms jostle for attention on restaurant menus. The hearty food of Dordogne, the rich dairy bounty of Poitou-Charentes, and shoals of succulent seafood from the Atlantic make for diversified table fare. The versatile wines of Bordeaux make fine accompaniments to most regional dishes. Cognac is de rigueur at the end of a meal; sweet, tangy *pineau des Charentes*—made from cognac and unfermented grape juice—at the beginning.

---

deaux, where fine shops invite exploration. To the south of the city center are the old docklands undergoing gradual renewal—one train station has now been transformed into a big multiplex cinema—but still a bit shady. As a whole, Bordeaux is a less exuberant city than many others in France. That noted, lively and stylish elements are making a dent in the city's conservative veneer, and the cleaned-up riverfront is said by some, after a bottle or two, to exude an elegance redolent of St. Petersburg. Some of that ambience, however, is currently under assault by the city's construction of a multibillion-euro tramway system, though at least the worst of the work, scheduled for completion in 2007, is now over. To get a feel for the historic port of Bordeaux, take the 90-minute boat trip that leaves quai Louis-XVIII every weekday afternoon, or the regular passenger ferry that plies the Garonne between Quai Richelieu and the Pont d'Aquitaine.

For a view of the picturesque quayside, stroll across the Garonne on the ❶ **Pont de Pierre,** the only bridge across the river until 1965; in calm weather you'll see a tethered balloon soaring 500 yards overhead, away

❷ to the left (€10). Return to the left bank and head north to **Place de la Bourse,** an open square (built 1730–55) ringed with large-windowed buildings designed by the era's most esteemed architect, Jacques-Ange Gabriel, who later worked for Marie-Antoinette at Versailles. A few blocks to the southeast of the place de la Bourse is the **place du Parlement,** also ringed by elegant 18th-century structures and packed with lively outdoor cafés. Just north of the Esplanade des Quinconces, a sprawling **❸** square, is the two-story **Musée d'Art Contemporain** (Contemporary Art Center), imaginatively housed in a converted 19th-century spice warehouse, the Entrepôt Lainé. Many shows here showcase cutting-edge artists who invariably festoon the huge expanse of the place with hanging ropes, ladders, and large video screens. ✉ *7 rue Ferrère* ☎ *05–56–00–81–50* 🖵 *€4* ☉ *Tues.–Sun. 11–6.*

need a break? The trendy **museum café,** next to the art library on the top floor of Musée d'Art Contemporain, offers a good choice of beverages and snacks, and fine views over the Bordeaux skyline. It's open Tuesday through Sunday, noon until six. ✉ *7 rue Ferrère.*

❹ Close by along the quayside is the **Musée des Chartrons,** in an 18th-century vintner's house, retracing the history of the wine trade through a fine collection of old barrels and antique bottles. ✉ *41 rue Borie* ☎ *05–57–87–50–60* 🖵 *€3.10* ☉ *Weekdays 2–6.*

Turn back along the Garonne and cross Esplanade des Quinconces to **★❺** tree-lined cours du XXX-Juillet and the **Maison du Vin,** run by the CIVB (Conseil Interprofessionnel des Vins de Bordeaux), the headquarters of the Bordeaux wine trade. Before you set out to explore the regional wine country, stop here to gain clues from the staff (some are English-speaking) on the art of *dégustation* and pointers for where to go; their publication *Vineyards and Wine Cellars in the Bordeaux Area* is helpful. More important, tasting a red (like Pauillac or St-Émilion), a dry white (like an Entre-Deux-Mers or Côtes de Blaye), and a sweet white (like Sauternes or Loupiac) will help you decide which of the seven wine regions to explore. Remember: Before visiting any country château vineyard, always call ahead to see if the tasting is free and whether you need an appointment—the staff here can help with these questions. You can also make purchases at the **Vinothèque** opposite. ✉ *1 cours du XXX-Juillet* ☎ *05–56–00–22–66* ⊕ *www.la-vinotheque.com* 🖵 *Free.*

❻ One block south is the city's leading 18th-century monument: the **Grand Théâtre,** designed by Victor Louis and built between 1773 and 1780. It's the pride of the city, with an elegant exterior ringed by graceful Corinthian columns and a dazzling foyer with a two-winged staircase and a cupola. The theater hall has a frescoed ceiling with a shimmering chandelier composed of 14,000 Bohemian crystals. ✉ *Pl. de la Comédie* ☎ *05–56–00–66–00* ⊕ *www.opera-bordeaux.com* 🖵 *€5* ☞ *Contact tourist office for guided tours.*

Continue south on rue Ste-Catherine, then turn right on cours d'Alsace **❼** to reach the **Cathédrale St-André** (✉ Pl. Pey-Berland). This hefty edifice isn't one of France's finer Gothic cathedrals, but the intricate 14th-

Bordeaux, Dordogne & Poitou-Charentes

Atlantic Ocean

Bay of Biscay

0 — 20 miles

0 — 30 km

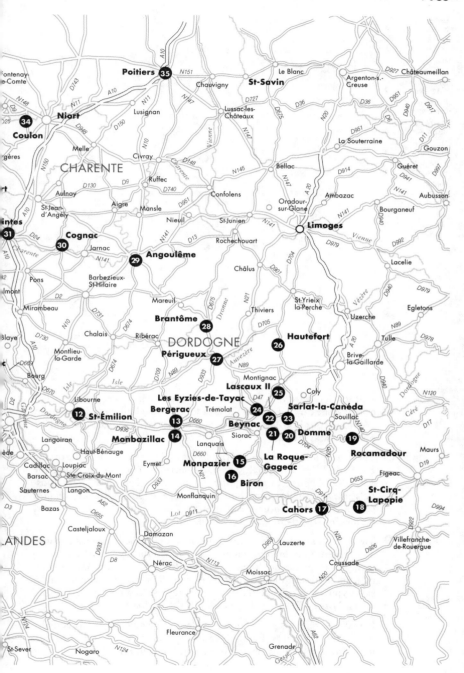

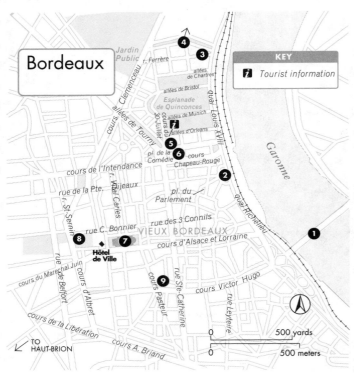

century chancel makes an interesting contrast with the earlier nave. Excellent stone carvings adorn the facade. You can climb the 15th-century, 160-foot **Tour Pey-Berland** for a view of the city; cost is €2.50, and it's open Tuesday–Sunday 10–noon and 2–5.

❽ The nearby **Musée des Beaux-Arts,** across tidy gardens behind the ornate Hôtel de Ville (town hall), has a collection of works spanning the 15th–20th centuries, with important paintings by Paolo Veronese (*Apostle's Head*), Camille Corot (*Bath of Diana*), and Odilon Redon (*Apollo's Chariot*), and sculptures by Auguste Rodin. ✉ *20 cours d'Albret* ☎ *05–56–10–20–56* 🎟 *€4* ⊙ *Wed.–Mon. 11–6.*

❾ Two blocks south of the Cathédrale St-André is the **Musée d'Aquitaine,** an excellent museum that takes you on a trip through Bordeaux's history, with emphases on Roman, medieval, Renaissance, port-harbor, colonial, and 20th-century daily life. The detailed prehistoric section almost saves you a trip to Lascaux II, which is reproduced here in part. ✉ *20 cours Pasteur* ☎ *05–56–01–51–00* 🎟 *€4* ⊙ *Tues.–Sun. 11–6.*

One of the region's most famous wine-producing châteaux is actually within the city limits: follow N250 southwest from central Bordeaux for 3 km (2 mi) to the district of Pessac, home to **Haut-Brion,** producer of the only non-Médoc wine to be ranked a *premier cru* (the most elite wine classification). The white château looks out over the celebrated pebbly soil. The wines produced at **La Mission–Haut Brion,** across the road, are almost as sought-after. ⊠ *133 av. Jean-Jaurès, 33600 Pessac* ☎ *05–56–00–29–31* ⊕ *www.chateau-haut-brion.tm.fr* ☜ *Free 1-hr visits by appointment, weekdays only, with tasting* ⊙ *Closed mid-July–mid-Aug.*

Where to Stay & Eat

Old Bordeaux has many small restaurants, particularly around the 18th-century place du Parlement, like bustling L'Ombrière (No. 14), with fairly priced steaks, and pricey Chez Philippe (No. 1), one of the city's top fish restaurants. What is lacking are charming hotels. You may want to consider staying outside Bordeaux: at Château Lamothe in St-Sulpice & Cameyrac, 20 km (12 mi) east of the city, for instance.

$$$$ ✕ **Le Chapon-Fin.** With all the laurels and stars thrown at Thierry Marx,
Fodor'sChoice the culinary wizard ensconced at Pauillac's Château Cordeillan-Bages,
★ it was just a matter of time before he would swoop in and give Bordeaux's own landmark restaurant an all-out re-energizing shot in the arm. It needed one: Founded in 1825, favored by such V.I.P.'s as Sarah Bernhardt, Toulouse-Lautrec, and Edward VII, and graced with an extraordinary decor (half winter-garden, half rococo-grotto), the Chapon-Fin had hardened with age. Marx's face-lift includes such nouvelle delights as foie gras on a bed of candied peaches with a sauce of reduced Port; lobster with sweet chestnuts and wild mushrooms; and Pauillac lamb grilled in a bordeaux sauce. Although Marx only spends two days a week here, Frank Feriguti, second in command, is good enough to also mastermind the restaurant's noted cooking school. You haven't really been to Bordeaux until you've been here—so book now. ⊠ *5 rue Montesquieu* ☎ *05–56–79–10–10* 🖶 *05–56–79–09–10* ☖ *Reservations essential* ☰ *AE, MC, V* ⊙ *Closed Sun. and Mon.*

★ **$$–$$$$** ✕ **La Tupina.** With much glory stolen by its noble cellars, Bordeaux has struggled mightily against its reputation as a culinary backwater. Happily, fine new chefs are arriving all the time and one of the best is Stéphane Gabrielly, whose earthy spins on *cuisine de terroir* are served up at this lovely restaurant set on one of Bordeaux's oldest streets. Inside, dried herbs hang from the ceiling, a Provençal grandfather clock ticks off the minutes, and an antique fireplace sports a grill bearing sizzling morsels of duck and chicken. Both the decor and the menu aspire to the *"nostalgie des anciennes menus"* and both succeed. On the same street (No. 34) is the owner's Bar-Cave, a cheaper bistro, with another fetching ambience. ⊠ *6 rue Porte de la Monnaie* ☎ *05–56–91–56–37* ⊕ *www.latupina.com* ☖ *Reservations essential* ☰ *AE, MC, V.*

★ **$$–$$$** ✕ **Le Vieux Bordeaux.** This lively, much-acclaimed nouvelle-cuisine haunt lies on the fringe of the *Vieille Ville* (Old Town). Chef Michel Bordage's menu is brief but of high quality, complemented by three prix-fixe menus. His fish dishes are particularly tasty, such as the grilled *bar* (bass) on a peppery *galette* of crab. ⊠ *27 rue Buhan* ☎ *05–56–52–94–36* ☰ *AE, DC, MC, V* ⊙ *Closed Sun., 2 wks Feb., 3 wks Aug. No lunch Sat. or Mon.*

$$ ✗ **L'Estaquade.** *Le tout Bordeaux* now congregates at this fashionable spot, spectacularly set in a pierlike structure right on the Garonne River. Enormous bay windows allow you to drink in a beautiful panorama of the 18th-century place de la Bourse on the opposite bank. The cuisine is creative (prawn risotto, mullet with trout roe); the wine list has few selections to offer other than young Bordeaux, but that seems only fitting. ⊠ *Quai des Queyries* ☎ *05–57–54–02–50* ▤ *MC, V.*

$–$$ ✗ **Gravelier.** Anne-Marie, daughter of Pierre Troisgros of Roanne, married Yves Gravelier, and they combine their culinary talents here. In sparse decor, full of light and openness, imaginative cuisine is served: fillets of *rouget* (red mullet) with foie gras, and pigeon potpie with Chinese cabbage. The €20 lunch menu is a good deal. ⊠ *114 cours de Verdun* ☎ *05–56–48–17–15* ▤ *AE, DC, MC, V* ☉ *Closed Sun. and 3 wks in Aug.*

$$$–$$$$ ✗▥ **Burdigala.** Of the three luxury hotels in Bordeaux, Burdigala (Latin for "Bordeaux") is the only one within walking distance of the center of town. Although the modern exterior is unappealing, the inside is comfortable. The soundproof rooms are smart and neat; No. 416 is especially quiet and sunny. Deluxe rooms have marble bathrooms with whirlpool baths. The Jardin du Burdigala restaurant serves nouvelle cuisine. ⊠ *115 rue Georges Bonnac, 33000* ☎ *05–56–90–16–16* 🖷 *05–56–93–15–06* ⊕ *www.burdigala.com* ⇌ *68 rooms, 15 suites* ⚭ *Restaurant, minibars, cable TV, Internet, some pets allowed (fee)* ▤ *AE, DC, MC, V* ▥ *MAP.*

$$–$$$ ▥ **Quality Hotel Sainte-Catherine.** This fully modernized hotel is in an 18th-century building in the old part of town. Service is limited, but the reception staff is helpful. The compact, pastel-tone rooms are decorated with light floral fabrics. ⊠ *27 rue du Parlement-Ste-Catherine, 33000* ☎ *05–56–81–95–12* 🖷 *05–56–44–50–51* ⊕ *www.bordeaux-hotelquality. com* ⇌ *82 rooms* ⚭ *Minibars, cable TV, bar, some pets allowed (fee)* ▤ *AE, DC, MC, V* ▥ *BP.*

$–$$ ▥ **Des Quatre Soeurs.** In an elegant 1840 town house near the Grand Théâtre, this hotel has sober, well-kept rooms of varying sizes, all with air-conditioning. It's changed a bit since Richard Wagner stayed here. ⊠ *6 cours du XXX-Juillet, 33000* ☎ *05–57–81–19–20* 🖷 *05–56–01–04–28* ⊕ *www.4soeurs.free.fr* ⇌ *29 rooms, 5 suites* ⚭ *Cable TV, Internet, some pets allowed (fee)* ▤ *AE, MC, V* ▥ *MAP.*

Nightlife & the Arts

A respected and long-established Bordeaux hangout, **Les Argentiers** (⊠ 33 rue des Argentiers) is the place for jazz. **L'Aztécal** (⊠ 61 rue du Pas-St-Georges) is a comfortable spot for a drink. **Sénéchal** (⊠ 57 bis quai de Paludate), near the station, is the place to dance the night away.

The **Grand Théâtre** (⊠ Pl. de la Comédie ☎ 05–56–00–85–95 ⊕ www. opera-bordeaux.com) puts on performances of French plays and occasionally operas. Bordeaux's four-day **Fête du Vin** (Wine Festival; ⊕ www.bordeaux-tourisme.com) at the end of June sees glass-clinking merriment along the banks of the Garonne. The tourist office Web site has the details.

Shopping

Between the cathedral and the Grand Théâtre are numerous pedestrian streets where stylish shops abound. For an exceptional selection of cheeses, go to **Jean d'Alos** (⊠ 4 rue Montesquieu). The **Vinothèque** (⊠ 8 cours du Juillet) sells top-ranked Bordeaux wines.

Route du Médoc

North of Bordeaux, the Route du Médoc wine road (D2)—sometimes called the Route des Châteaux—winds through the dusty Médoc Peninsula, past the townships of Margaux, St.-Julien, Pauillac, and St-Estèphe. Even the vines in Médoc look dusty, and so does the ugly town ⑩ of **Margaux,** the area's unofficial capital, 27 km (17 mi) northwest of Bordeaux. Yet **Château Margaux,** housed in a magnificent Neoclassical building from 1802, is recognized as a producer of premiers crus, whose wine qualifies with Graves's Haut-Brion as one of Bordeaux's top five reds. As with all the top Bordeaux châteaux, visits to Château Margaux are restricted to the wine chai through appointment on weekdays only (☎ 05–57–88–83–83). The well-informed, English-speaking staff at the **Margaux Maison du Vin** (☎ 05–57–88–70–82 or 05–57–88–38–27) can direct you to other châteaux such as **Lascombes** and **Palmer,** which have beautiful grounds, reasonably priced wines, and are open without reservations. In nearby Cussac, visit the winery and carriage museum at **Château Lanessan.**

★ ⑪ Some 90 km (56 mi) north of Bordeaux on highway D2 is **Pauillac,** home to the three wineries—Lafite-Rothschild, Latour, and Mouton-Rothschild—that produce Médoc's other top reds. Renowned **Château Latour** (☎ 05–56–73–19–80) sometimes requires reservations a month in advance. If the posh prices of these fabled *grands crus* are not for you, rent a bike from the tourist office at La Verrerie (☎ 05–56–59–03–08), and visit any of the less-expensive nearby wineries. Of all the towns and villages in the Médoc, Pauillac is the prettiest; you may want to stroll along the riverfront and stop for refreshments at one of its restaurants. A train line connects Pauillac to Bordeaux, running several times in the summer.

★ **Lafite-Rothschild** is among the most resonant names of the wine world. Even by the giddy standards of the Médoc, Lafite—owned by the Rothschild family since 1868 (but first recorded as making wine as early as 1234)—is a high temple of wine-making at its most memorable. Prices may be sky high but no one fortunate enough to sample one of the chateau's classic vintage will forget the experience in a hurry. Too bad you can't visit the family château on the grounds—its rooms are the defining examples of *le style Rothschild,* one of the most opulent styles of 19th-century interior decoration. ⊠ *33250 Pauillac* 🏠 🖃 *€5; with tasting, €11.50–13, depending on size of group of wines tasted* ☉ *By appointment only, reservations to be made at least two weeks in advance; closed Aug., Sept., and Oct.*

Most of the great vineyards in this area are strictly private (the owners, however, are usually receptive to inquiries about visits from bona fide

wine connoisseurs). One vineyard, however, has long boasted a welcoming
★ visitor center: **Mouton-Rothschild,** whose eponymous wine was brought
to perfection in the 1930s by that flamboyant figure Baron Philippe de
Rothschild, whose American-born wife, Pauline, was a great style-
maker of the 1950s. The baron's daughter, Philippine, continues to lavish money and love on this growth, so wine lovers should flock here for
either the one-hour visit, which includes a tour of the cellars, *chai*
(brandy warehouse), and museum, or the slightly longer visit that tops
off the tour with a tasting. ⊠ *Le Pouyalet, 33250 Pauillac*
☎ *05–56–73–21–29* 🔁 *€5; with tasting, €12.50* ⊘ *Apr.–Oct., daily*
9:30–11 and 2–4.

At the tip of the Gironde peninsula, near a memorial commemorating
the landing of U.S. troops in 1917, is the **Pointe de Grave,** where you
can take the *bac* (ferry) across the Gironde to Royan; it runs at least six
times daily and costs €20 per car and €3 per passenger. During the 20-
minute crossing, keep an eye out for the **Phare de Cordouan** on your
left, a lighthouse that looks as if it's emerging from the sea (at low tide,
its base is revealed to rest on a sandbank).

Where to Stay & Eat

★ **$$$–$$$$** ✕🖼 **Château Cordeillan-Bages.** This marble-face, single-story 17th-cen-
tury "chartreuse" just outside Pauillac is surrounded by the vines that
produce its own *cru bourgeois.* Paris-trained Thierry Marx is consid-
ered the highest-rated chef in Bordeaux—all the more valued as food
often takes second prize to wine in this region—and his fortes range from
local salt-meadow lamb and spit-roasted kid with shallots to smoked
eel with apple and crisp potato slices layered with oxtail and truffles.
Of course, who will be able to resist the accompaniment of one of the
1,000-plus Bordeauxs from the cellars? (The restaurant is closed Mon-
day other than for guests in the hotel, and Tuesday and Saturday lunch.)
The dining room decor is château-boring, but the guest rooms are cozy,
comfortable, and Relais-&-Châteaux stylish. ⊠ *61 rue des Vignerons,*
1½ km (1 mi) south of town, 33250 Pauillac ☎ *05–56–59–24–24*
🖨 *05–56–59–01–89* ⊕ *www.relaischateaux.com/cordeillan* ⇜ *25 rooms*
⟁ *Restaurant, minibars, cable TV, bar; no a/c in some rooms* ▭ *AE,*
DC, MC, V ⊘ *Closed mid-Dec.–mid-Feb.* ⍒ *MAP.*

$ 🖼 **France & Angleterre.** A convenient choice for those who wish to ex-
plore Pauillac's lovely streets, this low-key spot offers some doubles over-
looking the quaint waterfront. The restaurant is closed weekends late
fall to early spring. ⊠ *3 quai Albert-Pichon, 33250 Pauillac*
☎ *05–56–59–01–20* 🖨 *05–56–59–02–31* ⇜ *23 rooms* ⟁ *Restaurant;*
no a/c ▭ *AE, DC, MC, V* ⊘ *Closed mid-Dec.–mid-Jan.* ⍒ *MAP.*

Sports & the Outdoors

The **Médoc Marathon** (⊕ www.marathondumedoc.com), on the first or
second Saturday of September, is more than just a 42-km (26-mi) race
through the vineyards: 50 groups of musicians turn out to serenade the
runners, who can indulge in no fewer than 20 giant buffets en route,
and drink free wine from two dozen estates along the way. Speed is not
exactly of the essence for most taking part in the competition. 2005 sees
the 23rd running of this hybrid athletic-alcoholic event.

St-Émilion

⑫ *128 km (80 mi) southeast of Royan, 35 km (23 mi) east of Bordeaux.*

Suddenly the sun-fired flatlands of Pomerol break into hills and send you tumbling into St-Émilion. This jewel of a town has old buildings of golden stone, ruined town walls, well-kept ramparts offering magical views, and a church hewn into a cliff. Sloping vineyards invade from all sides, and thousands of tourists invade down the middle, many thirsting for the red wine and macaroons that bear the town's name. The medieval streets, delightfully cobblestoned (though often very steep), are filled with wine stores (St-Émilion reaches maturity earlier than other Bordeaux reds and often offers better value for the money than Médoc or Graves), crafts shops, bakeries, cafés, and restaurants.

The **Office de Tourisme** (Tourist Office; ⊠ Pl. des Créneaux ☎ 05–57–55–28–28 ⊕ www.saint-emilion-tourisme.com) hires out bikes (€14 per day) and organizes tours of the pretty local vineyards— the fabled **Château Pétrus** and **Cheval Blanc,** among others—including wine tastings and train rides through the vineyards. Note that it is best to hit the road on a weekday, when more châteaux are open.

A stroll along the 13th-century ramparts takes you to the **Château du Roi** (King's Castle), built by the English in the Henry III era (1216–72). From the castle ramparts, steps lead down to **Place du Marché,** a leafy square where cafés remain open late into the balmy summer night. Beware of the inflated prices charged at the café tables.

The **Église Monolithe** (Monolithic Church) is one of France's largest underground churches, hewn out of the rock face between the 9th and 12th centuries. The church was built by monks faithful to the memory of St-Émilion, an 8th-century hermit and miracle worker. Its spire-topped *clocher* (bell tower) rises out of the bedrock, dominating the center of town. ⊠ Pl. du Marché ⊠ €5.10 ۞ *Tours leave from tourist office, daily 10–11:30 and 2–5.*

Just south of the town walls is **Château Ausone,** an estate that is ranked with Cheval Blanc as a producer of St-Émilion's finest wines.

Where to Stay & Eat

$ ✕ **Chez Germaine.** Family cooking and regional dishes are the focus at this central St-Émilion eatery. The candlelit upstairs dining room and the terrace are both pleasant places to enjoy the reasonably priced set menus. Grilled meats and fish are house specialties; for dessert, go for the almond macaroons. ⊠ *13 pl. du Clocher* ☎ *05–57–74–49–34* ▤ *MC, V* ۞ *Closed mid-Dec.–mid-Jan.*

$$$–$$$$ ✕▥ **Grand Barrail.** This turn-of-the-20th-century luxury hotel just outside St-Émilion, flanked by a lake and vineyards, may seem a little stiff and heavy, but rooms are unusually large and smartly furnished; about half are in the transformed former stables. Talented chef Fabrice Giraud serves pumpkin soup, and calamari and goat-cheese risotto, in the Belle Epoque dining room (no dinner Sunday, no lunch Tuesday, closed Monday January and February). St-Émilions constitute at least 60% of the

impressive wine list. ⊠ *5 rue Marzelle, 4 km (2½ mi) northwest of St-Émilion on D243, 33330* ☎ *05–57–55–37–00* 🖷 *05–57–55–37–49* ⊕ *www.grand-barrail.com* 📨 *28 rooms* 🛆 *Restaurant, minibars, cable TV, pool, bar, Internet, some pets allowed (fee)* 🖃 *AE, DC, MC, V* ⊗ *Closed 3 wks Feb., late Nov.–mid-Dec.* ¶◎¶ *MAP.*

★ **$$$$**   ✕🏠 **L'Hostellerie de Plaisance.** Part of the Relais & Château group, this sumptuous hotel has long been considered the top address in St.-Emilion. Set next to the tourist office in the upper part of town and housed in a stunningly elegant limestone mansion, it's just across the way from the town's famous stone Eglise Monolithe. Rooms are warm and appealing and many come with terraces overlooking the tile roofs of the town; some, like the Descault Room, have excellent views of the vineyards. Dinner is often accompanied by St-Émilion wines; you need to pick and choose from the menu selections, but the crab stuffed with cabbage, pork with mango chutney, or the truffled bananas are all winners. ⊠ *5 pl. du Clocher, 33330* ☎ *05–57–55–07–55* 🖷 *05–57–74–41–11* ⊕ *www.hostellerie-plaisance.com* 📨 *19 rooms* 🛆 *Restaurant, some minibars, cable TV, some pets allowed (fee); a/c in some rooms only* 🖃*AE, DC, MC, V* ⊗ *Closed Jan.–mid-Feb.* ¶◎¶ *MAP.*

$$$$ 🏠 **Château Lamothe.** Many of St-Émilion's hotels are in-and-out tourist stops, while those in Bordeaux can lack charm. For something much more authentic, try this manor house located halfway between the two. The spacious guest rooms have large four-poster beds with soft cotton sheets; you may find them a little too frilly, but they are very comfortable. Owner Jacques Bastide speaks English and is extremely helpful with suggestions. ⊠ *6 rte. du Stade, 25 km (16 mi) west of St-Émilion, 20 km (12 mi) northeast of Bordeaux), 33450 St-Sulpice & Cameyrac* ☎ *05–56–30–82–16* 🖷 *05–56–30–88–33* 📨 *5 suites* 🛆 *Pool, fishing, Internet; no a/c* 🖃 *MC, V* ⊗ *Closed Nov.–Mar.* ¶◎¶ *BP.*

$–$$ 🏠 **Commanderie.** Close to the ramparts, this 19th-century two-story hotel has a garden and a view of the vineyards. Rooms are small but clean and individually decorated with colorful prints; some have exposed stonework. ⊠ *Rue des Cordeliers, 33300* ☎ *05–57–24–70–19* 🖷 *05–57–74–44–53* ⊕ *www.aubergedelacommanderie.com* 📨 *18 rooms* 🛆 *Cable TV, bar, Internet; no a/c in some rooms* 🖃 *MC, V* ⊗ *Closed mid-Jan.–mid-Feb.* ¶◎¶ *EP.*

DORDOGNE

What's not to love? Fairy-tale castles, geese flocks, storybook villages, prehistoric wonders, and medieval alleyways—little wonder the Dordogne has become one of the hottest destinations in France. Formerly one of those off-the-beaten-path regions, it's in danger of getting four-starred, boutiqued, and postcarded to death. Indeed, one sometimes has the sensation that visitors outnumber locals. But scratch the surface and you'll find one of the most authentic and appealing areas of rural France. What's more, and unlike the Loire Valley, for example, where attractions are often 20 mi apart, you can discover romantic riverside château after château with each kilometer traveled. The département centers on Sarlat, whose impeccably restored medieval buildings make it a great

BORDEAUX: A WINE-LOVER'S GAZETTEER

BARON PHILIPPE DE ROTHSCHILD, legendary owner of Bordeaux's famed Mouton-Rothschild vineyard, was known for his custom of drinking vin ordinaire at most lunches and dinners. Indeed, any French person knows you can't enjoy fine vintages at every meal. Still, if you're traveling to Bordeaux, you're going to want to enjoy some of the region's celebrated liquid fare. To find the best vineyards, just head in any direction from the city of Bordeaux. The city is at the hub of a patchwork of vineyards: the Médoc peninsula to the northwest; Bourg and Blaye across the estuary; St-Émilion inland to the east; then, as you wheel around clockwise, Entre-Deux-Mers, Sauternes, and Graves.

The nearest vineyard to Bordeaux itself is, ironically, one of the best: Haut-Brion, on the western outskirts of the city, and one of the five châteaux to be officially recognized as a premier cru or first growth. There are only five premiers crus in all, and Haut-Brion is the only one not in the Médoc (Château Mouton-Rothschild, Château Margaux, Château Latour, and Château Lafite-Rothschild complete the list). The Médoc is subdivided into various appellations, wine-growing districts with their own specific characteristics and taste. Pauillac and Margaux host premiers crus; St-Julien and St-Estèphe possess many domaines of almost equal quality, followed by Listrac and Moulis; wines not quite so good are classed as Haut-Médoc or, as you move farther north, Médoc, pure and simple. Wines from the Médoc are made predominantly from the cabernet sauvignon grape, and can taste dry, even austere, when young. The better ones often need 15 to 25 years before "opening up" to reveal their full spectrum of complex flavors. When considering lighter reds for earlier consumption, serious connoisseurs prefer to head southeast beyond Libourne to the stunning Vieille Ville of St-Émilion. The surrounding vineyards see the fruity merlot grape in control, and wines here often have more immediate appeal than those of the Médoc. There are several small appellations apart from St-Émilion itself, the most famous being Pomerol, whose Château Pétrus is the world's most expensive wine.

South of St-Émilion is the region known as Entre-Deux-Mers ("between two seas"— actually two rivers, the Dordogne and Garonne), whose dry white wine is particularly flavorsome if made from the vineyards near the ruined castle of Haut-Benauge. The picturesque villages of Loupiac and Sainte-Croix du Mont are sandwiched between the Garonne River and hillside vineyards producing sweet, not dry, white wine. But the best sweet wine produced hereabouts—some would say in the world—comes from across the Garonne and is made at Barsac and Sauternes. Nothing in the grubby village of Sauternes would suggest that mind-boggling wealth lurks amid the picturesque vine-laden slopes and hollows. The village has a wine shop where bottles gather dust on rickety shelves, next to handwritten price tags demanding small fortunes. Making Sauternes is a tricky business. Autumn mists steal up the valleys to promote Botrytis cinerea, a fungus known as pourriture noble or noble rot, which sucks moisture out of the grapes, leaving a high proportion of sugar. Heading back north toward Bordeaux you encounter the vineyards of the Graves region, so called because of its gravelly soil. Santé!

place to use as a base while exploring the region. Stretching along the Dordogne, Isle, Dronne, and Auvezère rivers, the Dordogne's wooded hills and valleys are packed with small villages. It's also one of the premier "prehistoric" areas in Europe, dotted with noted sites, including the incomparable Lascaux cavern paintings (today, in reality, the not-so-incomparable Lascaux II). These sites are centered in the region known as Les Eyzies. You may want to spend a week exploring the small country roads and picnicking on riverbanks, but hurry. Ever since the British discovered this area two decades ago and made it among their favored vacation spots in France, the buzz has grown and grown.

The 10-km (6-mi) stretch of the Dordogne river from Montfort to Beynac is easily accessible by car, bike, canoe, or on foot, and shouldn't be missed. Fields of sunflowers line the banks in season, and medieval châteaux perch high above the river. Another 30 km (19 mi) west, toward Bergerac, the land is dedicated to viticulture. All these attractions don't go unnoticed; in July and August even the smallest village is often packed with sightseers.

Bergerac

13 *57 km (36 mi) east of St-Émilion via D936, 88 km (55 mi) east of Bordeaux.*

Cyrano never lived here, but no matter—the town still claims the long-nosed swashbuckler as a local son (his family had roots here but he was actually a Parisian playwright who lived from 1619 to 1655). Bergerac is a lively town with ancient half-timber houses, narrow alleys, and colorful Wednesday and Saturday (the larger of the two) markets. It's also a fine railway hub, with trains often arriving from Bordeaux, Sarlat, and St-Emilion. Guided walking tours of the Vieille Ville (1 hour, €4) leave from the **tourist office** (⌧ 97 rue Neuve d'Argenson ☎ 05–53–57–03–11 ⊕ www.bergerac-tourisme.com). There are also hour-long cruises along the Dordogne (€6.50) in old wooden sailboats with **Périgord Gabarres** (☎ 05–53–24–58–80).

The **Cloître des Récollets**, a former convent, is in the wine business. The convent's stone-and-brick buildings range in date from the 12th to the 17th centuries and include galleries, a large vaulted cellar, and a cloister where the **Maison du Vin** (Wine Center) provides information on, and samples of, local vintages of sweet whites and fruity young reds. ⌧ *Quai Salvette* ☎ *05–53–63–57–55* ⌦ *Free* ☉ *Daily 10–12:30 and 1:30–6.*

You can learn about another local industry—tobacco growing—from its pre-Columbian origins to its spread worldwide, at the **Musée du Tabac** (National Tobacco Museum). It's housed in the 17th-century Maison Peyrarède, near the quayside. ⌧ *Pl. du Feu* ☎ *05–53–63–04–13* ⌦ *€3* ☉ *Tues.–Fri. 10–noon and 2–6, Sat. 10–noon and 2–5, Sun. 2:30–6:30.*

Where to Stay & Eat

$–$$ ✕▦ **Bordeaux.** One of the better hotels in town, the family-owned Bordeaux has contemporary furnishings and neat rooms. Request one on the garden courtyard or No. 22, which is slightly more spacious. Though you're not obliged to eat at the restaurant, Le Terroir (closed Friday–Saturday, November–March), it's difficult to refuse the marinated salmon in anisette and lime or the pan-fried *escalope de foie gras* (sautéed foie gras). The owner, Monsieur Maury, speaks fluent English. ⊠ *38 pl. Gambetta, 24100* ☎ *05–53–57–12–83* 🖷 *05–53–57–72–14* ⊕ *www.hotel-bordeaux-bergerac.com* ↰ *40 rooms* ⊛ *Restaurant, cable TV, pool, some pets allowed (fee); no a/c* ⊟ *AE, DC, MC, V* ☉ *Closed mid-Dec.–mid-Jan. and mid-Feb.–early Mar.* ⫩ *FAP.*

Monbazillac

⑭ *6 km (4 mi) south of Bergerac via D13.*

From the hilltop village of Monbazillac are spectacular views of the sweet wine–producing vineyards tumbling toward the Dordogne. The storybook corner towers of the beautifully proportioned 16th-century gray-stone **Château de Monbazillac** pay tribute to the fortress tradition of the Middle Ages, but the large windows and sloping roofs reveal a Renaissance influence. Regional furniture and an ornate early 17th-century bedchamber enliven the interior. A wine tasting is included to tempt you into buying a case or two of the famous but expensive bottles. The restaurant on the grounds serves expensive meals. ☎ *05–53–63–65–00 weekdays, 05–53–61–52–52 weekends* ⊕ *www.chateau-monbazillac.com* ▧ *€5.80* ☉ *June–Sept., daily 10–7; mid-Feb.–May and Oct.–Dec., Tues.–Sun. 10–noon and 2–5.*

Monpazier

⑮ *43 km (27 mi) southeast of Monbazillac via D14/D104.*

★ Monpazier, on the tiny Drot River, is one of France's best-preserved and most photographed bastide towns. It was built in ocher-color stone by English king Edward I in 1284 to protect the southern flank of his French possessions. The bastide has three stone gateways (of an original six), a large central square, and the church of **St-Dominique**, housing 35 carved-wood choir stalls and a would-be relic of the True Cross. Opposite the church is the finest medieval building in town, the **Maison du Chapître** (Chapter House), once used as a barn for storing grain. Its wood-beam roof is constructed of chestnut to repel insects.

Where to Stay & Eat

¢ ✕▥ **France.** Once an outbuilding on the estates of the Château de Biron, the Hôtel de France has never capitalized on its 13th-century heritage or its 15th-century staircase. Instead, it has remained a small, modest family-run hotel that caters less to tourists than to locals at its bar and restaurant, serving rich regional food. Rooms are a clutter of old furniture (with a plastic-cabinet shower and toilet squeezed into the corner); some are quite large. ⊠ *21 rue St-Jacques, 24540* ☎ *05–53–22–60–06* 🖷 *05–53–22–07–27* ↰ *10 rooms* ⊛ *Restaurant, bar; no a/c, no room TVs* ⊟ *MC, V* ⫩ *MAP.*

Biron

⑯ *8 km (5 mi) south of Monpazier via D2/D53.*

★ Stop in Biron to see its massive hilltop castle, the **Château de Biron**. Highlights of the château, which with its keep, square tower, and chapel dates from the Middle Ages, include monumental staircases, Renaissance-era apartments, the kitchen with its huge stone-slab floor, and a gigantic dungeon, replete with a collection of scarifying torture instruments. The classical buildings were completed in 1730. English Romantic poet Lord Byron (1788–1824) is claimed as a distant descendant of the Gontaut-Biron family, which lived here for 14 generations. ⌂ *221 bis route d'Angoulême* ☎ *05–53–35–50–40* ⌸ €5 ⊘ *Apr.–June, Sept. and Oct., Tues.–Sun. 10–12:30 and 2–6; July and Aug., daily 10–7.*

Cahors

⑰ *60 km (38 mi) southeast of Monpazier via D660.*

Less touristy and populated than the neighboring Dordogne, the Lot Valley has a subtler charm. The cluster of towns along the Lot River and the smaller rivers that cut through the dry, vineyard-covered plateau have a magical, abandoned feel. Just an hour north of southwestern France's main city, Toulouse, Cahors remains the Lot area's largest town and its information center and makes a fine base from which to explore the Lot River valley, a 50-km (31-mi) gorge punctuated by barely inhabited medieval villages. Here and on other routes—notably the GR46, which spans the interior of the Lot region, with breathtaking views of the limestone plateaus and quiet valleys between Rocamdour and St-Cirq-Lapopie—*cyclotourisme* (biking) rules supreme.

Modern Cahors encircles its *ville antique* (Old Town), which dates from 1 BC. Once an opulent Gallo-Roman town, Cahors, sitting snugly within a loop of the Lot River, is famous for its vin de Cahors, a tannic red wine known to the Romans as "black wine." Many of the small estates in the area offer tastings and the town tourist office on the place Mitterand can point you in the direction of some of the more notable vineyards of the area, including the Domaine de Lagrezette (in Caillac) and the Domaine de St-Didier (in Parnac). The town's finest sight is the 14th-century **Pont Valentré**, a bridge with three elegant towers that constitutes a spellbinding feat of medieval engineering. Also look for the fortresslike **Cathédrale St-Étienne** (⌂ Off rue du Maréchal-Joffre), with its cupolas and cloisters connecting to the courtyard of the archdeaconry, which is awash with Renaissance decoration and thronged with townsfolk who come for art exhibits.

FodorsChoice
★

The hour-long bike ride between Rocamadour and the Gouffre de Padirac might just be one of your most memorable experiences in France, as will day-long bike trips through the neighboring Célé valley and the 35-km (22-mi) trip to the **Grotte du Pech-Merle**, one of the finest caves with prehistoric drawings and carvings, located outside the town of Cabrerets. Happily, Cahors has plenty of places for bike rentals and picnic fixings (head for the town's covered and outdoor markets).

Where to Stay & Eat

$$$–$$$$ ✕▣ **Château de Mercuès.** The former home of the count-bishops of Cahors, on a rocky spur just outside town, has older rooms in baronial splendor (ask for one of these), as well as unappealing modern ones (which tend to attract midges). One of the best is "Tour," with a clever ceiling that slides back to expose the turret. Duck, lamb, and truffles reign in the restaurant, but the high prices lead you to expect more creativity from chef Philippe Combet than is delivered. The restaurant is closed Monday, and there's no lunch Tuesday–Thursday. ✉ *8 km (5 mi) northwest of Cahors on road to Villeneuve-sur-Lot, 46090 Mercuès* ☎*05–65–20–00–01* 🖷*05–65–20–05–72* ⊕ *www.relaischateaux.com/mercues* ➷ *22 rooms, 8 suites* ⚭ *Restaurant, minibars, cable TV, 2 tennis courts, pool, Internet, some pets allowed (fee); no a/c* ▤ *AE, DC, MC, V* ⊘ *Closed Nov.–Easter* ❏❙ *MAP.*

$$–$$$ ✕▣ **Terminus.** At this quaint ivy-covered hotel, only a two-minute walk from the train station, the Marre family goes out of its way to help guests. Rooms are tastefully done and up-to-date. The restaurant, La Balandre, is the town's best; truffles as well as exceptional *brandade* (puree of cod and potatoes) are served (closed Monday, no dinner Sunday). ✉ *5 av. Charles-de-Freycinet, 46000* ☎ *05–65–35–24–50* 🖷 *05–65–22–06–40* ➷ *22 rooms* ⚭ *Restaurant, minibars, bar, Internet* ▤ *AE, DC, MC, V* ⊘ *Closed 2 wks in Feb., 1 wk in June.*

St-Cirq-Lapopie

⑱ *32 km (20 mi) east of Cahors via D653, D662, and D40.*

Fodor'sChoice
★

The beautiful 13th-century village of St-Cirq (pronounced san-*sare*) is on a rocky spur 250 feet up, with nothing but a vertical drop to the Lot River below. Filled with artisans' workshops and not yet renovated à la Disney, the town has so many dramatic views you may end up spending several hours here. Traversing steep paths and alleyways among flower-filled balconies, you'll realize it deserves its description as one of the most beautiful villages in France. A mostly ruined château can be reached by a stiff walk along the path that starts near the Hôtel de Ville. Stop by the tourist office in the center of town for information on other points of interest in town and morning hikes in the misty gorges in the valley.

Where to Stay

$–$$ ▣ **Hôtel de la Pélissaria.** This intimate 16th-century hotel is small and simple but chock-full of atmosphere. The best rooms look out across the village or the valley and river; some rooms in the garden have less grand views (Nos. 3 and 4 are very small). The lounge is a snug place to relax in front of the fire in the evening. ✉ *46330 St-Cirq-Lapopie* ☎ *05–65–31–25–14* 🖷 *05–65–30–25–52* ✍ *lapelissariahotel@minitel. net* ➷ *10 rooms* ⚭ *Pool, bar, some pets allowed (fee); no a/c* ▤ *MC, V* ⊘ *Closed Nov.–Mar.* ❏❙ *MAP.*

Rocamadour

⑲ *72 km (45 mi) north of St-Cirq via Labastide-Murat.*

Rocamadour is a medieval village that seems to defy the laws of gravity; it surges out of a cliff 1,500 feet above the Alzou River gorge—an awe-inspiring sight that makes this one of the most-visited tourist spots in France. The town got its name after the discovery in 1166 of the 1,000-year-old body of St. Amadour "quite whole." The body was moved to the cathedral, where it began to work miracles. Legend has it that the saint was actually a publican named Zacheus, who, after the honor of entertaining Jesus in his home, came to Gaul after the crucifixion and, under the name of Amadour, established a private chapel in the cliff here. Pilgrims have long flocked to the site, climbing the 216 steps to the church on their knees, especially around August 15 (Assumption Day) and during the week of September 8 (the Virgin Mary's birthday). Making the climb on foot is sufficient reminder of the medieval penchant for agonizing penance; today an elevator lifts weary souls. Unfortunately, the summer influx of a million tourists has brought its own blight, judging by the dozens of tacky souvenir shops. Cars are not allowed; park in the lot below the town.

The town is split into three levels joined by steep stairs. The lowest level is occupied by the village of Rocamadour itself, and mainly accessed through the centuries-old Porte du Figuier (Fig Tree Gate). Past this portal, the **Cité Médiévale**, or the **Basse Ville**, though in parts grotesquely touristy, is full of beautifully restored structures, such as the 15th-century **Hôtel de Ville**, near the Porte Salmon, which houses the **tourist office** and an excellent collection of tapestries. 🖼 *Free* ⊙ *Mon.–Sat. 10–noon and 3–8.*

FodorśChoice
★
The Basse Ville's Rue Piétonne, the main pedestrian street, is lined with crêperies, tea salons, and hundreds of tourists, many of whom are heading heavenward by taking the **Grand Escalier** staircase or elevator (fee) from place de la Carreta up to the **Cité Religieuse**, set halfway up the cliff. If you walk, pause at the landing 141 steps up to admire the fort. Once up, you'll see tiny place St-Amadour and its seven sanctuaries: the basilica of **St-Sauveur** opposite the staircase; the **St-Amadour crypt** beneath the basilica; the chapel of **Notre-Dame** to the left; the chapels of **John the Baptist, St-Blaise**, and **Ste-Anne** to the right; and the Romanesque chapel of **St-Michel** built into an overhanging cliff. St-Michel's two 12th-century frescoes—depicting the Annunciation and the Visitation—have survived in superb condition. On the Parvis du Sanctuaire, the **Musée d'Art Sacré** has gilded reliquaires and chalices on view for a separate admission fee. ✉ *Centre d'Accueil Notre-Dame* 🖼 *Tips at visitors' discretion* ⊙ *Guided tours Mon.–Sat. 9–5* ☞ *English-speaking guide available.*

On the uppermost plateau stands the **Château de Rocamdaour**, a private residence of the church fathers. Open to the public for an admission fee are its ramparts, which have spectacular views of the gorge (however, you can enjoy the same views for free just by walking the **Chemin de la Croix** up to the castle).

Where to Stay & Eat

$$$$
FodorśChoice
★
✕🖼 **Château de la Treyne.** Certainly the most spectacular château-hotel in the Dordogne (and one of the most gorgeous and expensive in all France), this Xanadu sits in a picture-perfect perch on a cliff overlooking the Dordogne River. Part of the Relais & Châteaux group, set in Lacave, 6 km (3½ mi) northwest of Rocamadour, La Treyne has guarded the region since the 14th century. From the luxe and stylish rooms here,

you would never know that the castle's history was a tumultuous one: Nearly destroyed in the 16th-century Wars of Religion between Huguenot and Catholic forces, it was happily reconstructed under the reign of Louis XIII. Today, the Great Lounge restaurant is a symphony of chandeliers, delicate embroideries, oak panels, and Louis Treize chairs—but who can resist dining on the storybook terrace set with tables overlooking the river? Here you can feast on Fried Scallops on Chestnut Gallettes with a Cappuccino of Mushrooms, just one of the dishes featured in the hotel's special Menu St. Jacques de Compostelle, which pays homage to the castle's history as a stopping-off point for pilgrims on the ancient Compostela route to Spain. Or repair to the adjacent Music Lounge, with its gigantic fireplace and Old Master paintings or enjoy your after-dinner cognac with a stroll through the enchantingly Baroque formal gardens. Best of all are the astonishingly stylish guest rooms, ranging from the Louis XIII apartment (pink brocade, oak four-poster, parquet floors) to the Prison Doreé, or "Golden Prison" (set atop the castle tower, replete with centuries-old stone walls and panoramic views), or the most charming of all, the "Soleil Levant" (the former chapel, now glowing in historic limes and yellow). Apart from these showstoppers, there are numerous other rooms, all impressive essays in elegant style. The smallest, such as the Vendages, do come up short for their high price (rooms here range from €360 to €660 *but* include breakfast and dinner). There's also modern luxe to be had, as most rooms come complete with an array of facilities from Jacuzzis to minibars. For taste in every sense of the word (ooh, those scallops), La Treyne is tops. ⊠ *La Treyne, 46200 Lacave, 21 km (13 mi) northwest of Rocamadour* ☎ *05–65–27–60–60* 🖷 *05–65–27–60–70* 🛏 *14 rooms, 2 suites* 🛆 *Restaurant, minibars, tennis court, pool, sauna, Internet, some pets allowed (fee)* ⊟ *AE, DC, MC, V* ⊗ *Closed mid-Nov.–Christmas, Jan.–Apr.* ⑩ *MAP.*

$–$$ ✕⊡ **Beau Site.** This is the best of the few Vieille Ville hotels in Rocamadour. The charm of the ancient beams, exposed stone, and open hearth in the foyer ends, however, as you climb the stairs; rooms are modern and functional. The modern, large-window Jehan de Valon restaurant overlooks the canyon, serving foie gras, local lamb, and walnut gateau. Best of all, you can park inside Rocamadour if you stay here. ⊠ *Cité Médiévale, 46500* ☎ *05–65–33–63–08* 🖷 *05–65–33–65–23* ⊕ *www. bw-beausite.com* 🛏 *42 rooms* 🛆 *Restaurant, cable TV, bar, Internet, some pets allowed (fee); no a/c in some rooms* ⊟ *AE, DC, MC, V* ⊗ *Closed mid-Nov.–mid-Feb.* ⑩ *MAP.*

$ ⊡ **Lion d'Or.** In the center of Rocamadour, this gently priced hotel conveniently has a restaurant on the premises. ⊠ *Cité Médiévale, 46500* ☎ *05–65–33–62–04* 🖷 *05–65–33–72–54* ⊕ *www.liondor-rocamadour. com* 🛏 *35 rooms* 🛆 *Restaurant; no a/c, no room TVs* ⊟ *MC, V* ⊗ *Closed Nov.–Feb.* ⑩ *EP.*

Domme

⓴ *50 km (31 mi) west of Rocadamour via Payrac.*

The historic cliff-top village of Domme is famous for its **grottoes,** where prehistoric bison and rhinoceros bones have been discovered. You can visit the 500-yard-long illuminated galleries, which are lined with sta-lactites. ✉ *Pl. de la Halle* 🎟 €6 ☉ *Apr.–Sept., daily 10–noon and 2–6; Mar. and Oct., daily 2–6.*

La Roque-Gageac

㉑ *5 km (3 mi) northwest of Domme via D46/D703.*

Across the Dordogne from Domme, in the direction of Beynac, ro-mantically huddled beneath a cliff, is strikingly attractive La Roque-Gageac, one of the best-restored villages in the valley. Crafts shops line its narrow streets, dominated by the outlines of the 19th-century mock-medieval Château de Malartrie and the Manoir de Tarde, with its cylindrical turret. If you leave the main road and climb one of the steep cobblestone paths, you can check out the medieval houses on their natural perches and even hike up the mountain for a view down to the village.

Where to Stay & Eat

$–$$ ✕🏠 **La Plume d'Oie.** This small inn overlooks the river and the limestone cliffs. Rooms, in light fabrics and wicker furniture, vary in size and price. La Plume d'Oie's major raison d'être, however, is the stone-walled restaurant, at which you are expected to have at least one meal. Chef-owner Marc-Pierre Walker prepares classic regional cuisine, such as fil-let of beef cooked in red wine, and ragout of foie gras (the restaurant is closed Monday and does not serve lunch Tuesday). ✉ *24250 La Roque-Gageac* ☎ *05–53–29–57–05* 🖨 *05–53–31–04–81* ⇥ *4 rooms* ♿ *Restaurant; no a/c* ▭ *MC, V* ☉ *Closed Dec.–Feb.* ⊙|*EP.*

Beynac-et-Cazenac

㉒ *11 km (7 mi) west of La Roque-Gageac via D703.*

One of the most enchanting sights in the Dordogne is the medieval cas-tle that sits atop the wonderfully restored town of Beynac. Perched atop a sheer cliff face beside an abrupt bend in the Dordogne river, the FodorsChoice muscular 13th-century **Château de Beynac** has unforgettable views from ★ its battlements. During the Hundred Years' War this castle often faced off with forces massed directly across the way at the fort of Castenaud. Star of many films, Beynac was last featured in Luc Besson's 1999 life of Joan of Arc, *The Messenger*. Tours of the castle are in English as well as French. ☎ *05–53–29–50–40* 🎟 €6.55 ☉ *May–Sept. daily 10–6:30; Oct.–Apr. daily 10–6.*

With a fabulous mountaintop setting, the now-ruined castle of **Castle-naud,** containing a large collection of medieval arms, is just upstream from Beynac across the Dordogne; it's open May–October, daily 10–7, and admission is €6. Five kilometers (3 mi) from Castlenaud is the tur-★ reted **Château des Milandes** (☎ *05–53–59–31–21* ⊕ www.milandes. com), open April to mid-October, daily 9:30–7 (€7.50). Built around 1489 in Renaissance style, it has lovely terraces and gardens and was once owned by the American-born cabaret star of Roaring '20s Paris, Josephine Baker. Here she housed her "rainbow family," a large group of adopted children from many nationalities. Today, there's a museum devoted to her memory and, in summer, falconry displays. From here D53 (via Belvès) leads southwest to Monpazier.

Fodor'sChoice
★

One of the most regal yet picturesque sights in the Perigord Noir is the garden of the **Château de Marqueyssac**, set in Vézac, about 4 km (2 mi) south of Beynac-et-Cazenac. The park was founded in 1682 and its design, including an enchanting parterre of cut topiaries, was greatly influenced by the designs of André le Nôtre, the "green geometer" of Versailles. Shaded paths boarded by 150,000 hand-pruned boxwoods are graced with breathtaking viewpoints, rock gardens, waterfalls, and verdant glades. From the belvedere 400 feet above the river, there is an exceptional viewpoint of the Dordogne Valley, with its castles and beautiful villages such as Beynac, Fayrac, Castelnaud, Roque-Gageac, and Domme. A tea salon is open from May to September and is just the place to drink in the panoramic views from the parterre terrace. ⊠ *Belvédère de la Dordogne, Veazac, 9 km (5 mi) southwest of Sarlat* ☎ *05–53–31–36–36* ⊠ *€5.60* ⊗ *Apr.–Sept. daily 10–7; mid-Nov.–Feb. daily 2–5; otherwise daily 10–6.*

$$–$$$ ✕⌂ **Abbaye.** Named for the abbey of Augustinian friars that once stood on the spot, this historic hotel dating from the 18th century overlooks the pretty medieval village of St-Cyprien, midway between Sarlat and Les Eyzies. In the flagstone-detailed restaurant, with its floral-pattern tablecloths and exposed beams, Yvette Schaller serves up succulent local cuisine (set-price menus start at €24). Most rooms have reproduction furniture, stone walls, and beamed ceilings. Trees shade the small swimming pool, attractively sited with the village church visible in the distance. ⊠ *Rue de l'Abbaye, 10 km (6 mi) west of Beynac on D703, 24220 St-Cyprien* ☎ *05–53–29–20–48* ⊠ *05–53–29–15–85* ⇄ *23 rooms* ⚴ *Restaurant, cable TV, pool; no a/c* ⊟ *AE, DC, MC, V* ⊗ *Closed mid-Oct.–mid-Apr.* ⏃⌾ *EP.*

Sarlat-la-Canéda

㉓
Fodor'sChoice
★

10 km (6 mi) northeast of Beynac via D57, 74 km (46 mi) east of Bergerac.

Tucked among hills adorned with corn and wheat, Sarlat (as it is usually known) is a beautiful, well-preserved medieval town that attracts a lot of visitors but manages to retain some of its true character. With its storybook streets, Sarlat is filled most days with tour groups, and is especially hectic on Saturday, market day: all the geese on sale are proof of the local addiction to foie gras. To do justice to the town's goldenstone splendor, wander through its medieval streets in the later afternoon or early evening, aided by the tourist office's walking map. The tourist office also organizes walking tours, which for €4 give you an in-depth look at the town's medieval buildings. Trains arrive at Sarlat from Bordeaux about five times a day.

Of particular note is rue de la Liberté, which leads to **place du Peyrou,** anchored on one corner by the steep-gable Renaissance house where writer-orator Étienne de la Boétie (1530–63) was born. The elaborate turreted tower of the **Cathédrale St-Sacerdos** (⊠ Pl. du Peyrou), begun in the 12th century, is the oldest part of the building and, along with the choir, all that remains of the original Romanesque structure. The sloping garden behind the cathedral, the **cour de l'Évêché** (Bishop's Courtyard), contains a strange, conical tower known as the Lanterne des Morts (Lantern of the Dead), which was occasionally used as a funeral chapel. Rue d'Albusse, adjoining the garden behind the cathedral, and rue de la Salamandre are narrow, twisty streets that head to place de la Liberté and the 17th-century **Hôtel de Ville**. Opposite the town hall is the rickety former church of **Ste-Marie**, overlooking place des Oies. Ste-Marie points the way to Sarlat's most interesting street, **rue des Consuls**. Among its medieval buildings are the Hôtel Plamon, with broad windows that resemble those of a Gothic church, and, opposite, the 15th-century Hôtel de Vassal. Another winner is **rue Montaigne,** where the great 16th-century philosopher, Michel de Montaigne, once lived—some of the half-timbered houses that line this street define enchantment.

Where to Stay & Eat

★ $ ✕▦ **St-Albert & Montaigne.** The Garrigou family has two hotels on this delightful square in the center of town. The Montaigne is in a manor; ask for lovely Room 33, with exposed beams. The St-Albert has simply furnished rooms of varying size. Hearty regional fare is served by chef René Fontaine in the restaurant (closed Sunday and Monday). Over dinner, discuss your next day's itinerary with Monsieur Garrigou: he not only knows the region well but is also the town's backroom politician. ⊠ 10 pl. Pasteur, 24200 ☎ 05–53–31–55–55 🖷 05–53–59–19–99 ➟ 53 rooms ⚭ Restaurant, bar, Internet, some pets allowed (fee); no a/c in some rooms ☰ AE, MC, V ☺ Closed Nov.–Mar. ⦿I MAP.

Les Eyzies-de-Tayac

㉔ 21 km (13 mi) northwest of Sarlat via D47.

Sitting comfortably under a limestone cliff, Les Eyzies is the doorway to the prehistoric capital of France. Many signs of Cro-Magnon man have been discovered in this vicinity; a number of excavated caves and grottoes, some with wall paintings, are open for public viewing, including the Font de Gaume, just south of the town, with very faint drawings to be seen on a tour, and the Grotte de Combarelles. Stop by the town tourist office for the lowdown on all the caves in the area—the office also sells tickets for most sites and you should reserve here because a surprising number of tours sell out in advance (sometimes there are only six people allowed at any one time in a cave). At the **Grotte du Grand-Roc,** you can view weirdly shaped crystalline stalactites and stalagmites. ⊠ 48 av. de la Préhistoire ☎ 05–53–06–92–70 ⊕ www.grandroc.com ⊠ €6.50 ☺ Feb.–May and Sept.–mid-Nov., daily 10–6.

The **Musée National de Préhistoire** (National Museum of Prehistory), in a Renaissance château, attracts large crowds to its renowned collection of prehistoric artifacts, including primitive sculpture, furniture, and tools. You can also get ideas at the museum about excavation sites to visit in the region. ⊠ *Le Bourg* 🕿 *05–53–06–45–45* 🎫 *€4.50* ⊙ *Apr.–Oct., Wed.–Mon. 9:30–noon and 2–6; Nov.–Mar., Wed.–Mon. 9:30–noon and 2–5.*

Fodor's Choice
★

As you head north from Les Eyzies-de-Tayac toward Lascaux, stop off 7 km (4 mi) north of Les Eyzies near the village of Tursac to discover the enchanting troglodyte "lost village" of **La Madeleine,** found hidden in the Valley of Vézère at the foot of a ruined castle and overlooking the Vézère river. Human settlement here dates back to 15,000 BC, but what is most eye-catching now is its picturesque cliff-face chapel— seemingly half Cro-Magnon, half Gothic, it was constructed during the Middle Ages. The "Brigadoon" of the Dordogne, La Madeleine was abandoned once more in the 1920s. Guided visits tour the site (call ahead, English available). ⊠ *Tursac, 7 km (4 mi) north of Les Eyzies-de-Tayac* 🕿 *05–53–06–92–49* 🎫 *€5* ⊙ *Daily 10–6.*

Where to Stay & Eat

$$$–$$$$ ✕🏨 **La Centenaire.** Though it's also a stylish, modern hotel, Le Centenaire is known foremost as a restaurant. Chef Roland Mazère adds flair to the preparation of local delights: risotto with truffles or snails with ravioli and gazpacho. The dining room's golden stone and wood beams retain local character (on Thursday and on weekends, the restaurant serves lunch only; a jacket is required). ⊠ *24620 Les Eyzies-de-Tayac* 🕿 *05–53–06–68–68* 🖷 *05–53–06–92–41* ⊕ *www.hotelducentenaire. fr* ⮑ *14 rooms, 5 suites* ⬧ *Restaurant, minibars, cable TV, pool, health club, sauna, some pets allowed (fee)* ☰ *AE, DC, MC, V* ⊙ *Closed mid-Nov.–mid-Apr.* ❙⊙❙ *MAP.*

★ **$$$–$$$$** ✕🏨 **Le Vieux Logis.** Built around the most gorgeous dining room in the Dordogne, this vine-clad manor house on the edge of Trémolat remains one of the best hotels of the region. The warm guest rooms vary in size; most face the well-tended garden and a rushing brook. One favorite, No. 22, has a terra-cotta tile floor, exposed beams, stone walls, and a suitelike bathroom. Be sure to enjoy a meal in the restaurant, a stunning vision in half-timbering and pink and red *paisleys à la indiennes* fabrics. For dinner, the five-course Menu Vieux Logis (€45) might include the chef's forte, pigeon terrine (the restaurant is closed January and February; there's no lunch weekdays September–June). ⊠ *24 km (15 mi) west of Les Eyzies, 24510 Trémolat* 🕿 *05–53–22–80–06* 🖷 *05–53–22–84–89* ⮑ *19 rooms, 5 suites* ⬧ *Restaurant, minibars, cable TV, pool, Internet, some pets allowed (fee); no a/c* ☰ *AE, DC, MC, V* ❙⊙❙ *MAP.*

$$ 🏨 **Noyer.** This inn, in a steep-roofed 18th-century building west of Les Eyzies, is owned by Eric and Bettina Guilbert, who speak fluent English. The comfortable, provincial-style rooms are in the main building and in the former barn (avoid those on the ground floor: you can hear the upstairs plumbing). ⊠ *Le Reclaud, 5 km (3 mi) outside village; 11 km (7 mi) west of Les Eyzies, 24260 Le Bugue* 🕿 *05–53–07–49–35* 🖷 *05–53–54–57–44* ⊕ *www.perigord.com/aubergedunoyer* ⮑ *10 rooms* ⬧ *Pool; no a/c, no room TVs* ☰ *MC, V* ⊙ *Closed Nov.–Apr.* ❙⊙❙ *BP.*

Lascaux

㉕ *27 km (17 mi) northeast of Les Eyzies via D706.*

FodorsChoice The famous **Grotte de Lascaux** (Lascaux Caves), just outside Montignac,
★ contain hundreds of prehistoric wall paintings—thought to be at least
20,000 years old. The undulating horses, cow, black bulls, and unicorn
on their walls were discovered by chance in 1940. Although the caves
have been sealed off to prevent damage, two of the galleries and many
of the paintings have been reproduced in vivid detail in the Lascaux II
exhibition center nearby. The copy is almost as awe-inspiring as the original. Unlike caves marked with authentic prehistoric art, Lascaux II is
completely geared toward visitors, and you can watch a fancy presentation about cave art or take a tour in the language of your choice. Purchase tickets at the tourist office in Montignac before setting off. ⊠ *Rte.
de la Grotte* ☎ *05–53–51–95–03* ✇ *€7.70* ☉ *Feb. and Mar., Nov. and
Dec., Tues.–Sun. 10–noon and 2–5.30; Apr.–Sept., daily 9:30–6:30.*

Where to Stay & Eat

$$$ ✕▣ **Manoir d'Hautegente.** This old, ivy-covered manor (originally a
forge) enjoys a pastoral nook by the Vézère River. Inside, the modern-
ized rooms have beige-fabric wall coverings, and the colorful curtains
match the bedspreads. Chef Bernard Villain's specialties include cray-
fish in Pernod, duck with truffles, and chestnut mousse. The restaurant
is closed Monday through Wednesday and there's no lunch Thursday.
⊠ *Haute Gente, 12 km (7 mi) east of Lascaux), 24120 Coly*
☎ *05–53–51–68–03* 🖶 *05–53–50–38–52* ⊕ *www.manoir-hautegente.
com* ⇨ *15 rooms* ⌂ *Restaurant, minibars, cable TV, pool, Internet; no
a/c in some rooms* ▤ *DC, MC, V* ☉ *Closed Nov.–Easter* ¶◉¶ *EP.*

Hautefort

㉖ *32 km (20 mi) north of Lascaux via D704.*

★ The reason to come to Hautefort is to see its castle, which presents a
disarmingly arrogant face to the world. The silhouette of the **Château
de Hautefort** bristles with high roofs, domes, chimneys, and cupolas. The
square-lined Renaissance left wing clashes with the muscular, round tow-
ers of the right wing, as the only surviving section of the original me-
dieval castle—the gateway and drawbridge—plays referee in the middle.
Adorning the inside are 17th-century furniture and tapestries. ⊠ *Le Bourg*
☎ *05–53–50–51–23* ✇ *€6.50* ☉ *Apr.–Sept., daily 2–6; Oct. and Nov.,
Feb. and Mar., Sun. 2–6.*

Périgueux

㉗ *46 km (27 mi) west of Hautefort via D5, 120 km (75 mi) northeast of
Bordeaux.*

Périgueux is best known for its weird-looking cathedral. Finished in 1173
and restored in the 19th century, the **Cathédrale St-Front** looks like it might
be on loan from Istanbul, given its shallow-scale domes and elongated
conical cupolas sprouting from the roof like baby minarets. You may

be struck by similarities with the Byzantine-style Sacré-Coeur in Paris; that's no coincidence—architect Paul Abadie (1812–84) had a hand in the design of both. ⊠ *Pl. de la Clarté.*

Brantôme

28 *27 km (17 mi) north of Périgueux via D939.*

When the reclusive monks of the abbey of Brantôme decided the inhabitants of the village were getting too nosy, they dug a canal between themselves and the villagers, setting the *brantômois* adrift on an island in the middle of the river Dronne. How happy for them, or at least for us. Brantôme has been unable to outgrow its small-town status and remains one of the prettiest villages in France. Today it touts itself as the "Venice of Périgord." Enjoy a walk along the river or through the old, narrow streets. The meandering river follows you wherever you stroll. Cafés and small shops abound. At night the **Abbaye Benedictine** is romantically floodlighted. Possibly founded by Charlemagne in the 8th century, it has none of its original buildings left, but its bell tower has been hanging on since the 11th century (the secret of its success is that it is attached to the cliff rather than the abbey, and so withstood waves of invaders). Fifth-century Christians carved out much of the abbey and some rooms have sculpted reliefs of the Last Judgment. Also here is a small museum devoted to the 19th-century painter Fernand-Desmoulin. 🏛 *05–53–05–80–63* 🎫 *€3* 🕙 *July–Sept. 15, daily 9:30–6; Sept. 15–Oct., Apr.–June, Wed.–Mon. 10–noon and 2–6; Nov.–Mar., Wed.–Mon. 10–noon and 2–5.*

Where to Stay

$–$$ 🏨 **Château de La Borie.** This country château, set in 12 acres of grounds, is a step above your usual B&B. A long avenue of lime trees leads to the moat and handsome facade. Natty hostess Micheline "Dizzy" Duseau chats with all and offers advice on where to dine (one of these suggestions, the Terrace des Jardins, is below par). Rooms, furnished with hand-me-down antiques, are comfortable if a little stilted, though two rooms on the first floor are warmer and have fewer bourgeois pretensions. ⊠ *La Borie, 5 km (3 mi) north of Brantôme, 24530 Champagnac-de-Belair* 🏛 *05–53–54–22–99* 🖨 *05–53–08–53–78* 🛏 *5 rooms* ⚓ *Pool; no a/c, no room TVs* ▭ *No credit cards* ⦿ *BP.*

POITOU-CHARENTES

Poitou-Charentes occupies the northern part of the region covered in this chapter. Rural, rolling Poitou is named for the ancient town of Poitiers. Charentes refers to the two départements linked by the Charente River: Charente-Maritime, with its islands and sandy Atlantic beaches; and, inland, Charente. Highlights of Poitou-Charentes include the "Green Venice" of the Marais Poitevin and the town of Cognac, famed for its brandy, though almost wherever you go in the *deux* (two) Charentes you will find the ample vineyards that produce cognac grapes.

Angoulême

🟢 *59 km (37 mi) northwest of Brantôme via D939, 120 km (75 mi) northeast of Bordeaux.*

Angoulême is divided, like many other French towns, between an old, picturesque section around a hilltop cathedral and a modern, industrial area sprawling along the valley and railroad below. The 19th-century novelist Honoré de Balzac is one of the town's adopted sons; he described Angoulême in his meaty novel *Lost Illusions*. The Ville Haute (Upper Town), known as *Le Plateau*, has a warren of quaint old streets around the Hôtel de Ville (Town Hall) and stunning views from the ramparts. The 12th-century **Cathédrale St-Pierre** (✉ Pl. St-Pierre) bears little resemblance to the majority of its French counterparts because of the cupolas topping each of its three bays. The cathedral was partly destroyed by Calvinists in 1562, then restored in a heavy-handed manner in 1634 and 1866. Its main attraction is its magnificent Romanesque facade, whose layers of rounded arches bear 70 stone statues and bas-reliefs illustrating the *Last Judgment.*

Where to Stay & Eat

$ ✕ **La Tour des Valois.** Diagonally across from the market, this rustic 15th-century restaurant has a good choice of regional food. Sample one of Gérard André's veal dishes—the one using the local mustard from Jarnac is particularly good—and the locally made foie gras, served warm with plum and apple. ✉ *7 rue Massillon* ☎ *05–45–95–23–64* ▤ *AE, MC, V* ☉ *Closed part of Feb., mid-Aug.–early Sept., and Mon. No dinner Sun.* ❢❢ *MAP.*

$$$-$$$$ ✕▦ **Château de Nieuil.** If high-class bucolic bliss is to your taste rather than a hotel in Angoulême itself, this is the place to stay. It's an easy 35 km (20 mi) drive northeast from the city (follow the signs for La Rochefoucauld-Limoges, N141). An avenue of trees opening onto a circular lawn leads to this former hunting lodge—a huge Renaissance château with towers. Rooms vary: some have traditional furnishings and pastel blue fabric; others have a *petit salon* (small sitting area) or a garden view. If the reception area is small, the formidable dining room (no dinner Sunday; September to June closed Monday) has a large stone fireplace with sculpted family crests and a multifaceted chandelier. Enjoy Pascal Pressac's superb lamb (a regional specialty) or scallop of milk-fed veal with grapes. ✉ *Château de Nieuil, 16270 Nieuil* ☎ *05–45–71–36–38* 🖷 *05–45–71–46–45* ⊕ *www.chateaunieuilhotel. com* ↝ *11 rooms, 3 suites* ⚖ *Restaurant, minibars, cable TV, tennis court, pool, bar, baby-sitting, Internet, some pets allowed (fee)* ▤ *AE, DC, MC, V* ☉ *Closed Nov.–Apr.* ❢❢ *MAP.*

$$ ✕▦ **Mercure France.** On the edge of the Ville Haute, across from the covered market, this hotel has a traditional air. From the garden there are fine views of the city. Rooms lull in shades of pale blue with striped curtains and bedspreads. The staff is professional and accustomed to speaking English. The Jardins des Arceaux restaurant (closed for lunch on weekends) serves solid regional cuisine. ✉ *1 pl. des Halles-Centrales, 16000* ☎ *05–45–95–47–95, 0181/741–3100 in U.K., 800/637–2873 in*

U.S. 🏠 *05–45–92–02–70* 🕾 *89 rooms* ⟁ *Restaurant, bar, Internet, some pets allowed (fee)* ⊟ *AE, DC, MC, V* ⧖ *BP.*

Cognac

③⓪ *42 km (28 mi) west of Angoulême via N141.*

The black-walled town of Cognac seems an unlikely home for one of the world's most successful drinks trades. You may be disappointed initially by the town's unpretentious appearance but, like the drink, it tends to grow on you. Cognac owed its early development to the transport of salt and wine along the Charente River. When 16th-century Dutch merchants discovered that the local wine was both tastier and easier to transport if distilled, the town became the heart of the brandy industry. Most cognac houses organize visits of their premises and *chais,* the local name for cognac warehouses. Wherever you decide to go, you will literally be inhaling the atmosphere of cognac: 3% of the precious cask-bound liquid evaporates every year. It's known as *la part des anges,* the angels' share. This has two consequences: each chai smells delicious, and a small black fungus, which feeds on cognac's alcoholic fumes, forms on walls throughout the town.

The leading monument in Cognac is the former **Château François-I**ᵉʳ, now the premises of Otard Cognac. Volatile Renaissance monarch François I was born here in 1494. The remaining buildings are something of a hodgepodge, though the chunky towers recall the site's fortified origins. The tour of Otard Cognac combines slick propaganda with historical comment on the drink itself. At the end you get to sample free cognac, and you can buy some at reduced prices. ⊠ *127 bd. Denfert-Rochereau* 🕾 *05–45–35–72–68* ⊕ *www.otard.com* ⊠ *€4* ⊙ *Apr.–June, Sept. and Oct. daily 10–noon and 2–6, July and Aug. 10–noon and 1:30–7, Nov. and Dec. tours at 11, 2:30, 3:45, and 5.*

Hennessy, along the banks of the Charente and easily recognized by the company's mercenary emblem—an ax-wielding arm carved in stone—includes in its tour a cheerful jaunt across the Charente in old-fashioned barges. You begin at an historic warehouse, then boat over to a new Hennessy exhibition center designed by Jean-Michel Wilmotte. ⊠ *Quai Richard-Hennessy* 🕾 *05–45–35–72–68* ⊕ *www.hennessy-cognac.com* ⊠ *€5* ⊙ *June–Sept., daily 10–6; Oct.–Dec. and Mar.–May, daily 10–5.*

Among the Cognac houses, **Martell** gives the most polished guided tour and its chais are perhaps more picturesque than Hennessy's. ⊠ *7 pl. Édouard-Martell* 🕾 *05–45–36–33–33* ⊕ *www.martell.com* ⊠ *€4* ⊙ *June–Sept., weekdays 9:30–5, weekends 11–5; Oct. and Mar.–May, weekdays 9:30–noon and 2–5.*

Rue Saulnier, alongside the Hennessy premises, is the most atmospheric of the somber, sloping cobbled streets that compose the core of Cognac, dominated by the tower of **St-Léger** (⊠ Pl. d'Armes), a church with a notably large Flamboyant Gothic rose window.

Busy boulevard Denfert-Rochereau twines around the Vieille Ville, passing the town hall and the neighboring **Muséede Cognac** (Town Museum) with its collection of cognac posters, glasses, and other marketing artifacts. ✉ *48 bd. Denfert-Rochereau* ☎ *05–45–32–07–25* ⊕ *www.ville-cognac.fr* 📧 *€2.50* ☉ *June–Sept., Wed.–Mon. 10–noon and 2–6; Oct.–May, Wed.–Mon. 2–5:30.*

Where to Stay & Eat

★ **$$–$$$$** ✕🏨**Château de l'Yeuse.** For some, style and comfort may be reasons enough to stay in this lushly appointed hotel on Cognac's southern outskirts but, for most, it's the knock-out view of the Charente valley that is the real attraction. Built around a 19th-century château—picturesquely done up in red-and-white-stone stripes—this hotel has long been a regional lure (celebrities, from Alain Delon to Brian de Palma, love this place). Everyone agrees there are few more appealing places to sit and sip a cognac aperitif—"le long drink," to the French—on a summer evening. Alternatively, in winter, make yourself snug in the gloriously warm and wood-paneled Cognathèque. The mirror-lined, spaciously elegant restaurant is just the place to treat yourself to the "Havana" dessert, a crunchy confection made with cognac-flavor custard. Upstairs, guest rooms are flocked in designer fabrics and adorned with pretty accent pieces. ✉ *65 rue de Bellevuen, F-16100 Châteaubernard* ☎ *05–45–36–82–60* 🖨 *05–45–35–06–32* ⊕ *www.yeuse.fr* ↘ *24 rooms, 3 suites* ♻ *Restaurant, pool, health club, bar; no a/c* ▤ *AE, DC, MC, V* ⦿ *FAP.*

Nightlife & the Arts

La Maison Blanche (✉ 2 impasse de Moulins) is the place to party every night. Each September Cognac hosts a **crime film festival**.

Shopping

A bottle of old cognac makes a fine souvenir; try **La Cognathèque** (✉ 8 pl. Jean-Monnet), in Cognac itself, though you can usually find the same item infinitely cheaper at a local producer or in most regional supermarkets.

Saintes

③ *27 km (17 mi) northwest of Cognac via D24.*

On the banks of the Charente River, Saintes, littered with religious edifices and Roman ruins dating from the 1st century, exudes stately serenity. The town owes its development to the salt marshes that first attracted the Romans to the area some 2,000 years ago. The Romans left their mark with the impressive **Arènes** (Amphitheater; ✉ Rue Lacurie 📧 €1 ☉ Apr.–Oct., daily 9–7; Nov.–Mar., Tues.–Sun. 10–12:30 and 2–4:30). There are several better-preserved examples in France, but few as old—it dates from AD 40 and could hold 15,000. You'll find it to the west of the town center, close to the church of St-Eutrope with its mighty spire. On the bank of the Charente stands a grand Roman triumphal arch, the **Arc de Germanicus** (☎ 05–46–74–23–82 information), dedicated to Emperor Tiberius and built in AD 19 as the entry to Saintes on the old Roman road from Lyon (the arch was moved to its present site in the 19th century). Boats leave alongside for river trips in summer.

Climbing above the red roofs of the Vieille Ville is the **Cathédrale St-Pierre** (✉ Pl. du Synode), which seems to stagger beneath the weight of its stocky tower. Engineering caution foiled plans for the traditional pointed spire, so the tower was given a shallow dome—incongruous, perhaps, but distinctive. The austere 16th-century interior is lined with fat round pillars. The narrow pedestrian-only streets clustered around the cathedral contrast with the broad boulevards that sweep through the town and over the river.

Saintes's ecclesiastical pride and joy is the **Abbaye aux Dames** (Ladies' Abbey), consecrated in 1047. The abbey church is fronted by an exquisite, intricately carved, arcaded facade. Although the Romanesque choir remains largely in its original form, the rest of the interior is less harmonious, as the abbey fell on hard times after the death of the last abbess—the 30th—in 1792. It became a prison, then a barracks, and is now a cultural center for expositions. The brasserie opposite the abbey portals has inexpensive lunch menus (€10–€15). ⊠ *7 pl. de l'Abbaye* ☎ *05–46–97–48–48* ☜ *€3* ⊗ *Apr.–Sept., daily 10–12:30 and 2–7; Oct.–Mar., 10–12:30 and 2–7, Sun.–Tues., Thurs., and Fri. 2–6.*

La Rochelle

★ ③ *72 km (45 mi) northwest of Saintes via A610/ N137.*

La Rochelle is a vibrant, appealing town, with ancient streets and a picture-postcard harbor, the Vieux Port. Standing sentinel on either side of the harbor are two fortresslike 14th-century **towers,** the **Tour St-Nicolas** (to the left) and the **Tour de la Chaîne** (right); a third tower, the 15th-century **Tour de la Lanterne,** emerges a little farther along the quayside. You can climb to the top of any of them for a view of the bay toward Ile d'Aix. ☜ *Each tower €4; €9 all 3* ⊗ *Mid-May–mid-June and 1st 2 wks Sept., daily 10–1 and 2–6; July and Aug. daily 10–7; mid-Sept.–mid-May, Tues.–Sun. 10–12:30 and 2–5:30.*

Porte de la Grosse Horloge (Gate of the Giant Clock) is a massive stone gate marking the entrance to the narrow, bustling streets of the Vieille Ville. From Porte de la Grosse Horloge head down rue du Palais and onto rue Gargoulleau: halfway down on the left is the 18th-century Bishop's Palace, now the **Musée des Beaux-Arts** (Museum of Fine Arts). ⊠ *28 rue Gargoulleau* ☎ *05–46–41–64–65* ☜ *€3.50, joint ticket for all town museums €6.60* ⊗ *Wed.–Mon. 2–5.*

At the **Musée du Nouveau-Monde** (New World Museum), in an 18th-century building, old maps, engravings, watercolors, and even wallpaper evoke the commercial links between La Rochelle and the New World. ⊠ *10 rue Fleuriau* ☎ *05–46–41–46–50* ☜ *€3.50, joint ticket for all town museums €6.60* ⊗ *Wed.–Mon. 10:30–12:30 and 1:30–6, Sun. 3–6.*

In summer, boats operated by **Inter-Iles** leave La Rochelle harbor daily for cruises to **Ile de Ré, Ile d'Oléron, Ile d'Aix,** and **Fort Boyard.** ⊠ *Vieux Port* ☎ *05–46–50–51–88* ⊕ *www.inter-iles.com.*

Where to Stay & Eat

★ $$$–$$$$ ✕ **Richard Coutanceau.** Widely acknowledged as the region's premier chef, Richard Coutanceau deals imaginatively with fish and seafood in this sober, modern restaurant overlooking the bay and old port. Lobster, eel, bass with basil, and spider crab with asparagus number among his specialties. ⊠ *Plage de la Concurrence* ☎ *05–46–41–48–19* 🖃 *AE, DC, MC, V* ☺ *Closed Sun.*

$–$$ ✕ **Bar André.** The salty decor may be a bit excessive—with fishing nets fluttering from the ceiling—but the Bar Andre, in business since 1947, is a veritable La Rochelle institution. Food and service have such gusto that you'll be hard put to resist, especially if you order the monumental seafood platter and wash it down with a bottle of white Charentes wine. The three prix-fixe menus are priced from €20 to €30.50. ⊠ *7 rue St-Jean-du-Pérot* ☎ *05–46–41–28–24* ⊕ *www.bar-andre.com* 🖃 *AE, DC, MC, V.*

$–$$ 🏨 **Monnaie.** This 17th-century house by the Vieux Port has a wonderful lobby and cobblestone courtyard. Rooms are less inspiring; the quietest overlook the courtyard. Free parking is adjacent to the hotel, a definite plus as it's only a few minutes' walk from the harbor and town. ⊠ *3 rue de la Monnaie, 17000* ☎ *05–46–50–65–65* 🖶 *05–46–50–63–19* ⊕ *www.hotel-monnaie.com* ➥ *31 rooms, 4 suites* ⚹ *Cable TV, Internet, free parking, some pets allowed (fee)* 🖃 *AE, DC, MC, V* ⦿ *BP.*

¢–$ 🏨 **Tour de Nesle.** This 19th-century hotel is well situated near the Vieux Port. Rooms are a bit cramped but up-to-date—ask for one overlooking the port or the church of St-Sauveur across the canal. Solid value all round. ⊠ *2 quai Louis-Durand, 17000* ☎ *05–46–41–05–86* 🖶 *05–46–41–95–17* ⊕ *www.hotel-la-tour-nesle.com* ➥ *28 rooms* ⚹ *Some pets allowed (fee); no a/c* 🖃 *AE, DC, MC, V* ⦿ *EP.*

Ile de Ré

㉝ *11 km (7 mi) west of La Rochelle via Pont-Viaduc.*

L'Ile de Ré used to be a hush-hush, keep-it-quiet alternative to the Riviera. The few in the know enjoyed 30 mi of beaches with golden sand, an ornithological reserve, a citadel, a lighthouse, and great seafood, all baked by a sun that seems brighter here than anywhere else in France. But the secret is out and today the whole place smells more and more like burning money, with huge yachts in the old port towns, intellectuals splitting hairs in cafés, and Rolex watches jingling on the dance floors. A toll bridge curves across just north of La Rochelle to this cheerful island just 26 km (16 mi) long and never more than 6 km (4 mi) wide. Vineyards sweep over the eastern part of the island; oyster beds straddle the shallow waters to the west. The first village on the north coast reached from the mainland is **La Flotte.** The rectangular harbor hiding tiny fishing boats is surrounded by sturdy houses ready to stand against Atlantic gales. Ten kilometers (6 mi) farther on is the largest village on the island, **St-Martin de Ré** (population 3,000). It has a lively harbor and a citadel built by ace military architect Sébastien de Vauban in 1681. Many of its streets also date from the 17th century, and the villagers' low, white houses are typical of that period. **Ars,** a smaller village 10 km (6 mi) farther west, has a black-and-white church spire, a fine street market, and a cute harbor. If you go all the way to the northwestern end of Ile de Ré, be sure to climb up the **Phare de la Baleine** (Whale Lighthouse) for sweeping views of the Atlantic. At its foot is the **Café du Phare,** which has a surprising Art Deco setting full of artsy '30s lamps and serves a good *poutargue,* a local specialty made from smoked cod roe accompanied by shallots and sour cream.

Where to Stay & Eat

$$$$ ×⌂ **Richelieu.** Eat chef Dominique Bourgeois's seafood as you gaze at the ocean. Let lobster and smoked oysters spark your taste buds for the excellent grilled turbot in beurre blanc and superb wine. Guest rooms are innocuously furnished but have all the amenities, from bathrobes to balconies. A separate building houses masseurs, beauticians, and thalassotherapy equipment. A beach fronts the hotel, but it's better for strolling than lounging. ⊠ *44 av. de la Plage, 17630 La Flotte-en-Ré* ☎ *05–46–09–60–70* 🖷 *05–46–09–50–59* ⇥ *39 rooms, 3 suites* ⏦ *Restaurant, cable TV, 2 tennis courts, pool, hair salon, massage, spa, beach, some pets allowed (fee); no a/c* ⊟ *AE, DC, MC, V* ⊗ *Closed Jan.* ⑩ *MAP.*

en route | Head inland from La Rochelle along D9 and D20 northeast toward Marans, once a thriving seaport but now linked to the sea only by canal. The landscape is flat, barren, almost eerie: this is the **Marais Desséché** (Dry Marsh), and your first encounter with the Marais Poitevin. The verdant, tree-lined waterways that form the more scenic **Marais Mouillé** (Wet Marsh) gradually take over as you continue east. Take D114 from Marans, then a left on D116 just before Courçon and head north to Maillezais and its ruined abbey. Return south on D15 and turn left to Damvix, continuing along the pretty, canal-like Sèvre Niortaise to Arçais and Coulon.

Coulon

㉞ *60 km (38 mi) northeast of La Rochelle.*

The photogenic village of Coulon is the best base for exploring the Marais Poitevin. The ideal way to explore the Marais is by rowboat—or, more typically, on a *pigouille* (a flat, narrow boat maneuvered with a long pole). You can rent them in Coulon. They cost about €15 per hour per boat, maximum six persons, or you can hire a boat with a guide (for 45 minutes at €20) and get an earful of local lore as well. The town also has a lovely medieval church and a regional folk museum, the **Maison du Marais Mouillés.** ⊠ *Pl. de la Coutume* ☎ *05–49–35–81–04* ⊕ *www. parc-marais-poitevin.fr* 🎟 *€4.60* ⊗ *May, June, and Sept, weekdays 10–noon and 2–7, weekends 10–1 and 2–7; July and Aug., daily 10–8; Oct. and Dec.–Apr., Tues.–Sun. 10–noon and 2–7; Nov., daily 2–7.*

One of the best ways to explore the area is by bicycle (a detailed map is advisable), rented from **La Libellule** (⊠ 94 quai Louis-Tardy, ☎ 05–49–35–83–42).

Where to Stay & Eat

$–$$ ×⌂ **Central.** Just opposite the church on the town square, this hotel has a fine restaurant (closed Sunday evening and all day Monday) much favored by the local bourgeoisie, who enjoy an obsequious welcome from the blue-blazered owner. The fine choice of regional fare includes succulent lamb, eel fricassee, and warm oysters cooked with nettle leaves. Rooms are small and functional—good for an overnight stop, perhaps, but no longer. ☒ *4 rue d'Autremont, 79510* ☎ *05–49–35–90–20* 🖷 *05–49–35–81–07* ☜ *5 rooms* ⚴ *Restaurant; no a/c, no room TVs* ▤ *AE, MC, V* ☯ *Closed part of Oct. and Jan.* ⵏ⊙ⵏ *MAP.*

Poitiers

★ ㉟ *88 km (55 mi) northeast of Coulon via Niort/A10, 340 km (212 mi) southwest of Paris.*

Thanks to its majestic hilltop perch above the Clain River and its position halfway along the Bordeaux–Paris trade route, Poitiers became an important commercial, religious, and university town in the Middle Ages. Life quieted down after the 17th century, but tranquillity has resulted in excellent architectural preservation. For a taste of old Poitiers, explore the narrow streets of the Vieille Ville, most lined with weathered half-timbered buildings: Rue de la Chaîne, Rue des Veilles Boucheries, Rue du Marcheæ, and Grand'Rue. The church of **Notre-Dame-la-Grande** (☒ Pl. Charles-de-Gaulle), in the town center, is an impressive example of the Romanesque architecture so common in western France. Its 12th-century facade, framed by rounded arches and decorated with a multitude of bas-reliefs and sculptures, comes alive during a 15-minute light show that highlights the details in color every evening at 10:30 from mid-June through September.

The **Cathédrale St-Pierre** (☒ Pl. de la Cathédrale), a few hundred yards beyond Notre-Dame-la-Grande, was built between the 12th and the 14th centuries. With a huge portal showing plump gargoyles without and tremendous open space and luminosity within, the largest church in Poitiers has a distinctive facade marked by two asymmetrical towers. The imposing interior is noted for its late-18th-century organ, stained glass, and 13th-century wooden choir stalls, claimed as the oldest in France.

The **Musée Ste-Croix** houses archaeological discoveries, traditional regional crafts, and European paintings from the 15th to the 19th centuries. The **Musée Rupert-de-Chièvres** (☒ 9 rue Victor-Hugo ☎ 05–49–41–42–21) displays Renaissance furniture, ceramics, and Old Master paintings.

★ ☾ **Futuroscope,** just north of Poitiers, is a smorgasbord of cinema thrills that has attracted more than 20 million visitors since it opened in 1987, making it western France's leading tourist attraction. Choose between half-dome screens (L'Omnimax); high-resolution screens (Cinéma Haute Résolution); theaters with mechanical seat effects (Cinémas Dynamiques); the Cinéma 360°, where you stand in mid-theater as nine images, shot in a circle, re-create a surf-pounding trimaran ocean race; the Magic Carpet, where a huge front screen is synchronized with another below your feet; Destination Cosmos, featuring the giant Hubble telescope; or Solido, where a pair of stereoscopic shades send you on a virtual swim. ☒ *Exit 28 off A10, Jaunay-Clan* ☎ *05–49–49–59–84* ⊕ *www.planate-futuroscope.com* ▦ *1 day: adults, €21–€30; children, € 21–30. 2* *days: adults, € 40–€57; children, € 29–€40. All admission rates depend on season ⏲ Apr.–Sept., daily 10–10; Oct.–Mar., daily 10–6.*

Where to Stay & Eat

$$ ✕ **Maxime.** Reasonable prix-fixe menus and chef Christian Rougier's cooking have made Maxime a stylish crowd pleaser. Enjoy foie gras and duck salad in the pastel dining room lined with '30s-style frescoes. ✉ *4 rue St-Nicolas* ☎ *05–49–41–27–37* ✍ *Reservations essential* ▭ *AE, DC, MC, V* ⏲ *Closed weekends and mid-July to mid-Aug.* 🍴 *MAP.*

$ 🏨 **Europe.** An early-19th-century building with a modern extension houses this unpretentious hotel in the middle of town. Because it's off the main street and has a forecourt, rooms are quiet. It also has a pleasant garden in the back for an afternoon tea or an evening aperitif. ✉ *39 rue Carnot, 86000* ☎ *05–49–88–12–00* 📠 *05–49–88–97–30* *85 rooms* *Cable TV, Internet, some pets allowed; no a/c* ▭ *AE, DC, MC, V* 🍴 *EP.*

16

BORDEAUX, DORDOGNE & POITOU-CHARENTES A TO Z

To research prices, get advice from other travelers, and book travel arrangements, visit www.fodors.com.

AIR TRAVEL

Airlines & Contacts **Air France** ☎ 08-02-80-28-02.

AIRPORTS

Frequent daily flights on Air France link Bordeaux and the domestic airport at Limoges with Paris.

Airport Information **Aéroport de Bordeaux-Mérignac** ☎ 05-56-34-50-50 🌐 www.bordeaux.aeroport.

BUS TRAVEL

The regional bus operator is CITRAM; the main Gare Routière (bus terminal) in Bordeaux is on Allées de Chartres (by Esplanade des Quinconces), near the Garonne River. CITRAM buses cover towns in the wine country and beach areas not well served by rail (for instance, one or two buses run daily to St-Émilion and Pauillac). The Dordogne region is serviced by Trans-Périgord and CFTA; the region around La Rochelle by Océcars. Sarlat is a main bus hub, with connections to Les Eyzies, Périgueux, and Bordeaux. The Sarlat–Périgueux line has a stop at Montignac for the Lascaux Caves. CITRAM buses from Cognac end up in Angoulême. Coulon in the Marais Poitevin is serviced by Casa Buses. Bus service in and around Poitiers is offered by Société des Transports Poitevins.

Bus Information **Casa** ✉ 13 chemin Fief-Binard, 79000 Niort ☎ 05-49-24-93-47. **CFTA** ✉ Gare Routière, pl. Francheville, 24000 Périgueux ☎ 05-53-08-43-13. **CITRAM** ✉ 8 rue de Corneille, 33000 Bordeaux ☎ 05-56-43-68-43. **Océcars** ✉ 31 rue des Rameaux, 17000 La Rochelle ☎ 05-46-00-95-15. **Société des Transports Poitevins** ✉ 9 rue de Northampton, 86000 Poitiers ☎ 05-49-44-77-00. **Trans-Périgord** ✉ Cabarnat, 24250 Veyrines-de-Domme ☎ 05-53-28-52-20.

CAR RENTAL

🗐 Local Agencies **Avis** ✉ Gare St-Jean, Bordeaux ☎ 05-56-91-65-50 ✉ 133 bd. du Grand-Cerf, Poitiers ☎ 05-49-58-13-00 ✉ 166 bd. Joffre, La Rochelle ☎ 05-46-41-13-55. **Hertz** ✉ Pl. de la Gare, Bergerac ☎ 05-53-57-19-27 ✉ 105 bd. du Grand-Cerf, Poitiers ☎ 05-49-58-24-24.

CAR TRAVEL

As the capital of southwest France, Bordeaux has superb transport links with Paris, Spain, and even the Mediterranean (A62 expressway via Toulouse). The A10, the Paris–Bordeaux expressway, passes close to Poitiers, Niort (exit 33 for La Rochelle), and Saintes before continuing toward Spain as A63. Fast N137 connects La Rochelle with Saintes via Rochefort; Angoulême is linked to Bordeaux and Poitiers by N10; and D936 runs along the Dordogne Valley to Bergerac. N89 links Bordeaux to Périgueux.

EMERGENCIES

🗐 **Ambulance** ☎ 15. **Hôpital St-André** ✉ 1 rue Jean-Burguet, 33800 Bordeaux ☎ 05-56-79-56-79.

TOURS

The Office de Tourisme in Bordeaux organizes four-hour coach tours of the surrounding vineyards every Wednesday and Saturday afternoon. The office has information on other wine tours and tastings, and on local and regional sights; a round-the-clock phone service in English is available.

🗐 Fees & Schedules **Bordeaux Office de Tourisme** ✉ 12 cours du XXX-Juillet, cedex, 33080 Bordeaux ☎ 05-56-00-66-00.

TRAIN TRAVEL

The superfast TGV (Train à Grande Vitesse) Atlantique service links Paris (Gare Montparnasse) to Bordeaux—585 km (365 mi) in three hours—with stops at Poitiers and Angoulême (change for Cognac, and Saintes); and to La Rochelle—465 km (290 mi) in three hours—with a stop in Niort. Trains link Bordeaux to Lyon (8–9 hours) and Nice (eight hours) via Toulouse. Six trains daily make the 3½-hour, 400-km (250-mi) trip from Paris to Limoges.

Bordeaux is the region's major train hub. Trains run regularly from Bordeaux to Bergerac (80 minutes), with occasional stops at St-Émilion, and three times daily to Sarlat (nearly three hours). At least six trains daily make the 90-minute journey from Bordeaux to Périgueux, and four continue to Limoges (2 hours, 20 minutes). Poitiers is the connecting point for Niort, La Rochelle, and Rochefort; Angoulême is the connecting point for Jarnac, Cognac, and Saintes.

🗐 Train Information **SNCF** ☎ 08-36-35-35-35 🌐 www.ter-sncf.com/uk/poitou-charentes.

TRAVEL AGENCIES

🗐 Local Agent Referrals **American Express** ✉ 14 cours de l'Intendance, Bordeaux ☎ 05-56-00-63-33. **Carlson-Wagons-lit** ✉ 43 rue de la Porte-Dijeaux, Bordeaux ☎ 05-56-52-92-70.

VISITOR INFORMATION

🖪 Tourist Information **Angoulême** ✉ 7 bis rue du Chat ☎ 05-45-95-16-84 ⊕ www. tourisme.fr/angouleme. **Bergerac** ✉ 97 rue Neuve d'Argenson ☎ 05-53-57-03-11 ⊕ www.bergerac-tourisme.com. **Bordeaux** ✉ 12 cours du XXX-Juillet ☎ 05-56-00-66-00 ⊕ www.bordeaux-tourisme.com. **Cognac** ✉ 16 rue du XIV-Juillet ☎ 05-45-82-10-71 ⊕ www.tourism-cognac.com. **La Rochelle** ✉ Pl. de la Petite-Sirène ☎ 05-46-41-14-68 ⊕ www.larochelle-tourisme.com. **Pauillac** ✉ La Verrerie ☎ 05-56-59-03-08 ⊕ www. pauillac-Medoc.com. **Périgueux** ✉ 25 rue du Président-Wilson ☎ 05-53-35-50-24. **Poitiers** ✉ 8 rue des Grandes-Écoles ☎ 05-49-41-21-24 ⊕ www.ot-poitiers.fr. **Royan** ✉ Rond-Point de la Poste ☎ 05-46-05-04-71 ⊕ www.royan-tourisme.com. **St-Émilion** ✉ 15 rue du Clocher ☎ 05-57-55-28-28 ⊕ www.saint-emilion-tourisme.com. **Saintes** ✉ 62 cours National ☎ 05-46-74-23-82 ⊕ www.ot-saintes.fr. **Sarlat** ✉ Pl. de la Liberté ☎ 05-53-31-45-45.

UNDERSTANDING FRANCE

À LA FRANÇAISE

THERE IS AN OLD FAMILIAR SAYING: "Everyone has two countries, his or her own—and France." For France is the Land of Cockaigne, where every man and woman does what he or she pleases, where you can allow your personal idiosyncracies full play and apologize for them with complete acceptability by the simple remark, *Je suis comme ça.* I am like that. It's all that need be said. In France everyone has a right to be like him or herself. One needn't conform to the model of another.

It is this freedom that, millennia ago, made France the cultural—and hoopla—capital of the world; and it is this freedom that has given us Notre-Dame, Chartres, Versailles, and the Tour Eiffel; writers like Molière, Hugo, Balzac, and Proust; composers like Berlioz and Debussy; and painters like Georges de la Tour, Fragonard, Monet, Cézanne, and Matisse. Only when Picasso came to Paris from Spain did he become Picasso; only when van Gogh traveled to Provence from Holland did he become van Gogh. Clearly there are few other countries that can contribute so much to the spiritual development of the individual. If environment can add to a person's stature, the environment of France can be counted on to do it by virtue of the influence she brings to bear on everyone sensitive to beauty, measure, and intellectual stimulation. In addition to the roll-call listed above, the best witnesses to that are the many American and British expatriates who came to admire, and remained to praise.

For the expats France is neither too hot nor too cold, neither too wet nor too dry, neither too flat nor too crammed with inconvenient mountains. At any rate, that is what the French say. They will go on to tell you that countries should be hexagonal in shape and about 600 mi across. Spain is too square, Norway is frayed at the edges, l'Angleterre (which is what the French usually call Great Britain) is awkwardly surrounded by cold water, Switzerland is landlocked and too small, and the United States is too large.

Appropriately for les Français, France sits squarely in the middle of Western Europe; according to Francophiles, it might just as well be the center of the universe. The country has been the locus of European intellectual life ever since the founding of the Sorbonne in Paris in the 13th century. During the next few centuries the entire Western world began to adopt the French language and aspects of French culture. Then, with the French Revolution of 1789 and Napoléon's frolic over the European continent, France established itself as a world political, as well as cultural, power—a fact the proud French have not forgotten, and are always eager to remind you about.

In more recent years, the tables have turned, and foreign cultures have been invading France. And here "foreign" means American. For decades now, young French people have emulated Americans in the way they dress, the music they listen to, and even in their manner of speaking. Levi's go for $80 a pair and can be seen gracing the legs of any slick twentysomething, buskers sing Bob Dylan tunes in the streets, and teenagers hang out in the local MacDo (MacDonald's to the French), not in the corner café. And though they curse American movies to the death, the French love-hate relationship with Yankee films has let Hollywood win over the big screen.

But the French also fear the movement toward what they call *mondialisation* (globalization), which to many is a synonym for Americanization. The older generation in particular sees the infiltration of American fads and the country's integration into the European Union (EU) as eroding traditional French ways of life. Many grumble about the universality of the English language, which is commandeering World Wide Chats across the Internet and is the common parlance in international business deals. The Académie Française, tireless preserver of French culture, even set about to strike English words (like "le weekend" and "le parking") from the French vocabulary and establish 66% French music quotas for radio stations. The proposed changes stuck like wet Velcro when a cultural minister accidentally slipped an English word into his announcement speech. But even with the trend toward mondialisation, French culture remains, well, distinctly French. Paris is still the world center of the ultrastylish, and its cafés continue to be the breeding ground for smoking, coffee-drinking, armchair intellectuals. And in the French provinces, with their pastoral landscapes, stunning architecture, and delicious cuisine, there remains a determination to keep old-world charm uncompromising.

It's also important to remember, however, that there is not just one France: the country's geography is as diverse as the people who inhabit it. The Riviera attracts an international jet-set crowd to its famous strips of sand. In the south you can find an influx of recent immigrants and myriad cultures to match, a phenomenon that has met hostility from the steadily expanding Front National, France's ultraright party. In Provence the soil yields many gifts, and sunny pride blends with Spanish influence and Roman history to create an intriguing culture. In the southwest, along the Spanish border, the Basque people struggle to preserve their culture and their unique language, Euskera, in the face of trends toward centralization. Alsace-Lorraine, on the eastern edge of France, is almost as German as it is French. And in Brittany, one of the last regions to be incorporated into France, people still occasionally speak Breton and celebrate their Celtic heritage.

To really see France, you obviously must travel outside of Paris. In the small villages of the Loire Valley, Burgundy, and the Ile-de-France, you'll be surprised at how relaxed the pace is and at how much care goes into preparing a meal (and how much time is spent enjoying it). Venture off the Eurailpass trail and head to the Pyrénées at the Spanish border and the Alps at France's eastern edge to ski or mountainbike. Or head north through rolling farmland where you might not be awed by dramatic vistas, but where you will find plenty of locals willing to listen to your fumbling French and show you what "la belle vie française" is all about.

Let's look at the French timetable. Most city French folk are up early, gulping a café au lait and getting to work by 8. By 10, Parisian executives are fuming because their London contacts haven't yet answered the phone (it's only 9 in England). There's no coffee break. At noon, they are hungry. Work stops for two hours on occasion. Small shops close. Lunch, or *le déjeuner* (called *le dîner* in the country) is a sacred rite. Fast-food outlets have multiplied, but the norm is a proper meal, taking an hour and a half; a surprising number manage to get home for it. However, the increasing number of women at work means that six lunches out of ten are eaten at restaurants or canteens—substantial, freshly cooked affairs, eaten with serious critical attention. The French grew rich in the 1960s; back in 1920, they each ate nearly three pounds of bread a day—now it's just under a pound, with a corresponding increase in the consumption of meat, fish, and cheese. Less wine is drunk, but more of it is of higher quality.

The typical restaurant in your nearest market town (pop., let's say, 6,000) has only one menu: copious hors d'oeuvres, a fish dish or a light meat dish, a more serious meat dish, vegetables in season, a good cheese board, fruit or ice cream. It's always full by 12:30. A couple from San Francisco who stayed in a rented cottage in that village were hardly ever able to use it. They used to get up at 9 and were hopelessly out of phase with the commercial travelers (up at 6) who form the restaurant's main clientele. You can't start your lunch there at 1:30 or 2, and there are no doggie bags in France. When you are in the Midi (or South of France), an early start and a siesta prove convenient (many of the shops don't reopen until 3:30). However, the couple in question happily developed the picnic habit: France is God's own country for picnicking, if only you get to the *charcuterie* and the *boulangerie* and the *pâtisserie* well before they close at noon.

Back to work for another four-hour stretch. No tea or coffee break. Are the French mighty toilers? Yes and no. In the '90s, the average industrial worker put in 1,872 hours of work per year in the United States, 1,750 in Great Britain, but only 1,650 in France. Five weeks' paid vacation is the official minimum, and there are many public holidays. The French have become addicts of leisure in the past two decades. One family in 10 has a second house in the country, where they go on weekends and vacations, causing astounding traffic jams as they flee the cities.

If he finishes his day's work at 6 or 6:30, will our average Frenchman (or woman, of course) stop at his favorite café for a chat and an aperitif on his way home? Probably not, nowadays. In the past, the café was used as a sort of extra living room for meeting friends or professional contacts, or even for writing novels if you were Jean-Paul Sartre or Simone de Beauvoir. But today an average of two hours and 50 minutes is spent watching television at home, which reduces the time available for social life. This is sad. The number of cafés has diminished. Fortunately, there are still a lot left, and how convenient they are for the visitor! On the terrace of a French café you can bask in the sun or enjoy the shade of a multicolor parasol, sipping a cool beer and keeping an eye on life's passing show. A small black coffee entitles you to spend an hour or two—no hurry.

When one talks about the apéritif hour you are not only talking about cafés but about friendliness. Some people—notably Americans—complain that the French are inhospitable and standoffish. The fact is that they are great respecters of privacy. If the Englishman's home is his castle, the Frenchman's apartment or house is his lair. People simply do not pop into one another's lairs, drinking casual cups of coffee and borrowing half a pound of sugar. They need a neutral place in which to socialize. Britons come somewhere between typical French people and the American middle class. According to Paul Fussell (*Caste Marks,* 1983): "Among the [American] middles there's a convention that erecting a fence or even a tall hedge is an affront."

* * *

T'S DIFFERENT in France. People in the Midi, for instance, just love to talk, and even to listen. But village neighbors will prove timid about entering your house. If they want to ask you something, they will wait until you meet, or stay on the doorstep, or phone (from 50 yards away). They penetrate your house, and you penetrate theirs, when specifically invited. That is how they behave among themselves, too. It's not because we are foreigners.

When talking with the French, there are conventions that should be observed if you don't want to be thought a barbarian by people who are unaware of Anglo-Saxon attitudes. You must say *"Bonjour"* followed by *Monsieur, Madame, Mademoiselle, Messieurs, Mesdames,* or *Messieurs-dames* much more often than you would think necessary (on entering a small shop, for instance) and *"Au revoir, Monsieur"* (etc.). Hands are shaken frequently (by colleagues at work, morning and evening, and by the most casual acquaintances). *Bon appétit* can replace *au revoir* shortly before mealtimes. When you pass through a door, a certain amount of *après-vous*-ing is normal, with *pardon* if you go through first, turning your back. Getting on first-name terms is a sign of much greater intimacy than in England or the United States. Rush-hour Parisian life is more brutal, of course, and, as elsewhere in the world, the driving seat of a car exerts a malign influence. In England or the States, a headlight flash sometimes means "After you"; in France, it means either "After me" or "I am a criminal and I expect you are, too, so watch it, chum, the cops are round the corner."

* * *

B ACK HOME FROM the café, our typical French person, rich or poor, eats *le dîner* (called *le souper* in the country) around 8. It's a lighter meal than at midday, with soup replacing hors d'oeuvres. The movies, after a sharp fall as television established itself in every home, have resisted well. Except in Paris, films are dubbed into French, a practice deplored by intellectuals. Almost all employed people now have a two-day weekend, usually Saturday and Sunday, but Sunday and Monday for many shop workers. Schoolchildren have Wednesday free, but may attend Saturday morning instead. In recent years, the French have revolutionized their leisure habits: jogging, swimming, soccer, gymnastics, tennis, and vigorous bicycling (for fun, not transport) are practiced, mainly on weekends, by large numbers of all social classes.

The great Sunday ritual takes place at noon or soon after. Four out of 10 will visit friends or relations. Sixty percent of families do more cooking on Sunday than on other days. This is also a big day for restaurants that feature a special Sunday menu. Half the French end their Sunday lunch with a fresh fruit tart or some sort of gâteau, which is why the pastry shops are open in the morning and why you see Frenchmen carefully carrying flat cardboard boxes.

An essay such as this has to contain rash generalizations. Is there an average French person? Obviously not. There are the rich and the poor, for example. The poor in France like champagne, oysters, and foie gras, but they get them less often than do the rich. The same is true of other aspects of life. The gulf between one class and another is not one of tastes and aspirations; rich and poor are in broad agreement on what constitutes a pleasant life. The poor are simply further away from it than are the rich. The surge of prosperity in the '60s brought improvements to French life, with some drawbacks, but basic traditions die hard. The young ape foreign fashions, with a fast-food/motorcycle/mid-Atlantic pop noise/comic-strip culture, but they grow out of it. Official morality has changed. Contraception used to be forbidden; Paris was famed for its elegant brothels, but women had to go to London for diaphragms and to Switzerland for abortions. All that has gone. In 1988 the rise of AIDS caused a quickly smothered quarrel among bishops about the sinfulness of condoms, which are now readily available. *Le topless* is seen on most beaches, and total nakedness on some. But the family remains a powerful, cohesive unit.

In the end, there are those who love France and those who don't. It's a matter of taste and character. The former find it easy to slip into the French way of life for a week or a month or permanently. The latter are better off in Paris or on the Riviera. But really, the French are canny operators when it comes to enjoying *la douceur de vivre*, the sweetness of life. If you follow their example while in France, you can't go far wrong. (One way to go wrong would be to quote almost any paragraph from this essay to them; at any rate, it will start a vigorously French argument.)

BON APPÉTIT!: THE ART OF FRENCH COOKING

BORN BRITISH, NATURALIZED AMERICAN, I am an unabashed chauvinist about French food. To wander through a French open market, the vegetables overflowing from their crates, the fruits cascading in casual heaps on the counter, is a sensual pleasure. To linger outside a bakery in the early morning, to watch the fresh breads and croissants being lined up in regimental rows, awakens the most fickle appetite. Just to read the menu posted outside a modest café alerts the imagination to pleasures to come.

Best of all, the French are happy to share their enthusiasm for good food with others. There are more good restaurants and eating places in France than in any other European country; the streets are lined with delicatessens, butchers, cheese shops, bakeries, and pastry shops. And I have yet to find a Frenchman, cantankerous though he may be, who does not warm to anyone who shows an interest in his national passion for wines and fine cuisine.

Fine cuisine does not necessarily mean fancy cuisine. Masters though French chefs are of the soufflé and the butter sauce, the salmon in aspic, and the strawberry *feuilleté* (puff pastry), such delicacies are reserved for celebration. Everyday fare is much more likely to be roast chicken, steak, and *frites* (fries), an omelet, or a pork chop. Bread, eaten without butter, is mandatory at main meals, while the bottle of mineral water is almost as common as wine.

Where the French really score is in the variety and quality of their ingredients. Part of the credit must go to climate and geography—just look at the length of the French coastline and the part seafood plays in the cooking of Normandy, Brittany, and Provence. Count the number of rivers with fertile valleys for cattle and crops. Olives and fruit flourish in the Mediterranean sun, while the region from southwest of Paris running up north to the Belgian border is one of the great breadbaskets of Europe.

No one but the French identifies three basic styles of cuisine—classical, nouvelle, and regional. No other European nation pays so much attention to menus and recipes.

Most sophisticated are the sauces and soufflés, the mousselines and *macédoines* of classical cuisine. Since the 17th century, generations of chefs have lovingly documented their dishes, developing an intellectual discipline from what is an essentially practical art. As a style, classical cuisine is now outmoded, but its techniques form the basis of rigorous professional training in French cooking. In some measure, all other styles of cooking are based on its principles.

Nouvelle cuisine, for instance, is directly descended from the classics. Launched to worldwide acclaim in the late 1970s by such chefs as Michel Guérard, it takes a fresh, lighter approach, with simpler sauces and a colorful view of presentation. First-course salads, often with hot additions of shellfish, chicken liver, or bacon, have become routine. For a while cooks experimented with such way-out combinations as vanilla with lobster and chicken with raspberries, but now new-style cooking has its own classics. Typical are *magrets de canard* (boned duck breasts) sautéed like steak and served with a brown sauce of wine or green peppercorns and pot-au-feu made of fish rather than the usual beef.

Many cooks have made a refreshing return to country-style cooking. Indeed, many cooks never left it, for classical and nouvelle cuisines are almost exclusively the concern of professionals. However, regional dishes are cooked by everyone—at restaurants, at home, and in the café on the corner.

The city of Lyon exemplifies the best of regional cuisine. It features such local specialties as poached eggs in *meurette* (redwine sauce), *quenelles* (fish dumplings) in crayfish sauce, sausage with pistachios, and chocolate gâteau (cake). The Lyonnais hotly dispute Paris's title as gastronomic capital of France, pointing to the number of prestigious restaurants in their city. What is more, some of the world's finest wines are produced only 150 km (90 mi) north, in Burgundy.

Lyon may represent the best of French regional cooking, but there's plenty to look for elsewhere. Compare the sole of Normandy, cooked with mussels in cream sauce, with the sea bass of Provence, flamed with dried fennel or baked with tomatoes and thyme. Contrast the butter cakes of Brittany with the yeast breads of Alsace, the braised endive of Picardy with the gratin of cardoons (a type of artichoke) found in the south.

Authentic regional specialties are based on local products. They have a character that may depend on climate (cream cakes survive in Normandy but not in Provence) or geography (each mountain area has its own dried sausages and hams). History brought spice bread to Dijon, a legacy of the days when the dukes of Burgundy controlled Flanders and the spice trade. Ethnic heritage explains ravioli around Nice, near the Italian border, waffles in the north near Belgium, and dumplings close to Germany. Modern ethnic influences show up in cities, with many an Arab pastry shop started by Algerian immigrants and many a restaurant run by Vietnamese.

Fundamental to French existence is the baker, the *boulanger*. From medieval times legislation has governed the weight and content of loaves of bread, with stringent penalties for such crimes as adulteration with sand or sawdust. Today the government pegs the price of white bread, and

you'll find the famous long loaves a bargain compared with the price of brioche, croissants, or loaves of whole wheat (*pain complet*), rye (*pain de seigle*), and bran (*pain de son*). White bread can be bought as thin *flûtes* to slice for soup, as baguettes, or as the common, thicker loaves known simply as *pains*.

Since French bread stays fresh for only a few hours, it's baked in the morning for midday and baked again in the afternoon. A baker's day starts at 4 AM to give the dough time to rise. Sadly, there's a lack of recruits, so more and more French bread is being produced industrially, without the right nutty flavor and chew to the crisp crust. The clue to bread baked on the spot is the heady smell of fermenting yeast, so sniff out a neighborhood bakery before you buy.

If bread is the staff of French life, pastry is the sugar icing. The window of a city pastry shop (in the country, bakery and pastry shop are often combined) is a wonderland of éclairs and meringues, madeleines, puff pastry, spun sugar, and caramel. You'll find pies laden with seasonal fruit, nut cakes, and chocolate cakes, plus the baker's specialty, for he is certain to have one. Survey them with a sharp eye; they should be small (good ingredients are expensive) and impeccably alike in color and size (the sign of an expert craftsman). Last, the window should not be overflowing; because of the high cost, the temptation to cram the shelves with leftovers from the day before is strong.

The charcuterie is almost as French an institution as the bakery. *Chair cuite* means "cooked meat," and a charcuterie is a kind of delicatessen, specializing in pâtés, terrines, ham, and sausages. A charcuterie also sells long-lasting salads, such as cucumber, tomato, or grated carrot vinaigrette and root celery (celeriac) *rémoulade* (with mustard mayonnaise). Cooked "dishes of the day" may include coq au vin and *choucroute alsacienne* (sauerkraut with smoked pork hock). Often you'll also find such condiments as pickles, plus a modest selection of wines, cheeses, and desserts—rice pudding or baked apple, for example. Only bread is needed to complete the meal, and you're set for the world's best picnic!

French cheese deserves, and gets, close attention. Choosing a cheese is as delicate a matter as deciding on the right wine. In a good cheese shop you will be welcome to sample any of the cut cheeses, and assistants will gladly offer advice. One cardinal rule is to look for *fromage fermier* (farmhouse cheese), a rough equivalent of château-bottled wine. If the label says *lait cru* (raw milk)—even better; only when milk is unpasteurized does the flavor of some cheeses, Camembert, for example, develop properly. Try to keep a cheese cool without refrigeration and eat it as soon as you can. Delicate soft cheeses like Brie can become overripe within a matter of hours, one reason it's rare to find a wide-ranging selection of cheeses in a restaurant.

Many other kinds of specialty stores exist, often for local products. In Dijon, for instance, you'll find shops selling mustards in ornamental pots; in Gascony (near Bordeaux), it's foie gras and canned confit (preserved duck or goose). But the most famous concentration of food shops in the world must be clustered around place de la Madeleine in Paris. On one corner stands Fauchon, the dean of luxury food emporiums. Just across the square stands Hédiard, specializing in spices, rare fruits, and preserves.

The Madeleine crossroads may be unique, but with a bit of persistence, a more modest version can be found in most French towns in the weekly market, often held in a picturesque open hall that may be centuries old. Markets start early, typically around 8 AM, and often disband at noon. In Paris, street markets continue to thrive in almost every quarter, and although the main wholesale market of Les Halles has moved to the suburbs, the area around rue Coquillière is still worth exploring for its maze of truffle vendors, game purveyors, and professional kitchen-equipment outlets.

French markets are still dominated by the season—there's little or no sign of frozen produce and meats. The first baby lamb heralds Christmas; little chickens arrive around Easter, together with kid and asparagus. Autumn excitement comes with game—venison, pheasant, and wild boar. Even cheeses look and taste different according to the time of year.

If you're an early riser, there's a long wait until lunch, for snacks are not a French habit. The structure of a meal, its timing, and its content are taken seriously. The "grazing" phenomenon—minimeals snatched here and there throughout the day—is almost unheard of, and snacks are regarded as spoiling the appetite, not to mention being nutritionally unsound.

Still, the French light breakfast can come as no surprise; its unbeatable wake-up combination of croissant, brioche, or crusty roll with coffee has swept much of the world. Traditionally, the coffee comes as café au lait, milky and steaming in a wide two-handled bowl for dipping the bread.

At noon you'll be rewarded by what, for most French people, remains the main meal of the day. In much of the country, it's still true that everything stops for two hours; children return from school, and museums and businesses lock their doors. The pattern is much the same in provincial cities: Restaurants, bistros, and cafés are crammed with diners, most of whom eat at least two and often three or more courses. Unfortunately, however, quick lunches are becoming more and more the norm in larger cities like Paris.

A big lunch keeps French adults going until evening, but you may want to follow the example of schoolchildren, who are allowed a treat on the way home.

Often it's a *pain au chocolat* (chocolate croissant). By 8 you'll be ready for dinner and one of the greatest pleasures France has to offer.

The choice of restaurants in France is a feast in itself. At least once during your trip you may want to indulge in an outstanding occasion. But restaurants are just the beginning. You can also eat out in cafés, bistros, brasseries, fast-food outlets (they, too, have reached France), or auberges, which range from staid country inns to sybaritic hideaways.

Simplest is the café (where the espresso machine is king), offering drinks and such snacks as *croque monsieur* (toasted ham and cheese sandwich), *oeufs sur le plat* (fried eggs), *le hot dog,* and foot-long sandwiches of French bread. Larger-city cafés serve hot meals, such dishes as onion soup and braised beef with vegetables, consumed on marble-top tables to a background of cheerful banter. Like English pubs, French cafés are a way of life, a focal point for gossip and dominoes in practically every village.

The bistro, once interchangeable with the café, has taken a fashionable turn. In cities, instead of sawdust on the floor and a zinc-topped counter, you may find that a bistro is designer-decorated, serving new-style or fusion cuisine to a trendy, chattering crowd. If you're lucky, the food will be as witty and colorful as the clientele.

With few exceptions, brasseries remain unchanged—great bustling places with white-apron waiters and hearty food. Go to them for oysters on the half shell and other fine seafood, garlic snails, *boudin* (black pudding), sauerkraut, and vast ice cream desserts. Originally a brasserie brewed beer, and since many brewers came from Alsace on the borders of Germany, the cooking reflects their origins.

Training is an important factor in maintaining the standards of French cooking. Professional chefs begin their three-year apprenticeship at age 16, starting in baking, pastry, or cuisine and later branching out into such specialties as aspic work and sugar sculpture. To be a *chocolatier* is a career in itself. Much more than a manual trade, cooking in France aspires to being an art, and its exponents achieve celebrity status. Each decade has its stars, their rise and fall a constant source of eager speculation in the press and at the table.

The importance placed on food in France is echoed by the number of gastronomic societies, from the Chevaliers du Tastevin to the Chaîne des Rôtisseurs and the Confrérie des Cordons Bleus, to mention only three. The French believe that good eating, at whatever level, is an art that merits considerable time and attention. They have done the hard work, and as a traveler you can reap the benefits.

— Anne Willan

Anne Willan is president and founder of the École de Cuisine La Varenne in Paris. She has a series on PBS, Look and Cook with Anne Willan, and has written numerous books, including Cook It Right and La France Gastronomique.

FURTHER READING

Books on Paris alone can fill several libraries. Two titles that have recently hit the best-seller lists are *Paris to the Moon*, by Adam Gopnik—the distinguished Paris-based correspondent of the *New Yorker*—and *The Flâneur*, by Edmund White, the brilliant belletrist. For a look at American expatriates in Paris between the wars, read *Sylvia Beach and the Lost Generation*, by Noel R. Fitch, or *A Moveable Feast*, by Ernest Hemingway. George Orwell's *Down and Out in Paris and London* gives an account of life on a shoestring in these two European capitals. More essays about Paris are excerpted in *A Place in the World Called Paris*. Yet another anthology of essays on Paris is the *Travelers' Tales Guides: Paris*. For a visual feast, delight in John Russell's *Paris*—a compendium of city scenes painted by great masters accompanied by an illuminating text.

Three memoirs by Americans who have lived in Paris are Art Buchwald's *I'll Always Have Paris*, Edmund White's *The Flâneur*, and Stanley Karnow's *Paris in the Fifties*. *Paris Notebooks*, by Mavis Gallant, is her observations of Paris life. *Between Meals*, by A. J. Liebling, looks at the art of eating in Paris. *A Corner in the Marais: Memoir of a Paris Neighborhood* is Alex Karmel's history of the neighborhood. Edmund White and Hubert Sorin have also weighed in with *Our Paris: Sketches with Memory*.

The best introduction to modern France is John Ardagh's *France Today*. A witty but less complete survey of the country and its people is Theodore Zeldin's *The French*. Another entry on the list is Richard Bernstein's *Fragile Glory*. An immensely popular, if slightly satiric, introduction to French country life is provided by Peter Mayle's two autobiographical books on Provence, *A Year in Provence* and *Toujours Provence*, as well as his novel *Chasing Cézanne*.

Nancy Mitford's readable *The Sun King* covers the regal grandeur of the 17th century, while Alfred Cobban's workmanlike *History of Modern France* describes trends and events from the death of Louis XIV up to 1962. Another readable and fascinating book about French history is Barbara Tuchman's *A Distant Mirror*. Dorothy Carrington's classic work on Corsica, *Granite Island: A Portrait of Corsica*, is available at the library. For modern French history, particularly the Vichy era, a good bet is Robert Paxton's *Vichy France and the Jews*. For a scholarly study of Romanesque and Gothic architecture, read Henri Focillon's thoughtfully illustrated *The Art of the West*, available at the library.

Charles Dickens's *A Tale of Two Cities*, Flaubert's *Sentimental Education*, Henry James's *The Ambassadors*, Colette's *The Complete Claudine*, F. Scott Fitzgerald's *Tender Is the Night*, Hemingway's *The Sun Also Rises*, and Émile Zola's *La Curée*, *L'Assommoir*, *Nana*, and *La Débâcle* are just a handful of the classic novels set in France.

As for books about French wine and cuisine, Patricia Wells's *The Food Lover's Guide to Paris* and *The Food Lover's Guide to France* provide a good beginning. Waverly Root's *The Food of France* is a great accompaniment to any trip. Alexis Lichine's *Guide to Wines and Vineyards of France* is still the classic wine guide, though it's now only available from the library. For more books about French wine, try Robert M. Parker's *Bordeaux: A Comprehensive Guide to the Wines Produced from 1961–1997* and *Wines of the Rhône Valley*. A. J. Liebling's *Between Meals* provides a more literary look at the fine art of eating in France.

FRANCE AT A GLANCE

Fast Facts

Name in local language: France
Capital: Paris

If you are lucky enough to have lived in Paris as a young man, then wherever you go for the rest of your life it stays with you, for Paris is a moveable feast.
Ernest Hemingway, 1964

National anthem: "La Marseillaise" (The Song of Marseilles)
Type of government: Republic
Independence: A.D. 486 (unified by Clovis); Bastille Day celebrated on July 14th to commemorate the storming of the Bastille in 1789, which signified the end of the Monarchy and the beginning of the First Republic
Constitution: September 28, 1958
Legal system: Civil law system with indigenous concepts, review of administrative but not legislative acts

How can anyone govern a nation that has two hundred and forty different kinds of cheese?
General Charles de Gaulle, former President of France, 1962

Suffrage: 18 years of age
Population: 60,180,529
Population density: 110.30 persons per sq km (285.66 persons per sq mi)
Median age: Female 40, male 37
Life expectancy: Female 83, male 76
Infant mortality rate: 4.37 deaths per 1,000 live births
Literacy: 99%
Language: French (official), rapidly declining regional dialects and languages (Provencal, Breton, Alsatian, Corsican, Catalan, Basque, Flemish)

French is the language that turns dirt into romance.
Stephen King, 1986

Religion: Roman Catholic 83%–88%; Muslim 5%–10%; Protestant 2%; Jewish 1%; unaffiliated 4%
Discoveries & Inventions: Cassegrain telescope (1672), mayonnaise (1756), bicycle (1790), metric system (1790), Braille (1829), sewing machine (1830), aneroid barometer (1843), gyroscope (1852), dry cell battery (1870s), aqualung (1943)

Geography & Environment

Land area: 545,630 sq km (210,669 sq mi)
Coastline: 3,427 km (2,129 mi)
Terrain: Mostly flat plains or gently rolling hills in north and west; remainder is mountainous, especially Pyrenees in south, Alps in east
Natural hazards: Avalanches, drought, flooding, forest fires in south near Mediterranean, midwinter windstorms

Environmental issues: Agricultural runoff, air pollution, some forest damage from acid rain, water pollution

France has neither winter nor summer nor morals—apart from these drawbacks it is a fine country.
notebook entry, Mark Twain

Economy

Currency: Euro (€)
Exchange rate: 1.06 euros per U.S. dollar
GDP: €1.289 trillion ($1.558 trillion)
Per capita income: €21,513 ($26,000)
Inflation: 1.8%
Unemployment: 9.1%
Work force: 26.6 million (services 71%; agriculture 4%; industry 25%)
Debt: €87.78 billion ($106 billion)

Exports: €254.68 billion ($307.8 billion)
Export partners: Germany 15%; U.K. 9.8%; Spain 9%; Italy 9%; U.S. 7.8%; Belgium 6.9%
Imports: €251.29 billion ($303.7 billion)
Import partners: Germany 19.4%; Belgium 9.2%; Italy 8.8%; U.K. 7.3%; Netherlands 7%; U.S. 6.8%; Spain 6.7%

Did You Know?

• In France, chocolate was initially met with skepticism and was considered a barbarous, noxious drug. The French court accepted chocolate after the Paris faculty of medicine gave its approval.

• France and Italy produce over 40 percent of all wine consumed in the world.

• The "A-OK" gesture is widely accepted as the American "I'm in agreement" sign, but it means something quite different in other countries. In southern France, this fingers-circle sign signifies "worthless" or "zero."

• A "French kiss" in the English-speaking world is known as an "English kiss" in France.

• France has the highest per capita consumption of cheese.

• The 200-m (660-ft) long basilica of St. Pius X in Lourdes, France, holds up to 20,000 people—and the world's record for having the largest church capacity.

• Over a three-week period, more than 10,000,000 people cheer on the annual Tour de France cycling race, the greatest number of live spectators for any sporting event.

• France was the most popular tourist destination in 2001, according to the World Tourism Organization, attracting over 76.5 million international visitors that year (16 million more than the population of France itself!).

— Amy Wang

CHRONOLOGY

Here's a minihistory of France—an *aide mémoire* to monarchs and moments.

58–51 BC Julius Caesar conquers Gaul; writes up the war in *De Bello Gallico*.

52 BC Lutetia, later to become Paris, is built by the Gallo-Romans.

46 BC Roman amphitheater built at Arles.

14 BC Pont du Gard aqueduct at Nîmes is erected.

The Merovingian Dynasty

486–511 Clovis, king of the Franks (481–511), defeats the Roman governor of Gaul and founds the Merovingian dynasty. Great monasteries, such as those at Tours, Limoges, and Chartres, become centers of culture.

497 Franks convert to Christianity.

The Carolingian Dynasty

768–78 Charlemagne (768–814) becomes king of the Franks (768), conquers northern Italy (774), and is defeated by the Moors at Roncesvalles, Spain, after which he consolidates the Pyrénées border (778).

800 The pope crowns Charlemagne Holy Roman Emperor in Rome. Charlemagne expands the French kingdom far beyond its present borders and establishes a center for learning at his capital, Aix-la-Chapelle (Aachen, in present-day Germany).

The Capetian Dynasty

987 Hugh Capet (987–996) is made king of France and establishes the principle of hereditary rule for his descendants. Settled conditions and the increased power of the Church see the flowering of Romanesque architecture in the cathedrals of Autun and Angoulême.

1066 Norman conquest of England by William the Conqueror (1028–87).

1067 Work begins on the Romanesque Bayeux Tapestry, celebrating the Norman Conquest.

ca. 1100 First universities in Europe include one in Paris. Development of European vernacular verse: *Chanson de Roland*.

1140 The Gothic style of architecture first appears at St-Denis and later becomes fully developed at the cathedrals of Chartres, Reims, Amiens, and Paris's Notre-Dame.

ca. 1150 Struggle between the Anglo-Norman kings (Angevin empire) and the French; when Eleanor of Aquitaine switches husbands (from Louis VII of France to Henry II of England), her extensive lands pass to English rule.

The Valois Dynasty

1337–1453   Hundred Years' War between France and England: fighting for control of those areas of France gained by the English crown following the marriage of Eleanor of Aquitaine and Henry II.

1348–50   Black Death (plague) rages in France.

1428–31   Joan of Arc (1412–31), the Maid of Orléans, sparks the revival of French fortunes in the Hundred Years' War but is captured by the English and burned at the stake at Rouen.

1434   Johannes Gutenberg invents the printing press in Strasbourg, Alsace.

1453   France finally defeats England, terminating the Hundred Years' War and English claims to the French throne.

1475   Burgundy is at the height of its power under Charles the Bald.

1494   Italian wars: beginning of Franco-Hapsburg struggle for hegemony in Europe.

1515–47   Reign of François I, who imports Italian artists, including Leonardo da Vinci (1452–1519), and brings the Renaissance to France. The château of Fontainebleau is begun (1528).

1562–98   Wars of Religion: Catholics versus Huguenots (French Protestants).

The Bourbon Dynasty

1589   The first Bourbon king, Henri IV (1589–1610), is a Protestant who converts to Catholicism and achieves peace in France. He signs the Edict of Nantes, giving limited freedom of worship to Protestants. The development of Renaissance Paris begins.

1643–1715   Reign of Louis XIV, the Sun King, a monarch who builds the Baroque power base of Versailles and presents Europe with a glorious view of France. With his first minister, Colbert, Louis makes France, by force of arms, the most powerful nation-state in Europe.

1660   Classical period of French culture: dramatists Pierre Corneille (1606–84), Molière (1622–73), and Jean Racine (1639–99), and painter Nicolas Poussin (1594–1665).

ca. 1715   Rococo art and decoration develop in Parisian boudoirs and salons, typified by the painter Antoine Watteau (1684–1721) and, later, François Boucher (1703–70) and Jean-Honoré Fragonard (1732–1806).

1700–onward   Writer and pedagogue Voltaire (1694–1778) is a central figure in the French Enlightenment, along with Jean-Jacques Rousseau (1712–78) and Denis Diderot (1713–84), who in 1751 compiles the first modern encyclopedia. The ideals of the Enlightenment—for reason and scientific method and against social and political injustices—pave the way for the French Revolution.

1756–63 The Seven Years' War results in the loss by France of most of its overseas possessions and in the ascension of England as a world power.

1776 The French assist the Americans in the Revolutionary War.

The French Revolution

1789–1804 The Bastille is stormed on July 14, 1789. Following upon early republican ideals comes the Reign of Terror and the administration of the Directory under Robespierre. There are widespread political executions—Louis XVI and Marie-Antoinette are guillotined in 1793. Reaction sets in, and the instigators of the Terror are themselves executed (1794). Napoléon Bonaparte enters as Champion of the Directory (1795–99) and is installed as First Consul during the Consulate (1799–1804).

The First Empire

1804 Napoléon crowns himself emperor of France at Notre-Dame in the presence of the pope.

1805–12 Napoléon conquers most of Europe. The Napoleonic Age is marked by a Neoclassical artistic style called Empire as well as by the rise of Romanticism—characterized author Marie-Henri Stendhal (1783–1842) and painters Eugène Delacroix (1798–1863).

1812–14 Winter cold and Russian determination defeat Napoléon outside Moscow. The emperor abdicates and is transported to Elba.

Restoration of the Bourbons

1814–15 Louis XVIII, brother of the executed Louis XVI, regains the throne after the Congress of Vienna settles peace terms.

1815 The Hundred Days: Napoléon returns from Elba and musters an army on his march to the capital but lacks national support. He is defeated at Waterloo (June 18) and exiled to the island of St-Helena, in the south Atlantic.

1830 Bourbon king Charles X, locked into a pre-Revolutionary state of mind, abdicates. A brief upheaval (called Three Glorious Days) brings Louis-Philippe, the Citizen King, to the throne.

1846–48 Severe industrial and farming depression contributes to Louis-Philippe's abdication (1848).

Second Republic & Second Empire

1848–52 Louis-Napoléon (nephew and step-grandson of Napoléon I) is elected president of the short-lived Second Republic. He is declared emperor of France, taking the title Napoléon III.

ca. 1850 The ensuing period is characterized in the arts by the emergence of realist painters, such as Jean-François Millet (1814–75) and Gustave Courbet (1819–77), and late-Romantic writers, among them Honoré de Balzac (1799–1850) and Charles Baudelaire (1821–87).

1863 Napoléon III inaugurates the Salon des Refusés in response to critical opinion. It includes work by Édouard Manet (1832–83), Claude Monet (1840–1926), and Paul Cézanne (1839–1906), and is commonly regarded as the birthplace of Impressionism and of modern art in general.

The Third Republic

1870–71 The Franco-Prussian War sees Paris besieged by and then fall to the Germans. Napoléon III takes refuge in England.

1871–1914 Before World War I, France builds vast colonial empires in North Africa and Southeast Asia. Sculptor Auguste Rodin (1840–1917), composer Claude Debussy (1862–1918), and poets such as Stéphane Mallarmé (1842–98) and Paul Verlaine (1844–96) set the stage for modernism.

1889 The Eiffel Tower is built for the Paris World Exhibition.

1918–39 Between the wars, Paris attracts artists and writers, including Americans Ernest Hemingway (1899–1961) and Gertrude Stein (1874–1946). France nourishes major artistic and philosophical movements: Constructivism, Dadaism, Surrealism, and Existentialism.

1939–45 At the beginning of World War II, France sides with the Allies until invaded and defeated by Germany in 1940. The French government, under Marshal Philippe Pétain (1856–1951), moves to Vichy and cooperates with the Nazis.

1944 D-Day, June 6: The Allies land on the beaches of Normandy and successfully invade France. Additional Allied forces land in Provence. Paris is liberated in August 1944, and France declares full allegiance to the Allies.

1944–46 A provisional government takes power under General de Gaulle; American aid assists French recovery.

The Fourth Republic

1946 France adopts a new constitution; French women gain the right to vote.

1954–62 The Algerian War leads to Algeria's independence from France. Other French African colonies gain independence.

1957 The Treaty of Rome establishes the European Economic Community (now known as the European Union—EU), with France as one of its members.

The Fifth Republic

1958–69 De Gaulle is the first president under a new constitution; he resigns in 1969, a year after widespread disturbances begun by student riots in Paris.

1981 François Mitterrand (1916–1996) is elected the first Socialist president of France since World War II.

1994 The Channel Tunnel (or Chunnel) opens; trains link London to Paris in three hours.

1995 Jacques Chirac, mayor of Paris, is elected president.

2002 Throughout France, the widespread introduction of euro bills and coins goes off without a hitch.

FRENCH VOCABULARY

One of the trickiest French sounds to pronounce is the nasal final *n* sound (whether or not the *n* is actually the last letter of the word). You should try to pronounce it as a sort of nasal grunt—as in "huh." The vowel that precedes the *n* will govern the vowel sound of the word, and in this list we precede the final *n* with an *h* to remind you to be nasal.

Another problem sound is the ubiquitous but untransliterable *eu*, as in *bleu* (blue) or *deux* (two), and the very similar sound in *je* (I), *ce* (this), and *de* (of). The closest equivalent might be the vowel sound in "put," but rounded.

Words and Phrases

English	French	Pronunciation

Basics

English	French	Pronunciation
Yes/no	Oui/non	wee/nohn
Please	S'il vous plaît	seel voo **play**
Thank you	Merci	mair-**see**
You're welcome	De rien	deh ree-**ehn**
That's all right	Il n'y a pas de quoi	eel nee ah pah de **kwah**
Excuse me, sorry	Pardon	pahr-**dohn**
Sorry!	Désolé(e)	day-zoh-**lay**
Good morning/ afternoon	Bonjour	bohn-**zhoor**
Good evening	Bonsoir	bohn-**swahr**
Goodbye	Au revoir	o ruh-**vwahr**
Mr. (Sir)	Monsieur	muh-**syuh**
Mrs. (Ma'am)	Madame	ma-**dam**
Miss	Mademoiselle	mad-mwa-**zel**
Pleased to meet you	Enchanté(e)	ohn-shahn-**tay**
How are you?	Comment ça va?	kuh-mahn-sa-**va**
Very well, thanks	Très bien, merci	tray bee-ehn, mair-**see**
And you?	Et vous?	ay **voo**?

Numbers

English	French	Pronunciation
one	un	uhn
two	deux	deuh
three	trois	twah
four	quatre	**kaht**-ruh

five	cinq	sank
six	six	seess
seven	sept	set
eight	huit	wheat
nine	neuf	nuff
ten	dix	deess
eleven	onze	ohnz
twelve	douze	dooz
thirteen	treize	trehz
fourteen	quatorze	kah-**torz**
fifteen	quinze	kanz
sixteen	seize	sez
seventeen	dix-sept	deez-**set**
eighteen	dix-huit	deez-**wheat**
nineteen	dix-neuf	deez-**nuff**
twenty	vingt	vehn
twenty-one	vingt-et-un	vehnt-ay-**uhn**
thirty	trente	trahnt
forty	quarante	ka-**rahnt**
fifty	cinquante	sang-**kahnt**
sixty	soixante	swa-**sahnt**
seventy	soixante-dix	swa-sahnt-**deess**
eighty	quatre-vingts	kaht-ruh-**vehn**
ninety	quatre-vingt-dix	kaht-ruh-vehn-**deess**
one-hundred	cent	sahn
one-thousand	mille	meel

Colors

black	noir	nwahr
blue	bleu	bleuh
brown	brun/marron	bruhn/mar-**rohn**
green	vert	vair
orange	orange	o-**rahnj**
pink	rose	rose
red	rouge	rooje
violet	violette	vee-o-**let**
white	blanc	blahnk
yellow	jaune	zhone

Days of the Week

Sunday	dimanche	**dee**-mahnsh
Monday	lundi	**luhn**-dee
Tuesday	mardi	**mahr**-dee
Wednesday	mercredi	**mair**-kruh-dee
Thursday	jeudi	**zhuh**-dee
Friday	vendredi	**vawn**-druh-dee
Saturday	samedi	**sahm**-dee

Months

January	janvier	**zhahn**-vee-ay
February	février	**feh**-vree-ay
March	mars	marce
April	avril	a-**vreel**
May	mai	meh
June	juin	zhwehn
July	juillet	**zhwee**-ay
August	août	oot
September	septembre	sep-**tahm**-bruh
October	octobre	awk-**to**-bruh
November	novembre	no-**vahm**-bruh
December	décembre	day-**sahm**-bruh

Useful Phrases

Do you speak . . . English?	Parlez-vous . . . anglais?	par-lay **voo** **ahn**-glay
I don't speak . . . French	Je ne parle pas . . . français	zhuh nuh parl **pah** frahn-**say**
I don't understand	Je ne comprends pas	zhuh nuh kohm-prahn **pah**
I understand	Je comprends	zhuh kohm-**prahn**
I don't know	Je ne sais pas	zhuh nuh say **pah**
I'm American/ British	Je suis américain/ anglais	zhuh sweez a-may-ree-**kehn**/ahn-**glay**
What's your name?	Comment vous appelez-vous?	ko-mahn voo za-pell-ay-**voo**
My name is . . .	Je m'appelle . . .	zhuh ma-**pell** . . .
What time is it?	Quelle heure est-il?	kel air eh-**teel**
How?	Comment?	ko-**mahn**

When?	Quand?	kahn
Yesterday	Hier	yair
Today	Aujourd'hui	o-zhoor-**dwee**
Tomorrow	Demain	duh-**mehn**
This morning/ afternoon	Ce matin/cet après-midi	suh ma-**tehn**/set ah-pray-mee-**dee**
Tonight	Ce soir	suh **swahr**
What?	Quoi?	kwah
What is it?	Qu'est-ce que c'est?	kess-kuh-**say**
Why?	Pourquoi?	**poor**-kwa
Who?	Qui?	kee
Where is . . . the train station? the subway? station? the bus stop? the airport? the post office? the bank? the hotel? the store? the cashier? the museum? the hospital? the elevator? the telephone?	Où se trouve . . . la gare? la station de? métro? l'arrêt de bus? l'aérogare? la poste? la banque? l'hôtel? le magasin? la caisse? le musée? l'hôpital? l'ascenseur? le téléphone?	oo suh **troov** la gar la sta-**syon** duh may-**tro** la-**ray** duh **booss** lay-ro-**gar** la post la bahnk lo-**tel** luh ma-ga-**zehn** la **kess** luh mew-**zay** lo-pee-**tahl** la-sahn-**seuhr** luh tay-lay-**phone**
Where are the rest rooms?	Où sont les toilettes?	oo sohn lay twah-**let**
Here/there	Ici/là	ee-**see**/la
Left/right	A gauche/à droite	a goash/a drwaht
Straight ahead	Tout droit	too drwah
Is it near/far?	C'est près/loin?	say pray/lwehn
I'd like . . . a room the key a newspaper a stamp	Je voudrais . . . une chambre la clé un journal un timbre	zhuh voo-**dray** ewn **shahm**-bruh la clay uhn zhoor-**nahl** uhn **tam**-bruh
I'd like to buy . . . a cigar cigarettes matches	Je voudrais acheter . . . un cigare des cigarettes des allumettes	zhuh voo-**dray** **ahsh**-tay uhn see-**gar** day see-ga-**ret** days a-loo-**met**

dictionary	un dictionnaire	uhn deek-see-oh-**nare**
soap	du savon	dew sah-**vohn**
city map	un plan de ville	uhn plahn de **veel**
road map	une carte routière	ewn cart roo-tee-**air**
magazine	une revue	ewn reh-**vu**
envelopes	des enveloppes	dayz ahn-veh-**lope**
writing paper	du papier à lettres	dew pa-pee-**ay** a **let**-ruh
airmail writing paper	du papier avion	dew pa-pee-**ay** a-vee-**ohn**
postcard	une carte postale	ewn cart pos-**tal**
How much is it?	C'est combien?	say comb-bee-**ehn**
It's expensive/cheap	C'est cher/pas cher	say share/pa share
A little/a lot	Un peu/beaucoup	uhn peuh/bo-**koo**
More/less	Plus/moins	plu/mwehn
Enough/too (much)	Assez/trop	a-say/tro
I am ill/sick	Je suis malade	zhuh swee ma-**lahd**
Call a . . . doctor	Appelez un . . . médecin	a-play uhn mayd-**sehn**
Help!	Au secours!	o suh-**koor**
Stop!	Arrêtez!	a-reh-**tay**
Fire!	Au feu!	o fuh
Caution!/Look out!	Attention!	a-tahn-see-**ohn**

Dining Out

A bottle of . . .	une bouteille de . . .	ewn boo-**tay** duh
A cup of . . .	une tasse de . . .	ewn **tass** duh
A glass of . . .	un verre de . . .	uhn **vair** duh
Ashtray	un cendrier	uhn sahn-dree-**ay**
Bill/check	l'addition	la-dee-see-**ohn**
Bread	du pain	dew pan
Breakfast	le petit-déjeuner	luh puh-**tee** day-zhuh-**nay**
Butter	du beurre	dew burr
Cheers!	A votre santé!	ah vo-truh sahn-**tay**
Cocktail/aperitif	un apéritif	uhn ah-pay-ree-**teef**
Dinner	le dîner	luh dee-**nay**
Special of the day	le plat du jour	luh plah dew **zhoor**
Enjoy!	Bon appétit!	bohn a-pay-**tee**

Fixed-price menu	le menu	luh may-**new**
Fork	une fourchette	ewn four-**shet**
I am diabetic	Je suis diabétique	zhuh swee dee-ah-bay-**teek**
I am on a diet	Je suis au régime	zhuh sweez oray-**jeem**
I am vegetarian	Je suis végé-tarien(ne)	zhuh swee vay-zhay-ta-ree-**en**
I cannot eat . . .	Je ne peux pas manger de . . .	zhuh nuh **puh** pah mahn-**jay** deh
I'd like to order	Je voudrais commander	zhuh voo-**dray** ko-mahn-**day**
I'm hungry/thirsty	J'ai faim/soif	zhay fahm/swahf
Is service/the tip included?	Le service est-il compris?	luh sair-**veess** ay-teel com-**pree**
It's good/bad	C'est bon/mauvais	say bohn/mo-**vay**
It's hot/cold	C'est chaud/froid	say sho/frwah
Knife	un couteau	uhn koo-**toe**
Lunch	le déjeuner	luh day-zhuh-**nay**
Menu	la carte	la cart
Napkin	une serviette	ewn sair-vee-**et**
Pepper	du poivre	dew **pwah**-vruh
Plate	une assiette	ewn a-see-**et**
Please give me . . .	Merci de me donner . . .	Mair-**see** deh meh doe-**nay**
Salt	du sel	dew sell
Spoon	une cuillère	ewn kwee-**air**
Sugar	du sucre	dew **sook**-ruh
Waiter!/Waitress!	Monsieur!/Mademoiselle!	muh-**syuh**/mad-mwa-**zel**
Wine list	la carte des vins	la **cart** day van

MENU GUIDE

General Dining

French	English
Entrée	Appetizer/Starter
Garniture au choix	Choice of vegetable side
Selon arrivage	When available
Supplément/En sus	Extra charge
Sur commande	Made to order

Appetizers/Starters

French	English
Anchois	Anchovies
Andouille(tte)	Chitterling sausage
Assiette de charcuterie	Assorted pork products
Crudités	Mixed raw vegetable salad
Escargots	Snails
Jambon	Ham
Jambonneau	Cured pig's knuckle
Pâté	Liver puree blended with meat
Quenelles	Light dumplings
Saucisson	Dried sausage
Terrine	Pâté in an earthenware pot

Soups

French	English
Bisque	Shellfish soup
Bouillabaisse	Fish and seafood stew
Julienne	Vegetable soup
Potage/Soupe	Soup
Potage parmentier	Thick potato soup
Pot-au-feu	Stew of meat and vegetables
Soupe du jour	Soup of the day
Soupe à l'oignon gratinée	French onion soup
Soupe au pistou	Provençal vegetable soup
Velouté de . . .	Cream of . . .
Vichyssoise	Cold leek and potato cream soup

Fish and Seafood

French	English
Bar	Bass
Bourride	Fish stew from Marseilles
Brandade de morue	Creamed salt cod
Brochet	Pike
Cabillaud/Morue	Fresh cod
Calmar	Squid
Coquilles St-Jacques	Scallops

Crabe	Crab
Crevettes	Shrimp
Daurade	Sea bream
Écrevisses	Prawns/crayfish
Harengs	Herring
Homard	Lobster
Huîtres	Oysters
Langouste	Spiny lobster
Langoustine	Prawn/lobster
Lotte	Monkfish
Moules	Mussels
Palourdes	Clams
Rouget	Red mullet
Saumon	Salmon
Thon	Tuna
Truite	Trout

Meat

Agneau	Lamb
Ballotine	Boned, stuffed, and rolled
Blanquette de veau	Veal stew with a white-sauce base
Boeuf	Beef
Boeuf à la Bourguignonne	Beef stew
Boudin blanc	Sausage made with white meat
Boudin noir	Sausage made with pig's blood
Boulettes de viande	Meatballs
Brochette	Kabob
Cassoulet	Casserole of white beans, meat
Cervelle	Brains
Châteaubriand	Double fillet steak
Côtelettes	Chops
Choucroute garnie	Sausages and cured pork served with sauerkraut
Côte de boeuf	T-bone steak
Côte	Rib
Cuisses de grenouilles	Frogs' legs
Entrecôte	Rib or rib-eye steak
Épaule	Shoulder
Escalope	Cutlet
Foie	Liver
Gigot	Leg
Langue	Tongue
Médaillon	Tenderloin steak
Pavé	Thick slice of boned beef
Pieds de cochon	Pig's feet
Porc	Pork

Ragoût	Stew
Ris de veau	Veal sweetbreads
Rognons	Kidneys
Saucisses	Sausages
Selle	Saddle
Tournedos	Tenderloin of T-bone steak
Veau	Veal
Viande	Meat

Methods of Preparation

À point	Medium
À l'étouffée	Stewed
Au four	Baked
Bien cuit	Well-done
Bleu	Very rare
Bouilli	Boiled
Braisé	Braised
Frit	Fried
Grillé	Grilled
Rôti	Roast
Saignant	Rare
Sauté/poêlée	Sautéed

Game and Poultry

Blanc de volaille	Chicken breast
Caille	Quail
Canard/Caneton	Duck/duckling
Cerf/Chevreuil	Venison
Coq au vin	Chicken stewed in red wine
Dinde/Dindonneau	Turkey/Young turkey
Faisan	Pheasant
Lapin	Rabbit
Lièvre	Wild hare
Oie	Goose
Pigeon/Pigeonneau	Pigeon/Squab
Pintade/Pintadeau	Guinea fowl/Young guinea fowl
Poularde	Fattened pullet
Poulet/Poussin	Chicken/Spring chicken
Sanglier/Marcassin	Wild boar/Young wild boar
Volaille	Fowl

Vegetables

Artichaut	Artichoke
Asperge	Asparagus
Aubergine	Eggplant

Carottes	Carrots
Champignons	Mushrooms
Chou-fleur	Cauliflower
Chou (rouge)	Cabbage (red)
Choux de Bruxelles	Brussels sprouts
Courgette	Zucchini
Cresson	Watercress
Épinard	Spinach
Haricots blancs/verts	White kidney/green beans
Laitue	Lettuce
Lentilles	Lentils
Maïs	Corn
Oignons	Onions
Petits pois	Peas
Poireaux	Leeks
Poivrons	Peppers
Pomme de terre	Potato
Pommes frites	French fries
Tomates	Tomatoes

Desserts

Coupe (glacée)	Sundae
Crêpe	Thin pancake
Crème brûlée	Custard with caramelized topping
Crème caramel	Caramel-coated custard
Crème Chantilly	Whipped cream
Gâteau au chocolat	Chocolate cake
Glace	Ice cream
Mousse au chocolat	Chocolate mousse
Sabayon	Egg-and-wine-based custard
Tarte aux pommes	Apple pie
Tarte tatin	Caramelized apple tart
Tourte	Layer cake

Alcoholic Drinks

À l'eau	With water
Avec des glaçons	On the rocks
Kir	Chilled white wine mixed with black-currant syrup
Bière	Beer
blonde/brune	*light/dark*
Calvados	Apple brandy from Normandy
Eau-de-vie	Brandy
Liqueur	Cordial
Poire William	Pear brandy
Porto	Port

Vin	Wine
sec	*dry/neat*
brut	*very dry*
léger	*light*
doux	*sweet*
rouge	*red*
rosé	*rosé*
mousseux	*sparkling*
blanc	*white*

Nonalcoholic Drinks

Café	Coffee
noir	*black*
crème	*with steamed milk/cream*
au lait	*with steamed milk*
décaféiné	*caffeine-free*
Express	Espresso
Chocolat chaud	Hot chocolate
Eau minérale	Mineral water
gazeuse/non gazeuse	*carbonated/still*
Jus de . . .	. . . juice
Lait	Milk
Limonade	Lemonade
Thé	Tea
au lait/au citron	*with milk/lemon*
glacé	*Iced tea*
Tisane	Herb tea

INDEX

FODOR'S KEY TO THE GUIDES

America's guidebook leader publishes guides for every kind of traveler. Check out our many series and find your perfect match.

FODOR'S GOLD GUIDES
America's favorite travel-guide series offers the most detailed insider reviews of hotels, restaurants, and attractions in all price ranges, plus great background information, smart tips, and useful maps.

COMPASS AMERICAN GUIDES
Stunning guides from top local writers and photographers, with gorgeous photos, literary excerpts, and colorful anecdotes. A must-have for culture mavens, history buffs, and new residents.

FODOR'S CITYPACKS
Concise city coverage in a guide plus a foldout map. The right choice for urban travelers who want everything under one cover.

FODOR'S EXPLORING GUIDES
Hundreds of color photos bring your destination to life. Lively stories lend insight into the culture, history, and people.

FODOR'S TRAVEL HISTORIC AMERICA
For travelers who want to experience history firsthand, this series gives in-depth coverage of historic sights, plus nearby restaurants and hotels. Themes include the Thirteen Colonies, the Old West, and the Lewis and Clark Trail.

FODOR'S POCKET GUIDES
For travelers who need only the essentials. The best of Fodor's in pocket-size packages for just $9.95.

FODOR'S FLASHMAPS
Every resident's map guide, with dozens of easy-to-follow maps of public transit, restaurants, shopping, museums, and more.

FODOR'S CITYGUIDES
Sourcebooks for living in the city: thousands of in-the-know listings for restaurants, shops, sports, nightlife, and other city resources.

FODOR'S AROUND THE CITY WITH KIDS
Up to 68 great ideas for family days, recommended by resident parents. Perfect for exploring in your own backyard or on the road.

FODOR'S HOW TO GUIDES
Get tips from the pros on planning the perfect trip. Learn how to pack, fly hassle-free, plan a honeymoon or cruise, stay healthy on the road, and travel with your baby.

FODOR'S LANGUAGES FOR TRAVELERS
Practice the local language before you hit the road. Available in phrase books, cassette sets, and CD sets.

KAREN BROWN'S GUIDES
Engaging guides—many with easy-to-follow inn-to-inn itineraries—to the most charming inns and B&Bs in the U.S.A. and Europe.

BAEDEKER'S GUIDES
Comprehensive guides, trusted since 1829, packed with A–Z reviews and star ratings.

OTHER GREAT TITLES FROM FODOR'S
Baseball Vacations, The Complete Guide to the National Parks, Family Vacations, Golf Digest's Places to Play, Great American Drives of the East, Great American Drives of the West, Great American Vacations, Healthy Escapes, National Parks of the West, Skiing USA.

Linux IP Stacks
Commentary

Stephen T. Satchell
H.B.J. Clifford

President, CEO

Keith Weiskamp

Publisher

Steve Sayre

Acquisitions Editor

Stephanie Wall

Marketing Specialist

Diane Enger

Project Editor

Michelle Stroup

Technical Reviewer

Ivan McDonagh

Production Coordinator

Laura Wellander

Cover Designer

Jody Winkler

Layout Designer

April Nielsen

CD-ROM Developer

Robert Clarfield

The Coriolis Group, LLC
14455 N. Hayden Road, Suite 220
Scottsdale, Arizona 85260

480/483-0192
FAX 480/483-0193
http://www.coriolis.com

Library of Congress Cataloging-in-Publication Data
Satchell, Stephen T.
    Linux IP stacks commentary/by Stephen T. Satchell and H.B.J. Clifford
       p.   cm.
    Includes index.
    ISBN 1-57610-470-2
    1. Linux.   2. Operating systems (Computers)   3. Computer
networks. I. Title. II. Clifford, H.B.J.

QA76.76.O63 S3562   2000
005.4'4769–dc21

                                                           99-045280
                                                              CIP

Printed in the United States of America
10 9 8 7 6 5 4 3 2 1

14455 North Hayden Road • Suite 220 • Scottsdale, Arizona 85260

Dear Reader:

The CoriolisOpen™ Press was founded to create a very elite group of books: the ones you keep closest to your machine. Sure, everyone would like to have the Library of Congress at arm's reach, but in the real world, you have to choose the books you rely on every day *very* carefully.

To win a place for our books on that coveted shelf beside your PC, we guarantee several important qualities in every book we publish. These qualities are:

- *Technical accuracy*—It's no good if it doesn't work. Every CoriolisOpen™ Press book is reviewed by technical experts in the topic field, and is sent through several editing and proofreading passes in order to create the piece of work you now hold in your hands.

- *Innovative editorial design*—We've put years of research and refinement into the ways we present information in our books. Our books' editorial approach is uniquely designed to reflect the way people learn new technologies and search for solutions to technology problems.

- *Practical focus*—We put only pertinent information into our books and avoid any fluff. Every fact included between these two covers must serve the mission of the book as a whole.

- *Accessibility*—The information in a book is worthless unless you can find it quickly when you need it. We put a lot of effort into our indexes, and heavily cross-reference our chapters, to make it easy for you to move right to the information you need.

Here at The Coriolis Group we have been publishing and packaging books, technical journals, and training materials since 1989. We're programmers and authors ourselves, and we take an ongoing active role in defining what we publish and how we publish it. We have put a lot of thought into our books; please write to us at **ctp@coriolis.com** and let us know what you think. We hope that you're happy with the book in your hands, and that in the future, when you reach for software development and networking information, you'll turn to one of our books first.

Keith Weiskamp
President and CEO

Jeff Duntemann
VP and Editorial Director

Look For These Other Related Books From The Coriolis Group

Linux Core Kernel Commentary

Linux Install And Configuration Little Black Book

Linux Programming White Papers

Linux System Administration White Papers

Setting Up A Linux Intranet Server Visual Black Book

Also From CoriolisOpen™ Press

Apache Server For Windows Little Black Book

Apache Server Commentary

GIMP: The Official Handbook

Open Source Development With CVS

Perl Black Book

Perl Core Language Little Black Book

Samba Black Book

Dedicated to the memory of Jonathan B. Postel (1943–1998)

"Be conservative in what you do, be liberal in what you accept from others."

— Jon Postel, in numerous documents, letters, speeches,
arguments, and ad-hoc discussions…

*"Someone had to keep track of all the protocols, the identifiers, networks and addresses
and ultimately the names of all the things in the networked universe."*

—Vint Cerf French

*Jon Postel was the first keeper of the Requests for Comments (RFCs) for the ARPAnet
project and its successors. Working from UCLA, Mitre, and finally from his office at
the University of Southern California Information Sciences Institute (USC/ISI), he kept
the RFCs going for 27 years.*

*Much more than simply an editor or archivist, Jon was one of the primary movers,
shakers, and "Do it right, people"—sayers in networking.*

*RFC 2555 (included on the CD-ROM that accompanies this book) contains much more
information about this pivotal figure, his work, and his influence on today's Internet.*

and W. Richard Stevens (1951–1999)

"The gentleman who illustrated TCP/IP"

— Yahoo

*A reader of the original Lions' Commentary on Unix, Stevens wrote the textbooks that are
currently used as bibles by many students and practitioners of networking…including,
not least of all, Linux kernel developers. The Linux source code is liberally peppered
with comments acknowledging Stevens' suggestions about how the code might best
be implemented.*

*The Linux community owes a major debt to this man, whose books contain more "stories
around the campfire," and tell them better, than any other printed source.*

About The Authors

Since his early days on the ARPAnet project in 1972, **Stephen T. Satchell** has worked with an eclectic variety of information systems and applications. A nationally recognized expert in communications systems testing and analysis, he is currently developing commercial networking products that run under Linux.

As well as contributing over 400 articles to magazines (many of them with most-favored co-author H.B.J. Clifford), Stephen Satchell has contributed to a number of books. He is also one of the founding members of the Internet Press Guild (**www.netpress.org**), a group organized by journalists, pundits, and writers to improve the quality of reporting about the Internet in well-known weekly newsmagazines. Thanks to the efforts of the IPG, reporters around the world now have access to accurate information, and the mailing list serves as Rumor Control.

Stephen Satchell has contributed to a number of industry standards, including the first ANSI C programming language standard and the definitive standards for testing analog modems. He continues to be active in setting the standard for performance testing. He is active in local civic affairs (both online and off), contributing his expertise in theatrical sound recording, on the theory that whereas computing problems admit of only one right answer, in audio engineering there are no wrong answers.

Writer, editor, and translator **H.B.J. Clifford** has been active in computer journalism since the mid-1980s. Her work in that field includes stints as a beta-tester and longtime conference moderator on the pioneering Byte Information eXchange (BIX) teleconferencing system, technical editor at *VLSI Design*, associate reviews editor at *InfoWorld*, contributing editor to *Personal Workstation* magazine, and editor-in-chief of the *Hewlett-Packard PC Users' Quarterly*.

Although trained as a historian and musician, her (to say the least) eclectic background also includes a summer spent on a locked floor of Bellevue Hospital in New York, not as an inmate but as a resident redactor of the papers documenting an NYU School of Medicine research project on the computer simulation of visual signal processing in primates. Monkey see, 'puter too.

In addition to her frequent collaborations with Stephen Satchell, H.B.J. Clifford has written and/or translated books on database programming, the MIDI interface, and the Biblical Book of Revelation. Her English translation of an original Brazilian screenplay won critical acclaim at the 1999 Sundance Film Festival. She is also the uncredited co-author of two successful science-fiction adventure novels. In her copious free time she enjoys opera, rock-climbing, and teaching safe seamanship at a sailing club on San Francisco Bay.

Acknowledgments

No, this page isn't a dissertation on TCP packets that have the ACK bit set, although it serves somewhat the same purpose. This is where we thank all the people who made this book possible—some of whom didn't even know they were doing so. Any merit the book may have is due in very large part to their efforts.

Inseparable in our minds are our copy editor, Bill McManus, and our technical reviewer, Ivan McDonagh. Together they smoothed out our rough edges with admirable restraint, casting painstaking professional eyes over our manuscript while simultaneously holding their own (and more) in marginal-note repartee. They did exceptionally fine work, undeterred by threats of incipiently incontinent parrots and rampaging Hassocks.

Production coordinator Laura Wellander shepherded the book through the behind-the-scenes phases, from e-manuscript through typesetting, making those parts of the project completely transparent to us.

We extend grateful bows to Jody Winkler, for her elegantly understated cover design; April Nielsen, for her thoughtful and accessible book layout; and Robert Clarfield, for his attentive preparation of the accompanying CD-ROM.

Michelle Stroup was a marvelously patient project editor, tirelessly and with infinite good humor weaving the strands of the project into a coherent whole.

Acquisitions editor and general honcho Stephanie Wall kept a firm hand on the tiller, holding our little craft on course and bringing it to safe harbor after a long and sometimes arduous cruise.

Outside the immediate circle of the Coriolis Group, W. Richard Stevens made a major contribution through his wonderful book *TCP/IP Illustrated*, which helped us sort out some of the more abstruse and/or esoteric Standard-isms in the RFCs.

Amazon.com's overnight delivery of a cartful of network-routing references helped made Chapter 6 merely difficult, rather than next-to-impossible.

Two *very* deep bows go to Ellen and George Toto of the Wildflower Café in Incline Village, Nevada, for their generous contributions of meals when the writing sessions ran long, and much-appreciated "discussion space" when reserves of patience or co-auctorial regard ran short.

We can't leave this page without a heartfelt ACK to the Gang of Fur Times Two—Lady Boss Frank, AlexSasha, Bootsie, Sylvy Samantha, C.J., Ada Augusta, Cassidy the Mouser, and Miss Winnie—for the balance and perspective they bring to our lives. God bless you, little guys.

Table Of Contents

PART II   TCP/IP Stack Commentary

Chapter 1
Overview Of The TCP/IP Stack Commentary 453

Chapter 2
Background And Basic Concepts 455

Chapter 3
Linux And The ISO Model 461

Chapter 4
ICMP 469

Chapter 5
Sockets API Overview 477

Chapter 10
IP Firewall Support 571

Introduction

Linux IP Stacks Commentary offers programmers, network administrators, and students a series of in-depth analytical comments on a working implementation of the Transmission Control Protocol (TCP) and Internet Protocol (IP) suite whose source code (Linux Kernel release 2.0.34) is widely available. The authors' discussions of the functions and system calls contained in this kernel release are based on a detailed study of the TCP/IP kernel-resident code and of the implemented client and server programs that use the kernel-resident code.

Like others in the Coriolis Commentary series, this book was inspired by the vastly popular *Commentary on Unix*, written by John Lions in 1977. That archetypal document—whose original line-printed edition was the subject of now-legendary midnight sessions at the photocopier by successive classes of computer science undergraduates (and grad students as well)—provided what at the time was a unique elucidation of the inner workings of an early version (version 6) of AT&T's Unix operating system, as provided by that company to many universities in the United States.

Thus, in the spirit of Lions, the present authors hope that their study of the inner workings of TCP/IP will give readers insight into how to test the performance, reliability, and realtime responses of TCP/IP-based systems in general, and of Ethernet and TCP/IP-based modem telecommunications systems in particular.

Why, you may ask, does this book center around Linux Kernel release 2.0.34 rather than a later version? The answer goes back to mid-1999, when this project began. In order for the commentary to be as useful as possible to the largest number of readers, the authors and publisher agreed that it should address a popular and widely used version of the Linux operating system. Online research turned up a study (conducted by a group of crackers, and therefore more than averagely credible) based on a large-scale port scan of the Internet, which concluded that Linux release 2.0.34—greatly favored by both Internet Service Providers (ISPs) and end users—filled this bill.

At the end of 1999, as the writing for this edition of the book was being completed, the previously mentioned study hadn't been supplanted by more recent data. In fact, information gleaned from online newsgroups indicates that network administrators are still using "older" versions of Linux (such as release 2.0.34 or 2.0.35) and plan to stay with them until the need to upgrade becomes imperative. However, new server installations are being installed with current distributions, which means that systems using Kernel release 2.2.5 and its successors are starting to become more popular. The online extension of this book will monitor the progress of these releases (as described in the section entitled as "The Book Stops Here. . .Not," later in this introduction).

Portions of this book have been submitted, in the form of contributions (not unlike the Internet Requests for Comments), for consideration in connection with the development of various Standards for modem and network testing. These Standards are currently being developed by the technical subcommittees of the Telecommunications Industry Association (TIA) and the International Telecommunications Union (ITU).

What This Book Does

To fulfill its mission statement and be as useful as possible to its readers, this book:

- Provides a printed listing, with index numbers, of the Linux TCP/IP source code

- Introduces each protocol and its use, through a general overview and discussion

- Explores the implementation details for each protocol, through a close examination of the source code, with (where possible) expansions and (in some cases) corrections of the comments that appear in the source code

- Concentrates on how each function works within the context of the TCP/IP implementation, explaining not only how each protocol module works with the rest of the TCP/IP stack, the drivers, and the applications, but also why the modules were designed that way

- Correlates the contents of the source code with the Requests for Comments (RFCs) that define TCP/IP, and also with the requirements that must be met by host systems that are connected to the Internet

- Points out areas where certain functionalities can be improved, expanded, or added (especially areas that would benefit from an infusion of custom functionality)

Customization of the TCP/IP implementation is one of the strongest points of Linux, and the whole point of the "Open Source" programming philosophy. Unlike other operating systems (including other "free" operating systems, such as the BSD OS), Linux throws open to *everyone* the process of making changes to the kernel code. Even if a change that you want to make has a very narrow focus, you can still implement it. And if you think a change that you're contemplating may be generally useful, you can submit it (in the form of a kernel patch) for consideration to the Linux Kernel mailing list. More details about the process, along with information about obtaining the latest source code against which patches should be developed, are available at **http://www.linuxhq.com/** (the valid address when this book went to press).

Whom This Book Is For

As implied earlier in this introduction, this book is intended for students of TCP/IP who need complete working examples, experienced Linux enthusiasts who are curious about the inner workings of the kernel code, and network security administrators who need detailed information about TCP/IP in easy-to-grasp form.

Accordingly, this book assumes a few prerequisites:

- You have a working knowledge of the C programming language

- You are familiar with pointer-based data structures (and particularly with single- and double-link lists)

- You have some familiarity with the way integer values are represented within computer systems

- You really, truly want to understand how a fast, robust, attack-resistant networking OS implementation works

Although not a prerequisite, strictly speaking, the authors strongly and sincerely urge readers of this book to review its companion volume, *Linux Core Kernel Commentary*, by Scott Maxwell (The Coriolis Group, 1999; ISBN 1-57610-469-9), not only for its invaluable analysis of the kernel architecture but also for its essential background on Linux and valuable information about the Linux development process.

Contents: A Thumbnail Guide

Part I of this book reproduces a selected subset of the Linux kernel source code. The format is easy to read and the contents are cross referenced. Any line of code that is mentioned in the commentary section of the book is designated by a small graphic arrow that contains the page number on which the corresponding commentary appears.

The source code is followed by Part II (the commentary section), which contains the detailed discussions of the code. Each of the 10 chapters in this section addresses a specific protocol (including ICMP, TCP, and UDP) or topic (such as the application programming interface or the mapping of Linux TCP/IP into the standard ISO networking model). Extensive line references in the commentary point you back, by number, to the corresponding line in the source code, so that the source and the commentary can be approached from either direction.

Although the authors wouldn't object if you decided to read the entire commentary from cover to cover, you might find it more useful to head straight for the topics you're most interested in. We won't be offended. In fact, we wrote the code-commentary chapters, which are largely self-contained, with this approach in mind.

Appendix A, which appears in all Coriolis Open Press books, is the GNU license.

Appendix B contains a selection of the abbreviations and acronyms you're most likely to encounter as you explore the TCP/IP universe.

Appendix C discusses the Domain Name System and the *resolver*—the set of library routines that are used by networking applications when domain names (such as **www.coriolis.com**) need to be converted automatically to Internet addresses (such as 209.140.152.4). The DNS is a wonderful, and wonderfully useful, example of how the User Datagram Protocol (UDP) operates on the modern Internet.

Finally, the book is indexed. The authors and the publisher (not to mention serious readers) wouldn't have it any other way.

If you want to delve even more deeply into primary sources and first principles, the CD-ROM provided in the back of the book is for you. It contains the full text of the Linux Kernel release 2.0.34 source code, all the RFCs that were available at press time, and the scripts that were used to create the indexes for the source-code segments that appear in Part II of the book.

You may find the contents of the CD-ROM especially useful if you plan to investigate how file system support operates in the networking world (including, in particular, how the **select** and **poll** system calls interact with the networking implementation), or learn how other ports of Linux support computer systems that aren't built around Intel microprocessors.

The Book Stops Here . . . Not

The authors welcome your feedback. Please email your suggestions, questions, brickbats or bouquets to **satch@fluent-access.com** or to **hbjc@fluent-access.com**. A selection of your correspondence will be posted at **http://www.fluent-access.com/tcp-ip**, along with errata and supplemental information.

As we went to press, a quick look at the TCP/IP implementation for Kernel release 2.3.33 revealed that the networking code has metamorphosed extensively from the version (2.0.34) analyzed in this book. To keep up with the changes, the authors will be posting updated commentaries on the later releases. We invite you to visit the Web site for more details and to read the updated commentary as it becomes available.

A Final Word Or Three

One trademark of Satchell/Clifford collaborations is the phrase "full-tilt boogie," which appears at least once in each of their major articles and books. The first reader who accurately identifies every instance of the phrase in this book will receive a public acknowledgment on the book's Web site and a hand-embroidered, gilt-edged Certificate of Merit, suitable for framing or lining parrot cages.

Part I

Linux IP Stacks Code

usr/src/lib/resolv/herror.c

```
1    /*
2     * Copyright (c) 1987, 1993
3     *    The Regents of the University of California.  All
4    rights reserved.
5     *
6     * Redistribution and use in source and binary forms,
7    with or without
8     * modification, are permitted provided that the
9    following conditions
10    * are met:
11    * 1. Redistributions of source code must retain the
12   above copyright
13    *    notice, this list of conditions and the following
14   disclaimer.
15    * 2. Redistributions in binary form must reproduce the
16   above copyright
17    *    notice, this list of conditions and the following
18   disclaimer in the
19    *    documentation and/or other materials provided with
20   the distribution.
21    * 3. All advertising materials mentioning features or
22   use of this software
23    *    must display the following acknowledgement:
24    *  This product includes software developed by the
25   University of
26    *  California, Berkeley and its contributors.
27    * 4. Neither the name of the University nor the names
28   of its contributors
29    *    may be used to endorse or promote products derived
30   from this software
31    *    without specific prior written permission.
32    *
33    * THIS SOFTWARE IS PROVIDED BY THE REGENTS AND
34   CONTRIBUTORS "AS IS" AND
35    * ANY EXPRESS OR IMPLIED WARRANTIES, INCLUDING, BUT NOT
36   LIMITED TO, THE
37    * IMPLIED WARRANTIES OF MERCHANTABILITY AND FITNESS FOR
38   A PARTICULAR PURPOSE
39    * ARE DISCLAIMED.  IN NO EVENT SHALL THE REGENTS OR
40   CONTRIBUTORS BE LIABLE
41    * FOR ANY DIRECT, INDIRECT, INCIDENTAL, SPECIAL,
42   EXEMPLARY, OR CONSEQUENTIAL
43    * DAMAGES (INCLUDING, BUT NOT LIMITED TO, PROCUREMENT
44   OF SUBSTITUTE GOODS
45    * OR SERVICES; LOSS OF USE, DATA, OR PROFITS; OR
46   BUSINESS INTERRUPTION)
47    * HOWEVER CAUSED AND ON ANY THEORY OF LIABILITY,
48   WHETHER IN CONTRACT, STRICT
49    * LIABILITY, OR TORT (INCLUDING NEGLIGENCE OR
50   OTHERWISE) ARISING IN ANY WAY
51    * OUT OF THE USE OF THIS SOFTWARE, EVEN IF ADVISED OF
52   THE POSSIBILITY OF
53    * SUCH DAMAGE.
54    */
55
56    /*
57     * Portions Copyright (c) 1996 by Internet Software
58   Consortium.
59     *
60     * Permission to use, copy, modify, and distribute this
61   software for any
62     * purpose with or without fee is hereby granted,
63   provided that the above
64     * copyright notice and this permission notice appear in
65   all copies.
66     *
67     * THE SOFTWARE IS PROVIDED "AS IS" AND INTERNET
68   SOFTWARE CONSORTIUM DISCLAIMS
69     * ALL WARRANTIES WITH REGARD TO THIS SOFTWARE INCLUDING
70   ALL IMPLIED WARRANTIES
71     * OF MERCHANTABILITY AND FITNESS. IN NO EVENT SHALL
72   INTERNET SOFTWARE
73     * CONSORTIUM BE LIABLE FOR ANY SPECIAL, DIRECT,
74   INDIRECT, OR CONSEQUENTIAL
75     * DAMAGES OR ANY DAMAGES WHATSOEVER RESULTING FROM LOSS
76   OF USE, DATA OR
77     * PROFITS, WHETHER IN AN ACTION OF CONTRACT, NEGLIGENCE
78   OR OTHER TORTIOUS
79     * ACTION, ARISING OUT OF OR IN CONNECTION WITH THE USE
80   OR PERFORMANCE OF THIS
81     * SOFTWARE.
82     */
83
84   #if defined(LIBC_SCCS) && !defined(lint)
85   static char sccsid[] = "@(#)herror.c    8.1 (Berkeley)
86   6/4/93";
87   static char rcsid[] = "$Id: herror.c,v 8.7 1996/11/18
88   09:10:00 vixie Exp $";
89   #endif /* LIBC_SCCS and not lint */
90
91   #include "port_before.h"
92   #include <sys/types.h>
93   #include <sys/param.h>
94   #include <sys/uio.h>
95   #include <netdb.h>
```

```
 96      #include <string.h>
 97      #include <unistd.h>
 98      #include "port_after.h"
 99
100      const char *h_errlist[] = {
101          "Resolver Error 0 (no error)",
102          "Unknown host",             /* 1 HOST_NOT_FOUND */
103          "Host name lookup failure",    /* 2 TRY_AGAIN */
104          "Unknown server error",       /* 3 NO_RECOVERY */
105          "No address associated with name",  /* 4 NO_ADDRESS
106      */
107      };
108      int h_nerr = { sizeof h_errlist / sizeof h_errlist[0] };
109
110      int h_errno;
111
112      /*
113       * herror --
114       *  print the error indicated by the h_errno value.
115       */
116      void
117      herror(s)
118          const char *s;
119      {
120          struct iovec iov[4];
121          register struct iovec *v = iov;
122
123          if (s && *s) {
124              v->iov_base = (char *)s;
125              v->iov_len = strlen(s);
126              v++;
127              v->iov_base = ": ";
128              v->iov_len = 2;
129              v++;
130          }
131          v->iov_base = (char *)hstrerror(h_errno);
132          v->iov_len = strlen(v->iov_base);
133          v++;
134          v->iov_base = "\n";
135          v->iov_len = 1;
136          writev(STDERR_FILENO, iov, (v - iov) + 1);
137      }
138
139      const char *
140      hstrerror(err)
141          int err;
142      {
143          if (err < 0)
```

```
144              return ("Resolver internal error");
145          else if (err < h_nerr)
146              return (h_errlist[err]);
147          return ("Unknown resolver error");
148      }
```

usr/src/lib/resolv/res_comp.c

```
149      /*
150       * Copyright (c) 1985, 1993
151       *   The Regents of the University of California.  All
152       rights reserved.
153       *
154       * Redistribution and use in source and binary forms,
155       with or without
156       * modification, are permitted provided that the
157       following conditions
158       * are met:
159       * 1. Redistributions of source code must retain the
160       above copyright
161       *   notice, this list of conditions and the following
162       disclaimer.
163       * 2. Redistributions in binary form must reproduce the
164       above copyright
165       *   notice, this list of conditions and the following
166       disclaimer in the
167       *   documentation and/or other materials provided with
168       the distribution.
169       * 3. All advertising materials mentioning features or
170       use of this software
171       *   must display the following acknowledgement:
172       * This product includes software developed by the
173       University of
174       * California, Berkeley and its contributors.
175       * 4. Neither the name of the University nor the names
176       of its contributors
177       *   may be used to endorse or promote products derived
178       from this software
179       *   without specific prior written permission.
180       *
181       * THIS SOFTWARE IS PROVIDED BY THE REGENTS AND
182       CONTRIBUTORS "AS IS" AND
183       * ANY EXPRESS OR IMPLIED WARRANTIES, INCLUDING, BUT NOT
184       LIMITED TO, THE
185       * IMPLIED WARRANTIES OF MERCHANTABILITY AND FITNESS FOR
186       A PARTICULAR PURPOSE
187       * ARE DISCLAIMED.  IN NO EVENT SHALL THE REGENTS OR
188       CONTRIBUTORS BE LIABLE
189       * FOR ANY DIRECT, INDIRECT, INCIDENTAL, SPECIAL,
```

```
264
265    #if defined(LIBC_SCCS) && !defined(lint)
266    static char sccsid[] = "@(#)res_comp.c  8.1 (Berkeley)
267    6/4/93";
268    static char rcsid[] = "$Id: res_comp.c,v 8.11 1997/05/21
269    19:31:04 halley Exp $";
270    #endif /* LIBC_SCCS and not lint */
271
272    #include "port_before.h"
273    #include <sys/types.h>
274    #include <sys/param.h>
275    #include <netinet/in.h>
276    #include <arpa/nameser.h>
277    #include <ctype.h>
278    #include <resolv.h>
279    #include <stdio.h>
280    #include <string.h>
281    #include <unistd.h>
282    #include "port_after.h"
283
284    /*
```

```
285      * Expand compressed domain name 'comp_dn' to full
286     domain name.
287      * 'msg' is a pointer to the begining of the message,
288      * 'eomorig' points to the first location after the
289     message,
290      * 'exp_dn' is a pointer to a buffer of size 'length'
291     for the result.
292      * Return size of compressed name or -1 if there was an
293     error.
294      */
295     int
296     dn_expand(const u_char *msg, const u_char *eom, const
297     u_char *src,
298             char *dst, int dstsiz)
299     {
300         int n = ns_name_uncompress(msg, eom, src, dst,
301     (size_t)dstsiz);
302
303         if (n > 0 && dst[0] == '.')
304             dst[0] = '\0';
305         return (n);
306     }
307
308     /*
309      * Pack domain name 'exp_dn' in presentation form into
310     'comp_dn'.
311      * Return the size of the compressed name or -1.
312      * 'length' is the size of the array pointed to by
313     'comp_dn'.
314      */
315     int
316     dn_comp(const char *src, u_char *dst, int dstsiz,
317             u_char **dnptrs, u_char **lastdnptr)
318     {
319         return (ns_name_compress(src, dst, (size_t)dstsiz,
320                     (const u_char **)dnptrs,
321                     (const u_char **)lastdnptr));
322     }
323
324     /*
325      * Skip over a compressed domain name. Return the size
326     or -1.
327      */
328     int
329     dn_skipname(const u_char *ptr, const u_char *eom) {
330         const u_char *saveptr = ptr;
331
332         if (ns_name_skip(&ptr, eom) == -1)
```

```
333             return (-1);
334         return (ptr - saveptr);
335     }
336
337     /*
338      * Verify that a domain name uses an acceptable
339     character set.
340      */
341
342     /*
343      * Note the conspicuous absence of ctype macros in these
344     definitions.  On
345      * non-ASCII hosts, we can't depend on string literals
346     or ctype macros to
347      * tell us anything about network-format data.  The rest
348     of the BIND system
349      * is not careful about this, but for some reason, we're
350     doing it right here.
351      */
352     #define PERIOD 0x2e
353     #define hyphenchar(c) ((c) == 0x2d)
354     #define bslashchar(c) ((c) == 0x5c)
355     #define periodchar(c) ((c) == PERIOD)
356     #define asterchar(c) ((c) == 0x2a)
357     #define alphachar(c) (((c) >= 0x41 && (c) <= 0x5a) \
358             || ((c) >= 0x61 && (c) <= 0x7a))
359     #define digitchar(c) ((c) >= 0x30 && (c) <= 0x39)
360
361     #define borderchar(c) (alphachar(c) || digitchar(c))
362     #define middlechar(c) (borderchar(c) || hyphenchar(c))
363     #define domainchar(c) ((c) > 0x20 && (c) < 0x7f)
364
365     int
366     res_hnok(const char *dn) {
367         int ppch = '\0', pch = PERIOD, ch = *dn++;
368
369         while (ch != '\0') {
370             int nch = *dn++;
371
372             if (periodchar(ch)) {
373                 (void)NULL;
374             } else if (periodchar(pch)) {
375                 if (!borderchar(ch))
376                     return (0);
377             } else if (periodchar(nch) || nch == '\0') {
378                 if (!borderchar(ch))
379                     return (0);
380             } else {
```

```
381          if (!middlechar(ch))
382              return (0);
383          }
384          ppch = pch, pch = ch, ch = nch;
385       }
386       return (1);
387  }
388
389  /*
390   * hostname-like (A, MX, WKS) owners can have "*" as
391  their first label
392   * but must otherwise be as a host name.
393   */
394  int
395  res_ownok(const char *dn) {
396       if (asterchar(dn[0])) {
397          if (periodchar(dn[1]))
398              return (res_hnok(dn+2));
399          if (dn[1] == '\0')
400              return (1);
401       }
402       return (res_hnok(dn));
403  }
404
405  /*
406   * SOA RNAMEs and RP RNAMEs can have any printable
407  character in their first
408   * label, but the rest of the name has to look like a
409  host name.
410   */
411  int
412  res_mailok(const char *dn) {
413       int ch, escaped = 0;
414
415       /* "." is a valid missing representation */
416       if (*dn == '\0')
417          return (1);
418
419       /* otherwise <label>.<hostname> */
420       while ((ch = *dn++) != '\0') {
421          if (!domainchar(ch))
422              return (0);
423          if (!escaped && periodchar(ch))
424              break;
425          if (escaped)
426              escaped = 0;
427          else if (bslashchar(ch))
428              escaped = 1;
```

```
429          }
430       if (periodchar(ch))
431          return (res_hnok(dn));
432       return (0);
433  }
434
435  /*
436   * This function is quite liberal, since RFC 1034's
437  character sets are only
438   * recommendations.
439   */
440  int
441  res_dnok(const char *dn) {
442       int ch;
443
444       while ((ch = *dn++) != '\0')
445          if (!domainchar(ch))
446              return (0);
447       return (1);
448  }
449
450  #ifdef BIND_4_COMPAT
451  /*
452   * This module must export the following
453  externally-visible symbols:
454   *   ___putlong
455   *   ___putshort
456   *   __getlong
457   *   __getshort
458   * Note that one _ comes from C and the others come from
459  us.
460   */
461  void __putlong(u_int32_t src, u_char *dst) {
462  ns_put32(src, dst); }
463  void __putshort(u_int16_t src, u_char *dst) {
464  ns_put16(src, dst); }
465  u_int32_t _getlong(const u_char *src) { return
466  (ns_get32(src)); }
467  u_int16_t _getshort(const u_char *src) { return
468  (ns_get16(src)); }
469  #endif /*BIND_4_COMPAT*/
```

usr/src/lib/resolv/res_data.c

```
470  /*
471   * Copyright (c) 1995,1996 by Internet Software
472  Consortium.
473   *
474   * Permission to use, copy, modify, and distribute this
```

```
475    software for any
476     * purpose with or without fee is hereby granted,
477    provided that the above
478     * copyright notice and this permission notice appear in
479    all copies.
480     *
481     * THE SOFTWARE IS PROVIDED "AS IS" AND INTERNET
482    SOFTWARE CONSORTIUM DISCLAIMS
483     * ALL WARRANTIES WITH REGARD TO THIS SOFTWARE INCLUDING
484    ALL IMPLIED WARRANTIES
485     * OF MERCHANTABILITY AND FITNESS. IN NO EVENT SHALL
486    INTERNET SOFTWARE
487     * CONSORTIUM BE LIABLE FOR ANY SPECIAL, DIRECT,
488    INDIRECT, OR CONSEQUENTIAL
489     * DAMAGES OR ANY DAMAGES WHATSOEVER RESULTING FROM LOSS
490    OF USE, DATA OR
491     * PROFITS, WHETHER IN AN ACTION OF CONTRACT, NEGLIGENCE
492    OR OTHER TORTIOUS
493     * ACTION, ARISING OUT OF OR IN CONNECTION WITH THE USE
494    OR PERFORMANCE OF THIS
495     * SOFTWARE.
496     */
497
498    #if defined(LIBC_SCCS) && !defined(lint)
499    static char rcsid[] = "$Id: res_data.c,v 8.5 1996/11/18
500    09:10:02 vixie Exp $";
501    #endif /* LIBC_SCCS and not lint */
502
503    #include "port_before.h"
504    #include <sys/types.h>
505    #include <sys/param.h>
506    #include <sys/socket.h>
507    #include <sys/time.h>
508    #include <netinet/in.h>
509    #include <arpa/inet.h>
510    #include <arpa/nameser.h>
511    #include <ctype.h>
512    #include <resolv.h>
513    #include <stdio.h>
514    #include <stdlib.h>
515    #include <string.h>
516    #include <unistd.h>
517    #include "port_after.h"
518
519    const char *_res_opcodes[] = {
520        "QUERY",
521        "IQUERY",
522        "CQUERYM",
```

```
523        "CQUERYU",  /* experimental */
524        "NOTIFY",   /* experimental */
525        "UPDATE",
526        "6",
527        "7",
528        "8",
529        "9",
530        "10",
531        "11",
532        "12",
533        "13",
534        "ZONEINIT",
535        "ZONEREF",
536    };
537
538    const char *_res_resultcodes[] = {
539        "NOERROR",
540        "FORMERR",
541        "SERVFAIL",
542        "NXDOMAIN",
543        "NOTIMP",
544        "REFUSED",
545        "YXDOMAIN",
546        "YXRRSET",
547        "NXRRSET",
548        "NOTAUTH",
549        "ZONEERR",
550        "11",
551        "12",
552        "13",
553        "14",
554        "NOCHANGE",
555    };
556
557    #ifdef BIND_UPDATE
558    const char *_res_sectioncodes[] = {
559        "ZONE",
560        "PREREQUISITES",
561        "UPDATE",
562        "ADDITIONAL",
563    };
564    #endif
```

usr/src/lib/resolv/res_debug.c

```
565    /*
566     * Copyright (c) 1985
567     *    The Regents of the University of California.  All
568    rights reserved.
```

```
665    * not be used in connection with the marketing of any
666   product incorporating
667    * the Software or modifications thereof, without
668   specific, written prior
669    * permission.
670    *
671    * To the extent it has a right to do so, IBM grants an
672   immunity from suit
673    * under its patents, if any, for the use, sale or
674   manufacture of products to
675    * the extent that such products are used for performing
676   Domain Name System
677    * dynamic updates in TCP/IP networks by means of the
678   Software.  No immunity is
679    * granted for any product per se or for any other
680   function of any product.
681    *
682    * THE SOFTWARE IS PROVIDED "AS IS", AND IBM DISCLAIMS
683   ALL WARRANTIES,
684    * INCLUDING ALL IMPLIED WARRANTIES OF MERCHANTABILITY
685   AND FITNESS FOR A
686    * PARTICULAR PURPOSE.  IN NO EVENT SHALL IBM BE LIABLE
687   FOR ANY SPECIAL,
688    * DIRECT, INDIRECT, OR CONSEQUENTIAL DAMAGES OR ANY
689   DAMAGES WHATSOEVER ARISING
690    * OUT OF OR IN CONNECTION WITH THE USE OR PERFORMANCE
691   OF THIS SOFTWARE, EVEN
692    * IF IBM IS APPRISED OF THE POSSIBILITY OF SUCH DAMAGES.
693    */
694
695   /*
696    * Portions Copyright (c) 1996 by Internet Software
697   Consortium.
698    *
699    * Permission to use, copy, modify, and distribute this
700   software for any
701    * purpose with or without fee is hereby granted,
702   provided that the above
703    * copyright notice and this permission notice appear in
704   all copies.
705    *
706    * THE SOFTWARE IS PROVIDED "AS IS" AND INTERNET
707   SOFTWARE CONSORTIUM DISCLAIMS
708    * ALL WARRANTIES WITH REGARD TO THIS SOFTWARE INCLUDING
709   ALL IMPLIED WARRANTIES
710    * OF MERCHANTABILITY AND FITNESS. IN NO EVENT SHALL
711   INTERNET SOFTWARE
712    * CONSORTIUM BE LIABLE FOR ANY SPECIAL, DIRECT,
713   INDIRECT, OR CONSEQUENTIAL
714    * DAMAGES OR ANY DAMAGES WHATSOEVER RESULTING FROM LOSS
715   OF USE, DATA OR
716    * PROFITS, WHETHER IN AN ACTION OF CONTRACT, NEGLIGENCE
717   OR OTHER TORTIOUS
718    * ACTION, ARISING OUT OF OR IN CONNECTION WITH THE USE
719   OR PERFORMANCE OF THIS
720    * SOFTWARE.
721    */
722
723   #if defined(LIBC_SCCS) && !defined(lint)
724   static char sccsid[] = "@(#)res_debug.c 8.1 (Berkeley)
725   6/4/93";
726   static char rcsid[] = "$Id: res_debug.c,v 8.20
727   1998/02/13 01:11:34 halley Exp $";
728   #endif /* LIBC_SCCS and not lint */
729
730   #include "port_before.h"
731
732   #include <sys/types.h>
733   #include <sys/param.h>
734   #include <sys/socket.h>
735
736   #include <netinet/in.h>
737   #include <arpa/inet.h>
738   #include <arpa/nameser.h>
739
740   #include <ctype.h>
741   #include <errno.h>
742   #include <math.h>
743   #include <netdb.h>
744   #include <resolv.h>
745   #include <stdio.h>
746   #include <stdlib.h>
747   #include <string.h>
748   #include <time.h>
749
750   #include "port_after.h"
751
752   #ifdef SPRINTF_CHAR
753   # define SPRINTF(x) strlen(sprintf/**/x)
754   #else
755   # define SPRINTF(x) sprintf x
756   #endif
757
758   extern const char *_res_opcodes[];
759   extern const char *_res_resultcodes[];
760   extern const char *_res_sectioncodes[];
```

```
761
762      /*
763       * Print the current options.
764       */
765      void
766      fp_resstat(struct __res_state *statp, FILE *file) {
767          u_long mask;
768
769          fprintf(file, ";; res options:");
770          if (!statp)
771              statp = &_res;
772          for (mask = 1;  mask != 0;  mask <<= 1)
773              if (statp->options & mask)
774                  fprintf(file, " %s", p_option(mask));
775          putc('\n', file);
776      }
777
778      static void
779      do_section(ns_msg *handle, ns_sect section, int pflag,
780      FILE *file) {
781          int n, sflag, rrnum;
782          char buf[2048]; /* XXX need to malloc */
783          ns_opcode opcode;
784          ns_rr rr;
785
786          /*
787           * Print answer records.
788           */
789          sflag = (_res.pfcode & pflag);
790          if (_res.pfcode && !sflag)
791              return;
792
793          opcode = ns_msg_getflag(*handle, ns_f_opcode);
794          rrnum = 0;
795          for (;;) {
796              if (ns_parserr(handle, section, rrnum, &rr)) {
797                  if (errno != ENODEV)
798                      fprintf(file, ";; ns_parserr: %s\n",
799                          strerror(errno));
800                  else if (rrnum > 0 && sflag != 0 &&
801                      (_res.pfcode & RES_PRF_HEAD1))
802                      putc('\n', file);
803                  return;
804              }
805              if (rrnum == 0 && sflag != 0 && (_res.pfcode &
806      RES_PRF_HEAD1))
807                  fprintf(file, ";; %s SECTION:\n",
808                      p_section(section, opcode));
```

```
809              if (section == ns_s_qd)
810                  fprintf(file, ";;\t%s, type = %s, class =
811      %s\n",
812                      ns_rr_name(rr),
813                      p_type(ns_rr_type(rr)),
814                      p_class(ns_rr_class(rr)));
815              else {
816                  n = ns_sprintrr(handle, &rr, NULL, NULL,
817                          buf, sizeof buf);
818                  if (n < 0) {
819                      fprintf(file, ";; ns_sprintrr: %s\n",
820                          strerror(errno));
821                      return;
822                  }
823                  fputs(buf, file);
824                  fputc('\n', file);
825              }
826              rrnum++;
827          }
828      }
829
830      void
831      p_query(const u_char *msg) {
832          fp_query(msg, stdout);
833      }
834
835      void
836      fp_query(const u_char *msg, FILE *file) {
837          fp_nquery(msg, PACKETSZ, file);
838      }
839
840      /*
841       * Print the contents of a query.
842       * This is intended to be primarily a debugging routine.
843       */
844      void
845      fp_nquery(const u_char *msg, int len, FILE *file) {
846          ns_msg handle;
847          int n, qdcount, ancount, nscount, arcount;
848          u_int opcode, rcode, id;
849
850          if ((_res.options & RES_INIT) == 0 && res_init() ==
851      -1)
852              return;
853
854          if (ns_initparse(msg, len, &handle) < 0) {
855              fprintf(file, ";; ns_initparse: %s\n",
856      strerror(errno));
```

```
857            return;
858        }
859        opcode = ns_msg_getflag(handle, ns_f_opcode);
860        rcode = ns_msg_getflag(handle, ns_f_rcode);
861        id = ns_msg_id(handle);
862        qdcount = ns_msg_count(handle, ns_s_qd);
863        ancount = ns_msg_count(handle, ns_s_an);
864        nscount = ns_msg_count(handle, ns_s_ns);
865        arcount = ns_msg_count(handle, ns_s_ar);
866
867        /*
868         * Print header fields.
869         */
870        if ((!_res.pfcode) || (_res.pfcode & RES_PRF_HEADX)
871    || rcode)
872            fprintf(file,
873                ";; ->>HEADER<<- opcode: %s, status: %s, id:
874    %d\n",
875                _res_opcodes[opcode],
876    _res_resultcodes[rcode], id);
877        if ((!_res.pfcode) || (_res.pfcode & RES_PRF_HEADX))
878            putc(';', file);
879        if ((!_res.pfcode) || (_res.pfcode & RES_PRF_HEAD2))
880        {
881            fprintf(file, "; flags:");
882            if (ns_msg_getflag(handle, ns_f_qr))
883                fprintf(file, " qr");
884            if (ns_msg_getflag(handle, ns_f_aa))
885                fprintf(file, " aa");
886            if (ns_msg_getflag(handle, ns_f_tc))
887                fprintf(file, " tc");
888            if (ns_msg_getflag(handle, ns_f_rd))
889                fprintf(file, " rd");
890            if (ns_msg_getflag(handle, ns_f_ra))
891                fprintf(file, " ra");
892            if (ns_msg_getflag(handle, ns_f_z))
893                fprintf(file, " ??");
894            if (ns_msg_getflag(handle, ns_f_ad))
895                fprintf(file, " ad");
896            if (ns_msg_getflag(handle, ns_f_cd))
897                fprintf(file, " cd");
898        }
899        if ((!_res.pfcode) || (_res.pfcode & RES_PRF_HEAD1))
900        {
901            fprintf(file, "; %s: %d",
902                p_section(ns_s_qd, opcode), qdcount);
903            fprintf(file, ", %s: %d",
904                p_section(ns_s_an, opcode), ancount);
905            fprintf(file, ", %s: %d",
906                p_section(ns_s_ns, opcode), nscount);
907            fprintf(file, ", %s: %d",
908                p_section(ns_s_ar, opcode), arcount);
909        }
910        if ((!_res.pfcode) || (_res.pfcode &
911            (RES_PRF_HEADX | RES_PRF_HEAD2 |
912    RES_PRF_HEAD1))) {
913            putc('\n',file);
914        }
915        /*
916         * Print the various sections.
917         */
918        do_section(&handle, ns_s_qd, RES_PRF_QUES, file);
919        do_section(&handle, ns_s_an, RES_PRF_ANS, file);
920        do_section(&handle, ns_s_ns, RES_PRF_AUTH, file);
921        do_section(&handle, ns_s_ar, RES_PRF_ADD, file);
922        if (qdcount == 0 && ancount == 0 &&
923            nscount == 0 && arcount == 0)
924            putc('\n', file);
925    }
926
927    const u_char *
928    p_cdnname(const u_char *cp, const u_char *msg, int len,
929    FILE *file) {
930        char name[MAXDNAME];
931        int n;
932
933        if ((n = dn_expand(msg, msg + len, cp, name, sizeof
934    name)) < 0)
935            return (NULL);
936        if (name[0] == '\0')
937            putc('.', file);
938        else
939            fputs(name, file);
940        return (cp + n);
941    }
942
943    const u_char *
944    p_cdname(const u_char *cp, const u_char *msg, FILE
945    *file) {
946        return (p_cdnname(cp, msg, PACKETSZ, file));
947    }
948
949    /* Return a fully-qualified domain name from a
950    compressed name (with
951       length supplied).  */
952
```

```
953    const u_char *
954    p_fqnname(cp, msg, msglen, name, namelen)
955        const u_char *cp, *msg;
956        int msglen;
957        char *name;
958        int namelen;
959    {
960        int n, newlen;
961
962        if ((n = dn_expand(msg, cp + msglen, cp, name,
963    namelen)) < 0)
964            return (NULL);
965        newlen = strlen(name);
966        if (newlen == 0 || name[newlen - 1] != '.') {
967            if (newlen + 1 >= namelen)   /* Lack space for
968    final dot */
969                return (NULL);
970            else
971                strcpy(name + newlen, ".");
972        }
973        return (cp + n);
974    }
975
976    /* XXX: the rest of these functions need to become
977    length-limited, too. */
978
979    const u_char *
980    p_fqname(const u_char *cp, const u_char *msg, FILE
981    *file) {
982        char name[MAXDNAME];
983        const u_char *n;
984
985        n = p_fqnname(cp, msg, MAXCDNAME, name, sizeof name);
986        if (n == NULL)
987            return (NULL);
988        fputs(name, file);
989        return (n);
990    }
991
992    /*
993     * Names of RR classes and qclasses.  Classes and
994    qclasses are the same, except
995     * that C_ANY is a qclass but not a class.  (You can ask
996    for records of class
997     * C_ANY, but you can't have any records of that class
998    in the database.)
999     */
1000   const struct res_sym __p_class_syms[] = {
1001       {C_IN,      "IN"},
1002       {C_CHAOS,   "CHAOS"},
1003       {C_HS,      "HS"},
1004       {C_HS,      "HESIOD"},
1005       {C_ANY,     "ANY"},
1006       {C_NONE,    "NONE"},
1007       {C_IN,      (char *)0}
1008   };
1009
1010   /*
1011    * Names of message sections.
1012    */
1013   const struct res_sym __p_default_section_syms[] = {
1014       {ns_s_qd,   "QUERY"},
1015       {ns_s_an,   "ANSWER"},
1016       {ns_s_ns,   "AUTHORITY"},
1017       {ns_s_ar,   "ADDITIONAL"},
1018       {0,         (char *)0}
1019   };
1020
1021   const struct res_sym __p_update_section_syms[] = {
1022       {S_ZONE,    "ZONE"},
1023       {S_PREREQ,  "PREREQUISITE"},
1024       {S_UPDATE,  "UPDATE"},
1025       {S_ADDT,    "ADDITIONAL"},
1026       {0,         (char *)0}
1027   };
1028
1029   /*
1030    * Names of RR types and qtypes.  Types and qtypes are
1031   the same, except
1032    * that T_ANY is a qtype but not a type.  (You can ask
1033   for records of type
1034    * T_ANY, but you can't have any records of that type in
1035   the database.)
1036    */
1037   const struct res_sym __p_type_syms[] = {
1038       {T_A,       "A",        "address"},
1039       {T_NS,      "NS",       "name server"},
1040       {T_MD,      "MD",       "mail destination
1041   (deprecated)"},
1042       {T_MF,      "MF",       "mail forwarder
1043   (deprecated)"},
1044       {T_CNAME,   "CNAME",    "canonical name"},
1045       {T_SOA,     "SOA",      "start of authority"},
1046       {T_MB,      "MB",       "mailbox"},
1047       {T_MG,      "MG",       "mail group member"},
1048       {T_MR,      "MR",       "mail rename"},
```

```
1049        {T_NULL,     "NULL",      "null"},
1050        {T_WKS,      "WKS",       "well-known service
1051 (deprecated)"},
1052        {T_PTR,      "PTR",       "domain name pointer"},
1053        {T_HINFO,    "HINFO",     "host information"},
1054        {T_MINFO,    "MINFO",     "mailbox information"},
1055        {T_MX,       "MX",        "mail exchanger"},
1056        {T_TXT,      "TXT",       "text"},
1057        {T_RP,       "RP",        "responsible person"},
1058        {T_AFSDB,    "AFSDB",     "DCE or AFS server"},
1059        {T_X25,      "X25",       "X25 address"},
1060        {T_ISDN,     "ISDN",      "ISDN address"},
1061        {T_RT,       "RT",        "router"},
1062        {T_NSAP,     "NSAP",      "nsap address"},
1063        {T_NSAP_PTR, "NSAP_PTR", "domain name pointer"},
1064        {T_SIG,      "SIG",       "signature"},
1065        {T_KEY,      "KEY",       "key"},
1066        {T_PX,       "PX",        "mapping information"},
1067        {T_GPOS,     "GPOS",      "geographical position
1068 (withdrawn)"},
1069        {T_AAAA,     "AAAA",      "IPv6 address"},
1070        {T_LOC,      "LOC",       "location"},
1071        {T_NXT,      "NXT",       "next valid name
1072 (unimplemented)"},
1073        {T_EID,      "EID",       "endpoint identifier
1074 (unimplemented)"},
1075        {T_NIMLOC,   "NIMLOC",    "NIMROD locator
1076 (unimplemented)"},
1077        {T_SRV,      "SRV",       "server selection"},
1078        {T_ATMA,     "ATMA",      "ATM address
1079 (unimplemented)"},
1080        {T_IXFR,     "IXFR",      "incremental zone transfer"},
1081        {T_AXFR,     "AXFR",      "zone transfer"},
1082        {T_MAILB,    "MAILB",     "mailbox-related data
1083 (deprecated)"},
1084        {T_MAILA,    "MAILA",     "mail agent (deprecated)"},
1085        {T_NAPTR,    "NAPTR",     "URN Naming Authority"},
1086        {T_ANY,      "ANY",       "\"any\""},
1087        {0,          NULL,        NULL}
1088 };
1089
1090 int
1091 sym_ston(const struct res_sym *syms, const char *name,
1092 int *success) {
1093        for ((void)NULL; syms->name != 0; syms++) {
1094            if (strcasecmp (name, syms->name) == 0) {
1095                if (success)
1096                    *success = 1;
1097                return (syms->number);
1098            }
1099        }
1100        if (success)
1101            *success = 0;
1102        return (syms->number);        /* The default value. */
1103 }
1104
1105 const char *
1106 sym_ntos(const struct res_sym *syms, int number, int
1107 *success) {
1108        static char unname[20];
1109
1110        for ((void)NULL; syms->name != 0; syms++) {
1111            if (number == syms->number) {
1112                if (success)
1113                    *success = 1;
1114                return (syms->name);
1115            }
1116        }
1117
1118        sprintf(unname, "%d", number);
1119        if (success)
1120            *success = 0;
1121        return (unname);
1122 }
1123
1124 const char *
1125 sym_ntop(const struct res_sym *syms, int number, int
1126 *success) {
1127        static char unname[20];
1128
1129        for ((void)NULL; syms->name != 0; syms++) {
1130            if (number == syms->number) {
1131                if (success)
1132                    *success = 1;
1133                return (syms->humanname);
1134            }
1135        }
1136        sprintf(unname, "%d", number);
1137        if (success)
1138            *success = 0;
1139        return (unname);
1140 }
1141
1142 /*
1143  * Return a string for the type.
1144  */
```

```
1145  const char *
1146  p_type(int type) {
1147      return (sym_ntos(__p_type_syms, type, (int *)0));
1148  }
1149
1150  /*
1151   * Return a string for the type.
1152   */
1153  const char *
1154  p_section(int section, int opcode) {
1155      const struct res_sym *symbols;
1156
1157      switch (opcode) {
1158      case ns_o_update:
1159          symbols = __p_update_section_syms;
1160          break;
1161      default:
1162          symbols = __p_default_section_syms;
1163          break;
1164      }
1165      return (sym_ntos(symbols, section, (int *)0));
1166  }
1167
1168  /*
1169   * Return a mnemonic for class.
1170   */
1171  const char *
1172  p_class(int class) {
1173      return (sym_ntos(__p_class_syms, class, (int *)0));
1174  }
1175
1176  /*
1177   * Return a mnemonic for an option
1178   */
1179  const char *
1180  p_option(u_long option) {
1181      static char nbuf[40];
1182
1183      switch (option) {
1184      case RES_INIT:      return "init";
1185      case RES_DEBUG:     return "debug";
1186      case RES_AAONLY:    return "aaonly(unimpl)";
1187      case RES_USEVC:     return "usevc";
1188      case RES_PRIMARY:   return "primry(unimpl)";
1189      case RES_IGNTC:     return "igntc";
1190      case RES_RECURSE:   return "recurs";
1191      case RES_DEFNAMES:  return "defnam";
1192      case RES_STAYOPEN:  return "styopn";
1193      case RES_DNSRCH:    return "dnsrch";
1194      case RES_INSECURE1: return "insecure1";
1195      case RES_INSECURE2: return "insecure2";
1196      default:           sprintf(nbuf, "?0x%lx?",
1197  (u_long)option);
1198                  return (nbuf);
1199      }
1200  }
1201
1202  /*
1203   * Return a mnemonic for a time to live.
1204   */
1205  const char *
1206  p_time(u_int32_t value) {
1207      static char nbuf[40];
1208
1209      if (ns_format_ttl(value, nbuf, sizeof nbuf) < 0)
1210          sprintf(nbuf, "%u", value);
1211      return (nbuf);
1212  }
1213
1214
1215  /*
1216   * routines to convert between on-the-wire RR format and
1217  zone file format.
1218   * Does not contain conversion to/from decimal degrees;
1219  divide or multiply
1220   * by 60*60*1000 for that.
1221   */
1222
1223  static unsigned int poweroften[10] = {1, 10, 100, 1000,
1224  10000, 100000,
1225
1226  1000000,10000000,100000000,1000000000};
1227
1228  /* takes an XeY precision/size value, returns a string
1229  representation. */
1230  static const char *
1231  precsize_ntoa(prec)
1232      u_int8_t prec;
1233  {
1234      static char retbuf[sizeof "90000000.00"];
1235      unsigned long val;
1236      int mantissa, exponent;
1237
1238      mantissa = (int)((prec >> 4) & 0x0f) % 10;
1239      exponent = (int)((prec >> 0) & 0x0f) % 10;
1240
```

```
1241        val = mantissa * poweroften[exponent];
1242
1243        (void) sprintf(retbuf, "%ld.%.2ld", val/100,
1244    val%100);
1245        return (retbuf);
1246    }
1247
1248    /* converts ascii size/precision X * 10**Y(cm) to 0xXY.
1249    moves pointer. */
1250    static u_int8_t
1251    precsize_aton(strptr)
1252        char **strptr;
1253    {
1254        unsigned int mval = 0, cmval = 0;
1255        u_int8_t retval = 0;
1256        char *cp;
1257        int exponent;
1258        int mantissa;
1259
1260        cp = *strptr;
1261
1262        while (isdigit(*cp))
1263            mval = mval * 10 + (*cp++ - '0');
1264
1265        if (*cp == '.') {          /* centimeters */
1266            cp++;
1267            if (isdigit(*cp)) {
1268                cmval = (*cp++ - '0') * 10;
1269                if (isdigit(*cp)) {
1270                    cmval += (*cp++ - '0');
1271                }
1272            }
1273        }
1274        cmval = (mval * 100) + cmval;
1275
1276        for (exponent = 0; exponent < 9; exponent++)
1277            if (cmval < poweroften[exponent+1])
1278                break;
1279
1280        mantissa = cmval / poweroften[exponent];
1281        if (mantissa > 9)
1282            mantissa = 9;
1283
1284        retval = (mantissa << 4) | exponent;
1285
1286        *strptr = cp;
1287
1288        return (retval);
```

```
1289    }
1290
1291    /* converts ascii lat/lon to unsigned encoded 32-bit
1292    number. moves pointer. */
1293    static u_int32_t
1294    latlon2ul(latlonstrptr,which)
1295        char **latlonstrptr;
1296        int *which;
1297    {
1298        char *cp;
1299        u_int32_t retval;
1300        int deg = 0, min = 0, secs = 0, secsfrac = 0;
1301
1302        cp = *latlonstrptr;
1303
1304        while (isdigit(*cp))
1305            deg = deg * 10 + (*cp++ - '0');
1306
1307        while (isspace(*cp))
1308            cp++;
1309
1310        if (!(isdigit(*cp)))
1311            goto fndhemi;
1312
1313        while (isdigit(*cp))
1314            min = min * 10 + (*cp++ - '0');
1315
1316        while (isspace(*cp))
1317            cp++;
1318
1319        if (!(isdigit(*cp)))
1320            goto fndhemi;
1321
1322        while (isdigit(*cp))
1323            secs = secs * 10 + (*cp++ - '0');
1324
1325        if (*cp == '.') {          /* decimal seconds */
1326            cp++;
1327            if (isdigit(*cp)) {
1328                secsfrac = (*cp++ - '0') * 100;
1329                if (isdigit(*cp)) {
1330                    secsfrac += (*cp++ - '0') * 10;
1331                    if (isdigit(*cp)) {
1332                        secsfrac += (*cp++ - '0');
1333                    }
1334                }
1335            }
1336        }
```

```
1337
1338        while (!isspace(*cp))    /* if any trailing garbage */
1339            cp++;
1340
1341        while (isspace(*cp))
1342            cp++;
1343
1344    fndhemi:
1345        switch (*cp) {
1346        case 'N': case 'n':
1347        case 'E': case 'e':
1348            retval = ((unsigned)1<<31)
1349                + (((((deg * 60) + min) * 60) + secs) * 1000)
1350                + secsfrac;
1351            break;
1352        case 'S': case 's':
1353        case 'W': case 'w':
1354            retval = ((unsigned)1<<31)
1355                - (((((deg * 60) + min) * 60) + secs) * 1000)
1356                - secsfrac;
1357            break;
1358        default:
1359            retval = 0; /* invalid value -- indicates error
1360    */
1361            break;
1362        }
1363
1364        switch (*cp) {
1365        case 'N': case 'n':
1366        case 'S': case 's':
1367            *which = 1; /* latitude */
1368            break;
1369        case 'E': case 'e':
1370        case 'W': case 'w':
1371            *which = 2; /* longitude */
1372            break;
1373        default:
1374            *which = 0; /* error */
1375            break;
1376        }
1377
1378        cp++;            /* skip the hemisphere */
1379
1380        while (!isspace(*cp))    /* if any trailing garbage */
1381            cp++;
1382
1383        while (isspace(*cp))    /* move to next field */
1384            cp++;
```

```
1385
1386        *latlonstrptr = cp;
1387
1388        return (retval);
1389    }
1390
1391    /* converts a zone file representation in a string to an
1392    RDATA on-the-wire
1393     * representation. */
1394    int
1395    loc_aton(ascii, binary)
1396        const char *ascii;
1397        u_char *binary;
1398    {
1399        const char *cp, *maxcp;
1400        u_char *bcp;
1401
1402        u_int32_t latit = 0, longit = 0, alt = 0;
1403        u_int32_t lltemp1 = 0, lltemp2 = 0;
1404        int altmeters = 0, altfrac = 0, altsign = 1;
1405        u_int8_t hp = 0x16; /* default = 1e6 cm = 10000.00m
1406    = 10km */
1407        u_int8_t vp = 0x13; /* default = 1e3 cm = 10.00m */
1408        u_int8_t siz = 0x12;    /* default = 1e2 cm = 1.00m
1409    */
1410        int which1 = 0, which2 = 0;
1411
1412        cp = ascii;
1413        maxcp = cp + strlen(ascii);
1414
1415        lltemp1 = latlon2ul(&cp, &which1);
1416
1417        lltemp2 = latlon2ul(&cp, &which2);
1418
1419        switch (which1 + which2) {
1420        case 3:           /* 1 + 2, the only valid combination
1421    */
1422            if ((which1 == 1) && (which2 == 2)) { /* normal
1423    case */
1424                latit = lltemp1;
1425                longit = lltemp2;
1426            } else if ((which1 == 2) && (which2 == 1)) { /*
1427    reversed */
1428                longit = lltemp1;
1429                latit = lltemp2;
1430            } else {     /* some kind of brokenness */
1431                return (0);
1432            }
```

```
1433            break;
1434        default:        /* we didn't get one of each */
1435            return (0);
1436        }
1437
1438        /* altitude */
1439        if (*cp == '-') {
1440            altsign = -1;
1441            cp++;
1442        }
1443
1444        if (*cp == '+')
1445            cp++;
1446
1447        while (isdigit(*cp))
1448            altmeters = altmeters * 10 + (*cp++ - '0');
1449
1450        if (*cp == '.') {        /* decimal meters */
1451            cp++;
1452            if (isdigit(*cp)) {
1453                altfrac = (*cp++ - '0') * 10;
1454                if (isdigit(*cp)) {
1455                    altfrac += (*cp++ - '0');
1456                }
1457            }
1458        }
1459
1460        alt = (10000000 + (altsign * (altmeters * 100 +
1461    altfrac)));
1462
1463        while (!isspace(*cp) && (cp < maxcp)) /* if trailing
1464    garbage or m */
1465            cp++;
1466
1467        while (isspace(*cp) && (cp < maxcp))
1468            cp++;
1469
1470        if (cp >= maxcp)
1471            goto defaults;
1472
1473        siz = precsize_aton(&cp);
1474
1475        while (!isspace(*cp) && (cp < maxcp))   /* if
1476    trailing garbage or m */
1477            cp++;
1478
1479        while (isspace(*cp) && (cp < maxcp))
1480            cp++;

1481
1482        if (cp >= maxcp)
1483            goto defaults;
1484
1485        hp = precsize_aton(&cp);
1486
1487        while (!isspace(*cp) && (cp < maxcp))   /* if
1488    trailing garbage or m */
1489            cp++;
1490
1491        while (isspace(*cp) && (cp < maxcp))
1492            cp++;
1493
1494        if (cp >= maxcp)
1495            goto defaults;
1496
1497        vp = precsize_aton(&cp);
1498
1499    defaults:
1500
1501        bcp = binary;
1502        *bcp++ = (u_int8_t) 0;   /* version byte */
1503        *bcp++ = siz;
1504        *bcp++ = hp;
1505        *bcp++ = vp;
1506        PUTLONG(latit,bcp);
1507        PUTLONG(longit,bcp);
1508        PUTLONG(alt,bcp);
1509
1510        return (16);        /* size of RR in octets */
1511    }
1512
1513    /* takes an on-the-wire LOC RR and formats it in a human
1514    readable format. */
1515    const char *
1516    loc_ntoa(binary, ascii)
1517        const u_char *binary;
1518        char *ascii;
1519    {
1520        static char *error = "?";
1521        const u_char *cp = binary;
1522
1523        int latdeg, latmin, latsec, latsecfrac;
1524        int longdeg, longmin, longsec, longsecfrac;
1525        char northsouth, eastwest;
1526        int altmeters, altfrac, altsign;
1527
1528        const u_int32_t referencealt = 100000 * 100;
```

```
1529            int32_t latval, longval, altval;
1530            u_int32_t templ;
1531            u_int8_t sizeval, hpval, vpval, versionval;
1532
1533            char *sizestr, *hpstr, *vpstr;
1534
1535            versionval = *cp++;
1536
1537            if (versionval) {
1538                (void) sprintf(ascii, "; error: unknown LOC RR
1539    version");
1540                return (ascii);
1541            }
1542
1543            sizeval = *cp++;
1544
1545            hpval = *cp++;
1546            vpval = *cp++;
1547
1548            GETLONG(templ, cp);
1549            latval = (templ - ((unsigned)1<<31));
1550
1551            GETLONG(templ, cp);
1552            longval = (templ - ((unsigned)1<<31));
1553
1554            GETLONG(templ, cp);
1555            if (templ < referencealt) { /* below WGS 84 spheroid
1556    */
1557                altval = referencealt - templ;
1558                altsign = -1;
1559            } else {
1560                altval = templ - referencealt;
1561                altsign = 1;
1562            }
1563
1564            if (latval < 0) {
1565                northsouth = 'S';
1566                latval = -latval;
1567            } else
1568                northsouth = 'N';
1569
1570            latsecfrac = latval % 1000;
1571            latval = latval / 1000;
1572            latsec = latval % 60;
1573            latval = latval / 60;
1574            latmin = latval % 60;
1575            latval = latval / 60;
1576
1577            latdeg = latval;
1578
1579            if (longval < 0) {
1580                eastwest = 'W';
1581                longval = -longval;
1582            } else
1583                eastwest = 'E';
1584
1585            longsecfrac = longval % 1000;
1586            longval = longval / 1000;
1587            longsec = longval % 60;
1588            longval = longval / 60;
1589            longmin = longval % 60;
1590            longval = longval / 60;
1591            longdeg = longval;
1592
1593            altfrac = altval % 100;
1594            altmeters = (altval / 100) * altsign;
1595
1596            if ((sizestr = strdup(precsize_ntoa(sizeval))) ==
1597    NULL)
1598                sizestr = error;
1599            if ((hpstr = strdup(precsize_ntoa(hpval))) == NULL)
1600                hpstr = error;
1601            if ((vpstr = strdup(precsize_ntoa(vpval))) == NULL)
1602                vpstr = error;
1603
1604            sprintf(ascii,
1605                "%d %.2d %.2d.%.3d %c %d %.2d %.2d.%.3d %c
1606    %d.%.2dm %sm %sm %sm",
1607                latdeg, latmin, latsec, latsecfrac, northsouth,
1608                longdeg, longmin, longsec, longsecfrac, eastwest,
1609                altmeters, altfrac, sizestr, hpstr, vpstr);
1610
1611            if (sizestr != error)
1612                free(sizestr);
1613            if (hpstr != error)
1614                free(hpstr);
1615            if (vpstr != error)
1616                free(vpstr);
1617
1618            return (ascii);
1619    }
1620
1621
1622    /* Return the number of DNS hierarchy levels in the
1623    name. */
1624    int
```

```
1625   dn_count_labels(const char *name) {
1626       int i, len, count;
1627
1628       len = strlen(name);
1629       for (i = 0, count = 0; i < len; i++) {
1630           /* XXX need to check for \. or use named's
1631   nlabels(). */
1632           if (name[i] == '.')
1633               count++;
1634       }
1635
1636       /* don't count initial wildcard */
1637       if (name[0] == '*')
1638           if (count)
1639               count--;
1640
1641       /* don't count the null label for root. */
1642       /* if terminating '.' not found, must adjust */
1643       /* count to include last label */
1644       if (len > 0 && name[len-1] != '.')
1645           count++;
1646       return (count);
1647   }
1648
1649
1650   /*
1651    * Make dates expressed in seconds-since-Jan-1-1970 easy
1652   to read.
1653    * SIG records are required to be printed like this, by
1654   the Secure DNS RFC.
1655    */
1656   char *
1657   p_secstodate (u_long secs) {
1658       static char output[15];     /* YYYYMMDDHHMMSS and
1659   null */
1660       time_t clock = secs;
1661       struct tm *time;
1662
1663       time = gmtime(&clock);
1664       time->tm_year += 1900;
1665       time->tm_mon += 1;
1666       sprintf(output, "%04d%02d%02d%02d%02d%02d",
1667           time->tm_year, time->tm_mon, time->tm_mday,
1668           time->tm_hour, time->tm_min, time->tm_sec);
1669       return (output);
1670   }
```

usr/src/lib/resolv/res_init.c

```
1671   /*
1672    * Copyright (c) 1985, 1989, 1993
1673    *     The Regents of the University of California.  All
1674   rights reserved.
1675    *
1676    * Redistribution and use in source and binary forms,
1677   with or without
1678    * modification, are permitted provided that the
1679   following conditions
1680    * are met:
1681    * 1. Redistributions of source code must retain the
1682   above copyright
1683    *    notice, this list of conditions and the following
1684   disclaimer.
1685    * 2. Redistributions in binary form must reproduce the
1686   above copyright
1687    *    notice, this list of conditions and the following
1688   disclaimer in the
1689    *    documentation and/or other materials provided with
1690   the distribution.
1691    * 3. All advertising materials mentioning features or
1692   use of this software
1693    *    must display the following acknowledgement:
1694    * This product includes software developed by the
1695   University of
1696    * California, Berkeley and its contributors.
1697    * 4. Neither the name of the University nor the names
1698   of its contributors
1699    *    may be used to endorse or promote products derived
1700   from this software
1701    *    without specific prior written permission.
1702    *
1703    * THIS SOFTWARE IS PROVIDED BY THE REGENTS AND
1704   CONTRIBUTORS "AS IS" AND
1705    * ANY EXPRESS OR IMPLIED WARRANTIES, INCLUDING, BUT NOT
1706   LIMITED TO, THE
1707    * IMPLIED WARRANTIES OF MERCHANTABILITY AND FITNESS FOR
1708   A PARTICULAR PURPOSE
1709    * ARE DISCLAIMED.  IN NO EVENT SHALL THE REGENTS OR
1710   CONTRIBUTORS BE LIABLE
1711    * FOR ANY DIRECT, INDIRECT, INCIDENTAL, SPECIAL,
1712   EXEMPLARY, OR CONSEQUENTIAL
1713    * DAMAGES (INCLUDING, BUT NOT LIMITED TO, PROCUREMENT
1714   OF SUBSTITUTE GOODS
1715    * OR SERVICES; LOSS OF USE, DATA, OR PROFITS; OR
1716   BUSINESS INTERRUPTION)
1717    * HOWEVER CAUSED AND ON ANY THEORY OF LIABILITY,
1718   WHETHER IN CONTRACT, STRICT
```

```
1786
1787   #if defined(LIBC_SCCS) && !defined(lint)
1788   static char sccsid[] = "@(#)res_init.c  8.1 (Berkeley)
1789   6/7/93";
1790   static char rcsid[] = "$Id: res_init.c,v 8.7 1996/11/18
1791   09:10:04 vixie Exp $";
1792   #endif /* LIBC_SCCS and not lint */
1793
1794   #include "port_before.h"
1795   #include <sys/types.h>
1796   #include <sys/param.h>
1797   #include <sys/socket.h>
1798   #include <sys/time.h>
1799   #include <netinet/in.h>
1800   #include <arpa/inet.h>
1801   #include <arpa/nameser.h>
1802   #include <ctype.h>
1803   #include <resolv.h>
1804   #include <stdio.h>
1805   #include <stdlib.h>
1806   #include <string.h>
1807   #include <unistd.h>
1808   #include "port_after.h"
1809
1810   /* Options.  Should all be left alone. */
1811   #define RESOLVSORT
1812   #define RFC1535
1813   #define DEBUG
1814
```

```
1815    static void res_setoptions __P((char *, char *));
1816
1817    #ifdef RESOLVSORT
1818    static const char sort_mask[] = "/&";
1819    #define ISSORTMASK(ch) (strchr(sort_mask, ch) != NULL)
1820    static u_int32_t net_mask __P((struct in_addr));
1821    #endif
1822
1823    #if !defined(isascii)   /* XXX - could be a function */
1824    # define isascii(c) (!(c & 0200))
1825    #endif
1826
1827    /*
1828     * Resolver state default settings.
1829     */
1830
1831    struct __res_state _res
1832    # if defined(__BIND_RES_TEXT)
1833         = { RES_TIMEOUT, }   /* Motorola, et al. */
1834    # endif
1835             ;
1836
1837
1838    /*
1839     * Set up default settings.  If the configuration file
1840    exist, the values
1841     * there will have precedence.  Otherwise, the server
1842    address is set to
1843     * INADDR_ANY and the default domain name comes from the
1844    gethostname().
1845     *
1846     * An interim version of this code (BIND 4.9,
1847    pre-4.4BSD) used 127.0.0.1
1848     * rather than INADDR_ANY ("0.0.0.0") as the default
1849    name server address
1850     * since it was noted that INADDR_ANY actually meant
1851    "the first interface
1852     * you "ifconfig"'d at boot time'' and if this was a
1853    SLIP or PPP interface,
1854     * it had to be "up" in order for you to reach your own
1855    name server.  It
1856     * was later decided that since the recommended practice
1857    is to always
1858     * install local static routes through 127.0.0.1 for all
1859    your network
1860     * interfaces, that we could solve this problem without
1861    a code change.
1862     *
```

```
1863     * The configuration file should always be used, since
1864    it is the only way
1865     * to specify a default domain.  If you are running a
1866    server on your local
1867     * machine, you should say "nameserver 0.0.0.0" or
1868    "nameserver 127.0.0.1"
1869     * in the configuration file.
1870     *
1871     * Return 0 if completes successfully, -1 on error
1872     */
1873    int
1874    res_init() {
1875        register FILE *fp;
1876        register char *cp, **pp;
1877        register int n;
1878        char buf[BUFSIZ];
1879        int nserv = 0;     /* number of nameserver records
1880    read from file */
1881        int haveenv = 0;
1882        int havesearch = 0;
1883    #ifdef RESOLVSORT
1884        int nsort = 0;
1885        char *net;
1886    #endif
1887    #ifndef RFC1535
1888        int dots;
1889    #endif
1890
1891        /*
1892         * These three fields used to be statically
1893    initialized.  This made
1894         * it hard to use this code in a shared library.  It
1895    is necessary,
1896         * now that we're doing dynamic initialization here,
1897    that we preserve
1898         * the old semantics: if an application modifies one
1899    of these three
1900         * fields of _res before res_init() is called,
1901    res_init() will not
1902         * alter them.  Of course, if an application is
1903    setting them to
1904         * _zero_ before calling res_init(), hoping to
1905    override what used
1906         * to be the static default, we can't detect it and
1907    unexpected results
1908         * will follow.  Zero for any of these fields would
1909    make no sense,
1910         * so one can safely assume that the applications
```

```
1911    were already getting
1912         * unexpected results.
1913         *
1914         * _res.options is tricky since some apps were known
1915    to diddle the bits
1916         * before res_init() was first called. We can't
1917    replicate that semantic
1918         * with dynamic initialization (they may have turned
1919    bits off that are
1920         * set in RES_DEFAULT).  Our solution is to declare
1921    such applications
1922         * "broken".  They could fool us by setting RES_INIT
1923    but none do (yet).
1924         */
1925        if (!_res.retrans)
1926            _res.retrans = RES_TIMEOUT;
1927        if (!_res.retry)
1928            _res.retry = 4;
1929        if (!(_res.options & RES_INIT))
1930            _res.options = RES_DEFAULT;
1931
1932         /*
1933          * This one used to initialize implicitly to zero,
1934    so unless the app
1935          * has set it to something in particular, we can
1936    randomize it now.
1937          */
1938        if (!_res.id)
1939            _res.id = res_randomid();
1940
1941    #ifdef USELOOPBACK
1942        _res.nsaddr.sin_addr = inet_makeaddr(IN_LOOPBACKNET,
1943    1);
1944    #else
1945        _res.nsaddr.sin_addr.s_addr = INADDR_ANY;
1946    #endif
1947        _res.nsaddr.sin_family = AF_INET;
1948        _res.nsaddr.sin_port = htons(NAMESERVER_PORT);
1949        _res.nscount = 1;
1950        _res.ndots = 1;
1951        _res.pfcode = 0;
1952
1953        /* Allow user to override the local domain
1954    definition */
1955        if ((cp = getenv("LOCALDOMAIN")) != NULL) {
1956            (void)strncpy(_res.defdname, cp,
1957    sizeof(_res.defdname) - 1);
1958            haveenv++;
```

```
1959
1960            /*
1961             * Set search list to be blank-separated strings
1962             * from rest of env value.  Permits users of
1963    LOCALDOMAIN
1964             * to still have a search list, and anyone to
1965    set the
1966             * one that they want to use as an individual
1967    (even more
1968             * important now that the rfc1535 stuff
1969    restricts searches)
1970             */
1971            cp = _res.defdname;
1972            pp = _res.dnsrch;
1973            *pp++ = cp;
1974            for (n = 0; *cp && pp < _res.dnsrch + MAXDNSRCH;
1975    cp++) {
1976                if (*cp == '\n')      /* silly backwards
1977    compat */
1978                    break;
1979                else if (*cp == ' ' || *cp == '\t') {
1980                    *cp = 0;
1981                    n = 1;
1982                } else if (n) {
1983                    *pp++ = cp;
1984                    n = 0;
1985                    havesearch = 1;
1986                }
1987            }
1988            /* null terminate last domain if there are
1989    excess */
1990            while (*cp != '\0' && *cp != ' ' && *cp != '\t'
1991    && *cp != '\n')
1992                cp++;
1993            *cp = '\0';
1994            *pp++ = 0;
1995        }
1996
1997    #define MATCH(line, name) \
1998        (!strncmp(line, name, sizeof(name) - 1) && \
1999        (line[sizeof(name) - 1] == ' ' || \
2000         line[sizeof(name) - 1] == '\t'))
2001
2002        if ((fp = fopen(_PATH_RESCONF, "r")) != NULL) {
2003            /* read the config file */
2004            while (fgets(buf, sizeof(buf), fp) != NULL) {
2005                /* skip comments */
2006                if (*buf == ';' || *buf == '#')
```

```
2007                    continue;
2008            /* read default domain name */
2009            if (MATCH(buf, "domain")) {
2010                    if (haveenv)    /* skip if have from environ
2011    */
2012                            continue;
2013                    cp = buf + sizeof("domain") - 1;
2014                    while (*cp == ' ' || *cp == '\t')
2015                            cp++;
2016                    if ((*cp == '\0') || (*cp == '\n'))
2017                            continue;
2018                    strncpy(_res.defdname, cp,
2019    sizeof(_res.defdname) - 1);
2020                    if ((cp = strpbrk(_res.defdname, " \t\n"))
2021    != NULL)
2022                            *cp = '\0';
2023                    havesearch = 0;
2024                    continue;
2025            }
2026            /* set search list */
2027            if (MATCH(buf, "search")) {
2028                    if (haveenv)    /* skip if have from environ
2029    */
2030                            continue;
2031                    cp = buf + sizeof("search") - 1;
2032                    while (*cp == ' ' || *cp == '\t')
2033                            cp++;
2034                    if ((*cp == '\0') || (*cp == '\n'))
2035                            continue;
2036                    strncpy(_res.defdname, cp,
2037    sizeof(_res.defdname) - 1);
2038                    if ((cp = strchr(_res.defdname, '\n')) !=
2039    NULL)
2040                            *cp = '\0';
2041                    /*
2042                     * Set search list to be blank-separated
2043    strings
2044                     * on rest of line.
2045                     */
2046                    cp = _res.defdname;
2047                    pp = _res.dnsrch;
2048                    *pp++ = cp;
2049                    for (n = 0; *cp && pp < _res.dnsrch +
2050    MAXDNSRCH; cp++) {
2051                            if (*cp == ' ' || *cp == '\t') {
2052                                    *cp = 0;
2053                                    n = 1;
2054                            } else if (n) {
2055                                    *pp++ = cp;
2056                                    n = 0;
2057                            }
2058                    }
2059                    /* null terminate last domain if there are
2060    excess */
2061                    while (*cp != '\0' && *cp != ' ' && *cp !=
2062    '\t')
2063                            cp++;
2064                    *cp = '\0';
2065                    *pp++ = 0;
2066                    havesearch = 1;
2067                    continue;
2068            }
2069            /* read nameservers to query */
2070            if (MATCH(buf, "nameserver") && nserv < MAXNS) {
2071                    struct in_addr a;
2072
2073                    cp = buf + sizeof("nameserver") - 1;
2074                    while (*cp == ' ' || *cp == '\t')
2075                            cp++;
2076                    if ((*cp != '\0') && (*cp != '\n') &&
2077    inet_aton(cp, &a)) {
2078                            _res.nsaddr_list[nserv].sin_addr = a;
2079                            _res.nsaddr_list[nserv].sin_family = AF_INET;
2080                            _res.nsaddr_list[nserv].sin_port =
2081                                htons(NAMESERVER_PORT);
2082                            nserv++;
2083                    }
2084                    continue;
2085            }
2086    #ifdef RESOLVSORT
2087            if (MATCH(buf, "sortlist")) {
2088                    struct in_addr a;
2089
2090                    cp = buf + sizeof("sortlist") - 1;
2091                    while (nsort < MAXRESOLVSORT) {
2092                    while (*cp == ' ' || *cp == '\t')
2093                            cp++;
2094                    if (*cp == '\0' || *cp == '\n' || *cp == ';')
2095                            break;
2096                    net = cp;
2097                    while (*cp && !ISSORTMASK(*cp) && *cp != ';'
2098    &&
2099                            isascii(*cp) && !isspace(*cp))
2100                            cp++;
2101                    n = *cp;
2102                    *cp = 0;
```

```
2103              if (inet_aton(net, &a)) {
2104                  _res.sort_list[nsort].addr = a;
2105                  if (ISSORTMASK(n)) {
2106                      *cp++ = n;
2107                      net = cp;
2108                      while (*cp && *cp != ';' &&
2109                          isascii(*cp) && !isspace(*cp))
2110                          cp++;
2111                      n = *cp;
2112                      *cp = 0;
2113                      if (inet_aton(net, &a)) {
2114                          _res.sort_list[nsort].mask =
2115  a.s_addr;
2116                      } else {
2117                          _res.sort_list[nsort].mask =
2118                          net_mask(_res.sort_list[nsort].addr);
2119                      }
2120                  } else {
2121                      _res.sort_list[nsort].mask =
2122                      net_mask(_res.sort_list[nsort].addr);
2123                  }
2124                  nsort++;
2125              }
2126              *cp = n;
2127          }
2128          continue;
2129      }
2130  #endif
2131      if (MATCH(buf, "options")) {
2132          res_setoptions(buf + sizeof("options") - 1,
2133  "conf");
2134          continue;
2135      }
2136  }
2137  if (nserv > 1)
2138      _res.nscount = nserv;
2139  #ifdef RESOLVSORT
2140      _res.nsort = nsort;
2141  #endif
2142      (void) fclose(fp);
2143  }
2144  if (_res.defdname[0] == 0 &&
2145      gethostname(buf, sizeof(_res.defdname) - 1) == 0
2146  &&
2147      (cp = strchr(buf, '.')) != NULL)
2148      strcpy(_res.defdname, cp + 1);
2149
2150      /* find components of local domain that might be
2151  searched */
2152      if (havesearch == 0) {
2153          pp = _res.dnsrch;
2154          *pp++ = _res.defdname;
2155          *pp = NULL;
2156
2157  #ifndef RFC1535
2158          dots = 0;
2159          for (cp = _res.defdname; *cp; cp++)
2160              dots += (*cp == '.');
2161
2162          cp = _res.defdname;
2163          while (pp < _res.dnsrch + MAXDFLSRCH) {
2164              if (dots < LOCALDOMAINPARTS)
2165                  break;
2166              cp = strchr(cp, '.') + 1;    /* we know
2167  there is one */
2168              *pp++ = cp;
2169              dots--;
2170          }
2171          *pp = NULL;
2172  #ifdef DEBUG
2173          if (_res.options & RES_DEBUG) {
2174              printf(";; res_init()... default dnsrch
2175  list:\n");
2176              for (pp = _res.dnsrch; *pp; pp++)
2177                  printf(";;\t%s\n", *pp);
2178              printf(";;\t..END..\n");
2179          }
2180  #endif
2181  #endif /* !RFC1535 */
2182      }
2183
2184      if ((cp = getenv("RES_OPTIONS")) != NULL)
2185          res_setoptions(cp, "env");
2186      _res.options |= RES_INIT;
2187      return (0);
2188  }
2189
2190  static void
2191  res_setoptions(options, source)
2192      char *options, *source;
2193  {
2194      char *cp = options;
2195      int i;
2196
2197  #ifdef DEBUG
2198      if (_res.options & RES_DEBUG)
```

```
2199            printf(";; res_setoptions(\"%s\", \"%s\")...\n",
2200                    options, source);
2201    #endif
2202        while (*cp) {
2203            /* skip leading and inner runs of spaces */
2204            while (*cp == ' ' || *cp == '\t')
2205                cp++;
2206            /* search for and process individual options */
2207            if (!strncmp(cp, "ndots:", sizeof("ndots:") -
2208    1)) {
2209                i = atoi(cp + sizeof("ndots:") - 1);
2210                if (i <= RES_MAXNDOTS)
2211                    _res.ndots = i;
2212                else
2213                    _res.ndots = RES_MAXNDOTS;
2214    #ifdef DEBUG
2215                if (_res.options & RES_DEBUG)
2216                    printf(";;\tndots=%d\n", _res.ndots);
2217    #endif
2218            } else if (!strncmp(cp, "debug", sizeof("debug")
2219    - 1)) {
2220    #ifdef DEBUG
2221                if (!(_res.options & RES_DEBUG)) {
2222                    printf(";; res_setoptions(\"%s\",
2223    \"%s\")..\n",
2224                        options, source);
2225                    _res.options |= RES_DEBUG;
2226                }
2227                printf(";;\tdebug\n");
2228    #endif
2229            } else if (!strncmp(cp, "inet6", sizeof("inet6")
2230    - 1)) {
2231                _res.options |= RES_USE_INET6;
2232            } else {
2233                /* XXX - print a warning here? */
2234            }
2235            /* skip to next run of spaces */
2236            while (*cp && *cp != ' ' && *cp != '\t')
2237                cp++;
2238        }
2239    }
2240
2241    #ifdef RESOLVSORT
2242    /* XXX - should really support CIDR which means explicit
2243    masks always. */
2244    static u_int32_t
2245    net_mask(in)        /* XXX - should really use system's
2246    version of this */
2247    struct in_addr in;
2248    {
2249        register u_int32_t i = ntohl(in.s_addr);
2250
2251        if (IN_CLASSA(i))
2252            return (htonl(IN_CLASSA_NET));
2253        else if (IN_CLASSB(i))
2254            return (htonl(IN_CLASSB_NET));
2255        return (htonl(IN_CLASSC_NET));
2256    }
2257    #endif
2258
2259    u_int
2260    res_randomid()
2261    {
2262        struct timeval now;
2263
2264        gettimeofday(&now, NULL);
2265        return (0xffff & (now.tv_sec ^ now.tv_usec ^
2266    getpid())));
2267    }
```

usr/src/lib/resolv/res_mkquery.c

```
2268    /*
2269     * Copyright (c) 1985, 1993
2270     *    The Regents of the University of California.  All
2271    rights reserved.
2272     *
2273     * Redistribution and use in source and binary forms,
2274    with or without
2275     * modification, are permitted provided that the
2276    following conditions
2277     * are met:
2278     * 1. Redistributions of source code must retain the
2279    above copyright
2280     *    notice, this list of conditions and the following
2281    disclaimer.
2282     * 2. Redistributions in binary form must reproduce the
2283    above copyright
2284     *    notice, this list of conditions and the following
2285    disclaimer in the
2286     *    documentation and/or other materials provided with
2287    the distribution.
2288     * 3. All advertising materials mentioning features or
2289    use of this software
2290     *    must display the following acknowledgement:
2291     * This product includes software developed by the
2292    University of
```

```
2389    #endif /* LIBC_SCCS and not lint */
2390
2391    #include "port_before.h"
2392    #include <sys/types.h>
2393    #include <sys/param.h>
2394    #include <netinet/in.h>
2395    #include <arpa/nameser.h>
2396    #include <netdb.h>
2397    #include <resolv.h>
2398    #include <stdio.h>
2399    #include <string.h>
2400    #include "port_after.h"
2401
2402    /* Options.  Leave them on. */
2403    #define DEBUG
2404
2405    /*
2406     * Form all types of queries.
2407     * Returns the size of the result or -1.
2408     */
2409    int
2410    res_mkquery(op, dname, class, type, data, datalen,
2411    newrr_in, buf, buflen)
2412        int op;         /* opcode of query */
2413        const char *dname;  /* domain name */
2414        int class, type;    /* class and type of query */
2415        const u_char *data; /* resource record data */
2416        int datalen;        /* length of data */
2417        const u_char *newrr_in; /* new rr for modify or
2418    append */
2419        u_char *buf;        /* buffer to put query */
2420        int buflen;     /* size of buffer */
2421    {
2422        register HEADER *hp;
2423        register u_char *cp;
2424        register int n;
2425        u_char *dnptrs[20], **dpp, **lastdnptr;
2426
2427        if ((_res.options & RES_INIT) == 0 && res_init() ==
2428    -1) {
2429            h_errno = NETDB_INTERNAL;
2430            return (-1);
2431        }
2432    #ifdef DEBUG
2433        if (_res.options & RES_DEBUG)
2434            printf(";; res_mkquery(%d, %s, %d, %d)\n",
2435                op, dname, class, type);
2436    #endif
```

```
2437        /*
2438         * Initialize header fields.
2439         */
2440        if ((buf == NULL) || (buflen < HFIXEDSZ))
2441            return (-1);
2442        memset(buf, 0, HFIXEDSZ);
2443        hp = (HEADER *) buf;
2444        hp->id = htons(++_res.id);
2445        hp->opcode = op;
2446        hp->rd = (_res.options & RES_RECURSE) != 0;
2447        hp->rcode = NOERROR;
2448        cp = buf + HFIXEDSZ;
2449        buflen -= HFIXEDSZ;
2450        dpp = dnptrs;
2451        *dpp++ = buf;
2452        *dpp++ = NULL;
2453        lastdnptr = dnptrs + sizeof dnptrs / sizeof
2454    dnptrs[0];
2455        /*
2456         * perform opcode specific processing
2457         */
2458        switch (op) {
2459        case QUERY: /*FALLTHROUGH*/
2460        case NS_NOTIFY_OP:
2461            if ((buflen -= QFIXEDSZ) < 0)
2462                return (-1);
2463            if ((n = dn_comp(dname, cp, buflen, dnptrs,
2464    lastdnptr)) < 0)
2465                return (-1);
2466            cp += n;
2467            buflen -= n;
2468            __putshort(type, cp);
2469            cp += INT16SZ;
2470            __putshort(class, cp);
2471            cp += INT16SZ;
2472            hp->qdcount = htons(1);
2473            if (op == QUERY || data == NULL)
2474                break;
2475            /*
2476             * Make an additional record for completion
2477    domain.
2478             */
2479            buflen -= RRFIXEDSZ;
2480            n = dn_comp((char *)data, cp, buflen, dnptrs,
2481    lastdnptr);
2482            if (n < 0)
2483                return (-1);
2484            cp += n;
```

```
2485            buflen -= n;
2486            __putshort(T_NULL, cp);
2487            cp += INT16SZ;
2488            __putshort(class, cp);
2489            cp += INT16SZ;
2490            __putlong(0, cp);
2491            cp += INT32SZ;
2492            __putshort(0, cp);
2493            cp += INT16SZ;
2494            hp->arcount = htons(1);
2495            break;
2496
2497        case IQUERY:
2498            /*
2499             * Initialize answer section
2500             */
2501            if (buflen < 1 + RRFIXEDSZ + datalen)
2502                return (-1);
2503            *cp++ = '\0';    /* no domain name */
2504            __putshort(type, cp);
2505            cp += INT16SZ;
2506            __putshort(class, cp);
2507            cp += INT16SZ;
2508            __putlong(0, cp);
2509            cp += INT32SZ;
2510            __putshort(datalen, cp);
2511            cp += INT16SZ;
2512            if (datalen) {
2513                memcpy(cp, data, datalen);
2514                cp += datalen;
2515            }
2516            hp->ancount = htons(1);
2517            break;
2518
2519        default:
2520            return (-1);
2521        }
2522        return (cp - buf);
2523    }
```

usr/src/lib/resolv/res_mkupdate.c

```
2524    /*
2525     * Copyright (c) 1996 by Internet Software Consortium.
2526     *
2527     * Permission to use, copy, modify, and distribute this
2528    software for any
2529     * purpose with or without fee is hereby granted,
2530    provided that the above
2531     * copyright notice and this permission notice appear in
2532    all copies.
2533     *
2534     * THE SOFTWARE IS PROVIDED "AS IS" AND INTERNET
2535    SOFTWARE CONSORTIUM DISCLAIMS
2536     * ALL WARRANTIES WITH REGARD TO THIS SOFTWARE INCLUDING
2537    ALL IMPLIED WARRANTIES
2538     * OF MERCHANTABILITY AND FITNESS. IN NO EVENT SHALL
2539    INTERNET SOFTWARE
2540     * CONSORTIUM BE LIABLE FOR ANY SPECIAL, DIRECT,
2541    INDIRECT, OR CONSEQUENTIAL
2542     * DAMAGES OR ANY DAMAGES WHATSOEVER RESULTING FROM LOSS
2543    OF USE, DATA OR
2544     * PROFITS, WHETHER IN AN ACTION OF CONTRACT, NEGLIGENCE
2545    OR OTHER TORTIOUS
2546     * ACTION, ARISING OUT OF OR IN CONNECTION WITH THE USE
2547    OR PERFORMANCE OF THIS
2548     * SOFTWARE.
2549     */
2550
2551    /*
2552     * Based on the Dynamic DNS reference implementation by
2553    Viraj Bais
2554     * <viraj_bais@ccm.fm.intel.com>
2555     */
2556
2557    #if !defined(lint) && !defined(SABER)
2558    static char rcsid[] = "$Id: res_mkupdate.c,v 1.11
2559    1998/01/26 23:08:45 halley Exp $";
2560    #endif /* not lint */
2561
2562    #include "port_before.h"
2563
2564    #include <sys/types.h>
2565    #include <sys/param.h>
2566
2567    #include <netinet/in.h>
2568    #include <arpa/nameser.h>
2569    #include <arpa/inet.h>
2570
2571    #include <errno.h>
2572    #include <limits.h>
2573    #include <netdb.h>
2574    #include <resolv.h>
2575    #include <stdio.h>
2576    #include <stdlib.h>
2577    #include <string.h>
2578    #include <unistd.h>
```

```
2579    #include <ctype.h>
2580
2581    #include "port_after.h"
2582
2583    /* Options.  Leave them on. */
2584    #define DEBUG
2585
2586    static int getnum_str(u_char **, u_char *);
2587    static int getword_str(char *, int, u_char **, u_char *);
2588
2589    #define ShrinkBuffer(x)  if ((buflen -= x) < 0) return
2590    (-2);
2591
2592    /*
2593     * Form update packets.
2594     * Returns the size of the resulting packet if no error
2595     * On error,
2596     *   returns -1 if error in reading a word/number in rdata
2597     *          portion for update packets
2598     *       -2 if length of buffer passed is insufficient
2599     *       -3 if zone section is not the first section in
2600     *          the linked list, or section order has a
2601    problem
2602     *       -4 on a number overflow
2603     *       -5 unknown operation or no records
2604     */
2605    int
2606    res_mkupdate(ns_updrec *rrecp_in, u_char *buf, int
2607    buflen) {
2608        ns_updrec *rrecp_start = rrecp_in;
2609        HEADER *hp;
2610        u_char c, *cp, *cp1, *sp1, *sp2, *startp, *endp;
2611        int n, i, j, found, soanum, multiline;
2612        ns_updrec *rrecp, *tmprrecp, *recptr = NULL;
2613        struct in_addr ina;
2614            char buf2[MAXDNAME];
2615        int section, numrrs = 0, counts[ns_s_max];
2616        u_int16_t rtype, rclass;
2617        u_int32_t n1, rttl;
2618        u_char *dnptrs[20], **dpp, **lastdnptr;
2619
2620        if ((_res.options & RES_INIT) == 0 && res_init() ==
2621    -1) {
2622            h_errno = NETDB_INTERNAL;
2623            return (-1);
2624        }
2625
2626        /*
2627         * Initialize header fields.
2628         */
2629        if ((buf == NULL) || (buflen < HFIXEDSZ))
2630            return (-1);
2631        memset(buf, 0, HFIXEDSZ);
2632        hp = (HEADER *) buf;
2633        hp->id = htons(++_res.id);
2634        hp->opcode = ns_o_update;
2635        hp->rcode = NOERROR;
2636        sp1 = buf + 2*INT16SZ;   /* save pointer to zocount */
2637        cp = buf + HFIXEDSZ;
2638        buflen -= HFIXEDSZ;
2639        dpp = dnptrs;
2640        *dpp++ = buf;
2641        *dpp++ = NULL;
2642        lastdnptr = dnptrs + sizeof dnptrs / sizeof
2643    dnptrs[0];
2644
2645        if (rrecp_start == NULL)
2646            return (-5);
2647        else if (rrecp_start->r_section != S_ZONE)
2648            return (-3);
2649
2650        memset(counts, 0, sizeof counts);
2651        for (rrecp = rrecp_start; rrecp; rrecp =
2652    rrecp->r_grpnext) {
2653            numrrs++;
2654                section = rrecp->r_section;
2655            if (section < 0 || section >= ns_s_max)
2656                return (-1);
2657            counts[section]++;
2658            for (i = section + 1; i < ns_s_max; i++)
2659                if (counts[i])
2660                    return (-3);
2661            rtype = rrecp->r_type;
2662            rclass = rrecp->r_class;
2663            rttl = rrecp->r_ttl;
2664            /* overload class and type */
2665            if (section == S_PREREQ) {
2666                rttl = 0;
2667                switch (rrecp->r_opcode) {
2668                case YXDOMAIN:
2669                    rclass = C_ANY;
2670                    rtype = T_ANY;
2671                    rrecp->r_size = 0;
2672                    break;
2673                case NXDOMAIN:
2674                    rclass = C_NONE;
```

```
2675                    rtype = T_ANY;
2676                    rrecp->r_size = 0;
2677                    break;
2678                case NXRRSET:
2679                    rclass = C_NONE;
2680                    rrecp->r_size = 0;
2681                    break;
2682                case YXRRSET:
2683                    if (rrecp->r_size == 0)
2684                        rclass = C_ANY;
2685                    break;
2686                default:
2687                    fprintf(stderr,
2688                        "res_mkupdate: incorrect opcode:
2689    %d\n",
2690                        rrecp->r_opcode);
2691                    fflush(stderr);
2692                    return (-1);
2693                }
2694            } else if (section == S_UPDATE) {
2695                switch (rrecp->r_opcode) {
2696                case DELETE:
2697                    rclass = rrecp->r_size == 0 ? C_ANY :
2698    C_NONE;
2699                    break;
2700                case ADD:
2701                    break;
2702                default:
2703                    fprintf(stderr,
2704                        "res_mkupdate: incorrect opcode:
2705    %d\n",
2706                        rrecp->r_opcode);
2707                    fflush(stderr);
2708                    return (-1);
2709                }
2710            }
2711
2712            /*
2713             * XXX   appending default domain to owner name
2714    is omitted,
2715             *   fqdn must be provided
2716             */
2717            if ((n = dn_comp(rrecp->r_dname, cp, buflen,
2718    dnptrs,
2719                    lastdnptr)) < 0)
2720                return (-1);
2721            cp += n;
2722            ShrinkBuffer(n + 2*INT16SZ);
```

```
2723            PUTSHORT(rtype, cp);
2724            PUTSHORT(rclass, cp);
2725            if (section == S_ZONE) {
2726                if (numrrs != 1 || rrecp->r_type != T_SOA)
2727                    return (-3);
2728                continue;
2729            }
2730            ShrinkBuffer(INT32SZ + INT16SZ);
2731            PUTLONG(rttl, cp);
2732            sp2 = cp;  /* save pointer to length byte */
2733            cp += INT16SZ;
2734            if (rrecp->r_size == 0) {
2735                if (section == S_UPDATE && rclass != C_ANY)
2736                    return (-1);
2737                else {
2738                    PUTSHORT(0, sp2);
2739                    continue;
2740                }
2741            }
2742            startp = rrecp->r_data;
2743            endp = startp + rrecp->r_size - 1;
2744            /* XXX this should be done centrally. */
2745            switch (rrecp->r_type) {
2746            case T_A:
2747                if (!getword_str(buf2, sizeof buf2, &startp,
2748    endp))
2749                    return (-1);
2750                if (!inet_aton(buf2, &ina))
2751                    return (-1);
2752                n1 = ntohl(ina.s_addr);
2753                ShrinkBuffer(INT32SZ);
2754                PUTLONG(n1, cp);
2755                break;
2756            case T_CNAME:
2757            case T_MB:
2758            case T_MG:
2759            case T_MR:
2760            case T_NS:
2761            case T_PTR:
2762                if (!getword_str(buf2, sizeof buf2, &startp,
2763    endp))
2764                    return (-1);
2765                n = dn_comp(buf2, cp, buflen, dnptrs,
2766    lastdnptr);
2767                if (n < 0)
2768                    return (-1);
2769                cp += n;
2770                ShrinkBuffer(n);
```

```
2771                break;
2772          case T_MINFO:
2773          case T_SOA:
2774          case T_RP:
2775                for (i = 0; i < 2; i++) {
2776                     if (!getword_str(buf2, sizeof buf2,
2777    &startp,
2778                              endp))
2779                          return (-1);
2780                     n = dn_comp(buf2, cp, buflen,
2781                          dnptrs, lastdnptr);
2782                     if (n < 0)
2783                          return (-1);
2784                     cp += n;
2785                     ShrinkBuffer(n);
2786                }
2787                if (rrecp->r_type == T_SOA) {
2788                     ShrinkBuffer(5 * INT32SZ);
2789                     while (isspace(*startp) || !*startp)
2790                          startp++;
2791                     if (*startp == '(') {
2792                          multiline = 1;
2793                          startp++;
2794                     } else
2795                          multiline = 0;
2796                     /* serial, refresh, retry, expire,
2797    minimum */
2798                     for (i = 0; i < 5; i++) {
2799                          soanum = getnum_str(&startp, endp);
2800                          if (soanum < 0)
2801                               return (-1);
2802                          PUTLONG(soanum, cp);
2803                     }
2804                     if (multiline) {
2805                          while (isspace(*startp) || !*startp)
2806                               startp++;
2807                          if (*startp != ')')
2808                               return (-1);
2809                     }
2810                }
2811                break;
2812          case T_MX:
2813          case T_AFSDB:
2814          case T_RT:
2815                n = getnum_str(&startp, endp);
2816                if (n < 0)
2817                     return (-1);
2818                PUTSHORT(n, cp);
2819                ShrinkBuffer(INT16SZ);
2820                if (!getword_str(buf2, sizeof buf2, &startp,
2821    endp))
2822                     return (-1);
2823                n = dn_comp(buf2, cp, buflen, dnptrs,
2824    lastdnptr);
2825                if (n < 0)
2826                     return (-1);
2827                cp += n;
2828                ShrinkBuffer(n);
2829                break;
2830          case T_PX:
2831                n = getnum_str(&startp, endp);
2832                if (n < 0)
2833                     return (-1);
2834                PUTSHORT(n, cp);
2835                ShrinkBuffer(INT16SZ);
2836                for (i = 0; i < 2; i++) {
2837                     if (!getword_str(buf2, sizeof buf2,
2838    &startp,
2839                              endp))
2840                          return (-1);
2841                     n = dn_comp(buf2, cp, buflen, dnptrs,
2842                          lastdnptr);
2843                     if (n < 0)
2844                          return (-1);
2845                     cp += n;
2846                     ShrinkBuffer(n);
2847                }
2848                break;
2849          case T_WKS:
2850          case T_HINFO:
2851          case T_TXT:
2852          case T_X25:
2853          case T_ISDN:
2854          case T_NSAP:
2855          case T_LOC:
2856                /* XXX - more fine tuning needed here */
2857                ShrinkBuffer(rrecp->r_size);
2858                memcpy(cp, rrecp->r_data, rrecp->r_size);
2859                cp += rrecp->r_size;
2860                break;
2861          default:
2862                return (-1);
2863          } /*switch*/
2864          n = (u_int16_t)((cp - sp2) - INT16SZ);
2865          PUTSHORT(n, sp2);
2866     } /*for*/
```

```
2867
2868            hp->qdcount = htons(counts[0]);
2869            hp->ancount = htons(counts[1]);
2870            hp->nscount = htons(counts[2]);
2871            hp->arcount = htons(counts[3]);
2872            return (cp - buf);
2873     }
2874
2875     /*
2876      * Get a whitespace delimited word from a string (not
2877     file)
2878      * into buf. modify the start pointer to point after the
2879      * word in the string.
2880      */
2881     static int
2882     getword_str(char *buf, int size, u_char **startpp,
2883     u_char *endp) {
2884            char *cp;
2885            int c;
2886
2887            for (cp = buf; *startpp <= endp; ) {
2888                    c = **startpp;
2889                    if (isspace(c) || c == '\0') {
2890                            if (cp != buf) /* trailing
2891     whitespace */
2892                                    break;
2893                            else { /* leading whitespace */
2894                                    (*startpp)++;
2895                                    continue;
2896                            }
2897                    }
2898                    (*startpp)++;
2899                    if (cp >= buf+size-1)
2900                            break;
2901                    *cp++ = (u_char)c;
2902            }
2903            *cp = '\0';
2904            return (cp != buf);
2905     }
2906
2907     /*
2908      * Get a whitespace delimited number from a string (not
2909     file) into buf
2910      * update the start pointer to point after the number in
2911     the string.
2912      */
2913     static int
2914     getnum_str(u_char **startpp, u_char *endp) {
```

```
2915            int c, n;
2916            int seendigit = 0;
2917            int seendecimal = 0;
2918            int m = 0;
2919
2920            for (n = 0; *startpp <= endp; ) {
2921                    c = **startpp;
2922                    if (isspace(c) || c == '\0') {
2923                            if (seendigit) /* trailing
2924     whitespace */
2925                                    break;
2926                            else { /* leading whitespace */
2927                                    (*startpp)++;
2928                                    continue;
2929                            }
2930                    }
2931                    if (c == ';') {
2932                            while ((*startpp <= endp) &&
2933                            ((c = **startpp) != '\n'))
2934                            (*startpp)++;
2935                            if (seendigit)
2936                                    break;
2937                            continue;
2938                    }
2939                    if (!isdigit(c)) {
2940                            if (c == ')' && seendigit) {
2941                                    (*startpp)--;
2942                                    break;
2943                            }
2944                    return (-1);
2945                    }
2946                    (*startpp)++;
2947                    n = n * 10 + (c - '0');
2948                    seendigit = 1;
2949            }
2950            return (n + m);
2951     }
2952
2953     /*
2954      * Allocate a resource record buffer & save rr info.
2955      */
2956     ns_updrec *
2957     res_mkupdrec(int section, const char *dname,
2958            u_int class, u_int type, u_long ttl) {
2959        ns_updrec *rrecp = (ns_updrec *)calloc(1,
2960     sizeof(ns_updrec));
2961
2962        if (!rrecp || !(rrecp->r_dname = strdup(dname)))
```

```
2963          return (NULL);
2964      rrecp->r_class = class;
2965      rrecp->r_type = type;
2966      rrecp->r_ttl = ttl;
2967      rrecp->r_section = section;
2968      return (rrecp);
2969  }
2970
2971  /*
2972   * Free a resource record buffer created by res_mkupdrec.
2973   */
2974  void
2975  res_freeupdrec(ns_updrec *rrecp) {
2976      /* Note: freeing r_dp is the caller's
2977  responsibility. */
2978      if (rrecp->r_dname != NULL)
2979          free(rrecp->r_dname);
2980      free(rrecp);
2981  }
```

usr/src/lib/resolv/res_query.c

```
2982  /*
2983   * Copyright (c) 1988, 1993
2984   *    The Regents of the University of California.  All
2985  rights reserved.
2986   *
2987   * Redistribution and use in source and binary forms,
2988  with or without
2989   * modification, are permitted provided that the
2990  following conditions
2991   * are met:
2992   * 1. Redistributions of source code must retain the
2993  above copyright
2994   *    notice, this list of conditions and the following
2995  disclaimer.
2996   * 2. Redistributions in binary form must reproduce the
2997  above copyright
2998   *    notice, this list of conditions and the following
2999  disclaimer in the
3000   *    documentation and/or other materials provided with
3001  the distribution.
3002   * 3. All advertising materials mentioning features or
3003  use of this software
3004   *    must display the following acknowledgement:
3005   * This product includes software developed by the
3006  University of
3007   * California, Berkeley and its contributors.
3008   * 4. Neither the name of the University nor the names
3009  of its contributors
3010   *    may be used to endorse or promote products derived
3011  from this software
3012   *    without specific prior written permission.
3013   *
3014   * THIS SOFTWARE IS PROVIDED BY THE REGENTS AND
3015  CONTRIBUTORS "AS IS" AND
3016   * ANY EXPRESS OR IMPLIED WARRANTIES, INCLUDING, BUT NOT
3017  LIMITED TO, THE
3018   * IMPLIED WARRANTIES OF MERCHANTABILITY AND FITNESS FOR
3019  A PARTICULAR PURPOSE
3020   * ARE DISCLAIMED.  IN NO EVENT SHALL THE REGENTS OR
3021  CONTRIBUTORS BE LIABLE
3022   * FOR ANY DIRECT, INDIRECT, INCIDENTAL, SPECIAL,
3023  EXEMPLARY, OR CONSEQUENTIAL
3024   * DAMAGES (INCLUDING, BUT NOT LIMITED TO, PROCUREMENT
3025  OF SUBSTITUTE GOODS
3026   * OR SERVICES; LOSS OF USE, DATA, OR PROFITS; OR
3027  BUSINESS INTERRUPTION)
3028   * HOWEVER CAUSED AND ON ANY THEORY OF LIABILITY,
3029  WHETHER IN CONTRACT, STRICT
3030   * LIABILITY, OR TORT (INCLUDING NEGLIGENCE OR
3031  OTHERWISE) ARISING IN ANY WAY
3032   * OUT OF THE USE OF THIS SOFTWARE, EVEN IF ADVISED OF
3033  THE POSSIBILITY OF
3034   * SUCH DAMAGE.
3035   */
3036
3037  /*
3038   * Portions Copyright (c) 1993 by Digital Equipment
3039  Corporation.
3040   *
3041   * Permission to use, copy, modify, and distribute this
3042  software for any
3043   * purpose with or without fee is hereby granted,
3044  provided that the above
3045   * copyright notice and this permission notice appear in
3046  all copies, and that
3047   * the name of Digital Equipment Corporation not be used
3048  in advertising or
3049   * publicity pertaining to distribution of the document
3050  or software without
3051   * specific, written prior permission.
3052   *
3053   * THE SOFTWARE IS PROVIDED "AS IS" AND DIGITAL
3054  EQUIPMENT CORP. DISCLAIMS ALL
3055   * WARRANTIES WITH REGARD TO THIS SOFTWARE, INCLUDING
3056  ALL IMPLIED WARRANTIES
```

```
3057    * OF MERCHANTABILITY AND FITNESS.   IN NO EVENT SHALL
3058   DIGITAL EQUIPMENT
3059    * CORPORATION BE LIABLE FOR ANY SPECIAL, DIRECT,
3060   INDIRECT, OR CONSEQUENTIAL
3061    * DAMAGES OR ANY DAMAGES WHATSOEVER RESULTING FROM LOSS
3062   OF USE, DATA OR
3063    * PROFITS, WHETHER IN AN ACTION OF CONTRACT, NEGLIGENCE
3064   OR OTHER TORTIOUS
3065    * ACTION, ARISING OUT OF OR IN CONNECTION WITH THE USE
3066   OR PERFORMANCE OF THIS
3067    * SOFTWARE.
3068    */
3069
3070   /*
3071    * Portions Copyright (c) 1996 by Internet Software
3072   Consortium.
3073    *
3074    * Permission to use, copy, modify, and distribute this
3075   software for any
3076    * purpose with or without fee is hereby granted,
3077   provided that the above
3078    * copyright notice and this permission notice appear in
3079   all copies.
3080    *
3081    * THE SOFTWARE IS PROVIDED "AS IS" AND INTERNET
3082   SOFTWARE CONSORTIUM DISCLAIMS
3083    * ALL WARRANTIES WITH REGARD TO THIS SOFTWARE INCLUDING
3084   ALL IMPLIED WARRANTIES
3085    * OF MERCHANTABILITY AND FITNESS. IN NO EVENT SHALL
3086   INTERNET SOFTWARE
3087    * CONSORTIUM BE LIABLE FOR ANY SPECIAL, DIRECT,
3088   INDIRECT, OR CONSEQUENTIAL
3089    * DAMAGES OR ANY DAMAGES WHATSOEVER RESULTING FROM LOSS
3090   OF USE, DATA OR
3091    * PROFITS, WHETHER IN AN ACTION OF CONTRACT, NEGLIGENCE
3092   OR OTHER TORTIOUS
3093    * ACTION, ARISING OUT OF OR IN CONNECTION WITH THE USE
3094   OR PERFORMANCE OF THIS
3095    * SOFTWARE.
3096    */
3097
3098   #if defined(LIBC_SCCS) && !defined(lint)
3099   static char sccsid[] = "@(#)res_query.c 8.1 (Berkeley)
3100   6/4/93";
3101   static char rcsid[] = "$Id: res_query.c,v 8.14
3102   1997/06/09 17:47:05 halley Exp $";
3103   #endif /* LIBC_SCCS and not lint */
3104

3105   #include "port_before.h"
3106   #include <sys/types.h>
3107   #include <sys/param.h>
3108   #include <netinet/in.h>
3109   #include <arpa/inet.h>
3110   #include <arpa/nameser.h>
3111   #include <ctype.h>
3112   #include <errno.h>
3113   #include <netdb.h>
3114   #include <resolv.h>
3115   #include <stdio.h>
3116   #include <stdlib.h>
3117   #include <string.h>
3118   #include "port_after.h"
3119
3120   /* Options.  Leave them on. */
3121   #define DEBUG
3122
3123   #if PACKETSZ > 1024
3124   #define MAXPACKET   PACKETSZ
3125   #else
3126   #define MAXPACKET   1024
3127   #endif
3128
3129   /*
3130    * Formulate a normal query, send, and await answer.
3131    * Returned answer is placed in supplied buffer "answer".
3132    * Perform preliminary check of answer, returning
3133   success only
3134    * if no error is indicated and the answer count is
3135   nonzero.
3136    * Return the size of the response on success, -1 on
3137   error.
3138    * Error number is left in h_errno.
3139    *
3140    * Caller must parse answer and determine whether it
3141   answers the question.
3142    */
3143   int
3144   res_query(name, class, type, answer, anslen)
3145       const char *name;   /* domain name */
3146       int class, type;    /* class and type of query */
3147       u_char *answer;     /* buffer to put answer */
3148       int anslen;         /* size of answer buffer */
3149   {
3150       u_char buf[MAXPACKET];
3151       HEADER *hp = (HEADER *) answer;
3152       int n;
```

```
3153
3154        hp->rcode = NOERROR;      /* default */
3155
3156        if ((_res.options & RES_INIT) == 0 && res_init() ==
3157    -1) {
3158            h_errno = NETDB_INTERNAL;
3159            return (-1);
3160        }
3161    #ifdef DEBUG
3162        if (_res.options & RES_DEBUG)
3163            printf(";; res_query(%s, %d, %d)\n", name,
3164    class, type);
3165    #endif
3166
3167        n = res_mkquery(QUERY, name, class, type, NULL, 0,
3168    NULL,
3169                buf, sizeof(buf));
3170        if (n <= 0) {
3171    #ifdef DEBUG
3172        if (_res.options & RES_DEBUG)
3173            printf(";; res_query: mkquery failed\n");
3174    #endif
3175            h_errno = NO_RECOVERY;
3176            return (n);
3177        }
3178        n = res_send(buf, n, answer, anslen);
3179        if (n < 0) {
3180    #ifdef DEBUG
3181        if (_res.options & RES_DEBUG)
3182            printf(";; res_query: send error\n");
3183    #endif
3184            h_errno = TRY_AGAIN;
3185            return (n);
3186        }
3187
3188        if (hp->rcode != NOERROR || ntohs(hp->ancount) == 0)
3189    {
3190    #ifdef DEBUG
3191        if (_res.options & RES_DEBUG)
3192            printf(";; rcode = %d, ancount=%d\n",
3193    hp->rcode,
3194                ntohs(hp->ancount));
3195    #endif
3196        switch (hp->rcode) {
3197        case NXDOMAIN:
3198            h_errno = HOST_NOT_FOUND;
3199            break;
3200        case SERVFAIL:
3201            h_errno = TRY_AGAIN;
3202            break;
3203        case NOERROR:
3204            h_errno = NO_DATA;
3205            break;
3206        case FORMERR:
3207        case NOTIMP:
3208        case REFUSED:
3209        default:
3210            h_errno = NO_RECOVERY;
3211            break;
3212        }
3213        return (-1);
3214    }
3215    return (n);
3216 }
3217
3218 /*
3219  * Formulate a normal query, send, and retrieve answer
3220 in supplied buffer.
3221  * Return the size of the response on success, -1 on
3222 error.
3223  * If enabled, implement search rules until answer or
3224 unrecoverable failure
3225  * is detected.  Error code, if any, is left in h_errno.
3226  */
3227 int
3228 res_search(name, class, type, answer, anslen)
3229    const char *name;    /* domain name */
3230    int class, type;      /* class and type of query */
3231    u_char *answer;       /* buffer to put answer */
3232    int anslen;       /* size of answer */
3233 {
3234    const char *cp, * const *domain;
3235    HEADER *hp = (HEADER *) answer;
3236    u_int dots;
3237    int trailing_dot, ret, saved_herrno;
3238    int got_nodata = 0, got_servfail = 0, tried_as_is =
3239 0;
3240
3241    if ((_res.options & RES_INIT) == 0 && res_init() ==
3242 -1) {
3243            h_errno = NETDB_INTERNAL;
3244            return (-1);
3245    }
3246    errno = 0;
3247    h_errno = HOST_NOT_FOUND;   /* default, if we never
3248 query */
```

```
3249        dots = 0;
3250        for (cp = name; *cp; cp++)
3251            dots += (*cp == '.');
3252        trailing_dot = 0;
3253        if (cp > name && *--cp == '.')
3254            trailing_dot++;
3255
3256        /* If there aren't any dots, it could be a
3257    user-level alias. */
3258        if (!dots && (cp = hostalias(name)) != NULL)
3259            return (res_query(cp, class, type, answer,
3260    anslen));
3261
3262        /*
3263         * If there are dots in the name already, let's just
3264    give it a try
3265         * 'as is'.  The threshold can be set with the
3266    "ndots" option.
3267         */
3268        saved_herrno = -1;
3269        if (dots >= _res.ndots) {
3270            ret = res_querydomain(name, NULL, class, type,
3271    answer, anslen);
3272            if (ret > 0)
3273                return (ret);
3274            saved_herrno = h_errno;
3275            tried_as_is++;
3276        }
3277
3278        /*
3279         * We do at least one level of search if
3280         *  - there is no dot and RES_DEFNAME is set, or
3281         *  - there is at least one dot, there is no
3282    trailing dot,
3283         *      and RES_DNSRCH is set.
3284         */
3285        if ((!dots && (_res.options & RES_DEFNAMES)) ||
3286            (dots && !trailing_dot && (_res.options &
3287    RES_DNSRCH))) {
3288            int done = 0;
3289
3290            for (domain = (const char * const *)_res.dnsrch;
3291                *domain && !done;
3292                domain++) {
3293
3294                ret = res_querydomain(name, *domain, class,
3295    type,
3296                        answer, anslen);
```

```
3297            if (ret > 0)
3298                return (ret);
3299
3300            /*
3301             * If no server present, give up.
3302             * If name isn't found in this domain,
3303             * keep trying higher domains in the search
3304    list
3305             * (if that's enabled).
3306             * On a NO_DATA error, keep trying, otherwise
3307             * a wildcard entry of another type could
3308    keep us
3309             * from finding this entry higher in the
3310    domain.
3311             * If we get some other error (negative
3312    answer or
3313             * server failure), then stop searching up,
3314             * but try the input name below in case it's
3315             * fully-qualified.
3316             */
3317            if (errno == ECONNREFUSED) {
3318                h_errno = TRY_AGAIN;
3319                return (-1);
3320            }
3321
3322            switch (h_errno) {
3323            case NO_DATA:
3324                got_nodata++;
3325                /* FALLTHROUGH */
3326            case HOST_NOT_FOUND:
3327                /* keep trying */
3328                break;
3329            case TRY_AGAIN:
3330                if (hp->rcode == SERVFAIL) {
3331                    /* try next search element, if any */
3332                    got_servfail++;
3333                    break;
3334                }
3335                /* FALLTHROUGH */
3336            default:
3337                /* anything else implies that we're done
3338    */
3339                done++;
3340            }
3341
3342            /* if we got here for some reason other than
3343    DNSRCH,
3344             * we only wanted one iteration of the loop,
```

```
3345    so stop.
3346                    */
3347                if (!(_res.options & RES_DNSRCH))
3348                    done++;
3349            }
3350        }
3351
3352        /*
3353         * If we have not already tried the name "as is", do
3354    that now.
3355         * note that we do this regardless of how many dots
3356    were in the
3357         * name or whether it ends with a dot.
3358         */
3359        if (!tried_as_is) {
3360            ret = res_querydomain(name, NULL, class, type,
3361    answer, anslen);
3362            if (ret > 0)
3363                return (ret);
3364        }
3365
3366        /* if we got here, we didn't satisfy the search.
3367         * if we did an initial full query, return that
3368    query's h_errno
3369         * (note that we wouldn't be here if that query had
3370    succeeded).
3371         * else if we ever got a nodata, send that back as
3372    the reason.
3373         * else send back meaningless h_errno, that being
3374    the one from
3375         * the last DNSRCH we did.
3376         */
3377        if (saved_herrno != -1)
3378            h_errno = saved_herrno;
3379        else if (got_nodata)
3380            h_errno = NO_DATA;
3381        else if (got_servfail)
3382            h_errno = TRY_AGAIN;
3383        return (-1);
3384    }
3385
3386    /*
3387     * Perform a call on res_query on the concatenation of
3388    name and domain,
3389     * removing a trailing dot from name if domain is NULL.
3390     */
3391    int
3392    res_querydomain(name, domain, class, type, answer,
3393    anslen)
3394        const char *name, *domain;
3395        int class, type;     /* class and type of query */
3396        u_char *answer;      /* buffer to put answer */
3397        int anslen;      /* size of answer */
3398    {
3399        char nbuf[MAXDNAME];
3400        const char *longname = nbuf;
3401        int n, d;
3402
3403        if ((_res.options & RES_INIT) == 0 && res_init() ==
3404    -1) {
3405            h_errno = NETDB_INTERNAL;
3406            return (-1);
3407        }
3408    #ifdef DEBUG
3409        if (_res.options & RES_DEBUG)
3410            printf(";; res_querydomain(%s, %s, %d, %d)\n",
3411                name, domain?domain:"<Nil>", class, type);
3412    #endif
3413        if (domain == NULL) {
3414            /*
3415             * Check for trailing '.';
3416             * copy without '.' if present.
3417             */
3418            n = strlen(name);
3419            if (n >= MAXDNAME) {
3420                h_errno = NO_RECOVERY;
3421                return (-1);
3422            }
3423            n--;
3424            if (n >= 0 && name[n] == '.') {
3425                strncpy(nbuf, name, n);
3426                nbuf[n] = '\0';
3427            } else
3428                longname = name;
3429        } else {
3430            n = strlen(name);
3431            d = strlen(domain);
3432            if (n + d + 1 >= MAXDNAME) {
3433                h_errno = NO_RECOVERY;
3434                return (-1);
3435            }
3436            sprintf(nbuf, "%s.%s", name, domain);
3437        }
3438        return (res_query(longname, class, type, answer,
3439    anslen));
3440    }
```

```
3441
3442    const char *
3443    hostalias(const char *name) {
3444        char *cp1, *cp2;
3445        FILE *fp;
3446        char *file;
3447        char buf[BUFSIZ];
3448        static char abuf[MAXDNAME];
3449
3450        if (_res.options & RES_NOALIASES)
3451            return (NULL);
3452        file = getenv("HOSTALIASES");
3453        if (file == NULL || (fp = fopen(file, "r")) == NULL)
3454            return (NULL);
3455        setbuf(fp, NULL);
3456        buf[sizeof(buf) - 1] = '\0';
3457        while (fgets(buf, sizeof(buf), fp)) {
3458            for (cp1 = buf; *cp1 && !isspace(*cp1); ++cp1)
3459                ;
3460            if (!*cp1)
3461                break;
3462            *cp1 = '\0';
3463            if (!strcasecmp(buf, name)) {
3464                while (isspace(*++cp1))
3465                    ;
3466                if (!*cp1)
3467                    break;
3468                for (cp2 = cp1 + 1; *cp2 && !isspace(*cp2);
3469    ++cp2)
3470                    ;
3471                abuf[sizeof(abuf) - 1] = *cp2 = '\0';
3472                strncpy(abuf, cp1, sizeof(abuf) - 1);
3473                fclose(fp);
3474                return (abuf);
3475            }
3476        }
3477        fclose(fp);
3478        return (NULL);
3479    }
```

usr/src/lib/resolv/res_send.c

```
3535  /*
3536   * Portions Copyright (c) 1993 by Digital Equipment
3537  Corporation.
3538   *
3539   * Permission to use, copy, modify, and distribute this
3540  software for any
3541   * purpose with or without fee is hereby granted,
3542  provided that the above
3543   * copyright notice and this permission notice appear in
3544  all copies, and that
3545   * the name of Digital Equipment Corporation not be used
3546  in advertising or
3547   * publicity pertaining to distribution of the document
3548  or software without
3549   * specific, written prior permission.
3550   *
3551   * THE SOFTWARE IS PROVIDED "AS IS" AND DIGITAL
3552  EQUIPMENT CORP. DISCLAIMS ALL
3553   * WARRANTIES WITH REGARD TO THIS SOFTWARE, INCLUDING
3554  ALL IMPLIED WARRANTIES
3555   * OF MERCHANTABILITY AND FITNESS.   IN NO EVENT SHALL
3556  DIGITAL EQUIPMENT
3557   * CORPORATION BE LIABLE FOR ANY SPECIAL, DIRECT,
3558  INDIRECT, OR CONSEQUENTIAL
3559   * DAMAGES OR ANY DAMAGES WHATSOEVER RESULTING FROM LOSS
3560  OF USE, DATA OR
3561   * PROFITS, WHETHER IN AN ACTION OF CONTRACT, NEGLIGENCE
3562  OR OTHER TORTIOUS
3563   * ACTION, ARISING OUT OF OR IN CONNECTION WITH THE USE
3564  OR PERFORMANCE OF THIS
3565   * SOFTWARE.
3566   */
3567
3568  /*
3569   * Portions Copyright (c) 1996 by Internet Software
3570  Consortium.
3571   *
3572   * Permission to use, copy, modify, and distribute this
3573  software for any
3574   * purpose with or without fee is hereby granted,
3575  provided that the above
3576   * copyright notice and this permission notice appear in
3577  all copies.
3578   *
3579   * THE SOFTWARE IS PROVIDED "AS IS" AND INTERNET
3580  SOFTWARE CONSORTIUM DISCLAIMS
3581   * ALL WARRANTIES WITH REGARD TO THIS SOFTWARE INCLUDING
3582  ALL IMPLIED WARRANTIES
3583   * OF MERCHANTABILITY AND FITNESS. IN NO EVENT SHALL
3584  INTERNET SOFTWARE
3585   * CONSORTIUM BE LIABLE FOR ANY SPECIAL, DIRECT,
3586  INDIRECT, OR CONSEQUENTIAL
3587   * DAMAGES OR ANY DAMAGES WHATSOEVER RESULTING FROM LOSS
3588  OF USE, DATA OR
3589   * PROFITS, WHETHER IN AN ACTION OF CONTRACT, NEGLIGENCE
3590  OR OTHER TORTIOUS
3591   * ACTION, ARISING OUT OF OR IN CONNECTION WITH THE USE
3592  OR PERFORMANCE OF THIS
3593   * SOFTWARE.
3594   */
3595
3596  #if defined(LIBC_SCCS) && !defined(lint)
3597  static char sccsid[] = "@(#)res_send.c  8.1 (Berkeley)
3598  6/4/93";
3599  static char rcsid[] = "$Id: res_send.c,v 8.20 1998/04/06
3600  23:27:51 halley Exp $";
3601  #endif /* LIBC_SCCS and not lint */
3602
3603  /*
3604   * Send query to name server and wait for reply.
3605   */
3606
3607  #include "port_before.h"
3608  #include "fd_setsize.h"
3609
3610  #include <sys/types.h>
3611  #include <sys/param.h>
3612  #include <sys/time.h>
3613  #include <sys/socket.h>
3614  #include <sys/uio.h>
3615
3616  #include <netinet/in.h>
3617  #include <arpa/nameser.h>
3618  #include <arpa/inet.h>
3619
3620  #include <errno.h>
3621  #include <netdb.h>
3622  #include <resolv.h>
3623  #include <stdio.h>
3624  #include <stdlib.h>
3625  #include <string.h>
3626  #include <unistd.h>
3627
3628  #include "port_after.h"
3629
3630  /* Options.  Leave them on. */
```

```
3631    #define DEBUG
3632    #define CHECK_SRVR_ADDR
3633
3634    static int s = -1;        /* socket used for
3635    communications */
3636    static int connected = 0;    /* is the socket connected */
3637    static int vc = 0;        /* is the socket a virtual
3638    circuit? */
3639    static res_send_qhook Qhook = NULL;
3640    static res_send_rhook Rhook = NULL;
3641
3642
3643    #ifndef DEBUG
3644    #    define Dprint(cond, args) /*empty*/
3645    #    define DprintQ(cond, args, query, size) /*empty*/
3646    #    define Aerror(file, string, error, address) /*empty*/
3647    #    define Perror(file, string, error) /*empty*/
3648    #else
3649    #    define Dprint(cond, args) if (cond) {fprintf args;}
3650    else {}
3651    #    define DprintQ(cond, args, query, size) if (cond) {\
3652                fprintf args;\
3653                __fp_nquery(query, size, stdout);\
3654            } else {}
3655        static void
3656        Aerror(file, string, error, address)
3657        FILE *file;
3658        char *string;
3659        int error;
3660        struct sockaddr_in address;
3661        {
3662        int save = errno;
3663
3664        if (_res.options & RES_DEBUG) {
3665            fprintf(file, "res_send: %s ([%s].%u): %s\n",
3666                string,
3667                inet_ntoa(address.sin_addr),
3668                ntohs(address.sin_port),
3669                strerror(error));
3670        }
3671        errno = save;
3672        }
3673        static void
3674        Perror(file, string, error)
3675        FILE *file;
3676        char *string;
3677        int error;
3678        {
```

```
3679        int save = errno;
3680
3681        if (_res.options & RES_DEBUG) {
3682            fprintf(file, "res_send: %s: %s\n",
3683                string, strerror(error));
3684        }
3685        errno = save;
3686        }
3687    #endif
3688
3689    void
3690    res_send_setqhook(res_send_qhook hook) {
3691        Qhook = hook;
3692    }
3693
3694    void
3695    res_send_setrhook(res_send_rhook hook) {
3696        Rhook = hook;
3697    }
3698
3699    /* int
3700     * res_isourserver(ina)
3701     *    looks up "ina" in _res.ns_addr_list[]
3702     * returns:
3703     *    0  : not found
3704     *    >0 : found
3705     * author:
3706     *    paul vixie, 29may94
3707     */
3708    int
3709    res_isourserver(const struct sockaddr_in *inp) {
3710        struct sockaddr_in ina;
3711        int ns, ret;
3712
3713        ina = *inp;
3714        ret = 0;
3715        for (ns = 0;  ns < _res.nscount;  ns++) {
3716            const struct sockaddr_in *srv =
3717    &_res.nsaddr_list[ns];
3718
3719            if (srv->sin_family == ina.sin_family &&
3720                srv->sin_port == ina.sin_port &&
3721                (srv->sin_addr.s_addr == INADDR_ANY ||
3722                 srv->sin_addr.s_addr ==
3723    ina.sin_addr.s_addr)) {
3724                ret++;
3725                break;
3726            }
```

```
3727          }
3728          return (ret);
3729    }
3730
3731    /* int
3732     * res_nameinquery(name, type, class, buf, eom)
3733     *   look for (name,type,class) in the query section of
3734    packet (buf,eom)
3735     * requires:
3736     *   buf + HFIXEDSZ <= eom
3737     * returns:
3738     *   -1 : format error
3739     *   0  : not found
3740     *   >0 : found
3741     * author:
3742     *   paul vixie, 29may94
3743     */
3744    int
3745    res_nameinquery(const char *name, int type, int class,
3746            const u_char *buf, const u_char *eom)
3747    {
3748          const u_char *cp = buf + HFIXEDSZ;
3749          int qdcount = ntohs(((HEADER*)buf)->qdcount);
3750
3751          while (qdcount-- > 0) {
3752                char tname[MAXDNAME+1];
3753                int n, ttype, tclass;
3754
3755                n = dn_expand(buf, eom, cp, tname, sizeof tname);
3756                if (n < 0)
3757                      return (-1);
3758                cp += n;
3759                if (cp + 2 * INT16SZ > eom)
3760                      return (-1);
3761                ttype = ns_get16(cp); cp += INT16SZ;
3762                tclass = ns_get16(cp); cp += INT16SZ;
3763                if (ttype == type &&
3764                    tclass == class &&
3765                    strcasecmp(tname, name) == 0)
3766                      return (1);
3767          }
3768          return (0);
3769    }
3770
3771    /* int
3772     * res_queriesmatch(buf1, eom1, buf2, eom2)
3773     *   is there a 1:1 mapping of (name,type,class)
3774     *   in (buf1,eom1) and (buf2,eom2)?
3775     * returns:
3776     *   -1 : format error
3777     *   0  : not a 1:1 mapping
3778     *   >0 : is a 1:1 mapping
3779     * author:
3780     *   paul vixie, 29may94
3781     */
3782    int
3783    res_queriesmatch(const u_char *buf1, const u_char *eom1,
3784            const u_char *buf2, const u_char *eom2)
3785    {
3786          const u_char *cp = buf1 + HFIXEDSZ;
3787          int qdcount = ntohs(((HEADER*)buf1)->qdcount);
3788
3789          if (buf1 + HFIXEDSZ > eom1 || buf2 + HFIXEDSZ > eom2)
3790                return (-1);
3791
3792          /*
3793           * Only header section present in replies to
3794           * dynamic update packets.
3795           */
3796          if ( (((HEADER *)buf1)->opcode == ns_o_update) &&
3797               (((HEADER *)buf2)->opcode == ns_o_update) )
3798                return (1);
3799
3800          if (qdcount != ntohs(((HEADER*)buf2)->qdcount))
3801                return (0);
3802          while (qdcount-- > 0) {
3803                char tname[MAXDNAME+1];
3804                int n, ttype, tclass;
3805
3806                n = dn_expand(buf1, eom1, cp, tname, sizeof
3807    tname);
3808                if (n < 0)
3809                      return (-1);
3810                cp += n;
3811                if (cp + 2 * INT16SZ > eom1)
3812                      return (-1);
3813                ttype = ns_get16(cp);   cp += INT16SZ;
3814                tclass = ns_get16(cp); cp += INT16SZ;
3815                if (!res_nameinquery(tname, ttype, tclass, buf2,
3816    eom2))
3817                      return (0);
3818          }
3819          return (1);
3820    }
3821
3822    int
```

```
3823  res_send(const u_char *buf, int buflen, u_char *ans, int
3824  anssiz) {
3825      HEADER *hp = (HEADER *) buf;
3826      HEADER *anhp = (HEADER *) ans;
3827      int gotsomewhere, connreset, terrno, try, v_circuit,
3828  resplen, ns, n;
3829      u_int badns;    /* XXX NSMAX can't exceed #/bits in
3830  this variable */
3831
3832      if ((_res.options & RES_INIT) == 0 && res_init() ==
3833  -1) {
3834          /* errno should have been set by res_init() in
3835  this case. */
3836          return (-1);
3837      }
3838      if (anssiz < HFIXEDSZ) {
3839          errno = EINVAL;
3840          return (-1);
3841      }
3842      DprintQ((_res.options & RES_DEBUG) || (_res.pfcode &
3843  RES_PRF_QUERY),
3844          (stdout, ";; res_send()\n"), buf, buflen);
3845      v_circuit = (_res.options & RES_USEVC) || buflen >
3846  PACKETSZ;
3847      gotsomewhere = 0;
3848      connreset = 0;
3849      terrno = ETIMEDOUT;
3850      badns = 0;
3851
3852      /*
3853       * Send request, RETRY times, or until successful
3854       */
3855      for (try = 0; try < _res.retry; try++) {
3856          for (ns = 0; ns < _res.nscount; ns++) {
3857          struct sockaddr_in *nsap = &_res.nsaddr_list[ns];
3858  same_ns:
3859          if (badns & (1 << ns)) {
3860              res_close();
3861              goto next_ns;
3862          }
3863
3864          if (Qhook) {
3865              int done = 0, loops = 0;
3866
3867              do {
3868                  res_sendhookact act;
3869
3870                  act = (*Qhook)(&nsap, &buf, &buflen,
3871                      ans, anssiz, &resplen);
3872                  switch (act) {
3873                  case res_goahead:
3874                      done = 1;
3875                      break;
3876                  case res_nextns:
3877                      res_close();
3878                      goto next_ns;
3879                  case res_done:
3880                      return (resplen);
3881                  case res_modified:
3882                      /* give the hook another try */
3883                      if (++loops < 42) /*doug adams*/
3884                          break;
3885                      /*FALLTHROUGH*/
3886                  case res_error:
3887                      /*FALLTHROUGH*/
3888                  default:
3889                      return (-1);
3890                  }
3891              } while (!done);
3892          }
3893
3894          Dprint(_res.options & RES_DEBUG,
3895              (stdout, ";; Querying server (# %d)
3896  address = %s\n",
3897              ns + 1, inet_ntoa(nsap->sin_addr)));
3898
3899          if (v_circuit) {
3900              int truncated;
3901              struct iovec iov[2];
3902              u_short len;
3903              u_char *cp;
3904
3905              /*
3906               * Use virtual circuit;
3907               * at most one attempt per server.
3908               */
3909              try = _res.retry;
3910              truncated = 0;
3911              if (s < 0 || !vc || hp->opcode ==
3912  ns_o_update) {
3913                  if (s >= 0)
3914                      res_close();
3915
3916                  s = socket(PF_INET, SOCK_STREAM, 0);
3917                  if (s < 0) {
3918                      terrno = errno;
```

```
3919              Perror(stderr, "socket(vc)", errno);
3920              return (-1);
3921          }
3922          errno = 0;
3923          if (connect(s, (struct sockaddr *)nsap,
3924                  sizeof *nsap) < 0) {
3925              terrno = errno;
3926              Aerror(stderr, "connect/vc",
3927                      errno, *nsap);
3928              badns |= (1 << ns);
3929              res_close();
3930              goto next_ns;
3931          }
3932          vc = 1;
3933      }
3934      /*
3935       * Send length & message
3936       */
3937      putshort((u_short)buflen, (u_char*)&len);
3938      iov[0].iov_base = (caddr_t)&len;
3939      iov[0].iov_len = INT16SZ;
3940      iov[1].iov_base = (caddr_t)buf;
3941      iov[1].iov_len = buflen;
3942      if (writev(s, iov, 2) != (INT16SZ + buflen))
3943  {
3944          terrno = errno;
3945          Perror(stderr, "write failed", errno);
3946          badns |= (1 << ns);
3947          res_close();
3948          goto next_ns;
3949      }
3950      /*
3951       * Receive length & response
3952       */
3953  read_len:
3954      cp = ans;
3955      len = INT16SZ;
3956      while ((n = read(s, (char *)cp, (int)len)) >
3957  0) {
3958          cp += n;
3959          if ((len -= n) <= 0)
3960              break;
3961      }
3962      if (n <= 0) {
3963          terrno = errno;
3964          Perror(stderr, "read failed", errno);
3965          res_close();
3966          /*
```

```
3967       * A long running process might get its
3968 TCP
3969       * connection reset if the remote server
3970 was
3971       * restarted.  Requery the server
3972 instead of
3973       * trying a new one.  When there is only
3974 one
3975       * server, this means that a query might
3976 work
3977       * instead of failing.  We only allow
3978 one reset
3979       * per query to prevent looping.
3980       */
3981      if (terrno == ECONNRESET && !connreset) {
3982          connreset = 1;
3983          res_close();
3984          goto same_ns;
3985      }
3986      res_close();
3987      goto next_ns;
3988  }
3989  resplen = ns_get16(ans);
3990  if (resplen > anssiz) {
3991      Dprint(_res.options & RES_DEBUG,
3992              (stdout, ";; response
3993 truncated\n")
3994              );
3995      truncated = 1;
3996      len = anssiz;
3997  } else
3998      len = resplen;
3999  if (len < HFIXEDSZ) {
4000      /*
4001       * Undersized message.
4002       */
4003      Dprint(_res.options & RES_DEBUG,
4004              (stdout, ";; undersized: %d\n",
4005 len));
4006      terrno = EMSGSIZE;
4007      badns |= (1 << ns);
4008      res_close();
4009      goto next_ns;
4010  }
4011  cp = ans;
4012  while (len != 0 &&
4013          (n = read(s, (char *)cp, (int)len)) >
4014  0) {
```

```
4015                    cp += n;
4016                    len -= n;
4017                }
4018                if (n <= 0) {
4019                    terrno = errno;
4020                    Perror(stderr, "read(vc)", errno);
4021                    res_close();
4022                    goto next_ns;
4023                }
4024                if (truncated) {
4025                    /*
4026                     * Flush rest of answer
4027                     * so connection stays in synch.
4028                     */
4029                    anhp->tc = 1;
4030                    len = resplen - anssiz;
4031                    while (len != 0) {
4032                        char junk[PACKETSZ];
4033
4034                        n = (len > sizeof(junk)
4035                            ? sizeof(junk)
4036                            : len);
4037                        if ((n = read(s, junk, n)) > 0)
4038                            len -= n;
4039                        else
4040                            break;
4041                    }
4042                }
4043                /*
4044                 * The calling applicating has bailed out of
4045                 * a previous call and failed to arrange to
4046 have
4047                 * the circuit closed or the server has got
4048                 * itself confused. Anyway drop the packet
4049 and
4050                 * wait for the correct one.
4051                 */
4052                if (hp->id != anhp->id) {
4053                    DprintQ((_res.options & RES_DEBUG) ||
4054                        (_res.pfcode & RES_PRF_REPLY),
4055                        (stdout, ";; old answer
4056 (unexpected):\n"),
4057                        ans,
4058 (resplen>anssiz)?anssiz:resplen);
4059                    goto read_len;
4060                }
4061            } else {
4062                /*
4063                 * Use datagrams.
4064                 */
4065                struct timeval timeout;
4066                fd_set dsmask;
4067                struct sockaddr_in from;
4068                int fromlen;
4069
4070                if ((s < 0) || vc) {
4071                    if (vc)
4072                        res_close();
4073                    s = socket(PF_INET, SOCK_DGRAM, 0);
4074                    if (s < 0) {
4075 #ifndef CAN_RECONNECT
4076  bad_dg_sock:
4077 #endif
4078                        terrno = errno;
4079                        Perror(stderr, "socket(dg)", errno);
4080                        return (-1);
4081                    }
4082                    connected = 0;
4083                }
4084 #ifndef CANNOT_CONNECT_DGRAM
4085                /*
4086                 * On a 4.3BSD+ machine (client and server,
4087                 * actually), sending to a nameserver
4088 datagram
4089                 * port with no nameserver will cause an
4090                 * ICMP port unreachable message to be
4091 returned.
4092                 * If our datagram socket is "connected" to
4093 the
4094                 * server, we get an ECONNREFUSED error on
4095 the next
4096                 * socket operation, and select returns if
4097 the
4098                 * error message is received.  We can thus
4099 detect
4100                 * the absence of a nameserver without
4101 timing out.
4102                 * If we have sent queries to at least two
4103 servers,
4104                 * however, we don't want to remain
4105 connected,
4106                 * as we wish to receive answers from the
4107 first
4108                 * server to respond.
4109                 */
4110                if (_res.nscount == 1 || (try == 0 && ns ==
```

```
4111     0)) {
4112                          /*
4113                           * Connect only if we are sure we won't
4114                           * receive a response from another
4115     server.
4116                           */
4117                          if (!connected) {
4118                              if (connect(s, (struct sockaddr
4119     *)nsap,
4120                                  sizeof *nsap
4121                                  ) < 0) {
4122                                  Aerror(stderr,
4123                                      "connect(dg)",
4124                                      errno, *nsap);
4125                                  badns |= (1 << ns);
4126                                  res_close();
4127                                  goto next_ns;
4128                              }
4129                              connected = 1;
4130                          }
4131                          if (send(s, (char*)buf,
4132     buflen, 0) != buflen) {
4133                              Perror(stderr, "send", errno);
4134                              badns |= (1 << ns);
4135                              res_close();
4136                              goto next_ns;
4137                          }
4138                  } else {
4139                          /*
4140                           * Disconnect if we want to listen
4141                           * for responses from more than one
4142     server.
4143                           */
4144                          if (connected) {
4145     #ifdef CAN_RECONNECT
4146                              struct sockaddr_in no_addr;
4147
4148                              no_addr.sin_family = AF_INET;
4149                              no_addr.sin_addr.s_addr = INADDR_ANY;
4150                              no_addr.sin_port = 0;
4151                              (void) connect(s,
4152                                      (struct sockaddr *)
4153                                      &no_addr,
4154                                      sizeof no_addr);
4155     #else
4156                              int s1 = socket(PF_INET,
4157     SOCK_DGRAM,0);
4158                              if (s1 < 0)
```

```
4159                                  goto bad_dg_sock;
4160                              (void) dup2(s1, s);
4161                              (void) close(s1);
4162                              Dprint(_res.options & RES_DEBUG,
4163                                  (stdout, ";; new DG
4164     socket\n"))
4165     #endif /* CAN_RECONNECT */
4166                              connected = 0;
4167                              errno = 0;
4168                          }
4169     #endif /* !CANNOT_CONNECT_DGRAM */
4170                          if (sendto(s, (char*)buf, buflen, 0,
4171                                  (struct sockaddr *)nsap,
4172                                  sizeof *nsap)
4173                              != buflen) {
4174                              Aerror(stderr, "sendto", errno,
4175     *nsap);
4176                              badns |= (1 << ns);
4177                              res_close();
4178                              goto next_ns;
4179                          }
4180     #ifndef CANNOT_CONNECT_DGRAM
4181                  }
4182     #endif /* !CANNOT_CONNECT_DGRAM */
4183
4184                  /*
4185                   * Wait for reply
4186                   */
4187                  timeout.tv_sec = (_res.retrans << try);
4188                  if (try > 0)
4189                      timeout.tv_sec /= _res.nscount;
4190                  if ((long) timeout.tv_sec <= 0)
4191                      timeout.tv_sec = 1;
4192                  timeout.tv_usec = 0;
4193         wait:
4194                  if (s < 0 || s >= FD_SETSIZE) {
4195                      Perror(stderr, "s out-of-bounds",
4196     EMFILE);
4197                      res_close();
4198                      goto next_ns;
4199                  }
4200                  FD_ZERO(&dsmask);
4201                  FD_SET(s, &dsmask);
4202                  n = select(s+1, &dsmask, (fd_set *)NULL,
4203                      (fd_set *)NULL, &timeout);
4204                  if (n < 0) {
4205                      if (errno == EINTR)
4206                          goto wait;
```

```
4207                    Perror(stderr, "select", errno);
4208                    res_close();
4209                    goto next_ns;
4210                }
4211                if (n == 0) {
4212                    /*
4213                     * timeout
4214                     */
4215                    Dprint(_res.options & RES_DEBUG,
4216                        (stdout, ";; timeout\n"));
4217                    gotsomewhere = 1;
4218                    res_close();
4219                    goto next_ns;
4220                }
4221                errno = 0;
4222                fromlen = sizeof(struct sockaddr_in);
4223                resplen = recvfrom(s, (char*)ans, anssiz, 0,
4224                    (struct sockaddr *)&from,
4225    &fromlen);
4226                if (resplen <= 0) {
4227                    Perror(stderr, "recvfrom", errno);
4228                    res_close();
4229                    goto next_ns;
4230                }
4231                gotsomewhere = 1;
4232                if (resplen < HFIXEDSZ) {
4233                    /*
4234                     * Undersized message.
4235                     */
4236                    Dprint(_res.options & RES_DEBUG,
4237                        (stdout, ";; undersized: %d\n",
4238                      resplen));
4239                    terrno = EMSGSIZE;
4240                    badns |= (1 << ns);
4241                    res_close();
4242                    goto next_ns;
4243                }
4244                if (hp->id != anhp->id) {
4245                    /*
4246                     * response from old query, ignore it.
4247                     * XXX - potential security hazard could
4248                     *   be detected here.
4249                     */
4250                    DprintQ((_res.options & RES_DEBUG) ||
4251                        (_res.pfcode & RES_PRF_REPLY),
4252                        (stdout, ";; old answer:\n"),
4253                        ans,
4254    (resplen>anssiz)?anssiz:resplen);
```

```
4255                    goto wait;
4256                }
4257    #ifdef CHECK_SRVR_ADDR
4258                if (!(_res.options & RES_INSECURE1) &&
4259                    !res_isourserver(&from)) {
4260                    /*
4261                     * response from wrong server? ignore it.
4262                     * XXX - potential security hazard could
4263                     *   be detected here.
4264                     */
4265                    DprintQ((_res.options & RES_DEBUG) ||
4266                        (_res.pfcode & RES_PRF_REPLY),
4267                        (stdout, ";; not our server:\n"),
4268                        ans,
4269    (resplen>anssiz)?anssiz:resplen);
4270                    goto wait;
4271                }
4272    #endif
4273                if (!(_res.options & RES_INSECURE2) &&
4274                    !res_queriesmatch(buf, buf + buflen,
4275                        ans, ans + anssiz)) {
4276                    /*
4277                     * response contains wrong query? ignore
4278    it.
4279                     * XXX - potential security hazard could
4280                     *   be detected here.
4281                     */
4282                    DprintQ((_res.options & RES_DEBUG) ||
4283                        (_res.pfcode & RES_PRF_REPLY),
4284                        (stdout, ";; wrong query name:\n"),
4285                        ans,
4286    (resplen>anssiz)?anssiz:resplen);
4287                    goto wait;
4288                }
4289                if (anhp->rcode == SERVFAIL ||
4290                    anhp->rcode == NOTIMP ||
4291                    anhp->rcode == REFUSED) {
4292                    DprintQ(_res.options & RES_DEBUG,
4293                        (stdout, "server rejected query:\n"),
4294                        ans,
4295    (resplen>anssiz)?anssiz:resplen);
4296                    badns |= (1 << ns);
4297                    res_close();
4298                    /* don't retry if called from dig */
4299                    if (!_res.pfcode)
4300                        goto next_ns;
4301                }
4302                if (!(_res.options & RES_IGNTC) && anhp->tc)
```

```
4303        {
4304                    /*
4305                     * get rest of answer;
4306                     * use TCP with same server.
4307                     */
4308                    Dprint(_res.options & RES_DEBUG,
4309                            (stdout, ";; truncated
4310    answer\n"));
4311                    v_circuit = 1;
4312                    res_close();
4313                    goto same_ns;
4314                }
4315            } /*if vc/dg*/
4316            Dprint((_res.options & RES_DEBUG) ||
4317                    ((_res.pfcode & RES_PRF_REPLY) &&
4318                (_res.pfcode & RES_PRF_HEAD1)),
4319                    (stdout, ";; got answer:\n"));
4320            DprintQ((_res.options & RES_DEBUG) ||
4321                (_res.pfcode & RES_PRF_REPLY),
4322                (stdout, ""),
4323                ans, (resplen>anssiz)?anssiz:resplen);
4324            /*
4325             * If using virtual circuits, we assume that the
4326    first server
4327             * is preferred over the rest (i.e. it is on the
4328    local
4329             * machine) and only keep that one open.
4330             * If we have temporarily opened a virtual
4331    circuit,
4332             * or if we haven't been asked to keep a socket
4333    open,
4334             * close the socket.
4335             */
4336            if ((v_circuit && (!(_res.options & RES_USEVC)
4337    || ns != 0)) ||
4338                !(_res.options & RES_STAYOPEN)) {
4339                res_close();
4340            }
4341            if (Rhook) {
4342                int done = 0, loops = 0;
4343
4344                do {
4345                    res_sendhookact act;
4346
4347                    act = (*Rhook)(nsap, buf, buflen,
4348                            ans, anssiz, &resplen);
4349                    switch (act) {
4350                    case res_goahead:
4351                    case res_done:
4352                        done = 1;
4353                        break;
4354                    case res_nextns:
4355                        res_close();
4356                        goto next_ns;
4357                    case res_modified:
4358                        /* give the hook another try */
4359                        if (++loops < 42) /*doug adams*/
4360                            break;
4361                        /*FALLTHROUGH*/
4362                    case res_error:
4363                        /*FALLTHROUGH*/
4364                    default:
4365                        return (-1);
4366                    }
4367                } while (!done);
4368
4369            }
4370            return (resplen);
4371    next_ns: ;
4372        } /*foreach ns*/
4373    } /*foreach retry*/
4374    res_close();
4375    if (!v_circuit) {
4376        if (!gotsomewhere)
4377            errno = ECONNREFUSED;   /* no nameservers
4378    found */
4379        else
4380            errno = ETIMEDOUT;   /* no answer obtained */
4381    } else
4382        errno = terrno;
4383    return (-1);
4384    }
4385
4386    /*
4387     * This routine is for closing the socket if a virtual
4388    circuit is used and
4389     * the program wants to close it.  This provides support
4390    for endhostent()
4391     * which expects to close the socket.
4392     *
4393     * This routine is not expected to be user visible.
4394     */
4395    void
4396    res_close() {
4397        if (s >= 0) {
4398            (void) close(s);
```

```
4399              s = -1;
4400              connected = 0;
4401              vc = 0;
4402         }
4403    }
```

usr/src/lib/resolv/res_update.c

```
4404    #if !defined(lint) && !defined(SABER)
4405    static char rcsid[] = "$Id: res_update.c,v 1.14
4406    1998/03/10 22:04:48 halley Exp $";
4407    #endif /* not lint */
4408
4409    /*
4410     * Copyright (c) 1996 by Internet Software Consortium.
4411     *
4412     * Permission to use, copy, modify, and distribute this
4413    software for any
4414     * purpose with or without fee is hereby granted,
4415    provided that the above
4416     * copyright notice and this permission notice appear in
4417    all copies.
4418     *
4419     * THE SOFTWARE IS PROVIDED "AS IS" AND INTERNET
4420    SOFTWARE CONSORTIUM DISCLAIMS
4421     * ALL WARRANTIES WITH REGARD TO THIS SOFTWARE INCLUDING
4422    ALL IMPLIED WARRANTIES
4423     * OF MERCHANTABILITY AND FITNESS. IN NO EVENT SHALL
4424    INTERNET SOFTWARE
4425     * CONSORTIUM BE LIABLE FOR ANY SPECIAL, DIRECT,
4426    INDIRECT, OR CONSEQUENTIAL
4427     * DAMAGES OR ANY DAMAGES WHATSOEVER RESULTING FROM LOSS
4428    OF USE, DATA OR
4429     * PROFITS, WHETHER IN AN ACTION OF CONTRACT, NEGLIGENCE
4430    OR OTHER TORTIOUS
4431     * ACTION, ARISING OUT OF OR IN CONNECTION WITH THE USE
4432    OR PERFORMANCE OF THIS
4433     * SOFTWARE.
4434     */
4435
4436    /*
4437     * Based on the Dynamic DNS reference implementation by
4438    Viraj Bais
4439     * <viraj_bais@ccm.fm.intel.com>
4440     */
4441
4442    #include "port_before.h"
4443    #include <sys/param.h>
4444    #include <sys/socket.h>
4445    #include <sys/time.h>
4446    #include <netinet/in.h>
4447    #include <arpa/inet.h>
4448    #include <arpa/nameser.h>
4449    #include <errno.h>
4450    #include <limits.h>
4451    #include <netdb.h>
4452    #include <resolv.h>
4453    #include <stdio.h>
4454    #include <stdlib.h>
4455    #include <string.h>
4456    #include "port_after.h"
4457
4458    /*
4459     * Separate a linked list of records into groups so that
4460    all records
4461     * in a group will belong to a single zone on the
4462    nameserver.
4463     * Create a dynamic update packet for each zone and send
4464    it to the
4465     * nameservers for that zone, and await answer.
4466     * Abort if error occurs in updating any zone.
4467     * Return the number of zones updated on success, < 0 on
4468    error.
4469     *
4470     * On error, caller must deal with the unsynchronized
4471    zones
4472     * eg. an A record might have been successfully added to
4473    the forward
4474     * zone but the corresponding PTR record would be
4475    missing if error
4476     * was encountered while updating the reverse zone.
4477     */
4478
4479    #define NSMAX 16
4480
4481    struct ns1 {
4482        char nsname[MAXDNAME];
4483        struct in_addr nsaddr1;
4484    };
4485
4486    struct zonegrp {
4487        char        z_origin[MAXDNAME];
4488        int16_t     z_class;
4489        char        z_soardata[MAXDNAME + 5 * INT32SZ];
4490        struct ns1  z_ns[NSMAX];
4491        int     z_nscount;
4492        ns_updrec * z_rr;
```

```
4493        struct zonegrp *z_next;
4494    };
4495
4496
4497    int
4498    res_update(ns_updrec *rrecp_in) {
4499        ns_updrec *rrecp, *tmprrecp;
4500        u_char buf[PACKETSZ], answer[PACKETSZ],
4501    packet[2*PACKETSZ];
4502        char name[MAXDNAME], zname[MAXDNAME],
4503    primary[MAXDNAME],
4504            mailaddr[MAXDNAME];
4505        u_char soardata[2*MAXCDNAME+5*INT32SZ];
4506        char *dname, *svdname, *cp1, *target;
4507        u_char *cp, *eom;
4508        HEADER *hp = (HEADER *) answer;
4509        struct zonegrp *zptr = NULL, *tmpzptr, *prevzptr,
4510    *zgrp_start = NULL;
4511        int i, j, k = 0, n, ancount, nscount, arcount,
4512    rcode, rdatasize,
4513            newgroup, done, myzone, seen_before, numzones =
4514    0;
4515        u_int16_t dlen, class, qclass, type, qtype;
4516        u_int32_t ttl;
4517
4518        if ((_res.options & RES_INIT) == 0 && res_init() ==
4519    -1) {
4520            h_errno = NETDB_INTERNAL;
4521            return (-1);
4522        }
4523
4524        for (rrecp = rrecp_in; rrecp; rrecp = rrecp->r_next)
4525    {
4526            dname = rrecp->r_dname;
4527            n = strlen(dname);
4528            if (dname[n-1] == '.')
4529                dname[n-1] = '\0';
4530            qtype = T_SOA;
4531            qclass = rrecp->r_class;
4532            done = 0;
4533            seen_before = 0;
4534
4535            while (!done && dname) {
4536                if (qtype == T_SOA) {
4537                    for (tmpzptr = zgrp_start;
4538                        tmpzptr && !seen_before;
4539                        tmpzptr = tmpzptr->z_next) {
4540                        if (strcasecmp(dname,
```

```
4541                            tmpzptr->z_origin) == 0 &&
4542                            tmpzptr->z_class == qclass)
4543                            seen_before++;
4544                    for (tmprrecp = tmpzptr->z_rr;
4545                        tmprrecp && !seen_before;
4546                        tmprrecp = tmprrecp->r_grpnext)
4547                        if (strcasecmp(dname, tmprrecp->r_dname)
4548    == 0
4549                            && tmprrecp->r_class == qclass) {
4550                            seen_before++;
4551                            break;
4552                        }
4553                    if (seen_before) {
4554                        /*
4555                         * Append to the end of
4556                         * current group.
4557                         */
4558                        for (tmprrecp = tmpzptr->z_rr;
4559                            tmprrecp->r_grpnext;
4560                            tmprrecp = tmprrecp->r_grpnext)
4561                            (void)NULL;
4562                        tmprrecp->r_grpnext = rrecp;
4563                        rrecp->r_grpnext = NULL;
4564                        done = 1;
4565                        break;
4566                    }
4567                }
4568            } else if (qtype == T_A) {
4569                for (tmpzptr = zgrp_start;
4570                    tmpzptr && !done;
4571                    tmpzptr = tmpzptr->z_next)
4572                    for (i = 0; i < tmpzptr->z_nscount; i++)
4573                        if (tmpzptr->z_class == qclass &&
4574                            strcasecmp(tmpzptr->z_ns[i].nsname,
4575                                dname) == 0 &&
4576                            tmpzptr->z_ns[i].nsaddr1.s_addr !=
4577    0) {
4578                            zptr->z_ns[k].nsaddr1.s_addr =
4579                                tmpzptr->z_ns[i].nsaddr1.s_addr;
4580                            done = 1;
4581                            break;
4582                        }
4583            }
4584            if (done)
4585                break;
4586            n = res_mkquery(QUERY, dname, qclass, qtype,
4587    NULL,
4588                0, NULL, buf, sizeof buf);
```

```
4589            if (n <= 0) {
4590                    fprintf(stderr, "res_update: mkquery
4591    failed\n");
4592                    return (n);
4593            }
4594            n = res_send(buf, n, answer, sizeof answer);
4595            if (n < 0) {
4596                    fprintf(stderr, "res_update: send error for
4597    %s\n",
4598                            rrecp->r_dname);
4599                    return (n);
4600            }
4601            if (n < HFIXEDSZ)
4602                    return (-1);
4603            ancount = ntohs(hp->ancount);
4604            nscount = ntohs(hp->nscount);
4605            arcount = ntohs(hp->arcount);
4606            rcode = hp->rcode;
4607            cp = answer + HFIXEDSZ;
4608            eom = answer + n;
4609            /* skip the question section */
4610            n = dn_skipname(cp, eom);
4611            if (n < 0 || cp + n + 2 * INT16SZ > eom)
4612                    return (-1);
4613            cp += n + 2 * INT16SZ;
4614
4615            if (qtype == T_SOA) {
4616                    if (ancount == 0 && nscount == 0 && arcount
4617    == 0) {
4618                            /*
4619                             * if (rcode == NOERROR) then the dname
4620    exists but
4621                             * has no soa record associated with it.
4622                             * if (rcode == NXDOMAIN) then the dname
4623    does not
4624                             * exist and the server is replying out of
4625    NCACHE.
4626                             * in either case, proceed with the next try
4627                             */
4628                            dname = strchr(dname, '.');
4629                            if (dname != NULL)
4630                                    dname++;
4631                            continue;
4632                    } else if ((rcode == NOERROR || rcode ==
4633    NXDOMAIN) &&
4634                                    ancount == 0 &&
4635                                    nscount == 1 && arcount == 0) {
4636                            /*
4637                             * name/data does not exist, soa record
4638    supplied in the
4639                             * authority section
4640                             */
4641                            /* authority section must contain the soa
4642    record */
4643                            if ((n = dn_expand(answer, eom, cp, zname,
4644                                    sizeof zname)) < 0)
4645                                    return (n);
4646                            cp += n;
4647                            if (cp + 2 * INT16SZ > eom)
4648                                    return (-1);
4649                            GETSHORT(type, cp);
4650                            GETSHORT(class, cp);
4651                            if (type != T_SOA || class != qclass) {
4652                                    fprintf(stderr, "unknown answer\n");
4653                                    return (-1);
4654                            }
4655                            myzone = 0;
4656                            svdname = dname;
4657                            while (dname)
4658                                    if (strcasecmp(dname, zname) == 0) {
4659                                            myzone = 1;
4660                                            break;
4661                                    } else if ((dname = strchr(dname, '.'))
4662    != NULL)
4663                                            dname++;
4664                            if (!myzone) {
4665                                    dname = strchr(svdname, '.');
4666                                    if (dname != NULL)
4667                                            dname++;
4668                                    continue;
4669                            }
4670                            nscount = 0;
4671                            /* fallthrough */
4672                    } else if (rcode == NOERROR && ancount == 1)
4673    {
4674                            /*
4675                             * found the zone name
4676                             * new servers will supply NS records for
4677    the zone
4678                             * in authority section and A records for
4679    those
4680                             * nameservers in the additional section
4681                             * older servers have to be explicitly
4682    queried for
4683                             * NS records for the zone
4684                             */
```

```
4685              /* answer section must contain the soa
4686      record */
4687              if ((n = dn_expand(answer, eom, cp, zname,
4688                          sizeof zname)) < 0)
4689                  return (n);
4690              else
4691                  cp += n;
4692              if (cp + 2 * INT16SZ > eom)
4693                  return (-1);
4694              GETSHORT(type, cp);
4695              GETSHORT(class, cp);
4696              if (type == T_CNAME) {
4697                  dname = strchr(dname, '.');
4698                  if (dname != NULL)
4699                      dname++;
4700                  continue;
4701              }
4702              if (strcasecmp(dname, zname) != 0 ||
4703                  type != T_SOA ||
4704                  class != rrecp->r_class) {
4705                  fprintf(stderr, "unknown answer\n");
4706                  return (-1);
4707              }
4708              /* FALLTHROUGH */
4709          } else {
4710              fprintf(stderr,
4711          "unknown response: ans=%d, auth=%d, add=%d,
4712      rcode=%d\n",
4713                  ancount, nscount, arcount, hp->rcode);
4714          return (-1);
4715          }
4716          if (cp + INT32SZ + INT16SZ > eom)
4717              return (-1);
4718          /* continue processing the soa record */
4719          GETLONG(ttl, cp);
4720          GETSHORT(dlen, cp);
4721          if (cp + dlen > eom)
4722              return (-1);
4723          newgroup = 1;
4724          zptr = zgrp_start;
4725          prevzptr = NULL;
4726          while (zptr) {
4727              if (strcasecmp(zname, zptr->z_origin) == 0 &&
4728                  type == T_SOA && class == qclass) {
4729                  newgroup = 0;
4730                  break;
4731              }
4732              prevzptr = zptr;
4733              zptr = zptr->z_next;
4734          }
4735          if (!newgroup) {
4736          for (tmprrecp = zptr->z_rr;
4737              tmprrecp->r_grpnext;
4738              tmprrecp = tmprrecp->r_grpnext)
4739                  ;
4740          tmprrecp->r_grpnext = rrecp;
4741          rrecp->r_grpnext = NULL;
4742          done = 1;
4743          cp += dlen;
4744          break;
4745          } else {
4746          if ((n = dn_expand(answer, eom, cp, primary,
4747                      sizeof primary)) < 0)
4748              return (n);
4749          cp += n;
4750          /*
4751           * We don't have to bounds check here
4752      because the
4753           * next use of 'cp' is in dn_expand().
4754           */
4755          cp1 = (char *)soardata;
4756          strcpy(cp1, primary);
4757          cp1 += strlen(cp1) + 1;
4758          if ((n = dn_expand(answer, eom, cp, mailaddr,
4759                      sizeof mailaddr)) < 0)
4760              return (n);
4761          cp += n;
4762          strcpy(cp1, mailaddr);
4763          cp1 += strlen(cp1) + 1;
4764          if (cp + 5*INT32SZ > eom)
4765              return (-1);
4766          memcpy(cp1, cp, 5*INT32SZ);
4767          cp += 5*INT32SZ;
4768          cp1 += 5*INT32SZ;
4769          rdatasize = (u_char *)cp1 - soardata;
4770          zptr = calloc(1, sizeof(struct zonegrp));
4771          if (zptr == NULL)
4772                  return (-1);
4773          if (zgrp_start == NULL)
4774              zgrp_start = zptr;
4775          else
4776              prevzptr->z_next = zptr;
4777          zptr->z_rr = rrecp;
4778          rrecp->r_grpnext = NULL;
4779          strcpy(zptr->z_origin, zname);
4780          zptr->z_class = class;
```

```
4781              memcpy(zptr->z_soardata, soardata,
4782    rdatasize);
4783              /* fallthrough to process NS and A records */
4784              }
4785        } else if (qtype == T_NS) {
4786            if (rcode == NOERROR && ancount > 0) {
4787            strcpy(zname, dname);
4788            for (zptr = zgrp_start; zptr; zptr =
4789    zptr->z_next) {
4790                if (strcasecmp(zname, zptr->z_origin) ==
4791    0)
4792                break;
4793            }
4794            if (zptr == NULL)
4795                /* should not happen */
4796                return (-1);
4797            if (nscount > 0) {
4798                /*
4799                 * answer and authority sections contain
4800                 * the same information, skip answer
4801    section
4802                 */
4803                for (j = 0; j < ancount; j++) {
4804                n = dn_skipname(cp, eom);
4805                if (n < 0)
4806                    return (-1);
4807                n += 2*INT16SZ + INT32SZ;
4808                if (cp + n + INT16SZ > eom)
4809                    return (-1);
4810                cp += n;
4811                GETSHORT(dlen, cp);
4812                cp += dlen;
4813                }
4814            } else
4815                nscount = ancount;
4816            /* fallthrough to process NS and A records */
4817        } else {
4818            fprintf(stderr, "cannot determine
4819    nameservers for %s:\
4820    ans=%d, auth=%d, add=%d, rcode=%d\n",
4821                dname, ancount, nscount, arcount,
4822    hp->rcode);
4823            return (-1);
4824            }
4825        } else if (qtype == T_A) {
4826            if (rcode == NOERROR && ancount > 0) {
4827            arcount = ancount;
4828            ancount = nscount = 0;
4829            /* fallthrough to process A records */
4830            } else {
4831            fprintf(stderr, "cannot determine address
4832    for %s:\
4833    ans=%d, auth=%d, add=%d, rcode=%d\n",
4834                dname, ancount, nscount, arcount,
4835    hp->rcode);
4836            return (-1);
4837            }
4838        }
4839        /* process NS records for the zone */
4840        j = 0;
4841        for (i = 0; i < nscount; i++) {
4842            if ((n = dn_expand(answer, eom, cp, name,
4843                sizeof name)) < 0)
4844            return (n);
4845            cp += n;
4846            if (cp + 3 * INT16SZ + INT32SZ > eom)
4847                return (-1);
4848            GETSHORT(type, cp);
4849            GETSHORT(class, cp);
4850            GETLONG(ttl, cp);
4851            GETSHORT(dlen, cp);
4852            if (cp + dlen > eom)
4853            return (-1);
4854            if (strcasecmp(name, zname) == 0 &&
4855            type == T_NS && class == qclass) {
4856                if ((n = dn_expand(answer, eom, cp,
4857                    name, sizeof name)) < 0)
4858                    return (n);
4859                target = zptr->z_ns[j++].nsname;
4860                strcpy(target, name);
4861            }
4862            cp += dlen;
4863        }
4864        if (zptr->z_nscount == 0)
4865            zptr->z_nscount = j;
4866        /* get addresses for the nameservers */
4867        for (i = 0; i < arcount; i++) {
4868            if ((n = dn_expand(answer, eom, cp, name,
4869                sizeof name)) < 0)
4870            return (n);
4871            cp += n;
4872            if (cp + 3 * INT16SZ + INT32SZ > eom)
4873            return (-1);
4874            GETSHORT(type, cp);
4875            GETSHORT(class, cp);
4876            GETLONG(ttl, cp);
```

```
4877                  GETSHORT(dlen, cp);
4878                  if (cp + dlen > eom)
4879                      return (-1);
4880                  if (type == T_A && dlen == INT32SZ && class
4881  == qclass) {
4882                      for (j = 0; j < zptr->z_nscount; j++)
4883                          if (strcasecmp(name,
4884  zptr->z_ns[j].nsname) == 0) {
4885                              memcpy(&zptr->z_ns[j].nsaddr1.s_addr, cp,
4886                                  INT32SZ);
4887                              break;
4888                          }
4889                  }
4890                  cp += dlen;
4891              }
4892              if (zptr->z_nscount == 0) {
4893                  dname = zname;
4894                  qtype = T_NS;
4895                  continue;
4896              }
4897              done = 1;
4898              for (k = 0; k < zptr->z_nscount; k++)
4899                  if (zptr->z_ns[k].nsaddr1.s_addr == 0) {
4900                      done = 0;
4901                      dname = zptr->z_ns[k].nsname;
4902                      qtype = T_A;
4903                  }
4904
4905          } /* while */
4906      }
4907
4908      _res.options |= RES_DEBUG;
4909      for (zptr = zgrp_start; zptr; zptr = zptr->z_next) {
4910
4911          /* append zone section */
4912          rrecp = res_mkupdrec(ns_s_zn, zptr->z_origin,
4913                      zptr->z_class, ns_t_soa, 0);
4914          if (rrecp == NULL) {
4915              fprintf(stderr, "saverrec error\n");
4916              fflush(stderr);
4917              return (-1);
4918          }
4919          rrecp->r_grpnext = zptr->z_rr;
4920          zptr->z_rr = rrecp;
4921
4922          n = res_mkupdate(zptr->z_rr, packet, sizeof
4923  packet);
4924          if (n < 0) {
```

```
4925              fprintf(stderr, "res_mkupdate error\n");
4926              fflush(stderr);
4927              return (-1);
4928          } else
4929              fprintf(stdout, "res_mkupdate: packet size =
4930  %d\n", n);
4931
4932          /*
4933           * Override the list of NS records from
4934  res_init() with
4935           * the authoritative nameservers for the zone
4936  being updated.
4937           * Sort primary to be the first in the list of
4938  nameservers.
4939           */
4940          for (i = 0; i < zptr->z_nscount; i++) {
4941              if (strcasecmp(zptr->z_ns[i].nsname,
4942                      zptr->z_soardata) == 0) {
4943                  struct in_addr tmpaddr;
4944
4945                  if (i != 0) {
4946                      strcpy(zptr->z_ns[i].nsname,
4947                              zptr->z_ns[0].nsname);
4948                      strcpy(zptr->z_ns[0].nsname,
4949                              zptr->z_soardata);
4950                      tmpaddr = zptr->z_ns[i].nsaddr1;
4951                      zptr->z_ns[i].nsaddr1 =
4952                              zptr->z_ns[0].nsaddr1;
4953                      zptr->z_ns[0].nsaddr1 = tmpaddr;
4954                  }
4955                  break;
4956              }
4957          }
4958          for (i = 0; i < MAXNS; i++) {
4959              _res.nsaddr_list[i].sin_addr =
4960  zptr->z_ns[i].nsaddr1;
4961              _res.nsaddr_list[i].sin_family = AF_INET;
4962              _res.nsaddr_list[i].sin_port =
4963  htons(NAMESERVER_PORT);
4964          }
4965          _res.nscount = (zptr->z_nscount < MAXNS) ?
4966                  zptr->z_nscount : MAXNS;
4967          n = res_send(packet, n, answer, sizeof(answer));
4968          if (n < 0) {
4969              fprintf(stderr, "res_send: send error,
4970  n=%d\n", n);
4971              break;
4972          } else
```

```
4973              numzones++;
4974         }
4975
4976         /* free malloc'ed memory */
4977         while(zgrp_start) {
4978              zptr = zgrp_start;
4979              zgrp_start = zgrp_start->z_next;
4980              res_freeupdrec(zptr->z_rr);   /* Zone section we
4981    allocated. */
4982              free((char *)zptr);
4983         }
4984
4985         return (numzones);
4986    }
```

usr/src/linux/net/ipv4/af_inet.c

```
4987    /*
4988     * INET    An implementation of the TCP/IP protocol
4989    suite for the LINUX
4990     *    operating system.  INET is implemented using the
4991    BSD Socket
4992     *    interface as the means of communication with the
4993    user level.
4994     *
4995     *    AF_INET protocol family socket handler.
4996     *
4997     * Version: @(#)af_inet.c   (from sock.c) 1.0.17
4998    06/02/93
4999     *
5000     * Authors: Ross Biro, <bir7@leland.Stanford.Edu>
5001     *    Fred N. van Kempen, <waltje@uWalt.NL.Mugnet.ORG>
5002     *    Florian La Roche, <flla@stud.uni-sb.de>
5003     *    Alan Cox, <A.Cox@swansea.ac.uk>
5004     *
5005     * Changes (see also sock.c)
5006     *
5007     *    A.N.Kuznetsov   :   Socket death error in
5008    accept().
5009     *    John Richardson :   Fix non blocking error in
5010    connect()
5011     *                    so sockets that fail to connect
5012     *                    don't return -EINPROGRESS.
5013     *    Alan Cox    :   Asynchronous I/O support
5014     *    Alan Cox    :   Keep correct socket pointer on
5015    sock structures
5016     *                    when accept() ed
5017     *    Alan Cox    :   Semantics of SO_LINGER aren't
5018    state moved
5019     *                    to close when you look carefully.
5020    With
5021     *                    this fixed and the accept bug fixed
5022     *                    some RPC stuff seems happier.
5023     *    Niibe Yutaka  :   4.4BSD style write async I/O
5024     *    Alan Cox,
5025     *    Tony Gale   :   Fixed reuse semantics.
5026     *    Alan Cox    :   bind() shouldn't abort existing
5027    but dead
5028     *                    sockets. Stops FTP netin:.. I hope.
5029     *    Alan Cox    :   bind() works correctly for RAW
5030    sockets. Note
5031     *                    that FreeBSD at least was broken in
5032    this respect
5033     *                    so be careful with compatibility
5034    tests...
5035     *    Alan Cox    :   routing cache support
5036     *    Alan Cox    :   memzero the socket structure for
5037    compactness.
5038     *    Matt Day    :   nonblock connect error handler
5039     *    Alan Cox    :   Allow large numbers of pending
5040    sockets
5041     *                    (eg for big web sites), but only if
5042     *                    specifically application requested.
5043     *    Alan Cox    :   New buffering throughout IP.
5044    Used dumbly.
5045     *    Alan Cox    :   New buffering now used smartly.
5046     *    Alan Cox    :   BSD rather than common sense
5047    interpretation of
5048     *                    listen.
5049     *    Germano Caronni :   Assorted small races.
5050     *    Alan Cox    :   sendmsg/recvmsg basic support.
5051     *    Alan Cox    :   Only sendmsg/recvmsg now
5052    supported.
5053     *    Alan Cox    :   Locked down bind (see security
5054    list).
5055     *    Alan Cox    :   Loosened bind a little.
5056     *    Mike McLagan  :   ADD/DEL DLCI Ioctls
5057     * Willy Konynenberg  :   Transparent proxying support.
5058     *    David S. Miller :   New socket lookup
5059    architecture for ISS.
5060     *
5061     *    This program is free software; you can
5062    redistribute it and/or
5063     *    modify it under the terms of the GNU General
5064    Public License
5065     *    as published by the Free Software Foundation;
5066    either version
```

```
5067      *        2 of the License, or (at your option) any later
5068      version.
5069      */
5070
5071      #include <linux/config.h>
5072      #include <linux/errno.h>
5073      #include <linux/types.h>
5074      #include <linux/socket.h>
5075      #include <linux/in.h>
5076      #include <linux/kernel.h>
5077      #include <linux/major.h>
5078      #include <linux/sched.h>
5079      #include <linux/timer.h>
5080      #include <linux/string.h>
5081      #include <linux/sockios.h>
5082      #include <linux/net.h>
5083      #include <linux/fcntl.h>
5084      #include <linux/mm.h>
5085      #include <linux/interrupt.h>
5086      #include <linux/proc_fs.h>
5087      #include <linux/stat.h>
5088
5089      #include <asm/segment.h>
5090      #include <asm/system.h>
5091
5092      #include <linux/inet.h>
5093      #include <linux/netdevice.h>
5094      #include <net/ip.h>
5095      #include <net/protocol.h>
5096      #include <net/arp.h>
5097      #include <net/rarp.h>
5098      #include <net/route.h>
5099      #include <net/tcp.h>
5100      #include <net/udp.h>
5101      #include <linux/skbuff.h>
5102      #include <net/sock.h>
5103      #include <net/raw.h>
5104      #include <net/icmp.h>
5105      #include <linux/ip_fw.h>
5106      #ifdef CONFIG_IP_MASQUERADE
5107      #include <net/ip_masq.h>
5108      #endif
5109      #ifdef CONFIG_IP_ALIAS
5110      #include <net/ip_alias.h>
5111      #endif
5112      #ifdef CONFIG_BRIDGE
5113      #include <net/br.h>
5114      #endif
```

```
5115      #ifdef CONFIG_KERNELD
5116      #include <linux/kerneld.h>
5117      #endif
5118      #ifdef CONFIG_NET_RADIO
5119      #include <linux/wireless.h>
5120      #endif  /* CONFIG_NET_RADIO */
5121
5122      #define min(a,b)    ((a)<(b)?(a):(b))
5123
5124      extern struct proto packet_prot;
5125      extern int raw_get_info(char *, char **, off_t, int,
5126      int);
5127      extern int snmp_get_info(char *, char **, off_t, int,
5128      int);
5129      extern int afinet_get_info(char *, char **, off_t, int,
5130      int);
5131      extern int tcp_get_info(char *, char **, off_t, int,
5132      int);
5133      extern int udp_get_info(char *, char **, off_t, int,
5134      int);
5135
5136      #ifdef CONFIG_DLCI
5137      extern int dlci_ioctl(unsigned int, void*);
5138      #endif
5139
5140      #ifdef CONFIG_DLCI_MODULE
5141      int (*dlci_ioctl_hook)(unsigned int, void *) = NULL;
5142      #endif
5143
5144      int (*rarp_ioctl_hook)(unsigned int,void*) = NULL;
5145
5146      /*
5147       *  Destroy an AF_INET socket
5148       */
5149
5150      static __inline__ void kill_sk_queues(struct sock *sk)
5151      {
5152          struct sk_buff *skb;
5153
5154          while((skb = tcp_dequeue_partial(sk)) != NULL)
5155              kfree_skb(skb, FREE_WRITE);
5156
5157          /* Next, the write queue. */
5158          while((skb = skb_dequeue(&sk->write_queue)) != NULL)
5159              kfree_skb(skb, FREE_WRITE);
5160
5161          /* Then, the receive queue. */
5162          while((skb = skb_dequeue(&sk->receive_queue)) !=
```

```
5163    NULL) {
5164            /* This will take care of closing sockets that
5165    were
5166             * listening and didn't accept everything.
5167             */
5168            if (skb->sk != NULL && skb->sk != sk)
5169                skb->sk->prot->close(skb->sk, 0);
5170            kfree_skb(skb, FREE_READ);
5171        }
5172
5173        /*
5174         * Now we need to clean up the send head.
5175         */
5176
5177        cli();
5178        for(skb = sk->send_head; skb != NULL; )
5179        {
5180            struct sk_buff *skb2;
5181
5182            /*
5183             * We need to remove skb from the transmit queue,
5184             * or maybe the arp queue.
5185             */
5186            if (skb->next  && skb->prev)
5187            {
5188                IS_SKB(skb);
5189                skb_unlink(skb);
5190            }
5191            skb->dev = NULL;
5192            skb2 = skb->link3;
5193            kfree_skb(skb, FREE_WRITE);
5194            skb = skb2;
5195        }
5196        sk->send_head = NULL;
5197        sk->send_tail = NULL;
5198        sk->send_next = NULL;
5199        sti();
5200
5201        /* Finally, the backlog. */
5202        while((skb=skb_dequeue(&sk->back_log)) != NULL) {
5203            /* skb->sk = NULL; */
5204            kfree_skb(skb, FREE_READ);
5205        }
5206    }
5207
5208    static __inline__ void kill_sk_now(struct sock *sk)
5209    {
5210        /* No longer exists. */
```

```
5211        del_from_prot_sklist(sk);
5212
5213        /* This is gross, but needed for SOCK_PACKET -DaveM
5214    */
5215        if(sk->prot->unhash)
5216            sk->prot->unhash(sk);
5217
5218        if(sk->opt)
5219            kfree(sk->opt);
5220        ip_rt_put(sk->ip_route_cache);
5221        sk_free(sk);
5222    }
5223
5224    static __inline__ void kill_sk_later(struct sock *sk)
5225    {
5226        /* this should never happen. */
5227        /* actually it can if an ack has just been sent. */
5228        /*
5229         * It's more normal than that...
5230         * It can happen because a skb is still in the
5231    device queues
5232         * [PR]
5233         */
5234
5235        NETDEBUG(printk("Socket destroy delayed (r=%d
5236    w=%d)\n",
5237                sk->rmem_alloc, sk->wmem_alloc));
5238
5239        sk->destroy = 1;
5240        sk->ack_backlog = 0;
5241        release_sock(sk);
5242        reset_timer(sk, TIME_DESTROY, SOCK_DESTROY_TIME);
5243    }
5244
5245    void destroy_sock(struct sock *sk)
5246    {
5247        lock_sock(sk);          /* just to be safe. */
5248
5249        /*
5250         * Now we can no longer get new packets or once the
5251         * timers are killed, send them.
5252         */
5253
5254        delete_timer(sk);
5255        del_timer(&sk->delack_timer);
5256        del_timer(&sk->retransmit_timer);
5257
5258        kill_sk_queues(sk);
```

```
5259
5260        /*
5261         *  Now if it has a half accepted/ closed socket.
5262         */
5263
5264        if (sk->pair)
5265        {
5266            sk->pair->prot->close(sk->pair, 0);
5267            sk->pair = NULL;
5268        }
5269
5270        /*
5271         * Now if everything is gone we can free the socket
5272         * structure, otherwise we need to keep it around
5273    until
5274         * everything is gone.
5275         */
5276
5277        if (sk->rmem_alloc == 0 && sk->wmem_alloc == 0)
5278            kill_sk_now(sk);
5279        else
5280            kill_sk_later(sk);
5281    }
5282
5283    /*
5284     *  The routines beyond this point handle the behaviour
5285    of an AF_INET
5286     *  socket object. Mostly it punts to the subprotocols
5287    of IP to do
5288     *  the work.
5289     */
5290
5291    static int inet_fcntl(struct socket *sock, unsigned int
5292    cmd, unsigned long arg)
5293    {
5294        struct sock *sk;
5295
5296        sk = (struct sock *) sock->data;
5297
5298        switch(cmd)
5299        {
5300            case F_SETOWN:
5301                /*
5302                 * This is a little restrictive, but it's
5303    the only
5304                 * way to make sure that you can't send a
5305    sigurg to
5306                 * another process.
5307                 */
5308                if (!suser() && current->pgrp != -arg &&
5309                    current->pid != arg) return(-EPERM);
5310                sk->proc = arg;
5311                return(0);
5312            case F_GETOWN:
5313                return(sk->proc);
5314            default:
5315                return(-EINVAL);
5316        }
5317    }
5318
5319    /*
5320     *  Set socket options on an inet socket.
5321     */
5322
5323    static int inet_setsockopt(struct socket *sock, int
5324    level, int optname,
5325                char *optval, int optlen)
5326    {
5327        struct sock *sk = (struct sock *) sock->data;
5328        if (level == SOL_SOCKET)
5329            return
5330    sock_setsockopt(sk,level,optname,optval,optlen);
5331        if (sk->prot->setsockopt==NULL)
5332            return(-EOPNOTSUPP);
5333        else
5334            return
5335    sk->prot->setsockopt(sk,level,optname,optval,optlen);
5336    }
5337
5338    /*
5339     *  Get a socket option on an AF_INET socket.
5340     */
5341
5342    static int inet_getsockopt(struct socket *sock, int
5343    level, int optname,
5344                char *optval, int *optlen)
5345    {
5346        struct sock *sk = (struct sock *) sock->data;
5347        if (level == SOL_SOCKET)
5348            return
5349    sock_getsockopt(sk,level,optname,optval,optlen);
5350        if(sk->prot->getsockopt==NULL)
5351            return(-EOPNOTSUPP);
5352        else
5353            return
5354    sk->prot->getsockopt(sk,level,optname,optval,optlen);
```

```
5355        }
5356
5357        /*
5358         *  Automatically bind an unbound socket.
5359         */
5360
5361        static int inet_autobind(struct sock *sk)
5362        {
5363            /* We may need to bind the socket. */
5364            if (sk->num == 0) {
5365                sk->num = sk->prot->good_socknum();
5366                if (sk->num == 0)
5367                    return(-EAGAIN);
5368                sk->dummy_th.source = ntohs(sk->num);
5369                sk->prot->rehash(sk);
5370                add_to_prot_sklist(sk);
5371            }
5372            return 0;
5373        }
5374
5375        /*
5376         *  Move a socket into listening state.
5377         */
5378
5379        static int inet_listen(struct socket *sock, int backlog)
5380        {
5381            struct sock *sk = (struct sock *) sock->data;
5382
5383            if(inet_autobind(sk) != 0)
5384                return -EAGAIN;
5385
5386            /* We might as well re use these. */
5387            /*
5388             * note that the backlog is "unsigned char", so
5389        truncate it
5390             * somewhere. We might as well truncate it to what
5391        everybody
5392             * else does..
5393             * Now truncate to 128 not 5.
5394             *
5395             * This was wrong, truncate both cases to SOMAXCONN.
5396        -DaveM
5397             */
5398            if (((unsigned) backlog == 0) || ((unsigned) backlog
5399        > SOMAXCONN))
5400                backlog = SOMAXCONN;
5401            sk->max_ack_backlog = backlog;
5402            if (sk->state != TCP_LISTEN) {
```

```
5403                sk->ack_backlog = 0;
5404                sk->state = TCP_LISTEN;
5405                sk->prot->rehash(sk);
5406                add_to_prot_sklist(sk);
5407            }
5408            return(0);
5409        }
5410
5411        /*
5412         *  Default callbacks for user INET sockets. These just
5413        wake up
5414         *  the user owning the socket.
5415         */
5416
5417        static void def_callback1(struct sock *sk)
5418        {
5419            if(!sk->dead)
5420                wake_up_interruptible(sk->sleep);
5421        }
5422
5423        static void def_callback2(struct sock *sk,int len)
5424        {
5425            if(!sk->dead)
5426            {
5427                wake_up_interruptible(sk->sleep);
5428                sock_wake_async(sk->socket, 1);
5429            }
5430        }
5431
5432        static void def_callback3(struct sock *sk)
5433        {
5434            if(!sk->dead && sk->wmem_alloc*2 <= sk->sndbuf)
5435            {
5436                wake_up_interruptible(sk->sleep);
5437                sock_wake_async(sk->socket, 2);
5438            }
5439        }
5440
5441        /*
5442         *  Create an inet socket.
5443         *
5444         *  FIXME: Gcc would generate much better code if we set
5445        the parameters
5446         *  up in in-memory structure order. Gcc68K even more so
5447         */
5448
5449        static int inet_create(struct socket *sock, int protocol)
5450        {
```

```
5451        struct sock *sk;
5452        struct proto *prot;
5453
5454        sk = sk_alloc(GFP_KERNEL);
5455        if (sk == NULL)
5456            goto do_oom;
5457 #if 0 /* sk_alloc() does this for us. -DaveM */
5458        memset(sk,0,sizeof(*sk));    /* Efficient way to set
5459 most fields to zero */
5460 #endif
5461        /*
5462         *  Note for tcp that also wiped the dummy_th block
5463 for us.
5464         */
5465        if(sock->type == SOCK_STREAM || sock->type ==
5466 SOCK_SEQPACKET) {
5467            if (protocol && protocol != IPPROTO_TCP)
5468                goto free_and_noproto;
5469            protocol = IPPROTO_TCP;
5470            sk->no_check = TCP_NO_CHECK;
5471            prot = &tcp_prot;
5472        } else if(sock->type == SOCK_DGRAM) {
5473            if (protocol && protocol != IPPROTO_UDP)
5474                goto free_and_noproto;
5475            protocol = IPPROTO_UDP;
5476            sk->no_check = UDP_NO_CHECK;
5477            prot=&udp_prot;
5478        } else if(sock->type == SOCK_RAW || sock->type ==
5479 SOCK_PACKET) {
5480            if (!suser())
5481                goto free_and_badperm;
5482            if (!protocol)
5483                goto free_and_noproto;
5484            prot = &raw_prot;
5485            prot = (sock->type == SOCK_RAW) ? &raw_prot :
5486 &packet_prot;
5487            sk->reuse = 1;
5488            sk->num = protocol;
5489        } else {
5490            goto free_and_badtype;
5491        }
5492
5493        sk->socket = sock;
5494 #ifdef CONFIG_TCP_NAGLE_OFF
5495        sk->nonagle = 1;
5496 #endif
5497        sk->type = sock->type;
5498        sk->protocol = protocol;
5499        sk->allocation = GFP_KERNEL;
5500        sk->sndbuf = SK_WMEM_MAX;
5501        sk->rcvbuf = SK_RMEM_MAX;
5502        sk->rto = TCP_TIMEOUT_INIT;      /*TCP_WRITE_TIME*/
5503        sk->cong_window = 1; /* start with only sending one
5504 packet at a time. */
5505        sk->ssthresh = 0x7fffffff;
5506        sk->priority = 1;
5507        sk->state = TCP_CLOSE;
5508
5509        /* this is how many unacked bytes we will accept for
5510 this socket.  */
5511        sk->max_unacked = 2048; /* needs to be at most 2
5512 full packets. */
5513        sk->delay_acks = 1;
5514        sk->max_ack_backlog = SOMAXCONN;
5515        skb_queue_head_init(&sk->write_queue);
5516        skb_queue_head_init(&sk->receive_queue);
5517        sk->mtu = 576;
5518        sk->prot = prot;
5519        sk->sleep = sock->wait;
5520        init_timer(&sk->timer);
5521        init_timer(&sk->delack_timer);
5522        init_timer(&sk->retransmit_timer);
5523        sk->timer.data = (unsigned long)sk;
5524        sk->timer.function = &net_timer;
5525        skb_queue_head_init(&sk->back_log);
5526        sock->data =(void *) sk;
5527        sk->ip_ttl=ip_statistics.IpDefaultTTL;
5528        if(sk->type==SOCK_RAW && protocol==IPPROTO_RAW)
5529            sk->ip_hdrincl=1;
5530        else
5531            sk->ip_hdrincl=0;
5532 #ifdef CONFIG_IP_MULTICAST
5533        sk->ip_mc_loop=1;
5534        sk->ip_mc_ttl=1;
5535        *sk->ip_mc_name=0;
5536        sk->ip_mc_list=NULL;
5537 #endif
5538        /*
5539         *  Speed up by setting some standard state for the
5540 dummy_th
5541         *  if TCP uses it (maybe move to tcp_init later)
5542         */
5543
5544        sk->dummy_th.ack=1;
5545        sk->dummy_th.doff=sizeof(struct tcphdr)>>2;
5546
```

```
5547        sk->state_change = def_callback1;
5548        sk->data_ready = def_callback2;
5549        sk->write_space = def_callback3;
5550        sk->error_report = def_callback1;
5551
5552        if (sk->num) {
5553            /* It assumes that any protocol which allows
5554             * the user to assign a number at socket
5555             * creation time automatically
5556             * shares.
5557             */
5558            sk->dummy_th.source = ntohs(sk->num);
5559
5560            /* This is gross, but needed for SOCK_PACKET
5561  -DaveM */
5562            if(sk->prot->hash)
5563                sk->prot->hash(sk);
5564            add_to_prot_sklist(sk);
5565        }
5566
5567        if (sk->prot->init) {
5568            int err = sk->prot->init(sk);
5569            if (err != 0) {
5570                destroy_sock(sk);
5571                return(err);
5572            }
5573        }
5574        return(0);
5575
5576  free_and_badtype:
5577        sk_free(sk);
5578        return -ESOCKTNOSUPPORT;
5579
5580  free_and_badperm:
5581        sk_free(sk);
5582        return -EPERM;
5583
5584  free_and_noproto:
5585        sk_free(sk);
5586        return -EPROTONOSUPPORT;
5587
5588  do_oom:
5589        return -ENOBUFS;
5590  }
5591
5592
5593  /*
5594   *  Duplicate a socket.
5595   */
5596
5597  static int inet_dup(struct socket *newsock, struct
5598  socket *oldsock)
5599  {
5600        return(inet_create(newsock,((struct sock
5601  *)(oldsock->data))->protocol));
5602  }
5603
5604  /*
5605   *  The peer socket should always be NULL (or else).
5606  When we call this
5607   *  function we are destroying the object and from then
5608  on nobody
5609   *  should refer to it.
5610   */
5611
5612  static int inet_release(struct socket *sock, struct
5613  socket *peer)
5614  {
5615        struct sock *sk = (struct sock *) sock->data;
5616
5617        if (sk) {
5618            unsigned long timeout;
5619
5620            sk->state_change(sk);
5621
5622            /* Start closing the connection.  This may take
5623  a while. */
5624
5625  #ifdef CONFIG_IP_MULTICAST
5626            /* Applications forget to leave groups before
5627  exiting */
5628            ip_mc_drop_socket(sk);
5629  #endif
5630            /*
5631             * If linger is set, we don't return until the
5632  close
5633             * is complete.  Otherwise we return
5634  immediately. The
5635             * actually closing is done the same either way.
5636             *
5637             * If the close is due to the process exiting,
5638  we never
5639             * linger..
5640             */
5641            timeout = 0;
5642            if (sk->linger && !(current->flags &
```

```
5643        PF_EXITING)) {
5644                if (sk->lingertime)
5645                        timeout = jiffies + HZ*sk->lingertime;
5646                }
5647
5648                sock->data = NULL;
5649                sk->socket = NULL;
5650
5651                sk->prot->close(sk, timeout);
5652        }
5653        return(0);
5654 }
5655
5656
5657 static int inet_bind(struct socket *sock, struct
5658 sockaddr *uaddr, int addr_len)
5659 {
5660        struct sockaddr_in *addr=(struct sockaddr_in *)uaddr;
5661        struct sock *sk=(struct sock *)sock->data;
5662        unsigned short snum;
5663        int chk_addr_ret;
5664
5665        /* If the socket has its own bind function then use
5666 it. (RAW AND PACKET) */
5667        if(sk->prot->bind)
5668                return sk->prot->bind(sk, uaddr, addr_len);
5669
5670        /* Check these errors (active socket, bad address
5671 length, double bind). */
5672        if ((sk->state != TCP_CLOSE)              ||
5673                (addr_len < sizeof(struct sockaddr_in)) ||
5674                (sk->num != 0))
5675                return -EINVAL;
5676
5677        snum = ntohs(addr->sin_port);
5678 #ifdef CONFIG_IP_MASQUERADE
5679        /* The kernel masquerader needs some ports. */
5680        if(snum>=PORT_MASQ_BEGIN && snum<=PORT_MASQ_END)
5681                return -EADDRINUSE;
5682 #endif
5683        if (snum == 0)
5684                snum = sk->prot->good_socknum();
5685        if (snum < PROT_SOCK) {
5686        if (!suser())
5687        return(-EACCES);
5688        if (snum == 0)
5689                return(-EAGAIN);
5690        }
5691
5692        chk_addr_ret = ip_chk_addr(addr->sin_addr.s_addr);
5693        if (addr->sin_addr.s_addr != 0 && chk_addr_ret !=
5694 IS_MYADDR &&
5695        chk_addr_ret != IS_MULTICAST && chk_addr_ret !=
5696 IS_BROADCAST) {
5697 #ifdef CONFIG_IP_TRANSPARENT_PROXY
5698        /* Superuser may bind to any address to allow
5699 transparent proxying. */
5700        if(!suser())
5701 #endif
5702                return(-EADDRNOTAVAIL); /* Source address
5703 MUST be ours! */
5704        }
5705
5706        /*
5707         *        We keep a pair of addresses. rcv_saddr is
5708 the one
5709         *        used by hash lookups, and saddr is used for
5710 transmit.
5711         *
5712         *        In the BSD API these are the same except
5713 where it
5714         *        would be illegal to use them
5715 (multicast/broadcast) in
5716         *        which case the sending device address is
5717 used.
5718         */
5719        sk->rcv_saddr = sk->saddr = addr->sin_addr.s_addr;
5720        if(chk_addr_ret == IS_MULTICAST || chk_addr_ret ==
5721 IS_BROADCAST)
5722                sk->saddr = 0;   /* Use device */
5723
5724        /* Make sure we are allowed to bind here. */
5725        if(sk->prot->verify_bind(sk, snum))
5726                return -EADDRINUSE;
5727
5728        sk->num = snum;
5729        sk->dummy_th.source = ntohs(sk->num);
5730        sk->daddr = 0;
5731        sk->dummy_th.dest = 0;
5732        sk->prot->rehash(sk);
5733        add_to_prot_sklist(sk);
5734
5735        ip_rt_put(sk->ip_route_cache);
5736        sk->ip_route_cache=NULL;
5737        return(0);
5738 }
```

```
5739
5740     /*
5741      *  Connect to a remote host. There is regrettably still
5742     a little
5743      *  TCP 'magic' in here.
5744      */
5745
5746     static int inet_connect(struct socket *sock, struct
5747     sockaddr * uaddr,
5748              int addr_len, int flags)
5749     {
5750         struct sock *sk=(struct sock *)sock->data;
5751         int err;
5752         sock->conn = NULL;
5753
5754         if (sock->state == SS_CONNECTING &&
5755     tcp_connected(sk->state)) {
5756             sock->state = SS_CONNECTED;
5757             /* Connection completing after a
5758     connect/EINPROGRESS/select/connect */
5759             return 0;   /* Rock and roll */
5760         }
5761
5762         if (sock->state == SS_CONNECTING && sk->protocol ==
5763     IPPROTO_TCP && (flags & O_NONBLOCK)) {
5764             if(sk->err!=0)
5765                 return sock_error(sk);
5766             return -EALREADY;   /* Connecting is currently
5767     in progress */
5768         }
5769
5770         if (sock->state != SS_CONNECTING) {
5771             /* We may need to bind the socket. */
5772             if(inet_autobind(sk) != 0)
5773                 return(-EAGAIN);
5774             if (sk->prot->connect == NULL)
5775                 return(-EOPNOTSUPP);
5776             err = sk->prot->connect(sk, (struct sockaddr_in
5777     *)uaddr, addr_len);
5778             if (err < 0)
5779                 return(err);
5780             sock->state = SS_CONNECTING;
5781         }
5782
5783         if (sk->state > TCP_FIN_WAIT2 &&
5784     sock->state==SS_CONNECTING) {
5785             sock->state=SS_UNCONNECTED;
5786             return sock_error(sk);
5787         }
5788
5789         if (sk->state != TCP_ESTABLISHED &&(flags &
5790     O_NONBLOCK))
5791             return(-EINPROGRESS);
5792
5793         cli(); /* avoid the race condition */
5794         while(sk->state == TCP_SYN_SENT || sk->state ==
5795     TCP_SYN_RECV) {
5796             interruptible_sleep_on(sk->sleep);
5797             if (current->signal & ~current->blocked) {
5798                 sti();
5799                 return(-ERESTARTSYS);
5800             }
5801             /* This fixes a nasty in the tcp/ip code. There
5802     is a hideous hassle with
5803             icmp error packets wanting to close a tcp or
5804     udp socket. */
5805             if(sk->err && sk->protocol == IPPROTO_TCP) {
5806                 sock->state = SS_UNCONNECTED;
5807                 sti();
5808                 return sock_error(sk); /* set by tcp_err() */
5809             }
5810         }
5811         sti();
5812         sock->state = SS_CONNECTED;
5813
5814         if (sk->state != TCP_ESTABLISHED && sk->err) {
5815             sock->state = SS_UNCONNECTED;
5816             return sock_error(sk);
5817         }
5818         return(0);
5819     }
5820
5821
5822     static int inet_socketpair(struct socket *sock1, struct
5823     socket *sock2)
5824     {
5825         return(-EOPNOTSUPP);
5826     }
5827
5828
5829     /*
5830      *  Accept a pending connection. The TCP layer now gives
5831     BSD semantics.
5832      */
5833
5834     static int inet_accept(struct socket *sock, struct
```

```
5835    socket *newsock, int flags)
5836    {
5837        struct sock *sk1, *sk2;
5838        int err;
5839
5840        sk1 = (struct sock *) sock->data;
5841
5842        /*
5843         *  We've been passed an extra socket.
5844         *  We need to free it up because the tcp module
5845    creates
5846         *  its own when it accepts one.
5847         */
5848
5849        if (newsock->data) {
5850            struct sock *sk=(struct sock *)newsock->data;
5851            newsock->data=NULL;
5852            destroy_sock(sk);
5853        }
5854
5855        if (sk1->prot->accept == NULL)
5856            return(-EOPNOTSUPP);
5857
5858        /*
5859         *  Restore the state if we have been interrupted,
5860    and then returned.
5861         */
5862
5863        if (sk1->pair != NULL) {
5864            sk2 = sk1->pair;
5865            sk1->pair = NULL;
5866        } else {
5867            sk2 = sk1->prot->accept(sk1,flags);
5868            if (sk2 == NULL)
5869                return sock_error(sk1);
5870        }
5871        newsock->data = (void *)sk2;
5872        sk2->sleep = newsock->wait;
5873        sk2->socket = newsock;
5874        newsock->conn = NULL;
5875        if (flags & O_NONBLOCK)
5876            return(0);
5877
5878        cli(); /* avoid the race. */
5879        while(sk2->state == TCP_SYN_RECV) {
5880            interruptible_sleep_on(sk2->sleep);
5881            if (current->signal & ~current->blocked) {
5882                sti();
5883                sk1->pair = sk2;
5884                sk2->sleep = NULL;
5885                sk2->socket=NULL;
5886                newsock->data = NULL;
5887                return(-ERESTARTSYS);
5888            }
5889        }
5890        sti();
5891
5892        if (sk2->state != TCP_ESTABLISHED && sk2->err > 0) {
5893            err = sock_error(sk2);
5894            destroy_sock(sk2);
5895            newsock->data = NULL;
5896            return err;
5897        }
5898
5899        if (sk2->state == TCP_CLOSE) {
5900            destroy_sock(sk2);
5901            newsock->data=NULL;
5902            return -ECONNABORTED;
5903        }
5904        newsock->state = SS_CONNECTED;
5905        return(0);
5906    }
5907
5908
5909    /*
5910     *  This does both peername and sockname.
5911     */
5912
5913    static int inet_getname(struct socket *sock, struct
5914    sockaddr *uaddr,
5915            int *uaddr_len, int peer)
5916    {
5917        struct sockaddr_in *sin=(struct sockaddr_in *)uaddr;
5918        struct sock *sk;
5919
5920        sin->sin_family = AF_INET;
5921        sk = (struct sock *) sock->data;
5922        if (peer) {
5923            if (!tcp_connected(sk->state))
5924                return(-ENOTCONN);
5925            sin->sin_port = sk->dummy_th.dest;
5926            sin->sin_addr.s_addr = sk->daddr;
5927        } else {
5928            __u32 addr = sk->rcv_saddr;
5929            if (!addr) {
5930                addr = sk->saddr;
```

```
5931              }
5932              sin->sin_port = sk->dummy_th.source;
5933              sin->sin_addr.s_addr = addr;
5934          }
5935          *uaddr_len = sizeof(*sin);
5936          return(0);
5937     }
5938
5939
5940
5941     static int inet_recvmsg(struct socket *sock, struct
5942     msghdr *ubuf, int size, int noblock,
5943              int flags, int *addr_len )
5944     {
5945          struct sock *sk = (struct sock *) sock->data;
5946
5947          if (sk->prot->recvmsg == NULL)
5948              return(-EOPNOTSUPP);
5949          if(sk->err)
5950              return sock_error(sk);
5951
5952          /* We may need to bind the socket. */
5953          if(inet_autobind(sk) != 0)
5954              return(-EAGAIN);
5955
5956          return(sk->prot->recvmsg(sk, ubuf, size, noblock,
5957     flags,addr_len));
5958     }
5959
5960
5961     static int inet_sendmsg(struct socket *sock, struct
5962     msghdr *msg, int size, int noblock,
5963              int flags)
5964     {
5965          struct sock *sk = (struct sock *) sock->data;
5966          if (sk->shutdown & SEND_SHUTDOWN) {
5967              send_sig(SIGPIPE, current, 1);
5968              return(-EPIPE);
5969          }
5970          if (sk->prot->sendmsg == NULL)
5971              return(-EOPNOTSUPP);
5972          if(sk->err)
5973              return sock_error(sk);
5974
5975          /* We may need to bind the socket. */
5976          if(inet_autobind(sk) != 0)
5977              return -EAGAIN;
5978
```

```
5979          return(sk->prot->sendmsg(sk, msg, size, noblock,
5980     flags));
5981
5982     }
5983
5984
5985     static int inet_shutdown(struct socket *sock, int how)
5986     {
5987          struct sock *sk=(struct sock*)sock->data;
5988
5989          /*
5990           * This should really check to make sure
5991           * the socket is a TCP socket. (WHY AC...)
5992           */
5993          how++; /* maps 0->1 has the advantage of making bit
5994     1 rcvs and
5995                       1->2 bit 2 snds.
5996                       2->3 */
5997          if ((how & ~SHUTDOWN_MASK) || how==0)   /* MAXINT->0
5998     */
5999              return(-EINVAL);
6000          if (sock->state == SS_CONNECTING && sk->state ==
6001     TCP_ESTABLISHED)
6002              sock->state = SS_CONNECTED;
6003          if (!sk || !tcp_connected(sk->state))
6004              return(-ENOTCONN);
6005          sk->shutdown |= how;
6006          if (sk->prot->shutdown)
6007              sk->prot->shutdown(sk, how);
6008          return(0);
6009     }
6010
6011
6012     static int inet_select(struct socket *sock, int
6013     sel_type, select_table *wait )
6014     {
6015          struct sock *sk=(struct sock *) sock->data;
6016          if (sk->prot->select == NULL)
6017              return(0);
6018
6019          return(sk->prot->select(sk, sel_type, wait));
6020     }
6021
6022     /*
6023      *  ioctl() calls you can issue on an INET socket. Most
6024     of these are
6025      *  device configuration and stuff and very rarely used.
6026     Some ioctls
```

```
6027        *   pass on to the socket itself.
6028        *
6029        *   NOTE: I like the idea of a module for the config
6030   stuff. ie ifconfig
6031        *   loads the devconfigure module does its configuring
6032   and unloads it.
6033        *   There's a good 20K of config code hanging around the
6034   kernel.
6035        */
6036
6037   static int inet_ioctl(struct socket *sock, unsigned int
6038   cmd, unsigned long arg)
6039   {
6040        struct sock *sk=(struct sock *)sock->data;
6041        int err;
6042        int pid;
6043
6044        switch(cmd)
6045        {
6046             case FIOSETOWN:
6047             case SIOCSPGRP:
6048                  err=verify_area(VERIFY_READ,(int
6049   *)arg,sizeof(long));
6050                  if(err)
6051                       return err;
6052                  pid = get_user((int *) arg);
6053                  /* see inet_fcntl */
6054                  if (current->pid != pid && current->pgrp !=
6055   -pid && !suser())
6056                       return -EPERM;
6057                  sk->proc = pid;
6058                  return(0);
6059             case FIOGETOWN:
6060             case SIOCGPGRP:
6061                  err=verify_area(VERIFY_WRITE,(void *) arg,
6062   sizeof(long));
6063                  if(err)
6064                       return err;
6065                  put_fs_long(sk->proc,(int *)arg);
6066                  return(0);
6067             case SIOCGSTAMP:
6068                  if(sk->stamp.tv_sec==0)
6069                       return -ENOENT;
6070                  err=verify_area(VERIFY_WRITE,(void
6071   *)arg,sizeof(struct timeval));
6072                  if(err)
6073                       return err;
6074                  memcpy_tofs((void
6075   *)arg,&sk->stamp,sizeof(struct timeval));
6076                  return 0;
6077             case SIOCADDRT:
6078             case SIOCDELRT:
6079                  return(ip_rt_ioctl(cmd,(void *) arg));
6080             case SIOCDARP:
6081             case SIOCGARP:
6082             case SIOCSARP:
6083             case OLD_SIOCDARP:
6084             case OLD_SIOCGARP:
6085             case OLD_SIOCSARP:
6086                  return(arp_ioctl(cmd,(void *)arg));
6087             case SIOCDRARP:
6088             case SIOCGRARP:
6089             case SIOCSRARP:
6090   #ifdef CONFIG_KERNELD
6091                  if (rarp_ioctl_hook == NULL)
6092                       request_module("rarp");
6093   #endif
6094                  if (rarp_ioctl_hook != NULL)
6095                       return(rarp_ioctl_hook(cmd,(void *)
6096   arg));
6097             case SIOCGIFCONF:
6098             case SIOCGIFFLAGS:
6099             case SIOCSIFFLAGS:
6100             case SIOCGIFADDR:
6101             case SIOCSIFADDR:
6102             case SIOCADDMULTI:
6103             case SIOCDELMULTI:
6104             case SIOCGIFDSTADDR:
6105             case SIOCSIFDSTADDR:
6106             case SIOCGIFBRDADDR:
6107             case SIOCSIFBRDADDR:
6108             case SIOCGIFNETMASK:
6109             case SIOCSIFNETMASK:
6110             case SIOCGIFMETRIC:
6111             case SIOCSIFMETRIC:
6112             case SIOCGIFMEM:
6113             case SIOCSIFMEM:
6114             case SIOCGIFMTU:
6115             case SIOCSIFMTU:
6116             case SIOCSIFLINK:
6117             case SIOCGIFHWADDR:
6118             case SIOCSIFHWADDR:
6119             case SIOCSIFMAP:
6120             case SIOCGIFMAP:
6121             case SIOCSIFSLAVE:
6122             case SIOCGIFSLAVE:
```

```
6123                    return(dev_ioctl(cmd,(void *) arg));
6124
6125             case SIOCGIFBR:
6126             case SIOCSIFBR:
6127    #ifdef CONFIG_BRIDGE
6128                    return(br_ioctl(cmd,(void *) arg));
6129    #else
6130                    return -ENOPKG;
6131    #endif
6132
6133             case SIOCADDDLCI:
6134             case SIOCDELDLCI:
6135    #ifdef CONFIG_DLCI
6136                    return(dlci_ioctl(cmd, (void *) arg));
6137    #endif
6138
6139    #ifdef CONFIG_DLCI_MODULE
6140
6141    #ifdef CONFIG_KERNELD
6142                    if (dlci_ioctl_hook == NULL)
6143                            request_module("dlci");
6144    #endif
6145
6146                    if (dlci_ioctl_hook)
6147                            return((*dlci_ioctl_hook)(cmd, (void *)
6148    arg));
6149    #endif
6150                    return -ENOPKG;
6151
6152             default:
6153                    if ((cmd >= SIOCDEVPRIVATE) &&
6154                        (cmd <= (SIOCDEVPRIVATE + 15)))
6155                            return(dev_ioctl(cmd,(void *) arg));
6156
6157    #ifdef CONFIG_NET_RADIO
6158                    if((cmd >= SIOCIWFIRST) &&
6159                       (cmd <= SIOCIWLAST))
6160                            return(dev_ioctl(cmd,(void *) arg));
6161    #endif  /* CONFIG_NET_RADIO */
6162
6163                    if (sk->prot->ioctl==NULL)
6164                            return(-EINVAL);
6165                    return(sk->prot->ioctl(sk, cmd, arg));
6166         }
6167     /*NOTREACHED*/
6168     return(0);
6169 }
6170
6171 static struct proto_ops inet_proto_ops = {
6172     AF_INET,
6173
6174     inet_create,
6175     inet_dup,
6176     inet_release,
6177     inet_bind,
6178     inet_connect,
6179     inet_socketpair,
6180     inet_accept,
6181     inet_getname,
6182     inet_select,
6183     inet_ioctl,
6184     inet_listen,
6185     inet_shutdown,
6186     inet_setsockopt,
6187     inet_getsockopt,
6188     inet_fcntl,
6189     inet_sendmsg,
6190     inet_recvmsg
6191 };
6192
6193 extern unsigned long seq_offset;
6194
6195 /*
6196  *  Called by socket.c on kernel startup.
6197  */
6198
6199 void inet_proto_init(struct net_proto *pro)
6200 {
6201     struct inet_protocol *p;
6202
6203     printk("Swansea University Computer Society TCP/IP
6204 for NET3.034\n");
6205
6206     /*
6207      *  Tell SOCKET that we are alive...
6208      */
6209
6210     (void) sock_register(inet_proto_ops.family,
6211 &inet_proto_ops);
6212
6213     seq_offset = CURRENT_TIME*250;
6214
6215     /*
6216      *  Add all the protocols.
6217      */
6218
```

```
6219        printk("IP Protocols: ");
6220        for(p = inet_protocol_base; p != NULL;)
6221        {
6222            struct inet_protocol *tmp = (struct
6223  inet_protocol *) p->next;
6224            inet_add_protocol(p);
6225            printk("%s%s",p->name,tmp?", ":"\n");
6226            p = tmp;
6227        }
6228
6229        /*
6230         *  Set the ARP module up
6231         */
6232        arp_init();
6233        /*
6234         *  Set the IP module up
6235         */
6236        ip_init();
6237        /*
6238         *  Set the ICMP layer up
6239         */
6240        icmp_init(&inet_proto_ops);
6241        /*
6242         *  Set the firewalling up
6243         */
6244  #if
6245  defined(CONFIG_IP_ACCT)||defined(CONFIG_IP_FIREWALL)|| \
6246        defined(CONFIG_IP_MASQUERADE)
6247        ip_fw_init();
6248  #endif
6249        /*
6250         *  Initialise the multicast router
6251         */
6252  #if defined(CONFIG_IP_MROUTE)
6253        ip_mr_init();
6254  #endif
6255
6256        /*
6257         *  Initialise AF_INET alias type (register
6258  net_alias_type)
6259         */
6260
6261  #if defined(CONFIG_IP_ALIAS)
6262        ip_alias_init();
6263  #endif
6264
6265  #ifdef CONFIG_INET_RARP
6266        rarp_ioctl_hook = rarp_ioctl;
6267  #endif
6268        /*
6269         *  Create all the /proc entries.
6270         */
6271
6272  #ifdef CONFIG_PROC_FS
6273
6274  #ifdef CONFIG_INET_RARP
6275        proc_net_register(&(struct proc_dir_entry) {
6276            PROC_NET_RARP, 4, "rarp",
6277            S_IFREG | S_IRUGO, 1, 0, 0,
6278            0, &proc_net_inode_operations,
6279            rarp_get_info
6280        });
6281  #endif        /* RARP */
6282
6283        proc_net_register(&(struct proc_dir_entry) {
6284            PROC_NET_RAW, 3, "raw",
6285            S_IFREG | S_IRUGO, 1, 0, 0,
6286            0, &proc_net_inode_operations,
6287            raw_get_info
6288        });
6289        proc_net_register(&(struct proc_dir_entry) {
6290            PROC_NET_SNMP, 4, "snmp",
6291            S_IFREG | S_IRUGO, 1, 0, 0,
6292            0, &proc_net_inode_operations,
6293            snmp_get_info
6294        });
6295        proc_net_register(&(struct proc_dir_entry) {
6296            PROC_NET_SOCKSTAT, 8, "sockstat",
6297            S_IFREG | S_IRUGO, 1, 0, 0,
6298            0, &proc_net_inode_operations,
6299            afinet_get_info
6300        });
6301        proc_net_register(&(struct proc_dir_entry) {
6302            PROC_NET_TCP, 3, "tcp",
6303            S_IFREG | S_IRUGO, 1, 0, 0,
6304            0, &proc_net_inode_operations,
6305            tcp_get_info
6306        });
6307        proc_net_register(&(struct proc_dir_entry) {
6308            PROC_NET_UDP, 3, "udp",
6309            S_IFREG | S_IRUGO, 1, 0, 0,
6310            0, &proc_net_inode_operations,
6311            udp_get_info
6312        });
6313        proc_net_register(&(struct proc_dir_entry) {
6314            PROC_NET_ROUTE, 5, "route",
```

```
6315            S_IFREG | S_IRUGO, 1, 0, 0,
6316            0, &proc_net_inode_operations,
6317            rt_get_info
6318        });
6319        proc_net_register(&(struct proc_dir_entry) {
6320            PROC_NET_RTCACHE, 8, "rt_cache",
6321            S_IFREG | S_IRUGO, 1, 0, 0,
6322            0, &proc_net_inode_operations,
6323            rt_cache_get_info
6324        });
6325    #endif        /* CONFIG_PROC_FS */
6326    }
```

usr/src/linux/net/ipv4/datagram.c

```
6327    /*
6328     *   SUCS NET3:
6329     *
6330     *   Generic datagram handling routines. These are
6331     generic for all protocols. Possibly a generic IP version
6332     on top
6333     *   of these would make sense. Not tonight however 8-).
6334     *   This is used because UDP, RAW, PACKET, DDP, IPX,
6335     AX.25 and NetROM layer all have identical select code
6336     and mostly
6337     *   identical recvmsg() code. So we share it here. The
6338     select was shared before but buried in udp.c so I moved
6339     it.
6340     *
6341     *   Authors:     Alan Cox <alan@cymru.net>.
6342     (datagram_select() from old udp.c code)
6343     *
6344     *   Fixes:
6345     *       Alan Cox    :    NULL return from skb_peek_copy()
6346     understood
6347     *       Alan Cox    :    Rewrote skb_read_datagram to
6348     avoid the skb_peek_copy stuff.
6349     *       Alan Cox    :    Added support for
6350     SOCK_SEQPACKET. IPX can no longer use the SO_TYPE hack
6351     but
6352     *                       AX.25 now works right, and SPX is
6353     feasible.
6354     *       Alan Cox    :    Fixed write select of non IP
6355     protocol crash.
6356     *       Florian  La Roche:  Changed for my new skbuff
6357     handling.
6358     *       Darryl Miles    :    Fixed non-blocking
6359     SOCK_SEQPACKET.
6360     *       Linus Torvalds  :    BSD semantic fixes.
6361     *       Alan Cox        :    Datagram iovec handling
6362     *       Darryl Miles    :    Fixed non-blocking
6363     SOCK_STREAM.
6364     *
6365     */
6366
6367    #include <linux/types.h>
6368    #include <linux/kernel.h>
6369    #include <asm/segment.h>
6370    #include <asm/system.h>
6371    #include <linux/mm.h>
6372    #include <linux/interrupt.h>
6373    #include <linux/in.h>
6374    #include <linux/errno.h>
6375    #include <linux/sched.h>
6376    #include <linux/inet.h>
6377    #include <linux/netdevice.h>
6378    #include <net/ip.h>
6379    #include <net/protocol.h>
6380    #include <net/route.h>
6381    #include <net/tcp.h>
6382    #include <net/udp.h>
6383    #include <linux/skbuff.h>
6384    #include <net/sock.h>
6385
6386
6387    /*
6388     * Wait for a packet..
6389     *
6390     * Interrupts off so that no packet arrives before we
6391     begin sleeping.
6392     * Otherwise we might miss our wake up
6393     */
6394
6395    static inline void wait_for_packet(struct sock * sk)
6396    {
6397        unsigned long flags;
6398
6399        release_sock(sk);
6400        save_flags(flags);
6401        cli();
6402        if (skb_peek(&sk->receive_queue) == NULL)
6403            interruptible_sleep_on(sk->sleep);
6404        restore_flags(flags);
6405        lock_sock(sk);
6406    }
6407
6408    /*
```

```
6409        *  Is a socket 'connection oriented' ?
6410        */
6411
6412       static inline int connection_based(struct sock *sk)
6413       {
6414           if(sk->type==SOCK_SEQPACKET || sk->type==SOCK_STREAM)
6415               return 1;
6416           return 0;
6417       }
6418
6419       /*
6420        *  Get a datagram skbuff, understands the peeking,
6421       nonblocking wakeups and possible
6422        *  races. This replaces identical code in packet,raw
6423       and udp, as well as the IPX
6424        *  AX.25 and Appletalk. It also finally fixes the long
6425       standing peek and read
6426        *  race for datagram sockets. If you alter this routine
6427       remember it must be
6428        *  re-entrant.
6429        *
6430        *  This function will lock the socket if a skb is
6431       returned, so the caller
6432        *  needs to unlock the socket in that case (usually by
6433       calling skb_free_datagram)
6434        */
6435
6436       struct sk_buff *skb_recv_datagram(struct sock *sk,
6437       unsigned flags, int noblock, int *err)
6438       {
6439           int error;
6440           struct sk_buff *skb;
6441
6442           lock_sock(sk);
6443       restart:
6444           while(skb_queue_empty(&sk->receive_queue))  /* No
6445       data */
6446           {
6447               /* Socket errors? */
6448               error = sock_error(sk);
6449               if (error)
6450                   goto no_packet;
6451
6452               /* Socket shut down? */
6453               if (sk->shutdown & RCV_SHUTDOWN)
6454                   goto no_packet;
6455
6456               /* Sequenced packets can come disconnected. If
```

```
6457       so we report the problem */
6458               error = -ENOTCONN;
6459               if(connection_based(sk) &&
6460       sk->state!=TCP_ESTABLISHED)
6461                   goto no_packet;
6462
6463               /* User doesn't want to wait */
6464               error = -EAGAIN;
6465               if (noblock)
6466                   goto no_packet;
6467
6468               /* handle signals */
6469               error = -ERESTARTSYS;
6470               if (current->signal & ~current->blocked)
6471                   goto no_packet;
6472
6473               wait_for_packet(sk);
6474           }
6475
6476           /* Again only user level code calls this function,
6477       so nothing interrupt level
6478             will suddenly eat the receive_queue */
6479           if (flags & MSG_PEEK)
6480           {
6481               unsigned long flags;
6482               save_flags(flags);
6483               cli();
6484               skb=skb_peek(&sk->receive_queue);
6485               if(skb!=NULL)
6486                   skb->users++;
6487               restore_flags(flags);
6488               if(skb==NULL)        /* shouldn't happen but .. */
6489                   goto restart;
6490               return skb;
6491           }
6492           skb = skb_dequeue(&sk->receive_queue);
6493           if (!skb)   /* Avoid race if someone beats us to the
6494       data */
6495               goto restart;
6496           skb->users++;
6497           return skb;
6498
6499       no_packet:
6500           release_sock(sk);
6501           *err = error;
6502           return NULL;
6503       }
6504
```

```
6505  void skb_free_datagram(struct sock * sk, struct sk_buff
6506  *skb)
6507  {
6508      unsigned long flags;
6509
6510      save_flags(flags);
6511      cli();
6512      skb->users--;
6513      if(skb->users <= 0) {
6514          /* See if it needs destroying */
6515          /* Been dequeued by someone - ie it's read */
6516          if(!skb->next && !skb->prev)
6517              kfree_skb(skb,FREE_READ);
6518      }
6519      restore_flags(flags);
6520      release_sock(sk);
6521  }
6522
6523  /*
6524   *  Copy a datagram to a linear buffer.
6525   */
6526
6527  void skb_copy_datagram(struct sk_buff *skb, int offset,
6528  char *to, int size)
6529  {
6530      memcpy_tofs(to,skb->h.raw+offset,size);
6531  }
6532
6533
6534  /*
6535   *  Copy a datagram to an iovec.
6536   */
6537
6538  void skb_copy_datagram_iovec(struct sk_buff *skb, int
6539  offset, struct iovec *to, int size)
6540  {
6541      memcpy_toiovec(to,skb->h.raw+offset,size);
6542  }
6543
6544  /*
6545   *  Datagram select: Again totally generic. Moved from
6546  udp.c
6547   *  Now does seqpacket.
6548   */
6549
6550  int datagram_select(struct sock *sk, int sel_type,
6551  select_table *wait)
6552  {
6553      select_wait(sk->sleep, wait);
6554      switch(sel_type)
6555      {
6556          case SEL_IN:
6557              if (sk->err)
6558                  return 1;
6559              if (sk->shutdown & RCV_SHUTDOWN)
6560                  return 1;
6561              if (connection_based(sk) &&
6562  sk->state==TCP_CLOSE)
6563              {
6564                  /* Connection closed: Wake up */
6565                  return(1);
6566              }
6567              if (skb_peek(&sk->receive_queue) != NULL)
6568              {   /* This appears to be consistent
6569                      with other stacks */
6570                  return(1);
6571              }
6572              return(0);
6573
6574          case SEL_OUT:
6575              if (sk->err)
6576                  return 1;
6577              if (sk->shutdown & SEND_SHUTDOWN)
6578                  return 1;
6579              if (connection_based(sk) &&
6580  sk->state==TCP_SYN_SENT)
6581              {
6582                  /* Connection still in progress */
6583                  break;
6584              }
6585              if (sk->prot && sock_wspace(sk) >=
6586  MIN_WRITE_SPACE)
6587              {
6588                  return(1);
6589              }
6590              if (sk->prot==NULL &&
6591  sk->sndbuf-sk->wmem_alloc >= MIN_WRITE_SPACE)
6592              {
6593                  return(1);
6594              }
6595              return(0);
6596
6597          case SEL_EX:
6598              if (sk->err)
6599                  return(1); /* Socket has gone into error
6600  state (eg icmp error) */
```

```
6601              return(0);
6602          }
6603      return(0);
6604  }
```

usr/src/linux/net/ipv4/dev.c

```
6605  /*
6606   *    NET3    Protocol independent device support routines.
6607   *
6608   *    This program is free software; you can
6609  redistribute it and/or
6610   *    modify it under the terms of the GNU General
6611  Public License
6612   *    as published by the Free Software Foundation;
6613  either version
6614   *    2 of the License, or (at your option) any later
6615  version.
6616   *
6617   *    Derived from the non IP parts of dev.c 1.0.19
6618   *    Authors:    Ross Biro, <bir7@leland.Stanford.Edu>
6619   *            Fred N. van Kempen,
6620  <waltje@uWalt.NL.Mugnet.ORG>
6621   *            Mark Evans, <evansmp@uhura.aston.ac.uk>
6622   *
6623   *    Additional Authors:
6624   *    Florian la Roche <rzsfl@rz.uni-sb.de>
6625   *    Alan Cox <gw4pts@gw4pts.ampr.org>
6626   *    David Hinds <dhinds@allegro.stanford.edu>
6627   *
6628   *    Changes:
6629   *        Alan Cox    :    device private ioctl copies
6630  fields back.
6631   *        Alan Cox    :    Transmit queue code does
6632  relevant stunts to
6633   *                keep the queue safe.
6634   *        Alan Cox    :    Fixed double lock.
6635   *        Alan Cox    :    Fixed promisc NULL pointer trap
6636   *        ????????    :    Support the full private ioctl
6637  range
6638   *        Alan Cox    :    Moved ioctl permission check
6639  into drivers
6640   *        Tim Kordas  :    SIOCADDMULTI/SIOCDELMULTI
6641   *        Alan Cox    :    100 backlog just doesn't cut it
6642  when
6643   *                you start doing multicast video 8)
6644   *        Alan Cox    :    Rewrote net_bh and list manager.
6645   *        Alan Cox    :    Fix ETH_P_ALL echoback lengths.
6646   *        Alan Cox    :    Took out transmit every packet
6647  pass
6648   *                Saved a few bytes in the ioctl
6649  handler
6650   *        Alan Cox    :    Network driver sets packet type
6651  before calling netif_rx. Saves
6652   *                a function call a packet.
6653   *        Alan Cox    :    Hashed net_bh()
6654   *        Richard Kooijman:    Timestamp fixes.
6655   *        Alan Cox    :    Wrong field in SIOCGIFDSTADDR
6656   *        Alan Cox    :    Device lock protection.
6657   *        Alan Cox    :    Fixed nasty side effect of
6658  device close changes.
6659   *        Rudi Cilibrasi    :    Pass the right thing to
6660  set_mac_address()
6661   *        Dave Miller    :    32bit quantity for the device
6662  lock to make it work out
6663   *                on a Sparc.
6664   *        Bjorn Ekwall    :    Added KERNELD hack.
6665   *        Alan Cox    :    Cleaned up the backlog
6666  initialise.
6667   *        Craig Metz    :    SIOCGIFCONF fix if space for
6668  under
6669   *                1 device.
6670   *        Thomas Bogendoerfer :    Return ENODEV for
6671  dev_open, if there
6672   *                is no device open function.
6673   *        Lawrence V. Stefani :    Changed set MTU ioctl to
6674  not assume
6675   *                min MTU of 68 bytes for devices
6676   *                that have change MTU functions.
6677   *
6678   */
6679
6680  #include <asm/segment.h>
6681  #include <asm/system.h>
6682  #include <asm/bitops.h>
6683  #include <linux/config.h>
6684  #include <linux/types.h>
6685  #include <linux/kernel.h>
6686  #include <linux/sched.h>
6687  #include <linux/string.h>
6688  #include <linux/mm.h>
6689  #include <linux/socket.h>
6690  #include <linux/sockios.h>
6691  #include <linux/in.h>
6692  #include <linux/errno.h>
6693  #include <linux/interrupt.h>
6694  #include <linux/if_ether.h>
```

```
6695    #include <linux/inet.h>
6696    #include <linux/netdevice.h>
6697    #include <linux/etherdevice.h>
6698    #include <linux/notifier.h>
6699    #include <net/ip.h>
6700    #include <net/route.h>
6701    #include <linux/skbuff.h>
6702    #include <net/sock.h>
6703    #include <net/arp.h>
6704    #include <net/slhc.h>
6705    #include <linux/proc_fs.h>
6706    #include <linux/stat.h>
6707    #include <net/br.h>
6708    #ifdef CONFIG_NET_ALIAS
6709    #include <linux/net_alias.h>
6710    #endif
6711    #ifdef CONFIG_KERNELD
6712    #include <linux/kerneld.h>
6713    #endif
6714    #ifdef CONFIG_NET_RADIO
6715    #include <linux/wireless.h>
6716    #endif  /* CONFIG_NET_RADIO */
6717
6718    /*
6719     *   The list of packet types we will receive (as opposed
6720    to discard)
6721     *   and the routines to invoke.
6722     */
6723
6724    struct packet_type *ptype_base[16];
6725    struct packet_type *ptype_all = NULL;        /* Taps */
6726
6727    /*
6728     *   Device list lock
6729     */
6730
6731    int dev_lockct=0;
6732
6733    /*
6734     *   Our notifier list
6735     */
6736
6737    struct notifier_block *netdev_chain=NULL;
6738
6739    /*
6740     *   Device drivers call our routines to queue packets
6741    here. We empty the
6742     *   queue in the bottom half handler.
```

```
6743     */
6744
6745    static struct sk_buff_head backlog;
6746
6747    /*
6748     *  We don't overdo the queue or we will thrash memory
6749    badly.
6750     */
6751
6752    static int backlog_size = 0;
6753
6754    /*
6755     *  Return the lesser of the two values.
6756     */
6757
6758    static __inline__ unsigned long min(unsigned long a,
6759    unsigned long b)
6760    {
6761        return (a < b)? a : b;
6762    }
6763
6764
6765    /***********************************************************
6766    *********************************
6767
6768           Protocol management and registration routines
6769
6770    ***********************************************************
6771    *********************************/
6772
6773    /*
6774     *  For efficiency
6775     */
6776
6777    static int dev_nit=0;
6778
6779    /*
6780     *  Add a protocol ID to the list. Now that the input
6781    handler is
6782     *  smarter we can dispense with all the messy stuff
6783    that used to be
6784     *  here.
6785     */
6786
6787    void dev_add_pack(struct packet_type *pt)
6788    {
6789        int hash;
6790        if(pt->type==htons(ETH_P_ALL))
```

```
6791        {
6792            dev_nit++;
6793            pt->next=ptype_all;
6794            ptype_all=pt;
6795        }
6796        else
6797        {
6798            hash=ntohs(pt->type)&15;
6799            pt->next = ptype_base[hash];
6800            ptype_base[hash] = pt;
6801        }
6802    }
6803
6804
6805    /*
6806     *  Remove a protocol ID from the list.
6807     */
6808
6809    void dev_remove_pack(struct packet_type *pt)
6810    {
6811        struct packet_type **pt1;
6812        if(pt->type==htons(ETH_P_ALL))
6813        {
6814            dev_nit--;
6815            pt1=&ptype_all;
6816        }
6817        else
6818            pt1=&ptype_base[ntohs(pt->type)&15];
6819        for(; (*pt1)!=NULL; pt1=&((*pt1)->next))
6820        {
6821            if(pt==(*pt1))
6822            {
6823                *pt1=pt->next;
6824                return;
6825            }
6826        }
6827        printk(KERN_WARNING "dev_remove_pack: %p not
6828    found.\n", pt);
6829    }
6830
6831    /***********************************************
6832    ********************************
6833
6834                    Device Interface Subroutines
6835
6836    ***********************************************
6837    ********************************/
6838
6839    /*
6840     *  Find an interface by name.
6841     */
6842
6843    struct device *dev_get(const char *name)
6844    {
6845        struct device *dev;
6846
6847        for (dev = dev_base; dev != NULL; dev = dev->next)
6848        {
6849            if (strcmp(dev->name, name) == 0)
6850                return(dev);
6851        }
6852        return NULL;
6853    }
6854
6855    /*
6856     *  Find and possibly load an interface.
6857     */
6858
6859    #ifdef CONFIG_KERNELD
6860
6861    extern __inline__ void dev_load(const char *name)
6862    {
6863        if(!dev_get(name) && suser()) {
6864    #ifdef CONFIG_NET_ALIAS
6865            const char *sptr;
6866
6867            for (sptr=name ; *sptr ; sptr++) if(*sptr==':')
6868    break;
6869            if (!(*sptr && *(sptr+1)))
6870    #endif
6871            request_module(name);
6872        }
6873    }
6874
6875    #endif
6876
6877    /*
6878     *  Prepare an interface for use.
6879     */
6880
6881    int dev_open(struct device *dev)
6882    {
6883        int ret = -ENODEV;
6884
6885        /*
6886         *  Call device private open method
```

```
6887        */
6888        if (dev->open)
6889            ret = dev->open(dev);
6890
6891        /*
6892         *   If it went open OK then set the flags
6893         */
6894
6895        if (ret == 0)
6896        {
6897            dev->flags |= (IFF_UP | IFF_RUNNING);
6898            /*
6899             *   Initialise multicasting status
6900             */
6901            dev_mc_upload(dev);
6902            notifier_call_chain(&netdev_chain, NETDEV_UP,
6903    dev);
6904        }
6905        return(ret);
6906    }
6907
6908
6909    /*
6910     *   Completely shutdown an interface.
6911     */
6912
6913    int dev_close(struct device *dev)
6914    {
6915        int ct=0;
6916
6917        /*
6918         *   Call the device specific close. This cannot fail.
6919         *   Only if device is UP
6920         */
6921
6922        if ((dev->flags & IFF_UP) && dev->stop)
6923            dev->stop(dev);
6924
6925        /*
6926         *   Device is now down.
6927         */
6928
6929        dev->flags&=~(IFF_UP|IFF_RUNNING);
6930
6931        /*
6932         *   Tell people we are going down
6933         */
6934        notifier_call_chain(&netdev_chain, NETDEV_DOWN, dev);
```

```
6935        /*
6936         *   Flush the multicast chain
6937         */
6938        dev_mc_discard(dev);
6939
6940        /*
6941         *   Purge any queued packets when we down the link
6942         */
6943        while(ct<DEV_NUMBUFFS)
6944        {
6945            struct sk_buff *skb;
6946            while((skb=skb_dequeue(&dev->buffs[ct]))!=NULL)
6947                if(skb->free)
6948                    kfree_skb(skb,FREE_WRITE);
6949            ct++;
6950        }
6951        return(0);
6952    }
6953
6954
6955    /*
6956     *   Device change register/unregister. These are not
6957    inline or static
6958     *   as we export them to the world.
6959     */
6960
6961    int register_netdevice_notifier(struct notifier_block
6962    *nb)
6963    {
6964        return notifier_chain_register(&netdev_chain, nb);
6965    }
6966
6967    int unregister_netdevice_notifier(struct notifier_block
6968    *nb)
6969    {
6970        return notifier_chain_unregister(&netdev_chain,nb);
6971    }
6972
6973    /*
6974     *   Send (or queue for sending) a packet.
6975     *
6976     *   IMPORTANT: When this is called to resend frames. The
6977    caller MUST
6978     *   already have locked the sk_buff. Apart from that we
6979    do the
6980     *   rest of the magic.
6981     */
6982
```

```
6983   static void do_dev_queue_xmit(struct sk_buff *skb,
6984   struct device *dev, int pri)
6985   {
6986       unsigned long flags;
6987       struct sk_buff_head *list;
6988       int retransmission = 0; /* used to say if the packet
6989   should go  */
6990                       /* at the front or the back of the  */
6991                       /* queue - front is a retransmit try
6992   */
6993
6994       if(pri>=0 && !skb_device_locked(skb))
6995           skb_device_lock(skb);   /* Shove a lock on the
6996   frame */
6997   #if CONFIG_SKB_CHECK
6998       IS_SKB(skb);
6999   #endif
7000       skb->dev = dev;
7001
7002       /*
7003        *  Negative priority is used to flag a frame that
7004   is being pulled from the
7005        *  queue front as a retransmit attempt. It
7006   therefore goes back on the queue
7007        *  start on a failure.
7008        */
7009
7010       if (pri < 0)
7011       {
7012           pri = -pri-1;
7013           retransmission = 1;
7014       }
7015
7016   #ifdef CONFIG_NET_DEBUG
7017       if (pri >= DEV_NUMBUFFS)
7018       {
7019           printk(KERN_WARNING "bad priority in
7020   dev_queue_xmit.\n");
7021           pri = 1;
7022       }
7023   #endif
7024
7025       /*
7026        *  If the address has not been resolved. Call the
7027   device header rebuilder.
7028        *  This can cover all protocols and technically not
7029   just ARP either.
7030        */
7031
7032       if (!skb->arp && dev->rebuild_header(skb->data, dev,
7033   skb->raddr, skb)) {
7034           return;
7035       }
7036
7037       /*
7038        *
7039        *  If dev is an alias, switch to its main device.
7040        *  "arp" resolution has been made with alias
7041   device, so
7042        *  arp entries refer to alias, not main.
7043        *
7044        */
7045
7046   #ifdef CONFIG_NET_ALIAS
7047       if (net_alias_is(dev))
7048           skb->dev = dev = net_alias_dev_tx(dev);
7049   #endif
7050
7051       /*
7052        *  If we are bridging and this is directly
7053   generated output
7054        *  pass the frame via the bridge.
7055        */
7056
7057   #ifdef CONFIG_BRIDGE
7058       if(skb->pkt_bridged!=IS_BRIDGED && br_stats.flags &
7059   BR_UP)
7060       {
7061           if(br_tx_frame(skb))
7062               return;
7063       }
7064   #endif
7065
7066       list = dev->buffs + pri;
7067
7068       save_flags(flags);
7069       /* if this isn't a retransmission, use the first
7070   packet instead... */
7071       if (!retransmission) {
7072           if (skb_queue_len(list)) {
7073               /* avoid overrunning the device queue.. */
7074               if (skb_queue_len(list) > dev->tx_queue_len)
7075   {
7076                   dev_kfree_skb(skb, FREE_WRITE);
7077                   return;
7078               }
```

```
7079                    }
7080
7081            /* copy outgoing packets to any sniffer packet
7082    handlers */
7083            if (dev_nit) {
7084                    struct packet_type *ptype;
7085                    skb->stamp=xtime;
7086                    for (ptype = ptype_all; ptype!=NULL; ptype =
7087    ptype->next)
7088                    {
7089                            /* Never send packets back to the socket
7090                             * they originated from - MvS
7091    (miquels@drinkel.ow.org)
7092                             */
7093                            if ((ptype->dev == dev || !ptype->dev) &&
7094                                    ((struct sock *)ptype->data !=
7095    skb->sk))
7096                            {
7097                                    struct sk_buff *skb2;
7098                                    if ((skb2 = skb_clone(skb,
7099    GFP_ATOMIC)) == NULL)
7100                                            break;
7101                                    /* FIXME?: Wrong when the
7102    hard_header_len
7103                                     * is an upper bound. Is this even
7104                                     * used anywhere?
7105                                     */
7106                                    skb2->h.raw = skb2->data +
7107    dev->hard_header_len;
7108                                    /* On soft header devices we
7109                                     * yank the header before mac.raw
7110                                     * back off. This is set by
7111                                     * dev->hard_header().
7112                                     */
7113                                    if (dev->flags&IFF_SOFTHEADERS)
7114
7115    skb_pull(skb2,skb2->mac.raw-skb2->data);
7116                                    skb2->mac.raw = skb2->data;
7117                                    ptype->func(skb2, skb->dev, ptype);
7118                            }
7119                    }
7120            }
7121
7122            if (skb_queue_len(list)) {
7123                    cli();
7124                    skb_device_unlock(skb);     /* Buffer is on
7125    the device queue and can be freed safely */
7126                    __skb_queue_tail(list, skb);
7127                    skb = __skb_dequeue(list);
7128                    skb_device_lock(skb);       /* New buffer
7129    needs locking down */
7130                    restore_flags(flags);
7131            }
7132    }
7133    if (dev->hard_start_xmit(skb, dev) == 0) {
7134            /*
7135             * Packet is now solely the responsibility of
7136    the driver
7137             */
7138            return;
7139    }
7140
7141    /*
7142     * Transmission failed, put skb back into a list.
7143    Once on the list it's safe and
7144     * no longer device locked (it can be freed safely
7145    from the device queue)
7146     */
7147    cli();
7148    skb_device_unlock(skb);
7149    __skb_queue_head(list,skb);
7150    restore_flags(flags);
7151    }
7152
7153    void dev_queue_xmit(struct sk_buff *skb, struct device
7154    *dev, int pri)
7155    {
7156            start_bh_atomic();
7157            do_dev_queue_xmit(skb, dev, pri);
7158            end_bh_atomic();
7159    }
7160
7161    /*
7162     * Receive a packet from a device driver and queue it
7163    for the upper
7164     * (protocol) levels.  It always succeeds. This is the
7165    recommended
7166     *  interface to use.
7167     */
7168
7169    void netif_rx(struct sk_buff *skb)
7170    {
7171            static int dropping = 0;
7172
7173            /*
7174             * Any received buffers are un-owned and should be
```

```
7175    discarded
7176        *   when freed. These will be updated later as the
7177    frames get
7178        *   owners.
7179        */
7180
7181        skb->sk = NULL;
7182        skb->free = 1;
7183        if(skb->stamp.tv_sec==0)
7184            skb->stamp = xtime;
7185
7186        /*
7187         *  Check that we aren't overdoing things.
7188         */
7189
7190        if (!backlog_size)
7191            dropping = 0;
7192        else if (backlog_size > 300)
7193            dropping = 1;
7194
7195        if (dropping)
7196        {
7197            kfree_skb(skb, FREE_READ);
7198            return;
7199        }
7200
7201        /*
7202         *  Add it to the "backlog" queue.
7203         */
7204    #if CONFIG_SKB_CHECK
7205        IS_SKB(skb);
7206    #endif
7207        skb_queue_tail(&backlog,skb);
7208        backlog_size++;
7209
7210        /*
7211         *  If any packet arrived, mark it for processing
7212    after the
7213         *  hardware interrupt returns.
7214         */
7215
7216        mark_bh(NET_BH);
7217        return;
7218    }
7219
7220    /*
7221     *  This routine causes all interfaces to try to send
7222    some data.
```

```
7223    */
7224
7225    static void dev_transmit(void)
7226    {
7227        struct device *dev;
7228
7229        for (dev = dev_base; dev != NULL; dev = dev->next)
7230        {
7231            if (dev->flags != 0 && !dev->tbusy) {
7232                /*
7233                 *  Kick the device
7234                 */
7235                dev_tint(dev);
7236            }
7237        }
7238    }
7239
7240
7241    /************************************************************
7242    *************************
7243
7244                    Receive Queue Processor
7245
7246    ************************************************************
7247    *************************/
7248
7249    /*
7250     *  When we are called the queue is ready to grab, the
7251    interrupts are
7252     *  on and hardware can interrupt and queue to the
7253    receive queue as we
7254     *  run with no problems.
7255     *  This is run as a bottom half after an interrupt
7256    handler that does
7257     *  mark_bh(NET_BH);
7258     */
7259
7260    void net_bh(void)
7261    {
7262        struct packet_type *ptype;
7263        struct packet_type *pt_prev;
7264        unsigned short type;
7265
7266        /*
7267         *  Can we send anything now? We want to clear the
7268         *  decks for any more sends that get done as we
7269         *  process the input. This also minimises the
7270         *  latency on a transmit interrupt bh.
```

```
7271          */
7272
7273          dev_transmit();
7274
7275          /*
7276           *   Any data left to process. This may occur because
7277   a
7278           *   mark_bh() is done after we empty the queue
7279   including
7280           *   that from the device which does a mark_bh() just
7281   after
7282           */
7283
7284          /*
7285           *   While the queue is not empty..
7286           *
7287           *   Note that the queue never shrinks due to
7288           *   an interrupt, so we can do this test without
7289           *   disabling interrupts.
7290           */
7291
7292          while (!skb_queue_empty(&backlog)) {
7293                  struct sk_buff * skb = backlog.next;
7294
7295                  /*
7296                   *   We have a packet. Therefore the queue has
7297   shrunk
7298                   */
7299                  cli();
7300                  __skb_unlink(skb, &backlog);
7301                  backlog_size--;
7302                  sti();
7303
7304
7305  #ifdef CONFIG_BRIDGE
7306
7307                  /*
7308                   *   If we are bridging then pass the frame up to
7309   the
7310                   *   bridging code. If it is bridged then move on
7311                   */
7312
7313                  if (br_stats.flags & BR_UP)
7314                  {
7315                          /*
7316                           *   We pass the bridge a complete frame.
7317   This means
7318                           *   recovering the MAC header first.
7319                           */
7320
7321                          int offset=skb->data-skb->mac.raw;
7322                          cli();
7323                          skb_push(skb,offset);   /* Put header back
7324  on for bridge */
7325                          if(br_receive_frame(skb))
7326                          {
7327                              sti();
7328                              continue;
7329                          }
7330                          /*
7331                           *   Pull the MAC header off for the copy
7332  going to
7333                           *   the upper layers.
7334                           */
7335                          skb_pull(skb,offset);
7336                          sti();
7337                  }
7338  #endif
7339
7340          /*
7341           *   Bump the pointer to the next structure.
7342           *
7343           *   On entry to the protocol layer. skb->data and
7344           *   skb->h.raw point to the MAC and encapsulated
7345  data
7346           */
7347
7348          skb->h.raw = skb->data;
7349
7350          /*
7351           *   Fetch the packet protocol ID.
7352           */
7353
7354          type = skb->protocol;
7355
7356          /*
7357           *   We got a packet ID.  Now loop over the
7358  "known protocols"
7359           *   list. There are two lists. The ptype_all
7360  list of taps (normally empty)
7361           *   and the main protocol list which is hashed
7362  perfectly for normal protocols.
7363           */
7364
7365          pt_prev = NULL;
7366          for (ptype = ptype_all; ptype!=NULL;
```

```
7367        ptype=ptype->next)
7368            {
7369                if(!ptype->dev || ptype->dev == skb->dev) {
7370                    if(pt_prev) {
7371                        struct sk_buff *skb2=skb_clone(skb,
7372    GFP_ATOMIC);
7373                        if(skb2)
7374                            pt_prev->func(skb2,skb->dev,
7375    pt_prev);
7376                    }
7377                    pt_prev=ptype;
7378                }
7379            }
7380
7381        for (ptype = ptype_base[ntohs(type)&15]; ptype
7382    != NULL; ptype = ptype->next)
7383            {
7384                if (ptype->type == type && (!ptype->dev ||
7385    ptype->dev==skb->dev))
7386                {
7387                    /*
7388                     *  We already have a match queued.
7389    Deliver
7390                     *  to it and then remember the new match
7391                     */
7392                    if(pt_prev)
7393                    {
7394                        struct sk_buff *skb2;
7395
7396                        skb2=skb_clone(skb, GFP_ATOMIC);
7397
7398                        /*
7399                         *  Kick the protocol handler. This
7400    should be fast
7401                         *  and efficient code.
7402                         */
7403
7404                        if(skb2)
7405                            pt_prev->func(skb2, skb->dev,
7406    pt_prev);
7407                    }
7408                    /* Remember the current last to do */
7409                    pt_prev=ptype;
7410                }
7411            } /* End of protocol list loop */
7412
7413            /*
7414             *  Is there a last item to send to ?
7415             */
7416
7417            if(pt_prev)
7418                pt_prev->func(skb, skb->dev, pt_prev);
7419            /*
7420             *  Has an unknown packet has been received ?
7421             */
7422
7423            else
7424                kfree_skb(skb, FREE_WRITE);
7425            /*
7426             *  Again, see if we can transmit anything now.
7427             *  [Ought to take this out judging by tests it
7428    slows
7429             *   us down not speeds us up]
7430             */
7431    #ifdef XMIT_EVERY
7432            dev_transmit();
7433    #endif
7434        }   /* End of queue loop */
7435
7436        /*
7437         *  We have emptied the queue
7438         */
7439
7440        /*
7441         *  One last output flush.
7442         */
7443
7444    #ifdef XMIT_AFTER
7445        dev_transmit();
7446    #endif
7447    }
7448
7449
7450    /*
7451     *  This routine is called when an device driver (i.e. an
7452     *  interface) is ready to transmit a packet.
7453     */
7454
7455    void dev_tint(struct device *dev)
7456    {
7457        int i;
7458        unsigned long flags;
7459        struct sk_buff_head * head;
7460
7461        /*
7462         * aliases do not transmit (for now :) )
```

```
7463        */
7464
7465    #ifdef CONFIG_NET_ALIAS
7466        if (net_alias_is(dev)) return;
7467    #endif
7468        head = dev->buffs;
7469        save_flags(flags);
7470        cli();
7471
7472        /*
7473         *  Work the queues in priority order
7474         */
7475        for(i = 0;i < DEV_NUMBUFFS; i++,head++)
7476        {
7477
7478            while (!skb_queue_empty(head)) {
7479                struct sk_buff *skb;
7480
7481                skb = head->next;
7482                __skb_unlink(skb, head);
7483                /*
7484                 *  Stop anyone freeing the buffer while we
7485    retransmit it
7486                 */
7487                skb_device_lock(skb);
7488                restore_flags(flags);
7489                /*
7490                 *  Feed them to the output stage and if it
7491    fails
7492                 *  indicate they re-queue at the front.
7493                 */
7494                do_dev_queue_xmit(skb,dev,-i - 1);
7495                /*
7496                 *  If we can take no more then stop here.
7497                 */
7498                if (dev->tbusy)
7499                    return;
7500                cli();
7501            }
7502        }
7503        restore_flags(flags);
7504    }
7505
7506
7507    /*
7508     *  Perform a SIOCGIFCONF call. This structure will
7509    change
7510     *  size shortly, and there is nothing I can do about it.
```

```
7511     *  Thus we will need a 'compatibility mode'.
7512     */
7513
7514    static int dev_ifconf(char *arg)
7515    {
7516        struct ifconf ifc;
7517        struct ifreq ifr;
7518        struct device *dev;
7519        char *pos;
7520        int len;
7521        int err;
7522
7523        /*
7524         *  Fetch the caller's info block.
7525         */
7526
7527        err=verify_area(VERIFY_WRITE, arg, sizeof(struct
7528    ifconf));
7529        if(err)
7530            return err;
7531        memcpy_fromfs(&ifc, arg, sizeof(struct ifconf));
7532        len = ifc.ifc_len;
7533        pos = ifc.ifc_buf;
7534
7535        /*
7536         *  We now walk the device list filling each active
7537    device
7538         *  into the array.
7539         */
7540
7541        err=verify_area(VERIFY_WRITE,pos,len);
7542        if(err)
7543            return err;
7544
7545        /*
7546         *  Loop over the interfaces, and write an info
7547    block for each.
7548         */
7549
7550        for (dev = dev_base; dev != NULL; dev = dev->next)
7551        {
7552            if(!(dev->flags & IFF_UP))  /* Downed devices
7553    don't count */
7554                continue;
7555            /*
7556             *  Have we run out of space here ?
7557             */
7558
```

```
7559            if (len < sizeof(struct ifreq))
7560                break;
7561
7562            memset(&ifr, 0, sizeof(struct ifreq));
7563            strcpy(ifr.ifr_name, dev->name);
7564            (*(struct sockaddr_in *)
7565        &ifr.ifr_addr).sin_family = dev->family;
7566            (*(struct sockaddr_in *)
7567        &ifr.ifr_addr).sin_addr.s_addr = dev->pa_addr;
7568
7569
7570            /*
7571             *  Write this block to the caller's space.
7572             */
7573
7574            memcpy_tofs(pos, &ifr, sizeof(struct ifreq));
7575            pos += sizeof(struct ifreq);
7576            len -= sizeof(struct ifreq);
7577        }
7578
7579        /*
7580         * All done.  Write the updated control block back
7581    to the caller.
7582         */
7583
7584        ifc.ifc_len = (pos - ifc.ifc_buf);
7585        ifc.ifc_req = (struct ifreq *) ifc.ifc_buf;
7586        memcpy_tofs(arg, &ifc, sizeof(struct ifconf));
7587
7588        /*
7589         *  Report how much was filled in
7590         */
7591
7592        return(pos - arg);
7593    }
7594
7595
7596    /*
7597     * This is invoked by the /proc filesystem handler to
7598    display a device
7599     *  in detail.
7600     */
7601
7602    #ifdef CONFIG_PROC_FS
7603    static int sprintf_stats(char *buffer, struct device
7604    *dev)
7605    {
7606        struct enet_statistics *stats = (dev->get_stats ?
```

```
7607    dev->get_stats(dev): NULL);
7608        int size;
7609
7610        if (stats)
7611            size = sprintf(buffer, "%6s:%7d %4d %4d %4d %4d
7612    %8d %4d %4d %4d %5d %4d\n",
7613                dev->name,
7614                stats->rx_packets, stats->rx_errors,
7615                stats->rx_dropped + stats->rx_missed_errors,
7616                stats->rx_fifo_errors,
7617                stats->rx_length_errors +
7618    stats->rx_over_errors
7619                + stats->rx_crc_errors +
7620    stats->rx_frame_errors,
7621                stats->tx_packets, stats->tx_errors,
7622    stats->tx_dropped,
7623                stats->tx_fifo_errors, stats->collisions,
7624                stats->tx_carrier_errors +
7625    stats->tx_aborted_errors
7626                + stats->tx_window_errors +
7627    stats->tx_heartbeat_errors);
7628        else
7629            size = sprintf(buffer, "%6s: No statistics
7630    available.\n", dev->name);
7631
7632        return size;
7633    }
7634
7635    /*
7636     *  Called from the PROCfs module. This now uses the new
7637    arbitrary sized /proc/net interface
7638     *  to create /proc/net/dev
7639     */
7640
7641    int dev_get_info(char *buffer, char **start, off_t
7642    offset, int length, int dummy)
7643    {
7644        int len=0;
7645        off_t begin=0;
7646        off_t pos=0;
7647        int size;
7648
7649        struct device *dev;
7650
7651
7652        size = sprintf(buffer, "Inter-|   Receive
7653          |  Transmit\n"
7654                    " face |packets errs drop fifo
```

```
7655    frame|packets errs drop fifo colls carrier\n");
7656
7657        pos+=size;
7658        len+=size;
7659
7660
7661        for (dev = dev_base; dev != NULL; dev = dev->next)
7662        {
7663            size = sprintf_stats(buffer+len, dev);
7664            len+=size;
7665            pos=begin+len;
7666
7667            if(pos<offset)
7668            {
7669                len=0;
7670                begin=pos;
7671            }
7672            if(pos>offset+length)
7673                break;
7674        }
7675
7676        *start=buffer+(offset-begin);    /* Start of wanted
7677    data */
7678        len-=(offset-begin);            /* Start slop */
7679        if(len>length)
7680            len=length;        /* Ending slop */
7681        return len;
7682    }
7683    #endif   /* CONFIG_PROC_FS */
7684
7685
7686    #ifdef CONFIG_NET_RADIO
7687    #ifdef CONFIG_PROC_FS
7688
7689    /*
7690     * Print one entry of /proc/net/wireless
7691     * This is a clone of /proc/net/dev (just above)
7692     */
7693    static int
7694    sprintf_wireless_stats(char *        buffer,
7695                    struct device *   dev)
7696    {
7697        /* Get stats from the driver */
7698        struct iw_statistics *stats =
7699    (dev->get_wireless_stats ?
7700                            dev->get_wireless_stats(dev) :
7701                            (struct iw_statistics *) NULL);
7702        int size;
```

```
7703
7704        if(stats != (struct iw_statistics *) NULL)
7705            size = sprintf(buffer,
7706                    "%6s: %02x   %3d%c %3d%c   %3d%c %5d
7707    %5d %5d\n",
7708                    dev->name,
7709                    stats->status,
7710                    stats->qual.qual,
7711                    stats->qual.updated & 1 ? '.' : ' ',
7712                    stats->qual.level,
7713                    stats->qual.updated & 2 ? '.' : ' ',
7714                    stats->qual.noise,
7715                    stats->qual.updated & 3 ? '.' : ' ',
7716                    stats->discard.nwid,
7717                    stats->discard.code,
7718                    stats->discard.misc);
7719        else
7720            size = 0;
7721
7722        return size;
7723    }
7724
7725    /*
7726     * Print info for /proc/net/wireless (print all entries)
7727     * This is a clone of /proc/net/dev (just above)
7728     */
7729    int
7730    dev_get_wireless_info(char *      buffer,
7731                    char **    start,
7732                    off_t offset,
7733                    int    length,
7734                    int    dummy)
7735    {
7736        int    len = 0;
7737        off_t      begin = 0;
7738        off_t      pos = 0;
7739        int    size;
7740
7741        struct device * dev;
7742
7743        size = sprintf(buffer,
7744                    "Inter-|sta|   Quality      |   Discarded
7745    packets\n"
7746                    " face |tus|link level noise| nwid crypt
7747    misc\n");
7748
7749        pos+=size;
7750        len+=size;
```

```
7751
7752
7753        for(dev = dev_base; dev != NULL; dev = dev->next)
7754        {
7755            size = sprintf_wireless_stats(buffer+len, dev);
7756            len+=size;
7757            pos=begin+len;
7758
7759            if(pos < offset)
7760            {
7761                len=0;
7762                begin=pos;
7763            }
7764            if(pos > offset + length)
7765                break;
7766        }
7767
7768        *start = buffer + (offset - begin); /* Start of
7769    wanted data */
7770        len -= (offset - begin);        /* Start slop */
7771        if(len > length)
7772            len = length;       /* Ending slop */
7773
7774        return len;
7775    }
7776    #endif  /* CONFIG_PROC_FS */
7777    #endif  /* CONFIG_NET_RADIO */
7778
7779
7780    /*
7781     *  This checks bitmasks for the ioctl calls for devices.
7782     */
7783
7784    static inline int bad_mask(unsigned long mask, unsigned
7785    long addr)
7786    {
7787        if (addr & (mask = ~mask))
7788            return 1;
7789        mask = ntohl(mask);
7790        if (mask & (mask+1))
7791            return 1;
7792        return 0;
7793    }
7794
7795    /*
7796     *  Perform the SIOCxIFxxx calls.
7797     *
7798     *  The socket layer has seen an ioctl the address
```

```
7799    family thinks is
7800     *  for the device. At this point we get invoked to make
7801    a decision
7802     */
7803
7804    static int dev_ifsioc(void *arg, unsigned int getset)
7805    {
7806        struct ifreq ifr;
7807        struct device *dev;
7808        int ret;
7809
7810        /*
7811         *  Fetch the caller's info block into kernel space
7812         */
7813
7814        int err=verify_area(VERIFY_WRITE, arg, sizeof(struct
7815    ifreq));
7816        if(err)
7817            return err;
7818
7819        memcpy_fromfs(&ifr, arg, sizeof(struct ifreq));
7820
7821        /*
7822         *  See which interface the caller is talking about.
7823         */
7824
7825        /*
7826         *
7827         *  net_alias_dev_get(): dev_get() with added alias
7828    naming magic.
7829         *  only allow alias creation/deletion if
7830    (getset==SIOCSIFADDR)
7831         *
7832         */
7833
7834    #ifdef CONFIG_KERNELD
7835        dev_load(ifr.ifr_name);
7836    #endif
7837
7838    #ifdef CONFIG_NET_ALIAS
7839        if ((dev = net_alias_dev_get(ifr.ifr_name, getset ==
7840    SIOCSIFADDR, &err, NULL, NULL)) == NULL)
7841            return(err);
7842    #else
7843        if ((dev = dev_get(ifr.ifr_name)) == NULL)
7844            return(-ENODEV);
7845    #endif
7846        switch(getset)
```

```
7847            {
7848                case SIOCGIFFLAGS:  /* Get interface flags */
7849                    ifr.ifr_flags = (dev->flags &
7850     ~IFF_SOFTHEADERS);
7851                    goto rarok;
7852
7853                case SIOCSIFFLAGS:  /* Set interface flags */
7854                    {
7855                        int old_flags = dev->flags;
7856
7857                        if(securelevel>0)
7858                            ifr.ifr_flags&=~IFF_PROMISC;
7859                        /*
7860                         *  We are not allowed to potentially
7861     close/unload
7862                         *  a device until we get this lock.
7863                         */
7864
7865                        dev_lock_wait();
7866
7867                        /*
7868                         *  Set the flags on our device.
7869                         */
7870
7871                        dev->flags = (ifr.ifr_flags & (
7872                            IFF_BROADCAST | IFF_DEBUG |
7873     IFF_LOOPBACK |
7874                            IFF_POINTOPOINT | IFF_NOTRAILERS |
7875     IFF_RUNNING |
7876                            IFF_NOARP | IFF_PROMISC |
7877     IFF_ALLMULTI | IFF_SLAVE | IFF_MASTER
7878                            | IFF_MULTICAST)) | (dev->flags &
7879     (IFF_SOFTHEADERS|IFF_UP));
7880                        /*
7881                         *  Load in the correct multicast list
7882     now the flags have changed.
7883                         */
7884
7885                        dev_mc_upload(dev);
7886
7887                        /*
7888                         *  Have we downed the interface. We
7889     handle IFF_UP ourselves
7890                         *  according to user attempts to set
7891     it, rather than blindly
7892                         *  setting it.
7893                         */
7894
7895                        if ((old_flags^ifr.ifr_flags)&IFF_UP)
7896     /* Bit is different  ? */
7897                        {
7898                            if(old_flags&IFF_UP)        /* Gone
7899     down */
7900                                ret=dev_close(dev);
7901                            else                /* Come up */
7902                            {
7903                                ret=dev_open(dev);
7904                                if(ret<0)
7905                                    dev->flags&=~IFF_UP;    /*
7906     Open failed */
7907                            }
7908                        }
7909                        else
7910                            ret=0;
7911                        /*
7912                         *  Load in the correct multicast list
7913     now the flags have changed.
7914                         */
7915
7916                        dev_mc_upload(dev);
7917                    }
7918                    break;
7919
7920                case SIOCGIFADDR:   /* Get interface address
7921     (and family) */
7922                    if(ifr.ifr_addr.sa_family==AF_UNSPEC)
7923                    {
7924
7925     memcpy(ifr.ifr_hwaddr.sa_data,dev->dev_addr,
7926     MAX_ADDR_LEN);
7927                        ifr.ifr_hwaddr.sa_family=dev->type;
7928
7929                        goto rarok;
7930                    }
7931                    else
7932                    {
7933                        (*(struct sockaddr_in *)
7934                            &ifr.ifr_addr).sin_addr.s_addr =
7935     dev->pa_addr;
7936                        (*(struct sockaddr_in *)
7937                            &ifr.ifr_addr).sin_family =
7938     dev->family;
7939                        (*(struct sockaddr_in *)
7940                            &ifr.ifr_addr).sin_port = 0;
7941                    }
7942                    goto rarok;
```

```
7943                 case SIOCSIFADDR:   /* Set interface address
7944     (and family) */
7945
7946                     /*
7947                      * BSDism. SIOCSIFADDR family=AF_UNSPEC
7948     sets the
7949                      * physical address. We can cope with this
7950     now.
7951                      */
7952
7953                     if(ifr.ifr_addr.sa_family==AF_UNSPEC)
7954                     {
7955                         if(dev->set_mac_address==NULL)
7956                             return -EOPNOTSUPP;
7957                         if(securelevel>0)
7958                             return -EPERM;
7959
7960     ret=dev->set_mac_address(dev,&ifr.ifr_addr);
7961                     }
7962                     else
7963                     {
7964                         u32 new_pa_addr = (*(struct sockaddr_in
7965     *)
7966                             &ifr.ifr_addr).sin_addr.s_addr;
7967                         u16 new_family = ifr.ifr_addr.sa_family;
7968
7969                         if (new_family == dev->family &&
7970                             new_pa_addr == dev->pa_addr) {
7971                             ret =0;
7972                             break;
7973                         }
7974                         if (dev->flags & IFF_UP)
7975                             notifier_call_chain(&netdev_chain,
7976     NETDEV_DOWN, dev);
7977
7978                         /*
7979                          * if dev is an alias, must rehash to
7980     update
7981                          * address change
7982                          */
7983
7984     #ifdef CONFIG_NET_ALIAS
7985                         if (net_alias_is(dev))
7986                             net_alias_dev_rehash(dev
7987     ,&ifr.ifr_addr);
7988     #endif
7989                         dev->pa_addr = new_pa_addr;
```

```
7991                         dev->family = new_family;
7992
7993     #ifdef CONFIG_INET
7994                         /* This is naughty. When net-032e comes
7995     out It wants moving into the net032
7996                         code not the kernel. Till then it can
7997     sit here (SIGH) */
7998                         if (!dev->pa_mask)
7999                             dev->pa_mask =
8000     ip_get_mask(dev->pa_addr);
8001     #endif
8002                         if (!dev->pa_brdaddr)
8003                             dev->pa_brdaddr = dev->pa_addr |
8004     ~dev->pa_mask;
8005                         if (dev->flags & IFF_UP)
8006                             notifier_call_chain(&netdev_chain,
8007     NETDEV_UP, dev);
8008                         ret = 0;
8009                     }
8010                     break;
8011
8012             case SIOCGIFBRDADDR:    /* Get the broadcast
8013     address */
8014                     (*(struct sockaddr_in *)
8015                         &ifr.ifr_broadaddr).sin_addr.s_addr =
8016     dev->pa_brdaddr;
8017                     (*(struct sockaddr_in *)
8018                         &ifr.ifr_broadaddr).sin_family =
8019     dev->family;
8020                     (*(struct sockaddr_in *)
8021                         &ifr.ifr_broadaddr).sin_port = 0;
8022                     goto rarok;
8023
8024             case SIOCSIFBRDADDR:    /* Set the broadcast
8025     address */
8026                     dev->pa_brdaddr = (*(struct sockaddr_in *)
8027                         &ifr.ifr_broadaddr).sin_addr.s_addr;
8028                     ret = 0;
8029                     break;
8030
8031             case SIOCGIFDSTADDR:    /* Get the destination
8032     address (for point-to-point links) */
8033                     (*(struct sockaddr_in *)
8034                         &ifr.ifr_dstaddr).sin_addr.s_addr =
8035     dev->pa_dstaddr;
8036                     (*(struct sockaddr_in *)
8037                         &ifr.ifr_dstaddr).sin_family =
8038     dev->family;
```

```
8039              (*(struct sockaddr_in *)
8040                    &ifr.ifr_dstaddr).sin_port = 0;
8041              goto rarok;
8042
8043          case SIOCSIFDSTADDR:      /* Set the destination
8044 address (for point-to-point links) */
8045                  dev->pa_dstaddr = (*(struct sockaddr_in *)
8046                    &ifr.ifr_dstaddr).sin_addr.s_addr;
8047              ret = 0;
8048              break;
8049
8050          case SIOCGIFNETMASK:       /* Get the netmask for
8051 the interface */
8052                  (*(struct sockaddr_in *)
8053                    &ifr.ifr_netmask).sin_addr.s_addr =
8054 dev->pa_mask;
8055                  (*(struct sockaddr_in *)
8056                    &ifr.ifr_netmask).sin_family =
8057 dev->family;
8058                  (*(struct sockaddr_in *)
8059                    &ifr.ifr_netmask).sin_port = 0;
8060              goto rarok;
8061
8062          case SIOCSIFNETMASK:       /* Set the netmask for
8063 the interface */
8064              {
8065                  unsigned long mask = (*(struct
8066 sockaddr_in *)
8067                    &ifr.ifr_netmask).sin_addr.s_addr;
8068              ret = -EINVAL;
8069              /*
8070               *  The mask we set must be legal.
8071               */
8072              if (bad_mask(mask,0))
8073                  break;
8074              dev->pa_mask = mask;
8075              ret = 0;
8076              }
8077          break;
8078
8079          case SIOCGIFMETRIC: /* Get the metric on the
8080 interface (currently unused) */
8081
8082              ifr.ifr_metric = dev->metric;
8083              goto  rarok;
8084
8085          case SIOCSIFMETRIC: /* Set the metric on the
8086 interface (currently unused) */
```

```
8087              dev->metric = ifr.ifr_metric;
8088              ret=0;
8089              break;
8090
8091          case SIOCGIFMTU:     /* Get the MTU of a device */
8092              ifr.ifr_mtu = dev->mtu;
8093              goto rarok;
8094
8095          case SIOCSIFMTU:     /* Set the MTU of a device */
8096
8097              if (dev->change_mtu)
8098                  ret = dev->change_mtu(dev, ifr.ifr_mtu);
8099              else
8100              {
8101                  /*
8102                   *  MTU must be positive.
8103                   */
8104
8105                  if(ifr.ifr_mtu<68)
8106                      return -EINVAL;
8107
8108                  dev->mtu = ifr.ifr_mtu;
8109                  ret = 0;
8110              }
8111          break;
8112
8113          case SIOCGIFMEM:     /* Get the per device memory
8114 space. We can add this but currently
8115                       do not support it */
8116              ret = -EINVAL;
8117              break;
8118
8119          case SIOCSIFMEM:     /* Set the per device memory
8120 buffer space. Not applicable in our case */
8121              ret = -EINVAL;
8122              break;
8123
8124          case SIOCGIFHWADDR:
8125              memcpy(ifr.ifr_hwaddr.sa_data,dev->dev_addr,
8126 MAX_ADDR_LEN);
8127              ifr.ifr_hwaddr.sa_family=dev->type;
8128              goto rarok;
8129
8130          case SIOCSIFHWADDR:
8131              if(dev->set_mac_address==NULL)
8132                  return -EOPNOTSUPP;
8133              if(securelevel > 0)
8134                  return -EPERM;
```

```
8135                if(ifr.ifr_hwaddr.sa_family!=dev->type)
8136                    return -EINVAL;
8137
8138      ret=dev->set_mac_address(dev,&ifr.ifr_hwaddr);
8139                break;
8140
8141          case SIOCGIFMAP:
8142                ifr.ifr_map.mem_start=dev->mem_start;
8143                ifr.ifr_map.mem_end=dev->mem_end;
8144                ifr.ifr_map.base_addr=dev->base_addr;
8145                ifr.ifr_map.irq=dev->irq;
8146                ifr.ifr_map.dma=dev->dma;
8147                ifr.ifr_map.port=dev->if_port;
8148                goto rarok;
8149
8150          case SIOCSIFMAP:
8151                if(dev->set_config==NULL)
8152                    return -EOPNOTSUPP;
8153                return dev->set_config(dev,&ifr.ifr_map);
8154
8155          case SIOCADDMULTI:
8156                if(dev->set_multicast_list==NULL)
8157                    return -EINVAL;
8158                if(ifr.ifr_hwaddr.sa_family!=AF_UNSPEC)
8159                    return -EINVAL;
8160                dev_mc_add(dev,ifr.ifr_hwaddr.sa_data,
8161      dev->addr_len, 1);
8162                return 0;
8163
8164          case SIOCDELMULTI:
8165                if(dev->set_multicast_list==NULL)
8166                    return -EINVAL;
8167                if(ifr.ifr_hwaddr.sa_family!=AF_UNSPEC)
8168                    return -EINVAL;
8169
8170      dev_mc_delete(dev,ifr.ifr_hwaddr.sa_data,dev->addr_len,
8171      1);
8172                return 0;
8173          /*
8174           *  Unknown or private ioctl
8175           */
8176
8177          default:
8178                if((getset >= SIOCDEVPRIVATE) &&
8179                    (getset <= (SIOCDEVPRIVATE + 15))) {
8180                    if(dev->do_ioctl==NULL)
8181                        return -EOPNOTSUPP;
8182                    ret=dev->do_ioctl(dev, &ifr, getset);
8183                    memcpy_tofs(arg,&ifr,sizeof(struct
8184      ifreq));
8185                    break;
8186                }
8187
8188  #ifdef CONFIG_NET_RADIO
8189                if((getset >= SIOCIWFIRST) &&
8190                    (getset <= SIOCIWLAST))
8191                {
8192                    if(dev->do_ioctl==NULL)
8193                        return -EOPNOTSUPP;
8194                    /* Perform the ioctl */
8195                    ret=dev->do_ioctl(dev, &ifr, getset);
8196                    /* If return args... */
8197                    if(IW_IS_GET(getset))
8198                        memcpy_tofs(arg, &ifr,
8199                                sizeof(struct ifreq));
8200                    break;
8201                }
8202  #endif  /* CONFIG_NET_RADIO */
8203
8204                ret = -EINVAL;
8205          }
8206      return(ret);
8207  /*
8208   *  The load of calls that return an ifreq and ok (saves
8209  memory).
8210   */
8211  rarok:
8212      memcpy_tofs(arg, &ifr, sizeof(struct ifreq));
8213      return 0;
8214  }
8215
8216
8217  /*
8218   *  This function handles all "interface"-type I/O
8219  control requests. The actual
8220   *  'doing' part of this is dev_ifsioc above.
8221   */
8222
8223  int dev_ioctl(unsigned int cmd, void *arg)
8224  {
8225      switch(cmd)
8226      {
8227          case SIOCGIFCONF:
8228                (void) dev_ifconf((char *) arg);
8229                return 0;
8230
```

```
8231            /*
8232             *  Ioctl calls that can be done by all.
8233             */
8234
8235            case SIOCGIFFLAGS:
8236            case SIOCGIFADDR:
8237            case SIOCGIFDSTADDR:
8238            case SIOCGIFBRDADDR:
8239            case SIOCGIFNETMASK:
8240            case SIOCGIFMETRIC:
8241            case SIOCGIFMTU:
8242            case SIOCGIFMEM:
8243            case SIOCGIFHWADDR:
8244            case SIOCGIFSLAVE:
8245            case SIOCGIFMAP:
8246                return dev_ifsioc(arg, cmd);
8247
8248            /*
8249             *  Ioctl calls requiring the power of a
8250    superuser
8251             */
8252
8253            case SIOCSIFFLAGS:
8254            case SIOCSIFADDR:
8255            case SIOCSIFDSTADDR:
8256            case SIOCSIFBRDADDR:
8257            case SIOCSIFNETMASK:
8258            case SIOCSIFMETRIC:
8259            case SIOCSIFMTU:
8260            case SIOCSIFMEM:
8261            case SIOCSIFHWADDR:
8262            case SIOCSIFMAP:
8263            case SIOCSIFSLAVE:
8264            case SIOCADDMULTI:
8265            case SIOCDELMULTI:
8266                if (!suser())
8267                    return -EPERM;
8268                return dev_ifsioc(arg, cmd);
8269
8270            case SIOCSIFLINK:
8271                return -EINVAL;
8272
8273            /*
8274             *  Unknown or private ioctl.
8275             */
8276
8277            default:
8278                if((cmd >= SIOCDEVPRIVATE) &&
8279                   (cmd <= (SIOCDEVPRIVATE + 15))) {
8280                    return dev_ifsioc(arg, cmd);
8281                }
8282    #ifdef CONFIG_NET_RADIO
8283                if((cmd >= SIOCIWFIRST) &&
8284                   (cmd <= SIOCIWLAST))
8285                {
8286                    if((IW_IS_SET(cmd)) && (!suser()))
8287                        return -EPERM;
8288                    return dev_ifsioc(arg, cmd);
8289                }
8290    #endif  /* CONFIG_NET_RADIO */
8291                return -EINVAL;
8292        }
8293    }
8294
8295
8296    /*
8297     *  Initialize the DEV module. At boot time this walks
8298    the device list and
8299     *  unhooks any devices that fail to initialise
8300    (normally hardware not
8301     *  present) and leaves us with a valid list of present
8302    and active devices.
8303     *
8304     */
8305    extern int lance_init(void);
8306    extern int pi_init(void);
8307    extern void sdla_setup(void);
8308    extern int dlci_setup(void);
8309
8310    int net_dev_init(void)
8311    {
8312        struct device *dev, **dp;
8313
8314        /*
8315         *  Initialise the packet receive queue.
8316         */
8317
8318        skb_queue_head_init(&backlog);
8319
8320        /*
8321         *  The bridge has to be up before the devices
8322         */
8323
8324    #ifdef CONFIG_BRIDGE
8325        br_init();
8326    #endif
```

```
8327
8328        /*
8329         * This is Very Ugly(tm).
8330         *
8331         * Some devices want to be initialized early..
8332         */
8333   #if defined(CONFIG_PI)
8334        pi_init();
8335   #endif
8336   #if defined(CONFIG_PT)
8337        pt_init();
8338   #endif
8339   #if defined(CONFIG_DLCI)
8340        dlci_setup();
8341   #endif
8342   #if defined(CONFIG_SDLA)
8343        sdla_setup();
8344   #endif
8345        /*
8346         *   SLHC if present needs attaching so other people
8347   see it
8348         *   even if not opened.
8349         */
8350   #if (defined(CONFIG_SLIP) &&
8351   defined(CONFIG_SLIP_COMPRESSED)) \
8352        || defined(CONFIG_PPP) \
8353        || (defined(CONFIG_ISDN) && defined(CONFIG_ISDN_PPP))
8354        slhc_install();
8355   #endif
8356
8357        /*
8358         * Add the devices.
8359         * If the call to dev->init fails, the dev is
8360   removed
8361         * from the chain disconnecting the device until the
8362         * next reboot.
8363         */
8364
8365        dp = &dev_base;
8366        while ((dev = *dp) != NULL)
8367        {
8368            int i;
8369            for (i = 0; i < DEV_NUMBUFFS; i++) {
8370                skb_queue_head_init(dev->buffs + i);
8371            }
8372
8373            if (dev->init && dev->init(dev))
8374            {
8375                /*
8376                 *  It failed to come up. Unhook it.
8377                 */
8378                *dp = dev->next;
8379            }
8380            else
8381            {
8382                dp = &dev->next;
8383            }
8384        }
8385
8386   #ifdef CONFIG_PROC_FS
8387        proc_net_register(&(struct proc_dir_entry) {
8388            PROC_NET_DEV, 3, "dev",
8389            S_IFREG | S_IRUGO, 1, 0, 0,
8390            0, &proc_net_inode_operations,
8391            dev_get_info
8392        });
8393   #endif
8394
8395   #ifdef CONFIG_NET_RADIO
8396   #ifdef CONFIG_PROC_FS
8397        proc_net_register(&(struct proc_dir_entry) {
8398            PROC_NET_WIRELESS, 8, "wireless",
8399            S_IFREG | S_IRUGO, 1, 0, 0,
8400            0, &proc_net_inode_operations,
8401            dev_get_wireless_info
8402        });
8403   #endif   /* CONFIG_PROC_FS */
8404   #endif   /* CONFIG_NET_RADIO */
8405
8406        /*
8407         *   Initialise net_alias engine
8408         *
8409         *       - register net_alias device notifier
8410         *       - register proc entries:
8411   /proc/net/alias_types
8412         *                                    /proc/net/aliases
8413         */
8414
8415   #ifdef CONFIG_NET_ALIAS
8416        net_alias_init();
8417   #endif
8418
8419        init_bh(NET_BH, net_bh);
8420        return 0;
8421   }
```

usr/src/linux/net/ipv4/dev_mcast.c

```
8422    /*
8423     *   Linux NET3: Multicast List maintenance.
8424     *
8425     *   Authors:
8426     *       Tim Kordas <tjk@nostromo.eeap.cwru.edu>
8427     *       Richard Underwood <richard@wuzz.demon.co.uk>
8428     *
8429     *   Stir fried together from the IP multicast and CAP
8430    patches above
8431     *       Alan Cox <Alan.Cox@linux.org>
8432     *
8433     *   Fixes:
8434     *       Alan Cox    :   Update the device on a real
8435    delete
8436     *                       rather than any time but...
8437     *       Alan Cox    :   IFF_ALLMULTI support.
8438     *       Alan Cox    :   New format set_multicast_list()
8439    calls.
8440     *
8441     *   This program is free software; you can redistribute
8442    it and/or
8443     *   modify it under the terms of the GNU General Public
8444    License
8445     *   as published by the Free Software Foundation; either
8446    version
8447     *   2 of the License, or (at your option) any later
8448    version.
8449     */
8450
8451    #include <asm/segment.h>
8452    #include <asm/system.h>
8453    #include <asm/bitops.h>
8454    #include <linux/types.h>
8455    #include <linux/kernel.h>
8456    #include <linux/sched.h>
8457    #include <linux/string.h>
8458    #include <linux/mm.h>
8459    #include <linux/socket.h>
8460    #include <linux/sockios.h>
8461    #include <linux/in.h>
8462    #include <linux/errno.h>
8463    #include <linux/interrupt.h>
8464    #include <linux/if_ether.h>
8465    #include <linux/inet.h>
8466    #include <linux/netdevice.h>
8467    #include <linux/etherdevice.h>
8468    #include <net/ip.h>
8469    #include <net/route.h>
8470    #include <linux/skbuff.h>
8471    #include <net/sock.h>
8472    #include <net/arp.h>
8473
8474
8475    /*
8476     *   Device multicast list maintenance. This knows about
8477    such little matters as promiscuous mode and
8478     *   converting from the list to the array the drivers
8479    use. At least until I fix the drivers up.
8480     *
8481     *   This is used both by IP and by the user level
8482    maintenance functions. Unlike BSD we maintain a usage
8483    count
8484     *   on a given multicast address so that a casual user
8485    application can add/delete multicasts used by protocols
8486     *   without doing damage to the protocols when it
8487    deletes the entries. It also helps IP as it tracks
8488    overlapping
8489     *   maps.
8490     */
8491
8492
8493    /*
8494     *   Update the multicast list into the physical NIC
8495    controller.
8496     */
8497
8498    void dev_mc_upload(struct device *dev)
8499    {
8500        /* Don't do anything till we up the interface
8501            [dev_open will call this function so the list will
8502            stay sane] */
8503
8504        if(!(dev->flags&IFF_UP))
8505            return;
8506
8507        /*
8508         *   Devices with no set multicast don't get set
8509         */
8510
8511        if(dev->set_multicast_list==NULL)
8512            return;
8513
8514        dev->set_multicast_list(dev);
8515    }
8516
```

```
8517     /*
8518      *  Delete a device level multicast
8519      */
8520
8521     void dev_mc_delete(struct device *dev, void *addr, int
8522     alen, int all)
8523     {
8524         struct dev_mc_list **dmi;
8525         for(dmi=&dev->mc_list;*dmi!=NULL;dmi=&(*dmi)->next)
8526         {
8527
8528     if(memcmp((*dmi)->dmi_addr,addr,(*dmi)->dmi_addrlen)==0
8529     && alen==(*dmi)->dmi_addrlen)
8530             {
8531                 struct dev_mc_list *tmp= *dmi;
8532                 if(--(*dmi)->dmi_users && !all)
8533                     return;
8534                 *dmi=(*dmi)->next;
8535                 dev->mc_count--;
8536                 kfree_s(tmp,sizeof(*tmp));
8537                 dev_mc_upload(dev);
8538                 return;
8539             }
8540         }
8541     }
8542
8543     /*
8544      *  Add a device level multicast
8545      */
8546
8547     void dev_mc_add(struct device *dev, void *addr, int
8548     alen, int newonly)
8549     {
8550         struct dev_mc_list *dmi;
8551         for(dmi=dev->mc_list;dmi!=NULL;dmi=dmi->next)
8552         {
8553
8554     if(memcmp(dmi->dmi_addr,addr,dmi->dmi_addrlen)==0 &&
8555     dmi->dmi_addrlen==alen)
8556             {
8557                 if(!newonly)
8558                     dmi->dmi_users++;
8559                 return;
8560             }
8561         }
8562         dmi=(struct dev_mc_list
8563     *)kmalloc(sizeof(*dmi),GFP_KERNEL);
8564         if(dmi==NULL)
8565             return; /* GFP_KERNEL so can't happen anyway */
8566         memcpy(dmi->dmi_addr, addr, alen);
8567         dmi->dmi_addrlen=alen;
8568         dmi->next=dev->mc_list;
8569         dmi->dmi_users=1;
8570         dev->mc_list=dmi;
8571         dev->mc_count++;
8572         dev_mc_upload(dev);
8573     }
8574
8575     /*
8576      *  Discard multicast list when a device is downed
8577      */
8578
8579     void dev_mc_discard(struct device *dev)
8580     {
8581         while(dev->mc_list!=NULL)
8582         {
8583             struct dev_mc_list *tmp=dev->mc_list;
8584             dev->mc_list=dev->mc_list->next;
8585             kfree_s(tmp,sizeof(*tmp));
8586         }
8587         dev->mc_count=0;
8588     }
```

usr/src/linux/net/ipv4/devinet.c

```
8589     /*
8590      *  NET3    IP device support routines.
8591      *
8592      *      This program is free software; you can
8593     redistribute it and/or
8594      *      modify it under the terms of the GNU General
8595     Public License
8596      *      as published by the Free Software Foundation;
8597     either version
8598      *      2 of the License, or (at your option) any later
8599     version.
8600      *
8601      *  Derived from the IP parts of dev.c 1.0.19
8602      *      Authors:    Ross Biro, <bir7@leland.Stanford.Edu>
8603      *              Fred N. van Kempen,
8604     <waltje@uWalt.NL.Mugnet.ORG>
8605      *              Mark Evans, <evansmp@uhura.aston.ac.uk>
8606      *
8607      *  Additional Authors:
8608      *      Alan Cox, <gw4pts@gw4pts.ampr.org>
8609      */
8610
```

```
8611    #include <linux/config.h>    /* For CONFIG_IP_CLASSLESS */
8612
8613    #include <asm/segment.h>
8614    #include <asm/system.h>
8615    #include <asm/bitops.h>
8616    #include <linux/types.h>
8617    #include <linux/kernel.h>
8618    #include <linux/sched.h>
8619    #include <linux/string.h>
8620    #include <linux/mm.h>
8621    #include <linux/socket.h>
8622    #include <linux/sockios.h>
8623    #include <linux/in.h>
8624    #include <linux/errno.h>
8625    #include <linux/interrupt.h>
8626    #include <linux/if_ether.h>
8627    #include <linux/inet.h>
8628    #include <linux/netdevice.h>
8629    #include <linux/etherdevice.h>
8630    #include <net/ip.h>
8631    #include <net/route.h>
8632    #include <net/protocol.h>
8633    #include <net/tcp.h>
8634    #include <linux/skbuff.h>
8635    #include <net/sock.h>
8636    #include <net/arp.h>
8637
8638    /*
8639     *  Determine a default network mask, based on the IP
8640    address.
8641     */
8642
8643    unsigned long ip_get_mask(unsigned long addr)
8644    {
8645        unsigned long dst;
8646
8647        if (addr == 0L)
8648            return(0L); /* special case */
8649
8650        dst = ntohl(addr);
8651        if (IN_CLASSA(dst))
8652            return(htonl(IN_CLASSA_NET));
8653        if (IN_CLASSB(dst))
8654            return(htonl(IN_CLASSB_NET));
8655        if (IN_CLASSC(dst))
8656            return(htonl(IN_CLASSC_NET));
8657
8658        /*
8659         *  Something else, probably a multicast.
8660         */
8661
8662        return(0);
8663    }
8664
8665    /*
8666     *  Check the address for our address, broadcasts, etc.
8667     *
8668     *  I intend to fix this to at the very least cache the
8669    last
8670     *  resolved entry.
8671     */
8672
8673    int ip_chk_addr(unsigned long addr)
8674    {
8675        struct device *dev;
8676    #ifndef CONFIG_IP_CLASSLESS
8677        unsigned long mask;
8678    #endif
8679
8680        /*
8681         *  Accept both 'all ones' and 'all zeros' as
8682    BROADCAST.
8683         *  (Support old BSD in other words). This old BSD
8684         *  support will go very soon as it messes other
8685    things
8686         *  up.
8687         *  Also accept 'loopback broadcast' as BROADCAST.
8688         */
8689
8690        if (addr == INADDR_ANY || addr == INADDR_BROADCAST ||
8691            addr == htonl(0x7FFFFFFFL))
8692            return IS_BROADCAST;
8693
8694    #ifndef  CONFIG_IP_CLASSLESS
8695        mask = ip_get_mask(addr);
8696
8697        /*
8698         *  Accept all of the 'loopback' class A net.
8699         */
8700
8701        if ((addr & mask) == htonl(0x7F000000L))
8702            return IS_MYADDR;
8703    #else
8704        if ((addr & htonl(0x7F000000L)) ==
8705    htonl(0x7F000000L))
8706            return IS_MYADDR;
```

```
8707    #endif
8708
8709        /*
8710         *  OK, now check the interface addresses. We could
8711         *  speed this by keeping a dev and a dev_up chain.
8712         */
8713
8714        for (dev = dev_base; dev != NULL; dev = dev->next)
8715        {
8716            if ((!(dev->flags & IFF_UP)) ||
8717    dev->family!=AF_INET)
8718                continue;
8719            /*
8720             *  If the protocol address of the device is 0
8721    this is special
8722             *  and means we are address hunting (eg bootp).
8723             */
8724
8725            if (dev->pa_addr == 0)
8726                return IS_MYADDR;
8727            /*
8728             *  Is it the exact IP address?
8729             */
8730
8731            if (addr == dev->pa_addr)
8732                return IS_MYADDR;
8733            /*
8734             *  Is it our broadcast address?
8735             */
8736
8737            if ((dev->flags & IFF_BROADCAST) && addr ==
8738    dev->pa_brdaddr)
8739                return IS_BROADCAST;
8740            /*
8741             *  Nope. Check for a subnetwork broadcast.
8742             */
8743
8744            if (((addr ^ dev->pa_addr) & dev->pa_mask) == 0)
8745            {
8746                if ((addr & ~dev->pa_mask) == 0)
8747                    return IS_BROADCAST;
8748                if ((addr & ~dev->pa_mask) == ~dev->pa_mask)
8749                    return IS_BROADCAST;
8750            }
8751
8752    #ifndef CONFIG_IP_CLASSLESS
8753            /*
8754             *  Nope. Check for Network broadcast.
8755             */
8756
8757            if (((addr ^ dev->pa_addr) & mask) == 0)
8758            {
8759                if ((addr & ~mask) == 0)
8760                    return IS_BROADCAST;
8761                if ((addr & ~mask) == ~mask)
8762                    return IS_BROADCAST;
8763            }
8764    #endif
8765        }
8766        if(IN_MULTICAST(ntohl(addr)))
8767            return IS_MULTICAST;
8768        return 0;        /* no match at all */
8769    }
8770
8771
8772    /*
8773     *  Retrieve our own address.
8774     *
8775     *  Because the loopback address (127.0.0.1) is already
8776    recognized
8777     *  automatically, we can use the loopback interface's
8778    address as
8779     *  our "primary" interface.  This is the address used
8780    by IP et
8781     *  al when it doesn't know which address to use (i.e.
8782    it does not
8783     *  yet know from or to which interface to go...).
8784     */
8785
8786    unsigned long ip_my_addr(void)
8787    {
8788        struct device *dev;
8789
8790        for (dev = dev_base; dev != NULL; dev = dev->next)
8791        {
8792            if (dev->flags & IFF_LOOPBACK)
8793                return(dev->pa_addr);
8794        }
8795        return(0);
8796    }
8797
8798    /*
8799     *  Find an interface that can handle addresses for a
8800    certain address.
8801     */
8802
```

```
8803   struct device * ip_dev_bynet(unsigned long addr,
8804   unsigned long mask)
8805   {
8806       struct device *dev;
8807       struct device *best_dev = NULL;
8808       __u32 best_mask = mask;
8809
8810       for (dev = dev_base; dev; dev = dev->next)
8811       {
8812           if (!(dev->flags & IFF_UP))
8813               continue;
8814           if (dev->flags & IFF_POINTOPOINT)
8815           {
8816               if (addr == dev->pa_dstaddr)
8817                   return dev;
8818               continue;
8819           }
8820           if (dev->pa_mask & (addr ^ dev->pa_addr))
8821               continue;
8822           if (mask == dev->pa_mask)
8823               return dev;
8824           if (best_dev && (best_mask & dev->pa_mask) !=
8825   best_mask)
8826               continue;
8827           best_dev = dev;
8828           best_mask = dev->pa_mask;
8829       }
8830       return best_dev;
8831   }
8832
8833   /*
8834    *  Find the first device with a given source address.
8835    */
8836
8837   struct device *ip_dev_find(unsigned long addr)
8838   {
8839       struct device *dev;
8840       for(dev = dev_base; dev; dev=dev->next)
8841       {
8842           if((dev->flags&IFF_UP) && dev->pa_addr==addr)
8843               return dev;
8844       }
8845       return NULL;
8846   }
8847
8848   struct device *dev_getbytype(unsigned short type)
8849   {
8850       struct device *dev;
```

```
8851
8852       for (dev = dev_base; dev != NULL; dev = dev->next)
8853       {
8854           if (dev->type == type &&
8855   !(dev->flags&(IFF_LOOPBACK|IFF_NOARP)))
8856               return(dev);
8857       }
8858       return(NULL);
8859   }
8860
```

usr/src/linux/net/ipv4/icmp.c

```
8861   /*
8862    *  NET3:   Implementation of the ICMP protocol layer.
8863    *
8864    *      Alan Cox, <alan@cymru.net>
8865    *
8866    *  This program is free software; you can redistribute
8867   it and/or
8868    *  modify it under the terms of the GNU General Public
8869   License
8870    *  as published by the Free Software Foundation; either
8871   version
8872    *  2 of the License, or (at your option) any later
8873   version.
8874    *
8875    *  Some of the function names and the icmp unreach
8876   table for this
8877    *  module were derived from [icmp.c 1.0.11 06/02/93] by
8878    *  Ross Biro, Fred N. van Kempen, Mark Evans, Alan Cox,
8879   Gerhard Koerting.
8880    *  Other than that this module is a complete rewrite.
8881    *
8882    *  Fixes:
8883    *      Mike Shaver :   RFC1122 checks.
8884    *      Alan Cox    :   Multicast ping reply as self.
8885    *      Alan Cox    :   Fix atomicity lockup in
8886   ip_build_xmit
8887    *              call.
8888    *      Alan Cox    :   Added 216,128 byte paths to the
8889   MTU
8890    *              code.
8891    *      Martin Mares    :   RFC1812 checks.
8892    *      Martin Mares    :   Can be configured to follow
8893   redirects
8894    *              if acting as a router _without_ a
8895    *              routing protocol (RFC 1812).
8896    *      Martin Mares    :   Echo requests may be
```

```
8897  configured to
8898  *                     be ignored (RFC 1812).
8899  *       Martin Mares    :    Limitation of ICMP error
8900  message
8901  *                     transmit rate (RFC 1812).
8902  *       Martin Mares    :    TOS and Precedence set
8903  correctly
8904  *                     (RFC 1812).
8905  *       Martin Mares    :    Now copying as much data
8906  from the
8907  *                     original packet as we can without
8908  *                     exceeding 576 bytes (RFC 1812).
8909  *  Willy Konynenberg    :    Transparent proxying support.
8910  *       Keith Owens :    RFC1191 correction for 4.2BSD
8911  based
8912  *                     path MTU bug.
8913  *       Thomas Quinot    :    ICMP Dest Unreach codes up
8914  to 15 are
8915  *                     valid (RFC 1812).
8916  *       Alan Cox    :    Spoofing and junk icmp
8917  protections.
8918  *             Elliot Poger    :         Added support
8919  for SO_BINDTODEVICE.
8920  *  Willy Konynenberg    :    Transparent proxy adapted to
8921  new
8922  *                     socket hash code.
8923  *
8924  *
8925  * RFC1122 (Host Requirements -- Comm. Layer) Status:
8926  * (boy, are there a lot of rules for ICMP)
8927  *  3.2.2 (Generic ICMP stuff)
8928  *    MUST discard messages of unknown type. (OK)
8929  *    MUST copy at least the first 8 bytes from the
8930  offending packet
8931  *      when sending ICMP errors. (OBSOLETE -- see
8932  RFC1812)
8933  *    MUST pass received ICMP errors up to protocol
8934  level. (OK)
8935  *    SHOULD send ICMP errors with TOS == 0. (OBSOLETE --
8936  see RFC1812)
8937  *    MUST NOT send ICMP errors in reply to:
8938  *      ICMP errors (OK)
8939  *      Broadcast/multicast datagrams (OK)
8940  *      MAC broadcasts (OK)
8941  *      Non-initial fragments (OK)
8942  *      Datagram with a source address that isn't a
8943  single host. (OK)
8944  *  3.2.2.1 (Destination Unreachable)
```

```
8945  *   All the rules govern the IP layer, and are dealt
8946  with in ip.c, not here.
8947  * 3.2.2.2 (Redirect)
8948  *   Host SHOULD NOT send ICMP_REDIRECTs.  (OK)
8949  *   MUST update routing table in response to host or
8950  network redirects.
8951  *     (host OK, network OBSOLETE)
8952  *   SHOULD drop redirects if they're not from directly
8953  connected gateway
8954  *     (OK -- we drop it if it's not from our old
8955  gateway, which is close
8956  *       enough)
8957  * 3.2.2.3 (Source Quench)
8958  *   MUST pass incoming SOURCE_QUENCHs to transport
8959  layer (OK)
8960  *   Other requirements are dealt with at the transport
8961  layer.
8962  * 3.2.2.4 (Time Exceeded)
8963  *   MUST pass TIME_EXCEEDED to transport layer (OK)
8964  *   Other requirements dealt with at IP (generating
8965  TIME_EXCEEDED).
8966  * 3.2.2.5 (Parameter Problem)
8967  *   SHOULD generate these (OK)
8968  *   MUST pass received PARAMPROBLEM to transport layer
8969  (NOT YET)
8970  *     [Solaris 2.X seems to assert EPROTO when this
8971  occurs] -- AC
8972  * 3.2.2.6 (Echo Request/Reply)
8973  *   MUST reply to ECHO_REQUEST, and give app to do ECHO
8974  stuff (OK, OK)
8975  *   MAY discard broadcast ECHO_REQUESTs. (We don't, but
8976  that's OK.)
8977  *   MUST reply using same source address as the request
8978  was sent to.
8979  *     We're OK for unicast ECHOs, and it doesn't say
8980  anything about
8981  *      how to handle broadcast ones, since it's optional.
8982  *   MUST copy data from REQUEST to REPLY (OK)
8983  *      unless it would require illegal fragmentation (OK)
8984  *   MUST pass REPLYs to transport/user layer (OK)
8985  *   MUST use any provided source route (reversed) for
8986  REPLY. (NOT YET)
8987  * 3.2.2.7 (Information Request/Reply)
8988  *   MUST NOT implement this. (I guess that means
8989  silently discard...?) (OK)
8990  * 3.2.2.8 (Timestamp Request/Reply)
8991  *   MAY implement (OK)
8992  *   SHOULD be in-kernel for "minimum variability" (OK)
```

```
8993      *   MAY discard broadcast REQUESTs.  (OK, but see
8994   source for inconsistency)
8995      *   MUST reply using same source address as the request
8996   was sent to. (OK)
8997      *   MUST reverse source route, as per ECHO (NOT YET)
8998      *   MUST pass REPLYs to transport/user layer (requires
8999   RAW, just like
9000      *   ECHO) (OK)
9001      *   MUST update clock for timestamp at least 15
9002   times/sec (OK)
9003      *   MUST be "correct within a few minutes" (OK)
9004      * 3.2.2.9 (Address Mask Request/Reply)
9005      *   MAY implement (OK)
9006      *   MUST send a broadcast REQUEST if using this system
9007   to set netmask
9008      *     (OK... we don't use it)
9009      *   MUST discard received REPLYs if not using this
9010   system (OK)
9011      *   MUST NOT send replies unless specifically made
9012   agent for this sort
9013      *     of thing. (OK)
9014      *
9015      *
9016      * RFC 1812 (IPv4 Router Requirements) Status (even
9017   longer):
9018      * 4.3.2.1 (Unknown Message Types)
9019      *   MUST pass messages of unknown type to ICMP user
9020   iface or silently discard
9021      *     them (OK)
9022      * 4.3.2.2 (ICMP Message TTL)
9023      *   MUST initialize TTL when originating an ICMP
9024   message (OK)
9025      * 4.3.2.3 (Original Message Header)
9026      *   SHOULD copy as much data from the offending packet
9027   as possible without
9028      *     the length of the ICMP datagram exceeding 576
9029   bytes (OK)
9030      *   MUST leave original IP header of the offending
9031   packet, but we're not
9032      *     required to undo modifications made (OK)
9033      * 4.3.2.4 (Original Message Source Address)
9034      *   MUST use one of addresses for the interface the
9035   orig. packet arrived as
9036      *     source address (OK)
9037      * 4.3.2.5 (TOS and Precedence)
9038      *   SHOULD leave TOS set to the same value unless the
9039   packet would be
9040      *     discarded for that reason (OK)
```

```
9041      *   MUST use TOS=0 if not possible to leave original
9042   value (OK)
9043      *   MUST leave IP Precedence for Source Quench messages
9044   (OK -- not sent
9045      *   at all)
9046      *   SHOULD use IP Precedence = 6 (Internetwork Control)
9047   or 7 (Network Control)
9048      *     for all other error messages (OK, we use 6)
9049      *   MAY allow configuration of IP Precedence (OK -- not
9050   done)
9051      *   MUST leave IP Precedence and TOS for reply messages
9052   (OK)
9053      * 4.3.2.6 (Source Route)
9054      *   SHOULD use reverse source route UNLESS sending
9055   Parameter Problem on source
9056      *     routing and UNLESS the packet would be
9057   immediately discarded (NOT YET)
9058      * 4.3.2.7 (When Not to Send ICMP Errors)
9059      *   MUST NOT send ICMP errors in reply to:
9060      *     ICMP errors (OK)
9061      *     Packets failing IP header validation tests unless
9062   otherwise noted (OK)
9063      *     Broadcast/multicast datagrams (OK)
9064      *     MAC broadcasts (OK)
9065      *     Non-initial fragments (OK)
9066      *     Datagram with a source address that isn't a
9067   single host. (OK)
9068      * 4.3.2.8 (Rate Limiting)
9069      *   SHOULD be able to limit error message rate (OK)
9070      *   SHOULD allow setting of rate limits (OK, in the
9071   source)
9072      * 4.3.3.1 (Destination Unreachable)
9073      *   All the rules govern the IP layer, and are dealt
9074   with in ip.c, not here.
9075      * 4.3.3.2 (Redirect)
9076      *   MAY ignore ICMP Redirects if running a routing
9077   protocol or if forwarding
9078      *     is enabled on the interface (OK -- ignores)
9079      * 4.3.3.3 (Source Quench)
9080      *   SHOULD NOT originate SQ messages (OK)
9081      *   MUST be able to limit SQ rate if originates them
9082   (OK as we don't
9083      *   send them)
9084      *   MAY ignore SQ messages it receives (OK -- we don't)
9085      * 4.3.3.4 (Time Exceeded)
9086      *   Requirements dealt with at IP (generating
9087   TIME_EXCEEDED).
9088      * 4.3.3.5 (Parameter Problem)
```

```
9089    *    MUST generate these for all errors not covered by
9090    other messages (OK)
9091    *    MUST include original value of the value pointed by
9092    (OK)
9093    *    4.3.3.6 (Echo Request)
9094    *    MUST implement echo server function (OK)
9095    *    MUST process at ER of at least max(576, MTU) (OK)
9096    *    MAY reject broadcast/multicast ER's (We don't, but
9097    that's OK)
9098    *    SHOULD have a config option for silently ignoring
9099    ER's (OK)
9100    *    MUST have a default value for the above switch = NO
9101    (OK)
9102    *    MUST have application layer interface for Echo
9103    Request/Reply (OK)
9104    *    MUST reply using same source address as the request
9105    was sent to.
9106    *     We're OK for unicast ECHOs, and it doesn't say
9107    anything about
9108    *     how to handle broadcast ones, since it's optional.
9109    *    MUST copy data from Request to Reply (OK)
9110    *    SHOULD update Record Route / Timestamp options (??)
9111    *    MUST use reversed Source Route for Reply if
9112    possible (NOT YET)
9113    *    4.3.3.7 (Information Request/Reply)
9114    *    SHOULD NOT originate or respond to these (OK)
9115    *    4.3.3.8 (Timestamp / Timestamp Reply)
9116    *    MAY implement (OK)
9117    *    MUST reply to every Timestamp message received (OK)
9118    *    MAY discard broadcast REQUESTs.  (OK, but see
9119    source for inconsistency)
9120    *    MUST reply using same source address as the request
9121    was sent to. (OK)
9122    *    MUST use reversed Source Route if possible (NOT YET)
9123    *    SHOULD update Record Route / Timestamp options (??)
9124    *    MUST pass REPLYs to transport/user layer (requires
9125    RAW, just like
9126    *    ECHO) (OK)
9127    *    MUST update clock for timestamp at least 16
9128    times/sec (OK)
9129    *    MUST be "correct within a few minutes" (OK)
9130    *    4.3.3.9 (Address Mask Request/Reply)
9131    *    MUST have support for receiving AMRq and responding
9132    with AMRe (OK,
9133    *    but only as a compile-time option)
9134    *    SHOULD have option for each interface for AMRe's,
9135    MUST default to
9136    *    NO (NOT YET)
```

```
9137    *    MUST NOT reply to AMRq before knows the correct AM
9138    (OK)
9139    *    MUST NOT respond to AMRq with source address
9140    0.0.0.0 on physical
9141    *     interfaces having multiple logical i-faces with
9142    different masks
9143    *    (NOT YET)
9144    *    SHOULD examine all AMRe's it receives and check
9145    them (NOT YET)
9146    *    SHOULD log invalid AMRe's (AM+sender) (NOT YET)
9147    *    MUST NOT use contents of AMRe to determine correct
9148    AM (OK)
9149    *    MAY broadcast AMRe's after having configured
9150    address masks (OK -- doesn't)
9151    *    MUST NOT do broadcast AMRe's if not set by extra
9152    option (OK, no option)
9153    *    MUST use the { <NetPrefix>, -1 } form of broadcast
9154    addresses (OK)
9155    *    4.3.3.10 (Router Advertisement and Solicitations)
9156    *    MUST support router part of Router Discovery
9157    Protocol on all networks we
9158    *     support broadcast or multicast addressing. (OK --
9159    done by gated)
9160    *    MUST have all config parameters with the respective
9161    defaults (OK)
9162    *    5.2.7.1 (Destination Unreachable)
9163    *    MUST generate DU's (OK)
9164    *    SHOULD choose a best-match response code (OK)
9165    *    SHOULD NOT generate Host Isolated codes (OK)
9166    *    SHOULD use Communication Administratively
9167    Prohibited when administratively
9168    *     filtering packets (NOT YET -- bug-to-bug
9169    compatibility)
9170    *    MAY include config option for not generating the
9171    above and silently
9172    *    discard the packets instead (OK)
9173    *    MAY include config option for not generating
9174    Precedence Violation and
9175    *     Precedence Cutoff messages (OK as we don't
9176    generate them at all)
9177    *    MUST use Host Unreachable or Dest. Host Unknown
9178    codes whenever other hosts
9179    *     on the same network might be reachable (OK -- no
9180    net unreach's at all)
9181    *    MUST use new form of Fragmentation Needed and DF
9182    Set messages (OK)
9183    *    5.2.7.2 (Redirect)
9184    *    MUST NOT generate network redirects (OK)
```

```
9185     *    MUST be able to generate host redirects (OK)
9186     *    SHOULD be able to generate Host+TOS redirects (NO
9187   as we don't use TOS)
9188     *    MUST have an option to use Host redirects instead
9189   of Host+TOS ones (OK as
9190     *      no Host+TOS Redirects are used)
9191     *    MUST NOT generate redirects unless forwarding to
9192   the same i-face and the
9193     *      dest. address is on the same subnet as the src.
9194   address and no source
9195     *      routing is in use. (OK)
9196     *    MUST NOT follow redirects when using a routing
9197   protocol (OK)
9198     *    MAY use redirects if not using a routing protocol
9199   (OK, compile-time option)
9200     *    MUST comply to Host Requirements when not acting as
9201   a router (OK)
9202     *  5.2.7.3 (Time Exceeded)
9203     *    MUST generate Time Exceeded Code 0 when discarding
9204   packet due to TTL=0 (OK)
9205     *    MAY have a per-interface option to disable
9206   origination of TE messages, but
9207     *      it MUST default to "originate" (OK -- we don't
9208   support it)
9209     */
9210
9211   #include <linux/config.h>
9212   #include <linux/types.h>
9213   #include <linux/sched.h>
9214   #include <linux/kernel.h>
9215   #include <linux/fcntl.h>
9216   #include <linux/socket.h>
9217   #include <linux/in.h>
9218   #include <linux/inet.h>
9219   #include <linux/netdevice.h>
9220   #include <linux/string.h>
9221   #include <net/snmp.h>
9222   #include <net/ip.h>
9223   #include <net/route.h>
9224   #include <net/protocol.h>
9225   #include <net/icmp.h>
9226   #include <net/tcp.h>
9227   #include <net/udp.h>
9228   #include <net/snmp.h>
9229   #include <linux/skbuff.h>
9230   #include <net/sock.h>
9231   #include <linux/errno.h>
9232   #include <linux/timer.h>

9233   #include <asm/system.h>
9234   #include <asm/segment.h>
9235   #include <net/checksum.h>
9236
9237   #define min(a,b)     ((a)<(b)?(a):(b))
9238
9239   /*
9240    *  Statistics
9241    */
9242
9243   struct icmp_mib icmp_statistics;
9244
9245   /* An array of errno for error messages from dest
9246   unreach. */
9247   /* RFC 1122: 3.2.2.1 States that NET_UNREACH,
9248   HOS_UNREACH and SR_FAIELD MUST be considered 'transient
9249   errs'. */
9250
9251   struct icmp_err icmp_err_convert[] = {
9252     { ENETUNREACH,    0 },     /*  ICMP_NET_UNREACH    */
9253     { EHOSTUNREACH,   0 },     /*  ICMP_HOST_UNREACH   */
9254     { ENOPROTOOPT,    1 },     /*  ICMP_PROT_UNREACH   */
9255     { ECONNREFUSED,   1 },     /*  ICMP_PORT_UNREACH   */
9256     { EOPNOTSUPP,     0 },     /*  ICMP_FRAG_NEEDED    */
9257     { EOPNOTSUPP,     0 },     /*  ICMP_SR_FAILED      */
9258     { ENETUNREACH,    1 },     /*  ICMP_NET_UNKNOWN    */
9259     { EHOSTDOWN,      1 },     /*  ICMP_HOST_UNKNOWN   */
9260     { ENONET,     1 },    /*  ICMP_HOST_ISOLATED  */
9261     { ENETUNREACH,    1 },     /*  ICMP_NET_ANO        */
9262     { EHOSTUNREACH,   1 },     /*  ICMP_HOST_ANO       */
9263     { ENETUNREACH,    0 },     /*  ICMP_NET_UNR_TOS    */
9264     { EHOSTUNREACH,   0 },     /*  ICMP_HOST_UNR_TOS   */
9265     { EHOSTUNREACH,   1 },     /*  ICMP_PKT_FILTERED   */
9266     { EHOSTUNREACH,   1 },     /*  ICMP_PREC_VIOLATION */
9267     { EHOSTUNREACH,   1 } /*  ICMP_PREC_CUTOFF     */
9268   };
9269
9270   /*
9271    *  A spare long used to speed up statistics updating
9272    */
9273
9274   unsigned long dummy;
9275
9276   /*
9277    *  ICMP transmit rate limit control structures. We use
9278   a relatively simple
9279    *  approach to the problem: For each type of ICMP
9280   message with rate limit
```

```
9281     *  we count the number of messages sent during some
9282    time quantum. If this
9283     *  count exceeds given maximal value, we ignore all
9284    messages not separated
9285     *  from the last message sent at least by specified
9286    time.
9287     */
9288
9289    #define XRLIM_CACHE_SIZE 16     /* How many destination
9290    hosts do we cache */
9291
9292    struct icmp_xrl_cache           /* One entry of the ICMP
9293    rate cache */
9294    {
9295        __u32 daddr;            /* Destination address */
9296        unsigned long counter;      /* Message counter */
9297        unsigned long next_reset;   /* Time of next reset of
9298    the counter */
9299        unsigned long last_access;  /* Time of last access
9300    to this entry (LRU) */
9301        unsigned int restricted;    /* Set if we're in
9302    restricted mode */
9303        unsigned long next_packet;  /* When we'll allow a
9304    next packet if restricted */
9305    };
9306
9307    struct icmp_xrlim
9308    {
9309        unsigned long timeout;      /* Time quantum for rate
9310    measuring */
9311        unsigned long limit;        /* Maximal number of
9312    messages per time quantum allowed */
9313        unsigned long delay;        /* How long we wait
9314    between packets when restricting */
9315        struct icmp_xrl_cache cache[XRLIM_CACHE_SIZE];  /*
9316    Rate cache */
9317    };
9318
9319    /*
9320     *  ICMP control array. This specifies what to do with
9321    each ICMP.
9322     */
9323
9324    struct icmp_control
9325    {
9326        unsigned long *output;      /* Address to increment
9327    on output */
9328        unsigned long *input;       /* Address to increment

9329    on input */
9330        void (*handler)(struct icmphdr *icmph, struct
9331    sk_buff *skb, struct device *dev, __u32 saddr, __u32
9332    daddr, int len);
9333        unsigned long error;        /* This ICMP is classed
9334    as an error message */
9335        struct icmp_xrlim *xrlim;   /* Transmit rate limit
9336    control structure or NULL for no limits */
9337    };
9338
9339    static struct icmp_control icmp_pointers[19];
9340
9341    /*
9342     *  Build xmit assembly blocks
9343     */
9344
9345    struct icmp_bxm
9346    {
9347        void *data_ptr;
9348        int data_len;
9349        struct icmphdr icmph;
9350        unsigned long csum;
9351        struct options replyopts;
9352        unsigned char  optbuf[40];
9353    };
9354
9355    /*
9356     *  The ICMP socket. This is the most convenient way to
9357    flow control
9358     *  our ICMP output as well as maintain a clean
9359    interface throughout
9360     *  all layers. All Socketless IP sends will soon be
9361    gone.
9362     */
9363
9364    struct socket icmp_socket;
9365
9366    /*
9367     *  Send an ICMP frame.
9368     */
9369
9370
9371    /*
9372     *  Initialize the transmit rate limitation mechanism.
9373     */
9374
9375    #ifndef CONFIG_NO_ICMP_LIMIT
9376
```

```
9377    static void xrlim_init(void)
9378    {
9379        int type, entry;
9380        struct icmp_xrlim *xr;
9381
9382        for (type=0; type<=18; type++) {
9383            xr = icmp_pointers[type].xrlim;
9384            if (xr) {
9385                for (entry=0; entry<XRLIM_CACHE_SIZE;
9386    entry++)
9387                    xr->cache[entry].daddr = INADDR_NONE;
9388            }
9389        }
9390    }
9391
9392    /*
9393     *  Check transmit rate limitation for given message.
9394     *
9395     *  RFC 1812: 4.3.2.8 SHOULD be able to limit error
9396    message rate
9397     *           SHOULD allow setting of rate limits (we
9398    allow
9399     *           in the source)
9400     */
9401
9402    static int xrlim_allow(int type, __u32 addr)
9403    {
9404        struct icmp_xrlim *r;
9405        struct icmp_xrl_cache *c;
9406        unsigned long now;
9407
9408        if (type > 18)          /* No time limit present */
9409            return 1;
9410        r = icmp_pointers[type].xrlim;
9411        if (!r)
9412            return 1;
9413
9414        for (c = r->cache; c < &r->cache[XRLIM_CACHE_SIZE];
9415    c++)
9416            /* Cache lookup */
9417            if (c->daddr == addr)
9418                break;
9419
9420        now = jiffies;      /* Cache current time (saves
9421    accesses to volatile variable) */
9422
9423        if (c == &r->cache[XRLIM_CACHE_SIZE]) {     /* Cache
9424    miss */
```

```
9425        unsigned long oldest = now;      /* Find the
9426    oldest entry to replace */
9427            struct icmp_xrl_cache *d;
9428            c = r->cache;
9429            for (d = r->cache; d <
9430    &r->cache[XRLIM_CACHE_SIZE]; d++)
9431                if (!d->daddr) {          /* Unused entry */
9432                    c = d;
9433                    break;
9434                } else if (d->last_access < oldest) {
9435                    oldest = d->last_access;
9436                    c = d;
9437                }
9438            c->last_access = now;          /* Fill the
9439    entry with new data */
9440            c->daddr = addr;
9441            c->counter = 1;
9442            c->next_reset = now + r->timeout;
9443            c->restricted = 0;
9444            return 1;
9445        }
9446
9447        c->last_access = now;
9448        if (c->next_reset > now) {          /* Let's
9449    increment the counter */
9450            c->counter++;
9451            if (c->counter == r->limit) {      /* Limit
9452    exceeded, start restrictions */
9453                c->restricted = 1;
9454                c->next_packet = now + r->delay;
9455                return 0;
9456            }
9457            if (c->restricted) {          /* Any
9458    restrictions pending? */
9459                if (c->next_packet > now)
9460                    return 0;
9461                c->next_packet = now + r->delay;
9462                return 1;
9463            }
9464        } else {                    /* Reset the counter */
9465            if (c->counter < r->limit)     /* Switch off
9466    all restrictions */
9467                c->restricted = 0;
9468            c->next_reset = now + r->timeout;
9469            c->counter = 0;
9470        }
9471
9472        return 1;                /* Send the packet */
```

```
9473      }
9474
9475      #endif /* CONFIG_NO_ICMP_LIMIT */
9476
9477      /*
9478       *  Maintain the counters used in the SNMP statistics
9479      for outgoing ICMP
9480       */
9481
9482      static void icmp_out_count(int type)
9483      {
9484          if(type>18)
9485              return;
9486          (*icmp_pointers[type].output)++;
9487          icmp_statistics.IcmpOutMsgs++;
9488      }
9489
9490      /*
9491       *  Checksum each fragment, and on the first include the
9492      headers and final checksum.
9493       */
9494
9495      static void icmp_glue_bits(const void *p, __u32 saddr,
9496      char *to, unsigned int offset, unsigned int fraglen)
9497      {
9498          struct icmp_bxm *icmp_param = (struct icmp_bxm *)p;
9499          struct icmphdr *icmph;
9500          unsigned long csum;
9501
9502          if (offset) {
9503
9504      icmp_param->csum=csum_partial_copy(icmp_param->data_ptr+o
9505      ffset-sizeof(struct icmphdr),
9506                  to, fraglen,icmp_param->csum);
9507              return;
9508          }
9509
9510          /*
9511           *  First fragment includes header. Note that we've
9512      done
9513           *  the other fragments first, so that we get the
9514      checksum
9515           *  for the whole packet here.
9516           */
9517          csum = csum_partial_copy((void *)&icmp_param->icmph,
9518              to, sizeof(struct icmphdr),
9519              icmp_param->csum);
9520          csum = csum_partial_copy(icmp_param->data_ptr,
```

```
9521                  to+sizeof(struct icmphdr),
9522                  fraglen-sizeof(struct icmphdr), csum);
9523          icmph=(struct icmphdr *)to;
9524          icmph->checksum = csum_fold(csum);
9525      }
9526
9527      /*
9528       *  Driving logic for building and sending ICMP messages.
9529       */
9530
9531      static void icmp_build_xmit(struct icmp_bxm *icmp_param,
9532      __u32 saddr, __u32 daddr, __u8 tos)
9533      {
9534          struct sock *sk=icmp_socket.data;
9535          icmp_param->icmph.checksum=0;
9536          icmp_param->csum=0;
9537          icmp_out_count(icmp_param->icmph.type);
9538          sk->ip_tos = tos;
9539          ip_build_xmit(sk, icmp_glue_bits, icmp_param,
9540              icmp_param->data_len+sizeof(struct icmphdr),
9541              daddr, saddr, &icmp_param->replyopts, 0,
9542      IPPROTO_ICMP, 1);
9543      }
9544
9545
9546      /*
9547       *  Send an ICMP message in response to a situation
9548       *
9549       *  RFC 1122: 3.2.2 MUST send at least the IP header and
9550      8 bytes of header. MAY send more (we do).
9551       *          MUST NOT change this header information.
9552       *          MUST NOT reply to a multicast/broadcast IP
9553      address.
9554       *          MUST NOT reply to a multicast/broadcast MAC
9555      address.
9556       *          MUST reply to only the first fragment.
9557       */
9558
```

p 475
```
9559      void icmp_send(struct sk_buff *skb_in, int type, int
9560      code, unsigned long info, struct device *dev)
9561      {
9562          struct iphdr *iph;
9563          struct icmphdr *icmph;
9564          int atype, room;
9565          struct icmp_bxm icmp_param;
9566          __u32 saddr;
9567
9568          /*
```

```
9569          *  Find the original header
9570          */
9571
9572         iph = skb_in->ip_hdr;
9573
9574         /*
9575          *  No replies to physical multicast/broadcast
9576          */
9577
9578         if(skb_in->pkt_type!=PACKET_HOST)
9579             return;
9580
9581         /*
9582          *  Now check at the protocol level
9583          */
9584
9585         atype=ip_chk_addr(iph->daddr);
9586         if(atype==IS_BROADCAST||atype==IS_MULTICAST)
9587             return;
9588
9589         /*
9590          *  Only reply to fragment 0. We byte re-order the
9591 constant
9592          *  mask for efficiency.
9593          */
9594
9595         if(iph->frag_off&htons(IP_OFFSET))
9596             return;
9597
9598         /*
9599          *  If we send an ICMP error to an ICMP error a mess
9600 would result..
9601          */
9602
9603         if(icmp_pointers[type].error)
9604         {
9605             /*
9606              *  We are an error, check if we are replying to
9607 an ICMP error
9608              */
9609
9610             if(iph->protocol==IPPROTO_ICMP)
9611             {
9612                 icmph = (struct icmphdr *)((char *)iph +
9613 (iph->ihl<<2));
9614                 /*
9615                  *  Assume any unknown ICMP type is an
9616 error. This isn't
9617                  *  specified by the RFC, but think about
9618 it..
9619                  */
9620                 if(icmph->type>18 ||
9621 icmp_pointers[icmph->type].error)
9622                     return;
9623             }
9624         }
9625
9626         /*
9627          *  Check the rate limit
9628          */
9629
9630 #ifndef CONFIG_NO_ICMP_LIMIT
9631         if (!xrlim_allow(type, iph->saddr))
9632             return;
9633 #endif
9634
9635         /*
9636          *  Construct source address and options.
9637          */
9638
9639         saddr=iph->daddr;
9640         if(saddr!=dev->pa_addr &&
9641 ip_chk_addr(saddr)!=IS_MYADDR)
9642             saddr=dev->pa_addr;
9643         if(ip_options_echo(&icmp_param.replyopts, NULL,
9644 saddr, iph->saddr, skb_in))
9645             return;
9646
9647         /*
9648          *  Prepare data for ICMP header.
9649          */
9650
9651         icmp_param.icmph.type=type;
9652         icmp_param.icmph.code=code;
9653         icmp_param.icmph.un.gateway = info;
9654         icmp_param.data_ptr=iph;
9655         room = 576 - sizeof(struct iphdr) -
9656 icmp_param.replyopts.optlen;
9657         icmp_param.data_len=(iph->ihl<<2)+skb_in->len;   /*
9658 RFC says return as much as we can without exceeding 576
9659 bytes */
9660         if (icmp_param.data_len > room)
9661             icmp_param.data_len = room;
9662
9663         /*
9664          *  Build and send the packet.
```

```
9665            */
9666
9667            icmp_build_xmit(&icmp_param, saddr, iph->saddr,
9668                    icmp_pointers[type].error ?
9669                    (iph->tos & 0x1E) | 0xC0 : iph->tos);
9670    }
9671
9672
9673    /*
9674     *  Handle ICMP_DEST_UNREACH, ICMP_TIME_EXCEED, and
9675    ICMP_QUENCH.
9676     */
9677
9678    static void icmp_unreach(struct icmphdr *icmph, struct
9679    sk_buff *skb, struct device *dev, __u32 saddr, __u32
9680    daddr, int len)
9681    {
9682            struct iphdr *iph;
9683            int hash;
9684            struct inet_protocol *ipprot;
9685            unsigned char *dp;
9686            int match_addr=0;
9687
9688            if(len<sizeof(struct iphdr))
9689                goto flush_it;
9690
9691            iph = (struct iphdr *) (icmph + 1);
9692
9693            len-=iph->ihl<<2;
9694            if(len<0)
9695                goto flush_it;
9696
9697            dp= ((unsigned char *)iph)+(iph->ihl<<2);
9698
9699            if(icmph->type==ICMP_DEST_UNREACH)
9700            {
9701                switch(icmph->code & 15)
9702                {
9703                    case ICMP_NET_UNREACH:
9704                        break;
9705                    case ICMP_HOST_UNREACH:
9706                        break;
9707                    case ICMP_PROT_UNREACH:
9708                        NETDEBUG(printk(KERN_INFO "ICMP: %s:%d:
9709    protocol unreachable.\n",
9710                        in_ntoa(iph->daddr),
9711    (int)iph->protocol));
9712                        /* Drop through */
```

```
9713                    case ICMP_PORT_UNREACH:
9714                        match_addr=1;
9715                        break;
9716                    case ICMP_FRAG_NEEDED:
9717    #ifdef CONFIG_NO_PATH_MTU_DISCOVERY
9718                        NETDEBUG(printk(KERN_INFO "ICMP: %s:
9719    fragmentation needed and DF set.\n",
9720                                in_ntoa(iph->daddr)));
9721                        break;
9722    #else
9723                        {
9724                        unsigned short old_mtu =
9725    ntohs(iph->tot_len);
9726                        unsigned short new_mtu =
9727    ntohs(icmph->un.echo.sequence);
9728
9729                        /*
9730                         * RFC1191 5.  4.2BSD based router can
9731    return incorrect
9732                         * Total Length.  If current mtu is
9733    unknown or old_mtu
9734                         * is not less than current mtu, reduce
9735    old_mtu by 4 times
9736                         * the header length.
9737                         */
9738
9739                        if (skb->sk == NULL /* can this happen?
9740    */
9741                            || skb->sk->ip_route_cache == NULL
9742                            || skb->sk->ip_route_cache->rt_mtu
9743    <= old_mtu)
9744                        {
9745                            NETDEBUG(printk(KERN_INFO "4.2BSD
9746    based fragmenting router between here and %s, mtu
9747    corrected from %d", in_ntoa(iph->daddr), old_mtu));
9748                            old_mtu -= 4 * iph->ihl;
9749                            NETDEBUG(printk(" to %d\n",
9750    old_mtu));
9751                        }
9752
9753                        if (new_mtu < 68 || new_mtu >= old_mtu)
9754                        {
9755                            /*
9756                             *  It is either dumb router, which
9757    does not
9758                             *  understand Path MTU Disc.
9759    protocol
9760                             *  or broken (f.e. Linux<=1.3.37 8)
```

```
9761    router.
9762                            *    Try to guess...
9763                            *    The table is taken from RFC-1191.
9764                            */
9765                       if (old_mtu > 32000)
9766                           new_mtu = 32000;
9767                       else if (old_mtu > 17914)
9768                           new_mtu = 17914;
9769                       else if (old_mtu > 8166)
9770                           new_mtu = 8166;
9771                       else if (old_mtu > 4352)
9772                           new_mtu = 4352;
9773                       else if (old_mtu > 2002)
9774                           new_mtu = 2002;
9775                       else if (old_mtu > 1492)
9776                           new_mtu = 1492;
9777                       else if (old_mtu > 576)
9778                           new_mtu = 576;
9779                       else if (old_mtu > 296)
9780                           new_mtu = 296;
9781                       /*
9782                        *    These two are not from the RFC
9783    but
9784                        *    are needed for AMPRnet AX.25
9785    paths.
9786                        */
9787                       else if (old_mtu > 216)
9788                           new_mtu = 216;
9789                       else if (old_mtu > 128)
9790                           new_mtu = 128;
9791                       else
9792                       /*
9793                        *    Despair..
9794                        */
9795                           new_mtu = 68;
9796                   }
9797                   /*
9798                    * Ugly trick to pass MTU to protocol
9799    layer.
9800                    * Really we should add argument "info"
9801    to error handler.
9802                    */
9803                   iph->id = htons(new_mtu);
9804                   break;
9805               }
9806    #endif
9807           case ICMP_SR_FAILED:
9808               NETDEBUG(printk(KERN_INFO "ICMP: %s:
9809    Source Route Failed.\n", in_ntoa(iph->daddr)));
9810               break;
9811           default:
9812               break;
9813       }
9814       if(icmph->code>NR_ICMP_UNREACH) /* Invalid type
9815    */
9816           goto flush_it;
9817    }
9818
9819    /*
9820     *    Throw it at our lower layers
9821     *
9822     *    RFC 1122: 3.2.2 MUST extract the protocol ID
9823    from the passed header.
9824     *    RFC 1122: 3.2.2.1 MUST pass ICMP unreach
9825    messages to the transport layer.
9826     *    RFC 1122: 3.2.2.2 MUST pass ICMP time expired
9827    messages to transport layer.
9828     *
9829     *    Rule: Require port unreachable and protocol
9830    unreachable come
9831     *        from the host in question. Stop junk spoofs.
9832     */
9833
9834    if(!match_addr || saddr == iph->daddr)
9835    {
9836        /*
9837         *    Get the protocol(s).
9838         */
9839
9840        hash = iph->protocol & (MAX_INET_PROTOS -1);
9841
9842        /*
9843         *    This can't change while we are doing it.
9844         */
9845
9846        ipprot = (struct inet_protocol *)
9847    inet_protos[hash];
9848        while(ipprot != NULL)
9849        {
9850            struct inet_protocol *nextip;
9851
9852            nextip = (struct inet_protocol *)
9853    ipprot->next;
9854
9855            /*
9856             *    Pass it off to everyone who wants it.
```

```
9857                          */
9858
9859                  /* RFC1122: OK. Passes appropriate ICMP
9860     errors to the */
9861                  /* appropriate protocol layer (MUST), as per
9862     3.2.2. */
9863
9864                  if (iph->protocol == ipprot->protocol &&
9865     ipprot->err_handler)
9866                  {
9867                          ipprot->err_handler(icmph->type,
9868     icmph->code, dp,
9869                          iph->daddr, iph->saddr, ipprot,
9870     len);
9871                  }
9872
9873                  ipprot = nextip;
9874          }
9875      }
9876 flush_it:
9877      kfree_skb(skb, FREE_READ);
9878 }
9879
9880
9881 /*
9882  *  Handle ICMP_REDIRECT.
9883  */
9884
9885 static void icmp_redirect(struct icmphdr *icmph, struct
9886 sk_buff *skb, struct device *dev, __u32 source, __u32
9887 daddr, int len)
9888 {
9889      struct iphdr *iph;
9890      unsigned long ip;
9891
9892      /*
9893       *  Get the copied header of the packet that caused
9894      the redirect
9895       */
9896
9897      if(len<=sizeof(struct iphdr))
9898          goto flush_it;
9899
9900      iph = (struct iphdr *) (icmph + 1);
9901      ip = iph->daddr;
9902
9903      /*
9904       *  If we are a router and we run a routing
9905 protocol, we MUST NOT follow redirects.
9906       *  When using no routing protocol, we MAY follow
9907 redirects. (RFC 1812, 5.2.7.2)
9908       */
9909
9910 #if !defined(CONFIG_IP_DUMB_ROUTER)
9911      if (sysctl_ip_forward) {
9912          NETDEBUG(printk(KERN_INFO "icmp: ICMP redirect
9913 ignored. dest = %lX, "
9914              "orig gw = %lX, \"new\" gw = %lX, device =
9915 %s.\n", ntohl(ip),
9916              ntohl(source), ntohl(icmph->un.gateway),
9917 dev->name));
9918          goto flush_it;
9919      }
9920 #endif
9921      switch(icmph->code & 7)
9922      {
9923          case ICMP_REDIR_NET:
9924              /*
9925               *  This causes a problem with subnetted
9926 networks. What we should do
9927               *  is use ICMP_ADDRESS to get the subnet
9928 mask of the problem route
9929               *  and set both. But we don't.. [RFC1812
9930 says routers MUST NOT
9931               *  generate Network Redirects]
9932               */
9933 #ifdef not_a_good_idea
9934              ip_rt_add((RTF_DYNAMIC | RTF_MODIFIED |
9935 RTF_GATEWAY),
9936                  ip, 0, icmph->un.gateway, dev,0, 0, 0);
9937 #endif
9938              /*
9939               *  As per RFC recommendations now handle it
9940 as
9941               *  a host redirect.
9942               */
9943
9944          case ICMP_REDIR_HOST:
9945              /*
9946               *  Add better route to host.
9947               *  But first check that the redirect
9948               *  comes from the old gateway..
9949               *  And make sure it's an ok host address
9950               *  (not some confused thing sending our
9951               *  address)
9952               */
```

p 474

```
9953              NETDEBUG(printk(KERN_INFO "ICMP redirect
9954    from %s\n", in_ntoa(source)));
9955              ip_rt_redirect(source, ip,
9956    icmph->un.gateway, dev);
9957              break;
9958          case ICMP_REDIR_NETTOS:
9959          case ICMP_REDIR_HOSTTOS:
9960              NETDEBUG(printk(KERN_INFO "ICMP: cannot
9961    handle TOS redirects yet!\n"));
9962              break;
9963          default:
9964              break;
9965      }
9966
9967      /*
9968       *  Discard the original packet
9969       */
9970    flush_it:
9971      kfree_skb(skb, FREE_READ);
9972    }
9973
9974    /*
9975     *  Handle ICMP_ECHO ("ping") requests.
9976     *
9977     *  RFC 1122: 3.2.2.6 MUST have an echo server that
9978    answers ICMP echo requests.
9979     *  RFC 1122: 3.2.2.6 Data received in the ICMP_ECHO
9980    request MUST be included in the reply.
9981     *  RFC 1812: 4.3.3.6 SHOULD have a config option for
9982    silently ignoring echo requests, MUST have default=NOT.
9983     *  See also WRT handling of options once they are done
9984    and working.
9985     */
9986
9987    static void icmp_echo(struct icmphdr *icmph, struct
9988    sk_buff *skb, struct device *dev, __u32 saddr, __u32
9989    daddr, int len)
9990    {
9991    #ifndef CONFIG_IP_IGNORE_ECHO_REQUESTS
9992      struct icmp_bxm icmp_param;
9993      icmp_param.icmph=*icmph;
9994      icmp_param.icmph.type=ICMP_ECHOREPLY;
9995      icmp_param.data_ptr=(icmph+1);
9996      icmp_param.data_len=len;
9997      if (ip_options_echo(&icmp_param.replyopts, NULL,
9998    daddr, saddr, skb)==0)
9999          icmp_build_xmit(&icmp_param, daddr, saddr,
10000   skb->ip_hdr->tos);
```

```
10001   #endif
10002     kfree_skb(skb, FREE_READ);
10003   }
10004
10005   /*
10006    *  Handle ICMP Timestamp requests.
10007    *  RFC 1122: 3.2.2.8 MAY implement ICMP timestamp
10008   requests.
10009    *       SHOULD be in the kernel for minimum random
10010   latency.
10011    *       MUST be accurate to a few minutes.
10012    *       MUST be updated at least at 15Hz.
10013    */
10014
10015   static void icmp_timestamp(struct icmphdr *icmph, struct
10016   sk_buff *skb, struct device *dev, __u32 saddr, __u32
10017   daddr, int len)
10018   {
10019     __u32 times[3];      /* So the new timestamp works on
10020   ALPHA's.. */
10021     struct icmp_bxm icmp_param;
10022
10023     /*
10024      *  Too short.
10025      */
10026
10027     if(len<12)
10028     {
10029         icmp_statistics.IcmpInErrors++;
10030         kfree_skb(skb, FREE_READ);
10031         return;
10032     }
10033
10034     /*
10035      *  Fill in the current time as ms since midnight
10036   UT:
10037      */
10038
10039     {
10040         struct timeval tv;
10041         do_gettimeofday(&tv);
10042         times[1] = htonl((tv.tv_sec % 86400) * 1000 +
10043   tv.tv_usec / 1000);
10044     }
10045     times[2] = times[1];
10046     memcpy((void *)&times[0], icmph+1, 4);      /*
10047   Incoming stamp */
10048     icmp_param.icmph=*icmph;
```

p 474

```
10049        icmp_param.icmph.type=ICMP_TIMESTAMPREPLY;
10050        icmp_param.icmph.code=0;
10051        icmp_param.data_ptr=&times;
10052        icmp_param.data_len=12;
10053        if (ip_options_echo(&icmp_param.replyopts, NULL,
10054 daddr, saddr, skb)==0)
10055            icmp_build_xmit(&icmp_param, daddr, saddr,
10056 skb->ip_hdr->tos);
10057        kfree_skb(skb,FREE_READ);
10058 }
10059
10060
10061 /*
10062  *   Handle ICMP_ADDRESS_MASK requests.   (RFC950)
10063  *
10064  * RFC1122 (3.2.2.9).  A host MUST only send replies to
10065  * ADDRESS_MASK requests if it's been configured as an
10066 address mask
10067  * agent.  Receiving a request doesn't constitute
10068 implicit permission to
10069  * act as one. Of course, implementing this correctly
10070 requires (SHOULD)
10071  * a way to turn the functionality on and off.  Another
10072 one for sysctl(),
10073  * I guess. -- MS
10074  * Botched with a CONFIG option for now - Linus add scts
10075 sysctl please..
10076  */
10077
10078 static void icmp_address(struct icmphdr *icmph, struct
10079 sk_buff *skb, struct device *dev, __u32 saddr, __u32
10080 daddr, int len)
10081 {
10082 #ifdef CONFIG_IP_ADDR_AGENT /* Don't use, broken */
10083        struct icmp_bxm icmp_param;
10084        icmp_param.icmph.type=ICMP_ADDRESSREPLY;
10085        icmp_param.icmph.code=0;
10086        icmp_param.icmph.un.echo.id = icmph->un.echo.id;
10087        icmp_param.icmph.un.echo.sequence =
10088 icmph->un.echo.sequence;
10089        icmp_param.data_ptr=&dev->pa_mask;
10090        icmp_param.data_len=4;
10091        if (ip_options_echo(&icmp_param.replyopts, NULL,
10092 daddr, saddr, skb)==0)
10093            icmp_build_xmit(&icmp_param, daddr, saddr,
10094 skb->iph->tos);
10095 #endif
10096        kfree_skb(skb, FREE_READ);
10097 }
10098
10099 static void icmp_discard(struct icmphdr *icmph, struct      [p 472]
10100 sk_buff *skb, struct device *dev, __u32 saddr, __u32
10101 daddr, int len)
10102 {
10103        kfree_skb(skb, FREE_READ);
10104 }
10105
10106 #ifdef CONFIG_IP_TRANSPARENT_PROXY
10107 /*
10108  *   Check incoming icmp packets not addressed locally,
10109 to check whether
10110  *   they relate to a (proxying) socket on our system.
10111  *   Needed for transparent proxying.
10112  *
10113  *   This code is presently ugly and needs cleanup.
10114  *   Probably should add a chkaddr entry to ipprot to
10115 call a chk routine
10116  *   in udp.c or tcp.c...
10117  */
10118
10119 extern struct sock *tcp_v4_lookup(u32 saddr, u16 sport,
10120 u32 daddr, u16 dport, struct device *dev);
10121 extern struct sock *udp_v4_lookup(u32 saddr, u16 sport,
10122 u32 daddr, u16 dport, struct device *dev);
10123
10124 int icmp_chkaddr(struct sk_buff *skb)
10125 {
10126        struct icmphdr *icmph=(struct icmphdr *)(skb->h.raw
10127 + skb->h.iph->ihl*4);
10128        struct iphdr *iph = (struct iphdr *) (icmph + 1);
10129        void (*handler)(struct icmphdr *icmph, struct
10130 sk_buff *skb, struct device *dev, __u32 saddr, __u32
10131 daddr, int len) = icmp_pointers[icmph->type].handler;
10132
10133        if (handler == icmp_unreach || handler ==           [p 474]
10134 icmp_redirect) {
10135            struct sock *sk;
10136
10137            switch (iph->protocol) {
10138            case IPPROTO_TCP:
10139                {
10140                    struct tcphdr *th = (struct tcphdr
10141 *)(((unsigned char *)iph)+(iph->ihl<<2));
10142
10143                    sk = tcp_v4_lookup(iph->saddr, th->source,
10144 iph->daddr, th->dest, skb->dev);
```

```
10145            if (!sk) return 0;
10146            if (sk->saddr != iph->saddr) return 0;
10147            if (sk->daddr != iph->daddr) return 0;
10148            if (sk->dummy_th.dest != th->dest) return 0;
10149            /*
10150             * This packet came from us.
10151             */
10152            return 1;
10153            }
10154        case IPPROTO_UDP:
10155            {
10156            struct udphdr *uh = (struct udphdr
10157    *)(((unsigned char *)iph)+(iph->ihl<<2));
10158
10159            sk = udp_v4_lookup(iph->saddr, uh->source,
10160    iph->daddr, uh->dest, skb->dev);
10161            if (!sk) return 0;
10162            if (sk->saddr != iph->saddr &&
10163    ip_chk_addr(iph->saddr) != IS_MYADDR)
10164                return 0;
10165            /*
10166             * This packet may have come from us.
10167             * Assume it did.
10168             */
10169            return 1;
10170            }
10171        }
10172    }
10173    return 0;
10174 }
10175
10176 #endif
10177 /*
10178  *  Deal with incoming ICMP packets.
10179  */
10180
10181 int icmp_rcv(struct sk_buff *skb, struct device *dev,
10182 struct options *opt,
10183     __u32 daddr, unsigned short len,
10184     __u32 saddr, int redo, struct inet_protocol
10185 *protocol)
10186 {
10187    struct icmphdr *icmph=(void *)skb->h.raw;
10188 #ifdef CONFIG_IP_TRANSPARENT_PROXY
10189    int r;
10190 #endif
10191    icmp_statistics.IcmpInMsgs++;
10192
10193    if(len < sizeof(struct icmphdr))
10194    {
10195        icmp_statistics.IcmpInErrors++;
10196        NETDEBUG(printk(KERN_INFO "ICMP: runt
10197 packet\n"));
10198        kfree_skb(skb, FREE_READ);
10199        return 0;
10200    }
10201
10202    /*
10203     *  Validate the packet
10204     */
10205
10206    if (ip_compute_csum((unsigned char *) icmph, len))
10207    {
10208        /* Failed checksum! */
10209        icmp_statistics.IcmpInErrors++;
10210        NETDEBUG(printk(KERN_INFO "ICMP: failed checksum
10211 from %s!\n", in_ntoa(saddr)));
10212        kfree_skb(skb, FREE_READ);
10213        return(0);
10214    }
10215
10216    /*
10217     *  18 is the highest 'known' ICMP type. Anything
10218 else is a mystery
10219     *
10220     *  RFC 1122: 3.2.2  Unknown ICMP messages types
10221 MUST be silently discarded.
10222     */
10223
10224    if(icmph->type > 18)
10225    {
10226        icmp_statistics.IcmpInErrors++;        /* Is this
10227 right - or do we ignore ? */
10228        kfree_skb(skb,FREE_READ);
10229        return(0);
10230    }
10231
10232    /*
10233     *  Parse the ICMP message
10234     */
10235
10236 #ifdef CONFIG_IP_TRANSPARENT_PROXY
10237    /*
10238     *  We may get non-local addresses and still want to
10239 handle them
10240     *  locally, due to transparent proxying.
```

p 472

```
10241          *   Thus, narrow down the test to what is really
10242 meant.
10243          */
10244          if (daddr!=dev->pa_addr && ((r = ip_chk_addr(daddr))
10245 == IS_BROADCAST || r == IS_MULTICAST))
10246 #else
10247          if (daddr!=dev->pa_addr && ip_chk_addr(daddr) !=
10248 IS_MYADDR)
10249 #endif
10250      {
10251          /*
10252           *  RFC 1122: 3.2.2.6 An ICMP_ECHO to broadcast
10253 MAY be silently ignored (we don't as it is used
10254           *  by some network mapping tools).
10255           *  RFC 1122: 3.2.2.8 An ICMP_TIMESTAMP MAY be
10256 silently discarded if to broadcast/multicast.
10257           */
10258          if (icmph->type != ICMP_ECHO)
10259          {
10260              icmp_statistics.IcmpInErrors++;
10261              kfree_skb(skb, FREE_READ);
10262              return(0);
10263          }
10264          /*
10265           *  Reply the multicast/broadcast using a legal
10266           *  interface - in this case the device we got
10267           *  it from.
10268           */
10269          daddr=dev->pa_addr;
10270      }
10271
10272      len-=sizeof(struct icmphdr);
10273      (*icmp_pointers[icmph->type].input)++;
10274
10275 (icmp_pointers[icmph->type].handler)(icmph,skb,skb->dev,s
10276 addr,daddr,len);
10277      return 0;
10278 }
10279
10280 /*
10281  * This table defined limits of ICMP sending rate for
10282 various ICMP messages.
10283  */
10284
10285 static struct icmp_xrlim
10286      xrl_unreach = { 4*HZ, 80, HZ/4 },      /* Host
10287 Unreachable */
10288      xrl_redirect = { 2*HZ, 10, HZ/2 },      /* Redirect
10289 */
10290      xrl_generic = { 3*HZ, 30, HZ/4 };       /* All other
10291 errors */
10292
10293 /*
10294  * This table is the definition of how we handle ICMP.
10295  */
10296
10297 static struct icmp_control icmp_pointers[19] = {
10298 /* ECHO REPLY (0) */
10299    { &icmp_statistics.IcmpOutEchoReps,
10300 &icmp_statistics.IcmpInEchoReps, icmp_discard, 0, NULL },
10301    { &dummy, &icmp_statistics.IcmpInErrors, icmp_discard,
10302 1, NULL },
10303    { &dummy, &icmp_statistics.IcmpInErrors, icmp_discard,
10304 1, NULL },
10305 /* DEST UNREACH (3) */
10306    { &icmp_statistics.IcmpOutDestUnreachs,
10307 &icmp_statistics.IcmpInDestUnreachs, icmp_unreach, 1,
10308 &xrl_unreach },
10309 /* SOURCE QUENCH (4) */
10310    { &icmp_statistics.IcmpOutSrcQuenchs,
10311 &icmp_statistics.IcmpInSrcQuenchs, icmp_unreach, 1, NULL
10312 },
10313 /* REDIRECT (5) */
10314    { &icmp_statistics.IcmpOutRedirects,
10315 &icmp_statistics.IcmpInRedirects, icmp_redirect, 1,
10316 &xrl_redirect },
10317    { &dummy, &icmp_statistics.IcmpInErrors, icmp_discard,
10318 1, NULL },
10319    { &dummy, &icmp_statistics.IcmpInErrors, icmp_discard,
10320 1, NULL },
10321 /* ECHO (8) */
10322    { &icmp_statistics.IcmpOutEchos,
10323 &icmp_statistics.IcmpInEchos, icmp_echo, 0, NULL },
10324    { &dummy, &icmp_statistics.IcmpInErrors, icmp_discard,
10325 1, NULL },
10326    { &dummy, &icmp_statistics.IcmpInErrors, icmp_discard,
10327 1, NULL },
10328 /* TIME EXCEEDED (11) */
10329    { &icmp_statistics.IcmpOutTimeExcds,
10330 &icmp_statistics.IcmpInTimeExcds, icmp_unreach, 1,
10331 &xrl_generic },
10332 /* PARAMETER PROBLEM (12) */
10333 /* FIXME: RFC1122 3.2.2.5 - MUST pass PARAM_PROB
10334 messages to transport layer */
10335    { &icmp_statistics.IcmpOutParmProbs,
10336 &icmp_statistics.IcmpInParmProbs, icmp_discard, 1,
```

```
10337    &xrl_generic },
10338    /* TIMESTAMP (13) */
10339       { &icmp_statistics.IcmpOutTimestamps,
10340    &icmp_statistics.IcmpInTimestamps, icmp_timestamp, 0,
10341    NULL },
10342    /* TIMESTAMP REPLY (14) */
10343       { &icmp_statistics.IcmpOutTimestampReps,
10344    &icmp_statistics.IcmpInTimestampReps, icmp_discard, 0,
10345    NULL },
10346    /* INFO (15) */
10347       { &dummy, &dummy, icmp_discard, 0, NULL },
10348    /* INFO REPLY (16) */
10349       { &dummy, &dummy, icmp_discard, 0, NULL },
10350    /* ADDR MASK (17) */
10351       { &icmp_statistics.IcmpOutAddrMasks,
10352    &icmp_statistics.IcmpInAddrMasks, icmp_address, 0, NULL
10353    },
10354    /* ADDR MASK REPLY (18) */
10355       { &icmp_statistics.IcmpOutAddrMaskReps,
10356    &icmp_statistics.IcmpInAddrMaskReps, icmp_discard, 0,
10357    NULL }
10358    };
10359
10360    void icmp_init(struct proto_ops *ops)
10361    {
10362       struct sock *sk;
10363       int err;
10364       icmp_socket.type=SOCK_RAW;
10365       icmp_socket.ops=ops;
10366       if((err=ops->create(&icmp_socket, IPPROTO_ICMP))<0)
10367          panic("Failed to create the ICMP control
10368    socket.\n");
10369       sk=icmp_socket.data;
10370       sk->allocation=GFP_ATOMIC;
10371       sk->num = 256;          /* Don't receive any data */
10372    #ifndef CONFIG_NO_ICMP_LIMIT
10373       xrlim_init();
10374    #endif
10375    }
10376
```

usr/src/linux/net/ipv4/igmp.c

```
10377    /*
10378     *    Linux NET3: Internet Group Management Protocol
10379    [IGMP]
10380     *
10381     *    This code implements the IGMP protocol as defined in
10382    RFC1112. There has
10383     *    been a further revision of this protocol since which
10384    is now supported.
10385     *
10386     *    If you have trouble with this module be careful what
10387    gcc you have used,
10388     *    the older version didn't come out right using gcc
10389    2.5.8, the newer one
10390     *    seems to fall out with gcc 2.6.2.
10391     *
10392     *    Authors:
10393     *        Alan Cox <Alan.Cox@linux.org>
10394     *
10395     *    This program is free software; you can redistribute
10396    it and/or
10397     *    modify it under the terms of the GNU General Public
10398    License
10399     *    as published by the Free Software Foundation; either
10400    version
10401     *    2 of the License, or (at your option) any later
10402    version.
10403     *
10404     *    Fixes:
10405     *
10406     *        Alan Cox    :    Added lots of __inline__ to
10407    optimise
10408     *                         the memory usage of all the tiny
10409    little
10410     *                         functions.
10411     *        Alan Cox    :    Dumped the header building
10412    experiment.
10413     *        Alan Cox    :    Minor tweaks ready for multicast
10414    routing
10415     *                         and extended IGMP protocol.
10416     *        Alan Cox    :    Removed a load of inline
10417    directives. Gcc 2.5.8
10418     *                         writes utterly bogus code otherwise
10419    (sigh)
10420     *                         fixed IGMP loopback to behave in the
10421    manner
10422     *                         desired by mrouted, fixed the fact
10423    it has been
10424     *                         broken since 1.3.6 and cleaned up a
10425    few minor
10426     *                         points.
10427     *
10428     *        Chih-Jen Chang  :   Tried to revise IGMP to
10429    Version 2
10430     *        Tsu-Sheng Tsao       E-mail: chihjenc@scf.usc.edu
```

```
10431  and tsusheng@scf.usc.edu
10432  *                   The enhancements are mainly based on
10433  Steve Deering's
10434  *                   ipmulti-3.5 source code.
10435  *         Chih-Jen Chang  :   Added the
10436  igmp_get_mrouter_info and
10437  *         Tsu-Sheng Tsao      igmp_set_mrouter_info to
10438  keep track of
10439  *                   the mrouted version on that device.
10440  *         Chih-Jen Chang  :   Added the max_resp_time
10441  parameter to
10442  *         Tsu-Sheng Tsao      igmp_heard_query(). Using
10443  this parameter
10444  *                   to identify the multicast router
10445  version
10446  *                   and do what the IGMP version 2
10447  specified.
10448  *         Chih-Jen Chang  :   Added a timer to revert to
10449  IGMP V2 router
10450  *         Tsu-Sheng Tsao      if the specified time
10451  expired.
10452  *         Alan Cox     :   Stop IGMP from 0.0.0.0 being
10453  accepted.
10454  *         Alan Cox     :   Use GFP_ATOMIC in the right
10455  places.
10456  *         Christian Daudt :   igmp timer wasn't set for
10457  local group
10458  *                   memberships but was being deleted,
10459  *                   which caused a "del_timer() called
10460  *                   from %p with timer not initialized\n"
10461  *                   message (960131).
10462  *         Christian Daudt :   removed del_timer from
10463  *                   igmp_timer_expire function (960205).
10464  *         Christian Daudt :       igmp_heard_report
10465  now only calls
10466  *                           igmp_timer_expire
10467  if tm->running is
10468  *                           true (960216).
10469  *         Malcolm Beattie :   ttl comparison wrong in
10470  igmp_rcv made
10471  *                   igmp_heard_query never trigger.
10472  Expiry
10473  *                   miscalculation fixed in
10474  igmp_heard_query
10475  *                   and random() made to return unsigned
10476  to
10477  *                   prevent negative expiry times.
10478  *         Alexey Kuznetsov:   Wrong group leaving
10479  behaviour, backport
10480  *                   fix from pending 2.1.x patches.
10481  *         Alan Cox:       Forget to enable FDDI support
10482  earlier.
10483  *         Elena Apolinario Fdez de Sousa,: IGMP Leave
10484  Messages must be sent to
10485  *         Juan-Mariano de Goyeneche       the "all
10486  routers" group, not the group
10487  *                   group being left.
10488  */
10489
10490
10491  #include <asm/segment.h>
10492  #include <asm/system.h>
10493  #include <linux/types.h>
10494  #include <linux/kernel.h>
10495  #include <linux/sched.h>
10496  #include <linux/string.h>
10497  #include <linux/config.h>
10498  #include <linux/socket.h>
10499  #include <linux/sockios.h>
10500  #include <linux/in.h>
10501  #include <linux/inet.h>
10502  #include <linux/netdevice.h>
10503  #include <linux/if_arp.h>
10504  #include <net/ip.h>
10505  #include <net/protocol.h>
10506  #include <net/route.h>
10507  #include <linux/skbuff.h>
10508  #include <net/sock.h>
10509  #include <linux/igmp.h>
10510  #include <net/checksum.h>
10511
10512  #ifdef CONFIG_IP_MULTICAST
10513
10514
10515  /*
10516   * If time expired, change the router type to
10517  IGMP_NEW_ROUTER.
10518   */
10519
10520  static void ip_router_timer_expire(unsigned long data)
10521  {
10522      struct ip_router_info *i=(struct ip_router_info
10523  *)data;
10524
10525      del_timer(&i->timer);
10526      i->type=IGMP_NEW_ROUTER;    /* Revert to new
```

```
10527   multicast router */
10528       i->time=0;
10529   }
10530
10531   /*
10532    *  Multicast router info manager
10533    */
10534
10535   struct  ip_router_info  *ip_router_info_head=(struct
10536   ip_router_info *)0;
10537
10538   /*
10539    *  Get the multicast router info on that device
10540    */
10541
10542   static  struct  ip_router_info
10543   *igmp_get_mrouter_info(struct device *dev)
10544   {
10545       register struct ip_router_info *i;
10546
10547       for(i=ip_router_info_head;i!=NULL;i=i->next)
10548       {
10549           if (i->dev == dev)
10550           {
10551               return i;
10552           }
10553       }
10554
10555       /*
10556        *  Not found. Create a new entry. The default is
10557   IGMP V2 router
10558        */
10559
10560       i=(struct ip_router_info *)kmalloc(sizeof(*i),
10561   GFP_ATOMIC);
10562       if(i==NULL)
10563           return NULL;
10564       i->dev = dev;
10565       i->type = IGMP_NEW_ROUTER;
10566       i->time = IGMP_AGE_THRESHOLD;
10567       i->next = ip_router_info_head;
10568       ip_router_info_head = i;
10569
10570       init_timer(&i->timer);
10571       i->timer.data=(unsigned long)i;
10572       i->timer.function=&ip_router_timer_expire;
10573
10574       return i;
```

```
10575   }
10576
10577   /*
10578    *  Set the multicast router info on that device
10579    */
10580
10581   static  struct  ip_router_info
10582   *igmp_set_mrouter_info(struct device *dev,int type,int
10583   time)
10584   {
10585       register struct ip_router_info *i;
10586
10587       for(i=ip_router_info_head;i!=NULL;i=i->next)
10588       {
10589           if (i->dev == dev)
10590           {
10591               if(i->type==IGMP_OLD_ROUTER)
10592               {
10593                   del_timer(&i->timer);
10594               }
10595
10596               i->type = type;
10597               i->time = time;
10598
10599               if(i->type==IGMP_OLD_ROUTER)
10600               {
10601                   i->timer.expires=jiffies+i->time*HZ;
10602                   add_timer(&i->timer);
10603               }
10604               return i;
10605           }
10606       }
10607
10608       /*
10609        *  Not found. Create a new entry.
10610        */
10611       i=(struct ip_router_info *)kmalloc(sizeof(*i),
10612   GFP_ATOMIC);
10613       if(i==NULL)
10614           return NULL;
10615       i->dev = dev;
10616       i->type = type;
10617       i->time = time;
10618       i->next = ip_router_info_head;
10619       ip_router_info_head = i;
10620
10621       init_timer(&i->timer);
10622       i->timer.data=(unsigned long)i;
```

```
10623        i->timer.function=&ip_router_timer_expire;
10624        if(i->type==IGMP_OLD_ROUTER)
10625        {
10626              i->timer.expires=jiffies+i->time*HZ;
10627              add_timer(&i->timer);
10628        }
10629
10630        return i;
10631    }
10632
10633
10634    /*
10635     *  Timer management
10636     */
10637
10638    static void igmp_stop_timer(struct ip_mc_list *im)
10639    {
10640      if (im->tm_running) {
10641        del_timer(&im->timer);
10642        im->tm_running=0;
10643      }
10644      else {
10645        printk(KERN_ERR "igmp_stop_timer() called with timer
10646    not running by %p\n",__builtin_return_address(0));
10647      }
10648    }
10649
10650    extern __inline__ unsigned int random(void)
10651    {
10652        static unsigned long seed=152L;
10653        seed=seed*69069L+1;
10654        return seed^jiffies;
10655    }
10656
10657    /*
10658     *  Inlined as it's only called once.
10659     */
10660
10661    static void igmp_start_timer(struct ip_mc_list
10662    *im,unsigned char max_resp_time)
10663    {
10664        int tv;
10665        if(im->tm_running)
10666            return;
10667        tv=random()%(max_resp_time*HZ/IGMP_TIMER_SCALE); /*
10668    Pick a number any number 8) */
10669        im->timer.expires=jiffies+tv;
10670        im->tm_running=1;
```

```
10671        add_timer(&im->timer);
10672    }
10673
10674    /*
10675     *  Send an IGMP report.
10676     */
10677
10678    #define MAX_IGMP_SIZE (sizeof(struct
10679    igmphdr)+sizeof(struct iphdr)+64)
10680
10681    static void igmp_send_report(struct device *dev,
10682    unsigned long address, int type)
10683    {
10684        struct sk_buff *skb=alloc_skb(MAX_IGMP_SIZE,
10685    GFP_ATOMIC);
10686        int tmp;
10687        struct igmphdr *ih;
10688
10689        if(skb==NULL)
10690            return;
10691        tmp=ip_build_header(skb, dev->pa_addr, address,
10692    &dev, IPPROTO_IGMP, NULL,
10693                28 , 0, 1, NULL);
10694        if(tmp<0)
10695        {
10696            kfree_skb(skb, FREE_WRITE);
10697            return;
10698        }
10699        ih=(struct igmphdr *)skb_put(skb,sizeof(struct
10700    igmphdr));
10701        ih->type=type;
10702        ih->code=0;
10703        ih->csum=0;
10704        ih->group=address;
10705        ih->csum=ip_compute_csum((void *)ih,sizeof(struct
10706    igmphdr));    /* Checksum fill */
10707        ip_queue_xmit(NULL,dev,skb,1);
10708    }
10709
10710
10711    static void igmp_timer_expire(unsigned long data)
10712    {
10713        struct ip_mc_list *im=(struct ip_mc_list *)data;
10714        struct ip_router_info *r;
10715
10716        im->tm_running=0;
10717        r=igmp_get_mrouter_info(im->interface);
10718        if(r==NULL)
```

```
10719            return;
10720        if(r->type==IGMP_NEW_ROUTER)
10721            igmp_send_report(im->interface, im->multiaddr,
10722    IGMP_HOST_NEW_MEMBERSHIP_REPORT);
10723        else
10724            igmp_send_report(im->interface, im->multiaddr,
10725    IGMP_HOST_MEMBERSHIP_REPORT);
10726        im->reporter=1;
10727    }
10728
10729    static void igmp_init_timer(struct ip_mc_list *im)
10730    {
10731        im->tm_running=0;
10732        init_timer(&im->timer);
10733        im->timer.data=(unsigned long)im;
10734        im->timer.function=&igmp_timer_expire;
10735    }
10736
10737
10738    static void igmp_heard_report(struct device *dev, __u32
10739    address, __u32 src)
10740    {
10741        struct ip_mc_list *im;
10742
10743        if ((address & IGMP_LOCAL_GROUP_MASK) !=
10744    IGMP_LOCAL_GROUP)
10745        {
10746            /* Timers are only set for non-local groups */
10747            for(im=dev->ip_mc_list;im!=NULL;im=im->next)
10748            {
10749                if(im->multiaddr==address)
10750                {
10751                    if(im->tm_running)
10752                        igmp_stop_timer(im);
10753                    if(src!=dev->pa_addr)
10754                        im->reporter=0;
10755                    return;
10756                }
10757            }
10758        }
10759    }
10760
10761    static void igmp_heard_query(struct device *dev,unsigned
10762    char max_resp_time)
10763    {
10764        struct ip_mc_list *im;
10765        int mrouter_type;
10766

10767        /*
10768         *  The max_resp_time is in units of 1/10 second.
10769         */
10770        if(max_resp_time>0)
10771        {
10772            mrouter_type=IGMP_NEW_ROUTER;
10773
10774
10775        if(igmp_set_mrouter_info(dev,mrouter_type,0)==NULL)
10776                return;
10777            /*
10778             * - Start the timers in all of our membership
10779    records
10780             *    that the query applies to for the interface
10781    on
10782             *    which the query arrived excl. those that
10783    belong
10784             *    to a "local" group (224.0.0.X)
10785             * - For timers already running check if they
10786    need to
10787             *    be reset.
10788             * - Use the igmp->igmp_code field as the maximum
10789             *    delay possible
10790             */
10791            for(im=dev->ip_mc_list;im!=NULL;im=im->next)
10792            {
10793                if(im->tm_running)
10794                {
10795
10796    if(im->timer.expires>jiffies+max_resp_time*HZ/IGMP_TIMER_
10797    SCALE)
10798                    {
10799                        igmp_stop_timer(im);
10800                        igmp_start_timer(im,max_resp_time);
10801                    }
10802                }
10803                else
10804                {
10805                    if((im->multiaddr &
10806    IGMP_LOCAL_GROUP_MASK)!=IGMP_LOCAL_GROUP)
10807                        igmp_start_timer(im,max_resp_time);
10808                }
10809            }
10810        }
10811        else
10812        {
10813            mrouter_type=IGMP_OLD_ROUTER;
10814
```

```
10815   max_resp_time=IGMP_MAX_HOST_REPORT_DELAY*IGMP_TIMER_SCALE
10816   ;
10817
10818
10819   if(igmp_set_mrouter_info(dev,mrouter_type,IGMP_AGE_THRESH
10820   OLD)==NULL)
10821           return;
10822
10823           /*
10824            * Start the timers in all of our membership
10825   records for
10826            * the interface on which the query arrived,
10827   except those
10828            * that are already running and those that
10829   belong to a
10830            * "local" group (224.0.0.X).
10831            */
10832
10833           for(im=dev->ip_mc_list;im!=NULL;im=im->next)
10834           {
10835                   if(!im->tm_running && (im->multiaddr &
10836   IGMP_LOCAL_GROUP_MASK)!=IGMP_LOCAL_GROUP)
10837                           igmp_start_timer(im,max_resp_time);
10838           }
10839   }
10840   }
10841
10842   /*
10843    *  Map a multicast IP onto multicast MAC for type
10844   ethernet.
10845    */
10846
10847   extern __inline__ void ip_mc_map(unsigned long addr,
10848   char *buf)
10849   {
10850       addr=ntohl(addr);
10851       buf[0]=0x01;
10852       buf[1]=0x00;
10853       buf[2]=0x5e;
10854       buf[5]=addr&0xFF;
10855       addr>>=8;
10856       buf[4]=addr&0xFF;
10857       addr>>=8;
10858       buf[3]=addr&0x7F;
10859   }
10860
10861   /*
10862    *  Add a filter to a device
```

```
10863    */
10864
10865   void ip_mc_filter_add(struct device *dev, unsigned long
10866   addr)
10867   {
10868       char buf[6];
10869       if(dev->type!=ARPHRD_ETHER && dev->type!=ARPHRD_FDDI)
10870           return; /* Only do ethernet or FDDI for now */
10871       ip_mc_map(addr,buf);
10872       dev_mc_add(dev,buf,ETH_ALEN,0);
10873   }
10874
10875   /*
10876    *  Remove a filter from a device
10877    */
10878
10879   void ip_mc_filter_del(struct device *dev, unsigned long
10880   addr)
10881   {
10882       char buf[6];
10883       if(dev->type!=ARPHRD_ETHER && dev->type!=ARPHRD_FDDI)
10884           return; /* Only do ethernet or FDDI for now */
10885       ip_mc_map(addr,buf);
10886       dev_mc_delete(dev,buf,ETH_ALEN,0);
10887   }
10888
10889   extern __inline__ void igmp_group_dropped(struct
10890   ip_mc_list *im)
10891   {
10892       del_timer(&im->timer);
10893           /* It seems we have to send Leave Messages to
10894   224.0.0.2 and not to
10895            the group itself, to remain RFC 2236
10896   compliant... (jmel) */
10897           igmp_send_report(im->interface, IGMP_ALL_ROUTER,
10898   IGMP_HOST_LEAVE_MESSAGE);
10899       ip_mc_filter_del(im->interface, im->multiaddr);
10900   }
10901
10902   extern __inline__ void igmp_group_added(struct
10903   ip_mc_list *im)
10904   {
10905       struct ip_router_info *r;
10906       igmp_init_timer(im);
10907       ip_mc_filter_add(im->interface, im->multiaddr);
10908       r=igmp_get_mrouter_info(im->interface);
10909       if(r==NULL)
10910           return;
```

```
10911        if(r->type==IGMP_NEW_ROUTER)
10912            igmp_send_report(im->interface, im->multiaddr,
10913    IGMP_HOST_NEW_MEMBERSHIP_REPORT);
10914        else
10915            igmp_send_report(im->interface, im->multiaddr,
10916    IGMP_HOST_MEMBERSHIP_REPORT);
10917    }
10918
10919    int igmp_rcv(struct sk_buff *skb, struct device *dev,
10920    struct options *opt,
10921        __u32 daddr, unsigned short len, __u32 saddr, int
10922    redo,
10923        struct inet_protocol *protocol)
10924    {
10925        /* This basically follows the spec line by line --
10926    see RFC1112 */
10927        struct igmphdr *ih;
10928
10929        /*
10930         *    Mrouted needs to able to query local interfaces.
10931    So
10932         *    report for the device this was sent at. (Which
10933    can
10934         *    be the loopback this time)
10935         */
10936
10937        if(dev->flags&IFF_LOOPBACK)
10938        {
10939            dev=ip_dev_find(saddr);
10940            if(dev==NULL)
10941                dev=&loopback_dev;
10942        }
10943        ih=(struct igmphdr *)skb->h.raw;
10944
10945        if(len <sizeof(struct igmphdr) || skb->ip_hdr->ttl<1
10946    || ip_compute_csum((void *)skb->h.raw,sizeof(struct
10947    igmphdr)))
10948        {
10949            kfree_skb(skb, FREE_READ);
10950            return 0;
10951        }
10952
10953        /*
10954         *    I have a report that someone does this!
10955         */
10956
10957        if(saddr==0)
10958        {
```

```
10959            printk(KERN_INFO "Broken multicast host using
10960    0.0.0.0 heard on %s\n",
10961                dev->name);
10962            kfree_skb(skb, FREE_READ);
10963            return 0;
10964        }
10965
10966        if(ih->type==IGMP_HOST_MEMBERSHIP_QUERY &&
10967    daddr==IGMP_ALL_HOSTS)
10968            igmp_heard_query(dev,ih->code);
10969        if(ih->type==IGMP_HOST_MEMBERSHIP_REPORT &&
10970    daddr==ih->group)
10971            igmp_heard_report(dev,ih->group, saddr);
10972        if(ih->type==IGMP_HOST_NEW_MEMBERSHIP_REPORT &&
10973    daddr==ih->group)
10974            igmp_heard_report(dev,ih->group, saddr);
10975        kfree_skb(skb, FREE_READ);
10976        return 0;
10977    }
10978
10979    /*
10980     *    Multicast list managers
10981     */
10982
10983
10984    /*
10985     *    A socket has joined a multicast group on device dev.
10986     */
10987
10988    static void ip_mc_inc_group(struct device *dev, unsigned
10989    long addr)
10990    {
10991        struct ip_mc_list *i;
10992        for(i=dev->ip_mc_list;i!=NULL;i=i->next)
10993        {
10994            if(i->multiaddr==addr)
10995            {
10996                i->users++;
10997                return;
10998            }
10999        }
11000        i=(struct ip_mc_list *)kmalloc(sizeof(*i),
11001    GFP_KERNEL);
11002        if(!i)
11003            return;
11004        i->users=1;
11005        i->interface=dev;
11006        i->multiaddr=addr;
```

```
11007            i->next=dev->ip_mc_list;
11008            igmp_group_added(i);
11009            dev->ip_mc_list=i;
11010    }
11011
11012    /*
11013     *  A socket has left a multicast group on device dev
11014     */
11015
11016    static void ip_mc_dec_group(struct device *dev, unsigned
11017    long addr)
11018    {
11019            struct ip_mc_list **i;
11020            for(i=&(dev->ip_mc_list);(*i)!=NULL;i=&(*i)->next)
11021            {
11022                if((*i)->multiaddr==addr)
11023                {
11024                    if(--((*i)->users) == 0)
11025                    {
11026                        struct ip_mc_list *tmp= *i;
11027                        igmp_group_dropped(tmp);
11028                        *i=(*i)->next;
11029                        kfree_s(tmp,sizeof(*tmp));
11030                    }
11031                    return;
11032                }
11033            }
11034    }
11035
11036    /*
11037     *  Device going down: Clean up.
11038     */
11039
11040    void ip_mc_drop_device(struct device *dev)
11041    {
11042            struct ip_mc_list *i;
11043            struct ip_mc_list *j;
11044            for(i=dev->ip_mc_list;i!=NULL;i=j)
11045            {
11046                j=i->next;
11047                kfree_s(i,sizeof(*i));
11048            }
11049            dev->ip_mc_list=NULL;
11050    }
11051
11052    /*
11053     *  Device going up. Make sure it is in all hosts
11054     */
```

```
11055
11056    void ip_mc_allhost(struct device *dev)
11057    {
11058            struct ip_mc_list *i;
11059            for(i=dev->ip_mc_list;i!=NULL;i=i->next)
11060                if(i->multiaddr==IGMP_ALL_HOSTS)
11061                    return;
11062            i=(struct ip_mc_list *)kmalloc(sizeof(*i),
11063    GFP_KERNEL);
11064            if(!i)
11065                return;
11066            i->users=1;
11067            i->interface=dev;
11068            i->multiaddr=IGMP_ALL_HOSTS;
11069            i->tm_running=0;
11070            i->next=dev->ip_mc_list;
11071            dev->ip_mc_list=i;
11072            ip_mc_filter_add(i->interface, i->multiaddr);
11073
11074    }
11075
11076    /*
11077     *  Join a socket to a group
11078     */
11079
11080    int ip_mc_join_group(struct sock *sk , struct device
11081    *dev, unsigned long addr)
11082    {
11083            int unused= -1;
11084            int i;
11085            if(!MULTICAST(addr))
11086                return -EINVAL;
11087            if(!(dev->flags&IFF_MULTICAST))
11088                return -EADDRNOTAVAIL;
11089            if(sk->ip_mc_list==NULL)
11090            {
11091                if((sk->ip_mc_list=(struct ip_mc_socklist
11092    *)kmalloc(sizeof(*sk->ip_mc_list), GFP_KERNEL))==NULL)
11093                    return -ENOMEM;
11094
11095    memset(sk->ip_mc_list,'\0',sizeof(*sk->ip_mc_list));
11096            }
11097            for(i=0;i<IP_MAX_MEMBERSHIPS;i++)
11098            {
11099                if(sk->ip_mc_list->multiaddr[i]==addr &&
11100    sk->ip_mc_list->multidev[i]==dev)
11101                    return -EADDRINUSE;
11102                if(sk->ip_mc_list->multidev[i]==NULL)
```

```
11103              unused=i;
11104          }
11105
11106      if(unused==-1)
11107          return -ENOBUFS;
11108      sk->ip_mc_list->multiaddr[unused]=addr;
11109      sk->ip_mc_list->multidev[unused]=dev;
11110      ip_mc_inc_group(dev,addr);
11111      return 0;
11112  }
11113
11114  /*
11115   *  Ask a socket to leave a group.
11116   */
11117
11118  int ip_mc_leave_group(struct sock *sk, struct device
11119  *dev, unsigned long addr)
11120  {
11121      int i;
11122      if(!MULTICAST(addr))
11123          return -EINVAL;
11124      if(!(dev->flags&IFF_MULTICAST))
11125          return -EADDRNOTAVAIL;
11126      if(sk->ip_mc_list==NULL)
11127          return -EADDRNOTAVAIL;
11128
11129      for(i=0;i<IP_MAX_MEMBERSHIPS;i++)
11130      {
11131          if(sk->ip_mc_list->multiaddr[i]==addr &&
11132  sk->ip_mc_list->multidev[i]==dev)
11133          {
11134              sk->ip_mc_list->multidev[i]=NULL;
11135              ip_mc_dec_group(dev,addr);
11136              return 0;
11137          }
11138      }
11139      return -EADDRNOTAVAIL;
11140  }
11141
11142  /*
11143   *  A socket is closing.
11144   */
11145
11146  void ip_mc_drop_socket(struct sock *sk)
11147  {
11148      int i;
11149
11150      if(sk->ip_mc_list==NULL)
```

```
11151      return;
11152
11153      for(i=0;i<IP_MAX_MEMBERSHIPS;i++)
11154      {
11155          if(sk->ip_mc_list->multidev[i])
11156          {
11157              ip_mc_dec_group(sk->ip_mc_list->multidev[i],
11158  sk->ip_mc_list->multiaddr[i]);
11159              sk->ip_mc_list->multidev[i]=NULL;
11160          }
11161      }
11162      kfree_s(sk->ip_mc_list,sizeof(*sk->ip_mc_list));
11163      sk->ip_mc_list=NULL;
11164  }
11165
11166  #endif
```

usr/src/linux/net/ipv4/iovec.c

```
11167  /*
11168   *  iovec manipulation routines.
11169   *
11170   *
11171   *      This program is free software; you can
11172  redistribute it and/or
11173   *      modify it under the terms of the GNU General
11174  Public License
11175   *      as published by the Free Software Foundation;
11176  either version
11177   *      2 of the License, or (at your option) any later
11178  version.
11179   *
11180   *  Fixes:
11181   *      Andrew Lunn :   Errors in iovec copying.
11182   */
11183
11184
11185  #include <linux/errno.h>
11186  #include <linux/sched.h>
11187  #include <linux/kernel.h>
11188  #include <linux/mm.h>
11189  #include <linux/net.h>
11190  #include <asm/segment.h>
11191
11192
11193  extern inline int min(int x, int y)
11194  {
11195      return x>y?y:x;
11196  }
```

```
11197
11198    int verify_iovec(struct msghdr *m, struct iovec *iov,
11199    char *address, int mode)
11200    {
11201        int err=0;
11202        int len=0;
11203        int ct;
11204
11205        if(m->msg_name!=NULL)
11206        {
11207            if(mode==VERIFY_READ) {
11208                err=move_addr_to_kernel(m->msg_name,
11209    m->msg_namelen, address);
11210            } else
11211                err=verify_area(mode, m->msg_name,
11212    m->msg_namelen);
11213            if(err<0)
11214                return err;
11215            m->msg_name = address;
11216        }
11217        if(m->msg_control!=NULL)
11218        {
11219            err=verify_area(mode, m->msg_control,
11220    m->msg_controllen);
11221            if(err)
11222                return err;
11223        }
11224
11225        for(ct=0;ct<m->msg_iovlen;ct++)
11226        {
11227            err=verify_area(VERIFY_READ, &m->msg_iov[ct],
11228    sizeof(struct iovec));
11229            if(err)
11230                return err;
11231            memcpy_fromfs(&iov[ct], &m->msg_iov[ct],
11232    sizeof(struct iovec));
11233            err=verify_area(mode, iov[ct].iov_base,
11234    iov[ct].iov_len);
11235            if(err)
11236                return err;
11237            len+=iov[ct].iov_len;
11238        }
11239        m->msg_iov=&iov[0];
11240        return len;
11241    }
11242
11243    /*
11244     *    Copy kernel to iovec.
11245     */
11246
11247    void memcpy_toiovec(struct iovec *iov, unsigned char
11248    *kdata, int len)
11249    {
11250        while(len>0)
11251        {
11252            if(iov->iov_len)
11253            {
11254                int copy = min(iov->iov_len,len);
11255                memcpy_tofs(iov->iov_base,kdata,copy);
11256                kdata+=copy;
11257                len-=copy;
11258                iov->iov_len-=copy;
11259                iov->iov_base+=copy;
11260            }
11261            iov++;
11262        }
11263    }
11264
11265    /*
11266     *  Copy iovec to kernel.
11267     */
11268
11269    void memcpy_fromiovec(unsigned char *kdata, struct iovec
11270    *iov, int len)
11271    {
11272        while(len>0)
11273        {
11274            if(iov->iov_len)
11275            {
11276                int copy=min(len,iov->iov_len);
11277                memcpy_fromfs(kdata, iov->iov_base, copy);
11278                len-=copy;
11279                kdata+=copy;
11280                iov->iov_base+=copy;
11281                iov->iov_len-=copy;
11282            }
11283            iov++;
11284        }
11285    }
```

usr/src/linux/net/ipv4/ip_forward.c

```
11286    /*
11287     *  INET      An implementation of the TCP/IP protocol
11288    suite for the LINUX
11289     *        operating system.  INET is implemented using the
11290     BSD Socket
```

```
11291    *        interface as the means of communication with the
11292    user level.
11293    *
11294    *        The IP forwarding functionality.
11295    *
11296    * Authors: see ip.c
11297    *
11298    * Fixes:
11299    *        Many         :    Split from ip.c , see ip_input.c
11300    for
11301    *                      history.
11302    *        Dave Gregorich  :    NULL ip_rt_put fix for
11303    multicast
11304    *                      routing.
11305    *        Jos Vos      :    Add call_out_firewall before
11306    sending,
11307    *                      use output device for accounting.
11308    *        Jos Vos      :    Call forward firewall after
11309    routing
11310    *                      (always use output device).
11311    *        Philip Gladstone:   Add some missing ip_rt_put()
11312    */
11313
11314    #include <linux/config.h>
11315    #include <linux/types.h>
11316    #include <linux/mm.h>
11317    #include <linux/sched.h>
11318    #include <linux/skbuff.h>
11319    #include <linux/ip.h>
11320    #include <linux/icmp.h>
11321    #include <linux/netdevice.h>
11322    #include <net/sock.h>
11323    #include <net/ip.h>
11324    #include <net/icmp.h>
11325    #include <linux/tcp.h>
11326    #include <linux/udp.h>
11327    #include <linux/firewall.h>
11328    #include <linux/ip_fw.h>
11329    #ifdef CONFIG_IP_MASQUERADE
11330    #include <net/ip_masq.h>
11331    #endif
11332    #include <net/checksum.h>
11333    #include <linux/route.h>
11334    #include <net/route.h>
11335
11336    #ifdef CONFIG_IP_FORWARD /* set the default */
11337    int sysctl_ip_forward = 1;
11338    #else
```

```
11339    int sysctl_ip_forward = 0;
11340    #endif
11341
11342    #ifdef CONFIG_IP_MROUTE
11343
11344    /*
11345     *  Encapsulate a packet by attaching a valid IPIP
11346    header to it.
11347     *  This avoids tunnel drivers and other mess and gives
11348    us the speed so
11349     *  important for multicast video.
11350     */
11351
11352    static void ip_encap(struct sk_buff *skb, int len,
11353    struct device *out, __u32 daddr)
11354    {
11355        /*
11356         *  There is space for the IPIP header and MAC left.
11357         *
11358         *  Firstly push down and install the IPIP header.
11359         */
11360        struct iphdr *iph=(struct iphdr
11361    *)skb_push(skb,sizeof(struct iphdr));
11362
11363        if(len>65515)
11364            len=65515;
11365
11366
11367        iph->version    =    4;
11368        iph->tos        =    skb->ip_hdr->tos;
11369        iph->ttl        =    skb->ip_hdr->ttl;
11370        iph->frag_off   =    0;
11371        iph->daddr      =    daddr;
11372        iph->saddr      =    out->pa_addr;
11373        iph->protocol   =    IPPROTO_IPIP;
11374        iph->ihl        =    5;
11375        iph->tot_len    =    htons(skb->len + len);  /*
11376    Anand, ernet */
11377        iph->id         =    htons(ip_id_count++);
11378        ip_send_check(iph);
11379
11380        skb->dev = out;
11381        skb->arp = 1;
11382        skb->raddr=daddr;  /* Router address is not
11383    destination address. The
11384                   * correct value is given eventually. I
11385    have not
11386                   * removed this statement. But could
```

```
11387    have.
11388                        * Anand, ernet.
11389                        */
11390        /*
11391         *   Now add the physical header (driver will push it
11392    down).
11393         */
11394
11395        /* The last parameter of out->hard_header() needed
11396    skb->len + len.
11397         * Anand, ernet.
11398         */
11399        if (out->hard_header && out->hard_header(skb, out,
11400    ETH_P_IP, NULL, NULL,
11401        skb->len + len)<0)
11402                skb->arp=0;
11403        /*
11404         *   Read to queue for transmission.
11405         */
11406    }
11407
11408    #endif
11409
11410    /*
11411     *   Forward an IP datagram to its next destination.
11412     */
11413
11414    int ip_forward(struct sk_buff *skb, struct device *dev,
11415    int is_frag,
11416                __u32 target_addr)
11417    {
11418        struct device *dev2;    /* Output device */
11419        struct iphdr *iph;  /* Our header */
11420        struct sk_buff *skb2;   /* Output packet */
11421        struct rtable *rt = NULL;   /* Route we use */
11422        unsigned char *ptr; /* Data pointer */
11423        unsigned long raddr;    /* Router IP address */
11424        struct   options * opt  = (struct
11425    options*)skb->proto_priv;
11426        struct hh_cache *hh = NULL;
11427        int encap = 0;      /* Encap length */
11428    #ifdef CONFIG_FIREWALL
11429        int fw_res = 0;     /* Forwarding result */
11430    #ifdef CONFIG_IP_MASQUERADE
11431        struct sk_buff *skb_in = skb;   /* So we can
11432    remember if the masquerader did some swaps */
11433    #endif /* CONFIG_IP_MASQUERADE */
11434    #endif /* CONFIG_FIREWALL */
11435
11436        /*
11437         *   According to the RFC, we must first decrease the
11438    TTL field. If
11439         *   that reaches zero, we must reply an ICMP control
11440    message telling
11441         *   that the packet's lifetime expired.
11442         *
11443         *   Exception:
11444         *   We may not generate an ICMP for an ICMP.
11445    icmp_send does the
11446         *   enforcement of this so we can forget it here. It
11447    is however
11448         *   sometimes VERY important.
11449         */
11450
11451        iph = skb->h.iph;
11452        if (!(is_frag&IPFWD_NOTTLDEC))
11453        {
11454            unsigned long checksum = iph->check;
11455            iph->ttl--;
11456
11457        /*
11458         *   Re-compute the IP header checksum.
11459         *   This is efficient. We know what has happened to
11460    the header
11461         *   and can thus adjust the checksum as Phil Karn
11462    does in KA9Q
11463         *   except we do this in "network byte order".
11464         */
11465            checksum += htons(0x0100);
11466            /* carry overflow? */
11467            checksum += checksum >> 16;
11468            iph->check = checksum;
11469        }
11470
11471        if (iph->ttl <= 0)
11472        {
11473            /* Tell the sender its packet died... */
11474            icmp_send(skb, ICMP_TIME_EXCEEDED, ICMP_EXC_TTL,
11475    0, dev);
11476            return -1;
11477        }
11478
11479        /* If IPFWD_MULTITUNNEL flag is set, then we have to
11480    perform routing
11481         * decision so as to reach the other end of the
11482    tunnel. This condition
```

p 523

```
11483        * also means that we are dealing with a unicast IP
11484   packet "in a way".
11485        * Anand, ernet.
11486        */
11487
11488   #ifdef CONFIG_IP_MROUTE
11489       if(!(is_frag&IPFWD_MULTICASTING) ||
11490   (is_frag&IPFWD_MULTITUNNEL))
11491       {
11492   #endif
11493            /*
11494            * OK, the packet is still valid.  Fetch its
11495   destination address,
11496            * and give it to the IP sender for further
11497   processing.
11498            */
11499
11500            rt = ip_rt_route(target_addr, 0, NULL);
11501
11502            if (rt == NULL)
11503            {
11504                /*
11505                * Tell the sender its packet cannot be
11506   delivered. Again
11507                *  ICMP is screened later.
11508                */
11509                icmp_send(skb, ICMP_DEST_UNREACH,
11510   ICMP_NET_UNREACH, 0, dev);
11511                return -1;
11512            }
11513
11514
11515            /*
11516            * Gosh.  Not only is the packet valid; we even
11517   know how to
11518            * forward it onto its final destination.  Can
11519   we say this
11520            * is being plain lucky?
11521            * If the router told us that there is no GW,
11522   use the dest.
11523            * IP address itself- we seem to be connected
11524   directly...
11525            */
11526
11527            raddr = rt->rt_gateway;
11528
11529            if (opt->is_strictroute && (rt->rt_flags &
11530   RTF_GATEWAY)) {
```

```
11531            /*
11532            *  Strict routing permits no gatewaying
11533            */
11534
11535                ip_rt_put(rt);
11536                icmp_send(skb, ICMP_DEST_UNREACH,
11537   ICMP_SR_FAILED, 0, dev);
11538                return -1;
11539            }
11540
11541            /*
11542            *  Having picked a route we can now send the
11543   frame out
11544            *  after asking the firewall permission to do
11545   so.
11546            */
11547
11548            dev2 = rt->rt_dev;
11549            hh = rt->rt_hh;
11550            /*
11551            *  In IP you never have to forward a frame on
11552   the interface that it
11553            *  arrived upon. We now generate an ICMP HOST
11554   REDIRECT giving the route
11555            *  we calculated.
11556            */
11557   #ifndef CONFIG_IP_NO_ICMP_REDIRECT
11558            if (dev == dev2 &&
11559                !((iph->saddr^dev->pa_addr)&dev->pa_mask) &&
11560                /* The daddr!=raddr test isn't obvious -
11561   what it's doing
11562                    is avoiding sending a frame the receiver
11563   will not
11564                    believe anyway.. */
11565                iph->daddr != raddr/*ANK*/ && !opt->srr)
11566                icmp_send(skb, ICMP_REDIRECT,
11567   ICMP_REDIR_HOST, raddr, dev);
11568   #endif
11569   #ifdef CONFIG_IP_MROUTE
11570
11571        /* This is for ip encap. Anand, ernet.*/
11572
11573        if (is_frag&IPFWD_MULTITUNNEL)
11574        {
11575            encap=20;
11576        }
11577    }
11578    else
```

```
11579          {
11580              /*
11581               *  Multicast route forward. Routing is already
11582  done
11583               */
11584              dev2=skb->dev;
11585              raddr=skb->raddr;
11586              if(is_frag&IPFWD_MULTITUNNEL)   /* VIFF_TUNNEL
11587  mode */
11588                  encap=20;
11589              rt=NULL;
11590          }
11591  #endif
11592
11593          /*
11594           *  See if we are allowed to forward this.
11595           *  Note: demasqueraded fragments are always
11596  'back'warded.
11597           */
11598
11599  #ifdef CONFIG_FIREWALL
11600          if(!(is_frag&IPFWD_MASQUERADED))
11601          {
11602  #ifdef CONFIG_IP_MASQUERADE
11603              /*
11604               *  Check that any ICMP packets are not for a
11605               *  masqueraded connection.  If so rewrite them
11606               *  and skip the firewall checks
11607               */
11608              if (iph->protocol == IPPROTO_ICMP)
11609              {
11610  #ifdef CONFIG_IP_MASQUERADE_ICMP
11611  #define icmph ((struct icmphdr *)((char *)iph +
11612  (iph->ihl<<2)))
11613                  if
11614  ((icmph->type==ICMP_DEST_UNREACH)||
11615
11616  (icmph->type==ICMP_SOURCE_QUENCH)||
11617
11618  (icmph->type==ICMP_TIME_EXCEEDED))
11619                  {
11620  #endif
11621                      if ((fw_res = ip_fw_masq_icmp(&skb, dev2)) <
11622  0)
11623                      {
11624                          if (rt)
11625                              ip_rt_put(rt);
11626                          /* Problem - ie bad checksum */
```

```
11627                          return -1;
11628                      }
11629
11630                      if (fw_res)
11631                          /* ICMP matched - skip firewall */
11632                          goto skip_call_fw_firewall;
11633  #ifdef CONFIG_IP_MASQUERADE_ICMP             .
11634                  }
11635  #endif
11636              }
11637  #endif
11638          fw_res=call_fw_firewall(PF_INET, dev2, iph,
11639  NULL);
11640          switch (fw_res) {
11641          case FW_ACCEPT:
11642          case FW_MASQUERADE:
11643              break;
11644          case FW_REJECT:
11645              icmp_send(skb, ICMP_DEST_UNREACH,
11646  ICMP_HOST_UNREACH, 0, dev);
11647              /* fall thru */
11648          default:
11649              if (rt)
11650                  ip_rt_put(rt);
11651              return -1;
11652          }
11653
11654  #ifdef CONFIG_IP_MASQUERADE
11655          skip_call_fw_firewall:
11656  #endif
11657          }
11658  #endif
11659
11660          /*
11661           * We now may allocate a new buffer, and copy the
11662  datagram into it.
11663           * If the indicated interface is up and running,
11664  kick it.
11665           */
11666
11667          if (dev2->flags & IFF_UP)
11668          {
11669  #ifdef CONFIG_IP_MASQUERADE
11670              __u32    premasq_saddr = iph->saddr;
11671              __u16    premasq_sport = 0;
11672              __u16    *portptr=NULL;
11673              long     premasq_len_diff = skb->len;
11674
```

p 524

```
11675          if (iph->protocol==IPPROTO_UDP ||
11676                   iph->protocol==IPPROTO_TCP) {
11677              portptr = (__u16 *)&(((char
11678 *)iph)[iph->ihl*4]);
11679              premasq_sport = portptr[0];
11680          }
11681
11682          /*
11683           * If this fragment needs masquerading, make it
11684 so...
11685           * (Don't masquerade de-masqueraded fragments)
11686           */
11687          if (!(is_frag&IPFWD_MASQUERADED) &&
11688 fw_res==FW_MASQUERADE)
11689              if (ip_fw_masquerade(&skb, dev2) < 0)
11690              {
11691                  /*
11692                   * Masquerading failed; silently discard
11693 this packet.
11694                   */
11695                  if (rt)
11696                      ip_rt_put(rt);
11697                  return -1;
11698              }
11699 #endif
11700          IS_SKB(skb);
11701
11702          if (skb->len+encap > dev2->mtu && (iph->frag_off
11703 & htons(IP_DF)))
11704          {
11705              ip_statistics.IpFragFails++;
11706 #ifdef CONFIG_IP_MASQUERADE
11707              /* If we're demasquerading, put the correct
11708 daddr back */
11709              if (is_frag&IPFWD_MASQUERADED)
11710                  iph->daddr = dev->pa_addr;
11711
11712              /* If we're masquerading, put the correct
11713 source back */
11714              else if (fw_res==FW_MASQUERADE) {
11715                  iph->saddr = premasq_saddr;
11716                  if (premasq_sport)
11717                      portptr[0] = premasq_sport;
11718              }
11719
11720              /* If the packet has got larger and this has
11721 caused it to
11722                      exceed the MTU, then we'll claim that our
```

```
11723 MTU just got
11724                      smaller and hope it works */
11725                  premasq_len_diff -= skb->len;
11726
11727              if (premasq_len_diff < 0)
11728                  icmp_send(skb, ICMP_DEST_UNREACH,
11729 ICMP_FRAG_NEEDED,
11730                          htonl(dev2->mtu+premasq_len_diff),
11731 dev);
11732              else
11733 #endif
11734              icmp_send(skb, ICMP_DEST_UNREACH,
11735 ICMP_FRAG_NEEDED, htonl(dev2->mtu), dev);
11736              if(rt)
11737                  ip_rt_put(rt);
11738              return -1;
11739          }
11740
11741 #ifdef CONFIG_IP_MROUTE
11742          if(skb_headroom(skb)-encap<dev2->hard_header_len)
11743          {
11744              skb2 = alloc_skb(dev2->hard_header_len +
11745 skb->len + encap + 15, GFP_ATOMIC);
11746 #else
11747          if(skb_headroom(skb)<dev2->hard_header_len)
11748          {
11749              skb2 = alloc_skb(dev2->hard_header_len +
11750 skb->len + 15, GFP_ATOMIC);
11751 #endif
11752              /*
11753               * This is rare and since IP is tolerant of
11754 network failures
11755               * quite harmless.
11756               */
11757
11758              if (skb2 == NULL)
11759              {
11760                  NETDEBUG(printk("\nIP: No memory
11761 available for IP forward\n"));
11762                  if(rt)
11763                      ip_rt_put(rt);
11764                  return -1;
11765              }
11766
11767              IS_SKB(skb2);
11768              /*
11769               * Add the physical headers.
11770               */
```

```
11771              skb2->protocol=htons(ETH_P_IP);
11772  #ifdef CONFIG_IP_MROUTE
11773              if(is_frag&IPFWD_MULTITUNNEL)
11774              {
11775
11776  skb_reserve(skb2,(encap+dev2->hard_header_len+15)&~15);
11777  /* 16 byte aligned IP headers are good */
11778
11779  /* We need to pass on IP information of the incoming
11780  packet to ip_encap()
11781   * to fillin ttl, and tos fields.The destination should
11782  be target_addr.
11783   *  Anand, ernet.
11784   */
11785
11786                  skb2->ip_hdr = skb->ip_hdr;
11787
11788                  ip_encap(skb2,skb->len, dev2,
11789  target_addr);
11790
11791  /*  The router address is got earlier that to take us to
11792  the remote tunnel
11793   *  Anand, ernet.
11794   */
11795                  skb2->raddr = rt->rt_gateway;
11796              }
11797              else
11798  #endif
11799
11800  ip_send(rt,skb2,raddr,skb->len,dev2,dev2->pa_addr);
11801
11802              /*
11803               *  We have to copy the bytes over as the
11804  new header wouldn't fit
11805               *  the old buffer. This should be very rare.
11806               */
11807
11808              ptr = skb_put(skb2,skb->len);
11809              skb2->free = 1;
11810              skb2->h.raw = ptr;
11811              /*
11812               *  Copy the packet data into the new buffer.
11813               */
11814              memcpy(ptr, skb->h.raw, skb->len);
11815              memcpy(skb2->proto_priv, skb->proto_priv,
11816  sizeof(skb->proto_priv));
11817              iph = skb2->ip_hdr = skb2->h.iph;
11818          }
11819          else
11820          {
11821              /*
11822               *  Build a new MAC header.
11823               */
11824
11825              skb2 = skb;
11826              skb2->dev=dev2;
11827  #ifdef CONFIG_IP_MROUTE
11828              if(is_frag&IPFWD_MULTITUNNEL)
11829                  ip_encap(skb, 0, dev2, target_addr);
11830              else
11831              {
11832  #endif
11833              skb->arp=1;
11834              skb->raddr=raddr;
11835              if (hh)
11836              {
11837                  memcpy(skb_push(skb,
11838  dev2->hard_header_len), hh->hh_data,
11839  dev2->hard_header_len);
11840                  if (!hh->hh_uptodate)
11841                  {
11842  #if RT_CACHE_DEBUG >= 2
11843                      printk("ip_forward: hh miss %08x
11844  via %08x\n", target_addr, rt->rt_gateway);
11845  #endif
11846                      skb->arp = 0;
11847                  }
11848              }
11849              else if (dev2->hard_header)
11850              {
11851                  if(dev2->hard_header(skb, dev2,
11852  ETH_P_IP, NULL, NULL, skb->len)<0)
11853                      skb->arp=0;
11854              }
11855  #ifdef CONFIG_IP_MROUTE
11856              }
11857  #endif
11858          }
11859  #ifdef CONFIG_FIREWALL
11860          if((fw_res = call_out_firewall(PF_INET,
11861  skb2->dev, iph, NULL)) < FW_ACCEPT)
11862          {
11863              /* FW_ACCEPT and FW_MASQUERADE are treated
11864  equal:
11865               *  masquerading is only supported via
11866  forward rules */
```

```
11867            if (fw_res == FW_REJECT)
11868                icmp_send(skb2, ICMP_DEST_UNREACH,
11869 ICMP_HOST_UNREACH, 0, dev);
11870            if (skb != skb2)
11871                kfree_skb(skb2,FREE_WRITE);
11872            if (rt)
11873                ip_rt_put(rt);
11874            return -1;
11875        }
11876 #endif
11877        ip_statistics.IpForwDatagrams++;
11878
11879        if (opt->optlen)
11880        {
11881            unsigned char * optptr;
11882            if (opt->rr_needaddr)
11883            {
11884                optptr = (unsigned char *)iph + opt->rr;
11885                memcpy(&optptr[optptr[2]-5],
11886 &dev2->pa_addr, 4);
11887                opt->is_changed = 1;
11888            }
11889            if (opt->srr_is_hit)
11890            {
11891                int srrptr, srrspace;
11892
11893                optptr = (unsigned char *)iph + opt->srr;
11894
11895                for ( srrptr=optptr[2], srrspace =
11896 optptr[1];
11897                     srrptr <= srrspace;
11898                    srrptr += 4
11899                    )
11900                {
11901                    if (srrptr + 3 > srrspace)
11902                        break;
11903                    if (memcmp(&target_addr,
11904 &optptr[srrptr-1], 4) == 0)
11905                        break;
11906                }
11907                if (srrptr + 3 <= srrspace)
11908                {
11909                    opt->is_changed = 1;
11910                    memcpy(&optptr[srrptr-1],
11911 &dev2->pa_addr, 4);
11912                    iph->daddr = target_addr;
11913                    optptr[2] = srrptr+4;
11914                }
```

```
11915            else
11916                printk(KERN_CRIT "ip_forward():
11917 Argh! Destination lost!\n");
11918            }
11919            if (opt->ts_needaddr)
11920            {
11921                optptr = (unsigned char *)iph + opt->ts;
11922                memcpy(&optptr[optptr[2]-9],
11923 &dev2->pa_addr, 4);
11924                opt->is_changed = 1;
11925            }
11926            if (opt->is_changed)
11927            {
11928                opt->is_changed = 0;
11929                ip_send_check(iph);
11930            }
11931        }
11932 /*
11933  * ANK:  this is point of "no return", we cannot send an
11934 ICMP,
11935  *      because we changed SRR option.
11936  */
11937
11938        /*
11939         * See if it needs fragmenting. Note in ip_rcv
11940 we tagged
11941         * the fragment type. This must be right so that
11942         * the fragmenter does the right thing.
11943         */
11944
11945        if(skb2->len > dev2->mtu + dev2->hard_header_len)
11946        {
11947            ip_fragment(NULL,skb2,dev2, is_frag);
11948            kfree_skb(skb2,FREE_WRITE);
11949        }
11950        else
11951        {
11952 #ifdef CONFIG_IP_ACCT
11953        /*
11954         * Count mapping we shortcut
11955         */
11956
11957
11958 ip_fw_chk(iph,dev2,NULL,ip_acct_chain,0,IP_FW_MODE_ACCT_O
11959 UT);
11960 #endif
11961
11962        /*
```

```
11963              * Map service types to priority. We lie
11964  about
11965              * throughput being low priority, but it's
11966  a good
11967              * choice to help improve general usage.
11968              */
11969             if(iph->tos & IPTOS_LOWDELAY)
11970                 dev_queue_xmit(skb2, dev2,
11971  SOPRI_INTERACTIVE);
11972             else if(iph->tos & IPTOS_THROUGHPUT)
11973                 dev_queue_xmit(skb2, dev2,
11974  SOPRI_BACKGROUND);
11975             else
11976                 dev_queue_xmit(skb2, dev2, SOPRI_NORMAL);
11977         }
11978     }
11979     else
11980     {
11981         if(rt)
11982             ip_rt_put(rt);
11983         return -1;
11984     }
11985     if(rt)
11986         ip_rt_put(rt);
11987
11988     /*
11989      * Tell the caller if their buffer is free.
11990      */
11991
11992     if(skb==skb2)
11993         return 0;
11994
11995 #ifdef CONFIG_IP_MASQUERADE
11996     /*
11997      * The original is free. Free our copy and
11998      * tell the caller not to free.
11999      */
12000     if(skb!=skb_in)
12001     {
12002         kfree_skb(skb_in, FREE_WRITE);
12003         return 0;
12004     }
12005 #endif
12006     return 1;
12007 }
12008
12009
12010
```

```
12011
12012
```

usr/src/linux/net/ipv4/ip_fragment.c

```
12013 /*
12014  * INET      An implementation of the TCP/IP protocol
12015  suite for the LINUX
12016  *      operating system.  INET is implemented using the
12017  BSD Socket
12018  *      interface as the means of communication with the
12019  user level.
12020  *
12021  *      The IP fragmentation functionality.
12022  *
12023  * Authors: Fred N. van Kempen
12024  <waltje@uWalt.NL.Mugnet.ORG>
12025  *      Alan Cox <Alan.Cox@linux.org>
12026  *
12027  * Fixes:
12028  *      Alan Cox    :   Split from ip.c , see ip_input.c
12029  for history.
12030  *      Alan Cox    :   Handling oversized frames
12031  *      Uriel Maimon    :   Accounting errors in two
12032  fringe cases.
12033  */
12034
12035 #include <linux/types.h>
12036 #include <linux/mm.h>
12037 #include <linux/sched.h>
12038 #include <linux/skbuff.h>
12039 #include <linux/ip.h>
12040 #include <linux/icmp.h>
12041 #include <linux/netdevice.h>
12042 #include <net/sock.h>
12043 #include <net/ip.h>
12044 #include <net/icmp.h>
12045 #include <linux/tcp.h>
12046 #include <linux/udp.h>
12047 #include <linux/inet.h>
12048 #include <linux/firewall.h>
12049 #include <linux/ip_fw.h>
12050 #include <net/checksum.h>
12051
12052 /*
12053  * Fragment cache limits. We will commit 256K at one
12054  time. Should we
12055  * cross that limit we will prune down to 192K. This
12056  should cope with
```

```
12057    *  even the most extreme cases without allowing an
12058   attacker to measurably
12059    *  harm machine performance.
12060    */
12061
12062   #define IPFRAG_HIGH_THRESH      (256*1024)
12063   #define IPFRAG_LOW_THRESH       (192*1024)
12064
12065   /*
12066    *  This fragment handler is a bit of a heap. On the
12067   other hand it works quite
12068    *  happily and handles things quite well.
12069    */
12070
12071   static struct ipq *ipqueue = NULL;      /* IP fragment
12072   queue    */
12073
12074   atomic_t ip_frag_mem = 0;               /* Memory used for
12075   fragments */
12076
12077   char *in_ntoa(unsigned long in);
12078
12079   /*
12080    *  Memory Tracking Functions
12081    */
12082
12083   extern __inline__ void frag_kfree_skb(struct sk_buff
12084   *skb, int type)
12085   {
12086       atomic_sub(skb->truesize, &ip_frag_mem);
12087       kfree_skb(skb,type);
12088   }
12089
12090   extern __inline__ void frag_kfree_s(void *ptr, int len)
12091   {
12092       atomic_sub(len, &ip_frag_mem);
12093       kfree_s(ptr,len);
12094   }
12095
12096   extern __inline__ void *frag_kmalloc(int size, int pri)
12097   {
12098       void *vp=kmalloc(size,pri);
12099       if(!vp)
12100           return NULL;
12101       atomic_add(size, &ip_frag_mem);
12102       return vp;
12103   }
12104
```

```
12105   /*
12106    *  Create a new fragment entry.
12107    */
12108
12109   static struct ipfrag *ip_frag_create(int offset, int
12110   end, struct sk_buff *skb, unsigned char *ptr)
12111   {
12112       struct ipfrag *fp;
12113       unsigned long flags;
12114
12115       fp = (struct ipfrag *) frag_kmalloc(sizeof(struct
12116   ipfrag), GFP_ATOMIC);
12117       if (fp == NULL)
12118       {
12119           NETDEBUG(printk("IP: frag_create: no memory left
12120   !\n"));
12121           return(NULL);
12122       }
12123       memset(fp, 0, sizeof(struct ipfrag));
12124
12125       /* Fill in the structure. */
12126       fp->offset = offset;
12127       fp->end = end;
12128       fp->len = end - offset;
12129       fp->skb = skb;
12130       fp->ptr = ptr;
12131
12132       /*
12133        *  Charge for the SKB as well.
12134        */
12135
12136       save_flags(flags);
12137       cli();
12138       ip_frag_mem+=skb->truesize;
12139       restore_flags(flags);
12140
12141       return(fp);
12142   }
12143
12144
12145   /*
12146    *  Find the correct entry in the "incomplete datagrams"
12147   queue for
12148    *  this IP datagram, and return the queue entry address
12149   if found.
12150    */
12151
12152   static struct ipq *ip_find(struct iphdr *iph)
```

p 528
p 527

```
12153    {
12154        struct ipq *qp;
12155        struct ipq *qplast;
12156
12157        cli();
12158        qplast = NULL;
12159        for(qp = ipqueue; qp != NULL; qplast = qp, qp =
12160    qp->next)
12161            {
12162            if (iph->id== qp->iph->id && iph->saddr ==
12163    qp->iph->saddr &&
12164                iph->daddr == qp->iph->daddr &&
12165    iph->protocol == qp->iph->protocol)
12166                {
12167                del_timer(&qp->timer);  /* So it doesn't
12168    vanish on us. The timer will be reset anyway */
12169                sti();
12170                return(qp);
12171                }
12172            }
12173        sti();
12174        return(NULL);
12175    }
12176
12177
12178    /*
12179     *  Remove an entry from the "incomplete datagrams"
12180    queue, either
12181     *  because we completed, reassembled and processed it,
12182    or because
12183     *  it timed out.
12184     */
12185
12186    static void ip_free(struct ipq *qp)
12187    {
12188        struct ipfrag *fp;
12189        struct ipfrag *xp;
12190
12191        /*
12192         * Stop the timer for this entry.
12193         */
12194
12195        del_timer(&qp->timer);
12196
12197        /* Remove this entry from the "incomplete datagrams"
12198    queue. */
12199        cli();
12200        if (qp->prev == NULL)
```

p 527 (line 12186)

```
12201    {
12202        ipqueue = qp->next;
12203        if (ipqueue != NULL)
12204            ipqueue->prev = NULL;
12205    }
12206    else
12207    {
12208        qp->prev->next = qp->next;
12209        if (qp->next != NULL)
12210            qp->next->prev = qp->prev;
12211    }
12212
12213    /* Release all fragment data. */
12214
12215    fp = qp->fragments;
12216    while (fp != NULL)
12217    {
12218        xp = fp->next;
12219        IS_SKB(fp->skb);
12220        frag_kfree_skb(fp->skb,FREE_READ);
12221        frag_kfree_s(fp, sizeof(struct ipfrag));
12222        fp = xp;
12223    }
12224
12225    /* Release the IP header. */
12226    frag_kfree_s(qp->iph, 64 + 8);
12227
12228    /* Finally, release the queue descriptor itself. */
12229    frag_kfree_s(qp, sizeof(struct ipq));
12230    sti();
12231    }
12232
12233
12234    /*
12235     *  Oops- a fragment queue timed out.  Kill it and send
12236    an ICMP reply.
12237     */
12238
12239    static void ip_expire(unsigned long arg)
12240    {
12241        struct ipq *qp;
12242
12243        qp = (struct ipq *)arg;
12244
12245        /*
12246         *  Send an ICMP "Fragment Reassembly Timeout"
12247    message.
12248         */
```

p 528 (line 12239)

```
12249
12250        ip_statistics.IpReasmTimeout++;
12251        ip_statistics.IpReasmFails++;
12252        /* This if is always true... shrug */
12253        if(qp->fragments!=NULL)
12254            icmp_send(qp->fragments->skb,ICMP_TIME_EXCEEDED,
12255                    ICMP_EXC_FRAGTIME, 0, qp->dev);
12256
12257        /*
12258         *  Nuke the fragment queue.
12259         */
12260        ip_free(qp);
12261    }
12262
12263    /*
12264     *  Memory limiting on fragments. Evictor trashes the
12265    oldest
12266     *  fragment queue until we are back under the low
12267    threshold
12268     */
12269
12270    static void ip_evictor(void)
12271    {
12272        while(ip_frag_mem>IPFRAG_LOW_THRESH)
12273        {
12274            if(!ipqueue)
12275                panic("ip_evictor: memcount");
12276            ip_free(ipqueue);
12277        }
12278    }
12279
12280    /*
12281     *  Add an entry to the 'ipq' queue for a newly received
12282    IP datagram.
12283     *  We will (hopefully :-) receive all other fragments
12284    of this datagram
12285     *  in time, so we just create a queue for this
12286    datagram, in which we
12287     *  will insert the received fragments at their
12288    respective positions.
12289     */
12290
12291    static struct ipq *ip_create(struct sk_buff *skb, struct
12292    iphdr *iph, struct device *dev)
12293    {
12294        struct ipq *qp;
12295        int ihlen;
12296
12297        qp = (struct ipq *) frag_kmalloc(sizeof(struct ipq),
12298    GFP_ATOMIC);
12299        if (qp == NULL)
12300        {
12301            NETDEBUG(printk("IP: create: no memory left
12302    !\n"));
12303            return(NULL);
12304        }
12305        memset(qp, 0, sizeof(struct ipq));
12306
12307        /*
12308         *  Allocate memory for the IP header (plus 8 octets
12309    for ICMP).
12310         */
12311
12312        ihlen = iph->ihl * 4;
12313        qp->iph = (struct iphdr *) frag_kmalloc(64 + 8,
12314    GFP_ATOMIC);
12315        if (qp->iph == NULL)
12316        {
12317            NETDEBUG(printk("IP: create: no memory left
12318    !\n"));
12319            frag_kfree_s(qp, sizeof(struct ipq));
12320            return(NULL);
12321        }
12322
12323        memcpy(qp->iph, iph, ihlen + 8);
12324        qp->len = 0;
12325        qp->ihlen = ihlen;
12326        qp->fragments = NULL;
12327        qp->dev = dev;
12328
12329        /* Start a timer for this entry. */
12330        qp->timer.expires = jiffies + IP_FRAG_TIME; /* about
12331    30 seconds */
12332        qp->timer.data = (unsigned long) qp;         /*
12333    pointer to queue */
12334        qp->timer.function = ip_expire;          /* expire
12335    function  */
12336        add_timer(&qp->timer);
12337
12338        /* Add this entry to the queue. */
12339        qp->prev = NULL;
12340        cli();
12341        qp->next = ipqueue;
12342        if (qp->next != NULL)
12343            qp->next->prev = qp;
12344        ipqueue = qp;
```

```
12345        sti();
12346        return(qp);
12347    }
12348
12349
12350    /*
12351     *  See if a fragment queue is complete.
12352     */
12353
12354    static int ip_done(struct ipq *qp)
12355    {
12356        struct ipfrag *fp;
12357        int offset;
12358
12359        /* Only possible if we received the final fragment.
12360     */
12361        if (qp->len == 0)
12362            return(0);
12363
12364        /* Check all fragment offsets to see if they
12365    connect. */
12366        fp = qp->fragments;
12367        offset = 0;
12368        while (fp != NULL)
12369        {
12370            if (fp->offset > offset)
12371                return(0);  /* fragment(s) missing */
12372            offset = fp->end;
12373            fp = fp->next;
12374        }
12375
12376        /* All fragments are present. */
12377        return(1);
12378    }
12379
12380
12381    /*
12382     *  Build a new IP datagram from all its fragments.
12383     *
12384     *  FIXME: We copy here because we lack an effective way
12385    of handling lists
12386     *  of bits on input. Until the new skb data handling is
12387    in I'm not going
12388     *  to touch this with a bargepole.
12389     */
12390
12391    static struct sk_buff *ip_glue(struct ipq *qp)
12392    {
12393        struct sk_buff *skb;
12394        struct iphdr *iph;
12395        struct ipfrag *fp;
12396        unsigned char *ptr;
12397        int count, len;
12398
12399        /*
12400         *  Allocate a new buffer for the datagram.
12401         */
12402        len = qp->ihlen + qp->len;
12403
12404        if(len>65535)
12405        {
12406            NETDEBUG(printk("Oversized IP packet from
12407    %s.\n", in_ntoa(qp->iph->saddr)));
12408            ip_statistics.IpReasmFails++;
12409            ip_free(qp);
12410            return NULL;
12411        }
12412
12413        if ((skb = dev_alloc_skb(len)) == NULL)
12414        {
12415            ip_statistics.IpReasmFails++;
12416            NETDEBUG(printk("IP: queue_glue: no memory for
12417    gluing queue %p\n", qp));
12418            ip_free(qp);
12419            return(NULL);
12420        }
12421
12422        /* Fill in the basic details. */
12423        skb_put(skb,len);
12424        skb->h.raw = skb->data;
12425        skb->free = 1;
12426
12427        /* Copy the original IP headers into the new buffer.
12428     */
12429        ptr = (unsigned char *) skb->h.raw;
12430        memcpy(ptr, ((unsigned char *) qp->iph), qp->ihlen);
12431        ptr += qp->ihlen;
12432
12433        count = 0;
12434
12435        /* Copy the data portions of all fragments into the
12436    new buffer. */
12437        fp = qp->fragments;
12438        while(fp != NULL)
12439        {
12440            if (fp->len < 0 || fp->offset+qp->ihlen+fp->len
```

```
12441  > skb->len)
12442          {
12443                  NETDEBUG(printk("Invalid fragment list:
12444  Fragment over size.\n"));
12445                  ip_free(qp);
12446                  kfree_skb(skb,FREE_WRITE);
12447                  ip_statistics.IpReasmFails++;
12448                  return NULL;
12449          }
12450          memcpy((ptr + fp->offset), fp->ptr, fp->len);
12451          count += fp->len;
12452          fp = fp->next;
12453      }
12454
12455      skb->pkt_type = qp->fragments->skb->pkt_type;
12456      skb->protocol = qp->fragments->skb->protocol;
12457      /* We glued together all fragments, so remove the
12458  queue entry. */
12459      ip_free(qp);
12460
12461      /* Done with all fragments. Fixup the new IP header.
12462  */
12463      iph = skb->h.iph;
12464      iph->frag_off = 0;
12465      iph->tot_len = htons((iph->ihl * 4) + count);
12466      skb->ip_hdr = iph;
12467
12468      ip_statistics.IpReasmOKs++;
12469      return(skb);
12470  }
12471
12472
12473  /*
12474   *  Process an incoming IP datagram fragment.
12475   */
12476
12477  struct sk_buff *ip_defrag(struct iphdr *iph, struct
12478  sk_buff *skb, struct device *dev)
12479  {
12480      struct ipfrag *prev, *next, *tmp;
12481      struct ipfrag *tfp;
12482      struct ipq *qp;
12483      struct sk_buff *skb2;
12484      unsigned char *ptr;
12485      int flags, offset;
12486      int i, ihl, end;
12487
12488      ip_statistics.IpReasmReqds++;
```

```
12489
12490      /*
12491       *  Start by cleaning up the memory
12492       */
12493
12494      if(ip_frag_mem>IPFRAG_HIGH_THRESH)
12495          ip_evictor();
12496      /*
12497       *  Find the entry of this IP datagram in the
12498  "incomplete datagrams" queue.
12499       */
12500
12501      qp = ip_find(iph);
12502
12503      /* Is this a non-fragmented datagram? */
12504      offset = ntohs(iph->frag_off);
12505      flags = offset & ~IP_OFFSET;
12506      offset &= IP_OFFSET;
12507      if (((flags & IP_MF) == 0) && (offset == 0))
12508      {
12509          if (qp != NULL)
12510              ip_free(qp);      /* Fragmented frame replaced
12511  by full unfragmented copy */
12512          return(skb);
12513      }
12514
12515      offset <<= 3;          /* offset is in 8-byte chunks */
12516      ihl = iph->ihl * 4;
12517
12518      /*
12519       *  If the queue already existed, keep restarting its
12520  timer as long
12521       *  as we still are receiving fragments.  Otherwise,
12522  create a fresh
12523       *  queue entry.
12524       */
12525
12526      if (qp != NULL)
12527      {
12528          /* ANK. If the first fragment is received,
12529           * we should remember the correct IP header
12530  (with options)
12531           */
12532          if (offset == 0)
12533          {
12534              qp->ihlen = ihl;
12535              memcpy(qp->iph, iph, ihl+8);
12536          }
```

p 527

```
12537              del_timer(&qp->timer);
12538              qp->timer.expires = jiffies + IP_FRAG_TIME; /*
12539   about 30 seconds */
12540              qp->timer.data = (unsigned long) qp;     /*
12541   pointer to queue */
12542              qp->timer.function = ip_expire;     /* expire
12543   function */
12544              add_timer(&qp->timer);
12545          }
12546      else
12547      {
12548          /*
12549           *  If we failed to create it, then discard the
12550   frame
12551           */
12552          if ((qp = ip_create(skb, iph, dev)) == NULL)
12553          {
12554              skb->sk = NULL;
12555              kfree_skb(skb, FREE_READ);
12556              ip_statistics.IpReasmFails++;
12557              return NULL;
12558          }
12559      }
12560
12561      /*
12562       *  Attempt to construct an oversize packet.
12563       */
12564
12565      if(ntohs(iph->tot_len)+(int)offset>65535)
12566      {
12567          skb->sk = NULL;
12568          NETDEBUG(printk("Oversized packet received from
12569   %s\n",in_ntoa(iph->saddr)));
12570          kfree_skb(skb, FREE_READ);
12571          ip_statistics.IpReasmFails++;
12572          return NULL;
12573      }
12574
12575      /*
12576       *  Determine the position of this fragment.
12577       */
12578
12579      end = offset + ntohs(iph->tot_len) - ihl;
12580
12581      /*
12582       *  Point into the IP datagram 'data' part.
12583       */
12584

12585      ptr = skb->data + ihl;
12586
12587      /*
12588       *  Is this the final fragment?
12589       */
12590
12591      if ((flags & IP_MF) == 0)
12592          qp->len = end;
12593
12594      /*
12595       *  Find out which fragments are in front and at the
12596   back of us
12597       *  in the chain of fragments so far.  We must know
12598   where to put
12599       *  this fragment, right?
12600       */
12601
12602      prev = NULL;
12603      for(next = qp->fragments; next != NULL; next =
12604   next->next)
12605      {
12606          if (next->offset >= offset)
12607              break;  /* bingo! */
12608          prev = next;
12609      }
12610
12611      /*
12612       *  We found where to put this one.
12613       *  Check for overlap with preceding fragment, and,
12614   if needed,
12615       *  align things so that any overlaps are eliminated.
12616       */
12617      if (prev != NULL && offset < prev->end)
12618      {
12619          i = prev->end - offset;
12620          offset += i;    /* ptr into datagram */
12621          ptr += i;   /* ptr into fragment data */
12622      }
12623
12624      /*
12625       * Look for overlap with succeeding segments.
12626       * If we can merge fragments, do it.
12627       */
12628
12629      for(tmp=next; tmp != NULL; tmp = tfp)
12630      {
12631          tfp = tmp->next;
12632          if (tmp->offset >= end)
```

```
12633            break;      /* no overlaps at all */
12634
12635        i = end - next->offset;        /* overlap is
12636 'i' bytes */
12637        tmp->len -= i;              /* so reduce size of
12638    */
12639        tmp->offset += i;           /* next fragment
12640 */
12641        tmp->ptr += i;
12642        /*
12643         *  If we get a frag size of <= 0, remove it and
12644 the packet
12645         *  that it goes with.
12646         *
12647         *  We never throw the new frag away, so the
12648 frag being
12649         *  dumped has always been charged for.
12650         */
12651        if (tmp->len <= 0)
12652        {
12653            if (tmp->prev != NULL)
12654                tmp->prev->next = tmp->next;
12655            else
12656                qp->fragments = tmp->next;
12657
12658            if (tmp->next != NULL)
12659                tmp->next->prev = tmp->prev;
12660
12661            next=tfp;    /* We have killed the original
12662 next frame */
12663
12664            frag_kfree_skb(tmp->skb,FREE_READ);
12665            frag_kfree_s(tmp, sizeof(struct ipfrag));
12666        }
12667    }
12668
12669    /*
12670     *  Insert this fragment in the chain of fragments.
12671     */
12672
12673    tfp = NULL;
12674    tfp = ip_frag_create(offset, end, skb, ptr);
12675
12676    /*
12677     *  No memory to save the fragment - so throw the
12678 lot. If we
12679     *  failed the frag_create we haven't charged the
12680 queue.
12681     */
12682
12683    if (!tfp)
12684    {
12685        skb->sk = NULL;
12686        kfree_skb(skb, FREE_READ);
12687        return NULL;
12688    }
12689
12690    /*
12691     *  From now on our buffer is charged to the queues.
12692     */
12693
12694    tfp->prev = prev;
12695    tfp->next = next;
12696    if (prev != NULL)
12697        prev->next = tfp;
12698    else
12699        qp->fragments = tfp;
12700
12701    if (next != NULL)
12702        next->prev = tfp;
12703
12704    /*
12705     *  OK, so we inserted this new fragment into the
12706 chain.
12707     *  Check if we now have a full IP datagram which we
12708 can
12709     *  bump up to the IP layer...
12710     */
12711
12712    if (ip_done(qp))
12713    {
12714        skb2 = ip_glue(qp);      /* glue together the
12715 fragments */
12716        return(skb2);
12717    }
12718    return(NULL);
12719 }
12720
12721
12722 /*
12723  *  This IP datagram is too large to be sent in one
12724 piece.  Break it up into
12725  *  smaller pieces (each of size equal to the MAC header
12726 plus IP header plus
12727  *  a block of the data of the original IP data part)
12728 that will yet fit in a
```

```
12729    * single device frame, and queue such a frame for
12730   sending by calling the
12731    * ip_queue_xmit().  Note that this is recursion, and
12732   bad things will happen
12733    * if this function causes a loop...
12734    *
12735    * Yes this is inefficient, feel free to submit a
12736   quicker one.
12737    *
12738    */
12739
12740   void ip_fragment(struct sock *sk, struct sk_buff *skb,
12741   struct device *dev, int is_frag)
12742   {
12743       struct iphdr *iph;
12744       unsigned char *raw;
12745       unsigned char *ptr;
12746       struct sk_buff *skb2;
12747       int left, mtu, hlen, len;
12748       int offset;
12749
12750       unsigned short true_hard_header_len;
12751
12752       /*
12753        * Point into the IP datagram header.
12754        */
12755
12756       raw = skb->data;
12757   #if 0
12758       iph = (struct iphdr *) (raw + dev->hard_header_len);
12759
12760       skb->ip_hdr = iph;
12761   #else
12762       iph = skb->ip_hdr;
12763   #endif
12764
12765       /*
12766        * Calculate the length of the link-layer header
12767   appended to
12768        * the IP-packet.
12769        */
12770       true_hard_header_len = ((unsigned char *)iph) - raw;
12771
12772       /*
12773        * Setup starting values.
12774        */
12775
12776       hlen = iph->ihl * 4;
```

```
12777       left = ntohs(iph->tot_len) - hlen;   /* Space per
12778   frame */
12779       hlen += true_hard_header_len;
12780       mtu = (dev->mtu - hlen);           /* Size of data
12781   space */
12782       ptr = (raw + hlen);            /* Where to start from */
12783
12784       /*
12785        * Check for any "DF" flag. [DF means do not
12786   fragment]
12787        */
12788
12789       if (iph->frag_off & htons(IP_DF))
12790       {
12791           ip_statistics.IpFragFails++;
12792           NETDEBUG(printk("ip_queue_xmit: frag needed\n"));
12793           return;
12794       }
12795
12796       /*
12797        * The protocol doesn't seem to say what to do in
12798   the case that the
12799        * frame + options doesn't fit the mtu. As it used
12800   to fall down dead
12801        * in this case we were fortunate it didn't happen
12802        */
12803
12804       if(mtu<8)
12805       {
12806           /* It's wrong but it's better than nothing */
12807
12808   icmp_send(skb,ICMP_DEST_UNREACH,ICMP_FRAG_NEEDED,htons(de
12809   v->mtu), dev);
12810           ip_statistics.IpFragFails++;
12811           return;
12812       }
12813
12814       /*
12815        * Fragment the datagram.
12816        */
12817
12818       /*
12819        * The initial offset is 0 for a complete frame.
12820   When
12821        * fragmenting fragments it's wherever this one
12822   starts.
12823        */
12824
```

```
12825          if (is_frag & 2)
12826              offset = (ntohs(iph->frag_off) & IP_OFFSET) << 3;
12827          else
12828              offset = 0;
12829
12830
12831          /*
12832           *  Keep copying data until we run out.
12833           */
12834
12835          while(left > 0)
12836          {
12837              len = left;
12838              /* IF: it doesn't fit, use 'mtu' - the data
12839   space left */
12840              if (len > mtu)
12841                  len = mtu;
12842              /* IF: we are not sending upto and including the
12843   packet end
12844                  then align the next start on an eight byte
12845   boundary */
12846              if (len < left)
12847              {
12848                  len/=8;
12849                  len*=8;
12850              }
12851              /*
12852               *  Allocate buffer.
12853               */
12854
12855              if ((skb2 = alloc_skb(len + hlen+15,GFP_ATOMIC))
12856   == NULL)
12857              {
12858                  NETDEBUG(printk("IP: frag: no memory for new
12859   fragment!\n"));
12860                  ip_statistics.IpFragFails++;
12861                  return;
12862              }
12863
12864              /*
12865               *  Set up data on packet
12866               */
12867
12868              skb2->arp = skb->arp;
12869              skb2->protocol = htons(ETH_P_IP); /* Atleast PPP
12870   needs this */
12871   #if 0
12872              if(skb->free==0)
```

```
12873              printk(KERN_ERR "IP fragmenter: BUG free!=1
12874   in fragmenter\n");
12875   #endif
12876          skb2->free = 1;
12877          skb_put(skb2,len + hlen);
12878          skb2->h.raw=(char *) skb2->data;
12879          /*
12880           *  Charge the memory for the fragment to any
12881   owner
12882           *  it might possess
12883           */
12884
12885          if (sk)
12886          {
12887              atomic_add(skb2->truesize, &sk->wmem_alloc);
12888              skb2->sk=sk;
12889          }
12890          skb2->raddr = skb->raddr;    /* For
12891   rebuild_header - must be here */
12892
12893          /*
12894           *  Copy the packet header into the new buffer.
12895           */
12896
12897          memcpy(skb2->h.raw, raw, hlen);
12898
12899          /*
12900           *  Copy a block of the IP datagram.
12901           */
12902          memcpy(skb2->h.raw + hlen, ptr, len);
12903          left -= len;
12904
12905          skb2->h.raw+=true_hard_header_len;
12906
12907          /*
12908           *  Fill in the new header fields.
12909           */
12910          iph = (struct iphdr
12911   *)(skb2->h.raw/*+dev->hard_header_len*/);
12912          iph->frag_off = htons((offset >> 3));
12913          skb2->ip_hdr = iph;
12914
12915          /* ANK: dirty, but effective trick. Upgrade
12916   options only if
12917           *  the segment to be fragmented was THE FIRST
12918   (otherwise,
12919           *  options are already fixed) and make it ONCE
12920           *  on the initial skb, so that all the following
```

```
12921   fragments
12922           * will inherit fixed options.
12923           */
12924          if (offset == 0)
12925              ip_options_fragment(skb);
12926
12927          /*
12928           *  Added AC : If we are fragmenting a fragment
12929   that's not the
12930           *          last fragment then keep MF on each bit
12931           */
12932          if (left > 0 || (is_frag & 1))
12933              iph->frag_off |= htons(IP_MF);
12934          ptr += len;
12935          offset += len;
12936
12937          /*
12938           *  Put this fragment into the sending queue.
12939           */
12940
12941          ip_statistics.IpFragCreates++;
12942
12943          ip_queue_xmit(sk, dev, skb2, 2);
12944      }
12945      ip_statistics.IpFragOKs++;
12946  }
12947
12948
```

usr/src/linux/net/ipv4/ip_fw.c

```
12949  /*
12950   *  IP firewalling code. This is taken from 4.4BSD.
12951   Please note the
12952   *  copyright message below. As per the GPL it must be
12953   maintained
12954   *  and the licenses thus do not conflict. While this
12955   port is subject
12956   *  to the GPL I also place my modifications under the
12957   original
12958   *  license in recognition of the original copyright.
12959   *              -- Alan Cox.
12960   *
12961   *  Ported from BSD to Linux,
12962   *      Alan Cox 22/Nov/1994.
12963   *  Zeroing /proc and other additions
12964   *      Jos Vos 4/Feb/1995.
12965   *  Merged and included the FreeBSD-Current changes at
12966   Ugen's request
12967   *  (but hey it's a lot cleaner now). Ugen would prefer
12968   in some ways
12969   *  we waited for his final product but since Linux
12970   1.2.0 is about to
12971   *  appear it's not practical - Read: It works, it's not
12972   clean but please
12973   *  don't consider it to be his standard of finished
12974   work.
12975   *      Alan Cox 12/Feb/1995
12976   *  Porting bidirectional entries from BSD, fixing
12977   accounting issues,
12978   *  adding struct ip_fwpkt for checking packets with
12979   interface address
12980   *      Jos Vos 5/Mar/1995.
12981   *  Established connections (ACK check), ACK check on
12982   bidirectional rules,
12983   *  ICMP type check.
12984   *      Wilfred Mollenvanger 7/7/1995.
12985   *  TCP attack protection.
12986   *      Alan Cox 25/8/95, based on information from
12987   bugtraq.
12988   *  ICMP type printk, IP_FW_F_APPEND
12989   *      Bernd Eckenfels 1996-01-31
12990   *  Split blocking chain into input and output chains,
12991   add new "insert" and
12992   *  "append" commands to replace semi-intelligent "add"
12993   command, let "delete".
12994   *  only delete the first matching entry, use 0xFFFF
12995   (0xFF) as ports (ICMP
12996   *  types) when counting packets being 2nd and further
12997   fragments.
12998   *      Jos Vos <jos@xos.nl> 8/2/1996.
12999   *  Add support for matching on device names.
13000   *      Jos Vos <jos@xos.nl> 15/2/1996.
13001   *  Transparent proxying support.
13002   *      Willy Konynenberg <willy@xos.nl> 10/5/96.
13003   *  Make separate accounting on incoming and outgoing
13004   packets possible.
13005   *      Jos Vos <jos@xos.nl> 18/5/1996.
13006   *  Add timeout reprieve for idle control channels.
13007   *      Keith Owens <kaos@audio.apana.org.au> 05/07/1996.
13008   *
13009   *
13010   * Masquerading functionality
13011   *
13012   * Copyright (c) 1994 Pauline Middelink
13013   *
13014   * The pieces which added masquerading functionality are
```

```
13015   totally
13016    * my responsibility and have nothing to with the
13017   original authors
13018    * copyright or doing.
13019    *
13020    * Parts distributed under GPL.
13021    *
13022    * Fixes:
13023    *   Pauline Middelink    :    Added masquerading.
13024    *   Alan Cox        :    Fixed an error in the merge.
13025    *   Thomas Quinot      :    Fixed port spoofing.
13026    *   Alan Cox        :    Cleaned up retransmits in
13027   spoofing.
13028    *   Alan Cox        :    Cleaned up length setting.
13029    *   Wouter Gadeyne      :    Fixed masquerading support
13030   of ftp PORT commands
13031    *
13032    *   Juan Jose Ciarlante :    Masquerading code moved to
13033   ip_masq.c
13034    *
13035    *   All the real work was done by .....
13036    *
13037    */
13038
13039
13040   /*
13041    * Copyright (c) 1993 Daniel Boulet
13042    * Copyright (c) 1994 Ugen J.S.Antsilevich
13043    *
13044    * Redistribution and use in source forms, with and
13045   without modification,
13046    * are permitted provided that this entire comment
13047   appears intact.
13048    *
13049    * Redistribution in binary form may occur without any
13050   restrictions.
13051    * Obviously, it would be nice if you gave credit where
13052   credit is due
13053    * but requiring it would be too onerous.
13054    *
13055    * This software is provided "AS IS" without any
13056   warranties of any kind.
13057    */
13058
13059   #include <linux/config.h>
13060   #include <asm/segment.h>
13061   #include <asm/system.h>
13062   #include <linux/types.h>
13063   #include <linux/kernel.h>
13064   #include <linux/sched.h>
13065   #include <linux/string.h>
13066   #include <linux/errno.h>
13067   #include <linux/config.h>
13068
13069   #include <linux/socket.h>
13070   #include <linux/sockios.h>
13071   #include <linux/in.h>
13072   #include <linux/inet.h>
13073   #include <linux/netdevice.h>
13074   #include <linux/icmp.h>
13075   #include <linux/udp.h>
13076   #include <net/ip.h>
13077   #include <net/protocol.h>
13078   #include <net/route.h>
13079   #include <net/tcp.h>
13080   #include <net/udp.h>
13081   #include <net/sock.h>
13082   #include <net/icmp.h>
13083   #include <linux/firewall.h>
13084   #include <linux/ip_fw.h>
13085
13086   #ifdef CONFIG_IP_MASQUERADE
13087   #include <net/ip_masq.h>
13088   #endif
13089
13090   #include <net/checksum.h>
13091   #include <linux/proc_fs.h>
13092   #include <linux/stat.h>
13093
13094   /*
13095    *   Implement IP packet firewall
13096    */
13097
13098   #ifdef DEBUG_IP_FIREWALL
13099   #define dprintf1(a)       printk(a)
13100   #define dprintf2(a1,a2)      printk(a1,a2)
13101   #define dprintf3(a1,a2,a3)  printk(a1,a2,a3)
13102   #define dprintf4(a1,a2,a3,a4)    printk(a1,a2,a3,a4)
13103   #else
13104   #define dprintf1(a)
13105   #define dprintf2(a1,a2)
13106   #define dprintf3(a1,a2,a3)
13107   #define dprintf4(a1,a2,a3,a4)
13108   #endif
13109
13110   #define print_ip(a)
```

```
13111    printk("%ld.%ld.%ld.%ld",(ntohl(a)>>24)&0xFF,\
13112                             (ntohl(a)>>16)&0xFF,\
13113                             (ntohl(a)>>8)&0xFF,\
13114                             (ntohl(a))&0xFF);
13115
13116    #ifdef DEBUG_IP_FIREWALL
13117    #define dprint_ip(a)    print_ip(a)
13118    #else
13119    #define dprint_ip(a)
13120    #endif
13121
13122    #if defined(CONFIG_IP_ACCT) ||
13123    defined(CONFIG_IP_FIREWALL)
13124
13125    struct ip_fw *ip_fw_fwd_chain;
13126    struct ip_fw *ip_fw_in_chain;
13127    struct ip_fw *ip_fw_out_chain;
13128    struct ip_fw *ip_acct_chain;
13129
13130    static struct ip_fw **chains[] =
13131        {&ip_fw_fwd_chain, &ip_fw_in_chain,
13132    &ip_fw_out_chain, &ip_acct_chain};
13133
13134    int ip_fw_fwd_policy=IP_FW_F_ACCEPT;
13135    int ip_fw_in_policy=IP_FW_F_ACCEPT;
13136    int ip_fw_out_policy=IP_FW_F_ACCEPT;
13137
13138    static int *policies[] =
13139        {&ip_fw_fwd_policy, &ip_fw_in_policy,
13140    &ip_fw_out_policy};
13141
13142    #endif
13143
13144    /*
13145     *  Returns 1 if the port is matched by the vector, 0
13146    otherwise
13147     */
13148
13149    extern inline int port_match(unsigned short *portptr,int
13150    nports,unsigned short port,int range_flag)
13151    {
13152        if (!nports)
13153            return 1;
13154        if ( range_flag )
13155        {
13156            if ( portptr[0] <= port && port <= portptr[1] )
13157            {
13158                return( 1 );
```

```
13159            }
13160            nports -= 2;
13161            portptr += 2;
13162        }
13163        while ( nports-- > 0 )
13164        {
13165            if ( *portptr++ == port )
13166            {
13167                return( 1 );
13168            }
13169        }
13170        return(0);
13171    }
13172
13173    #if defined(CONFIG_IP_ACCT) ||
13174    defined(CONFIG_IP_FIREWALL)
13175
13176
13177    /*
13178     *  Returns one of the generic firewall policies, like
13179    FW_ACCEPT.
13180     *  Also does accounting so you can feed it the
13181    accounting chain.
13182     *
13183     *  The modes is either IP_FW_MODE_FW (normal firewall
13184    mode),
13185     *  IP_FW_MODE_ACCT_IN or IP_FW_MODE_ACCT_OUT
13186    (accounting mode,
13187     *  steps through the entire chain and handles fragments
13188     *  differently), or IP_FW_MODE_CHK (handles user-level
13189    check,
13190     *  counters are not updated).
13191     */
13192
13193
13194    int ip_fw_chk(struct iphdr *ip, struct device *rif,
13195    __u16 *redirport, struct ip_fw *chain, int policy, int
13196    mode)
13197    {
13198        struct ip_fw *f;
13199        struct tcphdr        *tcp=(struct tcphdr *)((__u32
13200    *)ip+ip->ihl);
13201        struct udphdr        *udp=(struct udphdr *)((__u32
13202    *)ip+ip->ihl);
13203        struct icmphdr       *icmp=(struct icmphdr *)((__u32
13204    *)ip+ip->ihl);
13205        __u32           src, dst;
13206        __u16           src_port=0xFFFF, dst_port=0xFFFF,
```

p 574

```
13207    icmp_type=0xFF;
13208        unsigned short      f_prt=0, prt;
13209        char                notcpsyn=0, notcpack=0, match;
13210        unsigned short      offset;
13211        int             answer;
13212        unsigned char       tosand, tosxor;
13213
13214        /*
13215         *   If the chain is empty follow policy. The BSD one
13216         *   accepts anything giving you a time window while
13217         *   flushing and rebuilding the tables.
13218         */
13219
13220        src = ip->saddr;
13221        dst = ip->daddr;
13222
13223        /*
13224         *   This way we handle fragmented packets.
13225         *   we ignore all fragments but the first one
13226         *   so the whole packet can't be reassembled.
13227         *   This way we relay on the full info which
13228         *   stored only in first packet.
13229         *
13230         *   Note that this theoretically allows partial
13231 packet
13232         *   spoofing. Not very dangerous but paranoid people
13233 may
13234         *   wish to play with this. It also allows the so
13235 called
13236         *   "fragment bomb" denial of service attack on some
13237 types
13238         *   of system.
13239         */
13240
13241        offset = ntohs(ip->frag_off) & IP_OFFSET;
13242
13243        /*
13244         *   Don't allow a fragment of TCP 8 bytes in. Nobody
13245         *   normal causes this. Its a cracker trying to break
13246         *   in by doing a flag overwrite to pass the
13247 direction
13248         *   checks.
13249         */
13250
13251        if (offset == 1 && ip->protocol == IPPROTO_TCP)
13252            return FW_BLOCK;
13253
13254        if (offset!=0 && !(mode &
13255 (IP_FW_MODE_ACCT_IN|IP_FW_MODE_ACCT_OUT)) &&
13256            (ip->protocol == IPPROTO_TCP || ip->protocol ==
13257 IPPROTO_UDP ||
13258            ip->protocol == IPPROTO_ICMP))
13259            return FW_ACCEPT;
13260
13261        /*
13262         *   Header fragment for TCP is too small to check
13263 the bits.
13264         */
13265
13266        if(ip->protocol==IPPROTO_TCP && (ip->ihl<<2)+16 >
13267 ntohs(ip->tot_len))
13268            return FW_BLOCK;
13269
13270        /*
13271         *   Too short.
13272         *
13273         *   But only too short for a packet with ports...
13274         */
13275
13276        else
13277 if((ntohs(ip->tot_len)<8+(ip->ihl<<2))&&(ip->protocol==IP
13278 PROTO_TCP || ip->protocol==IPPROTO_UDP))
13279            return FW_BLOCK;
13280
13281        src = ip->saddr;
13282        dst = ip->daddr;
13283
13284        /*
13285         *   If we got interface from which packet came
13286         *   we can use the address directly. This is unlike
13287         *   4.4BSD derived systems that have an address chain
13288         *   per device. We have a device per address with
13289 dummy
13290         *   devices instead.
13291         */
13292
13293        dprintf1("Packet ");
13294        switch(ip->protocol)
13295        {
13296            case IPPROTO_TCP:
13297                dprintf1("TCP ");
13298                /* ports stay 0xFFFF if it is not the first
13299 fragment */
13300                if (!offset) {
13301                    src_port=ntohs(tcp->source);
13302                    dst_port=ntohs(tcp->dest);
```

```
13303              if(!tcp->ack && !tcp->rst)
13304                  /* We do NOT have ACK, value TRUE */
13305                  notcpack=1;
13306              if(!tcp->syn || !notcpack)
13307                  /* We do NOT have SYN, value TRUE */
13308                  notcpsyn=1;
13309          }
13310          prt=IP_FW_F_TCP;
13311          break;
13312      case IPPROTO_UDP:
13313          dprintf1("UDP ");
13314          /* ports stay 0xFFFF if it is not the first
13315 fragment */
13316          if (!offset) {
13317              src_port=ntohs(udp->source);
13318              dst_port=ntohs(udp->dest);
13319          }
13320          prt=IP_FW_F_UDP;
13321          break;
13322      case IPPROTO_ICMP:
13323          /* icmp_type stays 255 if it is not the
13324 first fragment */
13325          if (!offset)
13326              icmp_type=(__u16)(icmp->type);
13327          dprintf2("ICMP:%d ",icmp_type);
13328          prt=IP_FW_F_ICMP;
13329          break;
13330      default:
13331          dprintf2("p=%d ",ip->protocol);
13332          prt=IP_FW_F_ALL;
13333          break;
13334  }
13335 #ifdef DEBUG_IP_FIREWALL
13336  dprint_ip(ip->saddr);
13337
13338  if (ip->protocol==IPPROTO_TCP ||
13339 ip->protocol==IPPROTO_UDP)
13340      /* This will print 65535 when it is not the
13341 first fragment! */
13342      dprintf2(":%d ", src_port);
13343  dprint_ip(ip->daddr);
13344  if (ip->protocol==IPPROTO_TCP ||
13345 ip->protocol==IPPROTO_UDP)
13346      /* This will print 65535 when it is not the
13347 first fragment! */
13348      dprintf2(":%d ",dst_port);
13349  dprintf1("\n");
13350 #endif
13351
13352  for (f=chain;f;f=f->fw_next)
13353  {
13354      /*
13355       *  This is a bit simpler as we don't have to
13356 walk
13357       *  an interface chain as you do in BSD - same
13358 logic
13359       *  however.
13360       */
13361
13362      /*
13363       *  Match can become 0x01 (a "normal" match was
13364 found),
13365       *  0x02 (a reverse match was found), and 0x03
13366 (the
13367       *  IP addresses match in both directions).
13368       *  Now we know in which direction(s) we should
13369 look
13370       *  for a match for the TCP/UDP ports.  Both
13371 directions
13372       *  might match (e.g., when both addresses are
13373 on the
13374       *  same network for which an address/mask is
13375 given), but
13376       *  the ports might only match in one direction.
13377       *  This was obviously wrong in the original BSD
13378 code.
13379       */
13380      match = 0x00;
13381
13382      if ((src&f->fw_smsk.s_addr)==f->fw_src.s_addr
13383      &&  (dst&f->fw_dmsk.s_addr)==f->fw_dst.s_addr)
13384          /* normal direction */
13385          match |= 0x01;
13386
13387      if ((f->fw_flg & IP_FW_F_BIDIR) &&
13388          (dst&f->fw_smsk.s_addr)==f->fw_src.s_addr
13389      &&  (src&f->fw_dmsk.s_addr)==f->fw_dst.s_addr)
13390          /* reverse direction */
13391          match |= 0x02;
13392
13393      if (!match)
13394          continue;
13395
13396      /*
13397       *  Look for a VIA address match
13398       */
```

```
13399          if(f->fw_via.s_addr && rif)
13400          {
13401              if(rif->pa_addr!=f->fw_via.s_addr)
13402                  continue;   /* Mismatch */
13403          }
13404
13405          /*
13406           *  Look for a VIA device match
13407           */
13408          if(f->fw_viadev)
13409          {
13410              if(rif!=f->fw_viadev)
13411                  continue;   /* Mismatch */
13412          }
13413
13414          /*
13415           *  Ok the chain addresses match.
13416           */
13417
13418 #ifdef CONFIG_IP_ACCT
13419          /*
13420           *  See if we're in accounting mode and only
13421 want to
13422           *  count incoming or outgoing packets.
13423           */
13424
13425          if (mode &
13426 (IP_FW_MODE_ACCT_IN|IP_FW_MODE_ACCT_OUT) &&
13427              ((mode == IP_FW_MODE_ACCT_IN &&
13428 f->fw_flg&IP_FW_F_ACCTOUT) ||
13429              (mode == IP_FW_MODE_ACCT_OUT &&
13430 f->fw_flg&IP_FW_F_ACCTIN)))
13431                  continue;
13432
13433 #endif
13434          /*
13435           * For all non-TCP packets and/or non-first
13436 fragments,
13437           * notcpsyn and notcpack will always be FALSE,
13438           * so the IP_FW_F_TCPSYN and IP_FW_F_TCPACK flags
13439           * are actually ignored for these packets.
13440           */
13441
13442          if((f->fw_flg&IP_FW_F_TCPSYN) && notcpsyn)
13443              continue;
13444
13445          if((f->fw_flg&IP_FW_F_TCPACK) && notcpack)
13446              continue;
```

```
13447
13448          f_prt=f->fw_flg&IP_FW_F_KIND;
13449          if (f_prt!=IP_FW_F_ALL)
13450          {
13451              /*
13452               *  Specific firewall - packet's protocol
13453               *  must match firewall's.
13454               */
13455
13456              if(prt!=f_prt)
13457                  continue;
13458
13459              if((prt==IP_FW_F_ICMP &&
13460                  ! port_match(&f->fw_pts[0], f->fw_nsp,
13461                      icmp_type,f->fw_flg&IP_FW_F_SRNG)) ||
13462                  !(prt==IP_FW_F_ICMP || ((match & 0x01) &&
13463                  port_match(&f->fw_pts[0], f->fw_nsp,
13464 src_port,
13465                      f->fw_flg&IP_FW_F_SRNG) &&
13466                  port_match(&f->fw_pts[f->fw_nsp],
13467 f->fw_ndp, dst_port,
13468                      f->fw_flg&IP_FW_F_DRNG)) || ((match
13469 & 0x02) &&
13470                  port_match(&f->fw_pts[0], f->fw_nsp,
13471 dst_port,
13472                      f->fw_flg&IP_FW_F_SRNG) &&
13473                  port_match(&f->fw_pts[f->fw_nsp],
13474 f->fw_ndp, src_port,
13475                      f->fw_flg&IP_FW_F_DRNG))))
13476              {
13477                  continue;
13478              }
13479          }
13480
13481 #ifdef CONFIG_IP_FIREWALL_VERBOSE
13482          /*
13483           * VERY ugly piece of code which actually
13484           * makes kernel printf for matching packets...
13485           */
13486
13487          if (f->fw_flg & IP_FW_F_PRN)
13488          {
13489              __u32 *opt = (__u32 *) (ip + 1);
13490              int opti;
13491
13492              if(mode == IP_FW_MODE_ACCT_IN)
13493                  printk(KERN_INFO "IP acct in ");
13494              else if(mode == IP_FW_MODE_ACCT_OUT)
```

```
13495                    printk(KERN_INFO "IP acct out ");
13496                else {
13497                    if(chain == ip_fw_fwd_chain)
13498                        printk(KERN_INFO "IP fw-fwd ");
13499                    else if(chain == ip_fw_in_chain)
13500                        printk(KERN_INFO "IP fw-in ");
13501                    else
13502                        printk(KERN_INFO "IP fw-out ");
13503                    if(f->fw_flg&IP_FW_F_ACCEPT) {
13504                        if(f->fw_flg&IP_FW_F_REDIR)
13505                            printk("acc/r%d ",
13506    f->fw_pts[f->fw_nsp+f->fw_ndp]);
13507                        else if(f->fw_flg&IP_FW_F_MASQ)
13508                            printk("acc/masq ");
13509                        else
13510                            printk("acc ");
13511                    } else if(f->fw_flg&IP_FW_F_ICMPRPL)
13512                        printk("rej ");
13513                    else
13514                        printk("deny ");
13515                }
13516                printk(rif ? rif->name : "-");
13517                switch(ip->protocol)
13518                {
13519                    case IPPROTO_TCP:
13520                        printk(" TCP ");
13521                        break;
13522                    case IPPROTO_UDP:
13523                        printk(" UDP ");
13524                        break;
13525                    case IPPROTO_ICMP:
13526                        printk(" ICMP/%d ", icmp_type);
13527                        break;
13528                    default:
13529                        printk(" PROTO=%d ", ip->protocol);
13530                        break;
13531                }
13532                print_ip(ip->saddr);
13533                if(ip->protocol == IPPROTO_TCP ||
13534    ip->protocol == IPPROTO_UDP)
13535                    printk(":%hu", src_port);
13536                printk(" ");
13537                print_ip(ip->daddr);
13538                if(ip->protocol == IPPROTO_TCP ||
13539    ip->protocol == IPPROTO_UDP)
13540                    printk(":%hu", dst_port);
13541                printk(" L=%hu S=0x%2.2hX I=%hu F=0x%4.4hX
13542    T=%hu",
```

```
13543                    ntohs(ip->tot_len), ip->tos,
13544    ntohs(ip->id),
13545                    ip->frag_off, ip->ttl);
13546                for (opti = 0; opti < (ip->ihl -
13547    sizeof(struct iphdr) / 4); opti++)
13548                    printk(" O=0x%8.8X", *opt++);
13549                printk("\n");
13550            }
13551    #endif
13552            if (mode != IP_FW_MODE_CHK) {
13553                f->fw_bcnt+=ntohs(ip->tot_len);
13554                f->fw_pcnt++;
13555            }
13556            if (!(mode &
13557    (IP_FW_MODE_ACCT_IN|IP_FW_MODE_ACCT_OUT)))
13558                break;
13559        } /* Loop */
13560
13561        if (!(mode &
13562    (IP_FW_MODE_ACCT_IN|IP_FW_MODE_ACCT_OUT))) {
13563
13564        /*
13565         * We rely on policy defined in the rejecting
13566    entry or, if no match
13567         * was found, we rely on the general policy
13568    variable for this type
13569         * of firewall.
13570         */
13571
13572        if (f!=NULL) {
13573            policy=f->fw_flg;
13574            tosand=f->fw_tosand;
13575            tosxor=f->fw_tosxor;
13576        } else {
13577            tosand=0xFF;
13578            tosxor=0x00;
13579        }
13580
13581        if (policy&IP_FW_F_ACCEPT) {
13582            /* Adjust priority and recompute checksum */
13583            __u8 old_tos = ip->tos;
13584            ip->tos = (old_tos & tosand) ^ tosxor;
13585            if (ip->tos != old_tos)
13586                ip_send_check(ip);
13587    #ifdef CONFIG_IP_TRANSPARENT_PROXY
13588            if (policy&IP_FW_F_REDIR) {
13589                if (redirport)
13590                    if ((*redirport =
```

p 574

```
13591    htons(f->fw_pts[f->fw_nsp+f->fw_ndp])) == 0) {
13592                            /* Wildcard redirection.
13593                             * Note that redirport will
13594    become
13595                             * OxFFFF for non-TCP/UDP
13596    packets.
13597                             */
13598                            *redirport = htons(dst_port);
13599                        }
13600                    answer = FW_REDIRECT;
13601                } else
13602    #endif
13603    #ifdef CONFIG_IP_MASQUERADE
13604                if (policy&IP_FW_F_MASQ)
13605                    answer = FW_MASQUERADE;
13606                else
13607    #endif
13608                    answer = FW_ACCEPT;
13609
13610            } else if(policy&IP_FW_F_ICMPRPL)
13611                answer = FW_REJECT;
13612            else
13613                answer = FW_BLOCK;
13614
13615            return answer;
13616        } else
13617            /* we're doing accounting, always ok */
13618            return 0;
13619    }
13620
13621
13622    static void zero_fw_chain(struct ip_fw *chainptr)
13623    {
13624        struct ip_fw *ctmp=chainptr;
13625        while(ctmp)
13626        {
13627            ctmp->fw_pcnt=0L;
13628            ctmp->fw_bcnt=0L;
13629            ctmp=ctmp->fw_next;
13630        }
13631    }
13632
13633    static void free_fw_chain(struct ip_fw *volatile*
13634    chainptr)
13635    {
13636        unsigned long flags;
13637        save_flags(flags);
13638        cli();
```

```
13639        while ( *chainptr != NULL )
13640        {
13641            struct ip_fw *ftmp;
13642            ftmp = *chainptr;
13643            *chainptr = ftmp->fw_next;
13644            kfree_s(ftmp,sizeof(*ftmp));
13645        }
13646        restore_flags(flags);
13647    }
13648
13649    /* Volatiles to keep some of the compiler versions
13650    amused */
13651
13652    static int insert_in_chain(struct ip_fw *volatile*
13653    chainptr, struct ip_fw *frwl,int len)
13654    {
13655        struct ip_fw *ftmp;
13656        unsigned long flags;
13657
13658        save_flags(flags);
13659
13660        ftmp = kmalloc( sizeof(struct ip_fw), GFP_ATOMIC );
13661        if ( ftmp == NULL )
13662        {
13663    #ifdef DEBUG_IP_FIREWALL
13664            printk("ip_fw_ctl:  malloc said no\n");
13665    #endif
13666            return( ENOMEM );
13667        }
13668
13669        memcpy(ftmp, frwl, len);
13670        /*
13671         *  Allow the more recent "minimise cost" flag to be
13672         *  set. [Rob van Nieuwkerk]
13673         */
13674        ftmp->fw_tosand |= 0x01;
13675        ftmp->fw_tosxor &= 0xFE;
13676        ftmp->fw_pcnt=0L;
13677        ftmp->fw_bcnt=0L;
13678
13679        cli();
13680
13681        if ((ftmp->fw_vianame)[0]) {
13682            if (!(ftmp->fw_viadev =
13683    dev_get(ftmp->fw_vianame)))
13684                ftmp->fw_viadev = (struct device *) -1;
13685        } else
13686            ftmp->fw_viadev = NULL;
```

```
13687
13688        ftmp->fw_next = *chainptr;
13689            *chainptr=ftmp;
13690        restore_flags(flags);
13691        return(0);
13692    }
13693
13694    static int append_to_chain(struct ip_fw *volatile*
13695    chainptr, struct ip_fw *frwl,int len)
13696    {
13697        struct ip_fw *ftmp;
13698        struct ip_fw *chtmp=NULL;
13699        struct ip_fw *volatile chtmp_prev=NULL;
13700        unsigned long flags;
13701
13702        save_flags(flags);
13703
13704        ftmp = kmalloc( sizeof(struct ip_fw), GFP_ATOMIC );
13705        if ( ftmp == NULL )
13706        {
13707    #ifdef DEBUG_IP_FIREWALL
13708            printk("ip_fw_ctl:  malloc said no\n");
13709    #endif
13710            return( ENOMEM );
13711        }
13712
13713        memcpy(ftmp, frwl, len);
13714        /*
13715         *  Allow the more recent "minimise cost" flag to be
13716         *  set. [Rob van Nieuwkerk]
13717         */
13718        ftmp->fw_tosand |= 0x01;
13719        ftmp->fw_tosxor &= 0xFE;
13720        ftmp->fw_pcnt=0L;
13721        ftmp->fw_bcnt=0L;
13722
13723        ftmp->fw_next = NULL;
13724
13725        cli();
13726
13727        if ((ftmp->fw_vianame)[0]) {
13728            if (!(ftmp->fw_viadev =
13729    dev_get(ftmp->fw_vianame)))
13730                ftmp->fw_viadev = (struct device *) -1;
13731        } else
13732            ftmp->fw_viadev = NULL;
13733
13734        chtmp_prev=NULL;
```

```
13735        for
13736    (chtmp=*chainptr;chtmp!=NULL;chtmp=chtmp->fw_next)
13737            chtmp_prev=chtmp;
13738
13739        if (chtmp_prev)
13740            chtmp_prev->fw_next=ftmp;
13741        else
13742            *chainptr=ftmp;
13743        restore_flags(flags);
13744        return(0);
13745    }
13746
13747    static int del_from_chain(struct ip_fw
13748    *volatile*chainptr, struct ip_fw *frwl)
13749    {
13750        struct ip_fw    *ftmp,*ltmp;
13751        unsigned short  tport1,tport2,tmpnum;
13752        char            matches,was_found;
13753        unsigned long   flags;
13754
13755        save_flags(flags);
13756        cli();
13757
13758        ftmp=*chainptr;
13759
13760        if ( ftmp == NULL )
13761        {
13762    #ifdef DEBUG_IP_FIREWALL
13763            printk("ip_fw_ctl:  chain is empty\n");
13764    #endif
13765            restore_flags(flags);
13766            return( EINVAL );
13767        }
13768
13769        ltmp=NULL;
13770        was_found=0;
13771
13772        while( !was_found && ftmp != NULL )
13773        {
13774            matches=1;
13775            if (ftmp->fw_src.s_addr!=frwl->fw_src.s_addr
13776                || ftmp->fw_dst.s_addr!=frwl->fw_dst.s_addr
13777                ||
13778    ftmp->fw_smsk.s_addr!=frwl->fw_smsk.s_addr
13779                ||
13780    ftmp->fw_dmsk.s_addr!=frwl->fw_dmsk.s_addr
13781                || ftmp->fw_via.s_addr!=frwl->fw_via.s_addr
13782                || ftmp->fw_flg!=frwl->fw_flg)
```

```
13783                    matches=0;
13784
13785            tport1=ftmp->fw_nsp+ftmp->fw_ndp;
13786            tport2=frwl->fw_nsp+frwl->fw_ndp;
13787            if (tport1!=tport2)
13788                    matches=0;
13789            else if (tport1!=0)
13790            {
13791                for (tmpnum=0;tmpnum < tport1 && tmpnum <
13792 IP_FW_MAX_PORTS;tmpnum++)
13793                    if
13794 (ftmp->fw_pts[tmpnum]!=frwl->fw_pts[tmpnum])
13795                    matches=0;
13796            }
13797            if (strncmp(ftmp->fw_vianame, frwl->fw_vianame,
13798 IFNAMSIZ))
13799                    matches=0;
13800        if(matches)
13801        {
13802            was_found=1;
13803            if (ltmp)
13804            {
13805                ltmp->fw_next=ftmp->fw_next;
13806                kfree_s(ftmp,sizeof(*ftmp));
13807                ftmp=ltmp->fw_next;
13808            }
13809            else
13810            {
13811                *chainptr=ftmp->fw_next;
13812                kfree_s(ftmp,sizeof(*ftmp));
13813                ftmp=*chainptr;
13814            }
13815        }
13816        else
13817        {
13818            ltmp = ftmp;
13819            ftmp = ftmp->fw_next;
13820          }
13821        }
13822    restore_flags(flags);
13823    if (was_found)
13824        return 0;
13825    else
13826        return(EINVAL);
13827 }
13828
13829 #endif   /* CONFIG_IP_ACCT || CONFIG_IP_FIREWALL */
13830
```

p 576

```
13831 struct ip_fw *check_ipfw_struct(struct ip_fw *frwl, int
13832 len)
13833 {
13834
13835     if ( len != sizeof(struct ip_fw) )
13836     {
13837 #ifdef DEBUG_IP_FIREWALL
13838        printk("ip_fw_ctl: len=%d, want %d\n",len,
13839 sizeof(struct ip_fw));
13840 #endif
13841        return(NULL);
13842     }
13843
13844     if ( (frwl->fw_flg & ~IP_FW_F_MASK) != 0 )
13845     {
13846 #ifdef DEBUG_IP_FIREWALL
13847        printk("ip_fw_ctl: undefined flag bits set
13848 (flags=%x)\n",
13849            frwl->fw_flg);
13850 #endif
13851        return(NULL);
13852     }
13853
13854 #ifndef CONFIG_IP_TRANSPARENT_PROXY
13855     if (frwl->fw_flg & IP_FW_F_REDIR) {
13856 #ifdef DEBUG_IP_FIREWALL
13857        printk("ip_fw_ctl: unsupported flag
13858 IP_FW_F_REDIR\n");
13859 #endif
13860        return(NULL);
13861     }
13862 #endif
13863
13864 #ifndef CONFIG_IP_MASQUERADE
13865     if (frwl->fw_flg & IP_FW_F_MASQ) {
13866 #ifdef DEBUG_IP_FIREWALL
13867        printk("ip_fw_ctl: unsupported flag
13868 IP_FW_F_MASQ\n");
13869 #endif
13870        return(NULL);
13871     }
13872 #endif
13873
13874     if ( (frwl->fw_flg & IP_FW_F_SRNG) && frwl->fw_nsp <
13875 2 )
13876     {
13877 #ifdef DEBUG_IP_FIREWALL
13878        printk("ip_fw_ctl: src range set but
```

```
13879         fw_nsp=%d\n",
13880                     frwl->fw_nsp);
13881  #endif
13882         return(NULL);
13883       }
13884
13885       if ( (frwl->fw_flg & IP_FW_F_DRNG) && frwl->fw_ndp <
13886  2 )
13887       {
13888  #ifdef DEBUG_IP_FIREWALL
13889         printk("ip_fw_ctl: dst range set but
13890  fw_ndp=%d\n",
13891                     frwl->fw_ndp);
13892  #endif
13893         return(NULL);
13894       }
13895
13896       if ( frwl->fw_nsp + frwl->fw_ndp > (frwl->fw_flg &
13897  IP_FW_F_REDIR ? IP_FW_MAX_PORTS - 1 : IP_FW_MAX_PORTS) )
13898       {
13899  #ifdef DEBUG_IP_FIREWALL
13900         printk("ip_fw_ctl: too many ports (%d+%d)\n",
13901                     frwl->fw_nsp,frwl->fw_ndp);
13902  #endif
13903         return(NULL);
13904       }
13905
13906       return frwl;
13907  }
13908
13909
13910
13911
13912  #ifdef CONFIG_IP_ACCT
13913
13914  int ip_acct_ctl(int stage, void *m, int len)
13915  {
13916       if ( stage == IP_ACCT_FLUSH )
13917       {
13918         free_fw_chain(&ip_acct_chain);
13919         return(0);
13920       }
13921       if ( stage == IP_ACCT_ZERO )
13922       {
13923         zero_fw_chain(ip_acct_chain);
13924         return(0);
13925       }
13926       if ( stage == IP_ACCT_INSERT || stage ==
```

p 576

```
13927  IP_ACCT_APPEND ||
13928                     stage == IP_ACCT_DELETE )
13929       {
13930         struct ip_fw *frwl;
13931
13932         if (!(frwl=check_ipfw_struct(m,len)))
13933           return (EINVAL);
13934
13935         switch (stage)
13936         {
13937           case IP_ACCT_INSERT:
13938             return(
13939  insert_in_chain(&ip_acct_chain,frwl,len));
13940           case IP_ACCT_APPEND:
13941             return(
13942  append_to_chain(&ip_acct_chain,frwl,len));
13943           case IP_ACCT_DELETE:
13944             return(
13945  del_from_chain(&ip_acct_chain,frwl));
13946           default:
13947             /*
13948              *   Should be panic but... (Why ??? - AC)
13949              */
13950  #ifdef DEBUG_IP_FIREWALL
13951             printk("ip_acct_ctl:  unknown request
13952  %d\n",stage);
13953  #endif
13954             return(EINVAL);
13955         }
13956       }
13957  #ifdef DEBUG_IP_FIREWALL
13958       printk("ip_acct_ctl:  unknown request %d\n",stage);
13959  #endif
13960       return(EINVAL);
13961  }
13962  #endif
13963
13964  #ifdef CONFIG_IP_MASQUERADE_IPAUTOFW
13965
13966  int ip_autofw_add(struct ip_autofw * af)
13967  {
13968       struct ip_autofw * newaf;
13969       init_timer(&af->timer);
13970       newaf = kmalloc( sizeof(struct ip_autofw),
13971  GFP_ATOMIC );
13972       if ( newaf == NULL )
13973       {
13974  #ifdef DEBUG_IP_FIREWALL
```

```
13975              printk("ip_autofw_add:  malloc said no\n");
13976  #endif
13977              return( ENOMEM );
13978          }
13979
13980      memcpy(newaf, af, sizeof(struct ip_autofw));
13981      newaf->timer.data = (unsigned long) newaf;
13982      newaf->timer.function = ip_autofw_expire;
13983      newaf->timer.expires = 0;
13984      newaf->lastcontact=0;
13985      newaf->next=ip_autofw_hosts;
13986      ip_autofw_hosts=newaf;
13987      return(0);
13988  }
13989
13990  int ip_autofw_del(struct ip_autofw * af)
13991  {
13992      struct ip_autofw * prev, * curr;
13993      prev=NULL;
13994      curr=ip_autofw_hosts;
13995      while (curr)
13996      {
13997          if (af->type    == curr->type &&
13998              af->low     == curr->low &&
13999              af->high    == curr->high &&
14000              af->hidden  == curr->hidden &&
14001              af->visible == curr->visible &&
14002              af->protocol == curr->protocol &&
14003              af->where   == curr->where &&
14004              af->ctlproto == curr->ctlproto &&
14005              af->ctlport == curr->ctlport)
14006          {
14007              if (prev)
14008              {
14009                  prev->next=curr->next;
14010                  kfree_s(curr,sizeof(struct ip_autofw));
14011                  return(0);
14012              }
14013              else
14014              {
14015                  kfree_s(ip_autofw_hosts,sizeof(struct
14016  ip_autofw));
14017                  ip_autofw_hosts=curr->next;
14018                  return(0);
14019              }
14020          }
14021          prev=curr;
14022          curr=curr->next;
```

```
14023      }
14024      return(EINVAL);
14025  }
14026
14027  int ip_autofw_flush(void)
14028  {
14029      struct ip_autofw * af;
14030      while (ip_autofw_hosts)
14031      {
14032          af=ip_autofw_hosts;
14033          ip_autofw_hosts=ip_autofw_hosts->next;
14034          kfree_s(af,sizeof(struct ip_autofw));
14035      }
14036      return(0);
14037  }
14038
14039  int ip_autofw_ctl(int stage, void *m, int len)
14040  {
14041      if (stage == IP_AUTOFW_ADD)
14042          return (ip_autofw_add((struct ip_autofw *) m));
14043
14044      if (stage == IP_AUTOFW_DEL)
14045          return (ip_autofw_del((struct ip_autofw *) m));
14046
14047      if (stage == IP_AUTOFW_FLUSH)
14048          return (ip_autofw_flush());
14049
14050      return(EINVAL);
14051  }
14052
14053  #endif /* CONFIG_IP_MASQUERADE_IPAUTOFW */
14054
14055  #ifdef CONFIG_IP_FIREWALL
14056  int ip_fw_ctl(int stage, void *m, int len)
14057  {
14058      int cmd, fwtype;
14059
14060      cmd = stage & IP_FW_COMMAND;
14061      fwtype = (stage & IP_FW_TYPE) >> IP_FW_SHIFT;
14062
14063      if ( cmd == IP_FW_FLUSH )
14064      {
14065          free_fw_chain(chains[fwtype]);
14066          return(0);
14067      }
14068
14069      if ( cmd == IP_FW_ZERO )
14070      {
```

p 576

```
14071          zero_fw_chain(*chains[fwtype]);
14072          return(0);
14073      }
14074
14075      if ( cmd == IP_FW_POLICY )
14076      {
14077          int *tmp_policy_ptr;
14078          tmp_policy_ptr=(int *)m;
14079          *policies[fwtype] = *tmp_policy_ptr;
14080          return 0;
14081      }
14082
14083      if ( cmd == IP_FW_CHECK )
14084      {
14085          struct device *viadev;
14086          struct ip_fwpkt *ipfwp;
14087          struct iphdr *ip;
14088
14089          if ( len != sizeof(struct ip_fwpkt) )
14090          {
14091  #ifdef DEBUG_IP_FIREWALL
14092              printk("ip_fw_ctl: length=%d, expected %d\n",
14093                  len, sizeof(struct ip_fwpkt));
14094  #endif
14095              return( EINVAL );
14096          }
14097
14098          ipfwp = (struct ip_fwpkt *)m;
14099          ip = &(ipfwp->fwp_iph);
14100
14101          if ( !(viadev = dev_get(ipfwp->fwp_vianame)) ) {
14102  #ifdef DEBUG_IP_FIREWALL
14103              printk("ip_fw_ctl: invalid device \"%s\"\n",
14104  ipfwp->fwp_vianame);
14105  #endif
14106              return(EINVAL);
14107          } else if ( viadev->pa_addr !=
14108  ipfwp->fwp_via.s_addr ) {
14109  #ifdef DEBUG_IP_FIREWALL
14110              printk("ip_fw_ctl: device \"%s\" has another
14111  IP address\n",
14112                  ipfwp->fwp_vianame);
14113  #endif
14114              return(EINVAL);
14115          } else if ( ip->ihl != sizeof(struct iphdr) /
14116  sizeof(int)) {
14117  #ifdef DEBUG_IP_FIREWALL
14118              printk("ip_fw_ctl: ip->ihl=%d, want
14119  %d\n",ip->ihl,
14120                  sizeof(struct iphdr)/sizeof(int));
14121  #endif
14122              return(EINVAL);
14123          }
14124
14125          switch (ip_fw_chk(ip, viadev, NULL,
14126  *chains[fwtype],
14127              *policies[fwtype], IP_FW_MODE_CHK))
14128          {
14129              case FW_ACCEPT:
14130                  return(0);
14131              case FW_REDIRECT:
14132                  return(ECONNABORTED);
14133              case FW_MASQUERADE:
14134                  return(ECONNRESET);
14135              case FW_REJECT:
14136                  return(ECONNREFUSED);
14137              default: /* FW_BLOCK */
14138                  return(ETIMEDOUT);
14139          }
14140      }
14141
14142      if ( cmd == IP_FW_MASQ_TIMEOUTS )
14143      {
14144  #ifdef CONFIG_IP_MASQUERADE
14145          struct ip_fw_masq *masq;
14146
14147          if ( len != sizeof(struct ip_fw_masq) )
14148          {
14149  #ifdef DEBUG_IP_FIREWALL
14150              printk("ip_fw_ctl (masq): length %d,
14151  expected %d\n",
14152                  len, sizeof(struct ip_fw_masq));
14153
14154  #endif
14155              return( EINVAL );
14156          }
14157
14158          masq = (struct ip_fw_masq *) m;
14159
14160          if (masq->tcp_timeout)
14161          {
14162              ip_masq_expire->tcp_timeout =
14163  masq->tcp_timeout;
14164          }
14165
14166          if (masq->tcp_fin_timeout)
```

```
14167              {
14168                    ip_masq_expire->tcp_fin_timeout =
14169    masq->tcp_fin_timeout;
14170              }
14171
14172              if (masq->udp_timeout)
14173              {
14174                    ip_masq_expire->udp_timeout =
14175    masq->udp_timeout;
14176              }
14177
14178              return 0;
14179    #else
14180              return( EINVAL );
14181    #endif
14182         }
14183
14184    /*
14185     *  Here we really working hard-adding new elements
14186     *  to blocking/forwarding chains or deleting 'em
14187     */
14188
14189        if ( cmd == IP_FW_INSERT || cmd == IP_FW_APPEND ||
14190    cmd == IP_FW_DELETE )
14191         {
14192              struct ip_fw *frwl;
14193              int fwtype;
14194
14195              frwl=check_ipfw_struct(m,len);
14196              if (frwl==NULL)
14197                    return (EINVAL);
14198              fwtype = (stage & IP_FW_TYPE) >> IP_FW_SHIFT;
14199
14200              switch (cmd)
14201              {
14202                    case IP_FW_INSERT:
14203
14204    return(insert_in_chain(chains[fwtype],frwl,len));
14205                    case IP_FW_APPEND:
14206
14207    return(append_to_chain(chains[fwtype],frwl,len));
14208                    case IP_FW_DELETE:
14209
14210    return(del_from_chain(chains[fwtype],frwl));
14211                    default:
14212                    /*
14213                     *  Should be panic but... (Why are BSD
14214    people panic obsessed ??)
```

```
14215              */
14216    #ifdef DEBUG_IP_FIREWALL
14217                    printk("ip_fw_ctl:  unknown request
14218    %d\n",stage);
14219    #endif
14220                    return(EINVAL);
14221         }
14222      }
14223
14224    #ifdef DEBUG_IP_FIREWALL
14225        printk("ip_fw_ctl:  unknown request %d\n",stage);
14226    #endif
14227        return(EINVAL);
14228    }
14229    #endif /* CONFIG_IP_FIREWALL */
14230
14231    #if defined(CONFIG_IP_FIREWALL) ||
14232    defined(CONFIG_IP_ACCT)
14233
14234    static int ip_chain_procinfo(int stage, char *buffer,
14235    char **start,
14236                    off_t offset, int length, int reset)
14237    {
14238        off_t pos=0, begin=0;
14239        struct ip_fw *i;
14240        unsigned long flags;
14241        int len, p;
14242        int last_len = 0;
14243
14244
14245        switch(stage)
14246        {
14247    #ifdef CONFIG_IP_FIREWALL
14248           case IP_FW_IN:
14249                i = ip_fw_in_chain;
14250                len=sprintf(buffer, "IP firewall input
14251    rules, default %d\n",
14252                    ip_fw_in_policy);
14253                break;
14254           case IP_FW_OUT:
14255                i = ip_fw_out_chain;
14256                len=sprintf(buffer, "IP firewall output
14257    rules, default %d\n",
14258                    ip_fw_out_policy);
14259                break;
14260           case IP_FW_FWD:
14261                i = ip_fw_fwd_chain;
14262                len=sprintf(buffer, "IP firewall forward
```

```
14263    rules, default %d\n",
14264                    ip_fw_fwd_policy);
14265            break;
14266  #endif
14267  #ifdef CONFIG_IP_ACCT
14268        case IP_FW_ACCT:
14269            i = ip_acct_chain;
14270            len=sprintf(buffer,"IP accounting rules\n");
14271            break;
14272  #endif
14273        default:
14274            /* this should never be reached, but safety
14275  first... */
14276            i = NULL;
14277            len=0;
14278            break;
14279        }
14280
14281    save_flags(flags);
14282    cli();
14283
14284    while(i!=NULL)
14285    {
14286
14287  len+=sprintf(buffer+len,"%08lX/%08lX->%08lX/%08lX %.16s
14288  %08lX %X ",
14289
14290  ntohl(i->fw_src.s_addr),ntohl(i->fw_smsk.s_addr),
14291
14292  ntohl(i->fw_dst.s_addr),ntohl(i->fw_dmsk.s_addr),
14293            (i->fw_vianame)[0] ? i->fw_vianame : "-",
14294            ntohl(i->fw_via.s_addr),i->fw_flg);
14295        len+=sprintf(buffer+len,"%u %u %-10lu %-10lu",
14296            i->fw_nsp,i->fw_ndp, i->fw_pcnt,i->fw_bcnt);
14297        for (p = 0; p < IP_FW_MAX_PORTS; p++)
14298            len+=sprintf(buffer+len, " %u",
14299  i->fw_pts[p]);
14300        len+=sprintf(buffer+len, " A%02X X%02X",
14301  i->fw_tosand, i->fw_tosxor);
14302        buffer[len++]='\n';
14303        buffer[len]='\0';
14304        pos=begin+len;
14305        if(pos<offset)
14306        {
14307            len=0;
14308            begin=pos;
14309        }
14310        else if(pos>offset+length)
14311        {
14312            len = last_len;
14313            break;
14314        }
14315        else if(reset)
14316        {
14317            /* This needs to be done at this specific
14318  place! */
14319            i->fw_pcnt=0L;
14320            i->fw_bcnt=0L;
14321        }
14322        last_len = len;
14323        i=i->fw_next;
14324    }
14325    restore_flags(flags);
14326    *start=buffer+(offset-begin);
14327    len-=(offset-begin);
14328    if(len>length)
14329        len=length;
14330    return len;
14331  }
14332  #endif
14333
14334  #ifdef CONFIG_IP_ACCT
14335
14336  static int ip_acct_procinfo(char *buffer, char **start,
14337  off_t offset,
14338                int length, int reset)
14339  {
14340      return ip_chain_procinfo(IP_FW_ACCT, buffer,start,
14341  offset,length,
14342                reset);
14343  }
14344
14345  #endif
14346
14347  #ifdef CONFIG_IP_FIREWALL
14348
14349  static int ip_fw_in_procinfo(char *buffer, char **start,
14350  off_t offset,
14351                int length, int reset)
14352  {
14353      return ip_chain_procinfo(IP_FW_IN,
14354  buffer,start,offset,length,
14355                reset);
14356  }
14357
14358  static int ip_fw_out_procinfo(char *buffer, char
```

```
14359    **start, off_t offset,
14360                        int length, int reset)
14361    {
14362        return ip_chain_procinfo(IP_FW_OUT,
14363    buffer,start,offset,length,
14364                        reset);
14365    }
14366
14367    static int ip_fw_fwd_procinfo(char *buffer, char
14368    **start, off_t offset,
14369                        int length, int reset)
14370    {
14371        return ip_chain_procinfo(IP_FW_FWD,
14372    buffer,start,offset,length,
14373                        reset);
14374    }
14375    #endif
14376
14377
14378    #ifdef CONFIG_IP_FIREWALL
14379    /*
14380     *  Interface to the generic firewall chains.
14381     */
14382
14383    int ipfw_input_check(struct firewall_ops *this, int pf,
14384    struct device *dev, void *phdr, void *arg)
14385    {
14386        return ip_fw_chk(phdr, dev, arg, ip_fw_in_chain,
14387    ip_fw_in_policy, IP_FW_MODE_FW);
14388    }
14389
14390    int ipfw_output_check(struct firewall_ops *this, int pf,
14391    struct device *dev, void *phdr, void *arg)
14392    {
14393        return ip_fw_chk(phdr, dev, arg, ip_fw_out_chain,
14394    ip_fw_out_policy, IP_FW_MODE_FW);
14395    }
14396
14397    int ipfw_forward_check(struct firewall_ops *this, int
14398    pf, struct device *dev, void *phdr, void *arg)
14399    {
14400        return ip_fw_chk(phdr, dev, arg, ip_fw_fwd_chain,
14401    ip_fw_fwd_policy, IP_FW_MODE_FW);
14402    }
14403
14404    struct firewall_ops ipfw_ops=
14405    {
14406        NULL,
```

```
14407        ipfw_forward_check,
14408        ipfw_input_check,
14409        ipfw_output_check,
14410        PF_INET,
14411        0    /* We don't even allow a fall through so we are
14412    last */
14413    };
14414
14415    #endif
14416
14417    #if defined(CONFIG_IP_ACCT) ||
14418    defined(CONFIG_IP_FIREWALL)
14419
14420    int ipfw_device_event(struct notifier_block *this,
14421    unsigned long event, void *ptr)
14422    {
14423        struct device *dev=ptr;
14424        char *devname = dev->name;
14425        unsigned long flags;
14426        struct ip_fw *fw;
14427        int chn;
14428
14429        save_flags(flags);
14430        cli();
14431
14432        if (event == NETDEV_UP) {
14433            for (chn = 0; chn < IP_FW_CHAINS; chn++)
14434                for (fw = *chains[chn]; fw; fw = fw->fw_next)
14435                    if ((fw->fw_vianame)[0] &&
14436    !strncmp(devname,
14437                        fw->fw_vianame, IFNAMSIZ))
14438                        fw->fw_viadev = dev;
14439        } else if (event == NETDEV_DOWN) {
14440            for (chn = 0; chn < IP_FW_CHAINS; chn++)
14441                for (fw = *chains[chn]; fw; fw = fw->fw_next)
14442                    /* we could compare just the pointers
14443    ... */
14444                    if ((fw->fw_vianame)[0] &&
14445    !strncmp(devname,
14446                        fw->fw_vianame, IFNAMSIZ))
14447                        fw->fw_viadev = (struct device *) -1;
14448        }
14449
14450        restore_flags(flags);
14451        return NOTIFY_DONE;
14452    }
14453
14454    static struct notifier_block ipfw_dev_notifier={
```

p 576

```
14455        ipfw_device_event,
14456        NULL,
14457        0
14458    };
14459
14460    #endif
14461
14462    void ip_fw_init(void)
14463    {
14464    #ifdef CONFIG_PROC_FS
14465    #ifdef CONFIG_IP_ACCT
14466        proc_net_register(&(struct proc_dir_entry) {
14467            PROC_NET_IPACCT, 7, "ip_acct",
14468            S_IFREG | S_IRUGO | S_IWUSR, 1, 0, 0,
14469            0, &proc_net_inode_operations,
14470            ip_acct_procinfo
14471        });
14472    #endif
14473    #endif
14474    #ifdef CONFIG_IP_FIREWALL
14475
14476        if(register_firewall(PF_INET,&ipfw_ops)<0)
14477            panic("Unable to register IP firewall.\n");
14478
14479    #ifdef CONFIG_PROC_FS
14480        proc_net_register(&(struct proc_dir_entry) {
14481            PROC_NET_IPFWIN, 8, "ip_input",
14482            S_IFREG | S_IRUGO | S_IWUSR, 1, 0, 0,
14483            0, &proc_net_inode_operations,
14484            ip_fw_in_procinfo
14485        });
14486        proc_net_register(&(struct proc_dir_entry) {
14487            PROC_NET_IPFWOUT, 9, "ip_output",
14488            S_IFREG | S_IRUGO | S_IWUSR, 1, 0, 0,
14489            0, &proc_net_inode_operations,
14490            ip_fw_out_procinfo
14491        });
14492        proc_net_register(&(struct proc_dir_entry) {
14493            PROC_NET_IPFWFWD, 10, "ip_forward",
14494            S_IFREG | S_IRUGO | S_IWUSR, 1, 0, 0,
14495            0, &proc_net_inode_operations,
14496            ip_fw_fwd_procinfo
14497        });
14498    #endif
14499    #endif
14500    #ifdef CONFIG_IP_MASQUERADE
14501
14502            /*
```

p 576 (at line 14462)

```
14503            *  Initialize masquerading.
14504            */
14505
14506            ip_masq_init();
14507    #endif
14508
14509    #if defined(CONFIG_IP_ACCT) ||
14510    defined(CONFIG_IP_FIREWALL)
14511        /* Register for device up/down reports */
14512        register_netdevice_notifier(&ipfw_dev_notifier);
14513    #endif
14514    }
```

usr/src/linux/net/ipv4/ip_input.c

```
14515    /*
14516     * INET      An implementation of the TCP/IP protocol
14517    suite for the LINUX
14518     *       operating system.  INET is implemented using the
14519    BSD Socket
14520     *       interface as the means of communication with the
14521    user level.
14522     *
14523     *       The Internet Protocol (IP) module.
14524     *
14525     * Version: @(#)ip.c     1.0.16b 9/1/93
14526     *
14527     * Authors: Ross Biro, <bir7@leland.Stanford.Edu>
14528     *       Fred N. van Kempen, <waltje@uWalt.NL.Mugnet.ORG>
14529     *       Donald Becker, <becker@super.org>
14530     *       Alan Cox, <Alan.Cox@linux.org>
14531     *       Richard Underwood
14532     *       Stefan Becker, <stefanb@yello.ping.de>
14533     *       Jorge Cwik, <jorge@laser.satlink.net>
14534     *       Arnt Gulbrandsen, <agulbra@nvg.unit.no>
14535     *
14536     *
14537     * Fixes:
14538     *       Alan Cox    :   Commented a couple of minor bits
14539    of surplus code
14540     *       Alan Cox    :   Undefining IP_FORWARD doesn't
14541    include the code
14542     *                      (just stops a compiler warning).
14543     *       Alan Cox    :   Frames with >=MAX_ROUTE record
14544    routes, strict routes or loose routes
14545     *                      are junked rather than corrupting
14546    things.
14547     *       Alan Cox    :   Frames to bad broadcast subnets
14548    are dumped
```

```
14549    *                  We used to process them non
14550 broadcast and
14551    *                  boy could that cause havoc.
14552    *       Alan Cox   :   ip_forward sets the free flag on
14553 the
14554    *                  new frame it queues. Still crap
14555 because
14556    *                  it copies the frame but at least it
14557    *                  doesn't eat memory too.
14558    *       Alan Cox   :   Generic queue code and memory
14559 fixes.
14560    *       Fred Van Kempen :   IP fragment support
14561 (borrowed from NET2E)
14562    *       Gerhard Koerting:   Forward fragmented frames
14563 correctly.
14564    *       Gerhard Koerting:   Fixes to my fix of the above
14565 8-).
14566    *       Gerhard Koerting:   IP interface addressing fix.
14567    *       Linus Torvalds :   More robustness checks
14568    *       Alan Cox   :   Even more checks: Still not as
14569 robust as it ought to be
14570    *       Alan Cox   :   Save IP header pointer for later
14571    *       Alan Cox   :   ip option setting
14572    *       Alan Cox   :   Use ip_tos/ip_ttl settings
14573    *       Alan Cox   :   Fragmentation bogosity removed
14574    *                  (Thanks to Mark.Bush@prg.ox.ac.uk)
14575    *       Dmitry Gorodchanin :   Send of a raw packet
14576 crash fix.
14577    *       Alan Cox   :   Silly ip bug when an overlength
14578    *                  fragment turns up. Now frees the
14579    *                  queue.
14580    *       Linus Torvalds/ :   Memory leakage on
14581 fragmentation
14582    *       Alan Cox   :   handling.
14583    *       Gerhard Koerting:   Forwarding uses IP priority
14584 hints
14585    *       Teemu Rantanen :   Fragment problems.
14586    *       Alan Cox   :   General cleanup, comments and
14587 reformat
14588    *       Alan Cox   :   SNMP statistics
14589    *       Alan Cox   :   BSD address rule semantics. Also
14590 see
14591    *                  UDP as there is a nasty checksum
14592 issue
14593    *                  if you do things the wrong way.
14594    *       Alan Cox   :   Always defrag, moved IP_FORWARD
14595 to the config.in file
14596    *       Alan Cox   :   IP options adjust sk->priority.
14597    *       Pedro Roque :   Fix mtu/length error in
14598 ip_forward.
14599    *       Alan Cox   :   Avoid ip_chk_addr when possible.
14600    *  Richard Underwood   :   IP multicasting.
14601    *       Alan Cox   :   Cleaned up multicast handlers.
14602    *       Alan Cox   :   RAW sockets demultiplex in the
14603 BSD style.
14604    *       Gunther Mayer :   Fix the SNMP reporting typo
14605    *       Alan Cox   :   Always in group 224.0.0.1
14606    *  Pauline Middelink   :   Fast ip_checksum update when
14607 forwarding
14608    *                  Masquerading support.
14609    *       Alan Cox   :   Multicast loopback error for
14610 224.0.0.1
14611    *       Alan Cox   :   IP_MULTICAST_LOOP option.
14612    *       Alan Cox   :   Use notifiers.
14613    *       Bjorn Ekwall :   Removed ip_csum (from slhc.c
14614 too)
14615    *       Bjorn Ekwall :   Moved ip_fast_csum to ip.h
14616 (inline!)
14617    *       Stefan Becker :   Send out ICMP HOST
14618 REDIRECT
14619    *  Arnt Gulbrandsen   :   ip_build_xmit
14620    *       Alan Cox   :   Per socket routing cache
14621    *       Alan Cox   :   Fixed routing cache, added
14622 header cache.
14623    *       Alan Cox   :   Loopback didn't work right in
14624 original ip_build_xmit - fixed it.
14625    *       Alan Cox   :   Only send ICMP_REDIRECT if
14626 src/dest are the same net.
14627    *       Alan Cox   :   Incoming IP option handling.
14628    *       Alan Cox   :   Set saddr on raw output frames
14629 as per BSD.
14630    *       Alan Cox   :   Stopped broadcast source route
14631 explosions.
14632    *       Alan Cox   :   Can disable source routing
14633    *       Takeshi Sone :   Masquerading didn't work.
14634    *  Dave Bonn,Alan Cox :   Faster IP forwarding
14635 whenever possible.
14636    *       Alan Cox   :   Memory leaks, tramples, misc
14637 debugging.
14638    *       Alan Cox   :   Fixed multicast (by popular
14639 demand 8))
14640    *       Alan Cox   :   Fixed forwarding (by even more
14641 popular demand 8))
14642    *       Alan Cox   :   Fixed SNMP statistics [I think]
14643    *  Gerhard Koerting   :   IP fragmentation forwarding
14644 fix
```

```
14645    *        Alan Cox    :    Device lock against page fault.
14646    *        Alan Cox    :    IP_HDRINCL facility.
14647    *   Werner Almesberger  :   Zero fragment bug
14648    *        Alan Cox    :    RAW IP frame length bug
14649    *        Alan Cox    :    Outgoing firewall on build_xmit
14650    *        A.N.Kuznetsov   :    IP_OPTIONS support
14651   throughout the kernel
14652    *        Alan Cox    :    Multicast routing hooks
14653    *        Jos Vos     :    Do accounting *before*
14654   call_in_firewall
14655    *   Willy Konynenberg   :    Transparent proxying support
14656    *
14657    *
14658    *
14659    * To Fix:
14660    *        IP fragmentation wants rewriting cleanly. The
14661   RFC815 algorithm is much more efficient
14662    *        and could be made very efficient with the
14663   addition of some virtual memory hacks to permit
14664    *        the allocation of a buffer that can then be
14665   'grown' by twiddling page tables.
14666    *        Output fragmentation wants updating along with
14667   the buffer management to use a single
14668    *        interleaved copy algorithm so that fragmenting
14669   has a one copy overhead. Actual packet
14670    *        output should probably do its own fragmentation
14671   at the UDP/RAW layer. TCP shouldn't cause
14672    *        fragmentation anyway.
14673    *
14674    *        FIXME: copy frag 0 iph to qp->iph
14675    *
14676    *        This program is free software; you can
14677   redistribute it and/or
14678    *        modify it under the terms of the GNU General
14679   Public License
14680    *        as published by the Free Software Foundation;
14681   either version
14682    *        2 of the License, or (at your option) any later
14683   version.
14684    */
14685
14686   #include <asm/segment.h>
14687   #include <asm/system.h>
14688   #include <linux/types.h>
14689   #include <linux/kernel.h>
14690   #include <linux/sched.h>
14691   #include <linux/mm.h>
14692   #include <linux/string.h>
```

```
14693   #include <linux/errno.h>
14694   #include <linux/config.h>
14695
14696   #include <linux/socket.h>
14697   #include <linux/sockios.h>
14698   #include <linux/in.h>
14699   #include <linux/inet.h>
14700   #include <linux/netdevice.h>
14701   #include <linux/etherdevice.h>
14702   #include <linux/proc_fs.h>
14703   #include <linux/stat.h>
14704
14705   #include <net/snmp.h>
14706   #include <net/ip.h>
14707   #include <net/protocol.h>
14708   #include <net/route.h>
14709   #include <net/tcp.h>
14710   #include <net/udp.h>
14711   #include <linux/skbuff.h>
14712   #include <net/sock.h>
14713   #include <net/arp.h>
14714   #include <net/icmp.h>
14715   #include <net/raw.h>
14716   #include <net/checksum.h>
14717   #include <linux/igmp.h>
14718   #include <linux/ip_fw.h>
14719   #ifdef CONFIG_IP_MASQUERADE
14720   #include <net/ip_masq.h>
14721   #endif
14722   #include <linux/firewall.h>
14723   #include <linux/mroute.h>
14724   #include <net/netlink.h>
14725   #ifdef CONFIG_NET_ALIAS
14726   #include <linux/net_alias.h>
14727   #endif
14728
14729   extern int last_retran;
14730   extern void sort_send(struct sock *sk);
14731
14732   #define min(a,b)    ((a)<(b)?(a):(b))
14733
14734   /*
14735    *   SNMP management statistics
14736    */
14737
14738   #ifdef CONFIG_IP_FORWARD
14739   struct ip_mib ip_statistics={1,64,};      /*
14740   Forwarding=Yes, Default TTL=64 */
```

```
14741  #else
14742  struct ip_mib ip_statistics={2,64,};      /*
14743  Forwarding=No, Default TTL=64 */
14744  #endif
14745
14746  /*
14747   *  Handle the issuing of an ioctl() request
14748   *  for the ip device. This is scheduled to
14749   *  disappear
14750   */
14751
14752  int ip_ioctl(struct sock *sk, int cmd, unsigned long arg)
14753  {
14754      switch(cmd)
14755      {
14756          default:
14757              return(-EINVAL);
14758      }
14759  }
14760
14761  #ifdef CONFIG_IP_TRANSPARENT_PROXY
14762  /*
14763   *  Check the packet against our socket administration
14764  to see
14765   *  if it is related to a connection on our system.
14766   *  Needed for transparent proxying.
14767   */
14768
14769  int ip_chksock(struct sk_buff *skb)
14770  {
14771      switch (skb->h.iph->protocol) {
14772      case IPPROTO_ICMP:
14773          return icmp_chkaddr(skb);
14774      case IPPROTO_TCP:
14775          return tcp_chkaddr(skb);
14776      case IPPROTO_UDP:
14777          return udp_chkaddr(skb);
14778      default:
14779          return 0;
14780      }
14781  }
14782  #endif
14783
14784
14785  /*
14786   *  This function receives all incoming IP datagrams.
14787   *
14788   *  On entry skb->data points to the start of the IP
```

```
14789  header and
14790   *  the MAC header has been removed.
14791   */
14792
14793  int ip_rcv(struct sk_buff *skb, struct device *dev,
14794  struct packet_type *pt)
14795  {
14796      struct iphdr *iph = skb->h.iph;
14797      struct sock *raw_sk=NULL;
14798      unsigned char hash;
14799      unsigned char flag = 0;
14800      struct inet_protocol *ipprot;
14801      int brd=IS_MYADDR;
14802      struct options * opt = NULL;
14803      int is_frag=0;
14804      __u32 daddr;
14805
14806  #ifdef CONFIG_FIREWALL
14807      int fwres;
14808      __u16 rport;
14809  #endif
14810  #ifdef CONFIG_IP_MROUTE
14811      int mroute_pkt=0;
14812  #endif
14813
14814  #ifdef CONFIG_NET_IPV6
14815      /*
14816       *  Intercept IPv6 frames. We dump ST-II and invalid
14817  types just below..
14818       */
14819
14820      if(iph->version == 6)
14821          return ipv6_rcv(skb,dev,pt);
14822  #endif
14823
14824      ip_statistics.IpInReceives++;
14825
14826      /*
14827       *  Account for the packet (even if the packet is
14828       *  not accepted by the firewall!).
14829       */
14830
14831  #ifdef CONFIG_IP_ACCT
14832
14833  ip_fw_chk(iph,dev,NULL,ip_acct_chain,0,IP_FW_MODE_ACCT_IN
14834  );
14835  #endif
14836
```

p 525

```
14837         /*
14838          * Tag the ip header of this packet so we can find
14839 it
14840          */
14841
14842         skb->ip_hdr = iph;
14843
14844         /*
14845          * RFC1122: 3.1.2.2 MUST silently discard any IP
14846 frame that fails the checksum.
14847          * RFC1122: 3.1.2.3 MUST discard a frame with
14848 invalid source address [NEEDS FIXING].
14849          *
14850          * Is the datagram acceptable?
14851          *
14852          * 1.  Length at least the size of an ip header
14853          * 2.  Version of 4
14854          * 3.  Checksums correctly. [Speed optimisation for
14855 later, skip loopback checksums]
14856          * 4.  Doesn't have a bogus length
14857          * (5. We ought to check for IP multicast addresses
14858 and undefined types.. does this matter ?)
14859          */
14860
14861         if (skb->len<sizeof(struct iphdr) || iph->ihl<5 ||
14862 iph->version != 4 || ip_fast_csum((unsigned char *)iph,
14863 iph->ihl) !=0
14864                 || skb->len < ntohs(iph->tot_len))
14865         {
14866                 ip_statistics.IpInHdrErrors++;
14867                 kfree_skb(skb, FREE_WRITE);
14868                 return(0);
14869         }
14870
14871         /*
14872          * Our transport medium may have padded the buffer
14873 out. Now we know it
14874          * is IP we can trim to the true length of the
14875 frame.
14876          * Note this now means skb->len holds
14877 ntohs(iph->tot_len).
14878          */
14879
14880         skb_trim(skb,ntohs(iph->tot_len));
14881
14882         /*
14883          * Try to select closest <src,dst> alias device, if
14884 any.
```

```
14885          * net_alias_dev_rx32 returns main device if it
14886          * fails to found other.
14887          *       If successful, also incr. alias rx count.
14888          *
14889          * Only makes sense for unicasts - Thanks ANK.
14890          */
14891
14892 #ifdef CONFIG_NET_ALIAS
14893         if (skb->pkt_type == PACKET_HOST && iph->daddr !=
14894 skb->dev->pa_addr && net_alias_has(skb->dev)) {
14895                 skb->dev = dev = net_alias_dev_rx32(skb->dev,
14896 AF_INET, iph->saddr, iph->daddr);
14897         }
14898 #endif
14899
14900         if (iph->ihl > 5)
14901         {
14902                 skb->ip_summed = 0;
14903                 if (ip_options_compile(NULL, skb))
14904                         return(0);
14905                 opt = (struct options*)skb->proto_priv;
14906 #ifdef CONFIG_IP_NOSR
14907                 if (opt->srr)
14908                 {
14909                         kfree_skb(skb, FREE_READ);
14910                         return -EINVAL;
14911                 }
14912 #endif
14913         }
14914
14915 #if defined(CONFIG_IP_TRANSPARENT_PROXY) &&
14916 !defined(CONFIG_IP_ALWAYS_DEFRAG)
14917 #define CONFIG_IP_ALWAYS_DEFRAG 1
14918 #endif
14919 #ifdef CONFIG_IP_ALWAYS_DEFRAG
14920         /*
14921          * Defragment all incoming traffic before even
14922 looking at it.
14923          * If you have forwarding enabled, this makes the
14924 system a
14925          * defragmenting router.  Not a common thing.
14926          * You probably DON'T want to enable this unless you
14927 have to.
14928          * You NEED to use this if you want to use
14929 transparent proxying,
14930          * otherwise, we can't vouch for your sanity.
14931          */
14932
```

```
14933        /*
14934         *  See if the frame is fragmented.
14935         */
14936
14937        if(iph->frag_off)
14938        {
14939            if (iph->frag_off & htons(IP_MF))
14940                is_frag|=IPFWD_FRAGMENT;
14941            /*
14942             *  Last fragment ?
14943             */
14944
14945            if (iph->frag_off & htons(IP_OFFSET))
14946                is_frag|=IPFWD_LASTFRAG;
14947
14948            /*
14949             *  Reassemble IP fragments.
14950             */
14951
14952            if(is_frag)
14953            {
14954                /* Defragment. Obtain the complete packet if
14955    there is one */
14956                skb=ip_defrag(iph,skb,dev);
14957                if(skb==NULL)
14958                    return 0;
14959                skb->dev = dev;
14960                iph=skb->h.iph;
14961                is_frag = 0;
14962                /*
14963                 * When the reassembled packet gets
14964    forwarded, the ip
14965                 * header checksum should be correct.
14966                 * For better performance, this should
14967    actually only
14968                 * be done in that particular case, i.e. set
14969    a flag
14970                 * here and calculate the checksum in
14971    ip_forward.
14972                 */
14973                ip_send_check(iph);
14974            }
14975        }
14976
14977    #endif
14978        /*
14979         *  See if the firewall wants to dispose of the
14980    packet.
14981         */
14982
14983    #ifdef  CONFIG_FIREWALL
14984
14985        if ((fwres=call_in_firewall(PF_INET, skb->dev, iph,
14986    &rport))<FW_ACCEPT)
14987        {
14988            if(fwres==FW_REJECT)
14989                icmp_send(skb, ICMP_DEST_UNREACH,
14990    ICMP_PORT_UNREACH, 0, dev);
14991            kfree_skb(skb, FREE_WRITE);
14992            return 0;
14993        }
14994
14995    #ifdef  CONFIG_IP_TRANSPARENT_PROXY
14996        if (fwres==FW_REDIRECT)
14997            skb->redirport = rport;
14998        else
14999    #endif
15000            skb->redirport = 0;
15001    #endif
15002
15003    #ifndef CONFIG_IP_ALWAYS_DEFRAG
15004        /*
15005         *  Remember if the frame is fragmented.
15006         */
15007
15008        if(iph->frag_off)
15009        {
15010            if (iph->frag_off & htons(IP_MF))
15011                is_frag|=IPFWD_FRAGMENT;
15012            /*
15013             *  Last fragment ?
15014             */
15015
15016            if (iph->frag_off & htons(IP_OFFSET))
15017                is_frag|=IPFWD_LASTFRAG;
15018        }
15019
15020    #endif
15021        /*
15022         *  Do any IP forwarding required.  chk_addr() is
15023    expensive -- avoid it someday.
15024         *
15025         *  This is inefficient. While finding out if it is
15026    for us we could also compute
15027         *  the routing table entry. This is where the great
15028    unified cache theory comes
```

```
15029            *   in as and when someone implements it
15030            *
15031            *   For most hosts over 99% of packets match the
15032    first conditional
15033            *   and don't go via ip_chk_addr. Note: brd is set
15034    to IS_MYADDR at
15035            *   function entry.
15036            */
15037           daddr = iph->daddr;
15038    #ifdef CONFIG_IP_TRANSPARENT_PROXY
15039            /*
15040            *   ip_chksock adds still more overhead for
15041    forwarded traffic...
15042            */
15043           if ( iph->daddr == skb->dev->pa_addr ||
15044    skb->redirport || (brd = ip_chk_addr(iph->daddr)) != 0
15045    || ip_chksock(skb))
15046    #else
15047           if ( iph->daddr == skb->dev->pa_addr || (brd =
15048    ip_chk_addr(iph->daddr)) != 0)
15049    #endif
15050           {
15051               if (opt && opt->srr)
15052               {
15053                   int srrspace, srrptr;
15054                   __u32 nexthop;
15055                   unsigned char * optptr = ((unsigned char
15056    *)iph) + opt->srr;
15057
15058                   if (brd != IS_MYADDR || skb->pkt_type !=
15059    PACKET_HOST)
15060                   {
15061                       kfree_skb(skb, FREE_WRITE);
15062                       return 0;
15063                   }
15064
15065                   for ( srrptr=optptr[2], srrspace = optptr[1];
15066                     srrptr <= srrspace;
15067                     srrptr += 4
15068                    )
15069                   {
15070                       int brd2;
15071                       if (srrptr + 3 > srrspace)
15072                       {
15073                           icmp_send(skb, ICMP_PARAMETERPROB,
15074    0, opt->srr+2,
15075                               skb->dev);
15076                           kfree_skb(skb, FREE_WRITE);
```

```
15077                           return 0;
15078                       }
15079                       memcpy(&nexthop, &optptr[srrptr-1], 4);
15080                       if ((brd2 = ip_chk_addr(nexthop)) == 0)
15081                           break;
15082                       if (brd2 != IS_MYADDR)
15083                       {
15084
15085                           /*
15086                           *   ANK: should we implement weak
15087    tunneling of multicasts?
15088                           *   Are they obsolete? DVMRP specs
15089    (RFC-1075) is old enough...
15090                           *   [They are obsolete]
15091                           */
15092                           kfree_skb(skb, FREE_WRITE);
15093                           return -EINVAL;
15094                       }
15095                       memcpy(&daddr, &optptr[srrptr-1], 4);
15096                   }
15097                   if (srrptr <= srrspace)
15098                   {
15099                       opt->srr_is_hit = 1;
15100                       opt->is_changed = 1;
15101                       if (sysctl_ip_forward) {
15102                           if (ip_forward(skb, dev, is_frag,
15103    nexthop))
15104                               kfree_skb(skb, FREE_WRITE);
15105                       } else {
15106                           ip_statistics.IpInAddrErrors++;
15107                           kfree_skb(skb, FREE_WRITE);
15108                       }
15109                       return 0;
15110                   }
15111               }
15112
15113    #ifdef CONFIG_IP_MULTICAST
15114           if(!(dev->flags&IFF_ALLMULTI) &&
15115    brd==IS_MULTICAST && iph->daddr!=IGMP_ALL_HOSTS &&
15116    !(dev->flags&IFF_LOOPBACK))
15117           {
15118               /*
15119               *   Check it is for one of our groups
15120               */
15121               struct ip_mc_list *ip_mc=dev->ip_mc_list;
15122               do
15123               {
15124                   if(ip_mc==NULL)
```

```
15125                    {
15126                        kfree_skb(skb, FREE_WRITE);
15127                        return 0;
15128                    }
15129                    if(ip_mc->multiaddr==iph->daddr)
15130                        break;
15131                    ip_mc=ip_mc->next;
15132                }
15133                while(1);
15134            }
15135    #endif
15136
15137    #ifndef CONFIG_IP_ALWAYS_DEFRAG
15138            /*
15139             *    Reassemble IP fragments.
15140             */
15141
15142            if(is_frag)
15143            {
15144                /* Defragment. Obtain the complete packet if
15145    there is one */
15146                skb=ip_defrag(iph,skb,dev);
15147                if(skb==NULL)
15148                    return 0;
15149                skb->dev = dev;
15150                iph=skb->h.iph;
15151            }
15152
15153    #endif
15154
15155    #ifdef CONFIG_IP_MASQUERADE
15156            /*
15157             * Do we need to de-masquerade this packet?
15158             */
15159            {
15160                int ret = ip_fw_demasquerade(&skb,dev);
15161                if (ret < 0) {
15162                    kfree_skb(skb, FREE_WRITE);
15163                    return 0;
15164                }
15165
15166                if (ret)
15167                {
15168                    struct iphdr *iph=skb->h.iph;
15169                    if (ip_forward(skb, dev,
15170    IPFWD_MASQUERADED, iph->daddr))
15171                        kfree_skb(skb, FREE_WRITE);
15172                    return 0;
```

```
15173                }
15174            }
15175    #endif
15176
15177            /*
15178             *    Point into the IP datagram, just past the
15179    header.
15180             */
15181
15182            skb->ip_hdr = iph;
15183            skb->h.raw += iph->ihl*4;
15184
15185    #ifdef CONFIG_IP_MROUTE
15186            /*
15187             *    Check the state on multicast routing
15188    (multicast and not 224.0.0.z)
15189             */
15190
15191            if(brd==IS_MULTICAST &&
15192    (iph->daddr&htonl(0xFFFFFF00))!=htonl(0xE0000000))
15193                mroute_pkt=1;
15194
15195    #endif
15196            /*
15197             *    Deliver to raw sockets. This is fun as to
15198    avoid copies we want to make no surplus copies.
15199             *
15200             *    RFC 1122: SHOULD pass TOS value up to the
15201    transport layer.
15202             */
15203
15204            /* Note: See raw.c and net/raw.h,
15205    RAWV4_HTABLE_SIZE==MAX_INET_PROTOS */
15206            hash = iph->protocol & (MAX_INET_PROTOS - 1);
15207
15208            /*
15209             *    If there maybe a raw socket we must check -
15210    if not we don't care less
15211             */
15212
15213            if((raw_sk = raw_v4_htable[hash]) != NULL) {
15214                struct sock *sknext = NULL;
15215                struct sk_buff *skb1;
15216
15217                raw_sk = raw_v4_lookup(raw_sk, iph->protocol,
15218                            iph->saddr, iph->daddr);
15219                if(raw_sk) {     /* Any raw sockets */
15220                    do {
```

```
15221                /* Find the next */
15222                sknext = raw_v4_lookup(raw_sk->next,
15223                               iph->protocol,
15224                               iph->saddr,
15225                               iph->daddr);
15226                   if(sknext)
15227                       skb1 = skb_clone(skb,
15228    GFP_ATOMIC);
15229                   else
15230                       break;  /* One pending raw
15231    socket left */
15232                   if(skb1)
15233                       raw_rcv(raw_sk, skb1, dev,
15234    iph->saddr,daddr);
15235                   raw_sk = sknext;
15236               } while(raw_sk!=NULL);
15237
15238               /*
15239                * Here either raw_sk is the last raw
15240    socket, or NULL if none
15241                */
15242
15243               /*
15244                * We deliver to the last raw socket
15245    AFTER the protocol checks as it avoids a surplus copy
15246                */
15247           }
15248       }
15249
15250       /*
15251        * skb->h.raw now points at the protocol beyond
15252    the IP header.
15253        */
15254
15255       for (ipprot = (struct inet_protocol
15256    *)inet_protos[hash];ipprot != NULL;ipprot=(struct
15257    inet_protocol *)ipprot->next)
15258       {
15259           struct sk_buff *skb2;
15260
15261           if (ipprot->protocol != iph->protocol)
15262               continue;
15263               /*
15264                * See if we need to make a copy of it.
15265    This will
15266                * only be set if more than one protocol
15267    wants it.
15268                * and then not for the last one. If there
```

```
15269    is a pending
15270                *   raw delivery wait for that
15271                */
15272
15273    #ifdef CONFIG_IP_MROUTE
15274           if (ipprot->copy || raw_sk || mroute_pkt)
15275    #else
15276           if (ipprot->copy || raw_sk)
15277    #endif
15278           {
15279               skb2 = skb_clone(skb, GFP_ATOMIC);
15280               if(skb2==NULL)
15281                   continue;
15282           }
15283           else
15284           {
15285               skb2 = skb;
15286           }
15287           flag = 1;
15288
15289           /*
15290            * Pass on the datagram to each protocol
15291    that wants it,
15292            * based on the datagram protocol.  We
15293    should really
15294            * check the protocol handler's return
15295    values here...
15296            */
15297
15298           ipprot->handler(skb2, dev, opt, daddr,
15299               (ntohs(iph->tot_len) - (iph->ihl * 4)),
15300               iph->saddr, 0, ipprot);
15301       }
15302
15303       /*
15304        * All protocols checked.
15305        * If this packet was a broadcast, we may *not*
15306    reply to it, since that
15307        * causes (proven, grin) ARP storms and a
15308    leakage of memory (i.e. all
15309        * ICMP reply messages get queued up for
15310    transmission...)
15311        */
15312
15313    #ifdef CONFIG_IP_MROUTE
15314       /*
15315        * Forward the last copy to the multicast
15316    router. If
```

```
15317          *   there is a pending raw delivery however make
15318   a copy
15319          *   and forward that.
15320          */
15321
15322          if(mroute_pkt)
15323          {
15324              flag=1;
15325              if(raw_sk==NULL)
15326                  ipmr_forward(skb, is_frag);
15327              else
15328              {
15329                  struct sk_buff *skb2=skb_clone(skb,
15330   GFP_ATOMIC);
15331                  if(skb2)
15332                  {
15333                      skb2->free=1;
15334                      ipmr_forward(skb2, is_frag);
15335                  }
15336              }
15337          }
15338   #endif
15339
15340          if(raw_sk!=NULL)      /* Shift to last raw user */
15341              raw_rcv(raw_sk, skb, dev, iph->saddr, daddr);
15342          else if (!flag)       /* Free and report errors */
15343          {
15344              if (brd != IS_BROADCAST && brd!=IS_MULTICAST)
15345                  icmp_send(skb, ICMP_DEST_UNREACH,
15346   ICMP_PROT_UNREACH, 0, dev);
15347              kfree_skb(skb, FREE_WRITE);
15348          }
15349
15350          return(0);
15351      }
15352
15353      /*
15354       *  Do any unicast IP forwarding required.
15355       */
15356
15357      /*
15358       *  Don't forward multicast or broadcast frames.
15359       */
15360
15361      if(skb->pkt_type!=PACKET_HOST || brd==IS_BROADCAST)
15362      {
15363          kfree_skb(skb,FREE_WRITE);
15364          return 0;
15365      }
15366
15367      /*
15368       *  The packet is for another target. Forward the
15369   frame
15370       */
15371
15372      if (sysctl_ip_forward) {
15373          if (opt && opt->is_strictroute)
15374          {
15375              icmp_send(skb, ICMP_PARAMETERPROB, 0, 16,
15376   skb->dev);
15377              kfree_skb(skb, FREE_WRITE);
15378              return -1;
15379          }
15380          if (ip_forward(skb, dev, is_frag, iph->daddr))
15381              kfree_skb(skb, FREE_WRITE);
15382      } else {
15383   /*  printk("Machine %lx tried to use us as a forwarder
15384   to %lx but we have forwarding disabled!\n",
15385              iph->saddr,iph->daddr);*/
15386          ip_statistics.IpInAddrErrors++;
15387          kfree_skb(skb, FREE_WRITE);
15388      }
15389      return(0);
15390   }
15391
15392
```

usr/src/linux/net/ipv4/ip_options.c

```
15393   /*
15394    * INET        An implementation of the TCP/IP protocol
15395   suite for the LINUX
15396    *        operating system.  INET is implemented using the
15397   BSD Socket
15398    *        interface as the means of communication with the
15399   user level.
15400    *
15401    *        The options processing module for ip.c
15402    *
15403    * Authors: A.N.Kuznetsov
15404    *
15405    */
15406
15407   #include <linux/types.h>
15408   #include <linux/skbuff.h>
15409   #include <linux/ip.h>
15410   #include <linux/icmp.h>
```

```
15411    #include <linux/netdevice.h>
15412    #include <net/sock.h>
15413    #include <net/ip.h>
15414    #include <net/icmp.h>
15415
15416    /*
15417     * Write options to IP header, record destination
15418    address to
15419     * source route option, address of outgoing interface
15420     * (we should already know it, so that this  function is
15421    allowed be
15422     * called only after routing decision) and timestamp,
15423     * if we originate this datagram.
15424     */
15425
15426    void ip_options_build(struct sk_buff * skb, struct
15427    options * opt,
15428                         __u32 daddr, __u32 saddr,
15429                         int is_frag)
15430    {
15431        unsigned char * iph = (unsigned char*)skb->ip_hdr;
15432
15433        memcpy(skb->proto_priv, opt, sizeof(struct options));
15434        memcpy(iph+sizeof(struct iphdr), opt->__data,
15435    opt->optlen);
15436        opt = (struct options*)skb->proto_priv;
15437        opt->is_data = 0;
15438
15439        if (opt->srr)
15440            memcpy(iph+opt->srr+iph[opt->srr+1]-4, &daddr,
15441    4);
15442
15443        if (!is_frag)
15444        {
15445            if (opt->rr_needaddr)
15446                memcpy(iph+opt->rr+iph[opt->rr+2]-5, &saddr,
15447    4);
15448            if (opt->ts_needaddr)
15449                memcpy(iph+opt->ts+iph[opt->ts+2]-9, &saddr,
15450    4);
15451            if (opt->ts_needtime)
15452            {
15453                struct timeval tv;
15454                __u32 midtime;
15455                do_gettimeofday(&tv);
15456                midtime = htonl((tv.tv_sec % 86400) * 1000 +
15457    tv.tv_usec / 1000);
15458                memcpy(iph+opt->ts+iph[opt->ts+2]-5,
```

```
15459    &midtime, 4);
15460            }
15461            return;
15462        }
15463        if (opt->rr)
15464        {
15465            memset(iph+opt->rr, IPOPT_NOP, iph[opt->rr+1]);
15466            opt->rr = 0;
15467            opt->rr_needaddr = 0;
15468        }
15469        if (opt->ts)
15470        {
15471            memset(iph+opt->ts, IPOPT_NOP, iph[opt->ts+1]);
15472            opt->ts = 0;
15473            opt->ts_needaddr = opt->ts_needtime = 0;
15474        }
15475    }
15476
15477    int ip_options_echo(struct options * dopt, struct
15478    options * sopt,
15479                 __u32 daddr, __u32 saddr,
15480                 struct sk_buff * skb)
15481    {
15482        unsigned char *sptr, *dptr;
15483        int soffset, doffset;
15484        int optlen;
15485
15486        memset(dopt, 0, sizeof(struct options));
15487
15488        dopt->is_data = 1;
15489
15490        if (!sopt)
15491            sopt = (struct options*)skb->proto_priv;
15492
15493        if (sopt->optlen == 0)
15494        {
15495            dopt->optlen = 0;
15496            return 0;
15497        }
15498
15499        sptr = (sopt->is_data ? sopt->__data - sizeof(struct
15500    iphdr) :
15501            (unsigned char *)skb->ip_hdr);
15502        dptr = dopt->__data;
15503
15504        if (sopt->rr)
15505        {
15506            optlen  = sptr[sopt->rr+1];
```

```
15507              soffset = sptr[sopt->rr+2];
15508              dopt->rr = dopt->optlen + sizeof(struct iphdr);
15509              memcpy(dptr, sptr+sopt->rr, optlen);
15510              if (sopt->rr_needaddr && soffset <= optlen) {
15511                  if (soffset + 3 > optlen)
15512                      return -EINVAL;
15513                  dptr[2] = soffset + 4;
15514                  dopt->rr_needaddr = 1;
15515              }
15516              dptr     += optlen;
15517              dopt->optlen += optlen;
15518          }
15519          if (sopt->ts)
15520          {
15521              optlen  = sptr[sopt->ts+1];
15522              soffset = sptr[sopt->ts+2];
15523              dopt->ts = dopt->optlen + sizeof(struct iphdr);
15524              memcpy(dptr, sptr+sopt->ts, optlen);
15525              if (soffset <= optlen)
15526              {
15527                  if (sopt->ts_needaddr)
15528                  {
15529                      if (soffset + 3 > optlen)
15530                          return -EINVAL;
15531                      dopt->ts_needaddr = 1;
15532                      soffset += 4;
15533                  }
15534                  if (sopt->ts_needtime)
15535                  {
15536                      if (soffset + 3 > optlen)
15537                          return -EINVAL;
15538                      dopt->ts_needtime = 1;
15539                      soffset += 4;
15540                  }
15541                  if (((struct timestamp*)(dptr+1))->flags ==
15542  IPOPT_TS_PRESPEC)
15543                  {
15544                      __u32 addr;
15545                      memcpy(&addr, sptr+soffset-9, 4);
15546                      if (ip_chk_addr(addr) == 0)
15547                      {
15548                          dopt->ts_needtime = 0;
15549                          dopt->ts_needaddr = 0;
15550                          soffset -= 8;
15551                      }
15552                  }
15553                  dptr[2] = soffset;
15554          }
15555              dptr += optlen;
15556              dopt->optlen += optlen;
15557          }
15558          if (sopt->srr)
15559          {
15560              unsigned char * start = sptr+sopt->srr;
15561              __u32 faddr;
15562
15563              optlen  = start[1];
15564              soffset = start[2];
15565              doffset = 0;
15566              if (soffset > optlen)
15567                  soffset = optlen + 1;
15568              soffset -= 4;
15569              if (soffset > 3)
15570              {
15571                  memcpy(&faddr, &start[soffset-1], 4);
15572                  for (soffset-=4, doffset=4; soffset > 3;
15573  soffset-=4, doffset+=4)
15574                      memcpy(&dptr[doffset-1],
15575  &start[soffset-1], 4);
15576                  /*
15577                   * RFC1812 requires to fix illegal source
15578  routes.
15579                   */
15580                  if (memcmp(&saddr, &start[soffset+3], 4) ==
15581  0)
15582                      doffset -= 4;
15583              }
15584              if (doffset > 3)
15585              {
15586                  memcpy(&start[doffset-1], &daddr, 4);
15587                  dopt->faddr = faddr;
15588                  dptr[0] = start[0];
15589                  dptr[1] = doffset+3;
15590                  dptr[2] = 4;
15591                  dptr += doffset+3;
15592                  dopt->srr = dopt->optlen + sizeof(struct
15593  iphdr);
15594                  dopt->optlen += doffset+3;
15595                  dopt->is_strictroute = sopt->is_strictroute;
15596              }
15597          }
15598      while (dopt->optlen & 3)
15599      {
15600          *dptr++ = IPOPT_END;
15601          dopt->optlen++;
15602      }
```

```
15603        return 0;
15604    }
15605
15606    void ip_options_fragment(struct sk_buff * skb)
15607    {
15608        unsigned char * optptr = (unsigned char*)skb->ip_hdr;
15609        struct options * opt = (struct
15610    options*)skb->proto_priv;
15611        int   l = opt->optlen;
15612        int   optlen;
15613
15614        while (l > 0)
15615        {
15616            switch (*optptr)
15617            {
15618                case IPOPT_END:
15619                return;
15620                case IPOPT_NOOP:
15621                l--;
15622                optptr++;
15623                continue;
15624            }
15625            optlen = optptr[1];
15626            if (optlen<2 || optlen>l)
15627                return;
15628            if (!(*optptr & 0x80))
15629                memset(optptr, IPOPT_NOOP, optlen);
15630            l -= optlen;
15631            optptr += optlen;
15632        }
15633        opt->ts = 0;
15634        opt->rr = 0;
15635        opt->rr_needaddr = 0;
15636        opt->ts_needaddr = 0;
15637        opt->ts_needtime = 0;
15638        return;
15639    }
15640
15641    /*
15642     * Verify options and fill pointers in struct options.
15643     * Caller should clear *opt, and set opt->data.
15644     * If opt == NULL, then skb->data should point to IP
15645    header.
15646     */
15647
15648    int ip_options_compile(struct options * opt, struct
15649    sk_buff * skb)
15650    {
```

```
15651        int l;
15652        unsigned char * iph;
15653        unsigned char * optptr;
15654        int optlen;
15655        unsigned char * pp_ptr = NULL;
15656
15657        if (!opt)
15658        {
15659            opt = (struct options*)skb->proto_priv;
15660            memset(opt, 0, sizeof(struct options));
15661            iph = (unsigned char*)skb->ip_hdr;
15662            opt->optlen = ((struct iphdr *)iph)->ihl*4 -
15663        sizeof(struct iphdr);
15664            optptr = iph + sizeof(struct iphdr);
15665            opt->is_data = 0;
15666        }
15667        else
15668        {
15669            optptr = opt->is_data ? opt->__data : (unsigned
15670        char*)&skb->ip_hdr[1];
15671            iph = optptr - sizeof(struct iphdr);
15672        }
15673
15674        for (l = opt->optlen; l > 0; )
15675        {
15676            switch (*optptr)
15677            {
15678                case IPOPT_END:
15679                for (optptr++, l--; l>0; l--)
15680                {
15681                    if (*optptr != IPOPT_END)
15682                    {
15683                        *optptr = IPOPT_END;
15684                        opt->is_changed = 1;
15685                    }
15686                }
15687                goto eol;
15688                case IPOPT_NOOP:
15689                l--;
15690                optptr++;
15691                continue;
15692            }
15693            optlen = optptr[1];
15694            if (optlen<2 || optlen>l)
15695            {
15696                pp_ptr = optptr;
15697                goto error;
15698            }
```

p 514 ► 15657

```
15699              switch (*optptr)
15700              {
15701                  case IPOPT_SSRR:
15702                  case IPOPT_LSRR:
15703              if (optlen < 3)
15704              {
15705                  pp_ptr = optptr + 1;
15706                  goto error;
15707              }
15708              if (optptr[2] < 4)
15709              {
15710                  pp_ptr = optptr + 2;
15711                  goto error;
15712              }
15713              /* NB: cf RFC-1812 5.2.4.1 */
15714              if (opt->srr)
15715              {
15716                  pp_ptr = optptr;
15717                  goto error;
15718              }
15719              if (!skb)
15720              {
15721                  if (optptr[2] != 4 || optlen < 7 ||
15722  ((optlen-3) & 3))
15723                  {
15724                      pp_ptr = optptr + 1;
15725                      goto error;
15726                  }
15727              memcpy(&opt->faddr, &optptr[3], 4);
15728              if (optlen > 7)
15729                  memmove(&optptr[3], &optptr[7],
15730  optlen-7);
15731              }
15732              opt->is_strictroute = (optptr[0] ==
15733  IPOPT_SSRR);
15734              opt->srr = optptr - iph;
15735              break;
15736                  case IPOPT_RR:
15737              if (opt->rr)
15738              {
15739                  pp_ptr = optptr;
15740                  goto error;
15741              }
15742              if (optlen < 3)
15743              {
15744                  pp_ptr = optptr + 1;
15745                  goto error;
15746              }
15747              if (optptr[2] < 4)
15748              {
15749                  pp_ptr = optptr + 2;
15750                  goto error;
15751              }
15752              if (optptr[2] <= optlen)
15753              {
15754                  if (optptr[2]+3 > optlen)
15755                  {
15756                      pp_ptr = optptr + 2;
15757                      goto error;
15758                  }
15759                  if (skb)
15760                  {
15761                      memcpy(&optptr[optptr[2]-1],
15762  &skb->dev->pa_addr, 4);
15763                      opt->is_changed = 1;
15764                  }
15765                  optptr[2] += 4;
15766                  opt->rr_needaddr = 1;
15767              }
15768              opt->rr = optptr - iph;
15769              break;
15770                  case IPOPT_TIMESTAMP:
15771              if (opt->ts)
15772              {
15773                  pp_ptr = optptr;
15774                  goto error;
15775              }
15776              if (optlen < 4)
15777              {
15778                  pp_ptr = optptr + 1;
15779                  goto error;
15780              }
15781              if (optptr[2] < 5)
15782              {
15783                  pp_ptr = optptr + 2;
15784                  goto error;
15785              }
15786              if (optptr[2] <= optlen)
15787              {
15788                  struct timestamp * ts = (struct
15789  timestamp*)(optptr+1);
15790                  __u32 * timeptr = NULL;
15791                  if (ts->ptr+3 > ts->len)
15792                  {
15793                      pp_ptr = optptr + 2;
15794                      goto error;
```

```
15795                       }
15796                   switch (ts->flags)
15797                   {
15798                       case IPOPT_TS_TSONLY:
15799                   opt->ts = optptr - iph;
15800                   if (skb)
15801                       timeptr =
15802 (__u32*)&optptr[ts->ptr-1];
15803                   opt->ts_needtime = 1;
15804                   ts->ptr += 4;
15805                   break;
15806                       case IPOPT_TS_TSANDADDR:
15807                   if (ts->ptr+7 > ts->len)
15808                   {
15809                       pp_ptr = optptr + 2;
15810                       goto error;
15811                   }
15812                   opt->ts = optptr - iph;
15813                   if (skb)
15814                   {
15815                       memcpy(&optptr[ts->ptr-1],
15816 &skb->dev->pa_addr, 4);
15817                       timeptr =
15818 (__u32*)&optptr[ts->ptr+3];
15819                   }
15820                   opt->ts_needaddr = 1;
15821                   opt->ts_needtime = 1;
15822                   ts->ptr += 8;
15823                   break;
15824                       case IPOPT_TS_PRESPEC:
15825                   if (ts->ptr+7 > ts->len)
15826                   {
15827                       pp_ptr = optptr + 2;
15828                       goto error;
15829                   }
15830                   opt->ts = optptr - iph;
15831                   {
15832                       __u32 addr;
15833                       memcpy(&addr,
15834 &optptr[ts->ptr-1], 4);
15835                       if (ip_chk_addr(addr) == 0)
15836                           break;
15837                       if (skb)
15838                           timeptr =
15839 (__u32*)&optptr[ts->ptr+3];
15840                   }
15841                   opt->ts_needaddr = 1;
15842                   opt->ts_needtime = 1;
15843                   ts->ptr += 8;
15844                   break;
15845                       default:
15846                   pp_ptr = optptr + 3;
15847                   goto error;
15848                   }
15849                   if (timeptr)
15850                   {
15851                       struct timeval tv;
15852                       __u32   midtime;
15853                       do_gettimeofday(&tv);
15854                       midtime = htonl((tv.tv_sec % 86400)
15855 * 1000 + tv.tv_usec / 1000);
15856                       memcpy(timeptr, &midtime,
15857 sizeof(__u32));
15858                       opt->is_changed = 1;
15859                   }
15860               }
15861               else
15862               {
15863                   struct timestamp * ts = (struct
15864 timestamp*)(optptr+1);
15865                   if (ts->overflow == 15)
15866                   {
15867                       pp_ptr = optptr + 3;
15868                       goto error;
15869                   }
15870                   opt->ts = optptr - iph;
15871                   if (skb)
15872                   {
15873                       ts->overflow++;
15874                       opt->is_changed = 1;
15875                   }
15876               }
15877               break;
15878                 case IPOPT_SEC:
15879                 case IPOPT_SID:
15880                 default:
15881               if (!skb)
15882               {
15883                   pp_ptr = optptr;
15884                   goto error;
15885               }
15886               break;
15887           }
15888           l -= optlen;
15889           optptr += optlen;
15890       }
```

```
15891
15892   eol:
15893       if (!pp_ptr)
15894           return 0;
15895
15896   error:
15897       if (skb)
15898       {
15899           icmp_send(skb, ICMP_PARAMETERPROB, 0,
15900   pp_ptr-iph, skb->dev);
15901           kfree_skb(skb, FREE_READ);
15902       }
15903       return -EINVAL;
15904   }
15905
```

usr/src/linux/net/ipv4/ip_output.c

```
15906   /*
15907    * INET       An implementation of the TCP/IP protocol
15908   suite for the LINUX
15909    *        operating system.  INET is implemented using the
15910   BSD Socket
15911    *        interface as the means of communication with the
15912   user level.
15913    *
15914    *        The Internet Protocol (IP) output module.
15915    *
15916    * Version: @(#)ip.c    1.0.16b 9/1/93
15917    *
15918    * Authors: Ross Biro, <bir7@leland.Stanford.Edu>
15919    *        Fred N. van Kempen, <waltje@uWalt.NL.Mugnet.ORG>
15920    *        Donald Becker, <becker@super.org>
15921    *        Alan Cox, <Alan.Cox@linux.org>
15922    *        Richard Underwood
15923    *        Stefan Becker, <stefanb@yello.ping.de>
15924    *        Jorge Cwik, <jorge@laser.satlink.net>
15925    *        Arnt Gulbrandsen, <agulbra@nvg.unit.no>
15926    *
15927    *  See ip_input.c for original log
15928    *
15929    *  Fixes:
15930    *        Alan Cox    :   Missing nonblock feature in
15931   ip_build_xmit.
15932    *        Mike Kilburn   :   htons() missing in
15933   ip_build_xmit.
15934    *        Bradford Johnson:   Fix faulty handling of some
15935   frames when
15936    *                 no route is found.
15937    *        Alexander Demenshin:   Missing sk/skb free in
15938   ip_queue_xmit
15939    *                 (in case if packet not accepted by
15940    *                 output firewall rules)
15941    *        Elliot Poger    :   Added support
15942   for SO_BINDTODEVICE.
15943    *        Juan Jose Ciarlante:   sk/skb source address
15944   rewriting
15945    * Elena Apolinario Fdez de Sousa,:ipmr_forward never
15946   received multicast
15947    *  Juan-Mariano de Goyeneche    traffic generated
15948   locally.
15949    */
15950
15951   #include <asm/segment.h>
15952   #include <asm/system.h>
15953   #include <linux/types.h>
15954   #include <linux/kernel.h>
15955   #include <linux/sched.h>
15956   #include <linux/mm.h>
15957   #include <linux/string.h>
15958   #include <linux/errno.h>
15959   #include <linux/config.h>
15960
15961   #include <linux/socket.h>
15962   #include <linux/sockios.h>
15963   #include <linux/in.h>
15964   #include <linux/inet.h>
15965   #include <linux/netdevice.h>
15966   #include <linux/etherdevice.h>
15967   #include <linux/proc_fs.h>
15968   #include <linux/stat.h>
15969
15970   #include <net/snmp.h>
15971   #include <net/ip.h>
15972   #include <net/protocol.h>
15973   #include <net/route.h>
15974   #include <net/tcp.h>
15975   #include <net/udp.h>
15976   #include <linux/skbuff.h>
15977   #include <net/sock.h>
15978   #include <net/arp.h>
15979   #include <net/icmp.h>
15980   #include <net/raw.h>
15981   #include <net/checksum.h>
15982   #include <linux/igmp.h>
15983   #include <linux/ip_fw.h>
15984   #include <linux/firewall.h>
```

```
15985   #include <linux/mroute.h>
15986   #include <net/netlink.h>
15987
15988   /*
15989    *   Allows dynamic re-writing of packet's addresses.
15990    *       value & 3    do rewrite
15991    *       value & 2    be verbose
15992    *       value & 4    rewrite connected sockets too
15993    *   Currently implemented:
15994    *       tcp_output.c   if sk->state!=TCP_SYN_SENT
15995    *       ip_masq.c      if no packet has been received by
15996   tunnel
15997    */
15998   int sysctl_ip_dynaddr = 0;
15999
16000   /*
16001    *   Very Promisc source address re-assignment.
16002    *   ONLY acceptable if socket is NOT connected yet.
16003    *       Caller already checked sysctl_ip_dynaddr & 3 and
16004   EITHER
16005    *       sysctl_ip_dynaddr & 4 OR consistent sk->state
16006    *   (TCP_SYN_SENT for tcp, udp-connect sockets are set
16007   TCP_ESTABLISHED)
16008    */
16009
16010   int ip_rewrite_addrs (struct sock *sk, struct sk_buff
16011   *skb, struct device *dev)
16012   {
16013       u32 new_saddr = dev->pa_addr;
16014       struct iphdr *iph;
16015
16016       /*
16017        *   Be carefull: new_saddr must be !0
16018        */
16019       if (!new_saddr) {
16020           printk(KERN_WARNING "ip_rewrite_addrs():
16021   NULL device \"%s\" addr\n",
16022                       dev->name);
16023           return 0;
16024       }
16025
16026       /*
16027        *   Ouch!, this should not happen.
16028        */
16029       if (!sk->saddr || !sk->rcv_saddr) {
16030           printk(KERN_WARNING "ip_rewrite_addrs():
16031   not valid sock addrs: saddr=%08lX rcv_saddr=%08lX",
16032                       ntohl(sk->saddr),
```

```
16033   ntohl(sk->rcv_saddr));
16034           return 0;
16035       }
16036
16037       /*
16038        *   Be verbose if sysctl value & 2
16039        */
16040       if (sysctl_ip_dynaddr & 2) {
16041           printk(KERN_INFO "ip_rewrite_addrs():
16042   shifting saddr from %s",
16043                       in_ntoa(skb->saddr));
16044           printk(" to %s (state %d)\n",
16045   in_ntoa(new_saddr), sk->state);
16046       }
16047
16048       iph = skb->ip_hdr;
16049
16050       if (new_saddr != iph->saddr) {
16051           iph->saddr = new_saddr;
16052           skb->saddr = new_saddr;
16053           ip_send_check(iph);
16054       } else if (sysctl_ip_dynaddr & 2) {
16055           printk(KERN_WARNING "ip_rewrite_addrs():
16056   skb already changed (???).\n");
16057           return 0;
16058       }
16059
16060       /*
16061        *   Maybe whe are in a skb chain loop and socket
16062   address has
16063        *   yet been 'damaged'.
16064        */
16065       if (new_saddr != sk->saddr) {
16066           sk->saddr = new_saddr;
16067           sk->rcv_saddr = new_saddr;
16068           sk->prot->rehash(sk);
16069       } else if (sysctl_ip_dynaddr & 2)
16070           printk(KERN_NOTICE "ip_rewrite_addrs():
16071   no change needed for sock\n");
16072       return 1;
16073   }
16074
16075   /*
16076    *   Loop a packet back to the sender.
16077    */
16078
16079   static void ip_loopback(struct device *old_dev, struct
16080   sk_buff *skb)
```

```
16081    {
16082        struct device *dev=&loopback_dev;
16083        int len=ntohs(skb->ip_hdr->tot_len);
16084        struct sk_buff
16085    *newskb=dev_alloc_skb(len+dev->hard_header_len+15);
16086
16087        if(newskb==NULL)
16088            return;
16089
16090        newskb->link3=NULL;
16091        newskb->sk=NULL;
16092        newskb->dev=dev;
16093        newskb->saddr=skb->saddr;
16094        newskb->daddr=skb->daddr;
16095        newskb->raddr=skb->raddr;
16096        newskb->free=1;
16097        newskb->lock=0;
16098        newskb->users=0;
16099        newskb->pkt_type=skb->pkt_type;
16100
16101        /*
16102         *   Put a MAC header on the packet
16103         */
16104        ip_send(NULL,newskb, skb->ip_hdr->daddr, len, dev,
16105    skb->ip_hdr->saddr);
16106        /*
16107         *   Add the rest of the data space.
16108         */
16109        newskb->ip_hdr=(struct iphdr *)skb_put(newskb, len);
16110        memcpy(newskb->proto_priv, skb->proto_priv,
16111    sizeof(skb->proto_priv));
16112
16113        /*
16114         *   Copy the data
16115         */
16116        memcpy(newskb->ip_hdr,skb->ip_hdr,len);
16117
16118        /* Recurse. The device check against IFF_LOOPBACK
16119    will stop infinite recursion */
16120
16121        /*printk("Loopback output queued [%lX to %lX].\n",
16122    newskb->ip_hdr->saddr,newskb->ip_hdr->daddr);*/
16123        ip_queue_xmit(NULL, dev, newskb, 2);
16124    }
16125
16126
16127
16128    /*
```

```
16129     *  Take an skb, and fill in the MAC header.
16130     */
16131
16132    int ip_send(struct rtable * rt, struct sk_buff *skb,
16133    __u32 daddr, int len, struct device *dev, __u32 saddr)
16134    {
16135        int mac = 0;
16136
16137        skb->dev = dev;
16138        skb->arp = 1;
16139        skb->protocol = htons(ETH_P_IP);
16140        skb_reserve(skb,(dev->hard_header_len+15)&~15); /*
16141    16 byte aligned IP headers are always good */
16142        if (dev->hard_header)
16143        {
16144            /*
16145             *  Build a hardware header. Source address is
16146    our mac, destination unknown
16147             *        (rebuild header will sort this out)
16148             */
16149            if (rt && dev == rt->rt_dev && rt->rt_hh)
16150            {
16151
16152    memcpy(skb_push(skb,dev->hard_header_len),rt->rt_hh->hh_d
16153    ata,dev->hard_header_len);
16154                if (rt->rt_hh->hh_uptodate)
16155                    return dev->hard_header_len;
16156    #if RT_CACHE_DEBUG >= 2
16157                printk("ip_send: hh miss %08x via %08x\n",
16158    daddr, rt->rt_gateway);
16159    #endif
16160                skb->arp = 0;
16161                skb->raddr = daddr;
16162                return dev->hard_header_len;
16163            }
16164            mac = dev->hard_header(skb, dev, ETH_P_IP, NULL,
16165    NULL, len);
16166            if (mac < 0)
16167            {
16168                mac = -mac;
16169                skb->arp = 0;
16170                skb->raddr = daddr; /* next routing address
16171    */
16172            }
16173        }
16174        return mac;
16175    }
16176
```

```
16177  static int ip_send_room(struct rtable * rt, struct
16178  sk_buff *skb, __u32 daddr, int len, struct device *dev,
16179  __u32 saddr)
16180  {
16181      int mac = 0;
16182
16183      skb->dev = dev;
16184      skb->arp = 1;
16185      skb->protocol = htons(ETH_P_IP);
16186      skb_reserve(skb,MAX_HEADER);
16187      if (dev->hard_header)
16188      {
16189          if (rt && dev == rt->rt_dev && rt->rt_hh)
16190          {
16191
16192  memcpy(skb_push(skb,dev->hard_header_len),rt->rt_hh->hh_d
16193  ata,dev->hard_header_len);
16194              if (rt->rt_hh->hh_uptodate)
16195                  return dev->hard_header_len;
16196  #if RT_CACHE_DEBUG >= 2
16197              printk("ip_send_room: hh miss %08x via
16198  %08x\n", daddr, rt->rt_gateway);
16199  #endif
16200              skb->arp = 0;
16201              skb->raddr = daddr;
16202              return dev->hard_header_len;
16203          }
16204          mac = dev->hard_header(skb, dev, ETH_P_IP, NULL,
16205  NULL, len);
16206          if (mac < 0)
16207          {
16208              mac = -mac;
16209              skb->arp = 0;
16210              skb->raddr = daddr; /* next routing address
16211  */
16212          }
16213      }
16214      return mac;
16215  }
16216
16217  int ip_id_count = 0;
16218
16219  /*
16220   * This routine builds the appropriate hardware/IP
16221  headers for
16222   * the routine.  It assumes that if *dev != NULL then the
16223   * protocol knows what it's doing, otherwise it uses the
16224   * routing/ARP tables to select a device struct.
16225   */
16226  int ip_build_header(struct sk_buff *skb, __u32 saddr,
16227  __u32 daddr,
16228          struct device **dev, int type, struct options
16229  *opt,
16230          int len, int tos, int ttl, struct rtable ** rp)
16231  {
16232      struct rtable *rt;
16233      __u32 raddr;
16234      int tmp;
16235      struct iphdr *iph;
16236      __u32 final_daddr = daddr;
16237
16238
16239      if (opt && opt->srr)
16240          daddr = opt->faddr;
16241
16242      /*
16243       * See if we need to look up the device.
16244       */
16245
16246  #ifdef CONFIG_IP_MULTICAST
16247      if(MULTICAST(daddr) && *dev==NULL && skb->sk &&
16248  *skb->sk->ip_mc_name)
16249          *dev=dev_get(skb->sk->ip_mc_name);
16250  #endif
16251      if (rp)
16252      {
16253          rt = ip_check_route(rp, daddr, skb->localroute,
16254  *dev);
16255          /*
16256           * If rp != NULL rt_put following below should
16257  not
16258           * release route, so that...
16259           */
16260          if (rt)
16261              atomic_inc(&rt->rt_refcnt);
16262      }
16263      else
16264          rt = ip_rt_route(daddr, skb->localroute, *dev);
16265
16266
16267      if (*dev == NULL)
16268      {
16269          if (rt == NULL)
16270          {
16271              ip_statistics.IpOutNoRoutes++;
16272              return(-ENETUNREACH);
```

```
16273                }
16274
16275            *dev = rt->rt_dev;
16276        }
16277
16278        if ((LOOPBACK(saddr) && !LOOPBACK(daddr)) || !saddr)
16279            saddr = rt ? rt->rt_src : (*dev)->pa_addr;
16280
16281    raddr = rt ? rt->rt_gateway : daddr;
16282
16283        if (opt && opt->is_strictroute && rt &&
16284  (rt->rt_flags & RTF_GATEWAY))
16285        {
16286            ip_rt_put(rt);
16287            ip_statistics.IpOutNoRoutes++;
16288            return -ENETUNREACH;
16289        }
16290
16291        /*
16292         *  Now build the MAC header.
16293         */
16294
16295        if (type==IPPROTO_TCP)
16296            tmp = ip_send_room(rt, skb, raddr, len, *dev,
16297  saddr);
16298        else
16299            tmp = ip_send(rt, skb, raddr, len, *dev, saddr);
16300
16301        ip_rt_put(rt);
16302
16303        /*
16304         *  Book keeping
16305         */
16306
16307        skb->dev = *dev;
16308        skb->saddr = saddr;
16309
16310        /*
16311         *  Now build the IP header.
16312         */
16313
16314        /*
16315         *  If we are using IPPROTO_RAW, then we don't need
16316  an IP header, since
16317         *  one is being supplied to us by the user
16318         */
16319
16320        if(type == IPPROTO_RAW)
```

```
16321            return (tmp);
16322
16323        /*
16324         *  Build the IP addresses
16325         */
16326
16327        if (opt)
16328            iph=(struct iphdr *)skb_put(skb,sizeof(struct
16329  iphdr) + opt->optlen);
16330        else
16331            iph=(struct iphdr *)skb_put(skb,sizeof(struct
16332  iphdr));
16333
16334        iph->version  = 4;
16335        iph->ihl      = 5;
16336        iph->tos      = tos;
16337        iph->frag_off = 0;
16338        iph->ttl      = ttl;
16339        iph->daddr    = daddr;
16340        iph->saddr    = saddr;
16341        iph->protocol = type;
16342        skb->ip_hdr   = iph;
16343
16344        if (!opt || !opt->optlen)
16345            return sizeof(struct iphdr) + tmp;
16346        iph->ihl += opt->optlen>>2;
16347        ip_options_build(skb, opt, final_daddr,
16348  (*dev)->pa_addr, 0);
16349        return iph->ihl*4 + tmp;
16350  }
16351
16352
16353  /*
16354   *  Generate a checksum for an outgoing IP datagram.
16355   */
16356
16357  void ip_send_check(struct iphdr *iph)
16358  {
16359      iph->check = 0;
16360      iph->check = ip_fast_csum((unsigned char *)iph,
16361  iph->ihl);
16362  }
16363
16364
16365  /*
16366   *  If a sender wishes the packet to remain unfreed
16367   *  we add it to his send queue. This arguably belongs
16368   *  in the TCP level since nobody else uses it. BUT
```

```
16369    *   remember IPng might change all the rules.
16370    */
16371   static inline void add_to_send_queue(struct sock * sk,
16372   struct sk_buff * skb)
16373   {
16374       unsigned long flags;
16375
16376       /* The socket now has more outstanding blocks */
16377       sk->packets_out++;
16378
16379       /* Protect the list for a moment */
16380       save_flags(flags);
16381       cli();
16382
16383       if (skb->link3 != NULL)
16384       {
16385           NETDEBUG(printk("ip.c: link3 != NULL\n"));
16386           skb->link3 = NULL;
16387       }
16388       if (sk->send_head == NULL)
16389       {
16390           sk->send_tail = skb;
16391           sk->send_head = skb;
16392           sk->send_next = skb;
16393       }
16394       else
16395       {
16396           sk->send_tail->link3 = skb;
16397           sk->send_tail = skb;
16398       }
16399       restore_flags(flags);
16400   }
16401
16402
16403   /*
16404    * Queues a packet to be sent, and starts the transmitter
16405    * if necessary.  if free = 1 then we free the block
16406   after
16407    * transmit, otherwise we don't. If free==2 we not only
16408    * free the block but also don't assign a new ip seq
16409   number.
16410    * This routine also needs to put in the total length,
16411    * and compute the checksum
16412    */
16413
16414   void ip_queue_xmit(struct sock *sk, struct device *dev,
16415               struct sk_buff *skb, int free)
16416   {
```

```
16417       unsigned int tot_len;
16418       struct iphdr *iph;
16419
16420       IS_SKB(skb);
16421
16422       /*
16423        * Do some book-keeping in the packet for later
16424        */
16425
16426       skb->sk = sk;
16427       skb->dev = dev;
16428       skb->when = jiffies;
16429
16430       /*
16431        * Find the IP header and set the length. This is
16432   bad
16433        * but once we get the skb data handling code in the
16434        * hardware will push its header sensibly and we
16435   will
16436        * set skb->ip_hdr to avoid this mess and the fixed
16437        * header length problem
16438        */
16439
16440       iph = skb->ip_hdr;
16441       tot_len = skb->len - (((unsigned char *)iph) -
16442   skb->data);
16443       iph->tot_len = htons(tot_len);
16444
16445       switch (free) {
16446           /* No reassigning numbers to fragments... */
16447           default:
16448               free = 1;
16449               break;
16450           case 0:
16451               add_to_send_queue(sk, skb);
16452               /* fall through */
16453           case 1:
16454               iph->id = htons(ip_id_count++);
16455       }
16456
16457       skb->free = free;
16458
16459       /* Sanity check */
16460       if (dev == NULL)
16461           goto no_device;
16462
16463   #ifdef CONFIG_FIREWALL
16464       if (call_out_firewall(PF_INET, skb->dev, iph, NULL)
```

```
16465    < FW_ACCEPT)
16466            goto out;
16467    #endif
16468
16469        /*
16470         *  Do we need to fragment. Again this is
16471    inefficient.
16472         *  We need to somehow lock the original buffer and
16473    use
16474         *  bits of it.
16475         */
16476
16477        if (tot_len > dev->mtu)
16478            goto fragment;
16479
16480        /*
16481         *  Add an IP checksum
16482         */
16483
16484        ip_send_check(iph);
16485
16486        /*
16487         *  More debugging. You cannot queue a packet
16488    already on a list
16489         *  Spot this and moan loudly.
16490         */
16491        if (skb->next != NULL)
16492        {
16493            NETDEBUG(printk("ip_queue_xmit: next !=
16494    NULL\n"));
16495            skb_unlink(skb);
16496        }
16497
16498        /*
16499         *  If the indicated interface is up and running,
16500    send the packet.
16501         */
16502
16503        ip_statistics.IpOutRequests++;
16504    #ifdef CONFIG_IP_ACCT
16505
16506    ip_fw_chk(iph,dev,NULL,ip_acct_chain,0,IP_FW_MODE_ACCT_OU
16507    T);
16508    #endif
16509
16510    #ifdef CONFIG_IP_MULTICAST
16511
16512        /*
16513         *  Multicasts are looped back for other local users
16514         */
16515
16516        if (MULTICAST(iph->daddr) &&
16517    !(dev->flags&IFF_LOOPBACK))
16518        {
16519            if(sk==NULL || sk->ip_mc_loop)
16520            {
16521                if(iph->daddr==IGMP_ALL_HOSTS ||
16522    (dev->flags&IFF_ALLMULTI))
16523                {
16524                    ip_loopback(dev,skb);
16525                }
16526                else
16527                {
16528                    struct ip_mc_list *imc=dev->ip_mc_list;
16529                    while(imc!=NULL)
16530                    {
16531                        if(imc->multiaddr==iph->daddr)
16532                        {
16533                            ip_loopback(dev,skb);
16534                            break;
16535                        }
16536                        imc=imc->next;
16537                    }
16538                }
16539            }
16540            /* Multicasts with ttl 0 must not go beyond the
16541    host */
16542
16543            if (iph->ttl==0)
16544                goto out;
16545        }
16546    #endif
16547        if ((dev->flags & IFF_BROADCAST) && !(dev->flags &
16548    IFF_LOOPBACK)
16549            && (iph->daddr==dev->pa_brdaddr ||
16550    iph->daddr==0xFFFFFFFF))
16551            ip_loopback(dev,skb);
16552
16553        if (dev->flags & IFF_UP)
16554        {
16555            /*
16556             *  If we have an owner use its priority setting,
16557             *  otherwise use NORMAL
16558             */
16559            int priority = SOPRI_NORMAL;
16560            if (sk)
```

```
16561              priority = sk->priority;
16562
16563          dev_queue_xmit(skb, dev, priority);
16564          return;
16565      }
16566      if(sk)
16567          sk->err = ENETDOWN;
16568      ip_statistics.IpOutDiscards++;
16569 out:
16570      if (free)
16571          kfree_skb(skb, FREE_WRITE);
16572      return;
16573
16574 no_device:
16575      NETDEBUG(printk("IP: ip_queue_xmit dev = NULL\n"));
16576      goto out;
16577
16578 fragment:
16579      ip_fragment(sk,skb,dev,0);
16580      goto out;
16581 }
16582
16583
16584 /*
16585  *  Build and send a packet, with as little as one copy
16586  *
16587  *  Doesn't care much about ip options... option length
16588 can be
16589  *  different for fragment at 0 and other fragments.
16590  *
16591  *  Note that the fragment at the highest offset is sent
16592 first,
16593  *  so the getfrag routine can fill in the TCP/UDP
16594 checksum header
16595  *  field in the last fragment it sends... actually it
16596 also helps
16597  *  the reassemblers, they can put most packets in at
16598 the head of
16599  *  the fragment queue, and they know the total size in
16600 advance. This
16601  *  last feature will measurable improve the Linux
16602 fragment handler.
16603  *
16604  *  The callback has five args, an arbitrary pointer
16605 (copy of frag),
16606  *  the source IP address (may depend on the routing
16607 table), the
16608  *  destination address (char *), the offset to copy
```

```
16609  from, and the
16610  *  length to be copied.
16611  *
16612  */
16613
16614 int ip_build_xmit(struct sock *sk,
16615          void getfrag (const void *,
16616              __u32,
16617              char *,
16618              unsigned int,
16619              unsigned int),
16620          const void *frag,
16621          unsigned short int length,
16622          __u32 daddr,
16623          __u32 user_saddr,
16624          struct options * opt,
16625          int flags,
16626          int type,
16627          int noblock)
16628 {
16629      struct rtable *rt;
16630      unsigned int fraglen, maxfraglen, fragheaderlen;
16631      int offset, mf;
16632      __u32 saddr;
16633      unsigned short id;
16634      struct iphdr *iph;
16635      __u32 raddr;
16636      struct device *dev = NULL;
16637      struct hh_cache * hh=NULL;
16638      int nfrags=0;
16639      __u32 true_daddr = daddr;
16640
16641      if (opt && opt->srr && !sk->ip_hdrincl)
16642          daddr = opt->faddr;
16643
16644      ip_statistics.IpOutRequests++;
16645
16646 #ifdef CONFIG_IP_MULTICAST
16647      if(MULTICAST(daddr) && *sk->ip_mc_name)
16648      {
16649          dev=dev_get(sk->ip_mc_name);
16650          if(!dev)
16651              return -ENODEV;
16652          rt=NULL;
16653          if (sk->saddr && (!LOOPBACK(sk->saddr) ||
16654 LOOPBACK(daddr)))
16655              saddr = sk->saddr;
16656          else
```

p 516 ▶ 16641

```
16657              saddr = dev->pa_addr;
16658          }
16659      else
16660      {
16661 #endif
16662          rt = ip_check_route(&sk->ip_route_cache, daddr,
16663                   sk->localroute ||
16664 (flags&MSG_DONTROUTE) ||
16665                      (opt && opt->is_strictroute),
16666 sk->bound_device);
16667          if (rt == NULL)
16668          {
16669              ip_statistics.IpOutNoRoutes++;
16670              return(-ENETUNREACH);
16671          }
16672          saddr = rt->rt_src;
16673
16674          hh = rt->rt_hh;
16675
16676          if (sk->saddr && (!LOOPBACK(sk->saddr) ||
16677 LOOPBACK(daddr)))
16678              saddr = sk->saddr;
16679
16680          dev=rt->rt_dev;
16681 #ifdef CONFIG_IP_MULTICAST
16682      }
16683      if (rt && !dev)
16684          dev = rt->rt_dev;
16685 #endif
16686      if (user_saddr)
16687          saddr = user_saddr;
16688
16689      raddr = rt ? rt->rt_gateway : daddr;
16690      /*
16691       *  Now compute the buffer space we require
16692       */
16693
16694      /*
16695       *  Try the simple case first. This leaves
16696 broadcast, multicast, fragmented frames, and by
16697       *  choice RAW frames within 20 bytes of maximum
16698 size(rare) to the long path
16699       */
16700
16701      if (!sk->ip_hdrincl) {
16702          length += sizeof(struct iphdr);
16703          if(opt) length += opt->optlen;
16704      }
```

```
16705
16706      if(length <= dev->mtu && !MULTICAST(daddr) &&
16707 daddr!=0xFFFFFFFF && daddr!=dev->pa_brdaddr)
16708      {
16709          int error;
16710          struct sk_buff *skb=sock_alloc_send_skb(sk,
16711 length+15+dev->hard_header_len,0, noblock, &error);
16712          if(skb==NULL)
16713          {
16714              ip_statistics.IpOutDiscards++;
16715              return error;
16716          }
16717          skb->dev=dev;
16718          skb->protocol = htons(ETH_P_IP);
16719          skb->free=1;
16720          skb->when=jiffies;
16721          skb->sk=sk;
16722          skb->arp=0;
16723          skb->saddr=saddr;
16724          skb->raddr = raddr;
16725          skb_reserve(skb,(dev->hard_header_len+15)&~15);
16726          if (hh)
16727          {
16728              skb->arp=1;
16729
16730 memcpy(skb_push(skb,dev->hard_header_len),hh->hh_data,dev
16731 ->hard_header_len);
16732              if (!hh->hh_uptodate)
16733              {
16734                  skb->arp = 0;
16735 #if RT_CACHE_DEBUG >= 2
16736                  printk("ip_build_xmit: hh miss %08x via
16737 %08x\n", rt->rt_dst, rt->rt_gateway);
16738 #endif
16739              }
16740          }
16741          else if(dev->hard_header)
16742          {
16743
16744 if(dev->hard_header(skb,dev,ETH_P_IP,NULL,NULL,0)>0)
16745                  skb->arp=1;
16746          }
16747          else
16748              skb->arp=1;
16749          skb->ip_hdr=iph=(struct iphdr
16750 *)skb_put(skb,length);
16751          dev_lock_list();
16752          if(!sk->ip_hdrincl)
```

p 517

```
16753                {
16754                    iph->version=4;
16755                    iph->ihl=5;
16756                    iph->tos=sk->ip_tos;
16757                    iph->tot_len = htons(length);
16758                    iph->id=htons(ip_id_count++);
16759                    iph->frag_off = 0;
16760                    iph->ttl=sk->ip_ttl;
16761                    iph->protocol=type;
16762                    iph->saddr=saddr;
16763                    iph->daddr=daddr;
16764                    if (opt)
16765                    {
16766                        iph->ihl += opt->optlen>>2;
16767                        ip_options_build(skb, opt,
16768                            true_daddr, dev->pa_addr, 0);
16769                    }
16770                    iph->check=0;
16771                    iph->check = ip_fast_csum((unsigned char
16772    *)iph, iph->ihl);
16773                    getfrag(frag,saddr,((char
16774    *)iph)+iph->ihl*4,0, length-iph->ihl*4);
16775                }
16776            else
16777                    getfrag(frag,saddr,(void *)iph,0,length);
16778            dev_unlock_list();
16779    #ifdef CONFIG_FIREWALL
16780            if(call_out_firewall(PF_INET, skb->dev, iph,
16781    NULL)< FW_ACCEPT)
16782            {
16783                    kfree_skb(skb, FREE_WRITE);
16784                    return -EPERM;
16785            }
16786    #endif
16787    #ifdef CONFIG_IP_ACCT
16788
16789    ip_fw_chk(iph,dev,NULL,ip_acct_chain,0,IP_FW_MODE_ACCT_OU
16790    T);
16791    #endif
16792            if(dev->flags&IFF_UP)
16793                    dev_queue_xmit(skb,dev,sk->priority);
16794            else
16795            {
16796                    ip_statistics.IpOutDiscards++;
16797                    kfree_skb(skb, FREE_WRITE);
16798            }
16799            return 0;
16800        }
```

```
16801        if (!sk->ip_hdrincl)
16802            length -= sizeof(struct iphdr);
16803
16804        if(opt)
16805        {
16806            length -= opt->optlen;
16807            fragheaderlen = dev->hard_header_len +
16808    sizeof(struct iphdr) + opt->optlen;
16809            maxfraglen = ((dev->mtu-sizeof(struct
16810    iphdr)-opt->optlen) & ~7) + fragheaderlen;
16811        }
16812        else
16813        {
16814            fragheaderlen = dev->hard_header_len;
16815            if(!sk->ip_hdrincl)
16816                fragheaderlen += 20;
16817
16818            /*
16819             *    Fragheaderlen is the size of 'overhead' on
16820    each buffer. Now work
16821             *    out the size of the frames to send.
16822             */
16823
16824            maxfraglen = ((dev->mtu-20) & ~7) +
16825    fragheaderlen;
16826        }
16827
16828        /*
16829         *    Start at the end of the frame by handling the
16830    remainder.
16831         */
16832
16833        offset = length - (length % (maxfraglen -
16834    fragheaderlen));
16835
16836        /*
16837         *    Amount of memory to allocate for final fragment.
16838         */
16839
16840        fraglen = length - offset + fragheaderlen;
16841
16842        if(length-offset==0)
16843        {
16844            fraglen = maxfraglen;
16845            offset -= maxfraglen-fragheaderlen;
16846        }
16847
16848
```

```
16849        /*
16850         *  The last fragment will not have MF (more
16851   fragments) set.
16852         */
16853
16854        mf = 0;
16855
16856        /*
16857         *  Can't fragment raw packets
16858         */
16859
16860        if (sk->ip_hdrincl && offset > 0)
16861            return(-EMSGSIZE);
16862
16863        /*
16864         *  Lock the device lists.
16865         */
16866
16867        dev_lock_list();
16868
16869        /*
16870         *  Get an identifier
16871         */
16872
16873        id = htons(ip_id_count++);
16874
16875        /*
16876         *  Being outputting the bytes.
16877         */
16878
16879        do
16880        {
16881            struct sk_buff * skb;
16882            int error;
16883            char *data;
16884
16885            /*
16886             *  Get the memory we require with some space
16887   left for alignment.
16888             */
16889
16890            skb = sock_alloc_send_skb(sk, fraglen+15, 0,
16891   noblock, &error);
16892            if (skb == NULL)
16893            {
16894                ip_statistics.IpOutDiscards++;
16895                if(nfrags>1)
16896                    ip_statistics.IpFragCreates++;
```

```
16897                dev_unlock_list();
16898                return(error);
16899            }
16900
16901            /*
16902             *  Fill in the control structures
16903             */
16904
16905            skb->dev = dev;
16906            skb->protocol = htons(ETH_P_IP);
16907            skb->when = jiffies;
16908            skb->free = 1; /* dubious, this one */
16909            skb->sk = sk;
16910            skb->arp = 0;
16911            skb->saddr = saddr;
16912            skb->daddr = daddr;
16913            skb->raddr = raddr;
16914            skb_reserve(skb,(dev->hard_header_len+15)&~15);
16915            data = skb_put(skb,
16916   fraglen-dev->hard_header_len);
16917
16918            /*
16919             *  Save us ARP and stuff. In the optimal case
16920   we do no route lookup (route cache ok)
16921             *  no ARP lookup (arp cache ok) and output. The
16922   cache checks are still too slow but
16923             *  this can be fixed later. For gateway routes
16924   we ought to have a rt->.. header cache
16925             *  pointer to speed header cache builds for
16926   identical targets.
16927             */
16928
16929            if (hh)
16930            {
16931                skb->arp=1;
16932
16933   memcpy(skb_push(skb,dev->hard_header_len),hh->hh_data,dev
16934   ->hard_header_len);
16935                if (!hh->hh_uptodate)
16936                {
16937                    skb->arp = 0;
16938   #if RT_CACHE_DEBUG >= 2
16939                    printk("ip_build_xmit: hh miss %08x via
16940   %08x\n", rt->rt_dst, rt->rt_gateway);
16941   #endif
16942                }
16943            }
16944            else if (dev->hard_header)
```

```
16945                {
16946                    if(dev->hard_header(skb, dev, ETH_P_IP,
16947                            NULL, NULL, 0)>0)
16948                        skb->arp=1;
16949                }
16950            else
16951                skb->arp = 1;
16952
16953            /*
16954             *  Find where to start putting bytes.
16955             */
16956
16957            skb->ip_hdr = iph = (struct iphdr *)data;
16958
16959            /*
16960             *  Only write IP header onto non-raw packets
16961             */
16962
16963            if(!sk->ip_hdrincl)
16964            {
16965
16966                iph->version = 4;
16967                iph->ihl = 5; /* ugh */
16968                if (opt) {
16969                    iph->ihl += opt->optlen>>2;
16970                    ip_options_build(skb, opt,
16971                            true_daddr, dev->pa_addr,
16972 offset);
16973                }
16974                iph->tos = sk->ip_tos;
16975                iph->tot_len = htons(fraglen - fragheaderlen
16976 + iph->ihl*4);
16977                iph->id = id;
16978                iph->frag_off = htons(offset>>3);
16979                iph->frag_off |= mf;
16980 #ifdef CONFIG_IP_MULTICAST
16981                if (MULTICAST(daddr))
16982                    iph->ttl = sk->ip_mc_ttl;
16983                else
16984 #endif
16985                    iph->ttl = sk->ip_ttl;
16986                iph->protocol = type;
16987                iph->check = 0;
16988                iph->saddr = saddr;
16989                iph->daddr = daddr;
16990                iph->check = ip_fast_csum((unsigned char
16991 *)iph, iph->ihl);
16992                data += iph->ihl*4;
```

```
16993
16994                /*
16995                 *  Any further fragments will have MF set.
16996                 */
16997
16998                mf = htons(IP_MF);
16999            }
17000
17001            /*
17002             *  User data callback
17003             */
17004
17005            getfrag(frag, saddr, data, offset,
17006 fraglen-fragheaderlen);
17007
17008            /*
17009             *  Account for the fragment.
17010             */
17011
17012 #ifdef CONFIG_FIREWALL
17013            if(!offset && call_out_firewall(PF_INET,
17014 skb->dev, iph, NULL) < FW_ACCEPT)
17015            {
17016                kfree_skb(skb, FREE_WRITE);
17017                dev_unlock_list();
17018                return -EPERM;
17019            }
17020 #endif
17021 #ifdef CONFIG_IP_ACCT
17022            ip_fw_chk(iph, dev, NULL, ip_acct_chain, 0,
17023 IP_FW_MODE_ACCT_OUT);
17024 #endif
17025            offset -= (maxfraglen-fragheaderlen);
17026            fraglen = maxfraglen;
17027
17028 #ifdef CONFIG_IP_MULTICAST
17029
17030            /*
17031             *  Multicasts are looped back for other local
17032 users
17033             */
17034
17035            if (MULTICAST(daddr) &&
17036 !(dev->flags&IFF_LOOPBACK))
17037            {
17038 #ifdef CONFIG_IP_MROUTE
17039                /* We need this so that mrouted "hears" packets
17040 sent from the
```

```
17041                    same host it is running on... (jmel) */
17042                  if
17043   (mroute_socket&&(iph->protocol!=IPPROTO_IGMP))
17044                    {
17045
17046   if((skb->ip_hdr->daddr&htonl(0xFFFFFF00))!=htonl(0xE00000
17047   00))
17048                      {
17049                        struct sk_buff* skb2=skb_clone(skb,
17050   GFP_ATOMIC);
17051                        if(skb2)
17052                          {
17053                            skb2->free=1;
17054                            ipmr_forward(skb2,
17055   0);
17056                          }
17057                      }
17058                    }
17059   #endif
17060                  /*
17061                   *  Loop back any frames. The check for
17062   IGMP_ALL_HOSTS is because
17063                   *  you are always magically a member of
17064   this group.
17065                   *
17066                   *  Always loop back all host messages when
17067   running as a multicast router.
17068                   */
17069
17070                  if(sk==NULL || sk->ip_mc_loop)
17071                    {
17072                      if(daddr==IGMP_ALL_HOSTS ||
17073   (dev->flags&IFF_ALLMULTI))
17074                        ip_loopback(dev,skb);
17075                      else
17076                        {
17077                          struct ip_mc_list
17078   *imc=dev->ip_mc_list;
17079                          while(imc!=NULL)
17080                            {
17081                              if(imc->multiaddr==daddr)
17082                                {
17083                                  ip_loopback(dev,skb);
17084                                  break;
17085                                }
17086                              imc=imc->next;
17087                            }
17088                        }
17089                    }
17090
17091                  /*
17092                   *  Multicasts with ttl 0 must not go beyond
17093   the host. Fixme: avoid the
17094                   *  extra clone.
17095                   */
17096
17097                  if(skb->ip_hdr->ttl==0)
17098                    {
17099                      kfree_skb(skb, FREE_WRITE);
17100                      nfrags++;
17101                      continue;
17102                    }
17103                }
17104   #endif
17105
17106          nfrags++;
17107
17108          /*
17109           *  BSD loops broadcasts
17110           */
17111
17112          if((dev->flags&IFF_BROADCAST) &&
17113   (daddr==0xFFFFFFFF || daddr==dev->pa_brdaddr) &&
17114   !(dev->flags&IFF_LOOPBACK))
17115              ip_loopback(dev,skb);
17116
17117          /*
17118           *  Now queue the bytes into the device.
17119           */
17120
17121          if (dev->flags & IFF_UP)
17122          {
17123              dev_queue_xmit(skb, dev, sk->priority);
17124          }
17125          else
17126          {
17127              /*
17128               *  Whoops...
17129               */
17130
17131              ip_statistics.IpOutDiscards++;
17132              if(nfrags>1)
17133                  ip_statistics.IpFragCreates+=nfrags;
17134              kfree_skb(skb, FREE_WRITE);
17135              dev_unlock_list();
17136              /*
```

```
17137              *   BSD behaviour.
17138              */
17139             if(sk!=NULL)
17140                 sk->err=ENETDOWN;
17141             return(0); /* lose rest of fragments */
17142         }
17143     }
17144     while (offset >= 0);
17145     if(nfrags>1)
17146         ip_statistics.IpFragCreates+=nfrags;
17147     dev_unlock_list();
17148     return(0);
17149 }
17150
17151
17152 /*
17153  *   IP protocol layer initialiser
17154  */
17155
17156 static struct packet_type ip_packet_type =
17157 {
17158     0,  /* MUTTER ntohs(ETH_P_IP),*/
17159     NULL,   /* All devices */
17160     ip_rcv,
17161     NULL,
17162     NULL,
17163 };
17164
17165 #ifdef CONFIG_RTNETLINK
17166
17167 /*
17168  *   Netlink hooks for IP
17169  */
17170
17171 void ip_netlink_msg(unsigned long msg, __u32 daddr,
17172 __u32 gw, __u32 mask, short flags, short metric, char
17173 *name)
17174 {
17175     struct sk_buff *skb=alloc_skb(sizeof(struct
17176 netlink_rtinfo), GFP_ATOMIC);
17177     struct netlink_rtinfo *nrt;
17178     struct sockaddr_in *s;
17179     if(skb==NULL)
17180         return;
17181     skb->free=1;
17182     nrt=(struct netlink_rtinfo *)skb_put(skb,
17183 sizeof(struct netlink_rtinfo));
17184     nrt->rtmsg_type=msg;
```

```
17185     s=(struct sockaddr_in *)&nrt->rtmsg_dst;
17186     s->sin_family=AF_INET;
17187     s->sin_addr.s_addr=daddr;
17188     s=(struct sockaddr_in *)&nrt->rtmsg_gateway;
17189     s->sin_family=AF_INET;
17190     s->sin_addr.s_addr=gw;
17191     s=(struct sockaddr_in *)&nrt->rtmsg_genmask;
17192     s->sin_family=AF_INET;
17193     s->sin_addr.s_addr=mask;
17194     nrt->rtmsg_flags=flags;
17195     nrt->rtmsg_metric=metric;
17196     strcpy(nrt->rtmsg_device,name);
17197     if (netlink_post(NETLINK_ROUTE, skb))
17198         kfree_skb(skb, FREE_WRITE);
17199 }
17200
17201 #endif
17202
17203 /*
17204  *   Device notifier
17205  */
17206
17207 static int ip_rt_event(struct notifier_block *this,
17208 unsigned long event, void *ptr)
17209 {
17210     struct device *dev=ptr;
17211     if(event==NETDEV_DOWN)
17212     {
17213         ip_netlink_msg(RTMSG_DELDEVICE,
17214 0,0,0,0,0,0,dev->name);
17215         ip_rt_flush(dev);
17216     }
17217 /*
17218  *   Join the initial group if multicast.
17219  */
17220     if(event==NETDEV_UP)
17221     {
17222 #ifdef CONFIG_IP_MULTICAST
17223         ip_mc_allhost(dev);
17224 #endif
17225         ip_netlink_msg(RTMSG_NEWDEVICE,
17226 0,0,0,0,0,dev->name);
17227         ip_rt_update(NETDEV_UP, dev);
17228     }
17229     return NOTIFY_DONE;
17230 }
17231
17232 struct notifier_block ip_rt_notifier={
```

p 528
p 528

```
17233        ip_rt_event,
17234        NULL,
17235        0
17236 };
17237
17238 /*
17239  *   IP registers the packet type and then calls the
17240 subprotocol initialisers
17241  */
17242
17243 void ip_init(void)
17244 {
17245        ip_packet_type.type=htons(ETH_P_IP);
17246        dev_add_pack(&ip_packet_type);
17247
17248        /* So we flush routes when a device is downed */
17249        register_netdevice_notifier(&ip_rt_notifier);
17250
17251 /*   ip_raw_init();
17252      ip_packet_init();
17253      ip_tcp_init();
17254      ip_udp_init();*/
17255
17256 #ifdef CONFIG_IP_MULTICAST
17257 #ifdef CONFIG_PROC_FS
17258      proc_net_register(&(struct proc_dir_entry) {
17259          PROC_NET_IGMP, 4, "igmp",
17260          S_IFREG | S_IRUGO, 1, 0, 0,
17261          0, &proc_net_inode_operations,
17262          ip_mc_procinfo
17263      });
17264 #endif
17265 #endif
17266 }
17267
```

usr/src/linux/net/ipv4/ip_sockglue.c

```
17268 /*
17269  * INET      An implementation of the TCP/IP protocol
17270 suite for the LINUX
17271  *          operating system.  INET is implemented using the
17272 BSD Socket
17273  *          interface as the means of communication with the
17274 user level.
17275  *
17276  *          The IP to API glue.
17277  *
17278  * Authors: see ip.c
```

```
17279  *
17280  * Fixes:
17281  *       Many          :   Split from ip.c , see ip.c for
17282 history.
17283  *       Martin Mares   :    TOS setting fixed.
17284  *       Alan Cox    :    Fixed a couple of oopses in
17285 Martin's
17286  *                         TOS tweaks.
17287  *       Elliot Poger    :         Added support
17288 for SO_BINDTODEVICE.
17289  */
17290
17291 #include <linux/config.h>
17292 #include <linux/types.h>
17293 #include <linux/mm.h>
17294 #include <linux/sched.h>
17295 #include <linux/skbuff.h>
17296 #include <linux/ip.h>
17297 #include <linux/icmp.h>
17298 #include <linux/netdevice.h>
17299 #include <net/sock.h>
17300 #include <net/ip.h>
17301 #include <net/icmp.h>
17302 #include <linux/tcp.h>
17303 #include <linux/udp.h>
17304 #include <linux/firewall.h>
17305 #include <linux/ip_fw.h>
17306 #include <net/checksum.h>
17307 #include <linux/route.h>
17308 #include <linux/mroute.h>
17309 #include <net/route.h>
17310
17311 #include <asm/segment.h>
17312
17313 #ifdef CONFIG_IP_MULTICAST
17314
17315 /*
17316  *  Write an multicast group list table for the IGMP
17317 daemon to
17318  *  read.
17319  */
17320
17321 int ip_mc_procinfo(char *buffer, char **start, off_t
17322 offset, int length, int dummy)
17323 {
17324     off_t pos=0, begin=0;
17325     struct ip_mc_list *im;
17326     unsigned long flags;
```

p 528

```
17327        int len=0;
17328        struct device *dev;
17329
17330        len=sprintf(buffer,"Device    : Count\tGroup
17331 Users Timer\n");
17332        save_flags(flags);
17333        cli();
17334
17335        for(dev = dev_base; dev; dev = dev->next)
17336        {
17337
17338 if((dev->flags&IFF_UP)&&(dev->flags&IFF_MULTICAST))
17339                {
17340                        len+=sprintf(buffer+len,"%-10s:
17341 %5d\n",
17342                    dev->name, dev->mc_count);
17343                        for(im = dev->ip_mc_list; im; im
17344 = im->next)
17345                    {
17346                            len+=sprintf(buffer+len,
17347            "\t\t\t%08lX %5d %d:%08lX\n",
17348                            im->multiaddr,
17349 im->users,
17350                    im->tm_running,
17351 im->timer.expires-jiffies);
17352                            pos=begin+len;
17353                            if(pos<offset)
17354                            {
17355                                len=0;
17356                                begin=pos;
17357                            }
17358                            if(pos>offset+length)
17359                                break;
17360                    }
17361                }
17362        }
17363        restore_flags(flags);
17364        *start=buffer+(offset-begin);
17365        len-=(offset-begin);
17366        if(len>length)
17367            len=length;
17368        return len;
17369 }
17370
17371
17372 /*
17373  *  Socket option code for IP. This is the end of the
17374 line after any TCP,UDP etc options on
17375  *  an IP socket.
17376  *
17377  *  We implement IP_TOS (type of service), IP_TTL (time
17378 to live).
17379  */
17380
17381 static struct device *ip_mc_find_devfor(unsigned long
17382 addr)
17383 {
17384    struct device *dev;
17385    for(dev = dev_base; dev; dev = dev->next)
17386    {
17387
17388 if((dev->flags&IFF_UP)&&(dev->flags&IFF_MULTICAST)&&
17389            (dev->pa_addr==addr))
17390            return dev;
17391    }
17392
17393    return NULL;
17394 }
17395
17396 #endif
17397
17398 int ip_setsockopt(struct sock *sk, int level, int
17399 optname, char *optval, int optlen)
17400 {
17401    int val,err;
17402    unsigned char ucval;
17403 #if defined(CONFIG_IP_FIREWALL) ||
17404 defined(CONFIG_IP_ACCT)
17405    struct ip_fw tmp_fw;
17406 #endif
17407    if (optval == NULL)
17408    {
17409        val=0;
17410        ucval=0;
17411    }
17412    else
17413    {
17414        err=verify_area(VERIFY_READ, optval,
17415 sizeof(int));
17416        if(err)
17417            return err;
17418        val = get_user((int *) optval);
17419        ucval=get_user((unsigned char *) optval);
17420    }
17421
17422    if(level!=SOL_IP)
```

```
17423          return -EOPNOTSUPP;
17424 #ifdef CONFIG_IP_MROUTE
17425     if(optname>=MRT_BASE && optname <=MRT_BASE+10)
17426     {
17427         return
17428 ip_mroute_setsockopt(sk,optname,optval,optlen);
17429     }
17430 #endif
17431
17432     switch(optname)
17433     {
17434         case IP_OPTIONS:
17435             {
17436                 struct options * opt = NULL;
17437                 struct options * old_opt;
17438                 if (optlen > 40 || optlen < 0)
17439                     return -EINVAL;
17440                 err = verify_area(VERIFY_READ, optval,
17441 optlen);
17442                 if (err)
17443                     return err;
17444                 opt = kmalloc(sizeof(struct
17445 options)+((optlen+3)&~3), GFP_KERNEL);
17446                 if (!opt)
17447                     return -ENOMEM;
17448                 memset(opt, 0, sizeof(struct options));
17449                 if (optlen)
17450                     memcpy_fromfs(opt->__data, optval,
17451 optlen);
17452                 while (optlen & 3)
17453                     opt->__data[optlen++] = IPOPT_END;
17454                 opt->optlen = optlen;
17455                 opt->is_data = 1;
17456                 opt->is_setbyuser = 1;
17457                 if (optlen && ip_options_compile(opt,
17458 NULL))
17459                     {
17460                         kfree_s(opt, sizeof(struct options) +
17461 optlen);
17462                         return -EINVAL;
17463                     }
17464                 /*
17465                  * ANK: I'm afraid that receive handler
17466 may change
17467                  * options from under us.
17468                  */
17469                 cli();
17470                 old_opt = sk->opt;
17471                 sk->opt = opt;
17472                 sti();
17473                 if (old_opt)
17474                     kfree_s(old_opt, sizeof(struct optlen) +
17475 old_opt->optlen);
17476                 return 0;
17477             }
17478         case IP_TOS:            /* This sets both TOS
17479 and Precedence */
17480             if (val & ~0xfe)      /* Reject setting of
17481 unused bits */
17482                 return -EINVAL;
17483             if ((val>>5) > 4 && !suser())   /* Only root
17484 can set Prec>4 */
17485                 return -EPERM;
17486             sk->ip_tos=val;
17487             switch (val & 0x1E) {
17488                 case IPTOS_LOWDELAY:
17489                     sk->priority=SOPRI_INTERACTIVE;
17490                     break;
17491                 case IPTOS_THROUGHPUT:
17492                 case IPTOS_MINCOST:
17493                     sk->priority=SOPRI_BACKGROUND;
17494                     break;
17495                 default:
17496                     sk->priority=SOPRI_NORMAL;
17497                     break;
17498             }
17499             return 0;
17500         case IP_TTL:
17501             if(val<1||val>255)
17502                 return -EINVAL;
17503             sk->ip_ttl=val;
17504             return 0;
17505         case IP_HDRINCL:
17506             if(sk->type!=SOCK_RAW)
17507                 return -ENOPROTOOPT;
17508             sk->ip_hdrincl=val?1:0;
17509             return 0;
17510 #ifdef CONFIG_IP_MULTICAST
17511         case IP_MULTICAST_TTL:
17512             {
17513                 sk->ip_mc_ttl=(int)ucval;
17514                 return 0;
17515             }
17516         case IP_MULTICAST_LOOP:
17517             {
17518                 if(ucval!=0 && ucval!=1)
```

```
17519                    return -EINVAL;
17520                sk->ip_mc_loop=(int)ucval;
17521                return 0;
17522            }
17523        case IP_MULTICAST_IF:
17524            {
17525            struct in_addr addr;
17526            struct device *dev=NULL;
17527
17528                /*
17529                 *  Check the arguments are allowable
17530                 */
17531
17532                err=verify_area(VERIFY_READ, optval,
17533        sizeof(addr));
17534                if(err)
17535                    return err;
17536
17537                memcpy_fromfs(&addr,optval,sizeof(addr));
17538
17539
17540                /*
17541                 *  What address has been requested
17542                 */
17543
17544                if(addr.s_addr==INADDR_ANY) /* Default */
17545                {
17546                    sk->ip_mc_name[0]=0;
17547                    return 0;
17548                }
17549
17550                /*
17551                 *  Find the device
17552                 */
17553
17554                dev=ip_mc_find_devfor(addr.s_addr);
17555
17556                /*
17557                 *  Did we find one
17558                 */
17559
17560                if(dev)
17561                {
17562                    strcpy(sk->ip_mc_name,dev->name);
17563                    return 0;
17564                }
17565                return -EADDRNOTAVAIL;
17566            }
```

p 512

```
17567
17568            case IP_ADD_MEMBERSHIP:
17569                {
17570
17571    /*
17572     *  FIXME: Add/Del membership should have a semaphore
17573    protecting them from re-entry
17574     */
17575                struct ip_mreq mreq;
17576                struct rtable *rt;
17577                struct device *dev=NULL;
17578
17579                /*
17580                 *  Check the arguments.
17581                 */
17582
17583                err=verify_area(VERIFY_READ, optval,
17584        sizeof(mreq));
17585                if(err)
17586                    return err;
17587
17588                memcpy_fromfs(&mreq,optval,sizeof(mreq));
17589
17590                /*
17591                 *  Get device for use later
17592                 */
17593
17594                if(mreq.imr_interface.s_addr==INADDR_ANY)
17595                {
17596                    /*
17597                     *  Not set so scan.
17598                     */
17599
17600    if((rt=ip_rt_route(mreq.imr_multiaddr.s_addr,0,sk->bound_
17601    device))!=NULL)
17602                    {
17603                        dev=rt->rt_dev;
17604                        atomic_dec(&rt->rt_use);
17605                        ip_rt_put(rt);
17606                    }
17607                }
17608                else
17609                {
17610                    /*
17611                     *  Find a suitable device.
17612                     */
17613
17614
```

```
17615  dev=ip_mc_find_devfor(mreq.imr_interface.s_addr);                17663                    }
17616            }                                                       17664                }
17617                                                                    17665            else
17618            /*                                                      17666            {
17619             *   No device, no cookies.                             17667
17620             */                                                     17668
17621                                                                    17669  dev=ip_mc_find_devfor(mreq.imr_interface.s_addr);
17622            if(!dev)                                                17670            }
17623                return -ENODEV;                                     17671
17624                                                                    17672            /*
17625            /*                                                      17673             *   Did we find a suitable device.
17626             *   Join group.                                        17674             */
17627             */                                                     17675
17628                                                                    17676            if(!dev)
17629            return                                                  17677                return -ENODEV;
17630  ip_mc_join_group(sk,dev,mreq.imr_multiaddr.s_addr);              17678
17631        }                                                           17679            /*
17632                                                                    17680             *   Leave group
17633        case IP_DROP_MEMBERSHIP:                                     17681             */
17634        {                                                           17682
17635            struct ip_mreq mreq;                                     17683            return
17636            struct rtable *rt;                                       17684  ip_mc_leave_group(sk,dev,mreq.imr_multiaddr.s_addr);
17637            struct device *dev=NULL;                                 17685        }
17638                                                                    17686  #endif
17639            /*                                                      17687  #ifdef CONFIG_IP_FIREWALL
17640             *   Check the arguments                                17688        case IP_FW_INSERT_IN:
17641             */                                                     17689        case IP_FW_INSERT_OUT:
17642                                                                    17690        case IP_FW_INSERT_FWD:
17643            err=verify_area(VERIFY_READ, optval,                    17691        case IP_FW_APPEND_IN:
17644  sizeof(mreq));                                                     17692        case IP_FW_APPEND_OUT:
17645            if(err)                                                 17693        case IP_FW_APPEND_FWD:
17646                return err;                                         17694        case IP_FW_DELETE_IN:
17647                                                                    17695        case IP_FW_DELETE_OUT:
17648            memcpy_fromfs(&mreq,optval,sizeof(mreq));               17696        case IP_FW_DELETE_FWD:
17649                                                                    17697        case IP_FW_CHECK_IN:
17650            /*                                                      17698        case IP_FW_CHECK_OUT:
17651             *   Get device for use later                           17699        case IP_FW_CHECK_FWD:
17652             */                                                     17700        case IP_FW_FLUSH_IN:
17653                                                                    17701        case IP_FW_FLUSH_OUT:
17654            if(mreq.imr_interface.s_addr==INADDR_ANY)               17702        case IP_FW_FLUSH_FWD:
17655            {                                                       17703        case IP_FW_ZERO_IN:
17656                                                                    17704        case IP_FW_ZERO_OUT:
17657  if((rt=ip_rt_route(mreq.imr_multiaddr.s_addr,0,sk->bound_         17705        case IP_FW_ZERO_FWD:
17658  device))!=NULL)                                                   17706        case IP_FW_POLICY_IN:
17659                    {                                               17707        case IP_FW_POLICY_OUT:
17660                    dev=rt->rt_dev;                                 17708        case IP_FW_POLICY_FWD:
17661                    atomic_dec(&rt->rt_use);                        17709        case IP_FW_MASQ_TIMEOUTS:
17662                    ip_rt_put(rt);                                  17710            if(!suser())
```

```
17711                return -EPERM;
17712            if(optlen>sizeof(tmp_fw) || optlen<1)
17713                return -EINVAL;
17714            err=verify_area(VERIFY_READ,optval,optlen);
17715            if(err)
17716                return err;
17717            memcpy_fromfs(&tmp_fw,optval,optlen);
17718            err=ip_fw_ctl(optname, &tmp_fw,optlen);
17719            return -err;     /* -0 is 0 after all */
17720
17721    #endif
17722    #ifdef CONFIG_IP_MASQUERADE_IPAUTOFW
17723        case IP_AUTOFW_ADD:
17724        case IP_AUTOFW_DEL:
17725        case IP_AUTOFW_FLUSH:
17726            if(!suser())
17727                return -EPERM;
17728            if(optlen>sizeof(tmp_fw) || optlen<1)
17729                return -EINVAL;
17730            err=verify_area(VERIFY_READ,optval,optlen);
17731            if(err)
17732                return err;
17733            memcpy_fromfs(&tmp_fw,optval,optlen);
17734            err=ip_autofw_ctl(optname, &tmp_fw,optlen);
17735            return -err;     /* -0 is 0 after all */
17736
17737    #endif
17738    #ifdef CONFIG_IP_ACCT
17739        case IP_ACCT_INSERT:
17740        case IP_ACCT_APPEND:
17741        case IP_ACCT_DELETE:
17742        case IP_ACCT_FLUSH:
17743        case IP_ACCT_ZERO:
17744            if(!suser())
17745                return -EPERM;
17746            if(optlen>sizeof(tmp_fw) || optlen<1)
17747                return -EINVAL;
17748            err=verify_area(VERIFY_READ,optval,optlen);
17749            if(err)
17750                return err;
17751            memcpy_fromfs(&tmp_fw, optval,optlen);
17752            err=ip_acct_ctl(optname, &tmp_fw,optlen);
17753            return -err;     /* -0 is 0 after all */
17754    #endif
17755        /* IP_OPTIONS and friends go here eventually */
17756        default:
17757            return(-ENOPROTOOPT);
17758        }
17759    }
17760
17761    /*
17762     *  Get the options. Note for future reference. The GET
17763     of IP options gets the
17764     *  _received_ ones. The set sets the _sent_ ones.
17765     */
17766
17767    int ip_getsockopt(struct sock *sk, int level, int
17768    optname, char *optval, int *optlen)
17769    {
17770        int val,err;
17771    #ifdef CONFIG_IP_MULTICAST
17772        int len;
17773    #endif
17774
17775        if(level!=SOL_IP)
17776            return -EOPNOTSUPP;
17777
17778    #ifdef CONFIG_IP_MROUTE
17779        if(optname>=MRT_BASE && optname <=MRT_BASE+10)
17780        {
17781            return
17782    ip_mroute_getsockopt(sk,optname,optval,optlen);
17783        }
17784    #endif
17785
17786        switch(optname)
17787        {
17788            case IP_OPTIONS:
17789                {
17790                    unsigned char optbuf[sizeof(struct
17791    options)+40];
17792                    struct options * opt = (struct
17793    options*)optbuf;
17794                    err = verify_area(VERIFY_WRITE, optlen,
17795    sizeof(int));
17796                    if (err)
17797                        return err;
17798                    cli();
17799                    opt->optlen = 0;
17800                    if (sk->opt)
17801                        memcpy(optbuf, sk->opt,
17802    sizeof(struct options)+sk->opt->optlen);
17803                    sti();
17804                    if (opt->optlen == 0)
17805                    {
17806                        put_fs_long(0,(unsigned long *)
```

p 512

```
17807  optlen);                                          17855          return 0;
17808                          return 0;                 17856      case IP_TOS:
17809                  }                                  17857          val=sk->ip_tos;
17810                  err = verify_area(VERIFY_WRITE, optval,  17858          break;
17811  opt->optlen);                                     17859      case IP_TTL:
17812                  if (err)                           17860          val=sk->ip_ttl;
17813                          return err;                17861          break;
17814  /*                                                17862      case IP_HDRINCL:
17815   * Now we should undo all the changes done by     17863          val=sk->ip_hdrincl;
17816  ip_options_compile().                             17864          break;
17817   */                                               17865  #ifdef CONFIG_IP_MULTICAST
17818                  if (opt->srr)                      17866      case IP_MULTICAST_TTL:
17819                  {                                  17867          val=sk->ip_mc_ttl;
17820                          unsigned  char * optptr =  17868          break;
17821  opt->__data+opt->srr-sizeof(struct  iphdr);       17869      case IP_MULTICAST_LOOP:
17822                          memmove(optptr+7, optptr+3,17870          val=sk->ip_mc_loop;
17823  optptr[1]-7);                                     17871          break;
17824                          memcpy(optptr+3, &opt->faddr, 4);  17872      case IP_MULTICAST_IF:
17825                  }                                  17873          err=verify_area(VERIFY_WRITE, optlen,
17826                  if (opt->rr_needaddr)              17874  sizeof(int));
17827                  {                                  17875          if(err)
17828                          unsigned  char * optptr =  17876              return err;
17829  opt->__data+opt->rr-sizeof(struct  iphdr);        17877          len=strlen(sk->ip_mc_name);
17830                          memset(&optptr[optptr[2]-1], 0, 4);  17878          err=verify_area(VERIFY_WRITE, optval, len);
17831                          optptr[2] -= 4;            17879          if(err)
17832                  }                                  17880              return err;
17833                  if (opt->ts)                       17881          put_user(len,(int *) optlen);
17834                  {                                  17882          memcpy_tofs((void *)optval,sk->ip_mc_name,
17835                          unsigned  char * optptr =  17883  len);
17836  opt->__data+opt->ts-sizeof(struct  iphdr);        17884          return 0;
17837                          if (opt->ts_needtime)      17885  #endif
17838                          {                          17886      default:
17839                              memset(&optptr[optptr[2]-1], 0,  17887          return(-ENOPROTOOPT);
17840  4);                                               17888      }
17841                              optptr[2] -= 4;        17889      err=verify_area(VERIFY_WRITE, optlen, sizeof(int));
17842                          }                          17890      if(err)
17843                          if (opt->ts_needaddr)      17891          return err;
17844                          {                          17892      put_user(sizeof(int),(int *) optlen);
17845                              memset(&optptr[optptr[2]-1], 0,  17893
17846  4);                                               17894      err=verify_area(VERIFY_WRITE, optval, sizeof(int));
17847                              optptr[2] -= 4;        17895      if(err)
17848                          }                          17896          return err;
17849                  }                                  17897      put_user(val,(int *) optval);
17850                  put_fs_long(opt->optlen, (unsigned long  17898
17851  *) optlen);                                       17899      return(0);
17852                  memcpy_tofs(optval, opt->__data,   17900  }
17853  opt->optlen);
17854                  }
```

usr/src/linux/net/ipv4/ipmr.c

```
17901  /*
17902   *      IP multicast routing support for mrouted 3.6/3.8
17903   *
17904   *      (c) 1995 Alan Cox, <alan@cymru.net>
17905   *      Linux Consultancy and Custom Driver Development
17906   *
17907   *      This program is free software; you can redistribute
17908  it and/or
17909   *      modify it under the terms of the GNU General Public
17910  License
17911   *      as published by the Free Software Foundation; either
17912  version
17913   *      2 of the License, or (at your option) any later
17914  version.
17915   *
17916   *
17917   *      Fixes:
17918   *      Michael Chastain    :    Incorrect size of copying.
17919   *      Alan Cox            :    Added the cache manager code.
17920   *      Alan Cox            :    Fixed the clone/copy bug and
17921  device race.
17922   *      Malcolm Beattie     :    Buffer handling fixes.
17923   *      Alexey Kuznetsov    :    Double buffer free and other
17924  fixes.
17925   *      SVR Anand           :    Fixed several multicast bugs and
17926  problems.
17927   *      Alexey Kuznetsov    :    Subset of bugfixes/changes
17928  pending for
17929   *                               2.1. Doesn't include Alexey's PIM
17930  support.
17931   *
17932   *      Status:
17933   *          Cache manager under test. Forwarding in vague
17934  test mode
17935   *      Todo:
17936   *          Flow control
17937   *          Finish Tunnels
17938   *          Debug cache ttl handling properly
17939   *          Resolve IFF_ALLMULTI for rest of cards
17940   */
17941
17942  #include <linux/config.h>
17943  #include <asm/system.h>
17944  #include <asm/segment.h>
17945  #include <linux/types.h>
17946  #include <linux/sched.h>
17947  #include <linux/errno.h>
17948  #include <linux/timer.h>
17949  #include <linux/mm.h>
17950  #include <linux/kernel.h>
17951  #include <linux/fcntl.h>
17952  #include <linux/stat.h>
17953  #include <linux/socket.h>
17954  #include <linux/in.h>
17955  #include <linux/inet.h>
17956  #include <linux/netdevice.h>
17957  #include <linux/proc_fs.h>
17958  #include <linux/mroute.h>
17959  #include <net/ip.h>
17960  #include <net/protocol.h>
17961  #include <linux/skbuff.h>
17962  #include <net/sock.h>
17963  #include <net/icmp.h>
17964  #include <net/udp.h>
17965  #include <linux/notifier.h>
17966  #include <net/checksum.h>
17967
17968  /*
17969   *      Multicast router control variables
17970   */
17971
17972  static struct vif_device vif_table[MAXVIFS];        /*
17973  Devices    */
17974  static unsigned long vifc_map;              /* Active
17975  device map    */
17976  int mroute_do_pim = 0;                      /* Set in PIM
17977  assert    */
17978  static struct mfc_cache *mfc_cache_array[MFC_LINES+1];
17979  /* Forwarding cache */
17980  #define cache_resolve_queue
17981  (mfc_cache_array[MFC_LINES])/* Unresolved cache      */
17982  int cache_resolve_queue_len = 0;            /* Size of
17983  unresolved    */
17984
17985  /*
17986   *      Delete a VIF entry
17987   */
17988
17989  static void vif_delete(struct vif_device *v)
17990  {
17991      if(!(v->flags&VIFF_TUNNEL))
17992      {
17993          v->dev->flags&=~IFF_ALLMULTI;
17994          dev_mc_upload(v->dev);
17995      }
```

```
17996        v->dev=NULL;
17997    }
17998
17999    /*
18000     *    Delete a multicast route cache entry
18001     */
18002
18003    static void ipmr_cache_delete(struct mfc_cache *cache)
18004    {
18005        struct sk_buff *skb;
18006        int line;
18007        struct mfc_cache **cp;
18008
18009        /*
18010         *    Find the right cache line
18011         */
18012
18013        if(cache->mfc_flags&MFC_QUEUED)
18014        {
18015            cp=&cache_resolve_queue;
18016            del_timer(&cache->mfc_timer);
18017        }
18018        else
18019        {
18020
18021    line=MFC_HASH(cache->mfc_mcastgrp,cache->mfc_origin);
18022            cp=&(mfc_cache_array[line]);
18023        }
18024
18025        /*
18026         *    Unlink the buffer
18027         */
18028
18029        while(*cp!=NULL)
18030        {
18031            if(*cp==cache)
18032            {
18033                *cp=cache->next;
18034                break;
18035            }
18036            cp=&((*cp)->next);
18037        }
18038
18039        /*
18040         *    Free the buffer. If it is a pending resolution
18041         *    clean up the other resources.
18042         */
18043
18044        if(cache->mfc_flags&MFC_QUEUED)
18045        {
18046            cache_resolve_queue_len--;
18047            while((skb=skb_dequeue(&cache->mfc_unresolved)))
18048                kfree_skb(skb, FREE_WRITE);
18049        }
18050        kfree_s(cache,sizeof(cache));
18051    }
18052
18053    /*
18054     *    Cache expiry timer
18055     */
18056
18057    static void ipmr_cache_timer(unsigned long data)
18058    {
18059        struct mfc_cache *cache=(struct mfc_cache *)data;
18060        ipmr_cache_delete(cache);
18061    }
18062
18063    /*
18064     *    Insert a multicast cache entry
18065     */
18066
18067    static void ipmr_cache_insert(struct mfc_cache *c)
18068    {
18069        int line=MFC_HASH(c->mfc_mcastgrp,c->mfc_origin);
18070        c->next=mfc_cache_array[line];
18071        mfc_cache_array[line]=c;
18072    }
18073
18074    /*
18075     *    Find a multicast cache entry
18076     */
18077
18078    struct mfc_cache *ipmr_cache_find(__u32 origin, __u32
18079    mcastgrp)
18080    {
18081        int line=MFC_HASH(mcastgrp,origin);
18082        struct mfc_cache *cache;
18083        cache=mfc_cache_array[line];
18084        while(cache!=NULL)
18085        {
18086            if(cache->mfc_origin==origin &&
18087    cache->mfc_mcastgrp==mcastgrp)
18088                return cache;
18089            cache=cache->next;
18090        }
18091        cache=cache_resolve_queue;
```

```
18092        while(cache!=NULL)
18093        {
18094            if(cache->mfc_origin==origin &&
18095  cache->mfc_mcastgrp==mcastgrp)
18096                return cache;
18097            cache=cache->next;
18098        }
18099        return NULL;
18100  }
18101
18102  /*
18103   *  Allocate a multicast cache entry
18104   */
18105
18106  static struct mfc_cache *ipmr_cache_alloc(int priority)
18107  {
18108      struct mfc_cache *c=(struct mfc_cache
18109  *)kmalloc(sizeof(struct mfc_cache), priority);
18110      if(c==NULL)
18111          return NULL;
18112      c->mfc_queuelen=0;
18113      skb_queue_head_init(&c->mfc_unresolved);
18114      init_timer(&c->mfc_timer);
18115      c->mfc_timer.data=(long)c;
18116      c->mfc_timer.function=ipmr_cache_timer;
18117      c->mfc_packets=0;
18118      c->mfc_bytes=0;
18119      return c;
18120  }
18121
18122  /*
18123   *  A cache entry has gone into a resolved state from
18124  queued
18125   */
18126
18127  static void ipmr_cache_resolve(struct mfc_cache *cache)
18128  {
18129      struct mfc_cache **p;
18130      struct sk_buff *skb;
18131      /*
18132       *  Kill the queue entry timer.
18133       */
18134      del_timer(&cache->mfc_timer);
18135      cache->mfc_flags&=~MFC_QUEUED;
18136      /*
18137       *  Remove from the resolve queue
18138       */
18139      p=&cache_resolve_queue;
```

```
18140        while((*p)!=NULL)
18141        {
18142            if((*p)==cache)
18143            {
18144                *p=cache->next;
18145                break;
18146            }
18147            p=&((*p)->next);
18148        }
18149        cache_resolve_queue_len--;
18150        sti();
18151        /*
18152         *  Insert into the main cache
18153         */
18154        ipmr_cache_insert(cache);
18155        /*
18156         *  Play the pending entries through our router
18157         */
18158        while((skb=skb_dequeue(&cache->mfc_unresolved)))
18159            ipmr_forward(skb, skb->protocol);
18160  }
18161
18162  /*
18163   *  Bounce a cache query up to mrouted. We could use
18164  netlink for this but mrouted
18165   *  expects the following bizarre scheme..
18166   */
18167
18168  static void ipmr_cache_report(struct sk_buff *pkt)
18169  {
18170      struct sk_buff *skb=alloc_skb(128, GFP_ATOMIC);
18171      int ihl=pkt->ip_hdr->ihl<<2;
18172      struct igmphdr *igmp;
18173      if(!skb)
18174          return;
18175
18176      skb->free=1;
18177
18178      /*
18179       *  Copy the IP header
18180       */
18181
18182      skb->ip_hdr=(struct iphdr *)skb_put(skb,ihl);
18183      skb->h.iph=skb->ip_hdr;
18184      memcpy(skb->data,pkt->data,ihl);
18185      skb->ip_hdr->protocol = 0;        /* Flag to the
18186  kernel this is a route add */
18187
```

```
18188        /*
18189         *   Add our header
18190         */
18191
18192        igmp=(struct igmphdr *)skb_put(skb,sizeof(struct
18193  igmphdr));
18194        igmp->type   =   IGMPMSG_NOCACHE;          /* non IGMP
18195  dummy message */
18196        igmp->code  =   0;
18197        skb->ip_hdr->tot_len=htons(skb->len);              /*
18198  Fix the length */
18199
18200        /*
18201         *   Deliver to mrouted
18202         */
18203        if(sock_queue_rcv_skb(mroute_socket,skb)<0)
18204        {
18205            skb->sk=NULL;
18206            kfree_skb(skb, FREE_READ);
18207        }
18208  }
18209
18210
18211  /*
18212   *   Queue a packet for resolution
18213   */
18214
18215  static void ipmr_cache_unresolved(struct mfc_cache
18216  *cache, vifi_t vifi, struct sk_buff *skb, int is_frag)
18217  {
18218      if(cache==NULL)
18219      {
18220          /*
18221           *   Create a new entry if allowable
18222           */
18223          if(cache_resolve_queue_len>=10 ||
18224  (cache=ipmr_cache_alloc(GFP_ATOMIC))==NULL)
18225          {
18226              kfree_skb(skb, FREE_WRITE);
18227              return;
18228          }
18229          /*
18230           *   Fill in the new cache entry
18231           */
18232          cache->mfc_parent=vifi;
18233          cache->mfc_origin=skb->ip_hdr->saddr;
18234          cache->mfc_mcastgrp=skb->ip_hdr->daddr;
18235          cache->mfc_flags=MFC_QUEUED;
```

```
18236          /*
18237           *   Link to the unresolved list
18238           */
18239          cache->next=cache_resolve_queue;
18240          cache_resolve_queue=cache;
18241          cache_resolve_queue_len++;
18242          /*
18243           *   Fire off the expiry timer
18244           */
18245          cache->mfc_timer.expires=jiffies+10*HZ;
18246          add_timer(&cache->mfc_timer);
18247          /*
18248           *   Reflect first query at mrouted.
18249           */
18250          if(mroute_socket)
18251              ipmr_cache_report(skb);
18252      }
18253      /*
18254       *   See if we can append the packet
18255       */
18256      if(cache->mfc_queuelen>3)
18257      {
18258          kfree_skb(skb, FREE_WRITE);
18259          return;
18260      }
18261      /*
18262       *   Add to our 'pending' list. Cache the is_frag data
18263       *   in skb->protocol now it is spare.
18264       */
18265      cache->mfc_queuelen++;
18266      skb->protocol=is_frag;
18267      skb_queue_tail(&cache->mfc_unresolved,skb);
18268  }
18269
18270  /*
18271   *   MFC cache manipulation by user space mroute daemon
18272   */
18273
18274  int ipmr_mfc_modify(int action, struct mfcctl *mfc)
18275  {
18276      struct mfc_cache *cache;
18277      if(!MULTICAST(mfc->mfcc_mcastgrp.s_addr))
18278          return -EINVAL;
18279      /*
18280       *   Find the cache line
18281       */
18282
18283      cli();
```

```
18284
18285
18286   cache=ipmr_cache_find(mfc->mfcc_origin.s_addr,mfc->mfcc_m
18287   castgrp.s_addr);
18288
18289         /*
18290          *  Delete an entry
18291          */
18292         if(action==MRT_DEL_MFC)
18293         {
18294             if(cache)
18295             {
18296                 ipmr_cache_delete(cache);
18297                 sti();
18298                 return 0;
18299             }
18300             sti();
18301             return -ENOENT;
18302         }
18303         if(cache)
18304         {
18305             /*
18306              *  Update the cache, see if it frees a pending
18307   queue
18308              */
18309
18310             cache->mfc_flags|=MFC_RESOLVED;
18311             cache->mfc_parent=mfc->mfcc_parent;
18312
18313             memcpy(cache->mfc_ttls,
18314   mfc->mfcc_ttls,sizeof(cache->mfc_ttls));
18315
18316             /*
18317              *  Check to see if we resolved a queued list.
18318   If so we
18319              *  need to send on the frames and tidy up.
18320              */
18321
18322             if(cache->mfc_flags&MFC_QUEUED)
18323                 ipmr_cache_resolve(cache);  /* Unhook & send
18324   the frames */
18325             sti();
18326             return 0;
18327         }
18328         /*
18329          *  Unsolicited update - that's ok, add anyway.
18330          */
18331
18332
18333         cache=ipmr_cache_alloc(GFP_ATOMIC);
18334         if(cache==NULL)
18335         {
18336             sti();
18337             return -ENOMEM;
18338         }
18339         cache->mfc_flags=MFC_RESOLVED;
18340         cache->mfc_origin=mfc->mfcc_origin.s_addr;
18341         cache->mfc_mcastgrp=mfc->mfcc_mcastgrp.s_addr;
18342         cache->mfc_parent=mfc->mfcc_parent;
18343         memcpy(cache->mfc_ttls,
18344   mfc->mfcc_ttls,sizeof(cache->mfc_ttls));
18345         ipmr_cache_insert(cache);
18346         sti();
18347         return 0;
18348   }
18349
18350   /*
18351    *  Socket options and virtual interface manipulation.
18352   The whole
18353    *  virtual interface system is a complete heap, but
18354   unfortunately
18355    *  that's how BSD mrouted happens to think. Maybe one
18356   day with a proper
18357    *  MOSPF/PIM router set up we can clean this up.
18358    */
18359
18360   int ip_mroute_setsockopt(struct sock *sk,int
18361   optname,char *optval,int optlen)
18362   {
18363       int err;
18364       struct vifctl vif;
18365       struct mfcctl mfc;
18366
18367       if(optname!=MRT_INIT)
18368       {
18369           if(sk!=mroute_socket)
18370               return -EACCES;
18371       }
18372
18373       switch(optname)
18374       {
18375           case MRT_INIT:
18376               if(sk->type!=SOCK_RAW ||
18377   sk->num!=IPPROTO_IGMP)
18378                   return -EOPNOTSUPP;
18379               if(optlen!=sizeof(int))
```

```
18380              return -ENOPROTOOPT;
18381
18382    if((err=verify_area(VERIFY_READ,optval,sizeof(int)))<0)
18383              return err;
18384          if(get_user((int *)optval)!=1)
18385              return -ENOPROTOOPT;
18386          if(mroute_socket)
18387              return -EADDRINUSE;
18388          mroute_socket=sk;
18389          /* Initialise state */
18390          return 0;
18391      case MRT_DONE:
18392          mroute_close(sk);
18393          mroute_socket=NULL;
18394          return 0;
18395      case MRT_ADD_VIF:
18396      case MRT_DEL_VIF:
18397          if(optlen!=sizeof(vif))
18398              return -EINVAL;
18399          if((err=verify_area(VERIFY_READ, optval,
18400    sizeof(vif)))<0)
18401              return err;
18402          memcpy_fromfs(&vif,optval,sizeof(vif));
18403          if(vif.vifc_vifi > MAXVIFS)
18404              return -ENFILE;
18405          if(optname==MRT_ADD_VIF)
18406          {
18407              struct vif_device
18408    *v=&vif_table[vif.vifc_vifi];
18409              struct device *dev;
18410              /* Empty vif ? */
18411              if(vifc_map&(1<<vif.vifc_vifi))
18412                  return -EADDRINUSE;
18413              /* Find the interface */
18414
18415    dev=ip_dev_find(vif.vifc_lcl_addr.s_addr);
18416              if(!dev)
18417                  return -EADDRNOTAVAIL;
18418              /* Must be tunnelled or multicastable */
18419              if(vif.vifc_flags&VIFF_TUNNEL)
18420              {
18421                  if(vif.vifc_flags&VIFF_SRCRT)
18422                      return -EOPNOTSUPP;
18423                  /* IPIP will do all the work */
18424              }
18425              else
18426              {
18427                  if(dev->flags&IFF_MULTICAST)
```

```
18428              {
18429                  /* Most ethernet cards don't know
18430                      how to do this yet.. */
18431                  dev->flags|=IFF_ALLMULTI;
18432                  dev_mc_upload(dev);
18433              }
18434              else
18435              {
18436                  /* We are stuck.. */
18437                  return -EOPNOTSUPP;
18438              }
18439          }
18440          /*
18441           *  Fill in the VIF structures
18442           */
18443          cli();
18444          v->rate_limit=vif.vifc_rate_limit;
18445          v->local=vif.vifc_lcl_addr.s_addr;
18446          v->remote=vif.vifc_rmt_addr.s_addr;
18447          v->flags=vif.vifc_flags;
18448          v->threshold=vif.vifc_threshold;
18449          v->dev=dev;
18450          v->bytes_in = 0;
18451          v->bytes_out = 0;
18452          v->pkt_in = 0;
18453          v->pkt_out = 0;
18454          vifc_map|=(1<<vif.vifc_vifi);
18455          sti();
18456          return 0;
18457      }
18458      else
18459      /*
18460       *  VIF deletion
18461       */
18462      {
18463          struct vif_device
18464    *v=&vif_table[vif.vifc_vifi];
18465          if(vifc_map&(1<<vif.vifc_vifi))
18466          {
18467              vif_delete(v);
18468              vifc_map&=~(1<<vif.vifc_vifi);
18469              return 0;
18470          }
18471          else
18472              return -EADDRNOTAVAIL;
18473      }
18474      /*
18475       *  Manipulate the forwarding caches. These live
```

```
18476              *   in a sort of kernel/user symbiosis.
18477              */
18478             case MRT_ADD_MFC:
18479             case MRT_DEL_MFC:
18480                 err=verify_area(VERIFY_READ, optval,
18481 sizeof(mfc));
18482                 if(err)
18483                     return err;
18484                 memcpy_fromfs(&mfc,optval, sizeof(mfc));
18485                 return ipmr_mfc_modify(optname, &mfc);
18486             /*
18487              *   Control PIM assert.
18488              */
18489             case MRT_ASSERT:
18490                 if(optlen!=sizeof(int))
18491                     return -EINVAL;
18492                 if((err=verify_area(VERIFY_READ,
18493 optval,sizeof(int)))<0)
18494                     return err;
18495                 mroute_do_pim= get_user((int *)optval)?1:0;
18496                 return 0;
18497             /*
18498              *   Spurious command, or MRT_VERSION which you
18499 cannot
18500              *   set.
18501              */
18502             default:
18503                 return -EOPNOTSUPP;
18504         }
18505 }
18506
18507 /*
18508  *   Getsock opt support for the multicast routing system.
18509  */
18510
18511 int ip_mroute_getsockopt(struct sock *sk,int
18512 optname,char *optval,int *optlen)
18513 {
18514     int olr;
18515     int err;
18516
18517     if(sk!=mroute_socket)
18518         return -EACCES;
18519     if(optname!=MRT_VERSION && optname!=MRT_ASSERT)
18520         return -EOPNOTSUPP;
18521
18522     olr=get_user(optlen);
18523     if(olr!=sizeof(int))
18524         return -EINVAL;
18525     err=verify_area(VERIFY_WRITE, optval,sizeof(int));
18526     if(err)
18527         return err;
18528     put_user(sizeof(int),optlen);
18529     if(optname==MRT_VERSION)
18530         put_user(0x0305,(int *)optval);
18531     else
18532         put_user(mroute_do_pim,(int *)optval);
18533     return 0;
18534 }
18535
18536 /*
18537  *   The IP multicast ioctl support routines.
18538  */
18539
18540 int ipmr_ioctl(struct sock *sk, int cmd, unsigned long
18541 arg)
18542 {
18543     int err;
18544     struct sioc_sg_req sr;
18545     struct sioc_vif_req vr;
18546     struct vif_device *vif;
18547     struct mfc_cache *cl;
18548
18549     switch(cmd)
18550     {
18551         case SIOCGETVIFCNT:
18552             err=verify_area(VERIFY_WRITE, (void *)arg,
18553 sizeof(vr));
18554             if(err)
18555                 return err;
18556             memcpy_fromfs(&vr,(void *)arg,sizeof(vr));
18557             if(vr.vifi>=MAXVIFS)
18558                 return -EINVAL;
18559             vif=&vif_table[vr.vifi];
18560             if(vifc_map&(1<<vr.vifi))
18561             {
18562                 vr.icount=vif->pkt_in;
18563                 vr.ocount=vif->pkt_out;
18564                 vr.ibytes=vif->bytes_in;
18565                 vr.obytes=vif->bytes_out;
18566                 memcpy_tofs((void *)arg,&vr,sizeof(vr));
18567                 return 0;
18568             }
18569             return -EADDRNOTAVAIL;
18570         case SIOCGETSGCNT:
18571             err=verify_area(VERIFY_WRITE, (void *)arg,
```

```
18572    sizeof(sr));
18573                if(err)
18574                    return err;
18575                memcpy_fromfs(&sr,(void *)arg,sizeof(sr));
18576
18577    cl=ipmr_cache_find(sr.src.s_addr,sr.grp.s_addr);
18578                if(cl==NULL)
18579                {
18580                    sr.pktcnt=0;
18581                    sr.bytecnt=0;
18582                    sr.wrong_if=0;
18583                }
18584                else
18585                {
18586                    sr.pktcnt=cl->mfc_packets;
18587                    sr.bytecnt=cl->mfc_bytes;
18588                    sr.wrong_if=0;
18589                }
18590                memcpy_tofs((void *)arg,&sr,sizeof(sr));
18591                return 0;
18592            default:
18593                return -EINVAL;
18594        }
18595    }
18596
18597    /*
18598     *    Close the multicast socket, and clear the vif tables
18599    etc
18600     */
18601
18602    void mroute_close(struct sock *sk)
18603    {
18604        int i;
18605        struct vif_device *v=&vif_table[0];
18606
18607        /*
18608         *    Shut down all active vif entries
18609         */
18610
18611        for(i=0;i<MAXVIFS;i++)
18612        {
18613            if(vifc_map&(1<<i))
18614            {
18615                if(!(v->flags&VIFF_TUNNEL))
18616                {
18617                    v->dev->flags&=~IFF_ALLMULTI;
18618                    dev_mc_upload(v->dev);
18619                }
18620            }
18621            v++;
18622        }
18623        vifc_map=0;
18624        /*
18625         *    Wipe the cache
18626         */
18627        for(i=0;i<MFC_LINES;i++)
18628        {
18629            while(mfc_cache_array[i]!=NULL)
18630                ipmr_cache_delete(mfc_cache_array[i]);
18631        }
18632        /* The timer will clear any 'pending' stuff */
18633    }
18634
18635    static int ipmr_device_event(struct notifier_block
18636    *this, unsigned long event, void *ptr)
18637    {
18638        struct vif_device *v;
18639        int ct;
18640        if(event!=NETDEV_DOWN)
18641            return NOTIFY_DONE;
18642        v=&vif_table[0];
18643        for(ct=0;ct<MAXVIFS;ct++)
18644        {
18645            if((vifc_map&(1<<ct)) && v->dev==ptr)
18646            {
18647                vif_delete(v);
18648                vifc_map&=~(1<<ct);
18649            }
18650            v++;
18651        }
18652        return NOTIFY_DONE;
18653    }
18654
18655
18656    static struct notifier_block ip_mr_notifier={
18657        ipmr_device_event,
18658        NULL,
18659        0
18660    };
18661
18662    /*
18663     *    Processing handlers for ipmr_forward
18664     */
18665
18666    static void ipmr_queue_xmit(struct sk_buff *skb, struct
18667    vif_device *vif, struct device *in_dev, int frag)
```

```
18668  {
18669      int tunnel=0;
18670      __u32 raddr=skb->raddr;
18671      if(vif->flags&VIFF_TUNNEL)
18672      {
18673          tunnel=IPFWD_MULTITUNNEL;
18674          raddr=vif->remote;
18675      }
18676      vif->pkt_out++;
18677      vif->bytes_out+=skb->len;
18678      skb->dev=vif->dev;
18679      skb->raddr=skb->h.iph->daddr;
18680      /*
18681       *  If the vif went down as we were forwarding..
18682  just throw the
18683       *  frame.
18684       */
18685      if(vif->dev==NULL || ip_forward(skb, in_dev,
18686  frag|IPFWD_MULTICASTING|tunnel, raddr)==-1)
18687          kfree_skb(skb, FREE_WRITE);
18688  }
18689
18690  /*
18691   *  Multicast packets for forwarding arrive here
18692   */
18693
18694  void ipmr_forward(struct sk_buff *skb, int is_frag)
18695  {
18696      struct mfc_cache *cache;
18697      struct sk_buff *skb2;
18698      int psend = -1;
18699      int vif,ct=0;
18700
18701      /*
18702       *  Without the following addition, skb->h.iph
18703  points to something
18704       *  different that is not the ip header.
18705       */
18706
18707      skb->h.iph = skb->ip_hdr;  /* Anand, ernet. */
18708
18709
18710  cache=ipmr_cache_find(skb->ip_hdr->saddr,skb->ip_hdr->dad
18711  dr);
18712
18713      /*
18714       *  No usable cache entry
18715       */
```

```
18716
18717      if(cache==NULL || (cache->mfc_flags&MFC_QUEUED))
18718      {
18719          ipmr_cache_unresolved(cache,ALL_VIFS,skb,
18720  is_frag);
18721          return;
18722      }
18723
18724      vif=cache->mfc_parent;
18725
18726      if(vif>=MAXVIFS || !(vifc_map&(1<<vif)) ||
18727          vif_table[vif].dev != skb->dev)
18728      {
18729          kfree_skb(skb, FREE_READ);
18730          return;
18731      }
18732
18733      vif_table[vif].pkt_in++;
18734      vif_table[vif].bytes_in+=skb->len;
18735      cache->mfc_packets++;
18736      cache->mfc_bytes+=skb->len;
18737
18738      /*
18739       *  Forward the frame
18740       */
18741
18742      while(ct<MAXVIFS)
18743      {
18744          /*
18745           *  0 means don't do it. Silly idea, 255 as
18746  don't do it would be cleaner!
18747           */
18748          if(skb->ip_hdr->ttl > cache->mfc_ttls[ct] &&
18749  cache->mfc_ttls[ct]>0)
18750          {
18751              if(psend!=-1)
18752              {
18753                  /*
18754                   *  May get variant mac headers
18755                   *  so must copy -- boo hoo.
18756                   */
18757                  skb2=skb_copy(skb, GFP_ATOMIC);
18758                  if(skb2)
18759                  {
18760                      skb2->free=1;
18761                      ipmr_queue_xmit(skb2,
18762  &vif_table[psend], skb->dev, is_frag);
18763                  }
```

```
18764                    }
18765                    psend=ct;
18766                }
18767                ct++;
18768            }
18769            if(psend==-1)
18770                kfree_skb(skb, FREE_WRITE);
18771            else
18772                ipmr_queue_xmit(skb, &vif_table[psend],
18773    skb->dev, is_frag);
18774    }
18775
18776    /*
18777     *  The /proc interfaces to multicast routing
18778    /proc/ip_mr_cache /proc/ip_mr_vif
18779     */
18780
18781    int ipmr_vif_info(char *buffer, char **start, off_t
18782    offset, int length, int dummy)
18783    {
18784        struct vif_device *vif;
18785        int len=0;
18786        off_t pos=0;
18787        off_t begin=0;
18788        int size;
18789        int ct;
18790
18791        len += sprintf(buffer,
18792            "Interface   Bytes In  Pkts In  Bytes Out  Pkts
18793    Out  Flags Local   Remote\n");
18794        pos=len;
18795
18796        for (ct=0;ct<MAXVIFS;ct++)
18797        {
18798            vif=&vif_table[ct];
18799            if(!(vifc_map&(1<<ct)))
18800                continue;
18801            if(vif->dev==NULL)
18802                continue;
18803            size = sprintf(buffer+len, "%-10s %8ld  %7ld
18804    %8ld   %7ld   %05X %08lX %08lX\n",
18805                    vif->dev->name,vif->bytes_in,
18806    vif->pkt_in, vif->bytes_out,vif->pkt_out,
18807                    vif->flags, vif->local, vif->remote);
18808            len+=size;
18809            pos+=size;
18810            if(pos<offset)
18811            {
18812                len=0;
18813                begin=pos;
18814            }
18815            if(pos>offset+length)
18816                break;
18817        }
18818
18819        *start=buffer+(offset-begin);
18820        len-=(offset-begin);
18821        if(len>length)
18822            len=length;
18823        return len;
18824    }
18825
18826    int ipmr_mfc_info(char *buffer, char **start, off_t
18827    offset, int length, int dummy)
18828    {
18829        struct mfc_cache *mfc;
18830        int len=0;
18831        off_t pos=0;
18832        off_t begin=0;
18833        int size;
18834        int ct;
18835
18836        len += sprintf(buffer,
18837            "Group    Origin   SrcIface VifTtls\n");
18838        pos=len;
18839
18840        for (ct=0;ct<MFC_LINES+1;ct++)
18841        {
18842            cli();
18843            mfc=mfc_cache_array[ct];
18844            while(mfc!=NULL)
18845            {
18846                char *name="none";
18847                int n;
18848                /*
18849                 *  Device name
18850                 */
18851                if(mfc->mfc_parent < MAXVIFS &&
18852    vifc_map&(1<<mfc->mfc_parent))
18853
18854    name=vif_table[mfc->mfc_parent].dev->name;
18855
18856                size = sprintf(buffer+len, "%08lX %08lX
18857    %-8s",
18858                    (unsigned long)mfc->mfc_mcastgrp,
18859                    (unsigned long)mfc->mfc_origin,
```

```
18860                name);
18861
18862            for(n=0;n<MAXVIFS;n++)
18863            {
18864                if(vifc_map&(1<<n))
18865                    size+=sprintf(buffer+len+size,
18866                        " %-3d", mfc->mfc_ttls[n]);
18867                else
18868                    size+=sprintf(buffer+len+size,
18869                        " -- ");
18870            }
18871            size+=sprintf(buffer+len+size,"\n");
18872            len+=size;
18873            pos+=size;
18874            if(pos<offset)
18875            {
18876                len=0;
18877                begin=pos;
18878            }
18879            if(pos>offset+length)
18880            {
18881                sti();
18882                goto done;
18883            }
18884            mfc=mfc->next;
18885        }
18886        sti();
18887    }
18888 done:
18889    *start=buffer+(offset-begin);
18890    len-=(offset-begin);
18891    if(len>length)
18892        len=length;
18893    return len;
18894 }
18895
18896 /*
18897  *    Setup for IP multicast routing
18898  */
18899
18900 void ip_mr_init(void)
18901 {
18902    printk(KERN_INFO "Linux IP multicast router
18903 0.07.\n");
18904    register_netdevice_notifier(&ip_mr_notifier);
18905 #ifdef CONFIG_PROC_FS
18906    proc_net_register(&(struct proc_dir_entry) {
18907        PROC_NET_IPMR_VIF, 9 ,"ip_mr_vif",
```

```
18908        S_IFREG | S_IRUGO, 1, 0, 0,
18909        0, &proc_net_inode_operations,
18910        ipmr_vif_info
18911    });
18912    proc_net_register(&(struct proc_dir_entry) {
18913        PROC_NET_IPMR_MFC, 11 ,"ip_mr_cache",
18914        S_IFREG | S_IRUGO, 1, 0, 0,
18915        0, &proc_net_inode_operations,
18916        ipmr_mfc_info
18917    });
18918 #endif
18919 }
```

usr/src/linux/net/ipv4/raw.c

```
18920 /*
18921  * INET      An implementation of the TCP/IP protocol
18922 suite for the LINUX
18923  *        operating system.  INET is implemented using the
18924 BSD Socket
18925  *        interface as the means of communication with the
18926 user level.
18927  *
18928  *        RAW - implementation of IP "raw" sockets.
18929  *
18930  * Version: @(#)raw.c    1.0.4    05/25/93
18931  *
18932  * Authors: Ross Biro, <bir7@leland.Stanford.Edu>
18933  *        Fred N. van Kempen, <waltje@uWalt.NL.Mugnet.ORG>
18934  *
18935  * Fixes:
18936  *        Alan Cox    :    verify_area() fixed up
18937  *        Alan Cox    :    ICMP error handling
18938  *        Alan Cox    :    EMSGSIZE if you send too big a
18939 packet
18940  *        Alan Cox    :    Now uses generic datagrams and
18941 shared skbuff
18942  *                    library. No more peek crashes, no
18943 more backlogs
18944  *        Alan Cox    :    Checks sk->broadcast.
18945  *        Alan Cox    :    Uses
18946 skb_free_datagram/skb_copy_datagram
18947  *        Alan Cox    :    Raw passes ip options too
18948  *        Alan Cox    :    Setsocketopt added
18949  *        Alan Cox    :    Fixed error return for broadcasts
18950  *        Alan Cox    :    Removed wake_up calls
18951  *        Alan Cox    :    Use ttl/tos
18952  *        Alan Cox    :    Cleaned up old debugging
18953  *        Alan Cox    :    Use new kernel side addresses
```

```
18954    *  Arnt Gulbrandsen    :   Fixed MSG_DONTROUTE in raw
18955   sockets.
18956    *       Alan Cox    :   BSD style RAW socket
18957   demultiplexing.
18958    *       Alan Cox    :   Beginnings of mrouted support.
18959    *       Alan Cox    :   Added IP_HDRINCL option.
18960    *       Alan Cox    :   Skip broadcast check if BSDism
18961   set.
18962    *       David S. Miller :   New socket lookup
18963   architecture for ISS.
18964    *
18965    *       This program is free software; you can
18966   redistribute it and/or
18967    *       modify it under the terms of the GNU General
18968   Public License
18969    *       as published by the Free Software Foundation;
18970   either version
18971    *       2 of the License, or (at your option) any later
18972   version.
18973    */
18974
18975   #include <linux/config.h>
18976   #include <asm/system.h>
18977   #include <asm/segment.h>
18978   #include <linux/types.h>
18979   #include <linux/sched.h>
18980   #include <linux/errno.h>
18981   #include <linux/timer.h>
18982   #include <linux/mm.h>
18983   #include <linux/kernel.h>
18984   #include <linux/fcntl.h>
18985   #include <linux/socket.h>
18986   #include <linux/in.h>
18987   #include <linux/inet.h>
18988   #include <linux/netdevice.h>
18989   #include <linux/mroute.h>
18990   #include <net/ip.h>
18991   #include <net/protocol.h>
18992   #include <linux/skbuff.h>
18993   #include <net/sock.h>
18994   #include <net/icmp.h>
18995   #include <net/udp.h>
18996   #include <net/raw.h>
18997   #include <net/checksum.h>
18998
18999   #ifdef CONFIG_IP_MROUTE
19000   struct sock *mroute_socket=NULL;
19001   #endif
```

```
19002
19003   struct sock *raw_v4_htable[RAWV4_HTABLE_SIZE];
19004
19005   static void raw_v4_hash(struct sock *sk)
19006   {
19007       struct sock **skp;
19008       int num = sk->num;
19009
19010       num &= (RAWV4_HTABLE_SIZE - 1);
19011       skp = &raw_v4_htable[num];
19012       SOCKHASH_LOCK();
19013       sk->next = *skp;
19014       *skp = sk;
19015       sk->hashent = num;
19016       SOCKHASH_UNLOCK();
19017   }
19018
19019   static void raw_v4_unhash(struct sock *sk)
19020   {
19021       struct sock **skp;
19022       int num = sk->num;
19023
19024       num &= (RAWV4_HTABLE_SIZE - 1);
19025       skp = &raw_v4_htable[num];
19026
19027       SOCKHASH_LOCK();
19028       while(*skp != NULL) {
19029           if(*skp == sk) {
19030               *skp = sk->next;
19031               break;
19032           }
19033           skp = &((*skp)->next);
19034       }
19035       SOCKHASH_UNLOCK();
19036   }
19037
19038   static void raw_v4_rehash(struct sock *sk)
19039   {
19040       struct sock **skp;
19041       int num = sk->num;
19042       int oldnum = sk->hashent;
19043
19044       num &= (RAWV4_HTABLE_SIZE - 1);
19045       skp = &raw_v4_htable[oldnum];
19046
19047       SOCKHASH_LOCK();
19048       while(*skp != NULL) {
19049           if(*skp == sk) {
```

```
19050              *skp = sk->next;
19051              break;
19052          }
19053          skp = &((*skp)->next);
19054      }
19055      sk->next = raw_v4_htable[num];
19056      raw_v4_htable[num] = sk;
19057      sk->hashent = num;
19058      SOCKHASH_UNLOCK();
19059  }
19060
19061  /* Grumble... icmp and ip_input want to get at this... */
19062  struct sock *raw_v4_lookup(struct sock *sk, unsigned
19063  short num,
19064                  unsigned long raddr, unsigned long laddr)
19065  {
19066      struct sock *s = sk;
19067
19068      SOCKHASH_LOCK();
19069      for(s = sk; s; s = s->next) {
19070          if((s->num == num)                &&
19071              !(s->dead && (s->state == TCP_CLOSE))    &&
19072              !(s->daddr && s->daddr != raddr)        &&
19073              !(s->rcv_saddr && s->rcv_saddr != laddr))
19074               break; /* gotcha */
19075          }
19076      SOCKHASH_UNLOCK();
19077      return s;
19078  }
19079
19080  static inline unsigned long min(unsigned long a,
19081  unsigned long b)
19082  {
19083      if (a < b)
19084          return(a);
19085      return(b);
19086  }
19087
19088
19089  /*
19090   * Raw_err does not currently get called by the icmp
19091  module - FIXME:
19092   */
19093
19094  void raw_err (int type, int code, unsigned char *header,
19095  __u32 daddr,
19096      __u32 saddr, struct inet_protocol *protocol)
19097  {
19098      struct sock *sk;
19099
19100      if (protocol == NULL)
19101          return;
19102      sk = (struct sock *) protocol->data;
19103      if (sk == NULL)
19104          return;
19105
19106      /* This is meaningless in raw sockets. */
19107      if (type == ICMP_SOURCE_QUENCH)
19108      {
19109          if (sk->cong_window > 1) sk->cong_window =
19110  sk->cong_window/2;
19111          return;
19112      }
19113
19114      if(type == ICMP_PARAMETERPROB)
19115      {
19116          sk->err = EPROTO;
19117          sk->error_report(sk);
19118      }
19119
19120      if(code<=NR_ICMP_UNREACH)
19121      {
19122          sk->err = icmp_err_convert[code & 0xff].errno;
19123          sk->error_report(sk);
19124      }
19125
19126      return;
19127  }
19128
19129  static inline void raw_rcv_skb(struct sock * sk, struct
19130  sk_buff * skb)
19131  {
19132      /* Charge it to the socket. */
19133
19134      if (__sock_queue_rcv_skb(sk,skb)<0)
19135      {
19136          ip_statistics.IpInDiscards++;
19137          skb->sk=NULL;
19138          kfree_skb(skb, FREE_READ);
19139          return;
19140      }
19141
19142      ip_statistics.IpInDelivers++;
19143  }
19144
19145  /*
```

```
19146    * This is the prot->rcv() function. It's called when we
19147   have
19148    * backlogged packets from core/sock.c if we couldn't
19149   receive it
19150    * when the packet arrived.
19151    */
19152   static int raw_rcv_redo(struct sk_buff *skb, struct
19153   device *dev, struct options *opt,
19154       __u32 daddr, unsigned short len,
19155       __u32 saddr, int redo, struct inet_protocol *
19156   protocol)
19157   {
19158       raw_rcv_skb(skb->sk, skb);
19159       return 0;
19160   }
19161
19162   /* This gets rid of all the nasties in af_inet. -DaveM */
19163   static int raw_bind(struct sock *sk, struct sockaddr
19164   *uaddr, int addr_len)
19165   {
19166       struct sockaddr_in *addr = (struct sockaddr_in *)
19167   uaddr;
19168       int chk_addr_ret;
19169
19170       if((sk->state != TCP_CLOSE) || (addr_len <
19171   sizeof(struct sockaddr_in)))
19172           return -EINVAL;
19173       chk_addr_ret = ip_chk_addr(addr->sin_addr.s_addr);
19174       if(addr->sin_addr.s_addr != 0 && chk_addr_ret !=
19175   IS_MYADDR &&
19176           chk_addr_ret != IS_MULTICAST && chk_addr_ret !=
19177   IS_BROADCAST) {
19178   #ifdef CONFIG_IP_TRANSPARENT_PROXY
19179           /* Superuser may bind to any address to allow
19180   transparent proxying. */
19181           if(!suser())
19182   #endif
19183               return -EADDRNOTAVAIL;
19184       }
19185       sk->rcv_saddr = sk->saddr = addr->sin_addr.s_addr;
19186       if(chk_addr_ret == IS_MULTICAST || chk_addr_ret ==
19187   IS_BROADCAST)
19188           sk->saddr = 0;   /* Use device */
19189       ip_rt_put(sk->ip_route_cache);
19190       sk->ip_route_cache = NULL;
19191       return 0;
19192   }
19193
19194   /*
19195    *  This should be the easiest of all, all we do is
19196    *  copy it into a buffer. All demultiplexing is done
19197    *  in ip.c
19198    */
19199
19200   int raw_rcv(struct sock *sk, struct sk_buff *skb, struct
19201   device *dev, __u32 saddr, __u32 daddr)
19202   {
19203       /* Now we need to copy this into memory. */
19204       skb->sk = sk;
19205       skb_trim(skb,ntohs(skb->ip_hdr->tot_len));
19206
19207       skb->h.raw = (unsigned char *) skb->ip_hdr;
19208       skb->dev = dev;
19209       skb->saddr = daddr;
19210       skb->daddr = saddr;
19211
19212   #if 0
19213       /*
19214        *  For no adequately explained reasons BSD likes to
19215   mess up the header of
19216        *  the received frame.
19217        */
19218
19219       if(sk->bsdism)
19220
19221   skb->ip_hdr->tot_len=ntohs(skb->ip_hdr->tot_len-4*skb->ip
19222   _hdr->ihl);
19223   #endif
19224
19225       if (sk->users) {
19226           __skb_queue_tail(&sk->back_log, skb);
19227           return 0;
19228       }
19229       raw_rcv_skb(sk, skb);
19230       return 0;
19231   }
19232
19233   /*
19234    *  Send a RAW IP packet.
19235    */
19236
19237   /*
19238    *  Callback support is trivial for SOCK_RAW
19239    */
19240
19241   static void raw_getfrag(const void *p, __u32 saddr, char
```

```
19242  *to, unsigned int offset, unsigned int fraglen)
19243  {
19244      memcpy_fromfs(to, (const unsigned char *)p+offset,
19245  fraglen);
19246  }
19247
19248  /*
19249   *  IPPROTO_RAW needs extra work.
19250   */
19251
19252  static void raw_getrawfrag(const void *p, __u32 saddr,
19253  char *to, unsigned int offset, unsigned int fraglen)
19254  {
19255      memcpy_fromfs(to, (const unsigned char *)p+offset,
19256  fraglen);
19257      if(offset==0)
19258      {
19259          struct iphdr *iph=(struct iphdr *)to;
19260          if(!iph->saddr)
19261              iph->saddr=saddr;
19262          iph->check=0;
19263          iph->tot_len=htons(fraglen);    /* This is right
19264  as you can't frag
19265                      RAW packets */
19266          /*
19267           *  Deliberate breach of modularity to keep
19268           *  ip_build_xmit clean (well less messy).
19269           */
19270          if (!iph->id)
19271              iph->id = htons(ip_id_count++);
19272          iph->check=ip_fast_csum((unsigned char *)iph,
19273  iph->ihl);
19274      }
19275  }
19276
19277  static int raw_sendto(struct sock *sk, const unsigned
19278  char *from,
19279      int len, int noblock, unsigned flags, struct
19280  sockaddr_in *usin, int addr_len)
19281  {
19282      int err;
19283      struct sockaddr_in sin;
19284
19285      /*
19286       *  Check the flags. Only MSG_DONTROUTE is permitted.
19287       */
19288
19289      if (flags & MSG_OOB)        /* Mirror BSD error
19290  message compatibility */
19291          return -EOPNOTSUPP;
19292
19293      if (flags & ~MSG_DONTROUTE)
19294          return(-EINVAL);
19295      /*
19296       *  Get and verify the address.
19297       */
19298
19299      if (usin)
19300      {
19301          if (addr_len < sizeof(sin))
19302              return(-EINVAL);
19303          memcpy(&sin, usin, sizeof(sin));
19304          if (sin.sin_family && sin.sin_family != AF_INET)
19305              return(-EINVAL);
19306          /*
19307           *  Protocol type is host ordered byte.
19308           */
19309          sin.sin_port=ntohs(sin.sin_port);
19310      }
19311      else
19312      {
19313          if (sk->state != TCP_ESTABLISHED)
19314              return(-EINVAL);
19315          sin.sin_family = AF_INET;
19316          sin.sin_port = sk->num;
19317          sin.sin_addr.s_addr = sk->daddr;
19318      }
19319      if (sin.sin_port == 0)
19320          sin.sin_port = sk->num;
19321
19322      if (sin.sin_addr.s_addr == INADDR_ANY)
19323          sin.sin_addr.s_addr = ip_my_addr();
19324
19325      /*
19326       *  BSD raw sockets forget to check SO_BROADCAST ....
19327       */
19328
19329      if (!sk->bsdism && sk->broadcast == 0 &&
19330  ip_chk_addr(sin.sin_addr.s_addr)==IS_BROADCAST)
19331          return -EACCES;
19332
19333      if(sk->ip_hdrincl)
19334      {
19335          if(len>65535)
19336              return -EMSGSIZE;
19337          err=ip_build_xmit(sk, raw_getrawfrag, from, len,
```

```
19338    sin.sin_addr.s_addr, 0, sk->opt, flags, sin.sin_port,
19339    noblock);
19340        }
19341        else
19342        {
19343            if(len>65535-sizeof(struct iphdr))
19344                return -EMSGSIZE;
19345            err=ip_build_xmit(sk, raw_getfrag, from, len,
19346    sin.sin_addr.s_addr, 0, sk->opt, flags, sin.sin_port,
19347    noblock);
19348        }
19349        return err<0?err:len;
19350    }
19351
19352    /*
19353     *  Temporary
19354     */
19355
19356    static int raw_sendmsg(struct sock *sk, struct msghdr
19357    *msg, int len, int noblock,
19358        int flags)
19359    {
19360        if(msg->msg_iovlen==1)
19361            return
19362    raw_sendto(sk,msg->msg_iov[0].iov_base,len, noblock,
19363    flags, msg->msg_name, msg->msg_namelen);
19364        else
19365        {
19366            /*
19367             *  For awkward cases we linearise the buffer
19368    first. In theory this is only frames
19369             *  whose iovec's don't split on 4 byte
19370    boundaries, and soon encrypted stuff (to keep
19371             *  skip happy). We are a bit more general about
19372    it.
19373             */
19374
19375            unsigned char *buf;
19376            int fs;
19377            int err;
19378            if(len>65515)
19379                return -EMSGSIZE;
19380            buf=kmalloc(len, GFP_KERNEL);
19381            if(buf==NULL)
19382                return -ENOBUFS;
19383            memcpy_fromiovec(buf, msg->msg_iov, len);
19384            fs=get_fs();
19385            set_fs(get_ds());
```

```
19386            err=raw_sendto(sk,buf,len, noblock, flags,
19387    msg->msg_name, msg->msg_namelen);
19388            set_fs(fs);
19389            kfree_s(buf,len);
19390            return err;
19391        }
19392    }
19393
19394    static void raw_close(struct sock *sk, unsigned long
19395    timeout)
19396    {
19397        sk->state = TCP_CLOSE;
19398    #ifdef CONFIG_IP_MROUTE
19399        if(sk==mroute_socket)
19400        {
19401            mroute_close(sk);
19402            mroute_socket=NULL;
19403        }
19404    #endif
19405        sk->dead=1;
19406        destroy_sock(sk);
19407    }
19408
19409
19410    static int raw_init(struct sock *sk)
19411    {
19412        return(0);
19413    }
19414
19415
19416    /*
19417     *  This should be easy, if there is something there
19418     *  we return it, otherwise we block.
19419     */
19420
19421    int raw_recvmsg(struct sock *sk, struct msghdr *msg, int
19422    len,
19423        int noblock, int flags,int *addr_len)
19424    {
19425        int copied=0;
19426        struct sk_buff *skb;
19427        int err;
19428        struct sockaddr_in *sin=(struct sockaddr_in
19429    *)msg->msg_name;
19430
19431        if (flags & MSG_OOB)
19432            return -EOPNOTSUPP;
19433
```

```
19434        if (sk->shutdown & RCV_SHUTDOWN)
19435            return(0);
19436
19437        if (addr_len)
19438            *addr_len=sizeof(*sin);
19439
19440        skb=skb_recv_datagram(sk,flags,noblock,&err);
19441        if(skb==NULL)
19442            return err;
19443
19444        copied = min(len, skb->len);
19445
19446        skb_copy_datagram_iovec(skb, 0, msg->msg_iov,
19447    copied);
19448        sk->stamp=skb->stamp;
19449
19450        /* Copy the address. */
19451        if (sin)
19452        {
19453            sin->sin_family = AF_INET;
19454            sin->sin_addr.s_addr = skb->daddr;
19455        }
19456        skb_free_datagram(sk, skb);
19457        return (copied);
19458    }
19459
19460
19461    struct proto raw_prot = {
19462        (struct sock *)&raw_prot,    /* sklist_next */
19463        (struct sock *)&raw_prot,    /* sklist_prev */
19464        raw_close,              /* close */
19465        ip_build_header,        /* build_header */
19466        udp_connect,            /* connect */
19467        NULL,                   /* accept */
19468        ip_queue_xmit,          /* queue_xmit */
19469        NULL,                   /* retransmit */
19470        NULL,                   /* write_wakeup */
19471        NULL,                   /* read_wakeup */
19472        raw_rcv_redo,           /* rcv */
19473        datagram_select,        /* select */
19474    #ifdef CONFIG_IP_MROUTE
19475        ipmr_ioctl,             /* ioctl */
19476    #else
19477        NULL,                   /* ioctl */
19478    #endif
19479        raw_init,               /* init */
19480        NULL,                   /* shutdown */
19481        ip_setsockopt,          /* setsockopt */
```

```
19482        ip_getsockopt,          /* getsockopt */
19483        raw_sendmsg,            /* sendmsg */
19484        raw_recvmsg,            /* recvmsg */
19485        raw_bind,           /* bind */
19486        raw_v4_hash,            /* hash */
19487        raw_v4_unhash,          /* unhash */
19488        raw_v4_rehash,          /* rehash */
19489        NULL,               /* good_socknum */
19490        NULL,               /* verify_bind */
19491        128,                /* max_header */
19492        0,                  /* retransmits */
19493        "RAW",              /* name */
19494        0,                  /* inuse */
19495        0                   /* highestinuse */
19496    };
```

usr/src/linux/net/ipv4/route.c

```
19497    /*
19498     * INET       An implementation of the TCP/IP protocol
19499    suite for the LINUX
19500     *       operating system.  INET is implemented using the
19501    BSD Socket
19502     *       interface as the means of communication with the
19503    user level.
19504     *
19505     *       ROUTE - implementation of the IP router.
19506     *
19507     * Version: @(#)route.c 1.0.14   05/31/93
19508     *
19509     * Authors: Ross Biro, <bir7@leland.Stanford.Edu>
19510     *       Fred N. van Kempen, <waltje@uWalt.NL.Mugnet.ORG>
19511     *       Alan Cox, <gw4pts@gw4pts.ampr.org>
19512     *       Linus Torvalds, <Linus.Torvalds@helsinki.fi>
19513     *
19514     * Fixes:
19515     *       Alan Cox    :   Verify area fixes.
19516     *       Alan Cox    :   cli() protects routing changes
19517     *       Rui Oliveira    :   ICMP routing table updates
19518     *       (rco@di.uminho.pt)  Routing table insertion and
19519    update
19520     *       Linus Torvalds  :   Rewrote bits to be sensible
19521     *       Alan Cox    :   Added BSD route gw semantics
19522     *       Alan Cox    :   Super /proc >4K
19523     *       Alan Cox    :   MTU in route table
19524     *       Alan Cox    :   MSS actually. Also added the
19525    window
19526     *                   clamper.
19527     *       Sam Lantinga    :   Fixed route matching in
```

```
19528   rt_del()
19529   *         Alan Cox    :   Routing cache support.
19530   *         Alan Cox    :   Removed compatibility cruft.
19531   *         Alan Cox    :   RTF_REJECT support.
19532   *         Alan Cox    :   TCP irtt support.
19533   *         Jonathan Naylor :   Added Metric support.
19534   *  Miquel van Smoorenburg  :   BSD API fixes.
19535   *  Miquel van Smoorenburg  :   Metrics.
19536   *         Alan Cox    :   Use __u32 properly
19537   *         Alan Cox    :   Aligned routing errors more
19538   closely with BSD
19539   *                 our system is still very different.
19540   *         Alan Cox    :   Faster /proc handling
19541   *  Alexey Kuznetsov    :   Massive rework to support
19542   tree based routing,
19543   *                 routing caches and better behaviour.
19544   *
19545   *         Olaf Erb     :   irtt wasn't being copied right.
19546   *         Bjorn Ekwall    :   Kerneld route support.
19547   *         Alan Cox    :   Multicast fixed (I hope)
19548   *         Pavel Krauz :   Limited broadcast fixed
19549   *             Elliot Poger    :       Added support
19550   for SO_BINDTODEVICE.
19551   *         Andi Kleen  :   Don't send multicast addresses to
19552   *             kerneld.
19553   *         Wolfgang Walter :   make rt_free() non-static
19554   *
19555   *  Juan Jose Ciarlante    :   Added ip_rt_dev
19556   *     This program is free software; you can
19557   redistribute it and/or
19558   *     modify it under the terms of the GNU General
19559   Public License
19560   *     as published by the Free Software Foundation;
19561   either version
19562   *     2 of the License, or (at your option) any later
19563   version.
19564   */
19565
19566   #include <linux/config.h>
19567   #include <asm/segment.h>
19568   #include <asm/system.h>
19569   #include <asm/bitops.h>
19570   #include <linux/types.h>
19571   #include <linux/kernel.h>
19572   #include <linux/sched.h>
19573   #include <linux/mm.h>
19574   #include <linux/string.h>
19575   #include <linux/socket.h>
19576   #include <linux/sockios.h>
19577   #include <linux/errno.h>
19578   #include <linux/in.h>
19579   #include <linux/inet.h>
19580   #include <linux/netdevice.h>
19581   #include <linux/if_arp.h>
19582   #include <net/ip.h>
19583   #include <net/protocol.h>
19584   #include <net/route.h>
19585   #include <net/tcp.h>
19586   #include <linux/skbuff.h>
19587   #include <net/sock.h>
19588   #include <net/icmp.h>
19589   #include <net/netlink.h>
19590   #ifdef CONFIG_KERNELD
19591   #include <linux/kerneld.h>
19592   #endif
19593
19594   /*
19595    * Forwarding Information Base definitions.
19596    */
19597
19598   struct fib_node
19599   {
19600       struct fib_node     *fib_next;
19601       __u32           fib_dst;
19602       unsigned long       fib_use;
19603       struct fib_info     *fib_info;
19604       short           fib_metric;
19605       unsigned char       fib_tos;
19606   };
19607
19608   /*
19609    * This structure contains data shared by many of routes.
19610    */
19611
19612   struct fib_info
19613   {
19614       struct fib_info     *fib_next;
19615       struct fib_info     *fib_prev;
19616       __u32           fib_gateway;
19617       struct device       *fib_dev;
19618       int         fib_refcnt;
19619       unsigned long       fib_window;
19620       unsigned short      fib_flags;
19621       unsigned short      fib_mtu;
19622       unsigned short      fib_irtt;
19623   };
```

```
19624
19625    struct fib_zone
19626    {
19627        struct fib_zone *fz_next;
19628        struct fib_node **fz_hash_table;
19629        struct fib_node *fz_list;
19630        int     fz_nent;
19631        int     fz_logmask;
19632        __u32       fz_mask;
19633    };
19634
19635    static struct fib_zone  *fib_zones[33];
19636    static struct fib_zone  *fib_zone_list;
19637    static struct fib_node  *fib_loopback = NULL;
19638    static struct fib_info  *fib_info_list;
19639
19640    /*
19641     * Backlogging.
19642     */
19643
19644    #define RT_BH_REDIRECT       1
19645    #define RT_BH_GARBAGE_COLLECT   2
19646    #define RT_BH_FREE       4
19647
19648    struct rt_req
19649    {
19650        struct rt_req * rtr_next;
19651        struct device *dev;
19652        __u32 dst;
19653        __u32 gw;
19654        unsigned char tos;
19655    };
19656
19657    int         ip_rt_lock;
19658    unsigned        ip_rt_bh_mask;
19659    static struct rt_req    *rt_backlog;
19660
19661    /*
19662     * Route cache.
19663     */
19664
19665    struct rtable       *ip_rt_hash_table[RT_HASH_DIVISOR];
19666    static int      rt_cache_size;
19667    static struct rtable    *rt_free_queue;
19668    struct wait_queue   *rt_wait;
19669
19670    static void rt_kick_backlog(void);
19671    static void rt_cache_add(unsigned hash, struct rtable *
```

```
19672        rth);
19673    static void rt_cache_flush(void);
19674    static void rt_garbage_collect_1(void);
19675
19676    /*
19677     * Evaluate mask length.
19678     */
19679
p 499  19680    static __inline__ int rt_logmask(__u32 mask)
19681    {
19682        if (!(mask = ntohl(mask)))
19683            return 32;
19684        return ffz(~mask);
19685    }
19686
19687    /*
19688     * Create mask from length.
19689     */
19690
p 499  19691    static __inline__ __u32 rt_mask(int logmask)
19692    {
19693        if (logmask >= 32)
19694            return 0;
19695        return htonl(~((1<<logmask)-1));
19696    }
19697
19698    static __inline__ unsigned fz_hash_code(__u32 dst, int
19699    logmask)
19700    {
p 500  19701        return ip_rt_hash_code(ntohl(dst)>>logmask);
19702    }
19703
19704    /*
19705     * Free FIB node.
19706     */
19707
19708    static void fib_free_node(struct fib_node * f)
19709    {
19710        struct fib_info * fi = f->fib_info;
p 500  19711        if (!--fi->fib_refcnt)
19712        {
19713    #if RT_CACHE_DEBUG >= 2
19714            printk("fib_free_node: fi %08x/%s is free\n",
19715    fi->fib_gateway, fi->fib_dev->name);
19716    #endif
19717            if (fi->fib_next)
19718                fi->fib_next->fib_prev = fi->fib_prev;
19719            if (fi->fib_prev)
```

```
19720              fi->fib_prev->fib_next = fi->fib_next;
19721          if (fi == fib_info_list)
19722              fib_info_list = fi->fib_next;
19723          kfree_s(fi, sizeof(struct fib_info));
19724      }
19725      kfree_s(f, sizeof(struct fib_node));
19726 }
19727
19728 /*
19729  * Find gateway route by address.
19730  */
19731
19732 static struct fib_node * fib_lookup_gateway(__u32 dst)
19733 {
19734      struct fib_zone * fz;
19735      struct fib_node * f;
19736
19737      for (fz = fib_zone_list; fz; fz = fz->fz_next)
19738      {
19739          if (fz->fz_hash_table)
19740              f = fz->fz_hash_table[fz_hash_code(dst,
19741 fz->fz_logmask)];
19742          else
19743              f = fz->fz_list;
19744
19745          for ( ; f; f = f->fib_next)
19746          {
19747              if (((dst ^ f->fib_dst) & fz->fz_mask) ||
19748                   (f->fib_info->fib_flags & RTF_GATEWAY))
19749                  continue;
19750              return f;
19751          }
19752      }
19753      return NULL;
19754 }
19755
19756 /*
19757  * Find local route by address.
19758  * FIXME: I use "longest match" principle. If destination
19759  *   has some non-local route, I'll not search shorter
19760 matches.
19761  *   It's possible, I'm wrong, but I wanted to prevent
19762 following
19763  *   situation:
19764  *   route add 193.233.7.128 netmask 255.255.255.192 gw
19765 xxxxxx
19766  *   route add 193.233.7.0   netmask 255.255.255.0 eth1
19767  *    (Two ethernets connected by serial line, one is
```

```
19768 small and other is large)
19769  *    Host 193.233.7.129 is locally unreachable,
19770  *    but old (<=1.3.37) code will send packets destined
19771 for it to eth1.
19772  *
19773  * Calling routine can specify a particular interface by
19774 setting dev.  If dev==NULL,
19775  * any interface will do.
19776  */
19777
19778 static struct fib_node * fib_lookup_local(__u32 dst,
19779 struct device *dev)
19780 {
19781      struct fib_zone * fz;
19782      struct fib_node * f;
19783
19784      for (fz = fib_zone_list; fz; fz = fz->fz_next)
19785      {
19786          int longest_match_found = 0;
19787
19788          if (fz->fz_hash_table)
19789              f = fz->fz_hash_table[fz_hash_code(dst,
19790 fz->fz_logmask)];
19791          else
19792              f = fz->fz_list;
19793
19794          for ( ; f; f = f->fib_next)
19795          {
19796              if ((dst ^ f->fib_dst) & fz->fz_mask)
19797                  continue;
19798              if ( (dev != NULL) && (dev !=
19799 f->fib_info->fib_dev) )
19800                  continue;
19801              if (!(f->fib_info->fib_flags & RTF_GATEWAY))
19802                  return f;
19803              longest_match_found = 1;
19804          }
19805          if (longest_match_found)
19806              return NULL;
19807      }
19808      return NULL;
19809 }
19810
19811 /*
19812  * Main lookup routine.
19813  * IMPORTANT NOTE: this algorithm has small difference
19814 from <=1.3.37 visible
19815  * by user. It doesn't route non-CIDR broadcasts by
```

p 498
p 503

```
19816   default.
19817    *
19818    *  F.e.
19819    *      ifconfig eth0 193.233.7.65 netmask
19820   255.255.255.192 broadcast 193.233.7.255
19821    *  is valid, but if you really are not able (not
19822   allowed, do not want) to
19823    *  use CIDR compliant broadcast 193.233.7.127, you
19824   should add host route:
19825    *      route add -host 193.233.7.255 eth0
19826    */
19827
19828   static struct fib_node * fib_lookup(__u32 dst, struct
19829   device *dev)
19830   {
19831       struct fib_zone * fz;
19832       struct fib_node * f;
19833
19834       for (fz = fib_zone_list; fz; fz = fz->fz_next)
19835       {
19836           if (fz->fz_hash_table)
19837               f = fz->fz_hash_table[fz_hash_code(dst,
19838   fz->fz_logmask)];
19839           else
19840               f = fz->fz_list;
19841
19842           for ( ; f; f = f->fib_next)
19843           {
19844               if ((dst ^ f->fib_dst) & fz->fz_mask)
19845                   continue;
19846               if ( (dev != NULL) && (dev !=
19847   f->fib_info->fib_dev) )
19848                   continue;
19849               return f;
19850           }
19851       }
19852       return NULL;
19853   }
19854
19855   static __inline__ struct device * get_gw_dev(__u32 gw)
19856   {
19857       struct fib_node * f;
19858       f = fib_lookup_gateway(gw);
19859       if (f)
19860           return f->fib_info->fib_dev;
19861       return NULL;
19862   }
19863
19864   /*
19865    *  Check if a mask is acceptable.
19866    */
19867
19868   static inline int bad_mask(__u32 mask, __u32 addr)
19869   {
19870       if (addr & (mask = ~mask))
19871           return 1;
19872       mask = ntohl(mask);
19873       if (mask & (mask+1))
19874           return 1;
19875       return 0;
19876   }
19877
19878
19879   static int fib_del_list(struct fib_node **fp, __u32 dst,
19880           struct device * dev, __u32 gtw, short flags,
19881   short metric, __u32 mask)
19882   {
19883       struct fib_node *f;
19884       int found=0;
19885
19886       while((f = *fp) != NULL)
19887       {
19888           struct fib_info * fi = f->fib_info;
19889
19890           /*
19891            *  Make sure the destination and netmask match.
19892            *  metric, gateway and device are also checked
19893            *  if they were specified.
19894            */
19895           if (f->fib_dst != dst ||
19896               (gtw && fi->fib_gateway != gtw) ||
19897               (metric >= 0 && f->fib_metric != metric) ||
19898               (dev && fi->fib_dev != dev) )
19899           {
19900               fp = &f->fib_next;
19901               continue;
19902           }
19903           cli();
19904           *fp = f->fib_next;
19905           if (fib_loopback == f)
19906               fib_loopback = NULL;
19907           sti();
19908           ip_netlink_msg(RTMSG_DELROUTE, dst, gtw, mask,
19909   flags, metric, fi->fib_dev->name);
19910           fib_free_node(f);
19911           found++;
```

p 497 (line 19868)
p 500 (line 19879)
p 503 (line 19834)
p 498 (line 19858)

```
19912        }
19913     return found;
19914  }
19915
19916  static __inline__ int fib_del_1(__u32 dst, __u32 mask,
19917          struct device * dev, __u32 gtw, short flags,
19918  short metric)
19919  {
19920     struct fib_node **fp;
19921     struct fib_zone *fz;
19922     int found=0;
19923
19924     if (!mask)
19925     {
19926        for (fz=fib_zone_list; fz; fz = fz->fz_next)
19927        {
19928           int tmp;
19929           if (fz->fz_hash_table)
19930              fp =
19931  &fz->fz_hash_table[fz_hash_code(dst, fz->fz_logmask)];
19932           else
19933              fp = &fz->fz_list;
19934
19935           tmp = fib_del_list(fp, dst, dev, gtw, flags,
19936  metric, mask);
19937           fz->fz_nent -= tmp;
19938           found += tmp;
19939        }
19940     }
19941     else
19942     {
19943        if ((fz = fib_zones[rt_logmask(mask)]) != NULL)
19944        {
19945           if (fz->fz_hash_table)
19946              fp =
19947  &fz->fz_hash_table[fz_hash_code(dst, fz->fz_logmask)];
19948           else
19949              fp = &fz->fz_list;
19950
19951           found = fib_del_list(fp, dst, dev, gtw,
19952  flags, metric, mask);
19953           fz->fz_nent -= found;
19954        }
19955     }
19956
19957     if (found)
19958     {
19959        rt_cache_flush();
```

```
19960        return 0;
19961     }
19962     return -ESRCH;
19963  }
19964
19965
19966  static struct fib_info * fib_create_info(__u32 gw,
19967  struct device * dev,
19968                        unsigned short flags, unsigned
19969  short mss,
19970                        unsigned long window, unsigned
19971  short irtt)
19972  {
19973     struct fib_info * fi;
19974
19975     if (!(flags & RTF_MSS))
19976     {
19977        mss = dev->mtu;
19978  #ifdef CONFIG_NO_PATH_MTU_DISCOVERY
19979        /*
19980         *  If MTU was not specified, use default.
19981         *  If you want to increase MTU for some net
19982  (local subnet)
19983         *  use "route add .... mss xxx".
19984         *
19985         *  The MTU isn't currently always used and
19986  computed as it
19987         *  should be as far as I can tell. [Still
19988  verifying this is right]
19989         */
19990        if ((flags & RTF_GATEWAY) && mss > 576)
19991           mss = 576;
19992  #endif
19993     }
19994     if (!(flags & RTF_WINDOW))
19995        window = 0;
19996     if (!(flags & RTF_IRTT))
19997        irtt = 0;
19998
19999     for (fi=fib_info_list; fi; fi = fi->fib_next)
20000     {
20001        if (fi->fib_gateway != gw ||
20002           fi->fib_dev != dev  ||
20003           fi->fib_flags != flags ||
20004           fi->fib_mtu != mss ||
20005           fi->fib_window != window ||
20006           fi->fib_irtt != irtt)
20007           continue;
```

```
20008            fi->fib_refcnt++;
20009    #if RT_CACHE_DEBUG >= 2
20010            printk("fib_create_info: fi %08x/%s is
20011    duplicate\n", fi->fib_gateway, fi->fib_dev->name);
20012    #endif
20013            return fi;
20014        }
20015        fi = (struct fib_info*)kmalloc(sizeof(struct
20016    fib_info), GFP_KERNEL);
20017        if (!fi)
20018            return NULL;
20019        memset(fi, 0, sizeof(struct fib_info));
20020        fi->fib_flags = flags;
20021        fi->fib_dev = dev;
20022        fi->fib_gateway = gw;
20023        fi->fib_mtu = mss;
20024        fi->fib_window = window;
20025        fi->fib_refcnt++;
20026        fi->fib_next = fib_info_list;
20027        fi->fib_prev = NULL;
20028        fi->fib_irtt = irtt;
20029        if (fib_info_list)
20030            fib_info_list->fib_prev = fi;
20031        fib_info_list = fi;
20032    #if RT_CACHE_DEBUG >= 2
20033        printk("fib_create_info: fi %08x/%s is created\n",
20034    fi->fib_gateway, fi->fib_dev->name);
20035    #endif
20036            return fi;
20037    }
20038
20039
20040    static __inline__ void fib_add_1(short flags, __u32 dst,
20041    __u32 mask,
20042        __u32 gw, struct device *dev, unsigned short mss,
20043        unsigned long window, unsigned short irtt, short
20044    metric)
20045    {
20046        struct fib_node *f, *f1;
20047        struct fib_node **fp;
20048        struct fib_node **dup_fp = NULL;
20049        struct fib_zone * fz;
20050        struct fib_info * fi;
20051        int logmask;
20052
20053        /*
20054         *  Allocate an entry and fill it in.
20055         */
20056
20057        f = (struct fib_node *) kmalloc(sizeof(struct
20058    fib_node), GFP_KERNEL);
20059        if (f == NULL)
20060            return;
20061
20062        memset(f, 0, sizeof(struct fib_node));
20063        f->fib_dst = dst;
20064        f->fib_metric = metric;
20065        f->fib_tos    = 0;
20066
20067        if ((fi = fib_create_info(gw, dev, flags, mss,
20068    window, irtt)) == NULL)
20069        {
20070            kfree_s(f, sizeof(struct fib_node));
20071            return;
20072        }
20073        f->fib_info = fi;
20074
20075        logmask = rt_logmask(mask);
20076        fz = fib_zones[logmask];
20077
20078
20079        if (!fz)
20080        {
20081            int i;
20082            fz = kmalloc(sizeof(struct fib_zone),
20083    GFP_KERNEL);
20084            if (!fz)
20085            {
20086                fib_free_node(f);
20087                return;
20088            }
20089            memset(fz, 0, sizeof(struct fib_zone));
20090            fz->fz_logmask = logmask;
20091            fz->fz_mask = mask;
20092            for (i=logmask-1; i>=0; i--)
20093                if (fib_zones[i])
20094                    break;
20095            cli();
20096            if (i<0)
20097            {
20098                fz->fz_next = fib_zone_list;
20099                fib_zone_list = fz;
20100            }
20101            else
20102            {
20103                fz->fz_next = fib_zones[i]->fz_next;
```

```
20104                fib_zones[i]->fz_next = fz;
20105            }
20106            fib_zones[logmask] = fz;
20107            sti();
20108        }
20109
20110        /*
20111         * If zone overgrows RTZ_HASHING_LIMIT, create hash
20112    table.
20113         */
20114
20115        if (fz->fz_nent >= RTZ_HASHING_LIMIT &&
20116    !fz->fz_hash_table && logmask<32)
20117        {
20118            struct fib_node ** ht;
20119    #if RT_CACHE_DEBUG >= 2
20120            printk("fib_add_1: hashing for zone %d
20121    started\n", logmask);
20122    #endif
20123            ht = kmalloc(RTZ_HASH_DIVISOR*sizeof(struct
20124    rtable*), GFP_KERNEL);
20125
20126            if (ht)
20127            {
20128                memset(ht, 0, RTZ_HASH_DIVISOR*sizeof(struct
20129    fib_node*));
20130                cli();
20131                f1 = fz->fz_list;
20132                while (f1)
20133                {
20134                    struct fib_node * next, **end;
20135                    unsigned hash =
20136    fz_hash_code(f1->fib_dst, logmask);
20137                    next = f1->fib_next;
20138                    f1->fib_next = NULL;
20139                    end = &ht[hash];
20140                    while(*end != NULL)
20141                        end = &(*end)->fib_next;
20142                    *end = f1;
20143                    f1 = next;
20144                }
20145                fz->fz_list = NULL;
20146                fz->fz_hash_table = ht;
20147                sti();
20148            }
20149        }
20150
20151        if (fz->fz_hash_table)
```

```
20152            fp = &fz->fz_hash_table[fz_hash_code(dst,
20153    logmask)];
20154        else
20155            fp = &fz->fz_list;
20156
20157        /*
20158         * Scan list to find the first route with the same
20159    destination
20160         */
20161        while ((f1 = *fp) != NULL)
20162        {
20163            if (f1->fib_dst == dst)
20164                break;
20165            fp = &f1->fib_next;
20166        }
20167
20168        /*
20169         * Find route with the same destination and less (or
20170    equal) metric.
20171         */
20172        while ((f1 = *fp) != NULL && f1->fib_dst == dst)
20173        {
20174            if (f1->fib_metric >= metric)
20175                break;
20176            /*
20177             *  Record route with the same destination and
20178    gateway,
20179             *  but less metric. We'll delete it
20180             *  after instantiation of new route.
20181             */
20182            if (f1->fib_info->fib_gateway == gw &&
20183                (gw || f1->fib_info->fib_dev == dev))
20184                dup_fp = fp;
20185            fp = &f1->fib_next;
20186        }
20187
20188        /*
20189         * Is it already present?
20190         */
20191
20192        if (f1 && f1->fib_metric == metric && f1->fib_info
20193    == fi)
20194        {
20195            fib_free_node(f);
20196            return;
20197        }
20198
20199        /*
```

```
20200        * Insert new entry to the list.
20201        */
20202
20203       cli();
20204       f->fib_next = f1;
20205       *fp = f;
20206       if (!fib_loopback && (fi->fib_dev->flags &
20207   IFF_LOOPBACK))
20208           fib_loopback = f;
20209       sti();
20210       fz->fz_nent++;
20211       ip_netlink_msg(RTMSG_NEWROUTE, dst, gw, mask, flags,
20212   metric, fi->fib_dev->name);
20213
20214       /*
20215        *  Delete route with the same destination and
20216   gateway.
20217        *  Note that we should have at most one such route.
20218        */
20219       if (dup_fp)
20220           fp = dup_fp;
20221       else
20222           fp = &f->fib_next;
20223
20224       while ((f1 = *fp) != NULL && f1->fib_dst == dst)
20225       {
20226           if (f1->fib_info->fib_gateway == gw &&
20227              (gw || f1->fib_info->fib_dev == dev))
20228           {
20229               cli();
20230               *fp = f1->fib_next;
20231               if (fib_loopback == f1)
20232                   fib_loopback = NULL;
20233               sti();
20234               ip_netlink_msg(RTMSG_DELROUTE, dst, gw,
20235   mask, flags, metric, f1->fib_info->fib_dev->name);
20236               fib_free_node(f1);
20237               fz->fz_nent--;
20238               break;
20239           }
20240           fp = &f1->fib_next;
20241       }
20242       rt_cache_flush();
20243       return;
20244   }
20245
20246   static int rt_flush_list(struct fib_node ** fp, struct
20247   device *dev)
20248   {
20249       int found = 0;
20250       struct fib_node *f;
20251
20252       while ((f = *fp) != NULL) {
20253   /*
20254    *  "Magic" device route is allowed to point to loopback,
20255    *  discard it too.
20256    */
20257           if (f->fib_info->fib_dev != dev &&
20258               (f->fib_info->fib_dev != &loopback_dev ||
20259   f->fib_dst != dev->pa_addr)) {
20260               fp = &f->fib_next;
20261               continue;
20262           }
20263           cli();
20264           *fp = f->fib_next;
20265           if (fib_loopback == f)
20266               fib_loopback = NULL;
20267           sti();
20268           fib_free_node(f);
20269           found++;
20270       }
20271       return found;
20272   }
20273
20274   static __inline__ void fib_flush_1(struct device *dev)
20275   {
20276       struct fib_zone *fz;
20277       int found = 0;
20278
20279       for (fz = fib_zone_list; fz; fz = fz->fz_next)
20280       {
20281           if (fz->fz_hash_table)
20282           {
20283               int i;
20284               int tmp = 0;
20285               for (i=0; i<RTZ_HASH_DIVISOR; i++)
20286                   tmp +=
20287   rt_flush_list(&fz->fz_hash_table[i], dev);
20288               fz->fz_nent -= tmp;
20289               found += tmp;
20290           }
20291           else
20292           {
20293               int tmp;
20294               tmp = rt_flush_list(&fz->fz_list, dev);
20295               fz->fz_nent -= tmp;
```

```
20296              found += tmp;
20297          }
20298      }
20299
20300      if (found)
20301          rt_cache_flush();
20302  }
20303
20304
20305  /*
20306   *  Called from the PROCfs module. This outputs
20307  /proc/net/route.
20308   *
20309   *  We preserve the old format but pad the buffers out.
20310  This means that
20311   *  we can spin over the other entries as we read them.
20312  Remember the
20313   *  gated BGP4 code could need to read 60,000+ routes on
20314  occasion (that's
20315   *  about 7Mb of data). To do that ok we will need to
20316  also cache the
20317   *  last route we got to (reads will generally be
20318  following on from
20319   *  one another without gaps).
20320   */
20321
20322  int rt_get_info(char *buffer, char **start, off_t
20323  offset, int length, int dummy)
20324  {
20325      struct fib_zone *fz;
20326      struct fib_node *f;
20327      int len=0;
20328      off_t pos=0;
20329      char temp[129];
20330      int i;
20331
20332      pos = 128;
20333
20334      if (offset<128)
20335      {
20336
20337  sprintf(buffer,"%-127s\n","Iface\tDestination\tGateway
20338  \tFlags\tRefCnt\tUse\tMetric\tMask\t\tMTU\tWindow\tIRTT")
20339  ;
20340          len = 128;
20341      }
20342
20343      while  (ip_rt_lock)
```

p 494

```
20344          sleep_on(&rt_wait);
20345      ip_rt_fast_lock();
20346
20347      for (fz=fib_zone_list; fz; fz = fz->fz_next)
20348      {
20349          int maxslot;
20350          struct fib_node ** fp;
20351
20352          if (fz->fz_nent == 0)
20353              continue;
20354
20355          if (pos + 128*fz->fz_nent <= offset)
20356          {
20357              pos += 128*fz->fz_nent;
20358              len = 0;
20359              continue;
20360          }
20361
20362          if (fz->fz_hash_table)
20363          {
20364              maxslot = RTZ_HASH_DIVISOR;
20365              fp  = fz->fz_hash_table;
20366          }
20367          else
20368          {
20369              maxslot = 1;
20370              fp  = &fz->fz_list;
20371          }
20372
20373          for (i=0; i < maxslot; i++, fp++)
20374          {
20375
20376              for (f = *fp; f; f = f->fib_next)
20377              {
20378                  struct fib_info * fi;
20379                  /*
20380                   *  Spin through entries until we are
20381  ready
20382                   */
20383                  pos += 128;
20384
20385                  if (pos <= offset)
20386                  {
20387                      len=0;
20388                      continue;
20389                  }
20390
20391                  fi = f->fib_info;
```

```
20392                   sprintf(temp,
20393   "%s\t%08lX\t%08lX\t%02X\t%d\t%lu\t%d\t%08lX\t%d\t%lu\t%u"
20394   ,
20395                   fi->fib_dev->name, (unsigned
20396   long)f->fib_dst, (unsigned long)fi->fib_gateway,
20397                   fi->fib_flags, 0, f->fib_use,
20398   f->fib_metric,
20399                   (unsigned long)fz->fz_mask,
20400   (int)fi->fib_mtu, fi->fib_window, (int)fi->fib_irtt);
20401                   sprintf(buffer+len,"%-127s\n",temp);
20402
20403                   len += 128;
20404                   if (pos >= offset+length)
20405                       goto done;
20406               }
20407           }
20408       }
20409
20410   done:
20411       ip_rt_unlock();
20412       wake_up(&rt_wait);
20413
20414       *start = buffer+len-(pos-offset);
20415       len = pos - offset;
20416       if (len>length)
20417           len = length;
20418       return len;
20419   }
20420
20421   int rt_cache_get_info(char *buffer, char **start, off_t
20422   offset, int length, int dummy)
20423   {
20424       int len=0;
20425       off_t pos=0;
20426       char temp[129];
20427       struct rtable *r;
20428       int i;
20429
20430       pos = 128;
20431
20432       if (offset<128)
20433       {
20434
20435   sprintf(buffer,"%-127s\n","Iface\tDestination\tGateway
20436   \tFlags\tRefCnt\tUse\tMetric\tSource\t\tMTU\tWindow\tIRTT
20437   \tHH\tARP");
20438           len = 128;
20439       }
```

```
20440
20441
20442       while (ip_rt_lock)
20443           sleep_on(&rt_wait);
20444       ip_rt_fast_lock();
20445
20446       for (i = 0; i<RT_HASH_DIVISOR; i++)
20447       {
20448           for (r = ip_rt_hash_table[i]; r; r = r->rt_next)
20449           {
20450               /*
20451                *  Spin through entries until we are ready
20452                */
20453               pos += 128;
20454
20455               if (pos <= offset)
20456               {
20457                   len = 0;
20458                   continue;
20459               }
20460
20461               sprintf(temp,
20462   "%s\t%08lX\t%08lX\t%02X\t%d\t%u\t%d\t%08lX\t%d\t%lu\t%u\t
20463   %d\t%1d",
20464               r->rt_dev->name, (unsigned
20465   long)r->rt_dst, (unsigned long)r->rt_gateway,
20466               r->rt_flags, r->rt_refcnt, r->rt_use, 0,
20467               (unsigned long)r->rt_src,
20468   (int)r->rt_mtu, r->rt_window, (int)r->rt_irtt, r->rt_hh
20469   ? r->rt_hh->hh_refcnt : -1, r->rt_hh ?
20470   r->rt_hh->hh_uptodate : 0);
20471               sprintf(buffer+len,"%-127s\n",temp);
20472               len += 128;
20473               if (pos >= offset+length)
20474                   goto done;
20475           }
20476       }
20477
20478   done:
20479       ip_rt_unlock();
20480       wake_up(&rt_wait);
20481
20482       *start = buffer+len-(pos-offset);
20483       len = pos-offset;
20484       if (len>length)
20485           len = length;
20486       return len;
20487   }
```

```
20488
20489
20490    void rt_free(struct rtable * rt)
20491    {
20492        unsigned long flags;
20493
20494        save_flags(flags);
20495        cli();
20496        if (!rt->rt_refcnt)
20497        {
20498            struct hh_cache * hh = rt->rt_hh;
20499            rt->rt_hh = NULL;
20500            restore_flags(flags);
20501            if (hh && atomic_dec_and_test(&hh->hh_refcnt))
20502                kfree_s(hh, sizeof(struct hh_cache));
20503            kfree_s(rt, sizeof(struct rtable));
20504            return;
20505        }
20506        rt->rt_next = rt_free_queue;
20507        rt->rt_flags &= ~RTF_UP;
20508        rt_free_queue = rt;
20509        ip_rt_bh_mask |= RT_BH_FREE;
20510    #if RT_CACHE_DEBUG >= 2
20511        printk("rt_free: %08x\n", rt->rt_dst);
20512    #endif
20513        restore_flags(flags);
20514    }
20515
20516    /*
20517     * RT "bottom half" handlers. Called with masked
20518    interrupts.
20519     */
20520
20521    static __inline__ void rt_kick_free_queue(void)
20522    {
20523        struct rtable *rt, **rtp;
20524
20525        ip_rt_bh_mask &= ~RT_BH_FREE;
20526
20527        rtp = &rt_free_queue;
20528
20529        while ((rt = *rtp) != NULL)
20530        {
20531            if (!rt->rt_refcnt)
20532            {
20533                struct hh_cache * hh = rt->rt_hh;
20534    #if RT_CACHE_DEBUG >= 2
20535                __u32 daddr = rt->rt_dst;
20536    #endif
20537                *rtp = rt->rt_next;
20538                rt->rt_hh = NULL;
20539                sti();
20540                if (hh &&
20541    atomic_dec_and_test(&hh->hh_refcnt))
20542                    kfree_s(hh, sizeof(struct hh_cache));
20543                kfree_s(rt, sizeof(struct rtable));
20544    #if RT_CACHE_DEBUG >= 2
20545                printk("rt_kick_free_queue: %08x is free\n",
20546    daddr);
20547    #endif
20548                cli();
20549                continue;
20550            }
20551            rtp = &rt->rt_next;
20552        }
20553    }
20554
20555    void ip_rt_run_bh()
20556    {
20557        unsigned long flags;
20558        save_flags(flags);
20559        cli();
20560        if (ip_rt_bh_mask && !ip_rt_lock)
20561        {
20562            if (ip_rt_bh_mask & RT_BH_REDIRECT)
20563                rt_kick_backlog();
20564
20565            if (ip_rt_bh_mask & RT_BH_GARBAGE_COLLECT)
20566            {
20567                ip_rt_fast_lock();
20568                ip_rt_bh_mask &= ~RT_BH_GARBAGE_COLLECT;
20569                sti();
20570                rt_garbage_collect_1();
20571                cli();
20572                ip_rt_fast_unlock();
20573            }
20574
20575            if (ip_rt_bh_mask & RT_BH_FREE)
20576                rt_kick_free_queue();
20577        }
20578        restore_flags(flags);
20579    }
20580
20581
20582    void ip_rt_check_expire()
20583    {
```

```
20584          ip_rt_fast_lock();
20585          if (ip_rt_lock == 1)
20586          {
20587              int i;
20588              struct rtable *rth, **rthp;
20589              unsigned long flags;
20590              unsigned long now = jiffies;
20591
20592              save_flags(flags);
20593              for (i=0; i<RT_HASH_DIVISOR; i++)
20594              {
20595                  rthp = &ip_rt_hash_table[i];
20596
20597                  while ((rth = *rthp) != NULL)
20598                  {
20599                      struct rtable * rth_next = rth->rt_next;
20600
20601                      /*
20602                       * Cleanup aged off entries.
20603                       */
20604
20605                      cli();
20606                      if (!rth->rt_refcnt && rth->rt_lastuse +
20607    RT_CACHE_TIMEOUT < now)
20608                      {
20609                          *rthp = rth_next;
20610                          sti();
20611                          rt_cache_size--;
20612    #if RT_CACHE_DEBUG >= 2
20613                          printk("rt_check_expire clean
20614    %02x@%08x\n", i, rth->rt_dst);
20615    #endif
20616                          rt_free(rth);
20617                          continue;
20618                      }
20619                      sti();
20620
20621                      if (!rth_next)
20622                          break;
20623
20624                      /*
20625                       * LRU ordering.
20626                       */
20627
20628                      if (rth->rt_lastuse +
20629    RT_CACHE_BUBBLE_THRESHOLD < rth_next->rt_lastuse ||
20630                          (rth->rt_lastuse <
20631    rth_next->rt_lastuse &&
```

```
20632                              rth->rt_use < rth_next->rt_use))
20633                      {
20634    #if RT_CACHE_DEBUG >= 2
20635                          printk("rt_check_expire bubbled
20636    %02x@%08x<->%08x\n", i, rth->rt_dst, rth_next->rt_dst);
20637    #endif
20638                          cli();
20639                          *rthp = rth_next;
20640                          rth->rt_next = rth_next->rt_next;
20641                          rth_next->rt_next = rth;
20642                          sti();
20643                          rthp = &rth_next->rt_next;
20644                          continue;
20645                      }
20646                      rthp = &rth->rt_next;
20647                  }
20648              }
20649              restore_flags(flags);
20650              rt_kick_free_queue();
20651          }
20652          ip_rt_unlock();
20653    }
20654
20655    static void rt_redirect_1(__u32 dst, __u32 gw, struct
20656    device *dev)
20657    {
20658        struct rtable *rt;
20659        unsigned long hash = ip_rt_hash_code(dst);
20660
20661        if (gw == dev->pa_addr)
20662            return;
20663        if (dev != get_gw_dev(gw))
20664            return;
20665        rt = (struct rtable *) kmalloc(sizeof(struct
20666    rtable), GFP_ATOMIC);
20667        if (rt == NULL)
20668            return;
20669        memset(rt, 0, sizeof(struct rtable));
20670        rt->rt_flags = RTF_DYNAMIC | RTF_MODIFIED | RTF_HOST
20671    | RTF_GATEWAY | RTF_UP;
20672        rt->rt_dst = dst;
20673        rt->rt_dev = dev;
20674        rt->rt_gateway = gw;
20675        rt->rt_src = dev->pa_addr;
20676        rt->rt_mtu = dev->mtu;
20677    #ifdef CONFIG_NO_PATH_MTU_DISCOVERY
20678        if (dev->mtu > 576)
20679            rt->rt_mtu = 576;
```

```
20680  #endif
20681      rt->rt_lastuse  = jiffies;
20682      rt->rt_refcnt   = 1;
20683      rt_cache_add(hash, rt);
20684      ip_rt_put(rt);
20685      return;
20686  }
20687
20688  static void rt_cache_flush(void)
20689  {
20690      int i;
20691      struct rtable * rth, * next;
20692
20693      for (i=0; i<RT_HASH_DIVISOR; i++)
20694      {
20695          int nr=0;
20696
20697          cli();
20698          if (!(rth = ip_rt_hash_table[i]))
20699          {
20700              sti();
20701              continue;
20702          }
20703
20704          ip_rt_hash_table[i] = NULL;
20705          sti();
20706
20707          for (; rth; rth=next)
20708          {
20709              next = rth->rt_next;
20710              rt_cache_size--;
20711              nr++;
20712              rth->rt_next = NULL;
20713              rt_free(rth);
20714          }
20715  #if RT_CACHE_DEBUG >= 2
20716          if (nr > 0)
20717              printk("rt_cache_flush: %d@%02x\n", nr, i);
20718  #endif
20719      }
20720  #if RT_CACHE_DEBUG >= 1
20721      if (rt_cache_size)
20722      {
20723          printk("rt_cache_flush: bug rt_cache_size=%d\n",
20724  rt_cache_size);
20725          rt_cache_size = 0;
20726      }
20727  #endif
```

```
20728  }
20729
20730  static void rt_garbage_collect_1(void)
20731  {
20732      int i;
20733      unsigned expire = RT_CACHE_TIMEOUT>>1;
20734      struct rtable * rth, **rthp;
20735      unsigned long now = jiffies;
20736
20737      for (;;)
20738      {
20739          for (i=0; i<RT_HASH_DIVISOR; i++)
20740          {
20741              if (!ip_rt_hash_table[i])
20742                  continue;
20743              for (rthp=&ip_rt_hash_table[i]; (rth=*rthp);
20744  rthp=&rth->rt_next)
20745              {
20746                  if (rth->rt_lastuse +
20747  expire*(rth->rt_refcnt+1) > now)
20748                      continue;
20749                  rt_cache_size--;
20750                  cli();
20751                  *rthp=rth->rt_next;
20752                  rth->rt_next = NULL;
20753                  sti();
20754                  rt_free(rth);
20755                  break;
20756              }
20757          }
20758          if (rt_cache_size < RT_CACHE_SIZE_MAX)
20759              return;
20760          expire >>= 1;
20761      }
20762  }
20763
20764  static __inline__ void rt_req_enqueue(struct rt_req **q,
20765  struct rt_req *rtr)
20766  {
20767      unsigned long flags;
20768      struct rt_req * tail;
20769
20770      save_flags(flags);
20771      cli();
20772      tail = *q;
20773      if (!tail)
20774          rtr->rtr_next = rtr;
20775      else
```

```
20776         {
20777             rtr->rtr_next = tail->rtr_next;
20778             tail->rtr_next = rtr;
20779         }
20780         *q = rtr;
20781         restore_flags(flags);
20782         return;
20783     }
20784
20785     /*
20786      * Caller should mask interrupts.
20787      */
20788
20789     static __inline__ struct rt_req * rt_req_dequeue(struct
20790     rt_req **q)
20791     {
20792         struct rt_req * rtr;
20793
20794         if (*q)
20795         {
20796             rtr = (*q)->rtr_next;
20797             (*q)->rtr_next = rtr->rtr_next;
20798             if (rtr->rtr_next == rtr)
20799                 *q = NULL;
20800             rtr->rtr_next = NULL;
20801             return rtr;
20802         }
20803         return NULL;
20804     }
20805
20806     /*
20807        Called with masked interrupts
20808      */
20809
20810     static void rt_kick_backlog()
20811     {
20812         if (!ip_rt_lock)
20813         {
20814             struct rt_req * rtr;
20815
20816             ip_rt_fast_lock();
20817
20818             while ((rtr = rt_req_dequeue(&rt_backlog)) !=
20819     NULL)
20820             {
20821                 sti();
20822                 rt_redirect_1(rtr->dst, rtr->gw, rtr->dev);
20823                 kfree_s(rtr, sizeof(struct rt_req));
```

```
20824             cli();
20825         }
20826
20827         ip_rt_bh_mask &= ~RT_BH_REDIRECT;
20828
20829         ip_rt_fast_unlock();
20830     }
20831     }
20832
20833     /*
20834      * rt_{del|add|flush} called only from USER process.
20835     Waiting is OK.
20836      */
20837
20838     static int rt_del(__u32 dst, __u32 mask,
20839         struct device * dev, __u32 gtw, short rt_flags,
20840     short metric)
20841     {
20842         int retval;
20843
p 500  20844         while (ip_rt_lock)
20845             sleep_on(&rt_wait);
20846         ip_rt_fast_lock();
20847         retval = fib_del_1(dst, mask, dev, gtw, rt_flags,
20848     metric);
20849         ip_rt_unlock();
p 501  20850         wake_up(&rt_wait);
20851         return retval;
20852     }
20853
20854     static void rt_add(short flags, __u32 dst, __u32 mask,
20855         __u32 gw, struct device *dev, unsigned short mss,
20856         unsigned long window, unsigned short irtt, short
20857     metric)
20858     {
p 498  20859         while (ip_rt_lock)
20860             sleep_on(&rt_wait);
20861         ip_rt_fast_lock();
p 499  20862         fib_add_1(flags, dst, mask, gw, dev, mss, window,
20863     irtt, metric);
20864         ip_rt_unlock();
20865         wake_up(&rt_wait);
20866     }
20867
p 499  20868     void ip_rt_flush(struct device *dev)
20869     {
20870         while (ip_rt_lock)
20871             sleep_on(&rt_wait);
```

```
20872        ip_rt_fast_lock();
20873        fib_flush_1(dev);
20874        ip_rt_unlock();
20875        wake_up(&rt_wait);
20876    }
20877
20878    /*
20879        Called by ICMP module.
20880     */
20881
20882    void ip_rt_redirect(__u32 src, __u32 dst, __u32 gw,
20883    struct device *dev)
20884    {
20885        struct rt_req * rtr;
20886        struct rtable * rt;
20887
20888        rt = ip_rt_route(dst, 0, NULL);
20889        if (!rt)
20890            return;
20891
20892        if (rt->rt_gateway != src ||
20893            rt->rt_dev != dev ||
20894            ((gw^dev->pa_addr)&dev->pa_mask) ||
20895            ip_chk_addr(gw))
20896        {
20897            ip_rt_put(rt);
20898            return;
20899        }
20900        ip_rt_put(rt);
20901
20902        ip_rt_fast_lock();
20903        if (ip_rt_lock == 1)
20904        {
20905            rt_redirect_1(dst, gw, dev);
20906            ip_rt_unlock();
20907            return;
20908        }
20909
20910        rtr = kmalloc(sizeof(struct rt_req), GFP_ATOMIC);
20911        if (rtr)
20912        {
20913            rtr->dst = dst;
20914            rtr->gw = gw;
20915            rtr->dev = dev;
20916            rt_req_enqueue(&rt_backlog, rtr);
20917            ip_rt_bh_mask |= RT_BH_REDIRECT;
20918        }
20919        ip_rt_unlock();
20920    }
20921
20922
20923    static __inline__ void rt_garbage_collect(void)
20924    {
20925        if (ip_rt_lock == 1)
20926        {
20927            rt_garbage_collect_1();
20928            return;
20929        }
20930        ip_rt_bh_mask |= RT_BH_GARBAGE_COLLECT;
20931    }
20932
20933    static void rt_cache_add(unsigned hash, struct rtable *
20934    rth)
20935    {
20936        unsigned long    flags;
20937        struct rtable    **rthp;
20938        __u32            daddr = rth->rt_dst;
20939        unsigned long    now = jiffies;
20940
20941    #if RT_CACHE_DEBUG >= 2
20942        if (ip_rt_lock != 1)
20943        {
20944            printk("rt_cache_add: ip_rt_lock==%d\n",
20945    ip_rt_lock);
20946            return;
20947        }
20948    #endif
20949
20950        save_flags(flags);
20951
20952        if (rth->rt_dev->header_cache_bind)
20953        {
20954            struct rtable * rtg = rth;
20955
20956            if (rth->rt_gateway != daddr)
20957            {
20958                ip_rt_fast_unlock();
20959                rtg = ip_rt_route(rth->rt_gateway, 0, NULL);
20960                ip_rt_fast_lock();
20961            }
20962
20963            if (rtg)
20964            {
20965                if (rtg == rth)
20966
20967    rtg->rt_dev->header_cache_bind(&rtg->rt_hh, rtg->rt_dev,
```

p 496 (line 20888)
p 502 (line 20923)
p 501 (line 20942)

```
20968   ETH_P_IP, rtg->rt_dst);
20969           else
20970           {
20971               if (rtg->rt_hh)
20972                   atomic_inc(&rtg->rt_hh->hh_refcnt);
20973               rth->rt_hh = rtg->rt_hh;
20974               ip_rt_put(rtg);
20975           }
20976       }
20977   }
20978
20979       if (rt_cache_size >= RT_CACHE_SIZE_MAX)
20980           rt_garbage_collect();
20981
20982       cli();
20983       rth->rt_next = ip_rt_hash_table[hash];
20984   #if RT_CACHE_DEBUG >= 2
20985       if (rth->rt_next)
20986       {
20987           struct rtable * trth;
20988           printk("rt_cache @%02x: %08x", hash, daddr);
20989           for (trth=rth->rt_next; trth; trth=trth->rt_next)
20990               printk(" . %08x", trth->rt_dst);
20991           printk("\n");
20992       }
20993   #endif
20994       ip_rt_hash_table[hash] = rth;
20995       rthp = &rth->rt_next;
20996       sti();
20997       rt_cache_size++;
20998
20999       /*
21000        * Cleanup duplicate (and aged off) entries.
21001        */
21002
21003       while ((rth = *rthp) != NULL)
21004       {
21005
21006           cli();
21007           if ((!rth->rt_refcnt && rth->rt_lastuse +
21008   RT_CACHE_TIMEOUT < now)
21009               || rth->rt_dst == daddr)
21010           {
21011               *rthp = rth->rt_next;
21012               rt_cache_size--;
21013               sti();
21014   #if RT_CACHE_DEBUG >= 2
21015               printk("rt_cache clean %02x@%08x\n", hash,
```

```
21016   rth->rt_dst);
21017   #endif
21018               rt_free(rth);
21019               continue;
21020           }
21021           sti();
21022           rthp = &rth->rt_next;
21023       }
21024       restore_flags(flags);
21025   }
21026
21027   /*
21028       RT should be already locked.
21029
21030       We could improve this by keeping a chain of say 32
21031   struct rtable's
21032       last freed for fast recycling.
21033
21034    */
21035
21036   struct rtable * ip_rt_slow_route (__u32 daddr, int
21037   local, struct device *dev)
21038   {
21039       unsigned hash = ip_rt_hash_code(daddr)^local;
21040       struct rtable * rth;
21041       struct fib_node * f;
21042       struct fib_info * fi;
21043       __u32 saddr;
21044
21045   #if RT_CACHE_DEBUG >= 2
21046       printk("rt_cache miss @%08x\n", daddr);
21047   #endif
21048
21049       rth = kmalloc(sizeof(struct rtable), GFP_ATOMIC);
21050       if (!rth)
21051       {
21052           ip_rt_unlock();
21053           return NULL;
21054       }
21055
21056       if (local)
21057           f = fib_lookup_local(daddr, dev);
21058       else
21059           f = fib_lookup (daddr, dev);
21060
21061       if (f)
21062       {
21063           fi = f->fib_info;
```

p 503

```
21064            f->fib_use++;
21065        }
21066
21067     if (!f || (fi->fib_flags & RTF_REJECT))
21068     {
21069 #ifdef CONFIG_KERNELD
21070        char wanted_route[20];
21071 #endif
21072 #if RT_CACHE_DEBUG >= 2
21073        printk("rt_route failed @%08x\n", daddr);
21074 #endif
21075        ip_rt_unlock();
21076        kfree_s(rth, sizeof(struct rtable));
21077 #ifdef CONFIG_KERNELD
21078        if (MULTICAST(daddr))
21079            return NULL;
21080        daddr=ntohl(daddr);
21081        sprintf(wanted_route, "%d.%d.%d.%d",
21082            (int)(daddr >> 24) & 0xff, (int)(daddr >>
21083 16) & 0xff,
21084            (int)(daddr >> 8) & 0xff, (int)daddr & 0xff);
21085        kerneld_route(wanted_route);    /* Dynamic route
21086 request */
21087 #endif
21088        return NULL;
21089     }
21090
21091     saddr = fi->fib_dev->pa_addr;
21092
21093     if (daddr == fi->fib_dev->pa_addr)
21094     {
21095        f->fib_use--;
21096        if ((f = fib_loopback) != NULL)
21097        {
21098            f->fib_use++;
21099            fi = f->fib_info;
21100        }
21101     }
21102
21103     if (!f)
21104     {
21105        ip_rt_unlock();
21106        kfree_s(rth, sizeof(struct rtable));
21107        return NULL;
21108     }
21109
21110     rth->rt_dst = daddr;
21111     rth->rt_src = saddr;
21112     rth->rt_lastuse = jiffies;
21113     rth->rt_refcnt   = 1;
21114     rth->rt_use = 1;
21115     rth->rt_next     = NULL;
21116     rth->rt_hh   = NULL;
21117     rth->rt_gateway = fi->fib_gateway;
21118     rth->rt_dev = fi->fib_dev;
21119     rth->rt_mtu = fi->fib_mtu;
21120     rth->rt_window  = fi->fib_window;
21121     rth->rt_irtt    = fi->fib_irtt;
21122     rth->rt_tos = f->fib_tos;
21123     rth->rt_flags   = fi->fib_flags | RTF_HOST;
21124     if (local)
21125        rth->rt_flags   |= RTF_LOCAL;
21126
21127     if (!(rth->rt_flags & RTF_GATEWAY))
21128        rth->rt_gateway = rth->rt_dst;
21129     /*
21130      * Multicast or limited broadcast is never
21131 gatewayed.
21132      */
21133     if (MULTICAST(daddr) || daddr == 0xFFFFFFFF)
21134        rth->rt_gateway = rth->rt_dst;
21135
21136     if (ip_rt_lock == 1)
21137     {
21138        /* Don't add this to the rt_cache if a device
21139 was specified,
21140         * because we might have skipped better routes
21141 which didn't
21142         * point at the right device. */
21143        if (dev != NULL)
21144            rth->rt_flags |= RTF_NOTCACHED;
21145        else
21146            rt_cache_add(hash, rth);
21147     }
21148     else
21149     {
21150        rt_free(rth);
21151 #if RT_CACHE_DEBUG >= 1
21152        printk(KERN_DEBUG "rt_cache: route to %08x was
21153 born dead\n", daddr);
21154 #endif
21155     }
21156
21157     ip_rt_unlock();
21158     return rth;
21159 }
```

```
21160
21161    void ip_rt_put(struct rtable * rt)
21162    {
21163        if (rt)
21164            atomic_dec(&rt->rt_refcnt);
21165
21166        /* If this rtable entry is not in the cache, we'd
21167    better free it once the
21168         * refcnt goes to zero, because nobody else will...
21169    */
21170        if ( rt && (rt->rt_flags & RTF_NOTCACHED) &&
21171    (!rt->rt_refcnt) )
21172            rt_free(rt);
21173    }
21174
21175    /*
21176     *  Return routing dev for given address.
21177     *  Called by ip_alias module to avoid using ip_rt_route
21178    and
21179     *  generating hhs.
21180     */
21181    struct device * ip_rt_dev(__u32 addr)
21182    {
21183        struct fib_node *f;
21184        f = fib_lookup(addr, NULL);
21185        if (f)
21186            return f->fib_info->fib_dev;
21187        return NULL;
21188    }
21189
21190    struct rtable * ip_rt_route(__u32 daddr, int local,
21191    struct device *dev)
21192    {
21193        struct rtable * rth;
21194
21195        ip_rt_fast_lock();
21196
21197        for
21198    (rth=ip_rt_hash_table[ip_rt_hash_code(daddr)^local];
21199    rth; rth=rth->rt_next)
21200        {
21201            /* If a network device is specified, make sure
21202    this route points to it. */
21203            if ( (rth->rt_dst == daddr) && ((dev==NULL) ||
21204    (dev==rth->rt_dev)) )
21205            {
21206                rth->rt_lastuse = jiffies;
21207                atomic_inc(&rth->rt_use);
21208                atomic_inc(&rth->rt_refcnt);
21209                ip_rt_unlock();
21210                return rth;
21211            }
21212        }
21213        return ip_rt_slow_route (daddr, local, dev);
21214    }
21215
21216    /*
21217     *  Process a route add request from the user, or from a
21218    kernel
21219     *  task.
21220     */
21221
21222    int ip_rt_new(struct rtentry *r)
21223    {
21224        int err;
21225        char * devname;
21226        struct device * dev = NULL;
21227        unsigned long flags;
21228        __u32 daddr, mask, gw;
21229        short metric;
21230
21231        /*
21232         *  If a device is specified find it.
21233         */
21234
21235        if ((devname = r->rt_dev) != NULL)
21236        {
21237            err = getname(devname, &devname);
21238            if (err)
21239                return err;
21240            dev = dev_get(devname);
21241            putname(devname);
21242            if (!dev)
21243                return -ENODEV;
21244        }
21245
21246        /*
21247         *  If the device isn't INET, don't allow it
21248         */
21249
21250        if (r->rt_dst.sa_family != AF_INET)
21251            return -EAFNOSUPPORT;
21252
21253        /*
21254         *  Make local copies of the important bits
21255         *  We decrement the metric by one for BSD
```

```
21256    compatibility.
21257        */
21258
21259        flags = r->rt_flags;
21260        daddr = (__u32) ((struct sockaddr_in *)
21261    &r->rt_dst)->sin_addr.s_addr;
21262        mask  = (__u32) ((struct sockaddr_in *)
21263    &r->rt_genmask)->sin_addr.s_addr;
21264        gw    = (__u32) ((struct sockaddr_in *)
21265    &r->rt_gateway)->sin_addr.s_addr;
21266        metric = r->rt_metric > 0 ? r->rt_metric - 1 : 0;
21267
21268        /*
21269         *  BSD emulation: Permits route add someroute gw
21270    one-of-my-addresses
21271         *  to indicate which iface. Not as clean as the
21272    nice Linux dev technique
21273         *  but people keep using it...  (and gated likes it
21274    ;))
21275         */
21276
21277        if (!dev && (flags & RTF_GATEWAY))
21278        {
21279            struct device *dev2;
21280            for (dev2 = dev_base ; dev2 != NULL ; dev2 =
21281    dev2->next)
21282            {
21283                if ((dev2->flags & IFF_UP) && dev2->pa_addr
21284    == gw)
21285                {
21286                    flags &= ~RTF_GATEWAY;
21287                    dev = dev2;
21288                    break;
21289                }
21290            }
21291        }
21292
21293        if (flags & RTF_HOST)
21294            mask = 0xffffffff;
21295        else if (mask && r->rt_genmask.sa_family != AF_INET)
21296            return -EAFNOSUPPORT;
21297
21298        if (flags & RTF_GATEWAY)
21299        {
21300            if (r->rt_gateway.sa_family != AF_INET)
21301                return -EAFNOSUPPORT;
21302
21303            /*
21304             *  Don't try to add a gateway we can't reach..
21305             *  Tunnel devices are exempt from this rule.
21306             */
21307
21308            if (!dev)
21309                dev = get_gw_dev(gw);
21310            else if (dev != get_gw_dev(gw) && dev->type !=
21311    ARPHRD_TUNNEL)
21312                return -EINVAL;
21313            if (!dev)
21314                return -ENETUNREACH;
21315        }
21316        else
21317        {
21318            gw = 0;
21319            if (!dev)
21320                dev = ip_dev_bynet(daddr, mask);
21321            if (!dev)
21322                return -ENETUNREACH;
21323            if (!mask)
21324            {
21325                if (((daddr ^ dev->pa_addr) & dev->pa_mask)
21326    == 0)
21327                    mask = dev->pa_mask;
21328            }
21329        }
21330
21331    #ifndef CONFIG_IP_CLASSLESS
21332        if (!mask)
21333            mask = ip_get_mask(daddr);
21334    #endif
21335
21336        if (bad_mask(mask, daddr))
21337            return -EINVAL;
21338
21339        /*
21340         *  Add the route
21341         */
21342
21343        rt_add(flags, daddr, mask, gw, dev, r->rt_mss,
21344    r->rt_window, r->rt_irtt, metric);
21345        return 0;
21346    }
21347
21348
21349    /*
21350     *  Remove a route, as requested by the user.
21351     */
```

```
21352
21353   int ip_rt_kill(struct rtentry *r)
21354   {
21355       struct sockaddr_in *trg;
21356       struct sockaddr_in *msk;
21357       struct sockaddr_in *gtw;
21358       char *devname;
21359       int err;
21360       struct device * dev = NULL;
21361
21362       trg = (struct sockaddr_in *) &r->rt_dst;
21363       msk = (struct sockaddr_in *) &r->rt_genmask;
21364       gtw = (struct sockaddr_in *) &r->rt_gateway;
21365       if ((devname = r->rt_dev) != NULL)
21366       {
21367           err = getname(devname, &devname);
21368           if (err)
21369               return err;
21370           dev = dev_get(devname);
21371           putname(devname);
21372           if (!dev)
21373               return -ENODEV;
21374       }
21375       /*
21376        * metric can become negative here if it wasn't
21377   filled in
21378        * but that's a fortunate accident; we really use
21379   that in rt_del.
21380        */
21381       err=rt_del((__u32)trg->sin_addr.s_addr,
21382   (__u32)msk->sin_addr.s_addr, dev,
21383           (__u32)gtw->sin_addr.s_addr, r->rt_flags,
21384   r->rt_metric - 1);
21385       return err;
21386   }
21387
21388   /*
21389    * Handle IP routing ioctl calls. These are used to
21390   manipulate the routing tables
21391    */
21392
21393   int ip_rt_ioctl(unsigned int cmd, void *arg)
21394   {
21395       int err;
21396       struct rtentry rt;
21397
21398       switch(cmd)
21399       {
```

```
21400           case SIOCADDRT:    /* Add a route */
21401           case SIOCDELRT:    /* Delete a route */
21402               if (!suser())
21403                   return -EPERM;
21404               err=verify_area(VERIFY_READ, arg,
21405   sizeof(struct rtentry));
21406               if (err)
21407                   return err;
21408               memcpy_fromfs(&rt, arg, sizeof(struct
21409   rtentry));
21410               return (cmd == SIOCDELRT) ? ip_rt_kill(&rt)
21411   : ip_rt_new(&rt);
21412       }
21413
21414       return -EINVAL;
21415   }
21416
21417   void ip_rt_advice(struct rtable **rp, int advice)
21418   {
21419       /* Thanks! */
21420       return;
21421   }
21422
21423   void ip_rt_update(int event, struct device *dev)
21424   {
21425   /*
21426    *  This causes too much grief to do now.
21427    */
21428   #ifdef COMING_IN_2_1
21429       if (event == NETDEV_UP)
21430           rt_add(RTF_HOST|RTF_UP, dev->pa_addr, ~0, 0,
21431   dev, 0, 0, 0, 0);
21432       else if (event == NETDEV_DOWN)
21433           rt_del(dev->pa_addr, ~0, dev, 0,
21434   RTF_HOST|RTF_UP, 0);
21435   #endif
21436   }
```

usr/src/linux/net/ipv4/skbuff.c

```
21437   /*
21438    *  Routines having to do with the 'struct sk_buff'
21439   memory handlers.
21440    *
21441    *  Authors:    Alan Cox <iiitac@pyr.swan.ac.uk>
21442    *              Florian La Roche <rzsfl@rz.uni-sb.de>
21443    *
21444    *  Fixes:
21445    *      Alan Cox    :   Fixed the worst of the load
```

```
21446  balancer bugs.
21447   *       Dave Platt  :   Interrupt stacking fix.
21448   *  Richard Kooijman   :    Timestamp fixes.
21449   *       Alan Cox    :   Changed buffer format.
21450   *       Alan Cox    :   destructor hook for AF_UNIX etc.
21451   *       Linus Torvalds  :   Better skb_clone.
21452   *       Alan Cox    :   Added skb_copy.
21453   *       Alan Cox    :   Added all the changed routines
21454  Linus
21455   *               only put in the headers
21456   *       Ray VanTassle  :   Fixed --skb->lock in free
21457   *
21458   *  TO FIX:
21459   *       The __skb_ routines ought to check interrupts
21460  are disabled
21461   *  when called, and bitch like crazy if not.
21462  Unfortunately I don't think
21463   *  we currently have a portable way to check if
21464  interrupts are off -
21465   *  Linus ???
21466   *
21467   *  This program is free software; you can redistribute
21468  it and/or
21469   *  modify it under the terms of the GNU General Public
21470  License
21471   *  as published by the Free Software Foundation; either
21472  version
21473   *  2 of the License, or (at your option) any later
21474  version.
21475   */
21476
21477  /*
21478   *  The functions in this file will not compile
21479  correctly with gcc 2.4.x
21480   */
21481
21482  #include <linux/config.h>
21483  #include <linux/types.h>
21484  #include <linux/kernel.h>
21485  #include <linux/sched.h>
21486  #include <linux/mm.h>
21487  #include <linux/interrupt.h>
21488  #include <linux/in.h>
21489  #include <linux/inet.h>
21490  #include <linux/netdevice.h>
21491  #include <linux/malloc.h>
21492  #include <linux/string.h>
21493  #include <linux/skbuff.h>
```

```
21494
21495  #include <net/ip.h>
21496  #include <net/protocol.h>
21497  #include <net/route.h>
21498  #include <net/tcp.h>
21499  #include <net/udp.h>
21500  #include <net/sock.h>
21501
21502  #include <asm/segment.h>
21503  #include <asm/system.h>
21504
21505  /*
21506   *  Resource tracking variables
21507   */
21508
21509  atomic_t net_skbcount = 0;
21510  atomic_t net_locked = 0;
21511  atomic_t net_allocs = 0;
21512  atomic_t net_fails  = 0;
21513  atomic_t net_free_locked = 0;
21514
21515  extern atomic_t ip_frag_mem;
21516
21517  void show_net_buffers(void)
21518  {
21519      printk(KERN_INFO "Networking buffers in use
21520  : %u\n",net_skbcount);
21521      printk(KERN_INFO "Network buffers locked by drivers
21522  : %u\n",net_locked);
21523      printk(KERN_INFO "Total network buffer allocations
21524  : %u\n",net_allocs);
21525      printk(KERN_INFO "Total failed network buffer allocs
21526  : %u\n",net_fails);
21527      printk(KERN_INFO "Total free while locked events
21528  : %u\n",net_free_locked);
21529  #ifdef CONFIG_INET
21530      printk(KERN_INFO "IP fragment buffer size
21531  : %u\n",ip_frag_mem);
21532  #endif
21533  }
21534
21535  #if CONFIG_SKB_CHECK
21536
21537  /*
21538   *  Debugging paranoia. Can go later when this crud
21539  stack works
21540   */
21541
```

```
21542    int skb_check(struct sk_buff *skb, int head, int line,
21543    char *file)
21544    {
21545        if (head) {
21546            if (skb->magic_debug_cookie != SK_HEAD_SKB) {
21547                printk("File: %s Line %d, found a bad
21548    skb-head\n",
21549                    file,line);
21550                return -1;
21551            }
21552            if (!skb->next || !skb->prev) {
21553                printk("skb_check: head without next or
21554    prev\n");
21555                return -1;
21556            }
21557            if (skb->next->magic_debug_cookie != SK_HEAD_SKB
21558                && skb->next->magic_debug_cookie !=
21559    SK_GOOD_SKB) {
21560                printk("File: %s Line %d, bad next head-skb
21561    member\n",
21562                    file,line);
21563                return -1;
21564            }
21565            if (skb->prev->magic_debug_cookie != SK_HEAD_SKB
21566                && skb->prev->magic_debug_cookie !=
21567    SK_GOOD_SKB) {
21568                printk("File: %s Line %d, bad prev head-skb
21569    member\n",
21570                    file,line);
21571                return -1;
21572            }
21573    #if 0
21574            {
21575            struct sk_buff *skb2 = skb->next;
21576            int i = 0;
21577            while (skb2 != skb && i < 5) {
21578                if (skb_check(skb2, 0, line, file) < 0) {
21579                    printk("bad queue element in whole
21580    queue\n");
21581                    return -1;
21582                }
21583                i++;
21584                skb2 = skb2->next;
21585            }
21586            }
21587    #endif
21588            return 0;
21589        }
21590        if (skb->next != NULL &&
21591    skb->next->magic_debug_cookie != SK_HEAD_SKB
21592            && skb->next->magic_debug_cookie != SK_GOOD_SKB)
21593    {
21594            printk("File: %s Line %d, bad next skb member\n",
21595                file,line);
21596            return -1;
21597        }
21598        if (skb->prev != NULL &&
21599    skb->prev->magic_debug_cookie != SK_HEAD_SKB
21600            && skb->prev->magic_debug_cookie != SK_GOOD_SKB)
21601    {
21602            printk("File: %s Line %d, bad prev skb member\n",
21603                file,line);
21604            return -1;
21605        }


21608        if(skb->magic_debug_cookie==SK_FREED_SKB)
21609        {
21610            printk("File: %s Line %d, found a freed skb
21611    lurking in the undergrowth!\n",
21612                file,line);
21613            printk("skb=%p, real size=%d, free=%d\n",
21614                skb,skb->truesize,skb->free);
21615            return -1;
21616        }
21617        if(skb->magic_debug_cookie!=SK_GOOD_SKB)
21618        {
21619            printk("File: %s Line %d, passed a non skb!\n",
21620    file,line);
21621            printk("skb=%p, real size=%d, free=%d\n",
21622                skb,skb->truesize,skb->free);
21623            return -1;
21624        }
21625        if(skb->head>skb->data)
21626        {
21627            printk("File: %s Line %d, head > data !\n",
21628    file,line);
21629            printk("skb=%p, head=%p, data=%p\n",
21630                skb,skb->head,skb->data);
21631            return -1;
21632        }
21633        if(skb->tail>skb->end)
21634        {
21635            printk("File: %s Line %d, tail > end!\n",
21636    file,line);
21637            printk("skb=%p, tail=%p, end=%p\n",
```

```
21638              skb,skb->tail,skb->end);
21639          return -1;
21640      }
21641      if(skb->data>skb->tail)
21642      {
21643          printk("File: %s Line %d, data > tail!\n",
21644 file,line);
21645          printk("skb=%p, data=%p, tail=%p\n",
21646              skb,skb->data,skb->tail);
21647          return -1;
21648      }
21649      if(skb->tail-skb->data!=skb->len)
21650      {
21651          printk("File: %s Line %d, wrong length\n",
21652 file,line);
21653          printk("skb=%p, data=%p, end=%p len=%ld\n",
21654              skb,skb->data,skb->end,skb->len);
21655          return -1;
21656      }
21657      if((unsigned long) skb->end > (unsigned long) skb)
21658      {
21659          printk("File: %s Line %d, control overrun\n",
21660 file,line);
21661          printk("skb=%p, end=%p\n",
21662              skb,skb->end);
21663          return -1;
21664      }
21665
21666      /* Guess it might be acceptable then */
21667      return 0;
21668 }
21669 #endif
21670
21671
21672 #if CONFIG_SKB_CHECK
21673 void skb_queue_head_init(struct sk_buff_head *list)
21674 {
21675      list->prev = (struct sk_buff *)list;
21676      list->next = (struct sk_buff *)list;
21677      list->qlen = 0;
21678      list->magic_debug_cookie = SK_HEAD_SKB;
21679 }
21680
21681
21682 /*
21683  *  Insert an sk_buff at the start of a list.
21684  */
21685 void skb_queue_head(struct sk_buff_head *list_,struct
21686 sk_buff *newsk)
21687 {
21688      unsigned long flags;
21689      struct sk_buff *list = (struct sk_buff *)list_;
21690
21691      save_flags(flags);
21692      cli();
21693
21694      IS_SKB(newsk);
21695      IS_SKB_HEAD(list);
21696      if (newsk->next || newsk->prev)
21697          printk("Suspicious queue head: sk_buff on
21698 list!\n");
21699
21700      newsk->next = list->next;
21701      newsk->prev = list;
21702
21703      newsk->next->prev = newsk;
21704      newsk->prev->next = newsk;
21705      newsk->list = list_;
21706      list_->qlen++;
21707
21708      restore_flags(flags);
21709 }
21710
21711 void __skb_queue_head(struct sk_buff_head *list_,struct
21712 sk_buff *newsk)
21713 {
21714      struct sk_buff *list = (struct sk_buff *)list_;
21715
21716
21717      IS_SKB(newsk);
21718      IS_SKB_HEAD(list);
21719      if (newsk->next || newsk->prev)
21720          printk("Suspicious queue head: sk_buff on
21721 list!\n");
21722
21723      newsk->next = list->next;
21724      newsk->prev = list;
21725
21726      newsk->next->prev = newsk;
21727      newsk->prev->next = newsk;
21728      newsk->list = list_;
21729      list_->qlen++;
21730
21731 }
21732
21733 /*
```

```
21734    *  Insert an sk_buff at the end of a list.
21735    */
21736   void skb_queue_tail(struct sk_buff_head *list_, struct
21737   sk_buff *newsk)
21738   {
21739       unsigned long flags;
21740       struct sk_buff *list = (struct sk_buff *)list_;
21741
21742       save_flags(flags);
21743       cli();
21744
21745       if (newsk->next || newsk->prev)
21746           printk("Suspicious queue tail: sk_buff on
21747   list!\n");
21748       IS_SKB(newsk);
21749       IS_SKB_HEAD(list);
21750
21751       newsk->next = list;
21752       newsk->prev = list->prev;
21753
21754       newsk->next->prev = newsk;
21755       newsk->prev->next = newsk;
21756
21757       newsk->list = list_;
21758       list_->qlen++;
21759
21760       restore_flags(flags);
21761   }
21762
21763   void __skb_queue_tail(struct sk_buff_head *list_, struct
21764   sk_buff *newsk)
21765   {
21766       struct sk_buff *list = (struct sk_buff *)list_;
21767
21768       if (newsk->next || newsk->prev)
21769           printk("Suspicious queue tail: sk_buff on
21770   list!\n");
21771       IS_SKB(newsk);
21772       IS_SKB_HEAD(list);
21773
21774       newsk->next = list;
21775       newsk->prev = list->prev;
21776
21777       newsk->next->prev = newsk;
21778       newsk->prev->next = newsk;
21779
21780       newsk->list = list_;
21781       list_->qlen++;
```

```
21782   }
21783
21784   /*
21785    *  Remove an sk_buff from a list. This routine is also
21786   interrupt safe
21787    *  so you can grab read and free buffers as another
21788   process adds them.
21789    */
21790
21791   struct sk_buff *skb_dequeue(struct sk_buff_head *list_)
21792   {
21793       unsigned long flags;
21794       struct sk_buff *result;
21795       struct sk_buff *list = (struct sk_buff *)list_;
21796
21797       save_flags(flags);
21798       cli();
21799
21800       IS_SKB_HEAD(list);
21801
21802       result = list->next;
21803       if (result == list) {
21804           restore_flags(flags);
21805           return NULL;
21806       }
21807
21808       result->next->prev = list;
21809       list->next = result->next;
21810
21811       result->next = NULL;
21812       result->prev = NULL;
21813       list_->qlen--;
21814       result->list = NULL;
21815
21816       restore_flags(flags);
21817
21818       IS_SKB(result);
21819       return result;
21820   }
21821
21822   struct sk_buff *__skb_dequeue(struct sk_buff_head *list_)
21823   {
21824       struct sk_buff *result;
21825       struct sk_buff *list = (struct sk_buff *)list_;
21826
21827       IS_SKB_HEAD(list);
21828
21829       result = list->next;
```

```
21830        if (result == list) {
21831            return NULL;
21832        }
21833
21834        result->next->prev = list;
21835        list->next = result->next;
21836
21837        result->next = NULL;
21838        result->prev = NULL;
21839        list_->qlen--;
21840        result->list = NULL;
21841
21842        IS_SKB(result);
21843        return result;
21844 }
21845
21846 /*
21847  *   Insert a packet before another one in a list.
21848  */
21849 void skb_insert(struct sk_buff *old, struct sk_buff
21850 *newsk)
21851 {
21852     unsigned long flags;
21853
21854     IS_SKB(old);
21855     IS_SKB(newsk);
21856
21857     if(!old->next || !old->prev)
21858         printk("insert before unlisted item!\n");
21859     if(newsk->next || newsk->prev)
21860         printk("inserted item is already on a list.\n");
21861
21862     save_flags(flags);
21863     cli();
21864     newsk->next = old;
21865     newsk->prev = old->prev;
21866     old->prev = newsk;
21867     newsk->prev->next = newsk;
21868     newsk->list = old->list;
21869     newsk->list->qlen++;
21870
21871     restore_flags(flags);
21872 }
21873
21874 /*
21875  *   Insert a packet before another one in a list.
21876  */
21877
21878 void __skb_insert(struct sk_buff *newsk,
21879     struct sk_buff * prev, struct sk_buff *next,
21880     struct sk_buff_head * list)
21881 {
21882     IS_SKB(prev);
21883     IS_SKB(newsk);
21884     IS_SKB(next);
21885
21886     if(!prev->next || !prev->prev)
21887         printk("insert after unlisted item!\n");
21888     if(!next->next || !next->prev)
21889         printk("insert before unlisted item!\n");
21890     if(newsk->next || newsk->prev)
21891         printk("inserted item is already on a list.\n");
21892
21893     newsk->next = next;
21894     newsk->prev = prev;
21895     next->prev = newsk;
21896     prev->next = newsk;
21897     newsk->list = list;
21898     list->qlen++;
21899
21900 }
21901
21902 /*
21903  *   Place a packet after a given packet in a list.
21904  */
21905 void skb_append(struct sk_buff *old, struct sk_buff
21906 *newsk)
21907 {
21908     unsigned long flags;
21909
21910     IS_SKB(old);
21911     IS_SKB(newsk);
21912
21913     if(!old->next || !old->prev)
21914         printk("append before unlisted item!\n");
21915     if(newsk->next || newsk->prev)
21916         printk("append item is already on a list.\n");
21917
21918     save_flags(flags);
21919     cli();
21920
21921     newsk->prev = old;
21922     newsk->next = old->next;
21923     newsk->next->prev = newsk;
21924     old->next = newsk;
21925     newsk->list = old->list;
```

```
21926        newsk->list->qlen++;
21927
21928        restore_flags(flags);
21929 }
21930
21931 /*
21932  *  Remove an sk_buff from its list. Works even without
      knowing the list it
21933
21934  *  is sitting on, which can be handy at times. It also
      means that THE LIST
21935
21936  *  MUST EXIST when you unlink. Thus a list must have
      its contents unlinked
21937
21938  *  _FIRST_.
21939  */
21940 void skb_unlink(struct sk_buff *skb)
21941 {
21942     unsigned long flags;
21943
21944     save_flags(flags);
21945     cli();
21946
21947     IS_SKB(skb);
21948
21949     if(skb->list)
21950     {
21951         skb->list->qlen--;
21952         skb->next->prev = skb->prev;
21953         skb->prev->next = skb->next;
21954         skb->next = NULL;
21955         skb->prev = NULL;
21956         skb->list = NULL;
21957     }
21958 #ifdef PARANOID_BUGHUNT_MODE    /* This is legal but we
      sometimes want to watch it */
21959
21960     else
21961         printk("skb_unlink: not a linked element\n");
21962 #endif
21963     restore_flags(flags);
21964 }
21965
21966 void __skb_unlink(struct sk_buff *skb)
21967 {
21968     IS_SKB(skb);
21969
21970     if(skb->list)
21971     {
21972         skb->list->qlen--;
21973         skb->next->prev = skb->prev;
```

```
21974        skb->prev->next = skb->next;
21975        skb->next = NULL;
21976        skb->prev = NULL;
21977        skb->list = NULL;
21978    }
21979 #ifdef PARANOID_BUGHUNT_MODE    /* This is legal but we
      sometimes want to watch it */
21980
21981    else
21982        printk("skb_unlink: not a linked element\n");
21983 #endif
21984 }
21985
21986 /*
21987  *  Add data to an sk_buff
21988  */
21989
21990 unsigned char *skb_put(struct sk_buff *skb, int len)
21991 {
21992     unsigned char *tmp=skb->tail;
21993     IS_SKB(skb);
21994     skb->tail+=len;
21995     skb->len+=len;
21996     IS_SKB(skb);
21997     if(skb->tail>skb->end)
21998         panic("skput:over: %p:%d",
21999 __builtin_return_address(0),len);
22000     return tmp;
22001 }
22002
22003 unsigned char *skb_push(struct sk_buff *skb, int len)
22004 {
22005     IS_SKB(skb);
22006     skb->data-=len;
22007     skb->len+=len;
22008     IS_SKB(skb);
22009     if(skb->data<skb->head)
22010         panic("skpush:under: %p:%d",
22011 __builtin_return_address(0),len);
22012     return skb->data;
22013 }
22014
22015 unsigned char * skb_pull(struct sk_buff *skb, int len)
22016 {
22017     IS_SKB(skb);
22018     if(len>skb->len)
22019         return 0;
22020     skb->data+=len;
22021     skb->len-=len;
```

```
22022          return skb->data;
22023     }
22024
22025     int skb_headroom(struct sk_buff *skb)
22026     {
22027          IS_SKB(skb);
22028          return skb->data-skb->head;
22029     }
22030
22031     int skb_tailroom(struct sk_buff *skb)
22032     {
22033          IS_SKB(skb);
22034          return skb->end-skb->tail;
22035     }
22036
22037     void skb_reserve(struct sk_buff *skb, int len)
22038     {
22039          IS_SKB(skb);
22040          skb->data+=len;
22041          skb->tail+=len;
22042          if(skb->tail>skb->end)
22043              panic("sk_res: over");
22044          if(skb->data<skb->head)
22045              panic("sk_res: under");
22046          IS_SKB(skb);
22047     }
22048
22049     void skb_trim(struct sk_buff *skb, int len)
22050     {
22051          IS_SKB(skb);
22052          if(skb->len>len)
22053          {
22054              skb->len=len;
22055              skb->tail=skb->data+len;
22056          }
22057     }
22058
22059
22060
22061     #endif
22062
22063     /*
22064      *  Free an sk_buff. This still knows about things it should
22065
22066      *  not need to like protocols and sockets.
22067      */
22068
22069     void kfree_skb(struct sk_buff *skb, int rw)
22070     {
22071          if (skb == NULL)
22072          {
22073              printk(KERN_CRIT "kfree_skb: skb = NULL (from
22074     %p)\n",
22075                  __builtin_return_address(0));
22076              return;
22077          }
22078     #if CONFIG_SKB_CHECK
22079          IS_SKB(skb);
22080     #endif
22081          /* Check it twice, this is such a rare event and
22082     only occurs under
22083           * extremely high load, normal code path should not
22084     suffer from the
22085           * overhead of the cli.
22086           */
22087          if (skb->lock) {
22088              unsigned long flags;
22089
22090              save_flags(flags); cli();
22091              if(skb->lock) {
22092                  skb->free = 3;      /* Free when unlocked */
22093                  net_free_locked++;
22094                  restore_flags(flags);
22095                  return;
22096              }
22097              restore_flags(flags);
22098          }
22099
22100          if (skb->free == 2)
22101              printk(KERN_WARNING "Warning: kfree_skb passed
22102     an skb that nobody set the free flag on! (from %p)\n",
22103                  __builtin_return_address(0));
22104          if (skb->list)
22105              printk(KERN_WARNING "Warning: kfree_skb passed
22106     an skb still on a list (from %p).\n",
22107                  __builtin_return_address(0));
22108
22109          if(skb->destructor)
22110              skb->destructor(skb);
22111          if (skb->sk)
22112          {
22113              struct sock * sk = skb->sk;
22114              if(sk->prot!=NULL)
22115              {
22116                  if (rw)
22117                      sock_rfree(sk, skb);
```

```
22118                else
22119                    sock_wfree(sk, skb);
22120
22121            }
22122        else
22123        {
22124            if (rw)
22125                atomic_sub(skb->truesize,
22126  &sk->rmem_alloc);
22127            else {
22128                if(!sk->dead)
22129                    sk->write_space(sk);
22130                atomic_sub(skb->truesize,
22131  &sk->wmem_alloc);
22132            }
22133            kfree_skbmem(skb);
22134        }
22135    }
22136    else
22137        kfree_skbmem(skb);
22138 }
22139
22140 /*
22141  *  Allocate a new skbuff. We do this ourselves so we
22142 can fill in a few 'private'
22143  *  fields and also do memory statistics to find all the
22144 [BEEP] leaks.
22145  */
22146 struct sk_buff *alloc_skb(unsigned int size,int priority)
22147 {
22148    struct sk_buff *skb;
22149    int len=size;
22150    unsigned char *bptr;
22151
22152    if (intr_count && priority!=GFP_ATOMIC)
22153    {
22154        static int count = 0;
22155        if (++count < 5) {
22156            printk(KERN_ERR "alloc_skb called
22157 nonatomically from interrupt %p\n",
22158                __builtin_return_address(0));
22159            priority = GFP_ATOMIC;
22160        }
22161    }
22162
22163    size=(size+15)&~15;      /* Allow for alignments. */
22164 Make a multiple of 16 bytes */
22165    size+=sizeof(struct sk_buff);   /* And stick the
```

```
22166 control itself on the end */
22167
22168    /*
22169     *  Allocate some space
22170     */
22171
22172    bptr=(unsigned char *)kmalloc(size,priority);
22173    if (bptr == NULL)
22174    {
22175        net_fails++;
22176        return NULL;
22177    }
22178 #ifdef PARANOID_BUGHUNT_MODE
22179    if(skb->magic_debug_cookie == SK_GOOD_SKB)
22180        printk("Kernel kmalloc handed us an existing skb
22181 (%p)\n",skb);
22182 #endif
22183    /*
22184     *  Now we play a little game with the caches. Linux
22185 kmalloc is
22186     *  a bit cache dumb, in fact its just about
22187 maximally non
22188     *  optimal for typical kernel buffers. We actually
22189 run faster
22190     *  by doing the following. Which is to deliberately
22191 put the
22192     *  skb at the _end_ not the start of the memory
22193 block.
22194     */
22195    net_allocs++;
22196
22197    skb=(struct sk_buff *)(bptr+size)-1;
22198
22199    skb->count = 1;     /* only one reference to this */
22200    skb->data_skb = NULL;   /* and we're our own data
22201 skb */
22202
22203    skb->free = 2;  /* Invalid so we pick up forgetful
22204 users */
22205    skb->lock = 0;
22206    skb->pkt_type = PACKET_HOST;      /* Default type */
22207    skb->pkt_bridged = 0;        /* Not bridged */
22208    skb->prev = skb->next = skb->link3 = NULL;
22209    skb->list = NULL;
22210    skb->sk = NULL;
22211    skb->truesize=size;
22212    skb->localroute=0;
22213    skb->stamp.tv_sec=0;     /* No idea about time */
```

```
22214        skb->localroute = 0;
22215        skb->ip_summed = 0;
22216        memset(skb->proto_priv, 0, sizeof(skb->proto_priv));
22217        net_skbcount++;
22218 #if CONFIG_SKB_CHECK
22219        skb->magic_debug_cookie = SK_GOOD_SKB;
22220 #endif
22221        skb->users = 0;
22222        /* Load the data pointers */
22223        skb->head=bptr;
22224        skb->data=bptr;
22225        skb->tail=bptr;
22226        skb->end=bptr+len;
22227        skb->len=0;
22228        skb->destructor=NULL;
22229        return skb;
22230 }
22231
22232 /*
22233  *   Free an skbuff by memory
22234  */
22235
22236 static inline void __kfree_skbmem(struct sk_buff *skb)
22237 {
22238     /* don't do anything if somebody still uses us */
22239     if (atomic_dec_and_test(&skb->count)) {
22240         kfree(skb->head);
22241         atomic_dec(&net_skbcount);
22242     }
22243 }
22244
22245 void kfree_skbmem(struct sk_buff *skb)
22246 {
22247     void * addr = skb->head;
22248
22249     /* don't do anything if somebody still uses us */
22250     if (atomic_dec_and_test(&skb->count)) {
22251         /* free the skb that contains the actual data if
22252 we've clone()'d */
22253         if (skb->data_skb) {
22254             addr = skb;
22255             __kfree_skbmem(skb->data_skb);
22256         }
22257         kfree(addr);
22258         atomic_dec(&net_skbcount);
22259     }
22260 }
22261
22262 /*
22263  *   Duplicate an sk_buff. The new one is not owned by a
22264 socket or locked
22265  *   and will be freed on deletion.
22266  */
22267
22268 struct sk_buff *skb_clone(struct sk_buff *skb, int
22269 priority)
22270 {
22271     struct sk_buff *n;
22272
22273     IS_SKB(skb);
22274     n = kmalloc(sizeof(*n), priority);
22275     if (!n)
22276         return NULL;
22277     memcpy(n, skb, sizeof(*n));
22278     n->count = 1;
22279     if (skb->data_skb)
22280         skb = skb->data_skb;
22281     atomic_inc(&skb->count);
22282     atomic_inc(&net_allocs);
22283     atomic_inc(&net_skbcount);
22284     n->data_skb = skb;
22285     n->next = n->prev = n->link3 = NULL;
22286     n->list = NULL;
22287     n->sk = NULL;
22288     n->free = 1;
22289     n->tries = 0;
22290     n->lock = 0;
22291     n->users = 0;
22292     return n;
22293 }
22294
22295 /*
22296  *   This is slower, and copies the whole data area
22297  */
22298
22299 struct sk_buff *skb_copy(struct sk_buff *skb, int
22300 priority)
22301 {
22302     struct sk_buff *n;
22303     unsigned long offset;
22304
22305     /*
22306      *   Allocate the copy buffer
22307      */
22308
22309     IS_SKB(skb);
```

```
22310
22311        n=alloc_skb(skb->truesize-sizeof(struct
22312  sk_buff),priority);
22313        if(n==NULL)
22314            return NULL;
22315
22316        /*
22317         *  Shift between the two data areas in bytes
22318         */
22319
22320        offset=n->head-skb->head;
22321
22322        /* Set the data pointer */
22323        skb_reserve(n,skb->data-skb->head);
22324        /* Set the tail pointer and length */
22325        skb_put(n,skb->len);
22326        /* Copy the bytes */
22327        memcpy(n->head,skb->head,skb->end-skb->head);
22328        n->link3=NULL;
22329        n->list=NULL;
22330        n->sk=NULL;
22331        n->when=skb->when;
22332        n->dev=skb->dev;
22333        n->h.raw=skb->h.raw+offset;
22334        n->mac.raw=skb->mac.raw+offset;
22335        n->ip_hdr=(struct iphdr *)(((char
22336  *)skb->ip_hdr)+offset);
22337        n->saddr=skb->saddr;
22338        n->daddr=skb->daddr;
22339        n->raddr=skb->raddr;
22340        n->seq=skb->seq;
22341        n->end_seq=skb->end_seq;
22342        n->ack_seq=skb->ack_seq;
22343        n->acked=skb->acked;
22344        memcpy(n->proto_priv, skb->proto_priv,
22345  sizeof(skb->proto_priv));
22346        n->used=skb->used;
22347        n->free=1;
22348        n->arp=skb->arp;
22349        n->tries=0;
22350        n->lock=0;
22351        n->users=0;
22352        n->pkt_type=skb->pkt_type;
22353        n->stamp=skb->stamp;
22354
22355        IS_SKB(n);
22356        return n;
22357  }
```

```
22358
22359  /*
22360   *      Skbuff device locking
22361   */
22362
22363  void skb_device_lock(struct sk_buff *skb)
22364  {
22365      unsigned long flags;
22366
22367      save_flags(flags); cli();
22368      if(skb->lock)
22369          printk("double lock on device queue, lock=%d
22370  caller=%p\n",
22371              skb->lock, (&skb)[-1]);
22372      else
22373          net_locked++;
22374      skb->lock++;
22375      restore_flags(flags);
22376  }
22377
22378  void skb_device_unlock(struct sk_buff *skb)
22379  {
22380      unsigned long flags;
22381
22382      save_flags(flags); cli();
22383      if(skb->lock==0)
22384          printk("double unlock on device queue!\n");
22385      skb->lock--;
22386      if(skb->lock==0)
22387          net_locked--;
22388      restore_flags(flags);
22389  }
22390
22391  void dev_kfree_skb(struct sk_buff *skb, int mode)
22392  {
22393      unsigned long flags;
22394
22395      save_flags(flags);
22396      cli();
22397      if(skb->lock)
22398      {
22399          net_locked--;
22400          skb->lock--;
22401      }
22402      if (!skb->lock && (skb->free == 1 || skb->free == 3))
22403      {
22404          restore_flags(flags);
22405          kfree_skb(skb,mode);
```

```
22406          }
22407      else
22408          restore_flags(flags);
22409  }
22410
22411  struct sk_buff *dev_alloc_skb(unsigned int length)
22412  {
22413      struct sk_buff *skb;
22414
22415      skb = alloc_skb(length+16, GFP_ATOMIC);
22416      if (skb)
22417          skb_reserve(skb,16);
22418      return skb;
22419  }
22420
22421  int skb_device_locked(struct sk_buff *skb)
22422  {
22423      return skb->lock? 1 : 0;
22424  }
```

usr/src/linux/net/ipv4/sock.c

```
22425  /*
22426   * INET       An implementation of the TCP/IP protocol
22427  suite for the LINUX
22428   *         operating system.  INET is implemented using the
22429  BSD Socket
22430   *         interface as the means of communication with the
22431  user level.
22432   *
22433   *         Generic socket support routines. Memory
22434  allocators, socket lock/release
22435   *         handler for protocols to use and generic option
22436  handler.
22437   *
22438   *
22439   * Version: @(#)sock.c  1.0.17  06/02/93
22440   *
22441   * Authors: Ross Biro, <bir7@leland.Stanford.Edu>
22442   *       Fred N. van Kempen, <waltje@uWalt.NL.Mugnet.ORG>
22443   *       Florian La Roche, <flla@stud.uni-sb.de>
22444   *       Alan Cox, <A.Cox@swansea.ac.uk>
22445   *
22446   * Fixes:
22447   *       Alan Cox    :   Numerous verify_area() problems
22448   *       Alan Cox    :   Connecting on a connecting socket
22449   *                   now returns an error for tcp.
22450   *       Alan Cox    :   sock->protocol is set correctly.
22451   *                   and is not sometimes left as 0.
```

```
22452   *       Alan Cox    :   connect handles icmp errors on a
22453   *                   connect properly. Unfortunately there
22454   *                   is a restart syscall nasty there. I
22455   *                   can't match BSD without hacking the C
22456   *                   library. Ideas urgently sought!
22457   *       Alan Cox    :   Disallow bind() to addresses
22458  that are
22459   *                   not ours - especially broadcast
22460  ones!!
22461   *       Alan Cox    :   Socket 1024 _IS_ ok for users.
22462  (fencepost)
22463   *       Alan Cox    :   sock_wfree/sock_rfree don't
22464  destroy sockets,
22465   *                   instead they leave that for the
22466  DESTROY timer.
22467   *       Alan Cox    :   Clean up error flag in accept
22468   *       Alan Cox    :   TCP ack handling is buggy, the
22469  DESTROY timer
22470   *                   was buggy. Put a remove_sock() in
22471  the handler
22472   *                   for memory when we hit 0. Also
22473  altered the timer
22474   *                   code. The ACK stuff can wait and
22475  needs major
22476   *                   TCP layer surgery.
22477   *       Alan Cox    :   Fixed TCP ack bug, removed
22478  remove sock
22479   *                   and fixed timer/inet_bh race.
22480   *       Alan Cox    :   Added zapped flag for TCP
22481   *       Alan Cox    :   Move kfree_skb into skbuff.c and
22482  tidied up surplus code
22483   *       Alan Cox    :   for new sk_buff allocations
22484  wmalloc/rmalloc now call alloc_skb
22485   *       Alan Cox    :   kfree_s calls now are
22486  kfree_skbmem so we can track skb resources
22487   *       Alan Cox    :   Supports socket option broadcast
22488  now as does udp. Packet and raw need fixing.
22489   *       Alan Cox    :   Added RCVBUF,SNDBUF size
22490  setting. It suddenly occurred to me how easy it was so...
22491   *       Rick Sladkey :   Relaxed UDP rules for
22492  matching packets.
22493   *       C.E.Hawkins :   IFF_PROMISC/SIOCGHWADDR support
22494   * Pauline Middelink :   identd support
22495   *       Alan Cox    :   Fixed connect() taking signals I
22496  think.
22497   *       Alan Cox    :   SO_LINGER supported
22498   *       Alan Cox    :   Error reporting fixes
22499   *       Anonymous   :   inet_create tidied up (sk->reuse
```

```
22500   setting)
22501   *       Alan Cox    :    inet sockets don't set sk->type!
22502   *       Alan Cox    :    Split socket option code
22503   *       Alan Cox    :    Callbacks
22504   *       Alan Cox    :    Nagle flag for Charles &
22505   Johannes stuff
22506   *       Alex        :    Removed restriction on inet
22507   fioctl
22508   *       Alan Cox    :    Splitting INET from NET core
22509   *       Alan Cox    :    Fixed bogus SO_TYPE handling in
22510   getsockopt()
22511   *       Adam Caldwell    :    Missing return in
22512   SO_DONTROUTE/SO_DEBUG code
22513   *       Alan Cox    :    Split IP from generic code
22514   *       Alan Cox    :    New kfree_skbmem()
22515   *       Alan Cox    :    Make SO_DEBUG superuser only.
22516   *       Alan Cox    :    Allow anyone to clear SO_DEBUG
22517   *                        (compatibility fix)
22518   *       Alan Cox    :    Added optimistic memory grabbing
22519   for AF_UNIX throughput.
22520   *       Alan Cox    :    Allocator for a socket is
22521   settable.
22522   *       Alan Cox    :    SO_ERROR includes soft errors.
22523   *       Alan Cox    :    Allow NULL arguments on some SO_
22524   opts
22525   *       Alan Cox    :    Generic socket allocation to
22526   make hooks
22527   *                        easier (suggested by Craig Metz).
22528   *       Michael Pall    :    SO_ERROR returns positive
22529   errno again
22530   *           Elliot Poger    :       Added support
22531   for SO_BINDTODEVICE.
22532   *       Russell King    :    Add #ifdef CONFIG_INET to
22533   SO_BINDTODEVICE
22534   *
22535   * To Fix:
22536   *
22537   *
22538   *       This program is free software; you can
22539   redistribute it and/or
22540   *       modify it under the terms of the GNU General
22541   Public License
22542   *       as published by the Free Software Foundation;
22543   either version
22544   *       2 of the License, or (at your option) any later
22545   version.
22546   */
22547
```

```
22548   #include <linux/config.h>
22549   #include <linux/errno.h>
22550   #include <linux/types.h>
22551   #include <linux/socket.h>
22552   #include <linux/in.h>
22553   #include <linux/kernel.h>
22554   #include <linux/major.h>
22555   #include <linux/sched.h>
22556   #include <linux/timer.h>
22557   #include <linux/string.h>
22558   #include <linux/sockios.h>
22559   #include <linux/net.h>
22560   #include <linux/fcntl.h>
22561   #include <linux/mm.h>
22562   #include <linux/interrupt.h>
22563
22564   #include <asm/segment.h>
22565   #include <asm/system.h>
22566
22567   #include <linux/inet.h>
22568   #include <linux/netdevice.h>
22569   #include <net/ip.h>
22570   #include <net/protocol.h>
22571   #include <net/arp.h>
22572   #include <net/rarp.h>
22573   #include <net/route.h>
22574   #include <net/tcp.h>
22575   #include <net/udp.h>
22576   #include <linux/skbuff.h>
22577   #include <net/sock.h>
22578   #include <net/raw.h>
22579   #include <net/icmp.h>
22580
22581   #define min(a,b)    ((a)<(b)?(a):(b))
22582
22583   /*
22584    *  This is meant for all protocols to use and covers
22585   goings on
22586    *  at the socket level. Everything here is generic.
22587    */
22588
22589   int sock_setsockopt(struct sock *sk, int level, int
22590   optname,
22591           char *optval, int optlen)
22592   {
22593       int val;
22594       int valbool;
22595       int err;
```

```
22596          struct linger ling;
22597          struct ifreq req;
22598
22599          /*
22600           *  Options without arguments
22601           */
22602
22603   #ifdef SO_DONTLINGER          /* Compatibility item... */
22604          switch(optname)
22605          {
22606              case SO_DONTLINGER:
22607                  sk->linger=0;
22608                  return 0;
22609          }
22610   #endif
22611
22612          if (optval == NULL)
22613              return(-EINVAL);
22614
22615          err=verify_area(VERIFY_READ, optval, sizeof(int));
22616          if(err)
22617              return err;
22618
22619          val = get_user((int *)optval);
22620          valbool = val?1:0;
22621
22622          switch(optname)
22623          {
22624              case SO_DEBUG:
22625                  if(val && !suser())
22626                      return(-EPERM);
22627                  sk->debug=valbool;
22628                  return 0;
22629              case SO_REUSEADDR:
22630                  sk->reuse = valbool;
22631                  return(0);
22632              case SO_TYPE:
22633              case SO_ERROR:
22634                  return(-ENOPROTOOPT);
22635              case SO_DONTROUTE:
22636                  sk->localroute=valbool;
22637                  return 0;
22638              case SO_BROADCAST:
22639                  sk->broadcast=valbool;
22640                  return 0;
22641              case SO_SNDBUF:
22642                  if(val > SK_WMEM_MAX*2)
22643                      val = SK_WMEM_MAX*2;
22644                  if(val < 256)
22645                      val = 256;
22646                  if(val > 65535)
22647                      val = 65535;
22648                  sk->sndbuf = val;
22649                  return 0;
22650
22651              case SO_RCVBUF:
22652                  if(val > SK_RMEM_MAX*2)
22653                      val = SK_RMEM_MAX*2;
22654                  if(val < 256)
22655                      val = 256;
22656                  if(val > 65535)
22657                      val = 65535;
22658                  sk->rcvbuf = val;
22659                  return(0);
22660
22661              case SO_KEEPALIVE:
22662                  sk->keepopen = valbool;
22663                  return(0);
22664
22665              case SO_OOBINLINE:
22666                  sk->urginline = valbool;
22667                  return(0);
22668
22669              case SO_NO_CHECK:
22670                  sk->no_check = valbool;
22671                  return(0);
22672
22673              case SO_PRIORITY:
22674                  if (val >= 0 && val < DEV_NUMBUFFS)
22675                  {
22676                      sk->priority = val;
22677                  }
22678                  else
22679                  {
22680                      return(-EINVAL);
22681                  }
22682                  return(0);
22683
22684
22685              case SO_LINGER:
22686
22687   err=verify_area(VERIFY_READ,optval,sizeof(ling));
22688          if(err)
22689              return err;
22690          memcpy_fromfs(&ling,optval,sizeof(ling));
22691          if(ling.l_onoff==0)
```

```
22692              sk->linger=0;
22693          else
22694          {
22695              sk->lingertime=ling.l_linger;
22696              sk->linger=1;
22697          }
22698          return 0;
22699
22700      case SO_BSDCOMPAT:
22701          sk->bsdism = valbool;
22702          return 0;
22703
22704  #ifdef CONFIG_NET
22705      case SO_BINDTODEVICE:
22706          /* Bind this socket to a particular device
22707  like "eth0",
22708           * as specified in an ifreq structure.  If
22709  the device
22710           * is "", socket is NOT bound to a device. */
22711          if (!valbool) {
22712              sk->bound_device = NULL;
22713          } else {
22714
22715  err=verify_area(VERIFY_READ,optval,sizeof(req));
22716              if(err)
22717                  return err;
22718          memcpy_fromfs(&req,optval,sizeof(req));
22719  #ifdef CONFIG_INET
22720          /* Remove any cached route for this
22721  socket. */
22722          if (sk->ip_route_cache) {
22723              ip_rt_put(sk->ip_route_cache);
22724              sk->ip_route_cache=NULL;
22725          }
22726  #endif
22727          if (*(req.ifr_name) == '\0') {
22728              sk->bound_device = NULL;
22729          } else {
22730              sk->bound_device =
22731  dev_get(req.ifr_name);
22732              if (sk->bound_device == NULL)
22733                  return -EINVAL;
22734          }
22735          }
22736          return 0;
22737  #endif
22738
22739      default:
```

```
22740          return(-ENOPROTOOPT);
22741      }
22742  }
22743
22744
22745  int sock_getsockopt(struct sock *sk, int level, int
22746  optname,
22747          char *optval, int *optlen)
22748  {
22749      int val;
22750      int err;
22751      struct linger ling;
22752
22753      switch(optname)
22754      {
22755          case SO_DEBUG:
22756              val = sk->debug;
22757              break;
22758
22759          case SO_DONTROUTE:
22760              val = sk->localroute;
22761              break;
22762
22763          case SO_BROADCAST:
22764              val= sk->broadcast;
22765              break;
22766
22767          case SO_SNDBUF:
22768              val=sk->sndbuf;
22769              break;
22770
22771          case SO_RCVBUF:
22772              val =sk->rcvbuf;
22773              break;
22774
22775          case SO_REUSEADDR:
22776              val = sk->reuse;
22777              break;
22778
22779          case SO_KEEPALIVE:
22780              val = sk->keepopen;
22781              break;
22782
22783          case SO_TYPE:
22784              val = sk->type;
22785              break;
22786
22787          case SO_ERROR:
```

```
22788                val = -sock_error(sk);
22789                if(val==0)
22790                    val=xchg(&sk->err_soft,0);
22791                break;
22792
22793        case SO_OOBINLINE:
22794                val = sk->urginline;
22795                break;
22796
22797        case SO_NO_CHECK:
22798                val = sk->no_check;
22799                break;
22800
22801        case SO_PRIORITY:
22802                val = sk->priority;
22803                break;
22804
22805        case SO_LINGER:
22806
22807 err=verify_area(VERIFY_WRITE,optval,sizeof(ling));
22808                if(err)
22809                    return err;
22810
22811 err=verify_area(VERIFY_WRITE,optlen,sizeof(int));
22812                if(err)
22813                    return err;
22814                put_fs_long(sizeof(ling),(unsigned long
22815 *)optlen);
22816                ling.l_onoff=sk->linger;
22817                ling.l_linger=sk->lingertime;
22818                memcpy_tofs(optval,&ling,sizeof(ling));
22819                return 0;
22820
22821        case SO_BSDCOMPAT:
22822                val = sk->bsdism;
22823                break;
22824
22825 #ifdef CONFIG_NET
22826            case SO_BINDTODEVICE:
22827            {
22828                struct ifreq req;
22829
22830                        /* Return the bound device (if
22831 any) */
22832
22833 err=verify_area(VERIFY_WRITE,optval,sizeof(req));
22834                    if(err)
22835                        return err;
```

```
22836
22837                    memset((char *) &req, 0,
22838 sizeof(req));
22839
22840                    if (sk->bound_device) {
22841                        strncpy(req.ifr_name,
22842 sk->bound_device->name, sizeof(req.ifr_name));
22843                        (*(struct sockaddr_in *)
22844 &req.ifr_addr).sin_family = sk->bound_device->family;
22845                        (*(struct sockaddr_in *)
22846 &req.ifr_addr).sin_addr.s_addr =
22847 sk->bound_device->pa_addr;
22848                    }
22849                    memcpy_tofs(optval, &req,
22850 sizeof(req));
22851                    return 0;
22852            }
22853 #endif
22854
22855        default:
22856            return(-ENOPROTOOPT);
22857    }
22858    err=verify_area(VERIFY_WRITE, optlen, sizeof(int));
22859    if(err)
22860        return err;
22861    put_fs_long(sizeof(int),(unsigned long *) optlen);
22862
22863    err=verify_area(VERIFY_WRITE, optval, sizeof(int));
22864    if(err)
22865        return err;
22866    put_fs_long(val,(unsigned long *)optval);
22867
22868    return(0);
22869 }
22870
22871 struct sock *sk_alloc(int priority)
22872 {
22873    struct sock *sk=(struct sock *)kmalloc(sizeof(*sk),
22874 priority);
22875    if(!sk)
22876        return NULL;
22877    memset(sk, 0, sizeof(*sk));
22878    return sk;
22879 }
22880
22881 void sk_free(struct sock *sk)
22882 {
22883    kfree_s(sk,sizeof(*sk));
```

```
22884    }
22885
22886
22887    struct sk_buff *sock_wmalloc(struct sock *sk, unsigned
22888    long size, int force, int priority)
22889    {
22890        if (sk) {
22891            if (force || sk->wmem_alloc < sk->sndbuf) {
22892                struct sk_buff * skb = alloc_skb(size,
22893    priority);
22894                if (skb)
22895                    atomic_add(skb->truesize,
22896    &sk->wmem_alloc);
22897                return skb;
22898            }
22899            return NULL;
22900        }
22901        return alloc_skb(size, priority);
22902    }
22903
22904    struct sk_buff *sock_rmalloc(struct sock *sk, unsigned
22905    long size, int force, int priority)
22906    {
22907        if (sk) {
22908            if (force || sk->rmem_alloc < sk->rcvbuf) {
22909                struct sk_buff *skb = alloc_skb(size,
22910    priority);
22911                if (skb)
22912                    atomic_add(skb->truesize,
22913    &sk->rmem_alloc);
22914                return skb;
22915            }
22916            return NULL;
22917        }
22918        return alloc_skb(size, priority);
22919    }
22920
22921
22922    unsigned long sock_rspace(struct sock *sk)
22923    {
22924        int amt;
22925
22926        if (sk != NULL)
22927        {
22928            if (sk->rmem_alloc >= sk->rcvbuf-2*MIN_WINDOW)
22929                return(0);
22930            amt =
22931    min((sk->rcvbuf-sk->rmem_alloc)/2-MIN_WINDOW,
22932    MAX_WINDOW);
22933            if (amt < 0)
22934                return(0);
22935            return(amt);
22936        }
22937        return(0);
22938    }
22939
22940
22941    unsigned long sock_wspace(struct sock *sk)
22942    {
22943        if (sk != NULL)
22944        {
22945            if (sk->shutdown & SEND_SHUTDOWN)
22946                return(0);
22947            if (sk->wmem_alloc >= sk->sndbuf)
22948                return(0);
22949            return sk->sndbuf - sk->wmem_alloc;
22950        }
22951        return(0);
22952    }
22953
22954
22955    void sock_wfree(struct sock *sk, struct sk_buff *skb)
22956    {
22957        int s=skb->truesize;
22958    #if CONFIG_SKB_CHECK
22959        IS_SKB(skb);
22960    #endif
22961        kfree_skbmem(skb);
22962        if (sk)
22963        {
22964            /* In case it might be waiting for more memory.
22965    */
22966            sk->write_space(sk);
22967            atomic_sub(s, &sk->wmem_alloc);
22968        }
22969    }
22970
22971
22972    void sock_rfree(struct sock *sk, struct sk_buff *skb)
22973    {
22974        int s=skb->truesize;
22975    #if CONFIG_SKB_CHECK
22976        IS_SKB(skb);
22977    #endif
22978        kfree_skbmem(skb);
22979        if (sk)
```

```
22980        {
22981            atomic_sub(s, &sk->rmem_alloc);
22982        }
22983    }
22984
22985    /*
22986     *  Generic send/receive buffer handlers
22987     */
22988
22989    struct sk_buff *sock_alloc_send_skb(struct sock *sk,
22990    unsigned long size, unsigned long fallback, int noblock,
22991    int *errcode)
22992    {
22993        struct sk_buff *skb;
22994        int err;
22995        unsigned long mem;
22996        do
22997        {
22998            if(sk->err!=0)
22999            {
23000                cli();
23001                err= -sk->err;
23002                sk->err=0;
23003                sti();
23004                *errcode=err;
23005                return NULL;
23006            }
23007
23008            if(sk->shutdown&SEND_SHUTDOWN)
23009            {
23010                *errcode=-EPIPE;
23011                return NULL;
23012            }
23013
23014
23015            mem=sk->wmem_alloc;
23016
23017            if(!fallback)
23018                skb = sock_wmalloc(sk, size, 0,
23019    sk->allocation);
23020            else
23021            {
23022                /* The buffer get won't block, or use the
23023    atomic queue. It does
23024                    produce annoying no free page messages
23025    still.... */
23026                skb = sock_wmalloc(sk, size, 0 , GFP_IO);
23027                if(!skb)
23028                    skb=sock_wmalloc(sk, fallback, 0,
23029    GFP_KERNEL);
23030            }
23031
23032            /*
23033             *  This means we have too many buffers for this
23034    socket already.
23035             */
23036
23037            if(skb==NULL)
23038            {
23039                sk->socket->flags |= SO_NOSPACE;
23040                if(noblock)
23041                {
23042                    *errcode=-EAGAIN;
23043                    return NULL;
23044                }
23045                if(sk->shutdown&SEND_SHUTDOWN)
23046                {
23047                    *errcode=-EPIPE;
23048                    return NULL;
23049                }
23050                cli();
23051                if(sk->shutdown&SEND_SHUTDOWN)
23052                {
23053                    sti();
23054                    *errcode=-EPIPE;
23055                    return NULL;
23056                }
23057
23058                if (sk->wmem_alloc==mem)
23059                {
23060                    sk->socket->flags &= ~SO_NOSPACE;
23061                    interruptible_sleep_on(sk->sleep);
23062                    if (current->signal & ~current->blocked)
23063                    {
23064                        sti();
23065                        *errcode = -ERESTARTSYS;
23066                        return NULL;
23067                    }
23068                }
23069                sti();
23070            }
23071        }
23072        while(skb==NULL);
23073
23074        return skb;
23075    }
```

```
23076
23077
23078    void __release_sock(struct sock *sk)
23079    {
23080    #ifdef CONFIG_INET
23081        if (!sk->prot || !sk->prot->rcv)
23082            return;
23083
23084        /* See if we have any packets built up. */
23085        start_bh_atomic();
23086        while (!skb_queue_empty(&sk->back_log)) {
23087            struct sk_buff * skb = sk->back_log.next;
23088            __skb_unlink(skb, &sk->back_log);
23089            sk->prot->rcv(skb, skb->dev, (struct
23090    options*)skb->proto_priv,
23091                        skb->saddr, skb->len, skb->daddr, 1,
23092                /* Only used for/by raw sockets. */
23093                (struct inet_protocol *)sk->pair);
23094        }
23095        end_bh_atomic();
23096    #endif
23097    }
```

usr/src/linux/net/ipv4/sysctl_net_ipv4.c

```
23098    /* -*- linux-c -*-
23099     * sysctl_net_ipv4.c: sysctl interface to net IPV4
23100    subsystem.
23101     *
23102     * Begun April 1, 1996, Mike Shaver.
23103     * Added /proc/sys/net/ipv4 directory entry (empty =) ).
23104    [MS]
23105     */
23106
23107    #include <linux/mm.h>
23108    #include <linux/sysctl.h>
23109    #include <net/ip.h>
23110
23111    /* From arp.c */
23112    extern int sysctl_arp_res_time;
23113    extern int sysctl_arp_dead_res_time;
23114    extern int sysctl_arp_max_tries;
23115    extern int sysctl_arp_timeout;
23116    extern int sysctl_arp_check_interval;
23117    extern int sysctl_arp_confirm_interval;
23118    extern int sysctl_arp_confirm_timeout;
23119
23120    extern int sysctl_ip_forward;
23121    extern int sysctl_ip_dynaddr;
```

```
23122    static int proc_doipforward(ctl_table *ctl, int write,
23123    struct file *filp,
23124                    void *buffer, size_t *lenp)
23125    {
23126        int val = sysctl_ip_forward;
23127        int retv;
23128
23129        retv = proc_dointvec(ctl, write, filp, buffer, lenp);
23130        if (write) {
23131            if (sysctl_ip_forward && !val) {
23132                printk(KERN_INFO "sysctl: ip forwarding
23133    enabled\n");
23134                ip_statistics.IpForwarding = 1;
23135            }
23136            if (!sysctl_ip_forward && val) {
23137                printk(KERN_INFO "sysctl: ip forwarding off\n");
23138                ip_statistics.IpForwarding = 2;
23139            }
23140        }
23141        return retv;
23142    }
23143
23144    ctl_table ipv4_table[] = {
23145        {NET_IPV4_ARP_RES_TIME, "arp_res_time",
23146         &sysctl_arp_res_time, sizeof(int), 0644, NULL,
23147    &proc_dointvec},
23148        {NET_IPV4_ARP_DEAD_RES_TIME, "arp_dead_res_time",
23149         &sysctl_arp_dead_res_time, sizeof(int), 0644,
23150    NULL, &proc_dointvec},
23151        {NET_IPV4_ARP_MAX_TRIES, "arp_max_tries",
23152         &sysctl_arp_max_tries, sizeof(int), 0644, NULL,
23153    &proc_dointvec},
23154        {NET_IPV4_ARP_TIMEOUT, "arp_timeout",
23155         &sysctl_arp_timeout, sizeof(int), 0644, NULL,
23156    &proc_dointvec},
23157        {NET_IPV4_ARP_CHECK_INTERVAL,
23158    "arp_check_interval",
23159         &sysctl_arp_check_interval, sizeof(int), 0644,
23160    NULL, &proc_dointvec},
23161        {NET_IPV4_ARP_CONFIRM_INTERVAL,
23162    "arp_confirm_interval",
23163         &sysctl_arp_confirm_interval, sizeof(int),
23164    0644, NULL,
23165         &proc_dointvec},
23166        {NET_IPV4_ARP_CONFIRM_TIMEOUT,
23167    "arp_confirm_timeout",
23168         &sysctl_arp_confirm_timeout, sizeof(int), 0644,
23169    NULL,
```

```
23170            &proc_dointvec},
23171        {NET_IPV4_FORWARD, "ip_forward", &sysctl_ip_forward,
23172    sizeof(int),
23173            0644, NULL, &proc_doipforward },
23174            {NET_IPV4_DYNADDR, "ip_dynaddr",
23175            &sysctl_ip_dynaddr, sizeof(int), 0644, NULL,
23176    &proc_dointvec},
23177            {0}
23178    };
```

usr/src/linux/net/ipv4/tcp.c

```
23179    /*
23180     * INET      An implementation of the TCP/IP protocol
23181    suite for the LINUX
23182     *        operating system.  INET is implemented using the
23183    BSD Socket
23184     *        interface as the means of communication with the
23185    user level.
23186     *
23187     *        Implementation of the Transmission Control
23188    Protocol(TCP).
23189     *
23190     * Version: @(#)tcp.c    1.0.16   05/25/93
23191     *
23192     * Authors: Ross Biro, <bir7@leland.Stanford.Edu>
23193     *        Fred N. van Kempen, <waltje@uWalt.NL.Mugnet.ORG>
23194     *        Mark Evans, <evansmp@uhura.aston.ac.uk>
23195     *        Corey Minyard <wf-rch!minyard@relay.EU.net>
23196     *        Florian La Roche, <flla@stud.uni-sb.de>
23197     *        Charles Hedrick, <hedrick@klinzhai.rutgers.edu>
23198     *        Linus Torvalds, <torvalds@cs.helsinki.fi>
23199     *        Alan Cox, <gw4pts@gw4pts.ampr.org>
23200     *        Matthew Dillon, <dillon@apollo.west.oic.com>
23201     *        Arnt Gulbrandsen, <agulbra@nvg.unit.no>
23202     *        Jorge Cwik, <jorge@laser.satlink.net>
23203     *
23204     * Fixes:
23205     *        Alan Cox    :   Numerous verify_area() calls
23206     *        Alan Cox    :   Set the ACK bit on a reset
23207     *        Alan Cox    :   Stopped it crashing if it closed
23208    while
23209     *                  sk->inuse=1 and was trying to connect
23210     *                  (tcp_err()).
23211     *        Alan Cox    :   All icmp error handling was
23212    broken
23213     *                  pointers passed where wrong and the
23214     *                  socket was looked up backwards.
23215    Nobody
```

```
23216     *                  tested any icmp error code obviously.
23217     *        Alan Cox    :   tcp_err() now handled properly.
23218    It
23219     *                  wakes people on errors. select
23220     *                  behaves and the icmp error race
23221     *                  has gone by moving it into sock.c
23222     *        Alan Cox    :   tcp_send_reset() fixed to work
23223    for
23224     *                  everything not just packets for
23225     *                  unknown sockets.
23226     *        Alan Cox    :   tcp option processing.
23227     *        Alan Cox    :   Reset tweaked (still not 100%)
23228    [Had
23229     *                  syn rule wrong]
23230     *        Herp Rosmanith :   More reset fixes
23231     *        Alan Cox    :   No longer acks invalid rst
23232    frames.
23233     *                  Acking any kind of RST is right out.
23234     *        Alan Cox    :   Sets an ignore me flag on an rst
23235     *                  receive otherwise odd bits of prattle
23236     *                  escape still
23237     *        Alan Cox    :   Fixed another acking RST frame
23238    bug.
23239     *                  Should stop LAN workplace lockups.
23240     *        Alan Cox    :   Some tidyups using the new skb
23241    list
23242     *                  facilities
23243     *        Alan Cox    :   sk->keepopen now seems to work
23244     *        Alan Cox    :   Pulls options out correctly on
23245    accepts
23246     *        Alan Cox    :   Fixed assorted sk->rqueue->next
23247    errors
23248     *        Alan Cox    :   PSH doesn't end a TCP read.
23249    Switched a
23250     *                  bit to skb ops.
23251     *        Alan Cox    :   Tidied tcp_data to avoid a
23252    potential
23253     *                  nasty.
23254     *        Alan Cox    :   Added some better commenting, as
23255    the
23256     *                  tcp is hard to follow
23257     *        Alan Cox    :   Removed incorrect check for 20 *
23258    psh
23259     *        Michael O'Reilly  :   ack < copied bug fix.
23260     *        Johannes Stille  :   Misc tcp fixes (not all in
23261    yet).
23262     *        Alan Cox    :   FIN with no memory -> CRASH
23263     *        Alan Cox    :   Added socket option proto
```

```
23264   entries.
23265   *               Also added awareness of them to
23266   accept.
23267   *       Alan Cox    :   Added TCP options (SOL_TCP)
23268   *       Alan Cox    :   Switched wakeup calls to
23269   callbacks,
23270   *               so the kernel can layer network
23271   *               sockets.
23272   *       Alan Cox    :   Use ip_tos/ip_ttl settings.
23273   *       Alan Cox    :   Handle FIN (more) properly (we
23274   hope).
23275   *       Alan Cox    :   RST frames sent on unsynchronised
23276   *               state ack error.
23277   *       Alan Cox    :   Put in missing check for SYN bit.
23278   *       Alan Cox    :   Added tcp_select_window() aka
23279   NET2E
23280   *               window non shrink trick.
23281   *       Alan Cox    :   Added a couple of small NET2E
23282   timer
23283   *                   fixes
23284   *       Charles Hedrick :   TCP fixes
23285   *       Toomas Tamm :   TCP window fixes
23286   *       Alan Cox    :   Small URG fix to rlogin ^C ack
23287   fight
23288   *       Charles Hedrick :   Rewrote most of it to
23289   actually work
23290   *       Linus       :   Rewrote tcp_read() and URG
23291   handling
23292   *                   completely
23293   *       Gerhard Koerting:   Fixed some missing timer
23294   handling
23295   *       Matthew Dillon  :   Reworked TCP machine states
23296   as per RFC
23297   *       Gerhard Koerting:   PC/TCP workarounds
23298   *       Adam Caldwell   :   Assorted timer/timing errors
23299   *       Matthew Dillon  :   Fixed another RST bug
23300   *       Alan Cox    :   Move to kernel side addressing
23301   changes.
23302   *       Alan Cox    :   Beginning work on TCP fastpathing
23303   *                   (not yet usable)
23304   *       Arnt Gulbrandsen:   Turbocharged tcp_check()
23305   routine.
23306   *       Alan Cox    :   TCP fast path debugging
23307   *       Alan Cox    :   Window clamping
23308   *       Michael Riepe   :   Bug in tcp_check()
23309   *       Matt Dillon :   More TCP improvements and RST
23310   bug fixes
23311   *       Matt Dillon :   Yet more small nasties remove
23312   from the
23313   *               TCP code (Be very nice to this man if
23314   *               tcp finally works 100%) 8)
23315   *       Alan Cox    :   BSD accept semantics.
23316   *       Alan Cox    :   Reset on closedown bug.
23317   *   Peter De Schrijver :   ENOTCONN check missing in
23318   tcp_sendto().
23319   *       Michael Pall    :   Handle select() after URG
23320   properly in
23321   *               all cases.
23322   *       Michael Pall    :   Undo the last fix in
23323   tcp_read_urg()
23324   *               (multi URG PUSH broke rlogin).
23325   *       Michael Pall    :   Fix the multi URG PUSH
23326   problem in
23327   *               tcp_readable(), select() after URG
23328   *               works now.
23329   *       Michael Pall    :   recv(...,MSG_OOB) never
23330   blocks in the
23331   *               BSD api.
23332   *       Alan Cox    :   Changed the semantics of
23333   sk->socket to
23334   *               fix a race and a signal problem with
23335   *               accept() and async I/O.
23336   *       Alan Cox    :   Relaxed the rules on
23337   tcp_sendto().
23338   *       Yury Shevchuk   :   Really fixed accept()
23339   blocking problem.
23340   *       Craig I. Hagan  :   Allow for BSD compatible
23341   TIME_WAIT for
23342   *               clients/servers which listen in on
23343   *               fixed ports.
23344   *       Alan Cox    :   Cleaned the above up and shrank
23345   it to
23346   *               a sensible code size.
23347   *       Alan Cox    :   Self connect lockup fix.
23348   *       Alan Cox    :   No connect to multicast.
23349   *       Ross Biro   :   Close unaccepted children on
23350   master
23351   *               socket close.
23352   *       Alan Cox    :   Reset tracing code.
23353   *       Alan Cox    :   Spurious resets on shutdown.
23354   *       Alan Cox    :   Giant 15 minute/60 second timer
23355   error
23356   *       Alan Cox    :   Small whoops in selecting before
23357   an
23358   *               accept.
23359   *       Alan Cox    :   Kept the state trace facility
```

```
23360  since
23361  *                  it's handy for debugging.
23362  *      Alan Cox    :   More reset handler fixes.
23363  *      Alan Cox    :   Started rewriting the code based
23364  on
23365  *                  the RFC's for other useful protocol
23366  *                  references see: Comer, KA9Q NOS, and
23367  *                  for a reference on the difference
23368  *                  between specifications and how BSD
23369  *                  works see the 4.4lite source.
23370  *      A.N.Kuznetsov  :   Don't time wait on
23371  completion of tidy
23372  *                  close.
23373  *      Linus Torvalds  :   Fin/Shutdown & copied_seq
23374  changes.
23375  *      Linus Torvalds  :   Fixed BSD port reuse to work
23376  first syn
23377  *      Alan Cox    :   Reimplemented timers as per the
23378  RFC
23379  *                  and using multiple timers for sanity.
23380  *      Alan Cox    :   Small bug fixes, and a lot of new
23381  *                  comments.
23382  *      Alan Cox    :   Fixed dual reader crash by
23383  locking
23384  *                  the buffers (much like datagram.c)
23385  *      Alan Cox    :   Fixed stuck sockets in probe. A
23386  probe
23387  *                  now gets fed up of retrying without
23388  *                  (even a no space) answer.
23389  *      Alan Cox    :   Extracted closing code better
23390  *      Alan Cox    :   Fixed the closing state machine
23391  to
23392  *                  resemble the RFC.
23393  *      Alan Cox    :   More 'per spec' fixes.
23394  *      Jorge Cwik  :   Even faster checksumming.
23395  *      Alan Cox    :   tcp_data() doesn't ack illegal
23396  PSH
23397  *                  only frames. At least one pc tcp
23398  stack
23399  *                  generates them.
23400  *      Alan Cox    :   Cache last socket.
23401  *      Alan Cox    :   Per route irtt.
23402  *      Matt Day    :   Select() match BSD precisely on
23403  error
23404  *      Alan Cox    :   New buffers
23405  *      Marc Tamsky :   Various sk->prot->retransmits and
23406  *                  sk->retransmits misupdating fixed.
23407  *                  Fixed tcp_write_timeout: stuck close,
23408  *                  and TCP syn retries gets used now.
23409  *      Mark Yarvis :   In tcp_read_wakeup(), don't send
23410  an
23411  *                  ack if stat is TCP_CLOSED.
23412  *      Alan Cox    :   Look up device on a retransmit -
23413  routes may
23414  *                  change. Doesn't yet cope with MSS
23415  shrink right
23416  *                  but it's a start!
23417  *      Marc Tamsky :   Closing in closing fixes.
23418  *      Mike Shaver :   RFC1122 verifications.
23419  *      Alan Cox    :   rcv_saddr errors.
23420  *      Alan Cox    :   Block double connect().
23421  *      Alan Cox    :   Small hooks for enSKIP.
23422  *      Alexey Kuznetsov:   Path MTU discovery.
23423  *      Alan Cox    :   Support soft errors.
23424  *      Alan Cox    :   Fix MTU discovery pathological
23425  case
23426  *                  when the remote claims no mtu!
23427  *      Marc Tamsky :   TCP_CLOSE fix.
23428  *      Colin (G3TNE)   :   Send a reset on syn ack
23429  replies in
23430  *                  window but wrong (fixes NT lpd
23431  problems)
23432  *      Pedro Roque :   Better TCP window handling,
23433  delayed ack.
23434  *      Joerg Reuter    :   No modification of locked
23435  buffers in
23436  *                  tcp_do_retransmit()
23437  *      Eric Schenk :   Changed receiver side silly
23438  window
23439  *                  avoidance algorithm to BSD style
23440  *                  algorithm. This doubles throughput
23441  *                  against machines running Solaris,
23442  *                  and seems to result in general
23443  *                  improvement.
23444  *      Eric Schenk :   Changed receiver side silly
23445  window
23446  *                  avoidance algorithm to BSD style
23447  *                  algorithm. This doubles throughput
23448  *                  against machines running Solaris,
23449  *                  and seems to result in general
23450  *                  improvement.
23451  *  Stefan Magdalinski  :   adjusted tcp_readable() to
23452  fix FIONREAD
23453  *  Willy Konynenberg   :   Transparent proxying support.
23454  *      Theodore Ts'o   :   Do secure TCP sequence
23455  numbers.
```

```
23456    *        David S. Miller :   New socket lookup
23457  architecture for ISS.
23458    *                This code is dedicated to John Dyson.
23459    *        Elliot Poger   :   Added support for
23460  SO_BINDTODEVICE.
23461    *
23462    * To Fix:
23463    *        Fast path the code. Two things here - fix the
23464  window calculation
23465    *        so it doesn't iterate over the queue, also spot
23466  packets with no funny
23467    *        options arriving in order and process directly.
23468    *
23469    *        Rewrite output state machine to use a single
23470  queue.
23471    *        Speed up input assembly algorithm.
23472    *        RFC1323 - PAWS and window scaling. PAWS is
23473  required for IPv6 so we
23474    *        could do with it working on IPv4
23475    *        User settable/learned rtt/max window/mtu
23476    *
23477    *        Change the fundamental structure to a single
23478  send queue maintained
23479    *        by TCP (removing the bogus ip stuff [thus fixing
23480  mtu drops on
23481    *        active routes too]). Cut the queue off in
23482  tcp_retransmit/
23483    *        tcp_transmit.
23484    *        Change the receive queue to assemble as it goes.
23485  This lets us
23486    *        dispose of most of tcp_sequence, half of tcp_ack
23487  and chunks of
23488    *        tcp_data/tcp_read as well as the window shrink
23489  crud.
23490    *        Separate out duplicated code - tcp_alloc_skb,
23491  tcp_build_ack
23492    *        tcp_queue_skb seem obvious routines to extract.
23493    *
23494    *        This program is free software; you can
23495  redistribute it and/or
23496    *        modify it under the terms of the GNU General
23497  Public License
23498    *        as published by the Free Software Foundation;
23499  either version
23500    *        2 of the License, or(at your option) any later
23501  version.
23502    *
23503    * Description of States:
```

```
23504    *
23505    *  TCP_SYN_SENT      sent a connection request,
23506  waiting for ack
23507    *
23508    *  TCP_SYN_RECV      received a connection request,
23509  sent ack,
23510    *                waiting for final ack in three-way
23511  handshake.
23512    *
23513    *  TCP_ESTABLISHED   connection established
23514    *
23515    *  TCP_FIN_WAIT1     our side has shutdown, waiting
23516  to complete
23517    *                transmission of remaining buffered data
23518    *
23519    *  TCP_FIN_WAIT2     all buffered data sent, waiting
23520  for remote
23521    *                to shutdown
23522    *
23523    *  TCP_CLOSING       both sides have shutdown but we
23524  still have
23525    *                data we have to finish sending
23526    *
23527    *  TCP_TIME_WAIT     timeout to catch resent junk
23528  before entering
23529    *                closed, can only be entered from
23530  FIN_WAIT2
23531    *                or CLOSING.  Required because the other
23532  end
23533    *                may not have gotten our last ACK causing
23534  it
23535    *                to retransmit the data packet (which we
23536  ignore)
23537    *
23538    *  TCP_CLOSE_WAIT    remote side has shutdown and is
23539  waiting for
23540    *                us to finish writing our data and to
23541  shutdown
23542    *                (we have to close() to move on to
23543  LAST_ACK)
23544    *
23545    *  TCP_LAST_ACK      out side has shutdown after
23546  remote has
23547    *                shutdown.  There may still be data in our
23548    *                buffer that we have to finish sending
23549    *
23550    *  TCP_CLOSE         socket is finished
23551    */
```

```
23552
23553    /*
23554     * RFC1122 status:
23555     * NOTE: I'm not going to be doing comments in the code
23556    for this one except
23557     * for violations and the like.  tcp.c is just too
23558    big... If I say something
23559     * "does?" or "doesn't?", it means I'm not sure, and
23560    will have to hash it out
23561     * with Alan. -- MS 950903
23562     *
23563     * Use of PSH (4.2.2.2)
23564     *     MAY aggregate data sent without the PSH flag. (does)
23565     *     MAY queue data received without the PSH flag. (does)
23566     *     SHOULD collapse successive PSH flags when it
23567    packetizes data. (doesn't)
23568     *     MAY implement PSH on send calls. (doesn't, thus:)
23569     *       MUST NOT buffer data indefinitely (doesn't [1
23570    second])
23571     *       MUST set PSH on last segment (does)
23572     *     MAY pass received PSH to application layer (doesn't)
23573     *     SHOULD send maximum-sized segment whenever
23574    possible. (almost always does)
23575     *
23576     * Window Size (4.2.2.3, 4.2.2.16)
23577     *     MUST treat window size as an unsigned number (does)
23578     *     SHOULD treat window size as a 32-bit number (does
23579    not)
23580     *     MUST NOT shrink window once it is offered (does not
23581    normally)
23582     *
23583     * Urgent Pointer (4.2.2.4)
23584     * **MUST point urgent pointer to last byte of urgent
23585    data (not right
23586     *       after). (doesn't, to be like BSD)
23587     *     MUST inform application layer asynchronously of
23588    incoming urgent
23589     *       data. (does)
23590     *     MUST provide application with means of determining
23591    the amount of
23592     *       urgent data pending. (does)
23593     * **MUST support urgent data sequence of arbitrary
23594    length. (doesn't, but
23595     *     it's sort of tricky to fix, as urg_ptr is a 16-bit
23596    quantity)
23597     *     [Follows BSD 1 byte of urgent data]
23598     *
23599     * TCP Options (4.2.2.5)
```

```
23600     *     MUST be able to receive TCP options in any segment.
23601    (does)
23602     *     MUST ignore unsupported options (does)
23603     *
23604     * Maximum Segment Size Option (4.2.2.6)
23605     *     MUST implement both sending and receiving MSS.
23606    (does)
23607     *     SHOULD send an MSS with every SYN where receive MSS
23608    != 536 (MAY send
23609     *       it always). (does, even when MSS == 536, which is
23610    legal)
23611     *     MUST assume MSS == 536 if no MSS received at
23612    connection setup (does)
23613     *     MUST calculate "effective send MSS" correctly:
23614     *       min(physical_MTU, remote_MSS+20) - sizeof(tcphdr)
23615    - sizeof(ipopts)
23616     *       (does - but allows operator override)
23617     *
23618     * TCP Checksum (4.2.2.7)
23619     *     MUST generate and check TCP checksum. (does)
23620     *
23621     * Initial Sequence Number Selection (4.2.2.8)
23622     *     MUST use the RFC 793 clock selection mechanism.
23623    (doesn't, but it's
23624     *       OK: RFC 793 specifies a 250KHz clock, while we
23625    use 1MHz, which is
23626     *       necessary for 10Mbps networks - and harder than
23627    BSD to spoof!)
23628     *
23629     * Simultaneous Open Attempts (4.2.2.10)
23630     *     MUST support simultaneous open attempts (does)
23631     *
23632     * Recovery from Old Duplicate SYN (4.2.2.11)
23633     *     MUST keep track of active vs. passive open (does)
23634     *
23635     * RST segment (4.2.2.12)
23636     *     SHOULD allow an RST segment to contain data (does,
23637    but doesn't do
23638     *       anything with it, which is standard)
23639     *
23640     * Closing a Connection (4.2.2.13)
23641     *     MUST inform application of whether connection was
23642    closed by RST or
23643     *       normal close. (does)
23644     *     MAY allow "half-duplex" close (treat connection as
23645    closed for the
23646     *       local app, even before handshake is done). (does)
23647     *     MUST linger in TIME_WAIT for 2 * MSL (does)
```

```
23648    *
23649    * Retransmission Timeout (4.2.2.15)
23650    *    MUST implement Jacobson's slow start and congestion
23651 avoidance
23652    *      stuff. (does)
23653    *
23654    * Probing Zero Windows (4.2.2.17)
23655    *    MUST support probing of zero windows. (does)
23656    *    MAY keep offered window closed indefinitely. (does)
23657    *    MUST allow remote window to stay closed
23658 indefinitely. (does)
23659    *
23660    * Passive Open Calls (4.2.2.18)
23661    *    MUST NOT let new passive open affect other
23662 connections. (doesn't)
23663    *    MUST support passive opens (LISTENs) concurrently.
23664 (does)
23665    *
23666    * Time to Live (4.2.2.19)
23667    *    MUST make TCP TTL configurable. (does - IP_TTL
23668 option)
23669    *
23670    * Event Processing (4.2.2.20)
23671    *    SHOULD queue out-of-order segments. (does)
23672    *    MUST aggregate ACK segments whenever possible.
23673 (does but badly)
23674    *
23675    * Retransmission Timeout Calculation (4.2.3.1)
23676    *    MUST implement Karn's algorithm and Jacobson's
23677 algorithm for RTO
23678    *      calculation. (does, or at least explains them in
23679 the comments 8*b)
23680    *    SHOULD initialize RTO to 0 and RTT to 3. (does)
23681    *
23682    * When to Send an ACK Segment (4.2.3.2)
23683    *    SHOULD implement delayed ACK. (does)
23684    *    MUST keep ACK delay < 0.5 sec. (does)
23685    *
23686    * When to Send a Window Update (4.2.3.3)
23687    *    MUST implement receiver-side SWS. (does)
23688    *
23689    * When to Send Data (4.2.3.4)
23690    *    MUST implement sender-side SWS. (does)
23691    *    SHOULD implement Nagle algorithm. (does)
23692    *
23693    * TCP Connection Failures (4.2.3.5)
23694    *    MUST handle excessive retransmissions "properly"
23695 (see the RFC). (does)
```

```
23696    *    SHOULD inform application layer of soft errors.
23697 (does)
23698    *
23699    * TCP Keep-Alives (4.2.3.6)
23700    *    MAY provide keep-alives. (does)
23701    *    MUST make keep-alives configurable on a
23702 per-connection basis. (does)
23703    *    MUST default to no keep-alives. (does)
23704    * **MUST make keep-alive interval configurable.
23705 (doesn't)
23706    * **MUST make default keep-alive interval > 2 hours.
23707 (doesn't)
23708    *    MUST NOT interpret failure to ACK keep-alive packet
23709 as dead
23710    *      connection. (doesn't)
23711    *    SHOULD send keep-alive with no data. (does)
23712    *
23713    * TCP Multihoming (4.2.3.7)
23714    *    MUST get source address from IP layer before
23715 sending first
23716    *      SYN. (does)
23717    *    MUST use same local address for all segments of a
23718 connection. (does)
23719    *
23720    * IP Options (4.2.3.8)
23721    *    MUST ignore unsupported IP options. (does)
23722    *    MAY support Time Stamp and Record Route. (does)
23723    *    MUST allow application to specify a source route.
23724 (does)
23725    *    MUST allow received Source Route option to set
23726 route for all future
23727    *      segments on this connection. (does not (security
23728 issues))
23729    *
23730    * ICMP messages (4.2.3.9)
23731    *    MUST act on ICMP errors. (does)
23732    *    MUST slow transmission upon receipt of a Source
23733 Quench. (does)
23734    *    MUST NOT abort connection upon receipt of soft
23735 Destination
23736    *      Unreachables (0, 1, 5), Time Exceededs and
23737 Parameter
23738    *      Problems. (doesn't)
23739    *    SHOULD report soft Destination Unreachables etc. to
23740 the
23741    *      application. (does)
23742    *    SHOULD abort connection upon receipt of hard
23743 Destination Unreachable
```

```
23744    *       messages (2, 3, 4). (does)
23745    *
23746    * Remote Address Validation (4.2.3.10)
23747    *    MUST reject as an error OPEN for invalid remote IP
23748 address. (does)
23749    *    MUST ignore SYN with invalid source address. (does)
23750    *    MUST silently discard incoming SYN for
23751 broadcast/multicast
23752    *       address. (does)
23753    *
23754    * Asynchronous Reports (4.2.4.1)
23755    * MUST provide mechanism for reporting soft errors to
23756 application
23757    *       layer. (does)
23758    *
23759    * Type of Service (4.2.4.2)
23760    *    MUST allow application layer to set Type of
23761 Service. (does IP_TOS)
23762    *
23763    * (Whew. -- MS 950903)
23764    **/
23765
23766 #include <linux/config.h>
23767 #include <linux/types.h>
23768 #include <linux/fcntl.h>
23769 #include <linux/random.h>
23770
23771 #include <net/icmp.h>
23772 #include <net/tcp.h>
23773
23774 #include <asm/segment.h>
23775
23776 unsigned long seq_offset;
23777 struct tcp_mib  tcp_statistics;
23778
23779 /* This is for sockets with full identity only.  Sockets
23780 here will always
23781  * be without wildcards and will have the following
23782 invariant:
23783    *       TCP_ESTABLISHED <= sk->state < TCP_CLOSE
23784    */
23785 struct sock *tcp_established_hash[TCP_HTABLE_SIZE];
23786
23787 /* All sockets in TCP_LISTEN state will be in here.
23788 This is the only table
23789  * where wildcard'd TCP sockets can exist.  Hash
23790 function here is just local
23791  * port number.  XXX Fix or we'll lose with thousands of
```

```
23792 IP aliases...
23793  */
23794 struct sock *tcp_listening_hash[TCP_LHTABLE_SIZE];
23795
23796 /* Ok, let's try this, I give up, we do need a local
23797 binding
23798  * TCP hash as well as the others for fast bind/connect.
23799  */
23800 struct sock *tcp_bound_hash[TCP_BHTABLE_SIZE];
23801
23802 extern struct sock *tcp_v4_lookup(u32 saddr, u16 sport,
23803 u32 daddr, u16 dport);
23804
23805 static int tcp_v4_verify_bind(struct sock *sk, unsigned
23806 short snum)
23807 {
23808     struct sock *sk2;
23809     int retval = 0, sk_reuse = sk->reuse;
23810
23811     SOCKHASH_LOCK();
23812     sk2 = tcp_bound_hash[tcp_bhashfn(snum)];
23813     for(; sk2 != NULL; sk2 = sk2->bind_next) {
23814         if((sk2->num == snum) && (sk2 != sk)) {
23815             unsigned char state = sk2->state;
23816             int sk2_reuse = sk2->reuse;
23817
23818             /* Two sockets can be bound to the same port
23819 if they're
23820              * bound to different interfaces... */
23821             if (sk->bound_device != sk2->bound_device)
23822                 continue;
23823
23824             if(!sk2->rcv_saddr || !sk->rcv_saddr) {
23825                 if((!sk2_reuse)          ||
23826                    (!sk_reuse)           ||
23827                    (state == TCP_LISTEN)) {
23828                     retval = 1;
23829                     break;
23830                 }
23831             } else if(sk2->rcv_saddr == sk->rcv_saddr) {
23832                 if((!sk_reuse)           ||
23833                    (!sk2_reuse)          ||
23834                    (state == TCP_LISTEN)) {
23835                     retval = 1;
23836                     break;
23837                 }
23838             }
23839         }
```

p 548

```
23840              }
23841              SOCKHASH_UNLOCK();
23842
23843              return retval;
23844      }
23845
p 548 23846  static __inline__ int tcp_lport_inuse(int num)
23847  {
23848          struct sock *sk = tcp_bound_hash[tcp_bhashfn(num)];
23849
23850          for(; sk != NULL; sk = sk->bind_next) {
23851              if(sk->num == num)
23852                  return 1;
23853          }
23854          return 0;
23855  }
23856
23857  /* Find a "good" local port, this is family independant.
23858   * There are several strategies working in unison here to
23859   * get the best possible performance.  The current socket
23860   * load is kept track of, if it is zero there is a strong
23861   * likely hood that there is a zero length chain we will
23862   * find with a small amount of searching, else the load
23863  is
23864   * what we shoot for for when the chains all have at
23865  least
23866   * one entry.  The base helps us walk the chains in an
23867   * order such that a good chain is found as quickly as
23868  possible.  -DaveM
23869   */
p 549 23870  unsigned short tcp_good_socknum(void)
23871  {
23872          static int start = PROT_SOCK;
23873          static int binding_contour = 0;
23874          int best = 0;
23875          int size = 32767; /* a big num. */
23876          int retval = 0, i, end, bc;
23877
23878          SOCKHASH_LOCK();
23879          i = tcp_bhashfn(start);
23880          end = i + TCP_BHTABLE_SIZE;
23881          bc = binding_contour;
23882          do {
23883              struct sock *sk =
23884  tcp_bound_hash[i&(TCP_BHTABLE_SIZE-1)];
23885              if(!sk) {
23886                  /* find the smallest value no smaller than
23887  start
```

```
23888   * that has this hash value.
23889   */
23890              retval =
23891  tcp_bhashnext(start-1,i&(TCP_BHTABLE_SIZE-1));
23892
23893              /* Check for decreasing load. */
23894              if (bc != 0)
23895                  binding_contour = 0;
23896              goto done;
23897          } else {
23898              int j = 0;
23899              do { sk = sk->bind_next; } while (++j < size
23900  && sk);
23901              if (j < size) {
23902                  best = i&(TCP_BHTABLE_SIZE-1);
23903                  size = j;
23904                  if (bc && size <= bc) {
23905                      i = best;
23906                      goto verify;
23907                  }
23908              }
23909          }
23910      } while(++i != end);
23911      i = best;
23912
23913      /* Socket load is increasing, adjust our load
23914  average. */
23915      binding_contour = size;
23916  verify:
23917      if (size < binding_contour)
23918          binding_contour = size;
23919
23920      retval = tcp_bhashnext(start-1,i);
23921
23922      best = retval;  /* mark the starting point to avoid
23923  infinite loops */
23924      while(tcp_lport_inuse(retval)) {
23925          retval = tcp_bhashnext(retval,i);
23926          if (retval > 32767) /* Upper bound */
23927              retval = tcp_bhashnext(PROT_SOCK,i);
23928          if (retval == best) {
23929              /* This hash chain is full. No answer. */
23930              retval = 0;
23931              break;
23932          }
23933      }
23934
23935  done:
```

```
23936        start = (retval + 1);
23937        if (start > 32767 || start < PROT_SOCK)
23938            start = PROT_SOCK;
23939        SOCKHASH_UNLOCK();
23940
23941        return retval;
23942    }
23943
23944    void tcp_v4_hash(struct sock *sk)
23945    {
23946        unsigned char state;
23947
23948        SOCKHASH_LOCK();
23949        state = sk->state;
23950        if(state != TCP_CLOSE || !sk->dead) {
23951            struct sock **skp;
23952
23953            if(state == TCP_LISTEN)
23954                skp =
23955    &tcp_listening_hash[tcp_sk_listen_hashfn(sk)];
23956            else
23957                skp =
23958    &tcp_established_hash[tcp_sk_hashfn(sk)];
23959
23960            if((sk->next = *skp) != NULL)
23961                (*skp)->pprev = &sk->next;
23962            *skp = sk;
23963            sk->pprev = skp;
23964            tcp_sk_bindify(sk);
23965        }
23966        SOCKHASH_UNLOCK();
23967    }
23968
23969    void tcp_v4_unhash(struct sock *sk)
23970    {
23971        SOCKHASH_LOCK();
23972        if(sk->pprev) {
23973            if(sk->next)
23974                sk->next->pprev = sk->pprev;
23975            *sk->pprev = sk->next;
23976            sk->pprev = NULL;
23977            tcp_sk_unbindify(sk);
23978        }
23979        SOCKHASH_UNLOCK();
23980    }
23981
23982    void tcp_v4_rehash(struct sock *sk)
23983    {
```

```
23984        unsigned char state;
23985
23986        SOCKHASH_LOCK();
23987        state = sk->state;
23988        if(sk->pprev) {
23989            if(sk->next)
23990                sk->next->pprev = sk->pprev;
23991            *sk->pprev = sk->next;
23992            sk->pprev = NULL;
23993            tcp_sk_unbindify(sk);
23994        }
23995        if(state != TCP_CLOSE || !sk->dead) {
23996            struct sock **skp;
23997
23998            if(state == TCP_LISTEN)
23999                skp =
24000    &tcp_listening_hash[tcp_sk_listen_hashfn(sk)];
24001            else
24002                skp =
24003    &tcp_established_hash[tcp_sk_hashfn(sk)];
24004
24005            if((sk->next = *skp) != NULL)
24006                (*skp)->pprev = &sk->next;
24007            *skp = sk;
24008            sk->pprev = skp;
24009            tcp_sk_bindify(sk);
24010        }
24011        SOCKHASH_UNLOCK();
24012    }
24013
24014    static void tcp_close(struct sock *sk, unsigned long
24015    timeout);
24016
24017    /*
24018     * Find someone to 'accept'. Must be called with
24019     * the socket locked or with interrupts disabled
24020     */
24021
24022    static struct sk_buff *tcp_find_established(struct sock
24023    *s)
24024    {
24025        struct sk_buff *p=skb_peek(&s->receive_queue);
24026        if(p==NULL)
24027            return NULL;
24028        do
24029        {
24030            if(p->sk->state == TCP_ESTABLISHED ||
24031    p->sk->state >= TCP_FIN_WAIT1)
```

```
24032            return p;
24033         p=p->next;
24034       }
24035     while(p!=(struct sk_buff *)&s->receive_queue);
24036     return NULL;
24037 }
24038
24039 /*
24040  *  This routine closes sockets which have been at least
24041 partially
24042  *  opened, but not yet accepted. Currently it is only
24043 called by
24044  *  tcp_close, and timeout mirrors the value there.
24045  */
24046
24047 static void tcp_close_pending (struct sock *sk)
24048 {
24049     struct sk_buff *skb;
24050
24051     while ((skb = skb_dequeue(&sk->receive_queue)) !=
24052 NULL)
24053       {
24054         tcp_close(skb->sk, 0);
24055         kfree_skb(skb, FREE_READ);
24056       }
24057     return;
24058 }
24059
24060 /*
24061  *  Enter the time wait state.
24062  */
24063
24064 void tcp_time_wait(struct sock *sk)
24065 {
24066     tcp_set_state(sk,TCP_TIME_WAIT);
24067     sk->shutdown = SHUTDOWN_MASK;
24068     if (!sk->dead)
24069         sk->state_change(sk);
24070     tcp_reset_msl_timer(sk, TIME_CLOSE,
24071 TCP_TIMEWAIT_LEN);
24072 }
24073
24074
24075 /*
24076  * This routine is called by the ICMP module when it
24077 gets some
24078  * sort of error condition.  If err < 0 then the socket
24079 should
```

```
24080  * be closed and the error returned to the user.  If err
24081 > 0
24082  * it's just the icmp type << 8 | icmp code.  After
24083 adjustment
24084  * header points to the first 8 bytes of the tcp header.
24085 We need
24086  * to find the appropriate port.
24087  */
24088
24089 void tcp_err(int type, int code, unsigned char *header,
24090 __u32 daddr,
24091     __u32 saddr, struct inet_protocol *protocol, int len)
24092 {
24093     struct tcphdr *th = (struct tcphdr *)header;
24094     struct sock *sk;
24095
24096     /*
24097      *  This one is _WRONG_. FIXME urgently.
24098      */
24099 #ifndef CONFIG_NO_PATH_MTU_DISCOVERY
24100     struct iphdr *iph=(struct iphdr
24101 *)(header-sizeof(struct iphdr));
24102 #endif
24103     th =(struct tcphdr *)header;
24104
24105     if (len < 8)     /* NOT sizeof(struct tcphdr) */
24106         return;
24107
24108     sk = tcp_v4_lookup(daddr, th->dest, saddr,
24109 th->source);
24110     if (sk == NULL)
24111         return;
24112
24113     if (type == ICMP_SOURCE_QUENCH)
24114       {
24115         /* Current practice says these frames are bad,
24116 plus the drops
24117            will account right anyway. If we act on this
24118 we stall doubly */
24119         return;
24120       }
24121
24122     if (type == ICMP_PARAMETERPROB)
24123       {
24124         sk->err=EPROTO;
24125         sk->error_report(sk);
24126       }
24127
```

```
24128   #ifndef CONFIG_NO_PATH_MTU_DISCOVERY
24129       if (type == ICMP_DEST_UNREACH && code ==
24130   ICMP_FRAG_NEEDED)
24131           {
24132               struct rtable * rt;
24133               /*
24134                * Ugly trick to pass MTU to protocol layer.
24135                * Really we should add argument "info" to error
24136   handler.
24137                */
24138               unsigned short new_mtu = ntohs(iph->id);
24139
24140               if ((rt = sk->ip_route_cache) != NULL)
24141                   if (rt->rt_mtu > new_mtu)
24142                       rt->rt_mtu = new_mtu;
24143
24144               /*
24145                * FIXME::
24146                * Not the nicest of fixes: Lose a MTU update
24147   if the socket is
24148                * locked this instant. Not the right answer
24149   but will be best
24150                * for the production fix. Make 2.1 work right!
24151                */
24152
24153               if (sk->mtu > new_mtu - sizeof(struct iphdr) -
24154   sizeof(struct tcphdr)
24155                   && new_mtu > sizeof(struct
24156   iphdr)+sizeof(struct tcphdr) && !sk->users)
24157                   sk->mtu = new_mtu - sizeof(struct iphdr) -
24158   sizeof(struct tcphdr);
24159
24160               return;
24161           }
24162   #endif
24163
24164       /*
24165        * If we've already connected we will keep trying
24166        * until we time out, or the user gives up.
24167        */
24168
24169       if(code<=NR_ICMP_UNREACH)
24170       {
24171           if(icmp_err_convert[code].fatal || sk->state ==
24172   TCP_SYN_SENT || sk->state == TCP_SYN_RECV)
24173           {
24174               sk->err = icmp_err_convert[code].errno;
24175               if (sk->state == TCP_SYN_SENT || sk->state
```

```
24176   == TCP_SYN_RECV)
24177               {
24178                   tcp_statistics.TcpAttemptFails++;
24179                   tcp_set_state(sk,TCP_CLOSE);
24180                   sk->error_report(sk);       /* Wake
24181   people up to see the error (see connect in sock.c) */
24182               }
24183           }
24184           else     /* Only an error on timeout */
24185               sk->err_soft = icmp_err_convert[code].errno;
24186       }
24187   }
24188
24189
24190   /*
24191    * Walk down the receive queue counting readable data
24192   until we hit the end or we find a gap
24193    * in the received data queue (ie a frame missing that
24194   needs sending to us). Not
24195    * sorting using two queues as data arrives makes life
24196   so much harder.
24197    */
24198
24199   static int tcp_readable(struct sock *sk)
24200   {
24201       unsigned long counted;
24202       unsigned long amount;
24203       struct sk_buff *skb;
24204       int sum;
24205       unsigned long flags;
24206
24207       if(sk && sk->debug)
24208           printk("tcp_readable: %p - ",sk);
24209
24210       save_flags(flags);
24211       cli();
24212       if (sk == NULL || (skb =
24213   skb_peek(&sk->receive_queue)) == NULL)
24214       {
24215           restore_flags(flags);
24216           if(sk && sk->debug)
24217               printk("empty\n");
24218           return(0);
24219       }
24220
24221       counted = sk->copied_seq;   /* Where we are at the
24222   moment */
24223       amount = 0;
```

p 550

```
24224
24225      /*
24226       *   Do until a push or until we are out of data.
24227       */
24228
24229      do
24230      {
24231          if (before(counted, skb->seq))      /* Found a
24232 hole so stops here */
24233              break;
24234          sum = skb->len - (counted - skb->seq);   /*
24235 Length - header but start from where we are up to (avoid
24236 overlaps) */
24237          if (skb->h.th->syn)
24238              sum++;
24239          if (sum > 0)
24240          {                       /* Add it up, move on */
24241              amount += sum;
24242              if (skb->h.th->syn)
24243                  amount--;
24244              counted += sum;
24245          }
24246          /*
24247           * Don't count urg data ... but do it in the
24248 right place!
24249           * Consider: "old_data (ptr is here) URG PUSH
24250 data"
24251           * The old code would stop at the first push
24252 because
24253           * it counted the urg (amount==1) and then does
24254 amount--
24255           * *after* the loop.  This means tcp_readable()
24256 always
24257           * returned zero if any URG PUSH was in the
24258 queue, even
24259           * though there was normal data available. If we
24260 subtract
24261           * the urg data right here, we even get it to
24262 work for more
24263           * than one URG PUSH skb without normal data.
24264           * This means that select() finally works now
24265 with urg data
24266           * in the queue.  Note that rlogin was never
24267 affected
24268           * because it doesn't use select(); it uses two
24269 processes
24270           * and a blocking read().  And the queue scan in
24271 tcp_read()
24272           * was correct.  Mike <pall@rz.uni-karlsruhe.de>
24273           */
24274          if (skb->h.th->urg)
24275              amount--;   /* don't count urg data */
24276 /*       if (amount && skb->h.th->psh) break;*/
24277          skb = skb->next;
24278      }
24279      while(skb != (struct sk_buff *)&sk->receive_queue);
24280
24281      restore_flags(flags);
24282      if(sk->debug)
24283          printk("got %lu bytes.\n",amount);
24284      return(amount);
24285 }
24286
24287 /*
24288  * LISTEN is a special case for select..
24289  */
24290 static int tcp_listen_select(struct sock *sk, int
24291 sel_type, select_table *wait)
24292 {
24293      if (sel_type == SEL_IN) {
24294          struct sk_buff * skb;
24295
24296          lock_sock(sk);
24297          skb = tcp_find_established(sk);
24298          release_sock(sk);
24299          if (skb)
24300              return 1;
24301          select_wait(sk->sleep,wait);
24302          return 0;
24303      }
24304      return 0;
24305 }
24306
24307
24308 /*
24309  *  Wait for a TCP event.
24310  *
24311  *  Note that we don't need to lock the socket, as the
24312 upper select layers
24313  *  take care of normal races (between the test and the
24314 event) and we don't
24315  *  go look at any of the socket buffers directly.
24316  */
24317 static int tcp_select(struct sock *sk, int sel_type,
24318 select_table *wait)
24319 {
```

```
24320        if (sk->state == TCP_LISTEN)
24321            return tcp_listen_select(sk, sel_type, wait);
24322
24323        switch(sel_type) {
24324        case SEL_IN:
24325            if (sk->err)
24326                return 1;
24327            if (sk->state == TCP_SYN_SENT || sk->state ==
24328 TCP_SYN_RECV)
24329                break;
24330
24331            if (sk->shutdown & RCV_SHUTDOWN)
24332                return 1;
24333
24334            if (sk->acked_seq == sk->copied_seq)
24335                break;
24336
24337            if (sk->urg_seq != sk->copied_seq ||
24338                sk->acked_seq != sk->copied_seq+1 ||
24339                sk->urginline || !sk->urg_data)
24340                return 1;
24341            break;
24342
24343        case SEL_OUT:
24344            if (sk->err)
24345                return 1;
24346            if (sk->shutdown & SEND_SHUTDOWN)
24347                return 0;
24348            if (sk->state == TCP_SYN_SENT || sk->state ==
24349 TCP_SYN_RECV)
24350                break;
24351            if (sk->wmem_alloc*2 > sk->sndbuf)
24352                break;
24353            return 1;
24354
24355        case SEL_EX:
24356            if (sk->urg_data)
24357                return 1;
24358            break;
24359        }
24360        select_wait(sk->sleep, wait);
24361        return 0;
24362 }
24363
24364 int tcp_ioctl(struct sock *sk, int cmd, unsigned long
24365 arg)
24366 {
24367     int err;
```

```
24368     switch(cmd)
24369     {
24370
24371        case TIOCINQ:
24372 #ifdef FIXME    /* FIXME: */
24373        case FIONREAD:
24374 #endif
24375        {
24376            unsigned long amount;
24377
24378            if (sk->state == TCP_LISTEN)
24379                return(-EINVAL);
24380
24381            lock_sock(sk);
24382            amount = tcp_readable(sk);
24383            release_sock(sk);
24384            err=verify_area(VERIFY_WRITE,(void *)arg,
24385 sizeof(int));
24386            if(err)
24387                return err;
24388            put_user(amount, (int *)arg);
24389            return(0);
24390        }
24391        case SIOCATMARK:
24392        {
24393            int answ = sk->urg_data && sk->urg_seq ==
24394 sk->copied_seq;
24395
24396            err = verify_area(VERIFY_WRITE,(void *) arg,
24397 sizeof(int));
24398            if (err)
24399                return err;
24400            put_user(answ,(int *) arg);
24401            return(0);
24402        }
24403        case TIOCOUTQ:
24404        {
24405            unsigned long amount;
24406
24407            if (sk->state == TCP_LISTEN) return(-EINVAL);
24408            amount = sock_wspace(sk);
24409            err=verify_area(VERIFY_WRITE,(void *)arg,
24410 sizeof(int));
24411            if(err)
24412                return err;
24413            put_user(amount, (int *)arg);
24414            return(0);
24415        }
```

```
24416            default:
24417                return(-EINVAL);
24418        }
24419 }
24420
24421
24422 /*
24423  *  This routine computes a TCP checksum.
24424  *
24425  *  Modified January 1995 from a go-faster DOS routine by
24426  *  Jorge Cwik <jorge@laser.satlink.net>
24427  */
24428 #undef DEBUG_TCP_CHECK
24429 void tcp_send_check(struct tcphdr *th, unsigned long
24430 saddr,
24431          unsigned long daddr, int len, struct sk_buff
24432 *skb)
24433 {
24434 #ifdef DEBUG_TCP_CHECK
24435     u16 check;
24436 #endif
24437     th->check = 0;
24438     th->check = tcp_check(th, len, saddr, daddr,
24439         csum_partial((char *)th,sizeof(*th),skb->csum));
24440
24441 #ifdef DEBUG_TCP_CHECK
24442     check = th->check;
24443     th->check = 0;
24444     th->check = tcp_check(th, len, saddr, daddr,
24445         csum_partial((char *)th,len,0));
24446     if (check != th->check) {
24447         static int count = 0;
24448         if (++count < 10) {
24449             printk("Checksum %x (%x) from %p\n",
24450 th->check, check,
24451                 (&th)[-1]);
24452             printk("TCP=<off:%d a:%d s:%d f:%d>\n",
24453 th->doff*4, th->ack, th->syn, th->fin);
24454         }
24455     }
24456 #endif
24457 }
24458
24459
24460 /*
24461  *  This routine builds a generic TCP header.
24462  */
24463
24464 static inline int tcp_build_header(struct tcphdr *th,
24465 struct sock *sk, int push)
24466 {
24467     memcpy(th,(void *) &(sk->dummy_th), sizeof(*th));
24468     th->psh = (push == 0) ? 1 : 0;
24469     th->seq = htonl(sk->write_seq);
24470     th->ack_seq = htonl(sk->acked_seq);
24471     th->window = htons(tcp_select_window(sk));
24472
24473     return(sizeof(*th));
24474 }
24475
24476 /*
24477  *  Wait for a socket to get into the connected state
24478  */
24479 static void wait_for_tcp_connect(struct sock * sk)
24480 {
24481     release_sock(sk);
24482     cli();
24483     if (sk->state != TCP_ESTABLISHED && sk->state !=
24484 TCP_CLOSE_WAIT && sk->err == 0)
24485         {
24486         interruptible_sleep_on(sk->sleep);
24487     }
24488     sti();
24489     lock_sock(sk);
24490 }
24491
24492 static inline int tcp_memory_free(struct sock *sk)
24493 {
24494     return sk->wmem_alloc < sk->sndbuf;
24495 }
24496
24497 /*
24498  *  Wait for more memory for a socket
24499  */
24500 static void wait_for_tcp_memory(struct sock * sk)
24501 {
24502     release_sock(sk);
24503     if (!tcp_memory_free(sk)) {
24504         struct wait_queue wait = { current, NULL };
24505
24506         sk->socket->flags &= ~SO_NOSPACE;
24507         add_wait_queue(sk->sleep, &wait);
24508         for (;;) {
24509             if (current->signal & ~current->blocked)
24510                 break;
24511             current->state = TASK_INTERRUPTIBLE;
```

```
24512              if (tcp_memory_free(sk))
24513                  break;
24514              if (sk->shutdown & SEND_SHUTDOWN)
24515                  break;
24516              if (sk->err)
24517                  break;
24518              schedule();
24519          }
24520          current->state = TASK_RUNNING;
24521          remove_wait_queue(sk->sleep, &wait);
24522      }
24523      lock_sock(sk);
24524  }
24525
24526
24527  /*
24528   * This routine copies from a user buffer into a socket,
24529   * and starts the transmit system.
24530   */
24531
24532  static int do_tcp_sendmsg(struct sock *sk,
24533      int iovlen, struct iovec *iov,
24534      int len, int nonblock, int flags)
24535  {
24536      int copied = 0;
24537      struct device *dev = NULL;
24538
24539      /*
24540       *  Wait for a connection to finish.
24541       */
24542      while (sk->state != TCP_ESTABLISHED && sk->state !=
24543  TCP_CLOSE_WAIT)
24544      {
24545          if (sk->err)
24546              return sock_error(sk);
24547
24548          if (sk->state != TCP_SYN_SENT && sk->state !=
24549  TCP_SYN_RECV)
24550          {
24551              if (sk->keepopen)
24552                  send_sig(SIGPIPE, current, 0);
24553              return -EPIPE;
24554          }
24555
24556          if (nonblock)
24557              return -EAGAIN;
24558
24559          if (current->signal & ~current->blocked)
```

```
24560              return -ERESTARTSYS;
24561
24562          wait_for_tcp_connect(sk);
24563      }
24564
24565      /*
24566       *  Ok commence sending
24567       */
24568
24569      while (--iovlen >= 0)
24570      {
24571          int seglen=iov->iov_len;
24572          unsigned char * from=iov->iov_base;
24573          iov++;
24574
24575          while(seglen > 0)
24576          {
24577              int copy, delay;
24578              int tmp;
24579              struct sk_buff *skb;
24580
24581              /*
24582               * Stop on errors
24583               */
24584              if (sk->err)
24585              {
24586                  if (copied)
24587                      return copied;
24588                  return sock_error(sk);
24589              }
24590
24591              /*
24592               *  Make sure that we are established.
24593               */
24594              if (sk->shutdown & SEND_SHUTDOWN)
24595              {
24596                  if (copied)
24597                      return copied;
24598                  send_sig(SIGPIPE,current,0);
24599                  return -EPIPE;
24600              }
24601
24602              /*
24603               * The following code can result in copy <=
24604  if sk->mss is ever
24605               * decreased.  It shouldn't be.  sk->mss is
24606  min(sk->mtu, sk->max_window).
24607               * sk->mtu is constant once SYN processing
```

```
24608   is finished.  I.e. we
24609                   * had better not get here until we've seen
24610   his SYN and at least one
24611                   * valid ack.  (The SYN sets sk->mtu and the
24612   ack sets sk->max_window.)
24613                   * But ESTABLISHED should guarantee that.
24614   sk->max_window is by definition
24615                   * non-decreasing.  Note that any ioctl to
24616   set user_mss must be done
24617                   * before the exchange of SYN's.  If the
24618   initial ack from the other
24619                   * end has a window of 0, max_window and
24620   thus mss will both be 0.
24621                   */
24622
24623                   /*
24624                   *   Now we need to check if we have a half
24625   built packet.
24626                   */
24627   #ifndef CONFIG_NO_PATH_MTU_DISCOVERY
24628                   /*
24629                   *   Really, we should rebuild all the
24630   queues...
24631                   *   It's difficult. Temporary hack is to
24632   send all
24633                   *   queued segments with allowed
24634   fragmentation.
24635                   */
24636                   {
24637                       /*
24638                       *   new_mss may be zero. That indicates
24639                       *   we don't have a window estimate for
24640                       *   the remote box yet.
24641                       *      -- AC
24642                       */
24643
24644                       int new_mss = min(sk->mtu,
24645   sk->max_window);
24646                       if (new_mss && new_mss < sk->mss)
24647                       {
24648                           tcp_send_partial(sk);
24649                           sk->mss = new_mss;
24650                       }
24651                   }
24652   #endif
24653
24654                   /*
24655                   *   If there is a partly filled frame we can
24656   fill
24657                   *   out.
24658                   */
24659                   if ((skb = tcp_dequeue_partial(sk)) != NULL)
24660                   {
24661                       int tcp_size;
24662
24663                       tcp_size = skb->tail - (unsigned char
24664   *)(skb->h.th + 1);
24665
24666                       /* Add more stuff to the end of skb->len
24667   */
24668                       if (!(flags & MSG_OOB))
24669                       {
24670                           copy = min(sk->mss - tcp_size,
24671   seglen);
24672
24673                           /*
24674                           *   Now we may find the frame is as
24675   big, or too
24676                           *   big for our MSS. Thats all fine.
24677   It means the
24678                           *   MSS shrank (from an ICMP) after
24679   we allocated
24680                           *   this frame.
24681                           */
24682
24683                           if (copy <= 0)
24684                           {
24685                               /*
24686                               *   Send the now forced complete
24687   frame out.
24688                               *
24689                               *   Note for 2.1: The MSS reduce
24690   code ought to
24691                               *   flush any frames in partial
24692   that are now
24693                               *   full sized. Not serious,
24694   potential tiny
24695                               *   performance hit.
24696                               */
24697                               tcp_send_skb(sk,skb);
24698                               /*
24699                               *   Get a new buffer and try
24700   again.
24701                               */
24702                               continue;
24703                           }
```

```
24704                         /*
24705                          *  Otherwise continue to fill the
24706      buffer.
24707                          */
24708                         tcp_size += copy;
24709                         memcpy_fromfs(skb_put(skb,copy),
24710      from, copy);
24711                         skb->csum = csum_partial(skb->tail -
24712      tcp_size, tcp_size, 0);
24713                         from += copy;
24714                         copied += copy;
24715                         len -= copy;
24716                         sk->write_seq += copy;
24717                         seglen -= copy;
24718                     }
24719                     /* If we have a full packet or a new OOB
24720                      * message, we have to force this packet
24721      out.
24722                      */
24723                     if (tcp_size >= sk->mss || (flags &
24724      MSG_OOB))
24725                         tcp_send_skb(sk, skb);
24726                     else
24727                         tcp_enqueue_partial(skb, sk);
24728                     continue;
24729                 }
24730
24731             /*
24732              * We also need to worry about the window.
24733              * If window < 1/2 the maximum window we've seen
24734      from this
24735              *   host, don't use it.  This is sender side
24736              *   silly window prevention, as specified in
24737      RFC1122.
24738              *   (Note that this is different than earlier
24739      versions of
24740              *   SWS prevention, e.g. RFC813.).  What we
24741      actually do is
24742              *   use the whole MSS.  Since the results in
24743      the right
24744              *   edge of the packet being outside the
24745      window, it will
24746              *   be queued for later rather than sent.
24747              */
24748
24749                 copy = sk->window_seq - sk->write_seq;
24750                 if (copy <= 0 || copy < (sk->max_window >>
24751      1) || copy > sk->mss)
```

```
24752                     copy = sk->mss;
24753                 if (copy > seglen)
24754                     copy = seglen;
24755                 if (copy <= 0)
24756                 {
24757                     printk(KERN_CRIT "TCP: **bug**: copy=%d,
24758      sk->mss=%d\n", copy, sk->mss);
24759                     return -EFAULT;
24760                 }
24761
24762             /*
24763              *  We should really check the window here
24764      also.
24765              */
24766
24767                 delay = 0;
24768                 tmp = copy + sk->prot->max_header + 15;
24769                 /* If won't fill the current packet, and
24770      it's not an OOB message,
24771                  * then we might want to delay to allow data
24772      in the later parts
24773                  * of iov to fill this packet out. Note that
24774      if we aren't
24775                  * Nagling or there are no packets currently
24776      out then the top
24777                  * level code in tcp_sendmsg() will force
24778      any partial packets out
24779                  * after we finish building the largest
24780      packets this write allows.
24781              */
24782                 if (copy < sk->mss && !(flags & MSG_OOB)) {
24783                     tmp = tmp - copy + sk->mtu + 128;
24784                     delay = 1;
24785                 }
24786                 skb = sock_wmalloc(sk, tmp, 0, GFP_KERNEL);
24787
24788             /*
24789              *  If we didn't get any memory, we need to
24790      sleep.
24791              */
24792
24793                 if (skb == NULL)
24794                 {
24795                     sk->socket->flags |= SO_NOSPACE;
24796                     if (nonblock)
24797                     {
24798                         if (copied)
24799                             return copied;
```

```
24800                    return -EAGAIN;
24801                }
24802
24803                if (current->signal & ~current->blocked)
24804                {
24805                    if (copied)
24806                        return copied;
24807                    return -ERESTARTSYS;
24808                }
24809
24810                wait_for_tcp_memory(sk);
24811                continue;
24812            }
24813
24814            skb->sk = sk;
24815            skb->free = 0;
24816            skb->localroute =
24817    sk->localroute|(flags&MSG_DONTROUTE);
24818
24819            /*
24820             * FIXME: we need to optimize this.
24821             * Perhaps some hints here would be good.
24822             */
24823
24824            tmp = sk->prot->build_header(skb, sk->saddr,
24825    sk->daddr, &dev,
24826                    IPPROTO_TCP, sk->opt,
24827    skb->truesize,sk->ip_tos,sk->ip_ttl,&sk->ip_route_cache);
24828            if (tmp < 0 )
24829            {
24830                sock_wfree(sk, skb);
24831                if (copied)
24832                    return(copied);
24833                return(tmp);
24834            }
24835    #ifndef CONFIG_NO_PATH_MTU_DISCOVERY
24836            skb->ip_hdr->frag_off |= htons(IP_DF);
24837    #endif
24838            skb->dev = dev;
24839            skb->h.th =(struct tcphdr
24840    *)skb_put(skb,sizeof(struct tcphdr));
24841            tmp = tcp_build_header(skb->h.th, sk,
24842    seglen-copy);
24843            if (tmp < 0)
24844            {
24845                sock_wfree(sk, skb);
24846                if (copied)
24847                    return(copied);
```

```
24848                return(tmp);
24849            }
24850
24851            if (flags & MSG_OOB)
24852            {
24853                skb->h.th->urg = 1;
24854                skb->h.th->urg_ptr = ntohs(copy);
24855            }
24856
24857            skb->csum = csum_partial_copy_fromuser(from,
24858                skb_put(skb,copy), copy, 0);
24859
24860            from += copy;
24861            copied += copy;
24862            len -= copy;
24863            seglen -= copy;
24864            skb->free = 0;
24865            sk->write_seq += copy;
24866
24867            if (delay)
24868            {
24869                tcp_enqueue_partial(skb, sk);
24870                continue;
24871            }
24872            tcp_send_skb(sk, skb);
24873        }
24874    }
24875    sk->err = 0;
24876
24877    return copied;
24878 }
24879
24880
24881 static int tcp_sendmsg(struct sock *sk, struct msghdr
24882 *msg,
24883      int len, int nonblock, int flags)
24884 {
24885    int retval = -EINVAL;
24886
24887    /*
24888     *  Do sanity checking for sendmsg/sendto/send
24889     */
24890
24891    if (flags & ~(MSG_OOB|MSG_DONTROUTE))
24892        goto out;
24893    if (msg->msg_name) {
24894        struct sockaddr_in *addr=(struct sockaddr_in
24895 *)msg->msg_name;
```

p 554

```
24896
24897            if (msg->msg_namelen < sizeof(*addr))
24898                goto out;
24899            if (addr->sin_family && addr->sin_family !=
24900  AF_INET)
24901                goto out;
24902            retval = -ENOTCONN;
24903            if(sk->state == TCP_CLOSE)
24904                goto out;
24905            retval = -EISCONN;
24906            if (addr->sin_port != sk->dummy_th.dest)
24907                goto out;
24908            if (addr->sin_addr.s_addr != sk->daddr)
24909                goto out;
24910        }
24911
24912        lock_sock(sk);
24913        retval = do_tcp_sendmsg(sk, msg->msg_iovlen,
24914  msg->msg_iov, len, nonblock, flags);
24915
24916  /*
24917   *  Nagle's rule. Turn Nagle off with TCP_NODELAY for
24918  highly
24919   *  interactive fast network servers. It's meant to be
24920  on and
24921   *  it really improves the throughput though not the
24922  echo time
24923   *  on my slow slip link - Alan
24924   *
24925   *  If not nagling we can send on the before case too..
24926   */
24927
24928        if (sk->partial) {
24929            if (!sk->packets_out ||
24930                (sk->nonagle && before(sk->write_seq ,
24931  sk->window_seq))) {
24932                    tcp_send_partial(sk);
24933            }
24934        }
24935
24936        release_sock(sk);
24937
24938  out:
24939        return retval;
24940  }
24941
24942
24943  /*
```

```
24944   *  Send an ack if one is backlogged at this point.
24945   */
24946
24947  void tcp_read_wakeup(struct sock *sk)
24948  {
24949        if (!sk->ack_backlog)
24950            return;
24951
24952        /*
24953         * If we're closed, don't send an ack, or we'll get
24954  a RST
24955         * from the closed destination.
24956         */
24957        if ((sk->state == TCP_CLOSE) || (sk->state ==
24958  TCP_TIME_WAIT))
24959            return;
24960
24961        tcp_send_ack(sk);
24962  }
24963
24964
24965  /*
24966   *  Handle reading urgent data. BSD has very simple
24967  semantics for
24968   *  this, no blocking and very strange errors 8)
24969   */
24970
24971  static int tcp_recv_urg(struct sock * sk, int nonblock,
24972            struct msghdr *msg, int len, int flags, int
24973  *addr_len)
24974  {
24975        /*
24976         *  No URG data to read
24977         */
24978        if (sk->urginline || !sk->urg_data || sk->urg_data
24979  == URG_READ)
24980            return -EINVAL; /* Yes this is right ! */
24981
24982        if (sk->err)
24983            return sock_error(sk);
24984
24985        if (sk->state == TCP_CLOSE || sk->done)
24986        {
24987            if (!sk->done)
24988            {
24989                sk->done = 1;
24990                return 0;
24991            }
```

p 554 (line 24947)

p 554 (line 24978)

```
24992          return -ENOTCONN;
24993      }
24994
24995      if (sk->shutdown & RCV_SHUTDOWN)
24996      {
24997          sk->done = 1;
24998          return 0;
24999      }
25000      lock_sock(sk);
25001      if (sk->urg_data & URG_VALID)
25002      {
25003          char c = sk->urg_data;
25004          if (!(flags & MSG_PEEK))
25005              sk->urg_data = URG_READ;
25006          memcpy_toiovec(msg->msg_iov, &c, 1);
25007          if(msg->msg_name)
25008          {
25009              struct sockaddr_in *sin=(struct sockaddr_in
25010  *)msg->msg_name;
25011              sin->sin_family=AF_INET;
25012              sin->sin_addr.s_addr=sk->daddr;
25013              sin->sin_port=sk->dummy_th.dest;
25014          }
25015          if(addr_len)
25016              *addr_len=sizeof(struct sockaddr_in);
25017          release_sock(sk);
25018          return 1;
25019      }
25020      release_sock(sk);
25021
25022      /*
25023       * Fixed the recv(..., MSG_OOB) behaviour.  BSD docs
25024  and
25025       * the available implementations agree in this case:
25026       * this call should never block, independent of the
25027       * blocking state of the socket.
25028       * Mike <pall@rz.uni-karlsruhe.de>
25029       */
25030      return -EAGAIN;
25031  }
25032
25033  /*
25034   * Release a skb if it is no longer needed. This routine
25035   * must be called with interrupts disabled or with the
25036   * socket locked so that the sk_buff queue operation is
25037  ok.
25038   */
25039
```

```
          ▶ p 554  25040  static inline void tcp_eat_skb(struct sock *sk, struct
25041  sk_buff * skb)
25042  {
25043      skb->sk = sk;
25044      __skb_unlink(skb, &sk->receive_queue);
25045      kfree_skb(skb, FREE_READ);
25046  }
25047
25048  /*
25049   * FIXME:
25050   * This routine frees used buffers.
25051   * It should consider sending an ACK to let the
25052   * other end know we now have a bigger window.
25053   */
25054
          ▶ p 554  25055  static void cleanup_rbuf(struct sock *sk)
25056  {
25057      /*
25058       * NOTE! The socket must be locked, so that we don't
25059  get
25060       * a messed-up receive queue.
25061       */
25062      while (!skb_queue_empty(&sk->receive_queue)) {
25063          struct sk_buff *skb = sk->receive_queue.next;
25064          if (!skb->used || skb->users)
25065              break;
25066          tcp_eat_skb(sk, skb);
25067      }
25068
25069      /*
25070       * Tell the world if we raised the window.
25071       */
25072      if (tcp_raise_window(sk))
25073          tcp_send_ack(sk);
25074  }
25075
25076
25077  /*
25078   * This routine copies from a sock struct into the user
25079  buffer.
25080   */
25081
25082  static int tcp_recvmsg(struct sock *sk, struct msghdr
25083  *msg,
25084      int len, int nonblock, int flags, int *addr_len)
25085  {
25086      struct wait_queue wait = { current, NULL };
25087      int copied = 0;
```

```
25088          u32 peek_seq;
25089          volatile u32 *seq;  /* So gcc doesn't overoptimise */
25090          unsigned long used;
25091
25092          /*
25093           *  This error should be checked.
25094           */
25095
25096          if (sk->state == TCP_LISTEN)
25097              return -ENOTCONN;
25098
25099          /*
25100           *  Urgent data needs to be handled specially.
25101           */
25102
25103          if (flags & MSG_OOB)
25104              return tcp_recv_urg(sk, nonblock, msg, len,
25105      flags, addr_len);
25106
25107          /*
25108           *  Copying sequence to update. This is volatile to
25109      handle
25110           *  the multi-reader case neatly (memcpy_to/fromfs
25111      might be
25112           *  inline and thus not flush cached variables
25113      otherwise).
25114           */
25115
25116          peek_seq = sk->copied_seq;
25117          seq = &sk->copied_seq;
25118          if (flags & MSG_PEEK)
25119              seq = &peek_seq;
25120
25121          add_wait_queue(sk->sleep, &wait);
25122          lock_sock(sk);
25123          while (len > 0)
25124          {
25125              struct sk_buff * skb;
25126              u32 offset;
25127
25128              /*
25129               * Are we at urgent data? Stop if we have read
25130      anything.
25131               */
25132
25133              if (copied && sk->urg_data && sk->urg_seq ==
25134      *seq)
25135                      break;
```

```
25136
25137          /*
25138           * We need to check signals first, to get
25139      correct SIGURG
25140           * handling.
25141           */
25142          if (current->signal & ~current->blocked) {
25143              if (copied)
25144                  break;
25145              copied = -ERESTARTSYS;
25146              if (nonblock)
25147                  copied = -EAGAIN;
25148              break;
25149          }
25150
25151          /*
25152           *  Next get a buffer.
25153           */
25154
25155          current->state = TASK_INTERRUPTIBLE;
25156
25157          skb = sk->receive_queue.next;
25158          while (skb != (struct sk_buff
25159      *)&sk->receive_queue)
25160          {
25161              if (before(*seq, skb->seq))
25162                  break;
25163              offset = *seq - skb->seq;
25164              if (skb->h.th->syn)
25165                  offset--;
25166              if (offset < skb->len)
25167                  goto found_ok_skb;
25168              if (skb->h.th->fin)
25169                  goto found_fin_ok;
25170              if (!(flags & MSG_PEEK))
25171                  skb->used = 1;
25172              skb = skb->next;
25173          }
25174
25175          if (copied)
25176              break;
25177
25178          if (sk->err && !(flags&MSG_PEEK))
25179          {
25180              copied = sock_error(sk);
25181              break;
25182          }
25183
```

```
25184          if (sk->state == TCP_CLOSE)
25185          {
25186              if (!sk->done)
25187              {
25188                  sk->done = 1;
25189                  break;
25190              }
25191              copied = -ENOTCONN;
25192              break;
25193          }
25194
25195          if (sk->shutdown & RCV_SHUTDOWN)
25196          {
25197              sk->done = 1;
25198              break;
25199          }
25200
25201          if (nonblock)
25202          {
25203              copied = -EAGAIN;
25204              break;
25205          }
25206
25207          cleanup_rbuf(sk);
25208          release_sock(sk);
25209          sk->socket->flags |= SO_WAITDATA;
25210          schedule();
25211          sk->socket->flags &= ~SO_WAITDATA;
25212          lock_sock(sk);
25213          continue;
25214
25215      found_ok_skb:
25216          /*
25217           *  Lock the buffer. We can be fairly relaxed as
25218           *  an interrupt will never steal a buffer we are
25219           *  using unless I've missed something serious in
25220           *  tcp_data.
25221           */
25222
25223          skb->users++;
25224
25225          /*
25226           *  Ok so how much can we use ?
25227           */
25228
25229          used = skb->len - offset;
25230          if (len < used)
25231              used = len;
```

```
25232          /*
25233           *  Do we have urgent data here?
25234           */
25235
25236          if (sk->urg_data)
25237          {
25238              u32 urg_offset = sk->urg_seq - *seq;
25239              if (urg_offset < used)
25240              {
25241                  if (!urg_offset)
25242                  {
25243                      if (!sk->urginline)
25244                      {
25245                          ++*seq;
25246                          offset++;
25247                          used--;
25248                      }
25249                  }
25250                  else
25251                      used = urg_offset;
25252              }
25253          }
25254
25255          /*
25256           *  Copy it - We _MUST_ update *seq first so
25257      that we
25258           *  don't ever double read when we have dual
25259      readers
25260           */
25261
25262          *seq += used;
25263
25264          /*
25265           *  This memcpy_tofs can sleep. If it sleeps and
25266      we
25267           *  do a second read it relies on the skb->users
25268      to avoid
25269           *  a crash when cleanup_rbuf() gets called.
25270           */
25271
25272          memcpy_toiovec(msg->msg_iov,((unsigned char
25273      *)skb->h.th) +
25274              skb->h.th->doff*4 + offset, used);
25275          copied += used;
25276          len -= used;
25277
25278          /*
25279           *  We now will not sleep again until we are
```

```
25280  finished
25281          *   with skb. Sorry if you are doing the SMP port
25282          *   but you'll just have to fix it neatly ;)
25283          */
25284
25285          skb->users --;
25286
25287          if (after(sk->copied_seq,sk->urg_seq))
25288              sk->urg_data = 0;
25289          if (used + offset < skb->len)
25290              continue;
25291
25292          /*
25293           *   Process the FIN.
25294           */
25295
25296          if (skb->h.th->fin)
25297              goto found_fin_ok;
25298          if (flags & MSG_PEEK)
25299              continue;
25300          skb->used = 1;
25301          if (!skb->users)
25302              tcp_eat_skb(sk, skb);
25303          continue;
25304
25305      found_fin_ok:
25306          ++*seq;
25307          if (flags & MSG_PEEK)
25308              break;
25309
25310          /*
25311           *   All is done
25312           */
25313
25314          skb->used = 1;
25315          sk->shutdown |= RCV_SHUTDOWN;
25316          break;
25317
25318      }
25319
25320      if(copied>0 && msg->msg_name)
25321      {
25322          struct sockaddr_in *sin=(struct sockaddr_in
25323  *)msg->msg_name;
25324          sin->sin_family=AF_INET;
25325          sin->sin_addr.s_addr=sk->daddr;
25326          sin->sin_port=sk->dummy_th.dest;
25327      }
```

```
25328      if(addr_len)
25329          *addr_len=sizeof(struct sockaddr_in);
25330
25331      remove_wait_queue(sk->sleep, &wait);
25332      current->state = TASK_RUNNING;
25333
25334      /* Clean up data we have read: This will do ACK
25335  frames */
25336      cleanup_rbuf(sk);
25337      release_sock(sk);
25338      return copied;
25339  }
25340
25341
25342
25343  /*
25344   *  State processing on a close. This implements the
25345  state shift for
25346   *  sending our FIN frame. Note that we only send a FIN
25347  for some
25348   *  states. A shutdown() may have already sent the FIN,
25349  or we may be
25350   *  closed.
25351   */
25352
25353  static int tcp_close_state(struct sock *sk, int dead)
25354  {
25355      int ns=TCP_CLOSE;
25356      int send_fin=0;
25357      switch(sk->state)
25358      {
25359          case TCP_SYN_SENT:   /* No SYN back, no FIN
25360  needed */
25361              break;
25362          case TCP_SYN_RECV:
25363          case TCP_ESTABLISHED:    /* Closedown begin */
25364              ns=TCP_FIN_WAIT1;
25365              send_fin=1;
25366              break;
25367          case TCP_FIN_WAIT1: /* Already closing, or FIN
25368  sent: no change */
25369          case TCP_FIN_WAIT2:
25370          case TCP_CLOSING:
25371              ns=sk->state;
25372              break;
25373          case TCP_CLOSE:
25374          case TCP_LISTEN:
25375              break;
```

p 555

```
25376              case TCP_LAST_ACK:  /* Could have shutdown()
25377  then close().
25378                          Be careful not to send double
25379  fin. */
25380                  ns=TCP_LAST_ACK;
25381              break;
25382          case TCP_CLOSE_WAIT:    /* They have FIN'd us.
25383  We send our FIN and
25384                      wait only for the ACK */
25385                  ns=TCP_LAST_ACK;
25386              send_fin=1;
25387      }
25388
25389      tcp_set_state(sk,ns);
25390
25391      /*
25392       *  This is a (useful) BSD violating of the RFC.
25393  There is a
25394       *  problem with TCP as specified in that the other
25395  end could
25396       *  keep a socket open forever with no application
25397  left this end.
25398       *  We use a 3 minute timeout (about the same as
25399  BSD) then kill
25400       *  our end. If they send after that then tough -
25401  BUT: long enough
25402       *  that we won't make the old 4*rto = almost no
25403  time - whoops
25404       *  reset mistake.
25405       */
25406      if(dead && ns==TCP_FIN_WAIT2)
25407      {
25408          int timer_active=del_timer(&sk->timer);
25409          if(timer_active)
25410              add_timer(&sk->timer);
25411          else
25412              tcp_reset_msl_timer(sk, TIME_CLOSE,
25413  TCP_FIN_TIMEOUT);
25414      }
25415
25416      return send_fin;
25417  }
25418
25419  /*
25420   *  Shutdown the sending side of a connection. Much like
25421  close except
25422   *  that we don't receive shut down or set sk->dead.
25423   */
```

```
25424
25425  void tcp_shutdown(struct sock *sk, int how)
25426  {
25427      /*
25428       *  We need to grab some memory, and put together a
25429  FIN,
25430       *  and then put it into the queue to be sent.
25431       *      Tim MacKenzie(tym@dibbler.cs.monash.edu.au)
25432  4 Dec '92.
25433       */
25434
25435      if (!(how & SEND_SHUTDOWN))
25436          return;
25437
25438      /*
25439       *  If we've already sent a FIN, or it's a closed
25440  state
25441       */
25442
25443      if (sk->state == TCP_FIN_WAIT1 ||
25444          sk->state == TCP_FIN_WAIT2 ||
25445          sk->state == TCP_CLOSING ||
25446          sk->state == TCP_LAST_ACK ||
25447          sk->state == TCP_TIME_WAIT ||
25448          sk->state == TCP_CLOSE ||
25449          sk->state == TCP_LISTEN
25450        )
25451      {
25452          return;
25453      }
25454      lock_sock(sk);
25455
25456      /*
25457       * flag that the sender has shutdown
25458       */
25459
25460      sk->shutdown |= SEND_SHUTDOWN;
25461
25462      /*
25463       *  Clear out any half completed packets.
25464       */
25465
25466      if (sk->partial)
25467          tcp_send_partial(sk);
25468
25469      /*
25470       *  FIN if needed
25471       */
```

p 556

```
25472
25473        if (tcp_close_state(sk,0))
25474            tcp_send_fin(sk);
25475
25476        release_sock(sk);
25477    }
25478
25479
25480    /*
25481     *  Return 1 if we still have things to send in our
25482    buffers.
25483     */
25484
25485    static inline int closing(struct sock * sk)
25486    {
25487        switch (sk->state) {
25488            case TCP_FIN_WAIT1:
25489            case TCP_CLOSING:
25490            case TCP_LAST_ACK:
25491                return 1;
25492        }
25493        return 0;
25494    }
25495
25496
25497    static void tcp_close(struct sock *sk, unsigned long
25498    timeout)
25499    {
25500        struct sk_buff *skb;
25501
25502        /*
25503         * We need to grab some memory, and put together a
25504    FIN,
25505         * and then put it into the queue to be sent.
25506         */
25507
25508        lock_sock(sk);
25509
25510        if(sk->state == TCP_LISTEN)
25511        {
25512            /* Special case */
25513            tcp_set_state(sk, TCP_CLOSE);
25514            tcp_close_pending(sk);
25515            release_sock(sk);
25516            sk->dead = 1;
25517            tcp_v4_unhash(sk);
25518            return;
25519        }
```

```
25520
25521        sk->keepopen = 1;
25522        sk->shutdown = SHUTDOWN_MASK;
25523
25524        if (!sk->dead)
25525            sk->state_change(sk);
25526
25527        /*
25528         *  We need to flush the recv. buffs.  We do this
25529    only on the
25530         *  descriptor close, not protocol-sourced closes,
25531    because the
25532         *  reader process may not have drained the data yet!
25533         */
25534
25535        while((skb=skb_dequeue(&sk->receive_queue))!=NULL)
25536            kfree_skb(skb, FREE_READ);
25537
25538        /*
25539         *  Get rid off any half-completed packets.
25540         */
25541
25542        if (sk->partial)
25543            tcp_send_partial(sk);
25544
25545        /*
25546         *  Timeout is not the same thing - however the code
25547    likes
25548         *  to send both the same way (sigh).
25549         */
25550
25551        if (tcp_close_state(sk,1)==1)
25552        {
25553            tcp_send_fin(sk);
25554        }
25555
25556        if (timeout) {
25557            cli();
25558            release_sock(sk);
25559            current->timeout = timeout;
25560            while(closing(sk) && current->timeout)
25561            {
25562                interruptible_sleep_on(sk->sleep);
25563                if (current->signal & ~current->blocked)
25564                {
25565                    break;
25566                }
25567            }
```

```
25568              current->timeout=0;
25569              lock_sock(sk);
25570              sti();
25571          }
25572
25573          /* Now that the socket is dead, if we are in the
25574   FIN_WAIT2 state
25575           * we may need to set up a timer.
25576           */
25577          if (sk->state==TCP_FIN_WAIT2)
25578          {
25579              int timer_active=del_timer(&sk->timer);
25580              if(timer_active)
25581                  add_timer(&sk->timer);
25582              else
25583                  tcp_reset_msl_timer(sk, TIME_CLOSE,
25584   TCP_FIN_TIMEOUT);
25585          }
25586
25587          sk->dead = 1;
25588          release_sock(sk);
25589
25590          if(sk->state == TCP_CLOSE)
25591              tcp_v4_unhash(sk);
25592   }
25593
25594
25595   /*
25596    * Wait for a incoming connection, avoid race
25597    * conditions. This must be called with the socket
25598    * locked.
25599    */
25600   static struct sk_buff * wait_for_connect(struct sock *
25601   sk)
25602   {
25603       struct wait_queue wait = { current, NULL };
25604       struct sk_buff * skb = NULL;
25605
25606       add_wait_queue(sk->sleep, &wait);
25607       for (;;) {
25608           current->state = TASK_INTERRUPTIBLE;
25609           end_bh_atomic();
25610           release_sock(sk);
25611           schedule();
25612           lock_sock(sk);
25613           start_bh_atomic();
25614           skb = tcp_find_established(sk);
25615           if (skb)
```

```
25616               break;
25617           if (current->signal & ~current->blocked)
25618               break;
25619       }
25620       remove_wait_queue(sk->sleep, &wait);
25621       return skb;
25622   }
25623
25624   /*
25625    * This will accept the next outstanding connection.
25626    *
25627    * Be careful about race conditions here - this is
25628   subtle.
25629    */
25630
25631   static struct sock *tcp_accept(struct sock *sk, int
25632   flags)
25633   {
25634       int error;
25635       struct sk_buff *skb;
25636       struct sock *newsk = NULL;
25637
25638     /*
25639      * We need to make sure that this socket is listening,
25640      * and that it has something pending.
25641      */
25642
25643       error = EINVAL;
25644       if (sk->state != TCP_LISTEN)
25645           goto no_listen;
25646
25647       lock_sock(sk);start_bh_atomic();
25648
25649       skb = tcp_find_established(sk);
25650       if (skb) {
25651   got_new_connect:
25652           __skb_unlink(skb, &sk->receive_queue);
25653           newsk = skb->sk;
25654           kfree_skb(skb, FREE_READ);
25655           sk->ack_backlog--;
25656           error = 0;
25657   out:
25658           end_bh_atomic();
25659           release_sock(sk);
25660   no_listen:
25661           sk->err = error;
25662           return newsk;
25663       }
```

```
25664
25665        error = EAGAIN;
25666        if (flags & O_NONBLOCK)
25667            goto out;
25668        skb = wait_for_connect(sk);
25669        if (skb)
25670            goto got_new_connect;
25671        error = ERESTARTSYS;
25672        goto out;
25673    }
25674
25675    /*
25676     * Check that a TCP address is unique, don't allow
25677    multiple
25678     * connects to/from the same address
25679     */
25680    static int tcp_unique_address(u32 saddr, u16 snum, u32
25681    daddr, u16 dnum)
25682    {
25683        int retval = 1, hashent = tcp_hashfn(saddr, snum,
25684    daddr, dnum);
25685        struct sock * sk;
25686
25687        /* Make sure we are allowed to connect here.
25688         * But freeze the hash while we snoop around.
25689         */
25690        SOCKHASH_LOCK();
25691        sk = tcp_established_hash[hashent];
25692        for (; sk != NULL; sk = sk->next) {
25693            if(sk->daddr        == daddr        && /* remote
25694    address */
25695                sk->dummy_th.dest    == dnum        && /*
25696    remote port */
25697                sk->num        == snum        && /* local port
25698    */
25699                sk->saddr        == saddr) {        /* local
25700    address */
25701                    retval = 0;
25702                    break;
25703                }
25704        }
25705        SOCKHASH_UNLOCK();
25706        return retval;
25707    }
25708
25709
25710    /*
25711     * This will initiate an outgoing connection.
```

```
25712    */
25713
25714    static int tcp_connect(struct sock *sk, struct
25715    sockaddr_in *usin, int addr_len)
25716    {
25717        struct sk_buff *buff;
25718        struct device *dev=NULL;
25719        unsigned char *ptr;
25720        int tmp;
25721        int atype;
25722        struct tcphdr *t1;
25723        struct rtable *rt;
25724
25725        if (sk->state != TCP_CLOSE)
25726            return(-EISCONN);
25727
25728        /*
25729         * Don't allow a double connect.
25730         */
25731
25732        if(sk->daddr)
25733            return -EINVAL;
25734
25735        if (addr_len < 8)
25736            return(-EINVAL);
25737
25738        if (usin->sin_family && usin->sin_family != AF_INET)
25739            return(-EAFNOSUPPORT);
25740
25741        /*
25742         * connect() to INADDR_ANY means loopback (BSD'ism).
25743         */
25744
25745        if (usin->sin_addr.s_addr==INADDR_ANY)
25746            usin->sin_addr.s_addr=ip_my_addr();
25747
25748        /*
25749         * Don't want a TCP connection going to a broadcast
25750    address
25751         */
25752
25753        if ((atype=ip_chk_addr(usin->sin_addr.s_addr)) ==
25754    IS_BROADCAST || atype==IS_MULTICAST)
25755            return -ENETUNREACH;
25756
25757        if (!tcp_unique_address(sk->saddr, sk->num,
25758    usin->sin_addr.s_addr, usin->sin_port))
25759            return -EADDRNOTAVAIL;
```

p 556
p 556
p 557

```
25760
25761        lock_sock(sk);
25762        sk->daddr = usin->sin_addr.s_addr;
25763
25764        sk->rcv_ack_cnt = 1;
25765        sk->err = 0;
25766        sk->dummy_th.dest = usin->sin_port;
25767
25768        buff = sock_wmalloc(sk,MAX_SYN_SIZE,0, GFP_KERNEL);
25769        if (buff == NULL)
25770        {
25771            release_sock(sk);
25772            return(-ENOMEM);
25773        }
25774        buff->sk = sk;
25775        buff->free = 0;
25776        buff->localroute = sk->localroute;
25777
25778        /* If this socket is bound to a particular device,
25779    make sure we use it. */
25780        dev = sk->bound_device;
25781
25782        /*
25783         *  Put in the IP header and routing stuff.
25784         */
25785
25786        tmp = sk->prot->build_header(buff, sk->saddr,
25787    sk->daddr, &dev,
25788            IPPROTO_TCP, sk->opt,
25789    MAX_SYN_SIZE,sk->ip_tos,sk->ip_ttl,&sk->ip_route_cache);
25790        if (tmp < 0)
25791        {
25792            sock_wfree(sk, buff);
25793            release_sock(sk);
25794            return(-ENETUNREACH);
25795        }
25796        if ((rt = sk->ip_route_cache) != NULL && !sk->saddr)
25797            sk->saddr = rt->rt_src;
25798        sk->rcv_saddr = sk->saddr;
25799
25800        /*
25801         * Set up our outgoing TCP sequence number
25802         */
25803        sk->write_seq =
25804    secure_tcp_sequence_number(sk->saddr, sk->daddr,
25805                        sk->dummy_th.source,
25806                        usin->sin_port);
25807        sk->window_seq = sk->write_seq;
```

```
25808        sk->rcv_ack_seq = sk->write_seq -1;
25809
25810        t1 = (struct tcphdr *) skb_put(buff,sizeof(struct
25811    tcphdr));
25812
25813        memcpy(t1,(void *)&(sk->dummy_th), sizeof(*t1));
25814        buff->seq = sk->write_seq++;
25815        t1->seq = htonl(buff->seq);
25816        sk->sent_seq = sk->write_seq;
25817        buff->end_seq = sk->write_seq;
25818        t1->ack = 0;
25819        t1->window = 2;
25820        t1->syn = 1;
25821        t1->doff = 6;
25822        /* use 512 or whatever user asked for */
25823
25824        if(rt!=NULL && (rt->rt_flags&RTF_WINDOW))
25825            sk->window_clamp=rt->rt_window;
25826        else
25827            sk->window_clamp=0;
25828
25829        if (sk->user_mss)
25830            sk->mtu = sk->user_mss;
25831        else if (rt)
25832            sk->mtu = rt->rt_mtu - sizeof(struct iphdr) -
25833    sizeof(struct tcphdr);
25834        else
25835            sk->mtu = 576 - sizeof(struct iphdr) -
25836    sizeof(struct tcphdr);
25837
25838        /*
25839         *  but not bigger than device MTU
25840         */
25841
25842        sk->mtu = min(sk->mtu, dev->mtu - sizeof(struct
25843    iphdr) - sizeof(struct tcphdr));
25844
25845        /* Must check it here, just to be absolutely safe.
25846    If we end up
25847         * with an sk->mtu of zero, we can thus end up with
25848    an sk->mss
25849         * of zero, which causes us to bomb out in
25850    tcp_do_sendmsg. -DaveM
25851         */
25852        if(sk->mtu < 32)
25853            sk->mtu = 32;    /* Sanity limit */
25854
25855        /*
```

```
25856        *   Put in the TCP options to say MTU.
25857        */
25858
25859        ptr = skb_put(buff,4);
25860        ptr[0] = 2;
25861        ptr[1] = 4;
25862        ptr[2] = (sk->mtu) >> 8;
25863        ptr[3] = (sk->mtu) & 0xff;
25864        buff->csum = csum_partial(ptr, 4, 0);
25865        tcp_send_check(t1, sk->saddr, sk->daddr,
25866              sizeof(struct tcphdr) + 4, buff);
25867
25868        tcp_set_state(sk,TCP_SYN_SENT);
25869
25870        /* Socket identity change complete, no longer
25871         * in TCP_CLOSE, so rehash.
25872         */
25873        tcp_v4_rehash(sk);
25874
25875        if(rt&&rt->rt_flags&RTF_IRTT)
25876            sk->rto = rt->rt_irtt;
25877        else
25878            sk->rto = TCP_TIMEOUT_INIT;
25879        sk->delack_timer.function = tcp_delack_timer;
25880        sk->delack_timer.data = (unsigned long) sk;
25881        sk->retransmit_timer.function = tcp_retransmit_timer;
25882        sk->retransmit_timer.data = (unsigned long)sk;
25883        sk->retransmits = 0;
25884        sk->prot->queue_xmit(sk, dev, buff, 0);
25885        tcp_reset_xmit_timer(sk, TIME_WRITE, sk->rto);
25886        tcp_statistics.TcpActiveOpens++;
25887        tcp_statistics.TcpOutSegs++;
25888
25889        release_sock(sk);
25890        return(0);
25891    }
25892
25893    /*
25894     *  Socket option code for TCP.
25895     */
25896
25897    int tcp_setsockopt(struct sock *sk, int level, int
25898    optname, char *optval, int optlen)
25899    {
25900        int val,err;
25901
25902        if(level!=SOL_TCP)
25903            return
```

```
25904    ip_setsockopt(sk,level,optname,optval,optlen);
25905
25906        if (optval == NULL)
25907            return(-EINVAL);
25908
25909        err=verify_area(VERIFY_READ, optval, sizeof(int));
25910        if(err)
25911            return err;
25912
25913        val = get_user((int *)optval);
25914
25915        switch(optname)
25916        {
25917            case TCP_MAXSEG:
25918    /*
25919     * values greater than interface MTU won't take effect.
25920    however at
25921     * the point when this call is done we typically don't
25922    yet know
25923     * which interface is going to be used
25924     */
25925                if(val<1||val>MAX_WINDOW)
25926                    return -EINVAL;
25927                sk->user_mss=val;
25928                return 0;
25929            case TCP_NODELAY:
25930                sk->nonagle=(val==0)?0:1;
25931                return 0;
25932            default:
25933                return(-ENOPROTOOPT);
25934        }
25935    }
25936
25937    int tcp_getsockopt(struct sock *sk, int level, int
25938    optname, char *optval, int *optlen)
25939    {
25940        int val,err;
25941
25942        if(level!=SOL_TCP)
25943            return
25944    ip_getsockopt(sk,level,optname,optval,optlen);
25945
25946        switch(optname)
25947        {
25948            case TCP_MAXSEG:
25949                val=sk->user_mss;
25950                break;
25951            case TCP_NODELAY:
```

```
25952            val=sk->nonagle;
25953            break;
25954         default:
25955            return(-ENOPROTOOPT);
25956      }
25957      err=verify_area(VERIFY_WRITE, optlen, sizeof(int));
25958      if(err)
25959         return err;
25960      put_user(sizeof(int),(int *) optlen);
25961
25962      err=verify_area(VERIFY_WRITE, optval, sizeof(int));
25963      if(err)
25964         return err;
25965      put_user(val,(int *)optval);
25966
25967      return(0);
25968   }
25969
25970
25971   struct proto tcp_prot = {
25972      (struct sock *)&tcp_prot,   /* sklist_next */
25973      (struct sock *)&tcp_prot,   /* sklist_prev */
25974      tcp_close,         /* close */
25975      ip_build_header,      /* build_header */
25976      tcp_connect,       /* connect */
25977      tcp_accept,       /* accept */
25978      ip_queue_xmit,        /* queue_xmit */
25979      tcp_retransmit,      /* retransmit */
25980      tcp_write_wakeup,     /* write_wakeup */
25981      tcp_read_wakeup,      /* read_wakeup */
25982      tcp_rcv,        /* rcv */
25983      tcp_select,      /* select */
25984      tcp_ioctl,       /* ioctl */
25985      NULL,          /* init */
25986      tcp_shutdown,       /* shutdown */
25987      tcp_setsockopt,      /* setsockopt */
25988      tcp_getsockopt,      /* getsockopt */
25989      tcp_sendmsg,       /* sendmsg */
25990      tcp_recvmsg,       /* recvmsg */
25991      NULL,         /* bind */
25992      tcp_v4_hash,       /* hash */
25993      tcp_v4_unhash,      /* unhash */
25994      tcp_v4_rehash,      /* rehash */
25995      tcp_good_socknum,     /* good_socknum */
25996      tcp_v4_verify_bind,    /* verify_bind */
25997      128,          /* max_header */
25998      0,          /* retransmits */
25999      "TCP",        /* name */
26000      0,          /* inuse */
26001      0          /* highestinuse */
26002   };
```

usr/src/linux/net/ipv4/tcp_input.c

```
26003   /*
26004    * INET      An implementation of the TCP/IP protocol
26005   suite for the LINUX
26006    *       operating system.  INET is implemented using the
26007   BSD Socket
26008    *       interface as the means of communication with the
26009   user level.
26010    *
26011    *       Implementation of the Transmission Control
26012   Protocol(TCP).
26013    *
26014    * Version: @(#)tcp_input.c 1.0.16   05/25/93
26015    *
26016    * Authors: Ross Biro, <bir7@leland.Stanford.Edu>
26017    *     Fred N. van Kempen, <waltje@uWalt.NL.Mugnet.ORG>
26018    *     Mark Evans, <evansmp@uhura.aston.ac.uk>
26019    *     Corey Minyard <wf-rch!minyard@relay.EU.net>
26020    *     Florian La Roche, <flla@stud.uni-sb.de>
26021    *     Charles Hedrick, <hedrick@klinzhai.rutgers.edu>
26022    *     Linus Torvalds, <torvalds@cs.helsinki.fi>
26023    *     Alan Cox, <gw4pts@gw4pts.ampr.org>
26024    *     Matthew Dillon, <dillon@apollo.west.oic.com>
26025    *     Arnt Gulbrandsen, <agulbra@nvg.unit.no>
26026    *     Jorge Cwik, <jorge@laser.satlink.net>
26027    *
26028    * FIXES
26029    *     Pedro Roque :   Double ACK bug
26030    *     Eric Schenk :   Fixes to slow start algorithm.
26031    *     Eric Schenk :   Yet another double ACK bug.
26032    *     Eric Schenk :   Delayed ACK bug fixes.
26033    *     Eric Schenk :   Floyd style fast retrans war
26034   avoidance.
26035    *     Eric Schenk :   Skip fast retransmit on small
26036   windows.
26037    *     Eric Schenk :   Fixes to retransmission code to
26038    *           :   avoid extra retransmission.
26039    *     Theodore Ts'o :   Do secure TCP sequence
26040   numbers.
26041    *     Eric Schenk :   SYN and RST cookies for dealing
26042    *           :   with SYN flooding attacks.
26043    *     David S. Miller :   New socket lookup
26044   architecture for ISS.
26045    *           This code is dedicated to John Dyson.
```

```
26046    *            Elliot Poger    :       Added support
26047   for SO_BINDTODEVICE.
26048    *  Willy Konynenberg   :    Transparent proxy adapted to
26049   new
26050    *             socket hash code.
26051    */
26052
26053   #include <linux/config.h>
26054   #include <linux/types.h>
26055   #include <linux/random.h>
26056   #include <net/tcp.h>
26057
26058   /*
26059    *  Policy code extracted so it's now separate
26060    */
26061
26062   /*
26063    *  Called each time to estimate the delayed ack
26064   timeout. This is
26065    *  how it should be done so a fast link isn't impacted
26066   by ack delay.
26067    */
26068
26069   extern __inline__ void tcp_delack_estimator(struct sock
26070   *sk)
26071   {
26072       /*
26073        *  Delayed ACK time estimator.
26074        */
26075
26076       if (sk->lrcvtime == 0)
26077       {
26078           sk->lrcvtime = jiffies;
26079           sk->ato = HZ/3;
26080       }
26081       else
26082       {
26083           int m;
26084
26085           m = jiffies - sk->lrcvtime;
26086
26087           sk->lrcvtime = jiffies;
26088
26089           if (m <= 0)
26090               m = 1;
26091
26092           /* This used to test against sk->rtt.
26093            * On a purely receiving link, there is no rtt
```

```
26094   measure.
26095        * The result is that we lose delayed ACKs on
26096   one-way links.
26097        * Therefore we test against sk->rto, which will
26098   always
26099        * at least have a default value.
26100        */
26101       if (m > sk->rto)
26102       {
26103           sk->ato = sk->rto;
26104           /*
26105            * printk(KERN_DEBUG "ato: rtt %lu\n",
26106   sk->ato);
26107            */
26108       }
26109       else
26110       {
26111           /*
26112            * Very fast acting estimator.
26113            * May fluctuate too much. Probably we
26114   should be
26115            * doing something like the rtt estimator
26116   here.
26117            */
26118           sk->ato = (sk->ato >> 1) + m;
26119           /*
26120            * printk(KERN_DEBUG "ato: m %lu\n",
26121   sk->ato);
26122            */
26123       }
26124   }
26125   }
26126
26127   /*
26128    *  Called on frames that were known _not_ to have been
26129    *  retransmitted [see Karn/Partridge Proceedings
26130   SIGCOMM 87].
26131    *  The algorithm is from the SIGCOMM 88 piece by Van
26132   Jacobson.
26133    */
26134
26135   extern __inline__ void tcp_rtt_estimator(struct sock
26136   *sk, struct sk_buff *oskb)
26137   {
26138       long m;
26139       /*
26140        *  The following amusing code comes from Jacobson's
26141        *  article in SIGCOMM '88. Note that rtt and mdev
```

```
26142        *  are scaled versions of rtt and mean deviation.
26143        *  This is designed to be as fast as possible
26144        *  m stands for "measurement".
26145        */
26146
26147        m = jiffies - oskb->when;  /* RTT */
26148
26149        if (sk->rtt != 0) {
26150            if(m<=0)
26151                m=1;          /* IS THIS RIGHT FOR <0 ??? */
26152            m -= (sk->rtt >> 3);    /* m is now error in rtt
26153    est */
26154            sk->rtt += m;           /* rtt = 7/8 rtt + 1/8
26155    new */
26156            if (m < 0)
26157                m = -m;       /* m is now abs(error) */
26158            m -= (sk->mdev >> 2);   /* similar update on
26159    mdev */
26160            sk->mdev += m;          /* mdev = 3/4 mdev + 1/4
26161    new */
26162        } else {
26163            /* no previous measure. */
26164            sk->rtt = m<<3;     /* take the measured time to
26165    be rtt */
26166            sk->mdev = m<<1;    /* make sure rto = 3*rtt */
26167        }
26168
26169        /*
26170         *  Now update timeout.  Note that this removes any
26171    backoff.
26172         */
26173
26174        /* Jacobson's algorithm calls for rto = R + 4V.
26175         * We diverge from Jacobson's algorithm here. See
26176    the commentary
26177         * in tcp_ack to understand why.
26178         */
26179        sk->rto = (sk->rtt >> 3) + sk->mdev;
26180        sk->rto += (sk->rto>>2) + (sk->rto >>
26181    (sk->cong_window-1));
26182        if (sk->rto > 120*HZ)
26183            sk->rto = 120*HZ;
26184        if (sk->rto < HZ/5) /* Was 1*HZ - keep .2 as minimum
26185    cos of the BSD delayed acks */
26186            sk->rto = HZ/5;
26187        sk->backoff = 0;
26188    }
26189
```

```
26190    #if defined(CONFIG_RST_COOKIES)
26191
26192    /*
26193     * This code needs to be a bit more clever.
26194     * Does 300 second timeouts now. Still just a circular
26195    buffer.
26196     * At most 32 validations stored. New validations are
26197    ignored
26198     * if all 32 validations are currently valid. To do
26199    otherwise
26200     * allows a situation in which clearances are forgotten
26201    before
26202     * they can be used (provided valid traffic is coming
26203    fast enough).
26204     * The buffer should really be as long as the number of
26205    valid
26206     * connections we want to accept in an 300 second period.
26207     * 32 is maybe to small. On the other hand, the
26208    validation check
26209     * algorithm has to walk the whole table, which is also
26210    stupid.
26211     * It would be better to have a combined hash/circular
26212    buffer.
26213     * The hash could be used with chaining for fast lookup.
26214     * Really this is probably an argument against using RST
26215    cookies
26216     * at all, since they take up space for the clearances.
26217     */
26218
26219    static struct {
26220        u32 saddr;
26221        unsigned long tstamp;
26222    } clearances[32] = {
26223    {0,0},{0,0},{0,0},{0,0},{0,0},{0,0},{0,0},{0,0},
26224    {0,0},{0,0},{0,0},{0,0},{0,0},{0,0},{0,0},{0,0},
26225    {0,0},{0,0},{0,0},{0,0},{0,0},{0,0},{0,0},{0,0},
26226    {0,0},{0,0},{0,0},{0,0},{0,0},{0,0},{0,0},{0,0}};
26227
26228    static next_clearance = 0;
26229    /* Does the address saddr have an active security
26230    clearance? */
26231    int tcp_clearance(__u32 saddr)
26232    {
26233        int i;
26234        for (i = 0; i < 32; i++)
26235            if (clearances[i].saddr == saddr
26236                && clearances[i].tstamp > jiffies-HZ*300)
26237                return 1;
```

p 558

```
26238        return 0;
26239   }
26240
26241   void add_clearance(__u32 saddr)
26242   {
26243        /*
26244         * If expired then we can add a new entry.
26245         */
26246        if (clearances[next_clearance].tstamp <=
26247   jiffies-HZ*300) {
26248             clearances[next_clearance].saddr = saddr;
26249             clearances[next_clearance].tstamp = jiffies;
26250             next_clearance = (next_clearance+1)%32;
26251        }
26252   }
26253
26254   #endif
26255
26256   #ifdef CONFIG_SYN_COOKIES
26257   /*
26258    *  MTU values we can represent in fall back mode.
26259    *  These values are partially borrowed from Jeff
26260   Weisberg's SunOS
26261    *  implementation of SYNCOOKIES. I have added an extra
26262   limiting
26263    *  value of 64 to deal with the case of very small MTU
26264   values.
26265    *  (e.g. long delay packet radio links, 1200 baud
26266   modems.)
26267    */
26268   static __u32 cookie_mtu[8] = { 64, 256, 512, 536, 1024,
26269   1440, 1460, 4312 };
26270   unsigned int ui_c_send_cookies = 0;
26271   #endif
26272
26273   extern void tcp_v4_hash(struct sock *sk);
26274   extern void tcp_v4_unhash(struct sock *sk);
26275   extern void tcp_v4_rehash(struct sock *sk);
26276
26277   /* Don't inline this cruft.  Here are some nice
26278   properties to
26279    * exploit here.  The BSD API does not allow a listening
26280   TCP
26281    * to specify the remote port nor the remote address for
26282   the
26283    * connection.  So always assume those are both
26284   wildcarded
26285    * during the search since they can never be otherwise.
26286    */
26287   static struct sock *tcp_v4_lookup_longway(u32 daddr,
26288   unsigned short hnum,
26289                       struct device *dev)
26290   {
26291       struct sock *sk =
26292   tcp_listening_hash[tcp_lhashfn(hnum)];
26293       struct sock *result = NULL;
26294       int score, hiscore = 0;
26295
26296       for(; sk; sk = sk->next) {
26297           if(sk->num == hnum) {
26298               __u32 rcv_saddr = sk->rcv_saddr;
26299               score = 1;
26300
26301               /* If this socket is bound to a particular
26302   IP address,
26303                * does the dest IPaddr of the packet match
26304   it?
26305                */
26306               if(rcv_saddr) {
26307                   if(rcv_saddr != daddr)
26308                       continue;
26309                   score++;
26310               }
26311
26312               /* If this socket is bound to a particular
26313   interface,
26314                * did the packet come in on it? */
26315               if (sk->bound_device) {
26316                   if (dev != sk->bound_device)
26317                       continue;
26318                   score++;
26319               }
26320
26321               /* Check the score--max is 3. */
26322               if (score == 3)
26323                   return sk; /* Best possible match. */
26324               if (score > hiscore) {
26325                   hiscore = score;
26326                   result = sk;
26327               }
26328           }
26329       }
26330       return result;
26331   }
26332
26333   /* Sockets in TCP_CLOSE state are _always_ taken out of
```

```
26334  the hash, so
26335   * we need not check it for TCP lookups anymore, thanks
26336  Alexey. -DaveM
26337   */
26338  static inline struct sock *__tcp_v4_lookup(struct tcphdr
26339  *th,
26340                              u32 saddr, u16 sport, u32 daddr,
26341                              u16 dport, struct device *dev)
26342  {
26343      unsigned short hnum = ntohs(dport);
26344      struct sock *sk;
26345
26346      /* Optimize here for direct hit, only listening
26347  connections can
26348       * have wildcards anyways.  It is assumed that this
26349  code only
26350       * gets called from within NET_BH.
26351       */
26352      sk = tcp_established_hash[tcp_hashfn(daddr, hnum,
26353  saddr, sport)];
26354      for(; sk; sk = sk->next)
26355          if(sk->daddr         == saddr       && /* remote
26356  address */
26357              sk->dummy_th.dest  == sport       && /*
26358  remote port   */
26359              sk->num        == hnum        && /* local port
26360       */
26361              sk->rcv_saddr    == daddr       && /* local
26362  address   */
26363              ((sk->bound_device==NULL) ||
26364  (sk->bound_device==dev))   )
26365              goto hit; /* You sunk my battleship! */
26366      sk = tcp_v4_lookup_longway(daddr, hnum, dev);
26367  hit:
26368      return sk;
26369  }
26370
26371  __inline__ struct sock *tcp_v4_lookup(u32 saddr, u16
26372  sport, u32 daddr, u16 dport,
26373                              struct device *dev)
26374  {
26375      return __tcp_v4_lookup(0, saddr, sport, daddr,
26376  dport, dev);
26377  }
26378
26379  #ifdef CONFIG_IP_TRANSPARENT_PROXY
26380  /* I am not entirely sure this is fully equivalent to
26381  the old lookup code, but it does
```

```
26382   * look reasonable.  WFK
26383   */
26384  struct sock *tcp_v4_proxy_lookup(u32 saddr, u16 sport,
26385  u32 daddr, u16 dport, u32 paddr, u16 rport,
26386                      struct device *dev)
26387  {
26388      unsigned short hnum = ntohs(dport);
26389      unsigned short hrnum = ntohs(rport);
26390      struct sock *sk;
26391
26392      /* Optimize here for direct hit, only listening
26393  connections can
26394       * have wildcards anyways.  It is assumed that this
26395  code only
26396       * gets called from within NET_BH.
26397       */
26398      sk = tcp_established_hash[tcp_hashfn(daddr, hnum,
26399  saddr, sport)];
26400      for(; sk; sk = sk->next)
26401          if(sk->daddr         == saddr       && /* remote
26402  address */
26403              sk->dummy_th.dest  == sport       && /*
26404  remote port   */
26405              sk->num        == hnum        && /* local port
26406       */
26407              sk->rcv_saddr    == daddr       && /* local
26408  address   */
26409              ((sk->bound_device==NULL) ||
26410  (sk->bound_device==dev))   )
26411              goto hit; /* You sunk my battleship! */
26412      /* If we don't match on a bound socket, try to find
26413  one explicitly listening
26414       * on the remote address (a proxy bind).
26415       */
26416      sk = tcp_v4_lookup_longway(daddr, hnum, dev);
26417      /* If that didn't yield an exact match, look for a
26418  socket listening on the
26419       * redirect port.
26420       */
26421      if (!sk || sk->rcv_saddr != daddr) {
26422          sk = tcp_v4_lookup_longway(paddr, hrnum, dev);
26423      }
26424  hit:
26425      return sk;
26426  }
26427  #endif
26428
26429  /*
```

```
26430    * React to a out-of-window TCP sequence number in an
26431   incoming packet
26432    */
26433
26434   static void bad_tcp_sequence(struct sock *sk, struct
26435   tcphdr *th, u32 end_seq,
26436           struct device *dev)
26437   {
26438       if (th->rst)
26439           return;
26440
26441       /*
26442        *  Send a reset if we get something not ours and we
26443   are
26444        *  unsynchronized. Note: We don't do anything to
26445   our end. We
26446        *  are just killing the bogus remote connection
26447   then we will
26448        *  connect again and it will work (with luck).
26449        */
26450
26451       if (sk->state==TCP_SYN_SENT ||
26452   sk->state==TCP_SYN_RECV)
26453       {
26454
26455   tcp_send_reset(sk->saddr,sk->daddr,th,sk->prot,NULL,dev,0
26456   ,255);
26457           return;
26458       }
26459
26460       /*
26461        *  This packet is old news. Usually this is just a
26462   resend
26463        *  from the far end, but sometimes it means the far
26464   end lost
26465        *  an ACK we sent, so we better send an ACK.
26466        */
26467       /*
26468        *  BEWARE! Unconditional answering by ack to
26469   out-of-window ack
26470        *  can result in infinite exchange of empty acks.
26471        *  This check cures bug, found by Michiel Boland,
26472   but
26473        *  not another possible cases.
26474        *  If we are in TCP_TIME_WAIT, we have already
26475   received
26476        *  FIN, so that our peer need not window update. If
26477   our
```

```
26478        *  ACK were lost, peer would retransmit his FIN
26479   anyway. --ANK
26480        */
26481       if (sk->state != TCP_TIME_WAIT || ntohl(th->seq) !=
26482   end_seq)
26483           tcp_send_ack(sk);
26484   }
26485
26486   /*
26487    * This functions checks to see if the tcp header is
26488   actually acceptable.
26489    */
26490
26491   extern __inline__ int tcp_sequence(struct sock *sk, u32
26492   seq, u32 end_seq)
26493   {
26494       u32 end_window = sk->lastwin_seq + sk->window;
26495       return  /* if start is at end of window, end must be
26496   too (zero window) */
26497           (seq == end_window && seq == end_seq) ||
26498           /* if start is before end of window, check for
26499   interest */
26500           (before(seq, end_window) && !before(end_seq,
26501   sk->acked_seq));
26502   }
26503
26504
26505   /*
26506    * When we get a reset we do this. This probably is a
26507   tcp_output routine
26508    * really.
26509    */
26510   static int tcp_reset(struct sock *sk, struct sk_buff
26511   *skb)
26512   {
26513       sk->zapped = 1;
26514       /*
26515        * We want the right error as BSD sees it (and
26516   indeed as we do).
26517        */
26518       switch (sk->state) {
26519       case TCP_TIME_WAIT:
26520           break;
26521       case TCP_SYN_SENT:
26522           sk->err = ECONNREFUSED;
26523           break;
26524       case TCP_CLOSE_WAIT:
26525           sk->err = EPIPE;
```

```
26526              break;
26527          default:
26528              sk->err = ECONNRESET;
26529          }
26530  #ifdef CONFIG_TCP_RFC1337
26531      /*
26532       *  Time wait assassination protection [RFC1337]
26533       *
26534       *  This is a good idea, but causes more sockets to
26535  take time to close.
26536       *
26537       *  Ian Heavens has since shown this is an
26538  inadequate fix for the protocol
26539       *  bug in question.
26540       */
26541      if(sk->state!=TCP_TIME_WAIT)
26542      {
26543          tcp_set_state(sk,TCP_CLOSE);
26544          sk->shutdown = SHUTDOWN_MASK;
26545      }
26546  #else
26547      tcp_set_state(sk,TCP_CLOSE);
26548      sk->shutdown = SHUTDOWN_MASK;
26549  #endif
26550      if (!sk->dead)
26551          sk->state_change(sk);
26552      kfree_skb(skb, FREE_READ);
26553      return(0);
26554  }
26555
26556
26557  /*
26558   *  Look for tcp options. Parses everything but only
26559  knows about MSS.
26560   *  This routine is always called with the packet
26561  containing the SYN.
26562   *  However it may also be called with the ack to the
26563  SYN.  So you
26564   *  can't assume this is always the SYN.  It's always
26565  called after
26566   *  we have set up sk->mtu to our own MTU.
26567   *
26568   *  We need at minimum to add PAWS support here.
26569  Possibly large windows
26570   *  as Linux gets deployed on 100Mb/sec networks.
26571   */
26572
26573  static void tcp_options(struct sock *sk, struct tcphdr
```

```
26574  *th)
26575  {
26576      unsigned char *ptr;
26577      int length=(th->doff*4)-sizeof(struct tcphdr);
26578      int mss_seen = 0;
26579
26580      ptr = (unsigned char *)(th + 1);
26581
26582      while(length>0)
26583      {
26584          int opcode=*ptr++;
26585          int opsize=*ptr++;
26586          switch(opcode)
26587          {
26588              case TCPOPT_EOL:
26589                  goto ende;
26590              case TCPOPT_NOP:    /* Ref: RFC 793 section
26591  3.1 */
26592                  length--;
26593                  ptr--;     /* the opsize=*ptr++ above
26594  was a mistake */
26595                  continue;
26596
26597              default:
26598                  if(opsize<=2)    /* Avoid silly options
26599  looping forever */
26600                      goto ende;
26601                  switch(opcode)
26602                  {
26603                      case TCPOPT_MSS:
26604                          if(opsize==4 && th->syn)
26605                          {
26606
26607  sk->mtu=min(sk->mtu,ntohs(*(unsigned short *)ptr));
26608                              mss_seen = 1;
26609                          }
26610                          break;
26611                          /* Add other options here as
26612  people feel the urge to implement stuff like large
26613  windows */
26614                  }
26615                  ptr+=opsize-2;
26616                  length-=opsize;
26617          }
26618      }
26619  ende:   if (th->syn)
26620      {
26621          if (! mss_seen)
```

```
26622              sk->mtu=min(sk->mtu, 536);  /* default MSS
26623  if none sent */
26624      }
26625  #ifdef CONFIG_INET_PCTCP
26626      sk->mss = min(sk->max_window >> 1, sk->mtu);
26627  #else
26628      sk->mss = min(sk->max_window, sk->mtu);
26629      sk->max_unacked = 2 * sk->mss;
26630  #endif
26631  }
26632
26633
26634  /*
26635   *  This routine handles a connection request.
26636   *  It should make sure we haven't already responded.
26637   *  Because of the way BSD works, we have to send a
26638  syn/ack now.
26639   *  This also means it will be harder to close a socket
26640  which is
26641   *  listening.
26642   */
26643
26644  static void tcp_conn_request(struct sock *sk, struct
26645  sk_buff *skb,
26646          u32 daddr, u32 saddr, struct options *opt,
26647  struct device *dev, u32 seq)
26648  {
26649      struct sock *newsk;
26650      struct tcphdr *th;
26651      struct rtable *rt;
26652  #ifdef CONFIG_SYN_COOKIES
26653      int send_cookie = 0;
26654  #endif
26655
26656      th = skb->h.th;
26657
26658      /* If the socket is dead, don't accept the
26659  connection. */
26660      if (!sk->dead)
26661      {
26662          sk->data_ready(sk,0);
26663      }
26664      else
26665      {
26666          if(sk->debug)
26667              printk("Reset on %p: Connect on dead
26668  socket.\n",sk);
26669          tcp_send_reset(daddr, saddr, th, sk->prot, opt,
```

```
26670  dev, 0,255);
26671          tcp_statistics.TcpAttemptFails++;
26672          kfree_skb(skb, FREE_READ);
26673          return;
26674      }
26675
26676      /*
26677       *  Make sure we can accept more.  This will prevent
26678  a
26679       *  flurry of syns from eating up all our memory.
26680       *
26681       *  BSD does some funnies here and allows 3/2 times
26682  the
26683       *  set backlog as a fudge factor. That's just too
26684  gross.
26685       *
26686       *     Well, now I'm making things even grosser for
26687  dealing
26688       *  with SYNACK flooding.
26689       */
26690
26691      if (sk->ack_backlog >= sk->max_ack_backlog)
26692      {
26693  #if defined(CONFIG_RST_COOKIES) ||
26694  defined(CONFIG_SYN_COOKIES)
26695          static unsigned long warning_time = 0;
26696
26697          /* We may be experiencing SYNACK flooding.
26698           * We now must decide if we should accept this
26699  connection.   * If we have a security clearance for the
26700  incoming
26701           * packet, i.e. it is from a location we where
26702           * packet, i.e. it is from a location we where
26703  talking
26704           * to succesfully recently, or that has
26705  responded to
26706           * a security probe, then we go ahead and deal
26707  normally,
26708           * accepting up to 2*max in the backlog.
26709           * Otherwise, we send out either an RST security
26710  probe
26711           * or a SYN cookie, or both. (depending on
26712  configuration).
26713           * Note that we send out a cookie even if the
26714  backlog
26715           * is full up to 2*max, since the backlog may
26716  clear
26717           * by the time we get a response.
```

```
26718              * WARNING: This code changes the semantics of
26719   the backlog
26720              * a bit. I'm not entirely sure this is the
26721   right thing
26722              * to do here.
26723              */
26724          extern void tcp_send_synack_probe(unsigned long
26725   saddr,
26726                             unsigned long daddr, struct
26727   tcphdr *th,
26728                             struct proto *prot,
26729                             struct options *opt,
26730                             struct device *dev, int tos,
26731   int ttl);
26732
26733   #ifdef CONFIG_RST_COOKIES
26734          if (!tcp_clearance(saddr)) {
26735   #endif
26736              /* Only let this warning get printed once a
26737   minute. */
26738          if (jiffies - warning_time > HZ*60) {
26739              warning_time = jiffies;
26740              printk(KERN_INFO "Warning: possible SYN
26741   flood from %d.%d.%d.%d on %d.%d.%d.%d:%d.  Sending
26742   cookies.\n",
26743                     NIPQUAD(saddr), NIPQUAD(daddr),
26744   ntohs(th->dest));
26745          }
26746   #ifdef CONFIG_RST_COOKIES
26747          tcp_send_synack_probe(daddr, saddr, th,
26748   &tcp_prot,
26749              opt, dev, skb->ip_hdr->tos, 255);
26750   #endif
26751   #ifdef CONFIG_SYN_COOKIES
26752          send_cookie = 1;
26753          ui_c_send_cookies++;
26754   #else
26755              /* If we only have RST cookies we should
26756               * not drop through to the rest of the
26757   response code.
26758               */
26759          kfree_skb(skb, FREE_READ);
26760          return;
26761   #endif
26762   #ifdef CONFIG_RST_COOKIES
26763          } else if (sk->ack_backlog >=
26764   2*sk->max_ack_backlog) {
26765          tcp_statistics.TcpAttemptFails++;
```

```
26766              kfree_skb(skb, FREE_READ);
26767              return;
26768          }
26769   #endif
26770   #else
26771          tcp_statistics.TcpAttemptFails++;
26772          kfree_skb(skb, FREE_READ);
26773          return;
26774   #endif
26775      }
26776
26777      /*
26778       * We need to build a new sock struct.
26779       * It is sort of bad to have a socket without an
26780   inode attached
26781       * to it, but the wake_up's will just wake up the
26782   listening socket,
26783       * and if the listening socket is destroyed before
26784   this is taken
26785       * off of the queue, this will take care of it.
26786       */
26787
26788      newsk = (struct sock *) kmalloc(sizeof(struct sock),
26789   GFP_ATOMIC);
26790      if (newsk == NULL)
26791      {
26792          /* just ignore the syn.  It will get
26793   retransmitted. */
26794          tcp_statistics.TcpAttemptFails++;
26795          kfree_skb(skb, FREE_READ);
26796          return;
26797      }
26798
26799      memcpy(newsk, sk, sizeof(*newsk));
26800
26801      /* Or else we die! -DaveM */
26802      newsk->sklist_next = NULL;
26803      /* and die again -- erics */
26804      newsk->pprev = NULL;
26805
26806      newsk->opt = NULL;
26807      newsk->ip_route_cache  = NULL;
26808      if (opt && opt->optlen)
26809      {
26810          sk->opt = (struct options*)kmalloc(sizeof(struct
26811   options)+opt->optlen, GFP_ATOMIC);
26812          if (!sk->opt)
26813          {
```

p 560

```
26814                    kfree_s(newsk, sizeof(struct sock));
26815                    tcp_statistics.TcpAttemptFails++;
26816                    kfree_skb(skb, FREE_READ);
26817                    return;
26818               }
26819          if (ip_options_echo(sk->opt, opt, daddr, saddr,
26820     skb))
26821               {
26822                    kfree_s(sk->opt, sizeof(struct
26823     options)+opt->optlen);
26824                    kfree_s(newsk, sizeof(struct sock));
26825                    tcp_statistics.TcpAttemptFails++;
26826                    kfree_skb(skb, FREE_READ);
26827                    return;
26828               }
26829          }
26830
26831     skb->when = jiffies;     /* For timeout */
26832     skb_queue_head_init(&newsk->write_queue);
26833     skb_queue_head_init(&newsk->receive_queue);
26834     newsk->send_head = NULL;
26835     newsk->send_tail = NULL;
26836     newsk->send_next = NULL;
26837     skb_queue_head_init(&newsk->back_log);
26838     newsk->rtt = 0;
26839     newsk->rto = TCP_TIMEOUT_INIT;
26840     newsk->mdev = TCP_TIMEOUT_INIT;
26841     newsk->max_window = 32; /* It cannot be left at
26842     zero. -DaveM */
26843          /*
26844           * See draft-stevens-tcpca-spec-01 for discussion of
26845     the
26846           * initialization of these values.
26847           */
26848     newsk->cong_window = 1;
26849     newsk->cong_count = 0;
26850     newsk->ssthresh = 0x7fffffff;
26851
26852     newsk->lrcvtime = 0;
26853     newsk->idletime = 0;
26854     newsk->high_seq = 0;
26855     newsk->backoff = 0;
26856     newsk->blog = 0;
26857     newsk->intr = 0;
26858     newsk->proc = 0;
26859     newsk->done = 0;
26860     newsk->partial = NULL;
26861     newsk->pair = NULL;
26862     newsk->wmem_alloc = 0;
26863     newsk->rmem_alloc = 0;
26864     newsk->localroute = sk->localroute;
26865
26866     newsk->max_unacked = MAX_WINDOW - TCP_WINDOW_DIFF;
26867
26868     newsk->err = 0;
26869     newsk->shutdown = 0;
26870     newsk->ack_backlog = 0;
26871     newsk->acked_seq = skb->seq+1;
26872     newsk->lastwin_seq = skb->seq+1;
26873     newsk->delay_acks = 1;
26874     newsk->copied_seq = skb->seq+1;
26875     newsk->fin_seq = skb->seq;
26876     newsk->syn_seq = skb->seq;
26877     newsk->state = TCP_SYN_RECV;
26878     newsk->timeout = 0;
26879     newsk->ip_xmit_timeout = 0;
26880     newsk->urg_data = 0;
26881     newsk->retransmits = 0;
26882     newsk->linger=0;
26883     newsk->destroy = 0;
26884     init_timer(&newsk->timer);
26885     newsk->timer.data = (unsigned long)newsk;
26886     newsk->timer.function = &net_timer;
26887     init_timer(&newsk->delack_timer);
26888     newsk->delack_timer.data = (unsigned long)newsk;
26889     newsk->delack_timer.function = tcp_delack_timer;
26890     init_timer(&newsk->retransmit_timer);
26891     newsk->retransmit_timer.data = (unsigned long)newsk;
26892     newsk->retransmit_timer.function =
26893     tcp_retransmit_timer;
26894     newsk->dummy_th.source = skb->h.th->dest;
26895     newsk->dummy_th.dest = skb->h.th->source;
26896     newsk->users=0;
26897
26898     #ifdef CONFIG_IP_TRANSPARENT_PROXY
26899          /*
26900           *  Deal with possibly redirected traffic by setting
26901     num to
26902           *  the intended destination port of the received
26903     packet.
26904           */
26905     newsk->num = ntohs(skb->h.th->dest);
26906
26907     #endif
26908          /*
26909           *  Swap these two, they are from our point of view.
```

```
26910        */
26911
26912        newsk->daddr = saddr;
26913        newsk->saddr = daddr;
26914        newsk->rcv_saddr = daddr;
26915 #ifdef CONFIG_SYN_COOKIES
26916        /* Don't actually stuff the socket into the protocol
26917 lists
26918         * if we are going to just destroy it anyway. We
26919 don't want any
26920         * funnies happening if the next packet arrives
26921 before we get
26922         * a chance to clean this one up.
26923         */
26924        if (!send_cookie)
26925 #endif
26926        {
26927            tcp_v4_hash(newsk);
26928            add_to_prot_sklist(newsk);
26929        }
26930
26931        newsk->acked_seq = skb->seq + 1;
26932        newsk->copied_seq = skb->seq + 1;
26933        newsk->socket = NULL;
26934
26935        /*
26936         *  Grab the ttl and tos values and use them
26937         */
26938
26939        newsk->ip_ttl=sk->ip_ttl;
26940        newsk->ip_tos=skb->ip_hdr->tos;
26941
26942        /*
26943         *  Use 512 or whatever user asked for
26944         */
26945
26946        /*
26947         *  Note use of sk->user_mss, since user has no
26948 direct access to newsk
26949         */
26950
26951        rt = ip_rt_route(newsk->opt && newsk->opt->srr ?
26952 newsk->opt->faddr : saddr, 0,
26953                sk->bound_device);
26954        newsk->ip_route_cache = rt;
26955
26956        if(rt!=NULL && (rt->rt_flags&RTF_WINDOW))
26957            newsk->window_clamp = rt->rt_window;
```

```
26958        else
26959            newsk->window_clamp = 0;
26960
26961        if (sk->user_mss)
26962            newsk->mtu = sk->user_mss;
26963        else if (rt)
26964            newsk->mtu = rt->rt_mtu - sizeof(struct iphdr) -
26965 sizeof(struct tcphdr);
26966        else
26967            newsk->mtu = 576 - sizeof(struct iphdr) -
26968 sizeof(struct tcphdr);
26969
26970        /*
26971         *  But not bigger than device MTU
26972         */
26973
26974        newsk->mtu = min(newsk->mtu, dev->mtu -
26975 sizeof(struct iphdr) - sizeof(struct tcphdr));
26976
26977        /* Must check it here, just to be absolutely safe.
26978 If we end up
26979         * with a newsk->{max_window,mtu} of zero, we can
26980 thus end up with
26981         * a newsk->mss of zero, which causes us to bomb out
26982 in
26983         * tcp_do_sendmsg. -DaveM
26984         */
26985        if(newsk->mtu < 32)
26986            newsk->mtu = 32;
26987
26988 #ifdef CONFIG_SKIP
26989
26990        /*
26991         *  SKIP devices set their MTU to 65535. This is so
26992 they can take packets
26993         *  unfragmented to security process then fragment.
26994 They could lie to the
26995         *  TCP layer about a suitable MTU, but it's easier
26996 to let skip sort it out
26997         *  simply because the final package we want
26998 unfragmented is going to be
26999         *
27000         *  [IPHDR][IPSP][Security data][Modified TCP
27001 data][Security data]
27002         */
27003
27004        if(skip_pick_mtu!=NULL)      /* If SKIP is loaded.. */
27005            sk->mtu=skip_pick_mtu(sk->mtu,dev);
```

```
27006   #endif
27007       /*
27008        *   This will min with what arrived in the packet
27009        */
27010
27011       tcp_options(newsk,skb->h.th);
27012
27013   #ifdef CONFIG_SYN_COOKIES
27014       if (send_cookie) {
27015           int mtu_index = 0;
27016           /* Pick the largest MTU smaller than sk->mtu
27017   that we
27018            * can represent in a cookies bottom 3 bits.
27019            */
27020           while (newsk->mtu > cookie_mtu[mtu_index+1] &&
27021   mtu_index < 7)
27022               mtu_index++;
27023           newsk->mtu = cookie_mtu[mtu_index];
27024           /*
27025            * Choose a cookie.
27026            */
27027           seq = secure_tcp_syn_cookie(daddr,saddr,
27028
27029   ntohs(th->source),ntohs(th->dest),ntohl(th->seq),jiffies/
27030   (60*HZ));
27031           seq |= mtu_index;
27032       }
27033   #endif
27034
27035       /* Set up the right sequence numbers */
27036       newsk->write_seq = seq;
27037       newsk->window_seq = newsk->write_seq;
27038       newsk->rcv_ack_seq = newsk->write_seq;
27039
27040   #ifdef CONFIG_SYN_COOKIES
27041       tcp_send_synack(newsk, sk, skb, send_cookie);
27042   #else
27043       tcp_send_synack(newsk, sk, skb, 0);
27044   #endif
27045   }
27046
27047
27048   #ifdef CONFIG_SYN_COOKIES
27049   /*
27050    *  This routine handles a faked connection request as a
27051   result
27052    *  of a valid SYN cookie being seen. This sets up a
27053   socket in the
```

```
27054    *  SYN_SENT state.
27055    */
27056
```
p. 560
```
27057   static int tcp_conn_request_fake(struct sock *sk, struct
27058   sk_buff *skb,
27059           u32 daddr, u32 saddr, struct options *opt,
27060   struct device *dev, u32 seq, u32 mtu)
27061   {
27062       struct sock *newsk;
27063       struct sk_buff *newskb;
27064       struct rtable *rt;
27065
27066       /* If the socket is dead, don't accept the
27067   connection. */
27068       if (!sk->dead)
27069       {
27070           sk->data_ready(sk,0);
27071       }
27072       else
27073       {
27074           if(sk->debug)
27075               printk("Reset on %p: Connect on dead
27076   socket.\n",sk);
27077           tcp_statistics.TcpAttemptFails++;
27078           return 0;
27079       }
27080
27081       /*
27082        * We need to build a new sock struct.
27083        * It is sort of bad to have a socket without an
27084   inode attached
27085        * to it, but the wake_up's will just wake up the
27086   listening socket,
27087        * and if the listening socket is destroyed before
27088   this is taken
27089        * off of the queue, this will take care of it.
27090        */
27091
27092       newsk = (struct sock *) kmalloc(sizeof(struct sock),
27093   GFP_ATOMIC);
27094       if (newsk == NULL)
27095       {
27096           /* Bad juju. If we ignore things now the remote
27097   side
27098            * will be frozen. Really we should retrans the
27099   cookie,
27100            * but that's a no go also, since we don't have
27101   enough
```

```
27102                * memory to receive it either. So, we're stuck
27103   with
27104                * this bad case, and a few others further down.
27105                * We just have to hope it is a low probability
27106   event.
27107                * Also, to avoid a loop we must not go down into
27108                * the recursive call to tcp_rcv in the caller
27109   to this
27110                * routine, so we should let them know we failed.
27111                */
27112               tcp_statistics.TcpAttemptFails++;
27113               return 0;
27114           }
27115
27116       memcpy(newsk, sk, sizeof(*newsk));
27117
27118       /* Or else we die! -DaveM */
27119       newsk->sklist_next = NULL;
27120
27121       newsk->opt = NULL;
27122       newsk->ip_route_cache  = NULL;
27123       if (opt && opt->optlen)
27124       {
27125           sk->opt = (struct options*)kmalloc(sizeof(struct
27126   options)+opt->optlen, GFP_ATOMIC);
27127           if (!sk->opt)
27128           {
27129               /* More bad juju. */
27130               kfree_s(newsk, sizeof(struct sock));
27131               tcp_statistics.TcpAttemptFails++;
27132               return 0;
27133           }
27134           if (ip_options_echo(sk->opt, opt, daddr, saddr,
27135   skb))
27136           {
27137               /* More bad juju. */
27138               kfree_s(sk->opt, sizeof(struct
27139   options)+opt->optlen);
27140               kfree_s(newsk, sizeof(struct sock));
27141               tcp_statistics.TcpAttemptFails++;
27142               return 0;
27143           }
27144       }
27145
27146       skb_queue_head_init(&newsk->write_queue);
27147       skb_queue_head_init(&newsk->receive_queue);
27148       newsk->send_head = NULL;
27149       newsk->send_tail = NULL;
27150       newsk->send_next = NULL;
27151       skb_queue_head_init(&newsk->back_log);
27152       newsk->rtt = 0;
27153       newsk->rto = TCP_TIMEOUT_INIT;
27154       newsk->mdev = TCP_TIMEOUT_INIT;
27155       newsk->max_window = 32; /* It cannot be left at
27156   zero. -DaveM */
27157       /*
27158        * See draft-stevens-tcpca-spec-01 for discussion of
27159   the
27160        * initialization of these values.
27161        */
27162       newsk->cong_window = 1;
27163       newsk->cong_count = 0;
27164       newsk->ssthresh = 0x7fffffff;
27165
27166       newsk->lrcvtime = 0;
27167       newsk->idletime = 0;
27168       newsk->high_seq = 0;
27169       newsk->backoff = 0;
27170       newsk->blog = 0;
27171       newsk->intr = 0;
27172       newsk->proc = 0;
27173       newsk->done = 0;
27174       newsk->partial = NULL;
27175       newsk->pair = NULL;
27176       newsk->wmem_alloc = 0;
27177       newsk->rmem_alloc = 0;
27178       newsk->localroute = sk->localroute;
27179
27180       newsk->max_unacked = MAX_WINDOW - TCP_WINDOW_DIFF;
27181
27182       newsk->err = 0;
27183       newsk->shutdown = 0;
27184       newsk->ack_backlog = 0;
27185       newsk->acked_seq = skb->seq;
27186       newsk->lastwin_seq = skb->seq;
27187       newsk->delay_acks = 1;
27188       newsk->copied_seq = skb->seq;
27189       newsk->fin_seq = skb->seq-1;
27190       newsk->syn_seq = skb->seq-1;
27191       newsk->state = TCP_SYN_RECV;
27192       newsk->timeout = 0;
27193       newsk->ip_xmit_timeout = 0;
27194       newsk->urg_data = 0;
27195       newsk->retransmits = 0;
27196       newsk->linger=0;
27197       newsk->destroy = 0;
```

```
27198        init_timer(&newsk->timer);
27199        newsk->timer.data = (unsigned long)newsk;
27200        newsk->timer.function = &net_timer;
27201        init_timer(&newsk->delack_timer);
27202        newsk->delack_timer.data = (unsigned long)newsk;
27203        newsk->delack_timer.function = tcp_delack_timer;
27204        init_timer(&newsk->retransmit_timer);
27205        newsk->retransmit_timer.data = (unsigned long)newsk;
27206        newsk->retransmit_timer.function =
27207 tcp_retransmit_timer;
27208        newsk->dummy_th.source = skb->h.th->dest;
27209        newsk->dummy_th.dest = skb->h.th->source;
27210        newsk->users=0;
27211
27212 #ifdef CONFIG_IP_TRANSPARENT_PROXY
27213        /*
27214         *  Deal with possibly redirected traffic by setting
27215 num to
27216         *  the intended destination port of the received
27217 packet.
27218         */
27219        newsk->num = ntohs(skb->h.th->dest);
27220
27221 #endif
27222        /*
27223         *  Swap these two, they are from our point of view.
27224         */
27225
27226        newsk->daddr = saddr;
27227        newsk->saddr = daddr;
27228        newsk->rcv_saddr = daddr;
27229        tcp_v4_hash(newsk);
27230        add_to_prot_sklist(newsk);
27231
27232        newsk->acked_seq = skb->seq;
27233        newsk->copied_seq = skb->seq;
27234        newsk->socket = NULL;
27235
27236        /*
27237         *  Grab the ttl and tos values and use them
27238         */
27239
27240        newsk->ip_ttl=sk->ip_ttl;
27241        newsk->ip_tos=skb->ip_hdr->tos;
27242
27243        rt = ip_rt_route(newsk->opt && newsk->opt->srr ?
27244 newsk->opt->faddr : saddr, 0,
27245                sk->bound_device);
```

```
27246        newsk->ip_route_cache = rt;
27247
27248        if (rt!=NULL && (rt->rt_flags&RTF_WINDOW))
27249            newsk->window_clamp = rt->rt_window;
27250        else
27251            newsk->window_clamp = 0;
27252
27253        newsk->mtu = mtu;
27254
27255        /* Set up the right sequence numbers.
27256         * Note that we have to make sure write_seq is
27257 correct for having
27258         * sent off the handshake!
27259         */
27260        newsk->write_seq = seq+1;
27261        newsk->sent_seq = seq+1;
27262        newsk->window_seq = seq;
27263        newsk->rcv_ack_seq = seq;
27264        newsk->max_unacked = 2 * newsk->mss;
27265
27266        tcp_select_window(newsk);
27267
27268        /* We need to get something into the receive queue
27269 to enable an
27270         * accept. Possibly we should be faking up a SYN
27271 packet, but
27272         * as far as I can tell the contents of this skb
27273 don't matter,
27274         * so long as it points to our new socket.
27275         */
27276        newskb = skb_clone(skb,GFP_ATOMIC);
27277        newskb->sk = newsk;
27278        atomic_add(skb->truesize, &newsk->rmem_alloc);
27279        sk->ack_backlog++;
27280        skb_queue_tail(&sk->receive_queue,newskb);
27281        return 1;
27282 }
27283 #endif
27284
27285 /*
27286  * Handle a TCP window that shrunk on us. It shouldn't
27287 happen,
27288  * but..
27289  *
27290  * We may need to move packets from the send queue
27291  * to the write queue, if the window has been shrunk on
27292 us.
27293  * The RFC says you are not allowed to shrink your window
```

```
27294        * like this, but if the other end does, you must be able
27295        * to deal with it.
27296        */
27297   void tcp_window_shrunk(struct sock * sk, u32 window_seq)
27298   {
27299        struct sk_buff *skb;
27300        struct sk_buff *skb2;
27301        struct sk_buff *wskb = NULL;
27302
27303        skb2 = sk->send_head;
27304        sk->send_head = NULL;
27305        sk->send_tail = NULL;
27306        sk->send_next = NULL;
27307
27308        /*
27309         *  This is an artifact of a flawed concept. We want
27310   one
27311         *  queue and a smarter send routine when we send
27312   all.
27313         */
27314        cli();
27315        while (skb2 != NULL)
27316        {
27317            skb = skb2;
27318            skb2 = skb->link3;
27319            skb->link3 = NULL;
27320            if (after(skb->end_seq, window_seq))
27321            {
27322                if (sk->packets_out > 0)
27323                    sk->packets_out--;
27324                /* We may need to remove this from the dev
27325   send list. */
27326                if (skb->next != NULL)
27327                {
27328                    skb_unlink(skb);
27329                }
27330                /* Now add it to the write_queue. */
27331                if (wskb == NULL)
27332                    skb_queue_head(&sk->write_queue,skb);
27333                else
27334                    skb_append(wskb,skb);
27335                wskb = skb;
27336            }
27337            else
27338            {
27339                if (sk->send_head == NULL)
27340                {
27341                    sk->send_head = skb;
```

```
27342                    sk->send_tail = skb;
27343                    sk->send_next = skb;
27344                }
27345                else
27346                {
27347                    sk->send_tail->link3 = skb;
27348                    sk->send_tail = skb;
27349                }
27350                skb->link3 = NULL;
27351            }
27352        }
27353        sti();
27354   }
27355
27356
27357   /*
27358    *  This routine deals with incoming acks, but not
27359   outgoing ones.
27360    *
27361    *  This routine is totally _WRONG_. The list
27362   structuring is wrong,
27363    *  the algorithm is wrong, the code is wrong.
27364    */
27365
27366   static int tcp_ack(struct sock *sk, struct tcphdr *th,
27367   u32 ack, int len)
27368   {
27369        int flag = 0;
27370        u32 window_seq;
27371
27372        /*
27373         * 1 - there was data in packet as well as ack or
27374   new data is sent or
27375         *     in shutdown state
27376         * 2 - data from retransmit queue was acked and
27377   removed
27378         * 4 - window shrunk or data from retransmit queue
27379   was acked and removed
27380         */
27381
27382        if(sk->zapped)
27383            return(1);  /* Dead, can't ack any more so why
27384   bother */
27385
27386        /*
27387         *  We have dropped back to keepalive timeouts. Thus
27388   we have
27389         *  no retransmits pending.
```

```
27390        */
27391
27392        if (sk->ip_xmit_timeout == TIME_KEEPOPEN)
27393            sk->retransmits = 0;
27394
27395        /*
27396         * If the ack is newer than sent or older than
27397 previous acks
27398         * then we can probably ignore it.
27399         */
27400
27401        if (after(ack, sk->sent_seq) || before(ack,
27402 sk->rcv_ack_seq))
27403            goto uninteresting_ack;
27404
27405        /*
27406         * Have we discovered a larger window
27407         */
27408        window_seq = ntohs(th->window);
27409        if (window_seq > sk->max_window)
27410        {
27411            sk->max_window = window_seq;
27412 #ifdef CONFIG_INET_PCTCP
27413            /* Hack because we don't send partial packets to
27414 non SWS
27415               handling hosts */
27416            sk->mss = min(window_seq>>1, sk->mtu);
27417 #else
27418            sk->mss = min(window_seq, sk->mtu);
27419 #endif
27420        }
27421        window_seq += ack;
27422
27423        /*
27424         * See if our window has been shrunk.
27425         */
27426        if (after(sk->window_seq, window_seq))
27427            tcp_window_shrunk(sk, window_seq);
27428
27429        /*
27430         * Pipe has emptied
27431         */
27432        if (sk->send_tail == NULL || sk->send_head == NULL)
27433        {
27434            sk->send_head = NULL;
27435            sk->send_tail = NULL;
27436            sk->send_next = NULL;
27437            sk->packets_out= 0;
27438        }
27439
27440        /*
27441         * We don't want too many packets out there.
27442         */
27443
27444        if (sk->ip_xmit_timeout == TIME_WRITE &&
27445            sk->cong_window < 2048 && after(ack,
27446 sk->rcv_ack_seq))
27447        {
27448
27449            /*
27450             * This is Jacobson's slow start and congestion
27451 avoidance.
27452             * SIGCOMM '88, p. 328.  Because we keep
27453 cong_window in integral
27454             * mss's, we can't do cwnd += 1 / cwnd.
27455 Instead, maintain a
27456             * counter and increment it once every cwnd
27457 times.  It's possible
27458             * that this should be done only if
27459 sk->retransmits == 0.  I'm
27460             * interpreting "new data is acked" as including
27461 data that has
27462             * been retransmitted but is just now being
27463 acked.
27464             */
27465            if (sk->cong_window <= sk->ssthresh)
27466                /*
27467                 * In "safe" area, increase
27468                 */
27469                sk->cong_window++;
27470            else
27471            {
27472                /*
27473                 * In dangerous area, increase slowly.  In
27474 theory this is
27475                 *      sk->cong_window += 1 /
27476 sk->cong_window
27477                 */
27478                if (sk->cong_count >= sk->cong_window)
27479                {
27480                    sk->cong_window++;
27481                    sk->cong_count = 0;
27482                }
27483                else
27484                    sk->cong_count++;
27485            }
```

```
27486          }
27487
27488      /*
27489       *   Remember the highest ack received and update the
27490       *   right hand window edge of the host.
27491       *   We do a bit of work here to track number of
27492  times we've
27493       *   seen this ack without a change in the right edge
27494  of the
27495       *   window and no data in the packet.
27496       *   This will allow us to do fast retransmits.
27497       */
27498
27499      /* We are looking for duplicate ACKs here.
27500       * An ACK is a duplicate if:
27501       * (1) it has the same sequence number as the
27502  largest number we've seen,
27503       * (2) it has the same window as the last ACK,
27504       * (3) we have outstanding data that has not been
27505  ACKed
27506       * (4) The packet was not carrying any data.
27507       * (5) [From Floyd's paper on fast retransmit wars]
27508       *     The packet acked data after high_seq;
27509       * I've tried to order these in occurrence of most
27510  likely to fail
27511       * to least likely to fail.
27512       * [These are an extension of the rules BSD stacks
27513  use to
27514       *   determine if an ACK is a duplicate.]
27515       */
27516
27517      if (sk->rcv_ack_seq == ack
27518          && sk->window_seq == window_seq
27519          && len == th->doff*4
27520          && before(ack, sk->sent_seq)
27521          && after(ack, sk->high_seq))
27522      {
27523          /* Prevent counting of duplicate ACKs if the
27524  congestion
27525           * window is smaller than 3. Note that since we
27526  reduce
27527           * the congestion window when we do a fast
27528  retransmit,
27529           * we must be careful to keep counting if we
27530  were already
27531           * counting. The idea behind this is to avoid
27532  doing
27533           * fast retransmits if the congestion window is
```

```
27534  so small
27535           * that we cannot get 3 ACKs due to the loss of
27536  a packet
27537           * unless we are getting ACKs for retransmitted
27538  packets.
27539           */
27540          if (sk->cong_window >= 3 || sk->rcv_ack_cnt >
27541  MAX_DUP_ACKS+1)
27542              sk->rcv_ack_cnt++;
27543          /* See draft-stevens-tcpca-spec-01 for
27544  explanation
27545           * of what we are doing here.
27546           */
27547          if (sk->rcv_ack_cnt == MAX_DUP_ACKS+1) {
27548              int tmp;
27549
27550              /* We need to be a bit careful to preserve
27551  the
27552               * count of packets that are out in the
27553  system here.
27554               */
27555              sk->ssthresh = max(
27556                  min(sk->cong_window,
27557
27558  (sk->window_seq-sk->rcv_ack_seq)/max(sk->mss,1))
27559                      >> 1, 2);
27560              sk->cong_window =
27561  sk->ssthresh+MAX_DUP_ACKS+1;
27562              sk->cong_count = 0;
27563              tmp = sk->packets_out;
27564              tcp_do_retransmit(sk,0);
27565              sk->packets_out = tmp;
27566          } else if (sk->rcv_ack_cnt > MAX_DUP_ACKS+1) {
27567              sk->cong_window++;
27568              /*
27569               * At this point we are suppose to transmit a
27570  NEW
27571               * packet (not retransmit the missing packet,
27572               * this would only get us into a retransmit
27573  war.)
27574               * I think that having just adjusted
27575  cong_window
27576               * we will transmit the new packet below.
27577               */
27578          }
27579      }
27580      else
27581      {
```

p 562 (marker at line 27540)

```
27582            if (sk->rcv_ack_cnt > MAX_DUP_ACKS) {
27583                /* Don't allow congestion window to drop to
27584    zero. */
27585                sk->cong_window = max(sk->ssthresh, 1);
27586                sk->cong_count = 0;
27587            }
27588            sk->window_seq = window_seq;
27589            sk->rcv_ack_seq = ack;
27590            sk->rcv_ack_cnt = 1;
27591        }
27592
27593        /*
27594         *  We passed data and got it acked, remove any soft
27595    error
27596         *  log. Something worked...
27597         */
27598
27599        sk->err_soft = 0;
27600
27601        /*
27602         *  If this ack opens up a zero window, clear
27603    backoff.  It was
27604         *  being used to time the probes, and is probably
27605    far higher than
27606         *  it needs to be for normal retransmission.
27607         */
27608
27609        if (sk->ip_xmit_timeout == TIME_PROBE0)
27610        {
27611            sk->retransmits = 0;     /* Our probe was
27612    answered */
27613
27614            /*
27615             *  Was it a usable window open ?
27616             */
27617
27618            if (!skb_queue_empty(&sk->write_queue) &&    /*
27619    should always be true */
27620                ! before (sk->window_seq,
27621    sk->write_queue.next->end_seq))
27622            {
27623                sk->backoff = 0;
27624
27625                /*
27626                 *  Recompute rto from rtt.  this eliminates
27627    any backoff.
27628                 */
27629
27630                /*
27631                 * Appendix C of Van Jacobson's final
27632    version of
27633                 * the SIGCOMM 88 paper states that although
27634                 * the original paper suggested that
27635                 *  RTO = R*2V
27636                 * was the correct calculation experience
27637    showed
27638                 * better results using
27639                 *  RTO = R*4V
27640                 * In particular this gives better
27641    performance over
27642                 * slow links, and should not effect fast
27643    links.
27644                 *
27645                 * Note: Jacobson's algorithm is fine on BSD
27646    which
27647                 * has a 1/2 second granularity clock, but
27648    with our
27649                 * 1/100 second granularity clock we become
27650    too
27651                 * sensitive to minor changes in the round
27652    trip time.
27653                 * We add in two compensating factors.
27654                 * First we multiply by 5/4. For large
27655    congestion
27656                 * windows this allows us to tolerate burst
27657    traffic
27658                 * delaying up to 1/4 of our packets.
27659                 * We also add in a rtt / cong_window term.
27660                 * For small congestion windows this allows
27661                 * a single packet delay, but has negligible
27662    effect
27663                 * on the compensation for large windows.
27664                 */
27665                sk->rto = (sk->rtt >> 3) + sk->mdev;
27666                sk->rto += (sk->rto>>2) + (sk->rto >>
27667    (sk->cong_window-1));
27668                if (sk->rto > 120*HZ)
27669                    sk->rto = 120*HZ;
27670                if (sk->rto < HZ/5) /* Was 1*HZ, then 1 -
27671    turns out we must allow about
27672                                .2 of a second because of BSD
27673    delayed acks - on a 100Mb/sec link
27674                                .2 of a second is going to
27675    need huge windows (SIGH) */
27676                    sk->rto = HZ/5;
27677            }
```

```
27678        }
27679
27680        /*
27681         *  See if we can take anything off of the
27682 retransmit queue.
27683         */
27684
27685        for (;;) {
27686            int was_locked;
27687            struct sk_buff * skb = sk->send_head;
27688            if (!skb)
27689                break;
27690
27691            /* Check for a bug. */
27692            if (skb->link3 && after(skb->end_seq,
27693 skb->link3->end_seq))
27694                printk("INET: tcp.c: *** bug send_list out
27695 of order.\n");
27696
27697            /*
27698             *  If our packet is before the ack sequence we
27699 can
27700             *  discard it as it's confirmed to have arrived
27701 the other end.
27702             */
27703
27704            if (after(skb->end_seq, ack))
27705                break;
27706
27707            if (sk->retransmits)
27708            {
27709                /*
27710                 *  We were retransmitting.  don't count
27711 this in RTT est
27712                 */
27713                flag |= 2;
27714            }
27715
27716            if ((sk->send_head = skb->link3) == NULL)
27717            {
27718                sk->send_tail = NULL;
27719                sk->send_next = NULL;
27720                sk->retransmits = 0;
27721            }
27722
27723            /*
27724             * advance the send_next pointer if needed.
27725             */
```

```
27726            if (sk->send_next == skb)
27727                sk->send_next = sk->send_head;
27728
27729            /*
27730             * Note that we only reset backoff and rto in the
27731             * rtt recomputation code.  And that doesn't
27732 happen
27733             * if there were retransmissions in effect.  So
27734 the
27735             * first new packet after the retransmissions is
27736             * sent with the backoff still in effect.  Not
27737 until
27738             * we get an ack from a non-retransmitted packet
27739 do
27740             * we reset the backoff and rto.  This allows us
27741 to deal
27742             * with a situation where the network delay has
27743 increased
27744             * suddenly.  I.e. Karn's algorithm. (SIGCOMM
27745 '87, p5.)
27746             */
27747
27748            /*
27749             *  We have one less packet out there.
27750             */
27751
27752            if (sk->packets_out > 0)
27753                sk->packets_out --;
27754
27755            /* This is really only supposed to be called
27756 when we
27757             * are actually ACKing new data, which should
27758 exclude
27759             * the ACK handshake on an initial SYN packet as
27760 well.
27761             * Rather than introducing a new test here for
27762 this
27763             * special case, we just reset the initial
27764 values for
27765             * rtt immediately after we move to the
27766 established state.
27767             */
27768            if (!(flag&2))  /* Not retransmitting */
27769                tcp_rtt_estimator(sk,skb);
27770            IS_SKB(skb);
27771
27772            /*
27773             *  We may need to remove this from the dev send
```

```
27774  list.
27775           */
27776          cli();
27777          was_locked = skb_device_locked(skb);
27778
27779          if (was_locked) {
27780               /* In this case, we are relying on the fact
27781  that kfree_skb
27782                * will just set the free flag to be 3, and
27783  increment
27784                * a counter. It will not actually free
27785  anything, and
27786                * will not take much time
27787                */
27788               kfree_skb(skb, FREE_WRITE);
27789          } else {
27790               skb_unlink(skb);
27791          }
27792          sti();
27793
27794          if (!was_locked)
27795               kfree_skb(skb, FREE_WRITE); /* write. */
27796          if (!sk->dead)
27797               sk->write_space(sk);
27798     }
27799
27800     /*
27801      * Maybe we can take some stuff off of the write
27802  queue,
27803      * and put it onto the xmit queue.
27804      * There is bizarre case being tested here, to check
27805  if
27806      * the data at the head of the queue ends before the
27807  start of
27808      * the sequence we already ACKed. This is not an
27809  error,
27810      * it can occur when we send a packet directly off
27811  of the write_queue
27812      * in a zero window probe.
27813      */
27814
27815     if (!skb_queue_empty(&sk->write_queue) &&
27816          !before(sk->window_seq,
27817  sk->write_queue.next->end_seq) &&
27818          (sk->retransmits == 0 ||
27819          sk->ip_xmit_timeout != TIME_WRITE ||
27820          !after(sk->write_queue.next->end_seq,
27821  sk->rcv_ack_seq)) &&
27822          sk->packets_out < sk->cong_window)
27823     {
27824          /*
27825           *  Add more data to the send queue.
27826           */
27827          tcp_write_xmit(sk);
27828     }
27829
27830     /*
27831      * Reset timers to reflect the new state.
27832      *
27833      * from TIME_WAIT we stay in TIME_WAIT as long as we
27834  rx packets
27835      * from TCP_CLOSE we don't do anything
27836      *
27837      * from anything else, if there is queued data (or
27838  fin) pending,
27839      * we use a TIME_WRITE timeout, if there is data to
27840  write but
27841      * no room in the window we use TIME_PROBE0, else if
27842  keepalive
27843      * we reset to a KEEPALIVE timeout, else we delete
27844  the timer.
27845      *
27846      * We do not set flag for nominal write data,
27847  otherwise we may
27848      * force a state where we start to write itsy bitsy
27849  tidbits
27850      * of data.
27851      */
27852
27853     switch(sk->state) {
27854     case TCP_TIME_WAIT:
27855          /*
27856           * keep us in TIME_WAIT until we stop getting
27857  packets,
27858           * reset the timeout.
27859           */
27860          tcp_reset_msl_timer(sk, TIME_CLOSE,
27861  TCP_TIMEWAIT_LEN);
27862          break;
27863     case TCP_CLOSE:
27864          /*
27865           * don't touch the timer.
27866           */
27867          break;
27868     default:
27869          /*
```

```
27870             *  Must check send_head and write_queue
27871             *  to determine which timeout to use.
27872             */
27873         if (sk->send_head) {
27874              tcp_reset_xmit_timer(sk, TIME_WRITE,
27875  sk->rto);
27876         } else if (!skb_queue_empty(&sk->write_queue)
27877              && sk->ack_backlog == 0)
27878         {
27879              /*
27880               * if the write queue is not empty when we
27881  get here
27882               * then we failed to move any data to the
27883  retransmit
27884               * queue above. (If we had send_head would
27885  be non-NULL).
27886               * Furthermore, since the send_head is NULL
27887  here
27888               * we must not be in retransmit mode at this
27889  point.
27890               * This implies we have no packets in flight,
27891               * hence sk->packets_out < sk->cong_window.
27892               * Examining the conditions for the test to
27893  move
27894               * data to the retransmission queue we find
27895  that
27896               * we must therefore have a zero window.
27897               * Hence, if the ack_backlog is 0 we should
27898  initiate
27899               * a zero probe.
27900               * We don't do a zero probe if we have a
27901  delayed
27902               * ACK in hand since the other side may have
27903  a
27904               * window opening, but they are waiting to
27905  hear
27906               * from us before they tell us about it.
27907               * (They are applying Nagle's rule).
27908               * So, we don't set up the zero window probe
27909               * just yet. We do have to clear the timer
27910               * though in this case...
27911               */
27912              tcp_reset_xmit_timer(sk, TIME_PROBE0,
27913  sk->rto);
27914         } else if (sk->keepopen) {
27915              tcp_reset_xmit_timer(sk, TIME_KEEPOPEN,
27916  TCP_TIMEOUT_LEN);
27917         } else {
27918              del_timer(&sk->retransmit_timer);
27919              sk->ip_xmit_timeout = 0;
27920         }
27921         break;
27922    }
27923
27924    /*
27925     * In the LAST_ACK case, the other end FIN'd us.  We
27926  then FIN'd them, and
27927     * we are now waiting for an acknowledge to our FIN.
27928  The other end is
27929     * already in TIME_WAIT.
27930     *
27931     * Move to TCP_CLOSE on success.
27932     */
27933
27934    if (sk->state == TCP_LAST_ACK)
27935    {
27936         if (!sk->dead)
27937              sk->state_change(sk);
27938         if(sk->debug)
27939              printk("rcv_ack_seq: %X==%X, acked_seq:
27940  %X==%X\n",
27941
27942  sk->rcv_ack_seq,sk->write_seq,sk->acked_seq,sk->fin_seq);
27943         if (sk->rcv_ack_seq == sk->write_seq /*&&
27944  sk->acked_seq == sk->fin_seq*/)
27945         {
27946              sk->shutdown = SHUTDOWN_MASK;
27947              tcp_set_state(sk,TCP_CLOSE);
27948              return 1;
27949         }
27950    }
27951
27952    /*
27953     * Incoming ACK to a FIN we sent in the case of our
27954  initiating the close.
27955     *
27956     * Move to FIN_WAIT2 to await a FIN from the other
27957  end. Set
27958     * SEND_SHUTDOWN but not RCV_SHUTDOWN as data can
27959  still be coming in.
27960     */
27961
27962    if (sk->state == TCP_FIN_WAIT1)
27963    {
27964
27965         if (!sk->dead)
```

```
27966                sk->state_change(sk);
27967            if (sk->rcv_ack_seq == sk->write_seq)
27968            {
27969                sk->shutdown |= SEND_SHUTDOWN;
27970                tcp_set_state(sk, TCP_FIN_WAIT2);
27971                /* If the socket is dead, then there is no
27972                 * user process hanging around using it.
27973                 * We want to set up a FIN_WAIT2 timeout ala
27974 BSD.
27975                 */
27976                if (sk->dead)
27977                    tcp_reset_msl_timer(sk, TIME_CLOSE,
27978 TCP_FIN_TIMEOUT);
27979            }
27980        }
27981
27982        /*
27983         *    Incoming ACK to a FIN we sent in the case of a
27984 simultaneous close.
27985         *
27986         *    Move to TIME_WAIT
27987         */
27988
27989        if (sk->state == TCP_CLOSING)
27990        {
27991
27992            if (!sk->dead)
27993                sk->state_change(sk);
27994            if (sk->rcv_ack_seq == sk->write_seq)
27995            {
27996                tcp_time_wait(sk);
27997            }
27998        }
27999
28000        /*
28001         *    Final ack of a three way shake
28002         */
28003
28004        if (sk->state==TCP_SYN_RECV)
28005        {
28006            tcp_set_state(sk, TCP_ESTABLISHED);
28007
28008            /* Must check for peer advertising zero sized
28009 window
28010             * or else we get a sk->{mtu,mss} of zero and
28011 thus bomb out
28012             * in tcp_do_sendmsg. -DaveM
28013             */
28014            if(sk->max_window == 0)
28015                sk->max_window = 32;
28016
28017            tcp_options(sk,th);
28018
28019 #if 0
28020            sk->dummy_th.dest=th->source;
28021            tcp_v4_rehash(sk);
28022 #endif
28023
28024            sk->copied_seq = sk->acked_seq;
28025            if(!sk->dead)
28026                sk->state_change(sk);
28027
28028            /* Reset the RTT estimator to the initial
28029             * state rather than testing to avoid
28030             * updating it on the ACK to the SYN packet.
28031             */
28032            sk->rtt = 0;
28033            sk->rto = TCP_TIMEOUT_INIT;
28034            sk->mdev = TCP_TIMEOUT_INIT;
28035        }
28036
28037        /*
28038         * The following code has been greatly simplified
28039 from the
28040         * old hacked up stuff. The wonders of properly
28041 setting the
28042         * retransmission timeouts.
28043         *
28044         * If we are retransmitting, and we acked a packet
28045 on the retransmit
28046         * queue, and there is still something in the
28047 retransmit queue,
28048         * then we can output some retransmission packets.
28049         *
28050         * Note that we need to be a bit careful here about
28051 getting the
28052         * correct TIME_WRITE timer set. If we just got an
28053 ack of a
28054         * packet we where retransmitting, we will
28055 retransmit the next
28056         * packet in the retransmit queue below, and the
28057 timeout
28058         * should now start from the time we retransmitted
28059 that packet.
28060         * The resetting of the TIME_WRITE timer above will
28061 have set it
```

```
28062          * relative to the prior transmission time, which
28063     would be wrong.
28064          */
28065
28066          if (sk->send_head != NULL && (flag&2) &&
28067     sk->retransmits)
28068          {
28069               tcp_do_retransmit(sk, 1);
28070               tcp_reset_xmit_timer(sk, TIME_WRITE, sk->rto);
28071          }
28072
28073          return 1;
28074
28075     uninteresting_ack:
28076          if(sk->debug)
28077               printk("Ack ignored %u %u\n",ack,sk->sent_seq);
28078
28079          /*
28080           *  Keepalive processing.
28081           */
28082
28083          if (after(ack, sk->sent_seq))
28084          {
28085               return 0;
28086          }
28087
28088          /*
28089           *  Restart the keepalive timer.
28090           */
28091
28092          if (sk->keepopen)
28093          {
28094               if(sk->ip_xmit_timeout==TIME_KEEPOPEN)
28095                    tcp_reset_xmit_timer(sk, TIME_KEEPOPEN,
28096     TCP_TIMEOUT_LEN);
28097          }
28098          return 0;
28099     }
28100
28101
28102     /*
28103      *  Process the FIN bit. This now behaves as it is
28104     supposed to work
28105      *  and the FIN takes effect when it is validly part of
28106     sequence
28107      *  space. Not before when we get holes.
28108      *
28109      *  If we are ESTABLISHED, a received fin moves us to
28110     CLOSE-WAIT
28111      *  (and thence onto LAST-ACK and finally, CLOSE, we
28112     never enter
28113      *  TIME-WAIT)
28114      *
28115      *  If we are in FINWAIT-1, a received FIN indicates
28116     simultaneous
28117      *  close and we go into CLOSING (and later onto
28118     TIME-WAIT)
28119      *
28120      *  If we are in FINWAIT-2, a received FIN moves us to
28121     TIME-WAIT.
28122      *
28123      */
28124
28125     static int tcp_fin(struct sk_buff *skb, struct sock *sk,
28126     struct tcphdr *th)
28127     {
28128          sk->fin_seq = skb->end_seq;
28129
28130          if (!sk->dead)
28131          {
28132               sk->state_change(sk);
28133               sock_wake_async(sk->socket, 1);
28134          }
28135
28136          switch(sk->state)
28137          {
28138               case TCP_SYN_RECV:
28139               case TCP_SYN_SENT:
28140               case TCP_ESTABLISHED:
28141                    /*
28142                     * move to CLOSE_WAIT, tcp_data() already
28143     handled
28144                     * sending the ack.
28145                     */
28146                    tcp_set_state(sk,TCP_CLOSE_WAIT);
28147                    if (th->rst)
28148                         sk->shutdown = SHUTDOWN_MASK;
28149                    break;
28150
28151               case TCP_CLOSE_WAIT:
28152               case TCP_CLOSING:
28153                    /*
28154                     * received a retransmission of the FIN, do
28155                     * nothing.
28156                     */
28157                    break;
```

```
28158           case TCP_TIME_WAIT:
28159               /*
28160                * received a retransmission of the FIN,
28161                * restart the TIME_WAIT timer.
28162                */
28163               tcp_reset_msl_timer(sk, TIME_CLOSE,
28164 TCP_TIMEWAIT_LEN);
28165               return(0);
28166           case TCP_FIN_WAIT1:
28167               /*
28168                * This case occurs when a simultaneous close
28169                * happens, we must ack the received FIN and
28170                * enter the CLOSING state.
28171                *
28172                * This causes a WRITE timeout, which will
28173 either
28174                * move on to TIME_WAIT when we timeout, or
28175 resend
28176                * the FIN properly (maybe we get rid of
28177 that annoying
28178                * FIN lost hang). The TIME_WRITE code is
28179 already correct
28180                * for handling this timeout.
28181                */
28182
28183               if (sk->ip_xmit_timeout != TIME_WRITE) {
28184                   if (sk->send_head)
28185                       tcp_reset_xmit_timer(sk, TIME_WRITE,
28186 sk->rto);
28187                   else if (sk->ip_xmit_timeout !=
28188 TIME_PROBE0
28189                       || skb_queue_empty(&sk->write_queue)) {
28190                       /* BUG check case.
28191                        * We have a problem here if there
28192                        * is no timer running [leads to
28193                        * frozen socket] or no data in the
28194                        * write queue [means we sent a fin
28195                        * and lost it from the queue before
28196                        * changing the ack properly].
28197                        */
28198                       printk(KERN_ERR "Lost timer or fin
28199 packet in tcp_fin.\n");
28200                   }
28201               }
28202               tcp_set_state(sk,TCP_CLOSING);
28203               break;
28204           case TCP_FIN_WAIT2:
28205               /*
```

```
28206                * received a FIN -- send ACK and enter
28207 TIME_WAIT
28208                */
28209               tcp_reset_msl_timer(sk, TIME_CLOSE,
28210 TCP_TIMEWAIT_LEN);
28211               sk->shutdown|=SHUTDOWN_MASK;
28212               tcp_set_state(sk,TCP_TIME_WAIT);
28213               break;
28214           case TCP_CLOSE:
28215               /*
28216                * already in CLOSE
28217                */
28218               break;
28219           default:
28220               tcp_set_state(sk,TCP_LAST_ACK);
28221
28222               /* Start the timers. */
28223               tcp_reset_msl_timer(sk, TIME_CLOSE,
28224 TCP_TIMEWAIT_LEN);
28225               return(0);
28226       }
28227
28228       return(0);
28229 }
28230
28231 /*
28232  * Add a sk_buff to the TCP receive queue, calculating
28233  * the ACK sequence as we go..
28234  */
28235 static inline void tcp_insert_skb(struct sk_buff * skb,
28236 struct sk_buff_head * list)
28237 {
28238     struct sk_buff * prev, * next;
28239     u32 seq;
28240
28241     /*
28242      * Find where the new skb goes.. (This goes
28243 backwards,
28244      * on the assumption that we get the packets in
28245 order)
28246      */
28247     seq = skb->seq;
28248     prev = list->prev;
28249     next = (struct sk_buff *) list;
28250     for (;;) {
28251         if (prev == (struct sk_buff *) list ||
28252 !after(prev->seq, seq))
28253             break;
```

p. 563

```
28254            next = prev;
28255            prev = prev->prev;
28256        }
28257        __skb_insert(skb, prev, next, list);
28258    }
28259
28260    /*
28261     * Called for each packet when we find a new ACK
28262    endpoint sequence in it
28263     */
28264    static inline u32 tcp_queue_ack(struct sk_buff * skb,
28265    struct sock * sk)
28266    {
28267        /*
28268         *  When we ack the fin, we do the FIN
28269         *  processing.
28270         */
28271        skb->acked = 1;
28272        if (skb->h.th->fin)
28273            tcp_fin(skb,sk,skb->h.th);
28274        return skb->end_seq;
28275    }
28276
28277    static void tcp_queue(struct sk_buff * skb, struct sock
28278    * sk, struct tcphdr *th)
28279    {
28280        u32 ack_seq;
28281
28282        tcp_insert_skb(skb, &sk->receive_queue);
28283
28284        /*
28285         * Did we get anything new to ack?
28286         */
28287        ack_seq = sk->acked_seq;
28288
28289
28290        if (!after(skb->seq, ack_seq)) {
28291            if (after(skb->end_seq, ack_seq)) {
28292                /* the packet straddles our window end */
28293                struct sk_buff_head * list =
28294    &sk->receive_queue;
28295                struct sk_buff * next;
28296                ack_seq = tcp_queue_ack(skb, sk);
28297
28298                /*
28299                 * Do we have any old packets to ack that
28300    the above
28301                 * made visible? (Go forward from skb)
```

```
28302                 */
28303                next = skb->next;
28304                while (next != (struct sk_buff *) list) {
28305                    if (after(next->seq, ack_seq))
28306                        break;
28307                    if (after(next->end_seq, ack_seq))
28308                        ack_seq = tcp_queue_ack(next, sk);
28309                    next = next->next;
28310                }
28311
28312                /*
28313                 * Ok, we found new data, update acked_seq as
28314                 * necessary (and possibly send the actual
28315                 * ACK packet).
28316                 */
28317                sk->acked_seq = ack_seq;
28318
28319            } else {
28320                if (sk->debug)
28321                    printk("Ack duplicate packet.\n");
28322                tcp_send_ack(sk);
28323                return;
28324            }
28325
28326
28327            /*
28328             * Delay the ack if possible.  Send ack's to
28329             * fin frames immediately as there shouldn't be
28330             * anything more to come.
28331             */
28332            if (!sk->delay_acks || th->fin) {
28333                tcp_send_ack(sk);
28334            } else {
28335                /*
28336                 * If psh is set we assume it's an
28337                 * interactive session that wants quick
28338                 * acks to avoid nagling too much.
28339                 */
28340                int delay = HZ/2;
28341                if (th->psh)
28342                    delay = HZ/50;
28343                tcp_send_delayed_ack(sk, delay, sk->ato);
28344            }
28345
28346            /*
28347             *  Tell the user we have some more data.
28348             */
28349
```

```
28350            if (!sk->dead)
28351                sk->data_ready(sk,0);
28352
28353        }
28354        else
28355        {
28356            /*
28357             *  If we've missed a packet, send an ack.
28358             *  Also start a timer to send another.
28359             *
28360             *  4.3reno machines look for these kind of acks
28361    so
28362             *  they can do fast recovery. Three identical
28363    'old'
28364             *  acks lets it know that one frame has been
28365    lost
28366             *    and should be resent. Because this is
28367    before the
28368             *  whole window of data has timed out it can
28369    take
28370             *  one lost frame per window without stalling.
28371             *  [See Jacobson RFC1323, Stevens TCP/IP illus
28372    vol2]
28373             *
28374             *  We also should be spotting triple bad
28375    sequences.
28376             *  [We now do this.]
28377             *
28378             */
28379
28380            if (!skb->acked)
28381            {
28382                if(sk->debug)
28383                    printk("Ack past end of seq packet.\n");
28384                tcp_send_ack(sk);
28385                /*
28386                 * We need to be very careful here. We must
28387                 * not violate Jacobsons packet conservation
28388    condition.
28389                 * This means we should only send an ACK
28390    when a packet
28391                 * leaves the network. We can say a packet
28392    left the
28393                 * network when we see a packet leave the
28394    network, or
28395                 * when an rto measure expires.
28396                 */
28397                tcp_send_delayed_ack(sk,sk->rto,sk->rto);
28398            }
28399        }
28400    }
28401
28402
28403    /*
28404     *  This routine handles the data.  If there is room in
28405    the buffer,
28406     *  it will be have already been moved into it.  If
28407    there is no
28408     *  room, then we will just have to discard the packet.
28409     */
28410
28411    static int tcp_data(struct sk_buff *skb, struct sock
28412    *sk,
28413        unsigned long saddr, unsigned int len)
28414    {
28415        struct tcphdr *th;
28416        u32 new_seq, shut_seq;
28417
28418        th = skb->h.th;
28419        skb_pull(skb,th->doff*4);
28420        skb_trim(skb,len-(th->doff*4));
28421
28422        /*
28423         *  The bytes in the receive read/assembly queue has
28424    increased. Needed for the
28425         *  low memory discard algorithm
28426         */
28427
28428        sk->bytes_rcv += skb->len;
28429
28430        if (skb->len == 0 && !th->fin)
28431        {
28432            /*
28433             *  Don't want to keep passing ack's back and
28434    forth.
28435             *  (someone sent us dataless, boring frame)
28436             */
28437            if (!th->ack)
28438                tcp_send_ack(sk);
28439            kfree_skb(skb, FREE_READ);
28440            return(0);
28441        }
28442
28443
28444        /*
28445         *  We no longer have anyone receiving data on this
```

```
28446  connection.
28447      */
28448
28449  #ifndef TCP_DONT_RST_SHUTDOWN
28450
28451      if(sk->shutdown & RCV_SHUTDOWN)
28452      {
28453          /*
28454           *  FIXME: BSD has some magic to avoid sending
28455  resets to
28456           *  broken 4.2 BSD keepalives. Much to my
28457  surprise a few non
28458           *  BSD stacks still have broken keepalives so
28459  we want to
28460           *  cope with it.
28461           */
28462
28463          if(skb->len)    /* We don't care if it's just an
28464  ack or
28465                          a keepalive/window probe */
28466          {
28467              new_seq = skb->seq + skb->len + th->syn;
28468  /* Right edge of _data_ part of frame */
28469
28470              /* Do this the way 4.4BSD treats it. Not
28471  what I'd
28472                  regard as the meaning of the spec but
28473  it's what BSD
28474                  does and clearly they know everything 8)
28475  */
28476
28477              /*
28478               *  This is valid because of two things
28479               *
28480               *  a) The way tcp_data behaves at the
28481  bottom.
28482               *  b) A fin takes effect when read not when
28483  received.
28484               */
28485
28486              shut_seq = sk->acked_seq+1; /* Last byte */
28487
28488              if(after(new_seq,shut_seq))
28489              {
28490                  if(sk->debug)
28491                      printk("Data arrived on %p after
28492  close [Data right edge %X, Socket shut on %X] %d\n",
28493                          sk, new_seq, shut_seq, sk->blog);
28494                  if(sk->dead)
28495                  {
28496                      sk->acked_seq = new_seq + th->fin;
28497                      tcp_send_reset(sk->saddr, sk->daddr,
28498  skb->h.th,
28499                          sk->prot, NULL, skb->dev, 0,
28500  255);
28501                      tcp_statistics.TcpEstabResets++;
28502                      sk->err = EPIPE;
28503                      sk->error_report(sk);
28504                      sk->shutdown = SHUTDOWN_MASK;
28505                      tcp_set_state(sk,TCP_CLOSE);
28506                      kfree_skb(skb, FREE_READ);
28507                      return 0;
28508                  }
28509              }
28510          }
28511      }
28512
28513  #endif
28514
28515      /*
28516       * We should only call this if there is data in the
28517  frame.
28518       */
28519      tcp_delack_estimator(sk);
28520
28521      tcp_queue(skb, sk, th);
28522
28523      return(0);
28524  }
28525
28526
28527  /*
28528   *  This routine is only called when we have urgent data
28529   *  signalled. Its the 'slow' part of tcp_urg. It could
28530  be
28531   *  moved inline now as tcp_urg is only called from one
28532   *  place. We handle URGent data wrong. We have to - as
28533   *  BSD still doesn't use the correction from RFC961.
28534   *
28535   *  For 1003.1g we should support a new option
28536  TCP_STDURG to permit
28537   *  either form.
28538   */
28539
28540  static void tcp_check_urg(struct sock * sk, struct
28541  tcphdr * th)
```

p 564

```
28542  {
28543      u32 ptr = ntohs(th->urg_ptr);
28544
28545      if (ptr)
28546          ptr--;
28547      ptr += ntohl(th->seq);
28548
28549      /* ignore urgent data that we've already seen and
28550  read */
28551      if (after(sk->copied_seq, ptr))
28552          return;
28553
28554      /* do we already have a newer (or duplicate) urgent
28555  pointer? */
28556      if (sk->urg_data && !after(ptr, sk->urg_seq))
28557          return;
28558
28559      /* tell the world about our new urgent pointer */
28560      if (sk->proc != 0) {
28561          if (sk->proc > 0) {
28562              kill_proc(sk->proc, SIGURG, 1);
28563          } else {
28564              kill_pg(-sk->proc, SIGURG, 1);
28565          }
28566      }
28567      /*
28568       *  We may be adding urgent data when the last byte
28569  read was
28570       *  urgent. To do this requires some care. We cannot
28571  just ignore
28572       *  sk->copied_seq since we would read the last
28573  urgent byte again
28574       *  as data, nor can we alter copied_seq until this
28575  data arrives
28576       *  or we break the sematics of SIOCATMARK (and thus
28577  sockatmark())
28578       */
28579      if (sk->urg_seq == sk->copied_seq)
28580          sk->copied_seq++;   /* Move the copied sequence
28581  on correctly */
28582      sk->urg_data = URG_NOTYET;
28583      sk->urg_seq = ptr;
28584  }
28585
28586  /*
28587   *  This is the 'fast' part of urgent handling.
28588   */
28589
```

```
28590  static inline void tcp_urg(struct sock *sk, struct
28591  tcphdr *th, unsigned long len)
28592  {
28593      /*
28594       *  Check if we get a new urgent pointer - normally
28595  not
28596       */
28597
28598      if (th->urg)
28599          tcp_check_urg(sk,th);
28600
28601      /*
28602       *  Do we wait for any urgent data? - normally not
28603       */
28604
28605      if (sk->urg_data == URG_NOTYET) {
28606          u32 ptr;
28607
28608          /*
28609           *  Is the urgent pointer pointing into this
28610  packet?
28611           */
28612          ptr = sk->urg_seq - ntohl(th->seq) + th->doff*4;
28613          if (ptr < len) {
28614              sk->urg_data = URG_VALID | *(ptr + (unsigned
28615  char *) th);
28616              if (!sk->dead)
28617                  sk->data_ready(sk,0);
28618          }
28619      }
28620  }
28621
28622  /*
28623   * This should be a bit smarter and remove partially
28624   * overlapping stuff too, but this should be good
28625   * enough for any even remotely normal case (and the
28626   * worst that can happen is that we have a few
28627   * unnecessary packets in the receive queue).
28628   *
28629   * This function is never called with an empty list..
28630   */
28631  static inline void tcp_remove_dups(struct sk_buff_head *
28632  list)
28633  {
28634      struct sk_buff * next = list->next;
28635
28636      for (;;) {
28637          struct sk_buff * skb = next;
```

p 564

```
28638              next = next->next;
28639              if (next == (struct sk_buff *) list)
28640                  break;
28641              if (before(next->end_seq, skb->end_seq)) {
28642                  __skb_unlink(next, list);
28643                  kfree_skb(next, FREE_READ);
28644                  next = skb;
28645                  continue;
28646              }
28647              if (next->seq != skb->seq)
28648                  continue;
28649              __skb_unlink(skb, list);
28650              kfree_skb(skb, FREE_READ);
28651          }
28652      }
28653
28654      /*
28655       * Throw out all unnecessary packets: we've gone over the
28656       * receive queue limit. This shouldn't happen in a normal
28657       * TCP connection, but we might have gotten duplicates
28658      etc.
28659       */
28660      static void prune_queue(struct sk_buff_head * list)
28661      {
28662          for (;;) {
28663              struct sk_buff * skb = list->prev;
28664
28665              /* gone through it all? */
28666              if (skb == (struct sk_buff *) list)
28667                  break;
28668              if (!skb->acked) {
28669                  __skb_unlink(skb, list);
28670                  kfree_skb(skb, FREE_READ);
28671                  continue;
28672              }
28673              tcp_remove_dups(list);
28674              break;
28675          }
28676      }
28677
28678      #ifdef CONFIG_IP_TRANSPARENT_PROXY
28679      /*
28680       *  Check whether a received TCP packet might be for one
28681      of our
28682       *  connections.
28683       */
28684
28685      int tcp_chkaddr(struct sk_buff *skb)
```

```
28686      {
28687          struct iphdr *iph = skb->h.iph;
28688          struct tcphdr *th = (struct tcphdr *)(skb->h.raw +
28689      iph->ihl*4);
28690          struct sock *sk;
28691
28692          sk = tcp_v4_lookup(iph->saddr, th->source,
28693      iph->daddr, th->dest,
28694                  skb->dev);
28695          if (!sk)
28696              return 0;
28697          /* 0 means accept all LOCAL addresses here, not all
28698      the world... */
28699          if (sk->rcv_saddr == 0)
28700              return 0;
28701          return 1;
28702      }
28703      #endif
28704
28705      /*
28706       *  A TCP packet has arrived.
28707       *      skb->h.raw is the TCP header.
28708       */
28709
28710      int tcp_rcv(struct sk_buff *skb, struct device *dev,
28711      struct options *opt,
28712          __u32 daddr, unsigned short len,
28713          __u32 saddr, int redo, struct inet_protocol *
28714      protocol)
28715      {
28716          struct tcphdr *th;
28717          struct sock *sk;
28718          __u32 seq;
28719      #ifdef CONFIG_IP_TRANSPARENT_PROXY
28720          int r;
28721      #endif
28722
28723          /*
28724           * "redo" is 1 if we have already seen this skb but
28725      couldn't
28726           * use it at that time (the socket was locked).  In
28727      that case
28728           * we have already done a lot of the work (looked up
28729      the socket
28730           * etc).
28731           */
28732          th = skb->h.th;
28733          sk = skb->sk;
```

```
28734  #ifdef CONFIG_RST_COOKIES
28735      if (th->rst &&
28736  secure_tcp_probe_number(saddr,daddr,ntohs(th->source),nto
28737  hs(th->dest),ntohl(th->seq),1)) {
28738          add_clearance(saddr);
28739      }
28740  #endif
28741      if (!redo) {
28742          tcp_statistics.TcpInSegs++;
28743          if (skb->pkt_type!=PACKET_HOST)
28744              goto discard_it;
28745
28746          /*
28747           *  Pull up the IP header.
28748           */
28749
28750          skb_pull(skb, skb->h.raw-skb->data);
28751
28752          /*
28753           *  Try to use the device checksum if provided.
28754           */
28755          switch (skb->ip_summed)
28756          {
28757              case CHECKSUM_NONE:
28758                  skb->csum = csum_partial((char *)th,
28759  len, 0);
28760              case CHECKSUM_HW:
28761                  if (tcp_check(th, len, saddr, daddr,
28762  skb->csum))
28763                      goto discard_it;
28764              default:
28765                  /* CHECKSUM_UNNECESSARY */
28766          }
28767  #ifdef CONFIG_SYN_COOKIES
28768  retry_search:
28769  #endif
28770  #ifdef CONFIG_IP_TRANSPARENT_PROXY
28771          if (skb->redirport)
28772              sk = tcp_v4_proxy_lookup(saddr, th->source,
28773  daddr, th->dest, dev->pa_addr, skb->redirport, dev);
28774          else
28775  #endif
28776          sk = __tcp_v4_lookup(th, saddr, th->source,
28777  daddr, th->dest, dev);
28778          if (!sk)
28779              goto no_tcp_socket;
28780          skb->sk = sk;
28781          skb->seq = ntohl(th->seq);
```

```
28782          skb->end_seq = skb->seq + th->syn + th->fin +
28783  len - th->doff*4;
28784          skb->ack_seq = ntohl(th->ack_seq);
28785
28786          skb->acked = 0;
28787          skb->used = 0;
28788          skb->free = 1;
28789          skb->saddr = daddr;
28790          skb->daddr = saddr;
28791
28792          /*
28793           * We may need to add it to the backlog here.
28794           */
28795          if (sk->users)
28796          {
28797              __skb_queue_tail(&sk->back_log, skb);
28798              return(0);
28799          }
28800      }
28801
28802      /*
28803       *  If this socket has got a reset it's to all
28804  intents and purposes
28805       *  really dead. Count closed sockets as dead.
28806       *
28807       *  Note: BSD appears to have a bug here. A 'closed'
28808  TCP in BSD
28809       *  simply drops data. This seems incorrect as a
28810  'closed' TCP doesn't
28811       *  exist so should cause resets as if the port was
28812  unreachable.
28813       */
28814
28815      if (sk->zapped || sk->state==TCP_CLOSE) {
28816          goto no_tcp_socket;
28817      }
28818
28819      if (!sk->prot)
28820      {
28821          printk(KERN_CRIT "IMPOSSIBLE 3\n");
28822          return(0);
28823      }
28824
28825
28826      /*
28827       *  Charge the memory to the socket.
28828       */
28829
```

```
28830    skb->sk=sk;
28831    atomic_add(skb->truesize, &sk->rmem_alloc);
28832
28833        /*
28834         * Mark the time of the last received packet.
28835         */
28836        sk->idletime = jiffies;
28837
28838        /*
28839         *  We should now do header prediction.
28840         */
28841
28842        /*
28843         *  This basically follows the flow suggested by
28844    RFC793, with the corrections in RFC1122. We
28845         *  don't implement precedence and we process URG
28846    incorrectly (deliberately so) for BSD bug
28847         *  compatibility. We also set up variables more
28848    thoroughly [Karn notes in the
28849         *  KA9Q code the RFC793 incoming segment rules
28850    don't initialise the variables for all paths].
28851         */
28852
28853        if(sk->state!=TCP_ESTABLISHED)      /* Skip this lot
28854    for normal flow */
28855        {
28856
28857            /*
28858             *  Now deal with unusual cases.
28859             */
28860
28861            if(sk->state==TCP_LISTEN)
28862            {
28863                if (th->ack) {   /* These use the socket
28864    TOS.. might want to be the received TOS */
28865    #ifdef CONFIG_SYN_COOKIES
28866                    if (!th->syn && !th->rst) {
28867                        __u32 acked_seq =
28868    ntohl(th->ack_seq)-1;
28869                        int mtu_index = (acked_seq&0x7); /*
28870    extract MTU */
28871                        __u32 count = jiffies/(60*HZ);
28872
28873                        acked_seq = acked_seq&0xfffffff8;
28874
28875                        /* Any time in the last 2 minutes is
28876    OK */
28877                        if (acked_seq ==
28878    secure_tcp_syn_cookie(daddr,
28879
28880    saddr,ntohs(th->source),ntohs(th->dest),
28881                                ntohl(th->seq)-1,count)
28882                            || acked_seq ==
28883    secure_tcp_syn_cookie(daddr,
28884
28885    saddr,ntohs(th->source),ntohs(th->dest),
28886                                ntohl(th->seq)-1,count-1)
28887                            || acked_seq ==
28888    secure_tcp_syn_cookie(daddr,
28889
28890    saddr,ntohs(th->source),ntohs(th->dest),
28891                                ntohl(th->seq)-1,count-2)) {
28892                            /* If this passes, we need to
28893    fake up the
28894                             * new socket in TCP_SYN_SENT
28895    state and
28896                             * call ourselves recursively to
28897    handle
28898                             * the move to ESTABLISHED using
28899    the
28900                             * current packet. Nasty, but a
28901    cleaner
28902                             * solution would require major
28903    rewrites.
28904                             */
28905                            if (tcp_conn_request_fake(sk,
28906    skb, daddr, saddr, opt,
28907                                    dev,
28908    (acked_seq | mtu_index), cookie_mtu[mtu_index])) {
28909
28910                                goto retry_search;
28911                            }
28912                        }
28913                    }
28914    #endif
28915
28916    tcp_send_reset(daddr,saddr,th,sk->prot,opt,dev,0, 255);
28917                }
28918
28919                /*
28920                 * We don't care for RST, and non SYN are
28921    absorbed (old segments)
28922                 * Broadcast/multicast SYN isn't allowed.
28923    Note - bug if you change the
28924                 * netmask on a running connection it can
28925    go broadcast. Even Sun's have
```

```
28926                 *  this problem so I'm ignoring it
28927                 */
28928
28929      #ifdef CONFIG_IP_TRANSPARENT_PROXY
28930                 /*
28931                  * We may get non-local addresses and still
28932      want to
28933                  * handle them locally, due to transparent
28934      proxying.
28935                  * Thus, narrow down the test to what is
28936      really meant.
28937                  */
28938                 if(th->rst || !th->syn || th->ack || (r =
28939      ip_chk_addr(daddr)) == IS_BROADCAST || r == IS_MULTICAST)
28940      #else
28941                 if(th->rst || !th->syn || th->ack ||
28942      ip_chk_addr(daddr)!=IS_MYADDR)
28943      #endif
28944                 {
28945                     kfree_skb(skb, FREE_READ);
28946                     return 0;
28947                 }
28948
28949                 /*
28950                  * Guess we need to make a new socket up
28951                  */
28952                 seq = secure_tcp_sequence_number(saddr,
28953      daddr,
28954                          skb->h.th->dest,
28955                          skb->h.th->source);
28956                 tcp_conn_request(sk, skb, daddr, saddr, opt,
28957      dev, seq);
28958
28959                 /*
28960                  * Now we have several options: In theory
28961      there is nothing else
28962                  * in the frame. KA9Q has an option to send
28963      data with the syn,
28964                  * BSD accepts data with the syn up to the
28965      [to be] advertised window
28966                  * and Solaris 2.1 gives you a protocol
28967      error. For now we just ignore
28968                  * it, that fits the spec precisely and
28969      avoids incompatibilities. It
28970                  * would be nice in future to drop through
28971      and process the data.
28972                  *
28973                  * Now TTCP is starting to use we ought to
28974      queue this data.
28975                  */
28976
28977                 return 0;
28978             }
28979
28980             /*
28981              * Retransmitted SYN for our socket. This is
28982      uninteresting. If sk->state==TCP_LISTEN
28983              * then it's a new connection
28984              */
28985
28986             if (sk->state == TCP_SYN_RECV && th->syn &&
28987      skb->seq+1 == sk->acked_seq)
28988             {
28989                 kfree_skb(skb, FREE_READ);
28990                 return 0;
28991             }
28992
28993             /*
28994              * SYN sent means we have to look for a
28995      suitable ack and either reset
28996              * for bad matches or go to connected. The
28997      SYN_SENT case is unusual and should
28998              * not be in line code. [AC]
28999              */
29000
29001             if(sk->state==TCP_SYN_SENT)
29002             {
29003                 /* Crossed SYN or previous junk segment */
29004                 if(th->ack)
29005                 {
29006                     /* We got an ack, but it's not a good
29007      ack.
29008                      * We used to test this with a call to
29009      tcp_ack,
29010                      * but this loses, because it takes the
29011      SYN
29012                      * packet out of the send queue, even if
29013                      * the ACK doesn't have the SYN bit
29014      sent, and
29015                      * therefore isn't the one we are
29016      waiting for.
29017                      */
29018                     if (after(skb->ack_seq, sk->sent_seq) ||
29019      before(skb->ack_seq, sk->rcv_ack_seq))
29020                     {
29021                         /* Reset the ack - it's an ack from
```

```
29022  a
29023                          different connection  [ th->rst
29024  is checked in tcp_send_reset()] */
29025                          tcp_statistics.TcpAttemptFails++;
29026                          tcp_send_reset(daddr, saddr, th,
29027                              sk->prot, opt,dev,0,255);
29028                          kfree_skb(skb, FREE_READ);
29029                          return(0);
29030                      }
29031                  if(th->rst)
29032                      return tcp_reset(sk,skb);
29033                  if(!th->syn)
29034                  {
29035                      /* A valid ack from a different
29036  connection
29037                          start. Shouldn't happen but cover
29038  it */
29039                          tcp_statistics.TcpAttemptFails++;
29040
29041  tcp_send_reset(daddr, saddr, th,
29042                                      sk->prot,
29043  opt,dev,0,255);
29044                          kfree_skb(skb, FREE_READ);
29045                          return 0;
29046                  }
29047
29048                  /* process the ACK, get the SYN packet
29049  out
29050                      * of the send queue, do other initial
29051                      * processing stuff. [We know it's good,
29052  and
29053                      * we know it's the SYN,ACK we want.]
29054                      */
29055                  tcp_ack(sk,th,skb->ack_seq,len);
29056
29057                  /* We must check here (before
29058  tcp_options) whether
29059                      * peer advertised a zero sized window
29060  on us, else
29061                      * we end up with a zero sk->{mtu,mss}
29062  and thus bomb
29063                      * out in tcp_do_sendmsg. -DaveM
29064                      */
29065                  if(sk->max_window == 0)
29066                      sk->max_window = 32;
29067
29068                  /*
29069                    * Ok.. it's good. Set up sequence
29070  numbers and
29071                      *  move to established.
29072                      */
29073                  sk->acked_seq = skb->seq+1;
29074                  sk->lastwin_seq = skb->seq+1;
29075                  sk->fin_seq = skb->seq;
29076                  tcp_send_ack(sk);
29077                  tcp_set_state(sk, TCP_ESTABLISHED);
29078                  tcp_options(sk,th);
29079
29080  #if 0
29081                  sk->dummy_th.dest=th->source;
29082                  tcp_v4_rehash(sk);
29083  #endif
29084
29085                  sk->copied_seq = sk->acked_seq;
29086                  if(!sk->dead)
29087                  {
29088                      sk->state_change(sk);
29089                      sock_wake_async(sk->socket, 0);
29090                  }
29091
29092                  /* Reset the RTT estimator to the initial
29093                    * state rather than testing to avoid
29094                    * updating it on the ACK to the SYN
29095  packet.
29096                      */
29097                  sk->rtt = 0;
29098                  sk->rto = TCP_TIMEOUT_INIT;
29099                  sk->mdev = TCP_TIMEOUT_INIT;
29100              }
29101          else
29102          {
29103              /* See if SYN's cross. Drop if boring */
29104              if(th->syn && !th->rst)
29105              {
29106                  /* Crossed SYN's are fine - but
29107  talking to
29108                      yourself is right out... */
29109                  if(sk->saddr==saddr &&
29110  sk->daddr==daddr &&
29111                      sk->dummy_th.source==th->source
29112  &&
29113                      sk->dummy_th.dest==th->dest)
29114                  {
29115                      tcp_statistics.TcpAttemptFails++;
29116                      return tcp_reset(sk,skb);
29117                  }
```

```
29118                tcp_set_state(sk,TCP_SYN_RECV);
29119
29120                    /*
29121                     *  FIXME:
29122                     *  Must send SYN|ACK here
29123                     */
29124                }
29125                /* Discard junk segment */
29126                kfree_skb(skb, FREE_READ);
29127                return 0;
29128            }
29129            /*
29130             *  SYN_RECV with data maybe.. drop through
29131             */
29132            goto rfc_step6;
29133        }
29134
29135        /*
29136         *  BSD has a funny hack with TIME_WAIT and fast
29137    reuse of a port. There is
29138         *  a more complex suggestion for fixing these reuse
29139    issues in RFC1644
29140         *  but not yet ready for general use. Also see
29141    RFC1379.
29142         *
29143         *  Note the funny way we go back to the top of this
29144    function for
29145         *  this case ("goto try_next_socket").  That also
29146    takes care of
29147         *  checking "sk->users" for the new socket as well
29148    as doing all
29149         *  the normal tests on the packet.
29150         */
29151
29152    #define BSD_TIME_WAIT
29153    #ifdef BSD_TIME_WAIT
29154        if (sk->state == TCP_TIME_WAIT && th->syn &&
29155    sk->dead &&
29156            after(skb->seq, sk->acked_seq) && !th->rst)
29157        {
29158            u32 seq = sk->write_seq;
29159            if(sk->debug)
29160                printk("Doing a BSD time wait\n");
29161            tcp_statistics.TcpEstabResets++;
29162            atomic_sub(skb->truesize, &sk->rmem_alloc);
29163            skb->sk = NULL;
29164            sk->err=ECONNRESET;
29165            tcp_set_state(sk, TCP_CLOSE);
29166            sk->shutdown = SHUTDOWN_MASK;
29167    #ifdef CONFIG_IP_TRANSPARENT_PROXY
29168                /* What to do here?
29169                 * For the non-proxy case, this code is
29170    effectively almost a no-op,
29171                 * due to the sk = NULL.  Is that
29172    intentional?  If so, why shouldn't we
29173                 * do the same for the proxy case and get
29174    rid of some useless code?
29175                 */
29176                if (skb->redirport)
29177                    sk = tcp_v4_proxy_lookup(saddr,
29178    th->source, daddr, th->dest,
29179                            dev->pa_addr,
29180    skb->redirport, dev);
29181                else
29182    #endif
29183                sk = __tcp_v4_lookup(th, saddr, th->source,
29184    daddr, th->dest, dev);
29185                /* this is not really correct: we should
29186    check sk->users */
29187                if (sk && sk->state==TCP_LISTEN)
29188                {
29189                    skb->sk = sk;
29190                    atomic_add(skb->truesize,
29191    &sk->rmem_alloc);
29192                    /* FIXME: Is the sequence number addition
29193                     * of 128000 here enough for fast
29194    networks?
29195                     * Also, does this reduce the security of
29196                     * our tcp sequence numbers?
29197                     */
29198                    tcp_conn_request(sk, skb, daddr,
29199    saddr,opt, dev,seq+128000);
29200                    return 0;
29201                }
29202                kfree_skb(skb, FREE_READ);
29203                return 0;
29204        }
29205    #endif
29206        }
29207
29208        /*
29209         *  We are now in normal data flow (see the step
29210    list in the RFC)
29211         *  Note most of these are inline now. I'll inline
29212    the lot when
29213         *  I have time to test it hard and look at what gcc
```

```
29214   outputs
29215       */
29216
29217       if (!tcp_sequence(sk, skb->seq,
29218   skb->end_seq-th->syn))
29219       {
29220           bad_tcp_sequence(sk, th, skb->end_seq-th->syn,
29221   dev);
29222           kfree_skb(skb, FREE_READ);
29223           return 0;
29224       }
29225
29226       if(th->rst)
29227           return tcp_reset(sk,skb);
29228
29229       /*
29230        *  Check for a SYN, and ensure it matches the SYN
29231   we were
29232        *  first sent. We have to handle the rather unusual
29233   (but valid)
29234        *  sequence that KA9Q derived products may generate
29235   of
29236        *
29237        *  SYN
29238        *              SYN|ACK Data
29239        *  ACK (lost)
29240        *              SYN|ACK Data + More Data
29241        *  .. we must ACK not RST...
29242        *
29243        *  We keep syn_seq as the sequence space occupied
29244   by the
29245        *  original syn.
29246        */
29247
29248       if(th->syn && skb->seq!=sk->syn_seq)
29249       {
29250           tcp_send_reset(daddr,saddr,th, &tcp_prot, opt,
29251   dev,0, 255);
29252           return tcp_reset(sk,skb);
29253       }
29254
29255       /*
29256        *  Process the ACK
29257        */
29258
29259
29260       if(th->ack && !tcp_ack(sk,th,skb->ack_seq,len))
29261       {
```

```
29262           /*
29263            *  Our three way handshake failed.
29264            */
29265
29266           if(sk->state==TCP_SYN_RECV)
29267           {
29268               tcp_send_reset(daddr, saddr, th,sk->prot,
29269   opt, dev,0,255);
29270           }
29271           kfree_skb(skb, FREE_READ);
29272           return 0;
29273       }
29274
29275   rfc_step6:       /* I'll clean this up later */
29276
29277       /*
29278        *  If the accepted buffer put us over our queue
29279   size we
29280        *  now drop it (we must process the ack first to
29281   avoid
29282        *  deadlock cases).
29283        */
29284
29285       /*
29286        *  Process urgent data
29287        */
29288
29289       tcp_urg(sk, th, len);
29290
29291       /*
29292        *  Process the encapsulated data
29293        */
29294
29295       if(tcp_data(skb,sk, saddr, len))
29296           kfree_skb(skb, FREE_READ);
29297
29298       /*
29299        *  If we had a partial packet being help up due to
29300        *  application of Nagle's rule we are now free to
29301   send it.
29302        */
29303       if (th->ack
29304           && sk->packets_out == 0
29305           && sk->partial != NULL
29306           && skb_queue_empty(&sk->write_queue)
29307           && sk->send_head == NULL)
29308       {
29309           tcp_send_partial(sk);
```

p. 566

```
29310        }
29311
29312        /*
29313         *  If our receive queue has grown past its limits,
29314         *  try to prune away duplicates etc..
29315         */
29316        if (sk->rmem_alloc > sk->rcvbuf)
29317            prune_queue(&sk->receive_queue);
29318
29319        /*
29320         *  And done
29321         */
29322
29323        return 0;
29324
29325 no_tcp_socket:
29326        /*
29327         * No such TCB. If th->rst is 0 send a reset
29328 (checked in tcp_send_reset)
29329         */
29330        tcp_send_reset(daddr, saddr, th, &tcp_prot,
29331 opt,dev,0,255);
29332
29333 discard_it:
29334        /*
29335         *  Discard frame
29336         */
29337        skb->sk = NULL;
29338        kfree_skb(skb, FREE_READ);
29339        return 0;
29340 }
```

usr/src/linux/net/ipv4/tcp_output.c

```
29341 /*
29342  * INET       An implementation of the TCP/IP protocol
29343 suite for the LINUX
29344  *        operating system.  INET is implemented using the
29345 BSD Socket
29346  *        interface as the means of communication with the
29347 user level.
29348  *
29349  *        Implementation of the Transmission Control
29350 Protocol(TCP).
29351  *
29352  * Version: @(#)tcp_input.c 1.0.16   05/25/93
29353  *
29354  * Authors: Ross Biro, <bir7@leland.Stanford.Edu>
29355  *        Fred N. van Kempen, <waltje@uWalt.NL.Mugnet.ORG>
29356  *        Mark Evans, <evansmp@uhura.aston.ac.uk>
29357  *        Corey Minyard <wf-rch!minyard@relay.EU.net>
29358  *        Florian La Roche, <flla@stud.uni-sb.de>
29359  *        Charles Hedrick, <hedrick@klinzhai.rutgers.edu>
29360  *        Linus Torvalds, <torvalds@cs.helsinki.fi>
29361  *        Alan Cox, <gw4pts@gw4pts.ampr.org>
29362  *        Matthew Dillon, <dillon@apollo.west.oic.com>
29363  *        Arnt Gulbrandsen, <agulbra@nvg.unit.no>
29364  *        Jorge Cwik, <jorge@laser.satlink.net>
29365  *
29366  * Fixes:   Eric Schenk : avoid multiple retransmissions
29367 in one
29368  *                   : round trip timeout.
29369  *        Eric Schenk : tcp rst and syn cookies to deal
29370  *                   : with synflooding attacks.
29371  *        Eric Schenk : If a simultaneous close occurred,
29372 and the
29373  *                    connection was over an assymetric
29374 route, we
29375  *                    would lose badly if we dropped our
29376 outgoing
29377  *                    FIN because the route disappeared on
29378 us.
29379  *                    We now handle this case correctly.
29380  *        Eric Schenk : Handle the case where a route
29381 changes, and
29382  *                    thus the outgoing device does as well,
29383 when
29384  *                    skb's are on the retransmit queue
29385 which still
29386  *                    refer to the old obsolete destination.
29387  *        Elliot Poger   : Added support for
29388 SO_BINDTODEVICE.
29389  * Juan Jose Ciarlante : Added sock dynamic source
29390 address rewriting
29391  */
29392
29393 #include <linux/config.h>
29394 #include <net/tcp.h>
29395 #include <linux/ip_fw.h>
29396 #include <linux/firewall.h>
29397 #include <linux/interrupt.h>
29398 #ifdef CONFIG_RST_COOKIES
29399 #include <linux/random.h>
29400 #endif
29401
29402 /*
29403  * RFC 1122 says:
```

```
29404      *
29405      * "the suggested [SWS] avoidance algorithm for the
29406    receiver is to keep
29407      *   RECV.NEXT + RCV.WIN fixed until:
29408      *   RCV.BUFF - RCV.USER - RCV.WINDOW >= min(1/2
29409    RCV.BUFF, MSS)"
29410      *
29411      * We do BSD style SWS avoidance -- note that RFC1122
29412    only says we
29413      * must do silly window avoidance, it does not require
29414    that we use
29415      * the suggested algorithm. Following BSD avoids
29416    breaking header
29417      * prediction.
29418      *
29419      * The "rcvbuf" and "rmem_alloc" values are shifted by
29420    1, because
29421      * they also contain buffer handling overhead etc, so
29422    the window
29423      * we actually use is essentially based on only half
29424    those values.
29425      */
29426    int tcp_new_window(struct sock * sk)
29427    {
29428        unsigned long window = sk->window;
29429        unsigned long minwin, maxwin;
29430        unsigned long free_space;
29431
29432        /* Get minimum and maximum window values.. */
29433        minwin = sk->mss;
29434        if (!minwin)
29435            minwin = sk->mtu;
29436        if (!minwin) {
29437            printk(KERN_DEBUG "tcp_new_window: mss fell to
29438    0.\n");
29439            minwin = 1;
29440        }
29441        maxwin = sk->window_clamp;
29442        if (!maxwin)
29443            maxwin = MAX_WINDOW;
29444
29445        if (minwin > maxwin/2)
29446            minwin = maxwin/2;
29447
29448        /* Get current rcvbuf size.. */
29449        free_space = sk->rcvbuf/2;
29450        if (free_space < minwin) {
29451            sk->rcvbuf = minwin*2;
```

```
29452            free_space = minwin;
29453        }
29454
29455        /* Check rcvbuf against used and minimum window */
29456        free_space -= sk->rmem_alloc/2;
29457        if ((long)(free_space - minwin) < 0)         /* SWS
29458    avoidance */
29459            return 0;
29460
29461        /* Try to avoid the divide and multiply if we can */
29462        if (window <= free_space - minwin || window >
29463    free_space)
29464                window = (free_space/minwin)*minwin;
29465
29466        if (window > maxwin)
29467            window = maxwin;
29468        return window;
29469    }
29470
29471    /*
29472     * Get rid of any delayed acks, we sent one already..
29473     */
29474    static __inline__ void clear_delayed_acks(struct sock *
29475    sk)
29476    {
29477        sk->ack_timed = 0;
29478        sk->ack_backlog = 0;
29479        sk->bytes_rcv = 0;
29480        del_timer(&sk->delack_timer);
29481    }
29482
29483    /*
29484     * This is the main buffer sending routine. We queue
29485    the buffer
29486     * having checked it is sane seeming.
29487     */
29488
29489    void tcp_send_skb(struct sock *sk, struct sk_buff *skb)
29490    {
29491        int size;
29492        struct tcphdr * th = skb->h.th;
29493
29494        /*
29495         * length of packet (not counting length of pre-tcp
29496    headers)
29497         */
29498
29499        size = skb->len - ((unsigned char *) th - skb->data);
```

```
29500
29501        /*
29502         *   Sanity check it..
29503         */
29504
29505        if (size < sizeof(struct tcphdr) || size > skb->len)
29506        {
29507                printk(KERN_ERR "tcp_send_skb: bad skb (skb =
29508    %p, data = %p, th = %p, len = %lu)\n",
29509                    skb, skb->data, th, skb->len);
29510                kfree_skb(skb, FREE_WRITE);
29511                return;
29512        }
29513
29514        /*
29515         *   If we have queued a header size packet.. (these
29516    crash a few
29517         *   tcp stacks if ack is not set)
29518         */
29519
29520        if (size == sizeof(struct tcphdr))
29521        {
29522                /* If it's got a syn or fin it's notionally
29523    included in the size..*/
29524                if(!th->syn && !th->fin)
29525                {
29526                        printk(KERN_ERR "tcp_send_skb: attempt to
29527    queue a bogon.\n");
29528                        kfree_skb(skb,FREE_WRITE);
29529                        return;
29530                }
29531        }
29532
29533        /*
29534         *   Jacobson recommends this in the appendix of his
29535    SIGCOMM'88 paper.
29536         *   The idea is to do a slow start again if we
29537    haven't been doing
29538         *   anything for a long time, in which case we have
29539    no reason to
29540         *   believe that our congestion window is still
29541    correct.
29542         */
29543        if (sk->send_head == 0 && (jiffies - sk->idletime) >
29544    sk->rto) {
29545                sk->cong_window = 1;
29546                sk->cong_count = 0;
29547        }
```

```
29548
29549        /*
29550         *   Actual processing.
29551         */
29552
29553        tcp_statistics.TcpOutSegs++;
29554        skb->seq = ntohl(th->seq);
29555        skb->end_seq = skb->seq + size - 4*th->doff +
29556    th->fin;
29557
29558        /*
29559         *   We must queue if
29560         *
29561         *   a) The right edge of this frame exceeds the
29562    window
29563         *   b) We are retransmitting (Nagle's rule)
29564         *   c) We have too many packets 'in flight'
29565         */
29566
29567        if (after(skb->end_seq, sk->window_seq) ||
29568            (sk->retransmits && sk->ip_xmit_timeout ==
29569    TIME_WRITE) ||
29570                sk->packets_out >= sk->cong_window)
29571        {
29572                /* checksum will be supplied by tcp_write_xmit.
29573    So
29574                 * we shouldn't need to set it at all.  I'm
29575    being paranoid */
29576                th->check = 0;
29577                if (skb->next != NULL)
29578                {
29579                        printk(KERN_ERR "tcp_send_partial: next !=
29580    NULL\n");
29581                        skb_unlink(skb);
29582                }
29583                skb_queue_tail(&sk->write_queue, skb);
29584
29585                if (before(sk->window_seq,
29586    sk->write_queue.next->end_seq) &&
29587                        sk->send_head == NULL && sk->ack_backlog ==
29588    0)
29589                        tcp_reset_xmit_timer(sk, TIME_PROBE0,
29590    sk->rto);
29591        }
29592        else
29593        {
29594                /*
29595                 *   This is going straight out
```

```
29596              */
29597          clear_delayed_acks(sk);
29598          th->ack_seq = htonl(sk->acked_seq);
29599          th->window = htons(tcp_select_window(sk));
29600
29601          tcp_send_check(th, sk->saddr, sk->daddr, size,
29602   skb);
29603
29604          sk->sent_seq = sk->write_seq;
29605
29606          /*
29607           *  This is mad. The tcp retransmit queue is put
29608   together
29609           *  by the ip layer. This causes half the
29610   problems with
29611           *  unroutable FIN's and other things.
29612           */
29613
29614          sk->prot->queue_xmit(sk, skb->dev, skb, 0);
29615
29616          /*
29617           *  Set for next retransmit based on expected
29618   ACK time
29619           *  of the first packet in the resend queue.
29620           *  This is no longer a window behind.
29621           */
29622
29623          tcp_reset_xmit_timer(sk, TIME_WRITE, sk->rto);
29624      }
29625   }
29626
29627   /*
29628    *  Locking problems lead us to a messy situation where
29629   we can have
29630    *  multiple partially complete buffers queued up. This
29631   is really bad
29632    *  as we don't want to be sending partial buffers. Fix
29633   this with
29634    *  a semaphore or similar to lock tcp_write per socket.
29635    *
29636    *  These routines are pretty self descriptive.
29637    */
29638
29639   struct sk_buff * tcp_dequeue_partial(struct sock * sk)
29640   {
29641      struct sk_buff * skb;
29642      unsigned long flags;
29643
29644      save_flags(flags);
29645      cli();
29646      skb = sk->partial;
29647      if (skb) {
29648          sk->partial = NULL;
29649          del_timer(&sk->partial_timer);
29650      }
29651      restore_flags(flags);
29652      return skb;
29653   }
29654
29655   /*
29656    *  Empty the partial queue
29657    */
29658
29659   void tcp_send_partial(struct sock *sk)
29660   {
29661      struct sk_buff *skb;
29662
29663      if (sk == NULL)
29664          return;
29665      while ((skb = tcp_dequeue_partial(sk)) != NULL)
29666          tcp_send_skb(sk, skb);
29667   }
29668
29669   /*
29670    *  Queue a partial frame
29671    */
29672
29673   void tcp_enqueue_partial(struct sk_buff * skb, struct
29674   sock * sk)
29675   {
29676      struct sk_buff * tmp;
29677      unsigned long flags;
29678
29679      save_flags(flags);
29680      cli();
29681      tmp = sk->partial;
29682      if (tmp)
29683          del_timer(&sk->partial_timer);
29684      sk->partial = skb;
29685      init_timer(&sk->partial_timer);
29686      /*
29687       *  Wait up to 30 second for the buffer to fill.
29688       *  ( I have no idea why this timer is here!
29689       *    It seems to be sillyness for interactive
29690   response. Linus?
29691       *  )
```

```
29692          */
29693          sk->partial_timer.expires = jiffies+30*HZ;
29694          sk->partial_timer.function = (void (*)(unsigned
29695 long)) tcp_send_partial;
29696          sk->partial_timer.data = (unsigned long) sk;
29697          add_timer(&sk->partial_timer);
29698          restore_flags(flags);
29699          if (tmp)
29700                tcp_send_skb(sk, tmp);
29701 }
29702
29703 /*
29704  *  This routine takes stuff off of the write queue,
29705  *  and puts it in the xmit queue. This happens as
29706 incoming acks
29707  *  open up the remote window for us.
29708  */
29709
29710 void tcp_write_xmit(struct sock *sk)
29711 {
29712      struct sk_buff *skb;
29713
29714      /*
29715       *  The bytes will have to remain here. In time
29716 closedown will
29717       *  empty the write queue and all will be happy
29718       */
29719
29720      if(sk->zapped)
29721          return;
29722
29723      /*
29724       *  Anything on the transmit queue that fits the
29725 window can
29726       *  be added providing we are not
29727       *
29728       *  a) retransmitting (Nagle's rule)
29729       *  b) exceeding our congestion window.
29730       */
29731
29732      while((skb = skb_peek(&sk->write_queue)) != NULL &&
29733          !after(skb->end_seq, sk->window_seq) &&
29734          (sk->retransmits == 0 ||
29735           sk->ip_xmit_timeout != TIME_WRITE ||
29736           !after(skb->end_seq, sk->rcv_ack_seq))
29737          && sk->packets_out < sk->cong_window)
29738      {
29739          IS_SKB(skb);
```

```
29740          skb_unlink(skb);
29741
29742          /*
29743           *  See if we really need to send the whole
29744 packet.
29745           */
29746
29747          if (before(skb->end_seq, sk->rcv_ack_seq +1)) {
29748              /*
29749               *  This is acked data. We can discard it.
29750               *  This implies the packet was sent out
29751               *  of the write queue by a zero window
29752 probe.
29753               */
29754
29755              sk->retransmits = 0;
29756              kfree_skb(skb, FREE_WRITE);
29757              if (!sk->dead)
29758                  sk->write_space(sk);
29759          } else {
29760              struct tcphdr *th;
29761              struct iphdr *iph;
29762              int size;
29763
29764              iph = skb->ip_hdr;
29765              th = (struct tcphdr *)(((char *)iph)
29766 +(iph->ihl << 2));
29767
29768                          /* See if we need to shrink the
29769 leading packet on
29770                           * the retransmit queue.
29771 Strictly speaking, we
29772                           * should never need to do this,
29773 but some buggy TCP
29774                           * implementations get confused
29775 if you send them
29776                           * a packet that contains both
29777 old and new data. (Feh!)
29778                           * Soooo, we have this uglyness
29779 here.
29780                           */
29781              if (after(sk->rcv_ack_seq,skb->seq+th->syn))
29782                  tcp_shrink_skb(sk,skb,sk->rcv_ack_seq);
29783
29784              size = skb->len - (((unsigned char *) th) -
29785 skb->data);
29786 #ifndef CONFIG_NO_PATH_MTU_DISCOVERY
29787              if (size > sk->mtu - sizeof(struct iphdr))
```

p 567

```
29788                    {
29789                        iph->frag_off &= ~htons(IP_DF);
29790                        ip_send_check(iph);
29791                    }
29792    #endif
29793
29794    /*
29795     * put in the ack seq and window at this point rather
29796    than earlier,
29797     * in order to keep them monotonic.  We really want to
29798    avoid taking
29799     * back window allocations.  That's legal, but RFC1122
29800    says it's frowned on.
29801     * Ack and window will in general have changed since
29802    this packet was put
29803     * on the write queue.
29804     */
29805                    th->ack_seq = htonl(sk->acked_seq);
29806                    th->window = htons(tcp_select_window(sk));
29807
29808                    tcp_send_check(th, sk->saddr, sk->daddr,
29809    size, skb);
29810
29811                    sk->sent_seq = skb->end_seq;
29812
29813                    /*
29814                     *  IP manages our queue for some crazy
29815    reason
29816                     */
29817    #ifndef NO_DAVEM_FIX
29818                    sk->prot->queue_xmit(sk, skb->dev, skb, 0);
29819    #else
29820                    sk->prot->queue_xmit(sk, skb->dev, skb,
29821    skb->free);
29822    #endif
29823
29824                    clear_delayed_acks(sk);
29825
29826                    tcp_reset_xmit_timer(sk, TIME_WRITE,
29827    sk->rto);
29828                }
29829            }
29830    }
29831
29832
29833    /*
29834     * A socket has timed out on its send queue and wants
29835    to do a
```

```
29836     * little retransmitting. Currently this means TCP.
29837     */
29838
29839    void tcp_do_retransmit(struct sock *sk, int all)
29840    {
29841        struct sk_buff * skb;
29842        struct proto *prot;
29843        struct device *dev;
29844        struct rtable *rt;
29845
29846        prot = sk->prot;
29847        if (!all) {
29848            /*
29849             * If we are just retransmitting one packet reset
29850             * to the start of the queue.
29851             */
29852            sk->send_next = sk->send_head;
29853            sk->packets_out = 0;
29854        }
29855        skb = sk->send_next;
29856
29857        while (skb != NULL)
29858        {
29859            struct tcphdr *th;
29860            struct iphdr *iph;
29861            int size;
29862            unsigned long flags;
29863
29864            dev = skb->dev;
29865            IS_SKB(skb);
29866            skb->when = jiffies;
29867
29868            /* dl1bke 960201 - @%$$! Hope this cures strange
29869    race conditions    */
29870            /*          with AX.25 mode VC. (esp. DAMA)
29871       */
29872            /*          if the buffer is locked we should not
29873    retransmit */
29874            /*          anyway, so we don't need all the fuss
29875    to prepare */
29876            /*          the buffer in this case.
29877       */
29878            /*          (the skb_pull() changes skb->data
29879    while we may    */
29880            /*          actually try to send the data. Ouch.
29881    A side      */
29882            /*          effect is that we'll send some
29883    unnecessary data, */
```

p 567

```
29884            /*         but the alternative is disastrous...
29885     */
29886
29887         save_flags(flags);
29888         cli();
29889
29890         if (skb_device_locked(skb)) {
29891             restore_flags(flags);
29892             break;
29893         }
29894
29895         /* Unlink from any chain */
29896         skb_unlink(skb);
29897
29898         restore_flags(flags);
29899
29900         /*
29901          *  Discard the surplus MAC header
29902          */
29903
29904         skb_pull(skb,((unsigned char
29905 *)skb->ip_hdr)-skb->data);
29906
29907         /*
29908          * In general it's OK just to use the old
29909 packet.  However we
29910          * need to use the current ack and window
29911 fields.  Urg and
29912          * urg_ptr could possibly stand to be updated as
29913 well, but we
29914          * don't keep the necessary data.  That
29915 shouldn't be a problem,
29916          * if the other end is doing the right thing.
29917 Since we're
29918          * changing the packet, we have to issue a new
29919 IP identifier.
29920          */
29921
29922         iph = (struct iphdr *)skb->data;
29923         th = (struct tcphdr *)(((char *)iph) + (iph->ihl
29924 << 2));
29925
29926         /* See if we need to shrink the leading packet on
29927          * the retransmit queue. Strictly speaking, we
29928          * should never need to do this, but some buggy
29929 TCP
29930          * implementations get confused if you send them
29931          * a packet that contains both old and new data.
```

```
29932 (Feh!)
29933          * Soooo, we have this uglyness here.
29934          *
29935          * Is the && test needed here? If so, then it
29936 implies that
29937          * we might be retransmitting an acked packet.
29938 This code is
29939          * needed here to talk to Solaris 2.6 stack.
29940          */
29941         if (after(sk->rcv_ack_seq,skb->seq+th->syn) &&
29942 before(sk->rcv_ack_seq, skb->end_seq))
29943             tcp_shrink_skb(sk,skb,sk->rcv_ack_seq);
29944
29945         size = ntohs(iph->tot_len) - (iph->ihl<<2);
29946
29947         /*
29948          *  Note: We ought to check for window limits
29949 here but
29950          *  currently this is done (less efficiently)
29951 elsewhere.
29952          */
29953
29954         /*
29955          *  Put a MAC header back on (may cause ARPing)
29956          */
29957
29958         {
29959             /* ANK: UGLY, but the bug, that was here,
29960 should be fixed.
29961             */
29962             struct options * opt = (struct
29963 options*)skb->proto_priv;
29964             rt = ip_check_route(&sk->ip_route_cache,
29965 opt->srr?opt->faddr:iph->daddr,
29966                     skb->localroute,
29967 sk->bound_device);
29968         }
29969
29970         iph->id = htons(ip_id_count++);
29971 #ifndef CONFIG_NO_PATH_MTU_DISCOVERY
29972         if (rt && ntohs(iph->tot_len) > rt->rt_mtu)
29973             iph->frag_off &= ~htons(IP_DF);
29974 #endif
29975         ip_send_check(iph);
29976
29977         if (rt==NULL)   /* Deep poo */
29978         {
29979             if(skb->sk)
```

```
29980                    {
29981                        skb->sk->err_soft=ENETUNREACH;
29982                        skb->sk->error_report(skb->sk);
29983                    }
29984                    /* Can't transmit this packet, no reason
29985                     * to transmit the later ones, even if
29986                     * the congestion window allows.
29987                     */
29988                    break;
29989                }
29990                else
29991                {
29992                    dev=rt->rt_dev;
29993                    if (skb->dev != dev && skb->link3 == 0
29994                    && !skb_queue_empty(&sk->write_queue)) {
29995                        /* THIS IS UGLY. DON'T SHOW THIS TO YOUR
29996 MOTHER. --erics
29997                         * Route shifted devices.
29998                         * If this is the last packet in the
29999                         * retransmit queue, then we should walk
30000                         * the chain of packets in the
30001 write_queue
30002                         * that have the same device and
30003                         * fix routing on these packets as well.
30004                         * If we fail to do this, then every
30005 packet
30006                         * in the transmit queue will incurr a
30007                         * retransmit with the backed off
30008 retransmit
30009                         * timeout. This is very bad.
30010                         */
30011                        struct sk_buff *skb2 =
30012 sk->write_queue.next;
30013                        while (skb2 && skb2->dev == skb->dev) {
30014                            skb2->raddr=rt->rt_gateway;
30015                                                     if
30016 (sysctl_ip_dynaddr & 4 || (sk->state == TCP_SYN_SENT &&
30017 sysctl_ip_dynaddr & 3))
30018
30019 ip_rewrite_addrs (sk, skb2, dev);
30020                            skb_pull(skb2,((unsigned char
30021 *)skb2->ip_hdr)-skb2->data);
30022                            skb2->dev = dev;
30023                            skb2->arp=1;
30024                            if (rt->rt_hh)
30025                            {
30026
30027 memcpy(skb_push(skb2,dev->hard_header_len),rt->rt_hh->hh_
30028 data,dev->hard_header_len);
30029                                if (!rt->rt_hh->hh_uptodate)
30030                                {
30031                                    skb2->arp = 0;
30032 #if RT_CACHE_DEBUG >= 2
30033
30034 printk("tcp_do_retransmit(1): hh miss %08x via %08x\n",
30035 iph->daddr, rt->rt_gateway);
30036 #endif
30037                                }
30038                            }
30039                            else if (dev->hard_header)
30040                            {
30041                                if(dev->hard_header(skb2, dev,
30042 ETH_P_IP, NULL, NULL, skb2->len)<0)
30043                                    skb2->arp=0;
30044                            }
30045
30046                            skb2 = skb2->next;
30047                        }
30048                    }
30049                    skb->raddr=rt->rt_gateway;
30050                    if ((skb->dev !=dev || skb->dev->pa_addr !=
30051 skb->ip_hdr->saddr) && (sysctl_ip_dynaddr & 4 ||
30052 (sk->state == TCP_SYN_SENT && sysctl_ip_dynaddr & 3)))
30053                                         ip_rewrite_addrs(sk,
30054 skb, dev);
30055                    skb->dev=dev;
30056                    skb->arp=1;
30057 #ifdef CONFIG_FIREWALL
30058                    if (call_out_firewall(PF_INET, skb->dev,
30059 iph, NULL) < FW_ACCEPT) {
30060                        /* The firewall wants us to dump the
30061 packet.
30062                         * We have to check this here, because
30063                         * the drop in ip_queue_xmit only catches
30064 the
30065                         * first time we send it. We must drop on
30066                         * every resend as well.
30067                         */
30068                        break;
30069                    }
30070 #endif
30071                    if (rt->rt_hh)
30072                    {
30073
30074 memcpy(skb_push(skb,dev->hard_header_len),rt->rt_hh->hh_d
30075 ata,dev->hard_header_len);
```

```
30076                if (!rt->rt_hh->hh_uptodate)
30077                {
30078                    skb->arp = 0;
30079 #if RT_CACHE_DEBUG >= 2
30080                    printk("tcp_do_retransmit(2): hh
30081 miss %08x via %08x\n", iph->daddr, rt->rt_gateway);
30082 #endif
30083                }
30084            }
30085            else if (dev->hard_header)
30086            {
30087                if(dev->hard_header(skb, dev, ETH_P_IP,
30088 NULL, NULL, skb->len)<0)
30089                    skb->arp=0;
30090            }
30091
30092            /*
30093             *  This is not the right way to handle
30094 this. We have to
30095             *  issue an up to date window and ack
30096 report with this
30097             *  retransmit to keep the odd buggy tcp
30098 that relies on
30099             *  the fact BSD does this happy.
30100             *  We don't however need to recalculate the
30101 entire
30102             *  checksum, so someone wanting a small
30103 problem to play
30104             *  with might like to implement
30105 RFC1141/RFC1624 and speed
30106             *  this up by avoiding a full checksum.
30107             */
30108
30109            th->ack_seq = htonl(sk->acked_seq);
30110            clear_delayed_acks(sk);
30111            th->window = ntohs(tcp_select_window(sk));
30112            tcp_send_check(th, sk->saddr, sk->daddr,
30113 size, skb);
30114
30115            /*
30116             *  If the interface is (still) up and
30117 running, kick it.
30118             */
30119
30120            if (dev->flags & IFF_UP)
30121            {
30122                /*
30123                 *  If the packet is still being sent by
```

```
30124 the device/protocol
30125                 *  below then don't retransmit. This is
30126 both needed, and good -
30127                 *  especially with connected mode AX.25
30128 where it stops resends
30129                 *  occurring of an as yet unsent anyway
30130 frame!
30131                 *  We still add up the counts as the
30132 round trip time wants
30133                 *  adjusting.
30134                 */
30135                if (!skb_device_locked(skb))
30136                {
30137                    /* Now queue it */
30138                    ip_statistics.IpOutRequests++;
30139                    dev_queue_xmit(skb, dev,
30140 sk->priority);
30141                    sk->packets_out++;
30142                } else {
30143                    /* This shouldn't happen as we skip
30144 out above if the buffer is locked */
30145                    printk(KERN_WARNING
30146 "tcp_do_retransmit: sk_buff (%p) became locked\n", skb);
30147                }
30148            }
30149        }
30150
30151        /*
30152         *  Count retransmissions
30153         */
30154
30155        sk->prot->retransmits++;
30156        tcp_statistics.TcpRetransSegs++;
30157
30158        /*
30159         *  Record the high sequence number to help avoid
30160 doing
30161         *  to much fast retransmission.
30162         */
30163        if (sk->retransmits)
30164            sk->high_seq = sk->sent_seq;
30165
30166        /*
30167         *  Advance the send_next pointer so we don't
30168 keep
30169         *  retransmitting the same stuff every time we
30170 get an ACK.
30171         */
```

p 568 → 30155

```
30172              sk->send_next = skb->link3;
30173
30174          /*
30175           *  Only one retransmit requested.
30176           */
30177
30178          if (!all)
30179              break;
30180
30181          /*
30182           *  This should cut it off before we send too
30183    many packets.
30184           */
30185
30186          if (sk->packets_out >= sk->cong_window)
30187              break;
30188
30189          skb = skb->link3;
30190      }
30191  }
30192
30193  /*
30194   *  This routine will send an RST to the other tcp.
30195   */
30196
30197  void tcp_send_reset(unsigned long saddr, unsigned long
30198  daddr, struct tcphdr *th,
30199        struct proto *prot, struct options *opt, struct
30200  device *dev, int tos, int ttl)
30201  {
30202      struct sk_buff *buff;
30203      struct tcphdr *t1;
30204      int tmp;
30205      struct device *ndev=NULL;
30206
30207      /*
30208       *  Cannot reset a reset (Think about it).
30209       */
30210
30211      if(th->rst)
30212          return;
30213
30214      /*
30215       * We need to grab some memory, and put together an
30216  RST,
30217       * and then put it into the queue to be sent.
30218       */
30219
30220      buff = alloc_skb(MAX_RESET_SIZE, GFP_ATOMIC);
30221      if (buff == NULL)
30222          return;
30223
30224      buff->sk = NULL;
30225      buff->dev = dev;
30226      buff->localroute = 0;
30227      buff->csum = 0;
30228
30229      /*
30230       *  Put in the IP header and routing stuff.
30231       */
30232
30233      tmp = prot->build_header(buff, saddr, daddr, &ndev,
30234  IPPROTO_TCP, opt,
30235              sizeof(struct tcphdr),tos,ttl,NULL);
30236      if (tmp < 0)
30237      {
30238          buff->free = 1;
30239          sock_wfree(NULL, buff);
30240          return;
30241      }
30242
30243      t1 =(struct tcphdr *)skb_put(buff,sizeof(struct
30244  tcphdr));
30245      memset(t1, 0, sizeof(*t1));
30246
30247      /*
30248       *  Swap the send and the receive.
30249       */
30250
30251      t1->dest = th->source;
30252      t1->source = th->dest;
30253      t1->doff = sizeof(*t1)/4;
30254      t1->rst = 1;
30255
30256      if(th->ack)
30257      {
30258          t1->seq = th->ack_seq;
30259      }
30260      else
30261      {
30262          t1->ack = 1;
30263          if(!th->syn)
30264              t1->ack_seq = th->seq;
30265          else
30266              t1->ack_seq = htonl(ntohl(th->seq)+1);
30267      }
```

p 568

```
30268
30269        tcp_send_check(t1, saddr, daddr, sizeof(*t1), buff);
30270        prot->queue_xmit(NULL, ndev, buff, 1);
30271        tcp_statistics.TcpOutSegs++;
30272 }
30273
30274 #ifdef CONFIG_RST_COOKIES
30275 /*
30276  *  This routine will send a bad SYNACK to the remote tcp
30277  *  containing a secure sequence number.
30278  *  This should evoke a reset with a cookie, so we can
30279 verify
30280  *  the existence of the remote machine.
30281  */
30282
30283 void tcp_send_synack_probe(unsigned long saddr, unsigned
30284 long daddr, struct tcphdr *th,
30285       struct proto *prot, struct options *opt, struct
30286 device *dev, int tos, int ttl)
30287 {
30288        struct sk_buff *buff;
30289        struct tcphdr *t1;
30290        int tmp;
30291        struct device *ndev=NULL;
30292
30293        /*
30294         * We need to grab some memory, and put together a
30295 SYNACK,
30296         * and then put it into the queue to be sent.
30297         */
30298
30299        buff = alloc_skb(MAX_SYN_SIZE, GFP_ATOMIC);
30300        if (buff == NULL)
30301            return;
30302
30303        buff->sk = NULL;
30304        buff->dev = dev;
30305        buff->localroute = 0;
30306        buff->csum = 0;
30307
30308        /*
30309         *  Put in the IP header and routing stuff.
30310         */
30311
30312        tmp = prot->build_header(buff, saddr, daddr, &ndev,
30313 IPPROTO_TCP, opt,
30314                  sizeof(struct tcphdr),tos,ttl,NULL);
30315        if (tmp < 0)
```

```
30316        {
30317            buff->free = 1;
30318            sock_wfree(NULL, buff);
30319            return;
30320        }
30321
30322        t1 = (struct tcphdr *)skb_put(buff,sizeof(struct
30323 tcphdr));
30324
30325        memcpy(t1, th, sizeof(*t1));
30326        /*
30327         *  Swap the send and the receive.
30328         */
30329        t1->dest = th->source;
30330        t1->source = th->dest;
30331        t1->ack_seq = t1->seq =
30332 htonl(secure_tcp_probe_number(daddr,saddr,
30333
30334 ntohs(th->source),ntohs(th->dest),ntohl(th->seq),0));
30335        t1->window = htons(1024);    /* make up a window
30336 here. */
30337        t1->syn = 1;
30338        t1->ack = 1;
30339        t1->urg = 0;
30340        t1->rst = 0;
30341        t1->psh = 0;
30342        t1->fin = 0;          /* In case someone sent us a
30343 SYN|FIN frame! */
30344        t1->doff = sizeof(*t1)/4;
30345
30346        tcp_send_check(t1, saddr, daddr, sizeof(*t1), buff);
30347        prot->queue_xmit(NULL, ndev, buff, 1);
30348        tcp_statistics.TcpOutSegs++;
30349 }
30350 #endif
30351
30352 /*
30353  *  Send a fin.
30354  */
30355
30356 void tcp_send_fin(struct sock *sk)
30357 {
30358        struct proto *prot =(struct proto *)sk->prot;
30359        struct tcphdr *th =(struct tcphdr *)&sk->dummy_th;
30360        struct tcphdr *t1;
30361        struct sk_buff *buff;
30362        struct device *dev=NULL;
30363        int tmp;
```

p 568

```
30364
30365        buff = sock_wmalloc(sk, MAX_RESET_SIZE,1 ,
30366 GFP_KERNEL);
30367
30368        if (buff == NULL)
30369        {
30370              /* This is a disaster if it occurs */
30371              printk(KERN_CRIT "tcp_send_fin: Impossible
30372 malloc failure");
30373              return;
30374        }
30375
30376        /*
30377         *  Administrivia
30378         */
30379
30380        buff->sk = sk;
30381        buff->localroute = sk->localroute;
30382        buff->csum = 0;
30383
30384        /*
30385         *  Put in the IP header and routing stuff.
30386         */
30387
30388        tmp = prot->build_header(buff,sk->saddr, sk->daddr,
30389 &dev,
30390                    IPPROTO_TCP, sk->opt,
30391                    sizeof(struct
30392 tcphdr),sk->ip_tos,sk->ip_ttl,&sk->ip_route_cache);
30393        if (tmp < 0)
30394        {
30395              /* Oh oh. We couldn't route the packet, and we
30396 can't afford
30397               * to drop it from the queue, since we will fail
30398 to retransmit
30399               * then, and we never try to initiate a close
30400 again.
30401               * Drop it onto the loopback device. The worst
30402 thing that
30403               * happens is that the send gets droped when it
30404 comes out the
30405               * the other side. If we get lucky it might even
30406 get forward
30407               * to its real destination.
30408               * WARNING: there are a few subtle points here.
30409               * 1) We assume that if we build the header
30410 using the
30411               *    loopback we can not fail. The only way
30412 this can happen
30413               *    right now is if someone marks the loopback
30414 as
30415               *    a gateway. This should never happen. Be
30416 careful
30417               *    not to change that without taking this
30418 case into account.
30419               * 2) If we fail to queue up the FIN packet here
30420 we get
30421               *    bitten later when we receive a
30422 simultaneous FIN.
30423               *    See the comments in tcp_fin().
30424               */
30425              dev = &loopback_dev;
30426              tmp = prot->build_header(buff,sk->saddr,
30427 sk->daddr, &dev,
30428                    IPPROTO_TCP, sk->opt,
30429                    sizeof(struct
30430 tcphdr),sk->ip_tos,sk->ip_ttl,&sk->ip_route_cache);
30431              if (tmp < 0) {
30432                    printk(KERN_CRIT "tcp_send_fin: Impossible
30433 loopback failure");
30434                    return;
30435              }
30436        }
30437
30438        clear_delayed_acks(sk);
30439
30440        /*
30441         *  We ought to check if the end of the queue is a
30442 buffer and
30443         *  if so simply add the fin to that buffer, not
30444 send it ahead.
30445         */
30446
30447        t1 =(struct tcphdr *)skb_put(buff,sizeof(struct
30448 tcphdr));
30449        buff->dev = dev;
30450        memcpy(t1, th, sizeof(*t1));
30451        buff->seq = sk->write_seq;
30452        sk->write_seq++;
30453        buff->end_seq = sk->write_seq;
30454        t1->seq = htonl(buff->seq);
30455        t1->ack_seq = htonl(sk->acked_seq);
30456        t1->window = htons(tcp_select_window(sk));
30457        t1->fin = 1;
30458        tcp_send_check(t1, sk->saddr, sk->daddr,
30459 sizeof(*t1), buff);
```

```
30460
30461        /*
30462         * If there is data in the write queue, the fin must
30463  be appended to
30464         * the write queue.
30465         */
30466
30467        if (skb_peek(&sk->write_queue) != NULL)
30468        {
30469            buff->free = 0;
30470            if (buff->next != NULL)
30471            {
30472                printk(KERN_ERR "tcp_send_fin: next !=
30473  NULL\n");
30474                skb_unlink(buff);
30475            }
30476            skb_queue_tail(&sk->write_queue, buff);
30477        }
30478        else
30479        {
30480            sk->sent_seq = sk->write_seq;
30481            sk->prot->queue_xmit(sk, dev, buff, 0);
30482            tcp_reset_xmit_timer(sk, TIME_WRITE, sk->rto);
30483        }
30484  }
30485
30486
30487  void tcp_send_synack(struct sock * newsk, struct sock *
30488  sk, struct sk_buff * skb, int destroy)
30489  {
30490        struct tcphdr *t1;
30491        unsigned char *ptr;
30492        struct sk_buff * buff;
30493        struct device *ndev=NULL;
30494        int tmp;
30495
30496        buff = sock_wmalloc(newsk, MAX_SYN_SIZE, 1,
30497  GFP_ATOMIC);
30498        if (buff == NULL)
30499        {
30500            sk->err = ENOMEM;
30501            destroy_sock(newsk);
30502            kfree_skb(skb, FREE_READ);
30503            tcp_statistics.TcpAttemptFails++;
30504            return;
30505        }
30506
30507        buff->sk = newsk;
```

```
30508        buff->localroute = newsk->localroute;
30509
30510        /*
30511         *  Put in the IP header and routing stuff.
30512         */
30513
30514        tmp = sk->prot->build_header(buff, newsk->saddr,
30515  newsk->daddr, &ndev,
30516                      IPPROTO_TCP, newsk->opt,
30517  MAX_SYN_SIZE,sk->ip_tos,sk->ip_ttl,&newsk->ip_route_cache
30518  );
30519
30520        /*
30521         *  Something went wrong.
30522         */
30523
30524        if (tmp < 0)
30525        {
30526            sk->err = tmp;
30527            buff->free = 1;
30528            kfree_skb(buff,FREE_WRITE);
30529            destroy_sock(newsk);
30530            skb->sk = sk;
30531            kfree_skb(skb, FREE_READ);
30532            tcp_statistics.TcpAttemptFails++;
30533            return;
30534        }
30535
30536        t1 =(struct tcphdr *)skb_put(buff,sizeof(struct
30537  tcphdr));
30538
30539        memcpy(t1, skb->h.th, sizeof(*t1));
30540        buff->seq = newsk->write_seq++;
30541        buff->end_seq = newsk->write_seq;
30542        /*
30543         *  Swap the send and the receive.
30544         */
30545        t1->dest = skb->h.th->source;
30546        t1->source = newsk->dummy_th.source;
30547        t1->seq = ntohl(buff->seq);
30548        newsk->sent_seq = newsk->write_seq;
30549        t1->window = ntohs(tcp_select_window(newsk));
30550        t1->syn = 1;
30551        t1->ack = 1;
30552        t1->urg = 0;
30553        t1->rst = 0;
30554        t1->psh = 0;
30555        t1->ack_seq = htonl(newsk->acked_seq);
```

p 568

```
30556        t1->doff = sizeof(*t1)/4+1;
30557        ptr = skb_put(buff,4);
30558        ptr[0] = 2;
30559        ptr[1] = 4;
30560        ptr[2] = ((newsk->mtu) >> 8) & 0xff;
30561        ptr[3] =(newsk->mtu) & 0xff;
30562        buff->csum = csum_partial(ptr, 4, 0);
30563 #ifdef CONFIG_SYN_COOKIES
30564        /* Don't save buff on the newsk chain if we are
30565 going to destroy
30566         * newsk anyway in a second, it just delays getting
30567 rid of newsk.
30568         */
30569        if (destroy) {
30570            /* BUFF was charged to NEWSK, _this_ is what we
30571 want
30572             * to undo so the SYN cookie can be killed now.
30573 SKB
30574             * is charged to SK, below we will undo that when
30575             * we kfree SKB.
30576             */
30577            buff->sk = NULL;
30578            atomic_sub(buff->truesize, &newsk->wmem_alloc);
30579        }
30580 #endif
30581        tcp_send_check(t1, newsk->saddr, newsk->daddr,
30582 sizeof(*t1)+4, buff);
30583        if (destroy)
30584            newsk->prot->queue_xmit(NULL, ndev, buff, 1);
30585        else
30586            newsk->prot->queue_xmit(newsk, ndev, buff, 0);
30587
30588
30589 #ifdef CONFIG_SYN_COOKIES
30590        if (destroy) {
30591            /*
30592             * Get rid of the newsk structure if this was a
30593 cookie.
30594             */
30595            destroy_sock(newsk);
30596            skb->sk = sk;
30597            kfree_skb(skb, FREE_READ);
30598        } else {
30599 #endif
30600            tcp_reset_xmit_timer(newsk, TIME_WRITE ,
30601 TCP_TIMEOUT_INIT);
30602            skb->sk = newsk;
30603
30604        /*
30605         * Charge the sock_buff to newsk.
30606         */
30607        atomic_sub(skb->truesize, &sk->rmem_alloc);
30608        atomic_add(skb->truesize, &newsk->rmem_alloc);
30609
30610        skb_queue_tail(&sk->receive_queue,skb);
30611        sk->ack_backlog++;
30612 #ifdef CONFIG_SYN_COOKIES
30613    }
30614 #endif
30615    tcp_statistics.TcpOutSegs++;
30616 }
30617
30618 /*
30619  * Set up the timers for sending a delayed ack..
30620  *
30621  *      rules for delaying an ack:
30622  *      - delay time <= 0.5 HZ
30623  *      - must send at least every 2 full sized packets
30624  *      - we don't have a window update to send
30625  *
30626  * additional thoughts:
30627  * - we should not delay sending an ACK if we have ato
30628 > 0.5 HZ.
30629  *      My thinking about this is that in this case we
30630 will just be
30631  *      systematically skewing the RTT calculation. (The
30632 rule about
30633  *      sending every two full sized packets will never
30634 need to be
30635  *      invoked, the delayed ack will be sent before the
30636 ATO timeout
30637  *      every time. Of course, the relies on our having a
30638 good estimate
30639  *      for packet interarrival times.)
30640  */
30641 void tcp_send_delayed_ack(struct sock * sk, int
30642 max_timeout, unsigned long timeout)
30643 {
30644    /* Calculate new timeout */
30645    if (timeout > max_timeout)
30646        timeout = max_timeout;
30647    if (sk->bytes_rcv >= sk->max_unacked)
30648        timeout = 0;
30649    timeout += jiffies;
30650
30651    /* Use new timeout only if there wasn't a older one
```

p 568

```
30652    earlier  */
30653        if (!del_timer(&sk->delack_timer) || timeout <
30654    sk->delack_timer.expires)
30655            sk->delack_timer.expires = timeout;
30656
30657        sk->ack_backlog++;
30658        add_timer(&sk->delack_timer);
30659    }
30660
30661
30662
30663    /*
30664     *  This routine sends an ack and also updates the
30665    window.
30666     */
30667
30668    void tcp_send_ack(struct sock *sk)
30669    {
30670        struct sk_buff *buff;
30671        struct tcphdr *t1;
30672        struct device *dev = NULL;
30673        int tmp;
30674
30675        if(sk->zapped)
30676            return;      /* We have been reset, we may not
30677    send again */
30678
30679        /*
30680         *  If we have nothing queued for transmit and the
30681    transmit timer
30682         *  is on we are just doing an ACK timeout and need
30683    to switch
30684         *  to a keepalive.
30685         */
30686
30687        clear_delayed_acks(sk);
30688
30689        if (sk->send_head == NULL
30690            && skb_queue_empty(&sk->write_queue)
30691            && sk->ip_xmit_timeout == TIME_WRITE)
30692        {
30693            if (sk->keepopen)
30694
30695    tcp_reset_xmit_timer(sk,TIME_KEEPOPEN,TCP_TIMEOUT_LEN);
30696            else
30697                del_timer(&sk->retransmit_timer);
30698        }
30699
```

```
30700        /*
30701         * We need to grab some memory, and put together an
30702    ack,
30703         * and then put it into the queue to be sent.
30704         */
30705
30706        buff = sock_wmalloc(sk, MAX_ACK_SIZE, 1, GFP_ATOMIC);
30707        if (buff == NULL)
30708        {
30709            /*
30710             *  Force it to send an ack. We don't have to do
30711    this
30712             *  (ACK is unreliable) but it's much better use
30713    of
30714             *  bandwidth on slow links to send a spare ack
30715    than
30716             *  resend packets.
30717             */
30718
30719            tcp_send_delayed_ack(sk, HZ/2, HZ/2);
30720            return;
30721        }
30722
30723        /*
30724         *  Assemble a suitable TCP frame
30725         */
30726
30727        buff->sk = sk;
30728        buff->localroute = sk->localroute;
30729        buff->csum = 0;
30730
30731        /*
30732         *  Put in the IP header and routing stuff.
30733         */
30734
30735        tmp = sk->prot->build_header(buff, sk->saddr,
30736    sk->daddr, &dev,
30737                    IPPROTO_TCP, sk->opt,
30738    MAX_ACK_SIZE,sk->ip_tos,sk->ip_ttl,&sk->ip_route_cache);
30739        if (tmp < 0)
30740        {
30741            buff->free = 1;
30742            sock_wfree(sk, buff);
30743            return;
30744        }
30745
30746    #ifndef CONFIG_NO_PATH_MTU_DISCOVERY
30747        buff->ip_hdr->frag_off |= htons(IP_DF);
```

```
30748    #endif
30749
30750        t1 =(struct tcphdr *)skb_put(buff,sizeof(struct
30751    tcphdr));
30752
30753        /*
30754         *  Fill in the packet and send it
30755         */
30756
30757        memcpy(t1, &sk->dummy_th, sizeof(*t1));
30758        t1->seq    = htonl(sk->sent_seq);
30759        t1->ack_seq = htonl(sk->acked_seq);
30760        t1->window = htons(tcp_select_window(sk));
30761
30762        tcp_send_check(t1, sk->saddr, sk->daddr,
30763    sizeof(*t1), buff);
30764        if (sk->debug)
30765            printk(KERN_ERR "\rtcp_ack: seq %x ack %x\n",
30766    sk->sent_seq, sk->acked_seq);
30767        sk->prot->queue_xmit(sk, dev, buff, 1);
30768        tcp_statistics.TcpOutSegs++;
30769    }
30770
30771    /*
30772     *  This routine sends a packet with an out of date
30773    sequence
30774     *  number. It assumes the other end will try to ack it.
30775     */
30776
30777    void tcp_write_wakeup(struct sock *sk)
30778    {
30779        struct sk_buff *buff,*skb;
30780        struct tcphdr *t1;
30781        struct device *dev=NULL;
30782        int tmp;
30783
30784        if (sk->zapped)
30785            return; /* After a valid reset we can send no
30786    more */
30787
30788        /*
30789         *  Write data can still be
30790    transmitted/retransmitted in the
30791         *  following states.  If any other state is
30792    encountered, return.
30793         *  [listen/close will never occur here anyway]
30794         */
30795
30796        if (sk->state != TCP_ESTABLISHED &&
30797            sk->state != TCP_CLOSE_WAIT &&
30798            sk->state != TCP_FIN_WAIT1 &&
30799            sk->state != TCP_LAST_ACK &&
30800            sk->state != TCP_CLOSING
30801        )
30802        {
30803            return;
30804        }
30805        if ( before(sk->sent_seq, sk->window_seq) &&
30806            (skb=skb_peek(&sk->write_queue)))
30807        {
30808            /*
30809             *  We are probing the opening of a window
30810             *  but the window size is != 0
30811             *  must have been a result SWS avoidance (
30812    sender )
30813             */
30814
30815            struct iphdr *iph;
30816            struct tcphdr *th;
30817            struct tcphdr *nth;
30818            unsigned long win_size;
30819    #if 0
30820        unsigned long ow_size;
30821    #endif
30822
30823            /*
30824             *  Recover the buffer pointers
30825             */
30826
30827            iph = (struct iphdr *)skb->ip_hdr;
30828            th = (struct tcphdr *)(((char *)iph)
30829    +(iph->ihl << 2));
30830
30831            /*
30832             *  How many bytes can we send ?
30833             */
30834
30835            /* During window probes, don't try to send more
30836    than is
30837             *  actually in the skb we've taken off the send
30838    queue here.
30839             */
30840            win_size = skb->len - (((unsigned char *) th) -
30841    skb->data);
30842            win_size -= th->doff * 4;
30843
```

p 569

```
30844            /* Don't send more than the offered window! */
30845            win_size = min(win_size, sk->window_seq -
30846   sk->sent_seq);
30847
30848            /*
30849             *  Grab the data for a temporary frame
30850             */
30851
30852            buff = sock_wmalloc(sk, win_size + th->doff
30853   * 4 +
30854                    (iph->ihl << 2) +
30855                    sk->prot->max_header + 15,
30856                    1, GFP_ATOMIC);
30857            if ( buff == NULL )
30858                return;
30859
30860            /*
30861             *  If we strip the packet on the write queue we
30862   must
30863             *  be ready to retransmit this one
30864             */
30865
30866            buff->free = /*0*/1;
30867
30868            buff->sk = sk;
30869            buff->localroute = sk->localroute;
30870
30871            /*
30872             *  Put headers on the new packet
30873             */
30874
30875            tmp = sk->prot->build_header(buff,
30876   sk->saddr, sk->daddr, &dev,
30877                    IPPROTO_TCP, sk->opt,
30878   buff->truesize,
30879
30880   sk->ip_tos,sk->ip_ttl,&sk->ip_route_cache);
30881            if (tmp < 0)
30882            {
30883            sock_wfree(sk, buff);
30884            return;
30885        }
30886
30887            /*
30888             *  Move the TCP header over
30889             */
30890
30891        buff->dev = dev;
```

```
30892
30893            nth = (struct tcphdr *)
30894   skb_put(buff,sizeof(*th));
30895
30896        memcpy(nth, th, sizeof(*th));
30897
30898        /*
30899         *  Correct the new header
30900         */
30901
30902        nth->ack = 1;
30903        nth->ack_seq = htonl(sk->acked_seq);
30904        nth->window = htons(tcp_select_window(sk));
30905        nth->check = 0;
30906
30907        /*
30908         *  Copy TCP options and data start to our new
30909   buffer
30910         */
30911
30912        buff->csum = csum_partial_copy((void *)(th + 1),
30913   skb_put(buff,win_size),
30914            win_size + th->doff*4 - sizeof(*th), 0);
30915
30916    /*
30917     *  Remember our right edge sequence number.
30918     */
30919
30920        buff->end_seq = sk->sent_seq + win_size;
30921        sk->sent_seq = buff->end_seq;       /* Hack
30922   */
30923        if(th->urg && ntohs(th->urg_ptr) < win_size)
30924            nth->urg = 0;
30925
30926    /*
30927     *  Checksum the split buffer
30928     */
30929
30930        tcp_send_check(nth, sk->saddr, sk->daddr,
30931            nth->doff * 4 + win_size , buff);
30932    }
30933    else
30934    {
30935        buff = sock_wmalloc(sk,MAX_ACK_SIZE,1,
30936   GFP_ATOMIC);
30937        if (buff == NULL)
30938            return;
30939
```

```
30940            buff->free = 1;
30941            buff->sk = sk;
30942            buff->localroute = sk->localroute;
30943            buff->csum = 0;
30944
30945            /*
30946             *  Put in the IP header and routing stuff.
30947             */
30948
30949            tmp = sk->prot->build_header(buff, sk->saddr,
30950    sk->daddr, &dev,
30951                    IPPROTO_TCP, sk->opt,
30952    MAX_ACK_SIZE,sk->ip_tos,sk->ip_ttl,&sk->ip_route_cache);
30953            if (tmp < 0)
30954            {
30955                sock_wfree(sk, buff);
30956                return;
30957            }
30958
30959            t1 = (struct tcphdr *)skb_put(buff,sizeof(struct
30960    tcphdr));
30961            memcpy(t1,(void *) &sk->dummy_th, sizeof(*t1));
30962
30963            /*
30964             *  Use a previous sequence.
30965             *  This should cause the other end to send an
30966    ack.
30967             */
30968
30969            t1->seq = htonl(sk->sent_seq-1);
30970    /*      t1->fin = 0;     -- We are sending a 'previous'
30971    sequence, and 0 bytes of data - thus no FIN bit */
30972            t1->ack_seq = htonl(sk->acked_seq);
30973            t1->window = htons(tcp_select_window(sk));
30974            tcp_send_check(t1, sk->saddr, sk->daddr,
30975    sizeof(*t1), buff);
30976
30977        }
30978
30979        /*
30980         *  Send it.
30981         */
30982
30983        sk->prot->queue_xmit(sk, dev, buff, 1);
30984        tcp_statistics.TcpOutSegs++;
30985    }
30986
30987    /*
```

```
30988     *  A window probe timeout has occurred.
30989     */
30990
30991    void tcp_send_probe0(struct sock *sk)
30992    {
30993        if (sk->zapped)
30994            return;      /* After a valid reset we can send
30995    no more */
30996
30997        tcp_write_wakeup(sk);
30998
30999        sk->backoff++;
31000        sk->rto = min(sk->rto << 1, 120*HZ);
31001        sk->retransmits++;
31002        sk->prot->retransmits ++;
31003        tcp_reset_xmit_timer (sk, TIME_PROBE0, sk->rto);
31004    }
31005
31006    /*
31007     * Remove the portion of a packet that has already been
31008    sent.
31009     * Needed to deal with buggy TCP implementations that
31010    can't deal
31011     * with seeing a packet that contains some data that has
31012    already
31013     * been received.
31014     *
31015     * Note that the SYN sequence number is at the start of
31016    the packet
31017     * while the FIN is at the end. This means that we
31018    always clear out
31019     * the SYN bit, and never clear out the FIN bit.
31020     */
31021    void tcp_shrink_skb(struct sock *sk, struct sk_buff
31022    *skb, u32 ack)
31023    {
31024        struct iphdr *iph;
31025        struct tcphdr *th;
31026        unsigned char *old, *new;
31027        unsigned long len;
31028        int diff;
31029
31030        /*
31031         *  Recover the buffer pointers
31032         */
31033
31034        iph = (struct iphdr *)skb->ip_hdr;
31035        th = (struct tcphdr *)(((char *)iph) +(iph->ihl <<
```

p 569 (line 30991)
p 569 (line 31021)

```
31036    2));
31037
31038         /* how much data are we droping from the tcp frame */
31039         diff = ack - (skb->seq + th->syn);
31040         /* how much data are we keeping in the tcp frame */
31041         len = (skb->end_seq - th->fin) - ack;
31042
31043         /* pointers to new start of remaining data, and old
31044    start */
31045         new = (unsigned char *)th + th->doff*4;
31046         old = new+diff;
31047
31048         /* Update our starting seq number */
31049         skb->seq = ack;
31050         th->seq = htonl(ack);
31051         th->syn = 0;          /* Turn SYN off as it is
31052    logically at the start of the packet */
31053
31054         iph->tot_len = htons(ntohs(iph->tot_len)-diff);
31055         ip_send_check(iph);
31056
31057         /* Get the partial checksum for the IP options */
31058         if (th->doff*4 - sizeof(*th) > 0)
31059             skb->csum = csum_partial((void *)(th+1),
31060                     th->doff*4-sizeof(*th),0);
31061         else
31062             skb->csum = 0;
31063
31064         /* Copy the good data down and get it's checksum */
31065         skb->csum = csum_partial_copy((void *)old,(void
31066    *)new,len,skb->csum);
31067
31068         /* shorten the skb */
31069         skb_trim(skb,skb->len-diff);
31070
31071         /* Checksum the shrunk buffer */
31072         tcp_send_check(th, sk->saddr, sk->daddr,
31073                 th->doff * 4 + len , skb);
31074    }
```

usr/src/linux/net/ipv4/tcp_timer.c

```
31075    /*
31076     * INET      An implementation of the TCP/IP protocol
31077    suite for the LINUX
31078     *        operating system.  INET is implemented using the
31079    BSD Socket
31080     *        interface as the means of communication with the
31081    user level.
31082     *
31083     *        Implementation of the Transmission Control
31084    Protocol(TCP).
31085     *
31086     * Version: @(#)tcp.c    1.0.16   05/25/93
31087     *
31088     * Authors: Ross Biro, <bir7@leland.Stanford.Edu>
31089     *        Fred N. van Kempen, <waltje@uWalt.NL.Mugnet.ORG>
31090     *        Mark Evans, <evansmp@uhura.aston.ac.uk>
31091     *        Corey Minyard <wf-rch!minyard@relay.EU.net>
31092     *        Florian La Roche, <flla@stud.uni-sb.de>
31093     *        Charles Hedrick, <hedrick@klinzhai.rutgers.edu>
31094     *        Linus Torvalds, <torvalds@cs.helsinki.fi>
31095     *        Alan Cox, <gw4pts@gw4pts.ampr.org>
31096     *        Matthew Dillon, <dillon@apollo.west.oic.com>
31097     *        Arnt Gulbrandsen, <agulbra@nvg.unit.no>
31098     *        Jorge Cwik, <jorge@laser.satlink.net>
31099     *
31100     * Fixes:
31101     *
31102     *        Eric Schenk : Fix retransmission timeout
31103    counting.
31104     */
31105
31106    #include <net/tcp.h>
31107
31108    void tcp_delack_timer(unsigned long data)
31109    {
31110        tcp_send_ack((struct sock *) data);
31111    }
31112
31113    /*
31114     *  Reset the retransmission timer
31115     */
31116
31117    void tcp_reset_xmit_timer(struct sock *sk, int why,
31118    unsigned long when)
31119    {
31120        del_timer(&sk->retransmit_timer);
31121        sk->ip_xmit_timeout = why;
31122        if (why == TIME_WRITE) {
31123            /* In this case we want to timeout on the first
31124    packet
31125             * in the resend queue. If the resend queue is
31126    empty,
31127             * then the packet we are sending hasn't made it
31128    there yet,
31129             * so we timeout from the current time.
```

p 569 → 31108
p 569 → 31117

```
31130              */
31131          if (sk->send_head) {
31132              sk->retransmit_timer.expires =
31133                  sk->send_head->when + when;
31134          } else {
31135              /* This should never happen!
31136               */
31137              printk(KERN_ERR "Error: send_head NULL in
31138  xmit_timer\n");
31139              sk->ip_xmit_timeout = 0;
31140              return;
31141          }
31142      } else {
31143          sk->retransmit_timer.expires = jiffies+when;
31144      }
31145
31146      if (sk->retransmit_timer.expires < jiffies) {
31147          /* We can get here if we reset the timer on an
31148  event
31149           * that could not fire because the interrupts
31150  were disabled.
31151           * make sure it happens soon.
31152           */
31153          sk->retransmit_timer.expires = jiffies+2;
31154      }
31155      add_timer(&sk->retransmit_timer);
31156  }
31157
31158  /*
31159   *  POLICY:
31160   *
31161   *  This is the normal code called for timeouts.  It
31162  does the retransmission
31163   *  and then does backoff.  tcp_do_retransmit is
31164  separated out because
31165   *  tcp_ack needs to send stuff from the retransmit
31166  queue without
31167   *  initiating a backoff.
31168   */
31169
31170
31171  static void tcp_retransmit_time(struct sock *sk, int all)
31172  {
31173      /*
31174       * record how many times we've timed out.
31175       * This determines when we should quite trying.
31176       * This needs to be counted here, because we should
31177  not be
31178       * counting one per packet we send, but rather one
31179  per round
31180       * trip timeout.
31181       */
31182      sk->retransmits++;
31183
31184      tcp_do_retransmit(sk, all);
31185
31186      /*
31187       * Increase the timeout each time we retransmit.
31188  Note that
31189       * we do not increase the rtt estimate.  rto is
31190  initialized
31191       * from rtt, but increases here.  Jacobson (SIGCOMM
31192  88) suggests
31193       * that doubling rto each time is the least we can
31194  get away with.
31195       * In KA9Q, Karn uses this for the first few times,
31196  and then
31197       * goes to quadratic.  netBSD doubles, but only goes
31198  up to *64,
31199       * and clamps at 1 to 64 sec afterwards.  Note that
31200  120 sec is
31201       * defined in the protocol as the maximum possible
31202  RTT.  I guess
31203       * we'll have to use something other than TCP to
31204  talk to the
31205       * University of Mars.
31206       *
31207       * PAWS allows us longer timeouts and large windows,
31208  so once
31209       * implemented ftp to mars will work nicely. We will
31210  have to fix
31211       * the 120 second clamps though!
31212       */
31213
31214      sk->backoff++;
31215      sk->rto = min(sk->rto << 1, 120*HZ);
31216
31217      /* be paranoid about the data structure... */
31218      if (sk->send_head)
31219          tcp_reset_xmit_timer(sk, TIME_WRITE, sk->rto);
31220      else
31221          /* This should never happen! */
31222          printk(KERN_ERR "send_head NULL in
31223  tcp_retransmit_time\n");
31224  }
31225
```

```
31226    /*
31227     *  POLICY:
31228     *      Congestion control.
31229     *
31230     *  A timer event has trigger a tcp retransmit timeout.
31231  The
31232     *  socket xmit queue is ready and set up to send.
31233  Because
31234     *  the ack receive code keeps the queue straight we do
31235     *  nothing clever here.
31236     */
31237
31238  void tcp_retransmit(struct sock *sk, int all)
31239  {
31240      if (all)
31241      {
31242          tcp_retransmit_time(sk, all);
31243          return;
31244      }
31245
31246      /* remember window where we lost */
31247      sk->ssthresh = min(sk->cong_window,
31248
31249  (sk->window_seq-sk->rcv_ack_seq)/max(sk->mss,1)) >> 1;
31250      /* sk->ssthresh in theory can be zero.  I guess
31251  that's OK */
31252      sk->cong_count = 0;
31253      sk->cong_window = 1;
31254
31255      /* Do the actual retransmit. */
31256      tcp_retransmit_time(sk, all);
31257  }
31258
31259  /*
31260   *  A write timeout has occurred. Process the after
31261  effects. BROKEN (badly)
31262   */
31263
31264  static int tcp_write_timeout(struct sock *sk)
31265  {
31266      /*
31267       *  Look for a 'soft' timeout.
31268       */
31269      if ((sk->state == TCP_ESTABLISHED && sk->retransmits
31270  && !(sk->retransmits & 7))
31271          || (sk->state != TCP_ESTABLISHED &&
31272  sk->retransmits > TCP_RETR1))
31273      {
```

```
31274      /*
31275       *  Attempt to recover if arp has changed
31276  (unlikely!) or
31277       *  a route has shifted (not supported prior to
31278  1.3).
31279       */
31280      ip_rt_advice(&sk->ip_route_cache, 0);
31281      }
31282
31283      /*
31284       *  Have we tried to SYN too many times (repent
31285  repent 8))
31286       *  NOTE: we must be careful to do this test for both
31287       *  the SYN_SENT and SYN_RECV states, otherwise we
31288  take
31289       *  23 minutes to timeout on the SYN_RECV state,
31290  which
31291       *  leaves us (more) open to denial of service
31292  attacks
31293       *  than we would like.
31294       */
31295
31296      if (sk->retransmits > TCP_SYN_RETRIES
31297      && (sk->state==TCP_SYN_SENT ||
31298  sk->state==TCP_SYN_RECV))
31299      {
31300          if(sk->err_soft)
31301              sk->err=sk->err_soft;
31302          else
31303              sk->err=ETIMEDOUT;
31304          sk->error_report(sk);
31305          del_timer(&sk->retransmit_timer);
31306          tcp_statistics.TcpAttemptFails++;    /* Is this
31307  right ??? - FIXME - */
31308          tcp_set_state(sk,TCP_CLOSE);
31309          /* Don't FIN, we got nothing back */
31310          return 0;
31311      }
31312      /*
31313       *  Has it gone just too far ?
31314       */
31315      if (sk->retransmits > TCP_RETR2)
31316      {
31317          if(sk->err_soft)
31318              sk->err = sk->err_soft;
31319          else
31320              sk->err = ETIMEDOUT;
31321          sk->error_report(sk);
```

```
31322            del_timer(&sk->retransmit_timer);
31323            /*
31324             *  Time wait the socket
31325             */
31326            if (sk->state == TCP_FIN_WAIT1 || sk->state ==
31327    TCP_FIN_WAIT2 || sk->state == TCP_CLOSING )
31328            {
31329                 tcp_set_state(sk,TCP_TIME_WAIT);
31330                 tcp_reset_msl_timer (sk, TIME_CLOSE,
31331    TCP_TIMEWAIT_LEN);
31332            }
31333            else
31334            {
31335                 /*
31336                  *  Clean up time.
31337                  */
31338                 tcp_set_state(sk, TCP_CLOSE);
31339                 return 0;
31340            }
31341        }
31342        return 1;
31343  }
31344
31345  /*
31346   *  It could be we got here because we needed to send an
31347  ack,
31348   *  so we need to check for that and not just normal
31349  retransmit.
31350   */
31351  static void tcp_time_write_timeout(struct sock * sk)
31352  {
31353        /*
31354         *  Retransmission
31355         */
31356        sk->prot->retransmit (sk, 0);
31357        tcp_write_timeout(sk);
31358  }
31359
31360
31361  /*
31362   *  The TCP retransmit timer. This lacks a few small
31363  details.
31364   *
31365   *  1.  An initial rtt timeout on the probe0 should
31366  cause what we can
31367   *      of the first write queue buffer to be split and
31368  sent.
31369   *  2.  On a 'major timeout' as defined by RFC1122 we
```

```
31370  shouldn't report
31371   *      ETIMEDOUT if we know an additional 'soft' error
31372  caused this.
31373   *      tcp_err should save a 'soft error' for us.
31374   */
31375
31376  void tcp_retransmit_timer(unsigned long data)
31377  {
31378        struct sock *sk = (struct sock*)data;
31379        int why = sk->ip_xmit_timeout;
31380
31381        /*
31382         *  We are reset. We will send no more retransmits.
31383         */
31384
31385        if(sk->zapped)
31386            return;
31387
31388        /*
31389         *  Only process if socket is not in use
31390         */
31391
31392        if (sk->users)
31393        {
31394            /* Try again in 1 second */
31395            sk->retransmit_timer.expires = jiffies+HZ;
31396            add_timer(&sk->retransmit_timer);
31397            return;
31398        }
31399
31400        if (sk->ack_backlog && !sk->dead)
31401            sk->data_ready(sk,0);
31402
31403        /* Now we need to figure out why the socket was on
31404  the timer. */
31405
31406        switch (why)
31407        {
31408        /* Window probing */
31409        case TIME_PROBE0:
31410            tcp_send_probe0(sk);
31411            tcp_write_timeout(sk);
31412            break;
31413
31414        /* Retransmitting */
31415        case TIME_WRITE:
31416            tcp_time_write_timeout(sk);
31417            break;
```

```
31418
31419        /* Sending Keepalives */
31420        case TIME_KEEPOPEN:
31421            /*
31422             * this reset_timer() call is a hack, this is not
31423             * how KEEPOPEN is supposed to work.
31424             */
31425            tcp_reset_xmit_timer (sk, TIME_KEEPOPEN,
31426   TCP_TIMEOUT_LEN);
31427            /* Send something to keep the connection open. */
31428            if (sk->prot->write_wakeup)
31429                sk->prot->write_wakeup (sk);
31430            sk->retransmits++;
31431            sk->prot->retransmits++;
31432            tcp_write_timeout(sk);
31433            break;
31434
31435        default:
31436            printk (KERN_ERR "rexmit_timer: timer expired -
31437   reason unknown\n");
31438            break;
31439        }
31440   }
```

usr/src/linux/net/ipv4/timer.c

```
31441   /*
31442    * INET      An implementation of the TCP/IP protocol
31443   suite for the LINUX
31444    *         operating system.  INET is implemented using the
31445   BSD Socket
31446    *         interface as the means of communication with the
31447   user level.
31448    *
31449    *         TIMER - implementation of software timers for IP.
31450    *
31451    * Version: @(#)timer.c 1.0.7    05/25/93
31452    *
31453    * Authors: Ross Biro, <bir7@leland.Stanford.Edu>
31454    *         Fred N. van Kempen, <waltje@uWalt.NL.Mugnet.ORG>
31455    *         Corey Minyard <wf-rch!minyard@relay.EU.net>
31456    *         Fred Baumgarten,
31457   <dc6iq@insu1.etec.uni-karlsruhe.de>
31458    *         Florian La Roche, <flla@stud.uni-sb.de>
31459    *
31460    * Fixes:
31461    *         Alan Cox    :   To avoid destroying a wait queue
31462   as we use it
31463    *                         we defer destruction until the
```

```
31464   destroy timer goes
31465    *                         off.
31466    *         Alan Cox    :   Destroy socket doesn't write a
31467   status value to the
31468    *                         socket buffer _AFTER_ freeing it!
31469   Also sock ensures
31470    *                         the socket will get removed BEFORE
31471   this is called
31472    *                         otherwise if the timer TIME_DESTROY
31473   occurs inside
31474    *                         of inet_bh() with this socket being
31475   handled it goes
31476    *                         BOOM! Have to stop timer going off
31477   if net_bh is
31478    *                         active or the destroy causes crashes.
31479    *         Alan Cox    :   Cleaned up unused code.
31480    *
31481    *         This program is free software; you can
31482   redistribute it and/or
31483    *         modify it under the terms of the GNU General
31484   Public License
31485    *         as published by the Free Software Foundation;
31486   either version
31487    *         2 of the License, or (at your option) any later
31488   version.
31489    */
31490
31491   #include <linux/types.h>
31492   #include <linux/errno.h>
31493   #include <linux/socket.h>
31494   #include <linux/in.h>
31495   #include <linux/kernel.h>
31496   #include <linux/sched.h>
31497   #include <linux/timer.h>
31498   #include <asm/system.h>
31499   #include <linux/interrupt.h>
31500   #include <linux/inet.h>
31501   #include <linux/netdevice.h>
31502   #include <net/ip.h>
31503   #include <net/protocol.h>
31504   #include <net/tcp.h>
31505   #include <linux/skbuff.h>
31506   #include <net/sock.h>
31507   #include <net/arp.h>
31508
31509   void delete_timer (struct sock *t)
31510   {
31511       unsigned long flags;
```

p 552

```
31512
31513        save_flags (flags);
31514        cli();
31515
31516        t->timeout = 0;
31517        del_timer (&t->timer);
31518
31519        restore_flags (flags);
31520 }
31521
31522 void reset_timer (struct sock *t, int timeout, unsigned
31523 long len)
31524 {
31525        delete_timer (t);
31526        t->timeout = timeout;
31527 #if 1
31528   /* FIXME: ??? */
31529        if ((int) len < 0)  /* prevent close to infinite
31530 timers. THEY _DO_ */
31531          len = 3;     /* happen (negative values ?) -
31532 don't ask me why ! -FB */
31533 #endif
31534        t->timer.expires = jiffies+len;
31535        add_timer (&t->timer);
31536 }
31537
31538
31539 /*
31540  *  Now we will only be called whenever we need to do
31541  *  something, but we must be sure to process all of the
31542  *  sockets that need it.
31543  */
31544
31545 void net_timer (unsigned long data)
31546 {
31547        struct sock *sk = (struct sock*)data;
31548        int why = sk->timeout;
31549
31550        /*
31551         * only process if socket is not in use
31552         */
31553
31554        if (sk->users)
31555        {
31556            sk->timer.expires = jiffies+HZ;
31557            add_timer(&sk->timer);
31558            sti();
31559            return;
```

```
31560        }
31561
31562     /* Always see if we need to send an ack. */
31563
31564        if (sk->ack_backlog && !sk->zapped)
31565        {
31566            sk->prot->read_wakeup (sk);
31567            if (! sk->dead)
31568                sk->data_ready(sk,0);
31569        }
31570
31571     /* Now we need to figure out why the socket was on
31572 the timer. */
31573
31574        switch (why)
31575        {
31576            case TIME_DONE:
31577                /* If the socket hasn't been closed off,
31578 re-try a bit later */
31579                if (!sk->dead) {
31580                    reset_timer(sk, TIME_DONE,
31581 TCP_DONE_TIME);
31582                    break;
31583                }
31584
31585                if (sk->state != TCP_CLOSE)
31586                {
31587                    printk ("non CLOSE socket in
31588 time_done\n");
31589                    break;
31590                }
31591                destroy_sock (sk);
31592                break;
31593
31594            case TIME_DESTROY:
31595            /*
31596             *  We've waited for a while for all the memory
31597 associated with
31598             *  the socket to be freed.
31599             */
31600
31601                destroy_sock(sk);
31602                break;
31603
31604            case TIME_CLOSE:
31605                /* We've waited long enough, close the
31606 socket. */
31607                tcp_set_state(sk, TCP_CLOSE);
```

```
31608            if (!sk->dead)
31609                sk->state_change(sk);
31610            sk->shutdown = SHUTDOWN_MASK;
31611            break;
31612
31613        default:
31614            printk ("net_timer: timer expired - reason
31615 %d is unknown\n", why);
31616            break;
31617        }
31618 }
31619
```

usr/src/linux/net/ipv4/udp.c

```
31620 /*
31621  * INET      An implementation of the TCP/IP protocol
31622 suite for the LINUX
31623  *        operating system.  INET is implemented using the
31624 BSD Socket
31625  *        interface as the means of communication with the
31626 user level.
31627  *
31628  *        The User Datagram Protocol (UDP).
31629  *
31630  * Version: @(#)udp.c   1.0.13   06/02/93
31631  *
31632  * Authors: Ross Biro, <bir7@leland.Stanford.Edu>
31633  *        Fred N. van Kempen, <waltje@uWalt.NL.Mugnet.ORG>
31634  *        Arnt Gulbrandsen, <agulbra@nvg.unit.no>
31635  *        Alan Cox, <Alan.Cox@linux.org>
31636  *
31637  * Fixes:
31638  *        Alan Cox    :   verify_area() calls
31639  *        Alan Cox    :   stopped close while in use off
31640 icmp
31641  *                   messages. Not a fix but a botch that
31642  *                   for udp at least is 'valid'.
31643  *        Alan Cox    :   Fixed icmp handling properly
31644  *        Alan Cox    :   Correct error for oversized
31645 datagrams
31646  *        Alan Cox    :   Tidied select() semantics.
31647  *        Alan Cox    :   udp_err() fixed properly, also
31648 now
31649  *                   select and read wake correctly on
31650 errors
31651  *        Alan Cox    :   udp_send verify_area moved to
31652 avoid mem leak
31653  *        Alan Cox    :   UDP can count its memory
31654  *        Alan Cox    :   send to an unknown connection
31655 causes
31656  *                   an ECONNREFUSED off the icmp, but
31657  *                   does NOT close.
31658  *        Alan Cox    :   Switched to new sk_buff
31659 handlers. No more backlog!
31660  *        Alan Cox    :   Using generic datagram code.
31661 Even smaller and the PEEK
31662  *                   bug no longer crashes it.
31663  *        Fred Van Kempen :   Net2e support for
31664 sk->broadcast.
31665  *        Alan Cox    :   Uses skb_free_datagram
31666  *        Alan Cox    :   Added get/set sockopt support.
31667  *        Alan Cox    :   Broadcasting without option set
31668 returns EACCES.
31669  *        Alan Cox    :   No wakeup calls. Instead we now
31670 use the callbacks.
31671  *        Alan Cox    :   Use ip_tos and ip_ttl
31672  *        Alan Cox    :   SNMP Mibs
31673  *        Alan Cox    :   MSG_DONTROUTE, and 0.0.0.0
31674 support.
31675  *        Matt Dillon :   UDP length checks.
31676  *        Alan Cox    :   Smarter af_inet used properly.
31677  *        Alan Cox    :   Use new kernel side addressing.
31678  *        Alan Cox    :   Incorrect return on truncated
31679 datagram receive.
31680  * Arnt Gulbrandsen    :   New udp_send and stuff
31681  *        Alan Cox    :   Cache last socket
31682  *        Alan Cox    :   Route cache
31683  *        Jon Peatfield :   Minor efficiency fix to
31684 sendto().
31685  *        Mike Shaver :   RFC1122 checks.
31686  *        Alan Cox    :   Nonblocking error fix.
31687  * Willy Konynenberg  :   Transparent proxying support.
31688  *        David S. Miller :   New socket lookup
31689 architecture for ISS.
31690  *                   Last socket cache retained as it
31691  *                   does have a high hit rate.
31692  *        Elliot Poger :      Added support
31693 for SO_BINDTODEVICE.
31694  * Willy Konynenberg  :   Transparent proxy adapted to
31695 new
31696  *                   socket hash code.
31697  *        Philip Gladstone:   Added missing ip_rt_put
31698  *
31699  *
31700  *        This program is free software; you can
31701 redistribute it and/or
```

```
31702    *        modify it under the terms of the GNU General
31703  Public License
31704    *        as published by the Free Software Foundation;
31705  either version
31706    *        2 of the License, or (at your option) any later
31707  version.
31708    */
31709
31710  /* RFC1122 Status:
31711     4.1.3.1 (Ports):
31712       SHOULD send ICMP_PORT_UNREACHABLE in response to
31713  datagrams to
31714         an un-listened port. (OK)
31715     4.1.3.2 (IP Options)
31716       MUST pass IP options from IP -> application (OK)
31717       MUST allow application to specify IP options (OK)
31718     4.1.3.3 (ICMP Messages)
31719       MUST pass ICMP error messages to application (OK)
31720     4.1.3.4 (UDP Checksums)
31721       MUST provide facility for checksumming (OK)
31722       MAY allow application to control checksumming (OK)
31723       MUST default to checksumming on (OK)
31724       MUST discard silently datagrams with bad csums (OK)
31725     4.1.3.5 (UDP Multihoming)
31726       MUST allow application to specify source address
31727  (OK)
31728         SHOULD be able to communicate the chosen src addr
31729  up to application
31730         when application doesn't choose (NOT YET -
31731  doesn't seem to be in the BSD API)
31732         [Does opening a SOCK_PACKET and snooping your
31733  output count 8)]
31734     4.1.3.6 (Invalid Addresses)
31735       MUST discard invalid source addresses (NOT YET --
31736  will be implemented
31737         in IP, so UDP will eventually be OK.  Right now
31738  it's a violation.)
31739       MUST only send datagrams with one of our addresses
31740  (NOT YET - ought to be OK )
31741     950728 -- MS
31742  */
31743
31744  #include <asm/system.h>
31745  #include <asm/segment.h>
31746  #include <linux/types.h>
31747  #include <linux/sched.h>
31748  #include <linux/fcntl.h>
31749  #include <linux/socket.h>
```

```
31750  #include <linux/sockios.h>
31751  #include <linux/in.h>
31752  #include <linux/errno.h>
31753  #include <linux/timer.h>
31754  #include <linux/termios.h>
31755  #include <linux/mm.h>
31756  #include <linux/config.h>
31757  #include <linux/inet.h>
31758  #include <linux/netdevice.h>
31759  #include <net/snmp.h>
31760  #include <net/ip.h>
31761  #include <net/protocol.h>
31762  #include <net/tcp.h>
31763  #include <linux/skbuff.h>
31764  #include <net/sock.h>
31765  #include <net/udp.h>
31766  #include <net/icmp.h>
31767  #include <net/route.h>
31768  #include <net/checksum.h>
31769
31770  /*
31771   *  Snmp MIB for the UDP layer
31772   */
31773
31774  struct udp_mib        udp_statistics;
31775
31776  struct sock *udp_hash[UDP_HTABLE_SIZE];
31777
31778  static int udp_v4_verify_bind(struct sock *sk, unsigned
31779  short snum)
31780  {
31781      struct sock *sk2;
31782      int retval = 0, sk_reuse = sk->reuse;
31783
31784      SOCKHASH_LOCK();
31785      for(sk2 = udp_hash[snum & (UDP_HTABLE_SIZE - 1)];
31786  sk2 != NULL; sk2 = sk2->next) {
31787          if((sk2->num == snum) && (sk2 != sk)) {
31788              int sk2_reuse = sk2->reuse;
31789
31790              /* Two sockets can be bound to the same port
31791  if they're
31792               * bound to different interfaces... */
31793              if (sk->bound_device != sk2->bound_device)
31794                  continue;
31795
31796              if(!sk2->rcv_saddr || !sk->rcv_saddr) {
31797                  if((!sk2_reuse) || (!sk_reuse)) {
```

p 536 ▶ 31785

```
31798                    retval = 1;
31799                    break;
31800                }
31801            } else if(sk2->rcv_saddr == sk->rcv_saddr) {
31802                if((!sk_reuse) || (!sk2_reuse)) {
31803                    retval = 1;
31804                    break;
31805                }
31806            }
31807        }
31808    }
31809    SOCKHASH_UNLOCK();
31810    return retval;
31811 }
31812
31813 static inline int udp_lport_inuse(u16 num)
31814 {
31815     struct sock *sk = udp_hash[num & (UDP_HTABLE_SIZE -
31816 1)];
31817
31818     for(; sk != NULL; sk = sk->next) {
31819         if(sk->num == num)
31820             return 1;
31821     }
31822     return 0;
31823 }
31824
31825 /* Shared by v4/v6 tcp. */
31826 unsigned short udp_good_socknum(void)
31827 {
31828     int result;
31829     static int start = 0;
31830     int i, best, best_size_so_far;
31831
31832     SOCKHASH_LOCK();
31833
31834     /* Select initial not-so-random "best" */
31835     best = PROT_SOCK + 1 + (start & 1023);
31836     best_size_so_far = 32767;   /* "big" num */
31837     result = best;
31838     for (i = 0; i < UDP_HTABLE_SIZE; i++, result++) {
31839         struct sock *sk;
31840         int size;
31841
31842         sk = udp_hash[result & (UDP_HTABLE_SIZE - 1)];
31843
31844         /* No clashes - take it */
31845         if (!sk)
```

`p 536` (marker pointing to line 31826)

```
31846            goto out;
31847
31848        /* Is this one better than our best so far? */
31849        size = 0;
31850        do {
31851            if(++size >= best_size_so_far)
31852                goto next;
31853        } while((sk = sk->next) != NULL);
31854        best_size_so_far = size;
31855        best = result;
31856 next:
31857    }
31858
31859    while (udp_lport_inuse(best))
31860        best += UDP_HTABLE_SIZE;
31861    result = best;
31862 out:
31863    start = result;
31864    SOCKHASH_UNLOCK();
31865    return result;
31866 }
31867
31868 static void udp_v4_hash(struct sock *sk)
31869 {
31870     struct sock **skp;
31871     int num = sk->num;
31872
31873     num &= (UDP_HTABLE_SIZE - 1);
31874     skp = &udp_hash[num];
31875
31876     SOCKHASH_LOCK();
31877     sk->next = *skp;
31878     *skp = sk;
31879     sk->hashent = num;
31880     SOCKHASH_UNLOCK();
31881 }
31882
31883 static void udp_v4_unhash(struct sock *sk)
31884 {
31885     struct sock **skp;
31886     int num = sk->num;
31887
31888     num &= (UDP_HTABLE_SIZE - 1);
31889     skp = &udp_hash[num];
31890
31891     SOCKHASH_LOCK();
31892     while(*skp != NULL) {
31893         if(*skp == sk) {
```

`p 535` (marker pointing to line 31868)

`p 535` (marker pointing to line 31883)

```
31894              *skp = sk->next;
31895              break;
31896          }
31897          skp = &((*skp)->next);
31898      }
31899      SOCKHASH_UNLOCK();
31900  }
31901
31902  static void udp_v4_rehash(struct sock *sk)
31903  {
31904      struct sock **skp;
31905      int num = sk->num;
31906      int oldnum = sk->hashent;
31907
31908      num &= (UDP_HTABLE_SIZE - 1);
31909      skp = &udp_hash[oldnum];
31910
31911      SOCKHASH_LOCK();
31912      while(*skp != NULL) {
31913          if(*skp == sk) {
31914              *skp = sk->next;
31915              break;
31916          }
31917          skp = &((*skp)->next);
31918      }
31919      sk->next = udp_hash[num];
31920      udp_hash[num] = sk;
31921      sk->hashent = num;
31922      SOCKHASH_UNLOCK();
31923  }
31924
31925  /* UDP is nearly always wildcards out the wazoo, it
31926  makes no sense to try
31927   * harder than this. -DaveM
31928   */
31929  __inline__ struct sock *udp_v4_lookup(u32 saddr, u16
31930  sport, u32 daddr, u16 dport,
31931                      struct device *dev)
31932  {
31933      struct sock *sk, *result = NULL;
31934      unsigned short hnum = ntohs(dport);
31935      int badness = -1;
31936
31937      for(sk = udp_hash[hnum & (UDP_HTABLE_SIZE - 1)]; sk
31938  != NULL; sk = sk->next) {
31939          if((sk->num == hnum) && !(sk->dead && (sk->state
31940  == TCP_CLOSE))) {
31941              int score = 0;
```

```
31942              if(sk->rcv_saddr) {
31943                  if(sk->rcv_saddr != daddr)
31944                      continue;
31945                  score++;
31946              }
31947              if(sk->daddr) {
31948                  if(sk->daddr != saddr)
31949                      continue;
31950                  score++;
31951              }
31952              if(sk->dummy_th.dest) {
31953                  if(sk->dummy_th.dest != sport)
31954                      continue;
31955                  score++;
31956              }
31957              /* If this socket is bound to a particular
31958  interface,
31959               * did the packet come in on it? */
31960              if (sk->bound_device) {
31961                  if (dev == sk->bound_device)
31962                      score++;
31963                  else
31964                      continue;  /* mismatch--not this
31965  sock */
31966              }
31967              if(score == 4) {
31968                  result = sk;
31969                  break;
31970              } else if(score > badness) {
31971                  result = sk;
31972                  badness = score;
31973              }
31974          }
31975      }
31976      return result;
31977  }
31978
31979  #ifdef CONFIG_IP_TRANSPARENT_PROXY
31980  struct sock *udp_v4_proxy_lookup(u32 saddr, u16 sport,
31981  u32 daddr, u16 dport, u32 paddr, u16 rport,
31982                  struct device *dev)
31983  {
31984      struct sock *hh[3], *sk, *result = NULL;
31985      int i;
31986      int badness = -1;
31987      unsigned short hnum = ntohs(dport);
31988      unsigned short hpnum = ntohs(rport);
31989
```

```
31990        SOCKHASH_LOCK();
31991        hh[0] = udp_hash[hnum & (UDP_HTABLE_SIZE - 1)];
31992        hh[1] = udp_hash[hpnum & (UDP_HTABLE_SIZE - 1)];
31993        for (i = 0; i < 2; i++) {
31994            for(sk = hh[i]; sk != NULL; sk = sk->next) {
31995                if(sk->num == hnum || sk->num == hpnum) {
31996                    int score = 0;
31997                    if(sk->dead && (sk->state == TCP_CLOSE))
31998                        continue;
31999                    if(sk->rcv_saddr) {
32000                        if((sk->num != hpnum ||
32001 sk->rcv_saddr != paddr) &&
32002                            (sk->num != hnum || sk->rcv_saddr
32003 != daddr))
32004                            continue;
32005                        score++;
32006                    }
32007                    if(sk->daddr) {
32008                        if(sk->daddr != saddr)
32009                            continue;
32010                        score++;
32011                    }
32012                    if(sk->dummy_th.dest) {
32013                        if(sk->dummy_th.dest != sport)
32014                            continue;
32015                        score++;
32016                    }
32017                    /* If this socket is bound to a
32018 particular interface,
32019                     * did the packet come in on it? */
32020                    if(sk->bound_device) {
32021                        if (sk->bound_device != dev)
32022                            continue;
32023                        score++;
32024                    }
32025                    if(score == 4 && sk->num == hnum) {
32026                        result = sk;
32027                        break;
32028                    } else if(score > badness && (sk->num ==
32029 hpnum || sk->rcv_saddr)) {
32030                        result = sk;
32031                        badness = score;
32032                    }
32033                }
32034            }
32035        }
32036        SOCKHASH_UNLOCK();
32037        return result;
```

```
32038 }
32039 #endif
32040
32041 static inline struct sock *udp_v4_mcast_next(struct sock
32042 *sk,
32043                     unsigned short num,
32044                     unsigned long raddr,
32045                     unsigned short rnum,
32046                     unsigned long laddr,
32047                     struct device *dev)
32048 {
32049     struct sock *s = sk;
32050     unsigned short hnum = ntohs(num);
32051     for(; s; s = s->next) {
32052         if ((s->num != hnum)                 ||
32053             (s->dead && (s->state == TCP_CLOSE))
32054 ||
32055             (s->daddr && s->daddr!=raddr)         ||
32056             (s->dummy_th.dest != rnum &&
32057 s->dummy_th.dest != 0) ||
32058             ((s->bound_device) &&
32059 (s->bound_device!=dev))         ||
32060             (s->rcv_saddr  && s->rcv_saddr != laddr))
32061             continue;
32062         break;
32063     }
32064     return s;
32065 }
32066
32067 #define min(a,b)     ((a)<(b)?(a):(b))
32068
32069
32070 /*
32071  * This routine is called by the ICMP module when it
32072 gets some
32073  * sort of error condition.  If err < 0 then the socket
32074 should
32075  * be closed and the error returned to the user.  If err
32076 > 0
32077  * it's just the icmp type << 8 | icmp code.
32078  * Header points to the ip header of the error packet.
32079 We move
32080  * on past this. Then (as it used to claim before
32081 adjustment)
32082  * header points to the first 8 bytes of the udp header.
32083 We need
32084  * to find the appropriate port.
32085  */
```

p 534

```
32086
32087    void udp_err(int type, int code, unsigned char *header,
32088    __u32 daddr,
32089        __u32 saddr, struct inet_protocol *protocol, int len)
32090    {
32091        struct udphdr *uh;
32092        struct sock *sk;
32093
32094        /*
32095         *  Find the 8 bytes of post IP header ICMP included
32096    for us
32097         */
32098
32099        if(len<sizeof(struct udphdr))
32100            return;
32101
32102        uh = (struct udphdr *)header;
32103
32104        sk = udp_v4_lookup(daddr, uh->dest, saddr,
32105    uh->source, NULL);
32106        if (sk == NULL)
32107            return; /* No socket for error */
32108
32109        if (type == ICMP_SOURCE_QUENCH)
32110        {   /* Slow down! */
32111            if (sk->cong_window > 1)
32112                sk->cong_window = sk->cong_window/2;
32113            return;
32114        }
32115
32116        if (type == ICMP_PARAMETERPROB)
32117        {
32118            sk->err = EPROTO;
32119            sk->error_report(sk);
32120            return;
32121        }
32122
32123        /*
32124         *  Various people wanted BSD UDP semantics. Well
32125    they've come
32126         *  back out because they slow down response to
32127    stuff like dead
32128         *  or unreachable name servers and they screw term
32129    users something
32130         *  chronic. Oh and it violates RFC1122. So
32131    basically fix your
32132         *  client code people.
32133         */
```

p 536

```
32134
32135        /* RFC1122: OK.  Passes ICMP errors back to
32136    application, as per */
32137        /* 4.1.3.3. */
32138        /* After the comment above, that should be no
32139    surprise. */
32140
32141        if(code<=NR_ICMP_UNREACH &&
32142    icmp_err_convert[code].fatal)
32143        {
32144            /*
32145             *  4.x BSD compatibility item. Break RFC1122 to
32146             *  get BSD socket semantics.
32147             */
32148            if(sk->bsdism && sk->state!=TCP_ESTABLISHED)
32149                return;
32150            sk->err = icmp_err_convert[code].errno;
32151            sk->error_report(sk);
32152        }
32153    }
32154
32155
32156    static unsigned short udp_check(struct udphdr *uh, int
32157    len, unsigned long saddr, unsigned long daddr, unsigned
32158    long base)
32159    {
32160        return(csum_tcpudp_magic(saddr, daddr, len,
32161    IPPROTO_UDP, base));
32162    }
32163
32164    struct udpfakehdr
32165    {
32166        struct udphdr uh;
32167        __u32 daddr;
32168        __u32 other;
32169        const char *from;
32170        __u32 wcheck;
32171    };
32172
32173    /*
32174     *  Copy and checksum a UDP packet from user space into
32175    a buffer. We still have to do the planning to
32176     *  get ip_build_xmit to spot direct transfer to network
32177    card and provide an additional callback mode
32178     *  for direct user->board I/O transfers. That one will
32179    be fun.
32180     */
32181
```

```
32182    static void udp_getfrag(const void *p, __u32 saddr, char
32183    * to, unsigned int offset, unsigned int fraglen)
32184    {
32185        struct udpfakehdr *ufh = (struct udpfakehdr *)p;
32186        const char *src;
32187        char *dst;
32188        unsigned int len;
32189
32190        if (offset)
32191        {
32192            len = fraglen;
32193            src = ufh->from+(offset-sizeof(struct udphdr));
32194            dst = to;
32195        }
32196        else
32197        {
32198            len = fraglen-sizeof(struct udphdr);
32199            src = ufh->from;
32200            dst = to+sizeof(struct udphdr);
32201        }
32202        ufh->wcheck = csum_partial_copy_fromuser(src, dst,
32203    len, ufh->wcheck);
32204        if (offset == 0)
32205        {
32206            ufh->wcheck = csum_partial((char *)ufh,
32207    sizeof(struct udphdr),
32208                            ufh->wcheck);
32209            ufh->uh.check = csum_tcpudp_magic(saddr,
32210    ufh->daddr,
32211                        ntohs(ufh->uh.len),
32212                        IPPROTO_UDP, ufh->wcheck);
32213            if (ufh->uh.check == 0)
32214                ufh->uh.check = -1;
32215            memcpy(to, ufh, sizeof(struct udphdr));
32216        }
32217    }
32218
32219    /*
32220     *  Unchecksummed UDP is sufficiently critical to stuff
32221    like ATM video conferencing
32222     *  that we use two routines for this for speed.
32223    Probably we ought to have a CONFIG_FAST_NET
32224     *  set for >10Mb/second boards to activate this sort of
32225    coding. Timing needed to verify if
32226     *  this is a valid decision.
32227     */
32228
32229    static void udp_getfrag_nosum(const void *p, __u32
```

```
32230    saddr, char * to, unsigned int offset, unsigned int
32231    fraglen)
32232    {
32233        struct udpfakehdr *ufh = (struct udpfakehdr *)p;
32234        const char *src;
32235        char *dst;
32236        unsigned int len;
32237
32238        if (offset)
32239        {
32240            len = fraglen;
32241            src = ufh->from+(offset-sizeof(struct udphdr));
32242            dst = to;
32243        }
32244        else
32245        {
32246            len = fraglen-sizeof(struct udphdr);
32247            src = ufh->from;
32248            dst = to+sizeof(struct udphdr);
32249        }
32250        memcpy_fromfs(dst,src,len);
32251        if (offset == 0)
32252            memcpy(to, ufh, sizeof(struct udphdr));
32253    }
32254
32255
32256    /*
32257     *  Send UDP frames.
32258     */
32259
32260    static int udp_send(struct sock *sk, struct sockaddr_in
32261    *sin,
32262                const unsigned char *from, int len, int rt,
32263            __u32 saddr, int noblock)
32264    {
32265        int ulen = len + sizeof(struct udphdr);
32266        int a;
32267        struct udpfakehdr ufh;
32268
32269        if(ulen>65535-sizeof(struct iphdr))
32270            return -EMSGSIZE;
32271
32272        ufh.uh.source = sk->dummy_th.source;
32273        ufh.uh.dest = sin->sin_port;
32274        ufh.uh.len = htons(ulen);
32275        ufh.uh.check = 0;
32276        ufh.daddr = sin->sin_addr.s_addr;
32277        ufh.other = (htons(ulen) << 16) + IPPROTO_UDP*256;
```

```
32278        ufh.from = from;
32279        ufh.wcheck = 0;
32280
32281   #ifdef CONFIG_IP_TRANSPARENT_PROXY
32282        if (rt&MSG_PROXY)
32283        {
32284            /*
32285             * We map the first 8 bytes of a second
32286   sockaddr_in
32287             * into the last 8 (unused) bytes of a
32288   sockaddr_in.
32289             * This _is_ ugly, but it's the only way to do it
32290             * easily, without adding system calls.
32291             */
32292            struct sockaddr_in *sinfrom =
32293                (struct sockaddr_in *) sin->sin_zero;
32294
32295            if (!suser())
32296                return(-EPERM);
32297            if (sinfrom->sin_family && sinfrom->sin_family
32298   != AF_INET)
32299                return(-EINVAL);
32300            if (sinfrom->sin_port == 0)
32301                return(-EINVAL);
32302            saddr = sinfrom->sin_addr.s_addr;
32303            ufh.uh.source = sinfrom->sin_port;
32304        }
32305   #endif
32306
32307        /* RFC1122: OK.  Provides the checksumming facility
32308   (MUST) as per */
32309        /* 4.1.3.4. It's configurable by the application via
32310   setsockopt() */
32311        /* (MAY) and it defaults to on (MUST).  Almost makes
32312   up for the */
32313        /* violation above. -- MS */
32314
32315        if(sk->no_check)
32316            a = ip_build_xmit(sk, udp_getfrag_nosum, &ufh,
32317   ulen,
32318                sin->sin_addr.s_addr, saddr, sk->opt, rt,
32319   IPPROTO_UDP, noblock);
32320        else
32321            a = ip_build_xmit(sk, udp_getfrag, &ufh, ulen,
32322                sin->sin_addr.s_addr, saddr, sk->opt, rt,
32323   IPPROTO_UDP, noblock);
32324        if(a<0)
32325            return a;
```

```
32326        udp_statistics.UdpOutDatagrams++;
32327        return len;
32328   }
32329
32330
32331   static int udp_sendto(struct sock *sk, const unsigned
32332   char *from, int len, int noblock,
32333        unsigned flags, struct sockaddr_in *usin, int
32334   addr_len)
32335   {
32336        struct sockaddr_in sin;
32337        int tmp;
32338        __u32 saddr=0;
32339
32340        /*
32341         * Check the flags. We support no flags for UDP
32342   sending
32343         */
32344
32345   #ifdef CONFIG_IP_TRANSPARENT_PROXY
32346        if (flags&~(MSG_DONTROUTE|MSG_PROXY))
32347   #else
32348        if (flags&~MSG_DONTROUTE)
32349   #endif
32350            return(-EINVAL);
32351        /*
32352         * Get and verify the address.
32353         */
32354
32355        if (usin)
32356        {
32357            if (addr_len < sizeof(sin))
32358                return(-EINVAL);
32359            if (usin->sin_family && usin->sin_family !=
32360   AF_INET)
32361                return(-EINVAL);
32362            if (usin->sin_port == 0)
32363                return(-EINVAL);
32364        }
32365        else
32366        {
32367   #ifdef CONFIG_IP_TRANSPARENT_PROXY
32368            /* We need to provide a sockaddr_in when using
32369   MSG_PROXY. */
32370            if (flags&MSG_PROXY)
32371                return(-EINVAL);
32372   #endif
32373            if (sk->state != TCP_ESTABLISHED)
```

p 531

```
32374            return(-EINVAL);
32375        sin.sin_family = AF_INET;
32376        sin.sin_port = sk->dummy_th.dest;
32377        sin.sin_addr.s_addr = sk->daddr;
32378        usin = &sin;
32379    }
32380
32381    /*
32382     *  BSD socket semantics. You must set SO_BROADCAST
32383 to permit
32384     *  broadcasting of data.
32385     */
32386
32387    /* RFC1122: OK.  Allows the application to select
32388 the specific */
32389    /* source address for an outgoing packet (MUST) as
32390 per 4.1.3.5. */
32391    /* Optional addition: a mechanism for telling the
32392 application what */
32393    /* address was used. (4.1.3.5, MAY) -- MS */
32394
32395    /* RFC1122: MUST ensure that all outgoing packets
32396 have one */
32397    /* of this host's addresses as a source
32398 addr.(4.1.3.6) - bind in  */
32399    /* af_inet.c checks these. It does need work to
32400 allow BSD style */
32401    /* bind to multicast as is done by xntpd         */
32402
32403    if(usin->sin_addr.s_addr==INADDR_ANY)
32404        usin->sin_addr.s_addr=ip_my_addr();
32405
32406    if(!sk->broadcast &&
32407 ip_chk_addr(usin->sin_addr.s_addr)==IS_BROADCAST)
32408            return -EACCES;           /* Must turn
32409 broadcast on first */
32410
32411    lock_sock(sk);
32412
32413    /* Send the packet. */
32414    tmp = udp_send(sk, usin, from, len, flags, saddr,
32415 noblock);
32416
32417    /* The datagram has been sent off.  Release the
32418 socket. */
32419    release_sock(sk);
32420    return(tmp);
32421 }
```

p 532 *(line 32403)*

```
32422
32423 /*
32424  *  Temporary
32425  */
32426
32427 static int udp_sendmsg(struct sock *sk, struct msghdr
32428 *msg, int len, int noblock,
32429    int flags)
32430 {
32431    if(msg->msg_iovlen==1)
32432        return
32433 udp_sendto(sk,msg->msg_iov[0].iov_base,len, noblock,
32434 flags, msg->msg_name, msg->msg_namelen);
32435    else
32436    {
32437        /*
32438         *  For awkward cases we linearise the buffer
32439 first. In theory this is only frames
32440         *  whose iovec's don't split on 4 byte
32441 boundaries, and soon encrypted stuff (to keep
32442         *  skip happy). We are a bit more general about
32443 it.
32444         */
32445
32446        unsigned char *buf;
32447        int fs;
32448        int err;
32449        if(len>65515)
32450            return -EMSGSIZE;
32451        buf=kmalloc(len, GFP_KERNEL);
32452        if(buf==NULL)
32453            return -ENOBUFS;
32454        memcpy_fromiovec(buf, msg->msg_iov, len);
32455        fs=get_fs();
32456        set_fs(get_ds());
32457        err=udp_sendto(sk,buf,len, noblock, flags,
32458 msg->msg_name, msg->msg_namelen);
32459        set_fs(fs);
32460        kfree_s(buf,len);
32461        return err;
32462    }
32463 }
32464
32465 /*
32466  *  IOCTL requests applicable to the UDP protocol
32467  */
32468
32469 int udp_ioctl(struct sock *sk, int cmd, unsigned long
```

p 532 *(line 32431)*

```
32470   arg)
32471   {
32472       int err;
32473       switch(cmd)
32474       {
32475           case TIOCOUTQ:
32476           {
32477               unsigned long amount;
32478
32479               if (sk->state == TCP_LISTEN) return(-EINVAL);
32480               amount = sock_wspace(sk);
32481               err=verify_area(VERIFY_WRITE,(void *)arg,
32482                       sizeof(unsigned long));
32483               if(err)
32484                   return(err);
32485               put_fs_long(amount,(unsigned long *)arg);
32486               return(0);
32487           }
32488
32489           case TIOCINQ:
32490           {
32491               struct sk_buff *skb;
32492               unsigned long amount;
32493
32494               if (sk->state == TCP_LISTEN) return(-EINVAL);
32495               amount = 0;
32496               skb = skb_peek(&sk->receive_queue);
32497               if (skb != NULL) {
32498                   /*
32499                    * We will only return the amount
32500                    * of this packet since that is all
32501                    * that will be read.
32502                    */
32503                   amount = skb->len-sizeof(struct udphdr);
32504               }
32505               err=verify_area(VERIFY_WRITE,(void *)arg,
32506                       sizeof(unsigned long));
32507               if(err)
32508                   return(err);
32509               put_fs_long(amount,(unsigned long *)arg);
32510               return(0);
32511           }
32512
32513           default:
32514               return(-EINVAL);
32515       }
32516       return(0);
32517   }
```

```
32518
32519
32520   /*
32521    *  This should be easy, if there is something there we\
32522    *  return it, otherwise we block.
32523    */
32524
32525   int udp_recvmsg(struct sock *sk, struct msghdr *msg, int
32526   len,
32527           int noblock, int flags,int *addr_len)
32528   {
32529       int copied = 0;
32530       int truesize;
32531       struct sk_buff *skb;
32532       int er;
32533       struct sockaddr_in *sin=(struct sockaddr_in
32534   *)msg->msg_name;
32535
32536       /*
32537        *  Check any passed addresses
32538        */
32539
32540       if (addr_len)
32541           *addr_len=sizeof(*sin);
32542
32543       /*
32544        *  From here the generic datagram does a lot of the
32545   work. Come
32546        *  the finished NET3, it will do _ALL_ the work!
32547        */
32548
32549       skb=skb_recv_datagram(sk,flags,noblock,&er);
32550       if(skb==NULL)
32551           return er;
32552
32553       truesize = skb->len - sizeof(struct udphdr);
32554       copied = min(len, truesize);
32555
32556       /*
32557        *  FIXME : should use udp header size info value
32558        */
32559
32560       skb_copy_datagram_iovec(skb,sizeof(struct
32561   udphdr),msg->msg_iov,copied);
32562       sk->stamp=skb->stamp;
32563
32564       /* Copy the address. */
32565       if (sin)
```

P 535 →

```
32566        {
32567            sin->sin_family = AF_INET;
32568            sin->sin_port = skb->h.uh->source;
32569            sin->sin_addr.s_addr = skb->daddr;
32570   #ifdef CONFIG_IP_TRANSPARENT_PROXY
32571            if (flags&MSG_PROXY)
32572            {
32573                /*
32574                 * We map the first 8 bytes of a second
32575   sockaddr_in
32576                 * into the last 8 (unused) bytes of a
32577   sockaddr_in.
32578                 * This _is_ ugly, but it's the only way to
32579   do it
32580                 * easily,  without adding system calls.
32581                 */
32582                struct sockaddr_in *sinto =
32583                    (struct sockaddr_in *) sin->sin_zero;
32584
32585                sinto->sin_family = AF_INET;
32586                sinto->sin_port = skb->h.uh->dest;
32587                sinto->sin_addr.s_addr = skb->saddr;
32588            }
32589   #endif
32590        }
32591
32592        skb_free_datagram(sk, skb);
32593        return(copied);
32594   }
32595
32596   int udp_connect(struct sock *sk, struct sockaddr_in
32597   *usin, int addr_len)
32598   {
32599        struct rtable *rt;
32600        if (addr_len < sizeof(*usin))
32601            return(-EINVAL);
32602
32603        if (usin->sin_family && usin->sin_family != AF_INET)
32604            return(-EAFNOSUPPORT);
32605        if (usin->sin_addr.s_addr==INADDR_ANY)
32606            usin->sin_addr.s_addr=ip_my_addr();
32607
32608        if(!sk->broadcast &&
32609   ip_chk_addr(usin->sin_addr.s_addr)==IS_BROADCAST)
32610            return -EACCES;          /* Must turn broadcast
32611   on first */
32612
32613        rt=ip_rt_route((__u32)usin->sin_addr.s_addr,
```

```
32614   sk->localroute, sk->bound_device);
32615        if (rt==NULL)
32616            return -ENETUNREACH;
32617        if(!sk->saddr)
32618            sk->saddr = rt->rt_src;       /* Update source
32619   address */
32620        if(!sk->rcv_saddr)
32621            sk->rcv_saddr = rt->rt_src;
32622        sk->daddr = usin->sin_addr.s_addr;
32623        sk->dummy_th.dest = usin->sin_port;
32624        sk->state = TCP_ESTABLISHED;
32625        if (sk->ip_route_cache)
32626            ip_rt_put(sk->ip_route_cache);
32627        sk->ip_route_cache = rt;
32628        return(0);
32629   }
32630
32631
32632   static void udp_close(struct sock *sk, unsigned long
32633   timeout)
32634   {
32635        lock_sock(sk);
32636        sk->state = TCP_CLOSE;
32637        sk->dead = 1;
32638        release_sock(sk);
32639        udp_v4_unhash(sk);
32640        destroy_sock(sk);
32641   }
32642
32643   static inline void udp_queue_rcv_skb(struct sock * sk,
32644   struct sk_buff *skb)
32645   {
32646        /*
32647         * Charge it to the socket, dropping if the queue
32648   is full.
32649         */
32650
32651        /* I assume this includes the IP options, as per
32652   RFC1122 (4.1.3.2). */
32653        /* If not, please let me know. -- MS */
32654
32655        if (__sock_queue_rcv_skb(sk,skb)<0) {
32656            udp_statistics.UdpInErrors++;
32657            ip_statistics.IpInDiscards++;
32658            ip_statistics.IpInDelivers--;
32659            skb->sk = NULL;
32660            kfree_skb(skb, FREE_WRITE);
32661            return;
```

```
32662            }
32663            udp_statistics.UdpInDatagrams++;
32664    }
32665
32666
32667    static inline void udp_deliver(struct sock *sk, struct
32668    sk_buff *skb)
32669    {
32670            skb->sk = sk;
32671
32672            if (sk->users) {
32673                    __skb_queue_tail(&sk->back_log, skb);
32674                    return;
32675            }
32676            udp_queue_rcv_skb(sk, skb);
32677    }
32678
32679    #ifdef CONFIG_IP_TRANSPARENT_PROXY
32680    /*
32681     *  Check whether a received UDP packet might be for one
32682    of our
32683     *  sockets.
32684     */
32685
32686    int udp_chkaddr(struct sk_buff *skb)
32687    {
32688            struct iphdr *iph = skb->h.iph;
32689            struct udphdr *uh = (struct udphdr *)(skb->h.raw +
32690    iph->ihl*4);
32691            struct sock *sk;
32692
32693            sk = udp_v4_lookup(iph->saddr, uh->source,
32694    iph->daddr, uh->dest,
32695                    skb->dev);
32696            if (!sk)
32697                    return 0;
32698            /* 0 means accept all LOCAL addresses here, not all
32699    the world... */
32700            if (sk->rcv_saddr == 0)
32701                    return 0;
32702            return 1;
32703    }
32704    #endif
32705
32706    #ifdef CONFIG_IP_MULTICAST
32707    /*
32708     *  Multicasts and broadcasts go to each listener.
32709     */
```

```
32710    static int udp_v4_mcast_deliver(struct sk_buff *skb,
32711    struct udphdr *uh,
32712                    u32 saddr, u32 daddr)
32713    {
32714            struct sock *sk;
32715            int given = 0;
32716
32717            SOCKHASH_LOCK();
32718            sk = udp_hash[ntohs(uh->dest) & (UDP_HTABLE_SIZE -
32719    1)];
32720            sk = udp_v4_mcast_next(sk, uh->dest, saddr,
32721    uh->source, daddr, skb->dev);
32722            if(sk) {
32723                    struct sock *sknext = NULL;
32724
32725                    do {
32726                            struct sk_buff *skb1 = skb;
32727
32728                            sknext = udp_v4_mcast_next(sk->next,
32729    uh->dest, saddr,
32730                                    uh->source, daddr, skb->dev);
32731                            if(sknext)
32732                                    skb1 = skb_clone(skb, GFP_ATOMIC);
32733
32734                            if(skb1)
32735                                    udp_deliver(sk, skb1);
32736                            sk = sknext;
32737                    } while(sknext);
32738                    given = 1;
32739            }
32740            SOCKHASH_UNLOCK();
32741            if(!given)
32742                    kfree_skb(skb, FREE_READ);
32743            return 0;
32744    }
32745    #endif
32746
32747    /*
32748     *  All we need to do is get the socket, and then do a
32749    checksum.
32750     */
32751
32752    int udp_rcv(struct sk_buff *skb, struct device *dev,
32753    struct options *opt,
32754            __u32 daddr, unsigned short len,
32755            __u32 saddr, int redo, struct inet_protocol
32756    *protocol)
32757    {
```

```
32758        struct sock *sk;
32759        struct udphdr *uh;
32760        unsigned short ulen;
32761        int addr_type;
32762
32763        /*
32764         * If we're doing a "redo" (the socket was busy last
32765  time
32766         * around), we can just queue the packet now..
32767         */
32768        if (redo) {
32769            udp_queue_rcv_skb(skb->sk, skb);
32770            return 0;
32771        }
32772
32773        /*
32774         * First time through the loop.. Do all the setup
32775  stuff
32776         * (including finding out the socket we go to etc)
32777         */
32778
32779        addr_type = IS_MYADDR;
32780        if(!dev || dev->pa_addr!=daddr)
32781            addr_type=ip_chk_addr(daddr);
32782
32783        /*
32784         *  Get the header.
32785         */
32786
32787        uh = (struct udphdr *) skb->h.uh;
32788
32789        ip_statistics.IpInDelivers++;
32790
32791        /*
32792         *  Validate the packet and the UDP length.
32793         */
32794
32795        ulen = ntohs(uh->len);
32796
32797        if (ulen > len || len < sizeof(*uh) || ulen <
32798  sizeof(*uh))
32799        {
32800            NETDEBUG(printk("UDP: short packet: %d/%d\n",
32801  ulen, len));
32802            udp_statistics.UdpInErrors++;
32803            kfree_skb(skb, FREE_WRITE);
32804            return(0);
32805        }
```

```
32806
32807        /* RFC1122 warning: According to 4.1.3.6, we MUST
32808  discard any */
32809        /* datagram which has an invalid source address,
32810  either here or */
32811        /* in IP. */
32812        /* Right now, IP isn't doing it, and neither is UDP.
32813  It's on the */
32814        /* FIXME list for IP, though, so I wouldn't worry
32815  about it. */
32816        /* (That's the Right Place to do it, IMHO.) -- MS */
32817
32818        if (uh->check && (
32819            ( (skb->ip_summed == CHECKSUM_HW) &&
32820  udp_check(uh, len, saddr, daddr, skb->csum ) ) ||
32821            ( (skb->ip_summed == CHECKSUM_NONE) &&
32822  udp_check(uh, len, saddr, daddr,csum_partial((char*)uh,
32823  len, 0)))
32824                    /* skip if CHECKSUM_UNNECESSARY */
32825                )
32826            )
32827        {
32828            /* <mea@utu.fi> wants to know, who sent it, to
32829              go and stomp on the garbage sender... */
32830
32831            /* RFC1122: OK.  Discards the bad packet silently
32832  (as far as */
32833            /* the network is concerned, anyway) as per
32834  4.1.3.4 (MUST). */
32835
32836            NETDEBUG(printk("UDP: bad checksum. From
32837  %08lX:%d to %08lX:%d ulen %d\n",
32838                ntohl(saddr),ntohs(uh->source),
32839                ntohl(daddr),ntohs(uh->dest),
32840                ulen));
32841            udp_statistics.UdpInErrors++;
32842            kfree_skb(skb, FREE_WRITE);
32843            return(0);
32844        }
32845
32846        /*
32847         *  These are supposed to be switched.
32848         */
32849
32850        skb->daddr = saddr;
32851        skb->saddr = daddr;
32852
32853        len=ulen;
```

```
32854
32855        skb->dev = dev;
32856        skb_trim(skb,len);
32857
32858   #ifdef CONFIG_IP_MULTICAST
32859        if (addr_type==IS_BROADCAST ||
32860   addr_type==IS_MULTICAST)
32861            return udp_v4_mcast_deliver(skb, uh, saddr,
32862   daddr);
32863   #endif
32864   #ifdef CONFIG_IP_TRANSPARENT_PROXY
32865        if(skb->redirport)
32866            sk = udp_v4_proxy_lookup(saddr, uh->source,
32867   daddr, uh->dest,
32868                       dev->pa_addr, skb->redirport, dev);
32869        else
32870   #endif
32871        sk = udp_v4_lookup(saddr, uh->source, daddr,
32872   uh->dest, dev);
32873
32874        if (sk == NULL)
32875        {
32876            udp_statistics.UdpNoPorts++;
32877            if (addr_type != IS_BROADCAST && addr_type !=
32878   IS_MULTICAST)
32879            {
32880                icmp_send(skb, ICMP_DEST_UNREACH,
32881   ICMP_PORT_UNREACH, 0, dev);
32882            }
32883            /*
32884             * Hmm.  We got an UDP broadcast to a port to
32885   which we
32886             * don't wanna listen.  Ignore it.
32887             */
32888            skb->sk = NULL;
32889            kfree_skb(skb, FREE_WRITE);
32890            return(0);
32891        }
32892        udp_deliver(sk, skb);
32893        return 0;
32894   }
32895
32896   struct proto udp_prot = {
32897        (struct sock *)&udp_prot,    /* sklist_next */
32898        (struct sock *)&udp_prot,    /* sklist_prev */
32899        udp_close,          /* close */
32900        ip_build_header,       /* build_header */
32901        udp_connect,            /* connect */
```

```
32902        NULL,              /* accept */
32903        ip_queue_xmit,       /* queue_xmit */
32904        NULL,              /* retransmit */
32905        NULL,              /* write_wakeup */
32906        NULL,              /* read_wakeup */
32907        udp_rcv,           /* rcv */
32908        datagram_select,     /* select */
32909        udp_ioctl,         /* ioctl */
32910        NULL,              /* init */
32911        NULL,              /* shutdown */
32912        ip_setsockopt,       /* setsockopt */
32913        ip_getsockopt,       /* getsockopt */
32914        udp_sendmsg,         /* sendmsg */
32915        udp_recvmsg,         /* recvmsg */
32916        NULL,            /* bind */
32917        udp_v4_hash,       /* hash */
32918        udp_v4_unhash,       /* unhash */
32919        udp_v4_rehash,       /* rehash */
32920        udp_good_socknum,    /* good_socknum */
32921        udp_v4_verify_bind,    /* verify_bind */
32922        128,             /* max_header */
32923        0,            /* retransmits */
32924        "UDP",          /* name */
32925        0,            /* inuse */
32926        0             /* highestinuse */
32927   };
```

usr/src/linux/net/ipv4/utils.c

```
32928   /*
32929    * INET     An implementation of the TCP/IP protocol
32930   suite for the LINUX
32931    *       operating system.  INET is implemented using the
32932   BSD Socket
32933    *       interface as the means of communication with the
32934   user level.
32935    *
32936    *       Various kernel-resident INET utility functions;
32937   mainly
32938    *       for format conversion and debugging output.
32939    *
32940    * Version: @(#)utils.c 1.0.7   05/18/93
32941    *
32942    * Author:  Fred N. van Kempen,
32943   <waltje@uWalt.NL.Mugnet.ORG>
32944    *
32945    * Fixes:
32946    *       Alan Cox    :    verify_area check.
32947    *       Alan Cox    :    removed old debugging.
```

```
32948   *
32949   *
32950   *       This program is free software; you can
32951   redistribute it and/or
32952   *       modify it under the terms of the GNU General
32953   Public License
32954   *       as published by the Free Software Foundation;
32955   either version
32956   *       2 of the License, or (at your option) any later
32957   version.
32958   */
32959
32960   #include <asm/segment.h>
32961   #include <asm/system.h>
32962   #include <linux/types.h>
32963   #include <linux/kernel.h>
32964   #include <linux/sched.h>
32965   #include <linux/string.h>
32966   #include <linux/mm.h>
32967   #include <linux/socket.h>
32968   #include <linux/in.h>
32969   #include <linux/errno.h>
32970   #include <linux/stat.h>
32971   #include <stdarg.h>
32972   #include <linux/inet.h>
32973   #include <linux/netdevice.h>
32974   #include <linux/etherdevice.h>
32975   #include <net/ip.h>
32976   #include <net/protocol.h>
32977   #include <net/tcp.h>
32978   #include <linux/skbuff.h>
32979
32980
32981   /*
32982    *  Display an IP address in readable format.
32983    */
32984
32985   char *in_ntoa(unsigned long in)
32986   {
32987       static char buff[18];
32988       char *p;
32989
32990       p = (char *) &in;
32991       sprintf(buff, "%d.%d.%d.%d",
32992           (p[0] & 255), (p[1] & 255), (p[2] & 255), (p[3]
32993   & 255));
32994       return(buff);
32995   }
```

```
32996
32997
32998   /*
32999    *  Convert an ASCII string to binary IP.
33000    */
33001
33002   unsigned long in_aton(const char *str)
33003   {
33004       unsigned long l;
33005       unsigned int val;
33006       int i;
33007
33008       l = 0;
33009       for (i = 0; i < 4; i++)
33010       {
33011           l <<= 8;
33012           if (*str != '\0')
33013           {
33014               val = 0;
33015               while (*str != '\0' && *str != '.')
33016               {
33017                   val *= 10;
33018                   val += *str - '0';
33019                   str++;
33020               }
33021               l |= val;
33022               if (*str != '\0')
33023                   str++;
33024           }
33025       }
33026       return(htonl(l));
33027   }
33028
```

usr/src/linux/net/protocol.c

```
33029   /*
33030    * INET      An implementation of the TCP/IP protocol
33031   suite for the LINUX
33032    *      operating system.  INET is implemented using the
33033   BSD Socket
33034    *      interface as the means of communication with the
33035   user level.
33036    *
33037    *      INET protocol dispatch tables.
33038    *
33039    * Version: @(#)protocol.c  1.0.5   05/25/93
33040    *
33041    * Authors: Ross Biro, <bir7@leland.Stanford.Edu>
```

```
33042    *        Fred N. van Kempen, <waltje@uWalt.NL.Mugnet.ORG>
33043    *
33044    * Fixes:
33045    *       Alan Cox    : Ahah! udp icmp errors don't work
33046  because
33047    *              udp_err is never called!
33048    *       Alan Cox    : Added new fields for init and
33049  ready for
33050    *              proper fragmentation (_NO_ 4K limits!)
33051    *       Richard Colella : Hang on hash collision
33052    *
33053    *       This program is free software; you can
33054  redistribute it and/or
33055    *       modify it under the terms of the GNU General
33056  Public License
33057    *       as published by the Free Software Foundation;
33058  either version
33059    *       2 of the License, or (at your option) any later
33060  version.
33061    */
33062
33063  #include <asm/segment.h>
33064  #include <asm/system.h>
33065  #include <linux/types.h>
33066  #include <linux/kernel.h>
33067  #include <linux/sched.h>
33068  #include <linux/string.h>
33069  #include <linux/config.h>
33070  #include <linux/socket.h>
33071  #include <linux/in.h>
33072  #include <linux/inet.h>
33073  #include <linux/netdevice.h>
33074  #include <linux/timer.h>
33075  #include <net/ip.h>
33076  #include <net/protocol.h>
33077  #include <net/tcp.h>
33078  #include <linux/skbuff.h>
33079  #include <net/sock.h>
33080  #include <net/icmp.h>
33081  #include <net/udp.h>
33082  #include <net/ipip.h>
33083  #include <linux/igmp.h>
33084
33085
33086  #ifdef CONFIG_NET_IPIP
33087
33088  static struct inet_protocol ipip_protocol =
33089  {
33090      ipip_rcv,           /* IPIP handler          */
33091      NULL,               /* TUNNEL error control    */
33092      0,                  /* next             */
33093      IPPROTO_IPIP,       /* protocol ID          */
33094      0,                  /* copy             */
33095      NULL,               /* data             */
33096      "IPIP"              /* name             */
33097  };
33098
33099
33100  #endif
33101
33102  static struct inet_protocol tcp_protocol =
33103  {
33104      tcp_rcv,        /* TCP handler       */
33105      tcp_err,        /* TCP error control    */
33106  #if defined(CONFIG_NET_IPIP)
33107      &ipip_protocol,
33108  #else
33109      NULL,           /* next             */
33110  #endif
33111      IPPROTO_TCP,        /* protocol ID      */
33112      0,          /* copy         */
33113      NULL,           /* data         */
33114      "TCP"           /* name         */
33115  };
33116
33117
33118  static struct inet_protocol udp_protocol =
33119  {
33120      udp_rcv,        /* UDP handler       */
33121      udp_err,        /* UDP error control    */
33122      &tcp_protocol,      /* next         */
33123      IPPROTO_UDP,        /* protocol ID      */
33124      0,          /* copy         */
33125      NULL,           /* data         */
33126      "UDP"           /* name         */
33127  };
33128
33129
33130  static struct inet_protocol icmp_protocol =
33131  {
33132      icmp_rcv,       /* ICMP handler      */
33133      NULL,           /* ICMP error control   */
33134      &udp_protocol,      /* next         */
33135      IPPROTO_ICMP,       /* protocol ID      */
33136      0,          /* copy         */
33137      NULL,           /* data         */
```

```
33138        "ICMP"              /* name          */
33139    };
33140
33141    #ifndef CONFIG_IP_MULTICAST
33142    struct inet_protocol *inet_protocol_base =
33143    &icmp_protocol;
33144    #else
33145    static struct inet_protocol igmp_protocol =
33146    {
33147        igmp_rcv,        /* IGMP handler     */
33148        NULL,            /* IGMP error control   */
33149        &icmp_protocol,    /* next          */
33150        IPPROTO_IGMP,        /* protocol ID      */
33151        0,           /* copy         */
33152        NULL,            /* data         */
33153        "IGMP"           /* name         */
33154    };
33155
33156    struct inet_protocol *inet_protocol_base =
33157    &igmp_protocol;
33158    #endif
33159
33160    struct inet_protocol *inet_protos[MAX_INET_PROTOS] =
33161    {
33162        NULL
33163    };
33164
33165
33166    /*
33167     *  Find a protocol in the protocol tables given its
33168     *  IP type.
33169     */
33170
33171    struct inet_protocol *inet_get_protocol(unsigned char
33172    prot)
33173    {
33174        unsigned char hash;
33175        struct inet_protocol *p;
33176
33177        hash = prot & (MAX_INET_PROTOS - 1);
33178        for (p = inet_protos[hash] ; p != NULL; p=p->next)
33179        {
33180            if (p->protocol == prot)
33181                return((struct inet_protocol *) p);
33182        }
33183        return(NULL);
33184    }
33185
33186    /*
33187     *  Add a protocol handler to the hash tables
33188     */
33189
33190    void inet_add_protocol(struct inet_protocol *prot)
33191    {
33192        unsigned char hash;
33193        struct inet_protocol *p2;
33194
33195        hash = prot->protocol & (MAX_INET_PROTOS - 1);
33196        prot ->next = inet_protos[hash];
33197        inet_protos[hash] = prot;
33198        prot->copy = 0;
33199
33200        /*
33201         *  Set the copy bit if we need to.
33202         */
33203
33204        p2 = (struct inet_protocol *) prot->next;
33205        while(p2 != NULL)
33206        {
33207            if (p2->protocol == prot->protocol)
33208            {
33209                prot->copy = 1;
33210                break;
33211            }
33212            p2 = (struct inet_protocol *) p2->next;
33213        }
33214    }
33215
33216    /*
33217     *  Remove a protocol from the hash tables.
33218     */
33219
33220    int inet_del_protocol(struct inet_protocol *prot)
33221    {
33222        struct inet_protocol *p;
33223        struct inet_protocol *lp = NULL;
33224        unsigned char hash;
33225
33226        hash = prot->protocol & (MAX_INET_PROTOS - 1);
33227        if (prot == inet_protos[hash])
33228        {
33229            inet_protos[hash] = (struct inet_protocol *)
33230    inet_protos[hash]->next;
33231            return(0);
33232        }
33233
```

```
33234        p = (struct inet_protocol *) inet_protos[hash];
33235        while(p != NULL)
33236        {
33237            /*
33238             * We have to worry if the protocol being
33239    deleted is
33240             * the last one on the list, then we may need to
33241    reset
33242             * someone's copied bit.
33243             */
33244            if (p->next != NULL && p->next == prot)
33245            {
33246                /*
33247                 * if we are the last one with this protocol
33248    and
33249                 * there is a previous one, reset its copy
33250    bit.
33251                 */
33252                if (p->copy == 0 && lp != NULL)
33253                    lp->copy = 0;
33254                p->next = prot->next;
33255                return(0);
33256            }
33257            if (p->next != NULL && p->next->protocol ==
33258    prot->protocol)
33259                lp = p;
33260
33261            p = (struct inet_protocol *) p->next;
33262        }
33263        return(-1);
33264    }
```

usr/src/linux/net/socket.c

```
33265    /*
33266     * NET      An implementation of the SOCKET network
33267    access protocol.
33268     *
33269     * Version:  @(#)socket.c    1.1.93   18/02/95
33270     *
33271     * Authors:  Orest Zborowski, <obz@Kodak.COM>
33272     *           Ross Biro, <bir7@leland.Stanford.Edu>
33273     *           Fred N. van Kempen, <waltje@uWalt.NL.Mugnet.ORG>
33274     *
33275     * Fixes:
33276     *           Anonymous    :   NOTSOCK/BADF cleanup. Error fix
33277    in
33278     *                            shutdown()
33279     *           Alan Cox     :   verify_area() fixes
33280     *           Alan Cox     :   Removed DDI
33281     *           Jonathan Kamens :  SOCK_DGRAM reconnect bug
33282     *           Alan Cox     :   Moved a load of checks to the
33283    very
33284     *                            top level.
33285     *           Alan Cox     :   Move address structures to/from
33286    user
33287     *                            mode above the protocol layers.
33288     *           Rob Janssen  :   Allow 0 length sends.
33289     *           Alan Cox     :   Asynchronous I/O support
33290    (cribbed from the
33291     *                            tty drivers).
33292     *           Niibe Yutaka :   Asynchronous I/O for writes
33293    (4.4BSD style)
33294     *           Jeff Uphoff  :   Made max number of sockets
33295    command-line
33296     *                            configurable.
33297     *           Matti Aarnio :   Made the number of sockets
33298    dynamic,
33299     *                            to be allocated when needed, and mr.
33300     *                            Uphoff's max is used as max to be
33301     *                            allowed to allocate.
33302     *           Linus        :   Argh. removed all the socket
33303    allocation
33304     *                            altogether: it's in the inode now.
33305     *           Alan Cox     :   Made sock_alloc()/sock_release()
33306    public
33307     *                            for NetROM and future kernel nfsd
33308    type
33309     *                            stuff.
33310     *           Alan Cox     :   sendmsg/recvmsg basics.
33311     *           Tom Dyas     :   Export net symbols.
33312     *           Marcin Dalecki  :   Fixed problems with
33313    CONFIG_NET="n".
33314     *
33315     *
33316     *     This program is free software; you can
33317    redistribute it and/or
33318     *     modify it under the terms of the GNU General
33319    Public License
33320     *     as published by the Free Software Foundation;
33321    either version
33322     *     2 of the License, or (at your option) any later
33323    version.
33324     *
33325     *
33326     * This module is effectively the top level interface
33327    to the BSD socket
```

```
33328    *  paradigm. Because it is very simple it works well
33329   for Unix domain sockets,
33330    *  but requires a whole layer of substructure for the
33331   other protocols.
33332    *
33333    *  In addition it lacks an effective kernel -> kernel
33334   interface to go with
33335    *  the user one.
33336    */
33337
33338   #include <linux/config.h>
33339   #include <linux/signal.h>
33340   #include <linux/errno.h>
33341   #include <linux/sched.h>
33342   #include <linux/mm.h>
33343   #include <linux/kernel.h>
33344   #include <linux/major.h>
33345   #include <linux/stat.h>
33346   #include <linux/socket.h>
33347   #include <linux/fcntl.h>
33348   #include <linux/net.h>
33349   #include <linux/interrupt.h>
33350   #include <linux/netdevice.h>
33351   #include <linux/proc_fs.h>
33352   #include <linux/firewall.h>
33353
33354   #ifdef CONFIG_KERNELD
33355   #include <linux/kerneld.h>
33356   #endif
33357
33358   #include <net/netlink.h>
33359
33360   #include <asm/system.h>
33361   #include <asm/segment.h>
33362
33363   #if defined(CONFIG_MODULES) && defined(CONFIG_NET)
33364   extern void export_net_symbols(void);
33365   #endif
33366
33367   static int sock_lseek(struct inode *inode, struct file
33368   *file, off_t offset,
33369                   int whence);
33370   static int sock_read(struct inode *inode, struct file
33371   *file, char *buf,
33372                   int size);
33373   static int sock_write(struct inode *inode, struct file
33374   *file, const char *buf,
33375                   int size);
```

```
33376
33377   static void sock_close(struct inode *inode, struct file
33378   *file);
33379   static int sock_select(struct inode *inode, struct file
33380   *file, int which, select_table *seltable);
33381   static int sock_ioctl(struct inode *inode, struct file
33382   *file,
33383                   unsigned int cmd, unsigned long arg);
33384   static int sock_fasync(struct inode *inode, struct file
33385   *filp, int on);
33386
33387
33388   /*
33389    *  Socket files have a set of 'special' operations as
33390   well as the generic file ones. These don't appear
33391    *  in the operation structures but are done directly
33392   via the socketcall() multiplexor.
33393    */
33394
33395   static struct file_operations socket_file_ops = {
33396       sock_lseek,
33397       sock_read,
33398       sock_write,
33399       NULL,           /* readdir */
33400       sock_select,
33401       sock_ioctl,
33402       NULL,           /* mmap */
33403       NULL,           /* no special open code... */
33404       sock_close,
33405       NULL,           /* no fsync */
33406       sock_fasync
33407   };
33408
33409   /*
33410    *  The protocol list. Each protocol is registered in
33411   here.
33412    */
33413   static struct proto_ops *pops[NPROTO];
33414   /*
33415    *  Statistics counters of the socket lists
33416    */
33417   static int sockets_in_use  = 0;
33418
33419   /*
33420    *  Support routines. Move socket addresses back and
33421   forth across the kernel/user
33422    *  divide and look after the messy bits.
33423    */
```

```
33424
33425    #define MAX_SOCK_ADDR    128      /* 108 for Unix domain -
33426    16 for IP, 16 for IPX, about 80 for AX.25 */
33427
33428    int move_addr_to_kernel(void *uaddr, int ulen, void
33429    *kaddr)
33430    {
33431        int err;
33432        if(ulen<0||ulen>MAX_SOCK_ADDR)
33433            return -EINVAL;
33434        if(ulen==0)
33435            return 0;
33436        if((err=verify_area(VERIFY_READ,uaddr,ulen))<0)
33437            return err;
33438        memcpy_fromfs(kaddr,uaddr,ulen);
33439        return 0;
33440    }
33441
33442    int move_addr_to_user(void *kaddr, int klen, void
33443    *uaddr, int *ulen)
33444    {
33445        int err;
33446        int len;
33447
33448
33449
33450    if((err=verify_area(VERIFY_WRITE,ulen,sizeof(*ulen)))<0)
33451            return err;
33452        len=get_user(ulen);
33453        if(len>klen)
33454            len=klen;
33455        if(len<0 || len> MAX_SOCK_ADDR)
33456            return -EINVAL;
33457        if(len)
33458        {
33459            if((err=verify_area(VERIFY_WRITE,uaddr,len))<0)
33460                return err;
33461            memcpy_tofs(uaddr,kaddr,len);
33462        }
33463        put_user(len,ulen);
33464        return 0;
33465    }
33466
33467    /*
33468     *  Obtains the first available file descriptor and sets
33469     it up for use.
33470     */
33471
33472    static int get_fd(struct inode *inode)
33473    {
33474        int fd;
33475
33476        /*
33477         *  Find a file descriptor suitable for return to
33478         the user.
33479         */
33480
33481        fd = get_unused_fd();
33482        if (fd >= 0) {
33483            struct file *file = get_empty_filp();
33484
33485            if (!file) {
33486                put_unused_fd(fd);
33487                return -ENFILE;
33488            }
33489
33490            current->files->fd[fd] = file;
33491            file->f_op = &socket_file_ops;
33492            file->f_mode = 3;
33493            file->f_flags = O_RDWR;
33494            file->f_count = 1;
33495            file->f_inode = inode;
33496            if (inode)
33497                inode->i_count++;
33498            file->f_pos = 0;
33499        }
33500        return fd;
33501    }
33502
33503
33504    /*
33505     *  Go from an inode to its socket slot.
33506     *
33507     *  The original socket implementation wasn't very
33508     clever, which is
33509     *  why this exists at all..
33510     */
33511
33512    __inline struct socket *socki_lookup(struct inode *inode)
33513    {
33514        return &inode->u.socket_i;
33515    }
33516
33517    /*
33518     *  Go from a file number to its socket slot.
33519     */
```

```
33520
33521    extern __inline struct socket *sockfd_lookup(int fd,
33522    struct file **pfile)
33523    {
33524        struct file *file;
33525        struct inode *inode;
33526
33527        if (fd < 0 || fd >= NR_OPEN || !(file =
33528    current->files->fd[fd]))
33529            return NULL;
33530
33531        inode = file->f_inode;
33532        if (!inode || !inode->i_sock)
33533            return NULL;
33534
33535        if (pfile)
33536            *pfile = file;
33537
33538        return socki_lookup(inode);
33539    }
33540
33541    /*
33542     *  Allocate a socket.
33543     */
33544
33545    struct socket *sock_alloc(void)
33546    {
33547        struct inode * inode;
33548        struct socket * sock;
33549
33550        inode = get_empty_inode();
33551        if (!inode)
33552            return NULL;
33553
33554        inode->i_mode = S_IFSOCK;
33555        inode->i_sock = 1;
33556        inode->i_uid = current->uid;
33557        inode->i_gid = current->gid;
33558
33559        sock = &inode->u.socket_i;
33560        sock->state = SS_UNCONNECTED;
33561        sock->flags = 0;
33562        sock->ops = NULL;
33563        sock->data = NULL;
33564        sock->conn = NULL;
33565        sock->iconn = NULL;
33566        sock->next = NULL;
33567        sock->file = NULL;
```

```
33568        sock->wait = &inode->i_wait;
33569        sock->inode = inode;          /* "backlink": we could
33570    use pointer arithmetic instead */
33571        sock->fasync_list = NULL;
33572        sockets_in_use++;
33573        return sock;
33574    }
33575
33576    /*
33577     *  Release a socket.
33578     */
33579
33580    static inline void sock_release_peer(struct socket *peer)
33581    {
33582        peer->state = SS_DISCONNECTING;
33583        wake_up_interruptible(peer->wait);
33584        sock_wake_async(peer, 1);
33585    }
33586
33587    void sock_release(struct socket *sock)
33588    {
33589        int oldstate;
33590        struct socket *peersock, *nextsock;
33591
33592        if ((oldstate = sock->state) != SS_UNCONNECTED)
33593            sock->state = SS_DISCONNECTING;
33594
33595        /*
33596         *  Wake up anyone waiting for connections.
33597         */
33598
33599        for (peersock = sock->iconn; peersock; peersock =
33600    nextsock)
33601        {
33602            nextsock = peersock->next;
33603            sock_release_peer(peersock);
33604        }
33605
33606        /*
33607         * Wake up anyone we're connected to. First, we
33608    release the
33609         * protocol, to give it a chance to flush data, etc.
33610         */
33611
33612        peersock = (oldstate == SS_CONNECTED) ? sock->conn :
33613    NULL;
33614        if (sock->ops)
33615            sock->ops->release(sock, peersock);
```

```
33616        if (peersock)
33617            sock_release_peer(peersock);
33618        --sockets_in_use;     /* Bookkeeping.. */
33619        sock->file=NULL;
33620        iput(SOCK_INODE(sock));
33621    }
33622
33623    /*
33624     *  Sockets are not seekable.
33625     */
33626
33627    static int sock_lseek(struct inode *inode, struct file
33628    *file, off_t offset, int whence)
33629    {
33630        return(-ESPIPE);
33631    }
33632
33633    /*
33634     *  Read data from a socket. ubuf is a user mode
33635    pointer. We make sure the user
33636     *  area ubuf...ubuf+size-1 is writable before asking
33637    the protocol.
33638     */
33639
33640    static int sock_read(struct inode *inode, struct file
33641    *file, char *ubuf, int size)
33642    {
33643        struct socket *sock;
33644        int err;
33645        struct iovec iov;
33646        struct msghdr msg;
33647
33648        sock = socki_lookup(inode);
33649        if (sock->flags & SO_ACCEPTCON)
33650            return(-EINVAL);
33651
33652        if(size<0)
33653            return -EINVAL;
33654        if(size==0)     /* Match SYS5 behaviour */
33655            return 0;
33656        if ((err=verify_area(VERIFY_WRITE,ubuf,size))<0)
33657            return err;
33658        msg.msg_name=NULL;
33659        msg.msg_iov=&iov;
33660        msg.msg_iovlen=1;
33661        msg.msg_control=NULL;
33662        iov.iov_base=ubuf;
33663        iov.iov_len=size;
33664
33665        return(sock->ops->recvmsg(sock, &msg,
33666    size,(file->f_flags & O_NONBLOCK), 0,&msg.msg_namelen));
33667    }
33668
33669    /*
33670     *  Write data to a socket. We verify that the user area
33671    ubuf..ubuf+size-1 is
33672     *  readable by the user process.
33673     */
33674
33675    static int sock_write(struct inode *inode, struct file
33676    *file, const char *ubuf, int size)
33677    {
33678        struct socket *sock;
33679        int err;
33680        struct msghdr msg;
33681        struct iovec iov;
33682
33683        sock = socki_lookup(inode);
33684
33685        if (sock->flags & SO_ACCEPTCON)
33686            return(-EINVAL);
33687
33688        if(size<0)
33689            return -EINVAL;
33690        if(size==0)     /* Match SYS5 behaviour */
33691            return 0;
33692
33693        if ((err=verify_area(VERIFY_READ,ubuf,size))<0)
33694            return err;
33695
33696        msg.msg_name=NULL;
33697        msg.msg_iov=&iov;
33698        msg.msg_iovlen=1;
33699        msg.msg_control=NULL;
33700        iov.iov_base=(void *)ubuf;
33701        iov.iov_len=size;
33702
33703        return(sock->ops->sendmsg(sock, &msg,
33704    size,(file->f_flags & O_NONBLOCK),0));
33705    }
33706
33707    /*
33708     *  With an ioctl arg may well be a user mode pointer,
33709    but we don't know what to do
33710     *  with it - that's up to the protocol still.
33711     */
```

```
33712
33713   int sock_ioctl(struct inode *inode, struct file *file,
33714   unsigned int cmd,
33715           unsigned long arg)
33716   {
33717       struct socket *sock;
33718       sock = socki_lookup(inode);
33719       return(sock->ops->ioctl(sock, cmd, arg));
33720   }
33721
33722
33723   static int sock_select(struct inode *inode, struct file
33724   *file, int sel_type, select_table * wait)
33725   {
33726       struct socket *sock;
33727
33728       sock = socki_lookup(inode);
33729
33730       /*
33731        *  We can't return errors to select, so it's either
33732   yes or no.
33733        */
33734
33735       if (sock->ops->select)
33736           return(sock->ops->select(sock, sel_type, wait));
33737       return(0);
33738   }
33739
33740
33741   void sock_close(struct inode *inode, struct file *filp)
33742   {
33743       /*
33744        *  It's possible the inode is NULL if we're closing
33745   an unfinished socket.
33746        */
33747
33748       if (!inode)
33749           return;
33750       sock_fasync(inode, filp, 0);
33751       sock_release(socki_lookup(inode));
33752   }
33753
33754   /*
33755    *  Update the socket async list
33756    */
33757
33758   static int sock_fasync(struct inode *inode, struct file
33759   *filp, int on)
33760   {
33761       struct fasync_struct *fa, *fna=NULL, **prev;
33762       struct socket *sock;
33763       unsigned long flags;
33764
33765       if (on)
33766       {
33767           fna=(struct fasync_struct
33768   *)kmalloc(sizeof(struct fasync_struct), GFP_KERNEL);
33769           if(fna==NULL)
33770               return -ENOMEM;
33771       }
33772
33773       sock = socki_lookup(inode);
33774
33775       prev=&(sock->fasync_list);
33776
33777       save_flags(flags);
33778       cli();
33779
33780       for(fa=*prev; fa!=NULL; prev=&fa->fa_next,fa=*prev)
33781           if(fa->fa_file==filp)
33782               break;
33783
33784       if(on)
33785       {
33786           if(fa!=NULL)
33787           {
33788               kfree_s(fna,sizeof(struct fasync_struct));
33789               restore_flags(flags);
33790               return 0;
33791           }
33792           fna->fa_file=filp;
33793           fna->magic=FASYNC_MAGIC;
33794           fna->fa_next=sock->fasync_list;
33795           sock->fasync_list=fna;
33796       }
33797       else
33798       {
33799           if(fa!=NULL)
33800           {
33801               *prev=fa->fa_next;
33802               kfree_s(fa,sizeof(struct fasync_struct));
33803           }
33804       }
33805       restore_flags(flags);
33806       return 0;
33807   }
```

```
33808
33809    int sock_wake_async(struct socket *sock, int how)
33810    {
33811        if (!sock || !sock->fasync_list)
33812            return -1;
33813        switch (how)
33814        {
33815            case 0:
33816                kill_fasync(sock->fasync_list, SIGIO);
33817                break;
33818            case 1:
33819                if (!(sock->flags & SO_WAITDATA))
33820                    kill_fasync(sock->fasync_list, SIGIO);
33821                break;
33822            case 2:
33823                if (sock->flags & SO_NOSPACE)
33824                {
33825                    kill_fasync(sock->fasync_list, SIGIO);
33826                    sock->flags &= ~SO_NOSPACE;
33827                }
33828                break;
33829        }
33830        return 0;
33831    }
33832
33833
33834    /*
33835     * Perform the socket system call. we locate the
33836    appropriate
33837     * family, then create a fresh socket.
33838     */
33839
33840    static int find_protocol_family(int family)
33841    {
33842        register int i;
33843        for (i = 0; i < NPROTO; i++)
33844        {
33845            if (pops[i] == NULL)
33846                continue;
33847            if (pops[i]->family == family)
33848                return i;
33849        }
33850        return -1;
33851    }
33852
33853    asmlinkage int sys_socket(int family, int type, int
33854    protocol)
33855    {
33856        int i, fd;
33857        struct socket *sock;
33858        struct proto_ops *ops;
33859
33860        /* Locate the correct protocol family. */
33861        i = find_protocol_family(family);
33862
33863    #ifdef CONFIG_KERNELD
33864        /* Attempt to load a protocol module if the find
33865    failed. */
33866        if (i < 0)
33867        {
33868            char module_name[30];
33869            sprintf(module_name,"net-pf-%d",family);
33870            request_module(module_name);
33871            i = find_protocol_family(family);
33872        }
33873    #endif
33874
33875        if (i < 0)
33876        {
33877            return -EINVAL;
33878        }
33879
33880        ops = pops[i];
33881
33882    /*
33883     * Check that this is a type that we know how to
33884    manipulate and
33885     * the protocol makes sense here. The family can still
33886    reject the
33887     * protocol later.
33888     */
33889
33890        if ((type != SOCK_STREAM && type != SOCK_DGRAM &&
33891            type != SOCK_SEQPACKET && type != SOCK_RAW &&
33892            type != SOCK_PACKET) || protocol < 0)
33893                return(-EINVAL);
33894
33895    /*
33896     * Allocate the socket and allow the family to set
33897    things up. if
33898     * the protocol is 0, the family is instructed to
33899    select an appropriate
33900     * default.
33901     */
33902
33903        if (!(sock = sock_alloc()))
```

```
33904          {
33905                  printk(KERN_WARNING "socket: no more sockets\n");
33906                  return(-ENOSR); /* Was: EAGAIN, but we are out of
33907                          system resources! */
33908          }
33909
33910          sock->type = type;
33911          sock->ops = ops;
33912          if ((i = sock->ops->create(sock, protocol)) < 0)
33913          {
33914              sock_release(sock);
33915              return(i);
33916          }
33917
33918          if ((fd = get_fd(SOCK_INODE(sock))) < 0)
33919          {
33920              sock_release(sock);
33921              return fd;
33922          }
33923
33924          sock->file=current->files->fd[fd];
33925
33926          return(fd);
33927 }
33928
33929 /*
33930  *  Create a pair of connected sockets.
33931  */
33932
33933 asmlinkage int sys_socketpair(int family, int type, int
33934 protocol, int usockvec[2])
33935 {
33936      int fd1, fd2, i;
33937      struct socket *sock1, *sock2;
33938      int er;
33939
33940      /*
33941       * Obtain the first socket and check if the
33942 underlying protocol
33943       * supports the socketpair call.
33944       */
33945
33946      if ((fd1 = sys_socket(family, type, protocol)) < 0)
33947          return(fd1);
33948      sock1 = sockfd_lookup(fd1, NULL);
33949      if (!sock1->ops->socketpair)
33950      {
33951          sys_close(fd1);
33952          return(-EINVAL);
33953      }
33954
33955      /*
33956       *  Now grab another socket and try to connect the
33957 two together.
33958       */
33959
33960      if ((fd2 = sys_socket(family, type, protocol)) < 0)
33961      {
33962          sys_close(fd1);
33963          return(-EINVAL);
33964      }
33965
33966      sock2 = sockfd_lookup(fd2, NULL);
33967      if ((i = sock1->ops->socketpair(sock1, sock2)) < 0)
33968      {
33969          sys_close(fd1);
33970          sys_close(fd2);
33971          return(i);
33972      }
33973
33974      sock1->conn = sock2;
33975      sock2->conn = sock1;
33976      sock1->state = SS_CONNECTED;
33977      sock2->state = SS_CONNECTED;
33978
33979      er=verify_area(VERIFY_WRITE, usockvec,
33980 sizeof(usockvec));
33981      if(er)
33982      {
33983          sys_close(fd1);
33984          sys_close(fd2);
33985          return er;
33986      }
33987      put_user(fd1, &usockvec[0]);
33988      put_user(fd2, &usockvec[1]);
33989
33990      return(0);
33991 }
33992
33993
33994 /*
33995  *  Bind a name to a socket. Nothing much to do here
33996 since it's
33997  *  the protocol's responsibility to handle the local
33998 address.
33999  *
```

```
34000    *  We move the socket address to kernel space before we
34001  call
34002    *  the protocol layer (having also checked the address
34003  is ok).
34004    */
34005
34006  asmlinkage int sys_bind(int fd, struct sockaddr
34007  *umyaddr, int addrlen)
34008  {
34009      struct socket *sock;
34010      int i;
34011      char address[MAX_SOCK_ADDR];
34012      int err;
34013
34014      if (fd < 0 || fd >= NR_OPEN ||
34015  current->files->fd[fd] == NULL)
34016          return(-EBADF);
34017
34018      if (!(sock = sockfd_lookup(fd, NULL)))
34019          return(-ENOTSOCK);
34020
34021
34022  if((err=move_addr_to_kernel(umyaddr,addrlen,address))<0)
34023          return err;
34024
34025      if ((i = sock->ops->bind(sock, (struct sockaddr
34026  *)address, addrlen)) < 0)
34027          {
34028          return(i);
34029          }
34030      return(0);
34031  }
34032
34033
34034  /*
34035    *  Perform a listen. Basically, we allow the protocol
34036  to do anything
34037    *  necessary for a listen, and if that works, we mark
34038  the socket as
34039    *  ready for listening.
34040    */
34041
34042  asmlinkage int sys_listen(int fd, int backlog)
34043  {
34044      struct socket *sock;
34045      int err=-EOPNOTSUPP;
34046
34047      if (fd < 0 || fd >= NR_OPEN ||
```

```
34048  current->files->fd[fd] == NULL)
34049          return(-EBADF);
34050      if (!(sock = sockfd_lookup(fd, NULL)))
34051          return(-ENOTSOCK);
34052
34053      if (sock->state != SS_UNCONNECTED)
34054          return(-EINVAL);
34055
34056      if (sock->ops && sock->ops->listen)
34057          {
34058          err=sock->ops->listen(sock, backlog);
34059          if(!err)
34060              sock->flags |= SO_ACCEPTCON;
34061          }
34062      return(err);
34063  }
34064
34065
34066  /*
34067    *  For accept, we attempt to create a new socket, set
34068  up the link
34069    *  with the client, wake up the client, then return the
34070  new
34071    *  connected fd. We collect the address of the
34072  connector in kernel
34073    *  space and move it to user at the very end. This is
34074  buggy because
34075    *  we open the socket then return an error.
34076    */
34077
34078  asmlinkage int sys_accept(int fd, struct sockaddr
34079  *upeer_sockaddr, int *upeer_addrlen)
34080  {
34081      struct file *file;
34082      struct socket *sock, *newsock;
34083      int i;
34084      char address[MAX_SOCK_ADDR];
34085      int len;
34086
34087      if (fd < 0 || fd >= NR_OPEN || ((file =
34088  current->files->fd[fd]) == NULL))
34089          return(-EBADF);
34090      if (!(sock = sockfd_lookup(fd, &file)))
34091          return(-ENOTSOCK);
34092      if (sock->state != SS_UNCONNECTED)
34093          {
34094          return(-EINVAL);
34095          }
```

```
34096        if (!(sock->flags & SO_ACCEPTCON))
34097        {
34098            return(-EINVAL);
34099        }
34100
34101        if (!(newsock = sock_alloc()))
34102        {
34103            printk(KERN_WARNING "accept: no more sockets\n");
34104            return(-ENOSR); /* Was: EAGAIN, but we are out
34105 of system
34106                          resources! */
34107        }
34108        newsock->type = sock->type;
34109        newsock->ops = sock->ops;
34110        if ((i = sock->ops->dup(newsock, sock)) < 0)
34111        {
34112            sock_release(newsock);
34113            return(i);
34114        }
34115
34116        i = newsock->ops->accept(sock, newsock,
34117 file->f_flags);
34118        if ( i < 0)
34119        {
34120            sock_release(newsock);
34121            return(i);
34122        }
34123
34124        if ((fd = get_fd(SOCK_INODE(newsock))) < 0)
34125        {
34126            sock_release(newsock);
34127            return(-EINVAL);
34128        }
34129        newsock->file=current->files->fd[fd];
34130
34131        if (upeer_sockaddr)
34132        {
34133            newsock->ops->getname(newsock, (struct sockaddr
34134 *)address, &len, 1);
34135            move_addr_to_user(address,len, upeer_sockaddr,
34136 upeer_addrlen);
34137        }
34138        return(fd);
34139 }
34140
34141
34142 /*
34143  *  Attempt to connect to a socket with the server
34144 address.  The address
34145  *  is in user space so we verify it is OK and move it
34146 to kernel space.
34147  */
34148
34149 asmlinkage int sys_connect(int fd, struct sockaddr
34150 *uservaddr, int addrlen)
34151 {
34152     struct socket *sock;
34153     struct file *file;
34154     int i;
34155     char address[MAX_SOCK_ADDR];
34156     int err;
34157
34158     if (fd < 0 || fd >= NR_OPEN ||
34159 (file=current->files->fd[fd]) == NULL)
34160         return(-EBADF);
34161     if (!(sock = sockfd_lookup(fd, &file)))
34162         return(-ENOTSOCK);
34163
34164
34165 if((err=move_addr_to_kernel(uservaddr,addrlen,address))<0
34166 )
34167         return err;
34168
34169     switch(sock->state)
34170     {
34171         case SS_UNCONNECTED:
34172             /* This is ok... continue with connect */
34173             break;
34174         case SS_CONNECTED:
34175             /* Socket is already connected */
34176             if(sock->type == SOCK_DGRAM) /* Hack for now
34177 - move this all into the protocol */
34178                 break;
34179             return -EISCONN;
34180         case SS_CONNECTING:
34181             /* Not yet connected... we will check this.
34182 */
34183
34184             /*
34185              * FIXME:  for all protocols what happens
34186 if you start
34187              * an async connect fork and both children
34188 connect. Clean
34189              * this up in the protocols!
34190              */
34191             break;
```

```
34192              default:
34193                  return(-EINVAL);
34194          }
34195          i = sock->ops->connect(sock, (struct sockaddr
34196  *)address, addrlen, file->f_flags);
34197          if (i < 0)
34198          {
34199              return(i);
34200          }
34201          return(0);
34202  }
34203
34204  /*
34205   *  Get the local address ('name') of a socket object.
34206  Move the obtained
34207   *  name to user space.
34208   */
34209
34210  asmlinkage int sys_getsockname(int fd, struct sockaddr
34211  *usockaddr, int *usockaddr_len)
34212  {
34213      struct socket *sock;
34214      char address[MAX_SOCK_ADDR];
34215      int len;
34216      int err;
34217
34218          if (fd < 0 || fd >= NR_OPEN ||
34219  current->files->fd[fd] == NULL)
34220              return(-EBADF);
34221          if (!(sock = sockfd_lookup(fd, NULL)))
34222              return(-ENOTSOCK);
34223
34224          err=sock->ops->getname(sock, (struct sockaddr
34225  *)address, &len, 0);
34226          if(err)
34227              return err;
34228          if((err=move_addr_to_user(address,len, usockaddr,
34229  usockaddr_len))<0)
34230              return err;
34231          return 0;
34232  }
34233
34234  /*
34235   *  Get the remote address ('name') of a socket object.
34236  Move the obtained
34237   *  name to user space.
34238   */
34239
34240  asmlinkage int sys_getpeername(int fd, struct sockaddr
34241  *usockaddr, int *usockaddr_len)
34242  {
34243      struct socket *sock;
34244      char address[MAX_SOCK_ADDR];
34245      int len;
34246      int err;
34247
34248          if (fd < 0 || fd >= NR_OPEN ||
34249  current->files->fd[fd] == NULL)
34250              return(-EBADF);
34251          if (!(sock = sockfd_lookup(fd, NULL)))
34252              return(-ENOTSOCK);
34253
34254          err=sock->ops->getname(sock, (struct sockaddr
34255  *)address, &len, 1);
34256          if(err)
34257              return err;
34258          if((err=move_addr_to_user(address,len, usockaddr,
34259  usockaddr_len))<0)
34260              return err;
34261          return 0;
34262  }
34263
34264  /*
34265   *  Send a datagram down a socket. The datagram as with
34266  write() is
34267   *  in user space. We check it can be read.
34268   */
34269
34270  asmlinkage int sys_send(int fd, void * buff, int len,
34271  unsigned flags)
34272  {
34273      struct socket *sock;
34274      struct file *file;
34275      int err;
34276      struct msghdr msg;
34277      struct iovec iov;
34278
34279          if (fd < 0 || fd >= NR_OPEN || ((file =
34280  current->files->fd[fd]) == NULL))
34281              return(-EBADF);
34282          if (!(sock = sockfd_lookup(fd, NULL)))
34283              return(-ENOTSOCK);
34284
34285          if(len<0)
34286              return -EINVAL;
34287          err=verify_area(VERIFY_READ, buff, len);
```

```
34288        if(err)
34289            return err;
34290
34291        iov.iov_base=buff;
34292        iov.iov_len=len;
34293        msg.msg_name=NULL;
34294        msg.msg_iov=&iov;
34295        msg.msg_iovlen=1;
34296        msg.msg_control=NULL;
34297        return(sock->ops->sendmsg(sock, &msg, len,
34298    (file->f_flags & O_NONBLOCK), flags));
34299    }
34300
34301    /*
34302     *  Send a datagram to a given address. We move the
34303    address into kernel
34304     *  space and check the user space data area is readable
34305    before invoking
34306     *  the protocol.
34307     */
34308
34309    asmlinkage int sys_sendto(int fd, void * buff, int len,
34310    unsigned flags,
34311            struct sockaddr *addr, int addr_len)
34312    {
34313        struct socket *sock;
34314        struct file *file;
34315        char address[MAX_SOCK_ADDR];
34316        int err;
34317        struct msghdr msg;
34318        struct iovec iov;
34319
34320        if (fd < 0 || fd >= NR_OPEN || ((file =
34321    current->files->fd[fd]) == NULL))
34322            return(-EBADF);
34323        if (!(sock = sockfd_lookup(fd, NULL)))
34324            return(-ENOTSOCK);
34325
34326        if(len<0)
34327            return -EINVAL;
34328        err=verify_area(VERIFY_READ,buff,len);
34329        if(err)
34330            return err;
34331
34332        iov.iov_base=buff;
34333        iov.iov_len=len;
34334        msg.msg_name = NULL;
34335        msg.msg_namelen = 0;
```

```
34336        msg.msg_iov=&iov;
34337        msg.msg_iovlen=1;
34338        msg.msg_control=NULL;
34339        if (addr && addr_len) {
34340            err=move_addr_to_kernel(addr,addr_len,address);
34341            if (err < 0)
34342                return err;
34343            msg.msg_name=address;
34344            msg.msg_namelen=addr_len;
34345        }
34346
34347        return(sock->ops->sendmsg(sock, &msg, len,
34348    (file->f_flags & O_NONBLOCK),
34349            flags));
34350    }
34351
34352
34353    /*
34354     *  Receive a datagram from a socket. Call the protocol
34355    recvmsg method
34356     */
34357
34358    asmlinkage int sys_recv(int fd, void * ubuf, int size,
34359    unsigned flags)
34360    {
34361        struct iovec iov;
34362        struct msghdr msg;
34363        struct socket *sock;
34364        struct file *file;
34365        int err;
34366
34367        if (fd < 0 || fd >= NR_OPEN || ((file =
34368    current->files->fd[fd]) == NULL))
34369            return(-EBADF);
34370
34371        if (!(sock = sockfd_lookup(fd, NULL)))
34372            return(-ENOTSOCK);
34373
34374        if(size<0)
34375            return -EINVAL;
34376        if(size==0)
34377            return 0;
34378        err=verify_area(VERIFY_WRITE, ubuf, size);
34379        if(err)
34380            return err;
34381
34382        msg.msg_name=NULL;
34383        msg.msg_iov=&iov;
```

```
34384         msg.msg_iovlen=1;
34385         msg.msg_control=NULL;
34386         iov.iov_base=ubuf;
34387         iov.iov_len=size;
34388
34389         return(sock->ops->recvmsg(sock, &msg,
34390    size,(file->f_flags & O_NONBLOCK),
34391    flags,&msg.msg_namelen));
34392    }
34393
34394    /*
34395     *  Receive a frame from the socket and optionally
34396    record the address of the
34397     *  sender. We verify the buffers are writable and if
34398    needed move the
34399     *  sender address from kernel to user space.
34400     */
34401
34402    asmlinkage int sys_recvfrom(int fd, void * ubuf, int
34403    size, unsigned flags,
34404              struct sockaddr *addr, int *addr_len)
34405    {
34406        struct socket *sock;
34407        struct file *file;
34408        struct iovec iov;
34409        struct msghdr msg;
34410        char address[MAX_SOCK_ADDR];
34411        int err;
34412        int alen;
34413        if (fd < 0 || fd >= NR_OPEN || ((file =
34414    current->files->fd[fd]) == NULL))
34415              return(-EBADF);
34416        if (!(sock = sockfd_lookup(fd, NULL)))
34417              return(-ENOTSOCK);
34418        if(size<0)
34419              return -EINVAL;
34420        if(size==0)
34421              return 0;
34422
34423        err=verify_area(VERIFY_WRITE,ubuf,size);
34424        if(err)
34425              return err;
34426
34427        msg.msg_control=NULL;
34428        msg.msg_iovlen=1;
34429        msg.msg_iov=&iov;
34430        iov.iov_len=size;
34431        iov.iov_base=ubuf;
```

```
34432         msg.msg_name=address;
34433         msg.msg_namelen=MAX_SOCK_ADDR;
34434         size=sock->ops->recvmsg(sock, &msg, size,
34435    (file->f_flags & O_NONBLOCK),
34436              flags, &alen);
34437
34438        if(size<0)
34439              return size;
34440        if(addr!=NULL &&
34441    (err=move_addr_to_user(address,alen, addr, addr_len))<0)
34442              return err;
34443
34444        return size;
34445    }
34446
34447    /*
34448     *  Set a socket option. Because we don't know the
34449    option lengths we have
34450     *  to pass the user mode parameter for the protocols to
34451    sort out.
34452     */
34453
34454    asmlinkage int sys_setsockopt(int fd, int level, int
34455    optname, char *optval, int optlen)
34456    {
34457        struct socket *sock;
34458        struct file *file;
34459
34460        if (fd < 0 || fd >= NR_OPEN || ((file =
34461    current->files->fd[fd]) == NULL))
34462              return(-EBADF);
34463        if (!(sock = sockfd_lookup(fd, NULL)))
34464              return(-ENOTSOCK);
34465
34466        return(sock->ops->setsockopt(sock, level, optname,
34467    optval, optlen));
34468    }
34469
34470    /*
34471     *  Get a socket option. Because we don't know the
34472    option lengths we have
34473     *  to pass a user mode parameter for the protocols to
34474    sort out.
34475     */
34476
34477    asmlinkage int sys_getsockopt(int fd, int level, int
34478    optname, char *optval, int *optlen)
34479    {
```

```
34480        struct socket *sock;
34481        struct file *file;
34482
34483        if (fd < 0 || fd >= NR_OPEN || ((file =
34484    current->files->fd[fd]) == NULL))
34485            return(-EBADF);
34486        if (!(sock = sockfd_lookup(fd, NULL)))
34487            return(-ENOTSOCK);
34488
34489        if (!sock->ops->getsockopt)
34490            return(0);
34491        return(sock->ops->getsockopt(sock, level, optname,
34492    optval, optlen));
34493    }
34494
34495
34496    /*
34497     *  Shutdown a socket.
34498     */
34499
34500    asmlinkage int sys_shutdown(int fd, int how)
34501    {
34502        struct socket *sock;
34503        struct file *file;
34504
34505        if (fd < 0 || fd >= NR_OPEN || ((file =
34506    current->files->fd[fd]) == NULL))
34507            return(-EBADF);
34508        if (!(sock = sockfd_lookup(fd, NULL)))
34509            return(-ENOTSOCK);
34510
34511        return(sock->ops->shutdown(sock, how));
34512    }
34513
34514    /*
34515     *  BSD sendmsg interface
34516     */
34517
34518    asmlinkage int sys_sendmsg(int fd, struct msghdr *msg,
34519    unsigned int flags)
34520    {
34521        struct socket *sock;
34522        struct file *file;
34523        char address[MAX_SOCK_ADDR];
34524        struct iovec iov[UIO_MAXIOV];
34525        struct msghdr msg_sys;
34526        int err;
34527        int total_len;
```

```
34528
34529        if (fd < 0 || fd >= NR_OPEN || ((file =
34530    current->files->fd[fd]) == NULL))
34531            return(-EBADF);
34532        if (!(sock = sockfd_lookup(fd, NULL)))
34533            return(-ENOTSOCK);
34534
34535        if(sock->ops->sendmsg==NULL)
34536            return -EOPNOTSUPP;
34537
34538
34539        err=verify_area(VERIFY_READ, msg,sizeof(struct
34540    msghdr));
34541        if(err)
34542            return err;
34543
34544        memcpy_fromfs(&msg_sys,msg,sizeof(struct msghdr));
34545
34546        /* do not move before msg_sys is valid */
34547        if(msg_sys.msg_iovlen>UIO_MAXIOV)
34548            return -EINVAL;
34549
34550        /* This will also move the address data into kernel
34551    space */
34552        err = verify_iovec(&msg_sys, iov, address,
34553    VERIFY_READ);
34554        if (err < 0)
34555            return err;
34556        total_len=err;
34557
34558        return sock->ops->sendmsg(sock, &msg_sys, total_len,
34559    (file->f_flags&O_NONBLOCK), flags);
34560    }
34561
34562    /*
34563     *  BSD recvmsg interface
34564     */
34565
34566    asmlinkage int sys_recvmsg(int fd, struct msghdr *msg,
34567    unsigned int flags)
34568    {
34569        struct socket *sock;
34570        struct file *file;
34571        struct iovec iov[UIO_MAXIOV];
34572        struct msghdr msg_sys;
34573        int err;
34574        int total_len;
34575        int len;
```

```
34576
34577        /* kernel mode address */
34578        char addr[MAX_SOCK_ADDR];
34579        int addr_len;
34580
34581        /* user mode address pointers */
34582        struct sockaddr *uaddr;
34583        int *uaddr_len;
34584
34585        if (fd < 0 || fd >= NR_OPEN || ((file =
34586   current->files->fd[fd]) == NULL))
34587            return(-EBADF);
34588        if (!(sock = sockfd_lookup(fd, NULL)))
34589            return(-ENOTSOCK);
34590
34591        err=verify_area(VERIFY_READ, msg,sizeof(struct
34592   msghdr));
34593        if(err)
34594            return err;
34595        memcpy_fromfs(&msg_sys,msg,sizeof(struct msghdr));
34596        if(msg_sys.msg_iovlen>UIO_MAXIOV)
34597            return -EINVAL;
34598
34599        /*
34600         * save the user-mode address (verify_iovec will
34601   change the
34602         * kernel msghdr to use the kernel address space)
34603         */
34604        uaddr = msg_sys.msg_name;
34605        uaddr_len = &msg->msg_namelen;
34606        err=verify_iovec(&msg_sys,iov,addr, VERIFY_WRITE);
34607        if(err<0)
34608            return err;
34609
34610        total_len=err;
34611
34612        if(sock->ops->recvmsg==NULL)
34613            return -EOPNOTSUPP;
34614        len=sock->ops->recvmsg(sock, &msg_sys, total_len,
34615   (file->f_flags&O_NONBLOCK), flags, &addr_len);
34616        if(len<0)
34617            return len;
34618
34619        if (uaddr != NULL) {
34620            err = move_addr_to_user(addr, addr_len, uaddr,
34621   uaddr_len);
34622            if (err)
34623                return err;
```

```
34624        }
34625        return len;
34626   }
34627
34628
34629   /*
34630    *  Perform a file control on a socket file descriptor.
34631    */
34632
34633   int sock_fcntl(struct file *filp, unsigned int cmd,
34634   unsigned long arg)
34635   {
34636        struct socket *sock;
34637
34638        sock = socki_lookup (filp->f_inode);
34639        if (sock != NULL && sock->ops != NULL &&
34640   sock->ops->fcntl != NULL)
34641            return(sock->ops->fcntl(sock, cmd, arg));
34642        return(-EINVAL);
34643   }
34644
34645
34646   /*
34647    *  System call vectors. Since I (RIB) want to rewrite
34648   sockets as streams,
34649    *  we have this level of indirection. Not a lot of
34650   overhead, since more of
34651    *  the work is done via read/write/select directly.
34652    *
34653    *  I'm now expanding this up to a higher level to
34654   separate the assorted
34655    *  kernel/user space manipulations and global
34656   assumptions from the protocol
34657    *  layers proper - AC.
34658    *
34659    *  Argument checking cleaned up. Saved 20% in size.
34660    */
34661
34662   asmlinkage int sys_socketcall(int call, unsigned long
34663   *args)
34664   {
34665        int er;
34666        unsigned char nargs[18]={0,3,3,3,2,3,3,3,
34667                    4,4,4,6,6,2,5,5,3,3};
34668
34669        unsigned long a0,a1;
34670
34671        if(call<1||call>SYS_RECVMSG)
```

```
34672            return -EINVAL;
34673
34674        er=verify_area(VERIFY_READ, args, nargs[call] *
34675    sizeof(unsigned long));
34676        if(er)
34677            return er;
34678
34679        a0=get_user(args);
34680        a1=get_user(args+1);
34681
34682
34683        switch(call)
34684        {
34685            case SYS_SOCKET:
34686                return(sys_socket(a0,a1,get_user(args+2)));
34687            case SYS_BIND:
34688                return(sys_bind(a0,(struct sockaddr *)a1,
34689                        get_user(args+2)));
34690            case SYS_CONNECT:
34691                return(sys_connect(a0, (struct sockaddr *)a1,
34692                        get_user(args+2)));
34693            case SYS_LISTEN:
34694                return(sys_listen(a0,a1));
34695            case SYS_ACCEPT:
34696                return(sys_accept(a0,(struct sockaddr *)a1,
34697                        (int *)get_user(args+2)));
34698            case SYS_GETSOCKNAME:
34699                return(sys_getsockname(a0,(struct sockaddr
34700    *)a1,
34701                        (int *)get_user(args+2)));
34702            case SYS_GETPEERNAME:
34703                return(sys_getpeername(a0, (struct sockaddr
34704    *)a1,
34705                        (int *)get_user(args+2)));
34706            case SYS_SOCKETPAIR:
34707                return(sys_socketpair(a0,a1,
34708                        get_user(args+2),
34709                        (int *)get_user(args+3)));
34710            case SYS_SEND:
34711                return(sys_send(a0,
34712                    (void *)a1,
34713                    get_user(args+2),
34714                    get_user(args+3)));
34715            case SYS_SENDTO:
34716                return(sys_sendto(a0,(void *)a1,
34717                    get_user(args+2),
34718                    get_user(args+3),
34719                    (struct sockaddr *)get_user(args+4),
34720                    get_user(args+5)));
34721            case SYS_RECV:
34722                return(sys_recv(a0,
34723                    (void *)a1,
34724                    get_user(args+2),
34725                    get_user(args+3)));
34726            case SYS_RECVFROM:
34727                return(sys_recvfrom(a0,
34728                    (void *)a1,
34729                    get_user(args+2),
34730                    get_user(args+3),
34731                    (struct sockaddr *)get_user(args+4),
34732                    (int *)get_user(args+5)));
34733            case SYS_SHUTDOWN:
34734                return(sys_shutdown(a0,a1));
34735            case SYS_SETSOCKOPT:
34736                return(sys_setsockopt(a0,
34737                    a1,
34738                    get_user(args+2),
34739                    (char *)get_user(args+3),
34740                    get_user(args+4)));
34741            case SYS_GETSOCKOPT:
34742                return(sys_getsockopt(a0,
34743                    a1,
34744                    get_user(args+2),
34745                    (char *)get_user(args+3),
34746                    (int *)get_user(args+4)));
34747            case SYS_SENDMSG:
34748                return sys_sendmsg(a0,
34749                    (struct msghdr *) a1,
34750                    get_user(args+2));
34751            case SYS_RECVMSG:
34752                return sys_recvmsg(a0,
34753                    (struct msghdr *) a1,
34754                    get_user(args+2));
34755        }
34756        return -EINVAL; /* to keep gcc happy */
34757    }
34758
34759    /*
34760     * This function is called by a protocol handler that
34761    wants to
34762     * advertise its address family, and have it linked
34763    into the
34764     * SOCKET module.
34765     */
34766
34767    int sock_register(int family, struct proto_ops *ops)
```

```
34768   {
34769       int i;
34770
34771       cli();
34772       for(i = 0; i < NPROTO; i++)
34773       {
34774           if (pops[i] != NULL)
34775               continue;
34776           pops[i] = ops;
34777           pops[i]->family = family;
34778           sti();
34779           return(i);
34780       }
34781       sti();
34782       return(-ENOMEM);
34783   }
34784
34785   /*
34786    * This function is called by a protocol handler that
34787   wants to
34788    * remove its address family, and have it unlinked from
34789   the
34790    * SOCKET module.
34791    */
34792
34793   int sock_unregister(int family)
34794   {
34795       int i;
34796
34797       cli();
34798       for(i = 0; i < NPROTO; i++)
34799       {
34800           if (pops[i] == NULL)
34801               continue;
34802           if (pops[i]->family == family)
34803           {
34804               pops[i]=NULL;
34805               sti();
34806               return(i);
34807           }
34808       }
34809       sti();
34810       return(-ENOENT);
34811   }
34812
34813   void proto_init(void)
34814   {
34815       extern struct net_proto protocols[];    /* Network
34816   protocols */
34817       struct net_proto *pro;
34818
34819       /* Kick all configured protocols. */
34820       pro = protocols;
34821       while (pro->name != NULL)
34822       {
34823           (*pro->init_func)(pro);
34824           pro++;
34825       }
34826       /* We're all done... */
34827   }
34828
34829
34830   void sock_init(void)
34831   {
34832       int i;
34833
34834       printk(KERN_INFO "Swansea University Computer
34835   Society NET3.035 for Linux 2.0\n");
34836
34837       /*
34838        * Initialize all address (protocol) families.
34839        */
34840
34841       for (i = 0; i < NPROTO; ++i) pops[i] = NULL;
34842
34843       /*
34844        * The netlink device handler may be needed early.
34845        */
34846
34847   #ifdef CONFIG_NETLINK
34848       init_netlink();
34849   #endif
34850       /*
34851        * Attach the routing/device information port.
34852        */
34853
34854   #if defined(CONFIG_RTNETLINK)
34855       netlink_attach(NETLINK_ROUTE, netlink_donothing);
34856   #endif
34857
34858       /*
34859        * Attach the firewall module if configured
34860        */
34861
34862   #ifdef CONFIG_FIREWALL
34863       fwchain_init();
```

```
34864  #endif
34865
34866      /*
34867       *  Initialize the protocols module.
34868       */
34869
34870      proto_init();
34871
34872      /*
34873       *  Export networking symbols to the world.
34874       */
34875
34876  #if defined(CONFIG_MODULES) && defined(CONFIG_NET)
34877      export_net_symbols();
34878  #endif
34879  }
34880
34881  int socket_get_info(char *buffer, char **start, off_t
34882  offset, int length)
34883  {
34884      int len = sprintf(buffer, "sockets: used %d\n",
34885  sockets_in_use);
34886      if (offset >= len)
34887      {
34888          *start = buffer;
34889          return 0;
34890      }
34891      *start = buffer + offset;
34892      len -= offset;
34893      if (len > length)
34894          len = length;
34895      return len;
34896  }
```

usr/src/linux/net/sysctl_net.c

```
34897  /* -*- linux-c -*-
34898   * sysctl_net.c: sysctl interface to net subsystem.
34899   *
34900   * Begun April 1, 1996, Mike Shaver.
34901   * Added /proc/sys/net directories for each protocol
34902  family. [MS]
34903   *
34904   * $Log: sysctl_net.c,v $
34905   * Revision 1.2  1996/05/08  20:24:40  shaver
34906   * Added bits for NET_BRIDGE and the NET_IPV4_ARP stuff
34907  and
34908   * NET_IPV4_IP_FORWARD.
34909   *
34910   *
34911   */
34912
34913  #include <linux/config.h>
34914  #include <linux/mm.h>
34915  #include <linux/sysctl.h>
34916
34917  #ifdef CONFIG_INET
34918  extern ctl_table ipv4_table[];
34919  #endif
34920
34921  #ifdef CONFIG_IPX
34922  extern ctl_table ipx_table[];
34923  #endif
34924
34925  #ifdef CONFIG_ATALK
34926  extern ctl_table atalk_table[];
34927  #endif
34928
34929  #ifdef CONFIG_NETROM
34930  extern ctl_table netrom_table[];
34931  #endif
34932
34933  #ifdef CONFIG_AX25
34934  extern ctl_table ax25_table[];
34935  #endif
34936
34937  extern ctl_table core_table[], unix_table[];
34938
34939  #ifdef CONFIG_NET
34940  extern ctl_table ether_table[], e802_table[];
34941  #endif
34942
34943  #ifdef CONFIG_BRIDGE
34944  extern ctl_table bridge_table[];
34945  #endif
34946
34947  ctl_table net_table[] = {
34948      {NET_CORE,   "core",      NULL, 0, 0555,
34949  core_table},
34950          {NET_UNIX,   "unix",      NULL, 0, 0555,
34951  unix_table},
34952  #ifdef CONFIG_NET
34953      {NET_802,    "802",       NULL, 0, 0555, e802_table},
34954      {NET_ETHER, "ethernet",  NULL, 0, 0555,
34955  ether_table},
34956  #endif
34957  #ifdef CONFIG_INET
```

```
34958        {NET_IPV4,   "ipv4",      NULL, 0, 0555, ipv4_table},
34959    #endif
34960    #ifdef CONFIG_IPX
34961        {NET_IPX,    "ipx",       NULL, 0, 0555,
34962    ipx_table},
34963    #endif
34964    #ifdef CONFIG_ATALK
34965        {NET_ATALK, "appletalk", NULL, 0, 0555,
34966    atalk_table},
34967    #endif
34968    #ifdef CONFIG_NETROM
34969        {NET_NETROM, "netrom",    NULL, 0, 0555,
34970    netrom_table},
34971    #endif
34972    #ifdef CONFIG_AX25
34973        {NET_AX25,   "ax25",      NULL, 0, 0555, ax25_table},
34974    #endif
34975    #ifdef CONFIG_BRIDGE
34976        {NET_BRIDGE, "bridge",    NULL, 0, 0555,
34977    bridge_table},
34978    #endif
34979        {0}
34980    };
```

usr/include/arpa/nameser.h

```
34981    /*
34982     * ++Copyright++ 1983, 1989, 1993
34983     * -
34984     * Copyright (c) 1983, 1989, 1993
34985     *    The Regents of the University of California.  All
34986    rights reserved.
34987     *
34988     * Redistribution and use in source and binary forms,
34989    with or without
34990     * modification, are permitted provided that the
34991    following conditions
34992     * are met:
34993     * 1. Redistributions of source code must retain the
34994    above copyright
34995     *    notice, this list of conditions and the following
34996    disclaimer.
34997     * 2. Redistributions in binary form must reproduce the
34998    above copyright
34999     *    notice, this list of conditions and the following
35000    disclaimer in the
35001     *    documentation and/or other materials provided with
35002    the distribution.
35003     * 3. All advertising materials mentioning features or
35004    use of this software
35005     *    must display the following acknowledgement:
35006     * This product includes software developed by the
35007    University of
35008     * California, Berkeley and its contributors.
35009     * 4. Neither the name of the University nor the names
35010    of its contributors
35011     *    may be used to endorse or promote products derived
35012    from this software
35013     *    without specific prior written permission.
35014     *
35015     * THIS SOFTWARE IS PROVIDED BY THE REGENTS AND
35016    CONTRIBUTORS "AS IS" AND
35017     * ANY EXPRESS OR IMPLIED WARRANTIES, INCLUDING, BUT NOT
35018    LIMITED TO, THE
35019     * IMPLIED WARRANTIES OF MERCHANTABILITY AND FITNESS FOR
35020    A PARTICULAR PURPOSE
35021     * ARE DISCLAIMED.  IN NO EVENT SHALL THE REGENTS OR
35022    CONTRIBUTORS BE LIABLE
35023     * FOR ANY DIRECT, INDIRECT, INCIDENTAL, SPECIAL,
35024    EXEMPLARY, OR CONSEQUENTIAL
35025     * DAMAGES (INCLUDING, BUT NOT LIMITED TO, PROCUREMENT
35026    OF SUBSTITUTE GOODS
35027     * OR SERVICES; LOSS OF USE, DATA, OR PROFITS; OR
35028    BUSINESS INTERRUPTION)
35029     * HOWEVER CAUSED AND ON ANY THEORY OF LIABILITY,
35030    WHETHER IN CONTRACT, STRICT
35031     * LIABILITY, OR TORT (INCLUDING NEGLIGENCE OR
35032    OTHERWISE) ARISING IN ANY WAY
35033     * OUT OF THE USE OF THIS SOFTWARE, EVEN IF ADVISED OF
35034    THE POSSIBILITY OF
35035     * SUCH DAMAGE.
35036     * -
35037     * Portions Copyright (c) 1993 by Digital Equipment
35038    Corporation.
35039     *
35040     * Permission to use, copy, modify, and distribute this
35041    software for any
35042     * purpose with or without fee is hereby granted,
35043    provided that the above
35044     * copyright notice and this permission notice appear in
35045    all copies, and that
35046     * the name of Digital Equipment Corporation not be used
35047    in advertising or
35048     * publicity pertaining to distribution of the document
35049    or software without
35050     * specific, written prior permission.
35051     *
```

```
35052    * THE SOFTWARE IS PROVIDED "AS IS" AND DIGITAL
35053    EQUIPMENT CORP. DISCLAIMS ALL
35054    * WARRANTIES WITH REGARD TO THIS SOFTWARE, INCLUDING
35055    ALL IMPLIED WARRANTIES
35056    * OF MERCHANTABILITY AND FITNESS.    IN NO EVENT SHALL
35057    DIGITAL EQUIPMENT
35058    * CORPORATION BE LIABLE FOR ANY SPECIAL, DIRECT,
35059    INDIRECT, OR CONSEQUENTIAL
35060    * DAMAGES OR ANY DAMAGES WHATSOEVER RESULTING FROM LOSS
35061    OF USE, DATA OR
35062    * PROFITS, WHETHER IN AN ACTION OF CONTRACT, NEGLIGENCE
35063    OR OTHER TORTIOUS
35064    * ACTION, ARISING OUT OF OR IN CONNECTION WITH THE USE
35065    OR PERFORMANCE OF THIS
35066    * SOFTWARE.
35067    * -
35068    * --Copyright--
35069    */
35070
35071    /*
35072    *        @(#)nameser.h    8.1 (Berkeley) 6/2/93
35073    *    nameser.h,v 1.2 1995/05/06 14:23:54 hjl Exp
35074    */
35075
35076    #ifndef _NAMESER_H_
35077    #define _NAMESER_H_
35078
35079    #include <sys/param.h>
35080    #if (!defined(BSD)) || (BSD < 199306)
35081    # include <sys/bitypes.h>
35082    #else
35083    # include <sys/types.h>
35084    #endif
35085    #include <sys/cdefs.h>
35086
35087    /*
35088    * revision information. this is the release date in
35089    YYYYMMDD format.
35090    * it can change every day so the right thing to do with
35091    it is use it
35092    * in preprocessor commands such as "#if (__BIND >
35093    19931104)".  do not
35094    * compare for equality; rather, use it to determine
35095    whether your resolver
35096    * is new enough to contain a certain feature.
35097    */
35098
35099    #define __BIND        19940417    /* interface version
```

```
35100    stamp */
35101
35102    /*
35103    * Define constants based on rfc883
35104    */
35105    #define PACKETSZ      512      /* maximum packet size */
35106    #define MAXDNAME      256      /* maximum domain name */
35107    #define MAXCDNAME     255      /* maximum compressed domain
35108    name */
35109    #define MAXLABEL      63       /* maximum length of domain
35110    label */
35111    #define HFIXEDSZ      12       /* #/bytes of fixed data in
35112    header */
35113    #define QFIXEDSZ      4        /* #/bytes of fixed data in
35114    query */
35115    #define RRFIXEDSZ     10       /* #/bytes of fixed data in
35116    r record */
35117    #define INT32SZ       4        /* for systems without
35118    32-bit ints */
35119    #define INT16SZ       2        /* for systems without
35120    16-bit ints */
35121    #define INADDRSZ      4        /* for sizeof(struct inaddr)
35122    != 4 */
35123
35124    /*
35125    * Internet nameserver port number
35126    */
35127    #define NAMESERVER_PORT 53
35128
35129    /*
35130    * Currently defined opcodes
35131    */
35132    #define QUERY         0x0      /* standard query */
35133    #define IQUERY        0x1      /* inverse query */
35134    #define STATUS        0x2      /* nameserver status query */
35135    /*#define xxx          0x3      *//* 0x3 reserved */
35136    #define NS_NOTIFY_OP     0x4      /* notify secondary of
35137    SOA change */
35138    #ifdef ALLOW_UPDATES
35139        /* non standard - supports ALLOW_UPDATES stuff from
35140    Mike Schwartz */
35141    # define UPDATEA      0x9      /* add resource record */
35142    # define UPDATED      0xa      /* delete a specific
35143    resource record */
35144    # define UPDATEDA     0xb      /* delete all named resource
35145    record */
35146    # define UPDATEM      0xc      /* modify a specific
35147    resource record */
```

```
35148  # define UPDATEMA   0xd     /* modify all named resource
35149  record */
35150  # define ZONEINIT   0xe     /* initial zone transfer */
35151  # define ZONEREF    0xf     /* incremental zone referesh
35152  */
35153  #endif
35154
35155  /*
35156   * Currently defined response codes
35157   */
35158  #define NOERROR      0       /* no error */
35159  #define FORMERR      1       /* format error */
35160  #define SERVFAIL     2       /* server failure */
35161  #define NXDOMAIN     3       /* non existent domain */
35162  #define NOTIMP       4       /* not implemented */
35163  #define REFUSED      5       /* query refused */
35164  #ifdef ALLOW_UPDATES
35165      /* non standard */
35166  # define NOCHANGE   0xf     /* update failed to change
35167  db */
35168  #endif
35169
35170  /*
35171   * Type values for resources and queries
35172   */
35173  #define T_A       1        /* host address */
35174  #define T_NS        2       /* authoritative server */
35175  #define T_MD        3       /* mail destination */
35176  #define T_MF        4       /* mail forwarder */
35177  #define T_CNAME     5       /* canonical name */
35178  #define T_SOA       6       /* start of authority zone */
35179  #define T_MB        7       /* mailbox domain name */
35180  #define T_MG        8       /* mail group member */
35181  #define T_MR        9       /* mail rename name */
35182  #define T_NULL      10      /* null resource record */
35183  #define T_WKS       11      /* well known service */
35184  #define T_PTR       12      /* domain name pointer */
35185  #define T_HINFO     13      /* host information */
35186  #define T_MINFO     14      /* mailbox information */
35187  #define T_MX        15      /* mail routing information
35188  */
35189  #define T_TXT       16      /* text strings */
35190  #define T_RP        17      /* responsible person */
35191  #define T_AFSDB     18      /* AFS cell database */
35192  #define T_X25       19      /* X_25 calling address */
35193  #define T_ISDN      20      /* ISDN calling address */
35194  #define T_RT        21      /* router */
35195  #define T_NSAP      22      /* NSAP address */
```

```
35196  #define T_NSAP_PTR 23      /* reverse NSAP lookup
35197  (deprecated) */
35198  #define T_SIG       24      /* security signature */
35199  #define T_KEY       25      /* security key */
35200  #define T_PX        26      /* X.400 mail mapping */
35201  #define T_GPOS      27      /* geographical position
35202  (withdrawn) */
35203  #define T_AAAA      28      /* IP6 Address */
35204  #define T_LOC       29      /* Location Information */
35205      /* non standard */
35206  #define T_UINFO     100     /* user (finger) information
35207  */
35208  #define T_UID       101     /* user ID */
35209  #define T_GID       102     /* group ID */
35210  #define T_UNSPEC    103     /* Unspecified format
35211  (binary data) */
35212      /* Query type values which do not appear in resource
35213  records */
35214  #define T_AXFR      252     /* transfer zone of
35215  authority */
35216  #define T_MAILB     253     /* transfer mailbox records
35217  */
35218  #define T_MAILA     254     /* transfer mail agent
35219  records */
35220  #define T_ANY       255     /* wildcard match */
35221
35222  /*
35223   * Values for class field
35224   */
35225
35226  #define C_IN        1       /* the arpa internet */
35227  #define C_CHAOS     3       /* for chaos net (MIT) */
35228  #define C_HS        4       /* for Hesiod name server
35229  (MIT) (XXX) */
35230      /* Query class values which do not appear in
35231  resource records */
35232  #define C_ANY       255     /* wildcard match */
35233
35234  /*
35235   * Status return codes for T_UNSPEC conversion routines
35236   */
35237  #define CONV_SUCCESS    0
35238  #define CONV_OVERFLOW   (-1)
35239  #define CONV_BADFMT (-2)
35240  #define CONV_BADCKSUM   (-3)
35241  #define CONV_BADBUFLEN  (-4)
35242
35243  #ifndef __BYTE_ORDER
```

```
35244  #if (BSD >= 199103)
35245  # include <machine/endian.h>
35246  #else
35247  #ifdef linux
35248  # include <endian.h>
35249  #else
35250  #define __LITTLE_ENDIAN 1234    /* least-significant
35251  byte first (vax, pc) */
35252  #define __BIG_ENDIAN    4321    /* most-significant byte
35253  first (IBM, net) */
35254  #define __PDP_ENDIAN    3412    /* LSB first in word,
35255  MSW first in long (pdp)*/
35256
35257  #if defined(vax) || defined(ns32000) || defined(sun386)
35258  || defined(i386) || \
35259      defined(MIPSEL) || defined(_MIPSEL) ||
35260  defined(BIT_ZERO_ON_RIGHT) || \
35261      defined(__alpha__) || defined(__alpha)
35262  #define __BYTE_ORDER    __LITTLE_ENDIAN
35263  #endif
35264
35265  #if defined(sel) || defined(pyr) || defined(mc68000) ||
35266  defined(sparc) || \
35267      defined(is68k) || defined(tahoe) || defined(ibm032)
35268  || defined(ibm370) || \
35269      defined(MIPSEB) || defined(_MIPSEB) ||
35270  defined(_IBMR2) || defined(DGUX) ||\
35271      defined(apollo) || defined(__convex__) ||
35272  defined(_CRAY) || \
35273      defined(__hppa) || defined(__hp9000) || \
35274      defined(__hp9000s300) || defined(__hp9000s700) || \
35275      defined (BIT_ZERO_ON_LEFT) || defined(m68k)
35276  #define __BYTE_ORDER    __BIG_ENDIAN
35277  #endif
35278  #endif /* linux */
35279  #endif /* BSD */
35280  #endif /* __BYTE_ORDER */
35281
35282  #if !defined(__BYTE_ORDER) || \
35283      (__BYTE_ORDER != __BIG_ENDIAN && __BYTE_ORDER !=
35284  __LITTLE_ENDIAN && \
35285      __BYTE_ORDER != __PDP_ENDIAN)
35286      /* you must determine what the correct bit order is
35287  for
35288      * your compiler - the next line is an intentional
35289  error
35290      * which will force your compiles to bomb until you
35291  fix
35292      * the above macros.
35293      */
35294    error "Undefined or invalid __BYTE_ORDER";
35295  #endif
35296
35297  /*
35298   * Structure for query header.  The order of the fields
35299  is machine- and
35300   * compiler-dependent, depending on the byte/bit order
35301  and the layout
35302   * of bit fields.  We use bit fields only in int
35303  variables, as this
35304   * is all ANSI requires.  This requires a somewhat
35305  confusing rearrangement.
35306   */
35307
35308  typedef struct {
35309      unsigned    id :16;      /* query identification
35310  number */
35311  #if __BYTE_ORDER == __BIG_ENDIAN
35312              /* fields in third byte */
35313      unsigned    qr: 1;      /* response flag */
35314      unsigned    opcode: 4;  /* purpose of message */
35315      unsigned    aa: 1;      /* authoritive answer */
35316      unsigned    tc: 1;      /* truncated message */
35317      unsigned    rd: 1;      /* recursion desired */
35318              /* fields in fourth byte */
35319      unsigned    ra: 1;      /* recursion available */
35320      unsigned    pr: 1;      /* primary server req'd
35321  (!standard) */
35322      unsigned    unused :2;  /* unused bits (MBZ as of
35323  4.9.3a3) */
35324      unsigned    rcode :4;   /* response code */
35325  #endif
35326  #if __BYTE_ORDER == __LITTLE_ENDIAN || __BYTE_ORDER ==
35327  __PDP_ENDIAN
35328              /* fields in third byte */
35329      unsigned    rd :1;      /* recursion desired */
35330      unsigned    tc :1;      /* truncated message */
35331      unsigned    aa :1;      /* authoritive answer */
35332      unsigned    opcode :4;  /* purpose of message */
35333      unsigned    qr :1;      /* response flag */
35334              /* fields in fourth byte */
35335      unsigned    rcode :4;   /* response code */
35336      unsigned    unused :2;  /* unused bits (MBZ as of
35337  4.9.3a3) */
35338      unsigned    pr :1;      /* primary server req'd
35339  (!standard) */
```

```
35340        unsigned    ra :1;        /* recursion available */
35341    #endif
35342                    /* remaining bytes */
35343        unsigned    qdcount :16;      /* number of question
35344    entries */
35345        unsigned    ancount :16;      /* number of answer
35346    entries */
35347        unsigned    nscount :16;      /* number of authority
35348    entries */
35349        unsigned    arcount :16;      /* number of resource
35350    entries */
35351    } HEADER;
35352
35353    /*
35354     * Defines for handling compressed domain names
35355     */
35356    #define INDIR_MASK  0xc0
35357
35358    /*
35359     * Structure for passing resource records around.
35360     */
35361    struct rrec {
35362        int16_t     r_zone;        /* zone number */
35363        int16_t     r_class;       /* class number */
35364        int16_t     r_type;        /* type number */
35365        u_int32_t   r_ttl;         /* time to live */
35366        int     r_size;        /* size of data area */
35367        char        *r_data;       /* pointer to data */
35368    };
35369
35370    extern  u_int16_t   _getshort __P((const u_char *));
35371    extern  u_int32_t   _getlong __P((const u_char *));
35372
35373    /*
35374     * Inline versions of get/put short/long.  Pointer is
35375    advanced.
35376     *
35377     * These macros demonstrate the property of C whereby it
35378    can be
35379     * portable or it can be elegant but rarely both.
35380     */
35381    #define GETSHORT(s, cp) { \
35382        register u_char *t_cp = (u_char *)(cp); \
35383        (s) = ((u_int16_t)t_cp[0] << 8) \
35384            | ((u_int16_t)t_cp[1]) \
35385            ; \
35386        (cp) += INT16SZ; \
35387    }
```

```
35388
35389    #define GETLONG(l, cp) { \
35390        register u_char *t_cp = (u_char *)(cp); \
35391        (l) = ((u_int32_t)t_cp[0] << 24) \
35392            | ((u_int32_t)t_cp[1] << 16) \
35393            | ((u_int32_t)t_cp[2] << 8) \
35394            | ((u_int32_t)t_cp[3]) \
35395            ; \
35396        (cp) += INT32SZ; \
35397    }
35398
35399    #define PUTSHORT(s, cp) { \
35400        register u_int16_t t_s = (u_int16_t)(s); \
35401        register u_char *t_cp = (u_char *)(cp); \
35402        *t_cp++ = t_s >> 8; \
35403        *t_cp   = t_s; \
35404        (cp) += INT16SZ; \
35405    }
35406
35407    #define PUTLONG(l, cp) { \
35408        register u_int32_t t_l = (u_int32_t)(l); \
35409        register u_char *t_cp = (u_char *)(cp); \
35410        *t_cp++ = t_l >> 24; \
35411        *t_cp++ = t_l >> 16; \
35412        *t_cp++ = t_l >> 8; \
35413        *t_cp   = t_l; \
35414        (cp) += INT32SZ; \
35415    }
35416
35417    #endif /* !_NAMESER_H_ */
```

usr/include/asm/byteorder.h

```
35418    #ifndef _I386_BYTEORDER_H
35419    #define _I386_BYTEORDER_H
35420
35421    #undef ntohl
35422    #undef ntohs
35423    #undef htonl
35424    #undef htons
35425
35426    #ifndef __LITTLE_ENDIAN
35427    #define __LITTLE_ENDIAN 1234
35428    #endif
35429
35430    #ifndef __LITTLE_ENDIAN_BITFIELD
35431    #define __LITTLE_ENDIAN_BITFIELD
35432    #endif
35433
```

```
35434   /* For avoiding bswap on i386 */
35435   #ifdef __KERNEL__
35436   #include <linux/config.h>
35437   #endif
35438
35439   extern unsigned long int    ntohl(unsigned long int);
35440   extern unsigned short int    ntohs(unsigned short int);
35441   extern unsigned long int    htonl(unsigned long int);
35442   extern unsigned short int    htons(unsigned short int);
35443
35444   extern __inline__ unsigned long int __ntohl(unsigned
35445   long int);
35446   extern __inline__ unsigned short int    __ntohs(unsigned
35447   short int);
35448   extern __inline__ unsigned long int
35449   __constant_ntohl(unsigned long int);
35450   extern __inline__ unsigned short int
35451   __constant_ntohs(unsigned short int);
35452
35453   extern __inline__ unsigned long int
35454   __ntohl(unsigned long int x)
35455   {
35456   #if defined(__KERNEL__) && !defined(CONFIG_M386)
35457       __asm__("bswap %0" : "=r" (x) : "0" (x));
35458   #else
35459       __asm__("xchgb %b0,%h0\n\t" /* swap lower bytes */
35460           "rorl $16,%0\n\t"    /* swap words       */
35461           "xchgb %b0,%h0"     /* swap higher bytes   */
35462           :"=q" (x)
35463           : "0" (x));
35464   #endif
35465       return x;
35466   }
35467
35468   #define __constant_ntohl(x) \
35469       ((unsigned long int)(((((unsigned long int)(x) &
35470   0x000000ffU) << 24) | \
35471                   (((unsigned long int)(x) & 0x0000ff00U)
35472   << 8) | \
35473                   (((unsigned long int)(x) & 0x00ff0000U)
35474   >> 8) | \
35475                   (((unsigned long int)(x) & 0xff000000U)
35476   >> 24)))
35477
35478   extern __inline__ unsigned short int
35479   __ntohs(unsigned short int x)
35480   {
35481       __asm__("xchgb %b0,%h0"     /* swap bytes      */
35482           : "=q" (x)
35483           : "0" (x));
35484       return x;
35485   }
35486
35487   #define __constant_ntohs(x) \
35488       ((unsigned short int)((((unsigned short int)(x) &
35489   0x00ff) << 8) | \
35490               (((unsigned short int)(x) & 0xff00) >>
35491   8))) \
35492
35493   #define __htonl(x) __ntohl(x)
35494   #define __htons(x) __ntohs(x)
35495   #define __constant_htonl(x) __constant_ntohl(x)
35496   #define __constant_htons(x) __constant_ntohs(x)
35497
35498   #ifdef __OPTIMIZE__
35499   #  define ntohl(x) \
35500   (__builtin_constant_p((long)(x)) ? \
35501    __constant_ntohl((x)) : \
35502    __ntohl((x)))
35503   #  define ntohs(x) \
35504   (__builtin_constant_p((short)(x)) ? \
35505    __constant_ntohs((x)) : \
35506    __ntohs((x)))
35507   #  define htonl(x) \
35508   (__builtin_constant_p((long)(x)) ? \
35509    __constant_htonl((x)) : \
35510    __htonl((x)))
35511   #  define htons(x) \
35512   (__builtin_constant_p((short)(x)) ? \
35513    __constant_htons((x)) : \
35514    __htons((x)))
35515   #endif
35516
35517   #endif
```

usr/include/asm/checksum.h

```
35518   #ifndef _I386_CHECKSUM_H
35519   #define _I386_CHECKSUM_H
35520
35521   /*
35522    * computes the checksum of a memory block at buff,
35523    length len,
35524    * and adds in "sum" (32-bit)
35525    *
35526    * returns a 32-bit number suitable for feeding into
35527    itself
```

```
35528        * or csum_tcpudp_magic
35529        *
35530        * this function must be called with even lengths, except
35531        * for the last fragment, which may be odd
35532        *
35533        * it's best to have buff aligned on a 32-bit boundary
35534        */
35535       unsigned int csum_partial(const unsigned char * buff,
35536       int len, unsigned int sum);
35537
35538       /*
35539        * the same as csum_partial, but copies from src while it
35540        * checksums
35541        *
35542        * here even more important to align src and dst on a
35543       32-bit (or even
35544        * better 64-bit) boundary
35545        */
35546
35547       unsigned int csum_partial_copy( const char *src, char
35548       *dst, int len, int sum);
35549
35550
35551       /*
35552        * the same as csum_partial_copy, but copies from user
35553       space.
35554        *
35555        * here even more important to align src and dst on a
35556       32-bit (or even
35557        * better 64-bit) boundary
35558        */
35559
35560       unsigned int csum_partial_copy_fromuser(const char *src,
35561       char *dst, int len, int sum);
35562
35563       /*
35564        *  This is a version of ip_compute_csum() optimized for
35565       IP headers,
35566        *  which always checksum on 4 octet boundaries.
35567        *
35568        *  By Jorge Cwik <jorge@laser.satlink.net>, adapted for
35569       linux by
35570        *  Arnt Gulbrandsen.
35571        */
35572       static inline unsigned short ip_fast_csum(unsigned char
35573       * iph,
35574                                unsigned int ihl) {
35575           unsigned int sum;
```

```
35576
35577           __asm__ __volatile__("
35578               movl (%1), %0
35579               subl $4, %2
35580               jbe 2f
35581               addl 4(%1), %0
35582               adcl 8(%1), %0
35583               adcl 12(%1), %0
35584       1:      adcl 16(%1), %0
35585               lea 4(%1), %1
35586               decl %2
35587               jne 1b
35588               adcl $0, %0
35589               movl %0, %2
35590               shrl $16, %0
35591               addw %w2, %w0
35592               adcl $0, %0
35593               notl %0
35594       2:
35595                       "
35596           /* Since the input registers which are loaded with
35597       iph and ipl
35598               are modified, we must also specify them as
35599       outputs, or gcc
35600               will assume they contain their original values. */
35601           : "=r" (sum), "=r" (iph), "=r" (ihl)
35602           : "1" (iph), "2" (ihl));
35603           return(sum);
35604       }
35605
35606       /*
35607        *  Fold a partial checksum
35608        */
35609
35610       static inline unsigned int csum_fold(unsigned int sum)
35611       {
35612           __asm__("
35613               addl %1, %0
35614               adcl $0xffff, %0
35615               "
35616           : "=r" (sum)
35617           : "r" (sum << 16), "0" (sum & 0xffff0000)
35618           );
35619           return (~sum) >> 16;
35620       }
35621
35622       /*
35623        * computes the checksum of the TCP/UDP pseudo-header
```

```
35624      * returns a 16-bit checksum, already complemented
35625      */
35626
35627     static inline unsigned short int
35628     csum_tcpudp_magic(unsigned long saddr,
35629                                 unsigned long daddr,
35630                                 unsigned short len,
35631                                 unsigned short proto,
35632                                 unsigned int sum) {
35633         __asm__("
35634         addl %1, %0
35635         adcl %2, %0
35636         adcl %3, %0
35637         adcl $0, %0
35638         "
35639         : "=r" (sum)
35640         : "g" (daddr), "g"(saddr),
35641     "g"((ntohs(len)<<16)+proto*256), "0"(sum));
35642         return csum_fold(sum);
35643     }
35644     /*
35645      * this routine is used for miscellaneous IP-like
35646     checksums, mainly
35647      * in icmp.c
35648      */
35649
35650     static inline unsigned short ip_compute_csum(unsigned
35651     char * buff, int len) {
35652         return csum_fold (csum_partial(buff, len, 0));
35653     }
35654
35655     #endif
```

usr/include/asm/errno.h

```
35656     #ifndef _I386_ERRNO_H
35657     #define _I386_ERRNO_H
35658
35659     #define EPERM         1   /* Operation not permitted */
35660     #define ENOENT        2   /* No such file or directory */
35661     #define ESRCH         3   /* No such process */
35662     #define EINTR         4   /* Interrupted system call */
35663     #define EIO          5   /* I/O error */
35664     #define ENXIO         6   /* No such device or address */
35665     #define E2BIG         7   /* Arg list too long */
35666     #define ENOEXEC       8   /* Exec format error */
35667     #define EBADF         9   /* Bad file number */
35668     #define ECHILD       10   /* No child processes */
35669     #define EAGAIN       11   /* Try again */
35670     #define ENOMEM       12   /* Out of memory */
35671     #define EACCES       13   /* Permission denied */
35672     #define EFAULT       14   /* Bad address */
35673     #define ENOTBLK      15   /* Block device required */
35674     #define EBUSY        16   /* Device or resource busy */
35675     #define EEXIST       17   /* File exists */
35676     #define EXDEV        18   /* Cross-device link */
35677     #define ENODEV       19   /* No such device */
35678     #define ENOTDIR      20   /* Not a directory */
35679     #define EISDIR       21   /* Is a directory */
35680     #define EINVAL       22   /* Invalid argument */
35681     #define ENFILE       23   /* File table overflow */
35682     #define EMFILE       24   /* Too many open files */
35683     #define ENOTTY       25   /* Not a typewriter */
35684     #define ETXTBSY      26   /* Text file busy */
35685     #define EFBIG        27   /* File too large */
35686     #define ENOSPC       28   /* No space left on device */
35687     #define ESPIPE       29   /* Illegal seek */
35688     #define EROFS        30   /* Read-only file system */
35689     #define EMLINK       31   /* Too many links */
35690     #define EPIPE        32   /* Broken pipe */
35691     #define EDOM         33   /* Math argument out of domain
35692     of func */
35693     #define ERANGE       34   /* Math result not representable
35694     */
35695     #define EDEADLK      35   /* Resource deadlock would occur
35696     */
35697     #define ENAMETOOLONG  36  /* File name too long */
35698     #define ENOLCK       37   /* No record locks available */
35699     #define ENOSYS       38   /* Function not implemented */
35700     #define ENOTEMPTY    39   /* Directory not empty */
35701     #define ELOOP        40   /* Too many symbolic links
35702     encountered */
35703     #define EWOULDBLOCK EAGAIN  /* Operation would block */
35704     #define ENOMSG       42   /* No message of desired type */
35705     #define EIDRM        43   /* Identifier removed */
35706     #define ECHRNG       44   /* Channel number out of range */
35707     #define EL2NSYNC     45   /* Level 2 not synchronized */
35708     #define EL3HLT       46   /* Level 3 halted */
35709     #define EL3RST       47   /* Level 3 reset */
35710     #define ELNRNG       48   /* Link number out of range */
35711     #define EUNATCH      49   /* Protocol driver not attached
35712     */
35713     #define ENOCSI       50   /* No CSI structure available */
35714     #define EL2HLT       51   /* Level 2 halted */
35715     #define EBADE        52   /* Invalid exchange */
35716     #define EBADR        53   /* Invalid request descriptor */
35717     #define EXFULL       54   /* Exchange full */
```

```
35718  #define ENOANO       55   /* No anode */
35719  #define EBADRQC      56   /* Invalid request code */
35720  #define EBADSLT      57   /* Invalid slot */
35721
35722  #define EDEADLOCK       EDEADLK
35723
35724  #define EBFONT       59   /* Bad font file format */
35725  #define ENOSTR       60   /* Device not a stream */
35726  #define ENODATA      61   /* No data available */
35727  #define ETIME        62   /* Timer expired */
35728  #define ENOSR        63   /* Out of streams resources */
35729  #define ENONET       64   /* Machine is not on the network
35730  */
35731  #define ENOPKG       65   /* Package not installed */
35732  #define EREMOTE      66   /* Object is remote */
35733  #define ENOLINK      67   /* Link has been severed */
35734  #define EADV         68   /* Advertise error */
35735  #define ESRMNT       69   /* Srmount error */
35736  #define ECOMM        70   /* Communication error on send */
35737  #define EPROTO       71   /* Protocol error */
35738  #define EMULTIHOP    72   /* Multihop attempted */
35739  #define EDOTDOT      73   /* RFS specific error */
35740  #define EBADMSG      74   /* Not a data message */
35741  #define EOVERFLOW    75   /* Value too large for defined
35742  data type */
35743  #define ENOTUNIQ     76   /* Name not unique on network */
35744  #define EBADFD       77   /* File descriptor in bad state
35745  */
35746  #define EREMCHG      78   /* Remote address changed */
35747  #define ELIBACC      79   /* Can not access a needed
35748  shared library */
35749  #define ELIBBAD      80   /* Accessing a corrupted shared
35750  library */
35751  #define ELIBSCN      81   /* .lib section in a.out
35752  corrupted */
35753  #define ELIBMAX      82   /* Attempting to link in too
35754  many shared libraries */
35755  #define ELIBEXEC     83   /* Cannot exec a shared library
35756  directly */
35757  #define EILSEQ       84   /* Illegal byte sequence */
35758  #define ERESTART     85   /* Interrupted system call
35759  should be restarted */
35760  #define ESTRPIPE     86   /* Streams pipe error */
35761  #define EUSERS       87   /* Too many users */
35762  #define ENOTSOCK     88   /* Socket operation on
35763  non-socket */
35764  #define EDESTADDRREQ    89   /* Destination address
35765  required */
```

```
35766  #define EMSGSIZE     90   /* Message too long */
35767  #define EPROTOTYPE   91   /* Protocol wrong type for
35768  socket */
35769  #define ENOPROTOOPT 92   /* Protocol not available */
35770  #define EPROTONOSUPPORT 93  /* Protocol not supported */
35771  #define ESOCKTNOSUPPORT 94  /* Socket type not supported
35772  */
35773  #define EOPNOTSUPP   95   /* Operation not supported on
35774  transport endpoint */
35775  #define EPFNOSUPPORT    96   /* Protocol family not
35776  supported */
35777  #define EAFNOSUPPORT    97   /* Address family not
35778  supported by protocol */
35779  #define EADDRINUSE  98   /* Address already in use */
35780  #define EADDRNOTAVAIL   99   /* Cannot assign requested
35781  address */
35782  #define ENETDOWN    100 /* Network is down */
35783  #define ENETUNREACH 101 /* Network is unreachable */
35784  #define ENETRESET   102 /* Network dropped connection
35785  because of reset */
35786  #define ECONNABORTED    103 /* Software caused
35787  connection abort */
35788  #define ECONNRESET  104 /* Connection reset by peer */
35789  #define ENOBUFS     105 /* No buffer space available */
35790  #define EISCONN     106 /* Transport endpoint is already
35791  connected */
35792  #define ENOTCONN    107 /* Transport endpoint is not
35793  connected */
35794  #define ESHUTDOWN   108 /* Cannot send after transport
35795  endpoint shutdown */
35796  #define ETOOMANYREFS    109 /* Too many references:
35797  cannot splice */
35798  #define ETIMEDOUT   110 /* Connection timed out */
35799  #define ECONNREFUSED    111 /* Connection refused */
35800  #define EHOSTDOWN   112 /* Host is down */
35801  #define EHOSTUNREACH    113 /* No route to host */
35802  #define EALREADY    114 /* Operation already in progress
35803  */
35804  #define EINPROGRESS 115 /* Operation now in progress */
35805  #define ESTALE      116 /* Stale NFS file handle */
35806  #define EUCLEAN     117 /* Structure needs cleaning */
35807  #define ENOTNAM     118 /* Not a XENIX named type file */
35808  #define ENAVAIL     119 /* No XENIX semaphores available
35809  */
35810  #define EISNAM      120 /* Is a named type file */
35811  #define EREMOTEIO   121 /* Remote I/O error */
35812  #define EDQUOT      122 /* Quota exceeded */
35813
```

```
35814    #define ENOMEDIUM   123 /* No medium found */
35815    #define EMEDIUMTYPE 124 /* Wrong medium type */
35816
35817    #endif
```

usr/include/asm/signal.h

```
35818    #ifndef _ASMi386_SIGNAL_H
35819    #define _ASMi386_SIGNAL_H
35820
35821    typedef unsigned long sigset_t;        /* at least 32 bits
35822    */
35823
35824    #define _NSIG                  32
35825    #define NSIG           _NSIG
35826
35827    #define SIGHUP         1
35828    #define SIGINT         2
35829    #define SIGQUIT        3
35830    #define SIGILL         4
35831    #define SIGTRAP        5
35832    #define SIGABRT        6
35833    #define SIGIOT         6
35834    #define SIGBUS         7
35835    #define SIGFPE         8
35836    #define SIGKILL        9
35837    #define SIGUSR1        10
35838    #define SIGSEGV        11
35839    #define SIGUSR2        12
35840    #define SIGPIPE        13
35841    #define SIGALRM        14
35842    #define SIGTERM        15
35843    #define SIGSTKFLT      16
35844    #define SIGCHLD        17
35845    #define SIGCONT        18
35846    #define SIGSTOP        19
35847    #define SIGTSTP        20
35848    #define SIGTTIN        21
35849    #define SIGTTOU        22
35850    #define SIGURG         23
35851    #define SIGXCPU        24
35852    #define SIGXFSZ        25
35853    #define SIGVTALRM      26
35854    #define SIGPROF        27
35855    #define SIGWINCH       28
35856    #define SIGIO          29
35857    #define SIGPOLL        SIGIO
35858    /*
35859    #define SIGLOST        29
```

```
35860    */
35861    #define SIGPWR         30
35862    #define SIGUNUSED      31
35863
35864    /*
35865     * sa_flags values: SA_STACK is not currently supported,
35866    but will allow the
35867     * usage of signal stacks by using the (now obsolete)
35868    sa_restorer field in
35869     * the sigaction structure as a stack pointer. This is
35870    now possible due to
35871     * the changes in signal handling. LBT 010493.
35872     * SA_INTERRUPT is a no-op, but left due to historical
35873    reasons. Use the
35874     * SA_RESTART flag to get restarting signals (which were
35875    the default long ago)
35876     * SA_SHIRQ flag is for shared interrupt support on PCI
35877    and EISA.
35878     */
35879    #define SA_NOCLDSTOP      1
35880    #define SA_SHIRQ     0x04000000
35881    #define SA_STACK     0x08000000
35882    #define SA_RESTART   0x10000000
35883    #define SA_INTERRUPT    0x20000000
35884    #define SA_NOMASK    0x40000000
35885    #define SA_ONESHOT   0x80000000
35886
35887    #ifdef __KERNEL__
35888    /*
35889     * These values of sa_flags are used only by the kernel
35890    as part of the
35891     * irq handling routines.
35892     *
35893     * SA_INTERRUPT is also used by the irq handling
35894    routines.
35895     */
35896    #define SA_PROBE SA_ONESHOT
35897    #define SA_SAMPLE_RANDOM SA_RESTART
35898    #endif
35899
35900
35901    #define SIG_BLOCK         0     /* for blocking signals
35902    */
35903    #define SIG_UNBLOCK       1     /* for unblocking
35904    signals */
35905    #define SIG_SETMASK       2     /* for setting the
35906    signal mask */
35907
```

```
35908   /* Type of a signal handler.  */
35909   typedef void (*__sighandler_t)(int);
35910
35911   #define SIG_DFL ((__sighandler_t)0) /* default signal
35912   handling */
35913   #define SIG_IGN ((__sighandler_t)1) /* ignore signal */
35914   #define SIG_ERR ((__sighandler_t)-1)    /* error return
35915   from signal */
35916
35917   struct sigaction {
35918       __sighandler_t sa_handler;
35919       sigset_t sa_mask;
35920       unsigned long sa_flags;
35921       void (*sa_restorer)(void);
35922   };
35923
35924   #ifdef __KERNEL__
35925   #include <asm/sigcontext.h>
35926   #endif
35927
35928   #endif
```

usr/include/asm/socket.h

```
35929   #ifndef _ASM_SOCKET_H
35930   #define _ASM_SOCKET_H
35931
35932   #include <asm/sockios.h>
35933
35934   /* For setsockoptions(2) */
35935   #define SOL_SOCKET  1
35936
35937   #define SO_DEBUG    1
35938   #define SO_REUSEADDR    2
35939   #define SO_TYPE     3
35940   #define SO_ERROR    4
35941   #define SO_DONTROUTE    5
35942   #define SO_BROADCAST    6
35943   #define SO_SNDBUF   7
35944   #define SO_RCVBUF   8
35945   #define SO_KEEPALIVE    9
35946   #define SO_OOBINLINE    10
35947   #define SO_NO_CHECK 11
35948   #define SO_PRIORITY 12
35949   #define SO_LINGER   13
35950   #define SO_BSDCOMPAT    14
35951   /* To add :#define SO_REUSEPORT 15 */
35952
35953   #define SO_BINDTODEVICE 25
```

```
35954
35955   #endif /* _ASM_SOCKET_H */
```

usr/include/asm/sockios.h

```
35956   #ifndef __ARCH_I386_SOCKIOS__
35957   #define __ARCH_I386_SOCKIOS__
35958
35959   /* Socket-level I/O control calls. */
35960   #define FIOSETOWN   0x8901
35961   #define SIOCSPGRP   0x8902
35962   #define FIOGETOWN   0x8903
35963   #define SIOCGPGRP   0x8904
35964   #define SIOCATMARK  0x8905
35965   #define SIOCGSTAMP  0x8906      /* Get stamp */
35966
35967   #endif
```

usr/include/asm/types.h

```
35968   #ifndef _I386_TYPES_H
35969   #define _I386_TYPES_H
35970
35971   typedef unsigned short umode_t;
35972
35973   /*
35974    * __xx is ok: it doesn't pollute the POSIX namespace.
35975   Use these in the
35976    * header files exported to user space
35977    */
35978
35979   typedef __signed__ char __s8;
35980   typedef unsigned char __u8;
35981
35982   typedef __signed__ short __s16;
35983   typedef unsigned short __u16;
35984
35985   typedef __signed__ int __s32;
35986   typedef unsigned int __u32;
35987
35988   #if defined(__GNUC__) && !defined(__STRICT_ANSI__)
35989   typedef __signed__ long long __s64;
35990   typedef unsigned long long __u64;
35991   #endif
35992
35993   /*
35994    * These aren't exported outside the kernel to avoid
35995   name space clashes
35996    */
35997   #ifdef __KERNEL__
```

```
35998
35999    typedef signed char s8;
36000    typedef unsigned char u8;
36001
36002    typedef signed short s16;
36003    typedef unsigned short u16;
36004
36005    typedef signed int s32;
36006    typedef unsigned int u32;
36007
36008    typedef signed long long s64;
36009    typedef unsigned long long u64;
36010
36011    #endif /* __KERNEL__ */
36012
36013    #endif
```

usr/include/linux/fcntl.h

```
36014    #ifndef _LINUX_FCNTL_H
36015    #define _LINUX_FCNTL_H
36016
36017    #include <asm/fcntl.h>
36018
36019    #endif
```

usr/include/linux/icmp.h

```
36020    /*
36021     * INET      An implementation of the TCP/IP protocol
36022    suite for the LINUX
36023     *       operating system.  INET is implemented using the
36024    BSD Socket
36025     *       interface as the means of communication with the
36026    user level.
36027     *
36028     *       Definitions for the ICMP protocol.
36029     *
36030     * Version: @(#)icmp.h  1.0.3    04/28/93
36031     *
36032     * Author:  Fred N. van Kempen,
36033    <waltje@uWalt.NL.Mugnet.ORG>
36034     *
36035     *       This program is free software; you can
36036    redistribute it and/or
36037     *       modify it under the terms of the GNU General
36038    Public License
36039     *       as published by the Free Software Foundation;
36040    either version
36041     *       2 of the License, or (at your option) any later
```

```
36042    version.
36043     */
36044    #ifndef _LINUX_ICMP_H
36045    #define _LINUX_ICMP_H
36046
36047    #define ICMP_ECHOREPLY       0    /* Echo Reply
36048    */
36049    #define ICMP_DEST_UNREACH    3    /* Destination
36050    Unreachable  */
36051    #define ICMP_SOURCE_QUENCH   4    /* Source Quench
36052    */
36053    #define ICMP_REDIRECT        5    /* Redirect (change
36054    route)  */
36055    #define ICMP_ECHO            8    /* Echo Request          */
36056    #define ICMP_TIME_EXCEEDED   11   /* Time Exceeded
36057    */
36058    #define ICMP_PARAMETERPROB   12   /* Parameter Problem
36059      */
36060    #define ICMP_TIMESTAMP       13   /* Timestamp Request
36061      */
36062    #define ICMP_TIMESTAMPREPLY  14   /* Timestamp Reply
36063    */
36064    #define ICMP_INFO_REQUEST    15   /* Information Request
36065      */
36066    #define ICMP_INFO_REPLY      16   /* Information Reply
36067      */
36068    #define ICMP_ADDRESS         17   /* Address Mask Request
36069      */
36070    #define ICMP_ADDRESSREPLY    18   /* Address Mask Reply
36071      */
36072
36073
36074    /* Codes for UNREACH. */
36075    #define ICMP_NET_UNREACH     0    /* Network Unreachable
36076      */
36077    #define ICMP_HOST_UNREACH    1    /* Host Unreachable
36078    */
36079    #define ICMP_PROT_UNREACH    2    /* Protocol Unreachable
36080      */
36081    #define ICMP_PORT_UNREACH    3    /* Port Unreachable
36082    */
36083    #define ICMP_FRAG_NEEDED     4    /* Fragmentation
36084    Needed/DF set  */
36085    #define ICMP_SR_FAILED       5    /* Source Route failed
36086      */
36087    #define ICMP_NET_UNKNOWN     6
36088    #define ICMP_HOST_UNKNOWN    7
36089    #define ICMP_HOST_ISOLATED   8
```

```
36090   #define ICMP_NET_ANO        9
36091   #define ICMP_HOST_ANO       10
36092   #define ICMP_NET_UNR_TOS    11
36093   #define ICMP_HOST_UNR_TOS   12
36094   #define ICMP_PKT_FILTERED   13   /* Packet filtered */
36095   #define ICMP_PREC_VIOLATION 14   /* Precedence violation
36096   */
36097   #define ICMP_PREC_CUTOFF    15   /* Precedence cut off */
36098   #define NR_ICMP_UNREACH 15   /* instead of hardcoding
36099   immediate value */
36100
36101   /* Codes for REDIRECT. */
36102   #define ICMP_REDIR_NET      0    /* Redirect Net
36103   */
36104   #define ICMP_REDIR_HOST     1    /* Redirect Host
36105   */
36106   #define ICMP_REDIR_NETTOS   2    /* Redirect Net for TOS
36107     */
36108   #define ICMP_REDIR_HOSTTOS  3    /* Redirect Host for TOS
36109     */
36110
36111   /* Codes for TIME_EXCEEDED. */
36112   #define ICMP_EXC_TTL        0    /* TTL count exceeded
36113     */
36114   #define ICMP_EXC_FRAGTIME   1    /* Fragment Reass time
36115   exceeded */
36116
36117
36118   struct icmphdr {
36119     __u8      type;
36120     __u8      code;
36121     __u16     checksum;
36122     union {
36123       struct {
36124           __u16   id;
36125           __u16   sequence;
36126       } echo;
36127       __u32   gateway;
36128     } un;
36129   };
36130
36131
36132   struct icmp_err {
36133     int       errno;
36134     unsigned  fatal:1;
36135   };
36136
36137
```

```
36138   #endif  /* _LINUX_ICMP_H */
```

usr/include/linux/if.h

```
36139   /*
36140    * INET      An implementation of the TCP/IP protocol
36141   suite for the LINUX
36142    *      operating system.  INET is implemented using the
36143   BSD Socket
36144    *      interface as the means of communication with the
36145   user level.
36146    *
36147    *      Global definitions for the INET interface module.
36148    *
36149    * Version: @(#)if.h    1.0.2   04/18/93
36150    *
36151    * Authors: Original taken from Berkeley UNIX 4.3, (c)
36152   UCB 1982-1988
36153    *      Ross Biro, <bir7@leland.Stanford.Edu>
36154    *      Fred N. van Kempen, <waltje@uWalt.NL.Mugnet.ORG>
36155    *
36156    *      This program is free software; you can
36157   redistribute it and/or
36158    *      modify it under the terms of the GNU General
36159   Public License
36160    *      as published by the Free Software Foundation;
36161   either version
36162    *      2 of the License, or (at your option) any later
36163   version.
36164    */
36165   #ifndef _LINUX_IF_H
36166   #define _LINUX_IF_H
36167
36168   #include <linux/types.h>       /* for "caddr_t" et al
36169     */
36170   #include <linux/socket.h>      /* for "struct sockaddr"
36171   et al */
36172
36173   /* Standard interface flags. */
36174   #define IFF_UP      0x1    /* interface is up      */
36175   #define IFF_BROADCAST 0x2    /* broadcast address
36176   valid */
36177   #define IFF_DEBUG   0x4      /* turn on debugging
36178   */
36179   #define IFF_LOOPBACK    0x8      /* is a loopback net
36180     */
36181   #define IFF_POINTOPOINT 0x10       /* interface is has
36182   p-p link    */
36183   #define IFF_NOTRAILERS  0x20        /* avoid use of
```

```
36184    trailers   */
36185    #define IFF_RUNNING 0x40        /* resources allocated
36186        */
36187    #define IFF_NOARP   0x80        /* no ARP protocol
36188    */
36189    #define IFF_PROMISC 0x100       /* receive all packets
36190        */
36191    /* Not supported */
36192    #define IFF_ALLMULTI   0x200        /* receive all
36193    multicast packets*/
36194
36195    #define IFF_MASTER   0x400      /* master of a load
36196    balancer    */
36197    #define IFF_SLAVE    0x800      /* slave of a load
36198    balancer */
36199
36200    #define IFF_MULTICAST    0x1000        /* Supports
36201    multicast       */
36202    #define IFF_SOFTHEADERS 0x2000       /* Device cannot
36203    construct headers
36204                          * until broadcast time. Therefore
36205                          * SOCK_PACKET must call header
36206                          * construction. Private flag.
36207                          * Never visible outside of kernel.
36208                          */
36209
36210    /*
36211     * The ifaddr structure contains information about one
36212    address
36213     * of an interface.  They are maintained by the
36214    different address
36215     * families, are allocated and attached when an address
36216    is set,
36217     * and are linked together so all addresses for an
36218    interface can
36219     * be located.
36220     */
36221
36222    struct ifaddr
36223    {
36224        struct sockaddr ifa_addr;   /* address of interface
36225        */
36226        union {
36227            struct sockaddr ifu_broadaddr;
36228            struct sockaddr ifu_dstaddr;
36229        } ifa_ifu;
36230        struct iface        *ifa_ifp;   /* back-pointer to
36231    interface    */
```

```
36232        struct ifaddr        *ifa_next;  /* next address for
36233    interface   */
36234    };
36235
36236    #define ifa_broadaddr   ifa_ifu.ifu_broadaddr   /*
36237    broadcast address    */
36238    #define ifa_dstaddr ifa_ifu.ifu_dstaddr /* other end of
36239    link   */
36240
36241    /*
36242     * Device mapping structure. I'd just gone off and
36243    designed a
36244     * beautiful scheme using only loadable modules with
36245    arguments
36246     * for driver options and along come the PCMCIA people
36247    8)
36248     *
36249     * Ah well. The get() side of this is good for WDSETUP,
36250    and it'll
36251     * be handy for debugging things. The set side is fine
36252    for now and
36253     * being very small might be worth keeping for clean
36254    configuration.
36255     */
36256
36257    struct ifmap
36258    {
36259        unsigned long mem_start;
36260        unsigned long mem_end;
36261        unsigned short base_addr;
36262        unsigned char irq;
36263        unsigned char dma;
36264        unsigned char port;
36265        /* 3 bytes spare */
36266    };
36267
36268    /*
36269     * Interface request structure used for socket
36270     * ioctl's.  All interface ioctl's must have parameter
36271     * definitions which begin with ifr_name.   The
36272     * remainder may be interface specific.
36273     */
36274
36275    struct ifreq
36276    {
36277    #define IFHWADDRLEN 6
36278    #define IFNAMSIZ    16
36279        union
```

```
36280        {
36281            char    ifrn_name[IFNAMSIZ];        /* if name,
36282  e.g. "en0" */
36283        } ifr_ifrn;
36284
36285        union {
36286            struct  sockaddr ifru_addr;
36287            struct  sockaddr ifru_dstaddr;
36288            struct  sockaddr ifru_broadaddr;
36289            struct  sockaddr ifru_netmask;
36290            struct  sockaddr ifru_hwaddr;
36291            short   ifru_flags;
36292            int ifru_metric;
36293            int ifru_mtu;
36294            struct  ifmap ifru_map;
36295            char    ifru_slave[IFNAMSIZ];   /* Just fits the
36296  size */
36297            caddr_t ifru_data;
36298        } ifr_ifru;
36299  };
36300
36301  #define ifr_name    ifr_ifrn.ifrn_name /* interface
36302  name   */
36303  #define ifr_hwaddr  ifr_ifru.ifru_hwaddr    /* MAC
36304  address       */
36305  #define ifr_addr    ifr_ifru.ifru_addr /* address
36306  */
36307  #define ifr_dstaddr ifr_ifru.ifru_dstaddr   /* other end
36308  of p-p lnk */
36309  #define ifr_broadaddr   ifr_ifru.ifru_broadaddr /*
36310  broadcast address    */
36311  #define ifr_netmask ifr_ifru.ifru_netmask   /* interface
36312  net mask   */
36313  #define ifr_flags   ifr_ifru.ifru_flags /* flags
36314  */
36315  #define ifr_metric  ifr_ifru.ifru_metric    /* metric
36316     */
36317  #define ifr_mtu     ifr_ifru.ifru_mtu   /* mtu
36318  */
36319  #define ifr_map     ifr_ifru.ifru_map   /* device map
36320     */
36321  #define ifr_slave   ifr_ifru.ifru_slave /* slave device
36322     */
36323  #define ifr_data    ifr_ifru.ifru_data  /* for use by
36324  interface */
36325
36326  /*
36327   * Structure used in SIOCGIFCONF request.
```

```
36328   * Used to retrieve interface configuration
36329   * for machine (useful for programs which
36330   * must know all networks accessible).
36331   */
36332
36333  struct ifconf
36334  {
36335      int ifc_len;                /* size of buffer   */
36336      union
36337      {
36338          caddr_t ifcu_buf;
36339          struct  ifreq *ifcu_req;
36340      } ifc_ifcu;
36341  };
36342  #define ifc_buf ifc_ifcu.ifcu_buf       /* buffer
36343  address   */
36344  #define ifc_req ifc_ifcu.ifcu_req       /* array of
36345  structures */
36346
36347  #endif /* _LINUX_IF_H */
```

usr/include/linux/igmp.h

```
36348  /*
36349   * Linux NET3: Internet Group Management Protocol
36350  [IGMP]
36351   *
36352   * Authors:
36353   *      Alan Cox <Alan.Cox@linux.org>
36354   *
36355   * Extended to talk the BSD extended IGMP protocol of
36356  mrouted 3.6
36357   *
36358   *
36359   * This program is free software; you can redistribute
36360  it and/or
36361   * modify it under the terms of the GNU General Public
36362  License
36363   * as published by the Free Software Foundation; either
36364  version
36365   * 2 of the License, or (at your option) any later
36366  version.
36367   */
36368
36369  #ifndef _LINUX_IGMP_H
36370  #define _LINUX_IGMP_H
36371
36372  /*
36373   * IGMP protocol structures
```

```
36374    */
36375
36376    /*
36377     *   Header in on cable format
36378     */
36379
36380    struct igmphdr
36381    {
36382        __u8 type;
36383        __u8 code;        /* For newer IGMP */
36384        __u16 csum;
36385        __u32 group;
36386    };
36387
36388    #define IGMP_HOST_MEMBERSHIP_QUERY  0x11    /* From
36389    RFC1112 */
36390    #define IGMP_HOST_MEMBERSHIP_REPORT 0x12    /* Ditto */
36391    #define IGMP_DVMRP          0x13    /* DVMRP routing */
36392    #define IGMP_PIM            0x14    /* PIM routing */
36393    #define IGMP_TRACE          0x15    /* CISCO trace */
36394    #define IGMP_HOST_NEW_MEMBERSHIP_REPORT 0x16    /* New
36395    version of 0x11 */
36396    #define IGMP_HOST_LEAVE_MESSAGE     0x17    /* An extra
36397    BSD seems to send */
36398
36399    #define IGMP_MTRACE_RESP        0x1e
36400    #define IGMP_MTRACE         0x1f
36401
36402
36403    /*
36404     *   Use the BSD names for these for compatibility
36405     */
36406
36407    #define IGMP_DELAYING_MEMBER        0x01
36408    #define IGMP_IDLE_MEMBER        0x02
36409    #define IGMP_LAZY_MEMBER        0x03
36410    #define IGMP_SLEEPING_MEMBER        0x04
36411    #define IGMP_AWAKENING_MEMBER       0x05
36412
36413    #define IGMP_OLD_ROUTER         0x00
36414    #define IGMP_NEW_ROUTER         0x01
36415
36416    #define IGMP_MINLEN         8
36417
36418    #define IGMP_MAX_HOST_REPORT_DELAY  10  /* max delay for
36419    response to */
36420                        /* query (in seconds)   */
36421
36422    #define IGMP_TIMER_SCALE        10  /* denotes that the
36423    igmphdr->timer field */
36424                        /* specifies time in 10th of
36425    seconds      */
36426
36427    #define IGMP_AGE_THRESHOLD      540 /* If this host
36428    don't hear any IGMP V1  */
36429                        /* message in this period of
36430    time,  */
36431                        /* revert to IGMP v2 router.
36432     */
36433
36434    #define IGMP_ALL_HOSTS      htonl(0xE0000001L)
36435    #define IGMP_ALL_ROUTER     htonl(0xE0000002L)
36436    #define IGMP_LOCAL_GROUP        htonl(0xE0000000L)
36437    #define IGMP_LOCAL_GROUP_MASK   htonl(0xFFFFFF00L)
36438
36439    /*
36440     * struct for keeping the multicast list in
36441     */
36442
36443    #ifdef __KERNEL__
36444    struct ip_mc_socklist
36445    {
36446        unsigned long multiaddr[IP_MAX_MEMBERSHIPS];    /*
36447    This is a speed trade off */
36448        struct device *multidev[IP_MAX_MEMBERSHIPS];
36449    };
36450
36451    struct ip_mc_list
36452    {
36453        struct device *interface;
36454        unsigned long multiaddr;
36455        struct ip_mc_list *next;
36456        struct timer_list timer;
36457        short tm_running;
36458        short reporter;
36459        int users;
36460    };
36461
36462    struct ip_router_info
36463    {
36464        struct device *dev;
36465        int   type;    /* type of router which is querier
36466    on this interface */
36467        int   time;    /* # of slow timeouts since last old
36468    query */
36469        struct timer_list timer;
```

```
36470      struct ip_router_info *next;
36471    };
36472
36473    extern struct ip_mc_list *ip_mc_head;
36474
36475
36476    extern int igmp_rcv(struct sk_buff *, struct device *,
36477    struct options *, __u32, unsigned short,
36478        __u32, int , struct inet_protocol *);
36479    extern void ip_mc_drop_device(struct device *dev);
36480    extern int ip_mc_join_group(struct sock *sk, struct
36481    device *dev, unsigned long addr);
36482    extern int ip_mc_leave_group(struct sock *sk, struct
36483    device *dev,unsigned long addr);
36484    extern void ip_mc_drop_socket(struct sock *sk);
36485    extern void ip_mr_init(void);
36486    #endif
36487    #endif
```

usr/include/linux/in.h

```
36488    /*
36489     * INET      An implementation of the TCP/IP protocol
36490    suite for the LINUX
36491     *       operating system.  INET is implemented using the
36492    BSD Socket
36493     *       interface as the means of communication with the
36494    user level.
36495     *
36496     *       Definitions of the Internet Protocol.
36497     *
36498     * Version: @(#)in.h    1.0.1    04/21/93
36499     *
36500     * Authors: Original taken from the GNU Project
36501    <netinet/in.h> file.
36502     *       Fred N. van Kempen, <waltje@uWalt.NL.Mugnet.ORG>
36503     *
36504     *       This program is free software; you can
36505    redistribute it and/or
36506     *       modify it under the terms of the GNU General
36507    Public License
36508     *       as published by the Free Software Foundation;
36509    either version
36510     *       2 of the License, or (at your option) any later
36511    version.
36512     */
36513    #ifndef _LINUX_IN_H
36514    #define _LINUX_IN_H
36515
36516    #include <linux/types.h>
36517
36518    /* Standard well-defined IP protocols.  */
36519    enum {
36520      IPPROTO_IP = 0,       /* Dummy protocol for TCP
36521    */
36522      IPPROTO_ICMP = 1,     /* Internet Control Message
36523    Protocol    */
36524      IPPROTO_IGMP = 2,     /* Internet Group Management
36525    Protocol    */
36526      IPPROTO_IPIP = 4,     /* IPIP tunnels (older KA9Q
36527    tunnels use 94) */
36528      IPPROTO_TCP = 6,      /* Transmission Control Protocol
36529     */
36530      IPPROTO_EGP = 8,      /* Exterior Gateway Protocol
36531     */
36532      IPPROTO_PUP = 12,     /* PUP protocol             */
36533      IPPROTO_UDP = 17,     /* User Datagram Protocol
36534    */
36535      IPPROTO_IDP = 22,     /* XNS IDP protocol         */
36536
36537      IPPROTO_RAW = 255,       /* Raw IP packets
36538    */
36539      IPPROTO_MAX
36540    };
36541
36542
36543    /* Internet address. */
36544    struct in_addr {
36545        __u32    s_addr;
36546    };
36547
36548    /* Request struct for multicast socket ops */
36549
36550    struct ip_mreq
36551    {
36552        struct in_addr imr_multiaddr;   /* IP multicast
36553    address of group */
36554        struct in_addr imr_interface;   /* local IP address
36555    of interface */
36556    };
36557
36558
36559    /* Structure describing an Internet (IP) socket address.
36560    */
36561    #define __SOCK_SIZE__    16      /* sizeof(struct
36562    sockaddr) */
36563    struct sockaddr_in {
```

```
36564    short int      sin_family; /* Address family      */
36565    unsigned short int    sin_port;   /* Port number
36566     */
36567    struct in_addr    sin_addr;   /* Internet address
36568 */
36569
36570    /* Pad to size of 'struct sockaddr'. */
36571    unsigned char     __pad[__SOCK_SIZE__ - sizeof(short
36572 int) -
36573            sizeof(unsigned short int) - sizeof(struct
36574 in_addr)];
36575 };
36576 #define sin_zero    __pad        /* for BSD UNIX comp.
36577 -FvK */
36578
36579
36580 /*
36581  * Definitions of the bits in an Internet address
36582 integer.
36583  * On subnets, host and network parts are found according
36584  * to the subnet mask, not these masks.
36585  */
36586 #define IN_CLASSA(a)        ((((long int) (a)) &
36587 0x80000000) == 0)
36588 #define IN_CLASSA_NET       0xff000000
36589 #define IN_CLASSA_NSHIFT    24
36590 #define IN_CLASSA_HOST      (0xffffffff & ~IN_CLASSA_NET)
36591 #define IN_CLASSA_MAX       128
36592
36593 #define IN_CLASSB(a)        ((((long int) (a)) &
36594 0xc0000000) == 0x80000000)
36595 #define IN_CLASSB_NET       0xffff0000
36596 #define IN_CLASSB_NSHIFT    16
36597 #define IN_CLASSB_HOST      (0xffffffff & ~IN_CLASSB_NET)
36598 #define IN_CLASSB_MAX       65536
36599
36600 #define IN_CLASSC(a)        ((((long int) (a)) &
36601 0xe0000000) == 0xc0000000)
36602 #define IN_CLASSC_NET       0xffffff00
36603 #define IN_CLASSC_NSHIFT    8
36604 #define IN_CLASSC_HOST      (0xffffffff & ~IN_CLASSC_NET)
36605
36606 #define IN_CLASSD(a)        ((((long int) (a)) &
36607 0xf0000000) == 0xe0000000)
36608 #define IN_MULTICAST(a)     IN_CLASSD(a)
36609 #define IN_MULTICAST_NET    0xF0000000
36610
36611 #define IN_EXPERIMENTAL(a)  ((((long int) (a)) &
```

```
36612 0xe0000000) == 0xe0000000)
36613 #define IN_BADCLASS(a)        ((((long int) (a)) &
36614 0xf0000000) == 0xf0000000)
36615
36616 /* Address to accept any incoming messages. */
36617 #define INADDR_ANY      ((unsigned long int) 0x00000000)
36618
36619 /* Address to send to all hosts. */
36620 #define INADDR_BROADCAST    ((unsigned long int)
36621 0xffffffff)
36622
36623 /* Address indicating an error return. */
36624 #define INADDR_NONE     ((unsigned long int) 0xffffffff)
36625
36626 /* Network number for local host loopback. */
36627 #define IN_LOOPBACKNET      127
36628
36629 /* Address to loopback in software to local host.  */
36630 #define INADDR_LOOPBACK     0x7f000001  /* 127.0.0.1   */
36631 #define IN_LOOPBACK(a)      ((((long int) (a)) &
36632 0xff000000) == 0x7f000000)
36633
36634 /* Defines for Multicast INADDR */
36635 #define INADDR_UNSPEC_GROUP     0xe0000000      /*
36636 224.0.0.0   */
36637 #define INADDR_ALLHOSTS_GROUP   0xe0000001      /*
36638 224.0.0.1   */
36639 #define INADDR_MAX_LOCAL_GROUP  0xe00000ff      /*
36640 224.0.0.255 */
36641
36642 /* <asm/byteorder.h> contains the htonl type stuff.. */
36643
36644 #include <asm/byteorder.h>
36645
36646 /* Some random defines to make it easier in the kernel..
36647 */
36648 #ifdef __KERNEL__
36649
36650 #define LOOPBACK(x) (((x) & htonl(0xff000000)) ==
36651 htonl(0x7f000000))
36652 #define MULTICAST(x)    (((x) & htonl(0xf0000000)) ==
36653 htonl(0xe0000000))
36654
36655 #endif
36656
36657 /*
36658  * IPv6 definitions as we start to include them. This
36659 is just
```

```
36660      *   a beginning -- don't get excited 8)
36661      */
36662
36663     struct in_addr6
36664     {
36665         unsigned char s6_addr[16];
36666     };
36667
36668     struct sockaddr_in6
36669     {
36670         unsigned short sin6_family;
36671         unsigned short sin6_port;
36672         unsigned long sin6_flowinfo;
36673         struct in_addr6 sin6_addr;
36674     };
36675
36676
36677     #endif  /* _LINUX_IN_H */
```

usr/include/linux/inet.h

```
36678     /*
36679      *       Swansea University Computer Society NET3
36680      *
36681      *   This work is derived from NET2Debugged, which is in
36682     turn derived
36683      *   from NET2D which was written by:
36684      *       Fred N. van Kempen, <waltje@uWalt.NL.Mugnet.ORG>
36685      *
36686      *       This work was derived from Ross Biro's
36687     inspirational work
36688      *       for the LINUX operating system.  His version
36689     numbers were:
36690      *
36691      *       $Id: Space.c,v     0.8.4.5  1992/12/12 19:25:04
36692     bir7 Exp $
36693      *       $Id: arp.c,v       0.8.4.6  1993/01/28 22:30:00
36694     bir7 Exp $
36695      *       $Id: arp.h,v       0.8.4.6  1993/01/28 22:30:00
36696     bir7 Exp $
36697      *       $Id: dev.c,v       0.8.4.13 1993/01/23 18:00:11
36698     bir7 Exp $
36699      *       $Id: dev.h,v       0.8.4.7  1993/01/23 18:00:11
36700     bir7 Exp $
36701      *       $Id: eth.c,v       0.8.4.4  1993/01/22 23:21:38
36702     bir7 Exp $
36703      *       $Id: eth.h,v       0.8.4.1  1992/11/10 00:17:18
36704     bir7 Exp $
36705      *       $Id: icmp.c,v      0.8.4.9  1993/01/23 18:00:11
36706     bir7 Exp $
36707      *       $Id: icmp.h,v      0.8.4.2  1992/11/15 14:55:30
36708     bir7 Exp $
36709      *       $Id: ip.c,v        0.8.4.8  1992/12/12 19:25:04
36710     bir7 Exp $
36711      *       $Id: ip.h,v        0.8.4.2  1993/01/23 18:00:11
36712     bir7 Exp $
36713      *       $Id: loopback.c,v  0.8.4.8  1993/01/23 18:00:11
36714     bir7 Exp $
36715      *       $Id: packet.c,v    0.8.4.7  1993/01/26 22:04:00
36716     bir7 Exp $
36717      *       $Id: protocols.c,v 0.8.4.3  1992/11/15 14:55:30
36718     bir7 Exp $
36719      *       $Id: raw.c,v       0.8.4.12 1993/01/26 22:04:00
36720     bir7 Exp $
36721      *       $Id: sock.c,v      0.8.4.6  1993/01/28 22:30:00
36722     bir7 Exp $
36723      *       $Id: sock.h,v      0.8.4.7  1993/01/26 22:04:00
36724     bir7 Exp $
36725      *       $Id: tcp.c,v       0.8.4.16 1993/01/26 22:04:00
36726     bir7 Exp $
36727      *       $Id: tcp.h,v       0.8.4.7  1993/01/22 22:58:08
36728     bir7 Exp $
36729      *       $Id: timer.c,v     0.8.4.8  1993/01/23 18:00:11
36730     bir7 Exp $
36731      *       $Id: timer.h,v     0.8.4.2  1993/01/23 18:00:11
36732     bir7 Exp $
36733      *       $Id: udp.c,v       0.8.4.12 1993/01/26 22:04:00
36734     bir7 Exp $
36735      *       $Id: udp.h,v       0.8.4.1  1992/11/10 00:17:18
36736     bir7 Exp $
36737      *       $Id: we.c,v        0.8.4.10 1993/01/23 18:00:11
36738     bir7 Exp $
36739      *       $Id: wereg.h,v     0.8.4.1  1992/11/10 00:17:18
36740     bir7 Exp $
36741      *
36742      *       This program is free software; you can
36743     redistribute it and/or
36744      *       modify it under the terms of the GNU General
36745     Public License
36746      *       as published by the Free Software Foundation;
36747     either version
36748      *       2 of the License, or (at your option) any later
36749     version.
36750      */
36751     #ifndef _LINUX_INET_H
36752     #define _LINUX_INET_H
36753
```

```
36754    #ifdef __KERNEL__
36755
36756    extern void      inet_proto_init(struct net_proto *pro);
36757    extern char      *in_ntoa(unsigned long in);
36758    extern unsigned long    in_aton(const char *str);
36759
36760    #endif
36761    #endif  /* _LINUX_INET_H */
```

usr/include/linux/ioctl.h

```
36762    #ifndef _LINUX_IOCTL_H
36763    #define _LINUX_IOCTL_H
36764
36765    #include <asm/ioctl.h>
36766
36767    #endif /* _LINUX_IOCTL_H */
36768
```

usr/include/linux/ip.h

```
36769    /*
36770     * INET      An implementation of the TCP/IP protocol
36771    suite for the LINUX
36772     *         operating system.  INET is implemented using the
36773    BSD Socket
36774     *         interface as the means of communication with the
36775    user level.
36776     *
36777     *         Definitions for the IP protocol.
36778     *
36779     * Version: @(#)ip.h    1.0.2    04/28/93
36780     *
36781     * Authors: Fred N. van Kempen,
36782    <waltje@uWalt.NL.Mugnet.ORG>
36783     *
36784     *         This program is free software; you can
36785    redistribute it and/or
36786     *         modify it under the terms of the GNU General
36787    Public License
36788     *         as published by the Free Software Foundation;
36789    either version
36790     *         2 of the License, or (at your option) any later
36791    version.
36792     */
36793    #ifndef _LINUX_IP_H
36794    #define _LINUX_IP_H
36795    #include <asm/byteorder.h>
36796
36797    #define IPOPT_END    0
```

```
36798    #define IPOPT_NOOP   1
36799    #define IPOPT_SEC    130
36800    #define IPOPT_LSRR   131
36801    #define IPOPT_SSRR   137
36802    #define IPOPT_RR     7
36803    #define IPOPT_SID    136
36804    #define IPOPT_TIMESTAMP 68
36805
36806
36807    #define MAXTTL       255
36808
36809    struct timestamp {
36810        __u8    len;
36811        __u8    ptr;
36812    #if defined(__LITTLE_ENDIAN_BITFIELD)
36813        __u8    flags:4,
36814            overflow:4;
36815    #elif defined(__BIG_ENDIAN_BITFIELD)
36816        __u8    overflow:4,
36817            flags:4;
36818    #else
36819    #error  "Please fix <asm/byteorder.h>"
36820    #endif
36821        __u32   data[9];
36822    };
36823
36824
36825    #define MAX_ROUTE   16
36826
36827    struct route {
36828        char    route_size;
36829        char    pointer;
36830        unsigned long route[MAX_ROUTE];
36831    };
36832
36833    #define IPOPT_OPTVAL 0
36834    #define IPOPT_OLEN   1
36835    #define IPOPT_OFFSET 2
36836    #define IPOPT_MINOFF 4
36837    #define MAX_IPOPTLEN 40
36838    #define IPOPT_NOP IPOPT_NOOP
36839    #define IPOPT_EOL IPOPT_END
36840    #define IPOPT_TS  IPOPT_TIMESTAMP
36841
36842    #define IPOPT_TS_TSONLY    0       /* timestamps only */
36843    #define IPOPT_TS_TSANDADDR 1       /* timestamps and
36844    addresses */
36845    #define IPOPT_TS_PRESPEC   2       /* specified modules
```

```
36846  only */
36847
36848  struct options {
36849    __u32   faddr;              /* Saved first hop
36850  address */
36851    unsigned char optlen;
36852    unsigned char srr;
36853    unsigned char rr;
36854    unsigned char ts;
36855    unsigned char is_setbyuser:1,      /* Set by
36856  setsockopt?          */
36857                  is_data:1,       /* Options in
36858  __data, rather than skb  */
36859                  is_strictroute:1,    /* Strict source
36860  route          */
36861                  srr_is_hit:1,       /* Packet
36862  destination addr was our one  */
36863                  is_changed:1,       /* IP checksum
36864  more not valid     */
36865                  rr_needaddr:1,      /* Need to
36866  record addr of outgoing dev  */
36867                  ts_needtime:1,      /* Need to
36868  record timestamp     */
36869                  ts_needaddr:1;      /* Need to
36870  record addr of outgoing dev  */
36871    unsigned char __pad1;
36872    unsigned char __pad2;
36873    unsigned char __pad3;
36874    unsigned char __data[0];
36875  };
36876
36877  struct iphdr {
36878  #if defined(__LITTLE_ENDIAN_BITFIELD)
36879      __u8   ihl:4,
36880          version:4;
36881  #elif defined (__BIG_ENDIAN_BITFIELD)
36882      __u8   version:4,
36883          ihl:4;
36884  #else
36885  #error "Please fix <asm/byteorder.h>"
36886  #endif
36887      __u8   tos;
36888      __u16  tot_len;
36889      __u16  id;
36890      __u16  frag_off;
36891      __u8   ttl;
36892      __u8   protocol;
36893      __u16  check;
```

```
36894      __u32   saddr;
36895      __u32   daddr;
36896      /*The options start here. */
36897  };
36898
36899  #endif  /* _LINUX_IP_H */
```

usr/include/linux/kernel.h

```
36900  #ifndef _LINUX_KERNEL_H
36901  #define _LINUX_KERNEL_H
36902
36903  /*
36904   * 'kernel.h' contains some often-used function
36905  prototypes etc
36906   */
36907
36908  #ifdef __KERNEL__
36909
36910  #include <stdarg.h>
36911  #include <linux/linkage.h>
36912
36913  /* Optimization barrier */
36914  #define barrier() __asm__("": : :"memory")
36915
36916  #define INT_MAX      ((int)(~0U>>1))
36917  #define UINT_MAX     (~0U)
36918  #define LONG_MAX     ((long)(~0UL>>1))
36919  #define ULONG_MAX    (~0UL)
36920
36921  #define STACK_MAGIC 0xdeadbeef
36922
36923  #define KERN_EMERG  "<0>"   /* system is unusable
36924     */
36925  #define KERN_ALERT  "<1>"   /* action must be taken
36926  immediately */
36927  #define KERN_CRIT   "<2>"   /* critical conditions
36928     */
36929  #define KERN_ERR    "<3>"   /* error conditions
36930  */
36931  #define KERN_WARNING    "<4>"    /* warning conditions
36932       */
36933  #define KERN_NOTICE "<5>"   /* normal but significant
36934  condition */
36935  #define KERN_INFO   "<6>"   /* informational
36936  */
36937  #define KERN_DEBUG  "<7>"   /* debug-level messages
36938     */
36939
```

```
36940  # define NORET_TYPE     /**/
36941  # define ATTRIB_NORET  __attribute__((noreturn))
36942  # define NORET_AND      noreturn,
36943
36944  extern void math_error(void);
36945  NORET_TYPE void panic(const char * fmt, ...)
36946      __attribute__ ((NORET_AND format (printf, 1, 2)));
36947  NORET_TYPE void do_exit(long error_code)
36948      ATTRIB_NORET;
36949  extern unsigned long simple_strtoul(const char *,char
36950  **,unsigned int);
36951  extern int sprintf(char * buf, const char * fmt, ...);
36952  extern int vsprintf(char *buf, const char *, va_list);
36953
36954  extern int session_of_pgrp(int pgrp);
36955
36956  extern int kill_proc(int pid, int sig, int priv);
36957  extern int kill_pg(int pgrp, int sig, int priv);
36958  extern int kill_sl(int sess, int sig, int priv);
36959
36960  asmlinkage int printk(const char * fmt, ...)
36961      __attribute__ ((format (printf, 1, 2)));
36962
36963  #if DEBUG
36964  #define pr_debug(fmt,arg...) \
36965      printk(KERN_DEBUG fmt,##arg)
36966  #else
36967  #define pr_debug(fmt,arg...) \
36968      do { } while (0)
36969  #endif
36970
36971  #define pr_info(fmt,arg...) \
36972      printk(KERN_INFO fmt,##arg)
36973
36974  /*
36975   * "suser()" checks against the effective user id, while
36976  "fsuser()"
36977   * is used for file permission checking and checks
36978  against the fsuid..
36979   */
36980  #define fsuser() (current->fsuid == 0)
36981
36982  /*
36983   *      Display an IP address in readable format.
36984   */
36985
36986  #define NIPQUAD(addr) \
36987          (((addr) >> 0)  & 0xff), \
```

```
36988          (((addr) >> 8)  & 0xff), \
36989          (((addr) >> 16) & 0xff), \
36990          (((addr) >> 24) & 0xff)
36991
36992  #endif /* __KERNEL__ */
36993
36994  #define SI_LOAD_SHIFT   16
36995  struct sysinfo {
36996      long uptime;              /* Seconds since boot */
36997      unsigned long loads[3];   /* 1, 5, and 15 minute
36998  load averages */
36999      unsigned long totalram;    /* Total usable main
37000  memory size */
37001      unsigned long freeram;     /* Available memory size
37002  */
37003      unsigned long sharedram;   /* Amount of shared
37004  memory */
37005      unsigned long bufferram;   /* Memory used by
37006  buffers */
37007      unsigned long totalswap;   /* Total swap space size
37008  */
37009      unsigned long freeswap;    /* swap space still
37010  available */
37011      unsigned short procs;      /* Number of current
37012  processes */
37013      char _f[22];               /* Pads structure to 64
37014  bytes */
37015  };
37016
37017  #endif
```

usr/include/linux/lists.h

```
37018  /*
37019   * lists.h:  Simple list macros for Linux
37020   */
37021
37022  #define DLNODE(ptype)                               \
37023      struct {                        \
37024          ptype * dl_prev;          \
37025          ptype * dl_next;          \
37026      }
37027
37028  #define DNODE_SINGLE(node) {(node),(node)}
37029  #define DNODE_NULL {0,0}
37030
37031  #define DLIST_INIT(listnam)
37032      \
37033      (listnam).dl_prev = &(listnam);               \
```

```
37034        (listnam).dl_next = &(listnam);
37035
37036  #define DLIST_NEXT(listnam) listnam.dl_next
37037  #define DLIST_PREV(listnam) listnam.dl_prev
37038
37039  #define DLIST_INSERT_AFTER(node, new, listnam)  do {
37040      \
37041      (new)->listnam.dl_prev = (node);                    \
37042      (new)->listnam.dl_next = (node)->listnam.dl_next;   \
37043      (node)->listnam.dl_next->listnam.dl_prev = (new);   \
37044      (node)->listnam.dl_next = (new);                    \
37045      } while (0)
37046
37047  #define DLIST_INSERT_BEFORE(node, new, listnam) do {
37048      \
37049      (new)->listnam.dl_next = (node);                    \
37050      (new)->listnam.dl_prev = (node)->listnam.dl_prev;   \
37051      (node)->listnam.dl_prev->listnam.dl_next = (new);   \
37052      (node)->listnam.dl_prev = (new);                    \
37053      } while (0)
37054
37055  #define DLIST_DELETE(node, listnam) do {            \
37056      node->listnam.dl_prev->listnam.dl_next =        \
37057          node->listnam.dl_next;                      \
37058      node->listnam.dl_next->listnam.dl_prev =        \
37059          node->listnam.dl_prev;                      \
37060      } while (0)
37061
37062  /*
37063   * queue-style operations, which have a head and tail
37064   */
37065
37066  #define QUEUE_INIT(head, listnam, ptype)            \
37067      (head)->listnam.dl_prev = (head)->listnam.dl_next =
37068  (ptype)(head);
37069
37070  #define QUEUE_FIRST(head, listnam)
37071  (head)->DLIST_NEXT(listnam)
37072  #define QUEUE_LAST(head, listnam)
37073  (head)->DLIST_PREV(listnam)
37074  #define QUEUE_EMPTY(head, listnam) \
37075      ((QUEUE_FIRST(head, listnam) == QUEUE_LAST(head,
37076  listnam)) && \
37077      ((u_long)QUEUE_FIRST(head, listnam) ==
37078  (u_long)head))
37079
37080  #define QUEUE_ENTER(head, new, listnam, ptype) do {    \
37081      (new)->listnam.dl_prev = (ptype)(head);            \
```

```
37082      (new)->listnam.dl_next = (head)->listnam.dl_next;  \
37083      (head)->listnam.dl_next->listnam.dl_prev = (new);  \
37084      (head)->listnam.dl_next = (new);                   \
37085      } while (0)
37086
37087  #define QUEUE_REMOVE(head, node, listnam)
37088  DLIST_DELETE(node, listnam)
```

usr/include/linux/mm.h

```
37089  #ifndef _LINUX_MM_H
37090  #define _LINUX_MM_H
37091
37092  #include <linux/sched.h>
37093  #include <linux/errno.h>
37094  #include <linux/kernel.h>
37095
37096  #ifdef __KERNEL__
37097
37098  #include <linux/string.h>
37099
37100  extern unsigned long high_memory;
37101
37102  #include <asm/page.h>
37103  #include <asm/atomic.h>
37104
37105  #define VERIFY_READ 0
37106  #define VERIFY_WRITE 1
37107
37108  extern int verify_area(int, const void *, unsigned long);
37109
37110  /*
37111   * Linux kernel virtual memory manager primitives.
37112   * The idea being to have a "virtual" mm in the same way
37113   * we have a virtual fs - giving a cleaner interface to
37114  the
37115   * mm details, and allowing different kinds of memory
37116  mappings
37117   * (from shared memory to executable loading to arbitrary
37118   * mmap() functions).
37119   */
37120
37121  /*
37122   * This struct defines a memory VMM memory area. There
37123  is one of these
37124   * per VM-area/task.  A VM area is any part of the
37125  process virtual memory
37126   * space that has a special rule for the page-fault
37127  handlers (ie a shared
```

```
37128     * library, the executable area etc).
37129     */
37130    struct vm_area_struct {
37131        struct mm_struct * vm_mm;    /* VM area parameters */
37132        unsigned long vm_start;
37133        unsigned long vm_end;
37134        pgprot_t vm_page_prot;
37135        unsigned short vm_flags;
37136    /* AVL tree of VM areas per task, sorted by address */
37137        short vm_avl_height;
37138        struct vm_area_struct * vm_avl_left;
37139        struct vm_area_struct * vm_avl_right;
37140    /* linked list of VM areas per task, sorted by address */
37141        struct vm_area_struct * vm_next;
37142    /* for areas with inode, the circular list inode->i_mmap
37143    */
37144    /* for shm areas, the circular list of attaches */
37145    /* otherwise unused */
37146        struct vm_area_struct * vm_next_share;
37147        struct vm_area_struct * vm_prev_share;
37148    /* more */
37149        struct vm_operations_struct * vm_ops;
37150        unsigned long vm_offset;
37151        struct inode * vm_inode;
37152        unsigned long vm_pte;              /* shared mem */
37153    };
37154
37155    /*
37156     * vm_flags..
37157     */
37158    #define VM_READ      0x0001  /* currently active flags */
37159    #define VM_WRITE     0x0002
37160    #define VM_EXEC      0x0004
37161    #define VM_SHARED    0x0008
37162
37163    #define VM_MAYREAD  0x0010  /* limits for mprotect() etc
37164    */
37165    #define VM_MAYWRITE 0x0020
37166    #define VM_MAYEXEC  0x0040
37167    #define VM_MAYSHARE 0x0080
37168
37169    #define VM_GROWSDOWN    0x0100  /* general info on the
37170    segment */
37171    #define VM_GROWSUP  0x0200
37172    #define VM_SHM       0x0400  /* shared memory area, don't
37173    swap out */
37174    #define VM_DENYWRITE    0x0800  /* ETXTBSY on write
37175    attempts.. */
37176
37177    #define VM_EXECUTABLE   0x1000
37178    #define VM_LOCKED   0x2000
37179
37180    #define VM_STACK_FLAGS  0x0177
37181
37182    /*
37183     * mapping from the currently active vm_flags protection
37184    bits (the
37185     * low four bits) to a page protection mask..
37186     */
37187    extern pgprot_t protection_map[16];
37188
37189
37190    /*
37191     * These are the virtual MM functions - opening of an
37192    area, closing and
37193     * unmapping it (needed to keep files on disk up-to-date
37194    etc), pointer
37195     * to the functions called when a no-page or a wp-page
37196    exception occurs.
37197     */
37198    struct vm_operations_struct {
37199        void (*open)(struct vm_area_struct * area);
37200        void (*close)(struct vm_area_struct * area);
37201        void (*unmap)(struct vm_area_struct *area, unsigned
37202    long, size_t);
37203        void (*protect)(struct vm_area_struct *area,
37204    unsigned long, size_t, unsigned int newprot);
37205        int (*sync)(struct vm_area_struct *area, unsigned
37206    long, size_t, unsigned int flags);
37207        void (*advise)(struct vm_area_struct *area, unsigned
37208    long, size_t, unsigned int advise);
37209        unsigned long (*nopage)(struct vm_area_struct *
37210    area, unsigned long address, int write_access);
37211        unsigned long (*wppage)(struct vm_area_struct *
37212    area, unsigned long address,
37213            unsigned long page);
37214        int (*swapout)(struct vm_area_struct *,  unsigned
37215    long, pte_t *);
37216        pte_t (*swapin)(struct vm_area_struct *, unsigned
37217    long, unsigned long);
37218    };
37219
37220    /*
37221     * Try to keep the most commonly accessed fields in
37222    single cache lines
37223     * here (16 bytes or greater).  This ordering should be
```

```
37224  particularly
37225   * beneficial on 32-bit processors.
37226   *
37227   * The first line is data used in page cache lookup, the
37228  second line
37229   * is used for linear searches (eg. clock algorithm
37230  scans).
37231   */
37232  typedef struct page {
37233      /* these must be first (free area handling) */
37234      struct page *next;
37235      struct page *prev;
37236      struct inode *inode;
37237      unsigned long offset;
37238      struct page *next_hash;
37239      atomic_t count;
37240      unsigned flags;  /* atomic flags, some possibly
37241  updated asynchronously */
37242      unsigned dirty:16,
37243           age:8;
37244      struct wait_queue *wait;
37245      struct page *prev_hash;
37246      struct buffer_head * buffers;
37247      unsigned long swap_unlock_entry;
37248      unsigned long map_nr;   /* page->map_nr == page -
37249  mem_map */
37250  } mem_map_t;
37251
37252  /* Page flag bit values */
37253  #define PG_locked        0
37254  #define PG_error         1
37255  #define PG_referenced        2
37256  #define PG_uptodate      3
37257  #define PG_free_after        4
37258  #define PG_decr_after        5
37259  #define PG_swap_unlock_after     6
37260  #define PG_DMA           7
37261  #define PG_reserved      31
37262
37263  /* Make it prettier to test the above... */
37264  #define PageLocked(page)    (test_bit(PG_locked,
37265  &(page)->flags))
37266  #define PageError(page)     (test_bit(PG_error,
37267  &(page)->flags))
37268  #define PageReferenced(page)    (test_bit(PG_referenced,
37269  &(page)->flags))
37270  #define PageDirty(page)     (test_bit(PG_dirty,
37271  &(page)->flags))
37272  #define PageUptodate(page)  (test_bit(PG_uptodate,
37273  &(page)->flags))
37274  #define PageFreeAfter(page) (test_bit(PG_free_after,
37275  &(page)->flags))
37276  #define PageDecrAfter(page) (test_bit(PG_decr_after,
37277  &(page)->flags))
37278  #define PageSwapUnlockAfter(page)
37279  (test_bit(PG_swap_unlock_after, &(page)->flags))
37280  #define PageDMA(page)       (test_bit(PG_DMA,
37281  &(page)->flags))
37282  #define PageReserved(page)  (test_bit(PG_reserved,
37283  &(page)->flags))
37284
37285  /*
37286   * page->reserved denotes a page which must never be
37287  accessed (which
37288   * may not even be present).
37289   *
37290   * page->dma is set for those pages which lie in the
37291  range of
37292   * physical addresses capable of carrying DMA transfers.
37293   *
37294   * Multiple processes may "see" the same page. E.g. for
37295  untouched
37296   * mappings of /dev/null, all processes see the same
37297  page full of
37298   * zeroes, and text pages of executables and shared
37299  libraries have
37300   * only one copy in memory, at most, normally.
37301   *
37302   * For the non-reserved pages, page->count denotes a
37303  reference count.
37304   *   page->count == 0 means the page is free.
37305   *   page->count == 1 means the page is used for exactly
37306  one purpose
37307   *   (e.g. a private data page of one process).
37308   *
37309   * A page may be used for kmalloc() or anyone else who
37310  does a
37311   * get_free_page(). In this case the page->count is at
37312  least 1, and
37313   * all other fields are unused but should be 0 or NULL.
37314  The
37315   * management of this page is the responsibility of the
37316  one who uses
37317   * it.
37318   *
37319   * The other pages (we may call them "process pages")
```

```
37320    are completely
37321     * managed by the Linux memory manager: I/O, buffers,
37322    swapping etc.
37323     * The following discussion applies only to them.
37324     *
37325     * A page may belong to an inode's memory mapping. In
37326    this case,
37327     * page->inode is the inode, and page->offset is the
37328    file offset
37329     * of the page (not necessarily a multiple of PAGE_SIZE).
37330     *
37331     * A page may have buffers allocated to it. In this case,
37332     * page->buffers is a circular list of these buffer
37333    heads. Else,
37334     * page->buffers == NULL.
37335     *
37336     * For pages belonging to inodes, the page->count is the
37337    number of
37338     * attaches, plus 1 if buffers are allocated to the page.
37339     *
37340     * All pages belonging to an inode make up a doubly
37341    linked list
37342     * inode->i_pages, using the fields page->next and
37343    page->prev. (These
37344     * fields are also used for freelist management when
37345    page->count==0.)
37346     * There is also a hash table mapping (inode,offset) to
37347    the page
37348     * in memory if present. The lists for this hash table
37349    use the fields
37350     * page->next_hash and page->prev_hash.
37351     *
37352     * All process pages can do I/O:
37353     * - inode pages may need to be read from disk,
37354     * - inode pages which have been modified and are
37355    MAP_SHARED may need
37356     *    to be written to disk,
37357     * - private pages which have been modified may need to
37358    be swapped out
37359     *    to swap space and (later) to be read back into
37360    memory.
37361     * During disk I/O, page->locked is true. This bit is
37362    set before I/O
37363     * and reset when I/O completes. page->wait is a wait
37364    queue of all
37365     * tasks waiting for the I/O on this page to complete.
37366     * page->uptodate tells whether the page's contents is
37367    valid.
37368     * When a read completes, the page becomes uptodate,
37369    unless a disk I/O
37370     * error happened.
37371     * When a write completes, and page->free_after is true,
37372    the page is
37373     * freed without any further delay.
37374     *
37375     * For choosing which pages to swap out, inode pages
37376    carry a
37377     * page->referenced bit, which is set any time the
37378    system accesses
37379     * that page through the (inode,offset) hash table.
37380     * There is also the page->age counter, which implements
37381    a linear
37382     * decay (why not an exponential decay?), see swapctl.h.
37383     */
37384
37385    extern mem_map_t * mem_map;
37386
37387    /*
37388     * This is timing-critical - most of the time in getting
37389    a new page
37390     * goes to clearing the page. If you want a page without
37391    the clearing
37392     * overhead, just use __get_free_page() directly..
37393     */
37394    #define __get_free_page(priority)
37395    __get_free_pages((priority),0,0)
37396    #define __get_dma_pages(priority, order)
37397    __get_free_pages((priority),(order),1)
37398    extern unsigned long __get_free_pages(int priority,
37399    unsigned long gfporder, int dma);
37400
37401    extern inline unsigned long get_free_page(int priority)
37402    {
37403        unsigned long page;
37404
37405        page = __get_free_page(priority);
37406        if (page)
37407            memset((void *) page, 0, PAGE_SIZE);
37408        return page;
37409    }
37410
37411    /* memory.c & swap.c*/
37412
37413    #define free_page(addr) free_pages((addr),0)
37414    extern void free_pages(unsigned long addr, unsigned long
37415    order);
```

```
37416    extern void __free_page(struct page *);
37417
37418    extern void show_free_areas(void);
37419    extern unsigned long put_dirty_page(struct task_struct *
37420    tsk,unsigned long page,
37421        unsigned long address);
37422
37423    extern void free_page_tables(struct mm_struct * mm);
37424    extern void clear_page_tables(struct task_struct * tsk);
37425    extern int new_page_tables(struct task_struct * tsk);
37426    extern int copy_page_tables(struct task_struct * to);
37427
37428    extern int zap_page_range(struct mm_struct *mm, unsigned
37429    long address, unsigned long size);
37430    extern int copy_page_range(struct mm_struct *dst, struct
37431    mm_struct *src, struct vm_area_struct *vma);
37432    extern int remap_page_range(unsigned long from, unsigned
37433    long to, unsigned long size, pgprot_t prot);
37434    extern int zeromap_page_range(unsigned long from,
37435    unsigned long size, pgprot_t prot);
37436
37437    extern void vmtruncate(struct inode * inode, unsigned
37438    long offset);
37439    extern void handle_mm_fault(struct vm_area_struct *vma,
37440    unsigned long address, int write_access);
37441    extern void do_wp_page(struct task_struct * tsk, struct
37442    vm_area_struct * vma, unsigned long address, int
37443    write_access);
37444    extern void do_no_page(struct task_struct * tsk, struct
37445    vm_area_struct * vma, unsigned long address, int
37446    write_access);
37447
37448    extern unsigned long paging_init(unsigned long
37449    start_mem, unsigned long end_mem);
37450    extern void mem_init(unsigned long start_mem, unsigned
37451    long end_mem);
37452    extern void show_mem(void);
37453    extern void oom(struct task_struct * tsk);
37454    extern void si_meminfo(struct sysinfo * val);
37455
37456    /* vmalloc.c */
37457
37458    extern void * vmalloc(unsigned long size);
37459    extern void * vremap(unsigned long offset, unsigned long
37460    size);
37461    extern void vfree(void * addr);
37462    extern int vread(char *buf, char *addr, int count);
37463
37464    /* mmap.c */
37465    extern unsigned long do_mmap(struct file * file,
37466    unsigned long addr, unsigned long len,
37467        unsigned long prot, unsigned long flags, unsigned
37468    long off);
37469    extern void merge_segments(struct mm_struct *, unsigned
37470    long, unsigned long);
37471    extern void insert_vm_struct(struct mm_struct *, struct
37472    vm_area_struct *);
37473    extern void remove_shared_vm_struct(struct
37474    vm_area_struct *);
37475    extern void build_mmap_avl(struct mm_struct *);
37476    extern void exit_mmap(struct mm_struct *);
37477    extern int do_munmap(unsigned long, size_t);
37478    extern unsigned long get_unmapped_area(unsigned long,
37479    unsigned long);
37480
37481    /* filemap.c */
37482    extern unsigned long page_unuse(unsigned long);
37483    extern int shrink_mmap(int, int, int);
37484    extern void truncate_inode_pages(struct inode *,
37485    unsigned long);
37486
37487    #define GFP_BUFFER   0x00
37488    #define GFP_ATOMIC   0x01
37489    #define GFP_USER     0x02
37490    #define GFP_KERNEL   0x03
37491    #define GFP_NOBUFFER     0x04
37492    #define GFP_NFS      0x05
37493    #define GFP_IO       0x06
37494
37495    /* Flag - indicates that the buffer will be suitable for
37496    DMA.  Ignored on some
37497       platforms, used as appropriate on others */
37498
37499    #define GFP_DMA      0x80
37500
37501    #define GFP_LEVEL_MASK 0xf
37502
37503    /* vma is the first one with  address < vma->vm_end,
37504     * and even  address < vma->vm_start. Have to extend
37505    vma. */
37506    static inline int expand_stack(struct vm_area_struct *
37507    vma, unsigned long address)
37508    {
37509        unsigned long grow;
37510
37511        address &= PAGE_MASK;
```

```
37512        grow = vma->vm_start - address;
37513        if (vma->vm_end - address
37514            > (unsigned long)
37515    current->rlim[RLIMIT_STACK].rlim_cur ||
37516            (vma->vm_mm->total_vm << PAGE_SHIFT) + grow
37517            > (unsigned long)
37518    current->rlim[RLIMIT_AS].rlim_cur)
37519            return -ENOMEM;
37520        vma->vm_start = address;
37521        vma->vm_offset -= grow;
37522        vma->vm_mm->total_vm += grow >> PAGE_SHIFT;
37523        if (vma->vm_flags & VM_LOCKED)
37524            vma->vm_mm->locked_vm += grow >> PAGE_SHIFT;
37525        return 0;
37526    }
37527
37528    #define avl_empty    (struct vm_area_struct *) NULL
37529
37530    /* Look up the first VMA which satisfies  addr < vm_end,
37531     NULL if none. */
37532    static inline struct vm_area_struct * find_vma(struct
37533    mm_struct * mm, unsigned long addr)
37534    {
37535        struct vm_area_struct * result = NULL;
37536
37537        if (mm) {
37538            struct vm_area_struct * tree = mm->mmap_avl;
37539            for (;;) {
37540                if (tree == avl_empty)
37541                    break;
37542                if (tree->vm_end > addr) {
37543                    result = tree;
37544                    if (tree->vm_start <= addr)
37545                        break;
37546                    tree = tree->vm_avl_left;
37547                } else
37548                    tree = tree->vm_avl_right;
37549            }
37550        }
37551        return result;
37552    }
37553
37554    /* Look up the first VMA which intersects the interval
37555    start_addr..end_addr-1,
37556       NULL if none.  Assume start_addr < end_addr. */
37557    static inline struct vm_area_struct *
37558    find_vma_intersection(struct mm_struct * mm, unsigned
37559    long start_addr, unsigned long end_addr)
37560    {
37561        struct vm_area_struct * vma;
37562
37563        vma = find_vma(mm,start_addr);
37564        if (vma && end_addr <= vma->vm_start)
37565            vma = NULL;
37566        return vma;
37567    }
37568
37569    #endif /* __KERNEL__ */
37570
37571    #endif
```

usr/include/linux/mroute.h

```
37572    #ifndef __LINUX_MROUTE_H
37573    #define __LINUX_MROUTE_H
37574
37575    #include <linux/sockios.h>
37576    #include <linux/in.h>
37577
37578    /*
37579     *  Based on the MROUTING 3.5 defines primarily to keep
37580     *  source compatibility with BSD.
37581     *
37582     *  See the mrouted code for the original history.
37583     *
37584     */
37585
37586    #define MRT_BASE    200
37587    #define MRT_INIT    (MRT_BASE)   /* Activate the kernel
37588    mroute code  */
37589    #define MRT_DONE    (MRT_BASE+1)    /* Shutdown the
37590    kernel mroute      */
37591    #define MRT_ADD_VIF (MRT_BASE+2)    /* Add a virtual
37592    interface     */
37593    #define MRT_DEL_VIF (MRT_BASE+3)    /* Delete a virtual
37594    interface       */
37595    #define MRT_ADD_MFC (MRT_BASE+4)    /* Add a multicast
37596    forwarding entry */
37597    #define MRT_DEL_MFC (MRT_BASE+5)    /* Delete a
37598    multicast forwarding entry  */
37599    #define MRT_VERSION (MRT_BASE+6)    /* Get the kernel
37600    multicast version */
37601    #define MRT_ASSERT  (MRT_BASE+7)    /* Activate PIM
37602    assert mode      */
37603
37604    #define SIOCGETVIFCNT   SIOCPROTOPRIVATE    /* IP
37605    protocol privates */
```

```
37606  #define SIOCGETSGCNT   (SIOCPROTOPRIVATE+1)
37607
37608  #define MAXVIFS    32
37609  typedef unsigned long vifbitmap_t;  /* User mode code
37610  depends on this lot */
37611  typedef unsigned short vifi_t;
37612  #define ALL_VIFS   ((vifi_t)(-1))
37613
37614  /*
37615   *  Same idea as select
37616   */
37617
37618  #define VIFM_SET(n,m)    ((m)|=(1<<(n)))
37619  #define VIFM_CLR(n,m)    ((m)&=~(1<<(n)))
37620  #define VIFM_ISSET(n,m)  ((m)&(1<<(n)))
37621  #define VIFM_CLRALL(m)   ((m)=0)
37622  #define VIFM_COPY(mfrom,mto)    ((mto)=(mfrom))
37623  #define VIFM_SAME(m1,m2)    ((m1)==(m2))
37624
37625  /*
37626   *  Passed by mrouted for an MRT_ADD_VIF - again we use
37627  the
37628   *  mrouted 3.6 structures for compatibility
37629   */
37630
37631  struct vifctl {
37632      vifi_t  vifc_vifi;        /* Index of VIF */
37633      unsigned char vifc_flags;   /* VIFF_ flags */
37634      unsigned char vifc_threshold;   /* ttl limit */
37635      unsigned int vifc_rate_limit;   /* Rate limiter
37636  values (NI) */
37637      struct in_addr vifc_lcl_addr;   /* Our address */
37638      struct in_addr vifc_rmt_addr;   /* IPIP tunnel addr
37639  */
37640  };
37641
37642  #define VIFF_TUNNEL 0x1     /* IPIP tunnel */
37643  #define VIFF_SRCRT  0x02        /* NI */
37644
37645  /*
37646   *  Cache manipulation structures for mrouted
37647   */
37648
37649  struct mfcctl
37650  {
37651      struct in_addr mfcc_origin;    /* Origin of mcast
37652  */
37653      struct in_addr mfcc_mcastgrp;      /* Group in
```

```
37654  question   */
37655      vifi_t  mfcc_parent;            /* Where it arrived
37656  */
37657      unsigned char mfcc_ttls[MAXVIFS];   /* Where it is
37658  going    */
37659  };
37660
37661  /*
37662   *  Group count retrieval for mrouted
37663   */
37664
37665  struct sioc_sg_req
37666  {
37667      struct in_addr src;
37668      struct in_addr grp;
37669      unsigned long pktcnt;
37670      unsigned long bytecnt;
37671      unsigned long wrong_if;
37672  };
37673
37674  /*
37675   *  To get vif packet counts
37676   */
37677
37678  struct sioc_vif_req
37679  {
37680      vifi_t  vifi;        /* Which iface */
37681      unsigned long icount;   /* In packets */
37682      unsigned long ocount;   /* Out packets */
37683      unsigned long ibytes;   /* In bytes */
37684      unsigned long obytes;   /* Out bytes */
37685  };
37686
37687  /*
37688   *  This is the format the mroute daemon expects to see
37689  IGMP control
37690   *  data. Magically happens to be like an IP packet as
37691  per the original
37692   */
37693
37694  struct igmpmsg
37695  {
37696      unsigned long unused1,unused2;
37697      unsigned char im_msgtype;      /* What is this */
37698      unsigned char im_mbz;          /* Must be zero */
37699      unsigned char im_vif;          /* Interface (this
37700  ought to be a vifi_t!) */
37701      unsigned char unused3;
```

```
37702        struct in_addr im_src,im_dst;
37703    };
37704
37705    /*
37706     *  That's all usermode folks
37707     */
37708
37709    #ifdef __KERNEL__
37710    extern struct sock *mroute_socket;
37711    extern int ip_mroute_setsockopt(struct sock *, int, char
37712    *, int);
37713    extern int ip_mroute_getsockopt(struct sock *, int, char
37714    *, int *);
37715    extern int ipmr_ioctl(struct sock *sk, int cmd, unsigned
37716    long arg);
37717    extern void mroute_close(struct sock *sk);
37718    extern void ipmr_forward(struct sk_buff *skb, int
37719    is_frag);
37720
37721
37722    struct vif_device
37723    {
37724        struct device    *dev;          /* Device we are
37725    using */
37726        struct route     *rt_cache;     /* Tunnel route
37727    cache */
37728        unsigned long    bytes_in,bytes_out;
37729        unsigned long    pkt_in,pkt_out;     /* Statistics
37730        */
37731        unsigned long    rate_limit;    /* Traffic shaping
37732    (NI)     */
37733        unsigned char    threshold;     /* TTL threshold
37734    */
37735        unsigned short   flags;         /* Control flags
37736    */
37737        unsigned long    local,remote;       /*
37738    Addresses(remote for tunnels)*/
37739    };
37740
37741    struct mfc_cache
37742    {
37743        struct mfc_cache *next;         /* Next entry on
37744    cache line    */
37745        __u32 mfc_mcastgrp;         /* Group the entry
37746    belongs to   */
37747        __u32 mfc_origin;           /* Source of packet
37748    */
37749        vifi_t mfc_parent;          /* Source interface
```

```
37750    */
37751        struct timer_list mfc_timer;        /* Expiry timer
37752        */
37753        int mfc_flags;              /* Flags on line
37754    */
37755        struct sk_buff_head mfc_unresolved; /* Unresolved
37756    buffers       */
37757        int mfc_queuelen;           /* Unresolved buffer
37758    counter    */
37759        unsigned char mfc_ttls[MAXVIFS];    /* TTL
37760    thresholds        */
37761        unsigned long mfc_packets;      /* Packets on this
37762    entry     */
37763        unsigned long mfc_bytes;        /* Bytes on this
37764    entry        */
37765    };
37766
37767    #define MFC_QUEUED       1
37768    #define MFC_RESOLVED        2
37769
37770
37771    #define MFC_LINES        64
37772
37773    #ifdef __BIG_ENDIAN
37774    #define MFC_HASH(a,b)
37775    ((((a)>>24)^((b)>>26))&(MFC_LINES-1))
37776    #else
37777    #define MFC_HASH(a,b)    (((a)^((b)>>2))&(MFC_LINES-1))
37778    #endif
37779
37780    #endif
37781
37782    /*
37783     *  Pseudo messages used by mrouted
37784     */
37785
37786    #define IGMPMSG_NOCACHE      1       /* Kernel cache fill
37787    request to mrouted */
37788    #define IGMPMSG_WRONGVIF     2       /* For PIM assert
37789    processing (unused) */
37790
37791    #endif
```

usr/include/linux/net.h

```
37792    /*
37793     *  NET      An implementation of the SOCKET network
37794    access protocol.
37795     *      This is the master header file for the Linux NET
```

```
37796  layer,
37797  *      or, in plain English: the networking handling
37798  part of the
37799  *      kernel.
37800  *
37801  * Version: @(#)net.h  1.0.3   05/25/93
37802  *
37803  * Authors: Orest Zborowski, <obz@Kodak.COM>
37804  *      Ross Biro, <bir7@leland.Stanford.Edu>
37805  *      Fred N. van Kempen, <waltje@uWalt.NL.Mugnet.ORG>
37806  *
37807  *      This program is free software; you can
37808  redistribute it and/or
37809  *      modify it under the terms of the GNU General
37810  Public License
37811  *      as published by the Free Software Foundation;
37812  either version
37813  *      2 of the License, or (at your option) any later
37814  version.
37815  */
37816  #ifndef _LINUX_NET_H
37817  #define _LINUX_NET_H
37818
37819
37820  #include <linux/wait.h>
37821  #include <linux/socket.h>
37822
37823  #define NPROTO     16    /* should be enough for
37824  now..  */
37825
37826
37827  #define SYS_SOCKET  1     /* sys_socket(2)      */
37828  #define SYS_BIND    2     /* sys_bind(2)        */
37829  #define SYS_CONNECT 3     /* sys_connect(2)     */
37830  #define SYS_LISTEN  4     /* sys_listen(2)      */
37831  #define SYS_ACCEPT  5     /* sys_accept(2)      */
37832  #define SYS_GETSOCKNAME 6     /* sys_getsockname(2)
37833      */
37834  #define SYS_GETPEERNAME 7     /* sys_getpeername(2)
37835      */
37836  #define SYS_SOCKETPAIR  8     /* sys_socketpair(2)
37837      */
37838  #define SYS_SEND    9     /* sys_send(2)        */
37839  #define SYS_RECV    10    /* sys_recv(2)        */
37840  #define SYS_SENDTO  11    /* sys_sendto(2)      */
37841  #define SYS_RECVFROM    12    /* sys_recvfrom(2)
37842  */
37843  #define SYS_SHUTDOWN    13    /* sys_shutdown(2)
37844  */
37845  #define SYS_SETSOCKOPT  14    /* sys_setsockopt(2)
37846      */
37847  #define SYS_GETSOCKOPT  15    /* sys_getsockopt(2)
37848      */
37849  #define SYS_SENDMSG 16    /* sys_sendmsg(2)      */
37850  #define SYS_RECVMSG 17    /* sys_recvmsg(2)      */
37851
37852
37853  typedef enum {
37854      SS_FREE = 0,        /* not allocated        */
37855      SS_UNCONNECTED,     /* unconnected to any socket
37856      */
37857      SS_CONNECTING,      /* in process of connecting
37858  */
37859      SS_CONNECTED,       /* connected to socket
37860  */
37861      SS_DISCONNECTING    /* in process of
37862  disconnecting */
37863  } socket_state;
37864
37865  #define SO_ACCEPTCON    (1<<16)    /* performed a
37866  listen     */
37867  #define SO_WAITDATA (1<<17)    /* wait data to read
37868      */
37869  #define SO_NOSPACE  (1<<18)    /* no space to write
37870      */
37871
37872  #ifdef __KERNEL__
37873  /*
37874  * Internal representation of a socket. not all the
37875  fields are used by
37876  * all configurations:
37877  *
37878  *      server          client
37879  * conn     client connected to server connected to
37880  * iconn    list of clients    -unused-
37881  *      awaiting connections
37882  * wait     sleep for clients,  sleep for connection,
37883  *      sleep for i/o       sleep for i/o
37884  */
37885  struct socket {
37886      short       type;        /* SOCK_STREAM, ...      */
37887      socket_state    state;
37888      long        flags;
37889      struct proto_ops *ops;       /* protocols do most
37890  everything */
37891      void        *data;     /* protocol data         */
```

```
37892    struct socket      *conn;       /* server socket
37893  connected to    */
37894    struct socket      *iconn;      /* incomplete client
37895  conn.s */
37896    struct socket      *next;
37897    struct wait_queue **wait;       /* ptr to place to wait
37898  on */
37899    struct inode       *inode;
37900    struct fasync_struct *fasync_list;   /* Asynchronous
37901  wake up list    */
37902    struct file        *file;       /* File back pointer for
37903  gc */
37904  };
37905
37906  #define SOCK_INODE(S)    ((S)->inode)
37907
37908  struct proto_ops {
37909    int    family;
37910
37911    int    (*create)    (struct socket *sock, int protocol);
37912    int    (*dup)       (struct socket *newsock, struct
37913  socket *oldsock);
37914    int    (*release)   (struct socket *sock, struct socket
37915  *peer);
37916    int    (*bind)      (struct socket *sock, struct
37917  sockaddr *umyaddr,
37918             int sockaddr_len);
37919    int    (*connect)  (struct socket *sock, struct
37920  sockaddr *uservaddr,
37921             int sockaddr_len, int flags);
37922    int    (*socketpair)  (struct socket *sock1, struct
37923  socket *sock2);
37924    int    (*accept)   (struct socket *sock, struct socket
37925  *newsock,
37926             int flags);
37927    int    (*getname) (struct socket *sock, struct
37928  sockaddr *uaddr,
37929             int *usockaddr_len, int peer);
37930    int    (*select)  (struct socket *sock, int sel_type,
37931             select_table *wait);
37932    int    (*ioctl)   (struct socket *sock, unsigned int
37933  cmd,
37934             unsigned long arg);
37935    int    (*listen)  (struct socket *sock, int len);
37936    int    (*shutdown) (struct socket *sock, int flags);
37937    int    (*setsockopt)  (struct socket *sock, int level,
37938  int optname,
37939             char *optval, int optlen);
```

```
37940    int    (*getsockopt)  (struct socket *sock, int level,
37941  int optname,
37942             char *optval, int *optlen);
37943    int    (*fcntl)   (struct socket *sock, unsigned int
37944  cmd,
37945             unsigned long arg);
37946    int    (*sendmsg) (struct socket *sock, struct msghdr
37947  *m, int total_len, int nonblock, int flags);
37948    int    (*recvmsg) (struct socket *sock, struct msghdr
37949  *m, int total_len, int nonblock, int flags, int
37950  *addr_len);
37951  };
37952
37953  struct net_proto {
37954    const char *name;           /* Protocol name */
37955    void (*init_func)(struct net_proto *);   /* Bootstrap
37956  */
37957  };
37958
37959  extern int  sock_wake_async(struct socket *sock, int
37960  how);
37961  extern int  sock_register(int family, struct proto_ops
37962  *ops);
37963  extern int  sock_unregister(int family);
37964  extern struct socket *sock_alloc(void);
37965  extern void sock_release(struct socket *sock);
37966  #endif /* __KERNEL__ */
37967  #endif  /* _LINUX_NET_H */
```

usr/include/linux/net_alias.h

```
37968  /*
37969   *        NET_ALIAS network device aliasing definitions.
37970   *
37971   *
37972   * Version: @(#)net_alias.h 0.50    4/20/97
37973   *
37974   * Author:  Juan Jose Ciarlante,
37975   <jjciarla@raiz.uncu.edu.ar>
37976   *
37977   *
37978   * This program is free software; you can redistribute
37979  it and/or
37980   * modify it under the terms of the GNU General Public
37981  License
37982   * as published by the Free Software Foundation; either
37983  version
37984   * 2 of the License, or (at your option) any later
37985  version.
```

```
37986     *
37987     * Fixes:
37988     *    Juan Jose Ciarlante :    Added tx/rx stats for
37989     aliases.
37990     *    Juan Jose Ciarlante    :    hash_tab size now in
37991     net_alias.c
37992     *    Juan Jose Ciarlante :    added sysctl interface
37993     */
37994
37995     #ifndef _NET_ALIAS_H
37996     #define _NET_ALIAS_H
37997
37998     #include <linux/types.h>
37999     #include <linux/if.h>
38000     #include <linux/netdevice.h>
38001
38002     struct net_alias;
38003     struct net_alias_info;
38004     struct net_alias_type;
38005
38006
38007     /*
38008      * main alias structure
38009      * note that *defines* dev & devname
38010      */
38011
38012     struct net_alias
38013     {
38014       struct device dev;       /* alias device defn*/
38015       char name[IFNAMSIZ];     /* device name defn */
38016       unsigned hash;         /* my hash value: for quick
38017     rehash */
38018       unsigned slot;         /* slot number */
38019       void *data;            /* private data */
38020       struct device *main_dev; /* pointer to main device */
38021       struct net_alias_type *nat;   /* alias type object
38022     bound */
38023       struct net_alias *next;   /* next alias (hashed linked
38024     list) */
38025       unsigned long rx_lookups;     /* 'fake' rx pkts */
38026       unsigned long tx_lookups;     /* 'fake' tx pkts */
38027     };
38028
38029
38030     /*
38031      *  alias structure pointed by main device
38032      *  it holds main device's alias hash table
38033      */
38034
38035     struct net_alias_info
38036     {
38037       int n_aliases;          /* num aliases */
38038       int truesize;                 /* actual malloc size
38039     for struct + hashtab */
38040       struct device *taildev;   /* my last (alias) device */
38041       int max_aliases;              /* max aliases allowed
38042     for main device */
38043       unsigned hash_tab_size;       /* hash_tab size in
38044     elements */
38045       struct net_alias *hash_tab[0]; /* hashed alias table */
38046     };
38047
38048     /*
38049      * net_alias_type class
38050      * declares a generic (AF_ independent) structure that
38051     will
38052      * manage generic to family-specific behavior.
38053      */
38054
38055     struct net_alias_type
38056     {
38057       int type;          /* aliasing type: address family */
38058       int n_attach;         /* number of aliases attached */
38059       char name[16];        /* af_name */
38060       __u32 (*get_addr32)      /* get __u32 addr
38061     'representation'*/
38062         (struct net_alias_type *this, struct sockaddr*);
38063       int (*dev_addr_chk)      /* address checking func: */
38064         (struct net_alias_type *this, struct device *,
38065     struct sockaddr *);
38066       struct device * (*dev_select) /* closest alias
38067     selector*/
38068         (struct net_alias_type *this, struct device *,
38069     struct sockaddr *sa);
38070       int (*alias_init_1)      /* called after alias
38071     creation: */
38072         (struct net_alias_type *this,struct net_alias
38073     *alias, struct sockaddr *sa);
38074       int (*alias_done_1)      /* called before alias
38075     deletion */
38076         (struct net_alias_type *this, struct net_alias
38077     *alias);
38078       int (*alias_print_1)
38079         (struct net_alias_type *this, struct net_alias
38080     *alias, char *buf, int len);
38081       struct net_alias_type *next;  /* link */
```

```
38082    };
38083
38084
38085    /*
38086     * is dev an alias?
38087     */
38088
38089    static __inline__ int
38090    net_alias_is(struct device *dev)
38091    {
38092      return (dev->my_alias != NULL);
38093    }
38094
38095
38096    /*
38097     * does dev have aliases?
38098     */
38099
38100    static __inline__ int
38101    net_alias_has(struct device *dev)
38102    {
38103      return (dev->alias_info != NULL);
38104    }
38105
38106    /*
38107     *  Initialise net_alias module
38108     */
38109    extern void net_alias_init(void);
38110
38111    /*
38112     * dev_get() with added aliasing magic
38113     */
38114    extern struct device * net_alias_dev_get(char *dev_name,
38115    int aliasing_ok, int *err, struct sockaddr *sa, void
38116    *data);
38117    extern int net_alias_dev_rehash(struct device *dev,
38118    struct sockaddr *sa);
38119
38120    /*
38121     *  PROC_FS entries
38122     */
38123    extern int net_alias_getinfo(char *buf, char **, off_t ,
38124    int , int );
38125    extern int net_alias_types_getinfo(char *buf, char **,
38126    off_t , int , int );
38127
38128    /*
38129     *  net_alias_type (address family) registration
```

```
38130    */
38131    extern int register_net_alias_type(struct net_alias_type
38132    *nat, int type);
38133    extern int unregister_net_alias_type(struct
38134    net_alias_type *nat);
38135
38136    /*
38137     *  get alias device _with_ specified address
38138     */
38139    extern struct device * net_alias_dev_chk(struct device
38140    *main_dev, struct sockaddr *sa, int flags_on, int
38141    flags_off);
38142    extern struct device * net_alias_dev_chk32(struct device
38143    *main_dev, int family, __u32 addr32, int flags_on, int
38144    flags_off);
38145
38146    /*
38147     *  get 'closest' device to specified address (returns
38148    main_dev if
38149     *  nothing better)
38150     *  if succesfull, also increment rx stats.
38151     */
38152    extern struct device * net_alias_dev_rx(struct device
38153    *main_dev, struct sockaddr *sa_src, struct sockaddr
38154    *sa_dst);
38155    extern struct device * net_alias_dev_rx32(struct device
38156    *main_dev, int family, __u32 src, __u32 dst);
38157
38158
38159    /*
38160     * returns MY 'true' main device
38161     * intended for alias devices
38162     */
38163
38164    static __inline__ struct device
38165    *net_alias_main_dev(struct device *dev)
38166    {
38167      return (net_alias_is(dev))? dev->my_alias->main_dev :
38168    dev;
38169    }
38170
38171
38172    /*
38173     * returns NEXT 'true' device
38174     * intended for true devices
38175     */
38176
38177    static __inline__ struct device *
```

```
38178    net_alias_nextdev(struct device *dev)
38179    {
38180      return (dev->alias_info)?
38181    dev->alias_info->taildev->next : dev->next;
38182    }
38183
38184
38185    /*
38186     * sets NEXT 'true' device
38187     * intended for main devices (treat main device as
38188    block: dev+aliases).
38189     */
38190
38191    static __inline__ struct device *
38192    net_alias_nextdev_set(struct device *dev, struct device
38193    *nextdev)
38194    {
38195      struct device *pdev = dev;
38196      if (net_alias_has(dev))
38197      {
38198        pdev = dev->alias_info->taildev; /* point to last
38199    dev alias */
38200      }
38201      pdev->next = nextdev;
38202      return nextdev;
38203    }
38204
38205    /*
38206     *  lookup counters (used for alias devices stats)
38207     */
38208    static __inline__ void net_alias_inc_rx(struct net_alias
38209    *alias)
38210    {
38211          if (alias != NULL) alias->rx_lookups++;
38212    }
38213    static __inline__ void net_alias_inc_tx(struct net_alias
38214    *alias)
38215    {
38216          if (alias != NULL) alias->tx_lookups++;
38217    }
38218
38219    /*
38220     *  To be called when passing down a pkt, to _switch_
38221    from alias device
38222     *  to actual device, also incr. alias tx counter.
38223     */
38224    static __inline__ struct device *net_alias_dev_tx(struct
38225    device *dev)
```

```
38226    {
38227            struct net_alias *alias = dev->my_alias;
38228            if (alias) {
38229                    net_alias_inc_tx(alias);
38230                    return alias->main_dev;
38231            }
38232            return dev;
38233    }
38234
38235    #endif  /* _NET_ALIAS_H */
```

usr/include/linux/netdevice.h

```
38236    /*
38237     * INET      An implementation of the TCP/IP protocol
38238    suite for the LINUX
38239     *      operating system.  INET is implemented using the
38240    BSD Socket
38241     *      interface as the means of communication with the
38242    user level.
38243     *
38244     *      Definitions for the Interfaces handler.
38245     *
38246     * Version: @(#)dev.h   1.0.11  07/31/96
38247     *
38248     * Authors: Ross Biro, <bir7@leland.Stanford.Edu>
38249     *      Fred N. van Kempen, <waltje@uWalt.NL.Mugnet.ORG>
38250     *      Corey Minyard <wf-rch!minyard@relay.EU.net>
38251     *      Donald J. Becker, <becker@super.org>
38252     *      Alan Cox, <A.Cox@swansea.ac.uk>
38253     *      Bjorn Ekwall. <bj0rn@blox.se>
38254     *      Lawrence V. Stefani, <stefani@lkg.dec.com>
38255     *
38256     *      This program is free software; you can
38257    redistribute it and/or
38258     *      modify it under the terms of the GNU General
38259    Public License
38260     *      as published by the Free Software Foundation;
38261    either version
38262     *      2 of the License, or (at your option) any later
38263    version.
38264     *
38265     *      Moved to /usr/include/linux for NET3
38266     *      Added extern for fddi_setup()
38267     */
38268    #ifndef _LINUX_NETDEVICE_H
38269    #define _LINUX_NETDEVICE_H
38270
38271    #include <linux/config.h>
```

```
38272    #include <linux/if.h>
38273    #include <linux/if_ether.h>
38274
38275    /* for future expansion when we will have different
38276    priorities. */
38277    #define DEV_NUMBUFFS    3
38278    #define MAX_ADDR_LEN    7
38279    #ifndef CONFIG_AX25
38280    #ifndef CONFIG_TR
38281    #if !defined(CONFIG_NET_IPIP) &&
38282    !defined(CONFIG_NET_IPIP_MODULE)
38283    #define MAX_HEADER 32        /* We really need about 18
38284    worst case .. so 32 is aligned */
38285    #else
38286    #define MAX_HEADER  80       /* We need to allow for
38287    having tunnel headers */
38288    #endif   /* IPIP */
38289    #else
38290    #define MAX_HEADER  48       /* Token Ring header needs
38291    40 bytes ... 48 is aligned */
38292    #endif /* TR */
38293    #else
38294    #define MAX_HEADER  96       /* AX.25 + NetROM */
38295    #endif /* AX25 */
38296
38297    #define IS_MYADDR   1        /* address is (one of) our
38298    own  */
38299    #define IS_LOOPBACK 2        /* address is for LOOPBACK
38300    */
38301    #define IS_BROADCAST    3       /* address is a valid
38302    broadcast */
38303    #define IS_INVBCAST 4        /* Wrong netmask bcast not
38304    for us (unused)*/
38305    #define IS_MULTICAST    5       /* Multicast IP address
38306    */
38307
38308    #ifdef __KERNEL__
38309
38310    #include <linux/skbuff.h>
38311
38312    /*
38313     *  We tag multicasts with these structures.
38314     */
38315
38316    struct dev_mc_list
38317    {
38318        struct dev_mc_list *next;
38319        char dmi_addr[MAX_ADDR_LEN];
38320        unsigned short dmi_addrlen;
38321        unsigned short dmi_users;
38322    };
38323
38324    struct hh_cache
38325    {
38326        struct hh_cache *hh_next;
38327        void        *hh_arp;     /* Opaque pointer, used by
38328                        * any address resolution module,
38329                        * not only ARP.
38330                        */
38331        int     hh_refcnt;  /* number of users */
38332        unsigned short  hh_type;    /* protocol identifier,
38333    f.e ETH_P_IP */
38334        char        hh_uptodate;    /* hh_data is valid */
38335        char        hh_data[16];    /* cached hardware
38336    header */
38337    };
38338
38339    /*
38340     * The DEVICE structure.
38341     * Actually, this whole structure is a big mistake.  It
38342    mixes I/O
38343     * data with strictly "high-level" data, and it has to
38344    know about
38345     * almost every data structure used in the INET module.
38346     */
38347    struct device
38348    {
38349
38350      /*
38351       * This is the first field of the "visible" part of
38352    this structure
38353       * (i.e. as seen by users in the "Space.c" file).  It
38354    is the name
38355       * the interface.
38356       */
38357      char            *name;
38358
38359      /* I/O specific fields - FIXME: Merge these and struct
38360    ifmap into one */
38361      unsigned long       rmem_end;       /* shmem "recv" end
38362    */
38363      unsigned long       rmem_start;     /* shmem "recv"
38364    start   */
38365      unsigned long       mem_end;        /* shared mem end
38366    */
38367      unsigned long       mem_start;      /* shared mem
```

```
38368    start */
38369    unsigned long        base_addr;        /* device I/0
38370    address   */
38371    unsigned char        irq;              /* device IRQ number
38372     */
38373
38374    /* Low-level status flags. */
38375    volatile unsigned char  start,        /* start an
38376    operation   */
38377                            interrupt;    /* interrupt
38378    arrived   */
38379    unsigned long        tbusy;          /* transmitter busy
38380    must be long for bitops */
38381
38382    struct device        *next;
38383
38384    /* The device initialization function. Called only
38385    once. */
38386    int              (*init)(struct device *dev);
38387
38388    /* Some hardware also needs these fields, but they are
38389    not part of the
38390       usual set specified in Space.c. */
38391    unsigned char        if_port;        /* Selectable AUI,
38392    TP,..*/
38393    unsigned char        dma;            /* DMA channel
38394    */
38395
38396    struct enet_statistics* (*get_stats)(struct device
38397    *dev);
38398
38399    /*
38400     * This marks the end of the "visible" part of the
38401    structure. All
38402     * fields hereafter are internal to the system, and
38403    may change at
38404     * will (read: may be cleaned up at will).
38405     */
38406
38407    /* These may be needed for future network-power-down
38408    code. */
38409    unsigned long        trans_start;    /* Time (in jiffies)
38410    of last Tx */
38411    unsigned long        last_rx;        /* Time of last Rx
38412    */
38413
38414    unsigned short       flags;          /* interface flags (a la
38415    BSD)   */
```

```
38416    unsigned short       family;      /* address family ID
38417    (AF_INET)  */
38418    unsigned short       metric;      /* routing metric (not
38419    used)   */
38420    unsigned short       mtu;         /* interface MTU value
38421     */
38422    unsigned short       type;        /* interface hardware
38423    type */
38424    unsigned short       hard_header_len;  /* hardware hdr
38425    length */
38426    void                *priv;      /* pointer to private data
38427    */
38428
38429    /* Interface address info. */
38430    unsigned char        broadcast[MAX_ADDR_LEN];  /* hw
38431    bcast add */
38432    unsigned char        pad;              /* make dev_addr
38433    aligned to 8 bytes */
38434    unsigned char        dev_addr[MAX_ADDR_LEN];   /* hw
38435    address   */
38436    unsigned char        addr_len; /* hardware address
38437    length  */
38438    unsigned long        pa_addr;  /* protocol address
38439    */
38440    unsigned long        pa_brdaddr;   /* protocol
38441    broadcast addr  */
38442    unsigned long        pa_dstaddr;   /* protocol P-P
38443    other side addr */
38444    unsigned long        pa_mask;  /* protocol netmask
38445    */
38446    unsigned short       pa_alen;  /* protocol address
38447    length  */
38448
38449    struct dev_mc_list    *mc_list;  /* Multicast mac
38450    addresses */
38451    int              mc_count;  /* Number of installed
38452    mcasts  */
38453
38454    struct ip_mc_list *ip_mc_list;  /* IP multicast
38455    filter chain   */
38456    __u32            tx_queue_len;   /* Max frames per queue
38457    allowed */
38458
38459    /* For load balancing driver pair support */
38460
38461    unsigned long        pkt_queue;  /* Packets queued */
38462    struct device        *slave;  /* Slave device */
38463    struct net_alias_info    *alias_info;   /* main dev
```

```
38464  alias info */
38465    struct net_alias      *my_alias;  /* alias devs */
38466
38467    /* Pointer to the interface buffers. */
38468    struct sk_buff_head    buffs[DEV_NUMBUFFS];
38469
38470    /* Pointers to interface service routines. */
38471    int              (*open)(struct device *dev);
38472    int              (*stop)(struct device *dev);
38473    int              (*hard_start_xmit) (struct sk_buff
38474  *skb,
38475                         struct device *dev);
38476    int              (*hard_header) (struct sk_buff *skb,
38477                     struct device *dev,
38478                     unsigned short type,
38479                     void *daddr,
38480                     void *saddr,
38481                     unsigned len);
38482    int              (*rebuild_header)(void *eth, struct
38483  device *dev,
38484                     unsigned long raddr, struct sk_buff
38485  *skb);
38486  #define HAVE_MULTICAST
38487    void             (*set_multicast_list)(struct device
38488  *dev);
38489  #define HAVE_SET_MAC_ADDR
38490    int              (*set_mac_address)(struct device *dev,
38491  void *addr);
38492  #define HAVE_PRIVATE_IOCTL
38493    int              (*do_ioctl)(struct device *dev, struct
38494  ifreq *ifr, int cmd);
38495  #define HAVE_SET_CONFIG
38496    int              (*set_config)(struct device *dev,
38497  struct ifmap *map);
38498  #define HAVE_HEADER_CACHE
38499    void             (*header_cache_bind)(struct hh_cache
38500  **hhp, struct device *dev, unsigned short htype, __u32
38501  daddr);
38502    void             (*header_cache_update)(struct hh_cache
38503  *hh, struct device *dev, unsigned char *  haddr);
38504  #define HAVE_CHANGE_MTU
38505    int              (*change_mtu)(struct device *dev, int
38506  new_mtu);
38507
38508    struct iw_statistics*  (*get_wireless_stats)(struct
38509  device *dev);
38510  };
38511
```

```
38512
38513  struct packet_type {
38514    unsigned short    type;    /* This is really
38515  htons(ether_type). */
38516    struct device *  dev;
38517    int              (*func) (struct sk_buff *, struct device
38518  *,
38519                     struct packet_type *);
38520    void          *data;
38521    struct packet_type    *next;
38522  };
38523
38524
38525  #include <linux/interrupt.h>
38526  #include <linux/notifier.h>
38527
38528  /* Used by dev_rint */
38529  #define IN_SKBUFF   1
38530
38531  extern volatile unsigned long in_bh;
38532
38533  extern struct device    loopback_dev;
38534  extern struct device    *dev_base;
38535  extern struct packet_type *ptype_base[16];
38536
38537
38538  extern int      ip_addr_match(unsigned long addr1,
38539  unsigned long addr2);
38540  extern int      ip_chk_addr(unsigned long addr);
38541  extern struct device    *ip_dev_bynet(unsigned long
38542  daddr, unsigned long mask);
38543  extern unsigned long    ip_my_addr(void);
38544  extern unsigned long    ip_get_mask(unsigned long addr);
38545  extern struct device    *ip_dev_find(unsigned long addr);
38546  extern struct device    *dev_getbytype(unsigned short
38547  type);
38548
38549  extern void     dev_add_pack(struct packet_type *pt);
38550  extern void     dev_remove_pack(struct packet_type *pt);
38551  extern struct device    *dev_get(const char *name);
38552  extern int      dev_open(struct device *dev);
38553  extern int      dev_close(struct device *dev);
38554  extern void     dev_queue_xmit(struct sk_buff *skb,
38555  struct device *dev,
38556                     int pri);
38557
38558  #define HAVE_NETIF_RX 1
38559  extern void     netif_rx(struct sk_buff *skb);
```

```
38560   extern void     net_bh(void);
38561   extern void     dev_tint(struct device *dev);
38562   extern int      dev_get_info(char *buffer, char **start,
38563   off_t offset, int length, int dummy);
38564   extern int      dev_ioctl(unsigned int cmd, void *);
38565
38566   extern void     dev_init(void);
38567
38568   /* Locking protection for page faults during outputs to
38569   devices unloaded during the fault */
38570
38571   extern int      dev_lockct;
38572
38573   /*
38574    * These two don't currently need to be interrupt-safe
38575    * but they may do soon. Do it properly anyway.
38576    */
38577
38578   extern __inline__ void  dev_lock_list(void)
38579   {
38580       unsigned long flags;
38581       save_flags(flags);
38582       cli();
38583       dev_lockct++;
38584       restore_flags(flags);
38585   }
38586
38587   extern __inline__ void  dev_unlock_list(void)
38588   {
38589       unsigned long flags;
38590       save_flags(flags);
38591       cli();
38592       dev_lockct--;
38593       restore_flags(flags);
38594   }
38595
38596   /*
38597    * This almost never occurs, isn't in performance
38598   critical paths
38599    * and we can thus be relaxed about it
38600    */
38601
38602   extern __inline__ void dev_lock_wait(void)
38603   {
38604       while(dev_lockct)
38605           schedule();
38606   }
38607
38608
38609   /* These functions live elsewhere
38610   (drivers/net/net_init.c, but related) */
38611
38612   extern void     ether_setup(struct device *dev);
38613   extern void     tr_setup(struct device *dev);
38614   extern void     fddi_setup(struct device *dev);
38615   extern int      ether_config(struct device *dev, struct
38616   ifmap *map);
38617   /* Support for loadable net-drivers */
38618   extern int      register_netdev(struct device *dev);
38619   extern void     unregister_netdev(struct device *dev);
38620   extern int      register_netdevice_notifier(struct
38621   notifier_block *nb);
38622   extern int      unregister_netdevice_notifier(struct
38623   notifier_block *nb);
38624   /* Functions used for multicast support */
38625   extern void     dev_mc_upload(struct device *dev);
38626   extern void     dev_mc_delete(struct device *dev,
38627   void *addr, int alen, int all);
38628   extern void     dev_mc_add(struct device *dev, void
38629   *addr, int alen, int newonly);
38630   extern void     dev_mc_discard(struct device *dev);
38631   /* This is the wrong place but it'll do for the moment */
38632   extern void     ip_mc_allhost(struct device *dev);
38633   #endif /* __KERNEL__ */
38634
38635   #endif  /* _LINUX_DEV_H */
```

usr/include/linux/param.h

```
38636   #ifndef _LINUX_PARAM_H
38637   #define _LINUX_PARAM_H
38638
38639   #include <asm/param.h>
38640
38641   #endif
```

usr/include/linux/route.h

```
38642   /*
38643    * INET      An implementation of the TCP/IP protocol
38644   suite for the LINUX
38645    *       operating system.  INET is implemented using the
38646   BSD Socket
38647    *       interface as the means of communication with the
38648   user level.
38649    *
38650    *       Global definitions for the IP router interface.
38651    *
```

```
38652    * Version: @(#)route.h 1.0.3    05/27/93
38653    *
38654    * Authors: Original taken from Berkeley UNIX 4.3, (c)
38655    UCB 1986-1988
38656    *      for the purposes of compatibility only.
38657    *
38658    *      Fred N. van Kempen, <waltje@uWalt.NL.Mugnet.ORG>
38659    *
38660    *      This program is free software; you can
38661    redistribute it and/or
38662    *      modify it under the terms of the GNU General
38663    Public License
38664    *      as published by the Free Software Foundation;
38665    either version
38666    *      2 of the License, or (at your option) any later
38667    version.
38668    */
38669    #ifndef _LINUX_ROUTE_H
38670    #define _LINUX_ROUTE_H
38671
38672    #include <linux/if.h>
38673
38674
38675    /* This structure gets passed by the SIOCADDRT and
38676    SIOCDELRT calls. */
38677    struct rtentry
38678    {
38679        unsigned long    rt_hash;    /* hash key for lookups
38680      */
38681        struct sockaddr rt_dst;      /* target address
38682    */
38683        struct sockaddr rt_gateway; /* gateway addr
38684    (RTF_GATEWAY)    */
38685        struct sockaddr rt_genmask; /* target network mask
38686    (IP) */
38687        short        rt_flags;
38688        short        rt_refcnt;
38689        unsigned long    rt_use;
38690        struct ifnet    *rt_ifp;
38691        short        rt_metric;   /* +1 for binary
38692    compatibility! */
38693        char        *rt_dev;      /* forcing the device at add
38694      */
38695        unsigned long    rt_mss;     /* per route MTU/Window
38696      */
38697        unsigned long    rt_window;  /* Window clamping
38698    */
38699        unsigned short  rt_irtt;    /* Initial RTT
```

```
38700    */
38701    };
38702
38703
38704    #define RTF_UP        0x0001      /* route usable
38705     */
38706    #define RTF_GATEWAY 0x0002       /* destination is a
38707    gateway   */
38708    #define RTF_HOST      0x0004      /* host entry (net
38709    otherwise)    */
38710    #define RTF_REINSTATE    0x0008       /* reinstate route
38711    after tmout   */
38712    #define RTF_DYNAMIC 0x0010       /* created dyn. (by
38713    redirect)    */
38714    #define RTF_MODIFIED    0x0020       /* modified dyn. (by
38715    redirect)    */
38716    #define RTF_MSS       0x0040      /* specific MSS for this
38717    route   */
38718    #define RTF_WINDOW 0x0080        /* per route window
38719    clamping    */
38720    #define RTF_IRTT      0x0100      /* Initial round trip
38721    time   */
38722    #define RTF_REJECT 0x0200        /* Reject route
38723     */
38724    #define RTF_NOTCACHED    0x0400       /* this route isn't
38725    cached        */
38726
38727    /*
38728     * This structure is passed from the kernel to user
38729    space by netlink
38730     * routing/device announcements
38731     */
38732
38733    struct netlink_rtinfo
38734    {
38735        unsigned long    rtmsg_type;
38736        struct sockaddr rtmsg_dst;
38737        struct sockaddr rtmsg_gateway;
38738        struct sockaddr rtmsg_genmask;
38739        short        rtmsg_flags;
38740        short        rtmsg_metric;
38741        char        rtmsg_device[16];
38742    };
38743
38744    #define RTMSG_NEWROUTE        0x01
38745    #define RTMSG_DELROUTE        0x02
38746    #define RTMSG_NEWDEVICE       0x11
38747    #define RTMSG_DELDEVICE       0x12
```

p 493 (marker at line 38704)

```
38748
38749   #endif   /* _LINUX_ROUTE_H */
38750
```

usr/include/linux/skbuff.h

```
38751   /*
38752    *   Definitions for the 'struct sk_buff' memory handlers.
38753    *
38754    *   Authors:
38755    *       Alan Cox, <gw4pts@gw4pts.ampr.org>
38756    *       Florian La Roche, <rzsfl@rz.uni-sb.de>
38757    *
38758    *   This program is free software; you can redistribute
38759   it and/or
38760    *   modify it under the terms of the GNU General Public
38761   License
38762    *   as published by the Free Software Foundation; either
38763   version
38764    *   2 of the License, or (at your option) any later
38765   version.
38766    */
38767
38768   #ifndef _LINUX_SKBUFF_H
38769   #define _LINUX_SKBUFF_H
38770
38771   #include <linux/config.h>
38772   #include <linux/time.h>
38773
38774   #include <asm/atomic.h>
38775   #include <asm/types.h>
38776
38777   #define CONFIG_SKB_CHECK 0
38778
38779   #define HAVE_ALLOC_SKB      /* For the drivers to know */
38780   #define HAVE_ALIGNABLE_SKB  /* Ditto 8)          */
38781
38782
38783   #define FREE_READ   1
38784   #define FREE_WRITE  0
38785
38786   #define CHECKSUM_NONE 0
38787   #define CHECKSUM_HW 1
38788   #define CHECKSUM_UNNECESSARY 2
38789
38790   struct sk_buff_head
38791   {
38792       struct sk_buff  * next;
38793       struct sk_buff  * prev;
```

```
38794       __u32       qlen;       /* Must be same length as a
38795   pointer
38796                               for using debugging */
38797   #if CONFIG_SKB_CHECK
38798       int     magic_debug_cookie;
38799   #endif
38800   };
38801
38802
38803   struct sk_buff
38804   {
38805       struct sk_buff  * next;      /* Next buffer in
38806   list          */
38807       struct sk_buff  * prev;      /* Previous buffer
38808   in list         */
38809       struct sk_buff_head * list;  /* List we are on
38810           */
38811   #if CONFIG_SKB_CHECK
38812       int     magic_debug_cookie;
38813   #endif
38814       struct sk_buff  *link3;      /* Link for IP
38815   protocol level buffer chains    */
38816       struct sock *sk;            /* Socket we are owned
38817   by      */
38818       unsigned long   when;       /* used to compute
38819   rtt's         */
38820       struct timeval  stamp;      /* Time we arrived
38821           */
38822       struct device   *dev;       /* Device we arrived
38823   on/are leaving by    */
38824       union
38825       {
38826           struct tcphdr   *th;
38827           struct ethhdr   *eth;
38828           struct iphdr    *iph;
38829           struct udphdr   *uh;
38830           unsigned char   *raw;
38831           /* for passing file handles in a unix domain
38832   socket */
38833           void *filp;
38834       } h;
38835
38836       union
38837       {
38838           /* As yet incomplete physical layer views */
38839           unsigned char   *raw;
38840           struct ethhdr   *ethernet;
38841       } mac;
```

```
38842
38843     struct iphdr    *ip_hdr;        /* For IPPROTO_RAW
38844            */
38845     unsigned long   len;            /* Length of actual
38846 data          */
38847     unsigned long   csum;           /* Checksum
38848            */
38849     __u32       saddr;          /* IP source address
38850            */
38851     __u32       daddr;          /* IP target address
38852            */
38853     __u32       raddr;          /* IP next hop address
38854            */
38855     __u32       seq;            /* TCP sequence number
38856            */
38857     __u32       end_seq;        /* seq [+ fin] [+ syn] +
38858 datalen    */
38859     __u32       ack_seq;        /* TCP ack sequence
38860 number         */
38861     unsigned char   proto_priv[16];     /* Protocol
38862 private data           */
38863     volatile char   acked,          /* Are we acked ?
38864            */
38865             used,           /* Are we in use ?
38866     */
38867             free,           /* How to free this buffer
38868         */
38869             arp;            /* Has IP/ARP resolution
38870 finished       */
38871     unsigned char   tries,          /* Times tried
38872            */
38873             lock,           /* Are we locked ?
38874     */
38875             localroute,     /* Local routing asserted
38876 for this frame     */
38877             pkt_type,       /* Packet class
38878     */
38879             pkt_bridged,        /* Tracker for bridging
38880         */
38881             ip_summed;      /* Driver fed us an IP
38882 checksum       */
38883 #define PACKET_HOST      0      /* To us
38884     */
38885 #define PACKET_BROADCAST   1      /* To all
38886         */
38887 #define PACKET_MULTICAST   2      /* To group
38888         */
38889 #define PACKET_OTHERHOST   3      /* To someone else
38890         */
38891     unsigned short  users;          /* User count - see
38892 datagram.c,tcp.c       */
38893     unsigned short  protocol;       /* Packet protocol
38894 from driver.       */
38895     unsigned int    truesize;       /* Buffer size
38896         */
38897
38898     atomic_t    count;          /* reference count
38899     */
38900     struct sk_buff  *data_skb;      /* Link to the
38901 actual data skb        */
38902     unsigned char   *head;          /* Head of buffer
38903         */
38904     unsigned char   *data;          /* Data head pointer
38905             */
38906     unsigned char   *tail;          /* Tail pointer
38907         */
38908     unsigned char   *end;           /* End pointer
38909         */
38910     void        (*destructor)(struct sk_buff *);    /*
38911 Destruct function      */
38912     __u16       redirport;      /* Redirect port
38913     */
38914 };
38915
38916 #ifdef CONFIG_SKB_LARGE
38917 #define SK_WMEM_MAX 65535
38918 #define SK_RMEM_MAX 65535
38919 #else
38920 #define SK_WMEM_MAX 32767
38921 #define SK_RMEM_MAX 32767
38922 #endif
38923
38924 #if CONFIG_SKB_CHECK
38925 #define SK_FREED_SKB    0x0DE2C0DE
38926 #define SK_GOOD_SKB 0xDEC0DED1
38927 #define SK_HEAD_SKB 0x12231298
38928 #endif
38929
38930 #ifdef __KERNEL__
38931 /*
38932  * Handling routines are only of interest to the kernel
38933  */
38934 #include <linux/malloc.h>
38935
38936 #include <asm/system.h>
38937
```

```
38938  #if 0
38939  extern void          print_skb(struct sk_buff *);
38940  #endif
38941  extern void          kfree_skb(struct sk_buff *skb, int
38942  rw);
38943  extern void          skb_queue_head_init(struct
38944  sk_buff_head *list);
38945  extern void          skb_queue_head(struct sk_buff_head
38946  *list,struct sk_buff *buf);
38947  extern void          skb_queue_tail(struct sk_buff_head
38948  *list,struct sk_buff *buf);
38949  extern struct sk_buff *    skb_dequeue(struct
38950  sk_buff_head *list);
38951  extern void          skb_insert(struct sk_buff
38952  *old,struct sk_buff *newsk);
38953  extern void          skb_append(struct sk_buff
38954  *old,struct sk_buff *newsk);
38955  extern void          skb_unlink(struct sk_buff *buf);
38956  extern __u32         skb_queue_len(struct
38957  sk_buff_head *list);
38958  extern struct sk_buff *    skb_peek_copy(struct
38959  sk_buff_head *list);
38960  extern struct sk_buff *    alloc_skb(unsigned int size,
38961  int priority);
38962  extern struct sk_buff *    dev_alloc_skb(unsigned int
38963  size);
38964  extern void          kfree_skbmem(struct sk_buff *skb);
38965  extern struct sk_buff *    skb_clone(struct sk_buff
38966  *skb, int priority);
38967  extern struct sk_buff *    skb_copy(struct sk_buff
38968  *skb, int priority);
38969  extern void          skb_device_lock(struct sk_buff *skb);
38970  extern void          skb_device_unlock(struct sk_buff
38971  *skb);
38972  extern void          dev_kfree_skb(struct sk_buff *skb,
38973  int mode);
38974  extern int           skb_device_locked(struct sk_buff
38975  *skb);
38976  extern unsigned char *    skb_put(struct sk_buff *skb,
38977  int len);
38978  extern unsigned char *    skb_push(struct sk_buff
38979  *skb, int len);
38980  extern unsigned char *    skb_pull(struct sk_buff
38981  *skb, int len);
38982  extern int           skb_headroom(struct sk_buff *skb);
38983  extern int           skb_tailroom(struct sk_buff *skb);
38984  extern void          skb_reserve(struct sk_buff *skb, int
38985  len);
38986  extern void               skb_trim(struct sk_buff *skb,
38987  int len);
38988
38989  extern __inline__ int skb_queue_empty(struct
38990  sk_buff_head *list)
38991  {
38992      return (list->next == (struct sk_buff *) list);
38993  }
38994
38995  /*
38996   * Peek an sk_buff. Unlike most other operations you
38997  _MUST_
38998   * be careful with this one. A peek leaves the buffer
38999  on the
39000   * list and someone else may run off with it. For an
39001  interrupt
39002   * type system cli() peek the buffer copy the data and
39003  sti();
39004   */
39005  extern __inline__ struct sk_buff *skb_peek(struct
39006  sk_buff_head *list_)
39007  {
39008      struct sk_buff *list = ((struct sk_buff
39009  *)list_)->next;
39010      if (list == (struct sk_buff *)list_)
39011          list = NULL;
39012      return list;
39013  }
39014
39015  /*
39016   * Return the length of an sk_buff queue
39017   */
39018
39019  extern __inline__ __u32 skb_queue_len(struct
39020  sk_buff_head *list_)
39021  {
39022      return(list_->qlen);
39023  }
39024
39025  #if CONFIG_SKB_CHECK
39026  extern int           skb_check(struct sk_buff
39027  *skb,int,int, char *);
39028  #define IS_SKB(skb)      skb_check((skb), 0,
39029  __LINE__,__FILE__)
39030  #define IS_SKB_HEAD(skb)    skb_check((skb), 1,
39031  __LINE__,__FILE__)
39032  #else
39033  #define IS_SKB(skb)
```

```
39034    #define IS_SKB_HEAD(skb)
39035
39036    extern __inline__ void skb_queue_head_init(struct
39037    sk_buff_head *list)
39038    {
39039        list->prev = (struct sk_buff *)list;
39040        list->next = (struct sk_buff *)list;
39041        list->qlen = 0;
39042    }
39043
39044    /*
39045     *  Insert an sk_buff at the start of a list.
39046     *
39047     *  The "__skb_xxxx()" functions are the non-atomic ones
39048    that
39049     *  can only be called with interrupts disabled.
39050     */
39051
39052    extern __inline__ void __skb_queue_head(struct
39053    sk_buff_head *list, struct sk_buff *newsk)
39054    {
39055        struct sk_buff *prev, *next;
39056
39057        newsk->list = list;
39058        list->qlen++;
39059        prev = (struct sk_buff *)list;
39060        next = prev->next;
39061        newsk->next = next;
39062        newsk->prev = prev;
39063        next->prev = newsk;
39064        prev->next = newsk;
39065    }
39066
39067    extern __inline__ void skb_queue_head(struct
39068    sk_buff_head *list, struct sk_buff *newsk)
39069    {
39070        unsigned long flags;
39071
39072        save_flags(flags);
39073        cli();
39074        __skb_queue_head(list, newsk);
39075        restore_flags(flags);
39076    }
39077
39078    /*
39079     *  Insert an sk_buff at the end of a list.
39080     */
39081
39082    extern __inline__ void __skb_queue_tail(struct
39083    sk_buff_head *list, struct sk_buff *newsk)
39084    {
39085        struct sk_buff *prev, *next;
39086
39087        newsk->list = list;
39088        list->qlen++;
39089        next = (struct sk_buff *)list;
39090        prev = next->prev;
39091        newsk->next = next;
39092        newsk->prev = prev;
39093        next->prev = newsk;
39094        prev->next = newsk;
39095    }
39096
39097    extern __inline__ void skb_queue_tail(struct
39098    sk_buff_head *list, struct sk_buff *newsk)
39099    {
39100        unsigned long flags;
39101
39102        save_flags(flags);
39103        cli();
39104        __skb_queue_tail(list, newsk);
39105        restore_flags(flags);
39106    }
39107
39108    /*
39109     *  Remove an sk_buff from a list.
39110     */
39111
39112    extern __inline__ struct sk_buff *__skb_dequeue(struct
39113    sk_buff_head *list)
39114    {
39115        struct sk_buff *next, *prev, *result;
39116
39117        prev = (struct sk_buff *) list;
39118        next = prev->next;
39119        result = NULL;
39120        if (next != prev) {
39121            result = next;
39122            next = next->next;
39123            list->qlen--;
39124            next->prev = prev;
39125            prev->next = next;
39126            result->next = NULL;
39127            result->prev = NULL;
39128            result->list = NULL;
39129        }
```

```
39130        return result;
39131    }
39132
39133    extern __inline__ struct sk_buff *skb_dequeue(struct
39134    sk_buff_head *list)
39135    {
39136        long flags;
39137        struct sk_buff *result;
39138
39139        save_flags(flags);
39140        cli();
39141        result = __skb_dequeue(list);
39142        restore_flags(flags);
39143        return result;
39144    }
39145
39146    /*
39147     *  Insert a packet on a list.
39148     */
39149
39150    extern __inline__ void __skb_insert(struct sk_buff
39151    *newsk,
39152        struct sk_buff * prev, struct sk_buff *next,
39153        struct sk_buff_head * list)
39154    {
39155        newsk->next = next;
39156        newsk->prev = prev;
39157        next->prev = newsk;
39158        prev->next = newsk;
39159        newsk->list = list;
39160        list->qlen++;
39161    }
39162
39163    /*
39164     *  Place a packet before a given packet in a list
39165     */
39166    extern __inline__ void skb_insert(struct sk_buff *old,
39167    struct sk_buff *newsk)
39168    {
39169        unsigned long flags;
39170
39171        save_flags(flags);
39172        cli();
39173        __skb_insert(newsk, old->prev, old, old->list);
39174        restore_flags(flags);
39175    }
39176
39177    /*
39178     *  Place a packet after a given packet in a list.
39179     */
39180
39181    extern __inline__ void skb_append(struct sk_buff *old,
39182    struct sk_buff *newsk)
39183    {
39184        unsigned long flags;
39185
39186        save_flags(flags);
39187        cli();
39188        __skb_insert(newsk, old, old->next, old->list);
39189        restore_flags(flags);
39190    }
39191
39192    /*
39193     * remove sk_buff from list. _Must_ be called
39194     atomically, and with
39195     * the list known..
39196     */
39197    extern __inline__ void __skb_unlink(struct sk_buff *skb,
39198    struct sk_buff_head *list)
39199    {
39200        struct sk_buff * next, * prev;
39201
39202        list->qlen--;
39203        next = skb->next;
39204        prev = skb->prev;
39205        skb->next = NULL;
39206        skb->prev = NULL;
39207        skb->list = NULL;
39208        next->prev = prev;
39209        prev->next = next;
39210    }
39211
39212    /*
39213     *  Remove an sk_buff from its list. Works even without
39214     knowing the list it
39215     *  is sitting on, which can be handy at times. It also
39216     means that THE LIST
39217     *  MUST EXIST when you unlink. Thus a list must have
39218     its contents unlinked
39219     *  _FIRST_.
39220     */
39221
39222    extern __inline__ void skb_unlink(struct sk_buff *skb)
39223    {
39224        unsigned long flags;
39225
```

```
39226        save_flags(flags);
39227        cli();
39228        if(skb->list)
39229            __skb_unlink(skb, skb->list);
39230        restore_flags(flags);
39231    }
39232
39233    /*
39234     *  Add data to an sk_buff
39235     */
39236
39237    extern __inline__ unsigned char *skb_put(struct sk_buff
39238    *skb, int len)
39239    {
39240        unsigned char *tmp=skb->tail;
39241        skb->tail+=len;
39242        skb->len+=len;
39243        if(skb->tail>skb->end)
39244        {
39245            __label__ here;
39246            panic("skput:over: %p:%d", &&here,len);
39247    here:
39248        }
39249        return tmp;
39250    }
39251
39252    extern __inline__ unsigned char *skb_push(struct sk_buff
39253    *skb, int len)
39254    {
39255        skb->data-=len;
39256        skb->len+=len;
39257        if(skb->data<skb->head)
39258        {
39259            __label__ here;
39260            panic("skpush:under: %p:%d", &&here,len);
39261    here:
39262        }
39263        return skb->data;
39264    }
39265
39266    extern __inline__ unsigned char * skb_pull(struct
39267    sk_buff *skb, int len)
39268    {
39269        if(len > skb->len)
39270            return NULL;
39271        skb->data+=len;
39272        skb->len-=len;
39273        return skb->data;
```

```
39274    }
39275
39276    extern __inline__ int skb_headroom(struct sk_buff *skb)
39277    {
39278        return skb->data-skb->head;
39279    }
39280
39281    extern __inline__ int skb_tailroom(struct sk_buff *skb)
39282    {
39283        return skb->end-skb->tail;
39284    }
39285
39286    extern __inline__ void skb_reserve(struct sk_buff *skb,
39287    int len)
39288    {
39289        skb->data+=len;
39290        skb->tail+=len;
39291    }
39292
39293    extern __inline__ void skb_trim(struct sk_buff *skb, int
39294    len)
39295    {
39296        if(skb->len>len)
39297        {
39298            skb->len=len;
39299            skb->tail=skb->data+len;
39300        }
39301    }
39302
39303    #endif
39304
39305    extern struct sk_buff *     skb_recv_datagram(struct
39306    sock *sk,unsigned flags,int noblock, int *err);
39307    extern int              datagram_select(struct sock *sk, int
39308    sel_type, select_table *wait);
39309    extern void             skb_copy_datagram(struct sk_buff
39310    *from, int offset, char *to,int size);
39311    extern void             skb_copy_datagram_iovec(struct
39312    sk_buff *from, int offset, struct iovec *to,int size);
39313    extern void             skb_free_datagram(struct sock * sk,
39314    struct sk_buff *skb);
39315
39316    #endif  /* __KERNEL__ */
39317    #endif  /* _LINUX_SKBUFF_H */
```

usr/include/linux/socket.h

```
39318    #ifndef _LINUX_SOCKET_H
39319    #define _LINUX_SOCKET_H
```

```
39320
39321   #include <asm/socket.h>        /* arch-dependent
39322   defines   */
39323   #include <linux/sockios.h>     /* the SIOCxxx I/O
39324   controls */
39325   #include <linux/uio.h>         /* iovec support
39326   */
39327
39328   struct sockaddr
39329   {
39330       unsigned short  sa_family;  /* address family,
39331   AF_xxx   */
39332       char         sa_data[14];   /* 14 bytes of protocol
39333   address */
39334   };
39335
39336   struct linger {
39337       int     l_onoff;    /* Linger active        */
39338       int     l_linger;   /* How long to linger for   */
39339   };
39340
39341   /*
39342    *  As we do 4.4BSD message passing we use a 4.4BSD
39343   message passing
39344    *  system, not 4.3. Thus msg_accrights(len) are now
39345   missing. They
39346    *  belong in an obscure libc emulation or the bin.
39347    */
39348
39349   struct msghdr
39350   {
39351       void    *   msg_name;   /* Socket name        */
39352       int     msg_namelen;    /* Length of name     */
39353       struct iovec * msg_iov;    /* Data blocks
39354   */
39355       int     msg_iovlen; /* Number of blocks     */
39356       void    *   msg_control;    /* Per protocol magic
39357   (eg BSD file descriptor passing) */
39358       int     msg_controllen; /* Length of rights list */
39359       int     msg_flags;  /* 4.4 BSD item we dont use
39360   */
39361   };
39362
39363   /* Control Messages */
39364
39365   #define SCM_RIGHTS      1
39366
39367   /* Socket types. */
```

```
39368   #define SOCK_STREAM 1         /* stream (connection)
39369   socket   */
39370   #define SOCK_DGRAM  2         /* datagram (conn.less)
39371   socket */
39372   #define SOCK_RAW    3         /* raw socket           */
39373   #define SOCK_RDM    4         /* reliably-delivered
39374   message   */
39375   #define SOCK_SEQPACKET  5        /* sequential packet
39376   socket */
39377   #define SOCK_PACKET 10       /* linux specific way of
39378   */
39379                           /* getting packets at the dev   */
39380                           /* level. For writing rarp and */
39381                           /* other similar things on the  */
39382                           /* user level.          */
39383
39384   /* Supported address families. */
39385   #define AF_UNSPEC   0
39386   #define AF_UNIX     1    /* Unix domain sockets       */
39387   #define AF_INET     2    /* Internet IP Protocol      */
39388   #define AF_AX25     3    /* Amateur Radio AX.25       */
39389   #define AF_IPX      4    /* Novell IPX               */
39390   #define AF_APPLETALK    5    /* Appletalk DDP         */
39391   #define AF_NETROM   6    /* Amateur radio NetROM      */
39392   #define AF_BRIDGE   7    /* Multiprotocol bridge      */
39393   #define AF_AAL5     8    /* Reserved for Werner's ATM
39394   */
39395   #define AF_X25      9    /* Reserved for X.25 project
39396   */
39397   #ifdef LINUX_2_1_X
39398   #define AF_INET6    10   /* IP version 6            */
39399   #endif
39400   #define AF_MAX      12   /* For now.. */
39401
39402   /* Protocol families, same as address families. */
39403   #define PF_UNSPEC   AF_UNSPEC
39404   #define PF_UNIX     AF_UNIX
39405   #define PF_INET     AF_INET
39406   #define PF_AX25     AF_AX25
39407   #define PF_IPX      AF_IPX
39408   #define PF_APPLETALK    AF_APPLETALK
39409   #define PF_NETROM   AF_NETROM
39410   #define PF_BRIDGE   AF_BRIDGE
39411   #define PF_AAL5     AF_AAL5
39412   #define PF_X25      AF_X25
39413   #ifdef LINUX_2_1_X
39414   #define PF_INET6    AF_INET6
39415   #endif
```

```
39416   #define PF_MAX        AF_MAX
39417
39418   /* Maximum queue length specifiable by listen. */
39419   #define SOMAXCONN   128
39420
39421   /* Flags we can use with send/ and recv. */
39422   #define MSG_OOB       1
39423   #define MSG_PEEK      2
39424   #define MSG_DONTROUTE   4
39425   /*#define MSG_CTRUNC    8    - We need to support this
39426   for BSD oddments */
39427   #define MSG_PROXY   16  /* Supply or ask second address.
39428   */
39429
39430   /* Setsockoptions(2) level. Thanks to BSD these must
39431   match IPPROTO_xxx */
39432   #define SOL_IP      0
39433   #define SOL_IPX     256
39434   #define SOL_AX25    257
39435   #define SOL_ATALK   258
39436   #define SOL_NETROM  259
39437   #define SOL_TCP     6
39438   #define SOL_UDP     17
39439
39440   /* IP options */
39441   #define IP_TOS      1
39442   #define IPTOS_LOWDELAY      0x10
39443   #define IPTOS_THROUGHPUT    0x08
39444   #define IPTOS_RELIABILITY   0x04
39445   #define IPTOS_MINCOST       0x02
39446   #define IP_TTL      2
39447   #define IP_HDRINCL  3
39448   #define IP_OPTIONS  4
39449
39450   #define IP_MULTICAST_IF       32
39451   #define IP_MULTICAST_TTL      33
39452   #define IP_MULTICAST_LOOP     34
39453   #define IP_ADD_MEMBERSHIP     35
39454   #define IP_DROP_MEMBERSHIP    36
39455
39456   /* These need to appear somewhere around here */
39457   #define IP_DEFAULT_MULTICAST_TTL    1
39458   #define IP_DEFAULT_MULTICAST_LOOP   1
39459   #define IP_MAX_MEMBERSHIPS          20
39460
39461   /* IPX options */
39462   #define IPX_TYPE    1
39463
39464   /* TCP options - this way around because someone left a
39465   set in the c library includes */
39466   #define TCP_NODELAY 1
39467   #define TCP_MAXSEG  2
39468
39469   /* The various priorities. */
39470   #define SOPRI_INTERACTIVE   0
39471   #define SOPRI_NORMAL        1
39472   #define SOPRI_BACKGROUND    2
39473
39474   #ifdef __KERNEL__
39475   extern void memcpy_fromiovec(unsigned char *kdata,
39476   struct iovec *iov, int len);
39477   extern int verify_iovec(struct msghdr *m, struct iovec
39478   *iov, char *address, int mode);
39479   extern void memcpy_toiovec(struct iovec *v, unsigned
39480   char *kdata, int len);
39481   extern int move_addr_to_user(void *kaddr, int klen, void
39482   *uaddr, int *ulen);
39483   extern int move_addr_to_kernel(void *uaddr, int ulen,
39484   void *kaddr);
39485   #endif
39486   #endif /* _LINUX_SOCKET_H */
```

usr/include/linux/sockios.h

```
39487   /*
39488    * INET     An implementation of the TCP/IP protocol
39489   suite for the LINUX
39490    *       operating system.  INET is implemented using the
39491   BSD Socket
39492    *       interface as the means of communication with the
39493   user level.
39494    *
39495    *       Definitions of the socket-level I/O control
39496   calls.
39497    *
39498    * Version: @(#)sockios.h   1.0.2   03/09/93
39499    *
39500    * Authors: Ross Biro, <bir7@leland.Stanford.Edu>
39501    *       Fred N. van Kempen, <waltje@uWalt.NL.Mugnet.ORG>
39502    *
39503    *       This program is free software; you can
39504   redistribute it and/or
39505    *       modify it under the terms of the GNU General
39506   Public License
39507    *       as published by the Free Software Foundation;
39508   either version
39509    *       2 of the License, or (at your option) any later
```

```
39510   version.
39511    */
39512   #ifndef _LINUX_SOCKIOS_H
39513   #define _LINUX_SOCKIOS_H
39514
39515   #include <asm/sockios.h>
39516
39517   /* Routing table calls. */
39518   #define SIOCADDRT    0x890B      /* add routing table
39519   entry */
39520   #define SIOCDELRT    0x890C      /* delete routing table
39521   entry   */
39522
39523   /* Socket configuration controls. */
39524   #define SIOCGIFNAME 0x8910       /* get iface name
39525   */
39526   #define SIOCSIFLINK 0x8911       /* set iface channel
39527      */
39528   #define SIOCGIFCONF 0x8912       /* get iface list
39529   */
39530   #define SIOCGIFFLAGS    0x8913      /* get flags
39531      */
39532   #define SIOCSIFFLAGS    0x8914      /* set flags
39533      */
39534   #define SIOCGIFADDR 0x8915       /* get PA address
39535   */
39536   #define SIOCSIFADDR 0x8916       /* set PA address
39537   */
39538   #define SIOCGIFDSTADDR  0x8917      /* get remote PA
39539   address    */
39540   #define SIOCSIFDSTADDR  0x8918      /* set remote PA
39541   address    */
39542   #define SIOCGIFBRDADDR  0x8919      /* get broadcast PA
39543   address */
39544   #define SIOCSIFBRDADDR  0x891a      /* set broadcast PA
39545   address */
39546   #define SIOCGIFNETMASK  0x891b      /* get network PA
39547   mask       */
39548   #define SIOCSIFNETMASK  0x891c      /* set network PA
39549   mask       */
39550   #define SIOCGIFMETRIC   0x891d      /* get metric
39551      */
39552   #define SIOCSIFMETRIC   0x891e      /* set metric
39553      */
39554   #define SIOCGIFMEM  0x891f       /* get memory address
39555   (BSD) */
39556   #define SIOCSIFMEM  0x8920       /* set memory address
39557   (BSD) */
```

```
39558   #define SIOCGIFMTU  0x8921       /* get MTU size
39559   */
39560   #define SIOCSIFMTU  0x8922       /* set MTU size
39561   */
39562   #define SIOCSIFHWADDR    0x8924       /* set hardware
39563   address (NI)    */
39564   #define SIOCGIFENCAP     0x8925       /* get/set slip
39565   encapsulation    */
39566   #define SIOCSIFENCAP     0x8926
39567   #define SIOCGIFHWADDR    0x8927       /* Get hardware
39568   address      */
39569   #define SIOCGIFSLAVE     0x8929       /* Driver slaving
39570   support    */
39571   #define SIOCSIFSLAVE     0x8930
39572   #define SIOCADDMULTI     0x8931       /* Multicast address
39573   lists */
39574   #define SIOCDELMULTI     0x8932
39575
39576   #define SIOCGIFBR    0x8940      /* Bridging support
39577   */
39578   #define SIOCSIFBR    0x8941      /* Set bridging options
39579      */
39580
39581   /* ARP cache control calls. */
39582   #define OLD_SIOCDARP     0x8950       /* old delete ARP
39583   table entry    */
39584   #define OLD_SIOCGARP     0x8951       /* old get ARP table
39585   entry */
39586   #define OLD_SIOCSARP     0x8952       /* old set ARP table
39587   entry */
39588   #define SIOCDARP      0x8953      /* delete ARP table
39589   entry   */
39590   #define SIOCGARP      0x8954      /* get ARP table entry
39591      */
39592   #define SIOCSARP      0x8955      /* set ARP table entry
39593      */
39594
39595   /* RARP cache control calls. */
39596   #define SIOCDRARP     0x8960      /* delete RARP table
39597   entry */
39598   #define SIOCGRARP     0x8961      /* get RARP table entry
39599      */
39600   #define SIOCSRARP     0x8962      /* set RARP table entry
39601      */
39602
39603   /* Driver configuration calls */
39604
39605   #define SIOCGIFMAP  0x8970       /* Get device parameters
```

```
39606     */
39607   #define SIOCSIFMAP  0x8971      /* Set device parameters
39608     */
39609
39610   /* DLCI configuration calls */
39611
39612   #define SIOCADDDLCI 0x8980      /* Create new DLCI
39613   device   */
39614   #define SIOCDELDLCI 0x8981      /* Delete DLCI device
39615     */
39616
39617   /* Device private ioctl calls */
39618
39619   /*
39620    *  These 16 ioctls are available to devices via the
39621   do_ioctl() device
39622    *  vector. Each device should include this file and
39623   redefine these names
39624    *  as their own. Because these are device dependent it
39625   is a good idea
39626    *  _NOT_ to issue them to random objects and hope.
39627    */
39628
39629   #define SIOCDEVPRIVATE  0x89F0  /* to 89FF */
39630
39631   /*
39632    *  These 16 ioctl calls are protocol private
39633    */
39634
39635   #define SIOCPROTOPRIVATE 0x89E0 /* to 89EF */
39636   #endif  /* _LINUX_SOCKIOS_H */
```

usr/include/linux/tcp.h

```
39637   /*
39638    * INET     An implementation of the TCP/IP protocol
39639   suite for the LINUX
39640    *      operating system.  INET is implemented using the
39641   BSD Socket
39642    *      interface as the means of communication with the
39643   user level.
39644    *
39645    *      Definitions for the TCP protocol.
39646    *
39647    * Version: @(#)tcp.h   1.0.2   04/28/93
39648    *
39649    * Author:  Fred N. van Kempen,
39650   <waltje@uWalt.NL.Mugnet.ORG>
39651    *
39652    *      This program is free software; you can
39653   redistribute it and/or
39654    *      modify it under the terms of the GNU General
39655   Public License
39656    *      as published by the Free Software Foundation;
39657   either version
39658    *      2 of the License, or (at your option) any later
39659   version.
39660    */
39661   #ifndef _LINUX_TCP_H
39662   #define _LINUX_TCP_H
39663
39664   #include <linux/types.h>
39665   #include <asm/byteorder.h>
39666
39667   struct tcphdr {
39668       __u16    source;
39669       __u16    dest;
39670       __u32    seq;
39671       __u32    ack_seq;
39672   #if defined(__LITTLE_ENDIAN_BITFIELD)
39673       __u16    res1:4,
39674           doff:4,
39675           fin:1,
39676           syn:1,
39677           rst:1,
39678           psh:1,
39679           ack:1,
39680           urg:1,
39681           res2:2;
39682   #elif defined(__BIG_ENDIAN_BITFIELD)
39683       __u16    doff:4,
39684           res1:4,
39685           res2:2,
39686           urg:1,
39687           ack:1,
39688           psh:1,
39689           rst:1,
39690           syn:1,
39691           fin:1;
39692   #else
39693   #error  "Adjust your <asm/byteorder.h> defines"
39694   #endif
39695       __u16    window;
39696       __u16    check;
39697       __u16    urg_ptr;
39698   };
39699
```

```
39700
39701   enum {
39702     TCP_ESTABLISHED = 1,
39703     TCP_SYN_SENT,
39704     TCP_SYN_RECV,
39705     TCP_FIN_WAIT1,
39706     TCP_FIN_WAIT2,
39707     TCP_TIME_WAIT,
39708     TCP_CLOSE,
39709     TCP_CLOSE_WAIT,
39710     TCP_LAST_ACK,
39711     TCP_LISTEN,
39712     TCP_CLOSING   /* now a valid state */
39713   };
39714
39715   #endif  /* _LINUX_TCP_H */
```

usr/include/linux/udp.h

```
39716   /*
39717    * INET     An implementation of the TCP/IP protocol
39718   suite for the LINUX
39719    *      operating system.  INET is implemented using the
39720   BSD Socket
39721    *      interface as the means of communication with the
39722   user level.
39723    *
39724    *      Definitions for the UDP protocol.
39725    *
39726    * Version: @(#)udp.h   1.0.2   04/28/93
39727    *
39728    * Author:  Fred N. van Kempen,
39729   <waltje@uWalt.NL.Mugnet.ORG>
39730    *
39731    *      This program is free software; you can
39732   redistribute it and/or
39733    *      modify it under the terms of the GNU General
39734   Public License
39735    *      as published by the Free Software Foundation;
39736   either version
39737    *      2 of the License, or (at your option) any later
39738   version.
39739    */
39740   #ifndef _LINUX_UDP_H
39741   #define _LINUX_UDP_H
39742
39743
39744   struct udphdr {
39745     unsigned short    source;
39746     unsigned short    dest;
39747     unsigned short    len;
39748     unsigned short    check;
39749   };
39750
39751
39752   #endif  /* _LINUX_UDP_H */
```

usr/include/linux/uio.h

```
39753   #ifndef __LINUX_UIO_H
39754   #define __LINUX_UIO_H
39755
39756   /*
39757    *  Berkeley style UIO structures   -   Alan Cox 1994.
39758    *
39759    *      This program is free software; you can
39760   redistribute it and/or
39761    *      modify it under the terms of the GNU General
39762   Public License
39763    *      as published by the Free Software Foundation;
39764   either version
39765    *      2 of the License, or (at your option) any later
39766   version.
39767    */
39768
39769
39770   /* A word of warning: Our uio structure will clash with
39771   the C library one (which is now obsolete). Remove the C
39772     library one from sys/uio.h if you have a very old
39773   library set */
39774
39775   struct iovec
39776   {
39777     void *iov_base;     /* BSD uses caddr_t (same thing
39778   in effect) */
39779     int iov_len;
39780   };
39781
39782   #define UIO_MAXIOV  16  /* Maximum iovec's in one
39783   operation
39784                    16 matches BSD */
39785
39786   #endif
```

usr/include/netinet/in.h

```
39787   /* Copyright (C) 1991 Free Software Foundation, Inc.
39788   This file is part of the GNU C Library.
39789
```

```
39790   The GNU C Library is free software; you can redistribute
39791   it and/or modify
39792   it under the terms of the GNU General Public License as
39793   published by
39794   the Free Software Foundation; either version 1, or (at
39795   your option)
39796   any later version.
39797
39798   The GNU C Library is distributed in the hope that it
39799   will be useful,
39800   but WITHOUT ANY WARRANTY; without even the implied
39801   warranty of
39802   MERCHANTABILITY or FITNESS FOR A PARTICULAR PURPOSE.
39803   See the
39804   GNU General Public License for more details.
39805
39806   You should have received a copy of the GNU General
39807   Public License
39808   along with the GNU C Library; see the file COPYING.  If
39809   not, write to
39810   the Free Software Foundation, 675 Mass Ave, Cambridge,
39811   MA 02139, USA.  */
39812
39813   #ifndef _NETINET_IN_H
39814
39815   #define _NETINET_IN_H    1
39816   #include <features.h>
39817
39818   #include <endian.h>
39819   #include <sys/socket.h>
39820
39821   __BEGIN_DECLS
39822
39823   /* Standard well-known ports.  */
39824   enum
39825     {
39826       IPPORT_ECHO = 7,        /* Echo service.  */
39827       IPPORT_DISCARD = 9,     /* Discard transmissions
39828   service.  */
39829       IPPORT_SYSTAT = 11,     /* System status service.  */
39830       IPPORT_DAYTIME = 13,    /* Time of day service.  */
39831       IPPORT_NETSTAT = 15,    /* Network status service.
39832   */
39833       IPPORT_FTP = 21,        /* File Transfer Protocol.
39834   */
39835       IPPORT_TELNET = 23,     /* Telnet protocol.  */
39836       IPPORT_SMTP = 25,       /* Simple Mail Transfer
39837   Protocol.  */
```

```
39838       IPPORT_TIMESERVER = 37, /* Timeserver service.  */
39839       IPPORT_NAMESERVER = 42, /* Domain Name Service.  */
39840       IPPORT_WHOIS = 43,      /* Internet Whois service.
39841   */
39842       IPPORT_MTP = 57,
39843
39844       IPPORT_TFTP = 69,       /* Trivial File Transfer
39845   Protocol.  */
39846       IPPORT_RJE = 77,
39847       IPPORT_FINGER = 79,     /* Finger service.  */
39848       IPPORT_TTYLINK = 87,
39849       IPPORT_SUPDUP = 95,     /* SUPDUP protocol.  */
39850
39851
39852       IPPORT_EXECSERVER = 512,    /* execd service.  */
39853       IPPORT_LOGINSERVER = 513,   /* rlogind service.  */
39854       IPPORT_CMDSERVER = 514,
39855       IPPORT_EFSSERVER = 520,
39856
39857       /* UDP ports.  */
39858       IPPORT_BIFFUDP = 512,
39859       IPPORT_WHOSERVER = 513,
39860       IPPORT_ROUTESERVER = 520,
39861
39862       /* Ports less than this value are reserved for
39863   privileged processes.  */
39864       IPPORT_RESERVED = 1024,
39865
39866       /* Ports greater this value are reserved for
39867   (non-privileged) servers.  */
39868       IPPORT_USERRESERVED = 5000
39869     };
39870
39871
39872   /* Link numbers.  */
39873   #define IMPLINK_IP        155
39874   #define IMPLINK_LOWEXPER    156
39875   #define IMPLINK_HIGHEXPER   158
39876
39877
39878   /*
39879    * Many other definitions have been moved to
39880   <linux/in.h>,
39881    * because several parts of the kernel need them. -FvK
39882    */
39883   #include <linux/in.h>
39884
39885   /*
```

```
39886   * Bind a socket to a privileged IP port
39887   */
39888  extern int bindresvport __P ((int __sockfd,
39889         struct sockaddr_in * __sin));
39890
39891  __END_DECLS
39892
39893  #endif  /* netinet/in.h */
```

usr/include/netinet/ip_fw.h

```
39894  #include <linux/ip_fw.h>
```

usr/include/resolv.h

```
39895  /*
39896   * ++Copyright++ 1983, 1987, 1989, 1993
39897   * -
39898   * Copyright (c) 1983, 1987, 1989, 1993
39899   *    The Regents of the University of California.  All
39900  rights reserved.
39901   *
39902   * Redistribution and use in source and binary forms,
39903  with or without
39904   * modification, are permitted provided that the
39905  following conditions
39906   * are met:
39907   * 1. Redistributions of source code must retain the
39908  above copyright
39909   *    notice, this list of conditions and the following
39910  disclaimer.
39911   * 2. Redistributions in binary form must reproduce the
39912  above copyright
39913   *    notice, this list of conditions and the following
39914  disclaimer in the
39915   *    documentation and/or other materials provided with
39916  the distribution.
39917   * 3. All advertising materials mentioning features or
39918  use of this software
39919   *    must display the following acknowledgement:
39920   *  This product includes software developed by the
39921  University of
39922   *  California, Berkeley and its contributors.
39923   * 4. Neither the name of the University nor the names
39924  of its contributors
39925   *    may be used to endorse or promote products derived
39926  from this software
39927   *    without specific prior written permission.
39928   *
39929   * THIS SOFTWARE IS PROVIDED BY THE REGENTS AND
39930  CONTRIBUTORS "AS IS" AND
39931   * ANY EXPRESS OR IMPLIED WARRANTIES, INCLUDING, BUT NOT
39932  LIMITED TO, THE
39933   * IMPLIED WARRANTIES OF MERCHANTABILITY AND FITNESS FOR
39934  A PARTICULAR PURPOSE
39935   * ARE DISCLAIMED.  IN NO EVENT SHALL THE REGENTS OR
39936  CONTRIBUTORS BE LIABLE
39937   * FOR ANY DIRECT, INDIRECT, INCIDENTAL, SPECIAL,
39938  EXEMPLARY, OR CONSEQUENTIAL
39939   * DAMAGES (INCLUDING, BUT NOT LIMITED TO, PROCUREMENT
39940  OF SUBSTITUTE GOODS
39941   * OR SERVICES; LOSS OF USE, DATA, OR PROFITS; OR
39942  BUSINESS INTERRUPTION)
39943   * HOWEVER CAUSED AND ON ANY THEORY OF LIABILITY,
39944  WHETHER IN CONTRACT, STRICT
39945   * LIABILITY, OR TORT (INCLUDING NEGLIGENCE OR
39946  OTHERWISE) ARISING IN ANY WAY
39947   * OUT OF THE USE OF THIS SOFTWARE, EVEN IF ADVISED OF
39948  THE POSSIBILITY OF
39949   * SUCH DAMAGE.
39950   * -
39951   * Portions Copyright (c) 1993 by Digital Equipment
39952  Corporation.
39953   *
39954   * Permission to use, copy, modify, and distribute this
39955  software for any
39956   * purpose with or without fee is hereby granted,
39957  provided that the above
39958   * copyright notice and this permission notice appear in
39959  all copies, and that
39960   * the name of Digital Equipment Corporation not be used
39961  in advertising or
39962   * publicity pertaining to distribution of the document
39963  or software without
39964   * specific, written prior permission.
39965   *
39966   * THE SOFTWARE IS PROVIDED "AS IS" AND DIGITAL
39967  EQUIPMENT CORP. DISCLAIMS ALL
39968   * WARRANTIES WITH REGARD TO THIS SOFTWARE, INCLUDING
39969  ALL IMPLIED WARRANTIES
39970   * OF MERCHANTABILITY AND FITNESS.   IN NO EVENT SHALL
39971  DIGITAL EQUIPMENT
39972   * CORPORATION BE LIABLE FOR ANY SPECIAL, DIRECT,
39973  INDIRECT, OR CONSEQUENTIAL
39974   * DAMAGES OR ANY DAMAGES WHATSOEVER RESULTING FROM LOSS
39975  OF USE, DATA OR
39976   * PROFITS, WHETHER IN AN ACTION OF CONTRACT, NEGLIGENCE
39977  OR OTHER TORTIOUS
```

```
39978    * ACTION, ARISING OUT OF OR IN CONNECTION WITH THE USE
39979    OR PERFORMANCE OF THIS
39980    * SOFTWARE.
39981    * -
39982    * --Copyright--
39983    */
39984
39985    /*
39986    * @(#)resolv.h    8.1 (Berkeley) 6/2/93
39987    * resolv.h,v 1.5 1995/07/01 19:58:35 hjl Exp
39988    */
39989
39990    #ifndef _RESOLV_H_
39991    #define _RESOLV_H_
39992
39993    #include <sys/param.h>
39994    #if (!defined(BSD)) || (BSD < 199306)
39995    # include <sys/bitypes.h>
39996    #else
39997    # include <sys/types.h>
39998    #endif
39999    #include <sys/cdefs.h>
40000    #include <stdio.h>
40001
40002    #include <arpa/nameser.h>    /* For MAXDNAME */
40003    #include <netinet/in.h>      /* For struct sockaddr_in */
40004
40005    /*
40006    * revision information.  this is the release date in
40007    YYYYMMDD format.
40008    * it can change every day so the right thing to do with
40009    it is use it
40010    * in preprocessor commands such as "#if (__RES >
40011    19931104)".  do not
40012    * compare for equality; rather, use it to determine
40013    whether your resolver
40014    * is new enough to contain a certain feature.
40015    */
40016
40017    #define __RES    19950621
40018
40019    /*
40020    * Resolver configuration file.
40021    * Normally not present, but may contain the address of
40022    the
40023    * inital name server(s) to query and the domain search
40024    list.
40025    */
```

```
40026
40027    #ifndef _PATH_RESCONF
40028    #ifdef __linux__
40029    #include <netdb.h>
40030    #else
40031    #define _PATH_RESCONF         "/etc/resolv.conf"
40032    #endif
40033    #endif
40034
40035    /*
40036    * Global defines and variables for resolver stub.
40037    */
40038    #define MAXNS           3    /* max # name servers we'll
40039    track */
40040    #define MAXDFLSRCH      3    /* # default domain levels
40041    to try */
40042    #define MAXDNSRCH       6    /* max # domains in search
40043    path */
40044    #define LOCALDOMAINPARTS 2   /* min levels in name
40045    that is "local" */
40046
40047    #define RES_TIMEOUT     5    /* min. seconds between
40048    retries */
40049    #define MAXRESOLVSORT   10   /* number of net to sort
40050    on */
40051    #define RES_MAXNDOTS    15   /* should reflect bit
40052    field size */
40053
40054    struct __res_state {
40055        int retrans;        /* retransmition time interval */
40056        int retry;          /* number of times to retransmit
40057    */
40058        u_long  options;        /* option flags - see below.
40059    */
40060        int nscount;        /* number of name servers */
40061        struct sockaddr_in
40062            nsaddr_list[MAXNS]; /* address of name server */
40063    #define nsaddr  nsaddr_list[0]      /* for backward
40064    compatibility */
40065        u_short id;         /* current packet id */
40066        char    *dnsrch[MAXDNSRCH+1];   /* components of
40067    domain to search */
40068        char    defdname[MAXDNAME]; /* default domain */
40069        u_long  pfcode;         /* RES_PRF_ flags - see
40070    below. */
40071        unsigned ndots:4;       /* threshold for initial
40072    abs. query */
40073        unsigned nsort:4;       /* number of elements in
```

```
40074    sort_list[] */
40075        char    unused[3];
40076        struct {
40077            struct in_addr  addr;
40078            u_int32_t   mask;
40079        } sort_list[MAXRESOLVSORT];
40080    };
40081
40082    /*
40083     * Resolver options (keep these in synch with
40084    res_debug.c, please)
40085     */
40086    #define RES_INIT    0x00000001  /* address initialized */
40087    #define RES_DEBUG   0x00000002  /* print debug messages
40088    */
40089    #define RES_AAONLY  0x00000004  /* authoritative answers
40090    only (!IMPL)*/
40091    #define RES_USEVC   0x00000008  /* use virtual circuit */
40092    #define RES_PRIMARY 0x00000010  /* query primary server
40093    only (!IMPL) */
40094    #define RES_IGNTC   0x00000020  /* ignore trucation
40095    errors */
40096    #define RES_RECURSE 0x00000040  /* recursion desired */
40097    #define RES_DEFNAMES    0x00000080  /* use default
40098    domain name */
40099    #define RES_STAYOPEN    0x00000100  /* Keep TCP socket
40100    open */
40101    #define RES_DNSRCH  0x00000200  /* search up local
40102    domain tree */
40103    #define RES_INSECURE1   0x00000400  /* type 1 security
40104    disabled */
40105    #define RES_INSECURE2   0x00000800  /* type 2 security
40106    disabled */
40107    #define RES_NOALIASES   0x00001000  /* shuts off
40108    HOSTALIASES feature */
40109
40110    #define RES_DEFAULT (RES_RECURSE | RES_DEFNAMES |
40111    RES_DNSRCH)
40112
40113    /*
40114     * Resolver "pfcode" values.  Used by dig.
40115     */
40116    #define RES_PRF_STATS   0x00000001
40117    /*          0x00000002  */
40118    #define RES_PRF_CLASS   0x00000004
40119    #define RES_PRF_CMD 0x00000008
40120    #define RES_PRF_QUES    0x00000010
40121    #define RES_PRF_ANS 0x00000020
40122    #define RES_PRF_AUTH    0x00000040
40123    #define RES_PRF_ADD 0x00000080
40124    #define RES_PRF_HEAD1   0x00000100
40125    #define RES_PRF_HEAD2   0x00000200
40126    #define RES_PRF_TTLID   0x00000400
40127    #define RES_PRF_HEADX   0x00000800
40128    #define RES_PRF_QUERY   0x00001000
40129    #define RES_PRF_REPLY   0x00002000
40130    #define RES_PRF_INIT    0x00004000
40131    /*          0x00008000  */
40132
40133    /* hooks are still experimental as of 4.9.2 */
40134    typedef enum { res_goahead, res_nextns, res_modified,
40135    res_done, res_error }
40136        res_sendhookact;
40137
40138    typedef res_sendhookact (*res_send_qhook)__P((struct
40139    sockaddr_in * const *ns,
40140                    const u_char **query,
40141                    int *querylen,
40142                    u_char *ans,
40143                    int anssiz,
40144                    int *resplen));
40145
40146    typedef res_sendhookact (*res_send_rhook)__P((const
40147    struct sockaddr_in *ns,
40148                    const u_char *query,
40149                    int querylen,
40150                    u_char *ans,
40151                    int anssiz,
40152                    int *resplen));
40153
40154    #if 0
40155    /* Private routines shared between libc/net, named,
40156    nslookup and others. */
40157    #if 0
40158    #define dn_skipname __dn_skipname
40159    #define fp_query    __fp_query
40160    #define fp_nquery   __fp_nquery
40161    #define hostalias   __hostalias
40162    #define putlong     __putlong
40163    #define putshort    __putshort
40164    #define p_class     __p_class
40165    #define p_time      __p_time
40166    #define p_type      __p_type
40167    #define p_cdnname   __p_cdnname
40168    #define p_cdname    __p_cdname
40169    #define p_fqname    __p_fqname
```

```
40170  #define p_rr           __p_rr
40171  #define p_option       __p_option
40172  #define res_randomid      __res_randomid
40173  #define res_isourserver __res_isourserver
40174  #define res_nameinquery __res_nameinquery
40175  #define res_queriesmatch __res_queriesmatch
40176  #else
40177  #define __dn_skipname   dn_skipname
40178  #define __fp_query  fp_query
40179  #define __fp_nquery fp_nquery
40180  #define __hostalias hostalias
40181  #define __putlong   putlong
40182  #define __putshort  putshort
40183  #define __p_class   p_class
40184  #define __p_time    p_time
40185  #define __p_type    p_type
40186  #define __p_cdnname p_cdnname
40187  #define __p_cdname  p_cdname
40188  #define __p_fqname  p_fqname
40189  #define __p_rr      p_rr
40190  #define __p_option  p_option
40191  #define __res_randomid  res_randomid
40192  #define __p_query   p_query
40193  #define __fp_resstat    fp_resstat
40194  #define __res_isourserver res_isourserver
40195  #define __res_nameinquery res_nameinquery
40196  #define __res_queriesmatch res_queriesmatch
40197  #endif
40198  #endif
40199
40200  __BEGIN_DECLS
40201
40202  #if defined(_POSIX_THREAD_SAFE_FUNCTIONS) ||
40203  defined(_REENTRANT)
40204  struct __res_state *__res_status_location __P((void));
40205  #define _res           (*__res_status_location())
40206  #else
40207  extern struct __res_state _res;
40208  #endif
40209
40210  int  __dn_skipname __P((const u_char *, const u_char *));
40211  void    __fp_resstat __P((struct __res_state *, FILE
40212  *));
40213  void    __fp_query __P((const u_char *, FILE *));
40214  void    __fp_nquery __P((const u_char *, int, FILE *));
40215  char    *__hostalias __P((const char *));
40216  void    __putlong __P((u_int32_t, u_char *));
40217  void    __putshort __P((u_int16_t, u_char *));
40218  char    *__p_time __P((u_int32_t));
40219  void    __p_query __P((const u_char *));
40220  const u_char *__p_cdnname __P((const u_char *, const
40221  u_char *, int, FILE *));
40222  const u_char *__p_cdname __P((const u_char *, const
40223  u_char *, FILE *));
40224  const u_char *__p_fqname __P((const u_char *, const
40225  u_char *, FILE *));
40226  const u_char *__p_rr __P((const u_char *, const u_char
40227  *, FILE *));
40228  const char *__p_type __P((int));
40229  const char *__p_class __P((int));
40230  const char *__p_option __P((u_long option));
40231  int  dn_comp __P((const char *, u_char *, int, u_char
40232  **, u_char **));
40233  int  dn_expand __P((const u_char *, const u_char *,
40234  const u_char *,
40235            char *, int));
40236  int  res_init __P((void));
40237  u_int16_t res_randomid __P((void));
40238  int  res_query __P((const char *, int, int, u_char *,
40239  int));
40240  int  res_search __P((const char *, int, int, u_char *,
40241  int));
40242  int  res_querydomain __P((const char *, const char *,
40243  int, int,
40244            u_char *, int));
40245  int  res_mkquery __P((int, const char *, int, int, const
40246  u_char *, int,
40247            const u_char *, u_char *, int));
40248  int  res_send __P((const u_char *, int, u_char *, int));
40249  int  res_isourserver __P((const struct sockaddr_in *));
40250  int  res_nameinquery __P((const char *, int, int,
40251            const u_char *, const u_char *));
40252  int  res_queriesmatch __P((const u_char *, const u_char
40253  *,
40254            const u_char *, const u_char *));
40255  /* XXX - these last two don't belong in the resolver */
40256  u_int    inet_nsap_addr __P((const char *, u_char *, int
40257  maxlen));
40258  char    *inet_nsap_ntoa __P((int, const u_char *, char
40259  *ascii));
40260
40261  __END_DECLS
40262
40263  #endif /* !_RESOLV_H_ */
```

usr/src/lib/resolv/res_mkupdate.h

```
40264  #ifndef _RES_MKUPDATE_H_
40265  #define _RES_MKUPDATE_H_
40266
40267  __BEGIN_DECLS
40268  __END_DECLS
40269
40270  #endif /* _RES_MKUPDATE_H_ */
```

usr/src/linux/include/firewall.h

```
40271  #ifndef __LINUX_FIREWALL_H
40272  #define __LINUX_FIREWALL_H
40273
40274  /*
40275   *   Definitions for loadable firewall modules
40276   */
40277
40278  #define FW_BLOCK      0
40279  #define FW_ACCEPT     1
40280  #define FW_REJECT     (-1)
40281  #define FW_REDIRECT   2
40282  #define FW_MASQUERADE     3
40283  #define FW_SKIP       4
40284
40285  struct firewall_ops
40286  {
40287      struct firewall_ops *next;
40288      int (*fw_forward)(struct firewall_ops *this, int pf,
40289              struct device *dev, void *phdr, void *arg);
40290      int (*fw_input)(struct firewall_ops *this, int pf,
40291              struct device *dev, void *phdr, void *arg);
40292      int (*fw_output)(struct firewall_ops *this, int pf,
40293              struct device *dev, void *phdr, void *arg);
40294      /* Data falling in the second 486 cache line isn't
40295  used directly
40296          during a firewall call and scan, only by
40297  insert/delete and other
40298          unusual cases
40299       */
40300      int fw_pf;      /* Protocol family          */
40301      int fw_priority;   /* Priority of chosen firewalls
40302       */
40303  };
40304
40305  #ifdef __KERNEL__
40306  extern int register_firewall(int pf, struct firewall_ops
40307  *fw);
40308  extern int unregister_firewall(int pf, struct
```

```
40309  firewall_ops *fw);
40310  extern int call_fw_firewall(int pf, struct device *dev,
40311  void *phdr, void *arg);
40312  extern int call_in_firewall(int pf, struct device *dev,
40313  void *phdr, void *arg);
40314  extern int call_out_firewall(int pf, struct device *dev,
40315  void *phdr, void *arg);
40316  extern void fwchain_init(void);
40317  #endif
40318
40319  #endif
```

usr/src/linux/include/ip_fw.h

```
40320  /*
40321   *   IP firewalling code. This is taken from 4.4BSD.
40322  Please note the
40323   *   copyright message below. As per the GPL it must be
40324  maintained
40325   *   and the licenses thus do not conflict. While this
40326  port is subject
40327   *   to the GPL I also place my modifications under the
40328  original
40329   *   license in recognition of the original copyright.
40330   *
40331   *   Ported from BSD to Linux,
40332   *        Alan Cox 22/Nov/1994.
40333   *   Merged and included the FreeBSD-Current changes at
40334  Ugen's request
40335   *   (but hey it's a lot cleaner now). Ugen would prefer
40336  in some ways
40337   *   we waited for his final product but since Linux
40338  1.2.0 is about to
40339   *   appear it's not practical - Read: It works, it's not
40340  clean but please
40341   *   don't consider it to be his standard of finished
40342  work.
40343   *        Alan.
40344   *
40345   * Fixes:
40346   * Pauline Middelink   :   Added masquerading.
40347   * Jos Vos          :   Separate input  and output
40348  firewall
40349   *                  chains, new "insert" and "append"
40350   *                  commands to replace "add" commands,
40351   *                  add ICMP header to struct ip_fwpkt.
40352   * Jos Vos          :   Add support for matching device
40353  names.
40354   * Willy Konynenberg   :   Add transparent proxying
```

```
40355  support.
40356  *  Jos Vos        :   Add options for input/output
40357  accounting.
40358  *
40359  *  All the real work was done by .....
40360  */
40361
40362  /*
40363  * Copyright (c) 1993 Daniel Boulet
40364  * Copyright (c) 1994 Ugen J.S.Antsilevich
40365  *
40366  * Redistribution and use in source forms, with and
40367  without modification,
40368  * are permitted provided that this entire comment
40369  appears intact.
40370  *
40371  * Redistribution in binary form may occur without any
40372  restrictions.
40373  * Obviously, it would be nice if you gave credit where
40374  credit is due
40375  * but requiring it would be too onerous.
40376  *
40377  * This software is provided "AS IS" without any
40378  warranties of any kind.
40379  */
40380
40381  /*
40382  *  Format of an IP firewall descriptor
40383  *
40384  *  src, dst, src_mask, dst_mask are always stored in
40385  network byte order.
40386  *  flags and num_*_ports are stored in host byte order
40387  (of course).
40388  *  Port numbers are stored in HOST byte order.
40389  */
40390
40391  #ifndef _IP_FW_H
40392  #define _IP_FW_H
40393
40394  #include <linux/icmp.h>
40395  #include <linux/in.h>
40396  #include <linux/ip.h>
40397  #include <linux/tcp.h>
40398  #include <linux/udp.h>
40399  #include <linux/config.h>
40400
40401  struct ip_fw
40402  {
40403      struct ip_fw *fw_next;        /* Next firewall on
40404  chain */
40405      struct in_addr fw_src, fw_dst;    /* Source and
40406  destination IP addr */
40407      struct in_addr fw_smsk, fw_dmsk;   /* Mask for src
40408  and dest IP addr */
40409      struct in_addr fw_via;        /* IP address of
40410  interface "via" */
40411      struct device *fw_viadev;      /* device of
40412  interface "via" */
40413      unsigned short fw_flg;        /* Flags word */
40414      unsigned short fw_nsp, fw_ndp;       /* N'of src
40415  ports and # of dst ports */
40416                      /* in ports array (dst ports
40417  follow */
40418                      /* src ports; max of 10
40419  ports in all; */
40420                      /* count of 0 means match
40421  all ports) */
40422  #define IP_FW_MAX_PORTS 10        /* A reasonable
40423  maximum */
40424      unsigned short fw_pts[IP_FW_MAX_PORTS]; /* Array of
40425  port numbers to match */
40426      unsigned long  fw_pcnt,fw_bcnt;    /* Packet and
40427  byte counters */
40428      unsigned char  fw_tosand, fw_tosxor;   /* Revised
40429  packet priority */
40430      char       fw_vianame[IFNAMSIZ];   /* name of
40431  interface "via" */
40432  };
40433
40434  /*
40435  *  Values for "flags" field .
40436  */
40437
40438  #define IP_FW_F_ALL 0x0000  /* This is a universal
40439  packet firewall*/
40440  #define IP_FW_F_TCP 0x0001  /* This is a TCP packet
40441  firewall      */
40442  #define IP_FW_F_UDP 0x0002  /* This is a UDP packet
40443  firewall      */
40444  #define IP_FW_F_ICMP   0x0003  /* This is a ICMP packet
40445  firewall      */
40446  #define IP_FW_F_KIND   0x0003  /* Mask to isolate
40447  firewall kind      */
40448  #define IP_FW_F_ACCEPT 0x0004  /* This is an accept
40449  firewall (as      *
40450                      *      opposed to a deny firewall)*
```

```
40451                      *                           */
40452  #define IP_FW_F_SRNG    0x0008  /* The first two src
40453  ports are a min  *
40454                       * and max range (stored in host byte *
40455                       * order).                          *
40456                      *                           */
40457  #define IP_FW_F_DRNG    0x0010  /* The first two dst
40458  ports are a min  *
40459                       * and max range (stored in host byte *
40460                       * order).                          *
40461                       * (ports[0] <= port <= ports[1])   *
40462                      *                           */
40463  #define IP_FW_F_PRN 0x0020  /* In verbose mode print
40464  this firewall*/
40465  #define IP_FW_F_BIDIR    0x0040  /* For bidirectional
40466  firewalls        */
40467  #define IP_FW_F_TCPSYN 0x0080  /* For tcp packets-check
40468  SYN only     */
40469  #define IP_FW_F_ICMPRPL 0x0100  /* Send back icmp
40470  unreachable packet  */
40471  #define IP_FW_F_MASQ     0x0200  /* Masquerading
40472      */
40473  #define IP_FW_F_TCPACK 0x0400  /* For tcp-packets match
40474  if ACK is set*/
40475  #define IP_FW_F_REDIR    0x0800  /* Redirect to local
40476  port fw_pts[n]   */
40477  #define IP_FW_F_ACCTIN  0x1000  /* Account incoming
40478  packets only.     */
40479  #define IP_FW_F_ACCTOUT 0x2000  /* Account outgoing
40480  packets only.     */
40481
40482  #define IP_FW_F_MASK    0x3FFF  /* All possible flag
40483  bits mask        */
40484
40485  /*
40486   *  New IP firewall options for [gs]etsockopt at the RAW
40487  IP level.
40488   *  Unlike BSD Linux inherits IP options so you don't
40489  have to use
40490   *  a raw socket for this. Instead we check rights in
40491  the calls.
40492   */
40493
40494  #define IP_FW_BASE_CTL     64  /* base for firewall
40495  socket options */
40496
40497  #define IP_FW_COMMAND       0x00FF  /* mask for command
40498  without chain */
```

```
40499  #define IP_FW_TYPE      0x0300  /* mask for type (chain)
40500  */
40501  #define IP_FW_SHIFT     8   /* shift count for type
40502  (chain) */
40503
40504  #define IP_FW_FWD       0
40505  #define IP_FW_IN        1
40506  #define IP_FW_OUT       2
40507  #define IP_FW_ACCT      3
40508  #define IP_FW_CHAINS      4   /* total number of ip_fw
40509  chains */
40510  #ifdef CONFIG_IP_MASQUERADE_IPAUTOFW
40511  #define IP_FW_AUTOFW      5
40512  #endif
40513
40514  #define IP_FW_INSERT       (IP_FW_BASE_CTL)
40515  #define IP_FW_APPEND       (IP_FW_BASE_CTL+1)
40516  #define IP_FW_DELETE       (IP_FW_BASE_CTL+2)
40517  #define IP_FW_FLUSH     (IP_FW_BASE_CTL+3)
40518  #define IP_FW_ZERO      (IP_FW_BASE_CTL+4)
40519  #define IP_FW_POLICY       (IP_FW_BASE_CTL+5)
40520  #define IP_FW_CHECK     (IP_FW_BASE_CTL+6)
40521  #define IP_FW_MASQ_TIMEOUTS (IP_FW_BASE_CTL+7)
40522
40523  #define IP_FW_INSERT_FWD    (IP_FW_INSERT | (IP_FW_FWD
40524  << IP_FW_SHIFT))
40525  #define IP_FW_APPEND_FWD    (IP_FW_APPEND | (IP_FW_FWD
40526  << IP_FW_SHIFT))
40527  #define IP_FW_DELETE_FWD    (IP_FW_DELETE | (IP_FW_FWD
40528  << IP_FW_SHIFT))
40529  #define IP_FW_FLUSH_FWD     (IP_FW_FLUSH  | (IP_FW_FWD
40530  << IP_FW_SHIFT))
40531  #define IP_FW_ZERO_FWD      (IP_FW_ZERO   | (IP_FW_FWD
40532  << IP_FW_SHIFT))
40533  #define IP_FW_POLICY_FWD    (IP_FW_POLICY | (IP_FW_FWD
40534  << IP_FW_SHIFT))
40535  #define IP_FW_CHECK_FWD     (IP_FW_CHECK  | (IP_FW_FWD
40536  << IP_FW_SHIFT))
40537
40538  #define IP_FW_INSERT_IN     (IP_FW_INSERT | (IP_FW_IN <<
40539  IP_FW_SHIFT))
40540  #define IP_FW_APPEND_IN     (IP_FW_APPEND | (IP_FW_IN <<
40541  IP_FW_SHIFT))
40542  #define IP_FW_DELETE_IN     (IP_FW_DELETE | (IP_FW_IN <<
40543  IP_FW_SHIFT))
40544  #define IP_FW_FLUSH_IN      (IP_FW_FLUSH  | (IP_FW_IN <<
40545  IP_FW_SHIFT))
40546  #define IP_FW_ZERO_IN       (IP_FW_ZERO   | (IP_FW_IN <<
```

```
40547    IP_FW_SHIFT))
40548    #define IP_FW_POLICY_IN      (IP_FW_POLICY | (IP_FW_IN <<
40549    IP_FW_SHIFT))
40550    #define IP_FW_CHECK_IN       (IP_FW_CHECK | (IP_FW_IN <<
40551    IP_FW_SHIFT))
40552
40553    #define IP_FW_INSERT_OUT     (IP_FW_INSERT | (IP_FW_OUT
40554    << IP_FW_SHIFT))
40555    #define IP_FW_APPEND_OUT     (IP_FW_APPEND | (IP_FW_OUT
40556    << IP_FW_SHIFT))
40557    #define IP_FW_DELETE_OUT     (IP_FW_DELETE | (IP_FW_OUT
40558    << IP_FW_SHIFT))
40559    #define IP_FW_FLUSH_OUT      (IP_FW_FLUSH | (IP_FW_OUT
40560    << IP_FW_SHIFT))
40561    #define IP_FW_ZERO_OUT       (IP_FW_ZERO  | (IP_FW_OUT
40562    << IP_FW_SHIFT))
40563    #define IP_FW_POLICY_OUT     (IP_FW_POLICY | (IP_FW_OUT
40564    << IP_FW_SHIFT))
40565    #define IP_FW_CHECK_OUT      (IP_FW_CHECK | (IP_FW_OUT
40566    << IP_FW_SHIFT))
40567
40568    #define IP_ACCT_INSERT       (IP_FW_INSERT | (IP_FW_ACCT
40569    << IP_FW_SHIFT))
40570    #define IP_ACCT_APPEND       (IP_FW_APPEND | (IP_FW_ACCT
40571    << IP_FW_SHIFT))
40572    #define IP_ACCT_DELETE       (IP_FW_DELETE | (IP_FW_ACCT
40573    << IP_FW_SHIFT))
40574    #define IP_ACCT_FLUSH        (IP_FW_FLUSH | (IP_FW_ACCT
40575    << IP_FW_SHIFT))
40576    #define IP_ACCT_ZERO         (IP_FW_ZERO  | (IP_FW_ACCT
40577    << IP_FW_SHIFT))
40578
40579    #ifdef CONFIG_IP_MASQUERADE_IPAUTOFW
40580    #define IP_AUTOFW_ADD        (IP_FW_APPEND |
40581    (IP_FW_AUTOFW << IP_FW_SHIFT))
40582    #define IP_AUTOFW_DEL        (IP_FW_DELETE |
40583    (IP_FW_AUTOFW << IP_FW_SHIFT))
40584    #define IP_AUTOFW_FLUSH      (IP_FW_FLUSH |
40585    (IP_FW_AUTOFW << IP_FW_SHIFT))
40586    #endif /* CONFIG_IP_MASQUERADE_IPAUTOFW */
40587
40588    struct ip_fwpkt
40589    {
40590        struct iphdr fwp_iph;         /* IP header */
40591        union {
40592            struct tcphdr fwp_tcph;     /* TCP header or */
40593            struct udphdr fwp_udph;     /* UDP header */
40594            struct icmphdr fwp_icmph;   /* ICMP header */
40595        } fwp_protoh;
40596        struct in_addr fwp_via;         /* interface address
40597    */
40598        char         fwp_vianame[IFNAMSIZ];   /* interface
40599    name */
40600    };
40601
40602    /*
40603     * timeouts for ip masquerading
40604     */
40605
40606    struct ip_fw_masq;
40607
40608    /*
40609     * Main firewall chains definitions and global var's
40610    definitions.
40611     */
40612
40613    #ifdef __KERNEL__
40614
40615    /* Modes used in the ip_fw_chk() routine. */
40616    #define IP_FW_MODE_FW       0x00    /* kernel firewall
40617    check */
40618    #define IP_FW_MODE_ACCT_IN  0x01    /* accounting
40619    (incoming) */
40620    #define IP_FW_MODE_ACCT_OUT 0x02    /* accounting
40621    (outgoing) */
40622    #define IP_FW_MODE_CHK      0x04    /* check requested
40623    by user */
40624
40625    #ifdef CONFIG_IP_FIREWALL
40626    extern struct ip_fw *ip_fw_in_chain;
40627    extern struct ip_fw *ip_fw_out_chain;
40628    extern struct ip_fw *ip_fw_fwd_chain;
40629    extern int ip_fw_in_policy;
40630    extern int ip_fw_out_policy;
40631    extern int ip_fw_fwd_policy;
40632    extern int ip_fw_ctl(int, void *, int);
40633    #endif
40634    #ifdef CONFIG_IP_MASQUERADE_IPAUTOFW
40635    extern int ip_autofw_ctl(int, void *, int);
40636    #endif
40637    #ifdef CONFIG_IP_ACCT
40638    extern struct ip_fw *ip_acct_chain;
40639    extern int ip_acct_ctl(int, void *, int);
40640    #endif
40641
40642    extern int ip_fw_chk(struct iphdr *, struct device *,
```

```
40643   __u16 *, struct ip_fw *, int, int);
40644   extern void ip_fw_init(void);
40645   #endif /* KERNEL */
40646
40647   #ifdef CONFIG_IP_MASQUERADE_IPAUTOFW
40648   #define IP_FWD_RANGE      1
40649   #define IP_FWD_PORT     2
40650   #define IP_FWD_DIRECT       3
40651
40652   #define IP_AUTOFW_ACTIVE   1
40653   #define IP_AUTOFW_USETIME  2
40654   #define IP_AUTOFW_SECURE   4
40655
40656   struct ip_autofw {
40657       struct ip_autofw * next;
40658       __u16 type;
40659       __u16 low;
40660       __u16 hidden;
40661       __u16 high;
40662       __u16 visible;
40663       __u16 protocol;
40664       __u32 lastcontact;
40665       __u32 where;
40666       __u16 ctlproto;
40667       __u16 ctlport;
40668       __u16 flags;
40669       struct timer_list timer;
40670   };
40671   #endif /* CONFIG_IP_MASQUERADE_IPAUTOFW */
40672   #endif /* _IP_FW_H */
```

usr/src/linux/include/net/checksum.h

```
40673   /*
40674    * INET     An implementation of the TCP/IP protocol
40675   suite for the LINUX
40676    *       operating system.  INET is implemented using the
40677   BSD Socket
40678    *       interface as the means of communication with the
40679   user level.
40680    *
40681    *       Checksumming functions for IP, TCP, UDP and so on
40682    *
40683    * Authors: Jorge Cwik, <jorge@laser.satlink.net>
40684    *       Arnt Gulbrandsen, <agulbra@nvg.unit.no>
40685    *       Borrows very liberally from tcp.c and ip.c, see
40686   those
40687    *       files for more names.
40688    *
```

```
40689    *       This program is free software; you can
40690   redistribute it and/or
40691    *       modify it under the terms of the GNU General
40692   Public License
40693    *       as published by the Free Software Foundation;
40694   either version
40695    *       2 of the License, or (at your option) any later
40696   version.
40697    */
40698   #ifndef _CHECKSUM_H
40699   #define _CHECKSUM_H
40700
40701   #include <asm/byteorder.h>
40702   #include <net/ip.h>
40703   #include <asm/checksum.h>
40704
40705   #endif
```

usr/src/linux/include/net/icmp.h

```
40706   /*
40707    * INET     An implementation of the TCP/IP protocol
40708   suite for the LINUX
40709    *       operating system.  INET is implemented using the
40710   BSD Socket
40711    *       interface as the means of communication with the
40712   user level.
40713    *
40714    *       Definitions for the ICMP module.
40715    *
40716    * Version: @(#)icmp.h  1.0.4   05/13/93
40717    *
40718    * Authors: Ross Biro, <bir7@leland.Stanford.Edu>
40719    *       Fred N. van Kempen, <waltje@uWalt.NL.Mugnet.ORG>
40720    *
40721    *       This program is free software; you can
40722   redistribute it and/or
40723    *       modify it under the terms of the GNU General
40724   Public License
40725    *       as published by the Free Software Foundation;
40726   either version
40727    *       2 of the License, or (at your option) any later
40728   version.
40729    */
40730   #ifndef _ICMP_H
40731   #define _ICMP_H
40732
40733   #include <linux/icmp.h>
40734   #include <linux/skbuff.h>
```

```
40735
40736    #include <net/sock.h>
40737    #include <net/protocol.h>
40738
40739    extern struct icmp_err icmp_err_convert[];
40740    extern struct icmp_mib icmp_statistics;
40741
40742    extern void icmp_send(struct sk_buff *skb_in,  int type,
40743    int code,
40744              unsigned long info, struct device *dev);
40745    extern int  icmp_rcv(struct sk_buff *skb1, struct device
40746    *dev,
40747              struct options *opt, __u32 daddr,
40748              unsigned short len, __u32 saddr,
40749              int redo, struct inet_protocol *protocol);
40750    extern int  icmp_ioctl(struct sock *sk, int cmd,
40751              unsigned long arg);
40752    extern void icmp_init(struct proto_ops *ops);
40753
40754    /* CONFIG_IP_TRANSPARENT_PROXY */
40755    extern int  icmp_chkaddr(struct sk_buff *skb);
40756
40757    #endif  /* _ICMP_H */
```

usr/src/linux/include/net/ip.h

```
40758    /*
40759     * INET     An implementation of the TCP/IP protocol
40760    suite for the LINUX
40761     *        operating system.  INET is implemented using the
40762    BSD Socket
40763     *        interface as the means of communication with the
40764    user level.
40765     *
40766     *        Definitions for the IP module.
40767     *
40768     * Version: @(#)ip.h     1.0.2    05/07/93
40769     *
40770     * Authors: Ross Biro, <bir7@leland.Stanford.Edu>
40771     *        Fred N. van Kempen, <waltje@uWalt.NL.Mugnet.ORG>
40772     *        Alan Cox, <gw4pts@gw4pts.ampr.org>
40773     *
40774     *        This program is free software; you can
40775    redistribute it and/or
40776     *        modify it under the terms of the GNU General
40777    Public License
40778     *        as published by the Free Software Foundation;
40779    either version
40780     *        2 of the License, or (at your option) any later
```

```
40781    version.
40782     */
40783    #ifndef _IP_H
40784    #define _IP_H
40785
40786
40787    #include <linux/config.h>
40788    #include <linux/types.h>
40789    #include <linux/socket.h>
40790    #include <linux/ip.h>
40791    #include <linux/netdevice.h>
40792    #include <net/route.h>
40793
40794    #ifndef _SNMP_H
40795    #include <net/snmp.h>
40796    #endif
40797
40798    #include <net/sock.h>   /* struct sock */
40799
40800    /* IP flags. */
40801    #define IP_CE        0x8000       /* Flag: "Congestion"
40802     */
40803    #define IP_DF        0x4000       /* Flag: "Don't
40804    Fragment"   */
40805    #define IP_MF        0x2000       /* Flag: "More
40806    Fragments"   */
40807    #define IP_OFFSET    0x1FFF       /* "Fragment Offset"
40808    part   */
40809
40810    #define IP_FRAG_TIME   (30 * HZ)       /* fragment
40811    lifetime   */
40812
40813    #ifdef CONFIG_IP_MULTICAST
40814    extern void     ip_mc_dropsocket(struct sock *);
40815    extern void     ip_mc_dropdevice(struct device *dev);
40816    extern int      ip_mc_procinfo(char *, char **, off_t,
40817    int, int);
40818    #endif
40819
40820    #include <net/ip_forward.h>
40821
40822    /* Describe an IP fragment. */
40823    struct ipfrag
40824    {
40825        int     offset;     /* offset of fragment in IP
40826    datagram    */
40827        int     end;        /* last byte of data in datagram
40828        */
```

```
40829        int     len;       /* length of this fragment
40830 */
40831        struct sk_buff  *skb;      /* complete received
40832 fragment     */
40833        unsigned char   *ptr;      /* pointer into real
40834 fragment data  */
40835        struct ipfrag   *next;     /* linked list pointers
40836        */
40837        struct ipfrag   *prev;
40838 };
40839
40840 /*
40841  *  Describe an entry in the "incomplete datagrams"
40842 queue.
40843  */
40844
40845 struct ipq
40846 {
40847        unsigned char   *mac;      /* pointer to MAC header
40848        */
40849        struct iphdr    *iph;      /* pointer to IP header
40850        */
40851        int     len;       /* total length of original
40852 datagram   */
40853        short       ihlen;     /* length of the IP header
40854        */
40855        short       maclen;    /* length of the MAC header
40856        */
40857        struct timer_list timer;   /* when will this queue
40858 expire?   */
40859        struct ipfrag   *fragments; /* linked list of
40860 received fragments   */
40861        struct ipq  *next;     /* linked list pointers
40862        */
40863        struct ipq  *prev;
40864        struct device   *dev;      /* Device - for icmp
40865 replies */
40866 };
40867
40868 /*
40869  *  Functions provided by ip.c
40870  */
40871
40872 extern void     ip_print(const struct iphdr *ip);
40873 extern int      ip_ioctl(struct sock *sk, int cmd,
40874 unsigned long arg);
40875 extern void     ip_route_check(__u32 daddr);
40876 extern int      ip_send(struct rtable *rt, struct
```

```
40877 sk_buff *skb, __u32 daddr, int len, struct device *dev,
40878 __u32 saddr);
40879 extern int      ip_build_header(struct sk_buff *skb,
40880                __u32 saddr,
40881                __u32 daddr,
40882                struct device **dev, int type,
40883                struct options *opt, int len,
40884                int tos,int ttl,struct rtable **rp);
40885 extern int      ip_rcv(struct sk_buff *skb, struct
40886 device *dev,
40887                struct packet_type *pt);
40888 extern int      ip_options_echo(struct options * dopt,
40889 struct options * sopt,
40890                __u32 daddr, __u32 saddr,
40891                struct sk_buff * skb);
40892 extern int      ip_options_compile(struct options * opt,
40893 struct sk_buff * skb);
40894 extern void     ip_send_check(struct iphdr *ip);
40895 extern int      ip_id_count;
40896 extern void     ip_queue_xmit(struct sock *sk,
40897                struct device *dev, struct sk_buff
40898 *skb,
40899                int free);
40900 extern void     ip_init(void);
40901 extern int      ip_build_xmit(struct sock *sk,
40902                void getfrag (const void *,
40903                __u32,
40904                char *,
40905                unsigned int,
40906                unsigned int),
40907                const void *frag,
40908                unsigned short int length,
40909                __u32 daddr,
40910                __u32 saddr,
40911                struct options * opt,
40912                int flags,
40913                int type,
40914                int noblock);
40915
40916 extern struct ip_mib    ip_statistics;
40917
40918 extern int sysctl_ip_dynaddr;
40919 int ip_rewrite_addrs(struct sock *sk, struct sk_buff
40920 *skb, struct device *dev);
40921
40922 /*
40923  *  Functions provided by ip_fragment.o
40924  */
```

```
40925
40926   struct sk_buff *ip_defrag(struct iphdr *iph, struct
40927   sk_buff *skb, struct device *dev);
40928   void ip_fragment(struct sock *sk, struct sk_buff *skb,
40929   struct device *dev, int is_frag);
40930
40931   /*
40932    *  Functions provided by ip_forward.c
40933    */
40934
40935   extern int ip_forward(struct sk_buff *skb, struct device
40936   *dev, int is_frag, __u32 target_addr);
40937   extern int sysctl_ip_forward;
40938
40939
40940   /*
40941    *  Functions provided by ip_options.c
40942    */
40943
40944   extern void ip_options_build(struct sk_buff *skb, struct
40945   options *opt, __u32 daddr, __u32 saddr, int is_frag);
40946   extern int ip_options_echo(struct options *dopt, struct
40947   options *sopt, __u32 daddr, __u32 saddr, struct sk_buff
40948   *skb);
40949   extern void ip_options_fragment(struct sk_buff *skb);
40950   extern int ip_options_compile(struct options *opt,
40951   struct sk_buff *skb);
40952
40953   /*
40954    *  Functions provided by ip_sockglue.c
40955    */
40956
40957   extern int      ip_setsockopt(struct sock *sk, int
40958   level, int optname, char *optval, int optlen);
40959   extern int      ip_getsockopt(struct sock *sk, int
40960   level, int optname, char *optval, int *optlen);
40961
40962   #endif  /* _IP_H */
```

usr/src/linux/include/net/ip_alias.h

```
40963   /*
40964    *       IP_ALIAS (AF_INET) aliasing definitions.
40965    *
40966    *
40967    * Version: @(#)ip_alias.h  0.50   4/20/97
40968    *
40969    * Author:  Juan Jose Ciarlante,
40970    *          <jjciarla@raiz.uncu.edu.ar>
40971    *
40972    *
40973    * This program is free software; you can redistribute
40974   it and/or
40975    * modify it under the terms of the GNU General Public
40976   License
40977    * as published by the Free Software Foundation; either
40978   version
40979    * 2 of the License, or (at your option) any later
40980   version.
40981    *
40982    */
40983
40984   #ifndef _IP_ALIAS_H
40985   #define _IP_ALIAS_H
40986
40987   extern int ip_alias_init(void);
40988   extern int ip_alias_done(void);
40989
40990   #endif  /* _IP_ALIAS_H */
```

usr/src/linux/include/net/ip_forward.h

```
40991   #ifndef __NET_IP_FORWARD_H
40992   #define __NET_IP_FORWARD_H
40993
40994   #define IPFWD_FRAGMENT     1
40995   #define IPFWD_LASTFRAG     2
40996   #define IPFWD_MASQUERADED  4
40997   #define IPFWD_MULTICASTING 8
40998   #define IPFWD_MULTITUNNEL  0x10
40999   #define IPFWD_NOTTLDEC     0x20
41000
41001   #endif
```

usr/src/linux/include/net/netlink.h

```
41002   #ifndef __NET_NETLINK_H
41003   #define __NET_NETLINK_H
41004
41005   #define NET_MAJOR 36       /* Major 18 is reserved for
41006   networking              */
41007   #define MAX_LINKS 11       /* 18,0 for route updates,
41008   18,1 for SKIP, 18,2 debug tap 18,3 PPP reserved  */
41009               /* 4-7 are psi0-psi3  8 is arpd 9 is ppp
41010   */
41011               /* 10 is for IPSEC <John Ioannidis> */
41012   #define MAX_QBYTES 32768   /* Maximum bytes in the
41013   queue                  */
41014
```

```
41015   #include <linux/config.h>
41016
41017   extern int netlink_attach(int unit, int
41018   (*function)(struct sk_buff *skb));
41019   extern int netlink_donothing(struct sk_buff *skb);
41020   extern void netlink_detach(int unit);
41021   extern int netlink_post(int unit, struct sk_buff *skb);
41022   extern int init_netlink(void);
41023
41024   #define NETLINK_ROUTE       0    /* Routing/device hook
41025           */
41026   #define NETLINK_SKIP        1    /* Reserved for ENskip
41027           */
41028   #define NETLINK_USERSOCK    2    /* Reserved for user
41029   mode socket protocols */
41030   #define NETLINK_FIREWALL    3    /* Firewalling hook
41031       */
41032   #define NETLINK_PSI     4   /* PSI devices - 4 to 7 */
41033   #define NETLINK_ARPD        8
41034   #define NETLINK_NET_PPP     9    /* Non tty PPP devices */
41035   #define NETLINK_IPSEC      10    /* IPSEC */
41036
41037   #ifdef CONFIG_RTNETLINK
41038   extern void ip_netlink_msg(unsigned long, __u32, __u32,
41039   __u32, short, short, char *);
41040   #else
41041   #define ip_netlink_msg(a,b,c,d,e,f,g)
41042   #endif
41043   #endif
```

usr/src/linux/include/net/nrcall.h

```
41044   /* Separate to keep compilation of protocols.c simpler */
41045   extern void nr_proto_init(struct net_proto *pro);
```

usr/src/linux/include/net/protocol.h

```
41046   /*
41047    * INET     An implementation of the TCP/IP protocol
41048   suite for the LINUX
41049    *      operating system.  INET is implemented using the
41050   BSD Socket
41051    *      interface as the means of communication with the
41052   user level.
41053    *
41054    *      Definitions for the protocol dispatcher.
41055    *
41056    * Version: @(#)protocol.h  1.0.2   05/07/93
41057    *
41058    * Author:  Fred N. van Kempen,
41059   <waltje@uWalt.NL.Mugnet.ORG>
41060    *
41061    *      This program is free software; you can
41062   redistribute it and/or
41063    *      modify it under the terms of the GNU General
41064   Public License
41065    *      as published by the Free Software Foundation;
41066   either version
41067    *      2 of the License, or (at your option) any later
41068   version.
41069    *
41070    * Changes:
41071    *      Alan Cox    :  Added a name field and a frag
41072   handler
41073    *                      field for later.
41074    *      Alan Cox    :  Cleaned up, and sorted types.
41075    */
41076
41077   #ifndef _PROTOCOL_H
41078   #define _PROTOCOL_H
41079
41080   #define MAX_INET_PROTOS 32      /* Must be a power of 2
41081      */
41082
41083
41084   /* This is used to register protocols. */
41085   struct inet_protocol {
41086      int         (*handler)(struct sk_buff *skb, struct
41087   device *dev,
41088                  struct options *opt, __u32 daddr,
41089                  unsigned short len, __u32 saddr,
41090                  int redo, struct inet_protocol
41091   *protocol);
41092      void        (*err_handler)(int type, int code,
41093   unsigned char *buff,
41094                  __u32 daddr,
41095                  __u32 saddr,
41096                  struct inet_protocol *protocol,
41097   int len);
41098      struct inet_protocol *next;
41099      unsigned char    protocol;
41100      unsigned char    copy:1;
41101      void        *data;
41102      const char      *name;
41103   };
41104
41105
41106   extern struct inet_protocol *inet_protocol_base;
```

```
41107   extern struct inet_protocol
41108   *inet_protos[MAX_INET_PROTOS];
41109
41110
41111   extern void    inet_add_protocol(struct inet_protocol
41112   *prot);
41113   extern int     inet_del_protocol(struct inet_protocol
41114   *prot);
41115
41116
41117   #endif  /* _PROTOCOL_H */
```

usr/src/linux/include/net/raw.h

```
41118   /*
41119    * INET    An implementation of the TCP/IP protocol
41120   suite for the LINUX
41121    *      operating system.  INET is implemented using the
41122   BSD Socket
41123    *      interface as the means of communication with the
41124   user level.
41125    *
41126    *      Definitions for the RAW-IP module.
41127    *
41128    * Version: @(#)raw.h    1.0.2    05/07/93
41129    *
41130    * Author:  Fred N. van Kempen,
41131   <waltje@uWalt.NL.Mugnet.ORG>
41132    *
41133    *      This program is free software; you can
41134   redistribute it and/or
41135    *      modify it under the terms of the GNU General
41136   Public License
41137    *      as published by the Free Software Foundation;
41138   either version
41139    *      2 of the License, or (at your option) any later
41140   version.
41141    */
41142   #ifndef _RAW_H
41143   #define _RAW_H
41144
41145
41146   extern struct proto raw_prot;
41147
41148
41149   extern void raw_err(int type, int code, unsigned char
41150   *header, __u32 daddr,
41151                  __u32 saddr, struct inet_protocol *protocol);
41152   extern int  raw_recvfrom(struct sock *sk, unsigned char
```

```
41153   *to,
41154                   int len, int noblock, unsigned flags,
41155                   struct sockaddr_in *sin, int *addr_len);
41156   extern int  raw_read(struct sock *sk, unsigned char
41157   *buff,
41158                   int len, int noblock, unsigned flags);
41159   extern int  raw_rcv(struct sock *, struct sk_buff *,
41160   struct device *,
41161                   __u32, __u32);
41162
41163   /* Note: v4 ICMP wants to get at this stuff, if you
41164   change the
41165    *      hashing mechanism, make sure you update icmp.c
41166   as well.
41167    */
41168   #define RAWV4_HTABLE_SIZE   MAX_INET_PROTOS
41169   extern struct sock *raw_v4_htable[RAWV4_HTABLE_SIZE];
41170
41171
41172   extern struct sock *raw_v4_lookup(struct sock *sk,
41173   unsigned short num,
41174                   unsigned long raddr, unsigned long
41175   laddr);
41176
41177   #endif  /* _RAW_H */
```

usr/src/linux/include/net/route.h

```
41178   /*
41179    * INET    An implementation of the TCP/IP protocol
41180   suite for the LINUX
41181    *      operating system.  INET  is implemented using
41182   the  BSD Socket
41183    *      interface as the means of communication with the
41184   user level.
41185    *
41186    *      Definitions for the IP router.
41187    *
41188    * Version: @(#)route.h 1.0.4    05/27/93
41189    *
41190    * Authors: Ross Biro, <bir7@leland.Stanford.Edu>
41191    *      Fred N. van Kempen, <waltje@uWalt.NL.Mugnet.ORG>
41192    * Fixes:
41193    *      Alan Cox    :   Reformatted. Added ip_rt_local()
41194    *      Alan Cox    :   Support for TCP parameters.
41195    *      Alexey Kuznetsov:   Major changes for new
41196   routing code.
41197    *              Elliot Poger    :       Added support
41198   for SO_BINDTODEVICE.
```

```
41199    *       Wolfgang Walter,
41200    *       Daniel Ryde,
41201    *       Ingo Molinar   :   fixed bug in ip_rt_put
41202  introduced
41203    *               by SO_BINDTODEVICE support causing
41204    *               a memory leak
41205    *
41206    *  FIXME:
41207    *       Make atomic ops more generic and hide them in
41208  asm/...
41209    *
41210    *       This program is free software; you can
41211  redistribute it and/or
41212    *       modify it under the terms of the GNU General
41213  Public License
41214    *       as published by the Free Software Foundation;
41215  either version
41216    *       2 of the License, or (at your option) any later
41217  version.
41218    */
41219  #ifndef _ROUTE_H
41220  #define _ROUTE_H
41221
41222  #include <linux/config.h>
41223
41224  /*
41225   * 0 - no debugging messages
41226   * 1 - rare events and bugs situations (default)
41227   * 2 - trace mode.
41228   */
41229  #define RT_CACHE_DEBUG      0
41230
41231  #define RT_HASH_DIVISOR        256
41232  #define RT_CACHE_SIZE_MAX      256
41233
41234  #define RTZ_HASH_DIVISOR    256
41235
41236  #if RT_CACHE_DEBUG >= 2
41237  #define RTZ_HASHING_LIMIT 0
41238  #else
41239  #define RTZ_HASHING_LIMIT 16
41240  #endif
41241
41242  /*
41243   * Maximal time to live for unused entry.
41244   */
41245  #define RT_CACHE_TIMEOUT       (HZ*300)
41246
41247  /*
41248   * Prevents LRU trashing, entries considered equivalent,
41249   * if the difference between last use times is less then
41250  this number.
41251   */
41252  #define RT_CACHE_BUBBLE_THRESHOLD   (HZ*5)
41253
41254  #include <linux/route.h>
41255
41256  #ifdef __KERNEL__
41257  #define RTF_LOCAL 0x8000
41258  #endif
41259
41260  struct rtable
41261  {
41262      struct rtable      *rt_next;
41263      __u32              rt_dst;
41264      __u32              rt_src;
41265      __u32              rt_gateway;
41266      atomic_t           rt_refcnt;
41267      atomic_t           rt_use;
41268      unsigned long      rt_window;
41269      atomic_t           rt_lastuse;
41270      struct hh_cache    *rt_hh;
41271      struct device      *rt_dev;
41272      unsigned short     rt_flags;
41273      unsigned short     rt_mtu;
41274      unsigned short     rt_irtt;
41275      unsigned char      rt_tos;
41276  };
41277
41278  extern void     ip_rt_flush(struct device *dev);
41279  extern void     ip_rt_update(int event, struct device
41280  *dev);
41281  extern void     ip_rt_redirect(__u32 src, __u32 dst,
41282  __u32 gw, struct device *dev);
41283  extern struct rtable    *ip_rt_slow_route(__u32 daddr,
41284  int local, struct device *dev);
41285  extern struct device    *ip_rt_dev(__u32 addr);
41286  extern int      rt_get_info(char * buffer, char **start,
41287  off_t offset, int length, int dummy);
41288  extern int      rt_cache_get_info(char *buffer, char
41289  **start, off_t offset, int length, int dummy);
41290  extern int      ip_rt_ioctl(unsigned int cmd, void *arg);
41291  extern int      ip_rt_new(struct rtentry *rt);
41292  extern int      ip_rt_kill(struct rtentry *rt);
41293  extern void     ip_rt_check_expire(void);
41294  extern void     ip_rt_advice(struct rtable **rp, int
```

p 492 (near line 41260)

```
41295    advice);
41296
41297    extern void     ip_rt_run_bh(void);
41298    extern atomic_t        ip_rt_lock;
41299    extern unsigned    ip_rt_bh_mask;
41300    extern struct rtable
41301    *ip_rt_hash_table[RT_HASH_DIVISOR];
41302    extern void     rt_free(struct rtable * rt);
41303
41304    extern __inline__ void ip_rt_fast_lock(void)
41305    {
41306        atomic_inc(&ip_rt_lock);
41307    }
41308
41309    extern __inline__ void ip_rt_fast_unlock(void)
41310    {
41311        atomic_dec(&ip_rt_lock);
41312    }
41313
41314    extern __inline__ void ip_rt_unlock(void)
41315    {
41316        if (atomic_dec_and_test(&ip_rt_lock) &&
41317    ip_rt_bh_mask)
41318            ip_rt_run_bh();
41319    }
41320
41321    extern __inline__ unsigned ip_rt_hash_code(__u32 addr)
41322    {
41323        unsigned tmp = addr + (addr>>16);
41324        return (tmp + (tmp>>8)) & 0xFF;
41325    }
41326
41327
41328    extern __inline__ void ip_rt_put(struct rtable * rt)
41329    #ifndef MODULE
41330    {
41331        if (rt)
41332            atomic_dec(&rt->rt_refcnt);
41333
41334        /* If this rtable entry is not in the cache, we'd
41335    better free it once the
41336         * refcnt goes to zero, because nobody else will...
41337    */
41338        if ( rt && (rt->rt_flags & RTF_NOTCACHED) &&
41339    (!rt->rt_refcnt) )
41340            rt_free(rt);
41341    }
41342    #else
```

```
41343    ;
41344    #endif
41345
41346    #ifdef CONFIG_KERNELD
41347    extern struct rtable * ip_rt_route(__u32 daddr, int
41348    local, struct device *dev);
41349    #else
41350    extern __inline__ struct rtable * ip_rt_route(__u32
41351    daddr, int local, struct device *dev)
41352    #ifndef MODULE
41353    {
41354        struct rtable * rth;
41355
41356        ip_rt_fast_lock();
41357
41358        for
41359    (rth=ip_rt_hash_table[ip_rt_hash_code(daddr)^local];
41360    rth; rth=rth->rt_next)
41361        {
41362            /* If an interface is specified, make sure this
41363    route points to it. */
41364            if ( (rth->rt_dst == daddr) && ((dev==NULL) ||
41365    (dev==rth->rt_dev)) )
41366            {
41367                rth->rt_lastuse = jiffies;
41368                atomic_inc(&rth->rt_use);
41369                atomic_inc(&rth->rt_refcnt);
41370                ip_rt_unlock();
41371                return rth;
41372            }
41373        }
41374        return ip_rt_slow_route (daddr, local, dev);
41375    }
41376    #else
41377    ;
41378    #endif
41379    #endif
41380
41381    extern __inline__ struct rtable * ip_check_route(struct
41382    rtable ** rp, __u32 daddr,
41383                        int local, struct device *dev)
41384    {
41385        struct rtable * rt = *rp;
41386
41387        if (!rt || rt->rt_dst != daddr ||
41388    !(rt->rt_flags&RTF_UP) || (dev!=NULL)
41389            || ((local==1)^((rt->rt_flags&RTF_LOCAL) != 0)))
```

```
41390        {
41391            ip_rt_put(rt);
41392            rt = ip_rt_route(daddr, local, dev);
41393            *rp = rt;
41394        }
41395        return rt;
41396 }
41397
41398
41399 #endif  /* _ROUTE_H */
```

usr/src/linux/include/net/snmp.h

```
41400 /*
41401  *
41402  *      SNMP MIB entries for the IP subsystem.
41403  *
41404  *      Alan Cox <gw4pts@gw4pts.ampr.org>
41405  *
41406  *      We don't chose to implement SNMP in the kernel
41407 (this would
41408  *      be silly as SNMP is a pain in the backside in
41409 places). We do
41410  *      however need to collect the MIB statistics and
41411 export them
41412  *      out of /proc (eventually)
41413  *
41414  *      This program is free software; you can
41415 redistribute it and/or
41416  *      modify it under the terms of the GNU General
41417 Public License
41418  *      as published by the Free Software Foundation;
41419 either version
41420  *      2 of the License, or (at your option) any later
41421 version.
41422  *
41423  */
41424
41425 #ifndef _SNMP_H
41426 #define _SNMP_H
41427
41428 /*
41429  * We use all unsigned longs. Linux will soon be so
41430 reliable that even these
41431  * will rapidly get too small 8-). Seriously consider
41432 the IpInReceives count
41433  * on the 20Gb/s + networks people expect in a few
41434 years time!
41435  */
```

```
41436
41437 struct ip_mib
41438 {
41439        unsigned long   IpForwarding;
41440        unsigned long   IpDefaultTTL;
41441        unsigned long   IpInReceives;
41442        unsigned long   IpInHdrErrors;
41443        unsigned long   IpInAddrErrors;
41444        unsigned long   IpForwDatagrams;
41445        unsigned long   IpInUnknownProtos;
41446        unsigned long   IpInDiscards;
41447        unsigned long   IpInDelivers;
41448        unsigned long   IpOutRequests;
41449        unsigned long   IpOutDiscards;
41450        unsigned long   IpOutNoRoutes;
41451        unsigned long   IpReasmTimeout;
41452        unsigned long   IpReasmReqds;
41453        unsigned long   IpReasmOKs;
41454        unsigned long   IpReasmFails;
41455        unsigned long   IpFragOKs;
41456        unsigned long   IpFragFails;
41457        unsigned long   IpFragCreates;
41458 };
41459
41460
41461 struct icmp_mib
41462 {
41463        unsigned long   IcmpInMsgs;
41464        unsigned long   IcmpInErrors;
41465        unsigned long   IcmpInDestUnreachs;
41466        unsigned long   IcmpInTimeExcds;
41467        unsigned long   IcmpInParmProbs;
41468        unsigned long   IcmpInSrcQuenchs;
41469        unsigned long   IcmpInRedirects;
41470        unsigned long   IcmpInEchos;
41471        unsigned long   IcmpInEchoReps;
41472        unsigned long   IcmpInTimestamps;
41473        unsigned long   IcmpInTimestampReps;
41474        unsigned long   IcmpInAddrMasks;
41475        unsigned long   IcmpInAddrMaskReps;
41476        unsigned long   IcmpOutMsgs;
41477        unsigned long   IcmpOutErrors;
41478        unsigned long   IcmpOutDestUnreachs;
41479        unsigned long   IcmpOutTimeExcds;
41480        unsigned long   IcmpOutParmProbs;
41481        unsigned long   IcmpOutSrcQuenchs;
41482        unsigned long   IcmpOutRedirects;
41483        unsigned long   IcmpOutEchos;
```

```
41484        unsigned long    IcmpOutEchoReps;
41485        unsigned long    IcmpOutTimestamps;
41486        unsigned long    IcmpOutTimestampReps;
41487        unsigned long    IcmpOutAddrMasks;
41488        unsigned long    IcmpOutAddrMaskReps;
41489   };
41490
41491   struct tcp_mib
41492   {
41493        unsigned long    TcpRtoAlgorithm;
41494        unsigned long    TcpRtoMin;
41495        unsigned long    TcpRtoMax;
41496        unsigned long    TcpMaxConn;
41497        unsigned long    TcpActiveOpens;
41498        unsigned long    TcpPassiveOpens;
41499        unsigned long    TcpAttemptFails;
41500        unsigned long    TcpEstabResets;
41501        unsigned long    TcpCurrEstab;
41502        unsigned long    TcpInSegs;
41503        unsigned long    TcpOutSegs;
41504        unsigned long    TcpRetransSegs;
41505   };
41506
41507   struct udp_mib
41508   {
41509        unsigned long    UdpInDatagrams;
41510        unsigned long    UdpNoPorts;
41511        unsigned long    UdpInErrors;
41512        unsigned long    UdpOutDatagrams;
41513   };
41514
41515
41516   #endif
```

usr/src/linux/include/net/sock.h

```
41517   /*
41518    * INET      An implementation of the TCP/IP protocol
41519   suite for the LINUX
41520    *        operating system.  INET is implemented using the
41521   BSD Socket
41522    *        interface as the means of communication with the
41523   user level.
41524    *
41525    *        Definitions for the AF_INET socket handler.
41526    *
41527    * Version: @(#)sock.h  1.0.4   05/13/93
41528    *
41529    * Authors: Ross Biro, <bir7@leland.Stanford.Edu>
41530    *        Fred N. van Kempen, <waltje@uWalt.NL.Mugnet.ORG>
41531    *        Corey Minyard <wf-rch!minyard@relay.EU.net>
41532    *        Florian La Roche <flla@stud.uni-sb.de>
41533    *
41534    * Fixes:
41535    *        Alan Cox    :  Volatiles in skbuff pointers. See
41536    *                       skbuff comments. May be overdone,
41537    *                       better to prove they can be removed
41538    *                       than the reverse.
41539    *        Alan Cox    :  Added a zapped field for tcp to
41540   note
41541    *                       a socket is reset and must stay shut
41542   up
41543    *        Alan Cox    :  New fields for options
41544    * Pauline Middelink   :   identd support
41545    *        Alan Cox    :  Eliminate low level recv/recvfrom
41546    *        David S. Miller :  New socket lookup
41547   architecture for ISS.
41548    *            Elliot Poger    :       New field for
41549   SO_BINDTODEVICE option.
41550    *
41551    *        This program is free software; you can
41552   redistribute it and/or
41553    *        modify it under the terms of the GNU General
41554   Public License
41555    *        as published by the Free Software Foundation;
41556   either version
41557    *        2 of the License, or (at your option) any later
41558   version.
41559    */
41560   #ifndef _SOCK_H
41561   #define _SOCK_H
41562
41563   #include <linux/timer.h>
41564   #include <linux/ip.h>        /* struct options */
41565   #include <linux/in.h>        /* struct sockaddr_in */
41566   #include <linux/tcp.h>       /* struct tcphdr */
41567   #include <linux/config.h>
41568
41569   #include <linux/netdevice.h>
41570   #include <linux/skbuff.h>    /* struct sk_buff */
41571   #include <net/protocol.h>        /* struct inet_protocol
41572   */
41573   #ifdef CONFIG_AX25
41574   #include <net/ax25.h>
41575   #ifdef CONFIG_NETROM
41576   #include <net/netrom.h>
41577   #endif
```

```
41578    #endif
41579
41580    #if defined(CONFIG_IPX) || defined(CONFIG_IPX_MODULE)
41581    #include <net/ipx.h>
41582    #endif
41583
41584    #if defined(CONFIG_ATALK) || defined(CONFIG_ATALK_MODULE)
41585    #include <linux/atalk.h>
41586    #endif
41587
41588    #include <linux/igmp.h>
41589
41590    #include <asm/atomic.h>
41591
41592    /*
41593     *   The AF_UNIX specific socket options
41594     */
41595
41596    struct unix_opt
41597    {
41598        int             family;
41599        char *          name;
41600        int             locks;
41601        struct inode *      inode;
41602        struct semaphore    readsem;
41603        struct sock *       other;
41604        int             marksweep;
41605    #define MARKED          1
41606        int         inflight;
41607    };
41608
41609    /*
41610     *   IP packet socket options
41611     */
41612
41613    struct inet_packet_opt
41614    {
41615        struct notifier_block   notifier;       /* Used when
41616    bound */
41617        struct device       *bound_dev;
41618        unsigned long       dev_stamp;
41619        struct packet_type  *prot_hook;
41620        char            device_name[15];
41621    };
41622
41623    /*
41624     *   Once the IPX ncpd patches are in these are going
41625    into protinfo
```

```
41626     */
41627
41628    #if defined(CONFIG_IPX) || defined(CONFIG_IPX_MODULE)
41629    struct ipx_opt
41630    {
41631        ipx_address     dest_addr;
41632        ipx_interface       *intrfc;
41633        unsigned short      port;
41634    #ifdef CONFIG_IPX_INTERN
41635        unsigned char           node[IPX_NODE_LEN];
41636    #endif
41637        unsigned short      type;
41638    /*
41639     * To handle asynchronous messages from the NetWare
41640    server, we have to
41641     * know the connection this socket belongs to.
41642     */
41643        struct ncp_server       *ncp_server;
41644    /*
41645     * To handle special ncp connection-handling sockets for
41646    mars_nwe,
41647     * the connection number must be stored in the socket.
41648     */
41649        unsigned short      ipx_ncp_conn;
41650    };
41651    #endif
41652
41653    #ifdef CONFIG_NUTCP
41654    struct tcp_opt
41655    {
41656    /*
41657     * RFC793 variables by their proper names. This means
41658    you can
41659     * read the code and the spec side by side (and laugh
41660    ...)
41661     * See RFC793 and RFC1122. The RFC writes these in
41662    capitals.
41663     */
41664        __u32   rcv_nxt;    /* What we want to receive next
41665        */
41666        __u32   rcv_up;     /* The urgent point (may not be
41667    valid)  */
41668        __u32   rcv_wnd;    /* Current receiver window
41669    */
41670        __u32   snd_nxt;    /* Next sequence we send
41671    */
41672        __u32   snd_una;    /* First byte we want an ack for
41673        */
```

```
41674        __u32   snd_up;      /* Outgoing urgent pointer
41675   */
41676        __u32   snd_wl1;     /* Sequence for window update
41677     */
41678        __u32   snd_wl2;     /* Ack sequence for update
41679   */
41680   /*
41681    *  Slow start and congestion control (see also Nagle,
41682   and Karn & Partridge)
41683    */
41684        __u32   snd_cwnd;    /* Sending congestion window
41685     */
41686        __u32   snd_ssthresh;  /* Slow start size threshold
41687        */
41688   /*
41689    *  Timers used by the TCP protocol layer
41690    */
41691      struct timer_list   delack_timer;      /* Ack delay
41692     */
41693      struct timer_list   idle_timer;      /* Idle watch
41694   */
41695      struct timer_list   completion_timer;    /* Up/Down
41696   timer */
41697      struct timer_list   probe_timer;      /* Probes
41698   */
41699      struct timer_list   retransmit_timer;    /* Resend
41700   (no ack) */
41701   };
41702   #endif
41703
41704   /*
41705    * This structure really needs to be cleaned up.
41706    * Most of it is for TCP, and not used by any of
41707    * the other protocols.
41708    */
41709   struct sock
41710   {
41711      /* This must be first. */
41712      struct sock     *sklist_next;
41713      struct sock     *sklist_prev;
41714
41715      struct options     *opt;
41716      atomic_t     wmem_alloc;
41717      atomic_t     rmem_alloc;
41718      unsigned long     allocation;    /* Allocation
41719   mode */
41720        __u32     write_seq;
41721        __u32     sent_seq;
41722        __u32        acked_seq;
41723        __u32        copied_seq;
41724        __u32        rcv_ack_seq;
41725      unsigned short     rcv_ack_cnt;      /* count of
41726   same ack */
41727        __u32        window_seq;
41728        __u32        fin_seq;
41729        __u32        urg_seq;
41730        __u32        urg_data;
41731        __u32        syn_seq;
41732      int        users;        /* user count */
41733      /*
41734       *    Not all are volatile, but some are, so we
41735       *    might as well say they all are.
41736       */
41737      volatile char        dead,
41738            urginline,
41739            intr,
41740            blog,
41741            done,
41742            reuse,
41743            keepopen,
41744            linger,
41745            delay_acks,
41746            destroy,
41747            ack_timed,
41748            no_check,
41749            zapped, /* In ax25 & ipx means not
41750   linked */
41751            broadcast,
41752            nonagle,
41753            bsdism;
41754      struct device        * bound_device;
41755      unsigned long        lingertime;
41756      int        proc;
41757
41758      struct sock     *next;
41759      struct sock     **pprev;
41760      struct sock     *bind_next;
41761      struct sock     **bind_pprev;
41762      struct sock     *pair;
41763      int        hashent;
41764      struct sock     *prev;
41765      struct sk_buff     * volatile send_head;
41766      struct sk_buff     * volatile send_next;
41767      struct sk_buff     * volatile send_tail;
41768      struct sk_buff_head back_log;
41769      struct sk_buff        *partial;
```

```
41770        struct timer_list    partial_timer;
41771        long              retransmits;
41772        struct sk_buff_head write_queue,
41773                    receive_queue;
41774        struct proto        *prot;
41775        struct wait_queue   **sleep;
41776        __u32            daddr;
41777        __u32            saddr;      /* Sending source */
41778        __u32            rcv_saddr;  /* Bound address */
41779        unsigned short      max_unacked;
41780        unsigned short      window;
41781        __u32                    lastwin_seq;   /* sequence
41782  number when we last updated the window we offer */
41783        __u32            high_seq;   /* sequence number when
41784  we did current fast retransmit */
41785        volatile unsigned long  ato;        /* ack
41786  timeout */
41787        volatile unsigned long  lrcvtime;      /* jiffies
41788  at last data rcv */
41789        volatile unsigned long  idletime;      /* jiffies
41790  at last rcv */
41791        unsigned int         bytes_rcv;
41792  /*
41793   *  mss is min(mtu, max_window)
41794   */
41795        unsigned short       mtu;        /* mss negotiated in
41796  the syn's */
41797        volatile unsigned short mss;        /* current eff.
41798  mss - can change */
41799        volatile unsigned short user_mss;   /* mss requested
41800  by user in ioctl */
41801        volatile unsigned short max_window;
41802        unsigned long       window_clamp;
41803        unsigned int         ssthresh;
41804        unsigned short       num;
41805        volatile unsigned short cong_window;
41806        volatile unsigned short cong_count;
41807        volatile unsigned short packets_out;
41808        volatile unsigned short shutdown;
41809        volatile unsigned long  rtt;
41810        volatile unsigned long  mdev;
41811        volatile unsigned long  rto;
41812
41813  /*
41814   *  currently backoff isn't used, but I'm maintaining it
41815  in case
41816   *  we want to go back to a backoff formula that needs it
41817   */
41818
41819        volatile unsigned short backoff;
41820        int          err, err_soft;  /* Soft holds errors
41821  that don't
41822                          cause failure but are the
41823  cause
41824                          of a persistent failure not
41825  just
41826                          'timed out' */
41827        unsigned char        protocol;
41828        volatile unsigned char  state;
41829        unsigned short       ack_backlog;
41830        unsigned char        priority;
41831        unsigned char        debug;
41832        int          rcvbuf;
41833        int          sndbuf;
41834        unsigned short       type;
41835        unsigned char        localroute; /* Route locally
41836  only */
41837  #ifdef CONFIG_AX25
41838        ax25_cb          *ax25;
41839  #ifdef CONFIG_NETROM
41840        nr_cb            *nr;
41841  #endif
41842  #endif
41843
41844  /*
41845   *  This is where all the private (optional) areas that
41846  don't
41847   *  overlap will eventually live.
41848   */
41849
41850        union
41851        {
41852            struct unix_opt af_unix;
41853  #if defined(CONFIG_ATALK) || defined(CONFIG_ATALK_MODULE)
41854            struct atalk_sock   af_at;
41855  #endif
41856  #if defined(CONFIG_IPX) || defined(CONFIG_IPX_MODULE)
41857            struct ipx_opt      af_ipx;
41858  #endif
41859  #ifdef CONFIG_INET
41860            struct inet_packet_opt  af_packet;
41861  #ifdef CONFIG_NUTCP
41862            struct tcp_opt      af_tcp;
41863  #endif
41864  #endif
41865        } protinfo;
```

```
41866
41867    /*
41868     *   IP 'private area' or will be eventually
41869     */
41870        int         ip_ttl;          /* TTL setting */
41871        int         ip_tos;          /* TOS */
41872        struct tcphdr       dummy_th;
41873        struct timer_list   keepalive_timer;    /* TCP
41874    keepalive hack */
41875        struct timer_list   retransmit_timer;   /* TCP
41876    retransmit timer */
41877        struct timer_list   delack_timer;       /* TCP
41878    delayed ack timer */
41879        int         ip_xmit_timeout;    /* Why the timeout
41880    is running */
41881        struct rtable       *ip_route_cache;    /* Cached
41882    output route */
41883        unsigned char       ip_hdrincl;     /* Include
41884    headers ? */
41885    #ifdef CONFIG_IP_MULTICAST
41886        int         ip_mc_ttl;        /* Multicasting TTL */
41887        int         ip_mc_loop;       /* Loopback */
41888        char                ip_mc_name[MAX_ADDR_LEN];/*
41889    Multicast device name */
41890        struct ip_mc_socklist   *ip_mc_list;        /* Group
41891    array */
41892    #endif
41893
41894    /*
41895     * This part is used for the timeout functions
41896    (timer.c).
41897     */
41898
41899        int         timeout;     /* What are we waiting for?
41900    */
41901        struct timer_list   timer;       /* This is the
41902    TIME_WAIT/receive timer
41903                        * when we are doing IP
41904                        */
41905        struct timeval      stamp;
41906
41907     /*
41908      * Identd
41909      */
41910
41911        struct socket       *socket;
41912
41913      /*
41914      *       Callbacks
41915      */
41916
41917        void            (*state_change)(struct sock *sk);
41918        void            (*data_ready)(struct sock *sk,int
41919    bytes);
41920        void            (*write_space)(struct sock *sk);
41921        void            (*error_report)(struct sock *sk);
41922
41923      /*
41924      *       Moved solely for 2.0 to keep binary module
41925    compatibility stuff straight.
41926      */
41927
41928        unsigned short      max_ack_backlog;
41929    };
41930
41931    /*
41932     * IP protocol blocks we attach to sockets.
41933     */
41934
41935    struct proto
41936    {
41937        /* These must be first. */
41938        struct sock     *sklist_next;
41939        struct sock     *sklist_prev;
41940
41941        void            (*close)(struct sock *sk, unsigned
41942    long timeout);
41943        int         (*build_header)(struct sk_buff *skb,
41944                    __u32 saddr,
41945                    __u32 daddr,
41946                    struct device **dev, int type,
41947                    struct options *opt, int len,
41948                    int tos, int ttl, struct rtable **
41949    rp);
41950        int         (*connect)(struct sock *sk,
41951                    struct sockaddr_in *usin, int
41952    addr_len);
41953        struct sock *       (*accept) (struct sock *sk, int
41954    flags);
41955        void            (*queue_xmit)(struct sock *sk,
41956                    struct device *dev, struct
41957    sk_buff *skb,
41958                    int free);
41959        void            (*retransmit)(struct sock *sk, int
41960    all);
41961        void            (*write_wakeup)(struct sock *sk);
```

```
41962     void          (*read_wakeup)(struct sock *sk);
41963     int           (*rcv)(struct sk_buff *buff, struct
41964 device *dev,
41965                      struct options *opt, __u32 daddr,
41966                      unsigned short len, __u32 saddr,
41967                      int redo, struct inet_protocol
41968 *protocol);
41969     int           (*select)(struct sock *sk, int which,
41970                      select_table *wait);
41971     int           (*ioctl)(struct sock *sk, int cmd,
41972                      unsigned long arg);
41973     int           (*init)(struct sock *sk);
41974     void          (*shutdown)(struct sock *sk, int
41975 how);
41976     int           (*setsockopt)(struct sock *sk, int
41977 level, int optname,
41978                      char *optval, int optlen);
41979     int           (*getsockopt)(struct sock *sk, int
41980 level, int optname,
41981                      char *optval, int *option);
41982     int           (*sendmsg)(struct sock *sk, struct
41983 msghdr *msg, int len,
41984                      int noblock, int flags);
41985     int           (*recvmsg)(struct sock *sk, struct
41986 msghdr *msg, int len,
41987                      int noblock, int flags, int
41988 *addr_len);
41989     int           (*bind)(struct sock *sk, struct sockaddr
41990 *uaddr, int addr_len);
41991
41992     /* Keeping track of sk's, looking them up, and port
41993 selection methods. */
41994     void          (*hash)(struct sock *sk);
41995     void          (*unhash)(struct sock *sk);
41996     void          (*rehash)(struct sock *sk);
41997     unsigned short    (*good_socknum)(void);
41998     int           (*verify_bind)(struct sock *sk, unsigned
41999 short snum);
42000
42001     unsigned short    max_header;
42002     unsigned long     retransmits;
42003     char          name[32];
42004     int           inuse, highestinuse;
42005 };
42006
42007 #define TIME_WRITE    1
42008 #define TIME_CLOSE    2
42009 #define TIME_KEEPOPEN    3
42010 #define TIME_DESTROY     4
42011 #define TIME_DONE    5    /* Used to absorb those last few
42012 packets */
42013 #define TIME_PROBE0 6
42014
42015 /*
42016  * About 10 seconds
42017  */
42018
42019 #define SOCK_DESTROY_TIME (10*HZ)
42020
42021 /*
42022  * Sockets 0-1023 can't be bound to unless you are
42023 superuser
42024  */
42025
42026 #define PROT_SOCK    1024
42027
42028 #define SHUTDOWN_MASK    3
42029 #define RCV_SHUTDOWN    1
42030 #define SEND_SHUTDOWN    2
42031
42032 /* Per-protocol hash table implementations use this to
42033 make sure
42034  * nothing changes.
42035  */
42036 #define SOCKHASH_LOCK()    start_bh_atomic()
42037 #define SOCKHASH_UNLOCK()    end_bh_atomic()
42038
42039 /* Some things in the kernel just want to get at a
42040 protocols
42041  * entire socket list commensurate, thus...
42042  */
42043 static __inline__ void add_to_prot_sklist(struct sock
42044 *sk)
42045 {
42046     SOCKHASH_LOCK();
42047     if(!sk->sklist_next) {
42048         struct proto *p = sk->prot;
42049
42050         sk->sklist_prev = (struct sock *) p;
42051         sk->sklist_next = p->sklist_next;
42052         p->sklist_next->sklist_prev = sk;
42053         p->sklist_next = sk;
42054
42055         /* Charge the protocol. */
42056         sk->prot->inuse += 1;
42057         if(sk->prot->highestinuse < sk->prot->inuse)
```

```
42058            sk->prot->highestinuse = sk->prot->inuse;
42059        }
42060        SOCKHASH_UNLOCK();
42061    }
42062
42063    static __inline__ void del_from_prot_sklist(struct sock
42064    *sk)
42065    {
42066        SOCKHASH_LOCK();
42067        if(sk->sklist_next) {
42068            sk->sklist_next->sklist_prev = sk->sklist_prev;
42069            sk->sklist_prev->sklist_next = sk->sklist_next;
42070            sk->sklist_next = NULL;
42071            sk->prot->inuse--;
42072        }
42073        SOCKHASH_UNLOCK();
42074    }
42075
42076    /*
42077     * Used by processes to "lock" a socket state, so that
42078     * interrupts and bottom half handlers won't change it
42079     * from under us. It essentially blocks any incoming
42080     * packets, so that we won't get any new data or any
42081     * packets that change the state of the socket.
42082     *
42083     * Note the 'barrier()' calls: gcc may not move a lock
42084     * "downwards" or a unlock "upwards" when optimizing.
42085     */
42086    extern void __release_sock(struct sock *sk);
42087
42088    static inline void lock_sock(struct sock *sk)
42089    {
42090    #if 0
42091    /* debugging code: the test isn't even 100% correct, but
42092    it can catch bugs */
42093    /* Note that a double lock is ok in theory - it's just
42094    _usually_ a bug */
42095        if (sk->users) {
42096            __label__ here;
42097            printk("double lock on socket at %p\n", &&here);
42098    here:
42099        }
42100    #endif
42101        sk->users++;
42102        barrier();
42103    }
42104
42105    static inline void release_sock(struct sock *sk)
42106    {
42107        barrier();
42108    #if 0
42109    /* debugging code: remove me when ok */
42110        if (sk->users == 0) {
42111            __label__ here;
42112            sk->users = 1;
42113            printk("trying to unlock unlocked socket at
42114    %p\n", &&here);
42115    here:
42116        }
42117    #endif
42118        if ((sk->users = sk->users-1) == 0)
42119            __release_sock(sk);
42120    }
42121
42122
42123    extern struct sock *        sk_alloc(int priority);
42124    extern void         sk_free(struct sock *sk);
42125    extern void         destroy_sock(struct sock *sk);
42126
42127    extern struct sk_buff       *sock_wmalloc(struct sock
42128    *sk,
42129                        unsigned long size, int force,
42130                        int priority);
42131    extern struct sk_buff       *sock_rmalloc(struct sock
42132    *sk,
42133                        unsigned long size, int force,
42134                        int priority);
42135    extern void         sock_wfree(struct sock *sk,
42136                struct sk_buff *skb);
42137    extern void         sock_rfree(struct sock *sk,
42138                struct sk_buff *skb);
42139    extern unsigned long        sock_rspace(struct sock *sk);
42140    extern unsigned long        sock_wspace(struct sock *sk);
42141
42142    extern int          sock_setsockopt(struct sock *sk, int
42143    level,
42144                    int op, char *optval,
42145                    int optlen);
42146
42147    extern int          sock_getsockopt(struct sock *sk, int
42148    level,
42149                    int op, char *optval,
42150                    int *optlen);
42151    extern struct sk_buff       *sock_alloc_send_skb(struct
42152    sock *skb,
42153                        unsigned long size,
```

```
42154                                   unsigned long fallback,
42155                                   int noblock,
42156                                   int *errcode);
42157
42158   /*
42159    *  Queue a received datagram if it will fit. Stream and
42160   sequenced    .
42161    *  protocols can't normally use this as they need to
42162   fit buffers in
42163    *  and play with them.
42164    *
42165    *  Inlined as it's very short and called for pretty
42166   much every
42167    *  packet ever received.
42168    */
42169
42170   extern __inline__ int sock_queue_rcv_skb(struct sock
42171   *sk, struct sk_buff *skb)
42172   {
42173       if (sk->rmem_alloc + skb->truesize >= sk->rcvbuf)
42174           return -ENOMEM;
42175       atomic_add(skb->truesize, &sk->rmem_alloc);
42176       skb->sk=sk;
42177       skb_queue_tail(&sk->receive_queue,skb);
42178       if (!sk->dead)
42179           sk->data_ready(sk,skb->len);
42180       return 0;
42181   }
42182
42183   extern __inline__ int __sock_queue_rcv_skb(struct sock
42184   *sk, struct sk_buff *skb)
42185   {
42186       if (sk->rmem_alloc + skb->truesize >= sk->rcvbuf)
42187           return -ENOMEM;
42188       atomic_add(skb->truesize, &sk->rmem_alloc);
42189       skb->sk=sk;
42190       __skb_queue_tail(&sk->receive_queue,skb);
42191       if (!sk->dead)
42192           sk->data_ready(sk,skb->len);
42193       return 0;
42194   }
42195
42196   /*
42197    *  Recover an error report and clear atomically
42198    */
42199
42200   extern __inline__ int sock_error(struct sock *sk)
42201   {
```

```
42202       int err=xchg(&sk->err,0);
42203       return -err;
42204   }
42205
42206   /*
42207    *  Declarations from timer.c
42208    */
42209
42210   extern struct sock *timer_base;
42211
42212   extern void delete_timer (struct sock *);
42213   extern void reset_timer (struct sock *, int, unsigned
42214   long);
42215   extern void net_timer (unsigned long);
42216
42217
42218   /*
42219    *  Enable debug/info messages
42220    */
42221
42222   #define NETDEBUG(x) do { } while (0)
42223
42224   #endif  /* _SOCK_H */
```

usr/src/linux/include/net/tcp.h

```
42225   /*
42226    * INET      An implementation of the TCP/IP protocol
42227   suite for the LINUX
42228    *      operating system.  INET is implemented using the
42229   BSD Socket
42230    *      interface as the means of communication with the
42231   user level.
42232    *
42233    *      Definitions for the TCP module.
42234    *
42235    * Version: @(#)tcp.h   1.0.5   05/23/93
42236    *
42237    * Authors: Ross Biro, <bir7@leland.Stanford.Edu>
42238    *      Fred N. van Kempen, <waltje@uWalt.NL.Mugnet.ORG>
42239    *
42240    *      This program is free software; you can
42241   redistribute it and/or
42242    *      modify it under the terms of the GNU General
42243   Public License
42244    *      as published by the Free Software Foundation;
42245   either version
42246    *      2 of the License, or (at your option) any later
42247   version.
```

```
42248    */
42249    #ifndef _TCP_H
42250    #define _TCP_H
42251
42252    #include <linux/tcp.h>
42253    #include <net/checksum.h>
42254
42255    /* This is for all connections with a full identity, no
42256    wildcards. */
42257    #define TCP_HTABLE_SIZE    256
42258
42259    /* This is for listening sockets, thus all sockets which
42260    possess wildcards. */
42261    #define TCP_LHTABLE_SIZE    32   /* Yes, really, this is
42262    all you need. */
42263
42264    /* This is for all sockets, to keep track of the local
42265    port allocations. */
42266    #define TCP_BHTABLE_SIZE    64
42267
42268    /* tcp_ipv4.c: These need to be shared by v4 and v6
42269    because the lookup
42270     *            and hashing code needs to work with
42271    different AF's yet
42272     *            the port space is shared.
42273     */
42274    extern struct sock
42275    *tcp_established_hash[TCP_HTABLE_SIZE];
42276    extern struct sock *tcp_listening_hash[TCP_LHTABLE_SIZE];
42277    extern struct sock *tcp_bound_hash[TCP_BHTABLE_SIZE];
42278
42279    /* These are AF independant. */
42280    static __inline__ int tcp_bhashfn(__u16 lport)
42281    {
42282        return (lport ^ (lport >> 7)) & (TCP_BHTABLE_SIZE-1);
42283    }
42284
42285    /* Find the next port that hashes h that is larger than
42286    lport.
42287     * If you change the hash, change this function to
42288    match, or you will
42289     * break TCP port selection. This function must also NOT
42290    wrap around
42291     * when the next number exceeds the largest possible
42292    port (2^16-1).
42293     */
42294    static __inline__ int tcp_bhashnext(__u16 lport, __u16 h)
42295    {
```

```
42296        __u32 s;    /* don't change this to a smaller
42297    type! */
42298
42299        s = (lport ^ (h ^ tcp_bhashfn(lport)));
42300        if (s > lport)
42301            return s;
42302        s = lport + TCP_BHTABLE_SIZE;
42303        return (s ^ (h ^ tcp_bhashfn(s)));
42304    }
42305
42306    static __inline__ int tcp_sk_bhashfn(struct sock *sk)
42307    {
42308        __u16 lport = sk->num;
42309        return tcp_bhashfn(lport);
42310    }
42311
42312    /* These can have wildcards, don't try too hard.
42313     * XXX deal with thousands of IP aliases for listening
42314    ports later
42315     */
42316    static __inline__ int tcp_lhashfn(unsigned short num)
42317    {
42318        return num & (TCP_LHTABLE_SIZE - 1);
42319    }
42320
42321    static __inline__ int tcp_sk_listen_hashfn(struct sock
42322    *sk)
42323    {
42324        return tcp_lhashfn(sk->num);
42325    }
42326
42327    /* This is IPv4 specific. */
42328    static __inline__ int tcp_hashfn(__u32 laddr, __u16
42329    lport,
42330                  __u32 faddr, __u16 fport)
42331    {
42332        return ((laddr ^ lport) ^ (faddr ^ fport)) &
42333    (TCP_HTABLE_SIZE - 1);
42334    }
42335
42336    static __inline__ int tcp_sk_hashfn(struct sock *sk)
42337    {
42338        __u32 laddr = sk->rcv_saddr;
42339        __u16 lport = sk->num;
42340        __u32 faddr = sk->daddr;
42341        __u16 fport = sk->dummy_th.dest;
42342
42343        return tcp_hashfn(laddr, lport, faddr, fport);
```

```
42344    }
42345
42346    /* Only those holding the sockhash lock call these two
42347    things here.
42348     * Note the slightly gross overloading of sk->prev,
42349    AF_UNIX is the
42350     * only other main benefactor of that member of SK, so
42351    who cares.
42352     */
42353    static __inline__ void tcp_sk_bindify(struct sock *sk)
42354    {
42355        int hashent = tcp_sk_bhashfn(sk);
42356        struct sock **htable = &tcp_bound_hash[hashent];
42357
42358        if((sk->bind_next = *htable) != NULL)
42359            (*htable)->bind_pprev = &sk->bind_next;
42360        *htable = sk;
42361        sk->bind_pprev = htable;
42362    }
42363
42364    static __inline__ void tcp_sk_unbindify(struct sock *sk)
42365    {
42366        if(sk->bind_next)
42367            sk->bind_next->bind_pprev = sk->bind_pprev;
42368        *(sk->bind_pprev) = sk->bind_next;
42369    }
42370
42371    /*
42372     * 40 is maximal IP options size
42373     * 4  is TCP option size (MSS)
42374     */
42375    #define MAX_SYN_SIZE    (sizeof(struct iphdr) + 40 +
42376    sizeof(struct tcphdr) + 4 + MAX_HEADER + 15)
42377    #define MAX_FIN_SIZE    (sizeof(struct iphdr) + 40 +
42378    sizeof(struct tcphdr) + MAX_HEADER + 15)
42379    #define MAX_ACK_SIZE    (sizeof(struct iphdr) + 40 +
42380    sizeof(struct tcphdr) + MAX_HEADER + 15)
42381    #define MAX_RESET_SIZE  (sizeof(struct iphdr) + 40 +
42382    sizeof(struct tcphdr) + MAX_HEADER + 15)
42383
42384    #define MAX_WINDOW  32767     /* Never offer a window
42385    over 32767 without using
42386                              window scaling (not yet
42387    supported). Some poor
42388                              stacks do signed 16bit maths! */
42389    #define MIN_WINDOW  2048
42390    #define MAX_ACK_BACKLOG 2
42391    #define MAX_DUP_ACKS    3
42392    #define MIN_WRITE_SPACE 2048
42393    #define TCP_WINDOW_DIFF 2048
42394
42395    /* urg_data states */
42396    #define URG_VALID   0x0100
42397    #define URG_NOTYET  0x0200
42398    #define URG_READ    0x0400
42399
42400    #define TCP_RETR1   7    /*
42401                     * This is how many retries it does
42402    before it
42403                     * tries to figure out if the gateway is
42404                     * down.
42405                     */
42406
42407    #define TCP_RETR2   15   /*
42408                     * This should take at least
42409                     * 90 minutes to time out.
42410                     */
42411
42412    #define TCP_TIMEOUT_LEN (15*60*HZ) /* should be about 15
42413    mins     */
42414    #define TCP_TIMEWAIT_LEN (60*HZ) /* how long to wait to
42415    successfully
42416                     * close the socket, about 60 seconds
42417    */
42418    #define TCP_FIN_TIMEOUT (3*60*HZ) /* BSD style FIN_WAIT2
42419    deadlock breaker */
42420    #define TCP_ACK_TIME    (3*HZ)   /* time to delay before
42421    sending an ACK   */
42422    #define TCP_DONE_TIME   (5*HZ/2)/* maximum time to wait
42423    before actually
42424                     * destroying a socket         */
42425    #define TCP_WRITE_TIME  (30*HZ) /* initial time to wait
42426    for an ACK,
42427                     * after last transmit         */
42428    #define TCP_TIMEOUT_INIT (3*HZ) /* RFC 1122 initial
42429    timeout value   */
42430    #define TCP_SYN_RETRIES  5  /* number of times to retry
42431    opening a
42432                     * connection   (TCP_RETR2-....)   */
42433    #define TCP_PROBEWAIT_LEN (1*HZ)/* time to wait between
42434    probes when
42435                     * I've got something to write and
42436                     * there is no window          */
42437
42438    #define TCP_NO_CHECK    0    /* turn to one if you want
42439    the default
```

```
42440                    * to be no checksum            */
42441
42442
42443    /*
42444     *  TCP option
42445     */
42446
42447    #define TCPOPT_NOP      1    /* Padding */
42448    #define TCPOPT_EOL      0    /* End of options */
42449    #define TCPOPT_MSS      2    /* Segment size negotiating
42450    */
42451    /*
42452     *  We don't use these yet, but they are for PAWS and
42453    big windows
42454     */
42455    #define TCPOPT_WINDOW       3    /* Window scaling */
42456    #define TCPOPT_TIMESTAMP    8    /* Better RTT
42457    estimations/PAWS */
42458
42459
42460    /*
42461     * The next routines deal with comparing 32 bit unsigned
42462    ints
42463     * and worry about wraparound (automatic with unsigned
42464    arithmetic).
42465     */
42466
42467    extern __inline int before(__u32 seq1, __u32 seq2)
42468    {
42469            return (__s32)(seq1-seq2) < 0;
42470    }
42471
42472    extern __inline int after(__u32 seq1, __u32 seq2)
42473    {
42474        return (__s32)(seq2-seq1) < 0;
42475    }
42476
42477
42478    /* is s2<=s1<=s3 ? */
42479    extern __inline int between(__u32 seq1, __u32 seq2,
42480    __u32 seq3)
42481    {
42482        return (after(seq1+1, seq2) && before(seq1, seq3+1));
42483    }
42484
42485    static __inline__ int min(unsigned int a, unsigned int b)
42486    {
42487        if (a > b)
42488            a = b;
42489        return a;
42490    }
42491
42492    static __inline__ int max(unsigned int a, unsigned int b)
42493    {
42494        if (a < b)
42495            a = b;
42496        return a;
42497    }
42498
42499    extern struct proto tcp_prot;
42500    extern struct tcp_mib tcp_statistics;
42501
42502    extern unsigned short        tcp_good_socknum(void);
42503
42504    extern void tcp_err(int type, int code, unsigned char
42505    *header, __u32 daddr,
42506                __u32, struct inet_protocol *protocol, int
42507    len);
42508    extern void tcp_shutdown (struct sock *sk, int how);
42509    extern int  tcp_rcv(struct sk_buff *skb, struct device
42510    *dev,
42511                struct options *opt, __u32 daddr,
42512                unsigned short len, __u32 saddr, int redo,
42513                struct inet_protocol *protocol);
42514
42515    extern int tcp_ioctl(struct sock *sk, int cmd, unsigned
42516    long arg);
42517
42518    extern void tcp_v4_unhash(struct sock *sk);
42519
42520    extern void tcp_read_wakeup(struct sock *);
42521    extern void tcp_write_xmit(struct sock *);
42522    extern void tcp_time_wait(struct sock *);
42523    extern void tcp_retransmit(struct sock *, int);
42524    extern void tcp_do_retransmit(struct sock *, int);
42525    extern void tcp_send_check(struct tcphdr *th, unsigned
42526    long saddr,
42527            unsigned long daddr, int len, struct sk_buff
42528    *skb);
42529
42530    /* tcp_output.c */
42531
42532    extern void tcp_send_probe0(struct sock *);
42533    extern void tcp_send_partial(struct sock *);
42534    extern void tcp_write_wakeup(struct sock *);
42535    extern void tcp_send_fin(struct sock *sk);
```

```
42536    extern void tcp_send_synack(struct sock *, struct sock
42537    *, struct sk_buff *, int);
42538    extern void tcp_send_skb(struct sock *, struct sk_buff
42539    *);
42540    extern void tcp_send_ack(struct sock *sk);
42541    extern void tcp_send_delayed_ack(struct sock *sk, int
42542    max_timeout, unsigned long timeout);
42543    extern void tcp_send_reset(unsigned long saddr, unsigned
42544    long daddr, struct tcphdr *th,
42545         struct proto *prot, struct options *opt, struct
42546    device *dev, int tos, int ttl);
42547
42548    extern void tcp_enqueue_partial(struct sk_buff *, struct
42549    sock *);
42550    extern struct sk_buff * tcp_dequeue_partial(struct sock
42551    *);
42552    extern void tcp_shrink_skb(struct sock *,struct sk_buff
42553    *,u32);
42554
42555    /* CONFIG_IP_TRANSPARENT_PROXY */
42556    extern int tcp_chkaddr(struct sk_buff *);
42557
42558    /* tcp_timer.c */
42559    #define     tcp_reset_msl_timer(x,y,z)
42560    reset_timer(x,y,z)
42561    extern void tcp_reset_xmit_timer(struct sock *, int,
42562    unsigned long);
42563    extern void tcp_delack_timer(unsigned long);
42564    extern void tcp_retransmit_timer(unsigned long);
42565
42566    static __inline__ int tcp_old_window(struct sock * sk)
42567    {
42568         return sk->window - (sk->acked_seq -
42569    sk->lastwin_seq);
42570    }
42571
42572    extern int tcp_new_window(struct sock *);
42573
42574    /*
42575     * Return true if we should raise the window when we
42576     * have cleaned up the receive queue. We don't want to
42577     * do this normally, only if it makes sense to avoid
42578     * zero window probes..
42579     *
42580     * We do this only if we can raise the window noticeably.
42581     */
42582    static __inline__ int tcp_raise_window(struct sock * sk)
42583    {
42584         int new = tcp_new_window(sk);
42585         return new && (new >= 2*tcp_old_window(sk));
42586    }
42587
42588    static __inline__ unsigned short
42589    tcp_select_window(struct sock *sk)
42590    {
42591         int window = tcp_new_window(sk);
42592         int oldwin = tcp_old_window(sk);
42593
42594         /* Don't allow a shrinking window */
42595         if (window > oldwin) {
42596              sk->window = window;
42597              sk->lastwin_seq = sk->acked_seq;
42598              oldwin = window;
42599         }
42600         return oldwin;
42601    }
42602
42603    /*
42604     * List all states of a TCP socket that can be viewed as
42605    a "connected"
42606     * state.  This now includes TCP_SYN_RECV, although I am
42607    not yet fully
42608     * convinced that this is the solution for the
42609    'getpeername(2)'
42610     * problem. Thanks to Stephen A. Wood <saw@cebaf.gov>
42611    -FvK
42612     */
42613
42614    extern __inline const int tcp_connected(const int state)
42615    {
42616       return(state == TCP_ESTABLISHED || state ==
42617    TCP_CLOSE_WAIT ||
42618         state == TCP_FIN_WAIT1   || state == TCP_FIN_WAIT2
42619    ||
42620         state == TCP_SYN_RECV);
42621    }
42622
42623    /*
42624     * Calculate(/check) TCP checksum
42625     */
42626    static __inline__ u16 tcp_check(struct tcphdr *th, int
42627    len,
42628       unsigned long saddr, unsigned long daddr, unsigned
42629    long base)
42630    {
42631       return
```

```
42632    csum_tcpudp_magic(saddr,daddr,len,IPPROTO_TCP,base);
42633    }
42634
42635    #undef STATE_TRACE
42636
42637    #ifdef STATE_TRACE
42638    static char *statename[]={
42639        "Unused","Established","Syn Sent","Syn Recv",
42640        "Fin Wait 1","Fin Wait 2","Time Wait", "Close",
42641        "Close Wait","Last ACK","Listen","Closing"
42642    };
42643    #endif
42644
42645    static __inline__ void tcp_set_state(struct sock *sk,
42646    int state)
42647    {
42648        int oldstate = sk->state;
42649
42650        sk->state = state;
42651
42652    #ifdef STATE_TRACE
42653        if(sk->debug)
42654            printk("TCP sk=%p, State %s -> %s\n",sk,
42655    statename[oldstate],statename[state]);
42656    #endif
42657
42658        switch (state) {
42659        case TCP_ESTABLISHED:
42660            if (oldstate != TCP_ESTABLISHED) {
42661                tcp_statistics.TcpCurrEstab++;
42662            }
42663            break;
42664
42665        case TCP_CLOSE:
42666            /* Preserve the invariant */
42667            tcp_v4_unhash(sk);
42668            /* Should be about 2 rtt's */
42669            reset_timer(sk, TIME_DONE, min(sk->rtt * 2,
42670    TCP_DONE_TIME));
42671            /* fall through */
42672        default:
42673            if (oldstate==TCP_ESTABLISHED)
42674                tcp_statistics.TcpCurrEstab--;
42675        }
42676    }
42677
42678    #endif   /* _TCP_H */
```

usr/src/linux/include/net/udp.h

```
42679    /*
42680     * INET      An implementation of the TCP/IP protocol
42681    suite for the LINUX
42682     *       operating system.  INET is implemented using the
42683    BSD Socket
42684     *       interface as the means of communication with the
42685    user level.
42686     *
42687     *       Definitions for the UDP module.
42688     *
42689     * Version: @(#)udp.h    1.0.2    05/07/93
42690     *
42691     * Authors: Ross Biro, <bir7@leland.Stanford.Edu>
42692     *       Fred N. van Kempen, <waltje@uWalt.NL.Mugnet.ORG>
42693     *
42694     * Fixes:
42695     *       Alan Cox    : Turned on udp checksums. I don't
42696    want to
42697     *                  chase 'memory corruption' bugs that
42698    aren't!
42699     *
42700     *       This program is free software; you can
42701    redistribute it and/or
42702     *       modify it under the terms of the GNU General
42703    Public License
42704     *       as published by the Free Software Foundation;
42705    either version
42706     *       2 of the License, or (at your option) any later
42707    version.
42708     */
42709    #ifndef _UDP_H
42710    #define _UDP_H
42711
42712    #include <linux/udp.h>
42713
42714    #define UDP_HTABLE_SIZE     128
42715
42716    /* udp.c: This needs to be shared by v4 and v6 because
42717    the lookup
42718     *       and hashing code needs to work with different
42719    AF's yet
42720     *       the port space is shared.
42721     */
42722    extern struct sock *udp_hash[UDP_HTABLE_SIZE];
42723
42724    extern unsigned short udp_good_socknum(void);
42725
```

```
42726   #define UDP_NO_CHECK    0
42727
42728
42729   extern struct proto udp_prot;
42730
42731
42732   extern void udp_err(int type, int code, unsigned char
42733   *header, __u32 daddr,
42734               __u32 saddr, struct inet_protocol *protocol,
42735   int len);
42736   extern void udp_send_check(struct udphdr *uh, __u32
42737   saddr,
42738               __u32 daddr, int len, struct sock *sk);
42739   extern int  udp_recvfrom(struct sock *sk, unsigned char
42740   *to,
42741                   int len, int noblock, unsigned flags,
42742                   struct sockaddr_in *sin, int *addr_len);
42743   extern int  udp_read(struct sock *sk, unsigned char
42744   *buff,
42745                 int len, int noblock, unsigned flags);
42746   extern int  udp_connect(struct sock *sk,
42747               struct sockaddr_in *usin, int addr_len);
42748   extern int  udp_rcv(struct sk_buff *skb, struct device
42749   *dev,
42750           struct options *opt, __u32 daddr,
42751           unsigned short len, __u32 saddr, int redo,
42752           struct inet_protocol *protocol);
42753   extern int  udp_ioctl(struct sock *sk, int cmd, unsigned
42754   long arg);
42755
42756   /* CONFIG_IP_TRANSPARENT_PROXY */
42757   extern int  udp_chkaddr(struct sk_buff *skb);
42758
42759   #endif  /* _UDP_H */
```

Part II

TCP/IP Stack Commentary

Chapter 1

Overview Of The TCP/IP Stack Commentary

The various distributions of the Linux operating system ship with fully functional workstation and server capabilities. The kernel code, both directly and through loaded modules, provides the underlying communications layers:

- Drivers for the vast majority of Ethernet, token ring, and Fiber Distributed Data Interface (FDDI) interface boards

- Point-to-Point Protocol (PPP), Serial Line Internet Protocol (SLIP), and Compressed SLIP (CSLIP) link-layer drivers for communications via modems

- NetWare communications via Internetwork Packet Exchange (IPX)

- Amateur radio communications (AX25)

- AppleTalk communications (APPLETALK)

- Other link–layer communications methods

- Full Internet router support, including Router Information Protocol (RIP) router-to-router protocol, if needed

- Internet Control Message Protocol (ICMP)

- Internet Group Message Protocol (IGMP)

- Internet Protocol (IP)

- Transmission Control Protocol (TCP)

- User Datagram Protocol (UDP)

Servers are supported in Linux through a wide range of daemons (programs that run as processes, but without control terminals). The following list includes a few of the daemons used in networking that are either provided as part of a Linux distribution or can be easily obtained free of charge via the Internet. In almost every case, the name ends with the character "d," and the names are customarily pronounced as though the "d" were completely separate: "i-net-d," "apache-d," and "name-d," and so on. Here are some common daemons:

- **inetd** is the "front door" for many servers

- **named** is the Domain Name Service server

- **ftpd** is the FTP server

- **apached** is the World Wide Web server, which is one of the most popular servers in the world; see *Apache Server Commentary*, by Holden, Wells, and Keller (ISBN 1-57610-468-0), also published by The Coriolis Group, for an in-depth look at this server

- **nntpd** is one of several Usenet news servers that are available via the Internet

- **tftpd** is the Trivial File Transfer Protocol server, which is used to upload firmware to certain Internet devices and to download memory images to computers that don't have hard drives (such computers are also known as *thin systems*)

Literally hundreds of servers exist, from Internet Relay Chat (IRC) servers to game servers to multimedia servers—and any list of "all" of them would be obsolete the day after it is generated.

Just as many server programs are available *for* Linux, many client programs are also available *on* Linux. Here again, the following list is just a sample of the client programs that are available:

- **Telnet**, which was one of the first applications created for the ARPAnet, is a "network teletype"

- **FTP** is the File Transfer Protocol program

- **whois** is a program that queries the InterNIC database for owner and contact information about Internet domain names

- **Ping** is a program that uses ICMP Echo Request and Echo Reply packets to determine whether a given system is working and available

- **traceroute**, which uses one of the network diagnostic tools built into Linux, is a program that uses special features of TCP/IP to determine the path ("trace the route") that packets take from the local system to a specified remote system

- **Lynx** is a nongraphical Web browser

- **inn**, **tin**, and **slrn**, which are three of the many different newsreader packages that are available for Linux users, work with news servers to provide a bulletin-board-type service called Usenet

Experimenting with new protocols? Linux makes it easy, by letting you load modules that implement and link new protocols into the system, or even replace existing protocols, without having to recompile the kernel each time you make a new build of the protocol modules. Experimenting with new applications is even easier (as it is with most Unix-type systems), because building servers and clients that use either TCP or UDP as the Layer 4 protocol is a straightforward process that requires no kernel modification whatsoever.

Scope And Focus Of The Commentary

A complete treatment of all aspects of Linux networking communications would extend far beyond a single book. Therefore, this book concentrates on the following basic TCP/IP kernel services that come into play whenever TCP/IP is used: network routing, packet management, datagram, and datastream.

Chapter 2 provides some background into the concepts and history of TCP/IP, its development, and some of the twisty turns it took between its obscure start as a nuclear-event-survival thought-experiment and the mainstream big-dollar market it has become.

To place TCP/IP in an academic perspective, Chapter 3 of this book compares TCP/IP with the ISO model of the networking process. The ISO model provides a good theoretical basis for developing new strategies and procedures, and also helps explain why the communication layers are separated the way they are.

The packet management service takes care of transporting data packets through the network and is the responsibility of the Internet Protocol. IP receives help from ICMP and IGMP. ICMP is discussed in Chapter 4, and IP itself is described in detail in Chapter 7.

To help you understand why the code works as it does, Chapter 5 provides an application program's view of the networking facility. That chapter shows the system calls used by application programs to initiate, terminate, control, and feed connections. It also covers the options and their meaning (and whether they are supported in this particular TCP/IP implementation), thus showing the local-system "input" to the networking software.

The network routing service concentrates on taking packets that are provided by processes running on the local system (or packets that are received from other systems) and forwarding those packets to other systems. The routing services, which are the "rocket science" of TCP/IP, are covered in detail in Chapter 6.

The User Datagram Protocol (UDP) is intended for those applications that need simple transfer, need it only occasionally, and don't need (or want) the complexity of sophisticated error recovery. UDP is a popular way to handle domain-name (DNS) lookup requests, thin-system initialization, DHCP (which enables clients to learn the IP address they are to use), and network diagnostics. UDP is covered in Chapter 8, and a popular (not to say essential) implementation of it is described in Appendix C, which addresses the Domain Name System (DNS).

The heavy lifting is done with the Transmission Control Protocol. Virtually every common network application—Telnet, FTP, Gopher, Archie, the Web—uses TCP to carry data and commands. TCP sports a number of sophisticated algorithms for network management, flow management, and error control, to ensure that data gets to its destination as safely and as quickly as practical. TCP is the subject of Chapter 9.

No system connected to the Internet is immune from the activities of serious dark-side hackers. Even worse, though, are the "script kiddie" wannabes—that is, the many less-talented proto-malefactors who take the work of the few seriously talented crackers and play back those clever scripts against virtually every system on the Internet. Chapter 10 describes the Linux firewall code, which is designed to keep out the bad guys and the bad kids alike, and which comes with every modern Linux kernel.

As noted in the general introduction to this book, these chapters are designed as predominantly self-contained units, so you can go directly to the chapter or chapters that contain the information you need. But if you prefer to read the entire commentary straight through, by all means, be our guest.

Updates and errata notices relating to the contents of this book will be posted from time to time at the authors' Web site: **www.fluent-access.com/linux-tcpip/**.

You may also contact the authors directly. Please email brickbats and/or bouquets to **satch@fluent-access.com** or **hbjc@fluent-access.com**. We're looking forward to hearing from you.

Chapter 2

Background And Basic Concepts

net•work•ing (net'wûr'king) *n.* A supportive system of sharing information and services among individuals and groups having a common interest.

Computer networking as we know it today, and the telecommunications protocols implemented under the programming language featured in this book, are the lineal descendants of two entities whose first incarnations date back to the early years of the eighth decade of the twentieth century: the original Internet and the Unix operating system.

Internet networking is a supportive system that was originally designed to share information even in the face of cataclysmic events, up to and including limited thermonuclear warfare. Its matrix, the Internet, is a direct descendant of that unique product of the Cold War, the 1970s-era ARPAnet. That Internet has grown up—and after 30 years, has grown *out*—from its first incarnation as a single 100-node network to become what is often referred to as a "cooperative anarchy" consisting of thousands of networks that interconnect millions of individual computers.

At almost the same time that the ARPAnet was fledging its wings, the Unix operating system was born. It started life as a tiny "skunkworks" project at a certain branch of The Phone Company (TPC, popularized in the contemporaneous novel and film *The President's Analyst*)—specifically, at that company's research arm, Bell Labs.

This small group effort was originally undertaken to design a writing workbench tool for a group of lawyers. The purpose of the Unix system, and of the B programming language that was developed along with it, was to

put to use some cast-off DEC PDP-7 computer hardware, without requiring legions of programmers or shiploads of paperwork.

Many of self-styled "Bell Lab Rat" Ken Thompson's innovations—a simple file system, a simple but powerful permissions system, and the concept of *pipes*—were developed with the innocent aim of speeding up the development of writing tools by making applications easier to integrate. "Divide and conquer" had been the dominant programming philosophy for almost a decade prior to the start of this project, but Unix was one of the first operating systems to provide an efficient way to implement this philosophy at the applications level.

These two projects—the ARPAnet and Unix—shared one central element that was largely responsible for their success. Specifically, they were both deeply rooted in the concept of using *simple building blocks* to create a larger, more complex whole.

And what Unix did for programming with its "pop-bead" approach to systems, TCP/IP did for telecommunications by using small, well-defined, easy-to-understand layers of abstraction and a large number of small custom protocols that could be combined to form complex, reliable, and robust data links. Given these strong similarities, in retrospect, it was inevitable (dare we say kismet) that Unix programmers would be drawn to TCP/IP networking.

The ARPAnet was originally built with "big iron" hardware, because that's what developers had on hand: IBM mainframes, DEC supercomputers, and Burroughs and GE timesharing complexes. But by the late 1970s, Unix hardware had become much cheaper, and network implementers found that the necessary hardware interfaces were much easier to design and build for Unix minicomputers than they were for non-Unix mainframes.

In short, Unix was now within the grasp of almost all university research centers. Best of all, the Unix operating system was modular enough that network device drivers were easy to write, debug, and install. With the

C programming language (which succeeded, and greatly improved on, the original B language) the chore of writing protocol drivers that actually worked became a comparatively simple task. When you consider that, at the time, these drivers were usually ground out in assembly language, it's easy to see why minicomputers running Unix soon became wildly popular platforms for experiments in networking.

A number of Unix minicomputers were available at the University of California at Berkeley (UCB), which also had a well-qualified pool of undergraduates who were eager to tinker with the systems. Thanks to that swarm of brainpower, Berkeley was able to introduce a "rival" Unix-based operating system, known as the Berkeley System Distribution (or simply BSD Unix).

Because U.C. Berkeley was also a major participant in the ARPAnet project, the Network Control Protocol (NCP) concept of *sockets* became part of the networking software that the university incorporated into BSD Unix. AT&T tried to introduce a competing concept, called *streams*, into its own version of Unix (known as System V), but it never really caught on.

In short, the availability of Unix (of which Linux is a distant but faithful relation) and "cheap" hardware brought the concepts of computer networking out of obscurity and into the hands of students, who grabbed the ball and ran with it, full-tilt boogie.

The Dark Ages

In the ancient days of networks, which for our purposes were the 1960s, the means by which computers talked to each other were developed and monopolized by the members of a tiny technological priestly caste. Shielded by esoteric language, graduate-level academic courses, obtuse standards published by the pound by the International Telecommunications Union (a subagency of the United Nations, which status may account, at least in part, for the impenetrability of its documentation), and enough state diagrams to gift-wrap the Great Wall of China, the priests and acolytes of networking's inner sanctum hid their work from the common herd of users. The users, often without understanding exactly what they were doing, simply memorized the mantras that made the systems work.

Of course, from time to time, real information filtered out. The IBM Corporation actually gave away some (but by no means all) of the details of its computer-to-computer communications schemes—but only to client companies who could afford to hire in-house gurus to implement the maddeningly (and unnecessarily) complex language.

Obfuscation in the service of proprietary interests wasn't limited to the private sector. Many details of the ARPAnet—which was nominally a public project—were buried in inches-thick reports that were hard to find and, for the uninitiated, harder to read. Technical articles were sprinkled liberally across a broad spectrum of journals, some of which were so obscure that only the members of the technopriesthood even knew of their existence, let alone had copies of them.

During the early days of TCP/IP, and right up through the early 1990s, hard information about networking was scarce, even for members of the inner manufacturing and academic circles. Then, the explosive growth of the Internet led increasing numbers of novices...er, young people, into jobs that exposed them to the inner workings of networking software, and thus to the networking traps and pitfalls that await unwary protocol designers.

But even with the advent of microcomputers in 1977, the Apple-based "VisiCalc"-type systems of 1978, or even the IBM PC (that 1981 devil-spawn, responsible for a veritable tsunami of bad programmers, worse programs, and overdone demo-dollies at the biannual COMDEX shows), networking at large remained a dark mystery. A few brave souls tried to create TCP/IP stacks, but their efforts were hobbled by a shortage of RAM and, even more so, by a shortage of information.

Speaking of information deficits, in 1985, the present authors bought a copy of "hot off the press" networking specifications. The price of the three-volume *DDN Protocol Handbook* was $100—equivalent, in today's money, to $625. This paper-bound product of the Defense Communications Agency consisted of selected RFCs and other explanatory text, and featured truly primitive line-printer output that would have been an embarrassment 10 years earlier. But, given what other information was—and wasn't—available, the *Handbook* was pure gold.

Rivals, Fallen And Otherwise

Its military-industrial pedigree aside, part of the reason TCP/IP was so obscure was that it wasn't the only way to link computers into networks. Some potential TCP/IP users were lured away from it by other methods that didn't require the use of leased lines, the way the ARPAnet and the original Internet did.

One of these rival methods, which was developed at Bell Labs early in the life of Unix, was the uucp (Unix-to-Unix copy) program. Not content with simply copying files from one system to another, the links provided by uucp also provided a way for electronic mail protocols to be launched. As a result, Unix-based systems all over the United States, and in many other parts of the world, soon became linked by an informal network of dial-up connections that used the public telephone network: first at 1,200 bits per second, and then, as the technology advanced, at speeds up to 18,000 bps.

The original network news packages also used these links, in their case to form a distributed bulletin board. (This application lives on today, in the form of the network news system.) But the original uucp network gradually withered and (for all practical purposes) died, as the network of Telebit Trailblazer modems, which from 1985 to 1995 knit Unix systems together, was gradually replaced by increasingly inexpensive leased telephone lines.

Not to be outdone, in 1984 the microcomputer community formed its own network of computers, called *FidoNet*, which also operated over the public telephone network. The FidoNet system, which was the brainchild of skateboard fanatic Tom Jennings, implemented electronic-mail functions and also distributed its BBS functionality. At this writing, the FidoNet is still in operation, carrying information between the Internet and FidoNet's loyal but no doubt dwindling devotees. Woof.

Commercial Unix systems, such as Xenix and SCO Unix, which were designed to run on microcomputers, did include TCP/IP networking. However, the cost of Internet connections during the late 1980s was so high that most people used modems instead, accessing the Internet through so-called *shell accounts* running on minicomputer Unix systems, and then using simple protocols such as uucp, Xmodem, or Kermit to exchange data between the Unix box and their own microcomputers.

Ghu Said "Let Linux Be, And All Was Light"

The rather dismal situation described in the preceding section changed radically in the mid-1990s, with the confluence of half a dozen seemingly unrelated trends and events:

- The patents on **set-user-id** and other Unix innovations expired.

- Linus Torvalds launched the clean-room Unix reimplementation project that we now know as Linux.

- The GNU project, with Richard Stallman and the Free Software Foundation at the helm, spawned a number of standard utilities that Unix people soon came to love, a phenomenon amply documented in Scott Maxwell's *Linux Core Kernel Commentary* (The Coriolis Group, 1999; ISBN 1-57610-469-9).

- The cost of microcomputers plummeted, and their capabilities burgeoned.

- Leased-line connections to the Internet became less expensive.

- The cost of high-speed dial-up access to the Internet dropped below $100 per month.

The first fruits of these happy accidents was the Linux operating system.

Linux brings to the world a real-life, standards-compliant OS whose source code is available to anyone—*anyone*—who wants it. Better yet, Linux's feature set includes a real-life, standards-compliant TCP/IP networking system, whose source code is likewise available to anyone who wants it. When wedded with the standard networking tools that are available for Unix-style systems, Linux stands proudly head-to-head with any other OS available today.

This book describes TCP/IP's implementation in the C programming language. Other implementations have been written—in FORTRAN, ALGOL, Pascal, PL/1, and any number of assembler languages, as well as in the language of the application-specific integrated circuits (ASICs) that drive the so-called "silicon compilers," which generate physical devices that implement the protocol suite directly in hardware. Special languages have also been created that build TCP/IP stacks, either because no traditional compiler was available for the designated hardware, or simply because the implementer could do it.

Some implementations of TCP/IP have been around for 30 years, evolving to meet a changing world, while others are still in the teething stage. The Linux implementation of TCP/IP, which is written in the C language, is the one that the present commentary addresses. First released in 1993, it's well out of its infancy, if not yet quite into long pants.

Network Programming Precepts

Telecommunications is all about talking with other computers. TCP/IP telecommunications is all about talking with many different kinds of other computers: new ones and old ones, "back-words" and "fore-words," from palm-tops to building-fillers and everything in between.

Talking with other computers also means agreeing on the answers to certain basic questions, such as:

- How are bits transmitted?
- How are characters transmitted?
- How are bit fields defined?
- How are integer numbers transmitted?

Bits On A Wire

The first task any telecommunications system must perform is to decide which bits get sent first. Here, TCP/IP doesn't issue any edicts; instead, it leaves the answer to be reached by the drivers and the hardware. However, according to telecomm custom, the transmission of bits in a given data unit (usually the character) starts with the low-order bit.

The reason the low-order bit is sent first is, well, historical. Early teletype communications systems used a *parity bit* to determine whether a character that was being sent had been transferred correctly. When the low-order bit was sent first, followed sequentially by the remaining bits, the parity bit could be calculated on the fly and transmitted after the last bit in a character (that is, in a data unit) had been transmitted.

Alas, not all transmission systems are serial in nature. The IBM PC parallel port and the standard SCSI bus are two examples of communications devices that can transfer bits of data in parallel. Here again, the determination of which bit is sent on what wire is a matter of convention.

It's Just A Jump To The Left, And A Step To The Right

The customary way of sending characters, in order from left to right, was determined not by teletypes but by early stock-market tickers, in the years immediately following the U.S. Civil War. These were mechanical marvels that required several wires in order to work properly, but they did the job of transmitting quotations from the central stock exchanges to wherever the tickers were located. To make them useful to human readers, the tickers were set up so that, as information was transmitted, characters were printed on the tape in the natural left-to-right order. This way, the stock quotations could be read and understood as soon as the tape came out of the ticker. This "natural-order" approach also simplified the task of encoding the quotations at the sending end. Lastly, early stock tickers were run by the Western Union company, whose telegraph operators wouldn't hear of keying data any other way but from left to right.

As "printing telegraphs" were introduced into newspaper companies, the left-to-right order was maintained, because that method was the one that the typists who were keying the information were accustomed to using. This habit persisted throughout the duration of the teletype era, up through the mid-1980s.

In TCP/IP, information is transmitted in characters (*octets*, if you prefer the formal international Standards language) in left-to-right order. Accordingly, in many of the diagrams that illustrate packet formats, both in this book and elsewhere in the literature, the customary transmission order is from left to right, top row to bottom row.

Characters stored in a computer's memory are usually arranged in order, from low to high memory addresses. This way, a packet can be built in memory and then handed directly to the device driver and the hardware. Indeed, the C programming language virtually guarantees that its I/O model will behave this way.

Bitfields, Or Logical Operations?

As you'll see in the definitions of IP and TCP packet headers, the individual data bits in the headers have meaning above and beyond the meaning of the characters that they constitute. For example, in the thirteenth byte of the TCP packet header, the rightmost bit of the byte (2^0) is interpreted as the FIN bit. Each implementation must interpret the same bit in the same way.

The C programming language defines the concept of *bitfields* as a way to associate a symbolic name with a single bit or group of bits in a word. Unfortunately, in the original language as defined by Kernighan and Ritchie, the actual interpretation of bitfields was left up to each individual implementation. The ANSI standard perpetuates this ambiguity. Unfortunately, such ambiguity is simply unacceptable in telecommunications, in which every single implementation of a communications protocol must agree with every other implementation on the questions of which bit means what.

One popular way to avoid the problem is to use the logical AND and OR operators to manipulate individual bits. This workaround imposes a slightly heavier burden on the programmer. Moreover, when a computer defines bit-manipulator instructions as part of its instruction set, this workaround can eat up machine cycles unnecessarily. When the logical operators are used purely to manipulate characters, this approach is essentially painless. However, when integer quantities need to be manipulated, the operations are complicated by byte-ordering problems, as described in the next section.

Another way to circumvent the bit-definition problem is to experiment with the compiler and determine how it allocates bits in a bitfield. You can then define the individual bit or group of bits as part of a structure, and treat the resulting bitfield structure like any other integer variable.

The Linux TCP/IP implementation uses a blend of all these methods. The TCP packet-header code uses bitfields (with conditional compilation, to ensure that the bits are defined in the "correct" order) to define the six bits that indicate which fields are valid, while the IP header code uses logical calculations to set and test the don't-fragment and more-fragment bits.

Start At The Big End...No, At The Little End

As previously noted, the contents of buffers are transmitted one character at a time, starting with the characters that live at low memory addresses and ending with the characters that live at high memory addresses. This procedure works well with some machines but not with others, due to the way certain computers store integer values. Obviously, this is a nontrivial problem.

The TCP/IP stack contains many fields that store integer values. Many of these values are 16-bit values, while others are 32-bit values. In other words, in computers that use 8-bit characters, these integer values can be represented by groups of two or four characters, respectively, of information.

When information is stored in integer memory locations in Motorola 68000-based computers, the most significant 8 bits of the integer data are placed in the lowest memory address. This arrangement is known as *fore-word* or *big-endian* orientation. In contrast, however, in the Intel 80x86 and Pentium family of computers, the *least* significant 8 bits of the integer data are stored in the lowest memory address. Hence, the monikers *back-word* and *little-endian*.

This disagreement about how integer values should be stored has been going on for as long as binary computers have existed. Motorola and Intel are relative latecomers to this particular religious war. True, for most computer work, the integer-value storage method doesn't make any difference. It only becomes a headache when you need to move data electronically between computers that disagree about byte order.

By definition, TCP/IP uses the big-endian scheme to store numbers in buffers. In much of the literature, this order, which is known as *network order*, is fixed. Unfortunately, computers perform calculations in their own way, in a native mode called *host order*. Consequently, programmers must keep track of whether a particular integer value is being stored in network order or in host order.

To create portable code that takes this machine-specific behavior into consideration, the poor programmers have to use the library functions **htonl** and **htons** to convert a 32-bit or 16-bit value from host to network order, and use the inverse functions **ntohl** and **ntohs** to convert values from network to host order. In big-endian systems, such as the Motorola 68000, these functions do nothing, whereas in Intel 80x86 and Pentium systems, they swap the bytes as indicated.

The alternative, which consists of breaking down the integer values into character chunks, is comparatively more expensive in terms of the number of CPU cycles required. The use of the conversion functions is a reasonable tradeoff, because hand-tooled assembler code can be used to make the implemented functions run very, very fast.

The other aspect of handling integer values relates to the fact that some machines work with integer values only when those values are aligned on a "word" boundary. The IBM System/360 computer was famous for this quirk, but it was far from alone in this regard. Any attempt to manipulate word values at arbitrary boundaries on these machines would cause machine exceptions, which meant that the protocol routines had to either include exception processing routines to handle the exception or else simply not function properly. Fortunately, with more-modern computers, the use of such unaligned integer quantities just slows down the processing.

Even so, a shortsighted implementation of TCP/IP on one networked machine could conceivably cause a malfunction in another machine on that network. Therefore, TCP/IP implementations must very carefully align integer quantities on word boundaries in the TCP and IP option fields.

"Co-op-er-a-tion," Say The Muppets

The authors conclude this tour with one final philosophical observation. Network programming is different from virtually every other kind of programming. Some programmers make the mistake of assuming that a master-slave relationship exists between two ends of a communications connection, just as a master-slave relationship exists between a function and the functions it calls. Indeed, some Paleolithic communications systems (such as those built by IBM for its big-business customers) involved the equivalent of a feudal lord and a ring of serfs, with each lowly endpoint doing the bidding of the Master Control Program that lived up the hill in the manor...er, mainframe.

It's easy to see why some business types tried so hard to erect, in the cyberworld, a duplicate of the real world's corporate ladder. (Remember, these are the same people who transmuted the relatively simple concept of "data processing" to "management information" and then to "information technology," in much the same way that the straightforward term "insane asylum" was metastasized into "state mental hospital" and then into the dazzlingly euphemistic "correctional medical facility.")

But we digress. "Divide and conquer" is a success formula in the day-to-day take-no-prisoners business world, or in strategic warfare, but it doesn't work for diplomats. Consider two heads of state in two completely different cultures (say, for instance, the U.S. and China) who are trying to reach an agreement. The will to understand is there, but the ideological chasm between the two sides is wide and brimming with alligators. Negotiators in good faith on both sides need to work *together* to bridge the difficulties.

Similarly, in a successful communications environment, two programs running on two different machines need to *cooperate*, instead of competing for control. The programs aren't each other's enemies; instead, the ravine full of alligators...er, the communications channel, is the common enemy of both of them. When one program tries to dominate the other, chaos ensues. Clarity and chaos don't mix. And clarity, as always, is the goal.

Programs—and people—of good will could do much worse than take to heart Dr. Jon Postel's following suggestion: "Be conservative in what you do; be liberal in what you accept from others."

Chapter 3

Linux And The ISO Model

The last chapter traces the evolution of TCP/IP and explains how, under the aegis of the Defense Advanced Research Projects Agency (DARPA), it grew from a protocol for a single network into a protocol that can link many networks. Thanks to the solution provided by TCP/IP, the ARPAnet grew from a single network into a collective network that led eventually to today's Internet.

However, while DARPA's practical-minded engineers were busy devising a system that would let hundreds of university research departments and defense contractors swap information on a day-to-day basis, groups of theoreticians were equally busy building a conceptual model for computer networking in general. Such a model would give networking researchers and implementers a way to discuss their work without getting bogged down in proprietary details. In other words, it would provide a common design metalanguage that would stay valid until the arrival of the next paradigm-shifting breakthrough in communications theory (which, at this writing, we're still awaiting).

As it turned out, the networking world's answer to the Grand Unified Field Theory was actually unveiled long before TCP/IP had gelled as the practical choice for internetwork communications. Proving that concepts can travel faster than electrons, the International Organization for Standardization (ISO) introduced its model in 1974, while formal work on TCP/IP was still in its early days. In fact, considering that work on TCP/IP continued for another decade (it wasn't codified by the U.S. Department of Defense as a U.S. federal standard until 1985, and it is still being refined), we can safely assume that ISO's theoretical model actually had some effect on DARPA's practical method.

ISO And OSI

ISO, a federation of individual national standards agencies, was formally established in 1947 and is now based in Geneva, Switzerland. The name "ISO" is not an orthographically impaired abbreviation of "International Organization for Standardization." Instead, it's a neologism derived from the Greek *isos* ("equal"), which is the root of many words, such as *isometric* ("of equal measure or dimensions") and *isonomy* ("equality of laws," or "equality of people before the law"). In ISO's own words, "from 'equal' to 'standard,' the line of thinking that led to the choice of 'ISO'… is easy to follow." The use of "ISO" worldwide also avoids the host of abbreviations derived from the translation of the organization's name into the languages of its 130-odd member nations. Whatever the country, the name stays the same.

In a move destined to confuse future generations of computer communications neophytes, ISO named its brainchild the "Open Systems Interconnection (OSI) model." Although it owed much to existing mainframe-based networks, including in particular the System Network Architecture (SNA) developed by IBM, the OSI model was defined in a non-vendor-specific way. And many of its principles jibed surprisingly well, up to a point, with DARPA's minicomputer-based, TCP/IP-linked systems.

ISO's purpose in creating the OSI model was not only to provide a design metalanguage, as previously mentioned, but also to define standards for protocols that fit within the model. Unhappily for ISO, the OSI protocol definitions proved to be less than useful in the commercial world, which is why not much is heard about this aspect of the model today.

So, you may be wondering why we are bothering with the ISO/OSI model at all. Because, as the model's designers foresaw, a well-known benchmark not only gives network researchers and implementers a common language, but also makes improvements easier to integrate into existing systems. The OSI model is studied in every college-level course on computer networking, and every article on networking issues uses the model as a basis for discussion—despite the fact that when the time comes to implement a protocol built to fit the OSI model, the model turns out to be cumbersome at best.

However, a flawed model is not necessarily useless. The model of the atom developed by Niels Bohr still has its uses in chemistry today, even though the quantum model is "better" at making accurate predictions about what "real" matter will do. But not every chemist is always in the prediction business, and for most chemists' purposes, the Bohr model is still perfectly useful. In the same way, the ISO/OSI networking model is still a fine tool—in fact, the best tool we have—for understanding what all the various bits and pieces of any given network protocol are doing.

If you're already familiar with the ISO/OSI model, this chapter will give you a good overview of how TCP/IP fits into this standard framework. If you're a TCP/IP guru, the following discussion will provide a bridge between your intimate knowledge of the Internet and the contents of technical articles in the published literature. If you're new to networking, you'll find that the ISO/OSI model offers a divide-and-conquer approach that reduces the networking "elephant" to more easily digestible "byte-sized" pieces.

The fundamental difference between the OSI model and TCP/IP is that the model imposes rigid separations between networking functions, whereas TCP/IP does not. This isn't to say that there is no compartmentalization of functions in TCP/IP; simply that, in order to reduce computational overhead and thereby improve its performance, TCP/IP takes a less doctrinaire approach to this issue than the OSI model does. One particular TCP/IP implementation that is much more efficient than the OSI model is, of course, the Linux implementation.

As you'll see, the original ISO/OSI networking model discussed in this chapter does not include any paradigms for connectionless communications. These issues have been addressed by addendums to the model that have been incorporated over the years. However, because these addendums can be confusing, the following discussion sticks with the original model and deals with the exceptions separately.

The OSI Stack

The ISO/OSI networking model consists of seven layers of functions, arranged for convenience in the form of a vertical stack. The functions closest to the physical user live at the top of the stack, while the functions located closest to the communications hardware live at the bottom. When two computers are communicating, the software in each layer in one computer "talks" with the software in the corresponding layer in the other computer. Communications between any two corresponding layers always use the services performed by the lower layers in each stack, as shown in Figure 3.1.

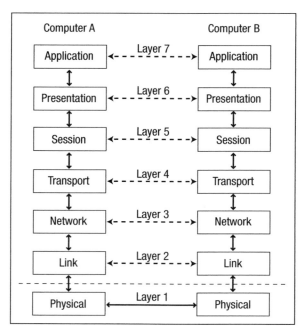

Figure 3.1   Logical versus physical data flow in the ISO model.

The solid line connecting the boxes marked "Physical" is the only physical connection between the computers (with the understanding that this *physical* connection may also be infrared or wireless). The arrows and dotted lines linking the other six levels, which are all implemented in software, show the logical data path. Imagine two colleagues, each of whom works in an office located high in one of the World Trade Center towers in New York City. To seal a deal with a personal handshake, one of them must travel down to ground level, walk across the plaza to the other tower, and ride up through all the intervening floors to his colleague's office. This route is exactly analogous to the pathway followed by the information sent by one network user to another, with the data traveling down the ISO stack to the physical layer in the first user's system, across to the physical layer in the second user's system, and up to the top of the ISO stack in that system.

The detailed descriptions of the layers in the OSI stack will be easier to understand if you have a conceptual framework to fit them into. You can start at the top of the stack, with user applications, not only because of their familiarity, but also because they contain all the functions and entities that live on the lower layers.

The applications that live on Layer 7 can be anything from order-entry systems or airline-reservations systems to library reference-information databases or museum catalog-exchange systems, to name just a few common examples. In terms of their OSI stack function, the applications define the data sets that are transferred and manipulated by the software on layers 6 through 2. The data sets consist of information, arranged in a format defined by the application, that is updated and examined over time.

With the data sets defined, you can step down to Layer 6, whose job is to ensure that the data can be interpreted properly by each type of system (hardware and OS) connected to the network. That's why Layer 6 is called the *presentation layer*. It deals with differences in the binary representation of floating-point operations, and

also with code-conversion issues involving ASCII, Extended Binary Coded Decimal Interchange Code (EBCDIC), Unicode, and special alphabet equivalencies. As you'll see later in this chapter, these responsibilities have recently been expanded to include encryption management.

Layer 5, the *session layer*, determines how each group of interactions between two or more computer systems is handled. Such a group of interactions might consist of, for example, the steps that have to be performed so that an order can be properly placed and tracked in an order-entry system.

Layer 5 is supported by Layer 4, the *transport layer*, which is responsible for ensuring that individual transactions are completed reliably. For example, in an order-entry application, an individual transaction might consist of issuing a notice about the availability of a particular item. Layer 4 is supposed to make sure that the notice is transported reliably from one system to another. If it can't do the job, Layer 4 must report its failure to the entity that requested the transaction.

Layer 3, the *network layer*, provides the data-transfer switching function that allows the messages sent by Layer 4 to reach the system they're supposed to reach. Mind you, Layer 3 doesn't actually *make sure* the messages reach their destination. Any number of bad things can keep that from happening. But, without the directions provided, traffic-cop style, by Layer 3, the messages have no chance of getting anywhere at all.

Layer 2, the *link layer*, oversees the transfer of messages between its own system and a neighboring, physically connected system. Of course, the neighboring system need not be the message's ultimate addressee; it could be just the first of many way stations en route to the final destination. Layer 2 "oversees" because, although it makes sure that an outgoing message is launched, it can't ensure that the message reaches its destination. Layer 2's other job is to capture incoming messages. However (as described later in the chapter),

Layer 2 doesn't take any steps to confirm either the accuracy of those messages or their freedom from errors.

At the bottom of the stack is the only nonsoftware layer. Layer 1 deals with the actual physical transmission of data—electrically, optically, or even (if the system uses conceptual carrier pigeons) ornithologically. (For the latter type, see RFC 1149, dated April 1, 1990.)

For convenience, in the following discussion, the term message refers to the individual elements of a conversation between systems. When humans converse, one person says something, and the other person replies. The "something" is an idea or thought, and a complete unit of meaning conveyed is a message. Most networking protocols work exactly the same way. So, in the remainder of this chapter, the one-way transfer of discrete ideas or thoughts is referred to as a *message*, with a conversation between two computers consisting of exchanges of messages. Assume, for example, that your computer wants to learn the Internet address of the machine **www.linux.org**. To do so, it engages in a series of message exchanges with name servers. The upshot of these message exchanges is that your computer is either told the address or informed that the address can't be found. This type of conversation also takes place when an FTP client system is receiving a file from an FTP server. The server sends data in a message, and the client says, "OK, I've got it; send me some more," and so on, until the server says, "There, you've got it all."

Now, take a closer look at each layer in the stack, from the bottom up.

Layer 1—The Physical Layer

The "street level" of the OSI stack is the physical layer, which handles the nuts-and-bolts business of passing bits between two computers. This layer contains the hardware, and sometimes some of the driver software, components that deal with the transmission and reception of digital bits or groups of bits, such as bytes or groups of bytes—up to, but usually *not* including, complete messages.

The physical layer also performs low-level conversions. In this area, it can convert an electron-based digital bitstream to analog signaling (as in a modem, ISDN terminal adapter, microwave transmission system, wireless link, or satellite link) or to light-based signaling (in fiber-optic or infrared transmission systems).

As noted earlier in this chapter, the OSI model isolates its functions with the zeal of a boarding-school proctor guarding her charges on a field trip. Nowhere is this isolation more evident than in the partition between the physical layer (the only hardware layer) and the link layer (the first of the six software layers). In practice, however, the isolation is breaking down, thanks to certain innovative devices. Some Ethernet chipsets are now so smart that the interface between the physical layer and higher layers is on the chips themselves, and not in the computer at all.

Layer 2—The Link Layer

The link layer is the first of the six software layers in the OSI stack. It handles the mechanics of launching messages over a physical connection to a neighboring computer, and of capturing messages that are received, over the same physical connection, from the neighboring computer. In the OSI model, the link layer does not have to guarantee the correct transfer of data. (Dealing with dropped or incorrect data is the job of the upper-layer software.) Nor does the connection path that the link layer uses have to be bidirectional: for instance, it may be a part of a ring system. Ideally, though, the network of pathways should let each computer talk to every other computer, one way or another.

Even though the link layer isn't required to transfer data reliably, implementations of link–level functionality are permitted to provide a degree of error control. In satellite links, for example, the transmission path is so long, and the likelihood of errors is so great, that some systems implement *forward error correction*. In this process, redundant data is added to the physical datastream so that errors can be caught (and, in many cases, corrected) at the receiving end with no further interaction. In practice, this capability can save significant amounts of expensive satellite-link time, because it can take as long as several seconds for a system to respond to a data-retransmission request issued at a higher level in the model. Closer to home, many modem links between individual computers and ISPs use International Telecommunications Union (ITU) Recommendation V.42 error control. The intent isn't primarily to obtain an error-free link, but rather to allow the use of data correction, as described in ITU Recommendation V.42 *bis*, to increase the capacity of the link. In this respect, reliability is a byproduct of the data-compression scheme.

Although link-layer protocols are supposed to deal with pairs of directly (physically) connected computers, some link-layer protocols allow connections among three or more computers over the same network. The most common of these multiple-endpoint systems is Ethernet, followed closely by Token Ring networking. The OSI model treats each pair of endpoints on a shared network as a separate link-layer connection. In other words, a connection with n computers will have a maximum of $n*(n-1)$ logical links.

Layer 3—The Network Layer

The network layer, which gave the Internet its name, is responsible for routing packets over multiple links on a single network and through gateways between two or more networks. If changes need to be made in packets of information so that the packets can travel across networks, those changes (such as changing that data in the header, or splitting packets to fit the capacity of the transmission path) are made here. In short, this layer's job is specifically to ensure that the data "gets through" the network(s). Any changes in the *form* of the data (such as character-set transformation or byte-order conversion) are the responsibility of the presentation layer.

The network layer is where the routing function lives. Whereas the routing function in a single host computer is straightforward, in a router, it is quite complex. So much so, in fact, that several very thick books have been written on the sole subject of routing over the Internet. Because we're not writing one of those books, our discussion of routing is limited to how it works in conjunction with Linux on desktop computers that are connected to the Internet.

We'd say that routing is the "rocket science" of the Internet, but that wouldn't be fair to rocket science, which is well-grounded and actually extremely rational (if not always intuitive). The "science" of routing is more analogous to the voodoo science of, say, economics—not least of which reasons is that they both offer arenas for the practical application of chaos theory and statistical analysis.

In short, the goal of Layer 3 is to take a message from an end-point computer and deliver it (if possible, intact) to the designated end-point computer, regardless of where the originating and receiving computers are located, and regardless of the Byzantine path the message may have to follow.

Layer 4—The Transport Layer

The transport layer is responsible for providing end-to-end connectivity between two specific computers on the network. This connectivity may consist of a stream of data or may be in the form of a single "connectionless" exchange of messages. The transport layer is the lowest layer in which the only peer entities involved are the peers that live in the source and destination computers, and not in any of the way-station systems used by Layer 3 to transfer messages over the network.

Consider the implications of that last statement. The implementation of the bottom two layers (Layer 1 and Layer 2) communicates on a point-to-point basis, computer to computer. The network layer (Layer 3) knits multiple point-to-point links into a path. The data stays at the network layer (or lower) until it reaches the destination computer. Only then does it travel to a higher layer in the OSI stack model. (Think of an underground pipeline, or a lawn-sprinkler conduit, that doesn't surface until it gets to the specified endpoint.)

What about your multicomputer LAN? Can it be thought of as a point-to-point connection? Conceptually, yes. A LAN provides a logical point-to-point connection between two machines, using a shared medium, and the LAN hardware functions in much the same way as the switch in a telephone system. Even though your voice call (network message) is handled by a potentially huge number of nodes, it appears to you that a direct private link exists between you (the source computer) and your interlocutor (the destination computer).

The protocols in the transport layer also have to worry about the Quality of Service (QoS) they provide to upper layers. The Quality of Service specification provides a handy way to characterize the most important aspects of data-transfer operations. The exact services that are needed may be different for each upper layer and for each Layer 7 application. For some applications, such as realtime audio, the timely arrival of data is more important than whether the data is error-free. For other applications, such as databases, accuracy and the proper sequencing of updates are far more important than the time it takes to complete a transaction. File transfers often occupy a middle ground. The error rate should be low and the connection should be robust, but the priority of the transfer is lower than that of a transfer of voice or music in real time. Alternatively, a file transfer may have been instructed to use the cheapest path rather than the fastest one. The following list summarizes (in alphabetical order) the QoS metrics that may or may not be important to specific types of data transactions over the network:

- Connection-establishment delay

- Connection-failure probability

- Connection robustness

- Data presentation order

- End-to-end transmission delay

- Error rate

- Priority

- Throughput

- Transfer-failure probability

The transport layer is the layer that's usually most concerned with the correction of transmission errors, because the error rate is a QoS issue. The actual error-correction scheme that the transport layer employs is also dictated by the QoS requested by the upper layers. Sometimes the transport layer simply has to indicate the presence of an error; other times, it has to "fix" the error, using whatever means it can find.

In a large network, such as the Internet, the transport layer is responsible for ensuring that, for streaming circuits, the data packets are presented to the upper layers on the receiving side in the same order in which they were presented to the transport layer on the sending side by the software residing on the upper layers.

Layer 5—The Session Layer

The session layer defines the format of the data that will be transmitted over the transport layer's connection, and also specifies the way in which the data will be exchanged.

A good example of a session-layer protocol is the Remote Procedure Call (RPC) protocol, as defined in the Xerox Network System (XNS) and replicated in several other networking systems (including the TCP/IP implementation of Linux). This protocol extends the concept of a function or subroutine call to a multiple-machine environment, allowing a program residing on one system to call a function or a subroutine residing on another system. The client-session protocol (the caller) makes a call to a remote procedure and passes parameters. The server-session protocol (the responder) then performs the remote procedure, returning a response to the call. Sun's Network File System (NFS) implementation uses RPCs to gain access to remote file systems, with each RPC performing a specific operation, such as Open, Close, Read, Write, Reposition (Seek), and Report Position (Tell), on a file.

Layer 6—The Presentation Layer

Early in the development of the model, ISO's researchers identified several data-exchange functions that warranted developing a general solution rather than forcing the applications to develop unique implementations of those functions. These functions live on the presentation layer of the stack. They include, for example, character-code conversion from one character set to another—usually between the EBCDIC and ASCII character sets. (This conversion is especially important when mainframes, which speak primarily EBCDIC, are exchanging data with scientific supercomputers, which seem to live in the world of ASCII.)

The compatibility and conversion issues go beyond character sets. For example, several different binary representations exist for floating-point numbers, each of which is incompatible with the others. In this context, the transfer of floating-point numbers very quickly becomes a question of data representation. For another example, data compression is very desirable in some applications, and the two sides of the conversation must agree on the details of this function.

The presentation layer, as defined by ISO, was intended to address the issue of encryption. However, in contemporary practice, particularly in the Virtual Private Network (VPN) world, encryption is implemented through the use of *tunnels*, in a technique that builds a second OSI stack on top of the main stack. Tunnels are also used to encapsulate the protocols of one networking system for transport through another networking system. Either way, in the ISO/OSI model, the tunnel is considered to be a presentation-layer protocol.

Layer 7—The Application Layer

The way in which users use a network is dictated by the applications that live on the linked systems. As befits their dominant role, the applications occupy the penthouse floor of the OSI model. As mentioned earlier, applications come in a range of flavors, limited only by the imagination and industriousness of their creators. Here are two examples:

- *Telnet*—Years ago, companies that couldn't afford their own computers would buy terminals and modems, using the modems for access to computers that offered services on a time-share basis. During the early days of the ARPAnet, researchers realized that this type of service needed to be provided between nodes on the ARPAnet. Thus was born the "network teletype" application known as Telnet. Using Telnet, a person connected to one computer via a terminal could ask that a call be made, via the network, to another computer. Through the resulting connection, the user could establish a terminal session on the remote machine, thereby relieving the user of the need to log off from the first computer to make a call, via modem, to the second computer.

- *Check processing*—A bank has several regional check-processing centers located around the state, with each processing center servicing the branches of the bank that are located within a radius of, say, 50 miles. Every night, couriers deliver the checks that were presented at the teller windows at the branches, and those checks are processed. As each check is read by the reader-sorter machines, information about it is transmitted via the network to the bank's state headquarters. Any exception conditions (stop payments, closed accounts, or special handling) are reported to the regional processing center so that specific checks can be handled manually. Meanwhile, during the same check-processing run, the account ledgers and the bank's general ledger (implemented, of course, as multicomputer databases) are updated. As a result, at the start of each business day, a customer can get up-to-date information about the status of an account by using the network from a teller station at any branch.

Mapping TCP/IP To The OSI Model

As noted at the beginning of this chapter, the ISO/OSI model was created in parallel with the early development of the ARPAnet, and was largely based on the design of centrally controlled mainframe networks. The surprise isn't how difficult it is to map TCP/IP, with its distributed-control orientation, to the OSI model; rather, the surprise is how well the OSI layers match up with specific TCP/IP equivalents.

The communications hardware and the device drivers in a typical TCP/IP system map to the physical and link layers of the network. TCP/IP doesn't worry about the exact dividing line between these layers, because the device drivers in Linux are nothing more than a data-transfer agent between the hardware (which has a surprising amount of smarts) and the caller (in this case, the Internet Protocol module).

The Address Resolution Protocol (ARP) and the Reverse Address Resolution Protocol (RARP) live at the boundary of the link and network layers. These protocols provide a way to bind physical LAN addresses (such as the Ethernet address) to IP addresses. Because this binding applies only to the local system and to directly connected LANs, these protocols live "below" the routing function. Because of its built-in routing function, IP implements the middle of the network layer.

Associated with IP in the network layer are the various routing protocols (RIP—Routing Information Protocol, BGP—Border Gateway Protocol, OSPF—Open Shortest Path First, and EGP—Exterior Gateway Protocol). Although all of these protocols may be present in a particular computer, the vast majority of Linux computers that are not being used specifically as routers usually have only RIP.

Taken collectively, all of these protocols maintain the routing table within the computer. This means that the protocols talk directly only to "neighboring" machines—

the ones with a physical connection to the machine on which the protocols live. (As mentioned earlier, every machine on a LAN is considered to be a neighboring machine, because of the logical direct connection between any given computer and each of the other computers on the LAN.)

The Internet Control Message Protocol (ICMP) and the Internet Group Message Protocol (IGMP) live at the top of the network layer. They provide information to other protocols that live at still-higher layers and, ultimately, to the server (or human user).

The Transmission Control Protocol (TCP) and the User Datagram Protocol (UDP) are the two transport-layer protocols. TCP provides virtual-connection services, while UDP provides connectionless services.

In the Linux implementation of TCP/IP, all the previously described protocols either reside in the kernel or are loaded as kernel modules. The protocols described next are implemented outside the kernel, usually either as a library routine built into the application or as a user process called a *daemon*.

The Secure Socket Layer (SSL) protocol is a session-layer protocol. Remote Procedure Call (RPC) is also a session-layer protocol; it rides on top of SSL, when SSL is present. In the TCP model, SSL becomes part of the top of the transport layer. RPC is treated as part of the Network File System application, because it's one of the few applications that uses RPC.

In the TCP/IP model, the presentation layer is empty. The functions that live there in the OSI model are subsumed under the design of the applications that use TCP/IP.

Lastly, the applications that use TCP/IP—FTP, Telnet, X, mail, the World Wide Web, rlogin, finger, rsh (Remote Shell), Network Time Protocol (NTP), to mention just a few—live on the application layer.

Loading session- and presentation-level protocol code into the applications has many practical advantages:

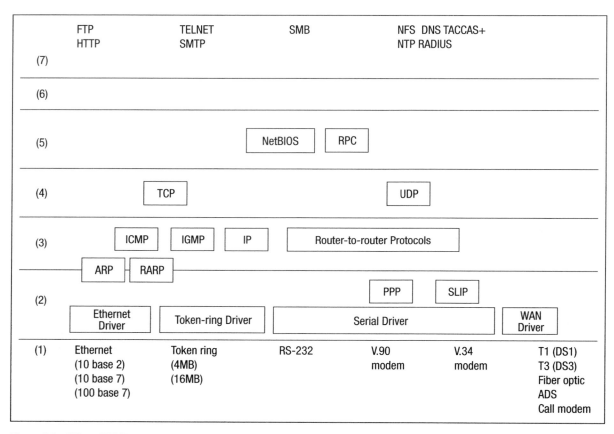

Figure 3.2   Where TCP/IP protocols sit in the ISO model.

- The basic TCP/IP implementation remains stable over time.

- The new protocols can be implemented on top of the existing transport protocols without requiring changes in the stack.

- Researchers can develop the protocols without having to hack the operating system, and their development work doesn't affect the system when the system is used for other purposes.

- An application's code can be tweaked much more easily than an operating system can be rebuilt. (On a 300MHz Pentium computer, it takes about 10 seconds to rebuild an experimental app and about 20 minutes to rebuild a kernel.)

- Application code can be debugged with a standard debugger.

The new protocols can be implemented as library routines, which can in turn be incorporated into programs, if the programs want them. The Transport Layer Security protocol (RFC 2246, also known as the Secure Sockets Layer Protocol) has been working its way into applications in exactly this way. Another protocol that has followed this path is Domain Name System (DNS), which began as an experiment in deleting static host tables and grew into a distributed namespace-management service. Every serious Internet application uses it, but in the form of a library routine, not as a service.

An overall advantage of having presentation-level protocols in the application is that the method of allocating time to them is decided by the application, rather than being a system-tuning issue. More importantly, the application can use the library-routine interface to control the QoS parameters with respect to the presentation-level protocols far more easily than if the application had to use the application programming interface (API) to set these parameters.

In conclusion, TCP/IP has been found to fit well enough into the ISO/OSI model to allow the model to be used successfully in the development of new and improved TCP/IP protocols. The descriptions of the layers are very useful in defining the structure of networking within TCP/IP. The differences are minor (and serve as great topics for master's theses). Most importantly, the theoretical structure of networking communications that was developed with the OSI model can be applied, with very few changes, to TCP/IP applications. This structure provides a foundation for continuing developments in TCP/IP networking, and also gives researchers the option of using TCP/IP as a workbench for testing and refining these developments.

Chapter 4

ICMP

The Internet Control Message Protocol is TCP/IP's one-trick pony. It was designed to do a single simple thing: provide a way for a system located anywhere on a network to report problems with packets that have been sent to it.

Using ICMP, any networked system can transmit a complaint to any other networked system that is generating faulty packets or asking for resources unavailable on the addressed system. The network path can contain as few as two systems or as many as several hundred. No matter how many hops the path involves, ICMP messages can still find their way back to the originating system—that is, they usually can. In other words, ICMP acknowledges Murphy's Third Law—"If anything can go wrong, it will"—and tries to enable prompt recovery from transient problems by letting the sending program know that a data packet is having trouble or causing problems.

The original intent of ICMP (which was introduced in the mid-1980s) was to provide error notification and some low-level network-testing mechanisms. Because ICMP was built into the system at the kernel level, it didn't need applications-level support. Nor did it require many system resources. Naturally, researchers and users soon came up with nifty new ideas for testing the network, and ICMP became somewhat bloated. At one point, attempts were even made to load more functions into ICMP. Fortunately, the functions that didn't refer specifically to network management were later properly moved to non-kernel protocols, such as BOOTP (Boot Protocol) and DHCP (Dynamic Host Configuration Protocol).

In addition to its error-message functions, ICMP still includes several services (which operate via query/response packets) that let a system administrator (whether human or cybernetic) track down problems on the network. These services are provided on the assumption that before a communications problem can be fixed, it first has to be found. And in order for it to be found, the network has to be diagnosed. ICMP's diagnostic tools, such as Ping and Timestamp, help system administrators do this.

But, you might ask, aren't ICMP packets themselves subject to diagnostics? The query/response packets are; the error packets aren't. Query/response packets are handled by the ICMP code in the same way as non-ICMP packets. But corrupted or defective ICMP error-report packets simply disappear. This is actually a good thing, because it would be difficult (not to mention wasteful of system resources) to try to track the permutations and combinations of layered error reports. It's much simpler, and in fact more effective, just to forget munged error packets.

Overall, ICMP is fairly compact and well focused—which makes it a good place to start this commentary. The protocols and the functions that implement them are relatively simple, so you can ease into seeing how Internet Protocol (IP) works in Linux.

Well-Mannered Messages

In contrast to almost every other error-detection and error-notification message system in computing (whose level of civility rarely rises above "Nyah-nyah, you goofed"), ICMP messages are like a polite tap on the shoulder ("Pardon me, but your slip is showing"). In other words, they are purely advisory. They have to be, because there's no guarantee that an ICMP message will get back to the originating system. ICMP packets are just as prone as any other Internet Protocol packet to being lost or mangled on their way through the Internet clouds. Thus, ICMP messages constitute a best-effort way to let an originating system know that something went wrong with a packet.

ICMP messages also help speed up error processing. If a computer system gets an ICMP message, it doesn't need to wait for a timeout before taking corrective action. Assume, for example, that System A sends a defective IP packet (such as one that specifies a TCP port number that isn't attached to a peer process in the remote system). The receiving system (System B) can either drop the packet (forget it), hazard a guess about what to do with the packet, or drop the packet and send back an ICMP error message telling the originating system what went wrong.

An ICMP error message contains the headers of a packet that was sent, so the ICMP message can correlate the error with a specific location in an IP packet header. For instance, suppose an IP packet is used to carry an Exterior Gateway Protocol (EGP) packet. System A is running EGP and directs an EGP packet (which is an IP packet that specifies the EGP in its header) to System B. But suppose System B isn't running EGP. System B will then generate an ICMP packet that contains a copy of the front (that is, the first 48 or so bytes) of the packet that triggered the error—this is so the system receiving the ICMP message can figure out which process and socket has the problem. This ICMP packet contains a pointer to the protocol field in the IP packet header, and the type code in the ICMP packet says, "Parameter problem," and the subtype (the "code") says, "IP header bad."

Most ICMP error messages are sent back to the ultimate, original source of the offending IP packet. However, there is one exception: the ICMP Redirect packet. When System A sends a packet to System B, and System B determines that the *only* route for the packet is back through System A, then not only does System B return the packet, but System B also sends an ICMP Redirect packet to System A to let System A know that System B thinks that System A has a problem in its routing tables—did you follow all that?

Figure 4.1 shows the layout of the ICMP packet and the values for specific fields within the packet, and Table 4.1 shows the values for the **type** and **code** fields for

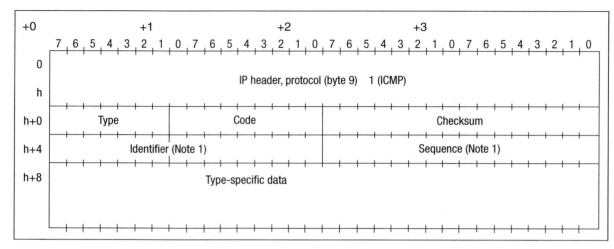

Figure 4.1 ICMP packet layout and field definitions.

each type of ICMP packet. No specific ports are associated with ICMP packets. The actual length of an ICMP packet depends on the implementation of the protocol that is running on the system that is sending the packet.

For the packet types marked with an asterisk (*) in Table 4.1, the type-specific data field contains at least the entire IP packet header plus the first 8 bytes of the IP packet payload. Some systems return exactly 8 bytes, while others return more data. The purpose for having at least 8 bytes of IP packet data is so that identifying information from an encapsulated TCP or UDP header is available to the software parsing the ICMP error packet. As you will see in Chapter 8 and Chapter 9, the first 8 bytes contain the source and destination ports for the packet, so that the ICMP packet can be associated with a unique socket object in the transmitting system.

In RFC 792, the amount of data to be returned in an ICMP error packet is specified in the following way:

"The internet header plus the first 64 bits of the original..."

Table 4.1 Type and code details.

TYPE	LEN	CODE	MEANING
0	>=h+8		Echo Request
		0	Remote system requests Echo Reply packet (type 8) (fixed)
3*	>=h+36		Destination Unreachable
		0	Net unreachable—remote subnet not accessible (obsolete)
		1	Host unreachable—the host identified by IP address not accessible
		2	Protocol unreachable—protocol module not available
		3	Port unreachable—the host has no connection to the address and port available
		4	Fragmentation blocked—packet too large and Don't Fragment flag set in IP header
		5	Source route failed—address on source route list not accessible
4*	>=h+36		Source Quench
		0	Slow down transmission rate (fixed)
5*	>=h+36		Redirect (redirect target IP address in h+4)

Table 4.1 Type and code details *(continued)*.

TYPE	LEN	CODE	MEANING
		0	Redirect network—in future, send datagrams for this network to target IP address
		1	Redirect host—in future, send datagrams for this host to target IP address
		2	Redirect network and TOS—in future, send datagrams for this network and TOS to target IP address
		3	Redirect host and TOS—in future, send datagrams for this host and TOS to target IP address
8	>=h+8		Echo Reply
		0	Copy of Echo Request packet (fixed)
11*	>=h+36		Time (hop count) Exceeded
		0	TTL (Time to Live) exceeded in transit
		1	Fragment reassembly time exceeded
12*	>=h+36		Parameter Problem
		0	Pointer [byte at h+8] to error field
			Pointer=1 problem with TOS
			Pointer=16 problem with destination address
			Pointer>=20 problem in IP options field
13	h+20		Timestamp Request
		0	(fixed)
14	h+20		Timestamp Reply
		0	(fixed)
15	h+8		Information Request (obsolete)
		0	Used to request "this" network number (fixed)
16	h+8		Information Reply (obsolete)
		0	Used to provide "this" network number to the requestor (fixed)
17	h+12		Address Mask Request
		0	(fixed)
18	h+12		Address Mask Response
		0	Packet contains network address of subnetwork (fixed)

*Types that return the first n bytes of the packet that caused the ICMP packet to be generated (see the discussion in the text).

(continued)

Some implementers casually misread the preceding statement and return the Internet header plus 64 *bytes* of the IP packet payload. This error, which has been observed on some Solaris systems, is benign.

For an exhaustive discussion of every combination of ICMP type and code, refer to RFC 792 (the base specification) and RFC 950 (the address mask query/response extension, both of which appear on the CD-ROM). Meanwhile, the notes in Table 4.1 provide a short description for each code.

For the packet types in Table 4.1 that are *not* marked with an asterisk, the packet is a query or a response to a query. These query-type packets allow problems in the Internet to be diagnosed in a uniform way, without causing huge increases in traffic or having to deal with details of implementation of diagnostic systems. (This does not keep a particular system from deploying its own diagnostic routines, but ICMP query/response packets provide a common set of test tools to the network administrator.)

Table 4.2 shows the ICMP functions listed by name, and Table 4.3 shows them listed by line number.

Table 4.2   Functions, listed by name.

Line	Function
10078	**icmp_address**
9531	**icmp_build_xmit**
10124	**icmp_chkaddr**
10099	**icmp_discard**
9987	**icmp_echo**
9495	**icmp_glue_bits**
10360	**icmp_init**
9482	**icmp_out_count**
10181	**icmp_rcv**
9885	**icmp_redirect**
9559	**icmp_send**
10015	**icmp_timestamp**
9678	**icmp_unreach**
9402	**xrlim_allow**
9377	**xrlim_init**

Table 4.3   Functions, listed by line number.

Line	Function
9377	**xrlim_init**
9402	**xrlim_allow**
9482	**icmp_out_count**
9495	**icmp_glue_bits**
9531	**icmp_build_xmit**
9559	**icmp_send**
9678	**icmp_unreach**
9885	**icmp_redirect**
9987	**icmp_echo**
10015	**icmp_timestamp**
10078	**icmp_address**
10099	**icmp_discard**
10124	**icmp_chkaddr**
10181	**icmp_rcv**
10360	**icmp_init**

The code consists of three groups of functions:

- *Incoming functions*—live in the local system and handle the ICMP packets that the system receives

- *Outgoing functions*—live in the local system and generate the ICMP packets destined for other systems

- *Housekeeping routines*—live in the source code and handle the startup procedures

Incoming Functions

To understand how ICMP packets are received, you first need to know how packets are received in the Linux system and how they get to the ICMP protocol modules. (The same general process also applies for all other TCP/IP protocols.) When a network device driver has collected a complete packet of data, the driver builds an **sk_buff** structure. This structure is then passed to the function **netfi_rx**, which is located in /usr/src/linux/net/core/dev.c (not included in the code listings in this book, but contained on this book's CD-ROM). The packet is then added to the queue that is anchored by the list head **backlog**, the flag for the backend handler is set, and control is returned to the driver that called **netfi_rx**.

Note that as of kernel release 2.0.34, the **netfi_rx** function allows only 300 packets to be backlogged. When the size of the backlog queue reaches 300 packets, any new packets that need to be placed in the queue are instead silently dropped. Unfortunately, this kernel release does not log the number of these overflow packets that have been dropped.

The function **net_bh** (at line 7260) is the backend handler. This routine first takes care of packet buffers that are queued for output and then starts processing the incoming packets, starting with the first one in the input queue. This might seem odd, but by passing on the packets to be output first, the physical device drivers can be sending the packets while the **net_bh** function handles the incoming ones, thereby increasing the parallel processing capability of the code. If bridging support has been configured, the packet is first handed to the bridge router code. If the bridge router code doesn't return the packet (that is, if the packet isn't an IP packet), processing continues with the next packet buffer. If the bridge router code does return the packet, the function **net_bh** performs more operations on it, as described at the end of this section. (Naturally, if bridging support hasn't been configured, the packet is processed directly.)

The driver sets the top-level protocol in the **sk_buff** structure. An example of this structure appears in Figure 4.2, which shows the contents of **sk_buff** for an Ethernet data frame. (Part of the data in this frame is a "protocol number" that refers to the Ethernet packet contents' protocol rather than to the IP protocol.)

The 16-bit type field contains the data value 0x0800 for an Internet Protocol packet. The other two values of the 16-bit type field used by Linux are 0x0806 (for an Address Resolution Protocol [ARP] request or reply packet) and 0x835 (for a Reverse Address Resolution Protocol [RARP] request and reply packet). These three types of packets are the only ones used in standard TCP/IP. The various Ethernet standards contain a long list of other 16-bit type codes, which you can find on the Web by using standard search techniques. Alternatively, see

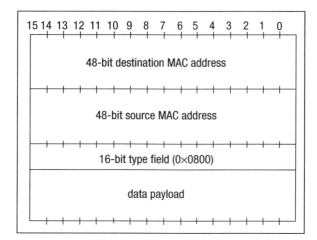

```
15 14 13 12 11 10  9  8  7  6  5  4  3  2  1  0

        48-bit destination MAC address

        48-bit source MAC address

        16-bit type field (0×0800)

        data payload
```

Figure 4.2   The structure of an IP Ethernet data frame.

the ETHER TYPES section of RFC 1700, which is included on the CD-ROM. Other link-level protocols (such as PPP) have similar mechanisms for identifying IP packets and segregating them from the other kinds of packets.

As previously noted, the driver sets the **protocol** field in the **sk_buff** structure. The **net_bh** function uses this value to find a matching protocol handler and then passes the packet to that handler. The handler examines the IP header in the packet buffer and plucks out the IP protocol number (that is, the high-order 16 bits of the second 32-bit word). Then, the handler looks up that number in the protocol registration tables. From there, the handler picks up the IP-protocol entry point (see /usr/src/linux/net/protocol.c, not included in this book) in the protocol steering structure and calls the entry-point routine. For ICMP, this routine is the function **icmp_rcv**.

icmp_rcv

The **icmp_rcv** function (line 10181) is called whenever an ICMP packet has been received and hasn't been sidetracked by another process (such as a firewall routine).

10191: Increment the incoming packet counter in the statistics table.

10193: If the packet is too small (a runt packet), purge it.

10206: If the packet checksum is incorrect, purge the packet and increment the packet-in-error statistics table counter.

10224: The highest known ICMP type value is 18. Anything higher than 18 "is a mystery" (as the comment on the code states). If the type value is too high, increment the packet-in-error statistics table counter and purge the packet.

10244: If transparent-proxy support has been compiled into the kernel, then check for a local address or a proxied address that is not a broadcast or multicast address. If this test fails and the packet is not an ICMP_ECHO packet, then increment the packet-in-error statistics table counter and purge the packet. If the packet is an ICMP_ECHO packet, then substitute the local machine's address and continue.

10247: If transparent-proxy support has not been compiled into the kernel, the packet is not for a local address, and the packet is not an ICMP_ECHO packet, then increment the packet-in-error statistics table counter and purge the packet. If the packet is an ICMP_ECHO packet, then substitute the local machine's address and continue.

10272: Calculate the length of the ICMP payload.

The following two comments refer to the structure definition **icmp_control** at line 9324 and the array-definition table **icmp_pointers[]** starting at line 10297. The SNMP MIP definition structure **icmp_mib**, which defines the ICMP counters, starts at line 41461.

10273: Increment the counter for the specific class of ICMP packet in the statistics table.

10275: Call the processing routine for this ICMP type; then, return 0 to the caller.

Table 4.4 shows the relationship between the ICMP **type** field and the routine called (taken from the table information at line 10297).

Table 4.4   ICMP type field values and the processing functions that handle packets having those type field values.

Type	Function
0	icmp_discard
1	icmp_discard
2	icmp_discard
3	icmp_unreach
4	icmp_unreach
5	icmp_redirect
6	icmp_discard
7	icmp_discard
8	icmp_echo
9	icmp_discard
10	icmp_discard
11	icmp_unreach
12	icmp_discard
13	icmp_timestamp
14	icmp_discard
15	icmp_discard
16	icmp_discard
17	icmp_address
18	icmp_discard

icmp_discard

The function **icmp_discard** (line 10099) is used when the only thing the ICMP module is supposed to do with a packet is to get rid of it. This function, which simply removes a packet from memory, is called for ICMP types 0, 1, 2, 6, 7, 9, 10, 12, 14, 15, 16, and 18.

icmp_unreach

The function **icmp_unreach** (line 9678) is called for ICMP types 3, 4, and 11. This code, when appropriate, is used in maximum transmission unit (MTU) discovery, which is the process used with TCP connections to sense the maximum packet size that can be transmitted through a path from one machine to another without fragmenting the packet. Finally, the function also passes the error information to any other module that wants this information.

9688:   If the packet is a runt packet, go to line 9876, flush the packet, and return. (Although many style guides allow the **goto** statement for error exits, this is one of the few places where it appears in the TCP/IP implementation in Linux.)

9691:   Calculate the start of the original IP packet header within the ICMP packet payload.

9693:   Calculate the length of the IP packet header. If the length field in the IP packet header is 0, then flush the packet and return.

9697:   Calculate the start of the original-IP payload, the data that was sent as part of the original IP packet that generated the ICMP message in the remote system. (This payload could be a UDP header or the first bytes of a TCP header.)

9699:   If the ICMP packet is type Destination Unreachable, then the code in the packet (the subtype) must be examined for additional information—and this job requires a lot of grungy code. If the ICMP packet isn't type Destination Unreachable, go to line 9817 and continue from there.

9701:   Examine the code associated with the packet. (Unfortunately, this code can be "spoofed," because the value of the code is masked to 4 bits by the expression in the switch statement. Fortunately, this boo-boo has no serious security implications.) Only two values are of real interest to this block of code: **type ICMP_PORT_UNREACH** and **type ICMP_FRAG_NEEDED**. For all other values, this code simply passes control to line 9814.

9713:   If the code value is equal to **ICMP_PORT_UNREACH**, pass control to line 9814.

9716:   If the code value is equal to **ICMP_FRAG_NEEDED**, a router somewhere on the path didn't like the size of the packet, and the packet that was sent had the Don't Fragment flag set in the IP header. The remainder of the code, from here to line 9817, addresses this condition.

9717:   If the operating system was compiled with the configuration option **CONFIG_NO_PATH_MTU_DISCOVERY** (an infrequently selected option, because MTU discovery can improve throughput by reducing the impact of losing a fragment packet), and if debug support was requested, a diagnostic message is issued and control is passed to line 9814.

9723:   If MTU path discovery has been configured, the process of determining a better trial MTU starts here. The old MTU is the length of the transmitted packet. The suggested MTU may be passed in the data portion of the ICMP packet.

9748:   When the sanity check of the hints in the ICMP packet fails, this code reduces the existing MTU value by four times the length of the header.

9753:   If the path MTU is too short (the limit is 68 bytes) or if the new MTU is larger than the old MTU, then it's time to guess at good values. The guessing happens in lines 9765 through 9795.

9803:   Because there is no good way to pass the MTU value back to protocols that want to know it, this code sticks the new MTU in a magic place: the ID field of the enclosed IP packet of the ICMP message.

9814:   After the code processing has been completed, check whether the value of the code field is too big. If it is, go to line 9876 to get rid of the packet. (Strictly speaking, this should have been done earlier, as input validation, before line 9701.)

9834:   This block of code calls each protocol handler that has registered an ICMP handler routine.

This routine is triggered when the code field has a value of ICMP Port Unreachable, or when the message refers to an error (which is manifested when the source address of the ICMP packet matches the destination [remote host] address of the original IP packet that caused the ICMP packet to be generated). The code picks up the root protocol (IP, or whatever) from the protocol hash table. The code then walks through the list of protocols associated with the main protocol, calling the error handler for each one. This process continues until the entire protocol chain has been processed. For IP, this means that the UDP and TCP protocols are contacted and passed the ICMP information.

9877:   The received ICMP packet is no longer needed. This code removes the packet from memory and from all the socket buffer chains. That's all there is to it!

icmp_redirect

The Internet, like any good social group, is held together by its gossips. In this case, the "gossips" are the routers, which carry tales about better ways to route packets. One mechanism for passing the rumors is the ICMP Redirect packet, which a router can use to tell its neighbor, "You really shouldn't send packets for address x to *me*, because I'll just hand them right back to you."

Now, if the system that is running this code is also running a routing protocol, then any ICMP redirects *must* be ignored, because the information returned by a downstream host may be out of date and therefore unreliable. In fact, for security reasons, many system administrators disable the recognition of all redirects on all of their machines—doing so prevents the redirection of packets toward a specific machine as part of a "man in the middle" attack. However, there is a purpose for ICMP redirects in smaller networks, so corporate LANs often enable them inside the campus, while blocking redirects that try to come in from the outside.

There are four types of redirects: network, host, network plus type-of-service, and host plus type-of-service. The code in this function that implements redirects worries about the first two types and ignores the type-of-service (TOS) redirects.

9934: Normally, the code that implements a network redirection is not compiled into the system, which is why the conditional compilation is based on the definition of the symbol **not_a_good_idea** in the module. If it is compiled into the system, this code passes the information contained in the ICMP packet to the router code (Chapter 6 describes what the **ip_rt_add** function does with the information) so that the routing table can be updated.

9955: On a host redirect, the information from the ICMP packet is sent to the **ip_rt_redirect** function (described in Chapter 6). The comments talk about performing many checks, but those checks are done in the routing code, not here.

9958: Any Redirect packets that involve type-of-service indications are discarded. When debug mode is turned on, the kernel will record that the TOS redirect was received and that nothing was done with it.

9971: After the ICMP packet information has been processed, the memory in which the packet was stored is released for other uses, and the function returns.

icmp_echo

One of the most important networking tools is a program called Ping, which sends out a "tickle" to an IP address. If and when the addressed system sees the tickle, it responds with a packet that contains the data from the original tickle packet. (Some very old documentation on the ICMP echo service refers to a "ping" packet and a "pong" packet. Modern documentation avoids this terminology.) Because the protocol is de-

signed to use as few resources as possible, this diagnostic aid minimizes the load on the network, hosts, and routers.

If the kernel has been compiled to respond to echo (which is the normal case), this code (at lines 9993 through 10000) changes the function to **ICMP_ECHO-REPLY**, checks to see whether echo is enabled, and sends the modified packet back toward the caller.

In any event, the memory for the original packet is released.

icmp_timestamp

The ICMP Timestamp packet was one of the early techniques for measuring the realtime performance of the Internet. It's still around.

The processing is fairly simple. Runt packets (packets that occupy fewer than 12 bytes of payload space) are discarded with no fanfare. The information from the received packet is copied into the Echo Reply packet, and the current time is put into its proper place in the reply. The new packet is then queued.

The memory for the original packet is released, and the function is done.

icmp_address

Linux can operate as a host or as a router. Routers always respond to address mask requests, whereas hosts have the option of responding. Linux's ability to respond to address mask requests while running as a host is a kernel-configuration option in release 2.0.34.

However, according to the comment at line 10082, this function in release 2.0.34 is broken and should not be used. An analysis of this failure is beyond the scope of this book; but when the function is eventually corrected, the following activities should take place: A reply packet should be built that contains the address mask for the subnet on which both the local system and the requesting system reside, and then the memory for the original packet should be released.

icmp_chkaddr

Because the Linux system can act as an intermediary between an untrusted network and a trusted network, the ICMP routines have to worry about ensuring that the ICMP packets are properly forwarded between the two networks. This is particularly true for *transparent-proxy* applications, in which the Linux box takes packets that were received on one interface and sends them onward to machines on another interface, transmitting those forwarded packets using the proxy machine's IP address, and then correctly steers all the return traffic (including ICMP notifications).

10133: If the ICMP handler routine that was selected was neither **icmp_unreach** nor **icmp_redirect**, then return 0 (saying, in effect, "No, that routine isn't one of ours").

10138: If the ICMP packet is handling a response to a TCP packet, test for the following conditions:

- The socket exists

- The socket source address matches the source of the packet

- The socket destination address matches the destination of the packet

If all three of these conditions are met, then return 1 (saying, in effect, "Yes, that packet is one of ours"); otherwise, return 0 to disavow all knowledge.

10154: Give UDP-triggered ICMP packets the same treatment that TCP-triggered packets got in the previous paragraph. The details differ somewhat, but the result is the same.

10173: When all else fails, tell the caller that we know nothing...nothing!

Outgoing Functions

When other parts of the system ask it to do so, the ICMP protocol handler builds the ICMP packets to be shipped to the other system. This centralization minimizes the need for UDP, TCP, and other protocols to "know" how to build ICMP packets. In essence, the calling routine identifies both the type of ICMP packet that is needed and the address of the system that ultimately needs to see the packet. The ICMP packets are usually found in the error-trapping routines in other protocols. Standard practice is to let many errors pass without comment, but when certain major blunders happen, the protocol handlers just have to rub the sender's nose in them.

icmp_xrlim_init

One way to launch a denial-of-service (DoS) attack on a system is to cause the system to generate ICMP messages. To help prevent DoS attacks, this routine initializes the transmission-rate limitation mechanism, which allows floods of ICMP messages to be stemmed.

This function walks through the table **icmp_pointers** and resets all the destination addresses within the pointer cache to the "none" address.

The next function implements the transmission-rate limitation.

icmp_xrlim_allow

This function determines whether the current packet scheduled to be transmitted should or should not be sent out of the system. If the packet should be dropped, the function returns 0. If the packet should be accepted for transmission, the function returns 1 (non–0).

9408: If the type code is unknown, tell the caller to ship it.

9410: If the type code has no limit cache, tell the caller to ship it.

9414: Search the cache for a matching destination address. If one is found, then stop searching.

9423: On a cache miss, use a least-recently used search to find a cache entry to create. Place the destination address in the hijacked cache entry, set the time to the current time (saved in line

9420), set the counter to 1, set the reset time to the timeout value for this type, kill the Too Much flag (which is a local variable), and tell the caller to ship the ICMP packet.

The following code section is supposed to limit the number of packets that are transmitted to a specific target address within a given time interval. Examination of the code shows that it's broken in subtle ways—specifically, it doesn't handle *jiffy wrap* (that is, the rollover of the master clock variable, named **jiffies**, from its maximum value to 0) well at all. ICMP messages to certain addresses could be blocked for all time! Fortunately, this wedge condition occurs only every 49.762 days.

9448: If the cache entry data hasn't expired, increment the counter and check for an overlimit condition. (The allotted number of this type of packet has already been sent.) When the counter is greater than the limit set for the ICMP **type** value, set the Too Much flag, set the time when the throttling code can start sending this type of ICMP packet again, and tell the caller to forget about sending the ICMP packet.

9457: If the cache entry has expired, and the throttling code has started restricting output, return forget-about-sending if the packet hold-off delay is still in effect. Otherwise, set the time when packets can be sent again and return OK-to-send. (Hey, we warned you this was convoluted!)

9464: If the cache entry has expired and if output hasn't been restricted, clear the entry down (that is, set the value of the entry to 0) and return OK-to-send.

icmp_out_count

This function maintains the output counters that are used to monitor system performance under the Simple Network Management Protocol (SNMP). This code increments the counter that records the number of ICMP messages that have been transmitted, and also increments a counter for each type of ICMP message transmitted.

icmp_build_xmt

Building a transmit packet for ICMP is like building a transmit packet for any other protocol in the TCP/IP suite: build the header, calculate the checksum for the header and for the payload, and launch the packet. This function uses the **ip_build_xmit** function to create the packet in a new socket buffer. The information to be transmitted is passed in the structure of type **icmp_bxm**. This information includes the address of the allocated socket buffer (the buffer that is allocated outside this routine).

icmp_send

This function, which starts at line 9559, takes the type, code, and payload information provided by the caller and builds the packet in the socket buffer object passed by the caller. The following filter conditions must be satisfied:

- No broadcast or multicast target addresses must exist.

- Any ICMP packet must refer to the first fragment of a fragmented IP packet.

- ICMP error packets are not sent in response to ICMP error packets (but reply packets are sent to non-error ICMP packets).

- ICMP packets of unknown type are not sent.

- If transmission limiting has been configured, a limit is placed on the number of packets of a particular type that are transmitted to a particular address.

- When ICMP Echo Reply packets are being suppressed, they are not sent.

When these filter conditions have been met (line 9639), the ICMP header is built. The payload is then copied, provided that the total length of the packet is less than 576 bytes (line 9655).

The function sends the whole mess to the **icmp_build_xmit** function for final construction details, and then returns to the caller.

Housekeeping Routines

The last routines in this chapter are ICMP's housekeeping routines, which all live under the umbrella of a single function, **icmp_init**. The **icmp_init** function resides on any system that will be generating and/or receiving ICMP packets. In essence, all this function does is hang out an electronic shingle that announces, "Complaints about bad packets are now being issued and accepted."

icmp_init

This little function registers the ICMP routine with the Linux system and creates a socket to which ICMP packet threads (for sending and receiving ICMP messages) can be hooked. If the function has been configured to do so, it also initializes the transfer-limitation routines.

Chapter 5

Sockets API Overview

In traditional programming—a database query application, for example—the user tells the program what he or she wants done. The application then follows those orders, executing library routines, subroutines, and operating system functions accordingly. In this context, a user's command is like a king's edict, which gets bounced down the power ladder to the poor serf at the bottom.

In contrast, network programming relies on cooperation. Users may think they're issuing commands, but the programs in the underlying application code in the networked computers cooperate with each other to get the job done. Chat programs, which enable two users to type messages to each other in realtime, are a good example of cooperative programming.

To understand the code in the Linux Transmission Control Protocol/Internet Protocol (TCP/IP) stack, you first need to know how applications interact with the Linux kernel. Assume, for example, that you're using a database program on a network. First, you enter a request through the application running on your computer, and then your computer cooperates with another computer, linked via the network, on which the database actually resides.

The API (application programming interface) for the network portion of an application suite provides the tools that let the *client* system and the *server* system work hand in hand. As with most operating services, the underlying implementation code for the API and the server do much of the grunt work for the application suite.

The information in this chapter is a "cheat sheet" for the API. It is not intended as a reference for writing network programs for Linux. Aspiring programmers in this area are strongly encouraged to seek out the book *Unix Network Programming: Volume 1, Networking APIs* by W. Richard Stevens (Prentice-Hall, 1998; ISBN 0-13-490012-X).

Each of the function calls in this chapter is followed by a brief description, a call template, a short explanation of each parameter, and a list of the information returned by the function.

The call templates in this chapter look slightly different from the call templates in the Linux man pages. In our templates, each parameter of a function call appears on a separate line. This line break, which provides visual separation, is especially useful for parameters that are defined as structure pointers.

Major Socket Functions

In the Linux operating system, all application-controlled network-related activities are associated with kernel control blocks. This book refers to each kernel control block as a *socket object*. In turn, socket objects are controlled by *functions*. The functions described in this section create socket objects, register them for specific purposes, use them to transfer data, and destroy them. These functions provide the basic building blocks for network-based applications.

Each socket object is created by a process and is referenced in the application by the file-descriptor (FD) number returned by the call to **socket** or to **accept** that creates that socket object. In Linux, an FD number can be any non-negative integer. The FD number space shares the spaces used for disk files, pipes, and other input/output objects. Each process has its own set of FD numbers, which may duplicate the set of FD numbers in another process. However, FD numbers in different processes can have different meanings. For example, FD "3" in one process may refer to a disk file, while FD "3" in another process may refer to a socket object.

An FD number can be used with the **select** and **poll** functions to allow an application to run as a single process that handles multiple file descriptors. The **select** function in Linux handles FD numbers ranging from 0 through 1,023. In contrast, the FD numbers used with the **poll** function are not limited in any way. For network programming, the **poll** function has the advantage of providing more information about the completion of an I/O transaction than the **select** function provides. (However, the authors have used the **select** function successfully in network applications they have written, in which other functions provide the information that would otherwise be provided by the **poll** function.)

Each socket object has an associated *reference count*. This count is created, with a value of 1, whenever the **socket** or **accept** function creates a new socket object. The reference count is incremented by 1 when the **fork**, **dup**, or **dup2** function is called, and is decremented by 1 when the **close** function is called. When the reference count is decremented to 0 (that is, after all references to the socket object have been removed), the socket object is destroyed.

socket

The **socket** function creates a socket object for a defined communications domain, communications type, and communications protocol. The following code constitutes the template for the call:

```
#include <sys/types.h>
#include <sys/socket.h>
#include <netinet/in.h> /* only need for
SOCK_RAW */
int socket (int domain,
        int type,
        int protocol)
```

In this book, the **domain** parameter is always coded as **AF_INET**. The **type** parameter is coded **SOCK_STREAM** for TCP connections, **SOCK_DGRAM** for User Datagram Protocol (UDP) connections, and **SOCK_RAW** for raw access to Version 4 of the Internet Protocol (IPv4). The **protocol** parameter is normally set to 0, except when **SOCK_RAW** is specified, in which instances the **protocol** parameter is set to **IPPORT_xxx**, or to values that can be found in the file /etc/protocols.

Note that the **type** parameter can also be coded as **SOCK_PACKET** for applications that run in superuser mode. This coding is used in utilities that monitor packet streams for diagnostic purposes. See **tcpdump** for an example of such a program.

If the function fails, −1 is returned. If the function succeeds, a nonnegative FD number is returned. This FD number is used by every other function call to specify the socket object created by the **socket** function.

connect

The **connect** function causes the TCP/IP stack to "open" a connection with a peer system. The action actually performed by the **connect** function depends on the domain and type of socket object referenced by the call. The following code constitutes the template for the call to this function:

```
#include <sys/types.h>
#include <sys/socket.h>
int connect (int sockfd,
        const struct sockaddr *serv_addr,
        int addrlen);
```

For **SOCK_STREAM** sockets, the **connect** call opens a connection to a peer system at the (remote) IP address and port number specified in the structure pointed to by **serv_addr**. The resulting connection stays open until the socket object is destroyed (through use of the **close** function).

For **SOCK_DGRAM** and **SOCK_RAW** sockets, this call creates an associative link between the local socket object (on one side) and the (remote) IP address and port number (on the other side). The application can use the **write**, **writev**, or **send** function (instead of the **sendto** function) to send a packet. The application can also use the **read**, **readv**, or **recv** function (instead of

the **recvfrom** function) to obtain data from the remote peer system. In practice, this means that data can be exchanged via a connected socket, with no need to specify a given IP address and port. Unlike **SOCK_STREAM** sockets, the **connect** function can be called multiple times, each time with a different address for the peer system. (The peer-system address can be set to the unassigned value by setting the IP address to 0.0.0.0.)

Note: This function is not used with **SOCK_PACKET** sockets.

If the function fails, −1 is returned, and the global variable **errno** is set accordingly. If the function succeeds, 0 is returned.

bind

The **bind** function creates an association between a local Internet address and port number, on the one hand, and the socket object, on the other hand. This function is commonly described as "assigning a name to a socket," even though the name is actually an address (instead of a name, such as **www.foo.bar.com**). The following code constitutes the template for the call to this function:

```
#include <sys/types.h>
#include <sys/socket.h>
int bind(int sockfd,
        const struct sockaddr *my_addr,
        int addrlen)
```

This function takes the IP address and port number contained in the structure pointed to by **my_addr** and sets the local address for the socket object specified by the parameter **sockfd**.

In most server systems, the application tells the **my_addr** structure to specify not only the well-known port, but also a wildcard IP address. Thanks to the wildcard IP address, a request for service (as submitted by a client system) can appear on any interface. However, if servers have multiple IP addresses, the server

application may be forced to accept requests for a specific IP address. In such a case, the call to **bind** dictates both the IP address and the port number. This situation often occurs when a public Web server is located at one IP address and a private Web server is at another address, and both addresses refer to the same physical machine. The wildcard option lets the operating system sort out the datastreams, instead of forcing the application to do this job.

In most client applications, the application tells the **my_addr** structure to specify not only a 0 port number, but also a wildcard IP address. When a connection is established, the wildcard IP address tells the system to select a port number from the range of *ephemeral port numbers*. In Linux, ephemeral port numbers are allocated from the set ranging from 1,024 through 32,766. A port number cannot be allocated if it is being used by another socket. If the function fails, −1 is returned, and the global variable **errno** is set accordingly. If the function succeeds, 0 is returned.

listen

The **listen** function converts an active TCP socket (a socket that will be used with the **connect** function) to a passive TCP socket (a socket that will be used with the **accept** function). The following code constitutes the template for the call to this function:

```
#include <sys/socket.h>
int listen(int sockfd,
        int backlog);
```

This function allocates memory for an incoming-connection queue that has at least as many elements as are specified in the parameter **backlog**, and associates that queue with the socket object specified by the parameter **sockfd**. This function should be used only on sockets of type **SOCK_STREAM**.

W.R. Stevens claimed to have discovered a Linux bug that allows any number of connections (limited only by the amount of memory available) to be made if an application specifies parameter **backlog** as 0. We will examine this claim during our analysis of the code.

If the function fails, −1 is returned, and the global variable **errno** is set accordingly. If the function succeeds, 0 is returned.

accept

The **accept** function examines the queue of completed connections for a specified socket object and creates a new socket object that includes not only the remote peer information, but also any parameters that have been negotiated for the new socket object. The following code constitutes the template for the call to this function:

```
#include <sys/types.h>
#include <sys/socket.h>
int accept(int sockfd,
        const struct sockaddr *addr,
        int *addrlen);
```

The **accept** function removes the next available connection from the incoming-connection queue associated with the socket specified by the parameter **sockfd**. If no connections are pending, then **accept** blocks the calling application until a connection is present or until a signal is caught.

When the new socket object is created, the **sockaddr** block pointed to by the parameter **addr** is filled in with the connection information, and the length of the information is placed in the integer variable pointed to by the parameter **addrlen**.

If the function fails, −1 is returned. If the function succeeds, a non-negative descriptor is returned.

read, readv

The **read** and **readv** functions accept data from TCP socket objects and UDP socket objects that are "connected" (via the **connect** function) to a remote peer sys-

tem. The difference between the two functions is that the **read** function specifies a single buffer, while the **readv** (read vector) function specifies up to 16 buffers into which data should be placed. The following two pieces of code constitute the templates for the calls to these functions:

```
#include <unistd.h>
ssize_t read(int sockfd,
        void *buf,
        size_t count);
```

```
#include <sys/uio.h>
int readv(int sockfd,
        const struct iovec *vector,
        size_t count);
```

Both of these functions read data associated with the socket object specified by the parameter **sockfd**. The **read** function reads bytes into the buffer pointed to by the parameter **buf**. (The number of bytes read into the buffer cannot exceed the number of bytes specified by the parameter **count**.) For the **readv** function, the parameter **vector** points to an array of address/length pairs. The **count** parameter specifies how many address/length pairs the array contains, and the function reads, at most, as many bytes into each of the buffers as are specified by the sum of the length members of the address/length pair.

If the function fails, −1 is returned, and the global variable **errno** is set accordingly. If the function succeeds, the total number of bytes read is returned.

If the **read** function is interrupted by a signal after any amount of data has been read, then the return indicates the number of bytes that were read before the interruption occurred. If the **read** or **readv** function is interrupted by a signal before any data has been read, the function returns −1 and sets the global variable **errno** to the value **EINTR**. A return of 0 indicates that the end-of-file (EOF) condition has been reached.

write, writev

The **write** and **writev** functions present data to be transmitted by TCP socket objects, as well as data to be transmitted by UDP socket objects that are "connected" (via the **connect** function) to a remote peer system. The difference between the two functions is that the **write** function specifies a single buffer whereas the **writev** (write vector) function specifies up to 16 buffers from which data is to be transmitted. The following pieces of code constitute the templates for the calls to these functions:

```
#include <unistd.h>
ssize_t write (int sockfd,
        const void *buf,
        size_t count);
```

```
#include <sys/uio.h>
int writev(sockfd,
        const struct iovec *vector,
        size_t count);
```

Both of these functions write data to buffers associated with the socket object specified by the parameter **sockfd**. For the **write** function, the number of bytes specified in the parameter **count** (which must be non-0) are written from the buffer pointed to by the parameter **buf**. For the **writev** function, the parameter **vector** points to an array of address/length pairs, and the **count** parameter specifies how many address/length pairs are in the array. The **writev** function writes, from each of the buffers, the number of bytes specified by the length member of the address/length pair.

If the function fails, −1 is returned, and the global variable **errno** is set accordingly. If the function succeeds, the total number of bytes written is returned.

If the **write** or **writev** function is interrupted by a signal after any amount of data has been read, then the return indicates the number of bytes that were read before the interruption occurred. If the **write** or **writev** function is interrupted by a signal before any data has been written, the function returns –1, and the global variable **errno** is set to **EINTR**.

When an application transmits data via a TCP socket, it is normal for a **write** (or **writev**) function to be incomplete when the amount of data being transmitted exceeds the capacity of the **SNDBUF** window.

shutdown

The **shutdown** function is used with a TCP socket object to inform the system that the transfer of data in one or both directions has been completed. This function provides a way to notify the remote peer system of the end of the datastream ("end of file") being sent to the remote peer system, or to warn the remote peer system that data will no longer be accepted on this socket. The following code constitutes the template for the call to this function:

```
#include <sys/socket.h>
int shutdown(int sockfd,
        int how)
```

This function applies only to TCP connections. The socket object described by the parameter **sockfd** is affected in various ways, depending on the value of the parameter **how**. If the value of **how** is 0, then the reception of data is prohibited. If the value of **how** is 1, then the transmission of data is prohibited, and the remote peer system sees what appears to be an end-of-file (EOF) condition. If the parameter **how** is set to 2, then the effect of this value is equivalent to the effect of value 0 and value 1 simultaneously. In other words, if the value of **how** is 2, then data reception and data transmission are both prohibited, and the remote peer system sees an apparent end-of-file condition. (Posix.1g defines three constants that can be used to define the **how** parameter: **SHUT_RD**, **SHUT_WR**, and **SHUT_RDWR**. However, as of the 2.0.34 release of the Linux kernel, these constants had not been defined for Linux.)

After a **shutdown** function has been applied to the read half of the connection, all data currently pending in the local system is discarded, along with any data that may subsequently be transmitted from the remote peer system.

A **shutdown** function, as applied to the write half of the connection, does not impose its will quite so abruptly. Instead it waits until all the data has been transmitted, and then causes a FIN packet to be transmitted to the remote peer system, to indicate that no more data is forthcoming.

If the function fails, –1 is returned, and the global variable **errno** is set accordingly. If the function succeeds, 0 is returned.

close (a socket object)

The **close** function, which is a standard part of the Linux I/O system, is used to dissociate a file-descriptor (FD) number from a socket object. When the last association has been broken, the socket object is destroyed. The following code constitutes the template for the call to this function:

```
#include <unistd.h>
int close(int sockfd);
```

The **close** function releases the file descriptor that specifies a socket object. If the FD is the last remaining one that points to a socket object (that is, when the reference count on the socket object changes from 1 to 0), then the socket object is closed out, the connection is terminated, and all resources are released. For TCP sockets, unless otherwise indicated by the **SO_LINGER** option, the system makes every effort to send any remaining data to the peer function.

If the function fails, –1 is returned, and the global variable **errno** is set accordingly. If the function succeeds, 0 is returned.

recv, recvfrom, recvmsg

These three functions, which are specific to certain socket objects, are used by most application programs to fetch packets of UDP data received by the Linux system. The following code constitutes the templates for the calls to these functions:

```
#include <sys/types.h>
#include <sys/socket.h>
int recv(int sockfd,
        void *buf,
        int len,
        unsigned flags);
int recvfrom(int sockfd,
        void *buf,
        int len,
        unsigned flags,
        struct sockaddr *from,
        int *fromlen);
int recvmsg(int sockfd,
        struct msghdr *msg,
        unsigned flags);
```

The **recv** function accepts data from a connected socket. This function is basically identical to the **read** function, but has the additional parameter **flags**, which lets the application specify one or more option flags (described later in this section).

The **recvfrom** function accepts data via unconnected sockets, returning the address information from the remote peer system in the data block pointed to by the **from** pointer. The length of the data in the block is returned in the integer pointed to by the **fromlen** parameter. When its parameter **from** is set to **NULL**, the **recvfrom** function is identical to the function **recv**.

The **recvmsg** function accepts data, using a pointer to a **msghdr** structure pointed to by the parameter **msg**, to receive the message, the address, and any return flags.

The **flags** parameter in each of these three functions can be set by OR'ing together one or more of the following constants: **MSG_DONTWAIT** (return immediately, regardless of whether data is present), **MSG_OOB** (receive out-of-band data), **MSG_PEEK** (read the data but don't dequeue it), and **MSG_WAITALL** (wait for all the data, as specified in the call).

Note that the **MSG_WAITALL** option is not implemented in the Linux 2.0.34 release.

For the **recvmsg** function, the TCP/IP code can return the following flags in the **msghdr** structure: **MSG_BCAST** (the message was in a broadcast datagram), **MSG_MCAST** (the message was in a multicast datagram), **MSG_TRUNC** (not all datagram data was returned), and **MSG_CTRUNC** (not all ancillary data was returned).

Note that the returned-flags field in the **msghdr** structure is not used in the Linux 2.0.34 release.

If the function fails, −1 is returned, and the global variable **errno** is set accordingly. If the function succeeds, the total number of bytes read is returned.

If one of these functions is interrupted by a signal after any amount of data has been read, then the return indicates the number of bytes that were read before the interruption occurred. If one of these functions is interrupted by a signal before any data has been read, −1 is returned, and the global variable **errno** is set to **EINTR**.

send, sendto, sendmsg

These three functions, which are specific to certain socket objects, are used by most application programs to send packets of UDP data from the Linux system to a remote peer system. The following code fragments constitute the templates for the calls to these functions:

```
#include <sys/types.h>
#include <sys/socket.h>
int send(int sockfd,
        const void *msg,
        int len, unsigned flags);
int sendto(int sockfd,
        const void *msg,
        int len,
```

```
        unsigned flags,
        struct sockaddr *to,
        int tolen);
int sendmsg(int sockfd,
        struct msghdr *msg,
        unsigned flags);
```

The **send** function transmits data via a connected socket. This function is basically identical to the **write** function, but has the additional parameter **flags**, which lets the application specify one or more option flags.

The **sendto** function transmits data via unconnected sockets, taking the address information for the remote peer from the data block pointed to by the **to** pointer. The length of the data in the block is returned in the integer pointed to by the **tolen** parameter.

The **sendmsg** function transmits data, using a pointer to a **msghdr** structure pointed to by the parameter **msg**, to specify the message and the remote peer-system address.

The **flags** parameter in each of these three functions can be set by OR'ing together one or more of the following constants: **MSG_DONTROUTE** (bypass routing), **MSG_OOB** (send out-of-band data), and **MSG_DONTWAIT** (return immediately).

For the **sendmsg** function, the flag field in the **msghdr** is ignored.

If the function fails, −1 is returned, and the global variable **errno** is set accordingly. If the function succeeds, the total number of bytes written is returned.

Socket Option Functions

Socket objects have many, many options that need to be set for particular applications. Some of the options are related to proper socket operation, while others are specific to a particular link and/or protocol. For the purposes of this book, we discuss only the options that apply to socket objects that have been created in the **AF_INET** domain.

In addition to the functions and options described in this section, application programs may also use the **ioctl** and **fcntl** system calls. The functions and parameters are not addressed here, but the options are discussed in the commentary for each module. Many of the options that are set using **ioctl** and **fcntl** can also be set via the **setsockopt** function, which is described later in this section.

getsockopt

The **getsockopt** function, which obtains the current option setting for a given socket object, is meant to be used by applications that inherit socket objects. For example, if the **inetd** process is listening for connections on behalf of a server, and launches the server when a connection is made, the server then needs information about the socket objects that it has inherited. It gets this information via the **getsockopt** function. The following code constitutes the template for the call to this function:

```
#include <sys/types.h>
#include <sys.socket.h>
int getsockopt(int sockfd,
        int level,
        int optname,
        void *optval,
        int *optlen);
```

The **getsockopt** function returns information about the current settings of a particular option for a specified socket object. The settings affect how the TCP/IP stack handles various conditions.

The option to be examined is specified using a combination of the parameter **level** and the parameter **optname**. In this book, we examine options whose **level** is specified as **SOL_SOCK**, **IPPROTO_IP**, or **IPPROTO_TCP**. The valid **optnames** are listed, by level, in the following subsections.

The **void** pointer to the buffer is specified in the parameter **optval**. The amount of data written to the buffer by the **getsockopt** function is reported, on return, by the integer value pointed to by the parameter **optlen**. The specific information that is returned depends on the option specified in the option **optname**, as qualified by the value to which the parameter **level** is set.

If the function fails, –1 is returned, and the global variable **errno** is set accordingly. If the function succeeds, 0 is returned.

setsockopt

The **setsockopt** function sets information about a setting of a particular option in the specified socket object. The settings affect how the TCP/IP stack handles various conditions. The following code constitutes the template for the call to this function:

```
#include <sys/types.h>
#include <sys/socket.h>
int setsockopt(int sockfd,
        int level,
        int optname,
        void *optval,
        int optlen);
```

The **void** pointer to the buffer is specified in the parameter **optval**, and the length of the data in the buffer is specified in the parameter **optlen**. The specific information passed to the function depends on the option specified in the option **optname**, as qualified by the value to which the parameter **level** is set.

The option to be set is specified by a combination of the parameter **level** and the parameter **optname**. In this book, we examine options whose **level** is specified as **SOL_SOCK**, **IPPROTO_IP**, or **IPPROTO_TCP**. The valid **optnames** are listed, by level, in the following subsections.

If the function fails, –1 is returned, and the global variable **errno** is set accordingly. If the function succeeds, 0 is returned.

Socket Options (SOL_SOCKET)

These options are used with the **getsockopt** and **setsockopt** functions previously described. In these calls, the parameter **level** should be coded as **SOL_SOCKET**. This section describes the format of the data that is being returned (via **getsockopt**) or that is being passed (via **setsockopt**).

We include options that do not appear in the Linux documentation but that are supported by the standard implementation of the Linux kernel code. When an option is available that uses another interface, that fact is mentioned.

We also include options that are defined in other TCP/IP implementations but that have not been implemented in the Linux 2.0.34 release. Based on our review of the commentary, we believe the list of unimplemented options described in this section provides strong hints as to when—and perhaps where—these options will be added to the Linux implementation.

SO_BINDTODEVICE

This option uses an instance of the structure **ifreq**. The **setsockopt** function reads (from the structure buffer) the null-terminated interface name from which all accesses should be serviced for the socket in question. The **setsockopt** function then saves this name in the socket object.

If an interface name has been specified, the **getsockopt** function returns (into the structure buffer) the null-terminated interface name that should be used with the socket object. Otherwise, the **getsockopt** function returns a zero-length string.

The default value is 0 (in other words, the socket object is not limited to a connection that uses a specific interface device).

Note that the man pages do not document the **SO_BINDTODEVICE** option.

SO_BROADCAST

This option uses a single integer value. A value of 0 blocks transmission of a broadcast packet using this socket object. Conversely, a non-0 value enables transmission of a broadcast packet.

The default value is 0 (in other words, no broadcast packets are allowed).

SO_BSDCOMPAT

This option uses a single integer value to indicate whether API responses are compatible with the Berkeley Software Distribution (BSD) implementation of Unix. A 0 value disables compatibility mode, whereas a non-0 value changes the way certain conditions are reported to the application.

Unless this option is enabled, Linux returns Internet Control Message Protocol (ICMP) Destination Unreachable messages to unconnected UDP sockets.

The default value is 0 (that is, BSD compatibility mode is disabled).

Note that the man pages do not document the **SO_BSDCOMPAT** option.

SO_DEBUG

This option, which applies only to TCP sockets, uses a single integer value to indicate whether debugging information is captured. A value of 0 disables the capture of debugging information, while a non-0 value enables this feature. When the debug feature is enabled, information about the TCP packets that have been sent or received is kept in a circular buffer located in the kernel. This buffer can be read by a utility.

The default value is 0 (that is, no debugging information is captured).

SO_DONTROUTE

This option uses a single integer value to change the routing followed by an outgoing packet. A value of 0 disables the use of nonstandard routing, while a non-0 value enables this feature. When the nonstandard routing feature is enabled, a packet being transmitted bypasses the normal routing protocol and (if possible) is sent to the appropriate local interface.

The default value is 0 (that is, all outgoing packets follow the standard routing).

SO_ERROR

This option, which uses a single integer value, is a read-only and read-once parameter. It returns the current value of the socket-object error member and is then set to 0. A return of 0 means that no function call has returned an error code since the last time this parameter was read. The return of a non-0 value indicates that an error has occurred, and the value of the integer corresponds to the error code.

SO_KEEPALIVE

This option, which uses a single integer value, applies only to TCP sockets. A 0 value disables the keep-alive feature, while a non-0 value enables it. When enabled, TCP exchanges a message with the remote peer system at regular intervals (by default, once every two hours). If the remote peer system does not respond within a given period (usually 12 minutes), the **SO_KEEPALIVE** option tells the application that the connection has been broken.

The default value is 0 (that is, no keep-alive signal is sent via the socket).

SO_LINGER

This option uses the structure **linger**, which can be found in /usr/include/linux/socket.h. The structure consists of two members: **l_onoff** and **l_linger**.

When the value of **l_onoff** is 0, the socket behaves normally when the **close** function is called. When the value of **l_onoff** is non-0, the socket uses an alternative action.

When the alternative action is enabled, a non-0 value of the **l_linger** member indicates how long the **close** function should wait for all data to be transmitted to the remote peer system before the **close** function closes the socket. A 0 value of the **l_linger** member causes the socket to be closed immediately after the **close** function has been called.

Note that according to Posix, the **l_linger** member of the **linger** structure must be interpreted such that the **l_linger** tick is counted in seconds. However, the man page for **setsockopt** and the Linux code both indicate that the **l_linger** tick is counted in hundredths of a second.

The default value is 0 (that is, a socket should be closed immediately after the **close** function is called).

Note that the **SO_LINGER** option is not implemented in the Linux 2.0.34 release.

SO_NO_CHECK

This option uses a single integer value to determine whether checksums are calculated. A value of 0 disables this feature, thereby causing checksums to be calculated, while a non-0 value enables this feature, instructing the underlying protocol module not to calculate checksums.

The default value is 0 (that is, checksums are calculated, if appropriate for the protocol).

SO_OOBINLINE

This option, which uses a single integer value, is disabled by a 0 value and enabled by a non-0 value. When the option is enabled, out-of-band data is placed in line with normal data, and use of the **recv**, **recvfrom**, or **recvmsg** functions with **MSG_OOB** in the **flags** parameter is prohibited.

The default value is 0 (indicating that out-of-band data is segregated).

SO_PRIORITY

This option, which uses a single integer value, sets the priority of a transmission. The three valid values are **SOPRI_BACKGROUND**, **SOPRI_NORMAL**, and **SOPRI_INTERACTIVE**.

Note that the **SO_PRIORITY** option is not documented in the man pages. The priority field in the socket object is normally set using the **IP_TOS** (Type Of Service specification) option.

SO_RCVBUF

This option uses a single integer value, which can range from a low of 256 bytes to a high of either 65,535 bytes or twice the value of **SK_RMEM_MAX** (usually 32,767), whichever is lower. This integer value defines the size, in bytes, of the receive buffer for the socket.

The default value is the value of **SK_RMEM_MAX**, which can be configured when the kernel is compiled.

SO_REUSEADDR

This option, which uses a single integer value, is disabled by a value of 0 and enabled by a non-0 value. When this option is enabled, the server application can reuse a given port even when connections specifying that port already exist, and even when other server applications exist that use the same port (provided, of course, that these applications have different IP addresses).

The default value is 0 (that is, addresses are not reused).

SO_RCVLOWAT

This option, which is not implemented in the Linux 2.0.34 release, represents the low-water mark or lower threshold for received data. In other words, when the amount of data indicated by this option is available, the **select** and **poll** functions will indicate that data is available.

If the amount of available data is less than the figure indicated by the **SO_RCVLOWAT** option, the **select** and **poll** functions will not indicate that data is available. The default value is 1. In other words, if a single byte of data is available, then the **select** and **poll** functions will indicate that data is available.

SO_RCVTIMEO

This option is not implemented in the Linux 2.0.34 release.

SO_REUSEPORT

This option, which is not implemented in the Linux 2.0.34 release, was introduced into Berkeley implementations for multicast support. **SO_REUSEADDR** is overloaded with the ability to bind multiple socket objects to the same port for multicast applications.

SO_SNDBUF

This option uses a single integer value, which can range from a low of 256 bytes to a high of either 65,535 bytes or twice the value of **SK_RMEM_MAX** (usually 32,767), whichever is lower. This value defines the size of the transmit buffer for the socket.

The default value is **SK_RMEM_MAX**, which can be configured when the kernel is compiled.

SO_SNDLOWAT

This option, which is not implemented in the Linux 2.0.34 release, represents the low-water mark or lower threshold for transmitted data. In other words, when the amount of buffer space indicated by this option is available, the **select** and **poll** functions will indicate okay-to-write.

If the amount of available buffer space is less than the figure indicated by the **SO_SNDLOWAT** option, the **select** and **poll** functions will not indicate okay-to-write. The standard default value is 2048; in other words, if 2,048 bytes of buffer space are available, then the **select** and **poll** functions will indicate okay-to-write.

SO_SNDTIMEO

This option is not implemented in the Linux 2.0.34 release.

SO_TYPE

This option uses a single integer value. This value, which is accessible via the **getsockopt** function, is a read-only value that returns the socket type. The valid values are those defined by **SOCK_xxx**.

IP Standard Options (IPPROTO_IP)

These options are used with the **getsockopt** and **setsockopt** functions previously described. In these calls, the parameter **level** should be coded as **IPPROTO_IP**.

We have included options that do not appear in the Linux documentation but are supported by the standard implementation of the Linux kernel code. When an option is available that uses another interface, that fact is mentioned.

The Slackware and Red Hat distributions do not document the **IPPROTO_IP** socket options on any man page. Other distributions may include documentation for these options.

IP_HDRINCL

This option, which uses a single integer value, applies only to sockets of type **SOCK_RAW**. The option is disabled by a 0 value and enabled by a non-0 value. When **IP_HDRINCL** is enabled, the application builds and provides the complete IP header for outgoing packets.

The default value is 0 (that is, the system builds the IP header).

Note that in the commentary, we discuss the various sources of the information that appears in IP headers.

IP_OPTIONS

This option uses a buffer containing up to 11 32-bit integers (44 bytes). The buffer contains the contents of the IPv4 options field in the packet. (This information is used for source routing, timestamping, route recording, and other optional IP facilities.) The **setsockopt** function records the buffer contents in the socket object, so that the buffered information can be placed in every packet that is transmitted.

For TCP sockets, the **getsockopt** function returns the source route that accompanied the SYN packet. For other sockets, the **getsockopt** function returns the same information that was stored by a prior **setsockopt** function on the socket object in question.

In the default setting, the options-field buffer is empty.

IP_RECVDSTADDR

This option is not implemented in the Linux 2.0.34 release. For UDP packets, this option lets an application

recover the destination address, in the local system, of a packet that has been received. This option serves as an alternative to the binding of multiple instances of a UDP server to specific IP addresses for a multi-address host.

IP_RECVIF

This option is not implemented in the Linux 2.0.34 release. For UDP packets, this option returns the identification of the interface from which a packet was received.

IP_TOS

This option uses a single integer value, which can be one of the following constant values: 0, **IPTOS_LOWDELAY**, **IPTOS_THROUGHPUT**, **IPTOS_RELIABILITY**, or **IP_MINCOST**. The integer value is inserted in the Type Of Service (TOS) field of transmitted IP packets.

The default value is 0 (in other words, the TOS is the normal one).

Note that the **IPTOS_RELIABILITY** constant is not used in the kernel as of the Linux 2.0.34 release.

IP_TTL

This option uses a single integer value. The time-to-live (TTL) value (which may be from 1 to 255, inclusive) represents the number of "hops" that a packet can make before the routers discard it.

The default values are 64 for TCP sockets, 64 for UDP sockets, and 0 for raw sockets (that is, sockets that were created via the **SOCK_RAW** option).

IP Multicast Options (IPPROTO_IP)

These options are used with the **getsockopt** and **setsockopt** functions described in the "Socket Option Functions" section, earlier in this chapter. In these calls, the parameter **level** should be coded as **IPPROTO_IP**.

These functions are described here in summary form.

Note that Linux includes support for these functions only if the kernel configuration is set to enable multicasting.

IP_ADD_MEMBERSHIP

This option passes the structure **ip_mreq**, to specify the multicast group that an application should join, or to inquire about the multicast group to which a given socket is joined. The members of the structure specify the multicast address and the local IP address.

IP_DROP_MEMBERSHIP

This option passes the structure **ip_mreq**, to specify the multicast group that an application should drop. The members of the structure specify the multicast address and the local IP address.

IP_MULTICAST_IF

This option passes the structure **in_addr**, to specify the interface that an application should use for outgoing packets.

IP_MULTICAST_LOOP

This option enables or disables local loopback of multicast messages. The default setting (enable) allows messages to be looped back.

IP_MULTICAST_TTL

This option specifies the hop count for multicast messages sent via this socket. The default value is 1 hop.

TCP Options (IPPROTO_TCP)

These options are used with the **getsockopt** and **setsockopt** functions previously described. In these calls, the parameter **level** should be coded as **IPPROTO_TCP**.

We have included options that do not appear in the Slackware Linux documentation but that are supported by the standard implementation of the Linux kernel code. When an option is available that uses another interface, that fact is mentioned.

The Slackware and Red Hat distributions do not document the **IPPROTO_TCP** socket options in any man page. Other distributions may include documentation for these options.

TCP_KEEPALIVE

This option is not implemented in the Linux 2.0.34 release. The **SO_KEEPALIVE** option (under **SOL_SOCKET**) is a useful alternative.

TCP_MAXRT

This option is not implemented in the Linux 2.0.34 release. This new parameter, which is defined in Posix.1g, indicates (in seconds) how long retransmission should be attempted before the socket is declared dead. A value of 0 indicates that the system default will be used, and the value −1 indicates that retries should be performed indefinitely.

TCP_MAXSEG

This option uses an integer buffer. The value is an integer, from 1 to **MAX_WINDOW** (32,767), that specifies the size of the largest window that can be published.

The default size depends on the segment size published by the remote peer system and the size that was defined when the kernel was compiled.

TCP_NODELAY

This option uses an integer buffer. A 0 value disables this feature, and a non-0 value enables it. When the feature is enabled, the algorithm used to reduce the number of small packets on the WAN is bypassed.

The default value is 0 (that is, the algorithm is enabled).

TCP_STDURG

This option is not implemented in the Linux 2.0.34 release.

Chapter 6

Routing

Communicating over a network means sending data from one computer to another. This sounds simple, and it is...when only two computers are involved...when those two computers are alike...when those two computers are physically near one another...and especially when the equipment doesn't fail.

Alas, few if any of these conditions are present on the Internet. Indeed, when an individual user of the Internet communicates with a popular server, the connection can involve dozens of intermediate computers, each with its own name, IP address, and designated duration. If you're curious about the number, you can use the **traceroute(1)** utility on your Linux computer (or the **tracert** program in a DOS window on a Microsoft system) to find out exactly how many other systems lie between you and a given destination site.

The **traceroute(1)** utility uses the Internet Control Message Protocol (ICMP) or User Datagram Protocol (UDP) facility of the Internet Protocol (IP) to determine how packets are transferred through the network, and to measure the transmission time required for each step of the journey.

For example, we often communicate with **www.linux.org**, starting from our connection to Nevada Bell's Internet site (**nvbell.net**). The following report (produced by the Windows **tracert** program) shows the path followed by our data packets, and the stops our packets make along that path, during their journey from our office to the server that hosts the Linux home page:

```
Tracing route to www.linux.org [198.182.196.56]
over 14 hops:
  1    33 ms     18 ms     19 ms
       adsl-216-101-13-254.dsl.renocs.pacbell.net
       [216.101.13.254]
  2    18 ms     19 ms     19 ms
       ign1-e45.renocs.nvbell.net
       [206.171.130.249]
  3    21 ms     19 ms     19 ms
       ign0-f00.renocs.nvbell.net
       [206.13.6.194]
  4    37 ms     41 ms     32 ms
       sfra1sr2-3-4.ca.us.ibm.net
       [165.87.225.30]
  5    29 ms     30 ms     32 ms
       165.87.160.193
  6    31 ms     29 ms     28 ms
       114.ATM3-0.XR1.SFO1.ALTER.NET
       [146.188.148.210]
  7    32 ms     34 ms     27 ms
       187.ATM2-0.TR1.SCL1.ALTER.NET
       [146.188.147.146]
  8    95 ms     98 ms    105 ms
       107.ATM6-0.TR1.DCA1.ALTER.NET
       [146.188.136.221]
  9    94 ms     94 ms    101 ms
       299.ATM6-0.XR1.TCO1.ALTER.NET
       [146.188.161.169]
 10   101 ms     91 ms     92 ms
       193.ATM9-0-0.GW2.TCO1.ALTER.NET
       [146.188.160.57]
 11   102 ms     96 ms     96 ms
       uu-peer.pos-4-oc12-core.ai.net
       [205.134.160.2]
 12   111 ms    112 ms    113 ms
       border-ai.invlogic.com
       [205.134.175.254]
 13   123 ms    109 ms    113 ms
       router.invlogic.com
       [198.182.196.1]
 14   158 ms    115 ms    165 ms
       www.linux.org [198.182.196.56]

Trace complete.
```

The report tells us that our data packets made 14 hops, starting at the end of our DSL link located at Nevada Bell's central office. The report then gives us information about each of the 14 hops: first, the round-trip duration (in milliseconds) of each of the three probes that the **tracert** program sends to each node in the series, and then the name (if available) and the IP address of each of those nodes.

Where did this arrangement come from, and why is it so complex? To answer these questions, we need to take a brief look at the history of distributed network computing.

The Legacy Of The ARPAnet

The granddaddy of today's Internet was an experimental communications system—the Advanced Research Projects Agency Network, or ARPAnet—conceived in the 1960s at the RAND Corporation on behalf of the U.S. Department of Defense (DOD), and launched in 1971 with four sites in the western United States. By 1976, the projected number of nodes in the ARPAnet had grown to an unmanageable figure (more than 250 of 'em), and a new way to connect them had to be found. Enter the *router*, which enabled the ARPAnet to double in size over the next few years, acquiring 200 host machines by 1981. In 1985, the ARPAnet broke the thousand-host barrier. By 1989, the experiment was over, and the ARPAnet as a system ceased to exist—leaving more than 100,000 machines interconnected via something called the "Internet."

Because of the circumstances envisioned for its use, the ARPAnet was required to heal itself whenever any single part of the network failed. (One type of failure contemplated by the DOD was the physical destruction of the ARPAnet's computers and communications links by nuclear events.) This requirement set the ARPAnet apart from the commercial computer networks of the day, which were centrally controlled. To prevent a single point of failure from bringing down the entire communications system, the ARPAnet's controlling functions had to be distributed, as evenly as possible, among computers physically located many miles apart.

Obviously, the number of possible failure points was huge. Moreover, because any given computer could, in theory, fail at any given time, the ARPAnet's designers also faced the daunting task of dealing with random changes in the topology of the network. These changes, the designers theorized, would be caused by nodes and links that not only disappeared, but, in the fashion of some subatomic particles, also *appeared* utterly unexpectedly and unpredictably—which, as it turned out, is exactly what happened.

The ARPAnet's protocol design was continually revised, based on an analysis of the hardware, telecommunications, and software failures that occurred. The changes that were made allowed the ARPAnet to cope with most failures automatically, finding alternate routes to keep data flowing even if several nodes or links went down. These workarounds are still part of the Internet today.

Here's how the ARPAnet's workarounds worked. Each connection node on the network, known as an *interface message processor (IMP)*, kept a living record of neighboring nodes and traded information with those nodes at regular intervals. The sum of each IMP's knowledge—including the list of neighboring nodes and a history of the information exchanged with those nodes—was stored in a dynamic structure known as a *routing table*. (Routing tables are still present, playing a more important role than ever, in today's Internet hosts. Entire books have been written about their design and use, and an in-depth discussion is beyond the scope of this book.)

From a cold standing start, all the nodes on the ARPAnet needed only a few minutes to learn enough about the network's topology to be able to send data to the proper destination. As the nodes built a history and exchanged data with each other, they "learned" the best data-transmission routes. In less than an hour, the nodes learned so much about ARPAnet routing that, when a glitch occurred (and glitches could range from a momentary interruption of transmission to the complete shutdown of a node), users rarely noticed it.

This learn-as-you-go technique is what the Internet uses today. As an example, consider how this technique helps your data get from your machine to a server located 12,000 miles away.

Before any data goes anywhere, it has to be properly "gift-wrapped." In the Internet, the bow-adorned object is an IP packet, which consists of a box with data inside, wrapping paper to ensure that the data stays together, and a tag that states who is sending the packet and who is supposed to receive it. Unlike the typical recipient of a holiday gift, the intended recipient of an IP packet can be miles or continents away, and the IP tag tells you absolutely nothing about how to get the package to the right giftee.

In a well-known experiment done in the 1960s, researchers found that a letter, addressed (by name only) to a randomly selected individual and entrusted to another randomly selected individual, reached the addressee after a remarkably small number of person-to-person transfers. (In fact, the researchers concluded that any living person could theoretically reach any other living person in six or fewer "hops.") The purpose of the experiment was to show how many people each human being knows directly and, by concatenation and extension, how interconnected all of humanity is.

However, computers aren't people, so the designers of the ARPAnet had to devise a less complex way to accomplish the same task; that is, determining a path between two random points without the help of a master directory. When the ARPAnet was small (with fewer than 64 nodes), each IMP kept a record of how far away and in what (logical) direction each host was located. As the ARPAnet evolved toward the Internet, network designers started to group hosts together, into *subnets*, to limit the amount of record-keeping data to a manageable size. Thanks to subnets, the amount of data that a pair of routers had to transfer to one another was also kept to a reasonable size. Today's Internet routers still operate this way, working in layers, so that each router's

task is relatively small—even if the number of hosts exceeds a billion. "Divide and conquer" (or "cut and control") could well be the Internet's motto.

Routing: What Makes The Internet The Internet

At its most elementary level, routing function means switching data through a series of ports located in a single physical unit so that the data gets from its source to its destination. For example, the routing box shown in Figure 6.1 has a total of nine ports: eight ports connected to remote computers or to other routing boxes, and one local connection within itself.

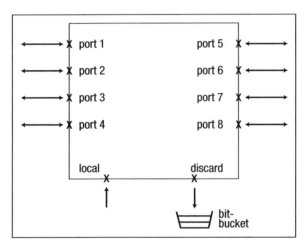

Figure 6.1   Block diagram of a router.

How does this router work? Assume that it receives a data packet at its local port. The routing software acquires the packet's destination address and, using the information stored in the router's internal routing tables, determines the best port from which the data packet should be sent.

In Figure 6.2, the routing software has determined that for the data packet to reach its destination efficiently, the packet should leave the router via port 6.

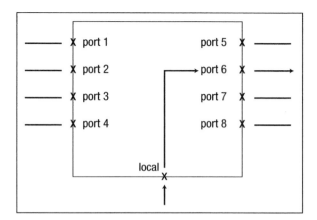

Figure 6.2 Schematic diagram of a router with data path for a specific packet.

Routers do not have an actual physical address to which they send data packets that are supposed to be discarded (for example, data packets for which no route can be found, or whose Time To Live (TTL) value has reached 0). However, a Linux kernel routine allows such doomed data packets to be removed from a router's memory, in an operation known familiarly as "sending the data to the bit-bucket."

A router follows the same steps each time it performs the analysis and port-assignment process. So, why doesn't the router always send out data packets via the same port? Because the port that the router ultimately selects depends on the information *stored in the routing table*, not on any change in the way the router performs its analysis of that information.

In short, then, the act of routing embraces the entire process of getting a message from, for example, the small (and very real) town of Truth or Consequences, New Mexico to its ultimate destination, the capital city of Ouagadougou, in the African nation of Burkina Faso.

The Data Packet Delivery Service

The router code that is the subject of this chapter uses information about the network (as collected by the IP

and ICMP protocol handlers and by other node-resident processes that exchange information with neighboring nodes) to decide how to handle a data packet that is being sent. However, in the router world, a data packet's destination is not necessarily a physically different machine. An internal process within a router is just as valid as an external destination, and routers often "send" packets to such internal processes.

The routing table is kept up to date by a set of pick-a-little talk-a-little router-to-router protocols. These protocols, which are implemented as *daemons* (programs that live in the computer, but are not part of the kernel), gossip continually with each other. By exchanging information this way, and especially by discarding obsolete information about traffic conditions and external nodes, they make the kernel code's task much easier. The kernel code, which uses the routing table several hundred times a second when data is being transferred, is appropriately grateful.

Back to your gift-wrapped data package. The IP packet starts out from its point of origin in Truth or Consequences, New Mexico. The first router that your packet reaches on the Internet contains a collection of hints in its routing table, gathered from its neighboring routers, that suggests the best way to forward a packet toward Ouagadougou. (In the data-transmission world, "best way" may mean any of several things. It might be either the fastest way to send information, the method that's cheapest in terms of resources or money, the route that's the least sensitive politically, or the pathway that's the least likely to damage the data.)

The first router sends your package to a second router, which, with luck, is located well along the way toward your package's destination. This second router then makes its best guess about how to pass the data, and speeds the package on its way toward the next router. The process continues until the package reaches its destination in Ouagadougou and the recipient opens it. In the very worst case, the package never gets to Ouagadougou. Instead, it hits a digital dead-end and is dumped unceremoniously into a bit-bucket.

In an ideal world, your package would travel as directly as possible to its destination. However, the data-transmission world is far from ideal. Just as on city streets or at airports, traffic congestion can affect a router's forwarding decision, such that packages are sent on detours around slow or stacked-up areas. Quite conceivably, your Africa-bound package could arrive in New York City or Casablanca, only to be turned around and routed back westward.

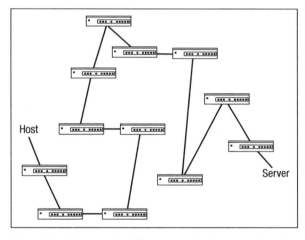

Figure 6.3 An example of the geographical progression of a packet route. This route depicts the physical path taken by a packet on a college campus circa 1987.

Or not. Sometimes, a router doesn't know that a path is congested and forwards an IP packet into a gridlock anyway. Remember, in selecting the outgoing path for a packet, a router bases its decision on the information it obtains from neighboring routers. When traffic conditions change, routers have no way of learning about the changes instantaneously. It takes time for the word to propagate outward from a congested node or link, and, in the meantime, a packet could arrive at a router and be sent onward, in all innocence, into trouble.

At its most frustrating, this slow spread of information among routers can cause an IP packet to travel in circles—in other words, in an *endless loop*. An endlessly looping packet eventually self-destructs, dying of old age. Unlike the U.S. Postal Service, the Internet has no Dead Letter Office for defunct datagrams. Instead, looping IP packets evaporate without a trace, considerately relieving the Internet of the need to dispose of them. (This wasn't always the case. In the early 1970s, the ARPAnet was sometimes very, very busy, but no data was getting through to users. The activity level was caused by packets that had invalid host addresses and therefore stayed alive—and undelivered—indefinitely in the network, like a subway passenger caught short by a fare increase, doomed to ride forever 'neath the streets of Boston—the datagram that never returned. That's when the network designers gave packets a finite lifespan.)

The routing tables are implemented in Linux as linked lists, and the elements of the list are defined in the structure described at line 41260. Although the tables are updated once or twice a minute, they are referenced many, many times—on a busy system, hundreds of times per second—by routing protocols, by certain free-running processes, and, most frequently of all, by the IP module in the kernel code.

The IP module's job is to handle packet routing requests, a process illustrated in Figure 6.4. Each packet is associated with its own routing request, which means that the IP module may have to process as many as 150,000 requests per second. Unfortunately, one routing request does not necessarily imply only one pass through the routing table. To handle a single routing request, for a single packet, the IP module may need to make several trips through the routing table. First, it looks for a specific host entry. If the host entry appears in the routing table, the IP module uses the designated port associated with that host. If the desired host doesn't appear in the list, then the IP module searches for the name of a

subnet that contains the host. If the IP module does find such a subnet, it sends the data out through the designated port for that subnet. If it doesn't find the right subnet, then it looks for a default port to which to send the data. If it finds the name of a default port, it sends the data to that port. Otherwise, it returns an error message and takes the appropriate action, depending on the source of the routing request.

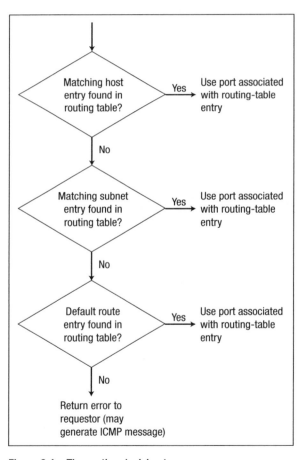

Figure 6.4   The routing decision tree.

Based on the information stored in the routing table, a data packet is directed to a specific interface on the computer. In the trivial case (when a router box has only one outgoing port), the packet is sent to a port (such as a modem or an Ethernet port) that leads to the outside world. When a router has two or more ports to the outside world, the decision process becomes more complex, but the result is the same—the IP module decides which port gets the packet.

For an idea of the amount of work a router does, consider a digital DS3 trunk operating at a speed of 44 megabits/second (Mbps). A router connected to such a trunk handles from 60,000 to 150,000 packets per second, virtually nonstop. In other words, this router has six whole microseconds (that is, 6 one-millionths of a second) to redirect each packet that comes in through any single port. If the redirection takes longer, the whole stream of packets may slow down, or even stop.

A T1 or ADSL (asymmetric digital subscriber line) channel is much slower, pouring in only 2,000 to 5,300 packets/second, whereas a 56-kilobyte/second (Kbps) modem or frame-relay connection drizzles just 75 to 180 packets/second into the router. But no matter how quickly or slowly the packets come in, the time required to make a routing decision directly affects a router's performance, even if the router lives in a single system. Indeed, packets can be lost when input buffers overflow, which can happen when a router's decisions are made too slowly. Fortunately, as you'll see in the commentary section of this chapter, the Linux code contains some timesaving tricks that keep the routing process from becoming a data bottleneck.

Of Packets And Checks

Messages travel through the Internet much the same way that checks flow through the commercial banking system. From the bottom up:

- Individual Internet surfers are analogous to businesses depositing checks that they've received from customers.

- Companies whose networks are completely internal (the *intranets*, used only by company employees and authorized guests) are analogous to small banks.

- A typical regional ISP is analogous to a standard bank.

- The *upstream providers* are analogous to bigger banks.

- The Internet has several nationwide ISPs, each with its own network, which are analogous to the multistate megabanks.

- At the very top of the heap, the similarity diverges slightly. Instead of a single analog of the U.S. Federal Reserve System, the Internet has several *backbone providers*, in the form of the companies who run the large networks that link the various regions of the United States. However, like the Fed, these companies are the lords of all they survey.

Checks fly in and out of banks in all directions. A few checks are deposited at a bank against accounts at that same bank—that's the easy case and is handled completely in-house. The vast majority of checks, though, are drawn on one bank and deposited at another. They come in through teller windows and ATM machines; from correspondent banks; and (for member banks) from the Fed itself. The incoming checks drawn on accounts at the bank itself are separated and processed, and then the checks drawn on other banks are sorted and sent on their way.

Analogously, data packets fly in and out of IP routers through a number of ports. When you log on to the Internet, your system receives packets confirming or denying your access. Those packets are sent to, and stay in, processes that live in your computer system. However, the great majority of packets that are sent out from your computer, via your modem or broadband link to the Internet, are processed at another system—usually a server of some kind—living at your ISP. A router box located at your ISP, at the upstream provider, or in the backbone can, in theory, have as few as three ports; however, most of these routers have several hundred ports

through which incoming packets arrive and reshuffled packets depart.

What makes the check-clearing analogy to the Internet so remarkable is that the decisions that govern how checks are routed are exactly the same decisions that are used to determine how data packets are steered. In the banking system, a check comes in and, based on its ABA/FRD (American Banking Association/Federal Reserve District) number, also known as the *routing number*, the bank decides where the check goes next (usually to another bank). On the Internet, a data packet comes in and, based on the Internet address in the packet header, the router decides where the packet goes next (usually to another router). In the banking system, the final decision is which truck a bag of checks should be tossed into. In an Internet router, the "ultimate decision" is the one that determines the I/O port to which the packet should be directed.

The major difference between the Internet and the U.S. check-clearing system lies in the acquisition of the information on which routing decisions are based. Relationships between banks are essentially static. A "Grand Opening" here or an unexpected bank failure there is a relatively small change, and is managed pretty much by exception. And in the banking world, mergers and takeovers don't "just happen." They're planned long in advance and often are heralded widely. In the online world, though, the network is constantly changing, with no fanfare at all. The beauty of the Internet is that it makes adjustments—automatically and continuously—that the banking system just couldn't handle.

Another difference between the banking system and the Internet is that every bundle of checks has to be accompanied by a *cash letter* that indicates the dollar value of each check in the bundle. In the Internet, as implemented in the United States, there is no accounting of any kind. That's not true in some other countries, where information transfers are billed by the kilopacket. In such cases, *least-cost routing* has a real monetary value, and mistakes can cost someone a bundle.

The Internet's paramount feature—flexibility—also makes it fast. For instance, if a courier company's truck is full, banks and the Fed won't ship a bag of checks on a different truck on a different route. Instead, the bag waits for the next truck on the usual route. In contrast, many Internet routers don't "wait for the next truck." Instead, they divert data packets to paths that are open (albeit sometimes basing that decision on the cost of the alternate paths, in terms of time or reliability).

This *dynamic routing*—with parts of a message being forwarded over different and sometimes wildly divergent routes—can cause packets in a TCP stream, or fragments of a UDP packet, to arrive at their destination in wildly scrambled order. Putting packets (and sometimes fragments of packets) back into their original, comprehensible order takes time and computational effort. But this effort is a small price to pay for coherent messages, even if some packets have to make detours, sometimes in rattly decrepit trucks over dusty back roads, to avoid fatal obstacles.

This matter of packet reassembly comes up again, with renewed significance, in connection with the IPv4 and TCP protocols, as you'll see in the following chapters. For now, though, the next section examines the Linux router code in detail.

Routing In Linux: Routing-Table Handling Routines

The routines in the source module route.c appear in arbitrary order and are not organized with any particular logic. To help you locate the modules in the code listings, Table 6.1 and Table 6.2 list the functions in the source module route.c.

Table 6.1   Functions, sorted by line number.

Number	Function
19680	rt_logmask
19691	rt_mask
19698	fz_hash_code

(continued)

Table 6.1   Functions, sorted by line number *(continued)*.

Number	Function
19708	fib_free_node
19732	fib_lookup_gateway
19778	fib_lookup_local
19828	fib_lookup
19855	get_gw_dev
19868	bad_mask
19879	fib_del_list
19916	fib_del_1
19966	fib_create_info
20040	fib_add_1
20246	rt_flush_list
20274	fib_flush_1
20322	rt_get_info
20421	rt_cache_get_info
20490	rt_free
20521	rt_kick_free_queue
20555	ip_rt_run_bh
20582	ip_rt_check_expire
20655	rt_redirect_1
20688	rt_cache_flush
20730	rt_garbage_collect_1
20764	rt_req_enqueue
20789	rt_req_dequeue
20810	rt_kick_backlog
20838	rt_del
20854	rt_add
20868	ip_rt_flush
20882	ip_rt_redirect
20923	rt_garbage_collect
20933	rt_cache_add
21036	ip_rt_slow_route
21161	ip_rt_put
21181	ip_rt_dev
21190	ip_rt_route
21222	ip_rt_new
21353	ip_rt_kill
21393	ip_rt_ioctl
21417	ip_rt_advice
21423	ip_rt_update

Table 6.2   Functions, listed alphabetically by name.

Number	Function
19868	bad_mask
20040	fib_add_1
19966	fib_create_info
19916	fib_del_1
19879	fib_del_list
20274	fib_flush_1
19708	fib_free_node
19828	fib_lookup
19732	fib_lookup_gateway
19778	fib_lookup_local
19698	fz_hash_code
19855	get_gw_dev
21417	ip_rt_advice
20582	ip_rt_check_expire
21181	ip_rt_dev
20868	ip_rt_flush
21393	ip_rt_ioctl
21353	ip_rt_kill
21222	ip_rt_new
21161	ip_rt_put
20882	ip_rt_redirect
21190	ip_rt_route
20555	ip_rt_run_bh
21036	ip_rt_slow_route
21423	ip_rt_update
20854	rt_add
20933	rt_cache_add
20688	rt_cache_flush
20421	rt_cache_get_info
20838	rt_del
20246	rt_flush_list
20490	rt_free
20923	rt_garbage_collect
20730	rt_garbage_collect_1
20322	rt_get_info
20810	rt_kick_backlog
20521	rt_kick_free_queue
19680	rt_logmask
19691	rt_mask

(continued)

Table 6.2   Functions, listed alphabetically by name *(continued)*.

Number	Function
20655	rt_redirect_1
20789	rt_req_dequeue
20764	rt_req_enqueue

Routing Table Structure

The routing table consists of a series of elements in a singly-linked list. The definition of the structure starts on line 41260. The following list describes the most important fields. (Other fields exist that are used internally by the router code, and yet other fields exist that are commonly used in routers, but not in the Linux implementation.)

41262: **rt_next**, the link to the next routing-table entry.

41263: **rt_dst**, the host or network address described by this entry.

41265: **rt_gateway**, the gateway address (the recommended immediate path to the destination address contained in **rt_dst**).

41266: **rt_refcnt**, the reference counter. When decremented to 0, this routing-table entry becomes a candidate for removal during garbage collection, so the memory space used by the routing-table entry element can be recovered.

41268: **rt_window**, the size of the TCP window that should be used for the destination described by this routing-table entry.

41271: **rt_dev**, the pointer to the name (a null-terminated ASCII string) of the device to be used to reach the destination described by this routing-table entry.

41272: **rt_flags**, the flags for this routing-table entry. The flags themselves are described separately, in the next section.

41273: **rt_mtu**, the maximum transmission unit (MTU) size, in bytes, from this host/router to the destination described by this routing-table entry.

41274: **rt_irtt**, the initial round-trip delay time that TCP shall assume exists between this host and the destination described by this routing-table entry.

The following bit flags may appear in the value contained in **rt_flags**:

38704: **RTF_UP**, which, when set, indicates that the route is usable.

38706: **RTF_GATEWAY**, indicates that the destination contained in **rt_dst** is a gateway (rather than a network or host).

38708: **RTF_HOST**, indicates that the destination contained in **rt_dst** is a host (not a network) with a possible gateway.

38712: **RTF_DYNAMIC**, indicates that this routing-table entry was created by an ICMP redirect packet received by the router/host.

38714: **RTF_MODIFIED**, indicates that this routing-table entry was modified dynamically by an ICMP redirect packet received by the router/host.

38716: **RTF_MSS**, instructs the code to use the maximum segment size contained in **rt_mtu** for this route.

38718: **RTF_WINDOW**, instructs the code to use the per-route window size maximum contained in **rt_window** for this route.

38720: **RTF_IRTT**, instructs the code to use the initial round-trip time contained in **rt_irtt** for this route.

38722: **RTF_REJECT**, indicates that the route is a "reject" route. If the search finds a match on this route, the assumption should be made that no route exists. This flag is used to block transfers involving port-to-private-network addresses

(and netmasks), such as 10.0.0.0 (255.0.0.0), 172.16.0.0 (255.240.0.0), and 192.168.0.0 (255.255.0.0).

38724: **RTF_NOTCACHED**, indicates that this route is not cached.

These same flags are used in the **rt_entry** structure, defined at line 38677, in the structure member **rt_flags** (line 38687).

The address of an instance of this structure is specified in the **argp** parameter. This parameter is copied from the corresponding parameter **ioctl** calls that specify the function requests **SIOCADDRT** (add route, at line 39518) and **SIOCDELRT** (delete route, at line 39520).

Although no explicit limit exists on the number of entries that a routing table can contain, a long list naturally takes longer to traverse than a short one.

/proc File System Support

In the Linux environment, users and many utility programs get information about the internal state of the system through the proc file system. This is a pseudo-file system, usually accessible through the directory /proc, that lets a user (via the shell and the **cat** utility) or an application (via standard file I/O) read the current condition of various internal processes.

The file system "files" are actually the output of executable routines, such as the ones in route.c that we will be reviewing, that report on the internal state of the system. In other portions of Linux, the "files" also accept data; as we'll see in other portions of the TCP/IP stack.

The routine **rt_get_info** is accessed via a pointer reference at line 6317, which in turn is referenced by the source file /usr/src/linux/fs/proc/net.c, which is a portion of the file system source (not included in this book). It outputs the contents of the main routing table. The routine outputs a header line followed by a line for each routing-table entry. Here is a sample of the output (with each physical line of output shown in the form of three lines):

Iface	Destination	Gateway		Flags	RefCnt
Use	Metric	Mask	MTU	Window	IRTT
eth0	0001010A	00000000		01	0
10	0	00FFFFFF	1500	0	0
10	0000007F	00000000		01	0
5	0	000000FF	3584	0	0

rt_cache_get_info is accessed via a pointer reference at line 6323. The routine outputs a header line followed by a line for each routing-table cache entry, as in this example (in which each physical line of output is shown in the form of three lines):

Iface	Destination	Gateway		Flags	RefCnt
Use	Metric	Source	MTU	Window	IRTT
HH	ARP				
eth0	FF01010A	FF01010A		05	0
1	0	1501010A	1500	0	0
1	1				
eth0	1401010A	1401010A		05	0
1	0	1501010A	1500	0	0
2	1				
10	1501010A	1501010A		05	1
2	0	1501010A	3584	0	0
-1	0				
eth0	1601010A	1601010A		05	0
1	0	1501010A	1500	0	0
2	1				
eth0	1701010A	1701010A		05	0
1	0	1501010A	1500	0	0
2	0				
eth0	8A01010A	8A01010A		05	0
1	0	1501010A	1500	0	0
2	1				

Later in this chapter, you'll see where each of these fields comes from.

To generate the routing-table cache shown here, we polled every computer on a small network and then immediately requested the dump just shown. After a few minutes, we asked for another cache dump. The result of the second request is shown here:

```
Iface  Destination  Gateway       Flags  RefCnt
Use    Metric Source        MTU    Window IRTT
HH     ARP

10     0100007F     0100007F      05     1
9      0       0100007F     3584    0      0
-1     0
```

All the entries we had generated earlier were cleared out of the cache very quickly. This speedy disposal makes sense, because the purpose of the cache is to speed up routing for active connections.

The formats for the output of these two pseudofiles are identical. The information in the lines forms a columnar database, with tab (\t) characters separating the fields. A database record is complete when the program sees a newline (\n) character or an end-of-file (EOF) condition. Because this data is intended to be read and manipulated by programs, the formatting of entries that are longer than the default tab width of the terminal (or other device, or printing protocol) becomes an issue. For example, the caching table contains what appears to be the phrase "Metric Source." This "phrase" actually refers to two separate columns. It is not a two-word description of a single column.

rt_get_info

This function is called multiple times. Based on the parameter **offset**, the function returns information in sequence about the routing table. The first time the function is called, the value of **offset** should be 0. Each subsequent time, the value of **offset** is incremented by the prior value of the offset plus the length of the information returned during the prior call. This way, the file

system routines can return a buffer of information for each call, without having to save significant state information for each process. (This technique also plugs a potential source of memory leaks.)

Although this technique increases the amount of processing to be performed, and also increases the risk of garbled data due to changes to the table that can occur between calls, it reduces the risk of other problems. For example, if you use the **cat** utility with a pipe to the **more** utility, early termination of the **more** utility will cause a *broken pipe* condition, which may prevent the rest of the output from ever being read.

20334: Output the header line to the buffer, if appropriate. Note that the **sprintf** call pads the output to 128 characters (including the new line), regardless of the actual length of the header.

20343: If necessary, wait for the **ip_rt_lock** semaphore.

20347: Go through the internal list of Forward Information Block (FIB) elements, one by one, from beginning to end.

20352: If no entries are associated with the current FIB element, then go to the next FIB element and try again.

20355: If the current FIB element is associated with a line that has already been printed, advance the virtual line pointer, go to the next FIB element, and try again.

20362: If a hash table is present for the current FIB element, then set the number of slots to the size of the hash table and point to the first list pointer. Otherwise, set the number of slots to 1 and position the pointer at the start of the list.

20373: Walk through the hash table (either one element or **RTZ_HASH_DIVISOR** elements).

20376: Walk through the current routing-table list.

20385: If this FIB has already been output, skip the entry.

20391: Prepare the line of information describing the route. (Table 6.3 shows the correspondence between the column label printed and the data field references.) The variable **f** is a pointer to the current block, while the variable **fz** points to the current zone; that is, to the current set of routes having a specific number of one-bits in the mask. (In the code, the variable **fi** is set to the pointer expression **f->fib_info**. The expression is expanded in the table, to clarify the path to the data.)

Table 6.3   Column heads and corresponding data sources.

Label	Data Source	Data Type
Iface	f->fib_info->fib_dev->name	char[]
Destination	f->fib_dst	unsigned long
Gateway	f->fib_info->fib_gateway	unsigned long
Flags	f->fib_info->fib_flags	unsigned short
RefCnt	(zero)	—
Use	f->fib_use	unsigned long
Metric	f->fib_metric	short
Mask	fz->fz_mask	unsigned long
MTU	f->fib_info->fib_mtu	unsigned short
Window	f->fib_info->fib_window	unsigned long
IRTT	f->fib_info->fib_irtt	unsigned short

20401: Take the prepared information (written to the temporary buffer) and output it in the form of a 128-byte line.

20403: Increment the position by 128 bytes. If the buffer passed by the caller is full, then break out of the loop prematurely (by branching to the program label **done**). The **goto done** instruction is the cleanest way to break out of all three loops at once, even if it makes structured-programming purists wince.

20406: These right braces close the loops started in line 20376, line 20373, and line 20347.

20410: The definition for the program label **done**.

20411: Free the lock and restart any processes that were waiting on the lock.

20414: Calculate and send back to the caller the starting offset for the next call, and return the length of the new data in the buffer.

rt_cache_get_info

This function is considerably simpler than the **rt_get_info** function, because the information is in a simple linked list. Each call returns a specified amount of information, with each call getting the next set of lines.

20432: If this is the first call, then write the column headers to the buffer.

20442: Wait for the semaphore **ip_rt_lock** to become available, and then lock it.

20446: Cycle through each of the cache table lists (the number of which is defined by the manifest constant **RT_HASH_DIVISOR**), taking the elements one at a time.

20455: If the element in question has been printed, then continue searching for the point at which to resume printing.

20461: Print the information for the cached route. (Table 6.4 shows the correspondence between the column label, as printed, and the data-field references.) The variable **r** is a pointer to the current block.

20471: Take the prepared information (written to the temporary buffer) and output it in the form of a 128-byte line.

20473: If the buffer is full, abort the loop (by branching to the program label **done**); otherwise, continue scanning the lists.

20475: The right braces close the list-traversing loop (line 20448) and hash-table scan loop (line 20446).

20479: Unlock the semaphore and restart any process that is waiting on this lock.

Table 6.4   Column heads and corresponding data sources.

Label	Data Source	Data Type
Iface	r->rt_dev->name	string
Destination	r->rt_dst	unsigned long
Gateway	r->rt_gateway	unsigned long
Flags	r->rt_flags	unsigned short
RefCnt	r->rt_refcnt	atomic_t (int)
Use	r->rt_use	atomic_t (int)
Metric	(zero)	—
Source	r->src	unsigned long
MTU	r->rt_mtu	unsigned short
Window	r->rt_window	unsigned long
IRTT	r->rt_irtt	unsigned short
HH	r->rt_hh->hh_refcnt	int
ARP	r->rt_hh->hh_uptodate	char (Boolean)

20482: Calculate and return the offset for the next call and then return the length of information for the buffer in this call.

The ioctl Handling Routine

External processes and some of the kernel routines talk to the routing system via the standard **ioctl** system call. This routine handles all requests for I/O control directed toward routes.

ip_rt_ioctl

This steering function takes a system call from a process and determines the proper routine for executing the request. This function also performs all necessary validation operations, so that memory isn't corrupted and no unexpected machine exceptions occur.

21393: This is the entry point called from the file /usr/src/linux/net/ipv4/af_inet.c (line 6079).

21398: This code selects one of the two permitted function requests for the **ioctl** call.

21402: The **ioctl** calls that affect routing-table entries must be made by a superuser process. This code checks for the superuser condition.

21404: To prevent panic (which can occur when a kernel routine causes a memory fault), the memory area used by the **ioctl** routine.

21408: The routing-table information is copied from the process space to local memory (allocated on the stack at line 21396). This operation speeds processing immensely and simply is a sensible thing to do.

21410: Depending on the function, a route is either killed or created/updated. For route creation, the function **ip_rt_new** is called. For route deletion, the function **ip_rt_kill** is called. In either case, when the applicable function is called, the local routing-table data is passed via a pointer, and the function's return value is propagated to the calling routine, from where it eventually returns to the process that started the entire operation.

Adding Routes To The Table

Before the routing system can be used, entries need to be placed in the routing table. This action is performed at system boot time, when the **route(8)** utility is used to install some basic routing information. The startup calls are located in various places, depending on the distribution of Linux being used. In Slackware, these calls are in the file /etc/rc.d/rc.inet1. In Red Hat, they're in /etc/sysconfig/network-scripts/ifup, with the parameters in /etc/sysconfig/network. Other distributions place the initial routes in other scripts.

Linux users on LANs will find routes for **localhost** and for the LAN itself. In many cases, the LAN will have a gateway to other networks, so the desired routes will be included in the static startup information. The system administrator enters these numbers manually when the Linux system is set up.

For Linux users who rely on dial-up modems and the Point-to-Point Protocol (PPP) for Internet access, the initial route at boot consists only of the **localhost** entry. The code that establishes PPP (or SLIP) connections then adds a route when the connection is made.

Boot time isn't the only time at which routes are added to the routing table. As you'll see (both later in this chapter and in Chapter 7), control messages can provide information that is placed in the routing table. In particular, *ICMP redirects* are used when an upstream router finds a route to a particular host that is better than the route provided in the default configuration. However, because ICMP redirects are a function of network complexity, you won't run into them unless you're running on a large intranet.

ip_rt_new

The **ip_rt_new** function creates a new route entry in the routing table. The new entry can replace (and, in practical terms, update) an existing routing entry.

21235: If the caller specified a device name in the structure **rt** (passed as **argp** in the **ioctl** call), this code block tries to find the device as named. The **getname** function is defined in the /usr/src/linux/fs/namei.c file.

21250: Check for the correct family value, which should be **AF_INET**.

21259: Copy the flags, target address, netmask, gateway address, and metric into local variables. This operation eliminates pointer dereferencing when these values are manipulated. (Note that the metric is decremented by 1 from the metric provided by the caller.)

21277: This code supports the case in which a gateway is being added to the table, but the gateway device is specified by IP address instead of by name. The code searches the device-block linked list for a working interface that has a matching IP address. The entries for the device-block linked list are defined by the **device** structure at line 38347. When a device is configured, the structure member **pa_addr** is filled with the IP address. If the address matches and the **IFF_UP** flag is also asserted, then a match has been found and the device name is used thereafter.

21293: If the **RTF_HOST** flag is set, this code overwrites the netmask for the request to all 1s.

21295: If a non-0 mask has been defined and if the socket isn't an **AF_INET** socket, then the balloon goes up and a "not-supported" return code is returned to the caller.

21300: Gateways are specific to Internet routes; so if this route isn't an Internet route, a "not-supported" return code is returned to the caller.

21308: Gateways are useless if you can't reach them. This code makes sure that the specified gateway is available.

21318: If this address is not a gateway (network or host), then zero out the gateway address. If no device was specified, then use the **ip_dev_bynet** function (line 8803) to find the device to use for this route. If no device can be found, then tell the caller that the designated network was unreachable. (We perform a routing operation whenever the caller doesn't tell us what he or she wants—even when we're creating routes.)

21323: If the caller didn't specify a mask, then copy the device's mask.

21332: The **ip_get_mask** function at line 8643 is used to set the mask to the correct mask for the address. This operation is performed if the working netmask is still 0 and if **CONFIG_IP_ CLASSLESS** was not defined.

21336: After all of this work, the mask may still be ill-formed. If so, it must be rejected, and an invalid-request return code must be sent back to the caller. The inline function **bad_mask** confirms that the mask is acceptable.

21343: The information in the request to add a route entry has passed muster, so now we call the routine that actually does the job. The function **rt_add** doesn't return a status, so we return 0 to the caller to indicate that that the job's been properly done.

ip_rt_redirect

This routine is called by ICMP handlers that have to deal with redirect requests. They do so by creating a new route and then deleting the old one.

20888: If no route exists for the destination, then kick the call back (that is, return the call, accompanied by an error code).

20892: If the information is not identical, create a new route record and return. (This operation is not a true redirection, but rather the publication of a route.)

20900: Create the modified route.

20903: If the semaphore can be captured, then perform the redirection now. Otherwise, queue up a request for service by the backend handlers (described later in this chapter).

ip_rt_update

This function isn't implemented in Linux kernel release 2.0.34. However, our crystal ball says that this function will automatically add a route to the device when it comes up, and will remove all routes for the device when it goes down. These events currently take place through configuration scripts, rather than happening all by themselves.

ip_rt_advice

This function is called by the **tcp_write_timeout** function in the file tcp_timer.c (described in Chapter 9).

21419: This function does nothing. The comment may amuse readers who appreciate programmer humor.

ip_rt_put

This routine handles the details of eliminating a reference to a routing element.

21163: Decrement the reference count.

21170: If the element has not been cached and if the reference count goes to 0, release the element (which has already been unlinked from any lists).

bad_mask

The **bad_mask** function takes a network address and a netmask and determines whether the address and mask are acceptable. It returns 0 if the mask is acceptable (not a bad mask) and non-0 if the mask is unacceptable (bad mask).

19868: The function **bad_mask** is expanded inline when it is encountered, so there is no call and no parameter passing. However, because it is used so often, it should be coded only once. This way, code can be executed faster without any undue expansion in size. The function returns FALSE (zero) if the mask is acceptable and returns NOT FALSE (non-zero) if the mask is ill-formed for the address.

19870: The address in question and the subnet address (obtained by taking the one's complement of the netmask) must yield a non-0 address.

19872: This function appears often when code performs arithmetic on addresses and masks. The information about addresses is stored in *network order*, which has the most significant byte in the leftmost position in byte-addressed storage. The Intel 8086 family of processors puts the most significant byte in the rightmost position in byte-addressed storage, which in Internet terminology is called *host-byte order*. The **ntohl** library function does the actual "byte swapping" when this operation is required.

19873: This is a tricky piece of code. For a mask (as passed originally into the inline function) to be valid, it must consist of a string of one-bits followed by a string of zero-bits. The one's complement reverses the state of the bits. When a constant (that is, the value 1) is added to the latter value, a valid mask is changed from a mass of one-bits to a single one-bit. The AND function checks for the occurrence of the change, to speed up the testing for this condition. If any bits survive the operation, then the mask is

invalid. Note that a mask consisting of all 1s is valid (that is, it signifies a host address), but a mask of all 0s is not. The latter result is the one we're looking for.

fib_add_1

20040: Note that this function extends to line 20224.

20057: Memory for the new node is allocated, and basic information is filled in.

20065: Note that the Type of Service field is set to 0, signifying the absence of any special considerations for sending packets. (No way exists to change the value in the routing table, which makes us wonder why the structure contains this member at all.)

20067: Now find (or create) an FIB (line 19966). If the FIB comes back as **NULL**, then release the new node allocated in line 20057.

20073: A pointer to the FIB node is placed in the routing-table block.

20075: The length of the host portion of the mask is calculated by the inline routine **rt_logmask**, based on the mask calculated thus far.

20076: Get the pointer to the FIB zone, based on the length of the mask. If no zone block is present, create one. (Can't create one? Then release the memory allocated for the FIB and get out.)

20089: Zero out the block and then fill it with the information available thus far.

20092: Find the insert point, such that the FIB zone list is in mask-length order.

20095: Turn off interrupts and then insert the FIB zone block into the proper place in the list.

20106: Put the pointer to the FIB zone block in the array and then turn the interrupts back on. It's remotely possible that two processes could cause a FIB block to be allocated more than once

(no semaphore), but both blocks would appear in the linked list (even though only one would have the pointer in the array **fib_zones**).

When the number of routine-table cache elements in a particular FIB zone exceeds a given limit (**RTZ_HASHING_LIMIT**, which, in production systems, is 16), a hashing table (consisting of 256 entries) is created for that zone. The idea is that a search for a particular record can be handled in fewer cycles if most of the list can be bypassed.

20115: The purpose of this code block is to convert a single zone list into 256 zone lists. Accordingly, if the number of entries in the FIB zone exceeds the hashing threshold, no hash table exists. If the mask indicates that the routing entry is not for a host, then create a hash table, initialize it, and stroll through the FIB node list to build sublists based on the calculated hash value. To preclude the possibility of race conditions, interrupts are turned off during the update process.

20146: Save the fact that a hashing table now exists.

20150: What happens if no memory is available for the creation of a hashing table? Why, nothing. Because the old FIB zone list is still there, many attempts will be made to create the hash table for that zone. These attempts will slow the proceedings, but won't bring them to a screeching halt.

20151: Find the proper head of the list to scan. If a hash list is present, point to the head of the sublist for the zone. Otherwise, point to the head of the zone itself.

20161: Scan the zone list for the desired destination address. Note that the routine will stop when it reaches a **NULL** pointer, while the rest of the list-scanning routines can handle a **NULL** flag.

20172: Continue scanning the list as long as the destination address still matches.

20174: Lower metric values are more desirable. Therefore, when you find a node with a metric whose value is equal to or higher than the metric value of the candidate node, the search is over.

20182: If the gateway addresses match and a matching gateway address or device has been specified, then save the pointer to the block pointer that meets these criteria.

20192: If the code already has a route with the same metric value, then dump the new block and return from the function.

20203 Insert the new FIB into the list. This operation lays the groundwork for an *insert sort* based on the destination and the metric value.

20210: Increment the zone entry count.

20211: Send to the peer a new route message. The **ip_netlink_msg** routine is at line 17171 in module **ip_output.c** (which is discussed in Chapter 7).

20219: If a route was marked at line 20184, start looking for duplicate routes at that point. Otherwise, start with the next route after the newly inserted route.

20224: Search the list until either the destinations don't match or the list is exhausted.

20226: Look for identical gateway addresses and device addresses. When one is found, remove the route from the list, free the node, and decrement the zone entry count. Then, break out of the loop. (At most, only one duplicate route should be in the routing table.)

20242: Because the structure of the routing table has changed, the general hash table is cleared out (via the **rt_cache_flush** routine at line 20688).

fib_create_info

The **fib_create_info** function allocates and fills in an FIB structure element (defined at line 19598). (The com-

ment in the code is that the FIB is "shared by many of the routes.")

19975: If the **RTF_MSS** flag is not set and if the kernel has been compiled not to discover the MTU for the path, then use the default MTU for the device. If the call defines a gateway (**RTF_GATEWAY**), then cap the maximum segment size at 576 bytes.

19994: If the **RTF_WINDOW** flag was not set, clear the window-size value.

19996: If the **RTF_IRTT** flag was not set, clear the initial round-trip time value.

19999: Search the FIB list, starting with the head point **fib_info_list** and continuing until a match is found or the end of the list (indicated by a **NULL**) is reached.

20008: If the gateway address, device, flags, maximum segment size, window size, and initial round-trip time all match, increment the reference count **fib_refcnt**, log the fact, and return the address of the reference FIB.

20015: If the FIB wasn't found, create an FIB by allocating memory from kernel memory. If no memory can be allocated, return **NULL**.

20020: Initialize the structure to all 0s and then fill in all the information that has been gathered so far. Lines 20026 and 20029 through 20031 add this new element to the beginning of the FIB list, so that the search order is last-in/first-found. Log this fact and return the address of the new FIB.

fib_lookup_gateway

This function searches the routing table for a gateway.

19737: For each element in the FIB zone list, find the list in which the destination address is most likely to be found. If the zone-list entry has a hash table, select the correct list by calculating the hash code for the destination and searching the appropriate sublist. Otherwise, use the zone's master list.

19745: Whenever the destination network doesn't match, or if the entry is marked as the default gateway, reject the current FIB entry and try the next one.

19750: A hit! Return the pointer to the Forward Information Block.

get_gw_dev

This inline function performs a route lookup based on the destination address. If the desired address is found, this function returns a pointer to the device name.

19858: Perform the search based on the destination address.

19859: If the desired address is found, return the pointer to the device name. Otherwise, return the **NULL** pointer.

rt_add

This function wraps the handling of the routing-table semaphore around the function **fib_add_1**, so that user processes won't step on each other.

20859: Only one process at a time is allowed to make changes in the routing table. If another process "holds the token" **ip_rt_lock**, then that process must be put to sleep until the other process (or processes) is finished with it. The **sleep_on** function lives in the /usr/src/linux/kernel/sched.c source file (which lies beyond the scope of this book).

20861: The **ip_rt_fast_lock** function (defined at line 41304) is a call to the function **atomic_inc**, which lives in the /usr/src/linux/include/asm-i386/atomic.h file (not included with this book). The **atomic_inc** function is written in assembler, so that it works properly in shared-memory multiprocessing systems. This way, nothing—not even other hardware operations—can interfere with the incrementing of the semaphore **ip_rt_lock**. (In older, 16-bit systems, such a function was needed to handle 32-bit numbers in environments with interrupts, because a 32-bit increment was implemented in two instructions, namely, a 16-bit increment followed by a 16-bit increment with carry. Intel 386, 486, Pentium, and clone chips have 32-bit pathways, so that such an incrementation scheme is no longer necessary. Multiprocessing systems keep them around.)

20862: This function incorporates the inline function **fib_add_1** (located at line 20040), which allocates the memory for the routing-table entry and fills the node. Note that this function does not provide an error return.

20864: The next two lines of code clear the semaphore flag and wake up any processes that may be waiting. Then, the function returns with no status.

rt_logmask

19680: This inline function returns the length of the low-order zero-bits in a mask. When the value is 0, the value 32 is returned. Otherwise, the value is changed from network-byte order to host-byte order, and the inline routine **ffz** ("find first zero bit"), located in file /usr/src/linux/include/asm-i386/bitops.h, is invoked. This routine executes a single 80386 bit-search operator, using a pattern such that 0xFFFFFFFF yields 0, 0xFFFFFFFE yields 1, and so on, until 0x80000000 yields 31.

rt_mask

19691: This inline function is the inverse of the **rt_logmask** function. It takes a number that represents the number of zero-bits to be generated at the low-order end of the network address. Any value greater than or equal to 32 yields a result of 0, while a value of 0 results in an all-ones mask. The mask is placed in network-byte order before it is returned.

Removing Routes From The Table

There are other ways to remove a route from a routing table, but this series of functions is the only one that

has the effect of removing a route explicitly. Such a deletion can be triggered by a network administrator who wants to make a change that reflects a modification of the physical network or who needs to remove an improperly added route that, because of the improper addition, makes a given host unreachable.

ip_rt_kill

This relatively small routine deletes routes from the routing table.

21362: This block of code copies information from the user's passed structure into local storage.

21365: If the caller told us the name of the interface (such as "eth0"), this routine gets the device information block for the device. Otherwise, it leaves the **NULL** pointer that was set in line 21360. If the caller made an error, the appropriate error code is returned.

21381: Call the routine **rt_del** (line 20838) that actually deletes the route, and propagate the return value from the deletion attempt.

21386: This code completes the function.

ip_rt_flush

This function is called when all routes for a device need to be cleaned out. Such a drastic action may be necessary, for example, when a device is taken to the Down state by the system operator, or when a PPP or SLIP connection is closed.

The **ip_rt_flush** routine is a user wrapper for the **fib_flush_1** routine. The code starts at line 20868.

ip_rt_check_expire

This function, which is called by the /usr/src/linux/net/core/arp.c module, checks the routing cache table for outdated entries. This action also has the effect of emptying outdated hardware handles, because the hh blocks are eliminated along with the cache entries.

20593: Run through the 256 lists for the cache, using the hash table as the starting point. Process each element in the list.

20606: If the element has reached its age limit, then remove the element completely and continue searching the list.

20628: The following code is a very complicated way to implement a fuzzy bubble sort. The idea is that if two adjacent elements are present for which the last-used timestamps are within **RT_CACHE_BUBBLE_THRESHOLD** time of each other (defined as five seconds), don't bother reordering the elements. Otherwise, if the physically earlier element is "newer" than the next element on the list, force these two elements to swap places. This swap puts the list in least-recently-used order, so that the oldest element is at the head of the list. This way, the relatively oldest element is the first to be pruned when the cache gets too big.

ip_rt_hash_code

This inline function calculates a hash value (returning a value from 0 through 255) whose purpose is to distribute IP address references evenly.

41323: Add the top 16 bits of the IP address to the bottom 16 bits of the IP address.

41324: Add bits 7 through 0 (counting the least significant bit as 0) to bits 8 through 15 of the previously calculated sum, and mask off all but the bottom 8 bits of the result. Return this result to the caller.

fib_del_1

This routine searches the FIB subsystem and deletes the references to this route contained in that subsystem.

19924: If the **mask** parameter is 0, then the reference is to a host, not to a network.

19926: This loop sweeps the FIB zone list from top to bottom.

19929: Set the local variable **fp** to the address of the FIB, as pointed to by the FIB zone block. (Note that this operation uses the hash-table entry, if any, that is attached to the FIB block.)

19935: Call the routine **fib_del_list** (line 19879) that extracts the FIB block from the database.

19937: If the deletion was acceptable, decrement the FIB zone block "contains" counter and increment the "number of blocks found" counter.

19941: If the mask is non-0, perform the following operations:

19943: If a route has the same length mask, then pick up the pointer to the list and traverse the list. (The list may be obtained from the zone table itself or from a hash table.)

19951: Release the appropriate entries from the list. The routine **fib_del_list** returns the number of elements freed.

19957: If any routing-table elements were indeed found and deleted, then flush the cache and return the success indicator (0).

19962: If no elements were removed from the routing table, return the appropriate error code.

fib_del_list

This routine takes the parameters for removing a route and traverses the list passed to it, performing deletions as it goes. It returns the number of elements removed.

19879: The beginning of the function. Because the list is a pointer to a pointer (usually referred to as a *handle*), the pointer needs to be doubly dereferenced before access can be gained to any internal element. Moreover, if necessary, the list head can be altered without causing major problems.

19886: Walk through the list, performing the steps on each element of it.

19895: If the following items do not match— destination, mask, metric (if specified), gateway (if specified), and device (if specified)—then go on to the next element.

19904: Remove the route block from the chain.

19905: If the route being removed is the loopback route, then set the shortcut to the route to the **NULL** pointer.

19908: Tell the neighboring systems that the route is being removed.

19910: Free the node.

19911: Increment the released-node counter.

19913: Return to the caller, indicating the number of routes that have been removed.

fib_flush_1

This routine kills off all routes for a given device. When it's done, it calls the cache flush function.

20279: Walk through the FIB zone list. If a hash table is present for the zone, then walk through all the lists pointed to by the hash table. Otherwise, just walk through the single list. For each list, call the function **rt_flush_list**.

20300: If any routes were removed, call **rt_cache_flush** to clean up the cache.

rt_flush_list

This routine kills off all the routes for a specific device.

20252: Search each node of the list passed by the caller.

20257: If the FIB element is for a different device, and if the block isn't pointing to the loopback device or if the FIB element isn't for the device's IP address, continue the search.

20264: Point to the next element.

20265: If the loopback device entry is being killed off, then reset the pointer.

20268: Free the node and increment the counter for the number of elements removed.

20271: When the list has been exhausted, return the number of elements that were freed.

fib_free_node

This function takes a routing-table element, removes it from the linked list, and frees the kernel memory associated with it. The function also checks the FIB associated with the route, to see whether the routing-table element contains any more references. If not, the FIB is also removed from the list and freed.

19711: If the reference counter in the FIB has been decremented by 1 and is not 0, then don't purge the FIB.

19717: Remove the FIB forward link.

19719: Remove the FIB backward link.

19721: If this block is the first one on the list, update the header pointer.

19723: Free the memory for the FIB.

19725: Free the memory for the router-table entry.

fz_hash_code

This inline function calculates a hash value (returning a value from 0 through 255) based on the network portion of the destination address. This function uses the inline function **ip_rt_hash_code** (line 41321).

19701: Return the 8-bit hash value of the network portion of the address. The parameter **logmask** is the number of zero-bits in the mask value. When **logmask** is shifted right by the number of zero-bits, the network portion of the address is right-aligned before the hash is calculated.

rt_del

This routine removes a specified route (or routes) from the routing table.

20844: This code implements a semaphore for a routing-table lock, to ensure that only a single process at a time manipulates the routing table.

20847: Call the routine **fib_del_1** (line 19916) that actually deletes the route.

20849: Remove the lock.

20850: Release any processes that may be waiting because of this lock.

20851: Propagate the return code to the caller.

rt_free

This routine handles the mechanics of freeing up a routing-table cache entry.

20494: Turn off interrupts. To do so, use the **save_flags** function to save the current CPU state, and then tell the system to disable device interrupts.

20496: Before doing anything else, confirm that the reference count for this entry is 0.

20498: Save the pointer to any hardware handle(s), and clear it from memory. (Strictly speaking, this step isn't necessary, because the memory will be going away anyway.)

20501: Decrement the reference count in the hardware handle. If the count is 0, then get rid of it.

20503: Delete the table entry.

20506: If the reference count isn't 0, add this route to the front of the free-element queue and reset the **RTF_UP** flag.

20509: Set a flag to indicate that the free-element queue contains an element.

Cache Management Routines

The designers of the Linux TCP/IP stack were well aware that network access is "session oriented"—in other words, that once two computers establish a conversation, the conversation lasts for a time and then ends. By recognizing and using the session-oriented nature of network access, the designers were able to implement techniques that led to significant improvements in the performance of network operations—which, on the Internet today, is overwhelmingly synonymous with Web browsing.

Web surfers look at sites one at a time. When surfers land on a site and find the first taste interesting, they tend to stay at that site—often to the exclusion of others—until they're satisfied or take a tangent to another, related site.

Yesterday's dominant application—file transfer—was even more narrowly focused, because there were no links to tempt users away from the FTP server they were using. Unlike Web surfing, which only requires that users specify the correct URL to access a page, FTP requires that users explicitly log onto the server. Consequently, users tend to milk the server they're currently using before moving on to the next one.

In the routing world, this "fixity of access" means that a route that has been used once is very, very likely to be used again in the near future. Conversely, a route that hasn't been used for a given length of time (say, 10 minutes) most likely will not be used again in the near future. These paired assumptions work equally well for routers and host systems, with the only difference lying in the size of the cache in which the recently accessed routes should be saved.

rt_cache_add

This function places in the routing cache a destination used by a routing request, and also performs a housekeeping task, by deleting the least recently used elements after a given number of elements have been placed in the cache.

20942: During development, this code checks to ensure that the value of the semaphore is exactly equal to 1. A semaphore value other than 1 means that the caller hasn't captured the semaphore, and that problems may therefore occur.

20952: If the device associated with the passed router-table entry has a bind routine, and if the gateway address is not the destination address, then search for the correct route. Note that the function **ip_rt_route** expects to be able to capture the semaphore. Therefore, before the call is made, this routine has to let the semaphore go and then snatch it back on return.

20963: If a route was found, and if the route is identical to the route that was passed by the caller, then call the device-bind routine.

20971: If the route is different, then update the hardware handle (if one is present) and copy the pointer from the original route to the new route. Then, call **ip_rt_put** to place the new route information in the cache.

20979: Caches work best when they're small. This code triggers a cleanup when the cache grows too large.

20983: Link the route into the hash table.

20994: Point the hash table to the new route (so that the most recently used route is at the head of the list).

21003: This loop walks through the list, checking for entries that have timed out (manifest constant **RT_CACHE_TIMEOUT**, currently 300 seconds) or that are duplicates of the previously checked route. If an entry is found that meets either of these conditions, then that element is removed and the cache-size counter is decremented. In any case, the search continues until all the elements have been checked.

21024: The CPU flags are restored to their previous state (the flag of interest is the interrupt-enable flag) and the function returns.

rt_cache_flush

This small routine cleans up the cache buffer.

20693: This loop cycles through all possible **RT_HASH_DIVISOR** cache lists.

20698: If the hash table points to nothing, then continue the loop.

20704: Wipe out the pointer to the hash-table entry. (The value of the pointer was saved earlier, in the variable **rth**.)

20707: Cycle through the link list and free up the elements.

20728: Complete the flushing of the routing cache table.

rt_garbage_collect_1

This routine swings through the FIB list and purges any element(s) that shouldn't be there.

20737: Continue through the process until the number of cache elements is below the limit defined by the manifest constant **RT_CACHE_SIZE_MAX** (256 elements).

20739: Run through the hash table and process each list entry.

20746: If the entry hasn't expired (based on the time of last use, adjusted by the number of routes using this entry), then continue searching.

20749: Decrement the cache-content count, adjust the list, and free the element. The **break** statement causes the code to start the search from the start of the hash table.

20758: When no candidates for removal remain, determine whether the garbage-collection operation was thorough enough. If not, decrease the expiration interval and go again. This way, enough elements will be deleted to reduce the cache to a reasonable size.

rt_garbage_collect

The purpose of this function (which is a wrapper for the function **rt_garbage_collect_1**) is to ensure that the routing-table semaphore is captured before the cleanup operation is performed. The function starts at line 20923.

Backend Handlers

Some jobs in route.c just can't be done when the original request comes in. To handle such instances, the Linux programmers set up queues and a flag word **ip_rt_bh_mask** to deal with the issues as they arise.

ip_rt_run_bh

This function is the entry point for the backend handlers. It is called when the lock is released (using **ip_rt_unlock**) and a backend job needs to be done. In one respect, this function is a wrapper for a series of functions that run with interrupts inhibited. Consequently, no way exists that the semaphore can be "stolen." When required (as indicated by bits in **ip_rt_bh_mask**), the following three routines are called: **rt_kick_backlog**, **rt_garbage_collect_1**, and **rt_kick_free_queue**.

When work needs to be deferred, the indicator flags are set by various routines in route.c.

rt_req_enqueue

This routine is used by **ip_rt_redirect** when a redirect request has to be queued. This simple interrupt-safe routine just adds a request to a request list.

rt_req_dequeue

This routine is used by **rt_kick_backlog** when a redirect request has to be removed from a queue. This simple interrupt-safe routine simply removes a request from a request list and returns it.

rt_kick_free_queue

This routine is a cleanup routine borrowed from **rt_free**, previously described. Any routing element that has a non-0 reference count and that was to be freed is handled here.

20525: Turn off (in other words, reset) the "gotta-do-it" flag.

20529: Walk through the free-element list. If the element now has a 0 reference count, remove the hardware-handle cache element and then remove the routing-table entry, too.

rt_kick_backlog

This routine goes through the list of requests for route redirection. Each previously queued request is processed (by calling **rt_redirect_1**, using the information about the request), and the request element is removed from memory.

rt_redirect_1

This routine accepts a call from ICMP. The call causes the routine to record a new route to a host, as determined by the ICMP message-processing code.

20661: If the gateway address is the desired interface, or if the device isn't accessible via the gateway address, forget it.

20665: Build a new routing-table element. Mark it as "dynamic", "modified", "host" (as opposed to "net"), "gateway address valid", and "up".

20684: Add the routing-table element to the queue.

Routing Request Handlers

This section is where the real action takes place. Although routing tables are read-mostly structures, because routes are supposed to change at a relatively slow rate, a busy host or router routinely has to handle thousands of routing requests.

ip_rt_route

Find the route for a particular destination. This routine examines the cache, because, as noted earlier, once a route is used, it tends to be used repeatedly for the life of a session.

21198: Select the correct cache list to examine for the route, and parse the list.

21203: Got a hit? That is, did the destination and any device qualifications match? If so, update the use time, increment the in-use and reference counts, and return to the caller. (Fast, huh?)

21213: Missed. Go look for the route the slow way.

ip_rt_dev

This routine is a wrapper for **fib_lookup**. The result is similar to that of **ip_rt_route**, except that the slow search is always used and no hardware handles are generated. This routine is used only by the ip_alias.c module when aliasing is compiled into the module.

ip_rt_slow_route

Okay, the code didn't find the route quickly, so now the code has to look for it the hard way. This routine searches for the best match in the routing table for a given destination, and an optional device qualification.

21049: Allocate memory for a routing-table entry. If not enough memory was available, then lie—say you didn't find the route.

21056: If this route request is a local lookup, use the faster routine **fib_lookup_local** to find the specific route. Otherwise, use **fib_lookup**.

21061: If you find a matching route, increment its in-use count.

21067: The route may be marked "reject." (This dodge is sometimes used to prevent the propagation of Internet Assigned Numbers Authority (IANA) private network addresses onto the public network.) Alternatively, it may have been not-found. In either case, release the memory that had been allocated for the routing-table entry.

21077: If the Linux kernel was configured for the kerneld.o module, then issue a dynamic route request.

21088: Return without a route-entry pointer.

21091: Set the source address to the interface address. This action associates the destination address with the gateway address that should be used. If the destination address is the gateway address, then decrement the use count for the FIB (except if it's the loopback address) and get the FIB for the gateway.

21103: Here's another chance to fail. If no route can be found, then free the memory and propagate the status of the search.

21110: Fill in all the information about the route.

21123: Mark this route as a host route (as opposed to a network route).

21136: If you have the semaphore, and if you didn't limit your search to a specific interface device, then add the route to the cache for next time (so that you can go fast, of course!). If you don't have the lock, then so much for speed, but better luck next time.

21158: Return the route information.

fib_lookup_local

This routine scans the entire routing table, looking for the "longest" match for the given destination. The idea here is that the route that "works" (in other words, the one with the most high-order one-bits in the netmask) is the route to pick. This approach gets around the problem, which existed in older code, of choosing a nonuseful route (documented in lines 19758 through 19775).

19784: Search each zone list, resetting the success flag at each return to 0 (no match). If a hash table is associated with the zone list, use the hashing function to find the head of the sublist that might contain the desired route. Otherwise, use the main list for the zone.

19794: Search the selected list. If the destination doesn't match the route's destination, go to the next element. Ditto if a device was specified and the devices don't match.

19801: If this route is a gateway route, the code can shout "Eureka!" and return with that route.

19803: Did the code match a non-gateway route? Then, remember this fact as the zone-list examination continues.

19805: If the code found a match in the zone list, don't bother looking in the next zone. The code already knows it's in trouble.

19808: If the code didn't find the destination at all, then it returns a failure report.

fib_lookup

This routine looks for any possible route to the destination. The primary difference between this routine and **fib_lookup_local** is that the route in the latter case is supposed to be on the local machine.

19834: Search the zone list. For each zone, if a hash table is present, use it to select the correct sublist for the desired destination. Otherwise, use the main list, and then scan the selected list.

19844: If the destination doesn't match the request, or if the device (if any) specified by the caller doesn't match the request, then go to the next element on the list.

19849: Was a matching destination found? If so, then report the success by returning the route pointer.

19852: Were no matching destinations found? If so, then report the failure by returning the **NULL** pointer.

Chapter 7

IPv4

The Internet Protocol (version 4) is the *IP* in *TCP/IP*. It performs most of the major tasks that enable the flow of information from system to system. In essence, the Internet Protocol is the "envelope" in which all user data is placed so that it can be transmitted anywhere on the Internet.

Like a paper envelope, IP has a destination address, a return address, and handling instructions aimed at the many entities that handle the data. IP even has an analog to the sorting of paper letters according to post-office boxes, so that data packets intended for TCP don't get mixed up with letters intended for UDP, and ICMP packets are kept segregated. (These are just 3 of the types of objects that IP can handle; another 252 types are possible, 97 of which are defined in RFC 1700.)

Unlike its physical counterpart—the U.S. Postal Service—IP doesn't believe there is any such thing as an oversized letter. When the amount of data to be transmitted is too large to fit into the "envelope," IP simply breaks the data down into chunks that are small enough for the data-transmission procedures to handle.

These chunks, called *fragments*, can be created at any point during the transfer of data from an originating system to a destination system. When all the fragments of a data packet have arrived at the destination system, the Internet Protocol reassembles them into a single large packet, and passes this packet up to the next-higher protocol layer.

This chapter examines the Linux source code that implements version 4 of the Internet Protocol (IPv4), which is the version that is used on the Internet today. IPv4 will eventually be replaced by IPv6, which, among other features, will offer a fourfold increase in address space

(just as the original IP provided a fourfold increase in address space over the original ARPAnet Network Control Protocol). For the moment, however, IPv4 is the version to know.

In brief, the IPv4 part of TCP/IP performs the following jobs:

- Packet fragmentation
- Packet reassembly
- Payload encapsulation
- Packet lifetime management
- Packet forwarding
- The dispatching of received and reassembled packets to upper-layer protocols

These tasks are closely linked with the format of Internet Protocol data packets, which are the subject of the following section.

Internet Protocol Packet Format

Figure 7.1 shows the general layout of an Internet Protocol packet. Such IP packets are transmitted via serial data-communications lines, with the 8-bit bytes shown in these illustrations being forwarded in order, from left to right and from top to bottom. Although the specific transmission method for the bits in each byte is defined by the underlying hardware, standard practice calls for the least-significant bit to be transmitted first.

The following subsections describe each of the fields in the Internet Protocol packet.

Version

The Version field (byte 0, bits 7 through 4) indicates the packet type. For IPv4 packets, this field contains the binary value 4.

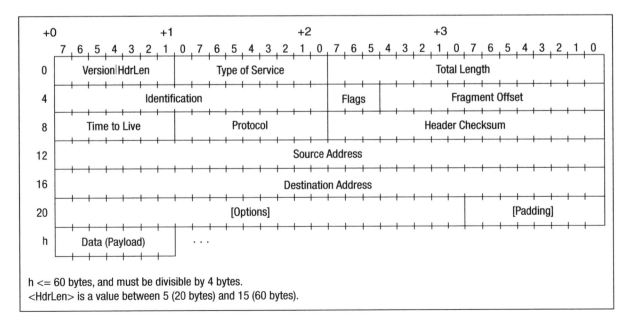

h <= 60 bytes, and must be divisible by 4 bytes.
<HdrLen> is a value between 5 (20 bytes) and 15 (60 bytes).

Figure 7.1   General format of an Internet Protocol packet (from RFC 791).

Header Length

The Header Length field (byte 0, bits 3 through 0, "HdrLen" in Figure 7.1) contains the number of 32-bit words in the IP packet header. Because the minimum header size is 20 bytes (that is, five 32-bit words), the minimum value of this field is 5. The only time this field has a value other than 5 is when the header contains IP options—which is a relatively rare occurrence on today's Internet.

Type Of Service

The Type of Service field (byte 1), also referred to widely in the literature as the *TOS field*, is illustrated in detail in Figure 7.2.

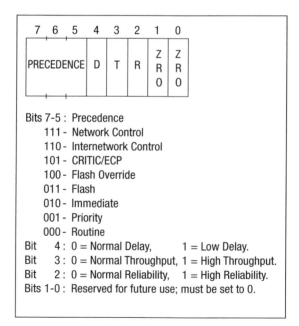

Bits 7-5 : Precedence
    111 - Network Control
    110 - Internetwork Control
    101 - CRITIC/ECP
    100 - Flash Override
    011 - Flash
    010 - Immediate
    001 - Priority
    000 - Routine
Bit   4 : 0 = Normal Delay,   1 = Low Delay.
Bit   3 : 0 = Normal Throughput, 1 = High Throughput.
Bit   2 : 0 = Normal Reliability, 1 = High Reliability.
Bits 1-0 : Reserved for future use; must be set to 0.

Figure 7.2   The Type of Service field, in detail (byte 1).

The first 3 bits define the *precedence classification* of the packet. The other 3 bits in this byte define the *preferred handling* of the packet within the precedence classification. The remaining 2 bits are reserved for future

use. The precedence classification, which is used in military networks, indicates the "importance" of the packet. This classification determines which packets are handled during peak loads and during overload conditions. The preferred handling bits allow routers to schedule the transport of packets in ways that improve the apparent (and actual) performance of network applications.

In the original U.S. Department of Defense (DOD) definition of TCP/IP, the contents of the Type of Service field were used to determine when certain packets should be sent ahead of other packets. RFC 795 (September 1981) describes how the information in this byte was mapped to the requirements of various datanet services that were in use at the time.

In military and government networks, the Precedence field is often very important. However, in the mostly civilian and commercially oriented data universe known as the Internet, this byte is largely ignored.

Total Length

The Total Length field (bytes 2 through 3) contains the length (in bytes) of the entire packet (that is, of the header, the IP options, and the data). This length field limits the maximum size of the packet to 65,535 bytes. Most of the protocols (such as ICMP, TCP, and UDP) that live on a layer above IP restrict themselves to packets whose size fits the *maximum transmission unit* (MTU) that can be sent over the path between the systems. (One notable exception is the Sun Network File System, commonly known as NFS, which in many implementations uses packets that contain 8,192 data bytes.)

Identification

The Identification field (bytes 4 through 5) contains a packet sequence number. When a data packet can be transmitted in its original form, with no modifications, this field is ignored. However, if a packet needs to be fragmented, the Identification field is used to identify all the resulting little pieces, so that they can be collected at the receiving end. The Identification field also allows the defragmentation algorithms at the receiving

end to reassemble, in proper order, multiple fragments derived from many large packets.

Fragment Control

The next two fields are used, in conjunction with the Identification field, to keep track of fragments of packets. Figure 7.3 shows the details of the Fragment field (bytes 6 and 7).

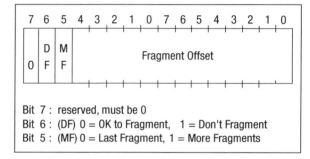

Bit 7 : reserved, must be 0
Bit 6 : (DF) 0 = OK to Fragment, 1 = Don't Fragment
Bit 5 : (MF) 0 = Last Fragment, 1 = More Fragments

Figure 7.3   The Fragment field, in detail (bytes 6 and 7).

When set, the Don't Fragment flag (byte 6, bit 6, also referred to in the commentary as the *DF flag*) indicates, to any router, that the packet in question should not be fragmented. This flag also indicates that the router in question should return an ICMP packet with a type value of 3 (destination unreachable) and code 4 (fragmentation needed and DF set). This flag is used when a system needs to discover the MTU of the path to a remote computer.

In this procedure, the originating system sends variously sized packets, with the DF bit set, to a remote receiving system. (The path traveled by these packets can go through any number of intermediate routers.) When the remote system finally responds, the originating system can infer the size of the MTU. Knowing the MTU, the sending system can tailor its transmission packets to use the path as effectively as possible, while also preventing packets from being fragmented.

When set, the More Fragments flag (byte 6, bit 5, also known as *MF*) indicates that the packet containing the set bit belongs to a given group of packet fragments. When the receiving system receives all the packet fragments in which bit 5 is set, plus one packet fragment in which bit 5 is clear, the receiving system can proceed with the reassembly of the fragments and the processing of the packet.

The Fragment Offset field (byte 6, bits 5 through 0, plus byte 7) indicates the starting position of the first data byte (that is, the first payload byte) in this IP packet, as this location appeared in the original unfragmented packet.

To locate the starting position in the reassembled packet in which the data from this packet needs to be placed, the receiving system must obtain a value known as the *byte offset*. To do so, the receiving system multiplies the contents of the Fragment Offset field by 8. This algorithm implies that fragment reassembly is governed by certain rules, to wit:

- For fragments other than the last fragment, the length of the data portion of the packet (that is, the payload) must be equal to a multiple of 8 bytes, and the length of the data portion plus the fragment offset must not exceed the length of the original unfragmented packet.

- For the last fragment, the sum total of the number of bytes in the data portion, plus the fragment offset, must not exceed the length of the original unfragmented packet. Some ill-intentioned system crackers have taken advantage of lax internal programming practices in order to perpetrate *buffer overrun* attacks, which are launched through packets that violate this length-limitation rule.

- For any fragment, the sum total of the number of bytes in the data portion, plus the fragment offset, must not exceed 65,535. Because this requirement forces the IP fragment reassembly code to write to astonishing locations in memory, it has given rise to the so-called *Ping of Death* packet, which is another, more insidious example of a buffer overrun attack. (Linux is a 32-bit operating system that runs on 32-bit comput-

ers, so the *bounds test*, which determines whether the specified number of bytes has been exceeded, can easily be performed. However, making this determination is not so easy on 16-bit machines. On these systems, programmers must be very, very careful if they don't want to be bitten by an undetected register overflow when this bounds check is performed.)

So, then, exactly how are packets reassembled? Well, first of all, the packet-reassembly algorithm collects the fragments, using the contents of the following four fields as index values:

- Source Address field

- Destination Address field

- Protocol field

- Identification field

After it has obtained the contents of these fields, the algorithm sorts the fragments into groups known as *collections*. When a collection is complete—with at least one fragment that covers each byte of the packet that is being reassembled—the original packet can be rebuilt and processed, and the fragments (which are no longer needed) can be discarded.

Strange things can happen on the Internet. Accordingly, the reassembly algorithm needs to be able to deal with fragments that are exact duplicates of packet fragments that have already been received. The reassembly algorithm might also have to deal with multiple copies of fragmented data, or with fragments that arrive in no discernible order—or even overlap each other. (Another game malicious system crackers play involves the generation of streams of bogus fragments, filled with data that differs from fragment instance to fragment instance, in an attempt to circumvent the packet-filtering rules in firewalls.)

The destination system can't reassemble an entire original packet unless all the constituent fragments are present. So, what can the reassembly algorithm do when a fragment is lost? The answer is rooted in time.

Incoming fragments must reach the reassembly algorithm within a given period of time, which can differ from system to system. Release 2.0.34 of the Linux kernel uses a deadline (known as a *timeout value*) of about 30 seconds. (As you'll see in the commentary section of this chapter, the source code is somewhat ambiguous about timeout values. For the moment, assume that the 30-second clock is restarted each time a fragment reaches the reassembly algorithm in the destination system.)

If one or more deadline periods have passed, such that the destination system concludes that it will probably never receive all the fragments that belong to a given packet, then the destination system will discard all the fragments that it has already received. Its next decision is whether to send an informative ICMP message (see Chapter 4) back to the originating system.

If the receiving system has acquired an incoming packet's IP header and at least the first 8 bytes of the packet's data portion, then it can generate an ICMP message to notify the originating system that a problem has occurred. If the receiving system has not acquired this minimum data, it cannot generate any ICMP messages, and the fragments in question quietly disappear into the bit-bucket.

Time To Live

The Time To Live field (TTL, byte 8) is initially set to the maximum number of routers that a packet can visit. As each router forwards the packet, the value contained in the TTL field is decremented by 1. If a router finds itself about to transmit an IP packet whose TTL value is 0, the router drops the packet and generates an ICMP packet with a type value of 11 (time exceeded) and a code value of 0 (TTL equals 0 during transit).

Here, the word *time* is a misnomer, because no way exists for today's routers to know exactly when a given packet was launched into the Internet. The initial meaning of the TTL value, which referred to clock time, now refers instead to the maximum number of routers through which a packet can be forwarded.

When an IP implementation fragments a packet (or fragments a packet fragment—this process can be iterative), each fragment that is generated by the router inherits the TTL value from the received packet that the router is fragmenting at that moment. For example, a system sends out a packet whose TTL value is 64. Over the course of this packet's travels, its TTL value is decremented by intermediate routers, such that when the packet arrives at the router in question, its TTL value is (for instance) 51. In this case, the TTL value that is inserted into the fragments is 51 minus 1, or 50. Because of this inherited TTL value, each fragment has a finite "lifetime" within which it must reach the destination system. In other words, fragmentation does not extend a packet's life expectancy.

Protocol

The Protocol field (byte 9) contains the identification of the next-higher-level protocol in the data portion (that is, the payload) of the IP packet. For example, the Protocol field contains the value 1 if the payload contains an ICMP packet; the value 6 if the payload contains a TCP packet; and the value 17 if the payload contains a UDP packet. RFC 1700 lists all the values that can appear in this field in the IP header.

Header Checksum

The Header Checksum field (bytes 10 and 11) contains the checksum of the entire IP header (but not of the payload). When an IP protocol handler receives a packet from a device driver, it can use this checksum to confirm that the header has not been damaged. The algorithm for calculating this checksum consists of the one's-complement sum of a certain number of values (usually from 10 to 30 of them), each of which contains 16 bits, with the checksum field initially set to 0.

The length of the header is obtained from the data that is being verified. Although at first glance this procedure may seem risky, closer examination of the possible error modes shows that the checksum verification will generate a true negative even if the length field itself is damaged.

The payload is *not* checksum-protected at this level. That task is left to the protocols (such as TCP or UDP) that process the payload.

Source And Destination Address

The Source Address field (bytes 12 through 15) and the Destination Address field (bytes 16 through 19) contain the IP address of the originator of the packet and the IP address of the intended recipient of the packet, respectively.

IP Packet Options

The Options field (bytes 20+) contains any IP options that may be present in the packet header. This part of the IP header can contain up to 40 bytes of additional information. Options can consist of a series of single bytes or a series of option data blocks, each of which is prefixed by a 2-byte option header. Each option can start at any byte position (not necessarily on a word boundary). If necessary, the Options field must be padded with end-of-list (0) codes until it reaches a 32-bit boundary. Figure 7.4 shows typical options that can be defined in this field.

None of these options is used regularly on the Internet today. Source routing is viewed as a security problem. The Security field is useful only in military networks. The SATNET Stream ID is useful only on SATNET. The Internet Timestamp and Record Route functions don't hold enough data, because the structure of the Internet virtually guarantees that your packets will pass through more than nine routers. RFC 791 contains more information about these options.

The major field of interest in Figure 7.4 is the column entitled Copy—because when a packet is being fragmented, only those options whose Copy bit has been set are copied to the fragments. (The sole exception—the pad byte—is always copied, because some systems use pad bytes to terminate certain options fields at 32-bit boundaries.)

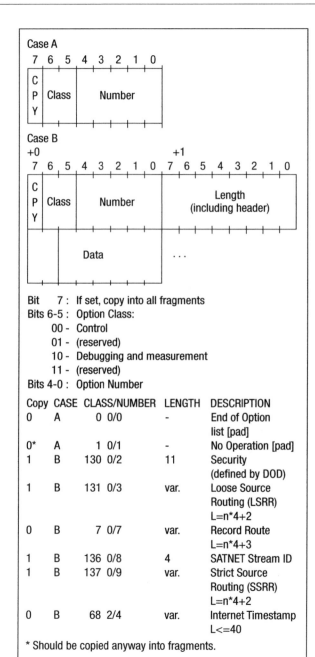

Bit 7 : If set, copy into all fragments
Bits 6-5 : Option Class:
    00 - Control
    01 - (reserved)
    10 - Debugging and measurement
    11 - (reserved)
Bits 4-0 : Option Number

Copy	CASE	CLASS/NUMBER		LENGTH	DESCRIPTION
0	A	0	0/0	-	End of Option list [pad]
0*	A	1	0/1	-	No Operation [pad]
1	B	130	0/2	11	Security (defined by DOD)
1	B	131	0/3	var.	Loose Source Routing (LSRR) L=n*4+2
0	B	7	0/7	var.	Record Route L=n*4+3
1	B	136	0/8	4	SATNET Stream ID
1	B	137	0/9	var.	Strict Source Routing (SSRR) L=n*4+2
0	B	68	2/4	var.	Internet Timestamp L<=40

* Should be copied anyway into fragments.

Figure 7.4 The Options field, in detail (bytes 20 and onward).

Implementation Do's and Don'ts

To flesh out the requirements of an Internet Protocol implementation, we must discuss RFC 1122. This document, entitled *Requirements for Internet Hosts—Communication Layers*, lists the "shoulds" and "musts" and "should nots" and "must nots" that are important in IP implementations.

RFC 1122 isn't just some random programmer's good idea. It is a standard, as defined by the computer industry, and therefore constitutes the widely accepted "word from on high."

At this point, some quotations are in order. Here are a few representative decrees from RFC 1122:

For incoming datagrams, the IP layer:

(1) Verifies that the datagram is correctly formatted;

(2) Verifies that it is destined to the local host;

(3) Processes options;

(4) Reassembles the datagram if necessary; and

(5) Passes the encapsulated message to the appropriate transport-layer protocol module.

For outgoing datagrams, the IP layer:

(1) Sets any fields not set by the transport layer;

(2) Selects the correct first hop on the connected network (a process called "routing");

(3) Fragments the datagram, if necessary and if intentional fragmentation is implemented (see Section 3.3.3); and

(4) Passes the packet(s) to the appropriate link-layer driver.

A datagram whose version number is not 4 MUST be silently discarded. [This requirement assumes that IPv6 has not been implemented, as is the case in Linux kernel release 2.0.34.]

A host MUST verify the IP header checksum on every received datagram and silently discard every datagram that has a bad checksum.

A host MUST silently discard an incoming datagram containing an IP source address that is invalid by the rules of this section. This validation could be done in either the IP layer or by each protocol in the transport layer.

A host MUST NOT discard a datagram just because it was received with TTL less than 2.

The IP layer must not crash as the result of an option length that is outside the possible range.

The foregoing excerpts are just a few of RFC 1122's many requirements. (The complete document appears on the CD-ROM that accompanies this book.) Note that RFC 1122 was written in 1989, and an update is long overdue. When the first edition of this book was written, no more recent document was available—not even in the form of an active Internet draft. The RFC index, as maintained by the Internet Engineering Task Force (IETF), will indicate whether RFC 1122 has been superseded since this book went to press.

Functions, Meet The Functions

The Linux implementation of IPv4 occupies a lot of code, most of which is fairly straightforward. Two notable exceptions are the routing code and the firewall code, which is why these two parts of IPv4 have chapters (6 and 10, respectively) of their own in this book.

Table 7.1 lists the IPv4 functions by name, and Table 7.2 lists them by line number.

Table 7.1   IPv4 functions, listed by name.

Line	Function
16371	add_to_send_queue
16226	ip_build_header
16614	ip_build_xmit

(continued)

Table 7.1   IPv4 functions, listed by name *(continued).*

Line	Function
14769	ip_chksock
12291	ip_create
12477	ip_defrag
12354	ip_done
11352	ip_encap
12270	ip_evictor
12239	ip_expire
12152	ip_find
11414	ip_forward
12109	ip_frag_create
12740	ip_fragment
12186	ip_free
17767	ip_getsockopt
12391	ip_glue
17243	ip_init
14752	ip_ioctl
16079	ip_loopback
17381	ip_mc_find_devfor
17321	ip_mc_procinfo
17171	ip_netlink_msg
15426	ip_options_build
15648	ip_options_compile
15477	ip_options_echo
15606	ip_options_fragment
16414	ip_queue_xmit
14793	ip_rcv
16010	ip_rewrite_addrs
17207	ip_rt_event
16132	ip_send
16357	ip_send_check
16177	ip_send_room
17398	ip_setsockopt

Table 7.2   IPv4 functions, listed by line number.

Line	Function
11352	ip_encap
11414	ip_forward
12109	ip_frag_create

(continued)

Table 7.2 IPv4 functions, listed by line number (continued).

Line	Function
12152	ip_find
12186	ip_free
12239	ip_expire
12270	ip_evictor
12291	ip_create
12354	ip_done
12391	ip_glue
12477	ip_defrag
12740	ip_fragment
14752	ip_ioctl
14769	ip_chksock
14793	ip_rcv
15426	ip_options_build
15477	ip_options_echo
15606	ip_options_fragment
15648	ip_options_compile
16010	ip_rewrite_addrs
16079	ip_loopback
16132	ip_send
16177	ip_send_room
16226	ip_build_header
16357	ip_send_check
16371	add_to_send_queue
16414	ip_queue_xmit
16614	ip_build_xmit
17171	ip_netlink_msg
17207	ip_rt_event
17243	ip_init
17321	ip_mc_procinfo
17381	ip_mc_find_devfor
17398	ip_setsockopt
17767	ip_getsockopt

The Other Side Of The API

Chapter 5 describes the application programming interface (API) functions, which set options and provide information about socket objects and their associated packets. The four control functions that implement the "other side" of the API—that is, the functions that pro-cess the application requests and return status information—are described here. In a nutshell:

- **ip_ioctl**—Receives all calls that are made to the system function **ioctl** and that specify I/O control functions related to IPv4.

- **ip_setsockopt**—Receives all calls that are made to the system function **setsockopt** and that refer to **IPPROTO_IP** options.

- **ip_getsockopt**—Receives all calls that are made to the system function **getsockopt** and that refer to **IPPROTO_IP** options.

- **ip_mc_find_devfor**—Provides a support service for the **setsockopt** function.

ip_ioctl

According to the comment at line 14747, the function is scheduled to disappear (at some unspecified future time). Therefore, this function is just a placeholder. It does not contain any code for processing the IP parameters that you might expect to be set via the **ioctl** system call. If any calls get through, regardless of the command(s) passed by the parameter(s), this function returns **EINVAL** status to the caller.

ip_setsockopt

When calls that specify IP options (**IPPROTO_IP**) are made to the system function **setsockopt**, this function (which starts at line 17398) accepts them. (Chapter 5 lists the valid IP option names that can be specified by these calls.) The **ip_setsockopt** function also modifies the socket-object parameters associated with IP options, as directed by the command(s) contained in the call(s) to the **setsockopt** system function. Socket objects contain information about option settings for IP, and also for higher-level protocols, such as TCP and UDP. Naturally, the code in the IPv4 modules only handles IP option names.

The "option names" previously referred to are in reality integer values. This use of an integer index (instead of a character string) makes for more efficient code execu-tion. And, as you will see next, the use of manifest constants makes the code readable by humans.

Many of the manifest constants used in the **ip_setsockopt** function appear in /usr/include/linux/socket.hm. The specific constants start at line 39431.

17407: If the pointer to the option value is 0 (**NULL**), then set to 0 both the internal version of the value and the data pointer. Otherwise, fetch the value, both as an integer and as an unsigned character pointer.

17422: If the parameter **level** (that is, the type of activity) does not have the expected value (**SOL_IP**), then the function was called in error and should return **EOPNOTSUPP** (operation not supported).

17424: If the option name lies within the range from **MRT_BASE** to **MRT_BASE+10**, inclusive, call the function **ip_mroute_setsockopt** (line 18360). These option names refer to multicast routing—a function that, in Linux, is handled primarily in user space. In turn, multicast routing supports the following option names:

- **MRT_INIT**

- **MRT_DONE**

- **MRT_ADD_VIF**

- **MRT_DEL_VIF**

- **MRT_ADD_MFC**

- **MRT_DEL_MFC**

17432: Select the code that implements the specified option name. The following option names are supported by this part of the code:

- **IP_OPTIONS** (line 17434)

- **IP_TOS** (line 17478)

- **IP_TTL** (line 17500)

- **IP_MULTICAST_TTL** (line 17511)
- **IP_ADD_MEMBERSHIP** (line 17568)
- **IP_DROP_MEMBERSHIP** (line 17633)
- **IP_FW_*** (line 17688) (for firewall options, see Chapter 10)
- **IP_AUTOFW_*** (line 17723) (automatic forwarding support for IP masquerade)
- **IP_ACCT_*** (line 17739) (IP accounting)

The handler for each of the preceding option names returns from the **ip_setsockopt** function. If the handler performs all of its tasks with no errors, **setsockopt** indicates success by returning to the calling routine with a status value of 0. If a handler runs into a problem, the standard response of **setsockopt** is to return an error code to the calling routine. If a request was rejected due to bad parameters, the value returned is **EINVAL**. If the request needed memory and the required memory space was not available, the value returned is **ENOMEM**.

The code for the **ip_setsockopt** function lives in the Linux kernel. Therefore, any attempt by the kernel code to write to (let alone read to) user memory must be validated beforehand. The **verify_area** memory management function, which is one of the core kernel routines (/usr/src/linux/mm/memory.c), performs this validation. If **verify_area** returns a non-0 value, then **setsockopt** reports the presence of a problem involving the address that was passed, doing so by propagating the error code back to the calling routine. The only error message that **verify_area** can return is **EFAULT**.

The switch statement at line 17432 uses the option name to specify the particular chunk of code that should be executed. In the following commentary, the **option name** indicates the beginning of each chunk of code.

17434: **IP_OPTIONS** tells the **setsockopt** function to read the option data (shown in Figure 7.4) that can be added to each IP packet. Because the option field is limited to 40 bytes, any request that exceeds this size must be rejected.

17444: Allocate enough memory for the option structure, the option data, the data copied into the option portion of the IP header, and up to 3 pad bytes (which are added to make the option-data header length a multiple of 4 bytes).

17457: If the check performed by the **ip_options_ compile** function (line 15648) indicates that the options list contains invalid data, then release the memory and reject the request.

17469: Get any existing buffer of saved option information (either from a previous **setsockopt** call or from the options in a packet that was received on this socket object), swap in the new option buffer, and release the old buffer (if there was one). (A **NULL** pointer indicates that there was no old option object.)

17476: Indicate success.

17478: **IP_TOS** asks **setsockopt** to set the Precedence-field value and the preferred-handling bits for the socket object. Any attempt to set the unused bits in the preferred-handling bitfield is rejected. Any attempt by nonsuperuser processes to set the Precedence field value to 5 or above is rejected.

17487: The value in the preferred-handling bitfield is translated into a three-level priority scheme. These levels, in descending order of priority, are *interactive*, *normal*, and *background*.

17499: Indicate success.

17500: **IP_TTL** asks **setsockobject** to set the Time to Live field for the socket object. Any value outside the range from 1 through 255 is rejected. Any value inside this range is stored in the socket object.

17504: Indicate success.

17505: **IP_HDRINCL**, which is used only with socket objects of type **SOCK_RAW**, sets a flag in the socket object. This flag indicates to the rest of the IP support system whether an application that is sending data will include the IP header that should be used, and whether an application that is receiving data will include the IP header in the data. If the socket object is not the right type, **IP_HDRINCL** indicates failure by returning **ENOPROTOOPT** to the calling routine. If the socket object is the right type, the flag is set according to the value that was passed as the option.

17509: Indicate success.

17511: **IP_MULTICAST_TTL**, which is valid only if the multicast configuration option was selected when the kernel was compiled, sets the multicast Time to Live field in the socket object. No bounds checking is performed on the value at this time.

17514: Indicate success.

17516: **IP_MULTICAST_LOOP**, which is valid only if the multicast configuration option was selected when the kernel was compiled, sets a flag to indicate whether transmitted packets should be "looped back" to the system in the same way in which standard broadcast packets that have been transmitted are received by the system. If the value is neither 0 nor 1, reject the request. If the value is either 0 or 1, save the value in the socket object.

17521: Indicate success.

17523: **IP_MULTICAST_IF**, which is valid only if the multicast configuration option was selected when the kernel was compiled, indicates which device (designated by its Internet address) should be used for this socket object. If this address is the wildcard address, then the name is set to the null string in the socket object, and success is indicated.

17554: Search for the device that matches the Internet address. If the device is not found, signal the failure by returning to the calling routine with status **EADDRNOTAVAIL**. If the device is found, copy the name of the device into the socket object.

17566: Indicate success. (This action actually happens at line 17563.)

17568: **IP_ADD_MEMBERSHIP**, which is valid only if the multicast configuration option was selected when the kernel was compiled, links the socket object to the membership of a multicast group, so that the socket object can send and receive packets to and from the multicast group. The address passed to this function by the caller is the Class D address that specifies the multicast address to which this socket object should be attached.

17594: If an address has been specified that refers to an interface, find this address in the routing tables. If no address has been specified, then find a suitable device for the Class D address that specifies the multicast group to which this socket object should be joined. If no suitable device can be found, return the error **ENODEV**.

17629: Return the status from the call that was made to **ip_mc_join_group** (line 11080).

17630: **IP_DROP_MEMBERSHIP**, which is valid only if the multicast configuration option was selected when the kernel was compiled, undoes the effect of the **IP_ADD_MEMBERSHIP** request. The processing that is done here is identical to the processing for the add-membership option, except that here the work is done by the function **ip_mc_leave_group** (line 11118).

17688: The **IP_FW_*** options, which are valid only if the firewall configuration option was selected when the kernel was compiled, control the stateless packet filter that comes with the standard kernel distribution. If the current process is not running as a superuser, reject the request and return the status **EPERM**. Reject any request in which the data block is too large (that is, larger than the structure **ip_fw**). (See Chapter 10 for details.)

17714: Fetch the user option block and call **ip_fw_ctl** (line 14056; see Chapter 10). Propagate the status from that function back to the calling routine.

17723: The **IP_AUTOFW_*** options (which are valid only if the masquerade configuration option was selected when the kernel was compiled) control the transparent proxy feature in Linux. This feature allows a computer that is connected to one subnetwork to communicate via another, separately connected subnetwork, by using the masquerade machine's IP addresses. This type of dynamic network-address translation prevents systems on an inside network from being accessed by an outside network—which is a useful security feature.

The processing done here is identical to the processing done in the **IP_FW_*** group, except that here the **ip_autofw_ctl** function (line 14039, discussed later in this section) is called.

17739: The **IP_ACCT_*** options, which are valid only if the IP accounting configuration option was selected when the kernel was compiled, control the accounting functions in the firewall-support code.

The processing done here is identical to the processing that is done in the **IP_FW_*** group, except that here the **ip_acct_ctl** function (line 13914; see Chapter 10) is called.

17756: Unknown options (or options that are specified but for which support hasn't been compiled into the kernel) end up here. The request unconditionally fails, and the status **ENOPROTOOPT** is returned.

ip_getsockopt

When calls that specify IP options (**IPPROTO_IP**) are made to the system function **getsockopt**, this function (which starts at line 17767) accepts them. (Chapter 5 lists the valid IP options that can be specified by these calls.) The **ip_setsockopt** function also queries the socket-object parameters associated with IP options. Socket objects contain information about option settings for IP and also for higher-level protocols, such as TCP and UDP. Naturally, the code in the IPv4 modules only handles IP options.

The **getsockopt** function almost always returns the same value that was set by default when the socket was opened (or the same value that was set when the socket was modified by a corresponding **setsockopt** call). The only time the **getsockopt** function returns a different value is when the **IP_OPTIONS** query returns a more recent event (such as an option that was set by the **setsockopt** function, or an option that was specified in an IP packet that was sent to the socket in question).

When the **getsockopt** function returns information to user space, the process it uses is very similar to the process that the **setsockopt** function uses to fetch information. The **verify_area** function checks whether the area in which the information is to be written is authorized to receive the information. If the area in question is not authorized to do so (that is, if the area cannot be modified by the current process), then the **verify_area** function returns **EPERM**. The **put_user** function actually places the data in the specified area in user space.

If the option name being queried lies in the range from **MRT_BASE** to **MRT_BASE+10**, inclusive, **getsockopt** calls the function **ip_mroute_getsockopt** (line 18511), which handles the following options:

- **MRT_VERSION**

- **MRT_ASSET**

To manipulate the IP options that are contained in IP socket objects, calls to **getsockopt** can specify the following option names (which are a subset of the option names that can be used by calls to **setsockopt**):

- **IP_OPTIONS**

- **IP_TOS**

- **IP_TTL**

- **IP_HDRINCL**

- **IP_MULTICAST_TTL**

- **IP_MULTICAST_LOOP**

- **IP_MULTICAST_IF**

ip_mc_find_devfor

In support of the **setsockopt** processing for IP, this function (which starts at line 17381) finds the device that corresponds to a given IP address. Starting with the device block pointed to by **dev_base**, the **ip_mc_find_devfor** function searches the device block chain for a device that is in an UP state, that supports multicasting, and whose interface address matches the address specified by the caller. If the function finds such a device, it returns the address of the device control block. Otherwise, it returns 0 (the **NULL** pointer).

Suiting Up

Regardless of where data comes from—ICMP packets, local programs, or a higher-level protocol—it can't be launched into the blue skies of the Internet without being properly dressed. In fact, without its binary "flight suit," which contains its guidance system, the Internet's data-forwarding functions wouldn't know where to send it.

The first supplemental layer that a bare datagram puts on is its virtual Nomex underwear—that is, its physical-

layer address and handling information, which are obtained from the device driver and added to the datagram as a prefix. Then, the datagram dons its outer protective layer, which consists of the information about where the data should ultimately be sent (even if the trip is a simple out-and-back to the point of origin). Once garbed in its flight suit, the datagram takes on a new name. Henceforth, it's known as an *IP packet*, with the configuration shown schematically in Figure 7.5.

These steps—prefixing the datagram with address and handling information, and determining where the packet should be sent—sound straightforward. However, they include some tedious details, which (because the details are where the deity resides) cannot be ignored. Many of these boring but necessary steps live in the **ip_build_header** function.

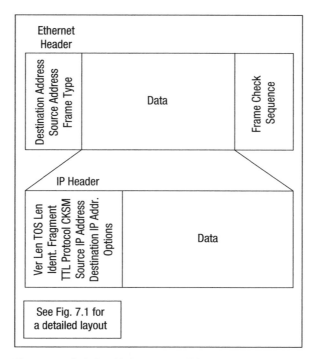

Figure 7.5   Relationship between an Ethernet packet and an Internet Protocol packet.

ip_build_header

This function (which starts at line 16226) is called from the various protocol handlers to construct a proper IP packet header from the information contained in the socket object, and place this header into the socket data buffer passed by the caller. The source code in this book contains references to this function at lines 10691 (igmp.c), 19465 (raw.c), 25975 (tcp.c), and 32900 (udp.c). All of those references are contained in **proto** structures. (The actual routine is called via the indirect routine named **build_header**.) Remember, one tenet of the "Linux Way" is to refrain from making unnecessarily formal separations between functional layers. This is why the individual protocol routines use the **ip_build_header** function (which can be thought of as a library function) to finish creating the IP header.

16239: If the IP header option list includes the strict source-routing options, use the first-hop address as the destination for this packet. The actual destination for the packet is listed as the last address in the option.

16247: If this packet is destined for a multicast (Class D) address, and no device was specified in the socket object, then obtain a suitable device address.

16251: The purpose of the handle **rp** (a *handle* is a pointer to a pointer) is to remember a route that was used earlier by the socket object. Use of the handle can speed up transmission, by eliminating a trip through the routing table when the previously selected routing-cache entry is still present. The call to **ip_check_route** performs this little task.

16267: If no route was found, then the function returns **ENETUNREACH** to the caller. That's it for this request.

16278: Set the source address to the source address in the routing-cache entry or to the device address being used. (When a packet is sent from multihomed systems, the packet's source address might not necessarily match the actual interface's source address.)

16281: Set the route address to the gateway address of the routing-cache entry. If no routing-cache entry is available, set the route address to the destination address.

16283: If a strict route was specified, and the first route in the list isn't associated with one of this system's interfaces, then the packet can't be transmitted: return **ENETUNREACH** to the calling routine.

16295: Build the MAC (media access control) address information in the packet. Two functions are provided to do this. For TCP packets, the **ip_send_room** function (line 16177) is used; for all other packets, the **ip_send** function (line 16132) is used.

16301: The routing-cache entry is marked as the "most-recently used" entry.

16307: Place the previously determined source address and device into the socket buffer.

16320: If the type of socket is **IPPROTO_RAW**, the work is done. Return the saved packet-size information.

16327: Allocate space in the socket buffer for the IP header, and save that address in the socket buffer header (at line 16342). Fill in the blanks. Return the size of the packet. Give yourself a pat for a job well done.

ip_send

This function (which starts at 16132) doesn't actually send any packets. Instead, it places the physical-layer header information in the socket buffer, as required by the device.

16139: Insert the Internet Protocol identification number **ETH_P_IP** (defined in /usr/src/linux/include/linux/if_ether.h) into the socket buffer header.

16140: Align the end of the socket buffer at a 16-byte boundary.

16142: If the device requires a hardware header, and the ARP (Address Resolution Protocol) cache contains the necessary information, then place the physical-layer header information in the socket buffer and return the length of the MAC header.

16164: If the device requires a hardware header, and no ARP cache entry exists, then call the device's header-building function. If the result returned by the call to the device's header-building function indicates that data is missing from the header, then indicate that ARP needs to get the hardware address that is associated with the destination IP address.

16174: Return the length of the MAC data.

ip_send_room

This function (which starts at line 16177) is identical to the **ip_send** function, except that instead of reserving a variable amount of space based on the device, it reserves a fixed amount of space specified by **MAX_HEADER** (defined at lines 38294 through 38294) in the call to **sk_reserve** (made at line 16186).

ip_options_build

This little function (which starts at line 15426) takes the IP options information located in the socket object and creates the IP options portion of the IP header.

15433: Copy the options, as passed by the caller, into the socket object.

15434: Copy the actual option data bytes from the options, as passed by the caller to the socket buffer, just after the fixed part of the IP header.

15439: If strict source routing has been specified as an option, then copy the destination address into the list.

15445: If the packet being built is not a fragment, and record-route is an option, then insert the source address into the option area.

15448: If the packet being built is not a fragment, and timestamping is an option, then copy the timestamp (expressed as the number of milliseconds since midnight) into the option area.

15461: The work is done. Return to the calling routine.

15463: If the packet being built is a fragment, and record-route is an option, then convert the record-route option to an NOP (no-operation).

15469: If the packet being built is a fragment, and timestamping is an option, then convert the timestamping option to a NOP.

15475: The work is done. Return to the calling routine.

ip_options_compile

The **ip_options_build** function (previously discussed) uses a "compiled" version of the options. The **ip_options_compile** function performs this compilation, by creating the data block that is loaded at the end of the IP packet header.

15657: If the pointer to the option block is 0 (**NULL**), then clear out the appropriate fields in the socket buffer.

15674: Walk through the option bytes, command by command, and process the options as you encounter them. (This gets very, very messy.)

15678: **IPOPT_END** indicates the end of the options. Walk through the rest of the option buffer, setting every byte to **IPOPT_END** and indicating that the option buffer has changed. Then, go to **eol**.

15688: **IPOPT_NOOP** is a placeholder. Ignore it and process the next byte.

15693: The rest of the options in the IP header have 1-byte length fields. Pick up the length field and go for the rest of them, unless the remaining length field **l** (the lowercase letter *l*, not the number 1) is less than the field length **optlen**. (The potential of confusing the number *1* and the lowercase letter *l* is very high—an excellent reason not to use these and certain other single-character identifiers in code.)

From this point until the end of this function, if a problem with an option is detected, control passes to the label **error** (at line 15896), and a parameter-problem ICMP is issued that points to the afflicted option.

15701: For **IPOPT_SSRR** and **IPOPT_LSRR**, if the field is too short, the pointer field is less than 4 bytes long, or either of these options has already been seen, then go to **error**.

15721: If a source routing is being compiled without a buffer packet (such as when **setsockopt** has been called), and the option already contains a source route, then go to **error**. Otherwise, copy the source-route address to **faddr** and then copy the source-routing information to the header buffer.

15732: If this option is a strict source-route option, set the corresponding flag.

15734: Save the offset of the source-route option in the option header.

15735: Process the next option field.

15736: **IPOPT_RR** is the record-route option. If a record-route option has already been seen, the option field is too short, the pointer-field value field is too small, or the pointer field points to data located beyond the end of the option's data area, then go to **error**. Otherwise, copy the record-route data and include its address.

15768: Save the offset of the record-route option in the option header.

15769: Process the next option field.

15770: **IPOPT_TIMESTAMP** is the record-timestamp option. If a timestamp option has already been seen, the option field is too short, or the pointer field is too small, then go to **error**. Otherwise, copy the existing timestamp data.

There are three possible variations of the timestamp option: *Record timestamps only*, *Record IP address and timestamp*, and *Record timestamp only if my* [that is, this system's] *address is in the option block*. The timestamp option header is accessed through the structure definition **timestamp** (at line 36809). The timestamp modifiers live at line 36842.

15798: *Timestamps only.* Point to the proper timestamp-insertion place in the options, and set a flag indicating that a timestamp request was received. Then, increment the pointer field. Fill in the time (if enough room exists) and then go handle the next option.

15806: *Timestamps and IP addresses.* Copy the device's IP address (at this point, the packet has already been routed) into the proper place in the option, and set a flag indicating that an address request was received. Point to the proper timestamp-insertion place in the options, and set a flag indicating that a timestamp request was received. Then, increment the pointer field. Fill in the time (if there's enough room) and then go handle the next option.

15824: *Timestamp if specific IP address.* Check whether the next address in the list is one of the addresses in this system. If not, this timestamp option is done. Go handle the next option. Otherwise, add the timestamp, increment the pointer field, and go handle the next option.

15845: If the timestamp flag field isn't recognized, go to **error**.

15865: If no room exists for the timestamp, and the overflow field is at its maximum value, then go to **error**.

15870: If no room exists for the timestamp, and the overflow field isn't at its maximum value, then increment it (to indicate that an attempt was made to add the timestamp, but was unsuccessful). Go handle the next option.

That's it for the timestamp option processing. Whew!

15878: **IPOPT_SEC** and **IPOPT_SID** (Security and Stream Identifier) are not handled by Linux kernel release 2.0.34. The **IPOPT_SEC** option includes military information, while the **IPOPT_SID** option provides support for a network that no longer exists. Go to **error**.

15888: If the option has been handled, or the option is unknown, then point past the current option and handle the next one. (If all the options have been handled, control falls through to label **eol**.)

15892: Label **eol**. If no errors were detected when the options were handled, then return success (0) to the calling routine.

15896: Label **error**. If a socket buffer is associated with this call, then generate an ICMP message telling the other end about any problems that were detected. In any case, return the failure code **EINVAL** to the calling routine.

Come Fly With Me, IP, Let's Fly Away

The IP packets are now fully suited up and have been informed of their destination. Next, they are belted into their cockpits and off they go.

Or not. Some of them may be too big for the cockpits of their flight articles. Fortunately, unlike real pilots, IP packets can be sliced and sectioned until they do fit into the designated cockpits of as many flight articles as may be needed. The packets are reassembled at the end of their flight...if all of their constituent pieces arrived at the designated destination.

In any event, the functions in this section launch the flights of the IP packets, whether solo or in echelon.

ip_build_xmit

This function, which includes an interesting callback routine, covers a lot of territory. As the flight operations chief for the IP packets, and thus the boss of all the other functions in this section, it oversees the sizing of the packets (with fragmentation, when necessary), calculates all checksums, and gets the packets launched. This function is, however, answerable to the firewall code, which serves as the chief of security. (With apologies to our neighbor, military technovelist extraordinaire Dale Brown.)

16641: If Internet packet options are present, and the option calls for strict source routing, then use the first forwarding address as the destination address.

16644: Update the SNMP (Simple Network Management Protocol) statistics counter for transmitted packets.

16647: If multicast support was compiled into the kernel, the packet is destined for a multicast address, and a device name is associated with the socket object, then find the device (returning **ENODEV** if the device is not found), forget the original route, and set the route address to the source address in the socket buffer (if a loopback is associated with either the source address or the destination address), or to the IP address associated with the physical device.

If multicast support was not compiled into the kernel, the packet is not destined for a multicast address, and no device name is associated with the socket object, then call **ip_check_route** to find a route (returning **ENETUNREACH** if no

route is found) and set the source address to the IP address associated with the device. If the source address is marked for loopback, then use the socket buffer's source address instead. In any case, save the pointer to the device descriptor.

16683: If multicast support was compiled into the kernel, a valid route is present, and no device is present, then use the device identification from the route.

16686: Got a source address, as passed from the caller? Then use it.

16689: Calculate the next-route IP address. If a route has been selected, use the gateway address from the route; otherwise, use the destination address.

16701: Figure out how much buffer space (over and above the length passed by the caller) is needed in the socket buffer. If the "header-included" flag (which is set or reset by **setsockopt**) is not set in the socket object, then add the length of the fixed portion of the IP header. If one or more IP options have been set, then add the length of the options string, as well.

16706: If the total length required is larger than the MTU, or if this packet is a multicast or broadcast packet, then go to line 16801. The result will be a packet that is built as a unicast packet, with no fragmentation.

16710: Allocate a socket buffer that is 15 bytes longer than the length requested by the caller (which length now includes the IP header) and the header length required by the device driver. Do so by calling the function **sock_alloc_send_skb** (line 22989). If a problem occurs, increment the SNMP counter (which tracks the packets that were discarded) and return the error code from **sock_alloc_send_skb**.

16717: Place in the socket buffer header all the information from the caller, from the socket object, and from other places (such as the **jiffies** variable, to timestamp the socket buffer).

16726: If a hardware hash entry is present, fill in the hardware header information and set a flag indicating that the hardware address (that is, the physical-layer address) has already been acquired. If the address isn't up to date, schedule a request to get an up-to-date binding of the IP address to the hardware address.

16744: If no hardware hash entry exists, but a hardware (physical layer) header for the device exists, then call the device's hardware-header generator and report that the hardware address has been acquired.

16748: If no hardware hash entry exists and no hardware header is required, then indicate that a hardware address has been acquired. (This step prevents the generation of any gratuitous ARP requests.)

16749: Set the socket buffer's IP-header pointer and the local equivalent variable **iph** to the beginning of the IP header field in the socket buffer. The function **sk_push** returns a pointer to the place where the header should be put, and keeps track of the location of the end of the buffer.

16751: Call the inline function **dev_lock_list** (line 38578). This function sets a semaphore that is tested in one place (line 7865, in dev.c). The semaphore blocks the setting of any device options via an **ioctl** system call that specifies the **SIOCSIFFLAGS** option. Specifically, this semaphore blocks the closing or unlocking of a device while packets are being built—an interesting condition that normally would occur only once in a blue moon. (Makes you wonder what bright spark discovered it.)

16752: If the caller is supposed to be creating the headers, then go to line 16777. (This code will be examined a little later in this section.)

16754: Fill in the IP header. (The IP header structure definition **iphdr** appears at line 36877.) Note that the fragment flags are not identified separately in the header definition, but rather are handled by logical operations.

16764: If IP options are associated with this packet, then calculate the extension to the IP header field and use the function **ip_options_build** (line 15426) to build the options into the packet.

16770: Calculate the checksum. (This process is described in depth in the commentary on the **ip_send_check** function.)

16773: Invoke the callback function **getfrag**, which performs any protocol-dependent post-processing activities. The following four functions are passed in the calling sequence and appear in this sequence as the **getfrag** function:

- **icmp_glue_bits** (line 9495)
- **upd_getfrag_nosum** (line 32229)
- **upd_getfrag** (line 32182)
- **raw_getrawfrag** (line 19252)

What about TCP, you ask? Good question. As you'll see, TCP uses the function **ip_build_header** to deal with the IP header. Does this constitute duplication of code? You decide.

16775: Head to line 16778, where processing resumes.

16777: If the header is included in the packet, invoke the callback function **getfrag**.

16778: Release the device semaphore. (Note that this particular spinlock does not try to signal a release.)

16780: If a firewall was compiled into the kernel, and the firewall says, "No," then release the packet. Return **KPERM**, to let the caller know that the output of the packet was blocked.

16789: If firewall accounting was compiled into this kernel, then let the firewall accountant know about the packet, so the firewall can count its beans...er, update its counters.

16792: Is the device available? If so, add the socket buffer to the device queue by calling **dev_queue_xmit** (line 7153). Then, return 0, to tell the caller that everything is fine.

16796: Is the device unavailable? If so, increment the SNMP discard count and get rid of the socket buffer. Then, lie to the caller. That's right—return 0 to tell the caller that everything is fine, even though it isn't.

The large block of statements that started with line 16706 ends here. Processing now resumes for the case in which the packet that is being built is intended for a broadcast or multicast address.

16801: If the socket indicates that the caller does *not* include the headers, then subtract the size of the fixed portion of the header from the overall length of the packet.

16804: If IP options are present, then subtract the length of the option header, as well. Then, calculate the fragment header length and the maximum payload size, based on the option size.

16814: If no IP options are present, then calculate the fragment header length and the maximum payload size based only on the fixed IP size. (At line 16816, a fixed constant of 20 is used instead of "**sizeof (struct iphdr)**". This substitution might cause problems later, when people try to maintain this code.)

16833: Fragments are built from the end of the packet toward the front, so that the last fragment contains the first data. Determine the offset for the last fragment. (If the data length is less than the maximum fragment size, a single packet is produced, essentially automatically.) Do the bookkeeping on the last fragment.

16860: If the packets are raw packets, and a fragment is indeed being generated, then just say, "No"—that is, return **EMSGSIZE** to the caller.

16867: Lock the device list (so that the device can't get yanked out from under this function) and get a new packet identifier from the global counter.

16879: Start building fragments. In the degenerate case, build one "fragment" that is a complete packet in and of itself. Continue until the offset of the generated packet is 0, indicating that this process has been completed.

The ensuing code forms a long, long loop. The final control structure doesn't appear until line 17144.

One preliminary observation: The code generates fragments, queuing them for transmission as they are successfully created, until all the data in the original request has been processed, or until the system runs out of memory. In other words, if Linux is running into resource limitations and some fool generates a lot of fragments, a lot of needless traffic will be produced on the Internet. Now, the system isn't supposed to run out of memory, so the likelihood of excess fragment generation due to lack of memory is remote. Nevertheless, the potential nuisance could have been avoided very easily, by allowing the fragments to be generated, saved in a list, and then presented (in the form of the list) to the device. Now, back to our regularly scheduled programming.

16890: Allocate the socket buffer. If the memory-allocation operation failed, then increment the SNMP counters, unlock the device semaphore, and propagate the error value returned by **sock_alloc_send_skb**.

16929: Perform the same hardware-hash activity that was performed in lines 16726 through 16748. (Why wasn't this activity implemented in a function?)

16957: Set the origin of the IP header in the socket buffer header, and also in the local variable that was set aside just for this purpose.

16963: If the caller provided the IP header in the data, then skip to line 16999.

16966: Fill in the IP header. This task has a few wrinkles. First, if the packet is a multicast packet, use a multicast time-to-live value. Second, the total length of the packet is for the fragment alone rather than for the full packet (unless the packet consists only of a single fragment). Then, add the flag **mf**, which is reset for the logically last, or only, fragment, but set to **htons(IP_MF)** for subsequent fragments.

17005: Invoke the callback routine **getfrag** (see the comments at line 16773).

17013: If the firewall says "No" to the fragment, then discard the fragment, unlock the device semaphore, and return.

This is where not keeping a queue of fragments can cause a lot of unnecessary traffic—and where unnecessary traffic can be caused by a sloppy sysadmin. The firewall system allows the sysadmin to define a rule that would permit true fragments to be transmitted, but block transmission of the first fragment (which contains the TCP, UDP, or ICMP header) when that packet fails a test. Because the generation rule is "back to front," and because fragments are queued on an as-you-go basis, fragments that have already been queued can't be "pulled back."

This problem may have been caught in later kernel releases. If not, the present authors will submit a patch.

17022: If firewall accounting was compiled into the kernel, then call the firewall accounting routines so that the fragment is suitably accounted for, based on the rules the sysadmin has in effect.

17035: If the packet is a multicast packet, and if the device does not loop back data by itself, then call **ip_loopback**. The determination of the need to call **ip_loopback** is governed by three conditions: if the packet is directed to the **IGMP_ALL_HOSTS** address, if the system is configured as a multicast router, or if any process is registered for the destination address. This function uses the function **skb_clone** to duplicate the packet.

17097: If the time-to-live value is 0, don't let this packet out of the box.

17106: Increment the number of fragments.

17112: If the device doesn't loop back packets and the packet in question is a broadcast packet, then call **ip_loopback** to loop back the packet.

17123: If the device is in the UP state, queue the fragment for transmission and continue with the fragment-building process, in which the loop continues at line 16890.

17131: The device is DOWN. Increment the SNMP counters, free the socket buffer memory, and release the device semaphore. If a socket object is present, save in it the fact the network is DOWN. Then, return 0 to indicate success. You don't need to worry that this process will die in the middle of the loop, because the device semaphore keeps the device status from changing.

17145: The fragment-creation process has been completed. If more than one fragment was created, increment the SNMP counter.

17147: Release the device semaphore and tell the caller that the process was completed and that no significant problems arose.

ip_queue_xmit

This function (which starts at line 16414) is called by the various upper-layer protocol functions. Its job is to launch an IP packet via the device driver, thereby getting the packet "out the door and off the ground." The major difference between **ip_queue_xmit** and **ip_build_xmit** is that the earlier routine creates a socket buffer to send the data, whereas **ip_queue_xmit** handles a preexisting socket buffer.

Why have two completely separate functions that do essentially the same thing? The main reason is to avoid having to copy memory contents.

Note that, according to a comment in the source code, the value of the variable **free** is either 1 or 2. But, in practice, the value that is actually passed by every call that references this variable is either 0 or 1. The comment at lines 16405–9 just doesn't jibe with the code as written.

16426: Bookkeeping. Save, in the socket buffer, pointers to the associated socket object and device. Also, add a timestamp indicating when this packet was processed.

16440: Find the IP header and then calculate the length of the packet. Place that length in the socket buffer and also in the IP header itself.

16445: If the value of the parameter **free** is 0, then call **add_send_queue** and assign a new packet identifier (ID number) to the packet. Then, place that packet ID in the IP header for the packet and set the socket-buffer **free** element to 0.

If the value of the parameter **free** is 1, then assign a new packet ID number to the packet.

Then, place that packet ID in the IP packet and set the socket-buffer **free** element to 1.

If the value of the parameter **free** is neither 0 nor 1, then set the socket-buffer element **free** to 1.

The next few commentary notes document code that is loaded with **goto** statements that implement error exits. Rather than force you to page back and forth in the source code, these notes follow the thread of the **goto** statements to their rightful ending point—namely, a **return** statement at line 16572.

16460: If no device was specified, then go to the label **no_device** (line 16574). If debugging is enabled, going to this label causes code to be executed that issues a debug message. Then, go to the label **out** (line 16570). If the socket buffer element **free** is non-0, the label **out** frees the buffer. In either case, the function now returns to the calling routine (line 16572).

16464: If firewall support was compiled in the kernel, ask whether the current IP packet should be sent. If not, go to the label **out** (line 16570). If the socket buffer element **free** is non-0, the label **out** frees the buffer. In any case, if the firewall says "No," then return to the caller (line 16572).

16477: If the packet is too large for the selected device's MTU, then go to the label **fragment** (line 16578). Going to this label executes code that calls the function **ip_fragment**. From there, go to the label **out** (line 16570). If the original socket buffer element **free** is non-0, the label **out** frees the buffer. In any case, if the packet was fragmented, control now returns to the caller (line 16572).

16484: Calculate the checksum for the IP header, by calling the function **ip_send_check** (line 16357).

16491: Here, an interesting question arises: Is this packet already on a list somewhere? If it is (and,

frankly, it shouldn't be), then unlink it. Use the **skb_unlink** function (line 21940) to do so.

16503: Increment the SNMP statistics counter for outgoing requests.

16506: If firewall accounting has been compiled into the kernel, call the accounting routines for the packet that's about to be output.

The following code (lines 16511 through 16545) is included only if multicast support was compiled into the kernel.

16516: If the packet is not being sent to a multicast IP address, or the interface is not configured to loop back requests, then go to line 16547.

16519: If the socket-object pointer is not **NULL**, and the socket is not marked for multicast loopback (**sk->ip_mc_loop** set to 0), then go to line 16543.

16521: If the destination address is the manifest constant **IGMP_ALL_HOSTS**, or the selected transmission device is flagged to accept all multicast packets, then call **ip_loopback** (line 16079) with this packet. If neither of these conditions applies, then walk through the list that starts with the element pointed to in the device block **ip_mc_list**. Search for the first multicast list element that matches the address specified in the destination. If this element is found, then call **ip_loopback** and stop searching. If the list has been exhausted, then simply stop searching, without calling the **ip_loopback** function.

16543: If the Time to Live field in the IP header is 0, then the packet should not leave this box. Go to the label **out** (line 16570). If the socket buffer element **free** is non-0, the label **out** frees the buffer. In any case, when the Time to Live field's value is 0, the function returns to the calling routine (line 16572).

16547: If the device has a broadcast mode, the device flags do not specify loopback, and the IP address

is a broadcast address, then call **ip_loopback** (line 16079). (For some networks, a broadcast address can be all 0s or all 1s. Therefore, the device block indicates whether the all-0s case should be interpreted as a broadcast.)

16553: If the device-up flag for the device is set, the packet will be transmitted. Set the priority to the priority value contained in the socket object (as set by **setsockopt**). If no socket object is associated with the socket buffer (as when the packet is being forwarded in this system), use priority **SOPRI_NORMAL**. Call **dev_queue_ xmit** to ship the packet to the device, and then return to the caller, secure in the knowledge that the IP packet has been successfully launched.

16566: If the device-up flag for the device has been reset (for instance, if the device was declared down, was disconnected, or was never successfully initialized), then the device is in the DOWN state. If a socket object is associated with the socket buffer being processed, store **ENETDOWN** as the last error, to indicate that the last transmission request encountered a downed network. Regardless of whether a socket object is or is not present, increment the SNMP discard count, release the buffer (if it is supposed to be freed, as indicated by a non-0 value for the element **free** in the socket buffer), and then return to the caller.

ip_loopback

Many network devices, and Ethernet devices in particular, receive data they are transmitting. In other words, if the device is transmitting a packet, and the destination address in that packet matches one of the addresses that the hardware is listening for, then the packet will be received by the hardware and presented back to the system.

No, this behavior is not a hardware bug. The purpose of this arrangement is to allow broadcast packets that are sent by one system to be received by all the systems on the network—including the system that sent the packets in the first place.

For example, consider PPP. If you use PPP to transmit a packet that contains a broadcast message, the PPP device driver may echo it back to the transmitting system...or it may not. If the driver doesn't loop back broadcast messages, it notifies the system of this fact via the device driver flag **IFF_LOOPBACK**.

The **ip_loopback** function fixes the problem presented by interfaces that can't (or won't) loop back broadcast (or multicast) messages.

16082:   The function allocates a socket buffer (if it can) and copies much (but not all) of the information from the original socket buffer.

16104:   Call **ip_send** (from line 16132) to fill in the physical-device header information. Actually, for the loopback device, this process just fills in a few socket buffer fields and then comes back.

16109:   Establish the start of the IP header.

16116:   Copy the packet, IP header and all.

16123:   Call **ip_queue_xmit**. This call causes recursion.

16124:   Return to the caller.

ip_send_check

This function (which starts at line 16357) is a self-contained function that calculates the checksum of an IP header. It does so by setting the checksum field to 0 and then calling the in-line function **ip_fast_csum** (line 35572), which consists of hand-optimized assembler code. (The version shown in this book is for Intel 80x86 processors.) Similar routines are provided for other platforms.

Warning: *Do not* try to read the following commentary on **ip_fast_csum** unless you already understand the GCC compiler conventions for in-line 80x86 assembler code!

35578:   The first four 32-bit words are added together, with carry. Note the cute way in which one of the additions for the loop is "reused."

35584:   Continue in a tight loop, adding the words together with carry, until the entire IP packet has been summed. This loop is executed at least once. The code for the 80x86 function has been organized so that you don't execute a single branch instruction for a regular IP header. As a result, the instruction fetch-ahead process is never broken, and execution is therefore sped up. This code is an example of low-level hacking at its best.

35588:   Add any remaining carry into the sum.

35589:   Copy the word into another register, shift one of the registers right by 16 bits, perform a 16-bit addition, and add in any remaining carry (lines 35589–35592). Take the complement of the result (line 35593) and return the checksum (line 35603).

Did you skip the last four paragraphs? Good. The authors wish they could have. Frankly, though, the pain of following GCC assembler is worth it: The reason the checksum operation is hand-coded in assembler, instead of being written in C, is that the GCC compiler's code generator would have generated "active" code to deal with word-width changes, rather than take advantage of the hardware's built-in word-access capabilities. Because this routine is performed so many times, hand-optimization can produce noticeably faster performance.

add_to_send_queue

This function (which starts at line 16371) adds a socket buffer to the queue of a socket object. The function runs with interrupts off, to ensure that no other process interrupts it.

If this socket buffer is the first one that is attached to the socket object, set the socket object fields **send_head**, **send_tail**, and **send_next** to point to the socket buffer.

If this socket buffer is not the first one that is attached to the socket object, set the forward link in the tail-socket buffer's field **link3** to point to the new socket buffer, and set the socket object's **send_tail** field to point to the newly appended socket buffer.

Restore the interrupt status (if interrupts were turned off earlier) and return to the caller.

ip_rewrite_addrs

"This is ugly, don't show this to your Mother." This comment, which appears in the TCP modules (at line 29995) pretty much sums up the present authors' feelings about the **ip_rewrite_addrs** function (which starts at line 16010). This process is required when a shift in devices occurs and the source addresses for the packets need to be updated. This can happen when a device goes into the DOWN state while TCP data is pending transmission.

The **ip_rewrite_addrs** function is called from only two places—line 30019 and line 30053—both of which reside in TCP.

Let's get it over with.

16020:   If the new IP address is 0, then do nothing. Just scream about it to the outside world (via the syslog function), and return 0 to the caller to say, "There's nothing I can do."

16029:   If the socket's source address is 0, then again do nothing. Just scream to the syslog and return 0 to the caller, to say, "No way."

16040:   If the sysadmin has written the value "2" to the pseudo-file /proc/sys/net/ipv4/ip_dynaddr, indicating that verbosity is required, then record in the syslog that an address is being redirected to another. Also, record the TCP (or UDP) state from the socket object.

16050:   If the address in the socket buffer should really be changed, both in the socket buffer header and in the IP header, then change it. If the change has already been made and the sysadmin has requested verbosity, then record the unusual event via the syslog. If the change has already been made and verbosity has not been requested, then take no further action. Just return 0 to the caller.

16065: If the address in the socket object should really be changed, then change it. If the change has already been made and the sysadmin has requested verbosity, then record the unusual event via the syslog.

16072: Return 1 to the caller, to indicate that the socket buffer has been changed.

ip_fragment

The **ip_fragment** function (which starts at line 12740) takes an existing packet that has been identified as being too large to be sent in one piece, and breaks it up into two or more chunks of palatable size. This action is useful primarily when a packet that has been received must be forwarded, and this packet is too big to be handled by the given device. (Both these conditions must be met.)

This function is the second implementation of packet fragmentation that has turned up in the code so far. Unlike the first implementation, in **ip_build_xmit**, this version of the fragmentation system outputs the packet fragments in order of *increasing* offset, whereas the first implementation outputs them "backward." The present authors believe that the rationale for producing fragments in reverse order, as presented in the *Linux Kernel Documentation*, is sufficiently persuasive that the way it's done here is...well, less than optimal. One last note: After having queued the packets, the **ip_fragment** function does not present these packets to the firewall. In each case, the packet being presented for fragmentation has *already* been presented to the firewall. The annoying upshot of this approach is that any attempt to count fragments accurately is thwarted.

12756: Do some bookkeeping. Point to the IP header, calculate the length of the physical-layer header, and set up to determine how to fragment the current packet.

12789: Hey, wait a minute! Is the packet marked "Do not fragment"? If so, then forget it and return. (At this point, no serious action has been taken. All we've done is waste a few CPU cycles.)

12797: It's not usually necessary to comment on a comment in the code. However, in this case, the comment in the code raises a good question: What happens when the IP header plus the IP options plus a minimum of 8 bytes of data don't fit in the MTU window?

To answer this question, first consider the actual amounts of data involved. The IP header can contain at most 60 bytes (4 times 15 bytes). Therefore, when an IP packet payload consists of 8 data bytes, the minimum payload in the physical-layer packet contains 68 bytes.

In Chapter 4, which examines the ICMP protocol, the code that implements **ICMP_FRAG_NEEDED** (line 9716) includes the MTU discovery code. In that code, the smallest MTU selected by the code is, surprise, 68 bytes. In reality, virtually every communications protocol that operates over "high-speed lines" (in 1985, 1,200 bits per second was considered high-speed) implements a payload capacity of at least 128 bytes. This capacity was present in protocols from Burroughs and IBM, and even in the super-simple but highly effective XMODEM protocol designed by Ward Christensen for use with bulletin-board systems and microcomputers that ran the CP/M operating system. Microcom Corporation's MNP protocol can step down to a physical frame size as low as 64 bytes per frame, but only in the face of very high line-error rates—and even so, this stepdown is transparent to the datastream that is being carried.

However, you don't need to worry about excessively small MTU values. Why not? Because of the "unit of transfer" in the mainframe-computer world, which was the punched-paper

card. In those early days of automation, any data-transmission system that was used with a mainframe had to be able to transmit, as an integral minimum, the contents (or "image") of one single card.

Most of IBM's tabulator machines and computer systems used the Hollerith card, which contained 80 punched columns. Remington Rand used a standard 45-column card, whose 2 characters per column yielded a 90-character record. In view of these historical precedents, no reason exists to believe that *any* physical-link layer would support an MTU of less than 80 bytes, which is comfortably over the 68-byte minimum.

And so, Virginia, that's why the code that would "fall down dead" never did so.

(But it's nice that the code was fixed to do *something*. This way, if someone implements the avian-link layer described in RFC 1149, the code will work properly.)

12804: If the MTU can't handle a standard IP frame, then generate a "destination unreachable" ICMP message. Then, return to the caller, as if nothing had happened.

12825: Determine the offset of the original packet. Note that this code could be fragmenting a fragment—this can happen when the network looks something like the arterial blood vessel system in your body. As you approach the endpoint, the pipe gets narrower and narrower.

12835: Now, as long as data remains to be sent (as determined by the working variable **left**), that data must be processed into fragments. This loop continues until line 12944.

12838: If the packet won't fit, then perform the procrustean operation of shortening it until it does.

12846: If the packet that is being built won't consume the whole of the remaining data, then shorten the packet's length to the nearest 8-byte boundary. (The code uses integer division followed by multiplication; how much nicer/cleaner this process would be if the code simply used a bit mask [such as **len &= ~7;**], to avoid the extra bit-fiddling.)

12855: Using the **alloc_skb** function (line 22146), try to allocate the socket buffer for the fragment. If this attempt fails, then increment the appropriate SNMP counter and return to the caller. This return aborts any further fragmentation operations.

12868: Continue with the bookkeeping for the socket buffer header. Copy the element **arp**, set the element **protocol**, and indicate that the socket buffer should be freed after the packet has been transmitted by the device driver.

12877: Set up the socket buffer data area, including the area for the IP header and the payload (as a "raw" packet).

12885: If a socket object is associated with this packet, then accumulate the memory usage within the socket object. This operation causes a subsequent call to the **write** system call, specifying this socket object, to block the calling process when a large number of packets has already been queued (so as not to eat up all the available memory).

12890: Copy the route IP address from the old socket buffer to the fragment socket buffer.

12897: Copy the IP header.

12902: Copy a portion of the data from the original packet into the fragment. To document the fact that the data was "eaten," decrement the amount of data that remains.

12905: Update the raw pointer to point past the physical-device header field to point to the IP

header. Update the offset and the header length in the new socket buffer.

12924: If the current fragment is the first fragment, as indicated by a fragment offset of 0, call the **ip_options_fragment** function (line 15606) to reprocess the options contained in the original IP header. This operation is performed after the fragment has been built, and only once, so that the second and subsequent fragments contain only those IP options that are appropriate for fragments.

12932: If the current fragment is not the last fragment, or a fragment is being fragmented, then set the flag that indicates that the current fragment is not the last fragment.

12934: Increment both the working offset and the pointer to the data in the original packet.

12941: Put the fragment in the transmit queue and increment the appropriate SNMP counter. Go make the next fragment, if one exists.

12945: The loop has been completed successfully; therefore, all the fragments created from the original packet have been processed. Update the appropriate SNMP counter and return to the caller.

ip_options_echo

This function takes IP options from an incoming packet and prepares an "echo" of those options for use in an outgoing IP packet. Both the source and the target memory areas are pointers to blocks of memory that are defined by the **options** structure definition (line 36848).

15486: Clear out the destination options area.

15490: If no source options block has been passed by the caller, then use the first word in the protocol private area **proto_priv**.

15493: If the source option length is 0 (that is, if there are no options at all), then set the destination option length to 0 and return to the caller.

15499: Set the source pointer for options according to the data flag in the options header. If the flag is set, the options follow the options structure; if the flag has been reset, the options are found in the IP header in the socket buffer. Set the target pointer to the location of the target IP header.

15504: If a record-route option is present, copy the options as passed in the source route, set the need-address flag, and increment the option field-pointer address. Then, increment the destination pointer flag and the length contained in the destination options.

15519: If a timestamp option is present, copy the options as passed in the source route, set a flag indicating whether the time needs to be recorded here, set a flag indicating whether the local IP address needs to be recorded here, and adjust the option field-pointer address. Then, increment the destination pointer flag and the length contained in the destination options. If the option indicates that the option has specified IP addresses, and if no address matches any of the system's addresses (as determined by the function **ip_chk_addr** at line 8673), then this code undoes all the work that previously was performed, as though the option was not present.

15558: If this route is a source route (either strict or loose), start by copying all the routes that have already been collected. Then, if appropriate, set up to have the system's address inserted. Copy the remainder of the source routing and duplicate the strict-route flag.

15598: Add one, two, or three pad characters, so that the options field ends at a 4-byte boundary.

15603: Return 0 to the caller, to indicate that the options were copied.

ip_options_fragment

This routine takes options that exist within a socket buffer's IP header and removes those options that are not supposed to be copied to second and subsequent fragments of a packet. This routine operates by scanning all the options and converting the ones that are not supposed to be copied to no-operation (NOP) codes. This operation doesn't change the size of the option field; instead, it just nulls out all the "inappropriate" option fields. The key is the "Copy" bit in the Option field, as shown in Figure 7.4. If this bit is set in the option identification field, the option is "appropriate"; if this bit is reset, this code overwrites the option.

Passing The Buck

Part of the Internet Protocol implementation of the network layer for TCP/IP involves the transparent forwarding of packets that are in transit (that is, packets that are received by a given computer but that are not intended for that computer). Here, the term *transparent* means that no application code and no higher-level protocol modules are involved. The only players here are the drivers and the ICMP, IGMP, and IP protocols.

Before a packet can be forwarded, it must first be received. (That operation is the subject of a separate section later in this chapter.) After the packet has been received and IP has determined that the packet's destination lies elsewhere, IP has to figure out what to do with it. Playing this game of hot potato, which is so crucial to the success of the Internet, is the job of the code described in this section and also in Chapter 6.

ip_forward

This function (which starts at line 11414) is called from the primary packet receive function **ip_rcv** (which lives at line 14793) and from the multicast transmit manager **ipmr_queue_xmit** (which lives at line 18685).

This code contains other complexities that go beyond the need to "just forward" packets. As an option, the code also supports IPIP (IP-within-IP encapsulation) Tunneling, in addition to providing the transparent proxy support ("masquerade") that allows systems on a trusted subnet to send and receive packets, with the masquerading system acting as an agent for these transfers.

The **ip_forward** function returns three values: –1, if the forwarding failed (that is, the socket buffer is now trash and should be discarded); 0, if the forwarding succeeded and the caller should not release the socket buffer; and 1, if the forwarding succeeded and the caller should release the socket buffer.

For discussion purposes and for the sake of (relative) simplicity, the present commentary assumes that all the many, many compile-time options are enabled. In practice, of course, references to firewall, masquerade, and tunneling functions are all optional, but the options interlace. As usual, when in doubt, "Use the Source, Luke!" Correlatively, it might also be wise to lay in an ample supply of your favorite programming fluid before embarking on a study of this 593-line function.

11451: If the flags from the caller say "decrement TTL," then decrement the Time to Live field in the header and adjust the checksum.

11471: If the TTL has reached 0 (the less-than-0 case is gratuitous, because the field is declared as an unsigned character), then issue an ICMP message telling the source system that the packet has breathed its last. Then, return to the caller, telling it that the packet has been discarded.

11489: If the caller said that this packet is a multicast forward or said that the packet is not a multicast tunnel, go to line 11578.

11500: Ask for a route. This task is performed via a call to the function **ip_rt_route** (line 21190, described in Chapter 6). If no route is found, then issue an ICMP message telling the source system that no route was found. Return to the caller, telling it that the packet should be discarded.

11527: Save the gateway address from the route. However, if a strict routing option is present, and the route is a gateway route, then the source routing failed. Strict source routine is supposed

to specify every hop on the way, and the route has to be operational. Sorry. Return to the caller, telling it that the packet should be discarded.

11558: If the packet selected by the routing protocol is going out the same device it came in on, then send a redirect-host ICMP packet to the system that gave us the packet we are handing back. This redirect notification will be sent in addition to the packet we send back—a two-for-one transaction that really shouldn't happen.

11575: If this packet is going into a tunnel, save the encapsulation header length (20 bytes). If this packet is not going into a tunnel, then the encapsulation header length is left set to 0 (set in line 11427).

11578: Go to line 11590. This code is the **else** from line 11489. (If the caller said that this packet is not a multicast forward or said that this packet is a multicast tunnel, continue from here.)

11584: In a multicast forward, the routing has already been done; therefore, just handle the bookkeeping. If this packet is a tunnel job, set the encapsulation header length, changing it to 20 (from the default value of 0). Don't forget to kill any route pointer(s) that may still be loitering around.

11590: End of the **if** statement.

11600: If this packet is not a masqueraded packet, go to line 11638.

11608: If the masqueraded packet is an ICMP packet, call the function **ip_fw_masq_icmp** (in /usr/src/linux/net/ipv4/ip_masq.c, which is on the accompanying CD-ROM) to handle the details of address translation. If the masquerade can't be done (that is, if the return value is less than 0), then tell the caller that the packet should be dropped. This condition can happen if a masquerade association has timed out.

11630: If the masquerade was successful, then go to label **skip_call_fw_firewall** to bypass the firewall check. (There's no need to ask; the masquerade obviously is okay.)

11638: Call the firewall and ask it what should be done with the packet to be forwarded. This call is made to the function **call_fw_firewall** (in /usr/src/linux/net/core/firewall.c, on the accompanying CD-ROM), which, for IP, ends up calling **ipfw_forward_check** (line 14397, described in Chapter 10).

11641: For **FW_ACCEPT** and **FW_MASQUERADE**, continue processing.

11644: For **FW_REJECT**, generate a "host unreachable" ICMP message and tell the caller that the packet has been rejected.

11648: For **FW_DENY** (or any other response), say nothing to the outside world, and tell the caller that the packet has been rejected. This action makes the system look like a "black hole" to the world, at least in terms of the service that is being blocked.

11667: Is a working device present? If not (looking now all the way down to line 11979), deal with the route and tell the caller that the packet is trash and hasn't been sent. (There's nothing like easy-to-read code, is there?)

11675: If the IP protocol is either UDP or TCP, get the premasquerade source port number from the TCP or UDP header. Otherwise, set the premasquerade source port to 0.

11687: If this packet needs to be masqueraded (that is, if the firewall returned a status of **FW_MASQUERADE**) and hasn't already been marked as a masqueraded packet, then ask **ip_fw_masquerade** to change the address information so that packets are steered properly. If **ip_fw_masquerade** can't do the job, return

to the caller, telling it that the packet is rubbish and should be discarded.

11702: Is the (possibly encapsulated) packet too big for the device to swallow, and is the don't-fragment flag set? If not, then go to line 11739 and continue processing the packet.

11709: Before anything else happens, the packet must be fixed up so that it has the original source and destination addresses. Otherwise, it will greatly confuse the poor remote ICMP handler that gets the need-to-fragment packet, and all the addresses will be weird. Select the correct information to include in the ICMP packet, add it, and ship off the packet. Then return, telling the poor caller that the packet is now just so much rubbish.

11742: If the socket buffer has the headroom for the physical headers and any associated encapsulation headers, then go to line 11819.

11743: The beginning of the buffer doesn't have enough room for the physical-layer header. Therefore, the socket buffer must be cloned, adding the needed headroom to the cloned socket buffer. Allocate the memory (returning an "aw-shucks" to the caller if the necessary memory can't be obtained), and add the physical headers.

11788: Call **ip_encap** (line 11352) if this packet is destined for an IPIP tunnel.

11800: If the packet is not destined for an IPIP tunnel, build the IP headers here, copy the data over, and then go to line 11858.

11819: Here's where we want to be, if we have the space in the original socket buffer to include the physical-layer headers.

11828: Call **ip_encap** (line 11352) if the packet is destined for an IPIP tunnel, and then go to line 11858.

11833: If a tunnel isn't in the packet's future, build a physical-layer header and deal with the hardware–hash list. (This hardware–hash list updating process has been described in detail, several times, in other chapters. No need to rehash it here.)

11860: Here's a packet to be shipped! First, ask the firewall what should be done with it. If the packet should be accepted, then continue processing the packet. If the packet should be rejected, send an ICMP message and tell the caller to trash the packet. If the packet should be denied, say nothing to anyone. Simply return to the caller, telling it that the packet is no longer useful.

11879: After performing the bookkeeping with the SNMP counters, process any options. Record any addresses or timestamps that still need to be added to the packet. The comment at line 11933 says it all: This is the "point of no return," after which an ICMP packet can no longer be sent back to the caller.

11945: If the packet is too big for the device, then call **ip_fragment** to break the packet into fragments. Then, dump the original packet. If the packet isn't too big for the device, then let the firewall accounting system update its counters.

11969: Queue the packet, in accordance with the indicated service requirements.

11992: If the packet that was passed by the caller is the same one that is queued to the device, then tell the caller not to dump the packet that was just put into the queue. Otherwise, clean up (we don't want to cause a memory leak) and return to the caller, telling the caller that the operation has been completed and that there is no further need for the socket buffer.

With this piece of spaghetti code now behind us, it's time for a drink and a well-deserved nap.

When Data Rains Upon Us

So far, you've seen how the Linux TCP/IP system sends data originating from in-system sources, and how any packets that are not destined for the local machine are forwarded via another interface. Now, it's time to see how packets get into the system from the outside.

Rather than try to trace all the ins and outs of the various combinations and permutations of options, this commentary assumes that every kernel option has been selected. If the commentary mentions a capability that you haven't compiled into the kernel, then check the source code to see whether the code in question is bracketed by #if/#endif gates.

ip_rcv

This function (which starts at line 14793) is the advertised entry point—the front door—for the reception of IP packets.

14820: If the version number of the IP header packet is 6 (indicating that the packet is an IPv6 packet), then shift the work over to the function **ipv6_rcv** and propagate the return value to the caller. (This function is not defined in the Slackware distribution of Linux kernel release 2.0.34.)

14824: Increment the appropriate SNMP counter.

14833: The firewall needs to do its accounting, even if it will later tell this code to dump the packet.

14842: Perform a sanity check on the IP header, confirming the presence of the following conditions:

- The packet is at least as long as the IP header

- The header is at least five 32-bit words long

- The version number in the IP packet is "4"

- The checksum for the header is correct

- The total length, as declared in the IP packet, fits within the socket buffer

If any of these conditions is not present, then release the socket buffer from memory and return to the caller with a status of 0 (failure).

14880: If the buffer is padded (as it is with Ethernet transmission systems, for example), this function calls **skb_trim** (line 22049). The **skb_trim** function adjusts the tail pointer for the socket buffer, so that this pointer reflects the actual length of the IP packet. (Why isn't this function an inline function? Your inquiring authors want to know.)

14893: If the packet type is **PACKET_HOST**, the packet's destination address isn't the same as the physical address, and the inline function **net_alias_has** (in /usr/src/linux/include/linux/net_alias.h) indicates that the device has aliases, then call the function **net_alias_dev_rx32** (in /usr/src/linux/net/core/net_alias.c) to obtain the pointer to the alias device.

14900: If the IP header contains options, run through these options to locate all the fields of interest. (If the options are defective, an ICMP packet stating that a parameter problem exists has already been sent; therefore, return to the caller with a status of 0.)

14907: If the kernel was configured to discard packets that have source routing (as is sometimes done as a security measure), and source routing is present, then release the socket buffer memory and return to the caller with **EINVAL** status.

14915: If the transparent-proxy option was selected and nothing was said about whether packets should always be defragmented, then indicate that packets should indeed always be defragmented.

14937: If the IP header fragment field is all 0s, go to line 14985.

14939: If the more-fragments bit in the IP header is set, then set the corresponding flag in the internal variable **flags**.

14945: If the 13-bit offset is non-0, then set a local "last fragment" flag. This implementation contains a bug, because, if this packet is the middle fragment in a series of three fragments, the local last-fragment flag is still set. However, this bug appears to be benign. The root cause of the problem is that the **else** verb is missing from between the two tests.

14952: If this packet is not a fragment, go to line 14985.

14956: The packet is a fragment. Call **ip_defrag** to handle the fragment, and see whether we now have a complete set of fragments that can be used to rebuild the original unfragmented packet. If we still are waiting for fragments, return to the caller.

14959: A complete packet has been reconstituted! Do the bookkeeping, including the recalculation of the IP checksum for the complete packet.

14985: If the input chain of the firewall rejects the packet, send an ICMP packet, free the packet, and return 0 to the caller. If the firewall denies the packet, just free the packet and return 0 to the caller. If the firewall accepts the packet (possibly with a redirect request), continue onward.

14996: If the input chain of the firewall decrees that the packet must be redirected, then set the redirect port identifier in the socket buffer. Otherwise, set the redirect port to 0 ("don't redirect").

15003: Set the packet fragment flags in exactly the same way as in lines 14939 through 14946. (This code is executed only if incoming packets are not always defragmented.)

15043: Test for any of the following conditions:

- The packet destination address matches the device address

- The packet is being redirected

- The destination IP address is one of the system's addresses (as checked by **ip_chk_addr** at line 8673)

- The destination IP address matches any socket object's address (as checked by **ip_chksock** at line 14769)

If the packet meets none of these conditions, then go to line 15361 to handle the transit packet.

15051: This packet is intended for the local system. If the packet contains a source-route option, and the packet is neither a host packet nor directed to this system, then discard the packet and return 0 to the caller.

15065: This packet is intended for this system, and a source route is present. Check whether the source route contains our address. If it doesn't, then release the packet and return 0 to the caller.

15095: This system is on the list. Save the next hop.

15097: If routes are still in the route list, then forward the packet (if forwarding is turned on). Otherwise, increment the statistics to indicate that we swallowed a packet. Then, release the packet and return 0 to the caller.

15114: Test for the following conditions:

- The device does *not* have the **IFF_ALL-MULTI** flag set

- The response from **ip_chk_addr** is **IS_MULTICAST**

- The destination address is not the all-hosts address

- The device does not automatically loop back packets

If the packet fails to meet any one of these conditions, then go to line 15142.

15122: If the local system has any process signed up to receive this type of multicast packet, then go to

line 15142. If we have no one listening for the multicast address, then release the memory for the packet and return 0 to the caller.

15137: (This code is executed if the option of always defragmenting packets before they are forwarded is *not* configured.) If all the fragments for the packet are present, reassemble them and continue. Otherwise, the defragmentation code saves the fragment, and 0 must be returned to the caller.

15160: Demasquerade the addressing in the packet, by calling the **ip_fw_demasquerade** function (located in /usr/src/linux/net/ipv4/ip_masq.c on the CD-ROM). This function searches for a proxy connection for the packet. If one is found, then the IP header is updated with the new address information, and the IP packet is forwarded. After the packet has been forwarded, the code returns 0 to the caller.

15191: If the packet is a multicast packet and does not occupy the first 256 address slots of the multicast address range, then document this fact via a local flag.

15213: For each raw socket that is listening on this address pair, queue up a copy of the packet so that the owner of the socket can see the complete IP packet—TOS field and all. This code satisfies a requirement published in RFC 1122. The code involves a little piece of trickery, in that the last raw socket doesn't get the packet until considerably later on (specifically, at line 15340).

15255: For each protocol (there can be more than one) that matches the IP header's protocol field and that wants a copy of the packet (as indicated when **ipprot->copy** is non-0), clone the packet and send it onward to the protocol's handler. Here again, if only one packet consumer is present, additional copies of the packet need not be made.

15322: If this packet is a multicast packet, then forward it. Clone the packet only if there is another consumer of the packet later on.

15340: Send the last copy of the packet onward to the raw socket, if there is a consumer for it.

15342: If the packet didn't have a home, send an ICMP packet back to the sender, and release the memory used by the socket buffer.

15350: Return 0 to the caller.

15361: This packet is a transit packet, as opposed to an on-us packet. (Odd, isn't it, how that check-processing analogy from Chapter 3 keeps turning up.) The processing comes here from line 15043. If the packet is a broadcast or multicast packet, don't forward the packet. Instead, release the memory and return 0 to the caller.

15372: If forwarding is not enabled (that is, if a 0 has been written to the pseudo-file /proc/sys/net/ipv4/ip_forward), then release the packet and return 0 to the caller. If both forwarding and strict source routing are enabled, send an ICMP packet pointing out the parameter problem. Then, release the memory that contains the socket buffer, and return 0 to the caller.

15380: Forward the packet, by calling the **ip_forward** function. Return 0 to the caller.

And that, gentle reader, is how IP packet input is processed. The **ip_rcv** routine has sent the packet buffers onward to the higher-level protocol identified by the IP header protocol field, and also to any raw sockets that are listening for the packet. In other words, everyone is happy.

ip_chksock

This function is included when transparent proxy support has been compiled into the kernel. Depending on the protocol, the **ip_chksock** function calls **icmp_chkaddr** (line 10124), **tcp_chkaddr** (line 28685), or **udp_chkaddr** (line 32686) functions. If the protocol in the IP header isn't one of these three protocols, the function returns 0.

If the protocol handler finds a socket, the function returns the value 1.

ip_defrag

In a few instances during input processing, we wanted to collect all the fragments and, after we had them all, return the reintegrated packets. The **ip_defrag** function (which starts at line 12477) is the front door to the process of fragment collection and integration.

Fragments are allowed to occupy only a certain amount of memory. The limit value, **IPFRAG_HIGH_THRESH**, which lives at line 12062, is defined as 256K.

Fragments also have lifetimes. They are discarded if completion isn't achieved within a certain number of clock ticks, as specified by the manifest constant **IP_FRAG_TIME**. The time period specified by this value (which is defined on line 40810) is approximately 30 seconds.

12494: If the fragment queues are occupying too much memory, call **ip_evictor** (line 12270) to reduce the load on the system's RAM.

12501: Locate the fragments that have been found so far for this datagram. To do so, use the function **ip_find** (line 12152).

12503: Does the datagram constitute a whole packet? If so, then discard the fragments being held in memory (because they're no longer needed) and return the whole packet in its original form. This operation becomes necessary when a single given packet takes two distinct paths: one with a small MTU and the other with a large MTU.

12526: If a fragment-queue entry is not present, go to line 12546.

12532: If the offset is 0 (that is, if the first fragment is present), then copy the IP header (which is complete in the first fragment) into the fragment-queue entry.

12537: Reset the timer for another 30-second timeout. When the bell rings, call the function **ip_expire**, whose task is to handle the then-dying queue entry. Go to line 12565.

12552: Use the function **ip_create** (at line 12291) to create a new queue entry. If **ip_create** can't do the job, then remove the socket buffer from memory and return **NULL** to the caller, to indicate that the task couldn't be performed.

12565: If this packet is a hostile packet of the Ping of Death type, destroy it and return **NULL** to the caller. In a 16-bit machine, this test would have to be crafted considerably more carefully, to avoid register overflow. Fortunately, Linux requires that **int** variables contain 32 bits; therefore, this attack fails with no special coding consideration.

12579: Insert this fragment into the fragment-queue entry, so that the offset values appear in increasing order as the list is traversed.

12617: Eliminate overlap (and duplication). When possible, merge adjoining fragments together. When older fragments in the queue are squeezed out and the memory is released, the accounting records for the amount of memory space that was occupied are maintained. When the old fragment or fragments are released, this function uses the inline functions **frag_kfree_skb** (defined at line 12083) and **frag_kfree_s** (defined at line 12090) not only to perform the **free** function, but also to track memory use.

12673: Create the fragment, by calling **ip_frag_create** (line 12109). If the fragment can't be created, then free the fragment's socket buffer and return **NULL** to the caller.

12694: Incorporate the new fragment-queue entry into the list. Then, use the function **ip_done** (line 12354) to check whether the packet is complete. If all the pieces have been received, then use **ip_glue** (line 12391) to stick the fragments

together. Then, return (to the caller) the pointer to the socket buffer that contains the complete packet.

12718: The fragments for a full packet still haven't all been collected. Return **NULL** to the caller, to indicate that more packets still need to be rounded up.

ip_evictor

This function (which starts at line 12270) walks through the fragment queue, discarding the fragments that have been collected so far, until the total amount of memory that is being used is below the authorized limit. As long as the memory limit is above the limit, this function calls the **ip_free** function (described in the next paragraph). The **ip_evictor** function can cause a kernel panic when the fragment queue is empty and the memory threshold is still exceeded, which means that the code didn't do its bookkeeping right.

ip_free

This function (which starts at line 12186) performs the mechanics of removing a fragment-queue element from the queue, releasing the socket buffers attached to that element, and then releasing the memory that had been allocated for the queue entry itself. First, it stops the timer associated with the queue element. Then, it unlinks the queue element from the queue. Next, it walks through the socket buffer list, releasing each socket buffer as it goes. The IP header that is associated with the overall packet is then released, and, finally, the queue element is released.

To prevent race conditions between the **ip_free** function and other system activities, the entire function runs with interrupts turned off.

ip_find

The **ip_find** function (which starts at line 12152) searches the fragment queue for a matching queue element. The specification fields in the desired element must match the following IP header fields of the fragment:

- Packet identifier number

- Source IP address

- Destination IP address

- IP protocol (TCP, UDP, ICMP, or whatever)

When a match is found, the timer associated with the queue element is deactivated and a pointer to the queue element is returned to the caller. (It's the caller's responsibility to restart the fragment expiration timer.) If the queue is exhausted before a match is found, the value **NULL** is returned to the caller.

ip_expire

The **ip_expire** function (which starts at line 12239) is called by the timer routines as a callback when a queue element's clock runs out. Because the remote system needs to recover from a packet timeout, this little function sends an ICMP message to the source system stating that some of the packets have been lost. (How that system responds to the ICMP message depends greatly on the system and its implementation of the protocols.) The queue element is then removed, via **ip_free** (line 12186).

ip_create

This function (which starts at line 12291) allocates memory for the queue entry. The allocated memory includes a separate block for the IP header and the first 8 bytes of the first fragment (when they arrive). The **ip_create** function uses the **frag_kmalloc** function (line 12096) to allocate the memory and to keep track of how much memory has been used (so that **ip_evictor** can be invoked if a spew of fragments occurs). The queue entry is filled in, the first socket buffer is linked to it, a timer is started on the queue entry (so that **ip_expire** can eliminate it after fragments have been lost), and the queue entry is added to the end of the fragment queue. To announce the successful creation of the queue entry, **ip_create** returns, to the caller, a pointer to the queue entry.

Whenever **ip_create** can't allocate memory, it backs out and returns **NULL** to the caller.

ip_frag_create

This function (which starts at line 12109) allocates a fragment control block for the socket buffer. It then fills

in the necessary information (including the pointer to the socket buffer), charges for the memory (including the socket buffer) against the total memory that can be used for fragment collection and reintegration (enforced by the **ip_evictor** function), and returns the pointer to the new fragment control block.

If any problems occur, **ip_frag_create** backs everything out and returns the **NULL** value to the caller.

ip_done

This function (which starts at line 12354) checks whether all fragments have been received for a collection of fragments. It walks through the fragment control blocks, first determining whether the last packet has been received, and then checking for gaps in the received data for the packet. If it finds any gaps, **ip_done** returns 0 to the caller. If all the data is there, **ip_done** returns 1 to the caller.

ip_glue

The **ip_glue** function (which starts at line 12391) is the paste-pot maven. It takes all the broken pieces of packets and sticks them back together. First, **ip_glue** allocates a new socket buffer for the complete packet. It then takes all the pieces and copies them into the new buffer. After these fragments have been stuck together, the fragments are released. The **ip_glue** function then does a little bookkeeping and returns, to the caller, the address of the socket buffer containing the packet that belies the old political nursery rhyme about what all the king's horses and all the king's men couldn't do for Humpty-Dumpty.

If at any point the **ip_glue** routine is blocked due to resource problems, the fragment-queue entry is released and **NULL** is returned to the caller.

Boring But Necessary Administrative Tasks

Nothing happens in this world without paperwork, and the Linux operating system is no exception. The three functions in this group handle the tedious clerical tasks. The **ip_init** function links the IP module into the sys-

tem; the **ip_rt_event** function catches device up/down event notifications; and the **ip_netlink_msg** function propagates the device up/down event notifications outward to non–kernel processes.

ip_init

During system initialization, the **ip_init** function (which starts at line 17243) is called so that it can install the Internet Protocol handlers into the system. The protocol control block for IP itself is added to the list of protocols via a call to **dev_add_pack**, and then the routing software's device state-change handling routine, **ip_rt_event** (which starts at line 17207), is linked into the system.

ip_rt_event

This function (which starts at line 17207) accepts notifications that the state of a device has changed.

When a device changes state to DOWN, this function first calls the **ip_netlink_msg** function (which starts at line 17171). Then, **ip_rt_event** tells the routing software to wipe out all the routes that are associated with the device (via **ip_rt_flush**, which starts at line 20868).

When a device changes state to UP, **ip_rt_event** joins the system to the "all host" multicast group on that device, calls **ip_netlink_msg** (which starts at line 17171), and informs the routing software that the device has come online.

ip_netlink_msg

This function (which starts at line 17171) generates netlink messages. It builds a socket buffer (if it can) and then fills this buffer with information about the device that just came up or went down. (The netlink system provides a way for user-space applications and kernel applications to communicate with each other. The Linux implementation of the netlink system is on the CD-ROM, in /usr/src/linux/net/netlink.c.)

Chapter 8

UDP

When you drop a letter into a slot at a post office, you're committing an act of faith. When an application uses the User Datagram Protocol (UDP), it commits a very similar act.

Unlike TCP, which requires a structured handshake to open a connection, and system resources to keep the connection open, UDP just sends data packets, one at a time, with no preliminaries, postliminaries, or fanfare of any kind—not even any confirmation that a data packet has actually *been* sent, let alone received. Much of TCP's other complexity (such as the slow-start algorithm, Nagle packet-stuffing algorithm, and lost-packet recovery algorithm) is likewise absent from UDP.

The absence of an error-recovery capability makes UDP the simplest of all the TCP/IP protocols. But, as always, simplicity has its price, and in this case, the price is paid by the application. Under the TCP protocol, "the system" handles recoveries from packet losses; with UDP's no-frills service, the application has to do this particular dirty job itself.

The UDP Packet Trajectory

If the user application is like an F-14 fighter jet, then sending a UDP message is like firing a Phoenix missile: point, shoot, and forget. The application puts together the data package, inserts the target IP address, and calls the appropriate outgoing-message function. The system sends back a status message telling the application that the message has taken off and has gone at least as far as the router. If the packet reaches its destination, fine. If it doesn't, the application—not the protocol—gets to decide what to do about it.

For applications, receiving a UDP packet is just a matter of waiting for a missile to land in the backyard. Applications don't anticipate what the missile may be carrying and deal only with missiles that hit the target. (Unlike real artillery projectiles, stray UDP "missiles" never cause collateral damage. They just nosedive into a bit-bucket.)

"Smart" missiles depend on their computer brains, and UDP depends on the "rocket science" of the Internet Protocol (IP) in general—and packet routing in particular—to deliver the message payloads as best it can. This means that the support code for UDP transmission is limited to preparing the UDP header and launching the data packets. As you'll see in the commentary portion of this chapter, UDP reception is somewhat trickier, because a receiving application has to call the **bind** function as a prerequisite to catching the packets.

UDP is used primarily for activities that require only infrequent interaction, where "infrequent" means that the interactions take place minutes, hours, or even days apart. One very common use of UDP transmissions is in the Domain Name System (DNS), which uses a distributed database and distributed servers to associate a human-friendly name (such as **www.linux.org**) with an IP address (such as 198.182.196.56—the associated IP address at the time this chapter was written). Using a library routine in a Linux system, an application discovers a *name binding* by sending a UDP packet to a DNS server and then waiting for a reply that contains the desired information. For example, a File Transfer Protocol (FTP) client may use UDP to send a human-readable address to a DNS server and get back an IP address. An FTP server may also use UDP to send an IP address to the DNS server and retrieve the human-readable address. Many contemporary systems use this technique (lookups in the in-addr.arpa. domain) as a security tool.

UDP is the only protocol that's used when information is sent to two or more destination computers, regardless of whether the recipients are limited to a group of registered computers (*multicasting*) or consist of every computer on a network (*broadcasting*).

Because of its simplicity, UDP has found favor with TCP/IP application protocols, such as Trivial File Transfer Protocol (TFTP), Bootstrap Protocol (BOOTP), and Dynamic Host Configuration Protocol (DHCP), which are all used at computer startup. In fact, BOOTP and DHCP *must* use UDP, because they rely on the broadcast mechanism to reach their respective servers or relay agents, which provide essential system-initialization information.

However, these three application-bootstrap protocols aren't always loaded from a hard disk drive. Sometimes, they're implemented in a computer's built-in read-only memory (ROM). This is the arrangement that makes possible *thin clients*—network computers that don't have their own individual hard drives. DHCP lets such a computer discover its IP address; BOOTP tells the computer where to find a load image; and TFTP actually transfers the load image to the computer. After the load image is installed, other TCP protocols can be used to finish the loading process. Note also that many of the routing support-related IP functions don't apply to the bootstrap applications; therefore, a ROM-based implementation of IP and UDP can be very simple indeed.

UDP is also used in Network File System (NFS) implementations, which date from the distant past of networking, now hardly remembered, when UDP was faster than TCP and had lower system overhead. True, older systems tended to transmit smaller blocks of data (usually 512 bytes) in each read or write operation, and the data transfers took place across comparatively small high-speed communications circuits (LANs and campus WANs). UDP's packet-exchange model fits well with the Remote Procedure Call (RPC) protocol (still used within NFS), which lets one computer execute a function call that was made from another computer.

Finally, UDP is used extensively by some routers to exchange information about the ever-mutating topology of the Internet. When such a router or a host wants to tell its neighbors about changes in the Internet, it employs the Router Information Protocol (RIP), which in turn uses UDP to transmit updated router-table information.

However, not all router protocols use UDP. Here are three that don't:

- *Open Shortest Path First (OSPF)*—Has its own IP protocol number and operates outside the TCP/IP domain.

- *Border Gateway Protocol (BGP)*—Uses TCP, not only because the amount of information BGP needs to transfer is greater than UDP can easily carry, but also because BGP-based routers sometimes want to use the TCP keep-alive feature to tell when a datalink has dropped.

- *Intermediate System to Intermediate System (IS-IS)*—Belongs to the ISO protocol family, which is a different family altogether.

In summary, although the use of UDP is far from universal, this protocol is very handy for systems in which only occasional exchanges are required and when the implementation has to be compact. UDP is also used in broadcast-based applications and in some router-to-router communications.

The UDP packet format is shown in Figure 8.1. As you see, the UDP packet header is actually smaller than the IP packet header. With its 4 fields and 8 bytes, a UDP packet is also much simpler than a TCP packet, which has 14 fields, a 20-byte basic header, and optional packet-header extensions.

Because of UDP's bare-bones nature, the amount of code devoted to it in Linux is comparatively small. From start to finish, not including the utilities common to all TCP/IP applications, it spans only about 1,150 lines.

Function Index

Tables 8.1 and 8.2 show the UDP functions and their line numbers. Table 8.1 shows the functions sorted by line number, and Table 8.2 shows the functions sorted by name.

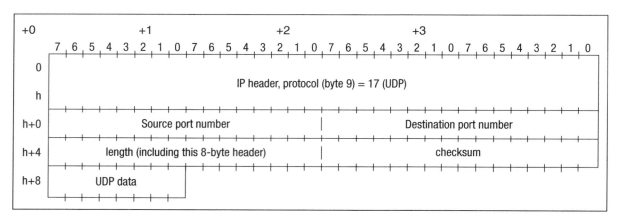

Figure 8.1   UDP packet format.

Table 8.1   UDP functions sorted by line number.

Line	Function
31778	**udp_v4_verify_bind**
31813	**udp_lport_inuse**
31826	**udp_good_socknum**
31868	**udp_v4_hash**
31883	**udp_v4_unhash**
31902	**udp_v4_rehash**
31929	**udp_v4_lookup**
31980	**udp_v4_proxy_lookup**
32041	**udp_v4_mcast_next**
32087	**udp_err**
32156	**udp_check**
32182	**udp_getfrag**
32229	**udp_getfrag_nosum**
32260	**udp_send**
32331	**udp_sendto**
32427	**udp_sendmsg**
32469	**udp_ioctl**
32525	**udp_recvmsg**
32596	**udp_connect**
32632	**udp_close**
32643	**udp_queue_rcv_skb**
32667	**udp_deliver**
32686	**udp_chkaddr**
32710	**udp_v4_mcast_deliver**
32752	**udp_rcv**

Table 8.2   UDP functions sorted alphabetically by name.

Line	Function
32156	**udp_check**
32686	**udp_chkaddr**
32632	**udp_close**
32596	**udp_connect**
32667	**udp_deliver**
32087	**udp_err**
32182	**udp_getfrag**
32229	**udp_getfrag_nosum**
31826	**udp_good_socknum**
32469	**udp_ioctl**
31813	**udp_lport_inuse**
32643	**udp_queue_rcv_skb**
32752	**udp_rcv**
32525	**udp_recvmsg**
32260	**udp_send**
32427	**udp_sendmsg**
32331	**udp_sendto**
31868	**udp_v4_hash**
31929	**udp_v4_lookup**
32710	**udp_v4_mcast_deliver**
32041	**udp_v4_mcast_next**
31980	**udp_v4_proxy_lookup**
31902	**udp_v4_rehash**
31883	**udp_v4_unhash**
31778	**udp_v4_verify_bind**

Sending A UDP Packet

An application can't send a UDP packet until after it completes two preliminary tasks: create a socket, and then call the bind(3) library package to set up the addressing for the socket. After these tasks are completed, the application is ready to send the UDP packet. At this point, however, the application has to decide which of the three possible outgoing-message functions it wants to call.

This choice depends both on what the application has already done and on what it wants to do next. When the socket is in a connected state (that is, when the application has called the **accept** function to fill in the target-address data field in the socket object), the application can call the **send** function. Otherwise, the application can call the **sendto** function, in which all the information is passed as parameters in the function call. Alternatively, the application can call the **sendmsg** function, which passes a single structure that contains all the information about the message.

Although each of these functions has its own advantages (and vocal partisans in the Linux community), they all share certain common behavior. Specifically, after a packet has been queued for transmission via any of the functions, each function returns 0 if it doesn't detect a parameter error, and returns –1 if it does detect a parameter error or a routing problem.

However, as noted in the discussion portion of this chapter, UDP has no error-recovery function, either before or after the packet leaves the system. This somewhat optimistic approach by the protocol leaves major room for doubt about whether a packet has actually traveled to another system at all.

In UDP, the function calls allow only the **MSG_DONTROUTE** and **MSG_PROXY** flags.

udp_send

This function is called when a call that has been made to the **send** function points to a socket object of type **SOCK_DGRAM**.

32265: Calculate the size of the packet that is being built.

32269: If this packet would contain more bytes than TCP/IP allows (that is, more than 65,535 bytes), then return the error **EMSGSIZE**.

32272: Build the pseudo-UDP header **ufh**, which is used later to calculate the UDP checksum value. The information contained in this header is always in network-byte order (HSB, 2SB, 3SB, LSB) instead of in Intel's machine order (LSB, 3SB, 2SB, HSB).

32281: This section of code is optional. It implements IP masquerade, so that when the masquerade code sees a responding UDP packet, the original address and port can be substituted for the masqueraded address and port (at line 32302).

32315: Turning off UDP checksumming is asking for trouble. However, this option is offered. Its purpose is to let the function **ip_build_xmit** (line 16614, described in Chapter 7) properly fill in the header packet, using as a "callback" function the routine **udp_getfrag_nosum**. If UDP checksum calculation is enabled, the same function is called with the same parameters, except that the callback function **udp_getfrag** is passed.

The code for the call to **ip_build_xmit** is the same regardless of whether UDP checksum is enabled. Except for the callback function, the parameters are almost identical. Depending on the optimizations that the compiler performs, some manual optimization can reduce, to a greater or lesser extent, the amount of code that is generated. Specifically, you can replace lines 32315 through 32323 with the following code:

```
a = ip_build_xmt(
  sk,
  ((sk->no_check) ? udp_getfrag
    _nosum: udp_getfrag),
  &ufh,
  ulen,
  sin->sin_addr.s_addr,
  saddr,
```

```
  sk->opt,
  rt,
  IPPROTO_UDP,
  noblock);
```

This substitution ensures that the same parameters are passed, except for the one that depends on the state of the flag.

32324: If an error was encountered, pass the error back up the chain until it reaches the caller.

32326: Increment the number of datagrams that are output.

32327: Return the length of the datagram that was sent. This returned value mirrors the value for the length of the datagram passed to the routine.

udp_sendto

This function is called when a call is made to the **sendto** function that involves a socket object of type UDP.

32345: Depending on whether proxy support is compiled into the kernel, check whether any flags other than **MSG_DONTROUTE** or **MSG_PROXY** have been specified. If they have, return an error status.

32357: Make sure that the address length is long enough, that the address family is correct, and (in nonproxy mode) that the application specified a port.

The following lines are executed only if the transparent proxy-configuration option was selected when the system kernel was built.

32370: If a proxy has been explicitly requested, return an error code.

32373: If the information about the connection isn't in the socket object, return an error code.

32375: Fill in the address information from the socket object.

That's it (for the moment) on transparent proxy support. Back to regular running mode.

32403: If the zero address (**INADDR_ANY**) is specified, then plug in the address of the system. Adding the address relieves the application of the need to discover "my" address before making calls. (Note that the function **ip_my_address** returns the address of the loopback port, 127.0.0.0—which is a synonym for "I want to talk to myself.")

32406: If the requested address is a broadcast address and the **SO_BROADCAST** socket option hasn't been specified, then return an error code.

Broadcasts tend to be expensive in terms of CPU resources and bandwidth. The check performed at this point in the code helps prevent the accidental broadcasting of packets due to a miscoded address or a malicious act on the part of some immature person. If an application really, *really* wants to send a UDP broadcast packet (and many do), then the application declares its intention by setting the socket option **SO_BROADCAST** before sending the broadcast packets.

32411: Set a semaphore so that the send-packet logic doesn't get into a race condition with another activity.

32414: Queue the packet.

32419: Release the semaphore.

32420: Return the error code, if any, from the queuing process.

udp_sendmsg

This function is similar to the **sendto** function, except that instead of passing a number of parameters, it passes a structure that contains all the information needed to process the call. System overhead is saved, because the code can perform a single user-to-kernel memory copy for the parameters instead of having to fetch the information several times over.

The comment at the beginning of the function indicates that this code is "temporary." This means that the function is implemented as a "wrapper" for the function

udp_sendto (in the sample case) and as a more complex wrapper (when an I/O buffer vector is used). In the latter case, all the buffer contents are copied into a single, allocated buffer.

32431: If the I/O vector length is 1 (single buffer entry), then convert the call directly to a **udp_sendmsg** call, returning a status code to the caller.

32449: We need to make one long buffer. Doing so is a copy operation, but that can't be helped. If the resulting buffer would be longer than a legal UDP packet, then tell the caller to forget it. (In this case, the request is discarded and an error code is returned.)

32451: Get a buffer, if possible; if you can. If not, return an error code that states, "No can do."

32454: Build the long buffer.

32455: The **get_fs**, **get_ds**, and **set_fs** functions are defined in /usr/src/linux/include/asm-i386/segment.h and are used to set the segmentation registers that allow addressing. These functions are used to ensure proper addressing of the data buffer that is newly allocated in kernel space.

32457: Convert the call to a **udp_sendmsg** call, using the newly formed buffer.

32460: The buffer has served its purpose; release it.

32461: Return the error code (if any) to the caller. The error code should be passed back to the using application.

udp_getfrag

This function is a callback function (from the function **ip_build_xmit**). Its job is to copy data and calculate the checksum of the UDP packet or packet fragment.

32190: If the parameter **offset** is non-0 (that is, if a fragment is being built that is not the first or only fragment), then calculate the source address for the data and copy the target address for the buffer. (A non-first or non-only fragment cannot contain a UDP header.)

32196: If the parameter **offset** is 0 (that is, if the fragment being built is the first or only fragment), then calculate the source address and the destination address. (A UDP header can appear only in the first or only fragment.)

32202: Copy the data from user space and perform a checksum on the copied data.

32204: If the fragment is the first or only fragment, also create the UDP header and perform a checksum on it.

The calculation of the checksum for the UDP header also includes information from the IP header. A structure called a *pseudo-UDP header* contains information from the IP header that also appears in the UDP header. This way, each end of the connection can ensure that the UDP packet has indeed been addressed properly.

The checksum itself is simple, consisting of the 16-bit exclusive-OR of each word of the packet, plus the 16-bit exclusive-OR of the pseudo-UDP header. If the packet length is not a multiple of 2 (which can happen with UDP packets), then the calculation uses 0 as a padding character.

32213: If the UDP checksum that is calculated by **csum_tcpudp_magic** returns a value of 0 (a rare case), this code converts the value to 0xFFFF, as specified in RFC 768, page 2, because an all-0-bits value tells the receiving UDP protocol handler that no checksum exists.

udp_getfrag_nosum

This function is a callback function (from the function **ip_build_xmit**). Its job is to copy data *without* calculating the checksum of the UDP packet or packet fragment. This isn't the place for a discussion of the pros and cons of using (and not using) checksums, so suffice it to say that valid reasons exist for checksumming UDP packets in some applications, but not checksumming them in others. We will leave further discussion to the newsgroups.

Interestingly, the code in lines 32229 through 32253 are *identical* to the code in the sister routines, except that line 32250 refers to **memcpy_fromfs** instead of **csum_partial_copy_fromuser**, and all the checksum calculations are missing (lines 32206 through 32214).

ioctl Interface—udp_ioctl

Two **ioctl** (input/output control) options apply to UDP. This section talks about the code that saves, in the socket object, the information about these options.

The **TIOCOUTQ** option asks for the quantity of data currently present in the output queue for the socket object. If the socket option state is **TCP_LISTEN** (line 32479), then this request cannot be fulfilled, and an error code is returned. Otherwise, all the buffers contained in the output queue are counted, their contents are summed, and the total size is returned to the caller.

The **IOUCINQ** option asks for the quantity of data currently present in the input queue for the socket object. If the socket option state is **TCP_LISTEN** (line 32494), then this option cannot be fulfilled, and an error code is returned. Otherwise, all the buffers contained in the input queue are counted, their contents are summed, and the total size is returned to the caller.

These **ioctl** calls are not part of the traditional UDP set. Moreover, the traditional UDP setting for the generation of checksums is handled at the socket level, through the specification of **SO_NO_CHECK** in a **setsockopt** call.

Receiving UDP Packets

Sending UDP packets is fairly easy; receiving them involves a little more work. Unlike TCP (discussed in Chapter 9), in which a standing connection is established, used, and then closed, UDP launches a packet with no assurance at all that a peer, or even a running system, is living at the other end.

Think of a game of badminton played using a standard net. You can see the presence and location of the other player, and see the shuttlecock as it leaves that player's racket. Now, consider playing the game with a 10-foot-high brick wall substituted for the net. You can't see the other player, so you have to be more alert for the service of the shuttlecock, because you don't know exactly when it will come sailing over the wall.

Before a program can receive a UDP packet, it has to express its desire to receive packets. To do so, the server application creates a socket object (using the **socket** function), registers the socket object to a set of addresses and a port (using the **bind** function), and then watches for packets (using the **recv**, **recvfrom**, or **recvmsg** function).

The same procedure applies for a UDP client, except that the **bind** function doesn't need to be called. (Please note that this brief summary is not intended as a replacement for an in-depth discussion of UDP programming. Specifically, such a discussion would address the steps that the two sides of the connection need to take when packets are lost in the network. Such a discussion appears in the book *Unix Network Programming: Volume 1, Networking APIs* by W. Richard Stevens (Prentice-Hall, 1998; ISBN 0-13-490012-X).

udp_rcv

This function is the external routine that handles incoming UDP packets. It is pointed to by the UDP protocol definition structure (which starts at line 32896), and is called when a packet that has been received is identified as a UDP packet. The function checks the packet for accuracy, and then places the packet on the socket-object input queue.

32768: If the data buffer for this socket couldn't be added (because the socket object was busy earlier), this code performs the queuing function. When a socket is locked, the flag is set in /usr/src/linux/fs/sysv/fsync.c.

32779: Determine the type of address. Possible values for **addr_type** are unknown address type (0), **IS_MYADDR** (1), **IS_LOOPBACK** (2), **IS_BROADCAST** (3), **IS_INVBCAST** (4), and **IS_MULTICAST** (5). This value is determined by the routine **ip_chk_addr**, located in /usr/src/linux/net/ipv4/devinet.c (line 8673).

32789: Increment the count for the number of UDP packets delivered to this module.

32795: Start the validation process. The declared length of the packet must be less than or equal to the size of the packet presented by the network layer, and must be larger than the size of the UDP header. If the packet fails any of these tests, increment the **UdpInErrors** counter and discard the packet.

32818: If the packet contains a checksum, check the checksum. If the checksum is wrong, increment **UdpInErrors** and discard the packet.

The variable **skb->ip_summed** is set to one of the following three possible values: **CHECKSUM_HW** (0), **CHECKSUM_NONE** (1), or **CHECKSUM_UNNECESSARY** (2). A cursory search of the source code reveals that for standard IPv4, the value is always **CHECKSUM_HW**, and a checksum value is returned in **skb->csum**.

32850: The source and destination addresses are swapped, so the connection information (in other words, the addresses) contained in the packet header appears in the same order as the connection information (the addresses) contained in the socket object.

32856: In many cases, the hardware buffer is much larger than the packet. The call to **skb_trim** (line 22049) sets the packet buffer length to the length of the data. Any excess buffer space is also tracked.

32859: If the multicast support option is enabled and the packet is a broadcast or multicast packet, then pass the work on to the function **udp_v4_mcast_deliver**.

32865: If the transparent proxy-configuration option is enabled and the buffer is marked as subject to redirection, then find the socket associated with the proxy connection.

32871: Find the socket that is bound to the source address and port.

A UDP server can listen for broadcast packets. This capability is necessary with some types of systems, such as BOOTP and DHCP servers and relay agents. In such a case, the match is limited to the port number.

32874: Nobody listening? If the packet isn't a broadcast or multicast packet, return an Internet Control Message Protocol (ICMP) Destination Unreachable message to the sender.

32888: Discard the packet and return from the routine.

32892: A socket was found, so let **udp_deliver** handle the task of saving the incoming packet.

udp_v4_lookup

To deliver a packet to a process, the packet has to be associated with the correct socket. This routine, which starts at line 31929, takes the packet presented to **udp_rcv** and finds the socket that is listening for it. The process of finding the appropriate socket is one of fuzzy logic, in which the "best" match returns. To reduce the amount of processing required for ideal UDP packet matches, a scoring system is used that allows an end-run around the analysis process if a socket earns a perfect score.

Before a candidate socket object can be selected for association with a packet, all the following conditions must be met:

- **sk->num** must match **uh->dest**

- The socket is not closed out (**sk->dead** is 0 or **sk->state** is not **TCP_CLOSE**)

- A non-wildcard **sk->daddr** matches **saddr**

- A non-wildcard **sk->dummy_th.dest** matches the source port **source**

- A non-wildcard **sk->bound_device** matches the device

- A non-wildcard **sk->rcv_saddr** matches the destination port **daddr**

For each nonwildcard match, the variable **score** is incremented. A perfect score (of 4) causes the socket object in question to be selected after the socket object has been found. Otherwise, the socket that has the highest score is selected after all of the socket objects have been searched. If two or more socket objects tie, then the *last* one that was checked is selected.

If no socket object is selected, then **NULL** is returned.

udp_deliver

This very simple little function (starting at line 32667) checks whether a socket object is locked. If so, the function adds the buffer to a backlog list and quits out. (Remember the **redo** parameter? This process of saving the buffer is how a recall is done to process the buffer after a socket is released.) Otherwise, the function makes a call to the function **udp_queue_rcv_skb**, described next, asking that the block be added to the receive queue.

udp_queue_rcv_skb

This function (line 32643) uses the inline function **__sock_queue_rcv_skb** (line 42183), which checks whether the socket has already exceeded its quota of data buffer space, as defined in **sk->rcvbuf** (which usually contains the value 65,535).

If the quota has been exceeded, the **UdpInErrors** counter and the **IpInDiscards** counter are incremented, and the buffer is dropped into the bit-bucket.

If the quota has not been exceeded, the buffer is added to the list of received buffers, the **UdpInDatagrams** counter is incremented, and the data-ready function associated with the socket object is called, so that the application can be told that data is waiting.

udp_v4_mcast_deliver

An interesting property of multicast support is that multiple socket objects may be bound to the multicast address and port. Thus, a single packet coming into a computer may be caught by multiple applications (assuming that this capability has been compiled into the kernel).

32717: Because the code has to walk through the UDP address list to pick up a number of codes, and because another process could come behind this

code and change things inappropriately, a semaphore locks out changes to the hash tables (actually, to *all* socket-related hash tables).

32720: Get a candidate socket object, based both on the source and destination addresses and on the device, by calling **udp_v4_mcast_next**. If the function returns a likely candidate, then continue. Otherwise, don't.

32725: Here, life degenerates into a complicated, interleaved mess. First, we have a socket (pointed to by **skb**) to which the buffer must be added. So, each time through the loop, we set the working pointer **skb1** to **skb**. Then, we search for the *next* socket. If we find the next socket, we then have *two* sockets that need the buffer. In this case, **skb1** is set to a clone of our packet buffer. (Otherwise, we still have the original buffer.) The code then calls the function **udp_deliver**, whose job is to add the (cloned) buffer to the socket's input queue and tell the process that owns the socket that data is available. This procedure continues until all the qualifying sockets have been processed.

32740: Release the semaphore.

32741: If the buffer was bound to a socket, then all is well. If no socket object matches the incoming packet, release the packet.

udp_v4_mcast_next

The preceding function needed a sieve to select the sockets that should receive packets. This function, which starts at line 32041, is that sieve.

All of the following variables and conditions must be met:

- **sk->num** matches **uh->dest**

- The socket is not closed out (**sk->dead** is 0 or **sk->state** is not equal to the manifest constant **TCP_CLOSE**)

- A non-wildcard **sk->daddr** matches **saddr**

- A non-wildcard **sk->dummy_th.dest** matches the source port **source**

- A non-wildcard **sk->bound_device** matches the device

- A non-wildcard **sk->rcv_saddr** matches the destination port **daddr**

The socket list is traversed until a suitable match (according to the foregoing criteria) is found or until the list is exhausted. The function either returns a pointer to a socket object or returns **NULL**.

udp_v4_proxy_lookup

This tour of the optional capabilities concludes with a look at the function that implements transparent proxy support for UDP. This function, which starts at line 31980, is responsible for the address and port translation for the packets that are received in response to a proxied request. In other words, if a UDP packet has been forwarded via a transparent proxy, the reply (if any) also has to be converted.

udp_connect

One way to receive (and send) UDP packets without requiring that every function know the address of the endpoints is to establish a virtual connection for a socket object. This way, UDP is almost as easy to use as TCP for tasks that, while requiring more than just one or two exchanges of data, don't need enough data exchanges to justify a full-blown TCP connection.

The caller specifies a remote address (in the form of an IP address and port) for the "other end," so that subsequent calls to **udp_send** will use this address and **udp_rcv** will steer incoming packets to the socket object indicated by the address.

The function (which starts on line 32596) performs the usual sanity checks on the request. It checks the size of the address, makes sure that the correct protocol family is specified, and (if the specified address is a broadcast address) confirms that the application issued a call to **setsockopt**, to turn on **SO_BROADCAST**.

The function then checks whether the specified address can be reached according to the routing table. (Frankly,

for most systems, this means that the routing table is checked for a default gateway entry. Very few system administrators put in deny-routes or other such niceties.)

After performing these sanity checks, the code saves the addresses in the socket, indicates the presence of a "connection," and returns control to the caller.

udp_close

This little function, which starts at line 32632, does housekeeping for the UDP socket. It undoes the effect of any call(s) that may have been made to **udp_connect**, and, using the **udp_v4_unhash** function, removes the socket object's information from the UDP hash tables. The function then sends the socket to socket heaven.

udp_unhash

Here's another small but necessary function, which starts at line 31883. It takes a socket object that has been placed in the UDP hash table and removes it from the hash-table list.

This function locates the list of socket objects from the hash table and then walks down the list until it finds the desired socket object. Then, it removes that object from the hash-table list.

udp_rehash

This function, which starts at line 31902, is a variation of the **udp_hash** and **udp_unhash** functions. It takes a socket object that has been placed in the UDP hash-table list, removes it from the list, and then adds it back to the list (or to a different list).

The routine locates the list of socket objects from the hash-table list, based on the old hash index, and then walks down the list until it finds the desired socket object. Then, it removes that object from the list, and the socket object is put at the head of the hash-table list, as indicated in the new hash index.

udp_hash

The **udp_hash** function, which starts at line 31868, completes this suite of functions. It takes a socket object and adds it to a hash list, as indicated by the contents of a hash index.

The routine places the socket object at the head of the hash-table list designated by the new hash index, and saves the hash-entry value for later dequeuing.

udp_recvmsg

To conclude the discussion of receiving UDP packets, this section looks at the routine that acquires the data that has been saved by all of the foregoing routines and returns that data to the using application. The story of this relatively simple but lengthy function starts at line 32525.

32540: If the address information is to be returned to the upper level, the length of the address field needs to be set.

32549: Call the routine that returns a saved datagram. If the parameter **noblock** is set, then the routine is guaranteed to return immediately. If no buffer was returned, then the error code is sent back to the caller of the function.

32553: Calculate the amount of data to be copied back into user space.

32560: The information in the data packet is copied back into user memory space, via the I/O vector mechanism, so that the packet can be distributed into multiple buffers. The copy operation can't be used to separate the various headers, because the IP header can vary in size, and no mechanism is provided that "guesses" the size of the IP packet beforehand.

32562: Save the packet's timestamp.

32565: If the caller passed a structure for receiving the addresses for the packet, copy all the information into that space. If the transparent proxy has been configured and the packet is marked for proxy, then the proxy information is copied into the "back half" of the address space.

32592: The data in the datagram has been passed to the caller, so bid the packet goodbye and release the memory.

32593: Return the number of bytes to the user.

IP Glue Routines

Although these functions are not a direct part of the UDP suite, they do provide services to other parts of the TCP/IP system that require input from the UDP module. Specifically, these routines make sure that the rest of the system doesn't need to know about the internal data structures of the UDP module—and that's a boon for program maintenance.

udp_chkaddr

This function, which starts at line 32686, checks whether a received packet is intended for a connected socket or for a bound socket. The function returns 0 if it doesn't find a socket or if the source address is 0, and returns 1 if the source address is non-0 and matches the socket found in the UDP list.

32693:   Search the UDP socket object list for a UDP socket whose address matches the desired address. This search uses the function **udp_v4_lookup**.

32696:   If no socket is found, return 0.

32700:   If the socket that is found has a wildcard source address, return 0.

32702:   The match is good, so return 1.

udp_check

This little function serves as a wrapper for the **csum_tcpudp_magic** checksum routine, customizing the routine for use in the creation of UDP packets. The **csum_tcpudp_magic** routine lives at line 35628, in the module /usr/include/asm/checksum.h.

udp_err

This module is called by the ICMP module when 1) an error condition is present and 2) the error was caused by a UDP packet.

32099:   If the packet is too short to be a UDP packet, ignore it.

32102:   Point to the UDP header and look for the socket object associated with the packet's addresses.

32106:   If no socket is found, stop here and go back to the caller.

32109:   If the other end is requesting slower transmission, shrink the window. However, when the window is shrunk, less data can be queued. This makes sense in UDP only when multiple packets are being transmitted. The window cannot shrink below 1; therefore, if the window is 2 or higher, divide the size of the window by 2. Return to the caller.

32116:   If an ICMP parameter problem is indicated, then pass the error back to the caller. The error is queued until the status is read out.

32141:   If the error code is within range and the array **icmp_err_convert** (at line 9251) indicates that the error is fatal, then continue working. Otherwise, go back to ICMP.

32148:   If the socket is not in a connected state, do nothing more. Otherwise, save the error and return an error code to the caller.

32153:   Return.

udp_v4_verify_bind

This function is used by the **bind** function call to make sure that two sockets are not bound to the same address at the same time. The function scans the hash list associated with the address in question, looking for a matching address on another socket object.

31785:   Start the search through the list of socket objects associated with the hash value.

31787:   Test for identical source port numbers and different socket objects. (Remember, this function can test a socket that is already bound or connected.) If the test fails, proceed immediately to the next socket in the list.

31793:   If the interfaces are different, obviously no collisions occurred. Continue.

31796:   If either source address is wildcarded and either socket object is *not* marked such that an address can be reused, indicate failure.

31801:   If either destination address is wildcarded and either socket object is *not* marked such that an address can be reused, indicate failure.

31810:   Return the result of the scan. A result of 0 (false) means that no collisions occurred.

udp_lport_inuse

This function, which starts at line 31813, searches the UDP hash lists for any occurrence of the port number passed by the caller. The reason for this search is that when an ephemeral port number is allocated, this port should not occur in a bound or connected socket. The search performed by this function confirms that this condition has been met.

The routine looks at the list in the hash table and scans the list of sockets for a matching port number. If the routine finds a matching port number (that is, if a collision occurred), the function returns 1. Otherwise (if no collision occurred), the function returns 0.

udp_good_socknum

This function, which starts at line 31826, selects a port number whose hash value points to the shortest list (or, ideally, to an empty list). Each call to this function remembers the result from the prior call and starts its search at one number past that result.

31838:   Loop through the hash table, trying each string in turn for the "best" fit.

31845:   If no sockets are associated with the hash value for the candidate port number, then stop the search now and use that result.

31850:   Count the number of socket objects in the hash-table list. Stop the loop if the earlier best result was better than the current result. (This approach avoids wasting time cycling through very long chains of socket objects.)

31859:   The shortest hash-table list has been found. Now, find an open port number that is a multiple of the hash-table value.

31862:   Save the port number that was found, and return it to the caller.

Chapter 9

TCP

This chapter brings us to the heart of the matter: Transmission Control Protocol, or TCP.

In Chapter 8, you saw how UDP treats data transfer as an occasional, *ad hoc*, as-needed event. In contrast, TCP treats data transfer as a continuous bidirectional stream of bytes that are exchanged between two systems. In further contrast, whereas UDP transfers are measured in seconds, TCP connections can stay open for minutes or even hours. Put another way, when faced with the task of moving messages from one side of a river to the other, UDP hires an individual boat and ferryman for each message, while TCP throws down a pontoon bridge and waves the traffic across.

Applications that use TCP range from Telnet (a relatively simple network teletype program) to World Wide Web browsers, router-to-router protocols, file transfer programs such as FTP, and PC remote-control applications.

These prepackaged applications aren't the only ones that like TCP. The protocol has also received a warm welcome from certain utilities, such as **netpipes**. Here, a bit of background is in order.

A simple but powerful concept implemented in Linux involves the use of a facility called *pipes*, which links the output of one program to the input of another program that is running on the same system. This way, large and useful systems of applications can be built and strings of programs can be assembled into a larger program—in much the same way that individual pop-beads are snapped together by a child to form a bracelet or necklace. In other words, simple modular building blocks are combined to form a single program that performs complex operations.

Back to the **netpipes** utility. A favorite of Linux programmers, it extends the concept of pipes to processes that are running on *separate* computers and that are connected via a network, so that multiple machines can participate in "piped" command lines.

This technique is often used in conjunction with the **tar** utility to move entire file systems from one computer to another. In such a transfer, the only place an intermediate copy needs to exist is on the network. Bringing matters full circle, **netpipes** makes extensive use of TCP.

Error-Free Error Control

Application programmers adore TCP because it lets "the system" take care of error detection and error recovery, allowing grateful programmers to pay more attention to the details of the code they're writing.

Why are error-control algorithms so unpopular? Well, because they're complex, tricky, and downright nasty to do right—especially when different implementations of a given error-control algorithm are supposed to work with each other. The early days of TCP's development were punctuated by several "TCP bake-offs" (see RFC 1025 on the CD-ROM), at which everyone would try to get their homegrown error-control algorithms to play nicely together ("bake-offs" would be echoed later in the "plug-fests" held regularly by the implementers of the Point-to-Point Protocol). When error control was developed as a system service, these pesky interactions were resolved once and for all, and the sighs of relieved code mavens were heard all 'round the Internet.

Application *users* adore TCP not only because it limits the opportunities for mistakes to be made in error control, but also because TCP gives them faster and more reliable access to complex applications, by making those programs easier to write and maintain. All in all, TCP is a palpable hit.

The View From Within

Because TCP is a system service, it uses the standard system interfaces. As you saw in Chapter 5, the application program interface (API) for TCP uses exactly the same I/O system calls that are used for disk files, serial ports, pipes, and the **read** and **write** system calls. The differences lie in how the "files" are opened. Disk files, pipes with specific names, and ports are all associated with file descriptors by means of the **open** system call. Unnamed pipes are created by means of the **pipe** system call. Applications that use TCP *socket connections* use the system calls **bind**, **connect**, **listen**, and **accept**. After a socket connection has been established between peer programs, the data stream on a TCP connection works exactly like a FIFO queue for data in each direction. In other words, it works exactly the same way as a pipe.

This scheme works so well that it's common for a process that is running on a given computer to talk to another process on the *same* computer, but to use the networking interface to do so. This way, the application doesn't have to know that its peer lives in the memory block right next door, instead of across the ocean.

The API for servers is straightforward. The server program makes a **bind** system call to register a listening socket with the system, specifying the IP address(es) and the TCP port number for which to listen for connections. The **listen** system call blocks execution until a connection request has been received for the socket. The **accept** system call signals the server's willingness to complete the connection and begin communication. The **read** and **write** system calls actually transfer data. The **shutdown** system call can be used to terminate one-half of the connection (for instance, to indicate that all of the available data has been transmitted). Finally, the **close** system call breaks the connection.

Here is a code fragment from a real server application written by your humble authors:

```
if((op ="socket",
    (g.well_known_socket =
     socket(AF_INET, SOCK_STREAM, 0))
     >=0)
  && (op = "setsockopt",
     setsockopt(g.well_known_socket,
SOL_SOCKET,
       SO_REUSEADDR, &yes, sizeof(int)) != -
1)
  && (op = "bind",
     (r = bind(g.well_known_socket,
      PIN(&s_in), sizeof(s_in))) != -1)
  && (op = "listen",
     (r = listen(g.well_known_socket, 0)) !=
-1)
  )
{
  printf("Server started on port %d\n",
g.port_number);
}
else
{
  printf("Server startup failed at
\"%s\"\n", op);
}
```

When a request comes in (as signaled by the **select** system call that is used when a connection is being awaited), the server then issues the call to the **accept** system function.

The API for the client program is even simpler. By making a **bind** system call, the client program creates a socket over which to establish a connection. The **connect** system call initiates the connection. After the **connect** system call succeeds, the client uses the **read**, **write**, and **shutdown** system calls to send, receive, and signal the exhaustion of data. (The purpose of the **close** system call is left as an exercise for the reader.)

```
if((op ="socket",
    (g.working_socket =
     socket(AF_INET, SOCK_STREAM, 0))
     >=0)
  && (op = "bind",
     (r = bind(g.working_socket,
      PIN(&s_in), sizeof(s_in))) != -1)
```

```
  && (op = "connect",
     (r = connect(g.working_socket,
      PIN(&remote_in), sizeof(remote_in)))
     != -1)
  )
{
  printf("Connected\n");
}
else
{
  printf("Connection failed at \"%s\"\n",
op);
}
```

The Chess Game

From the network's point of view, the life of a TCP connection has five distinct stages:

1. The two processes (which can reside on two different systems or on the same system) have not yet connected; however, they have taken the first steps toward a connection.

2. The processes negotiate the opening of the TCP connection.

3. The processes exchange data.

4. Both ends signal that they are through transferring data; any remaining dregs of data are discarded, and the connection is torn down.

5. All traces of the connection cease to exist, bringing us full circle.

A typical TCP connection establishment consists of a TCP SYN packet, a TCP SYN-ACK packet, and a TCP ACK packet. (In a *simultaneous open*, two processes can start to establish a connection at the same time. TCP is designed to handle this case, and, when it does so, it creates a single connection. This situation differs from the equivalent ISO function, in which *two* connections would be established.) This "ready, set, go!" three-way handshake performs three tasks: It synchronizes the control counters that are used to control data transfer, it exchanges some negotiated options between the two systems, and it opens the pipe between the processes.

After the pipe has been opened, the TCP connection becomes a full-duplex connection, in which data is transferred in both directions at the same time. Each half of the connection can be closed independently of the other direction (this is how processes signal that the end of a stream of data has been reached). When both directions have been closed, the TCP connection itself is considered closed, and the resources for the connection are released and returned to the operating system.

Next, the data is moved. In early communications systems, one end of the connection sent the data, the other end checked it and told the sender that all was well, and only then did the sender send the next batch of bytes. Under this arrangement, the data-transfer rate was limited by the transmission speed of the line and by the propagation delay over the communications channel.

Speaking of propagation delay, the late U.S. Navy Admiral Grace Hopper (a.k.a. "Grandma COBOL") would, during her lectures, hold up a foot-long piece of extruded copper that she called her "nanosecond of wire," so that the audience could put this abstract slice of time into concrete terms. (A nanosecond is 1×10^{-9} seconds, or a thousandth of a microsecond.) Now, consider a "wire" 15,840,000 feet long, or approximately the line-of-sight distance from Nantucket, Massachusetts to San Diego, California. Light in a vacuum would require about 16 milliseconds (16×10^{-3} seconds) to travel that distance. In a piece of wire, the speed of electrical signaling is a fraction of the speed of light, so an electrical impulse takes a bit longer to reach from one end to another—roughly 20 percent longer in high-speed communications cable—which means that the signaling time for our coast-to-coast cable is about 20 milliseconds.

During their research into optical computers, scientists at Bell Labs discovered that, because of the propagation-delay principle, an optical-computing-speed fiber-optic cable can be used as a surprisingly large storage medium, even to the point of allowing information about telephone calls to be stored on the same medium that is carrying the calls. A more prosaic T1/DS1 telephone circuit (commonly used in Internet connections) of that length "stores" more than 3,300 bytes in each direction on the wire itself.

The laws of physics aren't the only source of delay. The collision avoidance algorithm on an Ethernet can introduce delays when its exponential backoff method (which is used to deconflict frame collisions) goes to work. These delays may be as brief as 100 microseconds for a lightly loaded network, or as long as 30 milliseconds, or more, for a moderately loaded Ethernet. Add to that the time it takes to obtain a time slot, and a period of hundreds of milliseconds—or longer—may elapse before a packet is actually sent on its way. (Of course, if these delays happen often, your network administrator should be thinking about segmenting the Ethernet or moving to faster media; but until such a change is made, you'll have to live with what you have.)

Finally, very few coast-to-coast connections consist of a single long hop from source to destination. Instead, the connection is made over a series of links connected together by routers. These routers are *store-and-forward* devices, which means that they have to receive the packet completely, and then figure out where they go next before the packet can be sent on its way. Busy routers usually have a line of packets waiting to board the next-hop link. Each router can introduce between 1 and 250 milliseconds of delay for packets. (Complex router nests, such as those run by backbone providers, are knit together via Ethernet, too, so that source of delay rears its unlovely head again.)

Back now to TCP data transfers. The lock-step transfer of data described earlier works well when the connection is short and direct. When the wire gets longer, or complicated, or congested, the transmission must be uncoupled from the acknowledgment of data, so that data can be sent fast—even in the face of long realtime transfer delays. The classic technique (which TCP uses) is called *windowing*. In this technique, the receiving system guarantees that it can handle a certain amount of data that is sent from the other end. The sending system can then "fill the window" and wait for a response

from the receiving system. When the receiving system has processed the received data, it then sends as part of its acknowledgment a *window advertisement* stating that it can accept more data.

In the early days of TCP, the size of the window was limited to 65,535 bytes. With the growth of faster and faster communications systems—and with no repeal of the law of the speed of light currently in sight—systems can now negotiate larger windows by using the TCP *window scale* option to increase the amount of data that can be "in the pipe." When the two processes specify this option and provide the buffer space, the maximum size of the TCP window increases from 65,535 bytes to as much as 1,073,725,440 bytes.

Okay, you've transmitted the data. When one side has finished transmitting data, it can then shut down that direction by sending a FIN packet. This indicates to the other end that, after it has processed the data it has received, there will be no more. This is particularly important when TCP is used to emulate a Unix pipe—it's the only way to signal end-of-file to the remote end when the applications don't have their own in-band signaling mechanism in place.

When both sides have sent FIN packets, the connection is considered closed.

Open, transfer, close—sounds simple, doesn't it? The drudge, as you may suspect, is in the details, and TCP is no different in that regard than in any other enterprise. The complexity, though, is intended to refine and smooth the flow of data through the network, and to make TCP a good network neighbor in how it uses resources. These refinements, ranging from esoteric applications of queuing theory to some basic common-sense optimizations, carry such names as *slow-start* and the *Nagle algorithm*. These optimizations will be described as we go along—and you won't need a math degree to understand them.

Alas, not every system is a good neighbor. Just as a malicious programmer can abuse the features of IPv4, ICMP,

and UDP, so can TCP be abused. The commentary in this chapter points out some common tricks and swindles, and explains how the Linux implementation protects its system from would-be nefarious ill-wishers. Chapter 10 goes into further detail about how Linux protects itself (and you), including descriptions of the TCP-specific features built into the Linux firewall support.

Now, it's time to take a closer look at the issues the code has to contend with during the phases of the lifetime of a TCP connection. Bring out the chess board, and let the little game of "data, data, who has the data?" begin.

Setting Up The Board

"'Begin at the beginning,' the King said gravely, 'and go on till you come to the end; then stop.'" Wise advice from *Alice's Adventures in Wonderland*. But, before you can begin, you have to fall down the...er, establish a path so that communications can take place. The issue before us right now is the establishment, or *opening*, of the connection.

The job seems simple—exchange a few pleasantries, establish a few ground rules, and start exchanging data. The job *is* simple, when all goes right (as it does the vast majority of the time). But, this is the Internet, where anything can—and does—happen.

Let's review the basic job of opening a connection. The typical TCP connection establishment consists of a TCP SYN packet, a TCP SYN-ACK packet, and a TCP ACK packet, a "ready, set, go!" three-way handshake. Call the requestor A and the requestee B. The first packet, which is the SYN packet sent by A, provides the sequencing information for the A-to-B data direction. The second packet, the SYN-ACK packet sent by B, acknowledges the setting of the sequencing information in the A-to-B data direction, and at the same time provides the sequencing information in the B-to-A data direction. The third packet, the ACK packet sent by A, acknowledges the setting of the B-to-A sequencing information. At this point, both sides of the connection have identical copies of the two sequence numbers, and agree to any options that may have piggy-backed on the packets that set the sequence numbers.

This agreement means that data can now be transferred. Time to move on and transmit data.

But wait! Right off the bat, a nasty bit of business needs to be addressed. What happens when the second or third packet does not arrive? According to the TCP rules, when something should happen and it doesn't, you send *something* to let the other end know that you're confused. During the connection establishment sequence, the usual thing is to repeat, once or twice, the last packet that you sent. If you don't see an answer, you abandon the connection attempt as hopeless.

However, this approach has its consequences. During the opening process, the two systems have to create some control structures that may end up being useless and will therefore have to be released after a timer has expired. Different systems do different things, so the cost varies from one TCP implementation to another.

Regardless of the cost, this need to consume resources can be used to launch a denial-of-service attack. Consider the following scenario. Someone says to you, "Where shall we have lunch?" You reply with the name of the restaurant, and, with the expectation that lunch will be consumed there, you pack up to go to lunch. You wait for a "Let's go!" but you hear nothing. Indeed, when you look around, a lot of people are standing about waiting to go to lunch, but the person who made the query is nowhere to be seen. Pretty soon, everyone is standing about and no one is doing anything else. This is the essence of a *SYN flood* attack. An attacker sends the "ready" part (SYN packet) of the open exchange, in large numbers. The system being attacked responds to *every single one* of these connection bids with the "set" part (SYN-ACK packet) of the message, and also allocates the necessary control structures. The attacker never answers the second packet because it's being nasty.

As you'll see later in the code commentary, Linux implements several layers of defense against this sort of bad

behavior. The most obvious tactic is to limit the number of incomplete connections—particularly connections from a specific IP address—so that a digital delinquent can't (either by design or through stupidity) consume all the TCP connection slots. Another defensive tactic is to limit the lifetime of incomplete connections to a reasonable amount of time, on the theory that if the local system doesn't hear from the remote system by the time the alarm goes off, it probably won't hear from it at all. Other, more active, defensive measures are examined in the commentary.

Opening Gambits

Just as the tenor of a chess game can be set by the first move by White, so can the smoothness of data transfer be set by the first packets being sent. A chess master starts by moving pawns to establish a front position, and moving other pieces later, to project power onto the board. But, if you try to move more powerful pieces too soon, the result is a chaotic position and ultimately a complete mess and defeat. Try to push too much data onto the network, and the result is no less messy.

Sun-tzu, in *The Art of War*, put it more simply, "On the ground of intersecting highways, join hands with your allies." The metaphorical implications of this maxim as it relates to the Internet are considered in the following paragraphs.

When a TCP channel is opened for a file transfer (such as an FTP file transfer or a Web page download), the startup surge from the newly initiated transfer could swamp the ability of the channel to carry data, and thereby destabilize the links involved. This affects not only the transfer in question but also other transfers that are already in progress.

It's easy to visualize why this happens. Picture a major controlled-access highway in a metro area during rush hour. An existing stream of traffic is moving as fast as the road allows. Suddenly, a madman roars down an on-ramp and into the traffic flow. The usual results take

place: TV and radio traffic-reporting helicopters converge on the scene to report on the multivehicle accident caused by the rude injection of the careening car. The juggern aut(o) rarely survives, and the collateral damage can be extensive.

Now, electrons don't bruise that easily, and packets don't need trips to the body shop. What happens instead is that when a stream of packets is unleashed at full-tilt-boogie rates, the downstream routers can be overwhelmed to the point that buffers can't hold the traffic, and packets disappear over the guardrail. The packets that manage to keep a grip on the road find that they arrive at their destination considerably later than they would have if the reckless system had been more reasonable when it injected traffic into the network.

Indeed, the futility of being overzealous in sending data lies in the resulting delays in the transfer—or the loss—of that very data. Just as a highway will go into its "brake, accelerator, brake, accelerator, pound your fist upon the dashboard" mode when it has too many cars, so will the Internet have widely varying performance, tending toward crawling, when too many packets are crowding the pipeline.

A solution does exist, though. The *slow-start algorithm* is the TCP equivalent of the highway metering lights you see on so many highway on-ramps. At the beginning of a bulk-transfer connection, the TCP transmission algorithm sends a limited amount of data, receives the acknowledgments (ACKs) of the data, and—by performing on-the-fly analysis of the timing of the ACKs—decides when to shift to a faster traffic lane. By accelerating the rate of data transmission gradually, the rate of transfer increases steadily until the full bandwidth possible between the two systems has been reached and can be maintained. As the TCP transfer encounters traffic jams, it taps the brakes and backs off. Then, as traffic conditions warrant, it gradually speeds up.

In the Linux TCP code, the slow-start algorithm uses the concept of a *congestion window*. This window indicates the amount of data that has been successfully sent in the past without causing any hiccups. As data flows through the circuit with good ACK response times, the software will open this window wider and wider to increase the flow of data. When problems crop up, the window shrinks. When TCP's analysis suggests that the transfer is going as well as it can, the data rate stops accelerating. This way, the algorithm "hunts" for the best balance between throughput and stability. The servomechanism style of adjusting the transmission rate is tuned to balance reactivity to changes in the network path's capacity with stability in the rate of flow of the data.

The result of implementing this Type-B behavior is that TCP can get more data through the network on behalf of its client (which makes the client happy). Furthermore, the network itself handles far more data more smoothly (which makes the Internet Highway Patrol—and thus other users—happy).

As this book was going to press, the State of Nevada passed a law against aggressive automobile driving. A decade earlier than that, though, the Internet community mandated, in RFC 1122, that TCP implementations observe the slow-start rules. If only real-world motorists would learn this lesson.

Middle Game

The slow-start algorithm described in the last section smoothes the flow of data over the network. The rate of bulk transfer can also be throttled by the remote process not being able to handle the data bytes as fast as the source and the network can deliver them. By using window advertisements, the local system can keep the remote system from overwhelming the local system's RAM.

When TCP deals with interactive applications, such as Telnet, in which a human or some other slow process is involved in creating data to be sent, another optimization can be sent into the game. This optimization, the *Nagle algorithm*, tries to reduce the number of packets

that are transmitted, doing so by being clever about when data is sent.

Frankly, the overhead associated with sending a single character (such as when a human is at the keyboard) is atrocious. You need at least 20 bytes for the IP header and at least 20 bytes for the TCP header—all for *one measly byte of payload*. That's at best a 40:1 ratio of overhead to useful information! Add the overhead for the ACK packet (which lets the transmitting TCP know that the character was received), and you squander 81 bytes of network bandwidth to send just one lousy character. (At least Telnet is smart enough to eliminate the need for the receiving system to echo the character; otherwise, you'd be looking at a 160:1 ratio—a sure route to bandwidth bankruptcy.)

The grouping of characters in packets takes advantage of the characteristics displayed by humans at the keyboard. The average amateur typist can produce about 20 words a minute, or an average of 2 keyboard characters per second. In the distribution of typical keystrokes (especially by victims, er, veterans of high-school typing classes), characters are typed in very quick bursts of three to five. (The rest of the time is spent thinking, reading, or trying to find the backslash key.) For more skilled touch-typists, the "bursty" distribution of characters is the same, but the volume of keystrokes (that is, characters) per second is higher.

The Nagle algorithm capitalizes on the bursty nature of human typing by intentionally holding off sending a packet until the packet is "full," or until the first character in the packet gets painfully old. This *frame-forwarding strategy* is a lot like highway administrators' efforts to encourage people to carpool. It works like this: When you receive the first character for a packet, you set a timer for some reasonable amount of time (from 0.1 to 0.5 seconds). If you receive more characters in this window of time, you add the characters to the packet. When the timer dings, you launch the packet with as many characters as you have collected.

Using this system, the Nagle algorithm can easily cut the number of packets to less than half of the original volume. The better the typist, the higher the bandwidth savings. The realtime response of the remote systems isn't significantly affected, especially if the application knows about and deals with special characters (such as the Enter key) that have special meanings.

The Nagle algorithm isn't just for humans. Programs generate data in spurts as well. By combining the spurts, the Nagle algorithm can do a remarkable job of reducing the number of packets and the corresponding overhead. For example, the **ls** utility can output short segments of data as it outputs the file names from a directory. The Nagle algorithm can easily collect the short names and make a full packet out of them, thereby drastically reducing the overhead required to send the list of file names.

The Nagle algorithm is particularly important to people and companies who use certain European data networks. These networks charge their users by the packet (actually, by the kilopacket). In short, the Nagle algorithm isn't just for being nice; it saves money, too.

Unfortunately, some applications can't stand to have any delay imposed on transmission. Numeric control equipment, for example, might require that commands be issued at strict intervals (that is, with no distortion in transmission time). Certain interactive games require movements and weapon discharges to occur on command, and the Nagle algorithm would cause a *hang-fire* condition in those games. Although occasional hang-fires are realistic (ask any veteran ground-pounder), they're usually not part of the game design. For such applications, the API provides controls to turn off the algorithm. So, it's up to the application to package data appropriately, to avoid unnecessary overhead in data transmission and excessive charges for the poor user.

The economies enabled by the Nagle algorithm are not limited to reducing the number of data packets sent by the transmitting system. Savings are also achieved through a reduction in the number of ACK packets coming back from the other direction.

Speaking of ACK packets, there are possibilities for savings in traffic (and cost) over and above what the Nagle algorithm provides. The design of the protocol allows a single TCP ACK to indicate that virtually any number of data packets—as opposed to just one packet—was received properly. This means that the sending of an ACK packet can be delayed so that potentially more than one data packet can be acknowledged in a single 40-byte packet. Even better, the ACK can be combined with data going in the other direction so that instead of sending multiple packets—one containing the ACK information and one containing the data bytes—the sending system can collapse two packets into one.

The urge to conserve ACK packets must be tempered with the need to keep data flowing. The ACK packet serves two functions. First, it tells the sending TCP that data has been properly tucked away. Second, it tells the sending TCP that room exists for more data. If you send too few ACKs, the transmitter will run into what it thinks is a full-window condition, and the data transfer could be slowed.

The Push feature (not available in Linux release 2.0.34) is used by applications that use TCP to transfer transactions. Push lets the application tell the sending TCP code to send any buffered data, and to set the PSH flag in the TCP header of the last packet containing the data. In turn, the PSH flag in the TCP header tells the receiving TCP code to make the data available to the application now, instead of later. The purpose of the Push feature is to ensure that all the data involved in a transaction is presented, as soon as possible, to the receiving application. For example, when Telnet sees a line-ending character, it should send that line-ending character via a mechanism that triggers the invocation of the Push feature for that character. The TCP implementation then sends everything, up to and including the end-of-line character, to the remote system.

Instead of implementing the Push feature as an item supported by an application interface, the Linux implementation of TCP does not hold off transmission for long periods of time. Specifically, the use of the PSH flag in TCP packets follows the guidelines established in RFC 1122.

Disadvantageous Trades

The fact that a chess piece can move in several directions, sometimes even back and forth between two squares, doesn't mean that it's to the player's advantage to move it that way. Such silly moves can give your opponent an opportunity to improve her position, to the detriment of your own. Each move must be considered and must significantly advance your cause.

In TCP, lack of attention to simple conditions can lead to unnecessary network congestion and too much work for too little gain. Consider, for example, *Silly Window Syndrome*. This condition is caused when a TCP implementation makes small adjustments to its window advertisements, and the remote system reacts by sending small amounts of data to fill the window. The result is a huge and potentially costly stream of very-small-payload packets.

Even worse, inattention to the timing of the transmission of ACK packets can cause a blizzard of these packets. It can even lead to false detection of lost data, if the TCP code sees too many ACK packets. A good rule of thumb, according to RFC 1122, is to send an ACK no later than one-half second after the first packet received, or every 3,000 bytes or so of data, whichever comes first.

What happens if the receiver has advertised a 0-byte window, and, at a later time, advertises a non-0-byte window but the packet containing the advertisement is lost? The original TCP didn't implement a way to detect the loss of the advertisement of open space, so the connection would hang. Here's how the problem is fixed: Every so often, the sending side facing a 0-byte window will send 1 byte anyway. This action is guaranteed to generate an ACK packet, regardless of the window's

state. If the window is still closed, the ACK packet will show a 0-byte window and the same acknowledgment number as before, indicating that the 1 byte of data that was transmitted was rejected and should be sent again later. If the window opened up and the advertisement was lost, the persistence of the sending system is rewarded with a new window advertisement and the fact that the single byte of data was accepted.

Endgame

When the transmitting TCP receives a signal from the application (via the **shutdown** or **close** system function) that there is no more data to send, the TCP code expedites the transmission of any remaining data, setting the PSH and FIN flags in the last packet of the stream. If any of the concluding packets are lost, they may need to be retransmitted—so don't forget about them just yet.

When the receiving TCP receives a signal from the remote system that there is no more data to be received, the TCP code takes whatever data that is waiting for the application and makes it available to the application on request. After all the data has been sent and received, an end-of-file indication is returned to the application.

Checkmate

When both sides have indicated that they have exhausted their data sources, the connection is closed. But that's not the end of the game. Duplicate packets may still be out there, lost in the clouds—but not so lost that they can't eventually come home.

Like a noncompete clause in a bad employment contract, the connection record lives on, usually for about four minutes (the so-called *2MSL time*). During this period, random packets that arrive for transmission via the closed connection (rather like a commuter who dashes to the dock just as the ferry is pulling away) are silently discarded. The delay also ensures that the connection truly dies, and that all parties have agreed that the game is indeed over, with no last-ditch saves in the offing.

Sore Losers

Some people just can't seem to end a competitive encounter with good grace. The authors have encountered one particular brand of equipment whose TCP implementation refuses to close a connection "the right way," thereby causing any future attempted connection with that equipment to fail for the 2MSL time. In such cases, you may just have to break the rules and use the reset facility, "killing" the connection deader than dead—like a properly drowned, stirred, and redrowned campfire. This approach is highly discouraged, so much so, in fact, that the documented way to do it isn't even implemented in Linux release 2.0.34!

The reset option is also handy when both sides of the connection get hopelessly confused. It does happen, albeit not often.

The Lamp Test

No discussion of TCP would be complete without a brief discussion of RFC 1025. This document describes the "bake-off" that was held in the early days of TCP development, to test multiple implementations of the TCP algorithms against each other. The purpose of such events, which are common in the telecommunications field, is to ensure that the standards are written well enough to give programmers a fighting chance of creating an implementation that will work with other programmers' implementations.

One of the tests was designed to show what an implementation would do with one particular unusually formed packet, referred to by many names: Kamikaze packet, nastygram, Christmas tree packet, or (the authors' favorite) the lamp test packet. (The name *lamp test* comes from the key found on military aircraft, commercial airliners, and 1970s computers, which, when pressed, causes every lamp in the vehicle or system to light. The idea was to detect any burned-out bulbs, so operators could be sure that a lamp that was not lit wasn't simply burned out.)

This lamp test packet had a TCP header with the URG, PSH (EOL in RFC 1025), SYN, and FIN flags turned on. It also contained data. Any reasonable interpretation of RFC 793 in a data-processing environment would never generate such an unusual packet—clearly, this is an artificial test. (Kind of like setting a message in your code that, if all goes well, you should never see. "ESAD" is a popular one.)

Indeed, if you read RFC 793 closely, you'll see that the protocol designers inserted special rules into the processing of incoming packets to make the lamp test packet "legal." Removing those special rules has no effect on more common packet streams.

On further reflection, though, to the authors, the lamp test packet looks like the "group trigger" command, which is part of the IEEE-488 instrument-bus control specification. This capability could be extremely useful in military applications. (This could explain why Berkeley implementations of TCP/IP don't offer any way to generate such a packet. "What, me wargame?")

Here is the sequence of events, as described in RFC 793, that a TCP implementation goes through when it parses the lamp test packet (assuming the packet is directed toward a socket in the **LISTEN** state):

1. SYN seen; verify that the sequence number is acceptable (we assume it is), enter **SYN-RECEIVED** state, and continue processing the packet in the **SYN-RECEIVED** state.

2. Even though the advertised window is 0 (the socket isn't open yet), accept the packet because the URG flag is set. (Note that the Linux implementation determines a window advertisement early enough to avoid the need for the rule.)

3. Normally, the SYN bit would be an error, but in Step 1, part of the instruction is to skip the SYN and ACK tests. This is the special rule we talked about before.

4. In the URG bit checking, the **SYN-RECEIVED** state is not mentioned as a state in which processing is required, so nothing is done.

5. The text is discarded because no processing is defined for text processing while in the **SYN-RECEIVED** state.

6. Checking the FIN bit, signal to the user that the connection is closing (but, never signal to the user the connection was *open*), and enter the **CLOSE-WAIT** state.

7. You're done with the packet.

The net result: You have a bogus notification to the nonexistent user that the connection is closing; otherwise, nothing happens except that the connection finally goes into the **CLOSE-WAIT** state. The data is ignored, technically. So much for silly games.

Anatomy Of A Header

The overall structure of an Ethernet frame containing a TCP packet is shown in Figure 9.1. The format for the TCP header is shown in Figure 9.2. In the diagram, the value of h can vary from 20 through 60, depending on the IP options that are included in the IP header portion of the packet. For a TCP packet, the IP protocol field contains the binary value 6 to indicate that the payload of the IP packet contains TCP information.

The *source port number* field and *destination port number* field, in conjunction with the IP source and destination addresses in the IP packet header, identify the unique 96-bit identifier for the socket object associated with this packet. These port numbers are never either all 0-bits or all 1-bits. RFC 1700 identifies the *well-known port numbers* that can be used in these fields to create a connection with various services on remote systems. When appropriate, *ephemeral* (temporary) port numbers are allocated, so there are no conflicts with any other open socket objects on the system.

The *sequence number* field identifies the relative offset from an arbitrary starting point for the first data byte contained in the packet. If no data is contained in the packet, the sequence number field indicates where the

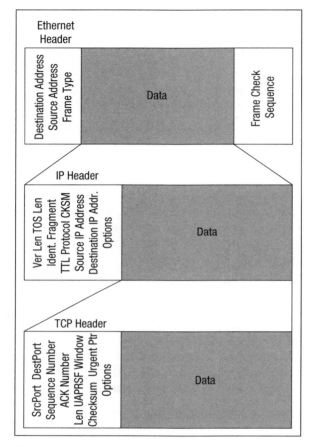

Figure 9.1 Overall structure of an Ethernet frame that contains a TCP packet.

next byte to be sent will be positioned in relation to that arbitrary starting point. Because packets can arrive in something other than their proper order, the sequence number identifies the relative position of the data contained in received packets. The sequence number field ensures that the data bytes can be presented to an application at the receiving end in the same order in which the application presented them at the sending end. If more than 2^{32} data bytes are transmitted, this 32-bit se-

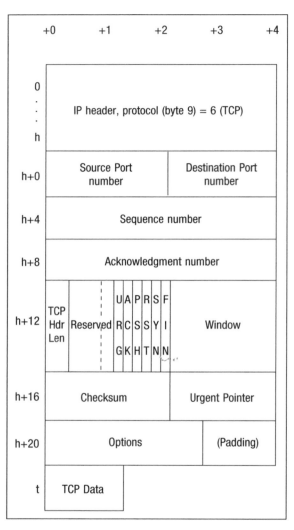

Figure 9.2 The TCP packet header, in detail.

quence-number field will wrap. The sequence numbers are independent in each transmission direction.

The *acknowledgment number* field identifies the next expected sequence number. The contents of this field

are valid only when the ACK flag (described later) is set. This field is included in every TCP header so that the TCP code at both ends has every opportunity to synchronize the state of the data transmission. The acknowledgment number is used in conjunction with the sequence number field in the packets that are travelling in the opposite direction.

Each end of a TCP connection has an independent sequence number s, which we will call s_A and s_B. Each end also has an acknowledgment number a, which we will call a_A and a_B. During the handshake process, system A transmits a packet with a sequence number s_A and the SYN flag set (described later); system B saves the value as a_B. System B does the same thing with s_B and the SYN flag set; system A saves the value as a_A. At the beginning of the connection, then, s_A equals a_B, and s_B equals a_A.

As system A transmits data, it places the current contents of s_A in the sequence-number field, and then increments s_A by the number of data bytes contained in the TCP packet payload. As system B receives the data, it increments a_B by the number of data bytes contained in the TCP packet. Now, when system B sends a TCP packet back to system A, it places the value contained in a_B into the acknowledgment number field. When system A sees the value of a_B, it knows what data has been successfully transferred and can be discarded from the holding buffers in system A.

Special processing is involved with the sequence and acknowledgment numbers when the SYN and FIN bits are set, which are described in this chapter's commentary section.

The *TCP header length* field (labeled TCP HdrLen in the diagram) contains a count of the number of 32-bit words in the TCP header, including any options. This value ranges from 5 through 15. In the commentary, this field is identified by the TCP header structure element **doff** (lines 39647 and 39683).

The field marked "reserved" in the diagram is a reserved field. It must be set to 0 when packets are built, and ignored when packets are examined.

The URG flag indicates that the urgent field (described shortly) contains valid data.

The ACK flag indicates that the acknowledgment number field contains valid data.

The PSH flag indicates that the data contained in the packet and in prior packets should be processed and provided to the application as quickly as is feasible. (This is the Push function described earlier in this chapter.) The original intent of this flag becomes clear when you check the early literature and see it referred to as the end-of-line (EOL) flag. Originally, the job of the EOL flag was to expedite the processing of data when a line-ending character was seen. This function stems from a feature in ITU Recommendation X.3, which allows the definition of certain characters, known as *forwarding characters*, that should be transmitted immediately instead of being buffered. Although TCP isn't data-sensitive (interpretation is left up to the application program), the PSH flag and its underlying functionality allow it to respond to the application program's interpretation.

The RST flag is the reset flag. It is used to close down unstable connections, such as those in which the sequence numbers are hopelessly out of synchronization and the connection needs to be restarted; to clean up the remnants of a connection in which one side has crashed and restarted and has forgotten all about the original connection; and to close a channel when the applications provide no in-band way for doing so.

The SYN flag is the synchronize flag. Used only when a connection is established, it sets the initial sequence number to be used for/in future communications.

The FIN flag is the finish flag. When set, it indicates that the data bytes (if any) are the final data bytes to be sent. (The PSH flag is usually also set.) After an application has received the data up to this point, the operating system is supposed to signal "end-of-file" to the application.

The *window* field describes the current window advertisement, which is the amount of data the receiver guarantees to the sender that the receiver can receive and store. The value in this field is multiplied by the window scale factor (described later when we describe the options field) to identify the size of the available window. This value can be 0, which tells the sender to not send anything. Like the acknowledgment number field, the window field is set by the system that receives the data.

The *checksum* field contains a checksum of the information in the TCP header plus selected information from the IP header plus the TCP payload. (See RFC 793, included on the CD-ROM, for a description of the checksum—it isn't bad, but it isn't simple, either.) The description of the **tcp_send_check** function also includes considerable information regarding the details for calculating a checksum for TCP packets. RFC 1071 (which appears on the CD-ROM) contains very useful information about calculating checksums, especially about how to do it quickly and how to use assembler code to extract the maximum possible performance from the checksum algorithm.

The *urgent pointer* field contains a 16-bit positive offset from the sequence number (contained in the sequence number field) to the sequence number of "urgent" data. This feature is used by several applications to provide a means for signaling interrupt conditions, even when TCP is advertising a 0-window size so that no data can be sent. It is used by some applications to simulate an out-of-band data channel for control data.

The interpretation of the urgent pointer is the "dirtiest" part of TCP. In the original RFC 793 (included on the CD-ROM), the definition in Section 3.1 states that the offset added to the sequence number field points *past* the last byte of urgent data. The documentation of the SEND pseudocode function (on page 56 of RFC 793) implies that the offset added to the sequence number field points *to* the last byte of urgent data. The Berkeley implementations of TCP use the prose definition, while

other implementations use the pseudocode definition. RFC 1122 has decreed that the latter interpretation is the "correct" one. That makes interoperation with Berkeley implementations tough. Linux fixes the problem by letting the application decide which interpretation to use. The app selects an interpretation by calling the **setsockopt** system call with the **SO_BSDCOMPAT** operation code. See Chapter 5 for details. (At least the default value for the option is to follow RFC 1122.) It's too bad that no code in Linux release 2.0.34 takes advantage of this **setsockopt** call.

New applications should be coded to assume that the sequence number of the urgent data (sequence number field plus option field) is the sequence number of the final byte (*octet* if you prefer the RFC language) of the urgent data.

Finally, the *options* field (which may be completely absent) contains a byte stream of options data. Figure 9.3 shows the format of the two types of options, the two single-byte options, and the general format for the rest of the options. Table 9.1 lists the options.

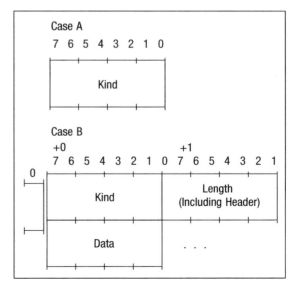

Figure 9.3   The TCP packet header options field, in detail.

Table 9.1   The TCP packet header options.

Case	Kind	Length	Description
A	0	-	End of option list
A	1	-	Nop (no operation)
B	2	4	Maximum segment size (16 bits)
B	3	3	Window scale factor (8 bits, values 0 through 14)
B	8	10	Timestamp

The maximum segment size (MSS) option overrides the default segment size for the purposes of performing the slow-start algorithm. The default is based on the path maximum transmission unit (MTU) and is calculated during MTU discovery, if discovery is needed.

The window scale factor contains the number of bits the window field should be shifted when calculating the number of bytes that can be transmitted. This value can range from 0 (the default) through 14 (which allows a 1GB window advertisement).

The timestamp option is analogous to the timestamp option in IPv4, except that it measures the interval only between the two TCP implementations; no router gets involved as with the IP option. RFC 1323 (included on the CD-ROM) contains more information on how this timestamp value can be used and some of the pitfalls in doing so.

The timestamp is considerably more valuable when used in conjunction with very-high-speed connections, as an extension to the sequence number to protect against the 32-bit sequence number wrapping too quickly. This is called PAWS (Protection Against Wrapped Sequence numbers). Because the channel can handle data so fast, the added overhead of carrying the sequence number is well worth the protection against too-early reuse of sequence numbers. (This problem won't turn into a monster until your systems are connected to gigabit-capacity telecomm lines.)

Other options are defined, so this table will grow as those options are added. As of Linux release 2.0.34, though,

Table 9.1 shows a complete-enough list. Indeed, the MSS option is the only one that release 2.0.34 supports.

As with IP options, any empty space in the options field needs to be filled with padding characters, so the options fit evenly into one or more 32-bit words.

You might ask how the computer knows how long the packet is and whether any data at all is in the payload of the TCP packet. The answer is that the length of the TCP header and the length of the total TCP packet (header plus payload) are included in the TCP header. Calculating the size of the payload is simple, after all.

Commentary

The entire foregoing discussion is preliminary to understanding what the code really does. Now, the chapter gets down to the true nitty-gritty, with almost a hundred TCP functions.

Unlike every other chapter in this book, the functions have not been reshuffled from their original source code order; instead, they (and the accompanying commentaries) appear in the order in which they are presented in the listings pages.

The major reason for this deviation from the customary style is that TCP is much better modularized than the other protocol handlers in the Linux TCP/IP stack. Consequently, when you run across a function that is used in a "later" routine, the fact that the functions appear in source line-number order makes the referencing function that much easier to locate.

That said, the index of functions in this chapter is still arranged by function name. When functions are referenced in the source code, the commentary makes copious use of line numbers.

Another departure-from-style note: The "we" that appears in much of the commentary is shorthand for "the system running the local instance of TCP code." For instance, the phrase "If we see a FIN packet..." means "If the TCP code running in the local machine sees a FIN

packet...." This usage is not an attempt to anthropomorphize (attribute human characteristics to) the code. Instead, it reflects a well-known telecommunications convention, in which the actions that take place on each side of the call are described in the terms used by bridge players—namely, "we" and "they." This convention emphasizes the ping-pong-game nature of telecommunications, as suggested in the example in the next paragraph, which describes the packet exchange required to open a TCP connection between a client (active open) and server (passive open):

"To open a TCP connection, we create a socket object in the **TCP_SYN_SENT** state and send a SYN packet. When they see our SYN packet, they create a socket in the **TCP_SYN_RECV** state, save our sequence number in it, and respond with a SYN/ACK packet containing an acknowledgment number of our initial sequence number plus one. When we see the TCP/ACK packet ACKing our starting sequence number, we in turn save their starting sequence number, set our socket object to **TCP_ESTABLISHED**, and riposte with the final ACK of their SYN/ACK packet containing an ACK number set to their initial sequence number plus one."

Using the we/they convention, the preceding 103-word description accurately encapsulates the entire TCP connection sequence, clearly showing what each end of the connection is supposed to be doing. If this description were written in a more conventional style, the clarity of who is doing what to whom would be lost, and the word count would grow big-bellied with the wanton wind.

Table 9.2 indexes the functions by name, while Table 9.3 indexes the functions by line number.

Table 9.2   Functions, listed by name.

Line	Function
26338	__tcp_v4_lookup
26241	add_clearance
26434	bad_tcp_sequence
25055	cleanup_rbuf

(continued)

Table 9.2 Functions, listed by name *(continued)*.

Line	Function
29474	clear_delayed_acks
25485	closing
31509	delete_timer
24532	do_tcp_sendmsg
31545	net_timer
28660	prune_queue
31522	reset_timer
25631	tcp_accept
27366	tcp_ack
24464	tcp_build_header
28540	tcp_check_urg
28685	tcp_chkaddr
26231	tcp_clearance
25497	tcp_close
24047	tcp_close_pending
25353	tcp_close_state
26644	tcp_conn_request
27057	tcp_conn_request_fake
25714	tcp_connect
28411	tcp_data
26069	tcp_delack_estimator
31108	tcp_delack_timer
29639	tcp_dequeue_partial
29839	tcp_do_retransmit
25040	tcp_eat_skb
29673	tcp_enqueue_partial
24089	tcp_err
28125	tcp_fin
24022	tcp_find_established
25937	tcp_getsockopt
23870	tcp_good_socknum
28235	tcp_insert_skb
24364	tcp_ioctl
24290	tcp_listen_select
23846	tcp_lport_inuse
24492	tcp_memory_free
29426	tcp_new_window
26573	tcp_options
28277	tcp_queue

(continued)

Table 9.2 Functions, listed by name *(continued)*.

Line	Function
28264	tcp_queue_ack
28710	tcp_rcv
24947	tcp_read_wakeup
24199	tcp_readable
24971	tcp_recv_urg
25082	tcp_recvmsg
28631	tcp_remove_dups
26510	tcp_reset
31117	tcp_reset_xmit_timer
31238	tcp_retransmit
31171	tcp_retransmit_time
31376	tcp_retransmit_timer
26135	tcp_rtt_estimator
24317	tcp_select
30668	tcp_send_ack
24429	tcp_send_check
30641	tcp_send_delayed_ack
30356	tcp_send_fin
29659	tcp_send_partial
30991	tcp_send_probe0
30197	tcp_send_reset
29489	tcp_send_skb
30487	tcp_send_synack
30283	tcp_send_synack_probe
24881	tcp_sendmsg
26491	tcp_sequence
25897	tcp_setsockopt
31021	tcp_shrink_skb
25425	tcp_shutdown
24064	tcp_time_wait
31351	tcp_time_write_timeout
25680	tcp_unique_address
28590	tcp_urg
23944	tcp_v4_hash
26371	tcp_v4_lookup
26287	tcp_v4_lookup_longway
26384	tcp_v4_proxy_lookup
23982	tcp_v4_rehash

(continued)

Table 9.2 Functions, listed by name *(continued)*.

Line	Function
23969	tcp_v4_unhash
23805	tcp_v4_verify_bind
27297	tcp_window_shrunk
31264	tcp_write_timeout
30777	tcp_write_wakeup
29710	tcp_write_xmit
25600	wait_for_connect
24479	wait_for_tcp_connect
24500	wait_for_tcp_memory

Table 9.3 Functions, listed by line number.

Line	Function
23805	tcp_v4_verify_bind
23846	tcp_lport_inuse
23870	tcp_good_socknum
23944	tcp_v4_hash
23969	tcp_v4_unhash
23982	tcp_v4_rehash
24022	tcp_find_established
24047	tcp_close_pending
24064	tcp_time_wait
24089	tcp_err
24199	tcp_readable
24290	tcp_listen_select
24317	tcp_select
24364	tcp_ioctl
24429	tcp_send_check
24464	tcp_build_header
24479	wait_for_tcp_connect
24492	tcp_memory_free
24500	wait_for_tcp_memory
24532	do_tcp_sendmsg
24881	tcp_sendmsg
24947	tcp_read_wakeup
24971	tcp_recv_urg
25040	tcp_eat_skb
25055	cleanup_rbuf

(continued)

Table 9.3   Functions, listed by line number *(continued)*.

Line	Function
25082	tcp_recvmsg
25353	tcp_close_state
25425	tcp_shutdown
25485	closing
25497	tcp_close
25600	wait_for_connect
25631	tcp_accept
25680	tcp_unique_address
25714	tcp_connect
25897	tcp_setsockopt
25937	tcp_getsockopt
26069	tcp_delack_estimator
26135	tcp_rtt_estimator
26231	tcp_clearance
26241	add_clearance
26287	tcp_v4_lookup_longway
26338	__tcp_v4_lookup
26371	tcp_v4_lookup
26384	tcp_v4_proxy_lookup
26434	bad_tcp_sequence
26491	tcp_sequence
26510	tcp_reset
26573	tcp_options
26644	tcp_conn_request
27057	tcp_conn_request_fake
27297	tcp_window_shrunk
27366	tcp_ack
28125	tcp_fin
28235	tcp_insert_skb
28264	tcp_queue_ack
28277	tcp_queue
28411	tcp_data
28540	tcp_check_urg
28590	tcp_urg
28631	tcp_remove_dups
28660	prune_queue
28685	tcp_chkaddr
28710	tcp_rcv

(continued)

Table 9.3   Functions, listed by line number *(continued)*.

Line	Function
29426	tcp_new_window
29474	clear_delayed_acks
29489	tcp_send_skb
29639	tcp_dequeue_partial
29659	tcp_send_partial
29673	tcp_enqueue_partial
29710	tcp_write_xmit
29839	tcp_do_retransmit
30197	tcp_send_reset
30283	tcp_send_synack_probe
30356	tcp_send_fin
30487	tcp_send_synack
30641	tcp_send_delayed_ack
30668	tcp_send_ack
30777	tcp_write_wakeup
30991	tcp_send_probe0
31021	tcp_shrink_skb
31108	tcp_delack_timer
31117	tcp_reset_xmit_timer
31171	tcp_retransmit_time
31238	tcp_retransmit
31264	tcp_write_timeout
31351	tcp_time_write_timeout
31376	tcp_retransmit_timer
31509	delete_timer
31522	reset_timer
31545	net_timer

tcp.c

The functions contained in the source module tcp.c implement features and capabilities that cannot readily be associated with input and output.

tcp_v4_verify_bind

This function, which starts at line 23805, takes the proposed port number **snum** and determines whether it is already in use. If it is, the function returns to the caller with the value 1 (TRUE). If the port number is free, the function returns to the caller with the value 0.

23811: Make sure no one changes the table while we're searching it.

23812: Use the inline function **tcp_bhashfn** (line 42280) to select one of the **TCP_BHTABLE_SIZE** (line 42266, defined as 64) TCP socket lists.

23813: Search until we either find a match or encounter a **NULL** forward pointer in the bind list. If we hit the end of the list, processing picks up at line 23841.

23814: If the source port numbers don't match, or we are looking at the socket passed to us, then process the next socket in the list.

23821: If the two sockets are bound to different devices, then reusing a port number is OK. Process the next socket in the list.

23824: If either socket is using the wildcard IP address for the source address, and if either socket does *not* have the **SO_REUSEADDR** bit set in the socket object or if the current state of the socket object being examined is **TCP_LISTEN**, then release the table lock and return 1 to the caller to indicate the port number is in use.

23831: If the two sockets have matching nonwildcard source addresses, and if either socket does *not* have the **SO_REUSEADDR** bit set in the socket object or if the current state of the socket object being examined is **TCP_LISTEN**, then release the table lock and return 1 to the caller to indicate the port number is in use.

23838: Continue the loop started in line 23813.

23841: Release the table lock and return the last saved status value saved in **retval**. When the list has been exhausted, the value returned to the caller is 0 to indicate the port number is available for use.

tcp_lport_inuse

This inline function (line 23846) determines if the TCP port number **num** is in use. It searches for a socket by having the inline function **tcp_bhashfn** calculate where in the array **tcp_bound_hash** the list of appropriate socket objects starts. It then scans the socket object list looking for a match. If one is found, the function returns 1 (TRUE) to the caller. If the end of the list is encountered, the function returns 0 (FALSE) to the caller.

tcp_good_socknum

This function (line 23870) selects a "good" ephemeral port to use for a TCP connection. The port is selected such that the lists pointed to by the array **tcp_bound_hash** are kept roughly equal in length; that is, no single list should be allowed to grow significantly longer than any other list by the operation of this function.

23872: The variables **start** and **binding_contour** are declared as **static** variables, which means that the starting port and probable shortest chain length will persist between calls.

23878: Lock out other people wanting to change the socket hash table. (This also indirectly protects the **start** and **binding_contour** variables by making this routine serial reusable.)

23879: Identify the start and end search points using the current value of **start**.

23883: Load a pointer to the head of the list of our candidate list.

23885: If the list is empty, return the port number larger than our start and hashes to this location, set the function to return this port number, and set the **binding_contour** variable to 0. Go to the label **done** on line 23935.

23898: Nonempty list. Count the number of socket elements at this point in the list, up to our current **size** value. If the current list is smaller than the one we found before, then set the variable **best** to remember this offset, and set **size** to the length of the (shorter) list.

23904: If the list size is lower than **bc** (originally taken from **binding_contour**), select this list and go to the label **verify** at line 23916. The intent of this code is to short-circuit having to search all the lists to find one that is "short enough."

23911: We have searched all 64 lists and found what we think is the best candidate. Remember the size of this list for next time.

23916: (Label **verify**)

23917: If the size of the list is smaller than the current value of **binding_contour**, remember the new size.

23920: Return a port number that hashes to our "best" list. Also, set the **best** value in case we have to go around again.

23924: Search for a port value that is not in use. If the code attempts to go above port 32767, then wrap to the port number above **PROT_SOCK** and continue the search. If the code searches all the port numbers (roughly 496 port numbers) without finding one open, set up to return port 0 (no port available). This makes sense, because the loop that started at line 23885 is designed to find the shortest list.

23935: (Label **done**)

23936: Save the new start point as one past the value we are returning. If the value is out of range (outside 1024 through 32767), then set the starting point for the port number to 1024 for next time. Unlock the table list and return the result saved in **retval**.

tcp_v4_hash

The **tcp_v4_hash** function (line 23944) takes a socket object and inserts it into the appropriate TCP hash list. First, it locks access to the hash tables so that no one else can change it. If the socket is in the **TCP_CLOSE** state and is marked dead, return without doing anything, not forgetting to release the access lock.

If the socket is in the **TCP_LISTEN** state, use the **tcp_sk_listen_hashfn** inline function (line 42321) to determine the appropriate hash list based on the contents of **tcp_listening_hash**. If the socket is not in the **TCP_LISTEN** state, use the **tcp_sk_hashfn** inline function (line 42336) to determine the appropriate hash list based on the contents of **tcp_established_hash**.

Add the socket to the head of the list. Then, call the **tcp_sk_bindify** inline function (line 42353) to add the socket to the hash list **tcp_bound_hash**.

Release the table lock and return to the caller.

tcp_v4_unhash

The **tcp_v4_unhash** function (line 23969) undoes the effect of the **tcp_v4_hash** function. It calls the inline function **tcp_sk_unbindify** (line 42364) to undo the effects of the call to the **tcp_sk_bindify** inline function.

tcp_v4_rehash

The **tcp_v4_rehash** function (line 23982) acts like a call to **tcp_v4_unhash** followed by a call to **tcp_v4_hash**. This function is called when a change in socket state would cause the socket to need to be moved from one hash list to another, or removed completely. The code in this function is identical to the code in the prior two functions.

tcp_find_established

The **tcp_find_established** function (line 24022) scans the receive queue of the passed socket object, looking for any socket buffer whose associated socket object is in the **TCP_ESTABLISHED** or **TCP_FIN_WAIT1** status. If one is found, return the pointer to the socket buffer. Otherwise, return **NULL** to indicate that no qualified socket buffer was found.

tcp_close_pending

The **tcp_close_pending** function (line 24047) will walk through the receive queue of the passed socket object. For each socket buffer in the list, the associated socket is closed, and the socket buffer's memory is released. This function is called by the **tcp_close** function for the special case in which a socket is being closed that was in the **TCP_LISTEN** state and there were requests that had not been accepted.

tcp_time_wait

The **tcp_time_wait** function (line 24064) sets the socket object into the **TCP_TIME_WAIT** state. The socket shutdown mask **shutdown** is set to indicate that both transmit and receive have been terminated. The **TIME_CLOSE** timer (line 42008, value 2) is set via a call to **tcp_reset_msl_timer** (line 42559), which converts via the macro to a call to **reset_timer** (line 31522).

tcp_err

The **tcp_err** function (line 24089) is called by the ICMP routines when an error notification regarding a TCP packet arrives. ICMP indicates just how serious the error is by whether or not the error code is negative.

24105: If there is insufficient information to ascertain the TCP port number, reject the message and return to the caller.

24108: Find the socket object associated with the IP address and TCP port addresses. Not found? Then, return to the caller.

24113: For Source Quench ICMP messages, do nothing and return to the caller.

24122: For Parameter Problem ICMP messages, save the error type in the socket object, and execute the callback routine to wake up any process waiting for error status on the socket object.

24129: If MTU path discovery isn't compiled into the kernel, and we get a fragmentation-required ICMP message, then perform a crude MTU size reduction.

24169: If the ICMP code is out of range, return to the caller now.

24171: If the ICMP code is considered fatal (based on the information in the structure **icmp_err_ convert** at line 9251), save the converted error message in the socket object (from **icmp_err_c onvert**). If the socket object is in either state

TCP_SYN_SENT or **TCP_SYN_RECV** (in an open-connection dialog), set the socket object state to **TCP_CLOSE** and wake up anyone waiting for error notifications on this socket.

24185: If the ICMP code is not considered fatal, save the converted error message in the soft-error variable in the socket object.

21487: Return to the caller.

tcp_readable

The **tcp_readable** function (line 24199) looks for the first "hole" in the data currently in the receive queue. The function returns the number of bytes waiting in the queue up to the hole. If there is no data, the function returns 0.

This code assumes that the socket buffers are placed into the socket object receive queue in sequence number order (modulo 2^{32}).

Any packet with the SYN flag set is considered to have 1 byte more than the amount of data in the packet; this has to do with the way TCP counts synchronize events. The occurrence of the SYN increment should affect the working sequence number, but not the amount of data returned by the function.

Duplicate packets and overlapping packets have to be handled as well. This is why the socket buffer sequence number can come "before" the working sequence number (line 24231).

Any packet with the URG flag set should not include the urgent byte in the amount available. (This code may be broken because it assumes the urgent pointer points to the end of the packet, and nothing in the TCP specifications or RFC 1122 precludes the urgent pointer from pointing elsewhere—even in a later segment.)

The comparison of the current working sequence number and the socket buffer's sequence number is performed modulo 2^{32} by the **before** inline function (line 42467). This is necessary for those occasions when the

sequence number wraps around from its maximum value through its minimum value.

When the receive queue has been processed, return the number of data bytes that can be processed to the caller. This return value is a nonnegative value.

tcp_listen_select

The **tcp_listen_select** function (line 24290) implements the **select** system call for those socket objects that are in the **TCP_LISTEN** state. This is called by **tcp_select**, described a little later.

This routine uses the inline function **select_wait** found in /usr/src/linux/include/linux/sched.h, which you can find on the CD-ROM.

If the type of select is not **SEL_IN**, return 0 (FALSE) to the caller immediately.

This routine uses the **tcp_find_establishment** function to see whether an active open is waiting for this socket. If so, this function returns 1 (TRUE) to the caller. If not, then the process is placed into sleep, and 0 (FALSE) is returned to the caller.

tcp_select

The **tcp_select** function (line 24317) implements the **select** system call for those socket objects that are not in the **TCP_LISTEN** state. In the commentary, the paragraphs will incorporate any actions taken after the **switch** statement in the processing.

24324: If the type of select (or poll) is not **SEL_IN**, go to line 24343.

24325: If there is an unprocessed error, return 1 (TRUE) to the caller to indicate to the application that there is something to do here.

24327: If the socket object is in either **TCP_SYN_SENT** or **TCP_SYN_RECV**—in the middle of a connection sequence—then call **select_wait** to queue the completion event and return 0 (FALSE) to the caller.

24331: If the socket object's shutdown state precludes receiving any more data, return 1 (TRUE) so that the application will process the end-of-file indication and remove this socket object's bit from the input-wait list.

24334: If TCP has ACKed all copied data, then there is nothing to read. Call **select_wait** to queue the completion event and return 0 (FALSE) to the caller.

24337: If urgent data is waiting, return 1 (TRUE) to the caller.

24341: Call **select_wait** to queue the completion event and return 0 (FALSE) to the caller.

24343: If the type of select (or poll) is not **SEL_OUT**, go to line 24355.

24344: If an error is waiting to be processed, return 1 (TRUE) to the caller so that the application can read and process the error.

24346: If the socket object's shutdown status precludes sending data, return 0 (FALSE) to the caller *without* calling **select_wait**.

24348: If the socket object is in either **TCP_SYN_SENT** or **TCP_SYN_RECV**—in the middle of a connection sequence—then call **select_wait** to queue the completion event and return 0 (FALSE) to the caller.

24351: If too much data is already queued up for transmission, call **select_wait** to queue the completion event and return 0 (FALSE) to the caller.

24353: Return 1 (TRUE) to the caller to indicate that the socket object can accept more data.

24355: If the type of select (or poll) is not **SEL_EX**, call **select_wait** to queue the completion event and return 0 (FALSE) to the caller. BUG: There should have been no call to **select_wait**.

24356: If urgent data is waiting, return 1 (TRUE) to the caller to signal to the caller.

24358: Call **select_wait** to queue the completion event and return 0 (FALSE) to the caller.

tcp_ioctl

The **tcp_ioctl** function (line 24364) implements the TCP implementation of certain operations requested via the **ioctl** system call. The operation codes allowed in the **ioctl** calls are **TIOCINQ** (input data waiting), **SIOCATMARK** (at urgent pointer), and **TIOCOUTQ** (output space available).

When the operation is **TIOCINQ**, the code uses the **tcp_readable** function (line 24199) to determine the number of bytes available for reading. After using **verify_area** to determine that the area passed by the caller is valid to receive data, the amount in bytes is returned to an integer buffer. Any error code (0 if no error) is returned to the caller.

When the operation is **TIOCOUTQ**, the code uses the **sock_wspace** function (line 22941) to determine the number of bytes available for writing. After using **verify_area** to determine that the area passed by the caller is valid to receive data, the amount in bytes is returned to an integer buffer. Any error code (0 if no error) is returned to the caller.

When the operation is **SIOCATMARK**, the value returned in the integer buffer is 0 if there is no urgent data or the next data byte to be read is not urgent data, and is 1 if the next data byte to be read is urgent data. After using **verify_area** to determine that the area passed by the caller is valid to receive data, the status value is returned to an integer buffer. Any error code (0 if no error) is returned to the caller.

When the operation is none of the preceding ones, the error code **EINVAL** is returned to the caller.

tcp_send_check

The **tcp_send_check** function (line 24429) calculates the TCP checkum. The inline function **tcp_check** (line 42626), which in turn uses the inline assembler function **csum_tcpudp_magic** (line 35627) and **csum_fold** (line 35610), does all the work to checksum the header.

The function **csum_partial** (in /usr/src/linux/arch/i386/lib/checksum.c, included on the CD-ROM) is the routine that handles the buffer itself. For other architectures, replace "i386" with the architecture-specific name.

The checksum algorithm is defined as the 1's complement of the 1's-complement sum of the TCP pseudo-header (defined as the IP source address, the IP destination address, the IP protocol field extended to 16 bits, and the length of the sum of the sizes of the TCP header and TCP payload), the TCP header, and the TCP payload.

RFC 1071, which is included on the CD-ROM, contains a wonderful explanation of how to calculate the checksum, along with various hints and techniques for speeding up the calculation, some of which are used in Linux. For the purposes of this discussion, though, the TCP algorithm can be expressed in the following pseudocode:

1. Zero the TCP header checksum field.

2. Using 32-bit arithmetic, accumulate the sum of the following: each 16-bit half of the source address; each 16-bit half of the destination address; the protocol number (6) expressed as a 16-bit value; the length of the TCP header; the length of the TCP payload; each 16-bit half of each TCP header word; each payload pair of bytes combined to form a 16-bit word; and, if the number of payload bytes is odd, the 16-bit word formed by multiplying the final byte by 256.

3. Take the top 16 bits of the accumulated sum and add it to the bottom 16 bits of the accumulator. This performs "end-around" carry of the 16-bit values. (This method implies a limit of 32,768 16-bit words that can be added together, because you can add 32,768 words of all-1-bit values without overflowing the accumulator.)

4. Take the 1's-complement of the result.

The following code fragment (borrowing liberally from RFC 1071) shows how the checksum algorithm could be implemented in pure C, if you assume that the entire area to be checksummed (including the pseudoheader) is in one block of memory:

```
unsigned general_checksum(unsigned count,
    unsigned char * buf)
{
  unsigned long sum = 0;
  if (!buf) {
    return 0;
  }
  while(count > 1)  {
    sum    += *((unsigned short *) buf);
    buf    += 2;
    count  -= 2;
  }
  if (count) {  /* if odd byte */
    unsigned short odd = 0;
    *((unsigned char *) odd) = *buf;
    sum += odd;  /* fixes byte order */
  }
  return ~((sum & 0xffff) + (sum >> 16));
}
```

The actual routines are written in GCC assembler instead of "plain C" to speed execution. These checksum routines are used so often that every microsecond saved means more performance out of the system. For example, using some of the tips from RFC 1071 and special features of the chip, the summation loop could be written for the 8086 family of chips using the REP instruction prefix so that the majority of the checksum is done in a single repeated instruction.

What Linux for the 8086 family does is use the 32-bit add with carry instructions to perform most of the operations. Instead of using loop control for the fixed portions of the headers, the loop is "unrolled" so that each addition is a separate instruction (lines 35364 through 35637).

In checksum.c for the Intel architecture, great pains are taken by the assembler code to use word-aligned fetches

and adds to keep the speed up. As long as it works, that's fine. The extra code at line 24335 and from line 24442 through 24455 is usually not included in production releases, but is there during debugging to be sure that the fast code works exactly the same as the slow-but-sure code.

tcp_build_header
The **tcp_build_header** function (line 24464) fills the header field with a template and then fills in the standard information for the header. The basic template is in the socket object in element **dummy_th**. The PSH flag is set based on the parameter passed by the caller. The sequence number and acknowledgment number come from the socket object, and represent the current values for these numbers.

The window advertisement is provided by the inline function **tcp_select_window** (line 42588). This references the inline function **tcp_old_window** (line 42566) and **tcp_new_window** (line 29426, described elsewhere). The use of **tcp_old_window** is to prevent the TCP code from shrinking the advertisement, which is a no-no, because the other end could have already filled the original advertisement.

This function returns the size of the TCP header.

wait_for_tcp_connect
The **wait_for_tcp_connect** function (line 24479) is used to block a process that is waiting for a connection on a socket object. The function will check whether the socket object is in a state other than **TCB_ESTABLISHED** or **TCB_CLOSE_WAIT**. If this is true and no error is pending, the process is put to sleep. Otherwise, control returns immediately without affecting the process.

tcp_memory_free
The **tcp_memory_free** function (line 24492) returns 0 (FALSE) if the socket object's buffer allocation exceeds the maximum allowed usage, or 1 (TRUE) if the socket object hasn't used up its quota of memory for socket buffers.

wait_for_tcp_memory
The **wait_for_tcp_memory** function (line 24500) causes a process to go to sleep until the socket object's usage of memory drops below the allocation limit.

24503: If **tcp_memory_free** says memory is available, return immediately. Otherwise, the socket has used too much memory, so reset the **SO_NO-SPACE** flag in the socket and add this process to the wait queue.

24508: This loop keeps processing from continuing in this process until conditions warrant it. The loop ends at 24520.

24509: If the process is not handling a signal or isn't blocked, escape from the loop and go to line 24520.

24511: Change the state of the process to **TASK_INTERRUPTABLE**.

24512: If memory is now available, the transmit side of the connection has been closed, or an error reported, then escape from the loop and go to line 24520.

24518: Select another process to run, because this one can't go any farther right now.

24520: The loop is ended. Set the state of the process to **TASK_RUNNING**, remove the process from the wait queue, and return to the caller.

do_tcp_sendmsg
The **do_tcp_sendmsg** function (line 24532), called only from **tcp_sendmsg**, handles the copying of data from a user buffer into the outgoing buffer associated with the socket object, and begins an output cycle.

24542: If the socket is in the **TCP_ESTABLISHED** or **TCP_CLOSE_WAIT** state (connection established, and not yet torn down), go to line 24569.

24545: If an unhandled error is present, return it to the caller via the **sock_error** inline function, defined at line 42200. The **sock_error** function uses the function **xchg** (in /usr/src/linux/include/asm-i386/system.h, included on the CD-ROM), which performs an atomic swap of the error code in the socket object with the constant value 0.

24548: If we aren't waiting for a TCP connection to become established on this socket, signal **SIGPIPE** and return **EPIPE** to the caller.

24556: If the socket is marked as nonblocking, return **EAGAIN** to the caller.

24559: If the process is running a signal processor and isn't blocked, return **ERESTARTSYS** to the caller. This will eventually turn into a signal for **SIGINT** and a status of **EINTR**, which signals the application to try again.

24562: Call **wait_for_tcp_connect** (line 24479) to wait for the TCP connection to be completed or aborted.

24569: Loop through the following code until the I/O vector **iov** has been processed. The loop ends at line 24874.

24575: Loop through the following until the segment has been processed. The loop ends at line 24873. If you are trying to queue enough data, the result of executing this loop multiple times is a series of packets that are the maximum segment size in length and queued for transmission, with a partial packet with an alarm set waiting in the wings.

24584: If we have an unprocessed error, return either the number of characters processed so far or, if 0, the error code, and then clear the error flag in the socket object.

24594: If we have shut down our transmitter, return the number of characters processed so far. If no characters have been processed during this call, raise the **SIGPIPE** condition and return **EPIPE** to the caller.

24627: If MTU path discovery wasn't compiled into the kernel, deal with the information at hand. If the MSS has shrunk, send the partial socket buffer and remember the shrunken MSS for next time.

24659: If we don't have a partially filled packet available (checked and dequeued via **tcp_dequeue_partial**, line 29639), go to line 24749. Otherwise, continue with the next paragraph.

24668: If the current **sendmsg** call has the **MSG_OOB** bit (really the urgent flag) set, go to line 24723.

24683: If the partial packet is now full, call **tcp_send_skb** (line 29489) to send it on its way, and continue with the loop by going to line 24575.

24708: Copy what additional data we can from user space into the buffer. Update all the accounting variables.

24723: If that makes for a full buffer, or if we have a request for the urgent pointer to be set, then call **tcp_send_skb** to send the packet on its way. Otherwise, call **tcp_enqueue_partial** (line 29673) to put the partial segment back on the socket object. In either case, continue with the loop by going to line 24575.

24749: Determine the size of the next segment, based on the **iov** element's length field, the maximum size of the segment, and the largest window advertisement seen from the other end. This is Silly Window Syndrome avoidance, from the transmitter side. Add in the size of the header.

24782: If the size of the next segment is less than the MSS and the urgent flag isn't to be set, consider building a partial segment and waiting for more data before sending the packet.

24786: Allocate a socket buffer. If we don't get one because of memory problems, indicate the problem in the socket object flags. If this socket is a nonblocking socket, return to the caller with **EAGAIN** status to tell the code to try again later.

If we are processing a signal and the process is not blocked, return to the caller with **ERESTARTSYS** status (which gets converted into an interrupt signal later). Otherwise, block waiting for memory and then restart the loop processing again at line 24575.

24814: Handle the bookkeeping for the new segment buffer. Build the IP header. If building the header failed, return to the caller. If any bytes were processed, return the count processed. Otherwise, return the error generated by the IP header build function.

24836: If MTU path discovery isn't compiled into the kernel, set the don't-fragment flag in the IP header offset field.

24838: Continue with the socket buffer bookkeeping.

24839: Allocate the space for the TCP header, and build the header using the **tcp_build_header** function (line 24464). If that function failed, return to the caller with the number of bytes processed; if the number of bytes processed is 0, return the error code returned by **tcp_build_header**.

24851: If the **MSG_OOB** flag is set, set the urgent pointer to the appropriate offset and turn on the URG flag in the TCP header.

24857: Set the checksum field of the TCP header. This uses the **csum_partial_copy_fromuser** function (line 35560), which combines the process of moving the data from user space and computing the checksum. This is recommended strongly by RFC 1025.

24860: Keep up that bookkeeping. If a delay was recommended at line 24782, call **tcp_enqueue_partial** to save the work so far, and continue with the loop. Otherwise, call **tcp_send_skb** to send the packet on its way, and continue with the loop.

24873: End of the **iov** element-processing loop.

24874: End of the **iov** list-processing loop.

24875: Wipe out any error that may have been sitting in the socket object, and return the number of bytes handled during the call. This is used by the application to figure out whether the entire buffer of data has been processed.

tcp_sendmsg

The **tcp_sendmsg** function (line 24881) is called from the system call **sendmsg**. It processes the data for the call and deals with the Nagle algorithm for grouping packets.

24891: If any call flags are set that shouldn't be, return to the caller with **EINVAL** status. (Try to be cute, you get your hand slapped.)

24893: If the IP address is passed in the **msg_name** element of the **msghdr** structure **msg**, save the pointer to the address. **msg_namelen** must be greater than or equal to the length of IP addresses, and the address family must be **AF_INET**; if either of these are not true, return to the caller with **EINVAL** status.

24903: If the state of the socket is **TCP_CLOSE**, return to the caller with **ENOTCONN** status.

24906: If the message name doesn't point to the same address and port as the socket object's binding, return to the caller with **EISCONN** status. Usually, a programmer writing to a TCP socket won't include the address, because the address is implied by the socket object.

24913: Process the data passed with the call by calling **do_tcp_sendmsg** (line 24532). Preserve the return value, which when nonnegative indicates the number of bytes handled by the call, and when negative indicates that no bytes were handled and there was an error condition.

24928: If we have a partial packet and there are no packets to send, send the partial packet by

calling **tcp_send_partial** (line 29659). If we have a partial packet, the Nagle algorithm has been disabled, and the packet fits in the window, then send the partial packet by calling **tcp_send_partial**.

24939: Return to the caller with the last developed return value, usually the number of bytes actually output.

tcp_read_wakeup

The **tcp_read_wakeup** function (line 24947) will send an ACK packet only if one is backlogged. If there is no ACK backlog, or if the connection is closed (**TCP_CLOSE** or **TCP_TIME_WAIT**), then don't do it. Otherwise, call **tcp_send_ack** (line 30668) to make it happen.

tcp_recv_urg

The **tcp_recv_urg** function (line 24971) deals with receiving urgent messages. It is called only from the **tcp_recvmsg** function, which may explain some of the strange comments and even stranger error returns. Indeed, the only time this function is called is when the application wants to pick up the urgent byte, which is why this code returns **EINVAL** if the urgent byte isn't the next byte ready to go.

24978: If urgent data is returned in line (as set by **setsockopt**), then no urgent data is waiting, or if the urgent data has already been read, then return to the caller with **EINVAL** status.

24982: If an error is pending on the socket object, return the error to the caller and clear the error indication.

24985: If the state of the socket object is **TCB_CLOSE** or if the socket **done** flag is set, then if the socket **done** flag is reset, then set it and return 0; otherwise, return **ENOTCONN** status.

24995: If receive has been shut down, set the socket **done** flag and return 0.

25001: If there is urgent data and the **URG_VALID** flag is set, return the urgent character to the user, set the urgent data indicator to show that the data has been read, and fill in the input address information if it was asked for. Then, return the value 1, because with urgent data, we return exactly one character to the caller.

25030: Return **EAGAIN** to the caller, because we never block the process on this condition.

tcp_eat_skb

The **tcp_eat_skb** function (line 25040) frees the socket buffer at the head of the socket's receive queue. That's all it does.

cleanup_rbuf

The **cleanup_rbuf** function (line 25055) walks through the receive buffer queue and releases any socket buffer that is marked "processed" and doesn't have any sockets using it.

tcp_recvmsg

The **tcp_recvmsg** function (line 25082) copies data from a socket buffer into user space. The convolutions stem from the code's need to check socket state and deal with the urgent feature.

25096: If the socket is in the **TCP_LISTEN** state, return **ENOTCONN** status.

25103: If the call includes the **MSG_OOB** flag, then the application should have gotten notification that an urgent byte is waiting, and this code calls **tcp_recv_urg** (line 24971) to get it. Propagate the return code back to the caller when returning to the caller.

25116: Determine whether *peek mode* is in effect. Peek mode is when an application takes a sneak preview of the data without actually removing it from the input buffers.

25121: Assume we are going to have to wait for data, so queue a wait now and avoid the winter-solstice rush.

25123: Loop while we have any dataspace left in the user's buffer. This loop ends at line 25318. (Nothing like huge multipage loops, is there?)

25133: If we have returned any data, and we have encountered the urgent byte (assuming there is one), then stop at this point.

25142: If we are in a signal handler and the process is not blocked, return the count of data read. If no data has been read, return **ERESTARTSYS** for blocking sockets and return **EAGAIN** for nonblocking sockets.

25157: Get the socket buffer at the forefront of the receive queue. Stop when we exhaust the receive queue. (The loop stops at line 25173.)

25161: If there is a hole in the input data, break out of this loop—we've done what we can.

25163: Calculate the offset of the first byte of the data based on the last sequence number. If the SYN flag is set, adjust the offset accordingly. If the offset is within the buffer, go to the label **found_ok_skb** at line 25215. If the FIN flag is set in the TCP header, go to the label **found_fin_skb** at line 25305. If we are not in peek mode, then mark the buffer as used, so that it will be cleaned up later.

25172: Check the next socket buffer.

25173: (End of the socket buffer loop)

25175: If we actually copied data to the user buffer, break from the loop (go to line 25318). If an error is pending and we aren't in peek mode, return the error to the caller and clear the error in the socket object.

25184: If the socket object is closed and the **done** flag is not set in the socket object, then set it and break from the loop (to line 25318). If the **done** flag was set, save the status **ENOTCONN** and break from the loop (to line 25318).

25193: If the receive side has been shut down, set the **done** flag and break from the loop (to line 25318).

25201: If the socket is a nonblocking one, save the status **EAGAIN** and break from the loop (to line 25318).

25207: Clean up any socket buffers we have processed, set the socket flags to indicate the process wait is for data, and wait for data to become available. When we get control again, undo the flag and go back through the loop.

25215: Label **found_ok_skb**. Increment the user count for the socket buffer. Calculate how much of the socket buffer we can use. If there is more data in the socket buffer than in the user's buffer, let's use the user buffer length.

25236: If we have urgent data, adjust the amount we can use by the amount available before the urgent data.

25262: Update the sequence number first, so that if we have two readers, they don't both get the data. Then, call **memcpy_toiovec** (line 11247) to move the data to user space. Finish the bookkeeping.

25287: If we have copied the urgent data, remove the fact that we have urgent data pending.

25289: If we haven't consumed the entire socket buffer, go around the loop again (line 25123).

25296: If the FIN flag in the TCP header is set, "receive" it by going to the label **found_fin_ok** at line 25305.

25298: Are we in peek mode? If so, continue the loop (line 25123).

25300: Mark the socket buffer used. If the use count for the socket buffer is 0, then eat it. Then, continue the loop (line 25123).

25305: Label **found_fin_ok**. Increment the sequence number (for the FIN) and exit the loop (line 25318) if we are in peek mode. Otherwise, mark the socket buffer as used and indicate that receive is shut down, and then break (line 25318).

25320: If we returned anything to the customer, and they provided a place to put a received address, then return the address information.

25331: Remove the task wait, make one more pass to release buffers, and return any error code or count of bytes returned to the user.

tcp_close_state

The **tcp_close_state** function (line 25353) sets the state of the TCP socket to the new proper state and determines whether a FIN packet needs to be transmitted. The following are the states and the new states and actions:

- *TCP_SYN_SENT*—New state **TCP_CLOSE**

- *TCP_SYN_RECV*—Send FIN, new state **TCP_FIN_WAIT1**

- *TCP_ESTABLISHED*—Send FIN, new state **TCP_FIN_WAIT1**

- *TCP_FIN_WAIT1*—No change

- *TCP_FIN_WAIT2*—No change

- *TCP_CLOSING*—No change

- *TCP_CLOSE*—No change

- *TCP_LISTEN*—New state **TCP_CLOSE**

- *TCP_LAST_ACK*—No change

- *TCP_CLOSE_WAIT*—Send FIN, new state **TCP_LAST_ACK**

Set the new TCP state, as indicated in the preceding list.

If the socket has been marked "dead" and the new state is **TCP_FIN_WAIT2**, then set the **TIME_CLOSE** timer (using the function **tcp_reset_msl_timer**, line 42559, which refers to **reset_timer** at line 31522).

Return with 0 if no FIN packet should be sent, or with 1 if a FIN packet should be sent.

tcp_shutdown

The **tcp_shutdown** function (line 25425) shuts down the transmit side of the connection. This is done based on the application calling the **shutdown** system function. If the parameter provided with the **shutdown** system function doesn't include the **SEND_SHUTDOWN** bit, or if we aren't in a proper state to accept the shutdown request, then return to the caller without doing anything.

Definitely send off any partial packet that has been built so far, and then call **tcp_close_state** to determine whether we should send the FIN packet and modify the socket's current TCP state. Return to the caller with the knowledge that the job was well-done.

closing

The **closing** function (line 25485) returns 1 (TRUE) if the TCP socket is in the **TCP_FIN_WAIT1**, **TCP_CLOSING**, or **TCP_LAST_ACK** state. Otherwise, return 0 (FALSE) to the caller.

tcp_close

The **tcp_close** function (line 25497) is the TCP implementation of the **close** system command, and handles the details of initiating a close of the connection. This function will block the current process until the close is complete, but will not wait for the 2MSL time to pass.

25510: If the socket is in the **TCP_LISTEN** state, handle the situation differently. Set the state to **TCP_CLOSE**, call **tcp_close_pending** (line 24047) to rid ourselves of any pending socket buffers (such as those asking for connection requests), indicate the socket is now dead, and remove the socket from the connection list so that incoming packets asking for a connection to the socket won't find it. Return to the caller.

25522: Indicate that both transmit and receive have been shut down.

25535: When an application makes a call to **close**, it implies that any data waiting should be discarded completely. This code discards any data in the receive queue without any further ado. We also get rid of any unsent packet fragments.

25551: Set the socket TCP state to the dead state (which is what the constant value 1 is). If this triggers a request for a FIN packet, call the **tcp_send_fin** function (line 30356) to make it so.

25556: For the caller-specified timeout period, wait for the socket to become closed, but don't wait for the 2MSL period.

25577: If the TCP socket is in the **TCP_FIN_WAIT2** state, set up the **TIME_CLOSE** timer using the **reset_timer** function (line 31522).

25587: Cleanup time. Mark the socket dead (it should be by now). If the socket is now really closed, remove it from the hash lists.

25592: Return to the caller.

wait_for_connect

The **wait_for_connect** function (line 25600) waits for an incoming connection request. When a packet arrives, the inner loop wakes up, and the code checks for a socket buffer. If there is one, return it to the caller. Otherwise, the code goes back to sleep.

tcp_accept

The **tcp_accept** function (line 25631) handles calls to the **accept** system call. Unfortunately, the coder got cute and used **goto** instructions instead of using proper structures. This isn't as bad as some of the spaghetti code that's in the TCP/IP stack, however.

25644: If the socket isn't in the **TCP_LISTEN** state, go to the label **no_listen**.

25649: If there is a connection to accept...

25651: (label **got_new_connection**)...unlink the connection record from the queue, create a new socket, decrease the backlog count, and clear the error value to 0.

25657: (label **out**)...and return the pointer to the new socket object for the fresh connection.

25660: (label **no_listen**) propagate any local error to the socket object, and return the new socket object, or **NULL** if there was no new socket object.

25665: If there is no new connection, and the socket object is marked as a nonblocking socket, then set the error **EAGAIN** in the socket object and return **NULL**.

25668: Wait for a connection to arrive. If one arrives, go to label **got_new_connect**.

25671: Set the status **ERESTARTSYS** into the socket object and return **NULL**.

tcp_unique_address

The **tcp_unique_address** function (line 25680) searches to see whether the socket identification is already in use. This compares the source IP address, destination IP address, source port number, and destination port number with every socket object associated with TCP. To speed the process, a hash function limits the search to one of 256 lists of sockets, as indicated by the inline function **tcb_hashfn** (line 42343).

The function returns 0 (FALSE) if the function is not unique. The function returns 1 (TRUE) if no socket contains these four addresses.

tcp_connect

The **tcp_connect** function (line 25714) initiates an outgoing connection. This is invoked as part of the processing of the **connect** system call.

25725: If the socket is not completely closed, return **EISCONN** to the caller.

25732: If a connection attempt has already been started on this socket, return **EINVAL** to the caller.

25735: If a net family is specified and it isn't **AF_INET**, return **EAFNOSUPPORT**.

25745: Handle the case where we are trying to connect to ourselves.

25753: If the address requested is a multicast or broadcast address, it's not allowed and must be stopped. Return **ENETUNREACH** to the caller.

25757: If the address requested is already in use, return **EADDNOTAVAIL**.

25762: Handle bookkeeping details. Save the destination address in the socket object, set the expected ACK number, and save the destination port.

25768: Allocate a socket buffer (note the use of the variable **buff** instead of the more common **skb** for the socket buffer pointer), but return **ENOMEM** if you can't get it.

25774: Handle bookkeeping. In the socket buffer, set the socket object address, the local route, and the device. Build an IP header in the socket object; if an error occurs while doing that, return **ENETUNREACH** to the caller (instead of the error status generated by **ip_build_header**) as the failure reason.

25803: Set the write sequence number based on the return from **secure_tcp_sequence_number** (/usr/src/linux/drivers/char/random.c, included on the CD-ROM), which generates a random number for the file starting point. The reason this needs to be as random as practical is to prevent certain *hijack attacks*, attacks that depend on being able to predict the starting sequence number, from succeeding. The number is calculated based on the source and destination addresses, plus "environmental noise from device drivers, &c." that "must be hard for outside attackers to observe."

25807: Set the original window advertisement to 0. Set the ACK number to the current write sequence number minus one. Allocate and set the pointer to the TCP header in the socket buffer, and copy the TCP header template from the socket object to the TCP header.

25814: Set the socket buffer sequence number to the write sequence number, and increment the sequence number (to account for the SYN flag to be set later). Set the sequence number in the TCP header.

25818: In the TCP header, the ACK number is set to 0, the window is set to 2, the SYN flag is set, and the header length (**doff**) is set to 6 because we put the MSS option in the table.

25824: If the routing entry is present and a window is defined for the route, use that window value as our initial value for **window_clamp**; otherwise, zero it. The only place this is referenced is in the **tcp_new_window** function at line 29426.

25829: Set the socket object MSS from the user-specified MSS, the route's MSS, or the default value of 576 minus the size of the headers. If the resulting MSS is larger than the device's MTU, cut the MSS back to fit. If the result is a segment size less than 32 bytes, stick 32 in there.

25859: Allocate space for the options word, and place the MSS into the TCP header. The "ready" (first SYN) packet is ready to go. Oh, don't forget to calculate the checksum and place the checksum in the TCP header first.

25868: Change the state of the socket to **TCP_SYN_SENT** (even though we haven't sent it yet). Because our socket has completely changed addresses, remove the socket from the hash list and do it again so that the hash lists reflect the new addresses.

25875: Initialize the route timeout to either the value from the routing table or the default value **TCP_TIMEOUT_INIT** (line 42428, about 3 seconds).

25879: More housekeeping. Set the timer fields in the socket object, zero the retransmit count, wave bye-bye to the nice ACK packet, reset the

transmission timer (via **tcp_reset_xmit_timer**, line 31117), keep the SNMP statistics, and return 0 to the caller.

tcp_setsockopt

The **tcp_setsockopt** function (line 25897) implements the TCP portion of the **setsockopt** system call. The options are handled in the same way for each TCP option—the value is read from user space and placed in the socket object in its appropriate place.

The code first checks to see whether the target of the call is **SOL_TCP**; if it is not, it passes the call to **ip_setsockopt** to process. Further, if the option value pointer is **NULL**, control returns to the caller with the status value **EINVAL**. Finally, if the memory area is not readable, the appropriate error status is propagated back to the caller.

The options are **TCP_MAXSEG** (set the socket object element **user_mss** to the user-specified MSS between 1 and 32767) and **TCP_NODELAY** (set the socket object element **nonagle** to 0 to turn on the Nagle algorithm, or to 1 to turn off the Nagle algorithm). Any other option causes the code to return the error status **ENOPROTOPT**. The successful completion of this function is signaled by 0 being returned to the caller.

tcp_getsockopt

The **tcp_getsockopt** function (line 25937) permits the application to read the values set by the **tcp_setsockopt**. If the target of the call is not **SOL_TCP**, the call is passed to **ip_getsockopt**. Otherwise, the appropriate value is picked up and stored, after the storage location is verified, in the user's memory space. The successful completion of this function is signaled by a return of 0 to the caller.

tcp_delack_estimator

The **tcp_delack_estimator** (line 26069) function is an inline function that calculates the timeout for a delayed ACK, so we can reduce the number of bare ACK packets we transmit. The estimation is based on the perceived realtime delay of the signal, so a fast link doesn't run out of window too quickly.

Here's a Rosetta stone: **rtt** is round-trip time, **rto** is retransmission timeout, and **ato** is acknowledgment timeout.

If we don't have a last-receive time yet, set one. Set the working acknowledgment timeout to 1/3 second and then return.

If we have a last-receive time, calculate the difference in jiffies between now and the last-receive time. If the time is 0, use 1. If our working time is greater than the retransmission timeout time, use the retransmission timeout time. Otherwise, use the prior acknowledgment timeout divided by two plus our new interval—this provides some adaptation in a small number of cycles, although it could fluctuate a bit more than a servoengineer might like. Return.

tcp_rtt_estimator

The inline function **tcp_rtt_estimator** (line 26135) estimates the round-trip time based on when a segment was sent and when its corresponding ACK was received. What complicates the calculation of the time based on TCP traffic is that an ACK may cover multiple transmitted segments, so the calculation needs to be made with the last segment transmitted.

26147: Calculate the difference in time between now and the time the socket buffer was transmitted.

26149: If we have a previous measurement of round-trip time, then ensure that our measurement is a nonnegative value, subtract the previously calculated round-trip time divided by eight, and add the difference to the round-trip time. This operation causes the new measurement to be weighted at one-eighth of the total.

26156: If we have a previous measurement of round-trip time, then take the previously calculated mean deviation, subtract one-fourth of that from the absolute value of the adjustment used in the prior calculation, and add it in. This causes the new mean deviation to be weighted one-fourth of the total.

26164: If there is no prior measurement, take the measurement and store one-eighth of the value in the round-trip time, and store one-half of the time as the mean deviation.

The remainder of the function takes the preceding metrics calculated above plus the algorithms in RFC 793 and calculates the retransmit timeout.

tcp_clearance

The **tcp_clearance** function (line 26231) is included only if RESET COOKIES support is compiled into the kernel. This function will see whether a source address is in the clearance list. If one is, the code returns 1 (TRUE); if one isn't, the code returns 0 (FALSE).

This is part of the SYN flood prevention for Linux.

add_clearance

The **add_clearance** function (line 26241) is included only if RESET COOKIES support is compiled into the kernel. This function will add a source address and timestamp to the clearance table. If the entry to be filled hasn't expired yet, the function doesn't file anything and fails to perform quietly. "Expire" is currently set for 300 seconds (5 minutes).

tcp_v4_lookup_longway

The **tcp_v4_lookup_longway** function (line 26287) searches for the socket object in the **TCP_LISTEN** state that matches a destination address, destination port (**hnum**), and device. This search uses "fuzzy" logic, so a partial match that doesn't involve a mismatch selects the socket object, but a perfect match stops the search and returns the socket-object pointer immediately.

For a socket to be considered, the port number must match, or the socket object is rejected immediately.

From there, the destination address is checked with any socket-object source address that may have been specified. If a target address was not wildcarded, and the destination address does not match, the socket object is discarded as a candidate. If it does match, the score is incremented. (If the socket-object source address was wildcarded, then no increment of the score takes place.)

If the socket was bound to a device, and the device passed down doesn't match, then the socket object is rejected immediately as a candidate. If the socket object was bound to the same device, the score is incremented. If the socket object was not bound to a device, the score is not incremented.

If the new score value is higher than the previously found score, save the pointer to the socket object that scored better. If the score is perfect, just return the pointer to the socket object now—further searching is useless.

After all the socket objects have been searched, return the address of the socket object that is the best match. If no suitable socket object was found, return **NULL**.

__tcp_v4_lookup

The **__tcp_v4_lookup** inline function (line 26338) looks for a socket object in the established state with the same source address, source port, destination address, and destination port. It also checks to see whether the packet came in from the device the socket object is bound to, if any.

If the function fails to find the right socket object on the established list, it searches the listening list by calling **tcp_v4_lookup_longway**.

The result is that the address of the socket object is returned; if no socket object was found, **NULL** is returned.

tcp_v4_lookup

The **tcp_v4_lookup** function (line 26371) is a wrapper function for the **__tcp_v4_lookup** function, specifying the wildcard address for the source.

tcp_v4_proxy_lookup

When the transparent proxy option is compiled, the **tcp_v4_proxy_lookup** function (line 26384) searches for a socket object in the established list that matches, a la **__tcp_v4_lookup**. Failing that, it looks for a socket object listening on the address by calling **tcp_v4_lookup_longway**. Failing that, it looks for a socket object listening on the redirect port by calling **tcp_v4_lookup_longway**, using the redirect port address. Failing that, it returns **NULL**.

bad_tcp_sequence

The **bad_tcp_sequence** function (line 26434) is called in reaction to a "bad" sequence number. How it reacts depends on the packet that caused this function to be invoked.

26438: Did the socket buffer's TCP header have the RST flag set? If so, ignore the problem and return to the caller, because RST packets don't have sequence numbers.

26451: Is the socket object waiting to complete the handshake? If so, send back an RST so that the other end tries to restart the handshake, and then return to the caller.

26481: If we aren't in **TCP_TIME_WAIT** or if the ending sequence number isn't in sync, send an ACK packet and return to the caller.

tcp_sequence

The inline function **tcp_sequence** (line 26491) looks to see whether the sequence number in the received packet sits within the currently advertised window.

If the packet buffer contains no data and has a sequence number equal to the end of the window, or if the starting sequence number lies within the window and the ending sequence number lies in the unACKed portion of the window, then return TRUE. Otherwise, return FALSE.

tcp_reset

The **tcp_reset** function (line 26510) is the reaction to receiving an RST flag from the other end.

26513: Set the **zapped** field in the socket object. (This is the only place this field is set, so "reset_seen" as a symbol name would have been more suitable, we think, if not as snappy.)

26518: Select the error code that should be sent to the application based on the current TCP state. For **TCP_TIME_WAIT**, no error code is required. For **TCP_SYN_SENT**, use **ECONNREFUSED**,

because an RST is the standard way to reject a connection attempt. For **TCP_CLOSE_WAIT**, use **EPIPE** (the pipe is busted, so this makes sense). For all other states, use **ECONNRESET**. In all cases, the error code goes into the socket object's error field.

26530: If RFC 1337 is implemented, don't let the RST flag abort the 2MSL wait time for those sockets sitting in the **TCP_TIME_WAIT** state. If RFC 1337 is not implemented (the usual case), change the state to **TCP_CLOSE**, shut down both directions of the connection, and perform appropriate cleanup of any hanging socket buffers.

26552: Free the socket buffer from memory, and return 0 to the caller.

tcp_options

The **tcp_options** function (line 26573) examines and acts on received TCP options. This code only acts on the MSS option. The comments indicate that in the future, the PAWS feature and the large-windows feature need to be added to this module.

26582: This loop processes all options. For those options that aren't processed by this code, the length field indicates to the loop control how to bypass the data in the options field. The loop ends at line 26618.

26588: For the list-end code, go to the label **ende** (line 26619, beyond the end of the loop).

26592: For the nop code, adjust the pointer so that only 1 byte is skipped, and continue with the loop (line 26582).

26598: Abort the scan if the length field is shorter than 2 bytes—this is the indication of a broken remote TCP implementation.

26604: For the MSS specification, select the minimum of the specified MSS from the remote end and

the MSS we calculated before. Set the result in the socket object as the MTU. Flag that we saw the MSS option.

26615: After processing (or not processing) the option, point past it and continue scanning.

26618: (end of loop)

26619: (label **ende**) If the SYN flag is set in the TCP header, and the MSS option was not seen, then use for the MTU the default MSS of 576 or the device's MTU minus headers, whichever is smaller.

26625: If PC TCP compatibility was configured into the kernel, select the MSS as one-half the size of the maximum window or the MTU, whichever is smaller. If PC compatibility was not configured, select the MSS as the smaller of the maximum window size or the MTU.

26631: Return to the caller.

tcp_conn_request

The **tcp_conn_request** function (line 26644) handles a connection request ("ready" or SYN packet) from the remote.

26660: If the socket has been marked dead, send a reset packet, free the socket buffer, and return to the caller. This tells the remote end that the connection request has been refused.

26662: Call the protocol data-ready function. For IP, this function is **def_callback2**, defined at line 5423. This function calls the **wake_up_interruptible** function (line 33582), followed by the **sock_wake_async** function (line 33809), both calls specify the socket passed in the call.

26691: If the current backlog of connect requests is less than the maximum backlog set in the socket object (currently **SOMAXCONN**, line 39414, value 128), head to line 26775.

Much of the following code has a number of conditional compilation tags around it, because the concept of SYN cookies and RST cookies is an option in Linux 2.0.34—an option that we authors think is a good thing to enable, given the current flood (if you'll pardon the pun) of script-kiddies and pranksters who view any vulnerable system as a target of opportunity. Therefore, we will assume that both SYN cookie support and RST cookie support have been requested.

26734: SYN/ACK flood may be in progress. If we have seen successful connections from this host before (this includes good responses to prior cookies), go to line 26763. Otherwise, print a warning message to the system log, send a probe (using **tcp_send_synack_probe**, line 30283), remember we had sent a cookie, release the socket buffer (we are discarding it), and return to the caller.

26763: If we have reset cookies compiled in, and the backlog is more than twice the limit, dump the packet and return to the caller. The idea here is that if we don't respond to the connection request with anything, the other end will time out its request and try again—perhaps by then the attacker will be stopped and legitimate connections will get through, or the attacker will grow tired of his play and quit.

26771: If we don't have either SYN cookie or RST cookie support compiled in, and the backlog is too big, drop the packets without doing anything else. This gives the system time to bring down the backlog if it can.

26788: Build a new socket. If we can't get the memory, ignore the SYN packet, because the requestor will just try again shortly, and by then we should have memory. If we do get memory, make the new socket a copy of the listening socket. Cloning the socket involves lots of bookkeeping, so get on with it. All the queues are set to initial

values by calls to **skb_queue_head_init** (line 21673), which sets up an empty queue with the proper "magic cookie" so that code that cares to check can see that it is a socket buffer queue list.

26808: The options portion of the socket deserves special attention. First, the options buffer has to be allocated. If it can't be, then we have memory problems again, so undo everything we've done and ignore the packet. Then, we call **ip_options_echo** (line 15477) to take the IP options (*not* the TCP options) from the SYN packet and place them in the socket object.

26884: The timers portion also deserves special attention. All the timers included in a socket are initialized using **init_timer** (/usr/src/linux/include/linux/timer.c, on the CD-ROM), and the data portion of each time is set to point to the socket. The callback functions for the sockets are set here as well: **net_timer** (line 31545) for the element **timer**, **tcp_delack_timer** (line 31108) for the element **delack_timer**, and **tcp_retransmit_timer** (line 31376) for the element **retransmit_timer**.

26905: Just in case this is a redirected transfer, save the destination port in the socket element **num**.

26912: Continue the bookkeeping. The source and destination addresses are reversed because the original packet has them from the remote's perspective, whereas the socket object needs them from our perspective. We also save the address used to open the socket, in case we end up using another device interface.

26924: If we either don't need to send a cookie or don't have cookie support compiled into the kernel, then add this socket to the hash list (so we can find it quickly) and also add it to the protocol socket list.

26936: Continue with the bookkeeping. Use the time to live and terms of service from the original socket for the new one.

26951: Determine the appropriate route for the new socket and save it in the socket object. Set the window clamp to the window associated with the route, or 0 if there is no route.

26961: Calculate the appropriate MSS, either from the user-specified size on the listen socket or based on the path MTU from the routing table. When all else fails, use an MSS based on an MTU of 576. In any case, the MSS can't exceed the MTU for the device. At the end, though, the floor for MSS is 32 bytes.

27004: If the SKIP device support is loaded, let that module set the MTU to use. This is a configurable option.

27011: Set the final MSS in the options packet.

27014: If cookie support was compiled into the kernel, and a cookie is needed, pick an MTU that can be supported by the 3-bit field in the cookies (see line 28268 for the values) and ship the cookie via the function **secure_tcp_syn_cookie** (line 27027).

27041: Send the "set," or SYN/ACK packet, with or without cookie to taste. Return to the caller.

tcp_conn_request_fake

The **tcp_conn_request_fake** function (line 27057) is included only when cookie support is compiled into the kernel. This permits the receipt of a SYN cookie to begin a connection. This is part of the SYN flood prevention code in Linux.

The code is virtually identical to **tcp_conn_request**, so in this section, the commentary concentrates on those few areas where **tcp_conn_request_fake** differs significantly. The first difference is that, because this routine is invoked in response to receiving a SYN cookie, there is no security issue.

The second and more significant difference revolves around what to do on a memory-resource exhaustion condition—and that's a problem. Running out of memory means that the connection essentially dies, and dies horribly, because without memory, there is no recourse. The other end may (or may not) resend the cookie to continue the connection attempt. If there has been screaming about this problem, the screams have been quiet.

tcp_window_shrunk

The **tcp_window_shrunk** function (line 27297) handles a condition that is *never* supposed to happen—the window advertisement changes so that the "right" edge of the window moves to the *left*. Visualize data placed with earlier data to the left, later data to the right, and available space to the far right. Now, think about how the edges of the areas continually move to the right as data is transferred. When the end of open space moves to the left instead of to the right, and not because of sequence number wrap, that is considered a shrinkage of the window.

Linux doesn't do this (at least the authors have not seen how Linux can do this), but other implementations can (and do) shrink windows even though they are not supposed to.

This emphasizes one of the rules of the Internet: When transmitting, stick as close to the rules as you can, but when receiving, permit a wide latitude in your reaction to the incoming data. This function is one of those "wide latitude" things.

The recovery in Linux is to move segments from the send queue (stuff that can be transmitted or has been transmitted) back to the write queue (stuff that could be transmitted if the window were large enough to accept it). This is a straightforward operation.

One thing that isn't straightforward is the need to unlink the socket buffers from the device transmission queues as well. The code at line 27326 takes care of this problem. The reason for this is that if we send data that

falls to the right of the window advertisement, at best, we have wasted bandwidth, and, at worse, we could be hit with an RST packet that kills the connection. (Yes, we know it's the other end's fault, but you live with what you have.)

tcp_ack

The humor in the **tcp_ack** function (line 27366) is rather interesting. "This routine is totally *WRONG* [emphasis in original]. The list structure is wrong. The algorithm is wrong. The code is wrong."

Seems to work, though. This is one case in which we will ignore the comments for the most part and instead look at what the code *does*.

It *is* big—759 lines. It's big because the ACK packet is one of the nexus points for the protocol. (The other nexus point is the transmit timeout.) From the ACK packet, so many different things can happen that it takes a lot of code to make it happen. An ACK packet can do the following:

- Confirm that data previously transmitted has been successfully received.

- Declare that data previously transmitted has been lost, by repeating that data reception made it *this* far and no farther. It's akin to being hit over the head with a two-by-four enough times that you get the idea you need to pay attention to something. After all, there is no NAK in TCP, and with packet reordering, there is no place for a NAK, either. This is how TCP differs from virtually every point-to-point protocol on the planet.

- Confirm that the connection is still alive.

- Confirm that the receive window is still closed, by rejecting the 1-byte probe this end sent a little while ago.

- Confirm that the receive window has opened and the original notice was lost in the shuffle.

So, because the function's source is big, let's wade right into it.

27382: If the socket has been reset (zapped), then return 1 to the caller.

27392: If the transmit timeout state **ip_xmit_timeout** is **TIME_KEEPOPEN**, then we are in keep-alive timeout mode. Make sure that we kill the retransmit flag in the socket object.

27401: If the ACK is out-of-bounds (to the left of the first sent packet or to the right of the window), go to label **uninteresting_ack** (line 28075).

27408: Handle window advertisements in which the window grows. Change the maximum segment size to fit the new window.

27426: If our window has shrunk, call **tcp_window_shrunk** (line 27297).

27432: Handle bookkeeping if we have exhausted our send queue. (This appears to be a piece of cruft held over from a hasty patch for a bug. The dequeue routines should have handled this detail properly.)

27444: Implement slow-start. The first part checks to see whether we are in a write-data mode, the congestion window is below 2,048 segments, and the ACK packet specifies a sequence number after our last transmitted packet.

When we are comfortably below the threshold of congestion, TCP increments its transmission congestion window by 1 for each ACK that is received in a timely manner. As the algorithm collects further information and we approach the capacity of the channel, the congestion window is incremented once for each n ACK packets, n defined as the current congestion window. At some point, the number of segments outstanding will match the channel capacity, at which point the congestion window will not grow further.

27517: Look for duplicate ACK packets that might signal a lost packet. The comments starting at line

27499 detail the conditions to look for. If we see three ACK packets in a row that meet the following five conditions, we have a candidate for a fast-recovery retransmission:

- They have the same acknowledgment number
- They have the same window advertisement
- The ACK packets are not carrying data
- The last-sent sequence number comes after the acknowledgment sequence number
- Data is waiting to be ACKed

27540: If our congestion window is greater than or equal to 3 (so we can have three outstanding segments) and there are more than **MAX_DUP_ACK** packets (line 42391, value 3), then increment the dry-ACK count.

27547: If the number of dry-ACK packets exceeds **MAX_DUP_ACK**, then we need to restart the transmission of packets that have been sent but not acknowledged. We do this by calling **tcp_do_retransmit** (line 29839), but specifying (via the 0 in the second argument) that only one packet is to be sent.

27566: If the number of dry-ACK packets doesn't exceed **MAX_DUP_ACK**, then transmit one new packet.

27581: If we don't have a duplicate ACK packet, deal with any old retransmit issues that may be outstanding, and then do the bookkeeping on the sequence numbers and ACK count.

27599: Remove any pending soft error—the ACK says that something happened right.

27609: If we were in a 0-window probe mode, then the probe was answered and we need to clear the retransmit flag. If a usable window was provided as well as a result of the probe, clear the backoff

flag, which was being used to time the probes, and then recalculate the retry timeout based on the latest ACK packet. Again, the comments contain all the details.

27685: This loop transmits anything sitting on the retransmission queue. It ends at line 27798.

27704: If the socket buffer's sequence number is before the ACK packet's acknowledgment number, we can discard the packet as sent. (In other words, clean up the trash.)

27752: Keep track of the number of packets we have emitted to the world.

27768: If we are not in a retransmitting mode, call **tcp_rtt_estimator** (line 26135) to estimate the round-trip time for this packet.

27776: Remove the socket buffer from the send list. If necessary, also remove it from the device transmit queue.

27798: Cycle the loop until the retransmission queue is empty.

27815: Here's an interesting condition: We have information on the write queue that has been transmitted before. This happens when a 0-window probe uses 1 byte of data to check whether the window is really closed. If this is the case, call **tcp_write_xmit** (line 29710) to send the complete segment. Don't worry about resending the 1 byte, because the remote TCP is supposed to be able to handle overlapping data.

27853: Depending on the existing TCP state, we manipulate timers in different ways.

27854: In the **TCP_TIME_WAIT** state, call **reset_timer** (line 31522) to set the **TIME_CLOSE** timer (line 42008, value 2) to **TCP_TIMEWAIT_LEN** (line 42414, value 60 seconds).

27863: In the **TCP_CLOSE** state, do nothing.

27874: In any other state, if we have data waiting to be sent, set the **TIME_WRITE** timer to the calculated retry timeout value.

27876: In any other state, with no data waiting to be sent, set the **TIME_PROBE0** timer to the calculated retry timeout value, to schedule a probe if we don't receive a window advertisement before the timeout.

27918: When none of the preceding conditions is true, delete the retransmission timer and go silent.

27934: Now, if we were in the **TCP_LAST_ACK** state, then this ACK should be for the FIN/FIN exchange. If the socket is not dead, call the socket state change routine (which, for TCP, should be **def_callback1** at line 5417). If the acknowledgment number is for the FIN packet, set the state to **TCP_CLOSE** and return to the caller.

27962: If we were in the **TCP_FIN_WAIT1** state—we sent a FIN but have not yet received a FIN—then move to state **TCP_FIN_WAIT2** if this ACK is for our original FIN. Set the **TIME_CLOSE** timeout to **TCP_FIN_TIMEOUT** (line 42418, value 3 minutes) if the socket is not marked dead.

27989: If we were in the **TCP_CLOSING** state, move to **TCP_TIME_WAIT** status (via **tcp_time_wait**, line 24064).

28004: If we were in the **TCP_SYN_RECV** state, then we have established our connection; move the socket to the **TCP_ESTABLISHED** state. Set the maximum window to a minimum value of 32, and copy the TCP options from the ACK socket buffer by calling **tcp_options** (line 26573). Do the sequence number bookkeeping, and also update the round-trip delay estimator variables for the new connection.

28066: TCP isn't done with the send queues. If stuff is waiting and we have retransmissions, then call **tcp_do_retransmit** (line 29839) and reset the **TIME_WRITE** timer to the current retransmission timeout value.

28073: Return 1 to the caller.

28075: (label **uninteresting_ack**)

28083: If the acknowledgement number is outside the sent-data window, return immediately with a value of 0.

28092: If the keep-alive option is selected for this socket object, restart the keep-alive timer by calling **tcp_reset_xmit_timer** to set the **TIME_KEEPOPEN** timer (line 42009, value 3) to **TCP_TIMEOUT_LEN** (line 42412, value 15 minutes).

28098: Return 0 to the caller.

tcp_fin

The **tcp_fin** function (line 28125) handles an incoming TCP packet with the FIN bit set.

28128: When we receive a FIN, we note the sequence number for the FIN.

28130: If the socket is not dead, indicate a state change and wake up the process waiting on this socket—it will want to pay attention.

28136: Process according to the current TCP state.

28138: If we are in the **TCP_SYN_RECV**, **TCP_SYN_SENT**, or **TCP_ESTABLISHED** state, then set the state to **TCP_CLOSE_WAIT** and shut down both directions of transfer.

28151: If we are in the **TCP_CLOSE_WAIT** or **TCP_CLOSING** state, then do nothing, because we received a retransmission of the FIN packet.

28158: If we are in the **TCP_TIME_WAIT** state, restart the **TIME_WAIT** timer by calling **reset_timer** (line 31522) with the value **TCP_TIMEWAIT_**

LEN (line 42414, value 60 seconds). Return 0 to the caller.

28166: If we are not in the **TCP_FIN_WAIT1** state, go to line 28204.

28183: If the write timer isn't in **TIME_WRITE** mode, and there is data to send, set the transmit time to **TIME_WRITE** mode and the interval to the retransmit timeout value calculated before.

28202: Change the state of the socket object to **TCP_CLOSING**.

28204: If the current state of the TCP socket is **TCP_FIN_WAIT2**, enter the **TIME_WAIT** state, and set up the timer in the **TIME_CLOSE** mode with a delay of **TCP_TIMEWAIT_LEN** (line 42414, value 60 seconds).

28214: If the current state of the TCP socket is **TCP_CLOSE**, do nothing—the socket is already closed.

28219: If the socket object is in any other state, set the state to **TCP_LAST_ACK**, and set the timer to **TIME_CLOSE** mode with a delay of **TCP_TIMEWAIT_LEN** (line 42414, value 60 seconds). Then, return 0 to the caller.

28228: Return 0 to the caller.

tcp_insert_skb

The **tcp_insert_skb** function (line 28235) takes a socket buffer and inserts it into a socket buffer list whose head is passed in the function. It starts looking from the end of the list, making the (questionable) assumption that it's more likely that we will get packets in order. After it finds the insert point, discovered by comparing the sequence numbers of the socket buffers, it links the socket buffer into the list.

The comment indicates that this is used to insert a socket buffer into the receive queue, but it can be used for the send queue as well.

tcp_queue_ack

The **tcp_queue_ack** function (line 28264) is called for each received packet with the ACK bit turned on. If the FIN bit is turned on, we call **tcp_fin** (line 28125) to process the FIN.

tcp_queue

The **tcp_queue** function (line 28277) takes an incoming data packet and places it on the receive queue.

28282: Call **tcp_insert_skb** (line 28235) to place the received packet in the receive queue in the proper place. Do the bookkeeping.

28290: If the acknowledgment number is after the last transmitted sequence number, go to line 28354.

28291: If the packet straddles the end of the window, then call **tcp_queue_ack** (line 28264) to schedule an ACK packet to be sent. Indeed, walk through the receive queue in case we got a packet out of order, and queue an ACK for any received packets that become useful because a hole has been filled.

28317: Update the sequence number of ACKed data in the socket object.

28319: If the ACK is for a duplicate, process the duplicate by calling **tcp_send_ack** (line 30668), which may eventually trigger the far end to realize that a packet may have been lost.

28332: If the current packet has the FIN flag set, or if there are no delayed ACKs waiting, then call **tcp_send_ack** (line 30668). Otherwise, wait either a half-second (not PSH flag) or 20 milliseconds (PSH flag) and call **tcp_send_delayed_ack** (line 30641) to schedule the transmission of an ACK packet. The shorter delay due to the PSH flag makes the assumption that the remote application is an interactive one.

28350: Send a wake-up call that data is available for the application.

28353: Return to the caller.

28380: If the socket buffer has not been ACKed, call **tcp_send_ack** (line 30668) to schedule an ACK, and call **tcp_send_delayed_ack** (line 30641) to schedule additional ACKs based on retransmission timeouts. Then, return to the caller.

tcp_data

The **tcp_data** function (line 28411) deals with the payload in the TCP packet.

28419: Remove the TCP header from the data portion of the socket buffer. This adjusts the **len** element of the socket buffer.

28430: If there is no data, and this isn't a FIN packet, then send the ACK and be done with the buffer. Return to the caller with 0 status.

28451: If the packet has been shut down for receive, avoid sending RST to a connection that has been closed but to which the remote keeps sending keep-alive packets. (This could happen when a socket has been half-closed and keep-alive is active). If there is data with the packet, though, ship a reset, put the error **EPIPE** in the socket object, and close the connection. Get rid of the incoming packet, too.

28519: For good data, call **tcp_delack_estimator** (line 26069) and **tcp_queue** to deal with the packet data. Return 0 to the caller.

tcp_check_urg

The **tcp_check_urg** function (line 28540) handles packets containing urgent data.

28545: In the BSD interpretation of the urgent pointer, the pointer points to the character beyond. In later versions, the pointer points to the character itself. Unfortunately, the code here assumes the BSD functionality without checking the **SO_BSDCOMPAT** flag first. This was fixed in later versions, but in Linux release 2.0.34, all applications had to assume the BSD interpretation.

28551: If we have seen and processed the urgent data, then return now. Ditto if we have either a duplicate or later urgent pointer (only one at a time, please).

28560: For new urgent data, we send the **SIGURG** signal to the process tied to this socket.

28568: The bookkeeping is tricky, as the comment starting at this line indicates. Return after the bookkeeping is complete.

tcp_urg

The **tcp_urg** function (line 28590) examines whether we have the URG flag set, and deals with the situation in which it is set by calling the function **tcp_check_urg** (line 28540). If the urgent offset pointer is pointing in this packet, wake up the process, too. Then, return to the caller.

tcp_remove_dups

The **tcp_remove_dups** function (line 28631) walks through the receive buffer and removes any duplicate packets, freeing memory as it goes.

prune_queue

The **prune_queue** function (line 28660) is called when too much data is sitting in the queue. The function will discard all socket buffers marked as ACKed, and then call **tcp_remove_dups** (line 28631) to remove any unACKed duplicates. Return to the caller when done.

tcp_chkaddr

The **tcp_chkaddr** function (line 28685) is compiled in when transparent proxy support is configured in the kernel. It calls **tcp_v4_lookup** (line 26338) to search for any matching address; if one is not found, return 0 to the caller. If one is found, check to see whether the source address is 0; if so, return 0 to the caller. Otherwise, return 1 to the caller to indicate that we have a match.

tcp_rcv

The **tcp_rcv** function (line 28710) is the open maw of TCP, into which all incoming packets are dumped. This master function is 630 lines long, and it does a bunch of

stuff. It's also spaghetti code. State machines based on rules are far easier to follow.

There are also a bunch of options, so we will assume that all options are configured except as noted in the commentary.

28735: If this is an RST packet and **secure_tcp_probe_number** (/usr/src/linux/drivers/char/random.c, on the CD-ROM) returns TRUE, then call **add_clearance** (line 26241) to vet the source address.

28741: If the processing of this socket buffer was previously interrupted by the socket object being locked, go to line 28800.

28743: If the packet is not for us, go to label **discard_it** (line 29333).

28755: If the TCP checksum doesn't match, go to label **discard_it** (line 29333).

28768: (label **retry_search**)

28770: Find the socket associated with this socket buffer. When transparent proxy support is compiled in the kernel, and the socket buffer is marked with the redirect flag, the function **tcp_v4_proxy_lookup** is called (line 26384); otherwise, the function **tcp_v4_lookup** is called (line 26338). In either case, if the socket can't be found, go to label **no_tcp_socket** (line 29325).

28795: If the socket buffer is in use by another process, then we need to add it to the backlog queue and return to the caller with 0 status.

28800: This takes care of the preliminaries.

28815: If the socket has been zapped (declared dead by the receipt of an RST packet) or the TCP state is **TCP_CLOSED**, then go to label **no_tcp_socket** (line 29325).

28830: Charge the memory usage to the socket. This prevents malicious attackers from eating up memory to a fare-thee-well in a denial-of-service attack on the TCP implementation.

28853: If the state of the socket object is **TCP_ESTAB-LISHED**, go to line 29217. This enables "normal" data packets to be processed quicker.

28861: If the TCP state of the socket object is not **TCP_LISTEN**, then go to line 28986.

28863: If the ACK flag is not set (acknowledgment number is not valid), go to line 28938.

28866: If both SYN and RST flags are reset, and SYN cookies are compiled, then verify that the address is in the security list and that the cookie was sent less than two minutes ago. This makes extensive use of the **secure_tcp_syn_cookie** function (/usr/src/linux/drivers/char/random.c, on the CD-ROM) to verify that the cookie is correct. If it is, create a new socket, via **tcp_conn_request_fake** (line 27057), and fall through. If the request failed, go to label **retry_search** (line 28768).

28916: **TCP_LISTEN** and ACK don't mix—send a reset packet.

28938: If the RST flag is on, the SYN flag is off, the ACK flag is on (proxy support installed), the destination address is either a broadcast or multicast address, or (no proxy support) the destination address is not my address, release the socket and return 0 to the caller.

28952: We have the beginnings of a new connection. Call **secure_tcp_sequence_number** (/usr/src/linux/drivers/char/random.c) to get a new starting sequence number, and call **tcp_conn_request** (line 26644) to clone the socket object. Return 0 to the caller.

28986: If the socket object is in state **TCP_SYN_RECV**, the SYN flag is set, and the sequence number matches the prior number in a SYN packet, then ignore the packet. Return to the caller with 0 status.

29001: If the socket object is not in state **TCP_SYN_SENT**, go to line 29113.

29004: If we don't have an ACK flag, go to line 29104.

29018: If the acknowledgment number is out of the allowable range, then this ACK packet is from another connection, and we need to send a reset packet, remove the packet from memory, and return 0 to the caller.

29031: If we have an RST flag, send a reset packet and return to the caller.

29033: If we don't have a SYN flag, we have another out-of-place packet. Send a reset packet, remove the packet from memory, and return 0 to the caller.

29055: It's the SYN/ACK packet we were expecting, so process it.

29065: If we currently have a 0-window advertisement, change it to 32.

29073: Save the sequence numbers, send the ACK packet (to complete the three-way handshake), set the TCP state to **TCP_ESTABLISHED**, and process the options in the SYN/ACK packet. Let the process associated with this socket know that something has happened. Set up the round-trip time estimator and go to line 29154.

29104: We have an ACK flag. If we have a SYN flag on and an RST flag off, then check to see whether the packet is our packet. (This shouldn't happen.) If it is our packet, then send a reset to ourselves, because we are hopelessly lost. Otherwise, set the socket state to **TCP_SYN_**

RECV. In either case, discard the packet (we're through with it) and return 0 to the caller. If we don't have the SYN flag on and the RST flag off, then go to label **rfc_step6** (line 29275).

29154: If the socket object's state is **TCP_TIME_WAIT**, we have a SYN, the socket was declared dead, the sequence number is after the last ACKed sequence number, and we don't have an RST flag, then continue with the next paragraph. Otherwise, go to line 29217.

29162: Don't charge this socket for the memory this socket takes, because eventually the memory will be charged against a new socket. Post the error **ECONNRESET** in the old socket. Force the socket to a closed state prematurely. Now, look for another socket with the correct information. If we find one, start a connection request and return to the caller with 0 status. No socket? Remove the packet from memory and return 0 to the caller.

29217: If the sequence number test fails (**tcp_sequence**, line 26491), report the bad sequence number (**bad_tcp_sequence**, line 26434), remove the packet buffer from memory, and return 0 to the caller.

29226: Reset flag set? If so, return to the caller with the status from **tcp_reset** (line 26510).

29248: If we have the SYN flag, but the sequence numbers differ from the first SYN, then call **tcp_send_reset** (line 30197). Then, return to the caller with the status from **tcp_reset** (line 2651).

29260: If the ACK flag is set and the function **tcp_ack** (line 27366) returns failure, then our three-way handshake failed, and, if we are in TCP state **TCP_SYN_RECV**, we need to send a reset, drop the packet, and return 0 to the caller.

29275: (label **rfc_step6**)

29289: Process any urgent data by calling **tcp_urg** (line 28590).

29295: Process the payload by calling **tcp_data** (line 28411). If the function returns TRUE, discard the packet.

29303: If we had a partial packet being built due to Nagle's algorithm, send it.

29316: If our memory allocation is over its limit, call **prune_queue** to try to reduce the memory load.

29323: Return 0 to the caller.

29325: (label **no_tcp_socket**)

29330: There is no socket object, so send a reset by calling **tcp_send_reset** (line 30197).

29333: (label **discard_it**)

29338: Remove the packet buffer from memory, and return 0 to the caller.

tcp_output.c

The functions in this source module are geared toward output services. Because the mechanics of building packets is repeated so many times, the commentaries refrain from engaging in endless repetition and, instead, focus on the significant deviations from normal packet-building practices.

Unlike the input functions, which need to use numerous state machines to trigger functions, the output functions tend to be straightforward in what they do.

tcp_new_window

The **tcp_new_window** function (line 29426) calculates the size of the new window to advertise to the other end. Because this process has so many dynamics, we will go through them step by step.

29433: Set the working minimum window size to the MSS. If this has fallen to 0, use the MTU. If *that* fell to 0, too, use 1 (and log a debug message to that effect).

29441: Set the maximum window size to the current socket **window_clamp** value—this is either 0 or the window size associated with the first route taken by packets from this socket. If that's 0, use **MAX_WINDOW** (line 42384, value 32767—the reason that we select this value for a maximum is that some stacks use signed 16-bit arithmetic, and using a larger window will break those stacks).

29445: If the minimum window size is more than half the size of the maximum window, pull the minimum window size back to half the size of the maximum window. In theory, the **window_clamp** element will never be less than 2, so the minimum window size will never drop to 0 because of this.

29449: Calculate the amount of free space in the receive buffer. This starts at one-half of the prior calculation. If this is below the minimum window previously calculated, then the socket object's receiver buffer size is set to twice the minimum window (we guarantee this is okay by making the maximum window at least double the size of the minimum window) and setting the free space to the minimum window size.

29456: If the amount of free space is less than the minimum window, then we have a possible case of Silly Window Syndrome and we need to advertise a 0-length window. Return 0 to the caller to do just that.

29462: If the original socket object window is smaller than or equal to half the buffer space available, or the old window value is greater than half the buffer space available, then pull back the window size to a multiple of the minimum window size.

29466: If the resulting window is larger than the maximum window, use the size of the maximum window.

29468: Return the window advertisement to the caller.

clear_delayed_acks

The **clear_delayed_acks** inline function (line 29474) is called to remove any delayed-ACK processing that may be pending. This clears the delayed-ACK bookkeeping variables and removes the delayed-ACK timer from the timer system.

tcp_send_skb

The **tcp_send_skb** function (line 29489) queues the buffer for transmission after checking it.

Because of the series of checklist checks, we will examine this function in detail.

29499: Calculate the size of the TCP packet. If the size is unreasonable (too small for a TCP header or too large for the socket buffer), eliminate the packet buffer from memory and return to the caller. Also, note the fact that we tried to transmit a bad SKB to the system log.

29520: If the packet is exactly the size of a TCP header, and neither the SYN nor FIN packet is set, then complain about a "bogon" packet, remove the packet buffer from memory, and return to the caller.

29543: If it has been a while since we sent data packets, reset the slow-start algorithm stuff so that we do it again. This is recommended to prevent a long pause from causing us to overload a data channel. "Long time" is defined as a delay longer than the retransmission timeout, initially three seconds and adjusted to about four times the round-trip time during other processing.

29567: If we need to hold off actually transmitting this packet—because it doesn't fit in the window advertisement from the other end, the packet is being retransmitted, or we have too many packets outstanding right now—then it's placed in the socket object's **write_queue**, the place where packets are placed in limbo for later transmission.

29597: If we can send the packet now, then call **clear_delayed_acks** (line 29474), because we piggyback the ACK in the data packet, set the ACK number and the window advertisement into the header, and call **tcp_send_check** (line 24429) to finish the packet. Update the sent sequence number in the socket object. Call the protocol's **queue_xmit** task—for TCP, this is **ip_queue_xmit** (line 16414). Then, reset the retransmission timer to **TIME_WRITE** with the current retransmission timeout value. Return to the caller.

tcp_dequeue_partial

The **tcp_dequeue_partial** function (line 29639) removes the list of partial packets from the socket object's queue for such things. It also kills the timer associated with partial packets, because we expect the caller to do something with the packets. Return **NULL** if there are no partial packets, or return the pointer to the first (or only) partial packet's socket buffer.

Apparently, the comments for this particular function are out-of-date, because in **tcp_enqueue_partial**, we see that any partial packet already in the socket object is transmitted immediately upon enqueuing the new partial object. This means that, in reality, only one partial packet at a time can be on the partial packet "queue."

tcp_send_partial

The **tcp_send_partial** function (line 29659) takes the list of partial packets, if any, and ships them by calling **tcp_send_skb** (line 29489). This function is called when the partial-packet timer expires. (See the following description of the **tcp_enqueue_partial** function for more details.)

tcp_enqueue_partial

The **tcp_enqueue_partial** function (line 29673) takes a partial packet and puts a pointer to it in the socket object. It also sets up a long delay (30 seconds) for that partial packet to be transmitted.

An interesting side effect of this function is that if there was a partial packet already here, it is queued for trans-

mission (using **tcp_send_skb**, line 29489) at the time the new partial packet is put on the socket list.

tcp_write_xmit

The **tcp_write_xmit** function (line 29710) uses incoming ACKs that open up the transmit window to trigger transmission of new data from the holding (**write_queue**) queue.

29720: If the socket object has been zapped by a reset, return now. Anything on the queues will be cleaned up later.

29732: If we have data pending to be written that fits in the transmit window, while we are not in a retransmission mode, and fits in the congestion window, then continue on. Otherwise, return to the caller.

29747: If the entire packet was previously transmitted and acknowledged, clean it off the list, signal the process that space has been opened up for writes, and return to the caller.

29781: If part of the packet was previously transmitted and acknowledged, call **tcp_shrink_skb** (line 31021) to eliminate the old data.

29787: If MTU path discovery isn't compiled into the kernel, then set the don't fragment flag so that TCP can do it.

29805: Put the acknowledge sequence number and window advertisement into the TCP header. Prepare the packet for shipment using **tcp_send_check** (line 24429). Call the protocol's **queue_xmit** task—for TCP, this is **ip_queue_xmit** (line 16414). Clear any delayed ACKs by calling **clear_delayed_acks** (line 29474). Finally, update the retransmission timer to function in the **TIME_WRITE** mode with a retransmission time of the retransmission timeout value calculated earlier. Return to the caller.

tcp_do_retransmit

The **tcp_do_retransmit** function (line 29839) is called when a transmission timeout occurs and it's time to try to recover from a packet loss (or worse).

29847: If the **all** parameter is 0, we are supposed to send just one packet. Prepare to process the first packet on the queue.

29857: Loop through the send queue. The loop ends at line 30190.

29890: If the device is locked, we can't do anything, so break out of the loop.

29896: Unlink the socket buffer from any queue. Remove any MAC header (this will be rebuilt later).

29941: If the packet has to be shrunk (because data was used from the packet to form a probe), then call the **tcp_shrink_skb** function (line 31021) to perform this task.

29964: Get an updated route and rebuild the IP and MAC headers for this packet. Because this packet may have been changed, we have to allocate a new ID for it. Calculate the IP checksum based on the new data—the TCP header hasn't changed, nor have any IP header fields that the TCP checksum uses, so we don't have to recalculate the TCP checksum.

29977: If we don't have a route, we're out of luck, at least for now. Set as a soft error **ENETUNREACH** and signal that there is a soft error. Break out of the loop, because there isn't much more we can do anyway.

29992: We have a route. If we have shifted devices, it gets ugly—we need to change every packet in the queues. The authors recommend strongly that you not look at the printed version of the code, but rather look at the original source on the CD-ROM (/usr/src/linux/net/ipv4tcpoutput.c) on a *very* wide screen (or on a landscape-oriented listing), because the code is nested very deeply. The mess stops at line 30149.

In summary, call **ip_rewrite_addrs** (line 16010), rebuild the hardware header, and check the send-firewall list (**call_out_firewall**, /usr/src/linux/net/core/firewall.h, on the CD-ROM) because the output device has changed, and the rules for one device may differ from rules for another device.

Clear any delayed ACKs, because any ACK will be carried in the data packet. Finish rebuilding the headers. As long as the device flags indicate that the device is up (connected), ship the retransmitted packets.

30155: Update the SNMP counters, update the transmitted sequence number high-water mark, and point to the next block.

30178: If we are not doing all the blocks, break out of this loop. If we have hit the congestion window limit, break out of the loop. Otherwise, point to the next packet in the list and loop back.

30191: Return to the caller.

tcp_send_reset

The **tcp_send_reset** function (line 30197) sends a reset packet.

If the packet has the RST flag on, return immediately, because we do not answer a reset with a reset. Otherwise, build a reset packet if you can, building the TCP and IP headers. Queue the buffer to the device and return to the caller.

tcp_send_synack_probe

The **tcp_send_synack_probe** function (line 30283), compiled only when cookie support has been compiled into the kernel, sends a probe to evoke a reset with a cookie.

This builds a SYN/ACK packet and ships it on its way. The window advertisement is bogus (the coder picked 1,024 bytes). After the packet is built, the function returns to the caller.

tcp_send_fin

The **tcp_send_fin** function (line 30356) sends a FIN packet based on the socket.

The major trick here is what happens when we can't find a route for the packet. The workaround is to drop the packet onto the loopback device. When the packet is read from the loopback device, then (with any luck) the packet will be forwarded to the correct place when a route becomes available.

As part of the process of sending the FIN packet, call **clear_delayed_acks** (line 29474) to clear any pending ACK packet transmission. Add the packet to the end of the write buffer (so that all data is transmitted before the FIN packet), or, if the write buffer is empty, ship the packet on directly and reset the retransmit timer to **TIME_WRITE** mode using for the interval the current retransmission timeout value. Then, return to the caller.

tcp_send_synack

The **tcp_send_synack** function (line 30487) builds and sends a SYN/ACK packet and creates the socket for the new connection. If anything goes wrong in doing this, everything is undone, the original SYN packet is removed, and control returns to the caller. The other end should send another SYN packet to try the connect again. By then, with any luck, any condition that caused us to not build the packet will have cleared.

30557: Add the MSS option to the TCP packet header.

30569: If the **destroy** parameter is non-0, we need to charge the memory allocation to the new socket object.

30590: If the **destroy** parameter is non-0, destroy the socket and release the passed socket buffer.

30616: Send the packet on its way (if **destroy** is 0), and return to the caller.

tcp_send_delayed_ack

The **tcp_send_delayed_ack** function (line 30641) sets up to send a delayed ACK if there wasn't an opportunity to send an ACK sooner.

First, the code calculates a new timeout value based on the parameters **timeout** and **max_timeout** such that the timeout doesn't exceed the maximum timeout value passed. If the number of bytes waiting to be ACKed exceeds the maximum threshold (2,048 bytes, or twice the maximum segment size; see lines 5511 and 26629), the timeout is zeroed.

From the result of the aforementioned calculation, the new timeout is calculated and the timer is updated (or started). Note that if there is a plethora of bytes to ACK, the timer will expire immediately, and an ACK will be generated very, very quickly.

When finished, return to the caller.

tcp_send_ack

The **tcp_send_ack** function (line 30668) sends an ACK packet and updates the window advertisement.

30675: If the socket object has been declared dead, return immediately without sending anything.

30687: Clear any pending delayed ACKs, because we are going to send one.

30689: If the transmit and write queues are empty (nothing to send, nothing to wait for) and the retransmission timer is in **TIME_WRITE** mode, then delete the retransmit timer. If the socket is marked as a "keep open" (by **setsockopt SO_KEEPALIVE**), then set the retransmission timer to **TIME_KEEPOPEN** mode with an interval of about 15 minutes (line 42412).

30706: Build an ACK packet, if we can. If successful, ship it using **queue_xmit** (really **ip_queue_xmit**, line 16414). Update the SNMP counters and return to the caller.

tcp_write_wakeup

The **tcp_write_wakeup** function (line 30777) is called when a write-data timeout is detected.

30784: If an RST packet was seen before for this socket, return now without doing anything.

30796: If this function is called in any state other than **TCP_ESTABLISHED**, **TCP_CLOSE_WAIT**, **TCP_FIN_WAIT1**, **TCP_LAST_ACK**, or **TCP_CLOSING**, then return now.

30805: If we don't have data waiting to be written or there is no space in the window, go to line 30935. Otherwise, we are in Silly Window Avoidance mode. Get the pointers to the various headers, and calculate how much data we can send based on the data in the socket buffer and the current window size.

Create the IP header, copy the TCP header, and update the information in the TCP header. Don't forget to copy the data for the short buffer and checksum the entire buffer. Go to line 30985.

30935: Otherwise, build a "special" ACK packet that has no data, and ACKs the byte prior to the actual high-water mark. This should elicit an ACK from the other end. In this way, we hope that we can get the prior response from the other end and also perhaps a window advertisement that will let us continue transmitting.

30985: Send whatever packet we have built, update the SNMP statistics, and return to the caller.

tcp_send_probe0

The **tcp_send_probe0** function (line 30991) is called when a window probe times out. The probe is re-sent (via **tcp_write_wakeup**, line 30777) and the retransmission timer is reset to the **TIME_PROBE0** state with an interval of the retransmission timeout calculated previously.

tcp_shrink_skb

The **tcp_shrink_skb** function (line 31021) takes a socket buffer and strips off data that has been transmitted and ACKed already. The sequence numbers are updated, and the data is moved and checksummed in place. The buffer is shortened using **skb_trim** (line 39293). When finished, control returns to the caller. The result is a packet with the first n bytes removed.

tcp_timer.c

The functions in this source module take care of the timing functions. In many cases, these functions perform simple manipulations of the timers in the socket objects, although the timeout callback wrappers have to figure out where to steer timeout signals in specific instances.

tcp_delack_timer

The **tcp_delack_timer** function (line 31108) is a callback wrapper for **tcp_send_ack**.

tcp_reset_xmit_timer

The **tcp_reset_xmit_timer** function (line 31117) restarts the retransmission timer and sets the mode for the timer. First, the timer is disabled, to cancel any timer event. The mode of the timer is saved. The expiry time is taken from the time stored in the first socket buffer in the resend queue plus the interval **when** that was passed to the function by the caller when the mode to be set is **TIME_WRITE**. For any other mode, the expiry time is the current time plus the interval **when**. If the time is already past, push it two clock ticks. Then, start the timer and return to the caller.

tcp_retransmit_time

The **tcp_retransmit_time** function (line 31171) is called from the timer callback routine **tcp_retransmit**. This function performs the backoff for retransmissions. See the comments starting at line 31187 for a description of the backoff algorithm. Basically, for each retransmission, the retransmission timeout is doubled, up to a maximum of 120 seconds. This is a network-friendly way

of working, but not exactly human-friendly, and is why an "interactive" program sometimes can appear to go to sleep for long periods of time, but still be working.

tcp_retransmit

The **tcp_retransmit** function (line 31238) is called from the timer callback function **tcp_time_write_timeout** (line 31351). This function resets the congestion control parameters to completely restart the slow-start algorithm, and triggers the retransmission of the data pending the receipt of an ACK.

tcp_write_timeout

The **tcp_write_timeout** function (line 31264) is called from the timer callback function **tcp_retransmit_timer** (line 31351) under certain circumstances. The function handles several different conditions.

31269: If we are in the **TCP_ESTABLISHED** state and we've either retried a multiple of 8 times or exceeded the retry limit **TCP_RETR1** (line 42400, value 7), check for a shifted route by calling **ip_route_advice** (line 21417).

31296: Have we retried too many times for a TCP open (states **TCP_SYN_SENT** and **TCP_SYN_RECV**), with "too many times" defined as **TCP_SYN_RETRIES** (line 42430, value 5)? If so, promote any soft error to a hard error or, if no soft error (the other end just isn't responding), set the hard error to **ETIMEDOUT**. Kill the timer, update the SNMP statistics, set the socket to the **TCP_CLOSE** state, and return to the caller now with 0 status.

31315: Is it time to just give up? If we have retried more than **TCP_RETR2** (line 42407, value 15) times, promote a soft error to a hard error, or, if no soft error exists, set a hard error to **ETIMEDOUT** and kill the timer.

31326: In giving up, if we are in the **TCP_FIN_WAIT1** or **TCP_FIN_WAIT2** state, switch to the **TCP_TIME_WAIT** state and set the retransmission timer in **TIME_CLOSE** mode with a one-minute interval. Otherwise, set the socket to the **TCP_CLOSE** state—there is no need to wait for a while, because the reason we are quitting is that the socket connection is already quite, quite dead.

31339: Return 0 to the caller.

31342: If we haven't given up, return 1 to the caller.

tcp_time_write_timeout

The **tcp_time_write_timeout** function (line 31351) is called by the timeout callback routine **tcp_retransmit_timer** (line 31376). This calls **retransmit** (which is **tcp_retransmit**, line 31238) and **tcp_write_timeout** (line 31264) to deal with ACKs as well as packets sent that haven't been acknowledged.

tcp_retransmit_timer

The **tcp_retransmit_timer** function (line 31376) is the callback function for the retransmission timer expiry.

31385: If the socket has been reset, return immediately.

31394: If the socket is in use, reschedule the timer for one second later.

31400: If backlogged ACKs are present and the socket isn't dead, call the protocol **data_ready** function (which for TCP is **def_callback2**, line 5423).

31409: If the timer mode is **TIME_PROBE0**, call **tcp_send_probe0** (line 30991), and then call **tcp_write_timeout** (line 31264) to restart the appropriate transmission. Then, return to the caller.

31415: If the timer mode is **TIME_WRITE**, call the **tcp_time_write_timeout** function (line 31264) and return to the caller.

31420: If the timer mode is **TIME_KEEPOPEN**, call **tcp_reset_xmit_timer** (line 31117) to reset the timer, and call **tcp_write_timeout** so that something (such as an ACK packet) gets written. Return to the caller.

31436: If the timer mode is none of the modes described earlier, write a syslog message and return to the caller.

timer.c

These three functions provide the timer functions needed by TCP in particular, and by the entire TCP/IP package in general. We include them with TCP because TCP depends on them so heavily. The functions in this routine use the system timer routines found in /usr/src/linux/kernel/sched.c (included on the CD-ROM).

In several places in the TCP code, there are calls to the kernel routine **add_timer**, which will take a timer and add it to the timer queue in sched.c.

delete_timer

The **delete_timer** function (line 31509) shuts off a timer, including zeroing the expiry time.

reset_timer

The **reset_timer** function (line 31522) shuts off a timer, calculates a new timeout value, and adds the newly set timer into the queue.

net_timer

The **net_timer** function (line 31545) is a general network system callback timer.

31554: If the socket is in use by a process, hold off the timer one second. Return to the timer routine.

31564: If we need to send an ACK on a live socket, call the protocol **read_wakeup** routine. If the socket hasn't been declared dead, call the protocol **data_ready** routine. These routines usually cause the process associated with the socket to wake up to check for newly unblocked access, or to process the system call **select** properly.

31576: If the reason for the timeout is **TIME_DONE** and the socket hasn't been closed off, then wait some more. Otherwise, destroy the socket by calling **destroy_sock** (line 5245) and return to the timer routine.

31594: If the reason for the timeout is **TIME_DESTROY**, call **destroy_sock** (line 5245) and return to the timer routine.

31604: If the reason for the timeout is **TIME_CLOSE**, we have waited long enough for stray packets to have been processed. Change the state to **TCP_CLOSE**, mark the packet as no longer accepting or sourcing data, and return to the timer routine.

31614: If we don't know why the timeout happened, print a message to the system log and return to the timer routine.

Chapter 10

IP Firewall Support

In BC (Before Computer) times, the term *firewall* meant only one thing: a physical barrier that keeps a physical fire from spreading from one physical space to another. You can find such firewalls in buildings (in the form of bricks, sand-filled concrete blocks, or thin vertical layers of poured cement) and in motor vehicles (in the form of a sturdy metal partition between the engine compartment and the passenger cabin). In either case, the firewall's job is to stay intact, until either the fire has been extinguished or the people and property at risk have been safely removed from the building or car.

Firewalls in a computer network also define separate spaces, but in a different way. Although network firewalls are often massive, they're not solid. Far from impenetrable, they have openings and passageways that allow traffic to circulate. These portals are tended by software that acts like sentries or gatekeepers, letting authorized data pass through while keeping unauthorized data out.

Unfortunately, the oxymoronic concept of a porous barrier didn't inspire confidence in business managers contemplating the new step of connecting company networks to the Internet. The reassuring term *firewall* was coined and, like most casual coinages, stuck.

So, although it's exciting to envision a stalwart band of crossbowmen atop a crenellated 30-foot wall defending your system against the siege towers and battering rams of the Ottoman Horde, a more realistic model of firewall protection would be a squad of Customs Office inspectors at the airport or on the shipping docks, on the lookout for counterfeit athletic shoes.

In a nutshell, if the Bad Guys really, *really* want access to your system, they *will* get in. Firewalls are simply a first line of defense. They can't protect you against ill-intentioned users who (like the medieval miners and sappers whose task was to tunnel under the city or castle walls) sneak into your system via browsers, mail programs, news readers, or other Internet applications. And, they certainly don't provide much protection against someone who physically breaks into your office and into your system. The most that a computer or network firewall can do is defeat remote, random, or casual attacks that aren't directed against a specific individual (you), but rather against so-called "targets of opportunity"—that is, any systems that happen to be connected to a given network at a given time. They're not personal, but that doesn't make them any less dangerous.

Passport, Please

When you get off the plane and collect your baggage after a trip abroad, the first people you meet will likely be a row of Customs Office inspectors. A simple glance can tell these officials a lot about you, based on your clothing and jewelry, your posture, your demeanor, your grooming, and even your expression. After examining your passport, visa, and declarations, the inspectors note how much luggage you're carrying and the size of each piece. Then, they decide whether you or your belongings merit more of their attention. Fairly or not, some travelers get through Customs with just a few questions, while others are searched thoroughly before being allowed to pass.

An Internet firewall behaves a lot like a Customs inspector. Depending on the firewall software and the options selected by the individual who established the firewall's permissions policy, every packet that reaches the firewall is examined for specific data. Depending on the contents of various fields in the IP header (such as the source address, destination address, packet size, and protocol number) and the presence or absence of IP options in the header, packets can be rejected, accepted, or subjected to more tests.

Some types of attacks on networked computers try to sneak around security measures by using packet fragments (described in Chapter 7). The firewall software, as implemented in Linux, includes many features that prevent packet fragments from becoming a security hazard.

Transmission Control Protocol (TCP) and User Datagram Protocol (UDP) packets (the two types of packets most widely used on the Internet) get special attention from the Linux firewall software. Besides helping the user set up the rules that govern how the packets will be handled, the source-port and destination-port numbers in TCP and UDP packets offer the firewall software more material on which to base its subsequent treatment of the packet. The software also checks TCP packets to determine whether they are part of an existing connection or part of a request for a new connection.

The Linux firewall software can also inspect Internet Control Message Protocol (ICMP) packets, to prevent certain attacks that use ICMP to do its dirty work.

Smuggling In Plain Sight

In a hoary old story, a man makes regular trips across the border between the United States and Mexico. His vehicle is a bicycle, and his cargo consists of a sack of sand. The U.S. Customs inspector always sifts the sand, searching for contraband, but never finds any. The trips continue, once a day, for several months. Then, some weeks later, when the man is passing through Customs in a car, the inspector recognizes him and says, "I won't arrest you now, but I just *know* you were smuggling something on all those trips. What was it?" The man grins and answers, "Bicycles."

IP packets that are otherwise perfectly harmless can contain hidden attacks on networked systems. A common attack is the so-called *buffer overrun* attack, which exploits ineptly programmed network software residing on the targeted system. In poorly written code, the amount of data placed into a buffer is not checked against the amount of memory allocated to the buffer. Consequently, if the program allows it, more data can be written to a buffer than the buffer is supposed to contain. The excess data spills over into memory areas that have been allocated for other data, overwriting that data and thereby causing the poorly written code to behave in an astonishing way. A clever attacker can tailor the invasive and hostile behavior to compromise the security of the target system.

In many instances, buffer overrun attacks are used to cause *denial of service*, in which use of the target system is compromised. However, as a more sophisticated variant, buffer overrun attacks can be used to perpetrate a *root compromise*, in which the intruder gains superuser (or, on Windows NT systems, Administrator) privileges on the target system.

In other cases, a perfectly legitimate-looking packet can have appalling side effects, because the underlying Internet protocol design (or a particular implementation of it) doesn't take proper steps to ensure system security. In a classic example, a *smurf attack* exploited a weakness in the original ICMP protocol that allowed bad guys to send a single packet into a network's broadcast address, causing all the systems on that network to respond at the same time. In the "best" case, the resulting packet storm degraded the performance of the target network, and in the worst case, it crashed one or more of the networked systems. This Achilles' heel in the ICMP protocol has since been dipped and presumably is as invulnerable to attack as the rest of the protocol.

Other attacks take advantage of specific options and features of TCP/IP or of a particular Internet protocol implementation. For example, the so-called *Ping of Death* attack misuses the fragmentation feature of IP, causing a too-trusting implementation of that protocol to write data wildly into memory. *Man in the middle* and *spoofing* attacks use the optional features of IP to misdirect packets to the attacking system, so that these packets can be monitored and/or modified.

This discussion is not meant as an essay on Internet security—whole books have been written on that subject—but rather as a brief overview, explaining why firewall code is provided as part of the standard Linux distribution. This chapter also introduces the features in this code that let you set up a perimeter defense against would-be intruders, and also strengthen any weak spots in your system citadel caused by buggy code.

Firewall Features

The following fact can't be emphasized enough: Firewalls are just one tool in the Linux system-security kit. They can't guarantee 100 percent protection. What firewalls *can* do is forestall direct attacks launched from the Internet against your system. This section offers a synoptic description of how the firewall code does its job.

The Linux firewall code implements a safety device known as a *stateless packet filter*. This filter inspects incoming packets discretely, one at a time, gleaning information and then immediately discarding it. As each packet arrives, the filter examines the data in the packet header, checking the data against a list of rules defined beforehand by the system administrator. Each rule specifies the data to be examined, the selection criteria for the data, and the action that the firewall filter should take when the data in the packet header meets the conditions specified in a given rule. The filter then keeps or discards the packet, depending on the outcome of the comparison.

Figure 10.1 shows the flow of packets through the Linux firewall. The firewall has three checkpoints:

- *The Input filter*—Where each incoming packet is examined

- *The Forwarding filter*—Where each packet that is to be routed is inspected

- *The Output filter*—Where each outgoing packet is checked

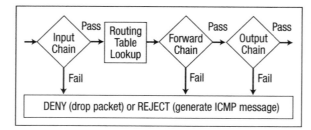

Figure 10.1   Data flow through the three checkpoints in the Linux firewall code.

For the sake of simplicity, Figure 10.1 doesn't show details, such as the flow of packets that are generated by, and sent back to, a single system, or the special hooks for IP masquerade (a feature that lets Linux implement a *transparent proxy* function, so that packets on a private network can be transmitted to an untrusted network).

When a packet is received from an external interface, such as an Ethernet card or a modem-based PPP connection, the packet is tested against the *input chain* of firewall rules. After the packet has passed all the corresponding tests, it is passed to the routing function. If the packet is intended to be forwarded, then it must satisfy the rules in the *forwarding chain* of rules. If the packet is to be sent out via an external interface, then it must satisfy the *output chain* before it can be presented to the Internet.

Some of the packet-filter rules are known as *accounting rules*. Unlike the rules that are actively applied when packets are filtered, the accounting rules are used simply to keep track of the number of bytes and packets that meet a given condition, so that the system administrator can measure and assess the flow of various types of packets.

The IP firewall code lives in a source module called ip_fw.c. This module consists primarily of administrative support code for adding, deleting, and changing the collections (*chains*) of packet-filter rules. The support code is actually lengthier than the packet-filter code, which is short and fairly simple. Brevity and simplicity are especially desirable qualities, because every single packet that is sent, received, or forwarded from one port to another has to pass through this code. Any extraneous processing instructions in the code would increase the CPU overhead significantly.

(Note that the IP firewall code in the 2.2.*x* kernels has been redesigned and expanded. The basic functions are the same, but are now more flexible. The maintenance tools have also been overhauled, so that the rules are now easier for users to define. The name of the new code, *IP Chains*, is taken from the name of one of the new maintenance tools, **ipchains**. To further confound the interested student, the 2.4.*x* kernels will have yet another implementation of firewall code, referred to as *IP Table* when this chapter was being written. Like most projects in the Open Source Systems arena, things move quickly, so who knows what firewalls will look like in kernel releases further down the road.)

Tables 10.1 and 10.2 list the function names and the line at which each function starts, respectively.

Table 10.1   Functions sorted alphabetically by name.

Line	Function Name
13694	append_to_chain
13831	check_ipfw_struct
13747	del_from_chain
13633	free_fw_chain
13652	insert_in_chain
13914	ip_acct_ctl
14336	ip_acct_procinfo
13966	ip_autofw_add
14039	ip_autofw_ctl
13990	ip_autofw_del
14027	ip_autofw_flush
14234	ip_chain_procinfo
13194	ip_fw_chk
14056	ip_fw_ctl
14367	ip_fw_fwd_procinfo
14349	ip_fw_in_procinfo
14462	ip_fw_init
14358	ip_fw_out_procinfo
14420	ipfw_device_event
14397	ipfw_forward_check
14383	ipfw_input_check
14390	ipfw_output_check
13622	zero_fw_chain

Table 10.2   Functions sorted by line number.

Line	Function Name
13194	ip_fw_chk
13622	zero_fw_chain
13633	free_fw_chain

(continued)

Table 10.2   Functions sorted by line number *(continued)*.

Line	Function Name
13652	insert_in_chain
13694	append_to_chain
13747	del_from_chain
13831	check_ipfw_struct
13914	ip_acct_ctl
13966	ip_autofw_add
13990	ip_autofw_del
14027	ip_autofw_flush
14039	ip_autofw_ctl
14056	ip_fw_ctl
14234	ip_chain_procinfo
14336	ip_acct_procinfo
14349	ip_fw_in_procinfo
14358	ip_fw_out_procinfo
14367	ip_fw_fwd_procinfo
14383	ipfw_input_check
14390	ipfw_output_check
14397	ipfw_forward_check
14420	ipfw_device_event
14462	ip_fw_init

Packet-Filter Routines

The administrative tools used by the firewall code will be easier to understand after a short look at how each packet-filter routine walks down the rule chains.

The firewall routines are called by the core network functions **call_in_firewall**, **call_fw_firewall**, and **call_out_firewall**, located in /usr/src/linux/net/core/firewall.c. The called firewall routines in turn call the functions **ipfw_input_check**, **ip_forward_check**, and **ipfw_output_check**. These routines (known as *glue routines*) are common to all packet types, not just IP packets. They check the return results against the manifest constant **FW_SKIP**. If the return value matches this constant, then the next rule is passed down to the firewall routine. If the return value doesn't match this constant, then the returned value is returned to the calling routine.

If a given chain contains no rules, or if the firewall function returns a value that matches **FW_SKIP** for every rule that is passed down, then the default policy for the firewall rule chain is returned to the calling routine.

The possible return values for the firewall function are defined at lines 40278 through 40283. A return value that matches either **FW_BLOCK** or **FW_REJECT** prevents the packet from going any further, removing it from memory and sending it to the bit-bucket. If the returned value matches **FW_SKIP**, the packet is examined further. Any of the other return values allows the processing of the packet to continue with no further rule-based inspections.

The rest of this section describes the operation of the packet-filter modules for the Internet Protocol.

ip_fw_chk

This routine performs the packet-filter check for each of the three check functions (input, forward, and output). The structure of the rule is defined starting at line 40401. Based on that definition, the list in Table 10.3 shows the packet information that is checked. Each of these fields has a "don't care" value, so that a rule includes information only on the fields that are to be checked.

The flags named in the rule field also indicate what the packet-filter code should do when the conditions stated in the rule are met. The filter code has three options: **ACCEPT** (packet processing continues), **DENY** (the packet is dropped without further comment), or **REJECT** (the packet is dropped, and an ICMP message is

Table 10.3   Parameters used in the rule table.

Packet source IP address (with netmask)
Packet destination IP address (with netmask)
Packet IP protocol number
Device IP address
Device name
Ports (up to 10) and ranges of ports
TCP SYN flag
TCP ACK flag

generated and sent back to the packet's source address; that is, to the calling system).

13199: Generate pointers for each of the most common IP packet protocols (TCP, UDP, and ICMP). Initialize the working stack variables to default values. These variables are updated with information from the packet at hand, depending on the nature of that packet.

13251: If the incoming packet appears to be coming from a "bad guy" who is trying to use packet fragments to break into the computer, return **BLOCK**. A return of **BLOCK** prevents packet assembly, so that when the packet reassembly timeout expires, the entire packet is flushed.

13254: Return **ACCEPT** if all three of these conditions are met:

- This packet is a fragment
- The rule isn't an accounting rule
- The packet is ICMP, TCP, or UDP

13266: If the header fragment is for the start of a TCP packet, and the packet itself is too short to be a proper TCP packet (that is, a *runt packet*), then return **DENY**.

13277: If the header fragment is too short to contain valid port information (in UDP) or type information (in ICMP), then return **DENY**.

13293: Start building the packet report. For each of the three packet types, if the packet is a fragment, then the value of each port number stays at –1. For TCP, flags are also set to indicate a SYN or ACK packet. If the packet is other than a TCP, UDP, or ICMP packet, a generic message is prepared.

13335: If debug is indicated, then the message prepared in the preceding step is printed to the system log, along with other pertinent information about the type of packet.

13352: Walk down the firewall rule chain. This step is located at this point in the process, rather than

earlier, to minimize the processing overhead. (The call- and function-setup overhead involved in using the loop in /usr/src/linux/net/core/firewall.c would markedly increase the amount of CPU time required to process the packet.)

13380: Indicate that no match has been found. The least-significant bit indicates that a normal match has been found, while the next-least-significant bit indicates that a reverse match has been found. This logical calculation is used with bidirectional rules.

13382: If the network source address (as modified by the rule's source netmask) matches the address given in the rule, and the destination address (as modified by the rule's destination netmask) matches the destination address stated in the rule, then indicate a forward match by logically adding 0x01 into **match**.

13387: Indicate a reverse match by logically adding 0x02 into **match**, if the following three conditions are met:

- This rule is a bidirectional rule
- The network destination address modified by the rule's source netmask matches the rule source address
- The network source address, as modified by the rule's destination netmask, matches the rule destination address

13393: If no address match is found, skip to the next rule.

13399: If the rule contains a device IP address, and the device IP address doesn't match the device IP address indicated in the rule, skip to the next rule.

13408: If the rule contains a device name, and the actual device name doesn't match the device name indicated in the rule, skip to the next rule.

13425: If this rule is only an accounting rule, and the calling routine has asked for IP accounting, then

determine whether this accounting rule is appropriate. If not, skip to the next rule.

13442: If this rule calls for TCP SYN and the packet is not a TCP SYN packet, skip to the next rule.

13445: If this rule calls for TCP ACK and the packet is not a TCP ACK packet, skip to the next rule.

13449: If the protocol is TCP, UDP, or ICMP, then perform protocol-specific checking (described in the next two commentary paragraphs). Otherwise, skip to line 13481.

13456: If the IP protocol type in the packet does not match the protocol type in the rule, skip to the next rule.

13459: If the IP protocol type is ICMP, and the port numbers (actually, the ICMP type and code fields) don't agree, skip to the next rule. The messiness of this particular code is due in part to the possibility that a match may be a forward or reverse match. (Alternatively, the author of the code *could* have broken the test down into its component parts, for greater ease in understanding what the code is doing.)

13481: This interesting block of code (to line 13551) outputs a message to the syslog file that a rule has matched, and provides information about the packet and what was done with it. (This code replicates in part the code that starts at line 13335.)

13552: If the call was for a packet check (instead of a test call used to debug chains), then increment the byte count and the packet count for the rule.

13556: If this rule is not an accounting rule, then break out of the loop now. If this rule is an accounting rule, then cycle back and check the next rule.

13561: If the matching rule is an accounting rule, and the calling routine requested accounting, then return 0 to the calling routine. (The return value is passed via the **else** clause at line 13616.)

13572: If the contents of the header of this packet match the specifications of the current rule, then pick up the policy and the type-of-service modifiers from this rule. If no rule matches the packet (a nonmatch is indicated by the **NULL** value for the current rule pointer), then use the default policy (passed by the calling routine) and make the type-of-service modifiers effectively "no operations."

13581: If the policy is **ACCEPT**, and if the type of service is being modified, then change the type of service and use the **ip_send_check** function to recompute the checksums.

13587: If transparent proxy support is compiled into the kernel, and the policy is to redirect the packet, then the redirection port is updated from the rule and **REDIRECT** status is returned.

13602: If IP masquerade support is compiled into the kernel, and the policy is to masquerade, then return **MASQ** status.

13610: If the policy is to reject the block, then return **REJECT** status.

13612: If the policy is to drop the block, then return **DENY** status.

Ipfw_input_check

This function, which is a wrapper for **ip_fw_chk**, specifies that the input rule chain is being applied.

Ipfw_forward_check

This function, which is a wrapper for **ip_fw_chk**, specifies that the forward rule chain is being applied.

Ipfw_output_check

This function, which is a wrapper for **ip_fw_chk**, specifies that the output rule chain is being applied.

/proc File System Support

If the proc file system support has been compiled into the kernel, the firewall implementation publishes the following four files in the /proc file system: /proc/net/ip_acct, /proc/net/ip_forward, /proc/net/ip_input, and /proc/net/ip_output. The four functions **ip_acct_procinfo**, **ip_fw_in_procinfo**, **ip_fw_fwd_procinfo**, and **ip_fw_out_procinfo** are wrapper functions for the **ip_chain_procinfo** common function.

The common function (which starts at line 14234) outputs the name of the chain and the default policy for that chain—in numeric rather than human-readable form—and then outputs a line that shows the definition of each rule contained in the chain. When all the rules have been output, the routine returns a buffer of length 0 to indicate "end of file."

The wrapper routines (which start at 14336) declare which rules should be printed.

The code in these functions is similar enough to the code in other proc file implementation functions described elsewhere in this book that a detailed look at these routines is not necessary. Suffice it to say that the code walks through the specified rules tree and prints the contents of each rule, observing buffer boundaries while doing so.

IP Masquerade Support

When a masquerade transfer is initiated, after the autoforwarding software (which is still experimental in the Linux 2.0.34 release) has been installed, the four routines **ip_autofw_add**, **ip_autofw_del**, **ip_autofw_flush**, and **ip_autofw_ctl** provide the code support for handling the masquerade of protocols that are not handled by protocol-specific modules. The add, delete, and flush routines implement the instructions provided by external routines for manipulation of the kernel-resident chain of autoforwarding blocks.

These routines are accessed through the **setsockopt** system call. Use of this system call means that applications can use these routines, and that a daemon program that does not reside in the kernel can oversee the autoforwarding task.

The **ip_autofw_add** routine creates a new autoforward block, fills in the information from the caller, and adds it to the chain (with the header **ip_autofw_hosts**). This routine returns 0 if the action was successful, or **ENOMEM** if the new block could not be allocated.

The **ip_autofw_del** routine searches the chain for the block that is identical to the information that was passed from the calling routine, removes the block from the chain, frees the memory, and returns a status of 0. If the block cannot be found, this routine returns a status of **EINVAL**.

The **ip_autofw_flush** routine walks through the autoforward chain, releases every block it finds, and then returns a status of 0.

The **ip_autofw_ctl** routine is the wrapper function that in turn calls the other three functions (**ip_autofw_add**, **ip_autofw_del**, and **ip_autofw_flush**).

Firewall Administration

Most of the Linux firewall code is devoted to the administration of the packet filter. As noted earlier in this chapter, each packet filter consists of a linked list of *rules*. Each rule contains a specification that describes the field in the packet to be examined, and indicates the values in the field that constitute a match. The administrative tools insert, append, and delete rules from specific individual packet-filter rule chains. These tools can also release an entire chain from memory, enabling that specific individual chain to be rebuilt.

Also associated with each chain is a default *policy*, which is simply an action that should be taken when no rule indicates how a packet should be handled. The policy may consist of accepting a packet for further processing, dropping the packet completely, or returning an ICMP message to the sender.

Associated with each rule are *counters* that let the system administrator see how many bytes and how many packets have been affected or counted by any given rule. These counters can be read and initialized to 0.

The implementations of the functions are simple and straightforward. Therefore, instead of analyzing the implementations line by line, the remainder of this section contains capsule descriptions of the functions.

zero_fw_chain

This function (which starts at line 13622) walks through the chain that was passed by the caller. For each node in the chain, the byte counter **fw_bcnt** and the packet counter **fw_pcnt** are set to 0.

free_fw_chain

This function (which starts at line 13633) also walks through the chain that was passed by the caller. The memory associated with each node in the chain is released. The pointer to the chain has the type "pointer to volatile pointer to structure **ip_fw**," so that the chain header can be updated while the chain is being removed from memory. This operation prevents a race condition from developing after the node has been freed, if the packet filter is invoked because a driver received a packet while this function was being executed. At no time does the packet-filter function **ip_fw_chk** use the stale contents of freed memory.

insert_in_chain

This function (which starts at line 13652) allocates memory for the new rule. First, it copies the rule information from the caller's buffer area (which information is passed in the structure pointed to by parameter **frwl**), and then links the new rule at the head of the chain. At line 13683, if a device name has been specified as part of the rule, the information about the device is obtained by the **dev_get** function.

To cause this routine to insert the new rule in the middle of the chain, the calling routine has the option of passing a pointer to the forward link of a rule's memory area as the chain header.

append_to_chain

This function (which starts at line 13694) is identical to the **insert_in_chain** function just described, except that the routine itself searches for the end of the chain and adds the new rule at the end of the chain. (Unfortunately, the author of the code didn't make this function a wrapper function that finds the end of the chain and then calls the **insert_in_chain** function. Doing so would have allowed existing code to be reused, with only a small overhead penalty in CPU time.)

del_from_chain

This function (which starts at line 13747) is interesting because it removes a matching rule from the chain, rather than depending on the calling routine to point to the rule that should be removed.

This function starts at the position passed by the calling routine. For each rule in the chain, the function checks all the information listed previously in Table 10.3, looking for a match. When it finds a match, the function removes the rule node from the chain and releases the memory.

check_ipfw_struct

This function (which starts at line 13831) examines a rule, looking for problems. If the rule is OK (that is, if no problems are detected), the function returns the address of the rule. If a problem is found, then the function returns the **NULL** address.

This function has one interesting side effect. If the **DEBUG_IP_FIREWALL** kernel configuration option was specified, a message describing the rule error is printed to the system's syslog file. This feature is useful not only to developers of firewall kernel code, but also to developers of support software that is written to use the administrative functions described in this section.

ip_acct_ctl

This function (which starts at line 13914) is a wrapper function for accounting rules. Depending on the function provided by the calling routine, it calls **free_fw_chain**, **zero_fw_chain**, **insert_in_chain**, **append_to_chain**, or **del_from_chain**, passing the address of the accounting chain to the called function.

ip_fw_ctl

This function (which starts at line 14056) is a wrapper function for the administration of firewall rules. Depending on the function provided by the calling routine, it calls **free_fw_chain**, **zero_fw_chain**, **insert_in_chain**, **append_to_chain**, or **del_from_chain**, passing the address of the accounting chain to the called function.

The **ip_acct_ctl** function serves a few additional purposes. If **IP_FW_POLICY** is specified for the parameter **stage**, then **ip_acct_ctl** sets the default policy for the chain in question (that is, it specifies the action to be returned if no rule in the chain matches a given packet).

If **IP_FW_CHECK** is passed by the calling routine for the parameter **stage**, then the packet passed by the calling function is submitted to the **ip_fw_chk** function for processing. The **ip_fw_chk** function then processes this packet (without updating any counters) as though it were a real packet, and returns the policy that should be applied to the packet. The function then converts the return of the **ip_fw_chk** function to one of the following specific error returns:

- **FW_ACCEPT** becomes 0

- **FW_REDIRECT** becomes **ECONNABORTED**

- **FW_MASQUARADE** becomes **ECONNRESET**

- **FW_REJECT** becomes **ECONNREFUSED**

- **FW_BLOCK** (or any other return) becomes **ETIMEDOUT**

This way, programmers can debug rule trees to confirm that a given set of packets has behaved as expected.

Finally, if the parameter **stage** is **IP_FW_MASQ_TIMEOUTS**, then the TCP and UDP timeouts are set to the values that are passed in the parameter block pointed to by parameter **m**.

ipfw_device_event

This function (which starts at line 14420) is called whenever a device is placed in either the UP or DOWN state. The routine examines all the rule chains and sets the device block pointer appropriately: either to the address of the **dev** structure for a newly UP device, or to a placeholder value of −1 for a newly DOWN device.

ip_fw_init

This function (which starts at line 14462) is called once, when the system is initialized. This function registers all the /proc file system entries, the entry point for device UP/DOWN notifications, and the entry points for the firewall lookup functions.

This function also calls the **ip_masq_init** function, to ensure that the masquerade support functions have been initialized by being set to a known state.

Appendix A

GNU General Public License

For your reference, we have included the GNU General Public License (GPL) as it applies to the software this book is about. However, the GPL does not apply to the text of this book.
Version 2, June 1991
Copyright (c) 1989, 1991 Free Software Foundation, Inc.
59 Temple Place, Suite 330, Boston, MA 02111-1307 USA

Everyone is permitted to copy and distribute verbatim copies of this license document, but changing it is not allowed.

Preamble

The licenses for most software are designed to take away your freedom to share and change it. By contrast, the GNU General Public License is intended to guarantee your freedom to share and change free software—to make sure the software is free for all its users. This General Public License applies to most of the Free Software Foundation's software and to any other program whose authors commit to using it. (Some other Free Software Foundation software is covered by the GNU Library General Public License instead.) You can apply it to your programs, too.

When we speak of free software, we are referring to freedom, not price. Our General Public Licenses are designed to make sure that you have the freedom to distribute copies of free software (and charge for this service if you wish), that you receive source code or can get it if you want it, that you can change the software or use pieces of it in new free programs; and that you know you can do these things.

To protect your rights, we need to make restrictions that forbid anyone to deny you these rights or to ask you to surrender the rights. These restrictions translate to certain responsibilities for you if you distribute copies of the software, or if you modify it.

For example, if you distribute copies of such a program, whether gratis or for a fee, you must give the recipients all the rights that you have. You must make sure that they, too, receive or can get the source code. And you must show them these terms so they know their rights.

We protect your rights with two steps: (1) copyright the software, and (2) offer you this license which gives you legal permission to copy, distribute and/or modify the software.

Also, for each author's protection and ours, we want to make certain that everyone understands that there is no warranty for this free software. If the software is modified by someone else and passed on, we want its recipients to know that what they have is not the original, so that any problems introduced by others will not reflect on the original authors' reputations.

Finally, any free program is threatened constantly by software patents. We wish to avoid the danger that redistributors of a free program will individually obtain patent licenses, in effect making the program proprietary. To prevent this, we have made it clear that any patent must be licensed for everyone's free use or not licensed at all.

The precise terms and conditions for copying, distribution and modification follow.

Terms And Conditions For Copying, Distribution And Modification

This License applies to any program or other work which contains a notice placed by the copyright holder saying it may be distributed under the terms of this General Public License. The "Program", below, refers to any such program or work, and a "work based on the Program" means either the Program or any derivative work under copyright law: that is to say, a work containing the Program or a portion of it, either verbatim or with modifications and/or translated into another language. (Hereinafter, translation is included without limitation in the term "modification".) Each licensee is addressed as "you".

Activities other than copying, distribution and modification are not covered by this License; they are outside its scope. The act of running the Program is not restricted, and the output from the Program is covered only if its contents constitute a work based on the Program (independent of having been made by running the Program). Whether that is true depends on what the Program does.

1. You may copy and distribute verbatim copies of the Program's source code as you receive it, in any medium, provided that you conspicuously and appropriately publish on each copy an appropriate copyright notice and disclaimer of warranty; keep intact all the notices that refer to this License and to the absence of any warranty; and give any other recipients of the Program a copy of this License along with the Program.

   You may charge a fee for the physical act of transferring a copy, and you may at your option offer warranty protection in exchange for a fee.

2. You may modify your copy or copies of the Program or any portion of it, thus forming a work based on the Program, and copy and distribute such modifications or work under the terms of Section 1 above, provided that you also meet all of these conditions:

   a) You must cause the modified files to carry prominent notices stating that you changed the files and the date of any change.

   b) You must cause any work that you distribute or publish, that in whole or in part contains or is derived from the Program or any part thereof, to be licensed as a whole at no charge to all third parties under the terms of this License.

c) If the modified program normally reads commands interactively when run, you must cause it, when started running for such interactive use in the most ordinary way, to print or display an announcement including an appropriate copyright notice and a notice that there is no warranty (or else, saying that you provide a warranty) and that users may redistribute the program under these conditions, and telling the user how to view a copy of this License. (Exception: if the Program itself is interactive but does not normally print such an announcement, your work based on the Program is not required to print an announcement.)

These requirements apply to the modified work as a whole. If identifiable sections of that work are not derived from the Program, and can be reasonably considered independent and separate works in themselves, then this License, and its terms, do not apply to those sections when you distribute them as separate works. But when you distribute the same sections as part of a whole which is a work based on the Program, the distribution of the whole must be on the terms of this License, whose permissions for other licensees extend to the entire whole, and thus to each and every part regardless of who wrote it.

Thus, it is not the intent of this section to claim rights or contest your rights to work written entirely by you; rather, the intent is to exercise the right to control the distribution of derivative or collective works based on the Program.

In addition, mere aggregation of another work not based on the Program with the Program (or with a work based on the Program) on a volume of a storage or distribution medium does not bring the other work under the scope of this License.

3. You may copy and distribute the Program (or a work based on it, under Section 2) in object code or executable form under the terms of Sections 1 and

2 above provided that you also do one of the following:

a) Accompany it with the complete corresponding machine-readable source code, which must be distributed under the terms of Sections 1 and 2 above on a medium customarily used for software interchange; or,

b) Accompany it with a written offer, valid for at least three years, to give any third party, for a charge no more than your cost of physically performing source distribution, a complete machine-readable copy of the corresponding source code, to be distributed under the terms of Sections 1 and 2 above on a medium customarily used for software interchange; or,

c) Accompany it with the information you received as to the offer to distribute corresponding source code. (This alternative is allowed only for non-commercial distribution and only if you received the program in object code or executable form with such an offer, in accord with Subsection b above.)

The source code for a work means the preferred form of the work for making modifications to it. For an executable work, complete source code means all the source code for all modules it contains, plus any associated interface definition files, plus the scripts used to control compilation and installation of the executable. However, as a special exception, the source code distributed need not include anything that is normally distributed (in either source or binary form) with the major components (compiler, kernel, and so on) of the operating system on which the executable runs, unless that component itself accompanies the executable.

If distribution of executable or object code is made by offering access to copy from a designated place, then offering equivalent access to copy the source code from the same place counts as distribution of

the source code, even though third parties are not compelled to copy the source along with the object code.

4. You may not copy, modify, sublicense, or distribute the Program except as expressly provided under this License. Any attempt otherwise to copy, modify, sublicense or distribute the Program is void, and will automatically terminate your rights under this License. However, parties who have received copies, or rights, from you under this License will not have their licenses terminated so long as such parties remain in full compliance.

5. You are not required to accept this License, since you have not signed it. However, nothing else grants you permission to modify or distribute the Program or its derivative works. These actions are prohibited by law if you do not accept this License. Therefore, by modifying or distributing the Program (or any work based on the Program), you indicate your acceptance of this License to do so, and all its terms and conditions for copying, distributing or modifying the Program or works based on it.

6. Each time you redistribute the Program (or any work based on the Program), the recipient automatically receives a license from the original licensor to copy, distribute or modify the Program subject to these terms and conditions. You may not impose any further restrictions on the recipients' exercise of the rights granted herein. You are not responsible for enforcing compliance by third parties to this License.

7. If, as a consequence of a court judgment or allegation of patent infringement or for any other reason (not limited to patent issues), conditions are imposed on you (whether by court order, agreement or otherwise) that contradict the conditions of this License, they do not excuse you from the conditions of this License. If you cannot distribute so as to satisfy simultaneously your obligations under this

License and any other pertinent obligations, then as a consequence you may not distribute the Program at all. For example, if a patent license would not permit royalty-free redistribution of the Program by all those who receive copies directly or indirectly through you, then the only way you could satisfy both it and this License would be to refrain entirely from distribution of the Program.

If any portion of this section is held invalid or unenforceable under any particular circumstance, the balance of the section is intended to apply and the section as a whole is intended to apply in other circumstances.

It is not the purpose of this section to induce you to infringe any patents or other property right claims or to contest validity of any such claims; this section has the sole purpose of protecting the integrity of the free software distribution system, which is implemented by public license practices. Many people have made generous contributions to the wide range of software distributed through that system in reliance on consistent application of that system; it is up to the author/donor to decide if he or she is willing to distribute software through any other system and a licensee cannot impose that choice.

This section is intended to make thoroughly clear what is believed to be a consequence of the rest of this License.

8. If the distribution and/or use of the Program is restricted in certain countries either by patents or by copyrighted interfaces, the original copyright holder who places the Program under this License may add an explicit geographical distribution limitation excluding those countries, so that distribution is permitted only in or among countries not thus excluded. In such case, this License incorporates the limitation as if written in the body of this License.

9. The Free Software Foundation may publish revised and/or new versions of the General Public License from time to time. Such new versions will be similar in spirit to the present version, but may differ in detail to address new problems or concerns.

Each version is given a distinguishing version number. If the Program specifies a version number of this License which applies to it and "any later version", you have the option of following the terms and conditions either of that version or of any later version published by the Free Software Foundation. If the Program does not specify a version number of this License, you may choose any version ever published by the Free Software Foundation.

10. If you wish to incorporate parts of the Program into other free programs whose distribution conditions are different, write to the author to ask for permission. For software which is copyrighted by the Free Software Foundation, write to the Free Software Foundation; we sometimes make exceptions for this. Our decision will be guided by the two goals of preserving the free status of all derivatives of our free software and of promoting the sharing and reuse of software generally.

No Warranty

11. BECAUSE THE PROGRAM IS LICENSED FREE OF CHARGE, THERE IS NO WARRANTY FOR THE PROGRAM, TO THE EXTENT PERMITTED BY APPLICABLE LAW. EXCEPT WHEN OTHERWISE STATED IN WRITING THE COPYRIGHT HOLDERS AND/OR OTHER PARTIES PROVIDE THE PROGRAM "AS IS" WITHOUT WARRANTY OF ANY KIND, EITHER EXPRESS OR IMPLIED, INCLUDING, BUT NOT LIMITED TO, THE IMPLIED WARRANTIES OF MERCHANTABILITY AND FITNESS FOR A PARTICULAR PURPOSE. THE ENTIRE RISK AS TO THE QUALITY AND PERFORMANCE OF THE PROGRAM IS WITH YOU. SHOULD THE PROGRAM PROVE DE-FECTIVE, YOU ASSUME THE COST OF ALL NECESSARY SERVICING, REPAIR OR CORRECTION.

12. IN NO EVENT UNLESS REQUIRED BY APPLICABLE LAW OR AGREED TO IN WRITING WILL ANY COPYRIGHT HOLDER, OR ANY OTHER PARTY WHO MAY MODIFY AND/OR REDISTRIBUTE THE PROGRAM AS PERMITTED ABOVE, BE LIABLE TO YOU FOR DAMAGES, INCLUDING ANY GENERAL, SPECIAL, INCIDENTAL OR CONSEQUENTIAL DAMAGES ARISING OUT OF THE USE OR INABILITY TO USE THE PROGRAM (INCLUDING BUT NOT LIMITED TO LOSS OF DATA OR DATA BEING RENDERED INACCURATE OR LOSSES SUSTAINED BY YOU OR THIRD PARTIES OR A FAILURE OF THE PROGRAM TO OPERATE WITH ANY OTHER PROGRAMS), EVEN IF SUCH HOLDER OR OTHER PARTY HAS BEEN ADVISED OF THE POSSIBILITY OF SUCH DAMAGES.

How To Apply These Terms To Your New Programs

If you develop a new program, and you want it to be of the greatest possible use to the public, the best way to achieve this is to make it free software which everyone can redistribute and change under these terms.

To do so, attach the following notices to the program. It is safest to attach them to the start of each source file to most effectively convey the exclusion of warranty; and each file should have at least the "copyright" line and a pointer to where the full notice is found.

```
<one line to give the program's name and
 a brief idea of what it does.>
Copyright (c) 20yy  <name of author>

This program is free software; you can
redistribute it and/or modify it under the
terms of the GNU General Public License as
```

```
published by the Free Software Foundation;
either version 2 of the License, or
(at your option) any later version.

This program is distributed in the hope that
it will be useful, but WITHOUT ANY WARRANTY;
without even the implied warranty of
MERCHANTABILITY or FITNESS FOR A PARTICULAR
PURPOSE.  See the GNU General Public License
for more details.

You should have received a copy of the GNU
General Public License along with this
program; if not, write to the Free Software
Foundation, Inc., 59 Temple Place, Suite 330,
Boston, MA  02111-1307  USA
```

Also add information on how to contact you by electronic and paper mail.

If the program is interactive, make it output a short notice like this when it starts in an interactive mode:

```
Gnomovision version 69, Copyright (c) 20yy
name of author Gnomovision comes with
ABSOLUTELY NO WARRANTY; for details type
'show w'. This is free software, and you are
welcome to redistribute it under certain
conditions; type 'show c' for details.
```

The hypothetical commands 'show w' and 'show c' should show the appropriate parts of the General Public License. Of course, the commands you use may be called something other than 'show w' and 'show c'; they could even be mouse-clicks or menu items—whatever suits your program.

You should also get your employer (if you work as a programmer) or your school, if any, to sign a "copyright disclaimer" for the program, if necessary. Here is a sample; alter the names:

```
Yoyodyne, Inc., hereby disclaims all copyright
interest in the program 'Gnomovision'
(which makes passes at compilers) written
by James Hacker.

<signature of Ty Coon>, 1 April 1989
Ty Coon, President of Vice
```

This General Public License does not permit incorporating your program into proprietary programs. If your program is a subroutine library, you may consider it more useful to permit linking proprietary applications with the library. If this is what you want to do, use the GNU Library General Public License instead of this License.

Appendix B

Abbreviations

To help forestall perplexity as you peruse this and other books about (and on) the Internet, the authors offer the following list of abbreviations that often appear in discussions of Internet systems, along with the expansions of those abbreviations:

ADSL—Asymmetric digital subscriber line

ANSI—American National Standards Institute

API—Application programming interface

ARP—Address Resolution Protocol

ARPA—Advanced Research Projects Agency (DoD)

ASCII—American Standard Code for Information Interchange

ATM—Asynchronous Transfer Mode

AUTH—Authentication Protocol

AWG—American Wire Gauge

BBN—Bolt Beranek and Newman (the original proto-Internet contractor)

BBS—Bulletin Board System

BER—Bit Error Rate

BGP—Border Gateway Protocol

BIND—Berkeley Internet Name Domain

BLER—Block Error Rate

BNF—Backus-Naur Form; Backus Normal Form

BOOTP—Bootstrap Protocol

BSD—Berkeley Software Distribution

CCITT—Consultative Committee for International Telegraphy and Telephony (or, in the original French, Comité Consultatif International Télégraphique et Téléphonique)

CD-ROM—Compact disc read-only memory

CHAP—Challenge Handshake Authentication Protocol

CIDR—Classless Inter-Domain Routing

CLNP—Connectionless Network Protocol

CRC—Cyclic redundancy check

CSLIP—Compressed Serial Line Internet Protocol

DES—Data Encryption Standard

DHCP—Dynamic Host Configuration Protocol

DID—Direct Inward Dialing

DNS—Domain Name System (or Service)

DoD—Department of Defense

DOD—Direct Outward Dialing

DoS—Denial of Service

DSL—Digital subscriber line

DVMRP—Distance Vector Multicast Routing Protocol

EBCDIC—Extended Binary Coded Decimal Interchange Code

EGP—Exterior Gateway Protocol

EIA—Electronic Industries Association

ETSI—European Telecommunication Standards Institute

FCS—Frame Check Sequence

FD—File descriptor

FDDI—Fiber Distributed Data Interface

FIB—Forward Information Base

FQDN—Fully qualified domain name

FTP—File Transfer Protocol

GGP—Gateway-to-Gateway Protocol

GPS—Global Positioning System

HDLC—High-level Data Link Control

HTML—Hypertext Markup Language

HTTP—Hypertext Transfer Protocol

IAB—Internet Architecture Board

IANA—Internet Assigned Numbers Authority

IAP—Internet Access Provider

ICMP—Internet Control Message Protocol

IDPR—Inter-Domain Policy Routing

IDRP—Inter-Domain Routing Protocol

IEEE—Institute of Electrical and Electronics Engineers

IESG—Internet Engineering Steering Group

IETF—Internet Engineering Task Force

IGMP—Internet Group Management Protocol

IGP—Interior Gateway Protocol

IMAP—Interim Mail Access Protocol

IMP—Interface message processor

INOC—Internet Network Operations Center

IP—Internet Protocol

IPIP—IP-within-IP Encapsulation Protocol

IPX—Internetwork Packet Exchange

IRC—Internet Relay Chat

IRTF—Internet Research Task Force

ISO—International Organization for Standardization

ISOC—Internet Society

ISP—Internet Service Provider

ITU—International Telecommunications Union

LAN—Local-area network

LCP—Link Control Protocol

LDAP—Lightweight Directory Access Protocol

LLC—Logical Link Control

LSRR—Loose Source and Record Route

MAC—Media Access Control

MIB—Management Information Base

MILNET—Military Network

MIME—Multipurpose Internet Mail Extensions

MQL—Maximum [permissible] queue length

MSS—Maximum segment size

MTU—Maximum transmission unit

NAP—Network Access Provider

NCP—Network Control Protocol

NetBIOS—Network Basic Input/Output System

NFS—Network File System

NIC—Network Information Center

NIC—Network interface card

NIST—National Institute of Standards and Technology

NNTP—Network News Transfer Protocol

NOP—No operation

NTP—Network Time Protocol

NWG—Network Working Group

OSF—Open Software Foundation

OSI—Open Systems Interconnection

OSPF—Open Shortest Path First

PAD—Packet assembler/disassembler

PAP—Password Authentication Protocol

PAWS—Protection Against Wrapped Sequence Numbers

PGP—Pretty Good Privacy

PING—Packet Internet Groper urban legend—the program name "ping" is actually derived from the sound made by underwater sonar

POP—Post Office Protocol

POSIX—Portable Operating System Interface

POTS—Plain Ol' Telephone Service

PPP—Point-to-Point Protocol

PVP—Packet Video Protocol

RAP—Route Access Protocol

RARP—Reverse Address Resolution Protocol

RFC—Request for Comments

RFNM—Request for Next Message

RIP—Routing Information Protocol

RJE—Remote job entry

RJOR—Remote job output retrieval

RPC—Remote procedure call

RR—Resource record

RSVP—Reservation Protocol

RTO—Retransmission Timeout

RTT—Round-trip time

SACK—Selective Acknowledgement

SCSI—Small Computer System Interface

SDLC—Synchronous Data Link Control

SDRP—Source Demand Routing Protocol

SGMP—Simple Gateway Monitoring Protocol

SLIP—Serial Line Internet Protocol

SMTP—Simple Mail Transfer Protocol

SNMP—Simple Network Management Protocol

SNPP—Simple Network Paging Protocol

SPX—Sequenced Packet Exchange

SQL—Structured Query Language

SSL—Secure Sockets Layer

SSRR—Strict Source and Record Route

SWISH—Simple Web Indexing System for Humans

SWS—Silly Window Syndrome

TACACS—Terminal Access Controller Access Control System

TCP—Transmission Control Protocol

Telnet—Teletype over the Network

TFTP—Trivial File Transfer Protocol

TIA—Telecommunications Industry Association

TLI—Transport layer interface

TOS—Type of Service

TTL—Time to Live

TTY—Teletype

TUBA—TCP and UDP over Bigger Addresses

UDP—User Datagram Protocol

URL—Universal Resource Locator (preferred); Uniform Resource Locator

UUCP—Unix-to-Unix Copy Program

VPN—Virtual Private Network

WAN—Wide-area network

WWW—World Wide Web

W3C—World Wide Web Consortium

XDMCP—X Display Manager Control Protocol

XNS—Xerox Network System

Appendix C

DNS

In Chapter 8, you learned about the User Datagram Protocol (UDP) and saw how its connections differ from standard TCP connections. This appendix describes one outstanding example of how UDP is used in day-to-day network communications.

Hostnames, Go Home

In virtually every network application that's written for use by human beings, hostnames have to be converted to Internet addresses. This task is so common and so pervasive that you'd expect it to be a built-in part of the great networking universe.

Not so. One of the basic tenets of Linux is to keep as many functions as possible *out* of the kernel code, leaving those tasks to the library lookup functions incorporated into applications.

One of the mechanisms that these library routines use is the *Domain Name System* (DNS, sometimes also referred to as the *Domain Name Service*), which is essentially a distributed database of hostnames in which the names are organized in the form of tree structures.

As part of its duties, DNS sends queries to servers on the network, packaging those queries as UDP packets (see Chapter 8). As such, DNS is a good example of a broad-based application that uses UDP, and whose use of UDP stems from the fact that DNS is based not on a client "program" but rather on a set of library functions that do the actual work.

You Are Number 6

The commentaries in this book refer often to 32-bit Internet Protocol addresses, each of which consists of a binary number. These numeric addresses, each of which is represented externally by four groups of three-digit decimal numbers, appear several times in every IP packet. They also appear in socket objects, as part of the information used by the socket objects in managing connections.

Alas, when human beings look up information, they tend not to think in terms of dozen-digit numbers. Instead, they think in terms of **www.yahoo.com**, **ftp.linux.org**, or **news.uu.net**. Consequently, one way or another, every single application that involves people uses names rather than numbers to identify services. Humans, in turn, rely on software applications that let computers do what computers do best—namely, the bookkeeping.

And what a task it is. Millions of names are currently in use for the "com" domain alone. Add the other domains ("org", "edu", "net", and the rest), and the number of endpoints is mind-boggling. A printed list would be as big as the New York City phone directories for all the five boroughs, and it would be obsolete the instant it hit your porch.

A centralized database would be just as obsolete, but even sooner. Worse still, the database would be prone to single-point failures, and the number of lookup operations that would have to be performed in response to inquiries from around the world would run to millions per second. How can such a workload be handled? The answer echoes the guiding principle of the Internet itself—distribute the task.

Several namespace management systems were devised during the development of the Internet, but the one that has gained universal acceptance is the Domain Name System (DNS), which was first implemented in 1985 in the Berkeley Internet Name Domain (BIND) software package. DNS simply distributes name information, using almost the same method that Internet Protocol routers use when they distribute information about the structure of the network—that is, neighbors talking to neighbors.

Almost, but not quite. To understand the difference, you need to get acquainted with the structure of a *domain name*, and then see how domain names relate to the rest of the network. This appendix contains a capsule summary of the process. For a more extensive description, see Paul Albitz and Cricket Liu's excellent book *DNS and BIND* (3rd ed., O'Reilly & Associates, September 1998; ISBN 1-56592-5122).

What's In A Name

Just as Unix has "directories" and Windows or Macintosh systems have "folders," DNS has "domains." A *domain name*, which defines the path through the DNS name tree, consists of several labels, separated by a period (.). A *fully qualified domain name (FQDN)*, such as "berkeley.edu." (note the period at the end of the string) defines an *absolute* name. Domain names can also be *relative*, just as a file name can be relative to the current directory or folder. Relative domain names don't have a period at the end.

A domain name can have any number of labels, and any label can appear in two or more domains. For example, the domains "berkeley.edu." and "berkeley.org." refer to two separate domains, in the same way file systems allow "/foo/bar" and "/heath/bar" to refer unambiguously to two separate files.

Name Structures: Root, Branch, And Leaf

In most OS file systems, each individual file name has the "leaf" of the name tree that appears at the rightmost end of the file name string, while the labels that appear to the left of the file name indicate the path back up the tree, from the leaf to the root node of the file system. Thus, for instance, the file name "/usr/src/linux" implies the tree structure shown in Figure C.1. The same tree structure would be implied in the Windows file name "C:\usr\src\linux" or in the Macintosh file name Hard Disk:Usr:Src:Linux. In other words, labels in file names are read and interpreted from left to right, from root to leaf.

Unfortunately, this convention isn't universally observed. Specifically, the DNS naming conventions read the la-

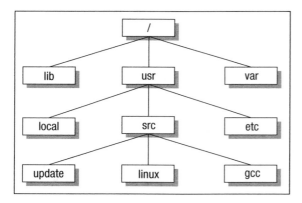

Figure C.1   File name tree for "/usr/src/linux".

bels in the reverse order—from right to left, from leaf to root. The tree structure shown in Figure C.2 is implied for the FQDN **ftp.berkeley.edu.**, which contains four labels: "ftp", "berkeley", "edu", and the empty string "".

Each domain customarily provides a name for a collection of networks, a collection of systems, or a collection of services on a host. The top-level domains, which consist of the common two-letter country codes (**us.** for the U.S., **ru.** for Russia, and so forth) and the three-letter global top-level domains (gTLDs, such as **com.**,

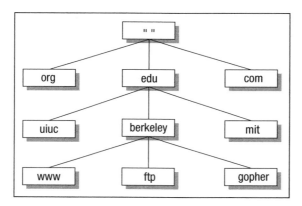

Figure C.2   Domain name tree for "ftp.berkeley.edu".

edu., and so forth), contain a mixture of network names and hostnames, with the actual structure of each domain being determined by how management is delegated as you go down the tree.

Divide And Conquer

As any consultant will tell you, no individual manager can handle dozens, let alone hundreds or thousands, of immediate subordinates ("direct reports"). Instead, authority must be delegated to subordinate managers who are closer to the workers. So it is with DNS.

Domains are actually defined on a handful of systems, known as *name servers*, that are known throughout the network. Although each name server originally resided in the domain that it defined, this practice is no longer rigidly followed. Name servers today can also define multiple domains.

Any changes made in a name server are eventually reflected throughout the network, because all the name servers talk to each other, either directly or indirectly. The only place where this procedure isn't followed is at the top-level domains, where name management is handled via email and postal mail.

Many *delegations* (that is, assignments of authority to secondary entities) are set up the same way, such that the contents of the DNS database are handled through the online update paradigm. As a result, management of the databases is so well distributed that no one entity is saddled with the whole task. Even better, the potential for a single-point failure is minimized or even eliminated.

Thanks to distributed maintenance, DNS protocols have access to mechanisms that let them duplicate—periodically and in many locations—the contents of the DNS database. This periodic duplication means that domain-name requests can be spread over a very large number of name servers, so failure of a single server—even a failure of the server of the designated DNS database maintainer—doesn't make names "disappear."

What's In A Database?

DNS contains a lot of detailed information about the endpoints of a network. The most important piece of information is the so-called "*A*" *record*, which describes the relationship between the name of a host and its Internet address. Meanwhile, the PTR record maintains the relation between the address of a host and its name. DNS also can hold information about the host, such as its hardware and software, and contact information for the system administrator. (For further details, see RFCs 974, 1034, 1035, and 2181 on the CD-ROM.)

DNS also stores information that is important to the e-mail systems used by users (or systems) who are not online all the time but have email addresses. This information is stored in the MX record.

If DNS seems to be just too simple, bear in mind that a given network or system can have more than one name, and a given name can refer to more than one IP address. This multiple-name situation occurs, for example, when a server is known by several aliases. The multiple-address situation occurs when a server is *multihomed* (that is, when it is connected to multiple independent networks) and can be reached from each one of those independent networks. In other words, each interface has its own IP address.

Each record in the DNS database has an associated *Time to Live (TTL)* parameter, which indicates how long a given entry should be assumed to be accurate. In associating a given name with a given address, a DNS server "remembers" an earlier request, so the request doesn't have to be repeated each time a client application needs the name. Because this function is part of the system or local network rather than part of the client application, a given name can be used by several applications, and only one query from the system group goes out over the network.

Please, Sir, May I Have A Name?

A *resolver* is a subroutine that asks name servers to report the association between an IP address and a given name. In most cases, this subroutine discovers the IP address of a name server (which may have been specified by the person who set up the system, or perhaps was provided as part of the automatic process of assigning an IP address using the DHCP protocol) and sends a name query to that server, via UDP. The server returns a response to the request. This response includes not only any IP addresses that are associated with the name, but also information about name servers that can return authoritative answers to the inquiring routine. (Here, the word *authoritative* means that the answer is provided directly by the system that defines the name. A *nonauthoritative* answer is one that is provided by a cached record, which may have been changed, even if the specified Time to Live hasn't expired.)

In rare instances, the client subroutine is forced to perform an iterative process, looking up name servers for each intermediate domain for the name in question, and ultimately submitting the desired name to the last enclosing domain. This iterative process is usually performed by the name server, on the theory that a server on a broadband link to the Internet is in a better position than the client system to perform the top-down search.

The library function that performs the name lookup on behalf of a client is **gethostbyname**. This function (as it pertains to UDP-based queries) takes a domain name (which can be either relative or fully qualified) and submits, to the name server, a request for resolution of the name to an address. After this task has been completed, a list of addresses is returned. The first address in this list is the one most likely to be the "closest" to the system.

The **gethostbyname** function builds a UDP packet that contains the desired name, sends the packet to the name server address contained in the resolver configuration

file (usually "/etc/resolv.conf"), and waits for a reply. If the server replies that it can't find information about the name, and if the name in question is a relative name, the function starts appending default domain names to the specified name and repeats the query of the server. It continues this process until it receives a response or until the list of searchable default domains has been exhausted.

Within **gethostbyname**, a temporary UDP connection is established with a name server in the list. The name servers listed in the resolver configuration file are queried, one by one, until one of them responds. Because UDP is a connectionless service, the function cannot send any requests until after it has registered a listening port. After a response has been received (or a timeout has indicated that the server isn't responding), the listening port must be closed.

The actual packets that are exchanged between the resolver routines and the name servers are described in detail in RFC 1035. RFC 1034 illustrates typical transactions. (Both of these RFCs appear on the accompanying CD-ROM.) Figure C.3 shows the general layout of a packet during the exchange procedure.

The *ID field* contains a 16-bit number used by the requesting program to match requests and responses.

The *QR bit* indicates whether the packet is a query (set to 0) or a response (set to 1).

The *Opcode field* contains a 4-bit value that is 0 for a standard query, 1 for an inverse query, or 2 for a server status request. The values 3 through 15 are reserved.

The *AA bit* indicates, in response packets, that the name server providing the information is an authority (master) for the domain name in the Question section.

The *TC bit* indicates that the message was truncated because it was too long to fit through the transmission channel.

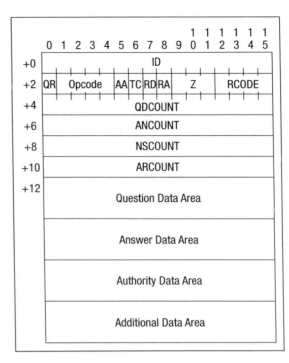

Figure C.3 Layout of the DNS request and response record.

The *RD bit* indicates, in request packets, that recursion is desired. (Specifically, the name server should initiate multiple queries, if necessary, instead of having the requesting program do so.) This bit is usually set by a resolver in a client system, rather than by a name server that is issuing requests. The RD bit is copied, unchanged, into response packets.

The *RA bit* indicates, in response packets, whether the name server supports recursive queries.

The bits in the *Z field* are reserved. They should be ignored when packets are examined and set to 0 when packets are built.

The *RCODE field* indicates, in response packets, the results of the query. 0 indicates no error, 1 indicates a format error, 2 indicates a server error, 3 indicates that the name in the question does not exist, 4 indicates that the query requested is not supported, and 5 indicates that, for policy reasons, the server refused to process the question. This response is used, for example, when a zone transfer (that is, a bulk transfer of name information) is requested by a system that is not authorized to receive such transfers.

The remaining four fixed fields are 16-bit counts of entries or resource records for the Question, Answer, Authority, and Additional-information sections, respectively. The data for the Question, Answer, Authority, and Additional-information data sections follows after the fixed header. The format of the data in these four data sections is explained in RFC 1035 (on the CD-ROM) and is not reproduced here.

One final note. Because the volume of information for some requests can exceed the size of the packets that are available for UDP, a resolver that wants this information has the option of opening a TCP connection to the name server in order to obtain it. This option is often implemented when a name server wants to download a copy of the information for a domain (a *zone*) from another server with the intention that the information be duplicated. The same request-and-response format is used, but a much, much larger amount of information can be transferred.

Index